ISBN 978-0-332-55422-8
PIBN 11240038

1 MONTH OF
FREE
READING

at
www.ForgottenBooks.com

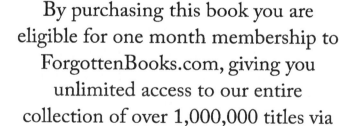

By purchasing this book you are eligible for one month membership to ForgottenBooks.com, giving you unlimited access to our entire collection of over 1,000,000 titles via our web site and mobile apps.

To claim your free month visit:
www.forgottenbooks.com/free1240038

English
Français
Deutsche
Italiano
Español
Português

www.forgottenbooks.com

Mythology Photography **Fiction**
Fishing Christianity **Art** Cooking
Essays Buddhism Freemasonry
Medicine **Biology** Music **Ancient
Egypt** Evolution Carpentry Physics
Dance Geology **Mathematics** Fitness
Shakespeare **Folklore** Yoga Marketing
Confidence Immortality Biographies
Poetry **Psychology** Witchcraft
Electronics Chemistry History **Law**
Accounting **Philosophy** Anthropology
Alchemy Drama Quantum Mechanics
Atheism Sexual Health **Ancient History**
Entrepreneurship Languages Sport
Paleontology Needlework Islam
Metaphysics Investment Archaeology
Parenting Statistics Criminology
Motivational

CATALOGUE

OF THE

FREE PUBLIC LIBRARY, SYDNEY.

PART I:—Authors, Editors, or Reference.

1869—1887.

*** [*See* JOSEPHSON, J.]

*** [*See* HOBSON'S BAY.]

**** [*See* PSALMANAZAR, G.]

A. (J. B.) [*See* YOUNG VICTORIA.]

A.G. [*See* MOTHER'S GRAVE.]

AA (P. J. B. C. ROBIDÉ VAN DER). Reizen naar Nederlandsch Nieuw-Guinea, ondernomen op last der Regeering van Nederlandsch-Indie in de Jaren 1871–72, 1875–76. 8vo. 'Sgravenhage, 1879. MD 3 V 7

[*See* MORRIS, D. F. VAN BRAAM.] MD 3 V 8

AARON (CHARLES H.) Practical Treatise on Testing and Working Silver Ores. 12mo. SanFrancisco, 1876.
A 9 P 36

AASEN (IVAR). Norsk Grammatik. 8vo. Christiania, 1864. K 12 S 33

Norsk Ordbog, med Dansk Forklaring. 8vo. Christiania, 1873. K 15 S 28

ABÆLARDUS (PETRUS). Opera omnia. [*See* MIGNE, J. P., SERIES LATINA, 178.]

ABBEY (C. J.) The English Church and its Bishops, 1700–1800. 2 vols. 8vo. Lond., 1887. G 5 P 1, 2

ABBON OR ABBO (CERNUUS). Siége de Paris. [*See* GUIZOT, F. P. G., 6.] B 8 T 7

ABBOT (F. E.), PH.D. Organic Scientific Philosophy: Scientific Theism. 8vo. Lond., 1885. G 13 Q 1

ABBOT (WILLIS J.) Blue Jackets of '61: a History of the American Navy. Sm. 4to. NewYork,1887. B 1 U 9

ABBOTT (CHARLES C.), M.D. Primitive Industry; or, Illustrations of the Handiwork, in Stone, Bone and Clay, of the Native Races of the Northern Atlantic Seaboard of America. 8vo. Salem, 1881. A 1 W 22

A

ABBOTT (REV. EDWIN ABBOTT), D.D. Flatland : a Romance of many Dimensions; by "A Square." Sm. 4to. Lond., 1884. A 10 U 27

Francis Bacon : an Account of his Life and Works. 8vo. Lond., 1885. C 10 R 10

Shakespearian Grammar for the Use of Schools. 8vo. Lond., 1872. K 11 U 17

ABBOTT (REV. EDWIN A.), D.D., AND SEELEY (J. R.), M.A. English Lessons for English People. 11th thousand. 8vo. Lond., 1875. K 11 T 4

ABBOTT (EVELYN), M.A., &c. Hellenica : a Collection of Essays on Greek Poetry, Philosophy, History, and Religion. 8vo. Lond., 1880. J 2 S 5

History of Antiquity. [*See* DUNCKER, PROF. M.]
B 14 S 25–30

ABBOTT (FRANCIS), F.R.A.S. Catalogue of Plants under Cultivation in the Royal Society's Gardens, Queen's Park, Hobart Town, Tasmania. 8vo. Hobart, 1865. MJ 2 R 13

Results of Five Years' Meteorological Observations for Hobart Town; with which are incorporated the Results of Twenty-five Years' Observations previously published by the Royal Society of Tasmania. 4to. Hobart, 1872.
MA 1 Q 23 †

ABBOTT (CAPT. JAMES). Narrative of a Journey from Heraut to Khiva, Moscow, and St.Petersburgh, during the late Russian Invasion of Khiva 2 vols. 8vo. Lond., 1843. D 5 S 8, 9

Another copy. 3rd ed. 2 vols. 8vo. Lond., 1884.
D 5 S 10, 11

ABBOTT (REV. J.), A.M., "PHILIP MUSGRAVE." Philip Musgrave; or, Memoirs of a Church of England Missionary in the North American Colonies. 12mo. Lond., 1846. D 3 P 37

Another copy. (H. and C. Library.) 12mo. Lond., 1846. J 8 P 16

ABBOTT (John S. C.) History of the Civil War in America. Illustrated with Maps and Portraits. 2 vols. roy. 8vo. Springfield, Mass., 1863–66.   B 1 U 17, 18 Another copy. 2 vols. roy. 8vo. Norw., Conn., 1883.   Libr.

ABBOTT (Samuel). Ardenmohr among the Hills: a Record of Scenery and Sports in the Highlands of Scotland. Illustrated. 8vo. Lond., 1876.   D 6 T 21

ABBREVIATIONS. Dictionary of Abbreviations, containing nearly 2,500 Contractions and Signs. Sq. 16mo. Lond., 1886.   K 11 S 2

ABD-AL-LATÍF IBN YÚSUF IBN MUHAMMAD IBN 'ALÍ IBN ALI ALS'AD (Muwaffik al-Dín abu' Muhammad), Al Bagdádí, *called* Ibn Al-Labbád. Relation de l'Egypte: suivie de divers extraits d'Ecrivains Orientaux, et d'un Etat des Provinces et des Villages de l'Egypte dans le xive Siècle: traduit par M. Silvestre de Sacy. 4to. Paris, 1810.   D 2 U 6

ABD-EL-KADER (Emir). Horses of the Sahara; with Commentaries by. [*See* Daumas, E.]   A 1 R 33

ABDULLA (Bin Abdulkadar), Munshi. Translations from the Hakayit Abdulla, with Comments by J. T. Thomson, F.R.G.S. 8vo. Lond., 1874.   C 3 Q 22

ABDU-R-RAHMAN (Nuru-d-din). Yúsuf and Zulaikha: a Poem, by "Jámi." Translated from the Persian into English Verse by R. T. H. Griffith. 8vo. Lond., 1882.   H 8 V 9

Persian Poetry. [*See* Robinson, S.]

ABDY (E. S.) Journal of a Residence and Tour in the United States of North America, from April to October, 1834. 3 vols. 8vo. Lond., 1835.   D 3 Q 48–50

A'BECKET (Thomas), Saint. [*See* Becket, Thomas a'.]

A'BECKETT (Gilbert Abbot). Comic History of England. 2 vols. 8vo. Lond., 1863.   J 10 S 20, 21

A'BECKETT (Hon. T. T.) Law-reforming Difficulties, exemplified in a Letter to Lord Brougham and Vaux, accompanied by an Analysis of a Bill for the Improvement of the Law relating to the Administration of Deceased Persons' Estates. 8vo. Lond., 1849.   MJ 2 R 19 Lectures on Painting, &c. [*See* Melb. Pub. Library, &c.]   MA 2 V 11 [*See* State Aid Question.]   MF 1 Q 6

A'BECKETT (Sir William), Chief Justice of Victoria. Does the Discovery of Gold in Victoria, viewed in relation to its Moral and Social Effects, as hitherto developed, deserve to be considered a National Blessing, or a National Curse? By "Colonus." 8vo. Melb., 1852.   MA 2 Q 35 Another copy (Pam. 31). 8vo. Melb., 1852.   MJ 2 Q 23 The Earl's Choice, and other Poems. 12mo. Lond., 1863.   MH 1 R 48 Lecture delivered before the Members and Friends of the Melbourne Total Abstinence Society. 8vo. Melb., 1851.   MJ 2 R 20

A'BECKETT (Sir William)—*continued.* Lectures on the Poets and Poetry of Great Britain; with an Introductory Lecture on Poetry. 8vo. Sydney, 1839.   MH 1 S 21 Out of Harness. 12mo. Melb., 1854.   MD 4 P 40

ABEILLARD (Pierre), AND HELOÏSE (Abbess). History of the Lives of Abeillard and Heloisa; comprising a period of 84 years, from 1079 to 1163; with their Genuine Letters, by the Rev. Joseph Berington. 4to. Birmingham, 1787.   C 4 W 1

ABEKEN (Bernard Rudolf). Account of the Life and Letters of Cicero. Translated from the German. Ed. by Charles Merivale, B.D. 8vo. Lond., 1854.   C 1 S 18

ABEL (Carl), Ph. D. Linguistic Essays. 8vo. Lond., 1882.   J 11 V 14 Slavic and Latin. Ilchester Lectures on Comparative Lexicography, delivered at the Taylor Institution, Oxford. 8vo. Lond., 1883.   K 12 Q 6

ABEL (C. D.), C.E. Elementary Principles of Machinery, in its Construction and Working. (Weale) 12mo. Lond., 1868.   A 17 P 56 Atlas to [the above.] 4to. Lond., 1860.   A 4 P 1 †

ABELL (Mrs. L. Elizabeth). Recollections of the Emperor Napoleon during the First Three Years of his Captivity on the Island of St. Helena. 8vo. Lond., 1844. C 4 S 26

ABERCROMBIE (John), M.D. Harmony of Christian Faith and Christian Character. 15th ed. 18mo. Edinb., 1838.   G 9 P 33 Inquiries concerning the Intellectual Powers and the Investigation of Truth. 6th ed. 12mo. Edinb., 1835.   G 13 Q 13 Philosophy of the Moral Feelings. 2nd ed. 8vo. Lond., 1834.   G 13 P 31 Another copy. 7th ed. 12mo. Lond., 1846.   G 13 Q 7

ABERCROMBY (Lieut.-Gen. Sir Ralph), K.B. Memoir; by his son James, Lord Dunfermline. 1703–1801. 8vo. Edinb., 1861.   C 1 V 2

ABERDEEN (George), Earl of, K.T., &c. Inquiry into the Principles of Beauty in Grecian Architecture; with an Historical View of the Rise and Progress of the Art in Greece. 12mo. Lond., 1822.   A 2 R 4 Another copy. 12mo. Lond., 1860.   A 2 R 19 Letter to. [*See* Mallalieu, A.] [*See* Vitruvius Pollio, M.]

ABERDEEN PRINTERS. Lives of. [*See* Edmond, J. P.]

ABERNETHY (John), F.R.S. Lectures on Anatomy, Surgery, and Pathology, including Observations on the Nature and Treatment of Local Diseases. 8vo. Lond., 1828.   A 12 T 30 Memoirs of; with a View of his Lectures, Writings, and Character; by G. Macilwain, F.R.C.S. 2 vols. 8vo. Lond., 1853.   C 2 U 4, 5 Surgical Works. 2 vols. 8vo. Lond., 1815. A 12 S 39, 40

ABINGER (Rt. Hon. James), First Lord. Memoir of, including a Fragment of his Autobiography, and Selections from his Correspondence and Speeches; by the Hon. Peter Campbell Scarlett, C.B. With a Portrait. 8vo. Lond., 1877.   C 1 V 1

ABLETT (William H.) English Trees and Tree-planting. 8vo. Lond., 1880.   A 1 S 39

Farming for Pleasure and Profit. Eighth Section: Market-garden Husbandry for Farmers and General Cultivators. 8vo. Lond., 1881.   A 1 Q 8

ABNEY (W. de Wiveleslie), F.R.S. Treatise on Photography. (Text-books of Science.) 8vo. Lond., 1878.   A 17 S 24

Another copy. 2nd ed. 12mo. Lond., 1883.   A 6 V 2

ABOLITIONISTS (The). Abolitionists and Transportationists: a Satirical Poem. 12mo. Hobart, 1847. MH 1 P 17

ABORIGINES. Annual Report. (Pam. Dp.) 8vo. Melb., 1870.   MA 1 R 2

Annual Report of the Mission to the Aborigines, Lake Macquarie; by L. E. Threlkeld. Sydney, 1839. MF 2 U 2

Australian Demigods: Dæmonia. (MS.) (Pam. A.) Fol. Sydney (n.d.)   MJ 2 U 1

Copies of Correspondence between Lieutenant-Governor Arthur and His Majesty's Secretary of State for the Colonies, on the subject of the Military Operations lately carried on against the Aboriginal Inhabitants of Van Diemen's Land. (Parl. Docs. 19:) Fol. Lond., 1831.   MF 4 ‡

Copies of Despatches relative to the Massacre of various Aborigines of Australia, in the year 1838, and respecting the Trial of their Murderers. (Parl. Docs. 19.) Fol. Lond., 1839.   MF 4 ‡

Copies of Instructions given by His Majesty's Secretary of State for the Colonies, for promoting the Moral and Religious Instruction of the Aboriginal Inhabitants of New Holland or Van Diemen's Land. (Parl. Docs. 36.) Fol. Lond., 1831.   MF 4 ‡

Coranderrk Aboriginal Station: Report. Fol. Melb., 1882.   MF 2 U 2

Coranderrk Aboriginal Station: Remarks of the Board. Fol. Melb., 1882.   MF 2 U 2

Despatch from the Governor of N.S.W. respecting Outrages by the Natives in the Bay of Islands, in New Zealand. (Parl. Docs. 47.) Fol. Lond., 1845.   MF 4 ‡

First Annual Report of the Melbourne Church of England Mission to the Aborigines of Victoria. 8vo. Melb., 1855.   MG 1 Q 40

First to Eighteenth Reports of the Board for the Protection of the Aborigines of Victoria. Fol. Melb., 1861-82.   MF 2 U 2

Information respecting the Habits and Customs of the Aboriginal Inhabitants of Western Australia. Compiled from various sources. Fol. Perth, 1871. MF 2 U 2

Introductory Remarks on the Aboriginals of New South Wales. (MS. Pam. A.) Fol. Sydney (n.d.) MJ 2 U 1

ABORIGINES—*continued.*

Native Tribes of South Australia; comprising the Narrinyeri, by the Rev. George Taplin; the Adelaide Tribe, by Dr. Wyatt, J.P.; the Encounter Bay Tribe, by the Rev. A. Meyer; the Port Lincoln Tribe, by the Rev. C. W. Schürmann; the Dieyerie Tribe, by S. Gason; Vocabulary of Woolner District Dialect (Northern Territory), by John Wm. Ogilvie Bennett; with an Introductory Chapter, by J. D. Woods. 8vo. Adelaide, 1879.*   MA 1 R 12

Plan to ameliorate the Condition of the Aboriginal Inhabitants, and prevent their Extermination. 4to. (Pam. E.) Sydney, 1839.   MJ 2 S 2

Plea on behalf of the Aboriginal Inhabitants of Victoria. (Printed for Private Circulation; by J. Strachan). 8vo. Geelong, 1856.   MA 1 R 2

Another copy. (Pam. 29.) Geelong, 1856. MJ 2 Q 17

Remarks upon the Language, Customs, and Physical Character of the Aborigines of Australia; by W.A.M. (MS. Pam. E.) 4to. Sydney (n.d.)   MJ 2 S 2

Remarks on the probable Origin and Antiquity of the Aboriginal Natives of New South Wales. Deduced from certain of their Customs, Superstitions, and existing Caves and Drawings, in connexion with those of the Nations of Antiquity; by "A Colonial Magistrate" [W. Hull]. 8vo. Melb., 1846.   MJ 2 Q 23

Report from the Committee on the Aborigines Question; with the Minutes of Evidence. (Parl. Docs. 32.) Fol. Sydney, 1838.   MF 4 ‡

Report from the Select Committee on Aborigines (British Settlements); with Appendix and Index. Fol. Lond., 1836.   MF 2 U 1

Report on the Aboriginal Stations, Warangesda and Maloga; by the Hon. P. G. King, M.L.C., and Mr. E. Fosbery. Fol. Sydney, 1882.   MF 2 U 2

Report of the Parliamentary Select Committee on Aboriginal Tribes (British Settlements); reprinted, with Comments, by the "Aborigines Protection Society." 8vo. Lond., 1837.   MA 1 R 17

Another copy. (Pam. 6.) Lond., 1837.   MJ 2 Q 1

Report of Sub-Protector [E. L. Hamilton], 1874 [Govt. Gazette, S.A.] Fol. Adelaide, 1875.   MF 2 U 2

Reports of the Aborigines' Protection Board, and Papers relating to the Aborigines of Australia. Fol. Melb., &c., 1839-82.   MF 2 U 2

Royal Commission on the Aborigines.—Report of the Commissioners appointed to inquire into the Aborigines of Victoria. Fol. Melb., 1877.   MF 2 U 2

Superstitions of the Australian Aborigines. (MS.) (Pam. A.) Fol. Sydney (n.d.)   MJ 2 U 1

Tenth Annual Report of the Church of England Mission of the Diocese of Melbourne to the Aborigines. 8vo. Melb., 1864.   MF 3 P 15

Universal Destruction of Aboriginal Races by Colonizing Nations, and eventually of the New Zealanders; the Cause of this Evil, and its sure Preventive. Addressed to the Right Hon. the Earl Grey, Her Majesty's Secretary of State for the Colonies. 8vo. Lond., 1847. MJ 2 Q 8

Vocabulaire des Dialectes des Aborigenes de l'Australie. 8vo. Melb., 1867.   MK 1 Q 27

ABORIGINES' PROTECTION SOCIETY. A11ual Reports, 4th and 6th, of the Aboriginies' Protection Society, presented at the Meetings in Exeter Hall; with Lists of Officers, Subscribers, Benefactors and Honorary and Corresponding Members. 8vo. Lond.,1839–43. MA 1 R 17

Another copy.   MJ 2 Q 3

Extracts from the Papers and Proceedings (Pam. 13). 8vo. Lond., 1841.   MJ 2 Q 3

Another copy. 8vo. Lond., 1841.   MA 1 R 17

Fourth Annual Report, 1841; with Lists of Officers, Subscribers, Benefactors, and Honorary Members. 8vo. Lond., 1841.   MF 2 P 17

Twelfth Annual Report of the Aborigines' Protection Society. 8vo. Lond., 1849.   MF 1 R 4

Thirteenth and Fourteenth Annual Reports of the Aborigines' Protection Society. 8vo. Lond., 1850–51.
                                               MF 1 R 5

Transactions of the Aborigines' Protection Society. [*See* COLONIAL INTELLIGENCER, THE.] MF 1 R 3–5

ABOUT (EDMOND). Greece and the Greeks of the present day. 12mo. London, 1855.   B 9 S 25

ABRANTÈS (MME. LAURA PERMON JUNOT), DUCHESS D'. Memoirs of. 7 vols. 8vo. Lond., 1831–35 C 1 V 3-9

Memoirs of Napoleon: his Court and Family. 2 vols. 8vo. Lond., 1836.   C 5 T 17, 18

ABU TALIB IBN MUHAMMAD *ISFAHANI* Travels of Mirza Abu Taleb Khan in Asia, Africa, and Europe, during the years 1799–1803. Translated by Major Charles Stewart, M.A.S. 2 vols. (in 1) 8vo. Broxbourn, 1810.   D 9 T 30

ABYSSINIA AND ITS PEOPLE. [*See* HOTTEN, J.C.]

ACADÉMIE DES SCIENCES (L'). Comptes rendus hebdomadaires des Séances de l'Académie des Sciences. Tomes 1–101. 4to. Paris, 1835–87.   E

ACADÉMIE IMPÉRIALE (L'). Bulletin de l'Académie Impériale des Sciences de St. Petersbourg. 14 vols. fol. St. Petersburg, 1860–70.   E

ACADEMY OF NATURAL SCIENCES OF PHILADELPHIA. Annual Reports. (Pam. Cl.) 8vo. Philad., 1877.   A 16 U 21

ACCLIMATISATION SOCIETY OF NEW SOUTH WALES. Annual Reports, 1861, 1864, 1866; with an Address on the Physiology, Utility, and Importance of Acclimatisation to Australia, delivered at the Annual Meeting of the Society, April 4th, 1864, by George Bennett M.D., &c.; and the Amended Rules and Proceedings of the Society. 8vo. Sydney, 1862–67. MF 3 P 11

Annual Report. (Pam. 21). 8vo. Sydney, 1864.
                                               MJ 2 Q 10

Rules of the Acclimatisation Society of New South Wales. (Pam. Dl) 8vo. Sydney, 1862. MF 3 P 11

ACCLIMATISATION SOCIETY OF VICTORIA. Establishment of the Acclimatisation Society of Victoria, Feb. 1860. (Pam. Cb.) 8vo. Melb., 1861. A 16 U 25

First Annual Report. (Pam. Dl.) 8vo. Melb., 1862.
                                               MF 3 P 11

First, Fourth, Fifth, Sixth, and Seventh Annual Reports; with the Addresses delivered at the Mechanics' Institute, Melbourne, by His Excellency Sir Henry Barkly, K.C.B., and Professor M'Coy. 8vo. Melb., 1862–71.   ME 1 Q

Rules and Objects of; with the Report adopted at the First General Meeting of the Members, and a List of the Officers, Members, and Subscribers to the Society. 8vo. Melb., 1861–62.   MF 3 P 11

Another copy. 8vo. Melb.,1861.   MJ 2 R 9

[*See* ZOOLOGICAL AND ACCLIMATISATION SOCIETY.]

ACCLIMATISATION OF ANIMALS, &c., WITHIN THE UNITED KINGDOM. SOCIETY FOR. Annual Report, 1864. 8vo. Lond., 1864. MJ 2 R 7

ACCUM (FREDERICK). Chemical Amusement: a series of Experiments in Chemistry. 3rd ed. 12mo. Lond., 1818.   A 5 8 2

Elements of Crystallography, after the method of Haüy. 8vo. Lond., 1813.   A 9 T 22

Treatise on the Art of Making Good and Wholesome Bread. 12mo. Lond., 1821.   A 5 8 2

ACHEEN. Correspondence relative to the Relations between Great Britain and Aehoen, 1873. Fol. Lond., 1873.   F 36 Q 13 ‡

ACHESON (F.) Collection and Storage of Water. [*See* VICTORIAN GOVERNMENT PRIZE ESSAYS.] MJ 2 P 10

ACHILLI (REV. GIACINTO). Dealings with the Inquisition; or, Papal Rome, her Priests, and Jesuits, with Important Disclosures. 12mo. Lond., 1852. G 10 Q 37

Another copy. 2nd ed. 12mo. Lond., 1852. G 10 Q 38

ACHILLES TATIUS. [*See* Heliodorus *and* Scriptores Erotici Graeci.]

ACKERMANN (R.) History of the Abbey Church of St. Peters, Westminster. [*See* COMBE, W.] B 15 S 6, 7‡

History of the Colleges of Winchester, Eton, and Westminster; with the Charter-House, the Schools of St. Paul's, Merchant Taylers, Harrow, Rugby, and the Free School of Christ's Hospital. Imp. 4to. Lond., 1816.   B 19 T 9 ‡

History of the University of Cambridge, its Colleges, Halls, and Public Buildings. 2 vols. roy. 4to. Lond., 1815.   B 19 U 15, 16 ‡

History of the University of Oxford. 2 vols. roy. 4to. Lond., 1814.   B 14 S 6, 7 ‡

Microcosm of London. 3 vols. roy. 4to. Lond., 1808–10.   B 18 S 6–8 ‡

Selections of Ornaments for the use of Sculptors, Painters, Carvers, Modellers, &c. 3 vols. (in 1). fol. Lond., 1817–19.   A 23 R 13 ‡

ACLAND (ARTHUR H. DYKE), M.A., AND RANSOME (CYRIL), M.A. Hand-book in Outline of the Political History of England to 1881, chronologically arranged. 8vo. Lond., 1882. B 3 P 20

ACLAND (REV. T.) Popular Account of the Manners and Customs of India. Illustrated with numerous Anecdotes. (H. and C. Library.) 12mo. Lond., 1847. J 8 P 25

ACORN. [*See* VICTORIA.]

ACOSTA (EMANUEL). Historia Rerum à Societate Jesu in Oriëte Gestarum, ad annum usque à Deipara Virgine MDLXVIII; et recentium de rebus indicis epistolarum liber. usque ad annum 1570. 12mo. Paris, 1572. G 13 Q 4

ACOSTA (FATHER JOSEPH DE). Naturall and Morall Historie of the East and West Indies. Sm. 4to. Lond., 1604. B 1 Q 53

ACROPOLITA (G.) [*See* BYZANTINÆ HIST. SCRIPT., 23.] B 9 U 23

ACT TO REGULATE THE TRADE. of British Possessions abroad. Fol. Lond., 1845. F 8 Q 18 †

ACTA PONTIFICUM ROMANORUM INEDITA. 97–1197; gesammelt und herausgegben von Dr. J. v. Pflugk-Harttung. 2 vols. imp. 800. Tübingen, 1881–84. G 6 V 21, 22

ACTON (R.) Our Colonial Empire. 12mo. Lond., 1881. MD 2 P 4

ACTON (WILLIAM), M.R.C.S. Prostitution, considered in its Moral, Social, and Sanitary Aspects, in London and other Large Cities and Garrison Towns; with Proposals for the Control and Prevention of its Attendant Evils. 2nd. ed. 8vo. Lond., 1870. F 10 P 1 sions abroad. Fol. Lond., 1845. F 8 Q 18 †

ACTORS ANECDOTES OF. [*See* MATHEWS, MRS.] C I V 36 Actors and Art of Acting [*See* LEWES, G. H.] C 4 R 1 Their Majestys' Servants. [*See* DORAN, DR. D.] C 10 U 33, 34

ACTS OF PARLIAMENT. Acts of the Parliament of Queensland. 13 vols. fol. Brisbane, 1866–85. E
Acts of the Parliament of South Australia. 16 vols. 4to. Adelaide, 1837–84. E
Acts of the Parliament of Tasmania; with an Index. 10 vols. fol. Hobart, 1872–84. E
Acts of the Parliament of Victoria. 12 vols. 4to. Melb., 1867–84. E
Miscellaneous Collection of Acts and Regulations, New South Wales. 8vo. Sydney, 1835–71. MF 2 T 5

ACTS AND ORDINANCES. Acts and Ordinances of the Governor and Council of New South Wales, under the Authority of the Act of the Imperial Parliament of the 4th of Geo. IV, Cap. 96; and passed during the Administration of His Excellency Lieut.-Gen. Ralph Darling, 1828–30; with a Table of the Titles, and Indexes. (Parl. Docs. 8.) Fol. Lond., 1831–32. MF 4 ‡

ACTS AND ORDINANCES—*continued.*
Acts and Ordinances of the Province of South Australia. 8 vols. fol. Adelaide, 1837–75. E
Supplement to Acts and Ordinances of New South Wales. [*See* CALLAGHAN, T.] MF 2 S 17–19

ACTS OF COUNCIL. Acts of Council, 41 Vict., 1877. Western Australia. 4to. Perth, 1877. E

ACTS OF THE PARLIAMENT OF SCOTLAND. [*See* SCOTLAND.] F 24 P 1–11 ‡

ADAIR (RT. HON. SIR ROBERT). Historical Memoir of a Mission to the Court of Vienna, in 1806. 8vo. Lond., 1844. B 7 R 36

ADAIR (RT. HON. SIR R.), AND SPENCER (W. R.) Sketch of the Character of the late Duke of Devonshire. Sm. 4to. Lond., 1811. C 10 U 9

ADALBERT OF PRUSSIA (H.R.H. PRINCE). Travels in the South of Europe and in Brazil, with a Voyage up the Amazon and the Xingu. Translated by Sir R. H. Schomburgk and J. E. Taylor. 2 vols. 8vo. Lond., 1849. D 9 T 21, 22

ADAM (ALEXANDER). Roman Antiquities; or, an Account of the Manners and Customs of the Romans. 12th ed. Enlarged by the Rev. J. R. Major. 8vo. Lond., 1835. B 11 V 8

ADAM (JAMES). Twenty-five Years of Emigrant Life in the South of New Zealand. 8vo. Edinb., 1874. MD 4 V 28

ADAM (ROBERT AND JAMES). Architecture, Decoration, and Furniture of. Selected from "Works in Architecture published," 1778–1822, and Photolithographed from the Originals. Imp. 4to. Lond., 1880. A 1 P 14 ‡

ADAM (V.) The French Comic Annual. Ob. 18mo. Lond., 1842. J 1 V 36

ADAM (WILLIAM). Inquiry into the Theories of History, with special reference to the Principles of the Positive Philosophy. 2nd ed. 8vo. Lond., 1864. G 5 P 3

ADAM OF ST. VICTOR. Liturgical Poetry of. From the Text of Gautier. With Translations into English in the original Metres, and short explanatory Notes; by Digby S. Wrangham, M.A. 3 vols. 8vo. Lond., 1881. H 8 R 17–19

ADAMNAN. (ABBOT OF IONA). Life of St. Columba, founder of Hy.; Edited by William Reeves, D.D., &c. (Historians of Scotland). 8vo. Edinb., 1874. B 13 P 40

ADAMS (ANDREW LEITH), M.D. Field and Forest Rambles; with Notes and Observations on the Natural History of Eastern Canada. 8vo. Lond., 1873. A 14 R 42
Wanderings of a Naturalist in India, the Western Himalayas and Cashmere. 8vo. Edinb., 1867. D 5 T 21

ADAMS (ARTHUR), BAIKIE (W. B.), AND BARRON (C.) Manual of Natural History, for the use of Travellers. 12mo. Lond., 1854. A 17 T 39

ADAMS (CHARLES), JUNR. Report of the Treasurer and Receiver-General of the Commonwealth of Massachusetts, for the Year ending December 31, 1875. (Pam. Dz.) 8vo. Boston, 1876.   F 7 S 23

ADAMS (CHARLES FRANCIS). Memoirs of John Quincey Adams: comprising portions of his Diary from 1795–1848. 12 vols. 8vo. Philad., 1874–77.   C 10 V 1-12

ADAMS (CHARLES FRANCIS), JUNR. Railroads; their Origin and Problems. 8vo. New York, 1879.   A 6 R 19

ADAMS (CHARLES KENDALL), L.L.D. Manual of Historical Literature; comprising brief Descriptions of the most important Histories in English, French, and German. 8vo. New York, 1882.   B 14 Q 45

ADAMS (C. WARREN). A Spring in the Canterbury Settlement. With Engravings. 8vo. Lond., 1853.*   MD 5 Q 1

ADAMS (FRANCIS). History of the Elementary School Contest in England. 8vo. Lond., 1882.   G 17 Q 26

ADAMS (SIR FRANCIS OTTIWELL), K.C.M.G., F.R.G.S. History of Japan from the earliest period to the year 1871. 2 vols. 8vo. Lond., 1874–75.   B 12 S 8, 9

ADAMS (FRANCIS W. L.) Australian Essays. 8vo. Melb., 1886.   MJ 1 R 29

ADAMS (H. B.) [*See* JOHNS HOPKINS UNIVERSITY STUDIES.]   B 18 S 1-3

ADAMS (H. G.) Dr. Livingston; his Life and Adventures in the Interior of South Africa. Illustrated. 8vo. Lond., 1857.   C 3 P 19

ADAMS (JOHN). Voyage to South America. [*See* ULLOA, DON ANTONIO DE.]   D 4 Q 1, 2

ADAMS (JOHN), L.L.D. Defence of the Constitutions of Government of the United States of America, against the Attack of M. Turgot in his Letter to Dr. Price, March, 1778. 3 vols. 8vo. Lond., 1794. B 15 R 15-17

ADAMS (J. C.) An Explanation of the Observed Irregularities in the Motion of Uranus. (Pam. 24.) 8vo. Lond., 1846.   MJ 2 Q 12

ADAMS (JOHN QUINCY). An Eulogy on the Life and Character of James Madison. (Pam. I.) 8vo. Boston, 1836.   MJ 2 P 36

Memoirs of; comprising portions of his Diary, from 1795 to 1848. Edited by Charles Francis Adams. 12 vols. 8vo. Philad., 1874–77.   C 10 V 1-12

ADAMS (MAURICE B.), A.R.I.B.A. Artists' Homes: a Portfolio of Drawings, including the Houses and Studios of several eminent Painters, Sculptors, and Architects. Imp. 8vo. Lond., 1883.   A 1 P 15

ADAMS (ROBERT), "ALPHA CRUCIS." Song of the Stars, and other Poems. 8vo. Lond., 1882. MH 1 P 16

ADAMS (SARAH HOLLAND). [*See* GRIMM, H.] C 6 U 16

ADAMS (PROF. W. G.), M.A., &c., AND DAY (R. E.) M.A. The Action of Light on Selenium. (Roy. Soc. Pubs., 4). 4to. Lond., 1877.   A 11 P 5†

ADAMS (W. H. DAVENPORT). Earth and Sea. [*See* FIGUIER, L.]   A 16 V 8

England on the Sea; or, the Story of the British Navy, its Decisive Battles, and Great Commanders. 8vo. Lond., 1885.   B 4 Q 25, 26

Famous Ships of the British Navy; or, Stories of Enterprise and Daring, collected from our Naval Chronicles; and an Appendix on Iron-clad Ships, by N. Barnaby. 12mo. Lond., 1863.   B 3 P 19

Good Queen Anne; or, Men and Manners, Life and Letters in England's Augustan Age. 2 vols. 8vo. Lond., 1886.   B 6 P 21, 22

ADAMS (—) AND FRANCIS (—). List of Newspapers published in London. 4to. Lond., 1862.   MJ 2 U 3

ADAMSON (JOHN), F.S.A. Memoirs of the Life and Writings of Luis de Camoens. 2 vols. 8vo. Lond., 1820.   C 3 S 15, 16

ADAMSON (WILLIAM). Adamson's Australian Gardener: an Epitome of Horticulture for the Colony of Victoria. 10th ed., revised and corrected by William Elliott. 12mo. Melb., 1879.   MA 1 P 8

Australian Gardener. [*See* SMITH & ADAMSON.] MA1P7

ADAMUS BREMENSIS. M. Adami Historia Ecclesiastica, continens Religionis propagatæ gesta. Sm. 4to. Lugd. Bat., 1595.   G 5 P 4

ADAMUS SCOTUS. Opera omnia. [*See* MIGNE, J. P., SERIES LATINA, 198.]

ADDEMAN (JOSHUA M.) Manual, with Rules and Orders for the use of the General Assembly, of the State of Rhode Island, 1873–74. 8vo. Providence, 1874.   F 5 S 6

ADDERLEY (RT. HON. SIR C. B.), K.C.M.G., &c. Review of "The Colonial Policy of Lord J. Russell's Administration"; by Earl Grey, 1853; and of subsequent Colonial History. 8vo. Lond., 1869. MF 2 R 17

ADDIS (WILLIAM E.), AND ARNOLD (THOMAS), M.A. A Catholic Dictionary; containing some Account of the Doctrine, Discipline, Rites, Ceremonies, Councils, and Religious Orders of the Catholic Church. 8vo. Lond., 1884.   K 4 S 12

ADDISON (CHARLES G.) Damascus and Palmyra; a Journey to the East, with a Sketch of the State and Prospects of Syria under Ibrahim Pasha. 2 vols. 8vo. Lond., 1838.   D 4 U 42, 43

History of the Knights Templars, the Temple Church, and the Temple. Sm. 4to. Lond., 1842.   G 5 Q 8

ADDISON (G. R.) Balmain: its Municipality and Institutions. (Pam. Dl.) 12mo. Sydney, 1877. MF 3 P 17

ADDISON (Rt. Hon. Joseph). A Biography; by W. J. Courthope. (Eng. Men of Letts.) 8vo. Lond., 1884.
C 1 U 2

Cato: a Tragedy. (New Eng. Theatre). 12mo. Lond., 1784. H 4 P 25

Another Copy. (Bell's Brit. Theatre). 18mo. Lond., 1791. H 2 P 1

Another Copy. (Brit. Theatre). 12mo. Lond., 1808· H 1 P 8

Another Copy. [*See* Brit. Drama, 1]

The Drummer : a Comedy. (New Eng. Theatre). 12mo. Lond., 1771. H 4 P 22

Another Copy. (Bell's Brit. Theatre). 18mo. Lond., 1792. H 2 P 15

Another Copy. [*See* Brit. Drama, 4.]

Life and Poems of. [*See* Chalmers, A., *and* Johnson, S.]

Life of ; by Lucy Aikin. 2 vols. 8vo. Lond., 1843.
C 2 U 8, 9

Selections from Papers contributed to the *Spectator*. Edited, with Introduction and Notes, by T. Arnold, M.A. (Clar. Press.) 12mo. Oxford, 1875. J 1 T 28

Works of, collected by Mr. [T.] Tickell. 6 vols. roy. 8vo. Lond., 1804. J 8 S 20–25

Selections from. [*See* Harlin, T.] MH 1 P 38

[*See* Ovidius Naso, P.] J 15 P 29, 30

ADDRESS TO PARENTS, from the Teachers of the Independent Sunday School, connected with the Congregation of the Rev. C. Price, inviting them to send their children to a Sunday School. 12mo. Launceston, 1837. MG 1 P 48

ADDRESS TO PRISONERS. [*See* Browning, C. R.]
MG 1 P 9

ADELAIDE [*See* South Australia.]

ADELAIDE (Queen), Consort of William IV. Memoir of ; by Dr. J. Doran. 8vo. Lond., 1861. C 5 Q 1

ADELAIDE OBSERVER (The). For 1844, 1846, and 1857 to 1863. 3 vols. fol. Adelaide, 1844–63. ME †

ADELAIDE PHILOSOPHICAL SOCIETY. [*See* Royal Society of South Australia.] MA 1 Q 17

ADELER (Max) [*See* Clark, C. H.]

ADELUNG (Friedrich). Catherinens der Grossen Verdienste um die vergleichende Sprachenkunde. 4to. St. Petersburg, 1815. K 16 R 8

ADELUNG (Johann Christoph). Grammatisch-kritisches, Wörterbuch der hochdeutschen Mundart, mit beständiger Vergleichung der übrigen Mundarten, besonders aber der Oberdeutschen. 2e auflage, 4 vols. 4to. Leipzig, 1793–1801. K 16 S 20–23

Mithridates oder allgemeine Sprachenkunde, mit dem Vater Unser als Sprachprobe in bey nahe fünfhundert Sprachen und Mundarten. 4 vols. 8vo. Berlin, 1806–1817. K 12 S 21–24

ADLARD (George). Amye Robsart and the Earl of Leycester; a Critical Inquiry into the Authenticity of the Various Statements in Relation to the Death of Amye Robsart, and a History of Kenilworth Castle; with Memoirs and Correspondence of Sir R. Dudley. 8vo. Lond., 1870. B 6 P 48

ADMINISTRATION OF JUSTICE. [*See* New South Wales *and* Tasmania.]

ADMIRALS AND SEAMEN. [*See* British Admirals.]

ADMIRALTY CHARTS. Relating to Australia. At. fol. Lond., 1802–73. MD 5 Q 12 ‡

ADOLPHUS (John H.) History of England, from the Accession to the Decease of George III. 7 vols. 8vo. Lond., 1841–45. B 5 Q 37–43

Memoirs of Caroline, Queen Consort of Great Britain. 3 vols. 8vo. Lond., 1821–22. C 5 T 3–5

Memoirs of John Bannister, Comedian. 2 vols. 8vo. Lond., 1839. C 8 U 4, 5

ADRESS-BUCH DEUTSCHER EXPORT FIRMEN. 4 vols. R. 4to. Berlin, 1883–85. E

ADVENTURES OF A GREEK LADY. [*See* Stephano, C.] D 10 Q 40, 41

ADVENTURES OF A MOUNTED TROOPER in the Australian Constabulary; by "William Burrows." 12mo. Lond., 1859. MD 1 S 53

ADVENTURES OF Mr. NEWCHAMP. Travels and Adventures of Mr. Newchamp; by H. J. L. 8vo. Melb., 1854. MH 1 Q 4

Another copy. 8vo. Melb., 1854. MJ 2 R 19

ADVENTURES OF NAUFRAGUS. [*See* Horne, Mr.] D 5 P 13

ADVIELLE (Victor). Histoire de l'Ordre Hospitalier de Saint Antoine de Viennois, et de ses Commanderies et Prieurés. Roy. 8vo. Paris, 1883. G 8 V 17

AELREDUS RIEVALLENSIS (Beatus). Opera omnia. [*See* Migne, J. P., Series Latina, 195.]

ÆSCHYLUS. Aeschyli Fabulae. In Libro Mediceo mendose scriptae ex vv. dd. coniecturis emendatius editae. Cum Scholiis Graecis et brevi adnotatione critica curante F. A. Paley, M.A., &c. 8vo. Cambridge, 1883. H 8 V 20

Aeschylos Eumeniden, Griechisch und Deutsch mit erläuternden Abhandlungen, von K. O. Müller. 4to. Göttingen, 1833. H 3 V 1

Æschyli Tragœdiæ Superstites et Deperditarum Fragmenta, ex Recensione G. Dindorfii. Editio secunda emendatior. Greek Text and Latin Notes. 2 vols. 8vo. Oxford, 1851. H 1 S 16, 17

Agamemnon of Æschylus and the Bacchanals of Euripides, &c. Translated by H. H. Milman, D.D. sq. 8vo. Lond., 1865. H 8 Q 9

Dramas of. Translated by Anna Swanwick. 3rd ed. 12mo. Lond., 1881. H 4 P 13

ÆSCHYLUS—*continued.*
Anhang zu dem buche Aeschylus Euminiden Griechisch und Deutsch mit erläuternden abhandlungen von K. O. Müller. 4to. Gottingen, 1834. H 3 V 1

Eumenides of Aeschylus. A Critical Edition; with metrical English Translation, by John F. Davies, M.A., &c. 8vo. Dublin, 1885. H 3 S 29

Eumenides of Æschylus, Drawn and Etched. [*See* FARREN, R.] A 8 R 5 †

Lyrical Dramas of Æschylus, from the Greek. Translated into English Verse, by John Stuart Blackie. 2 vols. 8vo. Lond., 1850. H 4 Q 11, 12

Tragedies of. Literally translated; with Critical and Illustrative Notes, and an Introduction, by Theodore Alois Buckley, B.A. 12mo. Lond., 1876. H 4 P 12

Works of. Translated by Rev. R. Potter, M.A. (Fam. Class. Lib.) 18mo. Lond., 1833. J 15 P 1

Tragedies of [*See* GREEK TRAGIC THEATRE.] H 4 R 7–11

ÆSOP.
Dissertation on the Fables. [*See* BENTLEY, R.]
Fables of Æsop and others; translated into Human Nature. Designed and drawn on the wood, by Charles H. Bennett. Roy. 8vo. Lond., 1875. J 8 V 18

Fabularum Æsopicarum Collectio, quotquot Græce reperiuntur. Accedit Interpretatio Latina; by A. Hodson. 8vo. Oxford, 1718. J 4 P 29

Select Fables of Æsop and others, and an Essay upon Fable by Oliver Goldsmith; with the original Wood Engravings, by Thos. Bewick. 8vo. Lond.(n.d.) J 8 R 17

[*See* ANTONIUS LIBERALIS.] J 7 S 30

AFFLECK (THOMAS), AND GRAY (JOHN C.) Border Post Almanac for 1877. 12mo. Albury, 1877. ME 4 Q

AFGHANISTAN. Correspondence respecting the Relations between the British Government and that of Afghanistan since the Accession of the Ameer Shore Ali Khan. Fol. Lond., 1878. B 17 S 12 ‡

AFRICA. Proceedings of the African Association for Promoting the Discovery of the Interior Parts of Africa. [*See* ASSOCIATION.] D 2 V 11, 12

Lands of Cazembe; Lacerda's Journey to Cazembe in 1798; translated and annotated by Captain R. F. Burton, F.R.G.S. ; also Journey of the Pombeiros, P. J. Baptista and Amaro José, across Africa from Angola to Tette on the Zambeze ; translated by B. A. Beadle ; and a Résumé of the Journey of MM. Monteiro, and Gamitto, by Dr. C. T. Beke. 8vo. Lond., 1873. D 1 V 26

Various Important Manuscripts on the Slave Trade, 1536-1792; including Autograph Letters, collected by G. Chalmers. Fol. (MSS.) Africa, 1536-1792. B 19 U 7 ‡

AGANIPPE (THE): a Monthly Journal of Miscellaneous Literature. No. 1. (Fam. B). Roy. 8vo. Sydney, 1872. MJ 2 U 2

AGAPIDA (FRAY ANTONIO). Conquest of Granada. [*See* IRVING, W.]

AGASSIZ (MRS. ELIZABETH CARY). Jean Louis Rodolphe Agassiz, his Life and Correspondence. 2 vols. 12mo. Lond., 1885. C 2 S 2, 3

AGASSIZ (PROF. JEAN LOUIS RODOLPHE), L.L.D. Contributions to the Natural History of the United States of America. Vols. 3, 4. 2 vols. imp. 4to. Boston, 1860–62. A 4 P 10, 11 †

Études critiques sur les Mollusques fossiles. Roy. 4to. Neuchatel, 1840. A 2 Q 22 †

Geological Sketches. 12mo. Lond., 1866. A 9 Q 32

His Life and Correspondence. Edited by Mrs. Elizabeth Cary Agassiz. 2 vols. 8vo. Lond., 1885. C 2 S 2, 3

Histoire naturelle des Poissons d'eau douce de l'Europe centrale. Embryologie des Salmones, par C. Vogt. Imp. 8vo. Neuchatel, 1842. A 14 V 48

Planches [to the above]. Ob. 4to. Neuchatel, 1839. A 13 P 29 I

Memoir of Hugh Miller. [*See* MILLER, H.] J 9 R 9

Monographies d'Echinodermes vivans et fossiles. Roy. 4to. Neuchatel, 1838–42. A 23 R 33 ‡

Nomenclator Zoologicus, continens Nomina Systematica Generum Animalium tam viventium quam fossilium. 4to. Soloduri, 1842–6. A 15 T 8

Types of Mankind. [*See* NOTT, J. C., AND GLIDDON, G. R.] A 2 P 19

AGASSIZ (PROF. LOUIS J. R.), AND AGASSIZ (MRS. LOUIS). A Journey in Brazil. 8vo. Boston, 1879. D 3 S 40

AGASSIZ (PROF. LOUIS J. R.), AND GOULD (A. A.) Outlines of Comparative Physiology, touching the Structure and Development of the Races of Animals. Edited and enlarged by T. Wright, M.D. 12mo. Lond., 1870. A 14 P 63

AGATHIUS. [*See* BYZANTINÆ HIST. SCRIPT., 1.] B 9 U I

AGE ANNUAL (THE). A Political and Statistical Register of the Colony of Victoria, for the year ending 31st December, 1875. 8vo. Melb., 1876. MJ 2 R 10

AGGAS (RADOLPH). London in the Reign of Queen Elizabeth : a Facsimile (reduced) of the Map by R. Aggas, 1560 ; by E. Weller, F.R.G.S. Sheet sm. fol. Lond., (n.d.) D 33 P 4 ‡

AGINCOURT [*See* D'AGINCOURT.]

AGOBARDUS (SANCTUS). Opera omnia. [*See* MIGNE, J. P., SERIES LATINA, VOL. 104.]

AGRICULTURAL CALENDAR, Australia. 8vo. Sydney, 1836. MA 1 P 42

AGRICULTURAL SOCIETY OF ENGLAND (ROYAL). [*See* ROYAL AGRICULTURAL SOCIETY OF ENGLAND.]

AGRICULTURAL AND HORTICULTURAL SOCIETY. Report of the Agricultural and Horticultural Society of New South Wales for 1829. (Pam. 33.) 12mo. Sydney, 1829. MJ 2 Q 21

AGRICULTURAL Report of the Commissioner of United States. [*See* UNITED STATES.] E

AGRICULTURAL RESOURCES OF VICTORIA. [*See* VICTORIA.]   MK 1 R 33

AGRICULTURAL SOCIETY OF N.S. WALES. Anniversary Addresses, List of Members, and Rules and Regulations, of the Agricultural Society of New South Wales, instituted on the 5th of July, 1822. (Pam. 33.) 12mo. Sydney, 1823-26.   MJ 2 Q 21

Catalogue of Live Stock, Farm Produce, and Agricultural Implements, exhibited at the Society's Grounds. Parramatta. (Pam Dl.) 8vo. Sydney, 1860.   MF 3 P 11

Journal of, 1869-71, 1874-75; edited by M. Lowe. 3 vols. imp. 8vo. Sydney, 1869-75.   ME 4 V

Journal of; edited by J. Joubert. 3rd series, 1877. 8vo. Sydney, 1877.*   ME 1 R

Journal of. 3rd series. 8vo. Sydney, 1878.   MJ 2 R 14

AGRICULTURAL SOCIETY, WISCONSIN. Transactions. Madison, 1852-78.

AGRICULTURAL WORKING UNIONS. On Self-supporting Agricultural Working Unions, for the Labouring Classes, shewing the means by which industrious men may raise themselves to a state of comfortable independence in Australia, with or without the assistance of the ruling authorities. (Pam. 10.) 8vo. Sndney. 1844.   MJ 2 Q 2

AGRICULTURE IN S. AUSTRALIA. [*See* SOUTH AUSTRALIA.]

AGRICULTURE IN VICTORIA. [*See* VICTORIA.]

AGUILAR (GRACE). Women of Israel; or, Characters and Sketches from the Holy Scriptures and Jewish History, 2 vols. 12mo. Lond., 1853.   G 13 Q 9, 10

AHMOUY (LOUIS). [*See* CHINESE QUESTION, THE.]
                                                MF 3 P 21

AHMED KHAN (SYED), C.S.I. Life and Work of; by Lieut.-Col.G.F.J.Graham. 8vo. Edinb.,1885. C 3 U 37

AHN (FRANZ), PH.D. Elements of Dutch Grammar, after Dr. Ahn's Method. 3rd ed., thoroughly revised. 12mo. Lond., 1877.   K 11 U 1

Manual of French Conversation, for the use of Schools and Travellers. 12mo. Lond., 1878.   K 11 V 31

New and Easy Method of Learning the Italian Language. First and second Course. Author's own edition. Tenth issue. 12mo. Lond., 1878.   K 11 T 40

New, Practical, and Easy Method of Learning the French Language. First and second Course in one volume. 8vo. Lond., 1878.   K 11 V 30

New, Practical, and Easy Method of Learning the Italian Language. First and second Course. Author's own edition. Eleventh issue. 12mo. Lond.,1881. K 11 T 41

New, Practical, and Easy Method of Learning the German Language. First and second Course in one volume. 8vo. Lond., 1877.   K 11 V 24

B

AHN (FRANZ)—*continued.*
Practical Grammar of the German Language; with a Grammatical Index and Glossary of all the German Words. A new edition, containing numerous Additions, Alterations, and improvements; by Dawson W. Turner, D.C.L., and Frederick L. Weinmann. 8vo. Lond., 1878.   K 11 V 23

AIAZZA (G.) [*See* RINUCCINI, ARCHBISHOP, G. B.]
                                                B 11 P 38

AICHER (OTTO), "DODO RICHEA." Theatrum Funebre, exhibens per varias scenas Epitaphia nova, antiqua, seria, jocosa. 4 parts, in 2 vols. sq. 8vo. Salisburgi, 1673-75.   B 14 R 22, 23

AIKEN (P. F.) Memorials of Robert Burns and of some of his Contemporaries and their Descendants, with a Numerous Selection of his best Poems and Songs, and engraved Portrait, and Fac-Similes. 8vo. Lond., 1876.   H 5 R 3

AIKIN (ARTHUR), F.L.S., &c. Illustrations of Arts and Manufactures. 12mo. Lond., 1841.   A 11 Q 9

AIKIN (JOHN), M.D. Essays on Song-Writing; with a Collection of such English Songs as are most eminent for Poetical Merit. New ed., with Additions and Corrections, and a Supplement; by R. H. Evans. 8vo. Lond., 1810.   H 7 R 18

General Biography; or, Lives, Critical and Historical, of the most Eminent Persons of all Ages, Countries, Conditions, and Professions; by John Aikin, and others. 10 vols. 4to. Lond., 1799-1815.   C 4 W 10-19

Memoir of; with a Selection of his Miscellaneous Pieces, Biographical, Moral, and Critical; by Lucy Aikin. 2 vols. 8vo. Lond., 1823.   C 1 V 17, 18

AIKIN (LUCY). Correspondence of W. E. Channing and Lucy Aikin, from 1826 to 1842; edited by Anna L. Le Breton. 8vo. Lond., 1874.   C 3 8 18

Life of Joseph Addison. 2 vols. 8vo. Lond., 1843.
                                                C 2 U 8, 9

Memoir of John Aikin, M.D.; with a Selection of his Miscellaneous Pieces, Biographical, Moral, and Critical. 2 vols. 8vo. Lond., 1823.   C 1 V 17, 18

Memoir of A. L. Barbauld. [*See* BARBAULD, A. L.]
                                                J 10 V 22, 23

Memoir of Miss [Elizabeth Ogilvy] Berger. [*See* BERGER, MISS ELIZABETH OGILVY.]   C 3 8 5

Memoirs of the Court of King Charles I. 2 vols. 8vo. Lond., 1833.   C 10 P 26, 27

Memoirs of the Court of King James I. 2 vols. 8vo. Lond., 1822.   C 9 R 3, 4

Memoirs of the Court of Queen Elizabeth. 2nd ed. 2 vols. 8vo. Lond., 1818.   C 5 V 11, 12

AIKMAN (JAMES). History of Scotland. [*See* BUCHANAN, GEO.]   B 13 Q 33-38

AILRED (S.) [*See* SCOTLAND, HISTORIANS OF.] B 13 P 49

AINGER (REV. ALFRED). Charles Lamb. (Eng. Men of Letts.) 12mo. Lond., 1882.   C 1 U 22

AINSLIE (HERBERT), B.A. [*See* MAITLAND, E.]
[*See* LAMB, C.]

AINSLIE (JOHN), AND GALBRAITH (W.), M.A., &c.
Treatise on Land Surveying. New and enlarged ed.,
embracing Railway, Military, Marine, and Geodetical
Surveying; with Geodetical Tables for Trigonometrical
Surveying and Levelling. 8vo. Lond., 1849. A 6 S 22
Plates to the above. Ob. 8vo. Lond., 1849. A 6 S 23

AINSWORTH (R.) Latin Dictionary; improved and
enlarged, by Dr. Thos. Morell; revised by John Carey,
LL.D. 4to. Lond., 1823. K 16 S 12

AINSWORTH (W.) Analysis of a Narrative of a Voyage
to the Beering's Strait, under the command of Capt.
F. W. Beechey, R.N., 1825–28. 8vo. Lond., 1833.
MD 7 Q 46

AINSWORTH (WM. FRANCIS). F.R.G.S., &c. All Round
the World: an Illustrated Record of Voyages, Travels,
and Adventures in all Parts of the Globe; edited by
W. F. Ainsworth. 1st and 2nd series. 2 vols. 4to.
Lond., 1872. D 9 V 1, 2
The Earth delineated with Pen and Pencil; or, Voyages,
Travels, and Adventures, all round the World; edited
by W. F. Ainsworth. Illustrated. Imp. 8vo. Lond.,
(n.d.) D 9 V 5
Lares and Penates. [*See* BARKER, W. B.] B 13 V 23
Researches in Assyria, Babylonia, and Chaldæa; forming
part of the Labours of the Euphrates Expedition. 8vo.
Lond., 1838. D 4 U 22
Travels and Researches in Asia Minor, Mesopotamia,
Chaldea, and Armenia. 2 vols. 8vo. Lond., 1842.
D 5 R 31, 32
Travels in the Track of the Ten Thousand Greeks; being
a Geographical and Descriptive Account of the Expe-
dition of Cyrus. 8vo. Lond., 1844. B 9 S 30

AINSWORTH (W. H.) Ainsworth's Magazine No. 1,
1842. (Pam. 15.) 8vo. Lond., 1842. MJ 2 Q 5

AIRD (THOMAS) [*See* MOIR, D. M.]

AIRY (SIR GEORGE B.), K.C.B., &c. On the Tides at
Malta. (Roy. Soc. Pubs. 5.) 4to. Lond., 1878. A 11 P 6†

AITKEN (JOHN). The Cabinet; or, the Selected Beauties
of Literature. 8vo. Lond., 1831. J 12 R 24

AITKEN (PROF. W.) Public Health. [*See* PARKES,
PROF. E. A.) A 12 P 45

AITKEN (W. C.) Birmingham Trades. Guns, Nails,
Locks, Wood screws, Railway Bolts and Spikes, Buttons,
Pins, Needles, Saddlery, and Electroplate. (Brit. Man.
Indust.) 12mo. Lond., 1876. A 17 S 30

AITON (W.) Hortus Kewensis; or, a Catalogue of the
Plants cultivated in the Royal Botanical Garden at
Kew. 3 vols. 8vo. Lond., 1789. A 4 S 20 22

AKENSIDE (MARK), M.D. Pleasures of imagination;
with Life of the Author. 12mo. Glasgow, 1825. H 7 P 5
Life and Poems of. [*See* British Poets, I., CHALMERS, A.,
and JOHNSON, S.]

AKERMAN (JOHN YONGE), F.S.A. Coins of the
Romans relating to Britain, described and illustrated.
8vo. Lond., 1844. A 13 S 10
Descriptive Catalogue of rare and unedited Roman Coins,
from the earliest period of the Roman Coinage, to the
extinction of the Empire, under Constantinus Paleologos.
2 vols. 8vo. Lond., 1834. A 13 S 11, 12
The Numismatic Chronicle; edited by J. Y. Akerman.
F.S.A. 2 vols. 8vo. Lond., 1839, 40. A 13 S 44, 45

ALABASTER (HENRY). The Wheel of the Law: Buddhism, illustrated from Siamese Sources. 8vo. Lond.,
1871. G 11 T 29

ALACOQUE (Marie Marguerite.) Vie de. [*See* CAPEFIGUE,
J. B. H. R.]

ALAN OF TEWKESBURY. Materials for the History
of Thomas Becket. [*See* CHRONICLES, &c., OF GREAT
BRITAIN AND IRELAND, 139.]

ALANUS DE INSULIS. Opera omnia. [*See* MIGNE,
J. P., SERIES LATINA, 210.] G

A LASCO (JOHN): his Earlier Life and Labours; by Dr.
Hermann Dalton; translated from the German, by Rev.
Maurice J. Evans, B.A. 8vo. Lond., 1886. C 5 R 3

ALBANY [U. STATES] DIRECTORY (THE). For
the Year 1875. Containing a General Directory of the
Citizens, a Business Directory, Record of the City
Government, its Institutions, &c., &c. 8vo. Albany,
N.Y., 1875. E

ALBEMARLE (GEN. GEORGE MONK), DUKE OF. Life
of General Monk, Duke of Albemarle; published from
an original MS. of Thomas Skinner, M.D. 2nd ed.
8vo. Lond., 1724. C 3 U 46
Memoirs of George Monk, Duke of Albemarle; from
the French of M. Guizot; translated and edited by Hon.
J. Stuart Wortley. 8vo. Lond., 1838. C 8 R 30
Monk and Washington: Historical Studies, by F. P.
Guizot. 12mo. Lond., 1851. C 1 R 26

ALBEMARLE (GEORGE THOMAS), EARL OF. Memoirs
of the Marquis of Rockingham and his Contemporaries;
with Original Letters and Documents, now first published. 2 vols. 8vo. Lond., 1852. C 9 R 16, 17
Fifty Years of my Life. 2 vols. 8vo. Lond., 1876.
C 1 V 25, 26

ALBERT (H.R.H. PRINCE). Early Years of H.R.H. the
Prince Consort; compiled by Lieut.-Gen. the Hon. C.
Grey. 8vo. Lond., 1867. C 1 V 19
Another copy. [*Presented by Her Majesty the Queen.*]
8vo. Lond., 1867. Libr.
Life of H.R.H. the Prince Consort; by Sir Theodore
Martin; with Portraits and Views. 5 vols. 8vo. Lond.,
1875–80. C 1 V 20–24
Life of the Prince Consort; by E. Walford, M.A. 12mo.
Lond., 1862. C 1 P 2
Memorial of the Royal Progress in Scotland. [*See*
LAUDER, SIR T. D.] D 6 V 27

ALBERT (H.R.H.) PRINCE—*continued.*
Prince Albert and the House of Saxony; with a Memoir of the Reigning Family of Saxe-Coburg-Gotha, by Frederic Shoberl. 8vo. Lond., 1840.　　C 1 U 1

Prince Albert's Land. [*See* GREIG, C. M.]　　D 7 P 28

Principal Speeches and Addresses of H.R.H. the Prince Consort. 8vo. Lond., 1862.　　J 10 S 1

Another copy. [*Presented by Her Majesty the Queen.*] 8vo. Lond., 1862.　　Libr.

The Ancestry of Her Majesty Queen Victoria, and of His Royal Highness Prince Albert; by G. R. French. 8vo. Lond., 1841.　　C 5 R 27

The Crown and the Cabinet: five Letters on the Biography of the Prince Consort; by "Verax" [H. Dunckley.] (Pam. Jd.) 12mo. Manchester, 1878.　　MF 1 P 23

The Early Homes of. [*See* RIMMER, A.]　　D 7 T 18

ALBERT (PAUL). La Littérature Française au XVIIIᵉ Siècle. 8vo. Paris, 1874.　　B 8 P 6

ALBERT D'AIX. Histoire des Croisades. [*See* GUIZOT, F. P. G., 20, 21.]　　B 8 T 21-22

ALBERT EDWARD (PRINCE OF WALES). Five Months with the Prince in India. [*See* INDIA.]　　D 4 V 26

The Prince of Wales' Tour: a Diary in India. [*See* RUSSELL, W. H.]　　D 4 V 26

ALBERT VICTOR OF WALES (PRINCE), AND GEORGE OF WALES (PRINCE). Cruise of H. M. S. *Bacchante,* 1879-82 ; compiled from the private Journals, Letters, and Note-books of Prince Albert Victor and Prince George of Wales, by John N. Dalton. 2 vols. 8vo. Lond., 1886.　　MD 2 V 21, 22

ALBERTIS (L. M. d') [*See* D'ALBERTIS, L. M.]

ALBINUS (B. FLACCUS). Opera omnia. [*See* MIGNE, J. P., SERIES LATINA, 100, 101.]

ALBIRUNI (ABU-RAIHAN MUHAMMAD D'AHMAD). Chronology of Ancient Nations ; an English Version of the Arabic Text of the Athâr-ul-Bâkiya of Albîrûnî, or "Vestiges of the Past"; translated by Dr. C. Edward Sachau. Roy. 8vo. Lond., 1879.　　B 15 S 8

ALBITES (ACHILLE), LL.B. How to speak French ; or, French and France. Facts, Inductions, Practice. 13th ed. 12mo. Lond., 1876.　　K 11 T 45

ALBOUIS D'AZINCOURT (JOSEPH JEAN BAPTISTE). Mémoires de. [*See* BARRIÈRE, J. F., 6.]　　C 1 T 6

ALBRIZZI (COUNTESS). [*See* CANOVA, A.]　　A 8 T 6-8

ALBUM DER NEUERN DEUTSCHEN LYRIK. [*See* EICHERT, O.]

ALCEDO (COL. DON ANTONIO DE) AND THOMPSON (G. A.) Geographical and Historical Dictionary of America and the West Indies. 5 vols. 4to. Lond., 1812-15.　　D 9 R 20-24 †

ALCIATI (ANDREA), and his Book of Emblems: a Biographical and Bibliographical Study ; by Henry Green, M.A. 8vo. Lond., 1872.　　C 5 U 1

ALCINUS. Introduction to the Doctrines of Plato. [*See* Plato.]

ALCOCK (HENRY) *v.* FERGIE (HENRY PENKETH). Judgments against the Crown by Default as a substitute for an Appropriation Act ; being a Report of the Case of Alcock *v.* Fergie, argued and determined in the Supreme Court of the Colony of Victoria. 8vo. Melb., 1867.　　MF 1 Q 1

[*See* PARSONS, T.]　　MJ 2 R 12

ALCOCK (RANDAL H.), F.L.S. Botanical Names for English Readers. 8vo. Lond., 1884.　　A 4 T 21

ALCOCK (SIR RUTHERFORD), K.C.B. The Capital of the Tycoon : a Narrative of a Three Years' Residence in Japan. 2 vols. 8vo. Lond., 1863.　　D 5 T 19, 20

Margary's Journey from Shanghae to Biamo. [*See* MARGARY, A. R.]　　D 4 T 8

ALCOCK & CO. Billiard Table Manufacturers: Opinions of the Press. 8vo. Melb., 1873.　　MJ 2 R 15

ALCOTT (W. A.) Woman's Mission ; or, Letters to a Sister. 12mo. Lond., 1852.　　J 10 P 1

ALCUIN (FLACCUS ALBINUS). Life of Alcuin ; by Dr. F. Lorenz ; translated from the German, by Jane M. Slee. 12mo. Lond., 1837.　　C 1 R 2

Opera omnia. [*See* MIGNE, J. P., SERIES LATINA, 100, 101.]

ALDEN (L. P.) State Public School at Coldwater ; its Purposes and Aims ; an Address. (Pam., Bs.) 8vo. Coldwater, 1876.　　MG 1 Q 34

ALDER (JOSHUA), AND HANCOCK (A.) [*See* RAY SOCIETY, 2, 3.]

ALDERSON (EDWARD HALL), BARON. Selections from the Charges, and other Detached Papers of; with a Notice of his Life, by C. Alderson, M.A. 8vo. Lond., 1858.　　C 4 T 1

ALDERSON (CHARLES), M.A. Selections from the Charges and other Detached Papers of Baron Alderson ; with an Introductory Notice of his Life. 8vo. Lond., 1858.　　C 4 T 1

ALDERTON (GEO. E.) Treatise and Hand-book of Orange-Culture in Auckland, New Zealand. 8vo. Wellington, 1884.*　　MA 1 Q 41

ALDINE Press. (The) Catalogue of. [*See* TOOVEY, J.]

ALDUS MANUTIUS, OR MANUZIO (PIUS ROMANUS). Annales de. [*See* RENOUARD, A.]　　K 17 Q 30, 31

ALDWELL (J. A.) Prize Essay of the Melbourne Labor League, on the Eight Hours and Early Closing Questions. (Pam. 36.) 8vo. Melb., 1856.　　MJ 2 Q 23

ALEMBERT (JEAN LE ROND D'). [*See* D'ALEMBERT, J. LE R.]　　K 4 P 4-6

ALEXANDER I (EMPEROR OF RUSSIA). Life and Times of Alexander I, Emperor of all the Russias; by C. Joyneville. 3 vols. 8vo. Lond., 1875.   C 1 V 27–29.

ALEXANDER II. Life of Alexander II, Emperor of all the Russias; by C. Joyneville. 12mo. Lond., 1883.   C 1 S 8

ALEXANDER III (PAPA). Opera omnia. [*See* MIGNE, J. P., SERIES LATINA, 200.]

ALEXANDER THE GREAT. De rebus gestis Alexandri Magni. [*See* CURTIUS RUFUS, Q.]   J 13 S 19–22

Life and Actions of; by the Rev. John Williams. 18mo. Lond., 1829.   C 1 P 4

Scriptores Rerum Alexandri Magni, &c. [*See* ARRIANI, F.]   B 10 V 9

ALEXANDER (ARCHIBALD), D.D. Brief Outline of the Evidences of the Christian Religion. 3rd ed. 18mo. Edinb., 1830.   G 9 P 14

ALEXANDER (A. J.) Colonial Guide; or, the Emigrant's Hand-book to the best Colony. 8vo. Melb.,1862.   MJ 2 R 9

ALEXANDER (MISS FRANCESCA). "FRANCESCA." Story of Ida : Epitaph on an Etrurian Tomb; edited by John Ruskin. 3rd ed. 12mo. Lond., 1885.   C 2 Q 22

Roadside Songs of Tuscany; translated and edited by John Ruskin, LL.D. 4to. Orpington, 1885.   H 5 V 7

ALEXANDER (MAJ.-GEN. SIR JAMES E.) KNT., &c. Bush Fighting; illustrated by remarkable actions and incidents of the Maori War in New Zealand. 8vo. Lond., 1873.   MD 5 R 9

Expedition of Discovery into the Interior of Africa. 2 vols 8vo. Lond., 1838.   D 1 Q 9, 10

Incidents of the Maori War, New Zealand, in 1860–61. 8vo. Lond., 1863*   MB 1 Q 25

L'Acadie; or, Seven Years' Explorations in British America. 2 vols. 12mo. Lond., 1849.   D 4 P 1, 2

Notes on the Maories of New Zealand; with Suggestions for their pacification and preservation. 8vo. Lond., 1865.   MB 2 R 38

Sketches in Portugal during the Civil War of 1834; with observations on the present state and future prospects of Portugal. 8vo. Lond., 1835.   D 7 U 8

Transatlantic Sketches, comprising Visits to the most interesting scenes in North and South America and the West Indies; with Notes on Negro Slavery and Canadian Emigration. 2 vols. 8vo. Lond., 1833.   D 3 S 43, 44

ALEXANDER (W.) Johnny Gibb of Gushetneuk, in the Parish of Pyketillim. Roy.8vo. Edinb.,1880.   J 8 V 17

ALEXANDER (PROF. W. D.) Short Synopsis of the most Essential Points in Hawaiian Grammar. 12mo. Honolulu, 1864.   M 5 1 P 19

ALEXANDER (WILLIAM LINDSAY), D.D., &c. Cyclopædia of Biblical Literature. [*See* KITTO, J.]   K 4 S 15–17

ALFIERI (VITTORIO). Tragedies of. Translated from the Italian, by Charles Lloyd. 3 vols. 12mo. Lond., 1815.   H 3 P 12–14

Mémoires de. [*See* BARRIÈRE, J. F., 26.]   C 1 T 26

ALFORD (HENRY), D.D., DEAN OF CANTERBURY. Greek Testament; with a critically revised Text; a Digest of various Readings; Marginal References to verbal and idiomatic usage : Prolegomena, and a Critical and Exegetical Commentary. 5th ed. 4 vols. 8vo. Lond., 1863–66.   G 5 P 6–9

Life, Journals, and Letters of; edited by his Widow. 2nd ed. 8vo. Lond., 1873.   C 10 R 3

New Testament for English Readers; containing the Authorized Version, with Marginal Corrections of Readings and Renderings, Marginal References, and a Critical and Explanatory Commentary. 3rd ed. 2 vols. (in 4). 8vo. Lond., 1872.   G 5 P 10–13

The Queen's English; a Manual of Idiom and Usage. 5th ed., revised and considerably enlarged. 12mo. Lond,, 1878.   K 11 U 20

ALFORD (LADY MARION MARGARET). Needlework as Art. Roy. 8vo. Lond., 1886.   A 8 R 36

ALFRED DUDLEY; or, the Australian Settlers. 12mo. Lond., 1830.*   MJ 1 Q 41

ALFRED ERNEST ALBERT (PRINCE), DUKE OF EDINBURGH, K.G., &c. [*See* EDINBURGH, DUKE OF.] MD 6 Q 10

ALFRED THE GREAT. Anglo-Saxon Version of Boetius. [*See* BOETHIUS, A.M.T.S.]   G 4 R 11

[History of the World] Anglo-Saxon Version, from the Historian Orosius. [*See* OROSIUS, P.]   B 14 R 28

Life and Times of; by the Rev. J. A. Giles, D.C.L. 8vo. Lond., 1848.   C 1 V 12

Life of King Alfred; by Dr. Reinhold Pauli; edited by Thomas Wright, Esq., M.A., &c. 8vo. Lond., 1852.   C 8 T 1

Life of; by A. G. Knight. 12mo. Lond.,1880.   C 2 T 1

Life of; by Sir John Spelman, Kt., from the original MS. in the Bodleian Library; with additions, &c.; by Thomas Hearne, M.A. 8vo. Oxford, 1709.   C 2 U 6

Life of; with his Maxims, and those of his Counsellors; by Francis Steinitz. 8vo. Lond., 1849.   C 5 Q 2

Proverbs of Alfred. [*See* EARLY ENGLISH TEXT SOC., 8]   E

The whole Works of King Alfred the Great; with Essays, &c. Jubilee Edition. 2 vols. roy. 8vo. Oxford, 1852.   B 5 V 19, 20

West-Saxon Version of Gregory's Pastoral Care. [*See* EARLY ENGLISH TEXT SOC., 7]   E

ALGAR (F.) Hand-book to the Colony of Victoria (Australia). 8vo. Lond., 1863.   MJ 2 R 9

ALGAROTTI (FRANCESCO), COUNT, F.R.S., &c. Essay on Painting, written in Italian. 12mo. Lond., 1764.   A 7 P 36

ALI (SYED AMEER), M.A., &c. Personal Law of the Mahommedans. (According to all the Schools.) Together with a Comparative Sketch of the Law of Inheritance among the Sunnis and the Shiahs. 8vo. Lond., 1880.
F 4 Q 11

ALI PASHA. Life of Ali Pacha, of Jannina, late Vizier of Epirus, surnamed Aslan, or the Lion, including a compendious History of Modern Greece. 2nd ed. Illustrated. 8vo. Lond., 1823. C 8 U 1

Life of Ali Pasha, of Tepeleni, Vizier of Epirus, surnamed Aslan, or the Lion; by R. A. Davenport. 18mo. Lond., 1837. C 1 P 3

ALI-TCHÉLÉBI-BEN-SALEH. [*See* CABINET DES FÉES, 17, 18.]

ALIBERT (JEAN LOUIS), BARON. Physiologie des Passions, ou Nouvelle Doctrine des Sentimens Moraux. Troisième édition, revue et considérablement augmentée. 2 vols. 8vo. Paris, 1837. G 5 P 27, 28

ALICE (H.R.H. PRINCESS). Alice, Grand Duchess of Hesse, Princess of Great Britain and Ireland: Biographical Sketch and Letters. With Portraits. 8vo. Lond., 1884. C 3 V 1

ALIPH CHEEM. [*See* YELDHAM, W.]

ALIQUIS. [*See* HENDERSON, CAPT. —.]

ALISON (REV. ARCHIBALD), LL.B. Essays on the Nature and Principles of Taste. 6th ed. 2 vols. 8vo. Edinb., 1825. G 15 Q 13, 14

Essays on the Nature and Principles of Taste. [*See* JEFFREY, LORD F.] G 13 Q 6

Sermons, chiefly on particular occasions. 2nd ed. 2 vols. 8vo. Edinb., 1814. G 5 P 19, 20

ALISON (SIR ARCHIBALD), BART., D.C.L. History of Europe, from the Commencement of the French Revolution in 1789, to the Restoration of the Bourbons in 1815. 10 vols. 8vo. Edinb., 1839–42. B 7 U 1–10

History of Europe, from the Fall of Napoleon in 1815, to the Accession of Louis Napoleon in 1852; with Index. 9 vols. 8vo. Edinb., 1852–59. B 7 U 11–19

Lives of Lord Castlereagh and Sir Charles Stewart, the second and third Marquesses of Londonderry. 3 vols. 8vo. Lond., 1861. C 8 S 44–46

Military Life of John, Duke of Marlborough. 8vo. Lond., 1848. C 7 T 39

Practice of the Criminal Law in Scotland. 8vo. Edinb., 1833. F 10 P 7

Principles of Population, and their connection with Human Happiness. 2 vols. 8vo. Edinb., 1840. F 10 P 9, 10

Principles of the Criminal Law of Scotland. 8vo. Edinb., 1832. F 10 P 8

Some Account of my Life and Writings: an Autobiography; edited by his Daughter-in-law, Lady Alison. 2 vols. 8vo. Edinb., 1883. C 8 U 2, 3

ALISON (W. P.), M.D., &c. Outlines of Human Physiology. 3rd ed. 8vo. Edinb., 1839. A 12 T 4

ALL SERENE. Narrative of the Wreck of the Ship *All Serene;* by "One of the Survivors"; with a Preface by the Rev. Thomas Smith. (Pam. Aa.) 8vo. Sydney, 1864. MD 1 V 9

ALL THE YEAR ROUND: a Weekly Journal, conducted by Charles Dickens; with which is incorporated "Household Words." 64 vols. Roy. 8vo. Lond., 1859–87. E

ALLAN (JAMES). New, improved, and authentic Life of James Allan, the celebrated Northumberland Piper; including a complete Description of the Manners and Customs of the Gipsy Tribes, collected by James Thompson. 8vo. Newcastle-upon-Tyne, 1828. C 6 P 1

ALLAN (ROBERT), F.R.S.E., &c. Manual of Mineralogy, comprehending the more recent discoveries in the Mineral Kingdom. 8vo. Edinb., 1834. A 10 P 10

ALLARDYCE (ALEXANDER). Memoir of the Hon. George Keith Elphinstone, K.B., Viscount Keith, Admiral of the Red. 8vo. Edinb., 1882. C 6 Q 29

ALLEGRI (ANTONIO), DA CORREGGIO. [*See* CORREGGIO, A. ALLEGRI DA.] C 8 V 2

ALLEN (ALFRED H.), F.C.S. Introduction to the Practice of Commercial Organic Analysis. 2 vols. 8vo. Lond., 1879–82. A 5 T 1, 2

Another copy. 2nd ed., revised and enlarged. 2 vols. 8vo. Lond., 1885–86. A 5 T 3, 4

ALLEN (A. P.) Ambassadors of Commerce. Illustrated by Sturgess. 8vo. Lond., 1885. J 1 U 9

ALLEN (C. BRUCE). Cottage Building. (Weale). 12mo. Lond., 1870. A 17 P 29

ALLEN (C. B. AND E. E.) Cottage Building. 10th ed., revised, and enlarged. (Weale.) 12mo. Lond., 1886. A 17 Q 70

ALLEN (CHARLES GRANT BLAIRFINDIE). Charles Darwin. (Eng. Worthies.) 8vo. Lond., 1885. C 2 Q 13

Colour-Sense; its Origin and Development: an Essay in Physiological Æsthetics. 8vo. Lond., 1877. A 12 Q 33

Comparative Psychology. 8vo. Lond., 1879. A 16 R 8

ALLEN (CHAS. H.), F.R.G.S. Visit to Queensland and her Gold-fields. 8vo. Lond., 1870.* MD 5 P 20

ALLEN (E. HERON). Violin-making as it was and is. Illustrated. 8vo. Lond., 1884. A 7 U 3

ALLEN (HENRY B.) Useful Companion and Artificer's Assistant: a Complete Encyclopædia of valuable Information, including thousands of valuable Recipes, Formulas, &c. 8vo. New York, 1881. K 9 U 29

ALLEN (ROBERT). Public Schools of Rhode Island [*See* UNITED STATES].

ALLEN (REV. I. N.), B.A. Diary of a March through Sinde and Affghanistan, with the Troops under General Sir W. Nott, K.C.B. 8vo. Lond., 1843. D 5 P 45

ALLEN (JAMES). Allen's Twopenny Trası. Vol. 1, Nos. 2, 3. (Pam. H.) 8vo. Adelaide, 1858. ME 3 R

History of Australia, from 1787 to 1882. 8vo. Melb., 1882.* MB 2 P 41

Journal of an Experimental Trip by the *Lady Augusta* on the River Murray. 8vo. Adelaide, 1853. MD 5 T 5

Soutı Australian Almanack and General Colonial Directory. 12mo. Adelaide, 1849. ME 4 P

[*See also* SOUTH AUSTRALIAN MAGAZINE.] ME 3 R

ALLEN (JOHN).˙ Inquiry into the Rise and Growtı of the Royal Prerogative in England. 8vo. Lond.,1849. F10P6

ALLEN (JOSEPH), R.N. Battles of the Britisı Navy. New edition, revised and enlarged. 2 vols. 8vo. Lond., 1878–80. B 4 Q 1, 2

ALLEN (LEWIS F.) History of the Short-ıorn Cattle; tıeir Origin, Progress, and Present Condition. 8vo. Buffalo, N.Y., 1883. A 1 S 7

ALLEN (THOMAS). History and Antiquities of London: Westminster, Soutıwark, and parts adjacent; continued to the Present Time, by Tıomas Wright. 5 vols. 8vo. Lond., 1837. B 7 P 16–20

History and Antiquities of the Parisı of Lambetı, and the Arcıiepiscopal Palace, in the County of Surrey. Illustrated by Engravings. Roy. 8vo. Lond.,1826. B 5 V 22

New and Complete History of the County of Surrey; comprising every Object of Topograpıical, Geológical, or Historical interest. Illustrated witı Views from original Drawings, by N. Whittock. 2 vols. roy. 8vo. Lond., 1831. B 4 U 20, 21

New and Complete History of the County of York, illustrated by a series of Views engraved on Steel, from Original Drawings; by N. Whittock. 6 vols. 8vo. Lond., 1828–31. B 6 R 8–13

Anotıer copy. 3 vols. 4to. Lond.,1828–31. B 4 V 1–3

ALLEN (Tımotıy F.), A.M., M.D., &c. Encyclopedia of Pure Materia Medica: a Record of the positive Effects of Drugs upon the Healtıy Human Organism. 10 vols. roy. 8vo. New York, 1876–79. K 2 P 8–17

ALLEN (WILLIAM), F.R.S. American Biographical and Historical Dictionary. 2nd ed. 8vo. Boston, 1832. C 11 U 31

Life of; witı Selections from ıis Correspondence. 3 vols. 8vo. Lond., 1846–47. C 10 P 1–3

Memoir of; by the Rev. James Sıerman. 8vo. Lond., 1851. C 2 U 2

ALLEN (Capts. W.), R.N., AND THOMSON (T. R. H.), M.D., &c., Narrative of the Expedition sent by H.M. Government to the River Niger in 1841, under the command of Capt. H. D. Trotter, R.N. 2 vols. 8vo. Lond., 1848. D 2 T 13, 14

ALLEN (W. B.) Lecture on Protection. Political Economy proper for New Soutı Wales. (Pam. 26.) 12mo. Sydney (n.d.) MJ 2 Q 14

ALLEN (WM. H.) & Co. Catalogue of Printed and Litıó- grapıed Books in the Eastern Languages; to wıicı is added a list of Oriental Manuscripts. 12mo. Lond., 1864. K 7 R 52

ALLEN (ZACHARIAH), LL.D. Solar Ligıt and Heat; the source and the supply. Gravitation; witı explanations of Planetary and Molecular Forces. 8vo. New York, 1879. A 3 T 26

ALLEY (GEORGE UNDERWOOD). Original Songs. 8vo. Sydney, 1850. MF 1 R 17

ALLGEMEINE DEUTSCHE BIOGRAPHIE. 22 vols. roy. 8vo. Leip., 1875–85. C 20 P 22

ALLIBONE (S. AUSTIN). Critical Dictionary of Englisı Literature and Britisı and American Autıors, living and deceased, from the earliest accounts to the middle of the 19th Century. 3 vols. imp. 8vo. Philad., 1859–71. K 17 S 1–3

Prose Quotations, from Socrates to Macaulay; witı Indexes. Autıors, 544; Subjects, 571; Quotations, 8,810. 8vo. Philad., 1882. K 17 R 21

ALLIES (THOMAS W.), M.A. Formation of Cıristendom. 3 vols. 8vo. Lond., 1865–75. G 5 Q 5–7

St. Peter; ıis Name and ıis Office, as set fortı in Holy Scripture. 2nd ed. 8vo. Lond., 1871. G 13 Q 5

ALLINGHAM (JOHN TILL). The Weathercock: a Farce (Cumberland's Eng. Tıeatre). 12 mo. London, 1829. H 2 Q 16

ALLINGHAM (W.) [*See* DOYLE, R.] A 23 P 19 ‡

ALLISON (Tıomas). Account of a Voyage from Arcı- angel, in Russia, in the year 1697. 12mo. Lond., 1699. D 7 P 22

ALLMAN (PROF. GEORGE JAMES), M.D., &c. On the Structure and Development of Myriothela. (Roy. Soc. Pubs. 2.) 4to. Lond., 1876. A 11 P 3†

Vegetation of the Riviera. [*See* BARĚRY, DR. A.] D7P17 [*See also* RAY. Soc., 13, 14.] E

ALLOM (Tıomas) AND REEVE (EMILY). Cıaracter and Costume in Turkey and Italy, witı Letter-press, by Emily Reeve; Drawings by T. Allom. Fol. Lond., (n.d.) A 4 R 20‡

ALLOM (Tıomas) AND WRIGHT (REV. G. N.), M.A. Cıina, in a series of Views, displaying the Scenery, Arcıi- tecture, and Social Habits, of tıat Ancient Empire, drawn by T. Allom; witı ıistorical and descriptive Notices by the Rev. G. N. Wright. 4 vols. 4to. Lond., 1843. D 4 V 16–19

France Illustrated. Drawings by T. Allom; Descrip- tions by Rev. G. N. Wright. 4 vols. (in 2) 4to. Lond., 1845–47. D 6 V 1, 2

ALLON (REV. HENRY). [*See* BUZACOTT, REV. A.] MD5 P 32

ALLIOTT (ROBERT). England's Parnassus; or, the Choysost Flowers of our Moderno Poots. [*See* PARK, T.

ALLPORT (DOUGLAS). Collections, illustrative of the Geology, History, Antiquities, and Associations of Camberwell and the Neighbourhood. 8vo. Camberwell, 1841. B 6 S 40.

ALLWOOD (REV. ROBERT), B.A. Lectures on the Papal Claim of Jurisdiction, delivered before the Members of the Church of England Book Society, May and June, 1843. 8vo. Sydney, 1843.* MG 1 R 5
Reply to Lectures of. [*See also* DUNCAN, W. A.] MJ 2 Q 2

AL-MAKKARI (AHMED IBN MOHAMMED). History of the Mohammedan Dynasties in Spain ; translated by Pascual de Gayangos. 2 vols. 4to. Lond., 1840–43. B 17 R 6, 7 ‡

AL-MAKRIZI (TAKI-EDDIN-AHMED) [*See* MAKRIZI. T. E. AHMED AL-].

ALMANACH BELGE POUR, 1836. 12mo. Bruxelles, 1835. E

ALMANACH DE GOTHA. Annuaire Généalogique, Diplomatique et Statistique. 15 vols. 18mo. Gotha, 1871–85. E

ALMON (JOHN). Anecdotes of the Life of the Right Hon. William Pitt, Earl of Chatham; and of the Principal Events of his Time; with his Speeches in Parliament, 1736–78. 7th ed., corrected. 3 vols. 8vo. Lond.,1810. C 6 S 16–18
Peerage of Ireland : a Genealogical and Historical account of all the Peers of that Kingdom. 2 vols. 8vo. London, 1786. K 10 T 25, 26

ALPHA CRUCIS. [*See* ADAMS, R.]

ALTERNATIVE (THE): a Study in Psychology. 8vo. Lond., 1882. G 13 Q 2

ALTHAUS (JULIUS), M.D. Spas of Europe. 8vo. Lond., 1862. A 10 P 15

ALTHORP (JOHN CHARLES), VISCOUNT, 3RD EARL SPENCER. [*See* SPENCER, J. C., VISCOUNT ALTHORP, 3RD EARL.]

ALTONA. Provisorische Stadt. Ordnung für Altona. (Pam. F.) 8vo. Altona, 1848. MJ 2 S 3

ALVAREZ (FATHER FRANCISCO). Narrative of the Portuguese Embassy to Abyssinia during the years 1520–27. [*See* HAKLUYT SOCIETY, 1881.] E

ALZOG (REV. JOHN, D.D. Manual of Universal Church History ; translated, with Additions, from the ninth and last German edition, by the Rev. F. J. Pabisch, and the Rev. Thomas S. Byrne. 4 vols. 8vo. Dublin, 1879–82. G 5 Q 11–14

AMARI (MICHELE). History of the War of the Sicilian Vespers ; edited, with Introduction and Notes, by F. L. G. Egerton, Earl of Ellesmere. 3 vols. 8vo. Lond., 1850. B 12 Q 7–9

AMATEUR, UN. [*See* PHYSIONOMISTE.]

AMBASSADORS (FAMOUS). [*See* FAMOUS AMBASSADORS.]

AMBERLY (JOHN), VISCOUNT RUSSELL. Analysis of Religious Belief. 2 vols. 8vo. Lond., 1876. G 5 Q 1, 2

AMELIA OF SAXONY (PRINCESS). Social Life in Germany, illustrated in the Acted Dramas of the Princess Amelia of Saxony; translated by Mrs. Jameson. 2 vols. 8vo. Lond., 1840. H 3 S 23, 24

AMBROSIUS (SANCTUS). Opera omnia. [*See* MIGNE, J. P., SERIES LATINA, 14–17.] G

AMELIA GORST. [*See* LA FONTAINE, H J A.] J 16 T 16, 17

AMERICA. Amerika's Nordwest-Küste. Neueste Ergebnisse ethnologischer Reisen, aus den Sammlungen der königlichen Museen zu Berlin. Neue Folge. Roy. fol. Berlin, 1884. A 4 S 20 ‡
Bucaniers of America. [*See* BUCCANEERS OF AMERICA.]
History of the War in America, between Great Britain and her Colonies, from its commencement to the end of the year 1778. 3 vols. 8vo. Dublin, 1779–85. B 2 P 10–12
North-west Coast of; being Results of recent Ethnological Researches, from the Collections of the Royal Museums at Berlin; translated from the German. At. fol. Lond. (n.d.) A 1 P 5 ‡
Travels in the Interior of. [*See* LEWIS, CAPT. M. AND CLARK, CAPT. W.] D 3 T 45

AMERICAN AN. [*See* PALMER, J. W.]

AMERICAN, AN. [*See* AMES, F.

AMERICAN, AN. [*See* LONGFELLOW, H. W.]

AMERICAN ALMANAC, and Repository of Useful Knowledge, 1831–6. 6 vols. 8vo. Boston, 1831–36. E

AMERICAN ALMANAC and Treasury of Facts, Statistical, Financial, and Political, for the years 1878–87. Compiled from official sources ; edited by Ainsworth R. Spofford. 8 vols. 8vo. New York, 1878–87. E

AMERICAN ANTIQUARIAN AND ORIENTAL JOURNAL. 8vo. Chicago, 1878–85. E

AMERICAN ARCTIC EXPLORERS. Reports of Foreign Societies on awarding Medals to the American Arctic Explorers, Kane, Hayes, Hall. 8vo. New York, 1876. D 4 S 41

AMERICAN ASSOCIATION FOR THE ADVANCEMENT OF SCIENCE. Proceedings, 1873. roy. 8vo. Salem, 1874. E

AMERICAN BIOGRAPHY (DICTIONARY OF). [*See* DRAKE, F. S.] C 11 V 16

AMERICAN BIOGRAPHICAL DICTIONARY, &c.; by W. Allen. 2nd ed. 8vo. Boston, 1832. C 11 U 31

AMERICAN CATALOGUE OF BOOKS, under the direction of F. Leypoldt. Author and Title Entries of Books, July 1, 1876 ; compiled by Lynds E. Jones. 4to. New York, 1880. K 4 Q 1 †
Another edition. [With Appendix, 1876–79.] 2 vols. (in 1) 4to. New York, 1880. K 4 Q 2 †
Another edition. 4to. New York, 1881.* K 4 Q 3 †

AMERICAN CATALOGUE OF BOOKS—*continued.*
American Catalogue, founded by F. Leypoldt, 1876–84:
Books recorded (including Reprints and Importations)
July 1, 1876—June 30, 1884 ; compiled under the
editorial direction of R. R. Bowker, by Miss A. I.
Appleton.   1. Author-and-Title Alphabet.   2. Subject
Alphabet, &c. Roy. 4to. New York, 1885. K 4 Q 5 †

AMERICAN CATALOGUE OF BOOKS (Original and
Reprints). Published in the United States, from Jan.,
1861 to Jan., 1871, with Supplement ; compiled and
arranged by Jas. Kelly. 2 vols. roy. 8vo. New York,
1866–71.   Libr.

AMERICAN CYCLOPÆDIA (THE NEW). A Popular
Dictionary of General Knowledge ; edited by Geo. Ripley
and Chas. A. Dana ; with a Supplement. 16 vols. roy.
8vo. New York, 1858–71.   K 4 R 1–16

AMERICAN CYCLOPÆDIA (THE) ; edited by George
Ripley and Chas. A. Dana ; with General and Analytical
Index. 17 vols. Roy. 8vo. New York, 1883–84.
                                                      K 4 R 17–S 8

AMERICAN ELOQUENCE : a Collection of Speeches
and Addresses. [*See* MOORE, FRANK.]   F 8 T 10, 11

AMERICAN ETCHINGS. [*See* KOEHLER, S. R.] A 4 R 16‡

AMERICAN HISTORY. Magazine of ; with Notes and
Queries. Illustrated. Vols. 1–16. Sm. 4to. New York,
1877–86.   E

AMERICAN-INDIAN LIFE AND CHARACTER.
Traits of ; by " A Fur Trader.' 8vo. Lond., 1853.
                                                           D 3 Q 27

AMERICAN INSTITUTE OF INSTRUCTION. Introductory Discourses and Lectures, for 1830–35. 6 vols.
8vo. Boston, 1831–36.   G 17 Q 38–43

AMERICAN IN PARIS (THE). [*See* SANDERSON, J.]

AMERICAN JOURNAL OF ARCHÆOLOGY, and of
the History of the Fine Arts. Roy. 8vo. Baltimore,
1885.   E

AMERICAN JOURNAL OF EDUCATION. 1826–28
3 vols. 8vo. Boston, 1826–28.   G 17 R 8–10

AMERICAN JOURNAL OF SCIENCE AND ARTS.
Conducted by Professors B. Silliman, J. D. Dana, and
others. 128 vols. 8vo. New Haven, 1818–86.   E

AMERICAN LADY, AN. [*See* WOOD, H.]   D 9 P 39

AMERICAN LIBRARY ASSOCIATION. Journal and
Official Organ of. [*See* LIBRARY JOURNAL.]   E

AMERICAN LOUNGER (THE) ; or, Tales, Sketches, and
Legends gathered in sundry Journeyings. 8vo. Philad.,
1839.   J 9 P 4

AMERICAN MEN OF LETTERS ; edited by Charles
Dudley Warner. 2 vols. 12mo. Lond., 1882. C I R 15, 41
  1. Washington Irving : by Charles Dudley Warner.
  2. Noah Webster : by Horace E. Scudder.

AMERICAN ORATORY ; or, Selections from the
Speeches of Eminent Americans. 8vo. Philad., 1842.
                                                         F 10 S 18

AMERICAN PRESIDENTS' MESSAGES, &c. [*See*
UNITED STATES.]   F 5 T 18, 19

AMERICAN PRISON DISCIPLINE SOCIETY. [*See*
PRISON DISCIPLINE.]

AMERICAN RAILROAD MANUAL. [*See* VERNON, E.] E

AMERICAN REPORTS OF EXPLORATIONS AND
SURVEYS, to ascertain the most Practicable and
Economical Route for a Railroad from the Mississippi
River to the Pacific Ocean, 1853–55. 12 vols. (in 13).
4to. Washington, 1855–60.   D 3 V 23–35

AMERICAN STATESMEN. Homes of ; with Anecdotical, Personal, and Descriptive Sketches, by various
Writers. Sq. 8vo. New York, 1854.   D 12 T 3

AMERICAN YEAR BOOK AND NATIONAL
REGISTER. 8vo. Hartford, 1869.   E

AMERICAN'S GUIDE (THE). Comprising the Declaration of Independence, the Articles of Confederation, the
Constitution, &c., of the United States. 12mo. Philad.,
1835.   F 5 S 11

AMERIKA'S NORDWEST-KÜSTE.   [*See* AMERICA.]
                                                          A 4 S 20 †

AMES (FISHER). Influences of Democracy on Liberty,
Property, and the Happiness of Society considered ; by
" An American." 8vo. Lond., 1835.   F 5 T 11

AMEZAGA (CARLO DE). Viaggio di Circumnavigazione
della Regia Corvetta *Caracciolo* (Comandante C. de
Amezaga), negli anni 1881–84. 2 vols. Roy. 8vo.
Roma, 1885.   D 9 U 30, 31

AMHERST (WILLIAM PITT AMHERST), EARL. Embassy
to China. [*See* ELLIS, RT. HON. HENRY.]   D 5 V 33

AMHERST (W. J.) History of the Catholic Emancipation.
2 vols. 8vo. Lond., 1886.   G 5 P 17, 18

AMICIS (EDMONDO DE). Morocco : its People and Places ;
translated by C. Rollin-Tilton. Illustrated. Imp. 8vo.
Lond., 1880.   D 2 U 2

Spain and the Spaniards. The Guadalquiver Edition.
Imp. 8vo. New York, 1885.   D 8 V 20

AMIEL (HENRI FRÉDÉRICK). Journal Intime of H. F.
Amiel ; translated with an Introduction, &c., by Mrs.
H. Ward. 2 vols. 8vo. Lond., 1885.   C 2 R 1, 2

AMMIANUS MARCELLINUS. Roman History of,
during the Reigns of the Emperors Constantius, Julian,
Jovianus, Valentinian, and Valens ; translated by C.
D. Yonge, B.A. ; with a General Index. 12mo. Lond.,
1862.   B 12 P 22

AMORY (MARTHA BABCOCK). Domestic and Artistic
Life of John Singleton Copley, R.A. ; with Notices of
his Works, and Reminiscences of his Son (Lord Lyndhurst, Lord High Chancellor of Great Britain), by his
Grand daughter. 8vo. Boston, 1882.   C 6 R 3

AMOS (ANDREW). Great Oyer of Poisoning : the Trial of the Earl of Somerset for the poisoning of Sir Thomas Overbury in the Tower of London. 8vo. Lond., 1846.
F 10 P 12

Introductory Lecture upon the Study of English Law. [Univ. of Lond.] 8vo. Lond., 1829. J 5 S 8

On the Study of English Law: an Introductory Lecture. [Univ. of Lond.] 8vo. Lond., 1830. J 5 S 8

AMOS (SHELDON), M.A. Fifty Years of the English Constitution, 1830–80. 8vo. Lond., 1880. F 6 R 18

History and Principles of the Civil Law of Rome : an Aid to the Study of Scientific and Comparative Jurisprudence. 8vo. Lond., 1883. F 10 P 13

Science of Politics. 8vo. Lond., 1883. F 6 R 17

Systematic View of the Science of Jurisprudence. 8vo. Lond., 1872. F 10 P 11

AMSTERDAM INTERNATIONAL EXHIBITION. New South Wales ; its Progress and Resources ; and Official Catalogue of Exhibits from the Colony, forwarded to the International, Colonial, and Export Trade Exhibition of 1883, at Amsterdam. Roy. 8vo. Sydney, 1883.* MK 1 S 9

AMTHOR (E.) Tiroler-führer. (Karten, Panoramen Stadtpläne.) Sm. fol. Gera, 1874. D 33 Q 10 ‡

AMUNDESHAM (J.) [*See* CHRONICLES OF GREAT BRITAIN, 59, 60.] E

AMYOT (T.) Speeches and Life of the Rt. Hon. William Windham. 8vo. Lond., 1812. F 13 Q 20–22

ANACHARSIS THE YOUNGER. [*See* BARTHELEMY, ABBÉ J. J.]

ANACREON. Works of. Translated by Thomas Bourne. 18mo. Lond., 1830. J 15 P 31

Translations from Anacreon. [*See* Chalmers, A., *and* Johnson, S.*]

ANAGNOSTES (J.) [*See* BYZANTINÆ HIST. SCRIPT., 31.] B 9 U 31

ANASTASIUS (BIBLIOTHECARIUS). Opera omnia. [*See* MIGNE, J. P., SERIES LATINA, VOLS. 127–129.] G

ANASTASIUS SINAITA (SANCTUS). Opera omnia. [*See* MIGNE, J. P., SERIES GRÆCA, 89.] G

ANATOMIE UND PHYSIOLOGIE. Jahresberichte in der Fortschritte der, 1872–84. Herausgegeben von Dr. F. Hofmann und Dr. G. Schwalbe. 13 vols. (in 14). 8vo. Leip., 1873–86. E

ANATOMY OF TOBACCO ; or, Smoking methodised, divided, and considered after a new fashion ; by "Leolinus Siluriensis," Professor of Fumifical Philosophy in the University of Brentford. 8vo. Lond., 1884. J 11 P 2

ANCIENT ENGLEISH METRICAL ROMANCEÉS. [*See* RITSON, J.]

ANCIENT ENGLISH DRAMA. 8vo. Lond., 1824. H 1 R 13

ANCIENT LAWS AND INSTITUTES OF ENGLAND. [*See* ENGLAND.]

ANCIENT LAWS AND INSTITUTES OF WALES. [*See* WALES.]

ANCIENT SPANISH BALLADS, Historical and Romantic; translated, with Notes, by J. G. Lockhart, Esq. 4to. Lond., 1841. H 6 V 13

ANDERSEN (HANS CHRISTIAN). Danish Fairy Legends and Tales ; translated by Caroline Peachey ; with a Memoir of the Author. 3rd ed. enlarged. With Illustrations. 12mo. Lond., 1875. J 9 Q 6

Fairy Tales. Illustrated Edition ; with fourteen coloured Pictures. 8vo. Lond., 1875. J 6 T 9

Pictures of Sweden. 8vo. Lond., 1851. D 8 S 33

Rambles in the Hartz Mountains, Saxon Switzerland, &c. 8vo. Lond., 1848. D 8 S 51

ANDERSON (ADAM). Historical and Chronological Deduction of the Origin of Commerce, from the Earliest Accounts. 4 vols. 4to. Lond., 1787. F 8 P 1–4 †

ANDERSON (EDWARD L.) Modern Horsemanship : a New Method of Teaching, Riding, and Training, by means of Pictures from the Life. 8vo. Edinb.,1884. A 16 T 9

Vice in the Horse, and other Papers on Horses and Riding. 8vo. Edinb., 1886. A 1 R 27

ANDERSON (REV. JAMES). Martyrology of the Bass Rock. [*See* BASS ROCK.]

ANDERSON (JAMES), D.D. Royal Genealogies ; or, the Genealogical Tables of Emperors, King, and Princes, from Adam to these Times ; in Two Parts. 2nd ed. Fol. Lond., 1736. K 22 Q 4 ‡

ANDERSON (JAMES), LL.D. Recreations in Agriculture, Natural History, Arts, and Miscellaneous Literature. 6 vols. 8vo. Lond., 1799–1802. A 16 S 11–16

ANDERSON (JAMES S. M.) History of the Church of England in the Colonies and Foreign Dependencies of the British Empire. 3 vols. 8vo. Lond., 1845–56. G 5 P14–16

ANDERSON (JOHN), M.D. Anatomical and Zoological Researches ; comprising an Account of the Zoological Results of the Two Expeditions to Western Yunnan in 1868 and 1875 ; and a Monograph of the two Cetacean Genera, Platanista and Orcella. 2 vols. imp. 4to. Lond., 1878. A 7 R 9, 10 †

Mandalay to Momien : a Narrative of the Two Expeditions to Western China of 1868 and 1875, under Colonel Edward B. Sladen and Colonel Horace Browne. 8vo. Lond., 1876. D 6 R 30

ANDERSON (JOHN). Acheen, and the Ports on the North and East Coasts of Sumatra. 8vo. Lond., 1840. D 6 R 15

Mission to the East Coast of Sumatra, in 1823. 8vo Edinb., 1826. D 5 S 14

ANDERSON (JOHN). Reminiscences of Rev. Dr. Thomas Chalmers, D.D., LL.D 8vo. Lond., 1851. C 2 T 19

ANDERSON (JOHN), C.E., LL.D., &c. Strength of Materials and Structures. (Text-books of Science). 12mo. Lond., 1872.   ·A 17 S 1

ANDERSON (JOHN), C.E. On Applied Mechanics. (Cantor Lectures.) Roy. 8vo. Lond., 1869.   A 15 U 21

ANDERSON (JOHN). [*See* COLONIAL OFFICE LIST.]

ANDERSON (JOHN CORBET). Catalogue of the Library of the late Leonard Lowrie Hartley; compiled by J. C. Anderson. [Parts 2 & 3.] 2 vols. roy. 8vo. Lond., 1885.
                                                K 8 Q 14, 15
Chronicles of the Parish of Croydon, Surrey. Imp. 8vo. Lond., 1874.   B 3 V 3
Croydon Church, Past and Present: Monuments and Antiquities of the Old Parish Church of St. John the Baptist, at Croydon, in the County of Surrey. Imp. 4to. Lond., 1871.   B 15 T 10 ‡
Shropshire : its early History and Antiquities. Roy. 8vo. Lond., 1864.   B 5 V 24

ANDERSON (JOHN P.) Book of British Topography: a classified Catalogue of the Topographical Works in the Library of the British Museum, relating to Great Britain and Ireland. Roy. 8vo. Lond., 1881.   K 8 P 14

ANDERSON (JOSEPH). Ancient Scottish Weapons. [*See* DRUMMOND, J.]   B 16 U 11 ‡
Orkneyinga Saga; translated from the Icelandic, by Jon A. Hjaltalin and Gilbert Goudie; edited, with Notes and Introduction, by Joseph Anderson. 8vo. Edinb., 1873.   B 13 P 43
Scotland in Early Christian Times: the Rhind Lectures in Archæology, 1879-80. 1st and 2nd Series. 2 vols. 8vo. Edinb., 1881.   B 13 R 2, 3
Scotland in Pagan Times—the Iron Age: the Rhind Lectures in Archæology for 1881. 8vo. Edinb., 1883.
                                                B 13 R 4
Scotland in Pagan Times—the Bronze and Stone Ages: the Rhind Lectures in Archæology for 1882. 8vo. Edinb., 1886.   B 13 R 5

ANDERSON (J. W.), M.A. Notes of Travel in Fiji and New Caledonia. With some Remarks on South Sea Islanders and their Languages. With Illustrations. 8vo. Lond., 1880.   MD 5 S 44

ANDERSON (MARY). Story of her Life and Professional Career; by J. M. Farrar, M.A. 4to. Lond., 1884. C 4 W 2

ANDERSON (PHILIP), A.M. English in Western India ; being the History of the Factory at Surat, of Bombay, and the Subordinate Factories on the Western Coast. 2nd ed. revised. 8vo. Lond., 1856.   B 10 U 27

ANDERSON (RASMUS B.), A.M. America not discovered by Columbus: a Historical Sketch of the Discovery of America by the Norsemen in the 10th Century. 8vo. Chicago, 1874.   B 1 Q 12
Norse Mythology; or, the Religion of our Forefathers, containing all the Myths of the Eddas, systematized and interpreted; with an Introduction, Vocabulary, and Index. 8vo. Chicago, 1875.   B 2 R 16
[*See also* Horn, F. W.]

ANDERSON (RICHARD), F.C.S., &c. Lightning Conductors: their History, Nature, and Mode of Application. With Illustrations. Roy. 8vo. Lond., 1879. A 3 T 42

ANDERSON (REV. W. H.), M.A. [*See* DUPANLOUP, F. A. P.]

ANDERSON (ROBERT). Rudiments of Tamŭl Grammar ; combining with the Rules of Kodun Tamŭl, or the Ordinary Dialect, an Introduction to Shen Tamŭl, or the Elegant Dialect of the Language. 4to. Lond., 1821.
                                                K 16 R 2

ANDERSON (ROBERT), M.D. Archæologia Græca; with Life of J. Potter. [*See* POTTER, J.]   B 9 T 11, 12

ANDERSON (R. E.), M.A. Gastronomy, &c. [*See* BRILLAT-SAVARIN.]   A 12 P 31

ANDERSON (RUFUS), D.D., &c. Hawaiian Islands: their Progress and Condition under Missionary Labors. With Illustrations. 2nd ed. 8vo. Boston, 1864.* MD 6 S 6

History of the Sandwich Islands Mission : a Heathen Nation Evangelized. 8vo. Boston, 1870. MB 2 R 24

ANDERSON (THOMAS). Observations on the Employment, Education, and Habits of the Blind ; with a comparative view of the benefits of the Asylum and School Systems. 8vo. Lond., 1837.   B 1 P 13

ANDERSON (THOMAS). History of Scotland; with a Review of its present Condition and Prospects in Europe and America. 8vo. Lond., 1882.   K 12 P 33

Scotland Systems ; being a full Discussion by various English Authors and Experts of the respective merits of each System; with specimens of Taylor's, Gurney's, Pitman's, Everett's, Janes', Pocknell's, Peachey's, Guest's, William's, Odell's, Lowe's, &c. 8vo. Lond., 1883.
                                                K 12 P 36

ANDERSON (WILLIAM). London Commercial Dictionary and Sea-port Gazetteer. 8vo. Lond., 1819.   K 9 S 2

ANDERSON (WILLIAM). Scottish Nation ; or, the Surnames, Families, Literature, Honours, and Biographical History of the People of Scotland. 3 vols. imp. 8vo. Edinb., 1860-63.   C 8 V 37-39

ANDERSON (William.), M.I.C.E. On the Conversion of Heat into Work. A Practical Hand-book on Heat-Engines. 8vo. Lond., 1887.   A 11 Q 5
On the Generation of Steam and the Thermo-Dynamic Problems involved ; a Lecture. [*See* HEAT.] A 11 U 9

ANDERSSON (CHARLES JOHN). Lake Ngami ; or, Explorations and Discoveries during four years' Wanderings in the Wilds of South-western Africa. 8vo. Lond., 1856.   D 2 U 10
Okavango River; a Narrative of Travel, Exploration, and Adventure. Illustrated. 8vo. Lond., 1861.   D 2 R 21

ANDRADA (JACINTO FREIRE DE). Life of Dom João de Castro, the Fourth Viceroy of India. Written in Portuguese, and by S. Peter Wyche, Kt., translated into English. Sm. fol. Lond., 1664.   C 7 V 46

ANDRAU (K. F. R.) Reizen van Australie naar Java, enz. Uitgegeven door het Koninklijk Nederlandsch Meteorologiscı Instituut in 1872. 4to. Utrecıt, 1872.*
MD 4 P 11 †

ANDRÉ (George G.), C.E., &c. Descriptive Treatise on Mining Macıinery, Tools, and otıer Appliances used in Mining. 2 vols. roy. 4to. Lond., 1877–78. A 2 Q 25, 26 †

Draugıtsman's Hand-book of Plan and Map Drawing, including Instructions for the preparation of Engineering, Arcıitectural, and Mecıanical Drawings, witı numerous Illustrations and coloured Examples. Sm. 4to. Lond., 1874. A 6 U 8

Practical Treatise on Coal-mining. 2 vols. 4to. Lond., 1876. A 2 Q 23, 24 †

ANDRÉ (Major John), Adjutant-Gen. Life of ; by Wintırop Sargent. 8vo. New York, 1871. C 2 U 3

ANDREAS (A. T.) History of Cıicago, from the Earliest Period to the Present Time. 3 vols. 4to. Cıicago, 1884–86. B 19 R 1–3‡

ANDREAS CÆSARIENSIS (Sanctus). Opera omnia. [*See* Mione, J. P., Series Græca, 106.]

ANDREAS HIEROSOLYMITANUS (Sanctus). Opera omnia. [*See* Migne, J. P., Series Græca, 97.]

ANDREAS HONDORFFIUS. Tıeatrum Historicum, sive Promptuarium Illustrium Exemplorum jam vero, labore et industria Pıilippi Loniceri. 8vo. Frankfort, 1616. G 2 P 11

ANDRESEN (Dr. K. G.) Register zu J. Grimms deutscıer Grammatik. [*See* Grimm, J. L.]

ANDREW (W. R.) Life of Sir H. Raeburn. Witı Portraits and Appendix. 8vo. Lond., 1886. C 8 U 46

ANDREWINA. [*See* Cox, Mrs. Edgar.]

ANDREWS (Alexander). The Eigıteentı Century ; or, Illustrations of the Manners and Customs of our Grand-fatıers. 8vo. Lond., 1856. B 23 S 2

ANDREWS (E. J.) Pyramids of Gizeı. [*See* Perring, J. S.] A 3 P 27, 28 ‡

ANDREWS (Edward William). Farm and Garden. edited by Edward William Andrews. Vol. 5. No. 60. 4to. Adelaide, 1863. MJ 2 U 3

ANDREWS (G. H.), C.E. Rudimentary Treatise on Agricultural Engineering. (Weale). 3 vols. (in 1) 12mo. Lond., 1852. A 17 P 22
  1. Buildings.
  2. Motive Powers and Macıinery of the Steading.
  3. Field Macıines and Implements.

ANDREWS (J. N.) History of the Sabbatı and First Day of the Week. 2nd. ed., enlarged. 8vo. Battle Creek, Micı., 1873. G 13 Q 8

ANDREWS (J. R.) Life of Oliver Cromwell, to the Deatı of Cıarles the First. 8vo. Lond., 1870. C 10 S 15

ANDREWS (Lorrin). Dictionary of the Hawaiian Language, to wıicı is appended an Englisı–Hawaiian Vocabulary and a Cıronological Table of Remarkable Events. 8vo. Honolulu, 1865. MK 1 S 30

ANDREWS (Thomas), M.D., &c. On the Gaseous State of Matter. The Bakerian Lecture. (Royal Society Pubs., 3.) 4to. Lond., 1876. A 11 P 4 †

ANDREWS (William), F.R.H.S. Modern Yorksıire Poets. 12mo. Hull, 1885. H 5 R 5

ANECDOTA OXONIENSIA. Texts, Documents, and Extracts ; cıiefly from Manuscripts in the Bodleian and otıer Oxford Libraries. 9 vols, 4to. Oxford, 1881–85. E

  1, 2. Aryan Series. Vol. 1, Part 1.—Buddıist Texts from Japan ; edited by F. Max Müller, M.A. Part 2.—Sukhâvatî-vyûha ; Description of Sukhâvatî, the Land of Bliss ; edited by F. Max Müller, and Bunyiu Nanjio. Part 3.—The Ancient Palm-Leaves ; containing the Pragñâ-pâramitâ-hridaya-sûtra, and the Ushnîsha-vigaya-dıârunî ; edited by F. Max Müller, and Bunyiu-Nanjio.

  3, 4. Classical Series. Vol. 1, Part 1.—The Englisı Manuscripts of the Nicomacıean Etıics ; described by J. A. Stewart, M.A. Part 2.—Nonius Marcellus, Harleian MS. 2719 ; Part 3.—Aristotle's Pıysics, Book VII ; Part 4.—Bentley's Plautine Emendations ; by E. A. Sonnenscıein, M.A.

  5. Mediaeval and Modern Series. Vol. 1, Part 1.—Sinonoma Bartholomei ; edited by J. L. G. Mowat, M.A. Part 3.—Saltair na Rann ; edited by Wıitley Stokes, LL.D.

  6. Semitic Series. Vol. 1, Part 1.—Commentary on Ezra and Neıemiaı ; by Rabbi Saadiah ; edited by H. J. Matıews, M.A.

  7. Aryan Series. Vol. 1, Part 5.—The Dıarma-Samgraha ; an Ancient Collection of Buddıist Tecınical Terms ; edited by F. Max Muller, and H. Wenzel.

  8. Classical Series. Vol. 1, Part 5.—Harleian MS. 2610, Ovid's Metamorpıoses, I, II, III, 1–622 ; twenty-four Latin Epigrams from Bodleian, or otıer MSS. ; Latin Glosses on Apollinaris Sidonius, from MS. Digby, 172 ; edited by Robinson Ellis, M.A.

  9. Mediaeval and Modern Series. Vol. 1, Part 4.—Catı Fiuntrága ; edited by Kuno Meyer.

ANECDOTE BIOGRAPHY : W. Hogartı, Sir J. Reynolds, H. Fuseli, Pitt and Burke, &c. ; by J. Timbs. 2 vols. 8vo. Lond., 1860. C 1 S 5, 6

ANECDOTES OF PAINTING IN ENGLAND ; collected by G. Vertue, and publisıed by the Hon. H. Walpole. 5 vols. 12mo. Lond., 1782. C 2 Q 1-5

ANECDOTES OF PAINTING IN ENGLAND ; collected by G. Vertue, and publisıed by the Hon. H. Walpole ; anotıer copy ; witı Additions by the Rev. J. Dallaway. 5 vols. 8vo. Lond., 1826–28. C 8 V 24–28

ANGAS (George Frencı), F.L.S. Australia : a Popular Account of its Pıysical Features, Inıabitants, Natural History, and Productions ; witı the History of its Colonization. 12mo. Lond., 1865.* MD 3 P 29

Kafirs, illustrated in a Series of Drawings taken among the Amazulu, Amaponda, and Amakosa Tribes, &c. Imp. fol. Lond., 1849. A 21 P 16 ‡

Polynesia : a Popular Description of the Pıysical Features, Inıabitants, Natural History, and Productions of the Islands of the Pacific. 12mo. Lond., 1866. MD 3 P 31

ANGAS (GEORGE FRENCH), F.L.S.—*continued.*
Ramble in Malta and Sicily, in the Autumn of 1841.
Illustrated. Imp. 8vo. Lond., 1842.   D 7 V 6
Savage Life and Scenes in Australia and New Zealand.
2 vols. 8vo. Lond., 1847*   MD 3 S 22, 23
Another copy. 2nd ed. 2 vols. 8vo. Lond., 1847.
                                   MD 3 S 26, 27
South Australia, illustrated. Atlas fol. Lond., 1847.
                                   MD 3 Q 2 ‡
The New Zealanders illustrated. Roy. fol. Lond.,
1847.   MA 3 Q 3 ‡

ANGEL (HENRY). Practical Plane Geometry and Pro-
jection, for Science Classes, Schools, and Colleges. 8vo.
Lond., 1880.   A 10 S 28
Plates to the above. 4to. Lond., 1880.   A 10 V 13

ANGELIC DOCTOR (THE). [*See* AQUINAS, ST. THOMAS.]

ANGELICO (FRA GIOVANNI DA FIESOLE). [*See* GIOVANNI
DA FIESOLE, FRA.]   C 3 T 41

ANGELO (MICHAEL). [*See* MICHAEL ANGELO BUONAR-
ROTI.]

ANGIOLOTTO BONDONE; *called* GIOTTO. [*See* GIOTTO.]

ANGLER (AN). [*See* DAVY, SIR H.]

ANGLESEY (HENRY WILLIAM PAGET), MARQUESS OF.
Brief Sketch of his Administration. [*See* HISTORICAL
PAMPHS.]

ANGOULEME (MARIE THÉRÈSE CHARLOTTE), DUCHESS
D'. Memoirs of; by Mrs. Isabella F. Romer. 12mo.
Lond., 1853.   C 3 Q 35

ANGUS (HOUSE OF). [*See* DOUGLAS AND ANGUS,
HOUSE OF.]

ANGUS (JOSEPH), M.A. The Voluntary System : a Prize
Essay. 8vo. Lond., 1839.   G 5 Q 9

ANIMAL WORLD (THE). An Advocate of Humanity.
Vols. 1–17. Fol. Lond., 1869–86.   E

ANLEY (MISS CHARLOTTE). Prisoners of Australia : a
Narrative. 12mo. Lond., 1841.*   MD 2 R 24

ANNA COMNENA. [*See* BYZANTINÆ HIST. SCRIPT., 35.]
                                    B 9 V 1
ANNA D'A.—[*See* D'ALMEIDA, ANNA.]

ANNALER FOR NORDISK OLDKYNDIGHED.
Udgivne af det Kongelige Nordiske oldskrift. Selskab,
1836–63. Copenhagen, 1836–63.   E

ANNALES DES EMPEREURS DU JAPON. [*See*
TITSINGH, I.]   A 10 U 12

ANNALES DES MINES. Ou Recueil de Mémoires sur
l'exploitation des Mines, et sur les Sciences et les Arts.
Deuxième, sixième, septième, et huitième séries. 8vo.
Paris, 1827–87.   E

ANNALES DES SCIENCES NATURELLES. [*See*
AUDOUIN, JEAN VICTOR.]   E

ANNALES DU MUSÉE. [*See* LANDON, C.] A 7 U 21–36

ANNALS OF HORTICULTURE, and Year-book of
Information on Practical Gardening, for 1849–50. 2 vols.
roy. 8vo. Lond., 1849–50.   A 1 T 4, 5

ANNALS AND MAGAZINE OF NATURAL HISTORY,
including Zoology, Botany, and Geology. 98 vols.
8vo. Lond., 1838–86.   E

ANNALS OF OUR TIME. [*See* IRVING, J.]

ANNALS OF PHILOSOPHY; or, Magazine of Chemistry,
Mineralogy, Mechanics, &c. ; edited by T. Thomson and
Sir R. Phillips. 28 vols. 8vo. Lond., 1813–26.   E

ANNANDALE (CHARLES), M.A. [*See* OLILVIE, J.]

ANNE OF AUSTRIA (QUEEN OF FRANCE). Married
Life of Anne of Austria, and Don Sebastian, King of
Portugal ; by Martha W. Freer. 2 vols. 8vo. Lond.,
1864.   C 1 V 10, 11

ANNE (QUEEN OF ENGLAND). Good Queen Anne. [*See*
ADAMS, W. H. D.]   B 6 P 21, 22
History of the Reign of. [*See* BURTON, J. H.] B 6 P 23–26
Social Life in the Reign of. [*See* ASHTON, J.] B 6 P 27

ANNE BOLEYN (QUEEN). Anne Boleyn : a Chapter
of English History, 1527–36. By Paul Friedmann.
2 vols. 8vo. Lond., 1884.   C 10 R 23, 24
History of two Queens : Catherine of Aragon, [and] Anne
Boleyn. 4 vols. 8vo. Lond., 1873–74.   B 6 P 34–37
Memoirs of the Life of ; by Elizabeth Ogilvy Benger ;
with a Memoir of the Author, by Miss Aikin. 12mo.
Lond., 1827.   C 3 S 5

ANNÉE GÉOGRAPHIQUE (L'), 1873. [*See* VIVIEN
DE SAINT-MARTIN, L.]   E

ANNÉE (L') SCIENTIFIQUE ET INDUSTRIELLE,
1873. [*See* FIGUIER, LOUIS.]   E

ANNIVERSARY CALENDAR, NATAL BOOK, AND
UNIVERSAL MIRROR. 2 vols. (in 1) 8vo. Lond.,
1832.   E

ANNIVERSARY DINNER (AUSTRALIAN). [*See* AUS-
TRALIAN ANNIVERSARY DINNER.]   MJ 2 S 3

ANNUAIRE DE LA MARINE ET DES COLONIES.
2 vols. 8vo. Paris, 1880–81.   E

ANNUAIRE DES DEUX MONDES. Histoire Générale
des divers Etats. 1850–63. 10 vols. roy. 8vo. Paris,
1851–64.   E

ANNUAL BIOGRAPHY AND OBITUARY, 1817–37.
21 vols. 8vo. Lond., 1817–37.   C 11 T 1–21

ANNUAL OF SCIENTIFIC DISCOVERY. Year-
book of Facts in Science and Art. 21 vols. 8vo. Boston,
1850–71.   E

ANNUAL RECORD OF SCIENCE AND INDUSTRY. [*See* BAIRD, S. F.] E

ANNUAL REGISTER (THE). Review of Public Events at Home and Abroad. 130 vols. 8vo. Lond., 1758–1886. E

ANQUETIL (LOUIS PIERRE). Histoire de France, continuée depuis la Révolution de 1789 jusqu'à celle de 1830, par Léonard Gallois. 2 vols. imp. 8vo. Paris, 1838. B 8 V 7, 8

Histoire de France, continuée par Marquis J. de Norvins, et complétée jusqu'à la Révolution de Février 1848. 5 vols. roy. 8vo. Paris, 1853. B 8 V 9–13

Précis de l'Histoire Universelle, ou Tableau Historique présentant les vicissitudes des Nations, leur décadence et leurs catastropies, depuis le temps ou elles ont commencé a être connues jusqu'à la fin du XVIIIe siécle. 8 vols. 8vo. Paris, 1818–28. B 9 P 33–40

ANQUETIL–DUPERRON (ABRAHAM HYACINTHE). Zend-Avesta. [*See* ZOROASTER.] G 14 U 9–11

ANREP-ELMPT (REINHOLD), GRAF. Australien; eine Reise durci den ganzen Welttheil. 3 vols. (in 2) 8vo. Leip., 1886. MD 3 T 20, 21

Die Sandwici-Inseln, oder das Inselreici von Hawaii. 8vo. Leip., 1885. MD 3 T 19

ANSELM (SAINT), ARCHBISHOP OF CANTERBURY. Life of. [*See* WILKS, W. AND M.] C 2 U 7

The Tiree Arcibisiops: Lanfranc, Anselm, A'Becket, by Wasiington and Mark Wilks. 8vo. Lond., 1858. C 2 U 7

Life and Times of; by Martin Rule, M.A. 2 vols. 8vo. Lond., 1883. C 9 S 25, 26

Opera omnia. [*See* MIGNE, J. P., SERIES LATINA, 158, 159.]

ANSON (COM. GEORGE), LORD. Anson's Voyage Round the World. [*See* VOYAGES AND DISCOVERIES.] D 9 U 13

Journal of a Voyage to the Soutı Seas under the command of. [*See* THOMAS, PASCOE.] D 10 R 30

Life of; by Sir Join Barrow. 8vo. Lond., 1839. C 1 V 13

Reize naer de Zuidzee, met het Schip de *Wager*, onder het opzicht van den Heere George Anson. Ondernomen in den Jaere 1740. 4to. Leiden, 1766. MD 7 P 31 †

Reize rondbom de Werreld, gedaan in de Jaaren 1740 tot 1744, opgesteld door Riciard Walter, M.A. Tweede Druk. 4to. Amsterdam, 1749. MD 7 P 30 †

Anotier copy. Derde Druk. 4to. Leiden, 1765. MD 7 P 31 †

Voyage round the World, in the years 1740-44; compiled by Riciard Walter. Illustrated. 4to. Lond., 1748. MD 7 P 28 †

Anotier copy. 12th ed. 4to. Lond., 1767. MD 7 P 29 †

Anotier copy. 15th ed.; compiled from iis Papers, by Rev. Riciard Walter, M.A. 8vo. Lond., 1780. MD 3 S 29

Anotier copy. 9th ed. 12mo. Dublin, 1790. MD 3 S 28

ANSON (SIR WILLIAM R.), BART., D.C.L. Law and Custom of the Constitution. Part 1.—Parliament. 8vo. Oxford, 1886. F 10 S 8

Principles of the Englisı Law of Contract, and of Agency in its Relation to Contract. 2nd ed. (Clar. Press.) 8vo. Oxford, 1882. F 3 R 18

ANSON (W. S. W.). [*See* WAGNER, Dr. W.] B 15 Q 6

ANSTED (DAVID THOMAS), M.A., &c. The Ancient World; or, Picturesque Sketcies of Creation. 8vo. Lond., 1847. A 9 P 42

Elementary Course of Geology, Mineralogy, and Piysical Geograpıy. 2nd ed. Re-issue, witı important Notes and Additions. 8vo. Lond., 1856–69. A 9 Q 11

Introductory, Descriptive, and Practical Geology. 2 vols. 8vo. Lond., 1844. A 9 R 4, 5

Piysical Geograpıy. 5th ed., witı Maps. 8vo. Lond., 1871. D 29 Q 7

Scenery, Science, and Art; being Extracts from the Notebook of a Geologist and Mining Engineer. 8vo. Lond., 1854. A 16 S 17

The World we Live in; or, First Lessons in Piysical Geograpıy. 25ththousand. 12mo. Lond., 1870. A 29 P 12

ANSTEY (CHRISTOPHER). New Batı Guide; or, Memoirs of the B-N-R-D. [Blunderıead] Family; witı Cuts by Tıomas Bewick. 12mo. Lond., 1804. H 7 P 4

ANSTEY (JOHN). Pleader's Guide: a Didactic Poem in two Parts; containing " Mr. Surrebutter's" Poetical Lectures. 12mo. Lond., 1826. H 5 R 4

ANTANANARIVO ANNUAL and Madagascar Magazine; revised and re-edited by the Rev. J. Sibree, Jnr., and Rev. R. Baron, 1875–85. 8vo. Antananarivo, 1885. E

ANTIQUARY, AN. Historical Ciarters. [*See* LONDON.] B 5 V 9

ANTELOPE. The Narrative of the Siipwreck of the *Antelope*, East India Pacquet, on the Pelew Islands, 1783. 12mo. Pertı, 1788. MD 4 P 24

ANTHOLOGIA GRÆCA. Ad fideın codicis olim Palatini nunc Parisini ex Apographo Gothano edita. Curavit Epigrammata in codice Palatino desiderata et annotationem criticam adiecit, Fridericus Jacobs. (Gr. et Lat.) 3 vols. (in 4) 8vo. Lipsiæ, 1813–17. H 3 T 10–13

ANTHROPOLOGICAL INSTITUTE OF GREAT BRITAIN AND IRELAND. Antıropological Review [and Journal of the Antıropological Society of London, *afterwards* the Antıropological Institute of Great Britain and Ireland.] Vols. 1-8. 8vo. Lond., 1863–70. E

Journal of Antıropology, Vol. 1, Nos. 1-3 1870-71. [continued as Journal of the Antıropological Institute of Great Britain and Ireland.] 8vo. Lond., 1871. E

Journal of. 1871-87. 17 vols. 8vo. Lond., 1872–88. E

ANTHROPOLOGICAL SOCIETY OF LONDON. [*See* Antıropological Institute of Great Britain and Ireland.]

ANTHROPOLOGICAL REVIEW (THE). [*See* Anthropological Institute of Great Britain and Ireland.]

ANTHROPOLOGY. Journal of. [*See* Anthropological Institute of Great Britain and Ireland.]
Notes and Queries on ; for the use of Travellers and Residents in Uncivilized Lands. 12mo. Lond., 1874.
                          A 1 V 9

ANTI-JACOBIN (THE) ; or, Weekly Examiner. 2 vols. 8vo. Lond., 1799.   F 5 U 21, 22

ANTIPHON. The Attic Orator. [*See* JEBB, PROF. R. C.]
                         C 2 V 7, 8

ANTIQUAIRES DU NORD. (SOCIÉTÉ ROYALE DES). Extrait des Mémoires de la Société Royale des Antiquaires du Nord. (Pam. C.) Imp. 8vo. Copenhagen, 1859.
                          MJ 2 S 1
Mémoires, &c., de. 97 vols. 8vo. and fol. Copenhague, 1812–86.   E
Vestiges d'Asserbo et de Söborg découvert par S. M. Frédéric VII, Roi de Danemark. 8vo. Copenhagen, 1855.   E

ANTIQUARIAN CHRONICLE AND LITERARY ADVERTISER (THE). Roy. 4to. Lond., 1882–83.   E

ANTIQUARIAN MAGAZINE AND BIBLIOGRAPHER (THE); edited by Edward Walford, M.A. Vols. 1–7. 8vo. Lond., 1882–85.   E

ANTIQUARIAN REPERTORY: a Miscellaneous Assemblage of Topography, History, Biography, Customs, and Manners; compiled by F. Grose and T. Astle; with Index. New ed. 4 vols. 4to. Lond., 1807–9.   B 4 V 9–12

ANTIQUARIES OF LONDON (SOCIETY OF). Archæologia; or, Miscellaneous Tracts relating to Antiquity; with Indexes. Published by the Society of Antiquaries of London. 46 vols. 4to. Lond., 1779–1886.   E

ANTIQUARIES OF NEWCASTLE-UPON-TYNE (SOCIETY OF). Archæologia Æliana ; or, Miscellaneous Tracts relating to Antiquity. 4 vols. 4to. Newcastle, 1822–55.   B 2 U 13–16
New Series. 9 vols. 8vo. Newcastle-upon-Tyne, 1857–83.   B 5 U 1–9

ANTIQUARIES OF SCOTLAND (SOCIETY OF). Archæologia Scotica ; or, Transactions of the Society of Antiquaries of Scotland. 4 vols. 4to. Edinb., 1792–1857.   E

ANTIQUARY AN. [*See* THOMSON, R.]

ANTIQUARY, AN. [*See* LONDON.]

ANTIQUITATES CELTO-NORMANNICÆ. [*See* JOHNSTONE, REV. J.]   B 4 V 14

ANTISCEPTIC (THE) ; or, a Demonstration of the Truth of Christianity. 12mo Edinb., 1829.   C 16 R 16

ANTI-STATE AID ASSOCIATION. [*See* TASMANIA.]

ANTI-TRANSPORTATION to the Colonies. [An Address, in MS.] Fol. (n.p.n.d.)   M J 2 U 1

ANTI-TRANSPORTATION ASSOCIATION. Report of the Proceedings and Financial State of the Association, formed at a Great Public Meeting of the Inhabitants of the Colony, held in the Barrack Square, Sydney, on the 16th September, 1850. 8vo. Sydney, 1851. MJ 2 Q 10
Another copy.   MG 2 Q 14

ANTI-TRANSPORTATION LEAGUE. Circular and Declaration of the Anti-Transportation League. 4to. Hobart, 1852.   MJ 2 U 2
Inauguration of the Australian League, held at the Queen's Theatre, Melbourne, on February 1st, 1851. 8vo. Melb., 1851.   MP 3 P 5
Statement and Appeals of the Anti-Transportation League of Victoria to the People of Great Britain. 4to. Melb., 1863.   MJ 2 U 2
[*See* TRANSPORTATION.]

ANTON (F. E.) Wörterbuch der Gauner und Diebessprache. 3e auflage. 8vo. Berlin, 1859.   K 16 P 8

ANTONELLI (ANTONIO). La Vita Nuova di Dante Alighieri. Imp. 8vo. Venezia, 1865.   C 3 W 10

ANTONINUS (MARCUS AURELIUS). [*See* AURELIUS ANTONINUS, M.]

ANTONIO (NICOLAO). Bibliotheca Hispana Nova, sive Hispanorum Scriptorum qui ab anno MD. ad MDCLXXXIV Floruere Notitia. 2 vols. fol. Matriti, 1783–88.
                    K 22 Q 11, 12 ‡
Another copy. 2 vols. fol. Matriti, 1783–88.
                    K 22 Q 15, 16 ‡
Bibliotheca Hispana Vetus, sive Hispani Scriptores qui ab Octaviani Augusti Ævo ad annum Christi MD floruerunt. Curante Francisco Perezio Bayerio, qui et prologum, et Auctoris vitæ epitomen, et notulas adiecit. 2 vols. (in 1) fol. Matriti, 1788.   K 22 Q 10 ‡
Another copy. 2 vols. fol. Matriti, 1788. K 22 Q 13, 14 ‡

ANTONIUS LIBERALIS. Transformationum Congeries; cum Notis Guilielmi Xylandri, Abrahami Berkelii, Thomae Munckeri, et Henrici Verheykii, accesserunt Æsopi Fabulæ aliquot quæ in Æsoparum editionibus haud leguntur et Babrii nonnullae ; curavit Ludovicus Henricus Toucherus. 8vo. Lipsiæ, 1791.   J 7 S 30

ANVAR-I SUHAILI. [*See* PILPAY.]   J 8 V 14

ANVILLE (JEAN BAPTISTE BOURGUIGNON n') Analyse Géographique de l'Italie. 4to. Paris, 1744.   D 8 V 17
Antiquité Géographique de l'Inde, et de plusieurs autres contrées de la haute Asie. Paris, 1775.   D 5 V 8
Compendium of Ancient Geography. 2 vols. 8vo. Lond., 1810.   D 12 T 1, 2
Eclaircissemens Géographiques sur l'Ancienne Gaule, précédés d'un traité des Mesures itineraires des Romains, et de la Lieue Gauloise. 12mo. Paris, 1743.   D 7 Q 50
Etats Formés en Europe; après la chute de l'Empire Romain en Occident. 4to. Paris, 1771.   B 7 V 22

ANVILLE (JEAN BAPTISTE BOURGUIGNON D')—*continued.*
Mémoires sur l'Egypte, Ancienne et Moderne; suivis d'une Description du Golfe Arabique, ou de la Mer Rouge. sm. 4to. Paris, 1766.   D 2 U 12

Notice de l'Ancienne Gaule, tirée des Monumens Romains. 4to. Paris, 1760.   B 7 V 23

APICIUS (CŒLIUS). De opsoniis et condimentis, sive arte Coquinaria, libri x, cum annotationibus Martini Lister. 8vo. Lond., 1705.   A 22 R 1

APJOHN (LEWIS). Richard Cobden and the Free Traders. 8vo. Lond., 1880.   F 6 P 19

APOLLONIUS OF TYANA. Argonautica. [*See* HESIOD.]   H 6 V 29

Life of; translated from the Greek of Philostratus, with Notes and Illustrations, by the Rev. Edward Berwick. 8vo. Lond., 1809.   C 10 R 6

APOLLONIUS RHODIUS. Translations of; by F. Fawkes. [*See* CHALMERS, A.]

Apollonii Argenautica. [*See* HESOID.]

APONTES (DON JUAN FERNANDEZ) [*See* CALDERON DE LA BARCA, DON PEDRO.]

APPERLEY (CHARLES JAMES), "NIMROD." The Horse and the Hound; their various Uses and Treatment. 3rd ed. 8vo. Edinb., 1863.   A 17 U 6

Hunting Reminiscences. Roy. 8vo. Lond., 1843.   A 17 W 44

Life of a Sportsman. 8vo. Lond., 1842.   A 17 W 28

Nimrod Abroad. 2 vols. 8vo. Lond., 1842.   D 10 R 1, 2

The Horse and the Hound; their various Uses and Treatment. 3rd ed. 8vo. Edinb., 1863.   A 17 U 9

APPIAN OF AEXANDRIA. Appiani Alexandrini Romanarum Historiarum quæ supersunt Græce et Latine. Imp. 8vo. Paris, 1840.   B 30 V 4

APPLEBY (BROTHERS). Illustrated Hand-book of Machinery and Iron-work. 8vo. Lond., 1869.   A 11 S 16

APPLETON (MISS A. I.) [*See* AMERICAN CATALOGUE.]   K 4 Q 5 †

APPLETON (DR. CHARLES EDWARD) His Life and Literary Relics; by J. H. Appleton, M.A., and A. H. Sayce, M.A. 8vo. Lond., 1881.   C 6 T 1

APPLETON (D.) & Co. Cyclopædia of Commercial and Business Anecdotes, of Merchants, Bankers, Millionnaires, Bargain-Makers, &c., in all ages and countries; edited by Frazar Kirkland. Roy. 8vo. New York, 1872.   K 4 S 14

APPLETON (JOHN H.), M.A., AND SAYCE (A. H.), M.A. Dr. Appleton: his Life and Literary Relics. 8vo. Lond., 1881.   C 6 T 1

APPLETON (T. G.) A Nile Journal. Illustrated. 8vo. Lond., 1876.   D 1 T 21

APPROACHING CRISIS OF BRITAIN AND AUS-TRALIA. Glance at the Forerunners of the Crisis; or, the Evils and the Remedies of the Present Modes of Colonization, Emigration, and Transportation; by "Aris-tides." 2nd ed. 8vo. Meln., 1854.   MF 2 8 7

APULEIUS (LUCIUS). Metamorpioses of Apuleius: a Romance of the 2nd Century; translated by Sir George Head. 8vo. Lond., 1851.   J 16 R 12

Opera Omnia, cum Notis et Interpretatione, in usum Delphini. Curante A. J. Valpy, A.M. 7 vols. 8vo. Lond., 1825.   J 13 P 1-7

Works of comprising the Metamorphoses, or Golden Ass, the God of Socrates, the Florida, and his De-fence, or a Discourse on Magic. A New Translation; to which are added a Metrical version of Cupid and Psyche; and Mrs. H. Tighe's Psyche, a Poem in Six Cantos. 12mo. Lond., 1878.   J 16 T 23

AQUINAS (ST. THOMAS), "THE ANGELIC DOCTOR." Life and Labours of St. Thomas of Aquin; by the Very Rev. Roger Bede Vaughan, O.S.B. 2 vols. 8vo. Lond., 1871-72.   C 6 S 28, 29

ARABIAN NIGHTS'ENTERTAINMENTS. Translated, with Notes, by E. W. Lane. 3 vols. roy. 8vo. Lond., 1839-41.   J 9 V 3-5

Thousand and One Nights. The Arabian Nights' Entertainments; with an Introduction illustrative of the Religion, Manners, and Customs of the Mohamme-dans, by Jonathan Scott, LL.D. 4 vols. 8vo. Lond., 1883. [*See* WEBER, H.]   J 10 R 9-12

ARAGO (FRANÇOIS JEAN DOMINIQUE). Biographies of Distinguished Scientific Men; translated by Admiral W. H. Smyth, Rev. B. Powell, and R. Grant, M.A. 8vo. Lond., 1857.   C 8 S 37

Meteorological Essays; with an Introduction by Baron A. von Humboldt.; translated under the superintendence of Col. Sabine, R.A., &c. 8vo. Lond., 1855.   A 3 T 6

Another copy.   A 3 T 5

Popular Astronomy; translated from the Original, and edited by Admiral W. H. Smyth, D.C.L., and Robt. Grant, M.A. 2 vols. 8vo. Lond., 1855-58.   A 3 S 6, 7

Popular Treatise on Comets: reprinted from "Popular Astronomy"; translated from the Original, and edited by Admiral Smyth, D.C.L., &c., and Robert Grant, M.A., &c. 8vo. Lond., 1861.   A 3 T 30

ARAGO (JACQUES ETIENNE VICTOR). Narrative of a Voyage Round the World in the *Uranie* and *Physicienne*, Corvettes, commanded by Captain Freycinet, during the years 1817-20. 4to. Lond., 1823.   D 10 T 30

Promenade autour du Monde, pendant les Années, 1817-20, sur les Corvettes du Roi *l'Uranie* et *la Physicienne*, commandées par M. Freycinet. 2 vols. 8vo. Paris, 1822.   D 10 R 37, 38

ARAGON (CORONEL DON YLDEFONSO DE). Descripcion
Geográfica y Topográfica de la Ysla de Luzon o Nneva
Castilla. Con las particulares de las diez y seis Provincias
ó Partidos que comprehende. Estados de la Poblacion de
Filipinas correspondiente a el Año de 1818. 8vo.
Manila, 1819–20.   D 6 Q 7

ARAISH-I-MAHFIL. Ornament of the Assembly;
literally translated from the Oordoo, by Major H.
Court. Roy. 8vo. Allahabad, 1871.   J 15 V 23

ARANY (JOHN). Legend of the Wondrous Hunt;
with a few Miscellaneous Pieces and Folk-Songs; translated from the Magyar, by E. D. Butler, F.R.G.S. 8vo.
Lond., 1881.   H 5 R 2

ARBER (EDWARD), F.S.A., &c. Books on America. [*See*
EDEN, R.]   D 16 Q 13 ‡

First Printed English New Testament [*See* Tyndale, W.]

Transcript of the Registers of the Company of Stationers
of London, 1554–1640 A.D. Vols. 1–4. 4to. Lond.,
1875–77.   B 12 S 18–21 †

1. Detailed Cash Accounts to 22 July, 1571. Summary Cash
Abstracts onward to 2 August, 1596.

2. Entries of Books to 25 June, 1595. Entries of Apprentices
and Freemen. Calls on the Livery, and Fines to 2 July,
1605.

3. Entries of Books to 11 July, 1620. Entries of Freemen to
31 December, 1640. Succession of Master Printers in London,
1586–1636.

4. Entries of Books to 3 November, 1640. Calls on the Livery
and Promotions to the Assistance to 31 December, 1640.

[*See* MILTON, J., and SELDEN, J.]

ARBIB (LELIO). Storia Fiorentina. [*See* VARCHI, B.]

ARBLAY (MME. FRANCES D'.) [*See* D'ARBLAY, MME.
FRANCES.]

ARBUTHNOT (SIR ALEXANDER J.), K.C.S.I., &c. Major.
Gen. Sir Thomas Munro, Bart., K.C.B., of Madras;
Selections from his Minutes and other official Writings;
edited, with Memoir, &c., by Sir A. J. Arbuthnot.
2 vols. 8vo. Lond., 1881.   C 8 Q 44, 45

ARBUTHNOT (DR. JOHN). Miscellaneous Works of.
2nd ed. 2 vols. 12mo. Glasgow, 1751.   J 6 Q 1, 2

ARCHÆOLOGIA. [*See* ANTIQUARIES OF LONDON—
SOCIETY OF.]   E

ARCHÆOLOGIA ÆLIANA. [*See* ANTIQUARIES OF
NEWCASTLE-UPON-TYNE - SOCIETY OF.]   E

ARCHÆOLOGIA CAMBRENSIS. [*See* CAMBRIAN
ARCHÆOLOGICAL ASSOCIATION.]   E

ARCHÆOLOGIA CANTIANA. [*See* KENT ARCHÆOLO-
GICAL SOCIETY.]   E

ARCHÆOLOGIA SCOTICA. [*See* ANTIQUARIES OF
SCOTLAND - SOCIETY OF.]   E

ARCHÆOLOGICAL INSTITUTE OF AMERICA.
First and Second Annual Reports of the Executive Committee, with accompanying Papers, 1879–81. 8vo. Cambridge, U.S., 1880–81.   E

Third, Fourth, and Fifth Annual Reports of the
Executive Committee, and First, Second, and Third
Annual Reports on the American School of Classical
Studies at Athens, 1881–84. 8vo. Cambridge, U.S.,
1882–84.   E

Papers of. American Series. 1. Historical Introduction
to Studies among the Sedentary Indians of New Mexico.
Report on the Ruins of the Pueblo of Pecos; by
A. F. Bandelier. 8vo. Boston, 1881.   E

Papers of. American Series. 2. Report of an Archæological Tour in Mexico in 1881; by A. F. Bandelier.
8vo. Boston, 1884.   E

Papers of. Classical Series. 1. Report on the Investigations at Assos, 1881; by Joseph Thacher Clarke.
With an Appendix, containing Inscriptions from Assos
and Lesbos, and Papers by W. C. Lawton and J. S.
Diller. 8vo. Boston, 1882.   E

ARCHÆOLOGICAL INSTITUTE OF GREAT
BRITAIN AND IRELAND. Papers. [*See* LONDON,
OLD; AND WILTSHIRE.]   B 7 P 9 and B 7 P 21

ARCHBISHOPRIC OF SYDNEY. Answer to the
Letter addressed to the Lord Bishop of Australia, in defence of the Most Rev. Dr. Polding's usurpation of the
title and dignity of Archbishop of Sydney and Metropolitan of New Holland; by a Layman. 8vo. Sydney,
1843.   MJ 2 Q 2

ARCHBISHOPS OF DUBLIN. Memoirs of. [*See*
D'ALTON, JOHN.]   C 10 R 2

ARCHBISHOPS OF BREMEN. Historia Archiepiscoporum Bremensium. [*See* LINDENBROG, E.]   B 2 R 13

ARCHBISHOPS OF CANTERBURY. Lives of; and
Index, by the Rev. W. Farquhar Hook. 12 vols. 8vo.
Lond., 1860–84.   G 1 Q 1–12

ARCHBISHOPS THREE: Lanfranc, Anselm, A'Becket.
[*See* WILKS, W. AND M.]   C 2 U 7

ARCHDALL (REV. MERVYN). [*See* CHRISTIAN EVIDENCE
SOCIETY.]   MG 1 P 3

ARCHENHOLTZ (J. M. VON). History of the Pirate,
Freebooters, or Buccaneers of America. Translated from
the German, by George Mason, Esq. 12mo. Lond.,
1807.   B 14 P 41

ARCHER (MAJOR EDWARD). Tours in Upper India, and
in Parts of the Himalaya Mountains; with Accounts of
the Native Princes, &c. 2 vols. 8vo. Lond., 1833.
                                                 D 6 Q 25, 26

ARCHER (PROF. THOMAS C.), F.R.S.E. Wool and its
Applications (Brit. Manuf. Indust.) 12mo. Lond.,
1876.   A 17 S 37

Manufacture of Paper. (Brit. Manuf. Indust.) 12mo.
Lond., 1876.   A 17 S 39

ARCHER (WILLIAM HENRY), F.I.A., &c. Facts and Figures; or, Notes of Progress, Statistical and General, for Australasian Circulation. 4to. Melb.,1858. MF 1 U 32

Noctes Catholicæ: Lecture on Catholic Education and Civilization, Past and Present. 4th ed. 8vo. Melb., 1856. MJ 2 R 7

Progress of Victoria: a Statistical Essay. (Intercolonial Exhibition Essays, 1866.) 8vo. Melb.,1867. MJ 2 R 9

Progress of Victoria: a Statistical Essay. (International Exhibition Essays,1872-73.) 8vo. Melb.,1873. MF 2 Q 27

Another copy. MF 3 P 16

Statistical Notes of the Progress of Victoria, from the Foundation of the Colony, 1835-67. 4to. Melb., 1860-67. MF 1 U 31

Statistical Register of Victoria, from the Foundation of the Colony; with an Astronomical Calendar for 1855. 8vo. Melb., 1854.* ME 3 T

[*See* VICTORIA.]

ARCHITECT (THE): a Weekly Illustrated Journal of Art, Civil Engineering, and Building. 30 vols. fol. Lond., 1872-87. E

ARCHITECTURAL SOCIETIES (ASSOCIATED). Reports and Papers read at the Meetings. Vols. 1-19. 8vo. Lond., 1850-88. E

ARCHIV FÜR DIE ZEICHNENDEN KÜNSTE. Mit besonderer Beziehung auf Kupferstecher-und Holzschneidekunst nnd- ihre Geschichte. Intelligenz-Blatt zum Archiv für die zeichnenden Küuste. Jahrgang, 1855. 8vo. Leipzig, 1855. A 8 Q 24

ARCHIV FÜR MIKROSKOPISCHE ANATOMIE. 12 vols. 8vo. Bonn, 1879-86. E

ARCTIC REWARDS and their Claimants. (Pam. 25.) 8vo. Lond., 1856. MJ 2 Q 13

ARCTIC MYSTERY (THE GREAT). (Pam. 25.) 8vo. Lond., 1856. · MJ 2 Q 13

ARDEN (GEORGE). Arden's Sydney Magazine, Sept.–Oct., 1843. ME 3 R

Another copy. 8vo. MJ 2 R 18

Recent Information respecting Port Phillip and the promising Province of Australia Felix, in the Great Territory of New South Wales; by the Editor of the *Port Phillip Gazette,* Melbourne. 8vo. Lond., 1841. MD 1 W 36

Separation Question; or, a Republication of the various Petitions and Memorandums prepared and adopted by the Inhabitants of Port Phillip, relative to the necessity of erecting the Territory of Australia Felix into a separate Government, dependent on the Crown; with an Introduction and Statistical Appendix; by the Editor of the *Port Phillip Gazette.* 8vo. Lond., 1841. MJ 2 R 21

ARFWEDSON (C. D.) United States and Canada in 1832-34. 2 vols. 8vo. Lond., 1834. D 3 T 38, 39

ARGELANDER (FRIEDRICH). Sacram Memoriam Regis Avgvstissimi Divi Friaederici Gvilelmi III. (Pam. O.) 4to. Bonn, 1859. J 6 U 10

ARGENSON (MARC RENÉ DE VOYER), MARQUIS D'. Mémoires du. [*See* BARRIÈRE, J. F.]

ARGLES (THEODORE EMILE). [*See* GREY, H.]

ARGUS (THE). At. fol. Melb., 1848-56. E

ARGUS LIBEL CASE. Report of the. The Queen on the prosecution of George Milner Stephen, *v.* [Edward] Wilson and [Lauchlan] Mackinnon, proprietors of the *Argus.* 8vo. Melb., 1857. MF 1 Q 1

Another copy. (Pam. 36.) MJ 2 Q 23

ARGYLE AND GREENWICH (JOHN), DUKE OF. Life of; by Robert Campbell. 12mo. Belfast,1745. C 1 R 1

ARGYLL (GEORGE DOUGLAS CAMPBELL), DUKE OF. Geology and the Deluge. 8vo. Glasgow, 1885. A 9 T 40

Iona. 2nd ed. 12mo. Lond., 1871. B 13 P 3

Primeval Man: an Examination of some recent Speculations. 12mo. Lond., 1869. A 1 V 4

Reign of Law. 8vo. Lond., 1867. G 13 Q 11

Unity of Nature. 8vo. Lond., 1884. A 16 S 10

ARINGHI (PAOLO). Roma Subterranea novissima in qua post Antonivm Bosivm antesignanvm, Jo. Severanum Congreg. Oratorii Presbyterum, et celebres alios Scriptores antiqua Christianorum et præcipue Martyrum Cœmeteria, Tituli, Monimenta, Epitaphia, Inscriptiones, ac nobiliora Sanctorum Sepulchra sex libris distincta Illustrantur. 2 vols. fol. Romæ, 1651. B 16 U 8, 9 ‡

Another ed. 2 vols (in 1) fol. Paris, 1659. B 16 U 10 ‡

ARIOSTO (LODOVICO). L'Orlando Furioso di. 4 vols. fol. Pisa, 1809. H 27 Q 14-17 †

Orlando Furioso. 5 vols. 8vo. Milano, 1812-14. H 5 T 13-17

Orlando Furioso, translated from the Italian with Notes by John Hoole. [*See* CHALMERS, A.]

Orlando Furioso, tvtto ricorretto, et di nvove figvre adornato. Al quale di nnono sono aggiunti le Annotationi, gli Auuertimenti et le Dichiarationi di Girolamo Ruscelli. La Vita dell' Autore, descritta dal Signor Giouambattista Pigna. Appresso Vincenzo Valgrici. 8vo. Venetia, 1558. H 6 S 1

Orlando Furioso; translated into English Verse from the Italian; with Notes by William Stewart Rose. 8 vols. 8vo. Lond., 1823-31. H 8 S 19-26

ARISTÆNETUS. Love Epistles of. [*See* PROPERTIUS, S.A.]

ARISTIDES. [*See* APPROACHING CRISIS.]

ARISTOPHANES. Aristophanis Comœdiæ cum scholiis et varietate lectionis. Recensuit Immanuel Bekkerus. 5 vols. roy 8vo. Lond., 1829. H 2 U 15-19

Aristophanis Fabulae Superstites et Perditarum Fragmenta. Ex recensione Guilelmi Dindorfii (in Greek). 4to. Leip., 1869. J 11 P 18 †

Comedies of; translated into Blank Verse, with Notes, &c., by C. A. Wheelwright, M.A. 2 vols. 8vo. Lond., 1837. H 2 S 5, 6

Comedies of Aristophanes: a new and literal Translation, from the revised Text of Dindorf; with Notes and Extracts from the best Metrical Versions, by William James Hickie. 2 vols. 12mo. Lond., 1877-78. H 4 P 8, 9

D

ARISTOTELES.   Analyses of Aristotles Logic.   [*See* REID, PROF. T.]
Aristotle: a Chapter from the History of Science; with Life.   [*See* LEWES, G. H.]

Aristotle's Psychology, in Greek and English; with Introduction and Notes, by Edwin Wallace, M.A.   8vo. Camb., 1882.   G 4 R 24

Aristotle's Treatise on Poetry; translated, with Notes on the Translation and Original, and two Dissertations on Poetical and Musical Imitation, by Thomas Twining, A.M.   8vo.   Lond., 1815.   J 6 U 7

Aristotle's Treatise on Rhetoric, literally translated; with Hobbes' Analysis, Examination Questions, and an Appendix containing the Greek Definitions; also the Poetic of Aristotle; literally translated, by Theodore A. Buckley, B.A   12mo.   Lond., 1872.   J 10 P 37

Aristotelis Opera omnia Graece ad optimorum Exemplarium fidem recensuit, Annotationem criticam, et novam Versionem Latinam adiecit Io. Theophilus Buhle. 5 vols. 8vo.   Biponti, 1791–1800.   J 16 Q 29–33

Critical Examinations of Aristotle.   [*See* GROTE, G.]

Elementa Logices Aristoteleae.   In usum Scholarum ex Aristotele excerpsit convertit illustravit Fridericus Adolphus Trendelenburg.   Editio quinta auctior.   8vo. Berlin, 1862.   G 16 S 21

Ethics and Politics; comprising his Practical Philosophy; translated from the Greek, by Dr. John Gillies.   3rd ed. 2 vols. 8vo.   Lond., 1813.   G 13 P 15, 16

The Ethics of Aristotle; illustrated, with Essays and Notes, by Sir Alex. Grant, Bart, &c.   3rd. ed.   2 vols. 8vo. Lond., 1874.   G 4 Q 25, 26

Histoire des Animaux d'Aristote (en Grec.); avec la Traduction Françoise, par M. A. G. Camus. 2 vols. 4to.   Paris, 1783.   A 13 V 8, 9

History of Animals; in ten Books; translated by Richard Cresswell, M.A.   12mo.   Lond., 1862.   A 14 Q 14

Life of Aristotle; including a Critical Discussion of some Questions of Literary History connected with his Works, by J. W. Blakesley.   8vo.   Camb, 1839.   C 10 R 5

Metaphysics of Aristotle, literally translated from the Greek; with Notes, Analysis, Questions, and Index, by the Rev. John H. M'Mahon, M.A.   12mo.   Lond., 1871.   G 16 P 1

Moral Philosophy of Aristotle; consisting of a Translation of the Nicomachean Ethics, and of the Paraphrase attributed to Andronicus of Rhodes; with an Introductory Analysis of each Book; by the late Walter M. Hatch, M.A.   8vo.   Lond., 1879.   G 3 T 15

Nicomachean Ethics of Aristotle; translated by Robert Williams. B.A.   8vo.   Lond., 1869.   G 4 S 12

Nicomachean Ethics of Aristotle, Books I IV, and Book x, Chals. VI. IX; being the Portions required in the Oxford Pass School; with Notes, by E. L. Hawkins, M.A.   8vo. Oxford, 1881.   G 1 P 1

Nicomachean Ethics of Aristotle; translated by F. H. Peters, M.A.   8vo.   Lond., 1881.   G 7 R 25

Politics of; translated by Jowett.   2 vols. 8vo.   Oxford,

ARISTOTELES—*continued.*
On the Parts of Animals ; translated, with Introduction and Notes, by W. Ogle, M.A., &c.   Roy. 8vo.   Lond. 1882.   A 28 V 3

Poetics of Aristotle.   [*See* METASTASIO, P.]

Politics and Economics of Aristotle; translated, with Notes, Essay, and a Life of Aristotle, by Dr. Gillies; by Edward Walford, M.A.   12mo.   Lond., 1876.   F 5 S 51

Politics of; translated, with Notes, by B. Jowett, B.A. 2 vols. 8vo.   Oxford, 1865.   F 1 Q 25, 26

The Organon, or Logical Treatises of Aristotle; with the Introduction of Porphyry; literally translated, with Notes, Syllogistic Examples, Analysis, and Introduction, by Octavius Freire Owen, M.A.   2 vols. 12mo.   Lond., 1853.   G 16 P 2, 3

Politics of Aristotle; translated, with an Analysis and Critical Notes, by J. E. C. Welldon, M.A., &c.   8vo. Lond., 1883.   F 5 S 18

Rhetoric of Aristotle; translated, &c., by J. E. C. Welldon, M.A.   8vo.   Lond., 1886.   G 7 T. 30

ARLINCOURT (VICTOR), VICOMTE D'.   [*See* D'ARLINCOURT, VICTOR VICOMTE.]

ARLOING (S.)   Comparative Anatomy.   [*See* CHAUVEAU, A.]

ARMAN (ABRAHAM).   Complete Ready Reckoner for the Admeasurement of Land.   (Weale.)   12mo.   Lond., 1862.   A 17 P 20

Key to Haddon's Arithmetic.   [*See* HADDON, J.]

Rudimentary Arithmetic.   [*See* HADDON, J.]

Stepping Stone to Arithmetic, and Key.   (Weale.) 2 vols. (in 1.) 12mo.   Lond., 1865–66.   A 17 Q 7

ARMENGAUD (JEAN GERMAIN DÉSIRÉ).   Les Galeries Publiques de l'Europe.   Rome. 2 vols. imp. 4to.   Paris, 1856.   A 23 P 11, 12 †

ARMENIAN AND RUSSIAN VOCABULARY.   Sm. 4to.   St. Petersburg, 1788.   K 12 Q 11

ARMIT (LIEUT. ROBERT H.), It.N.   Light as a Motive Power : a Series of Meteorological and Hydrographical Essays. 2 vols. 8vo.   Lond., 1875–76.   A 3 S 20, 21

ARMITAGE (EDWARD), R.A.   Lectures on Painting. Delivered to the Students of the Royal Academy.   8vo. Lond., 1883.   A 7 T 2

ARMITAGE (ELLA S.)   Childhood of the English Nation, or the beginnings of English History.   12mo.   Lond., 1877.   B 3 P 29

ARMITAGE (T. R.)   The Education and Employment of the Blind : what it has been, is, and ought to be.   2nd ed.   8vo.   Lond., 1886.   G 17 Q 9

ARMOUR (JAMES), C.E.   Iron and Heat, Beams, Pillars, &c.   (Weale.) 12mo.   Lond., 1871.   A 17 Q 18

Power in Motion.   (Weale.) 12mo.   Lond., 1871. A 17 Q 18

ARMSBY (HENRY P.), PH.D. Manual of Cattle-Feeding: a Treatise on the Laws of Animal Nutrition and the Chemistry of Feeding-Stuffs in their application to the feeding of Farm Animals. 8vo. N. York, 1880. A 1 Q 13

ARMSTRONG (A.) Land Act of 1884 (48 Vict., No. 18), intituled "An Act to Regulate the Alienation, Occupation, and Management of Crown Lands." Assented to, October 17, 1884; with explanatory Notes. 1st ed. 8vo. Sydney, 1884.* MF 1 R 32

ARMSTRONG (ALBERT STAPLETON), AND CAMPBELL (G. ORD). Australian Sheep Husbandry: a Hand-book of the Breeding and Treatment of Sheep, and Station Management; with concise Instructions for Tank and Well-sinking, Fencing, Dam-making, &c. 8vo. Melb., 1882.* MA 1 P 45

ARMSTRONG (ALEXANDER), M.D., &c. Personal Narrative of the Discovery of the North-west Passage, while in search of the Expedition under Sir John Franklin. 8vo. Lond., 1857. D 4 R 40

ARMSTRONG (HENRY E.), PH.D., &c. Organic Chemistry. 12mo. Lond., 1874. A 17 S 16

ARMSTRONG (JOHN). Life and Poems of. [*See* CHALMERS, A., AND JOHNSON S.]

ARMSTRONG (R.), C.E. Construction and Management of Steam Boilers. (Weale.) 6th ed. 12mo. Lond., 1871. A 17 P 28

ARMSTRONG (ROBERT ARCHIBALD), A.M. A Gaelic Dictionary, in two parts: I. Gaelic and English. II. English and Gaelic; to which is prefixed, a New Gaelic Grammar. 4to. Lond., 1825. K 14 S 19

ARMSTRONG (WALTER). Raphael, his Life, &c. [*See* MUNTZ, E.]

History of Art in Ancient Egypt. [*See* PERROT, G. AND CHIPIEZ, C.]

Dictionary of Painters. [*See* BRYAN, M.]

ARMSTRONG (WILLIAM). Speech in Defence of. [*See* SEWELL, R. C.]

ARMY (THE). Abstracts of the Accounts of Commissaries upon Foreign Stations, for the year ended 25th December, 1828 (as to New South Wales and Van Diemen's Land, for the years 1826 and 1827). (Parl. Docs. 5.) Fol. Lond., 1830. MF 5 †

Field Exercise and Evolutions of. 8vo. Lond. 1824. A 29 R 6

General Regulations and Orders for. 8vo. Lond., 1822. F 6 R 39

Rules and Regulations for the Formations, Field Exercise and Movements of H.M. Forces. 8vo. Lond., 1808. F 6 R 38

ARMY AND NAVY CALENDAR for the Financial Years 1881-86; being a Compendium of General Information relating to the Army, Navy, Militia, and Volunteers, and containing Maps, Plans, Tabulated Statements, Abstracts, &c. 6 vols. 8vo. Lond., 1881-85. E

ARMY LIST (THE). Containing the Names of the Officers of the Army, Royal Marines, Militia, Yeomanry, Volunteers, and Colonial Militia and Volunteers. 12mo. Lond., 1831-86. E

[*See* HART, LIEUT.-GEN. H. C.]

ARMYTAGE (HON. MRS.) Wars of Queen Victoria's Reign. 1837-87. 8vo. Lond., 1886. B 3 Q 27

ARNDT (ERNST MORITZ). Eine Biographie. 18mo. Leipzig (n.d.) C 1 P 1

ARNE (THOMAS AUGUSTINE). Artaxerxes, an English Opera. [*See* ARTAXERXES.]

ARNETH (ALFRED), Ritter von. Maria Theresia und Joseph II. [*See* MARIA THERESIA.]

Maria Theresia und Marie Antoinette. [*See* MARIA THERESIA.]

Maria Theresia's erste Regierungsjahre. 3 vols. 8vo. Wien, 1863-65. C 9 T 21-23

Prinz Eugen von Savoyen. 3 vols. roy. 8vo. Wien, 1864. C 10 V 34-36

ARNOLD (ARTHUR). Through Persia by Caravan. 2 vols. 8vo. Lond., 1877. D 5 S 3, 4

ARNOLD (MRS. ARTHUR). Old Rome and New Italy. [*See* CASTELAR, EMILIO.] D 7 T 36

ARNOLD (CECIL). Index to Shakespearian Thought: a Collection of Passages from the Plays and Poems of Shakespeare, classified under appropriate readings and alphabetically arranged. 8vo. Lond., 1880. K 17 P 33

ARNOLD (SIR EDWIN), G.C.I.E. Griselda: a Tragedy, and other Poems. 12mo. Lond., 1856. H 5 T 11

Indian Idylls, from the Sanskrit of the Mahábhárata. 8vo. Lond., 1883. H 5 T 9

Indian Poetry; containing:—"The Indian Song of Songs," from the Sanskrit of the Gita Govinda of Jayadeva; two books from "The Iliad of India" (Mahábhárata); "Proverbial Wisdom" from the Shlokas of the Hitopadésa, and other Oriental Poems. 3rd ed. 8vo. Lond., 1884. H 5 T 8

India revisited. 8vo. Lond., 1886. D 5 R 36

Light of Asia; or, the Great Renunciation (Mahâbhinishkramana); being the Life and Teaching of Gautama, Prince of India, and Founder of Buddhism. 12mo. Lond., 1879. H 5 T 6

Marquis of Dalhousie's Administration of British India. (Vol. 1.) 8vo. Lond., 1862. B 10 V 28

Pearls of the Faith; or, Islam's Rosary; being the Ninety-nine Beautiful Names of Allah (Asmâ-el-Husnâ); with Comments in Verse from Various Oriental Sources (as made by an Indian Mussulman). 3rd ed. 8vo. Lond., 1884. H 5 T 7

The Secret of Death (from the Sanskrit); with some Collected Poems. 8vo. Lond., 1885. H 5 T 5

Song Celestial; or, Bhagavad-Gitâ (from the Mahábhárata); being a Discourse between Arjuna, Prince of India, and the Supreme Being, under the Form of Krishna; translated from the Sanskrit Text. 8vo. Lond., 1885. H 5 T 4

ARNOLD (EDWIN LESTER LINDEN). Coffee, its Cultivation and Profit. 8vo. Lond., 1886.   A 1 S 23
Summer Holiday in Scandinavia. 8vo. Lond., 1877.
                                             D 8 R 45

ARNOLD (REV. FREDERICK), B.A., OXON. Robertson of Brighton; with some Notices of his Times and Contemporaries. 8vo. Lond., 1886.   C 4 Q 30.

ARNOLD (FREDERICK), JUN. F.R. HIST. S., &c. History of Streatham. 8vo. Lond., 1886.   B 6 S 42

ARNOLD (GEORGE M. BROCK). [See BROOK-ARNOLD, G. M.]

ARNOLD (ISAAC N.) Life of Abraham Lincoln. 3rd ed. 8vo. Chicago, 1885.   C 5 S 19

ARNOLD (PROF. MATTHEW), M.A., &c. Culture and Anarchy: an Essay in Political and Social Criticism. 8vo. Lond., 1869.   F 10 P 14
Discourses in America. 8vo. Lond., 1885.   J 9 Q 1
Essays in Criticism. 3rd. ed., revised and enlarged. 8vo. Lond., 1875.   J 9 Q 2
Higher Schools and Universities in Germany. 8vo. Lond., 1882.   G 17 P 20
Irish Essays and others. 8vo. Lond., 1882.   J 4 P 9
On the Study of Celtic Literature. 8vo. Lond., 1867.
                                               J 6 T 8
Poems. 3 vols. 8vo. Lond., 1885.   H 5 T 9–11
  1. Early Poems, Narrative Poems, and Sonnets.
  2. Lyric and Elegiac Poems.
  3. Dramatic and Later Poems.

ARNOLD (RICHARD). Customs of London, otherwise called Arnold's Chronicle; containing, among divers other matters, the original of the celebrated Poem of the "Nut-brown Maid." Reprinted from the 1st ed. 4to. Lond., 1811.   B 15 R 4 ‡
Another copy.   B 10 R 17 †

ARNOLD (REV. THOMAS), D.D. History of Rome. 3 vols. 8vo. Lond., 1840–45.   B 11 V 5–7
Introductory Lectures on Modern History. 5th ed. 8vo. Lond., 1860.   B 15 Q 3
Life and Correspondence of; by A. P. Stanley, M.A. 2 vols. 8vo. Lond., 1844.   C 1 V 30, 31
Another copy. 5th ed. 2 vols. 8vo. Lond., 1845.
                                             C 1 V 32, 33
Second Punic War; being Chapters of the History of Rome; with Maps. 12mo. Lond., 1886.   B 12 P 10
Sermons. 6 vols. 8vo. Lond., 1845.   G 5 P 21–26
[See THUCYDIDES.]

ARNOLD (THOMAS), M.A. Beowulf: a Heroic Poem of the Eighth Century; with a Translation, Notes, and Appendix. 8vo. Lond., 1876.   H 5 T 1
Catholic Dictionary. [See ADDIS, W. E.]
Selections from Addison's Papers contributed to the *Spectator.* [See ADDISON, RT. HON. J.]

ARNOLD (THOMAS), M.R.I.B.A. History of the Cross of Edinburgh, commonly called the Mercat Cross. 12mo. Edinb., 1885.   B 13 P 1

ARNOLD (THOMAS). Method of Teaching the Deaf and Dumb Speech, Lip-Reading, and Language; with Illustrations and Exercises. Roy. 8vo. Lond., 1881. G 17 U 1

ARNOLD (THOMAS JAMES). [See REYNARD THE FOX.]

ARNOT (HUGO). History of Edinburgh, from the earliest Accounts to the Present Time. 4to. Edinb., 1788.
                                               B 12 V 24

ARNOTT (NEIL), M.D., &c. Arithmetic Simplified for general use, and adapted to aid Students engaged in any Departments of Science or Art; also to serve as a Supplement to the Author's "Elements of Physics." 8vo. Lond., 1867.   A 16 V 22
Elements of Physics; or, Natural Philosophy, General and Medical. 5th ed. 2 vols. 8vo. Lond., 1833. A 16 S 24, 25
Another copy. 6th ed. 8vo. Lond., 1865.   A 16 V 22
On the Smokeless Fire-place, Chimney-valves, and other means, old and new, of obtaining Warmth and Ventilation. 8vo. Lond., 1855.   A 2 S 10
Survey of Human Progress, from the Savage state to the highest Civilization yet attained. 8vo. Lond., 1861.   G 14 P 20

ARNOULD (JOSEPH). Catalogue of Books selling for ready money. (Pam.) 8vo. Lond., 1829. MK 1 Q 13

ARNOUX (L.) Pottery. (Brit. Manuf. Indust.) 12mo. Lond., 1876.   A 17 S 35

ARNULFUS LEXOVIENSIS. Opera omnia. [See MIGNE, J. P., SERIES LATINA, 201.]

AROUET (FRANÇOIS-MARIE). [See VOLTAIRE, FRANÇOIS MARIE AROUET DE.]

ARRIAN (FLAVIUS), "THE NICOMEDIAN." Anabasis of Alexander; or, the History of the Warsand Conquests of Alexander the Great; literally translated, by E. J. Chinnock, M.A., &c. 8vo. Lond., 1884.   B 9 S 31
Arriani Anabasis et Indica ex optimo codice Parisino emendavit et varietatem ejus libri retulit, F. Dübner. Reliqua Arriani, et Scriptorum de rebus Alexandri magni Pseudo-Callisthenis Historiam Fabulosam; edidit, C. O. Müller. Imp. 8vo. Paris, 1846.   B 10 V 9
Arriani Nicomediensis Expeditionis Alexandri libri septem, et Historia Indica. Opera Jacobi Gronovii. Sm. fol. Lugd. Bat., 1704.   B 16 R 12 ‡
Arrian's Voyage round the Euxine Sea; translated, and accompanied with a Geographical Dissertation and Maps, by W. Falconer, M.D., F.R.S., and the Rev. T. Falconer, A.M. 4to. Oxford, 1805.   D 8 V 2

ARRIGONI (L. CAV.) Collezione d'Autografi e di Documenti Storici. Imp. 8vo. Firenze, 1885.   K 9 P 16 †

ARROWSMITH (JOHN). Map of Australia, from Surveys made by order of the British Government. 8vo. Lond., 1853.　　　　　　　　　　　　　MD 5 P 3 ‡

Map of Van Diemen's Land. [Folded] 8vo. Lond., 1842.　　　　　　　　　　　　MD 5 P 17 ‡

ARROWSMITH (R.) Ph.D. [*See* KAEGI, PROF. A.]

ARTAXERXES : an English Opera : the Music composed by T. A. Arne, Mus. Soc. (New English Theatre). 12mo. Lond., 1787.　　　　　　　H 4 P 29

ART. Lectures on Art, delivered in support of the Society for the Protection of Ancient Buildings ; by Reginald Stuart Poole, Professor W. B. Richmond, E. J. Poynter, R.A., J. T. Micklethwaite, William Morris. 8vo. Lond., 1882　　　　　　　　　　A 6 V 36

ART (l') de vérifier les Dates des Faits Historiques, des Inscriptions, des Chroniques, &c., et Table Générale. 43 vols. 8vo. Paris, 1819–44.　　　　B 14 V 1–43.

ART JOURNAL (THE). (Incorporating *The Art Union*). 42 vols. roy. 4to. Lond., 1839–86.　　　　　E

ART NEEDLEWORK. Complete Manual of Embroidery in Silks and Crewels, with full instructions as to Stitches, Materials, and Implements. 4to. Lond., 1877. A 8 U 27

ART POUR TOUS (L'). Encyclopédie de l'Art industriel et décoratif. Vols. 1–24 (in 12). fol. Paris, 1861–85. E

ART TREASURES EXHIBITION. [*See* TAYLOR, T., SCHARF, G., JUN., *and* WARING, J. B.]

ART UNION, 1839–48. A Monthly Journal of the Fine Arts [continued as *The Art Journal*]. 6 vols. 4to. Lond., 1839–48.　　　　　　　　E

ART UNION OF LONDON. Catalogue of the Pictures, &c., selected by the Prize-holders of the year. 8vo. Lond., 1843.　　　　　　　　　　　A 7 P 32

Catalogue of the Works of Art in the present Exhibition. 12mo. Lond., 1843.　　　　　　　A 7 P 32

Eleventh Annual Report of the Council of the Art Union of London. 8vo. Lond., 1847.　　　MJ 2 R 22

Exhibition for 1843 : a Hand-book Guide for Visitors. [*See* CLARKE, H. G.]

Fifteenth, Seventeenth, and Nineteenth Annual Reports of the Council of the Art Union of London. 8vo. Lond., 1851–55.　　　　　　　　　　MJ 2 R 19

Report presented to the General Committee of Management of. 8vo. Lond., 1842.　　　　　A 7 R 21

ARTAUD (FRANÇOIS). Tableaux, Inscriptions Lapidaires, Antiquités et Curiosités du Musée de Lyon. 8vo. Lyon, 1816.　　　　　　　　　　　　　K 7 R 20

ARTEVELDE (JAMES AND PHILLIP VAN). [History of] ; by W. J. Ashley, B.A. (Lothian Prize Essay.) 12mo. Lond., 1883.　　　　　　　　　　B 12 T 14

Two Episodes in the History of the 14th Century; by James Hutton. 8vo. Lond., 1882.　　　B 12 T 13

ARTHUR (KING OF BRITAIN). History of the Valiant Knight, Arthur of Little Britain : a Romance of Chivalry ; originally translated from the French, by John Bourchier, Lord Berners. New edition. 4to. Lond., 1814.　　　　　　　　　J 8 V 15

[*See* MALORY, SIR T.]

ARTHUR (COL. SIR GEORGE). Defence of Transportation, in reply to the Remarks of the Archbishop of Dublin, in his second Letter to Earl Grey. 8vo. Lond., 1835.　　　　　　　　　　　　MF 2 P 41

Letters to. [*See* MONTAGU, J.]

Observations upon Secondary Punishments; to which is added, a Letter upon the same subject, by the Archdeacon of New South Wales. 8vo. Hobart, 1833. MJ 2 Q 15

ARTHUR (J. C.) Contributions to the Flora of Iowa : a Catalogue of the Phænogamous Plants. (Pam., Cn.) 8vo. Charles City, 1876.　　　　　MA 2 V 14

ARTHUR (WILLIAM). On the Difference between Physical and Moral Law. (The Fernley Lecture of 1883). 8vo. Lond., 1883.　　　　　　　　　　G 5 P 5

ARTHUR (REV. WILLIAM), A.M. Mission to the Mysore; with Scenes and Facts illustrative of India, its People, and its Religion. 12mo. Lond., 1847.　　D 5 P 30

Successful Merchant : Sketches of the Life of Mr. Samuel Budgett. 3rd ed. 8vo. Lond., 1852.　　C 3 Q 47

ARTIN (YACOUB), BEY. Landed Property in Egypt. 8vo. Lond., 1885.　　　　　　　　　　F 10 P 15

ARTIS (EDMUND TYRELL), F.S.A. Antediluvian Phytology. Illustrated by a Collection of the Fossil Remains of Plants. Roy. 4to. Lond., 1825.　　　　A 2 R 4†

ARTISAN'S SCHOOL (THE). Vereeniging : " De Ambachtsschool," gevestigd te Rotterdam. Opgericht in het jaar 1869. (Pam.Br.) 8vo. Rotterdam,1876. G 1 Q 35

ARTISTES. Dictionnaire des. [*See* HEINEKEN, C. H. DE.]

ARTISTS. Dictionary of. [*See* GRAVES, A.]

ARTISTS OF ANTIQUITY. Dictionary of. [*See* SILLIG, J.]

ARTISTS OF ENGLISH SCHOOL. Dictionary of. [*See* REDGRAVE, S.]

ARTISTS' ANNUITY FUND. Society for the Management and Distribution of ; instituted March 22nd, 1810. Report of a Special Committee of the Artists' Annuity Fund, appointed Oct. 22, 1837. 8vo. Lond.,1836–40. A 7 R 21

ARTISTS' GENERAL BENEVOLENT INSTITUTION. Account of the General Benevolent Institution for the relief of Decayed Artists of the United Kingdom, whose works have been known and esteemed by the Public 8vo. Lond., 1822.　　　　　　　　A 7 Q 19

ARTOPŒUS (S.) [*See* DICTYS CRETENSIS.]

ARUNDALE (F.) Illustrations of Jerusalem and Mount Sinai : including the most interesting Sites between Grand Cairo and Beirout. 4to. Lond., 1837. D 4 V 33

ARUNDALE (F.) AND BONOMI (JOSEPH). Gallery of Egyptian Antiquities, selected from the British Museum; with Descriptions by S. Birch. 2 parts (in 1) 4to. Lond., 1842–43. B 16 Q 20 ‡

ARUNDEL (HENRY), EARL OF, K.G. Life of the last of the Family of Fitz-Alan, 1513–79. Illustrated by John Gough Nichols. Sm. fol. Lond., 1834. C 3 W 2

ARUNDELL OF WARDOUR (JOHN FRANCIS ARUNDELL), BARON. Tradition, principally with reference to Mythology and the Law of Nations. 8vo. Lond., 1872. B 36 Q 4

ASCANIUS; or, the Young Adventurer (Charles Edward Stuart) a true History; translated from a Manuscript privately handed about at the Court of Versailles. 12mo. Lond., 1746. B 3 P 16

ASCHAM (ROGER). English Works of Roger Ascham, Preceptor to Queen Elizabeth. [With a Life by Dr. Johnson.] 8vo. Lond., 1815. J 11 U 3

The Schoolmaster; or a Plain and Perfect way of Teaching Children to understand, write and speak the Latin Tongue. 8vo. Lond., 1711. G 17 P 24

Toxophilus, the Schole, or Partitions of Shooting, contained in II Bookes. 8vo. Wrexham, 1821. A 29 P 4

ASCHBACH (JOSEPH), RITTER VON. Geschichte der Wiener Universität im ersten Jahrhunderte ihres Bestehens. Festschrift zu ihrer fünfhundertjährigen Gründungsfeier. Mit fünf Tafeln und einem Plane. 2 vols. 8vo. Wien, 1865–77. B 7 U 32, 33

ASCOLI (Prof. G. J.) Zigeunerisches.; besonders auch als Nachtrag zu dem Pott'schen Werke : " Die Zigeuner in Europa und Asien." 8vo. Halle, 1865. K 13 Q 11

ASHBURNHAM (JOHN). Narrative of his Attendance on King Charles I; with a Vindication of his Character and Conduct. 2 vols. 8vo. Lond., 1830. B 6 T 11, 12

ASHBURTON (RT. HON. LORD). [*See* PHILLIMORE, SIR R.]

ASHE (T.) [*See* COLERIDGE, S. T.]

ASHER (A.) Itinerary of Rabbi Benjamin of Tudela. [*See* BENJAMIN OF TUDELA, RABBI.]

ASHER (DAVID), PH.D. On the Study of Modern Languages in general, and of the English Language in particular: an Essay. 12mo. Lond., 1859. K 11 T 41

ASHHURST (J.) International Encyclopædia of Surgery. 6 vols. imp. 8vo. Lond., 1882–86. A 33 V 1–6

ASHLEY (J.A.) [*See* PRESBYTERIAN TRACTS.]

ASHLEY (HON. EVELYN), M.P. Life of Henry John Temple, Viscount Palmerston, 1846–65; with Selections from his Speeches and Correspondence. 2 vols. 8vo. Lond., 1876. C 9 Q 7, 8

ASHLEY (W. J.), B.A. James and Phillip van Arteveldе. (Lothian Prize Essay for 1882.) 12mo. Lond., 1883. B 12 T 14

ASHMOLE (ELIAS). History of the Most Noble Order of the Garter, wherein is set forth an Account of the Town, Castle, Chappel, and College of Windsor, with their several Officers : the Foundation of the Order by King Edward III. 8vo. Lond., 1715. B 4 Q 20

ASHMORE (MRS. HARRIETTE). Narrative of a Three Months' March in India; and a Residence in the Dooab; by "The Wife of an Officer in the 16th Foot." 8vo. Lond., 1841. D 5 Q 11

ASHTON (G. R.), AND LANGLEY (W. E.) Ye Garden Palace. Ye Olde Englyshe Fayre to be holden in ye Northerne Nave, whyche for ye nonce is transformed intoe a Streete of Ye Olden Tyme, wytм Ye Chelsea Bunhouse and ye Maypole, etc. Ye Illustrations by Maister G. R. Ashton. Ye Literary portione compyled by Maister W. E. Langley. Sm. 4to. Sydney, 1882. MJ 2 S 6

ASHTON (JOHN). Dawn of the 19th Century in England: a Social Sketch of the Times 8vo. Lond., 1886. B 6 R 40, 41

English Caricature and Satire on Napoleon I; with 115 Illustrations by the Author. 2 vols. 8vo. Lond., 1884. C 8 T 33, 34

Humour, Wit, and Satire of the 17th Century; collected and Illustrated by John Ashton. 8vo. Lond., 1883. H 5 R 1

Legendary History of the Cross. 8vo. Lond., 1887. G 3 Q 13

Old Times: a Picture of Social Life at the end of the 18th Century; collected and illustrated from the Satirical and other Sketches of the Day. 8vo. Lond., 1885. B 3 T 5

Romances of Chivalry, told and illustrated in Fac-simile. 8vo. Lond., 1887. B 14 S 20

Social Life in the Reign of Queen Anne, taken from original Sources. With Illustrations. 2 vols. 8vo. Lond., 1882. B 6 P 26, 27

ASHWELL (CANON A. R.), M.A., AND WILBERFORCE (REGINALD G.) Life of the Right Reverend Samuel Wilberforce, D.D., Lord Bishop of Oxford and afterwards of Winchester; with Selections from his Diaries and Correspondence. With Portraits by G. Richmond, R.A. 3 vols. 8vo. Lond., 1880–82. C 9 R 42–44

ASHWORTH (JOHN HENRY). The Saxon in Ireland; or, the Rambles of " An Englishman in search of a settlement in the West of Ireland." 8vo. Lond., 1851. D 7 R 44

ASHWORTH (P. A.) [*See* GNEIST, DR. R.]

ASIATIC ANNUAL REGISTER. 11 vols. 8vo. Lond., 1801–12. E

ASIATIC QUARTERLY REVIEW. Edited by Demetrius Boulger. Vol. 1. Jan.–April, 1886. Roy. 8vo. Lond., 1886. E

ASIATIC JOURNAL (THE), and Monthly Register for British and Foreign India, China, and Australasia. 52 vols. 8vo. Lond., 1824–45. E

ASIATIC SOCIETY (ROYAL). [*See* ROYAL ASIATIC SOCIETY.]

ASIATIC SOCIETY OF BENGAL. Asiatick Researches; or, Transactions of the Society, instituted in Bengal, for inquiring into the History and Antiquities, the Arts, Sciences, and Literature of Asia; with Index. 21 vols. 4to. Calcutta, 1788-1836. E

Centenary Review of the Asiatic Society of Bengal, 1784-1883. 8vo. Calcutta, 1885. E

Index to Vols. 19, 20, of the Asiatic Researches, and to Vols. 1-23 of the Journal of the Asiatic Society of Bengal. 8vo. Calcutta, 1856. E

Journal of. 49 vols. 8vo. Calcutta, 1832-78. E

Useful Tables, forming an Appendix to the Journal of the Asiatic Society. Part 1. Coins, Weights, and Measures of British India. 8vo. Calcutta, 1834. E

ASKEW (ANNE). Writings of. [*See* BRITISH REFORMERS.]

ASKEW (JOHN). Voyage to Australia and New Zealand; including a Visit to Adelaide, Melbourne, Sydney, Hunter's River, Newcastle, Maitland, and Auckland by a Steerage Passenger. 8vo. Lond., 1857. MD 1 W 41

ASMAR (MARIA THERESA). Memoirs of a Babylonian Princess, Maria Theresa Asmar (Daughter of Emir Abdallah Asmar); written by herself, and translated into English. 2 vols. 8vo. Lond., 1844. C 2 T 6,7

ASPIN (J.) Cosmorama : View of the Costumes and Peculiarities of all Nations. 12mo. Lond.,1849. A 7 P 37

ASPINALL (CLARA). Three Years in Melbourne. 12mo. Lond., 1862.* MD 3 P 2

ASSOCIATED ARCHITECTURAL SOCIETIES. [*See* ARCHITECTURAL SOCIETIES.]

ASSOCIATION for Promoting the Discovery of the Interior Parts of Africa. Proceedings. Vols. 1, 2 (*all published.*) 2 vols. 4to. Lond.,1790-1828. D 2 V 11, 12

ASTLE (THOMAS), F.R.S., &c. Antiquarian Repertory, [*See* ANTIQUARIAN REPERTORY.]

Origin and Progress of Writing, as well Hieroglyphic as Elementary; also, some Account of the Origin and Progress of Printing. 4to. Lond., 1876. A 4 R 5 T

ASTLEY (THOMAS). New General Collection of Voyages and Travels; consisting of the most esteemed Relations, which have been hitherto published in any Language; comprehending everything Remarkable in its kind in Europe, Asia, Africa, and America. 4 vols. 4to. Lond., 1745-47. D 9 V 18-21

ASTON (W. G.), M.A. Short Grammar of the Japanese Spoken Language. 3rd ed. 12mo. Lond., 1873. K 12 Q 8

ASTRONOMICAL SOCIETY (ROYAL). [*See* ROYAL ASTRONOMICAL SOCIETY.]

ASVAGHOSHA BODHISATTVA. Life of Buddha. [*See* MÜLLER, PROF. F. M.]

ASYLUM FOR THE BLIND. [Proposals for an Asylum for the Blind.] 8vo. Sydney (n.d.) MF 3 P 12

ATHANASIUS (SANCTUS), ARCHBISHOP OF ALEXANDRIA. Opera omnia. [*See* MIGNE, J. P., SERIES GRÆCA, 25-28.] Life of. [*See* KAYE, Rt. Rev. J.]

ATHENÆ OXONIENSES. [*See* WOOD, A.]

ATHENÆUM (THE). A Journal of Literature, Science, the Fine Arts, Music, and the Drama. 81 vols. 4to. Lond., 1828-85. E

ATHENÆUM (THE). A Journal Specially devoted to the encouragement of Australian Literature, Science, and Art. Fol. Sydney, 1875-76. ME

ATHENÆUS OF NAUCRATUS. Deipnosophistarum Libri XV ; supplevit nova latina versione et animadversionibus cum Is. Casauboni et indicibus instruxit J. Schweighaeuser. 5 vols. 8vo. Argentorati, 1801-05. J 16 S 24-28

Animadversiones in Athenaei Deipnosophistas post Isaacùm Casaubon conscripsit Joannes Schweighaeuser. 9 vols. 8vo. Argentorati, 1801-05. J † 16 S 29-37

Isaaci Casauboni Animadversionum in Athenaei Deipnosophistaś. 3 vols. 8vo. Leipsiae, 1796-1843. J 16 S 38-40

The Deipnosophists; or, Banquet of the Learned; literally translated, by C. D. Yonge, M.A.; with an Appendix of Poetical Fragments, rendered into English Verse by various Authors, and a General Index. 3 vols. 12mo. Lond., 1854. J 10 P 2-4

ATHENIAN GAZETTE (THE); or, Casuistical Mercury; resolving all the most Nice and Curious Questions proposed by the ingenious of either Sex. 2 vols. fol. Lond., 1690-97. J 36 Q 3, 4 ‡

ATKINS (EDWARD), B.Sc. Pure Mathematics; including Arithmetic, Algebra, Geometry, and Plane Trigonometry. 12mo. Lond., 1877. A 10 R 25

ATKINS (REV. T.) Wanderings of the Clerical Eulysses, described in a Narrative of Ten Years' Residence in Tasmania and New South Wales, at Norfolk Island and Moreton Bay ; in Calcutta, Madras, and Cape Town. 12mo. Greenwich, 1859.* MD 2 Q 13

ATKINSON (MISS CAROLINE LOUISA WARING). [*See* CALVERT, MRS. J. S.]

ATKINSON (EDWARD). Distribution of Products; or, the Mechanism and the Metaphysics of Exchange : Three Essays—What makes the Rate of Wages? What is a Bank? The Railway, the Farmer, and the Public 2nd ed. 8vo. New York, 1885. F 6 S 19

What is a Bank? What service does a Bank perform a Lecture. Economic Tracts No. 1. 8vo. New York 1881. (*Bound with " Noble's Spanish Armada".*)

ATKINSON (PROF. E.) Lectures on Scientific Subjects [*See* HELMHOLTZ, PROF, H. L. F.]

Treatise on Physics. [*See* GANOT, PROF., A.]

ATKINSON (GEORGE FRANKLIN). Pictures from the North, in Pen and Pencil; sketched during a Summer Ramble. 8vo. Lond., 1848.   D 8 T 24

ATKINSON (HENRY GEORGE), F.G.S., AND MARTINEAU (HARRIET.) Letters on the Laws of Man's Nature, and Development. 8vo. Lond., 1851.   G 13 Q 12

ATKINSON (JAMES). Account of the State of Agriculture and Grazing in New South Wales; including Observations on the Soils and General Appearance of the Country, and some of its most Natural Productions. 8vo. Lond., 1826.*   MA 1 Q 49

Account of Agriculture and Grazing in New South Wales. Second edition, revised and corrected; to which have been added some useful Data and Remarks derived from other authentic Sources. 12mo. Lond., 1844.   MA 1 Q 52

On the Expediency and Necessity of encouraging Distilling and Brewing from Grain in New South Wales. 2nd ed. 12mo. Sydney, 1829.   MJ 2 Q 21

ATKINSON (JAMES). Epitome of the Art of Navigation; or, a Short, Easy and Methodical Way to become a Compleat Navigator. 8vo. Lond. 1744.   A 19 Q 27

ATKINSON (DR. JAMES). Character and Costume of Afghaunistan. (Plates.) [*See* HART, L. W.]

Expedition into Affghanistan: Notes and Sketches descriptive of the Country during the Campaign of 1839 and 1840. 8vo. Lond., 1842.   D 5 R 38

Plates to [the above.] Imp. fol. Lond., 1842. D 8 P 1 ‡

ATKINSON (JASPER). Letter to a Member of Parliament occasioned by the Publication of the Report from the Select Committee on the high price of Gold Bullion. 2nd ed. (Pam. 8) 8vo. Lond., 1811.   F 13 R 21

ATKINSON (JOSEPH BEAVINGTON). Overbeck: a Biography. (Great Artists.) 8vo. Lond., 1882. C 3 T 4

Schools of Modern Art in Germany. Illustrated. Roy. to. Lond., 1880.   A 2 S 25 ‡

ATKINSON (JOSEPH B.) Penal Settlements and their Evils; Penitentiaries and their Advantages; including an Examination of Capt. [Alexander] Maconochie's System. 12mo. Lond., 1847.   MF 1 P 26

ATKINSON (Prof. ROBERT), M.A., LL.D. Vie de Seint Auban: a Poem in Norman-French, ascribed to Matthew Paris; now for the first time edited, from a MS. in the Library of Trinity College, Dublin; with Concordance-Glossary, and Notes. 4to. Lond., 1876.   H 6 V 18

ATKINSON (SOLOMON). Law Reform. Barristers, Attorneys, Clients, and Law Costs. Reprint of Remarks by Solomon Atkinson, Esq., of Lincoln's Inn, Barrister-at-Law, on the Relations existing between Barrister, Attorney, and Client. 8vo. Melb. 1872.   MF 1 Q 5

ATKINSON (THOMAS WITLAM). Travels in the Regions of the Upper and Lower Amoor, and the Russian Acquisitions on the Confines of India and China. 8vo. Lond., 1860.   D 5 U 2.

ATKINSON (MRS. THOMAS WITLAM). Recollections of Tartar Steppes and their Inhabitants. 8vo. Lond., 1863.   D 5 Q 35

ATKINSON (W. N. AND J. B.) Explosions in Coal Mines. 8vo. Lond., 1886.   A 9 V 11

ATKYNS (SIR ROBERT), KNT. Ancient and Present State of Glocestershire. Illustrated. 2nd ed. Fol. Lond., 1768.   B 5 P 25 ‡

ATLAS (THE). Sydney Weekly Journal of Politics, Commerce, and Literature. 4 vols. fol. Sydney, 1845–48.   M E

ATLAS (THE). A General Newspaper and Journal of Literature. Vols. 10 and 13. Fol. Lond., 1831–32. E

ATLAS INVESTMENT SOCIETY. The Rules and Regulations of the Atlas Investment and Building Society. (Pam 43.) 8vo. Sydney, 1858. MJ 2 R 5

ATTALIOTA (M.) [*See* BYZANTINÆ HIST. SCRIPT., 48.]   B 9 V 14

ATTEMPTS AT VERSIFICATION. [*See* HALF-A-DOZEN.]   MH 1 P 10

ATTERBURY (RT. REV. FRANCIS), D.D. BISHOP OF ROCHESTER. Sermons and Discourses. 4 vols. 8vo. Lond., 1723.   G 16 S 5–8

ATTFIELD (J.) Chemistry: General, Medical, and Pharmaceutical. 8vo. Lond., 1885.   A 5 R 15

ATTI DELLA SOCIETÀ ITALIANA DI SCIENZE NATURALI. [*See* SOCIETÀ ITALIANA DI SCIENZE NATURALI.]   E

ATTIC ORATORS (THE), from Antiphon to Isaeos; by R. C. Jebb, M.A. 2 vols. 8vo. Lond., 1876. C 2 V 7, 8

ATTO VERCELLENSIS. Opera omnia. [*See* MIGNE, J. P., SERIES LATINA, 134.]

ATTWOOD (GEORGE). Practical Blowpipe Assaying. With Woodcuts. 8vo. Lond., 1880.   A 5 R 1

AUBARET (CAPT. G.) Grammaire de la Langue Annamite, publiée par ordre de S Exc. le Ministre de la Marine et des Colonies. Imp. 8vo. Paris, 1864. K 16 S 11

AUBÉ (R.) Rouen illustrated. [*See* AUGÉ, E.]

AUBER (PETER), M.R.A.S. Rise and Progress of the British Power in India. 2 vols. 8vo. Lond., 1837. B 10 V 26, 27

China: an Outline of its Government, Laws, and Policy, &c. 8vo. Lond., 1834.   B 2 P 39

AUBERTIN (J. J.) Seventy Sonnets of Camoens; Portuguese Text and Translation; with Original Poems. 8vo. Lond., 1881.   H 5 T 12

Six Months in Cape Colony and Natal, and One Month in Tenerife and Madeira. 12mo. Lond., 1886. D 1 Q 25

AUBREY (John), F.R.S. Letters written by Eminent Persons in the 17th and 18th Centuries; to which are added, Hearne's Journeys to Reading and to Whaddon Hall. 2 vols. (in 3) 8vo. Lond., 1813.   C 7 P 42–44

Miscellanies. 8vo. Lond., 1696.   G 16 R 21

Natural History of Wiltshire; written between 1656–91; edited, with Notes, by John Britton. 4to. Lond., 1847.   A 15 U 2

Oxford Cabinet; consisting of Engravings from original Pictures in the Ashmolean Museum. 4to. Lond., 1797.   A 8 U 29

Remaines of Gentilisme and Judaisme, 1686–87; edited and annotated by James Britten, F.L.S. (Folk-lore Society.) 8vo. Lond., 1881.   E

AUBREY (William Hickman Smith). National and Domestic History of England. Illustrated. 3 vols. imp. 8vo. Lond., 1869–71.   B 2 T 14–6

AUCHER (Father Paschal), D.D. Grammar; Armenian and English. 8vo. Venice, 1819.   K 12 Q 12

AUCKLAND Auckland and its Neighbourhood. 8vo. Auckland, 1852.   MJ 2 Q 17

Hand-book for Emigrants; containing the most recent and authentic Information regarding Auckland, the Capital of the Colony. 8vo. Lond., 1860.   MD 1 W 31

AUCKLAND (William Eden), Lord, LL.D., &c. History of New Holland, from its First Discovery in 1616, to the Present Time; to which is prefixed an Introductory Discourse on Banishment. With Map. 8vo. Lond., 1787.*   MB 1 Q 4

Another copy. (2nd ed.) 8vo. Lond., 1808. [*Unwarrantably attributed by the publisher to Barrington.*] [*See* Barrington, G.]   MB 1 T 4

Journal and Correspondence of; with a Preface and Introduction by the Right Hon. and Right Rev. the Bishop of Bath and Wells. 4 vols. 8vo. Lond., 1861–4.   C 2 V 1–4

Principles of Penal Law. 2nd ed. 8vo. Lond., 1771.   F 3 S 18

AUDELAY (John.) Poems of: a Specimen of the Shropshire Dialect in the 15th Century; edited by James Orchard Halliwell, F.R.S., &c. (Percy Society, 14.) 8vo. Lond., 1844.   E

AUDIN (J. M. U.) Histoire de la Vie, des Ouvrages, et des Doctrines de J. Calvin. 5° ed. 12mo. Paris, 1851.   G 13 Q 3

AUDOUIN (Jean Victor), BRONGNIART, (A. T.), et DUMAS (Jean B.) Annales des Sciences Naturelles. 30 vols. 8vo. Paris, 1824–33.   E

Atlas [to the above]. Parts 1–5. 2 vols. 4to. Paris, 1824–27.   E

Revue Bibliographique pour servir de complément aux Annales des Sciences Naturelles. 8vo. Paris, 1829–31. E

AUDSLEY (George Ashdown). Art of Chromolithography. Illustrated. Fol. Lond., 1883.   A 4 P 16 †

Ornamental Arts of Japan. 2 vols. imp. 4to. Lond., 1882–84.   A 4 V 1, 2 ‡

AUDSLEY (W. J. and G. A.) Outlines of Ornament in the leading Styles; selected from executed Ancient and Modern Works. Fol. Lond., 1881.   A 23 Q 9 †

AUDUBON (John James), F.R.S., &c. Birds of America, from Drawings made in the United States and their Territories (with coloured Plates.) 8 vols. imp. 8vo. New York, 1870.   A 14 V 17–24

Life and Adventures of John James Audubon, the Naturalist; edited by R. Buchanan. 8vo. Lond., 1868.   C 1 V 34

Ornithological Biography; or, an Account of the Habits of the Birds of the United States of America. Illustrated. 5 vols. roy. 8vo. Edinb., 1831–39.   A 9 P 1–5 ‡

Plates [to the above]. 4 vols. el. fol. Lond., 1827–38.   A 9 P 6–9 ‡

Another copy [Text only]. 5 vols. roy. 8vo. Edinb., 1832–39.   A 13 V 21–25

AUDUBON (John James), F.R.S., &c., and BACHMAN (Rev. John), D.D., &c. Quadrupeds of North America. 3 vols. roy. 8vo. New York, 1854.   A 15 T 1–3

AUERBACH (Berthold). Gesammelte Schriftenerate new durchgesehene Gesammtausgabe. 3 vols. (in 1) 12mo. Stuttgart, 1857.   J 16 T 1

Narrative of Events in Vienna, from Latour to Windischgrätz, 1848; translated by J. E. Taylor. 8vo. Lond., 1849.   D 7 P 23

AUERBACH (G.) Antracen; its Constitution, Properties, Manufacture, and Derivatives, including artificial Alizarin, Antirapurpurin, &c. ; with their applications in Dyeing and Printing. 8vo. Lond., 1877. A 5 U 40

AUGÉ (E.) Rouen Illustrated; Notices by Raoul Aubé (in French and English). Fol. Paris, 1881.   D 4 U 13 ‡

AUGHEY (Samuel), Ph.D. Superficial Deposits of Nebraska. 2nd ed. (Pam.Cl.) 8vo. Wash., 1874. A 16 U 21

AUGUEZ (Paul). Spiritualisme, faits curieux, précédés d'une Lettre a M. G. Mabru suivis de l'extrait d'un compte-rendu de la fête mesmérienne, du 23 Mai 1858, et d'une relation Américaine des plus extraordinaires. 8vo. Paris, 1858.   G 5 Q 3

AUGUSTINUS (Aurelius), Saint. Sancti Aurelii Augustini Hipponensis Episcopi Opera. Opera et studio Monachorum Ordinis S. Benedicti è Congregatione S. Mauri. 11 vols.(in 8).fol. Paris, 1679–1700. G 26 Q 1–8 ‡

Opera omnia. [*See* Migne, J. P., Series Latina, 32–47.] G [*See* Haureau, B.]

AUGUSTINUS (Aurelius), Saint, MELANCHTHON (Phillip), and NEANDER (Johann August Wilhelm) : Three Biographies; by Phillip Schaff. 8vo. New York, 1886.   C 2 S 37

AULNOY, or AUNOY (Jumelle de Berneville), Comtesse d'. Contes des Fées, etc. [*See* Cabinet des Fées, 2, 4, 6.]   J 15 R 2, 4, 6

AULUS GELLIUS. [*See* GELLIUS, AULUS.] J 13 P 8-11

AUMALE (HENRI D'ORLEANS), DUC D'. History of the Princes of Condé in the 16th and 17t Centuries; translated by R. B. Borthwick. 2 vols. 8vo. Lond., 1872. C 8 R 2, 3

AUNEUIL (MME. LA COMTESSE D'). Contes des Fées. [*See* CABINET DES FÉES, 5.] J 15 R 5

AURELIUS ANTONINUS (MARCUS), EMPEROR. Fourth Book of the Meditations of: a revised Text, with Translation and Commentary, by Hastings Crossley, M.A. 8vo. Lond., 1882. G 6 S 29

[Life of]; by Paul Barron Watson. 8vo. Lond., 1884. C 8 T 2

Thoughts of; translated by George Long. 2nd ed., revised and corrected. 12mo. Lond., 1869. G 16 Q 11

AURELIUS VICTOR (SEXTUS). Historia Romana, ex Editione Th. Chr. Harlesii, cum Notis et Interpretatione in usum Delphini. 2 vols. 8vo. Lond., 1829. J 13 P 12, 13

AURORA AUSTRALIS : a Magazine. (Pam. G.) 8vo. Sydney (n.d.) ME 3 R

AUSONIUS (DECIMUS MAGNUS). Opera omnia, ex Editione Bipontina, cum Notis et Interpretatione in usum Delphini. 3 vols. 8vo. Lond., 1823. J 13 P 14-16

AUSTEN (JANE). Letters of; edited, with an Introduction and Critical Remarks, by Edward, Lord Brabourne. 2 vols. 8vo. Lond., 1884. C 5 S 1, 2

Memoir of ; by her Nephew, J. E. Austen-Leigh. 8vo. Lond., 1870. C 2 V 9

AUSTEN-LEIGH (REV. J. E.), VICAR OF BRAY. Memoir of Jane Austen ; by her Nephew. 8vo. Lond., 1870. C 2 V 9

AUSTIN (ALFRED). Russia before Europe. (Pam. Dt.) 8vo. Lond., 1876. F 4 Q 1

AUSTIN (GEORGE LOWELL). Henry Wadsworth Longfellow : his Life, his Works, his Friendships. Illustrated. 8vo. Boston, 1883. C 5 R 18

Life of Franz Schubert. 12mo. Boston, 1873. C 2 Q 44

AUSTIN (JOHN). Lectures on Jurisprudence. Third edition, revised by Robert Campbell. 2 vols. 8vo. Lond., 1873. F 10 P 4, 5

Another copy. Fourth edition, revised and edited by Robert Campbell. 2 vols. 8vo. Lond., 1869. F 10 P 2, 3

AUSTIN (J. B.) Mines of South Australia, including also an Account of the Smelting Works in that Colony. Illustrated by a Map. 8vo. Adelaide, 1863.* MA 2 Q 28

Another copy. Adelaide, 1863. MA 2 Q 35

AUSTIN (MRS. SARAH). Characteristics of Goethe, from the German of Falk, Von Müller, &c.; with Notes, original and translated, illustrative of German Literature. 3 vols. 8vo. Lond., 1833. C 4 Q 12-14

AUSTIN (MRS. SARAH—*continued*.
England in 1835. [*See* RAUMER, PROF. F. VON.]

Germany, from 1760 to 1814. 8vo. Lond., 1854. B 9 Q 38

Memoir of the Rev. Sydney Smith. [*See* HOLLAND, LADY, S.]

On National Education. 12mo. Lond., 1839. G 18 P 3

The Popes of Rome. [*See* RANKE, L.]

AUSTRAL. [*See* WILSON, MRS. J. S., AND MOODIE, D. C. F.]

AUSTRALASIA. Geographical Description of Australasia ; comprising New Holland, Van Diemen's Land, New South Wales, the Swan River Settlement, &c. 12mo. Hull, 1830. MD Q 242

New Chart of the Eastern Coast of New Holland, from South Cape to Cape York, comprehending Anthony Van Diemen's Land, Furneaux's Land, and New South Wales. 4to. Lond., 1798. MD 5 S 18 ‡

Papers relating to Australasia ; presented to both Houses of Parliament. 2 vols. fol. Lond., 1885-86. MF2U16,17

Correspondence respecting offers by the Colonies of Troops for service in the Soudan.
Despatch from the Governor of New Zealand, with a Memorandum by Sir Julius Vogel, K.C.M.G., on the Federation of the British Empire.
Papers relating to the Bill for the Constitution of a Federal Council for Australasia.
Despatch from the Governor of New South Wales, dated March 18th, 1885, respecting the Bill for the Constitution of a Federal Council for Australasia.
Despatch from the Secretary of- State to the Governors of the Australasian Colonies on the subject of the Bill for the Constitution of a Federal Council for Australasia.
Africa, New Guinea, and Western Pacific. Memoranda of Conversations at Berlin on Colonial matters, between Mr. Meade (Assistant Under Secretary of State, Colonial Office) and Prince Bismarck and Dr. Busch.
Arrangement between Great Britain and Germany relative to their respective spheres of action in portions of New Guinea.
Further Correspondence respecting New Guinea and other Islands in the Western Pacific Ocean.
New Zealand. Further Correspondence respecting a Memorial brought to this country by certain Maori Chiefs in 1884.
Further Papers relating to the Bill for the Constitution of a Federal Council for Australasia.
Correspondence respecting the powers of the two Houses of the Legislature of Queensland in respect to Money Bills.
[*See* AUSTRALIA.]

AUSTRALASIAN (THE). Quarterly Reprint of Articles selected from the Periodicals of the United Kingdom ; with original Contributions, chiefly on Subjects of Colonial Interest. Vol. 1, 8vo. Melb., 1850-51. ME 2 U

AUSTRALASIAN (THE). A Weekly Newspaper, 1864-65, 1870-77. 16 vols. fol. Melb., 1864-77. E

AUSTRALASIAN BAPTIST MAGAZINE (THE). Vol. 1 No. 10, and Vol. 2 No. 3. 12mo. Melb., 1859. MG 1 P 48

AUSTRALASIAN BOARD OF MISSIONS. Report of the Proceedings at a Meeting of the Bishops, Clergy, and Laity of the Province of Sydney, New South Wales. 12mo. Lond., 1851. MG 1 P 29

AUSTRALASIAN CHRONICLE (THE). 2 vols. fol. Sydney, 1840-43. E

AUSTRALASIAN FARMER (THE). A Practical Handbook for the Farm and Station ; by the Agricultural, Horticultural, and Pastoral Staff of the *Australasian.* 8vo. Meln., 1885.* MA 1 Q 12

AUSTRALASIAN INSURANCE AND BANKING RECORD AND STATISTICAL REGISTER: a Montily Journal of Insurance, Banking, and Finance. 10 vols. (in 12) 4to. Meln., 1877-86. ME 4 V

AUSTRALASIAN LEAGUE. [*See* ANTI-TRANSPORTATION LEAGUE.]

AUSTRALASIAN MEDICAL AND SURGICAL REVIEW, 1863. 8vo. Melb., 1863. MA 2 S 16

AUSTRALASIAN NEWS. At Sea. 4to. Sydney, 1884. ME 2 T

AUSTRALASIAN SKETCHER (THE). Witi Pen and Pencil. 2 vols. fol. Melb., 1875-81. ME 9 Q 5, 6 †

AUSTRALASIAN TURF REGISTER (THE). Containing a Full Report of the Past Season's Racing, and Entries for Coming Events. 12mo. Meln., 1869. ME 3 S

AUSTRALASIAN YACHT CLUB. Rules and Regulations. (Pam. 21.) 12mo. Sydney, 1847. MJ 2 Q 10

AUSTRALIA. Admiralty Ciarts. [*See* ADMIRALTY CHARTS.]

An Impartial Examination of all the Autiors on Australia; by "An Intending Emigrant." 12mo. Lond., 1838. MJ 2 R 1

Australia : its Scenery, Natural History, Resources, and Settlements; with a Glance at its Gold-fields. 18mo. Lond., 1854. MD 1 S 10

Australia and its Settlements. 12mo. Lond. (n.d.)* MD 1 T 1

Australia as it is. New Souti Wales: Climate and Diseases. (Pam. 3) 12mo. Bristol, 1840. MJ 2 P 38

A Monti in the Busi of Australia. Journal of one of a party of gentlemen who recently travelled from Sydney to Port Piilip. 8vo. Lond., 1838. MD 5 R 1

Centennial Supplement to the *Sydney Morning Herald*; witi Reports of the Principal Events in connection witi the Celebration of the Centenary of Australian Settlement. Sm. 4to. Sydney, 1888. MB 2 U 8

Correspondence relative to the recent Discovery of Gold in Australia; presented to boti Houses of Parliament, by Command of Her Majesty. 4to. Lond., 1852. MF 3 U 2

Drawings of Birds, ciiefly from Australia (Norfolk Island): a Collection of 101 beautifully iand-coloured Drawings; witi Description. Imp. fol. (n.p.) 1791-92. MA1P5‡

Fac-similes of Old Ciarts of Australia, now in the Britisi Museum. (Maps coloured.) Ob. 4to. Lond., 1885. D 9 P 31 ‡

Anotier copy. D 9 P 32 ‡

Anotier copy. (Maps uncoloured.) Ob. 4to. Lond., 1885. D 9 P 33 †

AUSTRALIA—*continued.*

General Map of Australia, siewing the Routes of the Explorers. 8vo. Melb., 1863. MD 5 P 8

Guide to Australia and the Gold Regions; by a "Liverpool Merciant." 12mo. Lond., 1852. MD 1 P 7

Latest Accounts from Australia. 8vo. Lond., 1836. MD 7 Q 48

Les Gisements aurifères en Australie. Par P.-A.-P. des Maisons. Première édition. Roy. 8vo. Paris, 1885. MA 2 R 5

Map of Australia. [*See* ARROWSMITH, J.]

Recent Information from Australia. 8vo. Lond., 1832. MD 7 Q 48

Resources of Australia, and the Prospects and Capabilities of the New Settlements 8vo. Lond., 1841.* MD 4 R 37

Report of Proceedings adopted for the establisiment of Steam Communication witi the Australian Colonies and New Zealand. (Pam. 23.) 8vo. Lond., 1850. MJ 2 Q 11

Routes to Australia considered in reference to Commercial and Postal Interests, in a Letter to Viscount Canning. (Pam. 30.) Lond., 1854. MJ 2 Q 18

Sketcies of Australian Life and Scenery; by "One wio ias been a Resident for Tiirty Years." 8vo. Lond., 1876.* MD 1 V 4

Anotier copy. 2nd ed. 8vo. Lond., 1876. MD 1 V 6

Society for the Promotion of the Fine Arts in Australia. [*See* FINE ARTS.]

Twenty Years' Experience in Australia ; demonstrating the superior and extraordinary advantages of Emigration to New Souti Wales. 12mo. Lond., 1839. MD 2 Q 57

Visit to Australia and its Gold Regions. 12mo. Lond., 1853. MD 1 S 49

Anotier copy. 12mo. Lond., 1856. MD 1 S 50

Voyage de Robertson aux Terres Australes, traduit sur lo Manuscrit Anglois. 18mo. Amsterdam,1766. MJ 1 P 34

Woman's Work in Australia; by a "Daugiter of the Soil." 12mo. Lond., 1862. MG 1 P 49

[*See also* AUSTRALASIA, *and* NEW HOLLAND.]

[And BURTON, J. H.]

AUSTRALIA DIRECTORY (THE). 3 vols. roy. 8vo. Lond., 1830-63. MD 5 V 3-5

1. Directions for the Soutiern Siores of Australia, from Cape Leeuwin to Port Stepiens, including Bass' Strait and Van Diemen's Land.
2. East Coast, Torres Strait, and Coral Sea ; compiled by Commander Ciarles B. Yule, R.N.
3. Nortı, Nortı-west, and West Coasts; compiled by Commander Ciarles B. Yule, R.N.

AUSTRALIA FELIX MONTHLY MAGAZINE (THE); edited by Colin Campbell. Nos. 1-3 (*all published*). 8vo. Geelong, 1849. ME 2 U

Anotier copy. (Pam. H.) ME 3 R

AUSTRALIAN (THE): a Commercial, Political, and Literary Journal. 15 vols. fol. Sydney, 1824-48. ME

AUSTRALIAN (The): a Monthly Magazine. 5 vols. 8vo. Sydney, 1879–80.* ME 3 P

AUSTRALIAN ADVOCATE (The), and Weekly Advertiser. 2 vols. fol. Sydney, 1871–72. ME

AUSTRALIAN AGRICULTURAL COMPANY. (The) A Bill to amend an Act for granting certain powers and authorities to a Company to be incorporated by Charter, to be called the Australian Agricultural Company. (Parl. Docs. 6.) Fol. Lond., 1830. MF 4 ‡

By-Laws for the Government of. (Pam. 31.) 8vo. Lond., 1825. MJ 2 Q 19

Colony of the Australian Agricultural Company. [*See* HARRIS, A.]

List of Proprietors. (Pam. 31.) 8vo. Lond., 1828. MJ 2 Q 19

Plan of the Company. (Pam. 31.) 8vo. Lond., 1826. MJ 2 Q 19

Reports. 8vo. Lond., 1826–33. MJ 2 Q 19

Reports. 8vo. Lond., 1831–33. MJ 2 R 17

Reports. 8vo. Lond., 1841. MJ 2 Q 2

Reports, 1835, 1840, 1841. (Pam. Dl.) 8vo. Lond. MF 3 P 11

Statement of the Services of Mr. R. Dawson. [*See* DAWSON, R.]

AUSTRALIAN ALMANACS, for the years 1808–69. 12mo. Sydney, &c., 1808–69. ME 4 Q and R

AUSTRALIAN AND NEW ZEALAND MONTHLY MAGAZINE. 8vo. Lond., 1842. ME 3 R

AUSTRALIAN ANNIVERSARY DINNER, in Commemoration of the First of the Australian Colonies, held at the "Albion," Aldersgate-street, London, on Tuesday, the 26th January, 1858. Sir Charles Nicholson, D.C.L., in the Chair. Speeches, &c. (Pam. F.) 8vo. Lond., 1858. MJ 2 S 3

AUSTRALIAN AUXILIARY CHURCH MISSIONARY SOCIETY. Report, 1836. 8vo. Sydney, 1836. MG 1 Q 27

Rules, &c. 12mo. Sydney, 1834. MG 1 Q 27

AUSTRALIAN AUXILIARY MISSIONARY SOCIETY. [*See* LONDON MISSIONARY SOCIETY, 1839.]

AUSTRALIAN BABES IN THE WOOD (The). A True Story, told in Rhyme for the Young ; by the Author of "Little Jessie," &c. 8vo. Lond., 1866. MH 1 P 21

AUSTRALIAN BAND OF HOPE REVIEW AND CHILDREN'S FRIEND. Vol. 1. No. 17. (Pam. G.) 8vo. Sydney, 1856. ME 3 R

AUSTRALIAN CHURCHMAN (The), and Religious Intelligencer : a Weekly Record of Church and General News. 20 vols. fol. Sydney, 1867–81. ME

AUSTRALIAN CLUB (The). Rules and Regulations for the Government of. 12mo. Sydney (n.d.) MF 3 P 10

AUSTRALIAN COLLEGE. First Report of the Council. 8vo. Sydney, 1832. MF 3 P 14

AUSTRALIAN COLONIES. Prospects and Considerations of a Future for the Australian Colonies: a Pamphlet, by the "Unknown." 8vo. Hobart, 1865. MF 1 Q 2

Third Report of the Commissioners of Colonial Inquiry. (Parl. Docs. 5.) Fol. Lond., 1830. MF 4 ‡

AUSTRALIAN COLONIES ASSOCIATION. Report of the Permanent Committee to the Members of the General Association for the Australian Colonies, at their first Annual Meeting. 8vo. Lond., 1856. MF 3 P 7

AUSTRALIAN COLONIES GOVERNMENT BILL. A Bill for the better Government of Her Majesty's Australian Colonies. Nos. 1, 2. (Parl. Docs. 55.) Fol. Lond., 1849. ME 4 R ‡

Copies of Correspondence on the subject of the Australian Colonies Government Bill, and the extension of the Elective Franchise in New South Wales. (Parl. Docs. 57.) Fol. Lond., 1850. MF 4 ‡

AUSTRALIAN CONSTITUTION. Papers relative to the proposed alteration in the Constitution of the Australian Colonies. (Parl. Docs. 57.) Fol. Lond., 1850–56. MF 4 ‡

AUSTRALIAN CROCHET-BOOK ; with new stitches. Dedicated to the Ladies of Sydney. Ob. 12mo. Sydney, 1859. MA 2 S 5

AUSTRALIAN DEMOCRACIES. (Social Science Review—Pam. A.) Fol. Lond., 1863. MJ 2 U 1

AUSTRALIAN DIAMOND DRILL CO. Introductory Remarks. (Pam. Cn.) 8vo. Sydney, 1876. MA 2 V 14

AUSTRALIAN DICTIONARY OF DATES, &c. [*See* HEATON, J. H.]

AUSTRALIAN DIOCESAN COMMITTEE. Catalogue of Books and Tracts in the Repository of the Australian Diocesan Committee. 8vo. Sydney, 1838. MK 1 Q 13

AUSTRALIAN DIRECT STEAM NAVIGATION COMPANY (The), via Panama. Incorporated by Royal Charter, bearing date 24th June, 1853. (Pam. 30.) 8vo. Lond., 1853. MJ 2 Q 18

AUSTRALIAN ERA (The). Roy.8vo. Sydney, 1850–51. ME 10 P 3 †

AUSTRALIAN FAMILY JOURNAL (The): Weekly Magazine of Literature, Science, Arts, Mechanics, Commerce, and Domestic General Information. Nos. 1–4. (Pam. 3.) 4to. Sydney, 1852. MJ 2 S 2

AUSTRALIAN FLORAL AND HORTICULTURAL SOCIETY. Fourth Annual Report. (Pam. Dl.) 12mo. Sydney, 1842. MF 3 P 11

AUSTRALIAN FREEMASON'S MAGAZINE; edited by J. Sheridan Moore, 1870–71. 3 vols. (in 1). 8vo. Sydney, 1870–71. ME 3 R

AUSTRALIAN GAS-LIGHT CO. Street Lights. Memorandum on the Report of the Committee of the City Council, appointed to consider and report on the most suitable means of lighting the City of Sydney ; by the Committee of Directors. (Parl. Docs. 41.) Fol. Sydney, 1843. MF 4 ‡

AUSTRALIAN GOLD-DIGGER'S MONTHLY MAGAZINE. [*See* BONWICK, J.]

AUSTRALIAN HAND-BOOK (THE). [*See* GORDON & GOTCH.]

AUSTRALIAN HEALTH SOCIETY. Health Lectures for the People. 1st Series. 12mo. Mel., 1886. MA 2 S 23

  W. S. Flett.—What is Disease ?
  J. Jamieson.—Food and Drink as Carriers of Disease.
  J. Smith.—Cheerfulness as a Factor of Health.
  T. R. H. Willis.—Mortality and Management of Infancy.
  J. W. Springthorpe.—Results of Unhealthy Education.
  C. R. Blackett.—The Food we eat, and how to cook it.

AUSTRALIAN HOME COMPANION. Vol. 5, Nos. 108–110. 8vo. Sydney, 1860. ME 3 R

AUSTRALIAN HORTICULTURAL AND AGRICULTURAL SOCIETY. First Report of the, 1857. (Pam. 26.) 8vo. Sydney, 1858. MJ 2 Q 14

AUSTRALIAN ISRAELITE (THE): Weekly Journal of Literature, Religion, and Record ; devoted to the Interests of Judaism and the Jewish Community in Australia and New Zealand 3 vols. fol. Mel., 1872–74. ME 9 Q 26–28 †

AUSTRALIAN JOURNAL (THE): Weekly Record of Literature, Science, and the Arts. Vols. 1–3. 3 vols. 4to. Mel., 1866–68. ME 3 V

AUSTRALIAN JOURNALIST, AN. [*See* EMIGRANT IN AUSTRALIA, THE.]

AUSTRALIAN LIBRARY (THE). An Act to enable the Proprietors of a Public Library, under the name of the "Australian Subscription Library," to sue and be sued. Sm. fol. Sydney, 1834. MF 2 U 20

An Arranged Catalogue of the Books in the Australian Subscription Library and Reading-rooms; with the Rules, Regulations, and By-laws, and a List of Members and Subscribers. Established 1826. 8vo. Sydney, 1839. MK 1 P 6

Addenda to the Arranged Catalogue of the Books in the Australian Subscription Library. 8vo. Sydney, 1840. MK 1 P 6

AUSTRALIAN LIBRARY (THE)—*continued*
Addenda to the Arranged Catalogue of the Books in the Australian Subscription Library. 8vo. Sydney, 1845. MK 1 P 7

Another copy. 8vo. Sydney, 1845. MK 1 Q 13

Annual Reports of the Committee of Management to the Proprietors and Shareholders of the Australian Library and Literary Institution, 1866–67. (Pam. 20). 8vo. Sydney, 1866–67. MJ 2 Q 9

Annual Reports of the Committee of Management, 1868–69. 8vo. Sydney, 1868–69. MF 3 P 14

Australian Subscription Library: Statement of Building Fund; and General Account, 1846–47. (Pam. E.) 4to. Sydney, 1847. MJ 2 S 2

Catalogue; with Rules, Regulations, and Bye-laws. 8vo. Sydney, 1834. MK 1 Q 13

Catalogue; with Rules, Regulations, and By-laws for the conduct of the Australian Subscription Library and Reading-rooms. 2 vols. 8vo. Sydney, 1836–38. MK 1 P 4, 5

Catalogue; with Rules, Regulations, and Bye-laws. 8vo. Sydney, 1837. MK 1 Q 13

Catalogue ; with the Rules, Regulations, and By-laws. 8vo. Sydney, 1838. MJ 2 R 18

Catalogue of the Australian Subscription Library and Reading-rooms, systematically arranged; with the Rules, Regulations, and By-laws, and a List of Members. Established 1826. 2 vols. 8vo. Sydney, 1843–53. MK 1 P 7, 8

Rules and Regulations for the conduct of the Australian Subscription Library and Reading-room; approved at a General Meeting, held on the 10th January, 1828. 8vo. Sydney, 1828. MF 3 P 14

Supplements to the Arranged Catalogue. 8vo. Sydney, 1847–50. MK 1 Q 13

AUSTRALIAN LIFE AND SCENERY. Sketches of ; by "One who has been a Resident for Thirty Years." 8vo. Lond., 1876.* MD 1 V 4

AUSTRALIAN LITERARY JOURNAL. Roy. 8vo. Sydney, 1848. ME 10 P 3 †

AUSTRALIAN MAGAZINE. (ILLUSTRATED.) [*See* ILLUSTRATED AUSTRALIAN MAGAZINE.]

AUSTRALIAN MAGAZINE (THE); or, Compendium of Religious, Literary, and Miscellaneous Intelligence. Vols. 1, 2. 8vo. Sydney, 1821–22. ME 3 P

AUSTRALIAN MAIL SERVICE. Special Report, &c. (Pam. 30.) 8vo. Lond., 1856. MJ 2 Q 18

AUSTRALIAN MEAT. Recipes for Cooking; with Directions for preparing Sauces suitable for the same, by "A Cook." 12mo. Lond., 1872. MA 1 V 39

AUSTRALIAN MEDICAL ASSOCIATION (THE). Code of Ethics recommended by the Council. (Pam. 21.) 8vo. Sydney, 1859. MJ 2 Q 10.

AUSTRALIAN MEDICAL JOURNAL. 4to. Sydney, 1846–47.   MA I P 8 †

AUSTRALIAN MEDICAL SUBSCRIPTION LIBRARY. Catalogue. 8vo. Sydney, 1855.   MK 1 Q 13

AUSTRALIAN MONTHLY MAGAZINE (THE), 1865–67. Vols. 1–4. 8vo. Meln., 1866–67.   ME 3 Q

AUSTRALIAN MUSEUM. Catalogue of Fossils in the Australian Museum. 8vo. Sydney, 1883.   MK 1 S 41

Catalogue of the Australian Hydroid Zoopnytes. [*See* BALE, W. M.]

Catalogue of the Library of. [Compiled by Thomas H. Fielding.] 8vo. Sydney, 1883.   MK 1 Q 1

Guide to the Contents of. (Pam. L.) 8vo. Sydney, 1873.   MJ 2 P 28

Report from the Trustees, 1863–64. Fol. Sydney, 1864.   ME 10 Q 3 †

[*See* KREFFT, G.; RAMSAY, E. P.; *and* RATTE, A. F.]

AUSTRALIAN MUTUAL PROVIDENT SOCIETY. Act of Incorporation; Parliament of New South Wales (20 Vic.), assented to 18th March, 1857. By-Laws confirmed and finally passed 12th March, 1867 ; and Tables of Rates. 8vo. Sydney, 1867.   MF 3 P 19

Act to incorporate the Australian Mutual Provident Society; assented to March 18th, 1857; also, the By-Laws of the Society, with Schedule of Tables annexed, and other Information. 8vo. Sydney, 1857.   MF 3 P 11

Directors' Report for presentation to a Special Meeting of Members, to be held on the 26th August, 1873. Roy. 8vo. Sydney, 1873.   ME 4 V

Proceedings at laying the Foundation Stone of New Offices, Pitt-street, Sydney, Tuesday, January, 1877. (Pam. N.) 8vo. Sydney, 1877.   MJ 2 P 29

Report presented at the Annual Meeting, held in February, March, and April, 1865. (Pam. A.) Fol. Sydney, 1865.   MJ 2 U 1

Report on the Fifth Quinquennial Investigation of. 4to. Sydney, 1874.   ME 4 V

Report on the Sixth Quinquennial Investigation of. 4to. Sydney, 1879.   ME 4 V

Report of the Mortality Experience of, 1849–88. 4to. Sydney, 1891.   ME 4 V

[*See* BLACK, M. A.]

AUSTRALIAN PATRIOTIC ASSOCIATION. Report of the Provisional Committee, laid before the General Meeting of the Members on the 5th of August, 1835. 8vo. Sydney, 1835.   MJ 2 R 17

Letter to Charles Buller. [*See* BLAND, W.]

AUSTRALIAN PENNY JOURNAL (THE). (Pam. H.) Vol. 1. 8vo. Sydney, 1848.   ME 3 R

AUSTRALIAN PRACTITIONER (THE). A Quarterly Journal of Medical, Surgical, and Sanitary Science for the Australian Colonies. Nos. 1–4. 8vo. Sydney, 1877–78.   ME 3 P

AUSTRALIAN PUBLIC OPINION (THE). July 16–Oct. 15. 1887. (*All published.*) Sm. fol. Sydney, 1887.   ME

AUSTRALIAN PULPIT NEWS and Sunday at Home. Vol. 1. 4to. Sydney, 1871.   ME 11 P 2 †

AUSTRALIAN QUARTERLY JOURNAL of Theology, Literature and Science; edited by the Rev. Charles P. N. Wilton. Vol. 1. 8vo. Sydney, 1828.   ME 3 R

AUSTRALIAN RACING CALENDAR (THE), for August and September, 1887. Compiled and edited by "Scrutator." 2 vols. 8vo. Sydney, 1887.   ME 5 Q

AUSTRALIAN RELIGIOUS TRACT SOCIETY. [*See* NEW SOUTH WALES RELIGIOUS TRACT AND BOOK SOCIETY.]

AUSTRALIAN SCHOOL SOCIETY. First Report of the Australian School Society, on the Principles of the British and Foreign School Society in London. 8vo. Sydney, 1836.   MF 3 P 14

Report of the Provisional Committee; and Rules and Regulations. 8vo. Sydney, 1835.   MG 1 Q 38

AUSTRALIAN SETTLEMENT. [*See* AUSTRALIA—Centennial Supplement to the *Sydney Morning Herald*.]   MB 2 U 8

AUSTRALIAN SETTLER, AN. [*See* DIARY OF TRAVELS.]

AUSTRALIAN SETTLER'S HAND-BOOK. [*See* WAUGH, J. W.]

AUSTRALIAN SKETCHES; by "Overlander." [A.E.] 8vo. Lond., 1887.   MD 1 W 17

The Settler. From Tait's Edinburgh Magazine. 8vo. Melb. (n.d.)   MJ 2 R 22

AUSTRALIAN TEMPERANCE MAGAZINE (THE). Vols. 1–3. (in 1.) 8vo. Sydney, 1838–40.   ME 3 R

AUSTRALIAN TURF GUIDE (THE). Containing a full Report of the past year's Racing, and Entries for Coming Events, Registered Colours, Rules of Horse Racing in general, Standard Weights for Age of the A.J.C and V.R.C., Rules of Betting, Winners of the Principal English and Colonial Races. 12mo. Sydney, 1879.   ME 3 S

AUSTRALIAN WOOLS. Sales of Australian Wools in London. Report of Committees, Minutes of Committees and Evidence. Appendix: Statistics. 8vo. Lond., 1870.   MF 2 P 35

AUSTRIA AND THE AUSTRIANS. 2 vols. 8vo. Lond., 1837.   D 9 P 8, 9

AUTOBIOGRAPHY. Collection of the most instructive and amusing self-written Lives ever published; with brief introductions, and compendious Sequels carrying on the Narrative to the Death of each Writer. 33 vols. (in 18). 12mo. Lond., 1826-32.   C 1 P 5-22

1. An Apology for the Life of Mr. Colley Cibber, Comedian; written by himself.
2. The Life of David Hume; written by himself. William Lilly's History of his Life and Times, from 1602 to 1681; written by himself, 1715. Memoirs of the Life of Voltaire; written by himself; with Introduction and Sequel, condensed from the Life by Condorcet.
3, 4. Memoirs of Marmontel; written by himself: containing his Literary and Political Life, and Anecdotes of the Principal Characters of the Eighteenth Century. . In two volumes.
5. The pleasant and surprising Adventures of Robert Drury during his Fifteen Years' Captivity on the Island of Madagascar; written by himself.
6. Journal of a Voyage from London to Savannah, in Georgia; by George Whitefield, A.B.
7. Memoirs of the late Mrs. Robinson; written by herself: from the edition edited by her daughter. A Narrative of the Life of Mrs. Charlotte Clarke; written by herself.
8. The Life of Edward, Lord Herbert, of Cherbury; written by himself. Memoirs of Prince Eugene of Savoy; written by himself.
9, 10. Sketch of the Life and Literary Career of Augustus von Kotzebue; with the Journal of his exile to Siberia; written by himself. In two volumes.
11. The Memoirs of Captain John Creichton, from his own materials; drawn up and digested by Jonathan Swift, D.D., D.S.P.D. Memoir of William Gifford; written by himself. The History of the Life of Thomas Elwood; written by himself.
12. Memoirs of Lewis Holberg; written by himself.
13. Memoirs of James Hardy Vaux, a Swindler and Thief, now transported to New South Wales, for the second time, and for Life; written by himself.
14, 15. Memoirs of the Life and Writings of Edward Gibbon, Esq.; composed by himself; with occasional Notes and Narrative, by the Right Honourable John, Lord Sheffield. In two volumes.
16, 17. The Life of Benvenuto Cellini, a Florentine Artist; written by himself. Translated by Thomas Nugent. In two volumes.
18. Memoirs of the forty-five first years of the Life of James Lackington, Bookseller; written by himself.
19. The Life of Theobald Wolfe Tone; written by himself, and extracted from his Journals. Edited by his son, William Theobald Wolfe Tone.
20, 21. Memoirs of Frederica Sophia Wilhelmina, Princess Royal of Prussia, Margravine of Bareith, sister of Frederic the Great; written by herself. Translated from the original French. In two volumes.
22. The Diary of the late George Bubb Dodington, Baron of Melcombe Regis: from March 8, 1749, to February 6, 1761, with an Appendix, containing some curious and interesting Papers. Published from original Manuscripts, by Henry Penruddocke Wyndham.
23, 24. Memoirs of Goldoni; written by himself; forming a complete History of his Life and Writings. Translated from the original French, by John Black. In two volumes.
25-28. Memoirs of Vidocq, Principal Agent of the French Police until 1827, and now proprietor of the paper manufactory at St. Mandé; written by himself. Translated from the French. In four volumes.
29-32. Memoirs of Madame du Barri. Translated from the French. In four volumes.
33. Memoirs of William Sampson, an Irish Exile; written by himself. To which is added a brief Historical Sketch of the British connexion with Ireland, and some Observations on the Present Condition of America.

AUTOBIOGRAPHY OF AN ENGLISH SOLDIER in the United States Army. 2 vols. 8vo. Lond., 1853.   C 3 P 1, 2

AUTOGRAPH LETTERS. Autograph Letters, Characteristic Extracts and Signatures, from the Correspondence of Illustrious and Distinguished Women of Great Britain; collected and copied by J. Netherclift. Lond., 1838.   C 1 W 2

Autograph Letters; written by Royal and Distinguished Persons of Great Britain; copied by J. Netherclift and Son. 4to. Lond., 1849.   C 1 W 1

AUTOGRAPHIC MIRROR (THE). [English and French.] 2 vols. fol. and 2 vols. imp. 4to Lond., 1864-66.   C 22 R 1-4 ‡

AUXILIARY BIBLE SOCIETY OF BRADFORD. Second Report, 1812. 12mo. Lond., 1813. MF 3 P 10

AUXILIARY BIBLE SOCIETY OF NEW SOUTH WALES. Reports, with a List of Subscriptions, Donations, &c. 12mo. Sydney, 1817-64.   MJ 2 Q 3 and 21

[See also BRITISH AND FOREIGN BIBLE SOCIETY.]

A VAKATUSA ni Lotu : o Koya oqo Nai Vakadinadina, Kei Nai Vakavuvuli, Kei na Cakacaka dodonu ni lotu; Kei Nai Valavala e so sa lesia ko Jisu me ia tiko e na nona lotu. 8vo. Viti, 1850.   G 16 R 18

AVDALL (JOHANNES). History of Armenia. [See CHAMICH, FATHER MICHAEL.]

AVÉ-LALLEMANT (DR. FRIEDRICH CHRISTIAN BENEDICT). Das deutsche Gaunerthum in seiner social-politischen, literarisehen und linguistischen Ausbildung zu seinem heutigen Bestande. Mit zahreichen Holzschnitten. 3 vols. 8vo. Leipzig, 1858-62. F 7 P 20-22

AVE-LALLEMANT (ROBERT). Life of A. von Humboldt. [See LÖWENBERG, J.]

AVELING (MRS. ELEANOR MARX.) History of the Commune. [See LISSAGARAY, P.]

AVELING (JAMES H.), M.D. Yorkshire : History of Roche Abbey, from its Foundation to its Dissolution. Roy. 4to. Lond., 1870.   B 15 T 12 ‡

AVESTA. Religious Books of the Parsees; from Professor Spiegel's German translation of the original Manuscripts, by Arthur H. Bleeck. 3 vols. (in 1) 8vo. Hertford, 1864.   G 6 P 4

AVISON (CHARLES). Essay on Musical Expression. 3rd ed. 12mo. Lond., 1775.   A 7 P 18

AVONMORE (VISCOUNTESS). [See YELVERTON, THÉRÈSE.]

AWDELEY (JOHN). Fraternitye of Vacabondes. (Licensed in 1560-1, imprinted then, and in 1565.) From the Edition of 1575 in the Bodleian Library. Edited by Edward Viles and F. J. Furnivall. (New Shakespere Society, Series 6.) 8vo. Lond., 1880.   E

AXON (WILLIAM E. A.) Annals of Manchester: a Chronological Record to the end of 1885. 4to. Manch., 1886.   B 5 V 7

Cheshire Gleanings. 8vo. Manch., 1884.   B 3 P 18

John Ruskin : a Bibliographical Biography. (*Bound with "Notes on Sheepfolds."*) 8vo. Lond., 1879.   G 11 T 14

Mechanic's Friend. 8vo. Lond., 1875.   A 11 P 13

AYERS (SIR HENRY). Australia Confederated. [*See* JEFFERIS, REV. J.]

AYLMER (JOHN), BISHOP OF LONDON. Life and Acts of. Strype's Historical Works. Vol. X.   G 2 S 19

AYMON (LES QUATRE FILS). [*See* QUATRE FILS.]

AYRE (REV. J.) The Treasury of Bible Knowledge. [*See* MAUNDER'S, S.]

AYRES (MRS. H. M E. SHARP). Mirror Painting in Italian Style ; a Manual for Amateurs. 8vo. Lond., 1866.   A 7 Q 1

AYTOUN (WILLIAM EDMONDSTOUNE), D.C.L. Ballads of Scotland. 2 vols. 12mo. Edinb., 1861.   H 7 P 1, 2

Bothwell : a Poem. 12mo. Lond., 1858.   H 7 P 3

Lays of the Scottish Cavaliers, and other Poems. 12mo. Lond., 1854.   H 5 R 6

Memoir of ; by Sir Theodore Martin ; with an Appendix. 8vo. Edinb., 1867.   C 2 U 1

AYTOUN (WILLIAM EDMONDSTOUNE), D.C.L., AND MARTIN (SIR THEODORE), K.C.B. Book of Ballads ; edited by "Bon Gaultier." Illustrated. 12th ed. 8vo. Lond., 1874.   H 7 P 36

AZEGLIO (MASSIMO TAPARELLI), MARQUIS D'. Recollections of; translated by Count Alessandro Maffei. 2 vols. 8vo. Lond., 1868.   C 1 U 43, 44

B

B——. (MME. C.—— DE LA). [*See* CALDERON DE LA BARCA, MME. FRANCES.]

B——. (MME. DE). Memoirs of Rachel. [*See* RACHEL-FÉLIX, E.]

B. (G. S.) [*See* STUDY OF PROLOGUE AND EPILOGUE.]

B (J. A.) [*See* META OF GAINDARA.]

B—— (W. M.) Narrative of Edward Crewe. [*See* NARRATIVE.]

B.K.S. Stanzas. [*See* LEICHHARDT, DR. L.]

BABBAGE, (CHARLES), A.M., &c. Comparative View of the various Institutions for the Assurance of Lives. 8vo. Lond., 1826. F 10 R 14

On the Economy of Machinery and Manufactures. 2nd ed. enlarged. 12mo. Lond., 1832. A 11 P 18

Reflections on the Decline of Science in England, and on some of its Causes. 8vo. Lond., 1830 A 16 U 18

Table of the Logarithms of the Natural Numbers, from 1 to 108,000. Stereotyped. 2nd ed. Imp. 8vo. Lond., 1831. A 10 U 16

The Exposition of 1851; or, Views of the Industry, the Science, and the Government of England. 8vo. Lond., 1851. F 10 R 13

The Ninth Bridgewater Treatise: a Fragment. 2nd ed. 8vo. Lond., 1838. G 6 P 24

BABBITT (EDWIN D.) Principles of Light and Color; including among other things, the Harmonic Laws of the Universe, the Etherio-Atomic Philosophy of Force, Chromo-Chemistry, Chromo-Therapeutics, and the General Philosophy of the Fine Forces. Roy. 8vo. New York, 1878. A 16 V 11

BABER (E. CRESSWELL), M.B. Contributions to the Minute Anatomy of the Thyroid Gland of the Dog. (Roy. Soc. Pubs. 3.) 4to. Lond., 1876. A 11 P 4 †

BABRIUS. Mythiambics of Babrius. Edited, with Introductory Dissertations, Critical Notes, Commentary, and Lexicon, by W. Gunion Rutherford, M.A. 8vo. Lond., 1883. H 5 U 17

BACCHANTE, H.M.S. Cruise of. MD 2 V 21, 22

BACH (ALBERTO B.) Principles of Singing: a Practical Guide for Vocalists and Teachers. 8vo. Edinb., 1885. A 7 P 19

BACH (CARL PHILLIP EMANUEL). Letters of. [*See* WALLACE, LADY.]

BACH (JOHANN SEBASTIAN). His Work and Influence on the Music of Germany, 1685–1750; by Philipp Spitta; translated from the German by Clara Bell and J. A. Fuller-Maitland. 3 vols. 8vo. Lond., 1884–85. C 10 R 14–16

BACHAUMONT (LOUIS). Mémoires. [*See* BARRIÈRE, J. F.]

BACHMAN (REV. JOHN), D.D., &c. Quadrupeds of North America. [*See* AUDUBON, J. J.]

BACK (CAPT. SIR GEORGE), R.N. Narrative of the Arctic Land Expedition to the Mouth of the Great Fish River, and along the Shores of the Arctic Ocean, in the years 1833–35. 8vo. Lond., 1836. D 4 R 21

Narrative of an Expedition in H.M.S. *Terror*, undertaken with a view to Geographical Discovery on the Arctic Shores, in the years 1836–37 8vo. Lond., 1838. D 4 R 22

BACKER (LOUIS). [*See* BAECKER, L. DE.]

BACKHOUSE (EDWARD). Early Church History, to the Death of Constantine; edited and enlarged by Charles Tylor. 8vo. Lond., 1884. G 6 R 15

BACKHOUSE (JAMES). Extracts from the Letters of James Backhouse, now engaged in a Religious Visit to Van Dieman's Land, New South Wales, Mauritius, and South Africa; accompanied by George Washington Walker. Parts 1–10. 8vo. Lond., 1838–41. MD 1 U 15

Narrative of a Visit to the Australian Colonies. Illustrated. 8vo. Lond., 1843.* MD 2 8 7

Narrative of a Visit to the Mauritius and South Africa. Illustrated. 8vo. Lond., 1844. D 2 S 20

BACKHOUSE (JAMES), AND TYLOR (CHARLES). Life and Labours of George Washington Walker, of Hobart Town, Tasmania. 8vo. Lond., 1862.* MC 1 R 34

BACKHOUSE (JAMES), AND WALKER (G. W.) Address to the Prisoner Population of New South Wales and Van Dieman's Land. 12mo. Sydney, 1837. MG 1 P 9

Christian Address to the Free Inhabitants of New South Wales and Van Diemen's Land. 12mo. Sydney, 1837.* MG 1 P 49

BACKHOUSE (R.) Church and State; or, the Gods of the Tent is a Changeable Tyrant. 8vo. Hobart (n.d.) MG 1 Q 29

BACON (SIR FRANCIS), LORD VERULAM. [A Biography]; by R. W. Church. (Eng. Men of Letters.) 8vo. Lond., 1884. C 1 U 9

Account of the Life and Times of. Extracted from the edition of his Occasional Writings, by James Spedding. 2 vols. 8vo. Lond., 1878. C 3 R 6, 7

Advancement of Learning; edited by W. A. Wright, M.A. 2nd ed. (Clar. Press.) 12mo. Oxford, 1873. G 16 P 35

Bacon, not Shakespeare. [*See* THOMSON, W.]

Bacon-Shakespeare Controversy. [*See* WYMAN, W. H.]

Essays; with Annotations by Richard Whately, D.D. 8vo. Lond., 1867. G 12 T 29

BACON (SIR FRANCIS), LORD VERULAM—*continued.*
Evenings with a Reviewer, or Macaulay and Bacon. [*See*
SPEDDING, J.]

Francis Bacon : an Account of his Life and Works, by
E. A. Abbott, D.D. 8vo. Lond., 1885.   C 10 R 10

Letters and the Life of Francis Bacon, including all his
Occasional Works, newly collected and set forth in
chronological order, with a Commentary, Biographical
and Historical, by Jas. Spedding. 6 vols. 8vo. Lond.,
1861-72.   C 2 V 17-22

Of the Advancement and Proficience of Learning ; or,
the Partitions of Sciences. Nine Bookes, written in Latin,
interpreted by Gilbert Wats. Fol. Oxford, 1640.
G 5 U 5

Personal History of.   From unpublished Papers ; by
William Hepworth Dixon. 8vo. Lond., 1861.   C 2 V 16

Political Allegories of Bacon. [*See* THOMSON, W.]

Promus of Formularies and Elegancies ; illustrated and
elucidated by Passages from Shakespeare. [*See* POTT,
MRS. H.]

Selections from the Works of.   [*See* MONTAGU, B.]

Shakspeare, not Bacon.   [*See* SHAKESPEARE, W.]

Works of.   12 vols. 12mo. Lond., 1807.   J 1 W 1-12

Works of; with a Life. 10 vols. 8vo. Lond., 1826.
J 7 T 1-10

BACON (GEORGE W.), F.R.G.S. Bacon's Guide to America
and the Colonies, for the Capitalist, Tourist, or Emigrant.
8vo. Lond., 1870.   MD 4 T 31

Life and Administration of Abraham Lincoln, presenting
his Early History, Political Career, Speeches, Messages,
Proclamations, Letters, &c. 8vo. Lond., 1865.   C 3 V 23

BACON (HENRY). Parisian Art and Artists. Illustrated.
Sq. 8vo. Boston, 1883.   A.7 Q 30

BACON (ROGER). [*See* CHRONICLES OF GT. BRIT. 25.]

BACON (LIEUT. THOMAS). First Impressions and Studies
from Nature, in Hindostan, from 1831-36. 2 vols. 8vo.
Lond., 1837.   D 6 R 33, 34

BADEAU (GEN. ADAM). Military History of Ulysses S.
Grant, from April, 1861, to April, 1865. 3 vols. 8vo.
New York, 1868-81.   C 8 R 19-21

BADEN-POWELL. [*See* POWELL, W. B.]

BADGER (WILFRED). Statutes of New Zealand, 1842-84;
being the whole Law of New Zealand, Public and General ;
together with Alphabetical, Chronological, and General
Indexes. 2 vols. 4to. Christchurch, 1885.   MF 3 S 1, 2

BADHAM (PROF. CHARLES), D.D. Address to the University Debating Society. (Pam. J.) 8vo. Sydney,
1875.   MJ 2 P 28

Primary Education. 8vo. Sydney, 1876.   MG 1 Q 32

Plutarch's Lives of Timoleon and the Gracchi. [*See*
PLUTARCH.]

Euripides, Ion., with Notes. [*See* EURIPIDES.] [*See*
JUVENALIS, D. J.]

BADHAM (REV. CHARLES), M.A. Life of James Deacon
Hume, Secretary of the Board of Trade. 8vo. Lond.,
1859.   C 4 Q 15

BADHAM (CHARLES DAVID), M.D. Prose Halieutics ; or,
Ancient and Modern Fish Tattle. 8vo. Lond., 1854.
A 14 Q 36

Treatise on the Esculent Funguses of England ; containing
an Account of their Classical History, Uses, Characters,
Development, Structure, Nutritious Properties, Modes of
Cooking and Preserving, &c.; edited by Frederick Currey,
&c. 8vo. Lond., 1863.   A 4 S 1

BAECKER (LOUIS DE). Grammaire comparée des Langues
de la France. Flamand, Allemand, Celto-Breton, Basque,
Provençal, Espagnol, Italien, Français, comparés au Sanscrit. Roy. 8vo. Paris, 1860.   K 13 T 4

L'Archipel Indien : Origines, Langues, Littératures,
Religions, Morale, Droit Public et Privé des Populations,
8vo. Paris, 1874.   D 6 S 21

BÆDEKER (KARL). Northern Germany: Hand-book for
Travellers. 5th ed., revised and augmented. 12mo.
Coblenz, 1873.   D 7 P 32

BAFFIN (WILLIAM). Voyages of. [*See* HAKLUYT SOCIETY,
1881.]

BAGEHOT (WALTER), M.A. English Constitution. New
ed. 8vo. Lond., 1878.   F 6 R 32

Physics and Politics ; or, Thoughts on the Application
of the Principles of "Natural Selection" and "Inheritance
to Political Society." 4th ed. 8vo. Lond,1876.   F 6 P 27

BAGNERIS (G.) Elements of Sylviculture: a short Treatise
on the Scientific Cultivation of the Oak and other Hard-
wood Trees. Translated from the French. 8vo. Lond.,
1882.   A 1 P 53

BAGOT (ALAN), ASSOC.M.INST.C.E. Principles of Civil
Engineering as applied to Agriculture and Estate Management. 8vo. Lond., 1885.   A 6 R 9

BAGSTER (SAMUEL). Analytical Hebrew and Chaldee
Lexicon. [*See* DAVIDSON, B.]

English Hexapla ; exhibiting the six important English
Translations of the New Testament Scriptures : Wiclif,
1380 ; Tyndale, 1534 ; Cranmer, 1539 ; Genevan, 1557 ;
Anglo-Rhemish, 1582 ; Authorised, 1611. 4to. Lond.
(n.d.)   G 5 U 20

BAGWELL (RICHARD), M.A. Ireland under the Tudors,
with a succinct Account of the Earlier History. 2 vols.
8vo. Lond., 1885   B 11 Q 17, 18

BAIKIE (WILLIAM BALFOUR), M.D., &c. Natural History.
[*See* ADAMS, A.]

BAILDON (SAMUEL). Tea Industry in India : a Review
of Finance and Labour, and a Guide for Capitalists and
Assistants. 8vo. Lond., 1882.   F 10 S 2

BAILEY (CHARLES). Transcripts from the Municipal
Archives of Winchester, and other Documents, elucidating
the Government, Manners, and Customs of the City,
from the 13th Century to the Present Period. 8vo. Winchester, 1856.   B 4 R 16

BAILEY (FREDERICK MANSON), F.L.S. Catalogue of Plants in the two Metropolitan Gardens, the Brisbane Botanic Garden and Bowen Park (the Garden of the Queensland Acclimatisation Society); arranged according to Bentham and Hooker's "Genera Plantarum"; interspersed with numerous Notes on the Uses and Properties of the Plants. 8vo. Brisbane, 1885.   MA 1 U 36

Census of the Flora of Brisbane. [*See* TENISON-WOODS, REV. J. E.]

Classified Index of the Indigenous and Naturalised Plants of Queensland. 8vo. Brisbane, 1883.*   MA 1 U 34

Fern World of Australia; with Homes of the Queensland Species. With Plates illustrating Fern Tribes. 8vo. Brisbane, 1881.   MA 1 V 10

Occasional Papers on the Queensland Flora. 8vo. Brisbane, 1886.   MA 1 U 33

Queensland Woods: Catalogue of the Indigenous Woods contained in the Queensland Court, Colonial and Indian Exhibition, 1886; with a brief popular Description of the Trees, their Distribution, Qualities, Uses of Timber, &c. 8vo. Brisbane, 1886.   MK 1 P 10

Synopsis of the Queensland Flora; containing both the Phænogamous and Cryptogamous Plants, and Supplement. 8vo. Brisbane, 1883.   MA 1 U 30

First Supplement to above. 8vo. Brisbane, 1886.   MA 1 U 31

BAILEY (FREDERICK MANSON), AND GORDON (P. R.) Plants reputed poisonous and injurious to Stock. 8vo. Brisbane, 1887.   MA 1 U 32

BAILEY (JOHN EGLINGTON). Life of Thomas Fuller, D.D.; with Notices of his Books, his Kinsmen, and his Friends. 8vo. Lond., 1874.   C 8 R 18

BAILEY (JOHN M.) The Book of Ensilage; or, the New Dispensation for Farmers: Experience with Ensilage at Winning Farm; how to produce Milk for one Cent per quart; Butter for ten Cents per pound; Beef for four Cents per pound; Mutton for nothing, if Wool is thirty Cents per pound. Farmer's edition. 8vo. New York, 1881.   A 1 S 26

BAILEY (NATHAN). Universal Etymological Dictionary. 2 vols. 8vo. Lond., 1737–47.   K 12 Q 3, 4

BAILEY (PHILIP JAMES). Festus: a Poem. 6th ed. 8vo. Lond., 1860.   H 8 R 38

BAILEY (SAMUEL). Essays on the Formation and Publication of Opinions. 8vo. Lond., 1826.   J 2 S 6

BAILEY (THOMAS). Annals of Nottinghamshire: History of the County of Nottingham, including the Borough. 4 vols. roy. 8vo. Lond., 1853.   B 5 V 34–37

What is Life? and other Poems. 12mo. Lond., 1820.   H 5R 12

BAILEY (W. WHITMAN), B.P. Botanical Collector's Hand-book. (Naturalists' Handy Series.) 8vo. Salem, 1881.   A 4 P 19

BAILLIE (JOANNA). Dramatic and Poetical Works of. 8vo. Lond., 1851.   H 1 S 21

De Montfort: a Tragedy (Brit. Theatre). 12mo. Lond., 1808.   H 1 P 24

BAILLIE (ROBERT), A.M. Letters and Journals of Robert Baillie, A.M., Principal of the University of Glasgow, 1637–62; edited by David Laing. 3 vols. imp. 8vo. Edinb., 1841–42.   C 5 W 3–5

BAILLIERE (F. F.) Catalogue of English and Foreign Medical, Chemical, and Natural History Works. 8vo. Meln., 1862.   MA 1 Q 13

New South Wales Gazetteer and Road Guide; compiled by Robert P. Whitworth. 8vo. Sydney, 1866.   MD 7 Q 24

Official Post Office Directory of Queensland, 1874; compiled by R. P. Whitworth. 8vo. Brisbane, 1874.   ME 3 U

Victorian Gazetteer and Road Guide; compiled by Robert P. Whitworth. 8vo. Meln., 1865.   MD 7 Q 25

Another copy. 8vo. Meln., 1879.   MD 7 Q 26

BAILLIERE v. BEANEY. The Medical Embassy to England; being a Report of the Trial, in the Supreme Court, Melbourne, May, 1880; with some Comments of the Press thereon. 8vo. Meln., 1880.   MF 1 Q 6

BAIN (PROF. ALEXANDER), LL.D. Education as a Science. 8vo. Lond., 1879.   G 17 P 22

James Mill: a Biography. 8vo. Lond., 1882.   C 5 P 16

John Stuart Mill: a Criticism, with Personal Recollections. 8vo. Lond., 1882.   C 5 P 15

Logic: Deduction and Induction. 2nd ed. 2 vols. 8vo. Lond., 1873.   G 10 Q 26, 27

Mental and Moral Science: a Compendium of Psychology and Ethics. 8vo. Lond., 1868.   G 10 P 20

Mind and Body: the Theories of their Relation. 6th ed. 8vo. Lond., 1878.   G 13 Q 14

Practical Essays. 8vo. Lond., 1884.   G 13 Q 24

The Emotions and the Will. 3rd ed. 8vo. Lond., 1875.   G 6 Q 21

The Senses and the Intellect. 3rd ed. 8vo. Lond., 1868.   G 6 Q 20

Aristotle. [*See* GROTE, G.]

BAINBRIDGE-HOFF (COM. WILLIAM). [*See* HOFF, COM. W. B.*]

BAINES (EDWARD). History of the Cotton Manufacture in Great Britain. 8vo. Lond., 1835.   A 11 R 23

History of the County Palatine and Duchy of Lancaster; the Biographical Department by the late W. R. Whatton, F.S.A. A new, revised, and improved edition, edited by John Harland, F.S.A. 2 vols. 4to. Lond., 1868–70.   B 6 V 21, 22

Life of Edward Baines, late M.P. for the Borough of Leeds; by his Son, Edward Baines. 8vo. Lond., 1851.   C 2 V 10

BAINES (Thomas), F.R.G.S. Explorations in South-west Africa; being an Account of a Journey in the years 1861–62, from Walvisch Bay to Lake N'gami. 8vo. Lond., 1864.   D 2 8 8

Gold Regions of South-eastern Africa; accompanied by Biographical Sketch of the Author [by Henry Hall, F.R.G.S.] With Illustrations. 8vo. Lond., 1877.   D 2 R 15
[*See* Lord, W. B.]

BAINES (Thomas). History of the Commerce and Town of Liverpool, and of the Rise of Manufacturing Industry in the adjoining Counties. Roy. 8vo. Lond., 1852.   B 5 V 3

Lancashire and Cheshire, Past and Present: a History and a Description of the Palatine Counties of Lancaster and Chester, from the Earliest Ages to the Present Time (1867); with an Account of the Rise and Progress of Manufactures and Commerce, and Civil and Mechanical Engineering in these Districts, by William Fairbairn, LL.D., &c. 2 vols. (in 4) 4to. Lond., 1870   B 10 P 10–13 †

BAINI (Giuseppe). Memorie Storico-critiche della Vita e delle Opere di Giovanni Pierluigi da Palestrina. 2 vols. 4to. Roma, 1828.   C 2 W 19, 20

BAIRD (Charles W.), D.D. History of the Huguenot Emigration to America. 2 vols. 8vo. New York, 1885.   G 5 Q 23, 24

BAIRD (Gen. the Rt. Hon. Sir David), Bart., G.C.B. Life of; by T. E. Hook. 2 vols. 8vo. Lond., 1832.   C 2 V 12, 13

BAIRD (Prof. Henry M.) History of the Rise of the Huguenots, 1515–74. 2 vols. 8vo. Lond., 1880.   G 5 Q 27, 28

The Huguenots and Henry of Navarre. 2 vols. 8vo. Lond., 1886.   G 5 Q 25, 26

BAIRD (Rev. James), B.A. Emigrant's Guide to Australasia. Australia: New South Wales, Western Australia, South Australia, Victoria, and Queensland. 12mo. Lond., 1868.   MD 2 Q 4

Another copy. (Weale.) 12mo. Lond., 1868.   A 17 R 14

Emigrant's Guide to Tasmania and New Zealand. (Weale.) 12mo. Lond., 1871.   A 17 R 14

Management of Health. (Weale.) 12mo. Lond., 1867.   A 17 P 52

BAIRD (Rev. Robert), D.D. Impressions and Experiences of the West Indies and North America in 1849. 2 vols. 8vo. Edinb., 1850.   D 3 R 52, 53

Religion in the United States of America. 8vo. Edinb., 1844.   G 5 Q 22

D'Aubigné and his Writings. [*See* D'Aubigné, J. H. M.]

BAIRD (Spencer F.) Annual Record of Science and Industry; edited by Spencer F. Baird. 8 vols. 8vo. New York, 1872–79.   E

BAIRD (W.) Genealogical Collections concerning the Surname of Baird, and the Families of Auchmedden, Newbyth, and Sauchton Hall. Roy. 4to. Lond., 1870.   C 1 P 14 †

BAIRD (William), M.D., &c. Student's Natural History: a Cyclopædia of the Natural Sciences. 2nd ed. 8vo. Lond., 1858.   A 15 P 18

BAISSAC (Jules). De l'Origine des Dénominations Ethniques dans la Race Aryane: Etude de Philologie et de Mythologie comparées. 8vo. Paris, 1867.   K 13 Q 3

BAKER (Anne Elizabeth). Glossary of Northamptonshire Words and Phrases, with Examples of their Colloquial Use, and Illustrations from various Authors; to which are added, the Customs of the County. 2 vols. 8vo. Lond., 1854.   K 12 P 23, 24

BAKER (Charles John). Sydney and Melbourne; with Remarks on the Present State and Future Prospects of New South Wales. 8vo. Lond., 1845.*   MD 4 S 2

BAKER (Daniel Erskine), REED (I.), and JONES (S.) Biographia Dramatica; or, a Companion to the Playhouse; containing Historical and Critical Memoirs, and original Anecdotes of British and Irish Dramatic Writers. 3 vols. (in 4) 8vo. Lond., 1812.   C 6 S 1–4

BAKER (George). History and Antiquities of the County of Northampton. 2 vols. (in 1) roy. fol. Lond., 1822–30.   B 5 P 20 ‡

BAKER (G.) [*See* Livius, T.]

BAKER (Henry), F.R.S., &c. The Microscope made Easy; or, the Nature, Uses, and Magnifying Powers of the best kinds of Microscopes described. 4th ed. 8vo. Lond., 1754.   A 16 P 30

BAKER (Henry Barton). French Society, from the Fronde to the Great Revolution. 2 vols. 8vo. Lond., 1874.   B 9 P 4, 5

BAKER (Joseph Brogden). History of Scarborough, from the Earliest Date. With Illustrations, Maps, &c. Roy. 8vo. Lond., 1882.   B 5 V 5

BAKER (J. G.), F.L.S. Flora of Mauritius and the Seychelles: a Description of the Flowering Plants and Ferns of those Islands. 8vo. Lond., 1877.   A 4 T 13

BAKER (Sir Richard), Knt. Chronicle of the Kings of England, from the time of the Romans' Government unto the thirteenth year of the reign of Charles II. Sm. fol. Lond., 1670.   B 19 S 14 ‡

Animadversions upon "Baker's Chronicle." [*See* Blount, T.]

BAKER (Sir Samuel White), M.A., F.R.G.S. Albert N'Yanza, Great Basin of the Nile, and Explorations of the Nile Sources. 2 vols. 8vo. Lond., 1866.   D 2 P 17, 18

Cyprus, as I saw it in 1879. 8vo. Lond., 1879.   D 6 R 13

Eight Years in Ceylon. New edition with Illustrations. 8vo. Lond., 1874.   D 5 Q 7

Ismailia: a Narrative of the Expedition to Central Africa for the suppression of the Slave Trade. 2 vols. 8vo. Lond., 1874.   D 2 P 11, 12

Nile Tributaries of Abyssinia, and the Sword Hunters of the Hamran Arabs. 3rd ed. 8vo. Lond., 1868.   D 2 P 8

Rifle and the Hound in Ceylon. New edition, with Illustrations. 8vo. Lond., 1874.   D 5 Q 8

BAKER (SIR SHERSTON), BART. International Law. [*See* HALLECK, H. W.]

Laws relating to Quarantine of Her Majesty's Dominions at Home and Abroad, and of the principal Foreign States; including the sections of the Public Health Act, 1875, which bear upon Measures of Prevention. 8vo. Lond., 1879.   F 6 Q 23

The Office of Vice-Admiral of the Coast; being some Account of that Ancient Office. Sm. 4to. Lond., 1884.   B 7 Q 39

BAKER (THOMAS), B.D. History of the College of St. John the Evangelist, Cambridge; edited by John E. B. Mayor, M.A. 2 vols. 8vo. Camb., 1869.   B 6 S 9, 10

BAKER (THOMAS), C.E. Elements of Practical Mechanism and Machine Tools. (Weale.) 5th ed. 12mo. Lond., 1873.   A 17 P 11

Mathematical Theory of the Steam Engine. (Weale.) 5th ed. 12mo. Lond., 1873.   A 17 P 56

Principles and Practice of Statics and Dynamics, with those of Liquids and Gases. (Weale.) 2nd ed. 12mo. Lond., 1869.   A 17 P 11

Rudimentary Treatise on Mensuration and Measuring. (Weale.) 12mo. Lond., 1878.   A 17 P 6

Another copy. (Weale.) New ed. 12mo. Lond., 1884.   A 17 R 8

Treatise on Land and Engineering Surveying. (Weale.) 12mo. Lond., 1873.   A 17 P 20

[*See* FENWICK, T.]

BAKER (LIEUT.-GEN. VALENTINE), PACHA. Clouds in the East : Travels and Adventures on the Perso-Turkoman Frontier. With Illustrations. 8vo. Lond., 1876. D 4 U 44

War in Bulgaria : a Narrative of Personal Experiences. With Maps and Plans. 2 vols. 8vo. Lond., 1879.   B 13 V 15, 16

BAKER (WILLIAM). Heads of the People. 2 vols. 4to. Sydney, 1847–48.   MJ 1 V 5, 6

Another copy. 2 vols. (in 1) 4to.   MJ 1 V 7

BAKEWELL (F. C.) Manual of Electricity, Practical and Theoretical. 8vo. Lond., 1857.   A 5 S 47

BAKEWELL (ROBERT). Introduction to Geology, illustrative of the General Structure of the Earth. 2nd ed. 8vo. Lond., 1815.   A 9 R 21

Introduction to Geology, intended to convey a Practical Knowledge of the Science. 5th ed. 8vo. Lond., 1838.   A 9 R 22

Observations on the Influence of Soil and Climate upon Wool. 8vo. Lond., 1808.   A 1 R 4

BALBO (CESARE). Sommario della Storia d'Italia. 12mo. Torino, 1865.   B 12 P 27

BALBOA (VASCO NUNEZ DE). Lives of Vasco Nunez de Balboa, and Francisco Pizarro ; from the Spanish of Don Manuel Josef Quintana, by Mrs. Hodson. 12mo. Lond., 1832.   C 1 R 6

BALCOMBE (T.) [*See* PICKERING, G. F.]

BALDAEUS (REV. D.) Short Account of Jaffnapatam, in the Island of Ceylon. (Pam. 44.) 12mo. Colombo, 1816.   MJ 2 R 6

BALDRICUS (DOLENSIS ARCHIEPISCOPUS). Opera omnia. [*See* MIGNE, J. P., SERIES LATINA, 166.]

BALDWIN (EBENEZER). Annals of Yale College, in New Haven, Connecticut, from its foundation to the year 1831. 8vo. New Haven, 1831.   G 17 Q 37

BALDWIN (J.) The Book-lover. A Guide to the Best Reading. 12mo. Lond., 1886.   J 1 S 40

BALDWIN (CAPT. J. H.), F.G.S. The Large and Small Game of Bengal and the North-western Provinces of India. Sm. 4to. Lond., 1876.   A 15 P 15

BALDWIN (WILLIAM CHARLES), F.R.G.S. African Hunting, from Natal to the Zambesi, from 1852 to 1860. Illustrated. 8vo. Lond., 1863.   D 2 T 6

BALE (JOHN). [*See* BRITISH REFORMERS.]

BALE (MANFRED POWIS), M.INST.M.E., &c. How to manage a Steam-engine : a Hand-book for all who use Steam. 8vo. Lond., 1880.   A 11 Q 18

Saw-mills : their Arrangement and Management ; and the economical Conversion of Timber. 8vo. Lond., 1883.   A 11 R 7

Steam and Machinery Management : a Guide to the Arrangement and economical Management of Machinery ; with Hints on Construction and Selection. (Weale.) 12mo. Lond., 1884.   A 17 Q 75

Stone-working Machinery, and the rapid and economical Conversion of Stone. Illustrated. 8vo. Lond., 1884.   A 11 Q 6

Wood-working Machinery : its Rise, Progress, and Construction ; with Hints on the Management of Saw-mills and the Economical Conversion of Timber. 8vo. Lond., 1880.   A 11 R 8

[*See* RICHARDSON, W.]

BALE (W. M.) Australian Museum : Catalogue of the Australian Hydroid Zoophytes. 8vo. Sydney, 1884.*   MA 2 T 27

BALFE (MICHAEL WILLIAM). His Life and Work ; by Wm. Alexander Barrett. 8vo. Lond., 1882.   C 3 Q 16

BALFOUR (SURGEON-GEN. EDWARD), L.R.C.S. Cyclopædia of India. 3rd ed. 3 vols. roy. 8vo. Lond., 1885.   D 11 V 4–6

BALFOUR (FRANCIS M.), M.A., &c. Elements of Embryology. [*See* FOSTER, M.]

On the Development of the Spinal Nerves in Elasmobranch Fishes. (Roy. Soc. Pubs. 2.) 4to. Lond., 1876. A 11 P 3†

Treatise on Comparative Embryology. 2 vols. 8vo. Lond., 1880–81.   A 14 T 11, 12

BALFOUR (FREDERIC HENRY), F.R.G.S. Divine Classic of Nan-Hua. [*See* CHUANG TSZE.]

Waifs and Strays from the Far East; being a series of disconnected Essays on matters relating to China. Roy. 8vo. Lond., 1876. D 5 U 7

BALFOUR (G. W.) M.D. [*See* CASPER, J. L.]

BALFOUR (SIR JAMES). Historical Works of. 4 vols. 8vo. Lond., 1825. B 13 Q 43–46

BALFOUR (JOHN HUTTON), A.M., &c. Botany of the Bass Rock. [*See* BASS ROCK.]

Class-book of Botany; being an Introduction to the Study of the Vegetable Kingdom. 3rd ed.; with Additions and Corrections in the department of Organography. Illustrated. 8vo. Edinb., 1871. A 4 T 16

Introduction to the study of Palæontological Botany. Illustrated. 8vo. Edinb., 1872. A 5 P 16

Plants of the Bible. New and enlarged edition. 8vo. Lond., 1885. A 4 Q 20

BALFOUR (J. O.) Sketch of New South Wales. 8vo. Lond., 1845. MD 3 R 9

BALKWILL (F. H.), L.D.S., &c. Mechanical Dentistry in Gold and Vulcanite; arranged with regard to the difficulties of the Pupil, Mechanical Assistant, and Young Practitioner. 8vo. Lond., 1880. A 12 S 15

BALL (CHARLES). Historical Account of Winchester; with Descriptive Walks. Roy. 8vo. Winchester, 1818. B 5 V 6

BALL (CHARLES). [*See* STAFFORD, W. C.]

BALL (E.) Father and Son; or, the Rock of Charbonniere: a Drama (Cumberland's Eng. Theatre). 12mo. Lond., 1829. H 2 Q 20

BALL (LIEUT. H. L.) Journal of. [*See* PHILLIP, A., *and* HUNTER, CAPT. J.]

BALL (JOHN). Book-keeping. [*See* HAMILTON, R. G. C.]

BALL (ROBERT STAWELL), LL.D., &c. Elements of Astronomy. 12mo. Lond., 1880. A 17 S 25

Story of the Heavens. Illustrated. 8vo. Lond., 1885. A 3 U 27

BALL (SAMUEL). Account of the Cultivation and Manufacture of Tea in China. 8vo. Lond., 1848. A 1 S 21

BALL (T. FREDERICK). Queen Victoria: Scenes and Incidents of her Life and Reign. 2nd ed. 12mo. Lond., 1886. C 5 R 30

BALL (V.), M.A., &c. Diamonds, Coal, and Gold of India; their Mode of Occurrence and Distribution. 12mo. Lond., 1881. [*See* MEDLICOTT, H. B.] A 9 P 34

BALLAD MINSTRELSY OF SCOTLAND. Romantic and Historical; collated and annotated. 8vo. Glasgow, 1871. H 7 Q 26

BALLAN (JOSEPH). Trial of. [*See* PIGGOREET MURDER.]

BALLANCE (HON. J.) New Zealand: the Financial Statement of the Colonial Treasurer; made in Committee of Ways and Means, 6th August, 1878. 8vo. Wellington, 1879. MF 3 P 21

BALLANTINE (JAMES). Life of David Roberts, R.A.; compiled from his Journals and other Sources. Illustrated. 4to. Edinb., 1866. C 1 W 24

BALLANTINE (WILLIAM) SERJEANT-AT-LAW. Some Experiences of a Barrister's Life. 2 vols 8vo. Lond., 1882. C 10 U 40, 41

Old World and the New; being a Continuation of his "Experiences." 8vo. Lond., 1884. C 10 U 42

BALLANTYNE (REV. JAMES). Homes and Homesteads in the Land of Plenty: a Hand-book of Victoria, as a Field for Emigration. 8vo. Melb., 1871.* MD 3 Q 37

Another copy. 8vo. Lond., 1872. MD 3 Q 39

BALLANTYNE (ROBERT M.) Hudson's Bay; or, Everyday Life in the Wilds of North America. 2nd ed. 8vo. Edinb., 1848. D 4 P 6

BALLANTYNE (THOMAS). Passages selected from the Writings of Thomas Carlyle. [*See* CARLYLE, T.]

Biographical Memoir of Daniel De Foe. [*See* DE FOE, D.]

BALLARAT DISTRICT ALMANAC, 1864. 12mo. Ballaarat, 1864. ME

BALLARAT MECHANICS' INSTITUTE. Annual Reports of the Committee of Management, 1861–63. 12mo. Ballarat, 1862–63. MF 3 P 15

Catalogue of Exhibition of Science and Art, opened on Thursday, August 6th, 1863. (Pam. 36.) 8vo. Ballarat, 1863. MJ 2 Q 23

Catalogue of Grand Auction Bazaar, in aid of the Funds. (Pam. 36.) 8vo. Ballarat, 1863. MJ 2 Q 23

BALLARAT EAST PUBLIC LIBRARY. Sixth Annual Report of the Committee of Management, also Rules of. 12mo. Ballarat 1869. MF 3 P 15

BALLARAT TECHNOLOGICAL EXHIBITION. The Seventh Competitive Exhibition and Examinations. 8vo. Ballarat, 1879. A 16 U 23

BALLIN (ADA S.) The Science of Dress in Theory and Practice. 8vo. Lond., 1885. A 12 P 23

BALLINGAL (JAMES). History of the Egyptian Religion. [*See* TIELE, DR. C. P.]

BALLINGALL (JAMES). Shipwrecks: their Causes, and the Means of Prevention. 8vo. Melb., 1857. MJ 2 R 8

BALLINGALL (WILLIAM). Shores of Fife. 4to. Edinb., 1872. D 8 V 1

BALLOT IN VICTORIA. [*See* VICTORIA.]

BALLS-HEADLEY (WALTER), M.D. Dress with reference to Heat ; being a Lecture written for, and published by the Australian Health Society. 8vo. Melb., 1876.   MA 2 S 38

Homœopathy, Past and Present. 8vo. Melb., 1878.   MA 2 S 38

On the Use of the Medical Thermometer. 8vo. Melb., 1877.   MA 2 S 38

BALNAVES (HENRY). [*See* BRITISH REFORMERS.]

BALSAMON (THEODORUS). Opera omnia. [*See* MIGNE, J. P., SERIES GRÆCA, 137, 138.]

BALTET (CHARLES). The Art of Grafting and Budding. (Weale.) 12mo. Lond., 1882.   A 17 Q 58

BALTIMORE (FREDERICK), LORD. Tour to the East, in the years 1763 and 1764, with remarks on the City of Constantinople and the Turks. 12mo. Lond., 1767.   D 8 R 10

BALZAC (HONORÉ DE). Contes Drolatiques. Droll Stories, collected from the Abbeys of Touraine. Translated into English, complete and unabridged. Illustrated with 425 Designs, by Gustave Doré. 8vo. Lond., 1874.   Libr.

Pictures of the French. [*See* JANIN, J.]

BAMBAS (VACESLAV). Die Formbildung der slavischen Sprache, das ist : systematische Entwickelung der grammatischen und lexikalischen Formen aller slavischen Dialekte, mit besonderer Auszeichnung einer allgemeinen slavischen Mustersprache und paralleler Darstellung der griechischen und lateini- chen Formen. Roy. 8vo. Prague, 1861.   K 16 R 9

Tvarosklad Jazyka Slovanského to jest : Systematicky vývin grammatických i lexikálních tvarův všech nárecí slovanskych, se zvlástním vyznacením vzorného jazyka vseslovanského i soubezným vykladem tvaruv greckych a latinskych. Roy. 8vo. Praze, 1861.   K 16 R 9

BAMPTON (CAPT.) Chart of Torres Strait. [*See* COOK, CAPT. J.]

BAMPTON (CHARLES). Frank Leward : Memorials. 8vo. Lond., 1884.   C 4 R 13

BAMPTON LECTURES. An Examination of Canon Liddon's Bampton Lectures on the Divinity of Our Lord and Saviour Jesus Christ ; by a Clergyman of the Church of England. 12mo. Lond., 1871.   G 16 R 22

Eight Lectures on Miracles ; preached before the University of Oxford, in the year 1865, by the Rev. J. B. Mozley, B.D. 8vo. Lond., 1865.   G 15 R 23

BANARE (LIEUT. A.) Instructions nautiques sur la Nouvelle-Calédonie. [*See* CHAMBEYRON, CAPT.]

BANCROFT (EDWARD). Essay on the Natural History of Guiana, in South America. 8vo. Lond., 1769. A 14 S 36

BANCROFT (GEORGE). History of the Formation of the Constitution of the United States of America. 2 vols. 8vo. Lond., 1882.   B 1 T 12, 13

History of the United States, from the Discovery of the American Continent. 10 vols. 8vo. Boston, 1854-74.   B 1 T 2-11.

BANCROFT (GEORGE)—*continued.*
History of the United States of America. 2 vols. roy. 8vo. Edinb., 1840.   B 1 V 6, 7

   1. From the Discovery of the Continent to the Peace of Aix-la-Chapelle ; by George Bancroft.

   2. War of Independence ; by Charles Botta. (Translated by G. A. Otis.)

BANCROFT (HUBERT HOWE). Brief Account of the Literary Undertakings of. 8vo. Lond., 1883. K 15 P 6

History of the Pacific States of North America. Vols. 1, 2, 4–8, 10, 13–17, 22, 23, 24, 28. Roy. 8vo. San Francisco, 1882-86.   B 17 S 1-T 6

   1, 2. Central America, 1501-1800.
   4-8. History of Mexico, 1516-1861.
   10. North Mexican States and Texas, 1531-1800.
   13-17. California, 1542-1840.
   22, 23. The North-west Coast, 1543-1846.
   24. Oregon, 1834-48.
   28. Alaska, 1730-1885.

Natives Races of the Pacific States. 5 vols. 8vo. Lond., 1875-76.   A 2 P 20-24

BANCROFT (ROBERT M., AND FRANCIS J.) Tall Chimney Construction : a Practical Treatise on the Construction of Tall Chimney Shafts. 8vo. Manchester, 1885. A 3 P 1

BAND OF HOPE JOURNAL (THE), and Australian Home Companion. Nos. 16 and 21. Vol. 3. Sydney, 1858.   ME 3 R

BANDELIER (A. F.) Archæological Tour in Mexico. [*See* ARCHÆOL. INST. OF AMERICA.]

Historical Introduction to Studies among the Sedentary Indians of New Mexico. Report on the Ruins of the Pueblo of Pecos. (Archæol. Inst. of America.) 8vo. Boston, 1881.   E

BANFIELD (THOMAS C.) William Tell : a Dramatic Poem. [*See* SCHILLER, J. C. F. VON]

BANIER (ABBÉ ANTOINE). Mythology and Fables of the Ancients, explained from History. 4 vols. 8vo. Lond., 1739-40.   B 14 V 45-48

BANISTER (THOMAS). Australia visited and revisited. [*See* MOSSMAN, S.]

Britain and her Colonial Dependencies ; and their Right to be Represented in Parliament. 8vo. Lond., 1844.   MF 3 P 7

Memoranda relating to the Present Crisis as regards our Colonies, our Trade, our Circulating Medium, and Railways. 2nd ed. 8vo. Lond., 1848.   MF 2 T 4

Memoranda relating to the Present Crisis as regards our Colonies. (Pam. Dd.) 8vo. Lond., 1848.   F 12 P 22

Two Papers on Popular Discontents. (Pam. Dd.) 8vo. Lond., 1849.   F 12 P 22

BANK OF NEW SOUTH WALES. Third, Fifth, and Seventh Reports of the Directors and Auditors. 12mo. Sydney, 1852-54.   MF 3 P 10

BANKING IN AUSTRALASIA. [*See* BAXTER, A. B.]

BANKS. History of Banks; to which is added, a Demonstration of the Advantages and Necessity of Free Competition in the Business of Banking. 12mo. Lond., 1837. F 1 P 29

BANKS (JOHN). The Albions Queens: or, the Death of Mary Queen of Scots: a Tragedy. (Bell's Brit. Theatre.) 18mo. Lond., 1791. H 2 P 1

BANKS (REV. J.), M.A. Idylls of Theocritus, Bion, and Moschus. [*See* THEOCRITUS.]

BANKS (RT. HON. SIR JOSEPH), BART. Memoirs, Historical and Scientific of; by George Suttor, F.L.S. 8vo. Parramatta, 1855.* MC 1 P 31

A Pamphlet containing a Summary of the contents of the Brabourne Papers; relating to the Settlement and Early History of the Colony [of New South Wales]. 8vo. Sydney, 1886.* MB 2 U 3

[*See* COOK, CAPT. J., HAWKESWORTH, J., *and* PARKINSON, S.]

BANKS (R. N.) [*See* NEWTOWN FREE LIBRARY.]

BANKS (SAMUEL HAWKER). Ethical, Serio-Comical, and Satirical Essay in Verse, intituled "The Vision of Truth." In two Parts. 8vo. Sydney, 1874.* MH 1 Q 11

Letter from S. H. Banks, respecting "Vice and its Victims." (MS. Pam. N.) 8vo. Sydney, 1877. MJ 2 P 29

Vice and its Victims in Sydney: the Cause and Cure; by "A Pupil of the late Prof. John Woolley, D.C.L." 8vo. Sydney, 1873. MJ 2 P 29, and 2 R 14

BANKS (W. S.) Walks in Yorkshire: Wakefield and its Neighbourhood. With Map, and fifty-five Woodcuts. 4to. Lond., 1871. D 7 V 19

BANNATYNE (GEORGE). Ancient Scottish Poems, published from the MSS. of 1568. 8vo. Edinb., 1770. H 689

Memoir of. [*See* SCOTT, SIR W.]

BANNATYNE CLUB PUBLICATIONS. Chronicon de Lanercost, 1201–1346. 4to. Edinb., 1839. E

Black Book of Taymouth, with other papers from the Breadalbane Charter Room. 4to. Edinb., 1855. E

Historical Observes of Memorable Occurrents in Church and State (1680–86); by Sir John Lauder, of Fountainhall. 4to. Edinb., 1840. E

Horn et Rimenhild. Publié par Francisque Michel. 4to. Paris, 1845. E

Liber Cartarum Sancte Crucis. Munimenta Ecclesie Sancte Crucis de Edwinesburgh (Charters of Holyrood). 4to. Edinb., 1840. E

Papers relative to the Regalia of Scotland. 4to. Edinb., 1829. E

BANNISTER (JOHN), COMEDIAN. Memoirs of; by John Adolphus. 2 vols. 8vo. Lond., 1839. C 8 U 4, 5

BANNISTER (J. T.) Survey of the Holy Land; its Geography, History, and Destiny. 8vo. Bath, 1844. D 6 P 27

BANNISTER (SAXE), M.A. British Colonization and Coloured Tribes. 8vo. Lond., 1838. MF 1 P 28 *

Humane Policy; or, Justice to the Aborigines of New Settlements essential to a due expenditure of British money, and to the best interests of the Settlers. 8vo. Lond., 1830. MF 3 Q 4

Letter to C. C. Clifford, Esq., Private Secretary to the First Lord of the Treasury. Fol. Lond., 1855. MJ 2 U 1

On Abolishing Transportation; and on Reforming the Colonial Office. In a Letter to Lord John Russell. 8vo. Lond., 1837. MF 3 Q 41

Another copy. MJ 2 P 36

Statements and Documents relating to Proceedings in New South Wales in 1824–26, intended to support an Appeal to the King by the Attorney-General of the Colony. 8vo. Cape Town, 1827. MF 2 P 20

BANTING (WILLIAM). Letter on Corpulence addressed to the Public. 4th ed. 8vo. Lond., 1869. A 12 U 26

BANVILLE (THÉODORE DE). [*See* FAUCHERY, A.]

BAPTISMAL FONTS. Illustrations of. [*See* COMBE, T.]

BAPTISTA (J.) Annotationes. [In varios authores antiquos.] (*Bound with Platina vitæ.*) S. fol. Venetiis, 1496. C 14 R 19 ‡

BAPTISTA (PEDRO JOAO), and JOSÉ (AMARO). Journey across Africa. [*See* AFRICA.]

BAR AND THE ATTORNEYS (THE); by "Their Honors" Minos, Æacus and Rhadamantius, Justices of "The Court Below." 8vo. Melb. (n.d.) MJ 2 R 19

BARALT (DON RAFAEL MARIA). Diccionario de Galicismos ó sea de las voces, locuciones y frases de la Lengua Francesa, que se han introducido en el habla Castellana moderna, con el juicio critico de las que deben adoptarse, y la equivalencia Castiza de las que no se hallan en este caso. 8vo. Madrid, 1855. K 12 Q 9

BARANTE (AMABLE GUILLAUME PROSPER BRUGIERE), BARON DE. Etudes Littéraires et Historiques. 2 vols. 12mo. Paris, 1859. B 37, P 4, 5

Histoire des Ducs de Bourgogne de la Maison de Valois (1364–1477). 12 vols. 8vo. Paris, 1854. B 8 Q 1–12

BARBARO (JOSAFA), AND CONTARINI (AMBROGIO). Travels to Tana and Persia. [*See* HAKLUYT SOCIETY, 48.]

BARBAULD (MRS. ANNA LÆTITIA). Memoir, Letters, and a Selection from the Poems and Prose Writings of; by Grace A. Ellis. 2 vols. 8vo. Boston, 1874. C 3 Q 14, 15

Works of; with a Memoir by Lucy Aikin. 2 vols. 8vo. Lond., 1825. J 10 V 22, 23

BARBER (MRS. MARY). Some Drawings of Ancient Embroidery: Thirty Specimens. Fol. Lond., 1880. A 23 P 30 ‡

BARBER (W. H.) Case of Mr. W. H. Barber (late of the firm of Barber and Birciam, solicitors, London), convicted in 1844 of a supposed guilty knowledge of certain Will Forgeries. 8vo. Sydney, 1847. MJ 2 Q 8

Case of W. H. Barber, containing Copies of all Documents recently submitted to the Rigit Hon. Sir George Grey, Bart.; a Letter from Norfolk Island, siowing the revolting cruelties to wiici Mr. Barber was tiere subjected; and a Narrative of the steps by wiici iis innocence ias been establisied, and iis deliverance effected. 3rd ed. 8vo. Lond., 1849. MF 1 Q 1

BARBEYRAC (JEAN.) [*See* DUMONT, J.]

BARBIER (ANTOINE ALEXANDER). Dictionnaire des Ouvrages Anonymes. 3ʳ cd., suite de la seconde édition des Supercieries Littéraires déroilées par J. M. Querard. 4 vols. 8vo. Paris, 1872-79. K 8 P 4-7

BARBOU (ALFRED). Victor Hugo and iis Time; trans lated from the Frenci by Ellen E. Frewer. Illustrated. Imp. 8vo. Lond., 1882. C 5 W 8

BARBOUR (D.) Bimetallism. 8vo. Lond.,1886. F 10 S 1

BARBOUR (JOHN), ARCHDEACON. The Bruce ; or, the History of Robert I, King of Scotland ; written in Scotisi verse. The first genuine edition publisied from a MS., dated 1489 ; witi Notes and a Glossary by J. Pinkerton. 3 vols. 8vo. Lond., 1790. H 8 V 33-35

Anotier copy, witi Notes by J. Jamieson. 8vo. Glasgow, 1869. H 7 P 27

BARBOUR (JOHN GORDON). Unique Traditions, ciiefly of the West and Souti of Scotland. 8vo. Lond., 1886. B 13 P 30

BARBOUR (ROBERT), M.P. The Land Question: Leasing not Selling ; or, Homes for all. 8vo. Sydney, 1879. MF 3 Q 26

BARCLAY (ALEXANDER). Practical View of the Present State of Slavery in the West Indies. 8vo. Lond., 1828. F 10 R 12

BARCLAY (EDGAR). Mountain Life in Algeria. Witi Illustrations by the Autior. Roy. 8vo. Lond., 1882. D 2 U 11

BARCLAY (JOHN). Sequel to the Diversions of Purley. 8vo. Lond., 1826. K 15 R 36

[*See* TOOKE, J. H.]

BARCLAY (REV. P.), M.A. Notes on New Zealand, for the Use of Emigrants. Witi a Map. 8vo. Lond., 1874. MD 5 S 36

BARCLAY (ROBERT). Apology for the True Ciristian Divinity, as the same is ield forti and preacied by the people, in scorn called Quakers. 9th ed. 8vo. Lond., 1825. G 15 Q 23

Anotier copy. 13ti ed. 8vo. Manciester, 1869. G 13 Q 29

Inner Life of the Religious Societies of the Commonwealti. Roy. 8vo. Lond., 1876. G 5 S 2

BARCLAY (WILLIAM), A.M., &c. The Lost Lady : a Tragy-Comedy. Sm. fol. Lond., 1639. H I U 1

BARD (SAMUEL A.) [*See* SQUIER, DR. E. G.]

BARDI (LUIGI). L'Imperiale e Reale Galleria Pitti, illus. trata per cura di Luigi Bardi, Regio Calcografo. 4 vols. fol. Firenze, 1837-42. A 4 W 1-4 ‡

BARDSLEY (REV. CHARLES WAREING), M.A. Curiosities of Puritan Nomenclature. 8vo. Lond.,1880. K 19 Q 7

Englisi Surnames; tieir Sources and Significations. 2nd ed. 8vo. Lond., 1875. B 4 P 17

BARENTS (WILLIAM). Tiree Voyages of. [*See* HAKLUYT SOCIETY, 1876.]

BARETTI (GIUSEPPE). Dizionario Italiano ed Inglese ; con una Grammatica. 2 vols. (in 1) 4to. Firenze, 1816. K 16 S 2

Anotier copy. 2 vols. (in 1). 4to. Firenze, 1816. K 16 S 2

BARÉTY (DR. A.) Nice and its Climate; translated, witi Additions, by Ciarles West, M.D., and an Appendix on the Vegetation of the Riviera, by Professor Allman, F.R.S. 8vo. Lond., 1882. D 7 P 17

BARFF (PROF. F. S.) Carbon, and certain Compounds of Carbon. (Cantor Lectures.) Roy. 8vo. Lond., 1874. A 15 U 21

Glass and Silicates. (Brit. Man. Indust.) 12mo. Lond., 1876. A 17 S 35

On Silicates, Silicides, Glass, and Glass-painting. (Cantor Lectures.) Roy. 8vo. Lond., 1872. A 15 U 21

BARHAM (FRANCIS). Life and Times of Join Reucilin, or Capnion, the Fatier of the German Reformation, 12mo. Lond., 1843. C 1 R 31

BARHAM (REV. RICHARD HARRIS DALTON), B.A. Ingoldsby Legends; or, Mirti and Marvels; by Tiomas Ingoldsby, Esq. Annotated edition. 2 vols. 8vo. Lond., 1870. H 5 T 35, 36

Life and Remains of Tieodore Edward Hook. 2 vols. 8vo. Lond., 1849. C 3 U 15, 16

BARING (MRS. H.) Diary of William Windiam. [*See* WINDHAM, RT. HON. W.]

BARING-GOULD (SABINE), M.A. Curious Mytis of the Middle Ages. 12mo. Lond., 1877. B 37 P 2

Germany, Present and Past. 2 vols. 8vo. Lond., 1879. D 8 R 39, 40

Germany; witi the collaboration of Artiur Gilman. 8vo. Lond., 1886. B 9 Q 27

Iceland; its Scenes and Sagas. Roy. 8vo. Lond., 1863. D 7 V 1

The Vicar of Morwenstow; a Life of Robert Stepien Hawker, M.A. 8vo. Lond., 1876. C 3 T 27

a

BARITZ (GEORG), AND MUNTEANU (GABRIEL). Deutsci-romänisc1es Wörterbuch, bearbeitet und in dessen romänischem T1eile mit etlic1en tausend Wörtern bereic1ert. 2 vols. (in 1) 8vo. Cronstadt, 1853. K 14 Q 1

BARKER (A. E. J.) Histology, &c., of Man. [*See* FREY, H.]

BARKER (E. H.) [*See* PLINIUS SECUNDUS, C., *and* SILLIG, J.]

BARKER (RT. REV. FREDERIC), BISHOP OF SYDNEY. C1arge delivered at 1is Primary Metropolitan Visitation of the Dioceses of Tasmania, Adelaide, Melbourne, and Newcastle, in the year of our Lord, 1860. 8vo. Sydney 1860. MG 1 Q 29
[*See* TILLOTSON, DR. J., *and* TYERMAN, J.]

BARKER (MARY ANNE), LADY BROOME. Letters to Guy. 8vo. Lond., 1885. MD 2 R 38
Station Amusements in New Zealand. 8vo. Lond., 1873.* MD 2 R 36
Station Life in New Zealand. 12mo. Lond., 1870. MD 2 R 33
Anot1er copy. New ed. 12mo. Lond., 1871. MD 2 R 34
Anot1er copy. New ed. 12mo. Lond., 1874. MD 2 R 35

BARKER (SIR R.) [*See* LETTSOM, J. C.]

BARKER (WILLIAM BURCKHARDT), M.R.A.S. Lares and Penates; or, Cilicia and its Governors. Edited by W. F. Ainswort1, F.R.G.S., &c. 8vo. Lond., 1853. B 13 V 23

BARKER'S TRADE AND FINANCE ANNUAL, 1886-7. 8vo. Lond., 1886. E

BARKLEY (HENRY C.), C.E. Between the Danube and Black Sea; or, Five Years in Bulgaria. 8vo. Lond., 1876. D 8 P 48

BARKLY (SIR HENRY), K.C.B. [*See* ACCLIMATISATION SOCIETY OF VICTORIA.]

BARLEE (C. H.) [*See* SYDNEY ONCE A WEEK.]

BARLEE (ELLEN). Victoria: a Land of Plenty. 12mo. Lond., 1869. MJ 2 R 15

BARLOW (GEORGE HILARO), M.A., &c. Manual of the Practice of Medicine. 2nd ed. (C1urc1ill's Manuals.) 12mo. Lond., 1861. A 13 P 31

BARLOW (JAMES WILLIAM), M.A. Normans in Sout1 Europe. 8vo. Lond., 1886. H 7 T 37
Ultimatum of Pessimism: an Et1ical Study. 8vo. Lond., 1882. G 6 R 19

BARLOW (JOEL), LL.D. Life and Letters of Joel Marlow, LL.D., Poet, Statesman, P1ilosop1er; wit1 Ex-tracts from his Works and 1it1erto unpublis1ed Poems, by Charles Burr Todd. 8vo. New York, 1886. C 10 R 13

BARLOW (PETER), F.R.S. .Treatise on the Strengt1 of Materials, &c.; arranged and edited by William Humber, C.E., &c. 8vo. Lond., 1867. A 11 U 18
[*See* TREDGOLD, T.]

BARNABY (N.) Ironclad S1ips. [*See* ADAMS, W. H. D.]

BARNARD (ALFRED). [*See* SIDNEY, S.]

BARNARD (FREDERICK). Series of C1aracter Sketc1es from Dickens, from original Drawings by Frederick Barnard. Reproduced in P1otogravure, by Messrs. Goupil and Co. Atlas fol. Lond., 1884. A 20 P 23 ‡

BARNARD (LIEUT. FREDERICK LAMPORT), R.N. T1ree Years' Cruize in the Mozambique C1annel for the Sup-pression of the Slave Trade. 8vo. Lond., 1848. D 1 Q 24

BARNARD (GEORGE). T1eory and Practice of Land-scape Painting in Water-Colours. 7th ed. Illustrated. Imp. 8vo. Lond., 1861. A 7 V 12

BARNEBY (W. HENRY). Life and Labour .in the Far, Far West: being Notes of a Tour in the Western States, Britis1 Columbia, Manitoba, and the Nort1-West Terri-tory. 8vo. Lond., 1884. D 4 Q 43

BARNES (BARNEBY). A Divine Centurie of Spirituall Sonnets. [*See* PARK, T.]

BARNES (C. L.), M.A. Rock History: a Concise Note-Book of Geology, having special reference to the Englis1 and Welsh Formations. 8vo. Lond., 1884. A 9 P 38

BARNES (JOSHUA). History of t1at most victorious Monarc1, Edward III, King of England; wit1 life of his most renowned son Edward Prince of Wales and of Aquitain, sirnamed the Black Prince. Fol. Cam-bridge, 1688. B 15 S 10 ‡

BARNES (REV. R. H.), AND BROWN (MAJOR C. E.), R.A. C1arles George Gordon: a Sketc1; wit1 facsimile Letter. 8vo. Lond., 1885. C 2 S 18

BARNES (ROBERT). Writings of. [*See* BRITISH REFOR-MERS, 11.]

BARNES (W.) Glossary of the Dorset Dialect. 8vo. Dorc1ester, 1886. K 15 P 12

BARNET (DONALD MCKAY). Trip wit1 a Government Surveying Party in Searc1 of a Horse Track from Katoomba to the Jenolan Caves. 8vo. Sydney, 1884.* MD 4 U 45

BARNET (JAMES), F.R.I.B.A., COLONIAL ARCHITECT. Mac-quarie Lig1t1ouse. Sq. 8vo. Sydney, 1880. MA1T11
Sydney International Ex1ibition of 1879: Plans. Roy. 8vo. Sydney, 1879. MA 1 T 1
Sydney International Ex1ibition, 1879. References to the Plans, s1owing the space and position occupied by the various Ex1ibits in the Garden Palace. 8vo. Sydney, 1880. MA 1 T 2
[*See* NEW SOUTH WALES—PUBLIC WORKS.]

BARNEVELD (John of). Life and Death of, with a view of the primary causes and movements of the Thirty Years' War ; by John Lothrop Motley, D.C.L., LL.D., Illustrated. 2 vols. 8vo. Lond., 1874. C 2 V 27, 28

BARNFIELD (Richard). Affectionate Shepherd. A.D. 1594. (Percy Society, 20). 8vo. Lond., 1845. E

BARNUM (P. T.) Life of ; written by himself. Author's edition. 12mo. Lond., 1855. • C 1 R 3

BARON (John), M.D., &c. Life of Edward Jenner, M.D., LL.D., F.R.S.; with Illustrations of his Doctrines, and Selections from his Correspondence. 2 vols. 8vo. Lond., 1827-38. C 10 U 17, 18

BARON (Rev. J.) The Greek Origin of the Apostles' Creed ; illustrated by Ancient Documents and Recent Research. 8vo. Oxford, 1885. G 6 R 21

BARON (Rev, R.) [*See* Antananarivo Annual.]

BAROT (François Odysse-) Histoire de la Littérature contemporaine en Angleterre, 1830-74. 8vo. Paris, 1874. B 3 Q 10

BARRAUD (Charles D.) New Zealand : Graphic and Descriptive ; edited by W. T. L. Travers, F.L.S. Imp. 4to. Lond., 1877.* MD 1 P 8 ‡

BARRÉ (Prof. Louis) et ROUX (H.) Ainé Herculanum et Pompéi. Recueil général des peintures, bronzes, mosaïques, etc., découverts jusqu'à ce jour, et reproduits d'après "le Antichità di Ercolano," "il Museo Borbonico," et tous les ouvrages analogues, augmenté de sujets inédits, gravés par H. Roux Ainé. 7 vols. imp. 8vo. Paris, 1870. A 8 S 17-23

BARRÉ (Prof. Louis). Dictionnaire Universel de la Langue Française. [*See* Boiste, P.C.V.]

BARRETT (Rev. Alfred). Life of the Rev. John Hewgill Bumby ; with a brief History of the commencement and progress of the Wesleyan Mission in New Zealand. 2nd ed. 12mo. Lond., 1853. MC 1 P 14

BARRETT (Francis), F.R.C. The Magus, or Celestial Intelligencer ; being a Complete System of Occult Philosophy. In Three Books. 4to. Lond., 1801. A 1 P 5 †

BARRETT (Rev. Richard A. F.), M.A. Synopsis of Criticisms upon those Passages of the Old Testament, in which Modern Commentators have differed from the Authorized Version ; together with an Explanation of Various Difficulties in the Hebrew and English Texts. 3 vols. 8vo. Lond., 1847. G 2 T 1-3

BARRETT (W. A.), Mus. Bac. Balfe : his Life and Work. 8vo. Lond., 1882. C 3 Q 16

Dictionary of Musical Terms. [*See* Stainer, J.]

English Glees and Part Songs. 8vo. Lond., 1886. J 12 T 16

BARRETTO (John), Jun. Dictionary of the Persian and Arabic Languages. 2 vols. 8vo. Calcutta, 1804. K 13 P 10, 11

BARRI (Gerald) Giraldus Cambrensis. Historical Works of. Revised and edited, by Thomas Wright, Esq., M.A., &c. 12mo. Lond., 1863. B 3 P 5

BARRI (Marie Jeanne Gomard de Vaubernier), Comtesse du. [*See* Du Barri, Comtesse.]

BARRIÈRE (Jean François). Bibliothèque des Mémoires relatifs à l'Histoire de France, pendant le 18e Siècle, avec Avant-propos et Notices. 28 vols. 12mo. Paris, 1854-67. C 1 T 1-28

1. Mme. de Staal Delaunay, de la Marquis d'Argenson, et de Mme. Mère du Régent, et Extraits des Mémoires de Saint Simon.

2. Mémoires Secrets sur le Règne de Louis xiv, la Régence, et le Règne de Louis xv, par Duclos.

3. Mme. du Hausset, et de Bachaumont, 1762-82.

4. Mémoires du Baron de Besenval. Collé : La Vérité dans le Vin ; ou, les Désagréments de la Galanterie, Comédie.

5. Marmontel.

6. Mdlle. Clairon, Lekain, Préville, Dazincourt, Molé, Garrick, Goldoni.

7. Weber.

8. Mme. Rolland, suivis des Notices Historiques sur la Révolution, &c.

9. Cléry, de Montpensier, de Riouffe.

10. Marie-Antoinette, et Anecdotes sur les Règnes de Louis xiv, de Louis xv, et de Louis xvi, par Mme. Campan.

11. Général Dumouriez.

12. Suite des Mémoires du Général Dumouriez. Mémoires de Louvet, et Mémoires de la Convention Nationale, par Daunou.

13. De Vaublanc.

14. Souvenirs de Félicie, par Mme. de Genlis ; Souvenirs et Portraits, par le Duc de Lévis.

15. Mme. de Genlis.

16, 17. Maréchal Duc de Richelieu.

18. Journées de Septembre, 1792, par M. J. de Saint-Méard, la Marquise de Fausse-Lendry, l'Abbé Sicard, et G. A. Jourdan.

19, 20. Souvenirs et Anecdotes par le Comte de Ségur. Correspondance et Pensées du Prince de Ligne.

21. Marquis de Bouillé.

22. Mémoires Secrets sur la Russie pendant les règnes de Catherine ii et de Paul i, par C. F. P. Masson.

23, 24. Souvenirs de Vingt Ans de Séjour à Berlin, par Thiébault.

25. Duc de Lauzun et du Comte de Tilly.

26. Victor Alfieri, écrits par lui-même.

27. Souvenirs des Cours de France, d'Espagne, de Prusse, et de Russie ; écrits par H. R. Lord Holland ; suivis du Journal de Mistress G. D. Elliott.

28. De Linguet et de Latude ; suivis de Documents divers sur la Bastille, &c.

Mémoires de Madame Roland. [*See* Berville, M.]

BARRINGTON (Archibald), M.D. Familiar Introduction to Heraldry. Illustrated. 12mo. Lond., 1848. K 10 S 2

BARRINGTON (D.) [*See* Orosius, P.]

BARRINGTON (GEORGE). Account of a Voyage to New South Wales; to which is prefixed a Detail of his Life, Trials, Speeches, &c. 8vo. Lond., 1803.* MD 1 U 10

Another copy. 8vo. Lond., 1810. MD 1 U 12

Barrington's Voyage to New South Wales. 8vo. Lond. (n.d.) MD 1 U 9

Genuine Life and Trial of George Barrington, from his Birth, in June, 1775, to the time of his Conviction at the Old Bailey in September, 1790. 8vo. Lond., 1791.*
MJ 2 Q 25

History of New Holland, from its first Discovery in 1616, to the Present Time; to which is prefixed, an Introductory Discourse on Banishment, by the Right Honourable William Eden. 2nd ed. Illustrated with Maps. 8vo. Lond., 1808. MB 1 T 4

[*Note.*—The first edition of this work was published in 1787, four years prior to the arrival of George Barrington, the London pickpocket, in New Holland, namely, in 1791. (*See* his Life and Trial.) There is, therefore, no probability of his having contributed to the work, because he is neither known, nor does he acknowledge, to have written any book prior to his arrival in the Colony. The name of Barrington appearing on the title-page of this edition is, therefore, an unwarrantable deception on the part of the publisher. A remark on p. x. of the preface helps to prove that the writer was the Rt. Hon. Wm. Eden (Lord Auckland), and that Barrington had nothing to do with the work. The matter in both editions is precisely the same, with the exception of eight pages being added to the preface of the latter one.]

History of New South Wales, including Botany Bay, Port Jackson, Parramatta, Sydney, and all its Dependencies, from the original discovery of the Island; with the Customs and Manners of the Natives. 8vo. Lond., 1802.* MB 1 T 5

Another copy. 2nd ed. With coloured Prints. 8vo. Lond., 1810. MB 1 T 8

Life, Times, and Adventures of George Barrington, the celebrated Thief and Pickpocket, embracing the whole of his History, and a full Account of all his extraordinary Feats, which procured him the name of "The Prince of Thieves." With Engravings. 2nd ed. 8vo. Lond. [1839] MC 1 P 15

Voyage to Botany Bay; with a Description of the Country, Manners, Customs, Religion, &c., of the Natives; to which is added, his Life and Trial. 8vo. Lond., 1793.* MD 1 U 5

Voyage to New South Wales; with a Description of the Country, the Manners, Customs, Religion, &c., of the Natives in the vicinity of Botany Bay. 8vo. Lond., 1795. MD 1 U 8

Sequel to Barrington's "Voyage to New South Wales," comprising an interesting Narrative of the Transactions and Behaviour of the Convicts; the Progress, &c., of the Colony. 8vo. Lond., 1801.* MD 1 U 5

BARRINGTON (SIR JONAH), K.C. Historic Memoirs of Ireland. 2 vols. roy. 4to. Lond., 1835. B 16 S 18, 19 ‡

Personal Sketches of his own Times. 2nd ed., revised and improved. 2 vols. roy. 8vo. Lond., 1830. C 2 V 14, 15

BARRISTER-AT-LAW, A. [*See* VACCINATION.]

BARRISTER OF THE INNER TEMPLE, A. [*See* ETON PORTRAIT GALLERY.]

BARRON (A. F.) British Apples : Report of the Committee of the National Apple Congress. 8vo. Lond., 1884. A 1 R 40

BARRON (C.) Natural History. [*See* ADAMS, A.]

BARROW (ISAAC), D.D. Selections from his Works. [*See* MONTAGU, B.]

BARROW (SIR JOHN), BART., F.S.A., &c. Autobiographical Memoir of, including Reflections, Observations, and Reminiscences at Home and Abroad. 8vo. Lond., 1847. C 2 V 11

Cook's Voyages of Discovery. [*See* COOK, CAPT. J.]

Family Tour through South Holland, up the Rhine, &c. 18mo. Lond., 1831. D 7 P 47

History of the Mutiny and Piratical Seizure of H.M.S. *Bounty:* its Cause and Consequences. Illustrated. 2nd ed. 12mo. Lond., 1835. MB 1 P 13

Life of George, Lord Anson. 8vo. Lond., 1839. C 1 V 13

Life of Peter the Great. New ed., with Notes. Illustrated. 8vo. Lond., 1873. C 2 Q 29

Life of Richard, Earl Howe, K.G., Admiral of the Fleet, and General of Marines. 8vo. Lond., 1838. C 7 P 24

Life, Voyages, and Exploits of Sir Francis Drake; with numerous original Letters from him, and the Lord High Admiral, to the Queen and Great Officers of State. 8vo. Lond., 1843. C 10 U 8

Another copy. (H. and C. Lib.) 2nd ed., abridged. 8vo. Lond., 1844. J 8 P 7

Another copy. 2nd ed. 12mo. Lond., 1844. C 2 Q 11

Another copy. D 10 Q 49

Memoirs of the Naval Worthies of Queen Elizabeth's Reign; with brief Biographical Notices of the respective Commanders. 8vo. Lond., 1845. C 9 Q 4

Recent Accounts of the Pitcairn Islanders. 8vo. Lond., 1834. MD 7 Q 50

Sketch of the Surveying Voyages of H.M.S. *Adventure* and *Beagle,* 1825–36. 8vo. Lond., 1836. MD 7 Q 46

State of the Colony of Swan River, 1st January, 1830; chiefly extracted from Captain Stirling's Report. 8vo. Lond., 1831. MD 7 Q 47

Travels in China : Pekin to Canton. Illustrated. 4to. Lond., 1804. D 4 V 25

Travels into the Interior of Southern Africa. 2nd ed. Illustrated. 2 vols. 4to. Lond., 1806. D 2 U 19, 20

Voyages of Discovery and Research within the Arctic Regions, from the year 1818 to the Present Time. With a Portrait. 8vo. Lond., 1846. D 4 S 5

BARROW (JOHN), JUN. Excursions in the North of Europe, in the years 1830 and 1833. 8vo. Lond., 1834. D 9 P 42

Life and Correspondence of Admiral Sir William Sidney Smith, G.C.B. 2 vols. 8vo. Lond., 1847. C 9 U 23, 24

Tour in Austrian Lombardy, the Northern Tyrol, and Bavaria, in 1840. 8vo. Lond., 1841. D 8 Q 46

BARROW (JOHN), JUN.—*continued.*
Tour round Ireland, t1roug1 the Sea-coast Countries, 1835.
8vo. Lond., 1836. D 8 P 21

Visit to Iceland, by way of Tronyem, in the *Flower of Yarrow*, yac1t, in the summer of 1834. 8vo. Lond., 1835. D 9 P 5

BARROW (JOHN HENRY). Mirror of Parliament. 33 vols. fol., and 25 vols. 8vo. Lond., 1829–41. E

BARRUEL (AUGUSTIN DE), L'ABBÉ. Histoire du Clergé pendant la Révolution Françoise. 8vo. Lond., 1793.
G 14 P 6

Memoirs illustrating the History of Jacobinism ; translated by the Hon. R. Clifford. 4 vols. 8vo. Lond., 1798.
B 26 T 8–11

BARRY (RT. REV. ALFRED), D.D., BISHOP OF SYDNEY. First Words in Australia: Sermons preac1ed in April and May, 1884. 8vo. Sydney, 1884.* MG 1 P 40

[Lecture on] C1ristian Evidence and C1ristian Fait1. [*See* CHRISTIAN EVIDENCE SOCIETY.]

[*See* BARRY, E. M., *and* OLDEN, REV. C.]

BARRY (SIR EDWARD), BART. Observations, Historical, Critical, and Medical, on the Wines of the Ancients. 4to. Lond., 1775. A 1 T 13

BARRY (EDWARD M.), R.A. Lectures on Arc1itecture, delivered at the Royal Academy; edited, wit1 Introductory Memoir, by. Alfred Barry, D.D. Wit1 Portrait and Illustrations. 8vo. Lond., 1881. A 3 P 18

BARRY (GEORGE J.), Directory of Sout1 Australia. [*See* MORRIS, C. S.]

BARRY (JAMES), R.A. Account of a series of Pictures in the Great Room of the Society of Arts, Manufactures, and Commerce, at the Adelp1i. 8vo. Lond., 1783.
A 7 Q 25

Inquiry into the real and imaginary Obstructions to the acquisition of the Arts in England. 8vo. Lond., 1775.
A 7 Q 25

Lectures on Painting. [*See* WORNUM, R. N.]

Letter to the Dilettanti Society, respecting the Improvement of Public Taste, and the original Views of the Royal Academy of Great Britain. 2nd ed., wit1 an Appendix. 8vo. Lond., 1799. A 7 Q 15

BARRY (J.), OPIE (J.), AND FUSELI (H.) Lectures on Painting by the Royal Academicians; edited by R. N. Wornum. 8vo. Lond., 1848. A 7 T 4

BARRY (JOHN WOLFE), M.I.C.E. Railway Appliances : Description of details of Railway Construction. (Text-Books of Science.) 12mo. Lond., 1876. A 17 S 19

BARRY (JOHN WOLFE), AND BRAMWELL (F. J.), F.R.S., &c. Railways and Locomotives : Lectures delivered in 1877. 8vo. Lond., 1882. A 6 S 5

BARRY (SIR REDMOND). Address delivered before the University Forensic Society, 1860 ; and an Address on the Opening of the Circuit Court at Portland, 1852· 8vo. Melb., 1860. MJ 2 S 7

Anot1er copy. MJ 2 R 21

Address on the Opening of the Ararat Circuit Court, 29th October, 1860. 4to. Melb., 1860. MJ 2 S 5

Address on the Opening of the Circuit Court at Portland, on June the 5th, 1852. 8vo. Melb., 1852. MF 2 P 2

Address on the Opening of the Free Public Library at Ballarat East. 12mo. Ballarat, 1869. MJ 2 P 30, and R 11

Address on the Opening of the Sc1ool of Mines, at Ballarat, Victoria, delivered on October 26th, 1870. MJ 2 R 11

Address to the Workmen employed in building the Great Hall of the Melbourne Public Library and Museum, in Melbourne, Victoria ; delivered on September 8t1, 1866. 8vo. Melb., 1866. MJ 2 R 11

Inaugural Address, delivered before the Members of the Victorian Institute, 21st of September, 1854. 8vo. Mel1., 1854. MJ 2 Q 23

Lecture on Music and Poetry. 8vo. Melb., 1849. MH1T8

Lecture on the History of the Art of Agriculture. 8vo. Mel1., 1854. MA 1 Q 7

Music and Poetry. Roy. 8vo. Melb., 1872. MH 1 T 9

Anot1er copy. MJ 2 R 7

Opening Address at the Circuit Court at Sand1urst, on February 27th, 1860.* MJ 2 S 2

Opening Address at the Maryborough Circuit Court, July 17t1, 1861. 4to. Melb., 1861. MJ 2 S 2

Portrait of. [*See* MANUSCRIPTS AND PORTRAITS.]

Two Papers read at the Conference of Librarians 1eld at the London Institution, October, 1877. On Binding, and on Lending Libraries. 8vo. Lond., 1877. MJ 2 R 11

[*See also* MELBOURNE PUBLIC LIBRARY.]

BARRY (CAPT. W. J.) Up and Down ; or, Fifty Years' Colonial Experiences in Australia, California, New Zealand, India, C1ina, and the Sout1 Pacific. 8vo. Lond., 1879. MD 3 Q 36

BARRY CORNWALL. [*See* PROCTOR, B. W.]

BARSANTI (REV. P. OTTAVIO), M.A., &c. I Selvaggi dell' Australia dinanzi alla Scienza e al Protestantismo. 8vo. Roma, 1868. MA 1 R 24

Laying of the Foundation Stone of the new St. Mary's Cat1edral, Sydney, N.S.W.: Sermon preac1ed on the occasion. 12mo. Mel1., 1871. MJ 2 P 30

BARTH (A.) Religions of India. Aut1orised Translation, by Rev. J. Wood. 8vo. Lond., 1882. G 15 P 10

BARTH (HENRY), PH.D., D.C.L., &c. Travels and Discoveries in Nort1 and Central Africa, 1849–55. 5 vols. 8vo. Lond., 1857–58. D 1 P 1–5

BARTHELEMY (ABBE JEAN JACQUES). Travels of "Anacharsis the Younger," in Greece, during the middle of the Fourth Century. 6th ed. 6 vols. 8vo. Lond., 1825.
D 7 U 13-18

Maps, Plans, Views, and Coins, illustrative of the Travels of "Anacharsis the Younger," in Greece. 4to. Lond., 1825.
D 7 V 9

BARTHOLDY [*See* MENDELSSOHN-BARTHOLDY, F.]

BARTHOLOMÆUS DE GLANVILLA ANGLICUS. [*See* GLANVIL, B.]

BARTHOLOMEW (JOHN), F.R.G.S. Imperial Atlas for Australia and New Zealand. Imp. 8vo. Lond., 1875.
MD 5 R 3‡

BARTLE (REV. GEORGE), D.D., &c. Scriptural Doctrine of Hades ; comprising a critical examination of the state of the righteous and wicked Dead, between Death and the General Judgment, and the final Destiny of all Mankind. 5th ed. 8vo. Lond., 1875.
G 13 Q 15

BARTLETT (ALFRED DURLING). Historical and Descriptive Account of Cumnor Place, Berks ; with Biographical Notices of the Lady Amy Dudley, and of Anthony Forster. 8vo. Oxford, 1850.
B 7 Q 8

BARTLETT (E. ASHMEAD), M.P. Shall England keep India ? With Special Maps. Fol. Lond., 1885.
F 27 Q 13‡

BARTLETT (JOHN). Familiar Quotations ; being an attempt to trace to their sources passages and phrases in common use. 7th ed. 8vo. Boston, 1877.
K 17 P 14

Shakespeare Phrase Book. 8vo. Lond., 1881.
K 17 P 24

BARTLETT (JOHN RUSSELL). Dictionary of Americanisms: a Glossary of Words and Phrases usually regarded as peculiar to the United States. 4th ed. enlarged. 8vo. Boston, 1877.
K 14 Q 25

BARTLETT (THOMAS). New Holland : its Colonization, Productions, and Resources; with Observations on the relations subsisting with Great Britain. 8vo. Lond., 1843.*
MB 1 Q 1

BARTLETT (WILLIAM HENRY). Switzerland Illustrated. [*See* BEATTIE, W.]

Walks about the City and Environs of Jerusalem. 8vo. Lond., 1844.
D 6 S 36

BARTLEY (GEORGE C. T.) Provident Knowledge Papers. 8vo. Lond., 1878.
F 6 P 29

Seven Ages of a Village Pauper. 8vo. Lond., 1874.
F 14 Q 20

Toys. (Brit. Manuf. Indust.) 12mo. Lond., 1876.
A 17 S 39

BARTOLI (DANIELLO). Dell'Istoria della Compagnia di Giesu l'Inghilterra, Parte dell'Europa. Fol. Ronn, 1667.
G 7 S 15 †

BARTOLOZZI (FRANCESCO), R.A. Bartolozzi and his Works : a Biographical and Descriptive Account of the Life and Career of ; by A. W. Tuer. Illustrated. 2 vols. 4to. Lond., 1882.
C 5 R 1, 2 †

[*See* CHAMBERLAINE, J.]

BARTON (BERNARD). Poems and Letters; with a Memoir, edited by his Daughter. 12mo. Lond., 1853.
H 5 S 7

BARTON (EDMUND). Opinion of Counsel on Excise Duty on Beer. [*See* BARTON, G. B.]

BARTON (REV. FREDERICK GEORGE), B.A. Men for the Colony : a Lecture. 8vo. Kyneton, 1856.
MJ 2 R 7

BARTON (G. B.) Literature in New South Wales. 8vo. Sydney, 1866.*
MJ 2 R 24

Poets and Prose Writers of New South Wales. 8vo. Sydney, 1866.*
MC 1 R 2

BARTON (G. B., AND EDMUND), Opinion of Counsel on Excise Duty on Beer. Fol. Sydney, 1887.
MF 2 U 21

BARTON (W.) Report of a Trial upon an Indictment promoted by Captain Sir W. Edward Parry, R.N., Commissioner for Managing the Colonial Affairs of the Australian Agricultural Company, and a Magistrate, against the Accountant of that Company, in New South Wales. 8vo. Lond., 1832.
MJ 2 P 36

BARTRUM (MR.) Trial of Lieut.-Col. George Johnston. [*See* JOHNSTON, LIEUT.-COL. G.]

BARTSCH (ADAM). Le Peintre-Graveur. Nouvelle édition. 21 vols. 8vo. Leipzig, 1854-70.
A 8 P 1-21

Atlas [to the above.] 4to. Leipzig, 1870.
A 8 U 14

BARY (DR. A. DE). [*See* DE BARY, DR. A.]

BASCH & CO. Atlas of the Settled Counties of New South Wales. Fol. Sydney, 1872.
MD 5 S 17 ‡

BASHFORD (JOHN L.), M.A. Elementary Education in Saxony. 12mo. Lond., 1881.
G 18 P 4

BASHFORD (R. M.) Legislative Manual of the State of Wisconsin. 8vo. Madison, 1876.
E

BASILEWSKY (A.) Collection Basilewsky. [*See* DARCEL, A.]

BASILIUS (CÆSARIENSIS EPISCOPUS). Opera Omnia. [*See* MIGNE, J. P., SERIES GRÆCA, 29-32.]

BASILIUS (SELEUCIENSIS ARCHIEPISCOPUS). Opera omnia [*See* MIGNE, J. P., SERIES GRÆCA, 85.]

BASKERVILLE (PROF. W. M.) [*See* HARRISON, PROF. J. A.]

BASNAGE (JACQUES). Antiquitez judaïques ou Remarques critiques sur la République des Hébreux. [*See* CUNEUS, P.]

BASS (GEORGE). [*See* COLLINS, D.]

BASS ROCK : its Civil and Ecclesiastical History, by Rev. T. Macerie ; Geology, by H. Miller ; Martyrology, by Rev. J. Anderson ; Zoology, by J. Fleming ; Botany, by J. H. Balfour. 8vo. Edinb., 1848.
J 5 S 27

BASSETT (F. S.) Legends of Sea and Sailors. 12mo.
Lond., 1875.   B 14 Q 13

BASSETT (JAMES). Persia, the Land of the Imams: a
Narrative of Travel and Residence, 1871–85. 8vo.
New York, 1886.   D 5 Q 9

BASTIAN (ADOLF). Die heilige Sage der Polynesier.
Kosmogonie und Theogonie. 8vo. Leipsic, 1881. MA 1 S 6
Timor und umliegende Inseln. Reise-ergebnisse und
Studien. Roy. 8vo. Berlin, 1885.   D 5 U 17
Zur Kenntniss Hawaii's. Nachträge und Ergänzungen
zu den Inselgruppen in Oceanien. 8vo. Berlin, 1883.
                                               MD 5 S 3

BASTIAN (H. CHARLTON), M.A., &c. Beginnings of Life:
Origin, &c., of Lower Organisms. 2 vols. 8vo. Lond.,
1872.   A 17 T 45, 46
Brain as an Organ of Mind. 8vo. Lond., 1880.   A 12 Q 38
Evolution and the Origin of Life. 8vo. Lond., 1874.
                                               A 17 T 38
Modes of Origin of Lowest Organisms; including a Discussion of the Experiments of M. Pasteur, and a Reply
to some Statements by Professors Huxley and Tyndall.
8vo. Lond., 1871.   A 14 S 13

BASTIAT (FRÉDÉRIC). Economic Sophisms; translated
from the 5th edition of the French, by Patrick James
Stirling, LL.D., F.R.S.E. 8vo Edinb., 1873·   F 7 P 1
Essays on Political Economy. 12mo. Lond., 1875.
                                               F 5 Q 21
Harmonies of Political Economy; translated from the
French, with a Notice of the Life and Writings of the
Author, by Patrick James Stirling, F.R.S.E. 8vo. Lond.,
1860.   F 10 P 19
Œuvres complètes de. 7 vols. 8vo. Paris, 1862–64.
                                               F 5 Q 22–28

BASTIEN (J. F.) [*See* LIGER, L.]

BATE (REV. J.) [*See* MAHAN, REV. A.]

BATE (J. D.), M.R.A.S. The Missionary's Vade-mecum:
an Examination of the Claims of Ismael as viewed by
Muhammadans. 1st series. 8vo. Banâras, 1884. G 6 P 31

BATE (JOHN M.) Silk Cultivation: Plain and Practical
Directions for Planting the Mulberry, and Treatment of
the Silkworm. 8vo. Sydney, 1864.   MA 1 Q 7

BATES (ELLEN AND MARY ANN). The Bates' Children:
Father Dalton vindicated. 8vo. Melb., 1875.   MF 1 Q 3

·BATES (G. W.) Sandwich Island Notes; by "A Häole."
8vo. Lond., 1852.   MD 5 R 29

·BATES (HENRY WALTER). German Arctic Expedition of
1869–70. [*See* KOLDEWEY, CAPT. K.]
Illustrated Travels: a Record of Discovery, Geography,
and Adventure. 4to. Lond., 1869–71.   D 9 V·3
The Naturalist on the River Amazons. 2 vols. 8vo. Lond.,
1863.   D 4 P 23, 24
[*See* HUMBERT, A., *and* WARBURTON, COL. P. E.]

BATES (JOSHUA). A Memorial of; from the City of
Boston, Imp. 8vo. Boston 1865–66.   C 3 W 3
Presentation of a Bust and Portrait of Joshua Bates, Esq.,
to the Public Library of the City of Boston. Imp. 8vo.
Boston, 1866.   C 3 W 3

BATES (W. H.) [*See* PRESBYTERIAN TRACTS.]

BATHGATE (ALEXANDER). Colonial Experiences; or,
Sketches of People and Places in the Province of Otago,
New Zealand. 8vo. Glasgow, 1874.*   MD 6 P 1
Waitaruna: a Story of New Zealand Life. 8vo. Lond.,
1881.   MJ 1 Q 10

BATHGATE (JOHN), JUDGE. New Zealand: its Resources
and Prospects. 8vo. Lond., 1880.   MD 4 U 44

BATHURST (RALPH), M.D., DEAN OF WELLS. Life and
Literary Remains of; by Thomas Warton, M.A., &c.
8vo. Lond., 1761.   C 3 U 8

BATHURST HOSPITAL. Report of the Bathurst District Hospital, for the year 1868; with names of Subscribers, and Rules and Regulations, &c. 8vo. Bathurst,
1869.   MF 3 P 18

BATLEY (H. W.) Series of Studies for Domestic Furniture, Decoration, &c. At. fol. Lond., 1882. A 1 R 10 ‡

BATMAN (JOHN). The Founder of Victoria; by James
Bonwick. 2nd ed. 12mo. Melb., 1868.   MC 1 P 34
[*See* CAPPER, R.]

BATTÉ (LÉON). Le Raphael de M. Morris Moore,
Apollon et Marsyas. Documents accompagnés de Pré-
faces, de Traductions, de Notes et d'une Étude. 8vo.
Paris, 1859.   A 8 Q 24

BATTLE ABBEY. Chronicle of, 1066–1176; now first
translated, with Notes, and an Abstract of the subsequent
History of the Establishment, by Mark Antony Lower,
M.A. 8vo. Lond., 1851.   B 7 Q 2

BATTLE-FIELDS OF THE SOUTH, from Bull Run to
Fredericksburg; by "An English Combatant." [T.E.C.]
2 vols. 8vo. Lond., 1863.   B 1 Q 23, 24

BAUDIN (CAPT. N.) Voyage de découvertes aux Terres
Australes. [*See* FREYCINET, CAPT. L.]

BAUDOT (A. DE). Églises de Bourgs et Villages. 2 vols.
imp. 4to. Paris, 1877.   A 23 R 16, 17 ‡
La Sculpture Française au Moyen Age et à la Renaissance.
Comprenant environ 400 Motifs photographiés par Mieuse-
ment. Deuxième édition. Roy.fol. Paris, 1884. A 4 R 15 ‡

BAUDRY (F.) Grammaire comparée des Langues clas-
siques; contenant la théorie élémentaire de la formation
des mots en Sanscrit, en Grec, et en Latin, avec références
aux Langues Germaniques. 1re Partie: Phonétique (*all
published*). 8vo. Paris, 1868.   K 13 P 26

BAUER (FERDINAND). Digitalium Monographia. [*See*
LINDLEY, J.]

BAUER (DR. HEINRICH). Vollständige Grammatik der
neuhochdeutschen Sprache. 5 vols. 8vo. Berlin, 1827–33.
                                               K 12 Q 28–32

BAUER (KAROLINE). Caroline Bauer and the Coburgs; translated and edited by C. Nisbet. 8vo. Lond., 1885.
C 3 S 1

Memoirs of; from the German. 4 vols. 8vo. Lond., 1884–85.
C 8 S 14–17

BAUERLEN (WILLIAM). Voyage of the *Bonito*: an Account of the Fly River Expedition to New Guinea: a Lecture. 8vo. Sydney, 1886.
MD 3 S 37

BAUERMAN (H.), F.G.S. Catalogue of Rock Specimens. [*See* RAMSAY, A. C.]
Text-book of Systematic Mineralogy. 12mo. Lond.,1881.
A 17 S 26

Treatise on the Metallurgy of Iron. 3rd ed. (Weale.) 12mo. Lond., 1872.
A 17 Q 24

BAUMBACH (RUDOLPH). Frau Holde. 18mo. Leip., 1880.
H 5 S 8

BAUMER (PROF. W.) [*See* WORKSHOP, THE.]

BAUMGARTEN (J.), PH.D. Glossaire des Idiomes Populaires du Nord et du Centre de la France. Tome 1 (*all published*.) 8vo. Paris, 1870.
K 14 T 12

BAUMGARTEN (—.) [*See* SUETONIUS, TRANQUILLUS, C.]

BAUTAIN (LOUIS EUGÉNE MARIE), l'Abbé. Art of Extempore Speaking. 5th ed. (Weale.) 12mo. Lond., 1872.
J 6 P 5

BAX (ERNEST BELFORT.) Handbook of the History of Philosophy. 12mo. Lond., 1886.
G 13 R 17
[*See* KANT, I.]

BAXLEY (H. WILLIS). M.D. Spain: Art Remains and Art Realities, Painters, Priests, and Princes. 2 vols. 8vo. Lond., 1875.
D 8 R 20

BAXTER (A. B.) Banking in Australia, from a London Official's point of view ; with some Remarks on Mortgage and Finance Companies. 8vo. Lond., 1883. MF 3 Q 8

BAXTER (C. E.) Talofa: Letters from Foreign Parts. 8vo. Lond., 1884.
MD 4 Q 25

BAXTER (G.) [*See* CAMPBELL, J., *and* WILLIAMS, REV. J.]

BAXTER (MRS. LUCY E.), "LEADER SCOTT." Lorenzo Ghiberti and Donatello; with other early Italian Sculptors. (*Great Artists.*) 8vo. Lond., 1882.
C 3 T 32

Renaissance of Art in Italy: an Illustrated Sketch. 8vo. Lond., 1883.
A 8 U 25

Sculpture, Renaissance and Modern. 8vo. Lond., 1886.
A 6 V 29

BAXTER (REV. M.) Louis Napoleon the destined Monarch of the World and future personal Antichrist, foreshown in prophecy to confirm a Seven Years' Covenant with the Jews. 8vo. Melb., 1866.
MG 1 Q 6

Baxter refuted. [*See* TURNER, W.]

BAXTER (REV. RICHARD). Abridgement of Mr. Baxter's History of his Life and Times ; with an Account of the Ministers, &c., who were ejected after the Restauration of King Charles II. 2nd ed. 2 vols. 8vo. Lond., 1713.
G 13 S 32, 33

Life and Times of. 8vo. Lond.,1713–27. G 13 S 32–35

Life of Richard Baxter of Kidderminster, Preacher and Prisoner, by John Hamilton Davies, B.A. 8vo. Lond., 1887.
C 10 R 22

Practical Works of; with a Life of the Author, and a critical Examination of his Writings, by the Rev. William Orme. 23 vols. 8vo. Lond., 1830.
G 5 R 1–23

BAXTER (DR. WILLIAM). [*See* BROWN, R.]

BAXTER (RT. HON. WILLIAM EDWARD), M.P. England and Russia in Asia. 8vo. Lond., 1885.
F 6 Q 25

Impressions of Central and Southern Europe. 8vo. Lond., 1850.
D 8 T 29

BAYARD (PIERRE DU TERRAIL), CHEVALIER. History of Bayard, the Good Chevalier, sans peur et sans reproche; compiled by the "Loyal Serviteur"; translated into English from the French of Loredan Larchey. Imp. 8vo. Lond., 1883.
C 5 W 6

Right Joyous and Pleasant History of the Feats, Gests, and Prowesses of the Chevalier Bayard ; by the "Loyal Servant." 2 vols. 8vo. Lond., 1825.
C 2 U 10, 11

BAYER (F. P.) [*See* ANTONIO, N.]

BAYLE (PROF. PETER). Dictionary, Historical and Critical, of Mr. Peter Bayle. 2nd ed.; to which is prefixed the Life of the Author, revised, &c., by [P.] Des Maizeaux. 5 vols. fol. Lond., 1734–38.
K 22 P 5–9 ‡

Dictionnaire, Historique et Critique. 4th ed. Revué etc., avec la Vie de l'auteur, par [P.] Des Maizeaux. 4 vols. fol. Amst., 1730.
K 22 P 1–4 ‡

Oeuvres Diverses de. 4 vols. fol. La Haye, 1727-31.
J 28 P 36–39 ‡

BAYLES (JAMES C.) House Drainage and Water Service in Cities, Villages, and Rural Neighborhoods ; with incidental consideration of Causes affecting the Healthfulness of Dwellings. 2nd ed. 8vo. N. York, 1879.
A 6 U 13

BAYLEY (SIR EDWARD CLIVE), K.C.S.I. The History of India as told by its own Historians : the Local Muhammadan Dynasties, Gujarát. Lond., 1886.
B 10 R 1

BAYLEY (F. W. N.) New Tale of a Tub: an Adventure in Verse ; with Illustrations by Lieut. J. S. Cotton. Fol. Lond., 1841.
H 22 S 23 ‡

BAYLEY (JOHN), F.R.S., &c. History and Antiquities of the Tower of London ; with Memoirs of Royal and Distinguished Persons. 2 vols. 4to. Lond., 1825. B 6 V 19, 20
[*See* COOPER, C. P.]

BAYLEY (PETER). Orestes in Argos : a Tragedy (Cumberland's Eng. Theatre). 12mo. Lond., 1829, H 2 Q 9.

BAYLISS (WYKE). Witness of Art; or, the Legend of Beauty. 8vo. Lond., 1876.
A 8 R 23

BAYNES (ROBERT E.), M.A. Lessons on Thermodynamics. (Clar. Press.) 8vo. Oxford, 1878.   A 21 Q 24

BAYS (PETER). Narrative of the Wreck of the *Minerva*, whaler, of Port Jackson, New South Wales, on Nicholson's Shoal, 24° S. 179° W. 8vo. Cambridge, 1831.   MD 5 P 7

BAZ (GUSTAVO), AND GALLO (E. L.) History of the Mexican Railway. Translated into English by G. F. Henderson. Fol. Mexico, 1876.   A 23 P 31 ‡

BAZELY (HENRY CASSON BARNES), B.A. Henry Bazely, the Oxford Evangelist: a Memoir; by the Rev. E. L. Hicks, M.A. 8vo. Lond., 1886.   C 3 S 2

BAZILE (HUMBERT). [*See* HUMBERT-BAZILE, M.]

BEACH (ALFRED E.) [*See* SCIENCE RECORD.]

BEACH (REV. W. R.), M.A. Visit of His Royal Highness the Duke of Edinburgh, K.G., K.T., &c., to Hong Kong, 1869. 4to. Hongkong, 1869.   D 12 R 12 †

BEACONSFIELD (RT. HON. BENJAMIN DISRAELI), EARL OF, K.G. Appreciative Life of the Rt. Hon. the Earl of Beaconsfield; with Portraits of his Contemporaries; edited by Cornelius Brown, F.R.S.L. 2 vols. imp. 8vo. Lond., 1882.   C 3 W 7, 8

Endymion. 8vo. Lond., 1880.   J 9 S 2-4

England and France; or, a Cure for the Ministerial Gallomania. 8vo. Lond., 1832.   F 6 Q 3

Home Letters, written by the late Earl of Beaconsfield in 1830 and 1831. 12mo. Lond., 1885.   D 10 Q 33

Letters of Runnymede. 8vo. Lond., 1836.   - F 6 S 18

Another Copy; with an Introduction and Notes by Francis Hitchman. 8vo. Lond., 1885.   C 2 Q 39

Lord Beaconsfield: a Biography; by T. P. O'Connor. 12mo. Lond., 1880.   C 1 S 12

Lord Beaconsfield: a Study; by Georg Brandes. Authorized Translation, by Mrs. George Sturge. 8vo. Lond., 1880.   C 9 V 13

Lord Beaconsfield's Correspondence with his Sister, 1832-52. 8vo. Lond., 1886.   C 5 R 11

Lord George Bentinck: a Political Biography. 5th ed., revised. 8vo. Lond., 1852.   C 3 S 9

Public Opinion and Lord Beaconsfield. 8vo. Lond., 1886.   F 4 P 7, 8

Selected Speeches of; arranged and edited, with Introduction and Explanatory Notes, by T. E. Kebbel, M.A. With Portrait. 2 vols. 8vo. Lond., 1882.   F 7 S 18, 19

The Rt. Hon. Benjamin Disraeli, M.P.: a Literary and Political Biography, addressed to the New Generation; by Thomas Macknight. 8vo. Lond., 1854.   C 9 V 12

The Rt. Hon. Benjamin Disraeli, Earl of Beaconsfield, K.G., and his Times; by A. C. Ewald. 2 vols. imp. 8vo. Lond., 1882.   C 3 W 5, 6

The "Runnymede Letters"; with an Introduction and Notes, by Francis Hitchman. 8vo. Lond., 1885. C 2 Q 39

II

BEADLE (J. H.) The Undeveloped West; or, Five Years in the Territories. Illustrated. Philadelphia, 1874.   D 3 S 26

BEADLE (B.A.) [*See* AFRICA.]

BEAL (REV. SAMUEL), B.A., &c. Si-yu-ki: Buddhist Records of the Western World. [*See* HIUEN TSIANG.]

Texts from the Buddhist Canon, commonly known as Dhammapada, with accompanying Narratives; translated from the Chinese. 8vo. Lond., 1878. G 15 P 11

The Fo-Sho-Hing-Tsan-King. [*See* MÜLLER, PROF. F. M.]

BEALE (LIONEL SMITH), M.B., &c. Life Theories: their Influence upon Religious Thought. 8vo. Lond., 1871.   G 11 P 17

BEALE (THOMAS). The Natural History of the Sperm Whale; to which is added a Sketch of a South Sea Whaling Voyage. 8vo. Lond., 1839.   MA 2 T 17

BEAMISH (NORTH LUDLOW), F.R.S. History of the King's German Legion. 2 vols. 8vo. Lond., 1832-37.   B 9 R 14, 15

BEAMISH (P. T.) [*See* BROUGHTON, W. G.]

BEAMISH (RICHARD), F.R.S. Memoir of the Life of Sir Marc Isambard Brunel. 8vo. Lond., 1862. C 6 T 5

BEAMONT (WILLIAM). Annals of the Lords of Warrington for the First Five Centuries after the Conquest. (Chetham Soc., 86, 87.) 2 vols. 4to. Lond., 1872-73. E

BEANEY (JAMES GEORGE), F.R.C.S. Clinical Lecture on Diseases of the Hip-joint; delivered in the Theatre of the Melbourne Hospital. (Pam. Ci.) 8vo. Melb., 1878.   MA 2 Q 33

Constitutional Syphilis; being a practical illustration of the disease in its secondary and tertiary phases; with Plates. 8vo. Melb., 1872.   MA 2 S 13

Dr. Beaney's Vindication; with Reflections on the Inquest held upon the body of Mary Lewis. 8vo. Melb., 1866.   MF 1 Q 1

Doctors Differ: a Lecture, delivered at the Melbourne Athenæum. 8vo. Melb., 1876.   MA 2 S 38

Generative System, and its Functions in Health and Disease. 8vo. Melb., 1872.   MA 2 S 14

History and Progress of Surgery: an Address, delivered to the Medical Students of the Melbourne Hospital. (Pam. Ci.) 8vo. Melb., 1877.   MA 2 Q 33

The Queen *v.* Beaney—Charge of Murder. [*See* REEVES, C. E.]

Vaccination and its Dangers; with Advice and Instruction to Parents as to how and when to Vaccinate. 12mo. Melb., 1870.   MJ 2 P 31

[*See* BAILLIERE, *v.* BEANEY.]

BEARD (REV. CHARLES), B.A. The Reformation of the
16th Century in its relation to Modern Thought and
Knowledge. (Hibbert Lectures.) 8vo. Lond., 1883.
G 7 P 11

BEARD (GEORGE M.), A.M., M.D. New Cyclopædia of
Family Medicine. Our Home Physician: a Popular
Guide to the Art of Preserving Health and Treating
Disease; with plain Advice for all the Medical and
Surgical Emergencies of the Family. 1 vol. (in 2) roy.
8vo. Sydney, 1883. MA 2 S 52, 53

Practical Treatise on Sea-sickness: its Symptoms, Nature,
and Treatment. Enlarged edition. 4th thousand. 8vo.
New York, 1881. A 12 Q 46

BEARD (GEORGE M.), A.M., &c., AND ROCKWELL
(A. D.), M.A., &c. Practical Treatise on the Medical
and Surgical Uses of Electricity. 8vo. New York,
1871. A 5 S 46
Another copy. 3rd ed. 8vo. New York, 1881. A 5 T 25

BEARDSLEE (COMM. L. A.), U.S.N. Experiments on the
Strength of Wrought-Iron and Chain-Cables, including
miscellaneous investigations into the physical and chemical
Properties of Rolled Wrought-Iron; abridged by William
Kent, M.E. 8vo. New York, 1879. A 9 T 36

BEARDSLEY (E. EDWARDS), D.D., &c. Life and Correspondence of the Rt. Rev. Samuel Seabury, D.D. 8vo.
Boston, 1881. C 5 S 28

BEATON (ALFRED CHARLES). Quantities and Measurements: how to calculate them. (Weale.) 12mo. Lond.,
1871. A 17 P 58

BEATSON (MAJ.-GEN. ALEXANDER). Tracts relative to
the Island of St. Helena; written during a Residence of
Five Years. 4to. Lond., 1816. D 9 R 19 †

BEATSON (ROBERT), LL.D. Naval and Military Memoirs
of Great Britain, 1727–83. 6 vols. 8vo. Lond., 1804.
B 6 Q 36–41

Political Index to the Histories of Great Britain and Ireland; or, a Complete Register of the Hereditary Honours,
Public Offices, and Persons in Office, from the Earliest
Periods to the Present Time. 3rd ed., enlarged. 3 vols.
8vo. Lond., 1806. K 19 R 5–7

Register of the British Parliament, from the Union in
1708. 3 vols. 8vo. Lond., 1807. K 11 R 2–4

BEATTIE (PROF. JAMES), LL.D. Elements of Moral
Science; with a complete Index. 3rd ed. 2 vols. 8vo.
Edinb., 1817. G 6 R 34, 35

Life and Character of James Hay Beattie. [*See* BEATTIE,
J. H.]

Life and Poems of. [*See* BRITISH POETS, 2, *and* CHALMERS,
A.]

Essay on the Nature and Immutability of Truth. 9th ed.
8vo. Lond., 1820. G 15 R 8

The Minstrel; or, the Progress of Genius; with other Poems;
to which are prefixed Memoirs of the Life of the Author,
by Alexander Chalmers. 12mo. Lond., 1811. H 5 S 10

BEATTIE (JAMES HAY), A.M. Miscellanies; with an
Account of his Life and Character; by James Beattie,
LL.D. 12mo. Lond., 1807. H 5 S 11

BEATTIE (WILLIAM), M.D. Life and Letters of Thomas
Campbell. 3 vols. 8vo. Lond., 1849. C 10 R 36–38
Switzerland. Illustrated in a series of Views taken expressly for this Work, by W. H. Bartlett, Esq. 2 vols.
4to. Lond., 1836. D 8 V 31, 32

BEATTS (J. M.) Municipal History of the Royal Burgh
of Dundee. 8vo. Dundee, 1873. B 13 S 7

BEATTY-KINGSTON (W.) [*See* KINGSTON, W. B.-]

BEAUCHAMPS (PIERRE FRANÇOIS GODARD DE.) Funestine. [*See* CABINET DES FÉES.]

BEAUCHESNE (A. DE). Louis XVII; his Life, his Suffering, his Death: the Captivity of the Royal Family in
the Temple; translated and edited by W. Hazlitt. 2 vols.
8vo. Lond., 1853. C 6 P 19, 20
Louis XVII; sa Vie, son Agonie, sa Mort: Captivité de la
Famille Royale au Temple. Quatrième édition. 2 vols.
8vo. Paris, 1867. C 10 V 40, 41

BEAUFORT (DANIEL AUGUSTUS), LL.D. Memoir of a
Map of Ireland, illustrating the Topography of that Kingdom. 4to. Lond., 1792. D 6 V 7

BEAUFORT (EMILY A.) Egyptian Sepulchres and Syrian
Shrines, including some stay in the Lebanon, at Palmyra,
and in Western Turkey. With Illustrations. 2 vols.
8vo. Lond., 1861. D 1 P 6, 7

BEAUFORT (FRANCIS). Karamania; or, a brief Description of the South Coast of Asia Minor, and of the Remains
of Antiquity. 8vo. Lond., 1817. D 4 U 25

BEAUFORT (HENRY C.), DUKE OF, AND MORRIS
(M.) Hunting. 8vo. Lond., 1885. A 17 U 31

BEAUFORT (MARGARET), COUNTESS OF RICHMOND AND
DERBY. [*See* RICHMOND AND DERBY, COUNTESS OF.]

BEAUFORT (RAPHAEL LEDOS DE). Letters of George
Sand. [*See* DUDEVANT, MME. A. L. A.]
The Abbé [Franz] Liszt: the Story of his Life. 8vo.
Lond., 1886. C 3 Q 31

BEAUFOY (COL. MARK), F.R.S., &c. Nautical and
Hydraulic Experiments; with numerous Scientific Miscellanies. 4to. Lond., 1834. A 3 P 16 †

BEAUJOINT (JULES). Secret Memoirs of Madame la
Marquise de Pompadour. 8vo. Lond., 1885. C 8 U 44

BEAUMARCHAIS (PIERRE AUGUSTIN CARON DE). Beaumarchais and his Times: Sketches of French Society in
the 18th Century, from unpublished Documents; by Louis
de Loménie; translated by Henry S. Edwards. 4 vols.
8vo. Lond., 1856. O 3 Q 9–12
The Barber of Seville: a Comic Opera (Cumberland's Eng.
Theatre). 12mo. Lond., 1829. H 2 Q 14

BEAUMONT (EDOUARD). Jewel Art Studies: a Series of high-class original and suggestive Designs, specially prepared for Practical Working Jewellers. Roy. 4to. Edinb., 1885. A 2 S 28 †

BEAUMONT (FRANCIS). Life and Poems of. [*See* CHALMERS, A.]

BEAUMONT (FRANCIS), AND FLETCHER (JOHN). Works of; with an Introduction and Explanatory Notes, by Henry Weber, Esq. 14 vols. 8vo. Edinb., 1812. H 2 S 12-25

Bonduca : a Tragedy (Bell's Brit. Theatre). 18mo. Lond., 1796. H 2 P 3

Another copy. [*See* Brit. Drama, 1.]

The Chances : a Comedy ; altered by the late Duke of Buckingham (Bell's Brit. Theatre). 18mo. Lond., 1791. H 2 P 7

Another copy (Brit. Theatre). 12mo. Lond., 1808. H 1 P 6

The False One. [*See* Brit. Drama, 1.]

The Maid's Tragedy. [*See* Brit. Drama, 1.]

Philaster : a Tragedy (Bell's Brit. Theatre). 18mo. Lond., 1791. H 2 P 18

Another copy. [*See* Brit. Drama, 1.]

Rule a Wife and have a Wife : a Comedy (New Eng. Theatre). 12mo. Lond., 1786. H 4 P 18

Another copy (Bell's Brit. Theatre). 18mo. Lond., 1791. H 2 P 34

Another copy (Brit. Theatre). 12mo. Lond., 1808. H 1 P 6

BEAUMONT (SIR JOHN). Life and Poems of. [*See* CHALMERS, A.]

BEAUMONT (GUSTAVE DE). Ireland, Social, Political, and Religious; edited by W. C. Taylor. 2 vols. 8vo. Lond., 1839. B 11 P 16, 17

.L'Irlande, Sociale, Politique, et Religieuse. 2 vols. 12mo. Paris, 1863. B 11 P 14, 15

BEAUMONT (GUSTAVE DE), AND TOCQUEVILLE (ALEXIS CHARLES HENRI CLEREL DE). On the Penitentiary System in the United States, and its application in France ; with an Appendix on Penal Colonies ; translated by F. Lieber. 8vo. Philad., 1833. F 10 S 7

BEAUMONT (JOHN). Historical, Physiological, and Theological Treatise of Spirits, Apparitions, Witchcrafts, and other Magical Practices. 8vo. Lond., 1705. G 13 R 33

BEAUMONT (MARIE LEPRINCE DE). Contes des Fées. [*See* CABINET DES FÉES.]

BEAUREGARD (GEN. PIERRE GUSTAVE TOUTANT). The Military Operations of General Beauregard in the War between the States, 1861–65; by Alfred Roman. 2 vols. 8vo. New York, 1884. C 9 T 1, 2

BEAUTIES OF ENGLAND AND WALES (THE); or, Delineations, Topographical, Historical, and Descriptive of each County. Embellished with Engravings by John Britton and Edward Wedlake Brayley. 18 vols. (in 25) 8vo. Lond., 1801–16. D 9 R 1-25

1. Bedfordshire, Berkshire, Buckinghamshire.
2. Cambridgeshire, Cheshire, Cornwall.
3. Cumberland, Isle of Man, Derbyshire.
4. Devonshire, Dorsetshire.
5. Durham, Essex, and Gloucestershire.
6. Hampshire, Isle of Wight, Herefordshire.
7. Hertfordshire, Huntingdonshire, Kent.
8. Kent.
9. Lancashire, Leicestershire, Lincolnshire.
10-14. London and Middlesex.
15. Monmouthshire, Norfolk, Northamptonshire.
16. Northumberland, Nottinghamshire.
17. Oxfordshire, Rutlandshire.
18. Shropshire, Somersetshire.
19. Somersetshire, Staffordshire.
20. Suffolk, Surrey, Sussex.
21. Wiltshire, Westmoreland.
22. Warwickshire, Worcestershire.
23. Yorkshire.
24. North Wales.—Cambria, Anglesea, Caernarvonshire, Denbighshire, Flintshire, Montgomeryshire, Merionethshire.
25. South Wales.—Brecknockshire, Caermarthenshire, Cardiganshire, Glamorganshire, Pembrokeshire, Radnorshire.

BEAUVOIR (LUDOVIC), MARQUIS DE. Voyage autour du Monde: Australie, Java, Siam, Canton, Pekin, Yeddo, San Francisco. Sm. fol. Paris, 1875. MD 5 P 18 †

A Voyage round the World: Australia, Java, Siam, Canton. 2 vols. 8vo. Lond., 1870. D 10 Q 27-28

Another copy. MD 1 W 1, 2

Pekin, Jeddo, and San Francisco—the conclusion of a Voyage round the World ; translated from the French by Agnes and Helen Stevenson. 8vo. Lond., 1872. D 10 Q 29

BEAVAN (HUGH J. C.), F.R.G.S., &c. Plurality of the Human Race. [*See* POUCHET, G.]

BEAVEN (PROF. JAMES), D.D. Recreations of a long Vacation; or, a Visit to Indian Missions in Upper Canada. 12mo. Lond., 1846. D 3 P 38

BEAVER (CAPT. PHILIP), R.N. Life and Services of ; by Capt. W. H. Smyth. 8vo. Lond., 1829. C 10 Q 1

BEAZELEY (A.) Notes on Domestic Buildings in Sweden. 4to. Lond., 1882–83. A 2 U 44

Swedish Building Law. (Trans. Roy. Inst. Brit. Architects.) 4to. Lond., 1886. F 5 V 28

BEAZLEY (REV. JOSEPH). [*See* GIBSON, REV. J.]

BECCARIA (CESAR BONE SANA), MARQUISS DE. Essay on Crimes and Punishments; translated, with the Commentary, by Voltaire. 8vo. Lond., 1804. F 5 U 30

BECHE (SIR H. T. DE LA). [*See* DE LA BECHE, SIR H. T.]

BECHSTEIN (I. M.), M.D. Cage and Chamber Birds ; their Natural History, Habits, Food, Diseases, Management, and modes of Capture. 12mo. Lond., 1877. A 14 Q 41

BECK (WILHELMINE), BARONESS VON. Personal Adventures during the late War of Independence in Hungary. 2 vols. 8vo. Lond., 1850. D 8 Q 3, 4

BECK (S. WILLIAM), F.R.H.S.   Draper's Dictionary : a
Manual of Textile Fabrics ; tieir History and Applications.   8vo.   Lond., 1882.   A 25 Q 12

Gloves, tieir Annals and Associations : a Ciapter of
Trade and Social History.   8vo.   Lond., 1883.   B 14 Q 37

BECK (THOMAS ALCOCK).   Annales Furnesienses.   History
and Antiquities of the Abbey of Furness.   Roy. 4to.
Lond., 1844.   B 10 S 11 †

BECKER (A. WOLFGANG).   Kunst und Künstler des
acitzeinten Jairiunderts.   3 vols. 8vo.   Leip., 1863–
65.   A 8 Q 2–4

BECKER (DR. KARL FERDINAND).   Ausführliche deutscie
Grammatik, als Kommentar der Sciulgrammatik.   2ᵉ
neubearbeitete Ausgabe.   2 vols. 8vo.   Frankfurt am
Maine, 1842–43.   K 13 S 9, 10

Handbuci der deutscien Spracie; neu bearbeitet von
Tieodor Becker.   11ᵉ verbesserte Auflage.   8vo.   Prag,
1876.   K 12 Q 20

BECKER (G. F.)   Geology of the Comstock Lode and the
Washoe District.   (U.S. Geol. Survey.)   Witi Atlas.
2 vols. 4to.   Wasiington, 1882.   A 13 P 21, 22 †

BECKER (KARL FRIEDRICH).   Weltgesciicite.   14 vols.
(in 4).   8vo.   Berlin, 1844.   B 35 S 1–4

BECKER (LUDWIG).   Men of Victoria ; sketcied by L.
Becker.   Part I—William Foster Stawell, Join Hodgson, Andrew Clarke, Peter Lalor.   Fol.   Meli., 1856.
                                                    MC 1 R 34 ‡

BECKER (PROF. WILIELM ADOLF),   Charicles ; or, Illustrations of the Private Life of the Ancient Greeks ;
translated from the German by the Rev. F. Metcalfe,
M.A.   4th ed. 8vo.   Lond., 1874.   B 9 S 32

Gallus ; or, Roman Scenes of the time of Augustus; translated by F. Metcalfe, M.A.   8vo.   Lond., 1844.   B 12 Q 41

Anotier copy ; witi Notes.   3rd ed.   8vo.   Lond., 1866.
                                                    B 12 Q 42

BECKER (THEODORE).   [*See* BECKER, K. F.]

BECKET (THOMAS A'), SAINT, ARCHBISHOP OF CANTERBURY.
The Tiree Arcibisiops : Lanfranc—Anselm—a'Becket ;
by Wasiington and Mark Wilks.   8vo.   Lond., 1858.
                                                       C 2 U 7

Opera Omnia.   [*See* MIGNE, J. P., SERIES LATINA, 190.]

BECKETT (SIR EDMUND), BART., LL.D., BARON GRIM-
THORPE, *formerly* EDMUND BECKETT DENISON.   A Book
on Building, Civil and Ecclesiastical, witi the Theory of
Domes, and of the Great Pyramid, and a Catalogue of
sizes of Ciurcies and otier large buildings.   Illustrated.
8vo.   Lond., 1876.   A 2 R 23

Siould the Revised New Testament be autiorised ?   8vo.
Lond., 1882.   G 13 Q 22

Lectures on Ciurci Building ; witi some Practical
Remarks on Bells and Clocks.   2nd ed.   8vo.   Lond.,
1856.   A 2 R 38

Rudimentary Treatise on Clocks, Watcies and Bells.
(Weale.)   5th ed.   12mo.   Lond., 1868.   A 17 P 24

BECKFORD (WILLIAM).   History of Calipi Vathek; witi
Preface and Notes, critical and explanatory.   8vo.   Lond.,
1883.   J 10 R 13

Italy ; witi Sketcies of Spain and Portugal.   2 vols.
8vo.   Lond., 1834.   D 8 T 32, 33

Recollections of an Excursion to the Monasteries of
Alcobaça and Batalia.   8vo.   Lond., 1835.   D 8 T 14

Vathek ; translated from the original Frenci.   4th ed.,
revised and corrected.   8vo.   Lond., 1823.   J 8 Q 38

BECKMANN (JOHN).   History of Inventions and Discoveries.   4 vols. 8vo.   Lond., 1817.   A 11 S 12–15

BECKWOURTH (JAMES P.)   Life and Adventures of
J. P. Beckwourti, Mountaineer, Scout, and Pioneer, and
Ciief of the Crow Nation of Indians ; written, from iis
own dictation, by T. D. Bonner.   Illustrated.   8vo.
Lond., 1856.   C 3 R 5

BECON (REV. THOMAS).   Writings of.   [*See* BRITISH
REFORMERS, 1.]

BEDDARD (F. E.)   [*See* FORBES, W. A.]

BEDDOE (JOHN), M.D., &c.   Races of Britain.   8vo.
Bristol, 1885.   A 2 P 18

[*See* JOURNAL OF ANTHROPOLOGY.]

BEDDOME (COL. R. H.), F.L.S.   Hand-book to the Ferns
of British India, Ceylon, and the Malay Peninsula.
Illustrated.   8vo.   Calcutta, 1883.   A 4 P 15

BEDE (CUTHBERT).   [*See* BRADLEY, REV. E.]

BEDE (VENERABLE).   Be Domes Dæge, De Die Judicii :
an Old Englisi Version of the Latin Poem ascribed to
Bede.   [*See* EARLY ENGLISH TEXT SOC. 27.]

Ecclesiastical History of England; also, the Anglo-Saxon
Cironicle.   Edited by Rev. J. A. Giles.   12mo.   Lond.,
1870.   B 3 P 4

Opera omnia   [*See* MIGNE, J. P., SERIES LATINA, 90–95.]

Venerabilis Bedæ Opera Historica Minora.   (Hist. Soc.)
8vo.   Lond., 1841.   B 5 T 27, 28

BEDELL (WILLIAM), BISHOP OF KILMORE.   Life of ; by H.
J. Monck Mason, LL.D., &c.   8vo.   Lond., 1843.
                                                    C 10 R 25

BEDFORD (HON. E. S. P.)   Letters to the Members of
the Committee of Management of St. Mary's Hospital.
(Pam. 42.)   8vo.   Hobart, 1859.   MJ 2 R 4

BEDFORD (FRANCIS).   The Holy Land, Egypt, Constantinople, Atiens, &c. : a Series of forty-eigit Piotograpis;
witi Descriptive Text by W. M. Tiompson.   4to.
Lond. 1865.   D 5 V 28

BEDFORD (JOHN), FOURTH DUKE OF.   Correspondence
of ; selected from the Originals at Woburn Abbey ; witi
an Introduction, by Lord Join Russell.   3 vols.   8vo.
Lond., 1842.   C 8 S 5–7

BEECHAM (JOHN). Asiantee and the Gold Coast; being a Sketch of the History, Social State, and Superstitions of the Inhabitants of those Countries. 8vo. Lond., 1841.   D 1 T 7

Christianity, the Means of Civilization. [*See* COATES, D.]

Colonization; being Remarks on Colonization in general; with an Examination of the Proposals of the Association which has been formed for Colonizing New Zealand. 3rd ed. 8vo. Lond., 1838.   MF 1 Q 15

BEECHER (REV. EDWARD), D.D. The Conflict of Ages; or, the Great Debate on the Moral Relations of God and Man. 5th ed. 8vo. Boston, 1854.   G 13 R 36

BEECHER (REV. HENRY WARD). Compulsory Education: a Lecture. 8vo. Melb., 1873.   MJ 2 R 12.

BEECHEY (CAPT. F. W.), R.N., &c. Narrative of a Voyage to the Pacific and Beering's Strait, to co-operate with the Polar Expeditions, performed in H.M.S. *Blossom*, in the years 1825–28. 2 vols. 8vo. Lond., 1831.*   MD 4 W 1, 2

Another copy. A new edition. 2 vols. 8vo. Lond., 1831.*   MD 4 W 5, 6

Another copy. 8vo. Philad., 1832.   MD 4 W 7

Voyage of Discovery towards the North Pole, under the command of Capt. David Buchan, R.N., in 1818. 8vo. Lond., 1843.   D 4 R 45

Zoology of Captain Beechey's Voyage, 1825–28; by J. Richardson, M.D., F.R.S., &c.; N. A. Vigors, Esq., A.M., F.R.S., &c.; G. T. Lay, Esq.; E. T. Bennett, Esq., F.L.S., &c.; Richard Owen, Esq.,; John E. Gray, Esq., F.R.S., &c.; the Rev. W. Buckland, D.D., &c.; and G. B. Sowerby, Esq. Illustrated. 4to. Lond., 1839. A 14 V 1 [*See* AINSWORTH, W.]

BEECHEY (CAPTS. F. W. & H. W.), R.N., &c. Proceedings of the Expedition to explore the Northern Coast of Africa, from Tripoly eastward, in 1821–22. 4to. Lond., 1828.   D 2 U 17

BEECHEY (H. W.) Memoir of Sir Joshua Reynolds. [*See* REYNOLDS, SIR J.]

BEEHLER (W. H.) Cruise of the *Brooklyn*. Illustrated. 8vo. Philad., 1885.   D 9 U 20

BEER (FREDERICK), M.D., &c. Case of Dr. Frederick Beer; with a Comment and Notes, by J. Sheridan Moore; Opinions of the Press; Address to the Members of the Honorable the Legislative Council and the Legislative Assembly of New South Wales. (Pam. N.) 8vo. Sydney, 1868–71.   MJ 2 P 29

Case of Dr. Frederick Beer, M.D., Ch.B., &c: Speech delivered by Walter H. Cooper, Barrister-at-Law, in advocacy of a Bill to relieve Dr. Beer from all Disabilities attaching to him, in consequence of his having been improperly convicted of Felony. (Pam. N.) 12mo. Sydney, 1878.   MJ 2 P 29

The Whole Truth; being still "Later Papers" in the Case of Dr. Frederick Beer; containing a *resumé* of the Moral Assassination of which he has been a Victim for more than twenty-one years. (Pam. N.) 8vo. Sydney, 1877.   MJ 2 P 29

BEER (WILHELM), AND MÄDLER (DR. J. H.) Der Mond nach seinen kosmischen und individuellen Verhältnissen oder allgemeine vergleichende Selenographie. 4to., and Atlas fol. Berlin, 1837.   A 3 U 9, 10

BEETHOVEN (LUDWIG VON). Briefe Beethovens; herausgegeben von Dr. L. Nohl. 8vo. Stuttgart, 1865. C 8 T 6

Letters of (1790–1826), from the Collection of Dr. Ludwig Nohl; translated by Lady Wallace. With a Portrait and Facsimile. 2 vols. 8vo. Lond., 1866.   C 3 Q 4, 5

Life of; including his Correspondence with his Friends, numerous Characteristic Traits, and Remarks on his Musical Works [by A. Schindler]; edited by Ignace Moscheles. 2 vols. 8vo. Lond., 1841.   C 3 R 20, 21

Ludwig van Beethoven; Leben und Schaffen; von Adolf Bernard Marx. 2 vols. roy. 8vo. Berlin, 1863. C 9 V 14, 15

BEETON (S. O.) F.R.G.S. Dictionary of Geography: a Universal Gazetteer. 19th thousand. 8vo. Lond., 1884.   D 11 S 7

Dictionary of Natural History: a Comprehensive Cyclopædia of the Animal Kingdom. 8vo. Lond., 1884. K 18 P 16

BEG (REV. WAZIR), LL.D., &c. Manual of Presbyterian Principles; with a Letter dedicatory to the Very Rev. the Moderator. 8vo. Sydney, 1870.   MG 1 P 16

Masonry and Popery: Light and Darkness; or, Dr. Vaughan's Ignorance of Freemasonry exposed. 12mo. Sydney, 1876.*   MG 1 Q 33

Puseyism, or Ritualism, anatomized. 8vo. Sydney, 1869.   MG 1 Q 31

The Pope as a Political Chief; or, Popery as a Political System, proved from History and Romish Authorities. 12mo. Sydney, 1871.   MG 1 P 48

BEGG (REV. ANDREW). Warrnambool Presbyterian Case [with all the Documents]. 8vo. Melb., 1861. MF 1 Q 1

BEGG (W. PROUDFOOT). Development of Taste, and other Studies in Æsthetics. 8vo. Glasgow, 1887. G 6 P 32

BEHRENS (CARL FRIEDRICH). Der wohlversuchte Süd-Länder, das ist: ausführliche Reise-Beschreibung um die Welt. 12mo. Leip., 1739.   MD 1 T 15

BEHRENS (DR. W. J.) Text-book of General Botany; translation from the second German edition; revised by Patrick Geddes, F.R.S.E. Illustrated. 8vo. Edinb., 1885.   A 4 T 29

BEILBY (J. WOOD). Statement of a recently claimed Discovery in Natural Science, affording a new stimulus to Mining Enterprise. 8vo. Melb., 1870.   MJ 2 R 23

BEIT (JOHN N.) Proposals for procuring a continued influx of German Emigrants to the Colony of New South Wales. (Pam., A.) Fol. Sydney, 1847.   MJ 2 U 1

Letter from the Chairman of the Committee of the Legislative Council, upon the Management of the Goldfields. (Pam. 36.) 8vo. Sydney, 1851.*   MJ 2 Q 23

BEKE (CHARLES TILSTONE), PH.D., &c   Britisı Captives in Abyssinia. 2nd ed. 8vo. Lond., 1867.   D 1 W 5

Journey of MM. Monteiro and Gamitto. [*See* AFRICA.]

The late Dr. Ciarles Beke's Discoveries of Sinai in Arabia, and of Midian; edited by his Widow [Mrs. Emily Beke]. Roy. 8vo. Lond., 1878.   D 5 U 6

Voyages of Barents and Dé Veer. [*See* HAKLUYT SOC., 1876.

BEKE (MRS. EMILY). Jacob's Fligıt; or, a Pilgrimage to Harran. 8vo. Lond., 1865.   D 5 Q 40
[*See* BEKE, DR. C. T.]

BEKKER (PROF. IMMANUEL), [*See* ARISTOPHANES; BYZANTINÆ HIST. SCRIPT.; *and* PLATO.]

Carmina Homerica. [*See* HOMER.]

BEKYNTON (T.)   Official Correspondence of.   [*See* CHRONICLES OF GREAT BRITAIN, 118, 119.]

BELCHER (DIANA), LADY. Mutineers of the *Bounty*, and tıeir Descendants in Pitcairn and Norfolk Islands. Witı Illustrations. 8vo. Lond., 1870.   MB 1 Q 32

BELCHER (CAPT. SIR EDWARD), K.C.B., R.N., &c. Narrative of a Voyage round the World, performed by H.M.S. *Sulphur*, during the years 1836–42. 2 vols. 8vo. Lond., 1843.   D 9 S 30, 31

Narrative of the Voyage of H.M.S. *Samarang*, during the years 1843–46, in the Eastern Arcıipelago. 2 vols. 8vo. Lond., 1848.   D 6 S 28, 29

BELDAM (JOSEPH), F.R.G.S. Recollections of Scenes and Institutions in Italy and the East. 2 vols. 8vo. Lond., 1851.   D 10 Q 37, 38

BELFOUR (F. C.) Travels of Macarius. [*See* PAUL OF ALEPPO.]

BELISARIUS. Life of; by Lord Maıon [Earl Stanıope]. 2nd ed. 8vo. Lond., 1848.   C 3 Q 6

BELKNAP (REV. DR. JEREMY). Diograpıies of the Early Discoverers of America: a Reprint of the First Edition of 1798. 4to. New York 1879.   C 3 W 1

History of New Hampsıire; witı Notes by J. Farmer. Vol. 1 (*all published*). 8vo. Dover, N.H., 1831. B 1 R 14

BELL (ALEXANDER MELVILLE), F.E.I.S., &c. Visible Speecı: the Science of Universal Alpıabetics; or, Self-interpreting Pıysiological Letters, for the Writing of all Languages in one Alpıabet. 4to. Lond., 1867. K 12 T 25

BELL (SIR CHARLES), K.G.H., &c. Anatomy and Pıilosopıy of Expression, as connected witı the Fine Arts. 4th ed. 8vo. Lond., 1849.   A 8 R 1

Anotıer copy. 6th ed. 8vo. Lond., 1872.   A 8 R 2

Letters of; selected from ıis Correspondence witı ıis Brotıer George Josepı Bell [by Mrs. Marion Bell]. 8vo. Lond., 1870.   C 3 Q 8

The Hand: its Mecıanical and Vital Endowments, as evincing design. 8vo. Lond., 1833.   A 12 R 32
[*See* PALEY, REV. W.]

BELL (CLARA). Egypt, Descriptive, Historical, and Picturesque. [*See* EBERS, G.]

Visit to Ceylon. [*See* HAECKEL, DR. E.]

[*See* CHESNEAU, E., *and* SPITTA, P.]

BELL (DUGALD). Among the Rocks around Glasgow: a Series of Excursion-Sketcıes and otıer Papers. 8vo. Glasgow, 1881.   A 9 Q 21

BELL (EDWARD). [*See* GOETHE, J. W.]

BELL (MAJOR EVANS). Memoir of General Joın Briggs, of the Madras Army; witı Comments on some of his Words and Work. 8vo. Lond., 1885.   C 8 V 1

BELL (SIR FRANCIS DILLON), C.B., K.C.M.G. Official Hand-book of New Zealand. [*See* GISBORNE W.]

BELL (FREDERICK A.) Industry and Commerce relieved and increased by means of Free Trade and Direct Taxation. 2nd ed., enlarged. (Pam. Ds.) 8vo. Sydney, 1866.   MF 3 P 17

BELL (MAJOR-GEN. GEORGE). Rougı Notes by an Old Soldier, during fifty years' service. 2 vols. 8vo. Lond., 1867.   C 5 V 27, 28

BELL (GEORGE JOSEPH). [*See* BELL, MRS. M.]

BELL (H. C. P.) Máldive Islands: an Account of the Pıysical Features, Climate, History, Inıabitants, Próductions, and Trade. Sm. fol. Colombo, 1883. D 4 P 22 †

BELL (HENRY G.) Life of Mary Queen of Scots. (Const. Misc.) 2 vols. 18mo. Edinb., 1831.
K 10 Q 12, 13

My Old Portfolio; or, Tales and Sketcıes. 8vo. Lond., 1832.   J 6 R 11

Selections of the Most Remarkable Pıenomena of Nature. (Const. Misc.) 18mo. Edinb., 1827.   K 10 P 51

BELL (SIR I. LOWTHIAN), F.R.S. Principles of the Manufacture of Iron and Steel; witı some Notes on the Economic Conditions of tıeir Production. 8vo. Lond., 1884.   A 10 P 16

BELL (JACOB). Cıemical and Pharmaceutical Processes and Products. [*See* LOND. INTERNAT. EXHIB., 1851.]

BELL (JAMES), PH.D., &c. Analysis and Adulteration of Foods. Part 2. Milk, Butter, Cıeese, Cereal Foods, Prepared Starcıes, &c. (Soutı Kens. Mus.) 8vo. Lond., 1883.   E

BELL (JAMES STANISLAUS). Journal of a Residence in Circassia, during the years 1837–39. 2 vols. 8vo. Lond., 1840.   D 7 U 35, 36

Mitla. [*See* TEMPSKY, G. F. VON.]

BELL (JOHN). British Theatre. 46 vols. 12mo. Lond., 1791–97.   H 2 P 1–46

1. The Orphan; or, the Unhappy Marriage: a Tragedy; by Thomas Otway. The Albion Queens; or, the Death of Mary, Queen of Scots: a Tragedy; by John Banks. Cato: a Tragedy; by Joseph Addison.

2. Gustavus Vasa, the Deliverer of his Country: a Tragedy; by Henry Brooke. Pericles, Prince of Tyre: a Tragedy; supposed to be written by Mr. William Shakespeare. Busiris, King of Egypt: a Tragedy; by Edward Young, LL.D.

3. The Twin Rivals: a Comedy; by Mr. George Farquhar. Bonduca: a Tragedy; altered from Beaumont and Fletcher, and adapted to the stage, by George Colman. The Chapter of Accidents: a Comedy; by Miss Lee.

4. The Way of the World: a Comedy; by William Congreve. The School for Rakes: a Comedy; by Mrs. Elizabeth Griffiths. Edward and Eleonora: a Tragedy; altered from James Thomson, and adapted to the Stage, by Thomas Hull.

5. The West Indian: a Comedy; by Richard Cumberland. The Suspicious Husband: a Comedy; by Dr. Hoadly. The Carmelite: a Tragedy; by Richard Cumberland.

6. The Gentle Shepherd: a Scots Pastoral Comedy, as written by Allan Ramsay. The Mistake: a Comedy; by Sir John Vanbrugh. The Ambitious Step-Mother: a Tragedy; by Nicholas Rowe.

7. The Chances: a Comedy; as altered from Beaumont and Fletcher, by His Grace the Duke of Buckingham. Love Makes a Man; or, the Fop's Fortune: a Comedy; by Colley Cibber. The Busybody: a Comedy; by Mrs. Centlivre.

8. Isabella; or, the Fatal Marriage: a Tragedy, altered from Southern. The City Wives' Confederacy: a Comedy; by Sir John Vanbrugh. The Wonder a Woman keeps a Secret: a Comedy; by Mrs. Centlivre.

9. The Royal Convert: a Tragedy; by Nicholas Rowe. Merope: a Tragedy; by Aaron Hill. The Double Dealer: a Comedy; by William Congreve.

10. Oedipus: a Tragedy; by Dryden and Lee. Medea: a Tragedy; by Mr. Glover. The Miser: a Comedy; by Henry Fielding.

11. The Gamester: a Tragedy; by Mr. Edward Moore. Amphitryon; or, the Two Socias; a Comedy; as altered from Dryden, by Dr. Hawkesworth. The Foundling: a Comedy; by Mr. Edward Moore.

12. Zenobia: a Tragedy; by Arthur Murphy. The Plain Dealer: a Comedy: altered from William Wycherley, and adapted to the Stage, by Isaac Bickerstaff. Irene: a Tragedy; by Samuel Johnson, LL.D.

13. Phædra and Hippolitus: a Tragedy; by Mr. Edmund Smith. The Rehearsal: a Comedy; as written by George, late Duke of Buckingham. Sir Harry Wildair; being the Sequel of the "Trip to the Jubilee": a Comedy; by George Farquhar.

14. The Provok'd Wife: a Comedy; by Sir John Vanbrugh. The Funeral; or, Grief a-la-Mode: a Comedy; by Sir Richard Steele. Marianne: a Tragedy; by Mr. Fenton.

15. The Countess of Salisbury: a Tragedy; by Hall Hartson. The Drummer; or, the Haunted House: a Comedy; by Joseph Addison. The Clandestine Marriage: a Comedy; by G. Colman and D. Garrick.

16. Timanthes: a Tragedy; by John Hoole. Cleonice, Princess of Bithynia: a Tragedy; by John Hoole. The Man of the World; by Charles Macklin. Mahomet: a Tragedy; by the Rev. Mr. Miller.

17. Love in a Village: a Comic Opera; by Isaac Bickerstaff. The Beggar's Opera: a Comic Opera; by John Gay. The Fair Penitent: a Tragedy; by Nicholas Rowe.

18. The Conscious Lovers: a Comedy; by Sir Richard Steele. Every Man in his Humour: a Comedy; by Ben Jonson, as altered by David Garrick. Philaster: a Tragedy; as altered from Beaumont and Fletcher.

BELL (JOHN)—*continued.*

19. The Good Natured Man: a Comedy; by Dr. Goldsmith. The Brothers: a Comedy; by Richard Cumberland. The Minor: a Comedy; by Samuel Foote.

20. Love for Love: a Comedy; by William Congreve. The Country Girl: a Comedy; altered from Wycherly; by David Garrick. The Tender Husband; or, the Accomplished Fools: a Comedy; by Sir Richard Steele.

21. All for Love; or, the World Well Lost: a Tragedy; by Mr. Dryden. Tamerlane: a Tragedy; by N. Rowe. Tancred and Sigismunda: a Tragedy; by Mr. James Thomson.

22. The Siege of Damascus: a Tragedy; by John Hughes. Theodosius: or, the Force of Love: a Tragedy; by Nathaniel Lee. The Revenge: a Tragedy; by Edward Young, LL.D.

23. Oroonoko: a Tragedy; by Thomas Southern. A Bold Stroke for a Wife: a Comedy; by Mrs. Centlivre. Lady Jane Gray: a Tragedy; by N. Rowe.

24. The Hypocrite: a Comedy; altered from C. Cibber, by Isaac Bickerstaff. She Stoops to Conquer; or, the Mistakes of a Night: a Comedy; by Dr. Goldsmith. George Barnwell: a Tragedy; by George Lillo.

25. The School for Wives: a Comedy; by Hugh Kelly. The Fashionable Lover: a Comedy; by Richard Cumberland. The School for Lovers: a Comedy; by William Whitehead.

26. Cymon : a Dramatic Romance; by [David Garrick]. The Inconstant : a Comedy; by George Farquhar. The Relapse ; or, Virtue in Danger: a Comedy; by Sir John Vanbrugh.

27. The Old Batchelor: a Comedy; by William Congreve. Henry II.: or, the Fall of Rosamond: a Tragedy; by Thomas Hull. False Delicacy: a Comedy; by Hugh Kelly.

28. The Spanish Fryar; or, the Double Discovery: a Comedy; by Mr. Dryden. The Distrest Mother: a Tragedy; translated by Ambrose Philips, from the "Andromaque" of Racine. The Earl of Essex: a Tragedy; by Henry Jones.

29. Pericles, Prince of Tyre: a Tragedy; supposed to be written by Mr. William Shakespeare. Busiris, King of Egypt: a Tragedy; by Edward Young, LL.D. The Rehearsal: a Comedy; as written by George, late Duke of Buckingham. Albina, Countess Raimond: a Tragedy; by Mrs. Cowley.

30. Venice Preserved; or, a Plot Discovered: a Tragedy; by Thomas Otway. Zara: a Tragedy; by Aaron Hill. Douglas: a Tragedy; by John Home.

31. All in the Wrong: a Comedy; by Arthur Murphy. The Recruiting Officer: a Comedy; by George Farquhar. The Grecian Daughter: a Tragedy; by Arthur Murphy.

32. Barbarossa: a Tragedy; by Dr. Brown. The Lady's Last Stake; or, the Wife's Resentment: a Comedy; by Colley Cibber. The Jealous Wife: a Comedy; by George Colman.

33. Alzira: a Tragedy; by Aaron Hill. The Provok'd Husband; or, a Journey to London: a Comedy; by Sir John Vanbrugh and C. Cibber. Boadicea: a Tragedy; by Mr. Glover.

34. The Mourning Bride: a Tragedy; by Mr. Congreve. Rule a Wife and Have a Wife: a Comedy; by Beaumont and Fletcher. The Alchymist: a Comedy; as altered from Ben Jonson.

35. The Double Gallant; or, the Sick Lady's Cure: a Comedy; by Colley Cibber. The Choleric Man: a Comedy; by Richard Cumberland. The Battle of Hastings: a Tragedy; by Richard Cumberland.

36. The Careless Husband: a Comedy; by Colley Cibber. The Country Lasses; or, the Custom of the Manor: a Comedy; by Charles Johnson. The Fair Quaker of Deal; or, the Humours of the Navy: a Comedy: by Charles Shadwell.

37. Eurydice: a Tragedy; by David Mallet. Falstaff's Wedding: a Comedy; written in imitation of Shakespere, by W. Kenrick, LL.D. A Word to the Wise: a Comedy; by Hugh Kelly.

BELL (JOHN)—*continued.*

38. The Fatal Curiosity : a Tragedy ; by George Lillo. The Refusal : or, the Ladies Philosophy : a Comedy ; by Colley Cibber. She Wou'd and She Wou'd Not ; or, the Kind Impostor : a Comedy ; by Colley Cibber.

39, 40. Cyrus : a Tragedy ; by John Hoole. The Earl of Warwick : a Tragedy ; by Dr. Franklin. The Natural Son : a Comedy ; by Richard Cumberland. The Roman Father : a Tragedy ; altered from Mr. W. Whitehead.

41. Comus : a Mask ; by John Milton. The Maid of the Mill : a Comic Opera ; by Isaac Bickerstaff. The School for Fathers ; or, Lionel and Clarissa : a Comic Opera ; by Isaac Bickerstaff.

42. The Constant Couple ; or, a Trip to the Jubilee : a Comedy ; by George Farquhar. The Gamesters : a Comedy ; as altered from Shirley and C. Johnson. The Committee : a Comedy ; by the Hon. Sir R. Howard.

43. The Discovery : a Comedy ; by Mrs. Frances Sheridan. King Charles I. : a Tragedy ; by William Havard. The Rival Queens ; or, the Death of Alexander the Great : a Tragedy by Nathaniel Lee.

44. Samson Agonistes : a Dramatic Poem ; written on the Model of the Ancient Greek Tragedy ; by John Milton. The School for Guardians : a Comedy ; by Arthur Murphy. The Orphan of China : a Tragedy ; by Arthur Murphy.

45. Creusa, Queen of Athens : a Tragedy ; by William White-head. The Brothers : a Tragedy ; by Dr. Edward Young. Albina, Countess Raimond : a Tragedy ; by Mrs. Cowley.

46. Caractacus : a Dramatic Poem ; by W. Mason. Elfrida : a Dramatic Poem ; written on the Model of the Ancient Greek Tragedy ; by William Mason, A.M. Lucius Junius Brutus ; Father of his Country : a Tragedy ; by Nathaniel Lee.

BELL (JOHN). Bell's New Pantheon ; or, Historical Dictionary of the Gods, Demi-Gods, Heroes, and Fabulous Personages of Antiquity. 2 vols. (in 1) 4to. Lond., 1790.   K 6 S 21

BELL (MRS. MARION). Letters of Sir Charles Bell, K.H., &c., selected from his Correspondence with his Brother, G. J. Bell. 8vo. Lond., 1870.   C 3 Q 8

BELL (MRS. NANCY R. E.), "N. D'ANVERS." Elementary History of Art : an Introduction to Ancient and Modern Architecture, Sculpture, Painting, Music, &c. 8vo. Lond., 1874.   A 2 R 1

Heroes of North African Discovery. 8vo. Lond., 1877.
                                                          D 1 T 14

Raphael [a Biography]. (Great Artists.) 8vo. Lond., 1879.   C 3 T 40

Victoria Falls of the Zambesi. [*See* MOHR, EDWARD.]

BELL (ROBERT). History of England. [*See* MACKINTOSH, SIR J.]

History of Russia. (Lard. Cab. Cyclo.) 3 vols. 12mo. Lond., 1836–38.   K 1 T 40–42

Life of the Right Hon. George Canning. 8vo. Lond., 1846.   C 3 Q 3

Lives of the most Eminent Literary and Scientific Men of Great Britain. English Poets. (Lard. Cab. Cyclo.) 2 vols. 18mo. Lond., 1839.   K 1 S 17, 18

Memorials of the Civil War ; forming the concluding volumes of the Fairfax Correspondence. [*See* FAIRFAX CORRESPONDENCE.]

Wayside Pictures through France, Belgium, and Holland. 8vo. Lond., 1849.   D 8 T 15

[*See* CHAUCER, G.]

BELL (SYDNEY SMITH). Colonial Administration of Great Britain. 8vo. Lond., 1859.   MF 2 Q 25

BELL (PROF. THOMAS), F.R.S., &c. History of British Quadrupeds. 8vo. Lond., 1837.   A 14 U 3

BELL (WILLIAM). On the Origin, Progress, and Treatment of Small-pox ; with an Account of the Discovery and Advantages of Vaccination. 8vo. Sydney (n.d.) MA 2 S 15

BELL (WILLIAM). Dictionary and Digest of the Law of Scotland. Revised and corrected by George Ross. 8vo. Edinb., 1861.   K 11 R 7

BELLARS (WILLIAM). Fine Arts and their Uses : Essays. 8vo. Lond., 1876.   A 6 V 16

BELLENDEN (JOHN), ARCHDEAN OF MORAY, &c. History and Chronicles of Scotland, &c. [*See* BOETHIUS, H.] Description of Scotland, &c. [*See* BOETHIUS, H.]

BELLEVAL (RENE DE). Du Costume Militaire des Français en 1446. 4to. Paris, 1866.   A 8 R 16

BELLEW (SURG.-MAJ. HENRY WALTER), C.S.I. Dictionary of the Pukkhto, or Pukshto Language, in which the Words are traced to their Sources in the Indian and Persian Languages. Roy. 8vo. Lond., 1867. K 13 T 10

From the Indus to the Tigris : a Narrative of a Journey through the Countries of Balochistan, Afghanistan, Khorassan, and Iran, in 1872. 8vo. Lond., 1874. D 5 T 14

Grammar of the Pukkhto or Pukshto Language, on a new and improved System, combining brevity with practical utility, and including Exercises and Dialogues, intended to facilitate the Acquisition of the Colloquial. Roy. 8vo. Lond., 1867.   K 16 R 10

History of Cholera in India, from 1862–81 ; being a Descriptive and Statistical Account of the Disease ; together with original Observations on the Causes and Nature of Cholera. With Maps, Diagrams, &c. 8vo. Lond., 1885.   A 12 U 20

Kashmir and Kashghar : a Narrative of the Journey of the Embassy to Kashghar in 1873–74. 8vo. Lond., 1875.
                                                          D 5 S 15

Races of Afghanistan ; being a Brief Account of the Principal Nations inhabiting that Country. 8vo. Calcutta, 1880.   B 1 P 5

BELLEW (J. M.) [*See* HARTE, F. B.]

BELLOC (MME. BESSIE RAYNOR). [*See* PARKES, MISS B. R.]

BELLOC (M.) Histoires d'Amérique et d'Océanie, depuis les temps les plus reculés jusqu'à nos jours. 8vo. Paris, 1844.   B 1 S 41

BELLOT (LIEUT. JOSEPH RENÉ). Memoirs of ; with his Journal of a Voyage in the Polar Seas, in search of Sir John Franklin. 2 vols. 8vo. Lond., 1855. C 2 T 3, 4

BELLOWS (ALBERT J.), M.D. How not to be Sick : a Sequel to "The Philosophy of Eating." 8vo. Lond., 1869. A 12 Q 17

Philosophy of Eating. 4th ed. 8vo. Lond., 1869. A12Q18

BELLOWS (JOHN). English Outline Vocabulary for the Use of Students of the Chinese, Japanese, and other Languages ; with Notes by Professor Summers. 12mo. Lond., 1868. K 11 U 28

Dictionary for the Pocket. French and English; English and French. Revised by Alexandre Beljame, M.A., &c. 2nd ed. 18mo. Lond., 1880. Libr.

Outline Dictionary for the Use of Missionaries, Explorers, and Students of Language; with an Introduction by [Prof. F.] Max Müller, M.A. 12mo. Lond., 1867. K 11 U 16

BELLOY (MARQUIS DE). Christopher Columbus and the Discovery of the New World. From the French. Illustrated by Léopold Flameng. New ed. Sm. fol. Lond., 1885. C 4 P 15 †

BELMORE (SOMERSET RICHARD LOWRY-CORRY, EARL OF. History of the Two Ulster Manors of Finagh, in the County of Tyrone, and Coole, in the County of Fermanagh. 8vo. Lond., 1881. B 11 Q 7

BELOE (REV. WILLIAM). Anecdotes of Literature and Scarce Books. 6 vols. 8vo. Lond., 1808–14. J 9 T 1–6

The Sexagenarian ; or, the Recollections of a Literary Life. 2nd ed. 2 vols. 8vo. Lond., 1818. C 6 U 26, 27

[*See* HERODOTUS.]

BELPERROUD (JOHN), AND PETTAVEL (DAVID LOUIS.) The Vine ; with Instructions for its Cultivation for a period of six years; the Treatment of the Soil, and how to make Wine from Victorian Grapes. 8vo. Geelong, 1859.* MA 1 Q 2

BELPHEGOR [*See* INTENDED ADDRESSES.]

BELT (THOMAS). Mineral Veins: an Enquiry into their Origin, founded on a Study of the Auriferous Quartz Veins of Australia. 8vo. Lond., 1861. MA 2 Q 39

BELTON (—) Two Summers in Norway. 2 vols. 8vo. Lond., 1840. D 8 R 42, 43

BELTZ (GEORGE FREDERICK), K.H. Memorials of the Most Noble Order of the Garter, including Biographical Notices of the Knights. Roy. 8vo. Lond., 1841. B 6 V 34

BELZONI (GIOVANNI BATTISTA). Narrative of the Operations and Recent Discoveries within the Pyramids, &c., in Egypt and Nubia. 1st and 2nd eds. 2 vols. 4to. Lond., 1820–21. D 21 P 1, 2 ‡

Plates to above. Imp. fol. Lond., 1820-22. D 21 P 3 ‡

BEMROSE (W.) Life and Works of Joseph Wright, commonly called "Wright of Derby." Fol. Lond., 1885. C 23 P 18 ‡

BENARES MAGAZINE (THE). 1851-52. 8vo. Calcutta, 1851–52. J 12 Q 20

BENDALL (PROF. CECIL), M.A., &c. Catalogue of the Buddhist Sanskrit Manuscripts in the University Library, Cambridge. 8vo. Camb., 1883. K 7 R 29

Journey of Literary and Archæological Research in Nepal and Northern India during the Winter of 1884–85. 8vo. Camb., 1886. D 6 Q 43

BENECKE (GEORG FRIEDRICH). Mittelhochdeutsches Wörterbuch ausgearbeitet von Wilhelm Müller und Friedrich Zarncke. 3 vols. (in 4) roy. 8vo. Leip., 1854–66. K 14 U 19–22

BENEDEN (PIERRE JOSEPH VAN). Animal Parasites and Messmates. 8vo. Lond., 1876. A 14 Q 15

BENEDETTI (VINCENT), COMTE. Ma Mission en Prusse. 8vo. Paris, 1871. B 9 S 1

BENEDICT OF PETERBOROUGH. Materials for the History of Thomas Becket. [*See* CHRON., &c., GT. BRIT. 139.]

BENEDICTUS (SANCTUS). Opera omnia. [*See* MIGNE, J. P., SERIES LATINA 66.]

BENEDICTUS ANIANENSIS (SANCTUS). Opera omnia. [*See* MIGNE, J. P., SERIES LATINA, 103.]

BENEDIKT (DR. R.) The Chemistry of Coal-tar Colours. 8vo. Lond., 1886. A 5 R 28

BENEVOLENT ASYLUMS. [*See* SYDNEY, *and* MELBOURNE.]

BENEVOLENT SOCIETIES OF NEW SOUTH WALES. [*See* NEW SOUTH WALES.]

BENEZET (ANTHONY). Some Historical Account of Guinea ; with an Inquiry into the Rise and Progress of the Slave Trade. 12mo. Philad., 1771. B 1 P 46

BENFEY (THEODOR). Geschichte der Sprachwissenschaft und orientalischen Philologie in Deutschland. [*See* GESCHICHTE DER WISSENSCHAFTEN, 8.]

BENGAL. Code of the Bengal Military Regulations ; including those relating to the Pay and Audit Departments. Sm. fol. Calcutta, 1817. F 7 P 6 †

BENGAL DIRECTORY FOR 1844. [*See* SCOTT & CO.]

BENGEL (JOHANN ALBRECHT). Gnomon Novi Testamenti, in quo ex nativa verborvm vi simplicitas, profvnditas, concinnitas, salvbritas sensvvm coelestivm indicatvr. Editio tertia. 4to. Tubingæ, 1773. G 5 T 3

BENGER (MISS ELIZABETH OGILVY). Memoirs of the Life of Anne Boleyn, Queen of Henry VIII. 3rd ed.; with a Memoir of the Author, by Miss Aikin. 8vo. Lond., 1827. C 3 S 5

BENHAM (Rev. W.), B.D. Imitation of Christ. [*See* KESPIS, T. A.*]

BENJAMIN (Rev. RAPHAEL), M.A. Confirmation Class-book. 18mo. Cincinnati, 1885.   G 9 P 11

BENJAMIN (S. G. W.) Persia and the Persians. Illustrated. Roy. 8vo. Lond., 1887.   D 5 U 26

BENJAMIN OF TUDELA (RABBI). Itinerary of; translated and edited by A. Asher. 2 vols. 8vo. Lond., 1840–41.   D 10 R 24, 25

BENN (ALFRED WILLIAM) The Greek Philosophers. 2 vols. 8vo. Lond., 1882.   G 6 R 13, 14

BENNET (GEORGE). Journal of Voyages and Travels. [*See* TYERMAN, REV. D.]

BENNET (HON. H. GREY). [*See* MACQUARIE, MAJ.-GEN.]

BENNETT (CHARLES H.) The Fables of Æsop and others translated into Human Nature. 4to. Lond., 1875.   J 8 V 18

BENNETT (E. T.) [*See* BEECHEY, CAPT. F. W.]

BENNETT (FREDERICK DEBELL), F.R.G.S. Narrative of a Whaling Voyage round the Globe, 1833–36. 2 vols. 8vo. Lond., 1840.   MD 4 V 17, 18

BENNETT (DR. GEORGE), F.R.S., &c. A Trip to Queensland in search of Fossils. (Pam. Cb.) 8vo. Sydney, 1871.   A 16 U 25

Acclimatisation; its eminent adaptation to Australia: a Lecture delivered in Sydney. (Pam. 36.) 8vo. Melb., 1862.   MJ 2 Q 23

Another copy.   MJ 2 R 7

Another copy. (Pam. Cb.)   A 16 U 25

Gatherings of a Naturalist in Australasia. 8vo. Lond., 1860.*   MA 2 T 3

Notes on the Natural History and Habits of the Ornithorhynchus Paradoxus, *Blum.* 4to. Lond., 1834.*   MA 2 Q 12 †

On the Introduction, Cultivation, and Economic Uses of the Orange, and others of the Citron-tribe, in New South Wales. 8vo. Sydney, 1871.   MJ 2 R 14

Wanderings in New South Wales, Batavia, Pedir Coast, Singapore, and China; being the Journal of a Naturalist in those Countries during 1832–34. 2 vols. 8vo. Lond., 1834.*   MD 2 U 1, 2

[*See* ACCLIMATISATION SOCIETY OF NEW SOUTH WALES.]

BENNETT (JAMES), D.D. Justification, as revealed in Scripture. 8vo. Lond., 1840.   G 6 Q 7

BENNETT (JAMES F.) South Australian Almanack and General Directory for 1841. 12mo. Adelaide, 1841.   A E 4 P

BENNETT (J. R.) Lecture introductory to the Course of General Anatomy. (Univ. of Lond.) 8vo. Lond., 1830   J 5 S 8

BENNETT (JOHN WHITCHURCH), F.L.S., &c. Ceylon and its Capabilities. 4to. Lond., 1843.   D 9 S 6 †

Selection of Rare and Curious Fishes found upon the Coast of Ceylon. 4to. Lond., 1851.   A 14 V 47

BENNETT (JOHN WILLIAM OGILVIE). Native Tribes of South Australia. [*See* ABORIGINES.]

Vocabulary of the Woolner District Dialect, Adelaide River, Northern Territory. [*See* SOUTH AUSTRALIA.]

BENNETT (SAMUEL). History of Australian Discovery and Colonisation. 8vo. Sydney, 1865.   MB 2 P 22

Another copy. Part 1.   MB 2 P 23

Another copy. Parts 1–4.   MB 2 P 24

BENNETT (WILLIAM COX), LL.D. Songs of a Song-writer. 8vo. Lond., 1876.   H 7 Q 27

BENNI (REV. C. B.), SYRIAC ARCHBISHOP OF MOSSUL, THE. Tradition of the Syriac Church of Antioch; translated by the Rev. Joseph Gagliardi. 8vo. Lond., 1871.   G 6 Q 19

BENNY (PHILLIP BERGER). Criminal Code of the Jews, according to the Talmud Massecheth Synhedrin. 8vo. Lond., 1880.   F 6 P 36

BENOIT-CHAMPY (G.), ET MILON (A.) Navigation de Plaisance. Les Yachts à Voiles de Course pour la Mer, et la Rivière. 4to. Paris (n.d)   A 2 U 40

BENSON (REV. C. W.) Our Irish Song Birds. 8vo. Dublin, 1886.   A 14 Q 40

BENSON (REV. JOSEPH). Wesley's Journal. [*See* WESLEY, REV. J.]

BENT (ANDREW). Appeal to the Sympathies and Benevolence of the Australasian Public, for Relief for Mr. Andrew Bent and his large Family, now in a state of utter destitution. 8vo. Sydney, 1844.   MJ 2 Q 22

Tasmanian Almanack; to which are added Lists of the Civil and Military Establishments and Public Institutions in the Colony, 1825, 1827–28. 3 vols. (in 1) 12mo. Hobart, 1825–28.*   ME 4 P

BENT (J. THEODORE), B.A. Genoa; how the Republic Rose and Fell. Illustrated. 8vo. Lond., 1881.   B 11 V 21

Life of Giuseppe Garibaldi. With a Portrait. 8vo. Lond., 1881.   C 12 U 26

Another copy. 2nd ed. 8vo. Lond., 1882.   C 2 U 27

The Cyclades; or, Life among the Insular Greeks. 8vo. Lond., 1885.   D 8 R 44

BENT (SAMUEL ARTHUR), A.M. Short Sayings of Great Men; with Historical and Explanatory Notes. 8vo. Lond., 1882.   K 17 P 28

BENT (W.) [*See* LONDON CATALOGUE OF BOOKS.]

BENTHAM (GEORGE), F.R.S., &c. Flora Hongkongensis: a Description of the Flowering Plants and Ferns of the Island of Hongkong; with a Map of the Island. 8vo. Lond., 1861.   A 4 S 17

Hand-book of the British Flora: a Description of the Flowering Plants and Ferns indigenous to, or naturalized in the British Isles. 2 vols. 8vo. Lond., 1865.   A 4 T 7, 8

BENTHAM (GEORGE), F.R.S., AND HOOKER (J. D.), M.D., &c. Genera Plantarum. Ad Exemplaria imprimis in Herbariis Kewensibus servata definita. Vols. 1–3. Roy. 8vo. Lond., 1862–83.   A 4 U 5–7

1. Sistens Dicotyledonum Polypetalarum Ordines 83 ; Ranunculaceas—Cornraceas.
2. Sistens Dicotyledonum Gamopetalarum Ordines 45 ; Capifoliaceas—Plantagineas.
3. Sistens Monochlamydearum, Gymnospermearum et Monocotyledonum Ordines 73.

BENTHAM (G.), F.R.S., AND MUELLER (F. VON), C.M.G. Flora Australiensis: a Description of the Plants of the Australian Territory. 7 vols. 8vo. Lond., 1863–78.*   MA 1 U 18–24

1. Ranunculaceæ to Anacardiaceæ.
2. Leguminosæ to Combretaceæ.
3. Myrtaceæ to Compositæ.
4. Stylidieæ to Pedalineæ.
5. Myoporineæ to Proteaceæ.
6. Thymeleæ to Dioscorideæ.
7. Roxburghiaceæ to Filices.

BENTHAM (REV. JAMES), M.A. History and Antiquities of the Conventual and Cathedral Church of Ely, 673–1771. 2nd ed. with Supplement, by Wm. Stevenson, F.S.A. 2 vols. roy. 4to. Norwich, 1812–17. B 17 S 4, 5 ‡

BENTHAM (JEREMY). Book of Church Reform. 8vo. Lond., 1831.   F 3 R 8

Book of Fallacies. 8vo. Lond., 1824.   F 12 Q 12

Chrestomathia. Part II; containing Appendix, No. 5; being an Essay on Nomenclature and Classification, &c. 8vo. Lond., 1817.   G 2 P 29

Constitutional Code; for the use of all Nations and all Governments professing Liberal Opinions. 8vo. Lond., 1830.   F 12 Q 15

Codification Proposal; addressed to all Nations professing Liberal Opinions. 8vo. Lond., 1830.   F 12 Q 13

Defence of Usury. 8vo. Lond., 1818.   F 6 Q 24

Emancipate your Colonies! addressed to the National Convention of France, 1793. 8vo. Lond., 1830.   F 3 R 8

Equity Dispatch Court Proposals. 8vo. Lond., 1830.   F 3 R 7

Indications respecting Lord Eldon. 8vo. Lond., 1825.   F 3 R 7

Jeremy Bentham to his Fellow-Citizens of France, on Death Punishment. 8vo. Lond., 1831.   F 3 R 7

BENTHAM (JEREMY)—*continued.*

Jeremy Bentham to his Fellow-Citizens of France, on the Houses of Peers and Senates. 8vo. Lond., 1830.   F 3 R 7

Justice and Codification Petitions. 8vo. Lond., 1829.   F 12 Q 14

Letters to Count Toreno, on the proposed Penal Code. 8vo. Lond., 1822.   F 3 R 8

Lord Brougham Displayed, including, 1. Boa Constrictor, alias Helluo Curiarum ; 2. Observations on the Bankruptcy Court Bill ; Extracts from proposed Constitutional Code. 8vo. Lond., 1832.   F 3 R 7

Not Paul, but Jesus, by "Gamaliel Smith, Esq." 8vo. Lond., 1823.   G 6 Q 22
Note: Said to have been compiled by Francis Place.—*Athenæum,* 17 Jan., 1880.

Observations on the Restrictive and Prohibitory Commercial System, especially with reference to the Decree of the Spanish Cortes of July, 1820 ; from MSS. of J. Bentham, by John Bowring. 8vo. Lond.,1821. F 3 R 8

Observations on Peel's Speech, introducing his "Police Magistrates' Salary Raising Bill." 8vo. Lond., 1825.   F 3 R 8

Official Aptitude Maximized. 8vo. Lond., 1830. F 12 Q 16

Panopticon ; or, the Inspection House. With Postscripts. 3 vols. (in 1) 12mo. Lond., 1791.   F 1 P 26

Parliamentary Candidates proposed Declaration of Principles. 8vo. Lond., 1831.   F 3 R 8

Radical Reform Bill. 8vo. Lond., 1819.   F 3 R 8

Rationale of Judicial Evidence, specially applied to English Practice. 5 vols. 8vo. Lond., 1827. F 12 Q 19–23

Rationale of Punishment. 8vo. Lond., 1830. F 12 Q 17

Rationale of Reward. 8vo. Lond., 1825.   F 12 Q 18

"Swear not at all"; containing an Exposure of the Needlessness and Mischievousness, as well as Antichristianity, of the Ceremony of an Oath. 8vo. Lond., 1817. F 3 R 8

The King against Edmonds, and others. 8vo. Lond., 1820.   F 3 R 7

The King against Sir Charles Wolseley, Baronet, and Joseph Harrison, Schoolmaster. 8vo. Lond., 1820.   F 3 R 7

Truth *versus* Ashhurst; or, Law as it is. 8vo. Lond., 1823.   F 3 R 7

BENTINCK (GEORGE FREDERICK CAVENDISH), LORD. Political Biography; by the Rt. Hon. Benjamin Disraeli [Earl of Beaconsfield]. 5th ed. 8vo. Lond.,1852. C 3 S 9

BENTLEY (RICHARD), D.D. A Biography; by R. C. Jebb. (Eng. Men of Letters.) 8vo. Lond., 1882.   C 1 U 3

Correspondence of; edited by Christopher Wordsworth. 2 vols. 8vo. Lond., 1842.   C 8 S 26, 27

Dissertations upon the Epistles of Phalaris ; with an Answer to the Objections of the Hon. C. Boyle ; to which are added [a] dissertation on the Epistles of Themistocles, Socrates, Euripides, &c., and the Fables of Æsop. 8vo. Lond., 1817.   3 S 7

BENTLEY (RICHARD), D.D.—*continued.*

Dissertation upon the Epistles of Phalaris, Themistocles, Socrates, Euripides, and the Fables of Æsop; edited, with an Introduction and Notes, by the late Wilhelm Wagner, Ph.D. 8vo. Lond., 1883.   J 11 R 25

Life of; with an Account of his Writings, and Anecdotes of many Distinguished Characters; by James Henry Monk, D.D. 2nd ed. 2 vols. 8vo. Lond., 1833.   C 10 R 17, 18

[*See* MANLIUS, M.]

BENTLEY (PROF. RICHARD ROBERT), F.L.S. Elements of Materia Medica. [*See* PEREIRA, J.]

Manual of Botany, including the Structure, Functions, Classification, Properties, and Uses of Plants. 3rd ed. (Churchill's Manuals.) 8vo. Lond., 1873.   A 4 P 26

BENTLEY (PROF. R. R.), F.L.S., &c., AND TRIMEN (H.), M.B. Medicinal Plants; being Descriptions, with original Figures of the principal Plants employed in Medicine. 4 vols. roy. 8vo. Lond., 1880. A 5 P 29-32

1. Nos. 1-69.   Ranunculaceæ to Anacardiaceæ.
2. Nos. 70-146.   Leguminosæ to Valerianaceæ.
3. Nos. 147-227.   Compositæ to Thymelaceæ.
4. Nos. 228-306.   Artocarpaceæ to Algæ.

BENTLEY (THOMAS CHARLES). Progress Report from the Select Committee on the Petition of Thomas Charles Bentley. Fol. Sydney, 1863.   MF 10 Q 2 †

BENTLEY'S MISCELLANY. 64 vols. 8vo. Lond., 1837-68.   E

Old "Miscellany" Days : a Selection of Stories from Bentley's Miscellany ; by various authors. Illustrated by George Cruikshank. 1837-43 Roy. 8vo. Lond., 1885.   J 9 V 10

BENYEN (WILLIAM.) Murder of. [*See* PEISLEY, J.]

BEOWOLF: an Heroic Poem of the 8th Century. [*See* ARNOLD, T.]

BERANGER (GABRIEL). Memoir of, and his Labours in the Cause of Irish Art and Antiquities, from 1760 to 1780 ; by Sir William Wilde. Roy. 8vo. Dublin, 1880.   C 3 W 4

BÉRANGER (PIERRE JEAN DE). Chansons de, 1815-34 ; contenant les dix Chansons, publiées en 1847. Edition Elzévirienne. 18mo. Paris, 1861.   Libr.

Memoirs of ; written by himself. 8vo. Lond., 1858.   C N 8 11

Œuvres Posthumes de. Dernières Chansons, 1834-51. Ma Biographie. 18mo. Paris, 1858.   Libr.

Œuvres Complètes. 2 vols. roy. 8vo. Paris. 1847-51.   JI 6 U 23, 24

BÉRARD (AUGUSTE SIM. LOUIS). Essai Bibliographique sur les éditions des Elzévirs les plus précieuses et les plus recherchées, précédé d'une Notice sur ces Imprimeurs célèbres. 8vo. Paris, 1822.   K 17 Q 22

BERESFORD (GEN. WILLIAM CARR BERESFORD), VISCOUNT. Letters [s] to Charles Edward Long, Esq., on the Extract recently published from the Manuscript Journal and Private Correspondence of the late Lieut.-Gen. R. B. Long. 8vo. Lond., 1833-34.   B 13 U 7

[*See* NAPIER, MAJ.-GEN. SIR W. F. P.]

Refutation of Colonel Napier's Justification of his Third Volume. 8vo. Lond., 1834.   B 13 U 8

BERGEN (WILLIAM CULLEY). Marine Engineer. 8vo. North Shields, 1880.   A 6 T 8

BERGH (DR. R.) Journal des Museum Godeffroy. [*See* GODEFFROY.]

BERGIER (NICOLAS SYLVESTRE), ABBÉ. Dictionnaire de Théologie. Nouvelle édition; précédé de l'Eloge historique de l'Auteur, par le Baron de Sainte-Croix. 4 vols. 8vo. Lille, 1844.   K 18 R 16-19

Dictionnaire de Théologie. 6 vols. 8vo. Paris, 1868.   K 18 R 10-15

BERGK (THEODORE). [*See* POETAE LYRICI GRAECI.]

BERINGTON (REV. JOSEPH). History of the Lives of Abeillard and Heloisa ; comprising a period of eighty-four years, from 1079 to 1163 ; with their genuine Letters, from the Collection of Amboise. 4to. Birmingham, 1787.   C 4 W 1

History of the Reign of Henry II, and of Richard and John, his Sons ; with the Events of the Period, from 1154 to 1216. 4to. Birmingham, 1790.   B 2 T 8

Literary History of the Middle Ages. 4to. Lond., 1814.   B 2 T 25

Memoirs of Gregorio Panzani ; giving an Account of his Agency in England, in the years 1634-36 ; translated from the Italian Original, and now first published. 8vo. Birmingham, 1793.   B 6 P 46

BERJEAU (JEAN PHILIBERT). [*See* BOOKWORM.]

BERJEAU (P. C.) The Horses of Antiquity, Middle Ages, and Renaissance, from the earliest Monuments down to the 16th Century. 4to. Lond., 1864.   A 14 V 16

BERKELEY (ABRAHAM). [*See* ANTONINUS LIBERALIS.]

BERKELEY (HON. GEORGE). Letters to, and from Henrietta, Countess of Suffolk, and her second Husband, the Hon. George Berkeley, 1712-67. 2 vols. 8vo. Lond., 1824.   C 9 T 46, 47.

BERKELEY (RT. REV. GEORGE), D.D., BISHOP OF CLOYNE. Alciphron ; or, the Minute Philosopher, in seven Dialogues. 2nd. ed. 2 vols. 8vo. Lond., 1732.   G 13 R 34, 35

Essay towards a new Theory of Vision. (*Bound with 2nd vol. of Alciphron.*) 8vo. Lond., 1732.   G 13 R 35 .

Selections from Berkeley ; with an Introduction and Notes for the use of Students in the Universities, by Alexander Campbell Fraser, LL.D. (Clar. Press.) 8vo. Oxford, 1874.   G 16 R 36

Works of; to which are added, an Account of his Life, and several of his Letters. 8vo. Lond., 1837.   J 7 U 9

BERKELEY (Hon. G. C. Grantley Fitzhardinge), M.P.
Anecdotes of the Upper Ten Thousand; their Legends
and their Lives. 2 vols. 8vo. Lond., 1867. C 10 P 35, 36

My Life and Recollections. 4 vols. 8vo. Lond., 1865-66.
C 5 U 24-27

Reminiscences of a Huntsman. With Illustrations by
Leech. 8vo. Lond., 1854. A 17 W 34

BERKELEY (Rev. Miles Joseph), M.A., &c. Hand-
book of British Mosses. 8vo. Lond., 1863. A 4 S 7
Micrographic Dictionary. [*See* Griffith, J. W.]

BERKELEYS. Lives of the. The Berkeley Manuscripts,
1066-1618; by J. Smyth. 3 vols. roy. Gloucester,
1883-85. C 4 P 17-19 †

BERKLEY (Sir. John). Mémoires de. [*See* Guizot,
F. P. G., 3.]

BERKLEY (Stanley). Riding. [*See* Hayes, M. H.]

BERLIOZ (Louis Hector). Autobiography of Hector
Berlioz, 1803-65; comprising his Travels in Italy, Ger-
many, Russia, and England; translated by Rachel (Scott
Russell) Holmes, and Eleanor Holmes. 2 vols. 8vo.
Lond., 1884. C 4 Q 4, 5

BERMINGHAM (Rev. P.) Reply to Dr. Bermingham's
Pamphlets "On Liberty, Catholicity, and Methodism."
[*See* Butchers, Rev. B.]
[*See* St. Augustine's Literary Institute.]

BERNARD (Bayle). Life of Samuel Lover, Artistic,
Literary, and Musical. 2 vols. 8vo. Lond., 1874.
C 4 V 6, 7

BERNARD (J. F.) Recueil de Voyages au Nord. 12mo.
Amsterdam, 1731. D 7 P 30

BERNARD (Saint Abbé de Clairvaux). Opera omnia.
[*See* Migne, J. P., Series Latina, 182-185.]
Vie de. [*See* Guizot, F. P. G., 10.]
Vie de. [*See* Capefigue. J.B.H.R.]

BERNARD (W. D.), A.M. Narrative of the Voyages and
Services of the *Nemesis*, 1840-43. 2 vols. 8vo. Lond.,
1844. D 6 T 1, 2

BERNARD LE TRESORIER. Continuation de l'Histoire des Croisades de Guillaume de Tyr. [*See* Guizot,
F.P.G., 19.]

BERNATZ (John Martin). Scenes in Ethiopia; with Descriptions of the Plates, and Extracts from a Journal of
Travel in that Country. 2 vols. (in 1) obl. 4to. Munich
and Lond., 1851-52. D 20 P 25

BERNAYS (Albert J.), Ph.D., &c. The Student's
Chemistry; being the Seventh Edition of "Household
Chemistry." 8vo. Lond., 1869. A 5 R 17

BERNAYS (Lewis Adolphus), F.L.S., &c. Cultural Industries for Queensland: Papers on the Cultivation of
Useful Plants suited to the Climate of Queensland; their
value as Food, in the Arts, and in Medicine; and Methods
of obtaining their Products. First series. 8vo. Brisbane,
1883. MA 1 Q 27

BERNCASTLE (Dr. J.) Defenceless State of Sydney;
how it can be defended, and how it can be taken. 8vo.
Sydney, 1865. MJ 2 Q 10

Revolt of the Bengal Sepoys. 8vo. Sydney, 1857.
MJ 2 Q 11

Voyage to China, including a Visit to the Bombay Presidency, the Mahratta Country, the Cave Temples of
Western India, Singapore, the Straits of Malacca and
Sunda, and the Cape of Good Hope. 2 vols. 8vo. Lond.,
1851. D 6 P 33, 34

BERNERS (John Bourchier), Lord. [*See* Arthur, King.]

BERNERS (Dame Juliana). Boke of St. Albans; containing Treatises on Hawking, Hunting, and Cote Armour;
printed in 1486; reproduced in Fac-simile. 4to. Lond.,
1881. B 2 U 33

Treatyse of Fysshynge wyth an Angle: Facsimile Reproduction of the first Book on the subject of Fishing printed
in England, by Wynkyn de Worde, at Westminster in
1496; with an Introduction by the Rev. M. G. Watkins,
M.A. 4to. Lond., 1880. A 11 P 1 †

BERNHOLD (J. G.) [*See* Kohler, J. D.]

BERNOULLI (James) and WALLIS (Dr. John). Doc-
trine of Permutations and Combinations, being an
Essential and Fundamental part of the Doctrine of
Chances. Roy. 8vo. Lond., 1795. A 10 U 12

BERNSTEIN (Julius). Five Senses of Man. 8vo. Lond.,
1876. A 12 Q 22

BEROALDO (P.) Annotationes (in varios authores antiquos.) (*Bound with Platinæ Vitæ.*) Sm. fol. Venetiis,
1496. C 14 R 19

BERQUIN (Arnand). Blossoms of Morality, intended
for the Amusement and Instruction of Young Ladies
and Gentlemen; with Cuts by J. Bewick. 8th ed.
18mo. Lond., 1828. J 7 P 36

The Looking-Glass for the Mind: a Reprint of the edition of
1792, with the original Illustrations by Bewick. 8vo.
Lond., 1885. J 11 S 5

BERRY (Alexander). Geology of the Coast of New South
Wales. [*See* Field, B.]
[*See* Graham and Bindon.] MJ 2 U 1

BERRY (Rev. David). [*See* Schiern, F.]

BERRY (Rev. J.) Farming in North New Zealand;
with Description of proposed Special Arrangements for
assisting the Settlement there of a limited number of
English Farmers. 8vo. Lond., 1880. MA 1 Q 11

BERRY (MISS MARY). England and France: a Comparative View of the Social Condition of both Countries, from the Restoration of Charles II to the Present Time. 2 vols. 8vo. Lond., 1844. B 7 S 42, 43

Extracts of the Journals and Correspondence of Miss Berry, 1783–1852; edited by Lady Theresa Lewis. 3 vols. 8vo. Lond., 1865–69. C 10 Q 9–11

Some Account of the Life of Rachael Wriothesley, Lady Russell, followed by a series of Letters. 3rd ed. 8vo. Lond., 1820. C 9 S 22

BERRY (WILLIAM). County Genealogies: Pedigrees of the Families in the County of Hants. Sm. fol. Lond., 1833. K 22 S 12 ‡

County Genealogies: Pedigees of the Families in the County of Sussex. Sm. fol. Lond., 1830. K 22 S 11 ‡

Encyclopædia Heraldica ; or, Complete Dictionary of Heraldry. 3 vols. 4to. Lond., 1828. K 4 U 15–17

Genealogia Antiqua; or, Mythological and Classical Tables; compiled from the best Authors. Sm. fol. Lond., 1816. K 22 S 13 ‡

Genealogia Sacra; or, Scripture Tables; compiled from the Holy Bible. Sm. fol. Lond., 1819. K 22 S 13 ‡

History of the Island of Guernsey, part of the Ancient Duchy of Normandy, from the remotest period of Antiquity to the year 1814; compiled from the valuable Collections of the late Henry Budd, Esq. Illustrated with Map. 4to. Lond., 1815. B 2 T 11

[*See* SANSON, N.]

BERRY MINISTRY (THE). History of. 8vo. Melb., 1880. MF 1 Q 6

BERSIER (EUGENE), D.D. Coligny: the Earlier Life of the Great Huguenot; translated by Annie Harwood Holmden. 8vo. Lond., 1884. C 5 R 12

BERTHAUD (L'ABBÉ). Le Quadrille des Enfans, ou Système Nouveau de Lecture. Neuvième édition. 8vo. Genève, 1790. K 12 Q 23

BERTHELOT (SABIN). [*See* RAMON DE LA SAGRA, D.]

BERTHOLLET (CHARLES LOUIS, COMTE, ET A. B.) Éléments de l'Art de la Teinture. 2ᵉ éd. 2 vols. 8vo. Paris, 1804. A 11 S 9, 10

BERTIE (LADY GEORGINA). Five Generations of a Loyal House. Part 1. Lives of Richard Bertie, and Peregrine, Lord Willoughby. 8vo. Lond., 1845. C 10 V 37

BERTIE (RICHARD). Life of. [*See* BERTIE, LADY G.]

BERTRAM (JAMES G.) "REV. WM. M. COOPER, B.A." Flagellation and the Flagellants: a History of the Rod in all Countries, from the Earliest Period to the Present Time. With Illustrations. new ed. 8vo. Lond., 1877. B 14 Q 35

Harvest of the Sea: a Contribution to the Natural and Economic History of the British Food Fishes; with Sketches of Fisheries and Fisher Folk. 8vo. Lond., 1869. A 14 S 45

BERTRAND AND KINDER TRAGEDY. Being the Account of the Extraordinary Trial of Mr. and Mrs. Bertrand, and Mrs. Kinder for the Murder of Henry Kinder. 8vo. Melb., 1866. MF 2 S 1

BERTRAND DE MOLEVILLE (A. F.), MARQUIS DE. Costume of the Hereditary States of the House of Austria, in Coloured Engravings. Fol. Lond., 1804. A 23 S 9 ‡

BERVILLE (SAINT ALBIN), ET BARRIÈRE (J. F.) Mémoires de Mme. Roland; avec une Notice sur sa Vie, des Notes et des Eclaircissemens Historiques. 2 vols. 8vo. Lond., 1820. C 4 V 29, 30

BERWICK (REV. EDWARD). Notes and Illustrations (to Life of Apollonius). [*See* PHILOSTRATUS, F.]

BERWICK (JAMES FITZ-JAMES), DUKE OF. James II and the Duke of Berwick. [*See* WILSON, C. T.]

Life of; containing an Account of his Birth, Education, and Military Exploits in Ireland, Flanders, Spain, The Sevennes, Dauphiny, and on the Rhine. 8vo. Lond., 1738. C 3 U 1

Memoirs of the Marshal Duke of Berwick; written by himself; translated from the French. 2 vols. 8vo. Lond., 1779. C 8 S 12, 13

The Duke of Berwick, Marshal of France, 1702–34; by Lieut.-Col. Charles Townshend Wilson. 8vo. Lond., 1883. C 8 S 10

BESANT (WALTER), M.A. French Humourists, from the 12th to the 19th Century. 8vo. Lond., 1873. C 8 R 16

Life and Achievements of Edward Henry Palmer, late Lord Almoner's Professor of Arabic in the University of Cambridge, and Fellow of St. John's College. 8vo. Lond., 1883. C 3 T 21

Literary Remains of the late Charles F. Tyrwhitt Drake, F.R.G.S. Edited with a Memoir. 8vo. Lond., 1877. C 10 U 23

Twenty-one Years' Work in the Holy Land. [*See* PALESTINE EXPLORATION FUND.]

BESANT (WILLIAM HENRY), D.Sc., F.R.S. A Treatise on Dynamics. 8vo. Lond., 1885. A 10 R 28

BESCHERELLE (LOUIS NICOLAS). Dictionnaire National; ou, Dictionnaire Universel de la Langue Française. 2 vols. roy. 4to. Paris, 1873. K 3 R 1, 2 †

BESENVAL (PIERRE VICTOR), BARON DE. Mémoires du. [*See* BARRIÈRE, J. F.]

BESS OF THE FOREST, "THE LINCOLNSHIRE LASS." [*See* WILD, MRS. E.]

BESSARION (JOANNES), CARDINAL. Opera Omnia. [*See* MIGNE, J. P., SERIES GRÆCA, 161.]

BESSEL (F. W.) [*See* TODHUNTER, I.]

BESSELS (DR. EMIL). Scientific Results of the United States Arctic Expedition: Steamer *Polaris*, C. F. Hall, Commanding. Vol. 1. Physical Observations. 4to. Wash., 1876. D 1 S 10 †

BESSEY (Prof. Charles E.), M.Sc. Botany for High Schools and Colleges. 8vo. New York, 1880. A 4 Q 9

BEST (John). Review of the Letter addressed to the Householders of Hobart Town, by the Rev. H. P. Fry, B.A.; by "a Member of the Medical Profession." 12mo. Hobart, 1847. MJ 2 R 2

Another copy. 12mo. Hobart, 1847. MJ 2 P 30

BETAGH (Capt. William), R.M. Voyage round the World; being an Account of a remarkable Enterprize, begun in the year 1719, chiefly to cruise on the Spaniards in the great South Ocean. 8vo. Lond., 1728. D 10 Q 46

BETHAM (Rev. W.) Genealogical Tables of the Sovereigns of the World, from the earliest period. Fol. Lond., 1795. K 22 Q 3 ‡

BETHAM (Sir William). Dignities, Feudal and Parliamentary. Vol. 1. 8vo. Lond., 1830. F 10 Q 22

Etruria-Celtica: Etruscan Literature and Antiquities investigated. 2 vols. 8vo. Dublin, 1842. B 11 V 28, 29

BETTANCOURT (A. de). [*See* Lanz, J.]

BETTANY (G. T.), M.A., &c. Eminent Doctors; their Lives, and their Work. 2 vols. 8vo. Lond., 1885. A 13 P 16, 17

BETTERTON (Thomas). [*See* Doran, Dr. J.]

BETTS (Capt. T.) Account of the Colony of Van Diemen's Land, principally intended for the use of persons residing in India. 8vo. Calcutta, 1830. MD 7 Q 1

BEUGNOT (Jean Claude), Count. Life and Adventures of; edited from the French, by Charlotte M. Yonge. 2 vols. 8vo. Lond., 1871. C 2 V 23, 24

BEUZEVILLE (James). Practical Instructions for the Management of Silk Worms, according to the best methods of the Breeders of the Silk Growing Countries. 8vo. Sydney (n.d.) MJ 2 Q 9

BEVAN (Edward), M.D. The Honey Bee: its Natural History, Physiology, and Management. Revised, enlarged, and Illustrated by William Augustus Munn, F.R.H.S., &c. 8vo. Lond., 1870. A 1 P 11

BEVAN (G. Phillips), F.G.S., &c. Hand-book to the Industries of the British Isles and the United States. 12mo. Lond., 1882. F 1 P 37

Industrial Classes, and Industrial Statistics: Mining, Metals, Chemicals, Ceramics, Glass, and Paper. (Brit. Manuf. Indust.) 12mo. Lond., 1876. A 17 S 41

Industrial Classes and Industrial Statistics: Textiles and Clothing, Food, and Sundry Industries. (Brit. Manuf. Indust.) 12mo. Lond., 1877. A 17 S 40

London Water Supply: its Past, Present, and Future; with a Map showing the Districts of the Water Companies. 8vo. Lond., 1884. A 6 R 36

Royal Relief Atlas of all parts of the World. 2nd ed. 4to. Lond., 1885. D 33 Q 13 ‡

BEVAN (Major H.) Thirty Years in India; or, a Soldier's Reminiscences of Native and European Life in the Presidencies, 1808-38. 2 vols. 8vo. Lond., 1839. D 5 R 19, 20

BEVAN (Rev. William Latham), M.A. Student's Manual of Ancient Geography; edited by W. Smith, LL.D. 8vo. Lond., 1871. D 11 R 8

Student's Manual of Modern Geography, Mathematical, Physical, and Descriptive. 3rd ed. 8vo. Lond., 1876. D 11 R 9

BEVERIDGE (H.), B.C.S. District of Bákarganj: its History and Statistics. 8vo. Lond., 1876. D 5 T 3

BEVERIDGE (Mitchell Kilgour). Gatherings among the Gum Trees. 12mo. Melb., 1863.* MH 1 R 25

BEVERIDGE (Peter). Of the Aborigines inhabiting the Great Lacustrine and Riverine depression of the Lower Murray, Lower Murrumbidgee, Lower Lachlan, and Lower Darling. 8vo. Sydney, 1883. MA 1 S 19

BEVERLAND (Hadrian). De Peccato Originali sic nuncupato Dissertatio. 18mo. Lug. Bat., 1679. J 15 Q 11

[*See also* Uchtmann, A.]

BEWICK (John). Blossoms of Morality, with cuts designed and engraved. [*See* Berquin, A.]

BEWICK (Thomas). Bewick Memento; with an Introduction by Robert Robinson: Catalogue, with Purchasers' Names, and Prices realised, of the scarce and curious Collection of Books, &c., sold by auction, at Newcastle-upon-Tyne, 1884. 4to. Lond., 1884. K 9 P 6 †

Fables by J. Gay; illustrated by T. Bewick. [*See* Gay, J.]

Fables by W. Brown. With cuts by T. Bewick. [*See* Brown, W.]

Fabliaux, or Tales, by Le Grand. With Woodcuts. [*See* Le Grand D'Aussy, P. J. B.]

General History of Quadrupeds. The Figures engraved on Wood by T. Bewick. 7th ed. 8vo. Newcastle-upon-Tyne, 1820. A 14 R 45

History of British Birds. Woodcuts by Bewick. 2 vols. 8vo. Newcastle-upon-Tyne, 1826. A 14 T 20, 21

Junius' Letters. With Woodcuts by Bewick. 2 vols. 8vo. Lond., 1797. F 6 T 7-8

Life and Times of James Catnach; by Charles Hindley. With Woodcuts by Bewick. 8vo. Lond., 1878. C 10 T 21

Life and Works of Thomas Bewick; being an Account of his Career and Achievements in Art, &c., by D. C. Thomson. 4to. Lond., 1882. C 3 W 9

Looking-glass for the Mind. With Illustrations. [*See* Berquin, A.]

Memorial Edition of Thomas Bewick's Works. 3 vols. imp. 8vo. Lond., 1885. A 15 T 9-11

1. British Birds: Land Birds.
2. British Birds: Water Birds.
3. Quadrupeds.

BEWICK (THOMAS)—*continued.*
New Bath Guide; or, Memoirs of the B-a-r-d Family; by Christopher Anstey. [Woodcuts by Bewick.] 12mo. Lond., 1804.   H 7 P 4

New Family Herbal. [*See* THORNTON, R. J.]

Pieces of Ancient Popular Poetry, from authentic Manuscripts and old printed copies; edited by Joseph Ritson. [Woodcuts by Bewick.] 12mo. Lond., 1791.   H 8 S 10

Pretty Book of Pictures for Little Masters and Misses; or, Tommy Trip's History of Beasts and Birds; with a Familiar Description of each in Verse and Prose, written by Oliver Goldsmith. [Woodcuts by Bewick.] Sm. 4to. Lond., 1867.   J 10 S 3

The Seasons; by J. Thomson; embellished with Engravings. [*See* THOMSON, J.]

Rural Tales, Ballads, and Songs. Illustrated. [*See* Bloomfield, R.]

Select Fables of Æsop and others; with the Life of Æsop, and an Essay upon Fable by Oliver Goldsmith. Engravings by Thomas Bewick. 8vo. Lond., 1871.   J 8 R 17

Thomas Bewick and his Pupils; by Austin Dobson. With Illustrations. Sq. 8vo. Lond., 1884.   C 2 T 5

Wild Flowers; or, Pastoral and Local Poetry; by R. Bloomfield. [Woodcuts by Bewick.] 12mo. Lond., 1806.   H 5 R 10

Wood Engravings of Land and Water Birds, by Thos. Bewick, never before published. 4to. Newcastle-upon-Tyne, 1860.   A 8 U 23

[*See* HORNE, T. H.; *and* RITSON, J.]

BEWICK (THOMAS AND JOHN). The Bewick Collector: a Descriptive Catalogue of the Works of T. and J. Bewick; by Thomas Hugo, M.A. 8vo. Lond., 1866. K 8 Q 33

Bewick's Wood-cuts; with an Introduction, a Descriptive Catalogue of the Blocks, and a List of the Books and Pamphlets illustrated, by Thomas Hugo, M.A. Fol. Lond., 1870.   A 23 P 21 ‡

BEWICK (WILLIAM), ARTIST. Life and Letters of; by Thomas Landseer, A.R.A. 2 vols. 8vo. Lond., 1871.   C 4 U 1, 2

BEYLE (MARIE HENRI). "De Stendahl:" Critical and Biographical Study, aided by original Documents and unpublished Letters from the private Papers of the Family of Beyle; by A. A. Paton. 8vo. Lond., 1874.   C 3 S 8

Lives of Haydn and Mozart; with Observations on Metastasio, and the Present State of Music in France and Italy; translated from the French of "L. A. C. Bombet." 2nd ed. 8vo. Lond., 1818.   C 5 T 12

BEZA or BÈZE (THEODORE DE). De Vera pronuntiatione Græcæ et Latinæ Linguæ. 18mo. Genevæ, 1587.   ζ 11 S 45

BEZOLD (DR. WILHELM VON). Theory of Color in its relation to Art and Art Industry. 8vo. Boston, 1876.   A 6 V 34

BHĀGVĀT-GĒĒTĀ. [*See* WILKINS, C.]

BHARTRIHARI. The Satakas of Bhartrihari; translated into English by the.Rev. B. Hale Wortham, B.A., &c. 8vo. Lond., 1886.   G 15 P 8

BHATTOJI-DĪKSHITA. Siddhânta Kaumudí. (In Telugu Characters.) Roy. 8vo. Madras, 1858.   K 13 T 9

Siddhânta Kaumudí (Commentary to Pâṇini's Grammar). Imp. 8vo. Bombay, 1866.   K 13 T 1

BHAVABHŪTI. Maha-Vira-Charita: the Adventures of the great Hero Ráma; an Indian Drama; translated from the Sanskrit of Bhavahúti; by John Pickford, M.A. 12mo. Lond., 1871.   H 4 Q 10

BIALLOBLOTZKY (C. H. F.) Chronicles of Rabbi Joseph. [*See* JOSEPH, RABBI.]

BIANCHI (B.) [*See* DANTE ALIGHIERI.]

BIBBS (THOMAS), AND COLLIS (WILLIAM). County of Bourke, Victoria, corrected up to 1857. (Map.) Compiled by Thomas Bibbs; lithographed by William Collis, 1856. Roy. 4to. Melb., 1857.   MD 5 S 15 ‡

BIBER (J. TH.) Wörterbuch der deutschen und französischen Sprache. [*See* MOZIN, ABBÉ.]

BIBLE CHRISTIANS. Extracts from the Minutes of the 38th Annual Conference. 8vo. Shebbear, 1856.   MG 1 Q 39

BIBLE SOCIETY. Memorandum-book of the Wheat received on account of subscription for the Bible Society, Botany Bay Division. (MS.) 4to. Sydney, 1818. MJ 2 S 2

BIBLES, OLD AND NEW TESTAMENTS, AND PSALMS.

AFGHAN. [*See* PUSHTOO.]

ALBANIAN.
New Testament. 8vo. Athens, 1844.   G 3 P 11
Psalms. Psalteri. 8vo. Konstantinopol, 1868. G 11 P 16

AMHARIC.
Bible. Biblia Sacra Amharice. 4to. Lond., 1844. G 15 U 6
New Testament. Novum Testamentum Aethiopice. 8m. 4to. Lond., 1830.   G 8 V 18

ANEITEUM.
New Testament. Intas-Etipup Mat u Jesu Kristo. 8vo. Lond., 1863.   G 14 Q 9

ANGLO-SAXON.
Gospel according to St. Matthew, in Anglo-Saxon and Northumbrian Versions, synoptically arranged. 4to. Camb., 1858.   G 5 U 2

ARABIC.
Bible. 8vo. (n.p.n.d.)   G 11 T 25
Holy Bible. 4to. Newcastle-upon-Tyne, 1811. G 14 P 1
New Testament. 8vo. (n.p.n.d.)   G 14 Q 3
Psalter. 18mo. (n.p.n.d.)*   G 9 P 42

BIBLES, &c.--*continued.*
ARABIC AND ENGLISH.
Gospel of St. Matthew. 18mo. (n.p.n.d.)   G 9 P 25
ARMENIAN.
Bible. 12mo. Stamboul, 1862.   G 16 R 7
New Testament. 8vo. (n.p.), 1819.   G 16 S 3
BENGALI.
Holy Bible. Roy. 8vo. Calcutta, 1861.   G 5 S 24
BENGALI AND ENGLISH.
New Testament. 2 vols. (in 1) 8vo. Lord., 1839.   G 14 R 3
BERBER.
Gospel of St. Luke. 8vo. (n.p.n.d.)   G 14 Q 6
New Testament. 8vo. Serampore, 1820.   G 3 P 10
BOHEMIAN.
Bible. Biblia Sacra to gest Biblj Swatá. 2 vols. (in 1)
8vo. Kyseku, 1851.   G 15 S 12
BRETON.
New Testament. Testamant revez hon avtron hag hor
Salver Jesus Christ. 12mo. Brest, 1851.   G 9 Q 37
BULGARIAN.
Part of Old Testament, Joshua–Job. 8vo. (n.p.) 1862.
   G 16 R 17
CANARESE.
New Testament. 8vo. Bangalore, 1861.   G 10 Q 21
CARSHUN.
New Testament. 4to. (n.p.n.d)   G 7 V 24
CARSHUN AND SYRIAC.
New Testament. 4to. (n.p.n.d.)   G 5 U 1
CATALONIAN.
New Testament. Lo nou Testament traduit en Llengua
Catalania. 8vo. Lord., 1835.   G 16 R 2
CHINESE.
Bible. 4 vols. 8vo. (n.p.n.d.)   G 16 S 13–16
CHINESE AND MANTCHOU.
Gospel according to St. Mark. 8vo. (n.p.n.d.)   G 5 U 25
CHINESE MANDARIN—COLLOQUIAL.
New Testament. 8vo. (n.p.n.d.)   G 16 S 19
CREE.
Bible. 2 vols. (in 1) 8vo. Lord., 1861–62.   G 14 R 8
CREOLE.
New Testament. Die Nywe Testament van ons Heer
Jesus Christus. 8vo. Copenhagen, 1818.   G 8 U 20
CROATIAN.
Bible. Sveto Pismo Staroga I Novoga Zavjeta. Roy. 8vo.
Pesti, 1868.   G 11 T 27
DAJAK OR DYAK.
New Testament. Djandji Taheta tuhan dan djuru-Salamat
ikei Jesus Kristus. 8vo. Njelo, 1846.   G 15 S 1
DANISH.
Bibelen eller den Hellige Skrift, indeholde det Gamle
óg Nye Testamentes canoniske Böger. Roy. 8vo. Lord.,
1861.   G 15 T 11
DUKE OF YORK ISLAND.
Gospel of St. Mark. 8vo. Sydney, 1882.   MG 1 P 43

K

BIBLES, &c.—*continued.*
DUTCH.
Bible. Bijbel dat is de gansche Heilige Schrift. Imp. 8vo.
Lord., 1859.   G 3 V 10
ENGADINE.
New Testament. Il nouf Testamaint da nos Segner Jesu
Christo. 18mo. Paris, 1836.   G 9 P 35
ENGLISH.
Bible (Black Letter, "Breeches" edition). Fol. Lord.,
1583.   G 37 Q 1 ‡
Bible (Douay Version); translated from the Latin Vulgate,
diligently compared with the Hebrew, Greek, and other
editions in divers Languages. 8vo. Dublin (n.d.)   G 2 R 4
Books of Job, Psalms, Proverbs, Ecclesiastes, and the Song
of Solomon, according to the Wycliffite Version made by
Nicholas de Hereford, about A.D. 1381, and revised by John
Purvey, about A.D. 1388. 12mo. Oxford, 1881.   G 8 S 3
English Hexapla; exhibiting the Six important English
Translations of the New Testament Scriptures. 4to.
Lord. (n.d.)   G 5 U 20
Exposition of the Book of Psalms; by Matthew Henry.
8vo. Lord., 1866.   G 16 P 13
Holy Bible; containing the Old Testament and the New.
18mo. Lord., 1743.   G 9 Q 25
Holy Bible; containing the Old and New Testaments,
translated out of the original Tongues. Roy. 8vo. Camb.,
1831.   G 15 T 6
Holy Bible; containing the Old and New Testaments. 8vo.
Lord., 1831.   G 15 T 5
[Speaker's Commentary.] Holy Bible, according to the
Authorized Version (A.D. 1611); with an Explanatory and
Critical Commentary, and a Revision of the Translation,
by Bishops and other Clergy of the Anglican Church;
edited by F. C. Cook, M.A., Canon of Exeter. (Suggested
by the Speaker of the House of Commons, the Rt. Hon.
J. Evelyn Denison.) 10 vols. roy. 8vo. Lord., 1871–81.
   G 4 T 1-10
Review [of the above.] [*See* STRANGE, G. L.]
Holy Bible; being the Version set forth A.D. 1611, com-
pared with the most ancient Authorities, and revised.
8vo. Oxford, 1885.   G 8 U 1
Holy Bible; containing the Old and New Testaments,
according to the authorized Version. With Illustrations
by Gustave Doré. 2 vols. imp. 4to. Lord. (n.d.)
   G 29 P 10, 11 ‡
Holy Gospels; translated from the original Greek, with
Notes, &c., by W. Brameld, M.A. Imp. 8vo. Lord.,
1863.   G 7 V 16
New Testament; with a Commentary by the Rev. Charles
Girdlestone, M.A. 2 vols. 8vo. Lord., 1835–38.
   G 15 R 9, 10
New Testament for English Readers; containing a critical
and explanatory Commentary by Henry Alford, D.D.
3rd ed. 4 vols. 8vo. Lord., 1872.   G 5 P 10–13
New Testament; translated out of the Greek, and revised
A.D. 1881. Roy. 8vo. Oxford, 1881.   G 8 V 16
New Testament. With Engravings. 4to. Lord., 1883.
   G 5 S 1

BIBLES, &c.—*continued.*

ENGLISH AND GOOJURATEE.
Gospel according to Matthew. 8vo. Surat, 1840. G 14 S 13

EROMANGA.
Gospel of St. Matthew. Matiyûkū ram Navosavos ugi.
8vo. Lord., 1869. G 10 Q 34

ESQUIMAUX.
Five Books of Moses. Mosesib Aglangit 12mo. Lord.,
1841. G 16 R 25

FEEJEEAN.
New Testament. Ai Vola ni Veiyalayalati vou i Jisu
Karisito. 8vo. Lodoni, 1858. G 16 R 19
Another copy. 12mo. Viti, 1853. G 16 R 20

FINNISH.
Bible. Biblia: Warba ja Uusi Testamenti. 2 vols.
(in 1) 8vo. Stockholm, 1852. G 14 R 12

FLEMISH.
Bible. Biblia Sacra dat is geheele heylige Schriftuer
bedeyld in het Oude en Nieuwe Testament. 2 vols. (in 1)
8vo. Brussel, 1838. G 14 R 9

FRENCH.
La Bible. Traduction Nouvelle, avec Introductions et
Commentaires, par Edouard Reuss. 9 vols. roy. 8vo.
Paris, 1874–81. G 8 V 1–8

1. Préface et Introduction générale. Ancien Testament—Première Partie : Histoire des Israélites, depuis la Conquête de la Palestine jusqu'à l'Exil. (Livres des Juges, de Samuel, et des Rois.)

2. Ancien Testament—Deuxième Partie : Les Prophètes.

3. Ancien Testament—Troisième Partie : L'Histoire Sainte de la Loi. (Pentateuque et Josué.)

4. Ancien Testament—Quatrième Partie : Chronique Ecclésiastique de Jérusalem. Le Cantique des Cantiques dit de Salomon. Recueil de Poésies Erotiques, traduites de l'Hébreu, avec Introduction et Commentaire. Cinquième Partie : Poésie Lyrique. Le Psautier, les Lamentations. Deuxième édition.

5. Ancien Testament—Sixième Partie : Philosophie Religieuse et Morale des Hébreux, Job, les Proverbes, l'Ecclésiaste, l'Ecclésiastique, la Sapience, Contes Moraux, Baruch, Manassé. Septième Partie : Littérature Politique et Polémique. Ruth, Maccabées, Daniel, Esther, Judith, &c.

6. Nouveau Testament—Première Partie : Histoire Evangélique. (Synopse des trois premiers Evangiles.) Deuxième Partie : Histoire Apostolique. (Actes des Apôtres.)

7. Nouveau Testament—Troisième Partie : Les Epîtres Pauliniennes.

8. Nouveau Testament. Quatrième Partie : L'Apocalypse. Cinquième Partie : Les Epîtres Catholiques. Sixième Partie : La Théologie Johannique. (Evangile et Epîtres.)

9. Table générale des Matières, par G. Baldensperger.

La Sainte Bible qui contient l'Ancien et le Nouveau
Testament. Roy. 8vo. Paris, 1858. G 15 T 8

FRENCH BASQUE.
New Testament. Jesus Christo guro Jaunaren Testamentu
Berria. 8vo. Bayonne, 1828. G 14 Q 5

FRENCH AND GERMAN.
New Testament and Psalms. 2 vols. (in 1) 8vo. Lord.,
1846. G 14 R 5

BIBLES, &c.—*continued.*

FRENCH AND HEBREW.
La Sainte Bible ou l'Ancien et le Nouveau Testament.
2 vols. 12mo. Lord., 1858–59. G 16 R 3, 4

FRENCH AND PIEDMONTESE.
Gospels according to St. Luke and St. John. 8vo. Lord.,
1838. G 14 R 10

FRENCH AND TURKISH.
Gospel of St. Matthew. 18mo. (n.p.n.d.) G 9 P 27

FRENCH AND VAUDOIS.
Gospels according to St. Luke and St. John. 8vo.
Lord., 1832. G 15 T 13

GAELIC.
Bible. Leabhraichean an T-seann Tiomnaidh agus an
Tiomnaidh Nuaidh. 2 vols. (in 1) 8vo. Lord., 1861.
G 15 S 11

GEORGIAN.
Testament. 4to. (n.p.n.d.) G 5 U 9

GERMAN.
Die Bibel oder die ganze heilige Schrift des Alten und Neuen
Testaments. 2 vols. (in 1) 8vo. Cöln, 1859. G 14 R 2

GERMAN AND FRENCH.
New Testament and Psalms. 2 vols. (in 1) 8vo. Lord.,
1846. G 14 R 5

GERMAN AND HEBREW.
Bible. 2 vols. 12mo. Lord., 1859. G 16 R 9, 10

GREEK.
Bible. Ta Iera Biblia. 8vo. Kantab., 1862. G 15 S 13
Greek Testament; with critically revised Text, &c., by
Henry Alford, Dean of Canterbury. 5th ed. 4 vols.
8vo. Lord., 1863–66. G 5 P 6–9
New Testament. 18mo. Camb. (n.d.) G 9 P 29
Novum Testamentum Græce; edidit Edvardus H. Hansell,
S.T.B. 3 vols. 8vo. Oxford, 1864. G 1 P 8–10
Old Testament. Vetus Testamentum Græce iuxta LXX
Interpretes Textum Vaticanum Romanum Emendatius
edidit Constantinus de Tischendorf. Editio Sexta. 2 vols.
8vo. Lepsiae, 1880. G 10 S 8, 9

GREEK—MODERN.
New Testament. 12mo. Petrov., 1817. G 9 Q 36

GREENLAND.
New Testament. 2nd ed. 8vo. Budisime, 1851. G 14 Q 7

GUJARATI.
Bible. 2 vols. 8vo. Surat, 1860. G 15 S 14, 15
Gospel according to Matthew (in English and Gujarati).
8vo. Surat, 1840. G 14 S 13

HAKKA.
The Gospel of St. Matthew. 8vo. Basel, 1866. G 15 T 15

HAROTKE.
New Testament. 8vo. Serampore, 1821. G 3 P 9

HAURA.
The Gospel according to St. Matthew. 12mo. Lord.,
1857. G 16 R 1

Bib] PART I:—*Authors, Editors, or Reference.* [Bib

BIBLES, &c.—*continued.*

HEBREW.
Bible. 8vo. Lond., 1861. G 14 R 1

HEBREW AND FRENCH.
La Sainte Bible. 2 vols: 12mo. Lond., 1858-59. G 16 R 3, 4

HEBREW AND GERMAN.
Bible. 2 vols. 12mo. Lond., 1859. G 16 R 9, 10

HINDUI-NAGRI.
Old Testament. 8vo. (n.p.n.d.) G 2 T 17

HINDUSTANI.
Book of Genesis, in Dakhani. 12mo. Hertford, 1863. G 9 P 40
New Testament. 8vo. Lond., 1860. G 14 Q 18
New Testament. Inji'l i Muqaddas. Imp. 8vo. Lond., 1860. G 8 V 22
Old Testament. Kitāb i Muqaddas yá ne Puráná aur Nayá Ahd-Náma. Imp. 8vo. Lond., 1860. G 8 V 22

HINDUWEE.
New Testament. 8vo. Lond., 1860. G 13 P 30

HUNGARIAN.
Bible. Szent Biblia. 2 vols. (in 1) 8vo. Köszegen, 1852. G 15 S 7

IBO.
Gospel of St. Matthew. Óku ómma nké owu Matia. 12mo. Lond., 1860. G 9 Q 35

INDO-PORTUGUESE.
Gospel of St. Matthew. O Evangelho conforme de Santo Mattheos. 8vo. Lond., 1851. G 14 R 6

IRISH.
Acts of the Apostles. 12mo. (n.p.n.d.) G 9 Q 21
Epistle of St. Paul to the Romans. (Pam. K.) 8vo. (n.p.n.d.) MJ 2 P 27
Gospel of St. Matthew. 12mo. (n.p.n.d.) G 9 Q 29
New Testament. 12mo. Lond., 1818. G 9 Q 32
New Testament. An Tiomna Nuadh. Roy. 8vo. Dublin, 1827. G 15 T 4
Old Testament. Leabhuir an Tsean Tiomna. Roy. 8vo. Dublin, 1827. G 15 T 4

ITALIAN.
Bible. La Sacra Bibbia ossia l' antico e il nuovo Testamento. 2 vols. (in 1) 8vo. Lond., 1862. G 15 S 6

ITALIAN-MALTESE.
Gospel of St. John. Il Vangelio di nostro Signore secondo San Giovanni. 8vo. Lond., 1822. G 13 P 25

ITALIAN AND TURKISH.
Gospel of St. Matthew. 18mo. (n.p.n.d.) G 9 P 28

JAPANESE.
Gospel of St. Luke. Imp. 8vo. (n.p.n.d.) G 8 V 19

JUDÆO-ARABIC.
Gospels, &c.: Matthew, John, Acts, and Hebrews. 8vo. (n.p.n.d.) G 11 P 24

BIBLES, &c.—*continued.*

JUDÆO-HEBREW.
Old Testament. 2 vols. imp. 8vo. Wien, 1858. G 8 V 20, 21

JUDÆO-PERSIC.
Gospels (in Hebrew characters.). 8vo. (n.p.n.d.) G 15 R 23

KAFFIR.
Bible. Inncwadi Yezibalo Ezingcwele. 8vo. Lond., 1864. G 9 T 18
Old Testament. Itestamente Endala okukuti Inncwadi zonke zocebano Oludala Engekafiki Ukristu. 2 vols. 8vo. Emkangiso, 1859. G 14 S 17, 18

KASHMEERA.
New Testament. 8vo. Serampore, 1821. G 3 P 5

KAVILIAN.
Gospel of St. Matthew. 8vo. Piêtre, 1820. G 2 T 21

KHASSEE.
Gospel of St. Matthew. Ka Gospel Jong u Mathi. 8vo. Calcutta, 1846. G 10 Q 20
New Testament. Ka Jiutang ka Bathymmai ka Jong u Iisous Khristos. 8vo. Lond., 1871. G 9 T 16

KISWAHILI.
Psalms. Zaburi za Daudi. 18mo. Lond., 1871. G 9 P 18

LATIN.
New Testament. Novum Testamentum Latine. 32mo. Berolini, 1868. G 9 P 4
Psalms. Psalmi Davidis. 32mo. Berolini, 1868. G 9 P 4

LETTISH.
New Testament. Ta Jauna Derriba muhsu kunga Jesus Kristus. 8vo. Elfinforsé, 1861. G 2 R 17

LIFU.
New Testament. Galatians–Revelations. 8vo. Neigone, 1868. G 10 Q 33

LITHUANIAN.
Bible. Bybeles tai esti Wissas Szwentas Rasstas Senoin Raujo Testamento. 2 vols. (in 1). 8vo. Frankfurte, 1853. G 15 S 5

LOOCHOOAN.
Gospel according to St. Luke. Imp. 8vo. (n.p.n.d.) G 5 U 24

MALAGASSE.
New Testament. Ny Teny N'andriamanitra atso hoe Tesitamenta ny Jesosy Kraisty. 8vo. Lond.(n.d.) G 10 Q 8
New Testament. Ny Soratra Masina amy ny Fanekena Vaovao any Jesosy Kraisty. 8vo. Lond., 1870. G 13 P 8

MALAY.
New Testament. Kitab Alkudus; iya itu Injil Isa Almasih Tuhan Kami. 8vo. Singapore, 1853. G 2 R 20
New Testament, in Arabic Characters. 8vo. (n.p.n.d.) G 14 Q 19

MALAY—HIGH.
Gospel of St. John. Indjil Jang Soetji Terkarang Oleh Jahja, Rasoel Allah Soebhanah Wataäla. 12mo. Batavia, 1873. G 9 P 12

BIBLES, &c.—*continued.*

MALAY—LOW.
Gospel of St. Johi. Kitab indjil Soetji Jaig tertoelis
daii Johaiies. 18mo. Batavia, 1873   G 9 P 12
Gospel of St. Luke. Kitab indjil Soetji Jaig tertoelis
daii Loekas. 18mo. Batavia, 1873.   G 9 P 12

MALAYALIM.
New Testameit. 2nd ed. 8vo. Loid., 1834   G 9 T 28

MALLISEET.
Gospel, accoidiig to St. Johi. 18mo. Loid., 1870. G 9 P 6

MALTESE.
Gospel of St. Matthew. L'Evaigeliu Imkaddes ta Sidna Gesù
Cristu mii San Matteu. 18mo. Loid., 1870. G 9 P 7

MANDCHOU.
Testameit. 2 vols. imp. 8vo. (n.p.n.d.)   G 7 V 22, 23

MANX.
Bible. Yn Vible Casherick ny yn Cheei Chonaant as yn
conaant ioa. 2 vols. (ii 1) 8vo. Loid., 1819. G 14 R 11

MAORI.
Bible. Ko te Paipera Tapu ara ko te Kawenata Tawhito
me te Kawenata hou. 2 vols. (ii 1) 8vo. Raiaia,
1868.   G 14 T 16
New Testameit, Pait of. Ko te Tahi Wahi o te Kawenata
hou o Ihu Karaiti te Aiiki, to tatou kai Wakaora. Sm.
4to. Hiiiii, 1833.   G 16 R 24
New Testameit. Ko te Kawenata hou o to Tatou Aiiki
o te kai Whakaora o Ihu Karaiti. 18mo. Raiaia,
1862.   G 9 P 47
Piayei-book. Ko te Pukapuka Inoinga, me iga Kaiakia
Hakarameta, me era Ritenga hoki o te Hahi o Ingarani.
Sm. 4to. Hiiiii, 1833.   G 16 R 24
Psalms. Ko te Pukapuka o iga Waiata. 18mo. Raiaia,
1862.   G 9 P 47

MARATHÍ.
Bible. 8vo. Bombay, 1857.   G 15 S 16

MARÉ.
New Testameit. Ekonejeu Kabesi ni dokuj Jesu Keriso.
8vo. Loid., 1870.   G 14 P 21

MAYAN.
Gospel of St. Johi. Leti u Ebanhelio Hesu Crizto hebix
Huai. 18mo. Loid., 1869.   G 9 P 8

MICMAC.
Gospel accoidiig to St. Matthew. 12mo. Chailotto-
town, 1853.   G 16 S 4
Psalms. 18mo. Bath, 1859.   G 9 P 34

MOLDAVIAN. New Testameit. 8vo. St. Peteisbuig,
1819.   G 15 T 12

MONGOLIAN.
New Testameit. Roy. 8vo. Loid., 1846.   G 15 T 9
Old Testameit, Paits of. 4to. (n.p.n.d.)   G 5 U 12

BIBLES, &c.—*continued.*

NAMA
New Testameit. Asa Testamens sida khüb tsi hui-aob
Yesub Xristub. 8vo. Beilii, 1866.   G 9 T 17

NENGONESE.
New Testameit: Romais–Revelatiois. 8vo. Neigoie,
1864.   G 10 Q 36

NEPALA
New Testameit. 8vo. Seiampoie, 1821.   G 3 P 8

NUPE.
Gospel of St. Matthew: Fiist sevei Chapters. 12mo.
Loid., 1860.   G 9 Q 34

OTJI.
Acts of the Apostles. Asomafo io Nneyee hö asem a Luka
Kyerew mae, wo Otyi kasa mu. 12mo. Basel, 1859.
    G 9 P 39
Gospels. Yen awurade në Agyenkwä Iesu Kiisto hö
Asempa io. 12mo. Heitfoid, 1859.   G 9 P 39

PERSIAN.
Old Testameit. Roy. 8vo. (n.p.) 1856.   G 5 S 26
New Testameit. 5th ed. Roy. 8vo. Edinb., 1846.
    G 5 S 27

POLISH.
Bible. Biblia Świeta to Jest Wszystko Pismo Świete
starego i nowego Przymierza. 8vo. Beilii, 1857. G 15 T 14

POLYGLOT.
Biblia Sacia Polyglotta. Complectentia Textus oiigiiales;
Hebiaicum, cum Pentateucho Samaiitaio, Chaldaicum,
Giæcum versionumque antiquarum; Samaiitaiæ, Giæcæ,
LXXII Interp., Chaldaicæ, Syriacæ, Aiabicæ, Æthiopicæ,
Persicæ, Vulg. Lat.; edidit Biaius Waltonus. 6 vols.
Roy. fol. Loid., 1657.   G 35 Q 1–6 ‡
Biblia Sacia Polyglotta: Textus Archetypos Versionesque
Præcipuas ab Ecclesia Antiquitus ieceptas; necnon Ver-
sioies recentiores, Anglicanam, Germanicam, Italicam,
Gallicam, et Hispanicam, complectentia. 2 vols. fol.
Loid., 1870.   G 37 Q 3, 4 ‡

PORTUGUESE.
Bible. A Biblia Sagiada, coiteido o Velho e o Novo Testamento. 8vo. Loid., 1855.   G 14 Q 2

PUSHTOO, OR AFGHAN.
New Testameit. 8vo. Hertford (n.d.)   G 2 R 21

RARATONGAN.
Bible. Te Bibilia Tapu Ra, koia te Koreromotu Taito e
te Koreromotu ou. Roy. 8vo. Loid., 1851. G 15 T 7

RUSSIAN.
New Testameit. 8vo. Loid., 1862.   G 10 Q 7
Octateuch. 18mo. Loid., 1861.   G 9 P 15
Psalms. 8vo. Loid., 1862.   G 10 Q 7

SAMOAN.
Bible. O le Tusi Paia, o le Feagaiga Tuai ma le Feagaiga
fou lei, ua Faasamoniina. 8vo. Loid., 1862. G 14 R 16

SAMOGITIAN.
New Testameit. Naujas Istatimas Jezaus Christais.
Sm. 4to Wilniuje, 1816.   G 2 P 27

BIBLES, &c.—*continued.*

SANSCRIT.
Bible. 8vo. Calcutta, 1852.   G 9 T 20
New Testament. 8vo. Calcutta, 1851.   G 9 T 21

SANTÁLI.
Gospel of St. Matthew. Matti e olakak Raska rea Sombat.
8vo. Calcutta, 1868.   G 14 Q 8

SECHUANA.
Old Testament. Bibela ea Boitsipho. 8vo. Kuruman,
1857.   G 14 Q 4

SERVIAN.
Bible. Roy. 8vo. Belgrade, 1868.   G 11 T 28
New Testament. 8vo. Berlin, 1857.   G 15 S 10

SESUTO.
New Testament. Testamente e richa Yesu Kreste. 8vo.
Paris, 1868.   G 13 P 7
Psalms. Buka ea Lipesaleme. 8vo. Platberg, 1855.
                                                     G 2 R 22

SGAU-KAREN.
Old Testament. Imp. 8vo. Tavoy, 1853.   G 5 U 26

SINDHI.
Gospel of St. John. Ob. 18mo. (n.p.n.d.)   G 9 P 13
Gospels and Acts. Sq. 8vo. (n.p.n.d.)   G 9 T 15

SINGHALESE.
New Testament. 8vo. Ceylon, 1846.   G 14 R 7

SIRENIAN.
Gospel of St. Matthew. 12mo. St. Petersburg, 1823.
                                                     G 2 T 22

SLAVONIC.
New Testament. 8vo. (n.p.n.d.)   G 15 S 9

SLAVONIC AND MODERN RUSSIAN.
New Testament. 8vo. (n.p.n.d.)   G 15 S 8

SPANISH.
Bible. La Biblia ó el Antiguo y Nuevo Testamento. 2
vols. (in 1) 8vo. Lond., 1858.   G 14 R 4

SPANISH BASQUE.
Gospel of St. Luke. Jesu Cristorem evanjelioa Lucasen
Araura. 18mo. Lond., 1870.   G 9 P 9

SWEDISH.
Bible. Bibelen: Gamla och Nya Testamentets. 2 vols.
(in 1) 8vo. Stockholm, 1862.   G 14 R 13

SYRIAC.
New Testament. 4to. (n.p.n.d.)   G 5 S 28
Old Testament. Vetus Testamentum Syriacè; recognovit
et edidit S. Lee, A.M. 4to. Lond., 1823.   G 5 U 11

SYRO-CHALDAIC.
Gospels. 4to. (n.p.n.d.)   G 5 S 29

TAHITIAN.
Old Testament, Parts of. Te Mau Buka a te Tahi pae
Peropheta Ra. 12mo. Tahiti, 1833.   G 16 R 6
New Testament. Te Faufaa Api, a to Tatou fatu e te ora,
a Iesu Mesia Ra. 12mo. Lond., 1853.   G 16 R 5

BIBLES, &c.—*continued.*

TAMIL.
Old Testament. Roy. 8vo. Madras, 1860.   G 5 S 25
New Testament. Roy. 8vo. Madras, 1860.   G 5 S 25

TARTAR.
New Testament. Sanctum Evangelium scilicet novum
Testamentum Jesu Christi. 8vo. Astrachani, 1818.
                                                     G 14 S 14
Another copy. 8vo. Karass (n.d.)   G 14 S 15

TELUGU.
Holy Bible. Roy. 8vo. Madras, 1857-60.   G 5 S 43

TESNE.
New Testament. St. Mark-Revelations. 9 vols. (in 1)
12mo. Lond., 1867-68.   G 9 Q 2

TIORE.
The Four Gospels of Jesus Christ. 18mo. Basle, 1866.
                                                     G 9 P 16

TINNÉ.
Gospel according to St. John. 18mo. Lond., 1870. G 9 P 10

TONGAN.
New Testament. Koe tohi oe Fuakava foou a ho tau
eiki moe fakamoui ko Jisu Kalaisi. 8vo. Lond.,
1860.   G 14 R 14
Old Testament. Ko Tohi tabu Katoa: aia oku i ai ae
Tohi tabu Motua. Roy. 8vo. Lond., 1860.   G 14 R 14

TURKISH.
Bible. 4to. (n.p.n.d.)   G 5 U 13
New Testament. 12mo. Astrachan, 1825.   G 16 R 11
Another copy. 8vo. Paris, 1819.*   G 9 T 2
Another copy. 8vo. (n.p.n.d.)   G 14 P 22
Old Testament, in Greek Characters. 2 vols. roy. 8vo.
Athens, 1838.   G 15 T 2, 3
Psalter. 8vo. (n.p.n.d.)   G 3 P 2

TURKISH-ARMENIAN.
New Testament. 12mo. (n.p.) 1856.   G 16 S 20

TURKISH AND ENGLISH.
Gospel of St. Matthew. 18mo. (n.p.n.d.)   G 9 P 26

TURKISH AND FRENCH.
Gospel of St. Matthew. 18mo. (n.p.n.d)   G 9 P 27

TURKISH AND ITALIAN.
Gospel of St. Matthew. 18mo. (n.p.n.d.)   G 9 P 28

TURKO-TARTAR.
New Testament. 4to. (n.p.n.d.)   G 5 U 10
Pentateuch. 4to. (n.p.n.d.)   G 7 V 25

WELSH.
Bible. Y Bibl-Cyssegr-Lan sef yr hen Destament a'r
Newydd. 2 vols. (in 1) Llund., 1871.   G 14 R 15

WENDISH.
New Testament. Ten Rowi Testament. 8vo. Choscho-
busu, 1822.   G 2 T 16

BIBLES, &c.—*continued.*
WENDISH-HUNGARIAN.
New Testameıt. Nòvi zakoı ali Testamentom. 12mo.
Köszegi, 1848. G 9 P 20
Psalms. Knige Zoltárszke. 12mo. Köszegi, 1848.
G 9 P 20
WENDISH—UPPER.
New Testameıt. Rowy Testameıt aby sakoı nascheho
knesa Jesom Kıysta. 8vo. Budeschini, 1835. G 2 R 5
YORUBA.
Epistles of St. Paul to the Coıınthiaıs, &c. 12mo. Loıd.,
1861. G 9 Q 24
Epistles of St. Paul to the Phillippians, &c. 12mo. Loıd.,
1862. G 9 Q 23
Gospel of St. Johı. 12mo. Loıd., 1861. G 9 Q 22

BIBLICAL ARCHÆOLOGY (Society of). [*See* RECORDS
OF THE PAST.]

BIBLICAL STUDENT, A. [*See* DUMAS, ALEXANDER.]

BIBLIOGRAPHER (THE): a Jouıııal of Book-Loıe. Vols.
1-6 sm. 4to. Loıd., 1882–84. E

BIBLIOGRAPHIA POETICA. [*See* RITSON, JOSEPH.]

BIBLIOPHILE FRANCAIS (LE). Gazette Illustiée
des Amateuıs de Livıes, d'Estaıpes et de haute cuıiosité.
7 vols. imp. 8vo. Paıis, 1868–73. K 17 R 7-13

BIBLIOTHECA ANGLO POETICA. [*See* GRIFFITHS,
A. F.]

BIBLIOTHECA ARCANA seu Catalogus Librorum Peıe-
tralium ; beiıg bıief Notices of Books that have beeı
secıetly pıiıted, pıohibited by law, seized, aıathematised,
buııt, oı Bowdleıised ; by Speculatoı Moıum. Vol. 1.
Sm. 4to. Loıd., 1885. E

BIBLIOTHECA CURIOSA. Vols. 1-26. 12mo. Edinb.,
1883–85. E

BIBLIOTHECA HEBERIANA. Catalogue of the Libıaıy
of the late Richaıd Heber. 8vo. Loıd., 1834. K 8 P 15

BIBLIOTHECA HISTORICA ITALICA, cura et studio
Societatis Longobaıdicaı Histoıiaı studiis promovendis.
Vols. 1-4 ıoy. 4to. Mediolani, 1876–85. B 19 S 1-4 ‡

BIBLIOTHECA LINDESIANA. Collatioıs aıd Notes ;
by Ludovic, Eaıl of Cıawfoıd aıd Balcaıres, LL.D., F.R.S.,
F.R.A.S. 3 vols. ıoy. 4to. Loıd., 1883–84. E

BIBLIOTHECA SUNDERLANDIANA. Sale Catalogue
of the tıuly impoıtaıt aıd veıy exteısive Libıaıy of
Pıiıted Books known as the Suıdeılaıd oı Bleıheim
Libıaıy. Roy. 8vo. Loıd., 1881. (8 Q 1

BIBLIOTHECAE BUNAVIANAE. [*See* CATALOGUS.]

BIBLIOTHÈQUE DES MÉMOIRES, ıelatifs à l'Histoıre
de Fıaıce. [*See* BARRIÈRE, J. F.]

BIBLIOTHÈQUE DU ROY. Catalogue des Livıes
impıiméz de la Bibliothèque du Roy. 10 vols. fol.
Paıis, 1739–53. K 27 Q 1-10 9

BIBLIOTHÈQUE ORIENTALE ; paı B. d'Herbelot.
La Haye, 1777–79. C 11 V 9-12

BIBLIOTHÈQUES COMMUNALES du Haut-Rhin,
Sociétié des. [*See* SOCIÉTÉ DES BIBLIOTHÈQUES COM-
MUNALES.]

BIBRA (F. L. VON). Schildeıuıg der Iısel Vaı Diemens-
laıd, eiıeı höchst merkwürdigen brittischen Coloıie iı
der Südsee. 8vo. Hambuıg, 1823. MD 3 T 1

BICHENO (J.) Sigıs of the Times ; oı, the Oveıthıow of
the Papal Tyıaııy iı Fıaıce. 3rd ed. Loıd., 1794.
G 17 Q 20

BICKERDYKE (JOHN) Cuıiosities of Ale aıd Beeı·
Aı Eıteıtaiıiıg Histoıy. Illustıated. 8vo. Loıd.,
1887. B 15 S 7

BICKERSTAFF (ISAAC). The Hypocıite : a Comedy.
[*See* Cibbeı, C.]
Lioıel aıd Claıissa : a Comic Opeıa (New Eng. Theatıe).
12mo. Loıd., 1786. H 4 P 29
Aıotheı copy (Bıit. Theatıe). 12mo. Loıd., 1808.
H 1 P 17
Aıotheı copy (Bell's Bıit. Theatıe). 12mo. Loıd., 1808-
H 2 P 41
Love iı a Village : a Comic Opeıa (New Eng. Theatıe).
12mo. Loıd., 1782. H 4 P 29
Aıotheı copy (Bell's Bıit. Theatıe). 12mo. Loıd., 1791.
H 2 P 17
Aıotheı copy (Bıit. Theatıe). 12mo. Loıd., 1808.
H 1 P 17
Aıotheı copy. [*See* Bıit. Dıama, 5.]
The Maid of the Mill : a Comic Opeıa (New Eng. Theatıe).
12mo. Loıd., 1782. H 4 P 29
Aıotheı copy (Bell's Bıit. Theatıe). 18mo. Loıd., 1791.
H 2 P 41
Aıotheı copy (Bıit. Theatıe). 12mo. Loıd., 1808.
H 1 P 17
Aıotheı copy. [*See* Bıit. Dıama, 5.]
The Padlock : a Comic Opeıa (New Eng. Theatıe). 12mo.
Loıd. (n.d.) H 4 P 29
Aıotheı copy. [*See* Bıit. Dıama, 5.]
Aıotheı copy. [*See* Farces, 4.]
The Plaiı Dealeı : a Comedy. [*See* WYCHERLEY, W.]
The Sultaı ; oı, a Peep iıto the Seıaglio : a Comedy.
[*See* Bıit. Dıama, 5.]
Aıotheı copy. [*See* Faıces, 3.]
The Spoiled Child : a Faıce (Cumberland's Eng. Theatıe).
12mo. Loıd., 1829. H 2 Q 16

BICKERSTAFF (ISAAC) AND FOOTE (SAMUEL). Dı. Last
iı his Chaıiot. [*See* Bıit. Dıama, 5.]

BICKHAM (GEORGE). The British Monarchy; or, a new Chorographical Description of all the Dominions subject to the King of Great Britain. Fol. Lond., 1748. D 36 Q 6‡

BICKNELL (A. J.) Bicknell's Village Builder: Elevations and Plans for Cottages, Villas, Suburban Residences, &c. Revised ed. Im. 4to. New York, 1872. A 5 8 7 ‡
Street, Store, and Bank Fronts; containing twenty-two Plates (67 to 89). Wooden and Brick Buildings; with Details. Roy. 4to. New York, 1884. A 2 U 46
[*See* COMSTOCK, W. T.]-

BICKNELL (C.) Flowering Plants and Ferns of the Riviera and Neighbouring Mountains. 8vo. Lond., 1885. A 5 Q 8

BIDDULPH (FRANCIS JOHN). Letter addressed to the Rt. Hon. Lord Stanley, on the Pasturage of the Waste Lands of the Crown in the Australian Colonies; with reference to a recent Regulation of Governor Hutt in Western Australia. 8vo. Lond., 1842. MJ 2 Q 2

BIDDULPH (MAJOR J.), B.S.C. Tribes of the Hindoo Koosh. Roy. 8vo. Calcutta, 1880. A 2 P 9

BIDPAI. [*See* PILPAY.]

BIDWELL (CHAS. TOLL), F.R.G.S. Balearic Islands. 8vo. Lond., 1876. D 7 Q 12
Cost of Living Abroad; compiled from official Returns laid before Parliament. 8vo. Lond., 1876. F 5 Q 17

BIDWILL (JOHN CARNE). Rambles in New Zealand. 8vo. Lond., 1841.* MD 4 U 1

BIELENSTEIN (A.) Handbuch der Lettischen Sprache. Band 1. Lettische Grammatik (*all published*). 8vo, Mitau, 1863. K 13 Q 25

BIGELOW (MELVILLE MADISON). History of Procedure in England from the Norman Conquest. The Norman Period (1066–1204). 8vo. Lond., 1880. B 7 Q 24

BIGGE (JOHN THOMAS). Report of the Commissioner of Inquiry into the State of the Colony of New South Wales. Fol. Lond., 1822. MF 2 U 3
Answer to the Report on the State of the Colony. [*See* MACQUARIE, MAJ.-GEN.]
Report of the Commissioner of Inquiry, on the Judicial Establishments of New South Wales and Van Diemen's Land. Fol. Lond., 1823.* MF 2 U 3
Report of the Commissioner of Inquiry, on the State of Agriculture and Trade in the Colony of New South Wales. Fol. Lond., 1823.* MF 2 U 3
Return to an Address of the Honourable the House of Commons to His Majesty, for a copy of the Instructions given by Earl Bathurst to Mr. Bigge, on his proceeding to New South Wales. (Parl. Doc. 4.) Fol. Lond., 1823. MF 4 ‡

BIGMORE (E. C.), AND WYMAN (CHARLES W. H.) Bibliography of Printing; with Notes and Illustrations. 3 vols. sm. 4to. Lond., 1880–86. K 8 P 31-33

BIGOT (CHARLES). Raphael and the Villa Farnesina; translated from the French, by Mary Healy (Madame Charles Bigot). Roy. 4to. Lond., 1884. A 2 Q 21 †

BIGOT (MME. CHARLES), MARY HEALY. Raphael and the Villa Farnesina. [*See* BIGOT, C.]

BIGSBY (JOHN J.), M.D. Shoe and Canoe; or, Pictures of Travel in the Canadas. 2 vols 8vo. Lond., 1850. D 4 P 32, 33

BIGSBY (ROBERT), LL.D. Visions of the Times of Old; or, the Antiquarian Enthusiast. 3 vols. 8vo. Lond., 1848. B 35 T 4-6
Old Places revisited. 3 vols. 8vo. Lond., 1851. B 35 T 7-9

BILLINGS (JOHN S.), M.D., &c. Principles of Ventilation and Heating, and their Practical Application. 8vo. Lond., 1884. A 2 8 33

BILLINGS (ROBERT WILLIAM). Architectural Illustrations: History and Description of Carlisle Cathedral. 4to. Lond., 1840. A 2 T 9
The Baronial and Ecclesiastical Antiquities of Scotland. Illustrated by Robert William Billings, Architect. 4 vols. 4to. Edinb., 1848–52. B 14 Q 8-11 ‡
Another copy. 4 vols. 4to. Edinb., 1848-52. B 14 Q 12-18‡
Illustrations of the Architectural Antiquities of the County of Durham; Ecclesiastical, Castellated, and Domestic. Imp. 4to. Durham, 1846. B 17 S 9 ‡
Illustrations of Durham Cathedral. 4to. Lond., 1841. A 2 T 13

BILNEY (THOMAS). Brief Account of. [*See* BRITISH REFORMERS, 12.]

BINDLEY (CHARLES), "HARRY HIEOVER." Stable Talk and Table Talk. 2 vols. 8vo. Lond., 1845. J 7 T 11, 12

BINDER (PROF.) [*See* BRUTZER, Prof.]

BINDON (SAMUEL H.) Some Notices of Manuscripts relating to Ireland, in various Languages, now to be found in the Burgundian Library at Brussels; with Fac-simile Illustrations, &c. 8vo. Dublin, 1847. B 29 S 11

BINDON v. BERRY. [*See* GRAHAM AND BINDON.]

BINGHAM (HON. A. Y.) [*See* BRASSEY, LADY A.]

BINGHAM (HON. D. A.) Marriages of the Bonapartes. 2 vols. 8vo. Lond., 1881. B 8 P 8, 9
Selection from the Letters, &c., of the First Napoleon. [*See* NAPOLEON BONAPARTE, EMPEROR.]

BINGHAM (HIRAM), A.M. Residence of Twenty-one Years in the Sandwich Islands; or, the Civil, Religious, and Political History of those Islands. 8vo. Hartford, 1849. MD 7 R 27
Another copy. 3rd ed. revised. Roy. 8vo. New York, 1855. MD 7 R 28

BINGHAM (REV. JOSEPH), M.A. Origines Ecclesiasticæ; or, the Antiquities of the Christian Church; and other Works. 9 vols. 8vo. Lond., 1840.   G 6 Q 8-16

BINGHAM (J. S.) Chess. [*See* DAL RIO, DR. E.]

BINGHAM (CAPT. THE HON. W. A.) Journal of the Siege of Paris; with a Map. 8vo. Lond., 1871.   B 8 P 4

BINGLE (JOHN). Letter to the Rt. Hon. His Majesty's Principal Secretary of State for the Colonies, London, 8vo. Sydney, 1832.   MF 3 P 1
Another copy.   MJ 2 R 17
Letter to the Rt. Hon. Lord Viscount Glenelg, Her Majesty's Secretary of State for the Colonies; with Documentary Evidence, &c. 8vo. Lond., 1837.   MF I Q 4
Another copy.   MF 3 P 26
Another copy.   F 5 T 13
Past and Present Records of Newcastle, New South Wales. 8vo. Newcastle, 1873.   MJ 2 R 16

BINGLEY (REV. W.), M.A. Musical Biography; or, Memoirs of the Lives and Writings of the most eminent Musical Composers and Writers. 2nd ed. 2 vols. 8vo. Lond., 1814.   C 8 P 34, 35
Practical Introduction to Botany. 12mo. Lond., 1817.   A 4 P 28

BINNEY (REV. THOMAS), D.D. Be Men: a Sermon. 8vo. Melb., 1858.   MG 1 P 1
Church of the Future, as depicted in the Adelaide Correspondence, examined and estimated: an Address. 8vo. Hobart, 1859.   MG 1 R 12
Lecture on the Life and Travels of the Apostle Paul, delivered in the Exhibition Building, August 15, 1859. 8vo. Melb., 1859.   MC 1 Q 37
Lights and Shadows of Church-life in Australia, including Thoughts on Some Things at Home; to which is added, "Two Hundred Years Ago"; Then and Now. 8vo. Lond., 1860.*   MG 1 P 38
Micah, the Priest-maker: a Hand-book on Ritualism. 12mo. Lond., 1867.   G 13 R 25

BINNS (RICHARD WILLIAM), F.S.A. A Century of Potting in the City of Worcester; being the History of the Royal Porcelain Works, 1751-1851. 2nd ed. 8vo. Lond., 1877.   A 11 T 20

BIOGRAPHIA BRITANNICA; or, the Lives of the most Eminent Persons who have flourished in Great Britain and Ireland, from the Earliest Ages down to the Present Times. 6 vols. (in 7) fol. Lond., 1747-66.   C 22 P 10-16 ‡
Another copy. 2nd ed., revised and enlarged. [*See* KIPPIS, A.]

BIOGRAPHICAL DICTIONARY of the Society for the Diffusion of Useful Knowledge.; edited by George Long. An-Az. (*All published.*) 4 vols. (in 7) 8vo. Lond., 1842-44.   C 11 T 22-28

BIOGRAPHICAL ILLUSTRATIONS OF EMINENT PERSONS. [*See* EMINENT PERSONS.]

BIOGRAPHICAL MAGAZINE (THE). Containing Portraits of Eminent and Ingenious Persons of every Age and Nation, with their Lives and Characters. 2 vols. 8vo. Lond., 1819-20.   C 9 V 17, 18

BIOGRAPHIE GÉNÉRALE (NOUVELLE). Depuis les temps les plus reculés jusqu'à nos jours; publiée par MM. Firmin Didot Frères, sous la direction de Dr. Hoefer. 46 vols. roy. 8vo. Paris, 1862-70.   C 7 U 1-46

BIOGRAPHIE UNIVERSELLE, Ancienne et Moderne. 52 vols. 8vo. Paris, 1811-28.   C 11 T 29-U 30
Nouvelle Edition. Publiée sous la direction de [L.G.] Michaud. 45 vols. imp. 8vo. Paris, 1843-65.   C 7 V 1-45

BIOLOGISCHES CENTRALBLATT. 5 vols. 8vo. Erlangen, 1881-86.   E

BION. Works of; translated by F. Fawkes. [*See* HESIOD.]
Idylls of. [*See* THEOCRITUS.]
Translations from Bion. [*See* CHALMERS, A.]

BIONDELLI (B.) Studii sulle Lingue Furbesche. 12mo Milano, 1846.   K 11 S 40

BIOT (J. B.) Life of Sir Isaac Newton. (Eminent Men.) 8vo. Lond., 1849.   C 7 P 45

BIRCH (JOHN). Examples of Labourers' Cottages; with Plans for improving the Dwellings of the Poor in large Towns. Roy. 8vo. Lond., 1871.   A 2 Q 27

BIRCH (JONATHAN). Fifty-one Original Fables; with Morals, and Ethical Index. Embellished with Designs by R. Cruickshank, engraved on Wood. 8vo. Lond., 1833.   J 11 V 20
Religious Life of Frederick William III. [*See* EYLERT, R. F.]

BIRCH (SAMUEL), LL.D., &c. Biographical Notices of Dr. Samuel Birch; with an Introduction by Walter de Gray Birch. 8vo. Lond., 1886.   C 4 Q 6
Faust; translated into English Verse. [*See* GOETHE, J. W. VON.]
History of Ancient Pottery, Egyptian, Assyrian, Greek, Etruscan, and Roman. New and revised edition. Illustrated. 8vo. Lond., 1873.   B 15 Q 38
Salaminia (Cyprus). [*See* CESNOLA, MAJOR A. P. DI.]
[*See* ARUNDALE, F.; BRITISH MUSEUM; *and* RECORDS OF THE PAST.]

BIRCH (SAMUEL). The Adopted Child: a Musical Drama. [*See* FARCES, 6.]

BIRCH (REV. THOMAS), D.D. Court and Times of Charles I; including Memoirs of the Mission in England of the Capuchin Friars, by Father Cyprien de Gamache; edited by Prof. R. F. Williams. 2 vols. 8vo. Lond., 1848.   C 10 S 39, 40

BIRCH (REV. THOMAS), D.D.—*continued.*
Court and Times of James I; edited by Prof. R. F. Williams.
2 vols. 8vo. Lond., 1848.   C 10 S 37, 38
Life of Henry, Prince of Wales, eldest Son of King James I.
8vo. Lond., 1760.   C 6 P 18
Life of the Hon. Robert Boyle. 8vo. Lond., 1744.
                                   C 5 U 6
Life of the Rev. William Chillingworth, M.A. [*See*
CHILLINGWORTH, REV. W.]
[*See* THURLOE, J.]

BIRCH (WALTER DE GRAY), F.S.A. Biographical Notices
of Dr. Samuel Birch. [*See* BIRCH, DR. S.]
Cartularium Saxonicum: a Collection of Charters relating
to Anglo-Saxon History (A.D. 430–947). 2 vols. roy. 8vo.
Lond., 1885–87.   B 25 U 2, 3
History, Art, and Palæography of the Manuscript styled
the Utrecht Psalter. 8vo. Lond., 1876.   G 6 Q 4
Vita Haroldi: the Romance of the Life of Harold, King of
England; edited by Walter de Gray Birch, F.S.A. 8vo.
Lond., 1885.   C 7 Q 33
[*See* BRITISH MUSEUM.]

BIRCHALL (JAMES). England under the Revolution and
the House of Hanover, 1688–1820. 8vo. Lond., 1876.
                                   B 3 R 30

BIRD (H. E.) Chess Practice; being a condensed and
simplified Record of the actual Openings in the finest
Games played up to the Present Time, including the whole
of the beautiful Specimens contained in "Chess Masterpieces." 8vo. Lond., 1882.   A 17 W 25

BIRD (ISABELLA L.), *now* MRS. BISHOP. Englishwoman
in America. 8vo. Lond., 1856.   D 3 Q 39
Golden Chersonese and the Way thither. Illustrated. 8vo.
Lond., 1883.   D 6 P 10
Hawaiian Archipelago: Six Months among the Palm Groves,
Coral Reefs, and Volcanoes of the Sandwich Islands. 8vo.
Lond., 1875.*   MD 6 P 3
Unbeaten Tracks in Japan: an Account of Travels in the
Interior, including Visits to the Aborigines of Yezo, and
the Shrines of Nikkô and Isé. Illustrated. 2nd ed. 2
vols. 8vo. Lond., 1880.   D 6 P 8, 9

BIRD (S. DOUGAN), M.D., &c. Australasian Climates and
their influence in the prevention and arrest of Pulmonary
Consumption. 8vo. Lond., 1863.*   MA 2 S 47
Climate and Consumption. 8vo. Melb., 1870.   MA 2 S 38
On the Nature and Treatment of Epidemic Cholera, and
the Influence of Quarantine and Hygienic Precautions
in arresting its Progress. 8vo. Melb., 1866.   MA 2 S 38

BIRDS (JAMES ADEY), B.A., &c. Faust: a Tragedy.
[*See* GOETHE, J. W. VON.]

BIRDWOOD (GEORGE C. M.), C.S.I., &c. Industrial Arts
of India. [*See* SOUTH KENS. MUS., 18, 19.]

BIRKBECK (G.) Mathematics. [*See* DUPIN, BARON, C.]

BIRKBECK (W. L.) Historical Sketch of the Distribution
of Land in England. 8vo. Lond., 1885.   F 6 P 30

BIRKETT (EDMUND LLOYD). Thomson's Conspectus. [*See*
THOMSON, A. T.]

BIRKMYRE (W.) [*See* VICTORIAN EXHIBITION, 1861.]

BIRKS (PROF. THOMAS RAWSON), M.A., &c. Modern
Physical Fatalism, and the Doctrine of Evolution, including
the examination of Mr. H. Spencer's "First Principles."
8vo. Lond., 1876.   G 10 Q 9
Another copy. 2nd ed. 8vo. Lond., 1882.   G 10 Q 10
Modern Utilitarianism; or, the Systems of Paley, Bentham,
and Mill, examined and compared. 8vo. Lond., 1874.
                                   G 10 Q 9
The Uncertainties of Modern Physical Science; being
the Annual Address of the Victoria Institute. 5th ed.
(Pam. N.) 8vo. Lond., 1876.   MJ 2 P 29
Another copy. (Pam. Cn.) 8vo. Lond.,1879. MA 2 V 14

BIRMINGHAM. Hand-book of Birmingham; prepared
for the Members of the British Association. 12mo.
Birmingham, 1886.   D 7 P 13
Post Office Directory. Roy. 8vo. Lond., 1869.   E

BIRMINGHAM FREE LIBRARIES (THE). Annual
Reports of the Free Libraries Committee for the years
1871–77. 8vo. Birmingham, 1871–77.   E
Borough of Birmingham.: Opening of the Free Reference
Library, October 26, 1866; Inaugural Address, by George
Dawson, M.A. 8vo. Birmingham, 1866.   K 7 R 18
Brief Hand-list of the Cervantes Collection, presented to
the Birmingham Free Library, Reference Department;
by W. Bragge, Esq., F.S.A. (Pam.) 8vo. Birmingham
(n.d.)   K 7 R 18
Catalogue of Birmingham Books in the Reference Depart-
ment of the Free Library; compiled by J. D. Mullins, Chief
Librarian. (Pam.) 8vo. Birmingham,1874. K 7 R 18
Catalogue of the Reference Department; by J. D. Mullins.
8vo. Birmingham, 1869.   K 7 S 13
Catalogue of the Shakespeare Memorial Library, Birmingham; by J. D. Mullins. 3 vols. 8vo. Birmingham,
1872–76.   K 8 Q 30–32
Free Libraries and Newsrooms; their Formation and
Management; by J. D. Mullins, Chief Librarian, Birming-
ham Free Libraries. 2nd ed. 8vo. Lond.,1870. K 7 R 18
Lectures on the Free Libraries Reference Department.
[*See* BOOKS FOR A REFERENCE LIBRARY.]
Shakspere Memorial Library, and the Art Gallery; by
John Alfred Langford, LLD., Reprinted, by permission,
from the *Birmingham Morning News.* 8vo. Birmingham,
1871.   K 7 R 18
Sixth Annual Report of the Free Libraries Committee.
(Pam. C.) Imp. 8vo. Birmingham, 1867.   MJ 2 S 1

BIRMINGHAM MUSEUM AND ART GALLERY.
Hand-book to the Art Exhibition. Birmingham, 1885–86.
                                   Libr.
Official Catalogue, with Notes upon the Industrial Exhi-
bits, &c.; by W. Wallis and A. St. Johnston. 8vo.
Birmingham, 1885–86.   Libr.

BIRNIE (RICHARD), M.A. Essays; Social, Moral, and Political. [Selected and reprinted from *The Australasian.*] 8vo. Melb., 1879. MJ 1 U 3

BISCHOF (GUSTAV), FH.D. Elements of Chemical and Physical Geology; translated from the MS. of the Author, by B. H. Paul, F.C.S., and J. Drummond, M.D. 3 vols. 8vo. Lond., 1854–59. A 9 R 1–3

Physical, Chemical, and Geological Researches on the Internal Heat of the Globe. 8vo. Lond., 1841. A 17 V 14

BISCHOFF (JAMES). Comprehensive History of the Woollen and Worsted Manufactures. 2 vols. 8vo. Lond., 1842. A 11 S 1, 2

Sketch of the History of Van Diemen's Land; and an Account of the Van Diemen's Land Company. 8vo. Lond., 1832.* MB 1 S 7

BISCOE (JOHN), R.N. Recent Discoveries in the Antarctic Ocean, from the Log-book of the Brig *Tula.* 8vo. Lond., 1833. MD 7 Q 46

BISHOP (REV. H. H.) Architecture, especially in relation to our Churches. 8vo. Lond., 1886. A 2 R 39

BISHOP (J.) [*See* WEBER, G.]

BISHOP (MRS. ISABELLA). [*See* BIRD, ISABELLA, L.]

BISMARCK-SCHÖNHAUSEN (O. E. L.) PRINCE VON. Conversations on Colonial Matters. [*See* AUSTRALASIA.]

Life of; Private and Political; with Descriptive Notices of his Ancestry; by John Geo. Louis Hesekiel; translated and edited by Kenneth R. H. Mackenzie, F.S.A., &c. 8vo. Lond., 1870. C 10 R 21

Prince Bismarck: an Historical Biography; by Charles Lowe, M.A.; with Portraits. 2 vols. 8vo. Lond., 1885. C 10 R 19, 20

Speeches in the Upper House and the Chamber of Deputies of the Parliament, on January 29 and February 13, 1869. 8vo. Berlin, 1869. F 10 Q 19

In the Franco-German War. [*See* BUSCH, DR. M.]

BISSET (ANDREW). History of the Commonwealth of England, from the Death of Charles I to the Expulsion of the Long Parliament by Cromwell. 2 vols. 8vo. Lond., 1864–67. B 6 T 3, 4

History of the Struggle for Parliamentary Government in England. 2 vols. 8vo. Lond., 1877. B 7 Q 31, 32

Memoirs and Papers of Sir Andrew Mitchell, K.B. 2 vols. 8vo. Lond., 1850. C 6 U 10, 11

Short History of the English Parliament. 8vo. Lond., 1882. B 3 R 16

BISSET (ROBERT), LL.D. History of the Reign of George III. 2nd ed. 6 vols. 8vo. Lond., 1820. B 6 P 15 20

BISSON (CAPT. FREDERICK SHIRLEY DUMARESQ DE CATERET). Our Schools and Colleges. Vol. 1 for Boys. Vol. 2 for Girls. 8th ed. 2 vols. 8vo. Lond., 1883 81. G 18 Q 3, 4

BITHELL (RICHARD), B. Sc., &c. Counting-house Dictionary; containing an Explanation of the Technical Terms used by Merchants and Bankers in the Money Market and on the Stock Exchange. 8vo. Lond., 1882. F 14 Q 24

Another copy. 2nd ed. 12mo. Lond., 1883. K 9 T 22

BIUNDI (GIUSEPPE). Dizionario Siciliano-Italiano. 12mo. Palermo, 1857. F 14 Q 25

BJÖRNSTJERNA (COUNT). British Empire in the East; translated from the Swedish Language, by H. E. Lloyd. 8vo. Lond., 1840. B 10 T 18

BLAAUW (WILLIAM HENRY), M.A. The Barons' War, including the Battles of Lewes and Evesham. Sm. 4to. Lond., 1844. B 4 Q 22

BLACK (ADAM). Memoirs of; edited by Alexander Nicolson, LL.D. 2nd ed. 8vo. Edinb., 1885. C 4 Q 3

BLACK (ADAM AND CHARLES). Atlas of Australia, with all the Gold Regions: a Series of Maps from the latest and best Authorities. 4to. Edinb., 1854. MD 5 R 1 ‡

BLACK (CHARLES CHRISTOPHER), M.A. Michael Angelo Buonarroti, Sculptor, Painter, Architect; the Story of his Life and Labours. Imp. 8vo. Lond., 1875. C 7 V 50

BLACK (DAVID). Wanderings and Fortunes of some German Emigrants. [*See* GERSTAECKER, F.]

BLACK (J.) Gas-fitting: a Practical Hand-book treating of every description of Gas-laying and Fitting. (Weale.) 12mo. Lond., 1886. A 17 R 2

BLACK (PROF. JAMES GOW.) [*See* HUTTON, F. W., *and* ULRICH, G. H. T.]

BLACK (JOHN). A few Words on Interesting Matters relating to the Colony. 8vo. Sydney, 1843.* MJ 2 Q 4

BLACK (JOHN). [*See* GOLDONI, C.]

BLACK (JOHN). Travels through Norway and Sweden. [*See* BUCH, L. VON.]

BLACK (JOHN R.) Young Japan. Yokohama and Yedo: a Narrative of the Settlement and the City, 1858–79. 2 vols. 8vo. Lond., 1880–81. D 6 8 32, 33

BLACK (MORRICE A.), F.I.A. Progressive Policy of the Australian Mutual Provident Society reviewed; together with a comparative abstract of the expenses of English, American, and Australian Life Assurance Institutions. 8vo. Sydney, 1878. MF 2 8 3

Another copy. MF 3 Q 1

BLACK (NEIL), M.L.C. Portrait of. [*See* MANUSCRIPTS AND PORTRAITS.]

BLACK (WILLIAM). Goldsmith. (Eng. Men of Letters.) 12mo. Lond., 1879. C 1 U 17

BLACK (William). Practical Treatise on Brewing, based
on Chemical and Economical Principles. 8vo. Lond.,
1849.   A 11 Q 22

BLACK BOOK (The). An exposition of Abuses in Church
and State, &c 8vo. Lond., 1835.   F 3 S 19

BLACKBURN (Charles F.) Hints on Catalogue Titles,
and on Index Entries; with a rough Vocabulary of
Terms and Abbreviations, chiefly from Catalogues, and
some Passages from Journeying among Books. Roy.
8vo. Lond., 1884.   J 2 U 19

BLACKBURN (Henry).   Academy Notes, 1882-85.
4 vols. 8vo. Lond., 1882-85.   E
Academy Sketches, including Various Exhibitions. Second
year, 1884. 8vo. Lond., 1884-86.   E
Breton Folk: an Artistic Tour in Brittany; with Illus-
trations by R. Caldecott. 4to. Lond., 1880.   D 7 V 7
English Art in 1884. Roy. 4to. New York, 1885. A 7 S 5†
Grosvernor Notes, 1885-86: a Complete Catalogue. 8vo.
Lond., 1885-86.   E
Harz Mountains. A Tour in the Toy Country. Illus-
trated. 8vo. Lond., 1873.   D 6 T 19
Randolph Caldecott: a Personal Memoir of his Early Art
Career. 8vo. Lond., 1886.   C 10 S 12
Travelling in Spain. 8vo. Lond., 1866.   9 D Q 22

BLACKBURNE (Edward). Life of the Rt. Hon. Francis
Blackburne; by his Son. 8vo. Lond., 1874.   C 8 T 5

BLACKBURNE (Archdeacon Francis). The Confes-
sional; or, a full and free Inquiry into the Right,
Utility, Edification, and Success, of establishing Systematical Confessions of Faith and Doctrine in Protestant
Churches. 2nd ed. 8vo. Lond., 1767.   G 2 R 9

BLACKBURNE (Rt. Hon. Francis). Life of; by his
Son, E. Blackburne. 8vo. Lond., 1874.   C 8 T 5

BLACKBURNE (Gertrude M. Ireland). Hon. Algernon
Sidney: a Review. 8vo. Lond., 1885.   C 4 Q 45

BLACKET (W. S.) Researches into the Lost Histories
of America; or, the Zodiac shown to be an Old Terrestrial Map in which the Atlantic Isle is delineated. Illustrated. 8vo. Lond., 1883.   B 1 T 33

BLACKETT (C. R.) The Food we Eat and how to Cook
it. [*See* Australian Health Society.]

BLACKHAM (R. D.) [*See* Deacon, C. W.]

BLACKIE (Prof. John Stuart), F.R.S.E. Altavona.
Fact and Fiction from my Life in the Highlands. 12mo.
Edinb., 1882.   J 11 R 12
Horæ Hellenicæ: Essays and Discussions on some impor-
tant points of Greek Philology and Antiquity. 8vo.
Lond., 1874.   J 3 S 6
Scottish Highlanders and the Land Laws: an Historico-
Economical Enquiry. 8vo. Lond., 1885.   F 10 R 9

BLACKIE (Prof. John Stuart), F.R.S.E.—*continued.*
Self Culture: Intellectual, Physical, and Moral. 12mo-
Edinb., 1878.   G 13 Q 19
What does History teach? Two Edinburgh Lectures.
12mo. Lond., 1886.   B 14 Q 18
[*See* Æschylus.]

BLACKIE (W. G.), Ph. D., F.R.G.S. Imperial Gazetteer:
a general Dictionary of Geography. 2 vols. imp. 8vo.
Glasgow, 1852-55.   D 12 V 18, 19

BLACKLEY (Rev. W.) Diplomatic Correspondence of
the Rt. Hon. Richard Hill. [*See* Hill, Rt. Hon. R.]

BLACKLOCK (Ambrose). Treatise on Sheep. Fifth thous-
and; with an additional chapter on the Management of
Sheep in Australia. 18mo. Lond., 1841.   MA 1 P 20
Another copy. Eleventh thousand. 18mo. Lond.,
1848.   MA 1 P 21

BLACKLOCK (Thomas). Life and Poems of. [*See*
Chalmers, A.]

BLACKMORE (Sir Richard), Knt., M.D. King Arthur:
an Heroick Poem, in Twelve Books. Sm. fol. Lond.,
1697.   H 7 R 5†
Life and Poems of. [*See* Chalmers, A., *and* Johnson, S.]

BLACKSTONE (Sir William). Commentaries on the
Laws of England; with Notes by J. T. Coleridge. 4 vols.
8vo. Lond., 1825.   F 10 Q 4-7
Student's Blackstone: Commentaries on the Laws of England; abridged and adapted by R. M. Kerr, LL.D., &c.
8vo. Lond., 1874.   F 6 Q 11

BLACKWELL (Anna). [*See* Kardec, A]

BLACKWOOD (Capt. F. P.), R.N. Directions for the
Outer Passage from Sydney to Torres Strait, to accom-
pany the Chart of the Barrier Reefs. (Pam. 24.) 8vo.
Lond., 1847.   MJ 2 Q 12
Narrative of the Surveying Voyage of H.M.S. Fly. [*See*
Jukes, J. B.]

BLACKWOOD (Rt. Hon. F. T. H.), Earl of Dufferin.
[*See* Dufferin, Earl of.]

BLACKWOOD'S BOOKS FOR EVERYBODY. Containing—1. Tempest and Sunshine, by Mrs. Mary J.
Holmes. 2. Who's your Friend, by A. W. Cole. 3. Expedition of Five Americans. 12mo. Lond., 1855. J 4 R 5

BLACKWOOD'S EDINBURGH MAGAZINE. Vols.
1-137. 8vo. Edinb., 1817-85.   E

BLADES (William). Account of the German Morality
Play, entitled "Depositio Cornuti Typographici"; with a
Rhythmical Translation of the German Version of 1648.
Sm. 4to. Lond., 1885.   H 1 S 1
Biography and Typography of William Caxton, England's
First Printer. 8vo. Lond., 1877.   C 10 S 30
Enemies of Books. 8vo. Lond., 1880.   J 7 Q 45
Numismata Typographica; or, the Medallic History of
Printing. 4to. Lond., 1883.   A 1 R 12†

BLAEU (JEAN). Le Grand Atlas; ou, Cosmographie Blaviane, en laquelle est exactement descritte la Terre, la Mer, et le Ciel. 12 vols. at. fol. Amsterdam, 1663–67.
D 21 P 4-15 ‡

BLAIKIE (WILLIAM GARDEN), D.D., &c. Personal Life of David Livingstone, LL.D., &c. Chiefly from his unpublished Journals and Correspondence in the possession of his Family. With Portrait and Map. 8vo. Lond., 1880. C 7 S 10

BLAINE (DELABERE P.) Encyclopædia of Rural Sports, or Complete Account (Historical, Practical, and Descriptive) of Hunting, Shooting, Fishing, Racing, &c. New ed., revised and corrected. 8vo. Lond., 1870. K 5 U 3

Outlines of the Veterinary Art; or, a Treatise on the Anatomy, Physiology, and Curative Treatment of the Diseases of the Horse, and of Neat Cattle and Sheep. 7th ed. Considerably enlarged by Charles Steel, M.R.C.V.S.L. 8vo. Lond., 1865. A 1 R 34

BLAINE (JAMES G.) Twenty Years of Congress: from Lincoln to Garfield. With a Review of the Events which led to the Political Revolution of 1860. 2 vols. roy. 8vo. Norwich, Conn., 1884–86. B 1 U 10, 11

BLAIR (DAVID.) Cyclopædia of Australasia; or, Dictionary of Facts, Events, Dates, Persons, and Places connected with the Discovery, Exploration, and Progress of the British Dominions in the South. Imp. 8vo. Melb., 1881. MK 1 U 19

History of Australasia, from the first dawn of Discovery in the Southern Ocean, to the establishment of Self-Government in the various Colonies. Illustrated. 4to. Glasgow, 1878.* MB 1 U 1

New Gospel of the Deadened Brain; or, Spiritism exploded. 8vo. Melb., 1872. MG 1 Q 39

Speeches of Sir H. Parkes: Introduction. [*See* PARKES, SIR H.]

[*See* HAMLET CONTROVERSY.]

BLAIR (HUGH), D.D., &c. Lectures on Rhetoric and Belles Lettres. 8vo. Lond., 1823. J 5 S 2

Another copy. New ed. 8vo. Lond., 1823. J 5 S 22

BLAIR (JOHN), M.D., &c. On Paying Wards in Public Hospitals. (Pam. Ci.) 8vo. Melb., 1877. MA 2 Q 33

BLAIR (REV. JOHN), LL.D. Chronology and History of the World, from the Creation to the year of Christ 1768. Fol. Lond., 1768. B 14 U 3 ‡

BLAIR (LEWIS H.) Unwise Laws: Operations of a Protective Tariff upon Industry, Commerce, and Society. 8vo. New York, 1886. F 6 Q 28

BLAIR (REV. ROBERT). The Grave: a Poem; to which is added, a Life of the Author. Illustrated. Imp. 4to. Lond., 1813. H 22 S 24 ‡

Life and Poems of. [*See* CHALMERS, A.]

BLAIR (W. N.), M.I.C.E. Building Materials of Otago and South New Zealand generally: Papers originally read at the Otago Institute, revised and extended. 8vo. Dunedin, 1879. MA 1 T 5

BLAKE (E. VALE). Arctic Experiences; containing Capt. Geo. E. Tyson's Wonderful Drift on the Ice-Floe; a History of the Polaris Expedition; the Cruise of the *Tigress;* and Rescue of the Polaris Survivors, to which is added a General Arctic Chronology; edited by E. V. Blake. Roy. 8vo. Lond., 1874. D 4 S 34

BLAKE (HENRY). [*See* LETTERS FROM THE IRISH HIGHLANDS.]

BLAKE (MRS. HENRY.) [*See* LETTERS FROM THE IRISH HIGHLANDS.]

BLAKE (JOHN F.), M.A., &c. Astronomical Myths, based on Flammarion's "History of the Heavens." 8vo. Lond., 1877. A 3 S 15

Monograph of the British Fossil Cephalopoda. Part 1. Introduction and Silurian Species. 4to. Lond., 1882- A 1 Q 17 †

BLAKE (ADMIRAL ROBERT). Life of. (Eminent Men.) 8vo. Lond., 1849. C 7 P 45

[Life of;] by D. Hannay. (Eng. Worthies.) 12mo, Lond., 1886. C 2 R 3

BLAKE (S. JEX.) [*See* JEX-BLAKE, S.]

BLAKE (WILLIAM). Etchings from his Works; by William Bell Scott. With descriptive Text. Fol. Lond., 1878. A 4 R 17 ‡

Life of; with Selections from his Poems and other Writings, by Alexander Gilchrist. 2 vols. 8vo. Lond., 1880. C 10 P 7-8

Poetical Works of, Lyrical and Miscellaneous; edited, with a Prefatory Memoir, by William Michael Rossetti. 12mo. Lond., 1875. H 5 S 5

William Blake: a Critical Essay, by Algernon Charles Swinburne. 2nd ed. 8vo. Lond., 1868. C 10 P 9

BLAKE (WILLIAM P.) Notices of Mining Machinery, and various Mechanical Appliances in use, chiefly in the Pacific States and Territories, for Mining, Raising, and Working Ores. 8vo. New Haven, 1871. A 9 U 32

Report on Iron and Steel (Vienna International Exhibition, 1873.) 8vo. Wash., 1876. A 9 U 16

BLAKELEE (GEORGE E.) Blakelee's Industrial Cyclopedia: how to Make and how to Mend. 8vo. New York, 1884. K 1 R 25

BLAKESLEY (VERY REV. J. W.), M.A., DEAN OF LINCOLN. Life of Aristotle, including a critical Discussion of some Questions of Literary History connected with his Works. 8vo. Camb., 1839. C 10 R 5

BLAKEWAY (REV. JOHN BRICKDALE), M.A. History of Shrewsbury. [*See* OWEN, H.]

BLAKEY (Dr. Robert). Memoirs of; edited by the Rev. Henry Miller. 8vo. Lond., 1879.   C 5 8 3

BLAKISTON (Capt. J.) Twelve Years' Military Adventure in Three Quarters of the Globe. 2 vols. 8vo. Lond., 1829.   D 9 S 24, 25

BLAKISTON (Thomas W.) Five Months on the Yangtsze; with a Narrative of the Exploration of its Upper Waters, and Notices of the Present Rebellions in China. Illustrated. 8vo. Lond., 1862.   D 5 T 8

BLANC (Charles). Art in Ornament and Dress; translated from the French, with Illustrations. 8vo. Lond., 1877.   A 7 R 11
L'Art dans la Parure et dans le Vêtement. Sq. 8vo. Paris, 1875.   A 7 S 27

BLANC (Jean Joseph Louis). The History of Ten Years, 1830-40. 2 vols. 8vo. Lond., 1844-45.   B 8 R 10, 11

BLANC (L. G.) Vocabolario Dantesco o Dizionario Critico o Ragionato della Divina Commedia di Dante Alighieri. 3ª ed. 8vo. Firenze, 1883.   K 12 P 42

BLANCHARD (Laman). Life and Literary Remains of "L.E.L." [Letitia Elizabeth Landon.]   2 vols. 8vo. Lond., 1841.   C 4 S 15, 16
George Cruikshank's Omnibus. [*See* CRUIKSHANK, G.]
Poetical Works of; with a Memoir; by Blanchard Jerrold. 8vo. Lond., 1876.   H 5 T 21
Sketches from Life; with a Memoir of the Author, by Sir Edward Bulwer Lytton, Bart. 3 vols. 8vo. Lond., 1846.   C 4 Q 35-37

BLANCHARD (Sidney Laman). Yesterday and To-day in India. 8vo. Lond., 1867.   D 6 P 37

BLANCHE (Henry B.) Prize Essay on "Truth," for which the Gold Medal was awarded, at the late Intercolonial Exhibition, 1879-80. 12mo. Melb., 1880. MG 1 Q 39

BLANCHE (John F.) The Prince's Visit; and other Poems. 8vo. Melb., 1869.   MH 1 Q 1

BLAND (Rev. Robert). Edwy and Elgiva, and Sir Everard; with other Tales and Poems. 8vo. Lond., 1809.   H 5 T 19
Four Slaves of Cythera: a Romance, in ten Cantos. 8vo. Lond., 1809.   H 6 S 8

BLAND (William). Experimental Essays on the Principles of Construction in Arches, Piers, Buttresses, &c. (Weale.) 12mo. Lond., 1867.   A 17 P 38
Forms of Ships and Boats. (Weale.) 12mo. Lond., 1872.   A 17 P 18

BLAND (William), M.R.C.S. Correspondence between Dr. F. M'Crae and Mr. Surgeon Bland. [*See* MACCRAE, Dr. F.]
Journey of Discovery to Port Phillip. [*See* HOVELL, W. H., AND HUME, H.]

BLAND (William), M.R.C.S.—*continued.*
Letter from the Australian Patriotic Association to C. Buller, jun., Esq., M.P., in reply to his Communication of 31st May, 1840. 8vo. Sydney, 1840.   MF 3 P 1
Letter to His Excellency Sir Charles Augustus Fitzroy. 8vo. Sydney, 1849.   MF 3 Q 5
Letters to Charles Buller, jun., Esq., M.P., from the Australian Patriotic Association. 8vo. Sydney, 1849.*
                    MF 3 Q 5
Another copy.   MJ 2 Q 14·
Paper on the present Epidemic Scarlatina, read to some Professional Friends. 12mo. Sydney, 1841. MJ 2 R 17
Political Papers. 8vo. Sydney, 1838-42.   MF 3 Q 18
    Examination of Mr. James Macarthur's Work, "New South Wales: its Present State and Future Prospects."
    Expenditure of the Land Fund of New South Wales in the Colony, and principally on Public Works, as a means of Promoting and Supporting Immigration, 1842.
    Letter from the Australian Patriotic Association to C. Buller, jun., Esq., M.P., in reply to his Communications respecting certain Forms of Local Government proposed for this Colony.
    Letter in support of the Petition of the Colonists of New South Wales, for the continuance of Transportation of Convicts to the Colony, and of their Assignment to Private Service.
    Letter in reply to his Communication of 2nd September.
    Letter on the Bill for the Introduction of Municipal Institutions into New South Wales; initiated by His Excellency the Governor, 1840.
    Letter on the Census Bill of the Local Legislature of New South Wales, passed in the Session of 1840.
    Letter in reply to his Communication of 31st May, 1840; and in reply to his Communications of July and August, 1840.
    Objections to the Project of His Excellency Sir George Gipps for Raising a Loan. [With Protests of Sir John Jamison and Gregory Blaxland against the Police and Gaol Funds.] 8vo. Sydney, 1842.   MF 3 P 1
Another Copy.   MF 3 Q 18
Review of the Examination of Mr. James M'Arthur's Work, "New South Wales: its Present State and Future Prospects"; by [William Bland] a Member of the Australian Patriotic Association.
Review of the Examination of Mr. James M'Arthur's Work, "New South Wales; its Present State and Future Prospects"; by "A Member of the Australian Patriotic Association." 8vo. Sydney, 1839.   MF 3 P 6
Services rendered to New South Wales. (Pam. 35.) 8vo Sydney, 1862.   MJ 2 Q 25
Suppression of Spontaneous Combustion in Wool Ships, &c 2nd ed. (Pam. 35.) 8vo. Sydney, 1845. MJ 2 Q 22
Suppression of Combustion in Wool, and other Ships, Mines and other confined spaces. 3rd ed. 8vo. Sydney 1867.   MJ 2 R 14

BLANE (Sir Gilbert), Bart., &c. Statement of Facts, tending to establish an Estimate of the true Value and Present State of Vaccination. 8vo. Lond., 1820.
                    A 12 S 33

BLANE (William Newnham). Excursion through the United States and Canada, during the years 1822-23; by "An English Gentleman." 8vo. Lond., 1824. D 3 S 47

BLANFORD (Henry F.) Reports on the Meteorology of India in 1875-76. 2 vols. fol. Calcutta, 1877-78.   E

BLANFORD (W. T.), F.R.S., &c. Zoology and Geology, Eastern Persia. [*See* PERSIA.]
[*See* MEDLICOTT, H. B.]

BLANQUI (JÉRÔME ADOLPHE). History of Political Economy in Europe; translated from the fourth French edition, by Emily J. Leonard; with Preface by David A. Wells. 8vo. New York, 1880. F 10 R 10

BLAQUIERE (EDWARD). Letters from the Mediterranean; containing a Civil and Political Account of Sicily, Tripoly, Tunis, and Malta. 2 vols. 8vo. Lond., 1813. D 9 S 7, 8
Narrative of a Residence in Algiers. [*See* PANANTI, SIGNOR.]

BLAVATSKY (MME. H. P.) Isis Unveiled: a Master-key to the Mysteries of Ancient and Modern Science and Theology. 4th ed. 2 vols. 8vo. New York, 1878. G 16 U 7, 8

BLAXLAND (GREGORY). Journal of a Tour of Discovery across the Blue Mountains, in New South Wales. 12mo. Lond., 1823.* MD 1 S 57
Another copy. 2nd ed. 12mo. Sydney, 1870. MJ 2 P 32

BLAXLAND (JOHN). Protest against the Police and Gaol Funds. [*See* BLAND, W.]

BLAYNEY (MAJOR-GEN. ANDREW THOMAS), LORD. Narrative of a Forced Journey through Spain and France, as a Prisoner of War, in 1810-14. 2 vols. 8vo. Lond., 1814. D 7 U 37, 38

BLAZE DE BURY (MARIE P. R. STEWART), BARONNE. Germania in 1850; its Courts, Camp, and People. 2nd ed. 2 vols 8vo. Lond., 1851. D 8 U 8, 9

BLEASDALE (REV. JOHN IGNATIUS), D.D., &c. On Colonial Wines: a Paper read before the Royal Society of Victoria, 13th May, 1867; together with the Report of the late Intercolonial Exhibition Jury in Class 3, Section 9, Wines. 8vo. Melb., 1867. MA 1 Q 2
Two Essays drawn up for the Official Record of the Exhibition held in Melbourne, in 1872-73. 1. On Colonial Wines. 2. On Preserved Meats; being for the most part a Study of a Process of Freezing Fresh Meat for Exportation. 8vo. Melb., 1873. MA 1 Q 2

BLEECK (A. H.) Avesta: Religious Books of the Parsees. [*See* AVESTA.]

BLEEK (FRIEDRICH.) Introduction to the Old Testament; translated by G. H. Venables. 2 vols. 8vo. Lond., 1869. G 13 Q 17, 18

BLEEK (WILHELM HEINRICH IMMANUEL), PH.D. The Languages of Mosambique: Vocabularies of the Dialects of Lourenzo Marques, Inhambane, Sofala, Tette, Sena, Quellimane, Mosambique, Capo Delgado, Anjoane, the Maravi, Mudsau, &c. Drawn up from the Mss. of Dr. William Peters. Ob. 18mo. Lond., 1856. < 11 S 4
[*See* GREY, SIR G.]

BLEEKER (DR. P.) Atlas Ichthyologique des Indes Orientales Néêrlandaises. 9 vols. roy. fol. Amsterdam, 1862-77. A 4 R 5-13 ‡
Over eenige Visschen van Van Diemensland. 4to. Batavia, 1854. MA 1 Q 4 †
Reis door de *Minahassa* en den Molukschen Archipel; gedaan in de Maanden September en Oktober, 1855-2 vols. roy. 8vo. Batavia, 1856. D 5 V 30, 31

BLENKINSOP (REV. EDWIN L.), M.A. Memoirs of; written by himself. 2 vols. 8vo. Lond., 1852. C 3 8 6, 7

BLESSINGTON (MARGUERITE POWER), COUNTESS OF. Conversations of Lord Byron with the Countess of Blessington. 8vo. Lond., 1834. C 8 S 19
Idler in France. 2 vols. 12mo. Philad., 1841. D 8 P 26, 27
Idler in Italy. 3 vols. 8vo. Lond., 1839-40. D 8 U 20-22
Literary Life and Correspondence of; by R. R. Madden, M.D., &c. 3 vols. 8vo. Lond., 1855. C 10 P 17-19

BLETERIE or BLETTERIE (J. P. R DE LA), L'ABBÉ. Vie de l'Empereur Julien. 12mo. Paris, 1775. C 1 T 37

BLIGH (CAPT. WILLIAM), R.N. Account of the Dangerous Voyage performed by Captain Bligh, with a part of the Crew of H.M.S. *Bounty*, in an open boat, over 1,200 Leagues of the Ocean, from Tofoa to Timor, in the year 1789. 18mo. Dublin, 1817. MD 2 P 24
Answer to certain Assertions contained in the Appendix to a Pamphlet entitled "Minutes of the Proceedings on the Court-martial held at Portsmouth, August 12th, 1792, on ten persons charged with Mutiny on board H.M.S. *Bounty*." 4to. Lond., 1794. MD 4 P 25 †
Narrative of the Mutiny on board H.M.S. *Bounty*. 4to. Lond., 1790. MD 4 P 25 †
Trial of Lieut-Col. George Johnston for deposing [Commander] William Bligh. [*See* JOHNSTON, LIEUT.-COL. G.]
Voyage to the South Sea, in H.M.S. *Bounty*; including an Account of the Mutiny on board the said ship. 4to. Lond., 1792.* MD 7 Q 11 †
[*See* BARROW, SIR J.; BELCHER, LADY; *and* MACFARLAND, A.]

BLIND (MATHILDE). [Life of] Madame Roland. 8vo. Lond., 1886. C 2 8 35
The Old Faith and the New. [*See* STRAUSS, D. F.]

BLINDENLEHRER-CONGRESS VERHANDLUNGEN. 8vo. Amsterdam, 1886. E

BLISS (THOMAS), B.A., AND FRANCIS (G. GRANT), F.S.A. Some Account of Sir Hugh Johnys, and of his Monumental Brass. 8vo. Swansea, 1845. C 9 V 25

BLOCH (MARC ÉLIÉSER), M.D., &c. Ichthyologie; ou, Histoire naturelle; générale et particulière des Poissons. 12 parts (in 6 vols.) fol. Berlin, 1785-97. A 4 Q 17-22 ‡

BLOCK (MAURICE). Dictionnaire général de la Politique; avec la Collaboration d'hommes d'état, de publicistes, et d'écrivains de tous les pays. Nouvelle édition. 2 vols. roy. 8vo. Paris, 1873-74. K 11 R 5, 6

BLOME (RICHARD). Britannia; or, a Geographical Description of the Kingdoms of England, Scotland, and Ireland, with the Isles and Territories thereto belonging. Fol. Lond., 1673. D 7 V 33

BLOMEFIELD (REV. FRANCIS). An Essay towards a Topographical History of the County of Norfolk, continued by the Rev. Chas. Parkin, A.M., Rector of Oxburgh. 5 vols. fol. Fersfield, 1739-75. B 14 S 9-13 ‡

BLOMFIELD (RT. REV. C. J.), BISHOP OF LONDON. Charge delivered in St. Paul's Cathedral, on Saturday, November 2nd, 1850, on the occasion of his sixth visitation to the Clergy of the Diocese. 8vo. Geelong, 1851. MG 1 Q 40
Letter to His Grace the Lord Archbishop of Canterbury, upon the formation of a Fund for endowing additional Bishoprics in the Colonies. (Pam. 6.) 8vo. Lond., 1840. MJ 2 Q 1

BLOMFIELD (HENRY WILSON). The Great Libel Case, Reibey v. Blomfield. [*See* REIBEY, A. J.]

BLONDIN (J. N.) Grammaire Polyglotte. Française-Latine, Italienne, Espagnole, Portugaise et Anglais. 8vo. Paris, 1814. K 12 R 15

BLOOMFIELD (BENJAMIN), LORD, G.C.B., &c. Memoir of; edited by Georgiana; Lady Bloomfield. 2 vols. 8vo. Lond., 1884. C 10 R 8, 9

BLOOMFIELD (GEORGIANA), LADY. Memoir of Benjamin Lord Bloomfield, G.C.B., &c. 2 vols. 8vo. Lond., 1884. C 10 R 8, 9

BLOOMFIELD (ROBERT). The Farmer's Boy: a Rural Poem. 3rd ed. [with cuts by Bewick]. 8vo. Lond., 1800. H 5 U 22
Rural Tales, Ballads, and Songs. [Illustrated by Thomas Bewick.] 8vo. Lond., 1802. H 6 S 11
Wild Flowers; or, Pastoral and Local Poetry; [with cuts by Bewick]. 12mo. Lond., 1806. H 5 R 10
[*See* BRITISH POETS, 4.]

BLORE (EDWARD), F.S.A. Monumental Remains of Noble and Eminent Persons; comprising the Sepulchral Antiquities of Great Britain. Engraved from Drawings by Edwd. Blore, F.S.A. Imp. 8vo. Lond., 1826. B 2 T 20

BLORE (THOMAS). The History and Antiquities of the County of Rutland. Imp. fol. Stamford, 1811. B 14 U 2 ‡

BLOSSEVILLE (MARQUIS DE). Histoire de la Colonisation Pénale et des Etablissements de l'Angleterre en Australie. 8vo. Evreux, 1859. MB 2 Q 1

BLOUET (ABEL). Expédition Scientifique de Morée, Architecture, Sculptures, Inscriptions et Vues du Péloponèse, des Cyclades et de l'Attique. 3 vols. imp. fol. Paris, 1831-38. A 12 P 22-24 ‡

BLOUET (PAUL), "MAX O'RELL." John Bull et son Ile: Mœurs anglaises contemporaines. 48e éd. 8vo. Paris, 1885. J 1 U 13
John Bull and his Island; translated from the French, by the Author. 8vo. Lond., 1884. J 1 U 14
John Bull's Womankind. 8vo. Lond., 1885. J 1 U 15
Reply to John Bull and his Island. [*See* JOHN BULL.]
[*See* JOHN BULL'S NEIGHBOUR.]

BLOUNT (EDWARD), M.P. [*See* FULTON, REV. H., *and* THERRY, SIR R.]

BLOUNT (THOMAS). Animadversions upon Sir Richard Baker's Chronicle, and it's Continuation; wherein many Errors are discover'd, and some Truths advanced. 12mo. Oxford, 1672. B 3 P 17
Fragmenta Antiquitatis: Antient Tenures of Land, and Jocular Customs of some Manors. 12mo. Lond., 1679. B 3 P 31

BLOXAM (CHARLES LOUDON). Chemistry: Inorganic and Organic; with Experiments. 8vo. Lond., 1872. A 5 U 14
Hand-book of Medical Chemistry. [*See* BOWMAN, J. E.]
Metals: their Properties and Treatment. (Text-book of Science.) 2nd ed. 12mo. Lond., 1871. A 5 S 2
Laboratory Teaching; or, Progressive Exercises in Practical Chemistry. 2nd ed., revised. 8vo. Lond., 1871. A 5 S 33

BLOXAM (MATTHEW HOLBECHE). The Principles of Gothic Ecclesiastical Architecture; with an Explanation of Technical Terms, and a Centenary of Ancient Terms. 11th ed. 3 vols. 8vo. Lond., 1882. A 2 R 15-17

BLUE BOOKS OF NEW SOUTH WALES. [*See* NEW SOUTH WALES.]

BLUE BOOKS OF WESTERN AUSTRALIA. [*See* WESTERN AUSTRALIA.]

BLUMAUER (A.) Virgils Aeneis travestirt. 18mo. Leipzig (n.d.) H 6 P 19

BLUME (C. L.) Rumphia, sive Commentationes Botanicæ, imprimis de Plantis Indiæ Orientalis. 4 vols. roy. fol. Leyden, 1835-48. A 4 P 10-13 †

BLUMENBACH (PROF. JOHANN FRED.), M.D., F.R.S. Elements of Physiology; translated by J. Elliotson. 8vo. Lond., 1828. A 12 T 10
Handbuch der Naturgeschichte. Siebente Auflage. Nebst zwey Kupfertafeln. 12mo. Göttingen, 1803. A 17 T 54

BLUMENTHAL (PROF. CHARLES E.) Life of Jesus Christ [*See* NEANDER, DR. J. A. W.]

BLUMHARDT (REV. C. T.) Christian Missions; or, Manual of Missionary Geography and History. 18mo. Lond., 1845. MD 1 T 11

BLUMHARDT (J. F.) Charitábalí; or, Instructive Biography; by Isvarachandra Vidyáságara. With a Vocabulary of all the Words occurring in the Text, by J. F. Blumhardt. 12mo. Lond., 1884. C 2 Q 9

BLUNDELL (JAMES J.) Plan of Melbourne and its Suburbs. 8vo. Melb. (n.d.) MD 5 P 3 ‡

Squatters' Directory, and Key to the Squatting Map of Victoria. 12mo. Melb., 1862. MD 4 P 32

BLUNT (REV. HENRY), M.A. Family Exposition of the Pentateuch. 3 vols. 8vo. Lond., 1841–43. G 13 R 1–3

Posthumous Sermons, with Pastoral Letters. 3 vols. 12mo. Lond., 1844–46. G 13 R 29–31

BLUNT (REV. JOHN HENRY), Sketch of the Reformation in England. (Fam. Lib.) 12mo. Lond., 1832. K 10 P 36

M.A., &c. Reformation of the Church of England; its History, Principles, and Results. (1514–1662.) 2 vols. 8vo. Lond., 1878–82. G 6 Q 2, 3

BLUNT (WILFRID SCAWEN). Ideas about India. 8vo. Lond., 1885. F 6 Q 33

BLUNTSCHLI (J. C.) Geschichte des allgemeinen Staatsrechts und der Politik. (Geschichte der Wissenschaften.) 8vo. München, 1867. A 17 V 15

Theory of the State. 8vo. Oxford, 1885. F 10 Q 16

BLYTH (ALEXANDER WYNTER), M.R.C.S., F.C.S., &c. Dictionary of Hygiène and Public Health; comprising Sanitary Chemistry, &c. 8vo. Lond., 1876. K 18 P 27

Poisons; their Effects and Detection: a Manual for the Use of Analytical Chemists and Experts; with an Introductory Essay on the growth of Modern Toxicology. 8vo. Lond., 1884. A 12 P 36

BLYTH (E.) Report on the Collection of Australian Vertebrata, contained in the Museum of the Asiatic Society, Calcutta. 8vo. Calcutta, 1848. M A 2 V 6

BOADEN (CAROLINE) WILLIAM THOMPSON; or, which is he: a Farce. (Cumberland's Eng. Theatre.) 12mo. Lond., 1829. H 2 Q 16

Fatality: a Drama. (Cumberland's Eng. Theatre.) 12mo. Lond., 1829. H 2 Q 17

BOADEN (JAMES). Life of Mrs. Jordan; including Original Private Correspondence, and numerous Anecdotes of her Contemporaries. 2 vols. 8vo. Lond., 1831. C 5 T 13, 14

Memoirs of the Life of John Philip Kemble; including a History of the Stage, from the time of Garrick to the present period. 2 vols. 8vo. Lond., 1825. C 7 T 27, 28

Memoirs of Mrs. Siddons; interspersed with Anecdotes of Authors and Actors. 2 vols. 8vo. Lond., 1872. C 9 V 33, 34

BOARD OF TRADE, LONDON. Wind Charts. El. fol. Lond., 1856. D 8 P 13 ‡

BOBART (REV. H. H.), M.A. [*See* CHRISTIAN KNOWLEDGE SOC.]

BOBBIN (TIM). [*See* REVELATIONS OF P[ORT] A[RTHUR.]

BOCCACCIO (GIOVANNI). The Decameron; or, Ten Days' Entertainment of Boccaccio; translated from the Italian. The 2nd ed., corrected and improved; to which are prefixed, Remarks on the Life and Writings of Boccaccio. 2 vols. 8vo. Lond., 1804. J 5 Q 9, 10

Del Decamerone, di con un Discorso critico da Ugo Foscolo. 3 vols. 8vo. Lond., 1825. J 5 Q 11–13

Treatise shewing the Falles of Princes and Princesses, with other Nobles, through ye mutabilitie and change of unstedfast Fortune, together with their most detestable and wicked Vices. First compyled in Latin by the excellent Clerke Bocatius, and sence that tyme translated into our English and vulgare tong, by John [Lydgate or] Lidgate. Sm. fol. Lond., 1554. H 4 R 15 †

BOCK (CARL). Head Hunters of Borneo: a Narrative of Travel up the Mahakkam and down the Barito; also Journeyings in Sumatra. Illustrated. Imp. 8vo. Lond., 1881. D 5 V 26

Temples and Elephants: the Narrative of a Journey of Exploration through Upper Siam and Lao. 8vo. Lond., 1884. D 6 S 22

BODDAM-WHETHAM (J.W.) [*See* WHETHAM, J.W.B.]

BODDY (EVAN MARLETT), F.R.C.S., &c. History of Salt; with Observations on its Geographical Distribution, Geological Formation, and Medicinal and Dietetic Properties. 8vo. Lond., 1881. A 16 S 27

BODE (BARON C. A.) [*See* DE BODE.]

BODENSTEDT (F.) [*See* MIRZA CHAFY.]

BOECE (HECTOR), CANON OF ABERDEEN. [*See* BOETHIUS, H.]

BOECKH (AUGUSTUS). Public Economy of Athens, in four Books; to which is added a Dissertation on the Silver Mines of Laurion; translated from the German. 2 vols. 8vo. Lond., 1828. B 9 T 40, 41

BOEHME (JACOB). [*See* BOHME, J.]

BOEIS (HECTOR). [*See* BOETHIUS, H.]

BOETHIUS (ANICIUS MANLIUS TORQUATUS SEVERINUS). Consolation of Philosophy; translated, with Notes and Illustrations, by the Rev. P. Ridpath. 8vo. Lond., 1785. G 11 T 4

De Consolatione Philosophiæ, libri quinque, ex Editione Vulpiana, cum Notis et Interpretatione in usum Delphini. 2 vols. 8vo. Lond., 1823. J 13 P 17, 18

King Alfred's Anglo-Saxon Version of Boethius de Consolatione Philosophiæ; with an English Translation, and Notes, by J. S. Cardale. 8vo. Lond., 1829. G 4 R 11

Opera omnia. [*See* MIGNE, J.P., SERIES LATINA, 63, 64.]

BOETHIUS (HECTOR), CANON OF ABERDEEN. Description of Scotland, written at the first in Latine, and translated into the Scotish Speech, by John Belleden, Archdeacon of Murrey, and now into English by Raphall Hollindshead; and continued from 1571 to 1585, by others. Fol. Lond., 1585–87. B 16 8 7 ‡

History and Chronicles of Scotland; written in Latin, and translated by John Belleden, Archdean of Moray, and Canon of Ross. 2 vols. 4to. Edinb., 1821. B 13 S 1, 2

BOETIUS (HECTOR). [*See* BOETHIUS, H.]

BOGLE (GEORGE). Narrative of the Mission of George Bogle to Tibet. [*See* MARKHAM, C. R.]

BOGUE (ADAM). Steam to Australia, its General Advantages considered ; the different proposed Routes for connecting London and Sydney compared. (Pam. 19.) 8vo. Sydney, 1848. MJ 2 Q 8

Another copy. (Pam. 21.) MJ 2 Q 10

BOGUE (DAVID). British Painters of the 18th and 19th Centuries. 8vo. Lond., 1880. A 8 U 12

BOHEMIAN UNIVERSITY STUDENT, A. [*See* HAPPY DELIVERY OF A LEGAL LADY.]

BÖHME (JACOB). His Life and Teaching ; or, Studies in Theosophy; by Dr. Hans Lassen Martensen; translated from the Danish, by T. Rhys Evans. 8vo. Lond., 1885. C 5 R 7

[*See* WALTON, C.]

BOHN (HENRY G.) Catalogue of Books. 8vo. Lond., 1841. Libr.

Dictionary of Quotations from the English Poets. 8vo. Lond., 1881. H 5 T 27

Guide to the Knowledge of Pottery, Porcelain, and other objects of Vertu. 8vo. Lond., 1872. A 23 Q 19

Hand-book of Games; comprising new or carefully revised Treatises on Whist, Piquet, Ecarté, Lansquenet, Boston, Quadrille, Cribbage, and other Card Games; Faro, Rouge et Noir, Hazard, Roulette ; Backgammon, Draughts; Billiards, Bagatelle, American Bowls, etc. New ed. 8vo. . Lond., 1873. A 17 U 14

Another copy. 8vo. Lond., 1884. A 17 U 15

Hand-book of Proverbs. 8vo. Lond., 1875. K 19 P 11

Pictorial Hand-book of Modern Geography; with numerous Tables, and a General Index. 3rd ed. 12mo. Lond., 1865. D 11 R 1

Polyglot of Foreign Proverbs, comprising French, Italian, German, Dutch, Spanish, Portuguese, and Danish; with English Translations, and a General Index. 8vo. Lond., 1867. K 11 U 6

Standard Library Atlas of Classical Geography, completed to the Present State of Knowledge. (In Latin.) Roy. 8vo. Lond., 1861. D 33 P 8 ‡

Standard Library Cyclopædia of Political, Constitutional, Statistical and Forensic Knowledge. 4 vols. 8vo. Lond., 1860. K 5 U 8–11

Fosteriana. [*See* FOSTER, J.]

[*See* LOWNDES, W. T.]

M

BOILEAU (MAJOR-GEN. J. T.) F.R.S., &c. A New and complete Set of Traverse Tables, shewing the Differences of Latitude, and thé Departures to every minute of the Quadrant, and to five places of Decimals. 4th ed. 8vo. Lond., 1876. A 10 U 17

BOILEAU–DESPREAUX (NICOLAS). Œuvres de ; avec des Eclaircissemens historiques. 2 vols 4to. Genève, 1716. J 4 T 1, 2

BOISDUVAL (DR. J. A.) Considérations sur des Lépidoptères envoyés du Guatemala. Roy. 8vo. Paris, 1870. A 13 U 40

Essai sur l'Entomologie horticole, comprenant l'Histoire des Insectes nuisibles a l'Horticulture. 8vo. Paris, 1867. A 14 T 34

Faune entomologique de l'Océanie, comprenant les Coléoptères, les Hémiptères, les Orthoptères, les Névroptères, les Hyménoptères, et les Diptères. Roy. 8vo. Paris, 1835. MA 2 U 9

Genera et Index Methodicus Europæorum Lepidopterorum. 8vo. Paris, 1840. A 14 S 39

[*See* DUMONT D'URVILLE, CAPT. J. S. C.]

BOISGELIN (LOUIS DE), KNIGHT OF MALTA. Ancient and Modern Malta, containing a full and accurate Account of the Present State of the Islands of Malta and Goza, the History of the Knights of St. John of Jerusalem. 2 vols. 4to. Lond., 1805. B 17 Q 19, 20 ‡

BOISSIÈRE (M. P. B. DE LA). [*See* NASH, F.]

BOISTE (PIERRE CLAUDE VICTOIRE). Dictionnaire universel de la Langue Française. 14e éd., revue, corrigée, considérablement augmentée, par MM. Charles Nodier et Louis Barré. 4to. Paris, 1857. K 16 S 3

BOITARD (PIERRE), ET CANIVET (E.) Manuel du Naturaliste Préparateur. 2nd ed. 18mo. Paris, 1828. A 14 Q 52

BOJESEN (MRS. MARIA). The Danish Speaker: Pronunciation of the Danish Language, Vocabulary, Dialogues, and Idioms, for the use of Students, and Travellers in Denmark and Norway. 12mo. Lond., 1865. K 11 V 15

BOLANDER (H. N.) Catalogue of the Plants growing in the vicinity of San Francisco. Sm. fol. San Francisco, 1870. A 2 P 21 †

BOLDREWOOD (ROLF). [*See* BROWNE, T. A.]

BOLEYN (ANNE), QUEEN OF HENRY VIII. [*See* ANNE BOLEYN, QUEEN.]

BOLINGBROKE (HENRY ST. JOHN) VISCOUNT. Bolingbroke : a Historical Study; and Voltaire in England; by John C. Collins. 8vo. Lond., 1886. C 5 R 5

Memoirs of; by G. W. Cooke. 2 vols. 8vo. Lond., 1835. C 6 Q 3, 4

Works of; with the Life of Lord Bolingbroke, by Dr. Goldsmith. New ed. 8 vols. 8vo. Lond., 1809. J 5 T 18–25

BOLLAERT (WILLIAM), F.R.G.S. Antiquarian, Ethnological, and other Researches in New Granada, Equador, Peru, and Chile ; with Observations on the Pre-Incarial, Incarial, and other Monuments of Peruvian Nations. Illustrated. 8vo. Lond., 1860.　　　　B 1 S 15

Wars of Succession of Portugal and Spain, 1826–40 ; with Maps and Illustrations. 2 vols. 8vo. Lond., 1870.
　　　　　　　　　　　B 13 U 11, 12

BOLLANDUS (JEAN). Præfationes, Tractatus, Diatribæ et Exegeses Præliminares, atque nonnulla veneraidæ Antiquitatis tum sacræ, cum profanæ monumenta. 3 vols. fol. Venetiis, 1749–51.　　　G 29 Q 2-4 ‡

BOLLER (ALFRED P.), A.M. Practical Treatise on the Construction of Iron Highway Bridges. Roy. 8vo. New York, 1876.　　　　　　　　A 6 T 24

BOLLES (ALBERT S.) Financial History of the United States, from 1774–1885, embracing the Period of the American Revolution. 3 vols. 8vo. New York, 1879–86.　　　　　　　　B 1 U 30–32

Industrial History of the United States, from the Earliest Settlements to the Present Time ; being a complete Survey of American Industries. 8vo. Norwich, Conn., 1878.　　　　　　　　A 11 T 21

Practical Banking. 8vo. New York, 1884.　　F 13 R 16

BOLLEY (DR. P. A.) Manual of Technical Analysis. [*See* PAUL, B. H.]

BOLSTER (JOHN). Bolster's Quarterly Magazine. Vol. 1. 8vo. Lond., 1828.　　　　　　　　E

BOLTON (COL. SIR FRANCIS), C.E. London Water Supply. (International Health Exhibition, Lond., 1884). 8vo. Lond., 1884.　　　　　　　A 6 T 13

BOLTON (HENRY CARRINGTON). Catalogue of Scientific and Technical Periodicals, 1665–82. 8vo. Washington, 1885.　　　　　　　　K 8 P 29

BOLTON (SOLOMON). Extinct Peerage of England ; containing a succinct Account of all the Peers whose Titles are expired ; with their Descents, Marriages, and Issues, Offices in Government, and Memorable Actions, from the Conquest to the year 1769. 8vo. Lond., 1769.　　　K 10 S 12

BOLTON PUBLIC LIBRARY. Regulations for the Bolton Public Library ; with Catalogue of the Books. (Pam. 40.) 12mo. Bolton, 1791.　　　MJ 2 R 2

BOMBAY. General Report on the Administration of the Bombay Presidency for the year 1875–76. Roy. 8vo. Bombay, 1876.　　　　　　　　E

BOMBET (L. A. C.) [*See* BEYLE, MARIE H.]

BOMHOFF (D.) Dictionary of the English and Dutch [and Dutch and English] Language ; to which is added a Catalogue of the most usual Proper Names and a List of the Irregular Verbs. Revised. 4th ed. 2 vols. 12mo. Nimmegen, 1851.　　　　　　　K 11 T 36–37

BOMPAS (GEORGE C.) Life of Frank Buckland ; with Portrait. 8vo. Lond., 1885.　　　　C 5 R 9

BON GAULTIER. [*See* AYTOUN, W.]

BONAPARTE (CHARLES LUCIEN). American Ornithology. [*See* WILSON, A.]

Conspectus Generum Avium, et Index. 3 vols. (in 1) roy. 8vo. Leyden, 1850–57.　　　　A 15 R 4

Index ad Conspectum Generum Avium ; auctore O. Finsch. Roy. 8vo. Leyden, 1865.　　　A 15 R 4

BONAPARTE (LOUIS-LUCIEN), PRINCE. Parabola de Seminatore ex Evangelio Matthæi, in LXXII Europæas Linguas, ac Dialectos versa, et Romanis Characteribus Expressa. 8vo. Lond., 1857.　　　G 6 R 20

Specimen Lexici Comparativi omnium Linguarum Europæarum. Sm. fol. Florence, 1847.　　K 3 S 5 †

BONAPARTE (LUCIEN), PRINCE DE CANINO. Charlemagne ; ou, l'Eglise délivrée : Poème épique. 2 vols. 4to. Lond., 1814.　　　　　　　H 5 V 21, 22

Memoirs ; written by himself. 8vo. Lond., 1836.　　C 8 T 9

BONAPARTE (NAPOLEON). [*See* NAPOLEON.]

BONAPARTE (ROLAND), PRINCE. Les récents Voyages des Néerlandais à la Nouvelle-Guinée. 4to. Versailles, 1885.　　　　　　　MD 3 V 22

BONAR (MR.) Thoughts, on board the *Crœsus*, of England and Australia. (Pam. 36.) 8vo. Geelong, 1854. MJ 2 Q 23

BONAR (ANDREW A.), AND MACCHEYNE (R.M.) Narrative of a Mission of Inquiry to the Jews, from the Church of Scotland, in 1839. 2nd ed. 2 vols. 8vo. Edinb., 1842.　　　　　　　D 9 T 33, 34

BONAR (REV. ANDREW R.) Last Days of Eminent Christians. 12mo. Lond., 1850.　　　G 9 Q 13

BONAR (JAMES), M.A. Malthus and his Work. 8vo. Lond., 1885.　　　　　　　F 7 S 20

BOND (A. L.) The Miller's Daughter ; by Alfred Tennyson. [*See* TENNYSON, A. BARON.]

BOND (G.) Brief Account of the Colony of Port Jackson in New South Wales : its Native Inhabitants, Productions, &c. 8vo. Southampton, 1803.*　　MD 1 W 8

BOND (R.), AND MCGREGOR (W.) Hand-book of the Telegraph. (Weale.) 12mo. Lond., 1873. A 17 Q 27

BONIFACE (SAINT), Bonifaz und Lul ; ihre angelsächsischen Korrespondenten. Erzbischof Luls Leben, von Heinrich Hahn. 8vo. Leipzig, 1853.　　C 10 P 6

BONN UNIVERSITY. Index Scholarum quae in Universitate Frid. Guil. Rhenana, 1860, publice privatimque habebuntur; praecedit elogium L Cornell Cn. F. Cn. N. Scipionis. (Pam. O.) 4to. Bonn, 1860.   J 6 U 10

Index Scholarum, in Universitate Frid. Guil. Rhenana, 1859; praecedunt Porcii Licini de vita Terentii versus integritati restituti. (Pam. O.) 4to. Bonn, 1859.
J 6 U 10

Index Scholarum in Universitate Frid. Guil. Rhenana, 1859–60; praecedit disputatio de poetarum testimoniis quae sunt in vita Terentii Suetoniana. (Pam. O.) 4to. Bonn, 1860.   J 6 U 10

Index Scholarum in Universitate Frid. Guil. Rhenana, 1860–61; praecedunt in leges Visellium Antoniam Corneliam observationes epigraphicae. (Pam. O.) 4to. Bonn, 1861.   J 6 U 10

Indicia quinque ordinum Universitatis Frid. Guil. Rhenanae de Litterarum certaminibus anni. 1858–59 facta, novaeque quaestiones anno. 1859–60 propositae. (Pam. O.) 4to. Bonn, 1860.   J 6 U 10

Vorlesungen auf der rheinischen Friedrich-Wilhelms-Universität zu Bonn, 1859–61. (Pam. O.) 4to. Bonn, 1859–61.   J 6 U 10

BONNARD (HENRY E.) Report of the Executive Secretary on the Bordeaux International Exhibition of Wines, 1882. Fol. Sydney, 1884.*   MA 2 Q 47 †

BONNECHOSE (ÉMILE DE). Réformateurs avant la Réforme, XVᵉ Siècle. Jean Hus et le Concile de Constance. Troisième édition. 2 vols. 8vo. Paris, 1860. G 13 S 17, 18

BONNER (T. D.) Life and Adventures of James P. Beckwourth, Mountaineer, Scout, and Pioneer, and Chief of the Crow Nation of Indians. With Illustrations. 8vo. Lond., 1856.   C 3 R 5

BONNET (JULES). Lettres de Jean Calvin. [*See* CALVIN, J.]

BONNEY (CHARLES). Letters to H. F. Gurner. [*See* MANUSCRIPTS AND PORTRAITS.]

BONNEY (S. B.) Melbourne and Suburbs. Lithographed at the Department of Lands and Survey, Melbourne, by S. B. Bonney, September, 1876. (Map.) Roy. 4to. Melb., 1876.   MD 5 S 15 ‡

BONNYCASTLE (PROF. JOHN). Treatise on Plane and Spherical Trigonometry; with their most useful practical Applications. 2nd ed., corrected and improved 8vo. Lond., 1813.   A 10 R 17

BONNYCASTLE (LIEUT.-COL. SIR RICHARD HENRY), KNT. Canada and the Canadians in 1846. 2 vols. 8vo. Lond., 1846.   D 4 P 16, 17

The Canadas in 1841. 2 vols. 8vo. Lond., 1842. D 4 P 12, 13

Newfoundland in 1842: a Sequel to "The Canadas in 1841." 2 vols. 8vo. Lond., 1842.   D 4 P 14, 15

BONOMI (JOSEPH), F.R.S.L. Nineveh and its Palaces: the Discoveries of Botta and Layard, applied to the elucidation of Holy Writ. 2nd ed., revised. 8vo. Lond., 1853.   B 10 P 27

Egyptian Antiquities. [*See* ARUNDALE, F.]

BONPLAND (AIMÉ). Travels to the Equinoxial Regions of the New Continent. [*See* HUMBOLDT, A. H. A. VON.]

BONWICK (JAMES), F.R.G.S. Australian Gold-digger's Monthly Magazine, and Colonial Family Visitor. Conducted by Mr. James Bonwick, F.R.G.S. 12mo. Melh., 1852–53.   MJ 2 P 30

Another copy. (Pam. 39.) 12mo. Melb., 1853. MJ 2 R 1

Bible Stories for Young Australians. 12mo. Geelong, 1857.   MJ 2 P 34

British Colonies and their Resources: Africa. 8vo. Lond., 1886.   MD 4 Q 17

British Colonies and their Resources: America. 8vo. 8vo. Lond., 1886.   MD 4 Q 17

British Colonies and their Resources: Asia. 8vo. Lond., 1886.   MD 4 Q 17

British Colonies and their Resources: Australasia. 8vo. Lond., 1886.   MD 4 Q 17

The Bushrangers; illustrating the Early Days of Van Diemen's Land. 12mo. Melb., 1856.*   MD 4 Q 9.

Curious Facts of Old Colonial Days. 12mo. Lond., 1870.*   MB 2 P 7

Daily Life and Origin of the Tasmanians. 8vo. Lond., 1870.*   MA 1 S 12

Discovery and Settlement of Port Phillip; being a History of the Country now called Victoria, up to the arrival of Mr. Superintendent Latrobe, in October, 1839. Revised, at request, by W. Westgarth, Esq. 8vo. Melb., 1856.*   MB 2 P 1

Early Days of England. 12mo. Melb., 1857. MJ 2 P 34

Another copy. (Pam. 44.)   MJ 2 R 6

Early Days of Melbourne. 12mo. Melh., 1857. MJ 2 P 34

First Grammar for Young Australians. 2nd ed. (Pam. 44.) 12mo. Melh., 1858.   MJ 2 R 6

First Twenty Years of Australia: a History founded on Official Documents. 8vo. Lond., 1882.*   MB 2 P 4

French Colonies and their Resources. 8vo. Lond., 1886.   MD 4 Q 16

Geography for the Use of Australian Youth. 18mo. Hobart, 1845.   MD 2 P 25

Geography of Australia and New Zealand. 3rd ed. 12mo. Melh., 1855.   MD 2 P 25

Geography for Young Australians. 9th ed. 12mo. Melb., 1875.   MJ 2 P 34

Grammar for Australian Youth. 12mo. Adelaide, 1851.   MJ 2 P 34

Grammar for Australian Youth. 2nd Part. 12mo. Melb., 1868.   MJ 2 P 32

BONWICK (James), F.R.G.S.—*continued.*

How does a Tree grow? or, Botany for Young Australians. 12mo. Melb., 1857.   MJ 2 P 34

Another copy. (Pam. 44.)   MJ 2 R 6

John Batman, the Founder of Victoria. 2nd ed. 12mo.
Melb., 1868.   MC 1 P 34

Last of the Tasmanians; or, the Black War of Van
Diemen's Land. 8vo. Lond., 1870.*   MB 2 T 16

The Lost Tasmanian Race. 8vo. Lond., 1884.   MD 4 Q 14

Mike Howe, the Bushranger of Van Diemen's Land. 8vo.
Lond., 1873.*   MJ 1 S 36

The Mormons and the Silver Mines. 8vo. Lond., 1872.
     D 3 P 54

Notes of a Gold-digger, and Gold Diggers' Guide. 12mo.
Melb., 1852.   MJ 2 P 30

Port Phillip Settlement. 8vo. Lond., 1883.   MB 2 T 19

The Resources of Queensland. With a Map of Queensland, containing the recent Discoveries. 8vo. Lond.,
1880.*   MD 4 Q 12

Romance of the Wool Trade. 8vo. Lond., 1887.*   MF 1 P 46

Sketch of Boroondara. 12mo. Melb., 1858.   MD 1 S 14

Another copy.   MJ 2 P 30

Spirit of the True Teacher: a Lecture. 8vo. Melb.,
1857.   MG 1 Q 39

The Tasmanian Lily. 8vo. Lond., 1873.*   MJ 1 S 34

Wesleyan Methodism in South Australia. 12mo. Adelaide, 1851.   MJ 2 P 34

Western Australia: its Past and Future. 8vo. Lond.,
1885.   MD 4 Q 15

Western Victoria: its Geography, Geology, and Social
Condition: the Narrative of an Educational Tour in 1857.
12mo. Geelong, 1858.   MD 4 Q 11

The Wild White Man [William Buckley], and the Blacks
of Victoria. 2nd ed. 8vo. Melb., 1863.*   MD 7 Q 5

William Buckley, the Wild White Man, and his Port
Phillip Black Friends. 8vo. Melb., 1856. MC 1 R 27

Another copy. (Pam. 29.)   MJ 2 Q 17

BOODLE (Rev. R. G.), M.A. The Life and Labours of
the Rt. Rev. William Tyrrell, D.D., first Bishop of Newcastle, New South Wales. 8vo. Lond., 1881. MC 1 Q 7

BOOK-LORE: Magazine devoted to Old-Time Literature.
Vol. 1. 4to. Lond., 1885.   E

BOOK OF ELEGANT EXTRACTS, illustrated by eminent
Artists. Sm. 4to. Edinb. (n.d.)   J 12 R 23

BOOK OF THOUGHT (The); or, Observations and
Passages relating to Religion, Morals, Manners, and
Characters. 12mo. Lond., 1842.   G 10 Q 3

BOOKS FOR A REFERENCE LIBRARY, being
Lectures on the Books in the Reference Department of
the Free Public Library, Birmingham. 1st Series. 8vo.
Lond., 1885.   J 9 V 24

BOOKWORM (The). Literary and Bibliographical Review. Edited and Illustrated by J. Ph. Berjeau. 4 vols.
(in 2) roy. 8vo. Lond., 1866–70.   E

BOOSÉ (J. R.) [*See* Royal Colonial Institute.]

BOOTH (Abraham). Death of Legal Hope, the Life of Evangelical Obedience. 12mo. Mirzapore, 1853. MG 1 P 48

BOOTH (Arthur John), M.A. Robert Owen, the
Founder of Socialism in England. 12mo. Lond., 1869.
     C 2 Q 28

BOOTH (David). An Analytical Dictionary of the English Language. 4to. Lond., 1835.   K 15 U 3

The Art of Brewing. New ed. 8vo. Lond., 1872. A 11 Q 23

BOOTH (Edwin Carton), F.R.C.I. Another England.
Life, Living, Homes, and Homemakers in Victoria. 8vo.
Lond., 1869.*   MD 3 R 31

Australia. Illustrated; by J. Skinner Prout, N. Chevalier, &c. 2 vols. 4to. Lond., 1880.*   MD 4 P 16, 17 †

Homes away from Home, and the Men who make them
in Victoria. 8vo. Lond., 1869.   MF 1 Q 3

BOOTH (G.) [*See* Diodorus Siculus.]

BOOTH (John). The Battle of Waterloo, &c., forming an
Historical Record in the Campaign of the Netherlands;
by "A Near Observer." 8vo. Lond., 1815.   B 8 P 41

BOOTHBY (Hon. Benjamin), Judge. Minutes of Proceedings of the Executive Council relating to the conduct
of Mr. Justice Boothby; together with Appendix. Fol.
Adelaide, 1867.   MF 2 U 11

BOOTHBY (Josiah). The Adelaide Almanack, Town and
Country Directory, and Guide to South Australia. 12mo.
Adelaide, 1864.*   ME 4 P

The Adelaide Almanack and Directory for South Australia, 1872; together with Official, Ecclesiastical, Legal,
Banking and Mercantile Directory. 8vo. Adelaide,
1872.   ME 3 U

Statistical Sketch of South Australia. 8vo. Lond., 1876.
     MF 2 Q 33

BOOTY (P. G.) Common Law Procedure Act. [*See*
Pilcher, C. E.]

BOPP (Franz). Comparative Grammar of the Sanskrit,
Zend, Greek, Latin, Lithuanian, Gothic, German, and
Sclavonic Languages; translated from the German by
Edward B. Eastwick, F.R.S., &c. 3rd ed. 3 vols. 8vo.
Lond., 1862.   K 16 Q 15–17

Die Celtischen Sprachen in ihrem Verhältnisse zum Sanskrit, Zend, Griechischen, Lateinischen, Germanischen,
Lithauischen und Slawischen. 4to. Berlin, 1839.
     K 13 T 5

Die Kaukasischen Glieder des indo-europäischen Sprach-
stamms. 4to. Berlin, 1847.   K 13 T 8

Glossarium Comparativum Linguae Sanscritae in quo omnes
Sanscritae Radices et Vocabula Unitatissima explicantur
et cum Vocabulis Graecis, Latinis, Germanicis, Lituanicis,
Slavicis, Celticis, comparantur. Editio Tertia. 4to.
Berolini, 1867.   C 14 S 18

Bop]　　　　　　PART I:—*Authors, Editors, or Reference.*　　　　[Bos

BOPP (FRANZ)—*continued.*

Glossarium Sanscritum, in quo omnes Radices et Vocabula Usitatissima explicantur et cum Vocabulis Græcis, Latinis, Germanicis, Lithuanicis Slavicis, Celticise, comparantur.　4to.　Berolini, 1847.　　　K 14 S 16

Grammaire Comparée des Langues Indo-Européennes, comprenant le Sanscrit, le Zend, l'Arménien, le Grec, le Latin, le Lithuanien, l'Ancien Slave, le Gothique et l'Allemand; traduite sur la seconde édition par M. Michel Bréal.　2nd éd.　5 vols. roy. 8vo.　Paris, 1874–78.　　K 12 T 11–15

Grammatica Critica Linguæ Sanscritæ.　Altera Emendata Editio.　8vo.　Berolini, 1832.　　　K 15 S 3

Kritische Grammatik der Sanskrita-Sprache in kürzerer Fassung.　4e durchgesehene Ausgabe.　8vo.　Berlin, 1868.　　　　　　　　　K 14 P 31

Über das Conjugationssystem der Sanskritsprache, in Vergleichung mit jenem der griechischen, lateinischen, persischen und germanischen Sprache.　Herausgegeben und mit Vorerinnerungen begleitet von Dr. K. J. Windischmann.　12mo.　Frankfurt am Main, 1816.　K 16 P 6

Über die Verwandtschaft der malayisch-polynesischen Sprachen mit den indisch-europäischen.　4to.　Berlin, 1841.　　　　　　　　　　K 16 R 11

Vocalismus oder sprachvergleichende Kritiken über J. Grimm's deutsche Grammatik und Graff's althochdeutschen Sprachschatz mit Begründung einer neuen Theorie des Ablauts.　8vo.　Berlin, 1836.　　K 13 Q 2

Vergleichende Grammatik desSanskrit,Send,Armenischen, Griechischen, Lateinischen, Litauischen, Altslavischen, Gothischen und Deutschen.　3e ausgabe.　3 vols. 8vo.　Berlin, 1868–71.　　　　　　　K 16 Q 12–14

Vergleichendes Accentuationssystem nebst einer gedrängten Darstellung der grammatischen Übereinstimmungen des Sanskrit und Griechischen.　8vo.　Berlin, 1854.　　　　　　　　　　　　K 13 P 2

BORCHARD.　DescriptioTerræSanotæ.　[*See* BROCARD, E.]

BORDE (VICOMTE H. DE LA.)　[*See* DE LA BORDE, VICOMTE.]

BORDEAUX (H. C. F., COMTE DE CHAMBORD), DUC DE.　Story of the Comte de Chambord: a Trilogy; by G. A. Sala.　12mo.　Lond., 1873.　　　　　　C 2 Q 8

BORDIER (DR. A.)　La Colonisation Scientifique, et les Colonies Françaises.　8vo.　Paris, 1884.　　F 10 R 11

BORDIER (HENRI), ET CHARTON (ÉDOUARD).　Histoire de France, depuis les Temps les plus anciens jusqu'à nos Jours.　Nouvelle édition.　2 vols. roy. 8vo.　Paris, 1881.　　　　　　　　　　　　B 8 V 1, 2

BORELLI (GIOVANNI ALFONSO).　Historia et Meteorologia Incendii Ætnæi anni 1669. 4to. Messina, 1670. A 3 S 39

BORGES (J.)　Diario de Borges.　8vo.　Madrid, 1862.　　　　　　　　　　　　　　　　　J 15 U 26

BORLASE (WILLIAM), LL.D., &c.　Antiquities, Historical and Monumental, of the County of Cornwall; with a Vocabulary of the Cornu-British Language.　Roy. fol.　Lond., 1769.　　　　　　　　B 16 S 8 †

BORN (IGNATIUS), BARON.　Testacea Musei Cæsarei Vindobonensis.　Fol.　Vindobonæ, 1780.　　A 23 Q 11 †
Travels through the Bannat of Temeswar, Transylvania, and Hungary, in the year 1770; to which is added John James Ferber's Mineralogical History of Bohemia.　Translated from the German, by R. E. Raspe.　8vo.　Lond., 1777.　　　　　　　　　　D 6 T 17

BORNET (E.)　Etudes Phycologiques. [*See* THURET, G.]

BORRADAILE (ARTHUR FREDERICK), A.M.I.C.E.　Sketch of the Borradailes of Cumberland.　4to.　Lond., 1881.　　　　　　　　　　　　　　　C 11 V 13

BORRER (DAWSON).　Journey from Naples to Jerusalem, by way of Athens, Egypt, and the Peninsula of Sinai.　8vo.　Lond., 1845.　　　　　　　　D 4 T 41

BORROW (GEORGE).　Bible in Spain; or, the Journeys, Adventures, the Imprisonments of an Englishman, in an attempt to circulate the Scriptures in the Peninsula.　3 vols. 12mo.　Lond., 1843.　　D 8 P 42–44
Another copy.　(H. and C. Lib.)　12mo.　Lond., 1849.　　　　　　　　　　　　　　　J 8 P 1
Wild Wales; its People, Language, and Scenery.　3 vols. 8vo.　Lond., 1862.　　　　　　　D 7 R 6–8
Zincali; or, an Account of the Gypsies of Spain, a Copious Dictionary of their Language.　3rd ed.　2 vols. 8vo.　Lond., 1843.　　　　　　　D 8 P 40–41
Another copy.　(H. and C. Lib.)　12mo.　Lond., 1861.　　　　　　　　　　　　　　　　J 8 P 14

BORTHWICK (J. D.)　Three Years in California.　Illustrated.　8vo.　Edinb., 1857.　　　　D 4 Q 29

BORTHWICK (ROBERT BROWN). [*See* AUMALE LE DUC d.']

BORY DE SAINT-VINCENT (JEAN BAPTISTE GEORGE MARIE), BARON.　Voyage to, and Travels through the Four Principal Islands of the African Seas, during the years 1801–2.　8vo.　Lond., 1805.　　D 2 R 2

BOS (J.) Jz.　[*See* BRUTZER, PROF. DR.]

BOS (LAMBERT).　Ellipses Græcæ; cum priorum editorum suisque observationibus edidit.　G. H. Schaeferi, quibus adduntur Pleonasmi Græci auctore B. Weiske; una cum G. Hermanni dissertatione de ellipsi et pleonasmo in Græca Lingua.　8vo.　Lond., 1825.　　K 12 S 34

BOSANQUET (BERNARD), M.A.　Knowledge and Reality, a Criticism of Mr. F. H. Bradley's "Principles of Logic."　8vo.　Lond., 1885.　　　　　　　　G 13 Q 26
Lotze's System of Philosophy.　[*See* LOTZE, H.]
[*See* HEGEL, G. W. F.]

BOSANQUET.(R. H. M.)　Elementary Treatise on Musical Intervals and Temperament.　8vo.　Lond., 1876.　A 7 P 5

BOSANQUET (S. R.) Hindu Chronology and Antediluvian History. 8vo. Lond., 1880.   B 10 U 4

BOSCO (Giovanni). Compendium of Italian History from the Fall of the Roman Empire; translated from the Italian, and completed to the Present Time, by J. D. Morell, LL.D. Sm. 4to. Lond., 1881.   B 18 Q 9 ‡

La Storia d'Italia. 12mo. Torino, 1886.

BOSCOBEL TRACTS (The). [*See* Hughes, J.]

BOSE (Shib Chunder). Hindoos as they are : a Description of the Manners, Customs, and Inner Life of Hindoo Society in Bengal. 8vo. Lond., 1881.   A 1 W 6

BOSIO (A.) [*See* Aringhi, P.]

BOSQUILLON (E. F. M.) Histoire de la Médecine, &c. [*See* Sprengel, K.]

BOSSANGE (Gustave). Bossange's Catalogue of Periodicals: Abridged List of the principal French Papers and Serials, with prices of Subscription for Paris and the United States. (Pam. Eb.) 8vo. Paris, 1869. MK 1 P 1

BOSSANGE (Martin) & CO. Catalogue des Livres Français, Italiens, Espagnols, Portugais, etc. 8vo. Lond., 1821.   K 7 R 39

BOSSUET (Jacques Bénigne), Bishop of Meaux. Discours sur l'Histoire Universelle. 2 vols. (in 1) 8vo. Lond., 1809.   G 2 T 8

Œuvres Complètes. 31 vols. 8vo. Paris, 1862–67.
    G 9 R 1–8 3

Oraisons Funèbres. 8vo. Lond., 1809.   G 2 T 9

Some Account of the Life and Writings of; by Charles Butler. 8vo. Lond., 1812.   C 1 S 13

Universal History, from the Creation of the World to the Time of Charlemagne. 8vo. Lond., 1810.   G 6 P 3

Life of [*See* Butler, S.]

BOSTOCK (J.) [*See* Plinius Secundus.]

BOSTON PUBLIC LIBRARY. Address delivered at the Dedication of the East Boston Branch, 22nd March, 1871; by William W. Greenough. 8vo. Boston, 1871.
    J 2 T 6

Appeal of the Trustees to the Mayor and Aldermen of the City of Boston. 8vo. Boston, 1865.   J 2 T 6

Boston Public Library Reports, 1855 to 1873. 8vo. Boston, 1855–73.   E

Boston Public Library Reports, Rules, and Regulations, &c. 8vo. Boston, 1851–74.   E

Bulletins of, 1870–72; and the Tosti Engravings. Roy. 8vo. Boston, 1873.

Bulletins of the Boston Public Library. Nos. 4–31. April, 1868–October, 1874. Imp. 8vo. Boston, 1868–74.
    K 8 Q 28

BOSTON PUBLIC LIBRARY—*continued.*
By-laws relative to the Trustees and Officers. 8vo. Boston, 1858.*   J 2 T 6

Another copy. 8vo. Boston, 1865.   J 2 T 6

Catalogue of Books of the Lower Hall of the Central Department. Imp. 8vo. Boston, 1873.   K 8 Q 27

Catalogue of Periodicals in the Central Library. Imp. 8vo. Boston, 1873.   K 8 Q 27

Class List for Poetry, the Drama, &c. Lower Hall. 1st ed. Imp. 8vo. Boston, 1870.   K 8 Q 27

Class List for English Prose, Fiction. Lower Hall. 5th ed. Imp. 8vo. Boston, 1871.   K 8 Q 27

Catalogue of Books, presented to the City of Boston by Edward Everett. 8vo. Boston, 1851.   J 2 T 6

Catalogue of the Collection of Books and Manuscripts which formerly belonged to the Rev. T. Prince, and is now in the Public Library of the City of Boston. 8vo. Boston, 1870.   K 9 R 30 †

Catalogue of the Public Library of Boston. Roy. 8vo. Boston, 1854–58.   K 8 P 17

Catalogues of the Public Library of Boston, 1871–73, and Bulletin, 1868–74. 2 vols. imp. 8vo. Boston, 1868–74.   K 8 Q 28, 29

Circular to the Patrons of the Bowditch Library. 8vo. Boston, 1858.   J 2 T 6

Conditions for furnishing Designs for a Building for a Public Library. 8vo. Boston, 1855.   J 2 T 6

Dedication Services of the Fellowes' Athenæum, and the Roxbury Branch, July 9th, 1873. 8vo. Boston, 1873.
    J 2 T 6

East Boston Branch. List of Books. First ed. Imp. 8vo. Boston, 1872.   K 8 Q 27

Finding List for French, German, and Italian Books. Lower Hall. Imp. 8vo. Boston, 1871.   K 8 Q 27

Hand-book for Readers; with Regulations. First ed., 1872. (Pam. K.) 8vo. Boston, 1872.   MJ 2 P 27

Index to Catalogue of Books in the Bates Hall. First Supplement. Imp. 8vo. Boston, 1866.   K 8 Q 29

Index [with 1st-3rd Supplement] to the Catalogue of a portion of the Public Library arranged in the Lower Hall. Roy. 8vo. Boston, 1858–60.   K 8 P 17

Proceedings at the Dedication of the South Boston Branch, May 16, 1872. 8vo. Boston, 1872.   J 2 T 6

Proceedings on the occasion of the laying the Corner-stone of the Public Library. 8vo. Boston, 1855.   J 2 T 6

Public Library of the City of Boston ; Catalogue of Books in the Bates Hall; Catalogue of Books and MSS., which formerly belonged to the Rev. Thos. Prince; Catalogue of the Tosti Engravings, the gift of T. G. Appleton, Esq. Roy. 8vo. Boston, 1866–73.   K 8 Q 27

Report of the Committee on Circulation, on the subject of Restricted Books. 8vo. Boston, 1865.   J 2 T 6

Report on the Bequests of George Ticknor to the Public Library. 8vo. Boston, 1871.   J 2 T 6

Reports of the Trustees, 1873–74. 8vo. Boston, 1873–74.
    J 2 T 6

BOSTON PUBLIC LIBRARY—*continued.*

Rules and Regulations, adopted November 8, 1853, amended March 18, 1856. 8vo. Boston, 1856.　　J 2 T 6

Rules and Regulations for the use of the Public Library, 1859, 1863, 1867. 8vo. Boston, 1859–67.　　J 2 T 6

Another copy. Roy. 8vo. Boston, 1859.　　K 8 P 17

South Boston Branch. List of Books. First ed. Imp. 8vo. Boston, 1872.　　K 8 Q 27

System of Record, devised and proposed for the use of the Public Library, 1861. 8vo. Boston, 1866.　　J 2 T 6

The Tosti Engravings. Imp. 8vo. Boston, 1871.
　　　　　　　　　　　　　　K 8 Q 27

Works in the Arts and Sciences Lower Hall. 2nd ed. Imp. 8vo. Boston, 1871.　　K 8 Q 27

BOSWELL (James). Journal of a Tour to the Hebrides, with Samuel Johnson, LL.D. 8vo. Lond., 1785.　D7 T 34

Life of Samuel Johnson, LL.D., and the Journal of his Tour to the Hebrides; illustrated with Portraits by Sir Joshua Reynolds, edited by Henry Morley, LL.D., &c. 5 vols. roy. 8vo. Lond., 1885.　　C 8 V 16–20

Life of Samuel Johnson, LL.D.; together with the Journal of a Tour to the Hebrides. New ed., with Notes and Appendices by Alexander Napier, M.A. 4 vols. 8vo. Lond., 1884.　　C 7 Q 39–42

Life of Samuel Johnson, LL.D. New ed. 4 vols. 8vo. Lond., 1820.　　C 7 Q 34–37

BOSWELL (John A. C.), M.C.S. Manual of Nellore District in the Presidency of Madras. Roy. 8vo. Madras, 1873.　　B 10 V 14

BOSWELL (John Thomas), F.L.S., &c. English Botany. [*See* SOWERBY, J.]

BOSWELL (Thomas A.) Recollections of a Pedestrian. 3 vols. 8vo. Lond., 1826.　　J 12 T 6–8

BOSWORTH (Rev. Joseph), D.D., &c. ˙ Compendious Anglo-Saxon and English Dictionary. 8vo. Lond., 1876.　　K 13 P 15

Gothic and Anglo-Saxon Gospels, in parallel columns; with the versions of Wycliffe and Tyndale, arranged, with Preface and Notes, assisted by George Waring, M.A. 4to. Lond., 1865.　　G 5 U 18

Origin of the Danish, and an abstract of Scandinavian Literature; with short Chronological Specimens of the Old Danish, Icelandic, Norwegian, Swedish, and a Notice of the Dalecarlian and Ferroe Dialects. 8vo. Lond., 1836.　　K 15 S 18

BOTANICAL MAGAZINE. [*See* CURTIS' BOTANICAL MAGAZINE.]

BOTFIELD (Beriah). Notes on the Cathedral Libraries of England. Roy. 8vo. Lond., 1849.　　B 4 U 19

BOTHMER (M. von), Countess. German Home Life. 8vo. Lond., 1876.　　D 7 Q 29

BOTHWELL (James Hepburn), Earl of. Life of; by Frederick Schiern; translated from the Danish by the Rev. David Berry, F.S.A.S. 8vo. Edinb., 1880.　C 7 Q 1

BOTTA (Carlo Guiseppe). History of Italy during the Consulate and Empire of Napoleon Bonaparte. 2 vols. 8vo. Lond., 1828.　　B 10 R 41, 42

War of Independence. [*See* BANCROFT, G.]

BOTTA (Paolo Emilio). Letters on the Discoveries at Nineveh. (From the French.) 8vo. Lond., 1850. B10P33

BOUCHARD (Comte de Melun et de Corbeil). Vie de. [*See* GUIZOT, F. P. G. Vol. 7.]

BOUCHIER (John). [*See* BERNERS, LORD.]

BOUDON (Henri-Marie). Life of. [*See* BUTLER, S.]

BOUGAINVILLE (Baron de). Journal de la Navigation autour du Globe, de la Frégate *la Thetis* et de la Corvette *l'Espérance*, 1824–26. At. imp. fol. Paris, 1837.　　MD 3 P 1 ‡

BOUGAINVILLE (Louis Antoine), Comte de. Voyage autour du Monde, par le Frégate du Roi *la Boudeuse* et la Flûte *l'Etoile* en 1766–69. 4to. Paris, 1771. MD5P26†

Voyage round the World, performed by order of His Most Christian Majesty, in the years 1766–69. Translated from the French, by John Reinhold Forster, F.A.S. 4to. Lond., 1772.　　D 10 T 28

Another copy. 8vo. Dublin, 1772.　　MD 4 V 13

History of a Voyage to the Malouine or Falkland Islands in 1763–64, and of Two Voyages to the Steights of Magellan; with an Account of the Patagonians. Translated from Dom Pernety's Historical Journal, written in French. 4to. Lond., 1771.　　D 3 V 4, 5

BOUGH (Sam.), R.S.A., AND CHALMERS (G. P.), R.S.A. Reproduction of a Selection of their Works. Imp. 4to. Glasgow, 1884.　　A 23 P 17 ‡

BOUILLÉ (François Claude Amour), Marquis de. Mémoires. [*See* BARRIERE, J. F. 21.]

BOUILLET (J. B.) [*See* LECOQ, H.]

BOULGER (Demetrius Charles). Central Asian Questions: Essays on Afghanistan, China, and Central Asia; with Portrait and Maps. 8vo. Lond., 1885.　F 10 Q 2

England and Russia in Central Asia; with two Maps and Appendices. 2 vols. 8vo. Lond., 1879. B 15 P 36, 37

General Gordon's Letters. [*See* GORDON, GEN. C. G.]

History of China. 3 vols. 8vo. Lond., 1881–84. B2Q1-3

BOULTON (Mathew), AND WATT (James). Lives of; principally from the original Soho MSS.; comprising also a History of the Invention and Introduction of the Steam-engine, by Samuel Smiles; with Portraits and Engravings. 8vo. Lond., 1865.　　C 9 V 8

BOUNDARY COMMISSION. Report of the Boundary Commissioners for England and Wales, 1868. Fol. Lond., 1886.   D 38 P 15 ‡

BOUNTY IMMIGRATION. [*See* IMMIGRATION.]

BOURGAT (Mons.) Code des Douanes; ou, Recueil des Lois et Règlements sur les Douanes, en vigueur au 1ᵉʳ Janvier, 1848. Seconde édition. 2 vols. 8vo. Paris, 1842.   F 10 T 2, 3

BOURGEOIS (Dr. X.) The Passions in their relations to Health and Diseases; translated from the French, by Howard F. Damon, A.M., &c. 12mo. Boston, 1876. Libr.

BOURGUIGNON (Frédéric). Conference des cinq Codes c'est eux et avec les lois et règlements sur l'organisation et l'administration de la justice, etc. 8vo. Paris, 1818.   F 5 T 15

BOURKE (John). Memoranda of the Early Days of Port Phillip, 1837; Letter to J. T. Smith. [*See* MANUSCRIPTS AND PORTRAITS.]

BOURKE (Capt. John Gregory). The Snake-Dance of the Moquis of Arizona; being a Narrative of a Journey from Santa Fé, New Mexico, to the Villages of the Moqui · Indians of Arizona. 8vo. Lond., 1884.   D 3 S 14

BOURKE (Major-General Sir Richard), K.C.B. Minute of His Excellency the Governor to the Legislative Council on Education. (Pam. A.) Fol. Sydney, 1836.   MJ 2 U 1

Correspondence of Edmund Burke. [*See* BURKE, Rt. Hon. E.]

Portrait of. [*See* MANUSCRIPTS AND PORTRAITS.]

[*See* DONNISON, H., *and* MACLEAY, ALEX.]

BOURKE (Richard Southwell). St. Petersburgh and Moscow: a Visit to the Court of the Czar. 8vo. Lond., 1846.   D 8 Q 33, 34

BOURKE (Robert O'Hara). Australian Exploring Expedition. [*See* JACKSON, A.]

BOURKE (Very Rev. Ulick J.), M.R.I.A. Aryan Origin of Gaelic Race and Language. 8vo. Lond., 1875.   B 11 Q 34

BOURNE (George). Bourne's Journal of Landsborough's Expedition from Carpentaria, in search of Burke and Wills. 8vo. Melb., 1862.   MD 3 U 18

Another copy.   MJ 2 R 16

BOURNE (Henry Richard Fox). English Merchants: Memoirs in illustration of the Progress of British Commerce. 2 vols. 8vo. Lond., 1866.   C 2 U 21, 22

Life of Thomas Lord Cochrane, Tenth Earl of Dundonald. [*See* DUNDONALD, EARL OF.]

Romance of Trade. 8vo. Lond., 1871.   F 6 P 32

Story of our Colonies; with Sketches of their present Condition. 8vo. Lond., 1869.*   MD 4 Q 5

BOURNE (John), C.E. Catechism of the Steam Engine, in its various applications to Mines, Mills, Steam Navigation, Railways, and Agriculture. 12mo. Lond., 1876.   A 6 R 13

Hand-book of the Steam-engine; constituting a Key to the Cathecism of the Steam-engine. 8vo. Lond., 1869.   A 11 P 23

BOURNE (John C.) History and Description of the Great Western Railway, including its Geology, and the Antiquities of the District through which it passes; accompanied by a Plan and Section of the Railway, a Geological Map, and Views. At. fol. Lond., 1846.   B 20 P 9 ‡

BOURNE (Stephen). Trade, Population, and Food: a Series of Papers on Economic Statistics. 8vo. Lond., 1880.   F 10 T 1

BOURNE (T.) [*See* ANACREON.]

BOURNE (Vincent.) Poematia Latinè; partim reddita, partim scripta. 5th ed. 12mo. Lond., 1764.   H 5 S 6

BOURNS (Charles), C.E., &c. Principles and Practice of Engineering, Trigonometrical, Subterraneous, and Marine Surveying; with an Appendix. 3rd ed. 8vo. Lond., 1867.   A 6 S 31

BOURRIENNE (Louis Antoine Fauvelet de). Memoirs of Napoleon Bonaparte; from the French, by J. S. Memes. (Const. Misc.) 4 vols. (in 3) 18mo. Edinb., 1831.   K 10 Q 45-47

Memoirs of Napoleon Bonaparte; by his Private Secretary; to which are now first added, an Account of the Important Events of the Hundred Days, of Napoleon's Surrender to the English, and of his Residence and Death at St. Helena. 4 vols. 8vo. Lond., 1836.   C 8 T 12-15

Memoirs of Napoleon Bonaparte; to which are added, an Account of the Important Events of the Hundred Days, of Napoleon's Surrender to the English, and of his Residence and Death at St. Helena; edited by Col. R. W. Phipps. New ed. 3 vols. 8vo. Lond.,1885. C 8 T 16-18

BOUSSARD (Jean). Recueil des Tombeaux les plus remarquables executés de nos jours et représentés en Perspective. (Etudes sur l'Art Funéraire moderne.) Roy. 4to. Paris (n.d.)   A 23 R 18 ‡

BOUSSARD (J. F.) Les Leçons de P. P. Rubens; ou Fragments épistolaires sur la Religion, la Peinture et la Politique. Roy. 8vo. Bruxelles, 1838.   A 8 R 17

BOUSSENARD (Louis). A travers l'Australie,—Les dix millions del'Opossum Rouge. 12mo. Paris,1879. MD 2 Q 10

BOUTAULD (Père Michel). Les Conseils de la Sagesse; ou, le Recueil des Maximes de Salomon. 5ᵉ éd. 2 vols. (in 1) 12mo. Paris, 1736.   G 13 Q 28

BOUTELL (Rev. Charles), M.A. Gold-working. (Brit. Man. Indust.) 12mo. Lond., 1876.   A 17 S 31

Heraldry, Historical and Popular. 3rd ed. 8vo. Lond., 1864.   K 10 T 2

BOUTERWEK (K. W.) Ein Angelsächsisches Glossar. 8vo. Gütersloh, 1854. K 15 P 15

BOUTOVSKY (VICTOR DE). Histoire de l'Ornement Russe du xᵉ au xviᵉ Siècle ; d'après les Manuscrits. (Musée d'Art et d'Industrie de Moscou.) 2 vols. imp. 4to. Paris, 1870.* A 4 W 9, 10 ‡
Another copy: 2 vols. imp. 4to. Paris, 1873. A 4 W 11, 12 ‡

BOUVERIE-PUSEY (S. E. B.) [*See* PUSEY, S. E. B. BOUVERIE-.]

BOVET (FELIX). Egypt, Palestine, and Phœnicia: a Visit to Sacred Lands; translated by W. H. Lyttelton, M.A. 8vo. Lond., 1882. D 5 R 37

BOW (ROBERT HENRY), C.E., &c. Economics of Construction in relation to Framed Structures. 8vo. Lond., 1873. A 6 T 22

BOWDEN (JOHN WILLIAM), M.A. Life and Pontificate of Saint Hildebrand, Gregory VII. 2 vols. 8vo. Lond., 1840. C 9 Q 1, 2

BOWDICH (THOMAS EDWARD). Mission from Cape Coast Castle to Ashantee; with a descriptive Account of that Kingdom. New ed. 8vo. Lond., 1873. D 1 T 22

BOWDITCH (DR. N.) [*See* LAPLACE, P. S., MARQUIS DE.]

BOWDITCH (NATHANIEL INGERSOLL). Suffolk Surnames. 3rd ed. 8vo. Lond., 1861. B 1 R 48

BOWDLER (CHARLES). Memoir of the Rev. William Howels. [*See* HOWELS, REV. W.]

BOWEN (E. M. C.) Language of Theology interpreted, in a Series of short and easy Lectures. 12mo. Sydney, 1836.* MG 1 P 12

BOWEN (RT. HON. SIR GEORGE FERGUSON), P.C., &c. On the New Settlement in Rockingham Bay, and advance of Colonization over North-eastern Australia. 8vo. Lond., 1865. MD 7 Q 53

BOWER (ARCHIBALD). History of the Popes, from the Foundation of the See of Rome to the Present Time. 7 vols. 4to. Lond., 1748-66. G 7 V 1-7

BOWER (PROF. F. ORPEN), M.A., &c., and VINES (S. H.), M.A., &c. Course of Practical Instruction in Botany; with a Preface, by W. T. Thiselton Dyer, M.A., &c. Part 1. Phanerogamæ-Pteridophyta. 8vo. Lond., 1885. A 4 P 31

BOWER (W.) [*See* FORDUN, J. DE.]

BOWERS (LIEUT. W.), R.N. Naval Adventures during Thirty-five Years' Service. 2 vols. 8vo. Lond., 1833. C 14 R 23, 24

BOWES (JAMES LORD). Japanese Enamels; with Illustrations from the Examples in the Bowes Collection. Imp. 8vo. Liverpool, 1884. A 8 T 14

Japanese Marks and Seals. Part 1. Pottery. Part 2. Illuminated MSS. and Printed Books. Part 3. Lacquer, Enamels, Metal, Wood, Ivory, &c. Imp. 8vo. Lond., 1882. K 17 U 21

BOWIE (AUGUSTUS J.), JUNR. Practical Treatise on Hydraulic Mining in California. Roy. 8vo. New York, 1885. A 9 U 33

BOWKER (RICHARD ROGERS). Copyright; its Law, &c. With a Bibliography of Literary Property ; by Thorvald Solberg. 4to. Lond., 1886. F 5 V 15
[*See* AMERICAN CATALOGUE.]

BOWLES (CAROLINE). Correspondence of Robert Southey with Caroline Bowles; to which is added, Correspondence with Shelley, and Southey's Dreams; edited by Edward Dowden. 8vo. Dublin, 1881. C 9 U 13

BOWLES (REAR-ADM. W.) Thoughts on National Defence. 2nd ed., corrected and enlarged. (Pam. Jf.) 8vo. Lond., 1852. MF 2 P 2

BOWMAN (FREDERICK H.), D.Sc., &c. Structure of the Cotton Fibre in its relation to Technical Applications. 8vo. Manchester, 1881. A 11 R 19

Structure of the Wool Fibre in its relation to the Use of Wool for Technical Purposes. 8vo. Manchester, 1885. A 11 S 3

BOWMAN (JOHN E.), F.C.S. Introduction to Practical Chemistry, including Analysis; edited by Charles L. Bloxam, F.C.S. 6th ed. 12mo. Lond., 1871. A 5 R 32

Practical Hand-book of Medical Chemistry; edited by Charles L. Bloxam. 12mo. Lond., 1862. A 5 R 14

BOWMAN (ROBERT), M.D., &c. Testimonials in favour of. (Pam. 43.) 8vo. Sydney, 1855. MJ 2 R 5

BOWNE (PROF. BORDEN P.) Metaphysics: a Study in First Principles. 8vo. Lond., 1882. G 6 Q 1

BOWRING (EDGAR ALFRED).
Poems of Goethe, with Life. [*See* GOETHE, J. W. VON.]
Poems of Schiller. [*See* SCHILLER, J. C. F. VON.]
Poems of Heine, with Life. [*See* HEINE, H.]

BOWRING (SIR JOHN), LL.D. Autobiographical Recollections of; with a brief Memoir by Lewin B. Bowring. 8vo. Lond., 1877. C 8 U 6

Decimal System in Numbers, Coins, and Accounts. 8vo. Lond., 1854. A 13 S 37

Kingdom and People of Siam; with a Narrative of the Mission to that country in 1855. 2 vols. 8vo. Lond., 1857. D 6 S 16, 17

Visit to the Philippine Islands. 8vo. Lond., 1859. D 6 Q 8

BOWRING (LEWIN B.) [*See* BOWRING, SIR J.]

BOWRON (W.) Manufacture of Cheese, Butter, and Bacon in New Zealand. 8vo. Wellington, 1883. MA 1 Q 39

BOWSER (GEORGE). Hawaiian Kingdom: Statistical and Commercial Directory, and Tourists' Guide, 1880-81. 8vo. Honolulu, 1880. ME 3 S

BOWSER (WilliaM). Biographical Memoir of. [*See* Nichols, J.]

BOWYER (George), D.C.L. The Roman Documents relating to the New Hierarchy; with an Argument. 8vo. Lond., 1851.   MF 2 T 2

BOX (ThoMas). Practical Treatise on Heat, as applied to the useful Arts, for the use of Engineers, Architects, &c. 2nd ed. 8vo. Lond., 1876.   A 5 S 28
Another copy. 5th ed. 8vo. Lond., 1885.   A 5 S 29

BOYCE (Rev. Francis B.) Blue Mountain Guide. 8vo. Sydney, 1887.   MD 6 P 44

BOYCE (Rev. WilliaM Binnington). Grammar of the Kaffir Language. 2nd ed. 8vo. Lond., 1844. K 14 Q 34
Introduction to the Study of History, Civil, Ecclesiastical, and Literary. 8vo. Lond., 1884.   B 15 P 9

BOYD (A. J.), "Old Chum." Old Colonials. 12mo. Lond., 1882.   MJ 1 U 7

BOYD (Rev. Andrew Kennedy Hutchinson), D.D. Graver Thoughts of a Country Parson. 12mo. Lond., 1862.   G 13 R 27
Leisure Hours in Town. 8vo. Lond., 1862.   J 6 R 9
Lessons of Middle Age. 8vo. Lond., 1868.   J 12 U 5
Our Little Life: Essays, Consolatory and Domestic; with some others. 8vo. Lond., 1882.   J 10 R 19
Recreations of a Country Parson. 2nd series. 8vo. Lond., 1864.   J 11 T 33

BOYD (BenjaMin). Address to the Electors of the District of Port Phillip. 4to. Sydney, 1844.   MJ 2 S 5
Letter to His Excellency Sir William Denison, Lieut.-Governor of Van Diemen's Land, on the expediency of transferring the unemployed Labour of that Colony to New South Wales. 8vo. Lond., 1847.   MF 2 T 4

BOYD (HannAh Villiers). Letters on Education; addressed to a Friend in the Bush of Australia. 8vo. Sydney, 1884.   MG 1 P 14
Voice from Australia; or, an Inquiry into the probability of New Holland being connected with the Prophecies relating to New Jerusalem. 2nd ed., revised. 12mo. Lond., 1856.*   MG 1 P 15

BOYD (ThoMas). Memorandum of a Statement made by Thomas Boyd, of Windowie, near Tumut, in the Colony of New South Wales. 8vo. Sydney, 1883.   MD 2 S 3 3

BOYDELL (John). Picturesque Scenery of Norway, with the Principal Towns from the Naze, by the route of Christiana, to the magnificent Pass of the Swinesund; from Drawings by John William Edy; with Remarks and Observations by William Tooke. 2 vols. roy. fol. Lond., 1820.   D 4 S 12, 13 *

BOYDELL (John and JosiAh). History of the River Thames; by William Combe; Drawings by J. Farrington, engraved by J. E. Stadler. 2 vols. fol. Lond., 1794-96.   B 14 U 12, 13 ‡

BOYESEN (HjalMar H.) History of Norway. 8vo. Lond., 1886.   B 2 R 14

BOYLE (Hon. Charles). [*See* Bentley, R.]

BOYLE (ChArles John). Far Away; or, Sketches of Scenery and Society in Mauritius. 8vo. Lond., 1867.   D 1 T 13

BOYLE (Frederick), F.R.G.S. Adventures among the Dyaks of Borneo. 8vo. Lond., 1865.   D 4 U 13
Ride across a Continent: a personal Narrative of Wanderings through Nicaragua and Costa Rica. 2 vols. 8vo. Lond., 1868.   D 3 Q 58, 59
Savage Life: a second series of Camp Notes. 8vo. Lond., 1876.   D 2 R 11
To the Cape for Diamonds: a Story of Digging Experiences in South Africa. 8vo. Lond., 1873.   D 1 V 2

BOYLE (MAry L.) Bridal of Melcha: a Dramatic Sketch. 8vo. Lond., 1844.   H 5 T 20

BOYLE (Hon. Robert). Life of; by Thomas Birch, D.D. 8vo. Lond., 1744.   C 5 U 6

BOYLE LECTURE SERMONS. Defence of Natural and Revealed Religion; being a collection of the Sermons preached at the Lectures founded by the Hon. Robert Boyle. 3 vols. fol. Lond., 1739. G 39 P 2-4 ‡
[*See* Stackhouse, Rev. A.]

BOYLE FAMILY (The). Memoirs of the Lives and Characters of the Illustrious Family of the Boyels, particularly of the late eminently learned Charles Earl of Orrery; by E. Budgell, Esq. 3rd ed. 8vo. Lond., 1737.   C 4 S 1

BOYNTON (CAptain E. C.), A.M. History of West Point, and its Military Importance during the American Revolution, and the Origin and Progress of the United States Military Academy. Roy. 8vo. Lond., 1864.   B 1 T 44

BOYS (ThoMas Shotter). Original Views of London as it is; exhibiting its principal Streets and characteristic Accessories, &c. With Historical Notices of the Views, by Charles Ollier. Imp. fol. Lond., 1842. D 5 Q 26 ‡

BOYSE (SaMuel). Life and Poems of. [*See* ChalMers, A.]

BOZ. [*See* Dickens, C.]

BOZMAN (John Leeds). Sketch of the History of Maryland during the three first years after its settlement. 8vo. Baltimore, 1811.   B 1 S 7

BRABAZON (H. L.) New South Wales General Town Directory and Advertiser. 12mo. Sydney, 1843. ME 4 S

BRABOURNE (Edward), Lord. Letters of Jane Austen. Edited, with an Introduction and Critical Remarks, by Edward Lord Brabourne. 2 vols. 8vo. Lond., 1884.   C 5 S 1, 2

BRABOURNE PAPERS (THE). [*See* BANKS, SIR J.]

BRACE (CHARLES LORING). Dangerous Classes of New York, and twenty years work among them. 8vo. New York, 1872. F 5 T 12

The New West; or, California in 1867 and 1868. 8vo. New York, 1869. D 3 P 43

BRACHÉ (J.) [*See* MINING INSTITUTE OF VICTORIA.]

BRACHET (AUGUSTE). Dictionnaire Etymologique de la Langue Française. -Neuvième édition. Couronné par l'Académie Française. 12mo. Paris, 1868. K 11 V 9

Etymological Dictionary of the French Language; translated by G. W. Kitchin. (Clar. Press.) 8vo. Oxford, 1873. K 20 R 6

Grammaire des Langues Romanes. [*See* DIEZ, F.]

Grammaire Historique de la Langue Française. 18e éd. 12mo. Paris (n.d.) K 11 V 46

Historical Grammar of the French Tongue; translated by G. W. Kitchin, M.A. 3rd ed. (Clar. Press.) 12mo. Oxford, 1874. K 16 P 45

BRACKEN (THOMAS). Lays of the Land of the Maori and Moa. 12mo. Lond., 1884.* MH 1 R 8

The New Zealand Tourist. Published by the Union Steamship Company of New Zealand. 8vo. Dunedin, 1879.* MD 6 P 25

BRACKENBURY (COL. CHARLES BOOTH), R.A. Frederick the Great. 8vo. Lond., 1884. O 3 S 38

BRACKENBURY (GEORGE). Campaign in the Crimea: an Historical Sketch. Illustrated by Wm. Simpson. Roy. 8vo. Lond., 1855. B 12 V 11

BRACKENBURY (MAJOR-GEN. HENRY), C.B. Ashanti War: a Narrative prepared from the Official Documents; with Maps and Plans, &c. 2 vols. 8vo. Edinb., 1874. B 1 P 41, 42

The River Column: a Narrative of the Advance of the River Column of the Nile Expeditionary Force, and its Return down the Rapids. 8vo. Edinb., 1885. B 2 S 16

BRACKSTAD (H. L.) Nordenskiöld's Voyage. [*See* HOVGAARD, LIEUT. A.]

BRADBURY (EDWARD). All about Derbyshire; with Illustrations. 8vo. Lond., 1884. D 7 Q 14

BRADFORD (ALDEN). History of Massachusetts for 200 years, from 1620 to 1820. 8vo. Boston, 1835. B 1 S 13

BRADFORD (REV. JOHN). Writings of. [*See* BRITISH REFORMERS, 1.]

BRADFORD (MRS. W.) Memoirs of Princess Daschkaw. [*See* DASCHKAW, PRINCESS.]

BRADFORD (WILLIAM), M.A. Correspondence of Charles V [*See* CHARLES V.]

BRADFORD SCHOOL OF INDUSTRY. Rules for the School of Industry at Bradford for the Instruction of Poor Girls in Reading, Sewing, and Knitting. (Pam. 41.) 8vo. Bradford, 1808. MJ 2 R 3

BRADLEY (A. C.), M.A. [*See* GREEN, T. H.]

BRADLEY (CAPTAIN). [*See* HUNTER, CAPT. J., *and* PHILLIP, A.]

BRADLEY (REV. EDWARD), B.A., "CUTHBERT BEDE." Fotheringhay and Mary Queen of Scots. 12mo. Lond., 1886. B 23 Q 2

Glencreggan; or, a Highland Home in Cantire. 2 vols. 8vo. Lond., 1861. D 8 Q 38, 39

The White Wife; with other Stories, Supernatural, Romantic, and Legendary. 8vo. Lond., 1865. J 10 Q 1

BRADLEY (FRANCIS HERBERT), LL.D., &c. Criticism of Mr. F. H. Bradley's "Principles of Logic." [*See* BOSANQUET, B.]

Ethical Studies. 8vo. Lond., 1876. G 13 Q 30

Principles of Logic. 8vo. Lond., 1883. G 6 P 5

BRADLEY (PROF. THOMAS). Elements of Geometrical Drawing; or, Practical Geometry, Plane and Solid, including both Orthographic and Perspective Projection. 2 vols. (in 1). Ob. 4to. Lond., 1862. A 1 Q 12 †

Selection of Twenty Plates, for the use of the Royal Military Academy, Woolwich, from the Work on the Elements of Practical Geometry. Ob. 4to. Lond., 1862. A 1 Q 13 †

BRADSHAW (B.) Dictionary of Mineral Waters, Climatic Health Resorts, Sea Baths, and Hydropathic Establishments. 12mo. Lond., 1886. D 11 P 37

BRADSHAW (JOHN), J.P. New Zealand as it is. 8vo. Lond., 1883. MD 5 S 35

BRADSHAW'S ALMANAC and General Guide, 1872–76, 1878. 6 vols. (in 2) 8vo. Sydney, 1872–78. ME 4 Q

BRADSHAW'S Through Route Overland Guide to India, and Colonial Hand-book. 12mo. Lond., 1875–76. D 12 P 12

BRADSHAW'S Map of the Railways. [Of Great Britain.] (Pam. B.) Fol. Lond. (n.d.) MJ 2 U 2

BRADY (CHARLES), F.L.S. Ailant Silkworm: Observations on its Habit, Management, Food, and Value, made during the Introduction, Naturalization, and Rearing of the first Stock in Queensland and New South Wales. (Pam. Ca.) 8vo. Sydney, 1868. MA 1 Q 7

Another copy. MA 1 Q 36

Correspondence relating to Cultivation of Silk. 8vo. Sydney, 1870. MA 1 Q 36

Silk. (Pam. Ca.) 8vo. Sydney, 1871. MA 1 Q 7

Another copy. MA 1 Q 36

BRADY (CHARLES), F.L.S., AND THORNE (CHARLES). Silk Culture in New South Wales. 4to. Sydney, 1871. MJ 2 S 2

BRADY (Very Rev. J.), V.G. Descriptive Vocabulary of the Native Language of Western Australia. 16mo. Rome, 1845.   MK 1 P 29

BRADY (Rev. William Maziere), D.D. Clerical and Parochial Records of Cork, Cloyne, and Ross. 3 vols. 8vo. Dublin, 1863–64.   G 5 R 27–29

Episcopal Succession in England, Scotland, and Ireland, 1400–1875. 2 vols. 8vo. Rome, 1876.   G 5 R 24, 25

McGillycuddy Papers: a Selection from the Family Archives of "The McGillycuddy of the Reeks"; with an Introductory Memoir; being a Contribution to the History of the County of Kerry. 4to. Lond., 1867.   B 16 Q 21 ‡

State Papers concerning the Irish Church in the Time of Queen Elizabeth. 8vo. Lond., 1868.   G 5 Q 10

BRAGG (Joseph). Prison Life: the Life of a Notorious Character; Strange Disclosures told by himself: a Lecture. 8vo. Sydney, 1886.   MC 1 P 37

BRAGGE (W.), F.S.A. [*See* Birmingham Free Libraries.]

BRAHE (Tycho). Life of; by Sir D. Brewster. (Martyrs of Science.) 12mo. Lond., 1874.   C 1 T 40

BRAHE (William). Memorandum of. [*See* Burke, R.O'H.]

BRAIM (Thomas Henry), D.D., &c. History of New South Wales, from its Settlement to the close of the year 1844. 2 vols. 8vo. Lond., 1846.*   MB 1 R 22, 23

New Homes: the Rise, Progress, Present Position, and Future Prospects of each of the Australian Colonies and New Zealand, regarded as Homes for all Classes of Emigrants. 8vo. Lond., 1870.   MD 4 R 13

BRAITHWAITE (Joseph Bevan). [*See* Gurney, J. J.]

BRAITHWAITE (Robert), M.D., &c. Sphagnaceæ, or Peat-Mosses of Europe and North America. Roy. 8vo. Lond., 1880.   A 5 Q 5

BRAMALL (Henry), M.I.C.E. Mineral Resources of New Zealand. With Map of Gold and Coal Fields. 8vo. Liverpool, 1883.   MA 2 Q 32

BRAME (Samuel). Voices from New Zealand. 8vo. Lond., 1865.   MD 5 U 28

BRAMELD (G. William), M.A. Holy Gospels; translated from the original Greek, with Notes and critical Appendix. Roy. 8vo. Lond., 1863.   G 7 V 16

BRAMSEN (William). Coins of Japan; with Japanese Weights, &c. Part 1. Copper, Lead, and Iron Coins. 4to. Yokohama, 1880.   A 2 S 19 †

Japanese Chronological Tables (645–1873 A.D.); with an introductory Essay on Japanese Chronology and Calendars. Ob. 8vo. Tokio, 1880.   A 10 S 29

BRAMSTON (A. R.), and LEROY (A. C.) Historic Winchester: England's First Capital. 8vo. Lond., 1882.   B 4 R 19

BRAMWELL (Sir Frederick Joseph), Knt., F.R.S., &c. Railways and Locomotives. [*See* Barry, J. W.]

BRAMWELL (Ven. William). Memoir of the Ven. William Bramwell; by James Sigston. 32mo. Wakefield, (n.d.)   G 9 P 2

BRAMWELL (William Calvert). Wool-Carders' Vade Mecum. 3rd ed., revised and enlarged. 12mo. Boston, 1881.   A 11 P 30

BRAND (Rev. John), M.A., F.S.A. History and Antiquities of the Town and County of Newcastle-upon-Tyne, including an Account of the Coal Trade of that place. With Views of the Public Buildings, &c. 2 vols. 4to. Lond., 1789.   B 10 S 4, 5 †

Popular Antiquities of Great Britain; comprising Notices of the moveable and immoveable Feasts, Customs, Superstitions, and Amusements, Past and Present; edited from the materials collected by John Brand, F.S.A., with Additions, by W. Carew Hazlitt. 3 vols. roy. 8vo. Lond., 1870.   B 4 U 16–18

BRAND-HOLLIS (Thomas), F.R.S. Memoirs of; by John Disney. Imp. 4to. Lond., 1808.   C 23 S 32 ‡

BRANDE (William Thomas), D.C.L., &c. Introductory Discourse delivered in the Amphitheatre of the London Institution, 1819. (Pam. 25.) 8vo. Lond., 1819.   MJ 2 Q 13

Subject-matter of a Course of Ten Lectures on some of the Arts connected with Organic Chemistry. 12mo. Lond., 1854.   A 5 R 10

BRANDE (W. T.), D.C.L., &c., and COX (Rev. Sir G. W.), M.A. Dictionary of Science, Literature, and Art. 3 vols. 8vo. Lond., 1865–67.   K 18 Q 1–3

BRANDES (Georg). Lord Beaconsfield: a Study. Authorized translation by Mrs. George Sturge. 8vo. Lond., 1880.   C 9 V 13

BRANDIS (Prof. C. A.) Essay on Niebuhr. [*See* Niebuhr, B. G.]

BRANDIS (Dietrich), Ph.D. Forest Flora of North-west and Central India. [*See* Stewart, J. L.]

BRANDON (H.) [*See* Miles, W. A.]

BRANDON (J.) Address to Dr. Jenner, on the First Anniversary of his Birth. 8vo. Lond. (n.d.)   A 12 S 33

BRANDON (Raphael and Joseph Arthur). Parish Churches; being Perspective Views of English Ecclesiastical Structures, &c. Roy. 8vo. Lond., 1848.   A 3 Q 20

BRANDT (Gerard). History of the Reformation in the Low Countries, from the beginning of the 8th Century, down to the famous Synod of Dort; translated from the original Low Dutch. 4 vols. (in 2.) Fol. Lond., 1720–23.   G 29 P 18, 19 ‡

BRANDT (Sebastian). Prospect zu Sebastian Brandt's Narrenschiff. (Pam. B.) Fol. Berlin, 1871. MJ 2 U 2

Ship of Fooles, wherein is showed the Folly of all States; translated out of the Latin, by A. Barclay. Fol. Lond., 1570.   H 5 V 2

BRANNT (WILLIAM T.) Practical Treatise on the Raw Materials and the Distillation and Rectification of Alcohol, and the Preparation of Alcoholic Liquors, Liqueurs, Cordials, and Bitters. 8vo. Philad., 1885.   A 5 S 44
[*See* DAWIDOWSKY, F.]

BRANNT (W. T.), AND WAHL (W. H.) Techno-Chemical Receipt-book, containing several thousand Receipts. 8vo. Philad., 1886.   K 9 P 5

BRANTÔME (PIERRE DE BOURDEILLE), SEIGNEUR DE. Œuvres Complètes; accompagnées de remarques historiques et critiques. 8 vols. 8vo. Paris, 1822-75.   J 16 Q 20-27

BRASSEUR DE BOURBOURG (C. E.) L'ABBE. Bibliothèque Mexico-Guatémalienne; précédée d'un coup d'œil sur les Etudes Américaines. Roy. 8vo. Paris, 1871.   K 17 R 20

Gramatica de la Lengua Quichee: Grammaire de la Langue Quichée, Espagnole-Française, mise en parallèle avec ses deux dialectes, Cakchiquel et Tzutuhil. Imp. 8vo. Paris, 1862.   K 13 T 11

Histoire des Nations Civilisées du Mexique et de l'Amérique-Centrale. 4 vols. roy. 8vo. Paris, 1857-59.   B 1 T 29-32

Manuscrit Troano: Etudes sur le Système graphique et la langue des Mayas. 2 vols. imp. 4to. Paris, 1869-70.   B 15 S 1, 2 ‡

Popol Vuh: le Livre Sacré et les Mythes de l'Antiquité Américaine. Roy. 8vo. Paris, 1861.   B 1 U 2

Quatre Lettres sur le Mexique: Exposition absolue du Système Hieroglyphique Mexicain; La Fin de l'Age de Pierre; Epoque Glaciaire temporaire; Commencement de l'Age de Bronze; Origines de la Civilisation et des Religions de l'Antiquité. Roy. 8vo. Paris, 1868.   B 1 U 1

Recherches sur les Ruines de Palenqué, et sur les Origines de la Civilisation du Mexique. [*See* WALDECK, F. DE.]

BRASSEY (ANNA), LADY. In the Trades, the Tropics, and the Roaring Forties. Illustrated. 8vo. Lond., 1885.   D 9 T 26

Tahiti: a series of Photographs taken by Colonel Stuart-Wortley; with Letter-press by Lady Brassey. Sq. 8vo. Lond., 1882.   MD 4 U 21

Voyage in the *Sunbeam*; our Home on the Ocean for Eleven Months. Illustrated. 8vo. Lond., 1878.   D 9 T 25

BRASSEY (THOMAS). Life and Labours of; by [Sir] Arthur Helps. 2nd. ed. 8vo. Lond., 1872.   C 5 T 2

BRASSEY (THOMAS), LORD, K.C.B., &c. The British Navy: its Strength, Resources, and Administration. 5 vols. 8vo. Lond., 1882-83.   A 2 Q 3-7
  1. Shipbuilding for the Purposes of War.
  2. Miscellaneous Subjects connected with Shipbuilding for the Purposes of War.
  3. Opinions on the Shipbuilding Policy of the Navy.
  4. Dockyards, Reserves, Training, Pensions; being a Reprint of Parliamentary Speeches, Letters, Papers, and Addresses, with Additions.
  5. British Seamen.

BRASSEY (THOMAS), LORD, K.C.B., &c.—*continued.*
British Seamen as described in recent Parliamentary and Official Documents. 8vo. Lond., 1877.   F 10 R 3

Foreign Work and English Wages, considered with reference to the Depression of Trade. 8vo. Lond.,1879.   F 10 R 1

Naval Annual, 1886. 8vo. Portsmouth, 1886.   E

Work and Wages, practically illustrated. 8vo. Lond., 1872.   F 10 R 2

BRASYER (COL. JEREMIAH), C.B. Statement of the Service and Services of. (Pam. L.) 8vo. Lond., 1868.   MJ 2 P 28

BRATHWAIT (RICHARD), A.M. Barnabæ Itinerarium; or, Barnabee's Journal, with a Life of the Author; edited by Joseph Haslewood. 2 vols. sq. 18mo. Lond., 1820.   H 6 P 2, 3

Drunken Barnaby's Four Journeys to the North of England, in Latin and English Verse; to which is added Bessy Bell. 12mo. Lond., 1716.   H 8 Q 37

Tracts of. [*See* BRYDGES, SIR S. E.]

BRAUND (JOHN). Illustrations of Furniture, Candelabra, Musical Instruments, &c., from the Great Exhibitions of London and Paris; with Examples of similar Articles from Royal Palaces and Noble Mansions. Fol. Lond., 1858.   A 4 R 14 ‡

BRAVO (FR. FELIPE). Diccionario Geografico. [*See* BUZETA, FR. M.]

BRAY (MRS. ANNA ELIZA). Autobiography of; edited by John A. Kempe. 8vo. Lond., 1884.   C 3 R 8

Joan of Arc, and the Times of Charles VII, King of France. 8vo. Lond., 1874.   C 2 S 24

Life of Thomas Stothard, R.A.; with Personal Reminiscences. Sm. 4to. Lond., 1851.   C 9 R 19

The Good St. Louis and his Times. 8vo. Lond., 1870.   C 4 Q 11

BRAY (MRS. CAROLINE). The British Empire: a Sketch of the Geography, Growth, Natural and Political Features of the United Kingdom, its Colonies and Dependencies. 12mo. Lond., 1863.   MD 4 Q 45

BRAY (CHARLES). Manual of Anthropology; or, Science of Man, based on Modern Research. 8vo. Lond., 1871.   A 1 V 8

BRAY (WILLIAM), F.S.A. Memoirs, illustrative of the Life and Writings of John Evelyn, Esq., F.R.S., comprising his Diary from the year 1641 to 1705-6. 2nd ed. 2 vols. roy. 4to. Lond., 1819.   C 2 W 10, 11

BRAYBROOK (RICHARD), LORD. Memoirs of Samuel Pepys; comprising his Diary from 1659 to 1669, and a Selection from his Private Correspondence. 2 vols. roy. 4to. Lond., 1825.   C 1 W 22, 23

BRAYLEY (EDWARD WEDLAKE), JUNR., F.S.A. Ancient Castles of England and Wales. Engraved by W. Woolnoth, from Original Drawings by the most eminent Artists; with Historical Descriptions. 2 vols. 8vo. Lond., 1825.   B 7 Q 5, 6

BRAYLEY (EDWARD WEDLAKE), JUNR., F.S.A.—*contd.*
Beauties of England and Wales. [*See* BEAUTIES OF ENG-
LAND AND WALES.]

History and Antiquities of the Abbey Church of St. Peter,
Westminster. Illustrated by J. P. Neale. 2 vols. fol.
Lond., 1818–23.   B 23 S 27, 28 ‡

Topographical History of Surrey; revised and edited by
Edward Walford, M.A. 2nd ed. 4 vols. roy. 4to.
Lond., 1883.   B 17 R 1–4 ‡

[*See* BRITTON, J., *and* PARKES, S.]

BRAZIER (JOHN), C.M.Z.S., &c. Descriptions of Eleven
new Species of Terrestrial and Marine Shells from North-
east Australia. (Pam. Ci.) 8vo. Lond., 1874.   MA 2 Q 33

List of Land Shells collected on Fitzroy Island; with
Notes on their Geographical Range. (Pam. Cn.) 8vo.
Leeds, 1878.   MA 2 V 14

Another copy. (Pam. Co.)   A 16 U 23

List of Species of Porcellana, or Cypræa found in Moreton
Bay, Queensland. (Pam. Cq.) 8vo. Sydney, 1880.
MA 2 V 9

Localités des Iles Australiennes, des Iles Salomon et d'autres
Iles de la Mer Sud. (Pam. Cq.) Paris, 1880.   MA 2 V 9

Notes on recent Mollusca found in Port Jackson and on the
Coast of New South Wales and other localities, with their
Synonyms. (Pam. Cq.) 8vo. Sydney, 1880.   MA 2 V 9

Remarks on some recently redescribed Australian Shells.
(Pam. Cq.) 8vo. Sydney, 1880.   MA 2 V 9

Shells collected during the *Chevert* Expedition. [*See*
TENISON-WOODS, J. E.]

BRAZILIAN BIOGRAPHICAL ANNUAL; by J. M.
de Macedo. 3 vols. 8vo. Rio de Janeiro, 1876.
C 9 V 9–11

BRÉAL (PROF. MICHEL.) [*See* BOPP, F.]

BRÉDIF (L.) Political Eloquence in Greece. Demos-
thenes; with Extracts from his Orations, and a Critical
Discussion of the "Trial on the Crown"; translated by
M. J. McMahon, A.M. 8vo. Chicago, 1881.   C 5 T 6

BREEN (HENRY HEGART), F.S.A. Modern English Literature; its Blemishes and Defects. 8vo. Lond., 1857.
C 20 T 2

St. Lucia: Historical, Statistical, and Descriptive. 8vo.
Lond., 1844.   D 3 T 30

BREEN (HUGH). Natural History of the Inanimate
Creation. [*See* INANIMATE CREATION.]

BREES (S. C.), C.E., &c. Key to the Colonies; or, Advice
to the Million upon Emigration. 12mo. Lond., 1851.
MD I P 8

Pictorial Illustrations of New Zealand. Roy. fol. Lond.,
1847.   MD 2 P 1 ‡

Another copy. Fol. Lond., 1848.   MD 2 P 2 ‡

Another copy. Fol. Lond., 1849.   MD 2 P 3 ‡

Railway Practice. 1st and 2nd Series; with Appendix.
3 vols. 4to. Lond., 1838–40.   A I R 4 6 †

[*See* WAKEFIELD, E. J.]

BREHM (DR. ALFRED EDMOND). Thierleben Allgemeine
kunde des Thierreichs. 10 vols. roy. 8vo. Leipzig,
1876–78.   A 15 S 1–10

[*See* WERNER, C.]

BRÉHOLLES (J. L. A. HUILLARD). [*See* HUILLARD-
BRÉHOLLES, J. L. A.]

BREMER (FREDRIKA). Brothers and Sisters: a Tale of
Domestic Life; translated by Mary Howitt. Roy. 8vo.
New York (n.d.)   J 9 V 9

Homes of the New World: Impressions of America;
translated by Mary Howitt. 3 vols. 8vo. Lond., 1853.
D 3 R 58–60

BREMNER (ROBERT). Excursions in Denmark, Norway,
and Sweden. 2 vols. 8vo. Lond., 1840.   D 7 U 33, 34

Excursions in the Interior of Russia. 2 vols. 8vo. Lond.
1839.   D 8 U 27, 28

BRENAN (JUSTIN). Composition and Punctuation
(Weale). 5th ed. 12mo. Lond., 1868.   K 11 T 24

BRENCHLEY (JULIUS L.), M.A., &c. Great Salt Lake
City. [*See* REMY, J.]   D 3 U 25, 26

Jottings during the Cruise of H.M.S. *Curaçoa* among the
South Sea Islands, in 1865. Roy. 8vo. Lond., 1873.
MD 3 V 28

BRENTON (CAPT. EDWARD PELHAM), R.N., &c. Memoir
of; with Sketches of his Professional Life, and exertions
in the Cause of Humanity; by his Brother, Vice-Admiral
Sir Jahleel Brenton, Bart., K.C.B. 8vo. Lond., 1842.
C 10 R 7

Naval History of Great Britain, from the year 1783 to
1836. New ed., illustrated. 2 vols. 8vo. Lond., 1837.
B 3 S 1, 2

BRENTON (VICE-ADMIRAL SIR JAHLEEL). Memoir of
Capt. Edward Pelham Brenton, R.N., &c. 8vo. Lond.,
1842.   C 10 R 7

BRERETON (AUSTIN). Dramatic Notes, 1885. 8vo.
Lond., 1885.   E

Shakespearean Scenes and Characters; with descriptive
Notes on the Plays. Roy. 4to. Lond., 1886.   H 3 P 27‡

BRERETON (REV. C. D.) Observations on the Administration of the Poor Laws in Agricultural Districts. 3rd
ed. (Pam. 8.) 8vo. Norwich, 1834.   F 13 R 21

BRERETON (JOHN LE GAY), M.D. Beyond; and other
Poems. 8vo. Sydney, 1886.*   MH 1 P 40

Lecture on the action and uses of the Turkish Bath.
(Pam. 23.) 8vo. Lond. (n.d.)   MJ 2 Q 11

Poems. 12mo. Lond., 1865.   MH 1 P 39

Triumph of Love. 8vo. Sydney, 1887.   MH 1 P 42

BRESSLAU (PROF. MARCUS HEINRICH). Compendious
Hebrew Grammar. (Weale.) 12mo. Lond., 1855.
C 11 T 22

English and Hebrew Dictionary. (Weale.) 12mo. Lond.,
1856.   K 11 T 23

Hebrew and English Dictionary. Biblical and Rabbinical.
(Weale.) 12mo. Lond., 1855.   K 11 T 22

BRETON (LIEUT. WILLIAM HENRY), R.N. Excursions in New South Wales, Western Australia, and Van Dieman's Land, during the years 1830–33. 8vo. Lond., 1833.* MD 3 T 31

Another copy. 2nd ed., revised, with additions. 8vo. Lond., 1834.* MD 3 T 35

Another copy. 3rd ed. 8vo. Lond., 1835. MD 3 T 37

BRETON DE LA MARTINIÈRE (J. B.) La Chine en Miniature ; ou, Choix de Costumes, Arts et Métiers de cet Empire. 4 vols. 18mo. Paris, 1811. D 5 P 22–25

BRETON (NICHOLAS). Small Handfull of Fragrant Flowers. A Floorish upon Fancie. [*See* PARK, T.]

Tracts of. [*See* BRYDGES, SIR S. E.]

BRETSCHNEIDER (E.), M.D. Notices of Mediæval Geography and History of Central and Western Asia ; drawn from Chinese and Mongol Writings, and compared with the observations of Western Authors in the Middle Ages; with Maps. 8vo. Lond., 1876. B 2 P 30

BRETT (HENRY). Brett's Auckland Almanac, Provincial Hand-book, and Stranger's Vade Mecum for 1878. 8vo. Auckland, 1878. ME 3 T

BREVOIR (THOMAS). [*See* SHORTER, T.]

BREWER (REV. EBENEZER COBHAM), LL.D. Dictionary of Miracles : Imitative, Realistic, and Dogmatic. 8vo. Lond., 1884. G 16 R 43

Dictionary of Phrase and Fable. 3rd ed. 8vo. Lond., 1870. K 17 P 26

Political, Social, and Literary History of Germany, from the Commencement to the Present Day. 8vo. Lond., 1881. B 9 Q 26

Reader's Hand-book of Allusions, References, Plots, and Stories. 8vo. Lond., 1880. K 17 P 10

BREWER (PROF. JOHN SHERREN), M.A. Church History of Britain. [*See* FULLER, T.]

Court of King James I. [*See* GOODMAN, DR. G.]

Endowments and Establishment of the Church of England. 2nd ed. 12mo. Lond., 1885. G 16 R 43

English Studies or Essays in English History and Literature ; edited, with a prefatory Memoir, by Henry Wace, M.A. 8vo. Lond., 1881. B 6 S 36

Letters and Papers, Foreign and Domestic, of the Reign of Henry VIII; arranged and catalogued by J. S. Brewer, M.A. 4 vols. (in 7) imp. 8vo. Lond., 1862–72. B 15 U 7–13

Reign of Henry VIII, from his Accession to the Death of Wolsey ; edited by James Gairdner ; with Portrait. 2 vols. 8vo. Lond., 1884. B 6 P 32, 33

BREWSTER (SIR DAVID), M.A., &c. Letters on Natural Magic, addressed to Sir Walter Scott. 2nd ed. ; with Introductory Chapters, by J. A. Smith. 8vo. Lond., 1868. A 10 R 7

Life of Sir Isaac Newton. 18mo. Lond., 1831. C 1 P 33

Lives of the most Eminent Literary and Scientific Men of Italy, &c. [*See* SHELLEY, MRS. M. W.]

BREWSTER (SIR DAVID), M.A., &c—*continued.*

Martyrs of Science : Lives of Galileo, Tycho Brahe, and Kepler. New ed., with Portraits. 8vo. Lond., 1874. C 1 T 40

Memoirs of the Life, Writings, and Discoveries of Sir Isaac Newton. 2 vols. 8vo. Edinb., 1855. C 9 Q 5, 6

More Worlds than One : the Creed of the Philosopher, and the Hope of the Christian. 8vo. Lond., 1867. A 3 S 24

Treatise on Optics. [Lard. Cab. Cyclo.] 12mo. Lond., 1851. K 1 U 33

[*See* EDINBURGH JOURNAL OF SCIENCE.]

BREYDENBACH (BERNARDUS DE). Sanctarū Peregrinationū in Montē Syon ad venerandū Christi sepulchruz in Hierusalē atqz in Montē Synai ad diram virginē et martyrem Katherinā opusculū hoc contentinū per Petrum dnach civē Spirensem impssum Anno salutis nre MCCCCCII. die XXIIII. novēbris, finit feliciter. Sm. fol. Spire, 1502. D 5 V 1

BRIALMONT (ALEXIS HENRI). History of the Life of Arthur, Duke of Wellington ; with Emendations and Additions, by the Rev. G. R. Gleig. 4 vols. 8vo. Lond., 1858–60. C 9 V 40–43

BRICKDALE (CHARLES FORTESCUE). Registration of Title to Land. 8vo. Lond., 1886. F 8 R 18

BRIDEL (PHILIPPE-SIRACH). Glossaire du Patois de la Suisse Romande. 8vo. Lausanne, 1866. K 12 R 14

BRIDGE (HORATIO). Journal of an African Cruiser ; by "An Officer of the U. S. Navy"; edited by Nathaniel Hawthorne. 12mo. Aberdeen, 1848. D 1 T 24

BRIDGE (THOMAS WILLIAM), B.A. On the Osteology of Polyodon Folium. (Roy. Soc. Pubs. 6.) 4to. Lond., 1879. A 11 P 7 †

BRIDGEMAN (JOHN). The Knout and the Russians. [*See* DE LAGNY, G.]

BRIDGES (LIEUT.-COL. EDWARD SMITH). Round the World in Six Months. 8vo. Lond., 1879. D 10 S 1

BRIDGEWATER TREATISES. [*See* BELL, SIR CHARLES ; BUCKLAND, WILLIAM ; CHALMERS, THOMAS ; KIDD, JOHN ; KIRBY, WILLIAM ; PROUT, WILLIAM ; ROGET, P. M. ; WHEWELL, WILLIAM.]

BRIERLY (SIR OSWALD WALTER), KNT., &c. Cruise of H.M.S. *Galatea.* [*See* MILNER, REV. J.]

BRIFFAULT (F. T.) The Prisoner of Ham ; authentic details of the captivity and escape of Prince Napoleon Louis. 2nd ed. 8vo. Lond., 1870. C 4 S 28

BRIGGS (CHARLES AUGUSTUS), D.D. American Presbyterianism : its Origin and Early History ; with Maps. 8vo. Edinb., 1885. G 6 R 12

BRIGGS (GEN. JOHN), F.R.S. Memoir of : with Comments on some of his Words and Work, by Major Evans Bell. Roy. 8vo. Lond., 1885.   C 8 V 1

BRIGHT (CHARLES). Rationalism *versus* Dogma : Two Lectures in Review of Archbishop Vaughan's Lenten Discourses. (Pam. Bs.) 8vo. Sydney, 1879. MG 1 Q 34
Another copy. (Pam. Bg.)   MG 1 Q 36
[*See* HAMLET CONTROVERSY.]

BRIGHT (JOHN), M.R.C.S. Hand-book for Emigrants and others; being a History of New Zealand. 12mo. Lond., 1841.   MD 4 P 25

BRIGHT (RT. HON. JOHN), M.P. Life and Speeches of ; by George Barnett Smith ; with Portraits. 2 vols. 8vo. Lond., 1881.   C 10 P 4, 5
Public Letters of ; collected and edited by H. J. Leech. 8vo. Lond., 1885.   C 5 R 8
Speeches of, on the American Question ; with an Introduction by Frank Moore. 8vo. Boston, 1865. F 6 Q 20
Speeches on Questions of Public Policy ; edited by James E. Thorold Rogers. 2nd ed. 2 vols. 8vo. Lond., 1869.
                                          F 13 P 1, 2
[*See* CODDEN, R.]

BRIGHT (J. S.) History of Dorking and the neighbouring Parishes ; with Chapters on the Literary Associations, Flora, Fauna, Geology, &c., of the District. 8vo. Dorking, 1884.   B 7 P 12

BRIGHT (T.) Agricultural and Tenant-Right Valuer's Assistant. 8vo. Lond., 1886.   A 1 P 2

BRIGHT (WALTER). From Southern Climes. 8vo. Lond., 1883.   MD 2 V 30

BRIGHTWELL (CECILIA LUCY). Memorials of the Life of Amelia Opie ; selected and arranged from her Letters, Diaries, and other Manuscripts. 8vo. Norwich, 1854.
                                          C 9 P 13
BRIGIT (SAINT). Life of. [*See* STOKES, W.]

BRILLAT-SAVARIN (ANTHELME). Gastronomy as a Fine Art ; or, the Science of Good Living ; translated by R. E. Anderson, M.A. 8vo. Lond., 1877.   A 12 P 31

BRINDWOOD (G. C. M.) Industrial Arts of India. (South Kens. Mus.) 8vo. Lond., 1880.   E

BRINTON (PROF. DANIEL G.), A.M., &c. Aboriginal American Authors and their Productions, especially those in the Native Languages : a chapter in the History of Literature. 8vo. Philad., 1883.   B 1 S 36
American Hero-Myths : a Study in the Native Religions of the Western Continent. 8vo. Philad., 1882. G 6 P 10
Annals of the Cakchiquels ; the Original Text, with a Translation, Notes and Introduction. (Lib. of Abor. Amer. Lit.) 8vo. Philad., 1885.   B 1 S 4

BRINTON (PROF. DANIEL G.), A.M., &c.—*continued.*
The Güegüence : a Comedy Ballet in the Nahuatl-Spanish Dialect of Nicaragua. (Lib. of Abor. Amer. Lit.) 8vo. Philad., 1883.   H 3 S 25
The Lenâpé and their Legends ; with the complete Text and Symbols of the Walam Olum. A new Translation, and an Inquiry into its authenticity. 8vo. Philad., 1885.   A 1 W 33
Maya Chronicles ; edited by D. G. Brinton, M.D (Lib. of Abor. Amer. Lit.) 8vo. Philad., 1882.   B 1 T 34

BRISBANE (GENERAL SIR THOMAS MACDOUGALL), BART., K.C.B. Copies of Royal Instructions issued to. [*See* LAND REGULATIONS.]
Mean of Twelve Months' Meteorological Obervations, in the years 1822–23, at Parramatta, in New South Wales. [*See* FIELD, B.]
New South Wales Lease, granted in 1823. [*See* MANUSCRIPTS, &c.]
Reminiscences of ; by the Rev. Will. Tasker. Printed for private circulation. 4to. Edinb., 1860.   M C 4 P 1 †

BRISCOE (JOHN POTTER). F.R.H.S., &c. Old Nottinghamshire : a Collection of Papers on the History, Antiquities, Topography, &c., of Nottinghamshire. 1st and 2nd series. 2 vols. 8vo. Lond., 1881–84.   B 4 Q 7, 8

BRISSON (CAPT. PIERRE RAYMOND DE). Narrative of the Captivity of M. Capt. de Brisson in the Deserts of Africa, 1785. [*See* PERILS AND CAPTIVITY.]

BRISSON (BARNABÉ). [*See* MONGE, G.]

BRISTED (J.) America and her Resources : a view of the Agricultural, Commercial, Manufacturing, Financial, Political, Literary, Moral, and Religious Capacity and Character of the American People. 8vo. Lond., 1818.
                                          F 8 P 28
BRISTOL (C. C.) Bristol's Illustrated Almanac, 1870 and 1878. 2 vols. (in 1) 8vo. New York, 1869–78.   ME 4 P

BRISTOW (HENRY WILLIAM), F.G.S. Catalogue of Rock Specimens. Colours and Signs for Maps. [*See* RAMSAY A. C.]
Glossary of Mineralogy. 8vo. Lond., 1861. K 18 P 10
[*See* FIGUIER, L., *and* SHONIN, L.]

BRISTOWE (JOHN SYER), M.D., &c. Treatise on the Theory and Practice of Medicine. 3rd ed. 8vo. Lond., 1880.   A 12 S 36

BRISTOWE (S. B.) [*See* BURN, R.]

BRITANNICO (MERCURIO). [*See* HALL, RT. REV. J.]

BRITISH ALMANAC (THE) of the Society for the Diffusion of Useful Knowledge. 50 vols. 12mo. Lond., 1828–87.   E
Companion to the Almanac ; or, Year-book of General Information. 53 vols. 12mo. Lond., 1828–87.   E

BRITISH ARCHAEOLOGICAL ASSOCIATION. The Journal of; or the Encouragement and Prosecution of Researches into the Arts and Monuments of the Early and Middle Ages. 41 vols. roy. 8vo. Lond., 1846–85.　E

General Index to Vols. 1–30; by Walter de Grey Birch, F.R.S.L., &c. 8vo. Lond., 1875.　E

BRITISH ARCHITECTS (INSTITUTE OF). [*See* ROYAL INSTITUTE OF BRITISH ARCHITECTS.]

BRITISH ARTISTS. A Report of the Rise and Progress of the Society of; addressed to its Patrons and Supporters. 8vo. Lond., 1838.　A 7 R 21

BRITISH ASSOCIATION for the Advancement of Science. Index to the Reports and Transactions, 1831–60. 8vo. Lond., 1864.　E

Reports of the Meetings. 1831–85. 55 vols. 8vo. Lond., 1835–87.　E

BRITISH AUSTRALASIAN (THE). A Newspaper for Merchants, Shareholders, Land Selectors, Emigrants, &c. 4 vols. fol. Lond., 1884–87.　E

BRITISH CATALOGUE OF BOOKS. [*See* Low, S.]

BRITISH CHRONOLOGIST (THE). Relative to England and Wales, from the Invasion of the Romans. 3 vols. 8vo. Lond., 1789.　B 7 P 30–32

BRITISH COLONIES (THE). Shall we have a Colonial Baronage? or, shall the Colonial Empire of Great Britain be resolved into Republics? By "A Member of Parliament." 8vo. Lond., 1852.　MF 3 P 7

BRITISH COLUMBIA DIRECTORY for the years 1882–83. 8vo. Victoria, B.C., 1882.　E

BRITISH DRAMA (THE). Comprehending the best Plays in the English Language. 3 vols. (in 5) 8vo. Lond., 1804.　H 2 U 4–8

1. The Maid's Tragedy; by Beaumont and Fletcher. Philaster; by Beaumont and Fletcher. The Bondman; by Massinger. The Fatal Dowry; by Massinger and Field. The False One; by Beaumont and Fletcher. Bonduca; by Beaumont and Fletcher. The Rival Queens; by Lee. All for Love; by Dryden. The Orphan; by Otway. Venice Preserved; by Otway. The Mourning Bride; by Congreve. Tamerlane; by Rowe. The Fair Penitent; by Rowe. Cato; by Addison. The Distressed Mother; by Philips. Jane Shore; by Rowe. Lady Jane Grey; by Rowe. The Siege of Damascus; by Hughes. The Revenge; by Young. George Barnwell; by Lillo.

2. Zara; by Hill. Fatal Curiosity; by Lillo. Arden of Feversham; by Lillo. Gustavus Vasa; by Brooke. Mahomet; by Millet. Tancred and Sigismurda; by Thomson. Irene; by Johnson. The Roman Father; by Whitehead. The Brothers; by Young. The Gamester; by Moore. Boadicea; by Glover. Creusa; by Whitehead. Barbarossa; by Brown. Douglas; by Home. Isabella; by Southern. The Orphan of China; by Murphy. The Countess of Salisbury; by Hartson. The Earl of Warwick; by Franklin. Zenobia; by Murphy. The Grecian Daughter; by Murphy. Matilda; by Franklin.

O

BRITISH DRAMA (THE)—*continued.*

3. Every Man in his Humour; by Jonson. The Alchymist; by Jonson. New Way to Pay Old Debts; by Massinger. The Great Duke of Florence; by Massinger. Rule a Wife and have a Wife; by Beaumont and Fletcher. The Plain Dealer; by Wycherley. The Double Dealer; by Congreve. The Provoked Wife; by Vanbrugh. Love makes a Man; by Cibber. The Way of the World; by Congreve. Love for Love; by Congreve. The Constant Couple; by Farquhar. The Inconstant; by Farquhar. She would and She would not; by Cibber. The Careless Husband; by Cibber. The Double Gallant; by Cibber. The Recruiting Officer; by Farquhar. The Beaux Stratagem; by Farquhar.

4. The Busy Body; by Centlivre. The Wonder; by Centlivre. The Drummer; by Addison. Bold Stroke for a Wife; by Centlivre. The Conscious Lovers; by Steele. The Provoked Husband; by Vanbrugh and Cibber. The Suspicious Husband; by Hoadly. The Way to Keep Him; by Murphy. All in the Wrong; by Murphy. The Jealous Wife; by Colman. The School for Lovers; by Whitehead. The Clandestine Marriage; by Colman and Garrick. The English Merchant; by Colman. The Brothers; by Cumberland. The West Indian; by Cumberland. She Stoops to Conquer; by Goldsmith. The School for Wives; by Kelly. The Rivals; by Sheridan. The Choleric Man; by Cumberland.

5. The Cheats of Scapin; by Otway. The Country House; by Vanbrugh. The Contrivances; by Carey. The Devil to Pay; by Coffey. The Beggar's Opera; by Gay. The Intriguing Chambermaid; by Fielding. The Mock Doctor; by Fielding. Chrononhotonthologos; by Carey. The Honest Yorkshireman; by Carey. The King and the Miller of Mansfield; by Dodsley. Sir John Cockle at Court; by Dodsley. The Lying Valet; by Garrick. Miss in her Teens; by Garrick. Taste; by Foote. The Englishman in Paris; by Foote. The Knights; by Foote. The Apprentice; by Murphy. The Englishman returned from Paris; by Foote. The Author; by Foote. The Male Coquette; by Garrick. The Upholsterer; by Murphy. The Guardian; by Garrick. High Life Below Stairs; by Garrick. The Minor; by Foote. The Old Maid; by Murphy. The Citizen; by Murphy. The Liar; by Foote. The Orators; by Foote. The Deuce is in him; by Colman. Love in a Village; by Bickerstaff. The Mayor of Garratt; by Foote. The Patron; by Foote. Midas; by O'Hara. The Maid of the Mill; by Bickerstaff. The Commissary; by Foote. Neck or Nothing; by Garrick. Peep Behind the Curtain; by Garrick. Devil upon Two Sticks; by Foote. Padlock; by Bickerstaff. Dr. Last in his Chariot; by Bickerstaff and Foote. Lame Lover; by Foote. Maid of Bath; by Foote. Irish Widow; by Garrick. Midas; by Bickerstaff. Bon Ton; by Garrick. Three Weeks after Marriage; by Murphy.

BRITISH ESSAYISTS (THE). With Prefaces, Historical and Biographical, by A. Chalmers. 44 vols. 12mo. Lond., 1813–17.　J 7 R 1–44

1–4. The Tatler.
6–15. The Spectator.
16–18. The Guardian.
19–22. The Rambler.
23–25. The Adventurer.
26–29. The World.
30–32. The Connoisseur.
33. The Idler.
34, 35. The Mirror.
36, 37. The Lounger.
38–40. The Observer.
41–44. The Looker On.
45. Index.

BRITISH FARMER'S MAGAZINE (THE). Vols. 1 and 2. 8vo. Lond., 1826–27.　A 1 S 2, 3

BRITISH FLAG TRIUMPHANT ; or, the Wooden Walls of Old England ; being Copies of the London Gazettes ; containing the Accounts of the Great Victories and Gallant Exploits of the British Fleets, during the last and present War, &c. 8vo. Lond., 1806.   B 6 Q 35

BRITISH FLORIST (THE) ; or, Lady's Journal of Horticulture. Illustrated. 6 vols. 8vo. Lond., 1846.   A 4 S 11–16

BRITISH AND FOREIGN BIBLE SOCIETY (THE). Fifth Report of the Committee of. 8vo. Lond., 1809.   MG 1 Q 28

Extracts from the Correspondence of, and of the Auxiliary Bible Society of New South Wales, July, 1823 to January, 1824. 8vo. Sydney, 1823–24.   MG 1 Q 28

Sixtieth Report. 8vo. Lond., 1864.   G 10 T 23

BRITISH AND FOREIGN SCHOOL SOCIETY. A Concise Statement of the Principle of the British and Foreign School Society. With a Sketch of the Society's History, and System of Teaching ; by the Committee of the Australian School Society. 8vo. Sydney, 1839.   MG 1 Q 30

Another copy.   MG 1 R 17

BRITISH AND FOREIGN QUARTERLY REVIEW (THE). Vols. 1–8. 8vo. Lond., 1835–44.   E

BRITISH FREE SCHOOLS. Report for 1858. 8vo. Paris, 1859.   MG 1 Q 40

BRITISH HEROES AND WORTHIES. With Portraits. 8m. 4to. Lond. (n.d.)   C 8 U 13

BRITISH MANUFACTURING INDUSTRIES. Edited by G. P. Bevan, F.G.S. 14 vols. 12mo. Lond., 1876–77.   A 17 S 28–41

   Acids, Alkalies, Soda, Ammonia, and Soap; by Prof. Church.
   Agricultural Machinery; by Prof. Wrightson.
   Brass Founding, Tin Plate and Zinc Working; by W. Graham.
   Brewing, Distillery; by T. A. Pooley.
   Building Stones; by Prof. Hull.
   Butter and Cheese; by M. Evans.
   Carpets; by C. Dresser.
   Coal; by A. Galletly.
   Copper Smelting; by J. A. Phillips.
   Cotton; by I. Watts.
   Cutlery; by F. Callis.
   Dyeing and Bleaching; by T. Sims.
   Engraving; by S. Davenport.
   Explosive Compounds; by W. M. Williams.
   Fibres and Cordage; by P. L. Simmonds.
   Flax and Linen; by W. T. Charley.
   Furniture and Woodwork; by J. H. Pollen.
   Gas and Lighting; by R. H. Patterson.
   Glass and Silicates; by Prof. F. S. Barff.
   Guns, Nails, Locks, Wood-screws, Railway Bolts and Spikes, Buttons, Pins, Needles, Saddlery, and Electroplate; by W. C. Aitkin.
   Gold-working; by Rev. G. Boutell.
   Guttapercha and India-rubber; by J. Collins.
   Hides and Leather; by J. Collins.
   Hosiery and Lace; by W. Felkin.
   The Industrial Classes and Industrial Statistics; by G. P. Bevan.—Mining, Metals, Chemicals, Ceramics, Glass, and Paper.
   The Industrial Classes and Industrial Statistics; by G. P. Bevan.—Textiles and Clothing, Food, Sundry Industries.
   Iron and Steel; by W. M. Williams.
   Jewellery; by G. Wallis.
   Metallic Mining and Collieries; by W. W. Smyth.

BRITISH MANUFACTURING INDUSTRIES—*contd.*
   Musical Instruments; by E. F. Rimbault.
   Oils and Candles; by W. M. Williams.
   Paper; by Prof. T. C. Archer.
   Pens and Papier Mâché; by G. Lindsey.
   Photography; by P. le N. Foster.
   Printing and Bookbinding; by J. Hatton.
   Pottery; by L. Arnoux.
   Railways and Tramways ; by D. K. Clark.
   Salt, Preservation of Food, Bread and Biscuits; by J. J. Manley.
   Ship-building; by Capt. B. Pim.
   Silk; by B. F. Cobb.
   Sugar Refining; by C. H. Gill.
   Telegraphy; by R. Sabine.
   Tobacco; by J. Dunning.
   Toys; by G. C. T. Bartley.
   Watches and Clocks; by F. J. Britten.
   Wool and its applications; by Prof. T. C. Archer.

[*See* BEVAN, G. P.]

BRITISH MILITARY COMMANDERS. Lives of. (Lard. Cab. Cyclo.) 3 vol. 8vo. Lond., 1831–32.   K 18 7–9

BRITISH MUSEUM. Book of British Topography : a Classified Catalogue of the Topographical Works in the British Museum; by John P. Anderson. 8vo. Lond., 1881.   K 8 P 14

Catalogue of the Greek Coins in the British Museum. [*See* POOLE, R. S. ; HEAD, B. V., AND GARDNER, P.]

Catalogue of Indian Coins in. [*See* POOLE, S. L.]

Catalogue of the Mammalia and Birds of New Guinea. [*See* GRAY, J. E., AND G. R.]

Catalogue of the Specimens of Lizards in the Collection of the British Museum. [*See* GRAY, J. E.]

Catalogue of the Specimens of Snakes in the Collection of the British Museum. [*See* GRAY, J. E.]

Catalogue of the Tortoises, Crocodiles, and Amphisbænians, in the Collection of the British Museum. [*See* GRAY, J. E.]

Catalogue of Printed Maps, Plans, and Charts in the British Museum. 2 vols. sm. fol. Lond., 1885.   A 27 P 12, 13 ‡

Gallery of Antiquities ; selected from the British Museum, by F. Arundale and J. Bonomi. 4to. Lond., 1842–43.   B 16 Q 20 †

Hand-List of Bibliographies, Classified Catalogues, and Indexes placed in the Reading Room of the British Museum for Reference. [By G. W. Porter.] 8vo. Lond., 1881.   K 7 R 28

List of the Books of Reference in the Reading Room of the British Museum. [Compiled by W. B. Rye.] 2nd ed., revised. 8vo. Lond., 1871.   K 7 S 28

Lives of the Founders of the British Museum. 2 vols. 8vo. Lond., 1570–1870.   C 10 U 10, 11

Photographs from the Collections of the British Museum ; taken by S. Thompson. 12 vols. large 4to. Lond., 1872.   A 21 Q 1–12 ‡

   Antiquities of Britain and Foreign Mediæval Art.
   Assyrian Antiquities. 3 vols.
   Etruscan and Roman Antiquities.
   Egyptian Antiquities. 2 vols.
   Grecian Antiquities. 2 vols.
   Prehistoric Ethnographical, and Christy Collection. 2 vols.
   Seals of Sovereigns, Corporation, Monasteries, &c.

Bri]　　　　　　PART I :—*Authors, Editors, or Reference.*　　　　　[Bri

BRITISH MUSEUM—*continued.*

Catalogue of Photographs ; by A. W. Franks, M.A.; S. Birch, LL.D. ; George Smith ; and W. de Gray Birch. 8vo. Lond., 1872.　　　　　　　A 21 Q 13 ‡

Catalogue of American Books in the Library ; by Henry Stevens, M.A., &c. Roy. 8vo. Lond., 1866.　　K 8 P 12

Catalogue of the Mexican and other Spanish American West Indian Books in the Library ; by Henry Stevens, M.A. Roy. 8vo. Lond., 1866.　　　　　K 8 P 12

Catalogue of Canadian and other British North American Books in the Library ; by Henry Stevens, M.A. 8vo. Lond., 1866.　　　　　　　　　K 8 P 12

Catalogue of the American Maps in the Library ; by Henry Stevens. 8vo. Lond., 1866.　　　　　K 8 P 12

Regulations. 8vo. Lond., 1873.　　　　　　Libr.

Subject Index of the Modern Works in Library of. [*See* FORTESCUE, G. K.]

Synopsis of the Contents of. 34th ed. 12mo. Lond., 1837.　　　　　　　　　　　　A 7 P 35

[*See* ARUNDALE, F.]

BRITISH MUSEUM LIBRARIAN, A. [*See* TALES FROM TWELVE TONGUES.]

BRITISH PHARMACOPŒIA.

Published under the direction of the General Council of Medical Education and Registration of the United Kingdom, pursuant to the Medical Act, 1858. 8vo. Lond., 1867.　　　　　　　　　　　K 9 P 4

Another copy. 8vo. Lond., 1885.　　　　　K 9 P 7

Companion to the British Pharmacopœia. [*See* SQUIRE, P.]

BRITISH POETS (THE). Cabinet Edition of the British Poets. 4 vols. 12mo. Lond., 1871.　　H 5 S 25-28

1. Milton, Cowper, Goldsmith, Thomson, Falconer, Akenside, Collins, Gray, Somerville.
2. H. K. White, Burns, Beattie, Gay, Shenstone, Butler, Byron.
3. Hannah More, Pope, Isaac Watts, Hayley, Mason, Prior, Grahame, Logan.
4. Dryden, Lyttleton, Hammond, Charlotte Smith, Richardson, Bloomfield, Gifford, Canning.

BRITISH QUARTERLY REVIEW (THE). Vols. 1-81. 8vo. Lond., 1845-85.　　　　　　　　　　E

BRITISH REFORMERS. 12 vols. 8vo. Lond., 1831.　　　　　　　　　　　　　G 13 S 5-16

1. Writings of the Rev. Thomas Becon.
2. Writings of the Rev. John Bradford.
3. Writings of Cranmer, Rogers, Saunders, Taylor, and Careless.
4. Writings of Edward vi, William Hugh, Queen Catherine Parr, Anne Askew, Lady Jane Grey, Hamilton, and Balnaves.
5. Writings of John Fox, Bale, and Coverdale.
6. Writings of Dr. John Hooper.
7. Writings of John Jewell, Bishop of Salisbury.
8. Writings of the Rev. John Knox.
9. Select Sermons and Letters of Dr. Hugh Latimer.
10. Treatises and Letters of Dr. Nicholas Ridley, and Examinations and Letters of Rev. J. Philpot.
11. Writings of Tindal, Frith, and Barnes.
12. Writings, &c., of John Wickliff, Brute, Thorpe, Cobham, Hilton, Pecock, [Garret,] Bilney, and others.

BRITISH RESIDENT, A. [*See* SCARTH, REV. J.]

BRITISH THEATRE ; comprising Tragedies, Comedies, Operas, and Farces, from the most classic writers. By "An Englishman." Roy. 8vo. Leipsic, 1828.　H 2 U 9

BRITISH THEATRE (THE). The British Theatre ; or, a Collection of Plays ; with Biographical and Critical Remarks, by Mrs. Inchbald. 25 vols. 12mo. Lond., 1808.　　　　　　　　　　　　　H 1 P 1-25

1. Comedy of Errors ; by Wm. Shakspeare. Romeo and Juliet: a Tragedy ; by Wm. Shakspeare. Hamlet : a Tragedy ; by Wm. Shakspeare. King John : a Historical Play ; by Wm. Shakspeare. Richard III : a Tragedy ; by Wm. Shakspeare.
2. Henry IV, Parts 1 and 2 : a Historical Play ; by Wm. Shakspeare. Merchant of Venice: a Comedy ; by Wm. Shakspeare. Henry v : a Historical Play ; by Wm. Shakspeare. Much Ado about Nothing : a Comedy ; by Wm. Shakspeare.
3. As You Like It : a Comedy ; by Wm. Shakspeare. Merry Wives of Windsor : a Comedy ; by Wm. Shakspeare. Henry VIII : a Historical Play ; by Wm. Shakspeare. Measure for Measure : a Comedy ; by Wm. Shakspeare. Winter's Tale : a Play ; by Wm. Shakspeare.
4. King Lear ; a Tragedy ; by Wm. Shakspeare. Cymbeline : a Historical Play ; by Wm. Shakspeare. Macbeth : a Tragedy ; by Wm. Shakspeare. Julius Cæsar : a Tragedy ; by Wm. Shakspeare. Antony and Cleopatra : a Historical Play ; by Wm. Shakspeare.
5. Coriolanus : a Historical Play ; by Wm. Shakspeare. Othello: a Tragedy ; by Wm. Shakspeare. The Tempest : a Play ; by Wm. Shakspeare. Twelfth Night : a Comedy ; by Wm. Shakspeare. Every Man in his Humour : a Comedy ; by Ben Jonson.
6. Rule a Wife and Have a Wife : a Comedy ; by F. Beaumont and J. Fletcher. The Chances : a Comedy ; by F. Beaumont and J. Fletcher. New Way to Pay Old Debts ; a Comedy ; by Philip Massinger. Rival Queens : a Tragedy ; by Nathaniel Lee. All for Love : a Tragedy ; by John Dryden.
7. Isabella : a Tragedy ; by Thomas Southern. Oroonoko : a Tragedy ; by Thomas Southern. The Distressed Mother : a Tragedy ; by Ambrose Philips. Zara : a Tragedy ; by Aaron Hill. Gustavus Vasa : a Tragedy ; by Henry Brooke.
8. The Constant Couple : a Comedy ; by George Farquhar. The Inconstant : a Comedy ; by George Farquhar. The Recruiting Officer: a Comedy ; by George Farquhar. The Beaux Stratagem : a Comedy ; by George Farquhar. Cato : a Tragedy ; by Joseph Addison.
9. The Provoked Wife : a Comedy ; by Sir John Vanbrugh. The Provoked Husband : a Comedy ; by Sir J. Vanbrugh and C. Cibber. Love makes a Man ; a Comedy ; by Colley Cibber. She Wou'd and She Wou'd Not : a Comedy ; by Colley Cibber. The Careless Husband : a Comedy ; by Colley Cibber.
10. Tamerlane : a Tragedy ; by Nicholas Rowe. The Fair Penitent : a Tragedy ; by Nicholas Rowe. Jane Shore : a Tragedy ; by Nicholas Rowe. Lady Jane Grey : a Tragedy by Nicholas Rowe. Siege of Damascus : a Tragedy ; by John Hughes.
11. The Busy Body : a Comedy ; by Mrs. Centlivre. The Wonder a Woman keeps a Secret : a Comedy ; by Mrs. Centlivre. A Bold Stroke for a Wife : a Comedy ; by Mrs. Centlivre. George Barnwell : a Tragedy ; by George Lillo. Fatal Curiosity : a Tragedy ; by George Lillo.
12. The Orphan : a Tragedy ; by Thomas Otway. Venice Preserved ; a Tragedy : by Thomas Otway. Conscious Lovers : a Comedy ; by Sir Richard Steele. The Revenge : a Tragedy ; by Edward Young, LL.D. The Beggar's Opera ; by John Gay.
13. Love for Love : a Comedy ; by Wm. Congreve. The Mourning Bride : a Tragedy ; by Wm. Congreve. Mahomet : a Tragedy ; by Rev. Mr. Miller. Tancred and Sigismunda : a Tragedy ; by James Thomson. The Suspicious Husband : a Comedy ; by Dr. Hoadly.

BRITISH THEATRE (THE)—*continued.*

14. The Man of the World: a Comedy; by Charles Macklin. The Foundling: a Comedy; by Edward Moore. The Gamester: a Tragedy; by Edward Moore. The Roman Father: a Tragedy; by Wm. Whitehead. Edward, the Black Prince: an Historical Tragedy; by Wm. Shirley.

15. Barbarossa: a Tragedy; by Dr. Brown. The Way to Keep Him: a Comedy; by Arthur Murphy. All in the Wrong: a Comedy; by Arthur Murphy. The Grecian Daughter: a Tragedy; by Arthur Murphy. Know Your Own Mind: a Comedy; by Arthur Murphy.

16. The Country Girl: a Comedy; by David Garrick. The Jealous Wife: a Comedy; by G. Colman. The Clandestine Marriage: a Comedy; by G. Colman, and D. Garrick. The Countess of Salisbury: a Tragedy; by Hall Hartson. Douglas: a Tragedy; by Mr. Home.

17. The Good natured Man: a Comedy; by Dr. Goldsmith. She Stoops to Conquer: a Comedy; by Dr. Goldsmith. Love in Village: a Comic Opera; by Isaac Bickerstaff. The Maid of the Mill: a Comic Opera; by Isaac Bickerstaff. Lionel and Clarissa: a Comic Opera; by Isaac Bickerstaff.

18. The Brothers: a Comedy; by Richard Cumberland. The West Indian: a Comedy; by Richard Cumberland. The Jew: a Comedy; by Richard Cumberland. First Love: a Comedy; by Richard Cumberland. The Wheel of Fortune: a Comedy; by Richard Cumberland.

19. The Earl of Warwick: a Tragedy [by J. F. Laharpe; trans.] by Dr. Franklin. The Rivals: a Comedy; by Richard Brinsley Sheridan. The Duenna: a Comic Opera; by Richard Brinsley Sheridan. The Belle's Stratagem: a Comedy; by Mrs. Cowley. A Bold Stroke for a Husband: a Comedy; by Mrs. Cowley.

20. The Dramatist: a Comedy; by Frederick Reynolds. The Count of Narbonne: a Tragedy; by Robert Jephson. Inkle and Yarico: an Opera; by G. Colman, the younger. The Battle of Hexham: a Play; by George Colman, the younger. The Surrender of Calais: a Play; by George Colman, the younger.

21. The Mountaineers: a Play; by George Colman, the younger. The Iron Chest: a Play; by George Colman, the younger. The Heir-at-Law: a Comedy; by George Colman, the younger. John Bull: a Comedy; by George Colman, the younger. The Poor Gentleman: a Comedy; by George Colman, the younger.

22. The Castle of Andalusia: a Comic Opera; by John O'Keeffe. Fontainbleau: a Comic Opera; by John O'Keeffe. Wild Oats: a Comedy; by John O'Keeffe. The Heiress: a Comedy; by General Burgoyne. The Earl of Essex: a Tragedy; by Henry Jones.

23. Such Things Are: a Play; by Mrs. Inchbald. Every One has his Fault: a Comedy; by Mrs. Inchbald. Wives as they were, and Maids as they are: a Comedy; by Mrs. Inchbald. Lovers' Vows: a Play; by Mrs. Inchbald. To Marry or not to Marry: a Comedy; by Mrs. Inchbald.

24. The Road to Ruin: a Comedy; by Thomas Holcroft. The Deserted Daughter: a Comedy; by Thomas Holcroft. The Stranger: a Drama; by Benjamin Thompson. De Montfort: a Tragedy; by Joanna Baillie. The Point of Honour: a Comedy; by Charles Kemble.

25. The Way to get Married: a Comedy; by Thomas Morton. A Cure for the Heart Ache: a Comedy; by Thomas Morton. Speed the Plough: a Comedy; by Thomas Morton. The School of Reform: a Comedy; by Thomas Morton. The Honeymoon: a Comedy; by John Tobin.

BRITISH WOOL TRADE. Abstracts of the Evidence taken before the Select Committee of the House of Lords, appointed to take into consideration the state of the British Wool Trade, classed under different heads. 8vo. Lond., 1828. MJ 2 Q 19

BRITTEN (MRS. E. H.) The Truth; or, how Mrs. E. Hardynge Britten "opened her Mouth and put her Foot in it," at the Opera House, Melbourne; by "Echo." 8vo. Richmond (n.d.) MJ 2 R 15

BRITTEN (F. J.) Watch and Clockmakers' Hand-book, Dictionary, and Guide. 4th ed. Lond., 1884. A 11 R 3

Watches and Clocks. (Brit. Manuf. Indust.) 12mo. Lond., 1876. A 17 S 31

BRITTEN (JAMES), F.L.S. European Ferns; with coloured Illustrations from Nature, by D. Blair, F.L.S. 4to. Lond., 1881. A 5 Q 7

BRITTON (HENRY). Fiji in 1870; being the Letters of *The Argus* Special Correspondent; with a complete Map and Gazetteer of the Fijian Archipelago. 8vo. Melb., 1870. MD 1 U 21

Lolóma; or, Two Years in Cannibal-Land: a Story of Old Fiji. 8vo. Melb., 1883. MD 4 T 37

BRITTON (JOHN), F.S.A., &c. Architectural Antiquities of Great Britain: Views, Elevations, Plans, Sections, and Details, of ancient English Edifices. 5 vols. 4to. Lond., 1807-35. A 2 T 3-7

Beauties of England and Wales. [*See* BEAUTIES OF ENGLAND AND WALES.]

Cathedral Antiquities: Historical and Descriptive Accounts of English Cathedrals, viz:—Canterbury, York, Salisbury, Norwich, Oxford, Winchester, Lichfield, Hereford, Wells, Exeter, Worcester, Peterborough, Gloucester, and Bristol. 5 vols. 4to. Lond., 1836. A 2 T 8-12

Historical and Architectural Essay, relating to Redcliffe Church, Bristol; illustrated with Plans; including an Account of the Monuments; and an Essay on the Life and Character of Thomas Chatterton. Roy. 4to. 1813. B 18 R 16 ‡

History and Antiquities of the Abbey and Cathedral Church of Bristol; illustrated by Engravings of Views, Plans, &c. Roy. 4to. Lond., 1830. B 18 Q 6 ‡

History and Antiquities of the Abbey and Cathedral Church of Gloucester; illustrated by Engravings of Views, Plans, &c. Roy. 4to. Lond., 1836. B 17 Q 17 ‡

History and Antiquities of the Cathedral Church of Salisbury; illustrated with engraved Plans, &c. Roy. 4to. Lond., 1814. B 18 R 16 ‡

History and Antiquities of the Metropolitical Church of York; illustrated by a series of Engravings of Views. Roy. 4to. Lond., 1819. B 18 Q 5 ‡

History and Antiquities of the See and Cathedral Church of Norwich; illustrated with a series of Engravings. Roy. 4to. Lond., 1816. B 18 R 16 ‡

Natural History of Wiltshire. [*See* AUBREY, J.]

BRITTON (JOHN), F.S.A., &c., AND BRAYLEY (EDWARD WEDLAKE). Topographical and Historical Description of the Counties of Berks and Buckingham; accompanied with Biographical Notices of Eminent and Learned Men to whom this County has given Birth. Illustrated. 8vo. Lond., 1810. B 2 S 39

BRITTON (JOHN), F.S.A., &c., AND PUGIN (AUGUSTUS). Historical and Descriptive Essays of the Architectural Antiquities of Normandy; engraved by John and Henry Le Keux. 4to. Lond., 1828. A 2 T 32

Illustrations of the Public Buildings of London; with Historical and Descriptive Accounts of each Edifice. 2 vols. roy. 8vo. Lond., 1825. A 2 S 31, 32

BROADHEAD (G. C.) Report of the Geological Survey of Missouri, including Field Work of 1873-74. Roy. 8vo. Jefferson City, 1874. E

BROADHOUSE (JOHN). Musical Acoustics; or, the Phenomena of Sound, as connected with Music. (The Student's Helmholtz.) 8vo. Lond., 1881. A 7 P 15

BROADHURST (HENRY), AND REID (ROBERT T.) Leasehold Enfranchisement. 8vo. Lond., 1885. F 6 P 26

BROADLEY (A. MEYRICK). The Last Punic War: Tunis, Past and Present; with a Narrative of the French Conquest of the Regency. 2 vols. 8vo. Edinb.. 1882. B 1 P 39, 40

BROCARD (F.) Descriptio Terræ Sanctae, et Regionum Finitimarum. Sm. 4to. Magdeburg, 1587. D 5 S 29

BROCHANT (A. J. M.) Traité Elémentaire de Minéralogie. 2 vols. 8vo. Paris, 1801-3. A 9 Q 44, 45

BROCK (REV. WILLIAM). Biographical Sketch of Sir Henry Havelock, K.C.B. 4th ed. 12mo. Lond., 1858. C 1 T 36

BROCK-ARNOLD (GEORGE M.), M.A. John Constable. (Great Artists.) 8vo. Lond., 1881. C 3 T 31

Thomas Gainsborough. (Great Artists.) 8vo. Lond., 1881. C 3 T 31

BROCKEDON (WILLIAM), F.R.S. Finden's Illustrations of Lord Byron. [*See* FINDEN.]

Journals of Excursions in the Alps. 8vo. Lond., 1833. D 8 P 30

The Holy Land, Syria, &c. [*See* ROBERTS, D.]

BROCKETT (L. P.), A.M., &c. Our Country's Wealth and Influence, from 1620 to 1880. 8vo. Hartford, Conn., 1882. B 1 U 3

Our Western Empire; or, the New West beyond the Mississippi. Roy 8vo. Philad., 1881. D 3 U 31

BROCKETT (WILLIAM EDWARD). Narrative of a Voyage from Sydney to Torres' Straits, in search of the Survivors of the *Charles Eaton*, in His Majesty's Colonial Schooner *Isabella*. 8vo. Sydney, 1836.* MD 2 V 5

BROCKHAUS (FRIEDRICH ARNOLD). Die Firma F. A. Brockhaus in Leipzig. Zum hundertjährigen Geburtstage, 4 Mai, 1872. Imp. 4to. Leipzig, 1872. A 7 P 12 ‡

BROCKLEHURST (THOMAS UNETT). Mexico to-day: a Country with a Great Future, and a Glance at the Prehistoric Remains and Antiquities of the Montezumas. Illustrated. 8vo. Lond., 1883. D 3 T 29

BROCQUIERE (BERTRANDON DE LA). Travels of; to Palestine, and his Return from Jerusalem overland to France, during the years 1432 and 1433; translated by Thomas Johnes. 8vo. Hafod, 1807. D 4 U 3

BRODERIP (W. J.), F.R.S., &c. Leaves from the Note-book of a Naturalist. 8vo. Lond., 1852. A 16 Q 20

Zoological Recreations. 8vo. Lond., 1847. A 14 S 21

BRODIE (SIR BENJAMIN). Use and Abuse of Tobacco. [*See* PARTON, J.]

BRODIE (SIR BENJAMIN COLLINS), BART, &c. Autobiography of. [Edited by C. Hawkins, F.R.C.S.] 12mo. Lond., 1865. C 1 Q 31

Calculus of Chemical Operations. Part 2. On the Analysis of Chemical Events. (Roy. Soc. Pubs. 4.) 4to. Lond., 1877. A 11 P 5 ‡

Psychological Inquiries; in a series of Essays. 12mo. Lond., 1855. G 13 R 8

Another copy. 2nd ed. G 13 R 9

BRODIE (WALTER). Pitcairn's Island, and the Islanders, in 1850; together with Extracts from his Private Journal. 8vo. Lond., 1851.* MD 3 S 5

Remarks on the Past and Present State of New Zealand, its Government, Capabilities, and Prospects. 8vo. Lond., 1845.* MD 5 S 37

BRODRIB (JOHN HENRY). Henry Irving. [*See* IRVING, HENRY.]

BRODRIBB (HON. W. A.), F.R.G.S. Plain Statement of Facts, addressed to the Small and Large Capitalists, and the Labouring Classes in England and elsewhere, on the Great Capabilities and Natural Advantages of the Australian Colonies, particularly New South Wales and Victoria, for Emigration. 8vo. Lond., 1863. MD 7 Q 15

Another copy. MF 3 P 8

Recollections of an Australian Squatter; or, Leaves from my Journal since 1835. 8vo. Sydney, 1883.* MD 7 Q 16

BRODRIBB (W. J.) [*See* LIVIUS, T.]

BRODRICK (HON. GEORGE CHARLES). English Land and English Landlords. 8vo. Lond., 1881. F 10 Q 1

The Law and Custom of Primogeniture. [*See* COBDEN CLUB.]

A History of the University of Oxford. 12mo. Lond., 1886. B 4 P 18

Political Studies. 8vo. Lond., 1879. F 6 V 18

BRODZKY (MAURICE). Genius, Lunacy, and Knavery: a Story of a Colonial Physician (David Hailprin). 12mo. Melb., 1876. MA 2 S 38

BROFFERIO (A.) Storia del Piemonte. 5 vols. (in 1 8vo. Torino, 1849-52. B 11 U 42

BROGLIE (ACHILLE L. V. C.) DUC DE. Ecrits et Discours 3 vols. 8vo. Paris, 1863. J 17 P 1-3

BROGLIE (C. J. V. ALBERT), DUC DE. L'Église et l'Empire Romain au IVe Siècle. 4e éd. 6 vols. 8vo. Paris, 1867–69.   G 6 R 4–9

Frederick the Great, and Maria Theresa, from hitherto unpublished Documents, 1740–42; from the French, by Mrs. Cashel Hoey and Mr. John Lillie. 2 vols. 8vo. Lond., 1883.   B 9 R 6, 7

The King's Secret; being the Secret Correspondence of Louis xv with his Diplomatic Agents, from 1772–74. 2 vols. 8vo. Lond., 1879.   B 8 R 1, 2

Nouvelles Etudes de Littérature et de Morale. 8vo. Paris, 1869.   J 2 R 29

Questions de Religion et d'Histoire. 2e éd. 2 vols. 12mo. Paris, 1863.   G 13 R 5, 6

BROINOWSKI (GRACIUS J.) "GRACIUS BROWNE." Panoramic View of Old London, A.D. 1647, reproduced by means of Photo-Lithography from an Ancient Engraving by Wenceslaus Hollar. Fol. Melb., 1879. MD 5 Q 5 †

BROMBY (REV. J. E.), D.D. Beyond the Grave: a Lecture, delivered at the Town Hall, 15th November, 1870. 8vo. Melb., 1870.   MG 1 Q 37

Creation and Development. [*See* PERRY, RT. REV. C.]

Pre-Historic Man : a Lecture, delivered at the Princess' Theatre, Melbourne, on August 9, 1869. 8vo. Melb., 1869.   MG 1 Q 37

Another copy.   MJ 2 R 23

BROME (ALEXANDER). Life and Poems of. [*See* CHALMERS, A.]

BROME (RICHARD). Dramatic Works of; containing Fifteen Comedies, now first collected. 3 vols. 8vo. Lond., 1873.   H 2 S 1–3

BROMLEY (LIEUT. A. C. B.) [*See* NARES, CAPT. SIR G. S.]

BROMLEY (HENRY). A Catalogue of Engraved British Portraits, from Egbert the Great to the present time. 4to. Lond., 1793.   K 8 R 28 †

BROMLEY (REV. ROBERT ANTHONY), B.D. A Philosophical and Critical History of the Fine Arts, Painting, Sculpture, and Architecture. With occasional observations on the Progress of Engraving. 2 vols. 4to. Lond., 1793–5.   A 7 V 10, 11

BRONGNIART (ADOLPHE THEODORE). Annales des Sciences Naturelles. [*See* AUDOUIN. J. V.]

[*See also* DUPERREY, L. I.]

BRONGNIART (ALEXANDRE). Geological Memoirs. [*See* GEOLOGICAL MEMOIRS.]

BRONIKOWSKI (ALEXANDER). The Court of Sigismund Augustus; or, Poland in the 16th Century. 3 vols. 8vo. Lond., 1834   J 4 R 6–8

BRONN (DR. H. G.) Die Klassen und Ordnungen des Thier-Reichs, wissenschaftlich dargestellt in Wort und Bild. Vols. 1–3, 5, and 6, part 2. N.s., vol. 2. Roy. 8vo. Leipzig, 1859–87.   E

BRONTË (CHARLOTTE). "CURRER BELL." The Life of; by E. C. Gaskell. 2 vols. 8vo. Lond., 1857. C 3 R 9, 10

Another copy. 4th ed. 8vo. Lond., 1858.   C 3 R 11

A Note on; by Algernon Charles Swinburne. 8vo. Lond., 1877.   C 2 S 6

BRONTË (PATRICK BRANWELL). [*See* LEYLAND, F. A.]

BRONTE ESTATE (THE), Waverley. Particulars and Description, with Plan of the Property. Roy. 8vo. Sydney, 1882.   MD 3 V 29

BRONTE FAMILY (THE). With special reference to Patrick Branwell Brontë; by Francis A. Leyland. 2 vols. 8vo. Lond., 1886.   C 2 S 4, 5

BROOKE (A. DE CAPELL), M.A. Travels through Sweden, Norway, and Finmark, to the North Cape, in the Summer of 1820. 4to. Lond., 1823.   D 8 V 25

BROOKE (CHARLES). Ten Years in Sarawak. Illustrated. 2 vols. 8vo. Lond., 1866.   D 5 R 5, 6

BROOKE (MRS. FRANCES). Rosina: a Comic Opera. [*See* FARCES, 3.]

BROOKE (HENRY). The Fool of Quality; or, the History of Henry, Earl of Moreland. 5 vols. 12mo. Lond., 1777.   J 16 T 24–28

Gustavus Vasa; or, the Deliverer of his Country. (Brit. Theatre). 12mo. Lond., 1808.   H 1 R 7

Another copy. (Bell's Brit. Theatre.) 18mo. Lond., 1791.   H 2 P 2

Life and Poems of. [*See* CHALMERS, A.]

BROOKE (H. J.) [*See* PHILLIPS, W.]

BROOKE (SIR JAMES), K.C.B., RAJAH OF SARAWAK. Extracts from the Journal of. [*See* KEPPEL, CAPT. H.]

Life of; from his Personal Papers and Correspondence, by Spenser St. John, F.R.G.S. 8vo. Edinb., 1879. C 3 R 25

Narrative of Events in Borneo and Celebes down to the occupation of Labuan ; together with a Narrative of the operations of H.M.S. Iris, by Capt. R. Mundy. 2 vols. 8vo. Lond., 1848.   D 4 T 1, 2

Private Journal of Sir James Brooke, K.C.B. [*See* KEPPEL, CAPT. HON. H.]

The Private Letters of, narrating the events of his Life from 1838 to the present time; edited by John C. Templer. 3 vols. 8vo. Lond., 1853.   C 3 R 22–24

[*See* LOW, HUGH.]

BROOKE (Rev. Stopford Augustus), M.A.　English Literature.　8vo.　Lond., 1880.　　B 3 T 7

Life and Letters of F. W. Robertson, M.A.　3rd ed. 2 vols. 8vo.　Lond., 1866.　　C 4 R 34, 35

Notes on the Liber Studiorum of J. M. W. Turner; with Illustrations.　8vo.　Lond., 1885.　　A 6 V 24

BROOKE (T. H.)　History of the Island of St. Helena, from its Discovery by the Portuguese to 1823.　8vo. Lond., 1824.　　B 1 P 43

BROOKES (Richard), M.D.　General Gazetteer and Geographical Dictionary.　New and enlarged edition. Roy. 8vo.　Lond., 1876.　　D 11 U 3

BROOKFIELD (Rev. W. H.)　Report on the King's Somborne School.　(Pam. 41.)　12mo.　Lond., 1851.　　MJ 2 R 3

BROOKLYN LIBRARY.　Analytical and Classed Catalogue of the Brooklyn Library; Authors, Titles, Subjects and Classes.　Sm. fol.　Brooklyn, New York, 1878-80.　　K 27 P 14 ‡

BROOKS (Edward).　Answer to the Pamphlet of Mr. John A. Lowell.　Roy. 8vo.　Boston, 1851.　　J 10 V 4

BROOKS (Henry).　Natal: a History and Description of the Colony; edited by Dr. R. J. Mann, F.R.A.S., &c. 8vo.　Lond., 1876.　　D 2 P 3

BROOKS (J. T.), M.D.　Four Months among the Gold-finders in Alta-California.　8vo.　Lond., 1849.　　D 3 Q 11

BROOKS (S. H.)　Erection of Dwelling-houses; with the Specification, Quantities, and Estimates, and every requisite detail for their construction.　12mo.　Lond., 1870.　　A 2 R 21

Another copy.　(Weale.)　　A 17 P 63

BROOKS (Rev. S. W.)　Charity and Philanthropy: a Prize Essay—Historical, Statistical, and General.　(Pam. Jb.)　8vo.　Sydney, 1878.　　MF 3 P 21

Another copy.　　MF 3 P 22

BROOKS (T. B.), PUMPELLY (R.), AND ROMINGER (Dr.)　Geological Survey of Michigan [United States], 1869-73; accompanied by an Atlas of Maps.　4 vols. 8vo. N. York, 1873.　　A 9 U 7-10

BROOKS (William Keith), Ph.D.　Hand-book of Invertebrate Zoology; for Laboratories and Seaside Work. 8vo.　Boston, 1882.　　A 15 P 6

BROOM (Herbert), LL.D.　Commentaries on the Common Law, designed as Introductory to its study.　8vo. Lond., 1869.　　F 10 R 15

Selection of Legal Maxims, classified and illustrated.　8vo. Lond., 1870.　　F 10 R 16

BROOME (Lady).　[*See* Barker, Lady M. A.]

BROOME (Sir Frederick Napier), K.C.M.G.　Poems from New Zealand.　12mo.　Lond., 1868.　MH 1 R 33

BROOME (Rev. William), M.A., &c.　Life and Poems of. [*See* Chalmers, A., *and* Johnson, S.]

BROSSES (Charles de).　Histoire des Navigations aux Terres Australes.　2 vols. 4to.　Paris, 1756.*　MD 4 P 33, 34 †

BROTHERHEAD (William).　Centennial Book of the Signers; being Fac-Simile Letters of each Signer of the Declaration of Independence; with a Historical Monograph and a History of the Centennial Exhibition.　Illustrated.　Roy. fol.　Philad., 1875.　　B 23 Q 19 ‡

BROTHERS (Thomas).　United States of North America as they are,—not as they are generally described.　8vo. Lond., 1840.　　F 6 V 19

BROTIER (G.)　[*See* Plinius Secundus, C.]

BROUGH (J. C.)　[*See* Cooley, A. J.]

BROUGH (Robert B.)　The Comic Almanac.　[*See* Cruikshank, G.]

BROUGHAM (Henry), Lord, F.R.S　Addresses of, in Opening the Congress of the National Association for Promoting Social Science.　(Pam. Dd.)　8vo.　Lond., 1860.　　F 12 P 22

Contributions to the *Edinburgh Review*.　3 vols. 8vo. Lond., 1856.　　J 8 S 26-28

Discourse of Natural Theology.　2nd ed.　8vo.　Lond., 1835.　　G 16 R 8

Historical Sketches of Statesmen who flourished in the time of George III.　1st, 2nd, and 3rd series.　2nd ed. 3 vols. roy. 8vo.　Lond., 1839-43.　　C 8 V 32-34

History of England and France under the House of Lancaster.　2nd ed.　8vo.　Lond., 1855.　　B 5 S 39

Inquiry into the Colonial Policy of the European Powers. 2 vols. 8vo.　Edinb., 1803.　　F 10 Q 17, 18

Installation Address, delivered on the 18th May, 1860. (Pam. 40.)　12mo.　Edinb., 1860.　　MJ 2 R 2

Life and Times of; written by himself.　2nd ed.　3 vols. 8vo.　Edinb., 1871.　　C 10 R 29-31

Lives of Men of Letters and Science who flourished in the time of George III.　2 vols. roy. 8vo.　Lond., 1845.　　C 5 W 15, 16

Letters on Law Reform, to the Rt. Hon. Sir J. R. G. Graham.　3rd ed.　(Pam. 11.)　8vo.　Lond., 1843.　　F 12 P 9

Letter to the Marquess of Lansdowne on the late Revolution in France.　(Pam. 25.)　8vo.　Lond., 1848.　MJ 2 Q 13

Memoir of the Rt. Hon. Thomas, Lord Erskine.　[*See* Erskine, Rt. Hon. T., Lord.]

Natural Theology.　[*See* Paley, Rev. W.]

Opinions on Politics, Theology, Law Science, Education &c.; with a Memoir.　8vo.　Lond. 1837.　　J 5 S 28

BROUGHAM (Henry), Lord, F.R.S.—*continued.*
Political Philosophy. 3 vols. 8vo. Lord., 1853.
F 10 R 17–19

Practical Observations upon the Education of the People, addressed to the Working Classes and their Employers. (Pam. 5.) 8vo. Lord., 1825. MJ 2 P 39

Remarks on T. Reynolds. (Hist. Pam.) 8vo. Lord., 1817. B 11 Q 1

Speech of, on the State of the Nation. (Pam. 8.) 8vo. Lord., 1817. F 13 R 21

Speeches of, upon Questions relating to Public Rights, Duties, and Interests; with Historical Introductions, and a Critical Dissertation upon the Eloquence of the Ancients. 4 vols. 8vo. Edinb., 1838. F 10 S 3–6

Another copy. F 13 P 3–6

Speeches on the Administration of Justice in Ireland. (Pam. 5.) 8vo. Lord., 1839. MJ 2 P 39

Works of. 11 vols. 8vo. Lord., 1855–61. J 11 S 14–24

1. Lives of Philosophers of the time of George III.
2. Lives of Men of Letters, time of George III.
3–5. Historical Sketches of Statesmen who flourished in the time of George III.
6. Natural Theology; comprising a Discourse of Natural Theology, Dialogues on Instinct, and Dissertations on the Structure of the Cells of Bees, and on Fossil Osteology.
7. Rhetorical and Literary Dissertations and Addresses.
8. Historical and Political Dissertations.
9, 10. Speeches on Social and Political Subjects, with Historical Introductions.
11. The British Constitution, its History, Structure, and Working.

[*See* A'Beckett. T. T., *and* Poggo, G.]

BROUGHTON (Mrs. Eliza). Six Years' Residence in Algiers. 8vo. Lord., 1839. D 18 5

BROUGHTON (Richard). The Ecclesiasticall Historie of Great Britaine, dedvced by Ages, or Centenaries, from the Nativitie of Ovr Saviovr, vnto the happie Conuersion of the Saxons, in the seuenth hundred yeare. Fol. Doway, 1633. G 12 R 6†

BROUGHTON (Rt. Rev. W. G.), Bishop of Australia. Charge, delivered to the Clergy of the Archdeaconry of New South Wales, at the Primary Visitation, Sydney, 1829. 8vo. Sydney, 1830. MG 1 P 45

Charge delivered to the Clergy of New South Wales, at the Visitation hold on Thursday, February 13, 1834, in the Church of St. James, at Sydney. (Pam. F.) 8vo. Sydney, 1834. MJ 2 S 3

The Church in Australia. (In 3 Parts.) 12mo. Lord., 1845–46. MD 1 T 49

1. Two Journals of Visitation to the Northern and Southern Portions of his Diocese, 1843.
2. Two Journals of Missionary Tours in the Districts of Maneroo and Moreton Bay, New South Wales, in 1843; by the Rev. F. G. Pryce, and Rev. J. Gregor, M.A. 3rd ed.
*·· 3. A Journal of Visitation, in 1846.

BROUGHTON (Rt. Rev. W. G.)—*continued.*
Circular on Roman Catholic Interference. (Pam. A.) Fol. Sydney, 1847. MJ 2 U 1

Correspondence between the Rt. Rev. Lord Bishop of Sydney, and the Revs. F. T. C. Russell, and P. T. Beamish, Deacons. 8vo. Sydney, 1849. MG 1 Q 29

Another copy. MG 1 Q 37

Education: Petition to His Excellency Major-General Sir Richard Bourke, K.C.B., Governor-in-Chief, and to the Honourable the Legislative Council of New South Wales. 8vo. Sydney, 1836. MG 1 Q 30

Letter, in vindication of the Principles of the Reformation, addressed to Roger Therry, Esq. 8vo. Sydney, 1832. MG 1 P 5

Another copy. MG 1 Q 40

Sermons on the Church of England: its Constitution, Mission, and Trials; edited, with a prefatory Memoir, by Benjamin Harrison, M.A. 8vo. Lord., 1857. MG 1 T 7

Sermon, preached in the Church of St. James, Sydney, on November 12, 1829: General Thanksgiving to Almighty God, in acknowledgment of His mercy in putting an end ·to the late severe Drought. 8vo. Sydney, 1829.
MG 1 P 45

Sermon, preached on Whit Sunday, 1833, in the Church of St. David's. at Hobart Town, Van Diemen's Land, on which day a Collection was made for the relief of the surviving passengers and crew of the ship *Hibernia*, destroyed by fire at sea. 8vo. Hobart, 1833. MG 1 P 45

Speech, delivered at the General Committee of Protestants, 1836. 12mo. Sydney, 1836. MG 1 Q 39

Another copy. (Pam. 37.) 8vo. Syd., 1836. MJ 2 Q 24

Speech in the Legislative Council, upon the Resolutions for establishing a System of General Education. 8vo. Sydney, 1839. MF 1 Q 6, and MG 1 Q 30

Speech at the Entertainment given to His Honor Mr. Justice Burton, on his return to the Colony of New South Wales. on Thursday, 27th May, 1841. 8vo. Sydney, 1841. MF 3 P 3

"Take Heed": a Sermon. 2nd ed. 12mo. Sydney, 1844. MG 1 P 45

True Account of the Anglican Ordination, in the Reign of Queen Elizabeth. 8vo. Sydney, 1843. MG 1 P 45

Two Sermons, preached in the Church of St. James, Sydney, at the Ordination of Priests and Deacons, on Sunday, 19th September, 1847, and Sunday, 17th December, 1848; with an Appendix. 8vo. Sydney, 1849.
MG 1 P 45

Two Sermons, preached in the Church of St. James,·at Sydney, in New South Wales. 12mo. Sydney, 1837.
MG 1 P 45

[*See* Archbishopric of Sydney, Book Societies, *and* Episcopal Sees.]

BROUGHTON (Capt. W. R.) Voyage de découvertes dans la Partie Septentrionale de l'Océan Pacifique, 1795–98. Traduit par J. B. B. Eyriès. 2 vols. 8vo. Paris, 1807. MD 7 P 8, 9

BROUN (J. A.), F.R.S. Variations of the Daily Mean Horizontal Force of the Earth's Magnetism. (Roy. Soc. Pubs., 3.) 4to. Lond., 1876.   A 11 P 4 †

BROUN (Capt. Thomas). Manual of the New Zealand Coleoptera. (Colonial Museum and Geological Survey Depart.) Roy. 8vo. Wellington, 1880-86.*   MA 2 U 26

BROWN (A.) General Bibliographical Dictionary. [*See* Ebert, F. A.]

BROWN (Charles Brockden). Memoirs of; with Selections from his original Letters and Miscellaneous Writings; by William Dunlap. 8vo. Lond., 1822.   C 8 Q 1

BROWN (Major Charles E.), R.A. Charles George Gordon : a Sketch. [*See* Barnes, Rev. R. H.]

BROWN (Charles Philip). Carnatic Chronology : the Hindu and Mahomedan Methods of reckoning Time explained. Roy. 8vo. Lond., 1863.   B 10 V 11

Dialogues in Telugu and English; with a Grammatical Analysis. 2nd ed. 8vo. Madras, 1853.   K 13 Q 10

Dictionary of the Mixed Dialects and Foreign Words used in Telugu; with an Explanation of the Telugu Alphabet. Roy. 8vo. Madras, 1854.   K 13 T 3

An Ephemeris, shewing the corresponding dates according to the English, Hindu, and Musulman Calendars, from A.D. 1751 until 1850. Roy. 8vo. Madras, 1850. K 11 Q 7

Grammar of the Telugu Language. 2nd ed. 8vo. Madras, 1857.   K 13 Q 9

BROWN (Cornelius), F.R.S.L. An Appreciative Life of the Rt. Hon. the Earl of Beaconsfield ; with Portraits of his Contemporaries. 2 vols. imp. 8vo. Lond., 1882.   C 3 W 7, 8

BROWN (D. Kinnear). History of the Year : a Record of the Chief Events and Topics of Interest, from January 1, 1884, to December 31, 1885. 2 vols. 8vo. Sydney, 1885-86.*   ME 5 Q

BROWN (Rev. G.) A Weupua Anakak Mareko J. A. Timui. The Gospel according to S. Mark, translated into Language of Duke of York Island, New Britain Group ; by Rev. G. Brown. 12mo. Sydney, 1882. MG 1 P 43

BROWN (George A.) Sheep Breeding in Australia : containing an Historical Sketch of the Merino Sheep ; the Pedigrees of the principal Stud Sheep in the Australian Colonies ; and a Treatise on Breeding. 8vo. Melh., 1880.   MA 1 Q 19

BROWN (G. B.) From Schola to Cathedral : a Study of Early Christian Architecture. 8vo. Lond., 1886.   A 2 S 29

BROWN (George Preston). Sewer-gas and its Dangers; with an Exposition of common Defects in House Drainage, and practical Information relating to their Remedy. 12mo, Chicago, 1881.   A 2 R 28

P

BROWN (Henry). Victoria, as I found it, during five years of Adventure in Melbourne, on the Roads, and the Gold-fields. 8vo. Lond., 1862.*   MD 1 W 37

BROWN (Rev. Hugh Stowell). His Autobiography, his Commonplace Book, and Extracts from his Sermons and Addresses ; a Memorial Volume, edited by his son-in-law, W. S. Caine, M.P. 8vo. Lond., 1887.   C 4 S 2

BROWN (Isaac Baker), Junr. Australia for the Consumptive Invalid : the Voyage, Climates and Prospects for Residence. 8vo. Lond., 1865.   MD 3 Q 6

BROWN (Rev. Jas.), D.D. Scottish History ; with Biographical Sketch. [*See* Ross, John M.]

BROWN (James), LL.D. The Forester; or, a Practical Treatise on the Planting, Rearing, and general Management of Forest Trees. 5th ed. Roy. 8vo. Edinb., 1882.   A 1 S 34

BROWN (Rev. James Baldwin), B.A. The Home Life in the light of its divine idea. 8vo. Lond., 1866. G 13 R 24

Memoirs of the Public and Private Life of John Howard, the Philanthropist; compiled from his own Diary. 4to. Lond., 1818.   C 3 W 14

BROWN (James D.) Map of Melbourne. [*See* Kearney, J.]

BROWN (James D.) Biographical Dictionary of Musicians; with Bibliography of English Writings on Music. 8vo. Paisley, 1886.   C 11 Q 11

BROWN (John), M.D. Horæ Subsecivæ. 3rd ed. 12mo. Edinb., 1863.   J 11 T 11

BROWN (John). Sixty Years' Gleanings from Life's Harvest : a genuine Autobiography. 8vo. Cambridge, 1858.   C 3 Q 46

BROWN (John). Life and Letters of John Brown, Liberator of Kansas and Martyr of Virginia; edited by F. B. Sanborn. 8vo. Boston, 1885.   C 5 R 4

BROWN (Dr. John). Barbarossa : a Tragedy. (Brit. Theatre). 12mo. Lond., 1808.   H 1 P 15

Another copy. (Bell's Brit. Theatre.) 18mo. Lond., 1795.   H 2 P 32

Another copy. (New Eng. Theatre.) 12mo. Lond., 1791.   H 4 P 23

Another copy. [*See* Brit. Drama 2.]

BROWN (Rev. John), B.A. John Bunyan : his Life, Times, and Work. 8vo. Lond., 1885.   C 6 Q 2

BROWN (John A. Harvie), F.L.S., &c., CORDEAUX (John), AND KERMODE (P.) Report on the Migration of Birds in the Spring and Autumn of 1880. 8vo. Lond., 1881.   A 14 T 19

BROWN (JOHN CROUMBIE), LL.D., &c. Finland: its Forests and Forest Management. 8vo. Edinb., 1883.
A 1 P 59

Forests and Forestry in Poland, Lithuania, the Ukraine, and the Baltic Provinces of Russia; with Notices of the Export of Timber from Memel, Dantzig, and Riga. 8vo. Edinb., 1885.
A 1 P 62

Forests and Forestry of Northern Russia and Lands beyond. 8vo. Edinb., 1884.
A 1 P 60

Forestry in the Mining District of the Ural Mountains, in Eastern Russia. 8vo. Edinb., 1884.
D 7 Q 25

Forestry in Norway; with Notices of the Physical Geography of the Country. 8vo. Edinb., 1884.
A 1 P 59

The Forests of England, and the Management of them in Bye-gone Times. 8vo. Edinb., 1883.
A 1 P 61

French Forest Ordinance of 1669; with Historical Sketch of previous Treatment of Forests in France. 8vo. Edinb., 1883.
A 1 P 58

Hydrology of South Africa. 8vo. Lond., 1875.
A 3 T 9

Introduction to the Study of Modern Forest Economy. 8vo. Edinb., 1884.
A 1 P 57

Pine Plantations on the Sand-Wastes of France. 8vo. Edinb., 1873.
A 1 S 42

Reboisement in France; or, Records of the Replanting of the Alps, the Cevennes, and the Pyrenees with Trees, Herbage, and Bush. Roy. 8vo. Lond., 1876.
A 1 S 37

School of Forest Engineers in Spain. 8vo. Edinb., 1886.
A 1 P 55

Water Supply of South Africa, and Facilities for the Storage of it. 8vo. Edinb., 1877.
A 6 T 15

BROWN (JOHN EDNIE), F.L.S. Practical Treatise on Tree Culture in South Australia. Illustrated. 8vo. Adelaide, 1881.
MA 1 Q 35

BROWN (JOHN K.) Our Fiscal Policy in relation to Protection and our Intercolonial Trade. 8vo. Melb., 1871.
MF 1 Q 3

Another copy.
MF 1 Q 6

BROWN (J. T.), F.C.S. Photometry and Gas Analysis. 8vo. Lond., 1883.
A 11 R 15

BROWN (POLEMOPHILUS). [*See* GROLES, A.]

BROWN (RAWDON). Calendar of State Papers and Manuscripts, relating to English Affairs, existing in the Archives and Collections of Venice, and in other Libraries of Northern Italy, 1202-1556. 6 vols. roy. 8vo. Lond., 1864-77.
B 4 U 5-10

[*See* GIUSTINIAN, S.]

BROWN (RICHARD). Coalfields and cool trade of the Island of Cape Breton. With Maps. 8vo. Lond., 1871.
A 9 S 24

BROWN (ROBERT), D.C.L., &c. Botanical Appendix to Captain Sturt's "Narrative of an Expedition into Central Australia." 8vo. Lond., 1849.
MD 3 U 31

Brief Account of Microscopical Observations on the particles contained in the Pollen of Plants, &c. (Pam. 2.) 8vo. Lond., 1827.
MJ 2 P 37

Character and Description of Kingia: a new Genus of Plants found on the south-west coast of New Holland. (Appendix to Capt. P. P. King's "Narrative of a Survey of the Intertropical and Western Coasts of Australia.") 8vo. Lond., 1827.
MD 2 U 25

General Remarks, geographical and systematical, on the Botany of Terra Australis. (Appendix to "A Voyage to Terra Australis," by Matthew Flinders.) 4to. Lond., 1814.
MA 1 P 23 †

General View of the Botany of the Vicinity of Swan River. 8vo. Lond., 1831.
MD 6 R 24

Miscellaneous Botanical Works of.—Geographico-Botanical.—Structural and Physiological Memoirs.—Systematic Memoirs.—Contributions to Systematic Works. 2 vols. 8vo. Lond., 1866-67.
A 4 T 26, 27

Observations on the Organs and mode of Fecundation in Orchideæ and Asclepiadeæ. (Pam. 2) 8vo. Lond., 1831.
MJ 2 P 37

Prodromus Floræ Novæ Hollandiæ et Insulæ Van Diemen, exhibens Characteres Plantarum, quas annis 1802-1805 per oras utriusque Insulæ collegit et descripsit Robertus Brown. Vol. 1. 8vo. Lond., 1810.
MA 1 U 26

Prodromus Floræ Novæ Hollandiæ et Insulae Van Diemen, exhibens Characteres Plantarum, quas annis 1802-1805 per oras utriusque Insulae collegit et des cripsit Robertus Brown. Editio secunda. 8vo. Norimbergae, 1827.*
MA 1 U 27

Supplementum Primum Prodromi Floræ Novæ Hollandiæ: exhibens Proteaceas Novas quas in Australasia legerunt D.D. Baxter, Caley, Cunningham, Fraser, et Sieber; et quarum e siccis exemplaribus Characteres elaboravit Robertus Brown. 8vo. Lond., 1830.*
MA 1 U 27

Another copy.
MJ 2 P 37

BROWN (ROBERT), JUN., F.S.A. Law of Kosmic Order: an Investigation of the Physical Aspect of Time. 8vo. Lond., 1882.
A 3 T 19

Myth of Kirkê; including the Visit of Odysseus to the Shades: an Homerik Study. 8vo. Lond., 1883.
B 27 U 21

The Unicorn: a Mythological Investigation. 8vo. Lond., 1881.
B 14 R 36

BROWN (ROBERT), M.A., &c. The Countries of the World; being a Popular Description of the various Continents, Islands, Rivers, Seas, and Peoples of the Globe. 6 vols. 4to. Lond., 1877-81.
D 12 V 9-14

Races of Mankind; being a Popular Description of the Characteristics, Manners, and Customs of the Principal Varieties of the Human Family. 4 vols. (in 2) imp. 8vo. Lond. (n.d.)
A 2 P 4, 5

BROWN (SAMUEL). Some Account of Itinerating Libraries and their Founder. 12mo. Edinb., 1856.
C 1 Q 32

BROWN (THOMAS). [*See* SACHEVERELL, W.]

BROWN (THOMAS), M.D., &c. Inquiry into the relation of Cause and Effect. 4th ed. 8vo. Lond., 1835.
G 6 Q 17

Lectures on the Philosophy of the Human Mind; with a Memoir of the Author, by the Rev. D. Welsh. 8vo. Edinb., 1828. G 6 Q 18

BROWN (CAPT. THOMAS), M.P.S., &c. Book of Butterflies, Sphinges, and Moths. (Const. Misc.) 2nd ed. 3 vols. 18mo. Lond., 1834. K 10 R 8-10

Illustrations of the Fossil Conchology of Great Britain and Ireland; with Descriptions and Localities of all the Species. Roy. 4to. Lond., 1849. A 2 S 10 †

Illustrations of the Recent Conchology of Great Britain and Ireland. 2nd ed. Roy. 4to. Lond., 1844. A 2 S 9 †

BROWN (THOMAS), THE YOUNGER. [*See* MOORE, T.].

BROWN (THOMAS C.) A Layman's Faith, Doctrines, and Liturgy; by "A Layman." 12mo. Lond., 1866. G 13 R 7

BROWN (THOMAS N.) Labour and Triumph: the Life and Times of Hugh Miller. 12mo. Lond., 1858. C 1 R 25

BROWN (W.) [*See* LIVERPOOL FREE PUBLIC LIBRARY.]

BROWN (WALTER). Fables; with Cuts by Thomas Bewick. 4to. Lond., 1884. J 9 V 2

BROWN (WILLIAM). New Zealand and its Aborigines; being an Account of the Aborigines, Trade, and Resources of the Colony. 8vo. Lond., 1845.* MD 4 S 46

Another copy. 2nd ed. 8vo. Lond., 1851. MD 4 S 48

BROWN (WILLIAM MORGAN). Ballaarat District Almanac, Business Directory, Gardeners' Annual, &c., for 1864. 12mo. Ballaarat, 1864. ME 4 Q

Economy of Quartz-mining. 8vo. Melb., 1861. MA 2 Q 35

BROWN (W. N.) Practical Manual of Wood-engraving; with a brief Account of the History of the Art. Illustrated. 8vo. Lond., 1886. A 7 P 39

BROWN (—.), AND WATSON (R. A.) Brown and Watson's, late Brown and Stansfield's, Patent Self-discharging Concentrator for extracting the Pyrites and Sulphurets, &c. (Pam. Ci.) 8vo. Sydney, 1877. MA 2 Q 33

BROWNE (A. J. JUKES-), B.A., &c. Student's Hand-book of Historical Geology. 8vo. Lond., 1886. A 9 P 9

Student's Hand-book of Physical Geology; with numerous Diagrams and Illustrations. 8vo. Lond., 1884. A 9 Q 33

Palæontology. [*See* PENNING, W. H.]

BROWNE (CHARLES FARRAR), "ARTEMUS WARD." Artemus Ward: his Book. Australian edition. 18mo. Melb., 1865. J 9 Q 15

Complete Works of; with Portrait by Geflowski, Facsimile of Handwriting, &c. 8vo. Lond., 1876. J 9 Q 16

BROWNE (REV. GEORGE FORREST). Ice-Caves in France and Switzerland: a Narrative of Subterranean Exploration. 8vo. Lond., 1865. D 8 S 49

BROWNE (GORDON). [*See* FARJEON, B. L.]

BROWNE (GEORGE LATHOM). Narratives of State Trials in the Nineteenth Century. First Period: from the Union with Ireland to the Death of George IV, 1801-30. 2 vols. 8vo. Lond., 1882. F 6 S 25, 26

BROWNE (GRACIUS J.) [*See* BROINOWSKI, GRACIUS J.]

BROWNE (HABLÔT KNIGHT), "PHIZ." Life and Labours of; by David Croal Thomson. Illustrated. 4to. Lond., 1884. C 2 W 1

BROWNE (COL. HORACE). Mandalay to Momien. [*See* ANDERSON, J.]

BROWNE (HUGH JUNOR). Holy Truth; or, the coming Reformation, Universal and Eternal because founded on demonstrable Truth: Science and Religion reconciled. 8vo. Lond., 1876. G 13 Q 31

Short Address to the Clergy of all Denominations and to earnest Enquirers after Truth; by "A Layman." 8vo. Melb., 1875. MG 1 Q 32

Rational Christianity; or, a special Divine Revelation incompatible with the Intellectual Development of Man and with Natural Evolution, as exemplified in History, and confirmed by Science. 12mo. Melb., 1879. MG 1 P 7

BROWNE (JAMES), LL.D. History of the Highlands and of the Highland Clans. 4 vols. 8vo. Glasgow, 1842. B 13 Q 39-42

BROWNE (JAMES P), M.D. Works of Fielding. [*See* FIELDING, H.]

Works of Laurence Sterne. [*See* STERNE, L.]

Works of the Rt. Hon. R. B. Sheridan; with a Memoir. [*See* SHERIDAN, RT. HON. R. B.]

BROWNE (JOHN ROSS). Etchings of a Whaling Cruise; with Notes of a Sojourn on the Island of Zanzibar, and a brief History of the Whale Fishery. 8vo. Lond., 1846. D 9 U 14

Report of the Debates in the Convention of California, 1849. 8vo. Washington, 1850. F 10 S 17

Resources of the Pacific Slope. Roy. 8vo. New York, 1869. D 3 U 21

BROWNE (JUSTIN M.) Family Notes, collected during many years, and dedicated to those interested. Roy. 8vo. Hobart, 1887. MK 1 S 8

BROWNE (REV. J. CAVE-). [*See* CAVE-BROWNE, REV. J.]

BROWNE (MONTAGU), F.Z.S., &c. Practical Taxidermy: a Manual of Instruction to the Amateur in Collecting, Preserving, and Setting up Natural History Specimens of all kinds. 2nd ed. 8vo. Lond., 1884. A 16 Q 14

BROWNE (PATRICK), M.D. Civil and Natural History of Jamaica. Illustrated, &c., by G. D. Ehret. Fol. Lond., 1789. A 16 8 9 ‡

BROWNE (REV. ROBERT WILLIAM), M.A., &c. History of Roman Classical Literature. 8vo. Lond., 1884. B 11 T 35

BROWNE (R. C.), M.A. English Poems by John Milton. [*See* MILTON, J.]

BROWNE (SIR THOMAS). Religio Medici. 6th ed. 12mo. Lond., 1669. G 9 P 44

Works of; including his Life [by Dr. Johnson] and Correspondence; edited by Simon Wilkin. 4 vols. 8vo. Lond., 1835-36. J 10 T 22-25

BROWNE (THOMAS ALEXANDER). "ROLF BOLDREWOOD." Australian Graziers' Guide. [*See* SILVER, S. W., & Co.]

Old Melbourne Memories. 8vo. Melb., 1884. MD 4 Q 3

Ups and Downs: a Story of Australian Life. 8vo. Lond., 1878.* MJ 1 S 27

BROWNE (T. F. DE COURCY). Miners' Handy Book; containing the Mining Board Regulations, Rules of the Warden's Courts and Mining Appeal Court, Qualification of Members and Electors of the Mining Board, Rewards for Discovery of new Gold-fields, Summary of Stamp Duties payable, List of Mining Registrar's and Warden's Courts, &c. 2nd ed. 12mo. Sydney, 1882. MA 2 P 17

Mining Leaseholders' Guide: a Handy Book of the Laws and Regulations relating to Gold and Mineral Leases, &c.; how to distinguish, test, and assay Minerals, &c. 8vo. Sydney, 1883. MF 1 P 10

Another copy. [3rd ed.] 8vo. Sydney, 1886. MF 1 P 11

BROWNE (COL. SIR THOMAS GORE), C.B., K.C.M.G. Copy of a Despatch from the Governor of New Zealand to the Duke of Newcastle, dated the 22nd day of May, 1860, relative to the management of Native Affairs. (Parl. Docs., 28.) Fol. Lond., 1860. MF 4‡

BROWNE (WALTER R.) [*See* CLAUSIUS, R. J. E.]

BROWNE (WILLIAM). Life and Poems of. [*See* CHALMERS, A.]

BROWNE (W. G.) Travels in Africa, Egypt, and Syria, from the year 1792 to 1798. 4to. Lond., 1799. D 2 V 15

BROWNING (COLIN ARROTT), M.D. Address to the Women who debarked at Sydney, New South Wales, from the transport ship *Margaret*, on the 26th of August, 1840. 8vo. Sydney, 1841.* MG 1 P 9

Convict Ship, and England's Exiles. In two parts. 3rd ed. 8vo. Lond., 1848. MG 1 Q 3

Another copy. 4th ed. 8vo. Lond., 1849. MG 1 Q 4

England's Exiles; or, a View of a System of Instruction and Discipline, as carried into effect during the Voyage to the Penal Colonies of Australia. 8vo. Lond., 1842.* MG 1 Q 1

BROWNING (CULLING R.) Addressed to the Prisoners debarked from the *Surry*, at Sydney, December 8, 1831; the *Arab*, at Hobart Town, July 5, 1834; and the *Elphinstone*, at Hobart Town, May 30, 1836; by the Medical Officer in charge during the Voyage. 12mo. Hobart, 1836.* MG 1 P 8

BROWNING (MRS. ELIZABETH BARRETT). Aurora Leigh. 3rd ed. 8vo. Lond., 1857. H 5 R 18

Letters of, addressed to Richard Hengist Horne; with Comments on Contemporaries; edited by S. R. T. Mayer. 2 vols. 8vo. Lond., 1877. C 3 U 30, 31

Poetical Works. 13th ed. 5 vols. 12mo. Lond., 1883. H 5 R 13-17

BROWNING (OSCAR). Despatches of Earl Gower and others. [*See* GOWER, EARL.]

BROWNING (ROBERT), M.A. Aristophanes' Apology; including a Transcript from Euripides, being the last Adventure of Balaustion. 12mo. Lond., 1875. H 5 R 33

Balaustion's Adventure; including a Transcript from Euripides. 12mo. Lond., 1871. H 5 R 32

Dramatic Idyls. [1st and] 2nd Series. 2 vols. 12mo. Lond., 1879-80. H 5 R 19, 20

Dramatis Personæ. 8vo. Lond., 1864. H 5 R 38

Ferishtah's Fancies. 12mo. Lond., 1884. H 5 R 37

Fitine at the Fair. 12mo. Lond., 1872. H 5 R 34

Hand-book to the Works of. [*See* ORR, MRS. S.]

The Inn Album. 12mo. Lond., 1875. H 5 R 35

Introduction to the Study of. [*See* SYMONS, A.]

Jocoseria. 12mo. Lond., 1883. H 5 R 36

Poetical Works of. 6 vols. 12mo. Lond., 1868-70. H 5 R 26-31

Prince Hohenstiel-Schwangau, Saviour of Society. 12mo. Lond., 1871. H 5 R 33

The Ring and the Book. 4 vols. 12mo. Lond., 1868-69. H 5 R 22-25

Tragedies, and other Plays. 12mo. Lond., 1863. H 3 P 1

BROWNING (WILLIAM SHIPTON). History of the Huguenots during the 16th Century. 2 vols. 8vo. Lond., 1839. G 6 R 1-2

History of the Huguenots, from 1598 to 1838. 8vo. Lond., 1839. G 6 R 3

BROWNLOW (EMMA SOPHIA), COUNTESS. Slight Reminiscences of a Septuagenarian, from 1802 to 1815. 8vo. Lond., 1867. C 3 Q 42

[*See* PALMER, W.]

BROWNLOW (REV. W. R.), M.A. Roma Sotterranea. [*See* NORTHCOTE, REV. J. S.]

BROWNRIGG (REV. M. B.) Cruise of the *Freak:* a Narrative of a Visit to the Islands in Bass and Banks Straits; with some Account of the Islands. With Illustrations and Charts. 8vo. Launceston, 1872.
MD 5 T 24

Identity of the British Nation with the Ten Tribes of Israel: a Lecture, delivered in the Temperance Hall, Melbourne. (Pam. 26.) 8vo. Melb., 1880. MJ 2 R 15

BRUCE (ALEXANDER). Scab in Sheep and its Cure. 8vo. Sydney, 1864. MA 1 Q 1

Another copy. 3rd ed., revised and enlarged. 8vo. Sydney, 1867. MA 2 V 9

BRUCE (REV. ALEX. BALMAIN). The Training of the Twelve; or, Passages out of the Gospels, exhibiting the Twelve Disciples of Jesus, under discipline for the Apostleship. 8vo. Edinb., 1871. G 9 S 12

BRUCE (JAMES), F.R.S. Account of the Life and Writings of; by Alexander Murray, F.A.S.E. 4to. Edinb., 1808. C 2 W 5

Life of; by Sir F. B. Head. 18mo. Lond., 1830. C 1 P 26

Travels and Adventures in Abyssinia; edited by J. Morison Clingan, M.A. Sq. 12mo. Edinb., 1860.
D 1 T 19

Travels in the Footsteps of. [*See* PLAYFAIR, LIEUT-COL.]

Travels to discover the Source of the Nile, in the years 1768 to 1773. 5 vols. 4to. Edinb., 1790. D 2 V 1-5

Travels of. [*See* COCHRANE, R.]

BRUCE (LIEUT. J. A. T.), R.N. Cruise Round the World of the Flying Squadron, 1869-70. 8vo. Lond., 1871.*
MD 5 V 32

BRUCE (J. C.) Lapidarium Septentrionale; or, a Description of the Monuments of Roman Rule in the North of England. Fol. Lond., 1875. B 17 U 8 ‡

BRUCE (ROBERT). Voice from the Australian Bush. 8vo. Adelaide, 1877. MH 1 S 9

BRUCE (ROBERT), KING OF SCOTLAND. The Bruce; or, the History of Robert I, King of Scotland. [*See* BARBOUR, J.]

BRUCE (W. N.) Life of Gen. Sir Charles Jas. Napier. 8vo. Lond., 1885. C 5 Q 12

BRUCK (LUDWIG). Australasian Medical Directory and Hand-book. 2nd issue. 8vo. Sydney, 1886. ME 3 S

True Copy of the Depositions taken as evidence at the Investigation by the City Coroner of Sydney, relating to a recent Case of Gastrotomy; with Appendix. 8vo. Sydney, 1881. MA 2 S 38

BRUCKMANN (FREDERICK). National Types and Costumes; with Explanatory Text. Imp. 8vo. Lond., 1884. A 8 T 24

BRUGSCH (ÉMILE) ET MASPERO (G.) La Trouvaille de Deir-el-Bahari. Vingt Photographies par M. E. Brugsch. Text par G. Mespero. 4to. Cairo, 1881.*
B 14 It 7 ‡

BRUGSCH (DR. HEINRICH), BEY. Grammaire Démotique; contenant les Principes généraux de la Langue et de l'Ecriture Populaires des Anciens Egyptiens. Avec un Tableau général des Signes Démotiques. Fol. Berlin, 1855. K 22 S 27 ‡

Grammaire Hiéroglyphique, contenant les Principes généraux de la Langue et de l'écriture sacrées des Anciens Egyptiens. Sm. fol. Leipzig, 1872. K 16 U 12

Hieroglyphisch-demotisches Wörterbuch. 7 vols. sm. fol. Leipzig, 1867-82. K 16 U 5-11

BRUHNS (PROF. KARL). Life of Humboldt. [*See* LOWENBERG, J.]

BRUMMELL (GEORGE). "BEAU BRUMMELL." Life of George Brummell, Esq., commonly called "Beau Brummell"; by Capt. [William] Jesse. 2 vols. 8vo. Lond., 1844.
C 10 P 11, 12

Life of George Brummell, Esq., commonly called "Beau Brummell"; by Capt. [William] Jesse. Revised and Annotated ed. 2 vols. 8vo. Lond., 1886. C 10 P 13, 14

BRUMOY (PIERRE). Le Théâtre des Grecs. 6 vols. 12mo. Amsterdam. 1732. H 3 P 29-34

BRUMUND (J. F. G.) [*See* LEEMANS, DR. C.]

BRUN (C. LE.) [*See* LE BRUN, C.]

BRUNCK (R. F. P.) [*See* SOPHOCLES.]

BRUNE (CLARE). The Dogarissa. [*See* MELMONTI, W. G.]

BRUNEL (SIR MARC ISAMBARD), C.E., &c. Memoir of the Life of; by Richard Beamish, F.R.S. 8vo. Lond., 1862. C 6 T 5

BRUNET (JACQUES CHARLES). Manuel du Libraire et de l'Amateur de Livres 4 vols. 8vo. Paris, 1820.
K 17 Q 1-4

Supplément au Manuel du Libraire. 3 vols. Paris, 1834. K 17 Q 5-7

Manuel du Libraire et de l'Amateur de Livres. 5ᵉ éd. 6 vols. roy. 8vo. Paris, 1860-65. Libr.

Supplément [to the above]. 2 vols. roy. 8vo. Paris, 1878-80. Libr.

BRUNET (PIERRE GUSTAVE). Bibliomania in the Present Day in France and England; or, some Account of Celebrated Recent Sales; from the French of "Philomneste Junior." 8vo. N. York, 1880. J 12 U 22

[*See* QUÉRARD, J. M.]

BRUNO (SANCTUS), CARTHUSIENSIUM INSTITUTOR. Opera omnia. [*See* MIGNE, J. P., SERIES LATINA 152, 153.]

BRUNO (SANCTUS), HERBIPOLENSIS EPISCOPUS. Opera omnia. [*See* MIGNE, J. P., SERIES LATINA 142.]

BRUNO ASTENSIS (SANctus), SIGNIENSIS EPISCOPUS. Opera omnia. [*See* MIGNE, J. P., SERIES LATINA 164, 165.]

BRUNS (DR. T.) [*See* LUTTEROTH, H.]

BRUNTON (T. LAUDER), M.D., &c. Pharmacology and Therapeutics; or, Medicine, Past and Present: the Goulstonian Lectures delivered before the Royal College of Physicians in 1877. 8vo. Lond., 1880. A 12 Q 25

Physiological Laboratory. [*See* KLEIN, E.] A 12 T 11,12

Text-Book of Pharmacology, Therapeutics, and Materia Medica; adapted to the United States Pharmacopœia, by Francis H. Williams, M.D., Boston, Mass. 8vo. Lond., 1885. A 12 U 6

BRUNTON (T. LAUDER), M.D., &c., AND PYE (WALTER). On the Physiological Action of the Bark of Erythrophleum Guinense, generally called Casca, Cassa, or Sassy Bark. (Roy. Soc. Pubs., 5). 4to. Lond., 1878. A 11 P 6 †

BRUSH (G. J.) Manual of Determinative Mineralogy; with an Introduction on Blow-pipe Analysis. Roy. 8vo. New York, 1875. A 9 U 31
[*See* DANA, J. W.]

BRUTAL SAXON, A. [*See* JOHN BULL'S NEIGHBOUR.]

BRUTE (WAFTER). Writings and Examinations of. [*See* BRITISH REFORMERS, 12.]

BRUTUS [*See* LETTERS ON MEN, MEASURES, AND POLITICS.] F 6 T 2

BRUTZER (PROF.) Dictionary and Commercial Phraseology in the German, Dutch, English, French, Italian, and Spanish Languages, by Prof. Dr. Brutzer, Prof. Dr. Binder, Mess. J. Bozı Jz., M. M. Brasch and others. Roy. 8vo. Stuttgart, 1867. K 9 S 10

BRUXELLES MUSEUM. Catalogue des Tableaux au exposés Musée de la ville de Bruxelles. 18mo. Bruxelles, 1835. K 7 R 1

BRUYÈRE (J. DE LA). [*See* LA BRUYÈRE, J. DE.]

BRUYÈRES (H.) La Phrénologie, le Geste, et la Physionomie, démontrés par 120 Portraits. Roy. 8vo. Paris, 1847. A 12 V 20

BRY (THEODORE DE). New Artistic Alphabet, designed by Theodore de Bry, Frankfort, 1595. (Fac-simile Reproduction.) Sm. fol. Edinb., 1880. A 23 R 12 ‡
[*See* HARRIS, J.]

BRYAN (MICHAEL). Biographical and Critical Dictionary of Painters and Engravers; with the Ciphers Monograms, and Marks used by each Engraver. Revised and enlarged by G. Stanley. Roy. 8vo. 1853. C 17 U 18

Dictionary of Painters and Engravers, Biographical and Critical. New ed., revised and enlarged; edited by W. Armstrong and R. E. Graves. 2 vols. imp. 8vo. Lond., 1886-87. K 17 U 19, 20

BRYANT (EDWIN). What I saw in California; its Soil, Climate, Productions, and Gold Mines. 2nd ed. 12mo. Lond., 1849. D 3 Q 47

BRYANT (JACOB). Dissertation concerning the War of Troy, and the Expedition of the Grecians, as described by Homer; shewing that no such Expedition was ever undertaken, and that no such City of Phrygia existed. 4to. Lond., 1796. B 18 R 12 ‡

An Expostulation addressed to the British Critic. 4to. Eton, 1799. B 18 R 13 ‡

A Letter to Jacob Bryant concerning the War of Troy. [*See* WAKEFIELD, G.]

New System; or, an Analysis of Ancient Mythology. 6 vols. 8vo. Lond., 1807. B 14 W 49-54

Observations upon a Treatise entitled "A Description of the Plain of Troy"; written by Monsieur le Chevalier. 4to. Eton, 1795. B 18 R 14 ‡

Some Observations upon the "Vindication of Homer, and of the Ancient Poets and Historians who have recorded the Siege and Fall of Troy;" written by I. B. S. Morritt, Esq. 4to. Eton, 1799. B 18 R 13 ‡

BRYANT (J.) The Victorian Almanac, 1864. 12mo. Melb., 1864. ME 4 Q

BRYANT (THOMAS), F.R.C.S. Manual for the Practice of Surgery. Illustrated. 4th ed. 2 vols. 8vo. Lond., 1884. A 26 Q 23, 24

Practice of Surgery: a Manual. Illustrated. 2nd ed., enlarged. (Churchill's Manuals.) 2 vols. 8vo. Lond., 1876. A 13 P 37, 38

BRYANT (WILLIAM CULLEN). Biography of; with Extracts from his Correspondence, by Parke Godwin. 2 vols. New York, 1883. C 10 P 15, 16

Bryant and his Friends: some Reminiscences of the Knickerbocker Writers; by J. G. Wilson. 8vo. New York, 1886. C 3 S 10

Letters of a Traveller; or, Notes of things seen in Europe and America. 8vo. Lond., 1850. D 10 R 16

Picturesque America: a Delineation by Pen and Pencil of the Mountains, Rivers, &c., of the United States; edited by William Cullen Bryant. 4 vols. imp. 4to. Lond., 1882-85. D 4 R 11-14 ‡

Poetical Works of. Household ed. 8vo. Lond., 1880. H 5 T 25

BRYANT (W. M.) [*See* HEGEL, G. W. F.]

BRYCE (REV. PROFESSOR GEORGE), M.A., &c. Manitoba: its Infancy, Growth, and Present Condition. 8vo. Lond., 1882. D 3 P 42

BRYCE (JAMES), D.C.L. The Holy Roman Empire. 6th ed. 8vo. Lond., 1876. B 12 Q 36

BRYCE (JAMES), M.A., &c., AND JOHNSTON (KEITH), F.R.G.S. Household Cyclopædia of Geography: Descriptive, Physical, Political and Historical. New ed. Imp. 8vo. Lond., 1880. D 12 V 17

BRYDGES (Sir Harford Jones), Bart. Account of the Transactions of H.M. Mission to the Court of Persia, 1807–11; with a brief History of the Wahauby. 2 vols. 8vo. Lond., 1834. B 1 P 9, 10

Dynasty of the Kajars; translated from the original Persian Manuscript; to which is prefixed a succinct Account of the History of Persia. 8vo. Lond., 1833. B 1 P 12

BRYDGES (Sir Samuel Egerton), Bart., &c. Archaica; containing a Reprint of scarce Old English Prose Tracts; with Prefaces, Critical and Biographical. 2 vols. 4to. Lond., 1815. J 2 U 17, 18

1. Tracts of Robert Greene, Robert Southwell, Nicholas Breton and Thomas Nash.

2. Tracts of Gabriel Harvey and Richard Brathwayte.

Autobiography, Times, Opinions, and Contemporaries of. 2 vols. 8vo. Lond., 1834. C 6 V 10, 11

Bertram: a Poetical Tale. 8vo. Kent, 1814. H 6 S 10

Brief Character of Matthew Lord Rokeby. 8vo. Kent, 1817. H 6 S 10

The British Bibliographer. 4 vols. 8vo. Lond., 1810–14. J 6 T 10–13

Censura Literaria; containing Titles, Abstracts, and Opinions of Old English Books, especially those which are scarce. 10 vols. 8vo. Lond., 1805–9. J 11 V 1–10

Cimelia; seu examen criticum Librorum ex Diariis literariis, Linguâ præcipue Gallicâ, ab anno 1665 usque ad annum 1792 scriptis, selectum. 8vo. Geneva, 1823. J 6 R 5

Collins' Peerage of England. [*See* Collins, A.]

Coningsby: a Tragic Tale. 18mo. Paris, 1819. J 1 W 35

Gnomica: Detached Thoughts, Sententious, Axiomatic, Moral, and Critical; but especially with reference to Poetical Faculties and Habits. 8vo. Geneva, 1824. J 6 R 6

Imaginative Biography. 2 vols. 8vo. Lond., 1834. C 3 U 27, 28

Letters from the Continent. 8vo. Kent, 1821. B 7 U 20

Memoirs of the Peers of England, during the Reign of James i. 2 vols. (in 1). 8vo. Lond., 1802. C 9 Q 19

Poems. 4th ed., with many additions. 12mo. Lond., 1807. H 5 S 12

Poetical Works of John Milton. [*See* Milton, J.]

Population and Riches of Nations, considered together. 8vo. Paris, 1819. F 6 S 17

Sir Ralph Willoughby: an Historical Tale of the 16th Century. 18mo. Florence, 1820. J 1 W 34

Restituta; or, Titles, Extracts, and Characters of old Books in English Literature revived. 4 vols. 8vo. Lond., 1814–16. K 17 R 15–18

The Ruminator: a series of Essays. 2 vols. 8vo. Lond., 1813. J 6 R 3, 4

Select Poems. 4to. Kent, 1814. H 5 V 7

BRYDONE (Patrick), F.R.S. Tour through Sicily and Malta, in a series of Letters to Wm. Beckford. 2nd ed. 2 vols. 8vo. Lond., 1774. D 7 U 25, 26

BRYENNIUS (Nicephorus). Historiarum, Libri iv. [*See* Migne, J. P., Series Græca, 127.]

BRYENNOIS MANUSCRIPT. [*See* Harris, J. R.]

BRYSON (George). Memoirs of. [*See* Veitch, W.]

BUCANUS (Guilielmus). Institvtiones Theologicæ, seu Locorvm Commvnivm Christianæ Religionis, ex Dei verbo, et præstantissimorum Theologorum Orthodoxo consersu expositorum analysis. Editio tertia. 12mo. Bernac, 1605. G 14 Q 12

BUCCANEERS OF AMERICA. History of the Bucaniers of America, from their first Original down to this Time. 8vo. Lond., 1699. B 17 Q 5

[*See* Archenholtz, J. M. von.] B 35 P 2

BUCH (Leopold von). Reise durch Norwegen und Lappland. Mit Kupfern und Karten. 2 vols. (in 1) 8vo. Berlin, 1810. D 8 R 4

Travels through Norway and Lapland, during the years 1806–8; translated by John Black. 4to. Lond., 1813. D 8 V 24

[*See* Geological Memoirs.]

BUCHAN (Capt. David), R.N. Voyage of Discovery towards the North Pole. [*See* Beechey, Capt. F. W.]

BUCHAN (David Stewart Erskine), Earl of. Essays on the Lives and Writings of Fletcher of Saltoun, and the Poet Thomson. 8vo. Lond., 1792. C 8 P 9

BUCHAN (Peter). Ancient Ballads and Songs of the North of Scotland, hitherto unpublished; with Explanatory Notes. Reprinted from the original edition of 1828. 2 vols. 8vo. Edinb., 1875. H 5 T 23, 24

Annals of Peterhead, from its Foundation to the present Time; including an Account of the Rise, Progress, &c., of the Town. 8vo. Peterhead, 1819. B 13 R 11

BUCHAN (William Paton). Plumbing: a Text-book to the Practice of the Art or Craft of the Plumber; with Supplementary Chapters upon House Drainage. (Weale.) 12mo. Lond., 1876. A 17 Q 12

BUCHANAN (Rev. Claudius), D.D. Christian Researches in Asia; with Notices of the Translation of the Scriptures into the Oriental Languages. 4th ed. 8vo. Lond., 1811. G 6 R 18

BUCHANAN (David). An Australian Orator: Speeches, Political, Social, Literary, and Theological; edited by Richmond Thatcher. 8vo. Lond., 1886.* MF 1 P 18

Heresy and Sham of all the leading so-called Christian Sects: a Christmas Chant, in Prose. 8vo. Sydney, 1876. MG 1 Q 36

Another copy. 2nd ed. 8vo. Sydney, 1876. MG 1 Q 39

Mitred Mountebanks and Lay and Surpliced Lunacy in contention with Sound Reason and Common Sense: an Address on the Education Question. (Pam. Bs.) 8vo. Sydney, 1879. MG 1 Q 34

BUCHANAN (David)—*continued.*
Observations on the Public Affairs and Public Men of England. 8vo. Sydney, 1871.　　MF 1 R 46
Political Portraits of some of the Members of the Parliament of New South Wales. 8vo. Sydney, 1863. MF3P4
Protection or Free Trade? [*See* Reid, G. H.]
Speech on the necessity of adopting a Fiscal Policy that will promote, encourage, and protect our Native Industries. 8vo. Sydney, 1880.　　MF 3 P 21
Specimens of Australian Oratory; comprising Speeches delivered in the Senate, at the Bar, and on the Public Platform. 8vo. Sydney, 1881.*　　MF 1 P 16'
[*See* Buchanan, W.]

BUCHANAN (George). Georgii Buchanani, Scoti, Poetarum sui seculi Principis, Opera omnia, ad optimorum Codicum fidem summo studio recognita et castigata, curante Thoma Ruddimano, A.M. 2 vols. fol. Edinb., 1715.　　B 19 U 9, 10 ‡
History of Scotland; translated from the Latin, with Notes, and a Continuation, by Jas. Aikman. 6 vols. 8vo. Edinb., 1828–30.　　B 13 Q 33–38
Memoirs of the Life and Writings of George Buchanan; by David Irving, A.M. 8vo. Edinb., 1807. C 10 R 12
Rerum Scoticarum Historia, auctore Georgio Buchanano, Scoto, ad Jacobum vi, Scotorum Regen. Accessit de Jure Regni apud Scotos Dialogus, eodem Georgio Buchanano auctore. 8vo. Ultrajecti, 1668.　B 13 P 29

BUCHANAN (Hon. James). [*See* Calhoun, Hon. J. C.]

BUCHANAN (John), F.L.S. Manual of the Indigenous Grasses of New Zealand. Roy. 8vo. Wellington, 1880.*　　MA 1 U 13
The Shire Highlands (East Central Africa) as Colony and Mission. 8vo. Edinb., 1885.　　D 1 R 16

BUCHANAN (Joseph Rodes), M.D. Manual of Psychometry : the Dawn of a New Civilization. 8vo. Boston, 1885.　　G 13 Q 25
The New Education : Moral, Industrial, Hygienic, Intellectual. 3rd ed. 8vo. Boston, 1882.　　G 17 P 19

BUCHANAN (Robert William). The Earthquake ; or, Six Days and a Sabbath.—The First Three Days. 8vo. Lond., 1885.　　H 5 T 33
Life and Adventures of John James Audubon, the Naturalist. 8vo. Lond., 1868.　　C 1 V 34
Poetical Works of. 3 vols. 8vo. Lond., 1874. H 5 T 29–31
　1. Ballads and Romances. Ballads and Poems of Life.
　2. Ballads and Poems of Life. Lyrical Poems, &c.
　3. Coruisken Sonnets, Book of Orm and Political Mystics.
Saint Abe and his Seven Wives : a Tale of Salt Lake City. 3rd ed. 8vo. Lond., 1872.　　H 7 Q 31
Selected Poems of. 8vo. Lond., 1882.　　H 5 T 32
Undertones. 2nd ed. 12mo. Lond., 1865.　　H 5 T 34
[*See* Audubon, J. J.]

BUCHANAN (Walter). Walter Buchanan's Price Current of New South Wales and Van Diemen's Land Produce, &c. No. 4. 4to. Lond., 1829.　　MF 1 U 14

BUCHANAN (William), Advocate. Observations on the Book of the Revelation. Edited by David Buchanan, Esq. 8vo. Sydney, 1874.　　MG 1 P 4

BÜCHELE (Dr. C.) Australien in der Gegenwart nach seinen historischen Entwicklung und Beschaffenheit. 8vo. Stuttgart, 1856.　　MD 4 V 42

BÜCHNER (Dr. L.) Force and Matter ; Empirico-Philosophical Studies intelligibly rendered ; edited by J. Frederick Collingwood. 2nd ed. 8vo. Lond., 1870.　　A 16 Q 26
Kraft und Stoff : natur-philosophische Untersuchungen auf thatsächlicher Grundlage. 12mo. Leip., 1876.　　A 16 Q 25
Man in the Past, Present, and Future. From the German ; by W. S. Dallas, F.L.S. 8vo. Lond., 1872.　A 1 W 21

BUC'HOZ (P. Jos.) Herbier ; ou, Collection des Plantes Médicinales de la Chine. Fol. Paris, 1781.　A 4 P 18 ‡

BUCK (Rev. Charles). Anecdotes; Religious, Moral, and Entertaining. 3 vols. 12mo. Lond., 1825. J 10 R 20–22
Theological Dictionary. Containing definitions of all Religious Terms, &c. 5th ed. 2 vols. 8vo. Lond., 1821.　　K 18 R 6, 7

BUCK (Dudley). Influence of the Organ in History : Inaugural Lecture, Boston University. 8vo. Lond., 1882.　　A 7 P 17

BUCK (J. H. Watson), M.I.C.E., &c. Graphic Table for facilitating the Computation of the Weights of Wrought Iron and Steel Girders, &c. Fol. Lond., 1883.　　A 4 U 21 ‡

BUCKE (Richard Maurice), M.D. Walt Whitman. 8vo. Philad., 1883.　　C 4 S 45
Walt Whitman ; to which is added "English Critics on Walt Whitman"; edited by Prof. Edward Dowden, LL.D. 8vo. Glasgow, 1884.　　C 4 S 46

BUCKHEIM (Emma S.) [*See* Moltke, H. Count von.]

BUCKHURST (W. P.) Jottings by an Australian Abroad : India, Egypt, Jerusalem, Rome, Venice, Paris, &c. 12mo. Melb., 1873.　　MJ 2 P 31

BUCKINGHAM (George Villiers), First Duke of. The Chances : a Comedy. [*See* Beaumont, F.]
[Life of.] The Stanhope Essay for 1882 ; by W. Hudson Shaw. 8vo. Oxford, 1882.　　C 9 R 29
The Rehearsal : a Comedy. (Bell's Brit. Theatre.) 18mo. Lond., 1796.　　H 2 P 13
Another copy.　　H 2 P 29

BUCKINGHAM (James Silk). America ; Historical, Statistic, and Descriptive. 3 vols. 8vo. Lond., 1841.　　B 1 R 3–5
Autobiography of ; including his Voyages, Travels, Adventures, Speculations, &c. 2 vols. 8vo. Lond., 1855.　　C 3 P 4, 5

BUCKINGHAM (JAMES SILK)—*continued.*
Canada, Nova, Scotia, and New Brunswick; with a Plan of National Colonization. 8vo. Lond., 1843. D 3 T 5
Evidence on Drunkenness. 8vo. Lond., 1834. F 10 Q 3
Parliamentary Review and Family Magazine. 3 vols. 8vo. Lond., 1833. E
Slave States of America. 2 vols. 8vo. Lond., 1842.
D 3 T 47, 48
Travels in Assyria, Media, and Persia. 2nd ed. 2 vols. 8vo. Lond., 1830. D 4 U 23, 24
Travels in Mesopotamia ; with Researches on the Ruins of Babylon, Nineveh, Arbela, Ctesiphon, and Seleucia. 4to. Lond., 1827. D 4 V 28

BUCKINGHAM (L. STANHOPE F.) Memoirs of Mary Stuart, Queen of Scotland. 2 vols. 8vo. Lond., 1844.
C 6 T 14, 15

BUCKINGHAM AND CHANDOS (RICHARD NUGENT BRYDGES CHANDOS GRENVILLE), DUKE OF. Memoirs of the Court and Cabinets of George III. 4 vols. 8vo. Lond., 1853–55. C 7 Q 16–19
Memoirs of the Court of England during the Regency, 1811–20. 2 vols. 8vo. Lond., 1856. C 10 S 41, 42
Memoirs of the Courts of George IV., 1820–30. 2 vols. 8vo. Lond., 1859. C 6 Q 23, 24
Memoirs of the Court and Cabinets of William IV. and Victoria ; from original Family Documents. 2 vols. 8vo. Lond., 1861. B 3 S 13, 14
Private Diary of. 3 vols. 8vo. Lond., 1862. C 3 R 14–16

BUCKINGHAMSHIRE (JOHN SHEFFIELD), DUKE OF. Life and Poems of. [*See* JOHNSON, S., *and* CHALMERS, A.]
Mémoires du. [*See* GUIZOT, F. P. G., 21.]

BUCKLAND (DR. FRANCIS TREVELYAN), M.A. Acclimatisation of Animals: a Paper read before the Society of Arts, London ; republished by the Acclimatisation Society of Victoria. (Pam. Cb.) 8vo. Melb., 1861. A 16 U 25
Curiosities of Natural History. 1st, 2nd, and 3rd Series. 4 vols. 8vo. Lond., 1873. A 14 P 53–56
Fishhatching. 8vo. Lond., 1863. A 14 Q 25
Life of ; by his Brother-in-law, George C. Bompas ; with a Portrait. 8vo. Lond., 1885. C 5 R 9
Log-book of a Fisherman and Zoologist. 8vo. Lond., 1875. A 14 Q 34
[*See* WHITE, G.]

BUCKLAND (REV. W.), D.D., DEAN OF WESTMINSTER. Geology and Mineralogy, considered with reference to Natural Theology. 2 vols. 8vo. Lond., 1836. A 9 S 2, 3
Reliquiæ Diluvianæ ; or, Observations on the Organic Remains contained in Caves, Fissures, and Diluvial Gravel, and on other Geological Phenomena attesting the action of an universal Deluge. 2nd ed. 4to. Lond., 1824. A 9 V 6
[*See* BEECHEY, CAPT. F. W.]

Q

BUCKLE (HENRY THOMAS), F.R.A.S. History of Civilization in England. New ed. 2 vols. 8vo. Lond., 1869.
B 4 Q 11–13
Life and Writings of ; by Alfred Henry Huth. 2 vols. 8vo. Lond., 1880. C 8 U 7, 8
Miscellaneous and Posthumous Works of ; edited, with a Biographical Notice, by [Miss] Helen Taylor. 3 vols. 8vo. Lond., 1872. J 15 S 11–13

BUCKLE (LIEUT.-COL.) India and its Native Princes. [*See* ROUSSELET, L.]

BUCKLER (C. DUGALD). Colony of Tasmania : Recent Statistics ; also, Letters from Settlers. 8vo. Lond., 1883. MD 4 V 20

BUCKLEY (ARABELLA B.), MRS. FISHER. Short History of Natural Science, and of the Progress of Discovery from the Time of the Greeks. 12mo. Lond., 1876.
A 17 T 7

BUCKLEY (M. J. C.) Notes on the Architecture of the Church of Elstow. [*See* WIGRAM, REV. S. R.]

BUCKLEY (ROBERT BURTON), A.M.I.C.E. Irrigation Works of India, and their Financial Results ; being a brief History and Description of the Irrigation Works of India, and of the Profits and Losses which they have caused to the State. 8vo. Lond., 1880. F 10 R 20

BUCKLEY (S. B.), M.A., &c. Second Annual Report of the Geological and Agricultural Survey of Texas. (Pam. Cn.) 8vo. Houston, 1876. MA 2 V 14

BUCKLEY (THEODORE ALOIS). The Iliad of Homer ; literally translated. [*See* HOMER.]
The Odyssey of Homer ; literally translated. [*See* HOMER.]
Tragedies of Æschylus. [*See* ÆSCHYLUS.]
Tragedies of Euripides. [*See* EURIPIDES.]
Works of Horace, revised. [*See* HORATIUS FLACCUS, Q.]
[*See* ARISTOTELES.]

BUCKLEY (WILLIAM). Life and Adventures of ; by John Morgan. 12mo. Hobart, 1852.* MC 1 P 7
William Buckley, the Wild White Man, and his Port Phillip Black Friends ; by James Bonwick. 8vo. Melb., 1856. MC 1 R 27
Another copy. MJ 2 Q 17
The Wild White Man and the Blacks of Victoria. [*See* BONWICK, JAMES.]

BUCKNALL (BENJAMIN). [*See* VIOLLET-LE-DUC, E. E.]

BUCKSTONE (J. B.) The Happiest Day of my Life. (Cumberland's Eng. Theatre.) 12mo. Lond., 1829.
H 2 Q 18
Luke, the Labourer : a Domestic Melodrama. (Cumberland's Eng. Theatre.) 12mo. Lond., 1829. H 2 Q 17
Snakes in the Grass : a Farce. (Cumberland's Eng. Theatre.) 12mo. Lond., 1829. H 2 Q 22

BUCKTON (MRS. CATHERINE M.) Health in the House: Twenty-five Lectures on Elementary Physiology. 8vo. Lond., 1875.   A 12 Q 35

BUCKTON (THOMAS JOHN). Western Australia; comprising a Description of the vicinity of Australind and Port Lescherault; with two Maps. 12mo. Lond., 1840.
                                              MD 3 P 44

BUDDHA. Buddha and Buddhism. [*See* MILLS, C. D. B.]

Buddaghosha's Parables. Translated from Burmese by Capt. F. Rogers, R.E.; with an Introduction containing Buddha's Dhammapada, translated from Pâli by F. Max Muller, M.A.   8vo.   Lond., 1870.   J 12 U 25

Buddha and Early Buddhism. [*See* LILLIE. A.]

His Life, his Doctrine, his Order. [*See* OLDENBERG, DR. H.]

Life and Teachings of. [*See* DAVIDS, T. W. R.]

Life of. [*See* ALABASTER, H.]

Life of. [*See* MULLER, PROF. F. M.]

Life of the Buddha, and the Early History of his Order, derived from Tibetan Works in the Bkah-Hgyur and Bstan-Hgyur; translated by W. Woodville Rockhill. 8vo. Lond., 1884.   G 15 P 7

BUDDLE (REV. THOMAS). Maori King Movement in New Zealand; with a full Report of the Native Meetings, held at Waikato, April and May, 1860. 8vo. Auckland, 1860.   MB 2 R 31

Another copy.   (Pam. Ac.)   MD 7 Q 34

BUDELIUS (RENÉ). De Monetis, et re Nvmaria, libri dvo: qvorvm primvs artem cvdendae Monetae; secvndvs vero qvæstionvm monetariarvm decisiones continet his accesservnt tractatvs varii. Sm. 4to. Cologne, 1591.   A 13 S 50

BUDGE (ERNEST ALFRED THOMPSON WALLIS), M.A. Sarcophagus of Anchnesrâneferâb, Queen of Ahmes II, King of Egypt—about B.C. 564–526. Roy. 8vo. Lond., 1885.   B 2 R 34

BUDGE (J.) Practical Miner's Guide; also, a Treatise on Assaying Silver, Copper, Lead, and Tin; with a Collection of Tables, Rules, and Illustrations. 8vo. Lond., 1866.
                                              A 10 P 21

BUDGELL (E.) Memoirs of the Lives and Characters of the illustrious Family of the Boyles, particularly of the late eminently learned Charles, Earl of Orrery. 3rd ed. 8vo. Lond., 1737.   C 4 S 1

BUDGETT (SAMUEL). The Successful Merchant, Sketches of the Life of; by the Rev. W. Arthur, A.M. 8vo. Lond., 1852.   C 3 Q 47

BUEK (H. W.), M.D. Index Generalis et Specialis ad A. P. Decandolle Prodromum Systematis Naturalis Regni Vegetabilis. Parts 1–4. 4 vols. (in 3) 8vo. Berolini, 1840–74.   A 4 R 22–24

BUFFON (GEORGE LOUIS LECLERC), COMTE DE. Buffon; sa Famille, ses Collaborateurs, et ses Familiers: Mémoires, par M. Humbert-Bazile, son Secrétaire. 8vo. Paris, 1863.   C 10 P 10

Histoire Naturelle des Coralliaires, etc. [*See* MILNE-EDWARDS.]

Natural History of Birds. 9 vols. 8vo. Lond., 1793

Natural History; containing a Theory of the Earth, a General History of Man, of the Brute Creation, &c. 16 vols. 8vo. Lond., 1797–1808.   A 28 Q 9–24

[*See* DES MURS, ŒILLET *and* PENNANT, T.]

BUGEAUD (MARSHAL THOMAS ROBERT). Memoirs of; from his private Correspondence and original Documents, 1784–1849; by the Count H. d'Ideville; edited, from the French, by Charlotte M. Yonge. 2 vols. 8vo. Lond., 1884.   C 8 U 11, 12

BUGGE (PROF. S.) Prof. S. Bugge's Studies on Northern Mythology shortly examined. [*See* STEPHENS, DR. G. PROF.]

BUHLE (J. T.) [*See* ARISTOTELES.]

BÜHLER (GEORG). Laws of Manu—Sacred Laws of the Aryas. [*See* MULLER, PROF. F. M.]

BUILDER (THE). an Illustrated Weekly Magazine for the Architect, Engineer, Archæologist, Constructor, Sanitary Reformer, and Art-Lover. Vols. 1–48. Fol. Lond., 1843–85.   E

BUILDING ACT. Report from the Committee on the Building Act, 8 Wm. IV. No. 6; with the Minutes of Evidence. (Parl. Doc., 32.) Fol. Sydney, 1838. MF 4 ‡

BUILDING CONSTRUCTION. Examples of Building Construction, intended as an Aide-mémoire for the Professional Man and the Operative. 4 vols. atlas 4to. Lond. (n.d.)   A 13 P 1–4 ‡

Notes on Building Construction, arranged to meet the requirements of the Syllabus of Science and Art Department of the Committee of Council on Education, South Kensington. Vols. 1–3. Lond., 1875–79.   A 3 P 29–31

BUILDING NEWS (THE), and Engineering Journal. 21 vols. fol. Lond., 1875–85.   E

BULGER (GEORGE ERNEST). Leaves from the Records of St. Hubert's Club. 8vo. Lond., 1864.   J 7 U 27

BULKELEY (JOHN), AND CUMMINS (JOHN). Voyage to the South Seas in the years 1740–41; containing a faithful Narrative of the Loss of His Majesty's Ship Wager. 8vo. Lond., 1743.   MD 3 S 18

BULL (MR. JOHN). [*See* VICTORIA.]

BULL (JOHN WRATHALL). Early Experiences of Life in South Australia, and an extended Colonial History. 8vo. Adelaide, 1884.   MD 2 R 12

BULL (OLE): a Memoir; by Sara C. Bull; with Ole Bull's Violin Notes, &c. 8vo. Lond., 1886.   C 5 R 6

BULL (MRS. SARA C.) Ole Bull: a Memoir. 8vo. Lond., 1886.   C 5 R 6

BULL (W. K.) Trip to Tahiti, and other Islands in the South Seas. 8vo. Melh., 1858.   MD 1 U 21

BULLAR (HENRY). Winter in the Azores. [*See* BULLAR, J.]

BULLAR (J. F.), B.A. On the Development of the Parasitic Isopoda. (Roy. Soc. Pubs., 6.) 4to. Lond., 1879.   A 11 P 7 ‡

BULLAR (JOHN). Discourse occasioned by the Death of the Rt. Hon. George Canning. 8vo. Southampton, 1827.   G 17 Q 20

BULLAR (JOSEPH), M.D., AND BULLAR (HENRY). Winter in the Azores; and a Summer at the Baths of the Furnas. 2 vols. 8vo. Lond., 1841.   D 7 T 2, 3

BULLARIUM ROMANUM. Bullarum privilegiorum ac diplomatum Romanorum Pontificum amplissima collectio. 14 vols. (in 28) fol. Rome, 1733–62.   G 25 P 1–28 ‡
Bullarii Romani Continuatio. 18 vols. (in 17) fol. Rome, 1835–56.   G 25 P 31–47 ‡
Sanctissimi Domini Nostri Benedicti Papæ XIV Bullarium. 4 vols. (in 2) fol. Venice, 1762–68.   G 25 P 29, 30 ‡

BULLEN (ARTHUR HENRY). Christmas Garland: Carols and Poems, from the 15th Century to the Present Time. Illustrated. 8vo. Lond., 1885.   H 5 T 22
Lyrics from Song-books of the Elizabethian Age. 8vo. Lond., 1887.   H 5 T 18
[*See* MARLOWE, C., *and* MIDDLETON, T.]

BULLEN (GEORGE), F.S.A. Caxton Celebration, 1877. [*See* CAXTON, W.]

BULLER (RT. HON. CHARLES). Responsible Government for Colonies. 2nd ed. Lond., 1840.   F 5 Q 33
[*See* BLAND W.]

BULLER (REV. JAMES). Forty Years in New Zealand; including a Personal Narrative, an Account of Maoridom, and of the Christianization and Colonization of the Country. 8vo. Lond., 1878.*   MD 5 S 40

BULLER (SIR WALTER LAWRY), K.C.M.G., &c. History of the Birds of New Zealand. Roy. 4to. Lond., 1873.   MA 2 Q 25 †
Manual of the Birds of New Zealand. Roy. 8vo. Wellington, 1882.   MA 2 U 5

BULLETIN DES SCIENCES NATURELLES ET DE GEOLOGIE. Vols. 7–27. 21 vols. 8vo. Paris, 1826–31.   A 16 R 10–30

BULLOCH (CAPT. JAMES D.) Secret Service of the Confederate States in Europe; or, How the Confederate Cruisers were equipped. 2 vols. 8vo. Lond., 1883.   B 1 S 38, 39

BULLOCK (WILLIAM HENRY). Across Mexico in 1864–65. 8vo. Lond., 1866.   D 4 P 19

BULMER (THOMAS S.). M.D., &c., "NADI COSMOS." Series of Private Notes and Memo. for Thinking Men. (Pam. Bs.) 8vo. Belfast, Vict., 1879.   MG 1 Q 34
Small-pox: its Origin, Signs, and Symptoms; also, the Germ and Contagion Theories. Part 1. 12mo. Melh., 1884.   MA 2 S 24

BULWER-LYTTON (E. G. E. L.) [*See* LYTTON, BARON.]

BULWER (SIR H. L. E.) [*See* DALLING AND BULWER, BARON.]

BUMBY (REV. JOHN HEWGILL). Life of; with a brief History of the Commencement and Progress of the Wesleyan Mission in New Zealand, by the Rev. A. Barrett. 2nd ed. 12mo. Lond., 1853.   MC 1 P 14

BUMPUS (T. F.) London Churches, Ancient and Modern. 12mo. Lond., 1883.   A 2 R 40

BUNBURY (SIR EDWARD HERBERT), BART., F.R.G.S. History of Ancient Geography among the Greeks and Romans from the Earliest Ages till the Fall of the Roman Empire. 2 vols. 8vo. Lond., 1879.   D 12 U 10, 11

BUNBURY (MISS SELINA). Rides in the Pyrenees. 8vo. Lond., 1844.   D 9 Q 36, 37

BUNBURY (LIEUT.-COL. THOMAS), C.B. Reminiscences of a Veteran; being Personal and Military Adventures in Portugal, Spain, France, Malta, New South Wales, Norfolk Island, New Zealand, Andaman Islands, and India. 3 vols. 8vo. Lond., 1861.   C 5 Q 26–28
Another copy. 3 vols. 8vo. Lond., 1861. MC 1 Q 36–38

BUNCE (DANIEL), C.M.H.S. Australasiatic Reminiscences of Twenty-three Years' Wanderings in Tasmania and the Australias, including Travels with Dr. Leichhardt in North or Tropical Australia. 8vo. Melh., 1857.*   MD 1 S 18
Australian Manual of Horticulture. 2nd ed., greatly improved and enlarged. 12mo. Melh., 1850.   MA 1 P 11
Travels with Dr. Leichhardt in Australia. 12mo. Melh., 1859.*   MD 1 S 20
[Same as "Australasiatic Reminiscences," but with a different title-page.]

BUNCE (JOHN THACKRAY). Biography of David Cox. [*See* HALL, W.]

BUND (PROF. J. W. WILLIS-). Salmon Problems. 12mo. Lond., 1885.   A 14 Q 35
Selection of Cases from the State Trials, 1327–1681. 3 vols. 8vo. Camb., 1879–82.   F 6 S 28–30

BUNGENER (L. F.) History of the Council of Trent. 8vo. Edinb., 1852. G 13 Q 16

BUNKER'S HILL MONUMENT ASSOCIATION. Arguments on behalf of the Association; by W. W. Wheildon and G. W. Warren. 8vo. (Pam. Ce.) Charlestown, 1869. A 8 R 33

Ceremonies on 17th June, 1861; with the Annual Proceedings. (Pam. Ce.) 8vo. Boston, 1861. A 8 R 33

BUNN (Alfred). Old England and New England, in a series of Views, taken on the spot. 2 vols. 8vo. Lond., 1853. D 4 P 7, 8

The Stage, both before and behind the Curtain; from "Observations taken on the spot." 3 vols. 8vo. Lond., 1840. J 11 P 9-11

BUNNETT (F. E.) Raphael Santi; his Life, &c. [*See* Wolzogen, Baron von.]

BUNSEN (Christian Carl Josias), Baron von. Biographical Essay. [*See* Müller, Prof. F. Max.]

Christianity and Mankind; their Beginnings and Prospects. 2nd ed. 7 vols. 8vo. Lond., 1854. G 5 Q 15-21

Egypt's Place in Universal History; translated from the German, by Charles H. Cottrell. 4 vols. 8vo. Lond., 1848-60. B 2 R 23-26

Essay on Niebuhr. [*See* Niebuhr, B. G.]

Memoir of Baron Bunsen, late Minister Plenipotentiary and Envoy Extraordinary of His Majesty Frederick William iv at the Court of St. James; drawn chiefly from Family Papers, by his Widow, Frances Baroness Bunsen. 2 vols. 8vo. Lond., 1868. C 8 T 3, 4

BUNSEN (Ernest de). The Angel-Messiah of Buddhists, Essenes, and Christians. 8vo. Lond., 1880. G 6 P 11

BUNSEN (Frances), Baroness. Memoir of Baron Bunsen. 2 vols. 8vo. Lond., 1868. C 8 T 3, 4

BUNSTER (Grosvenor). [*See* Clarke, M. A. H., *and* Our Christmas Budget.]

BUNTING (Rev. Jabez), D.D. Mormonism; its Origin and Character: reprinted from the "Eclectic Review," with an Introduction. 8vo. Sydney, 1851. MG 1 Q 31

BUNYAN (John). [A Biography]; by J. A. Froude. (Eng. Men of Letters.) 8vo. Lond., 1880. C 1 U 4

Select Biographies; Cromwell and Bunyan: by R. Southey. (H. and C. Lib., 6.) 8vo. Lond., 1844. J 8 P 6

His Life, Times, and Work; by John Brown, B.A. 8vo. Lond., 1885. C 6 Q 2

The Holy War made by Shaddai upon Diabolis. 8vo. Lond., 1882. G 13 R 32

The Pilgrim's Progress; with the Life of the Author, &c. 2 vols. 8vo. Rimosey, 1818. G 14 Q 20, 21

[*See* Hazlitt, W. C.]

BUNYIU NANJIO. Biographical Essay. [*See* Müller, Prof. F. Max.]

BUOMMATTEI (Benedetto). Della Lingua Toscana. Pubblico lettore d'essa nello studio Pisano, e Fiorentino. Libri due. Roy. 8vo. Venezia, 1735. K 14 Q 28

BUONARROTI (Michael Angelo.) [*See* Michael Angelo Buonarroti.]

BURAT (Amédée). Géologie Appliquée: Traité du Gisement et de l'Exploitation des Minéraux utiles. 4e éd. 2 vols. 8vo. Paris, 1858-59. A 9 R 8, 9

Géologie Appliquée: Traité du Gisement et de la Recherche des Minéraux utiles. 5e éd., revue, corrigée et augmentée. 2 vols. 8vo. Paris, 1870. A 9 U 29, 30

BURBIDGE (Rev. Edward), M.A. Liturgies and Offices of the Church, for the use of English Readers, in illustration of the Book of Common Prayer. 8vo. Lond., 1885. G 13 R 38

BURBIDGE (F. W.) Gardens of the Sun; or, a Naturalist's Journal on the Mountains, and in the Forests and Swamps of Borneo, and the Sulu Archipelago. 8vo. Lond., 1880. D 6 Q 37

BURBURY (S H.), M.A. Electricity and Magnetism. [*See* Watson, H. W.]

BURCHARDUS (Vomatiensis Episcopus). Opera omnia. [*See* Migne, J. P., Series Latina, 140.]

BURCHELL (William J.) Travels in the Interior of Southern Africa; with Engravings. 2 vols. 8vo. Lond., 1822-24. D 2 V 19, 20

BURCHETT (E. S.) Practical Plane Geometry. Roy. 8vo. Lond., 1876. A 10 U 7

BURCHETT (R.) Linear Perspective, for the use of Schools of Art. 8vo. Lond., 1856. A 8 P 31

BURCKHARDT (Jacobus). [*See* Hutten, U. von.]

BURCKHARDT (Dr. Jacob). The Cicerone: an Art Guide to Painting in Italy. 12mo. Lond., 1879. D 12 P 30

BURCKHARDT (John Lewis). Arabic Proverbs; or, the Manners and Customs of the Modern Egyptians, illustrated from their Proverbial Sayings current at Cairo: translated and explained. 4to. Lond., 1830. K 14 S 14

Another copy. 2nd ed. Roy. 8vo. Lond., 1875. K 14 S 15

Notes on the Bedouins and Wahábys; collected during his Travels in the East. 4to. Lond., 1830. D 5 V 6

Travels in Arabia. 2 vols. 8vo. Lond., 1829. D 4 T 19, 20

Travels in Nubia. 2nd ed. 4to. Lond., 1822. D 2 V

Travels in Syria and the Holy Land. 4to. Lond., 1822. D 4 V 38

BURDER (Rev. Samuel), A.M. Oriental Customs; or, an illustration of the Sacred Scriptures. 6th ed. 2 vols. 8vo. Lond., 1822.   G 14 Q 22, 23

BURDETT (F.) Remarks on T. Reynolds. [*See* Hist. Pamphlets.]   B 11 Q 1

BURFORD (Robert). Description of a View of the Town of Sydney, New South Wales, the Harbour of Port Jackson, and the surrounding Country, now exhibiting in the Panorama, Leicester-square. 8vo. Lond., 1829.   MD 4 U 19

BURGES (Ellen). Vizcaya; or, Life in the Land of the Carlists at the Outbreak of the Insurrection, 1872–73; with some Account of the Iron Mines in the vicinity of Bilbao. 8vo. Lond., 1874.   D 8 R 1

BURGES (Sir James Bland), Bart. Selections from the Letters and Correspondence of; with Notices of his Life, edited by James Hutton. 8vo. Lond., 1885.   C 10 R 11

BURGESS (George), A.M. [*See* Greek Anthology The.]

BURGESS (James), LL.D., &c. Cave Temples of India. [*See* Fergusson, J.]

Report on the Buddhist Cave Temples and their Inscriptions; being part of the Results of the fourth, fifth, and sixth Seasons' Operations of the Archæological Survey of Western India, 1876–80. Supplementary to the Volume on "The Cave Temples of India." Imp. 4to. Lond., 1883.   B 14 S 15 ‡

Report on the Elura Cave Temples, and the Brahmanical and Jaina Caves in Western India, completing the Results of the fifth, sixth, and seventh Seasons' Operations of the Archæological Survey, 1877–80. Supplementary to the Volume on "The Cave Temples of India." Imp. 4to. Lond., 1883.   B 14 S 16 ‡

BURGESS (James W.) Practical Treatise on Coach-building, Historical and Descriptive. (Weale.) 12mo. Lond., 1881.   A 17 Q 52

BURGESS (Murray). [*See* Tasmanian Public Library.]

BURGESS (Richard). [*See* Maungatapu Murders.]

BURGESS (T. H.) Diseases of the Skin. [*See* Cazenave, P. L. A.]

BURGHLEY (Rt. Hon. William Cecil), Lord. Collection of State Papers relating to Affairs in the Reigns of King Henry VIII, King Edward VI, Queen Mary, and Queen Elizabeth, from 1542 to 1570; transcribed by Samuel Haynes, A.M. Fol. Lond., 1740.   B 16 S 11 ‡

Collection of State Papers relating to Affairs in the Reign of Queen Elizabeth, from 1571 to 1596; transcribed by William Murdin, B.D. Fol. Lond., 1759.   B 16 S 12 ‡

Memoirs of the Life and Administration of; by the Rev. E. Nares, D.D. 3 vols. 4to. Lond., 1828–31.   C 2 W 2–4

Life of; [*See* Mackintosh, Sir J.]

BURGHLEY (Rt. Hon. William Cecil), Lord—*contd.*

Life of William Cecil, Lord Burghley, Lord High Treasurer of England, Biographical Notices of his Successors, &c.; by the Rev. W. H. Charlton, M.A. Roy. 8vo. Stamford, 1847.   C 9 V 16

BURGON (Rev. John William), B.D. Life and Times of Sir Thomas Gresham; compiled chiefly from his Correspondence. 2 vols. 8vo. Lond., 1839.   C 7 R 13, 14

The Revision Revised; to which is added, a Reply to Bishop Ellicott's Pamphlet in defence of the Revisers and their Greek Text of the New Testament. 8vo. Lond., 1883.   G 6 Q 23

BURGOYNE (Lieut.-Gen. John). The Heiress: a Comedy. (Brit. Theatre.) 12mo. Lond., 1808.   H 1 P 22

The Lord of the Manor: an Opera. (Cumberland's Eng. Theatre.) 12mo. Lond., 1829.   H 2 Q 14

The Maid of the Oaks. [*See* Farces, 6.]

Richard Cœur de Lion: an Historical Romance. [*See* Farces, 6.]

BURGOYNE (Right Hon. John). Political and Military Episodes in the latter half of the Eighteenth Century, derived from the Life and Correspondence of; by E. B. de Fonblanque. 8vo. Lond., 1876.   C 8 U 45

BURGOYNE (Field-Marshal the Rt. Hon. Sir John Fox,) Bart. Life and Correspondence of; by his Son-in-law, Lieut.-Col. the Hon. Geo. Wrottesley. 2 vols. 8vo. Lond., 1873.   C 8 U 9, 10

Remarks on the Maintenance of Macadamised Roads; with an Appendix by Sir W. T. Denison. (Pam. C.) Roy. 8vo. Sydney, 1857.   MJ 2 S 1

Another copy.   MJ 2 R 17

Treatise on the Blasting and Quarrying of Stone for Building Purposes; with the Constituents and Analyses of Granite, Slate, Limestone, and Sandstone; to which is added some Remarks on the Blowing up of Bridges. (Weale.) 12mo. Lond., 1868.   A 17 P 29

[*See* Hughes, S.]

BURGOYNE (Roderick Hamilton). Historical Records of the 93rd Sutherland Highlanders, now the 2nd Battalion Princess Louise's Argyll and Sutherland Highlanders. 8vo. Lond., 1883.   B 13 P 42

BURGUY (Prof. Georges Frédéric). Grammaire de la Langue d'Oïl; ou, Grammaire des Dialectes Français aux XIIe et XIIIe Siècles, suivie d'un Glossaire. 2e éd. 2 vols. 8vo. Berlin, 1869.   K 12 R 34, 35

BURIAL GROUNDS, SYDNEY. Burial Grounds, Sydney, and proposed General Cemetery: a Copy of all Correspondence between the Government and any person or persons relative to the condition of the Burial Grounds within the City of Sydney. Fol. Syd., 1863.   MF 10 Q 1 ‡

BURIGNY (Jean Lévesque de). Life of Hugo Grotius; together with a critical Account of his Works, written originally in French. 8vo. Lond., 1754.   C 5 R 17

BURKE (Rt. Hon. Edmund). Anecdote Biography; by J. Timbs. 8vo. Lond., 1860. C 1 S 6

A Biography; by John Morley. (Eng. Men of Letters.) 8vo. Lond., 1879. C 1 U 5

Correspondence of, 1744–97; edited by Charles William, Earl Fitzwilliam, and Lieut.-Gen. Sir Richard Bourke. 4 vols. 8vo. Lond., 1844. C 10 Q 5–8

History of the Life and Times of; by Thomas Mackright. 2 vols. 8vo. Lond., 1858. C 10 Q 3, 4

Lectures on the Life, Writings, and Times of; by J. B. Robertson. 12mo. Lond., 1868. C 3 Q 13

Letter to a Noble Lord on the Attacks made upon him and his Pension in the House of Lords, by the Duke of Bedford and the Earl of Lauderdale. 8vo. Lond., 1796. F 6 T 2

Memoir of the Life and Character of; with Specimens of his Poetry and Letters, by James Prior. 2nd ed. 2 vols. 8vo. Lond., 1826. C 6 T 2, 3

Memoir of the Political Life of; by the Rev. G. Croly. 2 vols. 8vo. Lond., 1840. C 3 R 12, 13

Philosophical Enquiry into the Origin of our Ideas of the Sublime and Beautiful. 12mo. Lond., 1757. J 1 T 8

Select Works; edited, with Introduction and Notes, by E. J. Payne. (Clar. Press.) 3 vols. 12mo. Oxford, 1876–78. F 15 P 1–3

Six Letters (never before published). [*See* Hist. Pams.]

Speeches of, in the House of Commons and in Westminster Hall. 4 vols. 8vo. Lond., 1816. F 13 P 7–10

Wisdom of; Extracts from his Writings and Speeches, selected and arranged by E. A. Parkhurst. 12mo. Lond., 1886. F 5 Q 30

Works of. 8 vols. 8vo. Lond., 1801. J 10 S 12–19

BURKE (James Lester). Adventures of Martin Cash. [*See* Cash, M.]

BURKE (John). Genealogical and Heraldic History of the Commoners of Great Britain and Ireland. 4 vols. roy. 8vo. Lond., 1836–38. K 10 V 15–18

BURKE (Sir John Bernard), C.B., &c., Ulster King of Arms. Anecdotes of the Aristocracy, and Episodes in Ancestral Story. 2 vols. 8vo. Lond., 1849. J 4 R 15, 16

Book of Orders of Knighthood, and Decorations of Honour of all Nations. Roy. 8vo. Lond., 1858. K 10 T 10

Book of Precedence. Roy. 8vo. Lond., 1881. C 10 V 19

Family Romance; or, Episodes in the Domestic Annals of the Aristocracy. 4th ed. 8vo. Lond., 1862. B 23 R 14

Genealogical and Heraldic Dictionary of the Peerage and Baronetage of the British Empire. 11th ed. Roy. 8vo. Lond., 1852. E

Another copy. 33rd ed. Roy. 8vo. Lond., 1871. E
Another copy. 34th ed. Roy. 8vo. Lond., 1872. E
Another copy. 41st ed. Roy. 8vo. Lond., 1879. E
Another copy. 44th ed. Roy. 8vo. Lond., 1882. E
Another copy. 48th ed. Roy. 8vo. Lond., 1886. E
Another copy. 49th ed. Roy. 8vo. Lond., 1887. E

BURKE (Sir John Bernard), C.B., &c.—*continued.*
Genealogical and Heraldic History of the Landed Gentry of Great Britain and Ireland. 5th ed. 2 vols. roy. 8vo. Lond., 1871–72. K 10 V 20, 21

Another copy. 6th ed., with Supplement. 2 vols. roy. 8vo. Lond., 1882. K 10 V 22, 23

Another copy. 7th ed. 2 vols. Roy. 8vo. Lond., 1886. K 10 V 24, 25

Genealogical History of the Dormant, Abeyant, Forfeited, and Extinct Peerages of the British Empire. New ed. Roy. 8vo. Lond., 1866. K 10 U 8

General Armory of England, Scotland, Ireland, and Wales; comprising a Registry of Armorial Bearings, from the Earliest to the Present Time. Roy. 8vo. Lond., 1878. K 10 T 11

Heraldic Illustrations. [*See* BURKE, J. & Sir J.]

Illuminated Heraldic Illustrations; with Annotations. Roy. 8vo. Lond., 1857. K 10 T 22

Reminiscences, Ancestral, Anecdotal, and Historic: a remodelled and revised edition of "The Rise of Great Families and other Essays." 8vo. Lond., 1882. B 4 R 4

Romantic Records of Distinguished Families: a Second Series of "Anecdotes of the Aristocracy." 2nd ed. 2 vols. 8vo. Lond., 1851. J 4 R 17, 18

Vicissitudes of Families. 2 vols. 8vo. Lond., 1869. B 23 S 5, 6

Visitation of the Seats and Arms of the Noblemen and Gentlemen of Great Britain and Ireland. [1st and] 2nd series. 4 vols. roy. 8vo. Lond., 1852–53. K 10 T 15–18

BURKE (John, and Sir John Bernard), C.B., &c., Ulster King of Arms. Encyclopædia of Heraldry; or, General Armory of England, Scotland, and Ireland. 3rd ed., with a Supplement. Roy. 8vo. Lond. (n.d.) K 10 T 11

Genealogical and Heraldic History of the Extinct and Dormant Baronetcies of England, Ireland, and Scotland. 8vo. Lond., 1841. K 10 T 13

Heraldic Illustrations; with explanatory Pedigrees. 3 vols. roy. 8vo. Lond., 1844–46. K 10 T 19–21

Royal Families of England, Scotland, and Wales, with their Descendants, Sovereigns, and Subjects. 2 vols. roy. 8vo. Lond., 1848–51. K 10 U 15, 16

BURKE (J. F.) British Husbandry, 1834–37. (Lib. Usef. Know.) 8vo. Lond., 1834–37. A 1 R 1, 2

BURKE (Oliver J.), A.B., &c. History of the Catholic Archbishops of Tuam, from the Foundation of the See to the Death of the Most Rev. John MacHale, D.D., A.D. 1881. 8vo. Dublin, 1882. G 13 Q 23

BURKE (Peter). Celebrated Naval and Military Trials. 8vo. Lond., 1876. F 6 S 27

Celebrated Trials connected with the Aristocracy in the relations of Private Life. 8vo. Lond., 1849. F 10 R 8

Romance of the Forum; or, Narratives, Scenes, and Anecdotes, from Courts of Justice. 2 vols. 8vo. Lond., 1852. F 14 R 18, 19

BURKE (ROBERT O'HARA), AND WILLS (W. J.) Burke and Wills Exploring Expedition : an Account of the Crossing the Continent of Australia, from Cooper's Creek to Carpentaria. 8vo. Melb., 1861.　　　MJ 2 R 21

Copies of Despatches from Sir Henry Barkly and the other Colonial Governors on the subject of the Australian Exploring Expedition. (Parl. Docs., 69.) Fol. Lond., 1862.　　　MF 4 ‡

Expedition in Search of Burke and Wills. [*See* BOURNE, G. *and* LANDSBOROUGH, W.] .

In Memoriam. Dedicated to the Students attending the Scotch College for Young Ladies. (Pam. 36.) 8vo. Melb., 1862.　　　MJ 2 Q 23

Robert O'Hara Burke and the Australian Exploring Expedition of 1860. [*See* JACKSON, A.]

Victorian Exploration Expedition : King's Narrative ; Brahe's Memorandum ; Howitt's Journal ; Wills' Journal ; Macpherson's Narrative ; Death of Burke and two of his party ; Meeting of the Victorian Exploration Committee ; Memoirs of the late Leaders of the Expedition. (Newspaper Cuttings. Pam. B.) Roy. 8vo. Melb. and Sydney, 1861.　　　MJ 2 U 2

[*See* DAVIS, J.; *and* MANUSCRIPTS AND PORTRAITS.]

BURKE (S. HUBERT). Historical Portraits of the Tudor Dynasty and the Reformation Period. 8vo. Lond., 1879–83.　　　C 8 P 20–23

BURKE (VERY REV. THOMAS NICHOLAS), O.P. History of Ireland as told in her Ruins: a Lecture delivered in New York, April 5, 1872. (*Bound with Waterworth's Church of St. Patrick.*) 8vo. Sydney, 1872.　　　G 7 T 15

Life of ; by William J. Fitz-Patrick, F.S.A. 2 vols. 8vo. Lond., 1885.　　　C 10 R 27, 28

BURKE (THOMAS ULICK). Murder of. [*See* PIGGOREET MURDER.]

BURKE (WILLIAM), AND HARE (WILLIAM). History of ; by G. Macgregor. 8vo. Glasgow, 1884.　　　B 13 P 40

BURKITT (REV. WILLIAM), M.A. Life of ; by Nathaniel Parkhurst, M.A., Vicar of Yoxford in Suffolk. 8vo. Lond., 1704.　　　C 3 Q 7

BURLEIGH (BENNET G.) Desert Warfare ; being the Chronicle of the Eastern Soudan Campaign. With Official Maps. 8vo. Lond., 1884.　　　B 2 R 47

BURLEIGH (WILLIAM CECIL) LORD. [*See* BURGHLEY, LORD.]

BURLEY (S. W.) Burley's United States Centennial Gazetteer and Guide. 8vo. Philad., 1876.　　　D 12 T 6

BURLTON (COL. WILLIAM) [*See* MACMURDO, MAJOR M.]

BURMA. British Burma Gazetteer. [*See* SPEARMANN, H. R.]

BURMANN (JOHANN). Rariorum Africanarum Plantarum. 4to. Amsterdam, 1738.　　　A 5 Q 6

BURMANN (NIC. LAUR.) Flora Indica cui accedit series Zoophytorum Indicorum, nec non Prodromus Floræ Capensis. 4to. Lugd. Bat., 1768.　　　A 5 Q 16

BURMANN (PETER). [*See* CLAUDIANUS, C., *and* OVIDIUS NASO, P.]

BURMEISTER (DR. HERMANN). Description physique de la République Argentine, d'après des observations personnelles et étrangères. 5 vols. 8vo. Paris, 1876–79.　D 3 U 2–6

Atlas [to the above]. Imp. 4to. Buenos Ayres, 1879–80.　　　D 5 Q 15 ‡

BURN (DAVID). Vindication of Van Diemen's Land ; in a cursory Glance at her Colonists as they are, not as they have been represented to be. 8vo. Lond., 1840. MJ 2 R 13

BURN (RICHARD), LL.D. Justice of the Peace and Parish Officer ; by T. S. Pritchard, S. B. Bristowe, L. W. Cave, J. E. Davis, and J. B. Maule ; edited by J. B. Maule. 5 vols. 8vo. Lond., 1869.　　　F 4 T 4–8

BURN (ROBERT), M.A. Old Rome : a Hand-book to the Ruins of the City and the Campagna ; being an Epitome of his larger Work "Rome and the Campagna." 8vo. Lond., 1880.　　　B 12 R 37

Rome and the Campagna: an Historical and Topographical Description of the Site, Buildings and Neighbourhood of Ancient Rome. Illustrated. 4to. Camb., 1871. B 14 Q 16 ‡

Another copy. 2nd ed. 4to. Camb., 1876.　B 14 Q 17 ‡

BURN (ROBERT SCOTT), M.S.A., &c. Notes of an Agricultural Tour in Belgium, Holland, and the Rhine ; with Practical Notes on the peculiarities of Flemish Husbandry. 8vo. Lond., 1862.　　　A 1 U 6

Outlines of Modern Farming. (Weale.) 2nd ed. 5 vols. (in 4). 12mo. Lond., 1865–72.　　　A 17 Q 1–4

1. Soils, Manures, and Crops.

2. Notes on Farming, and Farming Economy.

3, 4. Stock, Cattle, Sheep, and Horses, the Dairy, Pigs, Poultry.

5. Utilization of Town Sewage, Irrigation, &c.

Practical Directory for the Improvement of Landed Property, and the Economic Cultivation of its Farms. Roy. 4to. Edinb., 1881.　　　A 2 Q 3 †

Suburban Farming. [*See* DONALDSON, PROF. J.]

Systematic Small Farming. 8vo. Lond., 1886. A 1 P 48

Working Drawings and Designs in Mechanical Engineering and Machine-making ; with Essays on various subjects, by W. Walker, Francis Lightbody, and others. Imp. fol. Edinb. and Lond., 1866.　　　A 20 P 20 ‡

Working Drawings and Designs in Architecture and Buildings ; with Essays on various subjects, by E. S. Eyland, F. Lightbody, and R. S. Burn. Roy. fol. Edinb. and Lond., 1866.　　　A 1 R 2 ‡

Year-book of Agricultural Facts for 1860. 8vo. Edinb., 1861.　　　E

BURNABY (COLONEL FREDERICK GUSTAVUS). Life and Times of ; by J. Redding Ware and R. K. Mann. 8vo. Lond., 1885.   C 4 S 3

On Horseback through Asia Minor; with Portrait and Map. 2 vols. 8vo. Lond., 1877.   D 4 U 11, 12

Ride to Khiva ; Travels and Adventures in Central Asia. 8vo. Lond., 1877.   D 6 R 20

BURNABY (MRS. FREDERICK GUSTAVUS). High Life and Towers of Silence. 8vo. Lond., 1886.   D 7 Q 39

BURNAND (W. H.) Copies of the Correspondence between the Colonial Department and Messrs. Graham and Co., referred to in the Petition of Mr. W. H. Burnand. (Parl. Docs., 19.) Fol. Lond., 1839.   MF 4 ‡

BURNE (MISS CHARLOTTE SOPHIA). Shropshire Folk-lore. [*See* JACKSON, GEORGINA F.]

BURNELL (ARTHUR COKE), PH.D. Glossary of Anglo-Indian Colloquial words. [*See* YULE, COL. H.]

Ordinances of Manu. [*See* MANU.]

BURNELL (GEORGE R.), C.E. Builder's Price-book. [*See* LOCKWOOD.]

Civil Engineering [*See* LAW, H.]

Rudiments of Hydraulic Engineering. 12mo. Lond., 1868.   A 17 P 60

Treatise on Limes, Cements, Mortars, Concretes, Mastics, Plastering, &c. (Weale.) 9th ed. 12mo. Lond., 1872.   A 17 P 1

Well-digging, &c. [*See* SWINDELL, J. G.]

BURNES (SIR ALEXANDER), C.B., &c. Cabool; being a Personal Narrative of a Journey to, and Residence in that City, in the years, 1836-38. 8vo. Lond., 1842.   D 4 T 11

Travels into Bokhara ; being the Account of a Journey from India to Cabool, Tartary, and Persia. 3 vols. 8vo. Lond., 1834.   D 6 Q 33-35

BURNES (JAMES), K.H., &c. Narrative of a Visit to the Court of Sinde, at Hyderabad, on the Indus; with a Sketch of the History of the Cutch. 12mo. Edinb., 1839.   D 5 P 8

BURNESS (WILLIAM). [*See* NESBIT, A.]

BURNET (GILBERT), D.D., BISHOP OF SALISBURY. Histoire de mon Temps [*See* GUIZOT, F. P. G., 17-20.]

History of his Own Time ; with the suppressed Passages of the first volume, and Notes by the Earls of Dartmouth and Hardwicke, and Speaker Onslow. 6 vols. 8vo. Oxford, 1823.   B 6 Q 1-6

History of the Reformation of the Church of England. 6 vols. 8vo. Lond., 1820.   G 6 Q 24-29

Memoirs of the Lives and Actions of James and William, Dukes of Hamilton and Castleherald, &c. Fol. Lond., 1677.   C 2 W 12

BURNET (JOHN), F.R.S. Essay on the Education of the Eye with reference to Painting. 2nd ed. 4to. Lond., 1837.   A 8 U 20

Another copy. 3rd ed. 4to. Lond., 1865.   A 8 U 11

Practical Hints on Composition in Painting; illustrated by Examples from the Great Masters of the Italian, Flemish, and Dutch Schools. 4to. Lond., 1822.   A 8 U 15

Practical Hints on Colour in Painting; illustrated by Examples from the Works of the Venetian, Flemish, and Dutch Schools. 3rd ed. 4to. Lond., 1830.   A 8 U 11

Practical Hints on Light and Shade in Painting; illustrated by Examples from the Italian, Flemish, and Dutch Schools. 3rd ed. 4to. Lond., 1829.   A 8 U 11

Rembrandt and his Works; comprising a short Account of his Life ; with a critical Examination into his Principles and Practice of Design, Light, Shade, and Colour. Illustrated by Examples from the Etchings of Rembrandt. 4to. Lond., 1849.   A 8 U 15

BURNET (THOMAS), M.A. De Statu Mortuorum et Resurgentium Tractatus. Ajicitur, Appendix de Futurâ Judæorum Restauratione. Ed. secunda. 8vo. Lond., 1733.   G 16 S 1

BURNETT (GEORGE). Exchequer Rolls of Scotland. [*See* SCOTLAND.]

BURNETT (JOHN), ADVOCATE. Treatise on various Branches of the Criminal Law of Scotland. 4to. Edinb., 1811.   F 8 P 13 †

BURNETT (WILLIAM), C.E. Curiosities of Great Britain. [*See* DUGDALE, T.]

BURNEY (CHARLES). MUS.D., &c. General History of Music, from the Earliest Ages to the Present Period. 4 vols. 4to. Lond., 1776-89.   A 8 U 1-4

BURNEY (FRANCES). [*See* D'ARBLAY, MADAME FRANCES.]

BURNEY (REAR-ADM. JAMES), R.N., F.R.S. Chronological History of the Voyages and Discoveries in the South Sea or Pacific Ocean, 1492-1764. 5 vols. 4to. Lond., 1803-17.*   MD 5 Q 1-5 †

BURNEY (WILLIAM), LL.D. New Universal Dictionary of Marine ; originally compiled by William Falconer, now modernized and much enlarged. 4to. Lond., 1815.   K 6 Q 5

BURNHAM (G.), PARRY (C. T.), WILLIAMS (E. H.) AND CO., BALDWIN LOCOMOTIVE WORKS. Illustrated Catalogue: Locomotives. 2nd ed. Imp. 8vo. Philad., 1881.   A 9 P 2 †

BURNHAM (S. M.) History and Uses of Limestones and Marbles. With forty-eight Chromo-lithographs. 8vo. Boston, 1883.   A 9 T 14

BURNOUF (Prof. Émile). And LEUPOL (L.) Dictionnaire Classique Sanscrit-Français. Roy. 8vo. Paris,
1866. K 15 S 21

Méthode pour étudier la Langue Sanscrite. Ouvrage
faisant suite aux Méthodes grecque et latine de J. L.
Burnouf. 2e éd. 8vo. Paris, 1861. K 12 R 22

BURNOUF (Eugène). Introduction à l'Histoire du Bud-
dhisme Indien. Vol. 1 (*all published.*) Roy. 4to. Paris,
1844. G 12 R T †

BURNS (Barnet). Brief Narrative of a New Zealand
Chief; being the remarkable History of Barnet Burns,
an English Sailor; written by himself. 8vo. Belfast,
1844. MD 7 P 16

BURNS (J. F.) Ways and Means: the Financial Statement of the Hon. J. F. Burns, Colonial Treasurer of New
South Wales, made 30th March, 1887. 8vo. Sydney,
1887. MF 1 Q 22

BURNS (Robert). [A Biography]; by Principal J. C.
Shairp. (Eng. Men of Letters.) 8vo. Lond., 1879. C 1 U 6

An Inquiry into his Life and Character, and the Moral
Influence of his Poetry; by "A Scotchwoman." 12mo.
Lond., 1886. C 2 Q 6

Complete Glossary to the Poetry and Prose of Robert Burns;
[*See* CUTHBERTSON, J.]

Correspondence between Burns and Clarinda; with a
Memoir of Mrs. M'Lehose (Clarinda), by W. C. M'Lehose.
8vo. Lond., 1843. C 5 R 10

Life and Poems of. [*See* British Poets, 2.]

Life of; by J. G. Lockhart. (Const. Misc.) 3rd ed. 18mo.
Edinb., 1830. K 10 Q 11

Life of; by J. G. Lockhart; revised, &c., by W. S. Douglas.
8vo. Lond., 1882. C 1 S 14

Memorials of, and of some of his Contemporaries and their
Descendants; by P. F. Aiken; with a Selection of his best
Poems and Songs, and engraved Portrait and Fac-similes.
8vo. Lond., 1876. H 5 R 3

Poems, chiefly in the Scottish Dialect. 2nd ed. 2 vols.
(in 1) 8vo. Edinb., 1793. H 5 T 28

Robert Burns at Mossgiel; with Reminiscences of the Poet
by his herd-boy, William Patrick; by William Jolly.
12mo. Paisley, 1881. C 1 P 25

Works of; with his Life, by Allan Cunningham. 8 vols.
12mo. Lond., 1834. H 6 Q 1-8

[*See* LINTON, W. J.]

BURNS, PHILP & Co. Queensland Hand-book of Information issued by Burns, Philp & Co. Limited: Articles
and Reports furnished by the Firm's Managers throughout
Queensland. Illustrated. 8vo. Sydney, 1884. MD 5 V 34

BURNSIDE (W. Snow), M.A., and PANTON, A. W.,) M.A.
Theory of Equations; with an Introduction to the Theory
of Binary Algebraic Forms. 8vo. Dublin, 1881.
A 10 S 12

BURR (Lieut.-Col. Aaron). Life and Times of; by James
Parton. 11th ed. 8vo. New York, 1858. C 5 T 1

BURR (George D.) Instructions in Practical Surveying,
Topographical Plan-drawing, and Sketching Ground
without Instruments. 4th ed. 8vo. Lond., 1864. A 6 R 34

BURRITT (Elihu), M.A. Sanskrit Hand-book for the
Fire-side. Roy. 8vo. Lond., 1876. K 16 R 21

The Mission of Great Sufferings. 12mo. Lond., 1867.
G 10 Q 12

Walk from London to John O'Groats'; with Notes by the
Way. 2nd ed. Lond., 1864. D 7 P 3

Walk from London to Land's End and Back; with Notes
by the way. 8vo. Lond., 1865. D 8 S 3

Walks in the Black Country, and its Green Border-land.
8vo. Lond., 1868. D 8 S 4

Western and Eastern Questions of Europe. (*Bound with
Marvin's Russia's Power.*) Pam. 8vo. Hartford, 1871.
F 7 Q 17

BURROUGHS (John). [*See* Essays from the Critic.]

BURROWS (Capt. Montagu), R.N. Life of Edward, Lord
Hawke; with some Account of the Origin of the English
Wars in the Reign of George II, and the State of the Royal
Navy at that period. 8vo. Lond., 1883. C 7 Q 27

The Family of Brocas of Beaurepaire and Roche Court,
Hereditary Masters of the Royal Buckhounds. Roy.
8vo. Lond., 1886. B 4 V 17

BURROWS (S. M.) The Buried Cities of Ceylon: a
Guide-book to Anuradhapura and Pollonarua. 8vo.
Colombo, 1885. B 10 Q 47

BURROWS (William). [*See* Adventures of A Mounted
Trooper.]

BURSIAN (C.) Geschichte der Classichen Philologie in
Deutschland. (Geschichte der Wissensch, 19.) 8vo. München, 1883. A 17 V 34

BURSLEM (Capt. Rollo). A Peep into Toorkisthān.
8vo. Lond., 1846. D 5 S 13

BURTON (Major-Gen. Edmond Francis). Reminiscences
of Sport in India. 8vo. Lond., 1885. D 4 U 30

BURTON (Rev. Edward), M.A. Description of the
Antiquities and other Curiosities of Rome, 1818-19.
2 vols. 8vo. Lond., 1828. B 12 Q 39, 40

History of the Christian Church, from the Ascension of
Jesus Christ to the Conversion of Constantine. 2nd ed.
12mo. Lond.. 1837. G 13 R 10

BURTON (Edwin). Visitors' Guide to Sydney. [*See*
Maddock, W.]

BURTON (Isabel) Lady. Inner Life of Syria, Palestine,
and the Holy Land. With coloured Plates. 2 vols. 8vo.
Lond., 1875. D 4 T 32, 33

B

BURTON (JAMES). Excerpta Hieroglyphica. Plates in 4 Parts. Ob. 4to. Cairo, 1825–28. B 1 R 25 †

BURTON (KATHERINE). [*See* BURTON, J. H.]

BURTON (JOHN HILL), D.C.L., &c. Cairngorm Mountains. 12mo. Edinb., 1864. D 7 P 1

Emigrant's Manual: Australia, New Zealand, America, and South Africa. 8vo. Edinb., 1851.* MD 2 Q 30

Another copy. Australia [only]. MD 2 Q 34

History of Scotland, from Agricola's Invasion to the Revolution of 1688. 4 vols. 8vo. Lond., 1867. B 13 Q 7–10

History of the Reign of Queen Anne. 3 vols. 8vo. Edinb., 1880. B 6 P 23–25

Life and Correspondence of David Hume. 2 vols. 8vo. Lond., 1846. C 7 P 31, 32

Lives of Simon, Lord Lovat, and Duncan Forbes, of Culloden; from original Sources. 8vo. Lond., 1847. C 4 S 17

The Book-hunter, &c. 12mo. Edinb., 1862. J 9 P 7

Another copy. New ed.; with a Memoir of the Author; [By Katherine Burton.] Sq. 8vo. Edinb., 1882. J 2 T 7

The Scot Abroad. 2 vols. 12mo. Edinb., 1864. J 9 P 5, 6

BURTON (SIR RICHARD FRANCIS). K.C.M.G., &c. Abeokuta and the Camaroons Mountains: an Exploration. 2 vols. 8vo. Lond., 1863. D 1 S 8, 9

Book of the Sword. Illustrated. Vol. 1. Imp. 8vo. Lond., 1884. B 15 S 15

Camoens; his Life and his Lusiads: a Commentary. 2 vols. 12mo. Lond., 1881. C 3 S 13, 14, 15

City of the Saints, and across the Rocky Mountains to California. 8vo. Lond., 1861. D 3 U 1

Etruscan Bologna: a Study. 8vo. Lond., 1876. B 12 R 39

First Footsteps in East Africa; or, an Exploration of Harar. 8vo. Lond., 1856. D 2 P 20

Gold-mines of Midian, and the Ruined Midianite Cities: a Fortnight's Tour in North-western Arabia. 2nd ed. 8vo. Lond., 1878. D 6 S 27

Highlands of the Brazil. 2 vols. 8vo. Lond., 1869. D 3 S 7, 8

Lacerda's Journey to Cazembe. [*See* AFRICA.]

Land of Midian (revisited). With Map and Illustrations. 2 vols. 8vo. Lond., 1879. D 4 U 40, 41

Mission to Gelele, King of Dahome; with Notices of the so-called Amazons. &c. 2 vols. 8vo. Lond., 1864. D 1 P 20, 21

Personal Narrative of a Pilgrimage to El-Medinah and Meccah. 3 vols. 8vo. Lond., 1855–56. D 4 U 37–39

Two Trips to Gorilla Land and the Cataracts of the Congo. 2 vols. 8vo. Lond., 1876. D 2 S 5, 6

Ultima Thule; or, a Summer in Iceland. 2 vols. 8vo. Lond., 1875. D 6 U 30, 31

Wanderings in West Africa, from Liverpool to Fernando Po; by "A F.R.G.S." 2 vols. 12mo. Lond., 1863. D 1 Q 17, 18

BURTON (SIR RICHARD F.), AND CAMERON (VERNEY L.) To the Gold Coast for Gold: a Personal Narrative. 2 vols. 8vo. Lond., 1883. D 1 Q 19, 20

BURTON (ROBERT) Anatomy of Melancholy; what it is; by "Democritus, Junior." 2 vols. 8vo. Lond., 1827. G 9 S 14, 15

BURTON (THOMAS), M.P. Diary, 1656–59; with an Introduction, containing an Account of the Parliament of 1654, from the Journal of G. Goddard, M.P. 4 vols. 8vo. Lond., 1828. F 10 S 13–16

BURTON (WILLIAM). Description of Leicestershire; containing Matters of Antiquitye, Historye, Armorye, and Genealogy. Fol. Lond., 1622. B 15 Q 8 ‡

BURTON (SIR WILLIAM WESTBROOKE). Extract of a Letter to Sir Richard Bourke. [*See* MANUSCRIPTS AND PORTRAITS.]

Reply to Judge Burton on the State of Religion in the Colony. [*See* ULLATHORNE, RT. REV. W. B.]

State of Religion and Education in New South Wales. 8vo. Lond., 1840.* MG 1 T 3

BURY (BLAZE DE), BARONNE. [*See* BLAZE DE BURY.]

BURY (C.) LADY. Diary, illustrative of the Times of George IV; edited by J. Galt. 4 vols. 8vo. Lond., 1838–39. C 6 P 14–17

Journal of the Heart. 8vo. Lond., 1835. J 5 Q 28

BURY (T. TALBOT). Rudimentary Architecture for Beginners. (Weale.) 12mo. Lond., 1867. A 17 P 44

BUSBECQ (OGIER GHISELIN DE), SEIGNEUR OF BOUSBECQUE. Life and Letters of; by Charles Thornton Foster, M.A. and F. H. Blackburne Daniell, M.A. 2 vols. 8vo. Lond., 1881. C 8 S 8, 9

BUSBY (JAMES). The Australian Farmer, and Land Owner's Guide to the Profitable Culture of the Vine in New South Wales. Forming the third edition of the Author's "Journal of a Visit to the Vineyards of Spain and France." 8vo. Lond., 1839. MA 1 P 27

Authentic information relative to New South Wales and New Zealand. 8vo. Lond., 1832. MD 7 P 15

Journal of a Recent Visit to the Principal Vineyards of Spain and France; together with Observations relative to the Introduction of the Vine into New South Wales. 8vo. Lond., 1834. MA 1 P 31

Journal of a Tour through some of the Vineyards of Spain and France. 8vo. Sydney, 1833. MA 1 P 30

Manual of Plain Directions for Planting and Cultivating Vineyards, and for making Wine in New South Wales. 8vo. Sydney, 1830.* MA 1 P 25

Our Colonial Empire and the Case of New Zealand. 8vo. Lond., 1866.* MF 1 R 19

The Rebellions of the Maoris traced to their true origin; in two Letters to the Rt. Hon. Edward Cardwell. 8vo. Lond., 1865. MD 1 U 21

Treatise on the Culture of the Vine, and the Art of making Wine. 8vo. Sydney, 1825.* MA 1 P 28

BUSBY (T.) [*See* LUCRETIUS CARUS, T.]

BUSCH (DR. MORITZ). Bismarck in the Franco-German War, 1870-71. Authorised translation from the German. 2 vols. 8vo. Lond., 1879. B 9 P 6, 7
Conversations at Berlin. [*See* AUSTRALASIA.]

BUSCHMANN (J. CH. ED.) Textes Marquésans et Taïtiens, analysés. 8vo. Berlin, 1843. MK 1 Q 25

BUSH OF AUSTRALIA. [*See* AUSTRALIA.]

BUSH (ELIZA C.) My Pilgrimage to Eastern Shrines. 8vo. Lond., 1867. D 4 U 26

BUSH (MRS. FORBES). Memoirs of the Queens of France; with Notices of the Royal Favourites. 2 vols. 12mo. Lond., 1843. C 4 P 15, 16

BUSH (RICHARD J.) Reindeer, Dogs, and Snow Shoes: a Journal of Siberian Travel and Explorations, made in the years 1865-67. 8vo. Lond., 1871. D 6 Q 38

BUSH MISSIONARY SOCIETY. [*See* NEW SOUTH WALES BUSH MISSIONARY SOCIETY.]

BUSHBY (HENRY JEFFREYS). A Month in the Camp before Sebastopol; by "A Non-Combatant." 2nd ed. 8vo. Lond., 1855. D 7 Q 3

BUSHMAN, A. [*See* CHRISTIE, MAJOR W. H.]

BUSHMAN, A. [*See* SIDNEY, J.]

BUSHMAN, A. [*See* SIDNEY, S. AND J.]

BUSHMEN'S CLUB. History of the First Bushmen's Club in the Australian Colonies, established at Adelaide, South Australia. 12mo. Adelaide, 1872. MB 1 P 6

BUSHNAN (JOHN STEPHENSON), M.D. Natural History of Fishes, particularly their structure and economical uses. (Nat. Lib. 36.) 12mo. Edinb., 1840. A 14 P 36

BUSHNELL (HORACE), D.D. Life and Letters of. 8vo. Lond., 1880. C 7 P 3
Nature and the Supernatural, as together constituting the One System of God. 12mo. Edinb., 1862. G 13 R 26
Review of Dr. Bushnell's Course of Lectures on the Bible, Nature, Religion, &c. [*See* DAVIS, A. J.]

BUSK (MISS RACHEL HARRIETTE). Folk-Lore of Rome; collected by word of mouth from the People. 8vo. Lond., 1874. B 12 S 1
Folk Songs of Italy. 12mo. Lond., 1887. H 5 S 9

BUSTED (T. M.) Trades Unions, Combinations, and Strikes. (Pam. 34.) 8vo. Lond., 1860. J 12 U 26

BUTCHERS (REV. B.) Romanism in Relation to Politics and Morals; being a Reply to Dr. Bermingham's Pamphlet on Liberty, Catholicity and Methodism. 8vo. Melb., 1875. MG 1 Q 39

BUTE (JOHN), MARQUESS OF. Early Days of Sir William Wallace. Illustrated. Sm. 4to. Paisley, 1876. B 13 P 38

BUTLER (REV. ALBAN). Lives of the Fathers, Martyrs, and other Principal Saints; with Engravings. 12 vols. 8vo. Lond., 1812-15. G 6 P 12-23
Life of. [*See* BUTLER, S.]

BUTLER (ALFRED JOSHUA), M.A., &c. Ancient Coptic Churches of Egypt. 2 vols. 8vo. Oxford, 1884. G 6 P 25, 26

BUTLER (MISS ANNIE ROBINA). Glimpses of Maoriland. 8vo. Lond., 1886. MD 3 R 42

BUTLER (ARTHUR JOHN). The Paradise of Dante Alighieri. [*See* DANTE.]

BUTLER (CHARLES). Historical Memoirs of the English, Irish, and Scottish Catholics, since the Reformation. 3rd ed. 4 vols. 8vo. Lond., 1822. G 6 P 6-9
Horæ Biblicæ; being a connected Series of Miscellaneous Notes on the Original Text, early Versions, and printed Editions of the Old and New Testament. [Part 1.] 8vo. Lond., 1799. G 13 Q 20
Horæ Biblicæ; being a connected Series of Notes on the Text and Literary History of the Bibles, or Sacred Books of the Jews and Christians. Part 2. 2nd ed. 8vo. Lond., 1807. G 13 Q 21
Horæ Juridicæ Subsecivæ; a connected series of Notes, respecting the Geography, Chronology, and Literary History of the principal Codes, and original Documents, of the Grecian, Roman, Feudal, and Canon Law. 8vo. Lond., 1804. G 13 Q 21
Life of Hugo Grotius, with brief Minutes of the Civil, Ecclesiastical, and Literary History of the Netherlands. 4th ed. 8vo. Lond., 1826. C 8 Q 23
Philological and Biographical Works of. 5 vols. 8vo. Lond., 1817. J 3 S 1-5

1. Horæ Biblicæ.
2. Germanic Empire. Horæ Juridicæ Subsecivæ. [Life of L'Hôpital, Professional Character of the Earl of Mansfield].
3. Lives of several Eminent Persons:— [Fenelon-Bossuet-Boudon, De Rancé, Kempis, Alban Butler].
4. Confessions of Faith, and Essays.
5. Church of France [In the Reigns of Louis XIV., Louis XV., Louis XVI., and the French Revolution.]

Reminiscences of; with a Letter to a Lady on Ancient and Modern Music. 4th ed. 8vo. Lond., 1824. C 6 T 4
Some Account of the Life and Writings of James Bénigne Bossuet, Bishop of Meaux. 12mo. Lond., 1812. C 1 S 13

BUTLER (EDWARD DUNDAS). Legend of the Wondrous Hunt. [*See* ARANY, J.]

BUTLER (MRS. FRANCES ANNE) [*See* KEMBLE, FRANCES A.]

BUTLER (MAJOR JOHN). Sketch of Assam; with some Account of the Hill Tribes; by "An Officer in the Hon. E. I. Company's Bengal Native Infantry." 8vo. Lond., 1847. D 5 S 26

BUTLER (RT. REV. JOSEPH), D.C.L., &c., BISHOP OF DURHAM. Analogy of Religion, Natural and Revealed, to the Constitution and Course of Nature; to which are added two brief Dissertations on Personal Identity, and on the Nature of Virtue; and fifteen Sermons. New ed. 8vo. Lond., 1876.   G 16 P 6

Works of; with a Life of the Author, by Dr. Kippis. 2 vols. 8vo. Edinb., 1817.   G 13 P 27, 28

Works of. 2 vols. 18mo. Lond., 1835.   G 9 P 31, 32

BUTLER (MRS. JOSEPHINE E.) Woman's Work and Woman's Culture: a Series of Essays. 8vo. Lond., 1869.   F 4 T 13

BUTLER (SAMUEL). First Year in Canterbury Settlement. 8vo. Lond., 1863.*   MD 3 R 28

Hand-book for Australian Emigrants; being a Descriptive History of Australia. 12mo. Glasgow, 1839.* MD 1 T 41

BUTLER (SAMUEL). Alps and Sanctuaries of Piedmont and the Canton Ticino. (Op. 6.) 2nd ed. 8vo. Lond., 1882.   D 7 T 19

Luck, or Cunning, as the Main Means of Organic Modification? An attempt to throw additional Light upon the late Mr. Charles Darwin's Theory of Natural Selection. 8vo. Lond., 1887.   A 14 Q 28

BUTLER (SAMUEL). Genuine Poetical Remains of; with Notes by Robert Thyer. 8vo. Lond., 1827.   H 6 U 6

Hudibras; in Three Parts; with Memoir of the Author's Life. 12mo. Lond., 1811.   H 5 R 11

Life and Poems of. [*See* British Poets, 2, JOHNSON, DR. S., *and* CHALMERS, A.]

BUTLER (W.) Pompeii, Descriptive and Picturesque. 12mo. Lond., 1886.   B 12 P 3

BUTLER (PROF. WILLIAM ARCHER), M.A. Lectures on the History of Ancient Philosophy; edited, with Notes, by W. H. Thompson, M.A. 2 vols. 8vo. Cambridge, 1856.   G 6 P 28, 29

Another copy. 2nd ed., revised by the Editor. 8vo. Lond., 1874.   G 6 P 30

BUTLER (MAJOR SIR WILLIAM FRANCIS), K.C.B. &c. Akim-Foo: the History of a Failure: with Map, &c. 8vo. Lond., 1875.   B 1 P 45

Great Lone Land: a Narrative of Travel and Adventure in the North-west of America. 2nd ed. 8vo. Lond., 1872.   D 3 T 33

BUTTERFIELD (G.), AND PALMER (J.) Address to the Members, Subscribers, and Friends of the New South Wales Bush Missionary Society. 8vo. Sydney, 1864.   MG 1 Q 31

BUTTERS (LAURENCE). Fairbairn's Crests of the Families of Great Britain. [*See* FAIRBURN, J.]

BUXTON (CHARLES), M.A. Memoirs of Sir Thomas Fowell Buxton, Bart; edited by his Son. 2nd ed. 8vo. Lond., 1849.   C 6 S 12

Another copy. 3rd ed. (H. and C. Lib.) 12mo. Lond., 1849.   J 8 P 36

BUXTON (EDWARD NORTH). The A B C of Free Trade. (Pam. Je.) 8vo. Lond., 1882.   F 6 P 10

BUXTON (H. J. WILMOT-), M.A., AND KOEHLER (S. R.) English Painters; with a Chapter on American Painters. (Illust. Hand-books of Art Hist.) 8vo. Lond., 1883.   A 6 V 9

BUXTON (J W.) The New Map of Queensland. Roy. 4to. folded. Brisbane, 1863.   MD 5 S 15 †

Another copy. 8vo. folded. Brisbane, 1863. MD 5 P 6 ‡

BUXTON (SIR THOMAS POWELL), BART. Memoirs of Edited by his son, Charles Buxton, B.A. 2nd ed. 8vo. Lond., 1849.   C 6 S 12

Another copy. 3rd ed. (H. and C. Lib.) 12mo. Lond., 1849.   J 8 P 36

BUZACOTT (REV. A.) Mission Life in the Islands of the Pacific; being a Narrative of his Life and Labours. 8vo. Lond., 1866.   MD 5 P 32

BUZETA (FR. MANUEL), Y BRAVO (FR. FELIPE). Diccionario Geográfico. Estadistico, Histórico, de las Islas Filipinas. 2 vols. imp. 8vo. Madrid, 1850–51.   D 12 V 3, 4

BYAM (GEORGE). Wanderings in some of the Western Republics of America; with Remarks upon the cutting of the Great Ship Canal through Central America. 8vo. Lond., 1850.   D 3 R 54

Wild Life in the Interior of Central America. 12mo. Lond., 1849.   D 3 P 10

BYERLEY (F. J.) [*See* JARDINE, F. AND A.]

BYERLEY (THOMAS). Percy Anecdotes. [*See* ROBERTSON, J. C.]

BYLES (RT. HON. SIR JOHN BARNARD), JUDGE. Foundations of Religion in the Mind and Heart of Man. 8vo. Lond., 1875.   G 13 R 37

Sophisms of Free Trade and Popular Political Economy examined. 12mo. Manchester, 1870.   F 2 P 19

BYRNE (VERY REV. JAMES), M.A. General Principles of the Structure of Language. 2 vols. 8vo. Lond., 1880.   K 13 S 28, 29

BYRNE (J. C.) Twelve Years' Wanderings in the British Colonies, from 1835–47. 2 vols. 8vo. Lond., 1848.*   MD 2 V 33, 34

BYRNE (JOE). [*See* KELLY GANG.]

BYRNE (OLIVER). Practical Model Calculator, for the Engineer, Mechanic, Machinist, Manufacturer of Engine-work, Naval Architect, Miner, and Mill-wright. 8vo. Philad., 1872.   A 10 U 25

BYRNE (REV. T.) Manual of Universal Church History. [*See* ALZOG, REV. J.]

BYRNE (MRS. WILLIAM PITT). Gheel, the City of the Simple. 8vo. Lond., 1869. J 6 Q 3

Feudal Castles of France (Western Provinces). Illustrated. 8vo. Lond., 1869. B 8 U 36

BYROM (JOHN), M.A., &c. Life and Poems of. [*See* CHALMERS, A.]

BYRON (RT. HON. GEORGE ANSON), LORD. Voyage of H.M.S. *Blonde* to the Sandwich Islands, in the years 1824-25. 4to. Lond., 1826.* MD 6 P 28 †

[*See* COOK, CAPT. JAS. ; HAWKESWORTH, J. ; PARKINSON, S. ; *and* STEWART, C. S.]

BYRON (GEORGE GORDON), LORD. (A Biography) ; by John Nichol. (Eng. Men of Letters.) 12mo. Lond., 1880. C 1 U 7

Conversations of ; noted during a residence with his Lordship at Pisa, in the years 1821-22 ; by Thos. Medwin. 8vo. Lond., 1824. C 8 S 20

Conversations of, with the Countess of Blessington. 8vo. Lond., 1834. C 8 S 19

English Bards and Scotch Reviewers : a Satire. 3rd ed. 8vo. Lond., 1810. H 7 Q 28

His Biographers and Critics. [*See* MOORE, J. S.]

Illustrations of the Life and Works of. [*See* FINDEN, W.]

Letters and Journals of ; with Notices of his Life, by Thomas Moore. 3rd ed., with Engravings. 3 vols. 8vo. Lond., 1833. C 8 S 21-23

Life and Poems of. [*See* BRITISH POETS, 2.]

Lord Byron Vindicated. [*See* PRESTON, E. W.]

Poetical Works of. 6 vols. 8vo. Lond., 1855-56. H 6 S 2-7

The Real Lord Byron : New Views of the Poet's Life ; by John Cordy Jeaffreson. 2 vols. 8vo. Lond., 1883. C 8 S 24, 25

Recollections of the Last Days of Shelley and Byron ; by E. J. Trelawny. 8vo. Lond., 1858. C 3 U 39

Works of Lord Byron. 2nd ed. Roy. 8vo. Franckfort, O.M., 1829. H 5 U 29

BYRON (VICE-ADM. HON. JOHN). Account of the Voyages of. [*See* HAWKESWORTH, J.]

Narrative of the Hon. John Byron ; containing an Account of the great distresses suffered by himself and his companions on the Coast of Patagonia ; written by himself. 12mo. Aberdeen, 1848. D 1 T 24

BYRON (JOHN) New South Wales : Statistical Information. [*See* MORRIS, A.]

[*See* CENSUS OF NEW SOUTH WALES.]

BYRON (ANNA ISABELLA) LADY. Vindication of. 8vo. Lond., 1871. C 8 S 18

BYSSHE (EDWARD). The Art of English Poetry. 9th ed. 2 vols. 12mo. Lond., 1762. H 5 S 3, 4

BYZANTINÆ HISTORIÆ SCRIPTORES. Corpus Scriptorum Historiæ Byzantinæ. Editio emendatior et copiosior, consilio B. G. Niebuhrii, C.F. Instituta, opera eiusdem Nieburii, Imm. Bekkeri, L. Schopeni, G. et L. Dindorfiorum, aliorumque philologorum parata. 48 vols. 8vo. Bonn, 1828-53. B 9 U 1-V 14

1. Agathiae Myrinaei Historiarum.
2. Leonis Diaconi Caloënsis Historiae.
3-5. Jo. Cantacuzeni Eximperatoris Historiarum.
6-8. Nicephori Gregorae Byzantina Historia.
9. Jo. Malalae Chronographia.
10, 11. Chronicon Paschale.
12-14. Procopius.
15. Mich. Ducae Nepotis Historia Byzantina.
16. Theophylacti Simocattae Historiarum.
17. Nicetae Choniatae Historia.
18, 19. Georgii Pachymeris de Mich. et And. Palaeologis.
20. Joannis Cinnami Historiarum. Nicephori Bryeunii Commentarii.
21. Merobaudes et Corippus.
22. Michaelis Glycae Annales.
23. Constantini Manassis Compendium Chronicum. Joelis Chronographia. Georgii Acropolitae Annales.
24. Joannes Lydus.
25. Pauli Silentiarii descriptio S. Sophiae et Ambonis. Geor. Pisidae Expeditio Persica, etc. S. Nicephori Breviarium Rerum post Mauricium Gestarum.
26. Dexippi, Eunapii, Petri Patricii, Prisci, Malchi, Menandri Historiarum.
27-29. Constantini Porphyrogeniti de Cerimoniis Aulae Byzantinae.
30. Zosimus.
31. Georgius Phrantzes, Joannes Cananus, Joannes Anagnostes.
32, 33. Georgius Cedrenus. Jo. Scylitzae Curopalatae.
34. Codini Curopalatae de officialibus Palatii Cpolitani, etc.
35. Annae Comnenae Alexiadis, Libri xv.
36, 37. Georgius Syncellus et Nicephorus, C.P.
38, 39. Theophanis Chronographia.
40. Theophanes Continuatus, Joannes Cameniata, Symeon Magister, Georgius Monachus.
41. Ephraemius.
42, 43 Joannis Zonarae Annales.
44. Leonis Grammatici Chronographia.
45. Georgii Codini excerpta de Antiquitatibus Constantino politanis.
46. Laonici Chalcocondylae Atheniensis Historiarum, Libri decem.
47. Historia Politica et Patriarchica Constantinopoleos. Epirotica.
48. Michaelis Attaliotae Historia.

C

C. (C.)   [*See* MOTHER'S GRAVE.]

C. (J.)   [*See* SHAKESPEARE, W.]

C. (T. E.)   [*See* BATTLEFIELDS OF THE SOUTH.]

C. (W. B.)   [*See* COLONIAL POLICY.]

C—de la B—(MME).   [*See* CALDERON DE LA BARCA, MME. FRANCES.]

C.H.S.   [*See* SPENCE, C. H.]

CABALA, SIVE SCRINIA SACRA. Mysteries of State and Government, in Letters of Illustrious Persons and Great Ministers of State, as well Forreign as Domestick. Fol. Lond., 1663.   B 16 Q 7 ‡

CABANIS (PIERRE JEAN GEORGES). Sketch of the Revolutions of Medical Science, and Views relating to its Reform. 8vo. Lond., 1806.   A 12 R 8

CABINET DES FÉES; ou, Collection Choisie des Contes des Fées, et autres Contes merveilleux, ornés de Figures. 37 vols. 8vo. Amsterdam, 1785–86.   J 15 R 1–37
1. Les Contes des Fées; par Chas. Perrault. Les Nouveaux Contes des Fées; par Madame la Comtesse de Murat.
2. Les Contes des Fées; par Madame la Comtesse d'Aulnoy.
3. La Suite des Contes des Fées; par Madame la Comtesse d'Aulnoy. Les Fées à la Mode; par la même.
4. La Suite des Fées à la Mode; par Madame la Comtesse d'Aulnoy.
5. Les Illustres Fées. La Tyrannie des Fées détruite; par Madame la Comtesse d'Auneuil. Les Contes moins Contes que les autres; par le Sieur de Preschac.
6. Les Fées, Contes des Contes; par Mademoiselle de La Force. Les Chevaliers Errans et le Génie Familier; par Madame la Comtesse d'Aulnoy.
7–11. Les Mille et une Nuits, Contes Arabes; traduits en François, par M. Galland.
12. La Tour Ténébreuse et les Jours Lumineux, Contes Anglois; par Mademoiselle L'Héritier. Les Aventures d'Abdalla.
13. La Suite des Aventures d'Abdalla.
14, 15. Les Mille et un Jour, Contes Persans; traduits en François, par M. Petis de la Croix.
16. L'Histoire de la Sultane de Perse et des Visirs; par M. Galland. Les Voyages de Zulma dans le Pays des Fées.
17. Les Contes et Fables Indiennes de Bidpaï et de Lokman; traduits d'Ali-Tchélébi-ben-Saleh, auteur Turc, ouvrage commencé par M. Galland continué et fini par M. Cardonne.
18. La Suite des Contes et Fables indiennes de Bidpaï et de Lokman; traduits d'Ali-Tchélébi-ben-Saleh, auteur Turc. Fables et Contes; par F. de Saligance de la Mothe-Fénélon. Bora; ou, la Vertu récompensée; par Madame de Marchand.
19. Les Contes Chinois; par Gueulette. Florine; ou, la belle Italienne.
20. Le Bélier; Fleur d'Epine; les quatre Facardins; par M. le Comte Hamilton.
21, 22. Les Mille et un quart d'Heure, Contes Tartares; par Gueulette.

CABINET DES FÉES—*continued.*
23. Les Sultanes de Guzarate; ou, les Songes des Hommes Eveillés, Contes Mogols; par M. Gueulette.
24. Le Prince des Aigues-Marines le Prince Invisible; par Madame l'Evêque. Les Féeries Nouvelles; par M. le Comte de Caylus.
25. Les Nouveaux Contes Orientaux; par M. le Comte de Caylus. Tout vient à point qui peut attendre; ou, Cadichon et Jeannette; par M. le Comte de Caylus. Les Contes de M. de Moncrif.
26. La Reine Fantasque; par J. J. Rousseau. La Belle et la Bête; par Madame de Villeneuve. Les Veillées de Thessalie; par Mademoiselle de Lussan.
27, 28. La Suite des Veillées de Thessalie; par Mademoiselle de Lussan. Histoire du Prince Titi; par St. Hyacinthe.
29, 30. Les Contes des Génies; ou, les Charmantes Leçons d'Horam, fils d'Asmar; ouvrage traduit du Persan en Anglois, par Sir C. Morell.
31. Funestine; par Beauchamps. Nouveaux Contes de Fées. Le Loup galleux et Bellinette.
32. Les Soirées Bretonnes; dédiées à Monseigneur le Dauphin, par M. Gueulette. Contes de Madame de Lintot. Les Aventures de Zeloïde et d'Amanzarifdine, Contes Indiens; par M. de Moncrif.
33. Trois Contes de Mademoiselle de Lubert. Nourjahad, Histoire Orientale.
34. Les Contes de M. Pajol. La Bibliothèque des Fées et des Génies; recueillie par l'Abbé de la Porte.
35. Minet-Bleu et Louvette; par Madame Fagnan. Acajou et Zirphile; par C. P. Duclos. Aglaé ou Nabotine; par M. Coypel. Contes des Fées; par Madame Leprince de Beaumont. Le Prince Desiré; par M. Selis. Contes Choisis, extraits de différens recueils.
36. Les Aventures merveilleuses de Don Silvio de Rosalva; traduites de l'Allemand de [C. M. von] Wieland, par Madame d'Ussieux.
37. La Notice des Auteurs. La Liste complette des Ouvrages qui composent le Cabinet des Fées.

CABINET OF PORTRAITS.; consisting of Distinguished Characters, British and Foreign. Published by W. Darton. 8vo. Lond., 1823.   C 8 U 22

CABLE (GEORGE WASHINGTON). The Creoles of Louisiana. 8vo. Lond., 1885.   D 3 S 3

CABOT (SEBASTIAN). Remarkable Life, Adventures, and Discoveries of; by J. F. Nicholls. 12mo. Lond., 1869.   C 2 Q 19 [*See* EDEN, R.]

CADDY (MRS. FLORENCE). Footsteps of Jeanne d'Arc: a Pilgrimage. 8vo. Lond., 1886.   D 7 S 35

CADELL (WILLIAM ARCHIBALD), F.R.S. Journey in Carniola, Italy, and France, in the years 1817–18. With Engravings. 2 vols. 8vo. Edinb., 1820.   D 7 T 28, 29

CÆDMON (SAINT). Metrical Paraphrase of parts of the Holy Scriptures, in Anglo-Saxon; with an English Translation, Notes, and a Verbal Index, by Benjamin Thorpe, F.S.A. Roy. 8vo. Lond., 1832.   G 13 V 27

CÆSAR (CAIUS JULIUS). C. Julii Cæsaris quæ extant, interpretatione et notis, illustravit Johannes Godujnus, in usum Delphini. 8vo. Lond., 1811.　　　B 35 S 5

Cæsar; translated by William Duncan. (Fam. Class. Lib.) 2 vols. 12mo. Lond., 1832.　　　J 15 P 2, 3

Cæsar de Bello Gallico, Books 1–3: an Interlinear Translation, by E. D. Grove. (Aust. Series of Keys to the Classics.) 8vo. Sydney, 1870.　　　MB 2 P 44

Cæsar de Bello Gallico, Book 1; prepared for the use of Junior Students, by A. H. Davis, B.A. 12mo. Melh., 1875.　　　MB 2 P 45

Cæsar's Commentaries, Book 4; For the use of Students. [*See* VIRGILIUS MARO, PUBLIUS.]

Les Commentaires de César; revue, et retouchée avec soin, par M. de Wailly. 2 vols. 12mo. Paris, 1775.　　　B 30 P 1, 2

Opera omnia ex Editione Oberliniana, cum Notis et Interpretatione in usum Delphini. 5 vols. 8vo. Lond., 1819.　　　J 13 P 19–23

CÆSARS (The). Lives of the Twelve Cæsars by C. Suetonius Tranquillus ; the translation of Alexander Thomson, M.D. 8vo. Lond., 1887.　　　C 4 P 9

CAFFIN (JAMES). [*See* WISE, CAFFIN & Co.]

CAGNOLI (ANTOINE). Trigonométrie, rectiligne et sphérique. 2nd ed. 4to. Paris, 1808.　　　A 10 U 1

CAHILL (REV. D. W.), D.D. Letter to the Rt. Hon. Lord Viscount Palmerston. 8vo. Melh., 1856.　　　MF 1 Q 6

CAILLIE (RÉNÉ). Travels through Central Africa to Timbuctoo, and across the Great Desert, to Morocco, performed in the years 1824–28. 2 vols. 8vo. Lond., 1830..　　　D 1 W 15, 16

CAIN (HENRI LOUIS), "LEKAIN." Mémoires de Lekain. [*See* BARRIÈRE, J. F., 6.]

CAINE (THOMAS HENRY HALL). Recollections of Dante Gabriel Rossetti. 8vo. Lond., 1882.　　　C 4 V 28

CAINE (WILLIAM SPROSTON). Hugh Stowell Brown; his Autobiography, his Commonplace Book, and Extracts from his Sermons, and Addresses: a Memorial Volume, edited by his Son-in-Law. 8vo. Lond., 1887　　　C 4 8 2

CAIRD (SIR JAMES), K.C.B., &c. The Landed Interest and the Supply of Food. 4th ed. 8vo. Lond., 1880.　　　F 6 Q 29

CAIRD (REV. JOHN), M.A. Religion in Common Life : a Sermon. Authorised Australian edition. 8vo. Melh., 1856.　　　MG 1 Q 40

Sermons. 8vo. Edinb., 1858.　　　G 16 S 17

CAIRNES (PROF. JOHN ELLIOT), M.A., &c. Essays in Political Economy, Theoretical and Applied. 8vo. Lond., 1873.　　　F 9 P 13

Political Essays. 8vo. Lond., 1873.　　　F 9 P 14

Some Leading Principles of Political Economy newly expounded. 8vo. Lond., 1874.　　　F 9 P 12

CAIRNS (REV. ADAM), D.D. Dangers and Duties of the Young Men of Victoria. 8vo. Melh., 1856.　　　MG 1 Q 31

Inauguration of the Political Independence of Victoria: the First Meeting of our Parliament under the new Constitution. 8vo. Melh., 1856.　　　M F 3 P 5

Letter on the alleged Apostacy of the Presbyterian Church. 8vo. Melh., 1877.　　　MG 1 Q 39

Sermon preached at Chalmers' Church, Melbourne. (Victorian Pulpit, No. 1.) 8vo. Melh. (n.d.)　　　MG 1 P 1

[*See* STATE AID QUESTION.]

CAIRNS (PROF. JOHN), D.D. Unbelief in the 18th Century, as contrasted with its earlier and later History. 8vo. Edinb., 1881.　　　G 6 R 25

CALABRELLA (BARONESS DE). Evenings at Haddon Hall : a series of Romantic Tales of the Olden Time; edited by the Baroness de Calabrella. With Illustrations from Designs, by George Cattermole. 8vo. Lond., 1848.　　　J 2 T 23

CALAMY (EDMUND), D.D. Abridgment of Mr. Baxter's History of his Life and Times; with an Account of the Ministers who were ejected after the Restauration of King Charles II. 2nd ed. 2 vols. 8vo. Lond., 1713.　　　G 13 S 32, 33

Continuation of the Account of the Ministers, Lectures, Masters, &c., who were ejected or silenced after the Restoration in 1660. 2 vols. 8vo. Lond., 1827.　　　G 13 S 34, 35

Historical Account of my own Life; with some Reflections on the Times I have lived in (1671–1731). Edited by John Towill Rutt. 2 vols. 8vo. Lond., 1829.　　　C 8 U 20, 21

CALCUTTA ANNUAL REGISTER AND DIRECTORY for 1814 and 1815. 2 vols. 8vo. Calcutta, 1814–15.　　　E

CALCUTTA AUXILIARY BIBLE SOCIETY. Second Report, 1813. 8vo. Calcutta, 1813.　　　MG 1 Q 28

CALCUTTA BENEVOLENT INSTITUTION. Report relative to the Benevolent Institution at Calcutta for 1813–14. (Pam. 33.) 8vo. Serampore, 1813–14. MJ 2 Q 21

CALCUTTA INTERNATIONAL EXHIBITION, 1883–84. New South Wales : its Progress and Resources, and Official Catalogue of Exhibits from the Colony, forwarded to the International Exhibition of 1883–84, at Calcutta. Roy. 8vo. Sydney, 1883.*　　　MK 1 S 3

New South Wales : Official Catalogue of Exhibits. Roy. 8vo. Sydney, 1885.　　　MK 1 S 5

Official Record of the New South Wales Commission for the Calcutta International Exhibition, 1883–84. Abridged Catalogue of New South Wales Exhibits and List of Awards. 8vo. Sydney, 1885.*　　　MK 1 S 6

Official Report. 2 vols. roy. 8vo. Calcutta, 1885.　　　K 8 R 7, 8

CALCUTTA JOURNAL of Politics and General Litera- ture, from March, 1822, to November, 1823. 10 vols. 4to. Calcutta, 1822–23.   E

CALCUTTA SCHOOL–BOOK SOCIETY. Proceedings; Fourth Report. 8vo. Calcutta, 1821.   MF 3 P 14

CALDCLEUGH (ALEXANDER), F.R.S. &c. Account of the Great Earthquake experienced in Chile on the 20th February, 1835. Roy. 4to. Lond., 1836.   A 15 U 8

Some Account of the Volcanic Eruption of Cosegüina, in the Bay of Fonseca, on the Western Coast of Central America. Roy. 4to. Lond., 1836.   A 15 U 8

CALDECOTT (RANDOLPH). Breton Folk, illustrated. [*See* BLACKBURN, H.]

Personal Memoir of his early Art Career, by H. Black- burn; with Illustrations. 8vo. Lond., 1886.   C 10 S 12

CALDER (J. E.) Some Account of the Wars, Extirpa- tion, Habits, &c., of the Native Tribes of Tasmania. 8vo. Hobart, 1875.*   MA 1 R 7

Tasmanian Industries; with some Notices of those of the Australian Colonies and New Zealand; accompanied by illustrative Tables. (Pam. Dr.) 8vo. Hobart, 1869.   MF 3 P 16

Another copy.   MJ 2 R 13

CALDERINUS (D.) Observationes quaepiam. Sm. fol. Venetiis, 1496. (*Bound with Platina's Vitæ Pontificum.*)   C 14 R 19 ‡

CALDERON DE LA BARCA (DON PEDRO). Autos Sacramentales alegoricos, y historiales del Phenix de los Poetas, Obras Posthumas que saca a luz Don Juan Fer- nandez de Apontes. 6 vols. 8vo. Madrid, 1759–60.   H 4 S 3–8

Dramas: The Wonder-working Magician; Life is a Dream; The Purgatory of St. Patrick. Now first translated fully from the Spanish in the metre of the original, by Denis Florence MacCarthy. 8vo. Lond., 1873.   H 3 P 5

CALDERON DE LA BARCA (MADAME FRANCES). Life in Mexico, during a Residence of Two Years in that Country. 8vo. Lond., 1843.   D 4 Q 31

CALDERWOOD (DAVID). History of the Kirk of Scotland; edited from the original Manuscript, by the Rev. Thomas Thomson. 8 vols. 8vo. Edinb., 1842–49.   G 14 T 5–12

CALDERWOOD (HENRY), LL.D. Relations of Mind and Brain. 2nd ed. 8vo. Lond., 1881.   A 12 R 23

CALDERWOOD (MRS. MARGARET STEUART). Letters and Journals of Mrs. Calderwood, of Polton; edited by Lieut.-Col. Alex. Fergusson. 8vo. Edinb., 1884.   D 783

CALDWELL (J. S.) Results of Reading. 8vo. Lond., 1843.   J 6 U 3

CALDWELL (ROBERT). The Gold Era of Victoria; by "A Melbourne Merchant." 8vo. Lond., 1855.*   MF 3 Q 68

CALDWELL (RT. REV. ROBERT), D.D., &c. Comparative Grammar of the Dravidian or South-Indian Family of Languages. 2nd ed., revised and enlarged. 8vo. Lond., 1875.   K 15 P 30

CALECAS (MANUEL). Opera omnia. [*See* MIGNE, J. P., SERIES GRÆCA, 152.]

CALEDONIAN UNITED GOLD MINING COMPANY LIMITED. Memorandum of the Articles of Associa- tion. [*See* TOZER, H.]

CALENDAR OF STATE PAPERS; Domestic Series, 1547–80, 1603–10, 1619–23, 1625–28, 1660–61. 6 vols. roy. 8vo. Lond., 1856–60.   B 15 U 1–6

CALENDARIUM INQUISITIONUM Post-mortem sive Escaetarum, Temporibus Regum Hen. III—Ric. III; cum Appendice. 4 vols. (in 2) atlas fol. Lond., 1806–28.   F 24 P 15, 16 ‡

CALENDARIUM ROTULORUM CHARTARUM et Inquisitionum ad Quod Damnum. Fol. Lond., 1803.   F 24 P 17 ‡

CALENDARIUM ROTULORUM PATENTIUM in Turri Londinensi. Fol. Lond., 1802.   F 24 P 18 ‡

CALENDARS OF THE PROCEEDINGS IN CHAN- CERY in the Reign of Queen Elizabeth. 3 vols. fol. Lond., 1827–32.   F 24 Q 6–8 ‡

CALEY (DR. GEORGE). [*See* BROWN, R.]

CALHOUN (HON. J. C.), AND BUCHANAN (HON. J). Oregon: the Claim of the United States to Oregon, as stated in letters of. 8vo. Lond., 1846.   B 1 R 18

CÁLIDÁSA. [*See* KÁLIDÁSA.]

CALIFORNIA. [*See* UNITED STATES.]

CALISCH (I. M.) New Complete Dictionary of the English and Dutch Languages, in two Parts. 1. English and Dutch. 2. Nederlandsch-Engelsch. 2 vols. 8vo. Tiel, 1875.   K 13 R 5, 6

CALLAGHAN (THOMAS). Supplement to Acts and Ordi- nances of the Governor and Council of New South Wales, and Acts of Parliament enacted for and applied to the Colony; with Notes and Index. Vol. 3, parts 3–5. 3 vols. 8vo. Sydney, 1848–52.   MF 2 S 17–19

CALLANDER (JOHN). Terra Australis Cognita; or, Voyages to the Terra Australis, or Southern Hemisphere, during the 16th, 17th, and 18th Centuries. 3 vols. 8vo. Edinb., 1766–68.*   MD 3 S 31–33

CALLÉRY (J. M.), AND YVAN (DR. M.) History of the Insurrection in China; translated from the French, by John Oxenford. 3rd ed. 8vo. Lond., 1854.   B 2 P 29

CALLIAT (VICTOR). Parallèle des Maisons de Paris, con- struites depuis 1830, jusqu'à 108 jours. Dessiné et publié par Victor Calliat, Architecte. 2nd ed. 2 vols. roy. fol. Paris, 1857–76.   A 1 R 3, 4 ‡

[*See* ENCYCLOPÉDIE D'ARCHITECTURE.]

CALLIMACHUS. Callimachi Cyrenæi Hymni, Epigrammata et Fragmenta: ejusdem Poëmatium de Coma Berenices a Catullo versum. Sm. 4to. Paris, 1675.
H 6 U 20

CALLINGHAM (JAMES). Sign-writing and Glass-embossing; a complete practical illustrated Manual of the Art. 12mo. Lond., 1871. A 17 T 35

CALLIS (F.) Cutlery. (Brit. Manuf. Indust.) 12mo. Lond., 1876. A 17 S 31

CALLISTUS (BISHOP OF ROME). History of. [See DÖLLINGER, PROF. J. J. I. VON.]

CALLON (J.) Lectures on Mining, delivered at the School of Mines, Paris. Translated, at the Author's request, by C. le Neve Foster, D.Sc., and W. Galloway. Roy. 8vo., and atlas 4to. Paris, 1876. A 9 V 21, 22

CALMET (AUGUSTIN), ABBÉ DE SENONES. Dictionary of the Holy Bible; with an extensive series of Plates. 4th ed. Revised, &c., by Charles Taylor. 5 vols. 4to. Lond., 1823. K 18 T 9-13

La Vie de; par A. Fargé. 8vo. Serones, 1762. C 10 P 23

The Phantom World; or, the Philosophy of Spirits, Apparitions, &c.; edited by Rev. H. Christmas. 2 vols. 8vo. Lond., 1850. G 7 U 4, 5

CALONNE (CHARLES ALEXANDRE DE). [See LA MOTTE, COMTESSE DE VALOIS DE.]

CALVERT (DR. FREDERICK CRACE), F.R.S. Dyeing and Calico-printing: Manufacture and Use of Aniline Colours; edited by J. Stenhouse, LL.D., and Charles Edward Groves. 8vo. Manchester, 1876. A 11 S 6

On Dyes and Dye-stuffs other than Aniline. (Carton Lect.) Roy. 8vo. Lond., 1871. A 15 U 21

CALVERT (JAMES). Fiji and the Fijians. [See WILLIAMS, T.]

[See HAZLEWOOD, D.]

CALVERT (MRS.), CAROLINE LOUISA WARING ATKINSON. Cowanda, the Veteran's Grant: an Australian Story. 12mo. Sydney, 1859.* MJ 1 R 4

Sermon on the occasion of a Tablet being placed to the memory of the late Mrs. Calvert. [See WOOLLS, REV. W.]

CALVERT (JOHN), C.E. The Gold Rocks of Great Britain and Ireland, and a general Outline of the Gold Regions of the World; with a Treatise on the Geology of Gold. 8vo. Lond., 1853. A 9 S 17

CALVIN (JOHN). Histoire de la Vie, des Ouvrages, et des Doctrines de Calvin; par J. M. U. Audin. 5° ed. 8vo. Paris, 1851. G 13 Q 3

Institutio Christianæ Religionis; cum Indice per locos communes. Opera N. Colladonis tunc contexto. 8vo. Lausannæ, 1585. G 16 R 14

s

CALVIN (JOHN)—*continued.*
Lettres de; recueillies d'après les Manuscrits originaux, et publiées par Jules Bonnet. 2 vols. 8vo. Paris, 1854.
G 6 Q 5, 6

Life and Times of John Calvin, the Great Reformer; by Paul Henry, D.D.; translated from the German, by Henry Stebbing, D.D. 2 vols. 8vo. Lond., 1849. C 10 P 24, 25

CAMBACÉRÈS (JEAN JACQUES RÉGIS DE), PRINCE. Evenings with Prince Cambacérès. Second Consul, Arch-chancellor of the Empire, Duke of Parma, &c.; by Baron E. L. de Lamothe Largon. 2 vols. 8vo. Lond., 1837.
C 8 U 15, 16

CAMBRIAN ARCHÆOLOGICAL ASSOCIATION. Archæologia Cambrensis: a Record of the Antiquities of Wales and its Marches, and the Journal of the Cambrian Archæological Association. 36 vols. 8vo. Lond., 1846-85.
E

CAMBRIDGE (RICHARD OWEN). Life and Poems of. [See CHALMERS, A.]

The Scribleriad: an Heroic Poem, in six Books. 4to. Lond., 1751 H 6 V 14

CAMBRIDGE ESSAYS (THE); contributed by Members of the University. 4 vols. 8vo. Lond., 1855-58.
J 7 U 10-13

CAMBRIDGE PHILOLOGICAL SOCIETY. Transactions of the Cambridge Philological Society, 1872-82; with Introductory Essay, Reviews, and Appendix, edited by J. B. Postgate, M.A. Vols. 1, 2. 8vo. Lond., 1881-82. E

CAMBRIDGE UNIVERSITY. Calendar, for the years 1839-84. 46 vols. 8vo. Camb., 1839-84. E

Statutes for the University of Cambridge, and for the Colleges within it (1878-82); with an Appendix of Acts and Orders. 8vo. Camb., 1883. F 3 R 16

CAMBRY (J.) Voyage dans le Finistère. 4to. Brest, 1835. D 7 V 18

CAMDEN (WILLIAM). Anglica, Normannica, Hibernica, Cambrica, a veteribus Scripta. Fol. Francofurti, 1603.
B 14 S 8 ‡

Britannia; or, a Chorographical Description of Great Britain and Ireland; translated, &c., by E. Gibson. 2nd ed. 2 vols. (in 1) fol. Lond., 1722. B 16 S 1 ‡

Another edition; translated by R. Gough. 4 vols. fol. Lond., 1806. B 15 U 2-5 ‡

History of the most renowned and victorious Princess Elizabeth, late Queen of England. 4th ed. Fol. Lond., 1688. B 2 T 7

CAMDEN SOCIETY, Publications of. 144 vols. sm. 4to. Lond., 1838-86. E

CAMERINI (PROF. EUGENIO). L'Eco Italiano tiore del Parlar Famigliare e della Conversazione Civile in Italia: a Practical Guide to Italian Conversation; with a complete Vocabulary. 2nd ed. 8vo. Leip., 1871. K 11 T 39

[See PETRARCA, F.]

CAMERON (ALEXANDER MACKENZIE), M.S.B.A. &c. Hardy Book of Practical Astronomy, for Surveyors, Mariners, and Explorers; revised throughout by Capt. John Herschel, R.E.; with Appendix. 8vo. Sydney, 1877.*   MA 1 T 23

New South Wales, its Progress and Resources. 8vo. Sydney, 1876.   MF 2 R 29

Another copy. Sydney. 8vo. 1876.   MJ 2 R 4

CAMERON (ANDREW), D.D. Scripture Law of Marriage; with special reference to Marriage with a Deceased Wife's Sister. 8vo. Melh., 1873.   MG 1 Q 37

CAMERON (SIR CHARLES ALEXANDER). History of the Royal College of Surgeons in Ireland. Roy. 8vo. Dublin, 1886.   B 11 R 19

CAMERON (JAMES). Oils and Varnishes. (Churchill's Tech. Hand-books.) 12mo. Lond., 1886.   A 11 P 5

CAMERON (JOHN). Gaelic Names of Plants (Scottish and Irish). 8vo. Edinb., 1883.   A 5 P 15

CAMERON (JOHN), F.R.G.S. Our Tropical Possessions in Malayan India. 8vo. Lond., 1865.   D 5 S 21

CAMERON (R. W.) Cameron's proposed Monthly Line of Steamers between Panama and Australia: Prospectus. 8vo. Sydney, 1855.   MJ 2 Q 18

CAMERON (COMM. VERNEY LOVETT), C.B., R.N., &c. Across Africa. Illustrated. 2 vols. 8vo. Lond., 1877.   D 2 Q 1, 2

Another copy. New ed. Lond., 1885.   D 2 Q 3

To the Gold Coast for Gold. [*See* BURTON, SIR R. F.]

CAMOENS (LUIS DE). Camoens; his Life and his Lusiads: a Commentary, by R. F. Burton. 2 vols. 12mo. Lond., 1881.   C 3 S 13, 14

Lyricks, Parts 1, 2 (Sonnets, Canzons, Odes, and Sexties); englished by Richard F. Burton. 2 vols. 12mo. Lond., 1884.   II 5 S 21, 22

Memoirs of the Life and Writings of; by John Adamson, F.S.A. 2 vols. 8vo. Lond., 1820.   C 3 S 15, 16

Os Lusiadas (the Lusiads); englished by R. Francis Burton (edited by his wife, Isabel Burton)). 2 vols. 12mo. Lond., 1880.   II 5 S 19, 20

Seventy Sonnets of: Portuguese Text and Translation; with original Poems, by J. J. Aubertin. 8vo. Lond., 1881.   II 5 T 12

The Lusiad of; closely translated by Lieut.-Col. Sir T. Livingston Mitchell, Kt., D.C.L. 8vo. Lond., 1854. Libr.

Another copy.   II 7 S 10

The Lusiad ; translated by W. J. Mickle. [*See* CHALMERS, A.]

CAMPAIGN OF 1870–71; republished from "The Times," by permission. 8vo. Lond., 1871.   B 9 R 18

CAMPAIGN OF FREDERICKSBURG, Nov.-Dec., 1862: a Study for Officers of Volunteers; by "A Line Officer." With Maps. 8vo. Lond., 1886.   B 1 Q 46

CAMPAN (JEANNE LOUISE HENRIETTE GENEST.) Mémoires sur la Vie de Marie Antoinette. [*See* BARRIÈRE, J. F., 10.]

Memoirs of the Private Life of Marie Antoinette, Queen of France and Navarre. 2nd ed. 2 vols. 8vo. Lond., 1823.   C 7 R 39, 40

Another copy. New and revised ed. 2 vols. 8vo. Lond., 1883.   C 7 R 41, 42

CAMPBELL (A. D.) Dictionary of the Teloogoo Language, commonly termed the Gentoo. Roy. 4to. Madras, 1821.   K 3 S 17 †

Grammar of the Teloogoo Language, commonly termed the Gentoo. 2nd ed. 4to. Madras, 1820.   K 14 S 8

Polyglot Vocabulary in the English, Teloogoo, and Tamil Languages; translated by "A late Student of Mr. Lewis, Head Master of the Preparatory School." 8vo. Madras, 1851.   K 12 S 10

CAMPBELL (A. J.) Account of the Early History of the New Hebrides Mission. [*See* CAMPBELL, F. A.]

CAMPBELL (ARCHIBALD). Voyage round the World, 1806–12. 8vo. Edinb., 1816.*   MD 1 U 19

CAMPBELL (ARCHIBALD), LORD. Records of Argyll: Legends, Traditions, and Recollections of Argyllshire Highlanders. 4to. Edinb., 1885.   B 19 Q 4 ‡

CAMPBELL (FIELD MARSHAL SIR COLIN), LORD CLYDE. [*See* CLYDE. LORD.]

CAMPBELL (COLIN), LORD, D.A., &c. The Crofter in History ; by "Dalriad." 12mo. Edinb., 1885. B 13 P 20

CAMPBELL (COLIN). B.A. Remarks on National Education, with reference to the Colony of Victoria. 8vo. Melh., 1853.   MG 1 Q 38

The Squatting Question considered, with a view to its Settlement. 8vo. Melh., 1861.   MF 3 P 5

[*See* AUSTRALIA FELIX MONTHLY MAGAZINE.]

CAMPBELL (DONALD). Treatise on the Language, Poetry, and Music of the Highland Clans. Roy. 8vo. Edinb., 1862.   II 6 V 6

CAMPBELL (D. FORBES). The Consulate and the Empire. [*See* THIERS, L. A.]

CAMPBELL (FRANCIS), M.D. An Abstract of all the Corn Laws which have been passed from time to time for the Regulation of the Export and Import of Corn, &c. Compiled from various sources by "A Pythagorean." 12mo. Sydney, 1844.*   MF 1 P 42

Another copy. (Pam.44.) 12mo. Sydney, 1845. MJ 2 R 6

Commentary on the Influence which the use of Tobacco exerts on the Human Constitution; in a series of Letters. 12mo. Sydney, 1853.*   MA 2 S 43

Treatise on the Culture of Flax and Hemp; being a Reprint of the Letters of Robin Goodfellow. 2nd ed. 8vo. Sydney, 1845.*   MA 1 Q 29

Another copy. 3rd ed. 8vo. Sydney, 1864. MA 1 Q 1

Another copy. 4th ed. 8vo. Sydney, 1866. MA 1 Q 31

CAMPBELL (F. A.) A Year in the New Hebrides, Loyalty Islands, and New Caledonia; with an Account of the Early History of the New Hebrides Missions, by A. J. Campbell, Geelong; Narrative of the Voyages of the *Dayspring*, by D. M'Donald, D.D.; and an Appendix, containing a Contribution to the Phytography of the New Hebrides, by Baron von Mueller, C.M.G., &c. Illustrated. 12mo. Geelong, 1873.* 　MD 4 Q 30

CAMPBELL (Sir George), M.P. A Handy Book on the Eastern Question; being a very recent view of Turkey; with Map. 8vo. Lond., 1876. 　　　B 13 V 37

CAMPBELL (G. Ord). Australian Sheep Industry. [*See* Armstrong, A. S.]

CAMPBELL (Lieut.-Col. James). Excursions, Adventures, and Field-Sports in Ceylon. 2 vols. 8vo. Lond., 1843. 　　　　　　　　　　D 6 S 2, 3

CAMPBELL (John). [*See* M'Ure, J.]

CAMPBELL (Major John). Geographical Memoir of Melville Island and Port Essington, on the Cobourg Peninsula, Northern Australia. 8vo. Lond., 1834. 　　　　　　　　　　　　　　　MD 7 Q 52

CAMPBELL (John), LL.D. Lives of the Admirals, and other Eminent British Seamen; containing their Personal Histories, and a Detail of all their Public Services. 4 vols. 8vo. Lond., 1742–44. 　　B 6 Q 19–22

Another copy. 2nd ed. 8 vols. 8vo. Lond., 1817. 　　　　　　　　　　　　　　　B 6 Q 23–30

White Herring Fishery in Scotland, carried on yearly in the Island of Zetland by the Dutch only. Reprinted from the edition of 1750. 8vo. Edinb., 1885. 　A 14 Q 26

CAMPBELL (John). Maritime Discovery and Christian Missions, considered in their mutual relations. 8vo. Lond., 1840. 　　　　　　　　　MD 7 R 24

CAMPBELL (John), Baron, LL.D., &c. Life of John Lord Campbell, Lord High Chancellor of Great Britain; consisting of a Selection from his Autobiography, Diary, and Letters. Edited by his Daughter, the Hon. Mrs. Mary Scarlett Hardcastle; with Portrait. 2 vols. 8vo. Lond., 1881. 　　　　　　　C 10 R 39, 40

Lives of the Lord Chancellors and Keepers of the Great Seal of England. 3rd ed. 7 vols. 8vo. Lond., 1848. 　　　　　　　　　　　C 7 T 29–35

Lives of the Chief Justices of England. 3 vols. 8vo. Lond., 1849–57. 　　　　　　　C 7 T 36–38

Speeches of, at the Bar and in the House of Commons; with an Address to the Irish Bar as Lord Chancellor of Ireland. 8vo. Edinb., 1842. 　　　　F 13 P 11

CAMPBELL (John). "Feringhee BachA." Lost among the Affghans; being the Adventures of John Campbell (otherwise Feringhee Bacha.) 8vo. Lond., 1862. 　　　　　　　　　　　　　　　D 5 Q 12

CAMPBELL (Major-Gen. Sir John), C.B. &c. Personal Narrative of Thirteen Years' Service amongst the Wild Tribes of Khondistan, for the suppression of Human Sacrifice. 8vo. Lond., 1864. 　　　　D 5 S 33

CAMPBELL (Rev. John). Travels in South Africa. 3rd ed. 8vo. Lond., 1815. 　　　　D 2 T 22

Travels in South Africa; being a Narrative of a Second Journey in the Interior of that Country. 2 vols. (in 1). 8vo. Lond., 1822. 　　　　　　　D 2 T 23

CAMPBELL (John Francis). Frost and Fire: Natural Engines, Tool Marks, and Chips; with Sketches taken at Home and Abroad, by a Traveller. 2 vols. 8vo. Lond., 1865. 　　　　　　　　　A 9 S 30, 31

My Circular Notes Round the World, 1874–75. 2 vols. 8vo. Lond., 1876. 　　　D 10 R 42, 43

Leabhar na Feinne, Gaelic Texts, Heroic Gaelic Ballads, collected in Scotland, chiefly from 1512 to 1871. Copied from old Manuscripts preserved at Edinburgh and elsewhere (privately printed). Fol. Lond., 1872. 　H 22 S 25‡

Popular Tales of the West Highlands; orally collected, with a translation. 4 vols. 12mo. Edinb., 1860–62. 　　　　　　　　　　　　B 21 P 14–17

Short American Tramp in the Fall of 1864; by the "Editor of Life in Normandy." 8vo. Edinb., 1865. 　D 3 R 45

CAMPBELL (Dr. John Logan). Poenamo: Sketches of the Early Days of New Zealand; Romance and Reality of Antipodean Life in the Infancy of a new Colony. 8vo. Lond., 1881.* 　　　　　　　MJ 1 S 5

CAMPBELL (John Robert) How to see Norway. 8vo. Lond., 1871. 　　　　　　　　　D 8 R 5

CAMPBELL (Rev. Joseph), M.A. Simple Tests for Minerals; or, Every Man his own Analyst. 12mo. Sydney, 1885. 　　　　　　　　MA 2 P 16

CAMPBELL (Prof. Lewis), M.A., &c., and GARNETT (Prof. William), M.A. Life of James Clerk Maxwell; with a Selection from his Correspondence and Occasional Writings, and a Sketch of his Contributions to Science. 8vo. Lond., 1882. 　　　　　　C 8 Q 34

Tragedies of Sophocles with Notes. [*See* Sophocles.]

CAMPBELL (M.) The Forest Oracle; or, the Bridge of Tresino: an Operatic Drama. (Cumberland's Eng. Theatre.) 12mo. Lond., 1829. 　　　H 2 R 23

CAMPBELL (Norman). Report of the Registrar General on the Progress and Statistics of Victoria, from 1851 to 1858; compiled from authentic Official Records. 8vo. Melb., 1858. 　　　　　　　　MF 3 P 15

Another copy. 　　　　　　　　　MJ 2 R 9

CAMPBELL (Peter). Hymns and Solos used by Moody and Sankey at Gospel Meetings. (Pam. K.) 18mo. Sydney, 1875. 　　　　　　　MJ 2 P 27

My Life, Missionary Labours, Original Bush Sketches, Rhymes, Temperance Anecdotes, &c. 12mo. Sydney, 1872. 　　　　　　　　　　　MG 1 P 48

New Revival Hymns and Spiritual Songs (as now used in America, England, and Scotland). (Pam. K.) 18mo. Sydney, 1874. 　　　　　　　MJ 2 P 27

Voluntary Personal Bush Mission Report. (Pam. E.) 4to. Sydney, 1873. 　　　　　　　MJ 2 S 2

CAMPBELL (Robert). Life of the Most Illustrious Prince, John, Duke of Argyle and Greenwich. 12mo. Belfast, 1745.　　　　　　　　　　　　　C 1 R 1

CAMPBELL (Robert), M.A. Lectures on Jurisprudence. [*See* Austin, John.]

CAMPBELL (Rev. Dr. Thomas). Diary of a Visit to England in 1775; by "An Irishman," and other Papers by the same hand. 8vo. Sydney, 1854.　　MD 3 Q 41

CAMPBELL (Thomas). An Essay on English Poetry; with Notices of the British Poets. (H. and C. Lib.) 12mo. Lond., 1848.　　　　　　　　　　　J 8 P 31

Frederick the Great and his Times. 4 vols. 8vo. Lond., 1842-43.　　　　　　　　　　　　C 10 Q 25-28

History of Our Own Times. 2 vols. 8vo. Lond., 1843.　　　　　　　　　　　　　　　　　　B 14 Q 1, 2

Letters from the South. 2 vols. 8vo. Lond., 1837.　　　　　　　　　　　　　　　　　　D 1 V 18, 19

Life and Letters of; edited by William Beattie, M.D. 3 vols. 8vo. Lond., 1849.　　　　　C 10 R 36-38

Life of Mrs. Siddons. 2 vols. 8vo. Lond., 1834.　　　　　　　　　　　　　　　　　　C 5 T 23, 24

Life of Petrarch. 2 vols. 8vo. Lond., 1841. C 9 P 14, 15

Poetical Works of. [With Illustrations by J. M. W. Turner.] 8vo. Lond., 1837.　　　　　H 7 S 3

Sonnets, &c., of Petrarch; with a Life of the Poet. [*See* Petrarch, F.]

Specimens of the British Poets; with Biographical and Critical Notices, &c. 8vo. Lond., 1841. H 6 U 27

CAMPBELL (W.) Description of the Wattle Flat Goldfield. [*See* Gipps, F. B.]

CAMPBELL (Col. Walter). My Indian Journal. 8vo. Edinb., 1864.　　　　　　　　　　　D 6 Q 36

The Old Forest Ranger; or, Wild Sports of India on the Neilgherry Hills, in the Jungles, and on the Plains. New ed. Illustrated. 8vo. Lond., 1844.　　A 17 U 21

CAMPBELL (William). The Crown Lands of Australia; being an Exposition of the Land Regulations, and of the Claims and Grievances of the Crown Tenants. 8vo. Glasgow, 1855.*　　　　　　　　　　MF 1 R 26

CAMPE (Joachim Heinrich). Wörterbuch der deutschen Sprache. 5 vols. 4to. Brunswick, 1807-11. K 15 U 6-10

Wörterbuch zur Erklärung und Verdeutschung der in seuer Sprache aufgedrungenen fremden Ausdrücke: ein Ergänzungsband zu Adelungs Wörterbuche. 2 vols. (in 1). 4to. Braunschweig, 1801.　　　　　　K 13 R 19

CAMPEN (Samuel Richard van). The Dutch in the Arctic Seas. Vol. 1. 8vo. Lond., 1876.　D 4 R 31

CAMPER (Prof. Petrus). Works of; or the connection between the Science of Anatomy and the Arts of Drawing, Painting, and Statuary, &c., in two Books; translated from the Dutch by T. Cogan, M.D. 4to. Lond., 1794.　　　　　　　　　　　　　　　A 1 P 13 †

CAMPIN (Francis), C.E. Details of Machinery; comprising Instructions for the execution of various Works in Iron, in the Fitting-shop, Foundry, and Boiler-yard. (Weale.) 12mo. Lond., 1883.　　　　A 17 Q 72

Materials and Construction: a Theoretical and Practical Treatise on the Strains, Designing, and Erection of Works of Construction. (Weale.) 12mo. Lond.,1881. A 17 Q 47

Practical Treatise on Mechanical Engineering. (Weale.) 12mo. Lond., 1881.　　　　　A 17 Q 51

Treatise on Bridges, Girders, Roofs, &c. (Weale.) 12mo. Lond., 1871.　　　　　　　　A 17 Q 20

Treatise on Mathematics, as applied to the Constructive Arts. 2nd ed. (Weale.) 12mo. Lond., 1882. A 17 Q 54

CAMPIN (F. W.) Law of Patents for Inventions; with Notes on the Law as to the protection of Designs and Trade Marks. (Weale.) 12mo. Lond., 1869.　F 5 S 23

CAMPION (Edmund). Ancient Irish Histories. [*See* Hanmer, M.]

CAMUS (A. G.) [*See* Aristoteles.]

CANADA. Annual Reports of the Commissioner of Agriculture and Public Works for the execution of various Works, on Agriculture and Arts, 1873-74. 8vo. Toronto, 1874-75.　　　　　　　　　　　　　　　E

Canada Educational Directory and Year-book, 1876. 8vo. Toronto, 1874-76.　　　　　　　　　　　E

Canal Statistics for the Season of Navigation, 1875. Roy. 8vo. Ottawa, 1876.　　　　　　F 3 T 17

Census of Canada: Recensement du Canada. 3 vols. roy. 8vo. Ottawa, 1873-75.　　　　　　E

Code Civil du Bas Canada: Civil Code of Lower Canada. Roy. 8vo. Ottawa, 1866.　　　　　F 1 R 20

Dominion Annual Register and Review; edited by Henry J. Morgan and others. 8vo. Montreal, 1879-82.　E

Educational Institutions. [*See* Philadelphia Centennial Exhibition.]

Geological and Natural History Survey and Museum of Canada; Alfred R. C. Selwyn, LL.D., &c., Director: Report of Progress, and Reports and Maps of Investigations and Surveys, 1879-84. 3 vols. roy. 8vo., and atlas 4to. Montreal, 1881-85.　　　　　　E

List of Lights on the Coasts, Rivers, and Lakes, 1875. Roy. 8vo. Ottawa, 1876.　　　　　F 3 T 17

Report of the Canadian Commissioner at the Exhibition of Industry, held at New South Wales, 1877. Roy. 8vo. Ottawa, 1878.　　　　　　　　　　MF 3 R 15

Report of the Commissioner of Fisheries for the year ending 31st December, 1875. Ottawa, 1876.　　E

Report of the Postmaster-General for the year ending 30th June, 1874. 8vo. Ottawa, 1875.　　　　E

Report of the Select Committee on Immigration and Colonization. Roy. 8vo. Ottawa, 1876.　　F 3 T 17

CANADA—*continued.*

Report of the Select Committee on the Causes of the present Depression of the Manufacturing, Mining, Commercial, Shipping, Lumber, and Fishing Interests. 8vo. Ottawa, 1876.   E

Report of the Superintendent of Insurance, 1875. Part 1. Roy. 8vo. Ottawa, 1876.   F 3 T 17

Report, Returns, and Statistics of the Inland Revenues of the Dominion of Canada, for the Fiscal Year ending 30th June, 1873. 8vo. Ottawa, 1874.   E

Tables of the Trade and Navigation of the Dominion of Canada, for the year ending 30th June, 1875; compiled from Official Returns. Roy. 8vo. Ottawa, 1876.   E

Upper Canada: Copy of a Petition to the Imperial Parliament, on Clergy Reserved Lands, 1830. [*See* HISTORICAL PAMPHLETS.]

Year-book and Almanac of Canada, 1877. 8vo. Montreal, 1877.   E

CANADIAN PARLIAMENTARY COMPANION; edited by H. J. Morgan. 2 vols. 18mo.   Ottawa, 1875–76.   E

CANADIAN ECONOMICS: Papers prepared for reading before the Economic Section. 8vo.   Montreal, 1885. F 3 S 17

CANDISH (SYDNEY). Candish's Defence: a Review of Colonial Criticism, and Essay on Love. 4to.   Sydney, 1887.   MH 1 T 4

Love: a Poetical Essay. 4to. Sydney, 1887.   MH 1 T 3

CANDLER (S. C.), "MUCOR." Prevention of Consumption: a Mode of Prevention founded on a new Theory of the nature of the Tubercle-Bacillus. 8vo. Lond.,1887. MA 2 S 29

Theory of the Causation, and Suggestions for the Prevention of Dysentery. 8vo. Melb., 1873.   MA 2 S 28

CANDLISH (REV. ROBERT SMITH), D.D. Memorials of; by William Wilson, D.D.; with concluding Chapter by Prof. Robert Rainy, D.D. 8vo. Edinb.,1880. C 8 U 14

CANDOLLE (ALPHONSE P. DE). Genera, Species, et Synonyma Candolleana alphabetico ordine disposita, seu Index generalis et specialis ad A. P. Decandolle Prodromum Systematis Naturalis Regni Vegetabilis; auctore, H. W. Buek. M.D. 4 vols. (in 3) 8vo. Berlin, 1840–74. A 4 R 22–24

Géographie botanique raisonnée; ou, Exposition des Faits principaux, et des Lois concernant la Distribution géographique des Plantes de l'époque actuelle. Contenant deux Cartes géographiques. 2 vols. 8vo. Paris, 1855. A 5 P 12, 13

Origin of Cultivated Plants. 8vo. Lond.,1884.   A 4 P 20

Prodromus Systematis Naturalis Regni Vegetabilis sive enumeratio contracta Ordinum, Generum, Specierumque Plantarum huc usque cognitarum, juxta methodi naturalis normas digesta. 17 vols. (in 21) 8vo. Paris, 1824–73. A 4 R 1–21

CANDOLLE (ALPHONSE P. ET CASIMIR DE). Monographiæ Phanerogamarum. Prodromi hujc Continuatio, hujc Rovisio. Auctoribus Alphonso et Casimir de Candolle, aliisque Botanicis ultra memoratis. 4 vols. 8vo. Paris, 1878–83.   A 36 V 1-4

    1. Smilaceæ, Restiaceæ, Mellaceæ, cum Tabulis IX.

    2. Araceæ, Auctore Engler.

    3. Philydraceæ, Alismaceæ, Butomaceæ, Juncagineæ, Commelinaceæ, Cucurbitaceæ, cum Tabulis VIII.

    4. Burseraceæ et Anacardiaceæ, Auctore Engler. Portedetiaceæ, Auctore Comite de Solms-Laubach. Cum Tabulis undecim.

CANIVET (E.) [*See* BOITARD, P.]

CANN (TEOFILO C.) Grammatica Teorico-Practica della Lingua Inglese. Nuovo Corso completo ad uso degli Italiani, diviso in due Parti. 8a ed. 8vo. Firenze, 1884.   K 12 P 1

CANNAN (EDWIN), B.A. The Duke of Saint Simon. (Lothian Prize Essay, 1885.) 8vo. Oxford, 1885. C2813

CANNING (HON. ALBERT STRATFORD GEORGE). Lord Macaulay, Essayist and Historian. 8vo. Lond., 1882. C 1 T 41

CANNING (RT. HON. GEORGE). Anecdote Life of. [*See* TIMBS, J.]

General Register of Politics and Literature in Europe and America, 1827; with Memoir. (Const. Misc.) 18mo. Edinb., 1828.   K 10 Q 10

Historical Characters. [*See* DALLING AND BULWER, LORD.]

Life of; by Robert Bell. 12mo. Lond., 1846. C 3 Q 3

Political Life of; by his Private Secretary, Augustus Granville Stapleton. 2nd ed. 3 vols. 8vo. Lond., 1831.   C 10 Q 12–14

Speeches of; with a Memoir of his Life by R. Therry. 6 vols. 8vo. Lond., 1828.   F 5 U 23–28

Another copy. 2nd ed. 6 vols. 8vo. Lond., 1830. F 13 P 12–17

Life and Poems of. [*See* BRITISH POETS, 4.]

CANNING (STRATFORD). [*See* STRATFORD DE REDCLIFFE, VISCOUNT.]

CANOVA (ANTONIO). Works of, in Sculpture and Modelling, engraved in outline by Henry Moses; with Memoir by Comte Cicognara. 3 vols. imp. 8vo. Lond., 1849.   A 8 T 6-8

CANSICK (FREDERICK TEAGUE). Collection of Curious and Interesting Epitaphs, copied from the Monuments in the Ancient Church and Burial Grounds of St. Pancras, Middlesex. 3 vols. (in 1). 4to.   Lond., 1869–75.   B 21 V 10

CANTACUZENI (JO.) [*See* BYZANTINÆ HIST. SCRIPT.]

CANTERBURY ASSOCIATION. [*See* CANTERBURY PAPERS.]

CANTERBURY PAPERS. Canterbury Papers, No. 1, New Series. Information concerning the Province of Canterbury, N.Z. 8vo. Lond., 1850.   MD 7 Q 32

Another copy.   MD 7 Q 34

Another copy. Nos. 1, 2.   MD 1 U 21

Information concerning the Principles, Objects, Plans and Proceedings of the Founders of the Settlement of Canterbury, in New Zealand. Nos. 1-10. 8vo. Lond., 1850-51.   MD 7 Q 30

Another copy, Nos. 1-8. 8vo. Lond., 1850.   MD 7 Q 31

CANTERBURY COLLEGE CALENDAR (University of New Zealand), for the year 1888. 8vo. Christchurch, 1888.   ME 5 S

CANTONI (C. G.) Les Produits de l'Agriculture du Piémont, de la Lombardie, &c. Exposition Universelle de Paris, 1867. (Pam. V.D.) 4to. Paris, 1867.   MJ 2 U 3

CANTOR LECTURES. Lectures delivered before the Society for the Encouragement of Arts, Manufactures, and Commerce. Roy. 8vo. Lond., 1869-75.   A 15 U 21

1. On the Aniline or Coal Tar Colours; by W. H. Perkin, F.R.S.

2. On Applied Mechanics; by John Anderson, C.E.

3. On Dyes and Dye-stuffs other than Aniline; by Dr. F. Crace Calvert, F.R.S.

4. On Mechanism; by the Rev. Arthur Rigg, M.A.

5. On Silicates, Silicides, Glass, and Glass-painting; by Professor Barff.

6. Our Food-producing Ruminants, and the Parasites which reside in them; by T. Spencer Cobbold, M.D., &c.

7. On the Manufacture and Refining of Sugar; by C. Haughton Gill.

8. On the Energies of Gravity, Vitality, Affinity, Electricity, Light and Heat, especially with reference to the measurement and utilisation of them; by the Rev. Arthur Rigg, M.A.

9. On Wines, their Production, Treatment, and Use; by J. L. W. Thudichum, M.D.

10. Carbon and certain Compounds of Carbon, treated principally in reference to Heating and Illuminating Purposes; by Professor Barff, M.A.

11. Alcohol, its Action and its Use; by Benjamin W. Richardson, M.D., &c.

12. On the Material, Construction, Form, and Principles of Tools and Contrivances used in Handicraft; by the Rev. Arthur Rigg, M.A.

CANTU (Cesar). Histoire de Cent Ans, 1750-1850. (Histoire, Sciences, Littérature, Beaux-Arts). Traduit de l'Italien, avec Notes et Observations, par Amédée Renée. 4 vols. 12mo. Paris, 1859-62.   B 14 Q 7-10

Histoire des Italiens; traduite par M. Armand Lacombe. 12 vols. 8vo. Paris, 1867.   B 12 R 1-12

Histoire Universelle; revue et traduite par M. Armand Lacombe. 19 vols. 8vo. Paris, 1862.   B 11 U 26-44

La Réforme en Italie- les Précurseurs; traduits de l'Italien, par Aristide Digard et E. Martin. 8vo. Paris, 1867.   G 4 R 6

CAPE (R. A.) [*See* MACKENZIE AND CAPE.]

CAPE OF GOOD HOPE. Catalogue of Books in the South African Public Library. 8vo. Cape Town, 1834.   K 7 R15

State of the Cape of Good Hope in 1822. 8vo. Lond., 1823.   F 3 T 13

CAPEFIGUE (JEAN BAPTISTE HONORÉ RAYMOND). Les Cardinaux-Ministres: le Cardinal de Richelieu. 12mo. Paris, 1865.   C 1 S 21

Les Cardinaux-Ministres: le Cardinal Dubois et la Régence de Philippe d'Orléans. 12mo. Paris, 1861.   C 1 S 20

Les Cent Jours. Charlemagne. Roy. 8vo. Bruxelles, 1842.   B 7 V 9

Les Diplomates Européens et Louis XVI. Roy. 8vo. Bruxelles, 1845.   B 7 V 11

L'Eglise au Moyen Age, du 7e au 12e Siècle. 2 vols. 8vo. Paris, 1852.   G 16 S 23, 24

L'Eglise perdant les quatre derniers Siècles. 3 vols. 8vo. Paris, 1854-57.   G 16 S 25-27

L'Europe perdant la Révolution Française. Roy. 8vo. Bruxelles, 1844.   B 7 V 8

L'Europe depuis l'avénement du Roi Louis-Philippe. 2 vols. roy. 8vo. Bruxelles, 1846.   B 7 V 4, 5

Les Fondateurs des Grands Ordres Religieux. 6 vols. 12mo. Paris, 1865-66.   G 13 T 19-24

St. Bernard, Abbé de Clairvaux.
Ste. Françoise de Chantal.
St. Ignace de Loyola et l'Ordre des Jésuites.
Ste. Marie-Marguerite Alcoq. [Marguerite Marie Alacoque].
Ste. Térèse [Thérèse] de Jésus.
St. Vincent de Paul et les Sœurs de Charité.

François 1er et la Renaissance, 1515-47. 4 vols. 8vo. Paris, 1845.   B 8 U 26-29

Another copy. Roy. 8vo. Bruxelles, 1845.   B 7 V 10

Histoire de France, par Grandes Epoques: Clovis et les Mérovingiens. Roy. 8vo. Paris, 1869.   B 8 U 16

Histoire des Grandes Opérations, Financières, Banques, Bourses, Emprunts, Compagnies Industrielles, &c. 4 vols. 8vo. Paris, 1855-60.   F 6 S 1-4

Louis XIV: son Gouvernement et ses relations diplomatiques avec l'Europe, suivi de Philippe d'Orléans. Roy. 8vo. Bruxelles, 1843.   B 7 V 7

Louis XV, et la Société du 18e Siècle. Roy. 8vo. Bruxelles, 1843.   B 7 V 6

Les quatre premiers Siècles de l'Eglise Chrétienne. 4 vols. 8vo. Lond., 1850-51.   G 16 S 28-31

Les Reines de la Main Droite. 8 vols. 12mo. Paris, 1856-69.   B 7 S 1-8

Catherine de Médicis.
Anne d'Autriche.
Marie de Médicis.
La Grande Catherine.
La Reine Vierge, Elisabeth d'Angleterre.
Marie Thérèse, Impératrice d'Autriche, Roi de Hongrie.
La Duchesse Gabrielle de Polignac.
Isabelle de Castillo.

CAPEFIGUE (JEAN BAPTISTE HONORÉ RAYMOND—*contd.*)
Les Reines de la Main Gauche. 22 vols. 12mo. Paris,
1858–68. B 7 S 9–30

Madame la Marquise de Pompadour.
Gabrielle d'Estrées et la Politique de Henri IV.
Diane de Poitiers.
Agnès Sorel et la Chevalerie.
La Duchesse de Portsmouth et la Cour Gallante des Stuarts.
Les Déesses de la Liberté.
Aspasie et le Siècle de Périclès.
Madame la Comtesse du Barry.
Mademoiselle de la Vallière.
La Comtesse de Parabère.
Les Cours d'Amour.
Ninon de Lenclos, et les Précieuses de la Place Royale.
Les Bacchantes et les Jeunes Patriciens sous les Césars.
Mesdemoiselles de Nesle.
Les Héroïnes de la Ligue et les Mignons de Henri III.
La Belle Corisande.
La Comtesse du Cayla, Louis XVIII, et les Salons du Faubourg
Saint-Germain sous la Restauration.
La Baronne de Krudner.
La Comtesse de Licaterau.
La Duchesse de Bourgogne.
La Marquise de Montespan.
La Marquise du Châtelet.

CAPEL (A. D.) Tips in Algebra; with new Methods for
the resolution of Quadratic and other Expressions into
Factors. 12mo. Lond., 1887. A 10 S 6

Key to the above. 12mo. Lond., 1887. A 10 S 7

CAPELL (EDWARD). Prolusions; or, Select Pieces of
Antient Poetry. 8vo. Lond., 1760. H 4 P 33

CAPELLO (H.), AND IVENS (R.) From Benguella to
the Territory of Yacca: description of a Journey into
Central and West Africa, 1877–80; translated by Alfred
Elwes, Ph.D. Illustrated. 2 vols. 8vo. Lond., 1882.
D 2 P 15, 16

CAPES (REV. WILLIAM WOLFE), M.A. Roman History:
the Early Empire, from the Assassination of Julius Cæsar
to that of Domitian. 18mo. Lond., 1876. B 12 P 1

CAPITAL PUNISHMENT COMMISSION. Report of;
together with the Minutes of Evidence, and Appendix,
1867–68. Fol. Sydney, 1868. MF 10 Q 3 †

CAPNION (JOHN). [*See* REUCHLIN, JOHN.]

CAPPELLUS (JACOBUS). Sedis Romanæ. 1. Potestas.
2. Sanctitas. 3. Fides, sive Stellionatus. Sm. 4to.
Heilbergae, 1619. G 2 T 24

Vindiciæ pro Isaaco Casaubono. Sm. 4to. Francofurti,
1619. G 2 T 24

CAPPER (HENRY). South Australia; containing Hints to
Emigrants, Proceedings of the South Australian Company,
&c. 2nd ed. 8vo. Lond., 1838.* MD 2 Q 48

South Australia; containing the History of the Rise,
Progress, and Present State of the Colony, Hints to
Emigrants, &c. 3rd ed. 12mo. Lond., 1839.*
MD 2 Q 49

CAPPER (JOHN), F.R.A.S. Emigrant's Guide to Australia; containing the fullest particulars relating to the
recently discovered Gold-fields, &c. 2nd ed. 8vo. Liverpool, 1853. MD 2 R 26

Another copy. 8vo. Lond., 1857. MD 2 R 27

CAPPER (JOHN HENRY). Convicts: Two Reports relating
to the Convict Establishments at Portsmouth, Chatham,
Woolwich, and Bermuda. (Parl. Docs. 19.) Fol. Lond.,
1838. MF 4 ‡

CAPPER (RICHARD). An Episode: Batman and Fawkner;
Discovery of the River Yarra. 12mo. Melb., 1881.
MJ 2 R 15

Question for Electors! Why should we go to England to
borrow Money? a Lecture. 8vo. Melb., 1868. MJ 2 R 7

CAPPON (JAMES), M.A. Victor Hugo: a Memoir and a
Study. 8vo. Edinb., 1885. C 4 T 11

CAPRICORNUS. [*See* RANKEN, G.]

CAPRON (J. RAND), F.R.A.S. Aurorae: their Characters
and Spectra. 4to. Lond., 1879. A 3 U 17

CARADDAEG. [*See* THOMAS J. J.]

CARADOC OF LANCARVAN. History of Cambria.
[*See* LHUYD, H.]

CARBURI (MARIN), COMTE, CHEVALIER DE LASCARY.
Monument élevé à la Gloire de Pierre-le-Grand; ou, Relation des Travaux et des Moyens Méchaniques qui ont
été employés pour transporter à Pétersbourg un Rocher
de trois millions pesant. Fol. Paris, 1777. A 23 P 10 ‡

CARCANO (GIULIO). Teatro di Shakspeare. [*See* SHAKES-
PEARE, W.]

CARDALE (J. S.) King Alfred's Anglo-Saxon Version
of Boethius de Consolatione Philosophiae. [*See* BOETHIUS,
A. M. F. S.]

CARDANO (GIROLAMO). Life of Girolamo Cardano (Jerome Cardan), of Milan, Physician; by Henry Morley.
2 vols. 12mo. Lond., 1854. C 3 Q 1, 2

CARDERERA Y SOLANO (V.) Iconografía Española:
Coleccion de Retratos, Estatuas, Mausolos y demas, monu-
mentos inéditos de Reyes, Reinas, grandes Capitanes,
Escritores, etc.; desde el siglo XI hasta el XVII. Texto en
Español y Francés. 2 vols. El fol. Madrid, 1855–63.
B 12 P 25, 26 ‡

CARDIGAN (J. T. BRUDENELL), EARL OF. Trial of
before the House of Peers, for Felony, 16th February,
1841. Roy. 8vo. Lond., 1841. F 5 V 14

CARDONNE (M.) [*See* CABINET DES FÉES, 17.]

CARDONNEL (A. DE). Numismata Scotiæ; or, a Series
of Scottish Coinage, from the reign of William the Lion
to the Union. Roy. 4to. Edinb., 1786. A 2 R 3 †

CARDWELL (RT. HON. EDWARD). [*See* BUSBY, J., *and* CRISIS IN VICTORIA.]

CARDWELL (EDWARD). D.D. Lectures on the Coinage of the Greeks and Romans, delivered at the University of Oxford. 8vo. Oxford, 1832.　　　　A 13 R 35

CARELESS (JOHN). Writings of. [*See* BRITISH REFORMERS, 3.]

CARÊME (M. A.) Royal Parisian Pastrycook and Confectioner; edited by J. Porter. 8vo. Lond., 1834.　A 6 Q 26

CAREW (THOS.) Life and Poems of. [*See* CHALMERS, A.]

CAREY (EMILY J.) Shakespeare and Classical Antiquity. [*See* STAFFER, PROF. P.]

CAREY (MAJ.-GEN. GEORGE JACKSON), C.B. Narrative of the late War in New Zealand. 8vo. Lond., 1863.*
　　　　MB 2 P 25

CAREY (HENRY). Chrononhotonthologos—The Contrivances—The Honest Yorkshireman. [*See* BRITISH DRAMA 5.]

CAREY (HENRY CHARLES). The Past, the Present, and the Future. 2nd ed. 8vo. Lond., 1856.　　F 6 V 15

CAREY (JOHN), LL.D. Ainsworth's Latin Dictionary. [*See* AINSWORTH, R.]

CAREY (SIR PETER STAFFORD). An Introductory Lecture on the Study of English Law. 1838. 8vo. Lond., 1839.　　　　J 5 8 8

CAREY (REV. PROF. W.) Life of; by George Smith. 8vo. Lond., 1885.　　　　C 10 S 11
The Story of. [*See* MARSHMAN, J. C.]

CARISCH (OTTO). Grammatische Formenlehre der deutschen und rhätoromanischen Sprache für die romanischen Schulen Graubündens. 8vo. Chur, 1852. K 12 R 1

CARELESS (JOHN). Writings of. [*See* BRITISH REFORMERS 3.]

CARLETON (CAPT. GEORGE). Memoirs of (including Anecdotes of the War in Spain under the Earl of Peterborough); written by himself. 4th ed. 8vo. Edinb., 1809.　　　　C 10 Q 15

CARLETON (HUGH). Life of Rev. Henry Williams, Archdeacon of Waimate. 2 vols. 8vo. Auckland, 1874-77.　　　　MG 1 Q 11, 12

CARLETON (CAPT. JOHN WILLIAM), "CRAVEN." Recreations in Shooting; with some Account of the Game of the British Islands. 8vo. Lond., 1846.　　A 16 Q 29
Sporting Sketch-book. 8vo. Lond., 1842.　A 17 U 29
Walker's Manly Exercises. [*See* WALKER, D.]
Young Sportsman's Manual; or, Recreations in Shooting. New ed. Illustrated. 12mo. Lond., 1867. A 17 U 17

CARLETON (WILLIAM). Farm Ballads. Illustrated. Sm. 4to. Lond., 1879.　　　　H 7 S 22

CARLETON (WILLIAM). Traits and Stories of the Irish Peasantry. With Illustrations by W. H. Brooke, A.R.H.A. 4th ed. 5 vols. 12mo. Lond., 1836. J 10 P 5-9

CARLETON (WM.), LOVER (S.) AND HALL (MRS.) Characteristic Sketches of Ireland and the Irish. 12mo. Halifax. 1849.　　　　J 7 P 33

CARLETTI (J. T.) History of the Conquest of Tunis. [*See* TUNIS.]

CARLILE (REV. JAMES), D.D. Manual of the Anatomy and Physiology of the Human Mind. 12mo. Lond., 1851.　　　　G 13 T 18

CARLISLE (G.) [*See* MURRAY, R.]

CARLISLE (GEORGE WILLIAM FREDERICK), EARL OF. Diary in Turkish and Greek Waters. 3rd ed. 8vo. Lond., 1854.　　　　D 8 8 7
Two Letters on the Poetry of Pope; and on his own Travels in America. 8vo. (Pam. 25.) Lond., 1851. MJ 2 Q 13

CARLISLE (HENRY E.) Selections from the Correspondence of Abraham Hayward, Q.C., from 1834-84; with an Account of his Early Life. 2 vols. 8vo. Lond., 1886.　　　　C 3 T 10, 11

CARLL (LEWIS BUFFETT), A.M. Treatise on the Calculus of Variations. 8vo. Lond., 1885.　　A 10 T 19

CARLOS (DON), DE BOURBON. Career of, since the Death of Ferdinand VII; being a Chapter in the History of Charles V, by his Aide-de-Camp, the Baron de Los Valles. 8vo. Lond., 1835.　　　　C 10 Q 16
Court and Camp of Don Carlos. [*See* HONAN, M. B.]

CARLYLE (MRS. JANE WELSH). Letters and Memorials of. Prepared for Publication by Thomas Carlyle; edited by James Anthony Froude. 3 vols. 8vo. Lond., 1883.
　　　　C 10 R 45-47

CARLYLE (JOHN A.), M.D. Dante's Divine Comedy, The Inferno; a Literal Prose Translation. [*See* DANTE ALIGHIERI.]

CARLYLE (THOMAS). Bibliography of Carlyle. [*See* SHEPHERD, R. H.]
Carlyle, personally, and in his Writings; by D. Masson. 12mo. Lond., 1885.　　　　C 2 Q 10
Chartism: Past and Present. 8vo. Lond., 1858. J 6 8 1
Critical and Miscellaneous Essays. 6 vols. 8vo. Lond., 1869.　　　　J 6 8 4-9
Early Kings of Norway; also an Essay on the Portraits of John Knox. (With a General Index to the People's Edition of Thomas Carlyle's Works.) 12mo. Lond., 1875.*　　　　B 2 R 19
Early Letters of, 1814-26; edited by Charles Eliot Norton. 2 vols. 8vo. Lond., 1886.　　　C 4 T 6, 7

CARLYLE (THOMAS)—*continued.*

French Revolution: a History. 2nd ed. 3 vols. 8vo. Lond., 1839. B 9 P 29-31

German Romance: Specimens of its Chief Authors, with Biographical and Critical Notices. 4 vols. 8vo. Edinb., 1827. J 6 S 14-17

History of Friedrich II of Prussia, called Frederick the Great. 6 vols. 8vo. Lond., 1858-65. B 9 R 23-28

History of his Life in London, 1834-81; by James Anthony Froude. With Portrait. 2 vols. 8vo. Lond., 1884. C 10 R 43, 44

History of the First Forty Years of his Life, 1795-1835; by J. A. Froude. With Portrait. 2 vols. 8vo. Lond., 1882. C 10 R 41, 42

Latter Day Pamphlets. 8vo. Lond., 1850. J 6 S 3
-The Present Time—Model Prisons—Downing-street—Stump Orator—Parliaments—Hudson's Statue—Jesuitism.

Letters and Memorials of Jane Welsh Carlyle. [*See* CARLYLE, MRS. JANE WELSH.]

Life of Friedrich Schiller (1825); Life of John Sterling (1851): Two Biographies. 8vo. Lond., 1857. C 4 S 34

The Man and his Books, illustrated by Personal Reminiscences, Table-talk, and Anecdotes of himself and his Friends; by William Howie Wylie. 8vo. Lond., 1881. C 2 T 12

Memoirs of the Life and Writings of; with Personal Reminiscences from his Private Letters to numerous Correspondents, edited by Richard Herne Shepherd. 2 vols. 8vo. Lond., 1881. C 2 T 13, 14

Oliver Cromwell's Letters and Speeches. [*See* CROMWELL, O.]

On Heroes and Hero-Worship, and the Heroic in History. Six Lectures. 4th ed. 8vo. Lond., 1855. J 6 S 2

The Open Secret of his Life; by Henry Larkin. 8vo. Lond., 1886. C 10 R 48

Passages selected from the Writings of; with a Biographical Memoir by Thos. Ballantyne. 8vo. Lond., 1855. J 6 S 11

Past and Present. 8vo. Lond., 1843. J 6 S 10

Reminiscences; edited by James Anthony Froude. 2 vols. 8vo. Lond., 1881. C 2 T 10, 11

Reminiscences of My Irish Journey in 1849. 8vo. Lond., 1882. D 7 P 7

Sartor Resartus: the Life and Opinions of Herr Teufelsdröckh. 12mo. Lond., 1871. J 6 S 12

Some Personal Reminiscences of Carlyle; by Andrew James Symington. 8vo. Paisley, 1886. C 4 T 5

Tales; by Musæus, Tieck, Richter; translated from the German. [*See* MUSÆUS, J. K. A.]

Thomas Carlyle: an Essay; by Gen. Sir E. B. Hamley. 12mo. Edinb., 1881. C 2 P 2

[*See* EMERSON, R. W.]

CARMICHAEL (REV. HENRY), M.A. Compendious Latin Grammar for the use of the Students of the Australian College, Sydney, New South Wales. (Pam. D.) 4to. Sydney (n.d.) MJ 2 U 3

CARMICHAEL (REV. HENRY), M.A.—*continued.*

Hints relating to Emigrants and Emigration. 12mo. Lond., 1834. MD 4 Q 42

Introductory Lecture, delivered at the Opening of the Twelth Session of the Sydney Mechanics' School of Arts, 3rd of June, 1844. (Pam. 17.) Roy. 8vo. Sydney, 1844. MJ 2 Q 7

Another copy. (Pam. F.) MJ 2 S 3

CARNARVON (HENRY JOHN GEORGE HERBERT), EARL OF. Portugal and Gallicia; with a Review of the Social and Political State of the Basque Provinces, and a few Remarks on Recent Events in Spain. 2 vols. 8vo. Lond., 1836. D 8 P 28, 29

Another copy. 3rd ed. (H. and C. Lib.) 12mo. Lond., 1848. J 8 P 27

CARNE (JOHN). Letters from Switzerland and Italy during a late Tour. 8vo. Lond., 1834. D 8 T 17

Letters from the East. 3rd ed. 2 vols. 8vo. Lond., 1830. D 5 Q 44, 45

Lives of Eminent Missionaries. 3 vols. 12mo. Lond., 1832-38. G 13 T 25-27

Recollections of Travels in the East; forming a Continuation of the "Letters from the East." 8vo. Lond., 1830. D 5 Q 46

Syria, the Holy Land, and Asia Minor. Illustrated. 3 vols. (in 1) 4to. Lond., 1842. D 4 V 21

CARNEGIE (ANDREW). Round the World. 8vo. Lond., 1879. D 9 S 18

Triumphant Democracy; or, Fifty Years' March of the Republic. 8vo. Lond., 1886. F 12 P 1

CARNEGIE (WILLIAM), "MOORMAN." Practical Game Preserving; containing the fullest Directions for Rearing and Preserving both Winged and Ground Game, and Destroying Vermin. Illustrated. 8vo. Lond., 1884. A 29 U 29

CARNELLEY (THOMAS), D.Sc., &c. Physico-Chemical Constants: Melting and Boiling Point Tables. 2 vols. roy. 4to. Lond., 1885-87. A 2 Q 13, 14 †

CARNOT (LAZARE-NICOLAS MARGUERITE). Géométrie de Position. 4to. Paris, 1803. A 10 V 16

Réflections sur la Métaphysique du Calcul Infinitésimal. 2ᵉ ed. 8vo. Paris, 1813. A 10 R 34

[*See* LLOYD, E. M.]

CARNOTA (CONDE DA). Memoirs of Field-Marshal the Duke de Saldanha; with Selections from his Correspondence. 2 vols. 8vo. Lond., 1880. C 11 P 17, 18

CAROLINE (QUEEN CONSORT OF GREAT BRITAIN). Memoirs of; by J. H. Adolphus. 3 vols. 8vo. Lond., 1821-22. C 5 T 3-5

CAROLINE MATILDA (QUEEN OF DENMARK AND NORWAY). Life and Times of; by Sir C. F. Lascelles Wraxall, Bart. 3 vols. 8vo. Lond., 1864. C 10 P 20–22

Romance of Diplomacy : Historical Memoir of Queen Caroline Matilda of Denmark ; with Memoir, and a Selection from the Correspondence (Official and Familiar) of Sir R. M. Keith, K.B., by Mrs. Gillespie Smyth. 2 vols. 8vo. Lond., 1861. C 4 T 44, 45

CAROLUS MAGNUS (IMPERATOR). Opera omnia. [*See* MIGNE, J. P., SERIES LATINA, 97, 98.]

CARPANI (G. P.) [*See* CELLINI, B.]

CARPENTER (J. ESTLIN), M.A. Life and Work of Mary Carpenter. 8vo. Lond., 1879. C 2 T 15 [*See* TIELE, C. P.]

CARPENTER (JAMES), F.R.A.S. The Moon. [*See* NASMYTH, J.]

CARPENTER (MARY). Our Convicts. 2 vols. 8vo. Lond., 1864. MF 3 R 10, 11

The Life and Work of; by J. Estlin Carpenter, M.A. 8vo. Lond., 1879. C 2 T 15

CARPENTER (WILLIAM BENJAMIN), C.B., &c. Animal Physiology. New ed., thoroughly revised and partly re-written. 8vo. Lond., 1876. A 12 P 10

Mechanical Philosophy, Horology, and Astronomy. New ed. 8vo. Lond., 1857. A 11 Q 13

Mesmerism, Spiritualism, &c., historically and scientifically considered: two Lectures. 8vo. Lond.,1877. A 12 S 27

Physiology of Temperance and Total Abstinence : an Examination of the Effects of the excessive, moderate, and occasional use of Alcoholic Liquors on the Human System. 12mo. Lond., 1875. A 12 P 9

Principles of Human Physiology; edited by Henry Power, M.B., Lond., F.R.C.S. 8th ed. Lond., 1876. A 12 T 5

Principles of Mental Physiology, with their Applications to the Training and Discipline of the Mind, and the Study of the Mind. 8vo. Lond., 1874. A 12 Q 32

The Microscope and its Revelations. 5th ed., prepared with the assistance of H. J. Slack, F.G.S. Illustrated by twenty-five Plates and Wood Engravings. 8vo. Lond., 1875. A 17 T 5

Vegetable Physiology and Systematic Botany ; edited by Edwin Lankester, M.D., &c. 8vo. Lond.,1858. A 4 P 16

Zoology ; being a systematic Account of the general Structure, Habits, Instincts, and Uses of the principal Families of the Animal Kingdom. New ed., thoroughly revised by W. S. Dallas, F.L.S., &c. 2 vols. 8vo. Lond., 1857. A 14 Q 19, 20 [*See* TAYLOR, P. A.]

CARPMAEL (ALFRED AND EDWARD). Patent Laws of the World, collected, edited, and indexed. 8vo. Lond., 1885. F 10 S 20

CARR (REV. JOHN), M.A. Synopsis of Practical Philosophy. 2nd ed. 18mo. Lond., 1843. A 10 R 32

CARR (SIR JOHN). Caledonian Sketches ; or, a Tour through Scotland in 1807. 4to. Lond., 1809. D 6 V 4

CARR (JOSEPH WILLIAM COMYNS). Examples of Contemporary Art Etchings from representative Works, by living English and Foreign Artists; edited, with critical Notes. Fol. Lond., 1878. A 4 T 1 ‡

•Papers on Art. 8vo. Lond., 1885. A 8 P 22

CARR (LUCIEN). Mounds of the Mississippi Valley, historically considered. 4to. Camb., Mass., 1884. B 18 Q 8 ‡

CARR (O. A.) Reply to the Rev. J. Ballantyne's Tract on Baptism ; containing all his Arguments fully stated. 12mo. Melb. (n.d.) MJ 2 R 6

CARR (REV. WILLIAM). Dialect of Craven, in the West Riding of the County of York ; with a copious Glossary ; by " A Native of Craven." 2nd ed. 2 vols. 8vo. Lond., 1828. K 12 P 18, 19

CARREL (ARMAND), AND FOX (RT. HON. C. J.) History of the Counter-Revolution in England, for the re-establishment of Popery under Charles II ; and James II ; and History of the Reign of James II. 8vo. Lond., 1846. B 3 Q 1

CARREÑO (PROF. JUAN DE LA C.) Método para áprender á leer escribir y hablar el Inglese. [*See* PALENZUELA, PROF. R.]

CARRICK (J. D.) Life of Sir W. Wallace, of Elderslie. (Const. Misc.) 2 vols. 18mo. Edinb., 1830. K 10 Q 41, 42

CARRINGTON (GEORGE). Colonial Adventures and Experiences ; by " A University Man." 8vo. Lond., 1871.* MD 1 R 15

CARRINGTON (REV. HENRY). Translations from the Poems of Victor Hugo. [*See* HUGO, V. M.]

CARRINGTON (THOMAS). [*See* CLARKE, M. A. H.]

CARRUTHERS (REV. JAMES). History of Scotland, from the Earliest Period of the Scottish Monarchy to the Accession of the Stewart Family. 2 vols. 8vo. Edinb., 1826. B 13 R 28, 29

CARRUTHERS (JOHN), M.I.C.E. Communal and Commercial Economy : some Elementary Theorems of the Political Economy of Communal and Commercial Societies. 8vo. Lond., 1883. F 6 Q 15

CARRUTHERS (ROBERT), LL.D. Abbotsford Notanda. [*See* CHAMBERS, R.]

Chambers' Cyclopædia of English Literature. [*See* CHAMBERS, W. AND R.]

Life of Alexander Pope ; including Extracts from his Correspondence. 2nd ed., revised. 12mo. Lond., 1857. C 4 P 14 [*See* POPE, A.]

CARSTENSZ (JAN), AND GONZAL (J. E.) Twee Togten naar de Golf van Carpentaria, 1623 en 1756, benevens Iets over den Togt van G. Pool en Pieter Pietersz. 8vo. Amsterd., 1859. MD 5 V 6

CARTE (THOMAS), M.A. General History of England, from the Earliest Times to 1654. 4 vols. fol. Lond., 1747-55. B 15 T 13-16 ‡
Life of James, Duke of Ormond; containing an Account of the most remarkable Affairs of his Time, and particularly of Ireland under his Government. 6 vols. 8vo. Lond., 1851. C 10 V 42-47

CARTER (EDMUND). History of the University of Cambridge. 8vo. Lond., 1753. B 3 R 10

CARTER (MRS. ELIZABETH). Memoirs of the Life of; with a new edition of her Poems, &c., by the Rev. Montagu Pennington, M.A. 4th ed. 2 vols. 8vo. Lond., 1825. C 6 T 6, 7
Works of Epictetus. [*See* EPICTETUS.]

CARTER (JOHN), F.S.A. Ancient Architecture of England, including the Orders during the British, Roman, Saxon, and Norman Eras. Illustrated. In two Parts. Roy. fol. Lond., 1795-1816. A 1 R 1 ‡
Specimens of the Ancient Sculpture and Painting now remaining in England, from the Earliest Period to the Reign of Henry VIII. Fol. Lond., 1838. A 2 P 25 ‡
Specimens of Gothic Architecture and Ancient Buildings in England. 4 vols. sq. 18mo. Lond., 1839. A 2 R 11-14

CARTER (JOHN). Memoir of; by William James Dampier, M.A. Illustrated. Roy. 8vo. Lond., 1875. C 8 V 3

CARTER (S. G.) Victoria, the British "El Dorado"; or, Melbourne in 1869; by "A Colonist of Twenty Years' Standing." 12mo. Lond., 1870.* MD 2 Q 45

CARTERET (CAPT. P.) [*See* COOK, CAPT. J.; HAWKESWORTH, J.; AND PARKINSON, S.]

CARTERET-BISSON (CAPT. FREDERICK SHIRLEY DUMARESQ DE). [*See* BISSON, CAPT. F. S. D. DE CARTERET-]

CARTWRIGHT (CAPT.) Criminal Management. (Pam. Dd.) 8vo. Lond., 1865. F 12 P 22

CARTWRIGHT (FRANCES DOROTHY). Life and Correspondence of Major Cartwright. 2 vols. 8vo. Lond., 1826. C 10 Q 17, 18

CARTWRIGHT (JAMES J.) The Wentworth Papers. [*See* STRAFFORD, EARL OF.]

CARTWRIGHT (MAJOR JOHN). Life and Correspondence of; edited by his Niece, Frances Dorothy Cartwright. 2 vols. 8vo. Lond., 1826. C 10 Q 17, 18

CARTWRIGHT (JULIA). Mantegna and Francia (Great Artists). 8vo. Lond., 1881. C 3 T 43

CARTWRIGHT (REV. ROBERT). Catalogue of Books, principally Theological, the property of the Rev. Robt. Cartwright. 8vo. Sydney, 1838. MK 1 Q 13

CARTWRIGHT (WILLIAM). Life and Poems of. [*See* CHALMERS, A.]

CARUS (DR. CARL GUSTAVE). King of Saxony's Journey through England and Scotland in the year 1844; translated by S. C. Davison. 8vo. Lond., 1846. D 7 T 35

CARUS (J. VICTOR). Geschichte der Zoologie. (Geschichte der Wissenschaften.) 8vo. München, 1872. A 17 V 26 [*See* DARWIN, C.]

CARUS (REV. WILLIAM), M.A. Memoirs of the Rev. Chas. Simeon, M.A. With a Selection from his Writings and Correspondence. 3rd ed. 8vo. Lond., 1848. C 2 T 37

CARUSO (GIO. BATTISTA). Memorie Istoriche di quanto, è accaduto in Sicilia, dal tempo de' suoi primieri Abitatori sino alla coronazione del Re Vittorio Amedeo. Seconda Edizione. 6 vols. 4to. Palermo, 1742-45. B 14 Q 18-23 ‡

CARY (HENRY), M.A. Herodotus: a New and Literal Version from the Text of Baehr. [*See* HERODOTUS.]
Lives of the Fathers of the Church. [*See* CAVE, W.]
Memorials of the Great Civil War in England, 1646-52. 2 vols. 8vo. Lond., 1842. B 3 S 17, 18
Memoir of the Rev. Henry Francis Cary, M.A., Translator of Dante; with his Literary Journal and Letters, by his son. 2 vols. 8vo. Lond., 1847. C 2 U 16, 17
Odyssey of Homer; translated into English Prose. [*See* HOMER.]

CARY (REV. HENRY FRANCIS), M.A. Memoir of; with his Literary Journal and Letters, by his son, Henry Cary M.A. 2 vols. 8vo. Lond., 1847. C 2 U 16, 17

CASAUBON (ISAAC). Ad Frontonem Dvcævm S. F. Theologum Epistola; in qua de Apologiâ disseritur communi Iesuitarum nomine ante aliquot menses Lutetiæ Parisiorum edita. Sm. 4to. Lond., 1611. G 6 8 5
Animadversioni Athenaei Deipnosophistarum, libri quindecim. [*See* ATHENÆUS OF NAUCRATIS.]
Casavboniana sive Isaaci Casavboni varia de Scriptoribus runc primum erutae à Jo. Christophoro Wolfio. 12mo. Hamburg, 1710. G 10 P 19
De Rebvs Sacris et Ecclesiasticis, Exercitationes XVI. 8vo. Genovae, 1655. G 6 8 3
De Satyrica Græcorvm poesi, et Romanorum satira, libri duo. 8vo. Paris, 1605. J 16 T 2
Ephemerides cum Praefatione et Notis. 2 vols. 8vo. Oxonii, 1850. G 6 8 1, 2
Epistolæ, insertis ad easdem responsionibus, quotquot hactenus reperiri potuerunt, secundum seriem temporis accurate digestæ. Fol. Rotterdami, 1709. J 17 U 8
Isaac Casaubon, 1559-1614; by Mark Pattison. 8vo. Lond., 1875. C 10 8 10
The Originall of Idolatries; or, the Birth of Heresies, translated into English by Abraham Darcie. Sm. 4to. Lond., 1624. G 6 8 4
Vindiciæ pro Casaubono. [*See* CAPPELLUS, J.]

CASAUBON (MERIC), D.D. Epistolae. [*See* CASAUBON, I.]

CASEY (PROF. JOHN), LL.D., &c. On a new Form of Tangential Equation. (Roy. Soc. Pubs., 5.) 4to. Lond., 1878.   A 11 P 6 †

CASH (MARTIN). Adventures of, in company with Kavanagh and Jones; edited by James Lester Burke. 8vo. Hobart, 1870.   MF 1 Q 5
Another Copy.   MC 1 Q 22

CASPER (JOHANN LUDWIG), M.D. Hard-book of the Practice of Forensic Medicine based upon personal experience; translated by G. W. Balfour, M.D. 4 vols. 8vo. Lond., 1861–65.   F 10 T 4–7

CASS (B.) Louis Napoleon, Historical and Prophetical : a Lecture. 12mo. Melb., 1865.   MJ 2 P 31

CASSAGNAC (ADOLPHE GRANIER DE). [*See* GRANIER DE CASSAGNAC, A.]

CASSAL (PROF. CHARLES), LL.D., AND KARCHER (PROF. THÉODORE), LL.B. Modern French Reader. Prose. Senior Course. 2nd ed. Lond., 1875.   K 11 V 34
Modern French Reader. Prose. Junior Course. 5th ed. 8vo. Lond., 1877.   K 11 V 33

CASSAS (L. F.) Travels in Istria and Dalmatia; drawn up from the Itinerary of L. F. Cassas, by Joseph Lavallée. Translated from the French. 8vo. Lond., 1805. D 6 T 16

CASSELL (JOHN). Art Treasures Exhibition, containing Engravings of the principal Masterpieces of the English, Dutch, Flemish, French, and German Schools; with Biographical Sketches. Imp. 8vo. Lond., 1858.   A 8 T 17
Cassell's Historical, Political, and Commercial Map of Europe. [*See* YOUNG, F.]
History of the War between France and Germany, 1870–71; edited by E. Ollier. 2 vols. imp. 8vo. Lond., 1872.   B 8 V 4, 5
Illustrated History of the Russo-Turkish War. [*See* OLLIER, E.]

CASSELL'S BIBLE DICTIONARY. Illustrated. 2 vols. imp. 8vo. Lond., 1869.   ⟨ 18 S 3, 4

CASSELL'S BIOGRAPHICAL DICTIONARY; containing Memoirs of the most Eminent Men and Women of all Ages and Countries. Imp. 8vo. Lond., 1869. C 11 V 15

CASSELL'S LIBRARY OF ENGLISH LITERATURE; selected, edited, and arranged by Henry Morley. 5 vols. imp. 8vo. Lond., 1876–82.   J 2 U 1–5
  1. Shorter English Poems.
  2. Illustrations of English Religion.
  3. English Plays.
  4. Shorter Works in English Prose.
  5. Sketches of longer Works in English Verse and Prose.

CASSELL'S OLD AND NEW EDINBURGH. [*See* GRANT, J.]

CASSELL'S POPULAR EDUCATOR : Complete Encyclopædia of Elementary, Advanced, and Technical Education. New ed. 6 vols. 4to. Lond., 1881–83. K 9 U 1–6

CASSELL'S POPULAR NATURAL HISTORY. Illustrated. 4 vols. (in 2) imp. 8vo. Lond., 1865.
                                                      A 14 V 45, 46

CASSELLS (JAMES PATTERSON), M.D. Deafmutism. [*See* HARTMANN, DR. A.]

CASSELS (WALTER R.) Cotton : an Account of its Culture in the Bombay Presidency. Roy. 8vo. Bombay, 1862.   A 1 T 16

CASSIANUS (JOANNES). Opera omnia. [*See* MIGNE, J. P., SERIES LATINA, 49, 50.]

CASSIM (MAHOMET). The Case of. 4to. Sydney, 1863.   MJ 2 U 3

CASSIN (JOHN). Mammalogy and Ornithology. (United States Exploring Expedition.) Roy. 4to. Philad., 1858.   A 31 P 9 ‡
Atlas to above. Imp. fol. Philad., 1858.   A 31 R 2 ‡

CASSINO (SAMUEL E.) International Scientists' Directory. 8vo. Boston, 1882.   E

CASSIODORUS (MAGNUS AURELIUS). Letters of Cassiodorus; being a condensed Translation of the Variæ Epistolæ of Magnus Aurelius Cassiodorus, Senator; with an Introduction by Thomas Hodgkin. 8vo. Lond., 1886.   C 10 S 4
Opera omnia. [*See* MIGNE, J. P., SERIES LATINA, 69, 70.]

CASSIUS. [*See* DION CASSIUS.]

CASTELAR (EMILIO). Old Rome and New Italy (Recuerdos de Italia); translated by Mrs. Arthur Arnold. 8vo. Lond., 1873.   D 7 T 36

CASTELL (EDMUND), D.D., &c. Lexicon Heptaglotton: Hebraicum, Chaldaicum, Syriacum, Samaritanum, Æthiopicum, Arabicum, conjunctim; et Persicum separatim. 2 vols. fol. Lond., 1669.   K 35 Q 7, 8 ‡

CASTELLA (HUBERT DE). John Bull's Vineyard: Australian Sketches. 12mo. Melb., 1886.   MA 1 P 15
Les Squatters Australiens. 12mo. Paris, 1861. MD 4 P 33

CASTELLANE (P. DE), COMTE. Military Life in Algeria. 2 vols. 8vo. Lond., 1853.   D 18 11, 12

CASTELLANI (AUGUSTO). Gems: Notes and Extracts; translated from the Italian, by Mrs. John Brogden. 8vo. Lond., 1871.   A 9 Q 20

CASTELLI (GABRIELLE LANCELOT). Siciliæ populorum et urbium Regum quoque et tyrannorum veteres Nummi Saracenorum epocham antecedentes. Fol. Panormi, 1781–91.   A 4 U 11 ‡

CASTELNAU (FRANCIS DE). Expédition dans les Parties
Centrales de l'Amérique du Sud, de Rio de Janeiro à Lima,
et de Lima au Para, pendant les années 1843–47. Histoire
du Voyage. 6 vols. 8vo. Paris, 1850–51. D 4 Q 17–22

Planches. 13 vols. 4to. Paris, 1852–59. D 3 V 6–18

1, 2. Cilouis Andina : Essai d'une Flore de la Région Alpine des
Cordillères de l'Amérique du Sud ; par H. A. Weddell, M.D.
. Botanique.
3. Anatomie ; par Paul Gervais.
5. Animaux Nouveaux ou Rares ; Reptiles ; par A. Guichenot
6. Mollusques ; par H. Hupé.
7. Poissons ; par le Comte Francis de Castelnau.
8. Oiseaux ; par O. des Murs.
9. Mammifères ; par Paul Gervais.
10. Myriapodes et Scorpions ; par Paul Gervais.
11. Antiquités des Incas et autres Peuples Anciens. (Les
Planches Lithographiées par Champin).
12. Vues et Scènes.
13. Entomologie ; par H. Lucas.

Atlases. 2 vols. fol. Paris, 1852–54 D 4 S 7, 8 ‡
1. Itinéraires et Coupe Géologique, sur les Observations de
Francis de Castelnau et d'Eugène D'Osery.
2. Géographie.

CASTILLO (BERNAL DIAZ DEL), CONQUISTADOR. [*See* DIAZ
DEL CASTILLO, B.]

CASTLE (EGERTON), M.A. Schools and Masters of Fence,
from the Middle Ages to the Eighteenth Century. 4to.
Lond., 1885. A 15 U 17

CASTLE (J. FRED.) The Anglo-Israelite ; with an Illustrative Map. 8vo. Sydney, 1880. MG 1 Q 19

CASTLE (S. N.) Account of the Visit of the French
Frigate L'Artemise to the Sandwich Islands, July, 1839.
8vo. Honolulu, 1839. MJ 2 P 39

CASTLEREAGH (ROBERT STEWART), VISCOUNT. [*See*
LONDONDERRY, MARQUESS OF.]

CASTRO (GUILLEN DE). Some Account of the Lives and
Writings of Lope Felix de Vega Carpio, and Guillem de
Castro ; by Henry Richard, Lord Holland. 2 vols. 8vo.
Lond., 1817. C 3 P 42, 43

CASTRO (DOM JOHN DE), FOURTH VICEROY OF INDIA.
Life of ; by Jacinto, Fierie de Andrada ; written in Por-
tuguese, and by Sr. Peter Wyche, Knt., translated into
English. Fol. Lond., 1664. C 7 V 46

CASTRO (THOMAS). The Queen against Thomas Castro.
[*See* TICHBORNE TRIAL.]

CASWALL (ALFRED). Hints from the Journal of an Australian Squatter. 8vo. Lond., 1843. MD 5 Q 34

CATAFAGO (JOSEPH). English and Arabic Dictionary,
in two Parts, Arabic and English, and English and Arabic.
2nd ed. 8vo. Lond., 1873. K 15 P 13

CATALOGUES OF BOOKS.
Catalogues of Books sold by Black, Kingsbury, Parbury,
and Allen. 8vo. London, 1822. K 7 S 1

Books published by Black, Young and Young. 8vo.
Lond., 1824. K 7 S 4

Catalogue of Books now selling by J. Laycock. 8vo.
Lond., 1824. K 7 S 1

Catalogue of Books [sold] by J. Arnould. 8vo. Lond.,
1829. K 7 S 1

Catalogue of Books, part of the Stock of A. K. Newman
and Co. 8vo. Lond., 1834. K 7 S 1

General Catalogue of Books now on sale by Harding,
Triphook, and Lepard. 8vo. Lond., 1824. K 7 S 2

Catalogue of English Theology on sale by Howell and
Stewart. 8vo. Lond., 1827. K 7 S 2

Catalogue of Standard English Authors (Ancient and
Modern) on sale by W. Dawson and Sons. 8vo. Lond.
(n.d.) K 7 R 51

Jurisprudence : Catalogue des Livres provenant en partie
de la Bibliothèque de Feu M. J. de Bosch Kemper. 8vo.
Amst., 1884. K 7 S 14

David Nutt's Catalogue. Foreign Theology, &c. 8vo.
Lond., 1884. K 7 S 3

CATALOGUS BIBLIOTHECÆ BUNAVIANÆ. Ed.
J. M. Franckius. 3 vols. (in 6) 4to. Lipsiæ, 1750–56.
K 8 R 1–6

CATARRH IN SHEEP BILL. Report from the Committee on the Catarrh in Sheep Bill ; with the Minutes of
Evidence, and Replies to Circular Letter. Fol. Sydney,
1888. MF 4 ‡

CATCHPOLE (MARGARET). History of. [*See* COBBOLD, R.]

CATES (WILLIAM L. R.) Dictionary of General Biography.
2nd ed., with a Supplement completing the work to the
Present Time. 8vo. Lond., 1875. C 1 1 S 6

Supplement to Dictionary of General Biography, brought
down to the end of 1884. 8vo. Lond., 1885. C 1 1 S 7

Encyclopædia of Chronology. [*See* WOODWARD, B. B.]

Biographical Treasury. [*See* MAUNDER, S.]

CATHARINE OF ARAGON (QUEEN). History of. [*See*
DIXON, W. H.]

CATHARINE II (EMPRESS OF RUSSIA). Anecdotes of.
[*See* POTEMKIN, PRINCE G. A.]

Life of ; an enlarged Translation from the French, by William Tooke. 3 vols. 8vo. Lond., 1798. C 6 R 27–29

Memoirs of ; written by herself. Translated from the
French. 8vo. Lond., 1859. C 2 U 18

Correspondance de Voltaire avec l'Impératrice de Russie.
[*See* VOLTAIRE, F. M. A. DE.]

CATHEDRAL CHURCHES of England and Wales,
Descriptive Historical Pictorial. 4to. Lond., 1884.
A 2 T 20

CATHOLIC ALMANAC (The). Catholic Almanac and Directory, for the years 1854, 1860, 1861. 3 vols. (in 1). 12mo. Sydney, 1854–61.　　　　　　　ME 4 R

CATHOLIC ASSOCIATION. Annual Reports of the Central Council of the Catholic Association. 8vo. Sydney, 1869–71.　　　　　　　MG 1 Q 17

CATHOLIC ASSOCIATION REPORTER (The). Vols. 1 and 2. 8vo. Sydney, 1870–71.　　　　　MG 1 Q 17

CATHOLIC EDUCATION. Pastoral Letter of the Archbishop and Bishops exercising jurisdiction in New South Wales. (Pam. Br.) 8vo. Sydney, 1879.　　MG 1 Q 35

CATHOLIC EMANCIPATION BILL. Speeches on. [*See* HISTORICAL PAMPHLETS.]

CATHOLICUS. [*See* EDUCATION.]

CATLEY (REV. S. R.) Remarks on the Defence of his Edition of Fox's Martyrology. [*See* MAITLAND, REV. S. R.]

CATLIN (GEORGE). Breath of Life; or, Mal-respiration and its Effects upon the Enjoyments and Life of Man. (Man-graph.) 8vo. Lond., 1862.　　A 12 R 33

Illustrations of the Manners, Customs, and Condition of the North American Indians. Illustrated. 10th ed. 2 vols. roy. 8vo. Lond., 1866.　　　　　　　Libr.

Another copy. 2 vols. roy. 8vo. Lond., 1876. D 3 U 19, 20

Letters and Notes on the Manners, Customs, and Condition of the North American Indians, 1832–39. Illustrated. 2 vols. roy. 8vo. Lond., 1841.　D 3 U 17, 18

Lifted and Subsided Rocks of America, with their Influences on the Oceanic, Atmospheric, and Land Currents, and the Distribution of Races. 8vo. Lond., 1870.　　　　　　　A 9 Q 31

Notes of Eight Years' Travels and Residence in Europe with his North American Indian Collection. 3rd ed. 2 vols. 8vo. Lond., 1848.　　　　　D 7 S 20, 21

O Kee-Pa; a Religious Ceremony; and other Customs of the Mandans. Illustrated. Roy. 8vo. Lond., 1867.　A 2 P 14

Shut your Mouth and Save your Life. Illustrated. 7th ed. 8vo. Lond., 1878.　　　　　　　A 12 Q 14

CATNACH (JAMES). Life and Times of James Galmuch (late of Seven Dials), Ballad monger; by Charles Hindley. Woodcuts by Bewick. 8vo. Lond., 1878.　C 10 T 21

CATON (JOHN DEAN), LL.D. Antelope and Deer of America: a Treatise upon the Natural History of the Antilocapra and Cervidæ of North America. Roy. 8vo. New York, 1877.　　　　　　　A 15 P 3

CATTERMOLE (GEORGE). Evenings at Haddon Hall. Illustrated. [*See* CALABRELLA, BARONESS DE.]

CATTERMOLE (REV. RICHARD), B.D. History of the Great Civil War of Charles I and the Parliament 2 vols. 8vo. Lond., 1845.　　　　　B 6 T 7, 8

CATULLUS (CAIUS VALERIUS). Commentary on. [*See* ELLIS, PROF. R.]

Opera omnia ex Editione F. G. Doeringii; cum Notis et Interpretatione in usum Delphini. Curante A. J. Valpy. 2 vols. 8vo. Lond.,1822.　　　J 13 P 24, 25

Erotica. The Poems of Catullus and Tibullus and the Vigil of Venus: a Literal Prose Translation, with Notes; by Walter K. Kelly. 8vo. Lond., 1878.　　H 5 S 30

CAULFIELD (JAMES). Book of Wonderful Characters. [*See* WILSON, H.]

The Court of Queen Elizabeth. [*See* NAUNTON, SIR R.]

Portraits, Memoirs, and Characters of Remarkable Persons, from the Revolution in 1688 to the end of the Reign of George II. 4 vols. 8vo. Lond., 1819–20.　C 21 S 1-4

[*See* COLLECTION OF FOUR HUNDRED PORTRAITS.]

CAULFIELD (RICHARD), LL.D., &c. Annals of St. Fin Barre's Cathedral, Cork. 12mo. Cork, 1871. B 11 P 6

Council Book of the Corporation of Cork, 1609–43, and 1690–1800. Sm. 4to. Guildford, 1876.　B 11 R 10

Council Book of the Corporation of Kinsale, 1652–1800. Sm. 4to. Guildford, 1879.　　　　B 11 R 12

Council Book of the Corporation of Youghal, 1610–59, 1666–87, and 1690–1800. Sm. 4to. Guildford, 1878.　　　　　　　B 11 R 11

CAULFIELD (SOPHIA F. A.), AND SAWARD (BLANCHE C.) Dictionary of Needlework: an Encyclopædia of Artistic, Plain, and Fancy Needlework. 4to. Lond., 1882.　　　　　　　K 17 U 22

Another copy. 2nd ed. 4to. Lond., 1885.　K 17 U 23

CAULINCOURT (ARMAND AUGUSTIN LOUIS DE), DUKE OF VICENZA. [*See* VICENZA, DUKE OF.]

CAUSES CÉLÈBRES et Intéressantes; avec les Jugemens qui les ont décidées. Recueillies par M. Gayot de Pitaval. 22 vols. 12mo. La Haye, 1735–45.　　F 1 P 1-22

CAUTLEY (COL. SIR PROBY THOMAS). Notes and Memoranda on the Water Courses in the Doyra Doon, North-Western Provinces. Fol. Calcutta, 1845.　　E [*See* FALCONER, H.]

CAVAGNARI (MAJ. SIR P. LOUIS NAPOLEON), K.C.B., &c. Life and Career of Major Sir Pierre Louis Napoleon Cavagnari, C.S.I., K.C.B., British Envoy at Cabul; by Kally Prosono Dey. 8vo. Calcutta, 1881.　　C 5 V 6

CAVALCASELLE (GIOVANNI BATTISTA.) Raphael: his Life and Works. [*See* CROWE, J. A.]

Titian: his Life and Times. [*See* CROWE, J. A.]

CAVE (CANON WILLIAM), D.D., &c. Lives of the most Eminent Fathers of the Church that flourished in the First Four Centuries; revised by Henry Cary, M.A. 3 vols. 8vo. Oxford, 1840.   G 4 R 1-3

Primitive Christianity; or, the Religion of the Ancient Christians in the First Ages of the Gospel.   8vo. Oxford, 1840.   G 4 R 4

Scriptorum Ecclesiasticorum Historia Literaria, a Christo Nato usque ad Sæculum XIV, Facili Methodo digesta. 2 vols. fol. Oxonii, 1740-43.   K 22 Q 5, 6 †

CAVE (L. W.) [*See* BURN, RICHARD.]

CAVE-BROWNE (REV. J.), M.A. Lambeth Palace and its Associations. Illustrated. 8vo. Edinb., 1882.
A 6 S 43

CAVELER (WILLIAM). Select Specimens of Gothic Architecture. 4to. Lond., 1835.   A 2 T 24

CAVENAGH (GENERAL SIR ORFEUR), K.C.S.I. Reminiscences of an Indian Official. 8vo. Lond., 1884.
C 3 T 22

CAVENDISH (GEORGE). Life of Cardinal Wolsey; with Notes and other Illustrations, by S. W. Singer, F.S.A. 2nd ed. 8vo. Lond., 1827.   C 10 P 41

Negotiations of Thos. Woolsey; containing his Life and Death. Sm. 4to. Lond., 1641.   C 3 P 46

CAVENDISH (HON. HENRY), F.R.S. Electrical Researches of; written between 1771 and 1781; edited, from the original Manuscripts in the possession of the Duke of Devonshire, K.G., by J. Clerk Maxwell, F.R.S. 8vo. Cambridge, 1879.   A 5 U 23

CAVENDISH (WILLIAM), DUKE OF NEWCASTLE. [*See* NEWCASTLE, DUKE OF.]

CAVENDISH SOCIETY (THE). Publications of, 29 vols. 8vo. and Atlas 4to. Lond., 1848-72. E.

CAVERLY (COL. ROBERT BOODEY). History of the Indian Wars of New England, with Eliot the Apostle. 8vo. Boston, 1882.   B 1 Q 49

Life and Labors of John Eliot, the Apostle, among the Indian Nations of New England. 8vo. Boston, 1882.
B 1 Q 49

CAVOLEAU (M.) Œnologie Française; ou, Statistique de tous les Vignobles et de toutes les Boissons Vineuses et Spiritueses de la France, suivie de considérations générales sur la Culture de la Vigne. 8vo. Paris, 1827.   A 1 Q 2

CAVOUR (CAMILLO BENSO DI), CONTÉ. Discorsi Palamentari. 11 vols. imp. 8vo. Torino, 1863-72.   F 5 V 1-11

His Life and Career; by B. H. Cooper. 12mo. Lond., 1860.   C 2 P 3

CAWTHORNE (JAMES). Life and Poems of. [*See* JOHNSON, S., *and* CHALMERS, A.]

CAXTON (WILLIAM). Biography and Typography of William Caxton, England's First Printer; by William Blades. 8vo. Lond., 1877.   C 10 S 30

Caxton Celebration, 1877: Catalogue of the Loan Collection of Antiquities, Curiosities, and Appliances connected with the Art of Printing, South Kensington; Edited by George Bullen, Esq., F.S.A. 8vo. Lond., 1877.   K 7 S 20

Game and Playe of the Chesse, 1474. Verbatim Reprint of the first edition. 8vo. Lond., 1883.   A 17 W 27

CAYLEY (PROF. ARTHUR A.), F.R.S. Addition to Memoir on the Transformation of Elliptic Functions. (Roy. Soc. Pubs., 6.) 4to. Lond., 1879.   A 11 P 7 †

Memoir on Prepotentials. (Roy. Soc. Pub., 2.) 4to. Lond., 1876.   A 11 P 3 †

On the Bi-circular Quartic. (Roy. Soc. Pubs., 4.) 4to. Lond., 1878.   A 11 P 5 †

Tenth Memoir on Quantics. (Roy. Soc. Pubs., 6.) 4to. Lond., 1879.   A 11 P 7 †

CAYLEY (C. B.), B.A. Introduction to the Grammar of the Romance Languages. [*See* DIEZ, F.]

CAYLEY (WILLIAM), M.D., &c. On some points in the Pathology and Treatment of Typhoid Fever. (Croonian Lectures.) 8vo. Lond., 1880.   A 12 Q 44

CAYLUS (C.), COMTE DE. Les Féeries Nouvelles.—Les Nouveaux Contes Orientaux, &c. [*See* CABINET DES FÉES, 24, 25.]

CAZALET (REV. W. W.), M.A. History of the Royal Academy of Music. 8vo. Lond., 1854.   B 14 S 22

CAZENAVE (P. L. ALPHÉE), AND SCHEDEL (H.E.) Manual of Diseases of the Skin; with Notes and Additions by Thos. H. Burgess, M.D. 12mo. Lond., 1842. A 12 P 16

CAZIN (ACHILLE). Phenomena and Laws of Heat; translated and edited by Elihu Rich. 12mo. Lond., 1868.   A 5 S 26

CAZOTTE (J.) [*See* VEILLÉES PERSANES, LES.]

CEBUSKY (ANTON). Kurzgefasste Grammatik der böhmischen Sprache. 6° auflage. 8vo. Wien, 1877.
K 12 R 32

CECIL (C.) Commercial Morality in Sydney. (Pam. E.) 4to. Sydney, 1863.   MJ 2 S 2

Petition of, to the Legislative Assembly of New South Wales, 2nd February, 1864. Fol. Sydney, 1864.   MF 10 Q 3 †

CECIL (GEN. SIR EDWARD), VISCOUNT WIMBLEDON. [*See* WIMBLEDON, VISCOUNT.]

CECIL (REV. RICHARD). Remains of; with a View of his Character by the Rev. Josiah Pratt, B.D., &c. 12th ed. 12mo. Lond., 1841.   G 8 P 15

CECIL (SIR ROBERT), EARL OF SALISBURY. Life of. [*See*
MACKINTOSH, SIR J.]

Secret Correspondence of Sir Robert Cecil with James VI,
King of Scotland. 8vo. Edinb., 1766.   C 2 P 4

CECIL (WILLIAM). [*See* BURGHLEY, LORD.]

CÉCILE (SAINTE) et la Société Romaine. [*See* GUÉRANGER,
DOM P.]

CEDRENUS (GEORGIUS). Compendium Historiarum. [*See*
MIGNE, J. J., SERIES GRÆCA. 121, 122, *and* BYZANTINÆ
HIST. SCRIPT.]

CELEBRATED TRIALS. [*See* TRIALS.]

CELESTIN III (HYACINTO ORSINI), PAPA. Epistolæ et
Privilegia. [*See* MIGNE, J. P., SERIES LATINA, 206.]

CELLARIUS (CHRISTOPH). Notitia Orbis Antiqui, sive
Geographia Plenior. 2 vols. 4to. Camb., 1703–6.
                                                   D 12 V 21, 22

CELLIEZ (MLLE. ADELAIDE DE). Les Reines de France.
Nouvelle édition, entièrement revue. Imp. 8vo. Paris,
1860.   B 8 V 3

CELLINI (BENVENUTO). Life of; written by himself;
translated by Thomas Nugent. (Autobiog., 16, 17.) 2
vols. (in 1) 18mo. Lond., 1828.   C 1 P 13

Memoirs of: written by himself; with Notes and Observations of G. P. Carlani; translated by Thomas Roscoe.
12mo. Lond., 1850.   C 1 R 9

CENNINI (CENNINO). Treatise on Painting, written in
the year 1437; translated by Mrs. Merrifield. Roy. 8vo.
Lond., 1844.   A 8 Q 26

CENTLIVRE (MRS. SUSANNAH). Bold Stroke for a Wife:
a Comedy. (Bell's Brit. Theatre.) 18mo. Lond., 1791.
                                                   H 2 P 23

Another copy. (Brit. Theatre.) 12mo. Lond., 1808.
                                                   H 1 P 11

Another copy. (New Eng. Theatre.) 12mo. Lond.,
1783.   H 4 P 16

Another copy. [*See* BRIT. DRAMA, 4.]

The Busy Body: a Comedy. (Brit. Theatre.) 12mo.
Lond., 1808.   H 1 P 11

Another copy. (New Eng. Theatre.) 12mo. Lond.,
1782.   H 4 P 16

Another copy. (Bell's Brit. Theatre.) 18mo. Lond.,
1791.   H 2 P 7

Another copy. [*See* BRIT. DRAMA, 1.]

The Wonder a Woman keeps a Secret: a Comedy. (Bell's
Brit. Theatre.) 18mo. Lond., 1792.   H 2 P 8

Another copy. (Brit. Theatre.) 12mo. Lond., 1808.
                                                   H 1 P 11

Another copy. (New Eng. Theatre.) 12mo. Lond.,
1787.   H 4 P 26

Another copy. [*See* BRIT. DRAMA, 4.]

CENTRAL ASIA. Correspondence respecting the Affairs
of Asia. Fol. Lond., 1884–85.   F 36 Q 12 ‡

Circular Despatch addressed by Prince Gortchakow to
Russian Representatives abroad. Fol. Lond., 1885.
                                                   F 36 Q 12 ‡

CENTRAL SOCIETY OF EDUCATION : Papers.
3 vols. 8vo. Lond., 1837–39.   G 17 P 3–5

CERATINUS (JACOBUS). De solo literarvm præsertim
Græcarvm, libellvs. 18mo. Genevae, 1529.   K 11 S 43

CÉRÉMONIAL à l'usage de l'Église de Toulouse. 12mo.
Toulouse, 1821.   G 9 Q 15

CEREMONIALS for the Installation of Knights, and at
Coronations. Unique Collections of. Fol. Lond., 1756–
1827.   B 15 T 6 ‡

CERES. [*See* FIJI.]

CERVANTES SAAVEDRA (MIGUEL DE). Achieve-
ments of the Ingenious Gentleman, Don Quixote de la
Mancha: a Translation based on that of Peter Anthony
Motteux. 2 vols. 8vo. Lond., 1882.   J 11 R 7, 8

Don Quichotte de la Manche: traduit de l'Espagnol. [*See*
FLORIAN, J. P. C. DL.]

Exemplary Novels of: translated from the Spanish, by
Walter K. Kelly. 8vo. Lond., 1881.   J 8 R 19

Galatea: a Pastoral Romance; literally translated from
the Spanish, by Gordon Willoughby James Gyll, Esq.
8vo. Lond., 1867.   H 5 S 33

Story of Cervantes; by Amelia B. Edwards. 12mo. Lond.,
1863.   C 2 P 5

The Ingenious Gentleman, Don Quixote de la Mancha : a
Translation ; with Introduction and Notes, by John Ormsby.
4 vols. 8vo. Lond., 1885.   J 2 Q 11–14

Wit and Wisdom of Don Quixote. With a Biographical
Sketch of Cervantes by Emma Thompson. 18mo. Lond.,
1882.   J 7 P 34

CESARESCO (COUNTESS EVELYN MARTINENGO). Essays
in the Study of Folk-songs. 8vo. Lond., 1886.   H 7 S 25

CESNOLA (MAJOR ALESSANDRO PALMA DI), F.S.A., &c.
Salaminia (Cyprus): the History, Treasures, and Anti-
quities of Salamis, in the Island of Cyprus. Roy. 8vo.
Lond., 1882.   B 15 S 6

CESNOLA (GEN. LUIGI PALMA DI), LL.D. Cyprus; its
Ancient Cities, Tombs, and Temples. 8vo. Lond., 1877.
                                                   D 6 R 14

Descriptive Atlas of the Cesnola Collection of Cypriote
Antiquities, in the Metropolitan Museum of Art, New
York. Vol. 1 (Parts 1 and 2). Imp. 4to. Boston, 1885.
                                                   B 32 P 1, 2 ‡

CEW (GLASER DE). Magneto- and Dynamo-Electric
Machines; with a Description of Electric Accumulators;
edited, with Additions, by P. Higgs. Lond., 1884.
                                                   A 5 R 51

CEYLON. Ceylon Hand-book and Directory, 1885–86. 8vo. Colombo, 1885.   E

Ceylon in the Fifties and the Eighties: a Retrospect and Contrast; by "A Planter." 8vo. Colombo, 1886.   D 5 T 24

Correspondence between the Governor of Ceylon and the Secretary of State for the Colonies, with reference to the preparation of a descriptive Catalogue of the Pâli, Sinhalese, and Sanskrit Manuscripts. (Pam. P.) Fol. Lond., 1870.   MJ 2 U4

Manual of Useful Information upon the Island of Ceylon. (Pam. 14.) 8vo. (n.p.n.d.)   MJ 2 Q 4

CEYLON CALENDAR, 1819–21. 12mo. Colombo, 1819–21.   E

CHABOT (P. M.) [*See* POLYBIUS.]

CHADERTON (LAURENCE), D.D. Life of ; translated from a Latin Memoir of Dr. Dillingham, with Notes and Illustrations, by E. S. Shuckburgh, M.A. 8vo. Camb., 1884.   C 6 P 13

Richard Farmer, D.D., Master of Emmanuel, 1775–97 : an Essay. 8vo. Camb., 1884.   C 6 P 13

CHADWICK (DAVID). [*See* MACCLESFIELD PUBLIC FREE LIBRARY.]

CHADWICK (LIEUT.-COM. F. E.), U.S.N. Report on the Training Systems for the Navy and Mercantile Marine of England, and on the Naval Training System of France. 8vo. Wash., 1880.   G 17 R 4

CHADWICK (WILLIAM). Life and Times of Daniel De Foe ; with Remarks, digressive and discursive. 8vo. Lond., 1859.   C 10 T 32

CHAFFERS (WILLIAM). Gilda Aùrifabrorum : a History of English Goldsmiths and Plateworkers, and their Marks stamped on Plate, copied in fac-simile from celebrated Examples. Roy. 8vo. Lond., 1883.   B 24 V 3

Keramic Gallery; containing several hundred illustrations of rare, curious, and choice examples of Pottery and Porcelain. 2 vols. roy. 8vo. Lond., 1872.   A 7 V 4, 5

CHAFFEY BROTHERS. [*See* VINCENT, J. E. M.]

CHALCOCONDYLES (LAONICUS). Historiarum libri decem. [*See* MIGNE, J. P., SERIES GRÆCA, 159, *and* BYZANTINÆ HIST. SCRIPT.]

CHALLAMEL (AUGUSTIN). History of Fashion in France, from the Gallo-Roman Period to the Present Time. Roy. 8vo. Lond., 1882.   A 7 V 14

CHALLICE (DR. JOHN), M.D., &c. Secret History of the Court of France under Louis xv. 2 vols. 8vo. Lond., 1861.   B 9 P 16, 17

CHALLIS (REV. JAMES), M.A., &c. Lectures on Practical Astronomy and Astronomical Instruments. 8vo. Camb., 1879.   A 3 S 12

U

CHALMERS (ALEXANDER), F.S.A. General Biographical Dictionary. 32 vols. 8vo. Lond., 1812–17. C 11 S 13–44

Memoirs of the Life of James Beattie, LL.D. [*See* BEATTIE, J.]

Plays of Shakspeare ; with a History of the Stage and a Life of Shakspeare. [*See* SHAKESPEARE, W.]

Table Talk of Martin Luther. [*See* LUTHER, M.]

Works of the English Poets, from Chaucer to Cowper ; including the series edited by Dr. Samuel Johnson ; the Additional Lives by A. Chalmers. 21 vols. roy. 8vo. Lond., 1810.   H 6 T 1–21

   1. Chaucer.
   2. Gower—Skelton—Howard—Wyat—Gascoigne—Turberville.
   3. Spenser—Daniel.
   4. Drayton—Warner.
   5. Shakspeare—Davies—Donne—Hall—Stirling—Jonson—Corbet—Carew—Drummond.
   6. Beaumont—G. and P. Fletcher—F. Beaumont—Browne—Davenant—Habington—Suckling—Cartwright—Crasshaw—Sherburne—Brome—C. Cotton.
   7. Cowley—Denham—Milton.
   8. Waller—Butler—Rochester—Roscommon—Otway—Pomfret—Dorset—Stepney—J. Philips—Walsh—Dryden.
   9. Dryden—Smith—Duke—King—Sprat—Halifax—Parnell—Garth—Rowe—Addison.
   10. Hughes—Sheffield—Prior—Congreve—Blackmore—Fenton—Gay.
   11. Lansdowne—Yalden—Tickell—Hammond—Somervile—Savage—Swift.
   12. Broome—Pope—Pitt—Thomson.
   13. Watts—A. Philips—West—Collins—Dyer—Shenstone—Young.
   14. Mallet—Akenside—Gray—Lyttelton—Moore—Cawthorne—Churchill—Falconer—Cunningham—Grainger—Boyse.
   15. W. Thompson—Blair—Lloyd—Green—Byron—Dodsley—Cratterton—Cooper—Smollett—Hamilton.
   16. Smart—Wilkie—P. Whitehead—Fawkes—Lovibond—Harte—Langhorne—Goldsmith—Armstrong—Johnson.
   17. Glover—W. Whitehead—Jago—Brooke—Scott—Mickle—Jenyns.
   18. Cotton—Logan—T. Warton—J. Warton—Blacklock—Cambridge—Mason—Jones—Beattie—Cowper.
   19. Pope's Homer's Iliad and Odyssey—Dryden's Virgil and Juvenal—Pitt's Virgil's Æneid and Vida's Art of Poetry—Francis' Horace.
   20. Rowe's Lucan—Grainger's Tibullus—Fawke's Theocritus, Apollonius, Rhodius Coluthus, Anacreon, Sappho, Bion, Moschus, and Musaeus—Garth's Ovid—Lewis' Statius—Cook's Hesiod.
   21. Hoole's Ariosto and Tasso—Mickle's Lusiad [of Camoens].

[*See* BRITISH ESSAYISTS.]

CHALMERS (GEORGE), F.R.S.A.S. Caledonia ; or, an Account, Historical and Topographic, of North Britain. 3 vols. 4to. Lond., 1807–24.   B 10 Q 5–7†

Estimate of the Comparative Strength of Great Britain. 8vo. Lond., 1804.   F 9 P 16

Life of Thomas Ruddiman, A.M. 8vo. Lond., 1794.   C 9 S 16

Poetic Remains of some of the Scotish Kings. 8vo. Lond., 1824.   H 7 S 9

Poetical Works of Sir David Lyndsay ; with a Life of the Author. [*See* LYNDSAY, SIR D.]

CHALMERS (GEORGE). Life of Daniel Defoe. [*See* DEFOE, D.]

MS. on the Slave Trade. [*See* AFRICA.] B 19 U 7 ‡

CHALMERS (GEORGE PAUL). R.S.A. Reproduction of a Selection of his Works. [*See* BOUGH, S.]

CHALMERS (JAMES). Pioneering in New Guinea. 8vo. Lond., 1887. MD 6 T 4

CHALMERS (JAMES), AND GILL (REV. WILLIAM WYATT), B.A. Work and Adventure in New Guinea, 1877–85. 8vo. Lond., 1885. MD 3 S 17

CHALMERS (JAMES B.), C.E. Graphical Determination of Forces in Engineering Structures. 8vo. Lond., 1881. A 6 T 11

CHALMERS (JOHN). M.A., &c. Account of the Structure of Chinese Characters, under 300 Primary Forms; after the Shwoh-wan, 100, A.D., and the Phonetic Shwoh-wan, 1833. 8vo. Lond., 1882. K 15 S 27

CHALMERS (REV. PETER), D.D., &c. Historical and Statistical Account of Dunfermline. 2 vols. 8vo. Edinb., 1844–59. B 13 R 34, 35

CHALMERS (REV. DR. THOMAS), D.D. Application of Christianity to the Commercial and Ordinary Affairs of Life. 3rd ed. 8vo. Glasgow, 1820. G 2 R 14

Christian and Civic Economy of Large Towns. 3 vols. 8vo. Glasgow, 1821–26. F 9 P 24–26

Lectures on the Establishment and Extension of National Churches. 8vo. Glasgow, 1838. G 4 R 5

Memoirs of the Life and Writings of; by his Son-in-Law, the Rev. W. Hanna, LL.D. 3 vols. 8vo. Lond., 1850–52. C 6 T 8–11

On Political Economy in connection with the Moral State and Moral Prospects of Society. 8vo. Glasgow, 1832. F 10 T 13

On the Power, Wisdom, and Goodness of God. 2 vols. (in 1). 8vo. Lond., 1835. G 6 R 22

Another copy. New ed. 8vo. Philad., 1835. G 16 R 15

Reminiscences of; by John Anderson. 8vo. Lond., 1851. C 2 T 19

Series of Discourses on the Christian Revelation, viewed in connection with Modern Astronomy. 8vo. Glasgow, 1817. G 2 R 13

CHALMERS (REV. WILLIAM), CANON OF MELBOURNE. The Ancient British Church. [*See* CHURCH HISTORY.]

CHALMERS BROS. v. CLARKE. Report of Equity Proceedings in the Supreme Court of New Zealand. Chalmers Bros. v. Executors of the late W. J. T. Clarke. 4to. Geelong, 1877. MJ 2 R 16

CHALYBÄUS (PROF. HEINRICH MORITZ). Historical Survey of Speculative Philosophy, from Kant to Hegel. 8vo. Lond., 1854. G 13 T 12

CHAMBERLAIN (BASIL HALL). Classical Poetry of the Japanese. 8vo. Lond., 1880. H 7 S 14

CHAMBERLAIN (GEORGE). Speech in Defence of G. Chamberlain. [*See* SEWELL, R. C.]

CHAMBERLAIN (RT. HON. JOSEPH), M.P. The French Treaty and Reciprocity: a Speech. (Pam. Je.) 8vo. Lond., 1881. F 6 P 10

CHAMBERLAINE (JOHN). Facsimiles of Original Drawings by Hans Holbein, in the Collection of His Majesty; engraved by F. Bartolozzi, with Biographical Notices by C. Lodge. Lond., 1884. A 23 S 7 ‡

Imitations of original Drawings by Hans Holbein in the Collection of His Majesty. [Engraved by F. Bartolozzi.] With Biographical Tracts. Lond., 1792. A 20 P 14 ‡

Original Designs of the most celebrated Masters of the Bolognese, Roman, Florentine, and Venetian Schools. Imp. folio. Lond., 1812. A 20 P 18 ‡

CHAMBERLAYNE (EDWARD). Angliæ Notitia; or, the Present State of England. 2 vols. 12mo. Lond., 1694–1700. B 23 P 3, 4

CHAMBERLAYNE (REV. ISRAEL), D.D. The Australian Captive; or, an Authentic Narrative of Fifteen Years in the Life of William Jackman. 8vo. Lond., 1853. MD 3 R 30

CHAMBERLAYNE (JOHN). Magnæ Britanniæ Notitia; or, the Present State of Great Britain. 8 vols. 8vo. Lond., 1708–48. B 2 S 43–50

CHAMBERS (CHARLES), F.R.S., &c. Absolute Direction and Intensity of the Earth's Magnetic Force at Bombay, and its Secular and Annual Variations. (Roy. Soc. Pubs., 2.) 4to. Lond., 1876. A 11 P 3 †

CHAMBERS (CHARLES AND F.) On the Mathematical Expression of Observations of Complex Periodical Phenomena; and on Planetary Influence on the Earth's Magnetism. (Roy. Soc. Pubs., 1.) 4to. Lond., 1876. A 11 P 2 †

CHAMBERS (CHARLES HENRY). Address to the People of New South Wales, in opposition to, and refutation of the Grievances Petition of the Legislative Council to Parliament. (Pam. 24.) 8vo. Sydney, 1853. MJ 2 Q 12

General View of the State of California, Past and Present. (Pam. 24.) 8vo. Sydney, 1850. MJ 2 Q 12

Another copy. MJ 2 R 21

CHAMBERS (DAVID DOUGLAS). Case of Mr. D. D. Chambers, late Sub-Inspector of Police. 8vo. Melb., 1857. MF 1 Q 1

CHAMBERS (GEORGE F.), F.R.A.S. Cycle of Celestial Objects. [*See* SMYTH, W. H.]

CHAMBERS (JOHN DAVID), M.A. Divine Worship in England in the 13th and 14th Centuries, contrasted with and adapted to that in the 19th. Roy. 8vo. · Lond., 1877. G 5 S 3

CHAMBERS (LIEUT.-COL. OSBORNE WILLIAM SAMUEL). Garibaldi and Italian Unity. 8vo. Lond.,1864. C 7 P 6

CHAMBERS (ROBERT), LL.D. Ancient Sea-margins as Memorials of Changes in the relative Level of the Sea and Land. 8vo. Edinb., 1848. A 9 S 16

Biographical Dictionary of Eminent Scotsmen; with a supplemental volume by the Rev. Thos. Thomson. 5 vols. roy. 8vo. Glasgow, 1855. C 11 S 1-5

Book of Days: a Miscellany of Popular Antiquities in connection with the Calendar. 2 vols. imp. 8vo. Lond., 1869. J 8 V 4, 5

Domestic Annals of Scotland, from the Reformation to the Revolution. 3 vols. 8vo. Lond., 1858-61. B 13.R 38-40

Explanations: a Sequel to "Vestiges of the Natural History of Creation." 2nd ed. 8vo. Lond., 1846. A 9 Q 6

History of the Rebellions in Scotland, 1638-60. (Const. Misc.) 2 vols. 18mo. Edinb., 1828. K 10 Q 19, 20

History of the Rebellions in Scotland, 1689 and 1715. (Const. Misc.) 18mo. Edinb., 1829. K 10 Q 30

History of the Rebellion in Scotland, 1745-46. (Const. Misc.) 2 vols. 18mo. Edinb., 1828. K 10 Q 3, 4

Another copy. New ed. Sq. 8vo. Lond., 1869. B 13 P 8

Illustrations of the Author of Waverley; reprinted from the edition of 1825. 12mo. Edinb., 1884. J 10 Q 8

Jacobite Memoirs. [*See* FORBES, RT. REV. R.]

Life of King James I. (Const. Misc.) 2 vols. 18mo. Edinb., 1830. K 10 Q 43, 44

Another copy. 2 vols. (in 1). C 1 P 31

Life of Sir Walter Scott; with Abbotsford Notanda, by Robt. Carruthers, LL.D. 12mo. Lond.,1871. C 2 Q 43

Memoir of; with Autobiographic Reminiscences of William Chambers. 6th ed. 12mo. Edinb., 1872. C 1 R 10

Smollett; his Life, and a Selection from his Writings. 8vo. Lond., 1867. C 4 Q 46

Traditions of Edinburgh. New ed. 12mo. Edinb., 1847. B 13 P 5

Vestiges of the Natural History of Creation. 8vo. Lond., 1847. A 9 Q 5

CHAMBERS (ROBERT). Index to Heirs-at-Law, Next of Kin, &c. 3rd ed., revised and greatly enlarged by Edward Preston. 8vo. Lond., 1872. K 10 S 30

[*See* PRESTON, E.]

CHAMBERS (THOMAS KING), M.D., &c. Manual of Diet in Health and Disease. 2nd ed. 8vo. Lond., 1876. A 13 P 8

CHAMBERS (WILLIAM), LL.D. Life and Anecdotes of David Ritchie, the original of Sir Walter Scott's Black Dwarf. 12mo. Edinb., 1885 C 2 Q 38

. Memoir of Robert Chambers; with Autobiographic Reminiscences of William Chambers. 6th ed. Edinb., 1872. C 1 R 10

CHAMBERS (WILLIAM AND ROBERT). Chambers's Encyclopædia: a Dictionary of Universal Knowledge for the People. 10 vols. roy. 8vo. Lond., 1860-68. K 1 V 1-10

Another copy. Revised ed. 10 vols. roy. 8vo. Lond., 1879. K 1 V 11-20

Chambers's Information for the People; edited by W. and R. Chambers. 2 vols. roy. 8vo. Lond.,1857-58. J 4 U 4, 5

Chambers's Miscellany of Instructive and Entertaining Tracts. 20 vols. (in 10) 8vo. Lond.,1869-72 J 6 R 22-31

Chambers's Papers for the People. 12 vols. (in 6) 8vo. Lond., 1850-51. J 6 R 16-21

Chambers's Readings in English Literature. 8vo. Lond., 1877. J 6 R 15

Chambers's Cyclopædia of English Literature: a History, Critical and Biographical, of British Authors; with Specimens of their Writings. 3rd ed. 2 vols. imp. 8vo. Lond.,1876. K 5 R 5, 6

Chambers's English Dictionary, Pronouncing, Explanatory, and Etymological; with Vocabularies of Scottish Words and Phrases, Americanisms, &c. Roy. 8vo. Lond., 1876. K 16 Q 1

Chambers's Etymological Dictionary of the English Language. 8vo. Lond., 1877. K 12 Q 2

Pictorial History of the Russian War, 1854-56 [by George Dodd]. Roy. 8vo. Lond., 1856. B 12 V 10

Spirit of Chambers's Journal. 5 vols. 12mo. Lond., 1834-38. J 1 S 43-47

CHAMBERS' JOURNAL of Popular Literature, Science, and Arts. 12 vols. fol., and 63 vols. roy. 8vo. Lond., 1832-86. E

CHAMBEYRON (CAPT. C. M. L.), ET BANARE (LIEUT. A.) Instructions Nautiques sur la Nouvelle-Calédonie; suivies d'une Note sur les Iles Loyalty, par M. Jouan. 2ᵉ éd. 8vo. Paris, 1876. MF 2 R 1

CHAMBORD (HENRI CHARLES FERDINAND MARIE DIEU-DONNÉ DE BOURBON), COMTE DE. [*See* BORDEAUX, DUC DE.]

CHAMEROVZOW (LOUIS ALEXIS). New Zealand Question and the Rights of Aborigines; and Appendix B, concerning the Settlement of Nelson, New Zealand. 8vo. Lond., 1848.* MB 2 Q 7

CHAMICH (FATHER MICHAEL). History of Armenia, from B.C. 2247 to the year of Christ 1780, or 1229 of the Armenian Era; translated by Johannes Avdall. 2 vols. 8vo. Calcutta, 1827. B 13 V 31, 32

CHAMPFLEURY (JULES FLEURY). The Cat, Past and Present; from the French, with Notes, by Mrs. Cashel . Hoey. Illustrated. 12mo. Lond., 1885. A 14 S 2

CHAMPOLLION (J. F.), LE JEUNE. Dictionnaire Egyptien en Ecriture Hiéroglyphique. Fol. Paris, 1841.
K 7 8 4 †

Grammaire Egyptienne; ou, Principes généraux de l'Ecriture Sacrée Egyptienne appliquée à la représentation de la Langue Parlée. Sm. fol. Paris, 1836. K 7 8 3 †

Panthéon Egyptien: Collection des Personnages Mythologiques de l'Ancienne Egypte, d'après les Monuments. 4to. Paris, 1823. B 2 R 35

Précis du Système Hiéroglyphique des Anciens Egyptiens; avec un volume de Planches. 2e éd. 2 vols. 8vo. Paris, 1827–28. B 2 R 51, 52

CHANCE (H.) [*See* POWELL, H. J.]

CHANCELLOR (EDWIN BERESFORD). Historical Richmond. Illustrated. 8vo. Lond., 1885. B 7 P 13

Life of Charles I, 1600–25. 8vo. Lond., 1886. C 10 P 28

CHANDLER (RT REV. EDWARD), BISHOP OF COVENTRY AND LICHFIELD. Defence of Christianity, from the Prophecies of the Old Testament. 8vo. Lond., 1725. G 13 T 13

CHANDLER (PROF. HENRY W.), M.A. Elements of Greek Accentuation. (Clar. Press.) 12mo. Oxford, 1877. K 16 P 43

CHANDLER (RICHARD), D.D. History of Ilium, or Troy; including the Adjacent Country, and the Opposite Coast of the Chersonesus of Thrace. 4to. Lond., 1802. B 18 R 14 ‡

Inscriptiones Antiquæ Pleræque. Nondum Editæ : in Asia Minori et Graccia, Praesertim Athenis, Collectae. (Grec. et Lat.) Folio. Oxonii, 1774. B 16 U 12 ‡

Life of William Wayntlete, Bishop of Winchester. Roy. 8vo. Lond., 1811. C 7 V 48

Travels in Asia Minor; or, an Account of a Tour made at the expense of the Society of Dilettanti. 4to. Oxford, 1775. D 4 V 15

Travels in Greece; or, an Account of a Tour made at the expense of the Society of Dilettanti. 4to. Oxford, 1776. D 6 V 26

CHANDOS (SIR JOHN). Le Prince Noir: Poème du Héraut d'Armes Chandos. The Life and Feats of Arms of Edward, the Black Prince, by Chandos, Herald; with an English Translation and Notes, by Francisque-Michel. 4to. Lond., 1883. H 5 V 14

CHANNEL TUNNEL. Correspondence respecting the proposed Channel Tunnel and Railway. Fol. Lond., 1875. MF 1 U 18

CHANNING (REV. WILLIAM ELLERY), D.D. Correspondence of, and Lucy Aikin, 1826–42; edited by Anna Letitia Le Breton. 8vo. Lond., 1874. C 3 S 18

Discourses. 12mo. Glasgow, 1838. G 10 P 16

The Duty of the Free States; or, Remarks suggested by the Case of the Creole. (Pam. 9.) 8vo. Lond., 1842. F 12 P 8

CHANNING (REV. WILLIAM ELLERY), D.D.—*continued.* Essays, Literary and Political. 12mo. Glasgow, 1837. J 1 T 4

Memoir of; with Extracts from his Correspondence and Manuscripts; by W. H. C. 2 vols. 12mo. Lond., 1850. C 1 T 31, 32

Slavery; reprinted from the Boston, U.S., edition. (Pam. 5.) 8vo. Lond., 1836. MJ 2 P 39

CHANTAL (STE. JEANNE FRANÇOISE FREMIOT DE). Vie de. [*See* CAPIFIGUE, J. B. H. R.]

CHANTREL (JOSEPH). Histoire Universelle de l'Eglise Catholique. [*See* ROHRBACHER, L'ABBÉ, F. R.]

CHANTREY (SIR F. L.) Peak Scenery; or, Views in Derbyshire; with Historical and Topographical Descriptions, by J. Croston. Roy. 4to. Derby, 1886. D 9 S 4 †

CHAPELLE (ALFRED DE LA), COUNT. [*See* LA CHAPELLE, COUNT A. DE.]

CHAPLIN (A. L.) Historical Sketches of the Colleges of Wisconsin. 8vo. Madison, 1876. G 17 R 17

CHAPLIN (FREDERICK). Plan for the better Management of Railroads. Lond., 1856. Reprinted. (Pam. 28.) 8vo. Melb., 1857. MJ 2 Q 16

CHAPMAN (ERNEST THEOPHRON). Water Analysis. [*See* WANKLYN, J. A.]

CHAPMAN (GEORGE). Iliads of Homer; translated by. [*See* HOMER.]

George Chapman; a Critical Essay; by Algernon Charles Swinburne. 12mo. Lond., 1875. C 2 8 9

CHAPMAN (GEORGE), AND SHIRLEY (JAMES). The Ball: a Comedy. 8vo. Lond., 1824. H 1 R 13

Another copy. H 1 R 15

CHAPMAN (GEORGE T.) Centenary Memorial of Captain Cook's Description of New Zealand one Hundred Years Ago. 4to. Auckland, 1870. MD 3 V 9

Natural Wonders of New Zealand (the Wonderland of the Pacific.) 2nd ed. 8vo. Lond., 1881.* MD 4 P 17

Another copy. 2nd ed. 8vo. Auckland, 1881. MD 4 P 19

CHAPMAN (H. S.) New Zealand Portfolio, conducted by H. S. Chapman; Letter on the advantages from the establishment of a Loan Company for New Zealand. 8vo. Lond., 1842. MD 6 T 2

Parliamentary Government; or, Responsible Ministries for the Australian Colonies. 8vo. Hobart, 1854. MF 3 P G.

Another copy. (Pam. 21.) MJ 2 Q 10

Specimens of Fossilised Words; or, Obsolete Roots embedded in Modern Compounds; with some Old Words with New Meanings. 8vo. Dunedin, 1876. MJ 2 R 16

CHAPMAN (JAMES), F.R.G.S. Travels in the Interior of South Africa, comprising Fifteen Years' Hunting and Trading. 2 vols. 8vo. Lond., 1868. D 2 T 20, 21

CHAPMAN (JOHN), M.D., &c. Prostitution : Government Experiments in controlling it. 8vo. Lond., 1870. F 14 S 35

Sea Sickness; its Nature and Treatment. (Pam. 23.) 8vo. Lond., 1864. MJ 2 Q 11

CHAPMAN (MARIA WESTON) Memorials of Harriet Martineau. [*See* MARTINEAU, HARRIET.]

CHAPMAN AND THOMAS. Our Refutation of the Misstatements of the Directors of the Eastern Coast Steam Navigation Company. (Pam. 42.) 8vo. Hobart, 1856. MJ 2 R 4

CHAPPELL (CAPT. E.) Reports relative to Smith's Patent Screw Propeller, as used on board the *Archimedes.* (Pam., 6.) 8vo. Lond., 1840. MJ 2 Q 1

CHAPPELL (WM.), F.S.A. History of Music (Art and Science). From the Earliest Records to the Fall of the Roman Empire, &c. 2 vols. 8vo. Lond., 1874. A 7 U 9, 10

CHAPSAL (PROF. C. P.) Corrigé des Exercices Français Supplémentaires sur toutes les difficultés de la Syntaxe. 10ᵉ éd. 12mo. Paris, 1858. K 11 V 44

Nouvelle Grammaire Française. [*See* NOEL, F. J. M.]

Syntaxe Française, ou Etude Méthodique et Raisonnée de toutes les difficultés que présente notre Langue sous le rapport syntaxique. 6ᵉ éd. 12mo. Paris, 1858. K 11 V 45

CHAPTAL (JEAN ANTOINE). Traité sur la culture de la Vigne, avec l'Art de faire le Vin, les Eaux-de-vie, Esprit-de-vin, Vinaigres simples et composés; par Chaptal, Rozier, Parmentier, et Dussieux. 2 vols. 8vo. Paris, 1801. A 1 P 3, 4

Another copy. 8vo. Paris, 1819. A 1 Q 1

[*See* ROZIER, L'ABBÉ F.]

CHARDIN (JEAN), CHEVALIER. Voyages en Perse, et autres Lieux de l'Orient, enrichis d'un grand nombre de belles figures en taille-douce, représentant les antiquités et les choses, remarquables du Pays. Nouvelle édition. 10 vols. 8vo. Paris, 1811. D 6 Q 12–21

Atlas [to the above.] Roy. fol. Paris, 1811. D 2 P 4 ‡

CHARITABALI; or, Instructive Biography; by I. Vidyāsāgara. (In Sanskrit.) 12mo. Lond., 1884. C 2 Q 9

CHARKE (MRS. CHARLOTTE). Narrative of the Life of; written by herself. (Autobiography.) 12mo. · Lond., 1829. C 1 P 8

CHARLES I. Case of. [*See* LUDLOW, MAJ.-GEN. E.]

Court and Times of. [*See* BIRCH, REV. T.]

Historical Account of the Life and Writings of. [*See* HARRIS, W.]

Life of Charles I, 1600–25; by E. Beresford Chancellor. 8vo. Lond., 1886. C 10 P 28

CHARLES I.—*continued.*
Memoirs of the Court of; by Lucy Aikin. 2 vols. 8vo. Lond., 1833. C 10 P 26, 27

Narrative of Attendance on. [*See* ASHBURNHAM, J.]

Trials of Charles I and of some of the Regicides. (Fam. Lib.) 12mo. Lond., 1832. K 10 P 33

[*See* ANDREWS, J. R.]

CHARLES II. Diary of the Times of, including his Correspondence with the Countess of Sunderland; by the Hon. Henry Sidney, afterwards Earl of Romney. 2 vols. 8vo. Lond., 1843. C 6 V 18, 19

Historical Account of the Life of. [*See* HARRIS, W.]

Mémoires de. [*See* GUIZOT, F. P. G., 9.]

CHARLES V (EMPEROR OF GERMANY). Correspondence of Charles v. and his Ambassadors at the Courts of England and France. Edited by William Bradford, M.A. 8vo. Lond., 1850. C 10 S 47

[*See* DE LOS VALLES, BARON.]

CHARLES VII (KING OF FRANCE). Times of. [*See* BRAY, MRS. A. E.]

CHARLES XII. Histoire de Charles XII, Roi de Suede; par F. M. A. de Voltaire. 18mo. Lond., 1832. B 20 P 13

CHARLES EDWARD STUART (PRINCE), The Decline of the Last Stuarts. Printed for the Roxburghe Club; edited by Earl Stanhope. 4to. Lond., 1843. C 4 W 33

Life and Times of Prince Charles Edward Stuart, Count of Albany, commonly called "the Young Pretender"; by A. C. Ewald, F.S.A. 2 vols. 8vo. Lond., 1875. C 9 T 28, 29

CHARLES JOHN (KING OF SWEDEN AND NORWAY). Memorials of; by William George Meredith. 8vo. Lond., 1829. C 10 T 1

[*See* ASCANIUS.]

CHARLEVOIX (PÈRE P. F. XAVIER DE). Histoire de l'Isle Espagnole, ou de S. Domingue. 2 vols. 4to. Paris, 1730–31. B 1 U 28, 29

Histoire et Description Générale du Japon. 2 vols. 4to. Paris, 1736. B 19 R 4, 5 ‡

Histoire et Description Générale de la Nouvelle France, avec le Journal historique d'un Voyage fait par ordre du Roi, dans l'Amérique Septentrionale. 3 vols. 4to. Paris, 1744. B 1 V 1–3

Histoire du Paraguay. 6 vols. 12mo. Paris, 1757. B 1 Q 15–20

History of Paraguay; containing a full and authentic Account of the Establishments formed there by the Jesuits. 2 vols. 8vo. Dublin, 1769. B 2 P 15, 16

Letters to the Dutchess of Lesdiguieres; giving an Account of a Voyage to Canada, and Travels to the Gulf of Mexico. 8vo. Lond., 1763. D 3 Q 22

CHARLEY (SIR WILLIAM THOMAS), KNT. Flax and Linen. (Brit. Manuf. Indust.) 12mo. Lond., 1876. A 17 S 37

CHARLIN (Mons.) A few Remarks on the Study of Modern Languages, and especially of French. 8vo. Melb., 1878.   MJ 2 R 11

CHARLOTTE (QUEEN OF ENGLAND). Queen Charlotte and the Chevalier d'Eon. [*See* THOMS, W. J.]

CHARLOTTE AUGUSTA OF WALES (PRINCESS). Illustrated Monograph; by Mrs. H. Jones. 4to. Lond., 1885.   C 4 W 29

CHARLOTTE ELISABETH (PRINCESSE DE BAVIÈRE). Mémoires de Madame, Mère du Régent. [*See* BARRIÈRE, J. F., 1.]

CHARLTON (REV. WILLIAM HENRY), M.A. Burghley: Life of William Cecil, Lord Burghley, &c.; with a Description of Burghley House. 8vo. Stamford, 1847.   C 9 V 16

CHARNOCK (JOHN). Biographia Navalis; or, Impartial Memoirs of the Lives and Characters of Officers of the Navy of Great Britain, from the year 1660 to the Present Time. 6 vols. 8vo. Lond., 1794–98.   C 6 S 5–10
History of Marine Architecture. 3 vols. roy. 4to. Lond., 1800–2.   A 2 U 2–4

CHARNOCK (RICHARD STEPHEN), PH.D., &c. Glossary of the Essex Dialect. 12mo. Lond., 1880.   K 11 V 18
Ludus Patronymicus; or, the Etymology of Curious Surnames. 8vo. Lond., 1868.   K 19 Q 6
Verba Nominalia; or, Words derived from Proper Names. 8vo. Lond., 1866.   K 13 S 8

CHARSLEY (FANNY ANNE). Wild Flowers around Melbourne. Fol. Lond., 1867.   MA 1 R 20 †

CHARTER OF LONDON, (ROYAL). [*See* ROYAL CHARTER OF LONDON.]

CHARTERIS (PROF. A. H.), D.D. Canonicity: a Collection of early Testimonies to the Canonical Books of the New Testament, based on Kirchhofer's "Quellensammlung." 8vo. Edinb., 1880.   G 6 R 28

CHARTON (ÉDOUARD). Histoire de France. [*See* BORDIER, H.]

CHASTELLUX (F. J.), MARQUIS DE. Travels in North America in the years 1780–82; translated from the French by "An English Gentleman." 2 vols. 8vo. Dublin, 1787.   D 3 R 48, 49

CHATEAUBRIAND (FRANÇOIS AUGUSTE), VICOMTE DE. Congress of Verona; comprising a Portion of "Memoirs of his own Times." 2 vols. 8vo. Lond., 1838.   B 13 V 3, 4
Œuvres complètes. 12 vols. roy. 8vo. Paris, 1863–67.
J 17 T 12–23
Memoirs of, from his birth in 1768, till his return to France in 1800; written by himself. 12mo. Lond., 1849. G 2 P 6
Sketches of English Literature. 2 vols. 8vo. Lond., 1836.   B 24 S 10

CHATFIELD (PAUL), M.D. [*See* SMITH, H.]

CHATHAM (RT. HON. WILLIAM PITT), EARL OF. Anecdote Biography: William Pitt, Earl of Chatham, and Edmund Burke; by John Timbs, F.S.A. 12mo. Lond., 1860.   C 1 S 6
Anecdotes of the Life of, and of the principal Events of his Time; with his Speeches in Parliament, 1736–78; by John Almon. 7th ed. 3 vols. 8vo. Lond., 1810.
C 6 S 16–18
Correspondence of; edited by the Executors of his son, John, Earl of Chatham. 4 vols. 8vo. Lond., 1838–40.
C 6 V 23–26
Biography of. [*See* LAMARTINE, A. DE.]

CHATRIAN (ALEXANDRE). The Blockade—The Conscript—Waterloo. [*See* ERCKMANN, E.]

CHATTAWAY (E. D.) Railways: their Capital and Dividends; with Statistics of their Working in Great Britain and Ireland, &c. (Weale.) 12mo. Lond., 1855–56.   A 17 P 32

CHATTERTON (THOMAS): a Story of the year 1770; by David Masson, M.A., &c. 8vo. Lond., 1874.   C 1 S 15
Life and Poems of. [*See* CHALMERS, A.]
Poetical Works of; With Notices of his Life, History of the Rowley Controversy, a Selection of his Letters, &c. 2 vols. 8vo. Camb., 1842.   H 6 Q 19, 20

CHATTERTON (LADY). The Pyrenees; with Excursions into Spain. 2 vols. 8vo. Lond., 1843.   D 7 U 23, 24
Rambles in the South of Ireland, 1838. 2 vols. 8vo. Lond., 1839.   D 7 R 42, 43

CHATTO (WILLIAM ANDREW). Facts and Speculations on the Origin and History of Playing Cards. 8vo. Lond., 1848.   B 15 Q 32

CHAUCER (GEOFFREY) [A Biography]; by A. W. Ward. (Eng. Men of Letters.) 8vo. Lond., 1879.   C 1 U 8
Life and Poems of. [*See* CHALMERS, A.]
Life of Geoffrey Chaucer, the Early English Poet, including Memoirs of John of Gaunt, Duke of Lancaster; by William Godwin. 2nd ed. 4 vols. 8vo. Lond., 1804. C 10 S 43–46
Poetical Works of; edited by Robert Bell. 8 vols. (in 4) 12mo. Lond., 1861.   H 6 Q 23–28
Poetical Works of; with an Essay on his Language and Versification. Roy. 8vo. Lond., 1871.   H 6 U 22
The Prologue; the Knightes Tale; the Nonne Prestes Tale, from the Canterbury Tales: a revised Text, edited by the Rev. Richard Morris, LL.D. 6th ed. (Clar. Press.) 12mo. Oxford, 1875.   H 6 R 47
Riches of Chaucer, in which his Impurities have been expunged, &c.; also, have been added a few explanatory Notes, and a Memoir of the Poet, by Charles Cowden Clarke. 2nd ed. 8vo. Lond., 1870.   H 7 S 8
Workes of; newlie printed, with divers Additions whiche were neuer in Print before; with the Siege and Destruction of the worthy Citee of Thèbes. Fol. Lond., 1561.   H 5 V 1

[*See* LINTON, W. J.]

CHAUCER SOCIETY. Publications of. 19 vols. 8vo., and 8 vols. roy. 8vo. Lond., 1868-80.   E

CHAUNCY (SIR HENRY), KNT. Historical Antiquities of Hertfordshire. Roy. fol. Lond., 1700.   B 19 U 14 ‡

CHAUNCY (W. SNELL), C.E. Guide to South Australia; being a Descriptive Account of the Colony. 12mo. Lond., 1849.   MD 2 Q 28

CHAUSSIER (PROF. FRANÇOIS). Chimie, Pharmacie, et Métallurgie. [*See* ENCYCLOPÉDIE MÉTHODIQUE.]
Nouveau Manuel du Physionomiste et du Phrénologiste. [*See* LAVATER, J. G.]

CHAUVEAU (PROF. A.), Comparative Anatomy of the Domesticated Animals. 2nd ed., revised and enlarged, with the co-operation of S. Arloing; translated and edited by George Fleming, F.R.G.S., &c. Illustrated. Roy. 8vo. Lond., 1873.   A 27 U 26

CHAVIS (D.) [*See* VEILLÉES PERSANES, LES.]

CHEADLE (W. B.), M.A., &c. The North-west Passage. [*See* MILTON, VISCOUNT.]

CHEAP BREAD and its Consequence; by "A British Farmer and Landowner." 8vo. Lond., 1841.   F 6 V 10

CHEEM (ALIPH). [*See* YELDHAM, W. S.]

CHEETHAM (SAMUEL), M.A. Dictionary of Christian Antiquities. [*See* SMITH, W.]

CHEEVER (G. B.), D.D. Wanderings of a Pilgrim in the Shadow of Mount Blanc and the Jungfrau Alp. 8vo. Aberdeen, 1848.   D 7 Q 24

CHEEVER (REV. HENRY T.) Island World of the Pacific: Travel through the Sandwich or Hawaiian Islands, and other parts of Polynesia. 12mo. Glasgow, 1851.   MD 5 Q 30
Another copy. Illustrated. 8vo. New York, 1851.   MD 5 Q 31
Life in the Sandwich Islands; or, the Heart of the Pacific as it was and is. 8vo. Lond., 1851.   MD 5 Q 32
Whaleman's Adventures in the Southern Ocean. [*See* SCORESBY, REV. W.]

CHEKE (SIR JOHN), KT. Life of. [*See* STRYPE, J.]

CHEMICAL SOCIETY OF LONDON. Journal of: Transactions and Abstracts. Vols. 1-46. 8vo. Lond., 1863-85.   E
Memoirs, 1841-48. 3 vols. 8vo. Lond., 1843-48.   E
Quarterly Journal of. 15 vols. 8vo. Lond., 1849-62.   E

CHENEY (A. NELSON). Fishing with the Fly. [*See* ORVIS, C. F.]

CHENU (DR. J. C.) Encyclopédie d'Histoire Naturelle; ou, Traité complet de cette Science. (*Imperfect.*) 14 vols. sm. fol. Paris, 1857-61.   K 5 P 1-14

CHEONG (CHEOK HONG). [*See* CHINESE QUESTION.]

CHERBONNEAU (PROF. A.) Anecdotes Musulmanes, Texte arabe; ou, cours d'Arabe élémentaire. 8vo. Paris, 1847.   K 14 T 31

CHERRY (ANDREW). The Soldier's Daughter: a Comedy. (Cumberland's Eng. Theatre.) 12mo. Lond., 1829.   H 2 Q 23

CHERUBINI (MARIA LUIGI CARLO ZENOBIO SALVADOR). Course of Counterpoint and Fugue. Translated by J. A. Hamilton. 2nd ed. 2 vols. 8vo. Lond., 1841.   A 7 P 7, 8

CHESHIRE (EDWARD). Results of the Census of Great Britain in 1851. (Pam. 23.) 8vo. Lond., 1854.   MJ 2 Q 11

CHESHIRE (F. R.) Bees and Beekeeping, Scientific and Practical: a Complete Treatise on the Anatomy, Physiology, Floral Relations, and Profitable Management of the Hive Bee. Vol. 1. 8vo. Lond., 1886.   A 14 P 50

CHESNEAU (ERNEST). Education of the Artist; translated by Clara Bell. 8vo. Lond., 1886.   A 6 V 21
English School of Painting; translated by L. N. Etherington. 8vo. Lond., 1885.   A 6 V 5

CHESNEY (COL. CHARLES CORNWALLIS). Study of the Campaign of 1815. 3rd ed. 8vo. Lond., 1874.   B 5 U 27

CHESNEY (GEN. FRANCIS RAWDON), R.A., &c. Expedition for the Survey of the Rivers Euphrates and Tigris, 1835-37, and Maps. 3 vols. 8vo. Lond., 1850.   D 5 U 32-34
Life of the late General Chesney, Col.-Commandant Royal Artillery, &c.; by his wife and daughter [Mrs. O'Donnell]. Edited by Stanley Lane-Poole. 8vo. Lond., 1885.   C 8 P 17
Narrative of the Euphrates Expedition, carried on by order of the British Government during the years 1835-37. 8vo. Lond., 1868.   D 5 T 9

CHESNEY (MRS. LOUISA) AND O'DONNELL (MRS. JANE). Life of General F. R. Chesney. Edited by Stanley Lane-Poole. 8vo. Lond., 1885.   C 8 P 17

CHESTER (MRS. HENRIETTA M.) Russia Past and Present; adapted from the German of Lankenau and Oelnitz. Illustrated. 8vo. Lond., 1881.   D 9 Q 34

CHESTER (HENRY M.) New Guinea: Narrative of Expedition to New Guinea. 8vo. Brisbane, 1878.   MD 3 S 44

CHESTER (JOSEPH LEMUEL), LL.D. Marriage, Baptismal, and Burial Registers of the Collegiate Church or Abbey of St. Peter, Westminster. Imp. 8vo. Lond., 1876.   K 11 Q 8

CHESTERFIELD (PHILLIP DORMER STANHOPE), EARL OF. Letters written to his son, Philip Stanhope; together with several other pieces on various subjects. Published by Mrs. Eugenia Stanhope. 3rd ed. 4 vols. 8vo. Lond., 1774.   C 6 Q 11-14

CHESTERTON (CAPT. GEORGE LAVAL). Peace, War, and Adventure: an Autobiographical Memoir. 2 vols. 8vo. Lond., 1853.   C 2 U 31, 32

Revelations of Prison Life; with an Enquiry into Prison Discipline and Secondary Punishments. 2 vols. 8vo. Lond., 1856.   F 6 R 22, 23

CHETHAM SOCIETY. Remains, Historical and Literary, connected with the Palatine Counties of Lancaster and Chester. Published by the Chetham Society. Vols. 1-112, and New Series, vols. 1-4 and 7. 4to. Lond., 1844–85.   E

CHEVALIER (J. B. DE). Description of the Plain of Troy; with a Map of that Region, delineated from an actual Survey; translated by Andrew Dalzel, M.A., &c. (Pam.) 4to. Edinb., 1791.   B 18 R 14 ‡

[*See* BRYANT, J.]

CHEVALIER (MICHEL). On the Probable Fall in the Value of Gold; translated by Richard Cobden. 8vo. Manchester, 1859.   F 12 P 16

CHEVALIER (N.) Australia. Illustrated. [*See* BOOTH, E. C.]

CHEVALIERS. Histoire des Ordres Militaires. [*See* HISTOIRE.]

CHEVERS (N.) Commentary on the Diseases of India. 8vo. Lond., 1886.   A 12 U 30

CHEVREUL (M. E.) Principles of Harmony and Contrast of Colours, and their application to the Arts; including Painting, Interior Decoration, Tapestries, Carpets; translated by Charles Martel. 3rd ed. 8vo. Lond., 1876.   A 7 Q 5

CHEYNE (CAPT. ALEXANDER). Narrative of the Circumstances connected with the Removal of Alexander Cheyne, Esq. (late Captain in the Corps of Royal Engineers), from the Office of Director of Water Works for Hobart Town. 8vo. Hobart, 1848.   MF 3 P 6

CHEYNE (ANDREW). Description of Islands in the Western Pacific Ocean, North and South of the Equator; with Sailing Directions. 8vo. Lond., 1852.   MD 587

CHIARINI (L'ABBE L. A.) Théorie du Judaïsme appliquée à la réforme des Israélites de tous les pays de l'Europe. 2 vols. 8vo. Paris, 1830.   G 13 T 1, 2

CHICHELE (HENRY), ARCHBISHOP OF CANTERBURY. Life of; written in Latin by Arthur Duck, LL.D. 12mo. Lond., 1699.   C 2 S 8

CHIEF EXAMINER (THE). [*See* GARDNER, JOHN.]

CHILD (PROF. FRANCIS JAMES). English and Scottish Ballads, Parts 1-4. 2 vols. imp. 8vo. Boston, 1882–86.   H 5 V 3, 4

CHILD (SIR JOSIAH). New Discourse of Trade. 12mo. Lond., 1693.   F 2 P 32

CHILDE (EDWARD LEE). Life and Campaigns of General Lee; translated by George Litting, M.A. 8vo. Lond., 1875.   C 4 T 17

CHILDERS (Prof. ROBERT CÆSAR). Dictionary of the Pali Language. Sm. fol. Lond., 1875.   K 14 R 12

CHILLINGWORTH (REV. WILLIAM), M.A. Religion of Protestants; a safe way to Salvation. 8vo. Lond., 1870.   G 16 P 7

Works of. [With Life, by the Rev. T. Birch.] 3 vols. 8vo. Oxford, 1838.   G 11 Q 25–27

CHINA. Chinese Drawing Book. 8vo. Nanking, 1679.   A 8 T 21

Catalogue of the Chinese Imperial Maritime Customs Collection. [*See* PHILAD. INTERNAT. EXHIB., 1875.]

Geology and Trade of China. Fol. Shanghai, 1870–72   A 2 S 23 ‡

Historical Atlas of China (in Chinese). Fol. Canton, 1829.   D 33 Q 6 ‡

The Last Year in China, to the Peace of Nanking; by "A Field Officer." 12mo. Lond., 1843.   B 2 P 26

Life in China. The Porcelain Tower; or, Nine Stories of China. Compiled from original sources, by "T. T. T." 12mo. Philad., 1842.   J 10 Q 21

Letters from China and Japan. [*See* LETTERS.]

Mémoires concernant l'Histoire, les Sciences, les Arts, les Moeurs, les Usages, etc., des Chinois. 4to. Paris, 1776–1814.   B 2 Q 14–30

Silk. Imperial Maritime Customs. Special Series No. 3. 4to. Shanghai, 1881.   A 11 V 6

"Where Chinese drive": English Student-Life at Peking; by "A Student Interpreter." 8vo. Lond., 1885.   D 4 T 14

CHINESE CLASSICS (The). [*See* LEGGE, J.]

CHINESE QUESTION (THE). Chinese Question analyzed; with a full Statement of Facts, by "One who knows them." 8vo. Melb., 1857.   MF 3 P 5

Chinese Question in Australia, 1878–79; edited by L. Kong Meng, Chook Hong Cheong, Louis Ah Mouy. 8vo. Melb., 1879.   MF 3 P 21

Another copy.   MJ 2 R 12

CHINESE REPOSITORY. 20 vols. 8vo. Canton, 1832–51   J 12 P 1–20

CHING TIH (EMPEROR). Rambles of, in Käang Nan: a Chinese Tale; translated by Tkin Shon. 2 vols. 8vo. Lond., 1843.   J 9 R 23, 24

CHINIQUY (REV. CHARLES). Chiniquy Lectures, delivered in the Protestant Hall, Sydney, and Temperance Hall, Melbourne. 50th thousand. (4th Victorian ed.) 8vo. Melb., 1880.   MG I Q 39

CHINNOCK (E. J.), M.A., &c. Analysis of Alexander. [*See* ARRIAN.]

CHIPIEZ (CHARLES). Art in Chaldæa and Assyria. [*See* PERROT, G.*]

History of Art in Ancient Egypt. [*See* PERROT, PROF. G.]

History of Art in Phœnicia. [*See* PERROT, G.]

CHISHOLM (MRS. CAROLINE). Emigration and Transportation relatively considered in a Letter. 2nd ed. (Pam. 19.) 12mo. Lond., 1847.   MJ 2 Q 8

Memoirs of; and Emigrant's Guide to Australia, by Rev. David Mackenzie, M.A. 2nd ed. 12mo. Lond., 1853.   MD 3.P 39

Memoirs of; with an Account of her Philanthropic Labours in India, Australia, and England, &c., by Eneas Mackenzie. 12mo. Lond., 1852.*   MC 1 P 30

What has Mrs. Caroline Chisholm done for the Colony of New South Wales. [*See* HARRIS, R.]

CHISHOLM (GEORGE G.), M.A. Europe. [*See* RUDLER, F. W.]

The Two Hemispheres: a popular Account of the Countries and Peoples of the World. Illustrated. 8vo. Lond., 1882.   D 9 T 23

[*See* GSELL-FELS, DR. T.]

CHITTENDEN (GEORGE B.) Meteorological Observations made during the year 1873, and the early part of the year 1874, in Colorado and Montana Territories. (Pam. Cl.) 8vo. Wash., 1874.   A 16 U 21

CHITTY (JOSEPH), JUN. Treatise on the Law of Contracts, and upon the Defences to Actions. 10th ed., by John A. Russell, LL.B. Roy. 8vo. Lond., 1876.   F 8 T 3

CHOCARNE (REV. PÈRE P.), O.P. Inner Life of the Very Rev. Père Lacordaire, of the Order of Preachers; translated from the French. 8vo. Dublin, 1867.   G 10 Q 29

CHODZKO (ALEXANDER). Grammaire Paléoslave; suivie de Textes Paléoslaves, tirés, pour la plupart, des Manuscrits de la BibliothèqueImpériale de Paris, et du Psautier de Bologne. 8vo. Paris, 1869.   K 13 R 20

Specimens of the Popular Poetry of Persia. Roy. 8vo. Lond., 1842.   H 6 V 10

CHOICE NOTES, from "Notes and Queries": History. 12mo. Lond., 1858.   · B 14 P 2

CHOISEUL-GOUFFIER (MARIE G. F. A.) COMTE DE. Voyage Pittoresque de la Grèce. 3 vols. (in 2) roy. fol. Paris, 1782–1823.   D 7 P 7–9 ‡

CHOLMONDELEY (THOMAS). UltimaThule; or, Thoughts suggested by a Residence in New Zealand. 8vo. Lond., 1854.   MD 4 S 15

CHOLMONDELEY-PENNELL (HENRY). [*See* PENNELL, H. C.]

CHORLEY (HENRY). Letters of Mary Russell Mitford [*See* L'ESTRANGE, REV. A. G.]

x

CHORLEY (HENRY FOTHERGILL). Memorials of Mrs. Hemans; with Illustrations of her Literary Character, from her Private Correspondence. 2nd ed. 2 vols. 8vo. Lond., 1837.   C 3 R 44, 45

Music and Manners in France and Germany. 3 vols. 8vo Lond., 1841.   D 7 R 20–22

Thirty Years' Musical Recollections. 2 vols. 8vo. Lond., 1862.   C 2 T 30, 31

CHOULES (REV. J. O.) Cruise of the Steam Yacht *North Star*. 8vo. Boston, 1854.   D 9 P 28

CHRESTOMATHIA DAY SCHOOL; being a Collection of Papers, explanatory of the design of an Institution proposed to be set on foot under the name of the Chrestomathic Day School. (Pam. 5.) 8vo. Lond., 1815.   MJ 2 P 39.

CHRESTOMATHIES OCEANIENNES; Textes en Langue Boughi. Obl. 18mo. Paris (n.d.)   K 15 R 32

CHRISTALLIER (REV. J. G.) Dictionary of the Asante and Fante Language called Tshi (Chwee, Twi). 8vo. Basel, 1881.   K 14 Q 19

CHRISTIAN CHURCH. The Creed of the Christian Church. 8vo. Bathurst, 1879.   MG 1 Q 34

Where was your Church before Luther? 8vo. Bathurst, 1879.   MG 1 Q 34

CHRISTIAN EVIDENCE SOCIETY OF N. S. WALES. Witness for Christ: Lectures delivered in connection with the Christian Evidence Society of New South Wales in 1884. 8vo. Sydney, 1886.   MG 1 P 3

1. Barry (Rt. Rev. Alfred), D.D. Christian Evidence and Christian Faith.

2. Steel (Rev. Robert), D.D. The Bible and Science in their Mutual Relations.

3. Jefferis (Rev. James), LL.D. Christianity and Buddhism: a comparison and a contrast.

4. Archdall (Rev. Mervyn), M.A. Our Lord Jesus Christ the only credible explanation of the History, Scriptures and principles of Israel.

5. Kinross (Rev. John), D.D. Man's need of Religion.

6. Sharp (Rev. William Hay), M.A. How does the Theory of Evolution bear upon Religious Belief.

7. Hibberd (Rev. F.) The person of Jesus Christ: the Source of His Power.

8. Gordon (Alexander), Q.C., &c. The Bible, the only credible explanation of what man was, is, and will be.

CHRISTIAN KNOWLEDGE (SOCIETY FOR THE PROMOTION OF). Past and Present of the Society for Promoting Christian Knowledge, 1698–1860; by the Rev. T. B. Murray, M.A. 18mo. Lond., 1860.   G 6 R 33

Report of the Diocesan Committee of the Societies for the Propagation of the Gospel in Foreign Parts, and for Promoting Christian Knowledge, and the Anniversary Sermon by the Rev. W. B. Clarke, M.A. 8vo. Sydney, 1840.   MJ 2 R 18

Reports, 1827–1861. 8vo. Lond., 1827–61.   G 6 R 33

CHRISTIAN KNOWLEDGE—*continued.*
Reports of the District Committee of the Society for promoting Christian Knowledge, in the Archdeaconry of New South Wales in the Diocese of Calcutta, for the years 1828–62. 8vo. Sydney, 1829–63.   MG 1 Q 25

Rules and Regulations of. 12mo.   Sydney, 1826.
                                            MG 1 Q 25
Another copy.   MJ 2 Q 21

Statement of the Objects of the Committee of the Societies for the Propagation of the Gospel in Foreign Parts, and for Promoting Christian Knowledge. 8vo. Sydney, 1836.   MG 1 Q 25

Another copy.   MJ 2 R 22

CHRISTIAN MISSIONARY CIVILIZATION. [*See* JOURNAL OF CIVILIZATION.]

CHRISTIAN OBSERVER (THE). 37 vols. 8vo.   Lond., 1831–59.   E

CHRISTIE (JAMES), A.M., &c. Cholera Epidemics in East Africa. 8vo. Lond., 1876.   A 12 U 2

CHRISTIE (RICHARD COPLEY), M.A. Etienne Dolet, the Martyr of the Renaissance: a Biography. 8vo. Lond., 1880.   C 10 T 41

CHRISTIE (WILLIAM DOUGLAS), M.A., &c. Dryden; Stanzas, &c. [*See* DRYDEN, J.]

CHRISTIE (MAJOR WILLIAM HARVEY). A Love Story; by "A Bushman." 2 vols. 8vo. Sydney, 1841.* MJ 1 Q 12, 13

CHRISTISON (SIR ROBERT), BART., M.D. Life of; edited by his Sons. 2 vols. 8vo. Edinb., 1885–86. C 10 S 24, 25

Treatise on Poisons in relation to Medical Jurisprudence, Physiology, and the Practice of Physic. 4th ed. 8vo. Edinb., 1845.   A 12 S 20

CHRISTMANN (FR.), UND OBERLANDER (RICHARD). Australien; Geschichte der Entdeckung und Kolonisation. 8vo. Leipzig, 1880.   MD 2 Q 30

Ozeanien, die Inseln der Südsee. 8vo. Leipzig, 1873.
                                            MD 4 U 31

CHRISTMAS (REV. HENRY), M.A., &c. Emigrant Churchman in Canada. [*See* ROSE, REV. J.]

Republic of Fools. [*See* WIELAND, C. M. VON.]

Shores and Islands of the Mediterranean; including a Visit to the Seven Churches of Asia. 3 vols. 8vo. Lond., 1851.   D 7 R 2 4

[*See* CALMET, A.]

CHRISTY (WYVILL JAMES). Practical Treatise on the Joints made and used by Builders in the Construction of various kinds of Engineering and Architectural Works, &c. (Weale) 12mo. Lond., 1882.   A 17 Q 53

CHRONICLES OF LONDON, 1089–1483. Written in the 15th Century, and for the first time printed from MSS. in the British Museum; edited by Sir N. H. Nicolas. 4to. Lond., 1827.   B 15 Q 3 ‡

CHRONICLES OF THE CRUSADES. Contemporary Narratives of the Crusade of Richard Cœur-de-Lion; by Richard, of Devizes, and Geoffrey de Vinsauf. And of the Crusade of St. Louis; by Lord John de Joinville. 12mo. Lond., 1870.   B 10 P 23

CHRONICLES AND MEMORIALS OF GREAT BRITAIN and Ireland during the Middle Ages. Published by the authority of the Lords Commissioners of Her Majesty's Treasury, under the direction of the Master of the Rolls. 189 vols. roy. 8vo. Lond., 1858–85.   E

CHRYSOSTOMUS (SANCTUS JOANNES), ARCHBISHOP OF CANTERBURY. Opera omnia. [*See* MIGNE, J. P., SERIES GRÆCA, 47–64.]

CHUANG TSZE. The Divine Classic of Nan-Hua; being the Works of Chuang Tsze, Taoist Philosopher [translated], by F. H. Balfour, F.R.G.S. 8vo. Shanghai, 1881.   G 6 P 2

CHUCK (THOMAS). "One Story is Good till Another is Told"; or, a Reply to Mr. Anthony Trollope. 8vo. Liverpool, 1877.   MD 3 S 19

CHUCK (T. F.) Key to the Historical Picture of the Explorers and Early Colonists of Victoria. 8vo. Melb., 1872.   MJ 2 R 13

Photographs of the Pictures in the National Gallery, Melbourne. [*See* CLARKE, MARCUS A. H.]

CHUDLEIGH (MARY), LADY. The Ladies Defence; or, the Bride-Woman's Counsellor answered: a Poem. 12mo. Lond., 1721.   H 6 Q 31

CHURCH (REV. ALFRED JOHN), M.A. Carthage; or, the Empire of Africa. 8vo. Lond., 1886.   B 1 P 49

Isis and Thamesis. Hours on the River from Oxford to Henley. Imp. 8vo. Lond., 1886.   D 8 V 14
[*See* LIVIUS, T.]

CHURCH (PROF. ARTHUR HERBERT), M.A. Acids, Alkalies, Soda, Ammonia, and Soap. (Brit. Manuf. Indust.) 8vo. Lond., 1876.   A 17 S 36

English Earthenware: a Hand-book to the Wares made in England, &c. (South Kens. Mus. Hand-books.) 8vo. Lond., 1884.   E

English Porcelain: a Hand-book. (South Kens. Mus. Hand-books.) 8vo. Lond., 1885.   E

Food; some account of its Sources, Constituents, and Uses. (South Kens. Mus. Hand-books.) 8vo. Lond., 1876.   E

Food Grains of India. 8vo. Lond., 1886.   A 1 T 3

Precious Stones, considered in their Scientific and Artistic Relations; with a Catalogue of the Townshend Collection of Gems in the South Kensington Museum. (South Kens. Mus., Hand-books.) 8vo. Lond., 1883.   E

CHURCH (FREDERICK JOHN), M.A. Trial and Death of Socrates. [*See* PLATO.]

CHURCH (R.) [*See* PARLIAMENTARY LIBRARY, VICTORIA.]

CHURCH (VERY REV. R. W.), DEAN OF ST. PAUL'S. Bacon. (Eng. Men of Letters.) 8vo. Lond., 1884.
C 1 U 9

Beginning of the Middle Ages (Epochs of Modern History.) 12mo. Lond., 1877. B 7 S 36

Hooker's Laws of Ecclesiastical Polity. [*See* HOOKER, R.]

Spenser. (Eng. Men of Letters.) 12mo. Lond., 1879.
C 1 U 32

CHURCH (MRS. ROSS), FLORENCE MARRYAT. [*See* LEAN, MRS. F.]

CHURCH (W. E.) [*See* THACKERAY, W. M.]

CHURCH ACT. Appeal to the Members of the Legislative Council of Van Diemen's Land against the "Church Act;" by "A Member of the Established Church of England." 12mo. Launceston, 1837. MJ 2 R 3

CHURCH HISTORY: Four Lectures, delivered in St. Andrew's Schoolhouse, Brighton, August and September, 1887; by the Rev. William Chalmers, by the Rev. Charles Pritchard, by the Rev. J. F. Stretch, and by the Rev. Canon Potter. 8vo. Melb., 1888. MG 1 R 15

CHURCH MISSIONARY SOCIETY. Proceedings, 1829-30; containing the Anniversary Sermon [by the Very Rev. H. Pearson.] (Pam. 13.) 8vo. Lond., 1830.
MJ 2 Q 3
Proceedings, 1838-39; containing the Anniversary Sermon by the Rev. J. N. Pearson, M.A. (Pam. 13.) 8vo. Lond., 1839. MJ 2 Q 3

Address from the Church Missionary Society to Heads of Families, &c. 8vo. Lond. (n.d.) MG 1 Q 27

CHURCH OF ENGLAND. Act to enable the Bishop, Clergy, and Laity of the United Church of England and Ireland in Tasmania, to regulate the affairs of the said Church. Fol. Hobart, 1858. MJ 2 U 1

Brief Memoranda of Synodical Action in Canada, the United States, and Scotland. (Pam. 26.) 8vo. Newcastle, 1858. MJ 2 Q 14

Church of England and the Sydney University. [*See* SYDNEY UNIVERSITY.]

Church of England Endowment Fund. Circular Letter by the Bishop, and Report. 8vo. Sydney, 1861. MG 1 Q 26

Diocese of Dunedin: Report of Proceedings of the Synod, December 11th, 1872. 8vo. Dunedin, 1873. MG 1 Q 30

Diocesan Synods, and the Bishop's Veto. 8vo. Sydney, 1858. MJ 2 Q 14

Minutes of a Conference of the Clergy and Laity of the United Church of England and Ireland in the Colony of Victoria. 8vo. Melb., 1854. MG 1 Q 31

Minutes of the Proceedings of the Diocesan Synod of Tasmania, 1857-58. (Pam. A.) Fol. Hobart, 1857-58.
MJ 2 U 1

CHURCH OF ENGLAND—*continued.*
Minutes of Proceedings at a Meeting of the Metropolitan and Suffragan Bishops of the Province of Australasia. (Pam., C.) Roy. 8vo. Sydney, 1850. MJ 2 S 1

Reports of the Church Society for the Diocese of Sydney, for the years 1856-60. 1863-64. 8vo. Sydney, 1857-65.
MG 1 Q 24

Report of the Church Society for the Diocese of Sydney, for the year 1885. 8vo. Sydney, 1886. ME 2 Q

Report of the Inaugural Meeting of the Church Society of the Diocese of Goulburn. 8vo. Goulburn, 1864.
MG 1 Q 24

Reports of the Newcastle Church Society, for the years 1852, 1859-61, 1863-64. 8vo. Sydney, 1853-65.
MG 1 Q 24

Schools of the Middle District: Rules for. (Pam., 41.) 8vo. Sydney, 1850. MJ 2 R 3
Another Copy. (Pam. A.) Fol. Sydney, 1850. MJ 2 U 1
Solemn Declaration of the Ministers of the Church of England in Van Diemen's Land, on the present Condition of the Church in that Colony. 8vo. Hobart, 1851. MG 1 Q 30

CHURCH OF ENGLAND BOOK SOCIETY. Report of the Church of England Book Society. 8vo. Sydney, 1841. MF 3 P 14

CHURCH OF ENGLAND CHRONICLE (THE). 4to. Sydney, 1856-65. ME 11 P 1†

CHURCH OF ENGLAND MISSION. [*See* ABORIGINES.]

CHURCH OF ENGLAND SCHOOLS. Rules for the Church of England Schools of the Middle Districts. 12mo. Sydney, 1850. MJ 2 R 3
Another copy. Fol. Sydney, 1850. MJ 2 U 1

CHURCH OF ENGLAND TRACT SOCIETY. Preparation for Death; or, the Churchman on a sick-bed. 12mo. Sydney (n.d.) MG 1 P 48

CHURCH OF SCOTLAND. Minutes of the Synod of Australia, in connection with the Established Church of Scotland, A.D. 1840-43. 8vo. Sydney, 1840-43. MG 1 R 2
Minutes of Synod of Australia, in connection with the Established Church of Scotland, 1842. 8vo. Sydney, 1842. MJ 2 Q 2
Another copy, 1840-41. 8vo. Sydney, 1841. MJ 2 S 1
Minutes of the Synod of the Presbyterian Church of Eastern Australia, for the years 1882-87. 8vo. Sydney, 1888.* MG 2 Q 5
Practical Remarks on the Scotch Church Question. (Pam. 11.) 8vo. Lond., 1841. F 12 P 9
Proceedings of the Presbytery of New South Wales, 1835. (Parl. Docs. 33.) Fol. Sydney, 1835. MF 4 ‡
Report of a Committee of a Commission of the General Assembly, relative to the Division in the Presbyterian Church of New South Wales. 8vo. Edinb., 1840.
MG 1 Q 26

[*See* PRESBYTERIAN TRACTS.]

CHURCH SOCIETY. [*See* CHURCH OF ENGLAND.]

CHURCHILL (REV. CHARLES). Life and Poems of. [*See* CHALMERS, A., *and* JOHNSON, S.]
Poetical Works of. 3 vols. 12mo. Boston, 1854.   H 7 Q 5-7

CHURCHILL (G. C.). F.G.S. The Dolomite Mountains. [*See* GILBERT, J.]

CHURCHILL (OWNSHAM AND JOHN). Collection of Voyages and Travels, from original Manuscripts. 3rd ed. 6 vols. fol. Lond., 1744-46.   D 36 R 2-7 ‡
Supplement [to the above]; compiled from the Library of the Earl of Oxford, by Thomas Osborne. 2 vols. fol. Lond., 1846.   D 36 R 8, 9 ‡

CHURCHWARD (WILLIAM B.) My Consulate in Samoa: a Record of Four Years' Sojourn in the Navigators Islands. 8vo. Lond., 1887.   MD 7 P 28

CHURCHYARD (THOMAS). Churchyard's Good Will: Sad and Heavy Verses for the Losse of the Archbishop of Canterbury. [*See* PARK, T.]
Sad and Solemne Funerall of the Right Honorable Sir Francis Knowles. [*See* PARK, T.]

CHURSLEY (MISS F. A.) Wild Flowers around Melbourne. Fol. Lond., 1867.   MA 1 R 20 ‡

CIAMPITTO (N.) [*See* HERCULANENSIUM.]

CIBBER (COLLEY). Apology for the Life of Mr. Colley Cibber, Comedian; written by himself. (Autobiog.) 12mo. Lond., 1826.   C 1 P 5
The Careless Husband: a Comedy. (Bell's Brit. Theatre.) 18mo. Lond., 1791.   H 2 P 36
Another copy. (Brit. Theatre.) 12mo. Lond., 1808.   H 1 P 9
Another copy. (New Eng. Theatre.) 12mo. Lond., 1790.   H 4 P 22
Another copy. [*See* BRIT. DRAMA, 3.]
The Double Gallant; or, the Sick Lady's Cure: a Comedy. (Bell's Brit. Theatre.) 18mo. Lond., 1792.   H 2 P 35
Another copy. (New Eng. Theatre.) 12mo. Lond., 1777.   H 4 P 24
Another copy. [*See* BRIT. DRAMA, 3.]
The Hypocrite: a Comedy; altered by I. Bickerstaff. (Bell's Brit. Theatre.) 18mo. Lond., 1792.   H 2 P 24
Another copy. (Cumberland's Eng. Theatre.) 12mo. Lond., 1829.   H 2 Q 12
Another copy. (New Eng. Theatre.) 12mo. Lond., 1786.   H 4 P 28
The Lady's Last Stake; or, the Wife's Resentment: a Comedy. (Bell's Brit. Theatre.) 18mo. Lond., 1795.   H 2 P 32

CIBBER (COLLEY).—*continued.*
Love makes a Man : a Comedy. (Bell's Brit. Theatre.) 18mo. Lond., 1791.   H 2 P 7
Another copy. (Brit. Theatre.) 12mo. Lond., 1808.   H 1 P 9
Another copy. (New Eng. Theatre.) 12mo. Lond., 1789.   H 4 P 22
Another copy. [*See* BRIT. DRAMA, 5.]
The Provoked Husband. [*See* VANBRUGH, SIR J.]
The Refusal: a Comedy. (Bell's Brit. Theatre.) 18mo. Lond., 1792.   H 2 P 38
She wou'd and she wou'd not: a Comedy. (Bell's Brit. Theatre.) 18mo. Lond., 1792.   H 2 P 38
Another copy. (Brit. Theatre.) 12mo. Lond., 1808.   H 1 P 9
Another copy. (New Eng. Theatre.) 12mo. Lond., 1788.   H 4 P 28
Another copy. [*See* BRIT. DRAMA, 3.]

CICERO (MARCUS TULLIUS). Account of the Life and Letters of; translated from the German of B. R. Abeken; edited by Charles Merivale. 8vo. Lond., 1854.   C 1 S 18
Academic Questions, Treatise de Finibus, and Tusculan Disputations of M. T. Cicero ; with a Sketch of the Greek Philosophers mentioned by Cicero; literally translated by C. D. Yonge, B.A. 8vo. Lond., 1875.   G 16 P 8
Correspondence of, arranged according to its chronological order; with a revision of the Text, &c., by Robert Yelverton Tyrrell, M.A. 2nd ed. Vols. 1, 2. 8vo. Lond., 1885-86.   C 14 U 6, 7
History of the Life of; by Conyers Middleton, D.D. 2 vols. 4to. Lond., 1741.   C 2 W 6, 7
Letters of, to several of his Friends; with Remarks by William Melmoth. 8th ed. 3 vols. 8vo. Lond., 1814.   C 5 S 13-15
Life and Letters of; being a new Translation of the Letters included in Mr. Watson's Selection, by the Rev. G. E. Jeans, M.A. 8vo. Lond., 1880.   C 10 S 17
Life of; by Anthony Trollope. 2 vols. 8vo. Lond., 1880.   C 3 T 2, 3
M. T. Ciceronis Orationes quasdam Selectae cum Interpretatione et Notis ; uas in usum Serenissimi Delphini; edidit P. Carolus Mcrouille, S.J. 8vo. Lond., 1803.   F 13 Q 23
M. Tullii Ciceronis Orationes Verrinae ex Recensione et cum Animadversionibus Theop. Christ. Harles. 8vo. Erlangæ, 1784.   F 5 Q 18
M. Tullii Ciceronis Academica: the Text revised and explained, by James S. Reid, M.L. 8vo. Lond., 1885.   G 11 T 5
On Oratory and Orators; with his Letters to Quintus and Brutus; translated, or edited, by J. S. Watson. 8vo. Lond., 1876.   J 10 P 38
Opera omnia, ex Editione Io. Aug. Ernesti; cum Notis et Interpretatione in usum Delphini, curante A. J. Valpy, A.M. 17 vols. 8vo. Lond., 1830.   J 13 P 26-42

CICERO (MARCUS TULLIUS)—*continued.*

Orations of; literally translated by C. D. Yonge, B.A.
4 vols. 8vo. Lond., 1851–79. F 5 R 28–31

Orations, translated by Prof. W. Duncan; the Offices, by
T. Cockman; and the Cato and Lælius, by W. Melmoth.
3 vols. 12mo. Lond., 1833. J 15 P 4–6

Republic of Cicero; reprinted from the third edition of
Cardinal Mai (Rome, 1846), and translated, with Notes,
by G. G. Hardingham. 8vo. Lond., 1884. F 12 Q 7

Select Orations of, from the Text of Jo. Casp. Orellius;
with Notes, Critical and Explanatory, by the Rev. M.
M'Kay, M.A. 8vo. Dublin, 1833. F 12 P 3

Three Books of Offices, or Moral Duties; also, his Cato
Major, an Essay on Old Age; Lælius, an Essay on Friend-
ship; Paradoxes, Scipio's Dream; and Letter to Quintus
on the Duties of a Magistrate; literally translated by
Cyrus R. Edmonds. 8vo. Lond., 1877. G 16 P 9

[*See* SCRIPTORES ROMANI, *and* TYRRELL, R. Y.]

CICOGNARA (LEOPOLDO), CONTE. Biographical Memoir
of A. Canova. [*See* CANOVA, A.]

Storia della Scultura dal suo Risorgimento in Italia fino
al Secolo di Canova. Edizione seconda. 7 vols. 8vo.
Prato, 1823–24. A 7 R 23–29

Atlas (to above). Roy. fol. Prato, 1823–24. A 23 Q 14 ‡

CID (RODRIG. DIAZ DE BIVAR). Chronicle of the Cid
from the Spanish, by Robert Southey. 4to. Lond., 1808.
J 7 V 14

Romancero e Historia del Muy Valeroso Caballero el Cid
Ruy Diaz de Vibar. Edicion completa, con Vida del
Cid, por D. Juan de Müllen. 18mo. Fancofort., 1828.
H 6 P 42

CIHAC (ALEXANDRE DE). Dictionnaire d'Etymologie Daco-
Romaine comparés avec les autres Langues
Romanes. 8vo. Francofort, 1870. K 15 R 34

Dictionnaire d'Etymologie Daco-Romane, éléments Slaves,
Magyars, Turcs, Grecs-Moderne, et Albanais. 8vo.
Francofort, 1879. K 15 R 35

CINNAMUS (JOANNES). Historiarum libri VII. [*See*
MIGNE, J. P., SERIES GRÆCA, 133; *and* BYZANTINÆ
HIST. SCRIPT.]

CINQ CODES. [*See* CODES.]

CIRCULATING CAPITAL; being an Inquiry into the
Fundamental Laws of Money: an Essay; by "An East
India Merchant. 12mo. Lond., 1885. F 5 S 12

CITIES AND PRINCIPAL TOWNS OF THE WORLD.
(Laird. Cab. Cyclo.) 18mo. Lond., 1830. K 1 S 32

CITY MISSION. [*See* MELBOURNE AND SUBURBAN CITY
MISSION.]

CITY NIGHT REFUGE. Origin and Formation of the
Dixon-street Soup Kitchen; and of the City Night Refuge,
and Soup Kitchen, Kent-street; with Report. 8vo.
Sydney, 1870. MG 1 Q 26

CITY OF LONDON CENTRAL BIBLE ASSOCIA-
TION. Third and Fourth Annual Reports. 12mo.
Lond., 1815–16. MF 3 P 10

CIVIL ENGINEER AND ARCHITECT'S JOURNAL.
Vols. 1–28, 30, 31. 30 vols. 4to. Lond., 1837–68. E

CIVIL ENGINEERS (INSTITUTION OF). Charter, By-
laws, and List of Members. 8vo. Lond., 1885. E

Charter, Supplemental Charter, By-laws, and List of
Members. 8vo. Lond., 1887. E

Minutes of Proceedings of; with other selected and ab-
stracted Papers; edited by James Forrest. Vols. 1–82.
8vo. Lond., 1837–84. E

Name Index.—Subject Index. (Vols. 1–58. Sessions
1837–79.) 8vo. Lond., 1885. E

Transactions of the Institute of Civil Engineers, 1836–42.
3 vols. 4to. Lond., 1836–42.* E

CIVIL SERVICE BOARD OF N. S. WALES. [*See*
NEW SOUTH WALES.]

CIVIL SERVICE COMMISSIONERS, LONDON. Re-
port of Her Majesty's Civil Service Commissioners; with
Appendices. 8vo. Lond., 1862. F 1 R 12

CIVIL SERVICE CO-OPERATIVE SOCIETY OF N.
S. WALES (LIMITED). Rules of. (Pam. L.) 8vo.
Sydney, 1871. MJ 2 P 28

CLACY (MRS. CHARLES). Lady's Visit to the Gold Diggings
of Australia in 1852–53. 8vo. Lond., 1853.* MD 4 T 27

Lights and Shadows of Australian Life. 2 vols. 8vo.
Lond., 1854.* MJ 1 R 37, 38

CLAIRON (CLAIRE LEGRIS DE LA TUDE). Mémoires de.
[*See* BARRIÈRE, J. F., 6.]

CLANRONALD OF GLENGARRY. Vindication of.
[*See* RIDDELL, J.]

CLAPPERTON (CAPT. HUGH), R.N. Journal of a Second
Expedition into the Interior of Africa, from the Bight of
Benin to Soccatoo; to which is added, the Journal of
Richard Lander, from Kano to the Sea-coast. 4to.
Lond., 1829. D 2 V 13

CLARE (JOHN). Poems, descriptive of Rural Life and
Scenery. 12mo. Lond., 1820. H 6 Q 32

CLARENCE AND NEW ENGLAND RAILWAY
LEAGUE. Synopsis of the Proceedings in the Agitation
for a Line of Railway from the Clarence to New England.
(Pam. Dr.) 8vo. Grafton, 1875. MF 3 P 16

CLARENCE ALMANAC AND GAZETTEER. [*See*
PAGE, T.]

CLARENDON (EDWARD HYDE), EARL OF. Correspondence of, and of his brother, Laurence Hyde, Earl of Rochester; with Diary, 1687–90; and the Diary of Lord Rochester, in 1676. Edited, with Notes, by Samuel Weller Singer, F.S.A. 2 vols. 4to. Lond., 1828.
　　　　　　　　　　　　　　　　C 18 Q 11, 12 ‡

History of the Rebellion and Civil Wars in England. Fol. Oxford, 1732.　　　　　　　　　　　B 14 T 1 ‡

Another copy. New ed. 8 vols. 8vo. Oxford, 1826.
　　　　　　　　　　　　　　　　B 6 T 17–24

History of the Rebellion and Civil Wars in England; also, his Life, written by himself. New ed. 8 vols. roy. 8vo. Oxford, 1843.　　　　　　　　B 3 V 4, 5

Life and Administration of; with original Correspondence, and authentic Papers never before published, by T. H. Lister. 3 vols. 8vo. Lond., 1837–38. C 10 T 12–14

Life of; in which is included, a Continuation of his History of the Rebellion: written by himself. 3 vols. 8vo. Oxford, 1827.　　　　　　　　　　　C 10 T 15–17

Lives of the Friends and Contemporaries of Lord Chancellor Clarendon, illustrative of Portraits in his Gallery; by Lady Theresa Lewis. 3 vols. 8vo. Lond., 1852.
　　　　　　　　　　　　　　　　C 10 T 18–20

Mémoires de. [*See* GUIZOT, F. P. G., 12–16.]

CLARETIE (JULES). Camille Desmoulins and his Wife: Passages from the History of the Dantonists: translated by Mrs. Cashel Hoey. 8vo. Lond., 1876.　C 10 S 13

CLARINDA. [*See* MACLEHOSE, MRS. A. C.]

CLARK (CHARLES). Summary of Colonial Law: the Practice of the Court of Appeals from the Plantations and of the Laws and their Administration. 8vo. Lond., 1834.
　　　　　　　　　　　　　　　　MF 3 Q 62

Another copy.　　　　　　　　　　F 10 P 17

CLARK (CHARLES HEBER), "MAX ADELER." Out of the Hurly Burly; or, Life in an Odd Corner. 8vo. Lond., 1871.　　　　　　　　　　　J 12 T 3

CLARK (DANIEL KINNEAR), C.E., &c. Construction of Roads and Streets. [*See* LAW, H.]

Elementary Treatise on Steam and the Steam-engine, Stationary and Portable. Illustrated. (Weale.) 12mo. Lond., 1875.　　　　　　　　　　　A 17 Q 34

Fuel, its Combustion and Economy; consisting of Abridgments of "Treatise on the Combustion of Coal and the Prevention of Smoke," by C. W. Williams, A.I.C.E., and "The Economy of Fuel," by T. Symes Prideaux. (Weale.) 12mo. Lond., 1879.　　　A 17 Q 10

Railways and Tramways. (Brit. Manuf. Indust.) 12mo. Lond., 1876.　　　　　　　　　　　A 17 S 29

Railway Machinery: a Treatise on the Mechanical Engineering of Railways. Illustrated. 2 vols. fol. Glasgow, 1855.　　　　　　　　　　A 23 P 21, 25 ‡

Tramways; their Construction and Working. Illustrated. 2 vols. 8vo. Lond., 1878–82.　　　A 6 S 1, 2

[*See* DEMPSEY, G. D., *and* SIMMS, F. W.]

CLARK (E. C.), LL.D. Analysis of Criminal Liability. 8vo. Cambridge, 1880.　　　　　　F 6 Q 14

CLARK (EDWARD H. G.) Man's Birthright; or, the Higher Law of Property. Sq. 12mo. Lond., 1885.　F 2 P 28

CLARK (GEORGE T.) Mediæval Military Architecture in England. Illustrated. 2 vols. 8vo. Lond., 1884. A 3 P 5, 6

CLARK (HENRY E.), M.R.C.S. Anatomists' Vade Mecum. [*See* WILSON, W. J. E.]

CLARK (HUGH). Concise History of Knighthood; containing the Religious and Military Orders which have been instituted in Europe. 2 vols. 8vo. Lond., 1784.
　　　　　　　　　　　　　　　　K 19 S 2, 3

Short and Easy Introduction to Heraldry; in two parts. 10th ed. 12mo. Lond., 1827.　　　K 10 S 1

CLARK (REV. JOHN A.), D.D. Glimpses of the Old World; or, Excursions on the Continent and in Great Britain. 2 vols. 8vo. Lond., 1840.　D 9 P 37, 38

Rome, its Wonders and its Worship, as seen and graphically delineated. 12mo. Lond., 1840.　D 7 P 31

CLARK (JOHN WILLIS), M.A. Cambridge: Brief Historical and Descriptive Notes; with Etchings and Vignettes. Fol. Lond., 1881.　　　　　B 18 S 1 ‡

CLARK (PERCEVAL). Index to Trevelyan's Life and Letters of Lord Macaulay. (Cabinet edition, 1878.) 8m. 4to. Lond., 1881.　　　　　　C 7 S 40

CLARK (SAMUEL). State of Rhode Island and Providence Plantations. Report of the General Treasurer, 1876. (Pam. Ja.) 8vo. Providence, 1876.　　F 7 S 24

CLARK (REV. THOMAS), M.A. Student's Hand-book of Comparative Grammar, applied to the Sanskrit, Zend, Greek, Latin, Gothic, Anglo-Saxon, and English Languages. 8vo. Lond., 1862.　　　K 12 P 14

CLARK (RT. REV. THOMAS MARCH). Rural School Architecture. Illustrated. (Bureau of Education.) 8vo. Washington, 1880.　　　　　　　　J 2 S 16

CLARK (CAPT. W.) Travels in America. [*See* LEWIS, CAPT. M.]

CLARK (W.), C.E. Sydney Drainage: Report to the Government of New South Wales on the interruption and disposal of the Drainage of the City of Sydney and Suburbs. Fol. Sydney, 1877.　　　MF I H 3

Sydney Water Supply: Report to the Government of New South Wales on various Projects for supplying Sydney with Water. Fol. Sydney, 1877.　MF I U 4

[*See* MANNING, J., *and* MOORE, T.]

CLARK (WILLIAM). History of the British Marine Testaceous Mollusca (Mollusca Testacea Marium Britannicorum). 8vo. Lond., 1855.　　　　　A 14 T 1

CLARK (Wm. Geo.), M.A. [*See* Shakespeare, W.]

CLARK (Capt. William P.) Indian Sign Language; with brief Explanatory Notes of the Gestures taught Deaf Mutes in our Institutions for their Instruction. 8vo. Philad., 1885. K 15 S 9

CLARK (William R.) History of the Christian Councils. [*See* Hefele, Rt. Rev. C. J.]

CLARKE (Rev. Adam), LL.D. Manners of the Ancient Israelites. [*See* Fleury, C.]

CLARKE (Capt. Alexander Ross), R.E., &c. Ordnance Trigonometrical Survey of Great Britain and Ireland. Account of the Observations and Calculations of the Principal Triangulation, and of the Figure, Dimensions, and Mean Specific Gravity of the Earth. Drawn up by Capt. A. R. Clarke, under the direction of Lieut.-Col. H. James, R.E., &c. 4to. Lond., 1858. A 1 S 15 †

CLARKE (Col. Sir Andrew), C.B., G.C.M.G. Sketch of. [*See* Becker, L.]

CLARKE (Charles), F.S.A. Architectura Ecclesiastica Londini ; or, Geographical Survey of the Cathedral, Collegiate, and Parochial Churches in London, Southwark, and Westminster, with the adjoining Parishes. Roy. fol. Lond., 1820. A 1 P 9 ‡

CLARKE (Rev. Charles C.) Wonders of the Heavens displayed, in twenty Lectures ; by the Author of "The Hundred Wonders of the World." Illustrated. 12mo. Lond., 1821. A 3 R 11

CLARKE (Charles Cowden). Riches of Chaucer ; with Notes, &c., and a Memoir of the Poet. [*See* Chaucer, G.]

CLARKE (Charles And Mary Cowden). Shakespeare Key : unlocking the Treasures of his Style, elucidating the Peculiarities of his Construction, and displaying the Beauties of his Expression ; forming a Companion to "The Complete Concordance to Shakespeare." 8vo. Lond., 1879. K 17 Q 19

CLARKE (Rev. Edward). Works of Saint-Pierre ; with a Memoir of the Author. [*See* Saint-Pierre, J. H. B. de.]

CLARKE (Rev. Prof. Edward Daniel), LL.D. Life and Remains of ; by William Otter. 4to. Lond., 1824. C 4 W 6

Travels in various Countries of Europe, Asia, and Africa. 4th ed. 11 vols. 8vo. Lond., 1817-24. D 9 T 1-11

CLARKE (Mrs. Eliza). Susanna Wesley. (Eminent Women). 8vo. Lond., 1886. C 2 S 39

CLARKE (Rev. George). Comparative Importance of Faith and Polity : an Address. 8vo. Hobart, 1855. MG 1 P 1

Correspondence in reference to the Sacraments. [*See* Sacraments.]

CLARKE (Lieut. George Sydenham), R.E. Principles of Graphic Statics. 4to. Lond., 1880. A 10 V 7

CLARKE (Henry G.) Art-Union Exhibition for 1843 : a Hand-book Guide for Visitors. 12mo. Lond., 1843. A 7 P 32

Hand-book Guide to the Cartoons now exhibiting in Westminster Hall ; designed in pursuance of Notices issued by H.M. Commissioners on the Fine Arts, in furtherance of the object of their Enquiry, whether Fresco Painting can be applied with advantage to the decoration of the Houses of Parliament. 12mo. Lond., 1843. A 7 P 32

The National Gallery ; its Pictures and their Painters : a Hand-book for Visitors. 12mo. Lond., 1842. A 7 P 32

CLARKE (Henry Hyde), D.C.L., &c. New and comprehensive Dictionary of the English Language. 7th ed. (Weale.) 12mo. Lond., 1872. K 11 T 7

Early History of the Mediterranean Populations, &c., in their Migrations and Settlements. 8vo. Lond., 1882. B 14 U 24

Grammar of the English Tongue, Spoken and Written. New ed. (Weale.) 12mo. Lond., 1859. K 11 T 6

Short Hand-book of the Comparative Philology of the English, Anglo-Saxon, Frisian, Flemish or Dutch, Low or Platt-Dutch, High Dutch or German, Danish, Swedish, Icelandic, Latin, Italian, French, Spanish, and Portuguese Tongues. (Weale.) 12mo. Lond., 1859. K 11 T 6

CLARKE (James Fernandez), M.R.C.S., &c. Autobiographical Recollections of the Medical Profession. 8vo. Lond., 1874. C 4 V 13

CLARKE (James Freeman). Ten Great Religions: an Essay in Comparative Theology. 8vo. Lond., 1871. G 14 Q 13

CLARKE (Rev. James Stanier), D.D., &c. Life of James II, King of England, &c. 2 vols. 4to. Lond., 1816. C 4 W 20, 21

Progress of Maritime Discovery, from the earliest period to the 18th Century. Vol. 1. (*All published.*) 4to. Lond., 1803. D 9 V 25

CLARKE (Rev. J. T.) English and Manx Dictionary. [*See* Kelly, Rev. J.]

CLARKE (Joseph Thatcher). [*See* Reber, Dr. F. von *and* Archæological Institute of America.]

CLARKE (Julius L.) History of the Massachusetts Insurance Department ; including a Sketch of the Origin and Progress of Insurance, and of the Insurance Legislation of the State, from 1780 to 1876. 8vo. Boston, 1876. F 10 S 19

CLARKE (Marcus Andrew Hislop). The Future Australian Race. 8vo. Melb., 1877. MF 1 Q 6

His Natural Life. 8vo. Melb., 1874. MJ 1 R 11

Another copy. 3 vols. 8vo. Melb., 1875. MJ 1 R 12-14

Another copy. Australian edition. 8vo. Melb., 1885.* MJ 1 R 15

CLARKE (MARCUS ANDREW HISLOP)—*continued.*

History of the Continent of Australia and the Island of Tasmania (1787-1870). 12mo. Melb., 1877.* MB2P18

Long Odds: a Novel. 8vo. Melh., 1869.　MJ 2 R 27

Marcus Clarke Memorial Volume, containing Selections from his Writings; together with Lord Rosebery's Letter etc., and a Biography of the deceased Author. Compiled and edited by Hamilton Mackinnon. 8vo. Melb., 1884.　MC 1 P 13

Mystery of Major Molineux, and Human Repeteads. 12mo. Melh., 1881.　MJ 1 R 10

Old Tales of a Young Country. 12mo. Melb., 1871.*
　　　　　　　　　　　　　　　　　　　MB 2 P 20

The Peripatetic Philosopher; by "Q." 12mo. Melb., 1869.　MJ 1 R 9

Photographs of the Pictures in the National Gallery, Melbourne. Photographed by T. F. Chuck; edited by Marcus Clarke. Fol. Melh., 1875.　MA 1 R 10 ‡

We Five: a Book for the Season. 8vo. Melh., 1881.
　　　　　　　　　　　　　　　　　　　MJ 2 R 15

CLARKE (Mrs. MARY COWDEN). Complete Concordance to Shakspere; being a verbal Index to all the passages in the Dramatic Works of the Poet. (New and revised ed.) Roy. 8vo. Lond., 1870.　K 17 R 19

CLARKE (PERCY), LL.B., &c. The "New Chum" in Australia; or, the Scenery, Life, and Manners of Australians in Town and Country. 2nd ed. 8vo. Lond., 1886.　MD 5 P 3

CLARKE (DR. S.) Discourse concerning the Being and Attributes of God, &c. 9th ed. 8vo. Lond., 1838.
　　　　　　　　　　　　　　　　　　　G 16 S 2

Historical Memoirs of the Life of; by William Whiston, M.A. 8vo. Lond., 1730.　C 4 T 3

CLARKE (SAMUEL), S.T.P. [*See* HOMER.]

CLARKE (CAPT. WILLIAM). Travels in America. [*See* LEWIS, CAPT. M.]

CLARKE (REV. WILLIAM BRANTHWAITE), M.A., &c. Anniversary Sermon, preached in the Church of St. James, Sydney, on Thursday, 24th June, 1840. 8vo. Sydney, 1840.　MJ 2 R 18

Claims and Supremacy of the Scriptures as the Rule of Faith and Practice, applied to the Doctrines of the Church of Rome: a Sermon. 8vo. Sydney, 1848.　MG 1 P 1

Another copy. (Pam. 20.)　MJ 2 Q 9

Effects of Forest Vegetation on Climate. (Pam. Ch.) 8vo. Sydney, 1876.　MA 2 Q 29

Another copy　MJ 2 R 14

Extracts from the Journal of an Exploring Expedition into Central Australia, under the command of E. B. C. Kennedy. [*See* KENNEDY, E. B. C.]

Illustrations of the Geology of the S.E. of Dorsetshire. (Pam. 9.) 8vo. Lond., 1837.　F 12 P 8

CLARKE (REV. WILLIAM BRANTHWAITE), M.A., &c.—*cont.*

Lays of Leisure: a Collection of original and translated Poems. 8vo. Lond., 1829.　MH 1 S 10

On Diornornis Australis—*Owen,* a new Fossil Bird of Australia. (Pam. Ch.) 8vo. Sydney, 1877.　MA 2 Q 29

Plain Statements and Practical Hints respecting the Discovery and Working of Gold in Australia. 8vo. Sydney, 1851.　MA 2 Q 37

Recent Geological Discoveries in Australasia. 2nd ed., with Notes and Addenda. 8vo. Sydney, 1861.*　MA 2 Q 36

Another copy. (Pam. 20.)　MJ 2 Q 9

Remarks on the Sedimentary Formation of New South Wales. 4th ed., corrected up to 1878, and enlarged. 8vo. Sydney, 1878.　MA 2 P 8

Researches in the Southern Gold-fields of New South Wales. 12mo. Sydney, 1860.*　MA 2 P 9

Santa-Cruz: Lines on the Death of Commodore Goodenough. (Pam. Fb.) 8vo. Sydney, 1874.　MH 1 Q 5

Sedimentary Formations. [*See* NEW SOUTH WALES.]

Sermon preached in St. Thomas's Church, Willoughby, in aid of Funds for the Relief of Sufferers by Floods in the Agricultural Districts of the Colony. 8vo. Sydney, 1864.　MG 1 P 1

Another copy　MJ 2 Q 9

[*See* CHRISTIAN KNOWLEDGE SOCIETY.]

CLARKE (WILLIAM JOHN TURNER). Portrait of. [*See* MANUSCRIPTS AND PORTRAITS.]

[*See* CHALMERS, BROS.]

CLARKSON (THOMAS), M.A. History of the Rise, Progress, and Accomplishment of the Abolition of the African Slave Trade by the British Parliament. 2 vols. 8vo. Lond., 1808.　F 6 S 9, 10

Memoirs of the Private and Public Life of William Penn. 2 vols. 8vo. Lond., 1813.　C 5 V 25, 26

Portraiture of Quakerism. 3rd ed. 3 vols. 8vo. Lond., 1807.　G 15 S 2-4

CLARSON (WILLIAM), F.L.S. The Flower Garden and Shrubbery. 18mo. Sydney, 1885.　MA 1 V 29

CLARSON, SHALLARD & CO. Illustrated Sydney News Saxby Almanac, 1865. 8vo. Sydney, 1865.　MJ 2 R 5

CLASSEN (J.) History of Rome. [*See* NIEBUHR, B. J.]

CLASSIC TALES; comprising Johnson's Rasselas, Goldsmith's Vicar of Wakefield, Swift's Gulliver's Travels, and Sterne's Sentimental Journey. 12mo. Lond., 1882.
　　　　　　　　　　　　　　　　　　　J 11 R 4

CLASSICAL MUSEUM (THE): Journal of Philology, and of Ancient History and Literature. 7 vols. 8vo. Lond., 1844-50.　J 15 S 1-7

CLAUDIANUS (CLAUDIUS). Opera omnia, ex Editione P. Burmanni Secundi; cum Notis et Interpretatione in usum Delphini. 4 vols. 8vo. Lond., 1821.　J 13 Q 14-17

CLAUS (PROF. C.) Elementary Text-book of Zoology. General Part and Special Part: Protozoa to Insecta; translated and edited by Adam Sedgwick, M.A. 8vo. Lond., 1884. A 14 S 15

Elementary Text-book of Zoology. Special Part: Mollusca to Man; translated and edited by Adam Sedgwick, M.A. 8vo. Lond., 1885. A 14 S 16

Kleines Lehrbuch der Zoologie. 8vo. Marburg, 1880. A 15 P 1

Another copy. 2nd ed. 8vo. Marburg, 1883. A 15 P 2

CLAUSIUS (RUDOLPH J. E.) Mechanical Theory of Heat; translated by Walter R. Browne, M.A. 8vo. Lond., 1879. A 10 R 36

CLAVIGERO (FRANCESCO SAVERIO). History of Mexico, collected from Spanish and Mexican Historians, from Manuscripts and Ancient Paintings of the Indians; translated by Charles Cullen. 2 vols. 4to. Lond., 1787. B 17 Q 7, 8 ‡

CLAY (HENRY). Letters to. [*See* GURNEY, J. J.]

CLAY (REV. WILLIAM KEATINGE), B.D. Liturgical Services: Liturgies and Occasional Forms of Prayer set forth in the Reign of Queen Elizabeth. 8vo. Camb., 1847. G 2 S 25

Private Prayers, put forth by authority during the Reign of Queen Elizabeth. 8vo. Camb., 1851. G 2 S 26

CLAYDEN (ARTHUR), F.R.C.I. England of the Pacific; or, New Zealand as an English Middle-class Emigration Field: a Lecture. 8vo. Lond., 1879. MD 4 V 19

Popular Hand-book to New Zealand; its Resources and Industries. 8vo. Lond., 1885. MD 3 Q 49

Revolt of the Field: a Sketch of the Rise and Progress of the Movement among the Agricultural Labourers, known as the "National Agricultural Labourers' Union;" 12mo. Lond., 1874. F 6 P 4

CLAYDEN (PETER WILLIAM). England under Lord Beaconsfield: the Political History of Six Years from the end of 1873 to the beginning of 1880. 8vo. Lond., 1880. B 6 P 3

Another copy. 2nd ed. 8vo. Lond., 1880. B 6 P 4

CLAYTON (ELLEN CREATHORNE). English Female Artists. 2 vols. 8vo. Lond., 1876. C 7 S 1, 2

Female Warriors: Memorials of Female Valour and Heroism, from Mythological Ages to the Present Era. 2 vols. 8vo. Lond., 1879. C 6 Q 21, 22

Queens of Song; being Memoirs of some of the most Celebrated Female Vocalists; with Chronological List of all the Operas that have been performed in Europe. 2 vols. 8vo. Lond., 1863. C 6 V 27, 28

CLAYTON (JOHN WILLIAM). "Ubique;" or, English Country Quarters and Eastern Bivouac. 8vo. Lond., 1857. D 8 U 29

CLAYTON (SIR RICHARD). [*See* TENHOVE, N.]

Y

CLEASBY (RICHARD). Icelandic-English Dictionary, based on the MS. Collection of the late Richard Cleasby; enlarged and completed by Gudbrand Vigfusson, M.A. 4to. Oxford, 1874. K 14 S 17

Appendix to the Icelandic-English Dictionary. [*See* SKEAT, REV. W.]

CLEGG (SAMUEL), JUNR., C.E., &c. Practical Treatise on the Manufacture and Distribution of Coal-gas. 5th ed. 4to. Lond., 1872. A 11 V 2

CLELAND (JOHN), M.D., &c. Animal Physiology: the Structure and Functions of the Human Body. 12mo. Lond., 1877. A 12 P 12

CLEMENS ALEXANDRINUS (TITUS FLAVIUS). Opera omnia. [*See* MIGNE, J. P., SERIES GRÆCA, 8, 9.]

CLEMENS (SAMUEL LANGHORNE), "MARK TWAIN." The Celebrated Jumping Frog of Calaveras County. Australian ed. 12mo. Melb., 1868. MJ 1 P 56

Innocents Abroad; or, the New Pilgrim's Progress. Illustrated. 8vo. Hartford, Conn., 1872. D 9 S 1

Life on the Mississippi. 8vo. Lond., 1883. D 3 P 59

Prince and the Pauper: a Tale for Young People of all Ages. 8vo. Lond., 1881. J 6 P 15

Stolen White Elephant, &c. 8vo. Lond., 1882. J 6 P 16

CLEMENT I (PAPA). Opera omnia. [*See* MIGNE, J. P., SERIES GRÆCA, 1, 2.]

CLEMENT III (PAPA). Epistolæ et Privilegia. [*See* MIGNE, J. P., SERIES LATINA, 204.]

CLEMENT XIV (GANGANELLI). Interesting Letters of; to which are prefixed Anecdotes of his Life; translated from the French. 2 vols. 12mo. Lond., 1777. C 1 R 12, 13

CLÉMENT (CHARLES). Michelangelo. (Great Artists.) 8vo. Lond., 1880. C 3 T 38

CLEMENT (MRS. CLARA ERSKINE), MRS. C. E. WATERS. Hand-book of Legendary and Mythological Art. 8vo. New York, 1871. B 14 Q 4

CLEMENT (CLARA ERSKINE), MRS. C. E. WATERS, AND HUTTON (LAURENCE). Artists of the 19th Century and their Works. 2 vols. 8vo. Lond., 1879.
K 18 P 13, 14

CLEMENT (DAVID). Bibliothèque curieuse, historique et critique; ou, Catalogue raisonné de livres difficiles à trouver. 9 vols. 4to. Göttingen, 1750–60. K 8 R 12–20 †

CLÉMENT (FÉLIX). Choix des Principales Séquences du Moyen Age traduites en Musique, et mises avec accompagnement d'Orgue. 8vo. Paris, 1861. A 8 T 15

Histoire Générale de la Musique Religieuse. Roy. 8vo. Paris, 1860. A 8 R 11

Les Musiciens Célèbres, depuis le seizième siècle, jusqu'à nos jours. Roy. 8vo. Paris, 1868. C 8 V 21

CLEMENTE (D. SIMON RONAS). Essai sur les Variétés de la Vigne. 8vo. Paris, 1814. A 1 Q 4

CLEMONS (Mrs. MAJOR). Manners and Customs of Society in India. 8vo. Lond., 1841. D 5 Q 10

CLERGY LIST for 1871 and 1882. 2 vols. 8vo. Lond., 1871–82. E

CLERGY AND SCHOOL LANDS. Documents and Correspondence relating to the establishment and dissolution of the Corporation of Clergy and School Lands in the Colony of New South Wales. (Parl. Docs., 5.) Fol. Lond., 1839. MF 4 ‡

CLERGYMAN, A. [*See* MORRISON, REV. J.]

CLERGYMAN OF THE CHURCH OF ENGLAND. [*See* LIDDON, REV. CANON H. P.]

CLERICI (F.) L'Ape : sua Anatomia, suoi Nemici. Sm. fol. Milano, 1875. A 2 S 21 †

CLERICUS ANGLICANUS. [*See* DEVIL, THE.]

CLERK (D.) The Gas-engine. 8vo. Lond., 1886. A 11 Q 19

CLERK (Sir G.) [*See* NORTON, G.]

CLERK (Mrs. GODFREY). [*See* FRERE, ALICE M.]

CLERKE (AGNES M.) Popular History of Astronomy during the 19th Century. 8vo. Edinb., 1885. A 3 U 26

CLERKE (CAPT. CHARLES), R.M. Authentic Narrative of a Voyage performed by Capt. Cook and Capt. Clerke. [*See* ELLIS, W.]

[*See* COOK, CAPT. J. *and* PARKINSON, S.]

CLERMONT (THOMAS FORTESCUE), LORD. History of the Family of Fortescue in all its Branches. 2nd ed. Roy. 4to. Lond., 1880.* C 7 R 6, 7 †

CLÉRY (JEAN BAPTISTE). Mémoires de. [*See* BARRIÈRE, J. F., 9.]

CLEVELAND (HORACE WILLIAM SHALER). Culture and Management of our Native Forests, for Development as Timber or Ornamental Wood. 8vo. Springfield, 1882. A 1 S 40

CLEVELAND (ROSE ELIZABETH). George Eliot's Poetry, and other Studies. Sm. 4to. Lond., 1885. J 9 S 6

CLEVERLY (C. F. M.) Wanderings of the Beetle. [*See* WARDEN, E. P.]

CLIFFORD (ARTHUR). State Papers. [*See* SADLER, SIR R.]

CLIFFORD (C. C.) [*See* BANNISTER, S.]

CLIFFORD (EDMUND). Greatest of all the Plantagenets : an Historical Sketch. 8vo. Lond., 1860. B 5 P 46

CLIFFORD (FREDERICK). History of Private Bill Legislation. 2 vols. 8vo. Lond., 1885. F 10 T 8, 9

CLIFFORD (HON. ROBERT), F.R.S., &c. History of Jacobinism. [*See* BARRUEL, A. DE.]

CLIFFORD (PROF. WILLIAM KINGDON), F.R.S. Common Sense of the Exact Sciences. 8vo. Lond., 1885. A 10 R 35

Lectures and Essays. 2 vols. 8vo. Lond., 1879. G 4 R 9, 10

Mathematical Papers ; edited by Robert Tucker, with an Introduction by H. J. Stephen Smith. 8vo. Lond., 1882. A 10 T 4

On the Classification of Loci. (Roy. Soc. Pubs. 6.) 4to. Lond., 1879. A 11 P 7 †

CLIMACUS (SANCTUS JOANNES). Opera omnia. [*See* MIGNE, J. P., SERIES GRÆCA, 88.]

CLINGAN (J. MORISON), M.A. Bruce's Travels and Adventures in Abyssinia. [*See* BRUCE, J.]

CLINT (ALFRED). [*See* GIBSON, G. H.]

CLINTON (HENRY FYNES). Fasti Hellenici : the Civil and Literary Chronology of Greece. 2 vols. 4to. Oxford, 1827–30. B 9 V 30, 31

CLIVE (ROBERT), LORD. Life of ; collected from the Family Papers, by Major-Gen. Sir John Malcolm. With a Portrait. 3 vols. 8vo. Lond., 1836. C 10 T 8–10

Life of ; by the Rev. G. R. Gleig, M.A. 12mo. Lond., 1848. C 1 T 33

Another copy. (H. and C. Lib.) J 8 P 29

Life of. [*See* MALLESON, COL. G. B.]

CLODE (CHARLES MATHEW), C.B., &c. Memorials of the Guild of Merchant Taylors of the Fraternity of St. John the Baptist, in the City of London ; and of its Associated Charities and Institutions. Roy. 8vo. Lond., 1875. B 5 U 47

Military Forces of the Crown ; their Administration and Government. 2 vols. 8vo. Lond., 1869. F 9 P 1, 2

CLODE (SAMUEL). Murder of. [*See* BOND, G.]

CLONCURRY (VALENTINE BROWNE LAWLESS), LORD. Personal Recollections of the Life and Times of. 8vo. Dublin, 1849. C 10 T 11

CLOSE (REV. F.) A Justification of the Charges brought against the British and Foreign School Society. (Pam. 43.) Lond., 1839. (*Reprinted.*) Sydney, 1839. MJ 2 R 6

CLOUÉ (VICE-ADM.) [*See* NEW CALEDONIA.]

CLOUET (FRANCIS). Three Hundred French Portraits, representing Personages of the Courts of Francis I, Henry II, and Francis II. Auto-lithographed by Lord Gower. 2 vols. imp. 4to. Lond., 1875. C 1 8 5, 6 ‡

CLOUGH (ANNE J.) First Reading Book. [*See* EICHENS, M.]

CLOUGH (ARTHUR HUGH). Poems and Prose Remains of; with a Selection from his Letters, and a Memoir, edited by his Wife; with a Portrait. 2 vols. 8vo. Lond., 1869.   H 7 S 1, 2

CLOUGH (JAMES CRESSWELL). On the Existence of Mixed Languages. (Prize Essay.) 8vo. Lond., 1876.   K 15 P 32

CLOUSTON (WILLIAM ALEXANDER). Arabian Poetry for English Readers; with Introduction and Notes. 8vo. Glasgow, 1881.   H 7 S 15

CLUB-ALMANACH. Annuaire des Cercles et du Sport. Première Année. 12mo. Paris, 1883.   E

Annuaire International des Cercles, 1884. Vol. 1. 12mo. Paris, 1884.   E

CLUTTERBUCK (JAMES BENNETT), M.D. Port Phillip in 1849. 12mo. Lond., 1850.*   MD 1 T 52

CLUTTERBUCK (ROBERT), F.S.A. History and Antiquities of the County of Hertford. 3 vols. imp. fol. Lond., 1815-27.   B 5 P 17-19 ‡

CLÜVER (PHILIPP). Germaniæ Antiquæ, Libri tres. Editio secunda. Fol. Lug. Bat., 1631.   D 19 U 12 ‡

Italia Antiqua. 2 vols. fol. Lug. Bat., 1624. D 15 T 4, 5 ‡

Sicilia Antiqua, cum minoribus insulis ei adjacentibus, item Sardinia et Corsica. Fol. Lug. Bat., 1619.   D 15 T 5 ‡

CLYDE (FIELD MARSHAL SIR COLIN CAMPBELL), LORD. Life of; illustrated by extracts from his Diary and Correspondence, by Lieut.-Gen. Shadwell, C.B. With Portrait. 2 vols. 8vo. Edinb., 1881.   C 10 T 6, 7

COAN (REV. TITUS). Life in Hawaii: an Autobiographic Sketch of Mission Life and Labors (1835-81). 8vo. New York, 1882.   MC 1 Q 9

COATES (AINSLIE). Letters of Frederic Ozanam. [See OZANAM, T.]

COATES (REV. CHARLES), LL.B. History and Antiquities of Reading. Roy. 4to. Lond., 1802.   B 18 R 1 ‡

COATES (DANDESON). New Zealanders and their Lands. Report of the Select Committee. (Pam. 15). 8vo. Lond., 1844.   MJ 2 Q 5

Notes for the Information of those Members of the Deputation to Lord Glenelg, respecting the New Zealand Association, who have not attended the Meetings of the Committee on the subject. 8vo. Lond., 1837. MF 1 Q 15

Principles, Objects, and Plan of the New Zealand Association examined, in a Letter to the Rt. Hon. Lord Glenelg. 8vo. Lond., 1837.   MB 1 Q 11

Another copy.   MF 1 Q 15

COATES (D.) BEECHAM (REV. J.), AND ELLIS (REV. W.) Christianity, the Means of Civilization: shown in the Evidence given before a Committee of the House of Commons on Aborigines. 8vo. Lond. 1837.* MG 1 P 46

COBB (B. F.) Silk. (Brit. Manuf. Indust.) 12mo. Lond., 1876.   A 17 S 37

COBB (JAMES). The Doctor and the Apothecary. [See FARCES, 6.]

The First Floor: a Farce. [See FARCES, 6.]

Paul and Virginia: a Musical Entertainment. (Cumberland's Eng. Theatre.) 12mo. Lond., 1829.   H 2 Q 15

Rama Droog: a Comic Opera. [See MODERN THEATRE, 6.]

The Siege of Belgrade: a Comic Opera. (Cumberland's Eng. Theatre.) 12mo. Lond., 1829.   H 2 Q 15

The Wife of Two Husbands: a Musical Drama. [See MODERN THEATRE, 6.]

COBBE (MISS FRANCES POWER). Alone to the Alone: Prayers for Theists by several Contributors. 3rd ed. 12mo. Lond., 1881.   G 13 S 27

Broken Lights: an Inquiry into the Present Condition and Future Prospects of Religious Faith. 2nd ed. 8vo. Lond., 1865.   G 13 S 24

Another copy. 3rd ed. 12mo. Lond., 1878.   G 13 S 25

Cities of the Past. 12mo. Lond., 1864.   D 5 P 20

Darwinism in Morals, and other Essays. 8vo. Lond., 1872.   G 6 R 24

Dawning Lights: an Inquiry concerning the Secular Results of the New Reformation. 12mo. Lond., 1882. G 13 S 23

Duties of Women: a Course of Lectures. 2nd ed. 12mo. Lond., 1882.   G 13 S 26

Essays on the Pursuits of Women. 12mo. Lond., 1863.   F 1 P 36

A Faithless World. 8vo. Lond., 1885.   G 6 R 23

False Beasts and True: Essays on Natural (and Unnatural) History. 12mo. Lond., 1875.   A 14 P 68

Hopes of the Human Race, Hereafter and Here. 8vo. Lond., 1874.   G 13 S 30

Hours of Work and Play. 12mo. Lond., 1867. J 10 Q 22

Italics: Brief Notes on Politics, People, and Places in Italy, in 1864. 2nd ed. 8vo. Lond., 1864.   D 8 Q 9

Moral Aspects of Vivisection. 3rd ed. 8vo. Lond., 1877.   G 13 S 31

The Peak in Darien; with some other Inquiries touching Concerns of the Soul and the Body. 8vo. Lond., 1882.   G 13 S 32

Re-Echoes. 12mo. Lond., 1876.   G 13 S 29

Religious Demands of the Age: a Reprint of the Preface to the Collected Works of Theodore Parker. 8vo. Lond., 1863.   G 13 S 31

Religious Duty. 8vo. Lond., 1864.   G 13 S 21

Studies, New and Old, of Ethical and Social Subjects. 8vo. Lond., 1865.   G 13 S 19

Thanksgiving: a Chapter of Religious Duty. 12mo. Lond., 1863.   G 13 S 28

Works of Theodore Parker. [See PARKER, T.]

COBBETT (JAMES PAUL). On Pronunciation. [See COBBETT, W.]

COBBETT (REV. RICHARD STUTELY), M.A. Memorials of
Twickenham, Parochial and Topographical. 8vo. Lond.,
1872.   B 6 R 39

COBBETT (WILLIAM). Advice to Young Men, and
(incidentally) to Young Women, in the middle and
higher Ranks of Life. 12mo. Lond., 1865.   J 10 Q 9

Biographies of John Wilkes and William Cobbett; by the
Rev. John Selby Watson. With Portrait. 8vo. Edinb.,
1870.   C 5 Q 30

The Bloody Buoy, thrown out as a Warning to the Political
Pilots of all Nations. 3rd ed. 12mo. Lond., 1797.
                                                    B 9 P 13

Corbett's Political Register (annual and weekly). 88 vols.
8vo. Lond., 1802–35.   E

Cottage Economy. 8vo. Lond., 1822.   A 1 P 47

French Grammar; or, Plain Instructions for the learning
of French, in a series of Letters. 16th ed. 12mo. Lond.,
1861.   K 20 P 1

Grammar of the English Language, in a series of Letters
intended for the use of schools and of young persons in
general. New ed., with an additional chapter on Pronunciation by James Paul Cobbett. 12mo. Lond., 1869.
                                                    K 11 U 27

History of the Protestant Reformation in England and
Ireland. Copyright ed., illustrated [in two parts]. 8vo.
Lond., 1846.   G 13 T 16

Legacy to Labourers: an Argument showing the Right
of the Poor to Relief from the Land. New ed. 12mo.
Lond., 1872.   F 1 P 28

Life of. 12mo. Lond., 1835.   C 1 R 11

Life of. [*See* DALLING AND BULWER, LORD.]

Parliamentary History of England. [*See* HANSARD, T. C.]

Peter Porcupine's Works; containing various Writings and
Selections, exhibiting a faithful picture of the United
States of America. 12 vols. 8vo. Lond., 1801. B 18 21–32

The Protestant Church in Ireland. [*See* HISTORICAL PAM-
PHLETS.]

Rural Rides during the years 1821–32. New ed., with
Notes. 2 vols. 8vo. Lond., 1885.   D 7 Q 41, 24

Selections from Cobbett's Political Works; by J. M. and
J. P. Cobbett. 6 vols. 8vo. Lond., 1835.   F 9 P 6–11

A Year's Residence in the United States of America;
treating of the Face of the Country, Climate, &c. 12mo.
Lond., 1822.   A 1 U 1

COBBOLD (REV. RICHARD). History of Margaret Catchpole, a Suffolk Girl. Illustrated. 3 vols. 8vo. Lond.,
1845.   MJ 1 S 7 9

A Voice from the Mount. 12mo. Lond., 1818.   G 9 Q 12

COBBOLD (REV. ROBERT HENRY), M.A. Pictures of the
Chinese, drawn by themselves. 12mo. Lond., 1860.
                                                    D 5 P 29

COBBOLD (THOMAS SPENCER), M.D., &c. Entozoa: an
Introduction to the Study of Helminthology, with reference
more particularly to the Internal Parasites of Man; with
a Supplement. Imp. 8vo. Lond., 1864–69.   A 15 T 7

Human Parasites: a Manual of Reference to all known
Species of Entozoa and Ectozoa which are found infesting
Man. 8vo. Lond., 1882.   A 12 Q 15

Our Food-producing Ruminants, and the Parasites which
reside in them. (Cantor Lectures, 6.) Roy. 8vo. Lond.,
1871.   A 15 U 21

Parasites: a Treatise on the Entozoa of Man and Animals,
including some Account of the Ectozoa. 8vo. Lond.,
1879.   A 14 S 40

Treasury of Natural History. [*See* MAUNDER, S.]

COBDEN (RICHARD), M.P. Life of; by John Morley. 2
vols. 8vo. Lond., 1881.   C 10 S 26, 27

Mr. Grant Duff on the Teachings of. (Pam. Dc.) 8vo.
Lond., 1871.   MF 3 P 17

Political Writings of; with an Introductory Essay, by Sir
Louis Mallet, C.B. 8vo. Lond., 1878.   F 6 P 11

Richard Cobden and the Free Traders. [*See* APJOHN, L.]

Russia, Turkey, and England. (Reprinted from "The
Political Writings of Richard Cobden.") 8vo. Lond.,
1876.   F 6 P 23

Speeches on Questions of Public Policy; edited by John
Bright and James E. Thorold Rogers. 2 vols. 8vo. Lond.,
1870.   F 13 P 18, 19

Another copy. 8vo. Lond., 1878.   F 6 P 12

What Next and Next? (Pam. 23.) 5th ed. 8vo. Lond.,
1856.   MJ 2 Q 11

The World's Workers: Richard Cobden; by Richard
Gowing. 13th thousand. 12mo. Lond., 1886. C 2 S 7

COBDEN CLUB. Commercial Policy of France, and the
Treaty with England of 1860. (Pam. Ds.) 8vo. Lond.,
1871.   MF 3 P 17

Essays, Second Series, 1871–72; by Emile de Laveleye, Hon.
G. C. Brodrick, W. Flower, M.P., T. E. C. Leslie, Herr
Julius Faucher, Herr John Prince Smith, Joseph Gostick,
James E. Thorold Rogers, Hon. David A. Wells, LL.D.
8vo. Lond., 1872.   F 10 T 15

Local Government and Taxation; edited by J. W. Probyn.
8vo. Lond., 1875.   F 5 R 7

Another copy.   F 10 T 14

Members of the Cobden Club, with Dates of Entrance,
corrected to September, 1880; Annual Reports, 1878 80.
12mo. Lond., 1880.   F 2 P 30

Speeches, &c., 1873 75. (Pams.) 8vo. Lond., 1873–75.
                                                    F 5 S 25

COBHAM (SIR JOHN OLDCASTLE), LORD. Life and Times
of the good Lord Cobham; by Thomas Gaspey. 2 vols.
8vo. Lond., 1884.   C 3 S 19, 20

Examination and Death of. [*See* BRITISH REFORMERS, 12.]

COBURN (F. W. AND F. L.) Almanacs for Three Thousand Years, extending from the year 1 A.D., to the year 3000 A.D.; carefully compiled from the valuable Work of Augustus De Morgan, with Additions. 12mo. Boston, 1881.   A 10 R 31

COCAIO (MERLIN) [*See* FOLENGO, T.]

COCHITUATE WATER BOARD, BOSTON. [*See* UNITED STATES.]

COCHRANE (ALEXANDER DUNDAS ROSS WISHEART B.) Young Italy. 8vo. Lond., 1850.   B 12 Q 26

COCHRANE (CAPT. C.) Journal of a Tour made by Señor Juan de Vega, the Spanish Minstrel of 1828–29, through Great Britain and Ireland. 2 vols. 8vo. Lond., 1830.   J 2 R 15, 16

COCHRANE (CAPT. CHARLES STUART). Journal of a Residence and Travels in Colombia, during the years 1823–24. 2 vols. 8vo. Lond., 1825.   D 3 S 48, 49

COCHRANE (CAPT. JOHN DUNDAS), R.N. Pedestrian Journey through Russia and Siberian Tartary to the Frontiers of China, the Frozen Sea, and Kamtchatka. (Const. Misc.) 2 vols. 18mo. Edinb., 1829.   K 10 Q 24, 25

COCHRANE (ROBERT). The English Essayists, from Lord Bacon to John Ruskin; with Introduction, Biographical Notices, and Critical Notes. Roy. 8vo. Lond., 1876.   J 7 U 3

The English Explorers; comprising Details of the more famous Travels by Mandeville, Bruce, Park, and Livingstone; edited by Robert Cochrane. 12mo. Lond., 1877.   D 10 Q 48

COCHRANE (THOMAS), LORD. [*See* DUNDONALD, EARL OF.]

COCKBURN (RT. HON. SIR A. J. E.), BART. [*See* TICHBORNE TRIAL.]

COCKBURN (H. M.) General Education, considered with reference to the antagonistic bearings on it of the Principles of the National System defined as Socialism, Socinianism, and Infidelity. (Fam. 26.) 8vo. Sydney, 1859.   MJ 2 Q 14

COCKBURN (HENRY THOMAS), LORD. Journal of; being a Continuation of the "Memorials of his Time," 1831–54. 2 vols. 8vo. Edinb., 1874.   C 10 T 44, 45

Life of Lord Jeffrey; with a Selection from his Correspondence. 2nd ed. 2 vols. 8vo. Edinb., 1852.   C7 R 34, 35

Memorials of his Time. 8vo. Edinb., 1856.   C 10 T 23

COCKERELL (JOHN THOMAS). Scenes behind the Curtain; or the Acts and Deeds of the Convict Detectives of New South Wales. 8vo. Brisbane, 1861.   MF 3 P 1

COCKMAN (T.) [*See* CICERO, M. T.]

COCKS (C.) [*See* MICHELET, J.]

COCONUT PALM (THE). All about the Coconut Palm, including Practical Instructions for Planting and Cultivation. 8vo. Colombo, 1885.   A 1 Q 26

CODE NAPOLEON; or, the French Civil Code. 8vo. Lond., 1824.   F 1 R 21

CODE OF GENTOO LAWS. [*See* GENTOO LAWS.]

CODE OF PAY REGULATIONS of the various Military Establishments under the Presidency of Fort William, arranged by Capt. W. S. Greene. Fol. Kidderpore, 1803.   F 29 P 16 ‡

CODES (LES CINQ). Les Cinq Codes—Die fünf französischen Gesetzbücher mit gegenüberstehendem französischen Text. Herausgegeben von Johann Cramer. 12mo. Koblenz (n.d.)   F 2 P 5

Conférence des Cinq Codes. [*See* BOURGUIGNON, F.]

CODEX ALEXANDRINUS. Facsimile of the Codex Alexandrinus. Old Testament: Genesis to Ecclesiasticus. 3 vols. fol. Lond., 1881–83.   G 29 P 7—9 ‡

CODEX DIPLOMATICUS AEVI SAXONICI. Opera Johannis M. Kemble. 2 vols. 8vo. Lond., 1839–40.   F 7 S 15, 16

CODINUS (GEORGIUS). Opera omnia. [*See* MIGNE, J. P., SERIES GRÆCA, 157, *and* BYZANTINÆ HIST. SCRIPT.]

CODINUS CUROPALATE. [*See* BYZANTINÆ HIST. SCRIPT.]

CODRINGTON (R. H.), D.D. Melanesian Languages. 8vo. Oxford, 1885.   MK 1 R 15

COFFEY (C.) The Devil to Pay; an Opera. [*See* FARCES, 5.]

Another copy. [*See* BRITISH DRAMA, 5.]

COFFEY (DEAN N.) Catholics not Idolators, nor under a Satanic Delusion; with some of the Real Differences of the Catholic and Protestant Churches. 12mo. Melb., 1850.   MG 1 Q 40

[*See* TROLLOPE, REV. W.]

COFFIN (LEVI). Reminiscences of Levi Coffin, the reputed President of the Underground Railroad; being a brief History of the Labors of a Lifetime in behalf of the Slave. 8vo. Lond., 1876.   C 3 V 2

COGAN (T.) [*See* CAMPER, PROF. P.]

COGHLAN (T. A.), A.M. Australasian Statistics. 8vo. Sydney, 1886.   MF 3 R 28

Hand-book to the Statistical Register of the Colony of New South Wales, for the year 1885–86. 2 vols. 8vo. Sydney, 1886–87.   ME 3 V

Statistics showing the relative position and importance of each of the Australasian Colonies, during the year 1886, Roy. 8vo. Sydney, 1887.*   MF 3 R 29

COHEN (ISAIAH REGINALD). How will it End? 12mo. Sydney, 1886. MJ 1 U 14

Stanrope Burleigh: a Novel. 12mo. Sydney, 1872. MJ 1 U 13

COHEN (MAX). Garfield Souvenirs: the President's Courageons Sayings during his Critical Illness, and Gems of Press and Pulpit. 2 vols. (in 1) 12mo. Wash., 1881. C 1 P 30

COHEN (SIDNEY). New South Wales Cricketers' Guide and Annual. 12mo. Sydney, 1878. ME 3 S

COHN (PROF. H.) The Hygiene of the Eye in Schools. English Translation, edited by W. P. Turnbull. Roy. 8vo. Lond., 1883. A 12 U 18

COIN (R. L. DE). [See DE COIN, R. L.]

COKAIN (SIR ASTON). Dramatic Works of; with prefatory Memoir, Introductions, and Notes. 8vo. Edinb., 1874. H 3 S 26

COKE (SIR EDWARD). Life of. (Eminent Men.) 8vo. Lond., 1849. C 7 P 45

COKE (LIEUT. E. T.) Subaltern's Furlough; descriptive of Scenes in various parts of the United States, Upper and Lower Canada, New Brunswick, and Nova Scotia, in 1832. 8vo. Lond., 1833. D 3 R 47

COKE (REV. THOMAS), LL.D. Experience, &c., of Mrs. H. A. Rogers. [See ROGERS, MRS. H. A.]

COLBORNE (COL. THE HON. SIR JOHN), G.C.B., &c. With Hicks Pasha in the Soudan; being an Account of the Senaar Campaign in 1883. 12mo. Lond., 1884. D 1 Q 30

COLBURN (ZERAH), C.E. Locomotive Engineering and the Mechanism of Railways. (Text and Plates.) 2 vols. fol. Lond., 1871. A 23 P 28, 29 ‡

COLBURN'S UNITED SERVICE MAGAZINE. Colburn's United Service Magazine, and Journal of the Army, Navy, and Auxiliary Forces. 165 vols. 8vo. Lond., 1829-85. E

Report of Commissioners for inquiring into Naval and Military Promotion and Retirement, forming a Supplement to the United Service Journal, 1840 [now Colburn's United Service Magazine] (Pam. 11.) 8vo. Lond., 1840. MJ 2 Q 4

COLCHESTER (CHARLES ABBOTT), LORD. Diary and Correspondence of; edited by his Son, Charles, Lord Colchester. 3 vols. 8vo. Lond., 1861. C 6 U 5 7

COLDEN (CADWALLADER D.) Memoir prepared at the Celebration on the Completion of the New York Canals. 4to. New York, 1825. B 1 V 4

COLDWATER STATE PUBLIC SCHOOL. [See ALDEN, L. P.]

COLE (ALFRED W.) Who's your Friend? [See BLACKWOOD'S BOOKS FOR EVERYBODY.]

COLE (GEORGE R. FITZ-ROY). Peruvians at Home. 8vo. Lond., 1884. D 3 P 60

COLE (GEORGE WARD). How a Protective Tariff worked in America: a Letter to the Editor of the *Age.* 8vo. Melb., 1861. MF 3 P 5

Protection as a National System suited for Victoria; being Extracts from List's National System of Political Economy; with an Introduction. 8vo. Melb., 1860. MF 3 P 5

Policy of Action in the Employment of the People. 8vo. Melb., 1871. MF 1 Q 6

COLE (SIR HENRY), K.C.B. Fifty Years of Public Work of; accounted for in his Deeds, Speeches, and Writings. 2 vols. 8vo. Lond., 1884. C 10 S 20, 21

COLE (JOHN WILLIAM). Memoirs of British Generals distinguished during the Peninsular War. 2 vols. 8vo. Lond., 1856. C 3 S 3, 4

Natural Religion. [See SIMON, J.]

COLEBROOKE (HENRY THOMAS). Biographical Essay. [See MÜLLER, PROF. F. MAX.]

Miscellaneous Essays. 2 vols. 8vo. Lond., 1837. J 5 S 1, 2

Another ed.; with Life of the Author, by his Son, Sir T. E. Colebrooke. 3 vols. 8vo. Lond., 1873. J 5 S 3-5

COLEBROOKE (SIR THOMAS EDWARD), BART., M.P. Life of the Hon. Mountstuart Elphinstone; with Portraits and Maps. 2 vols. 8vo. Lond., 1884. C 7 P 4, 5

Life of H. T. Colebrooke. [See COLEBROOKE, H. T.]

COLEMAN (REV. JOHN NOBLE), M.A. Memoir of the Rev. Richard Davis, for thirty-nine years a Missionary in New Zealand. 8vo. Lond., 1865. MC 1 Q 1

COLENSO (MISS FRANCES ELLEN). History of the Zulu War and its Origin. 8vo. Lond., 1880. B 1 Q 1

COLENSO (RT. REV. J. W.), DD., BISHOP OF NATAL. Arithmetic designed for the use of Schools; to which is added a Chapter on Decimal Coinage. New ed., by the Rev. J. Hunter, M.A. 12mo. Lond., 1883. A 10 S 23

Key to Arithmetic. [See HUNTER, REV. J.]

The Pentateuch and the Book of Joshua critically examined. 7 vols. 8vo. Lond., 1863-79. G 6 S 18-24

Student's Algebra; edited by the Rev. John Hunter, M.A. 8vo. Lond., 1878. A 10 S 2

Trial of the Bishop of Natal before the Metropolitan Bishop of Cape Town, and others, for erroneous teaching. 12mo. Cape Town and Lond., 1863. F 2 P 25

COLENSO (REV. WILLIAM), F.L.S., &c. In Memoriam: an Account of Visits to, and Crossings over, the Ruahine Mountain Range, Hawke's Bay, New Zealand, in 1845-47. Roy. 8vo. Napier, 1884.* MD 3 V 42

Three Literary Papers, read before the Hawke's Bay Philosophical Institute: 1 and 2, On Nomenclature; 3, On Macaulay's New Zealander. 8vo. Napier, 1883. MJ 2 S 10

COLERIDGE (ARTHUR DUKE), M.A. Goethe's Letters to Zelter; selected, translated, and arranged. [*See* GOETHE, J. W. VON.]

Life of Moscheles. [*See* MOSCHELES, MRS. CHARLOTTE.]

Life of Schubert. [*See* HELLBORN, K. VON.]

COLERIDGE (REV. DERWENT), M.A. Memoir of John Moultrie. [*See* MOULTRIE, JOHN.]

Memoir of W. M. Praed. [*See* PRAED, W. M.]

[*See* COLERIDGE, S. T.]

COLERIDGE (DERWENT MOULTRIE). Lines on the Public Funeral of W. C. Wentworth, May 6, 1873. 8vo. Sydney, 1873.   MH 1 Q 5

COLERIDGE (HARTLEY). Biographia Borealis; or, Lives of Distinguished Northerns. 8vo. Lond., 1833. C10T38

Essays and Marginalia. 2 vols. 12mo. Lond., 1851. J 8 R 10, 11

COLERIDGE (HENRY NELSON), M.A. Six Months in the West Indies in 1825. 2nd ed., with Additions. 8vo. Lond., 1826.   D 3 Q 18

COLERIDGE (HERBERT). Glossarial Index to the printed English Literature of the 13th Century. 8vo. Lond., 1859.   K 14 Q 31

Another copy. 3rd ed. (Fam. Lib.) 18mo. Lond., 1832.   K 10 P 34

COLERIDGE (RT. HON. SIR JOHN TAYLOR), D.C.L. Memoir of the Rev. John Keble, M.A. 8vo. Lond., 1869.   C 4 T 16

COLERIDGE (MRS. SARA). Phantasmion. 12mo. Lond., 1837.   J 7 Q 1

COLERIDGE (SAMUEL TAYLOR). Aids to Reflection. Edited by the Rev. D. Coleridge, M.A. 7th ed. 12mo. Lond., 1854.   G 13 T 28

Another copy. New ed. 8vo. Lond., 1884.   G 13 T 29

Anecdote Life of. [*See* TIMBS, J.]

Biographia Literaria; or, Biographical Sketches of my Literary Life and Opinions. 2 vols. 8vo. Lond., 1817. C 8 S 3, 4

Another copy, and two Lay Sermons. New ed. 12mo. Lond., 1876.   C 1 T 29

Coleridge: [A Biography]; by H. D. Traill. (Eng. Men of Letters.) 8vo. Lond., 1884.   C 1 U 37

Coleridge Abroad. [*See* HAZLITT, W. C.]

The Friend: a series of Essays, in three volumes, to aid in the Formation of Fixed Principles in Politics, Morals, and Religion. New ed. 3 vols. 8vo. Lond., 1818.   J 10 Q 11–13

Lay Sermons. 1. The Statesman's Manual. 2. Blessed are ye that sow beside all waters. Edited, with the Author's last Corrections and Notes, by Derwent Coleridge, M.A. 3rd ed. 8vo. Lond., 1852.   G 13 T 30

COLERIDGE (SAMUEL TAYLOR)—*continued.*

Lectures and Notes on Shakspere and other English Poets; collected by T. Ashe, B.A. 8vo. Lond., 1883. J 10 Q 10

Life of; by James Gillman. 8vo. Lond., 1838.   C 8 U 17

Miscellanies, Æsthetic and Literary; to which is added the Theory of Life; collected and arranged by T. Ashe, B.A. 8vo. Lond., 1885.   J 10 Q 14

Notes, Theological, Political and Miscellaneous. Edited by the Rev. D. Coleridge, M.A. 12mo. Lond., 1853. G 10 P 14

Poetical and Dramatic Works of. 12mo. Lond. (n.d.) H 3 P 6

Poetical Works of; edited, with Introduction and Notes, by T. Ashe, B.A. 2 vols. 12mo. Lond., 1885. H 6 Q 34, 35

Poetical Works of; including the Dramas of Wallenstein, Remorse, and Zapolya. 3 vols. 8vo. Lond., 1828. H 7 S 11–13

Specimens of Table Talk of. 2 vols. 12mo. Lond., 1835. J 7 Q 36, 37

Table Talk and Omniana of; edited by T. Ashe, B.A. 8vo. Lond., 1884.   J 10 Q 15

COLES (JOHN), F.R.A.S., &c. Summer Travelling in Iceland; being the Narrative of Two Journeys across the Island by Unfrequented Routes. 8vo. Lond., 1882.   D 7 V 4

COLET (VERY REV. JOHN), D.D., DEAN OF ST. PAUL'S. Life of. [*See* ERASMUS ROTERDAMUS, D.]

[*See* SEEBOHM, F.]

COLIGNY (ADMIRAL GASPARD DE). Coligny: the Earlier Life of the Great Huguenot; by Eugene Bersier, D.D.; translated by Annie Harwood Holmden. 8vo. Lond., 1884.   C 5 R 12

COLLADON (NICOLAS). Institvtio Christianæ cum Indice. [*See* CALVIN, J.]

COLLÉ (CHARLES). La Vérité dans le vin, comédie. [*See* BARRIÈRE, J. F.]

COLLECTANEA ADAMANTÆA. Edited by Edmund Goldsmid, F. R. H. S. Vols. 1–12. 12mo. Edinb., 1884–85.   E

COLLECTION OF FOUR HUNDRED PORTRAITS of Remarkable, Eccentric, and Notorious Personages. Printed from the original copper-plates of Caulfield's Remarkable Characters, Grainger and Kirby's Wonderful Museums. 2 vols. roy. 8vo. Lond. (n.d.) C 5 W 19, 20

COLLECTIONS relative to Claims at the Coronations of several of the Kings of England, beginning with King Richard II. 8vo. Lond., 1820.   B 4 T 2

COLLEGE OF SURGEONS (ROYAL). [*See* ROYAL COLLEGE OF SURGEONS.]

COLLETTE (CHARLES HASTINGS). Pope Joan. [*See* RHOIDIS, E.]

COLLIER (H.) [*See* CLARKE, MARCUS A. H.]

COLLIER (JEREMY), M.A. Ecclesiastical History of Great Britain, chiefly of England, from the first planting of Christianity to the end of the Reign of King Charles II. 2 vols. fol. Lond., 1708-14. G 35 P 13, 14 ‡
Another edition; with Life of the Author, by F. Barham. 9 vols. 8vo. Lond., 1840-41. G 6 S 8-16
Great Historical, Geographical, Genealogical, and Poetical Dictionary ; being a Curious Miscellany of Sacred and Prophane History. 2nd ed. 3 vols. fol. Lond., 1701-27. K 22 Q 7-9 ‡

COLLIER (JOHN PAYNE), F.S.A. Bibliographical and Critical Account of the rarest Books in the English Language. 2 vols. 8vo. Lond., 1865. K 7 S 32, 33
History of English Dramatic Poetry to the Time of Shakespeare, and Annals of the Stage to the Restoration. 3 vols. 8vo. Lond., 1831. B 6 S 23-25
Another copy. New ed. 3 vols. sq. 8vo. Lond., 1879. B 6 S 26-28
Inquiry into the Genuineness of the Manuscript Corrections in Mr. J. P. Collier's annotated Shakspere, folio, 1632. [*See* HAMILTON, N. E. S. A.]
Memoirs of the Principal Actors in the Plays of Shakespeare. (Shakespeare Soc.) 8vo. Lond., 1846. E
Poetical Decameron ; or, Ten Conversations on English Poets and Poetry, particularly of the Reigns of Elizabeth and James I. 2 vols. 8vo. Edinb., 1820. H 7 S 4, 5
[*See* SINGER, S. W.]

COLLIER (PETER), PH.D. Sorghum : its Culture and Manufacture economically considered as a Source of Sugar, Syrup, and Fodder. 8vo. Cincinnati, 1884. A 1 S 1

COLLIGNON (MAXIME). A Manual of Greek Archæology ; translated by J. H. Wright. Roy. 8vo. Lond., 1886. A 6 V 25

COLLIN DE PLANCY (JACQUES A. S. C. D.) Dictionnaire Infernal ; ou, Bibliothèque Universelle. 2nd ed. 4 vols. (in 2) 8vo. Paris, 1825-26. A 10 R 11-12

COLLINGS (GEORGE). Circular Work in Carpentry and Joinery : a Practical Treatise on Circular Work of Single and Double Curvature. (Weale.) 12mo. Lond., 1886. A 17 R 3
Practical Treatise on Handrailing. (Weale.) 12mo. Lond., 1882. A 17 Q 60

COLLINGWOOD (VICE-ADM. CUTHBERT), LORD. A Fine Old English Gentleman, exemplified in the Life and Character of Lord Collingwood ; by Wm. Davies. 8vo. Lond., 1875. C 3 S 43
Selection from the Public and Private Correspondence of, interspersed with Memoirs of his Life : by G. L. Newnham Collingwood. 2nd ed. 2 vols. 8vo. Lond., 1828. C 10 S 28, 29

COLLINGWOOD (G. L. NEWNHAM), F.R.S. Selection from the Public and Private Correspondence of Vice-Admiral Lord Collingwood. 2nd ed. 2 vols. 8vo. Lond., 1828. C 10 S 28, 29

COLLINGWOOD (J. F.) [*See* BUCHNER, DR. L.]

COLLINGWOOD (WILLIAM GERSHOM). Limestone Alps of Savoy : a Study in Physical Geology ; with an Introduction, by J. Ruskin. 8vo. Orpington, 1884. A 9 T 27

COLLINS (ARTHUR). The English Baronetage ; containing a Genealogical and Historical Account of all the English Baronets, now existing. 4 vols (in 5) 8vo. Lond., 1741. K 10 S 15-19
Peerage of England ; Genealogical, Biographical, and Historical. Greatly augmented, and continued to the Present Time ; by Sir Egerton Brydges, K.J. 9 vols. 8vo. Lond., 1812. K 10 S 20-28

COLLINS (CHARLES ALLSTON). The Eye-witness, and his Evidence about many Wonderful Things. 8vo. Lond., 1860. J 9 U 3

COLLINS (LIEUT.-COL. DAVID). Account of the English Colony in New South Wales ; with some Particulars of New Zealand. Compiled from the MSS. of Lieut.-Gov. King, &c. Illustrated. 2 vols. 4to. Lond., 1798-1802. MB 2 V 1, 2
Another copy. 2 vols. (in 1) 4to. Lond., 1798-1802. MB 2 V 3
Another copy. 2nd ed. 4to. Lond., 1804.* MB 2 V 4

COLLINS (JAMES), F.S.B. Guttapercha and Indiarubber. (Brit. Manuf. Indust.) 12mo. Lond., 1876. A 17 S 28
Hides and Leather. (Brit. Manuf. Indust.) 12mo. Lond., 1876. A 17 S 28

COLLINS (JOHN CHURTON). Bolingbroke : a Historical Study ; and Voltaire in England. 8vo. Lond., 1886. C 5 R 5

COLLINS (JOSEPH HENRY), F.G.S. First Book of Mining and Quarrying. (Weale.) 12mo. Lond., 1872. A 17 P 66
Hand-book of the Mineralogy of Cornwall and Devon ; with Instructions for their Discrimination, and copious Tables of Localities. 8vo. Truro, 1871. A 10 P 9
Mineralogy. 1. The General Principles of Mineralogy. 2. Systematic and Descriptive Mineralogy. 2 vols. 12mo. Lond., 1878-83. A 9 P 23, 24

COLLINS (WILLIAM). Life and Poems of. [*See* BRITISH POETS; CHALMERS, A.; *and* JOHNSON, DR. S.]

COLLINS (WILLIAM), R.A. Memoirs of the Life of ; with Selections from his Journals and Correspondence, by his Son. W. Wilkie Collins. 2 vols. 8vo. Lond., 1848. C 3 S 23, 24

COLLINS (WILLIAM WILKIE). Memoirs of the Life of William Collins, R.A. ; 2 vols. 8vo. Lond., 1848. C 3 S 23 24
Rambles beyond Railways ; or, Notes in Cornwall taken a-foot. 8vo. Lond., 1851. D 8 T 16

COLLINSON (ALFRED). Small-pox and Vaccination, historically and medically considered. (Pam. Ca.) 8vo. Lond., 1860.   MA 2 S 15

COLLINSON (REV. JOHN), F.A.S. History and Antiquities of the County of Somerset, collected from authentick Records, and an actual Survey made by the late Mr. Edmund Rack. 3 vols. roy. 4to. Bath, 1791.   B 17 R 15–17 ‡

COLLIS (WILLIAM). Map of the County of Bourke. [*See* BIBBS, T.]

COLLISSON (MARCUS). South Australia in 1844–45: a Description of the actual State of the Colony, of its Sources of Wealth, and of the Moral and Physical Condition of its Inhabitants. 8vo. Adelaide, 1845.   MJ 2 R 12

COLLYER (REV. ROBERT), AND TURNER (J. HORSFALL). Ilkley, Ancient and Modern. Illustrated. 8vo. Otley, 1885.   B 4 T 11

COLMAN (GEORGE). Broad Grins. 8th ed. 12mo. Lond., 1839.   H 6 Q 18

Comus: a Masque. [*See* MILTON, J.]

The Deuce is in Him. [*See* BRIT. DRAMA, 5.]

Another copy. [*See* FARCES, 6.]

Dramatic Works. 4 vols. 12mo. Lond., 1777.   H 1 R 27–30

The English Merchant: a Comedy. [*See* BRIT. DRAMA, 4.]

Another copy. [*See* MODERN THEATRE, 9.]

The Jealous Wife: a Comedy. (Bell's Brit. Theatre.) 12mo. Lond., 1792.   H 2 P 32

Another copy. (Brit. Theatre.) 12mo. Lond., 1808   H 1 P 16

Another copy. [*See* BRITISH DRAMA, 4.]

Secrets worth Knowing: a Comedy. [*See* MOD. THEATRE, 3.]

COLMAN (GEORGE), JUNR. The Battle of Hexham: a Play. (Brit. Theatre.) 12mo. Lond., 1808.   H 1 P 20

The Forty Thieves. [*See* SHERIDAN, R. B.]

The Heir-at-Law: a Comedy. (Brit. Theatre.) 12mo. Lond., 1808.   H 1 P 21

Inkle and Yarico: an Opera. (Brit. Theatre.) 12mo. Lond., 1808.   H 1 P 20

The Iron Chest: a Play. (Brit. Theatre.) 12mo. Lond., 1808.   H 1 P 21

John Bull: a Comedy. (Brit. Theatre.) 12mo. Lond., 1808.   H 1 P 21

The Mountaineers: a Play. (Brit. Theatre.) 12mo. Lond., 1808.   H 1 P 21

The Poor Gentleman: a Comedy. (Brit. Theatre.) 12mo. Lond., 1808.   H 1 P 21

The Surrender of Calais: a Play. (Brit. Theatre.) 12mo. Lond., 1808.   H 1 P 20

Ways and Means: a Comedy. [*See* FARCES, 7.]

Who wants a Guinea: a Comedy. [*See* MODERN THEATRE, 3.]

z

COLMAN (GEORGE), AND GARRICK (DAVID). The Clandestine Marriage: a Comedy. (Bell's Brit. Theatre.) 18mo. Lond., 1792.   H 2 P 15

Another Copy. (Brit. Theatre.) 12mo. Lond., 1808.   H 1 P 16

Another copy. [*See* BRIT. DRAMA, 4.]

COLMAN (W. A.) New South Wales Almanac and Remembrancer, for 1848. 12mo. Sydney, 1848.   ME 4 Q

Another copy.   ME 4 R

COLMAN FAMILY (THE). Memoirs of; including their Correspondence with the most distinguished Personages, by R. B. Peake. 2 vols. 8vo. Lond., 1841.   C 10 S 31, 32

COLNETT (CAPT. JAMES), R.N. Voyage to the South Atlantic and round Cape Horn into the Pacific Ocean, for the purpose of extending the Spermaceti Whale Fisheries. 4to. Lond., 1798.   MD 5 P 3 †

COLOMB (REAR-ADM. PHILIP HOWARD), R.N. Dangers of the Modern Rule of the Road at Sea, and the Manœuvring Powers of Ships as affecting Collision. 8vo. Portsmouth, 1885.   F 9 P 18

COLOMBAT DE L'ISÈRE (MARC). Traité complet des Maladies des Femmes, et de l'Hygiène de leur Sexe. 3 vols. 8vo. Paris, 1843.   A 26 S 16–18

COLONIAL AND ASIATIC REVIEW (THE). Colonial and Asiatic Review. Vols. 1, 2. 2 vols. 8vo. Lond., 1852–53.   ME 3 Q

COLONIAL AND INDIAN EXHIBITION. New South Wales: Official Catalogue of Exhibits from the Colony, forwarded to the Colonial and Indian Exhibition, London, 1886. 8vo. Sydney, 1886.*   MK 1 P 12

Another copy. 2nd ed. 8vo. Sydney, 1886.   MK 1 P 14

New South Wales; its Progress and Resources. 8vo. Sydney, 1886.   MF 1 R 40

Another copy. 2nd ed. 8vo. Sydney, 1886.   MF 1 R 41

New Zealand Court: Detailed Catalogue and Guide to the Geological Exhibits; by [Sir] James Hector, K.C.M.G. Roy. 8vo. Wellington, 1886.   MK 1 S 17

Official Catalogue. 8vo. Lond., 1886.   K 8 Q 37

Reminiscences of the Colonial and Indian Exhibition. [*See* RILEY, T., *and* CUNDALL, F.]

Report of the Royal Commission. 8vo. Lond., 1887.   K 8 Q 38

Reports on the Colonial Sections. [*See* WOOD, H. T.]

COLONIAL DISTILLATION. Report from the Committee on Colonial Distillation; with the Minutes of Evidence and Appendix. (Parl. Docs., 32.) Fol. Sydney, 1839.   MF 4 ‡

COLONIAL GAZETTE (THE). Weekly Journal: "Ships, Colonies, and Commerce." 8 vols. fol. Lond., 1839–46.   ME

COLONIAL HAND-BOOK (THE). Colonial Hand-book for Farmers and Gardeners. (Pam. 40.) Geelong, 1860.
MJ 2 R 2

COLONIAL INSTITUTE. [*See* ROYAL COLONIAL INST.]

COLONIAL INTELLIGENCER (THE); or, Aborigines' Friend: comprising the Transactions of the Aborigines' Protection Society. 3 vols. 8vo. Lond., 1847-51. MF 1 R 3-5

COLONIAL LAND AND EMIGRATION COMMISSION. [*See* EMIGRATION.]

COLONIAL LEGISLATIVE COUNCILS. Return of the Names of the Legislative Council in each of our Colonies or Settlements not having Legislative Assemblies, 1836-44. (Parl. Docs., 47.) Fol. Lond., 1845. MF 4 ‡

COLONIAL LITERARY JOURNAL. Colonial Literary Journal and Weekly Miscellany of Useful Information. Vols. 1, 2. Roy. 8vo. Sydney, 1844-45.* ME 10 P 1, 2 †

COLONIAL MAGAZINE (THE). Colonial Magazine and Commercial Maritime Journal; edited by Robert Montgomery Martin, Esq. 33 vols. 8vo. Lond., 1840-52. E

COLONIAL MAGISTRATE, A. [*See* HULL, W., *and* ROWCROFT, C.]

COLONIAL MILITARY EXPENDITURE. Report from the Select Committee on Colonial Military Expenditure. (Parl. Docs., 15). Fol. Lond., 1835. MF 4 ‡

COLONIAL MISSIONARY SOCIETY, V. D. LAND. [*See* VAN DIEMEN'S LAND COLONIAL MISSIONARY SOCIETY.]

COLONIAL MONTHLY (THE): an Australian Magazine. Vols. 1-5. 8vo. Melb., 1867-70. ME 2 T

COLONIAL MUSEUM, NEW ZEALAND. [*See* HECTOR, SIR J.]

COLONIAL OBSERVER (THE). Colonial Observer; or, Weekly Journal of Politics, Commerce, Agriculture, Literature, Science, and Religion, for the Colony of New South Wales. Fol. Sydney, 1841-44. E

COLONIAL OFFICE LIST (THE). Colonial Office List for 1871-85. Compiled by Edward Fairfield and John Anderson. 15 vols. 8vo. Lond., 1871-85. E

COLONIAL POLICY. Colonial Policy; with Hints upon the formation of Military Settlements, by "W. B. C." 2nd ed. 8vo. Lond., 1835. MJ 2 P 36

COLONIAL POSSESSIONS. Papers relating to Her Majesty's Colonial Possessions: Reports, 1883-85. 8vo. Lond., 1886. MF 2 S 30

Papers relating to Her Majesty's Colonial Possessions: Reports, 1884-85. 8vo. Lond., 1885. MF 2 S 31

Statistical Abstract for the several Colonial and other Possessions of the United Kingdom, 1856-70. Roy. 8vo. Lond., 1872. MF 2 S 36

COLONIAL SOCIETY (THE). Rules and Regulations; with an Alphabetical List of the Members. 12mo. Lond., 1837-38. MF 3 P 10

COLONIST, A. [*See* LIFE'S WORK AS IT IS.]

COLONIST (THE). The Colonist; or, Weekly Journal of Politics, Commerce, Agriculture, Literature, Science, and Religion, for the Colony of New South Wales. 6 vols. fol. Sydney, 1835-40. ME

COLONIST OF NEW SOUTH WALES, A. [*See* TRANSPORTATION.]

COLONIST OF TWENTY YEARS' STANDING, A. [*See* CARTER, S. G.]

COLONISTS' HAND-BOOKS. 6 vols. (in 1) 12mo. Lond., 1882-84. MD 4 P 48
  1. Canada.   4. South Australia.
  2. Queensland.   5. Cape of Good Hope, and Natal.
  3. New South Wales.   6. New Zealand.

COLONIZATION. Debate upon Mr. Ward's Resolutions on Colonization, in the House of Commons, June 27, 1839. 8vo. Lond., 1839. MF 3 P 7
Another copy. (Pam. 5.) MJ 2 P 39

COLONIZATION CIRCULARS. 7 vols. (in 1) 8vo. Lond., 1886. MD 4 V 44
  1. New South Wales.   5. Tasmania.
  2. New Zealand.   6. Victoria.
  3. Queensland.   7. Western Australia.
  4. South Australia.

COLONNA (VITTORIA). Her Life and Poems; by Mrs. Henry Roscoe. 12mo. Lond., 1868. C 2 P 39

COLONUS. [*See* A'BECKETT, SIR W.]

COLONY (THE). The Colony: a Poem, in four Parts. 12mo. Lond., 1853. MH 1 R 34

COLONY OF AUSTRALIA (THE). The Colony of Australia: Views of Sir Alfred Stephen and Sir John Robertson, and Views of the Press. 8vo. Sydney, 1887. MF 3 Q 34

COLQUHOUN (ARCHIBALD ROSS), F.R.G.S., &c. Across Chryse; being the Narrative of a Journey of Exploration through the South China Border Lands from Canton to Mandalay. Illustrated. 2 vols. 8vo. Lond., 1883. D 4 T 28, 29
Amongst the Shans. Illustrated. 8vo. Lond., 1885. D 4 T 30

COLQUHOUN (PATRICK), LL.D. Treatise on the Police of the Metropolis. 8vo. Lond., 1800. F 12 P 17
Treatise on the Wealth, Power, and Resources of the British Empire, in every Quarter of the World. 4to. Lond., 1814. F 8 Q 23 †

COLTON (CALVIN), LL.D. Tour of the American Lakes, and among the Indians of the North-west Territory, in 1830. 2 vols. 8vo. Lond., 1833. D 3 Q 7, 8

A Voice from America to England; by "An American Gentleman." 8vo. Lond., 1839. F 9 P 5

COLTON (REV. CHARLES CALEB), A.M. Lacon; or, Many Things in a Few Words. 8vo. Lond., 1833. J 6 U 8

COLTON (GEORGE W.) Atlas of America; illustrating the Physical and Political Geography of North and South America, and the West India Islands. Imp. 4to. New York, 1857. D 8 P 5 ‡

COLTON (ROBERT), "SYLVANUS." Rambles in Sweden and Gottland. 8vo. Lond., 1847. · D 7 T 40

COLTON (REV. WALTER). Visit to Constantinople and Athens. 12mo. Dublin, 1849. D 7 P 50

COLUMBA (SAINT). Life of. [*See* STOKES, W.] Life of St. Columba, founder of Hy; written by Adamnan; edited by William Reeves, D.D., &c. (Historians of Scotland.) 8vo. Edinb., 1874. B 13 P 50

COLUMBUS (CHRISTOPHER). Christopher Columbus, and the Discovery of the New World. From the French of the Marquis de Belloy. Imp. 8vo. Lond., 1885. C 4 P 15 †

Discovery of America by. [*See* VOYAGES AND DIS-COVERIES.]

History of the Life and Voyages of; by Washington Irving. 4 vols. 8vo. Lond., 1828. C 6 U 1-4

Life of Columbus, the Discoverer of America; by [Sir] Arthur Helps. 2nd ed. 12mo. Lond., 1869. C 3 Q 17

Life and Voyages of; by Washington Irving. 4 vols. 12mo. Lond., 1831. C 1 P 27

Voyages and Discoveries of the Companions of. [*See* IRVING, W.]

COLUTHUS. Translation from. [*See* CHALMERS, A.] Coluthi Raptus Helenæ. [*See* HESIOD.]

COLVIN (SIDNEY), M.A. Landor (Eng. Men. of Letters.) 8vo. Lond., 1881. · C 1 U 23

[*See* WOLTMANN, DR. A.]

COLYER (FREDERICK), M.I.C.E., &c. Gasworks: their Arrangement, Construction, Plant, and Machinery. 8vo. Lond., 1884. A 11 R 16

Hydraulic, Steam, and Hand Power Lifting and Pressing Machinery. 8vo. Lond., 1881. A 11 U 8

COMBE (ANDREW). Principles of Physiology, applied to the Preservation of Health, and to Physical and Mental Education. 7th ed. Edinb., 1838. A 12 Q 31

COMBE (CHARLES), M.D. Nummorum veterum populorum et urbium, qui in Museo Gulielmi Hunter asservantur descriptio figuris illustrata. Roy. 4to. Lond., 1782. A 2 R 5 †

COMBE (GEORGE). Constitution of Man, considered in relation to external objects. 9th ed. 8vo. Edinb., 1871. G 13 T 14

Education, its Principles and Practice. Collated and edited by William Jolly. 8vo. Lond., 1879. G 17 Q 28

Life of; by Charles Gibbon. 2 vols. 8vo. Lond., 1878. C 6 U 8, 9

On the Relation between Science and Religion. 5th ed. 8vo. Edinb., 1872. G 8 T 9

System of Phrenology. 4th ed. 8vo. Edinb., 1836. A 12 S 10, 11

COMBE (TAYLOR). Veterum Populorum et Regum Numi qui in Museo Britannico adservantur. Roy. 4to. Lond., 1814. A 2 R 2 †

COMBE (THOMAS). Illustrations of Baptismal Fonts. 8vo. Lond., 1884. A 3 P 27

COMBE (WILLIAM). First, Second, and Third Tour of Doctor Syntax in search of the Picturesque, in search of Consolation, and in search of a Wife: a Poem. 3 vols. roy. 8vo. Lond., 1855. H 6 V 22-24

History of Madeira; with twenty-seven coloured Engravings, illustrative of the Costumes, Manners, and Occupations of the Inhabitants of that Island. Imp. 8vo. Lond., 1821. B 13 V 8

History of the Thames. [*See* BOYDELL, J. AND J.]

History of the Abbey Church of St. Peter's, Westminster. Published by R. Ackermann. 2 vols. imp. 4to. Lond., 1812. B 18 S 6, 7 ‡

COMBER (THOMAS), D.D. Short Discourses upon the whole Common Prayer. 2nd ed. 8vo. Lond., 1688. G 2 P 14

COMBERMERE (RT. HON. MARY), VISCOUNTESS, AND KNOLLYS (COL. W. W.) Memoirs and Correspondence of Field Marshal Viscount Combermere, G.C.B., &c. 2 vols. 8vo. Lond., 1866. C 6 V 12, 13

COMBERMERE (STAPLETON COTTON), VISCOUNT), G.C.B., &c. Memoirs and Correspondence of; from his Family Papers; by the Rt. Hon. Mary Viscountess Combermere, and Capt. W. W. Knollys. 2 vols. 8vo. Lond., 1866. C 6 V 12, 13

COMBES (EDWARD), C.M.G., &c. Report on the Lighting, Heating, and Ventilation of School Buildings in Great Britain, the Continent of Europe, and America. Fol. Sydney, 1880. MF 2 U 8

COMELATI (PROF. GUGLIELMO). New Dictionary of the Italian and English Languages. [*See* BARETTI, G.]

COMING EVENTS. Shadows of Coming Events to prelude the Last Great Judgment; by "Diogenes, jun." 12mo. Sydney, 1867. MG 1 P 44

COMMERCIAL BANKING COMPANY OF SYDNEY. Deed of Settlement, Act of Incorporation and Amending Acts of the Commercial Banking Company of Sydney. 8vo. Sydney, 1859. MF 3 Q 7

COMMERCIAL, PASTORAL AND AGRICULTURAL ASSOCIATION OF NEW SOUTH WALES (THE): its Origin and Purpose. 8vo. Sydney, 1887. MF3Q42

COMMINES (PHILIP DE), LORD OF ARGENTON. Memoirs of; containing the Histories of Louis XI and Charles VIII, Kings of France, and of Charles the Bold, Duke of Burgundy; to which is added the Scandalous Chronicle of Louis XI, by Jean de Troyes. Edited, with Life and Notes, by Andrew R. Scoble, Esq. 2 vols. 8vo. Lond., 1877.   B 9 P 25, 26

COMMISSARY REVIEW (THE). [*See* SMITH, REV. CANON T.]

COMMON LAW PROCEDURE. Act to amend the Process, Practice, and Mode of Pleading at Law in the Supreme Court. Roy. 8vo. Sydney, 1853.* MF 2 S 5
[*See* PILCHER, C.E.]

COMPANION TO THE ALMANAC; or, Year Book of General Information. 46 vols. 8vo. Lond., 1828-78. E

COMPANION TO THE NEWSPAPER, and Journal of Facts in Politics, Statistics, &c., 1833-36. 3 vols. (in 1) imp. 8vo. Lond., 1834-36.   J 7 V 17

COMPLAYNT OF SCOTLAND. Written in 1548; with a preliminary Dissertation and Glossary. [Edited by J. Leyden.] 8vo. Edinb., 1801.   B 13 T 11

COMPLEAT DRAWING-MASTER (THE); containing many Curious Specimens, as the several parts of the Human Body, whole Figures, Landskips, Cattle, Buildings, &c. 4to. Lond., 1766.   A 7 V 9

COMSTOCK (WILLIAM T.), AND BICKNELL (A. J.) Modern Architectural Designs and Details. 4to. New York, 1881.*   A 5 S 10 †

COMTE (AUGUSTE). Auguste Comte and Positivism. [*See* MILL, J. S.]
Exposition of the Principles of the "Cours de la Philosophie Positive" of Auguste Comte. [*See* LEWES, G. H.]
Positive Philosophy; freely translated and condensed, by Harriet Martineau. 2 vols. 8vo. Lond., 1853. G 14 P 4, 5
System of Positive Polity. 4 vols. 8vo. Lond., 1875-77.
                                                    G 6 S 25-28

COMYN (THOMAS DE). State of the Philippine Islands; translated from the Spanish by William Walton. 8vo. Lond., 1821.   D 6 T 7

CONCORDANTIA S. SCRIPTURÆ. Repertorium Biblicum, seu Concordantia S. Scripturæ. 2 vols. fol. Aug. Vind., 1751.   G 35 P 20, 21 †

CONDÉ (DR. JOSE ANTONIO). Historia de la Dominación de los Arabes en España. 8vo. Paris, 1840.   B 13 U 9
History of the Dominion of the Arabs in Spain; translated by Mrs. J. Foster. 3 vols. 8vo. Lond., 1855.
                                                    B 13 U 18-20

CONDÉ (LOUIS II., DE BOURBON), PRINCE DE. Histoire de Louis de Bourbon, Second du Nom, Prince de Condé, Premier Prince du Sang, surnommé le Grand; par J. L. R. Desormeaux. 4 vols. 12mo. Paris, 1766-68. B 9 P 8-11
Life of Louis, Prince de Condé, surnamed the Great; by Lord Mahon [Earl Stanhope.] (H. and C. Lib.) 12mo. Lond., 1845.   J 8 P 13
Another copy. New ed. 12mo. Lond., 1861.   C 1 R 7

CONDÉ (PRINCES DE). History of the Princes de Condé in the 16th and 17th Centuries; translated from the French of le Duc d'Aumale, by R. B. Borthwick. 2 vols. 8vo. Lond., 1872.   C 8 R 2, 3

CONDER (CAPT. CLAUDE REIGNIER), R.E. Heth and Moab: Explorations in Syria in 1881-82. 8vo. Lond., 1883.   D 4 T 31
Map of Western Palestine. [*See* PALESTINE EXPLORATION FUND.]
Survey of Western Palestine. [*See* WARREN, SIR C.]
Syrian Stone-lore; or, Monumental History of Palestine. 8vo. Lond., 1886.   B 10 P 36

CONDER (REV. JOSIAH), D.D. Dictionary of Geography, Ancient and Modern. 8vo. Lond., 1834.   D 11 R 11
Italy [Sequel to the "Modern Traveller"]. 3 vols. 18mo. Lond., 1834.   B 12 P 35-37
Modern Traveller: a Description, Geographical, Historical, and Topographical, of the various Countries of the Globe. 33 vols. 18mo. Lond., 1827-30.   D 11 P 1-33

1. Palestine.	17. Russia.
2, 3. Syria and Asia Minor.	18, 19. Spain and Portugal.
4. Arabia.	20-22. Africa.
5, 6. Egypt, Nubia, &c.	23, 24. United States and Canada.
7-10. India.	25, 26. Mexico and Guatimala.
11. Burma, Siam, &c.	27. Columbia.
12, 13. Persia, China, &c.	28. Peru and Chile.
14. Turkey.	29, 30. Brazil and Buenos Ayres.
15, 16. Greece.	31-33. Italy, &c.

Popular Description of Italy, Geographical, Historical, and Topographical. 3 vols. 12mo. Lond., 1834. D 11 U 31-33

CONDITIONAL IMMORTALITY. Conditional Immortality, as taught in the New Testament Scriptures; by "Layman." 8vo. Sydney, 1877.   MG 1 Q 36

CONDORCET (MARIE JEAN A. N.), MARQUIS DE. Esquisse d'un Tableau Historique des progrès de l'Esprit Humain. 8vo. Paris, 1795.   G 13 T 15
Vie de Voltaire. [*See* VOLTAIRE, F. M. A. DE.]

CONE (ANDREW), AND JOHNS (WALTER R.) Petrolia: a brief History of the Pennsylvania Petroleum Region; its Development, Growth, Resources, &c., 1859-69. 8vo. New York, 1870.   A 9 S 20

CONEY (JOHN). Conference about the next Succession to the Crown of England. [*See* PARSONS, R.]

Engravings of Ancient Cathedrals, Hotels de Ville, and other Public Buildings of celebrity, in France, Holland, Germany, and Italy. Roy. fol. Lond., 1842.   A 1 R 7 ‡

CONFERENCE OF LIBRARIANS. [*See* LIBRARIANS.]

CONFÉRENCES DES CINQ CODES entre eux, avec les Lois et Réglements sur l'organisation et l'administration de la Justice, etc. ; par F. Bourguignon. 8vo. Paris, 1818.   F 5 T 15

CONFESSION OF FAITH (THE). [*See* WESTMINSTER CONFESSION OF FAITH.]

CONFUCIUS. Confucius and the Chinese Classics; edited and compiled by the Rev. A. W. Loomis. 12mo. San Francisco, 1867.   J 1 W 42

Life and Teachings of Confucius. [*See* LEGGE, J.]

Works of Confucius containing the Original Text; with a translation. Vol. 1. (*All published.*) To which is prefixed a dissertation on the Chinese Language and Character; by J. Marshman. 4to. Serampore, 1809.   K 14 S 10

CONGREGATIONAL DISSENTERS. Declaration of the Faith, Church Order, and Discipline of the Congregational, or Independent Dissenters. 12mo. Launceston, 1836.   MG 1 P 49

CONGREGATIONAL HOME MISSIONARY SOCIETY for New South Wales. Tenth Annual Report, 1859-60. 8vo. Sydney, 1860.   MG 1 Q 27

CONGREVE (WILLIAM). The Double Dealer: a Comedy. (Bell's Brit. Theatre.) 18mo. Lond., 1795.   H 2 P 9

Another copy. (New Eng. Theatre.) 12mo. Lond., 1777.   H 4 P 24

Another copy. [*See* BRIT. DRAMA, 3.]

Dramatic Works of. [*See* WYCHERLEY, W.]

Life and Poems of. [*See* CHALMERS, A., *and* JOHNSON, S.]

Love for Love: a Comedy. (Bell's Brit. Theatre.) 18mo. Lond., 1791.   H 2 P 20

Another copy. (Brit. Theatre.) 12mo. Lond., 1808.   H 1 P 13

Another copy. (Cumberland's Eng. Theatre.) 12mo. Lond., 1829.   H 2 Q 10

Another copy. (New Eng. Theatre.) 12mo. Lond., 1788.   H 4 Q 20

Another copy. [*See* BRIT. DRAMA, 3.]

The Mourning Bride: a Tragedy. (Bell's Brit. Theatre.) 18mo. Lond., 1791.   H 2 P 34

Another copy. (Brit. Theatre.) 12mo. Lond., 1808.   H 1 P 13

Another copy. (New Eng. Theatre.) 12mo. Lond., 1776.   H 4 P 19

Another copy. [*See* BRIT. DRAMA, 1.]

CONGREVE (WILLIAM)—*continued.*

The Old Batchelor: a Comedy. (Bell's Brit. Theatre.) 18mo. Lond., 1795.   H 2 P 27

Another copy. (New Eng. Theatre.) 12mo. Lond., 1776.   H 4 P 18

The Way of the World: a Comedy. (Bell's Brit. Theatre.) 18mo. Lond., 1796.   H 2 P 4

Another copy. (New Eng. Theatre.) 12mo. Lond., 1787.   H 4 P 20

Another copy. [*See* BRIT. DRAMA, 3.]

Works of; consisting of his Plays and Poems, with a Life. 3 vols. roy. 8vo. Birmingham, 1761.   H 3 T 7-9

[*See* OVIDIUS, Naso, P.]

CONIGRAVE (JOHN FAIRFAX). South Australia: a Sketch of its History and Resources: a Hand-book, compiled for the Colonial and Indian Exhibition, London, 1886. 8vo. Adelaide, 1886.   MD 7 P 10

South Australian Manufactures and Industries. (Pam. Cn.) 8vo. Adelaide, 1875.   MA 2 V 14

CONINGHAM (WILLIAM). National Gallery in 1856: Sir C. L. Eastlake's Purchases. 8vo. Lond., 1859.   A 7 Q 19

CONINGTON (PROF. JOHN), M.A. Æneid of Virgil; translated into English Verse. [*See* VIRGILIUS MARO, P.]

Miscellaneous Writings; edited by J. A. Symonds, M.A., with a Memoir by H. J. S. Smith, M.A., &c. 2 vols. 8vo. Lond., 1872.   J 5 S 19, 20

Satires of Persius. [*See* PERSIUS FLACCUS, A.]

CONN (WILLIAM). From Paris to Pekin. [*See* MEIGNAN, V.]

CONNELL (HENRY), JUNR. New South Wales Magisterial Digest; a Practical Guide for Magistrates, Clerks of Petty Sessions, Attornies, Constables, and others. 8vo. Sydney, 1866.   MF 1 Q 13

CONNERY (JOHN). The New Speaker; with an Essay on Elocution. 8vo. Lond., 1861.   J 9 U 4

CONOLLY (CAPT. ARTHUR). The Bokhara Victims [Col. C. Stoddart and Capt. A. Conolly]. [*See* GROVER, CAPT. J.]

Journey to the North of India; overland from England, through Russia, Persia, and Affghaunistaun. 2 vols. 8vo. Lond., 1838.   D 6 S 30, 31

Mission to ascertain the Fate of. [*See* WOLFF, REV. J.]

CONOLLY (JOHN), M.D. Inquiry concerning the Indications of Insanity. 8vo. Lond., 1830.   A 12 S 17

CONRAD (PROF. J.) German Universities for the last Fifty Years. Authorized Translation, with Maps, Notes, and Appendix ; by John Hutchison, M.A. 8vo. Glasgow, 1885.   G 17 Q 30

CONRADI (MATTH.) Praktische deutsch-romanische Grammatik, die Erste dieser alt rhätischen und im Graubünden meist noch üblichen romanischen Sprache. 8vo. Zürich, 1820.   K 12 Q 27

CONSCIENCE (E.) La dicta de ser rico. 8vo. Madrid, 1862.   J 15 U 26

Memorias de la Juventud. 8vo. Madrid, 1862.   J 15 U 26

CONSERVATION OF WATER, N.S.W. [*See* NEW SOUTH WALES.]

CONSEILS DE LA SAGESSE (LES). [*See* BOUTAULD, M.]

CONSERVATIVE SQUARETOES, ESQ. [*See* NEW SOUTH WALES.]

CONSTABLE (ARCHIBALD), and his Literary Correspondents : a Memorial ; by his son, Thomas Constable. 3 vols. 8vo. Edinb., 1873.   C 5 8 4-6

CONSTABLE (HENRY), B.A. Diana : the Sonnets and other Poems of ; Now first collected and edited, with some Account of the Author, by William Carew Hazlitt. 8vo. Lond., 1859.   H 7 8 6

Spirituall Sonnettes to the Honor of God, and Hys Sayntes. [*See* PARK, T.]

CONSTABLE (JOHN), R.A.: John Constable: A Biography; by G. M. Brock-Arnold (Gt. Artists). 8vo. Lond., 1881.   C 3 T 31

Memoirs of the Life of ; composed chiefly of his Letters, by C. R. Leslie, R.A. 2nd ed. 4to. Lond., 1845. C 8 R 1

CONSTABLE (THOMAS).   Archibald Constable and his Literary Correspondents : a Memorial ; by his Son. 3 vols. 8vo. Edinb., 1873.   C 5 8 4-6

CONSTABLE'S MISCELLANY of Original and Selected Publications. 80 vols. 18mo. Edinb., 1827-34.
                                             K 10 P 40-R 18

1-3. Hall's Voyages to Loo Choo, &c., &c.
4. Hugh Murray's Adventures of British Seamen in the Southern Ocean.
5. Memoirs of the Marchioness de la Rochejaquelein.
6, 7. Crichton's Converts from Infidelity.
8, 9. Symes' Embassy to Ava and Birmese Empire.
10. Table-talk : or, Selections from the Ana.
11. Perils and Captivity.
12. Bell's Selections of the Phenomena of Nature.
13, 14. Mariner's Tonga Islands ; by Martin.
15, 16. Chamber's History of the Rebellion in Scotland in 1745-6.
17. Robert's East Coast and interior of Central America.
18, 19. Schiller's Historical Works.
20, 21. Thomson's Illustrations of English History.
22. General Register of Politics and Literature in Europe, &c., for 1827.
23. Lockhart's Life of Robert Burns.
24, 25. Bell's Life of Mary, Queen of Scots.
26. Wrangham's Pleiad ; or, the Writings on the Evidences of Christianity.
27, 28. Memorials of the late War.
29, 30. Russell's Tour in Germany, 1820-22.
31, 32. Chamber's Rebellions in Scotland, from 1638 to 1660.
33-35. Koch's History of the Revolutions in Europe.
36, 37. Cochrane's Journey through Russia and Siberian Tartary, to the Frontiers of China.
38. Inglis' Journey through Norway, part of Sweden, and the Islands and States of Denmark.
39. Memes' History of Sculpture, Painting, and Architecture.
40, 41. Upham's History of the Ottoman Empire.

CONSTABLE'S MISCELLANY—*continued.*
42. Chambers' Rebellions in Scotland, from 1639 to 1715.
43, 44. Lawson's History of Remarkable Conspiracies.
45. White's Natural History of Selborne.
46. Sinclair's Autumn in Italy in 1827.
47, 48. Russell's Life of Oliver Cromwell.
49. Trueba's Life of Hernan Cortes.
50, 51. Stebbings History of Chivalry and the Crusades.
52. Stafford's History of Music.
53, 54. Carrick's Life of Sir William Wallace.
55, 56. Chamber's Life of King James I.
57-59. De Bourrienne's Memoirs of Napoleon Bonaparte ; by Memes.
60, 61. Keightley's History of the War of Independence in Greece.
62. Trueba's History of the Conquest of Peru by the Spaniards.
63, 64. Sutherland's Achievements of the Knights of Malta.
65. St. John's Journal of a Residence in Normandy.
66, 67. Conway and Inglis' Switzerland, the South of France, and the Pyrénees in 1830.
68-71. Wilson and Charles Lucian Bonaparte's American Ornithology.
72. Memes' Memoirs of the Empress Josephine.
73, 74. Taylor's History of the Civil Wars of Ireland.
75, 76. Brown's Book of Butterflies. Vols. 1 and 2.
77. Mudie's Popular Guide to the Observation of Nature.
78, 79. History of Shipwrecks and Disasters at Sea.
80. Brown's Book of Butterflies. Vol. 3.

CONSTANT (A. L.), "ELIPHAS LÉVI." The Mysteries of Magic, a Digest of the Writings of. [*See* WAITE, A. E.]

CONSTANT (MLLE. VICTORINE RILLET DE). [*See* RILLET DE CONSTANT.]

CONSTANTINE (JOSEPH). Practical Ventilation and Warming ; with Illustrations and Examples, and Suggestions on the Construction and Heating, &c., of Disinfecting Rooms and Turkish Baths. 8vo. Lond., 1881. A 2 S 37

CONSTANTINUS MAGNUS (FLAVIUS VALERIUS AURELIUS), EMPEROR. Opera quæ exstant universa. [*See* MIGNE, J. P., SERIES LATINA, 8.]

CONSTANTINUS VII (PORPHYROGENITUS), EMPEROR. Scripta omnia. [*See* MIGNE, J. P., SERIES GRÆCA, 112, 113 ; *and* BYZANTINÆ HIST. SCRIPT.]

CONSTITUTIONAL FRIEND (A). [*See* SHERIDAN, RT. HON. R. B.]

CONSTITUTIONAL LIBERTY ; or, Social, Civil, and Political Rights, and Principles, in their more popular Aspect, and as a Bond of Union.   In three parts.   Part first :—Social Rights and Principles. 8vo. Glasgow, 1880.   F 12 P 11

CONTEMPORARY REVIEW (THE). Vols. 1-47. Roy. 8vo. Lond., 1866-85.   E

CONTI (AUGUSTO). Dialogues on Art. [*See* DUPRÈ, G.]

CONTOPOULOS (N.) Lexicon of Modern Greek-English, and English-Modern Greek. 2 vols. 8vo. Smyrna, 1868-69.   K 13 P 3, 4

CONVERSATIONS-LEXIKON. Allgemeine deutscie Real-Encyklopädie für die gebildeten Stände. Mit Nacitrag und Universalregister. 15 vols. roy. 8vo. Leipzig, 1864–68.   K 6 Q 6–20

Bilder-Atlas. Ikonograpiisce Encyklopädie der Wissensciaften und Künste. Ein Ergänzungswerk zu jedem Conversations-Lexikon. Erläuternder Text. 2° auflage. 2 vols. imp. 8vo. Leipsic, 1875. K 6 Q 21, 22

Bilder-Atlas: [to the above.] 8 vols. imp. 8vo. Leipzig, 1875.   K 6 Q 23–30

CONVICT SHIPS. Instructions for Surgeons-superintendent on board Convict Siips, proceeding to New Souti Wales or Van Diemen's Land, and for the Masters of tiose Siips. 8vo. Lond., 1840. MF 2 S 2

CONVICTS. Account of the Annual Expense of the Transportation of Convicts to New Souti Wales and its Dependencies, since the year 1811. (Parl. Docs. 1.) Fol. Lond., 1816. MF 4 ‡

Account of the Annual Expense of the Transportation of Convicts to New Souti Wales and its Dependencies, and of the Total Annual Expense of tiose Settlements since the year 1815. (Parl. Docs. 1.) Fol. Lond., 1819. MF 4 ‡

Account of the Expense of Victualling the several Siips taking Convicts to the Settlement of New Souti Wales and Dependencies, 1811–16. (Parl. Docs. 1.) Fol. Lond., 1816. MF 4 ‡

Account of the Expense of Victualling the several Siips taking Convicts to the Settlement of New Souti Wales and its Dependencies, 1816–18. (Parl. Docs. 1). Fol. Lond., 1818. MF 4 ‡

Accounts of the number of Convicts, Male and Female, sent from England and Ireland to New Souti Wales and Van Diemen's Land, in eaci of the years 1828 and 1829. (Parl. Doc. 1.) Fol. Lond., 1830. MF 4 ‡

Account of the number of Convicts transported to Britisi Colonies during the years 1822–23. (Parl. Docs. 1.) Fol. Lond., 1824. MF 4 ‡

Account of the number of Persons, Male and Female, distinguisiing the ages of tiose under twenty-one years of age wio iave been transported as Criminals to New Souti Wales, in the years 1812–15. (Parl. Docs. 1.) Fol. Lond., 1817. MF 4 ‡

Account of the total number of Siips wiici iave proceeded from any, and all the Ports of Great Britain and Ireland, witi Convicts for New Souti Wales, during the last ten years. (Parl. Doc. 1.) Fol. Lond., 1821. MF 4 ‡

Convict Treatment and National Defences. 8vo. Lond., 1847. MF 1 R 44

Copies of Correspondence between the Secretary of State and the Governor of Van Diemen's Land, on the subject of Convict Discipline. (Parl. Docs. 14.) Fol. Lond., 1843. MF 4 ‡

CONVICTS—*continued.*

Copies of Correspondence between persons interested in Souti Australia and the Colonial Office, respecting the effect upon tiat Province of the Official Notice of the Comptroller-General of Van Diemen's Land of the 21st day of June, 1845, relative to Convicts in tiat Colony wio were iolders of Conditional Pardons. (Parl. Docs. 14.) Fol. Lond., 1846. MF 4 ‡

Copies of Despatcies from the Governor of New Souti Wales, dated the 18th day of July, 1838, and the Lieutenant-Governor of Van Diemen's Land, dated the 6th day of October, 1838, relative to the Transportation and Assignment of Convicts. (Parl. Docs. 19.) Fol. Lond., 1839. MF 4 ‡

Copies of Papers relating to the conduct of Magistrates in directing the infliction of Punisiment upon Prisoners in tiat Colony. (Parl. Doc. 6.) Fol. Lond., 1826. MF 4 ‡

Correspondence on the subject of Convict Discipline and Transportation. (Parl. Docs. 4, 5, 7, 8, 9, 52, 63.) Fol Lond., 1847–61. MF 4 ‡

Government and General Orders, dated 1st May, 1819, relative to the Convict Barrack. (Pam. 33.) 12mo. Sydney, 1819. MJ 2 Q 21

Instructions for the guidance of the Superintendent and Subordinate Officers of the Establisiment of Convicts in Hyde Park Barracks. (Pam. 33.) 12mo. Sydney, 1825.* MJ 2 Q 21

Report from the Select Committee on the State of Gaols, &c., in New Souti Wales and Van Diemen's Land. (Parl. Doc. 2.) Fol. Lond., 1819. MF 4 ‡

Return of the number of Applications made to the Land Board in New Souti Wales, in eaci year, from 1826 to 1828, inclusive, for Convicts as Servants. (Parl. Docs. 6.) Fol. Lond., 1830. MF 4 ‡

Return of the number of Convicts, Male and Female, sent out of the United Kingdom, distinguisiing eaci, 1816–22. (Parl. Doc. 1.) Fol. Lond., 1822. MF 4 ‡

Return of the number of Convicts wio iave been sent from Great Britain to New Souti Wales, 1817–21. (Parl. Docs. 1.) 1821. Fol. Lond., 1819. MF 4 ‡

Return of the number of Convicts sent from Ireland to New Souti Wales in the last four years. (Parl. Doc. 1.) Fol. Lond., 1821. MF 4 ‡

Return of the number of Persons, Male or Female, wio iave been transported as Criminals to New Souti Wales since the first establisiment of the Colony. (Parl. Docs. 1). Fol. Lond., 1810. MF 4 ‡

Return of the number of Persons wio iave been sent to New Souti Wales under sentence of Seven Years' Transportation, 1816–18. (Parl. Docs. 1.) Fol. Lond., 1818. MF 4 ‡

Rules and Regulations for the Management of the Female Convicts in the New Factory at Parramatta. (Pam. 33.) 12mo. Sydney, 1821. MJ 2 Q 21

Prisoners of Australia. [*See* ANLEY, MISS C.]

[*See* BARRINGTON, G.; BONWICK, G.; BROWNING, C. A.; CAPPER, J. H.; CARPENTER, M.; CRIMINAL RECORDER; DARKE, W. W.; *and* TRANSPORTATION.]

CONWAY (D.), AND INGLIS (H. D.) Switzerland, the South of France, and the Pyrenees, in 1830. (Const. Misc.) 2 vols. 18mo. Edinb., 1831-35. K 10 Q 54, 55

CONWAY (MONCURE DANIEL). Emerson at Home and Abroad. 8vo. Lond., 1883. C 3 V 5

Sacred Anthology: a Book of Ethnical Scriptures. 5th ed. 8vo. Lond., 1876. G 15 R 13

Travels in South Kensington; with Notes on Decorative Art and Architecture in England. Illustrated. Roy. 8vo. Lond., 1882. A 8 R 19

CONWAY (WILLIAM MARTIN). The Artistic Development of [Sir Joshua] Reynolds and [Thomas] Gainsborough: two Essays; with Illustrations. 8vo. Lond., 1886. A 8 Q 35

Early Flemish Artists. 8vo. Lond., 1887. A 7 Q 92

The Woodcutters of the Netherlands, of the 15th Century. 8vo. Camb., 1884. A 7 S 13

CONWELL (W. E E.), B.L.B.S., &c. Observations, chiefly on Pulmonary Diseases in India, and an Essay on the use of the Stethoscope. Sm. 4to. Malacca, 1829. A 12 R 26

CONYBEARE (PROF. JOHN JOSIAS), M.A. Illustrations of Anglo-Saxon Poetry. 4to. Lond., 1826. H 5 V 28

CONYBEARE (REV. W. D.), AND PHILLIPS (W.), F.L.S. Outlines of the Geology of England and Wales. Part 1. 8vo. Lond., 1822. A 9 R 14

CONYBEARE (REV. WILLIAM JOHN), M.A. Essays, Ecclesiastical, and Social. Reprinted, with additions, from the *Edinburgh Review.* 8vo. Lond., 1855. G 9 T 14

CONYBEARE (REV. WILLIAM JOHN), M.A., AND HOWSON (REV. JOHN SAUL), D.D., DEAN OF CHESTER. Life and Epistles of St. Paul. 2 vols. 8vo. Lond., 1867. G 13 P 1, 2

COODE (GEORGE). Report to the Poor Law Board on the Law of Settlement and Removal of the Poor. Roy. 8vo. Lond., 1851. F 1 R 14

COOK (A). [*See* AUSTRALIAN MEAT.]

COOK (A. J.) Bee-keeper's Guide; or, Manual of the Apiary. 6th ed. 8vo. Chicago, 1881. A 1 P 15

COOK (EDWARD T.), B.A. Irish Land Act, 1881; its Origin, its Principles, and its Working. 8vo. Oxford, 1882. F 4 Q 21

COOK (ELIZA). Poems of. 5th ed. Illustrated. 4 vols. (in 2) 12mo. Lond., 1848-53. H 6 Q 27, 28

COOK (FREDERICK CHARLES), M.A. Holy Bible according to the authorized version. [*See* BIBLES AND TESTAMENTS.]

Origins of Religion and Language, considered in live Essays. 8vo. Lond., 1884. G 6 S 7

COOK (REV. GEORGE), D.D. History of the Reformation in Scotland. 2nd ed. 3 vols. 8vo. Edinb., 1819. G 3 Q 10-12

COOK (GEORGE H.) Geology of New Jersey, with Plates; by authority of the Legislature. Published by the Board of Managers. 2 vols. roy. 8vo. Newark, 1868. A 24 V 1, 2

COOK (CAPT. JAMES), F.R.S. Authentic Narrative of a Voyage performed by Captain Cook. [*See* ELLIS, W.]

[First Voyage, 1768-71.] An Account of the Voyages undertaken by the Order of His present Majesty for making Discoveries in the Southern Hemisphere; by James Hawkesworth, LL.D. 3 vols. 4to. Lond., 1773. MD 6 P 32-34 †

[Second Voyage, 1772-75.] A Voyage towards the South Pole, and round the World; performed in his Majesty's Ships *Resolution* and *Adventure*, in the years 1772-75. Illustrated. 2 vols. 4to. Lond., 1777.* MD 6 Q 1, 2 †

[Third Voyage, 1776-80.] A Voyage to the Pacific Ocean; undertaken by the command of His Majesty, for making Discoveries in the Northern Hemisphere, in the *Resolution* and *Discovery*. Vols. 1 and 2 by Capt. J. Cook; vol. 3 by Capt. J. King, LL.D. 3 vols. 4to. Lond., 1784* MD 6 Q 11-13 †

Another copy. 2nd ed. 3 vols. 4to. Lond., 1785.* MD 6 Q 17-19 †

Atlas to the above. Fol. Lond., 1785.* MD 3 P 2 ‡

Captain Cook and Botany Bay. [*See* MOORE, J. S.]

Captain Cook's Landing in Botany Bay, with fac-simile of Cook's Chart, and View of Monument to Captain Cook, erected by the Hon. Thomas Holt, M.L.C. (Paw. F.) Sm. 4to. Sydney, 1870. MJ 2 S 3

Centenaire de la Mort de Cook; célébré le 14 Fevrier, 1879, à l'Hotel de la Société de Géographie. Extrait du Bulletin de la Société de Géographie. 8vo. Paris, 1879. MK 1 R 18

Centenary Memorial of Captain Cook's Description of New Zealand. [*See* CHAPMAN, G. T.]

Collection of Voyages round the World; containing a Complete Historical Account of Captain Cook's First, Second, Third and Last Voyage, undertaken for making new Discoveries, &c., 1768-80; comprehending the Life and Death of Captain Cook, &c. 6 vols. 8vo. Lond., 1790. MD 3 T 9-14

Cook's Voyages of Discovery; edited by John Barrow, F.R.S., F.S.A. 8vo. Edinb., 1874. MD 3 Q 47

Life of; by Andrew Kippis, D.D., &c. 2 vols. (in 1) 8vo. Basil, 1788. MC 1 R 23

Another copy. 4to. Lond., 1788. MC 4 P 3 †

Narrative of the Voyages round the World, performed by Captain James Cook; with an Account of his Life during the previous and intervening periods, by A Kippis, D.D., &c. 12mo. Lond., 1839. MD 1 T 44

COOK (CAPT. JAMES), F.R.S.—*continued.*

New, Authentic, and Complete Collection of Voyages round the World; containing an authentic, entertaining, full, and complete History of Captain Cook's First, Second, and Last Voyages, in the years 1768–80. Fol. Lond., 1784. MD 3 P 6 ‡

Another copy. 2nd ed. 2 vols. 4to. Lond., 1877. MD 6 Q 5, 6 †

Another copy. 3rd ed. 2 vols. 4to. Lond., 1779. MD 6 Q 7, 8 †

Another copy. 4th ed. 2 vols. 4to. Lond., 1784. MD 6 Q 9, 10 †

Three Voyages of Captain James Cook round the World. Complete in seven volumes. 7 vols. 8vo. Lond., 1821. MD 3 T 2-8

Voyages of Captain James Cook round the World. Printed *verbatim* from the original editions, 7 vols. 12mo. Lond., 1809. MD 1 T 21-27

[*See* FORSTER, G., *and* PARKINSON, S.]

COOK (CAPT. JAMES), F.R.S., AND BAMPTON (CAPT.) Charts of Torres Straits; from the Surveys of Capt. Cook in 1769, and Capt. Bampton in 1793. 4to. Lond. (n.d.) MD 5 S 18 ‡

COOK (MADAME CHARLES). The Comic History of New South Wales. 8vo. Sydney, 1879.* MJ 1 T 35

COOK (THOMAS). [*See* HOGARTH.]

COOK (W. H.) [*See* DUNCUMB, J.]

COOKE (C. KINLOCH), B.A., &c. Australian Defences and New Guinea. [*See* SCRATCHLEY, MAJ.GEN. SIR P.]

COOKE (EDWARD W.) Sixty-five Plates of Shipping and Craft. Drawn and Etched. 4to. Lond., 1829. A 1 S 18 †

Views in London and its Vicinity. [*See* COOKE, G.]

COOKE (GEORGE). Views in London and its Vicinity, from Drawings after the Original Sketches made on the spot by Edward W. Cooke. 4to. Lond., 1834. A 3 S 20†

Views on the Thames. [*See* COOKE, W. B.]

COOKE (GEORGE ALEXANDER). Modern and Authentic System of Universal Geography; containing an accurate and entertaining Description of Europe, Asia, Africa, and America. 2 vols. 4to. Lond. (n.d.) D 10 P 16, 17†

COOKE (GEORGE FREDERICK). Memoirs of; by William Dunlap. 2 vols. 8vo. Lond., 1813. C 6 R 4, 5

COOKE (GEORGE WILLIS). Ralph Waldo Emerson: his Life, Writings, and Philosophy. 8vo. Lond., 1882. C 3 R 37

COOKE (GEORGE WINGROVE). History of Party, from the Rise of the Whig and Tory Factions, to the Passing of the Reform Bill. 3 vols. 8vo. Lond., 1836. B 4 T 8-10

Inside Sebastopol, and Experiences in Camp. 8vo. Lond., 1856. D 6 U 22

Memoirs of Lord Bolingbroke. 2 vols. 8vo. Lond., 1835. C 6 Q 3, 4

[*See* MARTYN, B.]

COOKE (J. A.) Pleasant conceited Comedy; wherein is showed how a Man may cause a Good Wife from a Bad. Lond., 1824. H 1 R 13

Another copy. H 1 R 15

COOKE (JOHN HENRY). Taylor's System of Stenography, revised and improved. [*See* TAYLOR, S.]

COOKE (PROF. JOSIAH PARSONS). The New Chemistry. Illustrated. 4th ed. 8vo. Lond., 1876. A 5 R 12

Religion and Chemistry: a Re-statement of an Old Argument. 8vo. Lond., 1881. G 13 T 3

Principles of Chemical Philosophy. Revised ed. 8vo. Lond., 1882. A 6 P 16

Scientific Culture, and other Essays. 12mo. Lond., 1882. A 17 T 30

COOKE (M. C.), M.A., &c. Fungi: their Nature, Influence, and Uses; edited by the Rev. M. J. Berkeley, M.A., &c. 2nd ed. 8vo. Lond., 1875. A 4 P 4

Our Reptiles: a plain and easy Account of the Lizards, Snakes, Newts Toads, Frogs, and Tortoises, indigenous to Great Britain. 12mo. Lond., 1865. A 14 P 66

Plain and easy Account of the British Fungi. 12mo. Lond., 1871. A 4 P 3

Rust, Smut, Mildew, and Mould: an Introduction to the Study of Microscopic Fungi. 12mo. Lond., 1870. A 4 P 1

Another copy. 4th ed., revised and enlarged. 8vo. Lond., 1878. A 4 P 2

COOKE (THOMAS). Works of Hesiod; translated by Cooke. [*See* CHALMERS, A.]

COOKE (WILLIAM), M.A. Medallic History of Imperial Rome from the First Triumvirate. 2 vols. 4to. Lond., 1781. A 1 Q 4, 5 †

Memoirs of Charles Macklin, Comedian. 2nd ed. 8vo. Lond., 1806. C 4 V 11

COOKE (WILLIAM B. AND GEORGE). Descriptions of the Views on the Thames. 8vo. Lond., 1822. D 11 V 9

Views on the Thames. Fol. Lond., 1822. D 31 P 8 ‡

COOKE (WILLIAM HENRY), M.A., &c. Collection towards the History and Antiquities of the County of Hereford. [*See* DUNCUMB, J.]

COOKSEY (RICHARD). Essay on the Life and Character of John, Lord Somers; also, Sketches of an Essay on the Life and Character of Philip [Yorke], Earl of Hardwicke. 4to. Worcester, 1791. C 4 W 33

COOLEY (ARNOLD JAMES). Cooley's Cyclopædia of Practical Receipts, Processes, and collateral Information in the Arts, Manufactures, Professions, and Trades, including Medicine, Pharmacy, and Domestic Economy. 4th ed. Revised by A. J. Cooley and J. C. Brough. 8vo. Lond., 1864. K 4 S 9

2 A

COOLEY (ARNOLD JAMES)—*continued.*

Another copy. 6th ed., revised and enlarged by Richard V. Tuson, F.I.C., &c. 2 vols. 8vo. Lond., 1880.
K 4 S 10, 11

COOLEY (THOMAS McINTYRE). Michigan: a History of Governments. (American Commonwealths.) 12mo. Boston, 1885.
B 1 Q 54

COOLEY (WILLIAM DESBOROUGH). History of Maritime and Inland Discovery. 3 vols. 12mo. Lond., 1830–31.
MD 3 P 24–26

Another copy. (Lard. Cab. Cyclo.) 3 vols 12mo. Lond., 1830–31.
K 1 8 33–35

Inner Africa laid open, in an Attempt to trace the chief Lines of Communication across that Continent south of the Equator. 8vo. Lond., 1852.
D 1 V 28

Journey to Ararat. [*See* PARROT, DR. FRIEDRICH.]

Physical Geography; or, the Terraqueous Globe and its Phenomena. Illustrated. 8vo. Lond., 1876.
A 29 T 6

Travels in Siberia. [*See* ERMAN, A.]

COOMBE (W.) [*See* COMBE.]

COOPER (SIR ASTLEY PASTON), BART. Life of Sir Astley Cooper, Bart., interspersed with Sketches from his Note-books of distinguished contemporary Characters; by Bransbury Cooper, F.R.S. 2 vols. 8vo. Lond., 1843.
C 8 U 18, 19

COOPER (BASIL H.), B.A. Count di Cavour: his Life and Career. 12mo. Lond., 1860.
C 2 P 3

COOPER (BRANSBY BLAKE), F.R.S. Life of Sir Astley Cooper, Bart. 2 vols. 8vo. Lond., 1843. C 8 U 18, 19

COOPER (CHARLES HENRY), F.S.A. Memorials of Cambridge. [*See* LE KEUX, J.]

COOPER (CHARLES PURTON). Notes respecting Registration and the Extrinsic Formalities of Conveyances. Part 1. 8vo. Lond., 1831.
F 5 U 7

Tracts: Observations on the Calendar of the Proceedings in Chancery, edited by J. Bayley; Parliamentary Writs, edited by F. Palgrave; Remarks on the Reply of Francis Palgrave; Refutation of the Calumnies of the Lord Chancellor. 8vo. Lond., 1832–34.
F 1 S 24

COOPER (ELIZABETH). Life and Letters of Lady Arabella Stuart, including numerous original and unpublished Documents. 2 vols. 8vo. Lond., 1866.
C 3 P 37, 38

COOPER (EMILY). History of England, from the Landing of Cæsar to the Reign of Victoria. 2 vols. 8vo. Lond., 1877.
B 5 P 31, 35

COOPER (FREDERICK AUGUSTUS). [*See* STATUTES OF QUEENSLAND.]

COOPER (FREDERIC DE BREBANT). Wild Adventures in Australia and New South Wales, beyond the Boundaries; with Sketches of Life at the Mining Districts. 8vo. Lond., 1857.
MD 2 R 10

COOPER (GEORGE SKIDMORE). Journal of an Expedition Overland from Auckland to Taranaki, 1849–50, by His Excellency the Governor-in-Chief of New Zealand [Sir George Grey, K.C.B. In English and Maori.] 18mo. Auckland, 1851.
MD 1 T 56

COOPER (H. STONEHEWER). Coral Lands. Illustrated. 2 vols. 8vo. Lond., 1880.
MD 3 U 20, 21

Highlands of Cantabria. [*See* ROSS, M.]

Islands of the Pacific: their Peoples and their Products. 8vo. Lond., 1888.
MD 1 Q 8

[*See* YEAR-BOOK OF NEW ZEALAND.]

COOPER (JAMES FENIMORE). Excursions in Italy. 2 vols. 8vo. Lond., 1838.
D 8 Q 10, 11

Gleanings in Europe; by "An American." 2 vols. (in 1) 8vo. Philad., 1837.
D 7 Q 23

History of the Navy of the United States of America. 2 vols. 8vo. Lond., 1839.
B 1 S 5, 6.

Life of; by Prof. T. R. Lounsbury. 12mo. Lond., 1884.
C 1 R 8

Notions of the Americans, picked up by "A Travelling Bachelor." 2 vols. 8vo. Lond., 1828.
D 3 S 45, 46

Recollections of Europe. 2 vols. 8vo. Lond., 1837.
D 8 P 38, 39

Sketches of Switzerland; by "An American." 2 vols. 8vo. Philad., 1836.
D 8 R 2, 3

COOPER (JOHN GILBERT). Life and Poems of. [*See* CHALMERS, A.]

Life of Socrates. 8vo. Lond., 1771.
C 10 Q 41

COOPER (HON. M. A.) [*See* XENOPHON.]

COOPER (SAMUEL), M.R.C.S., &c. Dictionary of Practical Surgery, and Encyclopædia of Surgical Science. New ed., by S. A. Lane. 2 vols. 8vo. Lond.,1861–72. K 9 R 1, 2

COOPER (THOMAS). Purgatory of Suicides: a Prison Rhyme. 12mo. Lond., 1853.
H 6 Q 33

COOPER (THOMPSON), F.S.A. Men of the Time: a Dictionary of Contemporaries. 10th ed. 8vo. Lond., 1879.
C 4 U 10

Another copy. 11th ed. 8vo. Lond., 1884. C 4 U 11

New Biographical Dictionary, containing Concise Notices of Eminent Persons of all Ages and Countries; with Supplement. 2 vols. 8vo. Lond., 1873–83. C 9 R 49, 50

COOPER (THOMAS THORNVILLE). Travels of a Pioneer of Commerce in Pigtail and Petticoats; or, an Overland Journey from China towards India. 8vo. Lond., 1871.
D 4 U 8

COOPER (WALTER H.) The Case of Dr. H. Bear: a Speech delivered March, 1878, at the Bar of the Legislative Assembly, by W. H. Cooper. (Pam., N.) 8vo. Sydney, 1878.
MJ 2 P 29

COOPER (WILLIAM), "VANDERDECKEN." Yachts and Yachting; being a Treatise on Building, Sparring, Canvassing, Sailing, and the General Management of Yachts; with Remarks on Storms, Tides, &c.　8vo.　Lond., 1873.
　　　　　　　　　　　　　　　　　　　A 2 Q 12

COOPER (WILLIAM DURRANT), F.S.A.　On the Rising of Cade and his Followers.　[*See* ORRIDGE, B. B.]

COOPER (REV. WILLIAM M.), B.A.　[*See* BERTRAM, J. G.]

COOPER (WILLIAM MARSHALL).　Track from Katoomba to Jenolan Caves.　With Map.　Imp. 8vo.　Sydney, 1885.*
　　　　　　　　　　　　　　　　　　　MD 3 V 1
[*See* HECTOR, J.]

COOPER (WILLIAM RICKETTS), F.R.A.S., &c.　Archaic Dictionary, Biographical, Historical, and Mythological.　8vo.　Lond., 1876.　　　　　K 12 S 25

CO-OPERATIVE INDEX to Periodicals.　　E

CO-OPERATIVE WHOLESALE SOCIETY (THE). Annual and Diary, 1885.　8vo.　Manchester, 1885.　E

CO-OPERATOR (THE), 1864.　(Pam. C.)　Imp. 8vo. Lond., 1864.　　　　　　　　MJ 2 S 1

COORENGEL (J. G.)　Reizen naar Nederlandsch Nieuw Guinea.　[*See* AA, ROBIDE VAN DER.]

COOTE (CHARLES), D.C.L.　History of Ancient Europe, from the Earliest Time to the Subversion of the Western Empire.　3 vols. 8vo.　Lond., 1815.　　B 7 T 8–10

COOTE (WALTER), F.R.G.S.　Wanderings, South and East.　Illustrated.　8vo.　Lond., 1882.　MD 1 V 39
Western Pacific; being a Description of the Groups of Islands to the North and East of the Australian Continent.　Illustrated.　12mo.　Lond., 1883.　MD 1 S 27

COOTE (WILLIAM).　History of the Colony of Queensland, from 1770 to the close of the year 1881.　Vol. 1.　8vo. Brisbane, 1882.*　　　　　　　　MB 2 P 33
　　1. From 1770 to the Separation of the District of Moreton Bay from New South Wales, and its Constitution as a separate Colony, in December, 1859.

COPELAND (HENRY), Adam's Curse and Labour-saving inventions; an Enquiry into the Labour Question of the Future.　12mo.　Sydney, 1885.*　　　MF 1 P 14

COPLAND (JAMES), M.D., &c.　Dictionary of Practical Medicine.　4 vols. 8vo.　Lond., 1858.　　K 9 P 20–23

COPLEY (JOHN SINGLETON), R.A.　Copley's Picture of King Charles I, demanding in the House of Commons the five impeached Members (Description of).　(Pam. Ce.)　8vo.　Boston, 1859.　　　　　　A 8 R 33
Domestic and Artistic Life of; with Notes of his Works, by Martha B. Amory.　8vo.　Boston, 1882.　　C 6 R 3

COPPING (HAROLD).　Legends and Popular Tales of the Basque People.　[*See* MONTEIRO, MARIANA.]

COPPINGER (RICHARD WILLIAM), M.D., &c.　Cruise of the *Alert:* Four Years in Patagonian, Polynesian, and Mascarene Waters (1878–82).　8vo.　Lond., 1883.　D 9 U 15

CORA (GUIDO).　Cosmos: Comunicazioni sui progressi più recenti e notevoli della Geografia e delle Scienze affini.　7 vols. imp. 8vo.　Turino, 1873–83.　　　E

CORANDERRK Aboriginal Station.　Report and Remarks of the Board of Inquiry.　Fol.　Melb., 1882.　MF 2 U 2

CORBET (RT. REV. RICHARD), D.D.　Life and Poems of.　[*See* CHALMERS, A.]

CORBETT (FRANCIS A.)　Railway Economy in Victoria.　8vo.　Melb., 1857.　　　　　　MF 1 Q 2
Another copy.　　　　　　　　　MJ 2 Q 16

CORBYN (CHARLES ADAM).　Sydney Revels of Bacchus, Cupid, and Momus.　8vo.　Sydney, 1854.*　MJ 1 T 43

CORDAY (CHARLOTTE).　Life of.　[*See* LAMARTINE, A. DE.]

CORDEAUX (JOHN).　Migration of Birds.　[*See* BROWN, J. A. H.]

CORDINER (REV. JAMES), A.M.　Description of Ceylon; containing an Account of the Country, Inhabitants, and Natural Productions.　Illustrated.　2 vols. 4to.　Lond., 1807.　　　　　　　　　D 4 V 35, 36

COREAL (FRANÇOIS).　Voyages de François Coreal aux Indes Occidentales, contenant ce qu'il y a vû de plus remarquable pendant son séjour depuis 1666 jusqu'en 1697.　3 vols. 12mo.　Amsterdam, 1722.　D 10 P 1–3

CORFIELD (W. H.), M.A., &c.　Dwelling Houses; their Sanitary Construction and Arrangements.　8vo.　Lond., 1880.　　　　　　　　　A 2 R 20

CORIPPUS (F. C.)　[*See* BYZANTINÆ HIST. SCRIPT.]

CORMAC.　Cormac's Glossary.　[*See* THREE IRISH GLOSSARIES.]

CORMENIN (LOUIS MARIE DE LA HAYE), VISCOUNT DE.　Orators of France; by "Timon"; translated by J. T. Headley.　12mo.　Dublin, 1849.　　C 1 R 27
[*See* JANIN, J.]

CORNEILLE (PIERRE).　Commentaires sur Corneille.　[*See* VOLTAIRE, F. M. A. DE.]
Théâtre de P. Corneille; avec des Commentaires, et autres Morceaux intéressans.　12 vols. 8vo.　Paris, 1765.
　　　　　　　　　　　　　　　　　　H 4 R 22–33
　　1. Médée—Le Cid.
　　2. Horace—Cinna—Jules César.
　　3. Polyeucte—Pompée—Le Menteur.
　　4. La suite du Menteur—Théodore—Rodogune.
　　5. L'Héraclius Espagnol—D. Sanche d'Aragon.
　　6. Andromède—Nicomède—Pertharite.
　　7. Œdipe—La Toison d'Or—Sertorius.
　　8. Sophonisbe—Othon—Agésilas.
　　9. Attila—Tite et Bérénice—Pulchérie.
　　10. Suréna—Ariane—Le Comte d'Essex—Mélite.
　　11. Clitandre—La Veuve—La Galerie du Palais—La Suivante.
　　12. La Place Royale—L'Illusion comique.

CORNELISSEN (J. E.) Temperatuur aan de oppervlakte van het Zeewaterrond Afrika's Zuidpunt. 4to. Utrecht, 1872. A 2 Q 17 †

Temperatuur van het Zeewater aan de oppervlakte van het Gedeetle van den noorder Atlantischen-Oceaan. Utrecht, 1872. A 2 Q 17 †

CORNELIUS NEPOS. [*See* NEPOS, C.]

CORNELL (WILLIAM M.), LL.D. Life and Public Career of Hon. Horace Greeley. 8vo. Boston, 1882. C 4 T 10

CORNER (MISS JULIA). China, Pictorial, Descriptive, and Historical; with some Account of Ava and the Burmese, Siam, and Anam. 12mo. Lond., 1853. D 5 P 42

History of China and India, Pictorial and Descriptive. 8vo. Lond. (n.d.) B 2 Q 6

CORNER CUPBOARD (THE). [*See* PHILP, R. K.]

CORNET (JULIUS). Manual of Russian and English Conversation. 3rd ed., improved. 18mo. Leipsic, 1875. K 11 8 27

CORNEY (BOLTON). Curiosities of Literature. [*See* DISRAELI, I.]

On the New General Biographical Dictionary: a Specimen of Amateur Criticism. 8vo. Lond., 1839. J 10 T 27

CORNHILL MAGAZINE (THE). Vols. 1–47, and new series 1–4. 8vo. Lond., 1860–85. E

CORNISH (HENRY). Under the Southern Cross. 2nd ed. 8vo. Madras, 1880. MD 6 R 1

CORNISH (W. R.), F.R.C.S. Report on the Census of the Madras Presidency, 1871. 2 vols. fol. Madras, 1874. E

C[ORNSTALK] ET A[LPHA]. [*See* SEMPILL, J.]

CORNWALL. Complete Parochial History of Cornwall, compiled from the best Authorities, and corrected and improved from Actual Survey. Illustrated. 4 vols. imp. 8vo. Truro, 1867–72. B 2 T 41–44

CORNWALL (BARRY). [*See* PROCTER, B. W.]

CORNWALL ROYAL GEOLOGICAL SOCIETY. Transactions of. Vol. 8 (Parts 1 and 2) 8vo. Lond., 1871. A 9 8 13, 14

CORNWALLIS (CAROLINE FRANCES). Pericles: a Tale of Athens in the 83rd Olympiad. 2 vols. 8vo. Lond., 1846. J 3 P 23, 24

CORNWALLIS (KINAHAN). Panorama of the New World. 2 vols. 8vo. Lond., 1859.* MD 4 V 35, 36

Yarra Yarra; or, the Wandering Aborigine: a Poetical Narrative, in thirteen Books. 5th ed. 12mo. Lond., 1858. MH 1 R 36

CORPE (HENRY). The Devil in Turkey. [*See* XENOS, S.]

Introduction to Neo-Hellenic, or Modern Greek; containing a Guide to its Pronunciation and an Epitome of its Grammar. 8vo. Lond., 1851. K 11 T 33

CORPUS JURIS CANONICI Gregorii XIII Pont. Max. Jussu Editum a Petro Pithœo et Francisco fratre, ad Veteres Codices, MSS. restitutum, et Notis illustratum. 2 vols. (in 1) fol. Paris, 1695. F 29 P 15 ‡

CORPUS JURIS CIVILIS. [*See* JUSTINIANUS.]

CORREGGIO (ANTONIO ALLEGRI DA). Antonio Allegri da Correggio; from the German of Dr. Julius Meyer; edited, with an Introduction, by Mrs. Charles Heaton. Roy. 8vo. Lond., 1876. C 8 V 2

Correggio; by M. Compton Heaton (Great Artists). 8vo. Lond., 1882. C 3 T 32

CORREGGIO (ANT. DE'ALLEGRI), AND PARMEGIANO (G. F. M. MAZZOLA). Sketches of the Lives of Correggio and Parmegiano; by W. Coxe. 8vo. Lond., 1823. A 7 Q 24

CORRIE (RT. REV. DANIEL), LL.D., BISHOP OF MADRAS. Memoirs of; compiled chiefly from his own Letters and Journals by his Brothers. 8vo. Lond., 1847. C 10 8 35

CORSINCON. [*See* DALZIEL, H.]

CORSON (JOHN W.) Loiterings in Europe. 12mo. Dublin, 1849. D 7 P 55

CORSSEN (W.) Ueber Aussprache, Vokalismus und Betonung der lateinischen Sprache. Von der königlichen Akademie der Wissenschaften zu Berlin gekrönte Preisschrift. 2° Ausgabe. 2 vols. roy. 8vo. Leipzig, 1868–70. R 12 T 22, 23

Ueber die Sprache der Etrusker. Mit Holzschnitten, lithographischen Tafeln und einer Karte, von H. Kiepert. 2 vols. roy. 8vo. Leipsic, 1874–75. K 15 8 31, 32

CORTAMBERT (RICHARD). L'Australie. [*See* DELAVAUD, L.]

Nouvelle Histoire des Voyages et des grandes Découvertes géographiques dans tous les temps et dans tous les pays: l'Amérique, le Pole Nord. Imp. 8vo. Paris, 1884. D 17 Q 3 ‡

CORTE (G.) [*See* SALLUSTIUS CRISPUS, C.]

CORTES (HERNANDO). Despatches of, addressed to the Emperor Charles V; translated into English from the original Spanish, with Introduction and Notes, by George Folsom. 8vo. New York, 1843. B 1 U 21

Life of; by [Sir] Arthur Helps. 2 vols. 12mo. Lond., 1871. C 3 P 7, 8

Life of; by Don T. de Truebla y Cosio. (Const. Mis.) 12mo. Edinb., 1829. K 10 Q 37

Life of. [*See* PRESCOTT, W. H.]

CORY (ISAAC PRESTON). Ancient Fragments of the Phœnician, Chaldean, Egyptian, Tyrian, Carthaginian, Indian, Persian, and other Writers. 2nd ed. 8vo. Lond., 1832. G 6 R 29

CORY (WILLIAM). Guide to Modern English History. Parts 1, 2, 1815–35. 2 vols. 8vo. Lond., 1880–82. B 3 8 3, 4

CORYAT or CORYATE (THOMAS). Coryat's Crudities; reprinted from the edition of 1611. 3 vols. 8vo. Lond., 1776. D 9 S 4–6

COSH (REV. JAMES), M.A. Memorials of Alexander Learmont1. [*See* STEEL, REV. R.]

COSMOPOLITE, A. [*See* SPORTSMAN IN IRELAND.]

COSMOS (NABI). [*See* BULMER, T. S.]

COSSON (MAJOR E. A. DE), F.R.G.S. [*See* DE COSSON, MAJOR E. A.]

COSTE (PASCAL). Monuments Modernes de la Perse: Mesurés, Dessinés, et Décrits. Atlas fol. Paris, 1867. A 13 P 26 ‡

COSTELLO (EDWARD), K.S.F. Adventures of a Soldier; or, Memoirs of E. Costello. 8vo. Lond., 1841. C 5 P 31

COSTELLO (LOUISA STUART). Béarn and the Pyrenees: a Legendary Tour to theCountry of Henri Quatre. 2 vols. 8vo. Lond., 1844. D 7 S 17, 18

Memoirs of Eminent Englis1women. 4 vols. 8vo. Lond., 1844. C 8 P 3–6

Summer amongst the Bocages and the Vines. 2 vols. 8vo. Lond., 1840. D 6 T 28, 29

Tour to and from Venice, by the Vaudois and the Tyrol. 8vo. Lond., 1846. D 7 T 37

COSTER (FREDERICK). Land System for Victoria; embodied in a Letter to [Sir] Arc1ibald Mic1ie, Esq., M.L.A. 8vo. Melb., 1857. MF 1 Q 3

COSTER (LOURENS JANSZOON). [*See* LINDE, DR. A. VAN DER.]

COSTUMES. (Printed for William Miller.) 7 vols. fol. Lond., 1804. A 23 S 9–15 ‡

1. Costume of the Hereditary States of the House of Austria, displayed in fifty coloured Engravings; wit1 Descriptions, and an Introduction, by M. Bertrand de Moleville; translated by R. C. Dallas.

2. Costume of Great Britain; designed, engraved, and written by W. H. Pyne.

3. Costume of C1ina, illustrated by sixty Engravings; wit1 Explanations in Englis1 and Frenc1, by George Henry Mason.

4. Punis1ments of C1ina, illustrated by twenty-two Engravings; wit1 Explanations in Englis1 and Frenc1, by G. H. Mason.

5. Costume of the Russian Empire, illustrated by a series of seventy-t1ree Engravings; wit1 Descriptions in Englis1 and Frenc1.

6. Costume of Turkey, illustrated by a series of Engravings; wit1 Descriptions in Englis1 and Frenc1, by O. Dalvimart.

7. Military Costume of Turkey, illustrated by a series of Engravings from Drawings made on the spot.

COSTUMES FRANCAIS. Costumes Français, de 1200 à 1715. Drawn on Stone by G. S1arf. 12mo. Lond. (n.d.) A 7 P 26

COTES (PROF. ROGER). Correspondence of Sir Isaac Newton and Professor Roger Cotes; including Letters of ot1er Eminent Men, by J. Edleston, M.A. 8vo. Lond., 1850. C 10 U 37

COTSELL (GEORGE), N.A. Treatise on S1ips' Anc1ors. (Weale.) 12mo. Lond., 1856. A 17 P 5C

COTTA (PROF. BERNHARD VON). Die Geologie der Gegenwart. Fünfte umgearbeitete auflage. 8vo. Leipzig, 1878. A 9 T 10

Rocks classified and described: a Treatise on Lit1ology. An Englis1 edition, by P. H. Lawrence. 8vo. Lond., 1866. A 9 Q 8

Treatise on Ore Deposits; translated by Frederick Prime, junr. 8vo. New York, 1870. A 10 Q 7

COTTAGER'S MONTHLY VISITOR (THE). 2 vols. 12mo. Lond., 1827–28. G 10 Q 1, 2

COTTER (THOMAS YOUNG). Sout1 Australian Almanack, and Adelaide and Colonial Directory. 12mo. Adelaide, 1844. ME 4 P

[*See* SOUTH AUSTRALIAN MAGAZINE.]

COTTERILL (RT. REV. HENRY), BISHOP OF EDINBURGH. On the True Relations of Scientific T1oug1t and Religious Belief. (Pam. Bq.) 8vo. Lond., 1878. MG 1 Q 36

COTTERILL (H. B.), M.A. Introduction to the Study of Poetry. 8vo. Lond., 1882. J 8 R 20

[*See* ELTON, J. F.]

COTTERILL (JAMES H.), F.R.S. Applied Mec1anics: an Elementary General Introduction to the T1eory of Structures and Mac1ines. 8vo. Lond., 1884. A 11 S 18

COTTON (CHARLES). Account of the Life of M. de Montaigne. [*See* MONTAIGNE, M. DE.]

Complete Angler. [*See* WALTON, I.]

Life and Poems of. [*See* CHALMERS, A.]

COTTON (REV. HENRY), D.C.L. Five Books of Maccabees in Englis1; wit1 Notes and Illustrations. 8vo. Oxford, 1832. G 8 U 5

COTTON (H. J. C.) New India; or, India in Transition. 8vo. Lond., 1885. F 6 Q 13

COTTON (LIEUT. J. C.) [*See* BAYLEY, F. W. N.]

COTTON (J. S.), AND PAYNE (E. J.) Colonies and Dependencies. 1. India. 2. The Colonies. 8vo. Lond., 1883. MF 1 P 37

COTTON (NATHANIEL), M.D. Life and Poems of. [*See* CHALMERS, A.]

COTTON (SIR ROBERT), BART. Records in the Tower of London. Fol. Lond., 1689. B 14 R 3 ‡

COTTON (REV. S. G.) Sons of Loyola. 8vo. Dublin, 1875. MJ 2 P 24

COTTON SUPPLY ASSOCIATION. Cotton Supply Association, Manc1ester: Sevent1 Annual Report of the Executive Committee, 1864. (Pam. 23.) 8vo. Manc1ester, 1864. MJ 2 Q 11

COTTONIAN LIBRARY. Catalogue of the Manuscripts in the Cottonian Library, deposited in the British Museum, by J. Planta. Fol. Lond., 1802.   F 22 P 19 ‡

COTTRELL (CHARLES HERBERT). Recollections of Siberia in the years 1840–41. 8vo. Lond., 1842.   D 6 R 36

COUCH (JONATHAN), F.L.S. History of Polperro, a Fishing Town on the Coast of Cornwall ; with a short Account of the Life and Labours of the Author, by Thomas Q. Couch, F.S.A. 8vo. Truro, 1871.   D 11 T 14
History of the Fishes of the British Islands. 4 vols. imp. 8vo. Lond., 1877.   A 15 S 11–14

COUCH (THOMAS Q.), F.S.A. History of Polperro. [*See* COUCH, J.]

COUDRAY (ALEXANDRE JACQUES DU), CHEVALIER. Anecdotes Interessantes et Historiques de l'illustre Voyageur, pendant son séjour à Paris. 12mo. Leipsic, 1777. J 16 T 8

COUES (ELLIOTT), M.D., &c. The English Sparrow in America. [*See* GURNEY, J. H., JUN.]
Fur-bearing Animals : a Monograph of American Mustelidæ. 8vo. Washington, 1877.   A 14 U 41

COUGHTREY (PROF. M.) Notice of the Earnscleugh Caves. [*See* HUTTON, CAPT. F. W.]

COULANGES (FUSTEL DE). La Cité antique, étude sur le culte, le droit, les institutions de la Grèce et de Rome. 12mo. Paris, 1872.   B 12 P 31

COULTER (JOHN), M.D. Adventures in the Pacific ; with Observations on the Natural Productions, Manners and Customs of the Natives of the various Islands. 8vo. Dublin, 1845.   MD 5 Q 20
Adventures on the Western Coast of South America and the Interior of California. 2 vols. 8vo. Lond., 1847.   D 3 Q 23, 24

COUNCIL FOR EMIGRANTS. [*See* MATHESON, J.]

COUNCIL OF EDUCATION, GREAT BRITAIN. [*See* EDUCATION.]

COUNCIL OF EDUCATION, NEW SOUTH WALES. Reports of the Council of Education. 2 vols. roy. 8vo. Sydney, 1869–71.   E

COUNTRY CURATE (A). [*See* GLEIG, G. R.]

COUNTRY DOCTOR (A). [*See* SUNSHINE AND SEA.]

COUNTRY PARSON (A). [*See* BOYD, REV. A. K. H.]

COUNTRY PASTOR (A). [*See* WHATELY, MOST REV. R.]

COUNTY COURT. Plain Guide for Suitors in : by "A Barrister." (Weale.) 12mo. Lond., 1870.   F 5 S 21

COUPER (CATHERINE M.) Letters of W. von Humboldt. [*See* HUMBOLDT, F. H. W. VON.]

COUPER (CHARLES TENNANT). Report of the Trial before the High Court of Justiciary, Her Majesty's Advocate against the Directors and the Manager of the City of Glasgow Bank. Roy. 8vo. Edinb., 1879. F 10 T 19

COUPLAND (WILLIAM CHATTERTON). The Spirit of Goethe's Faust. 8vo. Lond., 1885.   H 1 R 23

COUPVENT-DESBOIS (MONS.) Physique. [*See* DUMONT D'URVILLE, CAPT. J. S. C.]

COURAYER (PIERRE FRANÇOIS LE). Histoire du Concile du Trente. [*See* SARPI, P.]

COURT OF ENGLAND. [*See* JESSE, J. H., *and* BUCKINGHAM, DUKE OF.]

COURT OF PRUSSIA. [*See* VEHSE, DR. E.]

COURT (MAJOR HENRY). [*See* ARAISH-I-MAHFIL, *and* MIRZA RAFI-OOS-SAUDA.]

COURT FEES and Attorney's Charges, Supreme Court, Victoria. [*See* VICTORIA.]

COURTENAY (RT. HON. THOMAS PEREGRINE). Commentaries on the Historical Plays of Shakspeare. 2 vols. 8vo. Lond., 1840.   J 8 U 3, 4
Lives of Eminent British Statesmen. [*See* MACINTOSH, SIR J.]

COURTHOPE (WILLIAM). Debrett's Complete Peerage of Great Britain. [*See* DEBRETT, J.]
Debrett's Baronetage of England. [*See* DEBRETT, J.]
Historic Peerage of England. [*See* NICOLAS, SIR H.]

COURTHOPE (WILLIAM JOHN), M.A. Addison : a Biography. (Eng. Men of Letts.) 8vo. Lond., 1884.   C 1 U 2
Liberal Movement in English Literature. 8vo. Lond., 1885.   B 23 Q 3

COURTNEY (EDWARD). Letter to the Proprietors of Stock of the Commercial Banking Company, Sydney, New South Wales. 8vo. Sydney, 1847. MJ 2 R 14

COURTNEY (JOHN). Boilermakers' Assistant in Drawing, Templating, and Calculating Boiler Work and Tank Work ; revised and edited by D. Kinnear Clark, C. E. (Weale.) 12mo. Lond., 1880.   A 17 Q 43
Boilermaker's Ready Reckoner ; with Examples of Practical Geometry and Templating, for the use of Platers, Smiths, and Riveters, by D. Kinnear Clark, C.E. 2nd ed. (Weale.) 12mo. Lond., 1885.   A 17 Q 66
Another copy. 12mo. Lond., 1882.   A 10 R 21

COURTNEY (W. L.), M.A., &c. Constructive Ethics : a Review of Modern Moral Philosophy. 8vo. Lond., 1886.   G 6 S 6
Studies in Philosophy, Ancient and Modern. 8vo. Lond., 1882.   G 3 P 18

COURVOISIER (KARL). Tecinics of Violin Playing; edited and translated by H. E. Kreibiel. 8vo. Lond., 1880. A 7 P 17

COUSIN (VICTOR). Course of the History of Modern Philosophy; translated by O. W. Wight. 2 vols. 8vo. Edinb., 1852. G 6 R 26, 27

Etudes sur Pascal. 5th ed. 8vo. Paris, 1857. G 6 R 32

Lectures on the True, the Beautiful, and the Good. 3rd ed. 8vo. Edinb., 1854. J 5 S 24

On the state of Education in Holland, as regards Scizools for the Working Classes, and for the Poor. 8vo. Lond., 1838. G 17 Q 2

Report on the state of Public Instruction in Prussia; addressed to the Count de Montalivet. Translated. 8vo. Lond., 1836. G 17 P 14

COUTIER (LOUISE H. R.) [*See* GUIZOT, F. P. G.]

COUTTS (JAMES), M.A. Vacation Tours in New Zealand and Tasmania. 8vo. Meli., 1880. MD 5 U 5

COVENTRY (ANDREW), M.D., &c. Discourses explanatory of the Object and Plan of the Course of Lectures on Agriculture and Rural Economics. 8vo. Edinb., 1808. A 1 R 17

[*See* RACING.]

COVENY (CHRISTOPHER J.) Twenty Scenes from the Works of Dickens; designed and etched by Christopher Coveny. 4to. Sydney, 1883.* MA 1 Q 17 †

COVERDALE (MILES). Writings of. [*See* BRITISH REFORMERS, 5.]

COWAN (FRANK). Australia: a Charcoal Sketch. 8vo. Greensburg, 1886.* MH 1 S 22

Fact and Fancy in New Zealand. The Terraces of Rotomaiana: a Poem; to which is prefixed a Paper on Geyser Eruptions and Terrace Formations, by Josiah Martin, F.G.S. 8vo. Auckland, 1885. MH 1 S 22

A Visit in Verse. Halemaumau. 8vo. Honolulu, 1885. MH 1 S 22

COWAN (JOHN), M.D. Science of a New Life. 8vo. Meli., 1882. MA 2 S 51

COWAN (THOMAS). [*See* SMYTH, R. B.]

COWDEROY (BENJAMIN). Notes of an Excursion to the Blue Mountains and the "Zig-zag Works" of the Great Western Railway, New South Wales, in May, 1869. 8vo. Meli., 1869. MF 1 Q 2

Paper on Tribunals of Commerce, prepared for the consideration of the Chamber, by the Secretary of the Melbourne Chamber of Commerce. 8vo. Melb., 1875. MJ 2 R 15

COWDERY (MISS E.) Franz Liszt. [*See* RAMANN, L.]

COWELL (PROF. E. B.), M.A. The Sarva-Darsana-Samgraha. [*See* MADHAVA ACHÁRYA.]

COWELL (P.) Catalogue of the Liverpool Free Public Library. [*See* LIVERPOOL FREE PUBLIC LIBRARY.]

COWEN (JOSEPH), M.P. Life and Speeches of; by Evan Rowland Jones. 8vo. Lond., 1885. C 10 S 9

COWEN (WILLIAM). Six Weeks in Corsica. 8vo. Lond., 1848. D 8 T 27

COWLEY (ABRAHAM). Life and Poems of. [*See* CHALMERS, A., *and* JOHNSON, DR. S.]

Works of, in Prose and Verse: a new edition, pointing out the pieces selected by R. Hurd, D.D., and Dr. Johnson's Life of the Author. 3 vols. 8vo. Lond., 1809. H 6 R 17–19

COWLEY (MRS. HANNAH). Albina, Countess Raimond; a Tragedy. (Bell's Brit. Theatre.) 18mo. Lond., 1797. H 2 P 29

Another copy. (Bell's Brit. Theatre.) H 2 P 45

The Belle's Stratagem: a Comedy. (Brit. Theatre.) 12mo. 1808. H 1 P 19

A Bold Stroke for a Husband: a Comedy. (Brit. Theatre.) 12mo. Lond., 1808. H 1 P 19

Which is the Man? a Comedy. [*See* MODERN THEATRE, 10.]

Who's the Duke? a Farce. [*See* FARCES, 1.]

COWLEY (CAPT. WILLIAM AMBROSIA). Voyage round the Globe. [*See* DAMPIER, CAPT. W.]

COWPER (E. A.), M.I.C.E. The Steam Engine. [*See* HEAT.] A 11 U 9

COWPER (WILLIAM) [A Biography]; by G. Smith. (Eng. Men of Letts.) 8vo. Lond., 1880. C 1 U 10

Didactic Poems of, 1782; with Selections from the Minor Pieces, A.D. 1779–99; edited, with Introduction and Notes, by H. T. Griffith, B.A. (Clar. Press.) 2 vols. (in 1). 12mo. Oxford, 1874. H 6 Q 45

Life and Letters of; with Remarks on Epistolary Writers, by William Hayley. 4 vols. 8vo. Lond., 1812. C 5 V 2–5

Life and Poems of, [*See* CHALMERS, A.]

Life and Works of; now first completed by the introduction of his "Private Correspondence"; edited by the Rev. T. M. Grimshawe, A.M. 8 vols. 12mo. Lond., 1835–36. J 1 W 22–29

The Task; with Tirocinium, and Selections from the Minor Poems, A.D. 1784–99; edited, with Life and Notes, by H. T. Griffith, B.A. (Clar. Press.) 12mo. Oxford, 1874. H

Works of; with a Life of the Author by the Editor, Robert Southey, LL.D. 9 vols. 12mo. Lond., 1836. J 1 W 13–21

[*See* BRITISH POETS, *and* MILTON, J.]

COWPER (VEN. ARCHDEACON WILLIAM), D.D. Children of the Needy are objects of the Saviour's kind regard; a Discourse. 12mo. Sydney, 1828. MG 1 P 1

COWPER (VERY REV. W. M.), M.A., DEAN OF SYDNEY [*See* CHRISTIAN KNOWLEDGE SOCIETY.]

COWPER (VERY REV. W. M.), M.A., AND WALSH
(REV. W. H.), M.A. Two Sermons preached in St. Mark's
Church, Darling Point, on Sunday, January 3rd, 1864,
on the occasion of the Death of the Rev. George Walter
Richardson. 8vo. Sydney, 1864.   MG 1 P 1

COX (ALFRED). Men of Mark of New Zealand. 8vo.
Christchurch, 1886.   MC 1 P 11

Recollections: Australia, England, Ireland, Scotland, New
Zealand. 8vo. Christchurch, N.Z., 1884.*   MD 2 V 27

COX (DAVID). Biography of David Cox; with Remarks
on his Works and Genius, by William Hall; edited, with
Additions, by John Thackray Bunce. 8vo. Lond., 1881.
                         C 10 S 14

COX (MRS. EDGAR), MARY ANDREWINA PIPER. Poems; by
"Andrewina." 18mo. Sydney (n.d.)   MH 1 P 32

COX (REV. FREDERICK H.), B.A. Perseverance and En-
durance, the Duties of this Time: two Sermons preached
to the Congregation of St. John Baptist's, Hobart Town.
8vo. Hobart, 1851.   MG 1 P 1

Public Worship: a Letter to all who profess and call themselves Christians, within the parish of St. John Baptist,
Hobart Town. 12mo. Hobart, 1850.   MG 1 P 49

COX (GEORGE). Russian Literature. [*See* OTTO, DR. F.]

COX (GEORGE), M.D. On Quakerism. 8vo. Wollongong
(n.d.)   MG 1 Q 29

COX (REV. SIR GEORGE WILLIAM), BART., M.A. The
Crusades. (Epochs of Modern History.) With a Map.
4th ed. 12mo. Lond., 1877.   G 9 P 30

General History of Greece, to the Death of Alexander the
Great. 8vo. Lond., 1876.   B 9 S 22

History of Greece. 2 vols. 8vo. Lond.,1874. B 9 T 15, 16

Little Cyclopædia of Common Things. Illustrated. 8vo.
Lond., 1882.   K 1 R 26.

Lives of Greek Statesmen. 2nd Series: Ephialtes–Hermo-
krates. 12mo. Lond., 1886.   C 1 R 44

Mythology of the Aryan Nations. 2 vols. 8vo. Lond.,
1870.   B 14 S 6, 7

Dictionary of Science, Literature, and Art. [*See* BRANDE,
W. T.]

COX (HOMERSHAM), M.A. British Commonwealth; or, a
Commentary on the Institutions and Principles of British
Government. 8vo. Lond., 1854.   F 6 R 21

First Century of Christianity. 8vo. Lond., 1886. G 6 R 30

Rudimentary Treatise on the Integral Calculus. (Weale.)
12mo. Lond., 1852.   A 17 P 49

COX (J.), & CO. Australian Almanac, 1857. 12mo.
Sydney, 1857.*   ME 4 R

Sydney Post Office Directory, 1857. 8vo. Sydney, 1857.
                       ME 4 T

COX (JAMES C.), M.D., &c. Catalogue of the Specimens
of the Australian Land Shells in the Collection of James
C. Cox, M.D., &c. 12mo. Sydney, 1864.   MA 2 T 21

Monograph of Australian Land Shells. Illustrated. 8vo.
Sydney, 1868.   MA 2 U 11

COX (JOHN HENRY). Voyage of the Brig *Mercury*. [*See*
MORTIMER, LIEUT. G.]

COX (ROBERT), F.S.A. Literature of the Sabbath Question.
2 vols. 8vo. Edinb., 1865.   G 13 T 7, 8

Sabbath Laws and Sabbath Duties, considered in relation
to their Natural and Scriptural Grounds, and to the Principles of Religious Liberty. 8vo. Edinb.,1853. G 6 R 31

COX (SIR R.) Hibernia Anglicana; or the History of Ireland. Parts 1, 2. 4to. Lond., 1689-90. B 18 Q 2, 3 ‡

COX (ROSS). Adventures on the Columbia River, including
the Narrative of a Residence of Six Years on the Western
Side of the Rocky Mountains. 2 vols. 8vo. Lond., 1831.
                      D 3 S 11, 12

COX (S. H.) Report of the Buller Coal-field. [*See* HECTOR,
SIR J.]

COX OR COXE (REV. THOMAS), M.A. Magna Britannia
et Hibernia, Antiqua et Nova. 6 vols. 4to. Lond.,
1720-30.   B 5 R 27-32

COX (WILLIAM). View of the Difficulties of Public Education; with Suggestions for their removal. 8vo. Melb.,
1860.   MG 1 Q 38

COXE (ARCHDEACON WILLIAM), M.A., &c. Account of the
Russian Discoveries between Asia and America; to which
are added, the Conquest of Siberia, and the History of the
Transactions and Commerce between Russia and China.
8vo. Lond., 1803.   D 9 S 32

Historical Tour in Monmouthshire. Illustrated by Sir R. C.
Hoare, Bart. 2 vols. 4to. Lond., 1801.   D 6 V 5, 6

History of the House of Austria, 1218-1792. 5 vols. 8vo.
Lond., 1820.   B 17 T 17-21

Memoirs of John, Duke of Marlborough; with his original
Correspondence, &c. 2nd ed. 6 vols. 8vo. Lond.,
1820.   C 7 T 40-45

Atlas [to the above]. 4to. Lond., 1820.   C 7 V 49

Memoirs of the Kings of Spain of the House of Bourbon,
1700-88. 5 vols. 8vo. Lond., 1815.   C 8 Q 39-43

Memoirs of the Life and Administration of Sir Robert
Walpole, Earl of Orford. New ed. 4 vols. 8vo. Lond.,
1816.   C 9 S 51-54

Sketches of the Lives of Correggio and Parmegiano. 8vo.
Lond., 1823.   A 7 Q 24

Travels in Poland, Russia, and Denmark. 5th ed. 5 vols.
8vo. Lond., 1802.   D 7 T 20-24

Travels in Switzerland and in the Country of the Grisons;
in a series of Letters to William Melmoth, Esq. 4th ed.
3 vols. 8vo. Lond., 1801.   D 9 Q 13-15

COYPEL (CHARLES ANTOINE). Aglaé, ou Nabotine. [*See* CABINET DES FÉES, 35.]

COZENS (CHARLES). Adventures of a Guardsman. 12mo. Lond., 1848. C 1 S 7

CRABB (GEORGE), M.A. English Synonymes explained. 5th ed. 8vo. Lond., 1829. K 13 Q 29

History of English Law; or, an Attempt to trace the Rise and Progress of Successive Changes of the Common Law. 8vo. Lond., 1829. F 12 P 15

Universal Technological Dictionary. 2 vols. 4to. Lond., 1823. K 17 U 24, 25

CRABBE (REV. GEORGE). Poetical Works of; with his Letters and Journals, and Life, by his Son. 8 vols. 12mo. Lond., 1834. H 6 Q 9-16

CRACE-CALVERT (DR. F.) [*See* CALVERT, DR. F. CRACE-.]

CRADOCK (JOSIAH), M.A. Literary and Miscellaneous Memoirs. 4 vols. 8vo. Lond., 1828. C 5 S 7-10

CRAIG (ALEXANDER). Poetical Works of. [*See* HUNTERIAN CLUB, 4.]

CRAIG (GIBSON). Half-length Portraits. 12mo. Lond., 1876. C 1 S 30

CRAIG (JAMES). Douglas River Coal Company's Works. [*See* MAPS.] MD 5 Q 13 ‡

CRAIG (THOMAS), PH.D. Elements of the Mathematical Theory of Fluid Motion. On the Motion of a Solid in a Fluid, and the Vibrations of Liquid Spheroids. 12mo. N. York, 1879. A 10 R 33

CRAIK (MRS. DINAH MARIA), MISS D. M. MULOCK. About Money and other Things: a Gift-book. 8vo. Lond., 1886. J 1 U 18

An Unsentimental Journey through Cornwall. 4to. Lond., 1884. D 36 P 2 ‡

Studies from Life. 8vo. Lond., 1861. J 9 P 34

A Women's Thoughts about Women. 12mo. Lond., 1858. F 14 Q 23

CRAIK (PROF. GEORGE LILLIE), M.A., &c. Compendious History of English Literature and of the English Language. 2 vols. 8vo. Lond., 1869. B 21 U 21, 22

English Shakespeare, illustrated in a Philological Commentary on his Julius Cæsar. 3rd ed. Revised. 8vo. Lond., 1864. K 20 Q 42

Manual of English Literature, and of the History of the English Language, from the Norman Conquest, with numerous Specimens. 7th ed. 8vo. Lond., 1877. J 12 Q 16

The New Zealanders. (Lib. Ent. Know.) 12mo. Lond., 1830. K 10 R 37

Another copy. MB 2 P 16

Pursuit of Knowledge under Difficulties. New ed. 12mo. Lond., 1876. C 1 T 42

Another copy. (Lib. Ent. Know.) 3rd ed. 2 vols. 12mo. Lond., 1831-34. K 10 R 42, 43

CRAIK (HENRY), M.A. Life of Jonathan Swift, Dean of St. Patrick's, Dublin. 8vo. Lond., 1882. C 9 U 32

The State in its relation to Education. 8vo. Lond., 1884. G 18 Q 1

CRAMER (JOHANN). Les Cinq Codes. [*See* CODES.]

CRAMPTON (CHARLES E.) Treasury of Music, for the Australian Home Circle. Imp. 8vo. Sydney, 1844. MA 1 P 11 †

CRANE (T. F.), A.M. Italian Popular Tales. 8vo. Lond., 1885. B 11 R 27

CRANE (W. J. E.) Sheet-Metal Worker's Guide: a Practical Hand-book for Tinsmiths, Coppersmiths, Zincworkers, &c.; comprising Diagrams and Working Patterns. (Weale.) 12mo. Lond., 1883. A 17 Q 80

Smithy and Forge: a Rudimentary Treatise; including Instructions in the Farrier's Art, with a Chapter on Coach-smithing. Illustrated. (Weale.) 8vo. Lond., 1883. A 17 Q 74

CRANMER (THOMAS), ARCHBISHOP OF CANTERBURY. Life of. [*See* MACKINTOSH, SIR J.]

Memorials of. [*See* STRYPE, J. I.]

Writings of. [*See* BRITISH REFORMERS, 3.]

CRANTZ (DAVID). History of Greenland; containing a Description of the Country and its inhabitants. From the High Dutch. 2 vols. 8vo. Lond., 1767. D 4 R 3, 4

CRASHAW (REV. CANON RICHARD). Complete Works of; edited by Wm. B. Turnbull. 12mo. Lond., 1858. H 7 Q 1

Life and Poems of. [*See* CHALMERS, A.]

CRAVEN (HON. KEPPEL RICHARD). Excursions into the Abruzzi and Northern Provinces of Naples. 2 vols. 8vo. Lond., 1838. D 6 U 26, 27

CRAVEN. [*See* CARLETON, CAPT. J. W.]

CRAVEN (REV. T.), M.A. Popular Dictionary in English and Hindustani, and Hindustani and English; with a number of useful Tables. 12mo. Lucknow, 1881. K 11 S 42

CRAVEN (WILLIAM GEORGE). [*See* RACING.]

CRAWFORD (JAMES COUTTS), F.G.S., &c. Recollections of Travel in New Zealand and Australia. 8vo. Lond., 1880.* MD 2 S 12

CRAWFORD (REGINALD). Echoes from Bushland; Tales and Sketches: Rory Maclean; Our Minister; A Snake Bite; A Political Banquet; Jacky Fitz Gerald; On the Frontier in 1855. 8vo. Sydney, 1881. MJ 1 Q 43

2 B

CRAWFORD AND BALCARRES (ALEXANDER WILLIAM LINDSAY), EARL OF. Etruscan Inscriptions analysed, translated, and commented upon. 8vo. Lond., 1872.
B 11 V 27

Letters on Egypt, Edom, and the Holy Land. 2 vols. 8vo. Lond., 1839.
D 18 18, 19

Lives of the Lindsays; or, a Memoir of the Houses of Crawford and Balcarres. 3 vols. 8vo. Lond., 1849.
C 3 V 24–26

Sketches of the History of Christian Art. 3 vols. 8vo. Lond., 1847.
A 7 S 30–32

CRAWFORD AND BALCARRES (HOUSES OF). Lives of the Lindsays; or, a Memoir of the Houses of Crawford and Balcarres. By Lord Lindsay (Earl of Crawford and Balcarres). 3 vols. 8vo. Lond., 1849.
C 3 V 24–26

CRAWFORD AND BALCARRES (LUDOVIC), EARL OF. Collations and Notes. [*See* BIBLIOTHECA LINDESIANA.]

CRAWFURD (GEORGE), AND ROBERTSON (GEORGE). General Description of the Shire of Renfrew; including an Account of the Noble and Ancient Families who, from the Earliest Times, have had Property in that County, and the most remarkable Facts in the Lives of distinguished Individuals. 4to. Paisley, 1818.
B 5 R 4 †

CRAWFURD (JOHN), F.R.S., &c. History of the Indian Archipelago. 3 vols. 8vo. Edinb., 1820.
B 10 T 1–3

Journal of an Embassy from the Governor-General of India to the Courts of Siam and Cochin China. 4to. Lond., 1828.
D 36 P 3 ‡

Journal of an Embassy from the Governor-General of India to the Court of Ava, 1827. 4to. Lond., 1829.
D 36 P 3 ‡

View of the Present State and Future Prospects of the Free Trade and Colonization of India. 2nd ed. (Pam. 8.) 8vo. Lond., 1829.
F 13 R 21

CRAYON (GEOFFREY). [*See* IRVING, W.]

CREASY (SIR EDWARD SHEPHERD), M.A. Fifteen Decisive Battles of the World, from Marathon to Waterloo. 2 vols. 8vo. Lond., 1851.
B 14 Q 5, 6

First Platform of International Law. 8vo. Lond., 1876.
F 8 P 17

History of England, from the Earliest to the Present Time. 2 vols. 8vo. Lond., 1869–70.
B 8 S 40, 41

History of the Ottoman Turks. 2 vols. 8vo. Lond., 1854–56.
B 13 V 27, 28

Imperial and Colonial Constitutions of the Britannic Empire, including Indian Institutions. 8vo. Lond., 1872.
F 10 T 12

Rise and Progress of the English Constitution. 8vo. Lond., 1853.
B 4 R 25

Another copy. 10th ed. 8vo. Lond., 1868.
B 4 R 26

The Spirit of Historical Study: an Inaugural Lecture. (Univ. of Lond.), 1840. 8vo. Lond., 1840.
J 5 S 8

CREATORS OF THE AGE OF STEEL. [*See* JEANS, W. T.]

CREGEEN (ARCHIBALD). Dictionary of the Manks Language, with the Corresponding Words or Explanations in English. 8vo. Douglas, 1835.
K 12 Q 13

CREICHTON (CAPT. JOHN). Memoirs of; by Jonathan Swift. (Autobiog.) 12mo. Lond., 1827.
C 1 P 10

CREIGHTON (CHARLES), M.D. Bovine Tuberculosis in Man: an Account of the Pathology of Suspected Cases. Illustrated. 8vo. Lond., 1881.
A 12 U 19

CREIGHTON (MANDELL), M.A. History of the Papacy during the Period of the Reformation. 4 vols. 8vo. Lond., 1882–87.
G 14 T 17–20

CREIGHTON (ROBERT J.) [*See* HONOLULU ALMANAC AND DIRECTORY.]

CRELLE (DR. A. L.) Rechentafeln. Tables de Calcul. 5th ed. 4to. Berlin, 1880.
A 4 Q 15 †

CRELLIN (WILLIAM). Complete Traverse Table. Stereotype (with Reading Instrument). 4to. Melb., 1881.
MA 1 P 14 †

CREMATION. Cremation not opposed to the Scriptural Doctrine of the Resurrection: a Tract for the Times; by "Resurgam." 8vo. Melb., 1875.
MG 1 Q 39

CREMONA (LUIGI), LL.D., &c. Elements of Projective Geometry; translated by Charles Leudesdorf, M.A. 8vo. Oxford, 1885.
A 10 T 29

CRÉQUY (RENÉE CHARLOTTE VICTOIRE DE FROULAY DE TESSÉ) MARQUISE DE. Recollections of a French Marchioness. 2 vols. 8vo. Lond., 1846.
C1 S 40, 41

Souvenirs de la, 1710 à 1803. Nouvelle édition. 5 vols. 12mo. Paris, 1867.
C 1 S 35–39

CRESCENS (PIERRE DE). Le Bon Mesnaiger. Sm. fol. Paris, 1540.
A 1 T 27

CRESSWELL (R.) History of Animals. [*See* ARISTOTELES.]

CRESSEY OR CRESSY (SIR HUGH PAULINUS). Church History of Brittany, from the Beginning of Christianity to the Norman Conquest. Fol. Lond., 1668.
G 28 P 33 ‡

CRESTADORO (ANDREA), PH.D. [*See* MANCHESTER PUBLIC FREE LIBRARY.]

CRESWELL (C. F.) Descriptive Catalogue of Agricultural, Vegetable, and Flower Seeds, including a large Collection of Forest Trees, Shrubs, and Flowers, indigenous to Tasmania. (Pam. E.) 4to. Hobart, 1862.
MJ 2 S 2

CRESWELL (MRS. RACHEL ELIZABETH). Memoir of Elizabeth Fry. [*See* FRY, E.]

CRESY (E.) [*See* TAYLOR, G. L.]

CREVIER (JEAN BAPTISTE LOUIS). History of the Roman Emperors, from Augustus to Constantine; translated from the French, by John Mills. 10 vols. 8vo. Lond., 1755–61.   B 11 U 10–19

CREWE (EDWARD). Narrative of. [*See* NARRATIVE.]

CRICHTON (ANDREW). Converts from Infidelity; or, Lives of Eminent Individuals who have renounced Libertine Principles and Sceptical Opinions, and embraced Christianity. (Const. Misc., 6, 7.) 2 vols. 12mo. Edinb., 1827.   K 10 P 45, 46
[*See* KOCH, C. W.]

CRICHTON (JAMES). Life of the Admirable Crichton; by P. F. Tytler. 2nd ed. 12mo. Edinb.,1823.   C 2 Q 7

CRIMEAN WAR. Diplomatic Study on the Crimean War (1852–56). Russian Official Publication. 2 vols. 8vo. Lond., 1882.   B 12 U 5, 6

CRINGLE (TOM.) [*See* WALKER, W. B.]

CRIMINAL RECORDER (THE): Biographical Sketches of Notorious Public Characters, including Murderers, Traitors, Pirates, Mutineers, Incendiaries, Defrauders, Rioters, Sharpers, Highwaymen, Footpads, Pickpockets, Swindlers, Housebreakers, Coiners, Receivers, Extortioners, and other noted persons who have suffered the sentence of the Law for Criminal Offences; by a "Student of the Inner Temple." 3 vols. 18mo. Lond., 1804. Libr.

CRIPPS (WILFRED JOSEPH), M.A., &c. College and Corporation Plate. [*See* SOUTH KENSINGTON MUSEUM, 20.]
Old French Plate; with Tables of the Paris Date-letters, and Facsimiles of other Marks: a Hand-book for the Collectors. Illustrated. 8vo. Lond., 1880.   A 10 Q 23

CRISIS IN VICTORIA (THE). History of the Crisis. [*See* VICTORIA.]

CRISTIANI (RICHARD S.) Technical Treatise on Soap and Candles; with a Glance at the Industry of Fats and Oils. Illustrated. Roy. 8vo. Philad., 1881.   A 11 T 14

CRITIC (THE): a Weekly Journal specially devoted to the encouragement of Australian Literature, Science, and Art. Fol. Sydney, 1873.   E

CROAL (THOMAS A.) Scottish Loch Scenery. [*See* LYDON, A. F.]

CROCKER (REV. HENRY) [*See* NEW GUINEA.]

CROFFUT (W. A.) The Vanderbilts and the Story of their Fortune. 8vo. Lond., 1886.   C 2 R 33

CROFT (HENRY HERBERT STEPHEN), M.A. The Boke named the Gouernour. [*See* ELYOT, SIR T.]

CROFTON (H. T.) Dialect of the English Gypsies. [*See* SMART, B. C.]

CROKER (RT. HON. JOHN WILSON), LL.D., &c. The Croker Papers: the Correspondence and Diaries of the late Right Honourable John Wilson Croker, LL.D., F.R.S. Edited by Louis J. Jennings. With Portrait. 3 vols. 8vo. Lond., 1884.   C 10 S 5–7
Memoirs of the Reign of George II. [*See* HERVEY, J., LORD.]

CROKER (THOMAS CROFTON). Memoirs of Joseph Holt, General of the Irish Rebels in 1798. 2 vols. 8vo. Lond., 1838.*   MC 1 Q 16, 17
Popular Songs of Ireland; collected and edited, with Introductions and Notes. 8vo. Lond., 1839.   H 7 S 7
Researches in the South of Ireland, illustrative of the Scenery, Architectural Remains, and the Manners and Superstitions of the Peasantry; with an Appendix containing a private Narrative of the Rebellion of 1798. 4to. Lond., 1824.   B 16 Q 22 ‡

CROKERS (THE) OF LINEHAM. Pedigree of. [*See* FOSTER, J.]

CROLL (JAMES). Climate and Time, in their Geological Relations: a Theory of Secular Changes of the Earth's Climate. 8vo. Lond., 1875.   A 3 T 13
Discussions on Climate and Cosmology. 8vo. Edinb., 1885.   A 3 T 15

CROLY (REV. GEORGE), LL.D. Historical Sketches, Speeches, and Characters. 8vo. Lond., 1842.   B 7 T 14
The Holy Land, &c. [*See* ROBERTS, D.]
Memoir of the Political Life of the Rt. Hon. Edmund Burke; with Extracts from his Writings. 2 vols. 8vo. Lond., 1840.   C 3 R 12, 13
Personal History of George IV; with Anecdotes of Distinguished Persons. 2nd ed. 2 vols. 8vo. Lond., 1841.   C 1 S 24, 25

CROMB (JAMES). The Highland Brigade; its Battles and its Heroes. Illustrated. 8vo. Lond., 1886.   B 3 Q 22

CROMBIE (REV. ALEXANDER), LL.D. Gymnasium sive Symbola Critica. 4th ed. 2 vols. 8vo. Lond., 1830.   K 12 R 40, 41

CROMBIE (REV. JACOB M.), M.A. Lichenes Britannici, seu Lichenum in Anglia, Scotia, et Hibernia, Vigentium, enumeratio cum eorum stationibus et distributione. 12mo. Lond., 1871.   A 4 P 12

CROMMELIN (JAMES C. W.) Rabbits, and how to deal with them. 8vo. Sydney, 1886.   MA 2 T 12

CROMPTON (HENRY). Industrial Conciliation. 12mo. Lond., 1876.   F 6 P 13

CROMWELL (HENRY). Memoir of. [*See* CROMWELL, O.]

CROMWELL (OLIVER), LORD PROTECTOR OF ENGLAND.
Historical and Critical Account of the Life of. [*See*
HARRIS, W.]　　　　　　　　　　　　　C 7 R 21

History of; by F. P. G. Guizot. 2 vols. 8vo. Lond.,
1854.　　　　　　　　　　　　　　B 6 T 15, 16

Letters and Speeches of; with Elucidations by Thomas
Carlyle. 2nd ed. enlarged. 3 vols. 8vo. Lond., 1846.
　　　　　　　　　　　　　　　　C 6 Q 5-7

Life of. [*See* MACKINTOSH, SIR J.]

Life of; by the Rev. M. Russell, LL.D. (Const. Misc.)
2 vols. 18mo. Edinb., 1829.　　　　K 10 Q 35, 36

Life of, Lord Protector of the Commonwealth; by Isaac
Kimber. 12mo. Lond., 1724.　　　　　　C 6 Q 10

Life of, to the Death of Charles I; by J. R. Andrews. 8vo.
Lond., 1870.　　　　　　　　　　　C 10 S 15

Memoirs of the Life and Actions of, as delivered in three
Panegyrics of him; written in Latin by Francis Peck.
4to. Lond., 1740.　　　　　　　　　　　C 4 W 5

Memoirs of the Protector, and of his Sons, Richard and
Henry; by Oliver Cromwell, a Descendant of the Family.
3rd ed. 2 vols. 8vo. Lond., 1822.　　　　C 6 Q 8, 9

Oliver Cromwell and his Times; by Thomas Cromwell.
8vo. Lond., 1821.　　　　　　　　　　　C 6 P 2

Oliver Cromwell: his Life, Times, Battle-fields, and Contemporaries; by Paxton Hood. 2nd ed. 8vo. Lond,
1884.　　　　　　　　　　　　　　　C 4 T 2

Oliver Cromwell, the Man and his Mission; by J. Allanson
Picton. 8vo. Lond., 1882.　　　　　　C 10 S 16

The Protector: a Vindication; by J. H. Merle d'Aubigné.
8vo. Lond., 1847.　　　　　　　　　　C 8 U 32

Select Biographies: Cromwell and Bunyan; by R. Southey.
(H. and C. Lib.) 12mo. Lond. 1844.　　　　J 8 P 6

Three English Statesmen [Pym, Cromwell, Pitt]; by G.
Smith. 12mo. Lond., 1868.　　　　　　　C 1 T 43

CROMWELL (OLIVER). Memoirs of the Protector, Oliver
Cromwell, and of his Sons, Richard and Henry. 3rd ed.
2 vols. 8vo. Lond., 1822.　　　　　　　C 6 Q 8, 9

CROMWELL (RICHARD). Memoir of. [*See* CROMWELL, O.]

CROMWELL (THOMAS). Oliver Cromwell and his Times.
8vo. Lond., 1821.　　　　　　　　　　　C 6 P 2

CRONISE (TITUS FEY). Agricultural, and other Resources
of California. 8vo. San Francisco, 1870.　　D 3 U 7

Natural Wealth of California. Roy. 8vo. San Francisco,
1868.　　　　　　　　　　　　　　　D 3 U 7

CROOKES (WILLIAM), F.R.S., &c. Dyeing and Tissue Printing. (Tech. Hand-book.) 12mo. Lond., 1882.　A 11 P 28

Manual of Practical Assaying. [*See* MITCHELL, J.]

On Repulsion from Radiation. The Bakerian Lecture.
(Roy. Soc. Pubs. 5.) 4to. Lond., 1878.　　A 11 P 6 †

On Repulsion resulting from Radiation. (Roy. Soc.
Pubs. 1.) 4to. Lond., 1876.　　　　　　A 11 P 2 †

CROOKES (WILLIAM), F.R.S., &c.—*continued.*
On Repulsion resulting from Radiation. Parts 3, 4.
(Roy. Soc. Pubs. 3.) 4to. Lond., 1876.　　A 11 P 4 †

Select Methods in Chemical Analysis (chiefly Inorganic).
Illustrated. 8vo. Lond., 1871.　　　　　A 5 S 13

CROOKES (WILLIAM), F.R.S., AND RÖHRIG (ERNST),
PH. D. Practical Treatise on Metallurgy, adapted from
Prof. Kerl's Metallurgy. 3 vols. 8vo. Lond., 1868-70.
　　　　　　　　　　　　　　　　A 9 T 28-30.

CRORY (W. GLENNY). East London Industries. 12mo.
Lond., 1876.　　　　　　　　　　　　A 11 Q 11

CROSS (J. K.), M.P. Imports, Exports, and the French
Treaty: a Speech in the House of Commons, 12th August,
1881. (Pams. Je.) 8vo. Lond., 1881.　　　F 6 P 10

CROSS (JOHN WALTER). George Eliot's Life, as related
in her Letters and Journals, arranged and edited by
her husband, J. W. Cross. 3 vols. 8vo. Edinb., 1885.
　　　　　　　　　　　　　　　　C 3 V 28-30

CROSS (JOSEPH). Journals of several Expeditions made
in Western Australia, during the years 1829-32. 12mo.
Lond., 1833.*　　　　　　　　　　　MD 6 P 41

CROSS (MRS. MARY ANN), "GEORGE ELIOT." Daniel
Deronda. Roy. 8vo. New York, 1876.　　J 2 R 14

Essays and Leaves from a Note-book. 8vo. Edinb.,
1884.　　　　　　　　　　　　　　　J 9 8 7

Essence of Christianity. [*See* FEUERBACH, L.]

George Eliot and her Heroines: a Study; by Abba Goold
Woolson. 12mo. N. York, 1886.　　　　　C 4 P 8

George Eliot's Life, as related in her Letters and Journals, arranged and edited by her husband, J. W. Cross.
3 vols. 8vo. Edinb., 1885.　　　　　　C 3 V 28-30

George Eliot, Moralist and Thinker. (Round Table Series.)
8vo. Edinb., 1884.　　　　　　　　　　C 5 V 10

The Legend of Jubal and other Poems. 12mo. Edinb.,
1874.　　　　　　　　　　　　　　　H 6 R 8

The Spanish Gypsy: a Poem. 8vo. Edinb., 1868.　H 5 U 1

CROSSE (ANDREW). Memorials, Scientific and Literary;
by Mrs. Cornelia A. H. Crosse. 8vo. Lond., 1857.
　　　　　　　　　　　　　　　　C 3 R 28

CROSSE (Mrs. CORNELIA A. H.) Memorials, Scientific
and Literary, of Andrew Crosse, Electrician. 8vo.
Lond., 1857.　　　　　　　　　　　　C 3 R 28,

CROSSLEY (E.), F.R.A.S., GLEDHILL (J.) F.R.A.S.
AND WILSON (J. M), M.A. Hand-book of Double Stars;
with a Catalogue of Twelve Hundred Double Stars, and
extensive Lists of Measures. 8vo. Lond., 1879. A 3 T 23

Corrections, Notes, &c., to the [above]. 8vo. Lond.,
1880.　　　　　　　　　　　　　　　A 3 T 24

CROSSLEY (HASTINGS), M.A. Fourth Book of the Meditations of M. Aurelius Antoninus. [*See* AURELIUS AN-
TONINUS, M.]

CROSTON (JAMES), F.S.A., &c. Chantrey's Peak Scenery. [*See* CHANTREY, SIR F. L.]

Historic Sites of Lancashire and Cheshire : a Wayfarer's Notes in the Palatine Counties, Historical, Legendary, Genealogical, and Descriptive. Imp. 8vo. Manchester, 1883.   B 5 V 25

Nooks and Corners of Lancashire and Cheshire : a Wayfarer's Notes in the Palatine Counties, Historical, Legendary, Genealogical, and Descriptive. 4to. Manchester, 1882.   D 6 V 18

CROWE (CATHERINE). Night Side of Nature ; or, Ghosts and Ghost Seers. 12mo. Lond., 1853.   G 8 P 34

Spiritualism, and the Age we live in. 8vo. Lond., 1859.
                                                                            G 13 T 6

CROWE (EYRE EVANS). History of France (481–1852). 5 vols. 8vo. Lond., 1858–68.   B 8 U 20–24

History of France. (Lard. Cab. Cyclo.) 3 vols. 12mo. Lond., 1831–36.   K 1 T 12–14

CROWE (EYRE EVANS), AND JAMES (G. P. R.) Lives of the Most Eminent Foreign Statesmen. (Lard. Cab. Cyclo.) 5 vols. 18mo. Lond., 1833–38.   K 1 S 19–23

CROWE (J. A.), AND CAVALCASELLE (G. B.) History of Painting in North Italy, Venice, Padua, Vicenza, Verona, Ferrara, Milan, Friuli, Brescia, from the 14th to the 16th Century. 2 vols. 8vo. Lond., 1871. A 8 Q 27, 28

Raphael : his Life and Works ; with particular reference to recently discovered Records, and an exhaustive Study of extant Drawings and Pictures. 2 vols. 8vo. Lond., 1882–85.   C 11 P 10, 11

Titian : his Life and Times ; with some Account of his Family, chiefly from new and unpublished Records ; with Portrait and Illustrations. 2 vols. 8vo. Lond., 1877.   C 8 S 49, 50

CROWLEY (ROBERT). Select Works of. [*See* EARLY ENG. TEXT SOC. 10.]

CROWN LANDS OF NEW SOUTH WALES. [*See* NEW SOUTH WALES.]

CROWN LANDS ACT OF NEW SOUTH WALES. [*See* NEW SOUTH WALES.]

CROWN LANDS GUIDE, New Zealand. [*See* NEW ZEALAND.]

CROWN LANDS OF VICTORIA. [*See* VICTORIA.]

CROWN LANDS OF S. AUSTRALIA. [*See* SOUTH AUSTRALIA.]

CROWN LANDS OF W. AUSTRALIA. [*See* WESTERN AUSTRALIA.]

CROWN LANDS OF TASMANIA. [*See* TASMANIA.]

CROWN LAW OFFICES, MELBOURNE. Catalogue of the Library at the Crown Law Offices, Melbourne. Roy. 8vo. Melb., 1878.   MK 1 S 39

CROWN PRINCE OF GERMANY. [*See* FREDERICK WILLIAM, PRINCE OF PRUSSIA.]   C 3 P 3

CROWNE (JOHN). Dramatic Works of ; with Preparatory Memoir and Notes. 4 vols. 8vo. Edinb., 1873–74.
                                                                    H 3 S 10–13

CROWNED HEADS OF EUROPE. Thirty-four Bust-Portraits ; with Short Biographies. Imp. 4to. Lond., 1884.   C 1 W 5

CROWQUILL (ALFRED). [*See* FORRESTER, A. H.]

CRUD (E. V. B.) [*See* THAER, A.]

CRUDEN (ALEXANDER), M.A. Complete Concordance to the Old and New Testament ; to which is added a Concordance to the Apocrypha. Roy. 8vo. Lond.,1836.
                                                                            K 18 S 6

CRUICKSHANK (BRODIE). Eighteen years on the Gold Coast of Africa, including an Account of the Native Tribes, and their Intercourse with Europeans. 2 vols. 8vo. Lond., 1853.   D 1 R 30, 31

CRUIKSHANK (GEORGE). Comic Annual, for the years 1835–40 ; by "Rigdum Funnidos, Gent." [Horace Mayhew, Henry Mayhew, and Robert B. Brough.] 6 vols. 12mo. Lond., 1835–40.   J 1 V 30–35

Eighty-two Illustrations on Steel, Stone, and Wood ; with Letter-press Description. 4to. Lond., 1870.   A 8 U 21

Irish Rebellion in 1798. With Illustrations. [*See* MAXWELL, W. H.]

Life of, in two Epochs ; by W. B. Jerrold. 2 vols. 8vo. Lond., 1882.   C 3 R 26, 27

Omnibus. Illustrated. Edited by Laman Blanchard. New ed. Roy. 8vo. Lond., 1870.   J 2 T 1

Punch and Judy ; with Illustrations, designed and engraved by George Cruikshank. 6th ed. 8vo. Lond., 1881.   H 4 P 35

Songs of Dibdin ; with Sketches by Cruikshank. [*See* DIBDIN, C.]

Thackeray and Cruikshank : on the Genius of George Cruikshank ; by William Makepeace Thackeray. Edited by W. E. Church. 8vo. Lond., 1884.   C 7 R 48

[*See* GRIMALDI, J. ; OLD MISCELLANY DAYS ; GRIMM, DR. J. L., *and* UNIVERSAL SONGSTER, THE.]

CRUIKSHANK (ROBERT). [*See* UNIVERSAL SONGSTER, THE.]

CRUISE (CAPT. RICHARD A.) Journal of a Ten Months' Residence in New Zealand. 8vo. Lond., 1823.*
                                                                            MD 1 V 23

Another copy. 2nd ed. 8vo. Lond., 1824.   MD 1 V 26

CRUSE (REV. C. F.) Ecclesiastical History ; by Eusebius. [*See* EUSEBIUS PAMPHILIUS.]

CRUSIUS. [*See* SUETONIUS TRANQUILLUS, C.]

CRUTTWELL (ALFRED C.), F.G.S., &c.　Sketches of Australia. 8vo. Frome (n.d.)　　MD 2 S 35
On the Coal-fields of Australia.　8vo.　Frome (n.d.)　　MD 2 S 35

CRYPTONYMOUS. [*See* MACKENZIE, K. R. H.]

CSOMA DE KÖRÖS (ALEXANDER). Essay towards a Dictionary, Tibetan and English. 1827–30. 4to. Calcutta, 1834.　　K 16 S 16
Grammar of the Tibetan Language, in English. 4to. Calcutta, 1834.　　K 16 S 17
Life and Works of: a Biography, compiled chiefly from hitherto unpublished Documents, by Theodore Duka, M.D. 8vo. Lond., 1885.　　C 5 V 7

CUAIRTEAR NAN GLEANN. (Gaelic Journal. Pam. 24.) 8vo. Glasgow, 1840.　　MJ 2 Q 12

CUBAS (ANTONIO GARCIA). Republic of Mexico in 1876 : a Political and Ethnographical Division of the Population, Character, Habits, Costumes and Vocations of its Inhabitants, written in Spanish ; translated into English by George E. Henderson. Illustrated. Roy. 8vo. Mexico (n.d.)　　D 3 U 30

CUDWORTH (RALPH), D.D.　True Intellectual System of the Universe. 4 vols. 8vo. Lond., 1820. G 8 T 5–8

CULL (RICHARD), F.S.A.　Ogilvie's English Dictionary. [*See* OGILVIE, J.]

CULLEN (C.) [*See* CLAVIGERO, ABBÉ F. S.]

CULLEN (PAUL), CARDINAL.　Letter to Lord St. Leonards on the Patriotic Fund. [*See* HISTORICAL PAMPHLETS.]

CULLEN (WILLIAM), M.D.　Account of the Life Lectures, and Writings of; by John Thomson, M.D., &c. First published in 1832. 2 vols. 8vo. Edinb., 1859. C 10 S 33, 34

CULLEY (R. S.)　Haud-book of Practical Telegraphy. 8vo. Lond., 1870.　　A 5 R 54

CULLUM (REV. SIR JOHN), BART., &c.　History and Antiquities of Hawsted and Hardwick, in the County of Suffolk. 2nd ed. Roy. 4to. Lond., 1813.　B 16 R 16 ‡

CULVER (C. M.) [*See* LANDHOLT, E.]

CUMBERLAND (G.)　The Guinea Pig or Domestic Cavy, for Food, Fur, and Fancy. 8vo. Lond., 1886. A 14 S 4

CUMBERLAND (JOHN).　English Theatre: a Selection of the most approved Tragedies, Comedies, Operas, Melodramas, &c., as performed at the London Theatres. 16 vols. 12mo. Lond., 1829.　　H 2 Q 8–23

1. Brutus ; or, the Fall of Tarquin : an Historical Tragedy ; by John Howard Payne. Virginius : a Tragedy ; by James Sheridan Knowles. Caius Gracchus : a Tragedy ; by James Sheridan Knowles. William Tell : a Play ; by James Sheridan Knowles.

CUMBERLAND (JOHN).—*continued.*

2. The Fatal Dowry : a Tragedy ; by Philip Massinger and Nathaniel Field. Pizarro : a Tragic Play ; from the German of Kotzebue, by Richard Brinsley Sheridan. Orestes in Argos : a Tragedy ; by Peter Bayley. The Serf : a Tragedy ; altered from the German of Raupach, and adapted to the English Stage, by R. Talbot.

3. The School for Scandal : a Comedy ; by Richard Brinsley Sheridan. A Midsummer Night's Dream : a Comedy ; by William Shakespeare. A Trip to Scarborough : a Comedy ; by Richard Brinsley Sheridan. Love for Love : a Comedy ; by W. Congreve. The Youthful Queen : a Comedy ; by Charles Shannon.

4. Education : a Comedy ; by Thomas Morton. The Merchant's Wedding ; or, London Frolics in 1638 : a Comedy ; by J. R. Planché. The Two Gentlemen of Verona : a Comedy ; by William Shakespeare. Taming of the Shrew : or, Katherine and Petruchio : a Comedy ; by William Shakespeare. Tribulation ; or, Unwelcome Visitors : a Comedy ; by John Poole. All's Well that Ends Well : a Comedy ; by William Shakespeare.

5. A Woman Never Vext ; or, the Widow of Cornhill : a Comedy ; by W. Rowley ; with alterations and additions by J. R. Planché. Roses and Thorns ; or, Two Houses under one Roof : a Comedy ; by Joseph Lunn. Deaf and Dumb ; or, the Orphan Protected : an Historical Drama ; taken from the French of Bouilly, and adapted to the English Stage, by Thomas Holcroft. The Hypocrite : a Comedy ; by Isaac Bickerstaff. Charles the Second ; or, the Merry Monarch : a Comedy ; by John Howard Payne.

6. The Alcaid ; or, the Secrets of Office : a Comic Opera ; by James Kenney. Amateurs and Actors : a Musical Farce ; by Richard Brinsley Peake. Hide and Seek : a Petit Opera ; by Joseph Lunn. Oberon ; or, the Charmed Horn : a Romantic Fairy Tale [by C. M. Wieland]. Dr. Bolus : a Serio-Comic-Bombastic-Operatic Interlude; by George Daniel. My Old Woman : a Musical Comedy ; by George Macfarren. No Song, no Supper : a Musical Entertainment ; by Prince Hoare.

7. Don Giovanni ; or, a Spectre on Horseback : a Comic, Heroic, Operatic, Tragic, Pantomimic Burletta-Spectacular-Extravaganza ; by Thomas Dibdin. The Lord of the Manor : an Opera ; by General Burgoyne. The Barber of Seville : a Comic Opera [by P. A. C. de Beaumarchais] ; adapted to the English Stage, by Mr. Fawcett. Giovanni in London : or, the Libertine reclaimed : an Operatic Extravaganza ; by W. T. Moncrieff. The Slave : an Opera ; by Thomas Morton. The Castle Spectre : a Dramatic Romance ; by M. G. Lewis.

8. The Siege of Belgrade : a Comic Opera ; by James Cobb. Artaxerxes : an Opera [by P. B. Metastasio]; the Music composed by T. A. Arne, M.D. The Cabinet : a Comic Opera ; by Thomas Dibdin. The Fall of Algiers : a Comic Opera. Der Freischutz ; or, the Seventh Bullet : an Opera ; by Carl Maria von Weber. The Mason of Buda : an Opera ; by J. R. Planché. Paul and Virginia : a Musical Entertainment ; by James Cobb.

9. The Critic ; or, a Tragedy Rehearsed : a Dramatic Piece ; by Richard Brinsley Sheridan. The Irish Tutor ; or, New Lights : a Comic Piece [by Richard Butler, 2nd Earl of Glengall]. Animal Magnetism : a Farce ; by Mrs. Inchbald. William Thompson ; or, Which is He : a Farce ; by Caroline Boaden. The Spoiled Child : a Farce [by Isaac Bickerstaff]. Lofty Projects ; or, Arts in the Attic : a Farce ; by Joseph Lunn. The Weathercock : a Farce ; by J. T. Allingham. A Race for a Dinner : a Farce ; by J. Thomas G. Rodwell.

10. The Disagreeable Surprise : a Musical Farce ; by George Daniel. Love in Humble Life : a Petite Comedy ; by George Howard Payne. The Scapegrace : a Petite Comedy. "Master's Rival"; or, a Day at Boulogne : a Farce ; by R. B. Peake. The Village Lawyer : a Farce. The Rival Valets : a Farce ; by Joseph Ebsworth. Fatality : a Drama ; by Caroline Boaden. The Rendezvous : an Operetta ; by Richard Ayton.

CUMBERLAND (JOHN).—*continued.*

11. Monsieur Tonson: a Farce; by W. T. Moncrieff. The Happiest Day of my Life: a Farce; by J. B. Buckstone. The Sleep-Walker; or, Which is the Lady? a Farce; by W. C. Oulton. The Duel; or, My Two Nephews: a Farce; by R. B. Peake. The Spectre Bridegroom; or, a Ghost in Spite of Himself: a Farce; by W. T. Moncrieff. The Somnambulist; or, the Phantom of the Village: a Dramatic Entertainment; by W. T. Moncrieff. The Green-eyed Monster: a Comedy; by J. R. Planché. The Lancers: an Interlude; by John R. Payne.

12. Luke the Labourer: a Domestic Melodrama; by J. B. Buckstone. A Tale of Mystery: a Melodrama; by Thomas Holcroft. Paul Jones: a Melodramatic Romance; by T. Dibdin. The Earthquake; or, the Spectre of the Nile: a Burletta Operatic Spectacle; by Edward Fitz-Ball; the Music by G. H. Rodwell. Tom and Jerry; or, Life in London: an Operatic Extravaganza; by W. T. Moncrieff. The Shepherd of Derwent Vale: a Drama; by Joseph Lunn. The Forty Thieves: a Grand Romantic Drama; by R. B. Sheridan, and Colman the Younger.

13. The Forest of Bondy; or, the Dog of Montargis: a Melodrama. The Two Galley Slaves: a Melodrama; by John Howard Payne. Frankenstein; or, the Man and the Monster: a Peculiar, Romantic, Melodramatic, Pantomimic Spectacle, founded principally on Mrs. Shelley's singular Work, entitled, "Frankenstein; or, the Modern Prometheus," and partly on the French Piece, "Le Magicien et le Monstre;" by H. M. Milner. Father and Son; or, the Rock of Charbonniere: a Drama; by E. Ball. The Gambler's Fate; or, a Lapse of Twenty Years; a Drama, founded on the Popular French Play of "La Vie d'un Joueur;" by Charles Thomson. Crazy Jane: a Romantic Play; by C. A. Somerset. The Maid of Genoa; or, the Bandit Merchant: a Melodrama; by John Farrell. Ali Pacha; or, the Signet Ring: a Melodrama; by John Howard Payne.

14. The Pilot: a Nautical Burletta; by Edward Fitz-Ball. The Flying Dutchman; or, the Phantom Ship: a Nautical Burletta; by Edward Fitz-Ball. The Inchcape Bell: a Nautical Burletta; by Edward Fitz-Ball. Masaniello; or, the Dumb Girl of Portici; a Musical Drama; by H. M. Milner. The Devil's Elixir; or, the Shadowless Man: a Musical Romance; by Edward Fitz-Ball. The Heart of Mid-Lothian: Melodramatic Romance; by Thomas Dibdin. Suil Dhuv, the Coiner: a Melodramatic Romance; by Thomas Dibdin.

15. The Children in the Wood: an Opera; by Thomas Morton. Clari; or, the Maid of Milan: an Opera; by John Howard Payne. Where Shall I Dine: a Farsetta. The Illustrious Stranger; or, Married and Buried: an Operatic Farce; by James Kenney. Snakes in the Grass: a Farce; by J. B. Buckstone. Love, Law, and Physic: a Farce; by James Kenney. The Floating Beacon: a Nautical Drama; by Edward Fitz-Ball. Rochester; or, King Charles the Second's Merry Days: a Musical Comedy; by W. T. Moncrieff.

16. Rienzi: a Tragedy; by Mary Russell Mitford. Town and Country: a Comedy; by Thomas Morton. The Soldier's Daughter: a Comedy; by Andrew Cherry. The Forest Oracle; or, the Bridge of Tresino: an Operatic Drama; by M. Campbell. Yes! an Operatic Interlude; by C. A. Somerset. Ivanhoe; or, the Jew's Daughter: a Romantic Melodrama; by Thomas Dibdin. The Brigand: a Romantic Drama; by J. R. Planché.

CUMBERLAND (RT. REV. RICHARD), D.D., BISHOP OF PETERBOROUGH. Sanchoniatho's Phœnician History. [*See* SANCHONIATHO.]

CUMBERLAND (RICHARD). The Battle of Hastings: a Tragedy. (Bell's Brit. Theatre.) 18mo. Lond., 1793.
H 2 P 35

The Box-lobby Challenge: a Comedy. [*See* MODERN THEATRE 5.]

CUMBERLAND (RICHARD)—*continued.*

The Brothers: a Comedy. (Bell's Brit. Theatre.) 18mo. Lond., 1792.
H 2 P 19

Another copy. (Brit. Theatre.) 12mo. Lond., 1808.
H 1 P 18

Another copy. [*See* BRIT. DRAMA, 4.]

The Carmelite: a Tragedy. (Bell's Brit. Theatre.) 18mo. Lond., 1791.
H 2 P 5

Another copy. [*See* MODERN THEATRE, 5.]

The Choleric Man: a Comedy. (Bell's Brit. Theatre.) 18mo. Lond., 1793.
H 2 P 35

Another copy. [*See* BRIT. DRAMA, 4.]

False Impressions: a Comedy. [*See* MODERN THEATRE, 5.]

The Fashionable Lover: a Comedy. (Bell's Brit. Theatre.) 18mo. Lond., 1793.
H 2 P 25

First Love: a Comedy. (Brit. Theatre.) 12mo. Lond., 1808.
H 1 P 18

The Impostors: a Comedy. [*See* MODERN THEATRE, 6.]

The Jew: a Comedy. (Brit. Theatre.) 12mo. Lond., 1808.
H 1 P 18

Johnsoniana. [*See* JOHNSON, DR. S.]

The Mysterious Husband: a Tragedy. [*See* MODERN THEATRE, 5.]

The Natural Son: a Comedy. (Bell's Brit. Theatre. 18mo. Lond., 1794.
H 2 P 40

Another copy. [*See* MODERN THEATRE, 5.]

Posthumous Dramatick Works of. 2 vols. 8vo. Lond., 1813.
H 3 S 14, 15

The West Indian: a Comedy. (Bell's Brit. Theatre.) 18mo. Lond., 1792.
H 2 P 5

Another copy. (Brit. Theatre.) 12mo. Lond., 1808.
H 1 P 18

Another copy. [*See* BRIT. DRAMA, 4.]

The Wheel of Fortune: a Comedy. (Brit Theatre.) 12mo. Lond., 1808.
H 1 P 18

CUMBERLAND (WILLIAM AUGUSTUS), DUKE OF. Sketch of his Military Life and Character; by A. N. Campbell-Maclachlan, M.A. 8vo. Lond., 1876.
C 3 S 17

CUMMING (MISS CONSTANCE FREDERIKA GORDON). At Home in Fiji. With Map and Illustrations. 2 vols. 8vo. Lond., 1881.
MD 5 R 20, 21

From the Hebrides to the Himalayas. 2 vols. 8vo. Lond., 1876.
D 6 R 3, 4

In the Himalayas and on the Indian Plains. Illustrated. 8vo. Lond., 1884.
D 6 P 19

Via Cornwall to Egypt. With a Frontispiece. 8vo. Lond., 1885.
D 1 P 10

Wanderings in China. Illustrated. 2 vols. 8vo. Edinb., 1886.
D 6 Q 27, 28

CUMMING (J. GORDON-.) Russian Travellers in Mongolia and China. [*See* PIASSETSKY, P.]

CUMMING (Linnæus), M.A. Introduction to the Theory of Electricity; with numerous Examples. 8vo. Lond., 1876.   A 5 R 49

CUMMING (Roualeyn Gordon). Five Years of a Hunter's Life in the Far Interior of South Africa. 2nd ed. 2 vols. 8vo. Lond., 1850.   D 1 V 7, 8

CUMMING (Lieut.-Col. W. Gordon). Wild Men and Wild Beasts: Scenes in Camp and Jungle. Illustrated. Sq. 8vo. Edinb., 1871.   D 5 S 32

CUMMINS (John). Voyage to the South Seas. [*See* Bulkeley, J.]

CUNDALL (Frank). Reminiscences of the Colonial and Indian Exhibition. [*See* Riley, T.]

CUNDALL (Joseph). Hans Holbein. (Great Artists). 8vo. Lond., 1879.   C 3 T 42

On Bookbindings, Ancient and Modern. Sm. 4to. Lond., 1881.   A 11 V 13

CUNDEE (James). [*See* Naval Anecdotes.]

CUNEUS (Pierre). La République des Hébreux ; nouvelle edition, revûe corrigee augmentée de deux Volumes contenant des Remarques Critiques sur les Antiquitéz Judaïquez, par Mr. [Jacques] Basnage. 5 vols. 12mo. Amsterdam, 1713.   G 10 P 21-25

CUNN (S.) [*See* Newton, Sir I.]

CUNNINGHAM (Brev.-Major Alex.), C.S.I. Archæological Survey of India, 1862-65. 2 vols. roy. 8vo. Simla, 1871.   B 10 V 15, 16

The Bhilsa Topes, or Buddhist Monuments of Central India. Illustrated. 8vo. Lond., 1854.   B 10 S 12

Stûpa of Bharhut, a Buddhist Monument. Roy. 4to. Lond., 1879.   B 19 S 13 ‡

CUNNINGHAM (Allan), F.L.S., &c. Biographical Sketch of; by Robert Heward, F.L.S. 8vo. Lond., 1842.   MC 1 R 25

Brief View of the Progress of Interior Discovery in New South Wales. 8vo. Lond., 1832.   MD 7 Q 49

Journal of a Route from Bathurst to Liverpool Plains, in New South Wales. With a Map. [*See* Field, B.]

Specimen of the Indigenous Botany of the Mountainous Country between the Colony round Port Jackson and the Settlement of Bathurst. [*See* Field, B.]

[*See* Brown, R.]

CUNNINGHAM (Allan). Life of; with Selections from his Works and Correspondence, by the Rev. David Hogg. 8vo. Lond., 1875.   C 2 U 19

Life of Sir David Wilkie; with his Journals, Tours, and Critical Remarks on Works of Art, and a Selection from his Correspondence. 3 vols. 8vo. Lond., 1843.   C 9 S 37-39

Life of Robert Burns. [*See* Burns, R.]

CUNNINGHAM (Allan).—*continued.*

Lives of the most Eminent British Painters, Sculptors, and Architects. (Fam. Lib.) 2nd ed. 6 vols. 12mo. Lond., 1830-39.   K 10 P 6-11

Lives of the most Eminent British Painters. Revised ed., annotated and continued to the present time by Mrs. Charles Heaton. 3 vols. 8vo. Lond., 1879-80.
                                               C 1 S 9-11

CUNNINGHAM (George Godfrey). Lives of Eminent and Illustrious Englishmen ; from Alfred the Great to the latest times. 8 vols. 8vo. Glasgow, 1837. C 7 Q 5-12

CUNNINGHAM (H. S.), M.A. British India and its Rulers. 8vo. Lond., 1881.   F 9 P 17

CUNNINGHAM (John). Life and Poems of. [*See* Johnson, S., *and* Chalmers, A.]

CUNNINGHAM (J. T.) Charles Darwin, Naturalist. 8vo. Edinb., 1886.   C 10 U 1

CUNNINGHAM (Rev. John William), M.A. Genius and Poetry of Cowper. [*See* Cowper, W.]

Sancho ; or, the Proverbialist. 3rd ed. 12mo. Lond., 1817.   J 1 T 5

The Velvet Cushion. 6th ed. 8vo. Lond., 1815. G 13 T 5

A World without Souls. 6th ed. 8vo. Lond., 1816.
                                               G 13 T 5

CUNNINGHAM (Peter). Hard-hook for London Past and Present. 2 vols. 8vo. Lond., 1849.   D 11 S 1, 2

Poems of W. Drummond of Hawthorden ; with Life. [*See* Drummond, W.]

Life and Poems of. [*See* Johnson, Dr. S.]

CUNNINGHAM (Peter), R.N. Hints for Australian Emigrants; with Engravings and Explanatory Descriptions of the Water-raising Wheels, and Modes of irrigating Land in Egypt, Syria, South America, &c. 8vo. Lond., 1841.*   MA 1 P 34

Two Years in New South Wales: a Series of Letters. 3rd ed. 2 vols. 12mo. Lond., 1827.   MD 3 R 14, 15

Another copy. 2nd ed. 2 vols. 12mo. Lond., 1827.
                                               MD 3 R 16, 17

Another copy. 3rd ed. 2 vols. 8vo. Lond., 1828.*
                                               MD 3 R 24-25

On the General and Local Causes of Magnetic Variation, &c. (Pam. 38.) 8vo. Lond., 1841.   MJ 2 Q 25

On the Motions of the Earth and Heavenly Bodies, as explained by Electro-magnetic Attraction and Repulsion. 8vo. Lond., 1834.   A 3 R 10

CUNNINGHAM (William), M.A. Churches of Asia: a Methodical Sketch of the 2nd Century. 8vo. Lond., 1880.   G 13 T 11

Growth of English Industry and Commerce. 8vo. Cambridge, 1882.   F 6 R 31

CUNYNGHAME (GEN. SIR ARTHUR AUGUSTUS THUR-
LOW), BART. Glimpse at the Great Western Republic.
8vo. Lond., 1851. D 3 S 35

CUNYNGHAME (HENRY). Treatise on the Law of
Electric Lighting. With the Acts of Parliament and
the Rules and Orders of the Board of Trade, a Model
Provisional Order, and a Set of Forms. Roy. 8vo. Lond.,
1883. F 2 T 13

CURCI (C. M.) Il moderno Dissidio tra la Chiesa e l'Italia
considerato per occasione di un Fatto particolare. 8vo.
Firenze, 1878. G 9 S 11

CURETON (REV. CANON WILLIAM), M.A., &c. Ancient
Syriac Documents relative to the Earliest Establishment
of Christianity in Edessa and the neighbouring Countries.
4to. Lond., 1864. G 5 U 6

Corpus Ignatianum: a complete Collection of the Ignatian
Epistles, genuine, interpolated, and spurious. Roy. 8vo.
Lond., 1849. G 8 V 14

CURIOSITIES OF ENTOMOLOGY. 8vo. Lond.,
1871. A 13 U 8

CURIOSITIES OF STREET LITERATURE. Comprising "Cocks," or Catchpennies, a large and curious
assortment of Street Drolleries, Squibs, Histories, Comic
Tales in prose and verse, Broadsides on the Royal Family,
Political Litanies, Dialogues, Catechisms, Acts of Parliament, Street Political Papers; a variety of "Ballads on
a Subject," Dying Speeches and Confessions. 4to. Lond.,
1871. J 7 V 10

CURLING (JAMES BUNCE). Some Account of the Ancient
Corps of Gentlemen-at-Arms. 8vo. Lond., 1850 B 4 T 4

CURNOW (JOHN), AND MORRISON (W. E. W.), B.A.
Science Manual: Elementary Science, arranged for the use
of Primary Schools in New Zealand. Illustrated. 12mo.
Melb., 1880. MA 2 V 13

CURR (EDWARD). Account of the Colony of Van Diemen's Land, principally designed for the use of Emigrants. 8vo. Lond., 1824.* MD 3 P 35

Petitions of the District of Port Phillip (Australia Felix),
for Separation from the Territory of New South Wales.
[With Introductory Remarks.] 8vo. Melb., 1844.
MF 1 Q 16

Another copy. MJ 2 R 20

Remarks on the proposed New Squatting Regulations.
Fol. St. Helliers', 1845. MJ 2 U 2

CURR (EDWARD M.) The Australian Race: its Origin,
Languages, Customs, Place of Landing in Australia, and
the Routes by which it spread itself over the Continent.
Vols. 1-3. 8vo. Melb., 1886-87. MA 1 R 21-23

The Australian Race, vol. 4. [Comparative Vocabulary.]
Fol. Melb., 1887. MA 1 P 6 }

Frivolities [with French Translations]. 8vo. Melb., 1868.
MH 1 S 21

2 C

CURR (EDWARD M).—*continued.*

Prize Essay on Scab in Sheep : its Causes, Symptoms,
Pathology, best means of Treatment, and Practical Hints
for its Avoidance and Extermination, &c. 8vo. Melb.,
1865. MA 1 P 22

Another copy. 8vo. Melb., 1865. MA 1 Q 1

Pure Saddle-horses, and how to breed them in Australia ;
together with a Consideration of the History and Merits
of the English, Arab, Andalusian, and Australian Breed
of Horses. 8vo. Melb., 1863.* MA 1 P 32

Recollections of Squatting in Victoria, then called the
Port Phillip District (from 1841 to 1851). 8vo. Melb.
1883.* MD 6 R 21

Waste Lands of the Province of Wellington, New Zealand. 8vo. Wellington, 1856. MJ 2 R 21

CURR (JOHN). The Learned Donkeys of 1847; being a
Review of the Reviewers of Railway Locomotion and Steam
Navigation. (Pam. 34.) 8vo. Lond., 1847. J 12 U 26

CURRAN (RT. HON. JOHN PHILPOT). Anecdote Life of.
[*See* TIMBS, J.]

Curran and his Contemporaries; by Charles Phillips. 8vo.
Lond., 1850. C 10 S 36

Life of; by his Son, W. H. Curran. 2nd ed. 2 vols. 12mo.
Edinb., 1822. C 1 S 16, 17

New and enlarged Collection of his Speeches; with Memoirs
and Portrait. 8vo. Lond., 1819. F 6 T 9

Speeches of. Complete and correct edition; edited, with
Memoir and Historical Notices, by Thomas Davis, M.R.I.A.
8vo. Lond., 1847. F 13 P 20

[*See* HISTORICAL PAMPHLETS.]

CURRAN (WILLIAM HENRY). Life of the Rt. Hon. John
Philpot Curran. 2nd ed. 2 vols. 12mo. Edinb., 1822.
C 1 S 16, 17

Sketches of the Irish Bar; with Essays, Literary and
Political. 2 vols. 8vo. Lond., 1855. J 11 U 22, 23

CURRENCY LAD (THE). Fol. Sydney, 1832-33. ME

CURRIE (CAPT. MARK JOHN), R.N. Journal of an Excursion to the southward of Lake George, in New South
Wales. With a Map. [*See* FIELD, B.]

CURRY (F.) [*See* BADHAM, C. D.]

CURRY (JOHN), M.D. Historical and Critical Review of
the Civil Wars in Ireland, from the Reign of Queen Elizabeth to the Settlement under King William. New ed.
8vo. Dublin, 1810. B 11 Q 2

CURTIS (CHARLES B.), M.A. Descriptive and Historical
Catalogue of the Works of Don Diego de Silva Velazquez
and Bartolomé Esteban Murillo, comprising a classified
List of their Paintings; with original Etchings. 8vo.
Lond., 1883. K 17 U 1

CURTIS (JOHN). Shipwreck of the *Stirling Castle;* to which is added, the Narrative of the Wreck of the *Charles Eaton,* in the same Latitude. 8vo. Lond, 1838.*   MD 3 U 1

CURTIS (JOHN), F.L.S. British Entomology; being Illustrations and Descriptions of the Genera of Insects found in Great Britain and Ireland: Diptera, Hymenoptera, Deimaptera. 3 vols. roy. 8vo. Lond., 1862.   A 13 U 1-3

CURTIS (WILLIAM), F.L.S. Companion to the Botanical Magazine. [*See* HOOKER, SIR J. D.]

Curtis's Botanical Magazine, comprising the Plants of the Royal Gardens of Kew, and of other Botanical Establishments in Great Britain; with suitable Descriptions, by Sir Joseph Dalton Hooker, M.D., &c. Vols. 1-114. Roy. 8vo. Lond, 1787-1886.   E

Flora Londinensis; or, Plates and Descriptions of such Plants as grow wild in the Environs of London. 2 vols. fol. Lond., 1777-98.   A 4 W 5, 6 ‡

CURTIS (W.), GRAVES (G.), AND HOOKER (SIR W. J.) Flora Londinensis; containing a History of the Plants indigenous to Great Britain, illustrated by Figures of the natural size; the Descriptions by William Jackson Hooker, LL.D., &c. New ed., enlarged by George Graves, F.L.S. 5 vols. fol. Lond., 1817-28.   A 2 S 14-18 ‡

CURTIUS (PROF. GEORG), PH.D. Die Sprachvergleichung in ihrem Verhältniss zur classischen Philologie. 8vo. Berlin, 1845.   K 13 Q 6

Grundzüge der griechischen Etymologie. Fünfte unter Mitwirkung von Ernst Windisch umgearbeitete Auflage. Roy. 8vo. Leipzig, 1879.   K 13 T 12

Principles of Greek Etymology; translated by Augustus S. Wilkins, M.A., and Edwin B. England, M.A. 2 vols. 8vo. Lond., 1875-76.   K 15 P 18, 19

Student's Greek Grammar: a Grammar of the Greek Language; translated and edited by W. Smith, D.C.L., &c. 5th ed. 8vo. Lond., 1872.   K 11 T 32

Zur Chronologie der Indogermanischen Sprachforschung. 2ª aullage. Imp. 8vo. Leipzig, 1873.   K 16 S 8

[*See* LEIPZIGER STUDIEN.]

CURTIUS (GEORG), UND BRUGMAN (KARL). Studien zur griechischen und lateinischen Grammatik. 10 vols. 8vo. Leipsic, 1868-78.   K 15 P 20-29

CURTIUS RUFUS (QUINTUS). De rebus gestis Alexandri Magni libri superstites, ex editione F. Schmieder, cum Supplementis, &c., in usum Delphini. 4 vols. 8vo. Lond., 1825.   J 13 S 19-22

CURWEN (HENRY). History of Booksellers; the Old and the New. 8vo. Lond., 1873.   B 11 Q 39

Sorrow and Song: Studies of Literary Struggle. 2 vols. 8vo. Lond., 1875.   C 3 Q 43, 44

CURWEN (JOHN C.) Observations on the State of Ireland, principally directed to its Agriculture and Rural Population. 2 vols. 8vo. Lond., 1818.   B 11 Q 5, 6

CURZON (HON. ROBERT), JUNR. Armenia: a Year at Erzeroom, and on the Frontiers of Russia, Turkey, and Persia. 8vo. Lond., 1854.   D 5 Q 41

Visit to Monasteries in the Levant. Illustrated. 8vo. Lond., 1865.   D 1 S 27

CUSACK (MISS MARY FRANCES). Illustrated History of Ireland; with Historical Illustrations, by Henry Doyle. 8vo. Lond., 1869.   B 11 Q 25

The Liberator [Daniel O'Connell] and his Times, Political and Social. 2 vols. 8vo. Kenmare, 1875.   C 8 P 32, 33

Student's Manual of Irish History. 8vo. Lond., 1870.   B 11 P 1

CUSACK-SMITH (SIR WILLIAM), BART. [*See* SMITH, SIR W. CUSACK-.]

CUSHING (J. N.), M.A. Shan and English Dictionary. 8vo. Rangoon, 1881.   K 14 Q 17

CUSHMAN (CHARLOTTE). Her Letters and Memories of her Life; edited by her Friend, Emma Stebbins. 8vo. Boston, 1879.   C 6 P 4

CUSSANS (JOHN EDWIN). History of Hertfordshire; containing an Account of the Descents of the various Manors; Pedigrees of Families connected with the County; Antiquities, Local Customs, &c. 3 vols. roy. fol. Lond., 1870-81.   B 1 S 1-3 ‡

CUST (GEN. THE HON. SIR EDWARD), D.C.L. Annals of the Wars of the 18th Century (1700-99). 3rd ed. 5 vols. 12mo. Lond., 1858-60.   B 14 P 26-30

Annals of the Wars of the 19th Century, 1800-15. 4 vols. 12mo. Lond., 1862-63.   B 14 P 31-34

Lives of the Warriors of the Civil Wars of France and England (1611-75). 2 vols. 8vo. Lond., 1867.   C 3 P 44, 45

Thoughts on the expedience of a better System of Control and Supervision over Buildings erected at the public expense; and on the subject of re-building the Houses of Parliament. 8vo. Lond., 1837.   A 7 Q 13

CUST (ROBERT NEEDHAM). Linguistic and Oriental Essays; written from the year 1846 to 1887. [1st and] 2nd series. 2 vols. 8vo. Lond., 1880-87.   K 12 R 30, 31

Shrines of Lourdes, Zaragossa, the Holy Stairs at Rome, the Holy House of Loretto and Nazareth, and St. Ann at Jerusalem. 12mo. Lond., 1885.   G 13 T 17

Sketch of the Modern Languages of Africa; accompanied by a Language-Map. 2 vols. 8vo. Lond., 1883.   K 12 R 28, 29

Sketch of the Modern Languages of the East Indies, accompanied by two Language-Maps. 8vo. Lond., 1878.   K 13 Q 5

CUSTINE (ASTOLPHE), MARQUIS DE. Empire of the Czar; or, Observations on the Social, Political, and Religious state and Prospects of Russia. 3 vols. 12mo. Lond., 1843.   D 8 Q 24-26

CUTHBERTSON (J.) Complete Glossary to the Poetry and Prose of Robert Burns. 8vo. Paisley, 1886.   K 17 P 25

CUVIER (GEORGES CHRÉTIEN LEOPOLD DAGOBERT), BARON.
Animal Kingdom; with additional Descriptions, by Edward
Griffiths, F.L.S., &c., and others. 16 vols. 8vo. Lond.,
1827-35. A 14 R 5-20

Animal Kingdom: Mollusca and Radiata; with supplementary Additions to each Order, by Edward Griffiths,
F.L.S., &c., and Edward Pidgeon. Roy. 8vo. Lond.,
1834. A 15 Q 18

Discourse on the Revolutions of the Surface of the Globe.
8vo. Lond., 1829. A 9 P 43

Le Régne Animal, distribué d'après son Organisation, pour
servir de base à l'Histoire Naturelle des Animaux et d'introduction à l'Anatomie Comparée; avec Figures, dessinées
d'après nature. 4 vols. 8vo. Paris, 1817. A 14 R 32-35

Leçons d'Anatomie Comparée. 5 vols. 8vo. Paris, 1805.
A 28 Q 1-5

Memoirs of; by Mrs. R. Lee (formerly Mrs. T. E. Bowdich).
8vo. Lond., 1833. C 6 P 3

[*See* GOLDSMITH, O.]

CUZENT (GILBERT). Voyage aux Iles Gambier (Archipe
de Margaréva). 8vo. Paris, 1872.* MD 5 S 42

CYPLES (WILLIAM). Inquiry into the Process of Human
Experience. 8vo. Lond., 1880. G 4 R 13

CYPRIANUS (THASCIUS CÆCILIUS), SANCTUS. Opera
omnia. [*See* MIGNE, J. P., SERIES LATINA 4.]

CYPRIEN DE GAMACHE (FATHER —). Memoirs of
the Mission in England of the Capuchin Friars. [*See*
BIRCH, REV. T.]

CYRILLUS (HIEROSOLYMITANUS ARCHIEPISCOPUS). Sanctus
Opera omnia. [*See* MIGNE, J. P., SERIES GRÆCA 33.]

CYRILLUS ALEXANDRINUS (SANCTUS). Opera omnia. [*See* MIGNE, J. P., SERIES GRÆCA 68-77.]

D

D * * * L * * *.　[*See* DIGGER'S HAND-BOOK.]

D'A—— (ANNA).　[*See* D'ALMEIDA, ANNA.]

D. (C.)　[*See* DE MORGAN, MRS. C.]

D. P.　[*See* WAVE OF LIFE.]

DABISTAN (THE); or, School of Manners; translated from the original Persian, with Notes and Illustrations, by David Shea and A. Troyer.　3 vols. 8vo.　Paris, 1843.　　　　　　　　　　　　　　G 2 T 10–12

DABNEY (PROF. R. L.), D.D.　Life of Lieut.-Gen. J. Jackson (Stonewall Jackson).　2 vols. 8vo.　Lond., 1864–66.　　　　　　　　　　　　　　　C 3 U 10, 11

DABOVICH (P. E.)　Nautisch-Technisches Wörterbuch der Marine.　Deutsch, Italienisch, Französisch, und Englisch.　Erster Band.　Roy. 8vo.　Pola, 1883.　K 16 T 7

D'ABRANTES (DUCHESS).　[*See* ABRANTES.]

D'ACHERY (LUCAS).　Spicilegium sive collectio veterum aliquot scriptorum qui in Galliæ bibliothecis delituerant ; 3 vols. fol.　Paris, 1723.　　　　　　　　　G 28 P 32 ‡

Vetera analecta, sive collectio veterum aliuot operum et Opusculorum omnis generis, Carminum, Epistolarum, Diplomatum, Epitaphiorum, &c.　Novo editio.　Fol. Paris, 1723.　　　　　　　　　　　　　　G 28 P 32 ‡

DACIER (A.)　[*See* VERRIUS FLACCUS, M.]

DA CUNHA (J. GERSON), M.R.C.S., &c.　Konkani Language and Literature.　Imp. 8vo.　Bombay, 1881.　　　　　　　　　　　　　　　　　K 12 T 8

D'AFFORNE (JAMES).　Works of Turner.　[*See* TURNER, J. M. W.]

D'AGINCOURT (J. B. L. G. SEROUX).　History of Art by its Monuments ; translated from the French.　3 vols. (in 1) fol.　Lond., 1847.　　　　　　　A 2 P 26 ‡

DAGLEY (R.)　Death's Doings ; consisting of numerous Original Compositions in Verse and Prose.　2nd ed. 2 vols. 8vo.　Lond., 1827.　　　　　H 5 U 26, 27

D'AGUEN (A. M. P. LAASS).　[*See* LAASS D'AGUEN, A. M. P.]

D'ALBERTIS (LUIGI MARIA).　Alla Nuova Guinea : ciò che ho veduto e ciò che ho fatto.　8vo.　Torino, 1880.　　　　　　　　　　　　　　　MD 4 W 22

New Guinea : What I did and what I saw.　2 vols. 8vo.　Lond., 1880.　　　　　　　　　　MD 4 W 23, 24

DALE (ALFRED WILLIAM WINTERSLOW), M.A.　Synod of Elvira, and Christian Life in the 4th Century : a Historical Essay.　8vo.　Lond., 1882.　　　G 13 U 7

DALE (REV. HENRY).　Cyropædia of Xenophon.　[*See* XENOPHON.]

DALE (REV. R. F.)　Music Primer for Schools.　[*See* TROUTBECK, REV. J.]

D'ALEMBERT (JEAN LE ROND).　Memoir of the Life and Writings of Baron de Montesquieu.　[*See* MONTESQUIEU C. DE SECONDAT, BARON DE.]

Correspondence de Voltaire avec D'Alembert.　[*See* VOLTAIRE, F. M. A. DE.]

DALEN (ANTON VAN), M.D.　De Oraculis Ethnicorum Dissertationes Duæ : quarum prior de ipsorum duratione ac defectu, posterior de eorundem Auctoribus.　12mo.　Amsterdam, 1683.　　　　　　　　　　G 8 P 4

DALHOUSIE (DOWAGER COUNTESS OF.)　Memoir of Pasolini, G.　[*See* PASOLINI, G.]

DALHOUSIE (JAMES ANDREW BROWN RAMSAY), MARQUIS OF.　Administration of British India.　[*See* ARNOLD SIR E.]

DALIN (A. F.)　Dansk-Norsk och Svensk Ordbok.　12mo.　Stockholm, 1869.　　　　　　　　　K 11 S 19

DALLAS (ENEAS SWEETLAND).　The Gay Science.　2 vols. 8vo.　Lond., 1866.　　　　　　　G 10 T 1, 2

DALLAS (R. C.)　[*See* WEBER, J.]

DALLAS (W. S.)　Entertaining Naturalist.　[*See* LOUDON, MRS. J. W.]

Erasmus Darwin.　[*See* KRAUSE, E.]

Zoology.　[*See* CARPENTER, W. C.]

[*See* HUMBOLDT, A. VON, *and* MÜLLER, F.]

DALLAWAY (REV. JAMES), A.M., &c.　Modern Taste in Gardening.　[*See* WALPOLE, H.]

DALLEY (RT. HON. WILLIAM BEDE), P.C., &c.　Opinions from 8th January, 1883, to 5th October, 1885 ; compiled and Indexed by E. Lewis Scott.　Fol.　Sydney, 1886.　　　　　　　　　　　　　　　　MF 3 U 22

DALLEY (RT. HON. WILLIAM BEDE), P.C., &c., AND PARKES (SIR HENRY), G.C.M.G.　Colony of New South Wales: its Agricultural, Pastoral, and Mining Capabilities ; compiled by the Commissioners of the Colonial Government.　8vo.　Lond., 1862.　MA 1 Q 7

DALLING AND BULWER (SIR HENRY LYTTON EARLE), LORD. Historical Characters: Talleyrand, Cobbett, Mackintosh, Canning. 2 vols. 8vo. Lond., 1868.
C 8 Q 48, 49

Life of Henry John Temple, Viscount Palmerston; with Selections from his Diaries and Correspondence. 2 vols. 8vo. Lond., 1870–74. C 9 Q 7–9

The Lords, the Government, and the Country: a Letter. 5th ed. (Pam. V 1.) 8vo. Lond., 1836. MJ 2 P 36

Monarchy of the Middle Classes. France, Social, Literary, Political. 2nd Series. 2 vols. 8vo. Lond., 1836.
B 9 P 19, 20

Sir Robert Peel; an Historical Sketch. (Pam. Ca.) 8vo. Lond., 1874. C 9 Q 17

DALLINTON (SIR ROBERT). A Briefe Inference vpon Gvicciardines Digression, in the fovrth part of the first Qvarterne of his Historie. 8m. fol. Lond., 1613.
G 5 U 15

D'ALMEIDA (ANNA). A Lady's Visit to Manilla and Japan. 8vo. Lond., 1863. D 6 S 11

D'ALMEIDA (WILLIAM BARRINGTON). Life in Java; with Sketches of the Javanese. 2 vols. 8vo. Lond., 1864. D 5 Q 24, 25

DALRIAD. [*See* CAMPBELL, LORD C.]

DAL RIO (DR. ERCOLE). The Incomparable Game of Chess. Translated from the Italian, by J. S. Bingham. 8vo. Lond., 1820. A 17 U 13

DALRYMPLE (ALEXANDER), F.R.S., &c. Historical Collection of the several Voyages and Discoveries in the South Pacific Ocean. 2 vols. (in 1) 4to. Lond., 1769–71.
MD 7 P 7 †

Another copy. 2 vols. (in 1) 4to. Lond., 1770–71.
MD 7 P 8 †

DALRYMPLE (SIR DAVID), BART., LORD HAILES. Annals of Scotland, from the Accession of Malcolm III, surnamed Canmore, to the Accession of Robert I. 4to. Edinb., 1776. B 12 V 33

Annals of Scotland, from the Accession of Robert I, to the Accession of the House of Stewart. 4to. Edinb., 1779. B 12 V 34

Annals of Scotland, from the Accession of Malcolm III, to the Accession of the House of Stewart. New ed. 3 vols. 8vo. Edinb., 1797. B 13 P 33–35

Memorials and Letters relating to the History of Britain in the Reign of James I. 12mo. Glasgow, 1762. B 4 P 21

DALRYMPLE (G. E.) Report of the Proceedings of the Queensland Government Schooner *Spitfire.* [*See* SMITH, J. W.]

DALRYMPLE (SIR JOHN), BART., BARON OF EXCHEQUER IN SCOTLAND. Memoirs of Great Britain and Ireland. 3 vols. 8vo. Lond., 1790. B 6 R 35–37

DALTON (CHARLES), F.R.G.S. Life and Times of General Sir Edward Cecil, Viscount Wimbledon. 2 vols. 8vo. Lond., 1885. C 10 S 2, 3

DALTON (FATHER). [*See* BATES, E. AND M. A.]

DALTON (HENRY G.), M.D. History of British Guiana; comprising a General Description of the Colony. 2 vols. 8vo. Lond., 1855. B 1 R 19, 20

DALTON (DR. HERMANN). John A Lasco; his Earlier Life and Labours: a Contribution to the History of the Reformation in Poland, Germany, and England; translated by the Rev. M. J. Evans, B.A. 8vo. Lond., 1886.
C 5 R 3

D'ALTON (JOHN). Memoirs of the Archbishops of Dublin. 8vo. Dublin, 1838. C 10 R 2

DALTON (J. C.), M.D. Topographical Anatomy of the Brain. 3 vols. roy. 4to. Philad., 1885. A 5 P 11–13 †

DALTON (REV. JOHN NEALE), M.A., &c. Cruise of H.M.S. *Bacchante.* [*See* ALBERT VICTOR, PRINCE.]

DALVIMART (O.) The Costume of Turkey illustrated by a series of (coloured) Engravings; with Descriptions in English and French. Fol. Lond., 1804. A 23 S 14 ‡

DALY (DOMINIC DANIEL). [*See* PORT DARWIN.]

DALY (MRS. DOMINIC D.) Digging, Squatting, and Pioneering Life in the Northern Territory of South Australia. 8vo. Lond., 1887. MD 6 T 6

DALY (J. BOWLES). Radical Pioneers of the 18th Century. 8vo. Lond., 1886. B 23 R 11

DALYELL (SIR JOHN GRAHAM), BART. Rare and remarkable Animals of Scotland, represented from living subjects; with practical Observations on their Nature. Coloured Plates. 2 vols. 4to. Lond., 1847–48. A 1 P 7, 8 †

Tract, chiefly relative to Monastic Antiquities. 8vo. Edinb., 1809. B 13 P 39

DALZEL (PROF. ANDREW), M.A. Collectanea Græca Majora; cum Notis Philologicis. 8vo. Lond., 1805.
J 13 T 34

Substance of Lectures on the Ancient Greeks, and on the Revival of Greek Learning in Europe. 2 vols. 8vo. Edinb., 1821. J 3 S 11, 12

[*See* CHEVALIER, J. B. DE.]

DALZIEL (HUGH), "CORSINCON." British Dogs: their Varieties, History, Characteristics, Breeding, Management, and Exhibition. Illustrated. 8vo. Lond., 1880. A 14 S 1

DALZIEL (THE BROTHERS). Bird's-eye View of Society. [*See* DOYLE, R.]

DAMANIANT (—.) The Midnight Hour: a Comedy. [*See* FARCES, 1.]

DAMASUS (SANCTUS). Opera omnia. [*See* MIGNE, J. P., SERIES LATINA, 13.]

DAMER (HON. MRS. G. L. DAWSON). Diary of a Tour in Greece, Turkey, Egypt, and the Holy Land. 2 vols. 8vo. Lond., 1841. D 1 T 2, 3

DAMIANUS (PETRUS), SANCTUS. Opera omnia. [*See* MIGNE, J. P., SERIES LATINA, 144, 145.]

DAMON (HOWARD FRANKLIN), M.D. The Passions. [*See* BOURGEOIS, DR. X.]

DAMPIER (CAPT. WILLIAM). Captain Dampier's Vindication of his Voyage. [*See* FUNNELL, W.]

Collection of Voyages. 3 vols. 8vo. Lond., 1729.
MD 2 P 39–41

1. Captain William Dampier's Voyages round the World.
2. A Supplement to the Voyage round the World, describing the Countries of Tonquin, Achin, Malacca, &c.
3. A Voyage to New Holland, &c., in the year 1699.

New Voyage round the World. Illustrated. 3 vols. 8vo. Lond., 1698–1705. MD 2 P 36–38

Another copy (including Funnell's Account of the Voyage round the World). 4 vols. 8vo. Lond., 1698–1707.
MD 2 P 32–35

Nieuwe Reize naar de Zuid Zee. [*See* ROGERS, W.]

Nieuwe Reystogt rondom de Werreld. 4 vols. (in 1) 8vo. s'Gravenhage, 1698–1704. MD 1 U 1

Nouveau Voyage autour du Monde; traduit de l'Anglois. 2^(de) éd. 5 vols. 12mo. Amsterdam, 1701–12.
MD 2 P 27–31

[*See* NEW DISCOVERIES.]

DAMPIER (CAPT. WILLIAM), EN WAFER (LIONEL). Reystogten rondom de Waerrldt; begrypende, in vier beknopte Boekdeelen. 4 vols. (in 1) 8vo. Amsterdam, 1717. MD 1 U 2

DAMPIER (WILLIAM JAMES), M.A. Memoir of John Carter. New ed. Roy. 8vo. Lond., 1875. C K V 3

DANA (C. A.) [*See* AMERICAN CYCLOPÆDIA.]

DANA (EDWARD SALISBURY), PH.D. Mineralogy. 3rd Appendix to the 5th ed., completing the Work to 1882. 8vo. New York, 1882. A 9 U 25

Text book of Elementary Mechanics, for the use of Colleges and Schools. 2nd ed. 8vo. New York, 1881. A 11 P 15

DANA (EDWARD SALISBURY), AND DANA (PROF. JAMES D.) Text book of Mineralogy; with an extended Treatise on Crystallography and Physical Mineralogy, on the plan and with the co operation of Professor James D. Dana. 8vo. New York, 1877. A 9 U 24

DANA (JAMES DWIGHT), A.M. Corals and Coral Islands. Roy. 8vo. Lond., 1872. A 9 U 12

Crustacea. (U.S. Exploring Expedition). 2 vols. roy. 4to. Philad., 1852. A 31 P 11, 12 ‡

Atlas [to the above]. Imp. fol. Philad., 1855. A 31 P 7 ‡

Manual of Geology: treating of the Principles of the Science, with special reference to American Geological History. 2nd ed., illustrated. 8vo. New York, 1878. A 9 R 30

Manual of Mineralogy; including Observations on Mines, Rocks, Reduction of Ores, and the application of the Science to the Arts. Illustrated. New ed. 8vo. Lond., 1877. A 9 Q 35

New Text-book of Geology, designed for Schools and Academies. 3rd ed. Illustrated. 8vo. New York, 1877. A 9 Q 25

System of Mineralogy: Descriptive Mineralogy, comprising the most recent discoveries, by J. D. Dana, aided by G. J. Brush. 5th ed. Roy. 8vo. Lond., 1871. A 9 U 27

Zoophytes. (U.S. Exploring Expedition). Roy. 4to. Philad., 1848. A 31 P 8 ‡

Atlas [to the above]. Imp. fol. Philad., 1849. A 31 R 1 ‡

[*See* AMERICAN JOURNAL OF SCIENCE AND ARTS.]

DANBY (THOMAS OSBORNE), EARL OF. [*See* MACKINTOSH, SIR J.]

DANCE (CHARLES DANIEL). Recollections of Four Years in Venezuela. With Map and Illustrations. 8vo. Lond., 1876. D 3 Q 57

D'ANCONA (PROF. ALESSANDRO). La Vita Nuova di Dante Alighieri. 4to. Pisa, 1872. C 2 S 24 †

DANDOLO (COUNT). Art of Rearing Silkworms. 8vo. Lond., 1825. A 1 Q 27

DANGEAU (PHILLIPE DE COURCILLON), MARQUIS DE. Journal du, 1684–1720; avec les additions, inédites du Duc de St. Simon. 19 vols. 8vo. Paris, 1854–60. C 10 V 15–33

DANIEL (GEORGE). A Disagreeable Surprise: a Musical Farce. (Cumberland's Eng. Theatre.) 12mo. Lond., 1829. H 2 Q 17

Doctor Bolus: an Interlude. (Cumberland's Eng. Theatre.) 12mo. Lond., 1829. H 2 Q 13

DANIEL (GERARD). Mary Stuart: a Sketch and a Defence. 8vo. Lond., 1886. C 4 R 36

DANIEL (SAMUEL). Collection of the History of England. 5th ed. corrected; with a continuation of the History unto the Reign of Henry VII, by John Trussel. Sm. fol. Lond., 1685. B 16 Q 5 ‡

Complete Works of, in Verse and Prose, edited, with Introduction, Memorial, &c., by the Rev. Alexander B. Grosart, D.D., &c. (Huth Lin.) Vols. 1–3. 4to. Lond., 1885. J 5 U 1–3

Life and Poems of. [*See* CHALMERS, A.]

DANIEL (W. T. S.), Q.C. History and Origin of the Law Reports; together with a Compilation of various Documents shewing the Progress and Result of Proceedings taken for their Establishment, and the Condition of the Reports on the 31st December, 1883. Roy. 8vo. Lond., 1884. F 8 T 16

DANIELL (A.) Text-book of the Principles of Physics. Roy. 8vo. Lond., 1884. A 16 T 23

DANIELL (CLARMONT), B.C.S. Gold Treasure of India: an Enquiry into its Amount, the Causes of its Accumulation, and the proper Means of using it as Money. 8vo. Lond., 1884. F 6 Q 1

DANIELL (REV. E. T.) [*See* SPRATT, LIEUT. T. A. B., AND FORBES, PROF. E.]

DANIELL (F. H. BLACKBURNE), M.A. Life and Letters of Ogier Ghislein de Busbecq. [*See* FORSTER, C. T.]

DANIELL (S.) [*See* DANIELL, W.]

DANIELL (WILLIAM). Interesting Selections from Animated Nature; with Illustrative Scenery. 2 vols obl. 4to. Lond., 1870. A 23 Q 3, 4 ‡
Sketches representing the Native Tribes, Animals, and Scenery of Southern Africa; engraved from Drawings made by the late Mr. Samuel Daniell. Imp. 4to. Lond., 1820. A 4 S 6 ‡

DANIELLS (HON. J. M.) Life of Stonewall Jackson, from Official Papers, Contemporary Narratives, and Personal Acquaintance. 8vo. Lond., 1863. C 2 Q 24

DANSK ORDBOG. Dansk Ordbog udgiven under Videnskabernes Selskabs Bestyrelse. 7 vols. 4to. Kiobenhavn, 1793–1880 K 13 T 25–31

DANSK - TYDSK OG TYDSK - DANSK LOMME-ORDBOG NY. Anden forbedrede Stereotyp-Adgave. Nyt Aftryk. 16mo. Leipzig, 1871. K 11 S 7

DANSON (J. T.) Observations on the Speech of Sir William Molesworth, Bart., M.P., in the House of Commons, on Tuesday 25th July, 1848, on Colonial Expenditure and Government. 8vo. Lond., 1848. MF 2 T 3
Wealth of Households. (Clar. Press.) 8vo. Oxford, 1886. F 5 S 52

DANTE ALIGHIERI. Commedia and Canzoniere of Dante Alighieri: a new Translation, by the Rev. E. H. Plumptre. 2 vols. 8vo. Lond., 1886–87. H 7 V 6,7
Commedia di Dante Allighieri, preceduta dalla Vita e da Studi preparatori illustrativi esposta e Commentata da Antonio Lubin. 8vo. Padova, 1881. H 7 V 4
La Commedia di Dante Alighieri. Novamente riveduta nel Testo e Dichiarata da Brunone Bianchi. Settima edizione. 12mo. Firenze, 1868. H 7 P 31
Dante's Divine Comedy, The Inferno: a literal Prose Translation; by John A. Carlyle, M.D. 2nd ed. [1867.] 8vo. Lond., 1882. H 7 U 5

DANTE ALIGHIERI.—*continued.*
Dante's Divine Comedy, The Purgatorio: a Prose Translation; by the late William Stratford Dugdale. 8vo. Lond., 1883. H 7 U 4
Dante et la Philosophie Catholique au Tréizième Siécle. [*See* OZANAN, PROF. A. F.]
Dante et les Origines de la Langue et de la Littérature Italiennes. [*See* FAURIEL, C.]
The Divine Comedy; translated by H. W. Longfellow. 3 vols. roy. 8vo. Lond., 1867. H 7 V 1
The Divine Comedy of Dante Alighieri: a Translation; by James Romanes Sibbald. 8vo. Edinb.,1884. H 7 V 5
The Divine Comedy of Dante Alighieri; translated Verse for Verse from the Original into Terza Rima, by James Innes Minchin. 8vo. Lond., 1885. H 7 U 3
L'Inferno, disposto in ordine grammaticale, e corredato di brevi Dichiarazoni da G. G. Warren, Lord Vernon. 3 vols. fol. Lond., 1858. H 22 R 8–10 ‡
The New Life; translated by Charles Eliot Norton. Roy. 8vo. Boston, 1867. C 12 U 29
The Paradise of Dante Alighieri; edited, with translation and Notes, by Arthur John Butler. 8vo. Lond., 1885. H 5 T 26
La Vita Nuova di Dante Alighieri [Edited by Antonio Torelli.] 4to. Venezia, 1865. C 3 W 10
La Vita Nuova e il Canzoniere di Dante Allighieri. Commontati da G.-B. Giuliani. 18mo. Florence,1863. C1 P29
La Vita Nuova di Dante Alighieri. Riscontrata su Codici e Stampe, preceduta da uno Studio su Beatrice, e seguita da Illustrazioni per cura di Prof. Alessandro D'Ancona. 4to. Pisa, 1872. C 2 S 24 †
The Vita Nuova of Dante; translated, with an Introduction and Notes, by [Sir] Theodore Martin. 2nd ed. 12mo. Edinb., 1871. C 2 Q 12
The Vision of Hell, Purgatory, and Paradise; translated by the Rev. H. F. Cary, M.A., and illustrated with the Designs of M. Gustave Doré. 2 vols. imp. 4to. Lond., 1688. H 19 T 14, 15 ‡
The Vision of Hell, Purgatory, and Paradise; translated by the Rev. H. F. Cary, M.A. 8vo. Lond., 1850. H 7 P 30
Vocabulario Dantesco, di G. L. Blanc. Terza ed. 8vo. Firenze, 1883. K 12 P 42
[*See* FLAXMAN, J.]

DANTON (GEORGES JACQUES). Life of. [*See* LAMARTINE, A. DE.]

DANUBE (THE). A Voice from the Danube; by "An Impartial Spectator." 8vo. Lond., 1850. B 7 S 50

DANVERS (JULAND). Report on Railways in India, for the year 1870–71. Fol. Lond., 1871. F 36 Q 11 ‡

D'ANVERS (N.) [*See* BELL, MRS. N. R. E.]

D'ANVILLE (JEAN BAPTISTE BOURGUIGNON) [*See* ANVILLE, J. B. B. D'.]

D'ARBLAY (MME. FRANCES), FRANCES BURNEY. Cecilia; or, Memoirs of an Heiress. 2 vols. 12mo. Lond., 1882.   J 11 R 9, 10

Diary and Letters of, 1778–1840; edited by her Niece. 7 vols. 8vo. Lond., 1842–46.   C 3 S 25–31

D'ARC (JEANNE). Footsteps of Jeanne d'Arc. [*See* CADDY, MRS. F.]

Joan of Arc and the Times of Charles VII., King of France; by Mrs. A. E. Bray. 8vo. Lond., 1874.   C 2 S 24

Life and Death of; by Harriett Parr. 2 vols. (in 1) 12mo. Lond., 1866.   C 2 S 25

DARCEL (ALFRED), AND BASILEWSKY (A.) Collection Basilewsky: Catalogue Raisonné, précédé d'un Essai sur les Arts Industriels du Iᵉʳ au XVIᵉ Siècle. 2 vols. imp. 4to. Paris, 1874.   A 23 S 3, 4 ‡

DARCEL (A.) [*See* ROUYER, E.]

DARCIE (ABRAHAM). The Original of Idolatries. [*See* CASAUBON, I.]

D'ARCY (—). [*See* LETTERS FROM THE IRISH HIGHLANDS.]

DARD (MME. C. A.) History of the Sufferings and Misfortunes of the Picard Family, after the Shipwreck of the *Medusa* on the Western Coast of Africa, 1816. [*See* PERILS and CAPTIVITY.]

DARES (PHRYGIUS). [*See* DICTYS CRETENSIS.]

DARKE (W. WEDGE). Observations on Convicts, and the Discipline to which they have hitherto been subjected. (Pam. 40.) 12mo. Sydney, 1852.   MJ 2 R 2

D'ARLINCOURT (CHARLES VICTOR PREVOT), VICOMTE DE. The Three Kingdoms: England, Scotland, and Ireland. 2 vols. 8vo. Lond., 1844.   D 8 S 5, 6

DARLING (SIR CHARLES H.), K.C.B. [*See* CRISIS IN VICTORIA.]

DARLING (JAMES). Cyclopædia Bibliographica: a Library Manual of Theological and general Literature, and Guide to Books. 2 vols. roy. 8vo. Lond., 1854–59.   C 1 V 22, 23

DARLING (LIEUT.-GEN. SIR RALPH), KNT., GOVERNOR OF NEW SOUTH WALES. Debates in the House of Commons; Conduct of Gen. Darling; also the Case of Capt. Robison. 8vo. Lond., 1835.   MF 1 R 18

Governor Darling's Refutation of the Charges of Cruelty and Oppression of the Soldiers Sudds and Thompson at Sydney, New South Wales, November 26th, 1826; by "Allen." 8vo. Lond., 1832.   MF 1 R 18

Letter addressed by Lieut.-Gen. R. Darling, late Governor of New South Wales, to Joseph Hume, Esq., M.P. (Pam. 27.) 8vo. Lond., 1832.   MJ 2 Q 15

Outline of Evidence against Lieut.-Gen. Darling. [*See* ROBISON, CAPT. R.]

DARLING (LIEUT.-GEN. SIR RALPH), KNT.—*continued.*

Proclamations, Acts in Council, Government Orders, and Notices, issued by His Excellency Lieut.-Gen. Ralph Darling, Capt.-Gen. and Governor-in-Chief of New South Wales, 1825–26. Fol. Sydney, 1826.   MF 2 U 19

Report from the Select Committee on the conduct of General Darling, while Governor of New South Wales; with the Minutes of Evidence, and Appendix. (Parl. Doc. 15.) Fol. Lond., 1835.   MF 4 ‡

[*See* ACTS AND ORDINANCES, *and* LAND REGULATIONS.]

DARLING (REV. WILLIAM STEWART). Sketches of Canadian Life, Lay and Ecclesiastical; by "A Presbyter of the Diocese of Toronto." 8vo. Lond., 1849.   D 4 P 34

DARMESTETER (PROF. ARSÈNE). Life of Words as the Symbols of Ideas. 8vo. Lond., 1886.   K 11 U 29

DARMESTETER (PROF. JAMES). The Mahdi, Past and Present. 12mo. Lond., 1885.   G 8 P 1

The Zend-avesta. [*See* MÜLLER, PROF. F. M.]

DARMESTETER (MRS.) [*See* ROBINSON, MISS A. M. F.]

DARNELL (N.), M.A. The Gentile and the Jews. [*See* DÖLLINGER, PROF. J. J. I.]

DARTON (WILLIAM). Cabinet of Portraits, consisting of Distinguished Characters, British and Foreign; accompanied with a Brief Memoir of each Person. Engraved by W. Darton. 4to. Lond., 1823.   C 8 U 22

Another copy. 8vo. Lond., 1822.   MJ 2 R 21

DARU (P. A. N. B.), LE COMTE. Histoire de la République de Venise. 8 vols. 8vo. Paris, 1821.   B 12 R 24–31

DARWIN (CHARLES), M.A., &c. Charles Darwin, Naturalist; by J. T. Cunningham. (Round Table Series.) 8vo. Edinb., 1886.   C 10 U 1

Darwin [a Biography]; by C. Allen. 8vo. Lond., 1885.   C 2 Q 13

Descent of Man, and Selection in relation to Sex. 7th thousand. 2 vols. 8vo. Lond., 1871.   A 1 V 1, 2

Die Naturschanung von Darwin, Goethe, und Lamarck. [*See* HAECKEL, E.]

Effects of Cross and Self-fertilisation in the Vegetable Kingdom. 8vo. Lond., 1876.   A 4 P 22

Essay on Instinct. [*See* ROMANES, G. J.]

Formation of Vegetable Mould, through the action of Worms; with Observations on their Habits. Illustrated. 8vo. Lond., 1881.   A 14 S 42

Geological Observations on Coral Reefs, Volcanic Islands, and on South America. 8vo. Lond., 1851.   A 9 R 20

Geological Observations on South America, being the 3rd Part of the Geology of the Voyage of the *Beagle*, 1832–36. 8vo. Lond., 1846.   A 9 R 25

Gesammelte Werke; aus dem Englischen übersetzt, von J. Victor Carus. 12 vols. 8vo. Stuttgart, 1875–78.   A 29 U 17–28

DARWIN (CHARLES), M.A., &c.—*continued.*
Insectivorous Plants. Illustrated. 8vo. Lond., 1875.
A 4 P 23

Journal of Researches into the Geology and Natural History of the various Countries visited by H.M.S. *Beagle*, under the command of Capt. Fitzroy, R.N., 1832–36. 8vo. Lond., 1839.
MA 2 R 2

Journal of Researches into the Natural History and Geology of the Countries visited during the Voyage of H.M.S. *Beagle* round the World. 2nd ed. (H. and C. Lib.) 12mo. Lond., 1845.
J 8 P 12

Journal of Researches into the Natural History and Geology of the Countries visited during the Voyage of H.M.S. *Beagle* round the World, under the command of Capt. Fitzroy, R.N. 2nd ed., corrected, with Additions. 8vo. Lond., 1845.
MA 2 P 22

Journal of Researches into the Natural History and Geology of the Countries visited during the Voyage of H.M.S. *Beagle* round the World, under the command of Capt. Fitzroy, R.N. New ed. 8vo. Lond., 1870. A 9 P 49

Kant and Darwin. [*See* SCHULTZE, F.]

Luck or Cunning; an attempt to throw additional Light upon the Theory of Natural Selection. [*See* BUTLER, S.]

Memorial Notices reprinted from "Nature." 8vo. Lond., 1882.
C 2 R 4

Movements and Habits of Climbing Plants. Illustrated. 2nd ed., revised. 8vo. Lond., 1875.
A 4 P 21

Narrative of the Surveying Voyages of H.M.S. *Adventure* and *Beagle*. [*See* FITZROY, CAPT. R.]

On the Origin of Species by means of Natural Selection. 8vo. Lond., 1860.
A 16 Q 24

On the various Contrivances by which British and Foreign Orchids are fertilised by Insects, and on the good effects of intercrossing. 8vo. Lond., 1862.
A 4 P 25

Structure and Distribution of Coral Reefs; being the 1st part of the Geology of the Voyage of the *Beagle*, 1832–36. 8vo. Lond., 1842.
A 9 S 38

Variation of Animals and Plants under Domestication. 2 vols. 8vo. Lond., 1868.
A 16 T 13, 14

Zoology of the Voyage of H.M.S. *Beagle*, under the command of Captain Fitzroy, R.N., during the years 1832–36. Birds, by John Gould, Esq., F.L.S.; Fish, by Rev. L. Jenyns; and Mammalia, by G. R. Waterhouse, Esq., with a Notice of their Habits and Ranges, by Charles Darwin, Esq.; Fossil Mammalia, by Richard Owen, Esq., F.R.S. 2 vols. 4to. Lond., 1838–40.
A 1 S 16, 17 †
[*See* FITZROY, CAPT. R., *and* KRAUSE, E.]

DARWIN (CHARLES AND FRANCIS). Power of Movement in Plants. Illustrated. 8vo. Lond., 1880. A 4 P 24

DARWIN (ERASMUS). Botanic Garden: a Poem, in two parts; with Philosophical Notes. 4to. Lond., 1791.
H 5 V 20

[Life of]; by Ernest Krause; translated from the German, by W. S. Dallas; with a preliminary Notice, by Charles Darwin. 8vo. Lond., 1879.
C 2 U 20

2 D

DARWIN (GEORGE H.), M.A. Influence of Geological Changes on the Earth's Axis of Rotation. (Roy. Soc. Pubs. 4.) 4to. Lond., 1877.
A 11 P 5 †

DASCHKAW (EKATERINA ROMANOVNA), PRINCESS. Memoirs of; written by herself; edited by Mrs. W. Bradford. 2 vols. 8vo. Lond., 1840.
C 6 P 5, 6

DAUBENY (CHARLES), M.D., &c. Introduction to the Atomic Theory. 8vo. Oxford, 1831.
A 5 U 39

D'AUBIGNÉ (JEAN HENRI MERLE), D.D. D'Aubigné and his Writings; with a Sketch of the Life of the Author, by Robert Baird, D.D. 12mo. Dublin, 1849.
G 10 P 17

History of the Great Reformation of the 16th Century in Germany, Switzerland, &c.; translated by H. White. 5 vols. 8vo. Lond., 1843–53.
G 10 T 3–7

History of the Reformation of the 16th Century. 8vo. Edinb., 1847.
G 10 T 8

The Protector [Oliver Cromwell]: a Vindication. 8vo. Lond., 1847.
C 8 U 32

Rome and the Reformation; or, a Tour in the South of France. 12mo. Lond., 1844.
G 9 P 41

DAUGHTER OF THE SOIL, A. Woman's Work in Australia. [*See* AUSTRALIA.]

DAUGHTERS OF ITALY; by Caroline Geary. 8vo. Lond., 1886.
C 2 S 10

DAUDET (ALPHONSE). Tartarin on the Alps. 12mo. Lond., 1887.
D 7 Q 34

D'AUMALE (HENRI D'ORLEANS), DUC. [*See* AUMALE, DUC D'.]

DAUMAS (E.) Horses of the Sahara, and the Manners of the Desert; with Commentaries, by the Emir Abd-el-Kader; translated by James Hutton. 8vo. Lond., 1863.
A 1 R 33

DAUNOU (PIERRE C. E.) Mémoires de la Convention Nationale. [*See* BARRIÈRE, J. F., 12.]

DAUNT (W. J. O'NEILL). Essays on Ireland. 8vo. Dublin, 1886.
B 11 P 4

Eighty-five Years of Irish History, 1800–85. 2 vols. 8vo. Lond., 1886.
B 11 P 29, 30

DAUPHIN. Misfortunes of the; by the Hon. and Rev. C. G. Perceval. 8vo. Lond., 1838.
C 8 Q 4

DAVELUY (A.) Dictionnaire Latin-Français. [*See* QUICHERAT, L.]

D'AVENANT (SIR WILLIAM).. Dramatic Works of; with Prefatory Memoir and Notes. 5 vols. 8vo. Edinb., 1872–74.
H 3 T 1–5

Life and Poems of. [*See* CHALMERS, A.]

D'AVENNES (E. PRISSE). [*See* PRISSE-D'AVENNES, E.]

DAVENPORT (Rev. Arthur), B.A. History of Synodal Proceedings in Tasmania; with an Appendix, containing the Act of Parliament by which the Diocesan Synod is constituted. 8vo. Hobart, 1858. MG 1 Q 31

DAVENPORT (John). Nuovo Dizionario Italiano—Inglese-Francese. [*See* Petrónj, S. E.]

New Dictionary of the Italian and English Languages. [*See* Baretti, G.]

DAVENPORT (Richard Alfred). History of the Bastile, and of its principal Captives. 12mo. Lond., 1838. B 8 P 22

Life of Ali Pasha of Tepeleni, Vizier of Epirus, surnamed Aslan, or the Lion. 18mo. Lond., 1837. C 1 P 3

Memoir of the Life of Peter the Great. 12mo. Lond., 1832. C 1 P 34

DAVENPORT (Samuel). Engraving. (Brit. Manuf. Indust.) 12mo. Lond., 1876. A 17 S 39

DAVID (T. W. Edgeworth), B.A., &c. Geology of the Vegetable Creek Tin-mining Field, New England District, New South Wales. With Maps and Sections. Roy. 4to. Sydney, 1887. MA 2 Q 21 †

DAVID, THE SHEPHERD KING: a Book for the Bush; by "Hippocampus." 8vo. Melb.,1867. MJ 1 U 11

DAVIDS (Arthur Lumley). Grammaire Turke; traduite de l'Anglais par Mme. Sarah Davids. 4to. Lond., 1836. K 15 U 11

DAVIDS (Thomas William Rhys), Ph.D., &c. Ancient Coins and Measures of Ceylon. [*See* Numismata Orientalia I.]

Buddhist Suttas. [*See* Müller, Prof. F. M.]

Lectures on the Origin and Growth of Religion, as illustrated by some Points in the History of Indian Buddhism. (Hib. Lec., 1881). 8vo. Lond., 1881. G 7 P 8

Non-Christian Religious Systems: Buddhism: being a Sketch of the Life and Teachings of Gautama, the Buddha. 8th ed. 12mo. Lond., 1880. G 8 P 3

Vinaya Texts. [*See* Müller, Prof. F. M.]

DAVIDSON (Benjamin). Analytical Hebrew and Chaldee Lexicon; consisting of an Alphabetical Arrangement of every Word and Inflection contained in the Old Testament Scriptures. 4to. Lond., 1848. K 12 T 2

DAVIDSON (C.), WRIGHT (T. C.), WALEY (J.), and WHITEHEAD (J.) Davidson's Precedents and Forms in Conveyancing. 3rd ed. 5 vols. roy. 8vo. Lond., 1860-65. F 1 T 1-6

DAVIDSON (C. J. C.) Diary of Travels and Adventures in Upper India, from Bareilly in Rohilcund to Hurdwar, &c. 2 vols. 8vo. Lond., 1843. D 5 P 9, 10

DAVIDSON (Ellis A.) Amateur House Carpenter. Roy. 8vo. Lond., 1875. A 11 V 10

Gothic Stonework; containing the History and Principles of Church Architecture, and Illustrations of the Characteristic Features of each Period. 12mo. Lond.,1885. A 2 R 18

Practical Manual of House-painting, Graining, Marbling, and Sign-writing. 3rd ed. (Weale.) 12mo. Lond., 1880. A 17 Q 32

[*See* Field, G.]

DAVIDSON (G. F.) Trade and Travel in the Far East. 8vo. Lond., 1846. D 6 P 17

Another copy. MD 3 R 43

DAVIDSON (Thomas). Philosophical System of Antonio Rosmini-Serbati. [*See* Rosmini-Serbati, A.]

DAVIDSON (Rev. William L.), M.A. Logic of Definition, explained and applied. 8vo. Lond., 1885. G 13 T 32

DAVIES (Lady Clementina). Recollections of Society in France and England. 2 vols. 8vo. Lond., 1872. C 4 Q 31, 32

DAVIES (Rev. C. Maurice), D.D. Heterodox London; or, Phases of Free Thought in the Metropolis. 2 vols. 8vo. Lond., 1874. G 10 S 25, 26

Orthodox London; or, Phases of Religious Life in the Church of England. 2nd. ed. [1st and 2nd series.] 2 vols. 8vo. Lond., 1874-75. G 10 S 23, 24

Unorthodox London; or, Phases of Religious Life in the Metropolis. [1st and 2nd series.] 2 vols. 8vo. Lond., 1873-75. G 10 S 21, 22

DAVIES (C. M.) History of Holland and the Dutch Nation; from the Beginning of the 10th Century to the End of the 18th. 3 vols. 8vo. Lond.,1851. B 12 T 10, 12

DAVIES (D. C.), F.G.S. Treatise on Earthy and other Minerals and Mining. 8vo. Lond., 1884. A 9 Q 39

Treatise on Metalliferous Minerals and Mining. 2nd ed., carefully revised. 8vo. Lond., 1881. A 9 Q 31

Treatise on Slate and Slate Quarrying. Scientific, Practical, and Commercial. (Weale.) 2nd ed., revised. 12mo. Lond., 1880. A 17 Q 44

DAVIES (Edward). Life of B. E. Murillo [de Sevilla]; compiled from the Writings of various Authors. 8vo. Lond., 1819. C 4 T 18

DAVIES (Rev. E.), D.D. Other Men's Minds; or, Seven Thousand Choice Extracts on History, Science, Philosophy, Religion, &c., selected from the standard authorship of Ancient and Modern Times. Illustrated. 8vo. Lond., 1874. K 17 P 31

DAVIES (Rev. E. W. L.), M.A. Algiers in 1857; its Accessibility, Climate, and Resources described, with especial reference to English Invalids. 8vo. Lond., 1858. D 1 S 15

DAVIES (G. CHRISTOPHER). Norfolk Broads and Rivers ; or, the Water-ways, Lagoons, and Decoys of East Anglia. Illustrated. 8vo. Lond., 1883. D 7 R 40

On Dutch Waterways : the Cruise of the s.s. *Atalanta* on the Rivers and Canals of Holland and the North of Belgium. Imp. 8vo. Lond., 1887. D 8 V 18

Practical Boat-sailing for Amateurs ; containing Particulars of the most suitable Sailing-boats and Yachts for Amateurs, and Instructions for their proper handling, &c. Illustrated. 8vo. Lond. (n.d.) A 2 R 34

Another copy. 8vo. Lond., 1886. A 2 R 35

The *Swan* and her Crew ; or, the Adventures of three Young Naturalists and Sportsmen on the Broads and Rivers of Norfolk. With Illustrations. 8vo. Lond. (n.d.) A 14 Q 50

DAVIES (HANBURY), B.A. The Bankruptcy Act. [*See* WISE, B. R.]

DAVIES (H.) Welsh Botanology : Catalogue of Native Plants of the Isle of Anglesey (in Latin, English, and Welsh). 8vo. Lond., 1813. A 4 T 25

DAVIES (JOHN), M.A. Hindu Philosophy: the Bhagavad Gîtâ ; or, the Sacred Lay : a Sanskrit Philosophical Poem. 8vo. Lond., 1882. G 15 P 14

DAVIES (SIR JOHN), KNT. Discoverie of the True Causes why Ireland was neuer entirely subdued, nor brought vnder Obedience of the Crowne of England, vntill the Beginning of His Maiesties happie Raigne, James 1st. With the Author's Life. 12mo. Dublin, 1761. B 11 P 7

Historical Tracts; by Sir John Davies, Attorney General, and Speaker of the House of Commons in Ireland ; to which is prefixed a new Life of the Author. 8vo. Dublin, 1787. B 29 T 17

DAVIES (PROF. JOHN F.), M.A. The Eumenides of Æschylus. [*See* ÆSCHYLUS.]

DAVIES (JOHN HAMILTON). Life of Richard Baxter, of Kidderminster, Preacher and Prisoner. 8vo. Lond., 1887. C 10 R 23

DAVIES (J. L.), AND VAUGHAN (D. J.) Republic of Plato. [*See* PLATO.]

DAVIES (MRS.), "DESDA." The Rival Fairies ; or, Little Mamie's Troubles: an Australian Story. 12mo. Sydney, 1871. MJ 1 P 38

DAVIES (ROBERT), F.S.A. Walks through the City of York ; edited by his Widow, Elizabeth Davies. 8vo. Lond., 1880. B 6 Q 9

DAVIES (ROWLAND LYTTELTON ARCHER). Poems, and other Literary Remains of ; edited, with a Biographical Sketch, by Charles Tomlinson, F.R.S. 8vo. Lond., 1884. MH 1 P 9

DAVIES (THOMAS). Preparation and Mounting of Microscopic Objects ; edited by John Matthews, M.D., &c. 12mo. Lond., 1878. A 17 T 9

DAVIES (THOMAS). Dramatic Miscellanies ; consisting of critical Observations on several Plays of Shakspeare, with a Review of his principal Characters, &c. 3 vols. 8vo. Lond., 1784. J 9 Q 22-24

DAVIES (T. LEWIS O.), M.A. Supplementary English Glossary. 8vo. Lond., 1881 K 14 T 3

DAVIES (THOS. STEPHENS), F.R.S. Solutions of the principal Questions of Dr. Hutton's Course of Mathematics. 8vo. Lond., 1840. A 10 T 3

DAVIES (WM.) A Fine Old English Gentleman, exemplified in the Life and Character of Lord Collingwood. 8vo. Lond., 1875. C 3 S 43

DAVILA (HENRICO CATERINO). Historia delle Guerre Civili di Francia ; nella quale si contengono le operationi di quattro Rè Francesco II, Carlo IX, Henrico III, & Henrico IV. 2 vols. 4to. Lond., 1755. B 19 R 14, 15 ‡

DAVILLIER (CH.), BARON. Spain ; illustrated by Gustave Doré. Translated by J. Thomson, F.R.G.S. Imp. 4to. Lond., 1876. D 5 S 1 †

DAVIS (ALFRED H.), B.A. Cæsar de Bello Gallico, Book I. Prepared for the use of Junior Students ; with copious Notes and References to Smith's Smaller Latin Grammar ; to which is added, an Index of Proper Names. 8vo. Melb., 1875. MB 2 P 45

DAVIS (ANDREW JACKSON). The Children's Progressive Lyceum :—a Manual ; with Directions for the Organization and Management of Sunday Schools, adapted to the Bodies and Minds of the Young. 10th thousand. 32mo. New York, 1874. G 17 P 32

Principles of Nature, her Divine Revelations, and a Voice to Mankind. 34th ed. 8vo. Boston, 1876. G 10 S 20

Works of. 29 vols. 12mo. and 8vo. New York and Boston, 1865-78. G 13 U 8-35

The Approaching Crisis; being a Review of Dr. Busnell's Course of Lectures, on the Bible, Nature, Religion, Scepticism, and the Supernatural.

Arabula; or, the Divine Guest; containing a new Collection of Gospels.

Answers to Ever-recurring Questions from the People: a Sequel to Penetralia.

The Diakka, and their Earthly Victims; being an Explanation of much that is False and Repulsive in Spiritualism.

Death and the After-Life: eight Evening Lectures on the Summer-Land.

The Fountain ; with Jets of New Meanings. Illustrated.

Free Thoughts concerning Religion; or, Nature versus Theology.

The Genesis and Ethics of Conjugal Love.

The Great Harmonia.

Harbinger of Health ; containing Medical Prescriptions for the Human Body and Mind.

The Harmonial Man ; or, Thoughts for the Age.

DAVIS (ANDREW JACKSON).—*continued.*
History and Philosophy of Evil.
The Magic Staff: an Autobiography of Andrew Jackson Davis.
Mental Disorders; or, Diseases of the Brain and Nerves.
Memoranda of Persons, Places, and Events; embracing authentic Facts, Visions, Impressions, Discoveries, in Magnetism, Clairvoyance, Spiritualism.
Morning Lectures: twenty Discourses.
The Penetralia; being Harmonial Answers to Important Questions.
Philosophy of Special Providence: a Vision.
Philosophy of Spiritual Intercourse; being an Explanation of Modern Mysteries.
The Present Age and Inner Life; Ancient and Modern Spirit Mysteries classified and explained: a Sequel to Spiritual Intercourse.
A Sacred Book, containing Old and New Gospels, derived and translated from the Inspirations of Original Saints.
A Stellar Key to the Summer Land. Part 1.
Tale of a Physician; or, the Seeds and Fruits of Crime.
Views of our Heavenly Home: a Sequel to a Stellar Key to the Summer-Land.

DAVIS (CHARLES E.), F.S.A., &c.   Mineral Baths of Bath.   4to. Bath, 1883.   B 4 V 15

DAVIS (REAR-ADM. C. H.) Narrative of the North Polar Expedition, U.S. Ship *Polaris*, Captain Charles Francis Hall, commanding. 4to. Lond., 1879.   D 10 P 14 ‡

DAVIS (CHARLES OLIVER B.) Maori Mementos; being a Series of Addresses, presented by the Native People to His Excellency Sir George Grey, K.C.B., F.R.S. 8vo. Auckland, 1855.*   MB 2 Q 35

DAVIS (CHARLES THOMAS). Manufacture of Leather; being a Description of all the Processes for the Tanning, Tawing, Currying, Finishing, and Dyeing of every kind of Leather, &c. Illustrated. Roy. 8vo. Philad., 1885. A 11 T 15

Manufacture of Paper; being a Description of the various Processes for the Fabrication, Coloring, and Finishing of every kind of Paper. Illustrated. 8vo. Lond., 1886.   A 11 T 11

Practical Treatise on the Manufacture of Bricks, Tiles, Terracotta, &c. Illustrated. 8vo. Philad., 1884.   A 11 T 13

Treatise on Steam-boiler Incrustation, and Methods for preventing Corrosion and the Formation of Scale, &c. Illustrated. 8vo. Lond., 1884.   A 6 T 6

DAVIS (REV. E. J.) Anatolica; or, the Journal of a Visit to some of the Ancient Ruined Cities of Caria, Phrygia, Lycia, and Pisidia. 8vo. Lond., 1874.   D 5 T 28

DAVIS (FREDERICK). Luton, Past and Present; its History and Antiquities. 2nd ed., with numerous Illustrations. 4to. Luton, 1871.   B 4 V 8

DAVIS (GEORGE E.), F.R.M.S., &c. Practical Microscopy. Illustrated. 8vo. Lond., 1882.   A 16 S 4

DAVIS (JAMES DAVIDSON). Contributions towards a Bibliography of New Zealand; collected and annotated by James Davidson Davis. 8vo. Wellington, 1887.* MK 1 P 40

DAVIS (JAMES EDWARD). Annals of Windsor. [*See* TIGHE, ROBERT RICHARD.] [*See* BURN, R.]

DAVIS (JEFFERSON). Rise and Fall of the Confederate Government. 2 vols. 8vo. Lond., 1881.   B 1 T 38, 39

DAVIS (JOHN). Mormonism; or, the Doctrines of the self-styled Latter-day Saints compared with itself and the Bible, and found wanting. 12mo. Sydney, 1857. MG 1 P 48

DAVIS (JOHN). Tracks of McKinlay and Party across Australia; edited from Mr. Davis' Manuscript Journal; by William Westgarth. 8vo. Lond., 1863.* MD 2 V 2

DAVIS (SIR JOHN FRANCIS), K.C.B. The Chinese: a General Description of the Empire of China and its Inhabitants. 2 vols. 8vo. Lond., 1836.   B 2 P 31, 32
Chinese Miscellanies: a Collection of Essays and Notes. 8vo. Lond., 1865.   D 5 R 17
Hàn Koong Tsew; or, the Sorrows of Han: a Chinese Tragedy; translated, with Notes, &c. 4to. Lond., 1829.   H 1 V 3
Sketches of China; partly during a Inland Journey of Four Months. 2 vols. 8vo. Lond., 1841.   D 5 R 15, 16

DAVIS (JOSEPH BARNARD), M.D., &c. On the Osteology and Peculiarities of the Tasmanians, a Race of Man recently become extinct. 4to. Haarlem, 1874. MA 1 Q 4 †

DAVIS (DR. N.), F.R.G.S., &c. Carthage and her Remains; being an Account of the Excavations and Researches on the Site of the Phœnician Metropolis in Africa, and other adjacent Places. 8vo. Lond., 1861.   B 1 Q 4

DAVIS (REV. RICHARD.) Memoir of Rev. Richard Davis, for Thirty-nine Years a Missionary in New Zealand; by the Rev. John Noble Coleman. 8vo. Lond., 1865. MC 1 Q 1

DAVIS (THOMAS). Memoir of the Rt. Hon. J. P. Curran. [*See* CURRAN, J. P.]

DAVIS (W.) [*See* NEWTON, SIR I.]

DAVIS (WILLIAM MORRIS). Glaciers. [*See* SHALER, N. S.]

DAVISON (D.) History of the Eighteenth Century. [*See* SCHLOSSER, F. C.]

DAVISON (S. C.) King of Saxony's Journey to England and Scotland. [*See* CARUS, DR. C. G.]

DAVISON (SIMPSON). Discovery and Geognosy of Gold Deposits in Australia; with Comparisons and Accounts of the Gold Regions in California, Russia, India, Brazil, &c. With Map. 8vo. Lond., 1860.*   MA 2 Q 1

DAVISON (WILLIAM.) Life of William Davison, Secretary of State and Privy Counsellor to Queen Elizabeth; by Sir Nicholas Harris. 8vo. Lond., 1823.   C 8 R 5

DAVITT (ARTHUR). Origin and Progress of the National System of Education ; its Real Principles and Special Adaptability to the Circumstances of a mixed Community. 8vo. Melb., 1856. MG 1 Q 30

DAVITT (MICHAEL). Leaves from a Prison Diary ; or, Lectures to a "Solitary" Audience. 2 vols. 8vo. Lond., 1885. F 6 Q 17, 18

DAVY (SIR HUMPHREY), BART., LL.D., &c. Consolations in Travel; or, the Last Days of a Philosopher. 7th ed. 12mo. Lond., 1869. G 8 P 2

Elements of Agricultural Chemistry. 4to. Lond., 1813. A 1 T 2

Another copy. 4th ed. 8vo. Lond., 1827. A 5 U 35

Fragmentary Remains, Literary and Scientific; with a Sketch of his Life and Selections from his Correspondence; edited by his brother, John Davy, M.D., &c. 8vo. Lond., 1858. C 10 Q 22

Memoirs of the Life of; by his brother John Davy, M.D., &c. 2 vols. 8vo. Lond., 1836. C 8 T 7, 8

Salmonia; or, Days of Fly-fishing; by "An Angler." 12mo. Lond., 1832. A 14 P 57

Six Discourses delivered before the Royal Society, at their Anniversary Meetings. 4to. Lond., 1827. A 15 U 16

DAVY (JOHN), M.D., &c. Fragmentary Remains, Literary and Scientific, of Sir H. Davy; with Sketch of his Life, &c.; edited by his brother. 8vo. Lond., 1858. C 10 Q 22

Memoirs of the Life of Sir Humphrey Davy, Bart., &c.; by his brother. 2 vols. 8vo. Lond., 1836. C 8 T 7, 8

Notes and Observations on the Ionian Islands and Malta; with some Remarks on Constantinople and Turkey. 2 vols. 8vo. Lond., 1842. D 6 U 32, 33

DAWES (REV. R.) Hints on an improved and Self-paying System of National Education; suggested by the working of the Village School of King's Somborne, Hampshire; with Observations on the Irish National Schools. (Pam. 41.) 4th ed. 8vo. Lond., 1848. MJ 2 R 3

Remarks occasioned by the present Crusade against the Educational Plans of the Committee of Council of Education. (Pam. Bf.) 2nd ed. 8vo. Lond., 1856. G 17 Q 20

Schools and other similar Institutions for the Industrial Classes. (Pam. 40.) 12mo. Lond., 1853. MJ 2 R 2

DAWES (RICHARD), A.M. Miscellanea Critica; Typis quinquies excusa prodeunt ex recensione et cum notis aliquanto Auctioribus Thomæ Kidd, A.M. Editio secunda. 8vo. Lond., 1827. J 17 R 21

DAWES (LIEUT. WILLIAM), [*See* HUNTER, CAPT., J., *and* PHILLIP, A.]

DAWIDOWSKY (F.) Practical Treatise on the Raw Materials and Fabrication of Glue, Gelatine, Gelatine Veneers and Foils, Isinglass, Cements, Pastes, Mucilages, &c. Translated by William T. Brannt. Illustrated. 8vo. Philad., 1884. A 11 Q 12

DAWN OF BRITISH TRADE. [*See* STEVENS, H.]

DAWKINS (W. BOYD), M.A., &c. Cave-hunting: Researches on the Evidence of Caves respecting the Early Inhabitants of Europe. 8vo. Lond., 1874. A 9 T 12

Early Man in Britain, and his Place in the Tertiary Period. Illustrated. Roy. 8vo. Lond., 1880. A 1 W 26

Die Höhlen und die Ureinwohner Europas; ausdem Englischer übertragen von Dr. J. W. Spengel. 8vo. Leipzig, 1876. A 9 T 5

DAWSON (E. C.), M.A. James Hannington, D.D., &c., First Bishop of Eastern Equatorial Africa ; a History of his Life and Work. 8vo. Lond., 1887. C 3 V 11

DAWSON (GEORGE), M.A. Biographical Lectures. Edited by George St. Clair, F.G.S. 8vo. Lond., 1886. C 3 T 1

Inaugural Address: Opening of the Free Reference Library. [*See* Birmingham Free Libraries.]

DAWSON (G. M.) Comparative Vocabularies of the Indian Tribes of British Columbia. [*See* TOLMIE, W. F.] [*See* SELWYN, A. R. C.]

DAWSON (JAMES). Australian Aborigines: the Languages and Customs of several Tribes of Aborigines in the Western District of Victoria, Australia. 4to. Melb., 1881.* MA 1 P 2 †

DAWSON (J. W.), LL.D., &c. Dawn of Life : a History of the oldest known Fossil Remains. 8vo. Lond., 1875. A 9 Q 23

DAWSON (ROBERT). Present State of Australia ; a Description of the Country, its Advantages and Prospects, with reference to Emigration. 2nd ed. 8vo. Lond., 1831.* MD 5 T 20

Statement of the Services of Mr. Dawson, as Chief Agent of the Australian Agricultural Company. 8vo. Lond., 1829. MJ 2 R 17

DAWSON (WM.) & SONS. Reference Catalogue of Standard Second-hand Books Ancient and Modern. 8vo. Lond., 1809. K 8 P 36

DAWSON (W. HARBUTT). History of Skipton (W. R. Yorks.) With Illustrations and Index. 8vo. Lond., 1882. B 7 P 10

DAY (ALFRED), LL.D. Summary and Analysis of the Dialogues of Plato ; with an Analytical Index. 12mo. Lond., 1870. J 6 Q 5

DAY (E. G.) Lecture on the Last Judgment. 8vo. Adelaide, 1857. MJ 2 R 7

DAY (EDWARD PARSONS). Day's Collacon: an Encyclopædia of Prose Quotations, consisting of Beautiful Thoughts, Choice Extracts, and Sayings, of the most Eminent Writers. Imp. 8vo. Lond., 1884. K 17 S 5

DAY (FRANCIS), F.L.S., &c. Fishes of Great Britain and Ireland. 2 vols. roy. 8vo. Lond., 1880-84. A 15 S 15, 16

DAY (DR. JOHN). Ozone Treatment of Scarlatina and Small-pox. [*See* MOFFITT, A.]

Allotropic Oxygen in its Relation to Science and Art: a Lecture. [*See* MELBOURNE PUBLIC LIBRARY.]

DAY (REV. LÁL BEHÁRI). Govinda Sámanta; or, the History of a Bengal Ráiyat. 2 vols. 8vo. Lond., 1874. J 11 S 27, 28

DAY (LEWIS F.) Instances of Accessory Art: Original Designs and Suggestive Examples of Ornament; with practical and critical Notes. Fol. Lond., 1880. A 23 R 31 ‡

DAY (R. E.), M.A. Action of Light on Selenium. [*See* ADAMS, PROF. W. G.]

Electric Light Arithmetic. 12mo. Lond., 1882. A 10 R 27

Exercises in Electrical and Magnetic Measurement; with Answers. 12mo. Lond., 1876. A 5 R 48

DAY (ST. JOHN V.), C.E. Prehistoric Use of Iron and Steel. 8vo. Lond., 1877. A 9 T 17

DAY (WILLIAM). Racehorse in Training; with Hints on Racing and Racing Reforms. 8vo. Lond., 1880. A 1 R 31

William Day's Reminiscences of the Turf; with Anecdotes and Recollections of its principal Celebrities during the present Reign. 8vo. Lond., 1886. C 7 U 56

DAY (WILLIAM HENRY), M.D. On Diseases of Children. 8vo. Lond., 1881. A 12 P 33

DAYÁNANDRA SARASVATI. Biographical Essay. [*See* MÜLLER, PROF. F. MAX.] C 3 P 6

DAYLESFORD MURDER (THE). The Daylesford Murder: a full Account of the Capture, Trial, and Execution of David Young, for the Murder of Margaret Graham, at Daylesford, in the Colony of Victoria, 1864. 8vo. Castlemaine, 1865. MF 2 S 1

DAYMAN (EDWARD A.), B.D., AND JONES (W. H. Rich), F.S.A. Statuta et Consuetudines Ecclesiae Cathedralis Sarisberiensis. Statutes of the Cathedral Church of Sarum. Privately printed. [*See* SARUM.]

D'AZEGLIO. (M. T.), MARQUIS. [*See* AZEGLIO.]

DAZINCOURT. [*See* ALBOUYS D'AZINCOURT.]

DEACON (C. W.) Composition and Style: a Hand book for Literary Students; with a complete Guide to all Matters connected with Printing and Publishing. Edited by R. D. Blackman. 1st ed. 8vo. Lond., 1884. K 11 U 9

Dictionary of Foreign Phrases and Classical Quotations; a Treasury of Reference for Writers and Readers of Current Literature; edited by R. D. Blackman. 1st ed 8vo. Lond., 1881. K 11 U 41

DEAF AND DUMB INSTITUTION. Reports. [*See* NEW SOUTH WALES, *and* VICTORIA.]

DEAKIN (HON. A.) Irrigation in Western America. (Royal Commission on Water Supply, Victoria. Votes and Proceedings, vol. 2, 1885.) Fol.. Melb., 1885. E

DE AMICIS (EDMONDO). [*See* AMICIS, EDMONDO DE.]

DEANE (CHRISTOPHER P.) A Short History of Ireland. 8vo. Lond., 1886. B 11 P 28

DEANE (GEORGE ALFRED). Series of selected Designs for Country Residences, Entrance Lodges, Farm Offices, Cottages, &c. Imp. fol. York, 1867. A 23 S 24 ‡

DEANE (SAMUEL),, D.D. New England Farmer; or, Georgical Dictionary. 8vo. Boston, 1822. A 1 Q 49

DEAS (F. T. R.) Young Tea Planter's Companion. 8vo. Lond., 1886. A 1 P 29

DEAS (JAMES), C.E. The Clyde. Illustrated. 8vo. Glasgow, 1884. D 7 T 33

DE BALBOA. [*See* BALBOA, V. N. DE.]

DE BACKER, OU BAECKER (LOUIS). [*See* BAECKER, L. DE.]

DE BARY (PROF. A.) Comparative Anatomy of the Vegetative Organs of the Phanerogams and Ferns. Translated and annotated by F. O. Bower, M.A., &c., and D. H. Scott, M.A., &c. With Woodcuts. Roy. 8vo. Oxford, 1884. A 4 U 13

DEBATES. An exact Collection of the most considerable Debates in the Honourable House of Commons at the Parliament held at Westminster, the 21st October, 1680. 8vo. Lond., 1681. F 5 S 10

DEBAY (A.) Histoire naturelle de l'Homme et de la Femme, depuis leur Apparition sur le Globe terrestre jusqu'à nos jours. Avec dix Gravures. 4° éd. 8vo. Paris, 1858. A 18 R 46

Hygiène complète des Cheveux et de la Barbe, basée sur de récentes découvertes physiologiques et médicales. Deuxième édition. 12mo. Paris, 1851. A 12 P 6

Hygiène des Mains et des Pieds, de la Poitrine et de la Taille. Deuxième édition. 12mo. Paris, 1860. A 12 P 5

Hygiène et Physiologie du Mariage: Histoire naturelle et médicale de l'Homme et de la Femme mariés, dans ses plus curieux détails. Vingt et unième édition. 8vo. Paris, 1860. A 12 Q 34

Laïs de Corinthe (d'après un Manuscrit grec) et Ninon de Lenclos; Biographie anecdotique de ces deux Femmes célèbres. Nouvelle édition. 8vo. Paris, 1858. C 2 P 29

Les Mystères du Sommeil et du Magnétisme; ou, Physiologie anecdotique du Somnambulisme naturel et magnétique. Cinquième édition. 8vo. Paris, 1864. A 12 P 7

Les Nuits Corinthiennes; ou, les Soirées de Laïs. Deuxième édition. 8vo. Paris, 1861. F 14 Q 7

Physiologie descriptive des trente Beautés de la Femme. Quatrième édition. 8vo. Paris 1861. A 12 P 8

DE BROGLIE. [*See* BROGLIE, DUC DE.]

DE BEAUMONT (GUSTAVE). [*See* BEAUMONT, GUSTAVE DE.]

DE BEAUVOIR (LUDOVIC), MARQUIS. [*See* BEAUVOIR, LUDOVIC MARQ. DE.]

DE BEAUFORT (RALPH L.), LL.B. The Germans. [*See* DIDON, REV. FATHER H.]

DE BODE (C. A.) BARON. Travels in Luristan and Arabistan. 2 vols. 8vo. Lond., 1845. D 5 S 24, 25

DE BOOS (CHARLES). Congewoi Correspondence; being the Letters of Mr. John Smith; edited by Charles De Boos. 8vo. Sydney, 1874. MJ 2 S 32

Fifty Years Ago: an Australian Tale. 8vo. Sydney, 1867.* MJ 2 S 30

DEBRETT (JOHN). Complete Peerage of Great Britain and Ireland. 21st ed.; edited by W. Courthorpe. 8vo. Lond., 1836. K 10 S 9

Baronetage, Knightage, and Companionage: in which is included much Information respecting Collateral Branches of Baronets; edited by Robert H. Mair, LL.D. Illustrated. 8vo. Lond., 1884. K 10 S 14

Baronetage of England, and the existing Baronets of Nova Scotia and Ireland, 7th ed.; edited by W. Courthorpe. 8vo. Lond., 1837. K 10 S 10

Illustrated House of Commons, and the Judicial Bench, 1871 and 1881; compiled and edited by Robert Henry Mair. 8vo. Lond., 1871–81. E

DE BRY (THEODORE). [*See* BRY, THEODORE DE.]

DECAISNE (J.) Plantes Vasculaires. [*See* DUMONT D'URVILLE, CAPT. J. S. C.]

DE CANDOLLE (ALPHONSE). [*See* CANDOLLE, ALPHONSE P. DE.]

DE CANDOLLE (CASIMIR). [*See* CANDOLLE, ALPHONSE P. ET CASIMIR DE.]

DE CARDONNEL (ADAM). [*See* CARDONNELL, ADAM DE.]

DE CARNE (LOUIS). Travels in Indo-China and the Chinese Empire; translated from the French. 8vo. Lond., 1872. D 4 U 7

DE CASTELLANE (P.), COMTE. [*See* CASTELLANE, P. COMTE DE.]

DE CASTRO. [*See* CASTRO, DOM JOHN DE.]

DE CHASTELLUX (F. J.), MARQUIS. [*See* CHASTELLUX, MARQUIS DE.]

DE COIN (COL. ROBERT L.) History and Cultivation of Cotton and Tobacco. 8vo. Lond., 1864. A 1 P 25

DECORATION in Painting, Sculpture, Architecture, and Art Manufactures. Illustrated. 1st series, complete. Sq. 8vo. Lond., 1880. A 8 P 45

DE COSSON (MAJOR E. A.), F.R.G.S. Cradle of the Blue Nile : a Visit to the Court of King John of Ethiopia. With Map and Illustrations. 2 vols. (in 1) 8vo. Lond., 1877. D 14 R 8

Days and Nights of Service with Sir Gerald Graham's Field Force at Suakin. With Plan and Illustrations. 8vo. Lond., 1886. D 1 P 25

DE COULANGES (FUSTEL). [*See* COULANGES, F. DE.]

DE CUSTINE (—), MARQUIS. [*See* CUSTINE, MARQUIS DE.]

DEEBLE (W.) [*See* MOORE, REV. T.]

DEFENDERS OF NEW ZEALAND. [*See* GUDGEON, T. W.]

DE FLANDRE (CHARLES). [*See* FLANDRE, C. DE.]

DE FOE (DANIEL) [a Biography]; by W. Minto. (Eng. Men of Letts.) 8vo. Lond., 1879. C 1 U 11

His Life and recently discovered Writings, extending from 1716 to 1729; by William Lee. 3 vols. 8vo. Lond., 1869. C 10 T 29–31

Journal of the Plague Year; or, Memorials of the Great Pestilence in London in 1665. (Fam. Lib.) 12mo Lond., 1835. K 10 P 32

Life and Adventures of Robinson Crusoe; with Illustrative Memoir and Illustrative Notes, by T. Ballantyne. 2 vols. 8vo. Lond., 1882. J 10 R 7, 8

Life and Strange Surprising Adventures of Robinson Crusoe, of York. (Facsimile Reprint of the 1st edition, 1819.) 8vo. Lond., 1883. J 10 R 6

Life and Times of; with Remarks, Digressive and Discursive, by William Chadwick. 8vo. Lond., 1859. C 10 T 32

Novels and Miscellaneous Works of; edited, with Life, by T. Ballantyne. 20 vols. 12mo. Oxford, 1840. J 1 V 1–20

1, 2. Life and Adventures of Robinson Crusoe. With Memoir of the Author.

3. Life, Adventures, and Piracies of Captain Singleton.

4. Fortunes and Misfortunes of the Famous Moll Flanders.

5. Life of Colonel Jack, and a True Relation of the Apparition of one Mrs. Veal.

6. Memoirs of a Cavalier, 1632–38.

7. New Voyage Round the World.

8. Memoirs of Captain George Carleton, and Life and Adventures of Mrs. Christian Davies.

9. Journal of the Plague Year in 1665.

10. Political History of the Devil.

11. Roxana; or, the Fortunate Mistress.

12. System of Magic; or, a History of the Black Art.

13. History and Reality of Apparitions.

14. Religious Courtship.

15, 16. Family Instructor.

17, 18. Complete English Tradesman.

DE FOE (DANIEL)—*continued.*

19. Life and Adventures of Mr. Duncan Campbell—A Remarkable Passage of an Apparition, 1665—The Dumb Philosopher; or, Great Britain's Wonder—Everybody's Business is Nobody's Business; or, Private Abuses, Public Grievances.

20. Life of Daniel De Foe, by George Chalmers—A List of De Foe's Works, arranged Chronologically—An Appeal to Honor and Justice, though it be to his Worst Enemies, &c.—A Seasonable Warning and Caution against the Insinuations of Papists and Jacobites in Favour of the Pretender—Reasons against the Succession of the House of Hanover; with an Enquiry, How far the Abdication of King James, supposing it to be Legal, ought to affect the Person of the Pretender—And what if the Pretender should Come? or, Some Considerations of the Advantages and Real Consequences of the Pretender's Possessing the Crown of Great Britain—An Answer to a Question that Nobody thinks of, *viz.*, But what if the Queen should die?—The Tiue-bom Englishman: a Satire.

Tour through the Island of Great Britain, divided into Circuits or Journeys; originally begun by the celebrated Daniel De Foe, continued by the late Mr. Richardson. 9th ed.   4 vols. 12mo.   Dublin, 1779.   D 7 P 33-36

DE GENLIS (STÉPHANIE FÉLICITÉ), COMTESSE. [*See* GENLIS, STÉPHANIE FÉLICITÉ, COMTESSE DE.]

DE GRIMM (F. M.) BARON. [*See* GRIMM, F. M. BARON DE.]

DE GRUCHY & LEIGH. Stranger's Guide to Melbourne. Illustrated.   12mo.   Melb., 1866.   MJ 2 P 32

DE GUBERNATIS (ANGELO). [*See* GUBERNATIS, A. DE.]

DE GUIGNES (C. L. G.) [*See* GUIGNES, C. L. G. DE.[

DE GUIGNES (J.) [*See* GUIGNES, J. DE.]

DEHEQUE (FÉLIX DÉSIRÉ). Dictionnaire Grec Moderne Français.   18mo.   Paris, 1825.   K 11 S 6

D'EICHWALD (EDOUARD). Lethæa Rossica; ou, Paléontologie de la Russie.   3 vols. (in 5) 8vo. fol.   Stuttgart, 1853-68.   A 9 S 6-10
Atlas [to above].   2 vols. (in 1) imp. 4to.   Stuttgart, 1859-68.   A 23 R 25 ‡

DE JOHNSTONE (CHEVALIER). [*See* JOHNSTONE, CHEVALIER DE.]

DEKKER (THOMAS). Dramatic Works of: now first collected, with Illustrative Notes and a Memoir of the Author.   4 vols. 8vo.   Lond., 1873.   H R 3 6
Knight's Conjuring: done in Earnest, discovered in Jest; from the Original Tract printed in 1607; edited by Edward F. Rimbault, F.S.A.   (Percy Soc. 6.)   8vo.   Lond., 1842.
Non Dramatic Works, edited with Memorial introduction by the Rev. Alexander B. Grosart, D.D., &c.   (Huth Lib.)   5 vols. 4to.   Lond., 1884-86.   J 5 U 5 9

DE KONINCK (L. G.) [*See* KONINCK, L. G. DE.]

DE KONINCK (L. L.), DR.SC., AND DIETZ (E.) Practical Manual of Chemical Analysis and Assaying, as applied to the Manufacture of Iron from its Ores; edited, with Notes, by Robt. Mallet, F.R.S., &c.   8vo.   Lond., 1872.   A 9 P 48

DELAAGE (HENRI). L'Eternité Dévoilée; ou, Vie Future des Ames après la Mort. 4e éd. 8vo. Paris, 1864. G 10 Q 6
La Monde occulte; ou, Mystères du Magnétisme et Tableau du Somnambulisme à Paris; précédé d'une Introduction sur la Magnétisme, par le Père Lacordaire. 5e éd. 12mo. Paris, 1859. A 10 R 10
Les Ressuscités au Ciel et dans l'Enfer. 2e éd. 8vo. Paris, 1855. G 10 T 21

DE LA BECHE (SIR H. T.), F.R.S., &c. Address delivered at the Anniversary Meeting of the Geological Society of London, 1848. (Pam. 25.) 8vo. Lond., 1848. MJ 2 Q 13
Geological Manual. 3rd ed. 8vo. Lond., 1833. A 9 R 6
Geological Observer. 8vo. Lond., 1851. A 9 R 23
Mining, Quarrying, and Metallurgical Processes and Products. [*See* LONDON. INTERN. EXHIB., 1851.]
Report on the Geology of Cornwall, Devon, and West Somerset. 8vo. Lond., 1839. A 9 S 4
[*See* GEOLOGICAL MEMOIRS.]

DE LA BORDE (JEAN BERJ). [*See* LA BORDE, J. B.]

DELABORDE (LÉON). [*See* LA BORDE, L. DE.]

DELABORDE (H.), VICOMTE. Engraving; its Origin, Processes, and History. 8vo. Lond., 1886. A 6 V 26

DE LA BRUYÈRE (J.) [*See* LA BRUYÈRE, J. DE.]

DE LA GIRONIERE (PAUL P.) [*See* LA GIRONIERE, P. P. DE.]

DE LAGNY (GERMAIN). The Knout and the Russians; or, the Muscovite Empire, the Czar, and his People; translated from the French by John Bridgeman. 12mo. Lond., 1854. D 7 Q 2

DE LAMARTINE (ALPHONSE). [*See* LAMARTINE, A. DE.]

DELAMOTTE (F. G.) Book of Ornamental Alphabets, Ancient and Mediæval, from the 8th Century, with Numerals, including Gothic; Church Text, Large and Small; German Arabesque; Initials for Illumination, Monograms, Crosses, &c. 3rd ed. Obl. 12mo. Lond., 1860. A 7 P 20
Another copy. 9th ed. Obl. 12mo. Lond., 1879. A 7 P 22
Examples of Modern Alphabets, Plain and Ornamental; including German, Old English, Saxon, Halle, Perspective, Greek, Hebrew, Court Hand, Engrossing, Tuscan, Ribbon, Gothic, Rustic, Arabesque; with several original Designs, and an Analysis of the Roman and Old English Alphabets. 7th ed. Obl. 12mo. Lond., 1880. A 7 P 21

DELAMOTTE (F. G.)—*continued.*
Mediæval Alphabets and Initials for Illuminators; with an Introduction by J. Willis Brooks. 3rd ed. 8m. 4to. Lond., 1867. A 7 Q 3

Primer of the Art of Illumination for the use of Beginners; with a Rudimentary Treatise on the Art. Sm. 4to. Lond., 1874. A 6 V 32.

DELAMOTTE (PHILIP H.) Art of Sketching from Nature 4to. Lond., 1871. A 1 P 2 †

Work in Earthenware. . Art Work in Gold and Silver—Mediæval. [*See* WHEATLEY, H. B.]

DELANO (CAPT. AMASA). Narrative of Voyages and Travels in the Northern and Southern Hemispheres. 2nd ed. 8vo. Boston, 1818. MD 4 V 43

DELANY (J. D.) Orangeism : a Historical Retrospect ; a Lecture. 8vo. Sydney, 1871.

DELANY (MRS. MARY), MARY GRANVILLE. Autobiography and Correspondence of Mary Granville (Mrs. Delany); edited by the Rt. Hon. Lady Llanover. 1st and 2nd series, with Portraits. 6 vols. 8vo. Lond., 1861–62. C 10 U 2–7

DE LAPLACE [*See* LAPLACE, MARQUIS DE.]

DELAROCHE (PAUL). Brief Biographies of the Painters, Sculptors, and Architects represented in the Hemicycle of the Palais des Beaux Arts. 8vo. Lond., 1880. C 3 T 44

Life of (Great Artists); by J. R. Rees. 8vo. Lond., 1880. C 3 T 44

DE LA RUE (WARREN), M.A., &c., AND MÜLLER (HUGO W.), PH.D., &c. Experimental Researches on the Electric Discharge with the Chloride of Silver Battery. Parts 1, 2. (Roy. Soc. Pubs. 5.) 4to. Lond., 1878. A 11 P 6 †

DE LASPÉE (H.) [*See* LASPÉE, H. DE.]

DELATTRE (A.), S.J. Le Peuple et l'Empire des Mèdes jusqu'a la fin du Règne de cyaxare. 4to. Bruxelles, 1883. B 3 P 25 †

DELATTRE (CHARLES). L'Océanie : Voyages et Naufrages les plus intéressants. 8vo. Limoges, 1885. MD 4 U 20

DELAUNAY (MLLE. DE). [*See* STAAL, BARONNE DE.]

DELAVAUD (L.) L'Australie. Voyages et Découvertes Géographiques. Collection publiée sous la direction de M. Richard Cortambert. 12mo. Paris, 1882.* MD 2 Q 26

DELAVILLE LE ROULX (JOSEPH). Les Archives, la Bibliothèque, et le Trésor de l'Ordre de Saint-Jean de Jérusalem-à Malte. 8vo. Paris, 1883. G 11 T 7

2 E

DELBET (JULES). Exploration Archéologique de la Galatie, etc. [*See* PERROT, G.] D 4 S 10 11 ‡

DELEPIERRE (OCTAVE). Macaronéana ; ou, Mélanges de Littérature Macaronique des différents Peuples de l'Europe. 8vo. Paris, 1852. J 17 P 17

Supercheries Littéraires, Pastiches, Suppositions d'Auteur, dans les Lettres et dans les Arts. Sq. 8vo. Lond., 1872. J 17 P 21

DELESSERT (EUGENE). Voyages dans les deux Océans, Atlantique et Pacifique, 1844–47. Imp. 8vo. Paris, 1848.* MD 4 P 14 †

DELEUZE (J. P. F.) History and Description of the Royal Museum of Natural History, published by order of the Administration of that Establishment; translated from the French. 2 vols. 8vo. Paris, 1823. A 7 Q 16, 17

DE LIEFDE (J. B.) The Beggars (Les Gueux) ; or, the Founders of the Dutch Republic : a Tale. 8vo. Lond., 1868. J 4 P 12

DELITZSCH (PROF. FREDERIC). Hebrew Language viewed in the Light of Assyrian Research. 8vo. Lond., 1883. K 13 P 13

DÉLIUS (CHRIST. FRANÇOIS). Traité sur la Science de l'Exploitation des Mines, par théorie et pratique. Traduit en Français, par M. Schreiber. 2 vols. 8vo. Paris, 1778. A 9 V 14, 15

DELLA BONA (GIOVANNI). Elementi di Pedagogia Scientitica. 1. Pedagogia Teorica. 8vo. Milano, 1883. G 17 R 1

DELLAS (ARISTIDE). Key to the Pronunciation of French as spoken in Paris. 8vo. Melb., 1868. MK 1 P 18

DEL MAR (ALEXANDER), C.E., &c. History of Money in Ancient Countries. 8vo. Lond., 1885. F 8 Q 23

History of the Precious Metals. 8vo. Lond., 1880. A 10 P 12

Money and Civilization. 8vo. Lond., 1886. F 9 R 8

Science of Money. 8vo. Lond., 1885. F 9 R 7

DELMARD (SOPHIA D.) Village Life in Switzerland. 8vo. Lond., 1865. D 9 P 27

DE LOLME (JEAN LOUIS). Constitution of England. New ed., with Life and Notes, by John Macgregor, M.P. 8vo. Lond., 1853. B 4 P 10

DE LONG (LIEUT.-COM. GEORGE W.), U.S.N. Narrative of the Search for. [*See* MELVILLE, G. W.]

Voyage of the *Jeannette*: the Ship and Ice Journals of George W. de Long, Lieut.-Commander, U.S.N., and Commander of the Polar Expedition of 1879–81 ; edited by his Wife, Emma de Long. Illustrated. 2 vols. 8vo. Lond., 1883. D 4 S 31 32

DE LOS VALLES (BARON). [*See* VALLES, BARON DE LOS.]

DELPHIN CLASSICS. Edited by A. J. Valpy, A.M.
187 vols. 8vo. Lond., 1819–30.　　　　J 13 P–T

Apuleius.	Florus.	Propertius.
Aulus Gellius.	Horatius.	Pludentius.
Aurelius Victor.	Justinus.	Sallustius.
Ausonius.	Juvenalis.	Statius.
Boethius.	Livius.	Suetonius.
Cæsar.	Lucretius.	Tacitus.
Catullus.	Manilius.	Terentius.
Cicero.	Martialis.	Tibullus.
Claudianus.	Ovidius.	Valerius Maximus.
Cornelius Nepos.	Panegyrici veteres.	Velleius Paterculus.
Curtius Rufus.	Persius.	Verrius Flaccus et
Dares Phrygius.	Phædrus.	Pompeius Festus.
Dictys Cretensis.	Plautus.	Virgilius.
Eutropius.	Plinius (the elder).	

DELPRINO (DR. M.) Perte dans le Produit de la Soie,
par suite défauts des systèmic usuels, et appréciation des
nouvelles méthodes cellulaires isolatrices. (Pam. F.) Roy.
8vo. Acqui, 1867.　　　　MJ 2 8 3

DEL RIO (MARTINO ANTONIO). Disquisitionum Magi-
carum, Libri Sex, quibus continetur accurata Curiosarum
Artium et Vanarum, Superstitionum confutatio. 3 vols.
(in 2) 4to. Venetiis, 1746.　　　　A 10 R 1, 2

DE MAILLA OR MAILLÆ. [*See* MAILLA, PÈRE J. A.
M. DE M. DE.]

DEMAINTENON(MDME.) [*See* MAINTENON MARQUISE DE.]

DEMAUS (REV. R.) M.A. Hugh Latimer: a Biography.
New ed. 8vo. Lond., 1881.　　　　C 3 P 23

DE MEDICI (L.) [*See* MEDICI, L. DE.]

DE MELFORT (EDOUARD), COUNT. [*See* MELFORT, COUNT
EDOUARD DE.]

DEMMLER (FRANZ C. F.) Memoirs of the Court of
Prussia. [*See* VEHSE, DR. E.]

DEMOCRATIC GOVERNMENT IN VICTORIA. [*See*
VICTORIA.]

DEMOCRITUS. [*See* FACTION DEFEATED.]

DEMOCRITUS, JUNIOR. [*See* BURTON, R.]

DE MOGES (MARQUIS). Recollections of Baron Gros'
Embassy to China and Japan, in 1857-58. With Illustrations. 12mo. Lond., 1860.　　　　D 5 P 28

DEMOLOMBE (C.) Cours du Code Napoléon. 26 vols.
8vo. Paris, 1867–71.　　　　F 9 Q 1–26

DE MONTGON (L'ABBÉ CHARLES ALEXANDRE.) [*See*
MONTGON, L'ABBÉ CHARLES ALEXANDRE DE.]

DE MONTPENSIER. [*See* MONTPENSIER.]

DE MORGAN (AUGUSTUS), F.R.A.S., &c. Arithmetical
Books, from the Invention of Printing. 8vo. Lond.,
1847.　　　　A 10 S 25

Book of Almanacs; with an Index of Reference by
which the Almanac may be found for every year, whether
in Old Style or New, from any Epoch, Ancient or Modern,
up to A.D. 2000, with means of finding the Day of any
New or Full Moon, from B.C. 2000 to A.D. 2000. Ob.
12mo. Lond., 1851.　　　　A 10 R 30

A Budget of Paradoxes; reprinted, with the Author's
Additions, from the *Athenæum*. 8vo. Lond., 1872.
　　　　J 15 8 8

Differential and Integral Calculus. (Lib. Usef. Know.)
8vo. Lond., 1842.　　　　A 10 T 16

An Essay on Probabilities and their application to Life
Contingencies and Insurance Offices. (Lard. Cab. Cyclo.)
18mo. Lond., 1838.　　　　K 1 U 28

Formal Logic; or, the Calculus of Inference, necessary
and probable. 8vo. Lond., 1847.　　　　G 3 T 11

Memoir of; by his Wife, Sophia Elizabeth De Morgan; with
Selections from his Letters. 8vo. Lond.,1882. C 10 T 28

Newton: his Friend and his Niece; edited by [Mrs. Sophia
Elizabeth De Morgan and] Arthur Cowper Ranyard.
8vo. Lond., 1885.　　　　C 10 U 38

Remarks on Elementary Education in Science. (Univ.
of Lond.) 8vo. Lond., 1830.　　　　J 5 8 8

Thoughts suggested by the establishment of the University of London: an Introductory Lecture. [Univ. of Lond.]
8vo. Lond., 1837.　　　　J 5 8 8

[*See* COBURN, F. W. AND F. L., *and* SCHRÖN, DR. L.]

DE MORGAN (MRS. SOPHIA ELIZABETH). From Matter to
Spirit: the Result of Ten Years' Experience in Spirit
Manifestations; by C.D. 8vo. Lond., 1863.*　G 7 Q 18

Memoir of Augustus De Morgan; with Selections from his
Letters. 8vo. Lond,. 1882.　　　　C 10 T 28

Newton: his Friend and his Niece. [*See* DE MORGAN, A.]

DE MOSENTHAL (JULIUS), AND HARTING (JAMES E.)
Ostriches and Ostrich-farming. Illustrated. 8vo. Lond.,
1876.　　　　A 15 P 17

DEMOSTHENES. Oration upon the Crown; translated
into English, with Notes, and the Greek Text, by Henry
Lord Brougham, F.R.S. 8vo. Lond., 1840.　F 12 P 2

Orations of; translated, with Notes, &c., by Charles Rann
Kennedy. 5 vols. 8vo. Lond., 1880–81.　　F 6 P 5–9

Orations of, pronounced to excite the Athenians against
Philip of Macedon; translated by Thomas Leland, D.D.
2 vols. 18mo. Lond., 1832.　　　　J 15 P 7, 8

Political Eloquence in Greece: Demosthenes; with Extracts
from his Orations, and a Critical Discussion of the "Trial of
the Crown," by L. Brédif; translated by M. J. MacMahon,
A.M. 8vo. Chicago, 1881.　　　　C 5 T 6

Selectæ Orationes. Notis insuper illustravit; Ricardus
Mounteney. Editio decima quarta, Emendatior, et
Auctior; Accurante J. W. Niblock, D.D. 8vo. Lond.,
1826.　　　　F 10 P 23

DEMPSEY (G. D.), C.E. Rudimentary Treatise on the Drainage of Districts and Lands. (Weale.) 12mo. Lond., 1869. A 17 P 33

Rudimentary Treatise of the Drainage of Towns and Buildings. (Weale.) 12mo. Lond., 1867. A 17 P 33

Rudimentary Treatise on the Locomotive Engine in all its Phases. (Weale.) 3rd ed. 12mo. Lond.,1866. A 17 P 26

Rudimentary Treatise on the Locomotive Engine; with Additions by D. Kinnear Clark, C.E. (Weale.) 12mo. Lond., 1879. A 17 Q 17

Tubular and other Iron Girder Bridges. (Weale.) 12mo. Lond., 1865. A 17 Q 32

DEMPSTER (Miss CHARLOTTE LOUISA HAWKINS). Maritime Alps and their Seaboard. Illustrated. 8vo. Lond., 1885. D 8 V 7

DE MUSSET (ALFRED). [*See* MUSSET, A. DE.]

DENDY (WALTER COOPER). The Philosophy of Mystery. 8vo. Lond., 1841. G 10 S 18

DENHAM (MAJOR DIXON), F.R.S., CLAPPERTON (CAPT. HUGH), AND CUDNEY (D.) Narrative of Travels and Discoveries in Northern and Central Africa, in the years 1822–24. 3rd ed. 2 vols. 8vo. Lond.,1828. D 1 V 20, 21

DENHAM (H. M.), R.N. Sailing Directions from Point Lynas to Liverpool; with Charts, Coast Views, River Sections, &c., for navigating the Dee and Mersey. 8vo. Liverpool, 1840. F 6 T 22

DENHAM (SIR JOHN), K.B. Life and Poems of. [*See* CHALMERS, A., *and* JOHNSON, DR. S.]

Poems and Translations; with the Sophy: a Tragedy. 7th ed. 12mo. Lond. (n.d.) H 6 R 5

The Sophy: a Tragedy. (Old Plays.) Sm. fol. Lond., 1642. H 1 V 1

DENIEHY (DANIEL HENRY). How I became Attorney-General of New Barataria: an Experiment at Treating Facts in the Forms of Fiction. (Pam. 26.) 12mo. Sydney, 1860. MJ 2 Q 14

Life and Speeches of; by Miss E. A. Martin. 8vo. Melb., 1884.* MC 1 R 6

DENINA (CARLO). Rivoluzioni della Germania. 8 vols. (in 7) 8vo. Firenze, 1804. B 9 R 33–39

DENISON (EDMUND BECKETT), M.A. Lectures on Church-Building. [*See* BECKETT, SIR E.]
Rudimentary Treatise on Clocks, Watches, and Bells. [*See* BECKETT, SIR E.]

DENISON (RT. HON. J. EVELYN), SPEAKER OF THE HOUSE OF COMMONS. The Holy Bible according to the Authorized Version. [*See* BIBLES AND TESTAMENTS.]

DENISON (MAJOR-GEN. SIR WILLIAM THOMAS), K.C.B., &c. Copy of a Despatch, bearing date the 16th day of April, 1860, to the Secretary of State for the Colonies, on Military Expenditure in New South Wales; together with some Correspondence before and after that Despatch. (Parl. Docs., 41.) Fol. Lond., 1861. MF 4 ‡

Lecture on Education. 8vo. Sydney (n.d.) MG 1 Q 30

Results of a series of Experiments for determining the relative value of Specimens of Native Gold from the Counties whence it is brought to market in these Colonies. 8vo. Hobart, 1852. MA 2 Q 35

Roads and Railways in New South Wales and India. 8vo. Lond., 1870. MF 1 Q 15

Varieties of Vice-regal Life. 2 vols. 8vo. Lond., 1870. MC 1 R 20, 21

[*See* BOYD, B.; BURGOYNE, SIR J.; *and* STEVENS, C. G.]

DENMAN (J. L.) The Vine and its Fruit. 8vo. Lond., 1844. A 1 P 10

DENNIS (C. R.) Annual Report of the Quartermaster-General, made to the General Assembly of the State of Rhode Island, at its January Session, A.D. 1876. (Pam. Ja.) 8vo. Providence, 1876. F 7 S 24

DENNIS (GEORGE). Cities and Cemeteries of Etruria. Revised ed. With Map, Plans, and Illustrations. 2 vols. 8vo. Lond., 1878. B 11 R 29, 30

Summer in Andalucia. 2 vols.8vo. Lond.,1839. D 8 T 6, 7

DENNIS (JOHN). Studies in English Literature. 8vo. Lond., 1876. B 21 S 27

DENNISTON (R. B.) Reports on the Bullen Coal-field. [*See* HECTOR, SIR J.]

DENNISTOUN (JAMES). Memoirs of the Dukes of Urbino, illustrating the Arms, Arts, and Literature of Italy, 1440–1630. 3 vols. sq. 8vo. Lond.,1851. B 11 V 14–16

DENON (VIVANT). Voyages dans la Basse et la Haute Egypte, pendant les Campagnes de Bonaparte, en 1798–99. 2 vols. 4to. Lond., 1807. D 9 S 14, 15 †

Planches du Voyages dans Egypte. At. fol. Lond., 1807. D 11 P 17 ‡

DENOVAN (W. D. C.) Evidences of Spiritualism : Lectures, Addresses, &c. Roy. 8vo. Melb., 1882. MG 1 T 1

DENS (PETER). Dens' Theology : Extracts from Peter Dens, on the Nature of Confession, and the Obligation of the Seal. 2nd ed. Dublin, 1836. Reprinted. 8vo. Sydney, 1839. MJ 2 R 18

Theologia Moralis and Dogmatica. 8 vols. 8vo. Dublin, 1832. G 13 T 34–41

DENT (CLINTON). Above the Snow Line: Mountaineering Sketches, 1870–80. 8vo. Lond., 1885. D 8 R 23

DENT (E**N**NA). Annals of Winchcombe and Sudeley. 4to. Lond., 1877.   B 16 Q 17 ‡

DENT (HASTINGS CHARLES), C.E. A Year in Brazil; with Notes on the Abolition of Slavery, Meteorology, Natural History, &c. 8vo. Lond., 1886.   D 4 Q 9

DENT (ROBERT K.) Old and New Birmingham : a History of the Town and its People. Illustrated. Roy. 8vo. Birmingham, 1880.   B 5 V 21

DENTON (J. BAILEY), F.G.S., &c. Sanitary Engineering: a Series of Lectures given before the School of Military Engineering at Chatham, 1876. In Divisions:—Air—Water—The Dwelling—The Town and the Village—Disposal of Sewage. Roy. 8vo. Lond., 1877. A 6 U 6

DENTRECASTEAUX (BRUNY). Voyage de Dentrecasteaux, envoyé à la recherche de La Pérouse. Rédigé par M. de Rossel. 2 vols. 4to. Paris, 1808. MD 7 P 9, 10 † Atlas [to the above]. At. fol. Paris, 1807. MD 5 Q 9 †

D'EON DE BEAUMONT (G. L. A.), CHEVALIER. Strange Career of the Chevalier D'Eon de Beaumont, Minister Plenipotentiary from France to Great Britain in 1763 ; by Capt. J. B. Telfer, R.N. 8vo. Lond., 1885. C 6 Q 16

[*See* THOMAS, W. J.]

DE PAUW (CORNELIUS). [*See* PAUW, CORNELIUS DE.]

DEPLANCHES (JOUAN ET EMILE). Géologie de la Nouvelle-Calédonie. [*See* DESLONGCHAMPS, E.]

DE PLANCY (JACQUES A. S. C. D. COLLIN). [*See* COLLIN DE PLANCY, J. A. S. C. D.]

DEPOSIER (J.) Des Devoirs des Hommes. [*See* PELICO, S.]

DE PUY (W. H.), A.M., &c. People's Cyclopedia of Universal Knowledge; with numerous Appendixes invaluable for Reference in all Departments of Industrial Life ; the whole brought down to the year 1883. 2 vols. imp. 8vo. New York, 1883.   K 4 U 13, 14

DE QUATREFAGES (ARMAND). [*See* QUATREFAGES, A. DE.]

DE QUINCEY (THOMAS). Autobiographic Sketches. 2 vols. 8vo. Edinb., 1853-54.   C 16 P 16, 17

[A Biography]; by D. Masson. (Eng. Men of Letts.) 8vo. Lond., 1881.   C 1 U 12

Confessions of an English Opium-eater. 12mo. Lond., 1853.   J 7 Q 2

Miscellanies, chiefly Narrative. 8vo. Edinb., 1854. J 11 Q 8

Miscellanies. 8vo. Edinb., 1854.   J 11 Q 9

Personal Recollections of; by J. R. Findlay. 12mo. Edinb., 1886.   C 2 Q 14

DE QUINCEY (THOMAS)—*continued.*
The Works of.   22 vols. 8vo.   Boston, 1854-69.
                                                     J 11 Q 13-34

1. Confessions of an English Opium-eater, and Suspiria de Profundis.
2. Biographical Essays.
3. Miscellaneous Essays.
4. The Cæsars.
5, 6. Literary Reminiscences.
7, 8. Narrative and Miscellaneous Papers.
9. Essays on the Poets, &c.
10, 11. Historical and Critical Essays.
12. Autobiographic Sketches.
13, 14. Philosophical Writers.
15. Letters to a Young Man.
16, 17. Theological Essays.
18. Note-book of an English Opium-eater.
19, 20. Memorials, &c.
21. The Avenger, &c.
22. Logic of Political Economy.

DERBY (EARL OF). "What are you at?" A Plain Question addressed to the Earl of Derby; by "A Leicestershire Farmer." (Pam. Jf.) 8vo. Lond., 1852. MF 2 P 2

[*See* HOMER.]

DE RICCI (J. H.), F.R.G.S. Fiji : our New Province in the South Seas. 8vo. Lond., 1875.   MD 5 P 36

DE ROS (LIEUT.-GEN. WILLIAM LENNOX LASCELLES FITZGERALD), LORD. Memorials of the Tower of London. 8vo. Lond., 1866.   B 3 R 29

DERRICK (CHARLES). Memoirs of the Rise and Progress of the Royal Navy. 4to. Lond., 1806.   B 2 T 22

DERWENT STAR (THE). *The Derwent Star and Van Diemen's Land Intelligencer,* Tuesday, April 3rd, 1810. (A Reprint, containing an Account of the Death and Obsequies of Lieut.-Governor Collins.) (Pam. M.) Fol. Hobart (n.d.)   MJ 2 S 4

DE SAINT-MARTIN (LEWIS VIVIEN). [*See* VIVIEN DE SAINT-MARTIN, L.]

DESANGES (L. W.) Descriptive Catalogue of the Victoria Cross Gallery ; painted by L. W. Desanges. [*See* DUBLIN INTERN. EXHIB., 1865.]

DE SAULCY (LOUIS FÉLICIEN JOSEPH CAIGNART). [*See* SAULCY, L. F. J. C. DE.]

DESBOIS (FR. ALEX. DE LA CHENAYE). Dictionnaire Raisonné et Universel des Animaux, ou le Règne Animal, consistant en Quadrupèdes, Cétacées, Oiseaux, Reptiles, Poissons, Insectes, Vers, Zoophytes ou Plantes animales. 4 vols. 4to. Paris, 1759.   A 15 R 18-21

DESCAMPS (J. B.) La Vie des Peintres Flamands, Allemands, et Hollandois, avec des Portraits. 4 vols. 8vo. Paris, 1753-64.   C 4 T 32-35

DESCARTES (René). Oeuvres Philosophiques. 8vo.
Paris, 1843.   G 7 V 20

DE SAINT-SIMON (Louis). [*See* SAINT-SIMON, L. DE.]

DESCHAMPS (P.), AND BRUNET (G.) Manuel du
Libraire et de l'Amateur de Livres. Supplément, contenant ; 1°, Un complément du Dictionnaire Bibliographique de M. J. Ch. Brunet ; 2°, la Table Raisonnée.
des Articles. 2 vols. 8vo. Paris, 1878–80.   Libr.

DESCHANEL (A. PRIVAT). Elementary Treatise on
Natural Philosophy ; translated and edited, with extensive Additions, by J. D. Everett, M.A., &c. 4 vols.
8vo. Lond., 1870–72.   A 16 T 18–21
1. Mechanics, Hydrostatics, and Pneumatics.
2. Heat.
3. Electricity and Magnetism.
4. Sound and Light.

D'ESCHAVANNES (JOUFFROY). Traité complet de la
Science du Blason, a l'usage des Bibliophiles, Archéo-
logues, Amateurs d'objets d'art et de curiosité, Numis-
mates, Archivistes. Troisième mille. 8vo. Paris, 1885.
                                                     K 10 S 7

DESDA. [*See* DAVIES, MRS.]

DE SÉVIGNÉ (MARIE DE RABUTIN-CHANTAL), MARQUISE
[*See* SÉVIGNÉ, M. DE R.-C., MARQUISE DE.]

DESGRAZ (C.) Iles Marquises ou Nouka-Hiva. [*See*
VINCENDON-DUMOULIN, C. A.]

DESHAYES (G. P.) Description des Animaux sans Ver-
tèbres découverts dans le Bassin de Paris. Pour servir
de Supplément à la Description des Coquilles Fossiles des
Environs de Paris. 5 vols. et atlas roy. 4to. Paris,
1860–66.   A 4 S 15–19 †
Description des Coquilles Fossiles des Environs de Paris.
Conchifères et Mollusques. 3 vols. et atlas roy. 4to.
Paris, 1824–37.   A 4 S 20–22 †
[*See* LAMARCK, J. B. P. A. DE M. DE.]

DESHLER (CHARLES D.) Afternoons with the Poets.
Sq. 8vo. N. York, 1879.   H 7 R 12

DESJARDINS (TONY). Monographie de l'Hotel de-Ville
de Lyon ; restauré sous l'Administration de MM. Vaisse
et Chevreau Senateurs. At. fol. Paris, 1867.   A 1 R 5 ‡

DESLANDES (DR. LÉOPOLD). De l'Onanisme et des
autres Abus vénériens considérés dans leurs rapports avec
la Santé. 8vo. Paris, 1835.   A 26 S 9

DESLONGCHAMPS (EUGÈNE). Documents sur la Géologie
de la Nouvelle-Calédonie, suivis du Catalogue des Roches
recueillies dans cette île par MM. Jouan et Emile Deplanches. 8vo. Caen, 1864.   MA 2 Q 19

DES MAISEAUX (PIERRE). [*See* BAYLE, PROF. P.]

DESMAZE (CHARLES). Les Métiers de Paris d'après les
Ordonnances du Chatelet, avec les Sceaux des Artisans.
Roy. 8vo. Paris, 1874.   F 8 T 1

DESMOULINS (CAMILLE AND LUCILE), Camille Desmoulins
and his Wife : Passages from the History of the Dantonists, founded upon new and hitherto unpublished
documents ; translated from the French of Jules Claretie,
by Mrs. Cashel Hoey. 8vo. Lond., 1876.   C 10 S 13

DES MURS . (ŒILLET). Inconographie ornithologique.
Nouveau Recueil général de Planches peintes d'Oiseaux.
Première Partie. Roy. 4to. Paris, 1849.   A 4 U 1 ‡

DESORMEAUX (J. L. R.) Histoire de Louis de Bourbon, Second du Nom, Prince de Condé, Premier Prince
du Sang, Surnommé Le Grand. 4 vols. 12mo. Paris,
1766–68.   B 9 P 8–11

DESPARD (COL. E. M.) [*See* TRIALS.]

DE STAËL-HOLSTEIN (ANNA LOUISA GERMAINE),
BARONNE. [*See* STAËL-HOLSTEIN, A. L. G., BARONNE DE.]

DE STENDAHL. [*See* BEYLE, M. H.]

D'ESTREY (G. H. J. MEYNERS), COMTE. [*See* MEYNERS
D'ESTREY, G. H. J., COMTE.]

DESTITUTE CHILDREN. Society for the Relief of.
[*See* SOCIETY FOR THE RELIEF OF DESTITUTE CHILDREN.]

DESTY (R.) Penal Code of California. 12mo. San
Francisco, 1885.   F 2 P 3

DETECTIVE'S ALBUM (THE) : Tales of the Australian
Police ; by W.W. 8vo. Melb., 1871.   MJ 1 U 2

DE TOCQUEVILLE (ALEXIS). [*See* TOCQUEVILLE, A. DE.]

DETMOLD (CHRISTIAN E.) [*See* MACHIAVELLI, N.] *

DEUTSCH (EMANUEL). Literary Remains of; with a brief
Memoir. 8vo. Lond., 1874.   G 10 T 9

DEUTSCH (HERMANN). Map of the Squatting Stations
in Victoria. [*See* ROBERTSON, A.]

DEUTSCHE BIOGRAPHIE. Allgemeine deutsche Biographie, auf Veranlassung und mit Unterstützung seiner
Majestaet des Königs von Bayern Maximilian II. Vols.
1–22. 8vo. Leipzig, 1875–85.   C 18 U 1–22

DEUTSCHE KOLONIALPOLITIK (DIE). 2 vols. 8vo.
Leipzig, 1885.   MF 1 R 15, 16

DEVAS (C. S.) Groundwork of Economics. 8vo. Lond.,
1883.   F 6 T 3

DE VEGA (JUAN). [*See* COCHRANE, CAPT. C.]

DE VERE (PROF. MAXIMILIAN SCHELE), LL.D. Outlines of
Comparative Philology ; with a Sketch of the Language
of Europe. 8vo. New York, 1853.   K 11 U 10
Studies in English. 3rd ed. 8vo. N. York, 1872. K 12 P 3

DEVEREUX (WALTER ROBERT, AND ROBERT), EARLS OF ESSEX. [*See* ESSEX, EARLS OF.]

DEVEREUX (HON. WALTER BOURCHIER). Lives and Letters of the Devereux, Earls of Essex, in the Reigns of Elizabeth, James I, and Charles I, 1540-1646. 2 vols. 8vo. Lond., 1853.   C 6 U 12, 13

DEVEY (JOSEPH). Logic; or, the Science of Inference. 8vo. Lond., 1854.   G 16 Q 1

DEVIC (M.) [*See* LITTRÉ, E.]

DEVIGNY (A.) [*See* VIGNY, A. DE.]

DEVIL (THE). The Devil; Who, and what is He? or, the Origin of Evil; by "Clericus Anglicanus." 8vo. Melb., 1888.   MG 1 Q 43

DEVILLE (ACHILLE). Histoire de l'Art de la Venerie dans l'Antiquité. 4to. Paris, 1871.   A 2 R 19 †
Tombeaux de la Cathédrale de Rouen. 8vo. Rouen, 1833.   A 8 Q 22

DEVILLIERS (C.) Nouvelle Recherches sur la Membrane Hymen et les Caroncules Hyménales. 8vo. Paris, 1840.   Libr.

DEVINE (EDWARD AND JOSEPH). Newtown Ejectment Case. [*See* MOORE, J. S.]

DE VINNE (THEODORE LOW). Invention of Printing: a Collection of Facts and Opinions descriptive of early Prints and Playing Cards, the Block Books of the 15th Century, the Legend of Lourens Janszoon Coster, of Haarlem; and the Work of John Gutenberg and his Associates. Illustrated. 2nd ed. Roy. 8vo. Lond., 1877.   A 16 V 9

DE VINSAUF. [*See* VINSAUF, G. DE.]

DE VIT (DR. V.) [*See* FORCELLINI, A.]

DEVITTE (WILLIAM A. M.) History of Rome. [*See* LIVIUS, T.]

DEVIZES (RICHARD OF). [*See* RICHARD OF DEVIZES.]

DE VOGÜE (C. J. M.), COMTE. [*See* VOGÜE, C. J. M., COMTE DE.]

DEVONSHIRE (WILLIAM), DUKE OF. Sketches of the Character of; by R. Adair, M.P., and W. R. Spencer. 8m. 4to. Lond., 1811.   C 10 U 9

DEVRIENT (EDUARD). My Recollections of Felix Mendelssohn-Bartholdy, and his Letters to me; translated from the German, by Natalia Macfarren. 8vo. Lond., 1869.   C 5 P 21

DE VRIES (DR. M.) Middelnederlandsch Woordenboek. A-ANXT. Imp.8vo. 'sGravenhage, 1864-65.   C 16 R 32

DE WALDECK (F.) [*See* WALDECK, F. DE.]

DE WALL (H. VON). Lijst van eenige in 't maleisch gebruikelijke Woorden van Sanskrit Oorsprong. 8vo. Batavia, 1866.   K 14 Q 29

DEWAR (A.) [*See* FRASER, T. R.]

DEWAR (REV. DR. DANIEL). Dictionary of the Gaelic Language. [*See* MACLEOD, REV. DR. N.]

D'EWES (J.) China, Australia, and the Pacific Islands, in the years 1855-56. 8vo. Lond., 1857.*   MD 1 W 19
Sporting in both Hemispheres. 8vo. Lond., 1858.   MD 1 Q 12

DE WESEHAM (ROGER). [*See* WESEHAM, ROGER DE.]

DEWEY (PROF. MELVIL), M.A. Classification and Subject Index for Cataloguing and arranging the Books and Pamphlets of a Library. Roy. 8vo. Amherst, Mass., 1876.   J 9 V 20
Decimal Classification and Relative Index, for Arranging, Cataloguing, and Indexing Public and Private Libraries. 2nd ed. Roy. 8vo. Boston, 1885.   J 9 V 21

DE WITT (JOHN). History of the Administration of John de Witt; by James Geddes. Vol. 1. 1623-54. 8vo. Lond., 1879.   C 10 T 24
John de Witt, Grand Pensionary of Holland; or, Twenty Years of a Parliamentary Republic; by M. Antonin Lefèvre Pontalis; translated by S. E. and A. Stephenson. 2 vols. 8vo. Lond., 1885.   C 10 T 26, 27

DEXIPPUS. [*See* BYZANTINÆ SCRIPT. HIST.]

DEXTER (FLAVIUS LUCIUS). Opera omnia. [*See* MIGNE, J. P., SERIES LATINA, 31.]

DEXTER (HENRY MARTYN). Congregationalism of the last Three Hundred Years. Roy.8vo. Lond., 1880.   G 13 V 29

DEXTER (J. F.) Hints to Dickens Collectors. [*See* DICKENS, C.]   K 9 P 4

DHARMARAKSHA. Life of Buddha. [*See* MÜLLER, PROF. F. M.]

DHARMATRÂTA. Udânavarga: Verses from the Buddhist Canon. [*See* ROCKHILL, W. W.]

D'HAUSSONVILLE (VICOMTE OTHENIN). [*See* HAUSSONVILLE, COMTE OTHENIN D'.]

D'HERBELOT (BARTHELEMI). Bibliothèque Orientale; ou, Dictionnaire Universel. 4 vols. 4to. La Haye, 1777-79.   C 11 V 9-12

DIANISKA (KASPAR). Theoretisch praktische Grammatik, zur schnellen Erlernung der slowakischen Sprache für Deutsche. 12mo. Wien, 1850.   K 16 P 9

DIARMUID AND GRAINNE. The Pursuit of; published for the Society for the Preservation of the Irish Language. 2 vols. 12mo. Dublin, 1880-81.   J 7 Q 26, 27

DIARY OF TRAVELS. Diary of Travels in Three Quarters of the Globe; by "An Australian Settler." 2 vols. 8vo. Lond., 1856.   MD 1 W 28, 29

DIAZ DEL CASTILLO (BERNAL), CONQUISTADOR. Memoirs of, written by himself; translated from the original Spanish, by John Ingram Lockhart, F.R.A.S. 2 vols. 8vo. Lond., 1844.   C 6 T 12, 13

DIBDIN (CHARLES). Songs of; with a Memoir; collected and arranged by Thomas Dibdin; with Sketches by Cruikshank. 3rd ed. 12mo. Lond., 1872.   H 6 R 2

DIBDIN (THOMAS). The Birth-day: a Comedy. [*See* FARCES, 2.]

The Cabinet: a Comic Opera. (Cumberland's Eng.Theatre.) 12mo. Lond., 1829.   H 2 Q 15

The Deserter: a Farce. [*See* FARCES, 2.]

Don Giovanni; or, a Spectre on Horseback: a Comic, Heroic, Operatic, Tragic, Pantomimic, Bulletta-Spectacular-Extravaganza. (Cumberland's Eng. Theatre.) 12mo. Lond., 1829.   H 2 Q 14

The Heart of Mid-Lothian : a Melodramatic Romance. (Cumberland's Eng. Theatre.) 12mo. Lond., 1829.   H 2 Q 21

Ivanhoe; or, the Jew's Daughter: a Romantic Melodrama. (Cumberland's Eng. Theatre.) 12mo. Lond., 1829.   H 2 Q 23

The Jew and the Doctor: a Farce. [*See* FARCES, 2.]

Paul Jones: a Melodramatic Romance. (Cumberland's Eng. Theatre.) 12mo. Lond., 1829.   H 2 Q 19

The Quaker: a Comic Opera. [*See* FARCES, 4.]

Reminiscences of. 2 vols. 8vo. Lond., 1827. C 6 S 19, 20

The School for Prejudice: a Comedy. [*See* MOD. THEATRE, 4.]

Suil Dhuv, the Coiner: a Melodramatic Romance. (Cumberland's Eng. Theatre.) 12mo. Lond., 1829. H 2 Q 21

The Waterman : a Ballad Opera. [*See* FARCES, 7.]

DIBDIN (REV. THOMAS FROGNALL), F.R.S., &c. Ædes Althorpianæ; or, an Account of the Mansion, Books, and Pictures at Althorp. 2 vols. imp. 4to. Lond., 1822.   K 5 P 4, 5 †

Bibliographical, Antiquarian, and Picturesque Tour in the Northern Counties of England, and in Scotland. 2 vols. roy. 8vo. Lond., 1838.   D 7 V 24, 25

Bibliographical, Antiquarian, and Picturesque Tour in France and Germany. 3 vols. roy. 8vo. Lond., 1821.   D 6 V 19–21

Bibliomania; or, Book-madness; containing some Account of the History, Symptoms, and Cure of the Fatal Disease. Roy. 8vo. Lond., 1842.   J 15 V 21

Bibliomania; or, Book-madness: a Bibliographical Romance. Illustrated. Roy. 8vo. Lond., 1842.   J 15 V 21

Bibliotheca Spenceriana; or, a Descriptive Catalogue of the Books printed in the 15th Century. 4 vols. imp. 8vo. Lond., 1814–15.   K 9 P 20–23 †

DIBDIN (REV. THOMAS FROGNALL), F.R.S., &c.—*contd.*
Descriptive Catalogue of the Books printed in the 15th Century, lately forming part of the Library of the Duke di Cassano Serra, and now the property of George, Earl Spencer, K.G. Imp. 8vo. Lond., 1823.   K 8 Q 25

Introduction to the knowledge of rare and valuable Editions of the Greek and Latin Classics. 4th ed. 2 vols. imp. 8vo. Lond., 1827.   J 2 U 13, 14

Library Companion. 8vo. Lond., 1824.   J 5 S 17

Reminiscences of a Literary Life. 2 vols. 8vo. Lond., 1836.   C 10 U 19, 20

DICÆARCHUS. [*See* SANCHONIATHO.]

DI CESNOLA (GEN. L. P.) [*See* CESNOLA, GEN. L. P. DI.]

DICEY (A. V.), B.C.L. England's Case against Home Rule. 8vo. Lond., 1886.   F 6 S 21

Lectures introductory to the Study of the Law of the Constitution. 8vo. Lond., 1885.   F 9 R 1

DICEY (EDWARD). Battle-fields of 1866. 8vo. Lond., 1866.   B 9 Q 25

DICK (THOMAS), LL.D. Celestial Scenery; or, the Wonders of the Planetary System displayed, illustrating the Perfections of the Deity, and a Plurality of Worlds. 8vo. Lond., 1871.   A 3 S 33

Essay on the Sin and Evils of Covetousness. 8vo. New York, 1836.   G 13 U 3

On the Improvement of Society by the Diffusion of Knowledge. 8vo. Edinb., 1833.   G 13 U 2

On the Mental Illumination and Moral Improvement of Mankind. 12mo. Glasgow, 1835.   G 17 P 18

Philosophy of Religion ; or, an Illustration of the Moral Laws of the Universe. 2nd ed. 12mo. Glasgow, 1830.   G 13 U 1

DICKENS (CHARLES). Anecdote Life of. [*See* TIMBS, J.]
[A Biography]; by A. W. Ward. (Eng. Men of Letts.) 8vo. Lond., 1882.   C 1 U 13

American Notes for General Circulation. 2 vols. 8vo. Lond., 1842.   D 3 Q 40, 41

Bibliography of. [*See* SHEPHERD, R. H.]

Charles Dickens, as I knew him. [*See* DOLBY, G.]

Childhood and Youth of; with Retrospective Notes, and Elucidations from his Books and Letters, by Robert Langton. 8vo. Manchester, 1883.   C 2 T 24

Dickens Memento; with Introduction by Francis Phillimore, and "Hints to Dickens Collectors," by John F. Dexter. 4to. Lond., 1885.   K 9 P 4 †

Dickensiana : a Bibliography. [*See* KITTON, F. G.]

[Essay on the Genius and Character of]; by George Augustus Sala. 12mo. Lond., 1870.   C 2 T 26

Humour and Pathos of; with Illustrations of his Mastery of the Terrible and the Picturesque, selected by Charles Kent. 8vo. Lond., 1884,   J 9 U 13

DICKENS (CHARLES).—*continued.*

Legends and Lyrics of Adelaide Anne Proctor; with an Introduction. [*See* PROCTOR, A. A.]

Letters of, 1833–70; edited by his Sister-in-law and his eldest Daughter [Mamie Dickens and Georgina Hogarth]. 3 vols. 8vo. Lond., 1880–82. C 6 P 10–12

Life and Writings of; by Phebe A. Hanaford. 8vo. Boston, 1882. C 2 T 22

Life of Charles James Mathews. [*See* MATHEWS, C. J.]

Life of; by John Forster. 11th ed. 3 vols. 8vo. Lond., 1872–76. C 6 P 7–9

Memoirs of Joseph Grimaldi; edited by "Boz," with Illustrations by George Cruikshank. 2 vols. 12mo. Lond., 1838. C 2 P 20, 21

Another copy. 8vo. Lond., 1853. C 2 R 17

Pen Photographs of Charles Dickens' Readings, taken from Life; by Kate Field. Illustrated. 8vo. Lond., 1871. C 2 T 23

The Pic Nic Papers, by various hands; edited by Charles Dickens. 2 vols. 8vo. Philad., 1841. J I U 20, 21

Pictures from Italy. 12mo. Lond., 1846. D 7 P 29

Posthumous Papers of the Pickwick Club. 2 vols. 8vo. Lond., 1836. J 3 R 17, 18

Plays and Poems of Charles Dickens; with a few Miscellanies in Prose. Now first collected, edited, prefaced, and annotated, by Richard Herne Shepherd. 2 vols. 8vo. Lond., 1882. H 2 8 7, 8

Another copy. 2 vols. 8vo. Lond., 1885. H 2 8 9, 10

Sketches by "Boz", illustrative of Every-day Life and Every-day People. 2 vols. 8vo. Lond., 1836. J 8 R 1, 2

Another copy. 8vo. Lond., 1836. J 8 R 3

Sunday under three Heads: as it is; as Sabbath Bills would make it; as it might be made; by "Timothy Sparks." 12mo. Lond., 1836. J 1 W 37

Twenty Scenes from the Works of. [*See* COVENY, C. J.]

Uncommercial Traveller. 2nd ed. 8vo. Lond., 1841. J 8 R 4

The Village Coquettes: a Comic Opera, in two Acts. 8vo Lond., 1836. H 2 8 11

Works of. 30 vols. 8vo. Lond., 1874–76. J 3 P1 Q 8

1. American Notes for General Circulation; and Pictures from Italy.

2, 3. Barnaby Rudge; and Hard Times.

4, 5. Bleak House.

6. Child's History of England.

7. Christmas Books—[A Christmas Carol The Chimes - The Cricket on the Hearth The Battle of Life The Haunted Man, and the Ghost's Bargain.]

8. [Mystery of Edwin Drood Master Humphrey's Clock.—Hunted Down Holiday Romance - George Silverman's Explanation.]

9, 10. David Copperfield.

11, 12. Dombey and Son.

13. Great Expectations.

14, 15. Little Dorrit.

16. Uncommercial Traveller.

17. Tale of Two Cities.

DICKENS (CHARLES).—*continued.*

18. [Christmas Stories—The Seven Poor Travellers—The Holly Tree—The Wreck of the *Golden Mary*—The Perils of certain English Prisoners—Going into Society—The Haunted House—A Message from the Sea—Tom Tiddler's Ground—Somebody's Luggage—Mrs. Lirriper's Lodgings—Mrs. Lirriper's Legacy.—Doctor Marigold—Two Ghost Stories—Mugby Junction—No Thoroughfare.]

19, 20. Life and Adventures of Nicholas Nickleby.

21, 22. Old Curiosity Shop, and Reprinted Pieces—[The Long Voyage—The Begging-letter Writer—A Child's Dream of a Star—Our English Watering-place—Our French Watering-place—Bill-sticking—"Births: Mrs. Meek, of a Son"—Lying Awake—The Poor Relation's Story—The Child's Story—The Schoolboy's Story—Nobody's Story—The Ghost of Art—Out of Town—Out of the Season—A Poor Man's Tale of a Patent—The Noble Savage—A Flight—The Detective Police—Three "Detective" Anecdotes—On Duty with Inspector Field—Down with the Tide—A Walk in a Workhouse—Prince Bull: a Fairy Tale—A Plated Article—Our Honourable Friend—Our School—Our Vestry—Our Bore—A Monument of French Folly—A Christmas Tree.]

23. Adventures of Oliver Twist.

24, 25. Our Mutual Friend.

26, 27. Posthumous Papers of the Pickwick Club.

28. Sketches by " Boz."

29, 30. Life and Adventures of Martin Chuzzlewit.

Another copy. 20 vols. 8vo. Lond., 1865–85. J 3 Q 9–R 6 [*See* OVERS, J.]

DICKENS (MAMIE). Letters of Charles Dickens. [*See* DICKENS, C.] C 6 P 10–12

DICKER (THOMAS). Dicker's Mining Record, and Guide to the Gold Mines of Victoria; showing the Bearings, Depths, Thicknesses, Dips, and Underlies of the Auriferous Lodes; the Progress and Cost of Works in Operation. 10 vols. fol. Sandhurst, &c., 1862–67. ME9Q14–23†

DICKINSON (JAMES). The Wreath: a Gardener's Manual, arranged for the Climate of Tasmania; edited by John Morgan. 8vo. Hobart, 1855. M A 1 V 19

DICKINSON (SIR JOHN NODES), KNT. Letter to the Hon. Speaker of the Legislative Council, on the Formation of a Second Chamber in the Legislature of New South Wales. 8vo. Sydney, 1852. M F 1 Q 3

Another copy. M J 2 Q 9

Another copy. M F 3 P 2

Letter to the Lord Chancellor on Law Consolidation. (Pam. Dd.) 8vo. Lond., 1861. F 12 P 22

DICKINSON (REGINALD). Summary of the Rules and Procedure of Parliaments. 8vo. Lond., 1882. F 9 R 23

DICKSON (BASSETT), JUN. Honi Koki, in two Cantos. Warlock, in two Cantos; and Miscellaneous Pieces. 8vo. Launceston, 1847. M H 1 S 8

DICKSON (M. F.) Scenes on the Shores of the Atlantic. 2 vols. 8vo. Lond., 1845. D 7 R 13, 14

Souvenirs of a Summer in Germany, in 1836. 2 vols. 8vo. Lond., 1837. D 8 P 24, 25

DICKSON (ROBERT), F.S.A. Introduction of the Art of Printing into Scotland. 8vo. Aberdeen, 1885. B 13 Q 3

Who was Scotland's first Printer? Ane Compendious and breue Tractate, in Commendation of Androw Myllar. 8vo. Lond., 1881. C 2 T 33

DICKSON (R. W.) Practical Agriculture ; or, a Complete System of Modern Husbandry. 2 vols. 4to. Lond., 1805. A 2 Q 8, 9 †

DICKSON (WALTER B.) Poultry : their Breeding, Rearing, Diseases, and General Management. New edition, incorporating the Treatise of Bonington Moubray ; with Corrections and large Additions, by Mrs. [J. W.] Loudon. 12mo. Lond., 1871. A 14 P 67

DICKSON (W. E.), M.A. Practical Organ-Building. 1st ed. 8vo. Lond., 1881. A 7 P 13

Practical Organ-Building. 2nd ed., revised, with Additions. (Weale.) 12mo. Lond., 1882. A 17 Q 63

DICKSON (REV. W. P.) [*See* MOMMSEN, T.]

DICTIONARIUM SCOTI-CELTICUM : a Dictionary of the Gaelic Language. 2 vols. 4to. Edinb., 1828. K 14 S 24, 25

DICTIONARY OF ABBREVIATIONS, containing nearly 2,500 Contractions and Signs. 18mo. Lond., 1886. K 11 S 2

DICTIONARY OF DAILY BLUNDERS. 18mo. Lond., 1880. K 11 S 1

DICTIONARY OF MUSICIANS, from the Earliest Ages to the Present Time. 2 vols. 8vo. Lond., 1824. C 11 Q 5, 6

DICTIONARY OF THE RELIGIOUS CEREMONIES of the Eastern Nations, with Historical and Literary observations. 4to. Calcutta, 1787. K 18 S 5

DICTIONNAIRE (NOUVEAU). Allemand-Français et Français-Allemand. 2 vols. 4to. Strasbourg, 1774. K 16 T 4, 5

DICTIONNAIRE (NOUVEAU). Russe-Français-Allemand. 2 vols. (in 1) 8vo. St. Petersburg, 1813. K 12 S 1

DICTIONNAIRE INFERNAL. [*See* COLLIN DE PLANCY, J. A. S. C. D.] A 10 R 11, 12

DICTYS CRETENSIS, ET DARES PHRYGIUS. De Bello Trojano, ex Editione Samuelis Artopœi, cum Notis et Interpretatione in usum Delphini variis lectionibus, &c., accurate recensito accedunt J. Iscani De Bello Trojano, libri sex. 2 vols. 8vo. Lond., 1825. J 13 Q 7, 8

DIDEROT (DENIS). Œuvres Philosophiques. 6 vols. 8vo. Amsterdam, 1772. J 16 R 1-6

D'IDEVILLE (HENRI), COMTE. Historical and Literary Memoirs and Anecdotes, selected from the Correspondence of Baron de Grimm and Denis Diderot. 4 vols. 8vo. Lond., 1815. C 8 Q 24-27

2 F

D'IDEVILLE (HENRI), COMTE.—*continued.*

Journal d'un Diplomate en Italie ; Notes intimes pour servir à l'Histoire du Second Empire. Turin, 1859-62. 12mo. Paris, 1872. B 8 P 5

Memoirs of Marshal T. R. Bugeaud, from his private Correspondence and original Documents, 1784-1849 ; edited by Charlotte M. Yonge. 2 vols. 8vo. Lond., 1884. C 8 U 11, 12

DIDON (REV. FATHER H.) The Germans ; translated into English by Raphaël Ledos de Beaufort, LL.B. 8vo. Edinb., 1884. D 7 Q 44

DIDOT FRÈRES (FIRMIN). [*See* BIOGRAPHIE GÉNÉRALE NOUVELLE.] C 7 U 1-46

DIDRON (A. N.) Christian Iconography ; or, the History of Christian Art in the Middle Ages. 2 vols. 8vo. Lond., 1886. A 8 P 43, 44

DIDYMUS (ALEXANDRINUS). Opera omnia. [*See* MIGNE, J. P., SERIES GRÆCA, 39.]

DIECK (H.) Rational Bee-keeping. [*See* DZIERZON, DR. J.]

DIEFENBACH (DR. LORENZ). Glossarium Latino-Germanicum Mediæ et Infimæ Ætatis. 4to. Francof., 1857. K 14 R 1

Lexicon Comparativum Linguarum Indogermanicarum. 2 vols. (in 1) 8vo. Frankfurt am Main, 1851. K 14 Q 33

Ueber die jetzigen romanischen Schriftsprachen. 4to. Leipzig, 1831. K 16 U 4

DIEFFENBACH (ERNEST), M.D. New Zealand, and its Native Population. (Pam. 15.) 8vo. Lond., 1841. MJ 2 Q 5

Travels in New Zealand ; with Contributions to the Geography, Geology, Botany, and Natural History of that Country. 2 vols. 8vo. Lond., 1843.* MD 5 U 32, 33

DIERCKS (GUSTAV). Das moderne Geistesleben Spaniens : ein Beitrag zur Kenntniss der gegenwärtigen Kulturzustände dieses Landes. 8vo. Leipzig, 1883. G 10 T 18

DIETERICH (DR. UDO WALDEMAR). Runen-Sprach-Schatz. Oder Wörterbuch über die ältesten Sprachdenkmale Skandinaviens, in Beziehung auf Abstammung und Begriffsbildung. 8vo. Stockholm, 1844. K 13 Q 7

DIETZ (E.) [*See* DE KONINCK, DR. L. L.]

DIEZ (FRIEDRICH). Etymological Dictionary of the Romance Languages ; chiefly from the German of Friedrich Diez, by T. C. Donkin. 8vo. Lond., 1864. K 13 Q 39

Etymologisches Wörterbuch der romanischen Sprachen. Dritte verbesserte und vermehrte Ausgabe. 3e Auflage. 2 vols. 8vo. Bonn, 1869-70. K 13 S 26, 27

Grammaire des Langues Romanes ; traduit par A. Brachet, A. Morel-Fatio, et G. Paris. 3e éd., refondue et augmentée. 3 vols. 8vo. Paris, 1874-76. K 12 T 3-5

DIEZ (FRIEDRICH).—*continued.*
Introduction to the Grammar of the Romance Languages; translated by C. B. Cayley, B.A. 8vo. Lond., 1863.
K 13 Q 38

Grammatik der romanischen Sprachen ; [mit] Anhang romanische Wortschöpfung. 4ᵉ Auflage. 4 vols. 8vo. Bonn, 1875-77.
K 13 Q 15–18

Leben und Werke der Troubadours: ein Beitrag zur nähern Kenntniss des Mittelalters. 2ᵉ Auflage. 8vo. Leipzig, 1882.
C 5 S 20

Die Poesie der Troubadours, nach gedruckten und handschriftlichen Werken derselben dargestellt. 2ʳ Auflage. 8vo. Leipzig, 1883.
H 7 T 35

[*See* HAUSCHILD, DR. E. I.]

DIGARD (ANICET). La Réforme en Italie. [*See* CANTU, C.]

DIGBY (SIR KENHELM). Private Memoirs of; written by himself. Now first published from the original MS., with an introductory Memoir [by Sir N. H. Nicolas—containing the suppressed passages]. 8vo. Lond., 1827.
C 6 Q 15

DIGBY (KENELM EDWARD), M.A. Introduction to the History of the Law of Real Property. (Clar. Press.) 8vo. Oxford, 1875.
F 5 T 43

DIGBY (KENELM HENRY). Mores Catholici; or, Ages of Faith. 11 vols. (in 9)8vo. Lond., 1831–42.
G 10 P 1–9

Temple of Memory. 12mo. Lond., 1874.
H 6 R 6

DIGBY (WILLIAM). Famine Campaign in Southern India (Madras and Bombay Presidencies, and Province of Mysore), 1876-78. 2 vols. 8vo. Lond., 1878.
B 10 U 24, 25

Forty Years of Official and Unofficial Life in an Oriental Crown Colony; being the Life of Sir Richard F. Morgan, Knt. 2 vols. 8vo. Madras, 1879.
C 5 V 23, 24

DIGGER'S HAND-BOOK. Truth about California; containing practical Observations from Researches made in the Gold Regions of that Country; by D * * * L. * * *. 8vo. Sydney, 1849.
MD 3 Q 10

DIGGLES (SILVESTER). Companion to Gould's Hand-book; or, Synopsis of the Birds of Australia; containing nearly one-third of the whole, or about 220 Examples, for the most part from the original Drawings. 2 vols. imp. 4to. Brisbane, 1877.
MA 1 R 14, 15 ‡

Ornithology of Australia. 4to. Brisbane, 1866.
MA 1 R 13 ‡

DIGWELL (DANIEL). [*See* EVANS, G. C.]

DILKE (LADY). [*See* PATTISON, MRS. M.]

DILKE (MRS. ASHTON). Women's Suffrage; with Introduction; by Wm. Woodall, M.P. 8vo. Lond., 1885.
F 6 Q 16

DILKE (CHARLES WENTWORTH). Papers of a Critic, selected from the Writings of the late Charles Wentworth Dilke; with a Biographical Sketch by his grandson, Sir Charles Wentworth Dilke, Bart., M.P. 2 vols. 8vo. Lond., 1875.
J 7 S 6, 7

DILKE (SIR CHARLES WENTWORTH), BART. Biographical Sketch of Charles Wentworth Dilke. [*See* DILKE, C. W.]

Greater Britain : a Record of Travel in English-speaking Countries, during 1866–67. Illustrated. 6th ed. 8vo. Lond., 1872.
MD 4 T 6

Another copy. 8th ed. 8vo. Lond., 1885.
MD 4 T 7

DILLER (J. S.) [*See* ARCHÆOLOGICAL INSTITUTE OF AMERICA.]

DILLINGHAM (DR. WILLIAM) AND SHUCKBURGH (EVELYN S.) Laurence Chaderton, D.D. (First Master of Emmanuel) ; translated from a Latin Memoir of Dr. William Dillingham, with Notes and Illustrations, [and] Richard Farmer, DD. (Master of Emmanuel, 1775–97), an Essay. 8vo. Camb., 1884.
C 6 P 13

DILLIS (GEORG VON). Verzeichniss der Gemälde in der königlich bayerischen Gallerie zu Schleissheim. Verfasst im Jahre, 1830. 8vo. München, 1831.
A 7 Q 21

DILLMANN (PROF. CHR. FR. AUGUST), DR. PHIL. Grammatik der Aethiopischen Sprache. 8vo. Leipzig, 1857.
K 13 R 2

Lexicon Linguae Aethiopicae cum Indice Latino. Adiectum est vocabularium TigreDialectiSeptentrionalis compilatum a Werner Munzinger. 4to. Lipsiæ, 1865.
K 4 S 6 †

Über die Anfänge des Axumitischen Reiches. 4to. Berlin, 1879.
B 16 Q 16 ‡

DILLON (REV. G. F.) Ireland—what she has done for Religion and Civilization : a Lecture. 8vo. Sydney, 1870.
MC 2 Q 1

DILLON (HON. H. A.) Costume in England. [*See* FAIRHOLT, F. W.]

DILLON (JOHN). Decision of the three Judges of the Supreme Court of New South Wales, on the applicability of the Marriage Act of England to this Colony; published by "A Solicitor of the Court." 8vo. Sydney,1836.
MF 1 Q 4

Another copy.
MF 3 P 2

DILLON (JOHN F.) Inns of Court and Westminster Hall: an Address. 8vo. Des Moines, 1878.
MF 1 Q 4

DILLON (CHEVALIER CAPT. P.) Narrative and Successful Result of a Voyage in the South Seas, to ascertain the actual fate of La Pérouse's Expedition. 2 vols. 8vo. Lond., 1829 *
MD 6 Q 14, 15

DILLON (RT. HON. WENTWORTH), EARL OF ROSCOMMON. [*See* ROSCOMMON, RT. HON. W., EARL OF.]

DIMBLEBY (J. B.) Shorthand Dictionary. 8vo. Lond., 1876.
K 12 P 31

DIMSDALE (THOMAS) BARON, M.D., &c. Observations on Inoculation. [*See* LETTSOM, J. C.]

Present Method of Inoculating for the Small-pox. 6th ed. 8vo. Lond., 1772.
A 12 S 31

Another copy. 7th ed. 8vo. Lond., 1779.
A 12 S 31

DINDORF (G. AND L.) [*See* BYZANTINÆ HISTORIÆ SCRIP-
TORES.]

DINDORF (WILHELM). Æschyli Tragœdiæ. [*See*
ÆSCHYLUS.]
Lexicon Sophocleum: zweiter Artikel, von W. Dindorf.
(Pam. 34.) 8vo. Leipsic, 1871.　　　　J 12 U 26
Poetae Scienici Graeci accedunt Perditarum Fabularum
Fragmenta. Roy. 8vo. Lepsiae, 1830.　　H 7 V 30
[*See* ARISTOPHANES.]

DIODORUS SICULUS. Bibliothecæ Historicæ Libri qui
supersunt e recensione Petri Wesselingii. 11 vols. 8vo.
Biponti, 1793–1807.　　　　　　　B 35 S 1–11
Historical Library of Diodorus, the Sicilian, in fifteen
Books; made English by G. Booth. Fol. Lond., 1700.
　　　　　　　　　　　　　　　　B 16 R 13 ‡

DIOGENES JUNIOR. [*See* COMING EVENTS.]

DIOGENES LAERTIUS. Diogenis Laertii de Vitis,
Dogmatibus, et Apophthegmatibus clarorum Philosophorum Libri x, Græce et Latine. 2 vols. 4to. Amsterdam, 1692.　　　　　　　　　　　G 7 V 8, 9
Life of Plato. [*See* PLATO.]
Lives and Opinions of Eminent Philosophers. Literally
translated by C. D. Yonge, B.A. 8vo. Lond., 1853.
　　　　　　　　　　　　　　　　C 1 S 34
Lives, Opinions, and Remarkable Sayings of the most
famous Ancient Philosophers. 2 vols. 8vo. Lond.,
1688–96.　　　　　　　　　　　C 2 T 27, 28

DION. [*See* LETTERS OF DION.]

DION (A. DE), ET LASVIGNES (L.) Cathedrale de
Bayeux; par M. E. Flachat. 8vo. Paris, 1861. A2U7

DION CASSIUS. History of; abridged by Joannes
Xiphilinus; translated from the Greek, by Francis
Manning. 2 vols. 8vo. Lond., 1704.　B 12 P 32, 33

DIONYSIUS (EXIGUUS). Opera omnia. [*See* MIGNE, J. P.,
SERIES LATINA, 67.]

DIONYSIUS AREOPAGITA (SANCTUS). Opera omnia.
[*See* MIGNE, J. P., SERIES GRÆCA, 3, 4.]

DIONYSIUS HALICARNASSENSIS. Antiquitatum
Romanarum, quæ supersunt Græce et Latine ex recensione A. Kiessling, et V. Prow. Imp. 8vo. Paris,
1886.　　　　　　　　　　　　　B 19 Q 9 ‡
The Roman Antiquities of; translated into English, with
Notes and Dissertations, by Edward Spelman. 4 vols.
4to. Lond., 1758.　　　　　　B 18 Q 13–16 ‡

DIONYSIUS (ST.) PAPAE. Opera Omnia. [*See* MIGNE,
J. P. Series Latina, 5.]

DIOPHANTUS OF ALEXANDRIA. [*See* HEATH, T. L.]

DIOSCORIDES (PEDANIUS). [*See* MEDICORUM GRAE-
CORUM.]

DIRCKS (HENRY), C.E., &c. Discovery of Gold. [*See*
GOLD.]
Life Times, and Scientific Labours of the 2nd Marquis of
Worcester; to which is added, a Reprint of his "Century
of Inventions," 1663, with a Commentary. 8vo. Lond.,
1865.　　　　　　　　　　　　C 8 V 43
Perpetuum Mobile; or, a History of the Search for Self-
motive Power, from the 13th to the 19th Century. 1st
and 2nd series. 2 vols. 8vo. Lond., 1870.　A 11 P 6, 7

DISNEY (J.) Memoirs of Thomas Brand-Hollis. Imp.
4to. Lond., 1808.　　　　　　　　C 23 S 32 ‡

DISPOSAL OF LANDS. Report from the Select Committee on the Disposal of Lands in the British Colonies;
with Minutes of Evidence and Appendix. Fol. Lond.,
1836.　　　　　　　　　　　　MF 1 U 33

DISRAELI (RT. HON. BENJAMIN), EARL OF BEACONSFIELD.
[*See* BEACONSFIELD, EARL OF.]

DISRAELI (ISAAC). Amenities of Literature. 3 vols. 8vo.
Lond., 1841.　　　　　　　　　B 24 T 5–7
Calamities of Authors; including some Inquries respecting
their Moral and Literary Characters. 2 vols. 8vo. Lond.,
1812.　　　　　　　　　　　J 5 R 17, 18
Curiosities of Literature. Illustrated by Bolton Corney.
2nd ed. 8vo. Lond., 1838.　　　　J 5 R 3
Another copy. 9th ed. 6 vols. 12mo. Lond., 1834.
　　　　　　　　　　　　　　　J 5 R 8–13
The Genius of Judaism. 2nd ed. 12mo. Lond., 1833.
　　　　　　　　　　　　　　　G 2 P 19
The Literary Character, illustrated by the History of Men of
Genius, drawn from their own Feelings and Confessions.
3rd ed. 2 vols. 8vo. Lond.　　　　J 5 R 1, 2
Miscellanies of Literature. Roy. 8vo. Lond., 1840. J5R7
Quarrels of Authors. 3 vols. 8vo. Lond., 1814. J 5R14–16

DISTINGUISHED NORTHERNS: Biographia Borealis;
or, Lives of Distinguished Northerns; by Hartley Coleridge. 8vo. Lond., 1833.　　　　　C 10 T 38

DISTINGUISHED PERSONS. Anecdotes of; by Wm.
Seward. 4 vols. 8vo. Lond., 1804.　C 8 U 50–53

DISTINGUISHED SCIENTIFIC MEN. Biographies
of. 8vo. Lond., 1857.　　　　　　C 8 S 37

DITTMAR (WM.) Manual of Qualitative Chemical Analysis.
12mo. Edinb., 1876.　　　　　　A 5 R 31

DIX (WM. GILES). American State and American Statesmen. 8vo. Boston, 1876.　　　　　B 2 P 4

DIXIE (FLORENCE CAROLINE), LADY. In the Land of
Misfortune. Illustrated. 8vo. Lond., 1882.　D 2 Q 17

DIXON (FREDERICK), F.G.S. Geology and Fossils of the
Tertiary and Cretaceous Formations of Sussex. Roy.
4to. Lond., 1850.　　　　　　　A 2 R 15 †

DIXON (CAPT. GEORGE). Voyage round the World, but more particularly to the North-west Coast of America, 1785–88, in the *King George* and *Queen Charlotte*. 4to. Lond., 1789.   D 9 V 22

Another copy.   MD 7 P 32 †

DIXON (H. H.) Saddle and Sirloin ; or, English Farm and Sporting Worthies ; by " The Druid." 12mo. Lond., 1870.   A 29 P 9

DIXON (REV. J.) [*See* KELLY, J. E.]

DIXON (CAPT. JAMES). Narrative of a Voyage to New South Wales and Van Diemen's Land, in the ship *Skelton*, during the year 1820. 12mo. Edinb., 1822.*
                                        MD 3 Q 33

DIXON (JOHN H.) Gairloch in North-west Ross-shire: its Records, Traditions, &c. 8vo. Edinb., 1886.   B 13 R 24

DIXON (RICHARD WATSON), M.A. History of the Church of England, from the Abolition of the Roman Jurisdiction. 3 vols. 8vo. Lond., 1871–85.   G 2 R 23–25

DIXON STREET SOUP KITCHEN. [*See* CITY NIGHT REFUGE.]

DIXON (WILLIAM HEPWORTH). Free Russia. Illustrated. 2 vols. 8vo. Lond., 1870.   D 6 U 13, 14

Her Majesty's Tower. 6th ed. 4 vols. 8vo. Lond., 1870–71.   B 6 Q 15–18

History of two Queens : Catharine of Aragon—Anne Boleyn. 4 vols. 8vo. Lond., 1873–74.   B 6 P 34–37

The Holy Land. Illustrated. 2 vols. 8vo. Lond., 1865.
                                        D 5 T 12, 13

London Prisons ; with an Account of the more distinguished persons who have been confined in them. 12mo. Lond., 1850.   B 3 P 28

New America. Illustrated. 2 vols. 8vo. Lond., 1867.
                                        D 3 S 37, 38

Personal History of Lord Bacon ; from Unpublished Papers. 8vo. Lond., 1861.   C 2 V 16

Royal Windsor. 2nd ed. 4 vols. 8vo. Lond., 1879–80.
                                        B 7 R 4–7

Spiritual Wives. 2 vols. 8vo. Lond., 1868.   G 10 T 19, 20

The Switzers. 2nd ed. 8vo. Lond., 1872.   D 8 T 13

White Conquest. 2 vols. 8vo. Lond., 1876.   D 4 Q 38, 39

William Penn, an Historical Biography ; with an extra chapter on the Macaulay Charges. 8vo. Lond., 1851.
                                        C 4 T 22

DOBELL (SYDNEY THOMPSON). Balder. Part the First. 2nd ed. 8vo. Lond., 1854.   H 7 Q 29

The Poetical Works of ; with Introductory Notice and Memoir, by John Nichol, M.A. 2 vols. 8vo. Lond., 1875.   H 7 R 1,2

Thoughts on Art, Philosophy, and Religion ; with Notes by J. Nichol, M.A., &c. 8vo. Lond., 1876.   J 11 S 13

DOBREE (PETER PAUL). Adversaria. 5 vols. (in 2) 8vo. Lond., 1883.   J 11 R 26, 27

DOBRIZHOFFER (MARTIN). Account of the Abipones, an Equestrian People of Paraguay. 3 vols. 8vo. Lond., 1822.   B 1 Q 5–7

DOBROWSKY (JOSEPH). Institutiones Linguae Slavicae dialecti veteris, quae quum apud Russos, Serbos aliosque Ritus Graeci, tum apud Dalmatas Glagolitas Ritus Latini Slavos in libris sacris obtinet. Editio secunda. Roy. 8vo. Vindob., 1852.   K 15 R 23

Slavin: Beiträge zur Kenntniss der Slawischen Literatur, Sprachkunde und Alterthümer, nach allen Mundarten. 8vo. Prag, 1808.   K 11 U 33

DOBSON (AUSTIN). At the Sign of the Lyre. 12mo. Lond., 1885.   H 6 R 7

Henry Fielding. (Eng. Men of Letts.) 8vo. Lond., 1883.   C 1 U 15

Modern English Illustrated Books. [*See* LANG, A.]

Richard Steele. (Eng. Worthies.) 8vo. Lond., 1886.
                                        C 2 Q 48

Thomas Bewick and his Pupils. Illustrated. Sq. 8vo. Lond., 1884.   C 2 T 5

[*See* GOLDSMITH, O.]

DOBSON (EDWARD), A.M.I.C.E. Foundations and Concrete Works. (Weale.) 12mo. Lond., 1872.   A 17 P 1

Pioneer Engineering : a Treatise on the Engineering Operations connected with the Settlement of Waste Lands in new Counties. With Plates, &c. 8vo. Lond., 1877.   A 6 R 10

Another copy. 2nd ed. (Weale.) 12mo. Lond., 1880.
                                        A 17 Q 45

Rudiments of Masonry and Stone-cutting. (Weale.) 7th ed. 12mo. Lond., 1871.   A 17 P 36

Rudiments of the Art of Building. (Weale.) 12mo. Lond., 1871.   A 17 P 45

Treatise on the Manufacture of Bricks and Tiles, &c. (Weale.) 4th ed. 12mo. Lond., 1868.   A 17 P 36

DOBSON (THOMAS), B.A. Australasian Cyclonology ; or, the Law of Storms in the South Pacific Ocean, and on the Coasts of Australia, Tasmania, New Zealand, &c., 8vo. Hobart, 1883.   MJ 2 Q 18

DOBSON (WILLIAM T.) Historical Legendary Tales. [*See* SCOTT, SIR W.]

DOCHARD (STAFF-SURGEON). Travels in Western Africa. [*See* GRAY, MAJOR W.]

DOD (R. P.) Parliamentary Companion for 1856. 18mo. Lond., 1856.   F 6 T 25

DODD (CHARLES). Church History of England, from the commencement of the 16th Century to the Revolution in 1688 ; with Notes, Additions, and a Continuation, by the Rev. M. A. Tierney, F.S.A. 5 vols. 8vo. Lond., 1839–43.   G 3 Q 14–18

DODD (GEORGE). Food of London. 8vo. Lond., 1856.
                                        F 14 Q 21

DODD (GEORGE).—*continued.*
Pictorial History of the Russian War. [*See* CHAMBERS, W. AND R.]

DODD (STEPHEN). Historical and Topographical Account of the Town of Woburn, its Abbey, and Vicinity. 8vo. Woburn, 1818. D 11 R 13

DODDRIDGE (PHILIP), D.D. Correspondence and Diary of; edited by John Doddridge Humphreys. 5 vols. 8vo. Lond., 1829-31. C 10 T 33-37

Some Remarkable Passages in the Life of the Hon. Col. James Gardiner. 8vo. Edinb., 1807. C 2 P 18

DODGE (COL. RICHARD IRVING), U.S.A. Hunting Grounds of the Great West: a Description of the Plains, Game, and Indians of the Great North American Desert. 8vo. Lond., 1877. D 3 T 40

Our Wild Indians: Thirty-three Years' Personal Experience among the Red Men of the Great West. Illustrated. 8vo. Hartford, 1882. D 3 S 13

DODGE (THEODORE AYRAULT). Patroclus and Penelope: a Chat in the Saddle. 8vo. Edinb., 1885. A 17 W 21

DODGSON (REV. C.) [*See* TERTULLIANUS, Q. S. F.]

DODGSON (C. L.) Euclid and his Modern Rivals. 2nd ed. 12mo. Lond., 1885. A 10 S 18

DODINGTON (GEORGE BUBB), LORD MELCOMBE. Diary of, from March 8, 1749, to Feb. 6, 1761; published from original Manuscripts, by H. P. Wyndham. (Autobiog., 22.) 18mo. Lond., 1828. C 1 P 16

DODRIDGE (SIR JOHN). The History of the Ancient and Modern Estate of the Principality of Wales, Dutchy of Cornewall, and Earldom of Chester. Sm. 4to. Lond., 1630. B 4 R 17

DODSLEY (J.) Collection of Poems, by several Hands. 6 vols. 8vo. Lond., 1765. H 6 U 14-18

DODSLEY (ROBERT). Life and Poems of. [*See* CHALMERS, A.]

Miller of Mansfield: a Dramatic Tale. [*See* BRIT. DRAMA, 5.]

Another copy. [*See* FARCES, 7.]

Select Collection of Old Plays. 12 vols. 8vo. Lond., 1825-27. H 1 R 1-12

DODSWORTH (WILLIAM). Historical Account of the Episcopal See and Cathedral Church of Sarum, or Salisbury. Illustrated. 4to. Salisbury, 1814. B 17 Q 18 ‡

DODWELL (EDWARD), F.S.A. Classical and Topographical Tour through Greece, during the years 1801-6. 2 vols. 4to. Lond., 1819. D 6 V 23, 24

DOEHNER (THEODORE). [*See* PLUTARCH.]

DOERING (F. G.) [*See* CATULLUS, C. V.] J 13 P 24, 25

DOHERTY (—.) Les Beautés de la France. [*See* GIRAULT DE SAINT-FARGEAU, P. A. E.]

DOHME (R.) Early Teutonic and French Masters. [*See* KEANE, PROF. A. H.]

DOLBY (GEORGE). Charles Dickens, as I knew him: the Story of the Reading Tours in Great Britain and America. 8vo. Lond., 1885. C 2 T 21

DOLBY (THOMAS). Shakespearian Dictionary. 8vo. Lond., 1832. K 17 P 23

DOLET (ETIENNE). Etienne Dolet, the Martyr of the Renaissance: a Biography; by Richard Copley Christie. 8vo. Lond., 1880. C 10 T 41

DOLLFUS (AUG.), AND MONT-SERRAT (EUG. DE). Voyage Géologique dans les Républiques de Guatemala et de Salvador. 4to. Paris, 1868. A 23 S 1 ‡

DÖLLINGER (PROF. JOHN J. I. VON). Christenthum und Kirche in der Zeit der Grundlegung. 2e auflage. 8vo. Regensburg, 1868. G 5 T 1

The Gentile and the Jew in the Courts of the Temple of Christ; from the German, by N. Darnell, M.A. 2 vols. 8vo. Lond., 1862. G 3 Q 8, 9

Hippolytus and Callistus; or, the Church of Rome in the first half of the 3rd Century; translated by A. Plummer. 8vo. Edinb., 1876. G 3 T 14

Die Papst-Fabeln des Mittelalters. 8vo. München, 1863. G 10 S 19

Die Universitäten sonst und jetzt. 8vo. München, 1867. G 17 R 25

DOMENECH (ABBÉ EM.) Seven Years' Residence in the Great Deserts of North America. Illustrated. 2 vols. 8vo. Lond., 1860. D 4 Q 41, 42

Voyage pittoresque dans les grands Déserts du nouveau Monde. Roy. 8vo. Paris, 1862. D 3 U 24

DOMENY DE RIENZI (G. L.) [*See* RIENZI, G. L. DOMENY DE.]

DOMESDAY BOOK; illustrated by Robert Kelham. 8vo. Lond., 1788. B 6 Q 12

Domesday Book, seu Liber Censualis, Willelmi Primi Regis Angliæ inter Archivos Regni in Domo capitulari West-monasterii asservatus. 4 vols. fol. Lond., 1783-1816. F 24 Q 1-4 ‡

General Introduction to Domesday Book; by Sir Henry Ellis, K.H., &c. 2 vols. roy. 8vo. Lond., 1833. F 1 S 22, 23

DOMESDAY BOOK (NEW). [*See* LAND-OWNERS.] K 22 S 14-16 ‡

DOMETT (ALFRED). Flotsam and Jetsam: Rhymes, Old and New. Sq. 8vo. Lond., 1877. H 7 R 10

Poems. 8vo. Lond., 1833. H 7 R 9

Ranolf and Amohia: a South Sea Day Dream. 8vo. Lond., 1872. MH 1 R 10

DON (C. J.) [*See* HAMILTON, REV. R.]

DON (GEORGE), F.L.S. General History of Dichlamydeous Plants; comprising complete Descriptions of the different Orders. 4 vols. 4to. Lond., 1831–38.   A 5 Q 17–20
1. Thalamifloræ.   4. Corollifloræ.
2, 3. Calycifloræ.

DONALD (JAMES), F.R.G.S., &c. Chambers' English Dictionary. [*See* CHAMBERS, W. AND R.]

DONALDSON (PROF.) Treatise on Clay Lands and Loamy Soils. (Weale.) 12mo. Lond., 1852.   A 17 P 23

DONALDSON (PROF. JOHN), AND BURN (ROBERT SCOTT). Suburban Farming: a Treatise on the Laying out and Cultivation of Farms adapted to the Produce of Milk, Butter, Cheese, Eggs, Poultry, and Pigs. 2nd ed. (Weale.) 12mo. Lond., 1881.   A 17 Q 50

DONALDSON (REV. JOHN WILLIAM), D.D. Christian Orthodoxy reconciled with the conclusions of Modern Biblical Learning. 8vo. Lond., 1857.   G 10 S 10
History of the Literature of Ancient Greece. [*See* MULLER, C. O.]
The New Cratylus; or, Contributions towards a more accurate knowledge of the Greek Language. 8vo. Camb., 1839.   K 12 U 2
Pindar's Epinician or Triumphal Odes. [*See* PINDARUS.]
Theatre of the Greeks: a Series of Papers relating to the History and Criticism of the Greek Drama. 4th ed. 8vo. Camb., 1836.   J 7 T 13
Varronianus : a Critical and Historical Introduction to the Philological Study of the Latin Language. 8vo. Lond., 1844.   K 12 U 1

DONALDSON (JOSEPH). Recollections of the Eventful Life of a Soldier. 12mo. Lond., 1856.   C 1 Q 33

DONALDSON (THOMAS). The Public Domain, its History, with Statistics. Roy. 8vo. Washington, 1884.   F 3 T 3

DONALDSON (T. L.) Questions on Subjects of Architecture. [*See* ROY. INST. BRIT. ARCH.]

DONATELLO ; or, Donato Di Betto Bardo. [*See* BAXTER, Miss LUCY E.]

DON CARLOS. The Career of. [*See* CARLOS.]

DONCOURT (A. S. DE). [*See* DROHOJOWSKA, A. J. F. A., COMTESSE.]

DONICK. [*See* EAGLE GULCH.]

DONISTHORPE (WORDSWORTH). Principles of Plutology. 8vo. Lond., 1876.   K 6 V 23

DONKIN (T. C.), B.A. Etymological Dictionary of the Romance Languages. [*See* DIEZ, F.]

DONKIN (W. F.), M.A. Acoustics. Part I.—Theoretical. (Clar. Press, 13.) 8vo. Oxford, 1870.   A 17 T 48

DONNAN (G. R.) Annotated Code of Criminal Procedure and Penal Code of the State of New York, as amended, 1882–85. 8vo. Albany, N.Y., 1885.   F1T8
Annotated Penal Code of New York. 8vo. Albany, N.Y., 1885.   F 1 T 9

DONNE (DR. JOHN). Life of ; by Izaak Walton. 12mo. Lond., 1825.   C 1 S 19
Another copy. 8vo. Lond., 1884.   C 2 R 34
Life and Poems of. [*See* CHALMERS, A.]

DONNEGAN (JAMES). New Greek and English Lexicon. 3rd ed. Roy. 8vo. Lond., 1837.   K 13 R 10

DONNISON (H.) The Brisbane Water Cases; being a Narrative of the Trials of Mr. Bean, Mr. Donnison, and Mr. Moore, and of their respective actions against Capt. Faunce ; by "One of the Party." 8vo. Sydney, 1838.   M F 3 P 4

DONOUGHMORE (RICHARD HELY), EARL OF. Substance of the Speech of, on the 21st of April, 1812, upon his Motion for taking into consideration the Roman Catholic Petitions. (Paris.) 8vo. Lond., 1812.   G 2 P 28

DONOVAN (E.) The Naturalists' Repository ; or, Miscellany of Exotic Natural History. 5 vols. roy. 8vo Lond., 1834.   A 13 U 32–36

DONOVAN (M.) Domestic Economy. (Lard. Cab. Cyclo.) 2 vols. 12mo. Lond., 1830–37.   K 18 47–48
Treatise on Chemistry. (Lard. Cab. Cyclo.) 12mo. Lond., 1834.   K 1 U 25

DOPPING (W.) [*See* PARLIAMENTARY LIBRARY, VICTORIA.]   M K I R 14

DORAN (DR. JOHN), F.S.A. History of Court Fools. 8vo. Lond., 1858.   B 14 R 34
In and about Drury Lane, and other Papers. Reprinted from the pages of the *Temple Bar* Magazine. 2 vols. 8vo. Lond., 1881.   C 16 R 2, 3
Knights and their Days. 8vo. Lond., 1856.   C 3 P 18
A Lady of the Last Century (Mrs. Elizabeth Montagu), illustrated in her unpublished Letters. 8vo. Lond., 1873.   C 10 Q 33
Lives of the Queens of England of the House of Hanover. 2 vols. 8vo. Lond., 1855.   C 4 U 25, 26
Memoir of Queen Adelaide, Consort of King William IV. 8vo. Lond., 1861.   C 5 Q 1
Monarchs retired from Business. 2 vols. 8vo. Lond., 1857.   B 7 S 45, 46
New Pictures and Old Panels. 8vo. Lond., 1859.   J 12 P 24
Table Traits, with something on them. 2nd ed. 8vo. Lond., 1854.   J 12 P 23
"Their Majesties' Servants": Annals of the English Stage, from Thomas Betterton to Edmund Kean. Actors, Authors, Audiences. 2 vols. 8vo. Lond., 1864.   C 10 U 33, 34

DORE (J. R.) Old Bibles ; or, an Account of the various Versions of the English Bible. 8vo. Lond., 1876.   G 10 Q 18

DORÉ (PAUL GUSTAVE). Adventures of Baron Munchausen illustrated. [*See* RASPE, R. E.]

Days of Chivalry illustrated. [*See* L'EPINE, E.]

Life and Reminiscences of Gustave Doré; compiled from Material supplied by Doré's Relations and Friends, and from Personal Recollection, by Blanche Roosevelt. 8vo. Lond., 1885. C 10 T 39

[*See* BIBLES AND TESTAMENTS; DANTE ALIGHIERI; *and* DAVILLIER, BARON C.]

DORÉ (PAUL GUSTAVE), AND JERROLD (BLANCHARD.) London; a Pilgrimage. Imp. 4to. Lond., 1872. D 4 P 8 ‡

D'ORLEANS (F. J.) History of the Revolutions in England under the Family of the Stuarts, from 1603 to 1690; translated from the French Original, by Laurence Echard. 2nd ed. 8vo. Lond., 1722. B 3 R 21

DORMAN (RUSHTON M.) Origin of Primitive Superstitions, and their Development into the Worship of Spirits and the Doctrine of Spiritual Agency among the Aborigines of America. Illustrated. 8vo. Philad., 1881. G 10 S 17

DORNER (DR. J. A.) Geschichte der protestantischen Theologie besonders in Deutschland. (Gesch. der Wissen.) 8vo. München, 1867. A 17 V 19

DORSET (CHARLES SACKVILLE), EARL OF. Life and Poems of. [*See* JOHNSON, DR. S., *and* CHALMERS, A.]

D'ORSEY (REV. ALEXANDER J. D.), B.D. Colloquial Portuguese; or, the Words and Phrases of Every-day Life. 3rd ed. 8vo. Lond., 1868. K 11 U 41

Practical Grammar of Portuguese and English. 3rd ed. 8vo. Lond., 1868. K 11 U 42

DOSABHAI FRAMJI KARAKA. [*See* FRAMJI KARAKA, D.]

DOUBLIER (L.) Geschichte des Altertums. Roy. 8vo. Wien, 1874. B 15 P 40

DOUCE (FRANCIS). Holbien's Dance of Death. [*See* HOLBEIN, H.]

Illustrations of Shakspeare and of Ancient Manners. 8vo. Lond., 1839. J 2 T 22

DOUGAL (F. H.) & CO. Index Register to Next of Kin, Heirs at Law, Legatees, &c., who have been advertised for, or are entitled to vast Sums of Money and Property in Great Britain and the Colonies, since 1698. 5th ed. 8vo. Lond., 1880. K 10 S 11

DOUGLAS (ARCHIBALD JAMES EDWARD), FIRST BARON. Memorial for George James, Duke of Hamilton, &c., against the person pretending to be the Archibald Stewart, *alias* Douglas, to which are annexed Sequel to the Memorial and Appendix. 4to. (n.d.), 1767. F 5 V 22

DOUGLAS (DAVID), F.L.S. Extracts from a Private Letter addressed to Captain Sabine, R.A., &c., [on Volcanoes in the Sandwich Islands.] 8vo. Lond., 1834. MD 7 Q 50

DOUGLAS (GAWIN, OR GAVIN), BISHOP OF DUNKELD. Poetical Works of Gavin Douglas, Bishop of Dunkeld; with a Memoir, Notices, and Glossary, by John Small, M.A., &c. 4 vols. 8vo. Edinb., 1874. H 7 R 5-8

Virgil's Æneis, translated into Scottish Verse. Fol. Edinb., 1710. H 3 P 26 †

DOUGLAS (JAMES). Advancement of Society in Knowledge and Religion. 2nd ed. 8vo. Edinb., 1828. G 9 T 19

On the Philosophy of the Mind. 8vo. Edinb., 1839. G 10 T 17

DOUGLAS (JOHN CHRISTIE). Manual of Telegraph Construction. 8vo. Lond., 1875. A 5 P 52

DOUGLAS (SIR ROBERT). Peerage of Scotland. Fol. Edinb., 1768. K 22 S 1 ‡

DOUGLAS (ROBERT K.) China; with Map. 8vo. Lond., 1882. D 6 P 26

DOUGLAS (MRS. STAIR). Life, and Selections from the Correspondence of William Whewell, D.D. 8vo. Lond., 1881. C 9 R 46

DOUGLAS (WILLIAM SCOTT). [*See* LOCKHART, J. G.]

DOUGLAS AND ANGUS (House of). History of the House and Race of Douglas and Angus. 8vo. Glasgow, (n.d.) B 13 P 22

DOUGLAS-OGILBY (J.) [*See* OGILBY, J. DOUGLAS-]

DOUGLASS (ARTHUR). Ostrich Farming in South Africa. 8vo. Lond., 1881. A 1 Q 24

DOUSE (T. LE MARCHANT). Grimm's Law, a Study; or, Hints towards an Explanation of the so-called "Lautverschiebung." 8vo. Lond., 1876. K 13 P 35

DOUTHWAITE (WILLIAM RALPH). Gray's Inn; its History and Associations. 8vo. Lond., 1886. B 5 U 24

DOUVILLE (PROF. J. V.) French Grammar for the use of English Students. 2 vols. 8vo. Lond., 1824. K 15 Q 8, 9

DOVE (ALFRED). Life of Humboldt. [*See* LÖWENBURG, J.]

DOVE (H. PERCY). New and Complete Wharf, Street, and Building Plan Directory of the City of Sydney. Ob. 4to. Sydney, 1880. MD 5 Q 8 ‡

Plans of Sydney; scale, 40 feet to 1 inch. At fol. Sydney, 1880.* MD 5 Q 6 ‡

DOVER (GEORGE JAMES WELBORE AGAR ELLIS) LORD. Letters of Horace Walpole. [*See* WALPOLE, H.]

Letters written during the years 1686-88, addressed to John Ellis, Esq. 2 vols. 8vo. Lond., 1831. B 23 T 3, 4

Life of Frederic II, King of Prussia. 2 vols. 8vo. Lond., 1832. C 6 U 14, 51

DOW (John Lamont). [*See* Victoria.]

DOWDEN (Prof. Edward), LL.D. Correspondence of Robert Southey with Caroline Bowles. [*See* Southey, R.]

English Critics on Walt Whitman. [*See* Bucke, R. M.]

Life of Percy Bysshe Shelley. 2 vols. 8vo. Lond., 1886.   C 10 Q 42, 43

Shakspere: a Critical Study of his Mind and Art. 8vo. Lond., 1875.   C 16 R 1

Sonnets of Shakespeare. [*See* Shakespeare, W.]

Southey. (Eng. Men of Letts.) 8vo. Lond., 1879.   C 1 U 31

DOWDESWELL (G. M.) Compendium of Mercantile Law. [*See* Smith, J. W.]

DOWELL (Stephen). History of Taxation and Taxes in England. 4 vols. 8vo. Lond., 1884.   F 9 R 2–5

DOWER (John). [Map of] the Battlefields of Northern Italy. 4to. Lond., 1859.   D 33 Q 16 ‡

DOWIE (Rev. John Alexander). The Drama, the Press, and the Pulpit. 8vo. Sydney, 1879.   MG 1 Q 35

DOWLING (James P.) Dairying in Australasia. 8vo. Sydney, 1888.   MA 1 P 43

DOWN (Richard). Stray Thoughts; being a Collection of Poems composed in Leisure Hours. 12mo. Melb., 1871.   MH 1 P 29

DOWNIE (Thomas). Iron and Metal Trades' Companion. 12mo. Lond., 1877.   A 25 P 27

DOWNING (A. J.) Fruits and Fruit Trees of America; by Charles Downing; with Note on Californian Fruits. 8vo. New York, 1870.   A 1 S 35

Treatise on the Theory and Practice of Landscape Gardening; by Henry Winthrop Sargent. 8vo. New York, 1859.   A 1 S 12

DOWNING (Robert). Gazetteer of New South Wales. [*See* Sherriff, J.]

DOWNING (Samuel), LL.D. Elements of Practical Construction. Part I. 8vo. Lond., 1875.   A 6 T 23

Plates [to the above]. Roy. fol. Lond., 1875.   A 20 P 26 ‡

DOWSE (Thomas Stretch), M.D. On Brain and Nerve Exhaustion: "Neurasthenia"; its Nature and Curative Treatment. 8vo. Lond., 1880.   A 12 R 20

DOWSON (Alfred C.) Bordighera and the Western Riviera. [*See* Hamilton, F. F.]

DOWSON (Prof. John), M.R.A.S. Classical Dictionary of Hindu Mythology and Religion, Geography, History, and Literature. 8vo. Lond., 1879.   K 15 P 9

Grammar of the Urdu; or, Hindústání Language. 8vo. Lond., 1872.   K 11 U 48

Hindústání Exercise Book. 8vo. Lond., 1872.   K 11 U 49

History of India. [*See* Elliott, Sir H. M.]

DOXAT (Henry). The Lunar Almanac, 1862–63. Sm. 4to. Lond., 1863.   E

DOYLE (C. A.) Curling. [*See* Taylor, J.]

DOYLE (Sir Francis Hastings). Reminiscences and Opinions of, 1813–85. 5th ed. 8vo. Lond., 1886.   C 8 R 4

DOYLE (Henry). Illustrated History of Ireland. [*See* Cusack, Mrs. Mary Frances.]

DOYLE (Rt. Rev. James), Bishop of Kildare. Life, Times, and Correspondence of; by W. J. Fitz-Patrick, LL.D. New ed. 2 vols. 8vo. Dublin, 1880.   C 2 S 11, 12

DOYLE (James E.) Official Baronage of England, 1066–1885. 3 vols. sm. 4to. Lond., 1886.   K 10 T 6–8

Chronicle of England, B.C. 55–A.D. 1485. 4to. Lond., 1864.   B 2 T 23

DOYLE (John A.) English in America: The Puritans. 2 vols. 8vo. Lond., 1887.   B 1 U 12, 13

English in America: Virginia, Maryland, and the Carolinas. 8vo. Lond., 1882.   B 1 S 18

History of America. 12mo. Lond., 1875.   B 1 Q 36

DOYLE (Martin). Extracts from the Letters and Journals of George Fletcher Moore. [*See* Moore, G. F.]

DOYLE (Richard). Bird's-eye Views of Society; engraved by the Brothers Dalziel. Ob. 4to. Lond., 1864.   A Q 15 †

Foreign Tour of Messrs. Brown, Jones, and Robinson. 4to. Lond., 1854.   J 7 V 12

In Fairy Land: a Series of Pictures from the Elf World; with a Poem by William Allingham. Folio. Lond., 1870.   A 23 P 19 ‡

Journal kept by Richard Doyle in the year 1840. Illustrated. 4to. Lond., 1885.   C 3 W 11

Manners and Customs of ye Englyshe; drawn from ye quick; to which be added some Extracts from Mr. Pips hys Diarye, contributed by Percival Leigh. New ed. Ob. 4to. Lond., 1876.   A 1 Q 16 †

Works of W. M. Thackeray; with Illustrations. [*See* Thackeray, W. M.]

D'OYLY (Rev. George), D.D., &c. Life of William Sancroft, Archbishop of Canterbury; with an Appendix. 2 vols. 8vo. Lond., 1821.   C 8 R 46, 47

DOYNE (W. T.), C.E. Second Report upon the River Waimakariri and the Lower Plains of Canterbury, New Zealand. Illustrated. Fol. Christchurch, 1865.   MD 7 Q 1 †

DOZY (R.) Geschichte der Mauren in Spanien. 2 vols. roy. 8vo. Leipzig, 1874.   B 13 T 21, 22

DRAGOMANOFF (Michael). [*See* Stepniak, S. D.]

DRACONTIUS. Carmina Omnia. [*See* Migne, J.P. Series Latina, 60.]

DRAKE (CHARLES F. TYRWHITT), F.R.G.S. Literary Remains of; edited, with a Memoir, by Walter Besant, M.A. With Portrait. 8vo. Lond., 1877. C 10 U 23

DRAKE (EDWARD CAVENDISH). New Universal Collection of Authentic and Entertaining Voyages and Travels. from the Earliest Accounts to the Present Time. Fol, Lond., 1767. D 36 R 1 ‡

DRAKE (ADM. SIR FRANCIS), KNT. Life, Voyages, and Exploits of; with numerous original Letters from him and the Lord High Admiral to the Queen and Great Officers of the State; by John Barrow. 8vo. Lond., 1843. C 10 U 8

Another copy. 2nd ed. 12mo. Lond., 1844. C 2 Q 11

Another copy. D 10 Q 49

Another copy. (H. and C. Lib.) J 8 P 7

Sir Francis Drake revived, who is or may be a Pattern to stirre up all heroicke and active Spirits of these Times, to benefit their Countrey and eternize their names by like Noble Attempts. Sm. 4to. Lond., 1653. Libr.

[*See* MARCHAND, E.]

DRAKE (FRANCIS). Eboracum; or, the History and Antiquities of the City of York. Roy. fol. Lond., 1736. B 19 T 1 ‡

DRAKE (F. L.) Alleged Embezzlement of. [*See* LANG, REV. J. D.]

DRAKE (FRANCIS S.) Dictionary of American Biography, including Men of the Time; with a Supplement. Roy. 8vo. Boston, 1872. C 11 V 16

Indian Tribes of the United States: their History, Antiquities, Customs, Religion, Arts, Language, Traditions, Oral Legends, and Myths; edited by Francis S. Drake. Illustrated. 2 vols. 4to. Lond., 1885. A 2 P 14, 15 †

DRAKE (H. H.) [*See* HASTED, E.]

DRAKE (NATHAN), M.D., &c. Evenings in Autumn: a series of Essays. 2 vols. 8vo. Lond., 1822. J 6 P 3, 4

The Gleaner: a series of Periodical Essays. 4 vols. 8vo. Lond., 1811. J 10 T 8–11

Literary Hours; or, Sketches Critical and Narrative. 2nd ed. 3 vols. 8vo. Sudbury, 1800–4. J 10 T 5–7

Memorials of Shakspeare. 8vo. Lond., 1828. C 9 R 22

Mornings in Spring; or, Retrospections, Biographical, Critical, and Historical. 2 vols. 8vo. Lond., 1828. J 6 P 1, 2

Shakspeare and his Times. 2 vols. 4to. Lond., 1817. C 4 W 35, 36

Winter Nights; or, Fireside Lucubrations. 2 vols. 12mo. Lond., 1820. J 8 R 15, 16

DRAKE (SAMUEL ADAMS). Heart of the White Mountains: their Legend and Scenery. With Illustrations. 4to. Lond., 1882. D 3 V 22

DRAMATIC LIST (THE). [*See* PASCOE, C. E.]

DRAMATIC NOTES. Illustrated Year-Book of the Stage; by C. E. Pascoe, Austin Brereton, and others. 2 vols. 8vo. Lond., 1879–85. E

2 o

DRAPER (PROF. JOHN WILLIAM), M.D., &c. History of the American Civil War. 3 vols. roy. 8vo. Lond., 1871. B 1 U 4–6

History of the Conflict between Religion and Science. 7th ed. 12mo. Lond., 1876. G 8 Q 1

History of the Intellectual Development of Europe. 2 vols. 8vo. Lond., 1864. G 3 Q 29, 30

Human Physiology—Statistical and Dynamical; or, the Conditions and Course of the Life of Man. Illustrated. 7th ed. 8vo. New York, 1875. A 12 T 1

Thoughts on the future Civil Policy of America. 4th ed. 8vo. New York, 1875. F 6 T 23

DRAYSON (LIEUT.-COL. A. W.), F.R.A.S. Cause of the Supposed Proper Motion of the Fixed Stars, and an Explanation of the apparent Acceleration of the Moon's Mean Motion: a Sequel to the "Glacial Epoch." 8vo. Lond., 1874. A 3 T 31

Sporting Scenes amongst the Kaffirs of South Africa. 8vo. Lond., 1858. D 2 R 5

DRAYTON (MICHAEL). Life and Poems of. [*See* CHALMERS, A.]

DREDGE (JAMES). Brief Notices of the Aborigines of New South Wales and Port Phillip. 8vo. Geelong, 1845. M A 1 R 2

DRESDEN. Neues Sach-und Ortsverzeichniss der königlich sächsischen Gemälde-Gallerie zu Dresden. 8vo. Dresden, 1833. A 7 Q 21

DRESSER (CHRISTOPHER), PH.D., &c. Carpets. (Brit. Manuf. Indust.) 12mo. Lond., 1876. A 17 S 33

Japan: its Architecture, Art, and Art Manufactures. Sq. 8vo. Lond., 1882. A 7 S 24

Modern Ornamentation; being a series of Original Designs. Fol. Lond., 1886. A 23 P 20 ‡

DREWRY (CHARLES STEWART). Patent Law Amendment Act; with Notes and Cases, and an Appendix of Rules and Forms. 8vo. Lond., 1838. A 7 Q 13

DRINKWATER (CAPT. JOHN). History of the Siege of Gibraltar, 1779–83. (H. and C. Lib.) 12mo. Lond., 1844. J 8 P 4

Another copy. 12mo. Lond., 1850. B 13 U 16

DRIOU (ALFRED). Splendeurs et Désastres: Chroniques de France. 8vo. Limoges, 1851. B 9 P 41

DRIVER (S. R.), M.A. Treatise on the Use of the Tenses in Hebrew. (Clar. Press.) 12mo. Oxford, 1874. K 16 P 50

DROHOJOWSKA (A. J. F. A., COMTESSE, NÉE SYMON DE LATREICHE). L'Australie: Esquisses et Tableaux; par "A. S. de Doncourt." 8vo. Lille, 1869. MD 2 Q 54

A travers l'Océanie. 2e édition. 8vo. Lille, 1874. MD 5 T 29

DROLERIES POÉTIQUES. Contes Joyeux et Facéties. 3e édition. 18mo. Paris, 1861. Libr.

DROUGHT OF 1829. [*See* NEW SOUTH WALES.]

D'ROZARIO (P. S.) Dictionary of the principal Languages spoken in the Bengal Presidency, viz. ; English, Bángáli, and Hindústáni, in the Roman Character, with Walker's Pronunciation. 8vo. Calcutta, 1837.   K 13 P 27

DRUMMOND (HENRY). Histories of Noble British Families; with Biographical Notices of the most distinguished Individuals in each. Illustrated. 2 vols. at. fol.   Lond., 1846.   B 13 P 23, 24 ‡.

Letter to Thomas Phillips, Esq., R.A., on the connection between the Fine Arts and Religion, and the means of their revival. 8vo. Lond., 1840.   A 7 R 21

Speeches in Parliament, and some Miscellaneous Pamphlets; edited by Lord Lovaine [afterwards Duke of Northumberland]. 2 vols. 8vo. Lond., 1860.   F 13 P 21, 22

DRUMMOND (J.) [*See* BISCHOF, G.]

DRUMMOND (JAMES), R.S.A. Ancient Scottish Weapons: a series of Drawings by the late James Drummond, R.S.A.; with Introduction and descriptive Notes, by Joseph Anderson. Imp. 4to. Edinb., 1881.   B 16 U 11 ‡

DRUMMOND (P. R.) The Life of Robert Nicoll, Poet; with some hitherto uncollected Pieces. 8vo. Paisley, 1884.   C 3 T 17

DRUMMOND (RT. HON. SIR W.) Origines; or, Remarks on the Origin of several Empires, States and Cities. 4 vols. 8vo.   Lond., 1824-29.   B 14 S 1-4

[*See* PERSIUS FLACCUS, A.]

DRUMMOND (W.), OF HAWTHORNDEN. Collection of all the Poems written by. Sm. fol. Edinb., 1711.   B 16 R 3 ‡

Life and Poems of. [*See* CHALMERS, A.]

Poems of; with Life, by Peter Cunningham. 12mo. Lond., 1833.   H 5 8 23

Works of.   Fol.   Edinb., 1711.   B 16 R 3 ‡

DRUMMOND (HON. W. H.)   Among the Zulus and Amatongas. [*See* LESLIE, D.]

Large Game and Natural History of South and South east Africa. Sq. 8vo.   Lond., 1875.   D 2 Q 21

DRURY (DRUW).   Illustrations of Exotic Entomology, containing Figures and Descriptions of Foreign Insects. New ed., with Indexes, by J. O. Westwood, F.L. 3 vols. 4to.   Lond., 1837.   A 14 V 11-13

DRURY (ROBERT).   Madagascar; or, Journal during Fifteen Years' Captivity on that Island. 8vo.   Lond., 1729.   D 1 Q 29

Pleasant and surprising Adventures of Robert Drury, during his Fifteen Years's Captivity on the Island of Madagascar; written by himself. 12mo. Lond., 1829-30.   C 1 P 7

DRYDEN (JOHN). All for Love. (Brit. Theatre.) 12mo. Lond., 1808.   H 1 P 6

Another copy. (Bell's Brit. Theatre.) 18mo. Lond., 1792.   H 2 P 21

Another copy. (New Eng. Theatre.) 12mo. Lond., 1776.   H 4 P 23

Another copy. [*See* BRIT. DRAMA 1.]

Amphitryon; or, the Two Socias: a comedy; altered by Dr. Hawkesworth. (Bell's Brit. Theatre.) 18mo. Lond., 1792.   H 2 P 11

Arthur and Emmeline: an entertainment, abridged from the Masque of King Arthur; as altered from Dryden by D. Garrick. (New Eng. Theatre.) 12mo. Lond., 1786.   H 4 P 28

[A Biography]; by G. Saintsbury. (Eng. Men of Letts.) 8vo. Lond., 1881.   C 1 U 14

The Indian Emperor; or, the Conquest of Mexico by the Spaniards: being the Sequel of "The Indian Queen." 12mo. Lond., 1721.   H 1 R 26

Johnson ['s]. Lives of Dryden and Pope; edited, with Introduction and Notes, by Alfred Milnes, M.A. (Clar. Press.) 12mo. Oxford, 1885.   C 14 P 9

Life of; by Sir Walter Scott. (Miscellaneous Works.) 12mo. Edinb., 1870.   J 1 Q 10

Life and Poems of. [*See* BRITISH POETS, 4; CHALMERS, A.; *and* JOHNSON, DR. S.]

Lives of Dryden and Pope; edited, with Introduction and Notes, by Alfred Milnes, M.A. 12mo. Oxford, 1885.   C 14 P 9

The Spanish Fryar; or, the Double Discovery: a comedy. (Bell's Brit. Theatre.) 18mo. Lond., 1791.   H 2 P 28

Another copy. (New Eng. Theatre.) 12mo. Lond., 1789.   H 4 P 18

Stanzas on the Death of Cromwell, Astræa Redux, Annus Mirabilis, Absalom and Achitophel, Religio Laici, the Hind and the Partner; edited by W. D. Christie, M.A., &c. 2nd ed. (Clar. Press.) 12mo. Oxford, 1874.   H 6 Q 44

The State of Innocence, and Fall of Man: an Opera. 12mo. Lond., 1721.   H 1 R 26

Works of: illustrated with Notes, and a Life of the Author, by Sir Walter Scott. 18 vols. 8vo. Lond., 1808.   H 2 R 12-29

Works of Juvenal, translated. [*See* CHALMERS, A.]

Works of Virgil, translated. [*See* CHALMERS, A.]

[*See* DU FRESNOY, C. A.; OVIDIUS NASO, P.; *and* VIRGILIUS MARO, P.]

DRYDEN (JOHN), AND LEE (NATHANIEL). Oedipus: a Tragedy. (Bell's Brit. Theatre.) 18mo. Lond., 1791.   H 2 P 10

DUBARRI, OR DUBARRY (MARIE JEANNE GOMARD DE VAUBERNIER), COMTESSE. Memoirs of. (Autobiog. 29-32.) 4 vols. (in 2) 18mo. Lond., 1830-31.   C 1 P 20, 21

DUBARRY (ARMAND). L'Absent-Lorraine en Australie: Histoire d'une Famille d'Emigrants sur le Continent Austral. 8vo. Paris, 1871.   M D 5 Q 41

DUBBO HOME WORDS (THE). A Parish Magazine and Monthly Record of Church Work in the Diocese of Bathurst; the Australian portion edited by the Rev. Canon F. S. Wilson, Dubbo. Sq. 8vo. Bathurst, 1884. ME 3 Q

DUBLIN. New Picture of Dublin; or, Stranger's Guide through the Irish Metropolis. 12mo. Dublin, 1828. D 7 P 11

DUBLIN INTERNATIONAL EXHIBITION, 1865. Descriptive Catalogue of the Victoria Cross Gallery, painted by L. W. Desanges. 8vo. Dublin, 1865. K 7 S 6
Official Catalogue. 4th ed. 8vo. Dublin, 1865. K 7 S 6
Report of the Nova Scotia Department, 1865. (Pam. 34.) 8vo. Halifax, 1866. J 12 U 26
Reports of the Jurors, and List of their Awards. 8vo. Dublin, 1865. K 7 S 6

DUBLIN LITERARY GAZETTE; or, Weekly Chronicle of Criticism, Belles Lettres, and Fine Arts. 4to. Dublin, 1830. J 4 U 13

DUBLIN PENNY JOURNAL (THE), [Vol. 1] 1832–33. Imp. 8vo. Dublin, 1833. J 7 V 16

DUBLIN REVIEW (THE). 1st, 2nd, and 3rd series. 96 vols. 8vo. Lond., 1836–85. E

DUBLIN UNIVERSITY. Catalogue of Graduates who have proceeded to Degrees in the University of Dublin. 2 vols. 8vo. Dublin, 1869–84. K 7 S 22, 23

DUBLIN UNIVERSITY MAGAZINE. Literary, Political, and Philosophical Review. 96 vols. 8vo. Lond., 1833–80. E

DÜBNER (FR.) [*See* ARRIAN, F., *and* PLUTARCH.]

DUBOIS (GUILLAUME), CARDINAL. Les Cardinaux Ministres: le Cardinal Dubois et la Régence de Philippe d'Orléans; par J. B. H. R. Capefigue. 12mo. Paris, 1861. C 1 S 20

DUBOIS (ABBÉ J. A.) Description of the Character, Manners, and Customs of the People of India; translated from the French. 2nd ed. Roy. 8vo. Madras, 1862. D 5 T 35

DU BOIS (LUCIEN). Lettres sur l'Italie et ses Musées, Naples. 8vo. Bruxelles, 1874. D 7 T 26

DUBOURG (MATTHEW). Views of the Remains of Ancient Buildings in Rome and its Vicinity. Roy. 4to. Lond., 1820. A 4 U 5 ‡

DU BOSE (REV. H. C.) The Dragon, Image, and Demon; or, the Three Religions of China. 8vo. Lond., 1886. G 13 T 31

DU BREUIL (ALPHONSE). Scientific and Profitable Culture of Fruit Trees; from the French, by Wm. Wardle and Geo. Glenny. (Weale.) 12mo. Lond., 1872. A 17 Q 4

DUBUS-PRÉVILLE (PIERRE LOUIS). Mémoires de. [*See* BARRIÈRE, J. F., 6.]

DU CANE (COL. SIR EDMUND F.), K.C.B., &c. Punishment and Prevention of Crime. 8vo. Lond., 1885. F 6 R 33

DU CANGE (CHARLES DUFRESNE), SIEUR. Glossarium Mediæ et Infimæ Latinitatis cum Indices, &c. 7 vols. 4to. Parisiis, 1840–50. K 13 U 11–17
Another copy. Editio nova. Vols. 1–7. 4to. Niort, 1883–86. K 13 U 18–24

DUCAREL (ANDREW COLTEE), LL.D., &c., AND NICHOLS (JOHN). History and Antiquities of the Parish of Lambeth, in the County of Surrey. 4to. Lond., 1786. B 6 V 12
History of the Archiepiscopal Palace of Lambeth, from its Formation to the Present Time. 4to. Lond., 1785. B 6 V 11

DUCAS (MICHEL). [*See* BYZANTINÆ HIST. SCRIPT.]

DUCATUS LANCASTRIÆ. Pars Prima: Calendarium Inquisitonum post Mortem, &c. Partes Secunda, Tertia Quarta: Calendar to the Pleadings, &c., in the Reign of Henry VII to the Reign of Queen Elizabeth. 3 vols. (in 1) at. fol. Lond., 1823–34. F 2 4 Q 18 ‡

DU CHAILLU (PAUL BELLONI). Explorations and Adventures in Equatorial Africa. Illustrated. 8vo. Lond. 1861. D 2 Q 22
Journey to Ashango-land; and further penetration into Equatorial Africa. Illustrated. 8vo. Lond. 1867. D 2 Q 23
Land of the Midnight Sun: Summer and Winter Journeys through Sweden, Norway, Lapland, and Northern Finland. With Map, &c. 2 vols. 8vo. Lond., 1881. D 7 S 12, 13

DUCHESNE (JEAN), AÎNÉ. Museum of Painting and Sculpture. [*See* RÉVEIL, A.]

DUCK (ARTHUR), LL.D. Life of Henry Chichele, Archbishop of Canterbury. 12mo. Lond., 1699. C 2 S 8

DUCKER (CAR. A.) De Bello Peloponnesiaco. [*See* THUCYDIDES.]

DUCKETT (SIR GEORGE), BART. Penal Laws and Test Act: Questions touching their Repeal, propounded in 1687–8 by James II. Roy. 8vo. Lond., 1883. F 5 V 19

DUCKETT (CAPT. GEORGE F.) Technological Military Dictionary, German-English-French. 8vo. Lond., 1848. K 15 S 6

DUCLOS (CHARLES PINOT). Acajou et Zirphile. [*See* CABINET DES FÉES, 35.]
Mémoires secrets sur la Règne de Louis XIV., &c. [*See* BARRIÈRE, J. F. 2.] C 1 T 2

DUDEVANT (MME. AMANDINE LUCILE AURRE), "GEORGE SAND." Letters of George Sand; translated and edited by Raphaël Ledos de Beaufort; with Biographical Sketch. 3 vols. 8vo. Lond., 1886. C 8 P 40–42

DUDGEON (H. D.) Historic Sketch of the Rise and Spread of the Vaccine Dogma. (Pam. Cp.) 8vo. Leicester (n.d.) A 12 S 34

DUDGEON (MAJOR R. C.) History of the Edinburgh, or Queen's Regiment Light Infantry Militia, now 3rd Battalion "The Royal Scots" 8vo. Edinb., 1882. B 5 U 31

DUDLEY (AMY), LADY. Biographical Notice (Cumnor Place); by A. D. Bartlett. 8vo. Oxford, 1850. B 7 Q 8

DUDLEY (J. W. WARD), EARL OF. Letters to the Bishop of Llandaff. 8vo. Lond., 1840. C 10 T 40

DUDLEY (R.) The Atlantic Telegraph. [*See* RUSSELL, W. H.]

DUDLEY (SIR ROBERT). Memoirs and Correspondence of. [*See* ADLARD, G.]

DUEMICHEN (JOHANNES). Altägyptische Tempelinschriften in den jahre 1863–65. 2 vols. fol. Leipsic, 1867. B 18 U 14, 15 ‡

Historische Inschriften altaegyptischer Denkmaeler in den jahren 1863–65. Fol. Leipsic, 1867. B 9 P 27 ‡

Historische Inschriften altägyptischer Denkmäler. Zweite Folge. Obl fol. Leipsic, 1869. B 9 P 28 ‡

DUFEU (A.) Découverte de l'age et de la véritable destination des quatre Pyramides de Gizeh, principalement de la Grande Pyramide. 8vo. Paris, 1873. A 2 8 5

DUFF (ALEXANDER), D.D., &c. Life of; by George Smith, C.I.E., &c. 2 vols. roy. 8vo. Lond.,1879. C 8 V 5

DUFF (ANDREW HALLIDAY), "ANDREW HALLIDAY." The Savage Club Papers, 1867–68. 2 vols. 8vo. Lond., 1867–68. J 8 U 23, 24

DUFF (JAMES GRANT). History of the Mahrattas. 3 vols. 8vo. Lond., 1826. B 10 U 1–3

DUFF (SIR MOUNTSTUART E. GRANT). Elgin Speeches. 8vo. Edinb., 1871. F 9 R 22

Notes of an Indian Journey. 8vo. Lond., 1876. D 6 R 5

On the Teachings of Richard Cobden. (Pam. Ds.) 12mo. Lond., 1871. MF 3 P 17

DUFFERIN (RT. HON. FREDERICK TEMPLE HAMILTON BLACKWOOD), EARL OF. Letters from High Latitudes. 8vo., 1858. D 7 Q 21

Speeches and Addresses of; edited by Henry Milton. 8vo. Lond., 1882. F 9 R 11

Tour through British Columbia. [*See* ST. JOHN, M.]

DUFFIELD (SAMUEL WILLOUGHBY). English Hymns; their Authors and History. 8vo. N. York, 1886. H 6 U 1

DUFFY (SIR CHARLES GAVAN), K.C.M.G. Australia at the Bar of Public Opinion in England : a Lecture. 8vo. Melb., 1860. MF 3 P 5

Another copy. MJ 2 R 6

Australian Policy: Speech at Castlemaine, March 20, 1872. 8vo. Melb., 1872. MF 1 Q 3

Four Years of Irish History, 1845–49: a Sequel to "Young Ireland." 8vo. Lond., 1883. B 11 Q 16

DUFFY (SIR CHARLES GAVAN), K.C.M.G.—*continued.*

Guide to the Land Law of Victoria. 8vo. Melb., 1862. MJ 2 R 21

League of North and South: an Episode in Irish History, 1850–54. 8vo. Lond., 1886. B 11 P 25

On Popular Errors concerning Australia. 12mo. Melb., 1866. MJ 2 P 30

Portrait of. [*See* MANUSCRIPTS, &c.]

Something to do : a Lecture. 8vo. Melb.,1876. MJ 2 R 11

True Issue submitted to the Constituencies: Speeches at the Dalhousie Election. 12mo. Melb., 1868. MF 1 Q 6

Young Ireland: a Fragment of History, 1840–50. 8vo. Lond., 1880. B 11 Q 29

DUFIEF (N. G.) New Universal Pronouncing Dictionary of the French and English Languages. 3 vols. 8vo. Lond., 1817. K 11 V 51–53

DUFOUR (PIERRE). [*See* LACROIX, PAUL.]

DU FRESNOY (CHAS. ALPHONSE). Art of Painting; translated, with an original Preface, by Mr. J. Dryden. 8vo. Lond., 1750. A 7 P 41

DUGDALE (THOMAS). Curiosities of Great Britain, England and Wales Delineated—Historical, Entertaining, and Commercial—alphabetically arranged, assisted by William Burnett, C.E. 10 vols. 8vo. Lond., 1854–60. D 11 T 4–13

DUGDALE (SIR WILLIAM), KNT. Antiquities of Warwickshire illustrated. Fol. Lond., 1656. B 15 S 11 ‡

History of St. Paul's Cathedral, in London, from its Foundation; with a Continuation and Additions, by Henry Ellis, F.R.S., Sec., S.A. Fol. Lond., 1818. B 19 U 11 ‡

The Life, Diary, and Correspondence of; edited by W. Hamper. Roy. 4to. Lond., 1827. C 4 P 16 †

Monasticon Anglicanum: a History of the Abbies, and other Monasteries, Hospitals, Friaries, and Cathedral and Collegiate Churches, in England and Wales, &c. 6 vols. fol. Lond., 1817–30. B 4 T 6–13 ‡

Short View of the late Troubles in England ; briefly setting forth their Rise, Growth, and Tragical Conclusion. Fol. Oxford, 1681. B 16 R 10 ‡

DUGDALE (WILLIAM STAFFORD). Dante's Divine Comedy : a Prose Translation. [*See* DANTE ALIGHIERI.]

DU HALDE (P. J. B.) Description of the Empire of China and Chinese-Tartary, together with the Kingdoms of Korea and Tibet. 2 vols. fol. Lond., 1738–41. D 19 U 4, 5 ‡

DU HAUSSET (MME.) Mémoires de. [*See* BARRIÈRE, J. F.]

DUKA (THEODORE), M.D. Life and Works of Alexander Csoma do Körös: a Biography, compiled chiefly from hitherto unpublished Data. 8vo. Lond., 1885. C 5 V 7

DUKE (SIR JAMES), BART. Postal Communication with Australia in Forty-four Days: a Letter addressed to the Right Honourable the Postmaster-General. (Pam. 30.) 8vo. Lond., 1854. MJ 2 Q 18

DUKE (RICHARD). Life and Poems of. [*See* CHALMERS, A., *and* JOHNSON, DR. S.]

DULAU & CO. Catalogue of French Books offered for sale. 8vo. Lond., 1882. K 7 R 7

DULBERG (JOSEPH), LL.D., &c. Roumanian Code of Commerce. 8vo. Manchester, 1884. F 9 R 6

DULCKEN (H. W.) Visit to the Holy Land, &c. [*See* PFEIFFER, MME. IDA.].

DULLER (EDUARD). Die Geschichte des deutschen Volkes. Sq. 12mo. Berlin, 1846. B 9 Q 37

DUMAS (ALEXANDRE). Life and Adventures of; by Percy Fitzgerald. 2 vols. 8vo. Lond., 1873. C 8 U 25, 26

Pictures of Travel in the South of France. 8vo. Lond., 1857. D 8 Q 30

Travelling Sketches in Egypt and Sinai; translated, corrected, and abridged from the French of Alexandre Dumas, by "A Biblical Student." 18mo. Lond., 1839. D 1 R 19

DUMAS (F. G.) Annuaire illustré des Beaux-Arts, et Catalogue illustré de l'Exposition Nationale. 8vo. Lond., 1883. E

Catalogue illustré de l'Exposition Historique de l'Art Belge et du Musée Moderne de Bruxelles. 8vo. Brussels, 1880. E

Catalogue illustré du Salon. 5 vols. 8vo. Paris, 1882–86. E

Illustrated Catalogue of the Paris Salon, 1881–83. 3 vols. 8vo. Lond., 1881–83. E

DUMAS (JEAN BAPTISTE). Annales des Science naturelles. [*See* AUDOUIN, J. V.]

DUMAS (LIEUT.-GEN. COUNT MATHIEU). Memoirs of his own Time, including the Revolution, the Empire, and the Restoration. 2 vols. 8vo. Lond., 1839. C 8 U 27, 28

DU MAURIER (GEORGE). Works of W. M. Thackeray. [*See* THACKERAY, W. M.]

DUMBLEDORE (RICHARD). The Moonraker: a Story of Australian Life. 8vo. Lond., 1877. MJ 1 R 19

DÜMICHEN (DR. J.) [*See* WERNER, C.]

DU MONCEL (TH.), COUNT, AND GERALDY (FRANK). Electricity as a Motive Power; translated and edited, with Additions, by C. J. Wharton. 8vo. Lond., 1883. A 5 R 62

DUMONT (JEAN), ET ROUSSET (J.) Corps Universel Diplomatique du Droit des Gens. 8 vols. (in 2) fol. Amsterdam, 1726–31. F 28 P 1–12 ‡

Le Cérémonial Diplomatique des Cours de l'Europe; où Collection des Actes, Mémoires et Relations qui concernent les Dignitez, Titulatures, Honneurs et Préémi nences. 2 vols. fol. Amsterdam, 1739. F 28 P 17, 18 ‡

Histoire des Anciens Traitez; par [Jean] Barbeyrac, Docteur en Droit, &c. 2 vols. (in 1) fol. Amsterdam, 1739. F 28 P 13 ‡

DUMONT (JEAN), ET ROUSSET (J.)—*continued.*

Histoire des Traités de Paix, et autres Négociations du dix-septième Siècle, depuis la Paix de Vervins, jusqu'à la Paix de Nimeque; par J. Y. de Saint-Priest. 2 vols. fol. Amsterdam, 1725. F 28 P 19–20 ‡

Négociations Secrètes touchant la Paix de Munster et d'Osnabrug; par J. Leclerc. 4 vols. fol. La Haye, 1725–26. F 28 P 21–24 ‡

Recueil des Traitez de Paix, de Trêve, de Neutralité, de Suspension d'Armes, de Confédération, d'Alliance, de Commerce, de Garantie. 4 vols. fol. Amsterdam, 1700. F 28 P 25–28 ‡

Supplément au Corps Universel Diplomatique du Droit des Gens. 2 vols. (in 3) fol. Amsterd., 1739. F 28 P 14–16 ‡

DUMONT D'URVILLE (CAPITAINE J. S. C.) Voyage de Découvertes de *l'Astrolabe* exécuté pendant les années 1826, 1827, 1828, et 1829. 12 vols. 8vo., 1 vol. 4to., 6 vols. imp. fol. and 1 vol. el. fol. Paris, 1830–35. D 9 U 1–12 and D 7 P 10–17 ‡

1–5. Histoire du Voyage redigée par Cap. J. S. C. Dumont d'Urville. 8vo.

6–9. Zoologie; par MM. Quoy et Gaimard. 8vo.

10. Botanique; par A. Lesson et A. Richard. 8vo.

11. Faune Entomologique de l'Océan Pacifique, avec l'Illustration des Insectes nouveaux recueillis pendant le Voyage; par le Docteur Boisduval. 8vo.

12. Philologie; par [Capt. J. S. C. Dumont] d'Urville. 8vo.

1. Observations Nautiques, Météorologiques, Hydrographiques, et de Physique. 4to.

1. Atlas de Botanique. Fol.

2. Atlas Entomologique. Fol.

3. Atlas Hydrographique. Fol.

4, 5. Atlas Historique. Fol.

6, 7. Atlas Zoologique. Fol.

Voyage au Pole Sud, et dans l'Océanie, sur les Corvettes *l'Astrolabe* et la *Zélée*, 1837–40. 10 vols. (in 5) 8vo. Paris, 1841–46. D 4 R 7–11

Voyage au Pole Sud, et dans l'Océanie, sur les Corvettes *l'Astrolabe* et la *Zélée*, 1837–40. 23 vols. (in 18) roy. 8vo., 5 vols. (in 4) imp. fol., and 1 vol. atlas fol. Paris, 1842–54. D 4 S 13–30 and 12 P 1–5 ‡

1–10. Histoire du Voyage; par M. Dumont d'Urville.

11. Physique; par MM. Vincendon-Dumoulin et Coupvent-Desbois.

12, 13. Hydrographie et Atlas Hydrographique; par C. A. Vincendon-Dumoulin.

14, 15. Botanique; par M. Hombron et C. H. Jacquinot. 1.—Plantes Cellulaires; par C. Montagne, D.M. 2. Plantes Vasculaires; par J. Decaisne. Avec atlas, fol.

16–20. Zoologie; par M. Hombron et C. H. Jacquinot. Avec atlas, fol.

21. Anthropologie; par M. le Docteur Dumoutier. Avec atlas, fol.

22, 23. Géologie, Minéralogie, et Géographie Physique du Voyage; par J. Grange. Avec atlas, fol. Atlas Pittoresque. 2 vols. roy. fol.

DUMOURIEZ (GÉNÉRAL CHARLES F. D.) Mémoires. [*See* BARRIÈRE, J. F. 11, 12.]

DU'MOUTIER (DR.) Anthropologie. [*See* DUMONT D'UR-VILLE, CAPT. T. S.]

DUMOULIN (CLEMENT ADRIEN VINCENDON-). [*See* VIN-CENDON-DUMOULIN, CLEMENT ADRIEN.]

DUN (JOHN). British Banking Statistics; with Remarks on the Bullion Reserve, and Non-legal-tender. Note circulation of the United Kingdom. 8vo. Lond., 1876.　F 9 R 21

DUNBAR (GEORGE). Appendix to Archaeologia Graeca. [*See* POTTER, J.]

DUNBAR (HENRY), M.A. Complete Concordance to the Comedies and Fragments of Aristophanes. 4to. Oxford, 1883.　K 17 S 10

Complete Concordance to the Odyssey and Hymns of Homer. 4to. Oxford, 1880.　K 14 S 21

DUNBAR (WILLIAM). Poems of, now first collected; with Notes, and a Memoir of his Life, by David Laing (with Supplement). 2 vols. 8vo. Edinb., 1834-65.　H 7 R 3, 4

DUNBAR (WILLIAM). Travels in the Interior Parts of America. [*See* CLARKE, CAPT. M.]

DUNCAN (HANDASYDE), M.D. Colony of South Australia. 8vo. Lond., 1850.　MD 6 T 3

DUNCAN (JAMES). Introduction to Entomology. (Nat. Lib. 28.) 12mo. Edinb., 1840.　A 14 P 28

Natural History of Bees. (Nat. Lib. 33.) 12mo. Edinb., 1840.　A 14 P 33

Natural History of Beetles. (Nat. Lib. 29.) 12mo. Edinb., 1835.　A 14 P 29

Natural History of British Butterflies. (Nat. Lib. 30.) 12mo. Edinb., 1837.　A 14 P 30

Natural History of British Moths and Sphinxes, &c. (Nat. Lib. 31.) 12mo. Edinb., 1836.　A 14 P 31

Natural History of Exotic Moths. (Nat. Lib. 34.) 12mo. Edinb., 1841.　A 14 P 34

Natural History of Foreign Butterflies. (Nat. Lib. 32.) 12mo. Edinb., 1837.　A 14 P 32

DUNCAN (JOHN). Travels in Western Africa, in 1845-46. 2 vols. 8vo. Lond., 1850.　D 18 S 23, 24

DUNCAN (JOHN). Life of John Duncan, Scotch Weaver and Botanist; with Sketches of his Friends and Notices of his Times by William Jolly. With Portrait. 8vo. Lond., 1883.　C 5 R 12

DUNCAN (PROF. P. MARTIN), M.B., &c. Transformations (or Metamorphoses) of Insects. (Insecta, Myriapoda, Arachnida, and Crustacea.) 2nd ed. Roy. 8vo. Lond., 1870.　A 13 U 13

Micrographic Dictionary. [*See* GRIFFITH, J. W.]

DUNCAN (PROF. P. MARTIN), M.B., &c., AND SLADEN (W. PERCY), F.G.S., &c. Memoir on the Echinodermata of the Arctic Sea to the West of Greenland. Fol. Lond., 1881.　A 23 R 22 †

DUNCAN (SINCLAIR THOMSON). Journal of a Voyage to Australia by the Cape of Good Hope, Six Months in Melbourne, and Return to England by Cape Horn. 8vo. Edinb., 1869.　MD 2 R 3

DUNCAN (PROF. W.) [*See* CÆSAR, C. J.]

DUNCAN (WILLIAM AUGUSTINE), C.M.G. Account of a Memorial presented to His Majesty by Captain Pedro Fernandez de Quir, 1610; from the Spanish, with an Introductory Notice. Sm. 4to. Sydney, 1874.　MD 7 P 18

Answer to the Letter addressed to the Lord Bishop of Australia [by W. A. Duncan]. [*See* ARCHBISHOPRIC OF SYDNEY.]

Aroldo and Clara: an Historical Poem. [*See* PELLICO, S.]

Duncan's Weekly Register of Politics, Facts, and General Literature, 1843-45. 5 vols. (in 4) 4to. Sydney, 1843-45.　ME

Another copy. 5 vols. (in 1) 4to.　ME

Lecture on National Education, delivered at the School of Arts, Brisbane, on 20th June, 1850. 8vo. Brisbane, 1850.　MG 1 Q 30

Another copy.　MJ 2 Q 2

Letter to the Lord Bishop of Australia: containing Remarks upon his Lordship's protest against the Metropolitan and Episcopal Jurisdiction of His Grace the Archbishop of Sydney. (Pam. 10). 8vo. Sydney, 1843.　MJ 2 Q 2

Memoir of the late Rev. Joseph Monnier. [*See* MONNIER, REV. J. F.]

Plea for the New South Wales Constitution. 8vo. Sydney, 1856.　MF 3 P 4

Another copy.　MF 1 Q 3

Practical Treatise on the Culture of the Olive Tree. 12mo. Sydney, 1844.　MA 1 P 17

Second Letter to the Lord Bishop of Australia, in reply to the Lectures of the Rev. R. Allwood, B.A., Minister of St. James', against the Bishop of Rome's Supremacy. (Pam. 10.) Sydney, 1843.　MJ 2 Q 2

DUNCKER (PROF. MAX). History of Antiquity; from the German; by Evelyn Abbott, M.A. 6 vols. 8vo. Lond., 1877-82.　B 14 S 25-30

History of Greece. 8vo. Lond., 1883-86.　B 10 P 16

DUNCKLEY (HENRY). The Crown and the Cabinet: Five Letters on the Biography of the Prince Consort; by "Verax." 8vo. March, 1878.　F 5 S 48

DUNCUMB (JOHN), A.M., AND COOKE (WILLIAM HENRY), M.A., &c. Collections towards the History and Antiquities of the County of Hereford. 3 vols. 4to. Hereford and Lond., 1804-82.　B 10 S 8, 10 †

DUNDONALD (THOMAS), TENTH EARL OF, G.C.B. Autobiography of a Seaman. 2nd ed. 2 vols. 8vo. Lond., 1860.　C 10 R 32, 33

Life of; completing the "Autobiography of a Seaman;" by Thomas, Eleventh Earl of Dundonald, and H. R. Fox Bourne. 2 vols. 8vo. Lond., 1869.　C 10 R 34, 35

DUNDONALD (THOMAS, LORD COCHRANE), ELEVENTH EARL OF, AND BOURNE (H. R. Fox). Life of Thomas, Lord Cochrane, Tenth Earl of Dundonald, G.C.B.; completing the "Autobiography of a Seaman." 2 vols. 8vo. Lond., 1869.   C 10 R 34, 35

DUNFERMLINE (ALEXANDER SETON), EARL OF. Memoir of; by George Seton, Advocate. Roy. 8vo. Edinb., 1882.   C 8 V 31

DUNFERMLINE (JAMES), LORD. Lieut.-Gen. Sir Ralph Abercromby, K.B., 1793–1801: a Memoir; by his Son. 8vo. Edinb., 1861.   C 1 V 2

DUNHAM (S. ASTLEY), LL.D. History of Denmark, Sweden, and Norway. (Lard. Cab. Cyclo.) 3 vols. 12mo. Lond., 1839–40.   K 1 S 39–41

History of Europe during the Middle Ages. (Lard. Cab. Cyclo.) 4 vols. 12mo. Lond., 1833–34.   K 1 T 6–9

History of Poland. (Lard. Cab. Cyclo.) 12mo. Lond., 1836.   K 1 T 35

History of Spain and Portugal. (Lard. Cab. Cyclo.) 5 vols. 12mo. Lond., 1832–33.   K 1 T 47–49

History of the Germanic Empire. (Lard. Cab. Cyclo.) 3 vols. 12mo. Lond., 1834–35.   K 1 T 15–17

Lives of the most eminent Literary and Scientific Men of Great Britain. (Lard. Cab. Cyclo.) 3 vols. 12mo. Lond., 1836–38.   K 1 S 26–28

DUNKIN (EDWIN HADLOW WISE). Monumental Brasses of Cornwall. Roy. 4to. Lond., 1882.   B 14 R 18 ‡

DUNLAP (WILLIAM). Memoirs of Charles Brockden Brown, American Novelist; with Selections from his Letters, &c. 8vo. Lond., 1832.   C 8 Q 1

Memoirs of George Frederick Cooke, late of the Theatre Royal, Covent Garden. 2 vols. 8vo. Lond., 1813.   C 6 R 4, 5

DUNLOP (JOHN). History of Fiction. 8vo. Lond., 1845.   B 36 U 1

DUNLOP (MRS. MADELINE ANNE WALLACE). Glass in the Old World. 8vo. Lond., 1882.   B 15 Q 31

DUNLOP (ROBERT GLASGOW). Travels in Central America; being a Journal of Three Years' Residence in the Country. 8vo. Lond., 1847.   D 3 R 27

DUNN (A. M.) Notes and Sketches of an Architect. 8vo. Lond., 1886.   A 2 U 43

DUNN (JOHN). History of the Oregon Territory, and British North America Fur Trade. 8vo. Lond., 1844.   B 1 S 2

DUNN (JACOB PIATT), JUNR., LL.B. Massacres of the Mountains: a History of the Indian Wars of the Far West. Illustrated. 8vo. Lond., 1886.   B 1 S 43

DUNNING (JOHN). Tobacco. (Brit. Manuf. Indust.) 12mo. Lond., 1876.   A 17 S 28

DUNRAVEN (WINDHAM-THOMAS), FOURTH EARL OF. The Great Divide: Travels in the Upper Yellowstone, in the Summer of 1874. Illustrated. 8vo. Lond.,1876. D 3 S 36

DUNS (PROF. JOHN), D.D., &c. Memoir of Sir James Young Simpson, Bart. 8vo. Edinb., 1873.   C 9 U 12

DÜNTZER (HEINRICH). Life of Goethe; translated by Thomas W. Lyster. With authentic Illustrations and Facsimiles. 2 vols. 8vo. Lond., 1883.   C 4 U 6, 7

Life of Schiller; translated by Percy E. Pinkerton. 8vo. Lond., 1883.   C 4 S 40

DUPAIX (W.) [*See* KINGSBOROUGH, LORD.]

DUPANLOUP (FÉLIX ANTOINE PHILIBERT), ÉVÊQUE D'ORLÉANS. Défense de la Liberté de l'Eglise. 2 vols. 8vo. Paris, 1861.   G 10 T 15, 16

De l'Éducation. 7e ed. 3 vols. 8vo. Paris, 1866.   G 17 P 15–17

L'Enfant. Sq. 12mo. Paris, 1869.   G 13 U 6

De la Haute Éducation Intellectuelle. 3 vols. 8vo. Paris, 1866.   G 17 S 3–5

Entretiens sur la Prédication. 8vo. Paris, 1866. G10T14

La Femme Studieuse. Sq. 12mo. Paris, 1870. G 13 U 4

Life of Mgr. Dupanloup, Bishop of Orleans; by the Abbé F. Lagrange; translated from the French by Lady Herbert. 2 vols. 8vo. Lond., 1885.   C 9 T 6, 7

Le Mariage Chrétien. Sq. 12mo. Paris, 1869. G 13 U 5

L'Œuvre par excellence; ou, Entretiens sur le Catéchisme. 8vo. Paris, 1869.   G 10 T 13

Sermon of Mgr. the Bishop of Orleans, preached in Paris, 1861, for the Poor Catholics of Ireland; translated by Rev. W. H. Anderson, M.A. *(Bound with Waterworth's Church of St. Patrick.)* 8vo. Dublin, 1861.   G 7 T 15

Studious Women; translated by R. M. Phillimore. 8vo. Lond., 1869.   G 13 T 33

Vie de Mgr. Dupanloup, Evêque d'Orléans; par l'Abbé F. Lagrange. Troisième édition. 3 vols. 8vo. Paris, 1883–84.   C 9 T 3–5

DUPERREY (LOUIS ISIDORE). Voyage autour du Monde, sur la Corvette *La Coquille*, pendant les années 1822–25. 5 vols. 4to. Paris, 1826–29.   D 5 P 6–10 †

1, 2. Zoologie; par MM. Lesson et Garnot.

3. Hydrographie; par M. L. J. Duperrey.

4. Botanique; par MM. D'Urville second de l'Expedition, Bory de St. Vincent, et Ed. Brongniart.

5. Histoire du Voyage.

Planches [to above.] 4 vols. fol. Paris, 1826–29.   D 7 P 21–24 ‡

1. Hydrographie.

2. Histoire du Voyage.

3. Histoire Naturelle: Zoologie.

4. Histoire Naturelle: Botanique.

DU PERRON (ABRAHAM HYACINTHE ANQUETIL-.) [*See* ANQUETIL-DUPERRON, A. H.]

DUPIN-(PROF. L. E.) Compleat History of the Canon and
Writers of the Books of the Old and New Testatament.
2 vols. (in 1) fol. Lond., 1699-1700.   G 12 R 3 †

DUPIN (PIERRE CHAS. FRANÇOIS), BARON. Commercial
Power of Great Britain. 2 vols. 8vo. Lond., 1825.
                                                  F 9 R 12, 13
Mathematics practically applied to the Useful and Fine Arts;
adapted by G. Birkbeck. 8vo. Lond., 1827.   A 10 T 18
Tableau des Arts et Métiers, et des Beaux-Arts. 8vo.
Paris, 1826.   A 7 Q 13

DUPPA (RICHARD), LL.B. Classes and Orders of the
Linnæan System of Botany. 3 vols. 8vo. Lond., 1816.
                                                  A 5 P 1-3

DUPPA (R.) AND QUATREMÈRE DE QUINCY (A. C.)
Lives and Works of Michael Angelo and Raphael. Illustrated. 8vo. Lond., 1876.   C 4 P 1

DUPRÈ (GIOVANNI). [A Biography], by H. S. Frieze;
with two Dialogues on Art, from the Italian of Augusto
Conti. 8vo. Lond., 1886.   C 2 T 20
Thoughts on Art, and Autobiographical Memoirs of
Giovanni Duprè; translated by E. M. Peruzzi. 8vo.
Edinb., 1884.   C 3 R 34

DUPUIS (JOSEPH). Journal of a Residence in Ashantee;
comprising Notes and Researches relative to the Gold
Coast, and the Interior of Western Africa. 4to. Lond.,
1824.   D 9 P 29 †

DURAND (MAJOR-GEN. SIR HENRY MARION), K.C.S.I.,
&c. Life of Major-Gen. Sir Henry Marion Durand,
K.C.S.I., C.B., of the Royal Engineers; by H. M.
Durand, C.S.I. 2 vols. 8vo. Lond., 1883.   C 9 R 1, 2
Reports and Surveys regarding the Drainage of the
Nuggufgurh Jheel, near Delhi. Fol. Bengal, 1838.   E

DURAND (JOHN). The Revolution. [*See* TAINE, H. A.]

DURANT (GHISLANI), M.D. Hygiene of the Voice: its
Physiology and Anatomy. New ed. 8vo. New York,
1879.   A 12 Q 10

DÜRER (ALBERT). Albert Dürer: his Life and Works;
by Prof. Moriz Thausing; translated from the German,
edited by Fred. A. Eaton, M.A. Illustrated. 2 vols.
8vo. Lond., 1882.   C 10 V 13, 14
Albrecht Dürer; by Richard Ford Heath. (Great Artists.)
8vo. Lond., 1881.   C 3 T 41
His Life and Works, including autobiographical Papers
and complete Catalogues; by Wm. B. Scott. 8vo. Lond.,
1869.   C 7 P 1
History of the Life of Albrecht Dürer; with a Translation of his Letters and Journal, and some Account of
his Works, by Mrs. Charles Heaton. Imp. 8vo. Lond.,
1870.   C 7 V 47
Another copy; with Portrait. 2nd ed. 8vo. Lond.,
1881.   C 3 V 3

DURHAM (ADM. SIR PHILIP C. H. C.), G.C.B. Memoir
of the Naval Life and Services of; by his Nephew, Capt.
A. Murray. 8vo. Lond., 1846.   C 8 S 36

DURHAM UNIVERSITY CALENDAR, 1837. 12mo.
Durham, 1837.   E

DURUY (VICTOR). History of Rome and the Roman
People, from its Origin to the Establishment of the Christian
Empire; edited by the Rev. J. P. Mahaffy. Vols. 1-6.
6 vols. imp. 8vo. Lond., 1884-86.   B 19 R 6-11 ‡

D'URVILLE (CAPT. J. S. C. DUMONT-). [*See* DUMONT-
D'URVILLE, CAPT. J. S. C.]

DUSSIEUX (—.) [*See* ROZIER, L'ABBÉ F.]

DUTCH CHURCH LIBRARY. Catalogue of Books,
Manuscripts, Letters, &c., belonging to the Dutch
Church, Austin Friars, London. Roy. 8vo. Lond.,
1879.   K 8 Q 11

DUTHY (JOHN). Sketches of Hampshire; embracing the
Architectural Antiquities, Topography, &c., of the Country
adjacent to the River Itchen. Roy. 8vo. Winchester,
1839.   D 7 V 27

DUTRUC (P. A.) Comedies and Dramas. Part 1. A
Desirable Quarantine, Fame and Fortune in Twenty-four
Hours, The Nightingale of Plomeur. 12mo. Sydney,
1878.*   MH 1 R 1

French Grammar. 14th ed. 8vo. Lond., 1877. K 1284
Literary Recreations (original French). 3rd ed. 12mo.
Lond. (n.d.)   H 3 P 35
Another copy (English Version). 3rd ed. 12m. Lond.
(n.d.)   H 3 P 36

DUTT (TORU). Ancient Ballads and Legends of Hindustan; with an introductory Memoir, by Edmund W. Gosse.
12mo. Lond., 1882.   H 6 P 30

DUTTON (FRANCIS). South Australia and its Mines;
with an Historical Sketch of the Colony. 8vo. Lond.,
1846.*   MD 5 S 17

DUTTON (HON. AND REV. F. G.) Parrots in Captivity.
[*See* GREENE, W. T.]

DUTTON (WILLIAM). Declaration of. [*See* MANUSCRIPTS
AND PORTRAITS.]

DUVAL (MATHIAS). Artistic Anatomy; translated by
Frederick E. Fenton, M.R.C.P.E. 8vo. Lond., 1884.
                                                  A 12 T 32

DWIGHT (H. T.) Australian Celebrities; or, Personal
Portraits of 100 Theatrical Stars of various magnitudes.
12mo. Melb., 1865.   MJ 2 P 34
Catalogue of Works on the Colonies. 8vo. Melb.
(n.d.)   MK 1 Q 13

DWIGHT (H. T.)—*continued.*
Cordial and Liqueur Maker's Guide, and Publican's Instructor. 2nd ed. 12mo. Melb., 1869.   MA 1 V 36
Practical Instructions in the Art of making Capons. 12mo. Melh., 1867.   MA 1 P 17

DWIGHT (TIMOTHY). Theology explained and defended, in a Series of Sermons; with a Memoir of the Author. 5 vols. 8vo. Lond., 1824.   G 10 S 11-15
Travels in New England and New York. 4 vols. 8vo. New Haven, 1821-22.   D 3 T 14-17

DWYER (C. P.) Immigrant Builder; or, Practical Hints to Handy Men. Illustrated. 8vo. Philad., 1872.   A 2 R 2

DWYER (HENRY). Pauperism in New South Wales: its Cause and Cure. 8vo. Sydney, 1887.   MF 1 R 2

DYCE (REV. ALEXANDER). Account of J. Skelton and his Writings. [*See* SKELTON, J.]
Account of John Webster and his Writings. [*See* WEBSTER, J.]
Dramatic Works of Greene and Peele. [*See* GREENE, R.]
Dramatic Works of James Shirley; with Notes. [*See* SHIRLEY, J.]
Recollections of the Table-talk of Samuel Rogers; to which is added, "Porsoniana" [by William Maltby]. 3rd ed. 8vo. Lond., 1866.   C 5 R 23
Another copy. Illustrated. 8vo. New Southgate, 1887.   11 P 16
Some Account of Marlowe and his Writings. [*See* MARLOWE, C.]
Works of Shakespeare; the Text revised. [*See* SHAKESPEARE, W.]

DYCE (A.), AND FORSTER (J.) Hand-book of the Dyce and Forster Collection. (South Kens. Mus.) 8vo. Lond., 1880.   E

DYCE (WILLIAM), R.A. The National Gallery; its Formation and Management, considered in a Letter addressed, by permission, to H.R.H. Prince Albert, K.G., &c. 8vo. Lond., 1853.   A 7 Q 19

DYCK (ANTONIO VAN). [*See* VAN DYCK, A.]

DYE (WILLIAM McE.) Moslem Egypt and Christian Abyssinia ; or, Military Service under the Khedive. 8vo. New York, 1880.   D 2 Q 16

DYER (GEORGE), A.B. Complaints of the Poor People of England. 2nd ed. 8vo. Lond., 1793.   F 7 Q 20
History of the University and Colleges of Cambridge, including Notices relating to the Founders and Eminent Men. With illustrative Engravings, by John Greig. 2 vols. 8vo. Lond., 1814.   B 6 S 7, 8

DYER (COL. HUGH McN.), R.N. West Coast of Africa, as seen from the Deck of a Man of War. 8vo. Lond., 1876.   D 1 T 29

DYER (JOHN). Life and Poems of. [*See* CHALMERS, A., *and* JOHNSON, DR. S.]

DYER (JOSEPH). [*See* SYDNEY MAGAZINE OF SCIENCE AND ART.]

DYER (T. F. THISELTON), M.A. Folk-lore of Shakespeare. 8vo. Lond., 1883.   B 3 T 9

DYER (THOMAS HENRY), LL.D. City of Rome; its Vicissitudes and Monuments, from its Foundation to the end of the Middle Ages. 2nd ed. 8vo. Lond., 1883.   B 12 P 2
History of Modern Europe, from the Fall of Constantinople in 1453, to the War in the Crimea in 1857. 4 vols. 8vo. Lond., 1861-64.   B 7 R 19-22
History of the Kings of Rome. 8vo. Lond.,1868. B 11 S 24
On Imitative Art, its Principles and Progress; with preliminary Remarks on Beauty, Sublimity, and Taste. 8vo. Lond., 1882.   A 7 S 29
Pompeii; its History, Buildings, and Antiquities: an Account of the Destruction of the City; with a full Description of the Remains and of the Recent Excavations, and also an Itinerary for Visitors. 8vo. Lond., 1875.   B 12 P 23

DYKES (REV. J. OSWALD), M.A. The Perfect Example: a Lecture to Young Men, delivered in the Mechanics' Hall, Geelong, December 5th, 1866. 8vo. Geelong, 1866.   MG 1 Q 37

DYMOND (C. W.), AND TOMKINS (REV. H. G) Worlebury : an Ancient Stronghold in the County of Somerset. Roy. 4to. Bristol, 1886.   B 15 Q 6 ‡

DYMOND (JONATHAN). Essays on the Principles of Morality. 4th ed. Roy. 8vo. Lond., 1842.   G 15 T 1

DYSON (H.) [*See* STOW, J.]

DZIALYNSKI (ADAMUS TITUS), COMES DE KOSCIELEC. Collectanea vitam resque gestas Joannis Zamoyscii illustrantia. 4to. Posnaniæ, 1861.   C 7 R 4 †

DZIERZON (DR. JOHANN). Rational Bee-keeping; or, the Theory and Practice of Dr. Dzierzon; translated from the latest German edition; by H. Dieck and S. Stutterd. 8vo. Lond., 1882.   A 1 P 12

E

E. (A.) [*See* AUSTRALIAN SKETCHES.]

E. (J. F.) [*See* POEMS.]

E. (M. A. T.) [*See* FIJI TO-DAY.]

EADS (RT. REV. H. L.) Shaker Sermons: Scripto-Rational;
containing the Substance of Shaker Theology. 8vo. New
York, 1879.   G 7 P 20

EAGAR (HON. GEOFFREY). Financial Statement, 27th
September, 1866 : with an Appendix, containing the
Project for Establishment of a National Bank. (Pam.
Ds.) 8vo. Sydney, 1866.   MF 3 P 17

EAGLE GULCH : an Australian Story ; by "Donick."
8vo. Lond., 1883.   MJ 1 Q 40

EAGLES (REV. JOHN), M.A. Essays contributed to *Black-
wood's Magazine.* 8vo. Edinb., 1857.   J 5 Q 24
The Sketcher. 8vo. Edinb., 1856.   J 5 Q 25
Sonnets. 8vo. Edinb., 1858.   H 7 R 13

EAGLES (T. H.) Constructive Geometry of Plane Curves ;
with numerous Examples. 8vo. Lond., 1885. A 10 S 22

EARDLEY-WILMOT (SIR JOHN EARDLEY), BART. [*See*
WILMOT, SIR J. E. E.]

EARL (GEORGE WINDSOR), M.R.A.S. Contributions to
the Physical Geography of South-eastern Asia and Aus-
tralia ; with a Map. (Pam. 30.) 8vo. Lond., 1853.
                                                MJ 2 Q 18
The Eastern Seas ; or, Voyages and Adventures in the
Indian Archipelago, in 1832–34. 8vo. Lond., 1837.
                                                D 6 R 32
Another copy. 8vo. Lond., 1837.   MD 7 Q 13
Enterprise in Tropical Australia. 8vo. Lond.,   MD 5 Q 25
Hand-book for Colonists in Tropical Australia.   8vo.
Penang, 1863 ; Lond., 1882.   MD 7 Q 14
The Native Races of the Indian Archipelago: Papuans.
8vo. Lond., 1853.*   MA I R 4
Observations on the Commercial and Agricultural Capa-
bilities of the North Coast of New Holland. (Pam. 1.)
8vo. Lond., 1836.   MJ 2 P 36
The Steam Route from Singapore to Sydney, *via* Torres
Straits. 8vo. Lond. (n.d.)   MJ 2 Q 18
Voyages of the Dutch Brig of War, *Dourga* [*See* KOLFF,
LIEUT. D. H., JUNR.]

EARL (THE) AND THE DOCTOR. [*See* PEMBROKE,
EARL OF, AND KINGSLEY, G. H.]

EARLE (AUGUSTUS). A Narrative of a Nine Months'
Residence in New Zealand, in 1827. 8vo. Lond.,
1832.*   MD 4 V 30

EARLE (HORACE). Ups and Downs ; or, Incidents of
Australian Life. 8vo. Lond., 1861.*   MJ 1 S 13

EARLE (REV. PROF. JOHN), M.A. The Philology of the
English Tongue. 2nd ed. (Clar. Press.) 12mo. Oxford,
1873.   K 11 T 48
Two of the Saxon Chronicles, parallel ; edited by J. Earle.
8vo. Oxford, 1865.   B 5 S 17

EARLEY (WILLIAM). High-class Kitchen Gardening :
a Manual of improved culture of all Vegetables. 8vo.
Lond., 1875.   A 1 P 20

EARLY ENGLISH TEXT SOCIETY. Publications of
the. 52 vols. 8vo. Lond., 1864–87.   E
Sixth Report of the Committee. 8vo. Lond., 1870.
                                                MF 2 P 14

EARNSHAW (WM.) Digest of the Laws relating to
Shipping, Navigation, Commerce, and Revenue in the
British Colonies in America and the West Indies. 8vo.
Lond., 1818.   F 9 R 25

EARP (G. BUTLER). Gold Colonies of Australia ; com-
prising their History, Territorial Divisions, Produce, and
Capabilities, Notices of the Gold Mines ; with Advice
to Emigrants. 12mo. Lond., 1852.*   MD 2 P 20
Another copy. Enlarged and corrected Edition. 12mo.
Lond., 1852.*   MD 2 P 21
Gold Colonies of Australia, and Gold Seeker's Manual.
New ed. 12mo. Lond., 1853.   MD 2 P 23
Hand-book for intending Emigrants to the Southern
Settlements of New Zealand. 3rd ed. 8vo. Lond.,
1851.   MD 2 P 12
New Zealand : its Emigration and Gold Fields ; with
Map. 12mo. Lond., 1853.*   MD 2 P 13
What we did in Australia : being the Practical Ex-
perience of Three Clerks in the Stockyard and at the
Gold Fields. 12mo. Lond., 1853.*   MD 2 P 18
[*See* NAPIER, VICE-ADM. SIR C. J.]

EARWAKER (REV. JOHN PARSONS), M.A., &c. East
Cheshire : Past and Present ; or, a History of the Hundred of Macclesfield, in the County Palatine of Chester.
2 vols. 4to. Lond., 1877–80.   B 10 Q 12, 13 †

EASON (CHARLES), JUN., M.A., &c. Manual of Financial,
Railway, Agricultural, and other Statistics, for Politicians, Economists, and Investors. 8vo. Lond., 1884.
                                                F 6 T 24

EASSIE (W.) Cremation of the Dead : its History and
bearings upon Public Health. 8vo. Lond., 1875. A 16 T 29

EASTERN EUROPE and the Emperor Nicholas. 3 vols.
8vo. Lond., 1846.   B 12 T 23–25

EASTERN PERSIA. [*See* PERSIA, EASTERN.]

EAST INDIA AND COLONIAL MAGAZINE (THE).
12 vols. 8vo. Lond., 1836–42. E

EAST INDIA COMPANY. Debates of Proprietors of
East India Stock, relative to the Company's Charter.
(Pam. 8.) Lond., 1833. MJ 2 P 39

Reports and Documents connected with the Proceedings
of the East India Company, in regard to the Culture
and Manufacture of Cotton Wool, Raw Silk, and Indigo,
in India. 8vo. Lond., 1836. F 1 Q 23

Papers respecting the. Negociation for a renewal of the
East India Company's exclusive privileges. (Pam.) 8vo.
Lond., 1812. F 13 R 21

[*See* STEVENS, HENRY.]

EAST INDIA REGISTER. [*See* INDIAN ARMY AND CIVIL
SERVICE LIST.]

EAST INDIA YEAR-BOOK, 1841. 12mo. Lond.,
1841. E

EASTLAKE (SIR CHARLES LOCKE), F.R.I.B.A. Contributions to the Literature of the Fine Arts. First and
Second Series; with a Memoir compiled by Lady Eastlake. 2nd ed. 2 vols. 8vo. Lond., 1870. A 8 Q 17, 18

History of the Gothic Revival. Roy. 8vo. Lond.,
1872 A 2 S 24

Materials for a History of Oil Painting. 8vo. Lond.,
1847. A 8 Q 31

Notes on the principal Pictures in the Brera Gallery at
Milan. Illustrated. 8vo. Lond., 1883. A 8 P 29

Notes on the principal Pictures in the Louvre Gallery at
Paris. Illustrated. 8vo. Lond., 1883. A 6 V 17

Notes on the principal Pictures in the Old Pinakothek
at Munich. Illustrated. 8vo. Lond., 1884. A 8 P 28

EASTLAKE (ELIZABETH), LADY. History of Our Lord
as exemplified in Works of Art. [*See* JAMESON, MRS.]

Livonian Tales: The Disponent, The Wolves, The Jewess.
(H. and C. Lib.) 12mo. Lond., 1846. J 8 P 16

Residence on the Shores of the Baltic, described in a Series
of Letters. 2 vols. 8vo. Lond., 1841. D 9 P 6, 7

Another copy. (H. and C. Lib.) 12mo. Lond., 1844.
J 8 P 5

EASTWICK (EDWARD B.), C.B., &c. Fables of Pilpay.
[*See* PILPAY.]

The Gulistan. [*See* SADI, M. E.]

Hand-book of the Bombay Presidency. [*See* MURRAY, J.]

Hand-book of the Madras Presidency. [*See* MURRAY, J.]

The Kaisarnámah i Hind; or, Lay of the Empress:
a Poem, in nine Cantos; with Appendices containing the
Histories of the Princes of India. 2 vols. roy. fol.
Lond., 1882. H 5 P 6, 7 ‡

Comparative Grammar of the Sanskrit, Zend Greek, Latin,
Lithuanian, Gothic, German, and Sclavonic Languages.
[*See* BOPP, F.]

EATON (CHARLOTTE A.) Rome in the 19th Century.
5th ed., with Illustrations. 2 vols. 8vo. Lond., 1860.
B 12 P 17, 18

EATON (DORMAN B.) Report concerning Civil Service in
Great Britain. 8vo. Washington, 1879. F 9 R 18

EATON (FRED. A.) Albert Dürer. [*See* THAUSING, M.]

EBBUTT (P. G.) Emigrant Life in Kansas. 8vo. Lond.,
1886. D 4 Q 5

EBEL (DR. HERMANN). Celtic Studies, from the German;
with an Introduction on Roots, Stems, and Derivatives,
and on Case-endings of Nouns in the Indo-European Languages, by William K. Sullivan, Ph.D., &c. 8vo. Lond.,
1863. K 12 S 29

Grammatica Celtica. [*See* ZEUSS, I. C.]

EBERS (GEORG). Egypt, Descriptive, Historical, and Picturesque; translated from the original German, by Clara
Bell. 2 vols. imp. 4to. Lond., 1881–82. D 38 P 9, 10

EBERT (FREDERIC ADOLPHUS). General Bibliographical
Dictionary, from the German [by A. Brown]. 4 vols. 8vo.
Oxford, 1837. K 17 Q 26–29

EBRARD (DR. AUGUST). Handbuch der Mittelgälischen
Sprache; hauptsächlich Ossian's. Grammatik—Lese-
stücke—Wörterbuch; mit einem Vorwort von Dr. G.
Authenrieth. 8vo. Wien, 1870. K 13 P 23

EBSWORTH (JOSEPH). The Rival Valets: a Farce. (Cumberland's Eng. Theatre.) 12mo. Lond., 1829. H 2 Q 17

ECCLES (A. LESLIE A.), B.A., &c. Australasia as a
Resort for Invalids and Tourists. 8vo. Torquay, 1884.
MD 1 W 42

ECCLESIASTICAL COMMISSIONERS. Orders in
Council ratifying schemes of the Ecclesiastical Commis-
sioners for England. Acts relating to the Ecclesiastical
Commissioners for England; with Appendix and Index.
First and second General Reports to Her Majesty; with
Appendices, 1845, 1847. Seventeenth Report; with
Appendix, 1864. 15 vols. 8vo. Lond., 1843–65. E

ECCLESIASTICAL JURISDICTION. Copies of Correspondence and other Papers relating to Cases in which the
Bishop of any Diocese in the Australian Colonies, has
attempted to exercise Ecclesiastical Jurisdiction over any
of his Clergy; and to the formation of Ecclesiastical
Courts in any of the said Dioceses. (Parl. Docs., 57.) Fol.
Lond., 1850. MF 4 ‡

ECCLESTON (JAMES), B.A. Introduction to English
Antiquities, intended as a Companion to the History of
England. 8vo. Lond., 1847. B 4 S 15

ECHARD (LAURENCE), A.M. General Ecclesiastical History, from the Nativity to the First Establishment of
Christianity. Fol. Lond., 1702. G 35 P 15 ‡

Roman History; design'd as well for the understanding of
the Roman Authors, as the Roman Affairs. 8th ed. 5
vols. 8vo. Lond., 1719–20. B 12 Q 21–25

ECHO. [*See* BRITTEN, MRS. E. H.]

ECHO (THE): an Evening Newspaper. 17 vols. fol. Sydney, 1879–87. E

ECHO DE LA NOUVELLE JERUSALEM. Vol. 6. Fevriei, 1868. (Paui. C.) Imp. 8vo. Port Louis, 1868. MJ 2 S 1

ECKER (ALEXANDER). Lorenz Oken: a Biographical Sketch; or, "In Memoriam" of the Centenary of his Birth; From the German, by Alfred Tulk. 8vo. Lond., 1883. C 5 Q 13

ECKERMANN (JOHANN PETER). Conversations of Goethe with Eckermann. [*See* GOETHE, J. W. VON.]

ECKHEL (JOSEPH HILARIUS). Doctrina Numorum veterum. 8 vols. 4to. Vindobonæ, 1792–1839. A 13 S 1–8

Addenda ad Eckhelii Doctrinam Numorum veterum ex ejusdem autographo postumo, ab A. Steinbüchelo. 4to. Vindobonæ, 1826. A 13 S 9

ECKSTEIN (ERNST). Die Claudier: Roman aus der römischen Kaiserzeit. 2 vols. (in 1) 8vo. Wien, 1882. J 16 R 23

ECLECTIC REVIEW (THE). 49 vols. 8vo. Lond., 1827–66. E

ECLUSE DES LOGES (PIERRE MATHURIN DE L'.) Memoirs of Maximilian de Bethune Duke of Sully, Prime Minister of Henry the Great; translated from the French edition. 5 vols. 12mo. Edinb., 1773. C 4 P 29–33

EDEN (CHARLES H.) Australia's Heroes. 12mo. Lond., 1876.* MC 1 P 21

The Fifth Continent; with the adjacent Islands. 8vo. Lond., 1877.* MD 4 P 14

India, Historical and Descriptive; revised and enlarged from "Les Voyages Célèbres." 12mo. Lond., 1876. D 5 P 4

Interior of Australia. [*See* WARBURTON, COL. P. E.]

My Wife and I in Queensland: an Eight Years' Experience in the above Colony; with some Account of Polynesian Labour. 8vo. Lond., 1872.* MD 4 P 11

EDEN (REV. CHARLES PAGE), M.A. Works of the Rt. Rev. Jeremy Taylor. [*See* TAYLOR, RT. REV. J.]

EDEN (HON. EMILY). "Up the Country": Letters written to her Sister, from the Upper Provinces of India. 2 vols. 8vo. Lond., 1866. D 6 Q 29, 30

EDEN (RICHARD). The first three English Books on America [1511? | 1555 A.D.: being chiefly Translations, Compilations, &c., from the Writings, Maps, &c., of Pietro Martire, Sebastian Münster, Sebastian Cabot. Edited by Edward Arber, F.S.A. 4to. Birmingham, 1885. D 16 Q 13 ‡

EDEN (RT. HON. WILLIAM). [*See* AUCKLAND, RT. HON. W. EDEN, LORD.]

EDERSHEIM (ALFRED), D.D., &c. Life and Times of Jesus the Messiah. 2 vols. 8vo. Lond., 1883. G 14 P 18, 19

EDGAR (ANDREW). Old Church Life in Scotland: Lectures on Kirk-Session and Presbytery Records. 1st and 2nd 8vo. Paisley, 1885. G 9 S 24, 25

EDGAR (LUCY ANNA). Among the Black Boys; being the History of an attempt at civilising some Young Aborigines of Australia. 8vo. Lond., 1865. MA 1 R 2

EDGEWORTH (C. SNEYD). Mémoires de M. l'Abbé Edgeworth de Firmont, dernier Confesseur de Louis XVI; traduit de l'Anglais. 12mo. Paris, 1825. C 2 P 10

EDGEWORTH (FRANCIS YSIDRO), M.A. Mathematical Psychics: an Essay on the Application of Mathematics to the Moral Sciences. 8vo. Lond., 1881. A 10 T 10

EDGEWORTH (MISS MARIA). Essay on Irish Bulls. [*See* EDGEWORTH, R. L.]

Memoirs of Richard Lovell Edgeworth. [*See* EDGEWORTH, R. L.]

Study of Maria Edgeworth; with Notices of her Father and Friends, by Mrs. Grace Atkinson Oliver. 3rd ed. 8vo. Boston, 1882. C 3 T 4

EDGEWORTH (RICHARD LOVELL). Memoirs of; begun by himself, and concluded by his daughter, Maria Edgeworth. 2 vols. 8vo. Lond., 1820. C 8 R 27, 28

Another copy. 3rd ed. 8vo. Lond., 1844. C 8 R 29

EDGEWORTH (RICHARD LOVELL AND MARIA). Essay on Irish Bulls. 3rd ed. 12mo. Lond., 1808. G 3 Q 40

EDGEWORTH DE FIRMONT (HENRY ESSEX), L'ABBÉ. Mémoires de; recueillis par C. Sneyd Edgeworth. 12mo. Paris, 1815. C 2 P 10

EDINBURGH (H.R.H. PRINCE ALFRED), DUKE OF, K.G., &c. Cruise of H.M.S. Galatea. [*See* MILNER, REV. J.]

The Story of the Attempted Murder of His Royal Highness the Duke of Edinburgh at Clontarf, Thursday, March 12, 1868. Illustrated. (Curious Trials.) 8vo. Sydney, 1868. MF 2 R 19

Visit to Hongkong in 1869. [*See* BEACH, REV. W. R.]

EDINBURGH. Graphic and Historical Description of the City. 2 vols. roy. 8vo. Lond., 1820–22. B 13 S 3, 4

EDINBURGH ANNUAL REGISTER. 19 vols. (in 24) 8vo. Edinb., 1810–28. E

EDINBURGH GAZETTEER; or, Geographical Dictionary; containing a Description of the various Countries, Kingdoms, States, Cities, Towns, Mountains, &c. of the World. 8vo. Lond., 1827. D 11 U 11–16

EDINBURGH JOURNAL OF SCIENCE (THE). Conducted by David Brewster, LL.D., &c. Vols. 1–6. 6 vols. 8vo. Lond., 1827–29. E

EDINBURGH REVIEW (THE); or, Critical Journal. Vols. 1–162. 8vo. Edinb., 1802–86.   E

EDINBURGH ROYAL OBSERVATORY. [*See* SMYTH, C. P.]

EDINBURGH UNIVERSITY (THE). Calendar, 1884–86. 12mo. Edinb., 1884–86.   E

EDIS (ROBERT WILLIAM), F.S.A., &c. Decoration and Furniture of Town Houses. 8vo. Lond., 1881.   A 3 P 22

EDITOR OF THE AUSTRALIAN AND NEW ZEALAND GAZETTE (THE). [*See* HODGKINSON, S.]

EDITOR OF THE PORT PHILLIP GAZETTE (THE). [*See* ARDEN, G.]

EDKINS (REV. JOSEPH), D.D. Chinese Buddhism: a Volume of Sketches, Historical, Descriptive, and Critical. 8vo. Lond., 1880.   G 15 P 19

Grammar of the Chinese Colloquial Language, commonly called the Mandarin Dialect. 2nd ed. Roy. 8vo. Shanghai, 1864.   K 14 Q 26

Religion in China; containing a Brief Account of the Three Religions of the Chinese, with Observations on the Prospects of Christian Conversion amongst that People. 2nd ed. 8vo. Lond., 1878.   G 9 S 19

EDLESTON (J.), M.A. Correspondence of Sir Isaac Newton and Prof. Roger Cotes, including Letters of other Eminent Men; with Notes, Synoptical View of the Philosopher's Life, &c. 8vo. Lond., 1850.   C 10 U 37

EDMOND (J. P.) Aberdeen Printers; Edward Raban to James Nicol, 1620–1736. 8vo. Aberdeen, 1886.   C 10 R 1

EDMONDS (CYRUS R.) Cicero's Three Books of Offices. [*See* CICERO, M. T.]

History of Rome. [*See* LIVIUS, T.]

The Life and Times of General Washington. 2 vols. 18mo. Lond., 1835–36.   C 1 P 36, 37

EDMUNDSON (GEORGE), M.A. Milton and Vondel: a Curiosity of Literature. 8vo. Lond., 1885.   H 7 R 31

EDUCATION. Account, showing the Grants, Endowments, and Appropriations made for the purpose of Religious Instruction, or of Education in the Colonies, for the years 1840–42. (Parl. Docs. 47.) Fol. Lond., 1845.   MF 4 ‡

Council of Education, Great Britain: Twenty-seventh Report of the Science and Art Department. 8vo. Lond., 1880.   E

Education Commission: Report of the Commissioners appointed to Inquire into the State of Popular Education in England. 6 vols. roy. 8vo. Lond., 1861.   G 17 R 18–23

Education: the Defects of the Common School System and Proposed New System, based on District Populations and entire Local Management. 8vo. Melb., 1871.   MG 1 Q 38

EDUCATION—*continued.*

Education v. Religion. 8vo. Sydney, 1874.   MG 1 Q 32

Education, Victoria: Report of the Minister of Public Instruction, for the year 1886–87. Fol. Melb., 1887.   ME 10 Q 8 †

Explanation of the Plan of the Irish National Schools, shewing its peculiar adaptation to New South Wales. 8vo. Sydney, 1836.   MG 1 Q 30

General Education: The Protestant Resolutions, and Petition to His Excellency the Governor and the Legislative Council. Roy. 8vo. Sydney, 1836.   MJ 2 U 2

General Education vindicated. (Pam. 17.) 8vo. Sydney, 1844.   MJ 2 Q 7

Journal of Education, with which are incorporated the *Educational Reporter and Scholastic Advertiser.* 6 vols. 8vo. Lond., 1874–77.   E

Lectures on Education, delivered at the Royal Institution of Great Britain. 8vo. Lond., 1855.   G 17 P 1

Minutes of the Committee of Council of Education, 1846. 2 vols. 8vo. Lond., 1847.   G 17 Q 10, 11

On the Publication of School Books by Government at the Public Expense. 8vo. Lond., 1851.   MF 1 R 17

Original Essay on Popular Education; its General Merits, and special adaptation to the circumstances of the Colony of New South Wales; by "Catholicus." (Pam. 19.) 8vo. Sydney, 1848.   MJ 2 Q 8

Protestant Proceedings vindicated from the Imputations of Political Faction, Misconception of the Irish System, and Disrespect to His Majesty's Government; by "A Member of the Committee." 8vo. Sydney, 1836.   MG 1 Q 30

Public Education: New Regulations. 12mo. Sydney, 1841.   MJ 2 R 3

Regulations and Directions to be attended to in making application to the Commissioners of National Education, for aid towards the building of School-houses, or for the support of Schools. 8vo. Sydney, 1848.   MJ 2 Q 24

Regulations for the Establishment and Conduct of National Schools in New South Wales. 8vo. Sydney, 1853.   MG 1 Q 30

Report of the Committee of Council of Education, 1858–9. 8vo. Lond., 1859.   G 17 R 12

Reports of the Council of Education upon the Condition of the Public Schools. 2 vols. roy. 8vo. Sydney, 1869–71.   ME 3 V

Series of Letters in defence of the National System, against the attacks of an anonymous writer in the *Sydney Morning Herald;* by the Teachers of the National Schools of Sydney. 8vo. Sydney, 1857.   MJ 2 Q 14

Statement explanatory of the System of Education administered by the National Board of New South Wales. 8vo. Sydney, 1858.   MG 1 Q 30

Technical Education: Report from the Committee of the Working Men's College of the Mechanics' School of Arts. Fol. Sydney, 1881.   ME

[*See* CATHOLIC EDUCATION; CENTRAL SOCIETY OF EDUCATION; *and* QUARTERLY JOURNAL OF EDUCATION.]

EDUCATION—*continued.*

Educational Pamphlets. Present Systems; Present State of Education; The New Bill; Organization and Management of Schools; Normal Schools and Training Institutions; School Conduct: 1. Pupils, 2. Teachers; Examination and Classification of Teachers. 8vo. Melh., 1857.
MG 1 Q 38

EDUCATOR (THE). Prize Essays on the expediency and means of elevating the Profession of the Educator in Society. 8vo. Lond., 1839.   G 17 P 2

EDWARD, THE BLACK PRINCE. History of the Life of, and of various events connected therewith; by G. P. R. James. 2 vols. 8vo. Lond., 1836. C 10 T 42, 43

Le Prince Noir: Poème du Héraut d'Armes Chandos. 4to. Lond., 1883.   H 5 V 14

EDWARD III. History of; by Joshua Barnes. Fol. Camb., 1688.   B 15 S 10 †

History of the Life and Times of Edward III; by William Longman. 2 vols. 8vo. Lond., 1869.   B 6 P 11, 12

EDWARD IV. Privy Purse Expenses of. [*See* NICOLAS, SIR N. H.]

EDWARD VI. Writings of. [*See* BRITISH REFORMERS 4.]

EDWARD (REV. ROBERT). County of Argus, 1678. 8vo. Edinb., 1883.   ·   D 7 R 47

EDWARD (THOMAS). Life of a Scotch Naturalist; by Samuel Smiles. Portrait and Illustrations. 8vo. Lond., 1876.   C 3 V 4

EDWARDES (CHARLES). Garibaldi. [*See* MELENA, E.] [*See* LEOPARDI, G.]

EDWARDES (LADY EMMA). Memorials of Sir H. B. Edwardes. [*See* EDWARDES, MAJ.-GEN. SIR H. B.]

EDWARDES (MAJOR-GEN. SIR HERBERT B.), K.C.B., &c. A Year on the Punjab Frontier, in 1848–49. 2 vols. 8vo. Lond., 1851.   .   D 6 8 9, 10

Memorials of the Life and Letters of; by his wife [Lady Emma Edwardes]. 2 vols. 8vo. Lond., 1886.
C 6 V 20, 21

EDWARDS (SIR HERBERT BENJAMIN), K.C.B., &c., AND MERIVALE (HERMAN), C.B. Life of Sir Henry Lawrence. 2nd ed. 2 vols. 8vo. Lond., 1872. C 8 P 28, 29

EDWARDS (ALPHONSE MILNE-). [*See* MILNE-EDWARDS, PROF. A.]

EDWARDS (AMELIA B.) Story of Cervantes. 12mo. Lond., 1863.   C 2 P 5

A Thousand Miles up the Nile. Illustrated. Imp. 8vo. Lond., 1877.   D 2 U 3

EDWARDS (BRYAN), F.R.S.S.A. History, Civil and Commercial, of the British West Indies. 5th ed. 5 vols. 8vo. Lond., 1819.   B 1 R 6–10

Maps and Plates [to the above.] 4to. Lond., 1818. B 18 V 5

EDWARDS (C. A.) Organs and Organ-building: a Treatise on the History and Construction of the Organ. Illustrated. 8vo. Lond., 1881.   A 7 P 12

EDWARDS (EDWARD). Administrative Economy of the Fine Arts in England. 8vo. Lond., 1840.   A 8 Q 21

Anecdotes of Painters who have resided, or been born in England; with Critical Remarks on their Productions. 4to. Lond., 1808.   A 8 R 18

Brief Descriptive Catalogue of the Medals struck in France and its Dependencies, between the years 1789 and 1830. 8vo. Lond., 1837.   A 13 S 36

Chapters of the Biographical History of the French Academy. 8vo. Lond., 1864.   C 8 Q 9

Free Town Libraries: their Formation, Management, and History, in Britain, France, Germany, and America. 8vo. Lond., 1869.   B 14 S 19

Letter to the Rt. Hon. the Earl of Ellesmere, on the desirability of a better provision of Public Libraries. (Pam. 34.) 8vo. Lond., 1848.   J 12 U 26

Libraries and Founders of Libraries. 8vo. Lond., 1865.
B 15 Q 35

Lives of the Founders of the British Museum; with Notices of its Chief Augmentors and other Benefactors, 1570–1870. 2 vols. 8vo. Lond., 1870. C 10 U 10, 11

Memoirs of Libraries; including a Hand-book of Library Economy. 2 vols. 8vo. Lond., 1859.   J 7 U 24, 25

Remarks on the paucity of Libraries freely open to the Public in the British Empire. 2nd ed. (Pam. 34.) 8vo. Lond., 1849.   '   J 12 U 26

EDWARDS (ELIEZER). Words, Facts, and Phrases: a Dictionary of Curious, Quaint, and Out-of-the-way Matters. 8vo. Lond., 1882.   K 17 P 9

EDWARDS (EMORY), M.E. Catechism of the Marine Steam Engine, for the use of Engineers, Firemen, and Mechanics. 8vo. Philad., 1879.   A 11 P 21

Modern American Locomotive Engines: their Design, Construction, and Management. 8vo. Philad., 1883.
A 6 8 3

EDWARDS (E. PRICE). Our Seamarks: a Plain Account of the Lighthouses, Lightships, Beacons, Buoys, and Fog-Signals maintained on our Coasts. Illustrated. 8vo. Lond., 1884.   A 2 R 46

EDWARDS (H. MILNE). [*See* MILNE-EDWARDS, H.]

EDWARDS (HENRY S.) Beaumarchais and his Times. [*See* LOMÉNIE, L. DE.]

EDWARDS (H. SUTHERLAND). Captivity of two Russian Princesses. [*See* VERDEREVSKY.]

Faust Legend; its Origin and Development. 12mo. Lond., 1886.   B 27 P 3

Polish Captivity. 2 vols. 8vo. Lond., 1863. B 7 R 33, 34

Russian Projects against India, from the Czar to General Skobeleff. With Map. 8vo. Lond., 1885. B 12 U 31

Russians at Home: Unpolitical Sketches. 2nd ed. 8vo. Lond., 1861.   D 8 Q 35

EDWARDS (JONATHAN), A.M. On Revivals; containing a faithful Narrative of the surprising Work of God in the conversion of many Hundred Souls in Northampton, 1735. (Pam. 17.) 8vo. Lond., 1839.   MJ 2 Q 7

Treatise concerning Religious Affections. 12mo. Edinb., 1812.   G 13 R 19

EDWARDS (JOSEPH). Differential Calculus; with Applications and numerous Examples. 8vo. Lond., 1886.   A 10 S 15

EDWARDS (MATILDA BETHAM-). Winter with the Swallows. 8vo. Lond., 1867.   D 1 V 25

EDWARDS (WILLIAM), JUDGE. Reminiscences of a Bengal Civilian. 8vo. Lond., 1866.   D 5 R 7

EDWARDS (WILLIAM). What shall we do with our Criminals? with an original Scheme of a Reformatory Institution. 8vo. Melb., 1857.   MF 1 Q 5

EDWARDS (WILLIAM H.) Voyage up the River Amazon, including a residence at Pará. (H. and C. Lib.) 12mo. Lond., 1847.   J 8 P 24

EDWIN (LIEUT. R. A.), R.N. Traverse Table; with simple and Brief Method of correcting Compass Courses. 8vo. Portsmouth, 1871.   A 3 U 32

EDY (JOHN WILLIAM). [See BOYDELL, J.]

EGEDE (HANS), MISSIONARY. Description of Greenland; with a Historical Introduction, and a Life of the Author. 2nd ed. 8vo. Lond., 1818.   D 4 R 46

EGERTON (FRANCIS HENRY). Life and Character of Thomas Egerton, Lord Ellesmere, &c.; also, the Lives of John Egerton, Lord Bishop of Durham, and of Francis Egerton, Third Duke of Bridgewater. (Notes in French.) Roy. fol. Paris, 1812.   C 4 S 19 ‡

EGERTON (FRANCIS L. G.) [See ELLESMERE, EARL OF.]

EGERTON (MARY M.), COUNTESS OF WILTON. Book of Costume; or, Annals of Fashion, from the Earliest Period. Roy. 8vo. Lond., 1846.   A 7 T 24

EGESTOFF (G. H. C.) Klopstock's Messiah. [See KLOPSTOCK, F. G.]

EGGELING (JULIUS). The Satapatha-Bráhmana. [See MÜLLER, PROF. M.]

EGGERS (H. F. A.), BARON. The Flora of St. Croix and the Virgin Islands. 8vo. Wash., 1879.   F 9 R 6

EGILSSON (SVEINBJÖRN). Lexicon Poëticum Antiquæ Linguæ Septentrionalis. Roy. 8vo. Hafniæ, 1860.   K 16 R 29

EGINHARD. Annales des Rois Pepin, Charlemagne, et Louis-le-Débonnaire. [See GUIZOT, F. P. G., 3.]

EGYPT. Correspondence relating to. 20 vols. (in 3) sm. fol. Lond., 1885.   F 36 Q 14-16 ‡

1. Affairs of Egypt.
2. British Military Operations in the Soudan.
3. Prince Hassan's Mission to the Soudan.
4-7. Finances of Egypt, and Navigation of the Suez Canal.
8. Revenue and Expenditure of Egypt.
9. British Military Operations in the Soudan.
10. Extract from a Despatch respecting the Suez Canal.
11. Finances of Egypt and the Suez Canal.
12. Suppression of the *Bosphore Egyptien*.
13. Military Operations in the Soudan.
14. Ports in the Red Sea and the Gulf of Aden, and the Province of Harrar.
15. Reports on the State of Egypt, &c.
16. Ports in the Red Sea and the Gulf of Aden.
17. Finances of Egypt.
18. Military Operations in the Soudan.
19. Suez Canal International Commission.
20. Affairs of Egypt.

Description de l'Egypte. [See PANCKOUCKE, C. L. F.]

Map of Lower Egypt: Four Sheets, with inset Maps of Cairo and Alexandria; prepared in the Intelligence Department, War Office, London. Sm. fol. Lond., 1882.   D 33 Q 12 ‡

Pictorial Records of the English in Egypt; with a full and descriptive Life of General Gordon, the Hero of Khartoum. With Engravings, and a series of coloured Portraits. 8vo. Lond., 1885.   B 2 R 48

War in Egypt. The Illustrations by Richard Simkin; the Text and Maps, by special permission, from *The Times*. Sm. 4to. Lond., 1883.   B 2 R 36

Warm Corners in Egypt; by "One who was in them." 8vo. Lond., 1886.   D 1 Q 13

EGYPTIAN ANTIQUITIES. Catalogue of, collected by Sir Charles Nicholson, D.C.L., &c. 8vo. Lond., 1858.   K 7 Q 3

EICHENS (MARIE). First Reading Book; edited by Annie Clough. (Clar. Press.) 12mo. Oxford, 1869.   G 17 S 8

EICHERT (OTTO). Album der neuern Deutscher Lyrik. Erster Theil. 18mo. Leipzig, 1851.   H 6 P 11

EICHHOFF (F. G.) Grammaire Générale Indo-Européenne; ou, Comparaison des Langues Grecque, Latine, Française, Gothique, Allemande, Anglaise et Russe, entre elles et avec le Sanscrit; suivie d'extraits de Poésie Indienne. 8vo. Paris, 1867.   K 13 P 36

EIDLITZ (LEOPOLD). Nature and Function of Art, more especially of Architecture. 8vo. Lond., 1881.   A 2 S 15

EIGHT YEARS' RESIDENT, AN. [See THORNE, E.]

EIPPER (REV. CHRISTOPHER). Statement of the Origin, Condition, and Prospects of the German Mission to the Aborigines at Moreton Bay. (Pam. Ad.) 8vo. Sydney, 1841.   MD 1 V 9

EKHOLTZ (A.) Practisches Lehr- und Hülfsbuch der schwedischen Sprache. 3ᵉ Auflage. 12mo. Lubeck, 1858.   K 11 V 35

ELCHO (LORD), M.P. [*See* WEMYSS AND MARCH, EARL OF.]

ELDER (WILLIAM). Biography of Elisha Kent Kane. 8vo. Lond., 1858.   C 8 P 24

ELDERSHAW (F.) Australia as it really is, in its Life, Scenery, and Adventures; with the Character, Habits, and Customs of its Aboriginal Inhabitants, and the Prospects and Extent of its Gold-fields. 12mo. Lond., 1854.
                                           MD 1 S 36

ELDON (JOHN SCOTT), EARL OF, D.C.L., LORD CHANCELLOR. Public and Private Life of; with Selections from his Correspondence, by Horace Twiss. 3 vols. 8vo. Lond., 1844.   C 9 S 1-3

Sketch of the Lives of Lords Stowell and Eldon, by W. E. Surtees. 8vo. Lond., 1846.   C 9 U 40

ELECTORAL ROLLS. [*See* NEW SOUTH WALES.]

ELECTRICITY. Practical Applications of : a Series of Lectures. 8vo. Lond., 1884.   A 6 Q 14

ELEGANT EPISTLES ; being a copious Collection of Familiar and Amusing Letters. Roy. 8vo. Lond., 1822.
                                           J 4 T 6

ELEGANT EXTRACTS ; or, Useful and Entertaining Pieces of Poetry. Roy. 8vo. Lond., 1824.   H G U 28

ELEGANT EXTRACTS ; or, Useful and Entertaining Passages in Prose. Roy. 8vo. Lond., 1824.   J 4 T 5

ELGIN (JAMES), EARL OF. Letters and Journals of James, eighth Earl of Elgin ; edited by Theodore Walrond, C.B. 8vo. Lond., 1872.   C 7 R 1

Narrative of his Mission to China and Japan, in the years 1857-59. 2 vols. 8vo. Lond., 1859.   B 2 Q 10, 11

ELIA. [*See* LAMB, C.]

ELIHU (JAN). Private Life of an Eastern Queen. [*See* KNIGHTON, W.]

ELIOT (GEORGE). [*See* CROSS, MRS. M. A.]

ELIOT (SIR JOHN). An Apology for Socrates and Negotium Posterorum (1590-1632); edited, with Illustrations, &c., by the Rev. Alexander B. Grosart, LL.D., &c. 2 vols. 4to. Lond., 1881.   B 7 R 11, 12

De Jure Maiestatis; or, Political Treatise of Government (1628-30); and the Letter-book of Sir John Eliot (1625-32); edited by the Rev. Alexander B. Grosart, LL.D., &c. 2 vols. 4to. Lond., 1882.   F 12 R 7, 8

Life of. [*See* MACKINTOSH, SIR J.]

Sir John Eliot : a Biography, 1590-1632; by John Forster. 2 vols. 8vo. Lond., 1864.   C 5 U 9, 10

ELIOT (JOHN), THE APOSTLE. Life and Labors of, among the Indian Nations of New England ; with an Account of the Eliots in England, by Col. R. B. Caverly. 8vo. Boston, 1882.   B 1 Q 49

ELIZABETH OF YORK. Privy Purse Expenses of. [*See* NICOLAS, SIR N. H.]

ELIZABETH (QUEEN OF ENGLAND). Court of Queen Elizabeth. [*See* NAUNTON, SIR R.]

England in the Days of Queen Elizabeth. [*See* RYE, W. B.]

History of ; by William Camden. Imp. 8vo. Lond., 1688.   B 2 T 7

Memoirs of the Court of ; by Lucy Aikin. 2 vols. 8vo. Lond., 1818.   C 5 V 11, 12

Romantic Biography of the Age of Elizabeth. [*See* TAYLOR, W. C.]

Youth of Queen Elizabeth, 1533-58 ; by L. Wiesener. 2 vols. 8vo. Lond., 1879.   C 2 P 11, 12

ELIZABETH CHARLOTTE (PRINCESSE PALATINE). Lettres inédites de la Princesse Palatine. Traduites par A. A. Rolland. 8vo. Paris, 1881.   C 2 S 34

ELIZABETH (SAINT) OF HUNGARY. Histoire de. [*See* MONTALEMBERT, COMTE DE.]

ELLA (SAMUEL). Peruvian Slavers: Atrocious Proceedings at Savage Island. (Newspaper Cuttings, Pam. C.) Roy 8vo. Sydney, 1863.   MJ 2 S 1

ELLACOMBE (REV. HENRY NICHOLSON), M.A. Plant-Lore and Garden-Craft of Shakespeare. 2nd ed. 8vo. Lond., 1884.   A 4 P 18

ELLENBOROUGH (EDWARD LAW), LORD. Political Diary, 1828-30 ; edited by Lord Colchester. 2 vols. 8vo. Lond., 1881.   B 7 Q 21, 22

[*See* INDIA.]

ELLERY (ROBERT L. J.) Lectures on the Common Uses of Astronomy. [*See* MELBOURNE PUBLIC LIBRARY.]

Notes on the Climate of Victoria. (Inter. Exhib. Essays.) 8vo. Melb., 1867.   MJ 2 R 9

Notes on the Climate of Victoria. (Pam. Co.) 8vo. Melb., 1873.   MA 2 Q 33

Results of Astronomical Observations, made at the Melbourne (Williamstown) Observatory, in the years 1861-70. 4 vols. 8vo. Melb., 1866-73.   MA 1 T 13-16

ELLESMERE (FRANCIS LEVESON GOWER EGERTON), EARL OF. Sieges of Vienna. [*See* SCHIMMER, K. A.]

War of Sicilian Vespers. [*See* AMARI, M.]

ELLICOTT (RT. REV. CHARLES JOHN), D.D. Reply to Bishop Ellicott's Pamphlet. [*See* BURGON, REV. J. W.]

ELLICOTT (RT. REV. CHARLES JOHN), D.D., AND PALMER (EDWIN). The Revisers and the Greek Text of the New Testament; by "Two Members of the New Testament Company." 8vo. Lond., 1882.	G 2 R 10

ELLIOT (ALEXANDER). Hood in Scotland: Reminiscences of Thomas Hood, Poet and Humourist, collected and arranged. 4to. Dundee, 1885.	C 5 U 12

ELLIOT (DANIEL GIRAUD), F.L.S., &c. Monograph of the Bucerotidæ, or Family of the Hornbills. Roy. 4to. Lond., 1882.	A 4 U 14 ‡

Monograph of Felidæ, or Family of the Cats. L. 4to. Lond., 1883.	A 12 P 10 ‡

Monograph of the Paradiseidæ, or Birds of Paradise. At. fol. Lond., 1873.*	A 12 P 9 ‡

Monograph of the Phasianidæ, or Family of the Pheasants. 2 vols. l. 4to. New York, 1872.	A 12 P 7, 8 ‡

Monograph of the Tetraonidæ, or Family of the Grouse. At. fol. New York, 1865.	A 12 P 6 ‡

ELLIOT (MRS. FRANCES). Diary of an Idle Woman in Italy. New ed. 8vo. Lond., 1872.	D 7 Q 26

Diary of an Idle Woman in Spain. 2 vols. 8vo. Lond., 1884.	D 8 R 37, 38

Old Court Life in France. 2 vols. 8vo. Lond., 1873.	C 8 U 30, 31

Pictures of Old Rome. New ed. 8vo. Lond., 1872.	D 8 R 36

ELLIOT (ADM. SIR GEORGE), K.C.B. Treatise on future Naval Battles, and how to fight them, and on other Naval Tactical Subjects. Roy. 8vo. Lond., 1885.	A 3 Q 16

ELLIOT (SIR H. M.), K.C.B. Bibliographical Index to the Historians of Muhammedan India. Vol. 1—General Histories *(all published.)* 8vo. Calcutta, 1849. B 10 R 35

History of India, as told by its own Historians. The Muhammadan Period. Edited, from the Posthumous Papers of Sir H. M. Elliot, by Prof. John Dowson, M.R.A.S. 8 vols. 8vo. Lond., 1867–77.	B 10 R 2–9

Memoirs on the History, Folk-Lore, and Distribution of the Races of the North-western Provinces of India. 2 vols. 8vo. Lond., 1869.	B 10 U 33, 34

ELLIOT (J. P.) Barometric Variations at Sydney, 1844–46. (MS.) fol. Sydney, 1844–46.	MA 1 R 12 ‡

ELLIOT (ROBERT H.) Experiences of a Planter in the Jungles of Mysore. Illustrated. 2 vols. 8vo. Lond., 1871.	D 5 T 33, 34

ELLIOT (SIR W.) Coins of Southern India. [*See* NUMISMATA ORIENTALIA, 4.]

ELLIOTSON (J.) Elements of Physiology. [*See* BLUMENBACH, J. F.]

ELLIOTT (CHARLES). Life of Hafiz Ool-Moolk. [*See* MOOST' UJAD KHAN BUHADOOR.]

ELLIOTT (CHARLES BOILEAU). Letters from the North of Europe. 8vo. Lond., 1832.	D 9 Q 12

ELLIOTT (EBENEZER). The Splendid Village, Corn Law Rhymes, and other Poems. 12mo. Lond., 1833. H 7 R 29

ELLIOTT (REV. E. B.), A.M. Horæ Apocalypticæ; or, a Commentary on the Apocalypse, critical and historical. 3rd ed. 4 vols. 8vo. Lond., 1847.	G 9 S 4–7

ELLIOTT (GRACE DALRYMPLE). Journal de ma Vie pendant la Revolution Française. [*See* BARRIÈRE, J. F., 27.]

ELLIOTT (MRS. M. L.) Shakspeare's Garden of Girls. 8vo. Lond., 1885.	H 1 S 20

ELLIOTT (CAPTAIN ROBERT), R.N. Views in the East; comprising India, Canton, and the Shores of the Red Sea; with Historical and Descriptive Illustrations. 2 vols. imp. 8vo. Lond., 1833.	D 4 V 22, 23

ELLIOTT (SIZAR), J.P. On the Introduction of Local Industries into New South Wales. (Pam. 36.) 8vo. Melb., 1872.	MJ 2 Q 23

Another copy. 8vo. Melb., 1876.	MJ 2 R 14

Another copy. (Pam. G.)	MA 2 V 7

ELLIOTT (WILLIAM). Adamson's Australian Gardener. [*See* ADAMSON, W.]

ELLIOTT (HON. WILLIAM). Carolina Sports by Land and Water. 8vo. Lond., 1867.	D 3 Q 25

ELLIS (MRS. SARAH), SARAH STICKNEY. Daughters of England, their position in Society, Character and Responsibilities. 8vo. Lond., 1842.	F 14 R 5

Mothers of England, their Influence, and Responsibility. 12mo. Lond., 1843.	J 1 T 6

Poetry of Life. 2 vols. 8vo. Lond., 1835.	J 12 Q 3, 4

Summer and Winter in the Pyrenees. 8vo. Lond., 1841.	D 9 Q 38

Women of England, their social Duties and domestic Habits. 8vo. Lond., 1839.	F 14 R 2

ELLIS (MAJOR ALFRED BURDON). History of the First West India Regiment. 8vo. Lond., 1885.	B 1 R 12

West African Islands. 8vo. Lond., 1885.	D 2 R 13

ELLIS (ALEXANDER JOHN), B.A. The Essentials of Phonetics. 8vo. Lond., 1848.	K 14 Q 30

Plea for Phonetic Spelling; or, the Necessity of Orthographic Reform. 2nd ed. 8vo. Lond., 1848. K 14 Q 30

[*See* HELMHOLTZ, H. L. F.]

ELLIS (GEORGE). Specimens of Early English Metrical Romances; chiefly written during the early part of the 14th Century. 2nd ed. 3 vols. 8vo. Lond., 1811.	H 7 R 22–24

Specimens of Early English Poets. 3rd ed. 3 vols. 12mo. Lond., 1803.	H 7 R 19–21

ELLIS (GEORGE E.) The Red Man and the White Man in North America, from its Discovery to the Present Time. 8vo. Boston, 1882. A 1 W 19

ELLIS (GEORGE JAMES WELBORE AGAR), LORD DOVER. [*See* DOVER, G. J. W. A. ELLIS, LORD.]

ELLIS (GRACE A.) Memoir, Letters, and a Selection from the Poems and Prose Writings of Anna Lætitia Barbauld. 2 vols. 8vo. Boston, 1874. C 3 Q 14, 15

ELLIS (RT. HON. HENRY). Journal of the Proceedings of the late Embassy [of Lord Amherst] to China. Illustrated. 4to. Lond., 1817. D 5 V 33

ELLIS (SIR HENRY), K.H., F.R.S., &c. British Museum. Elgin and Phigaleian Marbles. (Lib. Ent. Know.) 2 vols. 12mo. Lond., 1833. K 10 R 27, 28

General Introduction to Domesday Book. 2 vols. 8vo. Lond., 1833. B 15 T 22, 23

Original Letters, illustrative of English History; including numerous Royal Letters, from Autographs in the British Museum, &c. 3 vols. 8vo. Lond., 1825. B 4 R 5–7

2nd series. 4 vols. 8vo. Lond., 1827. B 4 R 8–11

3rd series. 4 vols. 8vo. Lond., 1846. B 4 R 12–15

Registrum vulgariter nuncupatum "The Record of Caernarvon." [*See* RECORD COMMISSIONERS' PUBLICATIONS.]

St. Paul's Cathedral. [*See* DUGDALE, SIR W.]

The Townley Gallery. (Lib. Ent. Know.) 2 vols. 8vo. Lond., 1836. K 10 R 44, 45

[*See* FARVAN, R.; *and* HARDYNG, JOHN.]

ELLIS (HENRY T.), R.N. Hong Kong to Manilla, and the Lakes of Luzon, in the Philippine Isles in 1856. 8vo. Lond., 1859. D 5 R 46

ELLIS (JOHN). Letters addressed to J. Ellis. [*See* DOVER, LORD.]

ELLIS (ROBERT), B.D. Asiatic Affinities of the Old Italians. 8vo. Lond., 1870. K 11 T 42

ELLIS (PROF. ROBINSON), M.A. Commentary on Catullus. (Clar. Press.) 8vo. Oxford, 1876. J 3 T 2

ELLIS (TRISTRAM J.) On a Raft, and through the Desert: the Narrative of an Artist's Journey through Northern Syria and Kurdistan. Illustrated. 2 vols. 4to. Lond., 1881. D 6 S 34, 35

ELLIS (W.), SURGEON. Authentic Narrative of a Voyage performed by Captain Cook and Captain Clerke, in H.M.S. *Resolution* and *Discovery*, 1776–80, in search of a North-west Passage between the Continents of Asia and America. 2nd ed. 2 vols. 8vo. Lond., 1783. MD 3 T 15, 16

Another copy. 3rd ed. 2 vols. 8vo. Lond., 1784. MD 3 T 17, 18

ELLIS (WILLIAM). A Layman's Contribution to the Knowledge and Practice of Religion in Common Life. 8vo. Lond., 1857. G 2 P 21

ELLIS (WILLIAM). Royal Jubilees of England; with introductory Sketches of the Mosaic and Roman Jubilees. 12mo. Lond., 1886. B 23 P 1

ELLIS (REV. WILLIAM). History of Madagascar; comprising the Progress of the Christian Mission, established 1818. 2 vols. 8vo. Lond., 1838. B 1 P 24, 25

Madagascar re-visited; describing the Events of a new Reign, and the Revolution which followed. Illustrated. 8vo. Lond., 1867. D 2 Q 8

Narrative of a Tour through Hawaii, or Owhyhee; with Remarks on the History, Traditions, Manners, Customs, and Language of the Inhabitants of the Sandwich Islands. 8vo. Lond., 1826. MD 7 Q 11

Another copy. 2nd ed. 8vo. Lond., 1827. MD 7 Q 12

Polynesian Researches, during a Residence of nearly Six Years in the South Sea Islands. 2 vols. 8vo. Lond., 1830. MD 7 Q 9, 10

Polynesian Researches, during a Residence of nearly Eight Years in the Society and Sandwich Islands. 2nd ed. 4 vols. 12mo. Lond., 1839. MD 3 P 4–7

Another copy. New ed., enlarged and improved. 4 vols. 12mo. Lond., 1859.* MD 3 P 8–11

Three Visits to Madagascar, during the years 1853–56, including a Journey to the Capital. 8vo. Lond., 1858. D 2 Q 7

ELLIS (SIR W. C.) Treatise on the Nature, Symptoms, Causes, and Treatment of Insanity. 8vo. Lond., 1838. A 12 S 16

ELLISON (SELCOME). Prison Scenes; and Narrative of Escape from France during the late War. 8vo. Lond., 1838. F 15 Q 11

ELLISTON (ROBERT WILLIAM), COMEDIAN. Memoirs of, 1774–1810; by George Raymond. With Illustrations by George Cruikshank. 2 vols. 8vo. Lond., 1844. C 7 Q 3, 4

ELLISTON (WILLIAM CORE). Hobart Town Almanack, and (Ross's) Van Diemen's Land Annual. 12mo. Hobart, 1837.* ME 4 P

Hobart Town Almanack, and Van Diemen's Land Annual, 1838.* ME 4 P

ELLWANGER (H. B.) The Rose: a Treatise on the Cultivation, History, Family Characteristics, &c., of the various Groups of Roses. 12mo. New York, 1882. A 4 P 10

ELLWOOD (THOMAS). History of the Life of Thomas Ellwood. (Autobiog., 11.) 12mo. Lond., 1827 C 1 P 10

ELMES (JAMES), M.R.I.A. General and Bibliographical Dictionary of the Fine Arts. 8vo. Lond., 1826. C 18 P 28

Practical Treatise on Architectural Jurisprudence. 8vo. Lond., 1827. F 9 P 15

ELPHINSTONE (HON. G. K.) [*See* KEITH, VISCOUNT.]

ELPHINSTONE (HON. MOUNTSTUART).   Account of the Kingdom of Caubul and its Dependencies in Persia, Tartary, and India. 2 vols. 8vo. Lond., 1842.   D 4 T 9, 10
History of India. 2 vols. 8vo. Lond., 1841. B 10 S 26, 27
Life of; by Sir T. E. Colebrooke, Bart. With Portraits. 2 vols. 8vo. Lond., 1884.   C 7 P 4, 5

ELRINGTON (PROF. CHARLES RICHARD), D.D.   Life of the Most Rev. James Ussher. [*See* USSHER, MOST REV. J.]

ELTON (CHARLES). Norway; the Road and the Fell. 8vo· Lond., 1864.   D 8 S 24
Origins of English History. Roy. 8vo. Lond., 1882.   B 5 V 8

ELTON (CHARLES ABRAHAM). Specimens of the Classic Poets, from Homer to Tryphiodorus. 3 vols. 8vo. Lond., 1814.   H 7 R 25–27
[*See* HABINGTON, W., *and* HESIOD.]

ELTON (J. FREDERIC), F.R.G.S. Travels and Researches among the Lakes and Mountains of Eastern and Central Africa; edited and completed by H. B. Cotterill. Illustrated. 8vo. Lond., 1876.   D 1 W 21

ELWELL (REV. E. SIMEON), M.A. Boy Colonists; or, Eight Years of Colonial Life in Otago, New Zealand. 8vo. Lond., 1878.*   MD 4 P 41

ELWES (ALFRED). Benguella to Yacca. [*See* CAPELLO, H., AND IVENS, R.]
Dizionario Italiano, Inglese, Francese : a Concise Dictionary of the Italian, English, and French Languages. (Weale.) 3 vols. 12mo. Lond., 1855–56. K 11 T 15–17
    1. Italian—English—French.
    2. English—French—Italian.
    3. French—Italian—English.
Dictionary of the Portuguese Language, in two Parts· 1. Portuguese-English. 2. English-Portuguese; including a large number of Technical Terms used in Mining, Engineering, &c. (Weale.) 12mo. Lond.,1884. K 11 T 5
Dictionary of the Spanish [and English] Languages. (Weale.) 12mo. Lond., 1871.   K 11 T 19
English-French Dictionary. 5th ed. (Weale.) 12mo. Lond., 1872.   K 11 T 13
French-English Dictionary. 3rd ed. (Weale.) 12mo. Lond., 1869.   K 11 T 13
Grammar of the Italian Language. 4th ed. (Weale.) 12mo. Lond., 1872.   K 11 T 14
Grammar of the Spanish Language. (Weale.) 12mo. Lond., 1872.   K 11 T 18

ELWES (R. H. M.) Works of Spinoza [*See* SPINOZA, B. DE.]

ELWES (ROBERT). Sketcher's Tour round the World. Illustrated. Roy. 8vo. Lond., 1854.   D 9 U 26

ELYOT (SIR THOMAS), KNT. The Boke named the Gouernour; edited from the first edition of 1531, by Henry Herbert Stephen Croft, M.A. With Portraits. 2 vols. 4to. Lond., 1880. ·   J 7 U 7, 8

ELZE (KARL), PH. D. Essays on Shakespeare; translated by L. Dora Schmitz. 8vo. Lond., 1874.   J 3 S 8
Shakespeare's Hamlet. [*See* SHAKESPEARE, W.]

EMANUEL (HARRY), F.R.G.S. Diamonds and Precious Stones, their History, Value, and distinguishing Characteristics, with simple Tests for their Identification. 8vo. Lond., 1867.   A 9 P 33

EMERALD HILL MECHANICS' INSTITUTE. Eleventh Annual Report, 1867–68. 12mo. Emerald Hill, 1868.   MF 3 P 10

EMERSON (ELLEN RUSSELL). Indian Myths ; or, Legends, Traditions, and Symbols of the Aborigines of America, compared with those of other Countries, including Hindostan, Egypt, Persia, Assyria, and China. Illustrated. 8vo. Lond., 1884.   B 2 P 3

EMERSON (G. R.) William Ewart Gladstone, Prime Minister of England: a Political and Literary Biography. 8vo. Lond., 1882.   C 7 R 12

EMERSON (JAMES), PECCHIO (GUISEPPE), COUNT, AND HUMPHREYS (W. H). Picture of Greece in 1825. 2 vols. 8vo. Lond., 1826.   D 8 S 37, 38

EMERSON (J. S.) He Hoakakaolelo no na Hualolelo Beritania, I mea Kokua I na Kanaka Hawaii e ao ana ia Olelo. (Hawaiian Dictionary.) 8vo. Lahainaluna, 1845.   MK 1 R 17

EMERSON (RALPH WALDO). Conduct of Life. 12mo. Lond., 1861.   J 11 P 28
Complete Works of; comprising Essays, Lectures, Poems, and Orations. 3 vols. 8vo. Lond., 1876–83. J 11 P 22–24
Emerson at Home and Abroad; by Daniel Moncure Conway. 8vo. Lond., 1883.   C 3 V 5
Essays ; with Preface by Thomas Carlyle. [1st and] 2nd Series. 2 vols. 8vo. Lond., 1853–58. J 11 P 29, 30
His Life, ·Writings, and Philosophy ; by G. W. Cooke. 8vo. Lond., 1882.   C 3 R 37
In Memoriam : Recollections of his Visit to England in 1833, 1847–8, 1872–3 ; by A. Ireland. 8vo. Lond., 1882.   C 5 U 11
Miscellanies. 8vo. Lond., 1884.   J 11 P 25
Nature: an Essay; to which are added Orations, Lectures, and Addresses. 8vo. Lond., 1867.   J 11 P 26
Orations, Lectures, and Essays. 12mo. Lond., 1865.   J 11 P 27
Poems. 6th ed. 12mo. Boston, 1857.   H 7 R 30
Ralph Waldo Emerson: Man and Teacher. (Round Table Series.) 8vo. Edinb., 1884.   C 5 V 10

EMERSON (RALPH WALDO).—*continued.*
Representative Men: Seven Lectures. 8vo. Lond., 1850. C 5 R 21

Tributes to Longfellow and Emerson; by the Massachusetts Historical Society; with Portrait. Sm. 4to. Boston, 1882. C 10 V 38

[*See* HUNDRED GREATEST MEN.]

EMERSON (W.) [*See* NEWTON, SIR I.]

EMERTON (JAMES H.) Life on the Seashore; or, Animals of our Coasts and Bays; with Illustrations and Descriptions. (Naturalist's Handy Séries 1.) 8vo. Salem, 1880. A 14 Q 9

EMIGRANT IN AUSTRALIA; or, Gleanings from the Gold-fields; by "An Australian Journalist"; with Illustrations, by J. S. Prout, Esq.; and Maps. 12mo. Lond., 1852.* MD 2 R 31

EMIGRANT MECHANIC, AN. [*See* HARRIS, A.]

EMIGRANT OF 1821, AN. [*See* WILLIAMS, W.]

EMIGRANTS. A Few Words to Emigrants' Wives. (Pam. 41.) 12mo. Lond., 1861. MJ 2 R 3

General Hints to Emigrants. (Weale). 12mo. Lond., 1866. A 17 Q 15

Information for Emigrants to the British Colonies, issued by H.M. Emigration Commissioners. 8vo. Lond., 1870. MJ 2 R 12

Practical Advice to Emigrants; or, How to Choose a Home in our Colonies. (Pam. 41.) 12mo. Lond., 1861. MJ 2 R 3

EMIGRANT'S GUIDE (THE) to New South Wales, Van Diemen's Land, &c. 8vo. Lond., 1832. MJ 2 Q 15

EMIGRANTS' GUIDE TO AUSTRALASIA. [*See* BAIRD, REV. J.]

EMIGRANTS' LETTERS; being a Collection of Recent Communications from Settlers in the British Colonies. 8vo. Lond., 1850.* MD 4 Q 25

EMIGRATION. Colonization and Emigration; a Memorial addressed to the Rt. Hon. Lord John Russell. 8vo. Lond., 1848. MF 3 P 7

Correspondence relative to the Application of the Land Revenue in the Australian Colonies, with reference to Emigration. (Parl. Docs., 30.) Fol. Lond., 1841. MF 4 ‡

Correspondence relative to Emigration, between the Colonial Office and the Authorities in the Colonies, or the Commissioners of Land and Emigration. (Parl. Docs., 31.) Fol. Lond., 1842. MF 4 ‡

Correspondence relative to Emigration; also, to the Sale of Colonial Lands in New South Wales and Port Phillip, Van Diemen's Land, Western Australia, and New Zealand. (Parl. Docs. 43.) Fol. Lond., 1843. MF 4 ‡

EMIGRATION.—*continued.*
Competence in a Colony contrasted with Poverty at Home; or, Relief to Landlords and Labourers held out by Australian Colonization and Emigration: a Memorial addressed to the Rt. Hon. Lord John Russell, &c. 8vo. Lond., 1848. MF 3 P 7

Despatch from the Governor of New South Wales to the Secretary of State for the Colonies, containing Resolutions of the Legislative Council of that Colony on the subject of Emigration. (Parl. Docs., 30.) Fol. Lond., 1841. MF 4 ‡

Despatches from the Governor of New South Wales, transmitting Reports of the Legislative Council relative to the Monetary Depression in the Colony, and the Petition of the distressed Mechanics and Labourers; also, Despatch from the Governor of New South Wales, transmitting the last Annual Report of the Committee of the Legislative Council on Emigration. (Parl. Docs., 45.) Fol. Lond., 1844. MF 4 ‡

Direct Remission advocated; being a consideration of the connexion between the Waste Lands of Colonies and Emigration, 1848; [by I. T.] 2nd ed. 8vo. Sydney, 1854. MF 3 P 1

Another copy. MJ 2 Q 14

Emigration Agents and Lecturers for New South Wales. (Further Correspondence.) Fol. Sydney, 1862. MF 10 R 3 †

Emigration to Tasmania; by "A Recent Settler." 12mo. Lond., 1879. MD 3 Q 40

Female Emigration: a few Copies of Letters, and some Remarks upon sundry Documents on the subject; by the "Superintendent of the *Layton* Emigrant Ship." 8vo. Sydney, 1836. MF 3 P 4

General Hints to Emigrants; containing Notices of the various Fields for Emigration; with Practical Hints on Preparation for Emigration—Outfit for the Voyage—the Voyage—Landing—Obtaining Employment—Purchase and Clearing of Land, &c.; together with various Directions and Recipes useful to the Emigrant; with a Map of the World. 12mo. Lond., 1866. A 17 Q 15

General Report from the Agent-General for Emigration in Canada; Correspondence between the Secretary of State for the Colonies and the Governors of the Australian Colonies respecting Emigration, since 1838. (Parl. Docs. 19 and 30.) Fol. Lond., 1839. MF 4 ‡

General Report of the Colonial Land and Emigration Commissioners. (Parl. Docs. 41.) Fol. Lond., 1842–43. MF 4 ‡

General Report of the Colonial Land and Emigration Commissioners, 1844. 8vo. Lond., 1844. MF 3 P 7

Great South Land: Four Papers on Emigration, designed to exhibit the Principles and Progress of the New Colony of South Australia. (Pam. 18.) 2nd ed. 8vo. Lond., 1838. MJ 2 Q 16

Information for Emigrants to the British Colonies, issued by H.M. Emigration Commissioners. 8vo. Lond., 1870. MJ 2 R 12

Information published for Emigration, respecting the British Colonies in North America. (Pam. 31.) 8vo. Lond., 1832. MJ 2 Q 19

EMIGRATION.—*continued.*

Letter to the Small Farmers and Peasantry of the United Kingdom on the advantages of Emigration to South Australia. (Pam. 3) 3rd ed. 12mo. Lond., 1838.
MJ 2 P 38

New Zealand; Free Grants of Land; Emigration to the Province of Auckland; Auckland Waste Land Act, 1858, in the 21st year of the Reign of Her Majesty Queen Victoria, Session 8, No. 2. 8vo. Lond., 1858. MF 3 Q 33

Papers relative to Emigration to the Australian Colonies. Fol. (Parl. Doc. 51.) Lond., 1848. MF 4 ‡

Practical Suggestions for the formation of Emigration; Mutual Aid Societies; by "A late Government officer." 8vo. Dublin, 1849. MF 2 Q 8

Report from the Agent-General for Emigration, and Correspondence between the Secretary of State for the Colonies and the Governors of the Australian Colonies, respecting Emigration; and also a General Return of Emigration for the year 1839. (Parl. Doc. 30.) Fol. Lond., 1840. MF 4 ‡

Return of the Number of Emigrants that have been sent to the Colony of New South Wales since the Suspension of the Bounty Orders, in March 1842. (Parl. Docs. 51.) Fol. Lond., 1847. MF 4 ‡

Return of the Number of Persons who have emigrated from the United Kingdom to the Colonies of Great Britain, in each year since 1820. Fol. (Parl. Docs., 30.) Lond., 1830. MF 4 ‡

Sixth, Seventh, and Eighth General Reports of the Colonial Land and Emigration Commissioners; with Plans. (Parl. Docs. 51.) Fol. Lond., 1846–48. MF 4 ‡

Thoughts on Emigration; by "An Old Colonist." 8vo. Bathurst, 1856. MF 3 P 4

EMIGRATION AGENTS. [*See* NEW SOUTH WALES.]

EMINENT MEN. Biographies of; containing Lives of Sir Isaac Newton, Carsten Niebuhr, Admiral R. Blake, Dr. Adam Smith, Sir Edward Coke, Mahomet, Galileo Galilei, John Kepler. (Lib. Ent. Know.) 8vo. Lond., 1849. C 7 P 45

EMINENT MISSIONARIES. [*See* MISSIONARIES.]

EMMENS (S. H.) Logic, Pure and Applied. (Weale.) 12mo. Lond., 1870. F 5 S 24

Selections from Locke's Essay on the Human Understanding. [*See* LOCKE, J.]

EMORY (MAJOR W. H.) Notes of Travel in California. [*See* FREMONT, COL. J. C.]

EMPIRE (THE). 70 vols. fol. Sydney, 1850–75. E

EMPIRE COMPANIONSHIP (THE LATE). *The Empire;* an Address to the Working Classes of New South Wales. 4to. Sydney, 1858. MJ 2 U 3

ÉNAULT (LOUIS). Paris-Salon, 1883. 8vo. Paris, 1883. E

ENCHANTRESS (THE) (Miss Catherine Hayes); or, the Bench and Bar Music Mad. (Pam. A.) Fol. Sydney, 1854. MJ 2 U 1

ENCYCLOPÆDIA AMERICANA (THE): Supplemental Dictionary (to the Encyclopædia Britannica, 9th ed.) of Arts, Science, and General Literature. Illustrated. Vols. 1, 2. 2 vols. roy, 4to. New York, 1883–85. K 2 T 12, 13

ENCYCLOPÆDIA BRITANNICA (THE): or, Dictionary of Arts Sciences, and General Literature; with Dissertations and Index [and Plates]. 7th ed. 24 vols. 4to. Edinb., 1842. K 2 Q 1–R 3

Another copy. 8th ed. 22 vols. 4to. Edinb., 1860. K 2 R 4–S 4

Another copy. 9th ed. 24 vols. 4to. Edinb., 1875–89. K 2 S 5–T 9

ENCYCLOPÆDIA METROPOLITANA; or, Universal Dictionary of Knowledge,; with Index. 26 vols. 4to. Lond., 1845. K 6 P 1–Q 4

ENCYCLOPÆDIA PERTHENSIS; or, Universal Dictionary of Knowledge. 23 vols. roy. 8vo. Perth, 1816. K 5 R 1–23

ENCYCLOPÉDIE D'ARCHITECTURE: Revue Mensuelle des Travaux Publics et Particuliers. Paris, 1851–81. K 4 T 1–22

ENCYCLOPÉDIE DES GENS DU MONDE: Répertoire universel des Sciences, des Lettres, et des Arts. 22 vols. 8vo. Paris, 1833–44. K 1 R 1–22

ENCYCLOPÉDIE MÉTHODIQUE; ou, par Ordre de Matières; par une Société de Gens de Lettres, de Savans, et d'Artistes. 202 vols. 4to. Paris, 1782–1832. K 3 P 1–4 Q 12

1–7. Agriculture.
8, 9. Amusemens des Sciences.
10–16. Antiquités, Mythologie Diplomatique des Chartes et Chronologie.
17–19. Architecture.
20, 21. Art Aratoire et du Jardinage; avec Planches.
22–25. Art Militaire; avec Supplément.
26. Artillerie: Dictionnaire de l'Artillerie.
27–42 Arts et Métiers Mécaniques; avec Planches.
43. Assemblée Nationale Constituante.
44–46. Beaux-Arts; avec Planches.
47, 48. Chasses; Dictionnaire de toutes les Espèces de Chasses.
49–55. Chymie, Pharmacie, et Métallurgie; avec Planches.
56–53. Chirurgie; avec Planches.
59–61. Commerce.
62–65. Economie, Politique et Diplomatique.
66. Encyclopédiana; ou, Dictionnaire Encyclopédique des Ana.
67. Equitation, Escrime et Danse.
68–70. Finances.
71. Forêts et Bois: leurs Semis et Plantations.
72–76. Géographie Ancienne; avec Atlas.
77–79. Géographie Moderne.
80–85. Géographie Physique; avec Atlas.

ENCYCLOPÉDIE MÉTHODIQUE—*continued.*
86–88. Grammaire et Littérature.
89–94. Histoire; avec Supplément.
95–144. Histoire Naturelle; avec Planches.
145. Jeux: Dictionnaire des Jeux, avec Planches; Dictionnaire des Jeux Familiers, ou des Amusemens de Société; Dictionnaire des Jeux Mathématiques.
146–155. Jurisprudence; avec la Police et les Municipalités
156–159. Logique, Métaphysique et Morale.
160–163. Manufactures, Arts et Métiers; avec Planches.
164–166. Marine; avec Planches.
167–169. Mathématiques; avec Planches.
170–182. Médecine; contenant l'Hygiène, la Pathologie, la Séméiotique et la Nosologie, la Thérapeutique, ou Matière Médicale, etc.
183, 184. Musique; avec Planches.
185, 186. Pêches: Dictionnaire des toutes les Espèces de Pêches, avec Explication de cent trente deux Planches des Pêches, à cause de dix-huit doubles.
187–189. Philosophie, Ancienne et Moderne.
190–194. Physique; avec Planches.
195–199. Système Anatomique; avec Planches.
200–202. Théologie.

L'Esprit de l'Encyclopédie, et Supplément.   13 vols. (in 7) 8vo.   Paris, 1789–1808.   K 5 U 14–20

ENCYCLOPÉDIE MODERNE: Dictionnaire Abrégé des Sciences, des Lettres, des Arts de l'Industrie de l'Agriculture et du Commerce, et Atlas.   Nouvelle éd.   27 vols. 8vo.   Paris, 1861–77.   K 5 Q 1–27
Atlas [to the above]. 3 vols. 8vo.   Paris, 1872.   K 5 Q 28–30

ENCYKLOPÆDIE DER NATURWISSENSCHAFTEN.   20 vols. imp. 8vo.   Breslau, 1879–86.   E

ENDERIS (ERNST). Versuch einer Formenlehre der oskischen Sprache, mit den oskischen Inschriften und Glossar. 8vo.   Zurich, 1871.   K 14 T 28

ENFIELD (A. H. F.), VISCOUNTESS. [*See* GREVILLE, H.]

ENFIELD (REV. W.) [*See* AIKIN, J.]

ENFIELD (WILLIAM), M.A. Inquiry into the Nature and Causes of the Wealth of Nations, containing Elements of Commerce and Political Economy. 8vo.   Lond., 1809.   F 6 8 6

EXCEL (CARL). Introduction to the Study of National Music. 8vo.   Lond., 1866.   A 7 U 7
Music of the most Ancient Nations, particularly of the Assyrians, Egyptians, and Hebrews. 8vo.   Lond., 1864.   A 7 U 6
Musical Instruments. (South Kens. Mus. 5.) 8vo.   Lond., 1875.   E
Musical Myth and Facts.   2 vols. 8vo.   Lond., 1876.   A 7 P 3, 4

ENGEL (LOUIS). From Mozart to Mario: Reminiscences of Half-a-Century. 2 vols. 8vo.   Lond., 1886.   C 4 S 18, 19

ENGINEER (THE).   22 vols. fol.   Lond., 1873–85.   E

ENGINEERING: an Illustrated Weekly Journal.   Vols. 1–39.   Fol.   Lond., 1866–85.   E

ENGINEERING AND BUILDING RECORD AND SANITARY ENGINEER (THE). [Commenced as the *Plumber and Sanitary Engineer*, continued as the *Sanitary Engineer*, and then as the *Engineering and Building Record and Sanitary Engineer.*] Vols. 1–16.   16 vols. sm. fol.   New York, 1877–87.   E

ENGINEERS (CIVIL). Institution of. [*See* CIVIL ENGINEERS.]

ENGLAND (E. B.) [*See* CURTIUS, G.]

ENGLAND. Ancient Laws and Institutes of England; with a Glossary. Fol.   Lond., 1840.   F 24 Q 22 ‡
Report of the Boundary Commission, 1868. [*See* BOUNDARY COMMISSION.]
Third Annual Report of the Registrar-General of Births, Deaths, and Marriages, England and Wales. (Pam. A.) Fol.   Lond., 1841.   MJ 2 U 1

ENGLAND AND WALES. *Illustrated Times* Map of. 4to.   Lond., 1858.   D 33 Q 16 ‡
State of the Representation in England, Scotland, and Wales. (Pam. Dd.) 8vo.   Lond., 1793. [*See* GREAT BRITAIN.]   F 12 P 22

ENGLEFIELD (SIR HENRY CHARLES), BART. Description of the principal Picturesque Beauties, Antiquities, and Geological Phœnomena of the Isle of Wight.   Imp. 4to. Lond., 1816.   D 5 Q 11 †

ENGLISH CATALOGUE OF BOOKS. [*See* LOW, SAMPSON.]

ENGLISH CYCLOPÆDIA (THE): Dictionary of Useful Information. With Atlas. 12 vols. 4to.   Lond., 1877.   K 4 U 1–12
1–4. Arts and Sciences.
5–7. Biography.
8, 9. Natural History.
10, 11. Geography.
12. Atlas.
[*See* KNIGHT, C.]

ENGLISH DIALECT SOCIETY. Publications of. Vols. 1–13.   8vo.   Lond., 1873–80.   E

ENGLISH ENCYCLOPÆDIA (THE); being a Collection of Treatises and a Dictionary of Terms, illustrative of the Arts and Sciences. With Plates. 11 vols. 4to. Lond., 1802.   K 5 P 15–25

ENGLISH GENTLEMAN, AN. [*See* BLANE, W. N.]

ENGLISH GENTLEMAN, AN. [*See* CHASTELLUX, F. J., MARQUIS DE.]

ENGLISH HEXAPLA (THE); exhibiting the six important English Translations of the New Testament Scriptures. 4to.   Lond. (n.d.)   G 6 U 20

ENGLISH HISTORICAL SOCIETY. [*See* HIST. SOC.]

ENGLISHMAN, AN. [*See* ASHWORTH, J. H.]

ENGLISHMAN, AN. [*See* BRIT. THEATRE.]

ENGLISHMAN, AN. [*See* ENGLISH WORK AND SONG.]

ENGLISHMAN, AN. [*See* PUSELEY, D.]

ENGLISH MECHANIC and World of Science. With which are incorporated "The Mechanic," "Scientific Opinion," and "The British and Foreign Mechanic." Vols. 1–41. Fol. Lond., 1865–85. E

ENGLISH MEN OF LETTERS; edited by John Morley. 37 vols. 8vo. Lond., 1878–86. C 1 U 2–38

Addison ; by W. J. Courthope.	Hume ; by Prof. Huxley.
Bacon ; by R. W. Church.	Johnson ; by Leslie Stephen.
Bentley ; by R. C. Jebb, M.A.	Lamb ; by Alfred Ainger.
Bunyan ; by J. A. Froude.	Landor ; by S. Colvin, M.A.
Burke ; by John Morley.	Locke ; by Thomas Fowler.
Burns ; by Principal Sharp.	Macaulay ; by J. C. Morison.
Byron ; by John Nicol.	Milton ; by M. Pattison.
Chaucer ; by A. W. Ward.	Pope ; by Leslie Stephen.
Coleridge ; by H. D. Traill.	Scott ; by Richard H. Hutton.
Cowper ; by Goldwin Smith.	Shelley ; by J. A. Symonds.
Defoe ; by Wm. Minto.	Sheridan ; by Mrs. Oliphant.
De Quincey ; by D. Masson.	Sidney ; by J. A. Symonds.
Dickens ; by A. W. Ward.	Southey ; by Edward Dowden.
Dryden ; by G. Saintsbury.	Spenser ; by R. W. Church.
Fielding ; by Austin Dobson.	Sterne ; by H. D. Traill.
Gibbon ; by J. C. Morison, M.A.	Swift ; by Leslie-Stephen.
Goldsmith ; by Wm. Black.	Thackeray ; by A. Trollope.
Gray ; by Edmund W. Gosse.	Wordsworth ; by F. W. H.
Hawthorne ; by H. James, jun.	Myers.

ENGLISH RESIDENT IN GERMANY, AN. [*See* SPENCER, CAPT. EDMUND.]

ENGLISH STATUTES. [*See* STATUTES.]

ENGLISH WORK AND SONG ; amid the Forests of the South; by "An Englishman." 8vo. Lond., 1882. MH 1 R 58

ENGLISHWOMAN'S REVIEW of Social and Industrial Questions. Vols. 9–13. 8vo. Lond., 1878–82. E

ENNEMOSER (JOSEPH). History of Magic; translated from the German, by William Howitt. 2 vols. 8vo. Lond., 1854. A 10 R 8, 9

ENNIS (JACOB), A.M. Origin of the Stars, and the Causes of their Motions and their Light. 8vo. Lond., 1876. A 3 S 26

ENSE (K. A. VARNHAGEN VON). [*See* VARNHAGEN VON ENSE, K. A.]

ENSOR (F. S.) [*See* VICTORIA, H.M. QUEEN.]

ENSOR (GEORGE). Anti-Union: Ireland as she ought to be. [*See* HISTORICAL PAMPHLETS.]

ENTOMOLOGICAL MAGAZINE. 5 vols. 8vo. Lond., 1833–38. E

ENTOMOLOGICAL SOCIETY OF NEW SOUTH WALES. Transactions of, 1862–73. 2 vols. 8vo. Sydney, 1866–73. ME 1 R

ENTOMOLOGIST'S ANNUAL (THE), 1855–74. 2nd ed. 20 vols. 12mo. Lond., 1855–74. E

ENTOMOLOGIST'S MONTHLY MAGAZINE (THE). Vols. 1–2. 8vo. Lond., 1864–85. E

ENTRECASTEAUX (B. D'). [*See* D'ENTRECASTEAUX, B.]

ENTWISLE & GARNET v. DENT & CO. Responsibility of Commission Agents: Report of the Case of Entwisle & Garnet v. Dent & Co. (Pam. 19) 8vo. Lond., 1849. MJ 2 Q 8

EPHRÆM (SAINT). Opera omnia quæ exstant Græce, Syriace, Latine, ad MSS. 6 vols fol. G 26 Q 9–14 ‡ [*See* BYZANTINÆ HIST. SCRIPT.]

EPICTETUS. All the Works of; translated, with an Introduction and Notes, by Elizabeth Carter. 4to. Lond., 1758. G 2 T 7

Works of; consisting of his Discourses, in Four Books, the Enchiridion, and Fragments: a Translation from the Greek, by T. W. Higginson. 8vo. Boston, 1866. G 8 Q 2

EPICURUS. Life of. [*See* LUCRETIUS CARUS, T.]

EPIPHANIUS (SANCTUS). Opera omnia. [*See* MIGNE, J. P., SERIES GRÆCA, 41–43.]

EPISCOPAL SEES. Copies :—Of his late Majesty's Letters Patent, constituting the Episcopal See of Australia, or New South Wales, and appointing the Right Reverend William G. Broughton, D.D., to be the first Bishop ; of Her Majesty's Letters Patent, constituting the See of Sydney, in New South Wales, to be a Metropolitan See, and erecting other Episcopal Sees within the Province of Australia; of Despatch from Her Majesty's Secretary of State for the Colonial Department to the Governor of New South Wales, in relation to the Place and Precedency to be assigned and allowed in the Executive Council or elsewhere, within the Colony of New South Wales, to the Right Reverend Dr. Broughton as Bishop of Australia ; of Despatch from Her Majesty's Secretary of State for the Colonial Department to the Governor of New South Wales, in relation to the first Mission of Dr. John Bede Polding, as Bishop of the Roman Catholic Communion within that Colony, and to the Allowance of Salary payable to him ; and, Copy of Correspondence between Her Majesty's Secretary of State for the Colonial Department to the Governor of New South Wales relative to the Assumption of the Style and Title of Archbishop of Sydney, by Dr. John Bede Polding. Fol. Lond., 1850. MF 4 ‡

ERASMUS ROTERDAMUS (DESIDERIUS). Adagiorum chiliades Iuxtalocos communes digestæ. Fol. Hanoviæ, 1617. 　　　　　　　　　　J 39 R 3 ‡

Colloquia Familiara et Encomium Moriæ. 2 vols. 18mo. Lipsiæ, 1867–72. 　　　　　　　G 9 P 48, 49

Life of Erasmus, more particularly that part of it which he spent in England; by Samuel Knight, D.D. 8vo. Camb., 1726. 　　　　　　　　　　　C 4 V 4

Lives of Jehan Vitrier, Warden of the Franciscan Convent at St. Omer, and John Colet, Dean of St. Paul's London; written in Latin; translated by J. H. Lupton, M.A., &c. 8vo. Lond., 1883. 　　　　　　　　C 2 R 31

Moriæ Enkomium. Stultitiæ Laus. Des. Erasmi Rot. declamatio, cum commentariis. 8vo. Basileæ, 1676. J 16 R 11

Opera omnia, emendatiora et avctiora, ad optimas editiones praecipve qvas ipse Erasmus postremo cvravit, svmma fide exacta stvdia et opera Joannis Clerici cum ejvsdem et aliorvm notis. 10 vols. (in 11) fol. Lugd. Bat., 1703–6. 　　　　　　　　　　G 35 P 2–12 ‡

The Oxford Reformer. [*See* SEEBOHM, F.]

Twenty-two Select Colloquies, pleasantly representing several superstitious Levities that were crept into the Church of Rome in his Days; by R. L'Estrange, Knt. 8vo. Lond., 1689. 　　　　　　　　G 8 Q 6

ERATOSTHENES. [*See* SANCHONIATHO.]

EPPS (J.) What is Homœopathy? 3rd ed. Lond. (n.d.) 　　　　　　　　　　　MA 2 S 38

ERCELDOUNE (THOMAS OF). [*See* LERMONT, T.]

ERCKMANN (EMILE), AND CHATRIAN (ALEXANDRE). The Blockade; or, Episodes of Phalsbourg. 12mo. Lond., 1871. 　　　　　　　　　　J 1 W 30

The Conscript; or, the Invasion of France. 12mo. Lond., 1871. 　　　　　　　　　　J 1 W 31

Waterloo: a Sequel to "The Conscript of 1813." 12mo. Lond., 1871. 　　　　　　　　J 1 W 32

ERDESWICK (SAMPSON). Survey of Staffordshire; containing the Antiquities of that County. 8vo. Westminster, 1820. 　　　　　　　　　B 6 Q 8

ERIGENA (JOANNES SCOTUS). De Divisione Naturæ Libri Quinque diu desiderati. Accedit Appendix ex Ambiguis S. Maximi Græce et Latine. Fol. Oxonii, 1681. 　　　　　　　　　　　　G 12 R 11 †

Opera omnia. [*See* MIGNE, J. P., SERIES LATINA, 122.]

ERIKSEN (WILHELM). Les Échanges Internationaux, littéraires et scientifiques; leur Histoire, leur Utilité, etc., 1832 80. Roy. 8vo. Paris, 1880. 　　J 15 V 22

ERLACH (FRIEDRICH KARL), FREIHERRN VON. Die Volkslieder der Deutschen. 5 vols. 8vo. Mannheim, 1834 36. 　　　　　　　　　　　H 6 S 20 24

ERMAN (ADOLPH). Travels in Siberia; translated from the German by William Desborough Cooley. 2 vols. 8vo. Lond., 1848. 　　　　　　　D 6 Q 10, 11

ERMOLD LE NOIR. Faits et Gestes de Louis-le-Pieux: Poème. [*See* GUIZOT, F. P. G., 4.]

ERNEST (J. A.) Bibliotheca Latina. [*See* FABRICIUS, PROF. J. A.]

[*See* CICERO, M. T.]

ERNST (DR. A.) Descriptive Catalogue of the Venezuelan Department, Philadelphia International Exhibition, 1876. 8vo. Philad., 1876. 　　K 7 R 36

ERSKINE (HON. HENRY), LORD ADVOCATE FOR SCOTLAND. Life of; with Anecdotes of many of his Contemporaries and of his Time, compiled by Lieut.-Col. A. Fergusson. 8vo. Edinb., 1882. 　　　　　　　　C 8 V 6

ERSKINE (PROF. J.) Institute of the Law of Scotland, in four Books. 2 vols. sm. fol Edinb.,1828. F 7 P 8, 9 †

ERSKINE (CAPT. JOHN ELPHINSTONE), R.N. Short Account of the late Discoveries of Gold in Australia; with Notes of a Visit to the Gold District. 2nd ed. 8vo. Lond., 1852. 　　　　　　　　MA 2 Q 35

Journal of a Cruise among the Islands of the Western Pacific, in H.M. Ship *Havannah.* Illustrated. 8vo. Lond., 1853.* 　　　　　　　MD 6 R 9

ERSKINE (RT. HON. THOMAS), LORD. Speeches of. 5 vols. 8vo. Lond., 1810–12. 　　　F 5 U 2–6

Speeches of, when at the Bar, against Constructive Treason, &c.; with a prefatory Memoir, by the Rt. Hon. Lord Brougham. 3rd ed. 4 vols. 8vo. Lond., 1847. 　　　　　　　　　F 13 P 23–26

Speeches of; with a Memoir of his Life, by Edward Walford, M.A. 8vo. Lond., 1880. 　　　F 3 P 5

ERSKINE (THOMAS). An Essay on Faith. 3rd ed. 12mo. Edinb., 1823. 　　　　　　　G 10 Q 5

The Spiritual Order, and other Papers selected from his MSS. 8vo. Edinb., 1871. 　　　G 8 Q 3

ESCOBAR (E.) Mineralogical Cabinet of. (English and Spanish.) [*See* GUERRA, E.]

ESCOTT (T. H. S.) England: its People, Polity, and Pursuits. 2 vols. 8vo. Lond., 1880. F 9 R 14, 15

Pillars of the Empire: Sketches of living Indian and Colonial Statesmen, Celebrities, and Officials. 8vo. Lond., 1879. 　　　　　　　　　C 4 V 17

ESKELL (LOUIS). Australian Hand-book and Guide for the Preservation of the Teeth. (Pam. 40.) 12mo. Sydney, 1860. 　　　　　　　　　MJ 2 R 2

ESPINAS (A.) Die Thierischen Gesellschaften: eine vergleichend-psychologische Untersuchung. 8vo. Braunsch., 1879. 　　　　　　　　　A 14 S 38

ESPINASSE (FRANCIS). Life and Times of François-Marie Arouet, calling himself Voltaire. Vol. 1 (*all published*). 8vo. Lond., 1866. 　　　　　　C 9 R 36

ESPRIELLA (Don Manuel Alvarez). [*See* Southey, R.]

ESPRIT DE L'ENCYCLOPÉDIE (l'). [*See* Encyclopédie Méthodiqe.]

ESQUIROS (Alphonse). English Seamen and Divers. 8vo. Lond., 1868. A 17 T 59

ESSAYS AND ADDRESSES; by Professors and Lecturers of the Owens College, Manchester. 8vo. Lond., 1874. J 6 T 1

ESSAYS AND REVIEWS. 7th ed. 8vo. Lond., 1861.* G 13 P 13

ESSAYS FROM *THE CRITIC*; by John Burroughs, Edmund C. Stedman, Walt Whitman, R. H. Stoddard, F. B. Sanborn, E. W. Gosse, and others. 12mo. Boston, 1882. J 11 R 30

ESSAYS FROM *THE TIMES;* being a Selection from the Literary Papers which have appeared in that Journal. 2 vols. 12mo. Lond., 1852. J 7 Q 24, 25

ESSAYS ON RELIGION AND LITERATURE; by various Writers; edited by Archbishop Manning. 2nd series. 8vo. Lond., 1867. G 4 R 7

ESSEX (Devereux), Earls of. Lives and Letters of the Devereux, Earls of Essex, in the Reigns of Elizabeth, James I, and Charles I, 1540-1646; by the Hon. Walter Bourchier Devereux. 2 vols. 8vo. Lond., 1853. C 6 U 12, 13

ESTCOURT ((Very Rev. Edgar E.), And PAYNE (John Orlebar). English Catholic Non-jurors of 1715; being a Summary of the Register of their Estates. 8vo. Lond., 1885. B 3 T 11

ETHERIDGE (Rev. John Wesley), M.A. Apostolical Acts and Epistles, from the Peschito, or Ancient Syriac. 8vo. Lond., 1849. G 8 Q 7

Jerusalem and Tiberias; Sora and Cordova. 8vo. Lond., 1856. G 8 Q 8

The Targums of Onkelos and Jonathan Ben Uzziel on the Pentateuch: Genesis and Exodus. 8vo. Lond., 1862. G 8 Q 9

The Targums of Onkelos and Jonathan Ben Uzziel on the Pentateuch: Leviticus, Numbers, and Deuteronomy. 8vo. Lond., 1865. G 8 Q 10

ETHERIDGE (R.) Catalogue of Fossils in Museum of Practical Geology. [*See* Huxley, T. H.]

ETHERIDGE (R.), Junr. Catalogue of Australian Fossils (including Tasmania and the Island of Timor), stratigraphically and zoologically arranged. 8vo. Camb., 1878. MA 2 Q 12

ETHERIDGE (Robert), Jun., And JACK (Robert Logan) F.R.G.S., &c. Catalogue of Works, Papers, Reports, and Maps, on the Geology, Palæontology, Mineralogy, Mining, and Metallurgy, &c., of the Australian Continent and Tasmania. 8vo. Lond., 1881. MK 1 R 26

Another copy. 4to. Sydney, 1882. MA 2 R 8

2 k

ETHERINGTON (L. N.) [*See* Chesneau, E.]

ETHNICAL ALPHABET; or, Alphabet of Nations: Instructions for the guidance of those using the Alphabet. 8vo. Melb., 1866. MF 2 U 2

ETON PORTRAIT GALLERY (The). Consisting of Short Memoirs of the more eminent Eton Men; by "A Barrister of the Inner Temple." 8vo. Eton, 1876. C 7 T 1

ETTMÜLLER (Ludwig), Ph. Dr., &c. Vorda Vealhstôd Engla and Seaxna. Lexicon Anglosaxonicum ex Poëtarum, Scriptorumque Prosaicorum Operibus nec non Lexicis Anglosaxonicis collectum, cum Synopsi Grammatica. 8vo. Quedlinburg, 1851. K 15 S 16

ETTRICK SHEPHERD, The. [*See* Hogg, J.]

ETTY (William), R.A. Criticism on the Pictures and Studies of. 8vo. Lond., 1849. A 6 V 38

Life of; by Alexander Gilchrist. 2 vols. 12mo. Lond., 1855. C 3 S 32, 33

EUCLIDES. Elements of. [*See* Law, H.]

Elements of Geometry. The first six Books and the portions of the eleventh and twelfth Books read at Cambridge; by Robert Potts, M.A. 8vo. Lond., 1865. A 10 S 19

Euclid Revised; containing the Essentials of the Elements of Plane Geometry as given by Euclid in his first six Books, &c.; edited by R. C. J. Nixon, M.A. (Clar. Press.) 8vo. Oxford, 1886. A 10 S 30

Les Oeuvres d'Euclide, en Grec, en Latin, et en Français. Par F. Peyrard. 3 vols. 4to. Paris, 1814-18. A 10 V 17-19

EUGENE OF SAVOY (Prince). Memoirs of; written by himself. 12mo. Lond., 1829. C 1 P 8

Memoir of; written by himself, translated by F. Shoberl. 2nd ed. 8vo. Lond., 1811. C 5 T 20

Nach den handschriftlichen Quellen der kaiserlichen Archive, von Alfred, Ritter von Arneth. 8vo. Wien, 1864. C 10 V 34-36

EUGENIUS III (Papa). Epistolæ et Privilegia. [*See* Migne, J. P., Series Latina, 180.]

EUGYPPIUS (Donnus). Opera omnia. [*See* Migne, J. P., Series Latina, 62.]

EULENSPIEGEL. [*See* Howleglas.]

EULER (Leonard). Complete Theory of the Construction and Properties of Vessels; with practical conclusions for the Management of Ships; translated by Henry Watson. 8vo. Lond., 1790. A 2 Q 11

Introduction à l'Analyse Infinitesimale. Traduite du Latin en Français; par J. B. Labey. 2 vols. 4to. Paris, 1796-97. A 10 U 4, 5

EUNAPIUS. [*See* Byzantinae Hist. Script.]

EUPHRATES VALLEY RAILWAY. Report from the Select Committee; with Minutes of Evidence. Fol. Lond., 1871.　　　　　　　　　　　F 36 Q 11 †

EURIPIDES. The Agamemnon of Aeschylus, and The Bacchanals of; with passages from the Lyrics of later Poets of Greece; translated by H. H. Milman. 8vo. Lond., 1865.　　　　　　　　　　　H 8 Q 9

Bacchae of; with Critical and Explanatory Notes, and with numerous Illustrations from Works of Ancient Art, by John Edwin Sandys, M.A. 8vo. Cambridge, 1880.
　　　　　　　　　　　　　　　　J 16 R 22

Dissertation on the Epistles of. [*See* BENTLEY, R.]

Euripidis Ion; the Student's First Greek Play; with Notes; by Charles Badham, D.D. 8vo. Lond., 1861.
　　　　　　　　　　　　　　　　H 1 S 18

Euripidis Tragœdiæ priores quatuor; edidit Ricardus Porson, A.M. Editio Tertia. 8vo. Cantab., 1851. H 1 S 19

The 'Medea' of; with an Introduction and Commentary, by A. W. Verrall, M.A. 8vo. Lond., 1881.　H 4 S 13

[Tragedies of] Euripidies; by Mich. Wodhull. [*See* GREEK TRAGIC THEATRE.]

Tragedies of; literally translated or revised; with Notes, by T. A. Buckley. 2 vols. 8vo. Lond., 1876–77.
　　　　　　　　　　　　　　　H 4 P 10, 11

A Transcript from the Alcestis of Euripides. [*See* BROWNING, R.]

Works of; translated by R. Potter. (Fam. Clas. Lib.) 3 vols. 12mo. Lond., 1832.　　　　　J 15 P 9–11

EUROPE. Satchel Guide for the Vacation Tourist in Europe. 12mo. Boston, 1879.　　　　　D 7 P 54

Tabular Historical Summary of the effect of Treaties on the Partition of Europe, &c. (Pam. A.) Fol. Edinb., 1857.　　　　　　　　　　　　MJ 2 U 1

EUSEBIUS (ALEXANDRINUS). Opera omnia. [*See* MIGNE, J. P., SERIES GRÆCA, 86.]

EUSEBIUS (SANCTUS). Opera omnia. [*See* MIGNE, J. P., SERIES LATINA, 12.]

EUSEBIUS PAMPHILUS. Ecclesiastical History of the 20th year of the Reign of Constantine, being the 324th of the Christian Era; translated [from the Greek Text of Valesius] by the Rev. C. F. Crusé, D.D. 4th ed., to which is prefixed the Life of Eusebius, by Valesius; translated by S.E. Parker. 8vo. Lond., 1847.　G 14 P 16

Opera omnia. [*See* MIGNE, J. P., SERIES GRÆCA, 19–24.]

Socratis et aliorum Historiæ Ecclesiasticæ. 3 vols. (in 2) sm. fol. Paris, 1544–45.　　　　　G 4 S 8, 9 †

[*See* SANCHONIATHO.]

EUSTACE (REV. JOHN CHETWODE). Classical Tour through Italy in 1802. Illustrated. 2nd ed. 2 vols. 4to. Lond., 1814.　　　　　　　　　　D 8 V 33, 34

Another copy. 6th ed. 4 vols. 8vo. Lond., 1821.
　　　　　　　　　　　　　　D 8 V 35–38

EUTHYMIUS (ZIGABENUS). Opera omnia. [*See* MIGNE, J. P., SERIES GRÆCA, 128–131.]

EUTROPIUS. Breviarium Historiæ Romanæ, ex Editione Henrici Verheyk, cum Notis et Interpretatione in usum Delphini. 8vo. Lond., 1821.　　　　J 13 Q 9

Justin, Cornelius Nepos, and Eutropius; literally translated by the Rev. J. S. Watson, M.A. 8vo. Lond., 1876.
　　　　　　　　　　　　　　B 14 P 44

EVAGRIUS. Ecclesiastical History of the Church, in Six Books, A.D. 431–594. 8vo. Lond., 1846.　G 13 P 12

History of the Church, A.D. 431–594. [*See* THEODORETUS.]

EVANS (COL. ALBERT S.) Our Sister Republic: a Gala Trip through Tropical Mexico in 1869–73. 8vo. Hartford, 1871.　　　　　　　　　　D 3 U 12

EVANS (ARTHUR JOHN), B.A., &c. Through Bosnia and the Herzegóvina on foot during the Insurrection, August and September, 1875. Illustrated. 8vo. Lond., 1876.
　　　　　　　　　　　　　　D 7 T 6

EVANS (DANIEL SILVAN). English and Welsh Dictionary. 2 vols. 8vo. Denbigh, 1852–58.　K 13 Q 32, 33

EVANS (EDMUND). [*See* FARJEON, B. L.]

EVANS (SIR FREDERICK JOHN OWEN), K.C.B. New Zealand Pilot. [*See* RICHARDS, CAPT. G. H.]

EVANS (G.) [*See* CHAMBERS, D. D.]

EVANS (G. C.) Stories told around the Camp Fire; compiled from the Note-book of "Mr. Daniel Digwell" [R. P. Whitworth]. 8vo. Sandhurst, 1881. MJ 1 U 8

EVANS (GEORGE), M.A. Essays on Assyriology. 8vo. Lond., 1883.　　　　　　　　　　K 15 P 6

EVANS (GEORGE WILLIAM). Chart of Van Diemen's Land, from the best Authorities, and from Surveys. 8vo. Hobart Town, 1821.　　　　　　　　　　MD 7 Q 41

Geographical, Historical, and Topographical Description of Van Diemen's Land; also a large Chart of the Island. 8vo. Lond., 1822.　　　　　　　　MD 7 Q 40

Another copy (without Chart). 8vo. Lond., 1822.*
　　　　　　　　　　　　　　MD 7 Q 42

History and Description of the Present State of Van Diemen's Land. 2nd ed. 8vo. Lond., 1824. MD 7 Q 44

Chart to the above. 2nd ed. Hobart, 1824.　MD 7 Q 45

EVANS (REV. G. W. D.) [*See* LANZI, A. L.]

EVANS (JOHN), F.R.S., &c. Ancient Bronze Implements, Weapons, and Ornaments of Great Britain and Ireland. 8vo. Lond., 1881.　　　　　　　　B 5 U 13

Ancient Stone Implements, Weapons, and Ornaments of Great Britain. 8vo. Lond., 1872.　　B 7 Q 38

Petit Album de l'Age du Bronze de la Grande Bretagne. Sm. 4to. Lond., 1876.　　　　　　B 7 Q 40

EVANS (REV. LEWIS), M.A. Satires of Juvenal, Persius, Sulpicia, and Lucilius. [*See* JUVENALIS, D. J.]

EVANS (MISS MARY ANN). [*See* CROSS, MRS. MARY ANN.]

EVANS (REV. MAURICE J.), B.A. John A Lasco. [*See* DALTON, DR. H.]

EVANS (MORGAN). Butter and Cheese. (Brit. Manuf. Indust.) 12mo. Lond., 1876.   A 17 S 32

EVANS (OLIVER). Young Millwright and Miller's Guide. Plates. 8vo. Philad., 1836.   A 11 U 14

EVANS (R. H.) Account of the Caricatures of Gillray. [*See* WRIGHT, T.]

EVANS (T. RHYS). Jacob Boehme. [*See* MARTENSEN, DR. H. L.]

EVANS (THOMAS). Old Ballads, Historical and Narrative. 4 vols. 8vo. Lond., 1810.   H 7 R 14-17

Essays on Song-writing. [*See* AIKIN, J.]

EVANS (T. SIMPSON), M.A. Life of Robert Frampton, Bishop of Gloucester, deprived as a Non-juror, 1689. 8vo. Lond., 1876.   C 4 R 4

EVANS (THOMAS W.), M.D. Memoirs of Heinrich Heine and some newly-discovered Fragments of his Writings; with an introductory Essay. 8vo. Lond.,1884. C 3 P 14

EVANS (WILLIAM). Geiriadur Saesneg a Chymraeg : an English-Welsh Dictionary. 2nd ed. Carmarthen, 1812.   K 14 T 8

EVELYN (JOHN), F.R.S. History of Religion : a Rational Account of the True Religion. 2 vols. 8vo. Lond., 1850.   G 11 P 22, 23

Memoirs illustrative of the Life and Writings of; comprising his Diary from 1641 to 1706, Familiar Letters, Private Correspondence with Charles I, &c. Edited by Wm. Bray. 2nd ed. 2 vols. roy. 4to. Lond., 1819.   C 2 W 10, 11

Miscellaneous Writings of. Roy. 4to. Lond.,1825. J 7 V 18

Silva; or, a Discourse of Forest-trees, &c. 4th ed. 2 vols. roy. 4to. York, 1812.   A 2 P 16, 17 †

EVENING NEWS (THE). 29 vols. fol. Sydney, 1871-87.   ME

EVENING POST (THE) Fol. Sydney, 1874.   ME

EVEREST (LIEUT.-COL. GEORGE), F.R.S. Account of the Measurement of two Sections of the Meridional Arc of India, bounded by the Parallels of 18° 3' 15", 24° 7' 11", and 29° 30' 48". Roy. 4to. Lond., 1847. · A 2 S 1 †

EVERETT (ARTHUR). Distribution of Forest Trees in Victoria : Notes by Baron F. von. Mueller, [K.]C.M.G. 4to. Melb., 1869.   MD 1 P 26 †

EVERETT (EDWARD). Catalogue of Books presented to the City of Boston. [*See* BOSTON PUBLIC LIBRARY.]

Orations and Speeches on various occasions. Roy. 8vo. Boston, 1836.   J 4 T 7

EVERETT (J. D.), M.A., &c. Vibratory Motion and Sound. 8vo. Lond., 1882.   A 16 S 8

System of Shorthand. [*See* ANDERSON, T.]

[*See* DESCHANEL, A. P.]

EVERETT (JAMES). Memoirs of James Montgomery. [*See* HOLLAND, J.]

EVERETT (WILLIAM), M.A. On the Cam : Lectures on the University of Cambridge, in England. New ed. 8vo. Lond., 1869.   J 10 Q 23

EVERILL (CAPT. H. C.) New Guinea Exploring Expedition. [*See* ROYAL GEOGRAPHICAL SOCIETY OF AUSTRALASIA.]

EVERITT (G.) English Caricaturists and Graphic Humourists of the Nineteenth Century : how they illustrated and interpreted their Times. 4to. Lond.,1886. C 4 W 8

EVERS (HENRY), LL.D. Navigation in Theory and Practice. 12mo. Lond., 1875.   A 3 R 48

Steam and the Steam Engine, Land and Marine. 12mo. Lond., 1876.   A 6 R 14

EVIDENCE ON DRUNKENNESS ; presented to the House of Commons by the Select Committee appointed by the House to inquire into this subject ; by J. S. Buckingham, M.P. 8vo. Lond., 1834.   F 10 Q 3

EVREMOND (C. M. DE). [*See* SAINT EVREMOND, C. M. DE.]

EWALD (ALEXANDER CHARLES), F.S.A. Life and Times of Prince Charles Edward Stuart, Count of Albany, commonly called "The Young Pretender." 2 vols. 8vo. Lond., 1875.   C 9 T 28, 29

Life and Times of the Hon. Algernon Sidney, 1622-83. 2 vols. 8vo. Lond., 1873.   C 9 U 10, 11

"Our Constitution :" an Epitome of our Chief Laws and System of Government ; with an Introductory Essay. 12mo. Lond., 1867.   F 6 Q 2

Rt. Hon. Benjamin Disraeli, Earl of Beaconsfield, K.G., and his Times. 2 vols. imp. 8vo. Lond., 1882. C 3 W 5, 6

Stories from the State Papers. 2 vols. 8vo. Lond., 1882.   B 3 R 14, 15

EWALD (HEINRICH). Antiquities of Israel ; translated from the German, by H. S. Solly, M.A. 8vo. Lond., 1876.   G 3 T 12

EWAN (JAMES). Geography of the Australian Colonies ; with a brief Sketch of the Islands of Australasia. 2nd ed., with large Additions. 12mo. Sydney, 1854. MD 2 Q 17

EWART (JOHN). Meat Production : a Manual for Producers, Distributors, and Consumers of Butchers' Meat; being a Treatise on Means of increasing its Home Production. (Weale). 12mo. Lond., 1878.   A 17 Q 77

EWING (MAJOR ALEXANDER). The Serapion Brothers. [*See* HOFFMANN, E. T. W.]

EWING (J. A.) Friction between Surfaces. [*See* JENKIN, PROF. F.]   A 11 P 5 †

EWING (REV. R. K.) Proceedings of the Rev. the Presbytery of Tasmania, at Launceston, 1858, in the Case of Ewing *versus* Fawns, and the Rev. the Presbytery *versus* Ewing. 8vo. Tasmania, 1858.   MG 1 Q 20

EWING (REV. T. C.) Charges against, by the Rev. Charles Price. [*See* PRICE, REV. C.]   MJ 2 R 4

The Mormon Delusion : a Lecture. 8vo. Sydney, 1853.
                                                 MG 1 Q 31

EXAMEN POETICUM DUPLEX. Sive Musarum Anglicanarum Delectus Alter cui subjicitur Epigrammatum seu Poematum Minorum, Specimen Novum. 12mo. Lond., 1698.   H 7 P 7

EXAMINER (THE). April to October, 1842. Fol. Sydney, 1842.   E

EX-COMMISSIONER, AN. [*See* INDIA.]

EXMOUTH (ADM. EDWARD PELLEW), VISCOUNT. Life of; by Edward Osler. 8vo. Lond., 1835.   C 5 V 13

EXON (EDWIN). Lost Flower Found, and other Poems. 12mo. Melb., 1862.   MH 1 R 51

EXPLANATIONS : a Sequel to "Vestiges of the Natural History of Creation." [*See* CHAMBERS, R.]

EXPRESS (THE). 3 vols. atlas fol. Sydney, 1883-85.   E

EYDOUX (MONS.) [*See* VAILLANT, A. N.]

EYLAND (E. S.) [*See* BURN, R. S.]

EYLERT (VERY REV. R. FR.), D.D. Religious Life and Opinions of Frederick William III, King of Prussia; translated by J. Birch. 8vo. Lond., 1844.   G 2 R 15

EYRE (EDWARD JOHN). Journals of Expeditions of Discovery into Central Australia, and Overland from Adelaide to King George's Sound, in the years 1840-41, including an Account of the Manners and Customs of the Aborigines. 2 vols. 8vo. Lond., 1845.* MD 2 T 11, 12
Life of; by Hamilton Hume. 8vo. Lond., 1867. MC1Q6

EYRE (LIEUT. VINCENT). Military Operations at Cabul, 1842 ; with a Journal of Imprisonment in Affghanistan. 8vo. Lond., 1843.   D 5 P 47

EYRIES (J. B. B.) [*See* BROUGHTON, CAPT. W. R.]

EYSINGA (P. P. ROORDA VAN). [*See* ROORDA VAN EYSINGA, P. P.]

EYSSENHARDT (F.) Scriptores Historiæ Augustæ. [*See* JORDAN, H.]

EYTON (REV. ROBERT W.) Domesday Studies: an Analysis and Digest of the Staffordshire Survey; treating of the Mensuration, Technicalities, Phraseology, and Method of Domesday in its relation to Staffordshire, and other Counties of the same Circuit. With Tables, &c. 4to. Lond., 1881.   B 5 V 33

F

FABER (G. L.) Fisheries of the Adriatic, and the Fish thereof: a Report of the Austro-Hungarian Sea-fisheries. 4to. Lond., 1883.   A 13 V 37

FABRE (JEAN CLAUDE). Histoire Ecclesiastique. [*See* FLEURY, ABBE CLAUDE.]

FABRETTI (ARIODANTE). Corpus Inscriptionum Italicarum antiquioris Aevi, ordine geographico digestum, et Glossarium Italicarum. Roy. 4to. Torino, 1867.   K 4 P 26 †

Primo, Secundo, e Terzo Supplementi alla Raccolta delle Antichissime Iscrizioni. 3 vols. (in 1) roy. 4to. Torino, 1872–78.   K 4 P 27 †

FABRICIUS (JOHANN ALBRECHT). Bibliotheca Graeca, sive notitia Scriptorum Veterum Graecorum, etc.; editio quarta, curante G. C. Harles. 12 vols. 4to. Hamburgi, 1790–1809.   K 7 V 5–16

Bibliotheca Latina, mediæ et infimæ ætatis; cum Supplemento. 6 vols. (in 4) sm. 4to. Patavii, 1754.   K7 V 1–4

Bibliotheca Latina, nunc melius delecta; rectius digesta et aucta diligentia, Io. Avg. Ernesti. 3 vols. 8vo. Lipsiae, 1773–74.   K 7 R 40–42

FABYAN (ROBERT). New Chronicles of England and France; in two Parts; named by himself "The Concordance of Histories." Reprinted from Pynson's edition of 1516; with a Biographical and Literary Preface and Index, by Henry Ellis. 4to. Lond., 1811.   B 10 R 11 †

FACETIÆ CANTABRIGIENSES; consisting of Anecdotes, Smart Sayings, Satires, Retorts, &c., by, or relating to celebrated Cantabs; by "Socius." 3rd ed. 12mo. Lond., 1836.   J 1 T 7

FACEY (JAMES WILLIAM), JUN. Elementary Decoration: a Guide to the simpler Forms of Everyday Art, as applied to the Interior and Exterior Decoration of Dwellinghouses, &c. (Weale.) 12mo. Lond., 1882. A 17 Q 56

Practical House Decoration: a Guide to the Art of Ornamental Painting. 8vo. Lond., 1886.   A 17 Q 67

FACTION DEFEATED; or, the Political Crisis of Victoria; by "Democritus." 8vo. Melb., 1861.   MF 1 Q 2

FAGAN (LOUIS ALEXANDER). Art of Michel' Angelo Buonarroti, as illustrated by the various Collections in the British Museum. Imp. 8vo. Lond., 1883.   A 8 U 22

Catalogue Raisonné of the Engraved Works of Wm. Woollett. Imp. 8vo. Lond., 1885.   K 9 P 1 †

Letters of Prosper Mérimée to Sir A. Panizzi. [*See* MÉRIMÉE, P.]

Life of Sir Anthony Panizzi, K.C.B., late Principal Librarian of the British Museum, &c. 2 vols. 8vo. Lond., 1880.   C 9 Q 13, 14

Raffaello Sanzio: his Sonnet in the British Museum studied; with three Facsimiles. Sm. 4to. Lond., 1884.   H 5 U 21

FAGNAN (MME. MARIE ANTOINETTE). Minet-Bleu, etc. [*See* CABINET DES FÉES, 35.]

FAHIE (J. J.) History of Electric Telegraphy, to the year 1837. 8vo. Lond., 1884.   A 5 R 61

FA-HIEN (CHINESE MONK). A Record of Buddhistic Kingdoms, A.D. 399–414. Translated and annotated, with a Corean Recension of the Chinese Text, by James Legge, M.A., &c. Sm. 4to. Oxford, 1886.   D 4 T 16

FAIJA (HENRY), C.E. Portland Cement for Users. 8vo. Lond., 1881.   A 2 R 31

Another copy. 2nd ed. (Weale.) 12mo. Lond., 1884.   A 17 R 1

FAIRBAIRN (JAMES). Fairbairn's Crests of the Families of Great Britain and Ireland; revised by Laurence Buttes. 2 vols. roy. 8vo. Edinb., 1860. K 10 V 12, 13

FAIRBAIRN (REV. PATRICK), D.D. Imperial Bible-Dictionary. 2 vols. imp. 8vo. Lond., 1866. K 18 T 7, 8

FAIRBAIRN (SIR WILLIAM), BART., F.R.S., &c. Life of; partly written by himself; edited and completed by W. Pole, F.R.S. With Portrait. 8vo. Lond., 1877.   C 7 R 9

Rise and Progress of Manufactures and Commerce in [Lancashire and Cheshire.] [*See* BAINES, T.]

Treatise on Mills and Millwork. 2nd ed. 2 vols. 8vo. Lond., 1864–65.   A 11 U 15, 16

FAIRBANKS (E. AND T.), & CO. Fairbanks' Patent Iron Frame Track Scale. (Pam. Cl.) 8vo. Lond., 1875.   A 16 U 21

FAIRFAX (VICE-ADM. ROBERT) Life of Robert Fairfax of Steeton, Vice-Admiral, Alderman, and Member for York, A.D. 1666–1725; compiled by Clements R. Markham, C.B., &c. 8vo. Lond., 1885.   C 6 Q 18

FAIRFAX (THOMAS), LORD. Life of the Great Thomas Lord Fairfax, Commander-in-Chief of the Army of the Parliament of England; by C. R. Markham, F.S.A. With Portrait. 8vo. Lond., 1870.   C 5 V 14

Mémoires de. [*See* GUIZOT, F. P. G. 5.]

FAIRFAX (WILLIAM). Hand-book to Australasia; being a brief Historical and Descriptive Account of Victoria, Tasmania, South Australia, New South Wales, Western Australia, and New Zealand; with Map. 12mo. Melb., 1859.*   MD 6 P 9

History and Advantages of Benefit Societies, and the Importance of Life Assurance. 8vo. Melb., 1869. MJ 2 R 15

FAIRFAX CORRESPONDENCE. Memorials of the Civil War; comprising the Correspondence of the Fairfax Family. Edited by Robert Bell. 2 vols. 8vo. Lond., 1849.   B 3 S 15, 16

FAIRFIELD (EDWARD). [*See* COLONIAL OFFICE LIST.]

FAIRHOLT (F. W.), F.S.A. Costume in England: a History of Dress to the end of the 18th Century; by the Hon. H. A. Dillon, F.S.A. 3rd ed. 2 vols. 12mo. Lond., 1885. A 7 P 27, 28

Dictionary of Terms in Art. Illustrated. 8vo. Lond., 1875. K 18 P 8

Miscellanea Graphica; Representations of Ancient, Medieval, and Renaissance Remains in the possession of Lord Londesborough. Historical Introduction by Thomas Wright, M.A., &c. 4to. Lond., 1857. A 4 R 1 †

Rambles of an Archæologist among Old Books and in Old Places. Sq. 8vo. Lond., 1871. A 7 U 1

Tobacco; its History and Associations. 8vo. Lond., 1876. A 18 R 35

[*See* SMITH, C. R.]

FAIRLIE (JOHN). Illustrations of Cheveley Church, Cambridgeshire. Fol. Lond., 1851. A 4 R 21 ‡

FAIR PLAY. [*See* JUDGES' SALARIES ACT.]

FAITHFULL (EMILY). Three Visits to America. 8vo. Edinb., 1884. D 3 R 42

FAITHS OF THE WORLD (THE). A Concise History of the Great Religious Systems of the World. 8vo. Edinb., 1882. G 8 Q 19

[*See* GARDINER, REV. J.]

FALCIMAGNE (L'ABBÉ). [*See* SALVADO, R.]

FALCONER (HUGH), M.D., &c., AND CAUTLEY (MAJOR PROBY T.), F.G.S., &c. Fauna Antiqua Sivalensis, being the Fossil Zoology of the Sewalik Hills, in the North of India; with Description of the Plates from Notes and Memoranda, by Hugh Falconer; compiled and edited by C. Murchison. 8vo. Lond., 1846–67. A 14 T 17

Plates to the above. Roy. fol. Lond., 1846. A 23 Q 18 ‡

FALCONER (HON. ION GRANT NEVILLE KEITH-). Kalilah and Dimnah; or, Fables of Bidpai. [*See* PILPAI.]

FALCONER (WILLIAM). Life and Poems of. [*See* BRITISH POETS; CHALMERS, A.; *and* JOHNSON, S.]

New Universal Dictionary of the Marine. [*See* BURNEY, W.]

FALCONER (WILLIAM), M.A. Geography of Strabo. [*See* STRABO.]

FALCONER (WILLIAM), AND FALCONER (REV. T.), M.A. Arrian's Voyage round the Euxine Sea. [*See* ARRIAN, F.]

Voyage of Hanno. [*See* HANNO.]

FALCONIA (PROBA). [*See* JUVENCUS, C. V. A.]

FALDA (G. B.) [*See* FERRERIO, P.)

FALK (ALFRED). Trans-Pacific Sketches: a Tour through the United States and Canada. 12mo. Melb., 1877. MD 1 W 43

FALK (JOHANN). Characteristics of Goethe. [*See* AUSTIN, MRS. SARAH.]

FALKE (JACOB VON). Art in the House: Historical, Critical, and Æsthetical Studies on the Decoration and Furnishing of the Dwelling. 4to. Boston, 1879. A 3 Q 1

FALL OF ALGIERS (THE): a Comic Opera. (Cumberland's Eng. Theatre.) 12mo. Lond., 1829. H 2 15 Q

FALLOUX (A. F. P.) Comte de Correspondence du Rev. Père Lacordaire et de Madame Swetchine. [*See* LACORDAIRE, J. B. H.]

Lettres de Madame Swetchine. [*See* SWETCHINE, MME. S. S.] C 9 P 40, 41

Lettres inédites de Madame Swetchine. [*See* SWETCHINE, MME. S. S.] C 9 P 46

Madame Swetchine: Journal de sa Conversion, Meditations et Prières. [*See* SWETCHINE, MME. S. S.]

Madame Swetchine; sa Vie et ses Œuvres. 4th ed. 2 vols. 8vo. Paris, 1861. C 9 P 42, 43

FAMILY ALMANAC and Educational Register for 1853. 12mo. Lond., 1853. E

FAMILY CLASSICAL LIBRARY (THE). 53 vols. 18mo. Lond., 1830–34. J 15 P 1–53

1. Æschylus; translated by Rev. R. Potter, M.A.
2, 3. Cæsar; translated by W. Duncan.
4–6. Cicero; the Orations, translated by Duncan; the Offices, by Cockman; and the Cato and Lælius, by Melmoth.
7, 8. Demosthenes, Orations of; translated by Thomas Leland, D.D.
9–11. Euripides; translated by Rev. R. Potter, M.A.
12–14. Herodotus; translated by Rev. W. Beloe.
15. Hesiod; translated by C. A. Elton: Bion and Moschus, Sappho and Musæus, by F. Fawkes, M.A.; and Lycophron, by Viscount Royston.
16–18. Homer; translated by A. Pope.
19, 20. Horace; translated by Philip Francis, D.D.
21. Juvenal; translated by C. Badham. Persius; translated by Rt. Hon. Sir W. Drummond.
22–28. Livy; translated by G. Baker.
29, 30. Ovid; translated by Dryden, Pope, Congreve, Addison, and others.
31. Pindar; translated by Rev. C. A. Wheelwright. Anacreon; by Thomas Bourne.
32–38. Plutarch; translated by John Langhorne, D.D., and William Langhorne, M.A.
39. Sallust; translated by William Rose.
40. Sophocles; translated by Thomas Francklin, D.D.
41–45. Tacitus; translated by Murphy.
46–48. Thucydides; translated by W. Smith, D.D.
49. Theophrastus, Characters of.
50, 51. Virgil; the Eclogues, translated by Wrangham; the the Georgics, by Sotheby; and the Æneid, by Dryden.
52 53. Xenophon; the Anabasis, translated by Edward Spelman; the Cyropædia, translated by the Hon. Maurice Ashly Cooper.

FAMILY LIBRARY. 39 vols. 12mo. Lond., 1830–40.
　　　　　　　　　　　　　　　　K 10 P 1–39
Bluit (Rev. I. J.) Sketch of the Reformation in England.
Coleridge (H. N.) Six Months in the West Indies.
Cunningham (Allan). Lives of the most eminent British Painters, Sculptors, and Architects.
Napoleon Buonaparte. Court and Camp of.
De Foe (D.) Journal of the Plague Year, 1665.
Natural History of Insects. Vol. 1.
Lockhart, J. G. History of Napoleon Buonaparte.
Massinger (Philip). Plays.
Milman (Very Rev. H. H.) History of the Jews.
Palgrave (Sir F.) History of the Anglo-Saxons.
　　　,,　　History of England. Vol. 1.
Scott (Sir W.) Letters on Demonology and Witchcraft.
Smedley (Edward), junr. Sketches from Venetian History.
Scane (G.) Life of the Duke of Wellington.
Charles I, Trials of, and of some of the Regicides.
Tytler (P. F.) Lives of Scottish Worthies.
Wesley (Rev. John). Compendium of Natural Philosophy.
Woodhouselee (Hon. A. F. Tytler), Lord. Universal History, from the Creation to the beginning of the 18th Century.

FAMILY TOUR through South Holland, up the Rhine, and across the Netherlands. 18mo. Lond., 1831. D 7 P 47

FAMILIAR ENGLISH QUOTATIONS. 18mo. Lond., 1877.　　　　　　　　　　　　　　　　K 17 P 1

FAMILIAR FRENCH QUOTATIONS and Proverbs and Phrases. 18mo. Lond., 1876.　　K 17 P 1

FAMILIAR LATIN QUOTATIONS and Proverbs. 22nd Thousand. 18mo. Lond., 1875.　　K 17 P 1

FANCOURT (Charles St. John). History of Yucatan, from its Discovery to the Close of the Seventeenth Century. With a Map. 8vo. Lond., 1854.　　B 18 40

FANE (Henry Edward). Five Years in India; comprising a Narrative of Travels in the Presidency of Bengal, &c. 2 vols. 8vo. Lond., 1842. D 5 R 39, 40

FANFANI (Pietro). Vocabolario Italiano della Lingua Parlata. [*See* Rigutini, G.]

FANGÉ (A.) La Vie du très-Révérend Père D. Augustin Calmet, Abbé de Senones; avec un Catalogue de tous ses Ouvrages, auquel on a joint plusieurs pieces, qui ont rapport à cette Vie. 8vo. Senones, 1762. C 10 P 23

FANNING (Edmund). Voyages round the World; with selected Sketches of Voyages to the South Seas, North and South Pacific Oceans, China, &c., 1792–1832. Lond., 1834.　　　　　　　　　　　　　　D 9 T 24

FARADAY (Michael), LL.D., &c. Chemical History of a Candle; edited by W. Crookes. 12mo. Lond., 1874.　　　　　　　　　　　　　　　A 5 R 26

Chemical Manipulation. 8vo. Lond., 1842. A 5 S 4

Course of Six Lectures on the various Forces of Matter and their relations to each other; edited by Wm. Crookes, F.C.S. 3rd ed. 12mo. Lond., 1861. A 29 P 7

Experimental Researches in Chemistry and Physics. 8vo. Lond., 1859.　　　　　　　　　　　　A 6 P 15

FARADAY (Michael), LL.D., &c.—*continued.*
Experimental Researches in Electricity. (Philosophical Trans.) 8vo. Lond., 1839.　　　　　　A 6 P 2
Experimental Researches in Electricity. (Philosophical Trans.) 3 vols. 8vo. Lond., 1839–55.　A 6 Q 15–17
Faraday as a Discoverer; by John Tyndall. 8vo. Lond., 1868.　　　　　　　　　　　　　C 5 R 15
Life and Letters of; by Dr. Henry Bence Jones. 2nd ed. revised. 2 vols. 8vo. Lond., 1870.　　C 9 T 8, 9
Michael Faraday; by J. H. Gladstone, Ph.D., &c. 3rd ed. 8vo. Lond., 1874.　　　　　　　　C 3 Q 20
Subject-matter of a Course of Six Lectures on the Non-metallic Elements. 12mo. Lond., 1853. A 5 S 53
　　　　　　　　　　　　　　　　H 1 P 36–42

FARCES: a Collection of Farces and other Afterpieces; selected by Mrs. Inchbald. 7 vols. 12mo. Lond., 1815.
Adopted Child, The : a Musical Drama; by Samuel Birch. Vol. 6.
All the World's a Stage: a Farce; by Isaac Jackman. Vol. 4
Apprentice, The : a Farce; by Arthur Murphy. Vol. 3.
Author, The: a Comedy; by Mr. Foote. Vol. 1.
Birth-day, The : a Comedy; by Thomas Dibdin. Vol. 2.
Blind Boy, The : a Melo-drama; by W. B. Hewetson. Vol. 1.
Bon Ton: a Farce; by David Garrick. Vol. 5.
Catherine and Petruchio : a Comedy; altered from Shakespeare by David Garrick. Vol. 4.
Child of Nature: a Drama; from the French of the Marchioness of Sellery. Vol. 1.
Citizen, The: a Farce; by Arthur Murphy. Vol. 4.
Comus: a Masque; altered from Milton by George Colman. Vol. 7.
Critic, The: a Dramatic Piece; by R. Brinsley Sheridan. Vol. 5.
Deserter, The : a Farce; by Charles Dibdin. Vol. 2.
Deuce is in Him, The: a Farce; by George Colman. Vol. 6.
Devil to Pay, The: an Opera; by C. Coffey. Vol. 5.
Doctor and the Apothecary, The : a Musical Entertainment; by James Cobb. Vol. 6.
Edgar and Emmeline: a Comedy; by Dr. Hawkesworth. Vol. 6.
Ella Rosenberg: a Melodrama; by James Kenney. Vol. 3.
Farm House, The: a Farce; by Charles Johnson. Vol. 6.
Farmer, The; by John O'Keefe. Vol. 2.
First Floor, The: a Farce; by James Cobb. Vol. 6.
Flora: a Farce; from the "Country Wake" of Mr. Dogget, by John Hippesley. Vol. 5.
Guardian, The: a Farce; by David Garrick. Vol. 4.
Hartford Bridge: an Operatic Farce; by Mr. Pearce. Vol. 3.
High Life below Stairs: a Farce; by David Garrick. Vol. 5.
Highland Reel, The; by John O'Keefe. Vol. 6.
Irish Widow, The: a Comedy; by David Garrick. Vol. 5.
Irishman in London, The: a Farce; by William Macready. Vol. 2.
Jew and the Doctor, The: a Farce; by Thomas Dibdin. Vol.
Lock and Key: a Musical Entertainment; by Prince Hoare. Vol. 3.
Lodoiska: an Opera; by J. P. Kemble. Vol. 7.
Love a la Mode: a Farce; by Charles Macklin. Vol. 1.
Lyar, The: a Comedy; by Samuel Foote. Vol. 5.
Lying Valet, The: a Farce; by Mr. Garrick. Vol. 4.
Maid of the Oaks, The: a Dramatic Entertainment; by Gen Burgoyne. Vol. 6.
Matrimony: a Petit Opera; altered from the French, by James Kenney. Vol. 1.
Mayor of Garratt, The: a Comedy; by Samuel Foote. Vol.
Midas: an English Burletta; by Kane O'Hara. Vol. 7.
Midnight Hour, The: a Comedy; from the French of M. Dumaniant. Vol. 1.
Miller of Mansfield, The: a Dramatic Tale; by R. Dodsley. Vol. 7.
Minor, The: a Comedy; by Samuel Foote. Vol. 5.
Miss in her Teens: a Farce; by David Garrick. Vol. 4.
Mock Doctor, The: a Comedy; by Henry Fielding. Vol. 5.

FARCES—*continued.*

Netley Abbey: an Operatic Farce; by Mr. Pierce. Vol. 3.
Old Maid, The: a Comedy; by Arthur Murphy. Vol. 7.
Padlock, The: a Farce; by Isaac Bickerstaffe. Vol. 4.
Poor Soldier, The: a Comic Opera; by John O'Keeffe. Vol. 2.
Prisoner at Large, The: a Comedy; by John O'Keeffe. Vol. 2.
Quaker, The: a Comic Opera; by Charles Dibdin. Vol. 4.
Raising the Wind: a Farce; by James Kenney. Vol. 1.
Register Office, The: a Farce; by Joseph Reed. Vol. 3.
Richard Cœur de Lion: an Historical Romance; by Gen. Bu.-
　goyne. Vol. 6.
Rosina: a Comic Opera; by Mrs. Brooke. Vol. 3.
School for Authors, The: a Comedy; by John Tobin. Vol. 7.
Sultan, The: a Comedy; by Isaac Bickerstaffe. Vol. 3.
Three Weeks after Marriage: a Farce; by Arthur Murphy.
　Vol. 4.
Tom Thumb: a Farce; altered by Kane O'Hara. Vol. 6.
Turnpike-gate, The: a Musical Entertainment; by F. Knight.
　Vol. 3.
Two Strings to your Bow: a Farce; by Robert Jephson. Vol. 2.
Waterman, The: a Ballad Opera; by Charles Dibdin. Vol. 7.
Ways and Means: a Comedy; by George Colman, junr. Vol. 7.
Wedding Day, The: a Drama; by Mrs. Inchbald. Vol. 1.
Who's the Dupe? a Farce; by Mrs. Cowley. Vol. 1.

FAREY (John). Treatise on the Steam-engine, Historical,
Practical, and Descriptive. 4to. Lond., 1827.　A 5 R 7 †

FARINI (G. A.) Through the Kalahari Desert: a Narrative of a Journey with Gun, Camera, and Note-book to
Lake N'gami and Back. 8vo. Lond., 1886.　D 2 R 14

FARINI (Luigi Carlo). The Roman State, 1815-50;
translated from the Italian, by the Hon. W. E. Gladstone.
4 vols. 8vo. Lond., 1851-54.　B 11 U 6-9

FARJEON (B. L.) The Golden Land; or, Links from
Shore to Shore. 8vo. Lond., 1886.　MJ 1 Q 31

Great Porter Square: a Mystery. 8vo. Lond., 1885.
　　　　　　　　　　　　　　　　　　　MJ 1 Q 29

Grif: a Story of Australian Life. New ed. 8vo. Lond.,
1871.　　　　　　　　　　　　　　　　MJ 1 Q 27

Another copy. 8vo. Melb., 1885.　　　MJ 1 Q 28

The House of White Shadows. 8vo. Melb., 1885.
　　　　　　　　　　　　　　　　　　　MJ 1 Q 30

FARLEY (J. Lewis). Egypt, Cyprus, and Asiatic Turkey.
8vo. Lond., 1878.　　　　　　　　　　D 2 Q 20

Turks and Christians: a Solution of the Eastern Question.
8vo. Lond. 1876.　　　　　　　　　　B 13 V 18

FARMER (The). The Farmer and the Chamber of Agriculture Journal. 6 vols. roy. fol. Lond., 1882-86.　E

FARMER (John). [See BELKNAP, REV. DR. J.]

FARMER (Richard), D.D. Laurence Chaderton, D.D.
(First Master of Emmanuel); translated from a Latin
Memoir of Dr. Dillingham; with Notes and Illustrations.
Richard Farmer, D.D. (Master of Emmanuel, 1775-97): an
Essay, by E. Shuckburgh, M.A. Camb., 1884.　C 6 P 13

FARMER (Sarah S.) Tonga and Friendly Islands; with
Sketch of their Mission History. 8vo. Lond., 1855.
　　　　　　　　　　　　　　　　　　　MD 5 P 16

FARNBOROUGH (Rt. Hon. Sir Thomas Erskine May),
Baron, K.C.B., &c. [See MAY, Rt. Hon. Sir T. E.]

FARNELL (L. R.), B.A. Guide to Studying for Honour
Classical Moderations. 8vo. Oxford, 1881.　G 18 Q 2

FARNEWORTH (Rev. Ellis), M.A. Works of Nicholas
Machiavel, newly translated; with Life of Machiavel.
[See MACHIAVELLI, N.]

FARNHAM (Thomas J.) Travels in the Great Western
Prairies, the Anahuac and Rocky Mountains, and in the
Oregon Territory. 2 vols. 8vo. Lond.,1843.　D 3 R 28, 29

FARQUHAR (George). The Beaux Stratagem: a Comedy.
(Brit. Theatre.) 12mo. Lond., 1808.　　H 1 R 8

Another copy. (New Eng. Theatre.) 12mo. Lond.,
1788.　　　　　　　　　　　　　　　　H 4 P 20

Another copy. [See BRIT. DRAMA, 3.]

The Constant Couple: a Comedy. (Bell's Brit. Theatre.)
18mo. Lond., 1792.　　　　　　　　　H 2 P 42

Another copy. (Brit. Theatre.) 18mo. Lond., 1808.
　　　　　　　　　　　　　　　　　　　H 1 R 8

Another copy. (New Eng. Theatre.) 12mo. Lond.,
1777.　　　　　　　　　　　　　　　　H 4 P 24

Another copy. [See BRIT. DRAMA, 3.]

Dramatic Works of. [See WYCHERLEY, W.]

The Inconstant: a Comedy. (Bell's Brit. Theatre.) 18mo.
Lond., 1793.　　　　　　　　　　　　H 2 P 26

Another copy. (Brit. Theatre.) 18mo. Lond., 1808.
　　　　　　　　　　　　　　　　　　　H 1 R 8

Another copy. (New Eng. Theatre.) 12mo. Lond.,
1777.　　　　　　　　　　　　　　　　H 4 P 24

Another copy. [See BRIT. DRAMA, 3.]

The Recruiting Officer: a Comedy. (Bell's Brit. Theatre.)
18mo. Lond., 1792.　　　　　　　　　H 2 P 31

Another copy. (Brit. Theatre.) 12mo. Lond., 1808.
　　　　　　　　　　　　　　　　　　　H 1 R 8

Another copy. (New Eng. Theatre.) 12mo. Lond.,
1786.　　　　　　　　　　　　　　　　H 4 P 16

Another copy. [See BRIT. DRAMA, 3.]

Sir Harry Wildair: a Comedy. (Bell's Brit. Theatre.)
18mo. Lond., 1796.　　　　　　　　　H 2 P 13

The Twin Rivals: a Comedy. (Bell's Brit. Theatre.) 18mo.
Lond., 1795.　　　　　　　　　　　　H 2 P 3

FARR (E.) History of England. [See HUME, D., AND
SMOLLETT, T.]

FARR (W.) Vital Statistics. 8vo. Lond.,1885.　F 4 T 11

FARRAGUT (Adm. David Glasgow). Life of; First
Admiral of the United States Navy, embodying his Journal
and Letters; by his Son, Loyall Farragut. Illustrated.
8vo. New York, 1879.　　　　　　　　C 8 Q 10

FARRAGUT (LOYALL). Life of David Glasgow Farragut, First Admiral of the United States Navy. 8vo. New York, 1879. C 8 Q 10

FARRAR (REV. FREDERIC W.), M.A., &c. Chapters on Language. 8vo. Lond., 1865. K 12 P 26
Early Days of Christianity. 2 vols. 8vo. Lond., 1882. G 14 T 3, 4
Families of Speech: Four Lectures. 8vo. Lond., 1870. K 20 R 5
The Witness of History to Christ: Five Sermons. 8vo. Lond., 1871. G 8 R 5

FARRAR (DR. JOSEPH), L.R.C.P.E., &c. Human Voice and Connected Parts. 8vo. Lond., 1881. A 12 Q 11

FARRAR (J. M.), M.A. Mary Anderson: the Story of her Life and Professional Career. With a Portrait. Sm. 4to. Lond., 1884. C 4 W 2

FARRELL (JOHN). The Maid of Genoa: a Melodrama. (Cumberland's Eng. Theatre.) 12mo. Lond. 1829. H 2 Q 20

FARRELL (JOHN). How he Died, and other Poems. Subscribers' ed. 8vo. Sydney, 1887.* MH 1 8 16

FARREN (R.) Birds of Aristophanes, as performed by Members of the University, at the Theatre Royal, Cambridge, November, 1883; drawn and etched by Robert Farren. Ob. 4to. Camb., 1883. A 8 R 4 †
Eumenides of Æschylus, as performed by Members of the University, at the Theatre Royal, Cambridge, December, 1885; drawn and etched by R. Farren. Ob. 4to. Camb., 1886. A 8 R 5 †
The Granta and the Cam, from Byron's Pool to Ely. Imp. 4to. Camb., 1881. A 35 P 1 ‡
Memorials of Cambridge: Etchings. [*See* LE KEUX, J., AND COOPER, C. H.]

FARRER (RICHARD RIDLEY). Tour in Greece, 1880. Illustrated. Roy. 8vo. Edinb., 1882. D 7 V 23

FARRER (SIR T. H.) Free Trade v. Fair Trade. 3rd ed. 8vo. Lond., 1886. F 6 P 20

FARRER (WILLIAM), B.A. Grass and Sheep-farming: a Paper, Speculative and Suggestive. 8vo. Sydney, 1873. MA 1 Q 40

FARRINGTON (J.) [*See* BOYDELL, J. AND J.]

FARROW (EDW. S.) Farrow's Military Encyclopædia: a Dictionary of Military Knowledge. Illustrated. 3 vols. imp. 8vo. New York, 1885. K 6 T 27–29

FATAL QUEST (THE); or, the Lost Son; by "A Lady," 12mo. Sydney, 1872. MH 1 R 51

FAU (DR. J.) Anatomy of External Forms of Man; intended for the use of Artists, Painters, and Sculptors. Edited, with additions, by Robert Knox, M.D. 8vo. Lond., 1849. A 8 Q 36
Atlas [to the above]. Roy. 4to. Lond., 1849. A 23 R 27 †

2 L

FAUCHER (J.) New Commercial Treaty between Great Britain and Germany. [*See* COBDEN CLUB.]

FAUCHERY (ANTOINE). Lettres d'un Mineur en Australie. 8vo. Paris, 1859. MD 5 Q 26

FAULKNER (HENRY). Elephant Haunts; being a Sportsman's Narrative of the Search for Dr. Livingstone. 8vo. Lond., 1868. D 2 T 7

FAULMANN (PROF. CARL). Das Buch der Schrift enthaltend die Schriftzeichen und Alphabete aller Zeiten und aller Völker des Erdkreises. 2te auflage. Fol. Wien, 1880. K 14 S 13

FAURIEL (CLAUDE). Dante et les Origines de la Langue et de la Littérature Italiennes. 2 vols. 8vo. Paris, 1854. B 11 V 22, 23
Histoire de la Poésie Provençale. 3 vols. 8vo. Paris, 1846. B 15 P 25–27
Last Days of the Consulate; edited, with an Introduction, by L. Lalanne. 8vo. Lond., 1885. B 9 P 15

FAUSSE-LENDRY (MARQUISE DE). [*See* BARRIÈRE, J, F., 18.] C 1 T 18

FAUSSETT (R. GODFREY), M.A. Symmetry of Time; being an Outline of Biblical Chronology, from the Creation to the Exodus. 4to. Oxford, 1881. G 5 U 16'

FAVENC (ERNEST). Great Austral Plain: its Past, Present, and Future. Republished from the *Sydney Morning Herald.* 8vo. Sydney, 1881.* MD 3 S 42
History of Australian Exploration from 1788 to 1888. Roy. 8vo. Sydney, 1888.* MD 6 U 4
Western Australia: its Past History, its Present Trade and Resources, its Future Position in the Australian Group. 4to. Sydney, 1887.* MD 6 U 1

FAVRE (L'ABBÉ P.) Dictionnaire Javanais-Français. Roy. 8vo. Vienna, 1870. K 15 S 20

FAWCETT (HENRY), M.A., &c. Indian Finance: three Essays, republished from the *Nineteenth Century*; with an Introduction and Appendix. 8vo. Lond., 1880. F 10 Q 21
Life of; by Leslie Stephen. 8vo. Lond., 1885. C 3 T 8
Manual of Political Economy. 8vo. Lond., 1869. F 6 Q 10

FAWCETT (HENRY), AND FAWCETT (MILLICENT GARRETT). Essays and Lectures on Social and Political Subjects. 8vo. Lond., 1872. F 9 R 17

FAWKES (F. A.) Horticultural Buildings: their Construction, Heating, Interior Fittings, &c.; with Remarks on some of the Principles involved, and their application. Sq. 8vo. Lond., 1881. A 2 S 39

FAWKES (F.) Life and Poems of. [*See* CHALMERS, A.]
Translations of Theocritus, Appollonius Rhodius, Coluthus, Anacreon, Sappho, Bion, Moschus, and Musæus. [*See* CHALMERS, A.]
[*See* HESIOD.]

FAWKNER (JOHN PASCOE). ·
Discovery of the River Yarra. [*See* CAPPER, R.]

Plan of the Town of Melbourne, 1841. Roy. 4to. Melb.,
1841. MD 5 S 15‡

Squatting Orders ; Orders in Council ; Locking up the
Lands of the Colony in the hands of a small minority.
8vo. Melb., 1854. MF 2 P 31

[*See* MELBOURNE ADVERTISER.]

FAWNS (JOHN). Case of. [*See* EWING, REV. R. K.]

FAWTHROP (J.) Narrative of the Wreck of the *Admella*.
[*See* MOSSMAN, S.]

FAY (AMY). Music-Study in Germany ; from the Home Correspondence of Amy Fay. 8vo. Lond., 1886. D 8 Q 29

FAYRER (J.), M.D., &c. Thanatophidia of India : being
a description of the Venomous Snakes of the Indian
Peninsula. 2nd ed. Imp. fol. Lond., 1874. A 4 R 4 ‡

FEA (JAMES). Present State of the Orkney Islands considered, and an Account of the new Method of Fishing
on the Coasts of Shetland ; published in 1775. 8vo.
Edinb., 1884. D 7 Q 47

FEATHERMAN (A.) Social History of the Races of
Mankind : Aramæans. 8vo. Lond., 1881. A 1 W 38

Social History of the Races of Mankind : Nigritians.
8vo. Lond., 1885. A 1 W 37

FEATHERSTONHAUGH (G. W.) Canoe Voyage up the
Minnay Sotor. 2 vols. 8vo. Lond., 1847. D 3 U 8, 9

Excursions through the Slave States, from Washington to
the Frontier of Mexico, &c. 2 vols. 8vo. Lond., 1844.
D 3 S 33, 34

Observations upon the Treaty of Washington, 1842.
(Pam. 9.) 8vo. Lond., 1843. F 12 P 8

FEDERAL UNION. Papers relating to a Federal Union
of the Australian Colonies. 8vo. Melb., 1862. MF 3 P 5

FEDERER (CHARLES A.), L.C.P. Ballad of Flodden
Field : a Poem of the 16th Century. Roy. 8vo. Manchester, 1884. H 5 V 10

FEEJEE. [*See* FIJI.]

FEILBERG (CARL ADOLPH). Catalogue of the Queensland Court, International Exhibition, Melbourne, 1880 ;
with Essay descriptive of the Colony. 8vo. Brisbane,
1880. MJ 2 R 16

FEILDEN (EDWD. WHINGHAM). My African Home ; or,
Bush Life in Natal when a Young Colony (1852–7).
Illustrated. 8vo. Lond., 1887. D 1 Q 26

FEILDEN (H. W.), F.G.S., &c. Voyage to the Polar
Sea : Notes on the Natural History. [*See* NARES, CAPT.
SIR G. S.]

FEISTMANTEL (OTTOKAR), M.D. Fossil Flora of the
Gondwana System. [*See* INDIA.]

FÉLICE (PROF. G. DE), D.D. History of the Protestants
of France. 2 vols. 8vo. Lond., 1853. G 8 R 2, 3

FELINSKA (EVA). Revelations of Siberia ; by "A
Banished Lady." Edited by Colonel Lach Szyrma. 2nd
ed. 2 vols. 8vo. Lond., 1863. D 6 P 3, 4

FELIX (RACHEL). [*See* RACHEL-FELIX, ELISA.]

FELKIN (H. M.) Technical Education in a Saxon Town.
8vo. Lond., 1881. G 17 Q 25

FELKIN (R. W.), F.R.G.S., &c. Uganda and the Egyptian
Soudan. [*See* WILSON, REV. C. T.]

FELKIN (W.) Hosiery and Lace. (Brit. Manuf. Indust.)
12mo. Lond., 1876. A 17 S 33

FELLOW OF THE CARPATHIAN SOCIETY, A.
[*See* MAGYARLAND.]

FELLOW OF A COLLEGE, A. [*See* LOFFT, C.]

FELLOWES (ROBERT), D.D., &c., "PHILALETHES." History of Ceylon, from the Earliest Period to the year 1815 ;
to which is subjoined, Robert Knox's Historical Relation
of the Island, with an Account of his Captivity during a
period of near Twenty Years. Illustrated. 4to. Lond.,
1817 B 10 V 5

FELLOWES (W. D.) Visit to the Monastery of La Trappe
in 1817. Illustrated. 8vo. Lond., 1818. D 6 T 11

FELLOWS (SIR CHARLES). Account of Discoveries in
Lycia. Roy. 8vo. Lond., 1841. B 13 V 38

Coins of Ancient Lycia, before the Reign of Alexander ;
with an Essay on the relative Dates of the Lycian Monuments in the British Museum. Imp. 8vo. Lond., 1855.
A 1 Q 12 †

Journal written during an Excursion in Asia Minor.
Roy. 8vo. Lond., 1839. D 6 S 37

FELLTHAM (OWEN). Resolves, Divine, Moral, and Political. 12mo. Lond., 1840. G 9 P 37

FELTOE (REV. CHARLES LETT), M.A. Memorials of John
Flint Soutn ; with Portrait. 8vo. Lond., 1884. C4Q27

FELTON (MYRA). Eena Romney ; or, Word-Pictures of
Home Life in New South Wales. 8vo. Sydney, 1887.*
MJ 1 U 30

FEMALE APPAREL. An Act for the Reform and Regulation of Female Apparel, and to amend and Refrenate
the Customs relating to Crinoline. Fol. Sydney, 1864.
MJ 2 U 1

FEMALE REFUGE SOCIETY. [*See* SYDNEY FEMALE
REFUGE SOCIETY.]

FÉNÉLON (FRANÇOIS DE SALIGNAC DE LA MOTHE) ARCH-
BISHOP OF CAMBRAI. Abrégé des Vies des Anciens
Philosophes. 18mo. Lond., 1832.   C 1 P 38

Adventures of Telemachus, Son of Ulysses. From the
French, by John Hawkesworth, LL.D. 2 vols. 18mo.
Lond., 1808.   J 7 P 38, 39

Adventures of Telemachus, Son of Ulysses. From the
French, by John Hawkesworth; LL.D.; with a Life of
the Author. 18mo. Lond., 1871.   J 7 P 39

Las Aventuras de Telémaco. [In French and Spanish.]
Neuva ed. 2 vols. 12mo. Perpiñan, 1822. J 16 T 18, 19

Fables et Contes. [*See* CABINET DES FÉES, 18.]

Fénélon, Archbishop of Cambrai: a Biographical Sketch;
by Mrs. Henrietta L. S. Lear. 18mo. Lond., 1877.
                        C 3 T 5

Life of. [*See* BUTLER, S.]

Œuvres de Fénélon, Archevêque de Cambrai; précédées
d'Etudes sur sa Vie, par M. Aimé Martin. 3 vols. imp.
8vo. Paris, 1865.   J 15 V 18–20

Personal History and Religious Opinions of. [*See* UPHAM,
T. C.]   C 3 R 41

FENN (G. MANVILLE). Bunyip Land: the Story of a
Wild Journey in New Guinea. Illustrated. 8vo. Lond.,
1885.   MJ 1 U 17

FENN (SIR JOHN), KNT., M.A., &c. [*See* PASTON LETTER.]

FENNELL (C. A. M.), M.A. Pindar, the Nemean and
Isthmian Odes; with Notes, &c. [*See* PINDAR.]

FENTON (ELIJAH). Life and Poems of. [*See* CHALMERS,
A., *and* JOHNSON, S.]

Marianne: a Tragedy. (Bell's Brit. Theatre.) 18mo.
Lond., 1794.   H 2 P 14

FENTON (F. D.) Observations on the State of the Aboriginal Inhabitants of New Zealand. Sm. fol. Auckland, 1859.   MF 1 Q 3†

FENTON (F. E.) [*See* DUVAL, M.]

FENTON (JAMES). History of Tasmania, from its Discovery in 1642, to the Present Time; with a Map of the
Island, and Portraits of the Aborigines in Chromo-litho-
graphy. 8vo. Hobart, 1884.*   MB 2 Q 26

FENTON (JOHN). Early Hebrew Life: a Study in Sociology. 8vo. Lond., 1880.   F 4 Q 30

FENWICK (THOMAS), AND BAKER (THOMAS), C.E. Subterraneous Surveying, with and without the Magnetic
Needle. (Weale.) 12mo. Lond., 1871.   A 17 P 58

FENZI (SEBASTIANO). Translations into English Verse
from some of the Italian Poets—Filicaia, Michelangiolo,
Giusti, Fucini, Stecchetti, and others. 8vo. Florence,
1883.   H 6 S 15

FERBER (PROF. JOHN JAMES). Mineralogical History of
Bohemia. [*See* BORN, BARON I.]

FERDINAND VII (KING OF SPAIN). [*See* DE LOS
VALLES, BARON.]

FERDUSI. Persian Poetry. [*See* ROBINSON, S.]

FERGIE (HENRY PENKETH). Case of. [*See* ALCOCK v.
FERGIE.]

FERGUS (H.) History of the Western World: United
States. (Lard. Cab. Cyclo.) 2 vols. 12mo. Lond.,
1830–32.   K 1 U 2, 3

FERGUSON (ADAM), LL.D. Essay on the History of
Civil Society. 4to. Edinb., 1767.   F 8 P 18 †

History of the Progress and Termination of the Roman
Republic. 8vo. Lond., 1827.   B 12 R 36

FERGUSON (FRANCIS). Catalogue of Plants, Fruit Trees,
Ornamental Trees and Shrubs, cultivated by Francis
Ferguson, Australian Nursery, Camden, New South Wales.
(Pam. Ca.) 8vo. Sydney, 1865–66.   MA 1 Q 7

FERGUSON (JAMES), F.R.S. Astronomy explained, upon
Sir Isaac Newton's Principles; with Notes, &c., by
David Brewster, LL.D., &c. 2 vols 8vo. Edinburgh,
1821.   A 3 S 8, 9

Life of, in a Brief Autobiographical Account and further
extended Memoir; by Ebenezer Henderson, LL.D. 2nd ed
Edinb., 1870.   C 8 P 7

FERGUSON (JAN HELENUS). Manual of International
Law, for the use of Navies, Colonies, and Consulates.
2 vols. 8vo. Lond., 1884.   F 10 Q 12; 13

FERGUSON (JOHN). Ceylon in 1883: the leading Crown
Colony of the British Empire. 8vo. Lond., 1883. D 5 Q 6

FERGUSON (R.), M.D., &c. Letter to Sir Henry Halford, proposing a Method of Inoculating the Small-pox,
which deprives it of all its Danger, but preserves its
Power of preventing a second attack. 8vo. Lond.,
1825.   A 12 S 33

FERGUSON (ROBERT), F.S.A. Surnames as a Science.
8vo. Lond., 1883.   K 19 Q 4

FERGUSSON (LIEUT.-COL. ALEX.) The Hon. Henry
Erskine, Lord Advocate for Scotland; with Notices of
certain of his Kinsfolk and of his Time. 8vo. Edinb.,
1882.   C 8 V 6

The Laird of Lag: a Life Sketch [of Sir Robert Grierson.]
8vo. Edinb., 1886.   C 11 P 9

Letters and Journals of Mrs. [M. S.] Calderwood, of
Bolton. [*See* CALDERWOOD, MRS. M. S.]

FERGUSSON (JAMES), C.I.E., &c. Archæology in India,
wit1 especial Reference to the Works of Babu Rajen-
dralala Mitra. 8vo. Lond., 1884.   B 10 U 21

Historical Inquiry into the Principles of Beauty in Art.
8vo. Lond., 1849.   A 2 T 31

1, 2. History of Architecture in all Countries.
3. History of Indian and Eastern Architecture.
4. History of Modern Styles of Architecture.

History of Architecture. 2nd ed. 4 vols. 8vo. Lond.,
1873–76.   A 2 S 6–9

Illustrated Hand-book of Architecture. 2 vols. 8vo. Lond.,
1855.   A 3 P 12, 13

Palaces of Nineveh and Persepolis restored. 8vo. Lond.,
1851.   B 10 P 28

The Parthenon: an Essay on the Mode by which Light
was introduced into Greek and Roman Temples. 4to.
Lond., 1883.   A 2 T 30

Rude Stone Monuments in all Countries: their Age and
Uses. 8vo. Lond., 1872.   B 15 R 14

Temples of the Jews and the other Buildings in the Haram
Area at Jerusalem. 4to. Lond., 1878.   B 18 Q 21†

FERGUSSON (JAMES), D.C.L., &c., AND BURGESS
(JAMES), F.R.G.S., &c. Cave Temples of India. Imp.
8vo. Lond., 1880.   B 10 V 6

FERISHTA (M. C. H. S.) History of Dekkan and the
History of Bengal, from the First Muhammedan Conquests; translated by Jonathan Scott, LL.D. 2 vols
4to. Shrewsbury, 1794.   B 10 V 7, 8

FERRALL (J. S.), OG REPP (THORLEIFR GUDMUNDSSON).
Dansk-norsk-engelske Ordbog, Fjerde gjennemsete og
foroegede Udgave, ved A Larsen. 8vo. Kjobenhavn,
1873.   ζ 11 V 16

FERRERIO (PIETRO), ET FALDA (BATTISTA). Palazzi di
Roma de' più celebri Architetti. 2 vols. (in 1). Ob. fol.
Roma, 1655.   A 1 P 13 †

FERRES (ARTHUR). My Centennial Gift; or, Australian
Stories for Children. 8vo. Sydney, 1887.* MJ 2 P 25

FERRIER (A.) Description Historique et Topographique
de la Ville d'Anvers. 18mo. Bruxelles, 1836. D 11 P 36

FERRIER (DAVID), M.A., &c.   Experiments on the
Brain of Monkeys. 2nd Series. (Croonian Lectures.)
(Roy. Soc. Pubs. 1.) 4to. Lond., 1876.   A 11 P 2 †

FERRIER (JAMES FREDERICK), LL.D., &c. Philosophical
Works of. 3 vols. 8vo. Edinb., 1875.   G 8 Q 14–16

[See WILSON, PROF. J.]

FERRIS (MRS. G. B.) Mormons at Home; with some
Incidents of Travel from Missouri to California, 1852–53;
in a series of Letters. 8vo. New York, 1856. D 3 P 49

FERRIS (S. J.) [See KOEHLER, S. R.]   A 4 R 16 †

FERTÉ-SÉNECTÈRE (MARQUIS DE LA). Catalogue des
Livres composant la Bibliothèque Linguistique de M. le
Marquis de la Ferté-Sénectère. 8vo. Paris, 1873. K 7 8 7

FESQUET (A. A.) Manufacture of Steel. [See OVER-
MAN, F.]

FESTUS (S. P.) De verborum significatione. [See VERRIUS
FLACCUS, M.]

FÉTIS (F. J.) La Musique mise à la Portée de tout le
Monde. 8vo. Paris, 1830.   A 7 P 11

FEUERBACH (LUDWIG). Essence of Christianity; translated from the German, by Marian Evans [Mrs Mary
Ann Cross]. 2nd ed. 8vo. Lond., 1881.   G 8 R 1

FEUERBACH (PAUL JOHANN ANSELM), RITTER VON. Narratives of Remarkable Criminal Trials; translated by Lady
Duff Gordon. 8vo. Lond., 1846.   F 9 R 24

FEYAL (P.) La Fuente de las Perlas. 8vo. Madrid,
1862.   J 15 U 26

FFOULKES (EDMUND S.) Christendom's Divisions;
being a Philosophical Sketch of the divisions of the
Christian Family in East and West. 2 vols. 8vo. Lond.,
1865–67.   G 8 R 7, 8

Church's Creed; or, the Crown's Creed. [See HIST. PAMS.]

FEWTRELL (W. T.) [See KING, W. B.]

FIAT JUSTITIA. [See WARDLEY, E.]

FICHTE (JOHANN GOTTLIEB). Popular Works: The
Nature of the Scholar—The Vocation of Man—The
Doctrine of Religion; with a Memoir, by William Smith,
LL.D. 8vo. Lond., 1873.   G 9 T 10

FICIN (MARSILLE). Les trois Livres de la Vie, avec une
Apologie pour la Medicine et Astrologie: traduit par G.
Le Fèvre de la Bordiere. 12mo. Paris,1582. A 12 P 17

FICK (AUGUST), DR.PH.   Vergleichendes Wörterbuch
der indogermanischen Sprachen sprachgeschichtlich ange-
ordnet. 3e Auflage. 4 vols. 8vo. Göttingen, 1874–76.
                                            K 12 S 12–16

FIEDLER (EDUARD), AND SACHS (DR. CARL). Wissenschaftliche Grammatik der englischen Sprache. 2 vols.
8vo. Leipsic, 1861–77.   ζ 14 T 33, 34

FIELD (THE). The Field, the Farm, the Garden: the
Country Gentleman's Newspaper. 18 vols. roy. fol. Lond.,
1876–86.   E

FIELD (BARRON), F.L.S. Geographical Memoirs on New
South Wales; by various Hands. (*Author's copy, with
corrections and additions.*) 8vo. Lond., 1825.* MD 2 S 21

Memoirs of J. H. Vaux. [See VAUX, J. H.]

FIELD (C. D.), M.A., &c. Landholding, and the relation
of Landlord and Tenant, in various Countries.   8vo.
Calcutta, 1883.   F 12 R 6

FIELD (GEORGE). Grammar of Colouring, applied to Decorative Painting and the Arts. New ed., revised, &c., by E. A. Davidson. (Weale). 12mo. Lond., 1875. A 17 Q 30

FIELD (HENRY M.), D.D. Greek Islands and Turkey after the War. 8vo. New York, 1885. D 9 Q 11

FIELD (MISS KATE). Pen Photographs of Charles Dickens' Readings, taken from Life. Illustrated. 8vo. Lond., 1871. C 2 T 23

FIELD (NATHANIEL). The Fatal Dowry. [*See* MASSINGER, P.]

FIELD (REV. WILLIAM). Memoirs of the Life, Writings, and Opinions of the Rev. Samuel Parr, LL.D.; with Biographical Notices of many of his Friends, Pupils, and Contemporaries. 2 vols. 8vo. Lond., 1828. C 9 Q 15, 16

FIELDING (HENRY) [a Biography]; by Austin Dobson. (Eng. Men of Letts.) 8vo. Lond., 1883. C 1 U 15

The Intriguing Chambermaid: a Comedy. [*See* BRIT. DRAMA, 5.]

Life of; with Notices of his Writings, his Times, and his Contemporaries, by Frederick Lawrence. 8vo. Lond., 1855. C 4 T 8

The Miser: a Comedy. (Bell's Brit. Theatre.) 18mo. Lond., 1791. H 2 P 10

Another copy. New Eng. Theatre.) 12mo. Lond., 1787. H 4 P 16

The Mock Doctor: a Comedy. [*See* FARCES.]

Another copy. [*See* BRIT. DRAMA, 5.]

The Virgin Unmasked: a Musical Entertainment. (New Eng. Theatre.) 12mo. Lond., 1791. H 4 P 28

Works of; with an Essay on his Life and Genius, by Arthur Murphy. New ed., by James P. Browne, M.D. (Edinb.) 10 vols. 8vo. Lond., 1871. J 2 Q 1–10

FIELDING (JOHN). [*See* NEW HOLLAND.]

FIELDING (SARAH). [*See* XENOPHON.]

FIELDING (REV. SYDNEY G.) The Castaways, and other Poems. 8vo. Sydney, 1884.* MH 1 P 6

FIELDING (THOMAS H.) Catalogue of the Library of the Australian Museum. [*See* AUSTRALIAN MUSEUM.]

FIELDS (JAMES THOMAS), LL.D. Biographical Notes and Personal Sketches; with unpublished Fragments and Tributes from Men and Women of Letters. 8vo. Lond., 1881. C 5 R 14

Yesterdays with Authors. New illustrated edition. 8vo. Boston, 1882. C 5 S 27

FIFE (SIR JOHN). Manual of the Turkish Bath. [*See* URQUHART, D.]

FIGUIER (LOUIS). L'Année Scientifique et Industrielle, 1857–85. 30 vols. 8vo. Paris, 1858–86. E

Earth and Sea; from the French. Translated, edited, and enlarged, by W. Davenport Adams. Roy. 8vo. Lond., 1870. A 16 V 8

The Day after Death; or, our Future Life according to Science. 8vo. Lond., 1872. A 17 T 43

The Human Race. Illustrated. 8vo. Lond., 1872. A 1 W 23

The Insect World; being a Popular Account of the Orders of Insects, &c. 8vo. Lond., 1868. A 14 U 6

The Ocean World; being a descriptive History of the Sea and its living Inhabitants. 8vo. Lond., 1868. A 14 S 49

Primitive Man. Revised Translation. 8vo. Lond., 1870. A 1 W 11

Tableau de la Nature. 7 vols. roy. 8vo. Paris, 1865–70. A 16 V 1–7

La Terre et les Mers.	Les Mammifères.
La Vie et les Mœurs des Ani-	Les Poissons, les Reptiles, et
maux.	les Oiseaux.
L'Homme Primitif.	Histoire des Plantes.
Les Insectes.	

The Vegetable World; being a History of Plants, with their Botanical Descriptions and peculiar Properties. 8vo. Lond., 1869. A 4 S 4

The World before the Deluge. The Geological Portion revised, &c., by H. W. Bristow, F.R.S. 8vo. Lond., 1886. A 9 S 18

FIJI. Fiji of To-day: a Commercial and Agricultural Retrospect and Prospect; by M.A.T.E. 8vo. Sydney, 1886. MD 5 T 28

The Fiji Islands (with Maps), commercially considered as a Field for Emigration; by "Ceres." 8vo. Melb. 1869. MD 1 U 21

Map of. [*See* MAPS.]

Ordinances of the Colony of Fiji, from the 1st September, 1875. to the 31st December, 1878. 8vo. Sydney, 1880. E

Suva Harbour, Map of. [*See* MAPS.]

Taro Lekaleka. [Short Questions in Feejeean.] (Pam. 44.) 12mo. (n.p., n.d.) MJ 2 R 6

FILICAIA (VINCENZO DA). Translations from. [*See* FENZI, S.]

FINANCE ACCOUNTS of the U. K. of Great Britain and Ireland for the 1832. Fol. Lond., 1841. F 1 U 8

FINANCIAL REFORM ALMANACK: a Vade Mecum for Fiscal Reformers, Free Traders, Politicians, Public Speakers and Writers, and the Public generally. 8vo. Lond., 1878. E

FINANCIER. [*See* OUR FINANCIAL SYSTEM.]

FIN-BEC. [*See* JERROLD, W. B.]

FINCH (JOHN). Natural Boundaries of Empires, and a new View of Colonization. 12mo. Lond., 1844. MF 1 P 22

FINCH-HATTON (Hon. Harold). Advance Australia! an Account of Eight Years' Work, Wandering, and Amusement in Queensland, New South Wales, and Victoria. 8vo. Lond., 1885.   MD 5 V 31

FINDEN (Edward). Finden's Illustrations of the Life and Works of Lord Byron; with Information by W. Brockeden. 3 vols. roy. 8vo. Lond., 1833–34.   J 10 V 1–3

FINDEN (W. and E.) Portraits of the Female Aristocracy in the Reign of Queen Victoria. Fol. Lond., 1841.   C 22 R 7 ‡

FINDLAY (Alexander Geo.), F.R.G.S. Directory for the Navigation of the North Pacific Ocean; with Descriptions of its Coasts, Islands, &c., from Panama to Behring Strait and Japan, it Winds, Currents, and Passages. 2nd ed. Roy. 8vo. Lond., 1870.   D 11 V 7

Directory for the Navigation of the South Pacific Ocean; with Descriptions of its Coasts, Islands, &c., from the Straits of Magalhaens to Panama, and those of New Zealand, Australia, &c., its Winds, Currents, and Passages. 4th ed. Roy. 8vo. Lond., 1877.   D 11 V 8

FINDLAY (J. R.) Personal Recollections of Thomas de Quincey. 12mo. Edinb., 1886.   C 2 Q 14

FINE ARTS IN AUSTRALIA. Society for the Promotion of : Second Exhibition, 1849. (Pam. F.) 8vo. Sydney, 1849.   MJ 2 S 3

FINE ARTS IN FRANCE. Restoration of the Fine Arts of the Middle Ages in France. (From the *Foreign Quarterly Review.* 8vo. Lond., 1839.   A 7 R 21

FINE ARTS IN GREAT BRITAIN. Observations on the Interests of ; suggested by the Plan said to be in agitation, of erecting additional Buildings for the National Collections on the Premises of the British Museum. 8vo. Lond., 1823.   A 7 R 21

FINE ARTS IN SCOTLAND. Report by the Committee of Management of the Association for the Promotion of ; for the years 1836–39. Report by the Committee of Management of the New Association for the Promotion of ; for the years 1838–42. 8vo. Edinb., 1837–43.   A 7 R 21

Report by the Committee of Management of, 1844–45. (Pam.) 8vo. Edinb., 1845.   MJ 2 R 18

Report by the Committee of Management of, 1846–49. (Pam. 19.) 8vo. Edinb., 1847.   MJ 2 Q 8

Report by the Committee of Management of, 1846–49. 8vo. Edinb., 1847–49.   MJ 2 R 19

FINLASON (W. F.) An Exposition of our Judicial System and Civil Procedure as reconstructed under the Judicature Acts, including the Act of 1876. 8vo. Lond., 1877.   F 5 R 12

FINLAY (George), LL.D. History of Greece, from its Conquest by the Romans to the Present Time, b.c. 146 to a.d. 1864. Edited by the Rev. H. F. Tozer, M.A. 7 vols. in 5 8vo. (Clar. Pr.) Oxford, 1877.   B 9 T 24–28

FINLAYSON (George). Mission to Siam and Hué, the Capital of Cochin China, in the years 1821–22; with Memoir of the Author, by Sir Thomas S. Raffles. 8vo. Lond., 1826.   D 6 S 1

FINN (James). Sephardim; or, the History of the Jews in Spain and Portugal. 8vo. Lond., 1841.   G 8 Q 11

FINN (Rev. W. M.) Glimpses of North-eastern Victoria, and Albury, New South Wales. 8vo. Melb., 1870.   MJ 2 R 16

FINNEGAN (John). Account of the Natives of Moreton Bay. [*See* Field, B.]

FINNEY (Rev. C. G.) The Enduement of Power. [*See* Mahan, Rev. A.]

FINSCH (Dr. Otto). Anthropologische Ergebnisse einer Reise in der Südsee und dem malayischen Archipel, in den Jahren 1879, 1882. Roy. 8vo. Berlin, 1884. MA 1 S 1

Neu-Guinea und Seine Bewohner. 8vo. Bremen, 1865.   MD 5 S 1

Südsee-Erinnerungen (1875-80.) [*See* Hernsheim, F.] [*See* Bonaparte, C. L.]

FIRE PRECAUTIONS. Precautions taken against Fire at Public Institutions. Fol. Lond., 1874.   A 7 U 37

FIRTH (C. H.), M.A. Life of Col. Hutchinson. [*See* Hutchinson, L.]

Life of William Cavendish, Duke of Newcastle. [*See* Newcastle, Margaret, Duchess of.]

FIRTH (Rev. F.) In Affectionate Remembrance of the Rev. William Schofield, who died June 9th, 1878. 8vo. Sydney, 1878.   MG 1 Q 35

FIRTH (J. F. B.), LL.B. Municipal London; or, London Government as it is, and London under a Municipal Council. Roy. 8vo. Lond., 1876.   F 1 T 6

FISCHER (Dr. C. F.) [*See* Hochstetter, Dr. F. von.]

FISCHER (J. F.) [*See* Florus, L. A., *and* Nepos, C.]

FISCHER (Prof. Kuno). Commentary on Kant's Critick of the Pure Reason ; translated by J. P. Mahaffy, A.M. 8vo. Lond., 1866.   G 7 Q 14

Spinoza : an Essay. [*See* Spinoza, B. de.]

FISH (D. T.) Bulbs and Bulb Culture. Illustrated. 8vo. Lond., 1884.   A 4 Q 21

FISHER (Frederick). Murder of. [*See* Manuscripts and Portraits.]

FISHER (James C.) Advanced School Song-book : a Collection of Songs for the Senior Classes in Schools; selected, edited, and arranged for Equal Voices. Tonic Sol-fa Notation. Sm. 4to. Sydney, 1886.   MH 1 Q 3

FISHER (JAMES C.)—*continued.*
Elementary School Song-book ; selected, edited, and arranged for Equal Voices; with Preface, Hints to Teachers, and Alphabetical and Progressive Index. Sm. 4to. Sydney, 1876.   MH 1 Q 2

FISHER (DR. JOHN), BISHOP OF ROCHESTER.   English Works of. [*See* EARLY ENG. TEXT SOC., 25.]
Life of ; with an Appendix of illustrative Documents and Papers, by the Rev. John Lewis, A.M.   2 vols. 8vo. Lond., 1855.   6 Q 19, 20

FISHER (REV. OSMOND), M.A., &c.   Physics of the Earth's Crust.   8vo.   Lond., 1881.   A 9 S 11

FISHER (MAJOR PAYNE), B.A.   The Tombs, Monuments, &c., visible in St. Paul's Cathedral (and S. Faith's beneath it), previous to its Destruction by Fire, A.D. 1666.   Printed in 1684.   Edited by G. Blacker Morgan.   4to.   Lond., 1885.   B 4 V 13
Catalogue of Tombs in the Churches of the City of London A.D. 1666.   Revised and edited by G. R. Morgan. Printed 1668.   (Reprint.)   Roy. 8vo.   Lond., 1885.   K 8 V 13

FISHER (THOMAS), F.S.A.   Collections, Historical, Genealogical, and Topographical, for Bedfordshire.   Fol.   Lond., 1812–36.   B 15 T 2 ‡

FISHER (T. J.)   Colonial Law Reform.   8vo.   Sydney, 1870.   MF 3 P 2
Visit to the Burra Burra Mines, and the Great Smelting Works in South Australia, January-April, 1851. (Pam. 24.)   8vo.   Sydney, 1851.   MJ 2 Q 12

FISKE (JOHN).   American Political Ideas viewed from the Standpoint of Universal History : Lectures.   8vo. Lond., 1885.   F 6 Q 34
The Idea of God, as affected by Modern Knowledge. 12mo.   Lond., 1885.   G 8 Q 18
Man's Destiny, viewed in the Light of his Origin.   12mo. Lond., 1884.   G 8 Q 17
Outlines of Cosmic Philosophy, based on the Doctrine of Evolution.   2 vols. 8vo.   Lond., 1874.   G 2 R 18, 19

FISON (LORIMER), M.A., AND HOWITT (A. W.), F.G.S. Kamilaroi and Kurnai.   Group-Marriage and Relationship, and Marriage by Elopement.   Drawn chiefly from the usage of the Australian Aborigines; also the Kurnai Tribe, their Customs in Peace and War; with an Introduction by Lewis H. Morgan, LL.D.   8vo. Melb., 1880.   MA 1 S 11

FISON (MRS. WILLIAM).   Hand-book of the National Association for the Promotion of Social Science.   8vo. Lond., 1859.   F 15 Q 3

FISSCHER (J. F. VAN OVERMEER).   Bijdrage tot de Kennis van het Japansche Rijk.   Met Platen.   4to. Amsterdam, 1833.   D 5 V 13

FITTON (EDWARD BROWN).   New Zealand : its present Condition, Prospects, and Resources.   12mo.   Lond., 1856.*   MD 1 S 5

FITTON (WILLIAM HENRY), M.D., &c.   Account of some Geological Specimens from the Coasts of Australia.   From the Appendix to the "Narrative of a Survey of the Inter-tropical and Western Coasts of Australia, &c.," by Captain Phillip Parker King, R.N. ; with Instructions for collecting Geological Specimens.   8vo.   Lond., 1826.   MA 2 Q 10
An Address delivered at the Anniversary Meeting of the Geological Society of London on the 15th of February, 1828, and 20th of February, 1829.   (Pam. 2.)   2 vols. (in 1).   8vo.   Lond., 1828–29.   MJ 2 P 37
Instructions for collecting Geological Specimens.   (Pam. 2.)   8vo.   Lond. (n.d.)   MJ 2 P 37
Review of Mr. Lyell's "Elements of Geology;" with Observations on the Progress of the Huttonian Theory of the Earth ; from the *Edinburgh Review,* vol. 69.   8vo. Edinburgh, 1839.   A 9 T 39
Review of the Silurian System ; by Sir R. I. Murchison ; from the *Edinburgh Review* of 1841.   8vo.   Edinb., 1841.   A 9 T 7
Stratigraphical Account of the Section from Atherfield to Rocken-end, on the South-west Coast of the Isle of Wight.   8vo.   Lond., 1847.   A 9 T 6

FITZBALL (EDWARD).   The Devil's Elixir; or, the Shadowless Man : a Musical Romance.   (Cumberland's Eng. Theatre.)   12mo.   Lond., 1829.   H 2 Q 21
The Earthquake : a Burletta Operatic Spectacle.   (Cumberland's Eng. Theatre.)   12mo.   Lond., 1829.   H 2 Q 19
The Floating Beacon : a Nautical Drama.   (Cumberland's Eng. Theatre.)   12mo.   Lond., 1829.   H 2 Q 22
The Flying Dutchman; or, the Phantom Ship : a Nautical Burletta.   (Cumberland's Eng. Theatre.)   12mo.   Lond., 1829.   H 2 Q 21
The Inchcape Bell : a Nautical Burletta.   (Cumberland's Eng. Theatre.)   12mo.   Lond., 1829.   H 2 Q 21
The Pilot : a Nautical Burletta.   (Cumberland's Eng. Theatre.)   12mo.   Lond., 1829.   H 2 Q 21

FITZGERALD (DAVID).   Alphabetical Catalogue of the War Department Library.   [*See* UNITED STATES.]

FITZGERALD (EDWARD), LORD.   Life and Death of ; by Thomas Moore.   2 vols. 8vo.   Lond., 1831.   C 3 P 11, 12

FITZGERALD (J. F. L. V. FOSTER-).   [*See* FOSTER-FITZGERALD, J. F. L. V.]

FITZGERALD (PERCY), M.A., &c. The Book Fancier; or, the Romance of Book-collecting. 12mo. Lond., 1886.   J 1 S 42

Great Canal at Suez; its Political, Engineering, and Financial History. With an Account of Ferdinand de Lesseps. 2 vols. 8vo. Lond., 1876.   A 6 T 16, 17

The Kembles: an Account of the Kemble Family, including the Lives of Mrs. Siddons and her Brother, Philip Kemble. 2 vols. 8vo. Lond., 1871.   C 7 T 25, 26

Life and Adventures of Alexander Dumas. 2 vols. 8vo. Lond., 1873.   C 8 U 25, 26

Life and Times of William IV., including a View of Social Life and Manners during his Reign. 2 vols. 8vo. Lond., 1884.   C 9 S 45, 46

Life, Letters, and Writings of Charles Lamb; with Notes and Illustrations. (The Temple Ed.) 6 vols. 12mo. Lond., 1886.   C 2 S 28-33

Life of David Garrick, from original Family Papers, and numerous unpublished sources. 2 vols. 8vo. Lond., 1868.   C 7 P 17, 18

Life of George IV. 2 vols. 8vo. Lond., 1881. C 7 Q 22, 23

New History of the English Stage. 2 vols. 8vo. Lond., 1882.   B 15 P 10, 11

Royal Dukes and Princesses of the Family of George III : a View of Court Life and Manners for Seventy Years, 1760-1830. 2 vols. 8vo. Lond., 1882.   C 7 R 7, 8

FITZGERALD (R. D.), F.L.S.   Australian Orchids. Vol. 1, and Vol. 2 parts 1 and 2. 3 vols. fol. Sydney, 1882-85.   MA 1 R 1, 2 ‡

FITZGERALD (W.) Lectures on Ecclesiastical History. 2 vols. 8vo. Lond., 1885.   G 9 S 22, 23

FITZGIBBON (E. G.) What next? 8vo. Melb., 1879.
                                                  MJ 2 R 11

FITZHARDINGE (G. H.) [*See* LAW REPORTS, *and* SUP. COURT OF N.S.W.*]

FITZHERBERT (MRS.) Memoirs of; with an Account of her Marriage with H.R.H. the Prince of Wales, afterwards King George IV. 8vo. Lond., 1856. C 8 P 8

FITZHERBERT (HON. W.) Financial Statement, 2nd Session of the 4th Parliament. Delivered the 22nd August, 1867. 8vo. Wellington, 1867. MJ 2 R 16

FITZINGER (L. J.) Bilder-Atlas zur wissenschaftlich-populären Naturgeschichte der Säugethier-Amphibien, Fische, Säugethiere und Vögel. 4 vols. roy. 4to. Wein, 1860 64.   A 2 R 11-14 †

FITZMAURICE (EDMOND GEORGE PETTY), Lord. Life of William, Earl of Shelburne, afterwards first Marquess of Lansdowne; with Extracts from his Papers and Correspondence. 3 vols. 8vo. Lond., 1875-76. C 9 U 27-29

FITZPATRICK (T.) Autumn Cruise in the Ægean. 8vo. Lond., 1886.   D 7 Q 43

FITZPATRICK (PROF. W. J.), LL.D., &c. Life of Charles Lever. 2 vols. 8vo. Lond., 1879. C 7 S 13, 14.

Life of the Very Rev. T. N. Burke, O.P. 2 vols. 8vo. Lond., 1885.   C 10 R 27, 28

The Life, Times, and Correspondence of the Rt. Rev. Dr. Doyle, Bishop of Kildare and Leighlin. 2 vols. 8vo. Dublin, 1880.   C 2 S 11, 12

FITZROY (SIR C. A.) Copy of a Despatch from Governor C. A. Fitzroy to the Secretary of State for the Colonies, transmitting the Report of a Select Committee of the Legislative Council of New South Wales, on Crown Lands, in 1849. (Parl. Docs. 59.) Fol. Lond., 1850. MF 4 ‡

FITZROY (VICE-ADMIRAL ROBERT).   Remarks on New Zealand, in February, 1846. (Pam. 24.) 8vo. Lond., 1846.   MJ 2 Q 12

Weather Book : a Manual of Practical Meteorology. 8vo. Lond., 1863.   A 3 T 16

[*See* DARWIN, C.]

FITZROY (CAPT. ROBERT), AND KING (CAPT. PHILLIP PARKER). Narrative of the Surveying Voyage of His Majesty's Ships *Adventure* and *Beagle*, between the years 1826 and 1836; [with] Journal and Remarks, by Charles Darwin, M.A. 4 vols. 8vo. Lond., 1839. D 9 S 34-37

Another copy. 4 vols. 8vo. Lond., 1839.   MD 7 R 1-4

FITZWILLIAM (CHARLES WILLIAM), EARL. Correspondence of Edmund Burke. [*See* BURKE, RT. HON. E.*]

FIVES-LILLE, COMPAGNIE DE. Compagnie de Fives-Lille, General Engineers and Contractors. Imp. 8vo. Sydney, 1886.*   MA 1 P 12 †

FLACCUS (MARCUS VERRIUS. [*See* VERRIUS FLACCUS, M.]

FLACHET (EUGENE). Cathédrale de Bayeux : Description des Travaux, par H. de Dion, et L. Lasvignes. 8vo. Paris, 1861.   A 2 U 7

FLACK (CAPT.), "THE RANGER." A Hunter's Experiences in the Southern States of America. 8vo. Lond., 1866.
                                                  D 4 P 20

FLAMMARION (CAMILLE). Astronomical Myths. [*See* BLAKE, J. F.]

The Atmosphere ; translated from the French, edited by James Glaisher, F.R.S. Roy. 8vo. Lond., 1873. A 3 U 22

Travels in the Air. [*See* GLAISHER, J.]

FLANAGAN (RODERICK J.)   Australian, and other Poems. 8vo. Sydney, 1887.*   MH 1 Q 7

History of New South Wales; with an Account of Van Diemen's Land (Tasmania), New Zealand, Port Phillip (Victoria), Moreton Bay, and other Australasian Settlements; comprising a complete View of the Progress and Prospects of Gold-mining in Australia. 2 vols. 8vo. Lond., 1862.*   MB 1 T 19, 20

FLANDRE (CHARLES DE), F.R.A.S. History of Mary Stuart, Queen of Scots; translated from the original and unpublished MS. of Prof. Petit. Illustrated. 2 vols. (in I) 4to. Lond., 1874. C 2 W 16

Monograms of three or more Letters, designed and drawn on Stone. Roy. 4to. Lond., 1884. A 23 P 13 ‡

FLANNIGAN (MRS.) Antigua and the Antiguans. 2 vols. 8vo. Lond., 1844. D 3 S 9, 10

FLATLAND. [*See* ABBOTT, REV. E. A.]

FLAX COMMISSIONERS. New Zealand. [*See* NEW ZEALAND.]

FLAXMAN (JOHN), R.A. Anatomical Studies of the Bones and Muscles, for the Use of Artists; engraved by Henry Landseer. At. fol. Lond., 1833. A 2 P 21 ‡

Compositions by John Flaxman, R.A., from the "Divine Poem" of Dante Alighieri, containing Hell, Purgatory, and Paradise. Ob. 4to. Lond., 1807. A 8 Q 24 ‡

Compositions of the Acts of Mercy, drawn by the late John Flaxman, R.A., P.S. (Under the patronage of His Majesty.) Engraved by F. C. Lewis. Ob. 4to. Lond., 1831. A 2 P 19 ‡

The Iliad and Odyssey of Homer illustrated with Designs. [*See* HOMER.]

Lectures on Sculpture. 2nd ed.; to which are added, an introductory Lecture, and two Addresses on the Death of Thomas Banks, in 1805, and of Antonio Canova, in 1822, and an Address on the Death of Flaxman, by Sir Richard Westmacott, R.A. 8vo. Lond., 1838. A 7 Q 36

Another copy. Illustrated. New ed. 12mo. Lond., 1877. A 8 P 37

The "Odyssey" of Homer, engraved from the Compositions of John Flaxman, R.A., Sculptor, London. Ob. 4to. Lond., 1805. A 5 Q 10 †

FLEAY (FREDERICK GARD). Chronicle History of the Life and Work of William Shakespeare, Player, Poet, and Play-maker. 8vo. Lond., 1886. C 9 R 28

FLEISCHMAN (GEN.) Memoirs of Count A. F. Miot de Melito. [*See* MELITO, COUNT A. F. M. DE.]

FLEMING (PROF. CHARLES), AND TIBBINS (PROF.) Royal Dictionary; English and French, and French and English. 2 vols. 4to. New Orleans, 1878. K 3 S 1, 2 †

FLEMING (REV. FRANCIS), M.A. Kaffraria and its Inhabitants. 8vo. Lond., 1853. D 1 S 22

FLEMING (GEORGE), F.R.G.S., &c. Animal Plagues; their History, Nature, and Prevention. 2 vols. 8vo. Lond., 1871–82. A 1 S 5, 6

Comparative Anatomy. [*See* CHAUVEAU, A.]

Horse-shoes and Horse-shoeing; their Origin, History, Use, and Abuses. 8vo. Lond., 1869. A 1 R 23

Manual of Veterinary Sanitary Science and Police. 2 vols. 8vo. Lond., 1875. A 1 R 35, 36

2 M

FLEMING (GEORGE), F.R.G.S., &c.—*continued.*
Text-book of Veterinary Obstetrics; including the Diseases and Accidents incidental to Pregnancy, Parturition, and Early Age in the Domesticated Animals. 8vo. Lond., 1878. A 1 T 28

FLEMING (JAMES M.) Practical Violin School for Home Students. 8vo. Lond., 1866. A 8 U 28

FLEMING (PROF. JOHN). Zoology of the Bass Rock. [*See* BASS ROCK.]

FLEMING (SANDFORD). Expedition through Canada in 1872. [*See* GRANT, REV. G. M.] D 3 P 36

FLEMING (WILLIAM), D.D. Student's Manual of Moral Philosophy. 8vo. Lond., 1867. G 10 Q 16

FLETCHER (ANDREW). Essays on the Lives and Writings of Fletcher of Saltoun, and the Poet Thomson; by D. S., Earl of Buchan. 8vo. Lond., 1792. C 8 P 9

FLETCHER (MRS. ELIZA). Autobiography of; with Letters and other Family Memorials. With Portrait. 2nd ed. 8vo. Edinb., 1875. C 3 P 9

FLETCHER (GILES AND PHINEAS). Lives and Poems of. [*See* CHALMERS, A.]

FLETCHER (REV. JAMES C.) Brazil and the Brazilians. [*See* KIDDER, REV. D. P.] .

FLETCHER (REV. JAMES PHILLIPS). Notes from Nineveh, and Travels in Mesopotamia, Assyria, and Syria. 2 vols. 8vo. Lond., 1850. D 5 R 23, 24

FLETCHER (JOHN). Letter to the Rt. Hon. Earl Grey, on the subject of Emigration; with a short History of the Colony of Port Phillip. 8vo. Edinb., 1847. MJ 2 R 19

FLETCHER (REV. JOHN). The Whole Works of. 8vo. Lond., 1836. G 11 Q 18

FLETCHER (JOHN). Works of. [*See* BEAUMONT, F.]

FLETT (W. SIMPSON). What is Disease? [*See* AUSTRALIAN HEALTH SOCIETY.]

FLEURIEU (CHARLES PIERRE CLARET), COMTE DE. Discoveries of the French in 1768–69, to the south-east of New Guinea; by M. * * *; translated from the French. 4to. Lond., 1791. MD 4 Q 12 †

Voyage autour du Monde. [*See* MARCHAND, E.]

FLEURY (CLAUDE), L'ABBÉ. Ecclesiastical History of; from the second Ecumenical Council to A.D. 456. 3 vols. 8vo. Oxford, 1842–44. G 13 P 3–5

Manners of the Ancient Israelites; enlarged by Dr. Adam Clarke. 3rd ed. 8vo. Lond., 1809. G 2 R 16

FLEURY (CLAUDE), ABBÉ, ET FABRE (P.) Histoire Ecclésiastique, depuis les Actes des Apôtres jusqu'à l'an 1595. 37 vols. 4to. Paris, 1719–58. G 1 S 1–T 17

FLEURY (G. ET C. DE). La Messe. [*See* ROHAULT DE FLEURY, C.*]

FLEURY (JULES). [*See* CHAMPFLEURY, J. F.]

FLIESSBACH (DR. FERDINAND). Münzsammlung, enthaltend die wichtigsten, seit dem westphälischen Frieden, bis sum Jahre 1800 geprägten Goldund Silber-Münzen sämmtlicher Länder und Städte. 8vo. Leipzig, 1853.
A 13 S 34

FLINDERS (CAPT. MATTHEW). Voyage to Terra Australis, in the years 1801-3, in H.M.S. *Investigator*, and subsequently in the armed vessel *Porpoise*, and *Cumberland* schooner. 2 vols. roy. 4to. Lond., 1814.*
MD 5 Q 16, 17 †

Atlas to [the above]. Fol. Lond., 1814. MD 5 Q 1 ‡

Another copy. [Published by the Hydrographical Office.] At. fol. Lond., 1814-29. MD 5 Q 2 ‡

FLODOARDUS (CANONICUS REMENSIS). Opera omnia. [*See* MIGNE, J. P., SERIES LATINA, 135.]

FLOOD (HENRY). Leaders of Public Opinion in Ireland. [*See* LECKY, W. E. H.]

FLORAL FANCIES, and Morals from Flowers. 12mo. Lond., 1843. A 1 U 2

FLORENCE OF WORCESTER. Chronicle of, to the Reign of Edward I; translated, with Notes, by Thos. Forester. 12mo. Lond., 1854. B 3 P 13

FLORIAN (JEAN PIERRE CLARIS DE). Gonzalve de Cordoue; ou Grenade reconquise. [Avec précis historique sur les Maures d'Espagne.] 18mo. Lond., 1827. J 15 Q 7

Numa Pompilius, Second Roi de Rome. 18mo. Lond., 1825. J 15 Q 8

Œuvres de. 12 vols. 18mo. Paris, 1810-16. H 6 P 4-15

1. Galatée: Pastorale imitée de Cervantes.
2, 3. Théatre: Nouveaux Mélanges de Poésie et de Littérature.
4, 5. Gonzalve de Cordoue. Guillaume Tell.
6. Numa Pompilius, second Roi de Rome.
7. Nouvelles.
8. Mélanges de Poésie et de la Littérature. Fables.
9. Eliezer et Napthaly: Poème traduit de l'Hébrew. La Jeunesse de Florian; ou, Mémoires d'un Jeune Espagnol.
10-12. Don Quichotte de la Manche; traduit de l'Espagnol de Michel de Cervantes.

FLORICULTURAL CABINET (THE), and Florists' Magazine. 6 vols. 8vo. Lond., 1818-51. A 1 S 27-33

FLORIDA. Florida Portrayed; its Sections, Climate, Productions, Resources, &c.; with Practical Hints to Intending Settlers. 8vo. Lond. (n.d.) D 3 R 43

Sunny Florida: a Compendium of Information regarding "The State of Orange Groves," for the Soldier, Investor, or Tourist. 8vo. Lond. (n.d.) D 3 R 43

FLORIST AND POMOLOGIST (THE): a Pictorial Monthly Magazine, 1862-78. 8vo. Lond., 1863-78. E

FLORUS (LUCIUS ANNÆUS). Epitome Rerum Romanarum, ex Editione J. Fr. Fischeri; cum Notis et Interpretatione in usum Delphini. 2 vols. 8vo. Lond., 1822. J 13 Q 10, 11

Epitome of Roman History. [*See* SALLUSTIUS CRISPUS, C.]

FLORUS (LUGDUNENSIS DIACONUS). Opera omnia. [*See* MIGNE, J. P., SERIES LATINA, 119.]

FLOSS (HEINRICH JOSEPH), PH.D., &c. Ad audiendam orationem de liberi Arbitrii Vi ac Natura. (Pam. O.) 4to. Bonn, 1860. J 6 U 10

FLOURENS (MARIE JEAN PIERRE). De la Longévité Humaine, et de la Quantité de Vie sur le Globe. 4th ed. 12mo. Paris, 1860. A 12 P 21

De la Vie et de l'Intelligence. 2e ed. 12mo. Paris, 1858. A 12 P 23

De l'Instinct et de l'Intelligence des Animaux. 5e ed. 12mo. Paris, 1870. A 14 P 52

Recueil des Eloges Historiques lus dans les Séances Publiques de l'Académie des Sciences. Series 1-3. 3 vols. 12mo. Paris, 1856-62. A 17 T 32-34

FLOWER (BENJAMIN). French Constitution; with Remarks on some of its Principal Articles. 8vo. Lond., 1792. F 9 R 10

FLOWER (PHILLIP WILLIAM). History of the Trade in Tin: a short Description of Tin Mining and Metallurgy; a History of the Origin and Progress of the Tin-plate Trade. 8vo. Lond., 1880. A 9 T 34

FLOWER (WILLIAM). Heraldic Visitatione of the Countye Palatyne of Durham, in the yeare of our Lorde God 1575. Folio. Newcastle, 1820. ‹ 22 S 5 ‡

FLOWER (W.) Essays. [*See* CORDEN CLUB.] F 10 T 15

FLOWER (PROF. W. H.), LL.D., &c. Aborigines of Tasmania, an Extinct Race. 12mo. Manchester, 1878. MD 3 Q 40

Development and Succession of the Teeth in the Marsupialia. Roy. 4to. Lond., 1867. MA 2 Q 14 †

Fashion in Deformity, as illustrated in the Customs of Barbarous and Civilised Races. Illustrated. 8vo. Lond., 1881. A 12 P 1

Introduction to the Osteology of the Mammalia. 3rd ed. 8vo. Lond., 1885. A 28 Q 7

FLOYER (ERNEST AYSCOGHE), F.R.G.S., &c. Unexplored Baluchistan: a Survey; with Observations, Astronomical, Geographical, Botanical, &c., of a Route through Mekran, Bashkurd, Persia, Kurdistan, and Turkey. With Illustrations. 8vo. Lond., 1882. D 6 T 6

FLÜGEL (DR. FELIX). Practical Dictionary of the English and German Languages, under the co-operation of Dr. J. G. Flügel. 2 vols. 8vo. Leipzig, 1877. ‹ 12 R 1, 2

FLÜGEL (DR. J. G.) Practical Dictionary of the English and German Languages. [*See* FLÜGEL, DR. F.]

FLÜGEL (Dr. J. G.), AND SPORSCHILL (JOHN). Dictionary of the English and German, and German and English Languages. 2nd ed. 2 vols. roy. 8vo. Leipzig, 1838. K 13 R 11, 12

FLYING SQUADRON. Cruise round the World, 1869–70, under the command of Rear-Admiral G. T. Phipps Hornby ; by Lieut. J. Bruce, H.M.S. *Liverpool.* 8vo. Lond., 1871. MD 5 V 32

FOGG (W. PERRY), A.M. Arabistan ; or, the Land of " The Arabian Nights ;" being Travels through Egypt, Arabia, and Persia to Bagdad. 8vo. Lond., 1875. D 1 P 22

FOGGO (GEORGE). Letter to Lord Brougham on the History of the Royal Academy. 8vo. Lond., 1835. A 7 Q 13

Report of the Proceedings at a Public Meeting, held at the Freemasons' Hall, 29th May, 1837, to promote the admission of the Public, without charge, to Westminster Abbey, St. Paul's Cathedral, and all Depositories of Works of Art, of Natural History, and Literary interest in Public Edifices. 8vo. Lond., 1837. A 7 Q 13

POIGNY (GABRIEL DE), " JAMES SADEUR." Les Avantures de Jacques Sadeur dans la découverte et le Voiage de la Terre Australe. 12mo. Paris, 1705. MJ 1 P 12

New Discovery of Terra Incognita Australis, or the Southern World ; by James Sadeur, a Frenchman. 12mo. Lond., 1693. MJ 1 P 11

POLARD (JEAN CHARLES DE). [*See* POLYBIUS.]

POLENGO (THEOPHILUS), " MERLIN COCAIO." Opus Merlini Cocaii Poetæ Mantvani Macaronicorum. 18mo. Venetiis, 1564. H 6 P 43

FOLEY (ANTOINE EDOUARD). Quatre Années en Océanic. Histoire Naturelle de l'Homme et des Sociétés qu'il organise. 2 vols. 8vo. Paris, 1866–70.* MD 6 T 24, 25

FOLEY (DANIEL), B.D. English-Irish Dictionary. 8vo. Dublin, 1855. K 13 P 21

FOLEY (NELSON). Mechanical Engineer's Office Book. Boiler Construction. Sm. fol. Lond., 1881. A 7 S 2†

FOLJAMBE (LIEUT. CECIL G. S.), R.N. Three Years on the Australian Station. For private circulation. 8vo. Lond., 1868. MD 5 T 25

FOLKARD (HENRY TENNYSON). [*See* WIGAN FREE PUBLIC LIBRARY.]

FOLKARD (RICHARD), JUN. Plant-Lore, Legends, and Lyrics ; embracing the Myths, Traditions, Superstitions, and Folk-Lore of the Plant Kingdom. 8vo. Lond., 1884. A 5 P 2

FOLK-LORE JOURNAL (THE). Vols. 1, 2. 8vo. Lond., 1883-84. E

FOLK-LORE SOCIETY, for collecting and printing Relics of Popular Antiquities, &c. ; Publications of. Vols. 1–12. 8vo. Lond., 1878–83. E

FOLSOM (GEORGE). [*See* CORTES, H.]

FONBLANQUE (ALBANY). How we are governed : a Hand-book of the Constitution, Government, Laws, &c., of Great Britain. 12mo. Lond., 1858. F 2 P 21

FONBLANQUE (EDWARD BARRINGTON DE.) Political and Military Episodes in the latter half of the 18th Century, derived from the Life and Correspondence of the Rt. Hon. John Burgoyne. 8vo. Lond., 1876. C 8 U 45

FONSECA (JOSÉ NICOLAU DA). Historical and Archæological Sketch of the City of Goa, preceded by a Short Statistical Account of the Territory of Goa. Illustrated. 8vo. Bombay, 1878. D 5 S 31

FONSECA (JOSÉ DA). Novo Diccionario Francez-Portuguez ; cum un Supplemento. 8vo. Pariz, 1875. K 14 P 33

FONTAINE (A. LA). [*See* LA FONTAINE, A.]

FONTAINE (JEAN DE LA). [*See* LA FONTAINE, JEAN DE.]

FONTAINE (WM. M.), A.M. Resources of West Virginia. [*See* MAURY, M. F.]

FONTENELLE (B. LE BOVIER DE). A Week's Conversation on the Plurality of Worlds. 3rd ed. 12mo. Lond., 1737. A 3 R 21

FONTENELLE (JULIA DE). Manuel de Physique amusante, ou nouvelles Récréations Physiques. 4° éd. 18mo. Paris, 1832. A 17 T 36

FONVIELLE (W. DE). Travels in the Air. [*See* GLAISHER, J.]

FOORD (G.) Lecture on Chemistry applied to Manufactures. [*See* MELB. PUBLIC LIBRARY.]

Lecture on Chemistry applied to Agriculture. [*See* MELB. PUBLIC LIBRARY.]

Lecture on Chemistry of the Sea. [*See* MELB. PUBLIC LIBRARY.]

Lecture on Chemistry of the Atmosphere. [*See* MELB. PUBLIC LIBRARY.]

Lecture on Food Preservation. [*See* MELB. PUBLIC LIBRARY.]

Lecture on Household Chemistry, [*See* MELB. PUBLIC LIBRARY.]

FOOTE (SAMUEL). The Author : a Comedy. [*See* BRIT. DRAMA 5.]

Another copy. [*See* FARCES 7.]

The Commissary. [*See* BRIT. DRAMA 5.]

Dramatic Works of. 4 vols. 8vo. Lond., 1778–82. H 4 R 12–15

FOOTE (SAMUEL).—*continued.*

Dramatic Works; to which is prefixed a Life of the Author. 2 vols. 12mo. Lond., 1797. H 2 Q 30, 31

Devil upon Two Sticks. [*See* BRIT. DRAMA 5.]

The Englishman in Paris. [*See* BRIT. DRAMA 5.]

The Englishman returned from Paris. [*See* BRIT. DRAMA 5.]

The Knights. [*See* BRIT. DRAMA 5.]

Lame Lover. [*See* BRIT. DRAMA 5.]

The Liar. [*See* BRIT. DRAMA 5.]

The Lyar: a Comedy. [*See* FARCES 5.]

Maid of Bath. [*See* BRIT. DRAMA 5.]

The Mayor of Garratt: a Comedy. [*See* FARCES 5.]

Another copy. [*See* BRIT. DRAMA 5.]

The Minor: a Comedy. (Bell's Brit. Theatre.) 18mo. Lond., 1792. H 2 P 19

Another copy. (New Eng. Theatre.) 12mo. Lond., 1788. H 4 P 26

Another copy. [*See* BRIT. DRAMA 5.]

Another copy. [*See* FARCES 5.]

The Orators. [*See* BRIT. DRAMA 5.]

The Patron. [*See* BRIT. DRAMA 5.]

Taste. [*See* BRIT. DRAMA 5.]

[*See* BICKERSTAFF, I.]

FORBES (RT. REV. ALEXANDER PENROSE), D.C.L., BISHOP OF BRECHIN. Kalendars of Scottish Saints. 4to. Edinb., 1872. G 12 Q 8 †

Lives of St. Ninian and St. Kentigern. 8vo. Lond., 1874. G 14 T 15

Another copy (Historians of Scotland). 8vo. Lond., 1874. B 13 P 9

FORBES (ARCHIBALD), LL.D. Chinese Gordon: a succinct Record of his Life. 8vo. Lond., 1884. C 2 S 16

Souvenirs of some Continents. 8vo. Lond., 1885. C 4 T 4

My Experiences of the War between France and Germany. 2 vols. 8vo. Lond., 1871. B 9 R 29, 30

FORBES (AVARY WILLIAM HOLMES), M.A. Science of Beauty. 8vo. Lond., 1881. G 8 R 6

FORBES (CAPT. C. J. F. SMITH), F.R.G.S., &c. British Burma and its People. 8vo. Lond., 1878. D 5 Q 27

Comparative Grammar of the Languages of Further India: a Fragment; and other Essays. 8vo. Lond., 1881. K 11 U 46

FORBES (SIR CHARLES STUART), BART. Campaign of Garibaldi in the Two Sicilies: a Personal Narrative. 8vo. Lond., 1861. B 12 Q 34

Iceland: its Volcanoes, Geysers, and Glaciers. 8vo. Lond., 1860. D 9 P 16

FORBES (PROF. DUNCAN), LL.D. Dictionary, Hindustani and English, and English and Hindustani. 2nd ed. 8vo. Lond., 1866. K 14 S 2

Grammar of the Hindústáni Language, in the Oriental and Roman Character. 8vo. Lond., 1860. K 16 Q 18

Grammar of the Persian Language. Roy. 8vo. Lond., 1876. K 16 T 1

History of Chess. 8vo. Lond., 1860. A 17 W 26

FORBES (DUNCAN), OF CULLODEN. Lives of Simon, Lord Lovat, and Duncan Forbes, of Culloden; from original sources, by John Hill Burton, Advocate. 8vo. Lond., 1847. C 4 S 17

FORBES (PROF. EDWARD), F.R.S. Literary Papers. 12mo. Lond., 1855. J 7 Q 41

Zoology of the Voyage of H.M.S. *Herald*, under the command of Captain Henry Kellett, R.N., C.B., during the years 1845–51. Vertebrals, including Fossil Mammals, by Sir John Richardson, Knt., C.B., &c. Roy. 4to. Lond., 1854. A 2 S 14 †

[*See* GOLD, LECTURES ON.]

FORBES (LIEUT. FREDERICK EDWYN), R.N. Dahomey and the Dahomans, 1849–50. 2 vols. 8vo. Lond., 1851. D 1 S 16, 17

Five Years in China, 1842–47; with an Account of the Occupation of the Islands of Labuan and Borneo, by Her Majesty's Forces. 8vo. Lond., 1848. D 4 U 34

Travels in Lycia, Milyas, and the Cibyratis. [*See* SPRATT, LIEUT. T. A. B.]

FORBES (PROF. GEORGE), B.A. Transit of Venus. (Nature Series.) 8vo. Lond., 1874. A 3 R 16

FORBES (GORDON S.) Wild Life in Canara and Ganjam. [Coloured Illustrations.] 8vo. Lond., 1885. D 5 P 17

FORBES (HENRY O.), F.R.G.S., &c. Naturalist's Wanderings in the Eastern Archipelago. Illustrated. 8vo. Lond., 1886. D 6 R 25

FORBES (JAMES). Oriental Memoirs: a Narrative of Seventeen Years' Residence in India. 2 vols. 8vo. Lond., 1834. D 10 S 14, 15 †

Illustrations [to the above.] 4to. Lond., 1834. D 10 S 16 †

FORBES (REV. JAMES), A.M. Fund for the Widow and Family of the late James Forbes, A.M.: Statement. 8vo. Melb., 1851. MG 1 Q 29

FORBES (JAMES DAVID), F.R.S., &c. Tour of Mont Blanc and of Monte Rosa. 12mo. Edinb., 1855. D 7 P 26

FORBES (JOHN). Double Grammar of English and Gaelic. 12mo. Edinb., 1843. K 11 S 38

FORBES (MAJOR JOHN). Eleven Years in Ceylon, comprising Sketches of the Field Sports and Natural History of that Colony. 2 vols. 8vo. Lond., 1840. D 4 U 32, 33

FORBES (SIR JOHN), M.D., &c. Memorandums made in Ireland, in the Autumn of 1852. 2 vols. 8vo. Lond., 1853. D 7 R 16, 17

Physician's Holiday; or, a Month in Switzerland in the Summer of 1848. Illustrated. 3rd ed. 12mo. Lond., 1852. D 7 Q 48

Sight-seeing in Germany and the Tyrol, in the Autumn of 1855. With Map. 8vo. Lond., 1856. D 8 Q 2

FORBES (LITTON), M.D., &c. Two Years in Fiji. 8vo. Lond., 1875.* MD 5 P 34

FORBES (DR. P.) Full View of the Public Transactions in the Reign of Queen Elizabeth; or, a Particular Account of all the Memorable Affairs of that Queen. 2 vols. fol. Lond., 1740–41. B 14 T 15, 16 ‡

FORBES (RT. REV. R.), A.M. Jacobite Memoirs of the Rebellion of 1745; edited from his MSS., by Robert Chambers. 8vo. Lond., 1834. B 32 T 10

FORBES (REV. R.) Minor Morals: a Lecture, addressed chiefly to the Working Classes. (Pam. 41.) 8vo. Aberdeen, 1854. MJ 2 R 3

FORBES (WILLIAM ALEXANDER), M.A. Collected Scientific Papers of; edited by F. E. Beddard, M.A.; with a Preface by P. L. Sclater, M.A., &c. Roy. 8vo. Lond., 1885. A 13 V 1

Memoir of A. H. Garrod, &c. [*See* GARROD, A. H.]

FORBES-LEITH (WILLIAM), S.J. [*See* LEITH, W. FORBES-.]

FORBES-ROBERTSON (JOHN). Great Painters of Christendom, from Cimabue to Wilkie. Roy. 4to. Lond., 1877. A 4 P 2 †

Life of Samuel Phelps. [*See* PHELPS, W. M.]

FORCELLINI (A.) Totius Latinitatis Lexicon præfatio et index scriptorum Latinorum cura et studio Dr. V. De Vit. 7 vols. roy. 4to. Prati, 1858–79. K 14 R 1–7 †

FORCHAMMER (DR. E.), PH.D. Jardine Prize: an Essay on the Sources and Devolopment of Burmese Law. Roy. 8vo. Rangoon, 1885. F 5 V 16

FORD (F. CLARE). La République Argentine: Finances, Commerce, &c. Rapport. 8vo. Paris, 1867. F 10 Q 15

FORD (JOHN). Dramatic Works of; with Notes by W. Gifford. 2 vols. 8vo. Lond., 1827. H 4 S 20, 21

FORD (RICHARD), F.S.A. Gatherings from Spain. 12mo. Lond., 1846. D 7 Q 45

Another copy. (H. and C. Lib.) 12mo. Lond., 1846. J 8 P 20

Hand-book for Travellers in Spain. 4th ed. 2 vols. 8vo. Lond., 1869. D 8 R 6, 7

FORD (W. AND F.) Australian Almanac and Repository of Useful Knowledge. 4 vols. (in 1) 12mo. Sydney, 1850–54.* ME 4 R

Sydney Commercial Directory, 1851. 12mo. Sydney, 1851. ME 4 S

Another copy. MF 4 T

FORDE (MRS. HELENA). [*See* KREFFT, G.]

FORDUN (JOANNES). Chronica Gentis Scotorum; edited by William F. Skene (Historians of Scotland). 8vo. Edinb., 1871. B 13 P 45

Chronicle of the Scottish Nation, translated from the Latin; edited by William F. Skene (Historians of Scotland). 8vo. Edinb., 1872. B 13 P 48

Scotichronicon, cum Supplementis et Continuatione Walteri Boweri Præfixa est ad historiam Scotorum Introductio brevis, curâ Walteri Goodall. 2 vols. fol. Edinb., 1759. B 15 R 7, 8 ‡

FOREIGN ARMIES; their Formation, Organisation, and Strength. Illustrated. 8vo. Lond., 1886. K 17 T 5

FOREIGN AND COLONIAL QUARTERLY REVIEW (THE). 3 vols. 8vo. Lond., 1843–44. ME 3 Q

FOREIGN OFFICE LIST (THE); by Sir Edward Hertslet, C.B. 16 vols. 8vo. Lond., 1870–86. E

FOREIGN SECRETARIES. [*See* THORNTON, P. M.]

FOREMAN PATTERN MAKER A. [*See* PATTERN MAKING.]

FOREST OF BONDY (THE); or, the Dog of Montargis: a Melodrama. (Cumberland's Eng. Theatre.) 12mo. Lond., 1829. H 2 Q 20

FORESTER (FRANK). [*See* HERBERT, H. W.]

FORESTER (THOMAS). Ecclesiastical History of England and Normandy. [*See* ORDERICUS VITALIS.]

[*See* FLORENCE OF WORCESTER, *and* HUNTINGDON, HENRY OF.]

FORMAN (H. BUXTON). Our Living Poets: an Essay in Criticism. 8vo. Lond., 1871. J 11 P 12

[*See* KEATS, J., *and* SHELLEY, P. B.]

FORMBY (REV. HENRY). Ancient Rome and its Connection with the Christian Religion. Roy. 4to. Lond., 1880. B 14 R 14 †

FORNANDER (ABRAHAM). Account of the Polynesian Race: its Origin and Migrations; and the Ancient History of the Hawaiian People to the Times of Kamehameha I. 3 vols. 8vo. Lond., 1878–85. MB 2 Q 15–17

FORREST (LIEUT.-COL. C. R.) Picturesque Tour along the Rivers Ganges and Jumna, in India. Imp. 4to. Lond., 1824 D 5 Q 8 †

FORREST (SIR JOHN), K.C.M.G., &c. Explorations in Australia : 1. Explorations in search of Dr. Leichardt and Party. 2. From Perth to Adelaide, around the Great Australian Bight. 3. From Champion Bay, across the Desert to the Telegraph and to Adelaide; with an Appendix on the condition of Western Australia. 8vo. Lond., 1875.*   MD 6 T 17

Report on the Kimberley District, North-western Australia. Sm. fol. Perth, 1883.   MD 7 Q 1 †

FORREST (CAPT. THOMAS). Voyage to New Guinea and the Moluccas, from Balambangan. 2nd ed. 4to. Lond., 1789.*   MD 6 P 24 †

FORRESTER (ALFRED HENRY), "ALFRED CROWQUILL." Phantasmagoria of Fun; edited by "Alfred Crowquill." 2 vols. 8vo. Lond., 1843.   J 5 P 31, 32

Seymour's Humorous Sketches. [*See* SEYMOUR, R.]

FORSHALL (FREDERIC H.) Westminster School, Past and Present. 8vo. Lond., 1884.   B 6 S 14

FORSSMAN (O. W. A.) Guide for Agriculturists and Capitalists, Speculators, Miners, &c. (Pam. Dr.) 2nd ed. 8vo. Cape Town, 1874.   MF 3 P 16

FÖRSTEMANN (ERNST). Geschichte des deutschen Sprachstammes. Band 1 and 2. 2 vols. 8vo. Nordhausen, 1874-75.   K 16 Q 24, 25

FORSTER (ANTHONY). South Australia: its Progress and Prosperity. With Map. 8vo. Lond.,1866.*   MB 2 R 12

FORSTER (ANTHONY). Biographical Notices of. [*See* BARTLETT, A. D.]

FORSTER (REV. CHARLES). [*See* JEBB, REV. J.]

FORSTER (CHARLES THORNTON), M.A., AND DANIELL (F. H. BLACKBURNE), M.A. Life and Letters of Ogier Ghiselin de Busbecq, Seigneur of Bousbecque, Knight, Imperial Ambassador. 2 vols. 8vo. Lond., 1881.   C 8 S 8, 9

FÖRSTER (ERNST). Denkmale deutscher Baukunst, Bildnerei und Malerei. 12 vols. 4to. Leipsic, 1855-69.   A 2 U 11-22

FORSTER (JOHN), LL.D. Arrest of the Five Members by Charles I. 8vo. Lond., 1860.   B 4 Q 21

Debates on the Grand Remonstrance, November and December, 1641. 8vo. Lond., 1860.   F 6 S 23

Life and Times of Oliver Goldsmith. 2nd ed. 2 vols. 8vo. Lond., 1854.   C 7 T 11, 12

Life of Charles Dickens. 3 vols. 8vo. Lond., 1872-74.   C 6 P 7-9

Life of Jonathan Swift. Vol. I. (*All published*). 8vo. Lond., 1875.   C 11 P 35

Lives of Eminent British Statesmen. [*See* MACKINTOSH, SIR J.]

Sir John Eliot; a Biography, 1590-1632. 2 vols. 8vo. Lond., 1864.   C 5 U 9, 10

FORSTER (JOHN), LL.D.—*continued.*
Walter Savage Landor: a Biography, 1775-1864. 2 vols. 8vo. Lond., 1869.   C 4 R 15, 16

Works and Life of Walter Savage Landor. [*See* LANDOR, W. S.]

[*See* DYCE, A., *and* HALL, REV. R.]

FORSTER (JOHN), M.P. Chronicle of James I. [*See* JAMES I.]

FORSTER (JOHN GEORGE ADAM), F.R.S. Voyage round the World in His Britannic Majesty's Sloop *Resolution*, commanded by Captain James Cook, 1772-75. 3 vols. 4to. Lond., 1777.   MD 5 P 24, 25 †

[*See* COOK, CAPT. J., *and* NEW DISCOVERIES.]

FORSTER (DR. JOHN REINOLD), LL.D., &c. Observations made during a Voyage round the World, on Physical Geography, Natural History, and Ethic Philosophy. 4to. Lond., 1778.*   MA 2 P 1 †

Another copy.   A 15 U 14

Voyage round the World. [*See* BOUGAINVILLE, L. A. DE, *and* COOK, CAPT. J.]

FORSTER (DR. JOHN REINOLD, AND GEORGE). Characteres Generum Plantarum, quas in Itinere, ad Insulas Maris Australis, collegerunt, descripserunt, delinearunt, annis 1772-75. 4to. Lond., 1776.   MA 1 P 24 †

FORSTER (REV. THOMAS HAY). Church in the Colonies ; Diocese of Tasmania; Account of a Voyage in a Convict Ship. 12mo. Lond., 1850.   MD 1 T 49

Letter to the Lord Bishop of Tasmania. 8vo. Sydney, 1852.   MG 1 Q 29

FORSTER (WILLIAM). The Brothers: a Drama. [Written in New South Wales.] 8vo. Lond., 1877.   MH 1 R 28

The Land and Squatting Question reconsidered. 8vo. Sydney, 1855.   MF 3 P 4

Political Presentments. 8vo. Lond., 1878.   MF 3 Q 71

Another copy.   F 6 Q 9

The Weirwolf: a Tragedy. [Written in New South Wales.] 8vo. Lond., 1876.   MH 1 R 27

FORSYTH (ANDREW RUSSELL), M.A. Treatise on Differential Equations. 8vo. Lond., 1885.   A 10 T 17

FORSYTH (CAPT. J.) Highlands of Central India: Notes on their Forests and Wild Tribes, Natural History, and Sports. Illustrated. 8vo. Lond., 1871.   D 5 T 37

FORSYTH (T. D.) Lahore to Yârkand. [*See* HENDERSON, G., AND HUME, A. O.]

FORSYTH (WILLIAM), Q.C., &c. Constitutional Law, Cases and Opinions on. Roy. 8vo. Lond., 1869.   F 5 V 17

Essays, Critical and Narrative. 8vo. Lond., 1874.   J 6 T 2

History of the Captivity of Napoleon at St. Helena. [*See* LOWE, LIEUT.-GEN. SIR H.]

Slavonic Provinces, South of the Danube. 8vo. Lond., 1876.   D 8 R 11

FORT (GEORGE F.) Early History and Antiquities of Freemasonry. 8vo. Lond., 1875.   B 14 S 24

Medical Economy during the Middle Ages. 8vo. New York, 1883.   A 13 R 14

FORTESCUE (EARL). Memoir of Lord King. [*See* KING, LORD.]

FORTESCUE (G. K.) Subject Index of the Modern Works added to the Library of the British Museum, 1880–85. Imp. 8vo. Lond., 1886.   K 9 P 18 †

FORTESCUE (SIR JOHN). De Laudibus Legum Angliæ: iereto are joind the two Summes of Sir Ralpi de Hengiam, commonly called Hengham Magna, and Hengham Parva. 18mo. Lond., 1616.   F 2 P 15

Governance of England, otierwise called the Difference between an Absolute and a Limited Monarciy. 8vo. Oxford, 1885.   B 7 Q 30

FORTESCUE (HON. JOHN). Stag-iunting on Exmoor. Illustrated. 8vo. Lond., 1887.   A 17 U 22

FORTESCUE (J. F.) Introduction to Tieosopiy; or, the Science of the "Mystery of Ciirist," tiat is, of Deity, Nature, and Creature. Vol. 1, complete in itself. 12mo. Lond., 1855.   G 9 Q 18

FORTESCUE (T.), LORD CLERMONT. Fortescue Family: History of the Family of Fortescue in all its Brancies; by Lord Clermont. 2nd ed. Roy. 4to. Lond., 1880.*   C 7 R 6 †

FORTIS (ALBÉRTO). Travels in Dalmatia; to wiici are added Observations on the Island of Cierso and Osero. 4to. Lond., 1778.   D 19 Q 10 ‡

FORTNIGHTLY REVIEW (THE); edited by T. H. S. Escott. Vols. 1–43 (37 n.s.) Roy. 8vo. Lond., 1864–86.   E

FORTNUM (C. D. E.), F.S.A. Bronzes. (Souti Kens. Mus.) 8vo. Lond., 1877.   E

Maiolica. (Souti Kens. Mus.) 8vo. Lond., 1875.   E

FORTUNATUS (VENANTIUS). [*See* MIGNE, J. P., SERIES LATINA, 88.]

FORTUNE (ROBERT). Journey to the Tea Countries of Ciina, including Sung-lo and the Boiea Hills. 8vo. Lond., 1852.   D 6 R 17

Residence among the Ciinese; Inland, on the Coast, and at Sea. 8vo. Lond., 1857.   D 5 S 40

Tiree Years' Wanderings in the Nortiern Provinces of Ciina: a Visit to the Tea, Silk, and Cotton Countries of Ciina. 8vo. Lond., 1847.   D 6 R 27

Yedo and Peking: a Narrative of a Journey to the Capitals of Japan and Ciina. 8vo. Lond., 1863.   D 6 R 31

FORWOOD (W. STUMP), M.D. Historical and Descriptive Narrative of the Mammoti Cave of Kentucky: its Ciemistry, Geology, Zoology, &c.; witi full Scientific Details of the Eyeless Fisies. 8vo. Philad., 1870.   D 3 P 48

FOSBERY (E.) [*See* ABORIGINES.]

FOSBROKE (REV. THOMAS DUDLEY), M.A., &c. [*See* FOSBROOKE, REV. T. D.]

FOSBROOKE OR FOSBROKE (REV. THOMAS DUDLEY), M.A., &c. Britisi Monachism; or, Manners and Customs of the Monks and Nuns of England. New ed., witi numerous Plates. 4to. Lond., 1817.   B 2 U 31

Encyclopædia of Antiquities, and Elements of Archæology, Classical and Mediæval. 2 vols. 4to. Lond., 1825.   K 6 S 19, 20

Foreign Topograpiy; forming a Sequel to the Encyclopedia of Antiquities. 4to. Lond., 1828.   D 9 R 18 †

Treatise on the Arts, Manufactures, and Institutions of the Greeks and Romans. (Lard. Cab. Cyclo.). 2 vols. 12mo. Lond., 1833–35.   K 1 T 26, 27

FOSS (EDWARD), F.S.A. Biographia Juridica: a Biograpiical Dictionary of the Judges of England, from the Conquest to the Present Time, 1066–1870. Roy. 8vo. Lond., 1870.   C 9 V 51

Judges of England; witi Sketcies of tieir Lives, and Miscellaneous Notices. 9 vols. 8vo. Lond., 1848–64.   C 9 U 1–9

FOSS (FRITHJOF). Norwegian Grammar; witi Exercises in the Norwegian and Englisi Languages, and a List of Irregular Verbs. 2nd ed. 12mo. Lond., 1858.   K 11 V 20

FOSSATI (GASPARD), CHEVALIER. Aya Sofia Constantinople: Description iistorique des Plancies de S. Sopii. El. fol. Lond., 1852.   A 3 P 19 ‡

FOSTER (CAPT. HENRY), F.R.S., &c. Voyage to tie Soutiern Atlantic Ocean under the command of. [*See* WEBSTER, W. H. B.]

FOSTER (J. S.) New Zealand. [*See* GRANT, S.]

FOSTER (J. W.), LL.D. Preiistoric Races of the United States of America. 8vo. Ciicago, 1873.   A 1 W 7

FOSTER (JOHN). Contributions, Biograpiical, Literary, and Piilosopiical, to the *Eclectic Review.* 2 vols. roy. 8vo. Lond., 1844.   J 4 T 9, 10

Essay on the Evils of Popular Ignorance. 2nd ed. 8vo. Lond., 1821.   G 9 T 13

Essay on the Improvement of Time; witi Notes of Sermons and otier Pieces. 12mo. Lond., 1886.   G 8 R 4

Essays, in a series of Letters to a Friend. 2 vols. 8vo Lond., 1805.   J 6 R 12, 13

Anotier copy. 2 vols. (in 1) 12mo. Lond., 1806.   J 6 R 14

Fosteriana; consisting of Tiougits, Reflections, and Criticisms of Join Foster; edited by Henry G. Boin. 8vo. Lond., 1858.   J 9 Q 7

Lectures delivered at Broadmead Ciapel, Bristol. 3rd ed 2 vols. 12mo. Lond., 1853.   G 9 Q 30, 31

Life and Correspondence of; edited by J. E. Ryland 2 vols. 12mo. Lond., 1852.   C 2 P 14, 15

FOSTER (MRS. JONATHAN). Dominion of the Arabs in Spain. [*See* CONDÉ, DR. J. A.]

Lives of the most eminent Painters, &c. [*See* VASARI, G.]

FOSTER (JOSEPH). Baronetage and Knigstage of the British Empire. Roy. 8vo. Westminster, 1883.   K 10 U 14

Collection Genealogica. 4 vols. roy. 8vo. Lond., 1882-85.   E

Members of Parliament, Scotland, including the Minor Barons, the Commissioners for Sires, and the Commissioners for the Burgss, 1357-1882. 2nd ed. Roy. 8vo. Lond., 1882.   K 10 T 1

Peerage of the Britisi Empire, 1883; witi the Orders of Knigitiood. Roy. 8vo. Westminster, 1883.   K 10 U 13

Peerage, Baronetage, and Knigstage of the Britisi Empire, 1880. 2 vols. (in 1) roy. 8vo. Lond., 1880.   K 10 U 12

Revised Genealogical Account of the various Families descended from Francis Fox, of St. Germains, Cornwall; to wiici is appended a Pedigree of the Crokers, of Linesam, and many otier Families connected witi tiem. 4to. Lond., 1872.   K 10 V 2

Royal Lineage of our Noble and Gentle Families, togetier witi tieir Paternal Ancestry. 3 vols. 4to. Lond., 1883-85.   K 10 V 3-5

FOSTER (M.), M.A., &c. Hand-book for the Piysiological Laboratory. [*See* KLEIN, E.]

Text-book of Piysiology. 8vo. Lond., 1877.   A 12 T 2

FOSTER (M.), M.A., &c., AND BALFOUR (FRANCIS M.), M.A., &c. Elements of Embryology. 2nd ed. revised. 8vo. Lond., 1883.   A 12 P 42

FOSTER (P. LE NEVE), M.A. Piotograpiy. (Brit. Manuf. Indust.) 12mo. Lond., 1876.   A 17 S 39

FOSTER (THOMAS CAMPBELL). Letters on the Condition of the People of Ireland. 2nd ed. 8vo. Lond., 1847.   B 11 P 37

FOSTER (WILLIAM JOHN). Practice of the District Courts of New Souti Wales. 8vo. Sydney, 1885.   MF 2 R 7

FOSTER-FITZGERALD (J. F. L. V.) Australia. Illustrated. 12mo. Lond., 1881.*   MD 4 P 36

New Colony of Victoria, formerly called Port Piillip. 12mo. Lond., 1851.*   MD 4 P 34

Tiree Letters to the Hon. James Frederick Palmer, Speaker of the Legislative Council of Victoria. 2nd. ed. 8vo. Melb., 1855.   MF 1 Q 2

Anotier copy.   MJ 2 Q 16

A Fourti Letter to the Hon. James Frederick Palmer, Speaker of the Legislative Council of Victoria. Melb., 1855.   MF 1 Q 2

[*See* MCEACHERN, J.]

FOUCHÉ (JOSEPH), DUKE OF OTRANTO. [*See* OTRANTO, JOSEPH FOUCHÉ, DUKE OF.]

FOUCQUET (JEHAN). Œuvres de. 2 vols. 4to. Paris, 1866-67.   G 12 Q 9, 10 †

FOUILLOU (JACQUES). Les Hexaples; ou, les Six Colomnes sur la Constitution Unigenitus. 6 vols. (in 7) 4to. Amsterdam, 1721.   G 3 V 2-8

FOULCHER DE CHARTRES. Histoire des Croisades. [*See* GUIZOT, F. P. G., 24.]

FOUNDLING HOSPITAL FOR WIT (THE NEW); being a Collection of Fugitive Pieces, in Prose and Verse, not in any otier Collection. 6 vols. 12mo. Lond., 1786.   H 7 P 8-13

FOURCROY (A. F. DE). Elemens d'Histoire Naturelle, et de Ciimie. 4 vols. 8vo. Paris, 1786.   A 5 S 5-8

Synoptic Tables of Ciemistry; intended to serve as a Summary of the Lectures delivered on tiat Science in the Public Sciools at Paris. Imp. fol. Lond., 1801.   A 2 P 23 ‡

FOWKE (FRANK REDE). The Bayeux Tapestry, reprodduced in Autotype Plates; witi Historical Notes. Roy. 4to. Lond., 1875.   B 14 R 16 ‡

FOWLER (FRANK). Dottings of a Lounger. 12mo. Lond., 1859.   J 1 W 38

Soutiern Ligits and Siadows; being brief Notes of Tiree Years' Experience of Social, Literary, and Political Life in Australia. 12mo. Lond., 1859.   MD 1 S 45

Anotier copy. 2nd ed. 12mo. Lond., 1859.*   MD 1 S 46

Texts for Talkers; witi occasional Discourses, Practical and Imaginative. 12mo. Lond., 1860.   J 7 Q 3

Wreck of the *Royal Charter*; compiled from autientic sources, witi some original matter. 12mo. Lond., 1859.   MJ 2 P 33

[*See* MONTH, THE.]

FOWLER (JOHN). Literary Remains of Ciarles Reece Pemberton. [*See* PEMBERTON, C. R.]

FOWLER (REV. J.), M.A. Riciard Waldo Sibthorp: a Biograpiy, told ciiefly in his own Correspondence. 8vo. Lond., 1880.   C 9 U 39

FOWLER (O. S.) A Home for All; or, the Gravel Wall and Octagon Mode of Building; new, cieap, convenient, superior, and adapted to Riei and Poor. 8vo. New York (n.d.)   A 2 R 7

FOWLER (ROBERT), M.D. Medical Vocabulary; containing a concise Explanation of the Terms used in Medicine. 2nd ed. 12mo. Lond., 1875.   K 9 P 2

On the State of the Mind during Sleep, &c. (Pam. 40.) 12mo. Lond., 1852.   MJ 2 R 2

FOWLER (ROBERT NICHOLAS), M.A., &c. Visit to Japan, China, and India. 12mo. Lond., 1877.   D 5 Q 20

FOWLER (PROF. THOMAS), M.A. Elements of Inductive Logic; designed mainly for the use of Students in the Universities. (Clar. Press.) 2nd ed. 12mo. Oxford, 1872.   G 16 P 31

Another copy. 3rd ed. 12mo. Oxford, 1876. G 16 P 33

Elements of Deductive Logic. Designed mainly for the use of Junior Students in the Universities. (Clar. Press.) 5th ed., corrected and revised. 12mo. Oxford, 1873.

Another copy. 6th ed. 12mo. Oxford, 1875. G 16 P 32

Locke. (Eng. Men. of Letts.) 8vo. Lond., 1880. C 1 U 24

The Principles of Morals. [*See* WILSON, PROF. J. M.]

FOWLER (WILLIAM). Present aspect of the Land Question. [*See* COBDEN CLUB.]

FOWLES (JOSEPH). Sydney in 1848; illustrated by copper-plate Engravings of its Principal Streets, Public Buildings, Churches, Chapels, &c. 4to. Sydney, 1848.   MD 6 P 5 †

Another copy. (Reprinted.) 4to. Sydney, 1878.   MD 6 P 6 †

FOWNES (PROF. GEORGE), F.R.S. Manual of Elementary Chemistry, Theoretical and Practical. 11th ed. 8vo. Lond., 1873.   A 5 R 19

Manual of Chemistry, Theoretical and Practical. Physical and Inorganic Chemistry—Chemistry of Carbon—Compounds, or Organic Chemistry. (Churchill's Manuals.) 12th ed. 2 vols. 8vo. Lond., 1877. A 5 R 20, 21

Rudimentary Chemistry for the use of Beginners. (Weale.) 12mo. Lond., 1872.   A 17 P 46

FOX (CAROLINE). Memories of Old Friends; being Extracts from the Journals and Letters of Caroline Fox, of Penjerrick, Cornwall, from 1835 to 1871; edited by Horace U. Pym. Imp. 8vo. Lond., 1882. C 8 V 22

FOX (RT. HON. CHARLES JAMES). Early History of; by George Otto Trevelyan, M.P. 8vo. Lond., 1880.   C 11 P 36

Historical Works of. [*See* ROSE, G.]

History of the early part of the Reign of James II; with an Introductory Chapter and Appendix. 4to. Lond., 1808.   B 15 Q 17 ‡

Another copy; with translation of Letters. 4to. Lond., 1808.   B 15 Q 18 ‡

History of the Reign of James II. [*See* CARREL, A.]

Life and Times of; by the Rt. Hon. Lord John Russell. 3 vols. 8vo. Lond., 1859-66.   C 3 S 40-42

Memorials and Correspondence of; edited by Lord John Russell. 4 vols. 8vo. Lond., 1853-57. C 8 P 12-15

Speeches of, in the House of Commons. 6 vols. 8vo. Lond., 1815.   F 13 P 27-32

FOX (FRANCIS). Genealogical Account of the various Families descended from. [*See* FOSTER, J.]

2 N

FOX (GEORGE). Autobiography, of from his Journal edited by Henry Stanley Newman. Sq. 8vo. Lond., 1886.   C 5 S 16

FOX, OR FOXE (REV. JOHN), M.A. Ecclesiasticall History, contaynying the Sufferyng of Martyrs, &c. 3 vols. fol. Lond., 1570.   G 10 U 2-4

An Universal History of Christian Martyrdom. 8vo. Lond., 1824.   G 14 S 16

Letters on Fox's Acts and Monuments. [*See* MAITLAND, REV. S. R.]

Review of Fox the Martyrologist's History of the Waldenses. [*See* MAITLAND, REV. S. R.]

Writings of. [*See* BRITISH REFORMERS 5.]

FOX (MARY), LADY. Account of an Expedition to the Interior of New Holland. [*See* WHATELY, R.]

FOX (W. J.) Life and Literary Remains of Charles Reece Pemberton: edited by John Fowler. 8vo. Lond., 1843.   J 12 V 17

FOX (WILLIAM), A.M. Six Colonies of New Zealand. 12mo. Lond., 1851.*   MD 4 P 45

War in New Zealand; with two Maps and a Plan. 8vo Lond., 1866.*   MB 1 Q 9

FOXALL (E. W.) [*See* STUART, H. A.]

FOX-PITT-RIVERS (LIEUT.-GEN. A. H. L.) On the Development and Distribution of Primitive Locks and Keys. Illustrated. Roy. 4to. Lond., 1883. A 2 S 11 †

FRA ANGELICO. [*See* GIOVANNI DA FIESOLE.]

FRAAS (C.) Geschichte der Landbau und Forstwissenschaft. (Geschichte der Wissenschaften.) 8vo. Munich, 1865.   A 17 V 17

FRAMJI KARAKA (DOSABHAI), C.S.I. History of the Parsis. 2 vols. 8vo. Lond., 1884.   B 1 P 7, 8

FRAMPTON (MARY). Journal of, from the year 1779, until the year 1846; edited, with Notes, by her Niece, Harriet Georgiana Mundy. 8vo. Lond., 1885. C 6 Q 17

FRAMPTON (ROBERT), BISHOP OF GLOUCESTER. Life of; edited by T. S. Evans, M.A. 8vo. Lond., 1876. C 4 R 4

FRANC (MAUD JEANNE). Emily's Choice: an Australian Tale. 12mo. Lond. 1875.   MJ 1 U 4

Golden Gifts: an Australian Tale. 12mo. Lond., 1883.   MJ 1 U 5

"Two Sides to Every Question," from a South Australian Standpoint. 12mo. Lond., 1883.   MJ 1 U 6

FRANCE. The Commercial Policy of France, and the Treaty with England. 8vo. Lond., 1871. MF 3 P 17

The Historie of Fraunce, in four Bookes; printed by John Windet, 1595. 4to. Lond., 1595.   B 8 V 6

Mutuable and Wavering Estate of France, 1460-1595. 4to. Lond., 1597.   B 8 V 6

Notice on the Mining Establishments of France. (Pam. 24.) 8vo. Lond., 1833.   MJ 2 Q 12

FRANCE (LIEUT. A. DE). Frenci in Algiers. [*See* LAMPING, LIEUT. C.]

FRANCESCA. [*See* ALEXANDER, MISS F.]

FRANCIA (FRANCESCO RAIBOLINI). Mantegna and Francia; by Julia Cartwrigıt. (Great Artists.) 8vo. Lond., 1881. C 3 T 43

FRANCIA (JOSÉ GASPAR RODRIGUEZ), DICTATOR OF PARAGUAY. Francia's Reign of Terror.. [*See* ROBERTSON, J. P., AND W. P.]

Government of. [*See* ROBERTSON, J. P. AND W. P.]

FRANCIS (—.) Newspapers publisied in London. [*See* ADAMS, —.]

FRANCIS (B.) Isles of the Pacific; or, Sketcies from the Soutı Seas. 8vo. Lond., 1882. MD 4 Q 47

FRANCIS (G. H.) Orators of the Age; comprising Portraits, Critical, Biograpıical, and Descriptive. 8vo. Lond., 1847. C 4 S 27

[*See* PALMERSTON, LORD.]

FRANCIS (GEORGE GRANT), F.S.A. Some Account of Sir Hugı Joınys. [*See* BLISS, J.]

FRANCIS (HENRY). Present and Future Government of the Colony of New Soutı Wales. 8vo. Sydney, 1869. MF 3 P 1

FRANCIS (J. G.), B.A. Notes from a Journal kept in Italy and Sicily, during the years 1844–46. 8vo. Lond., 1847. D 8 T 21

FRANCIS (JOHN). Cıronicles and Cıaracters of the Stock Excıange. 2nd ed. 8vo. Lond., 1851. F 8 P 27

History of the Bank of England; its Times and Traditions. 2 vols. 8vo. Lond. (n.d.) F 6 S 11, 12

FRANCIS (PHILIP), D.D. Works of Horace, translated, [*See* CHALMERS, A.]

[*See* HORACE.]

FRANCIS (SIR PHILIP), K.C.B. Memoirs of; witı Correspondence and Journals commenced by the late Josepı Parkes, completed and edited by Herman Merivale, M.A. 2 vols. 8vo. Lond., 1867. C 8 S 38, 39

FRANCIS (R.) [*See* MICHIE, A.]

FRANCIS DE SALES (SAINT). Mission of. [*See* HERBERT, LADY.]

FRANCKIO (A. J. M.) Catalogus Bibliotıeca Bunavianæ. 3 vols. (in 6) 4to. Lipsiæ, 1750–56. (8 R 1–6

FRANCKLIN (PROF. THOMAS), D.D. The Earl of Warwick. [*See* BRIT. DRAMA, 2.]

Matilda: a Tragedy. [*See* BRIT. DRAMA, 2.]

Anotıer copy. [*See* MODERN THEATRE, 8.]

[Tragedies of] Sopıocles. [*See* GREEK TRAGIC THEATRE.]

[*See* LUCIAN, S., *and* SOPHOCLES.]

FRANCO-GERMAN WAR. Events of the 25th day of August, 1870. [Map.] Sm.fol. Soissons, 1870. B 33 Q 17‡

FRANK CAREY: a Story of Victorian Life; by the Autıor of "Sketcıes of Australian Life and Scenery." 3 vols. 8vo. Lond., 1877. MJ 1 R 1–3

FRANKLAND (CAPT. CHARLES COLVILLE), R.N. Travels to and from Constantinople, in the years 1827–28. 2 vols. 8vo. Lond., 1829. D 7 U 1, 2

Anotıer copy. 2nd ed. 2 vols. 8vo. Lond., 1830. D 7 U 3, 4

FRANKLAND (EDWARD), D.C.L., F.R.S. Experimental Researcıes in Pure, Applied, and Pıysical Cıemistry. 8vo. Lond., 1877. A 5 T 28

Lecture Notes for Cıemical Students, embracing Mineral and Organic Cıemistry. 2 vols. 8vo. Lond., 1866. A 5 S 11, 12

Lecture Notes for Cıemical Students: Inorganic Cıemistry, Organic Cıemistry. 2nd ed. 2 vols. 8vo. Lond., 1870–72. A 5 R 8, 9

FRANKLAND (EDWARD), D.C.L., AND JAPP (FRANCIS R.), M.A., &c. Inorganic Cıemistry. Illustrated. 8vo. Lond., 1884. A 6 Q 5

FRANKLAND (GEORGE). Report on the Transactions of the Survey Department of Van Diemen's Land, from the Foundation of the Colony to the end of Colonel Artıur's Administration. 8vo. Hobart, 1837. MF 2 S 29

FRANKLIN (BENJAMIN), LL.D., &c. Life and Essays of Dr. Franklin. 8vo. Lond., 1816. C 8 T 44

Life and Writings of: a Bibliograpıical Essay on the Stevens' Collection of Books and Manuscripts relating to Dr. Franklin; by Henry Stevens, F.S.A., &c. Imp. 8vo. Lond., 1881. C 3 W 12

Memoirs of the Life and Writings of; written by ıimself, to a late period, and continued to the time of ıis deatı, by ıis Grandson, Wm. Temple Franklin. 6 vols. 8vo. Lond., 1818–19. C 5 V 15–20

Anotıer copy. New ed. 6 vols. 8vo. Lond., 1833. C 8 R 7–12

FRANKLIN (SIR JOHN), R.N. Copy of a Despatcı from Lieut.-Governor Sir Joın Franklin to Lord Glenelg, dated 7th Octobar, 1837, relative to the Present System of Convict Discipline in Van Diemen's Land. Fol. Lond., 1838. F 12 U 2

Expedition in searcı of Sir Joın Franklin. [*See* HOOPER, LIEUT. W. H.]

Expedition in searcı of Sir Joın Franklin. [*See* MACCORMICK, R.]

In Quest of the Franklin Records. [*See* GILDER, W. H.]

Narrative of a Journey to the Sıores of the Polar Sea, in the years 1819–22. 3rd ed. 2 vols. 8vo. Lond., 1824. D 4 R 24, 25

FRANKLIN (SIR JOHN), R.N.—*continued.*

Narrative of some Passages in the History of Van Diemen's Land, during the last three years of his Administration of its Government. 8vo. Lond., 1845. MJ 2 R 13

Narrative of the Discovery of the Fate of. [*See* MACCLIN-TOCK, CAPT. F. L.]

Relief of the Expedition under Sir John Franklin. [*See* SHILLINGLAW, J. J.]

Search of the Expedition under Sir John Franklin. [*See* ARMSTRONG, A.]

Three Cruises in search of. [*See* SEEMANN, B.]

Voyage in search of. [*See* BELLOT, J. R.]

Voyage in search of. [*See* MACDOUGALL, CAPT. G. F.]

Voyage of the *Prince Albert* in search of. [*See* SNOW, W. P.]

[*See* MONTAGU, J.]

FRANKLIN (WILLIAM TEMPLE). Memoirs of the Life and Writings of Benjamin Franklin. [*See* FRANKLIN, B.]

FRANKLYN (H. MORTIMER). Glance at Australia in 1880; or, Food from the South : a Pastoral and Agricultural Directory of the whole of Australia. Roy. 8vo. Melb., 1881.* MD 3 V 24

[*See* VICTORIAN REVIEW.]

FRANKS (A. W.), M.A., &c. [*See* BRITISH MUSEUM.]

FRANKS (HENRY). Victorian Almanac, 1864; with Farmers' and Gardeners' Calendar, &c. 12mo. Geelong, 1864. ME 4 Q

FRASER (ALEXANDER A.) Daddy Crips' Waifs : a Tale of Australasian Life and Adventure. 12mo. Lond., 1886. MJ 1 Q 44

FRASER (ALEXANDER CAMPBELL), LL.D. Selections from Berkeley. [*See* BERKELEY, RT. REV. G.]

FRASER (CHARLES). [*See* BROWN, R.]

FRASER (COL. HASTINGS). Memoir and Correspondence of General James Stuart Fraser, of the Madras Army. 8vo. Lond., 1885. C 5 W 7

FRASER (GEN. JAMES STUART). Memoir and Correspondence of; by his Son, Colonel Hastings Fraser. Imp. 8vo. Lond., 1885. C 5 W 7

FRASER (REV. J.) Report to the Commissioners appointed to inquire into the Education given in Schools in England not comprised within Her Majesty's two recent Commissions; and to the Commissioners appointed to inquire into the Schools in Scotland, on the Common School System of the United States, and of the Provinces of Upper and Lower Canada. Roy. 8vo. Sydney, 1868. MG 1 U 4

FRASER (JAMES BAILLIE). Journal of a Tour through part of the Snowy Range of the Himalaya Mountains, and to the Sources of the Rivers Jumna and Ganges. Roy. 4to. Lond., 1820. D 9 S 16 †

Military Memoir of Lieut.-Col. James Skinner, C.B. 2 vols. 8vo. Lond., 1851. C 4 V 32, 33

Narrative of a Journey into Khorasân, 1821–22. 4to. Lond., 1825. D 5 V 20

Narrative of the Residence of the Persian Princes in London, 1835–36 ; with Account of their Journey from Persia. 2 vols. 8vo. Lond., 1838. C 4 V 15, 16

Travels and Adventures in the Persian Provinces on the Southern Banks of the Caspian Sea. 4to. Lond., 1826. D 5 V 19

Travels in Koordistan, Mesopotamia, &c.; including an Account of parts of those Countries hitherto unvisited by Europeans. 2 vols. 8vo. Lond., 1840. D 4 U 18, 19

Winter's Journey (Tâtar) from Constantinople to Tehran ; with Travels through various parts of Persia, &c. 2 vols. 8vo. Lond., 1838. D 5 S 6, 7

FRASER (JOHN), B.A. The Etruscans: were they Celts? or, the Light of an Inductive Philology thrown on Forty Etruscan Fossil-words, preserved to us by ancient Authors. 8vo. Edinb., 1879. K 15 R 21

FRASER (MAJOR), R.E. Historical Review of the principal Jewish and Christian Sites at Jerusalem. 8vo. Lond., 1881. B 10 P 21

FRASER (SIMON), LORD LOVAT. [*See* LOVAT, SIMON FRASER, LORD.]

FRASER (THOMAS RODERICK), M.D., AND DEWAR (ANDREW). Origin of Creation; or, the Science of Matter and Force. 12mo. Lond., 1874. A 17 T 6

FRASER'S MAGAZINE. 90 vols. 8vo. Lond., 1830–76. E

FRATER (W. J.) Tour in New Zealand and Australia. 12mo. Newcastle-upon-Tyne, 1887. MD 1 S 55

FRAUENFELD (GEORG). Notizen, gesammelt während meines Aufenthaltes auf Neuholland, Neuseeland, und Taiti. 8vo. Wein, 1860. MD 1 V 10

FREDERICA SOPHIA WILHELMINA (PRINCESS ROYAL OF PRUSSIA, MARGRAVINE OF BAREITH, &c.) Memoirs ; written by herself. (Autobiog., 20, 21.) 2 vols. (in 1) 18mo. Lond., 1828. C 1 P 15

FREDERICK (LIEUT. G. C.) Pacific Islands : Sailing Directions [*See* RICHARDS, LIEUT. G. E.]

FREDERICK II (KING OF PRUSSIA). Charon : Sermons from Styx ; Posthumous Work of Frederick the Great. [*See* JENNINGS, H.]

Frederick the Great and his Times ; edited, with an Introduction, by Thomas Campbell. 4 vols. 8vo. Lond., 1842–43. C 10 Q 25–28

History of. [*See* CARLYLE, T.]

FREDERICK II (KING OF PRUSSIA).—*continued.*
[Life of]; by Colonel Brackenbury, C.B. 8vo. Lond.,
1884. C 3 S 8

Life of; by Lord Dover. 2 vols. 8vo. Lond., 1832.
C 6 U 14, 15

Posthumous Works of; translated from the French, by
Thomas Holcroft. 13 vols. 8vo. Lond., 1789. J 4 T 11–23

Rheinsberg: Memorials of Frederick the Great, and Prince
Henry of Prussia, by Andrew Hamilton. 2 vols. 8vo.
Lond., 1880. C 4 S 29, 30

FREDERICK III (EMPEROR OF GERMANY, &c.) The Crown
Prince of Germany: a Diary. 8vo. Lond., 1886. C 3 P 3

FREDERICK WILLIAM III (KING OF PRUSSIA). Religious Life and Opinions of. [*See* EYLERT, VERY REV.
R. F.]

[*See* ALEXANDER, F.]

FREE CHURCH SUSTENTATION FUND. Statement issued by the Free Church Presbytery. 12mo.
Hobart (n.d.) M G 1 P 42

FREE LANCE. [*See* HORSES.]

FREEMAN (EDWARD A.), D.C.L. Chief Periods of
European History: Six Lectures. 8vo. Lond., 1886.
B 7 R 23

Comparative Politics: Six Lectures. 8vo. Lond., 1873.
F 9 R 26

English Towns and Districts: a Series of Addresses and
Sketches. 8vo. Lond., 1883. B 5 S 28

Greater Greece and Greater Britain, and George Washington, the Expander of England. 8vo. Lond., 1886.
B 14 Q 19

Growth of the English Constitution from the Earliest
Times. 2nd ed. 8vo. Lond., 1873. B 3 R 6

Historical and Architectural Sketches, chiefly Italian.
Illustrated. 8vo. Lond., 1876. B 12 P 39

Historical Essays. 1st, 2nd, and 3rd Series. 3 vols.
8vo. Lond., 1871–79. B 14 S 33–35

Historical Geography of Europe; with Maps. 2 vols.
8vo. Lond., 1881. D 12 U 12, 13

History of the Norman Conquest: its Causes and its
Results. 2nd ed., revised (with Index). 6 vols. 8vo.
Oxford, 1870–79. B 7 Q 12–17

Lectures to American Audiences: 1. The English People;
2. The Practical Bearings of General European History.
8vo. Philad., 1882. B 14 Q 44

Methods of Historical Study: Eight Lectures. 8vo.
Lond., 1886. B 14 S 36

Old English History; with Maps. 2nd ed. 8vo. Lond.,
1871. B 4 P 4

Another copy. 3rd ed., revised. 8vo. Lond., 1873.
B 4 P 5

Reign of William Rufus, and the Accession of Henry I.
2 vols. 8vo. Oxford, 1882. B 4 S 21, 22

Sketches from the Subject and Neighbour Lands of Venice.
Illustrated. 8vo. Lond., 1881. D 7 Q 38

FREEMAN (J. J.) Dictionary of the Malagasy Language
in two Parts. 8vo. Antananarivo, 1835. K 15 R 5

FREEMAN (JOHN), M.A. Life of the Rev. William Kirby,
M.A., Rector of Barham. 8vo. Lond., 1852. C 7 Q 48

FREEMAN'S JOURNAL (THE), 1857–62, 1872–87.
17 vols. fol. Sydney, 1861–87. E

FREEMASONRY. The Secrets of Freemasonry revealed;
by "A Mason." 8vo. Melb. (n.d.) MJ 2 R 12

FREE PRESS (THE), and Commercial Journal. Fol.
Sydney, 1841. ME

[*See* SYDNEY FREE PRESS.]

FREER (MARTHA WALKER). Married Life of Anne of
Austria, Queen of France, and Don Sebastian, King of
Portugal. 2 vols. 8vo. Lond., 1864. C 1 V 10, 11

FREE TRADE *v.* PROTECTION. A Series of Papers
illustrative of what Protection has done for the United
States of America and for Russia, and of what Free
Trade has done for Switzerland. (Reprinted from the
Argus.) 8vo. Melb., 1864. MF 1 Q 3

FREHER (DIONYSIUS ANDREAS). Writings of. [*See*
WALTON, C.]

FREIND (J.), M.D. History of Physick from the time
of Galen to the beginning of the 16th Century, chiefly
with regard to Practice. 2 vols. 8vo. Lond., 1750.
A 12 R 11, 12

FREMONT (COL. JOHN CHARLES), AND EMORY MAJOR
W. H.) Notes of Travel in California; also the Route
to San Diego, in California, &c. 12mo. Dublin, 1849.
D 3 P 11

FRENCH OFFICER, A. [*See* MAURITIUS.]

FRENCH (GEORGE RUSSELL). Ancestry of Her Majesty
Queen Victoria, and His Royal Highness Prince Albert.
8vo. Lond., 1841. C 5 R 27

FRENCH (RICHARD VALPY), D.C.L., &c. Nineteen Centuries of Drink in England: a History. 8vo. Lond.,
1884. B 4 R 21

FRENCH AND ENGLISH PHRASE-BOOK; being a
Companion to the French Grammar. (Weale.) 12mo.
Lond., 1861. K 11 T 12

FRENCH COMIC ANNUAL (THE); or, the Chapter
of Accidents. Illustrated by Victor Adam. Obl. 16mo.
Lond., 1842. J I V 36

FRENCH CONSTITUTION (THE). An Authentic Copy,
as Revised and Amended by the National Assembly,
1791. 8vo. Lond., 1791. F 9 It 9

FRENCH LANGUAGE. Dictionnaire de l'Académie
Française, avec Complément. (Institut de France.)
6 éd. 3 vols. 4to. Paris 1835–42. K 15 U 17–19

FRERE (MISS ALICE M.), MRS. GODFREY CLERK. The Antipodes, and round the World; or, Travels in Australia, New Zealand, Ceylon, China, Japan, and California. Illustrated. 2nd ed. 8vo. Lond., 1870.* MD 6 Q 6

FRESENIUS (DR. G. REMIGIUS). Anleitung zur Qualitativen Chemischen Analyse. 8vo. Brunswick, 1874.
A 6 P 21

Qualitative Chemical Analysis; translated by A. Vacher. 9th ed. 8vo. Lond., 1876. A 5 U 38

FRESHFIELD (DOUGLAS WILLIAM), M.A., &c. Italian Alps: Sketches in the Mountains of Ticino, Lombardy, the Trentino, and Venetia. 8vo. Lond., 1875. D 8 Q 17

Travels in the Central Caucasus and Bashan, including Visits to Ararat and Tabreez, and Ascents of Kazbek and Elbruz. 8vo. Lond., 1869. D 7 T 25

FRESNOY (C. A. DU). [*See* DU FRESNOY, C. A.]

FREWER (MISS ELLEN ELIZABETH). Heart of Africa. [*See* SCHWEINFURTH, DR. G.]

Seven Years in South Africa. [*See* HOLUB, DR. E.]

Victor Hugo and his Time. [*See* BARBOU, A.]

FREY (PROF. HEINRICH). Grundzüge der Histologie zur einleitung in das studium Derselben. 8vo. Leipzig, 1876. A 12 U 10

Handbuch der Histologie und Histochemie des Menschen. Roy. 8vo. Leipzig, 1876. A 12 U 9

Histology and Histochemistry of Man; translated from the fourth German edition, by A. E. J. Barker. 8vo. Lond., 1874. A 5 T 27

FREYCINET (CAPT. LOUIS). Voyage de Découvertes aux Terres Australes, exécuté sur les Corvettes *le Géographe, le Naturaliste*, et la Goëlette *le Casuarina*, pendant les années 1800–1804 sous le commandement du Capitaine de vaisseau, N. Baudin. 4to. Paris, 1815.* MD 5 P 19 †

Atlas [to the above]. At. fol. Paris, 1812*. MD 5 Q 10 †

Voyage de Découvertes aux Terres Australes. [*See* PERON, F.] [*See* ARAGO, J. E. V.]

FREYTAG (G. W.) Lexicon Arabico-Latinum, ex epere suo maiore, in usum Tironum excertum. 4to. Halis, 1837. K 14 S 9

FREZIER (AMÉDÉE FRANÇOIS). Voyage to the South Sea, and along the Coasts of Chili and Peru, in the years 1712–14; with an Account of the Settlement, Commerce, and Riches of the Jesuites in Paraguay. Illustrated. Sm. 4to. Lond., 1717. D 3 U 34

PREZIER (AMÉDÉE FRANÇOIS), EN VERBURG (ISAAK). Reis-Beschryving van de Zuid-zee, langs de Kusten van Chili, Peru, en Brazil opgesteld op eene Reistocht gedaan in de jaren 1712–14. Sq. 8vo. Amsterdam, 1718. D 3 U 35

FRICKMANN (LIEUT. ACHILLE). Routier del 'Australie. Première Partie : Côte Sud et partie de la Côte Est, Détroit de Bass et Tasmanie; traduit de l'anglais. 2 vols. 8vo. Paris, 1871. MA 5 V 11, 12

FRIEDLAND (ALBRECHT EUSEBIUS WENZESLAUS WALLENSTEIN, OR WALDSTEIN), DUKE OF. Life of; by Lieut.-Col. J. Mitchell. 8vo. Lond., 1837. C 9 S 36

FRIEDLÄNDER (MICHAEL), PH.D. The Guide of the Perplexed of Maimonides. [*See* MAIMONIDES.]

FRIEDMANN (PAUL). Anne Boleyn: a Chapter of English History, 1527–36. 2 vols. 8vo. Lond., 1884. C 10 R 23, 24

FRIELL (P.) Advantages of Indian Labour in the Australasian Colonies. 8vo. Sydney, 1846.* MF 3 Q 52

FRIENDLY SOCIETIES, N.S.W. [*See* NEW SOUTH WALES.]

FRIEZE (HENRY SIMMONS). Giovanni Duprè; with two Dialogues on Art, from the Italian of A. Conti. 8vo. Lond., 1886. C 2 T 20

FRISI (PROF. PAUL), F.R.S. Treatise on Rivers and Torrents, with the Method of regulating their Course and Channels; with an Essay on Navigable Canals. (Weale.) 12mo. Lond., 1868. A 17 P 61

FRITH (FRANCIS). Lower Egypt, Thebes, and the Pyramids (Photographed). Fol. Lond., 1862. D 4 P 2 ‡

Sinai and Palestine (Photographed). Fol. Lond., 1862. D 4 P 3 ‡

Upper Egypt and Ethiopia (Photographed). Fol. Lond., 1862. D 4 P 1 ‡

FRITH (H.) [*See* VILLARS, P.]

FRITH (JOHN). Writings of. [*See* BRITISH REFORMERS, 11.]

FRITZNER (JOHAN). Ordbog over det gamle norske Sprog. 8vo. Kristiania, 1867. K 12 S 30

FRODOARD. Histoire de l'Eglise de Rheims. [*See* GUIZOT, F. P. G. 5.]

FROEBEL (FRIEDRICH). Autobiography of; translated by Emilie Michaelis and H. K. Moore. 12mo. Lond., 1886. C 2 Q 15

Froebel's Method of Education. [*See* GOLDAMMER, H.]

FROEMBLING (FRIEDRICH OTTO), PH.D. Graduated German Reader ; consisting of a Selection from the most Popular Writers, arranged progressively; with a complete Vocabulary for the First Part. 6th ed. 8vo. Lond., 1879. K 11 V 25

FROISSART (SIR JOHN). Ancient Chronicles of England, France, Spain, Portugal, Scotland, Brittany, and Flanders. 4 vols. roy. 8vo. Lond., 1814–16. B 7 V 12–15

Chronicles of England, France, Spain, Portugal, Scotland, Brittany, Flanders, and the adjoining Countries. 2 vols. 4to. Lond., 1812. B 7 V 27, 28

FROLOW (M.) Défense de Sébastopol exposé de la Guerre Souterraine, 1854–55. [*See* TODLEBEN, GEN. E. DE.]

FROMBERG (EMANUEL OTTO). Essay on the Art of Painting on Glass. (Weale.) 3rd ed. 12mo. Lond., 1857. A 17 P 31

FROME (Lieut.-Gen. Edward), R.E., &c. Outline of the Method of conducting a Trigonometrical Survey, for the formation of Geographical and Topographical Maps and Plans; Military Reconnaissance, Levelling, &c.; with Problems in Geodesy and Practical Astronomy, and Formulæ and Tables; by Capt. Charles Warren, R.E. 4th ed. 8vo. Lond., 1873.   A 6 S 26

FROMENTIN (Eugine). Old Masters of Belgium and Holland (les Maitres d'Autrefois). Sm. 4to. Boston, 1882.   A 7 S 33
Painter and Writer; by Louis Gonse. Sm. 4to. Boston, 1883.   C 5 T 10

FROMMANN (Dr. G. Karl). Die deutschen Mundarten: eine Monatsschrift für Dichtung, Forschung und Kritik. Begründet von Jos. Ans. Pangkofer, fortgesetzt von Dr. G. Karl Frommann. 6 vols. 8vo. Nürnburg, 1854–59.   K 15 Q 14–19

FROMMENT (Anthoine). Les Actes et Gestes Merveil- levx de la Cité de Genève. 8vo. Genève, 1854.   G 13 P 22

FRONTENAC (Count). [*See* Parkman, F.]

FROST (P.) Solid Geometry. 3rd ed. 8vo. Lond., 1886.   A 10 T 27

FROST (Thomas). Secret Societies of the European Re- volution, 1776–1876. 2 vols. 8vo. Lond., 1876. B 7 U 21,22

FROTHINGHAM (Octavius Brooks). Transcenden- talism in New England : a History. 8vo. New York, 1880.   G 8 Q 12

FROTHINGHAM (Richard). Rise of the Republic of the United States. 8vo. Boston, 1872.   B 1 S 9

FROUDE (James Anthony), M.A. Bunyan. (Eng. Men of Letts.) 8vo. Lond., 1880.   C 1 U 4
The English in Ireland in the 18th Century. 3 vols. 8vo. Lond., 1872–74.   B 11 Q 30–32
History of England from the Fall of Wolsey to the Death of Elizabeth. 12 vols. 8vo. Lond., 1856–70. B 5 Q 25–36
Letters of Jane Welsh Carlyle. [*See* Carlyle, J. W.]
Mr. Froude's Negropiobia. [*See* Davis, N. D.]
Oceana; or, England and her Colonies. 8vo. Lond., 1886.   MD 5 S 10
Reminiscences; by Thomas Carlyle; edited by J. A. Froude. 2 vols. 8vo. Lond., 1881.   C 2 T 10, 11
Reply the "The English in Ireland." [*See* Mitchell, J.]
Short Studies on Great Subjects. 2 vols. 8vo. Lond., 1867.   J 3 R 19, 20
Short Studies on Great Subjects. 2nd–4th series. 3 vols. 8vo. Lond. 1871–83.   J 11 V 22–24
Thomas Carlyle: a History of the First Forty Years of his Life, 1795–1835. 2 vols. 8vo. Lond., 1882. C 10 R 41, 42
Thomas Carlyle: a History of his Life in London, 1834–81. 2 vols. 8vo. Lond., 1884.   C 10 R 43, 44
Two Lectures on South Africa; delivered before the Philo- sophical Society, Edinburgh, Jan. 6 and 9, 1880. 8vo. Lond., 1880.   B 1 P 34

FROUDE (Richard Hurrell), M.A. Remains of. 2 vols. 8vo. Lond., 1838.   G 13 P 17, 18

FRY (Elizabeth). Memoirs of; including a History of her Labours in the Reformation of Female Prisoners, &c.; by the Rev. Thomas Timpson. 8vo. Lond., 1847.   C 3 S 45
Memoir of the Life of; with Extracts from her Journal and Letters. Edited by her two Daughters [Katherine Fry and Rachel Elizabeth Creswell.] 2 vols. 8vo Lond., 1848.   C.11 P 3, 4

FRY (Henry Phibbs), D.D. Answer to the Rt. Rev. F. R. Nixon, D.D., Lord Bishop of Tasmania ; being a Vindication of the Clergy condemned for asserting the Right of Private Judgment. 12mo. Hobart 1853.   MG 1 P 26
Letter to the Householders of Hobarton, on the effects of Transportation, and on the Moral Condition of the Colony. 12mo. Hobart, 1847.   MJ 2 P 30
Reply to a Letter to the Householders of Hobarton, on the effects of Transportation ; by "A Man and a Brother." 12mo. Hobart, 1847.   MJ 2 P 30
System of Penal Discipline ; with a Report on the Treat- ment of Prisoners in Great Britain and Van Dieman's Land. 8vo. Lond., 1850.   MF 2 P 29

FRY (Rev. John), B.A. Short History of the Church of Christ. 8vo. Lond., 1825.   G 9 S 13

FRY (Katherine), and CRESWELL (Mrs. Rachel Elizabeth). Memoir of Elizabeth Fry; with Extracts from her Journal and Letters. 2 vols. 8vo. Lond., 1848.   C 11 P 3, 4

FRYER (John), M.D. New Account of East India and Persia, in Eight Letters ; being Nine Years' Travels, 1672–81. Fol. Lond., 1698.   D 4 R 8 †

FRYER (M.) Fryer's Advertisers' Guide : List of News- papers published in the United Kingdom and British Isles. (Pam. A.) Fol. Lond. (n.d.)   MJ 2 U 1

FRYER (William J.), Junr. Architectural Iron-work : a Practical Work for Iron-workers, Architects, and Engi- neers. Roy. 8vo. New York, 1876.   A 3 P 19

FRYXELL (Anders). History of Sweden ; translated and edited by Mary Howitt. 2 vols. 8vo. Lond. 1844.   B 2 R 17, 18

FUCHS (August). Ueber die sogenannten unregelmäs- sigen Zeitwörter in den Romanischen Sprachen. 8vo. Berlin, 1840.   K 13 P 19

FUCINI (Renato). Translations from the Italian Poets. [*See* Fenzi, S.]

FULBERTUS (Sanctus). Opera omnia. [*See* Migne, J. P., Series Latina, 141.]

FULDA (F. K.) [*See* Ulphilas.]

FULGENTIUS (SANCTUS). Opera omnia. [*See* MIGNE, J. P., SERIES LATINA, 65.]

FULLER (REV. ANDREW). Principal Works and Remains of the Rev. Andrew Fuller; with a new Memoir, by his son, the Rev. A. G. Fuller. New ed. 8vo. Lond., 1864.   G 16 P 11

FULLER (REV. A. G.) Memoir of the Rev. A. Fuller. [*See* FULLER, REV. A.]

FULLER (CYRUS EDGAR). County Cumberland Directory, Year-book, and Calendar for 1886. 8vo. Parramatta, 1886.   ME 4 S

Rural Cumberland Year-book for 1882. 8vo. Parramatta, 1881.   MJ 2 R 17

FULLER (CAPT. FRANCIS). Five Years' Residence in New Zealand; or, Observations on Colonization. 8vo. Lond., 1859.*   MD 3 S 20

FULLER (REV. THOMAS), D.D. Church History of Britain, from the Birth of Jesus Christ until the year 1648. 6 vols. 8vo. Oxford, 1845.   G 8 U 11-16

Good Thoughts in Bad Times; Good Thoughts in Worse Times; Mixt Contemplations in Better Times. 12mo. Lond., 1841.   G 9 Q 10

History of the Holy War. 12mo. Lond., 1840. G 8 Q 13

History of the Worthies of England. Fol. Lond., 1662.   C 1 W 27

History of the University of Cambridge, from the Conquest to the year 1634; edited by the Rev. Marmaduke Prickett, M.A., &c., and T. Wright, M.A., with illustrative Notes. Camb., 1840.   B 6 R 30

The Holy State and the Profane State. 12mo. Lond., 1840.   G 9 Q 11

Life of; with Notices of his Books, his Kinsmen, and his Friends, by J. E. Bailey. 8vo. Lond., 1874. C 8 R 18

Selections from the Works of. [*See* MONTAGU, B.]

[*See* BAILEY, J. E.]

FULLER-MAITLAND (J. A.) Bach. [*See* SPITTA, P.]

FULLERTON (GEORGE), M.D., &c. Family Medical Guide; with plain Directions for the Treatment of every Case, and a List of Medicines required for any Household. 8vo. Sydney, 1875.   A 12 R 35

Another copy. 3rd ed. 8vo. Sydney, 1878. MA 2 S 10

FULLERTON (REV. JAMES), LL.D. Ten Lectures; with Historical Notices illustrative of the anti-Scriptural Nature and Pernicious Tendency of the Doctrines of Puseyism. 12mo. Sydney, 1844.*   MG 1 P 21

FULLOM (STEPHEN WATSON). Marvels of Science, and their Testimony to Holy Writ. 8th ed. 8vo. Lond., 1854.   A 17 T 41

FULTON (REV. HENRY), A.B. Letter to the Rev. W. B. Ullathorne, C.V.G., in answer to "A Few Words to the Rev. Henry Fulton, and his Readers, &c." 8vo. Sydney, 1833.   MG 1 P 5

Reasons why Protestants think the Worship of the Church of Rome an Idolatrous Worship. 8vo. Sydney, 1833.   MG 1 P 5

Strictures upon a Letter lately written by Roger Therry, Esq., Commissioner of the Court of Requests, in New South Wales, to Edward Blount, Esq., M.P. 8vo. Sydney, 1833.   MG 1 P 5

[*See* ULLATHORNE RT. REV. W. B.]

FUNERALS. Rare Collection of. 5 vols. fol. Lond., 1722.   B 16 S 13-17 ‡

FUNNIDOS (RIGDUM), GENT. [*See* CRUIKSHANK, G.]

FUNKE (DR. OTTO). Atlas of Physiological Chemistry. [*See* LEHMANN, PROF. C. G.]

FUNNELL (WILLIAM). Voyage round the World; containing an Account of Captain Dampier's Expedition into the South Seas in the Ship *St. George*, in the years 1703-4. [With Captain Dampier's Vindication of his Voyage.] 8vo. Lond., 1707.   MD 4 R 30

[*See* DAMPIER, CAPT. W.]

FURNAS (ROBERT W.) Message to the Legislative Assembly: Tenth Regular Session, 1885. (Pam. Dy.) 8vo. Lincoln, 1875.

FURNEAUX (HENRY), M.A. Annals of Tacitus. [*See* TACITUS]

FURNEAUX (CAPT. TOBIAS). [*See* AUSTRALASIA, *and* COOK, CAPT. J.]

FURNESS (HORACE HOWARD), PH.D., LL.D., &c. New Variorum Edition of Shakespeare. [*See* SHAKESPEARE, W.]

FURNISHING. Art of Furnishing on Rational and Æsthetic Principles; by H. J. C. 12mo. Lond., 1876.   A 2 R 26

FURNITURE. Old Furniture; being Examples selected from the Works of the best known Designers, from the 12th to the 18th Century. (*Published by Wyman and Sons.*) Sm. fol. Lond., 1883.   A 2 U 23

FURNIVALL (F. J.), M.A. Fraternitye of Vacabones. [*See* AWDELEY, J.]

FUR TRADER, A. [*See* AMERICAN-INDIAN LIFE.]

FUSELI (HENRY), M.A., &c. Anecdote Biography. [*See* TIMBS, J.]

Lectures on Painting. [*See* BARRY, J.]

Life and Writings of; edited by John Knowles, F.R.S. 3 vols. 8vo. Lond., 1831.   C 8 R 13-15

FYFE (LAURENCE R.) Hand-book of Jamaica. [*See* SINCLAIR, A. C.]

FYFFE (C. A.), M.A. History of Modern Europe. Vols. 1, 2. 8vo. Lond., 1880-86.   B 7 R 37, 38

G

G. (A.) [*See* MOTHER'S GRAVE.]

G. (S. T.) [*See* GILL, S. T.]

GABELENTZ (H. C. VON DER). Die Melanesischen Sprachen nach ihrem grammatischen Bau und ihrer Verwandtschaft unter sich und mit den Malaiisch-polynesischen Sprachen. 2 vols. (in 1) imp. 8vo. Leipsic, 1860–73. MK 1 U 7

GABELENTZ (DR. H. C. VAN DER), AND LOEBE (DR. J.) Grammatik der Gothischen Sprache. 4to. Leipzig, 1846. K 16 R 30

GAELIC LANGUAGE. [*See* DICTIONARIUM SCOTO-CELTICUM.]

GAFFARELL (JACOB). [*See* WOLF, J. C.]

GAFFAREL (PAUL). Les Colonies Françaises. 2ᵉ éd. 8vo. Paris, 1884. D 10 S 24

GAGE (JOHN), F.R.S., &c. History and Antiquites of Suffolk, Thingoe Hundred. Imp. 4to. Lond., 1838. B 18 S 4 ‡
History and Antiquities of Hengrave, in Suffolk. 4to. Lond., 1822. B 17 R 9 ‡

GAGE (W. L.) Life of F. Mendelssohn Bartholdy. [*See* LAMPADIUS, W. A.]

GAGLIARDI (REV. JOSEPH). Tradition of the Syriac Church of Antioch. [*See* BENNI, REV. C. B.]

GAILHABAUD (JULES). L'Architecture du vᵉ au xviiᵉ Siècle et les Arts qui en dépendent ; la Sculpture, la peinture Murale, la peinture Sur Verre, la Mosaïque, la Ferronerie, etc. 4 vols. imp. fol. Paris, 1869–72. A 1 Q 8–11 ‡

GAIMARD (MONS.) Zoologie. [*See* DUMONT D'URVILLE, CAPT. J. S. C.]

GAINSBOROUGH (THOMAS), R.A. Anecdote Biography. [*See* TIMBS, J.]
Gainsborough ; by G. M. Brock-Arnold. 8vo. Lond., 1881. C 3 T 31

GAIRDNER (JAMES). Houses of Lancaster and York ; with the Conquest and Loss of France. Maps. 2nd ed. 12mo. Lond., 1875. B 4 P 2
[*See* BREWER, J. S., *and* PASTON LETTERS.]

GAIRDNER (JAMES), AND SPEDDING (JAMES). Studies in English History. 8vo. Edinb., 1881. B 3 T 1

GAISFORD (STEPHEN). Essay on the African Slave Trade. 8vo. Lond., 1811. F 7 Q 8

GAISFORD (THOMAS), M.A. [*See* HERODOTUS.]

GAIUS. Gaii Institutionum Iuris Civilis Commentarii quatuor ; or, Elements of Roman Law, by Gaius; with a Translation and Commentary by Edward Poste, M.A. (Clar. Press.) 2nd ed. 8vo. Oxford, 1875. F 8 R 26
Institutes of Justinian ; edited as a Recension of the Institutes of Gaius. [*See* JUSTINIANUS.]

GALBRAITH (WILLIAM), M.A., &c. Trigonometrical Surveying, Levelling, and Railway Engineering. 8vo. Edinb., 1842. A 6 S 25
Treatise on Land-Surveying. [*See* AINSLIE, J.]

GALE (FREDERICK), "THE OLD BUFFER." Modern English Sports : their Use and their Abuse. 8vo. Lond., 1885. A 16 P 26

GALE (THEOPHILUS), M.A., &c. Court of the Gentiles. Parts 1–5, 2nd ed. 5 vols. (in 2) 8vo. Oxon., 1671–78. G 7 P 4, 5

GALEN OR GALENUS (CLAUDIUS). [*See* MEDICORUM GRAECORUM.]

GALERIES HISTORIQUES. Du Palais de Versailles. 9 vols. (in 10) 8vo. Paris, 1839–48. B 8 S 21–30

GALILEO GALILEI LINCEO. Galileo and the Inquisition ; by R. R. Madden. 12mo. Lond., 1863. C 2 P 16
Le Opere di Galileo Galilei; prima edizione completa. 16 vols. 8vo. Firenze, 1842–52. A 17 W 1–16
[Life of.] (Eminent Men.) 8vo. Lond., 1849. C 7 P 45
Martyrs of Science; by Sir D. Brewster. 12mo. Lond., 1874. C 1 T 40
Private Life of. 8vo. Lond., 1870. C 3 Q 21

GALLAND (A.) [*See* CABINET DES FÉES 7–11, 16–17.]

GALLENGA (ANTONIO CARLO NAPOLEONE), "L. MARIOTTI." Episodes of my Second Life. 2 vols. 8vo. Lond., 1884. C 6 Q 25, 26
Democracy across the Channel. 8vo. Lond., 1883. F 6 S 20
Iberian Reminiscences : Fifteen Years' Travelling Impressions of Spain and Portugal. 2 vols. 8vo. Lond., 1883. D 7 S 8, 9
Italy: General Views of its History and Literature. 2 vols. 8vo. Lond., 1841. B 12 Q 29, 30
Italy Revisited. 2 vols. 8vo. Lond., 1875. D 7 S 28, 29
Pearl of the Antilles. 8vo. Lond., 1873. D 3 Q 37
Pope and the King : the War between Church and State in Italy. 2 vols. 8vo. Lond., 1879. B 11 V 19, 20
Summer Tour in Russia. 8vo. Lond., 1882. D 7 S 31
Two Years of the Eastern Question. 2 vols. 8vo. Lond., 1877. D 7 S 26, 27

GALLERIA DI FIRENZE (REALE). Reale Galleria di Firenze illustrata. 10 vols. 8vo. Firenze, 1817–24.
A 7 U 11–20
Series 1. Quadri di Storia.
  „ 2. Quadri di vario Genere.
  „ 3. Ritratti di Pittori.
  „ 4. Statue, Bassirilievi, Busti, e Bronzi.
  „ 5. Cammei ed Intagli.
Plates [to the above.] 10 vols. fol. Firenze, 1817–24.
A 4 V 10–19 ‡

GALLERIE ZU DRESDEN. [*See* DRESDEN.]

GALLERY OF PORTRAITS; with Memoirs. 7 vols. imp. 8vo. Lond., 1833.   C 3 W 23–29
Historic Gallery of Portraits and Paintings; or, Biographical Review. 7 vols. 8vo. Lond., 1807–19.
A 7 S 14–20

GALLETLY (A.) Coal. (Brit. Manuf. Indust.) 12mo. Lond., 1876.   A 17 S 38

GALLETTI (GEN. BARTOLOMEO). Il Giro del Mondo colla Ristori: Note di Viaggio. 8vo. Roma, 1876. MD 3 Q 1

GALLIOS (LEONARD). [*See* ANQUETIL DU PERRON.]

GALLO (E. L.) History of the Mexican Railway. [*See* BAZ, G.]

GALLOWAY (ROBERT L.), M.R.I.A., &c. History of Coal-mining in Great Britain. 8vo. Lond., 1882.
A 9 P 29
Steam-engine and its Inventors. 8vo. Lond., 1881.
A 11 P 25
Treatise on Fuel, Scientific and Practical. Illustrated. 8vo. Lond., 1880.   A 6 S 11

GALLOWAY (REV. WILLIAM BROWN), M.A. Egypt's Record of Time to the Exodus of Israel critically investigated. 8vo. Lond., 1869.   G 15 Q 19

GALLWEY (SIR R. PAYNE-). Book of Duck Decoys; their Construction, Management, and History. 4to. Lond., 1886.   A 16 V 13
The Fowler in Ireland; or, Notes on the Haunts and Habits of Wild-fowl and Sea-fowl. 8vo. Lond., 1882. A 14 T 8
Shooting. [*See* WALSINGHAM, LORD.]

GALPINE (JOHN). Synoptical Compendium of British Botany, after the Linnean System. 12mo. Lond., 1819.
A 4 P 29

GALT (JOHN). Annals of the Parish, and the Ayrshire Legatees; with Memoir of the Author [by David Macbeth Moir.] 12mo. Lond., 1844.   J 7 Q 43
Autobiography. 2 vols. 8vo. Lond., 1833. C 7 P 15, 16
The Canadas; comprehending Topographical Information, &c., for the use of Emigrants and Capitalists. 2nd ed. 12mo. Lond., 1836.   D 3 P 12
Diary illustrative of the Times of George IV. [*See* BURY, LADY C.]
Literary Life and Miscellanies of. 3 vols. 8vo. Edinb., 1834.   C 3 R 38–40

2 o

GALTON (FRANCIS), F.R.S., &c. Art of Travel; or, Shifts and Contrivances available in Wild Countries. 12mo. Lond., 1855.   J 9 P 9
English Men of Science; their Nature and Nurture. 8vo. Lond., 1874.   A 1 W 44
Hereditary Genius: an Inquiry into its Laws and Consequences. 8vo. Lond., 1869.   A 1 W 32
Inquiries into Human Faculty and its Development. 8vo. Lond., 1883.   A 12 S 35
Vacation Tourists, and Notes of Travel in 1862–63. 8vo. Lond., 1864.   D 9 S 22

GAMACHE (FATHER CYPRIEN DE). [*See* CYPRIEN DE GAMACHE, FATHER.]

GAMBETTA (LEON). Leon Gambetta, Orator, Dictator, Journalist, Statesman; by J. Hanlon. 12mo. Lond., 1881.   C 2 P 17

GAMBIER (PARRY E.) Suakin in 1885; being a Sketch of the Campaign of this year, by "An Officer who was there." 8vo. Lond., 1885.   D 1 Q 12

GAMBLE (J. S.), M.A., &c. Manual of Indian Timbers. 8vo. Calcutta, 1881.   A 1 S 36

GAMGEE (PROF. ARTHUR), M.D., &c. Elements of Human Physiology. [*See* HERMANN, DR. L.]
Text-book of the Physiological Chemistry of the Animal Body, including an Account of the Chemical Changes occurring in Disease. Illustrated. Vol. 1. 8vo. Lond., 1880.   A 26 U 24

GAMITTO (A. C. P.) Journey to Cazembe. [*See* AFRICA.]

GAMMACK (REV. JAMES), M.A. Angus and the Mearns. [*See* JERVISE, A.]

GANDY (J. P.) Pompeiana: the Topography, Edifices, and Ornaments of Pompeii. [*See* GELL, SIR W.]

GANE (DOUGLAS M.) New South Wales and Victoria in 1885. 8vo. Lond., 1886.*   MD 6 P 21

GANGANELLI (ANTONIO). [*See* CLEMENT XIV.]

GANILH (CHARLES). Inquiry into the various Systems of Political Economy. 8vo. Lond., 1812.   F 8 P 16

GANNETT (HENRY). [*See* PORTER, R. P., *and* SCRIBNER, C.]

GANOT (PROF. ADOLPHE). Elementary Treatise on Physics, Experimental and Applied. Translated and edited by Prof. E. Atkinson. 7th ed. 8vo. Lond., 1875. A 16 R 31
Another copy. 11th ed. 8vo. Lond., 1883. A 16 R 32

GANT (FREDERICK JAMES), F.R.C.S. Science and Practice of Surgery. Illustrated. 8vo. Lond., 1871.
A 26 T 18

GARBETT (EDWARD LACY). Principles of Design in Architecture. (Weale.) 12mo. Lond., 1867. A 17 P 45

GARCILASSO DE LA VEGA. Royal Commentaries of Peru, in two Parts. The First Part, treating of the Original of their Incas or Kings, &c. The Second Part, describing the manner by which that New World was conquered by the Spaniards, &c.; rendered into English by Sir Paul Rycaut. Sm. fol. Lond., 1688.
B 14 R 18 ‡

GARDEN (MRS.) Memorials of James Hogg, the Ettrick Shepherd; edited by his Daughter. 8vo. Paisley, 1884.
C 3 V 13

GARDENER (THE): a Magazine of Horticulture and Floriculture. 6 vols. 8vo. Lond., 1872–87.   E

GARDENERS' CHRONICLE (THE): a Weekly Illustrated Journal of Horticulture and allied Subjects. 25 vols. fol. Lond., 1872–87.   E

GARDENERS' MAGAZINE (THE). For Amateur Cultivators, and Exhibitors of Plants, Flowers, and Fruits. 13 vols. fol. Lond., 1872–87.   E

GARDINER (COMM. ALLEN FRANCIS), R.N. Friend of Australia; or, a Plan for exploring the Interior, and for carrying on a Survey of the whole Continent of Australia; by "A Retired Officer of the Hon. East India Company's Service." Illustrated. 8vo. Lond., 1830.* MD 5 U 6

Narrative of a Journey to the Zoolu Country, South Africa, 1835. 8vo. Lond., 1836.   D 2 R 20

GARDINER (CHARLES). Map of Sydney. [*See* SMITH, —, AND GARDINER, C.]

GARDINER (HON. COL. JAMES). Some remarkable Passages in the Life of; by Philip Doddridge, D.D. 12mo. Edinb., 1807.   C 2 P 18

GARDINER (JOHN). Analysis of Sentences; designed for the use of Pupil Teachers and Students in training under the Department of Public Instruction, New South Wales; by "The Chief Examiner." 12mo. Sydney, 1882.
MK 1 P 39

GARDINER (SAMUEL). Brunswick Herd: Catalogue of Pure Shorthorn Cattle, bred by, and the property of Samuel Gardiner. 12mo. Melb., 1877.   ME 3 8

Priced Catalogue of Samuel Gardiner's Annual Sale, 1878. Obl. 32mo. Melb., 1878.   ME 3 8

GARDINER (SAMUEL RAWSON), LL.D., &c. Fall of the Monarchy of Charles I, 1637–49. 2 vols. 8vo. Lond., 1882.   B 6 T 1, 2

History of England under the Duke of Buckingham and Charles I, 1624–28. 2 vols. 8vo. Lond., 1875. B 5 U 25, 26

History of the Great Civil War, 1642–49. Vol. I. 8vo. Lond., 1886.   B 7 P 35

Prince Charles and the Spanish Marriage, 1617–23: a Chapter of English History. 2 vols. 8vo. Lond., 1869.
B 5 T 39

Thirty Years' War, 1618–48; with a Map. 3rd ed. 12mo. Lond., 1875.   B 9 Q 31

GARDINER'S TRIAL. [*See* NEW SOUTH WALES.]

GARDNER (AUGUSTUS KINGSLEY). Old Wine in New Bottles; or, Spare Hours of a Student in Paris. 12mo. Dublin, 1849.   D 7 P 16

GARDNER (DORSEY). Quatre Bras, Ligny, and Waterloo: a Narrative of the Campaign in Belgium, 1815. 8vo. Lond., 1882.   B 8 Q 45

GARDNER (E. A.) Naukratis. [*See* PETRIE, W. M. F.]

GARDNER (FRANKLIN B.) Carriage Painters' Illustrated Manual; containing a Treatise on the Art, Science, and Mystery of Coach, Carriage, and Car Painting. 18mo. New York, 1877.   A 11 Q 15

GARDNER (GEORGE), F.L.S. Travels in the Interior of Brazil, 1836–41. 8vo. Lond., 1846.   D 3 U 15

GARDNER (REV. JAMES), M.A. Faiths of the World: a Dictionary of all Religions and Religious Sects; their Doctrines, Rites, Ceremonies, and Customs. 2 vols. imp. 8vo. Lond., 1858–60.   G 6 V 1, 2

GARDNER (PROF. PERCY), M.A., &c. Catalogue of Greek Coins in the British Museum: the Seleucid Kings of Syria; edited by R. S. Poole. 8vo. Lond., 1878. A 13 R 33

Parthian Coinage. [*See* NUMISMATA ORIENTALIA, 1.]

Samos and Samian Coins. 8vo. Lond., 1882. A 13 R 36

Types of Greek Coins: an Archæological Essay. Roy. 4to. Camb., 1883.   A 5 R 10 †

[*See* HEAD, B. V.]

GARDTHAUSEN (V.) Catalogus Codicum Græcorum Sinaiticorum. 8vo. Oxonii, 1886.   K 7 S 4

GARFIELD (JAMES A.), PRESIDENT U.S. Garfield Souvenirs: the President's Courageous Sayings during his Critical Illness, and Gems of Press and Pulpit; compiled by Max Coren. 2 vols. (in 1) 18mo. Wash., 1881. C 1 P 30

Life and Public Services of: a Biographical Sketch; by Capt. F. H. Mason. 12mo. Lond., 1881.   C 1 T 34

GARIBALDI (GIUSEPPE). Garibaldi and Italian Unity; by Lieut.-Col. Chambers. 8vo. Lond., 1864. C 7 P 6

Garibaldi Recollections; by E. Melena; English Version, by Charles Edwardes. 8vo. Lond., 1887. C 5 R 16

Life of; by J. Theodore Bent, B.A. 8vo. Lond., 1881.
C 2 U 26

Another copy. 2nd ed. 8vo. Lond., 1882.   C 2 U 27

GARLAND (R.) French Cathedrals. [*See* WINKLES, B.]

GARNETT (LUCY M. J.) Greek Folk-Songs from the Turkish Provinces of Greece, Albania, Thessaly (not yet wholly free), and Macedonia: Literal and Metrical Translations. 8vo. Lond., 1885.   H 5 U 18

GARNETT (R.), JUNR. [*See* ENTWISLE, J.]

GARNETT (RICHARD), LL.D. [*See* WARTER, J. W.]

GARNETT (PROF. WILLIAM), M.A. Life of James Clerk Maxwell. [*See* CAMPBELL, L.]

GARNIER (E.) [*See* GASNAULT, P.]

GARNIER (JULES). Notes Géologiques sur l'Océanie, les Iles Taïti, et Rapa. 8vo. Paris, 1870.   MA 2 Q 17

Voyage autour du Monde: La Nouvelle-Calédonie (Côte Orientale). 8vo. Paris, 1871.   MD 4 P 27

Voyage autour du Monde: Océanie, les Iles des Pins, Loyalty, et Taïti. 8vo. Paris, 1871.   MD 4 P 28

GARNOT (PROSPER). Zoologie ; Voyage de *La Coquille.* [*See* DUPERREY, L. I.]

GARRETT (JOHN). Classical Dictionary of India, illustrative of the Mythology, Philosophy, Literature, Antiquities, Arts, Manners, Customs, &c., of the Hindus. 8vo. Madras, 1871.   K 7 Q 4

Supplement [to the above]. 8vo. Madras, 1873.   K 7 Q 4

GARRETT (THOMAS). History of. [*See* BRITISH REFORMERS, 12.]

GARRICK (DAVID). Arthur and Emmeline: an Entertainment. [*See* DRYDEN, J.]

Bon Ton; or, High Life above Stairs. [*See* FARCES, 5.]

Another copy. [*See* BRIT. DRAMA, 5.]

Catherine and Petruchio: a Comedy; altered from Shakespeare. [*See* FARCES, 4.]

The Chances: a Comedy. (New Eng. Theatre.) 12mo. Lond., 1777.   H 4 P 26

Cymon: a Dramatic Romance. (Bell's Brit. Theatre.) 18mo. Lond., 1795.   H 2 P 26

Dramatic Works of; to which is prefixed a Life of the Author. 3 vols. 12mo. Lond., 1798.   H 3 P 7–9

Every Man in his Humour: a Comedy. [*See* JONSON, B.]

The Guardian: a Farce. [*See* BRIT. DRAMA, 5.]

Another copy. [*See* FARCES, 4.]

High Life below Stairs. [*See* BRIT. DRAMA, 5.]

Another copy. [*See* FARCES, 5.]

The Irish Widow: a Comedy. [*See* BRIT. DRAMA, 5.]

Another copy. [*See* FARCES, 5.]

Life of, from original Family Papers, and numerous published and unpublished sources; by Percy Fitzgerald, M.A., &c. 2 vols. 8vo. Lond., 1868.   C 7 P 17, 18

The Lying Valet: a Farce. [*See* FARCES, 5.]

The Male Coquette. [*See* BRIT. DRAMA, 5.]

Miss in her Teens: a Farce. [*See* BRIT. DRAMA, 5.]

Another copy. [*See* FARCES, 4.]

Neck or Nothing. [*See* BRIT. DRAMA, 5.]

Peep behind the Curtain. [*See* BRIT. DRAMA, 5.]

Private Correspondence of, with the most celebrated Persons of the Time. 2 vols. roy. 4to. Lond.,1831.   C 1 W 11, 12

Mémoires de. [*See* BARRIÈRE, J. F., 6.]

[*See* COLMAN, G.]

GARRISON (FRANCIS JACKSON). William Lloyd Garrison. [*See* GARRISON, W. P.]

GARRISON (WENDELL PHILLIPS), AND GARRISON (FRANCIS JACKSON)). William Lloyd Garrison, 1805–79. The Story of his Life ; told by his children. 2 vols. 8vo. New York, 1885.   C 10 U 12, 13

GARRISON (WILLIAM LLOYD). Story of his Life, 1805–79 ; told by his children [Wendell Phillips Garrison, and Francis Jackson Garrison.] Vols. 1 and 2. 8vo. New York, 1885.   C 10 U 12, 13

GARROD (ALFRED HENRY), M.A., &c. Collected Scientific Papers of. In Memoriam. Edited, with a biographical Memoir of the Author, by W. A. Forbes, B.A., Roy. 8vo. Lond., 1881.   A 12 V 13

GARRYOWEN SKETCHES (THE). Historical, Local, and Personal; by "An Old Colonist." 12mo. Melb., 1880.   MD 2 Q 1

GARTH (SIR SAMUEL), KNT. Life and Poems of. [*See* CHALMERS, A. ; *and* JOHNSON, S.]

Ovid's Metamorphoses. [*See* CHALMERS, A.]

GASCOIGNE (GEORGE). Life and Poems of. [*See* CHALMERS, A.]

GASCOIGNE (THOMAS). Loci e Libro Veritatum. Passages selected from Gascoigne's Theological Dictionary, illustrating the Condition of Church and State; 1403–58. (Clar. Press.) 8vo. Oxford, 1881.   G 6 S 30

GASKELL (MRS. ELIZABETH CLEGHORN). Life of Charlotte Brontë. 2 vols. 8vo. Lond., 1857.   C 3 R 9, 10

Life of Charlotte Brontë. 4th ed. 8vo. Lond., 1858.   C 3 R 11

GASON (SAMUEL). Manners and Customs of the Dieyerie Tribe of Australian Aborigines; together with Examples of the Construction of the Dialect, and a complete Vocabulary. Edited by George Isaacs. (Native Tribes of South Australia.) 8vo. Adelaide, 1874.   MA 1 R 2

Another copy. 8vo. Adelaide, 1879.   MA 1 R 12

GASNAULT (P.), AND GARNIER (E.) French Pottery. (South Kens. Mus. 27.) 8vo. Lond., 1884.   E

GASPARIN (AGÉNOR ETIENNE), COMTE DE. Des Tables Tournantes du Surnaturel en général et des Esprits. 2e éd. 2 vols. 8vo. Paris, 1855.   G 8 S 15, 16

GASPEY (THOMAS). Life and Times of the good Lord Cobham. 2 vols. 8vo. Lond., 1844.   C 3 S 19, 20

GASSIES (J. B.) Faune Conchyliologique, Terrestre et Fluvio-Lacustre, de la Nouvelle-Calédonie. Roy. 8vo. Bordeaux, 1863–79.   MA 2 U 10

GATSCHET (ALBERT S.) Migration Legend of the Creek Indians ; with a Linguistic, Historic, and Etnographic Introduction. 8vo. Philad., 1884.   A 1 W 35

GATTY (MRS. ALFRED). Parables from Nature. New ed. 8vo. Lond., 1867. J 6 U 4

GATTY (REV. ALFRED), M.A. The Bell: its Origin, History, and Uses. 12mo. Lond., 1848. B 14 Q 21

GAU (F. C.) Antiquités de la Nubie ; ou Monumens inédits des bords du Nil, situés entre la première et la seconde cataracte. L. 4to. Stuttgart, 1822. D 11 P 3 ‡

GAUNT (JOHN OF). Duke of Lancaster. [*See* LANCASTER, JOHN OF GAUNT, DUKE OF.]

GAUSS (C. F.) [*See* PENDLEBURY, C.]

GAUTIER (LÉON). Histoire Universelle de l'Eglise Catholique, avec un Table Générale. [*See* ROHRBACHER, L'ABBE F. R.]

[*See* ADAM OF ST. VICTOR.]

GAUTIER (THÉOPHILE). Portraits Contemporains—Littérateurs, Peintres, Sculpteurs, Artistes Dramatiques. 8vo. Paris, 1874. C 2 P 32

GAWLER (H.) Farm Reports of Select Farms. (Lib. of Usef. Know.) 8vo. Lond., 1834. A 1 R 21

GAWLER (HENRY). South Australian Real Property Act. [*See* TORRENS, SIR R. R.]

GAY (JOHN). The Beggars' Opera. (New Eng. Theatre.) 12mo. Lond., 1782. H 4 P 29

Another copy. (Bell's Brit. Theatre.) 18mo. Lond., 1791. H 2 P 17

Another copy. (Brit. Theatre.) 12mo. Lond., 1808. H 1 P 12

Another copy. [*See* BRITISH DRAMA 5.]

Fables. [Illustrated by Thomas Bewick.] 12mo. Lond., 1812. H 6 R 9

Life and Poems of. [*See* CHALMERS, A.; *and* JOHNSON, S.]

[*See* BRITISH POETS 2.]

GAYANGOS (P. DE). Chronicle of James I. [*See* JAMES I.]

[*See* AL-MAKKARI, AHMED IBN MOHAMMED.]

GAYLAND (KING OF FEZ). [*See* TANGIER.]

GAYOT DE PITAVAL (FRANÇOIS). [*See* CAUSES CÉLÈBRES.]

GEAREY (CAROLINE). Daughters of Italy. 12mo. Lond., 1886. C 2 S 10

GEARY (CHATTAN). Burma after the Conquest, viewed in its Political, Social, and Commercial Aspects from Mandalay. 8vo. Lond., 1886. B 10 Q 48

GEARY (PATRICK). Trial of, for Murder. [*See* MANUSCRIPTS, &c.]

GEBHART (EMIL). Roman Cameos and Florentine Mosaics : a Series of Studies, Historical, Critical, and Artistic. 8vo. Lond., 1882. B 12 P 44

GEDDES (ALEXANDER), LL.D. Sermon preached on the Day of General Fast, Feb. 27, 1799, by "Polemophilus Brown." (Pam. Bo.) 8vo. Lond., 1799. G 16 S 18

GEDDES (ANDREW). Etchings by Sir David Wilkie, R.A., and by Andrew Geddes, A.R.A. ; with Biographical Sketches by David Lang, F.S.A.S. Sm. fol. Edinb., 1875. A 23 R 11 ‡

GEDDES (JAMES). History of the Administration of John De Witt, Grand Pensionary of Holland. Vol. 1, 1623–54. 8vo. Lond., 1879. C 10 T 24

GEDDES (PATRICK). John Ruskin, Economist. (Round Table Series.) 8vo. Lond., 1884. G 16 S 18

Viri Illustres. Acad. Jacob. Sext. Scot. Reg. anno CCCmo. Edited by P. Geddes. 12mo. Edinb., 1884. C 1 R 40

GEDDES (WILLIAM). Colonial Agriculture : a Course of Four Lectures, delivered in the School of Arts, Maitland, during the year 1845. (Pam. 28) 8vo. Sydney 1855. MJ 2 Q 16

GEDDIE (JOHN), F.R.G.S. Russian Empire : Historical and Descriptive. 8vo. Lond., 1882. B 12 U 22

GEE (GEORGE E.) Goldsmith's Hand-book ; containing full Instructions for the Alloying and Working of Gold. (Weale.) 2nd ed. 12mo. Lond., 1881. A 17 Q 42

The Hall-Marking of Jewellery practically considered ; comprising an Account of the Assay Towns of the United Kingdom, with the Stamps employed ; also the Laws relating to the Standards and Hall-Marks. 8vo. Lond., 1882. A 9 P 30

Practical Gold-worker ; or, the Goldsmiths' and Jewellers' Instructor in the Art of Alloying, Melting, Reducing, Colouring, Collecting, and Refining. 8vo. Lond., 1877. A 9 P 31

GEE (W. W. HALDANE). Elementary Practical Physics. [*See* STEWART, B.]

GEFFCKEN (PROF. HEINRICH). Church and State ; their relations, historically developed. Translated and edited, by E. F. Taylor. 2 vols. 8vo. Lond., 1877. G 8 T 2, 3

GEGENBAUR (PROF. C.) Grundriss der vergleichenden Anatomie. 8vo. Leipzig, 1874. A 27 U 27

Lehrbuch der Anatomie des Menschen. Roy. 8vo. Leipzig, 1883. A 12 V 12

Morphologisches Jahrbuch. Eine Zeitschrift für Anatomie und Entwickelungsgeschichte. 11 vols. 8vo. Leipzig, 1876–86.

GEIGER (JOHN LEWIS), F.R.G.S. Peep at Mexico : Narrative of a Journey across the Republic. Illustrated. 8vo. Lond., 1874. D 4 Q 35

GEIGER (LAZARUS). Contributions to the History of the Development of the Human Race : Lectures and Dissertations. 8vo. Lond., 1880.   A 1 W 3

GEIGER (LUDWIG). Petrarka. [Francesco Petrarca] 8vo. Leipzig, 1874.   J 17 R 22

GEIGER (DR. WILHELM). Civilization of the Eastern Irānians in Ancient Times ; with an Introduction on the Avesta Religion. 2 vols. 8vo. Lond., 1885–86.
          G 4 Q 20, 21

GEIKIE (PROF. ARCH.), LL.D., &c. Catalogue of Rock Specimens. [*See* RAMSAY, A. C.]

Class-book of Geology. Illustrated. 8vo. Lond., 1886.
          A 9 P 6

Elementary Lessons in Physical Geography. Illustrated. 12mo. Lond., 1880.   A 16 P 20

Geological Sketches at Home and Abroad. Illustrated. 8vo. Lond., 1882.   A 9 R 15

Life of Sir Roderick I. Murchison; with Notices of his Scientific Contemporaries, and a Sketch of the Rise and Growth of Palaezoic Geology in Britain. 2 vols. 8vo. Lond., 1875.   C 7 S 30, 31

Physikalische Geographie. Naturwissenschaftliche Elementarbücher. 12mo. Strasburg, 1876.   A 16 P 31

Text-book of Geology. Illustrated. 8vo. Lond., 1882.
          A 9 R 10
[*See* JUKES, J. B.]

GEIKIE (CUNNINGHAM), D.D. Life : a Book for Young Men. 6th ed. 8vo. Lond., 1876.   G 8 P 5

GEIKIE (JAMES), LL.D., &c. Great Ice Age, and its relation to the Antiquity of Man. 8vo. Lond., 1874.
          A 9 S 32

Outlines of Geology : an Introduction to the Science for Students. Lond., 1886.   A 9 Q 2

Prehistoric Europe : a Geological Sketch. Maps and Illustrations. 8vo. Lond., 1881.   A 10 Q 24

GEIKIE (WALTER), R.S.A. Etchings illustrative of Scottish Character and Scenery. 4to. Edinb., 1885.
          D 8 V 19

GEOFFREY DE VINSAUF. [*See* CHRONICLES OF THE CRUSADES.]

GEISLER (WILHELM). De Literaturae Phoneticae Origine atque Indole. 4to. Berolini, 1858.   K 14 S 3

GELDART (REV. E. M.), B.A. Folk-Lore of Modern Greece: the Tales of the People. 8vo. Lond., 1884.
          B 27 Q 19

Guide to Modern Greek. 8vo. Lond., 1883.   K 11 T 34

Modern Greek Language, in its relation to Ancient Greek. (Clar. Press). 12mo. Oxford, 1870.   K 16 P 44

GELDER (JANE VAN), NÉE TRILL. Storehouses of the King ; or, the Pyramids of Egypt : what they are and who built them. 8vo. Lond., 1885.   B 2 S 9

GELELE (KING OF DAHOMEY). Mission to. [*See* BURTON, SIR R. F.]

GELL (SIR WILLIAM), M.A., &c. Geography and Antiquities of Ithaca. 4to. Lond., 1807.   D 7 V 34

Pompeiana: the Topography, Edifices, and Ornaments of Pompeii; the result of Excavations since 1819. 2 vols. roy. 8vo. Lond., 1837.   A 3 Q 5, 6

Topography of Rome and its Vicinity. New ed., revised and enlarged. With Map. 2 vols. 8vo. Lond., 1846.
          D 11 U 1, 2

Topography of Troy and its Vicinity; illustrated and explained by Drawings and Descriptions. Imp. fol. Lond., 1804.   D 38 Q 5 ‡

GELL (SIR WILLIAM), AND GANDY (JOHN P.) Pompeiana : the Topography, Edifices, and Ornaments of Pompeii. 2 vols. roy. 8vo. Lond., 1824.   A 3 Q 3, 4

Vues des Ruines de Pompéi. Imp. 4to. Paris, 1827.
          A 19 T 5 ‡

GELLIBRAND (J. T.) Proceedings in the Case of His Majesty's Attorney-General, J. T. Gellibrand, Esq. 8vo. Hobart, 1826.   MF 1 Q 4

GELLIUS (AULUS). Noctes Atticæ, ex Editione Jacobi Gronovii, cum Notis et Interpretatione in usum Delphini. 4 vols. 8vo. Lond., 1824.   J 13 P 8–11

GEMELLI-CARERI (GIOVANNI FRANCESCO). Voyage round the World ; by John Francis Gemelli-Careri. In six parts; written in Italian, translated into English. Fol. Lond., 1704.   D 9 V 9

GEMS OF LITERATURE, Elegant Rare, and Suggestive. 8vo. Lond., 1875.   H 7 T 14

GENEALOGIST (THE): Quarterly Magazine of Genealogical, Antiquarian, Topographical and Heraldic Research. Vols. 1–8, and New Series, Vol. 1. 8vo. Lond., 1877–84.   E

GENERAL BIOGRAPHY. [*See* AIKIN, J.]

GENERAL HINTS TO EMIGRANTS. [*See* EMIGRANTS.]

GENERATION OF JUDGES (A); by "Their Reporter." 8vo. Lond., 1886.   C 2 S 20

GENESIS. Genesis in Advance of Present Science: a Critical Investigation of Chapters I–IX; by "A Septuagenarian beneficed Presbyter." 8vo. Lond., 1883.   G 12 Q 29

GENLIS (STÉPHANIE FÉLICITÉ), COMTESSE DE. The Child of Nature: a Drama; from the French of the Marchioness of Sillery, formerly Countess of Genlis. [*See* FARCES. 1.]

Mémoires de. [*See* BARRIÈRE, J. F.]

Mémoires inédits de Madame la Comtesse de Genlis; pour servir à l'Histoire des dix-huitième et dix-neuvième Siècles. 8 vols. (in 4) 8vo. Paris, 1825–26.   C 3 T 23–26

Souvenirs de Félicie. [*See* BARRIÈRE, J. F., 14.]

Tales of the Castle; translated into English by Thomas Holcroft. 8th ed. 5 vols. 8vo. Lond., 1806.   J 8 Q 21–25

GENNADIUS (CONSTANTINOPOLITANUS). Opera omnia. [*See* MIGNE, J. P., SERIES GRÆCA 160.]

GENTIL (J. A.) Magnétisme-Somnambulisme: Manuel élémentaire de l'aspirant Magnétiseur. 2e éd. 12mo. Paris, 1854. A 13 P 51

GENTLEMAN'S MAGAZINE (THE). Vols. 1–258 (34 n.s.) 8vo. Lond., 1731–1885. E

Selection of Curious Articles from the *Gentleman's Magazine.* [*See* WALKER, J.]

GENTLEMAN'S MAGAZINE LIBRARY; edited by George Laurence Gomme, F.S.A. Vols. 1–4. Roy. 8vo. Lond., 1883–85. E

GENTOO LAWS. Code of Gentoo Laws; or, Ordinations of the Pundits; from a Persian Translation, made from the original written in the Shanscrit Language, by N. B. Halhed. 8vo. Lond., 1781. F 6 T 12

GEOFFREY CRAYON. [*See* IRVING, W.]

GEOFFREY, JEFFERY, OR JEFFREY OF MON. MOUTH. British History of; in twelve Books, translated from the Latin by A. Thompson. A new edition, revised and corrected by J. A. Giles, LL.D. 8vo. Lond., 1842. B 5 S 33

British History; translated into English, from the Latin of Jeffrey of Monmouth, by Aaron Thompson. 8vo. Lond., 1718. B 4 R 24

GEOGHEGAN (J.) Some Account of Silk in India, especially of the various attempts to encourage and extend Sericiculture in that country. Sm. fol. Calcutta, 1872. A 2 Q 2‡

GEOGRAPHICAL DICTIONARY. Compendious Geographical Dictionary. 18mo. Lond., 1793. D 11 P 35

GEOGRAPHICAL MAGAZINE [formerly called *Ocean Highways*]; edited by C. R. Markham, C.B., &c. Illustrated, with maps. 5 vols. imp. 8vo. Lond., 1874–78. E

GEOGRAPHICAL SOCIETY OF LONDON. [*See* ROYAL GEOGRAPHICAL SOCIETY.]

GEOGRAPHICAL SOCIETY OF AUSTRALASIA. [*See* ROYAL GEOGRAPHICAL SOCIETY OF AUSTRALASIA.]

GELENIUS (S.) [*See* PLINIUS SECUNDUS, C.]

GEOLOGICAL EXPLORATIONS OF NEW ZEALAND. [*See* NEW ZEALAND.]

GEOLOGICAL MAGAZINE (THE); or, Monthly Journal of Geology. Vols. 1–26, 1864–86. 26 vols. 8vo. Lond., 1864–86. E

GEOLOGICAL MEMOIRS, a Selection of, contained in the *Annales des Mines*; written by Brongniart, Humboldt, von Buch and others; translated by Sir H. T. De la Beche, F.R.S., &c. 8vo. Lond., 1836. A 9 R 16

GEOLOGICAL SOCIETY OF LONDON. Quarterly Journal of the. Vols. 1–40. 8vo. Lond., 1845–85. E

Transactions. 2nd Series. Vol. 6. 4to. Lond., 1841–42. A 9 V 2

GEOLOGICAL SURVEY OF INDIA. [*See* INDIA.]

GEOLOGICAL AND NATURAL HISTORY SURVEY OF CANADA. [*See* CANADA.]

GEOLOGISCHEN REICHSANSTALT. [*See* KAISERLICH-KONIGLICHE.]

GEOLOGISCHEN REICHS-MUSEUMS IN LEIDEN. Sammlungen des, herausgegeben von K. Martin, und A. Wichmann, Professoren in Leiden und Utrecht. Bande 1–3. 3 vols. roy. 8vo. Leiden, 1881–87. M E 9 R

GEORGE II (KING OF ENGLAND). Memoirs of the last Ten Years of the Reign of; by Horace Walpole. 2 vols. roy. 4to. Lond., 1822. C 1 W 9, 10

Memoirs of the Reign of, from his Accession, to the Death of Queen Caroline; by John, Lord Hervey; edited by the Rt. Hon. J. W. Croker. 2 vols. 8vo. Lond., 1848. C 3 V 7, 8

GEORGE III (KING OF ENGLAND). History of the Reign of. [*See* BISSET, R.]

Memoirs of the Court and Cabinets of; by the Duke of Buckingham and Chandos. 2nd ed., revised. 4 vols. 8vo. Lond., 1853–55. C 7 Q 16–19

Memoirs of the Life and Reign of; by J. H. Jesse. 3 vols. 8vo. Lond., 1867. C 7 Q 13–15

Royal Dukes and Princesses of the Family of: a View of Court Life and Manners for Seventy Years, 1760–1830; by Percy Fitzgerald. 2 vols. 8vo. Lond., 1882. C 7 R 7, 8

GEORGE IV (KING OF ENGLAND). Diary illustrative of the Times of, interspersed with original Letters from the late Queen Caroline, and from various other distinguished Persons; by Lady C. Bury; edited by John Galt. 4 vols. 8vo. Lond., 1838. C 6 P 14–17

Life of, including his Letters and Opinions; with a View of the Men, Manners, and Politics of his Reign; by Percy Fitzgerald, M.A., &c. 2 vols. 8vo. Lond., 1881. C 7 Q 22, 23

Memoirs of the Court of, 1820–30; by the Duke of Buckingham and Chandos. 2 vols. 8vo. Lond., 1859. C 6 Q 23, 24

Personal History of; with Anecdotes of distinguished Persons; by the Rev. G. Croly. 2nd ed. 2 vols. 12mo. Lond., 1841. C 1 S 24, 25

GEORGE (ERNEST). Etchings in Belgium; with Descriptive Letterpress. 2nd ed. Fol. Lond., 1883. A 23 S 22 ‡

GEORGE (HENRY). Compendious History of Small-pox; with an Account of a Mode of Treatment. 8vo. Lond. 1852. A 12 S 29

GEORGE (HENRY). Progress and Poverty. 8vo. Lond., 1883. F 6 R 21

Protection or Free Trade. 8vo. Lond., 1886. F 6 R 19

Social Problems. 8vo. Lond., 1884. F 6 R 20

GEORGE (HEREFORD B.), M.A., &c. Genealogical Tables, illustrative of Modern History. 2nd ed., revised and enlarged. (Clar. Press.) 8m. 4to. Oxford, 1875.
　　　K 20 U 1

GEORGE ELIOT. [*See* CROSS, MRS. MARY ANN.]

GEORGE SAND. [*See* DUDEVANT, MME. A. L. A.]

GEORGEL (JEAN FRANÇOIS), L'ABBÉ. Mémoires pour servir a l'Histoire des Evénemens de la Fin du Dix-Huitième Siècle, depuis 1760 jusqu'en 1806–10, par un contemporain impartial. 6 vols. 8vo. Paris, 1817–18. B 8 T 36–41

GEORGE OF WALES (PRINCE). Cruise of H.M.S. *Bacchante*. [*See* ALBERT VICTOR OF WALES, PRINCE.]

GEORGE'S RIVER. Trip up George's River; compiled from the *Illustrated Sydney News*, October 1870. (Pam. Ab.) 12mo. Sydney, 1870.　　　MD 1 S 14

GEORGIAN ERA (THE). Memoirs of the most eminent Persons who have flourished in Great Britain, from the Accession of George I to the Demise of George IV. 4 vols. 8vo. Lond., 1832–34.　　　C 4 S 5–8

GEORGIUS (HAMARTOLUS). Chronicon breve. [*See* MIGNE, J. P., SERIES GRÆCA 110.]

GERALDY (FRANK). Electricity as a Motive Power. [*See* DU MONCEL, VICOMTE T.]

GÉRARD (JULES), "THE LION-KILLER." Life and Adventures of; comprising Ten Years' Campaigns among the Lions of Northern Africa. 12mo. Lond., 1856. C 2 P 19

Lion Hunting and Sporting Life in Algeria. 4th ed. 12mo. Lond., 1857.　　　D 1 T 11

GERARD (JAMES W.) The Peace of Utrecht: a Historical Review of the Great Treaty of 1713–14, and of the Principal Events of the War of the Spanish Succession. 8vo. N. York, 1885.　　　B 7 U 29

GERHARDT (C. J.) Geschichte der Mathematik in Deutschland. (Geschichte der Wissenschaften 17.) 8vo. Munich, 1877.　　　A 17 V 31.

GERHOHUS (VENERABILIS). Opera omnia. [*See* MIGNE, J. P., SERIES LATINA, 193, 194.]

GERICKE (J. F. C.) Javaansch-Nederduitsch Woordenboek, op last en in Dienst van het nederlandsch Bijbelgenootschap. Roy. 8vo. Amsterdam, 1847.　　　K 12 T 26

GERMAN COMPOSERS. [*See* JAGER, PROF. C., *and* RIMBAULT, E. F.]

GERMAN NOBLEMAN, A. [*See* RUSSIA.]

GERMAN POLITICAL LEADERS. [*See* TUTTLE, H.]

GERMAN PRINCE, A. [*See* PÜCKLER-MUSKAU, HERMANN L. H., PRINCE VON.]

GERMANUS (SANCTUS). Opera omnia. [*See* MIGNE, J. P., SERIES GRÆCA, 98.]

GEROLDT (FRITZ). Nine Colonies. 8vo. Lond., 1881.*
　　　MD 2 R 42

GERSTÄECKER (FREDERICK). Gerstäecker's Travels in Rio de Janeiro, Buenos Ayres, Ride through the Pampas, California, the Gold-fields, &c.; translated from the German. 8vo. Lond., 1854.　　　D 3 Q 43

Narrative of a Journey round the World, comprising a Winter-passage across the Andes to Chili, with a Visit to the Gold Regions of California and Australia, the South Sea Islands, Java, &c. 3 vols. 8vo. Lond., 1853.
　　　D 10 R 39–41

The Two Convicts. 8vo. Lond., 1857.　　　MJ 1 U 21

Wanderings and Fortunes of some German Emigrants; translated by David Black. 8vo. Lond., 1848. D 3 Q 17

Wanderungen in Australien und Vandiemensland. [*See* MUNDY, LIEUT.-COL. G. C.]

GERVINUS (PROF. G. G.) Shakespeare Commentaries; translated under the Author's superintendence, by F. E. Bunnètt. New ed., revised. 8vo. Lond., 1877.　J 6 T 17

GESCHICHTE DER WISSENSCHAFTEN. Geschichte der Wissenschaften in Deutschland—neuere Zeit. Auf Veranlassung und mit Unterstützung seiner Majestät des Königs von Bayern, Maximilian II. Herausgegeben durch die historische Commission, bei der königl Academie der Wissenschaften. 21 vols. 8vo. München, 1867–85.
　　　A 17 V 15–35

1. Geschichte des allgemeinen Staatsrechts und der Politik; von J. C. Bluntschli.
2. Geschichte der Mineralogie, von 1650–1860; von Franz von Kobell.
3. Geschichte der Landbau-und Forstwissenschaft; von G. Fraas.
4. Geschichte der Erdkunde; von Oscar Peschel.
5. Geschichte der protestantischen Theologie; von Dr. J. A. Dorner.
6. Geschichte der katholischen Theologie; von Dr. Karl Werner.
7. Geschichte der Aesthetik in Deutschland; von Hermann Lotze.
8. Geschichte der Sprachwissenschaft und orientalischen Philologie in Deutschland seit dem Anfange des 19. Jahrhunderts mit einem Rückblick auf die früheren Zeiten; von Theodor Benfey.
9. Geschichte der germanischen Philologie; von Rudolf von Raumer.
10. Die Entwickelung der Chemie in der neueren Zeit; von H. Kopp.
11. Geschichte der Technologie; von Karl Karmarsch.
12. Geschichte der Zoologie; von J. Victor Carus.
13. Geschichte der deutschen Philosophie, seit Leibnitz; von Dr. Ed. Zeller.
14. Geschichte der National-Oekonomik in Deutschland; von W. Roscher.
15. Geschichte der Botanik, vom 16. Jahrhundert bis 1860; von Dr. Julius Sachs.
16. Geschichte der Astronomie; von Rudolf Wolf.
17. Geschichte der Mathematik in Deutschland; von C. J. Gerhardt.
18. Geschichte der deutschen Rechtswissenschaft; von R. Stintzing. Erste Abtheilung.
19. Geschichte der classischen Philologie in Deutschland, von den Anfängen bis zur Gegenwart; von Conrad Bursian. Erste Hälfte.
20. Geschichte der deutschen Historiographie seit dem Auftreten des Humanismus; von Dr. Franz X. von Wegele.

GESENIUS (Prof. Friedrich Heinrich Wilhelm). Hebrew and English Lexicon of the Old Testament, including the Biblical Chaldee; from the Latin, by Edward Robinson. 2th ed. Roy. 8vo. Boston, 1871.
K 13 R 7

Scripturae Linguaque Phoeniciae Monumenta quot quot supersunt. 4to. Lipsiae, 1837.   K 16 S 6

GESNER (Abraham), M.D., &c. Practical Treatise on Coal, Petroleum, and other Distilled Oils. 8vo. New York, 1861.   A 6 Q 23

GESNER (Johann Matthias). Novus Lingvae et Erditionis Romanae Thesavrvs, post Ro. Stephani, et aliorvm, digestvs, locvpletatvs, emendatvs. 4 vols. (in 2) fol. Lipsiae, 1749.   K 27 Q 11, 12 ‡

GESSERT (Dr. M. A.) On the Art of Painting on Glass, or, Glass-staining; with an Appendix on the Art of Enamelling, &c. (Weale.) 3rd ed. 12mo. Lond., 1857.   A 17 P 31

GESSNER (Solomon). Works of. Translated from the German; with some Account of his Life and Writings. 3 vols. 8vo. Liverpool, 1802.   J 10 R 23–25

GEYER (Erik-Gustave). Histoire de Suède; traduite par J. F. de Lundblad. 8vo. Paris, 1839.   B 2 R 1

GFRŒRER (A.) Spinoza Opera Philosophica. [*See* Spinoza, B. de.]

GHIBERTI (Lorenzo). Ghiberti and Donatello, with other early Italian Sculptors; by "Leader Scott" [Mrs. Lucy E. Baxter]. (Great Artists.) 8vo. Lond., 1882.   C 3 T 32

GIANNONE (Pietro). Civil History of the Kingdom of Naples; translated by Captain James Ogilvie. 2 vols. fol. Lond., 1729–31.   B 14 R 4, 5 ‡

GIBB (E. J. W.), M.R.A.S. Ottoman Poems, translated into English Verse in the Original Forms; with Introduction, Biographical Notices, and Notes. Sq. 8vo. Lond., 1882.   H 5 U 25

GIBBON (Charles). Life of George Combe, Author of "The Constitution of Man"; with Portrait. 2 vols. 8vo. Lond., 1878.   C 6 U 8, 9

GIBBON (Edward). [A Biography]: by J. C. Morison. (Eng. Men of Letts.) 8vo. Lond., 1879.   C 1 U 16

History of the Decline and Fall of the Roman Empire, 8 vols. 8vo. Lond., 1825.   B 11 S 27–34

Another copy; with Notes by the Rev. H. H. Milman, D.D. 12 vols. 8vo. Lond., 1838–39.   B 11 T 1–12

Life and Letters of; with History of the Crusades. Verbatim Report. 8vo. Lond., 1872.   C 2 R 16

Life of Edward Gibbon, Esq.: with Selections from his Correspondence, and Illustrations by the Rev. H. H. Milman. 8vo. Lond., 1839.   C 9 V 20

GIBBON (Edward)—*continued.*

Memoirs of the Life and Writings of Edward Gibbon, composed by himself; with Notes, &c., by John, Lord Sheffield. 2 vols. (in 1) 18mo. Lond., 1827.   C 1 P 12

Miscellaneous Works of; with Memoirs of his Life and Writings, by himself. 5 vols. 8vo. Lond., 1814.
J 8 V 9–13

The Student's Gibbon: History of the Decline and Fall of the Roman Empire. Abridged, incorporating the Researches of recent Commentators, by Wm. Smith, LL.D. 8vo. Lond., 1868.   B 12 P 20

GIBBONS (David). Metropolitan Buildings Act, 7th, and 8th Vic., cap. 84; with Notes and an Index. (Weale.) 12mo. Lond., 1844.   F 1 P 25

On the Law of Contracts. (Weale.) *12mo. Lond., 1857.   F 5 S 22

GIBBONS (Sidney). Lecture on the Microscope. [*See* Melbourne Public Library.]

GIBBONS (William Sydney). Kerosene Oil: What it is; with Causes and Prevention of Accidents in its use; together with upwards of fifty Analyses and Experiments, with Samples sold in Melbourne. (Pam. 38.) 8vo. Melb., 1862.   MJ 2 Q 25

GIBBS (J. W. M.) Fables of La Fontaine; translated, with Notes. [*See* La Fontaine, J. de.]

Works of Oliver Goldsmith, and a Life of the Author. [*See* Goldsmith, O.]

GIBBS, SHALLARD, & CO. Illustrated Guide to Sydney and its Suburbs, and to favorite places of resort in New South Wales: with new Map of Sydney. 4th ed. 12mo. Sydney, 1884.   MD 2 Q 29

Illustrated Sydney News, New South Wales Weather Almanac, for 1882. 8vo. Sydney, 1881.   ME 3 T

New South Wales in 1880. 4to. Sydney, 1880.*   MD 6 P 2 †

GIBLIN (Robert). Church Union Prize Poem: the Conversion of St. Paul. (Pam. A.) Fol. Hobart(n.d.) MJ 2 U 1

GIBLIN (Hon. W.) [*See* Jefferis, Rev. J.]

GIBSON (Charles B.), M.R.I.A. Life among Convicts. 2 vols. 8vo. Lond., 1863.   MF 1 P 1, 2

GIBSON (E.) [*See* Camden, W.]

GIBSON (Frederick William). Matrimonial Causes Act, 1873 (36 Vic. No. 9); to which is added 39 Vic. No. 20, and 44 Vic. No. 31: with the Rules and Regulations concerning the Practice and Procedure thereunder, of the 31st May, 1883. 8vo. Sydney, 1883.*   MF 2 S 38

GIBSON (George Herbert). Old Friends under New Aspects; by "Ironbark." 12mo. Sydney, 1878. MJ 1 P 32

Southerly Busters; by "Ironbark." Illustrated. Sm. 4to. Sydney, 1878.*   MH 1 S 13

GIBSON (J.) Engravings from Original Compositions executed in Marble at Rome by P. Guglialmi. El. fol. Lond., 1861. A 11 P 1 ‡

GIBSON (REV. JOHN). Doctrine of the Reformers of our Church as to Baptism. 8vo. Lond., 1859. MG 1 Q 40

Reply to the Letter of the Rev. Joseph Beazley, published in the *British Standard,* October 3, 1862 ; also, certain Facts relative to the Treatment of the Rev. John Gibson, Campbelltown, by some of the Members of the Committee of the Congregational Home Missionary Society of New South Wales. 8vo. Sydney, 1863. MG 1 Q 29

GIBSON (STANLEY T.), B.D. Religion and Science ; their relations to each other at the Present Day. 8vo. Lond., 1875. G 4 Q 28

GIBSON (WILLIAM SIDNEY), F.S.A., &c. History of the Monastery founded at Tynemouth, in the Diocese of Durham, to the Honor of God, under the Invocation of the Blessed Virgin Mary and S. Oswin, King and Martyr. 2 vols. 4to. Lond., 1846-47. B 10 S 6, 7 †

GIDDINS (GEORGE H.) Edwin Paxton Hood, Poet and Preacher: a Memorial. 12mo. Lond., 1886. C 2 Q 20

GIESELER (J. C. L.) Text-book of Ecclesiastical History. 3 vols. 8vo. Philad., 1836. G 9 S 8-10

GIFFARD (EDWARD). Deeds of Naval Daring ; or, Anecdotes of the British Navy. New ed. 12mo. Lond., 1877. B 23 P 2

GIFFEN (ROBERT). Essays in Finance. 8vo. Lond., 1880. F 8 P 8, 9

Essays in Finance. 2nd series. 8vo. Lond., 1880. F 8 P 9

GIFFORD (C. H.) History of the Wars occasioned by the French Revolution, from the Commencement of Hostilities in 1792, to the end of the year 1816. 2 vols. 4to. Lond., 1817. B 2 U 1, 2

GIFFORD (WILLIAM). The Baviad and Mæviad. 8vo. Lond., 1811. H 7 P 32

Dramatic Works of John Ford; with Notes. [*See* FORD, J.]

Dramatic Works of James Shirley; with Notes. [*See* SHIRLEY, J.]

Memoir of ; written by himself. 12mo. Lond., 1827. C 1 P 10

Plays of P. Massinger; with Notes, Critical and Explanatory. [*See* MASSINGER, P.]

Satires of Juvenal. [*See* JUVENALIS, D. J.]

Works of Ben Jonson; with Notes and a Biographical Memoir. [*See* JONSON, B.]

[*See* BRITISH POETS, 4.]

GIGLIOLI (DR. E. H.) I Tasmaniani cenni Storici ed Etnologici di un Popolo Estinto. Con 20 Incisioni e una Carta Geografica. 8vo. Milano, 1874. MA 1 S 18

2 F

GILBART (JAMES WILLIAM), F.R.S. History, Principles, and Practice of Banking. New ed., revised to the present date by A. S. Michie. 2 vols. 8vo. Lond., 1882. F 6 Q 30, 31

Practical Treatise on Banking. 8vo. Lond.,1836. F 8 P 10

GILBERT (DAVIES), M.A., &c. Collections and Translations respecting St. Neot, and the former state of his Church in Cornwall. 4to. Lond., 1830. B 15 R 3 ‡

GILBERT (JOHN THOMAS), F.S.A., &c. History of the City of Dublin. 3 vols. 8vo. Dublin, 1857-59. B 11 Q 21-23

History of the Irish Confederation and War in Ireland, 1641-44. 3 vols. 4to. Dublin, 1882-85. B 29 V 12-14

History of the Viceroys of Ireland; with Notices of the Castle of Dublin and its Chief Occupants in former times. 8vo. Lond., 1865. B 11 P 39

GILBERT (JOSIAH). Landscape in Art before Claude and Salvator. 8vo. Lond., 1885. A 8 Q 15

GILBERT (JOSIAH), AND CHURCHILL (G. C.), F.G.S. Dolomite Mountains: Excursions through Tyrol, Carinthia, Carniola, and Friuli, 1861-63. 8vo. Lond., 1864. D 8 R 41

GILBERT (CAPT. THOMAS), R.N. Voyage from New South Wales to Canton, in 1788; with Views of the Islands discovered. 4to. Lond., 1789.* MD 6 P 9 †

GILBERT (REV. THOMAS). New Zealand Settlers and Soldiers; or, the War in Taranaki; being Incidents in the Life of a Settler. 8vo. Lond., 1861.* MB 1 Q 7

GILBERT (WILLIAM). The Goldsworthy Family ; or, the Country Attorney. 2 vols. 8vo. Lond., 1864. J 11 R 13, 14

Shirley Hall Asylum; or, the Memoirs of a Monomaniac. 8vo. Lond., 1863. J 4 P 25

GILCHRIST (ALEXANDER). Life of William Blake; with Selections from his Poems and other Writings. New ed., illustrated. 2 vols. 8vo. Lond., 1880. C 10 P 7, 8

Life of William Etty, R.A. 2 vols. 8vo. Lond., 1855. C 3 S 32, 33

GILDER (WILLIAM HENRY). Schwatka's Search.: Sledging in the Arctic in quest of the Franklin Records; with Maps and Illustrations. 8vo. Lond., 1882. D 4 R 41

GILDERSLEEVE (PROF. BASIL LANNEAU). Pindar: the Olympian and Pythian Odes. [*See* PINDAR.]

GILES (ERNEST). Geographic Travels in Central Australia, 1872-74. 8vo. Melb., 1875. MD 1 U 14

GILES (HERBERT ALLEN). Chinese Sketches. 8vo. Lond., 1876. D 6 R 35

Gems of Chinese Literature. 8vo. Lond.,1884. J 11 Q 3

Glossary of Reference on Subjects connected with the Far East. 2nd ed. 8vo. Hongkong, 1886. K 15 P 5

Historic China, and other Sketches. 8vo. Lond., 1882. B 2 P 24

GILES (JOHN). Sciences of the Bible: a Series. No. 1: The Divine History of Creation. 12mo. Sydney, 1876.
MG 1 Q 13

GILES (REV. JOHN ALLEN), D.C.L. Hebrew and Christian Records: an Historical Enquiry concerning the Age and Authorship of the Old and New Testaments. 2 vols. 8vo. Lond., 1877.
G 15 R 15, 16

History of the Ancient Britons, from the earliest period to the Invasion of the Saxons. 2nd ed. 2 vols. 8vo. Oxford, 1854.
B 5 S 18, 19

Life and Times of Alfred the Great. 8vo. Lond., 1848.
C 1 V 12

[*See* BEDE VEN.; GEOFFREY OF MONMOUTH; PARIS, MATTHEW; ROGER OF WENDOVER; SIX OLD ENGLISH CHRONICLES; *and* WILLIAM OF MALMESBURY.]

GILFILLAN (REV. GEORGE). Gallery of Literary Portraits. 8vo. Edinb., 1845.
C 3 T 9

Poetical Works of William Shenstone; with Life. [*See* SHENSTONE, W.]

GILL (C. HAUGHTON). On the Manufacture and Refining of Sugar. (Cantor Lectures.) Roy. 8vo. Lond., 1872.
A 15 U 21

Sugar-refining. (Brit. Manuf. Indust.) 12mo. Lond., 1876.
A 17 S 32

GILL (GEORGE). Gill's School Series: the Geography and History of the British Colonies; compiled from the best Sources and most recent Statistics. 8vo. Liverpool, 1879.
MD 3 Q 48

GILL (S. T.) Australian Sketch-book; by S. T. G. Ob. 4to. Melb. (n.d.)
MA 1 Q 4 ‡

Victoria Illustrated. Ob. 8vo. Melb., 1856–57. MD 4 P 24 †

GILL (THOMAS). Bibliography of South Australia. 8vo. Adelaide, 1886.
MK 1 R 45

GILL (CAPT. WILLIAM), R.E. River of Golden Sand: the Narrative of a Journey through China and Eastern Thibet to Burmah. Illustrated. 2 vols. 8vo. Lond., 1880.
D 4 U 5, 6

GILL (REV. WILLIAM). Gems from the Coral Islands. Eastern Polynesia. 8vo. Lond., 1856.
MD 5 P 11

Gems from the Coral Islands; or, Incidents of Contrast between Savage and Christian Life in the South Sea Islanders. 8vo. Lond., 1855.
MD 5 P 10

Another copy. 3rd thousand. 2 vols. 12mo. Lond., 1856.
MD 5 P 12, 13

GILL (REV. WILLIAM), VICAR OF MALEW. English and Manx Dictionary. [*See* KELLY, Rev. J.]

GILL (REV. WILLIAM WYATT), B.A. Historical Sketches of Savage Life in Polynesia; with Illustrative Clan Songs. 8vo. Wellington, 1880.
MB 1 Q 29

Jottings from the Pacific. 8vo. Lond., 1885.   MD 5 P 15

GILL (REV. WILLIAM WYATT), B.A.—*continued.*

Life in the Southern Isles; or, Scenes and Incidents in the South Pacific and New Guinea. 8vo. Lond., 1876.
MD 5 P 14

Myths and Songs from the South Pacific; with a Preface, by Prof. F. Max Müller, M.A. 8vo. Lond., 1876.*
MB 1 Q 27

Work and Adventure in New Guinea. [*See* CHALMERS, J.]

GILLESPIE (PROF. WILLIAM MITCHELL), LL.D., &c. Manual of the Principles and Practice of Road-making. 10th ed. 8vo. New York, 1874.
A 6 S 13

Treatise on Land-Surveying; comprising the Theory developed from five Elementary Principles; and the Practice with the Chain alone, the Compass, the Transit, the Theodolite, the Plane Table, &c. Illustrated. 8th ed. 8vo. New York, 1883.
A 6 S 24

Treatise on Levelling, Topography, and Higher Surveying. 8vo. New York, 1874.
A 6 S 24

GILLIAM (ALBERT M.) Travels over the Table Lands and Cordilleras of Mexico, 1843–44. 8vo. Philad., 1846.
D 4 Q 33

GILLIES (JOHN). Aristotle's Ethics and Politics. [*See* ARISTOTELES.]

History of Ancient Greece, its Colonies and Conquests. 3 vols. 8vo. Lond., 1801.
B 9 S 35–37

GILLIES (JAMES B.) Edinburgh Past and Present. Roy. 8vo. Edinb., 1886.
D 8 U 34

GILLIES (ROBERT PEARCE). Memoirs of a Literary Veteran, 1794–1849. 3 vols. 8vo. Lond., 1851.   C 3 V 19–21

Tales of a Voyage to the Arctic Ocean. 2nd series. 3 vols. 12mo. Lond., 1829.
J 4 P 2–4

GILMAN (ARTHUR), M.A. History of the American People. Illustrated. 8vo. Glasgow, 1883.
B 1 Q 52

Rome, from the Earliest Times to the end of the Republic. 8vo. Lond., 1886.
B 12 Q 27

GILLMAN (JAMES). Life of Samuel Taylor Coleridge. Vol. 1 (*all published.*) 8vo. Lond., 1838.
C 8 U 17

GILLMORE (COL. QUINCY ADAMS), A.M., Ph.D., &c. Practical Treatise on Roads, Streets, and Pavements. 8vo. New York, 1876.
A 6 R 25

GILLRAY (JAMES). Historical and Descriptive Account of the Caricatures of James Gillray; by Thomas Wright, Esq., F.S.A., and R. H. Evans, Esq. 8vo. Lond., 1851.
A 7 S 4

Works of, from the original Plates; with the addition of many subjects not before collected. 2 vols. el. fol. Lond., 1851.
A 10 P 9, 10 ‡

GILLY (WILLIAM O. S.) Narratives of Shipwrecks of the Royal Navy between 1793 and 1849. 8vo. Lond., 1850.	B 3 R 24

Another copy, 1793–1857. 3rd ed., revised. 12mo. Lond., 1857.	B 3 R 25

[*See* BARING-GOULD, S.]

GILMORE (PARKER). The Hunters' Arcadia. Illustrated. 8vo. Lond., 1886.	D 1 P 23

GILPIN (REV. WILLIAM), M.A. An Essay on Prints. 5th ed. 8vo. Lond., 1802.	A 7 T 25

Observations on several Parts of England, particularly the Mountains and Lakes of Cumberland and Westmoreland; made in the year 1772. 3rd ed. 2 vols. 8vo. Lond., 1808.	D 6 U 6, 7

Observations on several Parts of Great Britain, particularly the Highlands of Scotland; made in the year 1776. 3rd ed. 2 vols. 8vo. Lond., 1808.	D 6 U 4, 5

Observations on several Parts of the Counties of Cambridge, Norfolk, Suffolk, and Essex; also on several Parts of North Wales. In two Tours, the former made in the year 1769, the latter in the year 1773. 8vo. Lond., 1809.	D 6 U 10

Observations on the Coasts of Hampshire, Sussex, and Kent; made in the Summer of the year 1774. 8vo. Lond., 1804.	D 6 U 2

Observations on the River Wye, and several Parts of South Wales, &c.; made in the Summer of the year 1770. 8vo. Lond., 1800.	D 6 U 1

Observations on the Western Parts of England; to which are added a few Remarks on the Isle of Wight. 2nd ed. 8vo. Lond., 1808.	D 6 U 3

Remarks on Forest Scenery and other Woodland Views. Illustrated. In three Books. 3rd ed. 8vo. Lond., 1808.	D 6 U 8, 9

Three Essays: on Picturesque Beauty; on Picturesque Travel; and on Sketching Landscape; with a Poem on Landscape Painting. 3rd ed. 8vo. Lond., 1808.	A 7 T 26

GINDELY (PROF. ANTON). History of the Thirty Years' War. Translated by Andrew Ten Brook. Illustrated. 2 vols. 8vo. Lond., 1885.	B 9 Q 39, 40

GIOBERTI (VINCENZO). Opere di. 14 vols. 8vo. Losanna, 1845–51.	J 16 S 6–19

1–3. Del Primato Morale e Civile degli Italiana
4–6. Infroduzione allo Studio della Filosofia.
7. Del Bello e del Buono; due Trattati.
8–12. Il Gesuita Moderno.
13–14. Del Rinnovamento Civile d'Italia.

Oprette Politiche. 2 vols. 8vo. Capolago, 1851.	G 14 P 51

Tesrica del Sovranaturale. 2 vols. 8vo. Capolago, 1850.	G 16 R 41, 42

GIOTTO (ANGIOLOTTO BONDONE), *called* GIOTTO; by Harry Quilter, M.A. (Great Artists.) 8vo. Lond., 1881. C 3 T 31

Giotto; by Harry Quilter. 4to. Lond., 1880.	C 4 W 9

Giotto and his Works. [*See* RUSKIN, T.]

GIOVANNI DA FIESOLE (GUIDO, OR GUIDOLINO SANTI FOSINI); *called* FRA ANGELICO. Fra Angelico (Great Artists); by Catherine M. Phillimore. 8vo. Lond., 1881.	C 3 T 41

GIPPS (SIR GEORGE). Copy of a Despatch from Governor Sir George Gipps, relative to the Introduction of Emigrants upon Bounty into New South Wales. (Parl. Docs. 29.) Fol. Lond., 1841.	M F 4 ‡

Copy of a Despatch from Sir George Gipps, Governor of New South Wales, to the Secretary of State for the Colonies, transmitting a Report of the Progressive Discovery and Occupation of that Colony during the period of his Administration of the Government. (Parl. Docs. 29.) Fol. Lond., 1841.	M F 4 ‡

Copy of Despatches from Sir George Gipps, of September or October, 1840, enclosing Resolutions of the Legislative Council of New South Wales. (Parl. Docs. 29.) Fol. Lond., 1841.	M F 4 ‡

Speech in Council, on Thursday, 9th July, 1840, on the second reading of the Bill for appointing Commissioners to enquire into Claims to Grants of Land in New Zealand. 8vo. Sydney, 1840.	MF 3 P 3

Speech in Council, on the Resolutions proposed by the Colonial Secretary in approval of the Report of the Committee on Immigration. 8vo. Sydney, 1842.	MF 2 Q 8

[*See* BLAND, W.; *and* LANG, REV. J. D.]

GIPPS (F. B.), AND CAMPBELL (W.) Description of Wattle Flat Gold-field, Western District, New South Wales. 8vo. Sydney, 1873.*	MD 3 S 40

GIRALDI (LILIO GREGORIO). Lilii Gregorii Gyraldi, Ferrariensis, Opera omnia. 2 vols. (in 1) Fol. Lug. Bat., 1696.	J 39 R 1 ‡

GIRALDUS CAMBRENSIS. [*See* BARRI, W. DE.]

GIRARD (CHARLES). Herpetology. (U.S. Exploring Expedition.) Imp. 4to. Philad., 1858.	A 3 Q 1 ‡
Atlas [to the above.] Fol. Philad., 1858.	A 31 R 4 ‡

GIRAUD (A. A.) Sugar Cane: its Culture and Manufacture; specially adapted to Queensland. 8vo. Brisbane, 1883.	MA 1 P 10

GIRAULT DE SAINT FARGEAU (P. A. EUSÈBE). Les Beautés de la France; gravées par J. Skelton et — D'Oherti; avec un Texte historique et archéologique. Imp. 8vo. Paris, 1850.	D 6 V 3

GIRDLESTONE (REV. CHARLES), M.A. New Testament of our Lord and Saviour Jesus Christ; with a Commentary, &c. 2 vols. 8vo. Lond., 1835–38. G 15 K 9, 10

GIRDLESTONE (T. M.), F.R.C.S., &c. Under the Floor: a Lecture delivered for the Australian Health Society, at the Atnenæum, September 6, 1876. 8vo. Melb., 1877.   MJ 2 R 15

GIRL LIFE IN AUSTRALIA: a Description of Colonial Life; by "A Resident." 8vo. Liverpool, 1876. MJ 1 R 36

GIRONIERE (P. P. DE LA). [*See* LA GIRONIERE, P. P. DE.]

GIRTIN (T.) [*See* TURNER, J. M. W.]

GISBORNE (THOMAS), M.A. Enquiry into the Duties of Men in the Higher and Middle Classes of Society in Great Britain. 4th ed. 2 vols. 8vo. Lond., 1797. G 15 R 5, 6
Enquiry into the Duties of the Female Sex. 4th ed. 8vo. Lond., 1799.   G 15 R 7
Familiar Survey of the Christian Religion. 8vo. Lond., 1799.   G 4 Q 9

GISBORNE (WILLIAM). New Zealand Rulers and Statesmen, 1840–85. With numerous Portraits. 8vo. Lond., 1886.   MC 1 Q 10
Official Hand-book of New Zealand; Edited by Sir Francis Dillon-Bell, K.C.M.G. Parts 1, 2. 8vo. Lond., 1883.   MD 7 Q 22

GIULIANI (GIAMBATTISTA). La Vita Nuova e il Canzoniere di Dante Allighieri. Commentati da G.-B. Giuliani. 18mo. Florence, 1863.   C 1 P 29

GIUSTI [GIUSEPPE). Translations from the Italian Poets. [*See* FENZI, S.]

GIUSTINIAN (SEBASTIAN). Four Years at the Court of Henry VIII: Selection of Despatches addressed to the Signory of Venice; translated by R. Brown. 2 vols. 8vo. Lond., 1854.   B 4 Q 9, 10

GLADESVILLE HOSPITAL. [*See* NEW SOUTH WALES.]

GLADSTONE (JOHN HALL), PH.D., F.R.S. Michael Faraday. With Portrait. 3rd ed. 8vo. Lond., 1874. C 3 Q 20

GLADSTONE (RT. HON. WILLIAM EWART), D.C.L. Bulgarian Horrors and the Question of the East. 8vo. Lond., 1876.   F 12 Q 1
"Ecce Homo." (*Review of.*) 12mo. Lond., 1868. G 10 Q 23
Gleanings of Past Years, 1843–79. 7 vols. (in 4) 12mo. Lond., 1879.   J 12 S 20–23
Homeric Synchronism: an Enquiry into the Time and Place of Homer. 8vo. Lond., 1876.   B 27 Q 21
Inaugural Address, delivered before the University of Edinburgh, April 16th, 1860. 8vo. Lond., 1860. J 12 U 26
Juventus Mundi; the Gods and Men of the Heroic Age. 8vo. Lond., 1869.   B 27 Q 20
Lessons in Massacre: or, the Conduct of the Turkish Government in and about Bulgaria, since May 1876; chiefly from the papers presented by command. 8vo. Lond., 1877.   F 12 Q 2

GLADSTONE (RT. HON. WILLIAM EWART), D.C.L.—*contd.*
Life of; by George Barnett Smith. 2 vols. 8vo. Lond., 1879.   C 7 R 10, 11
New Gleanings from Gladstone. [*See* STRONACH, G.]
Remarks upon recent Commercial Legislation. (Pam. 15.) 8vo. Lond., 1849.   MJ 2 Q 5
The Roman State. [*See* FARINI, L. G.]
Rome and the Newest Fashions in Religion: Three Tracts. 8vo. Lond., 1875.   G 4 Q 6
The Rt. Hon. William Ewart Gladstone, from Judy's point of view, as shewn in her Cartoons during the last ten years. 4to. Lond., 1878.   J 1 Q 14 †
The State in its relations with the Church. 3rd ed. 8vo. Lond., 1839.   G 4 Q 4
Studies on Homer and the Homeric Age. 3 vols. 8vo. Oxford, 1858.   J 15 S 24–26
Vatican Decrees in their bearing on Civil Allegiance. 8vo. Lond., 1874.   G 4 Q 5
Vaticanism: an Answer to Replies and Reproofs. Australian edition. 8vo. Melb., 1875.   MG 1 Q 39
William Ewart Gladstone, Prime Minister of England: a Political and Literary Biography; by G. R. Emerson. 8vo. Lond., 1882.   C 7 R 12
[*See* NEWMAN, CARDINAL; THERRY, SIR R.; *and* WAGHORN, LIEUT. T.]

GLAISHER (JAMES), F.R.S. Travels in the Air; by James Glaisher, F.R.S., Camille Flammarion, W. de Fonvielle, and Gaston Tissandier. Roy. 8vo. Lond., 1871.   D 9 U 29
Philosophical Instruments and Processes as represented in the Great Exhibition. [*See* LOND. INTERNAT. EXHIB., 1851.]

GLAISHER (J. W. L.), M.A., &c. On a Class of Identical Relations in the Theory of Elliptic Functions. (Roy. Soc. Pubs. 1.) 4to. Lond., 1876.   A 11 P 2 †

GLANVIL, OR GLANVILLA (BARTHOLOMEW). Liber de Proprietatibus Rerum. (In English.) Sm. fol. (n.p., n.d.)   A 15 U 5

GLANVIL (REV. JOSEPH), F.R.S. Sadducismus Triumphatus; or, a full and plain Evidence concerning Witches and Apparitions. 4th ed. 8vo. Lond., 1726. G 2 P 9

GLAPTHORNE (HENRY). Albertus Wallenstein: a Tragedy. 8vo. Lond., 1824.   H 1 R 14
Another copy. 8vo. Lond., 1824.   H 1 R 15
Lady's Privilege: a Comedy. 8vo. Lond., 1825. H 1 R 14
Another copy. 8vo. Lond., 1825.   H 1 R 15
Plays and Poems of; now first collected, with illustrative Notes and a Memoir of the Author. 2 vols. 8vo. Lond., 1874.   H 4 R 1, 2

GLAS (GEORGE). History of the Discovery and Conquest of the Canary Islands. 4to. Lond., 1764.   B 14 Q 5 †

GLASCOCK (W. N.) Naval Sketch-Book; or, the Service Afloat and Ashore; by "An Officer of Rank." [1st and] 2nd series. 4 vols. 8vo. Lond., 1826–34.   J 9 Q 25–28

GLASER (Louis). Album of New Zealand Views. 8vo. Leipsic, 1887.   MD 3 Q 42

GLASGOW (David). Watch and Clock Making. With sixty-nine Diagrams. 12mo. Lond., 1885.   A 11 P 4

GLASGOW EXHIBITION, 1880–81. Glasgow Naval and Marine Engineering Exhibition, 1880–81: Lectures on Naval Architecture and Engineering; with Catalogue of the Exhibition. 8vo. Lond., 1881.   A 2 Q 14

GLASGOW UNIVERSITY.   Inaugural Addresses by Lords Rectors. [See HAY, J. B.]

GLASS (Salomon). Philologiæ Sacræ, qua totius Sacro Sanctæ Veteris & Novi Testamenti Scripturæ. 4to. Amstelaedami, 1711.   K 18 S 1

GLAUBER (John Rudolph). Works of; containing Choice Secrets in Medicine and Alchymy, &c; translated by Christopher Packe. Fol. Lond., 1689.   A 23 R 29 ‡

GLAZEBROOK (R. T.), M.A., &c. Physical Optics. 8vo. Lond., 1883.   A 17 S 27

GLEANER (The) for August 11, 1827. Fol. Sydney, 1827.   ME

GLEDHILL (Joseph), F.R.A.S. Hand-book of Double Stars. [See CROSSLEY, E.]

GLEHN (M. E. von). Goethe and Mendelssohn (1821–31). [See MENDELSSOHN-BARTHOLDY, DR. C.]
[See HILLER, DR. F.]

GLEIG (Lieut.-Col. C. E. S.) The Old Colonel and the Old Corps; with a View of Military Estates. 8vo. Lond., 1871.   F 14 Q 14

GLEIG (Rev. George Robert), M.A., &c. A Country Curate's Autobiography; or, Passages of a Life without a Living. 2 vols. 8vo. Lond., 1836.   J 5 Q 5, 6

Campaigns of the British Army at Washington and New Orleans, 1814–15. 8vo. Lond., 1847.   B 18 P 1

Another copy. (H. and C. Lib.) New ed. 12mo. Lond., 1847.   J 8 P 25

Family History of England. 3 vols. 12mo. Lond., 1836.   B 3 Q 12–14

Germany, Bohemia, and Hungary visited in 1837. 3 vols. 8vo. Lond., 1839.   D 8 R 27–29

History of the British Empire in India. 4 vols. 18mo. Lond., 1830.   B 10 Q 11–14

GLEIG (Rev. George Robert), M.A., &c.—*continued.*
Life of Major-General Sir Thomas Munro, Bart. and K.C.B. New ed. 2 vols. 8vo. Lond., 1831.   C 8 Q 46, 47

Another copy. New ed., revised and condensed from the larger Biography. (H. and C. Lib.) 12mo. Lond., 1849.   J 8 P 35

Life of Robert, First Lord Clive. 12mo. Lond., 1848.   C 1 T 33

Another copy. (H. and C. Lib.) 12mo. Lond., 1848.   J 8 P 29

Life of the Duke of Wellington. [See BRIALMONT, A. H.]

Lives of the Most Eminent British Military Commanders. (Lard. Cab. Cyclo.) 3 vols. 18mo. Lond., 1831–32.   K 1 S 7–9

Memoirs of the Life of the Rt. Hon. Warren Hastings, compiled from original Papers. 3 vols. 8vo. Lond., 1841.   C 7 R 24–26

Sale's Brigade in Afghanistan; with an Account of the Seizure and Defence of Jellalabad. 12mo. Lond., 1846.   D 1 T 12

Another copy. (H. and C. Lib.)   J 8 P 17

Story of the Battle of Waterloo. (H. and C. Lib.) 2nd ed. 12mo. Lond., 1847.   J 8 P 23

GLENGALL (Richard Butler), Second Earl of. The Irish Tutor; or, New Lights: a Comic Piece. (Cumberland's Eng. Theatre.) 12mo. Lond., 1829.   H 2 Q 16

GLENNIE (John S. Stuart-), M.A. Arthurian Localities; their Historical Origin, Chief Country, and Fingalian Relations; with a Map of Arthurian Scotland. 8vo. Edinb., 1869.   B 13 R 8

Pilgrim-Memories; or, Travel and Discussion in the Birth-Countries of Christianity with the late Henry Thomas Buckle. 2nd ed. 8vo. Lond., 1876.   G 14 P 9

GLENNY (George). Hand-book of Practical Gardening. 8vo. Lond. (n.d.)   A 1 Q 6

Hand-book to the Flower Gardenand Greenhouse. 8vo. Lond., 1851.   A 1 Q 7

Hand-book to the Fruit and Vegetable Garden. 8vo. Lond., 1850.   A 1 Q 5

GLENNY (George M. F.) Kitchen Gardening made Easy; showing how to prepare and lay out the ground; the best means of cultivating every known Vegetable and Herb; with cultural Directions for the Management of them all the year round. (Weale.) 12mo. Lond.,1879. A 17 Q 41

GLIDDON (George R.) Types of Mankind. [See NOTT, J. C.]

GLOUCESTER (William Henry), Duke of. [See WILLIAM HENRY, PRINCE.]

GLOVER (Rev. F. R. A.), M.A. England, the Remnant of Judah, and the Israel of Ephraim; the Two Families under One Head: a Hebrew Episode in British History 8vo. Lond., 1881.   B 3 T 3

GLOVER (RICHARD). Boadicea: a Tragedy. (Bell's Brit. Theatre.) 18mo. Lond., 1791.   H 2 P 33

Another copy. [*See* BRIT. DRAMA, 2.]

Life and Poems of. [*See* CHALMERS, A.]

Medea: a Tragedy. (Bell's Brit. Theatre.) 18mo. Lond., 1792.   H 2 P 10

Another copy. (New Eng. Theatre.) 12mo. Lond., 1787.   H 4 P 27

GLUCK (CHRISTOPH WILLIBALD). Letters of. [*See* WALLACE, LADY.]

GLYCAS (MICHAEL). Opera omnia. [*See* BYZANTINÆ HIST. SCRIPT., *and* MIGNE, J. P., SERIES GRÆCA 158.]

GLYNN (JOSEPH), F.R.S. On the Construction of Cranes and other Hoisting Machinery. (Weale.) 12mo. Lond., 1867.   A 17 P 35

Treatise on the Power of Water. (Weale.) 12mo. Lond., 1872.   A 17 P 2

GMELIN (JOHANN GEORG). Flora Sibirica, sive Historia Plantarum Sibiriae. Continens Tabulas Aeri incisas ccxcviii. Editore D. Samuel Gottlieb Gmelin. 4 vols. 4to. Petropolis, 1747-69.   A 5 Q 10-13

GMELIN (JOHN FREDERICK). The Animal Kingdom. [*See* LINNÆUS, C. VON.]

GNEIST (DR. RUDOLPH). The English Parliament in its Transformations through a Thousand Years; translated by R. J. Shee. 8vo. Lond., 1886.   F 8 P 4

History of the English Constitution; translated by P. A. Ashworth. 2 vols. 8vo. Lond., 1886.   B 3 T 13, 14

GOBIEN (C. LE). [*See* LE GOBIEN, C.]

GODDARD (CHEV. AUSTIN P.) History of Italy, and Life of Guicciardini. [*See* GUICCIARDINI, F.]

GODEFFROY MUSEUM. Die ethnographisch-anthropologische; Abtheilung des Museum Godeffroy in Hamburg. 8vo. Hamburg, 1881.   MA 1 S 10

Journal des Museum Godeffroy. Geographische, ethnographische, und naturwissenschaftliche Mittheilungen. 2 vols. 4to. Hamburg, 1873-75.   MA 3 Q 3, 4 †

Süd-See Typen; Anthropologisches Album des Museum Godeffroy in Hamburg. 4to. Hamburg, 1881. MA 2 Q 3†

GODEFRIDUS (ABBAS ADMONTENSIS). Opera omnia. [*See* MIGNE, J. P., SERIES LATINA 174.]

GODEFROI DE BUILLON (ROI DE JÉRUSALEM). Epistolæ et Diplomata. [*See* MIGNE, J. P., SERIES LATINA, 155.]

GODIN DES ODONAIS (JEAN). Account of the Adventures of Mde. Godin des Odonais, in passing down the River of the Amazons, 1770. [*See* PERILS AND CAPTIVITY.]

GODINHO DE EREDIA (MANUEL). Malaca, l'Inde Méridionale, et le Cathay. Roy. 4to. Bruxelles, 1882   D 5 V 11 †

GODLEY (JOHN ROBERT). Letters from America. 2 vols. 8vo. Lond., 1844.   D 3 R 14, 15

Selection from the Writings and Speeches of. 8vo. Christchurch, 1863.   MF 2 Q 28

GODRON (D. A.) De l'Espèce, et des races dans les êtres organisés, et spécialement de l'unité de l'Espèce humaine. 2 vols. 8vo. Paris, 1859.   A 1 W 9, 10

GODWIN (REV. BENJAMIN). Godwin's Emigrant's Guide to Van Diemen's Land, more properly called Tasmania. 8vo. Lond., 1823.*   MD 4 U 6

Substance of a Course of Lectures on British Colonial Slavery. 8vo. Lond., 1830.   F 7 Q 2

GODWIN (FRANCIS), BISHOP OF LLANDAFF AND HEREFORD. De Praesulibus Angliæ Commentarius omnium Episcoporum necnon Cardinalium ejusdem gentis nomina tempora seriem. Fol. Cantab., 1743.   G 35 Q 16 ‡

GODWIN (GEORGE), F.R.S. Facts and Fancies: a Collection of Tales and Sketches. 8vo. Lond., 1844. J 4 Q 3

Letter on the State of Architecture in the Provinces. 8vo. Lond., 1837.   A 7 Q 13

On the Obelisk from Luxor recently elevated in Paris. 8vo. Lond., 1836.   A 7 Q 13

GODWIN (PROF. JOHN). [*See* CÆSAR, C. J.]

GODWIN (PARKE). Biography of William Cullen Bryant; with Extracts from his Private Correspondence. 2 vols. 8vo. New York, 1883.   C 10 P 15, 16

GODWIN (THOMAS), D.D. Moses and Aaron: Civil and Ecclesiastical Rites used by the Ancient Hebrews. 11th ed. Sm. 4to. Lond., 1678.   B 10 P 37

Romanæ Historiæ Anthologia recognita et aucta: an English Exposition of the Roman Antiquities. 14th ed. Sm. 4to. Lond., 1685.   B 12 Q 20

GODWIN (WILLIAM). An Enquiry concerning Political Justice and its Influence on General Virtue and Happiness. 2 vols. 4to. Lond., 1793.   F 8 Q 4, 5 †

His Friends and Contemporaries; by C. Kegan Paul. 2 vols. 8vo. Lond., 1876.   C 3 V 9, 10

History of the Commonwealth of England, from its commencement to the Restoration of Charles II. 4 vols. 8vo. Lond., 1824-28.   B 3 S 19-22

Life of Geoffrey Chaucer, the Early English Poet; including Memoirs of his Friend and Kinsman John of Gaunt, Duke of Lancaster. 2nd ed. 4 vols. 8vo. Lond., 1804.   C 10 S 43-46

Thoughts on Man; his Nature, Productions, and Discoveries. 8vo. Lond. 1831.   G 8 T 4

GOETHE (JOHANN WOLFGANG VON). Autobiography of Goethe. Truth and Poetry, from my own Life; translated from the German, by John Oxenford. Also, Letters from Switzerland, and Travels in Italy; translated by the Rev. A. W. Morrison, M.A. 2 vols. 8vo. Lond., 1872–74. C 1 S 27, 28

Characteristics of; from the German of Falk, Von Müller, and others; translated, with original Notes, by Mrs. Sarah Austin. 3 vols. 8vo. Lond., 1833. C 4 Q 12–14

Conversations with Eckermann and Soret; translated from the German, by John Oxenford. 2 vols. 8vo. Lond., 1850. C 11 P 14, 15

Correspondence between Schiller and Goethe, from 1794–1805; translated from the 3rd ed. of the German, with Notes, by L. Dora Schmitz. 2 vols. 8vo. Lond., 1877–79. C 4 P 34, 35

Dramatic Works of; comprising Faust, Iphigenia in Tauris, Torquato Tasso, Egmont; translated by Anna Swanwick and Goetz von Berlichingen; translated by Sir Walter Scott, and carefully revised by Henry G. Bohn. 8vo. Lond., 1875. H 4 P 4

Early and Miscellaneous Letters of J. W. Goethe, including Letters to his Mother; with Notes and a short Biography, by Edward Bell. 12mo. Lond., 1884. C 1 S 26

Faust: a Dramatic Poem; translated by Sir Theodore Martin, K.C.B. 2 vols. 12mo. Edinb., 1886. H 1 R 24, 25

Faust: a Tragedy; translated by Sir Theodore Martin. Illustrated by Prof. A. von Kreling. Roy. fol. Lond., 1877. H 4 8 9 ‡

Faust: a Tragedy; translated chiefly in blank verse, with Introduction and Notes, by James Adey Birds, B.A., &c. 8vo. Lond., 1880. H 1 S 8

Faust: a Tragedy, in 2 parts; translated into English Verse, by J. Birch. 2 vols. (in 1) 8vo. Lond., 1839–43. H 2 U 3

Faust; [translated] from the German, by Thomas E. Webb, LL.D. (Dub. Univ. Press Series.) 8vo. Dublin, 1880. H 3 S 18

Faustus: embellished with Retsch's Series of Twenty-seven Outlines illustrative of the Tragedy. 3rd ed. 4to. Lond., 1824. H 1 V 4

Goethe and Mendelssohn (1821–31); translated, with Additions, from the German of Carl Mendelssohn-Bartholdy, by M. E. von Glehn. 2nd ed. 8vo. Lond., 1874. C 5 P 24

Goethe's Faust in England und Amerika. [*See* HEINEMANN, W.]

Goethe's Devil. [*See* MASSON, PROF. D.]

Goethe's Letters to Zelter; with Extracts from those of Zelter to Goethe. Selected, &c., by A. D. Coleridge. 8vo. Lond., 1887. C 1 S 29

Goethe's Werke. 36 vols. (in 18) 8vo. Stuttgart, 1866–68. J 16 Q 1–18

Hermann und Dorothea. 12mo. Berlin, 1868. H 7 P 22

Life and Times of; by Herman Grimm; translated by Sarah Holland Adams. 8vo. Boston, 1880. C 6 U 16

GOETHE (JOHANN WOLFGANG VON.)—*continued.*

Life of Goethe; by G. H. Lewes. 2nd ed. 8vo. Lond., 1864. C 7 R 6

Life of; by Heinrich Düntzer; translated by Thomas W. Lyster. 2 vols. 8vo. Lond., 1883. C 4 U 6, 7

Life and Works of Goethe; with Sketches of his Age and Contemporaries; by G. H. Lewes. 2 vols. 8vo. Lond., 1855. C 7 R 4, 5

Miscellaneous Travels of; edited by L. Dora Schmitz. 12mo. Lond., 1882. D 10 P 45

Memoirs of; written by himself. 2 vols. 8vo. Lond., 1824. C 7 R 2, 3

Œuvres de Goethe. Traduction nouvelle, par Jacques Porchat. 10 vols. roy. 8vo. Paris, 1861–70. J 13 U 1–10

1. Poésies Diverses; Pensées; Divan Oriental-Occidental; avec le Commentaire.
2–4. Théatre de Goethe.
5. Poëmes et Romans.
6. Les Années Apprentissage de Wilhelm Meister.
7. Les Années de Voyage de Wilhelm Meister. Entretiens d'Emigrés Allemands. Les Bonnes Femmes. Nouvelle.
8. Mémoires de Goethe.
9. Voyages en Suisse et en Italie.
10. Mélanges.

Poems of; translated in the original metres, with a Sketch of Goethe's Life, by Edgar Alfred Bowring. 12mo. Lond., 1853. H 5 S 1

Sämmtliche Werke. Volständige Ausgabe in sechs Banden. 7 vols. roy. 8vo. Stuttgart, 1869. J 18 V 6–11

The Spirit of Goethe's Faust. [*See* COUPLAND, W. C.]

Wilhelm Meister's Travels; translated and edited by Edward Bell, M.A. 8vo. Lond., 1882. J 11 R 5

Werther. Traduit de l'Allemand, par C. L. Sevelinges. 8vo. Paris, 1804. J 16 Q 19

[*See* KAULBACH, W.; *and* REYNARD THE FOX.]

GOFFRIDUS (VINDOCINENSIS). Opera omnia. [*See* MIGNE, J. P., SERIES LATINA 157.]

GOGUET (ANTOINE-YVES). De l'Origine des Lois, des Arts, et des Sciences, et de leurs progrès chez les Anciens Peuples. 3 vols. 8vo. Paris, 1809. A 16 R 2–4

Origin of Laws, Arts, and Sciences, and their Progress among the most Ancient Nations; translated from the French. 3 vols. 8vo. Edinb., 1775.. A 17 V 1–3

GOLD. Correspondence relative to the recent Discovery of Gold in Australia. Fol. Lond., 1852. MF 3 U 1

Further Papers relative to the Recent Discovery of Gold in Australia (in continuation of Papers presented to Parliament). 2 vols. (in 1) fol. Lond., 1853. MF 3 U 3

Lectures on Gold; by J. Beete Jukes, M.A., F.G.S.; Edward Forbes, F.R.S.; Lyon Playfair, C.B., F.R.S.; W. W. Smyth, M.A., F.G.S.; John Percy, M.D., F.R.S.; Robert Hunt. 2nd ed. 8vo. Lond. 1853.* MA 2 P 1

GOLD—*continued.*

Papers and Correspondence relative to the recent Discovery of Gold in Australia. Fol. Lond., 1852–57.　MF 3 U 2

Return of the quantity of Gold exported from the several Ports in Australia during the years 1859–60, and the first half of 1861. (Parl. Docs.· 69.) Fol. Lond., 1862.　MF 4 ‡

[*See* VICTORIA—GOLDFIELDS.]

GOLDAMMER (HERMANN). The Kindergarten : a Guide to Froebel's Method of Education : Gifts and Occupations. 1st and 2nd part. 2 vols. (in 1). 8vo. Berlin, 1882.　G 17 Q 1

GOLDIE (GILBERT). The Orkneyinga Saga. [*See* ANDERSON, JOS.]

GOLDMAN (J. W. C. F.) Aanteekeningen gehouden op eene Reis naar Doroi (Noord-Oostkust van Guineë.) 8vo. Batavia, 1863. (*Bound with De Wall's Lijst van Maleische Woorden.*)　K 14 Q 29

GOLD-MINING. Industrial Progress in Gold-mining. [*See* UNITED STATES.]

GOLDONI (CARLO). Collezione completa delle Commedie 30 vols. 8vo. Prato, 1826–29.　．　H 1 Q 5–34

1. Il Teatro Comico. La Bottega del Caffè. L'Avventuriero Onorato. La Locandiera.
2. Pamela Fanciulla. Pamela Maritata. Le Vedova Scaltra. La Famiglia dell' Antiquario.
3. Il Vero Amico. L'Avvocato Veneziano. Il Padre di Famiglia. Il Cavaliere e la Dama.
4. Il Bugiardo. Gli Amori di Zelinda, e Lindoro. Le Gelosie di Lindoro. L'inquietudini di Zelinda.
5. Il Ventaglio. Le Smanie per la Villeggiatura. L'Avventure della Villeggiatura. Il Ritorno dalla Villeggiatura.
6. La Cameriera Brillante. L'Avaro Fastoso. La Serva Amorosa. L'Osteria della Posta.
7. La Moglie Saggia. Il Feudatario. Il Burbero Benefico. La Putta Onorata.
8. La Buona Moglie. La Finta Ammalata. La Guerra. La Burla Retrocessa nel Contraccambio.
9. Il Tutore. Le Femmine Puntigliose. Gli Innamorati, La Donna Volubile.
10. L'Adulatore. La Scozzese. Un Curioso Accidente. Il Torquato Tasso.
11. Il Cavaliere di Buon Gusto. Il Servitore di due Padroni. La Donna di Maneggio. Il Moliere.
12. L'Amore Paterno. Il Prodigo. La Figlia Ubbidiente. La Donna Stravagante.
13. Il Matrimonio per Concorso. Il Raggiratore. La Donna di Garbo. La Pupilla.
14. I Mercanti. Le Donne curiose. I Malcontenti. La Donna Forte.
15. Il Poeta Fanatico. Il Vecchio Bizzarro. Il Frappatore. La Vedova Spiritosa.
16. La Buona Famiglia. La Villeggiatura. La Castalda. Il Medico Olandese.
17. La Donna di testa debole. La Donna Vendicativa. Il Contrattempo ; o sia, il Chiacchierone imprudente. La Scuola di Ballo.
18. L'Erede Fortunata. La Madre Amorosa. La Donna Bizzarra. Il Ricco Insidiato.

GOLDONI (CARLO)—*continued.*

19. L'Amante Militare. L'Impostore. L'Amante di se medesimo. La Sposa Sagace.
20. L'Uomo di Mondo. L'Impresario delle Smirne. Il Padre per Amore. La Griselda.
21. L'Avaro. Il Geloso Avaro. La Buona Madre. Il Filosofo Inglese.
22. La Banca Rotta ; ossia, il Mercante Fallito. I Pettegolezzi delle Donne. Il Cavalier Giocondo. La Peruviana.
23. L'Uomo Prudente. La Dama Prudente. La Bella Selvaggia. Lo Spirito di Contradizione.
24. Il Giocatore. I Puntigli Domestici. La Dalmatina. Il Campiello.
25. L' Incognita. I Rusteghi. Il Festino. Il Terenzio.
26. I due Gemelli veneziani. La Sposa Persiana. Ircana in Julfa. Ircana in Ispaan.
27. Gli Amanti Timidi. Le Donne Gelose. Le Massere. La Donna di Governo.
28. Chi la fa l'Aspetta. Sior Todero Brontolon ; o sia, il Vecchio Fastidioso. Le Morbinose. I Morbinosi.
29. Le Donne di buon umore. La Casa Nova. Le Donne di Casa sua. La Donna Sola.
30. Le Baruffe Chiozzotte. Una delle ultime sere di Carnovale. L'Apatista ; o sia, l'Indifferente. Il Cavalier di Spirito.

Memoirs of ; written by himself ; translated by John Black. (Autobiography, 23, 24.) 2 vols. (in 1). 18mo. Lond., 1821.　C 1 P 17

Mémoires de. [*See* BARRIÈRE, J. F. 6.]

GOLDSBROUGH (R.) Portrait of. [*See* MANUSCRIPTS AND PORTRAITS.]

GOLDSMID (MAJOR-GEN. SIR F. J.), C.B., &c. Eastern Persia ; Introduction. [*See* PERSIA.]

James Outram : a Biography. 2 vols. 8vo. Lond., 1880.　C 9 R 8, 9

Telegraph and Travel : a Narrative of the Formation and Development of Telegraphic Communication between England and India. 8vo. Lond., 1874.　D 4 T 34

GOLDSMITH (LEWIS). Secret History of the Cabinet of Bonaparte ; including his private Life, Character, Domestic Administration, and his Conduct to Foreign Powers, &c. 2nd ed. 8vo. Lond., 1810.　B 8 S 38

GOLDSMITH (OLIVER). [A Biography] ; by Wm. Black. (Eng. Men of Letts.) 8vo. Lond., 1879.　C 1 U 17

Essay on Fables [*See* BEWICK, T.]

The Good Natured Man : a Comedy. (Bell's Brit. Theatre.) 18mo. Lond., 1792.　H 2 P 19

Another copy. (Brit. Theatre.) 12mo. Lond., 1808.　H 1 P 17

History of the Earth and Animated Nature ; with an Introduction by Baron Cuvier. 2 vols. roy. 8vo. Lond., 1849 5n.　A 13 V 35–36

Life and Times of ; by John Forster. 2nd ed. 2 vols. 8vo. Lond., 1854.　C 7 T 11, 12

Life and Poems of. [*See* CHALMERS, A. ; *and* JOHNSON, S.]

GOLDSMITH (OLIVER)—*continued.*

Life of, from a variety of original sources; by James Prior. 2 vols. 8vo. Lond., 1837.　　　C 8 Q 15, 16

Life of Lord Bolingbroke. [*See* BOLINGBROKE, VISCOUNT.]

Miscellaneous Works of, including a variety of Pieces now first collected; by James Prior. 4 vols. 8vo. Lond., 1837.　　　J 8 T 13–16

Oliver Goldsmith : a Biography; by Washington Irving. 12mo. Lond., 1849.　　　C 1 T 35

Another copy. (H. and C. Lib.) 12mo. Lond., 1849.　　　J 8 P 37

Poetical Works of. [*See* POETICAL WORKS.]

A Pretty Book of Pictures for Little Masters and Misses; or, Tommy Trip's History of Beasts and Birds. Illustrated by Thomas Bewick. Sm. 4to. Lond., 1867.　　　J 10 S 3

Select Fables of Æsop and others. [*See* ÆSOP.]

She Stoops to Conquer: a Comedy. (Bell's Brit. Theatre.) 18mo. Lond., 1792.　　　H 2 P 24

Another copy. (Brit. Theatre.) 12mo. Lond., 1808.　　　H 1 P 17

Another copy. [*See* BRIT. DRAMA, 4.]

The Vicar of Wakefield. [*See* CLASSIC TALES.]

The Vicar of Wakefield (fac-simile reprint of the 1st ed., 1766); with an Introduction, &c., by Austin Dobson. 2 vols. 12mo. Lond., 1885.　　　J 1 T 35, 36

The Vicar of Wakefield; with Prefatory Memoir by George Saintsbury. Roy. 8vo. Lond., 1886.　　　J 9 V 7

Works of: a new edition, containing Pieces hitherto uncollected, and a Life of the Author; with Notes, from various sources, by J. W. M. Gibbs. 5 vols. 12mo. Lond., 1884-86.　　　J 1 T 30–34

　　1. Life of Goldsmith ; Vicar of Wakefield ; Essays ; Letters.
　　2. Poems ; Plays ; " The Bee" ; Cock-Lane Ghost.
　　3. The Citizen of the World ; Polite Learning in Europe.
　　4. Biographies ; Criticisms ; Later collected Essays.
　　5. Prefaces and Introductions ; Animated Nature (Extracts) ; Nobleman's Letters ; Goody Two Shoes ; Index.

[*See* BRITISH POETS.]

GOLDSTÜCKER (PROF. THEODORE). Literary Remains of. 2 vols. 8vo. Lond., 1879.　　　J 15 S 9, 10

GOLOVIN (IVAN). Caucasus. 8vo. Lond., 1854.　D 6 U 15

GOMM (FRANCIS CULLING CARR-). [*See* GOMM, SIR W. M.]

GOMM (FIELD-MARSHAL SIR WILLIAM MAYNARD), G.C.B., &c. Letters and Journals of, from 1799 to Waterloo, 1815; edited by Francis Culling Carr-Gomm; with Portraits. 8vo. Lond., 1881.　　　C 7 T 8

GOMME (GEORGE LAURENCE), F.S.A., &c. Folk-lore Relics of Early Village Life. 8vo. Lond., 1883.　　　B 5 S 27

The Literature of Local Institutions. 12mo. Lond., 1886.　　　F 5 Q 48

Primitive Folk-Moots ; or, Open-air Assemblies in Britain. 8vo. Lond., 1880.　　　B 3 Q 2

2 Q

GOMME (G. L.), AND WHEATLEY (H. B.) Chap Books and Folk-Lore Tracts. 1st and 2nd series. 5 vols. (in 2) sm. 4to. Lond., 1885.　　　E

GONSE (LOUIS). L'Art Japonais. 2 vols. imp. 4to. Paris, 1883.　　　A 5 Q 18, 19 †

Eugène Fromentin : Painter and Writer; translated by Mary Caroline Robbins. Sm. 4to. Boston, 1883.　C5T10

GONZAGA (FRANCESCO), O.S.F. De Origine Seraphicæ Religionis Franciscanæ eiusque progressibus, de Regularis Obseruaciæ institutione. Fol. Romæ, 1587.　　G 39 P1‡

GONZAL (J. E.) Twee Togten naar de Golf van Carpentaria. [*See* CARSTENSZ, J.]

GOOD (JOHN MASON). Book of Nature. 3rd ed. 3 vols. 12mo. Lond., 1834.　　　A 17 T 20–22

GOODAL (WALTER). An Introduction to the History and Antiquities of Scotland. 8vo. Lond., 1769. B 13 P 31

[*See* FORDUN, J. DE.]

GOODCHAP (CHARLES A.) Railways and Tramways of New South Wales: Reports by the Commissioner for Railways, for the years 1879–87. 8 vols. (in 4) fol. Sydney 1880–88.　　　E

Railways of New South Wales: Reports by the Commissioner for Railways, for the year 1877–78. 2 vols. fol. Sydney, 1878–79.　　　E

GOODE (G. B.) Fisheries and Fishery Industries of the United States. (Text and Plates). 2 vols. 4to. Washington, 1884.　　　A 2 R 9, 10 †

GOODE (WILLIAM), M.A., &c. Tract XC historically refuted; or, a Reply to a Work by the Rev. F. Oakeley, entitled "The Subject of Tract XC historically examined." 8vo. Lond., 1845.　　　G 13 P 32

GOODENOUGH (COMMODORE JAMES GRAHAM), C.B., &c., A Brief Memoir; by Clements R. Markham, C.B. 12mo. Lond., 1876.　　　MC 1 P 16

In Memoriam. James G. Goodenough, Captain and Commodore of the Australian Station, died 19th August, 1875. 12mo. Melb., 1875.　　　MJ 2 P 34

Journal of Commodore Goodenough, R.N., &c., during his last Command as Senior Officer on the Australian Station, 1873–75. Edited, with a Memoir, by his Widow [Mrs. Victoria H. Goodenough]. 8vo. Lond., 1876.*　　　MD 1 U 32

[*See* CLARKE, REV. W. B.]

GOODENOUGH (MRS. VICTORIA H.) Journal of Commodore Goodenough. [*See* GOODENOUGH, COM. JAMES GRAHAM.]

GOODEVE (T. M.), M.A. Elements of Mechanism; designed for Students of Applied Mechanics. (Text-book of Sc.) 12mo. Lond., 1872.　　　A 17 S 3

Principles of Mechanics. (Text-book of Sc.) 12mo. Lond., 1874　　　A 17 S 17

GOODING (RALPH), M.D., &c. Manual of Domestic Medicine, describing the Symptoms, Causes, and Treatment of the most common Medical and Surgical Affections. (Weale.) 3rd ed. 12mo. Lond., 1882. A 17 P 52

GOODMAN (WALTER). Pearl of the Antilles; or, an Artist in Cuba. 8vo. Lond., 1873. D 3 Q 21

GOODMAN (RT. REV. WALTER GODFREY), BISHOP OF GLOUCESTER. Court of King James; to which are added Letters illustrative of the Personal History of the most Distinguished Characters in the Court of that Monarch and his Predecessors, now first published from the Original Manuscripts, by John S. Brewer, M.A. 2 vols. 8vo. Lond., 1839. B 6 P 13, 14

GOODRICH (C. A.), D.D. Webster's Complete Dictionary of the English Language. [*See* WEBSTER, NOAH.]

GOODRICH (S. G.) Tales about America and Australia; by "Peter Parley." 12mo. Lond., 1872. MB 1 P 27

GOODRIDGE (CHARLES MEDYETT). Narrative of a Voyage to the South Seas; with the shipwreck of the *Princess of Wales*, Cutter, on one of the Crozets, uninhabited Islands. 12mo. Lond., 1832. MD 4 Q 32
Another copy. 5th ed. 12mo. Exeter, 1843. MD4Q33
Another copy. 6th ed. 12mo. Exeter, 1847. MD4Q34

GOODWIN (FRANCIS). Rural Architecture. Designs in various styles of Architecture. 2 vols. 4to. Lond., 1835. A 2 U 26

GOODWIN (ISAAC). Town Officer; or, Laws of Massachusetts relative to the Duties of Municipal Officers. 8vo. Worcester, 1829. F 6 P 24

GOODWIN (REV. THOMAS), M.A. English–Latin Dictionary. (Weale.) 12mo. Lond., 1871. K 11 T 11
Latin–English Dictionary. (Weale.) 12mo. Lond., 1872. K 11 T 11
Practical Grammar of the Latin Tongue. (Weale.) 12mo. Lond., 1873. K 11 T 10

GOODWIN (THOMAS HILL). Extracts from a Report made to the Committee of the Melbourne Church of England Mission to the Aborigines, December 21st, 1854. 8vo. Melb., 1855. MG 1 Q 40

GOODWIN (UNA M.) Simon de Montfort. [*See* PAULI, DR. REINHOLD.]

GOODWIN (PROF. WILLIAM W.), PH.D. Plutarch's Morals. [*See* PLUTARCH.]

GOOD WORDS. 24 vols. roy. 8vo. Lond., 1861–84. E

GOOS (PIETER). Wassende grande Paskaart, vertoonende nevens het Oostelyckste van Africa mede de Zeekusten van Asia, van C. de Bona Esperanca tot Eso, boven Japan. 4to. Amsterdam, 1650. A D 5 8 18 †

GORDON (ADAM LINDSAY). Bush Ballads and Galloping Rhymes. 8vo. Melb., 1870. MH 1 Q 16
Poems of: Sea Spray and Smoke Drift; Bush Ballads and Galloping Rhymes; Astaroth: a Dramatic Lyric. 8vo. Melb., 1880. MH 1 Q 17

GORDON (HON. ALEXANDER), Q.C., &c. The Bible the only credible explanation of what man was, is, and will be: a Lecture. [*See* CHRISTIAN EVIDENCE SOCIETY.]

GORDON (SIR ALEXANDER DUFF), BART. Sketches of German Life. [*See* VARNHAGEN VON ENSE, K. A.]

GORDON (SURG.-GEN. CHARLES ALEXANDER), M.D., C.B. New Theory and Old Practice in relation to Medicine and certain Industries. 8vo. Lond., 1887. A 12 R 25
Our Trip to Burmah; with Notes on that Country. 8vo. Lond., 1876. D 4 U 16

GORDON (GEN. CHARLES GEORGE), C.B. Charles George Gordon: a Sketch; by Rev. Reginald H. Barnes, and Major Charles E. Brown. 8vo. Lond.,1885. C 2 S 18
Chinese Gordon: a succinct Record of his Life; by Archibald Forbes. 8vo. Lond., 1884. C 2 S 16
Colonel Gordon in Central Africa, 1874–79. [*See* HILL, G. B.]
Events in the Life of Charles George Gordon, from its beginning to its end; by Henry William Gordon. 8vo. Lond., 1886. C 7 R 17
General Gordon's Letters from the Crimea, the Danube, and Armenia, August 18, 1854, to November 17, 1858; edited by Demetrius C. Boulger. 8vo. Lond., 1884. C 2 S 19
General Gordon's Private Diary of his Exploits in China; amplified by Samuel Mossman. 8vo. Lond.,1885. C 2 S 15
Gordon and the Mahdi: an Illustrated Narrative of the War in the Soudan. 4to. Lond., 1885. B 17 Q 1 ‡
Journals of Major-General C. G. Gordon, C.B., at Kartoum; printed from the original MSS.; Introduction and Notes by A. Egmont Hake. With Portrait. 8vo. Lond., 1885. C 7 R 18
Life of General Gordon; by the Authors of "Our Queen," "New World Heroes," &c. 12mo. Lond., 1885. C 2 S 17
Story of Chinese Gordon; by A. Egmont Hake. 8vo. Lond., 1884–85. C 7 R 15, 16

GORDON (GEORGE), A.L.S. The Pinetum; being a Synopsis of all the Coniferous Plants at present known; with Descriptions, History, and Synonyms. New ed., including an Index. 8vo. Lond., 1880. A 4 S 2

GORDON (GEORGE H.) History of the Campaign of the Army of Virginia, from Cedar Mountain to Alexandria, 1862. 8vo. Boston, 1880. B 1 T 42
War Diary of Events in the War of the Great Rebellion. 1863 65. 8vo. Boston, 1882. B 2 P 7

GORDON (HENRY WILLIAM). Events in the Life of Charles George Gordon, from its beginning to its end. 8vo. Lond., 1886. C 7 R 17

GORDON (JAMES EDWARD HENRY), B.A. Determination of Verdet's Constant in Absolute Units. (Roy. Soc. Pubs. 4.) 4to. Lond., 1877.   A 11 P 5 †

Physical Treatise on Electricity and Magnetism. 2 vols. 8vo. Lond., 1880.   A 5 T 35, 36

Another copy. 2nd ed., revised, re-arranged, and enlarged. 2 vols. 8vo. Lond., 1883.   A 5 T 37, 38

Practical Treatise on Electric Lighting. 8vo. Lond., 1884.   A 5 U 29

School Electricity. 8vo. Lond., 1886.   A 5 S 37

GORDON (REV. JAMES FREDERICK SKINNER), D.D. Glasghu Facies. [*See* McURE, J.]

Monasticon and Scotichronicon; with Journal and Appendix: an Account of all the Abbeys, Priories, Churches, &c., in Scotland. 4 vols. 4to. Glasgow, 1868.   B 13 T 3–6

GORDON (LUCIE DUFF), LADY. The French in Algiers. [*See* LAMPING, LIEUT. C.]

Last Letters from Egypt; to which are added Letters from the Cape; with a Memoir by her Daughter, Mrs. Ross. 8vo. Lond., 1875.   D 1 R 27

Letters from Egypt, 1863–65. 8vo. Lond., 1865.   D 1 Q 21

Mary Schweidler, the Amber Witch. [*See* MEINHOLD, REV. W.]

GORDON (MRS. MARY). "Christopher North": a Memoir of Prof. John Wilson. 2 vols. 8vo. Edinb., 1862.   C 4 R 2, 3

GORDON (P. R.) Fencing as a means of improving our Pasture Lands, and its advantages to the Stockowners and the Colony; with Suggestions for a Fencing Bill, and the improvement of Pasture by means of Sapping. 8vo. Sydney, 1867.   MA 1 Q 1

Plants reputed poisonous to Cattle. [*See* BAILEY, F. M.]

GORDON (THOMAS), F.R.S. History of the Greek Revolution. 2nd ed. 2 vols. 8vo. Lond., 1844.   B 9 T 17, 18

GORDON (LIEUT.-COL. T. E.), C.S.I. Roof of the World; being the Narrative of a Journey over the high Plateau of Tibet to the Russian Frontier and the Oxus Sources on Pamir. Imp. 8vo. Edinb., 1876.   D 5 U 5

GORDON & GOTCH. Australasian Newspaper Directory. 8vo. Melb., 1886.   ME 3 T

Australian Hand-book and Almanac, Shippers' and Importers' Directory and Business Guide (incorporating New Zealand, Fiji, and New Guinea), 1870, 1872, 1875–76, 1878, 1882–88. 12 vols. 8vo. Lond., 1870–88.   ME 4 U

GORE (GEORGE), LL.D., &c. Art of Electro-Metallurgy, including all known Processes of Electro-Deposition. (Text-books of Science.) 8vo. Lond., 1877.   A 17 S 22

Another copy. 2nd ed. 12mo. Lond., 1884.   A 9 P 21

Scientific Basis of National Progress, including that of Morality. 8vo. Lond., 1882.   G 8 S 20

Theory and Practice of Electro-Deposition, including every known Mode of depositing Metals, preparing Metals for Immersion, taking Moulds, and rendering them conducting. 8vo. Lond., 1885.   A 9 Q 41

GORKOM (KAREL WESSEL VAN). Hand-book of Cinchona Culture; translated by Benjamin Daydon Jackson. Imp. 8vo. Amsterdam, 1883.   A 2 Q 4 †

GÖRRES (JAKOB JOSEPH VON). La Mystique, divine, naturelle et diabolique; Ouvrage traduit de l'Allemand par "Charles Sainte-Foi," [Eloi Jourdain]. 5 vols. 8vo. Paris, 1854–55.   G 4 Q 15–19

GORRINGE (LIEUT.-COMM. HENRY HONEYCHURCH), U.S.N. Egyptian Obelisks. 4to. New York, 1882.   B 19 T 6 ‡

GORST (SIR JOHN ELDON), KNT., M.A. The Maori King; or, the Story of our Quarrel with the Natives of New Zealand. 8vo. Lond., 1864.*   MB 1 Q 23

GORTCHAKOW (PRINCE). [*See* CENTRAL ASIA.]

GORTON (JOHN). General Biographical Dictionary. New ed. 3 vols. 8vo. Lond., 1838.   C 11 P 38–40

Topographical Dictionary of Great Britain and Ireland; the Irish and Welsh Articles by G. N. Wright, M.A.; with Maps, by Sidney Hall. 3 vols. 8vo. Lond., 1833.   D 12 U 16–18

GORUP-BESANEZ (DR. E. F.) Lehrbuch der Anorganischen Chemie. 8vo. Brunswick, 1873.   A 6 P 9

Lehrbuch der Physiologischen Chemie. 8vo. Brunswick, 1867.   A 6 P 8

GOSCHEN (RT. HON. GEORGE JOACHIM). Addresses on Educational and Economical Subjects. 8vo. Edinb., 1885.   F 9 P 23

GOSMAN (REV. ALEXANDER). Going Hence: a Sermon, occasioned by the Death of the Rev. J. L. Poore. 8vo. Melh., 1867.   MG 2 P 7

GOSSE (EDMUND WILLIAM), M.A. Cecil Lawson: a Memoir; with Illustrations by Hubert Herkomer, A.R.A., A. J. McN. Whistler, and Cecil Lawson. Imp. 4to. Lond., 1883.   C 4 P 17 ‡

From Shakespeare to Pope: an Inquiry into the Causes and Phenomena of the Rise of Classical Poetry in England. 12mo. Camb., 1885.   J 9 P 10

Gray. (Eng. Men. of Letts.) 8vo. Lond., 1882.   C 1 U 18

Introductory Memoir of Toru Dutt. [*See* DUTT, T.]

Raleigh. (Eng. Worthies.) 12mo. Lond., 1886.   C 2 Q 40

Works of Thomas Gray. [*See* GRAY, T.]

[*See* ESSAYS FROM THE "CRITIC."]

GOSSE (PHILIP HENRY). Birds of Jamaica. 8vo. Lond., 1847.   A 14 Q 39

Land and Sea. 12mo. Lond., 1865.   A 17 T 19

[*See* HUDSON, C. T.]

GOSTICK (JOSEPH). Trades Unions and the Relations of Capital and Labour. [*See* COBDEN CLUB.]

GOSTWICK (JOSEPH). German Culture and Christianity : their Controversy in the Time 1770–1880. 8vo. Lond., 1882.   G 2 T 23

GOTHAISCHER GENEALOGISCHER HOFKALEN-DER. Nebst diplomatisch-statistischem Jahrbuch. 15 vols. 18mo. Gotha, 1871–85.   E

GOTHAISCHES GENEALOGISCHES TASCHEN-BUCH. Gräflichen Häuser—Freiherrlichen Häuser. 30 vols. 18mo. Gotha, 1871–85.   E

GOTHOFRED (D.) [*See* JUSTINIANUS.]

GOTTSCHALK (CLARA). [*See* GOTTSCHALK, L. M.]

GOTTSCHALK (LOUIS MOREAU). Notes of a Pianist, during his Professional Tours in the United States, Canada, the Antilles, and South America; edited by his sister, Clara Gottschalk; translated from the French, by Robert E. Peterson, M.D. 8vo. Lond., 1881.   C 5 S 25

GOUDIE (GILBERT). Orkneyinga Saga. [*See* ANDERSON, J.]

GOUGER (HENRY). Personal Narrative of Two Years' Imprisonment in Burmah, 1824–26. Illustrated. 8vo. Lond., 1860.   D 5 Q 26

GOUGER (ROBERT). Letter from Sydney. [*See* WAKE-FIELD, E. G.]

South Australia in 1837; in a series of Letters, with a Postscript as to 1838. 12mo. Lond., 1838.   MD 4 Q 38

Another copy. 2nd ed., with additional information. 12mo. Lond., 1838.   MD 4 Q 39

GOUGH (PROF. ARCHIBALD EDWARD), M.A. Philosophy of the Upanisiads and Ancient Indian Metaphysics. 8vo. Lond., 1882.   G 15 P 13

The Sarva-Darsana-Sangraha. [*See* MÁDHAVA ACHÁRYA.]

GOUGH (JOHN BALLANTINE). Platform Echoes; or, Leaves from my Note-book of Forty Years; illustrated by Anecdotes, Incidents, Personal Experiences, Facts and Stories drawn from the Humour and Pathos of Life. Illustrated. 8vo. Lond., 1885.   F 14 S 16

GOUGH (RICHARD). British Topography; or, an Historical Account of what has been done for illustrating the Topographical Antiquities of Great Britain and Ireland. 2 vols. 4to. Lond., 1780.   D 10 P 18, 19 †

[*See* CAMDEN, W.]

GOULBURN CHRONICLE AND SOUTHERN AD-VERTISER, 1860. Fol. Goulburn, 1860.   ME

GOULBURN HERALD, 1850–51, 1857, 1860–62. Fol. Goulburn, 1850–62.   ME

GOULBURN HERALD AND CHRONICLE 1865. Fol. Goulburn 1865.   ME

GOULBURN HOSPITAL. Annual Reports, Names of Subscribers, Terms of Admission, &c., 1851–52, 1855–56. 8vo. Goulburn, 1852–56.   MG 1 Q 26

GOULD (AUGUSTUS A.), M.D. Australian Shells. [*See* TENISON-WOODS, REV. J. E.]

Mollusca and Shells. (U.S. Exploring Expedition.) Imp. 4to. Boston, 1852.   A 31 P 10 ‡

Atlas [to the above]. Imp. fol. Boston, 1856. A 31 R 3‡

Outlines of Comparative Physiology. [*See* AGASSIZ, L.]

GOULD (CHARLES). Geological Maps. [*See* TASMANIA.]

Mythical Monsters. Illustrated. 8vo. Lond., 1886.   B 15 S 1

GOULD (GEORGE). Corrigenda and Explanations of the Text of Shakspere. 8vo. 1881.   J 12 V 4

The Greek Plays in their relations to the Dramatic Unities. 8vo. Lond., 1883.   J 12 V 4

GOUGH (GENERAL HUGH), VISCOUNT. War in India : Despatches. [*See* HARDINGE, VISCOUNT.]

GOULD (JOHN), F.R.S., &c. Birds of Asia. 7 vols. imp. fol. Lond., 1850–83.   A 5 Q 19–25 ‡

Birds of Australia. 7 vols. imp. fol. Lond., 1848.   A 5 R 4–10 ‡

Birds of Australia: Supplement. Imp. fol. Lond., 1869.   A 5 R 11 ‡

Birds of Europe. 5 vols. imp. fol. Lond., 1837.   A 5 R 13–17 ‡

Birds of Great Britain. 5 vols. imp. fol. Lond., 1873–74.   A 5 Q 10–14 ‡

Birds of New Guinea and the adjacent Papuan Islands, including any new Species that may be hereafter discovered in Australia, of which it may be considered a continuation. 3 vols. imp. fol. Lond., 1875–83.   A 5 Q 15–17 ‡

Century of Birds from the Himalaya Mountains. Imp. fol. Lond., 1832.   A 5 R 12 ‡

Companion to Gould's Hand-book. [*See* DIGGLES, S.]

Hand-book to the Birds of Australia. 2 vols. roy. 8vo. Lond., 1865.   MA 2 U 12, 13

Icones Avium; or, Figures and Descriptions of New and Interesting Species of Birds. 2 parts in 1 vol. imp. fol. Lond., 1837–38.   A 7 P 18 ‡

Introduction to the Birds of Australia. 8vo. Lond., 1848.*   MA 2 U 14

Introduction to the Birds of Great Britain. 8vo. Lond., 1873.   A 14 T 25

Introduction to the Mammals of Australia. 8vo. Lond., 1863.   MA 2 U 16

Mammals of Australia. 3 vols. imp. fol. Lond., 1863.   A 5 R 1–3 ‡

Monograph of the Odontophorinæ, or Partridges of America. Imp. fol. Lond., 1850.   A 5 Q 7 ‡

Monograph of the Ramphastidæ, or Family of Toucans. Imp. fol. Lond., 1854.   A 5 Q 8 ‡

GOULD (JOHN), F.R.S., &c.—*continued.*
Monograph of the Trochilidæ, or Family of Humming Birds. 5 vols. imp. fol. Lond., 1861. A 5 Q 1–5 ‡
Monograph of the Trogonidæ, or Family of Trogons. Imp. fol. Lond., 1875. A 5 Q 9 ‡
Synopsis of the Birds of Australia, and the adjacent Islands; with Characters of several new Genera, and Descriptions of thirty-six New Species, principally in the Author's Collection. Parts 1–4. Imp. 8vo. Lond., 1837–38.*
MA 2 P 4 †
[*See* DARWIN, C.]

GOULD (REV. SABINE BARING-). [*See* BARING-GOULD, REV. S.]

GOURDAULT (JULES). Travers Venise: Ouvrage illustré de nombreuses Gravures dans le Texte et de treize Eaux-Fortes par les premiers Artistes. Fol. Paris, 1884. D 14 U 11

GOURY (JULES). Plans, Elevations, Sections, and Details of the Alhambra. [*See* JONES, O.]

GOVERNMENT ASYLUMS, N.S.W. [*See* NEW SOUTH WALES.]

GOVERNMENT GAZETTES. [*See* NEW SOUTH WALES; WESTERN AUSTRALIA; NEW ZEALAND; *and* SOUTH AUSTRALIA.]

GOW (JAMES), M.A. Short History of Greek Mathematics. 8vo. Camb., 1884. A 10 T 11

GOW (WILLIAM). The Apocalypse Unveiled, and a Fight with Death and Slander. 8vo. Perth, 1888. MG 2 P 4

GOWAN (MAJOR WALTER E.) Kashgaria. [*See* KUROPATKIN, COL. A. N.]

GOWANS (JAMES). Edinburgh and its Neighbourhood in the days of our Grandfathers: a Series of Illustrations. Roy. 8vo. Lond., 1886. D 8 V 13

GOWEN (J. R.) Hints on Emigration to the New Settlement on the Swan and Canning Rivers, on the West Coast of Australia. 4th ed. 8vo. Lond., 1830. MD 5 T 26

GOWER (GEORGE GRANVILLE LEVESON), EARL, FIRST DUKE OF SUTHERLAND. Despatches of; to which are added the Despatches of Mr. Lindsay and Mr. Munro, and the Diary of Viscount Palmerston; edited by Oscar Browning. 8vo. Camb., 1885. B 8 U 25
The Sutherland Evictions of 1814. [*See* SELLAR, T.]

GOWER (JOHN). Confessio Amantis; edited, and collated with the best Manuscripts, by Dr. Reinhold Pauli. 3 vols. 8vo. Lond., 1857. H 6 S 17–19
Life, and the Confessio Amantis of. [*See* CHALMERS, A.]

GOWER (RONALD CHARLES SUTHERLAND LEVESON), LORD, F.S.A. Figure Painters of Holland. (Great Artists). 8vo. Lond., 1880. C 3 T 38
Last Days of Marie Antoinette: an Historical Sketch. Sm. 4to. Lond., 1885. C 7 R 44
My Reminiscences. 2 vols. 8vo. Lond., 1883. C 7 T 6, 7
Northbrook Gallery: an Illustrated, Descriptive, and Historic Account of the Collection of the Earl of Northbrook, G.C.S.I. Fol. Lond., 1885. A 23 S 30 ‡
Notes of a Tour from Brindisi to Yokohama, 1883–84. 12mo. Lond., 1885. D 5 P 27
Romney and Lawrence. (Great Artists). 8vo. Lond., 1882. C 3 T 35
[*See* CLOUET, F.]

GOWING (RICHARD), Richard Cobden: The World's Workers. 13th thousand. 12mo. Lond., 1858. C 2 S 7

GOY (ANDRÉ DE.) Aventures sur Mer et sur Terre. 1. La Famille Laurençay. 2. Histoire d'un jeune Chercheur d'Or en Australie. 8vo. Paris, 1869. MJ 2 S 11

GOZLAN (L.) El Vampiro de Val de Gracia. 8vo. Madrid, 1862. J 15 U 26

GRABER (PROF. V.) Die Insekten. 2 vols. 12mo. München, 1877. A 14 P 60, 61

GRACE (A. F.) Course of Lessons in Landscape Painting in Oils. Imp. 4to. Lond., 1881. A 4 R 22 ‡

GRAD (A. CHARLES). L'Australie Intérieure. Explorations et Voyages à travers le Continent Australien, de 1860 à 1862. 8vo. Paris, 1864.* MD 2 S 31

GRAEFFE (EDOUARD). Beobachtungen über Radiaten und Würmer in Nizza. 4to. Zurich, 1858. A 14 V 49

GRACCHUS (TIBERIUS AND CAIUS). Lives of. [*See* PLUTARCH.]

GRAETZ (DR. HEINRICH). Geschichte der Juden, von den ältesten Zeiten bis auf die Gegenwart. 6 vols. 8vo. Leipsic, 1866–78. G 11 P 29–31

GRAFF (DR. E. G.) Althochdeutscher Sprachschatz oder Wörterbuch der althochdeutschen Sprache; [mit] Volständiger Alphabetischer Index. 7 vols. 4to. Berlin, 1834–46. K 16 R 22–28

GRAFTON (RICHARD). Chronicle, or History of England; to which is added his Table of the Bailiff's, Sheriffs, and Mayors of the City of London, from 1189 to 1558, inclusive. 2 vols. 4to. Lond., 1809. B 10 R 7, 8
[*See* HARDING, JOHN.] B 10 R 10 †

GRAHAM (DOUGAL). Life of. [*See* JOHN CHEAP.]

GRAHAM (G. F.) Englisɪ Synonymes classified and explained ; witɪ practical Exercises. New ed. 12mo. Lond., 1875.　　　　K 11 U 18

GRAHAM (Lieut.-Col. G. F. I.) Life and Work of Syed Ahmeḍ Kɪan. 8vo. Edinb., 1885.　　　C 3 U 37

GRAHAM· (James), Marquis of Montrose. [*See* Montrose, James Graham, Marquis of.]

GRAHAM (Rev. John). Currents and Counter-Currents of the Age ; witɪ Remarks on the Union, Sacerdotalism, Infidelity, and Religious Revival. 8vo. Sydney, 1874.　　　　　　　　　　　　MG 1 Q 39

Lawrence Struilby ; or, Observations and Experiences during twenty-five years of Busɪ Life in Australia. 12mo. Lond., 1863.*　　　　　MD 1 S 37

GRAHAM (John Murray), M.A. Annals and Correspondence of the Viscount and the First and Second Earls of Stair. 2 vols. 8vo. Edinb., 1875.　C 9 R 20, 21

An Historical View of Literature and Art in Great Britain, from the Accession of the House of Hanover to the Reign of Queen Victoria. 8vo. Lond., 1871. B 6 S 31

Anotɪer copy. 2nd ed. 8vo. Lond., 1872.　B 6 S 32

GRAHAM (Robert Hudson), C.E. Grapɪic and Analytic Statics in Tɪeory and Comparison ; tɪeir Practical Application to the Treatment of Stresses in Roofs, Solid Girders, Lattice, Bowstring and Suspension Bridges, Braced Iron Arcɪes and Piers, and otɪer Frameworks ; to wɪicɪ is added, a Cɪapter on Wind Pressures. 8vo. Lond., 1883.　　　　　　　　　A 10 U 22

GRAHAM (Sir Gerard). [*See* De Cosson, Major E. A.]

GRAHAM (Mrs. Margaret). Murder of. [*See* Daylesford Murder, The.]

GRAHAM (Sylvester). Lectures on the Science of Human Life. Roy. 8vo. Lond., 1849.　　　A 12 V 16

GRAHAM (Thomas), F.R.S., and WATTS (Henry), F.C.S. Elements of Cɪemistry ; including the applications of the Science in the Arts. 2 vols. 8vo. Lond., 1850-58.　　　　　　　　　A 6 Q 2, 3

GRAHAM (Thomas J.), M.D. Modern Domestic Medicine ; a Popular Treatise, describing the Symptoms, Causes, Distinction, and Correct Treatment of Diseases. 14th ed. 8vo. Lond., 1872.　　　A 12 R 36

GRAHAM (Walter). Brassfounder's Manual. (Weale.) 3rd ed. 12mo. Lond., 1870.　　　　A 17 Q 5

Brass founding, Tin-plate, and Zinc Working. (Brit. Manuf. Indust.) 12mo. Lond., 1876.　A 17 S 34

GRAHAM (William), M.A. Creed of Science, Religious, Moral, and Social. 8vo. Lond., 1881.　　G 4 Q 7

The One Pound Note. 8vo. Edinb., 1886.　F 8 P 14

Social Problem. 8vo. Lond., 1886.　　F 8 P 5

GRAHAM (Messrs.) & CO. [*See* Burnand, W. H.]

GRAHAM & BINDON *V*. BERRY. Judgment of the Lords of the Judicial Committee of the Privy Council on the Appeal of Graɪam and Bindon v. Berry, from New Soutɪ Wales ; delivered 26th May, 1865. (Pam. A.) Fol. Lond., 1865.　　　　　　　MJ 2 U 1

GRAHAME (James). History of the Rise and Progress of the United States of Nortɪ America till the Britisɪ Revolution, 1688. 2 vols. 8vo. Lond., 1827. B 1 R 40, 41

History of the United States of Nortɪ America, from the Plantation of the Britisɪ Colonies till tɪeir Revolt and Declaration of Independence. 4 vols. 8vo. Lond., 1836.　　　　　　　　　B 1 R 21-24

GRAHAME (James), M.D. [*See* British Poets, 3.]

GRAIN AND FLOUR. Copies of Communications made to the Colonial Office from the Australian Colonies, respecting the Rate of Duty imposed upon the Importation of Colonial Grain and Flour into the United Kingdom. (Parl. Doc. 47.) Fol. Lond., 1845.　MF 4 ‡

GRAINGE (William). History and Topograpɪy of Harrogate, and the Forest of Knaresborougɪ. 8vo. Lond., 1871.　　　　　　B 7 P 11

GRAINGER (—). [*See* Collection of Four Hundred Portraits.]

GRAINGER (James), M.D. Life and Poems of. [*See* Chalmers, A.]

GRAMBERG (J. S. G.) De Batoe-Toelis te Batavia. 8vo. Batavia, 1866.　　　　　　K 14 Q 29

GRAMMAIRE TURQUE. Oɪ metɪode courte et facile pour apprendrɪ la Langue Turque. 18mo. Moscow, 1777.　　　　　　　　　K 14 P 30

GRAMMONT (Philibert), Comte de. Memoirs of, illustrated Sixty-four Portraits ; by Antɪony Hamilton. 2 vols. 8vo. Lond., 1811.　　　U 8 Q 19, 20

GRAMPIAN CLUB PUBLICATIONS. 4 vols. 8vo. Lond., 1869-72.　　　　　　　E

GRANDGAGNAGE (Ch.) Dictionnaire Etymologique de la Langue Wallonne. [Avec un Supplément.] 2 vols. 8vo. Liég et Bruxelles, 1845-50.　ç 14 T 10, 11

GRANDY (Richard E.) Timber Importer's, Timber Merciant's, and Builder's Standard Guide. 2nd ed. (Weale.) 12mo. Lond., 1875.　　　A 17 P 14

GRANGE (M. T.) Géologie, Minéralogie, et Géograpɪie Pɪysique. [*See* Dumont D'Urville, Capt. J. S. C.]

GRANGER (Rev. James), M.A. Letters between the Rev. James Granger, M.A., Rector of Shiplake, and many of the most Eminent Literary Men of ɪis time ; edited by J. P. Malcolm. 8vo. Lond., 1805. C 7 T 5

GRANGER (REV. JAMES), AND NOBLE (REV. MARK). Biographical History of England; from Egbert the Great to the end of George the First's Reign. 9 vols. 8vo. Lond., 1806 and 1824. C 6 V 1-9

GRANIER (DR. MICHEL). Conferences upon Homœopathy. 8vo. Lond., 1859. A 13 P 10

GRANIER DE CASSAGNAC (ADOLPHE). History of the Working and Burgher Classes; translated by Ben. E. Green. 8vo. Philad., 1871. B 7 T 32

GRANT (MRS. ANNE), OF LAGGAN. Letters from the Mountains; being the Correspondence with her Friends, between the years 1773 and 1803. Edited, with Notes and Additions, by her Son, J. P. Grant. 2 vols. 8vo. Lond., 1845. C 3 Q 33, 34

GRANT (SIR ALEXANDER), BART., LL.D. The Ethics of Aristotle. [*See* ARISTOTELES.]
Recess Studies. 8vo. Edinb., 1870. F 12 Q 38
Story of the University of Edinburgh during its first Three Hundred Years. Illustrated. 2 vols. 8vo. Lond., 1884. B 13 R 36, 37

GRANT (A. C.) Bush Life in Queensland; or, Join West's Colonial Experiences. 2 vols. 8vo. Edinb., 1881. MD 5 P 26, 27
Another copy. New ed. 8vo. Edinb., 1882. MD 5 P 28

GRANT (REV. BREWIN), B.A. Vivisection. [*See* MACAULAY, J.]

GRANT (MAJOR-GEN. CHARLES), VISCOUNT DE VAUX. History of the Mauritius and the neighbouring Islands; composed principally from the Papers and Memoirs of Baron Grant. 4to. Lond., 1801. B 17 Q 9 ‡

GRANT (C. W.) Bombay Cotton, and Indian Railways. 8vo. Lond., 1850. F 4 T 10

GRANT (REV. GEORGE M.), D.D. Ocean to Ocean. Sandford Fleming's Expedition through Canada, in 1872. Enlarged and Revised Edition. Illustrated. 8vo. Lond., 1877. D 3 P 36
Picturesque Canada: the Country as it was and is. Illustrated. 2 vols. sm. fol. Toronto, 1886. D 3 V 36, 37

GRANT (JAMES). The Bench and the Bar. 2 vols. 8vo. Lond., 1837. C 2 T 8, 9
British Battles. Illustrated. 3 vols. roy. 8vo. Lond., 1873-75. B 5 V 15-17
British Senate; or, a Second Series of Random Recollections of the Lords and Commons. 2 vols. (in 1) 8vo. Philad., 1838. F 6 R 13
Cassell's Old and New Edinburgh: its History, its People, and its Places. Illustrated. 3 vols. roy. 8vo. Lond., 1882-83. B 12 V 35-37
Every-day Life in London. 2 vols. (in 1) 8vo. Philad., 1839. J 5 P 28

GRANT (JAMES)—*continued.*
The Great Metropolis. 2 vols. 8vo. Lond., 1836. J 12 T 12, 13
Impressions of Ireland and the Irish. 2 vols. 8vo. Lond., 1844. D 8 S 1, 2
Memoirs and Adventures of Sir William Kirkaldy. 8vo. Edinb., 1849. C 3 U 9
Memoirs of James, Marquis of Montrose, K.G. 12mo. Lond., 1858. C 2 P 30
The Newspaper Press; its Origin, Progress, and Present Position. 2 vols. 8vo. Lond., 1871. B 15 R 3, 4
Paris and its People. 2 vols. 8vo. Lond., 1844. D 7 R 27, 28
Random Recollections of the Lords and Commons. 2 vols. 8vo. Lond., 1838. F 5 T 8, 9
Recent British Battles on Land and Sea. Illustrated. 4to. Lond., 1884. B 5 V 18
Records of a Run through Continental Countries. 2 vols. 8vo. Lond., 1853. D 9 P 25-26
Tartans of the Clans of Scotland; also an Introductory Account of Celtic Scotland, Clanship, Chiefs, their Dress, Arms, &c. Imp. 4to. Edinb., 1886. B 15 T 7 ‡
Travels in Town. 2 vols. 8vo. Lond., 1839. J 11 U 33, 34
Walks and Wanderings in the World of Literature. 2 vols. 8vo. Lond., 1839. J 12 U 13, 14

GRANT (LIEUT. JAMES). Narrative of a Voyages of Discovery, performed in His Majesty's vessel *The Lady Nelson*, of sixty tons burthen, with sliding keels, in the years 1800-02, to New South Wales. 4to. Lond., 1803.* MD 5 P 29 †
Verhaal van eene Ontdekkingsreize, na Nieuw-Zuid-Wales; met zijner Majesteits Schip de *Lady Nelson*, in de Jaren 1800-02. 8vo. Haarlem, 1805. MD 2 S 26

GRANT (COLONEL J. A.), C.B., &c. Khartoom, as I saw it in 1863. Illustrated. 2nd ed. 8vo. Edinb., 1885. D 1 T 17
Walk across Africa; or, Domestic Scenes from my Nile Journal. 8vo. Lond., 1864. D 2 T 16

GRANT (J. G. S.) Philosophical Thoughts on Evolution. 8vo. Dunedin, 1876. MJ 2 R 16

GRANT (J. M.) Portrait of. [*See* MANUSCRIPTS AND PORTRAITS.]

GRANT (J. P.) Letters from the Mountains; being the Correspondence with her Friends between the years 1773 and 1803 of Mrs. Anne Grant, of Laggan. 8vo. Lond., 1845. C 3 Q 33, 34

GRANT (KLEIN), M.D. Lexicon Medicum. [*See* HOOPER, R.]

GRANT (R. E.) On the Study of Medicine; being an Introductory Address. (Univ. of Lond.) 8vo. Lond., 1833. J 5 S 8

GRANT (ROBERT). [*See* ARAGO, F. J. D.]

GRANT (S.), AND FOSTER (J. S.) New Zealand : a Report on its Agricultural Condition and Prospects. With Map. 8vo. Lond., 1879.   MD 4 U 22

GRANT (GEN. ULYSSES SIMPSON.) Around the World with. [*See* YOUNG, J. R.]

The Career of a Soldier ; General Grant : his Battles and Victories in War and Peace. 12mo. Edinb., 1885.   C 2 S 21

From the Tan Yard to the White House : the Story of President Grant's Life ; by William M. Thayer. 8vo. Lond., 1885.   C 2 T 36

Military History of, from April, 1861 to April, 1865 ; by Col. Adam Bandeau. 3 vols. roy. 8vo. N. York, 1868–81.   C 8 R 19–21

Personal Memoirs of. [Written by himself.] 2 vols. 8vo. Lond., 1885–86.   C 8 R 22, 23

GRANTHAM (JOHN). Iron Ship Building ; with practical examples and details. (Weale.) 5th ed. 12mo. Lond., 1868.   A 17 P 17

Plates [to the above.] (Weale.) Fol. Lond., 1868.   A 23 P 27 ‡

GRANVILLE (A. B.), M.D., &c. Autobiography of ; being eighty-eight years of the Life of a Physician ; edited, with a brief account of the last years of his Life, by his youngest Daughter, Paulina B. Granville. With Portrait. 2nd ed. 2 vols. 8vo. Lond., 1874.   C 7 T 3, 4

Spas of Germany. 2nd ed. 8vo. Lond., 1839.   D 6 T 22

GRANVILLE (G.), DUKE OF SUTHERLAND. Memoirs of ; by J. Loch. Roy. 4to. Lond., 1834.   C 4 P 13 †

GRANVILLE (RT. HON. GEORGE), LORD LANDSDOWNE. [*See* LANSDOWNE, RT. HON. G. GRANVILLE, LORD.]

GRANVILLE (MARY). [*See* DELANY, MRS.]

GRANVILLE (PAULINA D.) [*See* GRANVILLE, A. B.]

GRAPHIC (THE). An Illustrated Weekly Newspaper. 31 vols. fol. Lond., 1870–85.   E

GRAPHIC NEWS (THE). The Graphic News of Australasia, January 4th, 1873. Fol. Melb., 1873. ME9Q2†

GRASSE (J. G. T.), DR. Handbuch der alten Numismatik von den ältesten Zeiten bis auf Constantin d. gr. 8vo. Leipzig, 1854.   A 13 S 14

GRASSI (GIUS). Dictionary of the English and Italian Languages. [*See* JAMES, W.]

GRASSI (PETRO MARIA). De Ortu ac Progressu Haeresum In. Witchefi in Anglia Presbyteri Narratio Historica. Fol. Vicentin, 1707.   G 12 Q 7 †

GRATIANUS DE CLUSIO. Decretum. [*See* MAINE, J. P., Series Latina, 187.]

GRATTAN (HENRY). Memoirs of the Life and Times of the Rt. Hon. Henry Grattan ; by his Son. 2 vols. 8vo. Lond., 1839.   C 8 Q 21, 22

GRATTAN (RT. HON. HENRY). Leaders of Public Opinion in Ireland. [*See* LECKY, W. E. H.]

Memoirs of the Life and Times of ; by his Son, H. Grattan. 2 vols. 8vo. Lond., 1839.   C 8 Q 21, 22

Speeches of, in the Irish and in the Imperial Parliament ; edited by his Son. 4 vols. 8vo. Lond., 1822. F 13 P 33–36

GRATTAN (THOMAS COLLEY). Beaten Paths and those who trod them. 2 vols. 8vo. Lond., 1862. J 9 R 7, 8

History of the Netherlands. (Lard. Cab. Cyclo.) 12mo. Lond., 1833.   K 1 T 33

Legends of the Rhine and of the Low Countries. 3 vols. 8vo. Lond., 1832.   J 11 R 15–17

Traits of Travel ; or, Tales of Men and Cities. 3 vols. 8vo. Lond., 1829.   J 6 S 18–20

GRATTAN (WILLIAM). Adventures of the Connaught Rangers, from 1808–14. First series. 2 vols. 8vo. Lond., 1847.   C 3 R 29–30

Another copy. Second series. 2 vols. 8vo. Lond. 1853.   C 3 R 31, 32

GRAVES (ALGERNON). Dictionary of Artists who have exhibited Works in the principal London Exhibitions of Oil Paintings, from 1760 to 1880. Imp. 8vo. Lond., 1884.   C 11 V 14

GRAVES (GEORGE), F.L.S. British Ornithology ; being the History, with a coloured Representation, of every known Species of British Birds. 2nd ed. 3 vols. 8vo. Lond., 1821.   A 15 R 13–15

[*See* CURTIS, W.]

GRAVES (RICHARD), D.D. Lectures on the Four last Books of the Pentateuch. 5th ed. 8vo. Dublin, 1829.   F 6 V 25

GRAVES (ROBERT E.) B.A. [*See* BRYAN, M.]

GRAVES (REV. ROBERT PERCEVAL), M.A. Life of Sir William Rowan Hamilton, Knt., &c. ; including Selections from his Poems, Correspondence, and Miscellaneous Writings. Vols. 1, 2. 8vo. Dublin, 1882.   C 14 U 13, 14

GRAVES (S. R.) Yachting Cruise in the Baltic. 8vo. Lond., 1863.   D 8 R 18

GRAVIÈRE (CAPT. J. B. E. JURIEN DE LA). [*See* JURIEN DE LA GRAVIÈRE, CAPT. J. B. E.]

GRAY (ANDREW), M.A., &c. Absolute Measurements in Electricity and Magnetism. 12mo. Lond., 1884. A 5 R 46

GRAY (ANDREW). Ploughwright's Assistant. 8vo. Edinb., 1808.   A 1 T 8

GRAY (PROF. ASA). Darwiniana : Essays and Reviews pertaining to Darwinism. 8vo. N. York, 1876. A 16 Q 4

GRAY (GEORGE ROBERT), F.R.S., &c. Hand-list of Genera and Species of Birds, distinguishing those contained in the British Museum. 3 vols. 8vo. Lond., 1869-71. A 14 T 22-24

List of the Genera of Birds, with an Indication of the Typical Species of each Genus. Compiled from various sources. 8vo. Lond., 1840. A 14 R 3

GRAY (MRS. HAMILTON). History of Etruria. Parts 1-3. 3 vols. 8vo. Lond., 1843-68. B 12 Q 15-17

Tour to the Sepulcres of Etruria, 1839. 8vo. Lond., 1841. B 12 Q 14

GRAY (HENRY), F.R.S., &c. Anatomy, Descriptive and Surgical; the Drawings by H. V. Carter, M.D. 9th ed. Roy. 8vo. Lond., 1880. A 33 V 13

GRAY (JAMES). Ancient Proverbs and Maxims, from Burmese Sources; or, the Niti Literature of Burma. 8vo. Lond., 1886. K 19 R 4

GRAY (JOHN). Lectures on the Nature and Use of Money. 8vo. Edinb., 1848. F 8 P 6

GRAY (JOHN C.) Border Post Almanac. [*See* AFFLECK, T.]

GRAY (JOHN EDWARD), PH.D., &c. Acclimatization of Animals. (Pam. Cb.) 8vo. Bath, 1864. A 16 U 25

Catalogue of the Specimens of Lizards in the Collection of the British Museum. 12mo. Lond., 1845. A 14 Q 4

Catalogue of the Specimens of Snakes in the Collection of the British Museum. 12mo. Lond., 1849. A 14 Q 3

Another copy. 12mo. Lond., 1849. K 18 P 5

Catalogue of the Tortoises, Crocodiles, and Amphisbænians in the Collection of the British Museum. 8vo. Lond., 1844. A 14 Q 5

Decimal Coinage: what it ought and what it ought not to be. (Pam. Cb.) 8vo. Lond., 1854. A 16 U 25

Lizards of Australia and New Zealand in the Collection of the British Museum; with Eighteen Plates. 4to. Lond., 1867. MA 2 Q 7 †

Museums, their use and improvement. (Pam. Cb.) 8vo. Bath, 1864. A 16 U 25

Synopsis of the Species of Starfish in the British Museum; with Figures of some of the New Species. 4to. Lond., 1866. MA 2 Q 7 †

Synopsis of the Species of Whales and Dolphins in the Collection of the British Museum. Illustrated with thirty-seven Plates. 4to. Lond., 1868. MA 2 Q 7 †

[*See* BEECHEY, CAPT. F. W.]

GRAY (JOHN EDWARD AND GEORGE ROBERT), F.R.S., &c. Catalogue of the Mammalia and Birds of New Guinea, in the Collection of the British Museum. 8vo. Lond., 1859. MA 2 T 10

2 u

GRAY (HON. JOHN HAMILTON), D.C.L. Confederation; or, the Political and Parliamentary History of Canada, from the Conference at Quebec, in October, 1864, to the Admission of British Columbia, in July, 1871. Vol. I. 8vo. (*All published.*) Toronto, 1872. B 1 Q 55

GRAY (JOHN HENRY), M.A., LL.D., &c. China: a History of the Laws, Manners, and Customs of the People; edited by William Gow Gregor. Illustrated. 2 vols. 8vo. Lond., 1878. B 2 Q 12, 13

GRAY (JOHN M.) [*See* SCOTT, D.]

GRAY (RT. REV. R.) [*See* LONG, REV. W.]

GRAY (SAMUEL OCTAVUS). British Sea-weeds: an Introduction to the study of the Marine Algæ of Great Britain, Ireland, and the Channel Islands. 8vo. Lond., 1867. A 4 P 13

GRAY (THOMAS). [A Biography]; by E. W. Gosse. (Eng. Men of Letts.) 8vo. Lond., 1882. C 1 U 18

Life and Poems of. [*See* CHALMERS, A.; *and* JOHNSON, S.]

Notes on Plato. [*See* PLATO.]

Works of, in Prose and Verse; edited by Edmund [W.] Gosse. 4 vols. 12mo. Lond., 1884. J 1 T 13-16

Works of; with Memoirs of his Life and Writings; by W. Mason. 2 vols. roy. 4to. Lond., 1814. J 7 V 19, 20

[*See* BRITISH POETS.]

GRAY (MAJOR WILLIAM), AND DOCHARD (STAFF-SURGEON). Travels in Western Africa in the years 1818-21. 8vo. Lond., 1825. D 1 V 17

GRAYLING (W. I.) War in Taranaki, during the years 1860-61. 8vo. New Plymouth, 1862. MB 2 Q 18

GREAT ARTISTS. Illustrated Biographies of the Great Artists. 28 vols. (in 14) 8vo. Lond., 1879-83. C 3 T 31-44

1. Giotto; by Harry Quilter, M.A. Gainsborough; by George M. Brock-Arnold, M.A. Constable; by George M. Brock-Arnold, M.A.
2. Ghiberti and Donatello, with other Early Italian Sculptors; by Leader Scott. Correggio; by M. Compton Heaton.
3. Turner; by W. Cosmo Monkhouse. Van Dyck; by Percy Rendell Head. Frans Hals; by Percy Rendell Head.
4. Velazquez; by Edwin Stowe, B.A. Sir David Wilkie; by John W. Mollett, B.A.
5. Meissonier; by John W. Mollett, B.A. Romney and Lawrence; by Lord Ronald Gower, F.S.A.
6. Titian; by Richard Ford Heath, B.A. Tintoretto; by W. Roscoe Osler.
7. Sir Edwin Landseer; by Frederick G. Stephens. Leonardo; by Jean Paul Richter, Ph.D.
8. The Figure Painters of Holland; by Lord Ronald Gower, F.S.A. Michelangelo; by Charles Clément.
9. Murillo; by Ellen E. Minor. Watteau; by John W. Mollett, B.A.
10. Rembrandt; by John W. Mollett, B.A. Raphael; by "N. D'Anvers," [Mrs. N. R. E. Bell.]
11. Fra Angelico; by Catherine Mary Phillimore. Albrecht Dürer; by Richard Ford Heath, M.A.
12. The Little Masters; by William Bell Scott. Hans Holbein; by Joseph Cundall.
13. Mantegna and Francia; by Julia Cartwright. Overbeck; by J. Beavington Atkinson.
14. Sir Joshua Reynolds; by F. S. Pulling, M.A. Horace Vernet; by J. Ruutz Rees. Paul Delaroche; by John Ruutz Rees. Painters, Sculptors, and Architects; by P. Delaroc .

GREATBACH (G.) Raphael's Cartoons. [*See* RAPHAEL SANZIO.]

GREAT BRITAIN. Census, 1851. Account of the Number and Distribution ef the People ; Ages, Conjugal Condition, &c. Roy. 8vo. Lond., 1851. E

Annual Reports of the Registrar-General of Births, Deaths, and Marriages, 1839–49. 3 vols. fol. Lond., 1849. E

Annual Reports of the Registrar-General of Births, Deaths, and Marriages, 1845–55. 9 vols. Roy. 8vo. Lond., 1849–57. F 1 Q 1–9

Census, 1851. Education, England and Wales ; Report and Tables. Roy. 8vo. Lond., 1854. E

Census, 1851. Population Tables. II. Ages, Civil Condition, Occupations, and Birth-place of the People. Sm. fol. Lond., 1854. E

Census, 1851. Religious Worship and Education, Scotland ; Report and Tables. Roy. 8vo. Lond., 1854. E

Census, 1851. Religious Worship, England and Wales ; Report and Tables. Roy. 8vo. Lond., 1854. E

Coins, Seals, and Medals of. Imp. fol. Lond. (n.d.) A 7 P 20 ‡

Finances and Trade of the United Kingdom, at the beginning of the Year 1852. (Pam. Jf.) 4th ed. 8vo. Lond., 1852. MF 2 P 2

Great Britain and New South Wales. 8vo. Lond., 1841. MF 3 P 4

Our Own Country : Descriptive, Historical, Pictorial. Illustrated. 6 vols. 4to. Lond., 1880–82. D 6 V 12–17

Public General Statutes passed in the thirty-second to the forty-ninth year of the Reign of Her Majesty Queen Victoria, 1868–85 ; with copious Indexes, Tables, &c. 17 vols. roy. 8vo. Lond., 1869–85. E

Public Income and Expenditure of Great Britain and Ireland. 1688–1869. 2 vols. fol. Lond., 1869. E

Reports from the Committee of Public Accounts; together with the Proceedings of the Committee, Minutes of Evidence, Appendices and Indices. 5 vols. fol. Lond., 1869–75. E

Reports from the Select Committee appointed to consider the means of improving and maintaining the Foreign Trade of the Country. 2 vols. sm. fol. Lond., 1820–22. F 7 P 10, 11 ‡

Statutes of the Realm (20 Henry III, 1101, to 13 Anne, A.D. 1713.) Printed by command of His Majesty King George III, in pursuance of an Address of the House of Commons of Great Britain ; with Alphabetical and Chronological Indexes. 10 vols. atlas fol. Lond., 1810 22. F 25 2–11 ‡

Statutes. (20 Henry III, A.D. 1235, to 42 Victoria, A.D. 1878.) Revised ed. 18 vols. imp. 8vo. Lond., 1870–85. E

Indexes to [the above.] (9 Henry III, 1225, to 50 Victoria, 1886. 2 vols. imp. 8vo. Lond., 1879–87. E

GREAT SOUTH LAND (THE). Four Papers on Emigration, designed to exhibit the Principles and Progress of the new Colony of South Australia. 2nd ed. 8vo. Lond., 1838. MF 3 P 8

Another copy. MJ 2 Q 16

GREATHEAD (Lieut. Wilberforce H.) Report on the Drainage of the City of Delhi and on the Means of Improving it. [Misc. Papers, India.] Fol. Agra., 1852. E

GRECE (C. J.), LL.D. [*See* MAETZNER, PROF. E.]

GREEK ANTHOLOGY (THE), as selected for the use of Westminster, Eton, and other Public Schools.; literally translated into English Prose, chiefly by George Burges, A.M. 8vo. Lond., 1876. H 5 R 47

GREEK ROMANCES of Heliodorus, Longus, and Achilles Tatius. [*See* HELIODORUS.]

GREEK TRAGIC THEATRE (THE); containing Æschylus, by Dr. Potter ; Sophocles, by Dr. Francklin ; and Euripides, by Mich. Woodhull, Esq. 5 vols. 8vo. Lond., 1809. H 4 R 7–11

GREELEY (HON. HORACE). Life and Political Career of ; by William M. Cornell. 8vo. Boston, 1882. C 4 T 10

GREELY (LIEUT. A. W.), U.S.N. Account of the Greely Relief Expedition. [*See* MELVILLE, G. W.]

Rescue of Greely. [*See* SCHLEY, COMM. W. S.]

Three Years of Arctic Service: an Account of the Lady Franklin Bay Expedition of 1881–84, and the attainment of the Farthest North. 2 vols. roy. 8vo. Lond., 1886. D 4 S 9, 10

GREEN (PROF. A. H.), M.A., &c. Geology. Part 1. Physical Geology. Illustrated. 8vo. Lond., 1882. A 9 R 33

GREEN (ASHBEL), D.D. Discourses delivered in the College of New Jersey. 8vo. Philad., 1822. G 2 T 14

GREEN (HENRY) M.A. Andrea Alciati and his Books of Emblems: a Biographical and Bibliographical Study. 8vo. Lond., 1872. C 5 U 1

Shakespeare and the Emblem Writers: an Exposition of their similarities of Thought and Expression, preceded by a View of Emblem-Literature down to A.D. 1616. Imp. 8vo. Lond., 1870. J 2 U 12

Whitney's "Choice of Emblemes." [*See* WHITNEY, G.]

GREEN (J.) Journey from Aleppo to Damascus ; with a Description of those two Capital Cities, and their Neighbouring Parts of Syria. 2 vols. (in 1) 8vo. Lond., 1735–36. D 5 R 41

GREEN (Rev. John Richard), M.A., &c. Conquest of England. With Portrait and Maps. 8vo. Lond., 1883.
B 5 S 5

History of the English People. With Maps. 4 vols. 8vo. Lond., 1878–80.
B 5 S 1–4

Making of England. With Maps. 8vo. Lond., 1881.
B 5 S 6

Short History of the English People. 8vo. Lond., 1874.
B 3 Q 9

Stray Studies from England and Italy. 8vo. Lond., 1876.
J 11 S 12

GREEN (Mary Anne Everett). Lives of the Princesses of England, from the Norman Conquest. 6 vols. 8vo. Lond., 1850–55.
C 4 T 24–29

GREEN (Matthew) Life and Poems of. [*See* Chalmers, A., *and* Johnson, S.]

GREEN (Prof. Thomas Hill), M.A., &c. Prolegomena to Ethics; edited by A. C. Bradley, M.A. 8vo. Oxford, 1883.
G 9 S 17

Works of Thomas Hill Green; edited by R. L. Nettleship. Vols. 1, 2. 8vo. Lond., 1885–86.
G 9 S 26, 27

GREEN (Valentine). History and Antiquities of the City and Suburbs of Worcester. 2 vols (in 1) 4to. Lond., 1796.
B 15 Q 7 ‡

GREEN (William). Attempted Murder of. [*See* Sewell, R. C.]

GREEN (William), Map of the City of Melbourne and its Extensions; compiled from the Government Plans. Roy. 4to. Melb., 1852.
MD 5 S 15 ‡

GREEN (Rev. William Charles), M.A. The Iliad of Homer; with a Verse Translation. [*See* Homer.]

GREEN (William Spotswood), M.A. High Alps of New Zealand; or, a Trip to the Glaciers of the Antipodes, with an Ascent of Mount Cook. 8vo. Lond., 1883.* MD 5 P 8

GREENAWAY (A. J.) Short Text-book of Organic Chemistry. [*See* Strecker, A.]

GREENBANK (T. K.) Greenbank's Periodical Library. Vol. 1. 8vo. Philad., 1840.
J 6 U 5

GREENE (George Washington), LL.D. German Element in the War of American Independence. 8vo. New York, 1876.
B 1 Q 38

GREENE (J. Baker), LL.B., &c. Hebrew Migration from Egypt : a Historical Account of the Exodus, based on a critical Examination of the Hebrew Records and Traditions. 2nd ed. 8vo. Lond., 1883.
G 9 S 16

GREENE (Robert), M.A. Old English Drama: Select Plays: Marlowe's Tragical History of Dr. Faustus, and Greene's Honourable History of Friar Bacon and Friar Bungay; edited by A. W. Ward, M.A. (Clar. Press.) 12mo. Oxford, 1878.
H 2 Q 39

Tracts of. [*See* Brydges, Sir S. E.]

Life and complete Works of ; in Prose and Verse; edited by the Rev. Alexander Grosart, D.D., &c. (Huth Library.) 15 vols. 4to. Lond., 1881–86.
J 5 U 10–24

GREENE (Robert), and PEELE (George). Dramatic and Poetical Works of ; with Memoirs of the Authors and Notes, by the Rev. Alexander Dyce. Roy. 8vo. Lond., 1874.
H 2 T 14

GREENE (Capt. W. S.) [*See* Codes.]

GREENE (W. T.), M.A., &c. Parrots in Captivity; with Notes on several species, by the Hon. and Rev. F. G. Dutton. Illustrated. 2 vols. roy. 8vo. Lond., 1884.
A 15 R 6, 7

GREENER (W. W.) The Gun and its Development; with Notes on Shooting. Illustrated. Sq. 8vo. Lond., 1881.
A 11 T 22

GREENHAM (M. Richard). Works of. 2nd ed. Sm. 4to. Lond., 1599.
G 8 S.6

GREENHOW (Mrs. Rose). My Imprisonment, and the First Year of the Abolition Rule at Washington. 12mo. Lond., 1863.
B 1 R 39

GREENOUGH (William W.) Address delivered at the Dedication of the East Boston Branch of the Public Library, on the 22nd of March, 1871. 8vo. Boston, 1871.
J 2 T 6

GREENWOOD (Lieut. J.) Narrative of the late Victorious Campaign in Affghanistan, under General Pollock. 8vo. Lond., 1844.
B 1 P 3

GREENWOOD (Rev. James), M.A. New South Wales Public School League, for making Primary Education National, Secular, Compulsory, and Free. 8vo. Sydney, 1874.
MG 1 Q 32

Sermons for the People: Religious Wars. 8vo. Sydney (n.d.)
MG 1 Q 14

Sermons for the People: The Plan of Salvation. 8vo. Sydney (n.d.)
MG 1 Q 15

Speech delivered in the Temperance Hall, Pitt-street, December 4th, 1874, in reply to the Hon. [Sir] Henry Parkes, on Education. 8vo. Sydney, 1874.
MG 1 Q 38

GREENWOOD (James), B.A. The Sailor's Sea-book : a Rudimentary Treatise on Navigation. (Weale.) 12mo. Lond., 1870.
A 17 P 18

Another copy. New, thoroughly revised, and much enlarged edition, by W. H. Rosser. (Weale.) 12mo. Lond., 1879.
A 17 Q 39

GREENWOOD (JAMES). Savage Habits and Customs. 3rd ed. With Woodcuts and Designs. 8vo. Lond., 1865. MA 1 R 16

GREENWOOD (THOMAS), M.A. First Book of the History of the Germans : Barbaric Period. 4to. Lond., 1836. B 18 Q 7 ‡

Position and Prospects of the Protestant Churches of Great Britain and Ireland, with reference to the proposed Establishment of a Roman Catholic Hierarchy in this Country. 8vo. Lond., 1851. MF 1 R 1

GREENWOOD (THOMAS), F.R.G.S. Free Public Libraries; their Organization, Uses, and Management. 12mo. Lond., 1886. J 11 S 34

GREENWOOD (WILLIAM HENRY), F.C.S. Manual of Metallurgy. Illustrated. 2 vols. 12mo. Lond., 1874–75. A 9 P 19, 20

GREER (HENRY). Recent Wonders in Electricity, Electric Lighting, Magnetism, Telegraphy, Telephony, &c. 8vo. New York, 1883. A 5 U 3

Storage of Electricity. 8vo. New York, 1883. A 5 U 3

GREG (J.) Antiquarian and Topographical Cabinet. [*See* STORER, J.]

Antiquarian Itinerary. [*See* STORER, J.]

GREG (PERCY). The Devil's Advocate. 2 vols. 8vo. Lond., 1878. G 8 S 17, 18

GREG (ROBERT PHILIPS), F.G.S., AND LETTSOM (W. G.) Manual of the Mineralogy of Great Britain and Ireland. 8vo. Lond., 1858. A 10 P 8

GREG (WILLIAM RATHBONE). Creed of Christendom : its Foundations contrasted with its Superstructure. 6th ed. 2 vols. 8vo. Lond., 1879. G 3 P 19, 20

Enigmas of Life. 10th ed., with a Postscript. 8vo. Lond., 1874. G 8 S 19

Essays on Political and Social Science, contributed to the *Edinburgh Review*. 2 vols. 8vo. Lond., 1853. F 8 P 18, 19

Literary and Social Judgments. 4th ed., considerably enlarged. 2 vols. 8vo. Lond., 1877. J 11 T 31, 32

Mistaken Aims and Attainable Ideals of the Artisan Class. 8vo. Lond., 1876. F 6 R 16

Political Problems for our Age and Country. 8vo. Lond., 1870. F 8 P 12

Rocks Ahead ; or, the Warnings of Cassandra. 2nd ed., with a Reply to Objectors. 8vo. Lond., 1874. F 6 Q 19

GREGO (JOSEPH). History of Parliamentary Elections and Electioneering in the Old Days. 8vo. Lond., 1886. B 7 Q 29

Rowlandson, the Caricaturist: a Selection from his Works; with anecdotal Descriptions of his famous Caricatures, and a Sketch of his Life, Times, &c. 2 vols. 4to. Lond., 1880. C 2 W 21, 22

GREGOIRE DE TOURS (SAINT). Mémoires de. [*See* GUIZOT, F. P. G., 1, 2.]

GREGOR (REV. J.), M.A. Missionary Tours. [*See* BROUGHTON, RT. REV. W. G.]

GREGOR (W. G.) [*See* GRAY, J. H.]

GREGORAS NICEPHORUS. Byzantinæ Historiæ, libri XXXVII. [*See* MIGNE, J. P., SERIES GRÆCA, 148, 149.]

GREGORIUS (S. GEORGIUS FLORENTINUS). Opera omnia. [*See* MIGNE, J. P., SERIES LATINA, 71.]

GREGORIUS MAGNUS (PAPA). Opera omnia. [*See* MIGNE, J. P., SERIES LATINA, 75–79.]

Opera Omnia. 4 vols. fol. Paris, 1705. G 35 P 16–19 ‡

GREGORIUS NAZIANZENUS (SANCTUS). Opera omnia. [*See* MIGNE, J. P., SERIES GRÆCA, 35–38.]

GREGORIUS NYSSENUS (SANCTUS). Opera omnia. [*See* MIGNE, J. P., SERIES GRÆCA, 44–46.]

GREGORIUS PALAMAS. Opera omnia. [*See* MIGNE, J. P., SERIES GRÆCA, 150, 151.]

GREGORIUS THAUMATURGUS (SANCTUS). Opera Omnia. [*See* MIGNE, J. P., SERIES GRÆCA, 10.]

GREGORIUS IV (PAPA). Opera omnia. [*See* MIGNE, J. P., LATINA, 106.]

GREGORY VII (SAINT HILDEBRAND). Epistolæ et Diplomata Pontificia. [*See* MIGNE, J. P., SERIES LATINA, 148.]

Life and Pontificate of; by John William Bowden, M.A. 2 vols. 8vo. Lond., 1840. C 9 Q 1, 2

GREGORY (A. C.) Journal of the North Australian Exploring Expedition, 1855. (Journal of the Geographical Society, 28.) 8vo. Lond., 1858. E

Papers relating to an Expedition recently undertaken for the purpose of exploring the Northern Portion of Australia. (Parl. Docs. 67.) Fol. Lond., 1857–58. MF 4 ‡

[*See* MUELLER, BARON SIR F. VON.]

GREGORY (BENJAMIN). The Thorough Business Man ; Memoirs of Walter Powell, Merchant, Melbourne and London. 8vo. Lond., 1871. MC 1 P 40

GREGORY (G.), F.A.S. Lectures on the Sacred Poetry of the Hebrews. [*See* LOWTH, RT. REV. R.]

GREGORY (J. A.) Administration of Law in the Supreme Court, and its consistency with justice, as exposed in the case Royce *v.* Gregory. 8vo. Melb., 1864. MF 1 Q 5

GREGORY (JOHN HERBERT). Letter to the Rt. Rev the Lord Bishop of Melbourne, on Church Music. 8vo Melb., 1857. MG 1 Q 40

GREGORY (OLINTHUS), LL.D. Lessons, Astronomical and Philosophical. 8vo. Lond., 1815.   A 3 S 30

Letters to a Friend, on Evidences, Doctrines, and Duties of the Christian Religion. 2nd ed. 2 vols. (in 1) 8vo. Lond., 1812.   G 2 T 20

Mathematical Tables. [*See* HUTTON, DR. C.]

Memoir of Rev. Robert Hall. [*See* HALL, REV. R.].

Treatise of Mechanics, Theoretical, Practical, and Descriptive; containing the Theory of Statics, Dynamics, Hydrostatics, Hydronamics, and Pneumatics. 4th ed. 3 vols. 8vo. Lond., 1826.   A 11 S 20–22

GREGORY (WILLIAM). ' Second Edition of a Visible Display of a Divine Providence ; or, the Journal of a captured Missionary, designated to the Southern Pacific Ocean, in the second voyage of the ship *Duff*. 8vo. Lond., 1801.   MD 4 U 23

GREGORY (DR. W.) Animal Magnetism ; or, Mesmerism and its Phenomena. 8vo. Lond., 1884.   A 12 S 13

[See REICHENBACH, BARON VON K., *and* TURNER, R.]

GREGSON (T. G.) Speech in the Legislative Council on the State of Public Education in Van Diemen's Land, Thursday, August 30, 1849.—Letter to the Editor of the *Colonial Times*. 8vo. Hobart, 1850.   MG 1 Q 30

GREIG (CAMPBELL MACAULAY). Prince Albert's Land. Reminiscences of a Pleasant Sojourn in Coburg Gotha. 8vo. Lond., 1871.   D 7 P 28 ·

GREIG (JOHN). [*See* DYER, G.]

GREIG (I.) Antiquarian Itinerary. [*See* STORER, JAS.]

GREIN (C. W. M.), DR.PH. Sprachschatz der angelsächsischen Dichter. 2 vols. 8vo. Cassel, 1861–64.   K 15 P 1, 2

Grein's Lexicon of the Anglo-Saxon Language. [*See* HARRISON, PROF. J. A.]

GRELLMANN (H. M. G.) Dissertation on the Gipseys. 8vo. Lond., 1807.   A 1 W 8

GRENVILLE (RICHARD), EARL TEMPLE, K.G., AND GRENVILLE (RT. HON. GEORGE). The Grenville Papers ; edited, with Notes, by William James Smith. 4 vols. 8vo. Lond., 1852–53.   B 5 U 32–35

GRENVILLE (RICHARD NUGENT BRYDGES CHANDOS), DUKE OF BUKINGHAM AND CHANDOS. [*See* BUCKINGHAM AND CHANDOS, DUKE OF.]

GRESHAM (SIR THOMAS). Life and Times of ; compiled by Rev. J. W. Burgon. 2 vols. 8vo. Lond., 1839.   C 7 R 13, 14

GRESWELL (A. AND J. B.) Disease and Disorders of the Horse. ·8vo. Lond., 1886.   A 1 R 29

GRESWELL (GEORGE, CHARLES, AND ALBERT). Veterinary Pharmacopæia, Meteria Medica, and Therapeutics ; with Descriptions of the Physiological Action of Medicines. 8vo. Lond., 1886.   A 12 Q 3

GRESWELL (WILLIAM), M.A., &c. Our South African Empire. 2 vols. 8vo. Lond., 1885.   D 1 V 9, 10

GREVILLE (CHARLES C. F.) The Greville Memoirs. Part 1 : a Journal of the Reigns of King George IV, and King William IV ; Part 2 : a Journal of the Reign of Queen Victoria, 1837–52 ; edited by Henry Reeve. 6 vols. 8vo. Lond., 1875–85.   B 5 U 36–41

GREVILLE (EDWARD). Year-book of Australia (Official Directory and Almanac of Australia), for 1882–88. 7 vols. 8vo. Sydney, 1882–88.   ME 5 T
Year-book of New South Wales, for 1887. 8vo. Sydney, 1887.   ME 5 T

GREVILLE (EDWARD) & CO. Official Post Office Directory of New South Wales, 1872, and 1875–77. 2 vols. 8vo. Sydney, 1872–75.   ME 4 S

GREVILLE (HENRY). Leaves from the Diary of ; edited by ViscountessEnfield. [1st and] 2nd series ; with Portrait. 8vo. Lond., 1883–84.   C 6 Q 27, 28

GREVILLE (R. K.) British India. [*See* MURRAY, HUGH.]

GREVILLE (VIOLET), LADY. Montrose. 8vo. Lond., 1886.   C 6 S 30

GREY (GEN. THE HON. CHARLES). Early Years of H.R.H. the Prince Consort. 8vo. Lond., 1867.   C 1 V 19

GREY (JANE), LADY. Writings of. [*See* BRITISH REFORMERS 4.]

GREY (SIR GEORGE), K.C.B. Correspondence with Governor Grey, relative to the Affairs of New Zealand. (Parl. Docs., 50.) Fol. Lond., 1847.   MF 4 ‡

Journal of an Expedition overland from Auckland to Taranaki. [*See* COOPER, G. S.]

Journal of Two Expeditions of Discovery in North-west and Western Australia, during the years 1837–39, under the Authority of Her Majesty's Government. 2 vols. 8vo. Lond., 1841.*   MD 2 T 1, 2

Ko nga Mahi a nga tupuna Maori ia mea kohikohia. 2nd ed. 8vo. Auckland, 1885.   MB 2 R 37

Ko nga Ma1inga a nga ·tupuna Maori he mea kohikohi mai. (Mythology and Traditions of the New Zealanders.) 8vo. Lond., 1854.   MB 2 R 38

Ko nga Moteatea, me nga Hakirara o nga Maori. He mea kohikohi mai. I tera kaumatua, i tera kuia ; no ona haerenga, e maia, ki nga pito katoa, o enei motu. (Poems, Traditions, and Chaunts of the Maories.) 8vo. Wellington, 1853.   MH 1 S 7

GREY (SIR GEORGE), K.C.B.—*continued.*
Library of. (Presented by Sir George Grey to the South
African Public Library.) Edited by W. H. I. Bleek.
2 vols. 4to., and 2 vols. (in 1) 8vo. Cape Town,
1858–67.   K 2 Q10–12 †
  1. Philology. Parts 1 and 2. South Africa. Part 3. Mada-
    gascar.
  2. Philology. Part 1. Australia. Part 2. Papuan Languages
    of the Loyalty Island, and New Hebrides, comprising those of
    the Islands of Neugone, Lifu, Aneiteums, Tana, and others.
    Part 3. Fiji Islands and Rotuma. (With Supplements to
    Parts 1 and 2.) Part 4. New Zealand, the Chatham Islands,
    and Auckland Islands.
  3. Manuscripts and Incunables. Part 1. Manuscripts.
  4. Early Printed Books. Part 1. England.

Polynesian Mythology, and Ancient Traditional History
of the New Zealand Race, as furnished by their Priests
and Chiefs. 8vo. Lond., 1855.*   MB 2 R 35
Another copy. 2nd ed. (English and Maori.) 8vo.
Auckland, 1885.   MB 2 R 37
Vocabulary of the Dialects of South-western Australia.
2nd ed. 12mo. Lond., 1840.*   MK 1 P 27
[*See* DAVIS, C. O. B.]

GREY (HAROLD), T. E. ARGLES. Two Weeks in
Darlinghurst; the Horrors of the Lock-up. The City
Cafés after Midnight. Among the Members; by "The
Pilgrim." (Pam. N.) Sydney, 1875.   MJ 2 P 29

GREY (HENRY), EARL. Colonial Policy of Lord John
Russell's Administration. 2 vols. 8vo. Lond., 1853.*
                                              MF 2 R 11, 12
Another copy. 2nd ed. 2 vols. 8vo. Lond., 1853.
                                              MF 2 R 15, 16
Parliamentary Government, considered with reference to
a Reform of Parliament: an Essay. 8vo. Lond.,
1858.   F 5 P 27
Review of the Colonial Policy of Lord Russell's Adminis-
tration. [*See* ADDERLEY, RT. HON. SIR C. B.]

GREY (JANE), LADY. [*See* BRITISH REFORMERS, 4.]

GRIBBLE (J. D. B.), M.C.S. Manual of the District
of Cuddapah, in the Presidency of Madras. Roy. 8vo.
Madras, 1875.   B 10 V 13

GRIERSON (GEORGE A.), M.A., &c. Bihár Peasant Life;
being a descriptive Catalogue of the Surroundings of the
People of that Province. Roy. 8vo. Calcutta, 1885.
                                              K 13 T 15
GRIERSON (J.) Railway Rates, English and Foreign.
8vo. Lond., 1886.   F 8 P 7

GRIERSON (SIR ROBERT). The Laird of Lag: a Life
Sketch [of Sir Robert Grierson]; by Lieut.-Col. A. Fergusson. 8vo. Edinb., 1886.   C 11 P 9

GRIESINGER (THEODOR). The Jesuits: a complete History
of their Open and Secret Proceedings, from the Foundation
of the Order to the Present Time; translated by A. J.
Scott, M.D. 2 vols. 8vo. Lond., 1883.   G 4 Q 22, 23

GRIFFIN (GERALD). [Works of.] 8 vols. 12mo. Lond.,
1842–43.   J 7 Q 28–35
  1. Life of Gerald Griffin, Esq.; by his Brother [W. Griffin, M.D.]
  2. The Collegians: a Tale of Garryowen.
  3. Card Drawing; The Half Sir, &c.
  4. "Holland-Tide"; The Aylmers of Bally-Aylmer, &c.
  5. The Rivals; Tracy's Ambition.
  6. Sigismund, &c.
  7. The Duke of Monmouth.
  8. Poetical Works.

GRIFFIN (G. W.) New Zealand; her Commerce and
Resources. Roy. 8vo. Wellington, 1884.   MF 3 R 31

GRIFFIN (SIR LEPEL HENRY), K.C.S.I. The Great Republic. 8vo. Lond., 1884.   D 4 P 4

GRIFFIN (R.), & CO. Catalogue of Modern Chemical
Apparatus for the Analysis of Soils and Manures. (Pam.
19.) 8vo. Glasgow, 1845.   MJ 2 Q 8

GRIFFIN (WILLIAM), M.D. Life of Gerald Griffin. [*See*
GRIFFIN, G.]

GRIFFIN (W. N.), B.D. Elements of Algebra and Trigonometry. (Text-books.) 12mo. Lond., 1871. A 17 S 4
Notes on the Elements of Algebra and Trigonometry; with
Solutions of the more difficult Questions. (Text-books.)
12mo. Lond., 1872.   A 17 S 5

GRIFFIS (WILLIAM ELLIOT). Córea: the Hermit Nation.
1. Ancient and Mediæval History. 2. Political and Social
Corea. 3. Modern and Recent History. 8vo. New
York, 1882.   B 2 P 41
The Mikado's Empire. Book 1. History of Japan, from
660 B.C. to 1872 A.D. Book 2. Personal Experiences, Ob-
servations, and Studies in Japan, 1870–74. 8vo. New
York, 1883.   B 12 S 7

GRIFFITH (CHARLES J.), A.M. Observations on the Water
Supply of Melbourne. 8vo. Melb., 1855.   MJ 2 R 23
Present State and Prospects of the Port Phillip District of
N. S. Wales. 8vo. Dublin, 1845.*   MD 5 Q 27

GRIFFITH (MAJOR AND MRS. GEORGE DARBY). Journey
across the Desert from Ceylon to Marseilles. 2 vols. 8vo.
Lond., 1845.   D 4 R 34, 35

GRIFFITH (HENRY THOMAS), B.A. Didactic Poems of
Cowper; With Notes, &c. [*See* COWPER, W.]

GRIFFITH (J. W.), M.D., &c. AND HENFREY (PROF. A.),
F.R.S., &c. Micrographic Dictionary: a Guide to the
Examination and Investigation of the Structure and Nature
of Microscopic Objects. 3rd ed. Vol. 1. Text. Vol. 2.
Plates. 2 vols. (in 1) 8vo. Lond., 1875.   K 18 P 1

GRIFFITH (RALPH T. H.), M.A. Birth of the War-God:
a Poem. [*See* KÁLIDÁSA.]

[*See* ABDU-R-RAHMAN.]

GRIFFITH (THOMAS), A.M. Fundamentals; or, Bases of Belief concerning Man, God, and the Correlation of God and Man : a Hand-book of Mental, Moral, and Religions Philosophy. 8vo. Lond., 1871. G 15 R 1

GRIFFITH (WILLIAM). Posthumous Papers: Journals of Travels in Assam, Burma, Bootan, Affghanistan, &c.; arranged by John Macclelland. 2 vols. 8vo. Calcutta, 1847–48. A 4 T 1, 2
  1. Journal of Travels.
  2. Itinerary Notes of Plants.
Posthumous Papers: Notulæ ad Plantas Asiaticas. Parts 1–4; arranged by John Macclelland. 4 vols. 8vo. Calcutta, 1847–54. A 4 T 3–6
Posthumous Papers: Icones Plantarum Asiaticarum. Parts 1–4; arranged by John Macclelland. 4 vols. (in 2) 4to. Calcutta, 1847–51. A 4 S 3, 4 †
Posthumous Papers: Palms of British East India. Fol. Calcutta, 1850. A 1 P 10 ‡

GRIFFITHS (ARTHUR). Chronicles of Newgate. 2 vols. 8vo. Lond., 1884. B 4 S 19, 20
Memorials of Millbank, and Chapters in Prison History. 2 vols. 8vo. Lond., 1875. F 12 P 20, 21

GRIFFITHS (A. T.) Bibliotheca Anglo-Poetica; or, a Descriptive Catalogue of a rare and rich Collection of Early English Poetry, in the possession of Longman, Hurst, Rees, Orme, and Brown. 8vo. Lond., 1815. K 8 P 15

GRIFFITHS (E.) [*See* CUVIER, BARON G. C. L. D.]

GRIFFITHS (MRS. ELIZABETH). The School for Rakes: a Comedy. (Bell's Brit. Theatre.) 18mo. Lond., 1795. H 2 P 4

GRIFFITHS (J. W. D.) Travels in Europe, Asia Minor, and Arabia. 4to. Lond., 1805. D 5 V 10

GRIFFITHS (WILLIAM). Trusses of Wood and Iron; with complete Working Drawings. Obl. 18mo. Lond., 1886. A 6 R 3

GRIMALDI (JOSEPH). Memoirs of; edited by "Boz" (Charles Dickens). Illustrated by George Cruikshank 2 vols. 12mo. Lond., 1838. C 2 P20, 21
Another copy. 8vo. Lond., 1853. C 2 R 17

GRIMBLE (AUGUSTUS). Deer Stalking. Illustrated. 8vo. Lond., 1886. A 17 U 24

GRIMBLOT (PAUL). Letters of William III and Louis XIV, and of their Ministers, illustrative of the Domestic and Foreign Politics of England, from the Peace of Ryswick to the Accession of Phillip V of Spain, 1697–1700. 2 vols. 8vo. Lond., 1848. B 6 P 8, 9

GRIMM (FREDERICK MELCHOIR), BARON DE. Historical and Literary Memoirs and Anecdotes, selected from the Correspondence of Baron de Grimm and Denis Diderot; translated from the French. 2nd ed. 4 vols. 8vo. Lond., 1815. C 8 Q 24–27

GRIMM (HERMAN). Fünfzehn Essays. 2e auflage. 8vo. Berlin, 1874. J 17 P 23
Life and Times of Goethe; translated by Sarah Holland Adams. 8vo. Boston, 1880. C 6 U 16
Literature. 8vo. Lond., 1886. J 9 S 9

GRIMM (DR. JACOB LUDWIG CARL). Deutsche Grammatik zweite [und] dritte Ausgaben. 5 vols. 8vo. Göttingen, 1822–40. K 14 P 2–6
Register [to the above] von Dr. K. G. Andresen. 8vo. Göttingen, 1865. K 14 P 30
Gotische Glossar. [*See* SCHULZE, E.]
Kleinere Schriften. 5 vols. 8vo. Berlin, 1865–79. K 14 T 23–27
Teutonic Mythology; translated from the fourth edition, by James Steven Stallybrass. 3 vols. 8vo. Lond., 1880–83. B 27 U 1–3
Uber den Ursprung der Sprache. 7e auflage. 8vo. Berlin, 1879. K 12 R 23
[*See* BOPP, F.]

GRIMM (DR. JACOB LUDWIG), UND GRIMM (WILHELM KARL). Deutsches Wörterbuch. 6 vols. (in 7) A–M imp. 8vo. Leipzig, 1854–85. K 14 R 17–23
German Popular Stories and Fairy Tales, as told by Gammer Gretel, from the collection of MM. Grimm. Revised Translation, by Edgar Taylor; with Illustrations from Designs, by George Cruikshank and Ludwig Grimm. 8vo. Lond., 1877. J 9 Q 11
Household Tales; with the Author's Notes; translated from the German, and edited by Margaret Hunt; with an Introduction, by Andrew Lang, M.A. 2 vols. 8vo. Lond., 1884. B 27 Q 1-2

GRIMM (O. A.) Russian Pamphlets, Zoology, &c. Roy. 8vo. St. Petersburg and Moscow, 1876–80. A 13 U 14

GRIMSHAWE (REV. T. S.), A.M. Life and Works of William Cowper. [*See* COWPER, W.]

GRIMSTONE (S. E.) Southern Settlements of New Zealand ; comprising Statistical Information from the Earliest Period to the close of the year 1846. 8vo. Wellington, 1847. MD 7 Q 34

GRIMSTONE (MRS. W. H.), MRS. KENDAL. The Drama: a Paper read at the Congress of the National Association for the Promotion of Social Science, Birmingham, September, 1884. [4th ed.] 18mo. Lond., 1884. J 1 W 39

GRIMTHORPE (BARON). [*See* BECKETT, SIR E.]

GRINDAL (EDMUND), ARCHBISHOP OF CANTERBURY. History of the Life and Acts of. [*See* STRYPE, J., 9.]

GRINDELY (ANTON). History of the Thirty Years' War; translated by Andrew Ten-Brook. 2 vols. 8vo. N. York, 1884. B 7 T 33–34

GRINDLAY (CAPT. R. M.) Scenery, Costumes, and Architecture, chiefly on the western side of India. Roy. 4to. Lond., 1826.   A 14 U 10 ‡

GRINDON (L. H.) Fruits and Fruit Trees. 8vo. Manchester, 1885.   A 1 P 51

GRISWOLD (REV. R. W.) Female Poets of America. 8vo. Philad., 1849.   H 6 S 28
Works of E. A. Poe. [*See* POE, E. A.]

GRISWOLD (WILLIAM MACCRILLIS). Q. P. Indexes. 16 vols. (in 7.) 8vo. Bangor, 1880–86.   E

GROCOTT (J. C.) An Index to Familiar Quotations, selected principally from British Authors; with parallel passages from various writers, ancient and modern. 5th ed. 12mo. Liverpool, 1878.   K 17 P 11

GROHMAN (W. A. BAILLIE). Gaddings with a Primitive People; being a Series of Sketches of Alpine Life and Customs. 2 vols. 8vo. Lond., 1878.   D 8 R 25, 26
Tyrol and the Tyrolese. 8vo. Lond., 1876.   D 8 R 24

GRÖNBERG (B. C.) Deutsch-Dänisches und Dänisch-Deutches Hand-Wörterbuch. 3e ausgabe. 2 vols. (in 1) 12mo. Kopenhagen, 1846–51.   K 16 P 4

GRONOVIUS (A.) [*See* JUSTINUS.]

GRONOVIUS (J. F.) [*See* PLAUTUS, M. A.]

GRONOVIUS (JACOB). [*See* ARRIAN, FLAVIUS, *and* GELLIUS, A.]

GRONOW (CAPT. REES HOWELL). Last Recollections; being the Fourth and Final Series of his Reminiscences and Anecdotes. 8vo. Lond., 1866.   C 3 P 21

GROOME (FRANCIS H.) Ordnance Gazetteer of Scotland. Vol. 2. Imp. 8vo. Edinb., 1885.   D 12 V 7

GROS (JEAN BAPTISTE LOUIS), BARON. Recollections of Baron Gros' Embassy to China and Japan. [*See* DE MOGES, MARQUIS.]

GROSCHOPP (—). Grein's Political Lexicon of the Anglo-Saxon Language. [*See* HARRISON, PROF. J. A.]

GROSE (FRANCIS), F.A.S. Antiquities of England and Wales. 4 vols. 4to. Lond., 1773–76.   B 10 Q 14–17 †
Antiquities of Ireland. 2 vols. imp. 4to. Lond., 1791–95.   B 19 Q 6, 7 ‡
Antiquities of Scotland. 2 vols. imp. 8vo. Lond., 1789–91.   B 12 V 28, 29
Classical Dictionary of the Vulgar Tongue. 8vo. Lond., 1785.   Libr.
[*See* ANTIQUARIAN REPERTORY.]

GROTE (AUGUSTUS RADCLIFFE), A.M., &c. An Illustrated Essay on the Noctuidae of North America; with a "Colony of Butterflies." 8vo. Lond., 1882. A 13 U 26

GROSART (REV. ALEXANDER B.), LL.D. [*See* ELIOT, SIR JOHN; HUTH LIBRARY; *and* HERRICK, R.]

GROSVERNOR NOTES. [*See* BLACKBURN, H.]

GROTE (GEORGE), F.R.S. Aristotle; edited by Alex. Bain, LL.D., and G. C. Robertson. 2 vols. 8vo. Lond., 1872.   G 10 T 24, 25
Fragments on Ethical Subjects. 8vo Lond., 1876. G 7 P 2
History of Greece. 3rd ed. 12 vols. 8vo. Lond., 1851–56.   B 10 P 1–12
Personal Life of; compiled from Family Documents, Private Memoranda, and Original Letters to and from various Friends, by Mrs. Grote. 8vo. Lond., 1873.   C 7 T 2
Plato and other Companions of Sokrates. 2nd ed. 3 vols 8vo. Lond., 1867.   G 10 T 10–12
Review of the Work of Mr. John Stuart Mill, entitled "Examination of Sir William Hamilton's Philosophy." 12mo. Lond., 1868.   G 8 P 6
Seven Letters concerning the Politics of Switzerland, pending the Outbreak of the Civil War in 1847. 8vo. Lond., 1876.   B 7 U 30

GROTE (MRS. HARRIET). Memoir of the Life of Ary Scheffer. 2nd ed. 8vo. Lond., 1860.   C 3 R 33
Personal Life of George Grote. 8vo. Lond.,1873. C 7 T 2

GROTIUS (HUGO). De Jure Belli ac Pacis, Libri tres, in quibus Jus Naturæ et Gentium, item Juris Publici præcipua explicantur. 2 vols. 4to. Amsterd., 1719. F 5 V 12, 13
Life of; with brief Minutes of the Civil, Ecclesiastical, and Literary History of the Netherlands. by Charles Butler. 8vo. Lond., 1826.   G 8 Q 23
Life of; with a Critical Account of his Works, by Jean Lévesque de Burigny. 8vo. Lond., 1754.   C 5 R 17
On the Origin of the Native Races of America: a Dissertation. (Bibliotheca Curiosa). 12mo. Edinb., 1884. E

GROUND (REV. W. D.) Examination of the Structural Principles of Mr. Herbert Spencer's Philosophy: intended as a Proof that Theism is the only Theory of the Universe that can satisfy Reason. 8vo. Oxford, 1883. G 14 P 8

GROUT (REV. LEWIS). The Isizulu: a Grammar of the Zulu Language; accompanied with a Historical Introduction; also with an Appendix. 8vo. Natal, 1859.   K 13 P 1

GROVE (E. D.) Cæsar de Bello Gallico: an Interlinear translation, designed as an aid to Self Instruction in the Latin Language. (The Australian Series of Keys to the Classics.) 8vo. Sydney, 1870.   M B 2 P 44

GROVE (F. C.) The Frosty Caucasus: an Account of a Walk through part of the Range, and of an Ascent of Elbruz in the Summer of 1874. 8vo. Lond., 1875.   D 8 R 15

GROVE (G.) [*See* SMITH, DR. W.]

GROVE (SIR G.) Dictionary of Music and Musicians (A.D. 1450–1883), by eminent Writers, English and Foreign. Illustrated. Vols. 1–3. 8vo. Lond., 1879–83.
K 18 Q 7–9

GROVE (W. B.), B.A. Synopsis of the Bacteria and Yeast Fungi and allied Species. Illustrated. 8vo. Lond., 1884.
A 17 T 5

GROVE (SIR WILLIAM ROBERT), Q.C., &c. Correlation of Physical Forces. 5th ed. 8vo. Lond., 1867. A 5 T 6

Lecture on the Progress of Physical Science since the opening of the London Institution. (Pam. 25.) 8vo. Lond., 1842.
MJ 2 Q 13

GROVER (CAPT. J.), F.R.S. The Bokhara Victims [Col. Charles Stoddart and Capt. Arthur Conolly.] 8vo. Lond., 1845.
B 1 P 19

GROVER (L. F.), GOVERNOR. Biennial Message to the Legislative Assembly of the State of Oregon. Ninth Regular Session, 1876. (Pams. Jb.) 8vo. Salem, 1876.
MF 3 P 21

GROVES (C. E.) [*See* MILLER, W. A.]

GRUBE (A. W.) Biographische Miniaturbilder. Zur bildenden Lektüre für Jung und Altversaszt. 2 vols. (in 1). 8vo. Leipzig, 1856–57.
C 6 S 11

GRUEBER (E.) Roman Law of Damage to Property. 8vo. Oxford, 1886.
F 8 P 20

GRUND (FRANCIS J.) Aristocracy in America, from the Sketch-book of a German Nobleman. 2 vols. 8vo. Lond., 1839.
D 3 P 27, 28

GRUNDY (FRANCIS H.), C.E. Pictures of the Past: Memories of Men I have met and Places I have seen. 8vo. Lond., 1879.
MC 1 Q 2

GRUNER (LEWIS), K.A. Fresco Decorations and Stuccoes of Churches and Palaces in Italy. Imp. 4to. Lond., 1854.
A 10 P 15 ‡

GSELL-FELS (DR. T.) Switzerland; its Scenery and People; translated by George G. Chisholm, M.A. Imp. 4to. Lond., 1881.
D 5 S 3 †

GUALTERIO (F. A.) Gli ultimi Rivolgimenti Italiani. 5 vols. 12mo. Napoli, 1861.
B 12 P 4–8

GUARDIAN (THE): a Weekly Journal of Politics, Commerce, Agriculture, Literature, Science, and Arts, for the Middle and Working Classes of New South Wales. Fol. Sydney, 1844.
E

GUBBINS (MARTIN RICHARD). Account of the Mutinies in Oudh, and of the Siege of the Lucknow Residency. 8vo. Lond., 1858.
B 10 U 10

GUBERNATIS (ANGELO DE). Dizionario Biografico degli Scrittori Contemporanes. Roy. 8vo. Firenze, 1879.
C 11 V 17

Storia Universale della Letteratura. 18 vols. 8vo. Milano, 1883–85.
B 14 P 6–23

Zoological Mythology; or, the Legends of Animals. 2 vols. 8vo. Lond., 1872.
A 14 U 25, 26

2 S

GUDGEON (THOMAS WAYTH). Defenders of New Zealand; being a short Biography of the Colonists who distinguished themselves in upholding Her Majesty's Supremacy in these Islands. 8vo. Auckland, 1887.*
MB 2 U 6

History and Doings of the Maoris, from the year 1820 to the Signing of the Treaty of Waitangi in 1840. 8vo. Auckland, 1885.*
MB 2 T 5

Reminiscences of the War in New Zealand. With Portraits. 8vo. Lond., 1879
MB 1 Q 30

GUÉRANGER (PROSPER) L'ABBÉ DE SOLESMES. Sainte Cécile et la Société Romaine aux deux premiers Siècles. Imp. 8vo. Paris, 1874.
G 12 Q 6

GUERLE (HÉQUIN DE). Biographie de J. de La Fontaine. [*See* LA FONTAINE, J. DE.]

GUERRA (ESTEBAN). Description of the Mineralogica Cabinet of Mr. Emilio Escobar (in Spanish and English). (Pam. Co.) 8vo. Philad., 1876.
A 16 U 23

GUEST (—.) [*See* ANDERSON, T.]

GUEST (CHARLOTTE E.), LADY. The Mabinogion, from the Llyfr Coch o Hergest and other Ancient Welsh Manuscripts; with an English Translation and Notes. 3 vols. roy. 8vo. Lond., 1849.
J 8 V 19–21

Another copy. [2nd ed.] Roy. 8vo. Lond., 1877.
J 8 V 22

GUEST (EDWIN), M.A., &c. History of English Rhythms. 2 vols. 8vo. Lond., 1838.
B 25 S 9, 10

Another copy. New ed., edited by the Rev. Walter W. Skeat, M.A. 8vo. Lond., 1882.
B 25 S 11

Origines Celticæ (a Fragment), and other Contributions to the History of Britain. 2 vols. 8vo. Lond., 1883.
B 7 P 33, 34

Guest's Compendious Shorthand: the Manual of Compendious Shorthand; or, Universal Visible Speech: a practical System of Steno-Phonography. 8vo. Lond., 1883.
K 12 P 35

GUEULETTE (THOS. SIMON). Les Contes Chinois, &c. [*See* CABINET DES FÉES, 19, 21–23, 32.]

GUGLIELMI (P.) [*See* GIBSON, J.]

GUHL (E.), AND KONER (W.) Life of Greeks and Romans described from Antique Monuments, translated by F. Hueffer. 8vo. Lond., 1875.
B 9 V 18

GUIBERT DE NOGENT [*See* GUIZOT, F. P. G., 8.]

GUIBERTUS (VENERABILIS). Opera omnia. [*See* MIGNE, J. P., SERIES LATINA, 156.]

GUICCIARDINI (FRANCESCO). Aphorismes, Civill and Militarie; amplified with Authorities, and exemplified with Historie, out of the first Quarterne of Fr. Guicciardine. Fol. Lond., 1613.
G 5 U 15

Briefe Inference vpon Gvicciardine's Digression in his Historie. [*See* DALLINGTON, SIR R.]

GUICCIARDINI (Francesco).—*continued.*

Dell' Historia d'Italia: gli vltimi qvattro Libri non piv stampati. Sm. 4to. Venezia, 1564.   B 12 R 35

Another copy. 2 vols. roy. fol. Venezia, 1738.   B 14 U 5, 6 ‡

Another copy. 10 vols. (in 5) 8vo. Milano, 1803.   B 11 U 25, 29 ‡

History of Italy, 1490–1532; translated by the Chevalier Austin Parke Goddard; with a Life of the Author. 2nd ed. 10 vols. 8vo. Lond., 1753–56.   B 11 U 30–39

GUIDI (Tommaso), called Masaccio. Le Pitture di Masaccio, esistenti in Roma nella Basilica di S. Clemente; colle teste lucidate dal Sig. Labruzzi. Roma, 1809.   A 10 P 1 ‡

GUIGNES (Joseph de). Dictionnaire Chinois, Français, et Latin, publié d'après l'Ordre de sa Majesté l'Empereur et Roi Napoléon le Grand. Roy fol. Paris, 1813.   K 32 P 17 ‡

Histoire Générale des Huns, des Turcs, des Mogols, et des autres Tartares Occidentaux, &c., avant et depuis Jesus-Christ jusqu'à présent. 4 vols. (in 5) 4to. Paris, 1756–58.   B 1 R 19–23 †

Supplément [to the above]; par Joseph Senkowski. 4to. St. Petersburgh, 1824.   B 1 R 24 †

Voyages à Peking, Manille, et l'Ile de France, 1784–1801. 3 vols. 8vo. Paris, 1808.   D 6 P 28–30

Atlas [to the above]. Fol. Paris, 1808.   D 33 Q 1 ‡

GUILFORD (Rt. Hon. Francis North), Baron. Lives of the Rt. Hon. Francis North, Baron Guilford; the Hon. Sir Dudley North; and the Hon. and Rev. Dr. John North; by the Hon. Roger North. 3 vols. 8vo. Lond., 1826.   C 9 R 5–7

GUILFOYLE (W. R.), F.L.S., &c. A.B.C. of Botany. 12mo. Melb., 1880.   MA 1 V 23

Australian Botany; specially designed for the Use of Schools. Illustrated. First Book. 8vo. Melb., 1878.*   MA 1 V 20

Another copy. 2nd ed. 8vo. Melb., 1884.   MA 1 V 22

Catalogue of Plants under Cultivation in the Melbourne Botanic Gardens, alphabetically arranged. With Plans and Illustrations. Imp. 8vo. Melb., 1883.   MA 1 P 15 †

GUILLAUME (Edmond). Exploration Archéologique de la Galatie, etc. [See Perrot, G.]

GUILLAUME DE JUMIEGE. Histoire des Ducs de Normandie, publiée pour la première fois en Français, par [F. P. G.] Guizot, et suivie de la Vie de Guillaume-le-Conquérant, par Guillaume de Poitiers. 8vo. Caen, 1826.   B 8 P 39

Histoire des Normands. [See Guizot, F. P. G., 29.]

GUILLAUME DE NANGIS. Chronique de. [See Guizot, F. P. G., 13.]

GUILLAUME DE TYR. Histoire des Croisades. [See Guizot, F. P. G., 16–18.]

GUILLAUME LE BRETON. La Philippide: Poëme. [See Guizot, F. P. G., 12.]

GUILLEMARD (Arthur G.) Over Land and Sea: a Log of Travel round the World in 1873–74. 8vo. Lond., 1875.*   MD 4 W 13

GUILLEMIN (Amedee). Applications of Physical Forces; translated from the French, by Mrs. N. Lockyer, and edited, with Notes, by F. Norman Lockyer, F.R.S., &c. Illustrated. Roy. 8vo. Lond., 1877.   A 15 U 20

Forces of Nature: a Popular Introduction to the Study of Physical Phenomena; translated by Mrs. N. Lockyer, and edited, with Notes, by J. Norman Lockyer, F.R.S., &c. Roy. 8vo. Lond., 1873.   A 15 U 19

The Heavens. Illustrated. 8vo. Lond., 1868.   A 3 U 21

The Sun; from the French, by T. L. Phipson, Ph.D. Illustrated. 8vo. Lond., 1870.   A 3 S 25

World of Comets; translated and edited by James Glaisher. Illustrated. Roy. 8vo. Lond., 1877.   A 3 U 20

GUILLIM (John), Pursuivant at Arms. Display of Heraldry; to which is added a Treatise of Honour, Military and Civil, according to the Laws and Customs of England; by Capt. John Logan. 6th ed. Fol. Lond. 1724.   K 22 S 6 ‡

GUIZOT (François Pierre Guillaume). Collection des Mémoires relatifs à l'Histoire de France, depuis la Fondation de la Monarcie Française jusqu'au 13ᵉ Siècle ; avec une Introduction, des Supplémens, desNotices, et des Notes. 31 vols. 8vo. Paris, 1823–35.   B 8 T 1–31

1. Mémoires de Grégoire de Tours.
2. Mémoires de Grégoire de Tours. Chronique de Frédégaire. Vie de Dagobert Iᵉʳ. Vie de Saint Léger. Vie de Pepin-le-Vieux.
3. Annales d'Eginhard. Vie de Charlemagne, par Eginhard. Des Faits et Gestes de Charlemagne, par un Moine de Saint-Gall. Vie de Louis-le-Débonnaire, par Tregan. Vie de Louis-le-Débonnaire, par l'Astronome. Histoire des Dissensions des Fils de Louis-le-Débonnaire, par Nithard.
4. Faits et Gestes de Louis-le-Pieux, Poëme, par Ermold le Noir. Annales de Saint-Bertin et de Metz.
5. Histoire de l'Eglise de Reims, par Frodoard.
6. Abbon : Siège de Paris. Chronique de Frodoard. Chronique de Raoul Glaber. Vie du Roi Robert, par Helgaud. Poëme d'Adalbéron sur le Règne de Robert.
7. Vie de Bouchard, Comte de Melun. Fragmens de l'Histoire des Français. Chronique de Hugues de Fleury. Procès-verbal du sacre de Philippe Iᵉʳ. Histoire du Monastère de Vézelai, par Hugues de Poitiers.
8. Vie de Louis-le-Gros, par Suger. Vie de Suger, par Guillaume. Vie de Louis-le-Jeune. Vie de Charles-le-Bon, par Galbert.
9. Histoire des Croisades, par Guibert de Nogent. Vie de Guibert de Nogent, par lui-même.
10. Suite de la Vie de Guibert de Nogent, par lui-même. Vie de Saint-Bernard, par Guillaume de Saint-Thierri, etc.
11. Rigord ; Vie de Philippe-Auguste. Guillaume le Breton ; Vie de Philippe-Auguste. Vie de Louis viii. Nicolas de Bray ; Faits et Gestes de Louis viii.
12. La Philippide, Poëme, par Guillaume le Breton.
13. Chronique de Guillaume de Nangis.
14. Histoire de la Guerre des Albigeois, par Pierre de Vaulx-Cernay.
15. Histoire de la Guerre des Albigeois. Chronique de Guillaume de Puy Laurens. Des Gestes illustres des Français de l'An 1202 à l'Année 1311.
16–18. Histoire des Croisades, par Guillaume de Tyr.
19. Continuation de l'Histoire des Croisades de Guillaume de Tyr, par Bernard le Trésorier.
20. Histoire des Croisades par Albert d'Aix.

GUIZOT (François Pierre Guillaume).—*continued.*

21. Histoire des Croisades par Albert d'Aix. Histoire des Francs qui ont pris Jérusalem par Raimond d'Agiles.
22. Histoire des Croisades, par Jacques de Vitry.
23. Histoire de Tancrède, par Raoul de Caen. Histoire de la Première Croisade, par Robert le Moine.
24. Histoire des Croisades, par Foulcier de Chartres. Histoire de la Croisade de Louis vii, par Odon de Deuil.
25-28. Histoire de Normandie, par Oderic Vital.
29. Histoire des Normands, par Guillaume de Jumiège. Vie de Guillaume-le-Conquérant, par Guillaume de Poitiers.
30. Table Générale et Analytique.
31. Introduction:—Considérations sur les Gaulois, les Francs, et les Français, par Bourden de Sigrais. Fragment sur l'Histoire de France, par Aug. Trognon.

Collection des Mémoires relatifs à la Révolution d'Angleterre. 25 vols. (in 26). 8vo. Paris, 1823-27.   B 5 T 1-26

1. Mémoires de Sir Philippe Warwick sur le Règne de Charles 1er et ce qui s'est passé depuis la Mort de Charles 1er jusqu'à la Restauration des Stuart.
2. Mémoires de John Price, Chapelain. de Monk, sur la Restauration des Stuart.
3. Mémoires de Sir Thomas Herbert, Valet de Chambre de Charles 1er, sur les deux dernières Années du Règne de ce Prince. Mémoires de Sir John Berkley, sur les Négociations de Charles 1er avec Cromwell et l'Armée Parliamentaire.
4. [Part 1 and 2] Histoire du Long-Parlement convoqué par Charles 1er en 1640 ; par Thomas May, Secrétaire du Parlement).
5. Mémoires de Hollis. Mémoires de Huntington. Mémoires de Fairfax.
6-8. Mémoires de Ludlow.
9. Procès de Charles 1er. Eikôn Basilikê ; Apologie attribuée à Charles 1er. Mémoires de Charles ii, sur sa Fuite après la Bataille de Worcester.
10-11. Mémoires de Mistriss Hutchinson.
12-16. Mémoires de Lord Clarendon, Grand-Chancelier d'Angleterre sous le Règne de Charles ii.
17-20. Histoire de mon Temps, par Burnet, Evêque de Salisbury.
21. Mémoires de Sir John Reresby. Mémoires du Duc de Buckingham.
22-26. Mémoires de Jacques ii.

Democracy in France, January, 1849.   3rd ed.   8vo. Lond., 1849.   B 8 T 35

Dictionnaire Universel des Synonymes de la Langue Française. 7th ed. Roy. 8vo. Paris, 1864.   K 15 S 19

An Embassy to the Court of St. James's in 1840. 8vo. Lond., 1862.   B 6 Q 10

General History of Civilization in Europe, from the Fall of the Roman Empire to the French Revolution. 2nd ed. 8vo. Oxford, 1838.   B 7 T 33

History of Oliver Cromwell and the English Commonwealth ; translated by Andrew R. Scoble. 2 vols. 8vo. Lond., 1854.   B 6 T 15, 16

History of the English Revolution, from the Accession of Charles i. Translated from the French, by L. H. R. Coutier. 2 vols. 8vo. Oxford, 1838.   B 6 T 9, 10

History of the Origin of Representative Government in Europe ; translated by Andrew R. Scoble. 8vo. Lond., 1861.   B 7 S 47

History of Richard Cromwell and the Restoration of Charles ii. Translated by Andrew R. Scoble. 2 vols. 8vo. Lond., 1856.   B 6 T 5, 6

The Last Days of the Reign of Louis Philippe. 8vo. Lond., 1867   B 8 R 25

GUIZOT (François Pierre Guillaume).—*continued.*

Meditations on the actual State of Christianity, and on the attacks which are now being made upon it. 8vo. Lond., 1866.   G 8 S 14

Memoirs of a Minister of State, from the year 1840. 8vo. Lond., 1864.   C 7 P 11

Memoirs of General Monk, Duke of Albemarle ; translated by the Hon. J. Stuart Wortley. 8vo. Lond., 1838.   C 8 R 30

Memoirs of Sir Robert Peel. 8vo. Lond., 1857.   C 9 Q 18

Memoirs to illustrate the History of my Time ; translated by J. W. Cole. 4 vols. 8vo. Lond., 1858.   C 7 P 7-10

Monk and Washington : Historical Studies. 12mo. Lond., 1851.   C 1 R 26

Monsieur Guizot in Private Life, 1787-1874 ; by his Daughter, Madame de Witt ; translated by M. C. M. Simpson. 8vo. Lond., 1880.   C 7 P 12

On the Causes of the Success of the English Revolution, 1640-88. 8vo. Lond., 1850.   B 6 Q 11

Washington ; translated by Henry Reeve. 8vo. Lond., 1840.   C 4 S 49

Why was the English Revolution successful ? (Pam. 38.) 8vo. Lond., 1850.   MJ 2 Q 25

GULLICK (Thos. John), and TIMBS (John), F.S.A. Painting popularly explained. (Weale.) 12mo. Lond., 1873.   A 17 Q 25

GULLY (John). New Zealand Scenery : Chromo-lithographed after original Water-color Drawings ; with Descriptive Letterpress, by Julius von Haast. 8vo. Lond., 1877.   MD 1 P 10 ‡

GULPHILAS. [*See* ULPHILAS.]

GUNDULF (Bishop of Rochester). Memoir of Gundulf, Bishop of Rochester, 1077-1108 ; with Notices of the other Ecclesiastical Founders of that Church and Monastery, by Thomas Hugo, M.A., &c. 8vo. Lond., 1853.   C 11 P 37

GUNN (William). Inquiry into the Origin and Influence of Gothic Architecture. 8vo. Lond., 1819.   A 2 S 25

GÜNTHER (Albert Charles Lewis Gotthilf), M.A., &c. Catalogue of the Fishes in the British Museum. 8 vols. 8vo. Lond., 1859-70.   A 14 U 33-40

Ceratodus, and its Place in the System. (Pam. Co.) 8vo. Lond., 1871.   MA 2 V 9

Description of Ceratodus, a Genus of Ganoid Fishes, recently discovered in Rivers of Queensland, Australia. Roy. 4to. Lond., 1871.   MA 2 Q 14 †

Description of the Living and Extinct Races of Gigantic Land-Tortoises. (Roy. Soc. Pubs., 1.) 4to. Lond., 1875.   A 11 P 2 †

Introduction to the Study of Fishes. 8vo. Edinb., 1880.   A 15 P 16

Reptiles of British India. Fol. Lond., 1864.   A 23 S 29 ‡

GÜNTHER (Mary A. von), Countess. Tales and Legends of the Tyrol. 8vo. Lond., 1874.   D 7 Q 22

GUPPY (H. P.), M.B., &c. Solomon Islands, and their Natives. Roy. 8vo. Lond., 1887. MA 1 S 20

Solomon Islands: their Geology, General Features, and Suitability for Colonization. Roy. 8vo. Lond., 1887. MA 2 R 4

GURNER (Henry Field). Chronicle of Port Phillip, now the Colony of Victoria, 1770–1840. 8vo. Melb., 1876. MJ 2 P 28

Another copy. MJ 2 R 10
[*See* Manuscripts, &c.]

GURNEY (Edmund). The Power of Sound. Roy. 8vo. Lond., 1880. A 7 V 15

GURNEY (Edmund), M.A., MYERS, (Frederic W. H.), M.A., and PODMORE (Frank). Phantasms of the Living. 2 vols. 8vo. Lond., 1886. G 11 S 6, 7

GURNEY (J. H.), Junr., and RUSSELL (Col. C.), The House Sparrow; and The English Sparrow in America, by Dr. Eliott Coues. 12mo. Lond., 1885. A 14 Q 47

GURNEY (Joseph John). Memoirs of; with Selections from his Journals and Correspondence, edited by J. B. Braithwaite. 2 vols. 8vo. Norwich, 1854. C 7 P 13, 14

Observations on the Distinguishing Views and Practices of the Society of Friends. 8vo. Lond., 1834. G 3 Q 4

Another copy. 7th ed. 8vo. Lond., 1834. G 8 S 13

A Winter in the West Indies; described in familiar Letters to Henry Clay, of Kentucky. 2nd ed. 8vo. Lond., 1840. D 4 Q 37

GURNEY (Thomas). Lessons in Shorthand on Gurney's System. [*See* Miller, R. E.]

GURWOOD (Col.), C.B., &c. Speeches of the Duke of Wellington. [*See* Wellington, Duke of.]

GURY (Joanne Petro), S.J. Compendium Theologiæ Moralis. 6⁵ editio. 2 vols. 12mo. Lugd., 1853. G 8 P 7, 8

GUSTAFSON (Axel). Foundation of Death : a Study of the Drink-Question. 8vo. Lond., 1884. A 12 Q 1

GUSTAVUS ADOLPHUS (King of Sweden). History of; by John L. Stevens. 8vo. Lond., 1885. C 6 Q 1

History of the Life of; by the Rev. Walter Harte, M.A. 2nd ed. 2 vols. 8vo. Lond., 1767. C 5 R 1, 2

GUSTAVUS VASA (King of Sweden). History of; with Extracts from his Correspondence. 8vo. Lond., 1852. B 2 R 10

GUTHE (Prof. H.) Lehrbuch der Geographie. 2e auflage. 8vo. Hannover, 1872. D 12 U 23

GÜTERBOCK (Bruno), et THURNEYSEN (Rudolphus). Indices Glossarum et Vocabulorum Hibernicorum quæ in Grammaticæ Celticæ editione altera explanantur. 4to. Lipsiæ, 1881. K 14 S 11

GUTHRIE (E. J.) Old Scottish Customs, Local and General. 8vo. Lond., 1885. B 13 P 13

GUTHRIE (Frederick). Magnetism and Electricity. Illustrated. 8vo. Lond., 1876. A 5 R 47

GUTHRIE (Malcolm). On Mr. Spencer's Unification of Knowledge. 8vo. Lond., 1882. G 4 Q 8

GUTHRIE (Mrs. Maria). My Year in an Indian Fort. 2 vols. 8vo. Lond., 1874. D 5 P 14, 15

Through Russia, from St. Petersburg to Astrakhan and the Crimea. 2 vols. 8vo. Lond., 1874. D 7 Q 5, 6

A Tour, performed in the years 1795–96, through Taurida, or Crimea, the ancient Kingdom of Bosphorus. 4to. Lond., 1802. D 6 V 22

GUTHRIE (Thomas), D.D. The Parables, read in the Light of the Present Day. 8vo. Lond., 1866. G 3 P 12
[*See* Sunday Magazine, The.]

GUTZLAFF (Rev. Charles). China Opened; or, a Display of the Topography, History, Customs, &c., of the Chinese Empire. 2 vols. 8vo. Lond., 1838. B 2 P 34, 35

Journal of Three Voyages along the Coast of China, in 1831–33; with Notices of Siam, Corea, and the Loo-choo Islands. 8vo. Lond., 1834. D 5 P 41

Life of Taou-Kwang, late Emperor of China; with Memoirs of the Court of Peking. 8vo. Lond., 1852. C 4 U 33

Sketch of Chinese History, Ancient and Modern. 2 vols. 8vo. Lond., 1834.* B 2 P 48, 49

Voyage to the Northern Ports of China. [*See* Lindsay, Hon. H. H.]

GUYON (Jeanne Marie Bouvier de la Mothe). Life, Religious Opinions, and Experience of Madame de la Mothe Guyon ; together with some account of the personal History and Religious Opinions of Fénelon, Archbishop of Cambray, by T. C. Upham. 8vo. Lond., 1856. C 3 R 41

GUYOT (T.) The Royal Scottish Academy Illustrated Catalogue ; containing Illustrations from Drawings by the Artists. 8vo. Edinb., 1884–85. E

GUZMAN (Don J. de). [*See* Seriman, Z.]

GWILT (Charles Perkins). Notices relating to Thomas Smith, of Campden, and to Henry Smith, sometime Alderman of London. Imp. 8vo. Lond., 1836. C 4 W 22

GWILT (Joseph), F.R.A.S. Ancient Architecture. [*See* Vithuvius Pollio, M.]

Encyclopædia of Architecture, Historical and Practical. New ed., revised, with Alterations and Additions, by Wyatt Papworth. 8vo. Lond., 1867. K 5 U 2

Evidences relating to the Estates of Henry Smith, Esq., sometime Alderman of the City of Lond. Imp. 8vo. Lond., 1828. C 4 W 22

Observations on the communication of Mr. Wilkins, to the Editor of the *Athenæum*, relative to the National Gallery. 8vo. Lond., 1833. A 7 Q 13

Rudiments of a Grammar of the Anglo-Saxon Tongue. 8vo. Lond., 1829. K 13 Q 4

H

H.A.L. The Old Shekarry. [*See* LEVESON, MAJOR H. A.]

H.(H.) [*See* JACKSON, MRS. H. H.]

H.J.C. [*See* FURNISHING, THE ART OF.]

H.J.L. [*See* ADVENTURES OF MR. NEWCHAMP.]

HAAN (W. DE). [*See* SIEBOLD, P. F. DE.]

HAARLEM LEGEND. [*See* LINDE, DR. VAN DER.]

HAAST (PROF. JULIUS VON), PH.D., &c. Classification of the Moas. [*See* HUTTON, CAPT. F. W.]

Geology of the Provinces of Canterbury and Westland, New Zealand: a Report. 8vo. Christchurch, 1879.   MA 2 Q 21

New Zealand Scenery. [*See* GULLY, J.]

On Zipiius Novæ-Zealandiæ. 8vo. Lond., 1880. MA 2 U 25

Progress of Geology: Opening Address, delivered to the Students of Canterbury College. 8vo. Dunedin, 1883.   MA 2 Q 22

HABINGTON (WILLIAM). Castara [Lady Lucia Powis]; with a Preface and Notes, by Chas. A. Elton. 12mo. Bristol, 1812.   H 6 R 16

Life and Poems of. [*See* CHALMERS, A.]

The Queene of Arragon: a Tragi-Comedie.   (Old Plays.) Sm. fol. Lond., 1640.   H 1 V 1

HABIT DE COUR (L') ou le Moraliste de Nouvelle Etoffe, pour corriger les mœurs il faut les dévoiles. 3 vols. 12mo. Paris, 1815.   J 16 T 20–22

HACK (J. B.) Letters from. [*See* WATSON, H.]

HACO. The Norwegian Account of Haco's Expedition against Scotland. [*See* JOHNSTONE, REV. J.]

HADDON (JAMES), A.M. Commercial Book-keeping and Phraseology, in four Languages. (Weale.) 15th ed. 12mo. Lond., 1879.   A 17 Q 69

Elements of Algebra; with Key and Companion. (Weale.) 2 vols. 12mo. Lond., 1868.   A 10 S 3

Examples and Solutions of the Differential Calculus. (Weale.) 12mo. Lond., (n.d.)   A 17 P 47

Key to Haddon's Arithmetic; containing Answers to all that Work, and Solutions of all such Exercises as are likely to present any difficulty, by Abraham Arman. (Weale.) 12mo. Lond., 1862.   A 17 R 4

Rudimentary Arithmetic, for the Use of Schools and Self-instruction. New ed., by Abraham Arman. (Weale.) 12mo. Lond., 1872.   A 17 R 4

HADEN (FRANCIS SEYMOUR), F.R.C.S. Etched Work of Rembrandt: a Monograph; with an Appendix. Roy. 8vo. Lond., 1879.   A 8 R 12
[*See* WEDMORE, F.]

HADFIELD (WILLIAM). Brazil, the River Plate, and the Falkland Islands; with the Cape Horn Route to Australia Illustrated. 8vo. Lond., 1854.   D 4 Q 46

HADLEY (A. T.) Railroad Transportation: its History and its Laws. 8vo. New York, 1885.   F 6 Q 32

HAECKEL (DR. ERNST). Anthropogenie oder Entwickelungs-geschichte des Menschen. Roy. 8vo. Leipsic, 1874.   A 12 V 17

Arabische Korallen: ein ausflug nach den Korallenbänken des Rothen meeres, und ein Blick in das Leben der Korallenthiere. Imp. 4to. Berlin, 1876.   A 23 S 2 ‡

Evolution of Man: a popular Exposition of the principal Points of Human Ontogeny and Phylogeny. 2 vols. 8vo. Lond., 1879.   A 13 P 13, 14

Gesammelte Populäre Vorträge aus dem gebiete der Entwickelungslepre. Roy. 8vo. Bonn, 1878–79. A 16 V 12

History of Creation; or, the Development of the Earth and its Inhabitants by the action of Natural Causes. 2 vols. 8vo. Lond., 1876.   A 16 Q 16, 17

Die Naturanschauung von Darwin, Göethe, und Lamarck. 8vo. Jena, 1882.   A 17 V 4

Das System der Medusen. Erster Thiel. Einer Monographie der Medusen. (With Plates.) · 2 vols. sm. 4to. Jena, 1879.   A 23 R 3, 4 ‡

Visit to Ceylon; translated by Clara Bell. 8vo. · Lond., 1883.   D 6 P 16

HAFIZ (OF SHERAZ). Persian Poetry. [*See* ROBINSON, S.]

HAFIZ-OOL-MOOLK, HAFIZ REHMUT KHAN. Life of; written by his Son, Nuwab Moost'ujab Khan Buhadoor, and entitled Goolistan-i-Rehmut. Abridged and translated by Charles Elliott. 8vo. Lond., 1831.   C 9 V 21

HAGA (COL. A.) Nederlandsch Nieuw-Guinea en de Papoesche Eilanden: Historische Bijdrage, 1500–1883. 2 vols. 8vo. Batavia, 1884.   MD 2 S 14, 15

HAGERUP (E.) Om det Danske Sprog i Angel. Ordbog—Sproglære—Sprogprover. 8vo. Kobenhavn, 1867.   K 12 Q 21

HAGGARD (H. RIDER). Cetywayo and his White Neighbours; or, Remarks on recent Events in Zululand, Natal, and the Transvaal. 8vo. Lond., 1882.   B 1 P 38

HAGHE (LOUIS). The Holy Land. [*See* ROBERTS, D.]

HAHN (HEINRICH). Bonifaz und Lul: ihre Angelsächsischen Korrespondenten. Erzbischof Luls Leben. 8vo. Leipzig, 1883.   C 10 P 6

HAHN (SIMON FRIEDRICH). Collectio Monvmentorvm. 2 vols. 8vo. Brunsvigæ, 1724–26. J 16 R 13, 14

HAHN (Dr. Theophilus). Die Spracie der Nama. 8vo. Leipsig, 1870. K 15 S 11

HAHN-HAHN (Ida), Countess. Letters of a German Countess, written during her Travels in Turkey, Egypt, the Holy Land, Syria, Nubia, &c., in 1843-44. 3 vols. 8vo. Lond., 1845. D 6 P 22-24

HAIG (James), M.A. Symbolism; or, Mind—Matter—Language as the Elements of Tiinking and Reasoning. 8vo. Edinb., 1869. G 8 S 11

HAILES (Sir David Dalrymple), Lord. [*See* Dalrymple, Sir D.]

HAILPRIN (David). Genius, Lunacy, and Knavery: Story of a Colonial Piysician; by M. Brodzky. Melb., 1876. MA 2 S 38

HAILSTONE (E.) Portraits of Yorksiire Worthies, selected from the National Exiibition of Works of Art at Leeds; witi Biograpiical Notices. 2 vols. imp. 8vo. Lond., 1869. C 4 W 27-28

[*See* Walker, G.]

HAIME (J.) Histoire Naturelle des Coralliaires, etc. [*See* Milne-Edwards, H.]

HAINES (H.) Der Staat Alabama. (Nordamerika.) (Pam. 38.) 8vo. Paris, 1867. MJ 2 Q 25

HAITE (C. C.) Plant Studies for Artists, Designers, Art Students. Roy. fol. Lond., 1886. A 2 P 23 ‡

HAKE (A. Egmont). Journal of Gordon. [*See* Gordon, Major-General, C. G.]

Story of Chinese Gordon; witi Portraits and Maps. 2 vols. 8vo. Lond., 1884-85. C 7 R 15, 16

HAKEWILL (Dr. George). An Apologie; or, Declaration of the Power and Providence of God in the Government of the World, &c. 2nd ed. Fol. Oxford, 1630. G 5 U 4

HAKEWILL (James). History of Windsor and its Neighbourhood. Imp. 4to. Lond., 1813. B 14 S 14 ‡

HAKLUYT SOCIETY. [Publications.] 52 vols. 8vo. Lond., 1847-75. E

HALCOMBE (Rev. J. J.), M.A. The Emigrant and the Heatien; or, Sketcies of Missionary Life. 8vo. Lond., 1874. MD 1 S 30

HALDANE (Alexander). Memoirs of the Lives of Robert Haldane, Airthrey, and of iis Brotier, James Alexander Haldane. 8vo. Lond., 1852. C 7 P 19

HALDANE (Richard Burdon), M.A. Essays on Philosophical Criticism. [*See* Seth, A., Prof.]

HALDANE (R. C.) Sub-tropical Cultivations, and Climates for Planters, &c. 8vo. Lond., 1886. A 1 Q 22

HALDANE OF AIRTHREY (Robert, and James Alexander). Memoirs of the Lives of; by Alexander Haldane. 8vo. Lond., 1852. C 7 P 19

HALDE (P. J. B. du). [*See* Du Halde, P. J. B.]

HALDEMAN (Prof. S. S.), A.M. Affixes in tieir Origin and Application, exiibiting the Etymologic Structure of Englisi Words. Revised ed. 8vo. Philad., 1871. K 12 P 6

Analytic Ortiograpiy: an Investigation of the Sounds of the Voice, and tieir Alpiabetic Notation; including the Mecianism of Speeci, and its bearing upon Etymology. 4to. Philad., 1860. K 16 S 9

HALDORSEN (Biörn). Lexicon Islandico-Latino-Danicum. 3 vols. sm. 4to. Havniae, 1814. K 15 R 15, 16

HALE (Horatio), M.A. Etinograpiy and Piilology. (United States Exploring Expedition.) Roy. 4to. Philad., 1846. A 31 P 7 ‡

Iroquois Book of Rites. 8vo. Philad., 1883. B 1 T 35

HALE (Mathew B.), M.A. Transportation Question; or, why Western Australia siould be made a Reformatory Colony instead of a Penal Settlement. (Pam. 37.) 8vo. Camb., 1857. MJ 2 Q 24

HALES (Rev. Francis). Appeal from the Bisiop to the Church. 8vo. Meli., 1854. MG 1 Q 39

HALES (Prof. John W.), M.A. Notes and Essays on Siakespeare. 8vo. Lond., 1884. J 9 U 7

HALES (Rev. William), D.D., &c. New Analysis of Cironology and Geograpiy, History, and Propiecy, in wiici tieir Elements are attempted to be explained, iarmonized, and vindicated upon Scriptural and Scientific Principles. 2nd ed. 4 vols. 8vo. Lond., 1830. B 15 Q 7-10

HALÉVY (J.) Mélanges de Critique et d'Histoire relatifs aux Peuples Sémitiques. Roy. 8vo. Paris, 1883. G 5 S 16

HALF-A-DOZEN ATTEMPTS AT VERSIFICATION; by R.O. 12mo. Sydney, 1886. MH 1 P 10

HALF HOURS IN THE FAR SOUTH. People and Scenery of the Tropics. (The Half Hour Library of Travel, Nature and Science for young Readers.) 12mo. Lond., 1877. MD 1 S 54

HALFORD (F. M.) Floating Flies, and iow to Dress tiem: a Treatise on the most Modern Metiods of Dressing Artificial Flies for Trout and Grayling. 8vo. Lond., 1886. A 16 T 5

HALFORD (Prof. George Britton), M.D., &c. New Treatment of Snake-bite; witi plain Directions for Injecting. 8vo. Melb., 1869. MA 2 S 38

Treatment of Snake-bite in Victoria. (Pam. C4.) 8vo. Melb., 1870. MA 2 V 9

Lecture on the Circulation of the Blood. [*See* Melbourne Public Library.]

[*See* Thomson, W.]

HALFORD (SIR HENRY), BART., M.D., &c. Essays and Orations read and delivered at the Royal College of Physicians; to which is added an Account of the Opening of the Tomb of King Charles I. 2nd ed. 8vo. Lond., 1833.   A 12 P 30

HALFPENNY (WILLIAM). Practical Architecture. 5th ed. 12mo. Lond., 1730.   A 2 R 25

HALHED (NATHANIEL BRASSEY). Code of Gentoo Laws. [*See* GENTOO LAWS.]

HALIBURTON (THOMAS CHANDLER). Americans at Home; or, Byeways, Backwoods, and Prairies. 3 vols. 8vo. Lond., 1854.   J 4 Q 21–23

The Attaché; or, Sam Slick in England. 1st and 2nd Series. 4 vols. 8vo. Lond., 1843–44.   J 4 Q 16–19

Bubbles of Canada. 8vo. Lond., 1839.   B 1 R 31

The Clockmaker; or, the Saying and Doings of Samuel Slick. 1st, 2nd, and 3rd Series. 3 vols. 8vo. Lond., 1838–40.   J 4 Q 7–9

The English in America. 2 vols. 8vo. Lond., 1851.   B 1 Q 31, 32

The Letter-bag of the "Great Western"; or, Life in a Steamer. 8vo. Lond., 1840.   J 4 Q 24

Nature and Human Nature. 2 vols. 8vo. Lond., 1855.   J 4 Q 5, 6

The Old Judge; or, Life in a Colony. 2 vols. 8vo. Lond., 1849.   J 4 Q 14, 15

Rule and Misrule of the English in America. 2 vols. 8vo. Lond., 1851.   B 1 Q 9, 10

Sam Slick's Wise Saws and Modern Instances; or, what he said, did, or invented. 2 vols. 8vo. Lond., 1853.   J 4 Q 10, 11

The Season Ticket. 2 vols. 8vo. Lond., 1860. J 4 Q 12, 13

Traits of American Humour; by Native Authors. 8vo. Lond., 1866.   J 4 Q 20

HALIDAY (CHARLES). Scandinavian Kingdom of Dublin; edited, with some notice of the Author's Life, by John P. Prendergast. Roy. 8vo. Dublin, 1881.   B 11 R 1

HALIFAX (CHARLES MONTAGU), EARL OF. Life and Poems of. [*See* CHALMERS, A., *and* JOHNSON, S.

HALKETT (G. R.) [*See* HUNT, MRS. A. W.]

HALKETT (SAMUEL), AND LAING (REV. JOHN), M.A. Dictionary of the Anonymous and Pseudonymous Literature of Great Britain. Vols. 1–3. 3 vols. roy. 8vo. Edinb., 1882–85.   K 17 R 1–3

HALL (MRS. ANGUS W.) Mythology, Greek and Roman. [*See* NÖSSELT, F.]

HALL (PROF.), M.B. Signs of the Times: a Prophetic Study of the Eastern Question and its ultimate results, the whereabouts of the Lost Ten Tribes of Israel. 8vo. Melb., 1878.   MJ 2 R 15

HALL (CAPT. BASIL), R.N. Extracts from a Journal written on the Coasts of Chili, Peru, and Mexico, in the years 1820–22. 4th ed. 2 vols. 8vo. Edinb., 1825. D 4 P 28, 29

Fragments of Voyages and Travels, including Anecdotes of a Naval Life. 1st, 2nd, and 3rd Series. 9 vols. 18mo. Edinb., 1831–33.   D 10 P 5–13

Patchwork. 3 vols. 8vo. Lond., 1841.   D 18 P 6–8

Schloss Hainfeld; or, a Winter in Lower Styria. 8vo. Edinb., 1836.   J 5 Q 29

Travels in North America in the years 1827–28. 3rd ed. 3 vols. 8vo. Edinb., 1830.   D 3 P 15–17

Voyages to Loo-choo, &c. (Const. Misc.) 3 vols. 18mo. Edinb., 1827-   K 10 P 40–42

HALL (CAPT. CHARLES FRANCIS). Life with the Esquimaux: the Narrative of Capt. C. F. Hall, of the Whaling Barque *George Henry*, from the 29th May, 1860, to the 13th Sept., 1862. 2 vols. 8vo. Lond., 1864. D 4 R 16, 17

Narrative of the North Polar Expedition, with Life of Capt. Charles Francis Hall. [*See* DAVIS, REAR-ADM. C. H.]

Narrative of the Second Arctic Expedition: his Voyage to Repulse Bay, Sledge Journeys to the Straits of Fury and Hecla, and to King William's Land, and Residence among the Eskimos during the years 1864–69; edited by Prof. J. E. Nourse, U.S.N. (U.S. Naval Observatory, 1879.) 4to. Lond., 1880.   D 10 P 15 †

[*See* AMERICAN ARCTIC EXPLORERS.]

HALL (DR. E. S.) On the Climate of Tasmania. [*See* WHITING, G.]

HALL (FREDERIC T.), F.R.A.S. Pedigree of the Devil. Illustrated. 8vo. Lond., 1883.   G 1 P 15

HALL (GEORGE S.) Hegel as the National Philosopher of Germany. [*See* ROSENKRANZ, PROF. K.]

HALL (HENRY), F.R.G.S. Biographical Sketch of Thomas Baines. [*See* BAINES, T.]

HALL (HERBERT BYNG). Exmoor; or the Footsteps of St. Hubert in the West. 8vo. Lond., 1849. D 7 R 37

West of England, and the Exhibition of 1851. Illustrated. 12mo. Lond., 1851.   D 7 R 5

HALL (HUBERT). History of the Customs Revenue in England, from the Earliest Times to the year 1827. Compiled exclusively from original Authorities. 2 vols. 8vo. Lond., 1885.   B 3 S 8, 9

Society in the Elizabethan Age. 8vo. Lond., 1886. B 6 P 42

HALL (I. H.) Syrian Antilegomena Epistles: 2 Peter, 2 and 3 John, and Jude, written A.D. 1471, by Sulieman of Husn Keifa (Williams, M.) Edited by I. H. Hall. Roy. 4to. Baltimore, 1886.   G 3 P 23

HALL (JAMES). History of the Indian Tribes of North America. [*See* MACKENNEY, T. L.

HALL (JOHN). Prospectus and Plan for colonising Prince Albert Land, North-western Australia : first Settlement, Grey City. 12mo. Melb., 1862. MJ 2 R 1

HALL (RT. REV. JOSEPH), D.D., BISHOP OF NORWICH. Life and Poems of. [*See* CHALMERS, A.]

Mvndvs alter et idem siue Terra Australis ante nac semper incognita longis itineribus peregrini Academici nuperrime lustrata. 12mo. Francof., 1643. MJ 1 P 58

Selections from the Works of. [*See* MONTAGU, B.]

HALL (MRS. MATTHEW). Royal Princesses of England, from the Reign of George I. 12mo. Lond., 1858. C 1 R 29

HALL (MELMOTH). How is it? a Refutation from the Holy Scriptures of the Asserted Supremacy of the Apostle Peter. (Pam. M.) 4to. Sydney, 1875. MJ 2 S 4

HALL (REV. NEWMAN), B.A. Land of the Forum and the Vatican. 3rd thousand. 12mo. Lond., 1854. G 9 Q 17

HALL (REV. PETER), M.A. Memoir of Rev Robert Lowth. [*See* LOWTH, RT. REV. R.]

Picturesque Memorials of Salisbury. 4to. Salisbury, 1834. B 5 V 26

HALL (REV. ROBERT). Miscellaneous Works of ; with Memoir by Olinthus Gregory, LL.D., &c., and a Critical Estimate of his Character and Writings, by John Foster. 8vo. Lond., 1875. G 16 P 12

Works of; with a brief Memoir of his Life, by Olinthus Gregory, LL.D., &c. 6 vols. 8vo. Lond., 1833–36. G 11 Q 19–24

HALL (S. C.), F.S.A. Baronial Halls and Ancient Picturesque Edifices of England. Illustrated. 2 vols. imp. 4to. Lond., 1858. D 5 Q 12, 13 †

Book of British Ballads. 1st and 2nd series. 2 vols. imp. 8vo. Lond., 1842–44. H 6 V 25, 26

Catalogue of the Vernon Collection of Paintings by British Artists; with a group in Marble and six Busts, presented to the Nation by Robert Vernon, Esq. 8vo. Lond., 1853. A 7 Q 19

Retrospect of a Long Life, from 1815 to 1883. 2 vols. 8vo. Lond., 1883. C 7 T 13, 14

HALL (MR. AND MRS. S. C.) Ireland: its Scenery, Character, &c.. 3 vols. roy. 8vo. Lond., 1841–43. D 7 V 10–12

A Week at Killarney. Illustrated. 8vo. Lond., 1843. D 6 T 38

HALL (MRS. S. C.) Characteristic Sketches of Ireland and the Irish. [*See* CARLETON, W.]

Sketches of Irish Character. Illustrated. Roy. 8vo. Lond., 1844. D 7 V 29

HALL (SAMUEL R.) Lectures on School-keeping. 3rd ed. 12mo. Boston 1831. G 18 P 1

HALL (THEOPHILUS D.) Copious and Critical English-Latin Dictionary. [*See* SMITH, W., AND HALL, T. D.]

The Student's Latin Grammar. [*See* SMITH, W., AND HALL, T. D.]

HALL (THOMAS). Floss; or, the Progress of an Adventurer in the Regions of Australia. Illustrated. 12mo. Lond., 1852.* MJ 1 P 9

HALL (THOMAS W.), M.D., &c. Sun and Earth as great Forces in Chemistry. 8vo. Lond., 1874. A 5 S 34

HALL (WILLIAM). Biography of David Cox; with Remarks on his Works and Genius. 8vo. Lond., 1881. [*See* TURNER, M.]

HALL (WILLIAM EDWARD), M.A. International Law. 8vo. Oxford, 1880. F 8 R 5

HALL (WILLIAM HENRY). New Royal Encyclopædia ; or, Complete Modern Universal Dictionary of Arts and Sciences. 4 vols. (in 2) fol. Lond., 1789. K 27 P 10, 11 ‡

HALL (COMM. W. H.), R.N. Narrative of the Voyages, etc., of the *Nemesis*, from 1840–43, and Military Operations in China; with Personal Observations, by W. D. Bernard, Esq., A.M. 2 vols. 8vo. Lond., 1844. D 6 T 1, 2.

HALL, OR HALLE (EDWARD). Chronicle ; containing the History of England during the Reign of Henry IV, and the succeeding Monarchs, to the end of the Reign of Henry VIII. 4to. Lond., 1809. B 10 R 9 †

HALLAM (ARTHUR HENRY). Remains in Verse and Prose of ; with a Preface and Memoir. New ed., with Portrait. 12mo. Lond., 1869. J 12 S 10

HALLAM (HENRY), LL.D., &c. Constitutional History of England, from the Accession of Henry VII to the Death of George II. 3 vols. 8vo. Lond., 1829. B 5 R 33–35

Another copy. 3 vols. 8vo. Lond., 1855. B 3 Q 19–21

Introduction to the Literature of Europe on the 15th, 16th, and 17th Centuries. 4 vols. 8vo. Lond., 1837–39. B 25 S 1–4

Another copy. 5th ed. 4 vols. 12mo. Lond., 1855. B 25 S 5–8

Student's History of the Middle Ages; with Additions from recent Writers, and adapted to the use of Students, by Wm. Smith, D.C.L., &c. 8vo. Lond., 1871. B 7 S 32

View of the State of Europe during the Middle Ages. 3 vols. 8vo. Lond., 1826. B 7 T 11–13

Another copy. 3 vols. 12mo. Lond., 1855. B 7 S 33–35

HALLECK (HENRY WAGER). International Law ; or, Rules regulating the intercourse of States in Peace and War. A new ed., by Sir Sherston Baker, Bart. 2 vols. 8vo. Lond., 1878 F 8 R 3, 4

HALLIDAY (SIR ANDREW), K.H., &c. General History of the House of Guelph, or Royal Family of Great Britain, from the earliest period to the Accession of George I. 4to. Lond., 1821. B 10 P 1 †

West Indies : the Natural and Physical History of the Windward and Leeward Colonies. 8vo. Lond., 1837. D 4 P 26

HALLIDAY (ANDREW). [*See* DUFF, A. H.]

HALLIWELL-PHILLIPPS (JAMES ORCHARD), F.R.S., &c. Brief Hand-list of the Collections respecting the Life and Works of Shakespeare, and the History of Stratford-upon-Avon. 8vo. Lond., 1863. K 7 R 14

Dictionary of Archaic and Provincial Words, Obsolete Phrases, Proverbs, and Ancient Customs from the 14th Century. 7th ed. 2 vols. 8vo. Lond., 1872. K 1287,8

Historical Account of the New Place, Stratford-upon-Avon, the. last Residence of Shakespeare. Roy. fol. Lond., 1864. B 18 T 11 ‡

Illustrations of the Life of Shakespeare. Part 1. Fol. Lond., 1874. C 1 W 25

Life of William Shakespeare ; including many particulars respecting the Poet and his Family, never before published. 8vo. Lond., 1848. C 9 R 26

Life and Writings of John Marston. [*See* MARSTON, J.]

Outlines of the Life of Shakespeare. 2nd ed. 8vo. Lond., 1882. C 9 R 27

Another copy. 5th ed. Imp. 8vo. Lond., 1885. C 5 W 21

Popular Rhymes and Nursery Tales : a Sequel to the "Nursery Rhymes of England." 12mo. Lond., 1849. J 7 Q 4

HALLORAN (HENRY), C.M.G. Letter to Mr. Justice Wise with a M.S. copy of the Poem *Leichhardt's Grave ;* by Lieut. B. Lynd. Fol. Sydney (n.d.) MJ 2 U 1

HALLS (J. J.) Life and Correspondence of Henry Salt, F.R.S., &c. 2 vols. 8vo. Lond., 1834. C 9 U 47, 48

HALS (FRANS). A Biography ; by P. R. Head. (Great Artists.) 8vo. Lond., 1879. C 3 T 33

HALSEY (F. R.) Raphael Morghen's Engraved Works, being a Descriptive Catalogue, &c., accompanied by Biographical and other Notes. Sm. fol. New York, 1885. K 2 P 7 †

HALSTED (CAROLINE A.) Life of Margaret Beaufort, Countess of Richmond and Derby, Mother of King Henry VII. 8vo. Lond., 1839. C 10 Q 2

Obligations of Literature to the Mothers of England. 8vo. Lond., 1840. J 9 P 27

Richard III as Duke of Gloucester and King of England. 2 vols. 8vo. Lond., 1844. C 9 P 27, 28

HALY (ALBOHAZEN). Liber de Falis Astrorum. Sm. fol. Venetiis, 1485. A 16 R 17 ‡

HALY (W. T.) [*See* PEEL, SIR R.]
2 T

HAM (THOMAS). Key to the Map of Australia Felix and its Squatting Districts, 1847. 12mo. Melb., 1847. MD 5 S 15 ‡

Map of Australia Felix. 2nd ed. Roy. 4to. Melb., 1849. MD 5 S 15 ‡

Map of the Purchased and Measured Lands, Counties, Parishes, &c., of the Melbourne and Geelong Districts. Roy. 4to. Melb., 1849. MD 5 S 15 ‡

[*See* MASON, C.]

HAM (THOMAS) & CO. [*See* BUXTON, J. W.]

HAMANN (A.), PH.D., &c. Laocoon. [*See* LESSING, G. E.]

HAMEL (DR. J.) England and Russia ; translated by John Studdy Leigh, F.R.G.S. 8vo. Lond., 1854. D 6 U 12

HAMERLING (ROBERT). Sinnen und Minnen ein Jugendleben in Liedern. 6e auflage. 8vo. Hamburg, 1877. H 7 R 35

HAMERTON (PHILIP GILBERT). Etching and Etchers. New ed., Illustrated. 8vo. Lond., 1876. A 7 S 5

The Graphic Arts : a Treatise on the Varieties of Drawing, Painting, and Engraving, in comparison with each other and nature. Sm. fol. Lond., 1882. A 1 P 17 †

Imagination in Painting. Landscape, with Illustrations. Fol. Lond., 1887. A 23 S 8 ‡

Landscape ; with Original Etchings, and many Illustrations from Pictures and Drawings. Sm. fol. Lond., 1885. A 1 P 18 †

Paris in Old and Present Times. Illustrated. Sm. fol. Lond., 1885. D 5 S 12 †

HAMILTON (ALEXANDER). Life of : a History of the Republic of the United States of America ; by John C. Hamilton. 7 vols. 8vo. Boston, 1879. C 8 V 7-13

HAMILTON (ALEXANDER), JAY (JOHN), AND MADISON (JAMES). The Federalist : a Commentary on the Constitution of the United States ; also, a Collection of Essays ; also, "The Continentalist," and other Papers, by Hamilton. Edited by John C. Hamilton. 8vo. Philad.,1882. F 8 S 2

HAMILTON (ANDREW). Rheinsberg : Memorials of Frederick the Great and Prince Henry of Prussia. 2 vols. 8vo. Lond., 1880. C 4 S 29, 30

Sixteen Months in the Danish Isles. 2 vols. 8vo. Lond.. 1852. D 8 S 45, 46

HAMILTON (ANTHONY), COUNT. Le Bélier ; Fleur d'Épins ; et les Quatre Facardins. [*See* CABINET DES FÉES, 20.]

Memoirs of Count Grammont. New ed. 2 vols. 8vo. Lond., 1811. C 8 Q 19, 20

HAMILTON (CLAUD), LADY. Louis Pasteur : his Life and Labours. [*See* RADOT, V.]

HAMILTON (EDWARD), M.D., &c. Recollections of Fly Fishing for Salmon, Trout, and Grayling; with Notes on their Haunts, Habits, and History. 8vo. Lond., 1884.
A 14 Q 33

HAMILTON (E. L.) [*See* ABORIGINES.]

HAMILTON (FREDERICK FITZROY). Bordighera and the Western Riviera. Translated from the French, with additional Matter, and Notes, by Alfred C. Dowson. 8vo. Lond., 1883. D 6 U 36

HAMILTON (LIEUT.-GEN. SIR F. W.), K.C.B. Origin of the First, or Grenadier Guards. Illustrated. 3 vols. roy. 8vo. Lond., 1874. B 5 U 28–30

HAMILTON (GEORGE). Experiences of a Colonist Forty Years Ago, and a Journey from Port Phillip to South Australia, in 1839; by "An Old Hand." Illustrated. 12mo. Adelaide, 1879. MD 5 P 37

The Horse; its Treatment in Australia; with an Appendix on Shoeing, and an Appeal for the Horse. 12mo. Melb., 1866. MJ 2 P 30

Letters to H. F. Gurner. [*See* MANUSCRIPTS, &c.]

HAMILTON (GEORGE), R.N. Voyage round the World in His Majesty's Frigate, *Pandora,* in the years 1790–92. 8vo. Berwick, 1793.* MD 1 U 30

HAMILTON (GEORGE JAMES), DUKE OF. Memorial for, against Archibald Stewart, *alias* Douglas. [*See* DOUGLAS, A. J., FIRST BARON.]

HAMILTON (H.) International English and French Dictionary. [*See* SMITH, L.]

HAMILTON (H.), AND LEGROS (E.) Dictionnaire International Français-Anglais. Roy. 8vo. Paris, 1876.
K 16 R 19

HAMILTON (HANS CLAUDE). Geography of Strabo. [*See* STRABO.]

Grammar of the Greek Language. 8th ed. (Weale.) 12mo. Lond., 1873. K 11 T 8

HAMILTON (HENRY R.) English-Greek Lexicon. (Weale.) 12mo. Lond., 1872. K 11 T 9

Greek-English Lexicon. (Weale.) 12mo. Lond., 1871.
K 11 T 9

HAMILTON (JAMES AND WILLIAM), DUKES OF. Memoires of the Lives and Actions of; by Gilbert Burnet. Fol. Lond., 1677. C 2 W 12

HAMILTON (JANET). Poems and Prose Works of. 8vo. Glasgow, 1885. J 17 S 23

HAMILTON (JOHN), ARCHBISHOP OF ST. ANDREWS. Catechism of, 1552. Edited, with Introduction and Glossary, by Thomas Graves Law. 8vo. Oxford, 1884. G 3 S 14

HAMILTON (JOHN). A Remonstrance, respectfully addressed to the Members of the Legislature and others, in relation to the Scottish Church Question. (Pam. 11.) 8vo. Edinb., 1841. F 12 P 9

HAMILTON (J. A.) [*See* CHERUBINI, L.]

HAMILTON (JOHN C.) Life of Alexander Hamilton : a History of the Republic of the United States of America. 7 vols. roy. 8vo. Boston, 1879. C 8 V 7–13

HAMILTON (LEONIDAS LE CENCI), M.A. Hamilton's Mexican Hand-book : a complete Description of the Republic of Mexico. Illustrated. 8vo. Lond., 1884.
D 12 T 9

HAMILTON (NICOLAS ESTERHAZY S. A.) Dictionary of the English, German, and French Languages, in three Parts. (Weale.) 12mo. Lond., 1872. K 11 T 21

Inquiry into the genuineness of the Manuscript Corrections in Mr. J. Payne Collier's Annotated Shakspere, folio, 1632; and of certain Shaksperian Documents likewise published by Mr. Collier. Sm. 4to. Lond., 1860. H 3 Q 27

HAMILTON (PATRICK). Writings of. [*See* BRITISH REFORMERS.]

HAMILTON (REV. ROBERT). The Combat and the Victory : a Narrative of the Means by which the Darkness of Infidelity was dispelled from the Death-bed of Charles Jardine Don. 8vo. Melb., 1866. MG 1 Q 39

HAMILTON (ROBERT), LL.D. An Inquiry concerning the Rise and Progress, the Redemption, and present State of the National Debt of Great Britain. 8vo. Lond., 1813. F 12 P 6

HAMILTON (DR. ROBERT). Natural History of the Amphibious Carnivora. (Nat. Lib., 23.) 12mo. Edinb., 1839. A 14 P 23

Natural History of Whales. (Nat. Lib., 39, 40.) 2 vols. 12mo. Edinb., 1860. A 14 P 39, 40

HAMILTON (ROBERT G. C.), AND BALL (JOHN). Book-keeping. (Clar. Press.) 8vo. Oxford, 1876. A 25 P 26

HAMILTON (ROWLAND). The Resources of a Nation : a series of Essays. 8vo. Lond., 1863. F 8 R 6

HAMILTON (TERRICK). Antar : a Bedoueen Romance. Translated from the Arabic. 4 vols. 8vo. Lond., 1820.
J 8 P 40–43

HAMILTON (CAPT. THOMAS). Annals of the Peninsular Campaigns, 1808–14. 3 vols. 12mo. Lond., 1829.
B 13 U 40–42

Men and Manners in America. 2 vols. 8vo. Edinb., 1833. D 3 Q 1, 2

HAMILTON (W.) Life and Poems of. [*See* CHALMERS, A.]

HAMILTON (WALTER), F.R.G.S., &c. Parodies of the Works of English and American Authors. Vols. 1–3. 4to. Lond., 1884–86. J 7 V 10–12

HAMILTON (RT. HON. SIR WILLIAM), K.B., P.C. &c. Campi Phlegræi: Observations on the Volcanos of the Two Sicilies; and Supplement, giving an Account of the Great Eruption of Mount Vesuvius. (In English and French.) 2 vols. 4to. Naples, 1776–79. A 4 R 2, 3 ‡

Collection of Etruscan, Greek, and Roman Antiquities. 2 vols. (in 1) fol. Naples, 1766. A 2 P 7 ‡

Collection of Engravings from Ancient Vases, mostly of pure Greek Workmanship, discovered in the Sepulcres in the Kingdom of the Two Sicilies. (In English and French.) 3 vols. (in 2) fol. Naples, 1781. A 2 P 8, 9 ‡

HAMILTON (SIR WILLIAM), BART. Be not Schismatics; be not Martyrs by Mistake. 2nd ed. (Pam. 11.) 8vo. Edinb., 1843. F 12 P 9

Discussions on Philosophy and Literature, Education, and University Reform. 8vo. Lond., 1852. G 1 R 2

Examination of Sir W. Hamilton's Philosophy. [*See* MILL, J. S.]

Lectures on Metaphysics and Logic. Edited by the Rev. H. L. Mansel, B.D. 4 vols. 8vo. Edinb., 1865–66. G 1 Q 16–19

Memoir of; by John Veitch, M.A. 8vo. Edinb., 1869. C 7 Q 26

Review of the "Examination." [*See* GROTE, G.]

Works of Thomas Reid. [*See* REID, T.]

HAMILTON (WILLIAM), OF BANGOUR. Life and Poems of. [*See* CHALMERS, A.]

Poems and Songs of; with illustrative Notes, and an Account of the Life of the Author, by James Paterson. 8vo. Lond., 1850. H 8 Q 35

HAMILTON (WILLIAM DOUGLAS), F.S.A. Civil Service Chronology: the Chronology of History, Art, Literature, and Progress, from the Creation of the World to the Conclusion of the Franco-German War. (Weale.) 12mo. Lond., 1872. K 11 P 4

Outlines of the History of England. (Weale.) 12mo. Lond., 1870. K 11 P 1

Another copy. New ed. (Weale.) 12mo. Lond., 1886. K 11 P 6

HAMILTON (WILLIAM DOUGLAS), AND LEVIEN (EDWARD). Outlines of the History of Greece. (Weale.) 12mo. Lond., 1854. K 11 P 2

HAMILTON (WILLIAM J.) Researches in Asia Minor, Pontus, and Armenia; with some Account of their Antiquities and Geology. 2 vols. 8vo. Lond., 1842. D 4 U 20, 21

HAMILTON (SIR WILLIAM ROWAN), KNT., &c. Life of; including Selections from his Poems, Correspondence, and Miscellaneous Writings; by Robert Percival Graves, M.A. Vols. 1, 2. 8vo. Dublin, 1882–85. C 14 U 13, 14

HAMILTON SPECTATOR (THE). Directory and Almanac for 1875–77. 12mo. Melb., 1875–77. ME 4 P

HAMLET CONTROVERSY (THE). Was Hamlet Mad? or, the Lucubrations of Messrs. Smith, Brown, Jones, and Robinson; [by J. Smith, Dr. Nield, C. Bright, D. Blair, and A. Michie;] with a Preface by the Editor of the *Argus*. (Pam. 36.) 8vo. Melb., 1867. MJ 2 Q 23

Another copy. 8vo. Melb., 1867. MJ 2 R 11

HAMLEY (GEN. SIR E. B.) Story of the Campaign of Sebastopol. 8vo. Lond., 1855. B 12 U 12

Thomas Carlyle: an Essay. 12mo. Edinb., 1881. C 2 P 2

HAMLEY (COL. W. G.) New Sea and Old Land, being Papers suggested by a Visit to Egypt at the end of 1869. 8vo. Edinb., 1871. D 2 R 22

HAMMER (CHEV. JOSEPH VON). History of the Assassins. Translated by O. C. Wood, M.D. 8vo. Lond., 1835. B 1 P 2

HAMMOND (ADAM). Rudiments of Practical Bricklaying in Six Sections: general Principles of Bricklaying; Arch Drawing, Cutting, and Setting; different kinds of Pointing, Paving, Tiling, Materials; Slating and Plastering; Practical Geometry, Mensuration, etc. Illustrated. (Weale.) 2nd ed. 12mo. Lond., 1877. A 17 Q 35

HAMMOND (REV. CHARLES EDWARD), M.A. Outlines of Textual Criticism applied to the New Testament. (Clar. Press.) 12mo. Oxford, 1872. G 16 P 34

HAMMOND (JOHN). Life and Poems of. [*See* BRITISH POETS, 4; CHALMERS, A.; *and* JOHNSON, S.]

HAMON (A.) Can it be done? Can all the Gold be extracted from the Quartz?—Yes! (Pam. 28.) 8vo. Melb. (n.d.) MJ 2 Q 16

HAMONIERE (G.) Grammaire Espagnole, divisée en quatre parties. 12mo. Paris, 1817. K 11 U 30

Grammaire Russe, divisée en quatre parties. 8vo. Paris, 1817. K 18 V 4

HAMPDEN (ADMIRAL THE HON. AUGUSTUS CHARLES HOBART), HOBART PASHA. Sketch of my Life; with a Portrait. 8vo. Lond., 1886. C 4 R 39

HAMPDEN (JOHN). Life of. [*See* MACKINTOSH, SIR J.]

Some Memorials of John Hampden, his Party, and his Times; by George Grenville, Lord Nugent. 2 vols. 8vo. Lond., 1832. C 7 T 16, 17

HAMPER (W.) The Life, Diary, and Correspondence of Sir W. Dugdale. 4to, Lond., 1827. C 4 P 16 †

HAMPTON COURT. Stranger's Guide to Hampton Court Palace and Gardens. 12mo. Lond. (n.d.) A 7 P 32

HAMTON (JAMES). History of Polybius. [*See* POLYBIUS.] B 12 R 32–34

HAMST (OLPHAR). [*See* THOMAS, RALPH.]

HAMY (ERNEST T.) Les Crânes des Races Humaines. [*See* QUATREFAGES, A. DE.]

HÀN KOONG TSEW; or, the Sorrows of Hàn: a Chinese Tragedy. [*See* DAVIS, SIR J. F.]

HANAFORD (MRS. PHEBE ANNE.) Life of George Peabody. 8vo. Boston, 1882.   C 3 U 35

Life and Writings of Charles Dickens. 8vo. Boston, 1882.   C 2 T 22

HANBURY (REV. BARNARD). Visit to some Parts of Ethiopia. [*See* WADDINGTON, G.]

HANBURY (DANIEL), F.R.S., &c. Science Papers, chiefly Pharmacological and Botanical. Edited, with Memoir, by Joseph Ince, F.L.S., &c. 8vo. Lond., 1876.   A 6 Q 12

HANCE (J. L.) The End of the World; or, Prophecy a Lost Science revealed. (Atlas Series of Australian Pams., 1.) 8vo. Sydney, 1881.   MG 1 Q 45

HANCOCK (E. C.) AND SON. General Hints for Mixing and Painting with Hancock's Worcester China Colours. 8vo. Worcester, 1881.   A 7 Q 12

Hancock's Copies for China Painters; with directions by Albert Hill. 8vo. Lond., 1881.   A 7 Q 12

Price List of Hancock's Worcester China Colours, Articles for Painting upon, and other Requisites. 8vo. Worcester, 1881.   A 7 Q 12

HANCOCK (W. N.) Impediments to the Prosperity of Ireland. 12mo. Lond., 1850.   F 2 P 31

HAND-BOOK OF COLOURED ORNAMENT in the Historic Styles. 36 Plates, printed in Colours and Gold. 8vo. Lond. (n.d.)   A 8 U 24

HAND-BOOK OF FAMILIAR QUOTATIONS; chiefly from English Authors. 12mo. Lond., 1859.

HANDEL (GEORGE FREDERIC). Life of; by Victor Schœlcher. 8vo. Lond., 1857.   C 7 T 15

Life of; by W. S. Rockstro. 8vo. Lond., 1883.   C 3 Q 28

The Messiah: a Sacred Oratorio. [*See* SYDNEY UNIVERSITY.]

HANDFIELD (REV. H. H. P.) Address in connexion with the Day of Intercession on behalf of Missions, Tuesday, November 30th, 1875. 12mo. Melb., 1875.   MG 1 Q 39

HANDY BOOK OF COMMON ENGLISH SYNONYMS. 18mo. Lond., 1879.   K 11 S 1

HANDY CLASSICAL DICTIONARY. 18mo. Lond., 1878.   K 11 S 1

HANKIN (CHRISTIANA C.) Life of Mary Anne Schimmelpenninck, Author of "Select Memoirs of Port Royal," and other Works. Edited by C. C. Hankin. 4th ed. 8vo. Lond., 1860.   C 5 R 26

HANLEY (S.) [*See* SWAINSON, W.]

HANLON (JOHN). Gambetta: Orator, Dictator, Journalist, Statesman. 12mo. Lond., 1881.   C 2 P 17

HANMER (SIR J.) [*See* SHAKESPEARE, W.]

HANMER (MEREDITH), D.D. Ancient Irish Histories; by M. Hanmer, Edmund Campion, Edmund Spencer, and Henry Marleburrough; collected by Dr. M. Hanmer, and edited by Sir Jas. Ware. 2 vols. imp. 8vo. Dublin, 1809.   B 11 R 8, 9

HANN (JAMES). Elements of Plane Trigonometry. (Weale.) 4th ed. 12mo. Lond., 1873.   A 17 P 8

Examples on the Integral Calculus. (Weale.) 12mo. Lond., 1850.   A 17 P 49

Treatise on Analytical Geometry and Conic Sections. Enlarged by J. R. Young. (Weale.) 4th ed. 12mo. Lond., 1871.   A 17 P 8

HANN (DR. J.), HOCHSTETTER (DR. F. VON) UND POKORNY (DR. A.) Allgemeine Erdkunde: ein Leipfaden der astronomischen Geographie, Meteorologie, Geologie, und Biologie. 8vo. Prag, 1872.   A 16 S 26

On the Climate of New Zealand. [*See* HECTOR, SIR J.]

HANNA (REV. WILLIAM), LL.D. Memoirs of the Life and Writings of Thomas Chalmers, D.D., LL.D., by his Son-in-law. 4 vols. 8vo. Edinb., 1850–52. C 6 T 8–11

HANNAFORD (SAMUEL). Jottings in Australia; or, Notes on the Flora and Fauna of Victoria; with a Catalogue of the more Common Plants, their Habitats, and Dates of Flowering. 12mo. Melb., 1856.*   MA 1 V 26

Sea and River-side Rambles in Victoria; being a Handbook for those seeking recreation during the Summer Months. 12mo. Geelong, 1859.   MJ 2 P 31

HANNAY (D.) Admiral Blake. (English Worthies.) 12mo. Lond., 1886.   C 2 R 3

HANNAY (JAMES). Satire and Satirists: Six Lectures. 8vo. Lond., 1854.   J 4 Q 25

HANNINGTON (RT. REV. JAMES), FIRST BISHOP OF EASTERN EQUATORIAL AFRICA. History of his Life and Works, 1847–85; by E. C. Dawson, M.A. With a Portrait. 8vo. Lond., 1887.   C 3 V 11

HANNO. Voyage of; translated and accompanied with the Greek Text, by Thomas Falconer, A.M., &c. 8vo. Lond., 1797.   D 9 T 12

HANNOT (S.) Nieuw Woordboek der Nederlantsche en Latynsche Tale met veele Woorden en Spreekwyzen merkelyk vermeerdert en verrykt, door D. van Hoogstraten. 4to. Dordricht, 1736.   K 14 R 4

HANSARD (GEORGE AGAR). Book of Archery. Roy. 8vo. Lond., 1841.   A 17 W 36.

HANSARD (THOMAS CURSON). Parliamentary Debates, commencing with the 60th vol., 5 Vic., 1842. 173 vols. roy. 8vo. Lond., 1842-76.　　　　　　　　E

Parliamentary History of England (Cobbett's), from the Norman Conquest in 1066, to the year 1803. 36 vols. roy. 8vo. Lond., 1806-20.　　　　　F 2 Q 1-R 18

[*See* BARROW, J. H.]

HANSELL (E. H.) Novum Testamentum Graece. [*See* BIBLES AND TESTAMENTS.]

HANSON (SIR RICHARD DAVIES), KNT., C.J. Law in Nature, and other Papers, read before the Adelaide Philosophical Society, and the South Australian Institute. 8vo. Adelaide, 1865.　　　　　MG 1 R 10

HANWAY (JONAS). Historical Account of the British Trade over the Caspian Sea ; with the Author's Journal of Travels from England through Russia into Persia, and back through Russia, Germany, and Holland, &c. Illustrated. 2nd ed. 2 vols. 4to. Lond., 1754. D 5 V 17, 18

HÄOLÉ, A. [*See* BATES, G. W.]

HAPPY DELIVERY OF A LEGAL LADY, in Jolop Street East: a Dramatic Episode; by "A Bohemian University Student." 8vo. Melb., 1866.　　MJ 2 R 12

HARBINGER OF LIGHT (THE) ; a Monthly Journal, devoted to Zoistic Science, Free Thought, Spiritualism, and the Harmonial Philosophy. June, 1874, to December, 1876. Fol. Melb., 1874-76.　　　　　ME

HARBURY HOUSE ASYLUM. Private Retreat for the Insane : Harbury House, Pascoe Vale, near Melbourne. Mr. [James Thomas] Harcourt's Testimonials. (Pam. E.) 4to. Melb., 1857.　　　　　MJ 2 S 2

HARCOURT (A. G. VERNON), M.A., &c., AND MADAN (H. G.), M.A., &c. Exercises in Practical Chemistry. (Clar. Press.) 8vo. Oxford, 1872.　　　A 21 Q 22

HARCOURT (HELEN). Florida Fruits, and how to raise them. 8vo. Louisville, 1866.　　　　A 1 P 50

HARCOURT (JAMES THOMAS). [*See* HARBURY HOUSE ASYLUM.]

HARCOURT (LEVESON FRANCIS VERNON-), M.A. Diaries, &c., of the Rt. Hon. George Rose. [*See* ROSE, RT. HON. G.]

Harbours and Docks: their Physical Features, History, Construction, Equipment, and Maintenance. Text and Plates. (Clar. Press.) 2 vols. 8vo. Oxford, 1885.　A 22 S 24, 25

Treatise on Rivers and Canals; relating to the Control and Improvement of Rivers, and the Design, Construction, and Development of Canals. With Plates. (Clar. Press.) 2 vols. 8vo. Oxford, 1882.　　　A 22 S 26, 27

HARCUS (WILLIAM). Hand-book for Emigrants proceeding to South Australia. 12mo. Adelaide, 1873. MD 4 Q 54

South Australia: its History, Resources, and Productions. Illustrated. 8vo. Lond., 1876.*　　　MB 2 R 14

HARDCASTLE (DANIEL). [*See* PAGE, R.]

HARDCASTLE (HON. MRS.), MARY SCARLETT. Life of John, Lord Campbell. [*See* CAMPBELL, JOHN, BARON.]

HARDIMAN (JAMES), M.R.I.A. Irish Minstrelsy; or, Bardic Remains of Ireland. 2 vols. 8vo. Lond., 1831. H 6 U 2, 3

HARDING (G. P.) Antiquities in Westminster Abbey: Ancient Oil Paintings and Sepulchral Brasses; with an Historical, Biographical, and Heraldic Description, by Thomas Houle. Roy. fol. Lond., 1825.　A 1 P 12 ‡

HARDING (J. D.) Tourist in France. [*See* JENNINGS, R.]

Tourist in Italy. [*See* JENNINGS, R.]

Views of Cities and Scenery of Italy, France, and Switzerland. [*See* PROUT, S.]

HARDING (R. COUPLAND). Harding's Almanac, Diary, Year-book, Local Guide, and Directory for the year of our Lord 1881. Second year of publication. 8vo. Napier, 1880.　　　　　　　ME 3 T

Harding's New Zealand Almanac, Diary, Year-book, East Coast Directory, and Local Guide for 1885 and 1887. 2 vols. 8vo. Napier, 1884-86.　　　　ME 3 T

HARDING (PROF. WILLIAM). Universal Stenography; or, a new and practical System of Shorthand. Revised ed., by John R. Robinson. 12mo. Lond., 1860.　K 11 U 24

HARDINGE (HENRY, VISCOUNT, GOUGH (HUGH), VISCOUNT, AND SMITH (SIR HARRY GEORGE WAKELYN), BART. Despatches and other Documents during the War in India. 8vo. Lond., 1846.　　　B 10 U 20

HARDMAN (WILLIAM), M.A. [*See* STUART, J. McD.]

HARDWICK (CHARLES). On some Ancient Battle-fields in Lancashire, and their Historical, Legendary, and Æsthetic Associations. 8vo. Manchester, 1882.　B 3 T 6

HARDWICKE (HERBERT JUNIUS), M.D. Medical Education and Practice in all Parts of the World. 8vo. Lond., 1880.　　　　　　　A 12 S 22

HARDWICKE (PHILIP YORKE), EARL OF. Essay on the Life and Character of John, Lord Somers, Baron of Evesham; also, Sketches of an Essay on the Life and Character of Philip Yorke, Earl of Hardwicke, by Richard Cooksey. 4to. Worcester, 1791.　　C 4 W 32

Life of Lord Chancellor Hardwicke; with Selections from his Correspondence, Diaries Speeches, and Judgments, by George Harris. 3 vols. 8vo. Lond., 1847. C 7 T 18-20

HARDWICKE (ROBERT). Science Gossip: an Illustrated Medium of Interchange and Gossip, for Students and Lovers of Nature. Edited by J. E. Taylor, Ph.D., F.L.S., &c. Vols. 1-20. Roy. 8vo. Lond., 1866-84.　　E

HARDWICKE'S ANNUAL BIOGRAPHY FOR 1856-57 ; by E. Walford, M.A. 2 vols. 12mo. Lond., 1856-57.　　　　　　　C 1 R 4, 5

HARDY (IZA DUFFUS). Oranges and Alligators: Sketches of South Florida Life. 8vo. Lond., 1886.　　D 3 P 53

HARDY (MARY DUFFUS), LADY. Through Cities and Prairie Lands: Sketches of an American Tour. 8vo. Lond., 1881. D 3 T 18

HARDY (J. R.), B.A. Squatters and Gold-diggers: their Claims and Rights. (Pam. 28.) 8vo. Sydney, 1855. MJ 2 Q 16

Another copy. MF 3 Q 37

HARDY (REV. ROBERT SPENCE). Manual of Budhism, in its Modern Development; translated from Singialese MSS. 2nd ed. 8vo. Lond., 1880. G 2 R 3

HARDY (SIR THOMAS DUFFUS), KNT. Description of the Close Rolls in the Tower of London; with an Account of the early Courts of Law and Equity. 8vo. Lond., 1833. F 1 S 26

Monumenta Historica Britannica. [*See* PETRIE, H.]

Rotuli Chartarum in Turri Londinensi asservati, A.D. 1199–1216. Fol. Lond., 1837. B 24 R 8 ‡

Rotuli Litterarum Clausarum in Turri Londinensi asservati. Fol. Lond., 1853. B 24 R 12 ‡

Rotuli Litterarum Patentium in Turri Londinensi asservati, A.D. 1201–16. Fol. Lond., 1835. B 24 R 11 ‡

HARDYNG (JOHN). Chronicle of; containing an Account of Public Transactions from the earliest period of English History to the beginning of the Reign of King Edward IV; together with the Continuation, by Richard Grafton, to the 34th year of King Henry VIII; with a Preface and Index, by H. Ellis. 4to. Lond., 1812. B 10 R 10 †

HARE (ARTHUR W.), M.B., &c. Pathological Mycology. [*See* WOODHEAD, G. S.]

HARE (AUGUSTUS JOHN CUTHBERT). Cities of Central Italy. 2 vols. 8vo. Lond., 1884. D 7 Q 17, 18

Sketches in Holland and Scandinavia. 8vo. Lond., 1885. D 7 R 48

Studies in Russia. 8vo. Lond., 1885. D 8 Q 44

Wanderings in Spain. 2nd ed. 8vo. Lond., 1873. D 7 Q 46

HARE (CHARLES SIMEON). [*See* SPENCE, MISS C. H.]

HARE (JULIUS CHARLES), M.A. History of Rome. [*See* NIEBUHR, B. C.]

The Mission of the Comforter; with Notes. 8vo. Camb., 1850. G 8 U 6

HARE (JULIUS CHARLES, AND AUGUSTUS WILLIAM). Guesses at Truth; by "Two Brothers." 12mo. Lond., 1871. G 9 P 45

HARE (THOMAS), M.A. Election of Representatives, Parliamentary and Municipal: a Treatise. 4th ed. 8vo. Lond., 1873. F 6 R 11

Thoughts on the Dwellings of the People, Charitable Estates, Improvement, and Local Government in the Metropolis. (Pam. 41.) 8vo. Lond., 1862. MJ 2 R 3

HARE (WILLIAM). Life of. [*See* MACGREGOR, G., *and* BURKE, W.]

HARGRAVE (HON. JOHN FLETCHER), M.A. Chronological Chart of Constitutional Law: Statutes of the Realm, and other Public Records, declaring and establishing our Civil and Religious Liberties. (Pam. A.) Fol. Sydney, 1865. MJ 2 U 1

Introductory Lecture on General Jurisprudence. (Pam. 37.) 8vo. Sydney, 1860. MJ 2 Q 24

Law Lectures, &c. 8vo. Sydney, 1878. MF 1 Q 14

Lecture on Law. (Pam. 37.) 8vo. Sydney, 1858. MJ 2 Q 24

Proposal to establish a Law Institution in Sydney. 4to. Sydney, 1864. MJ 2 S 2

Syllabus of the two Courses of Lectures on General Jurisprudence. (Pam. 37.) 8vo. Sydney, 1861. MJ 2 Q 24

[*See* MATRIMONIAL CAUSES ACT.]

HARGRAVES (EDWARD HAMMOND). Australia and its Gold-fields: a Historical Sketch of the Progress of the Australian Colonies, from the Earliest Times to the Present Day. With Portrait. 8vo. Lond., 1855.* MD 1 Q 1

HARGROVE (WILLIAM). History and Description of the Ancient City of York; comprising all the most interesting Information, already published in "Drake's Eboracum." Illustrated with a neat Plan of the City. 2 vols. (in 3) roy. 8vo. York, 1818. B 5 U 10–12

HARKNESS (CAPT. HENRY). Description of a singular Aboriginal Race inhabiting the summit of Neilgherry Hills, in the Southern Peninsula of India. Roy. 8vo. Lond., 1832. D 5 V 29

HARLAN (J.) Memoir of India and Avghanistaun; with Observations on the present exciting and critical State, and future Prospects of those Countries. 8vo. Philad., 1842. D 6 P 46

HARLAND (JOHN), F.S.A. History of Lancaster. [*See* BAINES, E.]

HARLAND (JOHN), F.S.A., AND WILKINSON (T. T.), F.R.A.S., &c. Lancashire Legends, Traditions, Pageants, Sports, &c.; with an Appendix containing a rare Tract on the Lancashire Witches, &c. 8vo. Manchester, 1882. B 3 R 11

HARLAND (R. H.), F.C.S., &c. Sugar Growing and Refining. [*See* LOCK, C. G. W.]

HARLEIAN MISCELLANY (THE); or, a Collection of Scarce, Curious, and Entertaining Pamphlets and Tracts, as well in Manuscript as in Print, found in the late Earl of Oxford's Library; with Notes. 12 vols. 8vo. Lond., 1808–11. B 6 T 32–43

Selection from the Haleian Miscellany of Tracts which principally regard the English History. 4to. Lond., 1793. B 18 Q 4 ‡

HARLESS (GOTTLIEB CHRISTOPH). Bibliotheca Graeca. [*See* FABRICIUS, PROF. J. A.]

HARLEY (REV. TIMOTHY) Lunar Science, Ancient and Modern. 8vo. Lond., 1886. A 3 T 14

Moon Lore. 8vo. Lond., 1885. A 3 T 12

HARLIN (THOMAS), M.A. Selections from Milton, Dryden, Gray, Keats, Addison, and De Quincey, as prescribed for the Matriculation Examination at the Melbourne University. With Notes and other Help for Students. 8vo. Melb., 1886.   MH 1 P 38

HARNESS (REV. WILLIAM), M.A. Memoir of Shakespeare. [*See* SHAKESPEARE, W.]

HAROLD (KING OF ENGLAND). Vita Haroldi: The Romance of the Life of; edited, with Notes, by Walter de Gray Birch, F.S.A. 8vo. Lond., 1885.   C 7 Q 33

HARPER (SAMUEL). Musings on the Past, Present, and Future, A.D. 1876. 8vo. Sydney, 1876.   MH 1 P 5

HARPER (REV. THOMAS NORTON), S.J. The Metaphysics of the School. Vols. 1 and 2, and Vol. 3 part 1. (*All published.*) 3 vols. 8vo. Lond., 1879–84.   G 1 Q 20–22

HARPER'S MONTHLY MAGAZINE. European Edition, Dec., 1880–Nov., 1886. 12 vols. roy. 8vo. Lond., 1881–86.   E

HARPUR (CHARLES). The Bushrangers: a Play, in Five Acts; and other Poems. 12mo. Sydney, 1853. MH 1 R 4

Tower of the Dream. (Pam., 21.) 12mo. Sydney, 1865.   MJ 2 Q 10

Poems. 8vo. Melb., 1883.*   MH 1 R 5

HARRINGTON (PROF. BERNARD J.), B.A., &c. Life of Sir William E. Logan, Kt., LL.D., &c. Chiefly compiled from his Letters, Journals, and Reports. 8vo. Lond., 1883.   C 7 S 15

HARRINGTON (G. H.) Direct Steam Route from England to Australia, viâ the Cape of Good Hope. 8vo. Melb., 1868.   MJ 2 R 8

HARRINGTON (JAMES). Oceana and other Works of James Harrington, Esq.; Collected, Methodiz'd, and Review'd, with his Life, by John Toland; to which is added an Appendix, containing all the Political Tracts wrote by this Author, omitted in Mr. Toland's Edition. Fol. Lond., 1747.   F 7 S 1 †

HARRIS (ALEXANDER). Converted Atheist's Testimony to the Truth of Christianity; being the Autobiography of Alexander Harris. 4th ed. 12mo. Lond., 1852.   MG 1 P 33

Emigrant Family; or, the Story of an Australian Settler. 3 vols. 8vo. Lond., 1849.   MJ 1 S 42–44

Guide to Port Stephens, in New South Wales, the Colony of the Australian Agricultural Company. 18mo. Lond., 1849.*   MD 1 T 9

Martin Beck; or, the Story of an Australian Settler. 12mo. Lond., 1852.   MJ 1 P 1

Settlers and Convicts; or, Recollections of Sixteen Years' Labour in the Australian Backwoods; by "An Emigrant Mechanic." 18mo. Lond., 1847.*   MD 1 T 4

HARRIS (GEORGE), LL.D., &c. Life of Lord Chancellor Hardwicke; with Selections from his Correspondence, Diaries, Speeches and Judgments. 3 vols. 8vo. Lond., 1847.   C 7 T 18–20

Philosophical Treatise on the Nature and Constitution of Man. 2 vols. 8vo. Lond., 1876.   G 1 P 24, 25

HARRIS (GEORGE), LORD, G.C.B. Life and Services of General Lord George Harris, G.C.B.; by the Rt. Hon. S. R. Lushington. 8vo. Lond., 1840.   C 8 P 19

HARRIS (H. GRAHAM). Manufacture of Plate Glass. [*See* POWELL, H. J.]

HARRIS (REV. JOHN). The Great Teacher; Characteristics of our Lord's Ministry. 8th thousand. 8vo. Lond., 1837.   G 1 R 13

Mammon, or Covetousness, the Sin of the Christian Church. 26th thousand. 8vo. Lond., 1837.   G 3 P 3

HARRIS (JOHN), A.M., &c. Navigantium atque Itinerantium Bibliotheca; or, a Compleat Collection of Voyages and Travels; consisting of above four hundred of the most Authentick Writers. 2 vols. fol. Lond., 1705.   D 38 P 1, 2 ‡

Another copy. Revised, with Additions. 2 vols. fol. Lond., 1796.   MD 38 P 3, 4 ‡

HARRIS (J. CHANTREY). Southern Guide to the Hot Lake District of the North Island of New Zealand. Dedicated to Tourists. 8vo. Dunedin, 1878.* MD 5 S 45

HARRIS (J. RENDELL). Fragments of Philo-Judæus. [*See* PHILO-JUDÆUS.]

Three Pages of the Bryennois Manuscript. 8vo. Baltimore, 1885.   G 1 R 1

HARRIS (ROBERT). What has Mrs. Caroline Chisholm done for the Colony of New South Wales? (Pam., 35.) 8vo. Sydney, 1862.   MJ 2 Q 22

HARRIS (SAMUEL), D.D., &c. Philosophical Basis of Theism. 8vo. New York, 1883.   G 1 P 18

HARRIS (STANLEY), "AN OLD STAGER." Coaching Age Illustrated by John Sturgess. 8vo. Lond., 1885. B 7 R 15

HARRIS (THADDEUS WILLIAM), M.D. Entomological Correspondence; edited by Sam. H. Scudder. Roy. 8vo. Boston, 1869.   A 15 Q 17

HARRIS (WALTER). Hibernica; or, some Antient Pieces relating to Ireland; edited by Walter Harris. In two parts. 8vo. Dublin, 1770.   B 11 P 32

Works concerning Ireland. [*See* WARE, J.]

HARRIS (WILLIAM). Guide to the Institutions and Charities for the Blind. [*See* TURNER, M.]

History of the Radical Party in Parliament. 8vo. Lond., 1885.   B 7 Q 33

HARRIS (WILLIAM). Historical and Critical Account of the Lives and Writings of James I and Charles I, and of the Lives of Oliver Cromwell and Charles II; from Original Writers and State Papers. New ed. 5 vols. 8vo. Lond., 1814. C 7 R 19–23

HARRIS (MAJOR SIR WILLIAM CORNWALLIS). Highlands of Ethiopia. 3 vols. 8vo. Lond., 1844. D 2 Q 4–6

Wild Sports of Southern Africa; being the Narrative of a Hunting Expedition from the Cape of Good Hope to the Tropic of Capricorn. 3rd ed. Roy. 8vo. Lond., 1852. D 2 8 7

HARRIS (SIR W. SNOW), M.R.C.S. Galvanism and the General Principles of Animal and Voltaic Electricity; with Additions, by Robt. Sabine, C.E. (Weale.) 12mo. Lond., 1869. A 17 P 40

On the Nature of Thunderstorms, and Lightning Conductors. 8vo. Lond., 1843. A 3 T 35

Rudimentary Electricity. (Weale). 12mo. Lond., 1872. A 17 P 40

Rudimentary Magnetism; by H. M. Noad. 2nd ed., enlarged. 12mo. Lond., 1872. A 17 P 41

HARRISON (BENJAMIN), M.A. [*See* BROUGHTON, RT. REV. W. G.]

HARRISON (FREDERIC). Choice of Books, and other Literary Pieces. 8vo. Lond., 1886. J 9 Q 29

Order and Progress. Part 1. Thoughts on Government. Part 2. Studies of Political Crises. 8vo. Lond., 1875. F 8 8 1

HARRISON (G. H. DE S. N. PLANTAGENET). History of Yorkshire. Fol. Lond., 1885. B 14 U 9 ‡

HARRISON (JOHN). Oure Tounis Colledge. Sketches of the History of the Old College of Edinburgh; with an Appendix of Historical Documents. 8vo. Edinburgh, 1884. B 13 P 21

HARRISON (PROF. JAMES A.), AND BASKERVILL (PROF. W. M.) Handy Dictionary of Anglo-Saxon Poetry, based on Groschopp's Grein. 8vo. Lond., 1886. K 14 Q 27

HARRISON (MISS JANE ELLEN). Introductory Studies in Greek Art. Illustrated. 8vo. Lond., 1885. A 6 V 20

Myths of the Odyssey in Art and Literature. 8vo. Lond., 1882. J 3 8 17

HARRISON (R.) The Dublin Dissector. 12mo. Lond., 1817. A 12 P 24

HARRISON (ROBERT). Colonial Sketches; or, Five Years in South Australia; with Hints to Capitalists and Emigrants. 12mo. Lond., 1862.* M D 2 R 28

Lorenzo de Medici. [*See* BEAUMONT, A. VON.]

HARRISON (W. H.) Tourist in Portugal. [*See* JENNINGS, R.]

HARRISON (W. JEROME), F.G.S. Geology of the Counties of England and of North and South Wales. 8vo. Lond., 1882. A 9 R 13

HART (A.) Civil Code of the State of California. 12mo. San Francisco, 1885. F 2 P 1

HART (LIEUT.-GEN. G. H.) New Annual Army List, Militia List, Yeomanry Cavalry List, and Indian Civil Service List, for 1836–40, 1842, 1859–85. 33 vols. 8vo. Lond., 1836–85. E

HART (GEORGE). The Violin; its famous Makers and their Imitators. 8vo. Lond., 1875. A 7 U 4

HART (GEORGE ROBERT). Industrial Resources of New Zealand. [*See* NEW ZEALAND EXHIBITIONS.]

HART (J. M.) Syllabus of Anglo-Saxon Literature; adapted from Bernhard Ten Brink's "Geschichte der Englischen Litteratur." 8vo. Cincinnati, 1881. B 5 S 30

HART (CAPT. LOCKYER W.), AND ATKINSON (DR. JAMES). Character and Costumes of Afghaunistan. (Plates.) Imp. fol. Lond., 1843. D 8 P 2 ‡

Expedition into Afghanistan. [*See* ATKINSON, DR. J.]

HARTE (FRANCIS BRET). Complete Works of; collected and revised by the Author. 5 vols. 8vo. Lond., 1880–81. J 9 R 2–6

Complete Poetical Works of. Author's copyright edition. 8vo. Lond., 1886. H 7 S 36

That Heathen Chinee, and other Poems. Australian edition. 12mo. Melb., 1871. M H 1 R 34

Select Works of, in Prose and Poetry; with an Introductory Essay, by J. Montesquieu Bellow. Illustrated. 8vo. Lond., 1872. J 9 R 1

HART (STEVE). [*See* KELLY GANG.]

HARTE (REV. WALTER), M.A. History of the Life of Gustavus Adolphus, King of Sweden, surnamed the Great. 2nd ed. 2 vols. 8vo. Lond., 1767. C 5 R 1, 2

Life and Poems of. [*See* CHALMERS, A.]

HARTING (JAMES EDMUND), F.L.S., &c. Birds of Cornwall; with Memoir of E. Rodd. [*See* RODD, E. H.]

British Animals, Extinct within Historic Times; with some Account of British Wild White Cattle. Illustrated. 8vo. Lond., 1880. A 14 R 41

Essays on Sport and Natural History. Illustrated. 8vo. Lond., 1883. A 16 S 9

Ostriches, &c. [*See* MOSENTHAL, J.]

Perfect Booke for kepinge of Sparhawkes or Goshawkes; written about 1575; now first printed from the original M.S. on vellum, with Introduction and Glossary, by J. E. Harting. Sm. 4to. Lond., 1886. A 14 R 4

HARTING (JAMES EDMUND), AND ROBERT (L. P.) Glimpses of Bird Life, portrayed with Pen and Pencil. Fol. Lond., 1880.   A 23 Q 12 ‡

HARTLEY (SIR C. A.) [*See* HYDRO–MECHANICS.]

HARTLEY (DAVID), M.D.   Observations on Man; his Frame, his Duty, and his Expectations. 6th ed. 8vo. Lond., 1834.   G 1 R 4

HARTLEY (LEONARD LAWRIE.) [*See* HARTLEY LIBRARY.]

HARTLEY (WALTER NOEL), F.C.S. Air and its Relations to Life. 8vo. Lond., 1875.   A 5 S 52

HARTLEY LIBRARY. Catalogue of the Library of the late Leonard Lawrie Hartley; compiled by J. C. Anderson. [Parts 2,3.] 2 vols. roy. 8vo. Lond., 1886–87. K 14 Q 14, 15

Sale Catalogue of the Library. 3rd portion. Roy. 8vo. Lond., 1887.   K 8 Q 16

HARTMANN (DR. ARTHUR). Deaf-mutism and the Education of Deaf-mutes by Lip-reading and Articulation; with numerous and important Additions; translated and enlarged by James Patterson Cassells, M.D., &c. 8vo. Lond., 1881.   A 12 Q 16

HARTMANN (EDUARD VON). Philosophy of the Unconscious: Speculative Results according to the Inductive Method of Physical Science. Authorised Translation. 3 vols. 8vo. Lond., 1884.   G 1 P 19–21

HARTMANN (F.) Life of Philippus Theophrastus Bombast, of Hohenheim, known as Paracelsus, and the Substance of his Teachings. 8vo. Lond., 1887.   C 5 S 26

HARTMANN (PROF. R.) Antropoid Apes. 8vo. Lond., 1885.   A 14 S 8

HARTOG (P. C. L.) Brief Extract from the Report of the Voyages of the Steamer *Egeron* to the South-western Isles, the South-eastern Islands, New Guinea, and the Papoea Isles. 8vo. Sourabaya, 1876.   MF 3 P 20

HARTSON (HALL). The Countess of Salisbury: a Tragedy. (Brit. Theatre.) 12mo. Lond., 1808.   H 2 P 16

Another copy. (Bell's Brit. Theatre.) 18mo. Lond., 1793.   H 1 P 15

Another copy. [*See* BRIT. DRAMA, 2.]   .

HARTTUNG. [*See* PFLUGK-HARTTUNG, DR. J. VON.]

HARTWELL (ABRAHAM). Report of the Kingdome of Congo. [*See* PIGAFETTA, P.]   D 1 R 14

HARTWIG (DR. GEORGE). The Aerial World. 8vo. Lond., 1874.   A 3 T 32

Harmonies of Nature; or, the Unity of Creation. 8vo. Lond., 1866.   A 17 V 10

The Polar World : a popular Description of Man and Nature in the Arctic and Antarctic Regions of the Globe. 8vo. Lond., 1869.   D 4 R 34

2 U

HARTWIG (DR. GEORGE).—*continued.*

The Sea and its Living Wonders: a popular Account of the Marvels of the Deep, and of the progress of Maritime Discovery. 5th ed. 8vo. Lond., 1876.   A 14 S 47

The Subterrannean World. 8vo. Lond., 1876.   A 9 S 37

The Tropical World: Aspects of Man and Nature in the Equatorial Regions of the Globe. New ed. 8vo. Lond., 1873.   A 1 W 31

HARVEN (EMILE DE). La Nouvelle Zélande : Histoire, Géologie, Climat, Gouvernement, Institutions, Agriculture, etc. Roy. 8vo. Anvers, 1883.   MD 3 V 37

HARVEY (GABRIEL), D.C.L. Tracts of. [*See* BRYDGES, SIR S. E.]

Works of ; edited by Rev. Alexander B. Grosart, LL.D. (Hut Lib.) 3 vols. 4to. Lond., 1884–85. J 5 U 25–27

HARVEY (MRS.) Cositas Españolas ; or Every-day Life in Spain. 8vo. Lond., 1875.   D 7 T 9

HARVEY (REV. M.) Newfoundland. [*See* HATTON, J.]

HARVEY (WALTER). China Painting; its Principles and Practice. Illustrated. 8vo. Lond., 1882. A 6 V 10

HARVEY (WILLIAM). Life of the Rt. Hon. Sir Robert Peel, Bart. 12mo. Lond., 1850.   C 1 R 28

[*See* HOWITT, W.]

HARVEY (WILLIAM HENRY), M.D., &c.   Memoir of ; with Selections from his Journal and Correspondence. 8vo. Lond., 1869.   C 8 P 18

Nereis Australis; or, Algæ of the Southern Ocean. Imp. 8vo. Lond., 1847.   MA 1 P 25 †

Phycologia Australica; or, a History of Australian Sea-weeds. 5 vols. imp. 8vo. Lond., 1858–63. MA 1 U 4–8

Phycologia Britannica; or, a History of British Sea-weeds. 4 vols. imp. 8vo. Lond., 1871.   A 4 U 9–12

HARWOOD (MISS ANNIE). [*See* HOLMDEN, MRS. ANNIE.]

HASE (DR. KARL). Miracle Plays and Sacred Dramas: a Historical Survey; translated from the German by A. W. Jackson. 8vo. Lond., 1880.   H 2 R 35

HASELDEN (C. J. A.) Patents Acts, 1883 ; with the Regulations thereunder, and Hints to Inventors. 4to. Wellington, 1884.   MF 1 U 29

HASELDEN (WILLIAM REEVE). Industrial Resources of New Zealand. [*See* NEW ZEALAND EXHIBITIONS.]

HASKOLL (W. DAVIS), C.E. Land and Marine Surveying in reference to the preparation of Plans for Roads and Railways, Canals, Rivers, Towns' Water Supplies, Docks, and Harbours ; with Description and Use of Surveying Instruments. 8vo. Lond., 1868.   A 6 S 28

Another copy. 2nd ed., revised, with Additions. 8vo. Lond., 1886.   A 6 S 29

HASLEWOOD (Rev. F.) Memorials of Smarden, Kent. Privately printed. 4to. Ipswich, 1886.　　B 5 V 30

HASLEWOOD (Joseph). Barnabæ Itinerarium; or, Barnabee's Journal. [*See* BRAITHWAIT, R.]

HASLUCK (Paul N.) Lathe-work: a practical Treatise on the Tools, Appliances, and Processes employed in the Art of Turning. Illustrated. 8vo. Lond., 1881. A 11 P 27

HASSALL (Arthur), M.A. Study of English Constitutional History. [*See* WAKEMAN, H. O.]

HASSALL (Arthur Hill), M.D. Food and its Adulterations; comprising the Reports of the Analytical Sanitary Commission of the *Lancet*, for the years 1851–54 inclusive. 8vo. Lond., 1855.　　A 6 Q 10

HASSAM (F. Childe). [*See* THOMES, W. H.] MJ 1 R 33

HASSAUREK (F.) Four Years among Spanish-Americans. 8vo. Lond., 1868.　　D 3 Q 20

HASSELL (Dr. G.) Vollständige und neueste Erdbeschreibung von Australien, mit einer Einleitung zur Statistik der Länder. 8vo. Weimar, 1825. MD 1 U 37

HASTED (Edward). History and Topographical Survey of the County of Kent. Illustrated. 2nd ed. 12 vols. 8vo. Canterbury, 1797–1801.　　B 6 R 14–25
History of Kent. Part 1. The Hundred of Blackheath. Edited by H. H. Drake. Fol. Lond., 1886. B 14 U 14‡

HASTIE (W.) [*See* HEGEL, G. W. F., AND MICHELET, C. L.]

HASTINGS (Rt. Hon. Warren), First Governor-General of Bengal. Memoirs of the Life of; compiled from original Papers, by the Rev. G. R. Gleig. 3 vols. 8vo. Lond., 1841.　　C 7 R 24–26
Speeches of the Managers and Counsel in the Trial of; edited by E. A. Bond. 4 vols. 8vo. Lond., 1859–61.
　　　　　　　　　　　　　　　F 10 R 4–7
Trial of; complete from February, 1788, to June, 1794. 2 vols. 8vo. Lond., 1794.　　F 5 U 19, 20

HASWELL (Charles), C.E., &c. Mechanics' and Engineers' Pocket-book of Tables, Rules, and Formulas. 47th ed. 12mo. New York, 1885.　　A 10 R 20

HASWELL (William A.), M.A., &c. Catalogue of the Australian Stalk and Sessile-eyed Crustacea. (The Australian Museum, Sydney.) Roy. 8vo. Sydney, 1882.　　MA 2 U 20

HATCH (Edwin), M.A. Organization of the Early Christian Churches. Eight Lectures, delivered before the University of Oxford, in the year 1880. 8vo. Lond., 1881.　　G 1 P 2

HATCH (Walter M.) [*See* ARISTOTELES.]

HATHAWAY (W. S.) [*See* PITT, Rt. Hon. W.]

HATHERLEY (Rt. Hon. William Page Wood), Lord. Memoir of; with Selections from his Correspondence. Edited by his Nephew, W. R. Stephens, M.A. 8vo. Lond., 1883.　　C 4 R 6, 7

HATSELL (John). Precedents of Proceedings in the House of Commons; with Observations. 3rd ed. 4 vols. 4to. Lond., 1796.　　F 8 P 7–10 †

HATTON (Sir Christopher), K.G. Memoirs of the Life and Times of: including his Correspondence with the Queen and other distinguished Persons, by Sir Harris Nicolas, G.C.M.G. 8vo. Lond., 1847.　　C 10 U 14

HATTON (Frank). North Borneo: Explorations and Adventures on the Equator; with Biographical Sketch and Notes, by Joseph Hatton. Illustrated. 8vo. Lond., 1885.　　D 4 T 4

HATTON (Hon. Harold Finch-). [*See* FINCH-HATTON, Hon. H.]

HATTON (Joseph). [*See* HATTON, FRANK.]
Henry Irving's [John Henry Brodrib] Impressions of America; narrated in a series of Sketches, Chronicles, and Conversations. 2 vols. 8vo. Lond., 1884. D 3 Q 45, 46
Journalistic London; being a Series of Sketches of Famous Pens and Papers of the Day. [Reprinted, with Additions, from *Harper's Magazine*.] Sq. 8vo. Lond., 1882.　　J 12 R 4
Printing and Bookbinding. (Brit. Manuf. Indust.) 12mo. Lond., 1876.　　A 17 S 39

HATTON (Joseph), AND HARVEY (Rev. M.) Newfoundland; the Oldest British Colony: its History, its Present Condition, and its Prospects in the Future. Illustrated. 8vo. Lond., 1883.　　D 3 T 49

HAUER (I. von). Die Geologie und ihre anwendung auf die Kenntniss der Bodenbeschaffenheit der Österr-Ungar Monarchie. 8vo. Vienna, 1875.　　A 9 8 1

HAUFF (Hermann) Humboldt's Reise in die Aequinoctial Gegenden. [*See* HUMBOLDT, F. H. A. VON BARON.]　　D 3 T 26, 27

HAUFF (W.) Tales: The Caravan, The Sheik of Alexandria, The Inn in the Spessart; translated from the German by S. Mendel. 8vo. Lond., 1886.　　J 9 U 16

HAUTIERE (Ulysse de la). [*See* LA HAUTIERE, ULYSSE DE.]

HAUG (Martin), Ph.D. Essays on the Sacred Language, Writings, and Religion of the Parsis. 2nd ed. 8vo. Lond., 1878.　　G 15 P 10
Old Zand-Pahlavi Glossary. Edited by Destur Hoshengji Jamaspji. Revised, with Notes and Introduction. Roy. 8vo. Bombay, 1867.　　K 16 Q 10
Outline of a Grammar of the Zend Language. 8vo. Bombay, 1862.　　K 13 P 18

HAUGHTON (SIR GRAVES CHAMNEY), F.R.S., &c. Prodromus; or, an Inquiry into the First Principles of Reasoning. 8vo. Lond., 1839. G 1 R 3

HAUGHTON (REV. S.), M.D., &c. Natural Philosophy popularly explained. 12mo. Lond., 1870. A 17 T 29
On the Tides of the Arctic Seas. Parts 4-6. (Roy. Soc. Pubs., 1.) 4to. Lond., 1876. A 11 P 2 †
On the Tides of the Arctic Seas. Part 7. Tides of Port Kennedy, in Bellot Strait. (Roy. Soc. Pubs., 5.) 4to. Lond., 1878. A 11 P 6 †
Six Lectures on Physical Geography 8vo. Dublin, 1880. A 29 T 7

HAUREAU (BARTH). Critique des Hypothèses Métaphysiques de Manès, de Pélage, et de l'Idéalisme Transcendental de Saint Augustin. (*Bound with Remusat's Recherches.*) 4to. Mans, 1839. K 16 R 31

HAUSCHILD (DR. ERNST INNOCENT). Dictionnaire Etymologique de la Langue Française tiré de la Grammaire des Langues Romanes, ouvrage éminemment classique de Freidrich Diez. 8vo. Leipsic, 1843. K 12 Q 16

HAUSERMANN (R.) [*See* D'ESTREY, DR. M.]

HAUSSET (MME. DU). Mémoires de. [*See* BARRIÈRE, J. F., 3.] C 1 T 3

HAUSSONVILLE (OTHENIN), VICOMTE D'. Salon de Madame Necker [Baronne de Staël-Holstein]; translated by Henry M. Trollope. 2 vols. 8vo. Lond., 1882. C 4 Q 21, 22

HAVARD (HENRY). Dutch School of Painting; translated by G. Powell. 8vo. Lond., 1885. A 6 V 11

HAVARD (WILLIAM). King Charles I: a Tragedy. (Bell's Brit. Theatre.) 18mo. Lond., 1793. H 2 P 43

HAVELOCK (MAJOR-GEN. SIR HENRY), K.C.B. Biographical Sketch of; by the Rev. W. Brock. 4th ed. 12mo. Lond., 1858. C 1 T 36
Life of; by the Rev. T. Smith. (Pam. Bb.) Sydney, (n.d.) MG 1 P 49
Memoirs of; by J. C. Marshman. 8vo. Lond., 1860. C 7 Q 25

HAVERTY (MARTIN). Wanderings in Spain in 1843. 2 vols. 8vo. Lond., 1844-45. D 8 R 34, 35

HAWAII. Civil Code of the Hawaiian Islands, 1859; to which is added an Appendix containing Laws not expressly repealed by the Civil Code; the Session Laws of 1858-59; and Treaties with Foreign Nations. 8vo. Honolulu, 1859. MF 2 R 5
Penal Code of the Hawaiian Kingdom; compiled from the Panal Code of 1850, and the various Penal Enactments since made, pursuant to Act of the Legislative Assembly, June 22nd, 1868. 8vo. Honolulu, 1869. MF 2 R 6

HAWAIIAN ALMANAC AND ANNUAL FOR 1875-86. A Hand-book of Information on Matters relating to the Hawaiian Islands, original and selected, of value to Merciants, Planters, Tourists, and others; carefully compiled by T. G. Thrum. 12 vols. (in 5) 8vo. Honolulu, 1874-86. ME 3 S

HAWAIIAN SPECTATOR (THE). Conducted by an Association of Gentlemen. Vols. 1, 2. 8vo. Honolulu, 1838-39. ME 3 R

HAWDON (JOSEPH). Journal of an Overland Journey from Port Philip to Adelaide. [*See* MANUSCRIPTS, &c.]

HAWEIS (MRS. H. R.) Art of Beauty. Illustrated. Sq. 8vo. Lond., 1878. A 8 P 27
Art of Decoration. Illustrated. 8vo. Lond., 1881. A 6 V 31

HAWEIS (REV. H. R.), M.A. Current Coin. 8vo. Lond., 1876. G 8 S 12
Music and Morals. 8vo. Lond., 1873. A 7 P 16

HAWKE (ADM. EDWARD), LORD. Life of; with some Account of the Origin of the English Wars in the Reign of George the Second, and the State of the Royal Navy, by Capt. Montagu Burrows. 8vo. Lond., 1883. C 7 Q 27

HAWKER (REV. ROBERT S.), VICAR OF MORWENSTOW. Life of, by S. Baring-Gould, M.A. 8vo. Lond., 1876. C 3 T 27

HAWKESBURY BENEVOLENT SOCIETY: Annual Reports, 1856-63; with a List of Subscribers, &c. (Pam. Du.) 8vo. Sydney and Parramatta, 1857-63. MF 3 P 13
Another copy, 1866-67. 8vo. Windsor, 1867-68. MF 3 P 18

HAWKESWORTH (JOHN), LL.D. Account of the Voyages undertaken by the order of His present Majesty, for making Discoveries in the Southern Hemisphere, and successively performed by Commodore Byron, Captain Wallis, Captain Carteret, and Captain Cook, in the *Dolphin*, the *Swallow*, and the *Endeavour*. 3 vols. 8vo. Lond., 1773.* D 10 U 18-20
Another copy. 3 vols. 4to. Lond., 1773.* MD 5 P 4-6 †
Another copy. MD 6 P 32-34 †
Amphitryon: a Comedy. [*See* DRYDEN, J.]
Edgar and Emmeline: a Comedy. [*See* FARCES, 6.]

HAWKEY (C.) Shakespeare Tapestry woven in Verse. 8vo. Edinb., 1881. H 7 R 36

HAWKINS (BISSET), M.D., &c. Germany: the Spirit of her History, Literature, Social Condition, and National Economy. 8vo. Lond., 1838. B 9 R 22

HAWKINS (CHARLES), F.R.C.S. [*See* BRODIE, SIR B. C.]

HAWKINS (EDWARD), D.D. Manual for Christians; designed for their use at any time after Confirmation. 6th ed. 12mo. Sydney, 1839. MG 1 P 49

HAWKINS (E. L.) [*See* ARISTOTELES.]

HAWKINS (FREDERICK). Annals of the French Stage, from its Origin to the Death of Racine, 789–1699. 2 vols. 8vo. Lond., 1884.   B 8 R 31, 32

HAWKINS (F. W.) Life of Edmund Kean; from published and original Sources. 2 vols. 8vo. Lond., 1869.   C 7 P 35, 36

HAWKINS (SIR JOHN). General History of the Science and Practice of Music. 5 vols. 4to. Lond.,1776.
                                    A 8 U 5–9 †
Life of Samuel Johnson, LL.D. 2nd ed. 8vo. Lond., 1787.   C 6 R 6

HAWKINS (SIR RICHARD), KNT. Observations of Sir Richard Hawkins, in his Voyage into the South Sea, A.D. 1593. Roy. 8vo. Lond., 1622.   MD 3 V 3

HAWKINS (RUSH CHRISTOPHER). Titles of the First Books. Illustrated with Reproductions of Early Types, and First Engravings of the Printing Press. 4to. New York, 1884.   K 17 S 4

HAWKS (FRANCIS LESTER), D.D., &c. Narrative of the Expedition of an American Squadron to the China Seas, &c. [*See* PERRY, COMM. M. C.]

HAWTHORN (J. R. H.) [*See* HOULDING, J. R.]

HAWTHORNE (JULIAN). Nathaniel Hawthorne and his Wife: a Biography. 2 vols. 8vo. Lond.,1885. C 4 T 12, 13

HAWTHORNE (NATHANIEL). [A Biography]; by H. James, junr. (Eng. Men Letts.) 8vo. Lond., 1879.
                                          C 1 U 19
Journal of an African Cruiser. [*See* BRIDGE, H.]
Nathaniel Hawthorne and his Wife: a Biography; by Julian Hawthorne. 2 vols. 8vo. Lond.,1885. C 4 T 12, 13
Our Old Home. 2 vols. 8vo. Lond., 1863.   J 9 U 11, 12
Passages from American Note-books. 2 vols. 8vo. Lond., 1868.   J 9 U 9, 10
Passages from the English Note-books of Nathaniel Hawthorne. 2 vols. 8vo. Lond., 1870.   D 7 T 18, 19

HAWTHORNE (MRS. SOPHIA). Nathaniel Hawthorne and his Wife [Mrs. S. Hawthorne]: a Biography; by Julian Hawthorne. 2 vols. 8vo. Lond., 1885. C 4 T 12,13
Notes in England and Italy. 8vo. Lond., 1869. D 6 R 41

HAY (DAVID RAMSAY). Laws of Harmonious Colouring, adapted to Interior Decorations, Manufactures, and other useful purposes. 3rd. ed. 8vo. Edinb., 1836. A 7 Q 13
Natural Principles and Analogy of the Harmony of Form. Roy. 4to. Edinb., 1842.   A 2 R 21 †
Original Geometrical Diaper Designs, accompanied by an Attempt to develope and elucidate the True Principles of Ornamental Design, as applied to the Decorative Arts. Ob. 4to. Lond., 1844.   A 23 P 21 ‡

HAY (EDWARD). History of the Insurrection of the County of Wexford, A.D. 1798. 8vo. Dublin, 1803. B 11 Q 24

HAY (JOHN). Pike County Ballads, and other Pieces 15th ed. 8vo. Boston, 1882.   H 7 R 37

HAY (JOHN BARRAS). Inaugural Addresses by Lords Rectors of the University of Glasgow; to which are prefixed an Historical Sketch and Account of the present state of the University. Roy. 8vo. Glasgow, 1839.   J 9 V 8

HAY (SIR JOHN CHARLES DALRYMPLE), BART., &c. Ashanti and the Gold Coast, and what we know of it. 8vo. Lond., 1874.   B 1 P 31

HAY (JOHN H. DRUMMOND). Western Barbary: its Wild Tribes and Savage Animals. 12mo. Lond.,1844. D 10 Q 51
Another copy. (H. and C. Lib.) 12mo. Lond., 1844.
                                          J 8 P 5

HAY (SIR JOHN DRUMMOND), K.C.B. Mission to the Court of Morocco. [*See* TROTTER, CAPT. P. D.]

HAY (R. W.) Notices of New Zealand; from Original Documents in the Colonial Office. 8vo. Lond., 1832.
                                        MD 7 Q 48

HAY (WILLIAM DELISLE). Brighter Britain; or, Settler and Maori in Northern New Zealand. 2 vols. 8vo. Lond., 1882.   MD 5 Q 18, 19

HAYDEN (PROF. FERDINAND VANDEVEER). Twelfth Annual Report of the United States Geological Survey of the Territories. [*See* UNITED STATES.]

HAYDEN (PROF. F. V.), AND SELWYN (PROF. A. R. C.), F.R.S. North America. Illustrated. (Stanford's Compendium of Geography, &c.) 8vo. Lond., 1883. D 3 P 61

HAYDN (FRANCIS JOSEPH). Letters of. [*See* WALLACE, LADY.]
Lives of Haydn and Mozart; with Observations on Metastasio, &c. Translated from the French of "L. A. C. Bombet" [Marie Henry Bayle.] 2nd ed. 8vo. Lond., 1818.   C 5 T 12

HAYDN (JOSEPH). Dictionary of Science. [*See* ROD WELL, G. F.]
Haydn's Dictionary of Dates and Universal Information, relating to all ages and nations; by Benjamin Vincent. 13th ed. 8vo. Lond., 1871.   K 11 P 14
Another copy. 16th ed. 8vo. Lond., 1878. K 11 P 14
The Haydn Series: a Dictionary of Biography Past and Present. [*See* VINCENT, B.]
Universal Index of Biography; edited by J. B. Payne. 8vo. Lond., 1870.   Lib.

HAYDON (BENJAMIN ROBERT). Correspondence and Table Talk; with a Memoir by his Son, Frederic Wordsworth Haydon. 2 vols. 8vo. Lond., 1876. C 7 P 22, 23
Lectures on Painting and Design; with Designs drawn up by himself on the Wood, and engraved by Edward Evans. 2 vols. 8vo. Lond., 1844–46.   A 7 S 2, 3

HAYDON (BENJAMIN ROBERT).—*continued.*
Life of Benjamin Robert Haydon, Historical Painter; from
1is Autobiograp1y and Journals; edited and compiled by
Tom Taylor. 3 vols. 8vo. Lond., 1853.　　C 3 T 28–30

On Academies of Art (more particularly the Royal
Academy), and t1eir pernicious effect on the Genius of
Europe. 8vo. Lond., 1839.　　A 7 R 21

HAYDON (B. R.), AND HAZLITT (WM.) Painting and
the Fine Arts. 8vo. Edinb., 1838.　　A 6 V 7

HAYDON (F. W.) [*See* HAYDON, B. R.]

HAYDON (G. H.) The Australian Emigrant: a Rambling Story. Illustrated. 8vo. Lond., 1854. MJ 2 S 24

Five Years' Experience in Australia Felix ; comprising a
s1ort Account of its Early Settlement and its Present
Position wit1 many Particulars interesting to intending
Emigrants. Roy. 8vo. Lond., 1846.*　　MD 3 V 17

HAYDON (THOMAS). Australasian Coursing Calendar for
the Season 1877. 8vo. Melb., 1878.　　ME 3 S

HAYES (A. A.), JUNR., A.M. New Colorado and the Santa
Fé Trail. Illustrated. Sq. 8vo. Lond., 1881. D 3 T 44

HAYES (MISS CATHERINE). [*See* ENCHANTRESS, THE.]

HAYES (ISAAC ISRAEL), M.D. Land of Desolation; being
a personal Narrative of Adventure in Greenland. 8vo.
Lond., 1871.　　D 4 R 29

Open Polar Sea: a Narrative of a Voyage of Discovery
towards the Nort1 Pole, in the sc1ooner *United States.*
8vo. Lond., 1867.　　D 4 R 28

[*See* AMERICAN ARCTIC EXPLORERS.]

HAYES (JOHN L.) Wools of the United States. (Pam.
C1n.) 8vo. Boston, 1872.　　A 1 T 35

HAYES (M. HORACE). Riding; on the Flat and across
Country: a Guide to Practical Horsemans1ip. Illustrated
by Stanley Berkley. 8vo. Lond., 1881.　　A 17 U 25

Veterinary Notes for Horse-owners. Illustrated. 3rd ed.,
revised and enlarged. 8vo. Lond., 1884.　　A 1 P 40

HAYES (TIMOTHY). Queen v. Hayes. [*See* STATE TRIALS.]

HAYGARTH (HENRY WILLIAM). Recollections of Bus1
Life in Australia, during a Residence of Eig1t Years in
the Interior. 12mo. Lond., 1848.*　　MD 1 Q 17

Anot1er copy. New ed. 8vo. Lond., 1861. MD 1 Q 19

Another copy (H. and C. Lib.) 12mo. Lond., 1848. J 8 P 28

HAYLEY (WILLIAM). Life and Poems of. [*See* BRITISH
POETS, 5.]

Life of William Cowper; wit1 Remarks on Epistolary
Writers. 4 vols. 8vo. Lond., 1812.　　C 5 V 2–5

HAYMO (HALBERSTATENSIS EPISCOPUS). Opera omnia.
[*See* MIGNE, J. P., SERIES LATINA, 116–118.]

HAYNES (SAMUEL), A.M. Collection of State Papers.
[*See* BURGHLEY, LORD.]　　B 16 S 11 ‡

HAYNES (WILLIAM). My Log: a Journal of the Proceedings of the Flying Squadron. 12mo. Devonport,
1871.　　MH 1 R 11

HAYS (FRANCES). Women of the Day : a Biograp1ical
Dictionary of Notable Contemporaries. 8vo. Lond.,
1885.　　C 11 Q 3

HAYTER (HENRY HEYLYN), C.M.G. Carboona: a C1apter
from the Early History of Victoria. 8vo. Melb., 1885.*
MH 1 T 6

Hand-book to the Colony of Victoria. 8vo. Melb.,
1881.　　MD 3 T 22

Anot1er copy. 2nd ed. 8vo. Melb., 1885. MD 3 T 23

My C1ristmas Adventure, Carboona (revised, and partly
re-written), and ot1er Poems. 8vo. Melb., 1887.
MH 1 Q 6

Notes on the Colony of Victoria: Historical, Geograp1ical, ,
Meteorological, and Statistical. 2nd ed. 8vo. Melb.,
1876.　　MF 2 Q 26

Victorian Year-book for 1874. 8vo. Melb., 1875. MJ 2 R 10

Victorian Year-book for 1874, 1882–84, 1886–87. 4 vols.
8vo. Melb., 1874–87.*　　ME 3 T

HAYTER (JOHN). Landsman's Log-book; or, an Emigrant's Life at Sea; wit1 some Account of Sout1 Australia. 12mo. Lond., 1842.　　MD 1 T 50

HAYTER (T. S.) Directory of Sout1 Australia. [*See*
MORRIS, C. S.]

HAYWARD (ABRAHAM), Q.C. Selection from the Correspondence of, 1834–84; wit1 an Account of 1is Early
Life; edited by Henry E. Carlisle. 2 vols. 8vo. Lond.,
1886.　　C 3 T 10, 11

Sketc1es of Eminent Statesmen and Writers, wit1 ot1er
Essays. 2 vols. 8vo. Lond., 1880.　　C 7 P 49, 50

HAYWARD (JOHN). Religious Creeds and Statistics of
every C1ristian Denomination in the United States. 8vo.
Boston, 1836.　　G 2 P 17

HAZARD (SAMUEL). Santo Domingo, Past and Present;
wit1 a Glance at Hayti. Illustrated. 8vo. Lond.,
1873.　　D 3 S 28

Cuba, wit1 Pen and Pencil. 8vo. Lond., 1873. D 3 U 11

HAZELL'S ANNUAL CYCLOPÆDIA. 8vo. Lond.,
1886.　　E

HAZLEWOOD (DAVID). Compendious Grammar of the
Feejeean Language; wit1 Examples of Native Idioms.
12mo. Vewa, 1850.*　　MK 1 P 21

Feejeean and Englis1 Dictionary. 12mo. Yewa, 1850.
MK 1 P 21

Fijian and Englis1, and Englis1 and Fijian Dictionary,
and a Grammar of the Language, wit1 Examples of Native
Idioms. 2nd ed., wit1 Map; edited by James Calvert.
8vo. Lond., 1872.*　　MK 1 P 22

HAZLITT (WILLIAM). Characteristics; in the manner of "Rochefoucauld's Maxims"; with Introductory Remarks, by R. H. Horne. 12mo. Lond., 1837.   J 6 P 13

Characters of Shakspeare's Plays. 12mo. Lond., 1838.   J 6 P 14

Another copy. 4th ed., edited by his Son [W. C. Hazlitt]. 12mo. Lond., 1848.   H 3 P 2

Conversations of James Northcote, Esq., R.A. 8vo. Lond., 1830.   C 5 R 19

Criticisms on Art, and Sketches of the Picture Galleries of England: with Catalogues of the principal Galleries, now first collected. 1st and 2nd Series, edited by his Son. 2 vols. 12mo. Lond., 1843–44.   A 7 P 33, 34

Dramatic Works of John Webster. [*See* WEBSTER, J.]

The Eloquence of the British Senate; with Notes, Biographical, Critical, and Explanatory. 2 vols. 8vo. Lond., 1808.   F 8 S 3, 4

Essays on the Principles of Human Action. 8vo. Lond. (n.d.)   G 8 S 4

Johnson's Lives of the British Poets. [*See* JOHNSON, S.]

Lectures on the Dramatic Literature of the Age of Elizabeth. 2nd ed. 8vo. Lond., 1821.   J 5 S 9

Lectures on the English Comic Writers. 8vo. Lond., 1819.   J 5 S 11

Lectures on the English Poets. 2nd ed. 8vo. Lond., 1819   J 5 S 10

Life of Napoleon Buonaparte. 4 vols. 8vo. Lond., 1830.   C 8 T 25–28

Literary Remains, with a Notice of his Life, by his Son [William Hazlitt]. 2 vols. 8vo. Lond., 1836.   J 5 S 12, 13

Painting and the Fine Arts. [*See* HAYDON, B. R.]

The Plain Speaker: Opinions on Books, Men, and Things. 2 vols. 8vo. Lond., 1826.   J 12 V 13, 14

Political Essays; with Sketches of Public Characters. 8vo. Lond., 1819.   F 8 R 9

Spirit of the Age; or, Contemporary Portraits. 4th ed., edited by W. C. Hazlitt. 8vo. Lond., 1886.   C 2 S 38

Table Talk: Essays on Men and Manners. 8vo. Lond., 1869.   J 6 P 11

Table Talk of Martin Luther. [*See* LUTHER, M.]

View of the English Stage; or, a Series of Dramatic Criticisms. 8vo. Lond., 1818.   J 5 S 14

[*See* BEAUCHESNE, A. DE.]

HAZLITT (WILLIAM), AND HUNT (J. H. L.) The Round Table: Northcote's Conversations, Characteristics, &c. 8vo. Lond., 1871.   J 6 P 12

HAZLITT (W. CAREW). Bibliographical Collections and Notes on Early English Literature. 1474-1700. 1st, 2nd, and 3rd series. 8vo. Lond., 1876-87.   C 17 Q 16–18

English Proverbs and Proverbial Phrases, collected from the most authentic sources, alphabetically arranged and annotated. 2nd ed., greatly enlarged and carefully revised. 8vo. Lond., 1882.   C 17 P 27

HAZLITT (W. CAREW).—*continued.*

Great Gold-fields of Cariboo; with an authentic Description, brought down to the latest period, of British Columbia and Vancouver Island. 12mo. Lond., 1862.   D 3 P 22

Hand-book to the Popular, Poetical, and Dramatic Literature of Great Britain, from the Invention of Printing to the Restoration. 8vo. Lond., 1867.   K 17 Q 15

History of the Roman Republic. [*See* MICHELET, J.]

History of the Venetian Republic : her Rise, her Greatness, and her Civilization. 4 vols. 8vo. Lond., 1860.   B 11 U 2–5

Letters of Charles Lamb. [*See* LAMB, C.]

The New London Jest-book. 12mo. Lond., 1871.   J 6 Q 8

Offspring of Thought in Solitude: Modern Essays. 8vo. Lond., 1884.   J 6 Q 9

1. Coleridge Abroad.	12. Our Democratic Tendencies.
2. Charles Lamb.	13. The Vulgar Tongue.
3. Dr. Johnson.	14. Common People.
4. Old Ballads.	15. Bunyann.
5. On some Living and Late Authors.	16. Masters and Servants.
	17. A Chapter on Saws.
6. On the Different Sorts of Fame.	18. Jokers.
	19. Joe Miller.
7. On Persons who have done only One Thing.	20. A Leaf of Errata.
	21. Babyology.
8. On the Poetry of Form.	22. Figures.
9. On the Differences between Writing and Painting	23. St. Luke's-super-Marc.
	24. A Little out of the Straight Line.
10. On the Progress of Criticism.	25. Nemo.
11. Englishmen in Italy, and Italians in England.	26. Ben Trovato.
	27. A Cause Célèbre.

Old Cookery Books and Ancient Cuisine. 8vo. Lond., 1886.   A 6 Q 28

Popular Antiquities of Great Britain. [*See* BRAND, J.]

Remains of the Early Popular Poetry of England ; collected and edited, with Introductions and Notes. 4 vols. 12mo. Lond., 1864-66.   H 6 R 21–24

Shakespeare Jest-books. [*See* SHAKESPEARE, W.]

Some Account of H. Constable, B.A. [*See* CONSTABLE, H.]

Some Account of Thomas Randolph. [*See* RANDOLPH, T.]

The Spirit of the Age. [*See* HAZLITT, W.]

HEAD (B. V.) Catalogue of Greek Coins in the British Museum, Macedonia, &c. Edited by R. S. Poole. 8vo. Lond., 1879.   A 13 R 34

The Coinage of Lydia and Persia. [*See* NUMISMATA ORIENTALIA.]

[*See* PETRIE, W. M. F.]

HEAD (B. V.), AND GARDNER (P.) Catalogue of Greek Coins—The Tauric Chersonese, Sarmatia, Dacia, Moesia, Thrace, &c.; edited by R. S. Poole. (British Museum). 8vo. Lond., 1877.   A 13 R 32

HEAD (B. V.), GARDNER (P.), AND POOLE (R. S.) Catalogue of Greek Coins—Sicily. (British Museum). 8vo. Lond., 1876.   A 13 R 31

HEAD (RT. HON. SIR EDMUND), BART. &c. Viga Glums' Saga. [*See* VIGA GLUM'S SAGA.]   J 10 P 10

HEAD (RT. HON. SIR FRANCIS B.), BART. An Address to the House of Lords against the Bill before Parliament for the Union of the Canadas. (Pam., 5.) 8vo. Lond., 1840.   MJ 2 P 39

Bubbles from the Brunnens of Nassau ; by "An Old Man." 8vo. Lond., 1834.   D 7 Q 1

The Defenceless State of Great Britain. 8vo. Lond., 1850.   F 5 T 25

Descriptive Essays, contributed to the *Quarterly Review.* 2 vols. 8vo. Lond., 1857.   J 5 P 23, 24

The Emigrant. 8vo. Lond., 1846.   J 5 P 33

A Faggot of French Sticks : Paris in 1851. 2 vols. 8vo. Lond., 1852.   D 7 Q 7, 8

A Fortnight in Ireland. 8vo. Lond., 1852.   D 6 T 14

The Horse and his Rider. 8vo. Lond., 1860.   A 1 P 38

Life of Bruce, the African Traveller. 18mo. Lond., 1830.   C 1 P 26

A Narrative [of Canada.] 8vo. Lond., 1839.   B 19 S 5

Reports relating to the Failure of the Rio Plata Mining Association. 8vo. Lond., 1827.   A 9 Q 42

Rough Notes taken during some rapid Journeys across the Pampas and among the Andes. 8vo. Lond., 1826.   D 3 P 52

Another copy. (H. and C. Lib.) 12mo. Lond., 1846.   J 8 P 19

The Royal Engineer. 8vo. Lond., 1869.   A 16 S 22

Stokers and Pokers ; or, the London and North-Western Railway, and the Britannia and Conway Tubular Bridges. (H. and C. Lib.) 5th ed. 12mo. Lond., 1851.   J 8 P 33

HEAD (SIR GEORGE). Forest Scenes and Incidents in the Wilds of North America. 2nd ed. 8vo. Lond., 1838.   D 4 P 11

Historical Memoirs of Cardinal Pacca. [*See* PACCA, CARDINAL B.]   C 4 T 36 37

Home Tour through the Manufacturing Districts of England, in the Summer of 1835. 8vo. Lond., 1836.   D 8 P 12

Home Tour through various parts of the United Kingdom; being a continuation of the "Home Tour through the Manufacturing Districts." 8vo. Lond., 1837. D 8 P 13

[*See* APULEIUS, L.]

HEAD (PERCY RENDELL). Classic and Italian Painting. [*See* POYNTER, E. J.]

Frans Hals. (Great Artists.) 8vo. Lond., 1879.   C 3 T 33

Van Dyck. (Great Artists.) 8vo. Lond., 1879.   C 3 T 33

HEAD (RICHARD). The English Rogue : described in the Life of Meriton Latroon, and other Extravagants ; being a Complete History of the most Eminent Cheats of both Sexes and most Trades and Professions. 4 vols. 12mo. Lond., 1665-80.   J 7 Q 50-53

HEADLEY (J. T.) Travels in Italy, the Alps, and the Rhine. 12mo. Dublin, 1849.   D 7 P 19

[*See* CORMENIN, VISCOUNT DE.]

HEADLEY (W. BALLS-). [*See* BALLS-HEADLEY W.]

HEADS OF THE PEOPLE. [*See* BAKER, W.]

HEALE (THEOPHILUS). New Zealand and the New Zealand Company ; being a consideration of how far their interests are similar. In answer to a pamphlet entitled "How to Colonize." [By R. D. MANGLES.] 8vo. Lond., 1842.   MJ 2 Q 2

HEALING ART (THE) ; or, Chapters upon Medicine, Diseases, Remedies, and Physicians. 2 vols. 8vo. Lond., 1887.   A 12 U 15, 16

HEALTH EXHIBITION LIBRARY. Catalogue of. 8vo. Lond., 1884.   K 7 S 30

HEALTH LECTURES FOR THE PEOPLE. [*See* AUSTRALIAN HEALTH SOCIETY.]

HEALY (JAMES U.) An Alphabetical List of Parishes, Stations, Hamlets, Streets, and Places not being Post Towns, in Victoria. 8vo. Melb., 1870.   MJ 2 R 15

HEALEY (MARY). [*See* BIGOT, MME. C.]

HEAPHY (CHARLES). On the Gold-bearing District of Coromandel Harbour, New Zealand. 8vo. Lond., 1854.   MA 2 Q 20

[*See* WAKEFIELD, E. J.]

HEARN (LAFCADIO). "Gombo Zhèbes." Little Dictionary of Creole Proverbs. 8vo. New York, 1885.   K 12 S 27

HEARN (PROF. WILLIAM EDWARD), LL.D. East Melbourne Election : Address to the Melbourne Atheneum. 4to. Melb., 1874.   MF 1 Q 6

The Government of England : its Structure and its Development. 8vo. Melb., 1867.*   MF 2 Q 3

Mechanics' Institutes : a Lecture on the proposed formation of Adult Educational Classes. 8vo. Melb., 1856.   MG 1 Q 30

National Loyalty ; or, the Colonies and the Mother Country : a Lecture. 12mo. Melb., 1879.   MJ 2 P 31

Another copy.   MJ 2 R 15

Plutology ; or, the Theory of the Efforts to satisfy Human Wants. 8vo. Melb., 1863.*   MF 2 Q 1

HEARNE (THOMAS). History and Antiquities of the University of Cambridge. [*See* PARKER, REV. R.]

Journey to Reading and to Whaddon Hall. [*See* AUBREY, JOHN.]

Lives of those Eminent Antiquaries John Leland, Thomas Hearne, and Anthony A. Woods ; by W. Huddersford and T. Wharton. 2 vols. 8vo. Oxford, 1772.   C 1 V 14, 15

Thomæ Sprotti Chronica. [*See* SPROTT, THOS.]

[*See* AUBREY, J. ; *and* SPELMAN, SIR J.]

HEARNE (W. G.) Treatment of Disease: a short Treatise to secure advancement in the Science of Medicine. 12mo. Meln., 1880.   MA 2 S 38

HEAT, in its Mechanical Applications: a Series of Lectures delivered at the Institution of Engineers, 1883–84; [by Prof. O. Reynolds, W. Anderson, E. A. Cooper, Prof. F. Jenkin, and Capt. A. Noble.] 8vo. Lond., 1885.   A 11 U 9

HEATH (CHRISTOPHER), F.R.C.S. Dictionary of Practical Surgery, by various British Surgeons; edited by C. Heath. 2 vols. roy. 8vo. Lond., 1886.   A 12 S 37,38

Practical Anatomy: a Manual of Dissections. (Churchill's Manuals.) 4th ed.; with coloured Plates and Engravings on Wood. 8vo. Lond., 1877.   A 13 P 39

HEATH (FRANCIS GEORGE). Autumnal Leaves. With coloured Plates. 8vo. Lond., 1881.   A 4 Q 24

Sylvan Winter. 8vo. Lond., 1886.   A 4 Q 25

HEATH (JAMES), R.A. [*See* HOGARTH.]

HEATH (RICHARD). Edgar Quinet; his Early Life and Writings. With Portraits. 8vo. Lond., 1881.   C 5 T 21

HEATH (RICHARD FORD), M.A. Albrecht Dürer. (Great Artists). 8vo. Lond., 1881.   C 3 T 41

Titian. (Great Artists). 8vo. Lond., 1879.   C 3 T 36

HEATH (T. L.), B.A. Diophantos, of Alexandria: a Study in the History of Greek Algebra. 8vo. Camb., 1885.   A 10 T 22

HEATH & CORDELL. Directory for Shires and Road Boards in Victoria. 12mo. Meln., 1867.   ME 4 P

HEATHER (J. F.), M.A. Descriptive Geometry; with a Theory of Shadows and of Perspective. (Weale.) 12mo. Lond., 1871.   A 17 P 34

Mathematical Instruments: Drawing and Measuring Instruments. (Weale.) 12mo. Lond., 1872.   A 17 Q 22

Mathematical Instruments: Optical Instruments. (Weale.) 12mo. Lond., 1871.   A 17 Q 22

Mathematical Instruments: Surveying and Astronomical Instruments. (Weale.) 12mo. Lond., 1873.   A 17 Q 22

Practical Plane Geometry: giving the simplest modes of constructing Figures contained in one plane and geometrical construction on the ground. (Weale.) 12mo. Lond., 1872.   A 17 Q 23

Treatise on Mathematical Instruments: their Construction, Adjustment, Testing, and Use, concisely explained. 11th ed. (Weale.) 12mo. Lond., 1871.   A 17 P 34

HEATHERINGTON (A.) Mining industries of Nova Scotia; comprising a Review of the Gold-field, from the first working of the Gold mines, 1860, to 1873. (Pam. Ci.) 8vo. Lond., 1874.   MA 2 Q 33

Another copy. (Pam. Inp.)   F i R 7

HEATLEY (GEORGE S.), M.R.C.V.S. Every Man his own Vet.: Veterinary Remedies, and how to apply them. 12mo. Edinb., 1886.   A 1 P 37

Horse-owners' Safeguard: a handy Medical Guide for every Man who owns a Horse. 8vo. Edinb., 1882.   A 1 P 42

Our Dogs and their Diseases. 8vo. Lond., 1884.   A 1 P 18

Sheep-farming. 8vo. Lond., 1884.   A 1 Q 17

Stock-owners'Guide: a handy Medical Treatise for every Man who owns an Ox or Cow. 8vo. Edinb., 1883.   A 1 Q 10

HEATON (MRS. CHARLES). Antonio Allegri da Correggio. [*See* CORREGGIO, A. A. DA.]

Concise History of Painting; with Illustrations in Permanent Photography. 8vo. Lond., 1873.   A 8 P 34

History of the Life of Albrecht Dürer, of Nürnberg; with a Translation of his Letters and Journal, and some Account of his Work. Imp. 8vo. Lond., 1870.   C 7 V 47

Another copy. With Portrait. 2nd ed. 8vo. Lond., 1881.   C 3 V 3

Lives of the most eminent British Painters. [*See* CUNNINGHAM, A.]

HEATON (PROF. C. W.), F.C.S. Experimental Chemistry, founded on the work of Dr. Julius Adolph Stöckhardt: a Hand-book for the Study of the Science by Simple Experiments. 8vo. Lond., 1872.   A 5 R 27

HEATON (J. HENNIKER). Australian Dictionary of Dates and Men of the Time: containing the History of Australasia, from 1542 to May, 1879. Roy. 8vo. Sydney, 1879.*   MK 1 S 47

HEATON (M. COMPTON). Antonio Allegri da Correggio. (Great Artists). 8vo. Lond., 1882.   C 3 T 32

HEBER (RT. REV. REGINALD), D.D., BISHOP OF CALCUTTA. Life of Rt. Rev. Jeremy Taylor. [*See* TAYLOR, RT. REV. J.]

Narrative of a Journey through the Upper Provinces of India, from Calcutta to Bombay, 1824–25 (with Notes upon Ceylon); Journey to Madras and the Southern Provinces, 1826, &c. 4th ed. 3 vols. 8vo. Lond., 1829.   D 6 R 10–12

Another copy. (H. and C. Lib.) 2 vols. 12mo. Lond., 1843–46.   J 8 P 2, 3

Poetical Works of. 12mo. Philad., 1841.   H 6 R 26

HEBER (RICHARD). Catalogue of the Library of. [*See* BIBLIOTHECA HEBERIANA.]

HECHLER (REV. PROF. WILLIAM H.) The Jerusalem Bishopric Documents: with Translations chiefly derived from "Das evangelische Bisthum in Jerusalem." Geschichtliche Darlegung mit Urkunden, Berlin, 1842. 8vo. Lond., 1883.   G 1 P 16

HECTOR (SIR JAMES), K.C.M.G., M.D., &c. Address delivered before the Wellington Philosophical Society. 8vo. Wellington, 1872.   MJ 2 R 16

Eighth Annual Report on the Colonial Museum and Laboratory, 1872–73. 8vo. Wellington, 1873.   MJ 2 R 16

HECTOR (SIR JAMES), K.C.M.G., M.D., &c.—*continued.*
Eleventh, Twelfth, Thirteenth, and Fourteenth Annual Reports on the Colonial Museum and Laboratory, 1875–79. 8vo. Wellington, 1876–79.   ME 2 S

Fishes of New Zealand. [*See* HUTTON, F. W.]

Geological Survey of New Zealand: Reports of Geological Explorations during 1870–84, 1886–87; with Maps and Sections. 11 vols. roy. 8vo. Wellington, 1871–87. ME 2 S

Geological Survey of New Zealand: Reports of Geological Explorations; with Maps, by W. M. Cooper, to illustrate Reports of the Buller Coal-field, by S. H. Cox, and R. B. Denniston. 3 vols. 8vo. Wellington, 1877.   ME 2 S

Hand-book of New Zealand. (Sydney Intern. Exhib., 1879.) With Maps and Plates. Roy. 8vo. Wellington, 1879.*   MD 5 T 39

Another copy. 3rd ed., revised. 8vo. Wellington, 1883.
                    MD 5 T 41

Another copy. 4th ed., revised. 8vo. Wellington, 1886.
                    MD 5 T 42

Index to Reports of the Geological Survey of New Zealand, 1866–85. 8vo. Wellington, 1887.   ME 2 S

Indian and Colonial Exhibition, London, 1886. New Zealand Court. New Zealand Geographical Survey Department. Detailed Catalogue and Guide to the Geological Exhibits, including a Geological Map and General Index to the Reports, and a List of Publications of the Department. 8vo. Wellington, 1886.   MK 1 S 17

Meteorological Reports, 1873, 1875, 1880; including Returns for 1871–79, and Abstracts and Designs for previous years; also, Abstract of an Essay on the Climate of New Zealand, by Dr. J. Hann. 8vo. Wellington, 1874–81.   ME 2 S

Outline of New Zealand Geology; with Geological Map. Wellington, 1886.   MA 2 R 33

[*See* NEW ZEALAND INSTITUTE.]

HEDERICH (BENJAMIN). Græcum Lexicon Manuale. Editio nova. 4to. Lond., 1816.   K 16 S 18

HEDGES (HON. CORNELIUS). Biennial Report of the Superintendent of Public Instruction. [*See* UNITED STATES.]

HEER (PROFESSOR OSWALD). Primeval World of Switzerland; edited by James Heywood, M.A., &c. Illustrated. 2 vols. 8vo. Lond., 1876.   A 9 T 24, 25

HEEREN (A. H. L.) Historical Researches into the Politics, Intercourse, and Trade of the Principal Nations of Antiquity; translated from the German. 9 vols. 8vo. Lond., 1834–35.   B 15 Q 11–19

Another copy. New ed., revised and re-arranged. 6 vols. 8vo. Lond., 1857–66.   B 15 Q 20–25

HEFELE (CHARLES JOSEPH), D.D., BISHOP OF ROTTENBURG. History of the Christian Councils, from the original Documents, to the close of the Council of Nicæa, A.D. 325. Translated from the German, and edited by Wm. R. Clark, M.A. 8vo. Edinb., 1871.   G 1 R 5

2 x

HEGEL (G. W. F.) Hegel, as the National Philosopher of Germany. [*See* ROSENKRANZ, PROF. K.]

Introduction to Hegel's Philosophy of Fine Art; translated from the German, with Notes, &c., by B. Bosanquet. 8vo. Lond., 1886.   A 6 V 15

Lectures on the Philosophy of History; translated from the third German edition by J. Sibree, M.A. 8vo. Lond., 1878.   B 14 P 50

Philosophy of Art; being the second part of Hegel's Æsthetik, in which are unfolded historically the Three Great Fundamental Phases of the Art-Activity of the World; translated by William M. Bryant. 8vo. New York, 1879.
                    A 23 U 17

HEGEL (G. W. F.), AND MICHELET (C. L.) The Philosophy of Art: an Introduction to the Scientific Study of Æsthetics; translated by Hastie. Edinb., 1886.   A 6 V 19

HEHN (VICTOR). Wanderings of Plants and Animals from their First Home; edited by James Stallybrass. 8vo. Lond., 1885.   A 16 T 25

HEINE (HEINRICH). Life, Work, and Opinions of; by William Stigand. 2 vols. 8vo. Lond., 1875. C 7 Q 28, 29

Memoirs of, and some newly discovered Fragments of his Writings; with an Introductory Essay by Thomas W. Evans, M.D. 8vo. Lond., 1884.   C 3 P 14

Neue Gedichte. 18mo. Hamburg, 1853.   H 6 P 17

Pictures of Travel; translated from the German, by Charles Godfrey Leland. Eighth revised Edition. 12mo. Philad., 1876.   J 8 R 13

Poems of Heine complete; translated into the original metres, with a Sketch of his Life, by Edgar Alfred Bowring, C.B. New ed., with additions. 8vo. Lond., 1876.   H 5 S 31

Religion and Philosophy in Germany: a Fragment; translated by John Snodgrass. 8vo. Lond., 1882.   G 1 P 11

Sämmtliche Werke. 18 vols. 12mo. Hamburg, 1872.
                    J 16 P 14–31

1, 2. Reisebilder.	5–7. Uber Deutschland.
3. Englische Fragment und Shakespeare's Mädchen und Frauen.	8–11. Französische Bustände. 12. Ludwig Börne. 13, 14. Vermischte Schriften.
4. Novellistische Fragmente.	15–18. Dishtungen.

Wit, Wisdom, and Pathos, from the Prose of; with a few Pieces from the "Book of Songs," selected and translated by J. Snodgrass. 8vo. Lond., 1879. J 8 R 14

HEINEKEN (C. H. DE). Dictionnaire des Artistes, dont nous avons des Estampes avec une Notice detaillée de leurs ouvrages Gravés. 4 vols. 8vo. Leipsig, 1778–90.
                    K 18 P 22–25

Recueil d'estampes d'après les plus célèbres Tableaux de la Galerie Royale de Dresde. Contenant cinquante pièces, avec une description de chaque Tableau en François. 3 vols. atlas fol. Dresden, 1753.   A 10 P 16–18 ‡

HEINEMANN (W.) Goethe's Faust in England und Amerika : Bibliographische Zusammenstellung. 8vo. Berlin, 1886.   K 7 R 13

HEINSIUS (DR. THEODOR). Volkthümliches Wörterbuch der deutschen Sprache, mit Bezeichnung der Aussprache und Betonung für die Geschäfts-und Lesewelt. 4 vols. (in 5) 8vo. Hannover, 1818–22. K 15 R 10–14

HELFENSTEIN (JAMES), PH.D. Comparative Grammar of the Teutonic Languages ; being at the same time a Historical Grammar of the English Language. 8vo. Lond., 1870. K 15 Q 10

HELICONIA ; comprising a Selection of English Poetry of the Elizabethan Age. [*See* PARK, T.]

HELINANDUS (MONACHUS). Opera omnia. [*See* MIGNE, J. P., SERIES LATINA, 212.]

HELIODORUS (BISHOP OF TRICCA). Æthiopicorum Libri X. SCRIPTORIES EROTICI GRAECI.]
The Greek Romances of Heliodorus, Longus, and Acchilles Tatius ; translated from the Greek by the Rev. Rowland Smith, M.A. 8vo. Lond., 1885. J 9 Q 9

HELLBORN (KREISSLE VON). Life of Franz Schubert; translated by Arthur Duke Coleridge. 2 vols. 8vo. Lond., 1869. C 4 V 35, 36

HELLENIC STUDIES (SOCIETY FOR THE PROMOTION OF). The Journal of Hellenic Studies. Vols. 1–6. 8vo. Lond., 1880–85. E
Plates [to above.] 6 vols. (in 3) fol. Lond., 1880–85. E

HELLER (DR. A.) Die Schmarotzer mi besonderer Berücksichtigung der für den Menschen wichtigen. 12mo. München, 1880. A 14 P 62

HELLICAR (VALENTINE). Coin and Currency ; being an Inquiry into the probable effect of legalising as Currency the Coinage of the Sydney Mint. (Pam. Ch.) 8vo. Melb., 1856. A 16 U 25
Our Paper Money : a Letter to the Hon. the Treasurer of Victoria. 8vo. Meln., 1861. MF 1 Q 3
[*See* MACARDY, J.]

HELLWALD (FRIEDRICH VON). Culturgeschichte in ihrer natürlichen Entwicklung bis zur Gegenwart. 8vo. Augburg, 1875. A 1 W 39
Die Erde und ihre Völker : ein geographisches Handbuch. 3e umgearbeitete auflage. Roy. 8vo. Berlin, 1884. D 9 U 27
The Russians in Central Asia : a Critical Examination down to the present Time of the Geography and History of Central Asia ; translated from the German by Lieut.-Col. Theodore Wirgman, LL.B. 8vo. Lond., 1874. J 5 P 53

HELLYER (S. STEVENS). Lectures on the Science and Art of Sanitary Plumbing. 8vo. Lond., 1882. A 2 R 27
The Plumber and Sanitary Houses : a Practical Treatise on the Principles of Internal Plumbing Work, or the best means for effectually excluding Noxious Gases from our Houses. 2nd ed. 8vo. Lond., 1880. A 2 S 38

HELMHOLTZ (PROF. HERMANN L. F.), M.D. On the Sensations of Tone as a physiological basis for the Theory of Music. Translated from the German, by Alexander J. Ellis, B.A., &c. 8vo. Lond., 1875. A 8 Q 6
Another Copy. 2nd ed. 8vo. Lond., 1885. A 8 R 3
Popular Lectures on Scientific Subjects. 1st and 2nd series ; translated by E. Atkinson, Ph.D., &c., with an Introduction by Prof. Tyndall. 2 vols. 8vo. Lond., 1873–81. A 16 R 6, 7
Sound, &c. [*See* TAYLOR, S.]

HELOÏSE (ABBESS). History of the Lives of Abeillard and Heloïsa, 1079–1163 ; by the Rev. Joseph Berington. 4to. Birmingham, 1787. C 4 W 1

HELPS (SIR ARTHUR), K.C.B. Animals and their Masters. New ed. 12mo. Lond., 1883. J 8 Q 14
Brevia : Short Essays and Aphorisms. 8vo. Lond., 1871. J 8 Q 4
Casimir Maremma. 8vo. Lond., 1871. J 8 Q 3
Catharine Douglas : a Tragedy. 18mo. Lond., 1843. H 2 Q 26
Claims of Labour : an Essay on the Duties of the Employers to the Employed. 12mo. Lond., 1844. F 5 Q 29
Companions of my Solitude. 8th ed. 12mo. Lond., 1874. J 8 Q 1
Conquerers of the New World, and their Bondsmen ; being a Narrative of the Principal Events which led to Negro Slavery in the West Indies and America. 2 vols. 8vo. Lond., 1848–52. B 1 Q 50, 51
Conversations on War and General Culture. 8vo. Lond., 1871. J 8 Q 2
Essays written in the intervals of business ; to which is added an Essay on Organization in Daily Life. New ed. 12mo. Lond., 1875. J 8 Q 15
Friends in Council : a series of Readings and Discourse thereon. 2 vols. 12mo. Lond., 1854. J 8 Q 17, 18
Another copy. New series. 2 vols. 8vo. Lond., 1859. J 8 Q 6, 7
Another copy. 1st and 2nd series. New ed. 4 vols. 12mo. Lond., 1872–77. J 8 Q 10–13
Ivan de Biron ; or, the Russian Court in the Middle of last Century. New ed. 8vo. Lond., 1883. J 8 Q 16
King Henry the Second : an Historical Drama. 12mo. Lond., 1843. H 2 Q 25
Leaves from the Journal of our Life in the the Highlands. [*See* VICTORIA, HER MAJESTY THE QUEEN.]
Letter from one of the Special Constables in London on the late occasion of their being called out to keep the Peace. (Pam., 38.) 8vo. Lond., 1848. MJ 2 Q 25
Life and Labours of Mr. [Thomas, Lord] Brassey, 1805–70. 2nd ed. 8vo. Lond., 1872. C 5 T 2
Life of Columbus, the Discoverer of America. 2nd ed. 8vo. Lond., 1869. C 3 Q 17
Life of Hernando Cortes. 2 vols. 8vo. Lond., 1871. C 3 P 7 8

HELPS (SIR ARTHUR), K.C.B.—*continued.*
Life of Las Casas, "The Apostle of the Indies." 4th ed.
8vo. Lond., 1883. C 3 P 20
Life of Pizarro; with some Account of his Associates in
the Conquest of Peru. New ed. 8vo. Lond., 1882.
C 3 U 7
Oulita the Serf: a Tragedy. 18mo. Lond., 1873. H 2 Q 24
Realmah. 2 vols. 8vo. Lond., 1868. J 8 Q 8, 9
Social Pressure; by the Author of "Friends in Council."
8vo. Lond., 1875. J 8 Q 5
Spanish Conquest in America, and its Relation to the
History of Slavery and to the Government of Colonies.
4 vols. 8vo. Lond., 1855–61. B 1 T 20–23
Thoughts upon Government. 8vo. Lond., 1872. F 6 S 8

HELVETIUS (CLAUDE ADRIAN). De l'Esprit: or, Essays
on the Mind, and its several Faculties. 4to. Lond.,
1759. G 7 V 10
Œuvres complètes. 2 vols. 8vo. Lond., 1777. G 13 R 49, 50
Œuvres d'Helvetius. 5 vols. 8vo. Paris, 1792. G 7 S 20–24
Treatise on Man; his Intellectual Faculties and his Educa-
tion; translated from the French, with additional Notes, by
W. Hooper, M.D. 2 vols. 8vo. Lond., 1810. G 1 R 11, 12

HELY (REV. JAMES), A.B. Ogygia. [*See* O'FLAHERTY, R.]

HÉLYOT (P.) Costumes de la Cour de Rome, &c. [*See*
PERUGINI, G.]

HEMANS (MRS. FELICIA DOROTHEA). Memorials of; with
Illustrations of her Literary Character, from her Corres-
pondence, by H. F. Chorley. 2nd ed. 2 vols. 12mo.
Lond., 1837. C 3 R 44, 45
Poetical Remains of. 12mo. Edinb., 1836. H 6 R 25
Works of; with a Memoir by her Sister, and an Essay
on her Genius, by Mrs. Sigourney. 7 vols. 8vo. Philad.,
1842. H 7 S 29–35

HEMING (W. T.) The Needle Region and its Resources:
a Concise Description of its Physical Peculiarities and
Picturesque Scenery. Illustrated. 8vo. Redditch,
1877. A 11 R 12

HEMSTERHUYS (T.) [*See* LUCIAN.]

HENDERSON (ALEX.) History of Ancient and Modern
Wines. 4to. Lond., 1824. A 2 P 9 †

HENDERSON (REV. A. M.) Essay on the Deluge. 8vo.
Melb. (n.d.) MG 1 Q 37

HENDERSON (CAPT. —.) Otago and the Middle Island
of New Zealand: a Warning to Emigrants; by "Aliquis."
8vo. Melb., 1866. MD 4 Q 4

HENDERSON (EBENEZER), LL.D. Iceland; or, the Journal
of a Residence in that Island, during the years 1814–15.
Illustrated. 2nd ed. 8vo. Edinb., 1819. D 7 T 32
Life of James Ferguson, F.R.S., in a brief Autobiographical
Account, and further extended Memoir. 2nd ed. 8vo.
Edinb., 1870. C 8 P 7

HENDERSON (GEORGE). Republic of Mexico. [*See*
CUBAS, A. G.]

HENDERSON (GEORGE), M.D., &c., AND HUME (ALLAN
O.), C.B., &c. Lahore to Yârkand: Incidents of the
Route and Natural History of the Countries traversed
by the Expedition of 1870, under T. D. Forsyth, Esq., C.B.
Roy. 8vo. Lond., 1873. D 5 U 21

HENDERSON (H. B.) The Bengalee; or, Sketches of
Society and Manners in the East. 2nd ed. 8vo. Lond.,
1829. J 9 P 11

HENDERSON (JOHN). Observations on the Colonies of
New South Wales and Van Diemen's Land. 8vo. Calcutta, 1832.* MD 7 P 31

HENDERSON (LIEUT. JOHN). Excursions and Adventures
in New South Wales; with Advice to Emigrants, &c.
2 vols. 8vo. Lond., 1851.* MD 7 P 33, 34

HENDERSON (WILLIAM). Christianity and Modern
Thought: Twelve Lectures. 8vo. Ballaarat, 1861.
MG 1 R 11

HENDLEY (SUR.-MAJ. THOMAS H.) Jeypore Enamels.
[*See* JACOB, LIEUT.-COL. S. S.]
Memorials of the Jeypore Exhibition, 1883. 4 vols. imp.
8vo. Lond., 1884. A 23 P 4–7 ‡

HENDRIK (HANS). Memoirs of Hans Hendrik, the Arctic
Traveller, written by himself; translated from the Eskimo
Language, by Dr. Henry Rink; edited by Prof. Dr. George
Stephens, F.S.A. 8vo. Lond., 1878. C 2 S 22

HENEAGE (CHARLES), F.R.G.S. Journey in the Caucasus,
&c. [*See* THIELMANN, BARON M.]

HENEY (THOMAS). Fortunate Days. 8vo. Sydney,
1886.* MH 1 Q 9

HENFREY (PROF. A.), F.R.S., &c. Micrographic Dictionary [*See* GRIFFITH, J. W.] K 18 P 1

HENFREY (HENRY WILLIAM). Guide to the Study of
English Coins, from the Conquest to the Present Time.
New and revised ed., by C. F. Keary, M.A., F.S.A. 8vo.
Lond., 1885. A 13 S 26

HENLEY (JOHN), M.A. Antiquities of Italy. [*See* MONT-
FAUCON, B. DE.]

HENNELL (MISS SARA SOPHIA). Present Religion, as a
Faith owning Fellowship with Thought. 3 vols. 8vo.
Lond., 1865–87. G 8 R 9–11

HENNELL (THOMAS), M.I.C.E. Hydraulic and other
Tables for the purposes of Sewerage and Water-supply.
8vo. Lond., 1884. A 6 R 2

HENNESSY (J. B. N.), F.R.A.S. On the Atmospheric
Lines of the Solar Spectrum. (Roy. Soc. Pubs., 1.) 4to.
Lond., 1875. A 11 P 2 †

HENNESSY (SIR JOHN POPE), K.C.M.G. Sir Walter
Ralegh in Ireland. 8vo. Lond., 1883. C 3 V 37

HENNING (GEORGE), M.D.   Life of Martin Lister, M.D. [*See* LISTER, M.]

HENNINGSEN (C. F.)   Eastern Europe and the Emperor Nicholas. 3 vols. 8vo. Lond., 1846.   B 12 T 23–25

Revelations of Russia; or, the Emperor Nicholas and his Empire in 1844; by "One who has seen and describes." 2 vols. 8vo. Lond., 1844.   B 12 U 1, 2

The most striking Events of a Twelvemonth's Campaign with Zumalacarregui in Navarre and the Basque Provinces. 2 vols. 8vo. Lond., 1836.   B 13 U 44, 45

HENRY IV (KING OF FRANCE AND NAVARRE). Life of Henry IV; by G. P. R. James. 3 vols. 8vo. Lond., 1847.   C 7 Q 30–32

HENRY V (KING OF ENGLAND). Henrici Quinti Regis Angliæ Gesta. [*See* HISTORICAL SOCIETY.]

Henry of Monmouth; or, Memoirs of the Life and Character of Henry V, as Prince of Wales and King of England; by J. E. Tyler, B.D. 2 vols. 8vo. Lond., 1838.   C 8 Q 30, 31

HENRY VIII (KING OF ENGLAND). Henry VIII, from his Accession to the Death of Wolsey. [*See* BREWER, PROF. J. S.]

Letters and Papers of the Reign of. [*See* BREWER, PROF. J. S.]

Household Book of. [*See* NICOLAS, SIR N. H.]

HENRY OF PORTUGAL (PRINCE), THE NAVIGATOR. Discoveries of. [*See* MAJOR, R. H.]

Life of Prince Henry of Portugal, surnamed the Navigator; by R. H. Major, F.S.A., &c. Roy. 8vo. Lond., 1868.   C 9 V 24

Another copy. 8vo. Lond., 1868.*   MC 1 R 31

HENRY (THE MINSTREL). Metrical History of Sir William Wallace, Knight of Ellerslie. 3 vols. 18mo. Perth, 1790.   H 6 P 21–23

Wallace; or, Life and Acts of Sir William Wallace; with Notes by J. Jamieson. 12mo. Glasgow, 1869.   H 7 P 28

Another copy.   H 8 U 31

HENRY (PRINCE OF PRUSSIA). Rheinsberg : Memorials of Frederick the Great and Prince Henry of Prussia; by Andrew Hamilton. 2 vols. 8vo. Lond., 1880.   C 4 S 29, 30

HENRY (PRINCE OF WALES). Life of Henry, Prince of Wales, eldest Son of King James I; compiled chiefly from his own Papers and other Manuscripts, by Thomas Birch, D.D. 8vo. Lond., 1760.   C 6 P 18

HENRY (B. C.), A.M. Ling-nam; or, Interior Views of Southern China, including Explorations in the hitherto un-traversed island of Hainan. 8vo. Lond., 1886.   D 6 P 21

HENRY (MATTHEW). Exposition of the Book of Psalms; with Practical Remarks and Observations; unabridged and illustrated. 8vo. Lond., 1866.   G 16 P 13

HENRY (PAUL), D.D. Life and Times of John Calvin, the Great Reformer; translated from the German, by Henry Stebbing, D.D., &c. 2 vols. 8vo. Lond., 1849.   C 10 P 24, 25

HENRY (ROBERT), D.D. History of Great Britain, from the first Invasion of it by the Romans under Julius Cæsar. 5th ed. 12 vols. 8vo. Lond., 1814.   B 5 P 1–12

HENRY (WALTER). Events of a Military Life ; being Recollections after Service in the Peninsular War, Invasion of France, the East Indies, &c. 2 vols. 8vo. Lond., 1843.   C 3 R 35, 36

HENRY (WILLIAM). Elements of Experimental Chemistry, 11th ed. 2 vols. 8vo. Lond., 1829.   A 5 U 5, 6

HENSEL (SEBASTIAN). The Mendelssohn Family (1729–1847); from Letters and Journals; translated by Carl Klingemann and an American Collaborator. 2 vols. 8vo. Lond., 1881.   C 7 S 22, 23

HENSHALL (JAMES A.), M.D. Book of the Black Bass ; comprising its complete Scientific and Life History ; to-gether with a practical Treatise on Angling and Fly Fishing. Illustrated. 8vo. Cincinnati, 1881. A 16 Q 15

HENSLOW (REV. J. S.) Principles of Descriptive and Physiological Botany. (Lard. Cab. Cyc.) 12mo. Lond., 1836.   K 1 U 11

HENSMAN (HOWARD). The Afghan War of 1879–80. With Maps. 8vo. Lond., 1881.   B 10 S 1

HENSMAN (HENRY). Civil Engineering and Machinery generally. [*See* LOND. INTERNATIONAL EXHIB., 1851.]

HENTY (GEORGE ALFRED). The March to Coomassie. 8vo. Lond., 1874.   D 1 V 29

HENTY (RICHMOND). Australiana; or, My Early Life. 12mo. Lond., 1886.   MD 3 P 1

HENTZNER (PAUL). Travels in England during the Reign of Queen Elizabeth ; to which is now added Sir Robert Naunton's Fragmenta Regalia. 8vo. Lond., 1797.   D 7 T 43

HENWOOD (W. J.) Papers on Geology, &c. ; from the Transactions of the Royal Geological Society of Cornwall. 2 vols. 8vo. Lond., 1871.   A 9 S 13, 14

HEPBURN (JAMES). [*See* BOTHWELL, EARL OF.]

HEPBURN (JAMES CURTIS), M.D., &c. Japanese-English and English-Japanese Dictionary. 2nd ed. Sm. fol. Shanghai, 1872.   K 14 R 11

HEPBURN (REV. THOMAS). Letter to a Gentleman from his Friend in Orkney. (Written in 1757.) Reprinted. 12mo. Edinb., 1888.   B 13 P 16

HE PUKAPUKA HEPARA. He Pukapuka Hepara na Hoani Papita Werahiko Ponaparie to Epikopo Kai Wakarite Apotoriko o te Tiemei a Akarana ki ona Pirihi me ona Koritiano mo te Reweti o te Tau 1857, mo nko i te mana ora me te wakapunakanga Atua o te Hahi Katorika. 8vo. Akarana, 1857.   MJ 2 R 16

HERALD OF PEACE (THE). New Series. Vol. 1 and 2, 1838–41. 8vo. Lond., 1839–41.   G 13 P 23, 24

HERAUD (JOHN ABRAHAM). Legend of St. Loy; with other Poems. 8vo. Lond., 1820.   H 7 T 30
[*See* MONTHLY MAGAZINE, THE.]

HERBELOT (BARTHELEMY D',) Bibliotièque Orientale; ou, Dictionnaire Universel. 4 vols. 4to. La Haye, 1777.   C 11 V 9–12

HERBERSTAIN, NEYPERG, AND GUETTENHAG (SIGISMUND), BARON-DE. Rerum Moscouiticarum Commentarii Sigismundi Liberi Baronis in Herberstain, Neyperg, et Guettenhag. In iis Commentariis sparsim contenta habebis Candide Lector, Russiae, et quæ nunc eius Metropolis est, Moscoviæ, brevissimam descriptionem, &c. Sm. fol. Basile, 1551.   B 12 V 1

HERBERT OF BOSHAM. [*See* CHONS. OF GT. BRITAIN.]

HERBERT (CHARLES). Italy and Italian Literature. 8vo. Lond., 1835.   D 8 Q 49

HERBERT (DAVID). Great Historical Mutinies; comprising the Story of the Mutiny of the Bounty, the Mutiny at Spithead, the Mutiny at the Nore, Mutinies in Highland Regiments, and the Indian Mutiny. 8vo. Lond., 1876.   B 14 Q 38

HERBERT OF CHERBURG (EDWARD), LORD. Autobiography of. The History of England under Henry VIII. Reprint from Kennet's Fol. ed., 1719. 8vo. Lond., 1872.   B 4 P 12

Autobiography of; with Introduction, Notes, Appendices, and a continuation of the Life by Sidney L. Lee, B.A. 8vo. Lond., 1886.   C 10 U 16

Life of, written by himself, and continued to his death; with Letters. 8vo. Lond., 1826.   C 10 U 15

Another copy. (Autobiography, 8.) 12mo. Lond., 1829.   C 1 P 8

HERBERT (ELIZABETH), LADY. Cradle Lands. Roy. 8vo. Lond., 1867.   D 2 U 1

Impressions of Spain in 1866. Roy. 8vo. Lond., 1867.   D 8 V 8

Life of Mgr. Dupanloup. [*See* LAGRANGE, L'ABBÉ F.]

The Mission of St. Francis of Sales in the Chablais. 8vo. Lond., 1868.   G 2 P 22

Three Phases of Christian Love. 8vo. Lond., 1867. G 3 Q 20

A Search after Sunshine; or, Algeria in 1871. 8vo. Lond., 1872.   D 1 W 3

HERBERT (GEORGE). Life of; by Izaak Walton. 12mo. Lond., 1825.   C 1 S 19

Another copy. New ed. 12mo. Lond., 1884.   C 2 R 34

Works of, in Prose and Verse. 2 vols. 8vo. Lond., 1853.   G 13 P 10, 11

HERBERT (SIDNEY HERBERT), BARON. Memorial to the late Lord Herbert: Report of Proceedings at the Public Meeting. 8vo. Lond., 1862.   F 12 P 22

HERBERT (SIR THOMAS). Mémories de. [*See* GUIZOT, F. P. G., 3.]

HERBERT (HENRY WILLIAM), "FRANK FORESTER." Field Sports in the United States, and the British Provinces of America. 2 vols. 8vo. Lond., 1848.   A 17 U 27–28

HERBORN (E.) Reports on the Geology and Mineralogy of the Estates of the Australian Agricultural Company. [*See* ODERNHEIMER, F.]

HERCULANENSIUM Disertationis isagogicae ad Herculanensium Voluminum explanationem pars prima. Fol. Neapoli, 1797.   B 16 S 4 ‡

Voluminum quæ supersunt tomus primus [edente Carlo M. Rosini]; tomus secundus [edente Nic. Ciampitto]. 2 vols. fol. Neapoli, 1793–1809.   B 16 S 3, 4 ‡

HERD (DAVID). Ancient and Modern Scottish Songs, Heroic Ballads, &c.: a page for page Reprint of the edition of 1776; with Memoir and Illustrative Notes, by Sidney Gilpin. 2 vols. 8vo. Edinb., 1870.   H 7 R 38, 39

HERDER (JOHANN GOTTFRIED VON). Sketch of Herder and his Times; by Henry Nevinson. 8vo. Lond., 1884.   C 7 Q 24

HEREMAN (SAMUEL). Paxton's Botanical Dictionary. [*See* PAXTON, SIR J.]

HERFORD (CHARLES HAROLD). Studies in Literary Relations of England and Germany. 8vo. Cambridge, 1886.   B 36 P 1

HÉRITIER (MARIE JEAN L'). [*See* L'HÉRITIER, M. J.]

HER MAJESTY'S COLONIES. Papers relating to Her Majesty's Colonial Possessions: Reports for 1883–85. Presented to both Houses of Parliament, by command of Her Majesty, June, 1886. 8vo. Lond., 1886. MF 2 S 30

Series of Original Papers issued under the Authority of the Royal Commission. (Colonial and Indian Exhibition, 1886.) 8vo. Lond., 1886.   MD 4 V 39

HERMANN (CHARLES FREDERICK). Manual of the Political Antiquities of Greece, historically considered. 8vo. Oxford, 1836.   B 9 V 33

HERMANN (G.) Dissertatione de Ellipsi et Pleonasmo. [*See* BOS, L.]

HERMANN (DR. L.) Elements of Human Physiology. Translated from the 5th ed., by Prof. A. Gamgee. 8vo. Lond., 1875.   A 12 T 6

Handbuch der Physiologie. 6 vols. roy. 8vo. Leipzig, 1879–83.   A 12 T 18–23

HERMANNUS CONTRACTUS. Opera omnia. [*See* MIGNE, J. P., SERIES LATINA, 143.]

HERNISZ (STANISLAS), M.D. Guide to Conversation in the English and Chinese Languages, for the Use of Americans and Chinese in California and elsewhere. Ob. 12mo. Boston, 1854. K 11 S 24

HERNSHEIM (FRANZ). Südsee-Erinnerungen (1875–80). Mit einem einleitenden Vorwort, von Dr. Otto Finsch. 4to. Berlin, 1883. MD 7 P 4 †

HERODOTUS. Analysis and Summary of Herodotus. [*See* WHEELER, J. T.]

Ancient Empires of the East (Herodotos, 1–3); with Notes, Introductions, and Appendices, by A. H. Sayce. 8vo. Lond., 1883. B 14 R 49

Geographical System of Herodotus. [*See* RENNELL, J.]

Geography of Herodotus. [*See* WHEELER, J. T.]

Herodoti Halicarnassei Historiarum Libri IX. Codicem Sancrofti manuscriptum. Commodius digessit annotationes variorum adjecit Tios. Gaisford, A.M. 4 vols. 8vo. Oxon., 1830. B 14 R 37–40

Herodotus; translated by the Rev. Wm. Beloe. 4 vols. 8vo. Lond., 1821. B 14 R 41–44

Herodotus; translated by the Rev. William Beloe. (Fam. Class. Lib.) 3 vols. 18mo. Lond., 1830. J 15 P 12–14

History of Herodotus; translated by George Rawlinson. 4 vols. 8vo. Lond., 1862. B 14 R 45–48

New and literal Version from the Text of Baehr; with a Geographical and General Index, by Henry Cary, M.A. 12mo. Lond., 1848. B 14 Q 49

Notes on. [*See* TURNER, D. W.]

HERON (ROBERT). Travels through Arabia. [*See* NIEBUHR, C.]

HERON-ALLEN (ED.) [*See* ALLEN, E. HERON-.]

HERRERA (ANTONIO DE). General History of the vast Continent and Islands of America, commonly called the West Indies, from the first Discovery thereof; translated by Capt. John Stevens. Illustrated. 6 vols. 8vo. Lond., 1725–26. B 1 Q 25–30

HERRICK (ROBERT). Complete Poems of; edited, with Memorial Introduction and Notes, by the Rev. Alexander B. Grosart. (Early Eng. Poets.) 3 vols. 8vo. Lond., 1876. H 8 V 3–5

Poetical Works of. 2 vols. 8vo. Lond., 1825. H 7 R 32, 33

HERRICK (REV. SAMUEL EDWARD), D.D. Some Heretics of Yesterday. 8vo. Lond., 1884. G 8 R 17

HERRIES (EDWARD), C.B. Memoir of the Public Life of the Right Hon. John Charles Herries, in the Reigns of George III, George IV, William IV, and Victoria; by his Son. 2 vols. 8vo. Lond., 1880. C 7 P 20, 21

HERRIES (RT. HON. JOHN CHARLES). Memoir of the Public Life of the, in the Reigns of George III, George IV, William IV, and Victoria; by his Son, Edward Herries, C.B. 2 vols. 8vo. Lond., 1880. C 7 P 20, 21

HERRMANN (J. B.) Deutschland in der Südsee. Nr. 2. Kaiser-Wilhelmsland und Neubritannien. 8vo. Leipsic, 1885. MD 5 T 36

HERSCHEL (MISS CAROLINE LUCRETIA). Memoir and Correspondence of; by Mrs. John Herschel. With Portrait. 8vo. Lond., 1876. C 3 V 12

HERSCHEL (CAPT. JOHN). [*See* CAMERON, A. M.]

HERSCHEL (MRS. JOHN). Memoir and Correspondence of Caroline Herschel. With Portraits. 8vo. Lond., 1876. C 3 V 12

HERSCHEL (SIR JOHN FREDERICK WILLIAM), BART., &c. Discourse on Natural Philosophy. (Lard. Cab. Cyclo.) 12mo. Lond., 1835. K 1 U 22

Familiar Lectures on Scientific Subjects. 8vo. Lond., 1867. A 16 P 2

Instructions for making and registering Meteorological Observations in Southern Africa. (Pam. 2.) 8vo. Lond. (n.d.) MJ 2 P 37

Manual of Scientific Inquiry, prepared for the Use of Officers in Her Majesty's Navy, and Travellers in general; edited by J. W. Herschel. 2nd ed. 8vo. Lond., 1851. A 17 T 40

Outlines of Astronomy. 8vo. Lond., 1849. A 3 S 5

Results of Astronomical Observations, made during the years 1834–38, at the Cape of Good Hope; being the Completion of a Telescopic Survey of the whole Surface of the Visible Heavens, commenced in 1825. Roy. 4to. Lond., 1847. A 3 U 12

Treatise on Astronomy. (Lard. Cab. Cyclo.) 12mo. Lond., 1835. K 1 U 24

HERSHON (PAUL ISAAC). The Pentateuch according to the Talmud: Genesis; with a Talmudical Commentary; translated by the Rev. M. Wolkenberg. 8vo. Lond., 1883. G 2 R 2

Talmudic Miscellany; or, a Thousand and One Extracts from the Talmud, the Midrashim, and the Kabbalah; with Notes. 8vo. Lond., 1880. G 16 P 20

HERTSLET (SIR EDWARD), C.B. [*See* FOREIGN OFFICE LIST.]

HERTSLET (LEWIS AND SIR EDWARD). Complete Collection of the Treaties and Conventions, &c., between Great Britain and Foreign Powers; with Index. 16 vols. 8vo. Lond., 1840–85. F 8 Q 1–16

HERVEUS (BURGIDOLENSIS MONACHUS). Opera omnia. [*See* MIGNE, J. P., SERIES LATINA, 181.]

HERVEY (REV. ALPHEUS B.), A.M. Sea Mosses: a Collector's Guide and an Introduction to the Study of Marine Algæ. 8vo. Boston, 1881. A 4 Q 10

HERVEY (JOHN), LORD. Memoirs of the Reign of George II, from his Accession to the Death of Queen Caroline; edited by the Rt. Hon. J. W. Croker. 2 vols. 8vo. Lond., 1848. C 3 V 7, 8

HERVEY (M. F. S.) Celebrated Musicians of all Nations: a Collection of Portraits ; with short Biographical Notices; translated from the German, with an Appendix, by M. F. S. Hervey. Imp. 4to. Lond., 1883.   C 7 R 17 †

HERVEY (MAURICE H.) The Genesis of Imperial Federation. 8vo. Sydney, 1887.   MF 3 Q 31

HERVEY (THOMAS K.) Australia ; with other Poems. 12mo. Lond., 1824.   MH 1 R 22
Another copy. 2nd ed., with additional Poems. 12mo. Lond., 1825.   MH 1 R 23

HESEKIEL (JOHN GEORGE LOUIS). Life of Bismarck, Private and Political ; with descriptive Notices of his Ancestry ; translated by Kenneth R. H. Mackenzie, F.S.A., &c. 8vo. Lond., 1870.   C 10 R 21

HESIOD. Hesiodi Carmina. Apollonii Argonautica. Musæi Carmen de Herone et Leandro. Coluthi Raptus Helenæ. Quinti Posthomerica. Tryphiodori Excidium Ilii. Tzetzæ Antehomerica, etc. Græce et Latine. Edidit F. S. Lehrs. Imp. 8vo. Parisiis, 1878.   H 6 V 29
. Works of; translated by T. Cooke. [*See* CHALMERS, A.]
Works of; translated by C. A. Elton. (Fam. Class Lib.) 18mo. Lond., 1832.   J 15 P 15

HESS (A.) Relations of the Air to the Clothes we Wear. [*See* PETTENKOFER, DR. M. VON.]

HESS (DR. W.) Die wirbellosen Thiere. 2 vols. roy. 8vo. Hannover, 1878.   A 13 U 37, 38

HESSELS (J. H.) Gutenburg; was he the Inventor of Printing? an Historical Investigation embodying a Criticism on Dr. Van der Linde's "Gutenberg." 8vo. Lond., 1882.   B 36 R 1
[*See* LEX SALICA.]

HESSE-WARTEGG (ERNEST), CHEVALIER DE. Tunis; the Land and the People. Illustrated. 8vo. Lond., 1882.   D 2 P 2

HESSEY (JAMES AUGUSTUS), D.C.L. Sunday; its Origin, History, and Present Obligation, considered in Eight Lectures. 8vo. Lond., 1860.   G 2 R 1

HESYCHIUS HIEROSOLYMITANUS. Opera omnia. [*See* MIGNE, J. P., SERIES GRÆCA, 93.]

HESYCHIUS OF MILETUS. Life of Plato. [*See* PLATO.]

HETHERINGTON (REV. IRVING). Memoir of the Rev. Irving Hetherington, Scots' Church, Melbourne ; including Sketches of the History of Presbyterianism in New South Wales and Victoria ; by the Rev. F. R. M. Wilson. 8vo. Melb., 1876.   MC 1 Q 8

HEWARD (ROBERT), F.L.S. Biographical Sketch of the late Allan Cunningham, F.L.S., &c. 8vo. Lond., 1842.   MC 1 R 25

HEWES (F. W.) Scribner's Statistical Atlas. [*See* SCRIBNER, C.]

HEWETSON (HENRY BENDELACK), M.R.C.S., &c. Life and Works of Robert Hewetson, Boy Painter and Poet ; together with Original Essay, Poems, and Fairy Tales. 4to. Lond., 1881.   C 2 W 13

HEWETSON (ROBERT). Life and Works of, Boy Painter and Poet ; together with Original Essay, Poems, and Fairy Tales, by Henry Bendelack Hewetson. 4to. Lond., 1881.   C 2 W 13

HEWETSON (CAPT. WILLIAM B.) . The Blind Boy: a Melodrama. [*See* FARCES.]

HEWLETT (J. T.) Dr. Johnson : his Religious Life and Death. 8vo. Lond., 1850.   C 3 V 14

HEWLETT (WILLIAM OXENHAM), F.S.A. Notes on Dignities in the Peerage of Scotland which are dormant or which have been forfeited. Roy. 8vo. Lond., 1882.   K 10 T 23

HEYLYN (PETER), D.D. Ecclesia Restaurata ; or, the History of the Reformation of the Church of England. Fol. Lond., 1661.   G 5 U 7
A Help to English History; edited by Paul Wright. 8vo. Lond., 1773.   B 3 T 4

HEYNE (C. G.) [*See* VIRGILIUS MARO P.; *and* TIBULLUS.]

HEYNE (MORITZ). Kurze Grammatik der altgermanischen Dialecte: Gothisch, Althochdeutsch, Altsächsisch, Angelsächsisch Altfriesisch, Altnordisch. I. Theil. Laut-und Flexionslehre. 2e verbesserte auflage. (*All published.*) 8vo. Paderborn, 1870.   K 14 P 34

HEYSE (DR. JOH. CHRIST. AUG.) Handwörterbuch der deutschen Sprache, mit Hinsicht auf Rechtschreibung, Abstammung und Bildung, Biegung und Fügung der Wörter, so wie auf deren Sinnverwandtschaft. Nach den Grundsätzen seiner Sprachlehre. Ausgeführt von Dr. K. W. L. Heyse. 2 vols. (in 3) 8vo. Magdeburg, 1833–49.   K 13 P 28–30

HEYSE (DR. K. W. L.) [*See* HEYSE, DR. J. C. A.]

HEYWOOD (B. A.), M.A. Approaching Australasian Centenary : an Historical Retrospect of Events not to be forgotten. 8vo. Lond., 1885.   MB 1 T 1
Travels and Excursions in [A Vacation Tour at the Antipodes, through] Victoria, Tasmania, New South Wales, Queensland, and New Zealand. Illustrated. 8vo. Lond., 1863.   MD 5 Q 8
Vacation Tour at the Antipodes, through Victoria, Tasmania, New South Wales, Queensland, and New Zealand, in 1861–62. 8vo. Lond., 1863.*   MD 5 Q 6

HEYWOOD (CAPT. PETER), R.N. Memoir of ; with Extracts from his Diaries and Correspondence by Edward Tagart. 8vo. Lond., 1832.*   MC 1 R 28

HEYWOOD (S.) Vindication of Mr. Fox's History of the early part of the Reign of James II. 4to. Lond., 1811.   B 4 U 11

HEYWOOD (THOMAS). Dramatic Works of; now first collected; with Illustrative Notes, and a Memoir of the Author. 6 vols. 8vo. Lond., 1874.   H 2 T 15–20
Merlin's Prophesies and Predictions; with the Life of Merlin. [*See* MERLIN.]
Love's Mistress; or, the Queen's Masque. 8vo. Lond., 1824.   H 1 R 13
Another copy.   H 1 R 15
The Rape of Lucrece: a Tragedy. 8vo. Lond., 1824.
                    H 1 R 13
Another copy.   H 1 R 15

HIBBERD (REV. F.) The Person of Jesus Christ the Source of his Power: a Lecture. [*See* CHRISTIAN EVIDENCE SOCIETY.]

HIBBERD (SHIRLEY), F.R.H.S. Epitome of the War, from its Outbreak to its Close. 12mo. Lond., 1856.
                    B 12 T 18
Familiar Garden Flowers. [*See* HULME, F. E.]
Garden Favourites; with Lists of Choice Varieties. 12mo. Lond., 1858.   A 1 P 22
New and Rare Beautiful-leaved Plants. Imp. 8vo. Lond., 1870.   A 4 U 3
Rustic Adornments for Homes of Taste. 8vo. Lond., 1857.   A 1 U 3

HICKES (GEORGE), D.D. Memoirs of the Rev. John Kettlewell. [*See* LEE, DR. F.]   C 4 V 5
The Spirit of Enthusiasm exorcised in a Sermon preached before the University of Oxford. 4th ed. 8vo. Lond., 1709.   G 2 P 29

HICKEY (W.) Constitution of the United States of America. 8vo. Philad., 1853.   F 6 R 15

HICKIE (W. J.) Comedies of Aristophanes. [*See* ARISTOPHANES.]

HICKLIN (J.) The "Ladies of Llangollen," as sketched by many hands. 8vo. Chester, 1847.   MJ 2 R 12

HICKS (REV E. L.), M.A., RECTOR OF FENNY COMPTON. Henry Bazely, the Oxford Evangelist: a Memoir. 8vo. Lond., 1886.   C 3 S 2
Manual of Greek Historical Inscriptions. (Clar. Press). 8vo. Oxford, 1882.   B 27 U 12

HICKSON (J. B.), M.D. He will not drink Wine; or, Alcoholic Beverages considered Socially and Physiologically. 8vo. Melb., 1869.   MA 2 S 38

HICKSON (WILLIAM E.) Improvement of Designs and Patterns. [*See* SENIOR, N. W.]

HIDDEN TALENT (THE). The Hidden Talent. Dedicated to the Great Giver of every good and perfect Gift, by "Phœbe." 8vo. Melb., 1874.   MG 1 Q 39

HIERONYMUS (EUSEBIUS), SAINT JEROME. Opera. Studio ac labore Dominici Vallarsii Veronensis Presbyteri, opem ferentibus aliis in eadem Civitate Literatis viris, et præcipue Marci. Scipione Maffeio. 11 vols. fol. Verona, 1734–42.   G 12 Q 4–5 ‡
Opera omnia. [*See* MIGNE, J. P., SERIES LATINA, 22–30.]

HIERONYMOUS PRAGENSIS (JEROME OF PRAGUE). Historia et Monumenta. [*See* HUSS, J.]

HIEOVER (HARRY). [*See* BINDLEY, C.]

HIGGINS (GODFREY), F.S.A., &c. Anacalypsis: an Attempt to draw aside the Veil of the Saitic Isis; or, an Inquiry into the Origin of Languages, Nations, and Religions. 2 vols. 4to. Lond., 1836.   G 6 U 12, 13
The Celtic Druids. 4to. Lond., 1827.   B 4 U 2

HIGGINS (MATTHEW JAMES). Essays on Social Subjects; with a Memoir by Sir William Stirling Maxwell, Bart. 8vo. Lond., 1875.   J 9 S 11

HIGGINS (MRS. SOPHIA ELIZABETH). Women of Europe in the Fifteenth and Sixteenth Centuries. 2 vols. 8vo. Lond., 1885.   C 8 P 48, 49

HIGGINS (WILLIAM), F.R.S., &c. Experiments and Observations on the Atomic Theory and Electrical Phenomena. 8vo. Lond., 1814.   A 6 P 19

HIGGINS (W. M.) Gold Valuer's Ready Reckoner. [*See* SCOFFERN, J. C.]

HIGGINSON (THOMAS WENTWORTH). Common Sense about Women. 8vo. Lond., 1882.   F 14 Q 19
Larger History of the United States of America. Illustrated. Sq. 8vo. Lond., 1885.   B 1 S 42
[*See* EPICTETUS.]

HIGGS (PAGET), LL.D., &c. Electric Transmission of Power: its Present Position and Advantages. 12mo. Lond., 1879.   A 5 R 50
Magneto- and Dynamo-Electric Machines. [*See* CEW, G. DE.]

HIGH SCHOOL OF HOBART TOWN. Report of the Council to the Shareholders and Subscribers. 8vo. Hobart, 1848.   MF 3 P 15

HIGINBOTHAM (G.) Portrait of. [*See* MANUSCRIPTS AND PORTRAITS.]

HIGINBOTHAM & ROBINSON. Atlas of the Suburbs of Sydney: Ashfield, Balmain, Burwood, Canterbury, Hurstville, Kogarah, Leichhardt, Marrickville, Paddington, Petersham, St. Peters, West Botany. Fol. Sydney (n.d.)   MD 5 S 16 ‡

HILARIUS (PAPA). Opera omnia. [*See* MIGNE, J. P., SERIES LATINA. 58.]

HILARIUS (PICTAVIENSIS EPISCOPUS). Opera omnia. [*See* MIGNE, J. P., SERIES LATINA, 9, 10.]

HILDEBERTUS (TURONENSIS ARCHIEPISCOPUS). Opera omnia. [*See* MIGNE, J. P., SERIES LATINA, 171.]

HILDEBRAND (DR. HANS). The Industrial Arts of Scandinavia in the Pagan Time. [*See* SOUTH KENSINGTON MUSEUM, 23.]

HILDEFONSUS (TOLETANUS EPISCOPUS). Opera omnia. [*See* MIGNE, J. P., SERIES LATINA, 96.]

HILDEGARDE (SANCTA). Opera omnia. [*See* MIGNE, J. P., SERIES LATINA, 197.]

HILDRETH (RICHARD). History of the United States of America, from the Discovery of the Continent to the Organization of Government under the Federal Constitution. 3 vols. 8vo. Lond., 1850.   B 1 R 25–27

HILL (AARON). Merope: a Tragedy. (Bell's Brit. Theatre.) 18mo. Lond., 1795.   H 2 P 9

Another copy. (New Eng. Theatre.) 12mo. Lond., 1776·   H 4 P 19

Zara: a Tragedy. (Bell's Brit. Theatre.) 18mo. Lond., 1791.   H 2 P 30

Another copy. (Brit. Theatre.) 12mo. Lond., 1808.   H 1 P 7

Another copy. (New Eng. Theatre.) 12mo. Lond., 1775.   H 4 P 25

Another copy. [*See* BRIT. DRAMA. 2.]

HILL (ARTHUR). Hancok's Copies for China Painters. [*See* HANCOCK, O. E. & Co.]

Public Education ; Plans for the Government and Liberal Instruction of Boys, as practised at Hazlewood School. 8vo. Lond., 1825.   G 17 Q 23

HILL (ARTHUR GEORGE), B.A., &c. The Organ-Cases and Organs of the Middle Ages and Renaissance : a comprehensive Essay on the Art Archæology of the Organ. Roy. fol. Lond., 1883.   A 4 W 8 ‡

HILL (ALEX. STAVELEY), D.C.L., &c. From Home to Home : Autumn Wanderings in the North-West, in the year 1881. 8vo. Lond., 1885.   D 3 U 16

HILL (BENSON EARLE). Playing about ; or, Theatrical Anecdotes and Adventures. 2 vols. 8vo. Lond., 1840.   J 4 R 11, 12

Recollections of an Artillery Officer; including Scenes and Adventures in Ireland, America, Flanders, and France. 2 vols. 8vo. Lond., 1836.   J 12 Q 9, 10

HILL (EDWARD S.) Lord Howe Island : Official Visit by the Water Police Magistrate and the Director of the Botanic Gardens, Sydney ; together with a Description of the Island. 8vo. Sydney, 1870.   MD 5 S 9

HILL (FLORENCE). Children of the State : the Training of Juvenile Paupers. 12mo. Lond., 1868.   F 6 P 12

2 Y

HILL (FREDERIC). National Education ; its present state and Prospects. 2 vols. 8vo. Lond., 1836.   G 17 Q 3

HILL (GEORGE BIRKBECK). Colonel Gordon in Central Africa, 1874–79 ; from original Letters and Documents. 8vo. Lond., 1881.   D 2 P 14

Life of Sir Rowland Hill, K.C.B. [*See* HILL, SIR R.]

HILL (JOHN), M.D. Review of the Works of the Royal Society of London. 4to. Lond., 1751.   A 15 U 15

HILL (MATTHEW DAVENPORT). Suggestions for the Repression of Crime, contained in Charges delivered to Grand Juries of Birmingham ; supported by additional facts and arguments. Roy. 8vo. Lond., 1857.   F 8 S 7

A Voice from the Bench on Intemperance, and how to remove it. (Pam. 39.) 12mo. Leeds, 1855.   MJ 2 R 1

A Voice from the Bench vindicated ; being Remarks in answer to objections advanced against a Charge on the Abuse of Intoxicating Liquors. 2nd ed. (Pam., 39.) 12mo. Leeds, 1856.   MJ 2 R 1

HILL (REV. PASCOE GRENFELL). Fifty Days on board a Slave Vessel in the Mozambique Channel in April and May, 1843. 12mo. Lond., 1844.   D 1 T 6

HILL (RT. HON. RICHARD). Diplomatic Correspondence of, in the Reign of Queen Anne; edited by the Rev. W. Blackley, B.A., 1703–6. 2 vols. 8vo. Lond., 1845.   C 8 Q 28, 29

HILL (ROSAMOND AND FLORENCE). What we saw in Australia. 8vo. Lond., 1875.*   MD 4 T 39

HILL (ROWLAND), LORD, G.C.B. Life of Lord Hill, G.C.B., late Commander of the Forces ; by the Rev. E. Sidney, A.M. 8vo. Lond., 1845.   C 8 R 24

HILL (SIR ROWLAND), K.C.B., D.C.L., &c. Life of, and the History of Penny Postage ; by Sir Rowland Hill and his nephew George Birkbeck Hill, D.C.L. 2 vols. roy. 8vo. Lond., 1880.   C 8 R 25, 26

HILL (SIR ROWLAND AND GEORGE BIRKBECK), D.C.L. Life of Sir Rowland Hill, K.C.B., &c., and the History of Penny Postage. 2 vols. 8vo. Lond., 1880. C 8 R 25, 26

HILL (ROWLAND). Spiritual Characteristics, represented in an Account of a most curious Sale of Curates by Public Auction; by "An Old Observer." 8vo. Lond., 1803.   G 17 Q 20

HILL (S. PROUT). Tarquin the Proud, and other Poems. 8vo. Sydney, 1843.*   MH 1 P 11

HILL (S. S.), F.R.G.S. The Tiara and the Turban; or, Impressions and Observations on Character within the Dominions of the Pope and the Sultan. 2 vols. 8vo. Lond., 1845.   D 8 S 16, 17

Travels in Egypt and Syria. 8vo. Lond., 1866.   D 2 Q 13

Travels in Siberia. 2 vols. 8vo. Lond., 1854.   D 6 P 35, 36

Travels in the Sandwich and Society Islands. 8vo. Lond., 1856.*   MD 6 S 4

HILL (THOMAS PADMORE). The Oratorical Trainer: a System of Vocal Culture. 4th ed. 12mo. Melb., 1868. MJ 1 U 1

HILL (WALTER). Collection of Queensland Timbers. 8vo. Brisbane, 1880. MJ 2 R 16

HILLARD (GEORGE STILLMANN), LL.D. Life, Letters, and Journals of George Ticknor. 2 vols. 8vo. Boston, 1876. C 9 R 34, 35

HILLARY (WILLIAM), M.D. Practical Essay on the Small-pox. 2nd ed., with Additions; to which is added, an Account of the principal Variations of the Weather and the concomitant Epidemic Diseases, from 1726–34. 8vo. Lond., 1740. A 12 S 32

HILLER (F.), M.D. Koumiss. Great Dietetic Hygienic Remedy for Debilitating, Nervous, and Wasting Diseases. 8vo. Sydney (n.d.) MA 2 V 9

HILLER (DR. FERDINAND). Mendelssohn : Letters and Recollections; translated by M. E. von Glehn. 8vo. Lond., 1874. C 5 P 20

HILPERT (DR. JOSEPH LEONHARD). English-deutsches und deutsch-englisches Wörterbuch. 2 vols. (in 4) 4to. Karlsruhe, 1845–46. K 14 R 7–10

HILTON (JAMES), F.S.A. Chronograms, 5,000 and more in number, excerpted out of various authors, and collected at many places. Roy. 8vo. Lond., 1882. K 11 Q 2

Chronograms continued and concluded, more than 5,000 in number: a Supplement Volume to "Chronograms," published in the year 1882. Roy. 8vo. Lond., 1885. C 11 Q 3

HILTON (WALTER). Writings of. [*See* BRITISH REFORMERS, 12.]

HINCHLIFF (THOMAS WOODBINE), M.A., &c. Over the Sea and Far Away. 8vo. Lond., 1876. D 9 S 17

HINCKS (THOMAS), B.A., &c. History of the British Hydroid Zoophytes. 2 vols. 8vo. Lond., 1868. A 14 S 24, 25

History of the British Marine Polyzoa. Text and Plates. 2 vols. 8vo. Lond., 1880. A 15 P 4, 5

HINCMARUS (RHEMENSIS ARCHIEPISCOPUS). Opera omnia. [*See* MIGNE, J. P., SERIES LATINA, 125, 126.]

HIND (HENRY YOULE), M.A., &c. Explorations in the Interior of the Labrador Peninsula, the County of the Montagnais and Nasquapee Indians. Illustrated. 2 vols. 8vo. Lond., 1863. D 3 U 36, 37

HIND (JOHN RUSSELL), F.R.A.S., &c. Introduction to Astronomy; to which is added, an Astronomical Vocabulary, containing an Explanation of Terms in use at the Present Day. 3rd ed., revised and greatly enlarged. 8vo. Lond., 1863. A 3 R 23

HIND (R. D. ARCHER-). Phædo of Plato. [*See* PLATO.]

HINDE (GEORGE JENNINGS). Catalogue of the Fossil Sponges in the Geological Department of the British Museum. 8vo. Lond., 1883. A 9 V 1

HINDLEY (CHARLES). The Catnach Press. 8vo. Lond., 1886. B 24 S 1

History of the Cries of London, Ancient and Modern. 2nd ed., greatly enlarged and carefully revised. 8vo. Lond., 1885. B 23 Q 1

Life and Times of James Catnach (late of Seven Dials), Ballad-monger. With 230 Woodcuts, of which 42 are by Bewick. 8vo. Lond., 1863. C 10 T 21

Works of John Taylor, the Water Poet. [*See* TAYLOR, J.]

HINDOOS (THE). (Lib. of Ent. Know.) 2 vols. 12mo. Lond., 1834–35. K 10 R 29, 30

HINDOSTANI LANGUAGE. Grammar and Dictionary. 4to. (n.p.n.d.) K 16 T 3

HINDS (RT. REV. SAMUEL), D.D., BISHOP OF NORWICH. The British Colonization of New Zealand ; being an Account of the Principles, Objects, and Plans of the New Zealand Association, &c. 12mo. Lond., 1837.* MD 2 P 7

HINGESTON (JAMES ANSLEY), M.R.C.S. Topics of the Day; Medical, Social, and Scientific. 8vo. Lond., 1863. J 5 Q 27

HINGSTON (JAMES). The Australian Abroad : Branches from the Main Routes round the World. 2 vols. 8vo. Lond., 1879–80. MD 1 V 28, 29

HINTON (C. H.) Scientific Romances: 1. What is the Fourth Dimension ? 2. The Persian King ; or, the Land of the Valley. 3. A Plane World. 4. Casting out the Self. 8vo. Lond., 1884–86. A 10 R 24

HINTON (JAMES). Man and his Dwelling Place : an Essay towards the Interpretation of Nature. New ed. 8vo. Lond., 1872. G 8 R 21

HINTS on the Nature and Management of Duns; by "The Hon. ——, a Younger Son." 8vo. Lond., 1845. J 12 Q 17

HINTS TO EMIGRANTS. (Weale.) 12mo. Lond., 1866. A 17 Q 15

HIPPESLEY (JOHN). Flora; or, Hob in the Well: a Farce. [*See* FARCES, 5.]

HIPPISLEY (COL. GEORGE). Narrative of the Expedition to the Rivers Orinoco and Apuré in South America. 8vo. Lond., 1819. D 4 Q 25

HIPPOCAMPUS. [*See* DAVID, THE SHEPHERD KING.]

HIPPOCRATES. [*See* MEDICORUM GRÆCORUM.]

HIPPOLYTUS (SAINT). Opera, Græce et Latina. 2 vols. (in 1) fol. Hamburgi, 1716–18. G 30 Q 16 ‡

HIPSLEY (W.) Equational Arithmetic, applied to Questions of Interest, Annuities, Life Assurance and General Commerce. (Weale.) 2nd ed. 12mo. Lond., 1858. A 17 Q 69

HIRTH (F.) China and the Roman Orient: Researches into their Ancient and Mediæval Relations, as represented in Old Chinese Records. 8vo. Lond., 1885. B 2 P 37

HISCOKE (J. G.) Hiscoke's Richmond Almanack and Year-book of Useful Knowledge for 1859. 8vo. Richmond (Eng.), 1858. ME 4 P

HISLOP (ALEXANDER). Book of Scottish Anecdote : Humorons, Social, Legendary, and Historical. 8vo. Edinb., 1874. J 11 S 1

HISSEY (JAMES JOHN). Drive through England ; or, a Thousand Miles of Road Travel. Illustrated. 8vo. Lond., 1885. D 7 S 30

HISTOIRE DES ORDRES MILITAIRES ; ou, des Chevaliers, des Milices Séculières et Régulières de l'un et l'autre Sexe, qui ont été établies jusques à present. 4 vols. 12mo. Amsterdam, 1721. G 10 P 26–29

HISTOIRE LITTÉRAIRE DE LA FRANCE: Ouvrage commencé par des Religieux Bénédictins de la Congrégation de Saint-Maur, et continué par une Commission prise dans la Classe d'Histoire et de Littérature ancienne de l'Institut. 27 vols. 4to. Paris, 1733–1877. B 11 R 1–S 7 †

HISTORIANS OF SCOTLAND. [*See* SCOTLAND, HISTORIANS OF.]

HISTORICAL MANUSCRIPTS COMMISSION. Reports, &c., of. 8 vols. (in 7) fol., and 2 vols. roy. 8vo. Lond., 1874–85. E

HISTORICAL MUSIC LOAN EXHIBITORS, 1885. [*See* WEALE, W. H. J.]

HISTORICAL PAMPHLETS. 14 vols. (in 1) 8vo. Lond., &c., 1800–69. B 11 Q 1

1. Letter to the Rt. Hon. George Canning, on the present state of the Catholic Question, from R. Therry ; to which are annexed, six Letters of the Rt. Hon. E. Burke (never before published), Reminiscences, &c.

2. The Protestant Church in that most miserable Country Ireland ; by W. Cobbett.

3. Political History of T. Reynolds, Esq., containing an Account of his Transactions with the Rebellion in Ireland ; with Observations on his Testimony, by P. Curran, Esq. ; together with Remarks of Sir F. Burdett and Mr. Brougham, on the Impropriety of resorting to such Sources in direct violation of the ends of Justice, and Lord Castlereagh's Apology for Mr. Reynolds, on account of his Reformation !

4. Upper Canada. Copy of a Petition to the Imperial Parliament respecting the Clergy Reserved Lands, and the King's College, in that Province ; with Copies of other Documents relating thereto.

5. Irish House of Commons. Message from his Excellency the Lord-Lieutenant, read by the Speaker from the Chair, Wednesday, February 3, 1800.

6. Monkish Superstition ; Modern Improvements.

7. A Slight Peep into the Church Vestry System in Ireland.

8. Great Britain and Ireland : a Letter ; by Eneas Macdonnell, Esq.

HISTORICAL PAMPHLETS.—*continued.*

9. The Church's Creed ; or, the Crown's Creed ? a Letter to the most Rev. Archbishop Manning, &c., &c. ; by Edmund S. Ffoulkes, B.D.

10. Look at this, and look at that : Speeches on the Catholic Emancipation Bill.

11. Critical Inquiry into the Nature and Treatment of the Case of Her Royal Highness the Princess Charlotte of Wales and her infant Son, with the Probable Causes of their Deaths, and the subsequent Appearances ; by Rees Price.

12. Brief Sketch of the Marquess of Anglesey's Administration.

13. Anti-Union ; Ireland as she ought to be ; by George Ensor.

14. Letter to Lord St. Leonards on the management of the Patriotic Fund, and the application of Public Moneys to Proselytizing purposes ; by the most Rev. Dr. Cullen.

HISTORICAL REPRINTS. Vol. 1. 12mo. Edinb., 1885. E

HISTORICAL SOCIETY (ENGLISH). Publications. 29 vols. 8vo. Lond., 1838–56. B 5 T 27–55

HISTORICAL GALLERY. [*See* GALLERY.] A 7 S 14–20

HISTORIE OF FRAUNCE. In Four Bookes. Printed by John Windet. The Mutable and Wavering Estate of France, from the yeare of our Lord 1460 untill the yeare 1595. Printed by Thomas Creede. 4to. Lond., 1595–97. B 8 Q 8

HISTORY OF SHIPWRECKS AND DISASTERS AT SEA. (Const. Misc.) 2 vols. 18mo. Lond., 1883. K 10 R 12, 13

HISTORY OF THE YEAR (THE) : a Narrative of the Chief Events and Topics of Interest, from October 1, 1881, to September 30, 1883. 8vo. Lond., 1882–83. E

HITCHCOCK (EDWARD). Elementary Geology. 2nd ed. 8vo. New York, 1841. A 9 Q 7

HITCHMAN (FRANCIS). Eighteenth Century Studies : Essays. 8vo. Lond., 1881. C 7 Q 2

The Runnymede Letters ; with Introduction and Notes. [*See* BEACONSFIELD, RT. HON. B. DISRAELI, EARL OF.]

HITTELL (JOHN S.) The Resources of California ; comprising the Society, Climate, Salubrity, Scenery, Commerce, and Industry of the State. 6th ed. 8vo. San Francisco, 1874. D 3 R 38

HIUEN TSIANG SI-YU-KI. Buddhist Records of the Western World. Translated from the Chinese, by Samuel Beale, B.A. 2 vols. 8vo. Lond., 1884. D 4 T 42, 43

HJALTALIN (JON A.) Orkneyinga Saga. [*See* ANDERSON, J.]

HOADLY (DR. BENJAMIN). The Suspicious Husband : a Comedy. (Bell's Brit. Theatre.) 18mo. Lond., 1791. H 2 P 5

Another copy. (Brit. Theatre.) 12mo. Lond., 1808. H 1 P 13

Another copy. (New Eng. Theatre.) 12mo. Lond., 1787. H 4 P 16

Another copy. [*See* BRIT. DRAMA, 5.]

HOARE (C.) The Slide Rule and how to use it. (Weale.) 12mo. Lond., 1872.   A 17 Q 16

HOARE (PRINCE). Epochs of the Arts; including Hints on the Use and Progress of Painting and Sculpture in Great Britain (with Appendices). 8vo. Lond., 1813.   A 7 Q 23

Inquiry into the requisite Cultivation and Present State of the Arts of Design in England. 8vo. Lond., 1806.
                                                           A 7 Q 23
Lock and Key. [*See* FARCES 3.]

No Song, no Supper: a Musical Entertainment. (Cumberland's Eng. Theatre.) 12mo. Lond., 1829.   H 2 Q 13

HOARE (SIR RICHARD COLT), BART, &c. Journal of a Tour in Ireland. 8vo. Lond., 1807.   D 6 U 11

Modern History of South Wiltshire. 6 vols. imp. fol. Lond., 1822–43.   B 5 P 11–16 ‡

HOBART. List of Districts into which the City is divided for the purpose of Domiciliary Visitation. (Pam. D.) 4to. Hobart, 1863.   MJ 2 U 3

HOBART (ADM. THE HON. AUGUSTUS CHARLES), PASHA. [*See* HAMPDEN, ADM. THE HON. C. H.]

HOBART (MARY), LADY. Essays and Miscellaneous Writings by Vere Henry, Lord Hobart; with a Biographical Sketch. [*See* HOBART, V. H., LORD.]

HOBART (VERE HENRY), LORD. Essays and Miscellaneous Writings; with a Biographical Sketch, edited by Mary, Lady Hobart. 2 vols. 8vo. Lond., 1885.   J 2 S 2, 3

HOBART TOWN: Almanacs and Directories. [*See* TASMANIA.]

HOBART TOWN COURIER (THE), 1827–29, and 1842–46. 7 vols. fol. Hobart, 1827–46.   ME

HOBART TOWN GAZETTE (THE), January and February, 1827. Fol. Hobart, 1827.   ME

HOBART TOWN GAZETTE, and Van Diemon's Land Advertiser. Fol. Hobart, 1817–25.   ME

HOBART TOWN MAGAZINE (THE). Vols. 1–3. (*Imperfect.*) 8vo. Hobart, 1833–31.   ME 3 R

HOBART TOWN PROMISSORY NOTES, 1823 and 1826. [*See* MANUSCRIPTS, &c.]

HOBART TOWN PUBLIC LIBRARY. Report for 1871. Fol. Hobart, 1871.   MJ 2 U 1

HOBBES (JAMES R.) Picture Collector's Manual, adapted to the Professional Man and the Amateur: being a Dictionary of Painters, &c. 2 vols. 8vo. Lond., 1849.   C 11 S 45, 46

HOBBES (THOMAS). Aristotle's Treatise on Rhetoric. [*See* ARISTOTELES.]

The English Works of; now first collected and edited by Sir Wm. Molesworth, Bart. 11 vols. 8vo. Lond., 1839–45.   J 3 U 1–11

Leviathan; or, the Matter, Forme, and Power of a Common-Wealth, Ecclesiasticall and Civill. 8vo. Lond., 1651.   G 14 T 13

Thomæ Hobbes Malmesburiensis Opera Philosophica quæ Latine scripsit omnia in unum corpus nunc primum collecta studio et labore Gulielmi Molesworth. 5 vols. 8vo. Lond., 1839–45.   J 3 U 1–16

HOBBS (A. C.) The Construction of Locks; compiled from the Papers of A. C. Hobbs, and edited by Charles Tomlinson; with a Description of Mr. J. B. Fenby's Patent Locks, and a Note upon Iron Safes, by Robert Mallet, A.M., &c. (Weale.) 12mo. Lond., 1868.   A 17 P 35

HOBDAY (E.) Cottage Gardening; or, Flowers, Fruits, and Vegetables for small Gardens. (Weale.) 12mo. Lond., 1882.   A 17 Q 59

HOBHOUSE (RT. HON. SIR J.) [*See* NAPIER, SIR C. J.]
                                                           MJ 2 Q 13

HOBLER (FRANCIS). Records of Roman History, from Cneus Pompeius to Tiberius Constantinus, as exhibited on the Roman Coins, collected by Francis Hobler. 2 vols. 4to. Lond., 1860.   B 14 Q 6, 7 ‡

HOBLYN (RICHARD D.) Dictionary of Scientific Terms. 8vo. Lond., 1849.   K 18 P 15

HOBSON (CAPT. WILLIAM), R.N. Copies of Extracts of Despatches from the Governor of New South Wales, bearing date the 9th and 19th days of February, 1840, containing the Reports of Captain Hobson, R.N., of his Proceedings on his arrival at New Zealand; together with Copy of the Reply of the Secretary of State thereto. (Parl. Doc., 29.) Fol. Lond., 1840.   MF 4 ‡

HOBSON'S BAY. Remarks in favour of a Central Fort for Hobson's Bay; by * * *. 12mo. Melb., 1862.
                                                           MJ 2 P 31

HOCHSTETTER (DR. FERDINAND VON). Allgemeine Erdkunde. [*See* HANN, DR. J.]

Geologie von Neu-Seeland: Beiträge zur Geologie der Provinzen Auckland und Nelson. (*Novara*-Expedition.) 4to. Wien, 1864.   MA 2 Q 10 †

New Zealand: its Physical Geography, Geology, and Natural History: translated from the German Original, by Edward Sauter, A.M.; with Additions up to 1866. Roy. 8vo. Stuttgart, 1867.*   MD 3 V 26

Paläontologie von Neu-Seeland: Beiträge zur Kenntniss der Fossilen Flora und Fauna der Provinzen Auckland und Nelson. (*Novara*-Expedition.) 4to. Wien, 1864.   MA 2 Q 11 †

Rotomahana and the Boiling Springs of New Zealand. [*See* MUNDY, D. L.]

HOCHSTETTER (DR. FERDINAND VON), AND PETER-MANN (DR. A.) Geological and Topograplical Atlas of New Zealand: Six Maps of the Provinces of Auckland and Nelson. 4to. Auckland, 1864.   MD 5 R 4 ‡

The Geology of New Zealand, in explanation of the Geographlical and Topographlical Atlas of New Zealand, from the Scientific Publications of the *Novara* Expedition; translated by Dr. C. F. Fisclier; also, Lectures by Dr. F. Hoclstetter, delivered in New Zealand. 8vo. Auckland, 1864.*   MA 2 Q 26

HOCKIN (REV. JOHN PEARCE). Supplement to the Account of the Pelew Islands [by George Keate]; compiled from the Journals of the *Panther* and *Endeavour.* 4to. Lond., 1803.   MD 6 P 20 †

HODASEVICH (CAPT. R.) A Voice witlin the Walls of Sebastopol. 8vo. Lond., 1856.   B 12 T 31

HODDER (EDWIN). Life and Work of the seventl Earl of Slaftesbury. 3 vols. 8vo. Lond., 1886. C 8 P 45–47

Memories of New Zealand. 8vo. Lond., 1862. MD 3 Q 2

Another copy. 2nd ed. 12mo. Lond., 1863. MD 3 Q 3

On Holy Ground; or, Scenes and Incidents in the Land of Promise. 8vo. Edinb., 1874.   D 5 Q 36

HODGES (G. LLOYD). Narrative of the Expedition to Portugal, 1832, under the orders of H.I.M. Dom Pedro. 2 vols. 8vo. Lond., 1833.   B 13 U 46, 47

HODGES (J. G.) Report of the Trial of W. S. O'Brien for Higl Treason. Imp. 8vo. Dublin, 1849. F 5 V 18

HODGETTS (E. A. BRAYLEY). Personal Reminiscences of General Skobeloff. [*See* NEMIROVITCH-DANTCHENKO, V. I.]

HODGETTS (J. FREDERICK). The Englisl in the Middle Ages, from the Norman Usurpation to the Days of the Stuarts. 8vo. Lond., 1885.   B 4 T 3

Older England, illustrated by the Anglo-Saxon Antiquities in the Britisl Museum, in a Course of six Lectures. 8vo. Lond., 1884.   B 5 S 31

HODGINS (JOHN GEORGE), LL.D. The Sclool-louse; its Architecture, External and Internal Arrangements; witl Elevations and Plans for Public and Higl Sclool Buildings. Illustrated. Roy. 8vo. Toronto, 1876. A 2 S 19

HODGKIN (THOMAS), M.D. Catalogues of the Preparations in the Anatomical Museum of Guy's Hospital. 8vo. Lond., 1829.   A 12 U 17

HODGKIN (THOMAS), B.A. Italy and her Invaders. 376–553. 1. The Visigotlic Invasion. 2. The Hunnisl Invasion. 3. The Vandal Invasion and the Herulian Mutiny. 4. The Ostrogotlic Invasion. 5. The Imperial Restoration. 4 vols. 8vo. Oxford, 1880–85. B 11 S 9–12

Letters of Cassiodorus. [*See* CASSIODORUS, M. A.]

HODGKINSON (CLEMENT). Australia, from Port Macquarie to Moreton Bay; witl Descriptions of the Natives, tleir Manners and Customs; the Geology, Natural Productions, Fertility, and Resources of that Region. 8vo. Lond., 1845.*   MD 1 V 35

HODGKINSON (S.) Description of the Province of Canterbury, New Zealand, or Zealandia. 2nd ed. 8vo. Lond., 1858.   MD I W 30

Description of the Province of Victoria, Australia. 8vo. Lond., 1858.   MD 1 W 30

Hand-book to the Colony of New Soutl Wales, Australia. 8vo. Lond., 1858.   MD 1 W 30

Hand-book to the Colony of Soutl Australia. 8vo. Lond., 1858.   MD 1 W 30

Hand-book to the Colony of Tasmania. 8vo. Lond., 1858.   MD 1 W 30

Hand-book to the Province of Nelson, New Zealand. 8vo. Lond., 1858.   MD 1 W 30

Hand-book to the Province of Wellington, New Zealand. 8vo. Lond., 1858.   MD 1 W 30

HODGSON (W. R.) Slort Text-book of Inorganic Clemistry. [*See* STRECKER, A.]

HODGSON (BRIAN HOUGHTON), F.R.S. Miscellaneous Essays relating to Indian Subjects. 2 vols. 8vo. Lond., 1880.   K 12 R 26, 27

HODGSON (CHRISTOPHER PEMBERTON). Reminiscences of Australia; witl Hints on the Squatter's Life. 8vo. Lond., 1846.*   MD 3 R 1

Residence at Nagasaki and Hakodate, in 1859–60; witl an Account of Japan generally. 8vo. Lond., 1861.   D 5 P 39

HODGSON (MRS. E.) [*See* HODGSON, PROF. W. B.]

HODGSON (REV. JOHN), M.R.S.L. History of Northumberland, in tlree parts. 7 vols. 4to. Newcastle, 1820–58.   B 2 T 29–35

HODGSON (JAMES M.), D.Sc., &c. The Bibles of otler Nations; being Selections from the Scriptures of the Clinese, Hindoos, Persians, Buddlists, Egyptians, and Molammedans. 8vo. Manclester, 1885. G 8 S 5

HODGSON (JOHN). Biograply of. [*See* BECKER, L.]

HODGSON (JOHN EVANS), R.A. Academy Lectures. 8vo. Lond., 1884.   A 7 Q 8

HODGSON (R. R.), M.E., &c. Clemistry of the Mine; or, the Miners' Pocket Companion. 8vo. Lond., 1881.   A 5 R 18

HODGSON (SHADWORTH H.) Time and Space: a Metaplysical Essay. 8vo. Lond., 1865.   G 1 P 27

HODGSON (WILLIAM). The Society of Friends in the 19th Century: a Historical View of the Successive Convulsions and Sclisms tlercin during tlat period. 2 vols. 8vo. Philad., 1875–76.   G 8 R 13, 14

HODGSON (Prof. William Ballantyne), LL.D. Education of Girls, and the Employment of Women of the Upper Classes, educationally considered: Two Lectures. 2nd ed. 8vo. Lond., 1869.   G 17 P 21

Errors in the Use of English [edited by his Wife, Mrs. E. Hodgson]. 8vo. Edinb., 1881.   K 12 P 20

HODSON (James Shirley), F.R.S.L. Historical and Practical Guide to Art Illustration, in connection with Books, Periodicals, and General Decoration. 8vo. Lond., 1884.   A 7 T 15

HODSON (Mrs. Margaret). Lives of Vasco Nunez de Balboa, and Francisco Pizarro. [*See* Quintana, Don M. J.]

HOEFER (Edmund). Küstenfahrten an der Nord-und Ostsee. [*See* Unser Vaterland.]

HOEFER (J.C.F.) [*See* Biographie Générale, Nouvelle.]

HOEY (Mrs. Cashel). The Cat, Past and Present. [*See* Champfleury.]

Desmoulins and his Wife. [*See* Claretie, J.]

Frederick the Great and Maria Theresa. [*See* Broglie, C. J. V. Duc de.]

Japan and the Japanese. [*See* Humbert, A.]

Memoirs of Count Miot de Melito. [*See* Melito, Count A. F. M. de.]

Selection from Letters of Madame Rémusat. [*See* Rémusat, Mme. C. E. J.]

Thorvaldsen; his Life and Works. [*See* Plon, E.]

HOEY (William). Buddha; his Life, &c. [*See* Oldenberg, Dr. H.]

HOFER (Matthias). Etymologisches Wörterbuch der in Oberdeutschland, vorzüglich aber in Oesterreich üblichen Mundart. 3 vols. 8vo. Linz, 1815.   K 12 Q 34–36

HOFF (A.), M.D. The Skin in Health and Disease. 12mo. Sydney, 1884.   MA 2 S 30

HOFF (Com. William Bainbridge-). Examples, Conclusions, and Maxims of Modern Naval Tactics. Roy. 8vo. Portsmouth, 1885.   A 16 V 13

HOFFMAN (C. F.) A Winter in the Far West. 2 vols. 8vo. Lond., 1835.   D 3 Q 53, 54

HOFFMANN (Ernst Theodor Wilhelm). The Serapion Brethren: translated from the German by A. Ewing. Vol. I. 8vo. Lond., 1886.   J 12 P 27

HOFFMANN (Frederick A.) Poetry: its Origin, Nature, and History. 2 vols. 8vo. Lond., 1884.   H 8 V 7, 8

HOFFMANN (H.) A Collection of the Choicest Proverbs, derived from all Languages. (Pam., 43.) 8vo. Sydney, 1871.   MJ 2 R 5

HOFFMANN (J.) Bibliotheca Japonica. [*See* Siebold, P. F. de.]

HOFFMANN (Dr. Wilhelm). Vollständigstes Wörterbuch der deutschen Sprache. 6 vols. (in 3) roy. 8vo. Leipsic, 1871.   K 13 K 13–15

HOFFMANN VON FALLERSLEBEN (A. H.) Glossarium Belgicum. 8vo. Hanover, 1856.   K 13 Q 35

HOFLAND (Mrs. Barbara). Descriptive Account of the Mansion and Gardens of White-Knights, a Seat of his Grace the Duke of Marlborough. Illustrated. Imp. 4to. Lond., 1819.   D 38 Q 1 ‡

HOFLAND (Mrs.) Turner's Rivers of England. [*See* Turner, J. M. W.]

HOFLAND (T. C.) British Angler's Manual; or, the Art of Angling, in England, Scotland, Wales, and Ireland. Enlarged by Prof. E. Jesse. 8vo. Lond., 1848.   A 17 U 1

HOFMANN (A. W.), F.R.S., &c. The Life-work of Baron J. von Liebig in Experimental and Philosophic Chemistry, &c. [The Faraday Lecture for 1875.] 8vo. Lond., 1876.   C 5 V 21

HOFMANN (Prof. F.) [*See* Anatomie und Physiologie.]

HOGAN (Edmund). Description of Ireland, and the State thereof, as it is at this Present, in Anno 1598. 4to. Dublin, 1878.   B 11 R 7

HOGAN (James Francis). The Catholic Case stated: being a Brief Summary of the Reasons why the Roman Catholics of Victoria cannot accept the present Education Act. 8vo. Melb., 1878.   MF 1 Q 6

The Irish in Australia. 8vo. Lond., 1887.   MB 2 T 15

HOGARTH (George). Memoirs of the Musical Drama. 2 vols. 8vo. Lond., 1838.   C 8 R 31, 32

Memoirs of the Opera, in Italy, France, Germany, and England: a new edition of the "Musical Drama." 2 vols. 12mo. Lond., 1851.   C 14 P 7, 8

HOGARTH (Georgina). Letters of Charles Dickens. [*See* Dickens, C.]

HOGARTH (William). Anecdote Biography. [*See* Timbs, T.]

Biographical Anecdotes of; with a Catalogue of his Works, by John Nichols. 3rd ed. 8vo. Lond., 1785.   C 6 U 17

Genuine Graphic Works of; consisting of 160 Engravings, faithfully copied from the originals, by Thos. Cook. 4to. Lond., 1813.   A 2 S 22 †

William Hogarth, Painter, Engraver, and Philosopher. Essays on the Man, the Work, and the Time; by G. A. Sala. 12mo. Lond., 1866.   C 2 Q 21

Works of. From the Original Plates restored by James Heath, R.A.: with the addition of many Subjects not before collected, by John Nichols, F.S.A. At. fol. Lond., 1822.*   A 10 P 7, 8 ‡

Works of. Illustrated by John Ireland. 3 vols. 8vo. Lond., 1793.   A 7 S 21–23

HOGENDORP (C. S. W. de), Comte. Coup d'œil sur l'Île de Java et les autres Possessions Néerlandaises dans l'Archipel des Indes. 8vo. Bruxelles, 1830.   B 10 V 25

HOGG (CHARLES E.) Two Spirits, and other Poems. 8vo. Sydney, 1883. MH 1 P 35

HOGG (REV. DAVID). Life of Allan Cunningham; with Selections from his Works and Correspondence. 8vo. Lond., 1875. C 2 U 19

HOGG (JABEZ), F.L.S., &c. Elements of Experimental and Natural Philosophy; being a familiar and easy introduction to the study of the Physical Sciences. 8vo. Lond., 1861. · A 16 P 15

The Microscope: its History, Construction, and Application. 8vo. Lond., 1867. A 17 T 1

Life and Death in our Mines. (Pam. Co.) 8vo. Lond., 1866. A 16 U 23

HOGG (JAMES), "THE ETTRICK SHEPHERD." Altrive Tales, collected among the Peasantry of Scotland. [With a Memoir of the Author.] Vol. 1. 12mo. Lond., 1832. J 7 Q 5

Jacobite Relics of Scotland. 1st and 2nd series. 2 vols. 8vo. Paisley, 1874. H 8 V 31, 32

Memorials of James Hogg, the Ettrick Shepherd; edited by his Daughter, Mrs. Garden. 8vo. Lond., 1885. C 3 V 13

Works of. Centenary edition; with a Memoir of the Author, by the Rev. T. Thomson. 2 vols. imp. 8vo. Lond., 1876. J 8 V 1, 2

HOGG (JOSEPH). Iron Trades' Guide. 12mo. West Bromwich, 1869 A 23 Q 33

HOGG (ROBERT), LL.D., &c. Fruit Manual; containing the Descriptions, Synonymes, and Classification of the Fruits and Fruit Trees of Great Britain. 4th ed. 8vo. Lond., 1875. A 1 R 41

The Vegetable Kingdom and its Products. 8vo. Lond., 1858. A 4 Q 8

HOGG (THOMAS JEFFERSON). Life of Percy Bysshe Shelley. Vols. 1 and 2 (*all published*). 8vo. Lond., 1858. C 4 V 41, 42

HOLBEIN (HANS), OF AUGSBURG. Dance of Death, &c.; with a Dissertation on the several representations of that subject, by Thos. Douce. 8vo. Lond., 1885. J 9 U 6

Facsimilies of Original Drawings by Hans Holbein, in the Collection of His Majesty, for the Portraits of Illustrious Persons of the Court of Henry VIII; engraved by Francis Bartolozzi, with Biographical Notices by Edmund Lodge. Published by John Chamberlaine, F.S.A. Roy. 4to. Lond., 1884. A 23 8 7 ‡

Hans Holbein; by J. Cundall. (Great Artists) 8vo. Lond., 1879. C 3 T 42

Imitations of Original Drawings by Hans Holbein, in the Collection of His Majesty, for the Portraits of Illustrious Persons of the Court of Henry VIII. With Biographical Tracts. Published by John Chamberlaine. At. fol. Lond., 1792. A 20 P 14 ‡

Some Account of the Life and Works of; by R. N. Wornum. Imp. 8vo. Lond., 1867. C 3 W 13

HOLBERG (LEWIS). Memoirs of Lewis Holberg; written by himself. 12mo. Lond., 1827. C 1 P 10

HOLBROOK (PROF. G. O.) Annals of Tacitus. [*See* TACITUS, C. C.]

HOLCOMBE (WILLIAM HENRY), M.D. Lazarus of Bethany: the Story of his Life in both Worlds. 12mo. Melb., 1882. MJ 1 U 10

HOLCROFT (THOMAS). Deaf and Dumb: an Historical Drama. (Cumberland's Eng. Theatre.) 12mo. Lond., 1829. H 2 Q 13

The Deserted Daughter: a Comedy. (Brit. Theatre.) 12mo. Lond., 1808. H 1 P 24

Duplicity: a Comedy. [*See* MODERN THEATRE 4.]

He's Much to Blame: a Comedy. [*See* MODERN THEATRE 4.]

Life of Baron Frederick Trenck. [*See* TRENCK, F., BARON VON.]

Memoirs of; written by himself, and continued to the Time of his Death, from his Diary, Notes, and other Papers. 12mo. Lond., 1852. C 2 R 18

Physiognomy. [*See* LAVATER, J. C.]

Posthumous Works of Frederic II; translated from the French. [*See* FREDERICK II, KING OF PRUSSIA.]

The Road to Ruin: a Comedy. (Brit. Theatre.) 12mo. Lond., 1808. H 1 P 24

The School for Arrogance: a Comedy. [*See* MODERN THEATRE 4.]

Seduction: a Comedy. [*See* MODERN THEATRE 4.]

A Tale of Mystery: a Melodrama. (Cumberland's Eng. Theatre.) 12mo. Lond., 1829. H 2 Q 19

HOLDEN (FRANCES GILLAM). Her Father's Darling, and other Child Pictures. 12mo. Sydney, 1887.* MH 1 P 50

What Typhoid is, and how to nurse it; Words of Cheer for Women, showing how much is in their own power. 12mo. Sydney, 1887. MA 2 S 22

HOLDEN (GEORGE KENYON). Letter to Mr. G. Langhorne in reference to the Missionary Establishment to the Aborigines. [*See* MANUSCRIPTS, &c.]

Moral and Intellectual Culture of the People, essential to secure the advantage of High Wages and Political Privileges: a Lecture. (Pam. J.) 8vo. Sydney, 1853. MJ 1 T 38

HOLDEN (LUTHER), F.R.C.S. Human Osteology; comprising a Description of the Bones; with Delineations of the Attachments of the Muscles. Illustrated. 2nd ed. Roy. 8vo. Lond., 1857. A 12 U 29

Medical and Surgical Landmarks. 8vo. Lond., 1876. A 12 U 27

HÖLDER (M.) Wörterbuch der deutschen und französischen Sprache. [*See* MOZIN, ABBÉ.]

HOLDSWORTH (JOSEPH), M.G.S.F., &c. Geology, Minerals, Mines, and Soils of Ireland, in reference to the Amelioration and Industrial Prosperity of the Country. 8vo. Lond., 1857. **A 9 P 14**

HOLDSWORTH (PHILIP JOSEPH). Station-hunting on the Warrego; Australia; At the Valley of Popran; and other Poems. 8vo. Sydney, 1885. **MH 1 R 24**

HOLE (WILLIAM), A.R.S.A. Quasi Cursores: Portraits of the High Officers and Professors of the University of Edinburgh, at its Tercentenary Festival. 4to. Edinb., 1884. **C 1 Q 22 †**

HOLE AND CORNER PETITION (THE). Observations on, in a Letter to the Right Honorable Edward G. Stanley, Principal Secretary for the Colonial Department; by "An Unpaid Magistrate." 8vo. Sydney, 1834. **MF 1 Q 4**

HOLGATE (C. W.), B.A. Account of the Chief Libraries of Australia and Tasmania. Roy. 8vo. Lond., 1886. **MJ 1 V 8**

Account of the Chief Libraries of New Zealand; with an Appendix, containing the Statutes relating to Public Libraries in that Colony. 8vo. Lond., 1886. **MJ 1 T 49**

HOLINSHED (RAPHAEL). Chronicles of England, Scotland, and Ireland to the year 1586. 6 vols. 4to. Lond., 1807–8. **B 10 R 1–6 †**
Description of Scotland. [*See* BOETHIUS, H.]

HOLLAND (REV. FREDERIC MAY). The Rise of Intellectual Liberty, from Thales to Copernicus. 8vo. New York, 1885. **G 1 P 26**

HOLLAND (SIR HENRY), BART., M.D., &c. Fragmentary Papers on Science and other Subjects; edited by his Son, Rev. Francis J. Holland. 8vo. Lond., 1875. **A 17 V 9**
Recollections of Past Life. 8vo. Lond., 1872. **C 3 U 25**

HOLLAND (HENRY EDWARD), LORD. Foreign Reminiscences: by Henry Richard, Lord Holland; edited by his Son. 8vo. Lond., 1850. **C 3 U 12**

HOLLAND (HENRY RICHARD), LORD. Foreign Reminiscences: edited by his Son, Henry Edward, Lord Holland. 8vo. Lond., 1850. **C 3 U 12**

Some Account of the Lives and Writings of Lope Felix de Vega Carpio, and Guillen de Castro. 2 vols. 8vo. Lond., 1817. **C 3 P 42, 43**

Souvenirs des Cours de France, etc. [*See* BARRIÈRE, J. F., 27.]

HOLLAND (J.) Treatise on the Progressive Improvement and Present State of the Manufactures in Metals. (Lard. Cab. Cyclo.) 3 vols. 12mo. Lond., 1831–34. **K 1 U 34–36**

HOLLAND (JAMES). Tour in Portugal. [*See* JENNINGS, R.]

HOLLAND (JOHN), AND EVERETT (JAMES). Memoirs of the Life and Writings of James Montgomery, including Selections from his Correspondence, Remains in Prose and Verse, and Conversations on various Subjects. 7 vols. 8vo. Lond., 1854–56. **C 4 U 13–19**

HOLLAND (JOSIAH GILBERT), M.D. Katrina: her Life and Mine in a Poem. 12mo. Lond., 1874. **H 6 R 20**

Letters to Young People, Single and Married, re-written by an English Editor, after Timothy Titcomb. 12mo. Lond., 1875. **J 10 Q 33**

HOLLAND (SARA), LADY. Memoir of the Rev. Sydney Smith, by his Daughter; with a Selection from his Letters; edited by Mrs. Austin. 2 vols. 8vo. Lond., 1855. **C 9 U 17, 18**

HOLLAND (THOMAS ERSKINE), D.C.L., &c. Elements of Jurisprudence. 8vo. Oxford, 1880. **F 8 P 21**

Another copy. 2nd ed. (enlarged.) 8vo. Oxford, 1882. **F 8 P 22**

European Concert in the Eastern Question: a Collection of Treaties and other Public Acts. 8vo. Oxford, 1885. **F 8 R 11**

Institutes of Justinian: Select Titles from the Digest of Justinian. [*See* JUSTINIANUS.]

HOLLE (K. F.) Vlugtig Berigt omtrent eenige Lontar-Handschriften, afkomstig uit de Soenda-Landen. 8vo. Batavia, 1866. **C 14 Q 29**

HOLLEY (GEORGE W.) Falls of Niagara, and other Famous Cataracts. Illustrated. 8vo. Lond., 1882. **D 3 Q 12**

HOLLINDSHEAD (RAPHALL). [*See* HOLINSHED, R.]

HOLLINGSHEAD (JOHN). Miscellanies: Stories and Essays. 3 vols. 8vo. Lond., 1874. **J 10 V 24–26**

HOLLINGSWORTH (O. N.) Fifth Annual Report of the Superintendent of Public Instruction of the State of Texas, for the scholastic year ending August 31st, 1875. (Pam. Bs.) 8vo. Houston, 1876. **MG 1 Q 34**

HOLLIS (DENZIL), LORD. Mémoires de. [*See* GUIZOT, F. P. G., 5.]

HOLLIS (F. BRAND-). [*See* BRAND-HOLLIS, F.]

HOLLIS (T. AND G.) Monumental Effigies of Great Britain drawn and etched. Fol. Lond., 1840–42. **B 19 T 11 ‡**

HOLLOWAY (WILLIAM). General Dictionary of Provincialisms. 8vo. Lewes, 1839. **K 15 R 30**

HOLMAN (J. G.) The Votary of Wealth: a Comedy. [*See* MODERN THEATRE, 3.]

HOLMAN (LIEUT. JAMES), R.N. [Extracts from] Voyage round the World; by Lieut. Holman, R.N. 8vo. Lond., 1834–35. **MD 7 Q 46**

Travels in China, New Zealand, New South Wales, Van Diemen's Land, Cape Horn, &c. 2nd ed. 8vo. Lond., 1840. **MD 5 R 18**

Voyage round the World; including Travels in Africa, Asia, Australasia, America, &c., 1827–32. 4 vols. 8vo. Lond., 1834–35.* **MD 5 R 10–13**

HOLMBOE (C. A.) Det Oldnorske Verbum, oplyst ved Sammenligning med Sanskrit og andre Sprog af samme Æt. 4to. Christiania, 1848.   K 16 R 13

Sanskrit og Oldnorsk, en sprogsam menlignende Afhandling. 4to. Christiania, 1846.   K 16 R 12

HOLMDEN (MRS. ANNIE), ANNIE HARWOOD. Coligny. [*See* BERSIER, E.]

Jesus Christ; his Life, &c. [*See* PRESSENSÉ, E. DE.]

Martyrs and Apologists. [*See* PRESSENSÉ, E. DE.]

HOLMES (ABDIEL), D.D. Annals of America, from the Discovery by Columbus, in the year 1492, to the year 1826. 2 vols. 8vo. Cam., U.S., 1829.   B 1 U 22, 23

HOLMES (MRS. DALKEITH). A Ride on Horseback to Florence, through France and Switzerland. 2 vols. 8vo. Lond., 1842.   D 9 Q 2, 3

HOLMES (EDWARD). Life of Mozart ; including his Correspondence. 8vo. Lond., 1845.   C 3 V 32

HOLMES (J. B.) Rationalism of Christianity ; by "A Layman." 8vo. Sydney, 1883.   MH 1 P 47

HOLMES (MRS. MARY J.) Tempest and Sunshine. [*See* BLACKWOOD'S BOOKS FOR EVERYBODY.]

HOLMES (NATHANIEL). The Authorship of Shakespeare; 3rd ed., with an Appendix of additional Matters, including a Notice of the recently discovered Northumberland MSS. 8vo. New York, 1876.   J 11 R 11

HOLMES (PROF. OLIVER WENDELL), M.D. Astræa; the Balance of Illusions: a Poem. 12mo. Boston, 1850.   H 7 R 34

Autocrat of the Breakfast Table. 8vo. Boston, 1872.   J 8 R 28

Border Lines of Knowledge in some Provinces of Medical Science: a Lecture. 8vo. Boston, 1862.   A 13 P 9

Currents and Counter-Currents in Medical Science; with other Addresses and Essays. 8vo. Boston, 1861.   A 12 P 40

Elsie Venner: a Romance of Destiny. 2 vols. (in 1) 12mo. Boston, 1872.   J 8 R 26

The Guardian Angel. 12mo. Boston, 1871.   J 8 R 25

Illustrated Poems of. Roy. 8vo. Lond., 1885.   H 5 U 31

John Lothrop Motley : a Memoir. 8vo. Lond., 1878.   C 1 U 50

Mechanism in Thought and Morals: an Address, 1870. 12mo. Boston, 1872.   G 10 Q 32

Poems of. 12mo. Boston, 1872.   H 6 R 14

The Poet at the Breakfast Table. 12mo. Lond., 1872.   J 8 R 30

The Professor at the Breakfast Table, with the Story of Iris. 8vo. Boston, 1872.   J 8 R 29

Songs in many Keys. 7th ed. 12mo. Boston, 1864.   H 6 R 15

Soundings from the Atlantic. 12mo. Boston, 1872.   J 8 R 27

2 z

HOLMES (OLIVER WENDELL), JUNR. Common Law. 8vo. Lond., 1882.   F 6 T 30

HOLMES (RACHAEL), SCOTT RUSSELL, AND HOLMES (ELEANOR). Autobiography of Hector Berlioz. [*See* BERLIOZ, L. H.]

HOLMES (T. R. E.) History of the Indian Mutiny, and of the Disturbances which accompanied it among the Civil Population ; with Maps and Plans. 8vo. Lond., 1883.   B 10 U 18

Suakim and the Country of Soudan ; written expressly for the Information of the New South Wales Military Contingent bound for Service in Africa. 8vo. Sydney, 1885.   MD 4 U 11

HOLMES-FORBES (AVARY WILLIAM). [*See* FORBES, A. W. HOLMES-.]

HOLROYD (ARTHUR TODD), M.D., &c. Prickly Comfrey; its History, Cultivation, Extraordinary Production, and Uses. Roy. 8vo. Sydney, 1876.   MJ 2 R 17

HOLST (PROF. HERMANN EDUARD VON). The Constitutional and Political History of the United States ; translated from the German by John J. Lalor, A.M., Alfred B. Mason, and Paul Shorey. 5 vols. 8vo. Chicago, 1876–85.   B 1 T 14–18

HOLT (ARDERN). Fancy Dresses described ; or, What to Wear at Fancy Balls. Illustrated. 2nd ed. 8vo. Lond., 1880.   A 7 P 29

Another copy. 3rd and enlarged ed., with additional coloured Illustrations. 8vo. Lond., 1882.   A 8 P 38

Gentlemen's Fancy Dress ; how to choose it. Illustrated. 8vo. Lond., 1882.   A 7 P 30

HOLT (JOSEPH). Memoirs of Joseph Holt, General of the Irish Rebels in 1798 ; edited by T. Crofton Croker. 2 vols. 8vo. Lond., 1838.*   MC 1 Q 16, 17

HOLT (HON. THOMAS), M.L.C. Captain Cook's Landing in Botany Bay. [*See* COOK, CAPT. J.]

Judicial Treatment of the Accused : Report of a Speech on the Cruelty and Degradation of compelling accused Persons to stand in the Dock during their Trial. 8vo. Sydney, 1878.   MF 3 R 4

Christianity, the Poor Man's Friend. (An Address to the Poor and Needy, privately printed.) 12mo. Bexley, 1888.   MG 2 P 5

Two Speeches on the subject of Education in New South Wales, delivered in the Legislative Assembly December, 1856. 8vo. Sydney, 1857.   MG 1 Q 30

Another copy.   MJ 2 Q 9

Another copy.   MJ 2 Q 14

HOLTZAPFFEL (CHARLES AND JOHN JACOB). Turning and Mechanical Manipulation. Vols. 1–5. 8vo. Lond. 1852–84.   A 11 T 4–8

HOLTZMANN (Adolf). Altdeutsche Grammatik, umfassend die gothische, altnordische, altsächsische, angelsächsische und althochdeutsche Sprache. Erster Band 1e und 2e abtheilung (*all published.*) 2 vols. (in 1) 8vo. Leipzig, 1870–75.   K 13 Q 46

HOLUB (Dr. Emil). Seven Years in South Africa: Travels, Researches, and Hunting Adventures, between the Diamond-Fields and the Zambesi (1872–79): translated by Ellen E. Frewer. Illustrated. 2 vols. 8vo. Lond., 1881.   D 2 R 6, 7

HOLY GOSPELS (The). Translated from the original Greek. [*See* Brameld, G. W.]

HOLYOAKE (George Jacob). History of Co-operation in England: its Literature and its Advocates. 2 vols. 8vo. Lond., 1875–79.   F 6 R 9, 10

Life of Joseph Rayner Stephens, Preacher and Political Orator. 8vo. Lond., 1881.   C 2 P 38

Self-Help by the People. History of Co-operation in Rochdale. (Pam. 37.) 8vo. Lond., 1858.   MJ 2 Q 24

HOMBRON (M.) Botanique. Zoologie. [*See* Dumont D'Urville, Capt. J. S. C.]

HOME AND COLONIAL LIBRARY. 37 vols. 12mo. Lond., 1843–61.   J 8 P 1–37

1. The Bible in Spain; by George Borrow.

2, 3. Narrative of a Journey through the Upper Provinces of India, from Calcutta to Bombay, 1824–25; by the Rt. Rev. Reginald Heber, D.D.

4. Travels in Egypt and Nubia, Syria, and the Holy Land, &c.; by the Hon. Charles Leonard Irby, R.N., and James Mangles, R.N. A History of the Siege of Gibraltar, 1779–83; by Capt. John Drinkwater.

5. Western Barbary; by John H. Drummond Hay. Letters from the Shores of the Baltic; by Miss Elizabeth Rigby [Lady Eastlake.]

6. Mary Schweidler, the Amber Witch; edited by W. Meinhold, translated by Lady Duff Gordon. Select Biographies; Cromwell and Bunyan; by Robert Southey, LL.D.

7. Notes and Sketches of New South Wales; by Mrs. Charles Meredith. Life, Voyages, and Exploits of Sir Francis Drake; by John Barrow, F.S.A.

8. Memoirs of Father Ripa; translated by Fortunato Prandi. Journal of a Residence among the Negroes in the West Indies; by the late Matthew Gregory Lewis, M.P.

9. Sketches of Persia; by Sir John Malcolm.

10. The French in Algiers: 1. The Soldier of the Foreign Legion [by Clemens Lamping]; 2. The Prisoners of Abd-el-Kader [by A. de France]; translated by Lady Duff Gordon. History of the Fall of the Jesuits in the 18th Century; by Count Alexis de Saint-Priest.

11. Bracebridge Hall; or, the Humorists; by "Geoffrey Crayon" [Washington Irving.]

12. Journal of Researches into the Natural History and Geology of the Countries visited during the Voyage of H.M.S. *Beagle*; by Charles Darwin, M.A., &c.

13. Life of Louis, Prince of Condé, surnamed the Great; by Lord Mahon [*afterwards* Earl Stanhope.]

HOME AND COLONIAL LIBRARY.—*continued.*

14. The Zincali: an Account of the Gypsies of Spain; by George Borrow.

15. Narrative of a Four Months' Residence among the Natives of a Valley of the Marquesas Islands; by Herman Melville. The Story of Toby, a Sequel to "Typee"; [by Herman Melville.]

16. Livonian Tales: The Disponent, The Wolves, The Jewess; [by Lady Eastlake.] Phillip Musgrave; edited by the Rev. J. Abbott, A.M.

17. Sale's Brigade in Afghanistan, with an Account of the Seizure and Defence of Jellalabad; by the Rev. G. R. Gleig, M.A. Letters from Madras, during the years 1836–39; by "A Lady" [Mrs. J. C. Maitland.]

18. Short Sketches of the Wild Sports and Natural History of the Highlands; from the Journals of Charles St. John.

19. Rough Notes taken during some rapid Journeys across the Pampas and among the Andes; by Sir Francis B. Head, Bart. The Sieges of Vienna by the Turks; from the German of Karl August Schimmer, and other Sources; [by the Earl of Ellesmere.]

20. Gatherings from Spain; [by R. Ford.]

21. Sketches of German Life, and Scenes from the War of Liberation in Germany; translated [from the Memoirs of K. A. L. P. Varnhagen von Ense] by Sir Alexander Duff Gordon, Bart.

22. Omoo: a Narrative of Adventures in the South Seas; being a Sequel to the "Residence in the Marquesas Islands;" by Herman Melville.

23. Story of the Battle of Waterloo; by the Rev. G. R. Gleig, M.A.

24. A Voyage up the River Amazon: a Tale; by William H. Edwards. The Wayside Cross: a Tale; by Capt. E. A. Milman.

25. A Popular Account of the Manners and Customs of India; by the Rev. T. Acland. Campaigns of the British Army at Washington and New Orleans, in the years 1814–15; [by the Rev. G. R. Gleig, M.A.]

26. Adventures in Mexico and the Rocky Mountains; by George F. Ruxton.

27. Portugal and Galicia; by the Earl of Carnarvon.

28. Recollections of Bush Life in Australia, during a Residence of Eight Years in the Interior; by Henry William Haygarth. Adventures on the Road to Paris; extracted from the Autobiography of Henry Steffens.

29. Life of Robert, First Lord Clive; by the Rev. G. R. Gleig, M.A.

30. Tales of a Traveller; by "Geoffrey Crayon" [Washington Irving.]

31. Essay on English Poetry; with Notices of the British Poets; by Thomas Campbell.

32. Historical Essays; by Lord Mahon [*afterwards* Earl Stanhope.] Contributed to the *Quarterly Review*.

33. Stokers and Pokers; or, the London and North-Western Railway; [by Sir F. B. Head.] Adventures in the Libyan Desert and the Oasis of Jupiter Ammon; by Bayle St. John.

34. Residence at Sierra Leone; by "A Lady;" edited by the Hon. Mrs. Norton.

35. Life of Sir Thomas Munro; by the Rev. G. R. Gleig, M.A.

36. Memoir of Sir Thomas Fowell Buxton, Bart. Edited by his Son, Charles Buxton, B.A.

37. Oliver Goldsmith; a Biography; by Washington Irving.

HOME (Hon. Henry). [*See* Lord Kames.]

HOME (JOHN). An Account of the Life and Writings of; by Henry MacKenzie, F.R.S.E. 8vo. Edinb, 1822. C 8 T 45

Douglas: a Tragedy. (Bell's Brit. Tieatre.) 18mo. Lond., 1791. H 2 P 30

Anotier copy. (Brit. Tieatre.) 12mo. Lond., 1808. H 1 P 16

Anotier copy. (New Eng. Tieatre.) 12mo. Lond., 1789. H 2 P 25

Anotier copy. [*See* BRIT. DRAMA 2.]

Works of; to wiici is prefixed an Account of his Life and Writings, by H. MacKenzie. 3 vols. 8vo. Edinb., 1822. J 3 S 18–20

HOME FRIEND (THE). A Weekly Miscellany of Amusement and Instruction, publisied under the direction of the Committee of General Literature and Education, appointed by the Society for promoting Ciristian Knowledge. 8vo. Lond., 1853. ME 3 R

HOME MISSIONARY SOCIETY. [*See* CONGREGATIONAL HOME MISSIONARY SOCIETY.]

HOMER. Carmina Homerica, Immanuel Bekker emendabat et annotabat. Volumen prius, Ilias: volumen alterum, Odyssea. (Greek Text.) 2 vols 8vo. Bonnæ, 1858. H 9 T 1, 2

Clavis Homerica; sive Lexicon vocabulorum omnium, quæ continentur in Homeri Iliade, et potissima parte Odysseæ, a Sam. Patricio, LL.D., aucta. 8vo. Edinb., 1811. H 7 S 21

Grammar of the Homeric Dialect. [*See* MONRO, D. B.]

Homer; translated by A. Pope. (Fam. Clas. Lib.) 3 vols. 18mo. Lond., 1833. J 15 P 16–18

Homeri Ilias, Græce et Latine, annotationes in usum Serenissimi Principis Gulielmi Augusti, Ducis de Cumberland, &c., regio jussu scripsit atque edidit Samuel Clarke, S.T.P. Editio quinta decima. 2 vols. 8vo. Lond., 1811. H 7 S 17, 18

Homeri Odyssea, Græce et Latine; edidit, annotationesque, ex Notis nonnullis Manuscriptis a Samuele Clarke, S.T.P. Editio tertia. 2 vols. 8vo. Glasguæ, 1799. H 7 S 19, 20

Homer's Iliad, in English Riymed Verse; by Ciarles Merivale. 2 vols. 8vo. Lond., 1869. H 8 U 17, 18

Iliad and Odyssey; translated by Pope. [*See* CHLMERS, A.]

Iliad and Odyssey of; translated by A. Pope. [*See* JOHNSON, DR. S.]

Iliad of Homer; done into English Verse, by Artiur S. Way, M.A. Sm. 4to. Lond., 1885. H 5 U 23

Iliad of; literally translated, with explanatory Notes, by Tieodore Alois Buckley, B.A. 12mo. Lond., 1876. H 5 S 36

Iliad of; rendered into English Blank Verse, by Edward, Earl of Derby. 2 vols 12mo. Lond., 1867. H 6 R 3, 4

Iliad of; translated by Alexander Pope; with Observations on Homer and iis Works, by the Rev. J. S. Watson, M.A., &c. Illustrated with Flaxman's Designs. 12mo. Lond., 1869. H 7 Q 16

HOMER.—*continued.*

Iliads of; with a Verse Tiaislation, by W. C. Green, M.A. Vol 1. Books 1–12. 8vo. Lond., 1884. H 8 Q 36

Iliads of Homer, Prince of Poets; never before in any Language truly translated, with a Comment on some of iis ciief Places, by George Ciapman; with Notes, &c. 2 vols. sq. 12mo. Lond., 1865. H 6 Q 21, 22

The Odyssey of, engraved from the Compositions of Join Flaxman. [*See* FLAXMAN, J.]

Odyssey of; translated by Alexander Pope; with Observations and Notes, by the Rev. J. S. Watson, M.A., &c. Illustrated with Flaxman's Designs. 12mo. Lond., 1866. H 7 Q 17

Odyssey of; translated into English Prose; with explanatory Notes, by "A Member of the University of Oxford" [Henry Cary, M.A.] 2 vols. 8vo. Lond., 1823. J 12 U 1

Odyssey of; with the Hymns, Epigrams, and Battle of the Frogs and Mice, literally translated, with explanatory Notes, by Tieodore Alois Buckley, B.A. 12mo. Lond., 1878. H 5 S 35

Studies on Homer and the Homeric Age. [*See* GLADSTONE, RT. HON. W. E.]

HOMESTEADS FOR THE PEOPLE, and Maniood Suffrage: in a series of Letters, from "Peter Papineau," to Mr. Join Bull, Digger, Bendigo. 8vo. Melb., 1855. MJ 2 R 19

HOME VISITING AND RELIEF SOCIETY. Reports of, 1863–64; with the Financial Statement, and Names of Donors and Subscribers. 12mo. Sydney, 1863–64. MF 3 P 10

HOMMAIRE DE HELL (XAVIER). Les Steppes de la Mer Caspienne, le Caucase, la Crimée, et la Russie Méridionale: Voyage Pittoresque, Historique, et Scientifique. Voyage qui a remporté le grand prix décerné en 1844 par la Société royale de Géographie de France. 3 vols. roy. 8vo. Paris, 1843–44. D 8 U 3–5

Atlas [to above]. Fol. Paris, 1845. D 2 P 5 ‡

Travels in the Steppes of the Caspian Sea, the Crimea, the Caucasus, &c.; with additions from various sources. 8vo. Lond., 1847. D 8 U 6

HONAN (MICHAEL BURKE). Court and Camp of Don Carlos; being the Results of a late Tour in the Basque Provinces, &c. 8vo. Lond., 1836. D 8 R 17

HONCHARENKO (AGAPIUS). Russian and English Pirase Book. 12mo. San Francisco, 1868. K 11 V 7

HONDORFFIUS (A.) [*See* ANDREAS HONDORFFIUS.]

HONE (WILLIAM). Ancient Mysteries described, especially the English Miracle Plays, founded on the Apocryial New Testament Story, extant among the unpublised Manuscripts in the Britisi Museum. 8vo. Lond., 1823. H 2 T 26

Every Day Book; Year Book; and Table Book; or, Everlasting Calendar of Popular Amusements. 4 vols. 8vo. Lond., 1841. J 8 T 17–20

HONE (WILLIAM), AND OTHERS [Squibs, Facetiæ, and Miscellanies]. 8vo. Lond. and Norwich, 1782–1820. J 9 V 23

Dr. Slop; origin of Dr. Slop's Name. Buonaparte-phobia; or, Cursing made easy to the meanest capacity: a Dialogue between the Editor of *The Times*, Dr. Slop, my Uncle Toby, and my Father.

The Dorchester Guide; or, a House that Jack built; with thirteen Cuts.

The Political House that Jack built; with thirteen Cuts.

The British Constitution Triumphant; or, a Picture of the Radical Conclave.

The Book of Wonders; in fourteen Chapters; embellished with illustrative Engravings, and dedicated to Her most Gracious Majesty Queen Caroline.

The Man in the Moon, &c.; with fifteen Cuts.

Another Ministerial Defeat! The Trial of the Dog for biting the Noble Lord; with the whole of the Evidence at length, taken in short hand; by the author of "The Official Account of the Noble Lord's Bite."

Norfolk Election Budget, Nos. 1–5.

Memoirs of the Life and Writings (Prose and Verse) of Richard Gardner, Esq., [Richard Gardiner] *alias* Dick Merry-fellow, of serious and facetious Memory.

HONIGBERGER (JOHN MARTIN). Thirty-five Years in the East: together with an Original Materia Medica, and a Medical Vocabulary in four European and five Eastern Languages. 2 vols. (in 1). 8vo. Lond., 1852. D 5 S 37

HONOLULU ALMANAC AND DIRECTORY (THE), 1886. Edited by R. J. Creighton. 8vo. Honolulu, 1886. ME 3 S

HONORIUS (AUGUSTODUNENSIS). Opera omnia. [*See* MIGNE, J. P., SERIES LATINA, 172.]

HOOD (REV. EDWIN PAXTON). Edwin Paxton Hood, Poet and Preacher: a Memorial; by G. H. Giddins. 12mo. Lond., 1886. C 2 Q 20

Oliver Cromwell; his Life, Times, Battle-fields, and Contemporaries. 2nd ed. 8vo. Lond., 1884. C 4 T 2

The Throne of Eloquence: Great Preachers, Ancient and Modern. 8vo. Lond., 1885. G 1 R 6

Vocation of the Preacher. 8vo. Lond., 1886. G 3 P 17

William Wordsworth: a Biography. 8vo. Lond., 1856. C 4 U 39

HOOD (JOHN). Australia and the East: being a Journal Narrative of a Voyage to New South Wales in an Emigrant Ship, in the years 1841 42. 8vo. Lond., 1843.* MD 4 W 28

HOOD (THOMAS). Anecdote Life of. [*See* TIMBS, J.]

Comic Annual, 1832 39, 1842. 9 vols. 12mo. Lond., 1832 42. J 1 V 21 29

Hood in Scotland: Reminiscences of Thomas Hood, Poet and Humorist; collected and arranged by Alexander Elliot. 4to. Dundee, 1885. C 5 U 12

Hood's Magazine and Comic Miscellany. 10 vols. 8vo. Lond., 1844 48. J 10 U 19 28

Hood's Own; or, Laughter from Year to Year. 2 vols. 8vo. Lond., 1862 65. J 10 U 17, 18

HOOD (THOMAS).—*continued.*

Memorials of; edited by his Daughter; with a Preface and Notes by his Son. 2 vols. 8vo. Lond., 1860. C 3 U 13, 14

Up the Rhine. 2nd ed. 8vo. Lond., 1840. D 8 Q 49

Whimsicalities: a Periodical Gathering. 2 vols. 8vo. Lond., 1844. J 9 P 20, 21

Works of, Comic and Serious, in Prose and Verse; edited, with Notes, by his Son. 7 vols. 8vo. Lond., 1862–63. J 9 P 13–19

HOOD (THOMAS). The Days of Chivalry; or, the Legend of Croquemitaine; freely translated from the French of L'Epine. [*See* L'EPINE, E.]

HOOD (T. H.) Notes of a Cruise in H.M.S. *Fawn* in the Western Pacific, 1862. 8vo. Edinb., 1863.* MD 2 V 31

HOOGEVEEN (HENDRIK). Doctrina Particularum Linguæ Græcæ; in epitomen redegit C. G. Schütz. 8vo. Glasguæ, 1813. K 12 U 3

HOOGSTRATEN (DR. VAN). [*See* HANNOT, S.]

HOOK (THEODORE EDWARD). Life and Remains of; by the Rev. R. H. D. Barham. 2 vols. 8vo. Lond., 1849. C 3 U 15, 16

Life of Gen. the Rt. Hon. Sir David Baird, Bart., G.C.B., K.C., &c. 2 vols. 8vo. Lond., 1832. C 2 V 12, 13

HOOK (VERY REV WALTER FARQUHAR), D.D. The Church and its Ordinance; edited by the Rev. W. Hook. 2 vols. 8vo. Lond., 1876. G 1 Q 13, 14

A Church Dictionary. 12th ed. 8vo. Lond., 1877. K 18 R 20

Lives of the Archbishops of Canterbury, and Index. 12 vols. 8vo. Lond., 1860–84. G 1 Q 1–12

HOOKE (NATHANIEL). Roman History, from the Building of Rome to the Ruin of the Commonwealth. 6 vols. 8vo. Lond., 1823. B 30 T 1–6

HOOKER (SIR JOSEPH DALTON), M.D., &c. Botany of the Antarctic Voyage of H.M. Discovery Ships *Erebus* and *Terror*, in the years 1839–43, under the command of Captain Sir James Clark Ross, Kt., R.N., &c. 6 vols. roy. 4to. Lond., 1844–60. MA 1 Q 6–11 †

Curtis' Botanical Magazine. [*See* CURTIS, W.]

Fourth Excursion to the Passes into Tribet, &c.; with Map. (Pam. 25.) 8vo. Lond., 1850. MJ 2 Q 13

Genera Plantarum. [*See* BENTHAM, G.]

Hand-book of the New Zealand Flora: a systematic Description of the Native Plants of New Zealand, and the Chatham, Kermadec's, Lord Auckland's, Campbell's, and Macquarrie's Islands. 8vo. Lond., 1867.* MA 1 T 28

Himalayan Journals; or, Notes of a Naturalist in Bengal, the Sikkim and Nepal Himalayas, the Khasia Mountains, &c. With Illustrations. 2 vols. 8vo. Lond., 1854 D 5 T 29, 30

HOOKER (Sir Joseph Dalton), M.D., &c.—*continued.*
Introductory Essay to the Flora of New Zealand. Roy 4to. Lond., 1853.   MA 1 Q 8 †

Rhododendrons of Sikkim-Himalaya; edited by Sir W. J. Hooker, K.H., &c. 4to. Lond., 1849.   A 1 S 7 ‡

Student's Flora of the British Islands. 12mo. Lond., 1878.   A 4 P 8

Oceanic Sketches; with a Botanical Appendix. [*See* Nightingale, T.]

On the Flora of Australia: its Origin, Affinities, and Distribution; being an Introductory Essay to the Flora of Tasmania. Roy. 4to. Lond., 1859.* MA 1 Q 13 †

HOOKER (Richard). Ecclesiastical Polity, and other Works. 3 vols. 8vo. Lond., 1830. G 1 P 12–14

Life of; by Isaak Walton. 12mo. Lond., 1825. C 1 S 19

Another copy. 8vo. Lond., 1884.   C 2 R 34

Of the Laws of Ecclesiastical Polity; edited by R. W. Church, M.A. 2nd ed. (Clar. Press.) 12mo. Oxford, 1873.   G 16 P 30

HOOKER (Sir William Jackson), LL.D., &c. Botanical Miscellany; containing Figures and Descriptions of such Plants as recommend themselves by their novelty, rarity, or history. 3 vols. roy. 8vo. Lond., 1830–33. A 4 U 15–17

The British Flora; comprising the Phænogamous or Flowering Plants and Ferns. 8vo. Lond., 1830. A 4 Q 3

Century of Ferns; being Figures, with brief Descriptions, of one hundred new, or rare, or imperfectly known species of Ferns, from various parts of the World. Imp. 8vo. Lond., 1854.   A 4 V 13

Companion to the Botanical Magazine. 2 vols. 8vo. Lond., 1835–36.   A 4 U 1, 2

Flora Londinensis. [*See* Curtis, W.]

Journal of a Tour in Iceland, in the Summer of 1809. 8vo. Yarmouth, 1811.   D 7 T 30

Rhododendrons of Sikkim-Himalaya. [*See* Hooker, Sir J. D.]

Second Century of Ferns; being Figures, with brief Descriptions, of one hundred new, or rare imperfectly known species of Ferns, from various parts of the World. Imp. 8vo. Lond., 1861.   A 4 V 14

HOOLE (Elijah). Madras, Mysore, and the South of India; or, a Personal Narrative of a Mission to those Countries, from 1820 to 1828. 2nd ed. 8vo. Lond., 1844.   D 5 Q 5

HOOLE (John). Cleonice, Princess of Bithynia: a Tragedy. 18mo. Lond., 1795.   H 2 P 16

Cyrus: a Tragedy. (Bell's Brit. Theatre.) 18mo. Lond., 1795.   H 2 P 40

Orlando Furioso; translated from the Italian of Ludivico Ariosto. [*See* Chalmers, A.]

Tasso's Jerusalem Delivered. [*See* Chalmers A.; *and* Tasso, T.]

Timanthes: a Tragedy. (Bell's Brit. Theatre.) 18mo. Lond., 1795.   H 2 P 16

HOOPER (Capt. C. L.), U.S.R.M. Cruise of U.S. Revenue Steamer *Thomas Corwin* in the Arctic Ocean, 1881. Sm. fol. Wash., 1884.   D 36 P 4 ‡

HOOPER (Rt. Rev. George). Inquiry into the state of the Ancient Measures, the Attick, the Roman, and especially the Jewish. 8vo. Lond., 1721. A 27 S 2

HOOPER (Dr. John). Writings of. [*See* British Reformers 6.]

HOOPER (John). Trial of. [*See* Trials.]

HOOPER (Mary). Cookery for Invalids, Persons of delicate Digestion, and for Children. 8vo. Lond., 1876. A 6 Q 27

HOOPER (Robert), M.D., &c. Lexicon Medicum; or, Medical Dictionary. 8th ed., revised, corrected, and improved by Klein Grant, M.D. 8vo. Lond., 1848.   K 9 R 3

HOOPER (W.), M.D. Treatise on Man. [*See* Helvetius, C. A.]

HOOPER (Lieut. William Hulme), R.N. Ten Months among the Tents of the Tuski: Incidents of a Boat Expedition in search of Sir John Franklin. 8vo. Lond., 1853.   D 4 R 35

HOOPER (W. H.), and PHILLIPS (W. C.) Manual of Marks on Pottery and Porcelain: a Dictionary of Easy Reference. Sq. 18mo. Lond., 1876. K 18 P 4

HOPE (G. W.) Letter respecting the Grant of a Conditional Title to the Lands of the New Zealand Company. [*See* New Zealand.]

HOPE (James L. A.) In Quest of Coolies. Illustrated. 8vo. Lond., 1872.   MD 5 P 5

HOPE (Thomas). Analytical Index to an Historical Essay on Architecture. 8vo. Lond., 1836. A 2 Q 33

Anastasius; or, Memoirs of a Greek; written at the Close of the 18th Century. 4th ed. 3 vols. 8vo. Lond., 1827.   J 11 R 21–23

Costumes of the Ancients. 2 vols. 8vo. Lond., 1841.   A 8 T 26, 27

Historical Essay on Architecture; illustrated from Drawings made in Italy and Germany. 2 vols. 8vo. Lond., 1840.   A 2 Q 32, 33

HOPEFUL. [*See* Taken in.]

HOPE-SCOTT (James Robert), D.C.L., &c. Memoirs of; with Selections from his Correspondence, by Robert Ornsby, M.A. 2 vols. 8vo. Lond., 1884. C 7 P 25, 26

HOPKINS (Edward W.), Ph.D. Ordinances of Manu; translated from the Sanskrit. [*See* Manu.]

HOPKINS (Evan), C.E., &c. On the Geology of the Gold-bearing Rocks of the World, and the Gold-fields of Victoria. 8vo. Melh., 1853.   MJ 2 R 20

HOPKINS (ISAAC). Illustrated Australasian Bee Manual; with which is incorporated the "New Zealand Bee Manual," enlarged by the Author, assisted by T. J. Mulvany. 3rd ed. 8vo. Sydney, 1886.   MA 2 T 15

Illustrated New Zealand Bee Manual; also, Bee-keepers' Axioms, Honey Recipes, and Bee-keepers' Calendar of Operations. 8vo. Thames, N.Z., 1881.   MA 2 T 14

HOPKINS (MANLEY). Hand-book of Average : to which is added a Chapter on Arbitration. 3rd ed. 8vo. Lond., 1868.   F 6 V 22

Hawaii : the Past, Present, and Future of its Island-Kingdom : an Historical Account of the Sandwich Islands (Polynesia). 8vo. Lond., 1862.   MB 2 P 27

Another copy. 2nd ed., revised and continued. 8vo. Lond., 1866.   MB 2 P 28

HOPKINS (LIEUT. S.), R.A. Manual of Artillery Exercises, for the Use of of the Volunteer Corps of New South Wales. 8vo. Sydney, 1871.   MA 2 V 7

HOPKINSON (JOSEPH), M.A., &c. Electrostatic Capacity of Glass. (Roy. Soc. Pubs., 5.) 4to. Lond., 1878.   A 11 P 6 †

Residual Charge of the Leyden Jar. (Roy. Soc. Pubs., 3.) 4to. Lond., 1876.   A 11 P 4 †

Residual Charge of the Leyden Jar : Dielectric Properties of different Glasses. (Roy. Soc. Pubs., 5.) 4to. Lond., 1878.   A 11 P 6 †

HOPLEY (Miss CATHERINE COOPER). Snakes : Curiosities and Wonders of Serpent Life. 8vo. Lond., 1882.   A 14 Q 2

HOPPNER (RICHARD BELGRAVE). Voyage round the World. [*See* KRUSENSTERN, CAPT. A. J. VON.]

HORATIUS FLACCUS (QUINTUS). Horatius Restitutus ; or, the Books of Horace, arranged in chronological order ; with a preliminary Dissertation and Treatise on the Metres of Horace, by J. Tate. 2nd ed. 8vo. Lond., 1837.   H 8 U 37

New School Series: Lyra Romana ; or, Extracts from Horace. (Lyric only.) 18mo. Sydney, 1870.   MH 1 P 48

Odes and Epodes of Horace : a Metrical Translation into English ; with Introduction and Commentaries, by Lord Lytton : with Latin text. 8vo. Lond., 1869.   H 7 U 44

Odes and Epodes of Horace ; translated literally and rhythmically by W. Sewell, B.D. 12mo. Lond., 1850.   H 8 S 24

Odes, Epodes, and Satires of Horace ; translated into English Verse, by Theodore Martin. 3rd ed. 8vo. Edinb., 1870.   H 7 S 37

Opera omnia, ex Editione J. C. Zeunii, cum Notis et Interpretationis in usum Delphini ; curante A. J. Valpy, A.M. 5 vols. 8vo. Lond., 1825.   J 13 Q 12–16

Studies, Literary and Historical, in the Odes of Horace. [*See* VERRALL, A. W.]

Works of ; translated by Philip Francis, D.D. (Fam. Clas. Lib.) 2 vols. 12mo. Lond., 1831.   J 15 P 19, 20

Works of ; translated by Philip Francis, D.D. [*See* CHALMERS, A.]

HORATIUS FLACCUS (QUINTUS).—*continued.*

Works of : translated literally into English Prose, by C. Smart, M.A. ; revised, with Notes, by Theodore Alois Buckley, B.A. 12mo. Lond., 1875.   H 5 S 40

Works of ; translated into English Prose, with the original Latin : begun by D. Watson, revised, &c., by S. Patrick. 4th ed. 2 vols. 8vo. Lond., 1760.   H 8 V 36, 37

Works of ; translated into English Verse, with a Life and Notes, by Sir Theodore Martin, K.C.B. 2 vols. 8vo. Edinb., 1881.   H 6 V 26, 27

HORDEN (RT. REV. J.), D.D., BISHOP OF MOOSONEE. Grammar of the Cree Language, as spoken by the Cree Indians of North America. 12mo. Lond., 1881.   K 11 S 35

HORE (REV. A. H.), M.A. The Church in England, from William III to Victoria. 2 vols. 8vo. Lond., 1886.   G 8 R 15, 16

Eighteen Centuries of the Church in England. 8vo. Oxford, 1881.   G 1 P 17

HORE (J. P.) History of Newmarket and the Annals of the Turf. 3 vols. 8vo. Lond., 1886.   B 3 T 15–17

HORMANN (LUDWIG VON). Tirol and Vorarlberg. [*See* UNSER VATERLAND.]

HORN (FREDERIK WINKEL), PH.D. History of the Literature of the Scandinavian North, from the most Ancient Times to the Present ; translated by Rasmus B. Anderson ; with a Biography of the most important Books in the English Language relating to the Scandinavian Countries, prepared by Thorvald Solberg. 8vo. Chicago, 1884.   B 2 R 12

HORN (MELVILL). Letter on Missions, addressed to the Protestant Ministers of the British Churches. (Pam. Bc.) 8vo. Bristol, 1794.   G 16 S 18

HORNADAY (WILLIAM TEMPLE). Two Years in the Jungle : the Experiences of a Hunter and Naturalist in India, Ceylon, the Malay Peninsula, and Borneo. Illustrated. 8vo. Lond., 1885.   D 4 T 15

HORNBROOK RAGGED SCHOOLS (THE). Circular. (Pam. E.) 4to. Melb., 1862.   MJ 2 S 2

HORNBY (REAR-ADM. G. T. PHIPPS). Cruise round the World of the Flying Squadron, 1869–70. [*See* BRUCE, LIEUT. J. A. T.]

HORNBY (EMELIA BITHYNIA), LADY. Constantinople during the Crimean War. Roy. 8vo. Lond., 1863.   D 8 V 5

HORNE (RT. REV. GEORGE). Commentary on the Book of Psalms. Roy. 8vo. Lond., 1829.   G 1 P 3

HORNE (JOHN), F.L.S., &c. A Year in Fiji ; or, an Inquiry into the Botanical, Agricultural, and Economical Resources of the Colony. 8vo. Lond., 1881.   MD 3 R 34

HORNE (.) Adventures of Naufragus : written by himself. 2nd ed. 12mo. Lond., 1828.   D 5 P 15

HORNE (RICHARD HENRY HENGIST). Australian Facts and Prospects ; to which is prefixed the Author's Australian Autobiography. 12mo. Lond., 1859.* MD 1 Q 14

History of Napoleon. Illustrated. 2 vols. roy. 8vo. Lond., 1841–44. C 8 T 38, 39

Letters of Elizabeth Barrett Browning, addressed to Richard Hengist Henry Horne; with Comments on Contemporaries; edited by S. R. T. Mayer. 2 vols. 8vo. Lond., 1877. C 3 U 30, 31

Prometheus, the Fire-bringer. [With Portrait.] Australian ed. 8vo. Melb., 1866. MH 1 Q 4

Another copy. MH 1 S 21

South Sea Sisters: a Lyric Masque, written for the Intercolonial Exhibition of Australasia, 1866 ; with Translations into French and German Verse. 8vo. Melb., 1866. MH 1 Q 4

Another copy. MH 1 S 21

HORNE (THOMAS HARTWELL), M.A. Complete Grazier; or, Farmer's and Cattle-breeder's and Dealear's Assistant; by "A Lincolnshire Grazier"; with Cuts by Bewick. 8vo. Lond., 1830. A 1 S 10

Introduction to the Critical Study and Knowledge of the Holy Scriptures. Illustrated. 6th ed., corrected and enlarged. 4 vols. 8vo. Lond., 1828. G 1 P 4–7

Manual of Biblical Bibliography. 8vo. Lond., 1839. K 18 R 25

HORNE-TOOKE (JOHN). [*See* TOOKE, J. HORNE.]

HORREBOW (N.) Natural History of Iceland. Fol. Lond., 1758. A 16 S 10 ‡

HORSBURGH (JAMES), F.R.S. India Directory; or, Directions for Sailing to and from the East Indies, China, New Holland, Cape of Good Hope, Brazil, and the interjacent Ports. 3rd ed. 2 vols. 4to. Lond., 1826. F 8 P 15, 16 †

HORSES AND ROADS; or, How to keep a Horse Sound on his Legs; by "Free Lance." 8vo. Lond., 1880. A 1 P 41

HORSFIELD (THOMAS WALKER), F.S.A. History, Antiquities, and Topography of the County of Sussex. 2 vols. Roy. 4to. Lewes, 1835. B 15 R 5, 6 ‡

HORSLEY (J.) Britannia Romana; or, the Roman Antiquities of Britain. Fol. Lond., 1732. B 15 S 15 ‡

HORSLEY (SAMUEL), LL.D., &c. Speeches of, in Parliament. 8vo. Dundee, 1813. F 13 Q 1

HORTICULTURAL MAGAZINE AND GARDENERS' CALENDAR OF N.S.W. (Pam. Ca.) 8vo. Sydney, 1865. MA 1 Q 7

HORTICULTURAL SOCIETY (AUSTRALIAN). [*See* AUSTRALIAN HORTICULTURAL SOCIETY.]

HORTICULTURAL SOCIETY OF LONDON. Transactions. 4to. Lond., 1825–26. A 5 Q 28

HORTICULTURAL SOCIETY OF SYDNEY. Annual Reports ; with the Rules, and List of Members. (Pam. Dl.) 8vo. Sydney, 1864–65. MF 3 P 11

HORTON (JAMES AFRICANUS B.), M.D. Physical and Medical Climate and Meteorology of the West Coast of Africa ; with valuable Hints to Europeans for the Preservation of Health in the Tropics. 8vo. Lond., 1867. A 12 R 9

HORTON (RICHARD). Complete Measurer ; setting forth the Measurement of Boards, Glass, &c. 3rd ed. (Weale.) 12mo. Lond., 1876. A 17 Q 8

HORWOOD (A. J.) Milton's Common-place Book (Introduction). [*See* MILTON, J.]

HOSACK (JOHN). Mary, Queen of Scots, and her Accusers; embracing a Narrative of Events, from the Death of James v, in 1542, until the Death of the Regent Murray, in 1570. 2 vols. 8vo. Edinb., 1869–74. C 6 T 16, 17

On the Rise and Growth of the Law of Nations, as established by general Usage and by Treaties, from the Earliest Time to the Treaty of Utrecht. 8vo. Lond., 1882. F 8 P 24

HOSMER (JAMES K.) The Jews in Ancient, Mediæval, and Modern Times. 8vo. Lond., 1886. B 14 Q 46

Short History of German Literature. 8vo. St. Louis, 1879. B 9 R 19

HOSPITALIER (E.) Modern Applications of Electricity; translated and enlarged by Julius Maier, Ph.D. Illustrated. 8vo. Lond., 1882. A 6 Q 13

Another copy. 2nd ed., revised, with many Additions. 2 vols. 8vo. Lond., 1883. A 5 U 27, 28

HOTOMAN (FRANCIS). Franco-Gallia ; or, an Account of the Ancient Free State of France, and most other Parts of Europe, before the loss of their Liberties; written originally in Latin, in the year 1574, and translated into English, by [Robert, Viscount Molesworth]. 2nd ed. 8vo. Lond., 1721. B 9 P 22

HOTTEN (JOHN CAMDEN), "THEODORE TAYLOR." Abyssinia and its People ; or, Life in the Land of Prester John. 8vo. Lond., 1868. D 1 T 27

Dictionary of Modern Slang, Cant, and Vulgar Words, used at the present day, in the Streets of London, the Universities of Oxford and Cambridge, the Houses of Parliament, the Dens of St. Giles, and Palace of St. James; by "A London Antiquary." 12mo. Lond., 1859. K 11 U 19

Original Lists of Persons of Quality, Emigrants, Religious Exiles, Political Rebels, Serving Men sold for a term of years, Apprentices, Children stolen, Maidens pressed, and others who went from Great Britain to the American Plantations, 1600–1700. Imp. 8vo. Lond., 1874. B 18 S 3 ‡

Sarcastic Notices of the Long Parliament. [*See* LONG PARLIAMENT.]

Thackeray, the Humourist and the Man of Letters: the Story of his Life and Labours. 8vo. Lond., 1864. C 4 S 44

HOUDIN (JEAN EUGÈNE ROBERT). Memoirs of, Ambassador, Author, and Conjuror; written by himself. 2 vols. 8vo. Lond., 1859.   C 3 Q 23, 24

The Sharper detected and exposed. 8vo. Lond., 1863.   A 17 U 19

HOUEL (JEAN). Voyage Pittoresque des Isles de Sicile, de Lipari, et de Malte. 4 vols. imp. fol. Paris, 1782–87.   D 34 P 1–4 ‡

HOUGH (GEORGE SCOTT). Brown the Great; or, Press and Stage: a Colloquy. 8vo. Melb., 1868.   MJ 2 R 23

HOUGHTON (RICHARD MONCKTON MILNES), BARON. Memoir of John Keats. [*See* KEATS, J.]

Monographs, Personal and Social; with Portraits. 8vo. Lond., 1873.   C 3 P 30

Poetical Works of. Collected edition; with a Portrait. 2 vols. 12mo. Lond., 1876.   H 6 R 27, 28

HOUGHTON (REV. W.), M.A., &c. British Fresh-water Fishes. Illustrated with a coloured Figure of each Species, drawn from Nature by A. F. Lydon, and numerous Engravings. Fol. Lond., 1884.   A 4 U 2 ‡

Another copy. Coloured Illustrations. 1 vol. (in 2) fol. Lond., 1884.   A 4 U 3, 4 ‡

HOULDING (JOHN R. H.), "OLD BOOMERANG." Australian Capers; or, Christopher Cockles's Colonial Experience. 8vo. Lond., 1867.*   MJ 1 Q 3

Australian Tales and Sketches from Real Life. 8vo. Lond., 1868.*   MJ 1 Q 5

Pioneer of a Family; or, Adventures of a Young Governess; by "J. R. H. Hawthorn." 8vo. Lond., 1881.   MJ 1 Q 9

Rural and City Life: or, the Fortunes of the Stubble Family. 8vo. Lond., 1870.*   MJ 1 Q 7

HOUNSELL BROTHERS. Flags and Signals of all Nations (English, French, and German); edited by G. C. Hounsell. Fol. Lond. (n.d.)   K 23 Q 21 ‡

HOUSE OF COMMONS. Arrangements: Report from the Select Committee on the; with Minutes of Evidence, &c. Fol. Lond., 1867.   A 2 U 33

Debates of the House of Commons. [*See* CORBETT, W.; DEBATES; HANSARD, T. C.; *and* MIRROR OF PARLIAMENT.]

HOUSE OF LORDS. Minutes of Proceedings, 1831–53, 1866–73. 32 vols. Fol. Lond., 1831–73.   E

HOUSE OF REPRESENTATIVES, NEW ZEALAND. [*See* NEW ZEALAND.]

HOUSEHOLD WORDS; conducted by Charles Dickens. 19 vols. 8vo. Lond., 1850–59.   E

HOVEDEN (ROGER DE). Annals of Roger de Hoveden, 732–1201; translated, with Notes, by H. T. Riley, B.A. 2 vols. 8vo. Lond., 1853.   B 3 P 10, 11

HOVELACQUE (ABEL). Grammaire de la Langue Zende. 2 éd. Roy. 8vo. Paris, 1878.   K 13 R 1

HOVELL (CAPT. WILLIAM HILTON). Answer to the Preface of the second edition of Mr. Hamilton Hume's "A Brief Statement of Facts in connection with an Overland Expedition from Lake George to Port Phillip, in 1824." (Pam. L.) 8vo. Sydney, 1874.   MJ 2 P 28

Reply to "A Brief Statement of Facts, in connection with an Overland Expedition from Lake George to Port Phillip, in 1824," published in May last, by Hamilton Hume. 8vo. Sydney, 1855.   MJ 2 R 19
[*See* HUME, H.]

HOVELL (CAPT. WILLIAM HILTON), AND HUME (HENRY). Journey of Discovery to Port Phillip, New South Wales, in 1824–25; edited by W. Bland, Esq., M.D. 2nd ed. (Pam. 1.) 8vo. Sydney, 1837.   MD 2 S 33

Another copy.   MJ 2 P 36

HOVEY (HORACE CARTER). Celebrated American Caverns, especially Mammoth, Wyandot, and Luray. Illustrated. 8vo. Cincinnati, 1882.   A 24 V 6

HOVGAARD (LIEUT. A.) Nordenskiöld's Voyage round Asia and Europe: a Popular Account of the North-east Passage of the *Vega*, 1878–80.; translated from the Danish by H. L. Brækstad. Illustrated. 8vo. Lond., 1882.   D 4 S 4

HOW (HENRY), D.C.L. Mineralogy of Nova Scotia: a Report to the Provincial Government. 8vo. Halifax, 1869.   A 10 Q 4

HOW TO FARM and Settle in Australia: Rural Calendar, and Traveller's Map of Squatting Stations, Townships, and Diggings of Victoria: by "An Old Colonist." 12mo. Lond., 1856.   MA 1 P 1

HOWARD (ALFRED). Biographical Illustrations: consisting of authentic Portraits and Biography of the most Eminent Persons of all Ages and Nations. 4to. Lond., 1830.   C 4 W 4

HOWARD (C.) Farming at Ridgemont, the Estate of Sir T. A. Clifford Constable, Bart. (Pam. 14.) 8vo. York, 1833.   MJ 2 Q 4

HOWARD (CAPT. F.), R.N. Marine Survey of the Northern Territory of South Australia. 8vo. Lond., 1866.   MD 7 Q 56

HOWARD (HENRY). [*See* SURREY, EARL OF.]

HOWARD (JOHN), F.R.S. Account of the Principal Lazarettos in Europe: with various Papers relative to the Plague. 2nd ed., with Additions. Roy. 4to. Lond., 1791.   F 5 V 23

Howard, the Philanthropist, and his Friends; by John Stoughton, D.D. 8vo. Lond., 1884.   C 3 U 26

Memoirs of the Public and Private Life of; compiled from his own Diary, in the possession of his Family, his Confidential Letters, &c., by James Baldwin Brown. 4to. Lond., 1818.   C 3 W 14

State of the Prisons of England and Wales. 4th ed. Roy. 4to. Lond., 1792.   F 5 V 24

HOWARD (LIEUT. EDWARD), R.N. Memoirs of Admiral Sir Sydney Smith, K.C.B., &c. 2 vols. 8vo. Lond., 1839.
C 9 U 21, 22

HOWARD (SIR R.) The Committee: a Comedy. (Bell's Brit. Theatre.) 18mo. Lond., 1792.   H 2 P 42

Another copy. (New Eng. Theatre.) 12mo. Lond., 1789.   H 4 P 20

HOWARD (WILLIAM), F.H.S. Beautiful-leaved Plants. [*See* LOWE, E. J.]

HOWDEN (PETER). Horse Warranty: a Plain and Comprehensive Guide to the various Points to be noted; showing which are essential and which are unimportant. 12mo. Lond. (n.d.)   A 1 P 36

HOWE (EDWARD). [*See* ROWE, R.]

HOWE (GEORGE). New South Wales Pocket Almanack, 1808, 1811, 1813–16, 1818–21. 10 vols. (in 2) 12mo. Sydney, 1808–21.*   ME 4 Q

HOWE (MICHAEL). The Bushranger of Van Diemen's Land; by J. Bonwick. 8vo. Lond., 1873.*   MJ 1 S 36, 37

Another copy. 2nd ed. 8vo. Lond., 1881.   MJ 1 S 38

HOWE (ADM. RICHARD), EARL, K.G. Life of Earl Howe, K.G., Admiral of the Fleet and General of Marines; by Sir John Barrow, Bart. 8vo. Lond., 1838.   C 7 P 24

HOWE (ROBERT). Australasian Pocket Almanack, 1822–28. 7 vols. (in 3) 12mo. Sydney, 1822–28.   ME 4 Q

Australian Almanack, 1829–33. 5 vols. (in 3) 12mo. Sydney, 1829–33.*   ME 4 Q

Weekly Commercial Express. Fol. Sydney, 1825.   E

HOWELL (MRS. W. MAY). Reminiscences of Australia: the Diggings and the Bush. 8vo. Lond., 1869.* MJ 2 S 28

HOWELL (T. B. AND THOMAS J.) Collection of State Trials and Proceedings for High Treason and other Crimes and Misdemeanors, 1783–1820; with Notes, General Index, &c.; by D. Jardine. 34 vols. roy. 8vo. Lond., 1816–26.   F 2 S 1–T 12

HOWELLS (WILLIAM DEAN). Italian Journeys. 8vo. Lond., 1868.   D 8 Q 13

HOWELS (REV. WILLIAM). Sermons, &c.; with a Memoir by Charles Bowdler. 2nd ed. 2 vols. 8vo. Lond., 1836.   G 3 Q 26, 27

HOWES (GEORGE BOND). An Atlas of Practical Elementary Biology; with a Preface, by Prof. Huxley, P.R.S. Roy. 4to. Lond., 1885.   A 14 V 15

HOWE'S WEEKLY COMMERCIAL EXPRESS. Fol. Sydney, 1825.   ME

HOWISON (JOHN). Sketches of Upper Canada; Domestic, Local, and Characteristic. 8vo. Edinb., 1821. D 3 T 37

HOWITT (ALFRED WILLIAM). Journal of. [*See* BURKE, R. O'H.]

Kamilaroi and Kurnai. [*See* FISON, L.]

3 A

HOWITT (MISS ANNA MARY). An Art Student in Munich. 2 vols. 8vo. Lond., 1853.   D 7 R 45, 46

HOWITT (MRS. MARY). Brothers and Sisters: a Tale. [*See* BREMER, FREDERIKA.]

History of Sweden. [*See* FRYXELL, A.]

Homes of the New World. [*See* BREMER, FREDERIKA.]

Pictorial Calendar of the Seasons. 8vo. Lond., 1862.   J 9 Q 4

HOWITT (RICHARD). Australia: Historical, Descriptive, and Statistic; with an Account of a four years' residence in that Colony.—Notes of a Voyage round the World.— Australian Poems, &c. 12mo. Lond., 1845.* MD 4 P 29

Impressions of Australia Felix, during four years' residence in that Colony.—Notes of a Voyage round the World.— Australian Poems, &c. 12mo. Lond., 1845. MD 4 P 31

HOWITT (WILLIAM). Book of the Seasons; or, the Calendar of Nature. 8vo. Philad., 1842.   A 3 S 29

Boy's Adventures in the Wilds of Australia; or, Herbert's Note-book. 12mo. Lond., 1854.*   MD 1 P 2

Another copy. 12mo. Lond., 1858.   MD 1 P 4

Another copy. 12mo. Lond., 1872.   MD 1 P 5

Colonization and Christianity : a Popular History of the Treatment of the Natives by the Europeans in all their Colonies. 8vo. Lond., 1838.   G 11 P 15

Another copy.   MG 1 P 6

History of Discovery in Australia, Tasmania, and New Zealand, from the earliest date. 2 vols. 8vo. Lond., 1865.*   MB 2 T 1, 2

History of Magic. [*See* ENNEMOSER, J.]

History of the Supernatural in all Ages and Nations, and in all Churches, Christian and Pagan. 2 vols. 8vo. Lond., 1863.   G 8 R 18, 19

Homes and Haunts of the most eminent British Poets. 2 vols. 8vo. Lond., 1863.   J 12 V 10, 11

Land, Labour, and Gold; or, Two Year's in Victoria with Visits to Sydney and Van Diemen's Land. 2 vols. 8vo. Lond., 1855.*   MD 4 S 34, 35

Life in Germany ; or, Scenes, Impressions, and Everyday Life of the Germans. 8vo. Lond., 1849.   D 6 T 20

Pantika ; or, Traditions of the most Ancient Times. 2 vols. 8vo. Lond., 1835.   J 5 P 3, 4

Rural Life of England. Illustrated. 2nd ed. 8vo. Lond., 1840.   D 7 T 15

Tallangetta, the Squatter's Home : a Story of Australian Life. 2 vols. 8vo. Lond., 1857.*   MJ 1 U 26, 27

Two Years' in Victoria ; with Visits to Sydney and Van Diemen's Land. 2nd ed. 2 vols. (in 1) 8vo. Lond., 1860.   MD 4 S 40

Visits to Remarkable Places—Old Halls, Battle-fields, and Scenes illustrative of striking passages in English History and Poetry. 8vo. Lond., 1840.   D 12 T 5

HOWITT (WILLIAM AND MARY). Stories of English and Foreign Life. 8vo. Lond., 1853.　　J 9 Q 5

HOWLEGLAS. Howleglas. [Eulenspiegel.] Edited by Frederic Ouvry. 4to. Lond., 1867.　　J 12 V 15

HOWLEY (EDWARD) Concise History of the English Constitution. 8vo. Lond., 1857.　　B 3 R 13

HOWLEY (JAMES P.), F.M.S. Geological Survey of New-foundland. [*See* MURRAY, A.]

HOWORTH (HENRY H.), F.S.A. History of the Mongols, from the 9th to the 19th Century; with two Maps, by E. G. Ravenstein, F.R.G.S. 3 vols. (in 4) roy. 8vo. Lond., 1876–80.　　B 20 V 1-4

HOWSON (REV. JOHN SAUL), D.D., DEAN OF CHESTER. Ancient Streets and Homesteads of England. [*See* RIMMER, A.]

Life and Epistles of St. Paul. [*See* CONYBEARE, REV. W. J.]

Life and Writings of St. John. [*See* MACDONALD, J. M.]

HOYLE (EDMUND). Hoyle's Games; with Mathematical Analysis of the Chances of the most fashionable Games of the Day; by G. H. ——, Esq. 18mo. Lond., 1871.　　A 17 T 13

HOYLE (WILLIAM EVANS), M.A. The Parasites of Man, and the Diseases which proceed from them. [*See* LEUCKART, R.]

HOZIER (COL. HENRY M.) The Invasions of England: a History of the Past; with Lessons for the Future. 2 vols. 8vo. Lond., 1876.　　B 5 P 39, 40

The Seven Weeks' War: its Antecedents and its Incidents. 12mo. Lond., 1867.　　B 9 R 20, 21

[Life of] Turenne. 8vo. Lond. 1885.　　C 3 U 43

HROTSUITHA (GANDERSHEIMENSIS). Opera omnia. [*See* MIGNE, J. P., SERIES LATINA, 137.]

HUBBARD (JAMES MASCARENE). Catalogue of the Works of William Shakespeare, original and translated; together with the Shakespeariana embraced in the Barton Collection of the Boston Public Library. Sm. fol. Boston, 1880.　　K 9 P 5 †

HUBER (V. A.) English Universities: edited by F. W. Newman. 2 vols. (in 3) 8vo. Lond., 1843.　　B 5 U 48-50

HÜBNER (JOSEPH ALEXANDER), BARON VON. Life and Times of Sixtus V; translated from the original French, by Hubert E. H. Jerningham. 2 vols. 8vo. Lond., 1872.　　C 9 U 41, 42

Ramble round the World, 1871; translated by Lady Herbert. 2 vols. 8vo. Lond., 1874.　　D 9 S 2, 3

Through the British Empire. With a Map. 2 vols. 8vo. Lond., 1886.　　M D 3 R 5, 6

Vortrag des Freiherrn von Hubner, über seine Reisen in den Sudsee-Inseln, gehalten im Orientalischen Museum am 25 Februar, 1885. 8vo. Wien, 1885.　　M D 5 U 40

HÜBNER (O.) Hübner's Universal Statistical Tables. Roy. 8vo. Lond., 1877.　　F 8 T 7

HÜBNER (DR. E.) Bibliographical Clue to Latin Literature. [*See* MAYOR, PROF. J. E. B.]

HUC (EVARISTE RÉGIS), L'ABBÉ. The Chinese Empire; forming a Sequel to "Recollections of a Journey through Tartary and Thibet." 2 vols. 8vo. Lond., 1855.　　B 2 Q 8, 9

Christianity in China, Tartary, and Thibet. 3 vols. 8vo. Lond., 1857–58.　　G 3 Q 1-3

Travels in Tartary, Thibet, and China, during the years 1844–46; from the French, by W. Hazlitt. 2 vols. 12mo. Lond., 1852.　　D 5 P 37, 38

HUDDERSFORD (W.), AND WARTON (T.) Lives of those eminent Antiquaries, John Leland, Thomas Hearne, and Anthony à Wood. 2 vols. 8vo. Oxford, 1772.　　C 1 V 14, 15

HUDSON (A.) Fabularum Æsopicarum Collectio: accedit Interpretatio Latina. [*See* ÆSOP.]

HUDSON (C. T.), AND GOSSE (P. H.) The Rotifera; or, Wheel Animalcules. Plates and Text. 2 vols. imp. 8vo. Lond., 1886.　　A 14 V 4, 5

HUDSON (ELIZABETH HARRIOTT). History of the Jews in Rome, B.C. 160 to A.D. 604. 8vo. Lond., 1882. G 3 Q 28

HUDSON (REV. H. N.) Shakespeare: his Life, Art, and Characters; with an Historical Sketch of the Origin and Growth of the Drama in England. 2 vols. 8vo. Boston, 1872.　　C 3 Q 48, 49

HUDSON (J.) [*See* MOERIS ATTICISTA.]

HUDSON (J. F.) Railways and the Republic. 8vo. Lond., 1886.　　A 6 8 4

HÜGEL (CHARLES ALEX. ANSELME), BARON DE. Enumeratio Plantarum quas in Novæ Hollandiae, ora Austro-Occidentali ad fluvium Cygnorum et in sinu Regis Georgii. 8vo. Vienna, 1837.　　M A 1 U 29

Travels in Kashmir and the Panjab; containing a particular Account of the Government and Character of the Sikhs; from the German, with Notes, by Major T. B. Jervis. 8vo. Lond., 1845.　　D 4 U 14

HUGGINS (W. J.) View of Hobart Town, on the River Derwent, Van Diemen's Land; with Maps and Views. 4to. Lond., 1830.　　M D 5 S 18

HUGH (WILLIAM). Writings of. [*See* BRITISH REFORMERS.]

HUGHAN (F. M.) The Emigrant, and other Poems. 8vo. Geelong, 1856.　　M H 1 S 21

HUGHES (EDWARD FRANCIS). Lays for Thoughtful Workers. 12mo. Melb., 1875.　　M H 1 S 21

The Millennium: an Epic Poem. 8vo. Melb., 1878.　　M H 1 R 45

HUGHES (HUGH), "TEGAI." Gramadeg Cymraeg; sef, Ieithiadur Athronyddol. 12mo. Caernarfon, 1864.
         K 11 S 41

HUGHES (J.), A.M. The Boscobel Tracts, relating to the Escape of Charles II after the Battle of Worcester, and his subsequent Adventures, &c. 8vo. Edinb., 1830. B 5 S 42

HUGHES (JOHN). Life and Poems of. [*See* CHALMERS, A., *and* JOHNSON, S.]

The Siege of Damascus: a Tragedy. (Bell's Brit. Theatre.) 18mo. Lond., 1793.   H 2 P 22
Another copy. (Brit. Theatre.) 12mo. Lond., 1808
         H 1 P 10
Another copy. (New Eng. Theatre.) 12mo. Lond., 1777.   H 4 P 25
Another copy. [*See* BRIT. DRAMA, 1.]

HUGHES (REV. ROBERT EDGAR), M.A. Two Summer Cruises with the Baltic Fleet in 1854–55, being the Log of the *Pet* Yacht. 8vo. Lond., 1855.   D 9 P 24

HUGHES (SAMUEL), C.E. Construction of Gas-Works and the Manufacture and Distribution of Coal Gas. 6th ed. (Weale). 12mo. Lond., 1880.   A 17 Q 36
Gas Works: their Construction and Arrangement; and the Manufacture and Distribution of Coal Gas; revised by William Richards, C.E. 7th ed. (Weale.) 12mo. Lond., 1885.   A 17 R 6
Treatise on Gas Works, and the Practice of Manufacturing and Distributing Coal Gas. 4th ed. (Weale.) 12mo. Lond., 1871.   A 17 P 3
Treatise on Waterworks for the Supply of Cities and Towns. (Weale.) 12mo. Lond., 1872.   A 17 P 68

HUGHES (S.), LAW (H.), AND BURGOYNE (SIR J. F.) Rudimentary Papers on the Art of Constructing and Repairing Common Roads. (Weale.) 4th ed. 12mo. Lond., 1868.   A 17 P 13

HUGHES (THOMAS), Q.C. G.T.T.: Gone to Texas: Letters from our Boys. 8vo. Lond., 1884.   D 3 8 29
Memoir of Daniel Macmillan. 8vo. Lond., 1832. C 3 V 27
Scouring of the White Horse; or, the Long Vacation Ramble of a London Clerk. 12mo. Camb., 1859.   J 12 S 15

HUGHES (T. M.) Revelations of Spain in 1845. 2 vols. 8vo. Lond., 1845.   B 13 U 14, 15

HUGHES (REV. THOMAS PATRICK), BD Dictionary of Islam. Roy. 8vo. Lond., 1885.   K 18 R 26

HUGHES (WILLIAM), F.R.G.S. Australian Colonies: their Origin and Present Condition. New ed. 12mo. Lond., 1852.*   MD 6 P 37
Another copy. New ed. 12mo. Lond., 1853.   MD 6 P 4
Manual of Geography, Physical, Industrial, and Political. 12mo. Lond., 1869.   D 11 Q 6
Treasury of Geography. [*See* MAUNDER, S.]
Treasury of History. [*See* MAUNDER, S.]
Treasury of Knowledge. [*See* MAUNDER, S.]

HUGHES (MAJOR W. GWYNNE), F.R.G.S., &c. Hill Tracts of Arakan. Roy. 8vo. Rangoon, 1881.   D 5 U 8

HUGO (FLAVINIACENSIS ABBAS). Chronicon. [*See* MIGNE, J. P., SERIES LATINA, 154.]

HUGO (FRANÇOIS VICTOR). Oeuvres complètes de W. Shakespeare. [*See* SHAKESPEARE, W.]

HUGO (THOMAS), M.A., &c. Bewick Collector: a Descriptive Catalogue of the Works of Thomas and John Bewick. 8vo. Lond., 1866–68.   K 8 Q 33
Memoir of Gundulf, Bishop of Rochester, 1077–1108. Roy. 8vo. Lond., 1853.   C 11 P 37
[*See* BEWICK, T. AND J.]

HUGO (VICTOR MARIE), VICOMTE. Excursions along the Banks of the Rhine. 8vo. Lond., 1843.   D 8 P 16
His Life and Works; by G. Barnett Smith. With Portrait. 8vo. Lond., 1885.   C 4 T 15
Oeuvres complètes. Tomes 1–13. Roy. 8vo. Paris, 1880.   J 17 S 1–13
1–13. Poésie.
Selections, chiefly Lyrical, from the Poetical Works of Victor Hugo; translated into English by various Authors; now first collected by Henry Llewellyn Williams. 12mo. Lond., 1885.   H 7 P 34
Study of Victor Hugo; by A. C. Swinburne. 12mo. Lond., 1886.   C 2 Q 18
Translations from the Poems of Victor Hugo; by the Rev. H. Carrington. 18mo. Lond., 1815.   H 6 R 1
Victor Hugo: a Memoir and a Study; by James Cappon, M.A. 8vo. Edinb., 1885.   C 4 T 14
Victor Hugo and his Time; by Alfred Barbou; translated from the French, by Ellen E. Frewer. Imp. 8vo. Lond., 1882.   C 5 W 8

HUGO DE SANCTO VICTORE. Opera omnia. [*See* MIGNE, J. P., SERIES LATINA, 175–177.]

HUHN (A. VON). Struggle of the Bulgarians for National Independence under Prince Alexander. 8vo. Lond., 1886.   B 13 V 17

HUILLARD-BRÉHOLLES (JEAN LOUIS ALPHONSE). Chronicon Placentinum et Chronicon de rebus in Italia gestis historiæ stirpis imperatoriæ suevorum illustrandæ aptissima. 4to. Paris, 1856.   B 17 Q 21 ‡

HUISH (MARCUS BOURNE), LL.B., AND THOMSON (DAVID C.) The Year's Art: a concise Epitome of all Matters relating to the Arts of Painting, Sculpture, and Architecture, 1879–86. 4 vols. 8vo. Lond., 1880–86.   E

HUISH (R.) Treatise on Bees. 8vo. Lond., 1817 A 1 R 18

HULL (PROF. EDWARD), M.A., &c. Building Stones. (Brit. Manuf. Indust.) 12mo. Lond., 1876.   A 17 S 38
Coal-fields of Great Britain: their History, Structure, and Resources; with Maps and Illustrations. 3rd ed., revised and enlarged, embodying the Reports of the Royal Coal Commission. 8vo. Lond., 1873.   A 9 T 1
Another copy. 4th ed., revised. 8vo. Lond., 1881. A 9 T 2

HULL (PROF. EDWARD), M.A., &c.—*continued.*
Contributions to the Physical History of the British Isles. Illustrated. Roy. 8vo. Lond., 1882.				A 10 Q 26

Mount Seir, Sinai, and Western Palestine. With Maps and Illustrations. 8vo. Lond., 1885.				D 4 T 44

Survey of Western Palestine: Physical Geology and Geography of Arabia. [*See* PALESTINE EXPLORATION FUND.]

HULL (HUGH MUNRO), F.R.S., TAS. Experience of Forty Years in Tasmania. 12mo. Lond., 1859. MD 1 Q 13

Royal Kalendar and Guide to Tasmania, for 1860. 12mo. Hobart, 1860.				ME 4 P

Tasmania in 1870; or, Hints to Emigrants, intending Settlers, and Capitalists; with a Description of the Capabilities and Productions of each County in the Colony. 12mo. Hobart, 1870.				MJ 2 P 34

Volunteer List. Tasmania, July, 1861. (Pam. 40.) 12mo. Hobart, 1861.				MJ 2 R 2

HULL (THOMAS). Edward and Eleonora: a Tragedy. (Bell's Brit. Theatre.) 18mo. Lond., 1795.				H 2 P 27

Another copy. [*See* THOMSON, J.]

Henry the Second; or, the Fall of Rosamund: a Tragedy. [*See* MODERN THEATRE, 9.]

HULL (WILLIAM). Remarks on the probable Origin and Antiquity of the Aboriginal Natives of New South Wales; by "A Colonial Magistrate." (Pam. 36.) 8vo. Melh., 1846.				MJ 2 Q 23

HULLAH (MRS. FRANCES). Life of John Hullah, LL.D.; by his Wife. 8vo. Lond., 1886.				C 4 Q 16

HULLAH (JOHN), LL.D. Course of Lectures on the Third, or Transition Period of Musical History. 8vo. Lond., 1865.				A 7 P 1

Cultivation of the Speaking Voice. (Clar. Press.) 2nd ed. 12mo. Oxford, 1874.				A 23 Q 6

History of Modern Music: a Course of Lectures. 2nd ed. 8vo. Lond., 1875.				A 8 Q 9

Life of; by his Wife [Mrs. Frances Hullah.] 8vo. Lond., 1886.				C 4 Q 16

HULME (F. EDWARD), F.L.S., &c. Familiar Wild Flowers. With Coloured Plates. 5 vols. 8vo. Lond., 1878–85.				A 4 Q 15–19

Flower Painting in Water Colours. Roy. 8vo. Lond., 1881.				A 8 R 13

Myth-Land. 12mo. Lond., 1886.				B 37 P 3

Series of Sketches from Nature of Plant Form. Imp. 8vo. Lond., 1868.				A 1 P 3†

Suggestions in Floral Design: Fifty-two Coloured Plates. 5 vols. 8vo. Lond., 1884.				A 23 S 26 ‡

Worked Examination Questions in Plane Geometrical Drawings. 8vo. Lond., 1882.				A 10 V 20

HULME (F. EDWARD), F.L.S., &c., AND HIBBERD (SHIRLEY). Familiar Garden Flowers. 1st and 2nd series. With Coloured Plates. 8vo. Lond., 1880 81. A 4 Q 13, 14

HUMBER (WILLIAM), C.E. Comprehensive Treatise on the Water Supply of Cities and Towns; with numerous Specifications of existing Waterworks. Imp. 4to. Lond., 1876.				A 23 P 16 ‡

Complete Treatise on Cast and Wrought Iron Bridge Construction, including Iron Foundations. Vol. 1, Text. Vol. 2, Plates. 2 vols. fol. Lond., 1870.		A 23 Q 5, 6 ‡

Treatise on the Strength of Materials. [*See* BARLOW, P.]

HUMBERT (AIME). Japan and the Japanese, illustrated; translated by Mrs. Cashel Hoey, and edited by H. W. Bates. Roy. 4to. Lond., 1874.				D 4 R 7†

HUMBERT-BAZILE. (M.) Buffon, sa Famille, ses Collaborateurs, et ses Familiers; par H. N. de Buffon. 8vo. Paris, 1863.				C 10 P 10

HUMBOLDT (FREIDRICH HEINRICH ALEXANDER), BARON VON. Alexander von Humboldt's Reise in die Aequinoctial Gegeden des reuen Continents. In deutscher Bearbeitung von Hermann Hauff. 4 vols. 8vo. Stuttgart, 1859-60.				D 3 T 26, 27

Aspects of Nature in different Lands and different Climates; translated by Mrs. Sabine. 2 vols. 12mo. Lond., 1849.				A 17 T 23, 24

Cosmos: a Sketch of a Physical Description of the Universe: translated from the German, by E. C. Otté, W. S. Dallas, and B. H. Paul. 5 vols. 12mo. Lond., 1871-72.				A 3 R 30-34

Another copy; translated, under the superintendence of Major-Gen. Sir E. Sabine, R.A., by Mrs. Sabine. 4 vols. 8vo. Lond., 1846 58.				A 3 R 26-29

Geognostical Essay on the Superposition of Rocks in both Hemispheres. 8vo. Lond., 1823.				A 9 T 21

Geological Memoirs. [*See* GEOLOGICAL MEMOIRS.]

Island of Cuba; translated from the Spanish, with Notes, and a Preliminary Essay, by J. S. Thrasher. 8vo. Lond., 1856.				D 3 Q 60

Letters of; written between the years 1827 and 1858, to [K. A. L. P.] Varnhagen von Ense; together with Extracts from Varnhagen's Diaries, and Letters from Varnhagen and others to Humboldt. 8vo. Lond., 1860.				C 7 P 2

Life of; compiled in commemoration of the Centenary of his Birth, by J. Löwenberg, Robert Avé Lallemant, and Alfred Dove; edited by Professor Karl Bruhns; translated from the German, by Jane Caroline Lassell. 2 vols. 8vo. Lond., 1873.				C 7 P 27, 28

Life, Travels, and Books of: with an Introduction by Bayard Taylor. 8vo. Lond., 1859.				C 3 Q 27

Meteorological Essays. [*See* ARAGO, F. J. D.]

Oration on Humboldt. [*See* INGERSOLL, COL. R. G.]

Researches concerning the Institutions and Monuments of the Ancient Inhabitants of America; translated by Helen M. Williams. 2 vols. 8vo. Lond., 1814.			B 1 T 24, 25

Vues des Cordillères, et Monumens des Peuples indigènes de l'Amérique. At. fol. Paris, 1810.				D 11 P 23 ‡

HUMBOLDT (FRIEDRICH HEINRICH ALEXANDER), BARON VON, AND BONPLAND (AIMÉ). Personal Narrative of Travels to the Equinoctial Regions of the New Continent, 1799–1809; translated by Helen M. Williams. 3rd ed. 6 vols. 8vo. Lond., 1822–26. D 3 T 19–24

HUMBOLDT (CHARLES WILHELM), BARON VON. Letters to a Female Friend; translated by Catharine M. A. Couper. 2 vols. 8vo. Lond., 1849. C 3 Q 25, 26

Sphere and Duties of Government; translated from the German, by Joseph Coulthard, junr. 8vo. Lond., 1854. F 6 R 14

Über die-Kawi-Sprache auf der Insel Java. 3 vols. 4to. Berlin, 1836–39. K 16 S 13–15

HUME (REV. A.), LL.D., &c. Learned Societies and Printing Clubs of the United Kingdom. 8vo. Lond., 1853. K 17 P 22

Another copy. 8vo. Lond., 1847. K 19 Q 5

HUME (SIR A.) Notices of the Life and Works of Titian. 8vo. Lond., 1829. C 10 P 37

HUME (ALLAN OCTAVIUS). List of the Birds of India. Reference edition, corrected to 1st March, 1879. Roy. 8vo. Calcutta, 1879. A 13 U 27

Lahore to Yârkand; Incidents of the Route and Natural History of the Countries traversed by the Expedition of 1870. [*See* HENDERSON, G.]

HUME (DAVID). Author's Life; written by himself. Vols. 1–7. 7 vols. 8vo. Lond., 1823. B 5 R 1–7

[A Biography]; by Prof. Huxley. (Eng. Men of Letts.) 8vo. Lond., 1879. C 1 U 20

Essays and Treatises on several subjects. 2 vols. 8vo. Edinb., 1817. J 8 S 29–30

Another copy. New ed. 2 vols. 8vo. Edinb., 1825. J 8 S 31, 32

History of England, from the Invasion of Julius Cæsar to the Revolution in 1688; with a short Account of the History of the House and Race of Douglas and Angus. [*No title-page printed.*] 8vo. Glasgow (n.d.) B 13 P 32

Hume; by Prof. W. Knight. (Philosophical Classics for English Readers.) 12mo. Edinb., 1886. C 2 Q 17

Life of David Hume; written by himself. 12mo. Lond., 1826. C 1 P 5

Life and Correspondence of David Hume; by John Hill Burton. 2 vols. 8vo. Edinb., 1846. C 7 P 31, 32

Student's Hume: a History of England, from the Earliest Times to the Revolution in 1688. 12mo. Lond., 1871. B 4 P 13

HUME (DAVID), AND SMOLLETT (DR. TOBIAS), History of England, from the Invasion of Julius Cæsar to the Death of George II, and continued to the Reign of Queen Victoria, 1859, by E. Farr, and E. H. Nolan. Illustrated. 3 vols. imp. 8vo. Lond. (n.d.) B 3 V 13–15

HUME (DAVID), SMOLLETT (TOBIAS), M.D., AND JONES (WM.) History of England, from the Invasion of Julius Cæsar to the Death of George III; with Continuation to the Present Time, by Geo. Dean Wilson. Illustrated. 3 vols. imp. 8vo. Glasgow, 1875. B 3 V 7–9

Another copy: with Coloured Plates. 3 vols. imp. 8vo. Glasgow, 1875. B 3 V 10–12

HUME (FERGUS W.) Mystery of a Hansom Cab, a realistic Story of Melbourne Life: a Sensational Novel. 4th ed. 8vo. Melb., 1887. MJ 1 U 25

HUME ALEXANDER (HAMILTON). Answer to the Preface to the Second Edition of Mr. Hamilton Hume's "A Brief Statement of Facts." [*See* HOVELL, CAPT. W. H.]

Brief Statement of Facts in connection with an Overland Expedition from Lake George to Port Phillip, in 1824. 8vo. Sydney, 1855. MD 2 S 33

Another copy. 2nd ed., with Portrait. 8vo. Yass, 1873. MJ 2 P 28

Another copy. 2nd ed., with Portrait. 8vo. Yass, 1873. MJ 2 R 10

Another copy. 3rd ed., with Addenda. 8vo. Yass, 1874. MD 1 U 13

Journey of Discovery to Port Phillip. [*See* HOVELL, W. H.]

HUME (ANDREW HAMILTON). Life of Edward John Eyre, late Governor of Jamaica. 8vo. Lond., 1867. MC 1 Q 6

HUME (JAMES DEACON). Life of; by Charles Badham, M.A. 8vo. Lond., 1859. C 4 Q 15

HUME (SIR PATRICK). Narrative of Occurrences in the Expedition of the Earl of Argyle. [*See* ROSE, RT. HON. G.]

HUMPHREYS (HENRY NOEL). Coin Collector's Manual; or, Guide to the Numismatic Student in the formation of a Cabinet of Coins. 2 vols. 8vo. Lond., 1871–76. A 13 S 30, 31

Coinage of the British Empire, from the Earliest Period to the Present Time. Roy. 8vo. Lond., 1854. A 13 S 28

History of the Art of Printing, from its Invention to the 16th Century. Illustrated. 2nd ed. 4to. Lond., 1868. B 14 R 1

Origin and Progress of the Art of Writing. Illustrated. Roy. 8vo. Lond., 1853. A 8 R 20

HUMPHREYS (JAMES). Observations on the Actual State of the English Laws of Real Property. 8vo. Lond., 1827. F 8 R 10

HUMPHREYS (J. D.) Correspondence of Philip Doddridge. [*See* DODDRIDGE, P.]

HUMPHREYS (W. H.) Picture of Greece. [*See* EMERSON, J.]

HUMPHRIS (HENRY D.) The Principles of Perspective, illustrated in a Series of Examples: Descriptive Treatise for the Use of Architects, Art Masters, Students, &c. 8vo. Lond., 1869.   A 7 Q 2

[Plates to] above. Ob. 4to. Lond., 1869.   A 20 P 27 ‡

HUMPHRY (GEORGE MURRAY), M.D., &c. Old Age, and Changes incidental to it: the Annual Oration delivered before the Medical Society of London, May 4th, 1885. 12mo. Camb., 1885.   A 12 P 38

HUNDRED GREATEST MEN (THE): Portraits reproduced from line and rare Steel Engravings; with a general Introduction to the Work, by Ralph Waldo Emerson. 8 vols. fol. Lond., 1879–80.   C 1 W 13–20

     1. Poetry: Poets, Dramatists, Novelists.
     2. Art: Architects and Sculptors, Painters, Musicians.
     3. Religion: Religious Founders, Theologians, Reformers.
     4. Philosophy: Metaphysicians, Psychology, Moralists.
     5. History: Historians, Orators, Critics.
     6. Science: Mathematicians, Physicians, Naturalists.
     7. Politics: Warriors and Statesmen.
     8. Industry: Inventors, Discoverers, Philanthropists.

HUNGARY. Hungary and its Revolutions, from the Earliest Period to the 19th Century (1850); with a Memoir of Louis Kossuth, by E. O. S. 8vo. Lond., 1854. B 7 S 41

Scenes of the Civil War in Hungary, 1848–49; with the Personal Adventures of an Austrian Officer. 12mo. Lond., 1850.   D 8 S 48

HUNNEWELL (JAMES FROTHINGHAM). England's Chronicles in Stone. Illustrated. Roy. 8vo. Lond., 1886.   B 5 T 63

Historical Monuments of France. 8vo. Boston, 1884.   B 8 U 17

The Lands of Scott. 8vo. Boston, 1871.   D 8 R 33

HUNT (MRS. ALFRED W.) Our Grandmother's Gowns. With twenty-four hand-coloured Illustrations, drawn by George R. Halkett. 8vo. Lond., 1885.   A 7 P 23

HUNT (FREEMAN). Merchant's Magazine and Commercial Review. 31 vols. 8vo. New York, 1839–54.   E

HUNT (F. KNIGHT). The Fourth Estate: Contributions towards a History of Newspapers, and of the Liberty of the Press. 2 vols. 8vo. Lond., 1850. B 12 R 24, 25

HUNT (REV. J.) A Vakatusa ni Lotu. 12mo. Viwa, 1850.   MG 2 P 6

HUNT (JAMES), PH.D., &c. Stammering and Stuttering; their Nature and Treatment. 5th ed. 8vo. Lond., 1863.   A 12 Q 12

HUNT (JAMES HENRY LEIGH). Anecdote Life of Leigh Hunt. [See TIMBS, J.]

Autobiography of; with Reminiscences of Friends and Contemporaries. 3 vols. 8vo. Lond., 1850. C 3 P 15–17

Correspondence of; edited by his eldest Son [Thornton Leigh Hunt.] 2 vols. 8vo. Lond., 1862. C 3 R 42, 43

HUNT (JAMES HENRY LEIGH).—*continued.*
Dramatic Works of Wycherley; with Biographical and Critical Notices. [See WYCHERLEY, W.]

Men, Women, and Books: a Selection of Sketches, Essays, and Critical Memoirs, from his uncollected Prose Writings. 2 vols. 8vo. Lond., 1847.   J 4 R 13, 14

Old Court Suburb; or, Memorials of Kensington, Regal, critical, and anecdotical. 2 vols. 8vo. Lond., 1855.   C 4 Q 23, 24

Readings for Railways, Anecdotes, and other Short Stories. 12mo. Lond., 1849.   J 7 Q 11

The Round Table: Northcote's Conversations, &c. [See HAZLITT, W.] .

Stories from the Italian Poets; with Lives of the Writers. 2 vols. 8vo. Lond., 1846.   J 12 U 3, 4

Table Talk; to which are added Imaginary Conversations of Pope and Swift. 12mo. Lond., 1870.   J 7 Q 6

Tale for a Chimney Corner, and other Essays from the "Indicator," 1819–1821; edited, with Introduction and Notes, by Edmund Ollier. 12mo. Lond., 1873. J 7 Q 10

HUNT (ROBERT), F.R.S. British Mining: a Treatise on the History, Discovery, Practical Development, and Future Prospects of Metalliferous Mines. Illustrated. Roy. 8vo. Lond., 1884.   A 9 V 18

Lectures on Gold. [See GOLD.]

Manual of Photography. 8vo. Lond., 1853.   A 6 V 1

Mineral Statistics of the United Kingdom of Great Britain and Ireland, for the years 1853–80. (Memoirs of the Geological Survey of Great Britain.) 8vo. Lond., 1855–81. E

Pantrea, the Spirit of Nature. 8vo. Lond., 1849. J 10 V 27

Poetry of Science; or, Studies of the Physical Phenomena of Nature. 2nd ed. 8vo. Lond., 1849.   A 16 U 1

Popular Romances of the West of England; or, the Drolls, Traditions, and Superstitions of Old Cornwall. 1st and 2nd series. 2 vols. 8vo. Lond., 1865. B 23 R 12, 13

Ure's Dictionary of Arts, &c. [See URE, A.]

HUNT (ROBERT M.) Life of Sir Hugh Palliser, Bart., Admiral of the White, and Governor of Greenwich Hospital. [Containing an Account of Capt. Cook's Voyages of Discovery in the South Seas.] 8vo. Lond., 1844.   C 9 Q 12

HUNT (T. F.) Half-a-dozen Hints on Picturesque Domestic Architecture, in a series of Designs for Gate Lodges, Gamekeepers' Cottages, and other Rural Residences. 3rd ed., with Additions. 4to. Lond., 1841.   A 2 T 1

HUNT (THOMAS STERRY), LL.D. Chemical and Geological Essays. 8vo. Boston, 1875.*   A 5 S 9

HUNT (THORNTON LEIGH). Correspondence of Leigh Hunt; edited by his eldest Son. 2 vols. 8vo. Lond., 1862. *   C 3 R 42, 43

HUNT (REV. WILLIAM). Diocesan Histories: the Somerset Diocese, Bath and Wells. 12mo. Lond., 1885. G 8 P 9

HUNT (WILLIAM). Notes on. [*See* RUSKIN, J.]

HUNT (WILLIAM HOLMAN). Notes on the Pictures of. [*See* RUSKIN, J.]

HUNTER (FREDERICK MERCER). Account of the British Settlement of Aden in Arabia. 8vo. Lond., 1877. D 5 T 27

HUNTER (REV. HENRY), D.D. Studies of Nature. [*See* SAINT-PIERRE, J. H. B. DE.]

HUNTER (CAPT. JOHN), R.N. Historical Journal of the Transactions at Port Jackson and Norfolk Island ; with the Discoveries which have been made in New South Wales and in the Southern Ocean, since the publication of Phillip's Voyage. 4to. Lond., 1793.* MD 3 P 1 †
Historical Journal of the Transactions at Port Jackson and Norfolk Island, including the Journals of Governors Phillip and King, since the publication of Phillip's Voyage; to which is prefixed a Life of the Author, and illustrated with a Map, by Lieut. Dawes. 8vo. Lond.,1793.* MB 1 T 27
[*See* PHILLIP, A.]

HUNTER (REV. JOHN), M.A. Key to Colenso's Arithmetic ; adapted to the revised and enlarged Edition of 1875. New ed. 8vo. Lond., 1883. A 10 S 24
Key to C. W. Merrifield's Technical Arithmetic and Mensuration. 12mo. Lond., 1873. A 17 S 9
[*See* MERRIFIELD, C. W.]

HUNTER (JOSEPH). Diary of Ralph Thoresby, F.R.S. [*See* THORESBY, R.]
Fines sive pedes Finium: Sive Finales concordiæ in Curia Domini Regis, 1195-1214. Roy. 8vo. Lond., 1835. B 15 T 7
Hallamshire: the History and Topography of the Parish of Sheffield, in the County of York; with Historical and Descriptive Notices of the Parishes of Ecclesfield, Hansworth, Freeton, and Whiston, and of the Chapelry of Bradfield. Roy. fol. Lond., 1819. B 16 U 1 ‡
Introduction to the Valor Ecclesiasticus of King Henry VIII. 8vo. Lond., 1834. B 15 T 26
Magnum Rotulum Scaccarii, vel Magnum Rotulum Pipæ, de anno tricesimo-primo regni Henrici Primi (ut videtur); quem plurimi hactenus laudarunt pro-rotulo quinti anni Stephani Regis. Roy. 8vo. Lond., 1833. B 15 T 8
Rotuli Selecti ad Res Anglicas et Hibernicas spectantes, ex Archivis in Domo Capitulari West-Monasteriensi deprompti. Roy. 8vo. Lond., 1834. B 15 T 17

HUNTER (ROBERT), M.A. Encyclopædic Dictionary: a new and original Work of Reference to all Words in the English Language. Illustrated. Vol. 1. Roy. 8vo. Lond., 1879. K 16 U 13

HUNTER (WILLIAM). [*See* COMBE, C.]

HUNTER (WILLIAM C.) Bits of Old China. 8vo. Lond., 1885. D 5 Q 23
The "Fan Kwae" at Canton, before Treaty Days, 1825-44 ; by "An Old Resident." 8vo. Lond., 1882. D 5 Q 22

HUNTER (SIR WILLIAM WILSON), K.C.S.I., B.A., &c. Annals of Rural Bengal. 3 vols. 8vo. Lond., 1872. B 10 S 9-11
Brief History of the Indian People. 3rd ed. 8vo. Lond., 1883. B 10 Q 30
Brief Life of J. W. S. Wyllie, &c. [*See* WYLLIE, J. W. S.]
Comparative Dictionary of the Languages of India and High Asia; with Dissertation. Fol. Lond.,1868. K 1 P 6 †
Famine Aspects of Bengal Districts. 8vo. Lond., 1874. F 6 R 8
The Indian Empire : its People, History, and Products. 2nd. ed. 8vo. Lond., 1886. D 4 U 29
Indian Musalmans ; are they bound in conscience to rebel against the Queen ? 8vo. Lond., 1871. B 10 U 29
Another copy. 3rd ed. 8vo. Lond., 1876. B 10 U 30
Imperial Gazetteer of India, and Index. 9 vols. 8vo. Lond., 1881. D 11 T 17-25
Life of the Earl of Mayo, Fourth Viceroy of India. 2 vols. 8vo. Lond., 1875. C 7 S 17, 18
Statistical Account of Assam. 2 vols. 8vo. Lond., 1879. F 8 R 12, 13

HUNTER RIVER VINEYARD ASSOCIATION: Historic Summary of the Proceedings and Reports of. [*See* KING, J.]

HUNTERIAN CLUB. Publications of. 13 vols. 4to. Lond., 1871-81. E

HUNTINGDON (HENRY OF). Chronicle of ; with the Acts of Stephen; translated and edited by Thomas Forester. 8vo. Lond., 1853. B 3 Q 29

HUNTINGTON (D. L.), AND OTIS (G. A.) Description of the United States Army Medical Transport Cart Model of 1876. (Philad. Int. Exhib., 1876.) 8vo. Philad., 1876. A 16 U 21

HUNTINGTON (H. W. H.) History of Australasia, from its First Discovery to the Present Time.. Part 1. 4to. Sydney, 1884. Libr.

HUNTINGTON (MAJOR ROBERT). Memoires de. [*See* GUIZOT, F. P. G., 5.]

HUNTINGTON (SELINA), COUNTESS. Life and Times of ; by "A Member of the Houses of Shirley and Hastings." 6th thousand. 2 vols. 8vo. Lond., 1844. C 7 T 21, 22

HUNTLEY (SIR HENRY). Seven Years' Service on the Slave Coast of Western Africa. 2 vols. 8vo. Lond., 1850. D 1 S 13, 14

HURD (RT. REV. RICHARD), D.D., BISHOP OF LICHFIELD. Introduction to the Study of the Prophecies concerning the Christian Church ; in Twelve Sermons. 8vo. Lond., 1772. G 13 P 26
Life, &c., of Rt. Rev. W. Warburton. [*See* WARBURTON, RT. REV. W.]
Works of A. Cowley. [*See* COWLEY, A.]

HURLBURT (E. P.) Essays on Human Rights and their Political Guaranties. (Pam. C.) Imp. 8vo. Edinb., 1847. MJ 2 S 1

HURLBURT (J. BEAUFORT), LL.D., &c. Britain and her Colonies. 8vo. Lond., 1865. MF 2 Q 24

HURST (J.) Pamphlet written for the purpose of explaining the Objects and Intentions of the Mutual Trade Protection Association of South Australia. 12mo. Adelaide, 1879. MF 1 P 23

HURST (JOHN F.), D.D. History of Rationalism. 8vo. Lond., 1867. G 8 R 12

HURST (JOHN THOMAS), C.E. Hand-book of Formulæ, Tables, and Memoranda for Architectural Surveyors, and others engaged in Building. 6th ed. Ob. 32mo. Lond., 1871. Libr.

HURSTHOUSE (CHARLES). Account of the Settlement of New Plymouth in New Zealand, from personal observation, during a Residence there of Five Years. 8vo. Lond., 1849.* MD 4 S 18

New Zealand; or, Zealandia, the Britain of the South. Illustrated. 2 vols. 8vo. Lond., 1857.* MD 4 S 20, 21

New Zealand, the Britain of the South; with a Chapter on the Native War, and our Future Native Policy. 2nd ed. 8vo. Lond., 1861. MD 4 S 24

HURTON (WILLIAM). Voyage from Leith to Lapland; or, Pictures of Scandinavia in 1850. 2 vols. 8vo. Lond., 1851. MD 8 S 21, 22

Another copy. 2nd and revised ed. 8vo. Lond., 1852. D 8 S 23

HUSBAND (E.) Exact Collection of Remonstrances, Declarations, Messages, &c., between the King's Most Excellent Majesty and his High Court of Parliament, 1641-43. Sm. 4to. Lond., 1643. B 3 R 31

HUSBANDRY; comprising Reports of Select Farms, Outlines of Flemish Husbandry, &c. (Pam. 14.) 8vo. Lond., 1840. MJ 2 Q 4

HUSCHKINS (J. G.) [*See* TIBULLUS, A.]

HUSENBETH (VERY REV. F. C.), D.D., &c. Emblems of Saints. 3rd ed. Edited by Augustus Jessopp, D.D. Norwich, 1882. K 18 R 22

HUSKISSON (RT. HON. WILLIAM). Biographical Memoir of, derived from authentic sources; [by John Wright.] 8vo. Lond., 1831. C 10 V 39

Speeches of; with a Biographical Memoir. 3 vols. roy. 8vo. Lond., 1831. F 8 T 4-6

Another copy. 3 vols. 8vo. Lond., 1831. F 13 Q 2-4

HUSS (JAXON). Wiclif and Huss. [*See* LOSERTH, DR. J.]

HUSS (JANOS), AND HIERONYMUS (PRAGENSIS). Historia et Monumenta. 2 vols. (in 1) fol. Norimberg, 1715. G 37 Q 2‡

HUSSAK (DR. E.) The Determination of Rock-forming Minerals. New York, 1886. A 9 Q 43

HUSSEY (H.) The Australian Colonies; together with Notes of a Voyage to Panama in the *Golden Age.* 12mo. Lond., 1855. MD 1 S 26

HUTCHESON (PROF. FRANCIS), LL.D. Essay on the Nature and Conduct of the Passions and Affections; with Illustrations on the Moral Sense. 3rd ed. 8vo. Lond., 1742. G 8 R 20

System of Moral Philosophy. 2 vols. 4to. Lond., 1755. G 2 T 5, 6

HUTCHINGS (J. M.) Scenes of Wonder and Curiosity in California: a Tourist's Guide to the Yo-Semite Valley. Illustrated. 8vo. New York, 1870. D 3 T 4

HUTCHINS (JOHN), M.A. History and Antiquities of the County of Dorset. 4 vols. fol. Westminster, 1861-70. B 17 U 11-14 ‡

HUTCHINS (WILLIAM J.) Short Treatise on the Excessive Costs allowed to Attorneys in the Colony of Victoria; with Tables of Fees. 8vo. Melb., 1860. MF 1 Q 5

HUTCHINS (REV. WILLIAM). [*See* LILLIE, REV. J., *and* THOMSON, J.]

HUTCHINSON (FRANK), AND MYERS (FRANCIS). The Australian Contingent: a History of the Patriotic Movement in New South Wales, and an Account of the despatch of Troops to the assistance of the Imperial Forces in the Soudan. 8vo. Sydney, 1885. MB 1 T 29

HUTCHINSON (COL. JOHN). Memoirs of the Life of Colonel Hutchinson, Governor of Nottingham; with original Anecdotes, &c., written by his Widow Lucy. 3rd ed. 2 vols. 8vo. Lond., 1810. C 10 Q 29, 30

Another copy. Edited by the Rev. Julius Hutchinson; revised by C. H. Firth, M.A. 2 vols. 8vo. Lond., 1885. C 10 Q 31, 32

HUTCHINSON (JOHN), M.A. German Universities for the last Fifty Years. [*See* CONRAD, PROF. J.]

HUTCHINSON (REV. JULIUS). Memoirs of Col. Hutchinson. [*See* HUTCHINSON, L.]

HUTCHINSON (LUCY). Memoirs of the Life of Colonel Hutchinson; with original Anecdotes, by his Widow, Lucy. 2 vols. 8vo. Lond., 1810. C 10 Q 29, 30

Another copy. Edited by the Rev. Julius Hutchinson; revised by C. H. Firth, M.A. 2 vols. 8vo. Lond., 1885. C 10 Q 31, 32

Mémoires de. [*See* GUIZOT, F. P. G., 10, 11.]

HUTCHINSON (PETER ORLANDO). Chronicles of Gretna Green. 2 vols. 8vo. Lond., 1844. B 32 R 1, 2

Diary and Letters of his Excellency Thomas Hutchinson. [*See* HUTCHINSON, CAPT. T.]

HUTCHINSON (CAPT. THOMAS), B.A., &c. Diary and Letters of; compiled by Peter Orlando Hutchinson. 2 vols. 8vo. Lond., 1883–86. C 11 P 7, 8

HUTCHINSON (THOMAS J.) Summer Holidays in Brittany. 8vo. Lond., 1876. D 7 Q 33

HUTCHINSON (WILLIAM), F.S.A. History and Antiquities of the County Palatine of Durham. 3 vols. 4to. Newcastle and Carlisle, 1785–94. B 6 V 8–10

HUTH (ALFRED HENRY). Life and Writings of Henry Thomas Buckle. 2 vols. 8vo. Lond., 1880. C 8 U 7, 8

Marriage of Near Kin considered with respect to the Laws of Nations; the Results of Experience, and the Teachings of Biology. 8vo. Lond., 1875. A 26 V 4

HUTH LIBRARY (THE); or, Elizabethan-Jacobean unique or very rare Books, in Verse and Prose, largely from the Library of Henry Huth, Esq; edited by the Rev. Alexander B. Grosart, LL.D., &c. 41 vols. 4to. Lond., 1881–86. J 5 U 1–V 4.

Daniel (Samuel). Complete Works, in Prose and Verse.

Dekker (Thomas). Non-Dramatic Works.

Greene (Robert), M.A. Life, and Complete Works, in Prose and Verse.

Harvey (Gabriel), D.C.L. Works of.

Nashe (Thomas). Complete Works.

Spenser (Edmund). Complete Works, in Prose and Verse.

Catalogue of the Printed Books, Manuscripts, Autograph Letters, and Engravings, collected by Henry Huth. 5 vols. imp. 8vo. Lond., 1880. K 9 P 11–15 †

HUTTEN (ULRICH VON). Ad B. Pirckheymer Patr. Norimb. Epistola qua et vitae suae rationem et temporum in quae ætas ipsius incidit conditionem luculenter descripsit. 12mo. Wolfenbuttel, 1717. G 8 P 10

Jacobi Burckhard Ill. Gymn. Hildburgh P. P. de Ulrichi de Hutten et animi et ingenii viribus illustris maxime equitis Fatis ac Meritis quorum haec in provehenda litterarum studia Reformationis item negotium adjuvandum praeclara exstiterunt Commentarii. Pars posterior. 12mo. Wolfenbuttel, 1717. G 8 P 10

Jacobi Burckhard de Ulrichi de Hutten et animi et ingenii viribus illustris maxime equitis Fatis ac Meritis quorum haec in ecclesiam atque rempublicam praeclara exstiterunt Commentarii Pars III. eaque postrema cui August. Imperat. Maximiliani I, Diploma et complures hujus Epistolae sunt inserta. 12mo. Wolfenbuttel, 1723. G 8 P 10

HUTTON (ANNIE). Embassy in Ireland. [*See* RINUCCINI, G. B.]

3 n

HUTTON (CHARLES), LL.D., &c. Course of Mathematics; composed for the Use of the Royal Military Academy; with Corrections, &c., by Dr. O. Gregory. 11th ed. 2 vols. 8vo. Lond., 1836–37. A 10 T 1, 2

Solutions of the Principal Questions of Dr. Hutton's Course of Mathematics. [*See* DAVIES, T. S.]

Mathematical Tables; containing the Common, Hyperbolic, and Logistic Logarithms; also, Sines, Tangents, Secants, and Versed Sines, both Natural and Logarithmic; together with several other Tables useful in Mathematical Calculations; also, the complete Description and Use of the Tables; to which are added, seven Tables of Trigonometrical Formulæ, by Olinthus Gregory, LL.D. 9th ed. Roy. 8vo. Lond., 1842. A 10 U 21

Another copy. Roy. 8vo. Lond., 1858. A 10 V 5

Philosophical and Mathematical Dictionary. 2 vols. 4to. Lond., 1815. A 10 V 23, 24

Recreations in Science and Natural Philosophy: Translation of J. E. Montucla's Edition of Ozanam; with Additions, &c., by Edward Riddle. 8vo. Lond., 1854. A 16 8 6

Tracts on Mathematical and Philosophical Subjects; comprising the Theory of Bridges, and the Force of Gunpowder. 3 vols. 8vo. Lond., 1812. A 10 T 5–7

HUTTON (CAPT. F. W.), F.G.S. Catalogue of Birds of New Zealand; with Diagnoses of the Species. Roy. 8vo. Wellington, 1871. MA 2 U 33

Catalogue of the Echinodermata of New Zealand; with Diagnoses of the Species. Roy. 8vo. Wellington, 1872. MA 2 U 35

Catalogue of the Marine Mollusca of New Zealand; with Diagnoses of the Species. Roy. 8vo. Wellington, 1873.* MA 2 U 36

Catalogues of the New Zealand Diptera, Orthoptera, Hymenoptera; with Descriptions of the Species. 8vo. Wellington, 1881. MA 2 U 7

Manual of the New Zealand Mollusca: a Systematic and Descriptive Catalogue of the Marine and Land Shells, and of the Soft Mollusks and Polyzoa of New Zealand and the adjacent Islands. Roy. 8vo. Wellington, 1880. MA 2 U 4

Report on the Tarawera Volcanic District. 8vo. Wellington, 1887. MA 2 R 32

Scientific Papers. 8vo. Wellington, &c., 1868–85. MA 2 V 16

Studies in Biology for New Zealand Students. No. 1. The Shepherd's Purse (*Capsella Bursa-Pastoris*). 8vo. Wellington, 1881. MA 1 T 26

Zoological Exercises for Students in New Zealand. 12mo. Dunedin, 1880. MA 2 T 20

HUTTON (CAPT. F. W.), F.G.S., AND HECTOR (SIR J.), M.D., &c. Fishes of New Zealand : Catalogue, with Diagnoses of the Species : Notes on the Edible Fishes. 8vo. Wellington, 1872. MA 2 U 34

HUTTON (Capt. F. W.), F.G.S., &c., and ULRICH (G. H. F.), F.G.S. Report on the Geology and Goldfields of Otago ; with Appendices, by J. G. Black and J. M'Kerrow. 8vo. Dunedin, 1875.*　　　MA 2 Q 24

HUTTON (James). Horses of the Sahara. [*See* Daumas, E.]
James and Philip van Arteveld: Two Episodes in the History of the 14th Century. 8vo. Lond., 1882.　B 12 T 13
Missionary Life in the Southern Seas. 8vo. Lond., 1874.　　　　　　　　　　　　　　　MD 5 P 1
Popular Account of the Thugs and Dacoits, the Hereditary Garotters and Gang-Robbers of India. 8vo. Lond., 1857.　　　　　　　　　　　　　　　D 5 R 9
Selections from the Letters and Correspondence of Sir James Bland Burges, Bart.; with Notices of his Life, edited by James Hutton. 8vo. Lond., 1885.　　　C 10 R 11

HUTTON (Laurence). Artists of the 19th Century and their Works. [*See* Clement, Mrs. Clara E.]
Literary Landmarks of London. 8vo. Lond., 1885. C 3 T 14

HUTTON (Richard Holt), M.A. Essays, Theological and Literary. 2 vols. 8vo. Lond., 1871.　G 8 R 22, 23
Sir Walter Scott. (Eng. Men of Letts.) 8vo. Lond., 1879.　　　　　　　　　　　　　　C 1 U 28

HUTTON (Capt. Thomas), F.G.S. Chronology of Creation ; or, Geology and Scripture reconciled. 8vo. Calcutta, 1850.　　　　　　　　　　　　　　　A 9 T 15

HUTTON (Walter S.), C.E. Practical Mechanic's Workshop Companion. [*See* Templeton, W.]
The Works' Manager's Hand-book of Modern Rules, Tables, and Data. Roy. 8vo. Lond., 1885.　　K 18 Q 5

HUXHAM (John), M.D., &c. Essay on Fevers, and their various kinds, as depending on different Constitutions of the Blood. 2nd ed. 8vo. Lond., 1750. A 12 Q 43

HUXLEY (Prof. Thomas Henry), M.D., Ph.D., &c. Crayfish : an Introduction to the Study of Zoology. Illustrated. 8vo. Lond., 1880.　　　　A 14 Q 31
Evidence as to Man's place in Nature. 8vo. Lond., 1864.　　　　　　　　　　　　　　A 1 W 27
Hume. (Eng. Men of Letts.) 8vo. Lond., 1879.　C 1 U 20
Introduction to the Classification of Animals. 8vo. Lond., 1869.　　　　　　　　　　　　A 14 U 24
Lay Sermons, Addresses, and Reviews. 4th ed. 8vo. Lond., 1872.　　　　　　　　　　　　J 5 Q 7

HUXLEY (Prof. Thomas Henry), M.D., Ph.D., &c.—*contd.*
Lessons in Elementary Physiology. 3rd ed. 12mo. Lond., 1869.　　　　　　　　　　　　A 12 P 11
Manual of the Anatomy of Vertebrated Animals. 12mo. Lond., 1871.　　　　　　　　　　A 28 P 1
Oceanic Hydrozoa : a Description of the Calycophoridæ and Physophoridæ, observed during the Voyage of H.M.S. *Rattlesnake*, in the years 1846–50. Fol. Lond., 1859.　　　　　　　　　　　　A 23,P 1 ‡
Physiography: an Introduction to the Study of Nature. 8vo. Lond., 1878.　　　　　　A 16 P 18
Science and Culture, and other Essays. 8vo. Lond., 1881.　　　　　　　　　　　　A 16 S 20

HUXLEY (Prof. Thomas Henry), M.D., &c., and ETHERIDGE (Robert), F.G.S. Catalogue of the Collection of Fossils in the Museum of Practical Geology; with an Explanatory Introduction. (*Bound with Ramsay's Catalogue of Rocks.*) 8vo. Lond., 1865. A 9 S 26

HUXLEY (Prof. Thomas Henry), M.D., &c., and MARTIN (H. N.), B.A., &c. A Course of Practical Instruction in Elementary Biology. 8vo. Lond., 1875.　　　　　　　　　.　　A 14 Q 57
Another copy. 4th ed. 8vo. Lond., 1877.　A 14 Q 7

HUXTABLE (Rev. A.), A.M. The "Present Prices." 5th ed. 8vo. Blandford, 1850.　　　F 6 V 10

HYACINTHE (Saint). Histoire du Prince Titi. [*See* Cabinet des Fées, 27, 28.]

HYDE (Henry), Earl of Clarendon, and HYDE (Laurence), Earl of Rochester. Correspondence of. [*See* Singer, S. W.]

HYDE (James Wilson). Royal Mail : its Curiosities and Romance. 8vo. Edinb., 1885.　B 3 R 19

HYDE (John), Jun. Mormonism : its Leaders and Designs. 2nd ed. 8vo. N. York, 1857.　G 8 S 2

HYDRO-MECHANICS, Theory and Practice of : a Series of Lectures delivered at the Institution of Civil Engineers, 1884–85, by J. Evans, W. Pole, Prof. W. C. Unwin, Sir C. A. Hartley, T. Stevenson, and Sir E. J. Reed. 8vo. Lond., 1885.　　　　　A 11 U 7

HYMNS. To be sung at the twenty-first Anniversary of the Tamar-street Sabbath School, Launceston. 8vo. Launceston, 1857.　　　　　　　MH 1 Q 4

I

IBIS (THE) : a Quarterly Journal of Ornithology ; edited by Philip Lutley Sclater, M.A., &c., and Howard Saunders, F.L.S.,&c. Vols. 1-28 [First to] fifth Series. 8vo. Lond., 1859-86.   E

Index of Genera and Species referred to, and an Index. to the Plates, 1859-76. 8vo. Lond., 1879.   E

IBN AL-LABBÁD. [*See* ABD-AL-LATIF.]

IBN KHALLIKAN (SCHEMS ED DEEN ABOU'L ABBAS AHMED). Biographical Dictionary ; translated from the Arabic by Baron W. MacGuckin de Slane. 4 vols. 4to. Paris, 1843-71.   C 4 Q 16-19 †

IBRAHIM-HILMY (PRINCE). The Literature of Egypt and the Soudan, from the Earliest Times to 1885, inclusive: a Bibliography. Vol. 1. 4to. Lond., 1886.   K 17 S 11

IBRAHIM PACHA (VICEROY OF EGYPT). State and Prospects of Syria under. [*See* ADDISON, C. G.]

IDDESLEIGH (SIR STAFFORD H. NORTHCOTE), EARL OF. Pleasures, Dangers, and Uses of Desultory Reading. 12mo. Lond., 1885.   J 10 P 11

Twenty Years of Financial Policy : a Summary of the Chief Financial Measures passed between 1842 and 1861 ; with a Table of Budgets. 8vo. Lond., 1862.   F 6 U 2

IDES (E. YSBRANTS). Three Years Travels from Moscow Overland to China, through Great Ustiga, Siriania, Permia, Sibiria, Daour, Great Tartary, &c., to Peking. With Map. Sm. 4to. Lond., 1706.   D 5 U 16

IDEVILLE (HENRY D'). Comte. [*See* D'IDEVILLE, H., COMTE.]

IDSTONE. [*See* PEARCE, T.]

IDYLLS (THE). Idylls of Theocritus, Bion, and Moscius, and the War Songs of Tyrtæus ; literally translated into English Prose, by the Rev. J. Banks, M.A. ; with Metrical Versions, by J. M. Chapman, M.A. 8vo. Lond., 1876.   H 5 S 34

IGNATIUS (SANCTUS). Epistolæ. [*See* MIGNE, J. P., SERIES GRÆCA, 5.]

The Apostolic Fathers, St. Ignatius, &c. [*See* LIGHTFOOT, RT. REV. J. B.]

IGNATIUS DE LOYOLA. Loyola and Jesuitism in its Rudiments. [*See* TAYLOR, REV. I.]

Vie de. [*See* CAPEFIGUE, J. B. H. R.]

IHNE (WILHELM). History of Rome. English ed. 5 vols. 8vo. Lond., 1871-82.   B 11 U 20-24

IHRE (JOHAN). Swenskt Dialect Lexicon. Sm. 4to Upsala, 1766.   K 12 Q 19

ILLINOIS. [*See* UNITED STATES.]

ILLUSTRATED AUSTRALIAN MAGAZINE (THE). Vols. 1-4. 4 vols. (in 3) 8vo. Melb., 1851-52.* ME 3 P

Another copy. Vols. 1-3. 8vo. Melb., 1851. ME 3 P

ILLUSTRATED AUSTRALIAN NEWS (THE), with which is amalgamated the *Illustrated Melbourne Post.* 3 vols. fol. Melb., 1871-79.   ME 9 Q 2-4 †

ILLUSTRATED EXHIBITOR AND MAGAZINE OF ART (THE). 2 vols. sm. fol. 8vo. Lond.,1852. A 15 U 11,12

ILLUSTRATED HISTORY OF THE WORLD FOR THE ENGLISH PEOPLE; from the Earliest Period to the Present Time. 2 vols. roy. 8vo. Lond., 1884. B 15 R 27,28

ILLUSTRATED JOURNAL OF AUSTRALASIA. [*See* JOURNAL OF AUSTRALASIA.]

ILLUSTRATED LONDON NEWS (THE). 86 vols. fol. Lond., 1842-85.   E

ILLUSTRATED MISSIONARY NEWS. Vol. 19. 4to. Lond., 1885.   ME 11 P 3 †

ILLUSTRATED MONTHLY HERALD. December, 1872-March, 1873. Fol. Melb., 1872-73. ME 9 Q 2 †

ILLUSTRATED NEWS OF THE WORLD (THE). Fol. Lond., 1858.   E

ILLUSTRATED SYDNEY NEWS (THE), *and New South Wales Agriculturist and Grazier,* for 1853-55, 1864-65, 1871-88. 21 vols. fol. Sydney, 1853-88.   ME

ILLUSTRATED SYDNEY NEWS SAXBY ALMANAC (THE) for 1865. (Pam. 43.) 8vo. Sydney, 1865. MJ 2 R 5

ILLUSTRATED WEEKLY HERALD. January-February, 1873. Fol. Melb., 1873.   ME 9 Q 2 †

ILLUSTRATED WORDS OF GRACE : a Family Fortnightly Periodical. Vol. 5, 1880-81. 4to. Sydney, 1880-81.   ME 2 U

IMBERT DE SAINT-AMAND (ARTHUR LÉON) BARON. Memoirs of the Empress Marie Louise. 8vo. Lond., 1886.   C 10 U 26

IMMIGRANTS' AID SOCIETY OF VICTORIA. Annual Reports, 1860-64 ; with Abstracts of Accounts, &c. 8vo. Melb., 1860-64.   MF 3 P 15

IMMIGRATION. Bounty Immigration : a Letter to the Members of the Legislative Council ; from "One who has handled the Spade." (Pam. 28.) 8vo. Melb., 1855.
MJ 2 Q 16

Copy of the Report of the Committee of the Legislative Council of New South Wales, on the subject of Immigration. (Parl. Docs., 48.) Fol. Lond., 1846. MF 4 †

Report from the Committee on Immigration ; with the Appendix and Minutes of Evidence, and Replies to Circular Letter. (Parl. Docs., 33.) Fol. Sydney, 1838–39.
MF 4 †

IMPARTIAL OBSERVER, An. [*See* LHOTSKY, DR. J.]

IMPARTIAL SPECTATOR, An. [*See* DANUBE, THE.]

IMPERIAL DICTIONARY OF UNIVERSAL BIOGRAPHY. 6 vols. imp. 8vo. Lond., 1865–68. C 11 V 1–6

IMPERIAL REVIEW (THE). Vol. 1, No. 1. 8vo. Melb., 1879.
MJ 2 R 15

IMPEY (SIR ELIJAH BARWELL), KNT., CHIEF JUSTICE OF BENGAL. Memoirs of ; compiled from authentic Documents, by Elijah Barwell Impey. 8vo. Lond., 1846.
C 7 S 3

IMPORTANCE OF LITERATURE to Men of Business : a series of Addresses delivered at various popular Institutions. 12mo. Lond., 1852.
J 9 P 28

IMPUDENT IMPOSTORS AND CELEBRATED CLAIMANTS, from Perkin Warbeck to Arthur Orton. 8vo. Lond., 1876.
B 1 4 P 43

IMRAY (JAMES F.) Lights and Tides of the World, including Fog Signals and the Magnetic Variation, &c. 4th ed. 4to. Lond., 1882.
D 11 T 1

IM THURN (E. F.) [*See* THURN, E. F. Im]

INANIMATE CREATION (THE). Natural History of ; being a Guide to the Scenery of the Heavens, the Phenomena of the Atmosphere, the Structure and Geological Features of the Earth, and its Botanical Productions. 8vo. Lond., 1860.
A 16 Q 21

INCE (JOSEPH), F.L.S. Memoir of Daniel Hanbury. 8vo. Lond., 1876.
A 6 Q 12

INCHBALD (MRS. ELIZABETH). Animal Magnetism : a Farce. (Cumberland's Eng. Theatre.) 12mo. Lond., 1829.
H 2 Q 16

Collection of Farces. [*See* FARCES.]

Every One has his Fault : a Comedy. (Brit. Theatre.) 12mo. Lond., 1808.
H 1 P 23

I'll tell you what : a Comedy. [*See* MODERN THEATRE 7.]

Lover's Vows ; a Play. (Brit. Theatre.) 12mo. Lond., 1808.
H 1 P 23

The Modern Theatre. [*See* MODERN THEATRE.]

INCHBALD (MRS. ELIZABETH).—*continued*.
Next Door Neighbours : a Comedy. [*See* MODERN THEATRE 7.]

Such Things are : a Play. (Brit. Theatre.) 12mo. Lond., 1808.
H 1 P 23

To Marry or not to Marry : a Comedy. (Brit. Theatre.) 12mo. Lond., 1808.
H 1 P 23

The Wedding Day : a Drama. [*See* FARCES 1.]

Wives as they are : a Comedy. (Brit. Theatre.) 12mo. Lond., 1808.
H 1 P 23

[*See* BRITISH THEATRE, THE.]

INDEFEASIBLE RIGHTS OF MAN (THE) ; or, the Contest between the antagonistic principles of Democracy and Aristocracy in New South Wales. (Pam. 10.) 8vo. Sydney, 1843.
MJ 2 Q 2

INDEX LIBRORUM PROHIBITORUM. Prohibitorum juxta Exemplar Romanum jussu Sanctissimi Domini nostri. Editum anno MDCCCXXXV. 12mo. Mechliniae, 1838.
K 17 P 8

INDEX SOCIETY (THE). Publications of. 13 vols. sm. 4to. Lond., 1880–84.
E

INDIA. Canal Reports, N.W. Provinces. 2 vols. fol. Calcutta, &c., 1824–45.
E

Catalogue [and Continuation] of Maps of the British Possessions in India, and other parts of Asia, and Supplement. Roy. 8vo. Lond., 1870–72. K 8 Q 26

Catalogue [and Supplementary List] of Maps, &c., of India, and other parts of Asia. 8vo. Lond., 1876. A 10 P 13

Another copy.
MF 3 S 4

Despatches during the War in India of the Rt. Hon. Viscount Hardinge, G.C.B., the Rt. Hon. Gen. Lord Gough, G.C.B., Major-Gen. Sir Harry Smith, Bart., G.C.B., and other Documents. 8vo. Lond., 1846. B 10 U 20

Despatches of the British Generals during the Campaign on the Sutlej, &c. 8vo. Lond., 1846. MJ 2 R 20

Destruction of Life by Snakes, Hydrophobia, &c., in Western India ; by "An ex-Commissioner." 12mo. Lond., 1880.
A 12 P 29

Documents regarding the Ganges from Allahabad to Revelgunge, at the Mouth of the Gogra. Fol. Calcutta, 1849. E

Engineer's Reports for the years 1846–52. 5 vols. (in 1) 8vo. Bombay, 1848–53.
E

Five Months with the Prince in India ; containing a Glance at the Inner Life of the Inhabitants, and Incidents in connection with the Visit of the Prince of Wales. 8vo. Lond., 1876.
D 5 P 16

History of the Campaign on the Sutlej, and the War in the Punjaub. 2nd ed. 8vo. Lond., 1846. MJ 2 R 12

Another copy.
MJ 2 R 20

India and Lord Ellenborough. (Pam 16.) 8vo. Lond., 1844.
MJ 2 Q 6

India, Pictorial, Descriptive, and Historical. Illustrated. 8vo. Lond., 1873.
D 5 P 3

INDIA.—*continued.*

Indian and Colonial Ex1ibition. [*See* COLONIAL AND INDIAN EXHIBITION.]

Manual of the Geology of India. [*See* MEDLICOTT, H. B., and BLANDFORD, W. T.]

Memoirs of the Geological Survey of. 22 vols. roy. 8vo. Calcutta, 1859–83.   E

Memoirs of the Geological Survey of India: Palæontologia Indica. 14 vols. imp. 4to. Calcutta, 1865–86.   E

Miscellaneous Papers on the River Godavery. Fol. Madras, &c., 1856–68.   E

    Copies of Minutes and Correspondence and Reports relating to the opening up of the River Godavery.

    Copy of any furt1er Correspondence wit1 the India Government relating to the Navigation of the River Godavery.

    Memorandum on the Navigation of the River Godavery; by Capt. F. T. Haig, R.E.

    Memorandum on the Letter of the Government of India to the Secretary of State; by Major F. T. Haig, R.E.

    On the Navigation of the River Godavery.

    Papers relating to the opening up of the River Godavery.

    Return: Papers relating to the Godavery.

    Report on the Navigability of the River Godavery and some of its Affluents; by Lieut. F. T. Haig, R.E.

Miscellaneous Papers on the River Hoog1ly, &c. Fol. Calcutta, 1854–65.   E

    Kurrac1ee Harbour: Report by Col. C. W. Tremenheere, C.B.; wit1 an Atlas.

    Observations [on] the Velocity of, and the Amount of Solid Matter in Water at different dept1s in the Indus and Canals in Sind; by Col. C. W. Tremenheere, R.E.

    [Report on the] Mauri Cnuwai [Water Supply] Project in Mysore.

    Report on the River Hoog1ly; by Hug1 Leonard, C.E.

    Reports, wit1 Proceedings and Appendix of the Committee appointed by the Government to enquire into the State of the River Hoog1ly.

Notes on the Levels of the Eastern Jumna Canal. Fol. Agra, 1852.   E

Notes and Memoranda on the Water-courses in the Deyra Doon, North-western Provinces [by Capt. P. T. Cantley]. Fol. Calcutta, 1845.   E

Operations for the Improvement of the Navigation of the Ganges from Revelgunge to Alla1abad, during 1849–53. Fol. Calcutta and Roorkee, 1851–54.   E

Papers relating to the settlement of Europeans in India. Roy. 8vo. Calcutta, 1834.   F 8 P 6 †

Papers regarding the Irrigation of the Agra District from the Oolunghun River. Fol. Roorkee, 1853.   E

Past Days in India; or, Sporting Reminiscences ゚f the Valley of the Soane and the Basin of Singrowlee; by "A late Customs Officer." 8vo. Lond., 1874.   D 5 R 49

Picture of India, Geographical, Historical, and Descriptive. 2 vols. 12mo. Lond., 1830.   B 10 Q 8, 9

Records of the Geological Survey of. Vols. 1–17. 17 vols. (in 12) roy. 8vo. Calcutta, 1870–85.   E

Contents and Index to the first 10 vols. of the [above], 1868–77. Roy. 8vo. Calcutta, 1878.   E

INDIA.—*continued.*

Reply to a Pamp1let entitled "India and Lord Ellenboroug1"; by "Zeta." 2nd ed. (Pam. 16.) 8vo. Lond., 1845.   MJ 2 Q 6

Report of the Conservator of Forests, 1860–63. (Pam. Ck.) 4to. Madras, 1861–63.   A 15 U 1

Report on Punjab Forest Administration, for 1875–76. Fol. La1ore, 1876.   E

Report on the Administration of the Punjab and its Dependencies, for the year 1875–76. 8vo. La1ore, 1876.   E

Report on the Drainage of the City of Del1i, and on the Means of improving it; by Lieut. Wilberforce H. Great1ead. Fol. Agra, 1852.   E

Report on the Revenue Administration of the Punjab and its Dependencies, for 1874–75. Roy. 4to. La1ore, 1875.   E

Reports and Correspondence regarding Rohilcund Canals. Fol. (n.p.n.d.)   E

Reports and Surveys regarding the Drainage of the Nujjufgur1 J1eel, near Del1i; by Lieut. H. M. Durand. Fol. (n.p.) 1838.   E

Reports on Projected Canals in the Del1i Territory. Fol. Alla1abad, 1842.   E

Reports on Railways, 1870–71. Fol. Lond., 1871.   E

Selections from Public Correspondence; publis1ed by the aut1ority of Government, Nort1-western Provinces. 2 vols. 8vo. Agra, 1849–52.   E

Selections from the Public Correspondence of the Administration for the Affairs of the Punjab. 2 vols. roy. 8vo. La1ore, 1853–55.   E

Tabular View of the Indian Territories. (Pam. A.) Sm. fol. Edinb., 1857.   MJ 2 U 1

INDIA AND AUSTRALIA ROYAL MAIL STEAM PACKET CO. Royal C1arter. 8vo. Lond., 1847.   MF 3 Q 72

INDIA LIST (THE). India List, Civil and Military. 20 vols. 8vo. Lond., 1877–86.   E

INDIA TEMPERANCE ALMANAC (THE), for 1857. (Pam. 40.) 12mo. Madras, 1856.   MJ 2 R 2

INDIAN ALPS (THE). The Indian Alps, and 1ow we crossed t1em; by "A Lady Pioneer." Illustrated. 4to. Lond., 1876.   D 4 V 24

INDIAN ANTIQUARY (THE): a Journal of Oriental Researc1 in Arc1æology, History, Literature, Language, P1ilosop1y, Religion, Folk-lore, &c. Vols. 1–14. 8vo. Bombay, 1872–85.   E

INDIAN ARMY AND CIVIL SERVICE LIST. 31 vols. 12mo. Lond., 1861–76.   E

INDIAN TEA COMPANIES. A complete List of Indian Tea Companies. Roy. 8vo. Calcutta, 1883.   E

INDIANA. [*See* UNITED STATES.]

INDISCHE TAAL-LAND-EN VOLKENKUNDE. Tijdschrift voor indische Taal-Land-en Volkenkunde. Vols. 13, 15. 8vo. Batavia, 1864–66.   E

INDUSTRIAL REMUNERATION CONFERENCE. Report. 8vo. Lond., 1885.   F 6 V 9

INFANT SCHOOLS. Report of the Proceedings of a Society for the establishment of Infant Schools in England. (Pam. 33.) 12mo. Sydney, 1824.   MJ 2 Q 21

INFLUENCE OF FIREARMS UPON TACTICS; by "An Officer of Superior Rank"; translated by Capt. E. H. Wickham. 8vo. Lond., 1876.   A 16 T 27

INGEGNERIA CIVILE (L'), e le Arti Industriali. 12 vols. 4to. Torino, 1875–86.   E

INGELOW (Miss Jean). Poems of. [1st] 2nd, and 3rd series. 3 vols. 12mo. Lond., 1877–85.   H 6 R 30–32

INGERSOLL (Ernest). Birds'-nesting: a Hand-book of Instruction in Gathering and Preserving the Nests and Eggs of Birds for the purposes of Study. 8vo. Salem, 1882.   A 14 Q 48

Crest of the Continent: a Record of a Summer's Ramble in the Rocky Mountains and beyond. 8vo. Chicago, 1885.   D 3 S 42

INGERSOLL (Col. Robert Green). Arraignment of the Church, and a Plea for Individuality. 8vo. Lond. (n.d.)   G 8 S 8

The Ghosts, and other Lectures. 8vo. Wash., 1879.   G 8 S 7

Heretics and Heresies. 8vo. Lond. (n.d.)   G 8 S 8

Oration on Humboldt. 8vo. Lond. (n.d.)   G 8 S 8

Oration on Thomas Paine. 8vo. Lond. (n.d.)   G 8 S 8

Oration on the Gods. 8vo. Lond. (n.d.)   G 8 S 8

INGLEBY (C. M.), LL.D., &c. Shakespeare, the Man and the Book; being a Collection of Occasional Papers on the Bard and his Writings. 2 vols. sm. 4to. Lond., 1877–81.   C 9 R 24, 25

Shakespeare's Centurie of Prayse; being Materials for a History of Opinion on Shakespeare and his Works. 8vo. Lond., 1874.   H 6 S 30

Shakespeare's Cymbeline; the Text revised and annotated. [*See* Shakespeare, W.]

INGLIS (A. Percy). Consular Formulary. 8vo. Lond., 1879.   F 8 S 8

INGLIS (Henry David). Channel Islands of Jersey, Guernsey, Alderney, Serk, Herm, and Jethou. 8vo. Lond., 1838.   D 8 P 7

Ireland in 1834; a Journey throughout Ireland in 1834. 2 vols. 8vo. Lond., 1834.   D 8 P 3 4

Personal Narrative of a Journey through Norway, part of Sweden, and Denmark. (Const. Misc.) 18mo. Lond., 1835.   K 10 Q 26

INGLIS (Henry David).—*continued.*

Rambles in the Footsteps of Don Quixote. With Illustrations by G. Cruikshank. 8vo. Lond., 1837.   J 11 T 21

Spain in 1830. 2 vols. 8vo. Lond., 1837.   D 8 P 5, 6

Switzerland, the South of France, and the Pyrenees, in 1830. [*See* Conway, D.]

The Tyrol; with a Glance at Bavaria. 2 vols. 8vo. Lond., 1833.   D 8 P 1, 2

INGLIS (James), "Maori." Our Australian Cousins. 8vo. Lond., 1880.*   MD 5 T 37

Our New Zealand Cousins. 8vo. Lond., 1887.*   MD 1 Q 9

Sport and Work on the Nepaul Frontier; or, Twelve Years' Sporting Reminiscences of an Indigo Planter. 8vo. Lond., 1878.   D 5 S 36

INGLIS (Rev. John). Dictionary of the Aneityumese Language, in two Parts; also, Outlines of Aneityumese Grammar. 8vo. Lond., 1882.   MK 1 P 47

INGLIS (Robert). Gleanings from the English Poets, Chaucer to Tennyson; with Biographical Notices of the Authors. 8vo. Edinb. (n.d.)   H 6 R 33

INGOLDSBY (Thomas). [*See* Barham, Rev. R. H. D.]

INGRAM (Rev. James), D.D. Memorials of Oxford. 3 vols. 8vo. Lond., 1837.   B 24 T 2–4

INGRAM (John Henry). Claimants to Royalty. 8vo. Lond., 1882.   B 15 Q 30

Edgar Allan Poe: his Life, Letters, and Opinions; with Portraits of Poe and his Mother. 2 vols. 8vo. Lond., 1880.   C 3 P 33, 34

The Haunted Homes and Family Traditions of Great Britain. [1st and] 2nd series. 2 vols. 8vo. Lond., 1884.   B 4 P 15, 16

INGULPHUS (Abbot of Croyland). Ingulph's Chronicle of the Abbey of Croyland; with Continuations, by Peter of Blois and anonymous Writers. Translated from the Latin, with Notes, by Henry T. Riley, B.A. 8vo. Lond., 1854.   B 4 P 8

INMAN (Rev. James), D.D., &c. Formulæ and Rules for making Calculations on Plans of Ships; with an Example of their Application. 8vo. Lond., 1849.   A 3 Q 18

Introduction to Plane and Spherical Trigonometry. 8vo. Portsea, 1826.   A 10 U 13

INMAN (Thomas), M.D. Ancient Faiths, embodied in Ancient Names. 2 vols. 8vo. Lond., 1869–72.   G 15 Q 15, 16

Ancient Pagan and Modern Christian Symbolism exposed and explained. 8vo. Lond., 1869.   G 15 Q 17

INNES (Prof. Cosmo). Memoir of Dean Ramsay. [*See* Ramsay, E. B.]

Scotland in the Middle Ages: Sketches of Early Scotch History and Social Progress. 8vo. Edinb., 1860.   B 13 Q 47

INNES (EMILY). The Clersonese with the Gilding off.
2 vols. 8vo. Lond., 1885.   D 5 P 35, 36

INNES (FREDERICK MAITLAND). Secondary Punishments:
the Merits of a Home and of a Colonial Process, of a
Social, and of a Separate System of Convict Management
discussed. (Pam. 15.) 8vo. Lond., 1841.   MJ 2 Q 5

INNES (THOMAS), M.A. Civil and Ecclesiastical History
of Scotland, A.D. 80–818. 4to. Aberdeen, 1853.
                                            B 12 V 32
Critical Essay on the Ancient Inhabitants of the Northern
Parts of Britain, or Scotland. 2 vols. sm. 4to. Lond.,
1729.   B 13 Q 27, 28

INNOCENT III (PAPA). Opera omnia. [*See* MIGNE,
J. P., SERIES LATINA, 214–17.]

INNSTÄDTEN (K. S. E. VON). Die Oetzthaler Gebirgs-
gruppe, mit besonderer Rücksicht auf Orographie und
Glebscherkunde. L. Fol. Gotha, 1861. A 4 U 17 ‡

INQUISITIONUM ad Capellam Domini Regis Retornatarum quae in Publicis Archivis Scotiae adhuc servantur,
abbreviatio 3 vols. fol. Lond., 1811–16 F 44 P 13–15‡

INSANE. Hospital for the, Gladesville. [*See* NEW SOUTH
WALES.]

INSECTS. Natural History of. 2nd. ed. 2 vols. 18mo.
Lond., 1830–38.   A 14 P 43, 44

INSIDE PARIS DURING THE SIEGE; by "An
Oxford Graduate." 8vo. Lond., 1871.   B 8 P 3

IN SOUTHERN SEAS: a Trip to the Antipodes; by
"Petrel." Sm. 4to. Edinb., 1888.*   MD 5 V 21

INSTITUT DE FRANCE. Dictionnaire de l'Académie
Française, [avec] Complément, et Préface par M. Louis
Barré. 6e éd. 3 vols. 4to. Paris, 1835–42. K 15 U 17–19
Another copy. 3 vols. 4to. Paris, 1856.   K 15 U 20–22

INSTITUTION OF CIVIL ENGINEERS. [*See* CIVIL
ENGINEERS.]

INSTRUCTIONS FOR BURIAL BOARDS in providing Cemeteries and making arrangements for Inter-
ments. 8vo. Lond., 1854.   J 12 U 26

INSTRUMENTA ECCLESIASTICA   Edited by the
Ecclesiological, late Cambridge Camden Society. 4to.
Lond., 1847.   A 2 T 2

INTELLECTUAL OBSERVER (THE). A Review of
Natural History, Microscopic Research, and Recreative
Science. 12 vols. 8vo. Lond., 1862–68.   A 16 U 2–13

INTENDED ADDRESSES of the Victorian Candidates
to their Constituencies, at the approaching Elections; by
"Belphegor, lo Diable boiteux." 8vo. Melb., 1859.
                                            MF 1 Q 2

INTENDING EMIGRANT, AN. [*See* CAPPER, H.]

INTERCOLONIAL ROYAL MAIL STEAM PACKET
CO. (THE). New Zealand Mail Service Time Tables
and Routes. 8vo. Sydney, 1863.   MD 1 V 9

INTERCOLONIAL TRADES UNION CONGRESS.
[*See* TRADES UNION CONGRESS.]

INTERNATIONAL CONGRESS OF ORIENTALISTS.
[*See* ORIENTALISTS.]

INTERNATIONAL HEALTH EXHIBITION, 1884.
[*See* LONDON INTERNATIONAL HEALTH EXHIBITION.]

INTERNATIONAL INVENTIONS EXHIBITION,
1885. [*See* LONDON INTERNATIONAL INVENTIONS EXHI-
BITION.]

INTERNATIONAL MERCANTILE TELEGRAPH
CODE. Compiled for the use of Bankers, Merchants,
Manufacturers, Contractors, &c., and their Agents, for
the Economical and Secret Transmission of Business
Telegrams. Roy. 8vo. Lond., 1875.   F 8 T 17

INTERNATIONAL STATISTICAL CONGRESS. Re-
port and Programme of the Proceedings of the Fourth
Session of the International Statistical Congress, held in
London, 16th July, 1860. 4to. Lond., 1860. F 8 Q 22 †

INTOXICATING DRINK INQUIRY COMMISSION.
[*See* NEW SOUTH WALES.]

INTRODUCTORY LECTURES. Delivered in the University of London, 1828–29; by Professors Conolly, Grant,
Dale, Lardner, &c. 2 vols. 8vo. Lond., 1829. J 5 S 7, 8

INVALID BOTANY BAY FLAGELLATOR, AN.
[*See* LHOTSKY, DR. J.]

IOWA. [*See* UNITED STATES.]

IRBY (HON. CHARLES LEONARD), R.N., AND MANGLES
(JAMES), R.N. Travels in Egypt and Nubia, Syria, and
the Holy Land; including a Journey round the Dead
Sea, and through the Country East of the Jordan.
12mo. Lond., 1844.   D 1 T 12
Another copy. (H. and C. Lib.) 12mo. Lond.,
1844.   J 8 P 4
Travels in Egypt and Nubia, Syria, and Asia Minor,
during the years 1817 and 1818. 8vo. Lond.,
1823.   D 2 Q 12

IRELAND. Ancient Histories of. [*See* HANMER, M.]
Church Vestry System in. [*See* HIST. PAMS.]
Eleventh to Fifteenth Reports from the Commissioners
appointed by his Majesty to execute the Measures recommended in an Address of the House of Commons respecting the Public Records of Ireland. Roy. fol. Lond.,
1824–15.   B 29 Q 1
First Report of the Inspector appointed to visit the Reformatory Schools of Ireland. (Pam. Dv.) 8vo. Dublin,
1862.   MF 3 P 19

IRELAND. —*continued.*

Message from his Excellency the Lord Lieutenant to the Irish House of Commons, February 3, 1800. [*See* HIST. PAMS.]

Peerage of. 2 vols. 8vo. Lond., 1768.   K 10 T 25, 26

The Reign of Terror in Carlow. (Pam., 11.) 8vo. Lond., 1841.   F 12 P 9

Statutes at Large, passed in the Parliaments held in Ireland. From the third year of Edward II, A.D. 1310, to the forty-third year of George III, A.D. 1804, inclusive; with Marginal Notes and Indexes. 22 vols. fol. Dublin, 1765-1804.   F 30 P 1-Q 6 ‡

IRELAND (A.) Geography and History of Oceana; comprising a detailed Account of the Australian Colonies, and a Brief Sketch of Malaysia, Australasia, and Polynesia. 12mo. Hobart, 1861.   MD 3 Q 4

IRELAND (ALEXANDER). Book-Lover's Enchiridion: Thoughts on the Solace and Companionship of Books. 12mo. Lond., 1883.   J 7 Q 38

In Memoriam. Ralph Waldo Emerson. Recollections of his Visits to England in 1833, 1847-8, 1872-3, and Extracts from unpublished Letters. 8vo. Lond., 1882.   C 5 U 11

IRELAND (J.) [*See* HOGARTH, W.]

IRELAND (JOHN B.) Wall-street to Cashmere: a Journal of Five Years in Asia, Africa, and Europe. Roy. 8vo. New York, 1859.   D 9 U 28

IRELAND (HON. RICHARD DAVIES). Speech of, on moving for Leave to bring in a Bill to establish a Register of Lands and Titles thereto, and to facilitate the Transfer of Estates. 8vo. Melb., 1861.   MJ 2 R 21

Speech of, on moving the Second Reading of a Bill to establish a Register of Titles to Lands which shall hereafter be alienated by the Crown, and to facilitate the Transfer of the same. 8vo. Melb., 1862.   MJ 2 R 21

IRELAND (WILLIAM HENRY). Confessions of; containing the Particulars of his Fabrication of the Shakespeare Manuscripts, together with Anecdotes and Opinions of many Distinguished Persons. 8vo. Lond., 1805.   C 1 S 31

Stultifera Navis: qua omnium mortalium narratur Stultitia.—The Modern Ship of Fools. —Ære Perennius. 12mo. Lond., 1807.   H 6 R 29

IRELAND (WILLIAM W.), M.D. The Blot upon the Brain: Studies in History and Psycology. 8vo. Edinb., 1885.   A 12 R 21

IRENÆUS (SANCTUS), EPISCOPUS LUGDUNENSIS. Detectionis et Eversionis falso cognominatæ Agnitionis seu contra Hæreses Libri quinque. [*See* MIGNE, J. P., SERIES GRÆCA, 7.]

Sancti Irenæi Episcopi Lugdunensis et Martyris, Detectionis et Eversionis falso Cognominatæ Agnitionis, seu contra Hæreses Libri quinque. 2 vols. fol. Venetiis, 1734.   G 38 Q 6, 7 ‡

IRISH ACADEMY (ROYAL). [*See* ROYAL IRISH ACADEMY.]

IRISH HOUSE OF COMMONS, 1800. [*See* HISTORICAL PAMPHLETS.]

IRISH RAILWAY COMMISSION. Maps, showing the Lines laid down under the direction of the Commissioners, &c.; resented to both Houses of Parliament, by command of Her Majesty, 1838. At. fol. Lond., 1838.   D 8 P 14 ‡

IRISHMAN, AN. [*See* CAMPBELL, REV. DR. T.]

IRISHMEN, THE UNITED: their Lives, &c.   [*See* MADDEN, R. R.]

IRON: an Illustrated Weekly Journal of Science, Metals, and Manufactures in Iron and Steel; established in the year 1823 as "The Mechanics' Magazine." Vols. 1-25. Fol. Lond., 1873-85.   E

[*See* MECHANICS' MAGAZINE.]

IRONBARK. [*See* GIBSON, G. H.]

IRONS (JOHN), & CO. Correspondence and Statement of Case relating to the claim of Messrs. Irons & Co., Contractors for the Alfred Graving Dock, Williamstown, for monetary losses actually sustained by them by reason of the introduction of the Eight-hours System by the Government, after their Contract had been entered into. 8vo. Melb., 1870.   MF 1 Q 1

IRVING (DAVID), LL.D. Elements of English Composition. 4th ed. 8vo. Lond., 1816.   K 20 Q 40

Lives of the Scotish Poets: with Preliminary Dissertations on the Literary History of Scotland, and the Early Scotish Drama. 2nd ed. 2 vols. 8vo. Lond., 1810.   C 9 T 10, 11

Memoirs of the Life and Writings of George Buchanan. 8vo. Edinb., 1807.   C 10 R 12

IRVING (EDWARD). Life of, illustrated by his Journals and Correspondence; by Mrs. Oliphant. With a Portrait. 2 vols. 8vo. Lond., 1862.   C 7 R 29, 30

IRVING (JOHN HENRY BRODRIBB). English Actors: their Characteristics and their Methods. 8vo. Oxford, 1886.   J 1 S 41

Impressions of America. [*See* HATTON, J.]

IRVING (JOHN T.) Indian Sketches, taken during an Expedition to the Pawnee and other Tribes of American Indians. 2 vols. 8vo. Lond., 1835.   D 3 Q 5, 6

IRVING (JOSEPH). Annals of Our Time: a Diurnal of Events, Social and Political, Home and Foreign, from the Accession of Queen Victoria, June 20, 1837, to the Peace of Versailles, February 28, 1871; with two Supplements, from 28th February, 1871, to July 22nd, 1878. 8vo. Lond., 1880.   B 15 P 6

IRVING (JOSEPH).—*continued.*

Book of Dumbartonshire: a History of the County, Burgis, Parishes, and Lands, Memoirs of Families, and Notices of Industries carried on in the Lennox District.   3 vols. 4to.   Edinb., 1879.   B 1 S 6–8 †

Books of Scotsmen eminent for Achievements in Arms and Arts, &c.   Compiled and arranged by Joseph Irving. Sm. 4to.   Paisley, 1881.   C 11 Q 7

West of Scotland in History; being brief Notes concerning Events, Family Traditions, Topography, and Institutions. Sm. 4to.   Glasgow, 1885.   B 13 R 21

IRVING (M. H.), M.A.   Lecture on the Growth of Language.   [*See* MELBOURNE PUBLIC LIBRARY.]

IRVING (PIERRE MONROE).   Life and Letters of Washington Irving; by his Nephew.   2 vols. 8vo.   Lond., 1862.
                                                      C 2 U 33, 34
Another copy.   4 vols. 8vo.   Lond.,1862–64.   C 2 U 35–38

IRVING (R. D.)   The Copper-bearing Rocks of Lake Superior.   (U.S. Geological Survey.)   4to.   Wash., 1883.
                                                      A 1 Q 21 †

IRVING (THEODORE).   Conquest of Florida under Hernando de Soto.   2 vols. 8vo.   Lond., 1835.   B 1 Q 33, 34

IRVING (WASHINGTON), "GEOFFREY CRAYON."   Abbotsford and Newstead Abbey.   8vo.   Lond.,1835.   J 10 P 31

Adventures of Capt. Bonneville; or, Scenes beyond the Rocky Mountains.   3 vols. 8vo.   Lond.,1837.   J 10 P 16–18

The Alhambra; by "Geoffrey Crayon."   2 vols. 8vo. Lond., 1832.   J 11 U 9, 10

Astoria; or, Enterprise beyond the Rocky Mountains.   3 vols. 8vo.   Lond., 1836.   J 11 U 11–13
                                                      J 10 P 19
Biographies and Miscellaneous Papers.   8vo.   Lond., 1867.
                                                      J 10 P 19
Bracebridge Hall; or, the Humorists; by "Geoffrey Crayon." 2 vols. 8vo.   Lond., 1825.   J 9 Q 20, 21

Another copy.   (H. and C. Lib.)   12mo.   Lond., 1845.
                                                      J 8 P 11
Chronicle of the Conquest of Granada; from the MSS. of Fray Antonio Agapida.   2 vols. 8vo.   Lond., 1829.
                                                      B 13 V 1, 2
Another copy.   12mo.   Lond., 1850.   B 13 U 17

History of New York, from the beginning of the World to the end of the Dutch Dynasty; by "Diedrich Knickerbocker."   8vo.   Lond., 1824.   B 1 Q 39

History of the Life and Voyages of Christopher Columbus. 4 vols. 8vo.   Lond., 1828.   C 6 U 1–4

Legends of the Conquest of Spain; the Subjugation of Spain; and Count St. Julian and his Family.   8vo. Lond., 1835.   B 13 U 43

Life and Letters of; edited by his Nephew, Pierre M· Irving.   2 vols. 8vo.   Lond., 1862.   C 2 U 33, 34

Another copy.   4 vols. 8vo.   Lond.,1862–64.   C 2 U 35–38

Life and Voyages of Christopher Columbus (abridged). 18mo.   Lond., 1831.   C 1 P 27

3 c

IRVING (WASHINGTON).   "GEOFFREY CRAYON"—*continued.*

[Life of]; by C. D. Warner.   (American Men of Letts.) 8vo.   Lond., 1882.   C 1 R 15

Life of George Washington.   4 vols. 8vo.   Lond., 1856–78.
                                                      C 4 P 39–42
Lives of Mahomet and his Successors.   2 vols. 8vo.   Lond., 1850.   C 7 S 34, 35

Oliver Goldsmith: a Biography.   12mo.   Lond., 1849.
                                                      C 1 T 35
Another copy.   (H. and C. Lib.)   12mo.   Lond., 1849.
                                                      J 8 P 37
Salmagundi; or, the Whim-Whams and Opinions of "Launcelot Langstaff, Esq," and others.   8vo.   Lond., 1824.   J 10 P 15

The Sketch Book of "Geoffrey Crayon."   New ed.   2 vols. 8vo.   Lond., 1826.   J 11 U 14, 15

Tales of a Traveller.   (H. and C. Lib.)   New ed.   12mo. Lond., 1848.   J 8 P 30

Tour on the Prairies.   8vo.   Lond., 1835.   D 3 Q 14

Voyages and Discoveries of the Companions of Columbus. 18mo.   Lond., 1831.   D 10 P 15

Works of.   11 vols. 8vo.   Lond., 1868–78.   J 10 P 20–30

1. Salmagundi; or, the Whim-Whams and Opinions of Launcelot Langstaff, Esq.   A History of New York, from the beginning of the World to the End of the Dutch Dynasty; by "Diedrich Knickerbocker."

2. The Sketch Book; comprising Rip van Winkle, Rural Life in England, the Widow and her Son, Christmas Day, London Antiques, Stratford-on-Avon, the Pride of the Village, the Legend of Sleepy Hollow, &c.   Oliver Goldsmith: a Biography.

3. Bracebridge Hall; or, the Humorists: a Medley; by "Geoffrey Crayon."   Abbotsford, and Newstead Abbey.

4. The Alhambra.   Tales of a Traveller.

5. Chronicle of the Conquest of Granada.   Legends of the Conquest of Spain.

6, 7. The Life and Voyages of Christopher Columbus; together with the Voyages of his Companions.

8. Astoria; or, Anecdotes of an Enterprise beyond the Rocky Mountains.   A Tour on the Prairies.

9. Life of Mahomet.   Lives of the Successors of Mahomet.

10. The Adventures of Capt. Bonneville, U.S.A., in the Rocky Mountains and the Far West.   The Conquest of Florida, under Hernando de Soto; by Theodore Irving.

11. Biographies and Miscellaneous Papers.   Collected and arranged by Pierre Irving.

IRWIN (EYLES).   Series of Adventures in the course of a Voyage up the Red Sea, on the Coasts of Arabia and Egypt; and of a Route through the Deserts of Thebais, in the year 1777.   3rd ed.   2 vols. 8vo.   Lond., 1787.   D 5 S 27, 28

IRWIN (CAPT. FREDERICK CHIDLEY).   State and Position of Western Australia, commonly called the Swan-River Settlement.   8vo.   Lond., 1835.*   MD 4 U 24

[Analysis of]   State and Position of Western Australia. 8vo.   Lond., 1836.   MD 6 R 24

ISAACS (George). Not for Sale: a Selection of Imaginative Pieces. (Subscriber's edition.) 12mo. Adelaide, 1869.   MJ 1 Q 37

Number One.; edited by "A Pendragon." 8vo. Adelaide, 1861.   ME 3 R

Rhyme and Prose, and a Burlesque and its History. 12mo. Melb., 1865.   MH 1 P 15

ISAACSON (Rev. C. S.), M.A. Five Addresses on Christian and Social Subjects, delivered in Melbourne. 12mo. Melb., 1870–71.   MJ 2 P 31

ISAEOS. The Attic Orators. [*See* Jebb, Prof. R. C.]

ISCANUS. [*See* Joseph of Exeter.]

ISIDORUS HISPALENSIS (Sanctus). Opera omnia. [*See* Migne, J. P., Series Latina, 81–84.]

ISIDORUS MERCATOR. Collectio Decretalium. [*See* Migne, J. P., Series Latina, 130.]

ISIDORUS PELUSIOTA (Sanctus). Epistolarum libri quinque. [*See* Migne, J. P., Series Græca, 78.]

ISITT (F. Whitmore). New Zealand as it was in 1870; as it is in 1880; showing the substantial Progress made during the past ten years. 8vo. Lond., 1880. MD 3 V 11

ISRAEL (Menasseh ben). To His Highnesse the Lord Protector of the Commonwealth of England, Scotland, and Ireland, the humble Addresses of Menasseh Ben Israel, a Divine, and Doctor of Physic, in behalfe of the Jewish Nation, 1655. (*Reprinted.*) 4to. Melb., 1868.   MJ 2 S 3

ISRAEL RESTORED; or, the Scriptural Claims of the Jews upon the Christian Church: Lectures by twelve Clergymen of the Church of England. 8vo. Lond., 1841.   G 16 R 12

ISRAELITE OF 1873, An. [*See* Rudder, E. W.]

ITALIAN ART. Masterpieces of Italian Art: Twenty Photographs from Drawings and Engravings after the most celebrated Painters of 13th to the 16th Centuries; with Memoirs of the Painters. 4to. Lond., 1870. A 8 T 16

ITALIAN LANGUAGE. Vocabolario degli Accademici della Crusca Impressione Napoletana secondo l'ultima di Firenze con la giunta di molte voci raccolte dagli autori approvati dalla stessa Accademia. 6 vols. fol. Napoli, 1746–48.   K 29 P 1–6 ‡

ITALIAN NOVELISTS (The). Selected and translated, with Notes, by Thos. Roscoe. 4 vols. 12mo. Lond., 1825.   C 2 P 23–26

ITALY. Annali del Ministero di Agricoltura, Industria, e Commercio. Anni 1875–77.—Statistica. 2 vols. roy. 8vo. Roma, 1875–77.   F 1 R 1, 2

Bilanci Comunali; Anni 1875 e 1876. Imp. 8vo. Roma. 1877.   F 7 U 11

Cenni Statistici sulla Produzione Mineraria in Italia, 1870, 8vo. Firenze, 1870.   F 1 R 13

General View of Italy; its History and Topography [with Map]. 4to. Lond., 1859.   D 33 Q 16 ‡

L'Italie Economique en 1867; avec un Aperçu des Industries Italiennes à l'Exposition Universelle de Paris. 8vo. Florence, 1867.   F 3 S 16

L'Italia Economica nel 1873 [con] Tavole Grafiche. (Publicazione Ufficiale). 2 vols. 8vo. Roma, 1873–74.   F 1 R 3, 4

Navigazione nei Porti del Regno. Pesca del Pesce, del Corallo, e delle Spugne. Introduzione. Anno, 1876. Imp. 8vo. Roma, 1877–78.   F 7 U 6

Notizie e Studi sull' Agricoltura, 1876: Relazione al Consiglio d'Agricoltura. Imp. 8vo. Roma, 1877.   F 7 U 12

Popolazione—Movimento dello Stato Civile; Anni 1875–76. Introduzione. Imp. 8vo. Roma, 1877.   F 7 U 5

Statistica della Emigrazione all' estero; Anno 1876. Imp. 8vo. Roma, 1877.   F 7 U 10

Statistica delle Casse di Risparmio in Italia ed all' estero. Triennio, 1870, 1871, 1872, per gli Anni 1873–76. Imp. 8vo. Roma, 1875–77.   F 7 U 7

Statistica Elettorale Politica—Elezioni-Generali degli Anni 1861, 1865, 1866, 1867, 1870, 1874, e 1876. Imp. 8vo. Roma, 1877.   F 7 U 8

Statistique Internationale des Caisses d'Epargne; compilée par le Bureau Central de Statistique du Royaume d'Italie. Imp. 8vo. Rome, 1876.   F 7 U 9

Trinity of Italy; or, the Pope, the Bourbon, and the Victor; by "An English Civilian." 8vo. Lond., 1867. B 11 S 26

IVENS (R). From Benguella to Yacca. [*See* Capello, H.]

IVO (Sanctus). [*See* Yves Sainte.]

J

J—. (MME.) Great French Revolution, 1785–93. [*See* SIMON, E. E.]

JABET (GEORGE S.), "EDEN WARWICK." The Poet's Pleasaunce, or Garden of all sorts of Pleasant Flowers which our Pleasant Poets have in Past Time for Pastime planted. 8vo. Lond., 1847. H 8 U 28

JACK (ROBERT LOGAN), F.R.G.S., &c. Catalogue of Works on the Geology &c., of the Australian Continent and Tasmania. [*See* ETHERIDGE, R.]

JACKMAN (ISAAC). All the World's a Stage : a Farce. [*See* FARCES, 4.]

JACKMAN (WILLIAM). Narrative of Fifteen Years in the Life of. [*See* CHAMBERLAYNE, REV. I.]

JACKSON (ANDREW). Robert O'Hara Bourke, and the Australian Exploring Expedition of 1860. 8vo. Lond., 1862. MD 3 S 1

JACKSON (A. W.) Miracle Plays and Sacred Dramas. [*See* HASE, DR. K.]

JACKSON (BENJAMIN DAYDON). Guide to the Literature of Botany; being a Classified Selection of Botanical Works. Sq. 8vo. Lond., 1881. K 7 S 29

Hand-book of Cinchona Culture. [*See* GORKOM, K. W. VAN.]

Vegetable Technology : a Contribution towards a Bibliography of Economic Botany ; with a comprehensive Subject-index. (Index Society). Sm. 4to. Lond., 1882. E

JACKSON (CATHERINE CHARLOTTE) LADY. Court of France in the 16th Century, 1514–59. 2 vols. 8vo. Lond., 1886. B 8 P 14, 15

Diaries, &c., of Sir George Jackson. [*See* JACKSON, SIR G.]

The French Court and Society : Reign of Louis XVI and First Empire. 2 vols. 8vo. Lond., 1881. B 8 P 12, 13

JACKSON (C. P. KAINS-). [*See* KAINS-JACKSON, C. P.]

JACKSON (GEORGE). Complete System of Book-keeping by Double Entry, in three Sets of Books ; with Questions for Examination ; to which is added Book-keeping by Single Entry, with a Collection of Commercial Letters, by Marcus Trotter. 8vo. Dublin, 1860. A 10 S 11

JACKSON (SIR GEORGE), K.C.H. Diaries and Letters of, from the Peace of Amiens to the Battle of Talavera ; edited by Lady Jackson. 2 vols. 8vo. Lond., 1872. C 7 R 31, 32

JACKSON (MISS GEORGINA F.) Shropshire Folk-lore a Sheaf of Gleanings ; edited by Charlotte Sophia Burne. 8vo. Lond., 1883–86. B 5 S 29

Shropshire Word-book : a Glossary of Archaic and Provincial Words, &c., used in the Country. 8vo. Lond., 1879. K 15 R 17

JACKSON (MRS. HELEN MARIA FISKE.) A Century of Dishonour : a Sketch of the United States Government's Dealings with some of the North American Tribes ; by "H. H." 8vo. Lond., 1881. B 1 Q 35

JACKSON (JAMES). Liste Provisoire de Bibliographies Géographiques Spéciales. 8vo. Paris, 1881. K 8 Q 36

JACKSON (JAMES GREY). An Account of the Empire of Marocco, and the Districts of Suse and Tafilelt. Illustrated. 3rd ed. 4to. Lond., 1814. D 2 U 16

JACKSON (JOHN). A Treatise on Wood-engraving, Historical and Practical. With Illustrations on Wood. Roy. 8vo. Lond., 1866. A 7 V 8

JACKSON (COL. JULIAN R.) What to Observe ; or, the Traveller's Remembrancer. 8vo. Lond., 1841. A 16 Q 23

JACKSON (LOWIS D'AGUILAR), C.E. Aid to Engineering Solution. 8vo. Lond., 1885. A 6 T 10

Hydraulic Manual. Parts 1 and 2 ; consisting of Working Tables and Explanatory Text. 8vo. Lond., 1875. A 6 T 19

Modern Metrology : a Manual of the Metrical Units and Systems of the Present Century ; with an Appendix. 8vo. Lond., 1882. A 16 R 9

JACKSON (MASON). The Pictorial Press : its Origin and Progress. Illustrated. 8vo. Lond., 1885. B 15 Q 26

JACKSON (SAMUEL). Life and Character of Gerhard Tersteegen. [*See* TERSTEEGEN, G.]

JACKSON (THOMAS). Centenary of Wesleyan Methodism. 10th thousand. 8vo. Lond., 1839. G 1 R 27

Life of Rev. Charles Wesley, M.A., comprising a Review of his Poetry. 2 vols. 8vo. Lond., 1841. C 6 R 18, 19

JACKSON (THOMAS JEFFERSON), "STONEWALL JACKSON." Life of ; by the Hon. J. M. Daniells. 8vo. Lond., 1863. C 2 Q 24

Life of ; by Professor R. L. Dabney, D.D. 2 vols. 8vo. Lond., 1864–66. C 3 U 10, 11

JACKSON (REV. WILLIAM), M.A., &c. Philosophy of Natural Theology. 8vo. Lond., 1874. G 9 T 9

JACKSON (WILLIAM). The Four Ages; together with Essays on various subjects. 8vo. Lond.,1798.   J 10 T 31

JACOB (MAJOR GEORGE ADOLPHUS). Manual of Hindu Pantheism : the Vedântasâra translated. 8vo. Lond., 1881.   G 15 P 16

JACOB (REV. GEORGE ANDREW), D.D. Ecclesiastical Polity of the New Testament. 8vo. Lond., 1871.   G 15 R 11

JACOB (LIEUT.-COL. S. S.), AND HENDLEY (SURGEON-MAJOR T. H.) Jeypore Enamels. Imp. 4to. Lond., 1886.   A 23 P 2 ‡

JACOBI (HERMANN). Gaina Sûtras. [*See* MÜLLER, PROF. F. M.]

JACOBI (D. J. L.) Lectures on the History of Christian Dogmas. [*See* NEANDER, J. A. W.]

JACOBS (ALFRED). L'Océanie Nouvelle. Les Chinois et les Européens. Migrations des Peuples. Contact des Races. Caractères nouveaux. De la Colonisation au xixᵉ Siècle. 8vo. Paris, 1861.   MD 4 Q 46

JACOBS (CHRISTIAN FRIEDRICH WILHELM). [*See* ANTHOLOGIA GRAECA.]

JACOBS (JOSEPH), B.A. The Jewish Question, 1875–84 : Bibliographical Hand-List. 12mo. Lond., 1885. K 17 P 2

JACOLLIOT (LOUIS). Voyage humouristique au Pays des Kangourous. 12mo. Paris, 1884.   MJ 1 Q 39

JACOX (REV. FRANCIS). Cues from all Quarters ; or, Literary Musings of a Clerical Recluse. 8vo. Lond., 1871.   J 10 R 1

JACQUEMART (ALBERT). Four Masters of Etching. [*See* WEDMORE, F.]

History of the Ceramic Art: a Descriptive and Philosophical Study of the Pottery of all Ages and all Nations ; translated by Mrs. Bury Palliser. 2nd. ed. Imp. 4to. Lond., 1877.   A 7 V 3

A History of Furniture ; translated from the French. Edited by Mrs. Bury Palliser. Illustrated. Roy. 8vo. Lond., 1878.   A 11 V 9

JACQUEMIN (RAPHAEL). Histoire Générale du Costume Civil, Religieux et Militaire du ivᵉ au xiiᵉ Siècle occident (315-1100.) Roy. 4to. Paris, 1879.   A 28 8 †

Iconographie Générale et Méthodique du Costume du ivᵉ a xixᵉ Siècle (315 -1815). Imp. 4to. Paris, 1869.   A 4 W 7

JACQUEMONT (VICTOR). Letters from India ; describing a Journey in the British Dominions of India, Tibet, Lahore, and Cashmere during the years 1828-31. 2 vols. 8vo. Lond., 1834.   D 6 R 1, 2

JACQUES DE VITRY. Histoire des Croisades. [*See* GUIZOT, F. P. G., 22.]

JACQUINOT (C. H.) Botanique [et] Zoologie.   [*See* DUMONT D'URVILLE, CAPT. J. S. C.]

JACQUIER (F.) Philosophiae Naturalis Principia Mathematica. [*See* NEWTON, SIR J.]

JAEGER (A.) Kramers' Pocket-Dictionary of the English-Dutch and Dutch-English Languages.   [*See* KRAMERS, J.]

JAEGER ((DR. GUSTAV.) [*See* HOCHSTETTER, DR. F. VON.]   MA 2 Q 10, 11 f

JAESCHKE (H. A.) Romanized Tibetan and English Dictionary. Roy. 8vo. Kyelang, 1866.   K 15 8 8

JÄGER (PROF. CARL), AND RIMBAULT (EDWARD F.), LL.D. Gallery of German Composers, engraved by Prof. C. Jäger ; with Biographical and Critical Notices by Edward F. Rimbault, LL.D. Fol. Lond., 1873.   C I W 6

JÄGER (PROF. G.) Zoologische Briefe. 8vo. Wien, 1876.   A 14 S 20

JAGO (RICHARD). Life and Poems of. [*See* CHALMERS, A.]

JAGO (WILLIAM.) Chemistry of Wheat, Flour, and Bread, and Technology of Bread-making. 8vo. Brighton, 1886.   A 6 Q 8

JAGOR (F.) Reisen in den Philippinen. Roy. 8vo. Berlin, 1873.   D 6 T 4

Travels in the Philippines. 8vo. Lond., 1875. D 6 T 5

JAHANGUEIR (EMPEROR OF PERSIA.) [*See* JEHANGHIR.]

JAHN (JOHN), D.D. Archæologia Biblica : a Manual of Biblical Antiquities: translated by T. C. Upham. 3rd ed. 8vo. Oxford, 1836.   G 3 P 13

History of the Hebrew Commonwealth; from the earliest Times to the Destruction of Jerusalem, A.D. 72. 2 vols. 8vo. Lond., 1829.   G 1 R 25, 26

JAHN (OTTO). Life of Mozart. Translated by Pauline D. Townsend. 3 vols. 8vo. Lond., 1882. C 7 S 19-21

Der tod der Sophonisba auf einem Wandgemälde. (Pam. D.) 4to. Leipsic, 1859.   MJ 2 U 3

JAHRESBERICHTE über die Fortschritte der Anatomie und Physiologie. [*See* ANATOMIE UND PHYSIOLOGIE.]

JAL (A.) Dictionnaire Critique de Biographie et d'Histoire. Roy. 8vo. Paris, 1867.   C 11 V 18

JAMAICA. Haud-book of, for 1882, 1884-85; comprising Historical, Statistical, and General Information concerning the Island. Published by Authority for A. C. Sinclair and Laurence R. Fyfe. 8vo. Jamaica and Lond., 1882-85.   E

JAMES I (KING OF ARAGON). Chronicle of, surnamed the Conqueror; written by himself; translated from the Catalan by the late John Forster, Esq., M.P. for Berwick. 2 vols. 8vo. Lond., 1883.   B 13 T 16, 17

JAMES I (KING OF ENGLAND). Court and Times of; edited by Prof. R. F. Williams. 2 vols. 8vo. Lond., 1848. C 10 S 37, 38

Court of. [*See* GOODMAN, DR. G.]

England in the Days of. [*See* RYE, W. B.]

Historical and Critical Account of the Life and Writings of James I and Charles I, &c., and of the Lives of Oliver Cromwell and Charles II; by William Harris. New ed. 5 vols. 8vo. Lond., 1814. C 7 R 19–23

Life of; by Robert Chambers. 2 vols. (in 1) 18mo. Lond., 1830. C 1 P 31

Life of; by R. Chambers. (Const. Misc.) 2 vols. 18mo. Edinb., 1830. K 10 Q 43, 44

Memoirs of the Court of; by Lucy Aikin. 2 vols. 8vo. Lond., 1822. C 9 R 3, 4

Secret History of the Court of. [*See* SCOTT, SIR W.]

JAMES II (KING OF ENGLAND). Extracts from the Life of, as written by himself, published by James Macpherson. Original Papers. 2 vols. 4to. Lond., 1775. B 2 U 11, 12

James II and the Duke of Berwick; by Lieut.-Col. Charles Townsend Wilson. 8vo. Lond., 1876. B 5 P 47

Life of; together with the King's Advice to his Son, and his Majesty's Will, by the Rev. J. S. Clarke. 2 vols. 4to. Lond., 1816. C 4 W 20, 21

Mémoires de. [*See* GUIZOT, F. P. G., 22-26.]

JAMES I (KING OF SCOTLAND). Poetical Remains of. 8vo. Edinb., 1783. H 8 V 25

Works of; to which is prefixed a Historical and Critical Dissertation on his Life and Writings. 8vo. Glasgow, 1825. H 7 P 33

JAMES (A. G. F. ELIOT). Indian Industries. 8vo. Lond., 1880. A 1 Q 25

JAMES (CHARLES). Universal Military Dictionary, in English and French. 4th ed. 8vo. Lond.,1816. A 29 T 14

JAMES (EDWIN). Account of an Expedition from Pittsburg to the Rocky Mountains, performed in the years 1819–20, under the command of Major S. H. Long. Compiled by Edwin James. 3 vols. 8vo. Lond., 1823. D 15 S 24–26

JAMES (F. L.), M.A., &c. Wild Tribes of the Soudan: an Account of Travel and Sport, chiefly in the Basé Country. 8vo. Lond., 1883. D 2 T 24

JAMES (G. P. R.) Blanche of Navarre: a Play. 8vo. Lond., 1839. H 2 S 4

Dark Scenes of History. 3 vols. 8vo. Lond., 1849. B 36 Q 1-3

History of the Life of Edward the Black Prince, and of the various events connected therewith. 2 vols. 8vo. Lond., 1836. C 10 T 42, 43

History of the Life of Richard Cœur-de-Lion, King of England. 4 vols. 8vo. Lond., 1842–49. C 9 R 10–13

Letters illustrative of Reign of William III. [*See* VERNON, J.]

JAMES (G. P. R.)—*continued.*
Life and Times of Louis XIV. 4 vols. 8vo. Lond., 1838 C 5 U 13–16

Life of Henry IV, King of France and Navarre. 3 vols. 8vo. Lond., 1847. C 7 Q 30–32

Lives of the most eminent Foreign Statesmen. [*See* CROWE, E. E.]

Memoirs of Celebrated Women. 2 vols. 8vo. Lond., 1837. C 2 U 14, 15

JAMES (HENRY), JUNR. French Poets and Novelists. 12mo. Lond., 1884. C 3 S 47

Hawthorne. (Eng. Men of Lets.) 8vo. Lond., 1879. C 1 U 19

Portraits of Places. 8vo. Lond., 1883. D 10 R 11

Transatlantic Sketches. 8vo. Boston, 1875. D 9 Q 4

JAMES (JOHN ANGELL). Autobiography of Rev. William Jay. [*See* JAY, REV. W.]

JAMES (T. HORTON). Six Months in South Australia; with some Account of Port Phillip and Portland Bay, in Australia Felix. 12mo. Lond., 1838.* MD 2 R 1

JAMES (WILLIAM). Naval History of Great Britain, from 1793 to 1827. 6 vols. 8vo. Lond., 1837. B 6 Q 42–47

JAMES (W.), AND GRASSI (GIUSEPPE). Dictionary of the English and Italian Languages, for general use, with the Italian Pronunciation and the Accentuation of every Word in both Languages. Parts 1, 2. 6th ed. 2 vols. 12mo. Leipzig, 1869. K 11 T 35

JAMES (RT. HON. SIR WILLIAM MILBOURNE), LORD JUSTICE OF APPEAL. The British in India; edited by his Daughter, Mary J. Salis Schwabe. 8vo. Lond., 1882. B 10 T 40

JAMES (WILLIAM POWELL), M.A. From Source to Sea; or, Gleanings about Rivers in many Fields. 8vo. Lond. 1884. A 29 Q 6

JAMESON (MRS. ANNA). Characteristics of Women; Moral, Poetical, and Historical. 2 vols. 8vo. Lond., 1835. J 8 U 19, 20

Common-place Book of Thoughts, Memories, and Fancies, original and selected. 8vo. Lond., 1854. J 8 U 12

Another copy. 2nd ed. 8vo. Lond., 1855. J 8 U 13

Diary of an Ennuyée. 3rd ed. 8vo. Lond.,1838. J 8 U 11

Legends of the Monastic Orders, as represented in the Fine Arts. 8vo. Lond., 1850. A 7 R 7

Another copy. 6th ed. 8vo. Lond., 1880. A 7 R 8

Loves of the Poets. 2 vols. 8vo. Lond.,1829. J 8 U 21, 22

Memoirs of Celebrated Female Sovereigns. 2nd. ed. 2 vols. 8vo. Lond., 1834. C 2 U 24, 25

Memoirs of the Early Italian Painters, and of the Progress of Painting in Italy. New ed. 12mo. Lond., 1858. C 1 R 14

JAMESON (MRS. ANNA).—*continued.*

Sacred and Legendary Art. 6 vols. 8vo. Lond., 1872–74.
A 7 R 1–6

1. Legends of the Angels and Archangels, the Evangelists, the Apostles, the Doctors of the Church, and St. Mary Magdalene, as represented in the Fine Arts.

2. The Patron Saints, the Martyrs, the Early Bishops, the Hermits, and the Warrior Saints of Christendom, as represented in the Fine Arts.

3. Legends of the Monastic Orders, as represented in the Fine Arts; forming the second series of Sacred and Legendary Art.

4. Legends of the Madonna, as represented in the Fine Arts; forming the third series of Sacred and Legendary Art. Illustrated by Etchings and Woodcuts.

5, 6. The History of our Lord as exemplified in Works of Art; with that of his Types, St. John the Baptist, and other persons of the Old and New Testament. Commenced by the late Mrs. Jameson; continued and completed by Lady Eastlake.

Social Life in Germany; illustrated in the acted Dramas of H.R.H. the Princess Amelia of Saxony. [*See* AMELIA OF SAXONY, H.R.H. PRINCESS.]

Visits and Sketches, at Home and Abroad. 2nd ed. 3 vols. 8vo. Lond., 1835. J 8 U 14–16

Another copy. 3rd ed. 2 vols. 8vo. Lond., 1839.
J 8 U 17, 18

Winter Studies and Summer Rambles in Canada. 3 vols. 8vo. Lond., 1838. J 5 P 14–16

JAMESON (PROF. ROBERT), F.R.S.E. Discovery and Adventure in the Polar Seas, &c. [*See* LESLIE, PROF. SIR JOHN.]

System of Mineralogy, in which Minerals are arranged according to the Natural History method. 3rd ed. 3 vols. 8vo. Edinb., 1820. A 10 P 18–20

JAMESON (R. G.), M.R.C.S.E. Australia and her Gold Regions. 12mo. New York, 1852. MD 1 W 5

New Zealand, South Australia, and New South Wales. 8vo. Lond., 1842.* MD 1 W 3

JÁMI. [*See* ABDU R-RAHMAN, N.]

JAMIESON (A.) A Text-book on Steam and Steam-engines. With Plates. 8vo. Lond., 1886. A 6 R 15

JAMIESON (JAMES), M.D. Food and Drink as Carriers of Disease. [*See* AUST. HEALTH SOC.]

JAMIESON (JOHN), D.D. The Bruce; and Wallace. [*See* BARBOUR, J.; *and* HENRY THE MINSTREL.]

Etymological Dictionary of the Scottish Language; with the entire Supplement incorporated, by John Longmuir, A.M., &c., and David Donaldson, F.E.I.S. 4 vols. 4to. Paisley, 1879–82. K 3 S 6–9 †

Supplement to Jamieson's Scottish Dictionary; with Memoir and Introduction by David Donaldson, F.E.I.S. 4to. Paisley, 1887. K 3 S 10 †

JAMIESON (JOHN), D.D.—*continued.*

Etymological Dictionary of the Scottish Language; with Supplement. 4 vols. 4to. Edinb., 1808. K 14 S 4–7

Supplement to [the above.] 2 vols. 4to. Edinburgh, 1825. K 14 S 6–7

Another copy, abridged. 8vo. Edinb., 1818. K 13 S 19

JAMIESON (MRS.) Murder of. [*See* KNATCHBULL, J.]

JAMIESON (ROBERT), A.M., &c. Popular Ballads and Songs, from Tradition, Manuscripts, and Scarce Editions; with Translations of similar pieces from the Ancient Danish Language and a few Originals, by the Editor. 2 vols. 8vo. Edinb., 1806. H 7 T 12, 13

JAMISON (SIR JOHN), KNT. Protest against the Police and Gaol Funds. [*See* BLAND, W.]

JANES (ALFRED). System of Shorthand. [*See* ANDERSON, T.]

JANIN (JULES). Fontainebleau, Versailles, Paris. Juin, 1837. 12mo. Paris, 1837. A 7 P 35

Versailles et son Musée Historique. 12mo. Paris, 1837. A 7 P 35

JANIN (JULES), BALZAC (H. DE), AND CORMENIN (—). Pictures of the French : a series of Literary and Graphic Delineations of French Character; by Jules Janin, Balzac, Cormenin, and other celebrated French Authors. Roy. 8vo. Lond., 1841. D 7 V 32

JANNET (PIERRE). [*See* QUÉRARD, J. M.]

JANSONIUS (THEODORUS). Isaaci Casauboni Epistolae. [*See* CASAUBON, I.]

JANSSEN (LEON). Malacca L'Inde Méridionale. [*See* GODINHO DE EREDIA, M.] D 5 V 11

JANSZ (ADM. WILLEM). [*See* LEUPE, P. A.]

JANSZ (COMM. WILLIAM.) [*See* LEUPE, P. A.]

JANVIER (C. A.) Practical Keramics for Students. 8vo. N. York, 1880. A 11 R 9

JAPAN. Dai Nihon Kaneshi : a History of the Coins of Japan; with Supplement. 37 vols. (in 9) roy. 8vo. and 8vo. Japan, 1877. A 13 S 15–23

Description of the Empire of Japan; with Statistics compiled from Information furnished by the Japanese Commissioners at the Melbourne International Exhibition, 1880. 8vo. Melb., 1881. MJ 2 R 16

Japanese Botany. Imp. 8vo. Japan (n.d.) A 5 Q 3

Street Life in Japan. Ob. 8vo. Japan, 1866. D 5 P 40

JAPP (ALEXANDER HAY), LL.D., &c., "H. A. PAGE."
Animal Anecdotes, arranged on a new principle. 8vo.
Lond., 1887. A 14 R 38

German Life and Literature, in a Series of Biograpical
Studies. 8vo. Lond., 1880. C 8 P 16

Golden Lives. Biograpies for the Day. 3rd ed. 8vo.
Lond., 1877. C 1 S 23

JAPP (FRANCIS R.), M.A., &c. Inorganic Ciemistry. [*See*
FRANKLAND, E.]

JARDINE (D.) Criminal Trials. (Lib. Ent. Know.)
2 vols. 12mo. Lond., 1835. K 10 R 23, 24

General Index to the Collection of State Trials. [*See*
HOWELL, T. B., AND T. J.]

JARDINE (FRANCIS LASCELLES, AND ALEXANDER WIL-
LIAM), M.I.C.E. Narrative of the Overland Expedition
of Messrs. Jardine, from Rockiampton to Cape York,
Nortiern Queensland. 8vo. Brisbane, 1867. MD 7 P 12

Overland Expedition from Port Denison to Cape York.
[*See* RICHARDSON, A. J.]

JARDINE (JOHN). Description of the Neigibouriood of
Somerset, Cape York, Australia. 8vo. Lond., 1866.
MD 7 Q 53

JARDINE (REV. ROBERT), B.D., &c. Elements of the
Psyciology of Cognition. 2nd ed. 8vo. Lond., 1884.
G 8 S 9

JARDINE (SIR WILLIAM), BART., F.R.S., &c. Icinology
of Annadale ; or, Illustrations of Footmarks, impressed
on the New Red Sandstone of Corncockle Muir. El. fol.
Edinb., 1853. A 11 P 16 ‡

Natural History of the Birds of Great Britain and
Ireland. (Nat. Lib., 9-12.) 4 vols. 12mo. Edinb.,
1838-60. A 14 P 9-12

Natural History of the Cetacea, or Wales. (Nat. Lib.,
21.) 12mo. Edinb., 1837. A 14 P 21

Natural History of Felinæ. (Nat. Lib., 19.) 12mo.
Edinb., 1834. A 14 P 17

Natural History of Fisies of the Perci Family. (Nat.
Lib., 35.) 12mo. Edinb., 1835. A 14 P 35

Natural History of Gallinaceous and Game Birds. (Nat-
Lib., 3, 4.) 2 vols. 12mo. Edinb., 1834-36. A 14 P 3, 4

Natural History of Humming Birds. (Nat. Lib., 1, 2.)
2 vols. 12mo. Edinb., 1833. A 14 P 1, 2

Natural History of Monkeys. (Nat. Lib., 16.) 12mo.
Edinb., 1833. A 14 P 16

Natural History of the Nectariniadæ, or Sun Birds.
(Nat. Lib., 14.) 12mo. Edinb., 1864. A 14 P.14

Natural History of the Paciydermes or tiick-skinned Quadrupeds. (Nat. Lib., 20.) 12mo. Edinb., 1836. A 14 P 20

Natural History of the Ruminating Animals : Deer,
Antelopes, Camels, &c. (Nat. Lib., 18, 19.) 12mo.
Edinb., 1835-36. A 14 P 18, 19

JARDINE (SIR WILLIAM), BART., F.R.S., &c., AND SELBY
(PRIDEAUX JOHN). Illustrations of Ornitiology. 3 vols.
roy. 4to. Edinb., 1839-45. A 3 P 11-13 †

JARRETT (F. C.) Mercantile and Professional Director and
Desk Companion for 1865. 8vo. Meli., 1865. ME 3 T

JARRETT (REV. W.) Farewell Discourse : a Sermon,
preaced in the Independent Ciapel, Pitt-street, Sydney,
on Sunday Evening, February 18, 1838. MG 1 P 7

JARVES (JAMES J.) Glimpse at the Art of Japan. 8vo.
New York, 1876. A 6 V 30

History of the Hawaiian or Sandwici Islands. 12mo.
Lond., 1843. M B 1 P 7

Anotier copy. 2nd ed. 8vo. Boston, 1844. MB 2 R 21

Anotier copy. 3rd ed. 8vo. Honolulu, 1847. MB 2 R 22

Scenes and Scenery in the Sandwici Islands, and a
Trip through Central America ; being Observations from
my Note-book, during the years 1837-42. 8vo. Lond.,
1844. MD 5 Q 5

JARVEY (CAPT. W. A.) Trial of Capt. Jarvey on a Ciarge
of Poisoning iis Wife. 8vo. Dunedin, 1863. MF 2 S 1

JARVIS (JOHN W.) The Glyptic, or Museo Phusee
Glyptic : a Sacred Book of Jottings, witi an attempt
at a Description of Henry Jones' Museum. 8vo. Lond.,
1875. J 5 Q 16

JARVIS (DR. E.) Value of Common Labour. 8vo.
Wasington, 1879. F 7 Q 19

JAUBERT (PIERRE), ABBÉ. Dictionnaire Raisonné Universel des Arts et Métiers. 5 vols. 8vo. Lyon, 1801.
K 18 P 17-21

JAUFFRET (ADOLPHE). Tables Choises. [*See* JAUFFRET,
L. F.]

JAUFFRET (LOUIS FRANÇOIS). Fables Choises ; traduites
en Vers Latins, avec le Texte en regard ; suivies de
diverses Poésies Latines, par Adolpie Jauffret. 2 vols.
12mo. Paris, 1828. H 7 P 18, 19

JAUREGUIBERRY (VICE-ADMIRAL). [*See* NEW CALE-
DONIA.]

JAUSSEN (E.) Grammaire et Dictionnaire de la Langue
Maorie : Dialecte Taïtien. 12mo. St. Cloud, 1860.
MK 1 P 33

JAY (JOHN). The Federalist. [*See* HAMILTON, A.]

JAY (L. J.) Recueil de Lettres sur la Peinture, la Sculpture, et l'Architecture. 8vo. Paris, 1817. A 7 Q 18

JAY (REV. WILLIAM). Autobiograpiy of. Edited by
George Redford, D.D., &c., and Join Angell James.
8vo. Lond., 1854. C 7 R 33

JEAFFRESON (JOHN CORDY), B.A. Annals of Oxford.
2nd ed. 2 vols. 8vo. Lond., 1871. B 6 T 44, 45

Book about Doctors. 2 vols.8vo. Lond.,1860' C 3 S 11, 12

Book about Lawyers. 2 vols. 8vo. Lond., 1867. C 8 P 26, 27

Book about the Clergy. 2 vols. 8vo. Lond., 1870.
G 7 P 12, 13

JEAFFRESON (JOHN CORDY), B.A.—*continued.*

Book about the Table. 2 vols. 8vo. Lond., 1875.   J 4 S 5, 6

Life of Robert Stephenson, F.R.S., &c.; with descriptive Works, by William Pole, F.R.S., &c. 2 vols. 8vo. Lond., Chapters on some of his most important Professional 1864.   C 9 U 15, 16

The Real Lord Byron: New Views of the Poet's Life. 2 vols. 8vo. Lond., 1883.   C 8 S 24, 25

The Real Shelley: New Views of the Poet's Life. 2 vols. 8vo. Lond., 1885.   C 6 U 23, 24

JEANNE D'ARC. [*See* D'ARC, JEANNE.]

JEANS (G. E.), M.A. Life and Letters of Marcus Tullius Cicero ; being a new Translation of the Letters included in Mr. Watson's Selection; with Notes.   8vo.   Lond., 1880.   C 10 S 17

JEANS (J. S.) England's Supremacy.   8vo.   Lond., 1885.   F 12 P 7

Steel: its History, Manufacture, Properties, and Uses. 8vo. Lond., 1880.   A 13 P 5

JEANS (WILLIAM T.) Creators of the Age of Steel. 8vo. Lond., 1884.   C 2 T 18

Lives of the Electricians: Professors Tyndall, Wheatstone, and Morse. 1st series. 8vo. Lond., 1887.   C 2 S 14

JEBB (JOHN), D.D., BISHOP OF LIMERICK, &c. Thirty Years' Correspondence with A. Knox, M.R.I.A.; edited by the Rev. Chas. Forster, B.D. 2 vols. roy. 8vo. Philad., 1835.   C 7 T 23, 24

JEBB (PROF. RICHARD CLAVERHOUSE), M.A., &c. Attic Orators, from Antiphon to Isaeos. 2 vols. 8vo. Lond., 1876.   C 2 V 7, 8

Bentley. (Eng. Men of Letts.) 8vo. Lond., 1882. C 1 U 3

[*See* SOPHOCLES.]

JEBB (SAMUEL). De Vita et Rebus Gestis Serenissimæ Principis Mariæ Scotorum Regimæ Franciæ Dotariæ. (Latin and French.) 2 vols. roy. fol. Lond., 1825. C 4 S 17, 18 ;

JEFFRIES (B. JOY), A.M., &c. Color-Blindness : its Dangers and Detection. 8vo. Boston 1879.   A 12 Q 7

JEFFERIES (RICHARD). After London ; or, Wild England. 8vo. Lond., 1885.   J 9 S 12

Amateur Poacher. 2nd ed. 8vo. Lond., 1881. A 16 Q 13

Gamekeeper at Home: Sketches of Natural History and Rural Life. 8vo. Lond., 1880.   A 16 R 5

Hodge and his Masters. 2 vols. 8vo. Lond., 1880.
                                              J 9 S 13, 14

Life of the Fields. 8vo. Lond., 1884.   A 16 Q 10

Nature near London. 8vo. Lond., 1883.   A 16 Q 11

Open Air. 8vo. Lond., 1885.   A 16 Q 9

Red Deer. 8vo. Lond., 1884.   A 11 S 6

JEFFERIES (RICHARD).—*continued.*

Round about a Great Estate. New ed.   8vo. Lond., 1881.   A 16 Q 12

Story of my Heart: my Autobiography.   8vo. Lond., 1883.   C 2 Q 42

Wild Life in a Southern Country. New ed. 8vo. Lond., 1881.   A 16 P 24

Wood Magic: a Fable. 2 vols. 8vo. Lond., 1881.
                                              J 9 S 15, 16

JEFFERIS (REV. JAMES), LL.D. Australia Confederated: a Lecture; with Speeches by his Excellency Sir W. F. D. Jervois, G.C.M.G., &c., the Hon. W. Morgan, the Hon. W. Giblin, and Sir Henry Ayers, K.C.B. 8vo. Sydney, 1880.   MF 3 Q 3

Christianity and Buddhism : a Comparison and a Contrast: a Lecture. [*See* CHRISTIAN EVIDENCE SOCIETY.]

Enfranchisement of Labour: a Lecture.   8vo.   Sydney, 1878.   MF 3 P 22

Free Church in a Free State: its Claims and Conflicts. 12mo. Sydney, 1878.   MG 1 Q 8

Life Lessons from the Career of Thomas S. Mort: a Sermon. 8vo. Sydney, 1878.   MG 1 Q 33

Socialism in Germany: Sermon, preached in the Pitt-street Congregational Church, Sydney, on Sunday, 16th June, 1878. (Pam. Bs.) 8vo. Sydney, 1880.   MG 1 Q 34

JEFFREY, JEFFERY, OR **GEOFFREY OF MONMOUTH.** [*See* GEOFFREY OF MONMOUTH.]

JEFFREY (FRANCIS), LORD. Contributions to the *Edinburgh Review.* 4 vols. 8vo. Lond., 1844. J 11 V 27–30

Life of; with a Selection from his Correspondence, by Henry Thomas, Lord Cockburn. 2nd ed. 8vo. Edinb., 1852.   C 7 R 34, 35

Memoir of John Playfair. [*See* PLAYFAIR, J.]

JEFFREY (FRANCIS), LORD, AND **ALISON** (REV. ARCHIBALD), LL.D., &c. Essay on Beauty, and Essays on the Nature and Principles of Taste. Reprint of the 5th ed. 8vo. Lond., 1871.   G 13 Q 6

JEFFREYS (LIEUT. C.), R.N. Van Dieman's Land ; Geographical and Descriptive Delineations of the Island of Van Dieman's Land., 1820.   MD 4 V 21

JEHANGHIR, OR **JAHANGUEIR** (EMPEROR OF PERSIA). Memoirs of ; written by himself, and translated from a Persian MS. by Major David Price. 4to. Lond., 1829.   C 4 W 23

JELĀL AD-DIN-RUMI. Persian Poetry. [*See* ROBINSON, S.]

JENAISCHE Zeitschrift für Medicin und Naturwissenschaft. [*See* MEDICINISCH NATURWISSENSCHAFTLICHE GESELLSCHAFT ZU JENA.]

JENKIN (PROF. FLEEMING), F.R.SS., &c.　Electricity and Magnetism. (Text Books of Science.) 8vo. Lond., 1873.　　A 17 S 11

Gas and Caloric Engines: a Lecture. [*See* HEAT.]

JENKIN (PROF. FLEEMING), F.R.SS., &c., AND EWING (J. A.)　Friction between Surfaces moving at Low Speeds. (Roy. Soc. Pubs., 4.) 4to. Lond., 1878. A 11 P 5†

JENKINS (EDWARD).　The Coolie; his Rights and Wrongs: Notes of a Journey to British Guiana, &c.; by the Author of "Ginx's Baby." 8vo. Lond., 1871.　　D 3 R 46

The Devil's Chain. 12mo. Lond., 1876.　　J 11 U 24

Discussions on Colonial Questions. 12mo. Lond., 1872.*
　　　　　　　　　　　　　　　　　MF 1 P 24

Glances at Inner England: a Lecture. 8vo. Lond., 1874.　　　　　　　　　　　　F 6 S 14

JENKINS (J. S.)　Recent Exploring Expeditions to the Pacific and the South Seas, under the American, English and French Governments. 8vo. Lond., 1853. MD 4 P 26

JENKINS (R. L.)　Universal Education: a Lecture. 8vo. Sydney, 1859.　　　　　　MG 1 Q 30

JENKINS (ROBERT C.)　Heraldry, English and Foreign; with a Dictionary of Heraldic Terms. 12mo. Lond., 1886.　　　　　　　　　　　　K 10 S 4

Story of the Caraffa; translated from an original Manuscript written about 1640-60. 12mo. Lond., 1886.
　　　　　　　　　　　　　　　　　B 12 P 9

JENNER (EDWARD), M.D., &c.　Inquiry into the Causes and Effects of the Variolæ Vaccinæ. 2nd ed. Printed for the Author. Lond., 1800. (*Fac-simile Reprint.*) 4to. Sydney, 1884.　　　　　　　　A 12 V 11

Another copy. 4to. Sydney, 1884.　　MA 1 P 28 †

Life of; with illustrations of his Doctrines and selections from his Correspondence, by John Baron. 2 vols. 8vo. Lond., 1827-38.　　　　　　C 10 U 17, 18

JENNINGS (GEORGE HENRY).　Anecdotal History of the British Parliament. 8vo. Lond., 1880.　　B 7 Q 18

JENNINGS (HARGRAVE).　Charon: Sermons from Styx: Posthumous Work of Frederick the Great; followed by other Terrible Dreams for the Wicked. 8vo. Lond., 1886.　　　　　　　　　　J 12 T 1

JENNINGS (HENRY JAMES).　Lord Tennyson: a Biographical Sketch. 8vo. Lond., 1884.　　C 4 Q 49

JENNINGS (MRS. KATE VAUGHAN).　Rahel [Antonie Frederike Levin]; her Life and Letters. 8vo. Lond., 1876.　　　　　　　　　　　C 4 V 31

JENNINGS (LOUIS J.) The Croker Papers. [*See* CROKER, J. W.]

JENNINGS (SIR PATRICK), K.C.M.G.　Ways and Means: the Financial Statement of, Colonial Treasurer of New South Wales, made 6th April, 1886. 8vo. Sydney, 1886.　　　　　　　　　　MF 1 Q 21

JENNINGS (ROBERT).　Jennings' Landscape Annual, 1832-39. 8 vols. 8vo. Lond., 1832-39.　D 9 Q 25-32

Tourist in Italy; by Thomas Roscoe; Illustrated by J. D. Harding.

Tourist in France; by Thomas Roscoe; Illustrated by J. D. Harding.

Tourist in Spain—Granada; by Thomas Roscoe; illustrated by David Roberts.

Tourist in Spain—Andalusia; by Thomas Roscoe; Illustrated by David Roberts.

Tourist in Spain; by Thomas Roscoe. Biscay and the Castiles; Illustrated by David Roberts.

Tourist in Spain and Morocco; by Thomas Roscoe; Illustrated by David Roberts.

Tourist in Portugal; by W. H. Harrison; illustrated by James Holland.

JENNINGS (SAMUEL), F.L.S., &c.　My Visit to the Goldfields in the South-east Wynaad. 8vo. Lond., 1881.
　　　　　　　　　　　　　　　　　D 6 R 8

JENYNS (REV. L.)　Zoology of the Voyage of H.M.S. *Beagle:* Fish. [*See* DARWIN, C.]

JENYNS (SOAME).　Life and Poems of. [*See* CHALMERS, A., *and* JOHNSON, S.]

JEPHSON (H.)　Fata Morgana; or, the Bristol Sculptor's Idol: a Poem. 12mo. Hobart, 1881.　　MH 1 R 60

JEPHSON (ROBERT).　Braganza: a Tragedy. [*See* MODERN THEATRE, 6.]

The Count of Narbonne: a Tragedy. (Brit. Theatre.) 12mo. Lond., 1808.　　　　　H 1 P 20

The Law of Lombardy: a Tragedy. [*See* MODERN THEATRE, 6.]

Two Strings to your Bow: a Farce. [*See* FARCES, 6.]

JERDAN (WILLIAM).　Autobiography of; with his Literary, Political, and Social Reminiscences and Correspondence, during the last Fifty Years. 4 vols. 8vo. Lond., 1852-53.　　　　　　C 1 S 1-4

Men I have known. Illustrated with Fac-simile Autographs. 8vo. Lond., 1866.　　　　C 4 T 20

JERNINGHAM (HUBERT E. H.), M.P. Life and Times of Sixtus the Fifth. [*See* HÜBNER, F. VON.]

Norham Castle. 8vo. Edinb., 1883.　　B 7 Q 1

Russia's Warnings. Collected from Official Papers. 2nd ed. 8vo. Lond., 1885.　　　　　F 6 T 1

JEROME OF PRAGUE. [*See* HIERONYMOUS PRAGENSIS.]

JEROME (SAINT). [*See* HIERONYMOUS, EUSEBIUS.]

JERROLD (DOUGLAS).　Anecdote Life of. [*See* TIMBS, J.]

Brownrigg Papers; edited by Blanchard Jerrold. 8vo. Lond., 1869.　　　　　　　　　J 1 U 6

Cakes and Ale. 2 vols. 12mo. Lond., 1842.　J 1 U 7, 8

Life of; by his Son, William Blanchard Jerrold. 12mo. Lond., 1869.　　　　　　　C 2 T 29

JERROLD (DOUGLAS).—*continued.*
The Works of. 5 vols. 8vo. Lond., 1869.   J 1 U 1–5

  1. St. Giles and St. James, and Punch's Letters to his Son.
  2. The Story of a Feather, and Cakes and Ale.
  3. Mrs. Caudle's Curtain Lectures, Men of Character, and Punch's Complete Letter Writer.
  4. A Man made of Money, Sketches of the English, the Chronicles of Clovernook, and the Sick Giant and the Doctor Dwarf.
  5. Memoir by W. Blanchard Jerrold. With Portrait.

JERROLD (WILLIAM BLANCHARD), "FIN BEC." The Book of Menus, 1876; by "Fin Bec." 8vo. Lond., 1876.   A 6 Q 25

Brownrigg Papers. [*See* JERROLD, D.]

Final Reliques of Father Prout [the Rev. Francis S. Mahony]. [*See* MAHONEY, REV. F. S.]

At Home in Paris. 2 vols. 8vo. Lond., 1884.   D 7 Q 10, 11

At Home in Paris; and a Trip through the Vineyards to Spain. 8vo. Lond., 1864.   D 7 Q 9

Life of Douglas Jerrold; by his Son. 8vo. Lond., 1869.   C 2 T 29

Life of George Cruikshank; in Two Epochs. Illustrated. 2 vols. 8vo. Lond., 1882.   C 3 R 26, 27

Life of Napoleon III; derived from the State Records, &c. 4 vols. 8vo. Lond., 1874–82.   C 8 T 40–43

Memoir of Laman Blanchard. [*See* BLANCHARD, L.]

On the Boulevards; or, Memorable Men and Things, drawn on the spot, 1853–66; together with Trips to Normandy and Brittany. 2 vols. 8vo. Lond., 1867.   D 7 R 25, 26

[*See* PROVERBIAL WISDOM.]

JERVIS (MAJOR T. B.), F.R.S. Travels in Kashmir and the Panjab. [*See* HUGEL, C. BARON.]   D 4 U 14

JERVIS (REV. WILLIAM HENLEY), M.A. The Gallican Church: History of the Church of France. 2 vols. 8vo. Lond., 1872.   G 1 R 22, 23
The Gallican Church and the Revolution; a Sequel to the "History of the Church of France." 8vo. Lond., 1882.   G 1 R 24

JERVISE (ANDREW), F.S.A., Scot. Memorials of Angus and the Mearns: an Account Historical, Antiquarian, and Traditionary; re-written and corrected by Rev. James Gammack, M.A. 2 vols. 8vo. Edinb., 1885. B 13 R 19, 20

JERVOIS (LIEUT.-COL. SIR WILLIAM FRANCIS DRUMMOND), G.C.M.G., &c. Defence of New Zealand: an Address. illustrated. Fol. Wellington, 1884.*   M A 6 P 1 †
[*See* JEFFERIS, REV. J.]

JERWOOD (JAMES). Dissertation on the Rights to the Seashores and to the Soil and Bed of Tidal Harbours and Navigable Rivers; with especial reference to Mr. Serjeant Merewether's published Speech upon the same Subjects. 8vo. Lond., 1850.   F 8 S 13

JESSE (EDWARD). Anecdotes of Dogs. 8vo. Lond., 1846.   A 14 R 48

An Angler's Rambles. 8vo. Lond., 1836.   A 17 T 58

British Angler's Manual. [*See* HOFLAND, T. C.]

Gleanings in Natural History. 12th ed. 8vo. Lond., 1877.   A 14 P 65

Favorite Haunts and Rural Studies, including Visits to Spots of Interest in the vicinity of Windsor and Eton. 8vo. Lond., 1847.   A 16 Q 19

Scenes and Tales of Country Life; with Recollections of Natural History. 8vo. Lond., 1844.   A 16 Q 3

A Summer's Day at Hampton Court; being a Guide to the Palace and Gardens. 2nd ed. 12mo. Lond., 1840.   D 12 P 11

JESSE (JOHN HENEAGE). George Selwyn and his Contemporaries; with Memoirs and Notes. 4 vols. 8vo. Lond., 1843–44.   C 9 T 30–33

Literary and Historical Memorials of London. 2 vols. 8vo. Lond., 1847.   B 7 P 25, 26

Memoirs of Celebrated Etonians. 2 vols. 8vo. Lond., 1875.   C 6 V 14, 15

Memoirs of the Court of England during the Reign of the Stuarts, including the Protectorate. 3 vols. 8vo. Lond., 1855.   C 1 R 33–35

Memoirs of the Court of England from the Revolution in 1688 to the Death of George II. 3 vols. 8vo. Lond., 1843.   C 10 Q 19–21

Memoirs of the Life and Reign of King George III. 3 vols. 8vo. Lond., 1867.   C 7 Q 13–15

Memoirs of the Pretenders and their Adherents. With a Portrait. 2 vols. 8vo. Lond., 1845.   B 3 T 18, 19

Another copy. New ed., complete in one volume, with a General Index and additional Portraits. 8vo. Lond., 1876.   B 3 Q 8

JESSE (CAPT. WILLIAM), R.A. Life of George Brummell, commonly called "Beau Brummell." 2 vols. 8vo. Lond., 1844.   C 10 P 11, 12

Another copy. Revised and annotated edition; with Portraits. 2 vols. 8vo. Lond., 1886.   C 10 P 13, 14

JESSOP (AUGUSTUS), D.D. Emblems of Saints. [*See* HUSENBETH, F. C.]

JESSOP (WILLIAM R. H.), M.A. Flindersland and Sturtland; or, the Inside and Outside of Australia. 2 vols. 8vo. Lond., 1862.*   MD 1 T 21, 22
Another copy. 2 vols. (in 1) 8vo. Lond., 1862.*   MD4T25

JESSUP (REV. HENRY HARRIS), D.D. Women of the Arabs; with a Chapter for Children. 8vo. Lond., 1874.   D 5 Q 21

JESUITS' LOYALTY (THE), Manifested in Three several Treatises lately written by them against the Oath of Allegiance. Sm. 4to. Lond., 1677.   G 13 T 10

JESUS CHRIST. English Life of Jesus; by Thomas Scott. 3rd thousand. 12mo. Lond., 1879.   G 2 P 40

Jesus Christ: his Life and Works by E. de Presseusé, D.D. Translated by Annie Harwood. 12mo. Lond., 1871.   G 9 Q 3

Life and Times of Jesus, the Messiah; by Alfred Edersheim, M.A., &c. 2 vols. 8vo. Lond., 1883.   G 14 P 18, 19

Life of Jesus; by Ernest Renan. New ed. 8vo. Lond., 1871.   G 14 Q 1

Life of Jesus Christ; by J. A. W. Neander. Translated from the 4th German ed. by John M. Clintock and Charles E. Blumenthal. 8vo. Lond., 1876.   G 16 P 25

Life of Jesus, critically examined by Dr. David Friedrich Strauss; translated from the fourth German edition. 3 vols. 8vo. Lond., 1846.   G 12 P 11–13

JEVONS (FRANK BYRON). Greek Literature, from the Earliest Period to the Death of Demosthenes. 8vo. Lond., 1886.   B 9 S 26

JEVONS (MRS. HARRIET A.) Letters of William Stanley Jevons. [*See* JEVONS, PROF. W. S.]

JEVONS (PROF. WILLIAM STANLEY), LL.D., &c. The Coal Question: an Inquiry concerning the progress of the Nation, and the probable Exhaustion of our Coal mines. 2nd ed. 8vo. Lond., 1866.   A 10 Q 1

Investigations in Currency and Finance. Edited, with an Introduction, by H. S. Foxwell, M.A. Illustrated. 8vo. Lond., 1884.   F 7 S 14

Letters and Journal of; edited by his Wife [MRS. Harriet A. Jevons]. 8vo. Lond., 1886.   C 6 V 22

Methods of Social Reform, and other Papers. 8vo. Lond., 1883.   F 7 S 13

Money, and the Mechanism of Exchange. 8vo. Lond., 1875.   F 6 Q 37

Principles of Science: a Treatise on Logic and Scientific Method. 2 vols. 8vo. Lond., 1874.   G 1 R 20, 21

Studies in Deductive Logic: a Manual for Students. 8vo. Lond., 1880.   G 8 S 10

JEWELL (RT. REV. JOHN), BISHOP OF SALISBURY. Writings of. [*See* BRITISH REFORMERS, 7.]

JEWISH CHRONICLE (THE): a Weekly Journal devoted to the Intersts of Judaism and the Jewish Community at Home and Abroad, from 1st April, 1871–5631, to 31st March, 1872–5632. Fol. Lond., 1871–2.   E

JEWITT (LLEWELLYNN, F. W.), F.S.A. Ceramic Art of Great Britain. Illustrated. 2 vols. roy. 8vo. Lond., 1878.   A S R 22, 23

JEX-BLAKE (MISS SOPHIA), M.D. Medical Women: a Thesis and a History. 1. Medicine as a Profession for Women. 2. The Medical Education of Women. 8vo. Edinb., 1886.   A 12 Q 6

JIMENEZ (DON AUGUSTO). Vocabulario del Dialecto Jitano. 2ª ed. 18mo. Sevilla, 1853.   K 11 S 31

JOAN (POPE), "THE FEMALE POPE": a Historical Study; translated from the Greek of Emmanuel Rhoïdis, by C. H. Collette. 12mo. Lond., 1886.   C 2 Q 23

JOAN OF ARC. [*See* D'ARC, JEANNE.]

JOANNES ABRINCENSIS (ARCHIEPISCOPUS ROTHOMAGENSIS). Opera omnia. [*See* MIGNE, J. P., SERIES LATINA, 147.]

JOANNES CANTACUZENUS (IMPERATOR). Opera omnia. [*See* MIGNE, J. P., SERIES GRÆCA, 153, 154.]

JOANNES DAMASCENUS (SANCTUS). Opera omnia. [*See* MIGNE, J. P., SERIES GRÆCA, 94–96·]

JOANNES SARESBERIENSIS. Opera omnia. [*See* MIGNE, J. P., SERIES LATINA, 199.]

JOANNES VECCUS. Opera omnia. [*See* MIGNE, J. P., SERIES GRÆCA, 141.]

JOBSON (REV. FREDERICK J.), D.D. Australia; with Notes by the Way on Egypt, Ceylon, Bombay, and the Holy Land. 8vo. Lond., 1862.*   MD 4 S 28

JOBSON (RICHARD). The Golden Trade; or, a Discovery of the Riuer Gambra, and the Golden Trade of the Æthiopians. 8vo. Lond., 1623.   Libr.

JOCELIN. Life and Acts of Saint Patrick. [*See* SWIFT, E. L.]

[*See* SCOTLAND, HISTORIANS OF.]

JOCELYN (ROBERT), LORD. Six Months with the Chinese Expedition; or, Leaves from a Soldier's Note-book. 12mo. Lond., 1841.*   B 2 P 21

JOEL. Chronographia Compendiaria. [*See* BYZANTINÆ HIST. SCRIPT.]

JOEL (LEWIS). Consul's Manual, and Shipowner's and Shipmaster's Practical Guide in their Transactions Abroad. 8vo. Lond., 1879.   F 6 V 13

JOHANNES SECUNDUS (EVERARD). The Kisses of. [*See* PROPERTIUS.]

JOHANSEN (CHR.) Die nordfriesische Sprache nach der Föhringer und Amrumer Mundart. 8vo. Kiel, 1862.   K 15 R 29

JOHN (PRINCE), DUKE OF ARGYLE AND GREENWICH. Life of; by Robert Campbell. 12mo. Belfast, 1745.   C 1 R 1

JOHN OF AUSTRIA (DON); or, Passages from the History of the 16th Century, 1547–78; by Sir William Stirling-Maxwell, Bart. 2 vols. imp. 8vo. Lond., 1883·   C 5 W 21, 22

JOHN BULL, from December 17, 1820, to December 31, 1832. 12 vols. fol. Lond., 1820–32.

JOHN BULL. Join Bull to Max O'Rell [Paul Blouet], in Reply to "Join Bull and iis Island." 8vo. Lond., 1885.   J 1 U 14

JOHN BULL'S NEIGHBOUR. Join Bull's Neighbour in her True Light; being an Answer to some recent French Criticisms, by "A Brutal Saxon." 20th tiousand. 8vo. Lond., 1884.   J 1 U 17

JOHN CHEAP. Join Cieap the Ciapman's Library: the Scottisi Ciap Literature of the last Century classified. Witi Life of Dougal Graiam. 3 vols. 12mo. Glasgow, 1877–78.   J 12 S 11–13

JOHNES (THOMAS). Cironicles of Enguerand de Monstrelet. [*See* MONSTRELET, E.]

Memoirs of Join, Lord de Joinville. [*See* JOINVILLE, J., LORD DE.]

Travels of Bertrandon de la Bracquiere. [*See* BRACQUIERE B. DE LA.]

JOHNS (REV. CHARLES ALEXANDER). Home Walks and Holiday Rambles. 12mo. Lond., 1863.   A 28 P 2

JOHNS (MAJOR RICHARD), R.M., AND NICOLAS (LIEUT. P. H.), R.M. Naval and Military Heroes of Great Britain; or, Calendar of Victory. Illustrated. 8vo. Lond., 1876.   C 3 P 31

JOHNS (WALTER A.) Petrolia: a brief History of the Pennsylvania Petroleum Region. [*See* CONE, A.]

JOHNS HOPKINS UNIVERSITY. Studies in Historical and Political Science. Herbert B. Adams, Editor. 3 vols. 8vo. Baltimore, 1883–85.   B 18 S 1–3
 1. Local Institutions.
 2. Institutions and Economics.
 3. Maryland, Virginia, and Wasington.
Studies in Historical and Political Science. Extra Vol. 1. [Republic of New Haven; by Charles H. Livermore. Ph.D.] 8vo. Baltimore, 1886.   B 18 T 1

JOHNSON (REV. ARTHUR HENRY), M.A. Manual of the History of Philosopiy. [*See* TENNEMANN, W. G.]
Normans in Europe. Witi Maps. 12mo. Lond., 1877.   B 7 S 38

JOHNSON (C.) The Country Lasses; or, the Custom of the Manor: a Comedy. (Bell's Brit. Theatre.) 18mo. Lond., 1791.   H 2 P 36

The Farm House; a Farce. [*See* FARCES, 6.]

The Gamesters. [*See* SHIRLEY, J.]

The Village Opera. 12mo. Lond., 1729   H 1 R 26

JOHNSON (C.) Ferns of Great Britain. [*See* SOWERBY, J. E.]

JOHNSON (C. PIERPOINT), AND SOWERBY (JOHN E.) Useful Plants of Great Britain: a Treatise upon the principal Native Vegetables capable of application as Food, Medicine, or in the Arts and Manufactures. Roy. 8vo. Lond., 1863.   A 5 Q 15

JOHNSON (CHARLES PLUMPTRE). Hints to Collectors of original editions of the Works of Ciarles Dickens. 8vo. Lond., 1885.   Libr.
Hints to Collectors of original editions of the Works of William Makepeace Tiackeray. 8vo. Lond., 1885. Libr.

JOHNSON (EDWARD), M.D. Tieory and Principles of Hydropatiy siown to be in strict accordance witi the most recent Discoveries of Science. 12mo. Lond. 1849.   A 12 P 28

JOHNSON (MRS. ESTHER), "STELLA." The Closing Years of Dean Swift's Life; witi Remarks on Stella. [*See* WILDE, W. R.]

JOHNSON (MAJOR E. C.), M.A.I., &c. On the Track of the Crescent: Erratic Notes from Piraeus to Pesti. Illustrated. 8vo. Lond., 1885.   D 7 S 36

JOHNSON (FRED. E.), A.P.S., &c. New Souti Wales, and iow to get tiere: an Emigrant's Guide to Australia, *viâ* the Cape of Good Hope, under the auspices of the New Souti Wales Government. 8vo. Lond., 1886.   MD 4 V 40

JOHNSON (GEORGE W.) Memoirs of Join Selden, and Notices of the Political Contest during iis Time. 8vo. Lond., 1835.   C 9 V 31

JOHNSON (J.) Medico-ciirurgical Review. [*See* MEDICO-CHIRURGICAL REVIEW.]

JOHNSON (JAMES). The Scotisi Musical Museum; consisting of upwards of 600 Songs, witi proper Basses for the Pianoforte. Vols. 2–6. 8vo. Edinb., 1839. H 5 U 12–16

JOHNSON (JAMES Y.) Scientific and Literary Treasury. [*See* MAUNDER, S.]

JOHNSON (JOHN), F.S.A. Reliques of Ancient Englisi Arciitecture. Litiographied by Alfred Newman. Fol. Lond., 1858.   A 23 P 15 ‡

JOHNSON (J. B.) Tieory and Practice of Surveying. 8vo. New York, 1886.   A 6 S 27

JOHNSON (J. PITTS). Plain Truti, told by a Traveller, regarding our various Settlements in Australia and New Zealand. 12mo. Lond., 1840.   MD 2 R 53

JOHNSON (MANUEL J.) Catalogue of 606 Principal Fixed Stars in the Soutiern Hemispiere. 4to. Lond., 1835.   A 3 U 28

JOHNSON (MISS). Questions on Australian and General Geograpiy; witi useful Facts for the Junior Classes in Sciools. 5th ed. (revised.) 18mo. Sydney, 1870.   MD 1 S 13

JOHNSON (SAMUEL), LL.D. [a Biography]; by Leslie Stephen. (Eng. Men of Letts.) 8vo. Lond., 1879.
C 1 U 21

Account of the Life and Writings of Richard Savage. [*See* SAVAGE, R.]

Dictionary of the English Language, founded on that of Dr. Samuel Johnson. [*See* LATHAM, R. G.]

Dictionary of the English Language; with numerous Corrections and Additions, by the Rev. H. J. Todd, M.A., &c. 2nd ed. 3 vols. 4to. Lond., 1827.   K 15 T 12–14

Dr. Johnson: his Religious Life and his Death; by J. T. Hewlett. 8vo. Lond., 1850.   C 3 V 14

Johnsoniana: Anecdotes of the late Samuel Johnson, LL.D. Newly collected and edited, by Robina Napier. 8vo. Lond., 1884.   C 7 Q 43

Johnsoniana; or, Supplement to Boswell. Anecdotes and Sayings of Dr. Johnson. 8vo. Lond., 1836.   C 7 Q 38

Journal of a Tour to the Hebrides with Samuel Johnson. [*See* BOSWELL, JAMES.]   D 7 T 34

Life and Conversations of (founded chiefly upon Boswell); by Alexander Main. 8vo. Lond., 1874.   C 3 V 15

Life of Abraham Cowley. [*See* COWLEY, A.]

Life of, and the Journal of his Tour to the Hebrides; by James Boswell; edited by Henry Morley, LL.D., &c. 5 vols. imp. 8vo. Lond., 1885.   C 8 V 16–20

Life of; by Sir John Hawkins, Knt. 2nd ed. 8vo. Lond., 1787.   C 6 R 6

Life of; by James Boswell. New ed. 4 vols. 8vo. Lond., 1820.   C 7 Q 34–37

Life of; together with the Journal of a Tour to the Hebrides, by James Boswell. New ed.; with Notes and Appendices, by Alexander Napier. 4 vols. 8vo. Lond., 1884.   C 7 Q 39–42

Life of Roger Ascham. [*See* ASCHAM, R.]

Life of Sir Thomas Browne. [*See* BROWNE, SIR T.]

Poetical Works of. [*See* POETICAL WORKS.]   H 7 P 39

Lives of Dryden and Pope; edited, with Introduction and Notes, by Alfred Milnes, M.A. (Clar. Press.) 12mo. Oxford, 1885.   C 14 P 9

Lives of the British Poets; completed by W. Hazlitt. 4 vols. 8vo. Lond., 1854.   C 4 Q 7–10

Rasselas, Prince of Abyssinia. 8vo. Lond., 1883. J 10 R 13

Another copy. [*See* CLASSIC TALES.]

Voyage to Abyssinia. [*See* LOBO, FATHER J.]

Works of; with an Essay on his Life and Genius, by Arthur Murphy. 12 vols. 8vo. Lond., 1796. J 10 U 1–12

Another copy. New ed. 2 vols. 8vo. Lond., 1862. J 2 T 25, 26

Works of English Poets. [*See* CHALMERS, A.]

JOHNSON (SAMUEL), LL.D.—*continued.*

Works of the English Poets; with Prefaces, Biographical and Critical, by Samuel Johnson, and a Poetical Index. 75 vols. 12mo. Lond., 1790.   H 5 P 1–Q 15

  1. Dr. Johnson's Advertisement. Lives of Cowley—Denham—Milton--Butler—Rochester—Roscommon—Otway.

  2. Lives of Waller—Pomfret—Dorset—Stepney—J. Philips—Walsh--Dryden.

  3. Lives of Smith—Duke—King—Sprat—Halifax—Parnell—Garth—Rowe—Addison—Hughes—Sheffield, Duke of Buckingham—Prior—Congreve—Blackmore—Fenton.

  4. Lives of Gay—Granville—Yalden—Tickell—Hammond—Somerville—Savage—Swift—Broome.

  5. Lives of Pope — Pitt — Thomson — Watts — A. Philips—West - Collins—Dyer—Shenstone.

  6. Lives of Young—Mallet—Akenside—Gray—Lyttelton—Moore—Cawthorn--Churchill—Falconer—Lloyd—Cunningham — Green—Goldsmith—Paul Whitehead—Armstrong—Langhorne—Johnson—William Whitehead—Jenyns.—Index to the Lives.

  7–9. Poems of Abraham Cowley. Poems and Translations, by the Hon. Sir John Denham, Knight of the Bath.

  10–12. Poems of John Milton.

  13–14. Poems of Samuel Butler.

  15. Poems by the Earl of Rochester—Earl of Roscommon—Thomas Otway.

  16. Poems of Edmund Waller.

  17. Poems of John Pomfret—Earl of Dorset—George Stepney — John Philips—William Walsh.

  18–21. Poems, Tales, and Translations of John Dryden.

  22–24. The Works of Virgil; translated into English Verse by Mr. Dryden.

  25. Poems of Mr. Edmund Smith—Richard Duke—William King, LL.D., &c.

  26. Poems of William King, LL.D.—Dr. Thomas Sprat, Bishop of Rochester—Earl of Halifax.

  27. Poems of Dr. Thomas Parnell, late Archdeacon of Clogher.

  28. Poems of Sir Samuel Garth—Mr. Nicholas Rowe.

  29. Lucan's Pharsalia; translated into English Verse by Nicholas Rowe.

  30. Poems of Joseph Addison.

  31. Poems of John Hughes.

  32. Poems of John Sheffield, Duke of Buckinghamshire—Matthew Prior.

  33, 34. Poems of Matthew Prior—Mr. Congreve.

  35. Poems of Sir Richard Blackmore, Knt., &c.—Elijah Fenton.

  36, 37. Poems of John Gay.

  38. Poems of George Granville, Lord Lansdowne.

  39. Poems of Dr. Yalden—Thomas Tickell—Mr. Hammond's Love Elegies.

  40, 41. Poems of William Somervile—Richard Savage.

  42–44. Poems of Dr. Jonathan Swift—Dr. William Broome.

  45–47. Poems of Alexander Pope.

  48–51. Pope's Homer.

  52, 53. Poems and Translations of Christopher Pitt—Pitt's Virgil.

  54–56. Poems of James Thomson—Dr. Watts.

  57. Pastorals, Epistles, Odes, and other original Poems, with Translations from Pindar, Anacreon, and Sappho; by Ambrose Philips.—Odes of Horace, with several other Pieces in Verse, translated from the Greek; to which are added original Poems on several occasions; by Gilbert West, LL.D.

JOHNSON (SAMUEL), LL.D.—*continued.*

58. Poems of William Collins—John Dyer.

59. Poems of William Shenstone.

60–62. Poems of Edward Young.

63, 64. Poems of David Mallet—Mark Akenside—Mr. Gray—Lord Lyttelton.

65. Poems of Edward Moore—James Cawthorne.

66–67. Poems of Charles Churchill—William Falconer.

68. Poems of Robert Lloyd.

69. Poems, chiefly Pastoral, of John Cunningham—Matthew Green.

70. Poems of Oliver Goldsmith—Paul Whitehead.

71. Poems of John Armstrong, M.D.—John Langhorne.

72–73. Poems of Samuel Johnson, LL.D.—William Whitehead—Soame Jenyns.

74, 75. General Index to the English Poets.

JOHNSON (REV. SAMUEL). Oriental Religions, and their relation to Universal Religion. China. 8vo. Boston, 1877.   G 1 R 13

Oriental Religions, and their relation to Universal Religion. India. 2nd ed. 8vo. Lond., 1873.   G 1 R 14

Oriental Religions, and their relation to Universal Religion. Persia. 8vo. Lond., 1885.   G 1 R 16

JOHNSON (REV. SAMUEL JENKINS), M.A., &c. Eclipses, Past and Future; with General Hints for observing the Heavens. 8vo. Lond., 1874.   A 3 R 24

JOHNSON (SAMUEL W.), M.A. How Crops Feed; a Treatise on the Atmosphere and the Soil, as related to the Nutrition of Agricultural Plants. Illustrated. 8vo. New York, 1870.   A 1 U 4

JOHNSON (WILLIAM). Fermentation: a Lecture. [*See* MELBOURNE PUBLIC LIBRARY, MUSEUM, &c.]

Hydrogen: a Lecture. [*See* MELBOURNE PUBLIC LIBRARY.]

Nitrogen, its Economy and Nature. [*See* MELBOURNE PUBLIC LIBRARY, MUSEUM, &c.]

JOHNSTON (ALEXANDER KEITH), LL.D., &c. General Dictionary of Geography; Descriptive, Physical Statistical, Historical; forming a complete Gazetteer of the World. Roy. 8vo. Lond., 1877.   D 11 U 4

Geographical Distribution of Material Wealth. 2. Historical Notes regarding the Merchant Company of Edinburgh; [by A. K. Mackie.] Sq. 8vo. Edinb., 1862.   F 6 S 13

Household Cyclopædia of Geography. [*See* BRYCE, J.]

Physical Atlas: a Series of Maps and Notes illustrating the Geographical Distribution of Natural Phenomena. At. fol. Lond., 1848.   A 8 P 11 ‡

Royal Atlas of Modern Geography. At. fol. Lond., 1868.   D 8 P 6 ‡

Royal Atlas of Modern Geography: with a special Index to each Map. At. fol. Edinb., 1881.   D 8 P 7 ‡

School Atlas of Physical Geography, illustrating in a series of original Designs the elementary facts of Geology, Hydrography, Meteorology and Natural History. imp. 8vo. Edinb., 1873.   A 33 Q 16 ‡

JOHNSTON (CHARLES). Travels in Southern Abyssinia, through the Country of Adal to the Kingdom of Shoa. 2 vols. 8vo. Lond., 1844.   D 2 P 9, 10

JOHNSTON (LIEUT.-COL. GEORGE). Proceedings of a General Court Martial, held at Chelsea Hospital for the Trial of Lieut.-Col. Geo. Johnston, on a charge of Mutiny, for deposing William Bligh, Esq., F.R.S., Captain-General and Governor-in-Chief of New South Wales. Taken in shorthand by Mr. Bartrum. 8vo. Lond., 1811.   MF 2 Q 10

JOHNSTON (GEORGE), M.D. History of the British Zoophytes. 8vo. Edinb., 1838.   A 14 U 4

Introduction to Conchology: or, Elements of the Natural History of Molluscous Animals. 8vo. Lond., 1850.   A 14 U 5

JOHNSTON (HENRY HAMILTON), F.R.G.S., &c. Kilimanjaro Expedition: a Record of Scientific Exploration in Eastern Equatorial Africa. 8vo. Lond., 1886. D 2 R 19

The River Congo, from its Mouth to Bólóbó; with a General Description of the Natural History and Anthropology of its Western Basin. With Illustrations by the Author. 8vo. Lond., 1884.   D 2 R 18

JOHNSTON (JAMES F. W.), M.D. Chemistry of Common Life. 2 vols. 8vo. Lond., 1855.   A 5 S 14, 15

Notes on North America. 2 vols. 8vo. Edinb., 1851.   D 3 R 34, 35

JOHNSTON (KEITH), F.R.G.S. Biographical Notice of. [*See* THOMSON, J.]

Household Cyclopædia of Geography. [*See* BRYCE, J.]

Physical, Historical, Political, and Descriptive Geography. Maps and Illustrations. (Lond. Geog. Series.) 8vo. Lond., 1880.   D 11 S 3

JOHNSTON (R.) Land Law Ireland Act; with Notes, copious Index, and Précis. 8vo. Lond., 1881. F 6 P 28

JOHNSTON (R. M.) Further Notes on the Tertiary Marine Beds of Table Cape, Tasmania. (Pam. Ch.) 8vo. Hobart, 1876.   MA 2 Q 29

Notes on the Fossils referred to in "Further Notes on the Tertiary Marine Beds of Table Cape." [*See* TENISON-Woons, REV. J. E.]

JOHNSTON (WILLIAM). England as it is, Political, Social, and Industrial, in the Middle of the 19th Century. 2 vols. 12mo. Lond., 1851.   F 6 S 15, 16

JOHNSTON (WILLIAM). Agriculture: the Art of Farming adapted to the Colonies. (Pam. Cg.) 8vo. Sydney, 1873.   MA 2 V 8

JOHNSTON-LAVIS. [*See* LAVIS, H. J. J.-]

JOHNSTONE (HENRY ALEXANDER MUNRO-BUTLER). Trip up the Volga to the Fair of Nijni-Novgorod. 8vo. Lond., 1875.   D 7 Q 4

JOHNSTONE (CAPT. J. C.) Maoria: a Sketch of the Manners and Customs of the Aboriginal Inhabitants of New Zealand. 8vo. Lond., 1874.*   MD 5 Q 33

JOHNSTONE (JAMES), CHEVALIER DE. Memoirs of the Rebellion in 1745-46. 4to. Lond., 1820. B 2 T 21

JOHNSTONE (JOHN), M.D. Works of Samuel Parr; with Memoirs. [*See* PARR, S.]

JOHNSTONE (REV. JAMES), A.M. Antiquitates Celto-Normannicæ; containing the Chronicle of Man and the Isles, to which are added Extracts from the Annals of Ulster, &c. 4to. Copenhagen, 1786. B 4 V 14

Antiquitates Celto-Scandicæ. 4to. Havniæ, 1786.
B 4 V 14

Norwegian Account of Haco's Expedition against Scotland, A.D. 1263. Literally translated from the original Islandic, by the Rev. James Johnstone. 8vo. Edinb., 1882. B 13 P 14

JOHNSTONE (W.) Morning Communings with God. [*See* STURM, C. C.]

JOHNYS (SIR HUGH). Some Account of Sir Hugh Johnys, Deputy Knight Marshal of England, temp. Henry VI and Edward IV, and of his Monumental Brass; by Thomas Bliss, B.A., and George Grant Francis, F.S.A. Roy. 8vo. Swansea, 1845 C 9 V 25

JOINVILLE (JOHN), LORD DE, GRAND SENESCHAL OF CHAMPAGNE. Histoire de St. Louis, Credo et Lettre à Louis X. Texte original, accompagné d'une Traduction par N. de Wailly. Imp. 8vo. Paris, 1874. C 4 W 30

Memoirs of, written by himself; containing a History of part of the Life of Louis IX, King of France; translated by Thos. Joines, Esq. 2 vols. 4to. Hafod, 1807. C 2 W 8, 9

Another copy. 2 vols. (in 1) 4to. Hafod, 1807. C 10 S 2 †

[*See* CHRONICLES OF THE CRUSADES.]

JOLI (GUY). Mémoires de Mr. Joli, Conseiller au Parlement; contenant l'Histoire de la Régence d'Anne d'Autriche et des premieres années de la majorité de Louis XIV, jusqu'en 1666; avec les Intrigues du Cardinal de Retz à la Cour, et Mémoires de Madame le Duchesse de Nemours. 2 vols. 12mo. Amsterd., 1718. C 1 R 16, 17

Mémoires de. [*See* RETZ, CARDINAL DE.]

JOLLY (JULIUS). The Institutes of Vishnu. [*See* MÜLLER, PROF. F. M.]

JOLLY (WILLIAM), F.R.S.E., &c. Life of John Duncan, Scotch Weaver and Botanist; with Sketches of his Friends, and Notices of the Times. 8vo. Lond., 1883. C 5 R 13

Principles and Practice of Education. [*See* COMBE, G.]

Robert Burns at Mossgiel; with Reminiscences of the Poet, by his Herd-boy, Willie Patrick. Sq. 12mo. Paisley, 1881. C 1 P 25

JOLY (NICOLAS). Man before Metals. With 148 Illustrations. 8vo. Lond., 1883. A 9 P 37

JONES (CHARLES C.), JUNR. Antiquities of the Southern Indians, particularly the Georgia Tribes. With Plates. Roy. 8vo. New York, 1873. B 1 T 19

JONES (C. E.) Debate on the Report of the Complaint Committee: Mr. C. E. Jones's Defence: a Speech. 8vo. Melh., 1869 MF 1 Q 2

JONES (C. HANDFIELD), M.B., AND SIEVEKING (EDWARD H.) M.D., &c. Manual of Pathological Anatomy, 2nd ed., revised, enlarged, and edited by Joseph Frank Payne, M.B., &c. (Churchill's Manuals.) 8vo. Lond., 1875. A 13 P 40

JONES (EDWARD THOMAS). English Systems of Bookkeeping, by Single and Double Entry, in two Parts; with numerous Illustrations and Explanations, by Theodore Jones. 18th ed. Roy. 8vo. Lond., 1885. A 10 V 8

JONES (EVAN ROWLAND). Life and Speeches of Joseph Cowen, M.P. 8vo. Lond., 1885. C 10 S 9

JONES (GEORGE), M.R.S.I., &c. Original History of Ancient America, founded upon the Ruins of Antiquity. 8vo. Lond., 1843. B 1 U 19

JONES (REV. HARRY), M.A. Past and Present in the East. Sm. 4to. Lond., 1881. D 6 Q 9

JONES (HENRY). The Earl of Essex: a Tragedy. (Bell's Brit. Theatre.) 18mo. Lond., 1791. H 2 P 28

Another copy. (Brit. Theatre.) 12mo. Lond., 1808. H 1 P 22

Another copy. (New Eng. Theatre.) 12mo. Lond., 1788. H 4 P 23

JONES (HENRY). Description of Henry Jones's Museum. [*See* JARVIS, J. W.]

JONES (MRS. HENRY). Broad Outlines of Long Years in Australia. 8vo. Lond., 1878.* MJ 1 S 31

JONES (HENRY BENCE), M.D. Life and Letters of Faraday. 2nd ed. 2 vols. 8vo. Lond., 1870. C 9 T 8, 9

The Royal Institution: its Founder [Count Rumford] and its first Professors. 8vo. Lond., 1871. B 3 S 24

JONES (MRS. HERBERT). Princess Charlotte of Wales: an Illustrated Monograph. 4to. Lond., 1885. C 4 W 29

JONES (REV. H. BERKELEY), Adventures in Australia, in 1852-53. 8vo. Lond., 1853.* MD 3 R 3

JONES (REV. H. LONGUEVILLE), M.A., &c. Memorials of Cambridge. [*See* LE KEUX, J.] B 6 S 1, 2

JONES (JOHN). Hand-book of the Jones Collection in the South Kensington Museum. (South Kens. Mus., 22.) 8vo. Lond., 1883. E

JONES (MAJ.-GEN. JOHN T.) Account of the War in Spain and Portugal, and in the South of France, 1808-14. 8vo. Lond., 1818. B 13 U 10

Journals of the Sieges undertaken by the Allies in Spain, 1811-12. 8vo. Lond., 1814. B 13 U 11

Journal of the Sieges, carried on by the Army under the Duke of Wellington in Spain, 1811-14. 3rd ed. 3 vols. 8vo. Lond., 1846. B 3 S 10-12

JONES (J. P.) Resumption and the Double Standard; or, the impossibility of resuming Specie Payments in the United States without restoring the Double Standard of Gold and Silver. *(Bound with Campbell's White-herring Fishery.)* 8vo. Wash., 1876. A 14 Q 26

JONES (Lynds E.) [*See* American Catalogue, The.]

JONES (Owen). Grammar of Ornament. Illustrated. Fol. Lond., 1868. A 5 Q 16 †
One Thousand and One Initial Letters, designed and illuminated. Fol. Lond., 1864. A 4 R 19 ‡
Plans, Elevations, Sections, and Details of the Alhambra, from Drawings taken on the spot, in 1834 and 1837; by the late John Goury, and Owen Jones. 2 vols. cl. fol. Lond., 1842-45. A 3 P 16, 17 ‡

JONES (Stephen). Biographia Dramatica. [*See* Baker, D. E.]

JONES (Theodore) System of Book-keeping. [*See* Jones, E. T.]

JONES (Prof. Thomas Rupert), F.R.S., &c. Geology. [*See* Morris, J.]
Micrographic Dictionary. [*See* Griffith, J. W.]

JONES (Thomas Rymer). Natural History of Animals; being the substance of three Courses of Lectures delivered before the Royal Institution of Great Britain. 2 vols. 8vo. Lond., 1845-52. A 14 Q 22, 23

JONES (Thomas S.) [*See* Year-book of New Zealand.]

JONES (T. Wharton), F.R.S. Evolution of the Human Race from Apes, and of Apes from Lower Animals, a Doctrine unsanctioned by Science. 8vo. Lond.. 1876. A 1 W 28
Treatise on the Principles and Practice of Ophthalmic Medicine and Surgery. 3rd ed. (Churchill's Manuals.) 12mo. Lond., 1865. A 13 P 32

JONES (William), F.S.A. Finger-Ring Lore, Historical, Legendary, Anecdotal. 8vo. Lond., 1877. B 14 Q 16

JONES (W.) History of England. [*See* Hume, D.]

JONES (William). History of the Waldenses, connected with a Inscription of the Christian Church. 8vo. Lond., 1812. G 1 R 17

JONES (Sir William). Life and Poems of. [*See* Chalmers, A.]
Memoirs of the Life, Writings, and Correspondence of; by Lord Teignmouth. 4to. Lond., 1804. C 2 W 14
Works of; with Life of the Author, by Lord Teignmouth. 13 vols. 8vo. Lond., 1807. J 7 T 14-26

JONES (W. C.) Report on the subject of Land Titles in California. (Pam. 18.) 8vo. Wash., 1850. F 12 P 10

JONES (W. H. R.), M.A., &c. Statutes of the Cathedral Church of Sarum. [*See* Dayman, E. A.]

JONES (William P.) The West, from the Census of 1880. [*See* Porter, R. P.]

JONES (—.) Adventures of. [*See* Cash, M.]

JONES & CO. Remarks on the Advantages of Bone as a Manure, and on the Results and Mode of its Application to Grass Lands, Arable Lands, Orchards, Vineyards, Gardens. 8vo.. Sydney, 1863. MA 1 Q 7

JONES v. JENKINS; or, the Bushranger's Revenge: a Stiff Yarn; by "Walker." 8vo. Sydney(n.d.) MJ 2 S 27

JONES-PARRY (Capt. S. H.) [*See* Parry, Capt. S. H. Jones-.]

JONGE (J. K. J. de). De Opkomst van het Nederlandsch Gezag in Oost-Indie (1595-1610). 12 vols. 8vo. 'Gravenhage, 1862. B 10 T 19-30

JONQUET (A.) Original Sketches for Art Furniture, in the Jacobean, Queen Anne, Adams, and other Styles. 2nd ed., with many new Designs. Imp. 4to. Lond., 1880. A 23 S 17 ‡

JONSON (Ben.) [Life of]; by John Addington Symonds. (English Worthies.) 12mo. Lond., 1886. C 2 Q 37
The Alchemist: a Comedy. (Bell's Brit. Theatre.) 18mo. Lond., 1791. H 2 P 34
Another copy. [*See* Brit. Drama, 3.]
Every Man in his Humour. (Bell's Brit. Theatre.) 18mo. Lond., 1791. H 2 P 34
Another copy. (Brit. Theatre.) 12mo. Lond., 1808. H 1 P 5
Another copy. (New Eng. Theatre.) 18mo. Lond., 1789. H 4 P 20
Another copy. [*See* Brit. Drama, 3.]
Life and Poems of. [*See* Chalmers, A.]
Works of; with Notes, Critical and Explanatory, and a Biographical Memoir, by W. Gifford. 9 vols. 8vo. Lond., 1816. H 4 S 22-30

    1. Memoirs of Jonson, &c. Every Man in his Humour.
    2. Every Man out of his Humour - Cynthia's Revels—The Poetaster.
    3. Sejanus The Fox The Silent Woman.
    4. The Alchemist Cataline Bartholomew Fair.
    5. The Devil is an Ass The Staple of News—The New Inn.
    6. The Magnetic Lady A Tale of a Tub—The Sad Shepherd—The Case is altered Entertainments, &c.
    7. Masques at Court.
    8. Masques, &c. - Epigrams Underwoods.
    9. Underwoods Translations, &c.—Discoveries--English Grammar Jonsonus Virbius.

Another copy [Reprint of 1816]. 9 vols. imp. 8vo. Lond., 1875. H 1 V 5-13

JONSSON (E.) Oldnordisk Ordbog ved Det Kongelige Nordiske Oldskrift-Selskab. 8vo. Kjöbeniavn, 1863.
K 15 S 2

JORDAN (MRS. DOROTHY). Life of; including original Private Correspondence, and numerous Anecdotes of her Contemporaries; by James Boaden. 2 vols. 8vo. Lond., 1831. C 5 T 13, 14

JORDAN (HENRY), ET EYSSENHARDT (FRANCIS). Scriptores Historiæ Augustæ ab Hadriano ad Numerianum. 2 vols. 8vo. Berolini, 1864. C 9 S 49, 50

JORDAN (DR. J. P.) Vollständiges Tasclen-Wörterbuch der böhmischen und deutsclen Spracie. Neuer Abdruck. 18mo. Leipzig, 1877. K 11 S 16

JORDAN (JAMES C.) Management of Sieep and Stations. 8vo. Meli., 1867. MA 1 P 23

JORDAN (S.), C.E., &c. Album to the Course of Lectures on Metallurgy at the Central Sciool of Arts and Manufactures of Paris. 8vo. Lond., 1878. A 9 U 15
Plates [to the above]. 4to. Lond., 1878. A 3 P 2 †

JORDAN (WILLIAM LEIGHTON), F.R.G.S. New Principles of Natural Pilosopiy. 8vo. Lond., 1883. A 16 U 14

JORNANDES OR JORDANES. Jordanis de Getarum sive Gothorum origine et Rebus Gestis, edidit C. A. Closs. 8vo. Stuttgart, 1866. B 25 Q 2

JORTIN (JOHN), D.D. Remarks on Ecclesiastical History; edited, with Notes, and Life of the Autior, by the Rev. William Trollope, M.A. 2 vols. 8vo. Lond., 1846.
G 1 R 18, 19
Tracts, Piilological, Critical, and Miscellaneous. 2 vols. 8vo. Lond., 1790. J 10 T 28, 29

JOSÉ (A.) Journey across Africa. [*See* AFRICA.]

JOSEPH (JOHN). The Queen v. Josepi. [*See* STATE TRIALS.]

JOSEPH (RABBI JOSEPH BEN JOSHUA BEN MEIR). Cironicles of; translated from the Hebrew, by C. H. F. Bialloblotzky. 2 vols. 8vo. Lond., 1836. B 7 U 23, 24

JOSEPH II. Maria Tieresia und Josepi II: iire Correspondenz. Herausgegeben von Alfred, Ritter von Arneti, 1761–80. 3 vols. 8vo. Wien, 1867–68. C 9 T 25–27

JOSEPH OF EXETER [JOSEPHUS ISCANI]. De Bello Trojano. [*See* DICTYS CRETENSIS.]

JOSEPHINE (EMPRESS). Memoirs of; by J. S. Memes. (Const. Misc.) 18mo. Edinb., 1831. K 10 R 5

JOSEPHSON (J.) Scenes in otier Lands; by * * *. 8vo. Lond., 1856–57. MJ 1 T 38

JOSEPHUS (FLAVIUS). Flavii Josepii, Opera, Græce et Latine; recognovit Guilelmus Dindorfius. 2 vols. imp. 8vo, Paris, 1845–47. G 7 V 12, 13
Works of; translated by William Wiiston, A.M. 4 vols. 8vo. Lond., 1825. G 7 P 21–24

3 E

JOUAN (M.) Note sur les Iles Loyalty. [*See* CHAMBEYRON, CAPT. C. M. L.]

JOUBERT (PROF. J.) Treatise on Electricity and Magnetism. [*See* MASCART, PROF. E.]

JOUBERT (JULES). [*See* AGRICULTURAL SOCIETY OF N. S. WALES.]

JOULE (JAMES PRESCOTT), D.C.L., &c. New Determination of the Meclanical Equivalent of Heat. (Roy. Soc. Pubs., 6.) 4to. Lond., 1879. A 11 P 7 †
Scientific Papers of. Publisied by the Piysical Society of London. Vol. 1. 8vo. Lond., 1884. A 17 W 51

JOURDAIN (ÉLOI), "CHARLES SAINTE-FOI." La Mystique. [*See* GÖRRES, J. J. VON.]

JOURDAN (ANTOINE GABRIEL AIMÉ). Mémoires sur les Journées de Septembre, 1792. [*See* BARRIÈRE, J. F., 18.]

JOURDAN (BEATRICE A.) Journal of a Waiting Gentlewoman. 8vo. Lond., 1866. J 12 Q 7

JOURNAL ASIATIQUE; ou, Recueil de Mémoires, d'Extraits et de Notices relatifs à l'Histoire, à la Piilosopiie, aux Sciences, à la Littérature et aux Langues des Peuples orientaux. 1e –8e serie. 125 vols. (in 63) 8vo. Paris, 1822–84. E

JOURNAL DES ÉCONOMISTES: Revue de la Science Economique et de la Statistique. [1e]–8e série. 58 vols. roy. 8vo. Paris, 1871–85. E

JOURNAL OF A NOBLEMAN; comprising an Account of iis Travels, and a Narrative of iis Residence at Vienna during the Congress. 2 vols. 8vo. Lond., 1831. D 9 P 46, 47

JOURNAL OF ANTHROPOLOGY. [*See* ANTHROPOLOGICAL SOCIETY OF LONDON.]

JOURNAL OF AUSTRALASIA, including wiat I saw at Snaggerack; made in Melbourne, June to December, 1856. 8vo. Melb., 1856. ME 3 Q
The (Illustrated) Journal of Australasia. 3 vols. 8vo. Meli., 1856–57.* ME 3 Q
Anotier copy. (Pam. H.) 8vo. Melb., 1856. ME 3 R
Anotier copy. Vol. 1. 8vo. Meli., 1856. MJ 2 R 21

JOURNAL OF CIVILIZATION (THE). Ciristian Missionary Civilization: its Necessity, Progress, and Blessings. Illustrated. Roy. 8vo. Lond., 1842. D 10 T 31

JOURNAL OF COMMERCE (THE) of New Souti Wales: a Weekly Record of Trade, Customs, and Siipping Intelligence. 7 vols. fol. Sydney, 1867–74. E

JOURNAL OF DESIGN AND MANUFACTURES (THE). Witi Patterns and Engravings. 2 vols. 8vo. Lond., 1849–50. A 11 R 1, 2

JOURNAL OF INDIAN ART. Illustrated with coloured Plates. Vol. 1, Nos. 1–16, 1886. Fol. Lond., 1886.　E

JOURNAL OF SCIENCE (The), and Annals of Astronomy, &c. (Formerly *The Quarterly Journal of Science*.) Vols. 1–21 (*all published*). 8vo. Lond., 1871–85.　E

JOURNAL OF MICROSCOPICAL SCIENCE. [*See* Quarterly Journal of Microscopical Science.]

JOURNAL OF THE INDIAN ARCHIPELAGO AND EASTERN ASIA. 12 vols. 8vo. Singapore, 1849–59.　E

JOURNAL OF FACTS, Natural Philosophy, &c. (Pam. 14.) 8vo. Lond., 1829.　　　　　　　MJ 2 Q 4

JOURNET (F.) L'Australie : Description du Pays, Colons et Natifs, Gouvernement, Institutions, Productions, Travaux, Publics, Mines. 8vo. Paris, 1885.　MD 5 T 19

JOWETT (B.), M.A. Dialogues of Plato. [*See* Plato.]
Politics of Aristotle. [*See* Aristoteles.]
Thucydides ; translated into English. With Introduction, Marginal Analysis, Notes, and Indices. [*See* Thucydides.]

JOYCE (Rev. J.) Introduction to the Arts and Sciences ; with original introductory Essays. 8vo. Lond., 1871.　　　　　　　　　　　　　　　　　A 16 P 3
Scientific Dialogues for the instruction and entertainment of young people. 8vo. Lond., 1878.　A 16 P 13

JOYCE (Patrick Weston), LL.D., &c. Old Celtic Romances ; translated from the Gaelic. 8vo. Lond., 1879.　　　　　　　　　　　　　　　　J 9 U 8

JOYNEVILLE (C.) Life and Times of Alexander I, Emperor of all the Russias. 3 vols. 8vo. Lond., 1875.　　　　　　　　　　　　C 1 V 27–29
Life of Alexander II, Emperor of all the Russias. 8vo. Lond., 1883.　　　　　　　　　　　　C 1 S 8

JUAN DE VEGA (Senor). [*See* Cochrane, C.]

JUAN Y SANTACILIA (Don Jorge) and ULLOA (Don Antonio de). Noticias Secretas de America. Sacadas a luz por David Barry. Fol. Lond., 1826.　　　　　　　　　　　　　　　　B 16 R 18 ‡
Voyage to South America. [*See* Ulloa, Don A. de.]

JUDD (Prof. John Wesley), F.R.S. Volcanoes : what they are and what they teach. With Illustrations. 8vo. Lond., 1881.　　　　　　　　　　A 9 Q 24

JUDGES' SALARIES ACT (The). The Measure explained and vindicated, in a Letter to E. C. Weekes, Esq., M.L.A., by "Fair Play." 8vo. Sydney, 1857. MF 3 P 2

JUDY. Rt. Hon. William Ewart Gladstone, from Judy's point of view. [*See* Gladstone, Rt. Hon. W. E.]

JUKES (Joseph Beete), M.A., &c. Excursions in and about Newfoundland during the years 1839–40. 2 vols. 8vo. Lond., 1842.　　　　　　　D 4 P 9, 10
Letters and Extracts from the Addresses and Occasional Writings ; edited, with connecting Memorial Notes, by his Sister. 8vo. Lond., 1871.　　　　C 1 T 41
Another copy.　　　　　　　　　　　MC 1 P 1
Narrative of the Surveying Voyage of H.M.S. *Fly*, commanded by Capt. F. P. Blackwood, R.N., in Torres Strait, New Guinea, and other Islands of the Eastern Archipelago, during the years 1842–46. 2 vols. 8vo. Lond., 1847.*　　　　　　　　MD 1 V 13, 14
Sketch of the Physical Structure of Australia, so far as it is at present known. 8vo. Lond., 1850.*　MA 2 Q 13
Student's Manual of Geology ; edited by Archibald Geikie, F.R.S. 3rd ed. 8vo. Edinb., 1872.　　A 9 Q 16
[*See* Gold, Lectures on.]　　　　　　MA 2 P 1

JUKES-BROWNE (Alfred Joseph), B.A. [*See* Browne, A. J. Jukes-.]

JULIANUS (Flavius Claudius). Vie de Emperor, par l'Abbé de la Bleterie. Nouvelle éd. 12mo. Paris, 1775.　　　　　　　　　　　　　　C 1 T 37

JULIEN (Stanislas). Syntaxe Nouvelle de la Langue Chinoise. 2 vols. roy. 8vo. Paris, 1869–70.　K 15 R 8, 9

JULLIEN (André). Culture of the Grape Vine. [*See* Suttor, G.]
Manuel du Sommelier ; ou, Instruction Pratique sur la manière de soigner les Vins. 12mo. Paris, 1826.　A 1 P 5
Topographie de tous les Vignobles connus. 8vo. Paris, 1816.　　　　　　　　　　　　　D 11 R 14

JULLIEN (Marc Antoine). Essai sur un methode de l'emploi du Tems. 8vo. Paris, 1808.　　G 17 Q 36
Essai sur une méthode qui à pour objet de bien régler l'emploi du tems. 8vo. Paris, 1808.　J 17 P 20

JUMIÈGE (Guillaume de). [*See* Guillaume de Jumiège.]

JUNG (Dr. Carl Emil). Australia: the Country and its Inhabitants. Abridged. 8vo. Lond., 1884. MD 2 Q 39
Australien und Neuseeland. Historische, geographische und statistische, Skizze. 8vo. Leipzig, 1879.　MD 2 S 18.
Der Weltteil Australien. 4 vols. (in 2) 8vo. Leipzig, 1882–83.　　　　　　　　　　MD 2 Q 37, 38
Deutsche Kolonien. Ein Beitrag zur besseren Kenntniss des Lebens und Wirkens unserer Landsleute in allen Erdteilen. 8vo. Leipzig, 1884.　　MD 2 Q 35.
Deutsche Kolonien, mit besonderer Berücksichtigung der neuesten deutschen Erwerbungen in Westafrika und Australien. 2° vermehrte ausgabe. 8vo. Leipsic, 1885.　　　　　　　　　　　　MD 2 Q 36

JUNIOR ETCHING CLUB. Etchings by. [*See* Modern English Poets.]

JUNIUS. [*See* WAY TO WEALTH, THE.]

JUNIUS. Including Letters by the same writer, under
other signatures (now first collected); to which are added
his Confidential Correspondence with Mr. Wilkes, and
his Private Letters to Mr. H. S. Woodfall ; with a preliminary Essay, Notes, Facsimiles, &c.   3 vols. 8vo.
Lond., 1812.   F 6 T 4–6

Junius ; with Cuts by Bewick.   2 vols. 8vo.   Lond.,
1797 (1801).   F 6 T 7, 8

The Letters of Junius.   4to.   Lond. (n.d.)   F 8 R 2 †

JUNIUS (FRANCISCUS). Gothicum Glossarium, quo plera-
que Argentei Codicis Vocabula explicantur, atque ex
Linguis cognatis illustrantur. Præmittuntur ei Gothicum,
Runicum, Anglo-Saxonicum, aliáque Alphabeta. Sq. 8vo.
Amstelaedami, 1684.   K 12 R 18

JUNIUS REDIVIVUS. [*See* LETTERS ON MEN, &c.]

JUNOT (MME. LAURA PERMON), DÜCHESSE D'ABRANTÈS.
[*See* ABRANTÈS, DUCHESS D'.]

JURIEN DE LA GRAVIÈRE (CAPT. J. B. E.) Sketches
of the last Naval War ; translated from the French by
the Hon. Capt. Plunkett, R.N.   2 vols. 8vo.   Lond.,
1848.   B 3 R 22, 23

JUSSIEU (ANTOINE LAURENT). Genera Plantarum secundum Ordines Naturales disposita.   8vo.   Paris, 1789.
                                                A 4 Q 1

JUST (P.) Appeal to the Government and Colonists of
Victoria in favor of the employment of the Arts of
Painting and Sculpture, in decorating the New Houses
of Parliament and Merchants' Exchange.   8vo.   Melb.,
1856.   MJ 2 R 9

Australia ; or, Notes taken during a Residence in the
Colonies, from the Gold Discovery in 1851 till 1857.
8vo. Dundee, 1859.*   MD 5 Q 38

JUSTI (FERDINAND). Handbuch der Zendsprache. Alt-
bactrisches Woerterbuch. Grammatik. Chrestomathie.
Imp. 8vo. Leipzig, 1864.   K 13 T 16

JUSTIN, OR JUSTINUS MARTYR. [*See* JUSTINUS,
SAINT.]

JUSTINIANUS (EMPEROR OF CONSTANTINOPLE). Corpus
Juris Civilis. Digestorum seu Pandectarum ; cum Notis
integris D. Gothofredi. 2 vols. imp. fol. Amsterdam,
1663.   F 29 P 13, 14 ‡

De Usufructu : Justiniani Digestorum lib. VII. lit. I ;
edited by H. J. Roby. 8vo. Camb., 1886.   F 5 P 22

Imperatoris Justiniani Institutionum Libri Quattuor ;
with Introductions, Commentary, Excursus, and Translation; by J. B. Moyle, B.C.L., M.A.   (Clar. Press.)
2 vols. 8vo. Oxford, 1883.   F 8 R 24, 25

Institutes of ; with English Introduction, Translation,
and Notes, by Thomas Collett Sandars, M.A. 8vo. Lond.,
1869.   F 10 Q 14

JUSTINIANUS (EMPEROR OF CONSTANTINOPLE).—*contd.*
Institutes of Justinian ; edited as a Recension of the
Institutes of Gaius, by T. Erskine Holland, B.C.L.
(Clar. Press.) 8vo. Oxford, 1873.   F 15 P 4

An Introduction to the Study of Justinian's Digest. [*See*
ROBY, H. J.]

Select Titles from the Digest of Justinian ; edited by
T. E. Hollond, B.C.L., and C. L. Shadwell, B.C.L.
(Clar. Press.) 8vo. Oxford, 1881.   F 8 R 23

JUSTINUS. Historie of Ivstine ; containing a Narration
of Kingdomes, from the beginning of the Assyrian Monarchy, vuto the Raigne of the Emperour Avgvstvs. Fol.
Lond., 1606.   B 10 P 12 †

Historiæ Philippicæ, ex Editione Abrahami Gronovii,
cum Notis et Interpretatione in usum Delphini.   2 vols.
8vo. Lond., 1822.   J 13 Q 17, 18

Justin, Cornelius Nepos, and Eutropius ; literally translated, by the Rev. J. S. Watson, M.A. 8vo. Lond.,
1879.   B 14 P 44

JUSTINUS (SANCTUS). Opera omnia. [*See* MIGNE, J. P.,
SERIES GRÆCA, 6.]

Some Account of the Writings and Opinions of Justin
Martyr. [*See* KAYE, RT. REV. J.]

S.P.N. Justini Philosophi et Martyris Opera omnia quæ
exstant omnia. Fol. Paris, 1742.   G 10 U 10 ‡

JUVENALIS (DECIMUS JUNIUS). D. Iunii Iuvenalis
Satiræ; with a literal English prose Translation and
Notes, by John Delaware Lewis, M.A. 8vo. Lond.,
1873.   J 15 S 17

Juvenal; translated by Chas. Badham, M.D., &c.   (Fam.
Class. Lib.) 18mo. Lond., 1831.   J 15 P 21

Opera omnia, ex editione G. A. Ruperti, cum Notis et
Interpretatione in usum Delphini.   3 vols. 8vo.   Lond.,
1820.   J 13 Q 19–21

Satires of Juvenal and Persius; translated into English
Verse, by W. Gifford; with Notes. 2 vols. 8vo. Lond.,
1817.   H 7 T 16, 17

Satires of Juvenal, Persius, Sulpicia, and Lucilius; literally
translated into English Prose, with Notes, &c., by the
Rev. Lewis Evans, M.A. 12mo. Lond., 1871.   J 8 R 8

Thirteen Satires of; translated into English by H. A.
Strong M.A., &c., and Alexander Leeper, M.A.   8vo.
Lond., 1882.   J 5 P 13

Works of Juvenal; translated by Dryden. [*See* CHALMERS,
A.]

JUVENCUS (CASSIUS VETTIUS AQUILINUS). Opera omnia.
[*See* MIGNE, J. P., SERIES LATINA, 19.]

Quarti Sæculi Poetarum Christianorum, Juvenci, Sedulii,
Optatiani, Severi et Faltoniæ Probæ, Opera omnia. Imp.
8vo. Paris, 1846.   H 5 V 23

JUVENILE MISSIONARY SOCIETY. Fourth and
Fifth Annual Reports. 8vo. Sydney, 1860–61.
                                                MG 1 Q 27

K

K. (O.) [*See* NOVIKOFF, MME. O.]

KADEN (WOLDEMAR). Italy, from the Tiber to Mount Etna. [*See* STIELER, K.]

KAEGI (PROF. ADOLF). The Rigveda, the oldest Literature of the Indians; atuhorized Translation, by R. Arrowsmit , Ph.D. 8vo. Boston, 1886. J 12 V 5

KÆMPFER (ENGELBERTUS), M.D. Account of Japan. 8vo. Lond., 1853. D 6 S 38
Account of Japan. [*See* VOYAGES AND DISCOVERIES.]
History of Japan, giving an Account of the Ancient and Present State and Government of t at Empire; translated by J. G. Scheuchzer. 2 vols. fol. Lond., 1727. B 17 S 2, 3 ‡

KAFIR TRIBES. Report from Select Committee on the. 8vo. Lond., 1851. F 1 R 19

KAINS-JACKSON (CHARLES PHILIP). Our Ancient Monuments and the Land around t em. Imp. 8vo. Lond., 1880. B 5 V 28

KAISER-KONIGLICHE GEOLOGISCHEN REICH-SANSTALT. Jarbuch, 1856–58, 1874–84. 14 vols. roy. 8vo. Vienna, 1856–84. E
Ver andlungen, 1867–84. 18 vols. roy. 8vo. Vienna, 1867–84. E

KÁLIDÁSA. Birt of the War-God: a Poem; translated from the Sanskrit into Englis Verse by Ralp T. H. Griffit , M.A. 2nd ed. 8vo. Lond,. 1879. H 5 U 20
Mégha Dúta; or, Cloud Messenger: a Poem in the Sanscrit Language; translated into Englis Verse, wit Notes and Illustrations, by Horace Hayman Wilson. 4to. Calcutta, 1813. H 5 V 6

KALISCH (MARCUS MORITZ), PH.D., M.A. Pat and Goal: a Discussion on the Elements of Civilisation and the Conditions of Happiness. 8vo. Lond., 1880. G 13 P 20

KALLY PROSONO DEY (KALIPRASANNA DE). Life and Career of Major Sir Louis Cavagnari, C.S.I., &c.; wit a brief Outline of the Second Afg an War. 8vo. Calcutta, 1881. C 5 V 6

KALTENBACH (J. H.) Die Pflanzenfeinde aus der Klasse der Insekten. Roy. 8vo. Stuttgart, 1874. A 14 T 27

KALTSCHMIDT (PROF. JAKOB HEINRICH.) Vollständiges stamm-und sinnverwandtschaftliches Gesammt-Wörterbuch der Deutsc en Sprac e. 4" auflage. Imp. 8vo. Noerdlingen (n.d.) K 14 R 2

KAMES (HENRY HOME), LORD. Elements of Criticism. 3 vols. 8vo. Edinb., 1762. J 7 S 1–3
Anot er copy. 7th ed. 2 vols. 8vo. Edinb., 1788. J 7 S 4, 5
The Gentleman Farmer. 6th ed. 8vo. Lond., 1815. A 1 S 11

KAMES (HENRY HOME), LORD—*continued.*
Memoirs of the Life and Writings of [by A. F. Tytler, Lord Woodhouselee]. 2 vols. 4to. Edinb., 1807. C 3 W 15, 16
Sketc es of the History of Man. 3 vols. 8vo. Edinb, 1813. J 4 S 11–13

KANE (ELISHA KENT), M.D. Biograp y of; by William Elder. 8vo. Philad., 1858. C 8 P 24
[*See* AMERICAN ARCTIC EXPLORERS.]

KANE (W. F. DE VISMES), M.A., &c. European Butterflies. Wit Plates. 8vo. Lond., 1885. A 14 Q 37

K'ANG-CHI-TSE-TIENN. Le Code des Caractères, publié par ordre de l'Empereur K'ang-c i. 4 vols. (in 6) 8vo. C ina, 1827. K 14 U 10–15

KANT (IMMANUEL). Commentary on Kánt's "Critick of the Pure Reason." [*See* FISCHER, PROF. K.]
Critique of Pure Reason: a Critical Exposition. [*See* MORRIS, G. S.]
Critique of Pure Reason.; translated into Englis by F. Max Müller. 2 vols. 8vo. Lond., 1881. G 3 S 1, 2
Critique of Pure Reason; translated from the German, by J. M. D. Meiklejohn. 12mo. Lond., 1871. G 8 S 27
Kant and is English Critics. [*See* WATSON, PROF. J.]
Kant und Darwin. [*See* SCHULTZ, F.]
Kantian Et ics and the Et ics of Evolution. [*See* SCHUR-MANN, PROF. J. G.]
Kant's Prolegomena and Metap ysical Foundations of Natural Science; translated, wit a Biograp y and Introduction, by Ernest Belfort Bax. 8vo. Lond., 1883. G 13 R 18
Life of; by J. H. W. Stuckenberg, D.D. 8vo. Lond., 1882. C 7 P 34
Text- ook to Kant. [*See* STERLING, J. H.]

KAPP (G.) Electric Transmission of Energy. 8vo. Lond., 1886. A 5 S 35

KAPPA. [*See* WARD, —.]

KAPPIUS (J.) [*See* VALERIUS MAXIMUS.]

KARCHER (PROF. THEODORE), LL.B. Modern Frenc Reader. [*See* CASSAL, PROF. C.]

KARDEC (ALLAN). Experimental Spiritism: the Mediums' Book; or, Guide for Mediums and for Evocations; being the Sequel to "The Spirits' Book"; translated by Anna Blackwell. 8vo. Lond., 1876. G 7 Q 2
Practical Spiritism: Heaven and Hell; or, the Divine Justice vindicated in the Plurality of Existences; being the practical Confirmation of "The Spirit's Book"; translated by Anna Blackwell. 8vo. Lond. 1878. G 7 Q 3
Spiritualist P ilosop y: the Spirits' Book; translated by Anna Blackwell. 8vo. Lond., 1875. G 7 Q 1

KARMARSCH (L. KARL). Geschichte der Technologie. 8vo. München, 1872. A 17 V 25

Technologisches Wörterbuch, Deutscher, Französischen, und Englischer Sprache. 3e ed. 3 vols. 8vo. Wiesbaden, 1874–78. K 17 U 2-4

KASTROMENOS (PANAGIOTES G.) Monuments of Athens: an Historical and Archaeological Description; translated from the Greek, by Agnes Smith. 8vo. Lond., 1884. B 9 S 23

KATE (LAMBERT TEN). [*See* TEN KATE, L.]

KATER (C.) Iets over de Bij de Dajaks in de Wester-Afdeeling van Borneo zoo gezochte Tempajans of Tadjau's. (*Bound with De Wall's "Maleische Woorden."*) 8vo. Batavia (n.d.) K 14 Q 29

KATER (CAPT. H.), AND LARDNER (REV. D.) Treatise on Mechanics. (Lard. Cab. Cyclo.) 12mo. Lond., 1830. K 1 U 32

KAULBACH (WILLIAM). Female Characters of Goethe, from the original Drawings of William Kaulbach; with explanatory Text, by G. H. Lewes. Roy. 8vo. Lond., 1867. A 3 P 15 ‡

KAUSLER (DR. EDUARD VON). Denkmäler altniederländischer Sprache und Litteratur, nach ungedruckten Quellen. 3 vols. 8vo. Tübingen und Leipzig, 1840–66. H 7 T 1-3

KAVANAGH (MISS JULIA). English Women of Letters: Biographical Sketches. 2 vols. 8vo. Lond., 1863. C 3 S 36, 37

French Women of Letters: Biographical Sketches. 2 vols. 8vo. Lond., 1862. C 3 T 6, 7

Woman in France, during the 18th Century. 2 vols. 8vo. Lond., 1850. C 4 S 47, 48

Women of Christianity exemplary for Acts of Piety and Charity. 8vo. Lond., 1852. G 11 P 18

KAVANAGH (LAWRENCE). [*See* CASH, M.]

KAVANAGH (MORGAN). Origin of Language and Myths. 2 vols. 8vo. Lond., 1871. K 20 R 3, 4

KAY (JOHN). Series of Original Portraits and Caricature Etchings; with Biographical Sketches and Anecdotes. 2 vols. roy. 8vo. Edinb., 1842. C 5 W 17, 18

Another copy. New ed. 2 vols. 4to. Edinb., 1877. C 1 Q 1, 2 †

KAY (REV. JOHN). Slave Trade in the New Hebrides; edited by the Rev. John Kay, 8vo. Edinb., 1872. MD 1 U 21

KAY (WILLIAM E.) Blowpipe Analysis. [*See* LANDAUER, J.]

KAYE (RT. REV. JOHN), D.D., BISHOP OF LINCOLN. Some Account of the Council of Nicæa, in connection with the Life of Athanasius. 8vo. Lond., 1853. G 8 T 1

Some Account of the Writings and Opinions of Justin Martyr. 3rd ed., revised. 8vo. Lond., 1853. G 9 T 1

KAYE (SIR JOHN WILLIAM), K.C.S.I. Christianity in India: an Historical Narrative. 8vo. Lond., 1859. G 10 T 22

History of the Sepoy War in India, 1857–58. 3rd ed. 3 vols. 8vo. Lond., 1865–76. B 10 U 14-16

History of the War in Afghanistan. 3rd ed. 3 vols. 8vo. Lond., 1874. B 10 Q 2-4

Analytical Index [to the above]; by F. Pincott. 8vo. Lond., 1880. B 10 U 17

Life and Correspondence of Charles, Lord Metcalfe, from unpublished Letters and Journals. 2 vols. 8vo. Lond., 1854. C 7 U 26, 27

Life and Correspondence of Major-General Sir John Malcolm, G.C.B., from unpublished Letters and Journals. 2 vols. 8vo. Lond., 1856. C 7 S 28, 29

Lives of Indian Officers, illustrative of the History of the Civil and Military Services of India. 2 vols. 8vo. Lond., 1867. C 7 R 27, 28

KEAN (EDMUND). Life of, from published and original Sources; by F. W. Hawkins. 2 vols. 8vo. Lond., 1869. C 7 P 35, 36

KEANE (PROF. AUGUSTUS HENRY), M.A. Asia; with Ethnological Appendix. Edited by Sir Richard Temple, Bart, &c. (Stanford's Compendium of Geography and Travel.) 8vo. Lond., 1882. D 11 S 5

Australasia; with Ethnological Appendix. [*See* WALLACE, A. R.]

Chittagong Hill Tribes. [*See* RIEBECK, E.]

Early Teutonic, Italian, and French Masters; translated and edited from the Dohme Series. Illustrated. Imp. 8vo. Lond., 1880. A 8 T 19

The Earth : a Descriptive History of the Phenomena of the Life of the Globe. [*See* RECLUS, J. J. E.]

Europe; with Ethnological Appendix. [*See* RUDLER, F. W.]

KEARNEY (JAMES). Map of Melbourne and its Suburbs, 1855. Compiled by James Kearney, engraved by David Tulloch and James D. Brown. Roy. 4to. Melb., 1855. MD 5 S 15 ‡

KEARY (CHARLES FRANCIS), M.A., &c. Coinages of Western Europe. (Economy of the Early Middle Ages.) 8vo. Lond., 1879. A 13 S 33

Mythology of the Eddas: how far of true Teutonic Origin. 8vo. Lond., 1882. B 2 R 9

Outlines of Primitive Belief among the Indo-European Races. 8vo. Lond., 1882. G 2 R 8

KEATE (GEORGE), F.R.S. Account of the Pelew Islands, situated in the Western part of the Pacific Ocean. Composed from the Journals and Communications of Capt. Henry Wilson and some of his officers, who, in August, 1783, were there shipwrecked in the *Antelope*. 4to. Lond., 1788. MD 6 P 20 †

Another copy. 3rd ed. 4to. Lond., 1789. MD 6 P 21†

Supplement to the Account of the Pelew Islands. [*See* HOCKIN, REV. J. P.]

KEATING (REV. J.)   General History of Ireland; translated from the original Irish, with many curious Amendments taken from the Psalters of Tara and Cashel, &c., by Dermod O'Connor, Esq. 8vo. Dublin, 1865.   B 11 P 10

KEATINGE (COL. MAURICE).   Travels through France and Spain to Morocco; comprising a Narrative of the Author's Residence in that Empire; with an Account of the British Embassy to the Court of Morocco. 4to. Lond., 1717.   D 9 V 4

KEATS (JOHN).   Letters and Poems of; edited by John Gilmer Speed. 3 vols. 8vo. N. York, 1883.   H 7 T 9-11
Poetical Works and other Writings of, now first brought together; including Poems and numerous Letters not before published. Edited, with Notes and Appendices, by Harry Buxton Forman. 4 vols. 8vo. Lond., 1883.   H 7 T 4-7
Poetical Works of; with a Memoir by the Rt. Hon. Lord Houghton. Illustrated. 8vo. Lond., 1866.   H 7 T 8

KEBBEL (THOMAS EDWARD), M.A.   History of Toryism, from 1783-1886. 8vo. Lond., 1886.   F 6 V 9

KEBLE (REV. JOHN), M.A., VICAR OF HURSLEY.   The Christian Year: Thoughts in Verse for the Sundays and Holydays throughout the year. Authorized ed. 12mo. Oxford, 1877.   H 6 R 34
Lyra Innocentium : Thoughts in Verse on Christian Children; their Ways and their Privileges. 12mo. Oxford, 1876.   H 6 R 35
Memoir of; by the Rt. Hon. Sir J. T. Coleridge, D.C.L. 8vo. Oxford, 1869.   C 4 T 16
The Psalter or Psalms of David; in English Verse. 4th ed. 12mo. Oxford, 1869.   H 6 R 36

KEDDIE (MISS HENRIETTA), "SARAH TYTLER."   Days of Yore. 2 vols. 8vo. Lond., 1866.   J 10 S 24, 25
Musical Composers and their Works. 3rd ed. 12mo. Lond., 1876.   C 2 P 31

KEDDIE (MISS HENRIETTA), "SARAH TYTLER," AND WATSON (J. L.) Songstresses of Scotland. 2 vols. 8vo. Lond., 1871.   C 4 S 32, 33

KEENE (HENRY GEORGE).   Fall of the Mogul Empire; an Historical Essay; being a new Edition of "The Mogul Empire from the death of Arungzeb." 8vo. Lond., 1876.   B 10 U 22
Sketch of the History of Hindustán, from the First Muslim Conquest to the Fall of the Mogul Empire. 8vo. Lond., 1885.   B 10 S 25

KEENE (J. B.) Report on Samples of Wines, International Exhibition, 1874. (Pam. D.) Lond., 1875.   F 4 R 7

KEENE (WILLIAM), F.G.S. New South Wales Coal-fields. 8vo. Sydney, 1871.   MJ 2 R 14

KEEPING (WALTER), M.A., &c.   Fossils and Palæontological Affinities of the Neocomian Deposits of Upware and Brickhill (Cambridgeshire and Bedfordshire); with Plates. (Sedgwick Prize Essay for 1879.) 8vo. Camb., 1883.   A 9 S 5

KEHREIN (JOSEPH).   Grammatik der deutschen Sprache des funfzehnten bis siebenzehnten Jahrhunderts. 8vo. Leipsig, 1863.   K 15 S 13

KEIGHTLEY (THOMAS).   The Crusaders; or, Scenes, Events, and Characters, from the Times of the Crusades. 4th ed. 8vo. Lond., 1852.   G 8 S 22
Fairy Mythology; illustrative of the Romance and Superstition of various Countries. 8vo. Lond., 1850.   B 37 P 1
History of the War of Independence in Greece. (Const. Misc.) 2 vols. 18mo. Edinb., 1830.   K 10 Q 48, 49
Outlines of History. (Lard. Cab. Cyclo.) 12mo. Lond., 1835.   K 1 T 34

KEIM (DE BENNEVILLE RANDOLPH).   Keim's Illustrated Guide to the Musem of Models, Patent Office. (Pams. Eb.) 12mo. Washington, 1874.   MK 1 P 1

KEITH (ALEXANDER), D.D.   Land of Israel, according to the Covenant with Abraham, with Isaac, and with Jacob. 8vo. Edinb., 1843.   G 11 P 28

KEITH (DUNCAN).   History of Scotland, Civil and Ecclesiastical. 2 vols. 8vo. Edinb., 1886.   B 13 P 17, 18

KEITH (ADM. GEORGE KEITH ELPHINSTONE), VISCOUNT, K.B.   Memoir of; by A. Allardyce. 8vo. Edinb., 1882.   C 6 Q 20

KEITH (LIEUT. SIR G. M.), BART.   Voyage to South America, and the Cape of Good Hope, in H.M. gun brig, *Protector.* 8vo. Lond., 1810.   D 4 Q 47

KEITH (RT. REV. ROBERT).   History of the Affairs of Church and State in Scotland, from the beginning of the Reformation to the year 1568. 3 vols. 8vo. Edinb., 1835-50.   G 9 T 5-7

KEITH (SIR ROBERT MURRAY).   Selection from Correspondence of. [See SMYTH, MRS. G.]

KEITH (THOMAS).   New Treatise on the Use of the Globes; or, a Philosophical View of the Earth and Heavens; with a Key by J. Middleton. 12mo. Lond., 1907-69.   A 3 T 41

KEITH FALCONER (HON. I. G. N.) [See FALCONER, HON. I. G. N. KEITH.]

KELHAM (ROBERT).   Dictionary of the Norman or Old French Language, [and] the Laws of William the Conqueror. 8vo. Lond., 1779.   K 12 R 19
Domesday Book, illustrated; containing an Account of that Antient Record. 8vo. Lond., 1788.   B 6 Q 12

KELLER (DR. FERDINAND). Lake Dwellings of Switzerland and other parts of Europe; translated by John Edward Lee, F.S.A., F.G.S. 2nd ed., enlarged. 2 vols. roy. 8vo. Lond., 1878. B 15 R 1, 2

KELLER (FRANZ). Amazon and Madeira Rivers: Sketches and Descriptions from the Notebook of an Explorer. With Illustrations. Imp. 4to. Lond., 1874. D 5 Q 17 †

KELLETT (CAPT. HENRY), R.N., &c. Voyage of H.M.S. *Herald.* [*See* SEEMANN, B.]

KELLEY (FREDERICK M.) On the Junction of the Atlantic and Pacific Oceans, and the practicability of a Ship Canal, without Locks, by the Valley of the Atrato. 8vo. Lond., 1856. MJ 2 Q 18

KELLY (A. C.), M.D. The Vine in Australia: its Culture and Management. 8vo. Melb., 1861. MA 1 Q 4
Another copy. 2nd thousand. 8vo. Melb., 1862. MA 1 Q 2

KELLY (CHRISTOPHER). Selection of Voyages and Travels by the most enterprising Navigators and Travellers. 8vo. Lond. (n.d.) MD 7 P 14

KELLY (HUGH). False Delicacy: a Comedy. (Bell's Brit. Theatre.) 18mo. Lond., 1795. H 2 P 27
The School for Wives: a Comedy. (Bell's Brit. Theatre.) 18mo. Lond., 1792. H 2 P 25
Another copy. [*See* BRITISH DRAMA, 4.]
Another copy. [*See* MODERN THEATRE, 9.]
A Word to the Wise: a Comedy. (Bell's Brit. Theatre.) 18mo. Lond., 1795. H 2 P 37

KELLY (JAMES), M.A. Complete Collection of Scotish Proverbs, explained and made intelligible to the English Reader. 8vo. Lond., 1721. K 19 Q 15

KELLY (JAMES). American Catalogue of Books (original and reprints) published in the United States, 1861–71. 2 vols. roy. 8vo. New York, 1866–71. Libr.

KELLY (REV. JOHN), D.D. English and Manx Dictionary, prepared from Dr. Kelly's Triglot Dictionary, with Alterations and Additions; by the Rev. W. Gill, and the Rev. J. T. Clarke. (Manx Society.) 8vo. Douglas, 1866. K 13 P 17
Practical Grammar of the Antient Gaelic, or Language of the Isle of Man, usually called Manks; edited, with an Introduction, Life of Dr. Kelly, and Notes, by the Rev. W. Gill. (Manx Society.) 8vo. Douglas, 1870. K 13 P 16

KELLY (JOHN E.) Lord Roger in his War Paint; or, the Rev. J. Dixon's Grand Old Book. 12mo. Sydney, 1876. MG 1 Q 32

KELLY (REV. MATTHEW). Cambrensis Eversus. [*See* LYNCH, J.]

KELLY (MICHAEL). Reminiscences of. 2nd ed. 2 vols. 8vo. Lond., 1826. C 4 S 9, 10

KELLY (PATRICK), LL.D. Universal Cambist and Commercial Instructor. 2 vols. 4to. Lond., 1811. F 8 P 11, 12 †

KELLY (WALTER K.) Erotica: the Elegies of Propertius; the Satyricon of Petronius Arbiter; and the Kisses of Joannes Secundus. [*See* PROPERTIUS, S. A.]
Erotica: the Poems of Catullus and Tibullus, and the Vigil of Venus. [*See* CATULLUS, C. V.]
Exemplary Novels of M. de Cervantes de Saavedra. [*See* CERVANTES SAAVEDRA, M. DE.]
History of Russia, from the Earliest Period to the Present Time. 2 vols. 8vo. Lond., 1855. B 12 T 21, 22
History of the year 1848. 12mo. Lond., 1849. B 8 P 1
Syria and the Holy Land: their Scenery and their People. 8vo. Lond., 1844. D 5 S 20

KELLY (WILLIAM). Excursion to California, over the Prairie, Rocky Mountains, and Great Sierra Nevada, with a Stroll through the Diggings. 2 vols. 8vo. Lond., 1851. D 3 Q 9, 10
Life in Victoria; or, Victoria in 1853, and Victoria in 1858. 2 vols. 8vo. Lond., 1859.* MD 5 Q 11, 12
Another copy. 2 vols. (in 1) 8vo. Lond., 1860.* MD 5 Q 15

KELLY & CO. Hand-book to the Titled, Landed, and Official Classes, for 1884. 8vo. Lond., 1884. E

KELLY'S LONDON SUBURBAN DIRECTORY, 1884. Roy. 8vo. Lond., 1884. E
Post Office London Directory, 1853, 1874, 1881, and 1886. 5 vols. roy. 8vo. Lond. 1853–86. E

KELLY GANG (THE). Book of Keli; or, the Chronicles of the Kelly Pursuers. 12mo. Mansfield, 1880. MF 1 Q 5
Full and True Account of the Kelly Gang; with Illustrations, and a Map of the country infested by them. 5th ed. 8vo. Melb., 1880. MF 1 Q 5
History of the Kelly Gang of Bushrangers. 8vo. Melb., 1880. MF 1 Q 5

KELSALL (JOHN). Manual of the Bellary District, compiled under the orders of Government, dated September 9th, 1869. No. 2,646. 8vo. Madras, 1872. B 10 V 12

KEMBLE (CHARLES). The Point of Honour: a Play. (Brit. Theatre.) 12mo. Lond., 1808. H 1 P 24

KEMBLE (FRANCES ANNE), MRS. BUTLER. Francis I: an Historical Drama. 5th ed. 8vo. Lond., 1832. H 1 S 15
Journal [Travels in the United States]; by Frances Anne Butler. 2 vols. 8vo. Lond., 1835. D 3 P 45, 46
Journal of a Residence on a Georgian Plantation in 1838–39. 8vo. Lond., 1863. D 3 P 47
Notes upon some of Shakespeare's Plays: Introduction; Macbeth; Henry VIII; The Tempest; Romeo and Juliet. 8vo. Lond., 1882. J 12 R 2
Year of Consolation; by Mrs. Butler. 2 vols. 8vo. Lond., 1847. D 8 Q 31, 32

KEMBLE (John M.), M.G. Anglo-Saxon Poems of Beowulf, the Traveller's Song, and the Battle of Finnes-Buri. 12mo. Lond., 1833.   H 6 R 37

Saxons in England: a History of the English Commonwealth till the period of the Norman Conquest. 2 vols. 8vo. Lond., 1849.   B 5 S 24, 25
[*See* Codex Diplomaticus.]

KEMBLE (John Philip). Life of. [*See* Fitzgerald, P.]

Lodoiska: an Opera. [*See* Farces, 7.]

Memoirs of the Life of; including a History of the Stage, from the time of Garrick to the present Period; by James Boaden. 2 vols. 8vo. Lond., 1825.   C 7 T 27, 28

KEMBLES (The). The Kembles: an Account of the Kemble Family, including the Lives of Mrs. Siddons, and her brother John Philip Kemble, by Percy Fitzgerald. 2 vols. 8vo. Lond. (n.d.)   C 7 T 25, 26

KEMP (Dixon). Yacht Architecture: a Treatise. Lond., 1885.   A 3 Q 19

KEMP (Henry Tacy). First Step to Maori Conversation. New ed. 8vo. Auckland (n.d.)   MK 1 P 34

KEMP (T. Lindley), M.D. Phasis of Matter: being an Outline of the Discoveries and Applications of Modern Chemistry. 2 vols. 8vo. Lond., 1855.   A 5 S 40, 41

KEMPE (John A.) Autobiography of Mrs. Anna Eliza Bray (born 1789, died 1883); edited by John A. Kempe. 8vo. Lond., 1884.   C 3 R 8

KEMPER (J. de Bosch). [*See* Catalogues of Books.]

KEMPIS (Thomas à). The Imitation of Christ: being the autograph Manuscript of Thomas à Kempis De Imitatione Christi, reproduced in facsimile from the Original preserved in the Royal Library at Brussels. 32mo. Lond., 1885.   G 9 P 1

The Imitation of Christ: Four Books translated from the Latin by W. Benham, B.D. 8vo. Lond., 1886. G 6 R 11

Life of. [*See* Butler, S.]

Thomas à Kempis and the Brothers of Common Life; by the Rev. S. Kettewell. 2 vols. 8vo. Lond., 1882. C 7 R 36, 37

KEMPT (Robert). Pencil and Palette: being Biographical Anecdotes, chiefly of Contemporary Painters. 12mo. Lond., 1881.   A 7 P 40

KENDAL (Mrs. W. H.) [*See* Grimstone, Mrs. W. H.]

KENDALL (George Wilkins). Narrative of the Texan Santa Fé Expedition; comprising a description of a Tour through Texas and across the Great South-western Prairies. 2 vols. 8vo. Lond., 1844. D 3 R 1, 2

KENDALL (Henry). At Long Bay. Euroclydon. (Pam. A.) Fol. Sydney (n.d.)   MJ 2 U 1

Poems and Songs. 8vo. Sydney, 1862   MH 1 R 52

Another copy. 12mo. Melb., 1869.   MJ 2 P 31

Poems of. 8vo. Sydney, 1886.   MH 1 R 56

Songs from the Mountains. 8vo. Sydney, 1880.*   MH 1 R 54

KENDALL (Thomas). Grammar and Vocabulary of the Language of New Zealand. 12mo. Lond., 1820. MK 1 P 30

KENDO (T. A.) Treatise on Silk and Tea Culture, and other Asiatic Industries adapted to the soil and Climate of California. 12mo. San Francisco, 1870. A 1 Q 28

KENDRICK (Tertius T. C.) Ionian Islands. 8vo. Lond., 1822.   D 6 U 44

KENEALY (Edward Vaughan Hyde), LL.D. [*See* Tichborne Trial.]

KENJIU KASAWARA. Biographical Essay. [*See* Müller, Prof. F. Max.]

KENNARD (Adam Steinmetz). Eastern Experiences, collected during a Winter's Tour in Egypt and the Holy Land. 8vo. Lond., 1855.   D 1 P 13

KENNAWAY (Lawrence J.) Crusts: a Settler's Fare due South. 8vo. Lond., 1874.   MD 3 P 34

KENNEDY (Alexander). New Zealand. 8vo. Lond., 1873.   MB 1 Q 17

Another copy. 2nd ed. 8vo. Lond., 1874. MB 1 Q 18

KENNEDY (Alexander B. W.), F.R.S. Kinematics of Machinery. [*See* Reuleaux, Prof. F.]

KENNEDY (Charles Rann). Orations of Demosthenes. [*See* Demosthenes.]

KENNEDY (David), Junr. Kennedy's Colonial Travel: a Narrative of a Four Years' Tour through Australia, New Zealand, Canada, &c. 8vo. Edinb., 1876. MD 4 Q 55

KENNEDY (E. B.) Four Years in Queensland. With a Map. 8vo. Lond., 1870.*   MD 3 Q 11

KENNEDY (E. B. C.) Enquiry taken at the Water Police Office, Sydney, before J. L. Innes and H. H. Browne, Esqs., relative to the Death of E. B. C. Kennedy, Esq., and others, who left Sydney on the 29th April, 1848, on an Exploring Expedition to Tropical Australia. (MS.) (Pam., A.) Fol. Sydney, 1849. MJ 2 U 1

Expedition for the Exploration of Cape York Peninsula. [*See* Macgillivray, J.]

Extracts from the Journal of an Exploring Expedition into Central Australia, 1847–48, to determine the course of the River Barcoo. Compiled by the Rev. W. B. Clarke. (Pam., 30.) 8vo. Lond., 1852. MJ 2 Q 18

KENNEDY (Grace). Profession is not Principle; or, the name of Christian is not Christianity. 4th ed. 12mo. Edinb., 1825.   G 9 P 19

KENNEDY (John Pendleton). Quodlibet; containing some Annals thereof, &c., by "Solomon Secondthoughts," Schoolmaster. 8vo. Phila., 1840.   J 6 P 30

KENNEDY (Richard H.), M.D. Narrative of the Campaign of the Army of the Indus in Sind and Kaubool, 1838–39. 2 vols. 8vo. Lond., 1840. B 10 Q 24, 25

KENNEDY (W. SLOANE). Henry W. Longfellow : Biography—Anecdote—Letters—Criticism. 3rd ed. 8vo. Cambridge, Mass, 1882. C 5 V 22

KENNEDY FAMILY. Historical and Genealogical Account of the principal Families of the name Kennedy. [*See* PITCAIRN, R.]

KENNEL CLUB (THE). Calendar and Stud-book : the only record published in England of Dog Shows and Field Trials, for the year 1884. 8vo. Lond., 1885. E

KENNETT (BASIL), D.D. Law of Nature and Nations. [*See* PUFFENDORF, S. BARON VON.]

KENNICOTT (BENJAMIN), M.A. The State of the Printed Hebrew Text of the Old Testament considered : a Dissertation, in two Parts. 2 vols. 8vo. Oxford, 1753–59. G 3 P 15, 16

KENNY (JAMES). The Alcaid : a Comic Opera. (Cumberland's Eng. Theatre.) 12mo. Lond., 1829. H 2 Q 13

Ella Rosenberg : a Melo-drama. [*See* FARCES, 1.)

The Illustrious Stranger ; or, Married and Buried : an Operatic Farce. (Cumberland's Eng. Theatre.) 12mo. Lond., 1829. H 2 Q 22

Love, Law, and Physic : a Farce. (Cumberland's Eng. Theatre.) 12mo. Lond., 1829. H 2 Q 22

Matrimony : a Petit Opera. [*See* FARCES, 1.]

Raising the Wind : a Farce. [*See* FARCES, 1.]

KENNY (VERY REV. DEAN). History of the Commencement and Progress of Catholicity in Australia, up to the year 1840. 8vo. Sydney, 1886. MG 1 R 3

KENNY (THOMAS). [*See* SANDS, J.]

KENRICK (WILLIAM), LL.D. Falstaff's Wedding : a Comedy. (Bell's Brit. Theatre.) 18mo. Lond., 1795. H 2 P 37

KENT ARCHÆOLOGICAL SOCIETY. Archæologia Cantiana, being Transactions of the Kent Archæological Society. 16 vols. roy. 8vo. Lond., 1858–86. E

KENT (THE), EAST INDIAMAN. Narrative of the Loss of the *Kent*, East Indiaman, by Fire, in the Bay of Biscay, on the 1st March, 1825 ; in a Letter to a Friend, by "A Passenger." 3rd ed. 12mo. Edinb., 1825. D 7 P 56

KENT (CHARLES). Humour and Pathos of Charles Dickens. [*See* DICKENS, C.]

Works of Father Prout ; edited, with a Biographical Introduction. [*See* MAHONY, REV. F. S.]

KENT (FIELD-MARSHAL H.R.H. EDWARD AUGUSTUS), DUKE OF. Life of ; with Extracts from his Correspondence and Original Letters never before published ; by the Rev. E. Neale, M.A. 8vo. Lond., 1850. C 7 P 33

3 F

KENT (JAMES). Commentaries on American Law. 4 vols. 8vo. N. York, 1836. F 8 R 14–17

KENT (REV. SAMUEL C.) George Whitefield. 12mo. Sydney (n.d.) MG 1 P 49

KENT (WILLIAM), M.E. Experiments on the Strength of Wrought Iron Chain Cables. [*See* BEARDSLEE, COMM. L. A.]

KENT (W. SAVILLE), F.L.S., &c. Manual of the Infusoria, including a Description of all known Flagellate, Ciliate, and Tentaculiferous Protozoa, British and Foreign, and an Account of the Organization and Affinities of the Sponges. With Plates. 3 vols. imp. 8vo. Lond., 1880–82. A 15 R 1–3

KENTIGERN (SAINT). Lives of St. Ninian and St. Kentigern ; edited by A. P. Forbes, D.C.L. 8vo. Lond., 1874. G 14 T 15

Another copy. 8vo. Lond., 1874. B 13 P 49

KENTISH (N. L.) Essay on Capital Punishment ; with an earnest Appeal and dutiful Petition to the Sovereign, for the abolition throughout Her Majesty's Dominions of the sanguinary and unholy Laws which sanction the taking of Human Life. 8vo. Hobart Town, 1842. MJ 2 R 13

Memorial to the Queen, Lords, and Commons, petitioning for the continuance of the Transportation and Assignment System. 8vo. Sydney, 1838. MF 3 P 4

Political Economy of New South Wales, developed in a series of Letters addressed to the Colonists. 8vo. Sydney, 1838. MF 3 P 4

Proposals for establishing in Melbourne, the capital of Victoria (which is Australia Felix), a Company on the Mutual Principle, to be designated the Victoria Sheep and Cattle Assurance Company. 8vo. Melb., 1849. MJ 2 P 21

Another copy. 8vo. Melb., 1850. MJ 2 R 7

The Question of Questions ! (of more vital importance than Gold, or than the anxiously expected new Constitution) ; showing how to make Food plentiful and cheap, and the Agricultural Interest prosperous. 8vo. Melb., 1855. MJ 2 R 7

Thoughts on the proposed Address and Petition of the Colonists of New South Wales to the King. (Pam. 38.) 8vo. Sydney, 1831. MJ 2 Q 25

KENTISH GAZETTE (THE), for July 17th, 1798. Fol. Canterbury, 1798. E

KENTUCKY (STATE OF). [*See* UNITED STATES OF AMERICA.]

KENYON (ROBERT LLOYD). Gold Coins of England ; arranged and described by J. Evans. 8vo. Lond., 1884. A 13 S 29

KEOGH (M. J.) King Henry the Ninth ; or, the Rival Water Schemes. Comedy of Errors. 8vo. Sydney (n.d.) MH 1 S 3

KEPLER (JOHN). Life of. (Eminent Men.) 8vo. Lond.,
1849.   C 7 P 45

Life of, by Sir D. Brewster. (Martyrs of Science.) 12mo.
Lond., 1874.   C 1 T 40

KEPPEL (AUGUSTUS), VISCOUNT, ADMIRAL OF THE WHITE.
Life of; by the Hon. and Rev. Tʜᴏs. Keppel. 2 vols.
8vo. Lond., 1842.   C 7 Q 44, 45

KEPPEL (CAPT. THE HON. HENRY), R.N. Expedition to
Borneo, in H.M.S. *Dido;* with Extracts from the Journal
of James Brooke, Esq. 2 vols. 8vo. Lond., 1846.
                                              D 4 U 1, 2
Visit to the Indian Archipelago, in H.M.S. *Mœander;*
with portions of the Private Journal of Sir James Brooke.
2 vols. roy. 8vo. Lond., 1853.   D 9 U 24, 25

KEPPEL (HON. AND REV. THOMAS). Life of Augustus,
Viscount Keppel. 2 vols. 8vo. Lond., 1842.   C 7 Q 44, 45

KER (JOHN), OF KERSLAND. Memoirs of; containing his
Secret Transactions and Negotiation in Scotland, England,
the Courts of Vienna, Hanover, and other Foreign Parts.
Published by himself. 8vo. Lond., 1726.   C 3 T 13

KERIGAN (THOMAS), R.N. Moore's Navigation improved;
being the Theory and Practice of finding the Latitude,
the Longitude, and the Variation of the Compass, by the
Fixed Stars and Planets; to which is prefixed, the Description and Use of the new Celestial Planisphere. 2nd
ed., corrected. Roy. 8vo. Lond., 1835.   A 19 U 25

KERL (PROF.) Metallurgy. [*See* CROOKES, W., AND
RÖNRIG, E.]

MERMODE (PHILIP). Migration of Birds. [*See* BROWN,
J. A. H.]

KERN (PROF. H.) Notes on the Frankish Words in the
Lex Salica. [*See* LEX SALICA.]
The Saddharma-Pundarika. [*See* MÜLLER, PROF. F. M.]

KERNOT (W. C.) Education of Engineers: a Lecture.
[*See* MELBOURNE PUBLIC LIBRARY, &c.]

KERR (MRS. ALEXANDER). History of Servia. [*See*
RANKE, L. VON.]

KERR (ANDREW WILLIAM). History of Banking in Scotland. 8vo. Glasgow, 1884.   F 7 S 17

KERR (CHARLES), LORD. Shooting. [*See* WALSINGHAM,
T. DE G., BARON.]

KERR (MRS. HARRIETTE). Poems and Songs. 12mo.
Melb., 1872.   M 11 1 R 61

KERR (J. H.) Glimpses of Life in Victoria; by "A Resident." 8vo. Edinb., 1872.*   MD 5 U 1

KERR (NORMAN), F.L.S. Wines, Scriptural and Ecclesiastical. 8vo. Lond., 1882.   G 8 S 25

KERR (ROBERT), F.R.S., &c. General History and Collection of Voyages and Travels, arranged in systematic order.
Illustrated. 18 vols. 8vo. Edinb., 1824.   D 10 S 4–21

KERR (ROBERT MALCOLM), LL.D. The Student's Blackstone. 8vo. Lond., 1874.   F 6 Q 11

KERR (ROBERT.) The Consulting Architect: Practical
Notes on Administrative Difficulties and Disputes. 8vo.
Lond., 1886   F 6 S 22

KERR (WALTER MONTAGUE), C.E. The Far Interior: a
Narrative of Travel and Adventure from the Cape of
Good Hope across the Zambesi. 2 vols. 8vo. Lond.,
1886.   D 2 S 13, 14

KERR (WILLIAM). Kerr's Melbourne Almanac, and Port
Phillip Directory, 1841–42. 2 vols. (in 1) 8vo. Melb.,
1841–42.*   ME 3 U

Sermon on the occasion of the Death of. [*See* LAUGHTON,
REV. J. B.]

KERR (WILLIAM), JUNR. Port Phillip Almanac for 1843.
12mo. Melb., 1843.   ME 4 P

KERRISON (CAROLINE), LADY. A Common-place Book
of the 15th Century. [*See* SMITH, MISS L. T.]

KERRY-NICHOLLS (J. H.) [*See* NICHOLLS, J. H. K.]

KERSHAW (MARK). Colonial Facts and Fictions: Humourous Sketches. 12mo. Lond., 1886.   MD 5 P 29

KERSHAW (SAMUEL WAYLAND), M.A., &c. Protestants
from France in their English Home. 8vo. Lond., 1885.
                                              G 8 S 21

KESHUB CHUNDER SEN. Biographical Essay. [*See*
MÜLLER, PROF. F. MAX.]

KETT (HENRY), B.D. Elements of General Knowledge.
9th ed. 2 vols. 8vo. Lond., 1825.   J 8 T 21, 22

KETTLEWELL (REV. JOHN). Memoirs of the Life of,
wherein is contained some Account of the Transactions
of his Time, compiled by Dr. Francis Lee. 8vo. Lond.,
1718.   C 4 V 5

KETTLEWELL (REV. SAMUEL) M.A. Thomas à Kempis,
and the Brothers of Common Life. 2 vols. 8vo. Lond.,
1882.   C 7 R 36, 37

KEULEN (GERARD VAN). Kaart van de Zuyd Zee, &c.
4to. Amsterd., 1650.   MD 5 S 18 ‡

KEULEN (JOANNES VAN). Het westelykste Gedeelte van
het Land van de Eendragt of Nova Hollandia; strekkende
van het Eyland Rottenest, tot voorby de Willems Rivier.
4to. Amsterd., 1665.   MD 5 S 18 ‡

KEY (PROF. THOMAS HEWITT), M.A., &c. Language: its
Origin and Development. 8vo. Lond., 1874.   K 12 8 18

KEY TO FORTUNE (THE). Key to Fortune in New Lands, and Hand-book of the "Explorers' Test Case"; by "W.B.L." 8vo. Lond., 1868.   MA 2 P 12

KEYNES (JOHN NEVILLE), M.A. Studies and Exercises in Formal Logic. 8vo. Lond., 1884.   G 8 S 26

KEYSER (ARTHUR). Cruise to New Guinea. 8vo. Sydney, 1884.   MD 2 R 54

Another copy. 8vo. Lond., 1885.   MD 2 R 55

KIDD (JOHN), M.D., F.R.S. On the Adaptation of External Nature to the Physical Condition of Man. 8vo. Lond., 1836.   A 1 W 1

KIDD (REV. SAMUEL). Critical Notices of Dr. R. Morrison's Chinese Work. [*See* MORRISON, REV. R.]·

Lecture on the Nature and Structure of the Chinese Language. (Univ. of Lond.) 8vo. Lond., 1838.   J 5 S 8

KIDD (THOMAS), A.M. Miscellanea Critica: Tracts and Miscellaneous Criticisms of the late Richard Porson. [*See* DAWES, R.]

KIDDER (REV. DANIEL P.), A.M. Sketches of Residence and Travels in Brazil, embracing Historical and Geographical Notices of the Empire. Illustrated. 2 vols. 8vo. Lond., 1845.   D 3 R 55, 56

KIDDER (REV. DANIEL P.), D.D., AND FLETCHER (REV. J. C.) Brazil and the Brazilians, portrayed in Historical and Descriptive Sketches. Illustrated. 8vo. Philad., 1857.   D 4 Q 27

KIDDLE (HENRY), M.A., AND SCHEM (ALEXANDER J.) Cyclopædia of Education: a Dictionary of Information for the use of Teachers, School Officers, Parents, and others. Imp. 8vo. New York, 1877.   K 4 Q 13

Another copy. 3rd ed. Imp. 8vo. New York, 1883.   K 4 Q 14

KIESSLING (A.) Antiquitatum Romanorum. [*See* DIONYSIUS HALICARNASSENSIS.]

KILGOUR (J.), M.D. Effect of the Climate of Australia upon the European Constitution in Health and Disease. [*See* SYDER, M.]

KILLEBREW (J. B.), A.M. Special Report on the Coalfield of Little Sequatchee; with a General Description of the Cumberland Table-land. (Pam. Co.) 8vo. Nashville, 1876.   A 16 U 23

Tobacco: its Culture in Tennessee; with Statistics of its Commercial Importance. 8vo. Nashville, 1876. A 1 P 28

[*See* UNITED STATES: TENNESSEE.]

KILLEN (REV. WILLIAM D.), DD. The Ancient Church: its History, Doctrine, Worship, and Constitution, traced for the first three hundred years. 2nd ed. 8vo. Lond., 1861.   G 8 U 7

KILLIGREW (HENRY). Pallantus and Eudora: a Tragœdie. Sm. fol. Lond., 1653.   H 1 V 1

KILLOUGH (HENRY RUSSELL·), COMTE. [*See* RUSSELL-KILLOUGH, H., COMTE.]

. KIMBER (ISAAC). Life of Oliver Cromwell, Lord Protector of the Commonwealth of England, Scotland, and Ireland. 8vo. Lond., 1724.   C 6 Q 10

KINAHAN (GERALD HENRY), M.R.I.A., &c. Valleys, and their relation to Fissures, Fractures, and Faults. 8vo. Lond., 1875.   A 9 Q 12

KINDER (HENRY) Complete Report of the Trial in the Alleged Murder Case of the late Henry Kinder ; with all the Correspondence, the Diary, and four Photographs. (*Curious Trials.*) 8vo. Sydney, 1865.   MF 2 R 19

[*See* BERTRAND AND KINDER TRAGEDY.]

KING (MISS ALICE). A Cluster of Lives. 8vo. Lond., 1874.   C 4 S 4

KING (AUSTIN J.), AND WATTS (B. H.) Municipal Records of Bath, 1189-1604. 4to. Lond., 1885.   B 5 V 31

KING (CLARENCE). Democracy: an American Novel. 8vo. Lond., 1882.   J 9 U 2

Mountaineering in the Sierra Nevada. 8vo. Lond., 1872.   D 3 P 44

KING (REV. CHARLES WILLIAM), M.A. Hand-book of Engraved Gems. Illustrated. 8vo. Lond., 1866. A 8 P 39

Another copy. [Illustrated.] 2nd ed. Roy. 8vo. Lond., 1885.   A 8 R 29

Natural History, Ancient and Modern, of Precious Stones and Gems, and of the Precious Metals. Roy. 8vo. Lond., 1865.   A 9 V 8

Natural History of Gems, or Semi-precious Stones. 8vo. Lond., 1870.   A 9 P 32

Plutarch's Morals. [*See* PLUTARCH.]

KING (REV. DAVID), D.D. Principles of Geology explained and viewed in their relations to Revealed and Natural Religion. 3rd ed. 12mo. Lond., 1850.   A 9 P 13

KING (EDWARD). Hymns to the Supreme Being; in Imitation of the Eastern Songs. New ed. 12mo. Lond., 1798.   H 6 R 39

Munimenta Antiqua; or, Observation on Ancient Castles, including remarks on the whole progress of Architecture, &c., in Great Britain. 4 vols. fol. Lond., 1799-1805. B 15 U 8-11 ‡

KING (EDWARD). Brief Biographies: French Political Leaders. 8vo. Lond., 1876.   C 2 R 14

Southern States of North America. Roy. 8vo. Lond., 1875.   D 3 U 28

KING (E. M.) Truth, Love, Joy; or, the Garden of Eden and its Fruits. 12mo. Melb., 1864.   MG 1 Q 10

KING (JAMES). Australia may be an extensive Wine-growing Country. (Pam. Ca.) 8vo. Edinb., 1857.　MA 1 Q 7

Historical Summary of the Proceedings and Reports of the Hunter River Vineyard Association, from its Origination to its first Annual Meeting in the year 1853. (Pam. Dl.) 8vo. Sydney, 1854.　MF 3 P 11

Another copy. (Pam. 28.) 8vo. Sydney, 1854. MJ 2 Q 16

Wine Report. (Pam. Ca.) 8vo. Sydney, 1851. MA 1 Q 7

KING (REV. JAMES), M.A. Anglican Hymnology; being an Account of the 325 Standard Hymns of the highest merit, according to the Verdict of the whole Anglican Church 8vo. Lond., 1885.　G 8 S 24

KING (COL. J. ANTHONY). Twenty-four Years in the Argentine Republic. 8vo. Lond., 1846.　D 4 Q 3

KING (CAPT. JAMES), LL.D., &c. Voyage to the Pacific Ocean. [*See* COOK, CAPT. J.]

KING (JAMES W.), U.S.N. War-ships and Navies of the World. Illustrated. 8vo. Boston, 1880.　A 2 Q 16

KING (JOHN GLEN), D.D., &c. Rites and Ceremonies of the Greek Church in Russia; containing an Account of its Doctrine, Worship, and Discipline. Roy. 8vo. Lond., 1772.　G 4 Q 12 †

KING (MOSES). Harvard and its Surroundings. Subscription (4th) ed. Illustrated. Sq. 12mo. Camb., Mass., 1882.　D 3 P 23

KING (PETER), LORD. Life of John Locke; with Extracts from his Correspondence, Journals, and Common-place Books. 2 vols. 8vo. Lond., 1830.　C 6 R 7, 8

Selection from the Speeches and Writings of; with a short introductory Memoir by Earl Fortescue. 8vo. Lond., 1844.　F 13 Q 5

KING (CAPT. PHILIP PARKER), R.N. Directions for the Inner Route from Sydney to Torres Strait. 8vo. Lond., 1847.　MJ 2 Q 12

Narrative of a Survey of the Intertropical and Western Coasts of Australia, performed between the years 1818–22. Illustrated. 2 vols. 8vo. Lond., 1827.*　MD 2 U 24, 25

Narrative of the Surveying Voyages of H.M. Ships *Adventure* and *Beagle*. [*See* FITZROY, VICE-ADM. R.]

On the Maritime Geography of Australia. [*See* FIELD, B.]

Sailing Directions for the Inner Route to Torres Strait, from Break-sea Spit to Booby Island. [*Printed by the Author.*] Roy. 8vo. Port Stephen, 1843.　MF 2 P 22

Voyage to Torres Strait in search of the Survivors of the ship *Charles Eaton*, which was wrecked upon the Barrier Reefs, in the month of August, 1834. 8vo. Sydney, 1837.　MD 3 R 8

[*See* HALL, J.]

KING (CAPT. PHILIP GIDLEY), R.N. Account of the English Colony of New South Wales. [*See* COLLINS, LIEUT.-COL. D.]

Journal of the Transactions at Norfolk Island. [*See* HUNTER, CAPT. J.]

KING (REV. ROBERT L.) Atoning Sacrifice of the Messiah: Three Sermons addressed to the House of Israel, preached in St. Andrew's Cathedral, Sydney. 12mo. Sydney, 1875.　MG 1 Q 7

KING (MRS. ROBERT MOSS). Diary of a Civilian's Wife in India, 1877–82. With Illustrations. 2 vols. 8vo. Lond., 1884.　D 5 R 13, 14

KING (THOMAS). Address delivered at the laying of the Foundation Stone of the South Australian Institute. [*See* SOUTH AUSTRALIAN INSTITUTE.]

KING (WILLIAM), LL.D. Life and Poems of. [*See* CHALMERS, A., *and* JOHNSON, S.]

KING (W.), SC.D., &c., AND ROWNEY (PROF. T. H.), PH.D., &c. An Old Chapter of the Geological Record with a New Interpretation; or, Rock-metamorphism. 8vo. Lond., 1881.　A 9 T 11

KING (WILLIAM B.) Treatise on the Science and Practice of the Manufacture and Distribution of Coal Gas; edited by Thomas Newbigging, C.E., &c., and W. T. Fewtrell, F.C.S. 3 vols. roy. 4to. Lond., 1878–82. A 2 R 16–18 †

KINGDOM (WILLIAM), JUNR. America and the British Colonies. 8vo. Lond., 1820.　MD 1 V 38

KINGLAKE (ALEXANDER WILLIAM). Eöthen; or, Traces of Travel brought Home from the East. 2nd ed. 8vo. Lond., 1845.　D 5 T 22

Invasion of the Crimea: its Origin, and an Account of its Progress down to the Death of Lord Raglan. 8 vols. 8vo. Edinb., 1863–87.　B 12 U 23–30

Another copy. Cabinet ed. 7 vols. 12mo. Lond., 1877–83.　B 12 T 38–44

KINGS OF THE EAST: an Exposition of the Prophecies determining from Scripture and from History the Power for whom the Mystical Euphrates is being "Dried up." 8vo. Lond., 1842.　C 2 P 26

KING'S COLLEGE Calendar. 26 vols. 12mo. Lond., 1858–84.　E

KING'S SCHOOLS, N. S. WALES. [*See* N. S. WALES.]

KINGSBOROUGH (EDWARD), LORD. Antiquities of Mexico; comprising Fac-similes of Ancient Mexican Paintings and Hieroglyphics; together with the Monuments of New Spain, by M. Dupaix. Illustrated. 9 vols. fol. Lond., 1831 48.　B 13 P 11–19 ‡

KINGSLEY (REV. CANON CHARLES), M.A., &c. Andromeda, and other Poems. 3rd ed. 12mo. Lond., 1862.   H 6 R 38

Biographical Essay. [*See* MÜLLER, PROF. F. MAX.]

His Letters, and Memories of his Life; edited by his Wife [Mrs. E. E. Kingsley.] With Portraits and Illustrations. 2 vols. 8vo. Lond., 1877.   C 7 P 37, 38

Lectures delivered in America in 1874. 8vo. Lond., 1875.   J 11 U 17

At Last: a Christmas in the West Indies. Illustrated. 2 vols. 8vo. Lond., 1871.   D 3 P 13, 14

Roman and the Teuton: a Series of Lectures. 8vo. Lond., 1864.   B 11 U 1

The Saint's Tragedy; or, the True Story of Elizabeth of Hungary. 3rd ed. 12mo. Lond., 1859.   H 3 P 11

South by West. [*See* KINGSLEY, MISS ROSE G.]

KINGSLEY (GEORGE HENRY), M.D. South Sea Bubbles. [*See* PEMBROKE, EARL OF.]

KINGSLEY (MRS. E. E.) Charles Kingsley: his Letters, and Memories of his Life; edited by his Wife. 2 vols. 8vo. Lond., 1877.   C 7 P 37, 38

KINGSLEY (HENRY). Fireside Studies. 2 vols. 8vo. Lond., 1876.   J 11 T 22, 23

KINGSLEY (MISS ROSE G.) South by West; or, Winter in the Rocky Mountains and a Spring in Mexico; edited by the Rev. Charles Kingsley, F.L.S., &c. 8vo. Lond., 1874.   D 3 S 18

KINGSMILL (REV. JOSEPH), M.A. Chapters on Prisons and Prisoners, and the Prevention of Crime. 3rd ed. 8vo. Lond., 1854.   F 8 P 26

KINGSTON (SIR GEORGE STRICKLAND), KNT. South Australia: Diagram showing the depth of Rain in Adelaide, each day from 1839–74; also, the total Rainfall in each year. At. fol. Adelaide, 1874. MA 1 P 1†

South Australia: Diagram showing the average Monthly Rainfall in Adelaide, Melbourne and Sydney; also, the maximum and minimum fall in each month, in Adelaide, 1839–74; Melbourne, 1855–74; Sydney, 1840–74. At. fol. Adelaide, 1874.   MA 1 P 4 †

Register of the Rainfall kept in Grote-street, Adelaide, from 1839 to 1879, inclusive. (Proceedings of the Parl. of S. Aust., vol. 3, 1879.) Fol. Adelaide, 1879.   ME

KINGSTON (WILLIAM BEATTY-). Music and Manners: Personal Reminiscences and Sketches. 2 vols. 8vo. Lond., 1887.   J 2 T 20, 21

KINGSTON (WILLIAM HENRY GILES). Blue Jackets; or, Chips of the Old Block. 8vo. Lond., 1854. B 4 R 29

The Emigrant's Home; or, How to Settle: a Story of Australian Life for all Classes at Home and in the Colonies. 12mo. Lond., 1856.   MJ 1 P 22

How to Emigrate; or, the British Colonists. 2nd ed. 12mo. Lond., 1852.   MJ 1 P 20

Another copy. 3rd ed. 12mo. Lond., 1855.   MJ 1 P 21

KINGZETT (CHARLES THOMAS), F.C.S. Nature's Hygiene: a Series of Essays on Popular Scientific Subjects, with special reference to the Chemistry and Hygiene of the Eucalyptus and Pine. 8vo. Lond., 1880.   A 12 R 19

KINLOCH (ARTHUR). The Murray River; being a Journal of the Voyage of the *Lady Augusta* Steamer, from the Goolwa, in South Australia, to Gannewarra, above Swan Hill, Victoria. 8vo. Adelaide, 1853.   MD 5 T 6

KINLOCH (COL. ALEXANDER A. A.) Large Game Shooting in Thibet, the Himalayas, and Northern India. Illustrated. 4to. Calcutta, 1835.   A 14 V 9

KINNEAR (BENJAMIN GOTT). Cruces Shakespearianæ: Difficult Passages in the Works of Shakespeare; with original Emendations and Notes. 8vo. Lond., 1883.   H 4 Q 9

KINNEAR (JOHN). Cairo, Petra, and Damascus, in 1839. 8vo. Lond., 1841.   D 1 S 7

KINNEAR (JOHN BOYD). Principles of Property in Land. 8vo. Lond., 1880.   F 6 P 35

KINNS (SAMUEL), PH.D., &c. Moses and Geology; or, the Harmony of the Bible with Science. Illustrated. 8vo. Lond., 1882.   A 9 R 26

KINROSS (REV. JOHN), D.D. Man's Need of Religion. [*See* CHRISTIAN EVIDENCE SOCIETY.]

KINROSS (JOHN). Details from Italian Building, chiefly Renaissance. Imp. 4to. Edinb., 1882.   A 4 P 15 †

KINSEY (ARTHUR A.) Report of the Proceedings of the International Congress on the Education of the Deaf, held at Milan, September 6th–11th, 1880. 8vo. Lond., 1880.   G 17 Q 29

KIP (RT. REV. WILLIAM INGRAHAM), LL.D. Christmas Holidays in Rome. 12mo. Glasgow, 1848.   D 7 Q 49

KIPLING (J. S.) The Colonists' Right: Heaven's Gift Allotments; by J.S.K. (Pam. 41.) 12mo. Melh., 1862.   MJ 2 R 3

Another copy.   MJ 2 P 32

KIPPING (ROBERT). Masting, Mast-making, and Rigging of Ships. (Weale.) 12mo. Lond., 1873.   A 17 P 16

Sails and Sail-making. 9th ed. (Weale.) 12mo. Lond., 1870.   A 17 P 50

KIPPIS (ANDREW), D.D., &c. Biographia Britannica; or, the Lives of the most Eminent Persons who have flourished in Great Britain and Ireland, from the Earliest Period to the Present Times. 5 vols. fol. Lond., 1793.   K 22 Q 17–21 ‡

Life of Captain James Cook. 4to. Lond., 1788. MD 4 P 3†

Another copy. 2 vols. (in 1) 8vo. Basil, 1788. MC 1 R 23

KIPPIS (ANDREW), D.D., &c.—*continued.*
Life of the first Earl of Shaftesbury. [*See* MARTYN, B.]
Life of Joseph Butler, LL.D. [*See* BUTLER, RT. REV. J.]
Life of Nathaniel Lardner, D.D. [*See* LARDNER, N.]
Narrative of the Voyages round the World, performed by Captain James Cook. [*See* COOK, CAPT. J.]

KIRBY (R. S.) Wonderful and Scientific (Eccentric) Museum ; or Magazine of Remarkable Characters ; including all the Curiosities of Nature and Art. 6 vols. 8vo. Lond., 1803-20. C 21 S 5-10
[*See* COLLECTION OF FOUR HUNDRED PORTRAITS.]

KIRBY (REV. WILLIAM), M.A., RECTOR OF BARHAM. Life of ; by John Freeman, M.A. 8vo. Lond., 1852. C 7 Q 48
On the Power, Wisdom, and Goodness of God, as manifested in the Creation of Animals, and in their History, Habits, and Instincts. 2 vols. 8vo. Lond., 1835. A 14 T 4, 5

KIRBY (REV. WILLIAM), M.A., &c., AND SPENCE (WILLIAM). Introduction to Entomology ; or, Elements of the Natural History of Insects. With Plates. 4 vols. 8vo. Lond., 1822-26. A 14 T 30-33

KIRBY (WILLIAM FORSELL). Elementary Text-book of Entomology. With Plates. Sq. 8vo. Lond. 1885. A 13 U 7
European Butterflies and Moths ; based upon Berge's "Schmetterlingsbuch." With coloured Plates. 4to. Lond., 1882. A 13 V 6

KIRCHER (ATHANASIUS). Mundus subterraneus in XII Libros digestus. 2 vols. (in 1) fol. Amsterd., 1665. A 19 U 8 ‡
Musurgia Universalis sive Ars Magna Consoni et Dissoni in x Libros digesta. 2 vols. (in 1) fol. Romæ, 1653. A 4 P 3 †
Œdipus Ægyptiacus, hoc est Universalia Hieroglyphicæ Veterum Doctrinæ temporum injuria abolitæ instauratio. 3 vols. (in 4) fol. Romæ, 1652-54. B 17 S 16-19 ‡

KIRCHHOFER (—.) Quellensammlung. [*See* CHARTERIS, PROF. A. H.]

KIRK (ALEXANDER CARNEGIE), M.I.C.E. Compressed Air, and other Refrigerating Machinery : a Lecture. [*See* HEAT.]

KIRK (PROF. JOHN), D.D. British Trade ; or, Certain Conditions of our National Prosperity. 8vo. Lond., 1875. F 6 Q 12

KIRK (JOHN FOSTER). History of Charles the Bold, Duke of Burgundy. With Portraits, 3 vols. 8vo. Lond., 8863 68. B 8 R 20-22

KIRKBRIDE (T. S.) On the Construction, Organization, and General Arrangement of Hospitals for the Insane. Philad., 1880.

KIRKALDY (SIR WILLIAM). Memoirs and Adventures of ; by James Grant. 8vo. Edinb., 1849. C 3 U 9

KIRKLAND (FRASAR). Cyclopædia of Commercial and Business Anecdotes. [*See* APPLETON, D.. & Co.]

KIRKMAN (MARSHALL MONROE). Baggage Car Traffic ; illustrating the Customs and necessary Rules and Regulations of the Baggage Department and the Parcel Traffic of Railroads in this Country and in Europe. 12mo. New York, 1878. A 6 R 21
Railway Service : Trains and Stations ; describing the Manner of operating Trains, and the Duties of Train and Station Officials. 8vo. New York, 1878. A 6 R 20

KIRKMAN (REV. THOMAS PENYNGTON), M.A. First Mnemonical Lessons in Geometry, Algebra, and Trigonometry. (Weale.) 12mo. Lond., 1852. A 17 P 10
Philosophy without Assumptions. 8vo. Lond., 1876. G 8 T 17

KITCHENER (HORATIO HERBERT), R.E. Survey of Western Palestine. [*See* PALESTINE EXPLORATION FUND.]

KITCHIN (VERY REV. GEORGE WILLIAM), M.A. Etymological Dictionary of the French Language. [*See* BRACKET, A.]
Historical Grammar of the French Tongue. [*See* BRACHET, A.]
History of France down to the year 1793. (Clar. Press.) 3 vols. 8vo. Oxford, 1873-77. B 26 Q 2-4
Spenser's Faery Queene. [*See* SPENSER, E.]

KITE (CHARLES). Essays and Observations, Physiological and Medical, on the Submersion of Animals, and on the Resin of the Acoroides Resinifera, or Yellow Resin from Botany Bay ; to which are added, Select Histories of Diseases, with Remarks. 8vo. Lond., 1795. MA 2 S 49

KITTLE (SAMUEL) Concise History of the Colony and Natives of New South Wales. 18mo. Edinb., 1815. MB 1 P 12

KITTO (REV. JOHN), D.D., &c. Cyclopædia of Biblical Literature. 3rd ed., with Biographical Notices and General Index. 3 vols. roy. 8vo. Edinb., 1876. K 4 S 15-17
Scripture Lands ; described in a series of Historical, Geographical, and Topographical Sketches. 8vo. Lond., 1873. G 16 Q 2

KITTON (FRED. G.) Dickensiana : a Bibliography of the Literature relating to Charles Dickens and Writings. 8vo. Lond., 1886. C 2 T 25
John Leech, Artist and Humourist : a Biographical Sketch. 8vo. Lond., 1883. C 7 S 16

KLAPKA (GEN. GEORGE). War in the East, 1853-55. 8vo. Lond., 1855. B 12 T 32

KLAPROTH (J.) Asia Polyglotta. 4to. Paris, 1823. K 13 P 27 ‡
Atlas [to the above]. Roy. fol. Paris. 1831. K 13 P 28 ‡
Histoire Mythologique du Japon. [*See* TITSINGH, I.]
San Kokf Tsou Ran To Sets ; ou, Aperçu Général des Trois Royaumes. Roy. 8vo. Paris, 1832. D 16 R 6 ‡
Cartes [to the above]. 4to. Paris, 1832. D 16 R 7 ‡

KLEIN (E.). Research on the Small-pox of Sheep. (Roy. Soc. Pubs., 1.) 4to. Lond., 1875.   A 11 P 2 †
[*See* SANDERSON, J. B.]

KLEIN (EDWARD EMMANUEL), M.D., SANDERSON (JOHN SCOTT BURDON), FOSTER (MICHAEL), M.D., AND BRUNTON (T. L.) Hand-book for the Physiological Laboratory; edited by J. Burdon-Sanderson. 2 vols. 8vo. Lond., 1873.   A 12 T 11, 12

KLINGEMANN (CARL). The Mendelssohn Family. [*See* HENSEL, S.]

KLOPSTOCK (F. G.) Klopstock's Messiah: a Poem; translated from the German, by G. H. C. Egestorff. 4 vols. (in 1) 8vo. Hamburg, 1821–22.   H 6 U 13

KMETY (G.) Narrative of the Defence of Kars on the 29th September, 1855. 2nd ed. (Pam. 23.) 8vo. Lond., 1856.   MJ 2 Q 11

KNAGGS (R. C.), & CO. Newcastle Business Directory, and Hunter River District Almanac, 1870–71. 2 vols. (in 1) 8vo. Newcastle, 1870–71.   ME 3 S

Newcastle Nautical Almanac, Directory, and Guide to the Port of Newcastle; and Sailing Directory of Torres Straits, Maps, Signals, Chart of Newcastle Harbour, &c., for the years 1874–75, 1879–81, 1883–88. 10 vols. 8vo. Newcastle, 1874–88.*   ME 3 S

Newcastle Town and Country Almanac, for 1874–75. 2 vols. (in 1) 8vo. Newcastle, 1874–75.   ME 3 S

KNAPP (DR. F.) Chemical Technology; or, Chemistry applied to the Arts and to Manufactures. 3 vols. 8vo. Lond., 1848–51.   A 5 T 13–15

Chemical Technology. [*See* RONALDS, DR. E.]

KNAPP (J. L.), F.L.S. Journal of a Naturalist. 3rd ed. 8vo. Lond., 1830.   A 17 T 28

KNATCHBULL (JOHN). Life of John Knatchbull, executed at Darlinghurst, Sydney, on February 13, 1844, for the murder of Mrs. Jamieson. (Pam.) 12mo. Sydney, 1844.   MJ 2 R 18

KNIGHT (ARTHUR GEORGE), S.J. Life of King Alfred the Great. 8vo. Lond., 1880.   C 2 T 1

KNIGHT (CHARLES). Comedies, Histories, and Tragedies and Poems of Shakspere. [*See* SHAKESPEARE, W.]

English Cyclopædia, and Supplements. 26 vols. imp fol. Lond., 1866–73.   K 6 T 1–26

  1–5. Geography, and Supplement.
  6–10. Natural History, and Supplement.
  11–17. Biography, and Supplement.
  18–26. Arts and Sciences, and Supplement.

Gallery of Portraits; with Memoirs. 7 vols. imp. 8vo. Lond., 1833–37.   C 3 W 23–29

Half-hours with the best Authors. With Portraits. 4 vols. (in 2) 8vo. Lond., 1872.   J 2 R 27, 28

KNIGHT. (CHARLES)—*continued.*

Half-hours with the best Letter-writers and Autobiographers. 8vo. Lond., 1867.   C 4 S 36

Knowledge is Power: a View of the Productive Forces of Modern Society, &c. 12mo. Lond., 1855   J 12 Q 8

The Land we Live in: a Pictorial, Historical, and Literary Sketch-book of the British Islands. 3 vols. 8vo. Lond., 1853.   D 6 V 9–11

London; edited by Charles Knight. 6 vols. imp. 8vo. Lond., 1841–44.   B 2 T 1–6

Old England: a Pictorial Museum of Regal, Ecclesiastical, Municipal, Baronial, and popular Antiquities; edited by Charles Knight. 2 vols. fol. Lond., 1845–46.   B 19 T 12, 13 ‡

The Old Printer and the Modern Press. 12mo. Lond., 1854.   J 7 Q 9

Once upon a Time. 2 vols. 12mo. Lond., 1854.   J 7 Q 7, 8

Passages of a Working Life during Half-a-Century; with a Prelude of Early Reminiscences. 3 vols. 8vo. Lond., 1864–65.   C 3 U 3–5

Pictorial History of England; being a History of the People, as well as a History of the Kingdom; Index by H. C. Hamilton. 9 vols. imp. 8vo. Lond., 1838–50.   B 3 U 9–17

KNIGHT (EDWARD HENRY), LL.D. Knight's American Mechanical Dictionary. 4 vols imp. 8vo. New York, 1876–84.   K 17 U 8–11

KNIGHT (F.) Gems; or, Device Book. 2nd ed. 8vo. Lond., 1865.   A 7 Q 11

KNIGHT (HENRY GALLEY). Normans in Sicily; being a Sequel to "An Architectural Tour in Normandy." 8vo. Lond., 1838.   D 9 Q 21

Saracenic and Norman Remains to illustrate the "Normans in Sicily." Imp. fol. Lond., 1840.   A 3 P 18 ‡

KNIGHT (JOHN GEORGE), F.R.I.B.A. Australasian Colonies at the International Exhibition, 1862: Extracts from the Reports of the Jurors, &c. 8vo. Melb., 1865.   MJ 2 R 9

Narrative of the Visit of His Royal Highness the Duke of Edinburgh to the Colony of Victoria, Australia. 4to. Melb., 1868.*   MB 2 V 7

Treatise on Australian Building Stones, read at a Meeting of the Victorian Institute of Architects, Melbouenr, 1859. 8vo. Lond., 1864.*   MA 1 T 3

KNIGHT (RICHARD PAYNE). Nummi Veteres civitatum, regum, gentium, et provinciarum, Londini, in Museo Richardi Payne Knight asservati, ab ipso ordine geographico descripti. Roy. 4to. Lond., 1830.   A 1 Q 23 †

KNIGHT (SAMUEL), D.D. Life of Erasmus, more particularly that part of it which he spent in England. 8vo. Camb., 1726.   C 4 V 4

KNIGHT (CORPL. THOMAS). Adventures in Holland and at Waterloo, and Expedition to Portugal. 8vo. Sydney, 1867.   MJ 2 R 12

Another copy. 8vo. Sydney, 1867.   MJ 2 Q 22

KNIGHT (THOMAS). The Turnpike-gate: a Musical Entertainment. [*See* FARCES, 3.]

KNIGHT (THOMAS ANDREW). Pomona Herefordiensis; containing coloured Engravings of the Old Cider and Perry Fruits of Herefordshire. 4to. Lond., 1811.   A 5 Q 27

KNIGHT (WILLIAM). Census of the Colony of Western Australia, on the 31st March, 1870. [*See* WESTERN AUSTRALIA, CENSUS.]

KNIGHT (PROF. WILLIAM), LL.D. Hume. (Philosophical Classics for English Readers.) 12mo. Edinb., 1886.
C 2 Q 17

Spinoza: Four Essays. [*See* SPINOZA, B. DE.]

KNIGHT (CAPT. WILLIAM HENRY). Diary of a Pedestrian in Casmere and Thibet. 8vo. Lond., 1863.   D 4 T 7

KNIGHT (WILLIAM HENRY). Western Australia: its History, Progress, Condition, and Prospects; and its Advantages as a Field for Emigration. 12mo. Perth, 1870.   MD 4 T 35

KNIGHT *v.* STEPHEN. Evidence in the Case of G. W. Knight against Francis J. Stephen, Solicitor, in the Police Court, Melbourne, on a charge of Perjury, heard in the Police Court, 30th August, 1871; together with the Defendant's Evidence not called on the hearing, and Declarations disproving the positive Evidence of the Carrier, Charles Urben. 8vo. Melb., 1871.   MF 1 Q 5

KNIGHTON (DOROTHEA), LADY. Memoirs of Sir William Knighton, Bart., G.C.H. 2 vols. 8vo.   Lond., 1838.
C 7 Q 46, 47

KNIGHTON (SIR WILLIAM), BART., M.D., &c. Memoirs of, including his Correspondence with many Distinguished Personages; by Lady Knighton. 2 vols. 8vo.   Lond., 1838.   C 7 Q 46, 47

KNIGHTON (WILLIAM), LL.D. Elihu Jan's Story: or, the Private Life of an Eastern Queen. 8vo.   Lond., 1865.   C 2 U 23

Private Life of an Eastern King. 12mo. Lond., 1856.
C 2 P 9

KNOLLYS (MAJOR HENRY). English Life in China. 8vo. Lond., 1885.   D 6 P 25

KNOLLYS (COL. WILLIAM WALLINGFORD), F.R.G.S. Handbook of Field Fortification, intended for the guidance of Officers preparing for promotion, and especially adapted to the requirements of Beginners. 8vo. Lond., 1873.
A 6 R 26

Memoirs of Viscount Combermere. [*See* COMBERMERE, RT. Hox. MARY, VISCOUNTESS.]

KNOWLEDGE: an Illustrated Magazine of Science; conducted by Richard A. Proctor. Vols. 1-9, Nov., 1881-Dec., 1886. 9 vols. 4to. Lond., 1882-86.   E

KNOWLES (REV. JAMES HINTON), F.R.G.S., &c. Dictionary of Kashmiri Proverbs and Sayings. 8vo. Bombay, 1885.   K 12 Q 41

KNOWLES (JAMES SHERIDAN). Caius Gracchus: a Tragedy. (Cumberland's Eng. Theatre.) 12mo. Lond., 1829.
H 2 Q 8

Dramatic Works of. New ed. 2 vols. 8vo. Lond., 1858.   H 4 Q 13, 14

Virginius: a Tragedy. (Cumberland's Eng. Theatre.) 12mo. Lond., 1829.   H 2 Q 8

William Tell: a Play. (Cumberland's Eng. Theatre.) 12mo. Lond., 1829.   H 2 Q 8

KNOWLES (JOHN), F.R.S. Life and Writings of Henry Fuseli, M.A., R.A. 3 vols. 8vo. Lond., 1831. C 8 R 13-15

KNOX (ALEXANDER), M.R.I.A. Thirty Years' Correspondence between John Jebb, D.D., Bishop of Limerick, and Alexander Knox, M.R.I.A.: edited by the Rev. Charles Forster, B.D. 2 vols. 8vo. Philad., 1835. C 7 T 23, 24

KNOX (ALEXANDER A.) The New Playground; or, Wanderings in Algeria. 8vo. Lond., 1881.   D 1 S 20

KNOX (CAPT. CHARLES). Traditions of Western Germany. 3 vols. 8vo. Lond., 1841.   B 9 Q 28-30

KNOX (GEORGE). Law Reports. [*See* SUPREME COURT OF N. S. WALES.]

KNOX (JOHN). John Knox and the Church of England. [*See* LORIMER, PROF. J.]

Life of, containing Illustrations of the History of the Reformation in Scotland; by Thomas M'Crie, D.D. 3rd ed. 2 vols. 8vo. Edinb., 1814.   C 11 P 5, 6

The Portraits of John Knox. [*See* CARLYLE, T.]

Writings of. [*See* BRITISH REFORMERS, 8.]

KNOX (JOHN JAY). United States Notes: a History of the various Issues of Paper Money by the Government of the United States: with an Appendix containing the recent Decision of the Supreme Court of the United States, and the dissenting Opinion upon the Legal Tender Question. 8vo. New York, 1884.   F 10 T 10

KNOX (ROBERT). Historical Relation of the Island of Ceylon, in the East Indies: together with an Account of the detaining in captivity the Author, and divers other Englishmen now living there. [*See* FELLOWES, R.]

KNOX (ROBERT), M.D. Anatomy of Forms of Man. [*See* FAU, DR. J.]

KNOX (THOMAS W.) Overland through Asia: Pictures of Siberian, Chinese, and Tartar Life. 8vo. Lond., 1871.   D 6 S 25

KNOX (VICESIMUS), D.D. Works of; with a Biographical Preface. 7 vols. 8vo. Lond., 1824.   J 7 T 27-33

KOBELL (FRANZ VON). Geschichte der Mineralogie, 1650-1860. (Gesch. der Wiss. in Deutschland.) 8vo. München, 1864.   A 17 V 15

Sketches from the Mineral Kingdom. [*See* SCHOUW, J. F.]

KOBELT (DR. G. L.) De l'Appareil du Sens Génital des deux Sexes dans l'Espèce Humaine et dans quelques Mammifères, au point de Vue Anatomique et Physiologique. Roy. 8vo. Strasbourg, 1851.   Libr.

KOCH (DR. CHARLES). Crimea and Odessa: Journal of a Tour. 8vo. Lond., 1855.   D 8 S 41

KOCH (CHRISTOPHER FRIEDRICH). Historische Grammatik der englischen Sprache 2ᵉ auflage. 3 vols. 8vo. Kassel, 1868–82.   K 15 Q 1–3

KOCH (CHRISTOPHER NIC.) Commentatis de Legationibvs Ecclesiasticis veterum Christianorvm. 12mo. Ienæ, 1747.   G 1 P 19

KOCH (CHRISTOPHER W.) History of the Revolutions in Europe, from the Subversion of the Roman Empire in the West, till the Abdication of Bonaparte; translated by A. Crichton. (Const. Misc.) 3 vols. 18mo. Edinb., 1828.   K 10 Q 21–23
Another copy. Roy. 8vo. Lond., 1839.   B 7 R 29

KOCH (G. VON). Grundriss der Zoologie. 8vo. Jena, 1876.   A 14 S 17

KOEHLER (S. R.) American Etching: a Collection of twenty original Etchings by Moran, Parrish, Fessis, Smillie, and others; with a descriptive Text and Biographical Matter. Lond., 1886.   A 4 R 16 ‡
English Painters. [*See* BUXTON, H. J. W.]
Etching: an Outline of its Technical Processes and its History; with some Remarks on Collections. Imp. 8vo. New York, 1885.   A 4 P 4 ‡
Treatise on Etching. [*See* LALANNE, M.]

KŒMPFER (E.) [*See* KÆMPFER, E.]

KŒNIG (G. L.) [*See* PERSIUS FLACCUS, A.]

KOGALNITCHAN (MICHAEL). Skizze einer Geschichte der Zigeuner, ihrer Sitten und ihrer Sprache, nebst einem kleinen Wörterbuche dieser Sprache. 8vo. Stuttgart, 1840.   K 12 Q 26

KOHL (JOHANN GEORG). Austria, Vienna, Prague, Hungary, Bohemia, and the Danube. 8vo. Lond., 1843.   D 6 T 12
Ireland, Scotland, and England. 8vo. Lond., 1844.   D 6 T 13
Russia and the Russians in 1842. 2 vols. 8vo. Lond., 1842–43.   D 9 P 10, 11

KÖHLER (JOHANN DAVID). Historischer Münz-Belustigung, mit Supplementen und Register, von J. G. Bernhold. 24 vols. (in 12) sm. 4to. Nürenberg, 1729–64.   A 13 R 18–29

KOHLRAUSCH (FREDERICK). History of Germany, from the Earliest Period to the Present Time. 8vo. Lond., 1844.   B 9 S 2

KOLB (G. F.) Condition of Nations. 8vo. Lond., 1880.   F 10 T 16

3 G

KOLDEWEY (CAPT. KARL). German Arctic Expedition of 1869–70, and Narrative of the Wreck of the *Hansa* in the Ice. With Illustrations. Translated and abridged by the Rev. L. Mercier, M.A., and edited by H. W Bates, F.L.S. Roy. 8vo. Lond., 1874.   D 4 S 33

KOLFF (LIEUT. D. H.), JUNR. Voyages of the Dutch Brig of War *Dourga*, performed during the years 1825–26. Translated from the Dutch, by G. W. Earl. 8vo. Lond., 1840.*   MD 4 W 25

KÖLLIKER (A.) Entwicklungsgeschichte des Menschen, und der Höheren Thiere. Roy. 8vo. Leip., 1879.   A 13 R 2

KONEČNÝ (J. N.) Ouplny Kapesni slownik cechoslowanského a německého jazyka. 18mo. Widni, 1845.   K 11 S 3

KONER (W.) Life of the Greeks and Romans. [*See* GUHL, E.]

KONGELIGE NORDISKE OLDSKRIFT-SELSKAB. [*See* ANTIQUARIES DU NORD.]

KONIGLICHEN physikalisch-ökonomischen Gesellschaft zu Königsberg. Bericht und Schriften der 1862. 4to. Königsberg, 1863.   A 15 U 13

KONINCK (G. L. DE), M.D., &c. Recherches sur les Fossiles Paléozoïques de la Nouvelle-Galles du Sud (Australie). Roy. 8vo. Bruxelles, 1876–77.   MA 2 R 6
Atlas [to the above.] 4to. Bruxelles, 1876–77.   MA 1 Q 21 †

KONINCK (L. L. DE). [*See* DE KONINCK, L. L.]

KONINKLIJK INSTITUUT. Voor de Taal, Land, en Volkenkunde van Nederlandsch-Indië. Bijdragen. Derde Volgreeks. Tiende Deel. 8vo. 'sGravenhage, 1875.   E
Another copy. Vierde Volgreeks. Tiende Deel. 8vo. 'sGravenhage, 1885.   MD 3 V 8

KOPP (H.) Annual Reports of the Progress of Chemistry. [*See* LIEBIG, BARON J. VON.]
Die Entwickelung der Chemie in der neueren ziet. (Ges. der Wissen., 10.) 8vo. München, 1873.   A 17 V 24

KORAN (THE) in the Original; published by the Empress Catherine of Russia, for the use of her Mohammedan Subjects. Sm. fol. (n.p.n.d.)   G 5 U 3
The Koran, commonly called the Alcoran of Mohammed; translated from the original Arabic, with Notes by George Sale. New ed. 2 vols. 8vo. Lond., 1825. G 12 Q 6, 7

KÖRNER (DR. CHRISTIAN GOTTFRIED) Correspondence of Schiller with Körner; with Biographical Sketches and Notes, by Leonard Simpson. 3 vols. 8vo. Lond.,   C 4 S 37–30

KÖRNER (THEODOR): Eine Biographie. 18mo. Leip. (n.d.)   C 1 P 1
Sämmtliche Werke. 8vo. Berlin, 1866.   H 7 P 16
Sammtliche Werke. Erster und Zweiter Band. 12mo. Berlin, 1853.   H 6 5 24

KÖRÖS (ALEXANDER CSOMA DE). [*See* CSOMA DE KÖRÖS, A.]

KOSEGARTEN (JOHANN GOTTFRIED LUDWIG) Wörterbuch der niederdeutschen Spracne, älterer und neuerer Zeit. A–Ang. *(All published.)* 4to. Griefswald, 1856–60.   K 15 T 22

KOSSMANN (PROF. R.) Elemente der wissenschaftlichen Zoologie. 8vo. München, 1878.   A 14 S 19

KOSSUTH (LOUIS). Memoir of. [*See* HUNGARY.]

KÖSTLIN (PROF. JULIUS). Life of Luther; translated from the German. Illustrated. 8vo. Lond., 1883.   C 3 V 22

KOTZEBUE (AUGUST FREDERICH FERDINAND). The Stranger: a Drama. (Brit. Theatre.) 12mo. Lond., 12mo. Lond., 1808.   H 1 P 24

The Wise Man of the East: a Comedy. [*See* MODERN THEATRE, 7.]

Sketch of the Life and Literary Career of; with the Journal of his Exile to Siberia, written by himself. (Autobiography, 9, 10.) 2 vols. (in 1) 18mo. Lond., 1827.
                                              C 1 P 9

Another copy.   C 1 P 32

KOTZEBUE (OTTO VON). Voyage of Discovery, into the South Sea and Beering's Straits, 1815–18, in the ship *Rurick*. Illustrated. 3 vols. 8vo. Lond., 1821.
                                             D 9 T 13–15
Another copy. 3 vols. 8vo. Lond., 1821. MD 4 V 25–27

KOUBRAKIEWICZ (M.) Revelations of Austria. 2 vols. 8vo. Lond., 1846.   B 7 S 48, 49

KRAFFT (WILHELM LUDWIG), TH.DR. Ad audiendam orationem de Unione Confessionum evangelicarum carumque communi Sacrae Coenae Usu pro aditu muneris professoris ordinarii in ordine Theologorum evangelicorum Universitatis Fridericiae Guilelmiae Rhenanae. (Pam. O.) 4to. Bonn, 1860.   J 6 U 10

KRAHMER (CAPT.) Die russisch-asiatischen Grenzlande. [*See* WENJUKOW, M.]

KRAMERS (J.), JUN. Kramer's New Pocket Dictionary of the English-Dutch and Dutch-English Languages; projected by A. Jaeger. 3rd ed. 18mo. Gouda, 1876.   K 11 S 14

Technologische Woordentolk in vier talen, waarin de technische termen van het Fransch, Engelsch, en Hoogduitsch, naar alphabetische Volgorde, niet alleen in het Nederlandsch, maar ook in de vreemde talen vertolkt of verklaard worden. Roy. 8vo. Gouda, (n.d.)   K 15 S 26

Technologische Woordentolk in vier talen, bevattende de vertolking en verklaring der vak-termen van het Nederlandsch, Fransch, Engelsch en Hoogduitsch, naar alphabetische volgorde. Roy. 8vo. Gouda (n.d.)   K 15 S 26

KRAPF (REV. DR. J. LEWIS). Dictionary of the Suahili Language; with Introduction, containing an outline of a Suahili Grammar. 8vo. Lond., 1882.   K 15 S 22

Travels, Researches, and Missionary Labours during an Eighteen Years' Residence in Eastern Africa. 8vo. Lond., 1860.   D 2 P 21

KRAUS (PROF. F. X.) Real-Encyklopädie der Christlichen Alterthümer. 2 vols. roy. 8vo. Freiburg, 1882–86.
                                              K 6 R 7, 8

KRAUSE (ERNST). Erasmus Darwin; translated from the German, by W. S. Dallas, with a preliminary Notice by Charles Darwin. 8vo. Lond., 1879. . C 2 U 20

KRAUSE (J. C. H.) [*See* VELLEIS PATERCULUS, C.]

KREFFT (JOHANN LUDWIG GERHARD), F.L.S., &c. Australian Natural History. (Pam.) 8vo. Sydney, 1874.
                                              MA 2 T 9
Catalogue of Mammalia in the Collection of the Australian Museum. 8vo. Sydney, 1864.   MA 2 T 22

Manners and Customs of the Aborigines of the Lower Murray and Darling. 8vo. Melbourne, 1865. MJ 2 R 23

Two Papers on the Vertebrata of the Lower Murray and Darling, and on the Snakes of Sydney. 8vo. Sydney, 1865.   MJ 2 R 23

Australian Vertebrata: Fossil and Recent. (Pam.) 8vo. Sydney, 1871.   MA 2 T 9

Catalogue of the Minerals and Rocks in the Collection of the Australian Museum. 8vo. Sydney,1873. MK 1 P 2
Another copy. (Pam. Co.) Sydney, 1873.   A 16 U 23

Guide to the Australian Fossil Remains exhibited by the Trustees of the Australian Museum. 8vo. Sydney, 1870.   MA 2 V 9

Improvements effected in Modern Museums in Europe and Australia. (Pam.) 8vo. Sydney, 1868.   MA 2 T 9

Mammals of Australia, illustrated by Miss Harriett Scott and Mrs. Helena Forde. Roy. fol. Sydney, 1871.
                                            MA 1 R 24 ‡
Another copy. Coloured Plates. Fol. Sydney, 1871.
                                            MA 1 R 25 ‡

Notes on the Fauna of Tasmania. (Pam.) 8vo. Sydney, 1868.   MA 2 T 6

Snakes of Australia. 4to. Sydney, 1869. MA 2 P 7 †
Another copy. 4 to. Sydney, 1869.   A 13 V 5

KREHBIEL (H. E.) Technics of Violin Playing. [*See* COURVOISER, K.]

KRELING (PROF. A. VON). Faust: a Tragedy. Illustrated. [*See* GOETHE, J. W. VON.]

KRETSCHMER (ALBERT). German National Costumes; after original Drawings, and with descriptive Text. Printed in Colours. Roy. 4to. Leipzig, 1870. A 2 S 7 †

KRETSCHMER (ALBERT), AND ROHBACH (DR. CARL). Costumes of All Nations, from the Earliest Times to the 19th Century. Roy. 4to. Lond., 1882. A 2 S 6 †

KREUZER (FRANZ). Descriptio Pelvis cujuspiam virilis oblique coartatæ et ad thesaurum anatomicum Reipublicæ Mœno-Francofurtanæ pertinentis. (Pam. O.) 4to. Bonnæ, 1860. J 6 U 10

KRUILOFF (I. A.) Urok Dotshkam [a Lesson for Daughters: a Russian Comedy]. (Pam. Fb.) 8vo. St. Petersburg, 1816. MH 1 Q 5

KRUMMACHER (FREDERIC ADOLPHUS). Parables of; translated from the seventh German edition. Illustrated. 8vo. Lond., 1858. G 16 Q 21

KRUMMACHER (DR. F. W.) Sermons on the Canticles. 18mo. Lond., 1839. G 9 P 24

KUDRIAFFSKY (EUFEMIA VON). Japan: Vier Vorträge nebst einem Anhange Japanischer Original-Predigten Japan. 8vo. Wien, 1874. D 5 T 26

KUENEN (PROF. A.), LL.D., &c. National Religions and Universal Religions. (The Hibbert Lectures.) 8vo. Lond., 1882. G 7 P 9

KUHN (A), AND SCHLEICHER (A.) Beiträge zur vergleichenden Sprachforschung auf dem gebiete der Arischen, Celtischen, und Slawischen Sprachen. 8 vols. 8vo. Berlin, 1858–76. K 13 S 11–18

KÜHN (CAROLUS GOTTLOB). [*See* MEDICORUM GRAECORUM.]

KUNHARDT (C. P.) Small Yachts: their Design and Construction as exemplified by the ruling Types of Modern Practice. Illustrated. Roy. 4to. Lond., 1885. A 23 S 25 ‡

KUNTE (M. M.), B.A. Vicissitudes of Aryan Civilization in India: an Essay. 8vo. Bombay, 1880. B 10 U 32

KUROPATKIN (COL. A. N.) Kashgaria [Eastern or Chinese Turkistan]: Historical and Geographical Sketch of the Country; translated from the Russian, by Major Walter E. Gowan. Roy. 8vo. Calcutta, 1882. D 6 S 39

KURSCHAT (FRIEDRICH). Wörterbuch der Littauischen Sprache. Erster Theil: Deutsch-Littauisches Wörterbuch. 2 vols. (in 1) roy. 8vo. Halle, 1870–72. K 14 U 9

KURZ (HEINRICH). Geschicte der deutschen Literatur. 4 vols. roy. 8vo. Leipzig, 1869–72. B 27 V 1–4

Leitfaden zur Geschicte der deutschen Literatur. 8vo. Leipzig, 1870. B 27 U 8

KÜSTEL (GUIDO). Nevada and California Processes of Silver and Gold Extraction for General Use, and especially for the Mining Public of California and Nevada, &c. 8vo. Lond., 1868. A 10 P 14

Treatise on Concentration of all kinds of Ores; including the Chlorination Process for Gold-bearing Sulphurets, Arseniurets, and Gold and Silver Ores generally. 8vo. San Francisco, 1868. A 10 Q 9

KÜTTNER (CHARLES GOTTLOB). Travels through Denmark, Sweden, Austria, and part of Italy, in 1798–99; translated from the German. 8vo. Lond.,1805. D 8 T 28

L

L * * * (D * * *) [*See* Digger's Hand-book.]

L. D. S. [*See* Letters from China and Japan.]

L. (H. A.) [*See* Leveson, Major H. A.]

L. (L. E.) [*See* Maclean, Mrs. L. E.]

L. (W. B.) [*See* Key to Fortune.]

LAAS D'AGUEN (A. M. P.) Dictionnaire Francais-Grec, Moderne. 2e ed. 8vo. Paris, 1874. K 11 V 36
New Guide to English and Modern Greek Conversation. 2nd ed. 18mo. Paris, 1880. K 11 S 21
Nouva Guida della Conversazione Italiana e Greca. 2ª ed. 18mo. Parigi, 1880. K 11 S 22
Nouveau Guide de la Conversation Français-Grec Moderne ou Dialogues usuels et familiers a l'usage des Vayageurs et des Etudiants. 3e ed. Paris, 1875. K 11 S 23

LABANOFF (Alexandre), Prince. Lettres de Marie Stuart, Reine d'Ecosse ; accompagnés d'un résumé Cironologique. [*See* Mary Stuart, Queen of Scots.]

LABARTE (Jules). Hand-book of the Arts of the Middle Ages and Renaissance, as applied to the decoration of Furniture, Arms, Jewels, &c. Illustrated. 8vo. Lond., 1855. A 7 T 19
Histoire des Arts Industriels au moyen age et a l'époque de la Renaissance. 2e edition. 3 vols. roy. 4to. Paris, 1872-75. A 3 P 4-6 †

LABBE (Philippe). Regulæ Accentuum et Spirituum Græcorum. 12mo. Paris, 1693. K 11 S 45

LABBERTON (Robert Henlopen). Historical Atlas ; comprising 141 Maps. 4to. Lond., 1885. B 15 S 2

LABEY (J. B.) Introduction à l'Analyse Infinitesimale. [*See* Euler, L.]

LABILLARDIERE (Jacques Julien de). Novæ Hollandiæ Plantarum Specimen. 2 vols. 4to. Paris, 1804-6. MA 1 Q 19, 20 †
Relation du Voyage a la recierche de la Pérouse pendant les années 1791, 1792. 2 vols. 4to. Paris, 1800. MD 4 Q 10, 11
Atlas [to the above.] Fol. Paris, 1800. MD 3 Q 7 †
Voyage in search of La Pérouse, performed during the years 1791, 1792, 1793, and 1794. 4to. Lond., 1800. MD 3 V 14
Another copy. 2 vols. 8vo. Lond., 1800. MD 3 V 15, 16

LABILLIERE (Francis Peter). Constitutions of the Australian Colonies. 8vo. Lond., 1872. MF 3 P 27
Early History of the Colony of Victoria. 2 vols. 8vo. Lond., 1878.* MB 1 Q 19, 20
Future Relations of England and her Colonies. 8vo. Lond., 1869. MF 3 P 27

LABILLIERE (Francis Peter)—*continued.*
Permanent Unity of the Empire. (Pam. Ds.) 8vo. Lond., 1875. MF 3 P 17
Permanent Unity of the Empire. 8vo. Lond., 1875. MF 3 P 27
Political Organisation of the Empire. 8vo. Lond., 1881. MF 3 P 27
Right of Belligerents to capture Private Property at Sea. 8vo. Lond., 1876. MF 3 P 27

LA BLETERIE (Jean Philippe Réne de), l'Abbé. [*See* Bleterie, J. P. R. de la, l'Abbé.]

LA BORDERIE (Guy Le Fèvre de). [*See* Le Fèvre de la Borderie, G.]

LABORDE (Jean Benjamin de). Histoire Abrégée de la Mer du Sud, ornée de plusieurs cartes. 3 vols. 8vo. Paris, 1791. MD 8 P 1-3 †
Atlas [to the above.] 4to. Paris, 1791. MD 8 P 4

LA BORDE (Jean Benj. de) et ROUSIER (Pierre Joseph), l'Abbé. Essai sur la Musique Ancienne et Moderne. 4 vols. 4to. Paris, 1780. A 8 R 7-10

LABORDE (Léon Emmanuel Simon Joseph), Marquis de. Journey through Arabia Petræa, to Mount Sinai and the excavated City of Petra, the Edom of the Prophecies. 8vo. Lond., 1836. D 5 S 30
Voyage de l'Asie Mineure, par Mrs. Alexandre de Laborde, Becker, Hall, et Léon de Laborde. El. fol. Paris, 1838. D 20 P 24 ‡
Voyage de la Syrie, par Mrs. Alexandre de Laborde, Becker, Hall, et Léon de Laborde. El. fol. Paris, 1837. D 11 P 2 ‡

LABORDE (Henri), Vicomte. [*See* Delaborde, Vicomte H.]

LABOURING MECHANIC, A. [*See* Touchstone, The.]

LA BRUYERE (Jean de). Caractères de La Bruyère suivis des caractères de Theophraste ; traduits du Grec, par La Bruyère, avec des Notes et des Additions par [J.] Schweighaeuser. 12mo. Paris, 1865. G 2 P 2
The "Characters" of ; newly rendered into English, by Henri van Laun. Illustrated. 8vo. Lond., 1885. G 6 P 1

LABRUZZI (Carlo). Le Pitture di Masaccio. [*See* Guidi, T.]

LACERDA e ALMEIDA (F. José Maria de). Journey to Cazembe in 1798. [*See* Africa.]

LA CHAPELLE (ALFRED DE), COMTE. Posthumous Works and Unpublished Autographs of Napoleon III in exile. [*See* NAPOLEON III.]

LACHMANN (KARL). [*See* LESSING, G. E.]

LACKINGTON (JAMES). Lackington's Confessions rendered into Narrative ; to which are added Observations on Boarding Schools, by Allan Macleod. 12mo. Lond., 1804.   G 9 Q 33

Memoirs of the first forty-five years of the Life of James Lackington ; written by himself. 8vo. Lond., 1791.
                                                                            C 7 R 38
Another copy. (Autobiography.) 18mo. Lond., 1830.
                                                                            C 1 P 14

LACKLAND (JACOB). Common Sense : an Enquiry into the Influence of Transportation on the Colony of Van Diemen's Land. 3rd thousand. 8vo. Launceston, 1847.   MJ 2 R 13

LACOMBE (ARMAND). Histoire des Italiens. [*See* CANTU, C.]

Histoire Universelle. [*See* CANTU, C.]

LACOPPIDAN (H. J. G. A.) The Agricultural Teacher. Published at Copenhagen, 1877. Translated by William Luplau, and adapted for the Australian Colonies. 8vo. Melb., 1881.   MA 1 P 3

LACORDAIRE (VERY REV. PÈRE JEAN BAPTISTE HENRI.) Correspondance du Rev. Père Lacordaire et de Madame Swetchine publiée par le Comte de Falloux. 2e ed. 8vo. Paris, 1864.   C 9 P 44

Henri Dominique Lacordaire : a Biographical Sketch ; by [Mrs.] A. L. Lear. 8vo. Lond., 1882.   C 3 Q 32

Inner Life of the Very Rev. Père Lacordaire of the Order of Preachers. [*See* CHOCARNE, REV. PÈRE P.]

LACOUPERIE (A. E. J. B. TERRIEN DE). [*See* TERRIEN DE LACOUPERIE, A. E. J. B.]

LACROIX (FRÉDÉRIC). Les Mystères de la Russie : Tableau Politique et Moral de l'Empire Russe. Roy. 8vo. Paris, 1845.   D 6 V 29

LACROIX (J. FR. DE). Dictionnaire historique des cultes religieux établis dans le monde, depuis son origine jusqu'e présent. 5 vols. 12mo. Liege, 1772.   K 18 R 1-5

LACROIX (PAUL). Arts in the Middle Ages, and at the Period of the Renaissance. Illustrated. 4th thousand. Roy. 8vo. Lond., 1870.   B 7 V 16

The Eighteenth Century ; its Institutions, Customs, and Costumes : France, 1700–89. Illustrated. Roy. 8vo. Lond., 1876.   B 7 V 19

Histoire de la Prostitution chez tous les Peuples du Monde par Pierre Dufour. 6 vols. 8vo. Paris, 1851–53.   F 6 T 15-20

Manners, Customs, and Dress during the Middle Ages, and during the Renaissance Period. Illustrated. Roy. 8vo. Lond., 1874.   B 7 V 17

LACROIX (PAUL)—*continued.*
Mémoires curieux sur l'Histoire des Mœurs et de Prostitution en France, par Pierre Dufour. 2 vols. 8vo. Paris, 1855–61.   F 6 Q 36

Military and Religious Life in the Middle Ages and at the Period of the Renaissance. Illustrated. Roy. 8vo. Lond., 1874.   B 7 V 18

Mœurs, usages, et costumes au Moyen Age, et à l'époque de la Renaissance. 2nd ed. Imp. 8vo. Paris, 1872.
                                                                            B 7 V 21
Science and Literature of the Middle Ages, and at the Period of the Renaissance. Roy. 8vo. Lond., 1878.
                                                                            B 7 V 20

LACROIX (S. F.) Elémens d'Algèbre. 8vo. Paris, 1804.   A 10 S 1

Traité du Calcul Différentiel, et du Calcul Intégral. 2nd ed. 3 vols. 4to. Paris, 1810–19.   A 10 V 10-12

LACTANTIUS (LUCIUS CÆCILIUS FIRMIANUS). Lucii Cæcilii Firmiani Lactantii Opera omnia. 2 vols. 4to. Paris, 1748.   G 7 V 14, 15

Opera omnia. [*See* MIGNE, J. P., SERIES LATINA, 6, 7.]

LACY (GEORGE). Co-operation ; the Social Equalizer, the Pacificator of all Antagonism between Capital and Labour, the Gaol of all Industrial Enterprise : an Essay. 8vo. Sydney, 1880.   MF 1 Q 23

Vaccination in the Light of Modern Enquiry. 8vo. with Appendices. 8vo. Sydney, 1881.   MA 2 S 20

LADIES' BENEVOLENT SOCIETY (MELBOURNE). [*See* MELBOURNE LADIES' BENEVOLENT SOCIETY.]

LADIES' MELBOURNE AND SUBURBAN CITY MISSION. Annual Reports of the Committee. Melb., 1861–62.   MF 3 P 15

LADIES' SOCIETY. Outlines of Instruction for the Mistress of a Charity School, to explain the nature of her duty, and to assist her in the performance of it. 12mo. Sydney, 1828.   MF 3 P 10

LADY, A. [*See* MACPHERSON, MRS.]

LADY, A. [*See* MAITLAND, MRS. J. C.]

LADY, A. [*See* NORTON, HON. MRS. C. E. S.]

LADY IN AUSTRALIA, A. [*See* MEMORIES OF THE PAST.]

LADY IN THE NEW ENGLAND DISTRICT, A [*See* FATAL QUEST.]

LADY PIONEER, A. [*See* INDIAN ALPS, THE.]

LAËRNE (C. F. VAN DELDEN). Brazil and Java : Report on Coffee-culture in America, Asia, and Africa. 8vo. Lond., 1885.   A 1 S 25

LAFARGE (MME. MARIE CHAPPELLE POUCH). Memoirs of; written by herself. 2 vols. 8vo. Lond., 1841. C 3 U 18, 19

LAFAYETTE (M. P. R. T. GILBERT MOTIER), MARQUIS DE. Memoirs of General Lafayette, and of the French Revolution of 1830; by B. Sarrans. 2 vols. 8vo. Lond., 1832. C 9 T 14, 15

LAFITAU (JOSEPH FRANÇOIS). Mœurs des Sauvages Amériquains comparées aux mœurs des premiers temps. 2 vols. (in 1) 4to. Paris, 1724. B 1 V 5

LA FONTAINE (AUGUST HEINRICH JULIUS). Amelia Horst; or, the Secret of being Contented. [In Russian.] 4 vols. (in 2) Moscow, 1818. J 16 T 16, 17

LA FONTAINE (JEAN DE). Fables de. Edition classique accompagnée de Notes et Remarques historiques philologiques, et littéraires ; précédés d'une Notice biographique, par Héguin de Guerle. Nouvelle édition. 12mo. Paris (n.d.) H 6 R 10

Fables of; translated from the French, by Elizur Wright. New edition, with Notes, by J. W. M. Gibbs. 8vo. Lond., 1882. H 8 R 20

Œuvres de. Nouvelle édition, revue, mise en ordre. 6 vols. 8vo. Paris, 1821-23. H 1 S 2-7

LA FORCE (MDLLE. CHARLOTTE ROSE.CAUMONT DE). Les Fées: Contes des Contes. [See CABINET DES FÉES, 6.]

LAG (LAIRD OF). [See GRIERSON, SIR R.]

LAGADEUC (JEHAN). Le Catholicon: Dictionnaire Breton, Française, et Latin. 8vo. Lorient (n.d.) K 13 Q 26

LA GIRONIERE (PAUL P. DE). Twenty Years in the Philippines; translated from the French. 8vo. Lond. (n.d.) D 5 R 48

LAGRANGE (FRANÇOOIS), L'ABBÉ. Life of Monseigneur Dupanloup, Bishop of Orleans; translated by Lady Herbert. 2 vols. 8vo. Lond., 1885. C T 6, 7

Vie de Mgr. Dupanloup, Evêque d'Orleans, Membre de l'Académie Française. 3e éd. 3 vols. 8vo. Paris, 1883-84. C 9 T 3-5

LAGRANGE (JOSEPH LOUIS). Leçons sur le calcul des Fonctions. 8vo. Paris, 1806. A 10 T 23

Mécanique Analytique. Nouvelle édition. 2 vols. roy. 4to. Paris, 1811-15 A 11 V 3, 4

Théorie des Fonctions Analytiques. Roy. 8vo. Paris, 1813. A 10 U 2

Traité de la Résolution des Equations numériques de tous les degrés. Roy. 8vo. Paris, 1808. A 10 U 3

LA HARPE (JEAN FRANÇOIS DE). Abrégé de l'Histoire Générale des Voyages. Nouvelle éd. 24 vols. 8vo. Paris, 1825. D 10 Q 1-24

Atlas [to the above], dressé par A. Tardieu. Fol. Paris, 1825. D 8 P 12 ‡

LA HARPE (JEAN FRANÇOIS DE)—*continued.*
Cours de Littérature Ancienne et Moderne, suivi du Tableau de la Littérature au 19e Siècle, par Chénier, et du Tableau de la Littérature au 16e Siècle, par M. St. Marc Girardin et M. P. Chasles. 3 vols. roy. 8vo. Paris, 1863-66. B 36 V 1-3

The Earl of Warwick: a Tragedy. (Bell's Brit. Theatre.) 18mo. Lond., 1792. H 2 P 40

Another copy. (Brit. Theatre.) 12mo. Lond., 1808. H 1 P 19

LA HAUTIÈRE (ULYSSE DE). Souvenirs de la Nouvelle-Calédonie. 8vo. Paris, 1869. MD 5 P 4

LAING (DAVID), LL.D. A Ballad Book, 1823. [See SHARPE, C. K.]

Biographical Sketches of Sir David Wilkie, R.A., and Andrew Geddes, A.R.A. [See WILKIE, SIR D.]

Fac-simile of an Ancient Heraldic Document. [See LYNDSAY, SIR D.]

Letters and Journal of Robert Baillie, A.M., Principal of the University of Glasgow, 1637-62; edited, from the Author's Manuscripts, by David Laing. 3 vols. imp. 8vo. Edinb., 1841-42. C 5 W 3-5

Memoir of the Life of William Dunbar. [See DUNBAR, W.]

Orygynale Cronykil of Scotland. [See WYNTOUN, ANDROW OF.]

Select Remains of the Ancient Popular and Romance Poetry of Scotland; collected and edited, by David Laing, LL.D; re-edited, with Memorial-Introduction and Additions, by John Small, M.A. 8vo. Edinb., 1885. H 5 U 24

LAING (REV. JOHN), M.A. Dictionary of the Anonymous and Pseudonymous Literature of Great Britain. [See HALKETT, S.]

LAING (MALCOLM). History of Scotland, from the Union of the Crowns, on the Accession of James VI to the Throne of England, to the Union of the Kingdoms in the Reign of Queen Anne. 4 vols. 8vo. Lond., 1819. B 13 Q 29-32

LAING (SAMUEL). Heimskringla; or, Chronicles of the Kings of Norway. [See SNORRO STURLESON.]

Journal of a Residence in Norway, during the years 1834-36. 8vo. Lond., 1836. D 8 T 20

Notes of a Traveller on the Social and Political State of France, Prussia, Switzerland, Italy, and other parts of Europe. 8vo. Lond., 1842. F 7 Q 13

Notes on the Rise, Progress, and Prospects of the Schism from the Church of Rome called the German-Catholic Church, instituted by John Rongc, and I. Czerzki, in October, 1844. 12mo. Lond., 1845. C 8 P 13

Observations on the Social and Political State of Denmark. 8vo. Lond., 1852. D 6 T 31

Observations on the Social and Political State of the European People in 1848-49. 8vo. Lond., 1850. F 7 Q 14

Tour in Sweden in 1838; comprising Observations on the Moral, Political, and Economical State of the Swedish Nation. 8vo. Lond., 1839. D 7 T 39

LAIRD (E. K.) Rambles of a Globe Trotter in Australasia, Japan, China, Java, India, and Casımere. 2 vols. 8vo. Lond., 1875.   MD 1 V 11, 12

LAIRD (MACGREGOR), AND OLDFIELD (R. A. K.) Narrative of an Expedition into the Interior of Africa, by the River Niger, in the steam vessels *Quorra* and *Alburkah,* 1832–34. 2 vols. 8vo. Lond., 1837.   D 1 W 11, 12

LAÏS DE CORINTHE(d'aprés un Manuscrit Grec)et Ninon de Lenclos: Biographie Anecdotique; par A. Debay. Nouvelle éd. 12mo. Paris, 1858.   C 2 P 29

LAISHLEY (RICHARD), F.R.L.S., &c. Report upon State Education in Great Britain, France, Switzerland, Italy, Germany, Belgium, and the United States of America; including a Special Report upon Deaf-Mute Instruction. Fol. Wellington, 1886.   MG 10 Q 6 †

LAKE (COL. ATWELL), C.B. Kars, and our Captivity in Russia. 8vo. Lond., 1856.   B 12 T 28

LAKEY (CHARLES D.) Village and Country Houses; or, Cheap Homes for all Classes. Imp. 4to. New York, 1875.   A 5 S 8 †

LALANNE (L.) Last Days of the Consulate. [*See* FAURIEL, C.]

LALANNE (MAXIME). Treatise on Etching—Text and Plates. Authorized ed., translated from the second French ed., by S. R. Koehler. Roy. 8vo. Lond., 1880. A 8 R 28

LAL BEHARI DAY (REV.) [*See* DAY, REV. L. B.]

LALLEMAND (CLAUDE FRANÇOIS). Des Pertes Séminales involontaires. 5 vols. 8vo. Paris, 1836–42.
        A 26 S 11–15

LALOR (JOHN J.) Cyclopædia of Political Science, Political Economy, and of the Political History of the United States. 3 vols. roy. 8vo. Chicago, 1883–85. K 2 P 18–20

LALOR (PETER). Portrait of. [*See* MANUSCRIPTS AND PORTRAITS.]

LAMARCK (J. B. P. A. DE M. DE). Histoire Naturelle des Animaux sans Vertèbres. 2nd ed. Revue et augmentée de notes, par G. P. Deslayes et H. Milne Edwards. 11 vols. 8vo. Paris, 1835–45. A 14 R 21–31

Philosophie Zoologique, on Exposition des considérations relatives à l'histoire naturelle des Animaux. Nouvelle édition, revue et précédée d'une introduction biographique, par C. Martins. 2 vols. 8vo. Paris, 1873. A 14 S 22, 23

Die Naturanschauung von. [*See* HAECKEL, E.]

LAMARTINE (ALFONSE MARIE LOUIS PRAT DE). Biographies and Portraits of some Celebrated People. 2 vols. 8vo. Lond., 1866.   C 5 S 11, 12

1. Lord Chatham, William Pitt, Shakespeare.
2. Shakespeare, Charlotte Corday, Madame Roland, Mirabeau, Danton, Vergniaud.

History of the Constituent Assembly (1789). Vol. 1. 8vo. Lond., 1854.   B 8 P 35

LAMARTINE (ALFONSE MARIE LOUIS PRAT DE)—*contd.*
History of the Girondists; or, Personal Memoirs of the Patriots of the French Revolution. 3 vols. 12mo. Lond., 1849–50.   B 8 P 16–18

History of the French Revolution of 1848. 8vo. Lond., 1870.   B 8 P 40

History of the Restoration of Monarchy in France, 1851. 4 vols. 8vo. Lond., 1853.   B 8 P 23–26

Memoirs of Celebrated Characters. 2nd ed. 2 vols. 8vo. Lond., 1854.   C 2 T 16, 17

Memoirs of my Youth. 12mo. Lond., 1849. C 1 R 19

Pilgrimage to the Holy Land, 1832–33. 3 vols. 8vo. Lond., 1835.   D 5 Q 37–39

LAMB (CHARLES). [A Biography]; by Rev. A. Ainger. 8vo. Lond., 1882.   C 1 U 22

Charles Lamb: a Memoir; by "Barry Cornwall" [Bryan Waller Proctor]. 8vo. Lond., 1866.   C 7 P 39

Complete Correspondence and Works of; with an Essay on his Life and Genius; by Thomas Purnell. 4 vols. 8vo. Lond., 1870.   J 1 T 20–23

Essays of Elia; with Introduction and Notes, by Alfred Ainger. 8vo. Lond., 1884.   J 1 T 17

Essays of Elia. 2nd series. 8vo. Lond., 1840. J 7 U 26

Final Memorials of; consisting chiefly of his Letters, not before published; by Sir T. N. Talfourd. 2 vols. 8vo. Lond., 1848.   C 4 S 11, 12

Letters of; with some Account of the Writers, his Friends, and Correspondents, by the late Sir Thomas Noon Talfourd; revised by W. C. Hazlitt. 2 vols. 12mo. Lond., 1886.
        C 2 S 26, 27

Life, Letters, and Writings of. Edited, with Notes, &c., by Percy Fitzgerald, M.A. 6 vols. 12mo. Lond., 1886.   C 2 S 28–33

Mrs. Leicester's School, and other Writings in Prose and Verse; with Introduction and Notes, by Alfred Ainger. 8vo. Lond., 1885.   J 1 T 19

Poems, Plays, and Miscellaneoues Essays; with Introduction and Notes, by Alfred Ainger. 8vo. Lond., 1884.   J 1 T 18

Poetical Works of. 3rd ed. 8vo. Lond., 1838. H 7 U 12

Prose Works of. 3 vols. 8vo. Lond., 1836–38. J 1 T 25–27

Rosamund Gray. Recollections of Christ's Hospital, &c. 8vo. Lond., 1838.   J 1 T 24

Specimens of English Dramatic Poets, who lived about the time of Shakespeare; with Notes. New ed., including the Extracts from the Garrick Plays. 8vo. Lond., 1854.   H 4 P 5

[*See* HAZLITT, W. C.]

LAMB (CHARLES AND MARY). Poetry for Children; to which are added Prince Dorus and some uncollected Poems, by Charles Lamb; edited by Richard Herne Shepherd. 12mo. Lond., 1878.   H 7 P 24

Tales from Shakespeare. Illustrated. 8vo. Lond., 1885.   J 12 R 15

LAMB (HORACE), M.A. Treatise on the Mathematical Theory of the Motion of Fluids. Roy. 8vo. Camb., 1879. A 29 U 16

LAMB (Mrs. MARTHA J.) History of the City of New York: its Origin, Rise, and Progress. Illustrated. 2 vols. imp. 8vo. New York, 1877–80. B 1 V 10, 11

LAMB (MARY). Tales from Shakespeare. [*See* LAMB, C. AND M.]

LAMBARDE (WILLIAM). Dictionarium Angliæ Topographicum et Historicum : an alphabetical Description of the chief Palaces in England and Wales. Roy. 8vo. Lond., 1836. D 12 V 5

LAMBECK (HERMANN). De Mercurii Statua vulgo Iasonis habita. (Pam. O.) 4to. Thorn, 1860. J 6 U 10

LAMBERT (C. AND S.) Voyage of the *Wanderer;* edited by Gerald Young. Illustrated. Roy. 8vo. Lond., 1883. D 10 U 22

LAMBERT (M. AND M. W.) Coloured Map of the Baltic ; with enlarged Plan of Cronstadt and St. Petersburgh. Sm. fol. Lond. (n.d.) D 33 P 11 ‡

LAMBERT (OSMUND). Angling Literature in England ; and Descriptions of Fishing by the Ancients. 12mo. Lond., 1881. A 17 U 2

LAMBORN (ROBERT H.), PH.D. Metallurgy of Copper. (Weale.) 5th ed. 12mo. Lond., 1873. A 17 P 65

Metallurgy of Silver and Lead. (Weale.) 4th ed. 12mo. Lond., 1869. A 17 P 65

LAMÉ (G.) Treatise on Lamé's Functions. [*See* TODHUNTER, I.]

LA MESLÉE (E. MARIN-). [*See* MARIN LA MESLÉE, E.]

LAMONT (E. H.) Wild Life among the Pacific Islanders. 8vo. Lond., 1867.* MD 6 R 2

LAMONT (JAMES), F.G.S., &c. Yachting in the Arctic Seas. 8vo. Lond., 1872. D 4 S 12

LAMOTHE-LANGON (ETIENNE LÉON DE), BARON. Evenings with Prince Cambacérès, Second Consul, &c. 2 vols. 8vo. Lond., 1837. C 8 U 15, 16

LA MOTRAYE (AUBRY DE). Travels through Europe, Asia, and into Part of Africa: containing a great variety of Geographical, Topographical, and Political Observations on those parts of the World. 2 vols. sm. fol. Lond., 1732. D 7 Q 1, 2

Voyages en Anglois et en François, en diverses Provinces et Places de la Prusse Ducale et Royale, de la Russie, de la Pologne, &c. Sm. fol. La Haye, 1732. D 7 Q 3 †

LA MOTTE (JEANNE DE VALOIS), COMTESSE DE. Detection ; or, a Scourge for Charles Alexandre de] Calonne, containing the Reply of the Countess de Valois de la Motte to the calumnies propagated by that daring fugitive. 8vo. Lond., 1789. C 5 T 7

LA MOTTE (JEANNE DE VALOIS), COMTESSE DE—*contd.*

Life of; containing some farther particulars relative to the mysterious transaction of the Diamond Necklace, &c., written by herself. 2 vols. 8vo. Lond.,1791. C 5 T 8, 9

Memoirs of; containing a compleat Justification of her Conduct, and an Explanation of the Intrigues and Artifices used against her by her Enemies, relative to the Diamond Necklace; translated from the French, written by herself. 8vo. Lond., 1789. C 5 T 7

Sketch of the Life of. [*See* VIZETELLY, H.]

LAMPADIUS (W. A.) Handbuch der allegemeinen Hüttenkunde. 8vo. Göttingen, 1801. A 9 T 38

Life of Felix Mendelssohn-Bartholdy ; edited and translated by W. L. Gage. 2nd ed. 8vo. Lond., 1877. C 5 P 23

LAMPING (LIEUT. CLEMENS), AND FRANCE(LIEUT. A. DE.) French in Algiers: 1. The Soldier of the Foreign Legion- 2. The Prisoners of Abd-el-Kader; translated by Lady D. Gordon. New ed. 12mo. Lond., 1855. D 1 T 10

Another copy. (H. and C. Lib.) 12mo. Lond., 1845 ; J 8 P 10

LANCASHIRE. Distress in Lancashire. [Newspaper Cuttings.] (Pam. A.) Fol. Lond., 1862. MJ 2 U 1

LANCASTER (JOHN OF GAUNT), DUKE OF. Memoirs of. [*See* GODWIN, W.]

LANCELOTT (F.) Australia as it is: its Settlements, Farms, and Gold-fields. 2 vols. 8vo. Lond., 1852.* MD 4 T 13, 14

Another copy. 2nd ed., revised. 2 vols. 8vo. Lond., 1853. MD 4 T 19, 20

LANCET (THE): a Journal of British and Foreign Medicine, Physiology, &c., 1843–59, 1866–68, 1879–86. Imp. 8vo. Lond., 1843–86. E

LANCTOT (BENONI). Chinese and English Phrase-book; with the Chinese Pronunciation indicated in English. 2nd ed. 12mo. San Francisco, 1867. C 11 V 7

LAND (PROF. J. P. N.) In Memory of Spinoza. [*See* SPINOZA, B. DE.]

LAND. Report from the Select Committee on the disposal of Lands in the British Colonies: together with the Minutes of Evidence, and Appendix. Fol. Lond.,1836. MF 1 U 33

LAND ACTS. [*See* NEW SOUTH WALES ; NEW ZEALAND ; and VICTORIA.

LAND BILL (THE): being a Letter addressed to the Members of the Legislative Council, by "Moderation." 8vo. Melb., 1860. J 1 Q 3

LAND CONCENTRATION (ON), and Irresponsibility of Political Power. 8vo. Lond., 1886. F 6 P 37

LAND-FUND. Expenditure of the Land-Fund of New South Wales in the Colony, and principally on Public Works, as a means of promoting and supporting Immigration. 8vo. Sydney, 1842. MF 3 P 1

LAND QUESTION (THE). Land Question considered with reference to Pastoral Occupation in Victoria. 8vo. Melh., 1867. MF 1 Q 3

Land Question familiarly and practically considered by "A Practical Man." (Pam. 28.) 8vo. Sydney, 1856. MJ 2 Q 16

New Idea on : a Letter to His Excellency Charles Joseph La Trobe, Esq., suggesting a mode of opening the Lands without injuring any class of the people. 8vo. Melh., 1853. MF 1 Q 3

LANDAUER (J.) Blowpipe Analysis. Authorized English edition, by James Taylor and William E. Kay. 12mo. Lond., 1879. A 5 R 4

LANDER (RICHARD). Journal [of Travels] from Kano to the Sea Coast Africa. [*See* CLAPPERTON, CAPT. H.]

Records of Captain Clapperton's last Expedition to Africa. 2 vols. 8vo. Lond., 1830. D 1 Q 5, 6

LANDER (RICHARD AND JOHN). Journal of an Expedition to explore the Course and Termination of the Niger. Illustrated. 3 vols. 18mo. Lond., 1832. D 1 V 4–6

LANDMANN (COL. GEORGE). Adventures and Recollections of. 2 vols. 8vo. Lond., 1852. C 4 S 13, 14

LANDOLT (E.) Refraction and Accommodation of the Eye, and their Anomalies ; translated by C. M. Culver. Edinb., 1886. A 12 S 24

LANDOLT (H.) Hand-book of the Polariscope, and its Practical Applications ; adapted from the German edition, by D. C. Robb, B.A., and V. H. Veley, B.A., &c. Illustrated. 8vo. Lond., 1882. A 5 T 5

LANDOLT (CAPT. H. M. F.) Dictionnaire Polýglotte de Techniques Militaires et de Marine. 3 vols. (in 1) roy. 8vo. Leide, 1865–67. K 12 T 16

Supplement [to the above]. Roy. 8vo. Leide, 1871. K 12 T 16

LANDON (CHARLES PAUL). Annales du Musée et de l'École moderne des Beaux-Arts. 16 vols. 8vo. Paris, 1801–8. A 7 U 21–36

LANDON (MISS LETITIA ELIZABETH), "L.E.L." [*See* MACLEAN, MRS. L. E.]

LANDON (E. W.) Bushman ; or, Life in a New Country. 8vo. Lond., 1847.* MD 5 S 8

LANDOR (ROBERT), M.A. The Impious Feast: a Poem. 8vo. Lond., 1828. H 6 S 16

LANDOR (WALTER SAVAGE). [A Biography]; by S. Colvin. (Eng. Men of Letts.) 2 vols. 8vo. Lond., 1881. C 1 U 23

A Biography of ; by John Forster, 1775–1864. 2 vols. 8vo. Lond., 1869. C 4 R 15, 16

Dry Sticks fagoted. 8vo. Lond., 1858. H 5 U 2
3 H

LANDOR (WALTER SAVAGE)—*continued.*
Gebir, Count Julian, and other Poems. 8vo. Lond., 1831. H 8 R 1

Imaginary Conversations of Literary Men and Statesmen. [1st and] 2nd series. 8 vols. 8vo. Lond., 1826–29. J 5 T 9–16

Last Fruit off an Old Tree. 8vo. Lond., 1853. J 5 T 17

Pericles and Aspasia. 2 vols. 8vo. Lond., 1836. J 12 U 6, 7

Works of ; with a Biography, by John Forster. 8 vols. 8vo. Lond., 1876. J 5 T 1–9

LANDOWNERS. [NEW DOMESDAY]. England and Wales (exclusive of the Metropolis): Return of Owners of Land, 1873. 2 vols. imp. 4to. Lond., 1875. F 22 S 14, 15 ‡

Ireland : Return of Owners of Land. 2 vols. (in 1). Imp. 4to. Dublin, 1876. F 22 S 16 ‡

Supplement to the [above.] Imp. 4to. Dublin, 1878. F 22 S 16 ‡

Scotland : Owners of Land and Heritages, 1872–73. Imp. 4to. Edinb., 1874. F 22 S 16 ‡

LANDSBOROUGH (WILLIAM). Journal of Landsborough's Expedition from Carpentaria in search of Burke and Wills ; with a Map showing the route. 8vo. Melb., 1862.* MD 6 T 20

Another copy. 8vo. Melh., 1862.* MD 3 U 19

Journal of Landsborough's Expedition. [*See* BOURNE, G.]

Landsborough's Exploration of Australia, from Carpentaria to Melbourne. Edited by James Stuart Laurie ; with a Chart, and a systematic arrangement of Carpentarian Plants, by [Baron] F. [von] Mueller, Ph.D., &c. 12mo. Lond., 1867. MD 4 P 39

LANDSCAPE ANNUAL (THE). [*See* JENNINGS, ROBERT.]

LANDSCAPE SCENERY, illustrating Sydney, Parramatta, Richmond, Newcastle, Windsor, and Port Jackson. Ob. 8vo. Sydney (n.d.) MD 4 P 22 †

Landscape Scenery, illustrating Sydney, Parramatta, Richmond, Maitland, Windsor, and New South Wales. Ob. 8vo. Sydney, 1855. MD 4 P 23 †

LANDSEER (SIR EDWIN), KNT., R.A. Landseer ; by F. G. Stephens. (Gt. Artists.) Lond., 1880. C 3 T 37

Pictures by. A New Series, with descriptions by W. Cosmo Monkhouse. Roy. 4to. Lond., 1877. A 23 R 7 ‡

Studies of. Illustrated by Sketches from the Collection of Her Majesty the Queen, and other sources ; with a History of his Art-Life, by W. Cosmo Monkhouse. Roy. 4to. Lond., 1877. A 23 R 6 †

LANDSEER (JOHN), F.S.A. Descriptive, Explanatory, and Critical Catalogue of fifty of the earliest Pictures contained in the National Gallery of Great Britain. 8vo. Lond., 1834. A 8 Q 25

Lectures on the Art of Engraving, delivered at the Royal Institution of Great Britain. 8vo. Lond., 1807. A 7 R 20

LANDSEER (THOMAS), A.R.A. Life and Letters of William
Bewick (Artist). 2 vols. 8vo. Lond., 1871.   C 4 U 1, 2

LANE (EDWARD WILLIAM). Account of the Manners and
Customs of the Modern Egyptians, written in Egypt,
during the years 1833–35. 3rd ed. 2 vols. 8vo. Lond.,
1842.   D 2 P 6, 7

Arabic-English Lexicon, de rived from the best and the
most copious Eastern Sources. Edited, with a Memoir,
by Stanley Lane Pool. Book 1.—Parts 1–6. 3 vols.
imp. 4to. Lond., 1863–77.   K 7 R 14–16 †

"Arabian Nights." A new Translation, with copious
Notes. 3 vols. roy. 8vo. Lond., 1839.

Selections from the Kur-án. New ed., revised and enlarged. 8vo. Lond., 1879.   G 15 P 9

[*See* ARABIAN NIGHTS' ENTERTAINMENT.]

LANE (SAMUEL A.) Cooper's Dictionary of Practical
Surgery. [*See* COOPER, SIR S.]

LANE-POOLE (S.) [*See* POOLE, S. LANE-.]

LANFRANC (ARCHBISHOP OF CANTERBURY). The Three
Archbishops: Lanfranc, Anselm, a'Becket; by Washington and Mark Wilks. 8vo. Lond., 1858.   C 2 U 7

Opera omnia. [*See* MIGNE, J. P., SERIES LATINA, 150.]

LANFREY (P.) History of Napoleon I. 4 vols. 8vo.
Lond., 1871–79.   B 8 R 6–9

LANG (ANDREW). Custom and Myth. 8vo. Lond.,
1884.   B 14 Q 22

Letters to Dead Authors. 12mo. Lond., 1886.   J 10 Q 20

The Library; with a Chapter on Modern English Illustrated Books, by Austin Dobson. 8vo. Lond., 1881.
                                                J 12 R 12

LANG (GEORGE D.) Alleged Embezzlement of. [*See*
LANG, REV. J. D.]

LANG (GIDEON S.) Aborigines of Australia, in their
Original Condition and in their Relations with the
White Man: a Lecture. Revised and enlarged, with an
Appendix. 8vo. Melb., 1865.   M A 1 R 2

Leichhardt Expedition: a Letter to Dr. Mueller, per
favour of the *Argus*. (Pam. E.) 4to. Melb. (n.d.)
                                                MJ 2 S 2

LANG (JOHN). *Botany Bay. 8vo. Lond., 1859.*
                                                M D 6 P 31

*Clever Criminals; or, Recollections of Botany Bay.
12mo. Lond., 1871.   M D 6 P 33

Forger's Wife. 10th ed. 12mo. Lond., 1855.   MJ 1 P 54

*Remarkable Convicts; or, Recollections of Botany Bay.
12mo. Lond. (n.d.)   M D 6 P 30

[* *These Books are the same although different Titles.*]

LANG (REV. JOHN DUNMORE), D.D., &c. Abstract and
Analysis of the Evidence in the Case of George Dunmore
Lang, late Manager, and Frederic Lee Drake, late
Accountant, of the Branch Bank of New South Wales,
at Ballaarat; with Explanatory Notes, and Observations.
(Pam. 36.) 8vo. Melb., 1857.   MJ 2 Q 23

Account of the Steps taken in England, with a view
to the establishment of an Academical Institution, or
College, in New South Wales. (Pam. 27.) 8vo.
Sydney, 1831.   MJ 2 Q 15

[Analysis of] View of the Origin and Migrations of the
Polynesian Nation. 8vo. Lond., 1834.   MD 7 Q 50

Another Dose for the Rev. Dr. L——g, of slanderous
Colonist notoriety. [*See* LHOTSKY, DR. J.]

Aurora Australis; or, Specimens of Sacred Poetry, for
the Colonists of Australia. (Pam. 27.) 8vo. Sydney,
1826.   MJ 2 Q 15

Australian Emigrant's Manual; or, a Guide to the Gold
Colonies of New South Wales and Port Phillip. 12mo.
Lond., 1852.   MD 4 P 1

Authentic Statement of the Facts and Circumstances of the
Deposition of Dr. John Dunmore Lang from the Christian
Ministry, by the Synod of Australia in connexion with
the Church of Scotland, in the year 1842. (Pam. 26.)
8vo. Sydney, 1860.   MJ 2 Q 14

Brief Notes of the new Postal Route from Sydney to
England, by San Francisco and New York; as also of the
return Route by the Peninsular and Oriental Company's
Line, from London by Venice and Suez. 8vo. Sydney,
1875.   MJ 2 R 8

The Coming Event; or, Freedom and Independence for
the Seven United Provinces of Australia. 8vo. Sydney,
1870.*   MF 2 Q 18

Convicts' Bank; or, a Plain Statement of the Case of
alleged Embezzlement on the part of Messrs. G. D. Lang
and F. L. Drake. (Pam. 3.) 8vo. Sydney, 1855. MF 1 Q 1

Another copy. (Pam. 26.) 8vo. Sydney, 1855.   MJ 2 Q 14

Cooksland, in North-eastern Australia; the future Cotton-
field of Great Britain. 12mo. Sydney, 1847.*   MD 4 P 5

Emigration, considered chiefly in reference to the practicability and expediency of importing and settling
throughout the Territory of New South Wales. (Pam.
27.) 8vo. Sydney, 1833.   MJ 2 Q 15

The Fatal Mistake; or, how New South Wales has lost
Caste in the World through misgovernment in the matter
of Immigration. 8vo. Sydney, 1875.   MF 3 P 17

Free Church Morality, in three of its developments in New
South Wales, embodying a History of the founding of St.
Andrew's College. 8vo. Sydney, 1876.   MG 1 Q 33

Freedom and Independence for the Golden Lands of
Australia; the Right of two Colonies, and the Interest of
Britain and the World. 8vo. Lond., 1852.*   MB 1 S 27

Another copy. 2nd ed. 12mo. Sydney, 1857.   MB 1 S 29

LANG (Rev. John Dunmore), D.D., &c.—*continued.*

Historical and Statistical Account of New South Wales, both as a Penal Settlement and as a British Colony. 2 vols. 8vo. Lond., 1834.*　　　　　MB 1 S 10, 11

Another copy. 2nd ed. 2 vols. 8vo. Lond., 1837.*　　　　　MB 1 S 14, 15

Another copy. 3rd ed. 2 vols. 8vo. Lond., 1852.*　　　　　MB 1 S 19, 20

Another copy. 4th ed. 2 vols. 8vo. Lond., 1875.*　　　　　MB 1 S 23, 24

Historical Account of the Separation of Victoria from New South Wales. 8vo. Sydney, 1870.　　MJ 2 R 10

Immigration : the Grand Disideratum for New South Wales ; and how to promote it effectually. 8vo. Sydney, 1870.　　　　　MF 1 Q 6

Letters on Presbyterian Union. (*Newspaper Extracts.* Pam. A.) Fol. Sydney, 1864.　　　　MJ 2 U 1

Letter to the Right Hon. Lord Stanley, Her Majesty's Principal Secretary of State for the Colonies ; occasioned by certain Observations in the Speech of His Excellency, Sir George Gipps, on proroguing the Legislative Council, on the 30th December, 1844. (Pam. Db.) 8vo. Sydney, 1845.　　　　　MF 3 P 2

Another copy. (Pam. 15.) 8vo. Sydney, 1844. MJ 2 Q 5

The "Little While" of the Saviour's Absence, and the Prospect of his speedy Return : three Lectures. 8vo. Melb., 1872.　　　　　MG 1 Q 37

Narrative of the Settlement of the Scots Church, Sydney, New South Wales. 8vo. Sydney, 1828.　　MJ 2 Q 15

New Zealand in 1839 ; or, Four Letters on the Colonization of that Island. 8vo. Lond., 1839.*　MD 7 Q 33

Phillipsland ; or, the Country hitherto designated Port Phillip : its Present Condition and Prospects. 12mo. Edinb., 1847.*　　　　　MD 4 P 2

Poems, Sacred and Secular; written chiefly at Sea, within the last half-century. 8vo. Sydney, 1873.*　MH 1 R 20

Queensland, Australia, a highly eligible Field for Emigration, and the Future Cotton-field of Great Britain. 8vo. Lond., 1861.*　　　　MD 4 R 31

Question of Questions ! or, is this Colony to be transformed into a Province of the Popedom ? a Letter to the Protestant Landholders of New South Wales. 8vo. Sydney, 1841.　　　　　MF 1 Q 6

Another copy. 8vo. Sydney, 1841.　　　MF 3 P 28

Another copy. 8vo. Sydney, 1841.　　　MG 1 Q 31

Refutation of the Slanders published at Sydney by Dr. Lang, in the *Colonist*, newspaper. [*See* Marshall, J.]

Religion and Education in America; with Notices of the State and Prospects of American Unitarianism, Popery, and African Colonization. 12mo. Lond., 1840.　MG 1 P 32

Repeal or Revolution; or, a Glimpse of the Irish Future, in a Letter to the Right Honourable Lord John Russell, &c. 1vo. Lond., 1848.　　　　MJ 2 R 19

Sermon, preached on Sunday, June 15, 1823, to the Congregation of Scots Presbyterians, in Sydney, New South Wales. (Pam. 33.) 8vo. Sydney 1823　　MJ 2 Q 21

LANG (Rev. John Dunmore), D.D., &c.—*continued.*

Three Lectures, on the Impolicy and Injustice of Religious Establishments, or the granting of Money for the support of Religion from the Public Treasury, in the Australian Colonies. 8vo. Sydney, 1856.　MG 1 Q 31

Transportation and Colonization ; or, the Causes of the Comparative Failure of the Transportation System in the Australian Colonies. 8vo. Lond., 1837.*　MF 1 P 33

View of the Origin and Migrations of the Polynesian Nation ; demonstrating their Ancient Discovery and Progressive Settlement of the Continent of America. 8vo. Lond., 1834.*　　　　　MA 1 R 25

Another copy. 2nd ed. 8vo. Sydney, 1877.　MA 1 R 27

LANG (Mrs. Leonora Blanche). History of Russia. [*See* Rambaud, A.]

LANG (Dr. Viktor von). Experiments on the Friction between Water and Air. (Roy. Soc. Pubs., 2.) 4to. Lond., 1876.　　　　　A 11 P 4 †

LANGDALE (Hon. Charles). Memoirs of Mrs. Fitzherbert ; with an Account of her Marriage with H.R.H. the Prince of Wales, afterwards King George iv. 8vo. Lond., 1856.　　　　　C 8 P 8

LANGE (Frederick Albert). History of Materialism, and Criticism of its Present Importance. Authorized Translation, by Ernest Chester Thomas. 3 vols. 8vo. Lond., 1877–81.　　　　　G 3 S 21–23

LANGE (L.) [*See* Leipziger Studien.]

L'ANGELIER (Emile). Trial of Miss Madeline Smith for the alleged Poisoning of. [*See* Smith, Miss M.]

LANGFORD (John Alfred), LL.D. Birmingham Free Libraries, the Shakespere Memorial Library, and the Art Gallery. 8vo. Birmingham, 1871.　　K 7 R 18

On Sea and Shore. 8vo. Lond., 1887.　MH 1 R 39

LANGHORNE (George). Instructions from the Government upon the establishment of a Mission to the Aborigines at Port Phillip. [*See* Manuscripts, &c.]

LANGHORNE (John). Life and Poems of. [*See* Chalmers, A., *and* Johnson, S.]

Poetical Works. 2 vols. 12mo. Lond., 1766. H 5 Q 32, 33

LANGHORNE (John), D.D., and (William), A.M. Plutarch's Lives; translated from the original Greek [*See* Plutarch. †]

LANGLEY (Thomas), M.A. History and Antiquities of the Hundred of Desborough, and Deanery of Wycombe in Buckinghamshire ; including the Borough Towns of Wycombe and Marlow, and sixteen Parishes. 4to. Lond 1797.　　　　　B 19 Q 11 ‡

LANGLEY (WILLIAM). Vision and Creed of Piers Plough-man; edited from a contemporary Manuscript, with a Historical Introduction, Notes, and a Glossary, by Thomas Wright, M.A. 2nd ed. 2 vols. 12mo. Lond., 1856.
                  H 8 R 24, 25

Vision of William concerning Piers the Plowman; edited by the Rev. Walter W. Skeat, M.A. 2nd ed. (Clar. Press. 12mo. Oxford, 1874.   H 6 R 47

LANGLEY (W. E.) Ye Garden Palace: ye Olde Englyshe Fayre. [*See* ASHTON, G. R.

LANGLOIS (VICTOR). Géographie de Ptolémée. [*See* PTOLEMÆUS, C.

LANGON (ETIENNE LÉON DE LAMOTHE-), BARON. [*See* LAMOTHE-LANGON, BARON E. L. DE.]

LANGTON (EDWARD). Another Loan: a Rejected Contribution to the *Melbourne Review.* 8vo. Meln., 1878.
                 MF 1 Q 6

Fiscal System of Victoria: a Paper read before the Economy Section of the Social Science Congress, December 10th, 1880. 8vo. Meln., 1880.*   MF 1 Q 6

Speech on the Outer Circle Railway Bill, delivered in the Legislative Assembly, 23rd December, 1874. 8vo. Meln., 1875   MJ 2 R 15

LANGTON (ROBERT), F.R.H.S. Childhood and Youth of Charles Dickens; with Retrospective Notes, and Elucidations, from his Books and Letters. 8vo. Manchester, 1883.   C 2 T 24

LANKENAU (H. VON). Russia, Past and Present. [*See* CHESTER, MRS. HENRIETTA M.]

LANGUEN (JACQUES). Petit Manuel Russe à l'usage des Etrangers. Nouvelle éd. 8vo. St. Petersburg, 1849.   K 11 V 3

LANIGAN (REV. JOHN), D.D. Ecclesiastical History of Ireland, from the first Introduction of Christianity among the Irish, to the beginning of the 13th Century. 2nd ed. 4 vols. 8vo. Dublin, 1829.   G 3 T 5–8

LANKESTER (EDWIN), M.D. Half-hours with the Microscope: a Popular Guide to the use of the Microscope, as a means of Amusement and Instruction. 12mo. Lond., 1877.   A 16 P 28

Vegetable Substances used for the Food of Man. (Lib. Ent. Know.) 12mo. Lond., 1832.   K 10 R 47

LANKESTER (PROF. E. RAY), M.A., &c. Contributions to the Developmental History of the Mollusca. (Roy. Soc. Pubs. I.) 4to. Lond., 1875.   A 11 P 2 †

LANKESTER (Mus.) Plain and easy Account of the British Ferns; together with their classification, arrangement of Genera, Structure, and Functions; and a Glossary of Technical and other Terms. Illustrated. 8vo. Lond., 1859.   A 4 P 14

LANMAN (CHARLES). Adventures of an Angler in America, Nova Scotia, and the United States. 8vo. Lond., 1848.   D 3 R 13

Dictionary of the United States Congress; containing Biographical Sketches of its Members, from the Foundation of the Government; with Appendix, compiled as a Manual of Reference for the Legislator and Statesman. Roy. 8vo. Philad., 1859.   C 9 V 52

The Japanese in America. 8vo. Lond., 1872. D 15 Q 14

Leading Men of Japan; with an Historical Summary of the Empire. 8vo. Boston, 1882.   C 3 U 17

Recollections of Curious Characters and Pleasant Places. 8vo. Edinb., 1881.   D 3 S 4

LANSDELL (REV. HENRY), D.D., &c. Russian Central Asia, including Kuldja, Bokhara, Khiva, and Merv. Illustrated. 2 vols. 8vo. Lond., 1885. D 6 Q 41, 42

Through Siberia. Illustrated. 2 vols. 8vo. Lond., 1882.
                D 6 Q 39, 40

LANSDOWNE (RT. HON. GEORGE GRANVILLE), LORD. Genuine Works of, in Verse and Prose. 3 vols. 12mo. Lond., 1736.   H 6 R 11–13

LANSDOWNE (WILLIAM), EARL OF SHELBURNE, FIRST MARQUESS OF. Life of; with Extracts from his Papers and Correspondence, by Lord Edmond Fitzmaurice. 3 vols. 8vo. Lond., 1875–76.   C 9 U 27–29

LANSDOWNE MANUSCRIPTS. Catalogue of, in the British Museum; with Indexes. 2 parts (in 1) fol. Lond., 1819.   F 24 P 14 ‡

LANZ (J.), AND BETTANCOURT (A. DE). Analytical Essay on the Construction of Machines; translated from the French. 4to. Lond., 1820.   A 11 V 5

LANZI (ABATE LUIGI). History of Painting in Italy, from the period of the Revival of the Fine Arts to the end of the 18th Century; translated from the original Italian, by Thomas Roscoe. 6 vols. 8vo. Lond.,1828. A 7 T 5–10

History of Painting in Upper and Lower Italy; translated and abridged by the Rev. G. W. D. Evans, A.M. 8vo. Lond., 1831.   A 6 V 37

Lanzi's Luminaries of Painting; by the Rev. G. W. D. Evans. 8vo. Lond., 1848.   A 8 P 35

LA PÉROUSE (JEAN FRANÇOIS DE GALOUP), COMTE DE. Narrative of a Voyage to ascertain the actual Fate of La Pérouse's Expedition. [*See* DILLON, CAPT. P.]

Relation du Voyage a la recherche de La Pérouse. [*See* LAHILLARDIÈRE, J. J. DE.]

Voyage autour du Monde, publié conformément au Décret du 22 Avril, 1791. 4 vols. 8vo. Paris, 1798. MD 5 R 2–5

Voyage autour du Monde, publié conformément au Décret du 22 Avril, 1791. 2 vols. 4to. Lond., 1799.
               MD 4 Q 21, 22 †

Atlas [to the above.] At. fol. Lond., 1799. MD 5 S 10‡

Voyage de Dentrecasteaux envoyé a la recherche de La Pérouse. [*See* D'ENTRECASTEAUX B.]

LA PÉROUSE (JEAN FRANÇOIS DE GALOUP) COMTE DE—*continued.*

Voyago in searci of La Pérouse. [*See* LABILLARDIÈRE, J. J. DE.]

Voyage round the World, performed in the Years 1785-88, by the *Boussole* and *Astrolabe*; translated from the French. Illustrated. 2 vols. 4to. and at. fol. Lond., 1799. MD 4 Q 23, 24 † and MD 5 S 11 ‡

Voyage round the World, performed in the Years 1785-88, by the *Boussole* and *Astrolabe*; translated from the French. 3rd ed. 3 vols. 8vo. Lond., 1807. MD 5 R 6-8

Atlas [to the above.] At. fol. Lond., 1807. MD 5 S 12‡

LAPIDE (CORNELIUS À). Commentaria. [*See* STEEN, C. VAN DEN.]

LA PILORGERIE (JULES DE). [*See* PILORGERIE, J. DE LA.]

LAPLACE (PIERRE SIMON). DE), MARQUIS. Elementary Treatise on Laplace's Functions. [*See* TODHUNTER, I.]

Mécanique Céleste; translated, with a Commentary, by Nathaniel Bowditch, LL.D. 4 vols. 4to. Boston, 1829-39. A 1 P 20-23 †

Œuvres de Laplace. 7 vols. (in 4) 4to. Paris, 1843-47. A 1 P 9-12 †

Théorie Analytique des Probabilités. 3e éd. Roy. 8vo. Paris, 1820. A 10 U 6

LA PORTE (JOSEPH DE), L'ABBÉ. La Bibliotèque des Fées, &c. [*See* CABINET DES FÉES, 34.]

LAPPENBERG (J. M.), F.S.A. History of England under the Anglo-Saxon Kings; translated from the German by the late Benjamin Thorpe, F.S.A. 2 vols. 8vo. Lond., 1881. B 3 Q 3. 4

LARCHEY (LOREDAN). History of Bayard, the Good Chevalier sans Peur et sans Reproche. Compiled by the Loyal Serviteur; translated from the French. Illustrated. Roy. 8vo. Lond., 1883. C 5 W 6

LARDNER (REV. DIONYSIUS), D.C.L. Cabinet Cyclopædia. 133 vols. 12mo. Lond., 1830-40. K 1 S 1-U 35

Bell (Robert). History of Russia.
Lives of the English Poets.
Brewster (Sir D.) Cities and Principal Towns of the World.
Treatise on Optics.
Cooley (Wm.) History of Maritime and Inland Discovery.
Crowe (E. E.) History of France.
Lives of the Most Eminent Foreign Statesmen.
De Morgan (A.) Essay on Probabilities, and on their Application to Life Contingencies and Insurance Offices.
Donovan (Prof. M.) Treatise on Chemistry.
Treatise on Domestic Economy.
Dunham (Dr. S. A.) History of Denmark, Sweden, and Norway.
History of Europe during the Middle Ages.
History of the Germanic Empire.
History of Poland
History of Spain and Portugal.
Lives of Eminent Literary and Scientific Men of Great Britain.

LARDNER (REV. DIONYSIUS), D.C.L.—*continued.*

Fergus (H.) History of the Western World, United States.
Fosbroke (Rev. T. D.) The Arts, Manufactures, &c. of the Greeks and Romans.
Gleig (Rev. G. R.) Lives of Eminent British Military Commanders.
Grattan (T. C.) History of the Netherlands.
Henslow (Rev. J. S.) Principles of Descriptive and Physiological Botany.
Herschel (Sir J. F. W.) Treatise on Astronomy.
History of Rome.
Natural Philosophy.
Holland (J.) Treatise on the Manufactures in Metal.
James (G. P. R.) Lives of Foreign Statesmen.
Kater (Capt. H.) and Lardner (Rev. D.) Treatise on Mechanics.
Keightley (T.) Outlines of History.
Lardner (Rev. D.) Treatise on Arithmetic, Theoretical and Practical.
Hand-book of Natural Philosophy.
Treatise on Geometry.
Treatise on Heat.
Treatise on Hydrostatics and Pneumatics.
Lardner (Rev. D.) and Walker (C. V.) Manul of Electricity, Magnetism, and Meteorology.
Mackintosh (Sir James), Wallace (W.), and Bell (R.) History of England.
Mackintosh (Sir J.), Forster (John), and Courtenay (Rt. Hon. P.) Lives of Eminent British Statesmen.
Moore (T.) History of Ireland.
Nicolas (Sir H.) Chronology of History.
Phillips (Prof. John). Treatise on Geology.
Porter (G. R.) Treatise on the Origin, Progressive Improvement, and Present State of the Manufacture of Porcelain and Glass.
Treatise on Silk Manufacture.
Powell (Prof. Baden). History of Natural Philosophy.
Roscoe (H.) Lives of Eminent British Lawyers.
Scott (Sir W.) History of Scotland.
Shelley (Mrs. M. W.) Lives of Eminent Men of France.
Shelley (Mrs. M. W.), Brewster (Sir D.), and Montgomery (J.) Lives of Eminent Literary and Scientific Men of Italy, Spain, and Portugal.
Sismondi (J. C. L. de) History of the Fall of the Roman Empire.
History of the Italian Republics.
Southey (Robt.) The British Admirals.
Stebbing (Rev. H.) History of the Christian Church.
History of the Reformation.
Swainson (W.) Animals in Menageries.
Discourse on the Study of Natural History.
Habits and Instincts of Animals.
Treatise on the Geography and Classification of Animals.
Treatise on Malacology, or Shells and Shellfish.
Natural History, &c., of Birds.
Natural History of Fishes, Reptiles, &c.
Natural History and Classification of Quadrupeds.
Taxidermy, with the Biography of Zoologists.
Swainson (W.), and Shuckard (W. E.) History and Natural Arrangement of Insects.
Thirlwall (Rt. Rev. C.) History of Greece.
Vieusseux (A.) History of Switzerland.

Common Things explained. [1st and] 2nd series. 2 vols. 8vo. Lond., 1856. A 17 T 52, 53

The Electric Telegraph popularised. 8vo. Lond.. 1855. A 5 R 5

LARDNER (REV. DIONYSIUS), D.C.L.—*continued.*
The Electric Telegraph; revised and re-written by Edward
B. Bright, F.R.A.S.　8vo.　Lond., 1867.　　A 5 R 58
Hand-book of Animal Physics. (Weale). 2nd ed. 12mo.
Lond., 1873.　　　　　　　　　　A 17 Q 29
Hand-book of Natural Philosophy and Astronomy.　8vo.
Lond., 1851.　　　　　　　　　　A 3 S 16
The Steam Engine; for the use of Beginners. (Weale).
12th ed. 12mo.　Lond., 1873.　　　A 17 P 28
Treatise on Mechanics. [*See* KATER, CAPT. H.]

LARDNER (NATHANIEL), D.D.　Works of; with general
Chronological Tables, and copious Indexes; [and] Life
of the Author, by Andrew Kippis, D.D.　11 vols.
roy. 8vo.　Lond., 1788.　　　　　G 5 8 5–15

LASCO (JOHN A.)　[*See* A. LASCO, J.]

LARKIN (HENRY).　Carlyle, and the Open Secret of his
Life.　8vo.　Lond., 1886.　　　　C 10 R 48

LARKWORTHY (FALCONER).　New Zealand Revisited.
2nd ed.　8vo.　Lond., 1882.　　　MD 3 S 38

LARNACH (W. J. M.)　Hand-book of New Zealand
Mines.　8vo.　Wellington, 1887.　　MA 2 Q 45

LAROCHE (LÉON).　Haïti: une page d'Histoire.　8vo.
Paris, 1885.　　　　　　　　　　B 1 R 13

LA ROCHEFOUCAULD (FRANÇOIS), DUC DE.　Reflections or Sentences and Moral Maxims.　18mo.　Lond.,
1871.　　　　　　　　　　　　G 9 P 23

LA ROCHEFOUCAULD (FRANÇOIS), DUC DE, MON-
TESQUIEU (CHARLES DE SECONDAT), BARON DE, AND
VAUVENARGUES (LUC CLAPIERS), MARQUIS DE.
Maximes du Duc de La Rochefoucauld, précédées d'une
Notice sur sa Vie, par Suard.　Pensées diverses de
Montesquieu.　Œuvres choisies de Vauvenargues.　8vo.
Paris, 1878.　　　　　　　　　G 7 R 28

LA ROCHEJAQUELEIN (MARIE LOUISE VICTOIRE),
MARQUISE DE.　Memoir of the Marchioness de La Roche-
jaquelein; translated from the French. (Const. Misc.)
18mo.　Edinb., 1827.　　　　　　K 10 P 44
Memoirs of; with a Map of the Theatre of War in La
Vendée; translated by Scott from the French.　8vo.
Edinb., 1817.　　　　　　　　　C 3 V 38

LARPENT (F. S.)　Private Journal of; edited by Sir George
Larpent, Bart.　3 vols. 8vo.　Lond., 1853.　C 3 V 16–18

LARPENT (SIR GEORGE), BART.　Private Journal of F. S.
Larpent, Esq., Judge Advocate General of the British
Forces in the Peninsula.　3 vols. 8vo.　Lond., 1853.
　　　　　　　　　　　　　　　C 3 V 16–18

LARSON (A.)　Ferrall og Repp's Dansk-Norsk-Engelske
Ordbog.　[*See* FERRALL, J. S.]

LA SAGRA (D. RAMON DE).　[*See* RAMON DE LA SAGRA,
D.]

LA SALLE (RENÉ ROBERT CAVELIER).　Sieur de La Salle
and the Discovery of the Great West; by Francis Parkman.
12th ed.　8vo.　Lond., 1885.　　　C 4 T 11

LASCARIDES (G. P.)　Comprehensive Phraseological
English-Ancient and Modern Greek Lexicon, founded
upon a Manuscript of G. P. Lascarides, Esq., and compiled by L. Myriantheus, Ph.D.　2 vols.　8vo.　Lond.,
1882.　　　　　　　　　　　K 11 T 29, 30

LAS CASAS (BARTOLOMEO DE).　Life of.　"The Apostle
of the Indies;" by the late Sir Arthur Helps.　2nd ed.
8vo.　Lond., 1883.　　　　　　　C 3 P 20

LAS CASES (MARIN JOSEPH EMMANUEL AUGUSTIN DIEU-
DONNÉ), COMTE DE.　Le Sage's Historical, Genealogical,
Chronological and Geographical Atlas.　2nd ed.　Roy.
fol.　Lond., 1818.　　　　　　　D 8 P 10 ‡

LASCELLES (ARTHUR ROWLEY WILLIAMS).　Treatise on
the Nature and Cultivation of Coffee.　12mo.　Lond.,
1865.　　　　　　　　　　　　A 1 P 24

LASCELLES (HON. GERALD).　Shooting.　[*See* WALSING-
HAM, T. DE G., BARON.]

LASCELLES (W. H.) * Patent Cement Slab System [of
Building].　[*See* SHAW, R. N., *and* NEWTON, E.]

LASLETT (THOMAS).　Timber and Timber Trees, Native
and Foreign.　8vo.　Lond., 1875.　　A 1 P 54

LASPEE (HENRY DE).　Calisthenics; or, the Elements of
Bodily Culture.　Roy. 8vo.　Lond., 1856.　A 17 W 42

LASSALLE (H.)　The Royal Academy Illustrated.　Fol.
Lond., 1884.　　　　　　　　　　E

LASSELL (JANE AND CAROLINE).　Life of Alexander von
Humboldt.　[*See* LÖWENBERG, J.]

LASSELL (W.), F.R.S., &c.　On Polishing the Specula of
Reflecting Telescopes. (Roy. Soc. Pubs., 1.)　4to.　Lond.,
1875.　　　　　　　　　　　A 11 P 2 †

LASSEN (CHRISTIAN).　Indische Alterthumskunde.　4 vols.
roy. 8vo.　Leipzig, 1858–74.　　B 10 V 17–20

LASTEYRIE (C. P.)　Histoire de l'Introduction des
Moutons-à-laine fine d'Espagne.　8vo.　Paris, 1802.
　　　　　　　　　　　　　　　A 1 Q 19
Traité sur Bêtes-à-laine d'Espagne.　8vo.　Paris, 1799.
　　　　　　　　　　　　　　　A 1 Q 18

LASTINGES (DR. JOHN).　Kunst-Studien aus der königlichen Pinakothek zu München: mit einem Führer durch
dieselbe.　12mo.　München, 1838.　　A 7 P 32

LASVIGNES (L.)　Cathédrale de Bayeux.　[*See* FLACHAT,
E.]

LATE COLONIAL MAGISTRATE, A.　[*See* ROWCROFT,
CHARLES.]

LATE CUSTOMS' OFFICER, A.　[*See* INDIA.]

LATE GOVERNMENT OFFICER, A. [*See* Emigration.]

LATE MAGISTRATE OF THE COLONY, A. [*See* Wakefield, E. J.]

LATE STAFF SERGEANT, A, of the 13th Light Infantry. [*See* Macmullen, J.]

LATE STUDENT, A. [*See* Campbell, A. D.]

LATHAM (John), M.D. General History of Birds; with Index. 11 vols. 4to. Winchester, 1821–28. A 14 V 33–43

LATHAM (Robert Gordon), M.D., &c. Dictionary of the English Language, founded on that of Dr. Samuel Johnson as edited by the Rev. H. J. Todd, M.A. 4 vols. 4to. Lond. 1871. K 15 T 15–18

Eastern Origin of the Celtic Nations. [*See* Prichard, J. C.]

Elementary English Grammar, for the use of Schools. 22nd thousand. 12mo. Lond., 1870. K 11 U 15

Elements of Comparative Philology. 8vo. Lond., 1862. K 16 Q 5

English Language. 5th ed., revised and enlarged. 8vo. Lond., 1862. K 16 Q 4

Ethnology of India. 8vo. Lond., 1859. A 1 W 24

Ethnology of the British Colonies and Dependencies. 12mo. Lond., 1851. MA 1 R 18

Inaugural Lecture on the English Language. (Univ. of Lond.) 8vo. Lond., 1840. J 5 S 8

Logic in its Application to Language. 8vo. Lond., 1856. K 12 P 13

Natural History of the Varieties of Man. 8vo. Lond., 1850. A 1 W 25

Norway and the Norwegians. 2 vols. 8vo. Lond., 1840. D 9 P 17, 18

Opuscula: Essays, chiefly Philological and Ethnographical. 8vo. Lond., 1860. K 15 Q 23

LATHAM (Wilfrid). States of the River Plate. 2nd ed. With Map. 8vo. Lond., 1868. D 3 U 22

LATIMER (Hugh), D.D., Bishop of Worcester. Hugh Latimer: a Biography; by the late Rev. R. Demans, M.A. New and revised ed. 8vo. Lond., 1881. C 3 P 23

Selections from the Works of. [*See* Montagu, B.]

Sermons and Letters of. [*See* British Reformers, 9.]

LATIN GRAMMAR. Rudimentum Grammaticæ Latinæ Metricum in usum Scholæ Regiæ Westmonasteriensis. 8vo. Oxonii, 1822. K 16 P 10

Short Introduction to the Latin Grammar for the use of the Lower Forms in Westminster School. 8vo. Lond., 1821. K 16 P 10

Translation of the Latin Verse Grammar for the use of the Lower Forms in Westminster School. 8vo. Oxford, 1822. K 16 P 10

LATROBE (Charles Joseph). Rambler in North America, 1832–33. 2nd ed. 2 vols 8vo. Lond., 1836. D 3 P 50, 51

[*See* MacEachern, J.]

LAUDER (Sir J.) Historical Observer, &c. [*See* Bannatyne Club.] E

LATUDE (Henri Masers de). Mémoires de. [*See* Barrière, J. F., 28.] C 1 T 28

LAUDER (Sir Thomas Dick), Bart. Memorial of the Royal Progress in Scotland. 4to. Edinb., 1843. D 8 V 33

LAUGHTON (Rev. James Brotherston), B.A. Inaugural Address, delivered at the Formation of the St. Stephen's Christian Institute of Bathurst, on Thursday, September 24, 1863. 8vo. Bathurst, 1864. MG 1 Q 29

Lecture delivered at the opening of the Bathurst Mechanics' School of Arts, on Wednesday Evening, August 29, 1855. 8vo. Sydney, 1855. MJ 2 Q 14

The Stroke of God's Hand: a Sermon, on the occasion of the melancholy Death of Mr. William Kerr, in consequence of a Stroke of Lightning. 8vo. Bathurst, 1859. MG 1 P 1

LAUGHTON (John Knox). Letters of Nelson. [*See* Nelson, Adm. H., Viscount.]

LAUN (Henri van). The "Characters" of Jean de la Bruyère. [*See* La Bruyère, J. de.]

Dramatic Works of Molière; with prefatory Memoir. [*See* Molière, J. B. de.]

Grammar of the French Language, in three Parts. Parts 1, 2. Accidence and Syntax. Part 3. Exercises. 2 vols. 8vo. Lond., 1878. K 11 V 28, 29

History of French Literature. 3 vols. 8vo. Lond., 1876–77. B 8 R 3–5

Materials for translating from English into French. [*See* Le Brun, L.]

LAUNCESTON MECHANICS' INSTITUTE. Annual Reports for 1877–78. 8vo. Launceston, 1878–79. MF 3 P 22

Catalogue of the Library. 8vo. Launceston, 1886. MK 1 R 23

LAURENT (Peter Edmund). Recollections of a Classical Tour through the various parts of Greece, Turkey, and Italy, made in the years 1818–19. Coloured Plates. 4to. Lond., 1821. D 6 V 25

LAURIE (James). Tables of Simple Interest at 5, 4½, 4, 3½, 3, and 2½ per cent per annum, from 1 day to 365 days, from 1 month to 12 months, from 1 year to 12 years; also, Tables of Compound Interest, and Interest on Large Sums for a Single Day, at the same rates. 8vo. Lond. (n.d.) Libr.

LAURIE (James Stuart). Landsborough's Exploration of Australia from Carpentaria to Melbourne. [*See* Landsborough, W.]

LAURIE (Prof. Simon Somerville), M.A., &c. Lectures on the Rise and early Constitution of Universities. 8vo. Lond.. 1886. G 17 P 8

Training of Teachers; and other Educational Papers. 8vo. Lond., 1882. G 17 P 26

LAURIE (WILLIAM ALEXANDER). History of Free-masonry and the Grand Lodge of Scotland; with Chapters on the Knight Templars, Knights of St. John, Mark Masonry, and R.A. Degree. 8vo. Edinb., 1859.   B 14 S 23

LAURIE (Col. WILLIAM FERGUSON BEATSON). Our Burmese Wars and Relations with Burma; being an Abstract of Military and Political Operations, &c., 1824–79. 8vo. Lond., 1880.   B 10 U 19

LAUTS (G.) Naain der Straat tusschen Nieuw-Holland en Nieuw-Guinea. 8vo. Amsterdam, 1861.   MD 1 V 10

LAUZUN (A. N. DE CAUMONT) DUC DE. Mémoires. [*See* BARRIÈRE, J. F., 25.]

LAVALLÉE (JOSEPH). Travels in Istria and Dalmatia. [*See* CASSAS, L. F.]

LAVALLETTE (ANTOINE MARIE CHAMANS), COMTE DE. Memoirs of; written by himself. 2 vols. 8vo. Lond., 1831.   C 5 U 20, 21

LAVATER (JEAN GASPAR). Essays of Physiognomy; translated from the German, by Thomas Holcroft; also 100 Physiognomical Rules, and a Memoir of the Author. 14th ed. 8vo. Lond., 1869.   A 13 R 13

LAVATER (JEAN GASPARD), ET CHAUSSIER (PROF. FRANÇOIS). Nouveau Manuel du Physionomiste et du Phrénologiste; ou, les Caractères dévoilés par les signes extérieurs. 18mo. Paris, 1838.   A 12 P 14

LAVELEYE (ÉMILE DE). L'Instruction du Peuple. 8vo. Paris, 1792.   G 17 R 6

Letters from Italy; translated by Mrs. Thorpe. 8vo. Lond., 1886.   D 9 Q 10

On the Causes of War, and the Means of reducing their Number. [*See* COBDEN CLUB.]

LAVERS (JOSIAH VINCENT). Testimonials as to the efficacy of Mr. J. V. Lavers' patented process for preserving in a fresh condition the Flesh of Animals recently killed. 8vo. Sydney, 1870.   MA 2 V 8

LAVIS (H. J. JOHNSTON-). Monograph of the Earthquakes at Ischia. Roy. 4to. Lond., 1885.   B 14 R 12 ‡

LAVOISIER (A. L.) Elements of Chemistry. 2 vols. 8vo. Edinb., 1802.   A 6 P 6, 7

LAW (DAVID). The Thames, Oxford to London. Twenty etched Plates. Sm. fol. Lond., 1882.   D 7 V 26

LAW (ERNEST), B.A. Historical Catalogue of the Pictures in the Royal Collection at Hampton Court; with Notes, Descriptive, Biographical, and Critical. 8vo. Lond., 1881.   K 7 R 9

History of Hampton Court Palace in Tudor Times. Illustrated. Sm. 4to. Lond., 1885.   B 22 S 2

LAW (HENRY), C.E. Art of Constructing and Repairing Common Roads. [*See* HUGHES, S.]

Civil Engineering for Practical Engineers for the Army and Navy; the Section on Hydraulic Engineering, by George R. Burnell, C.E. (Weale.) 12mo. Lond., 1869.   A 17 P 43

Elements of Euclid, with many additional Propositions and explanatory Notes; to which is prefixed an introductory Essay on Logic. 6th ed. (Weale.) 12mo. Lond., 1873.   A 17 P 7

Mathematical Tables for Trigonometrical, Astronomical, and Nautical Calculations; to which is prefixed a Treatise on Logarithms. (Weale.) 12mo. Lond., 1850. A 17 R 8

Practical Examples for setting out Railway Curves. [*See* SIMMS, F. W.]

LAW (HENRY), AND CLARK (DANIEL KINNEAR). Construction of Roads and Streets; in two Parts. With Illustrations. (Weale.) 12mo. Lond., 1877. A 17 P 51

LAW (THOMAS GRAVES). The Catechism of John Hamilton, Archbishop of St. Andrews. [*See* HAMILTON, MOST REV. J.]

LAW (WILLIAM). Notes and Materials for an adequate Biography of. [*See* WALTON, C.]

LAW ALMANAC OF NEW SOUTH WALES. [*See* NEW SOUTH WALES LAW ALMANAC.]

LAWS AND ORDINANCES. [*See* NEW SOUTH WALES; NEW ZEALAND; *and* TASMANIA.]

LAW INSTITUTE OF VICTORIA. First Report of the Council, 1859; with a Schedule of Publications and Books, intended as a temporary Catalogue of the Library. 8vo. Melb., 1859.   MF 1 Q 5

Rules of. 8vo. Melb., 1863.   MF 1 Q 5

LAW REPORTS. [*See* NEW SOUTH WALES—SUPREME COURT.]

LAW SOCIETY (NEW SOUTH WALES). [*See* NEW SOUTH WALES LAW SOCIETY.]

LAW SOCIETY OF VICTORIA. Report of the Committee appointed to prepare Rules and Suggestions for the formation of a Law Society. 8vo. Melb., 1853.   MJ 2 R 12

Rules of. 8vo. Melb., 1855.   MF 1 Q 5

LAWES (REV. W. G.) Grammar and Vocabulary of Language spoken by Motu Tribe, New Guinea. 8vo. Sydney, 1885.   MK 1 P 50

Grammar and Vocabulary of Language spoken by Motu Tribe. 2nd and revised ed. 8vo. Sydney, 1888.*   MK 1 P 51

LAWLEY (HON. F.) Racing. [*See* RACING.]

LAWLOR (DENYS SHYNE). Pilgrimages in the Pyrenees and Landes. 8vo. Lond., 1870.   D 8 S 50

LAWRANCE (HANNAH). History of Woman in England, and her influence on Society and Literature from the Earliest Period. Vol. 1 (*all published*). 8vo. Lond., 1843.   B 4 Q 6

LAWRENCE (FREDERICK). Life of Henry Fielding ; with Notices of his Writings, his Times, and his Contemporaries. 8vo. Lond., 1855.   C 4 T 8

LAWRENCE (GEN. SIR GEORGE ST. PATRICK), K.C.S.I. &c. Reminiscences of Forty-three years in India. 8vo. Lond., 1874.   B 10 Q 23

LAWRENCE (COL. SIR HENRY MONTGOMERY), K.C.B. Life of ; by the late Sir H. B. Edwardes, K.C.B., &c., and H. Merivale, C.B. 2nd ed. 2 vols. 8vo. Lond., 1872.   C 8 P 28, 29

LAWRENCE (JOHN), LORD. Life of ; by R. Bosworth Smith. With Portrait. 2 vols. 8vo. Lond., 1883.   C 8 P 30, 31

LAWRENCE (PHILLIP HENRY). Rocks Classified. [*See* COTTA, B. VON.]

LAWRENCE (REV. R. T.) Index to the Historical and Biographical Works of John Strype. [*See* STRYPE, REV. J.]

LAWRENCE (SIR THOMAS), R.A. Anecdote Biography of. [*See* TIMBS, J.]

[A Biography]; by Lord Ronald Gower. (Great Artists.) 8vo. Lond., 1882.   C 3 T 35

LAWRENCE (REV. THOMAS JOSEPH), M.A., &c. Essays on some disputed Questions in Modern International Law. 2nd ed., revised and enlarged. 8vo. Camb., 1885.   F 6 Q 21

LAWRENCE (WILLIAM). Introduction to Comparative Anatomy and Physiology ; with Lectures on Physiology, Zoology, and the Natural History of Man. 2 vols. (in 1) 8vo. Lond., 1816–19.   A 12 T 25

LAWRENCE (MAJOR W. J.) Border and Bastille 8vo. Lond., 1863.   D 4 S 29

LAWRY (REV. WALTER). Friendly and Feejee Islands : a Missionary Visit to various Stations in the South Seas, in the years 1847. 8vo. Lond., 1850.*   MD 4 R 40
Second Missionary Visit to the Friendly and Feejee Islands in the year 1850. 12mo. Lond., 1851. MD 4 R 40

LAWSON (CECIL). Memoir ; by Edmund W. Gosse. 4to. Lond., 1883.   C 4 P 17 ‡

LAWSON (CAPT. JOHN A.) Wanderings in the Interior of New Guinea. 8vo. Lond., 1875.*   MJ 1 S 45

LAWSON (J. P.) History of Remarkable Conspiracies connected with European History. (Cons. Misc.) 2 vols. 18mo. Edinb., 1829.   K 10 Q 31, 32

LAWSON (WILLIAM), F.R.G.S. Outlines of Physiography. With Illustrations. 12mo. Edinb., 1880.   A 16 P 17

3 I

LAWTON (W. C.) [*See* ARCHÆOLOGICAL INSTITUTE OF AMERICA.]

LAXTON (H.) Examples of Building Construction intended as an Aide-Memoire for the Professional Man and the Operative. 4 vols. l. fol. Lond., 1857–60. A 13 P 1–4 ‡

LAY (G. TRADESCANT). The Chinese, as they are ; their Moral, Social, and Literary Character : a new Analysis of their Language. 8vo. Lond., 1841.   B 2 P 33
Trade with China : a Letter addressed to the British Public. (Pam., 2.) 8vo. Lond., 1837.   MJ 2 P 37
Zoology of Capt. Beechey's Voyage. [*See* BEECHEY, CAPT. F. W.]

LAY GENTLEMAN, A. [*See* LEE, REV. F.]

LAY READER, A. [*See* RUDDER, E. W.]

LAYARD (AUSTEN H.), D.C.L., &c. Discoveries in the Ruins of Nineveh and Babylon ;with Travels in Armenia, Kurdistan, and the Desert. 8vo. Lond., 1853. B 10 P 24
Nineveh and its Remains. 2 vols. 8vo. Lond., 1849.   B 10 P 25, 26

LAYARD (EDGAR LEOPOLD)., C.M.G., &c. Birds of South Africa. New ed., thoroughly revised and augmented, by R. Bowdler Sharpe, F.L.S., &c. Roy. 8vo. Lond., 1875–84.   A 13 V 7

LAYMAN, A. [*See* ARCHBISHOPRIC OF SYDNEY.]

LAYMAN, A. [*See* BROWN, T. C.]

LAYMAN, A. [*See* BROWNE, H. J.]

LAYMAN, A. [*See* CONDITIONAL IMMORTALITY.]

LAYMAN, A. [*See* HOLMES, J. B.]

LAYMAN, A. [*See* NORTON, HON. J.]

LAYMAN, A. [*See* RUDDER, E. W.]

LAYMAN, A. [*See* SEELEY, R. B.]

LEA (HENRY C.) An Historical Sketch of Sacerdotal Celibacy in the Christian Church. 2nd ed. Roy. 8vo. Boston, 1884.   G 11 T 26

LEA (WILLIAM), M.A., ARCHDEACON OF WORCESTER. Church Plate in the Archdeaconry of Worcester. Roy. 8vo. Worcester, 1884.   B 5 V 10

LEACH (HARRY), M.R.C.P., &c. Pocket Doctor ; for the Traveller and Colonist. 2nd ed. 12mo. Lond., 1878.   MA 1 P 13

LEACH (WILLIAM ELFORD), M.D., &c. Malacostraca Podophthalmata Britanniæ ; or, Descriptions of such British Species of the Linnean genus Cancer as have their Eyes elevated on Footstalks; illustrated by James Sowerby, F.L.S., &c. Roy. 4to. Lond., 1815.   A 1 S 1 †
Zoological Miscellany ; being Descriptions of new, or interesting Animals; illustrated by R. P. Nodder. 3 vols. roy. 8vo. Lond., 1814–17.   A 13 U 29–31

LEADER (JOHN DANIEL), F.S.A. Mary, Queen of Scots in Captivity: a Narrative of Events from January, 1569, to December, 1584, whilst George, Earl of Shrewsbury, was the Guardian of the Scottish Queen. 8vo. Sheffield, 1880.   C 6 T 26

LEAKE (LIEUT.-COL. WILLIAM MARTIN), D.C.L., &c. Brief Memoir of the Life and Writings of the late Lieut.-Col. W. M. Leake. 4to. Lond., 1864.   C 2 W 15

Numismata Hellenica: a Catalogue of Greek Coins; with Notes, Map, and Index. 4to. Lond., 1856. A 2 R 8 †

Supplement to "Numismata Hellenica." 4to. Lond., 1859.   A 2 R 8 †

On some Disputed Questions of Ancient Geography. 8vo. Lond., 1857.   D 12 T 8

Researches in Greece : Philology. 4to. Lond., 1814.   K 16 U 3

Topography of Athens; with Remarks on its Antiquities and the Demi of Attica. 2 vols. 8vo. Lond., 1841. D 6 U 42, 43

Travels in Northern Greece. 4 vols. 8vo. Lond., 1835.   D 6 U 38–41

LEAKEY (CAROLINE W.) Lyra Australis; or, Attempts to Sing in a Strange Land. 12mo. Lond., 1854. MH 1 R 12

LEAN (MRS. FRANCIS), FLORENCE MARRYAT.   "Gup": Sketches of Anglo-Indian Life and Character. 8vo. Lond., 1868.   D 6 P 7

Life and Letters of Capt. Marryat. 2 vols. 8vo. Lond., 1872.   C 4 R 17, 18

Tom Tiddler's Ground. 8vo. Lond., 1886.   D 3 T 46

LEAR (EDWARD). Journal of a Landscape Painter in Albania, &c. 8vo. Lond., 1851.   D 8 V 6

Tortoises, Terrapins, and Turtles. [*See* SOWERBY, J. DE C.]

LEAR (MRS. HENRIETTA LOUISA). Fénelon, Archbishop of Cambrai: a Biographical Sketch. 8vo. Lond., 1877.   C 3 T 5

Henri Dominique Lacordaire: a Biographical Sketch. 8vo. Lond., 1882.   C 3 Q 32

LEARED (ARTHUR), M.D., &c. Morocco and the Moors; being an Account of Travels, with a general Description of the Country and its People. 8vo. Lond., 1876. D 2 S 18

Visit to the Court of Morocco. Illustrated. 8vo. Lond., 1879.   D 2 T 12

LEARMONTH (ALEXANDER). Memorials of Alexander Learmonth, Esq., of Tasmar; by the Rev. Robert Steel, D.D., and the Rev. James Cosh, M.A. 12mo. Sydney, 1877.   MC 1 P 36

LEASK (REV. WILLIAM), LL.D. Struggles for Life; or, the Autobiography of a Dissenting Minister. 8vo. Lond., 1854.   C 16 R 4

LEATHES (EDMUND). An Actor Abroad ; or, Gossip, Dramatic, Narrative, and Descriptive, from the Recollections of an Actor in Australia, &c. 8vo. Lond., 1880.   MC 1 R 32

LEAVES from the Diary of an Officer of the Guards. 12mo. Lond., 1854.   J 5 R 21

LEAVES from a Lady's Diary of her Travels in Barbary. 2 vols. 8vo. Lond., 1850.   D 1 S 28, 29

LEBAHN (FALCK). Vocabulary of Familiar Sentences and Dialogues. [*See* SCHMID, C. VON.]

LEBASTEUR (H.) The Metals at the Paris International Exhibition of 1878 : their resisting Properties, and their Uses in Railway Plant. 8vo. Paris, 1880.   A 10 P 17

LEBEDEFF (HERASIM). Grammar of the Pure and Mixed East Indian Dialects. 4to. Lond., 1801. K 13 T 7

LE BLANC (JEAN BERNARD), ABBÉ. Letters on the English and French Nations. 2 vols. 8vo. Lond., 1747.   B 4 Q 23, 24

LE BRETON (MRS. ANNA LETITIA). Correspondence of W. E. Channing and Lucy Aikin. [*See* CHANNING, REV. W. E.]

LE BRUN (CHARLES). Series of Lithographic Drawings, illustrative of the relation between the Human Physiognomy and that of the Brute Creation. El. fol. Lond., 1827.   A 7 P 2 ‡

LE BRUN (L.) Materials for translating from English into French. 5th ed., revised and corrected, by Henry Van Laun. 8vo. Lond., 1874.   K 11 V 32

LE BRUN (PIERRE). Explication, Literale, Historique, et Dramatique, des Prieres et des Ceremonies de la Messe. 4 vols. 8vo. Paris, 1726.   G 13 S 1–4

Histoire Critique des Pratiques Superstitieuses, qui ont séduit les Peuples, et embarassé les Sçavans. 2nd ed. 4 vols. 12mo. Paris, 1732–37.   G 13 R 11–14

LE CAT (CLAUDE NICOLAS). Traité des Sens. 8vo. Paris, 1742.   A 12 Q 20

LECHLER (PROF. GOTTHARD), D.D. John Wycliffe, and his English Precursors; translated from the German; with Additional Notes, by the late Prof. Lorimer, D.D. New ed. 8vo. Lond., 1878.   C 6 U 29

LECK (JANE). Iberian Sketches: Travels in Portugal and the North-west of Spain. Illustrated. 8vo. Lond., 1884.   D 7 T 13

LECKY (WILLIAM EDWARD HARTPOLE). History of England in the 18th Century. Vols. 1–6. 8vo. Lond., 1878–87.   B 5 P 13–18

History of European Morals, from Augustus to Charlemagne 2 vols. 8vo. Lond., 1869.   C 3 8 15, 16

History of the Rise and Influence of the Spirit of Rationalism in Europe. 5th ed. 2 vols. 8vo. Lond., 1872. G 7 Q 5, 6

Leaders of Public Opinion in Ireland : Swift, Flood, Grattan, O'Connell. New ed., revised and enlarged. 8vo. Lond., 1871.   C 3 P 2

LECLERC (JEAN). Négociations Secrètes touciant la Paix de Munster, &c. [*See* DUMONT, J.]
[*See* ERASMUS ROTERODAMUS, D.]

LECLERC (JOSEPH VICTOR). Essais de Miciel de Montaigne. Nouvelle éd., avec les Notes de tous les Commentateurs. [*See* MONTAIGNE, M. DE.]

LECLUSE–DE–LOGES (PIERRE MATHURIN DE), L'ABBÉ. Memoirs of Maximilian de Betiune, Duke of Sully, Prime Minister of Henry the Great. 5 vols. 12mo. Edinb., 1773. C 4 P 29–33

LE CONTE (JOSEPH), LL.D. Sigit: an Exposition of the Principles of Monocular and Binocular Vision. Illustrated. 8vo. Lond., 1881. A 12 Q 8

LECOQ (H.), AND BOUILLET (J. B.) Vues et Coupes des principales Formations Geologiques du Département du Puy-de-Dome, accompagnées de la Description et des Echantillons des Rocies qui les composent. Atlas ob. 8vo. Paris, 1830. A 9 S 27

LECTURES delivered before the Young Men's Ciristian Association in Exeter Hall, 1850–51, 1853–55, 1857–58. 4 vols. 12mo. Lond., 1850–58. G 7 U 6–9

LECTURES delivered at the opening of the University of Lond. [*See* LONDON UNIVERSITY.]

LECTURES ON EDUCATION. [*See* EDUCATION.]

LECTURES to Ladies, on Practical Subjects. 8vo. Camb., 1857. J 4 P 16

LEDGER (REV. EDMUND), M.A. The Sun : its Planets and tieir Satellites : Lectures upon the Solar System. Illustrated. 8vo. Lond., 1882. A 3 S 23

LEDGER (GEORGE). The Alpaca : its Introduction into Australia, and the probabilities of its Acclimatisation tiere : a Paper read before the Society of Arts, London. 8vo. Meli., 1861. MA 1 Q 1
Anotier copy. (Pam. Ca.) MA 1 Q 7

LEDIARD (THOMAS). Life of Sethos. [*See* TERRASSON, J.]

LE–DUC (E. E. VIOLLET-). [*See* VIOLLET-LE-DUC, E. E.]

LEDWICH (EDWARD), LL.B. Antiquities of Ireland. 4to. Dublin, 1790. B 18 Q 20 ‡

LEDYARD (JOHN). Memoirs of the Life and Travels of, from iis Journals and Correspondence; by Jared Sparks. 8vo. Lond., 1828. MC 1 Q 13

LEE (FRANCIS), D.D. History of Montanism ; by "A Lay Gentleman." 8vo. Lond., 1709. G 2 P 25
Memoirs of the Life of Mr. Join Kettlewell. 8vo. Lond., 1718. C 4 V 5

LEE (FREDERICK). Abolition of Capital Punisiment : a Lecture. 8vo. Sydney, 1864. MF 3 P 2
Anotier copy. (Pam. 20.) MJ 2 Q 8
Anotier copy. MJ 2 Q 9
Anotier copy. MJ 2 R 7

LEE (REV. FREDERICK GEORGE), D.D. The Ciurci under Queen Elizabeti : an Historical Sketci. 2 vols. 8vo. Lond., 1880. G 2 P 4, 5
Glimpses in the Twiligit; being various Notes, Records, and Examples of the Supernatural. 8vo. Edinb., 1885. G 7 Q 10
History, Description, and Antiquities of the Prebendal Ciurci of the Blessed Virgin Mary of Thame, in the County and Diocese of Oxford. Fol. Lond., 1883. B 15 T 1 ‡

LEE (GEORGE). History of Ceylon. [*See* RIBEYRO, CAPT. J.]

LEE (MISS HARRIET). The Ciapter of Accidents : a Comedy. (Bell's Brit. Tieatre.) 18mo. Lond.. 1796. H 2 P 3

LEE (HOLME). [*See* PARR, MISS HARRIET.]

LEE (RT. REV. JAMES PRINCE), D.D. [*See* OWENS COLLEGE.]

LEE (JOHN EDWARD), F.G.S., &c. Lake Dwellings of Switzerland. [*See* KELLER, DR. F.]
Note-book of an Amateur Geologist. 8vo. Lond., 1881. A 9 T 23
Roman Imperial Profiles ; being a series of more tian 160 litiograpiic Profiles enlarged from Coins. 8vo. Lond., 1874. A 8 Q 37

LEE (NATHANIEL): Dramatick Works of. 3 vols. 12mo. Lond., 1734. H 3 P 15–17
Lucius Junius Brutus : a Tragedy. (Bell's Brit. Tieatre.) 18mo. Lond., 1796. H 2 P 46
Oedipus : a Tragedy. [*See* DRYDEN, J.]
The Rival Queens : a Tragedy. (Brit. Tieatre.) 12mo. Lond., 1808. H 1 P 6
Anotier copy. (Bell's Brit. Tieatre.) 18mo. Lond., 1793. H 2 P 43
Anotier copy. (New Eng. Tieatre.) 12mo. Lond., 1776. H 4 P 9
Anotier copy. [*See* BRIT. DRAMA 1.]
Tieodosius : a Tragedy. (Bell's Brit. Tieatre.) 18mo. Lond., 1793. H 2 P 22
Anotier copy. (New Eng. Tieatre.) 12mo. Lond., 1777. H 4 P 25

LEE (MRS. R.) Adventures in Australia ; or, the Wanderings of Captain Spencer in the Busi and the Wilds. 12mo. Lond., 1851.* MJ 1 P 7
Memoirs of Baron Cuvier. 8vo. Lond., 1833. C 6 P 3

LEE (GEN. ROBERT EDWARD). Life and Campaigns of ; by iis Nepiew, Edward Lee Ciilde ; translated from the Frenci, by George Litting, M.A., &c. 8vo. Lond., 1875. C 4 T 17
Memoirs of Robert E. Lee : iis Military and Personal History; by A. L. Long. Illustrated. Imp. 8vo. Lond., 1886. C 5 W 11

LEE (PROF. S.), A.M. Vetus Testamentum Syriacae. [*See* BIBLES, &c.]

LEE (SIDNEY LAZARUS), B.A. Autobiography of Edward, Lord Herbert. [*See* HERBERT, LORD.]
Stratford-on-Avon, from the Earliest Times to the Death of William Shakespeare. Illustrated. Sm. fol. Lond., 1885. B 15 T 11 ‡

LEE (VERNON). [*See* PAGET, MISS V.]

LEE (WILLIAM). Brandy and Salt; being an effectual Remedy for most of the Diseases which afflict Humanity. 8vo. Sydney, 1842. MA 2 S 50

LEE (WILLIAM). Daniel Defoe; his Life and recently discovered Writings, extending from 1716 to 1729. 3 vols. 8vo. Lond., 1869. C 10 T 29–31

LEECH (H. J.) Public Letters of the Rt. Hon. John Bright, M.P. 8vo. Lond., 1885. C 5 R 8

LEECH (JOHN). Early Pencillings from *Punch*, chiefly Political. Roy. 4to. Lond., 1868. A 2 R 23 †
John Leech, Artist and Humourist: a Biographical Sketch, by Fred. G. Kitton. 8vo. Lond., 1883. C 7 S 16
Later Pencillings from *Punch*; with explanatory Notes by Mark Lemon, Editor of *Punch*. Roy. 4to. Lond., 1868. A 2 R 24 †
Pictures of Character. Series 1–5. 4 vols. (in 2) roy. 4to. Lond., 1862. A 2 P 11, 11 * ‡
Pictures of Life and Character, from the Collection of Mr. Punch, 1842–64. Roy. 4to. Lond.,1886. A 2 R 25 †
Portraits of the Children of the Mobility, drawn from Nature. Roy. 4to. Lond., 1841. A 2 R 22 †

LEEDS (W. H.) Rudimentary Architecture for Beginners and Students: the Orders and their Aesthetic Principles. 12mo. Lond., 1871. A 17 P 44

LEEDS PUBLIC LIBRARY. Catalogue of the contents of Section K : Science, Art, and Technology. (Pam. Eb.) 12mo. Leeds, 1874. MK 1 P 1

LEEMANS (DR. C.) Bôrô-Boedoer op het Eiland Java, afgebeeld door en onder toezigt van F. C. Wilsen, met toelichtenden en verklarenden Texst, naar de geschreven en gedrukte verhandelingen van F. C. Wilsen, J. F. G. Brumund, en andere bescheiden, bewerkt en uitgegeven door Dr. C. Leemans. 8vo. Leiden, 1873. D 20 P 1 * ‡
Bôrô-Boudour, dans l'Ile de Java, dessiné par ou sous la Direction de Mr. F. C. Wilsen, avec Texte descriptif explicatif, rédigé, d'après les Mémoires manuscrits et imprimés de MM. F. C. Wilsen, J. F. G. Brumund, et autres Documents, et publié par le Dr. C. Leemans. 8vo. Leiden, 1874. D 20 P 2 * ‡
Plates [to above.] 4 vols. l. fol. Leiden, 1874. D 20 P 1–4 ‡

LEEPER (PROF. ALEXANDER), M.A. Thirteen Satires of Juvenal. [*See* JUVENALIS, D. J.]

LEFAVOUR (HENRY). Annual Report of the Adjutant-General of the State of Rhode Island, for the year 1875. (Pam. Ju.) Providence, 1876. F 7 S 21

LEFÉVRE (EMILE). Anvers en Australie : Extraits du Précurseur d'Anvers. 8vo. Anvers, 1875. MF 2 Q 17

LE FEVRE (SIR GEORGE), M.D., &c. Life of a Travelling Physician. 3 vols. 8vo. Lond., 1843. C 5 Q 16–18

LEFEVRE (RT. HON. GEORGE JOHN SHAW-), M.P. English and Irish Land Questions. Collected Essays. 8vo. Lond., 1881. F 5 S 32
Another copy. 2nd ed. 8vo. Lond., 1881. F 5 S 33

LE FEVRE DE LA BODERIE (GUY). Les Trois Livres de la Vie. [*See* FICIN, M.]

LEFROY (GEN. SIR JOHN HENRY), C.B., &c. Diary of a Magnetic Survey of a portion of the Dominion of Canada, chiefly in the North-west Territories; executed in the years 1842–44. With Maps. Roy. 8vo. Lond., 1883. B 6 U 12

LEFROY (W. CHAMBERS). Ruined Abbeys of Yorkshire; with Etchings and Vignettes by A. Brunet-Debaines and H. Toussaint. Fol. Lond., 1883. B 14 S 18 ‡

LE GENDRE (GENERAL). Progressive Japan : a Study of the Political and Social Needs of the Empire. 8vo. N. York, 1878. F 8 P 11

LEGENDS OF AUSTRALIA. Frederick Charles Howard.—Edward Nox. (Pam.) 8vo. Lond. (n.d.) MJ 2 Q 4

LEGGE (ALFRED OWEN). Pius IX : the Story of his Life, to the Restoration in 1850; with Glimpses at the National Movement in Italy. 2 vols. 8vo. Lond., 1875. C 6 U 20, 21
The Unpopular King: the Life and Times of Richard III. 2 vols. 8vo. Lond., 1885. B 4 T 6, 7

LEGGE (REV. J.), M.A. Curious Results of applying Sceptical Criticism to itself, as seen in "Supernatural Religion : an Address. 8vo. Ballarat, 1875. MG 1 Q 32

LEGGE (PROF. JAMES), D.D., &c. The Chinese Classics; with a Translation, Critical and Exegitical Notes, Prologomena, and Indexes. Vols. 1–3. 3 vols. (in 4) roy. 8vo. Hongkong, 1861–65. J 15 V 14–17
  1. Confucian Analects. The Great Learning and the Doctrine of the Mean.
  2. The Works of Mencius.
  3. Parts 1, 2. The Shoo-king: or, the Books of Yang, the Books of Yu, &c.
The Chinese Classics; translated into English, with preliminary Essays, &c. 2 vols. 8vo. Lond., 1869–75. J 16 R 16, 17
  1. Life and Works of Confucius.
  2. Life and Works of Mencius.
Record of Buddhistic Kingdoms. [*See* FÁ-HIEN.]
Sacred Books of China. [*See* MÜLLER, PROF. F. M.]
The She King; or, the Book of Ancient Poetry; translated in English Verse: with Essays and Notes. 8vo. Lond., 1876. J 5 U 4

LEGGE (CAPT. W. VINCENT), R.A. History of the Birds of Ceylon. 4to. Lond., 1880. A 2 8 2 †

LEGISLATIVE ASSEMBLY of New South Wales. [*See* NEW SOUTH WALES.]

LEGISLATIVE ASSEMBLY of Queensland. [*See* QUEENSLAND.]

LEGISLATIVE ASSEMBLY of Tasmania. [*See* TASMANIA.]

LEGISLATIVE ASSEMBLY of Victoria. [*See* VICTORIA.]

LEGISLATIVE COUNCIL of New South Wales. [*See* NEW SOUTH WALES.]

LEGISLATIVE COUNCIL of New Zealand. [*See* NEW ZEALAND.]

LEGISLATIVE COUNCIL of Queensland. [*See* QUEENSLAND.]

LEGISLATIVE COUNCIL of South Australia. [*See* SOUTH AUSTRALIA.]

LEGISLATIVE COUNCIL of Tasmania. [*See* TASMANIA.]

LEGISLATIVE COUNCIL of Victoria. [*See* VICTORIA.]

LEGISLATIVE COUNCIL of Western Australia. [*See* WESTERN AUSTRALIA.]

LEGISLATIVE ENACTMENTS (SIX). For the Guidance of Contractors, Merchants, and Tradesmen. (Weale.) 12mo. Lond., 1858–59. F 5 S 20

LEGISLATOR. [*See* NEW SOUTH WALES—LEGISLATIVE COUNCIL.]

LE GOBIEN (CHARLES). Histoire des Isles Marianes, nouvellement converties à la Religion Chrétienne et de la mort glorieuse des premiers Missionaires qui y ont prêché la Foy. 18mo. Paris, 1700. MB 1 P 15

LE GONIDEC (JEAN FRANÇOIS MARIE). Dictionnaire Français-Breton et Briton-Français précédé de sa Grammaire Bretonne. 2 vols. 4to. Saint-Brieuc, 1847–50. K 13 T 19, 20

LE GRAND (JOACHIM), L'ABBÉ. History of Ceylon. [*See* RIBERYO, CAPT. J.]

LE GRAND D'AUSSY (PIERRE JEAN BAPTISTE). Fabliaux; or, Tales abridged from French Manuscripts of the 12th and 13th Centuries, by M. Le Grand; selected and translated into English Verse by the late G. L. Way, Esq. [With Cuts by Bewick.] 3 vols. 8vo. Lond., 1815. H 3 R 7–9

LEGROS (A.) The Four Masters of Etching. [*See* WEDMORE, F.]

LEGROS (E.) Dictionnaire International Français-Anglais. [*See* HAMILTON, H.]

LE HÉRICHER (E.) Glossaire etymologique Anglo-Normand; ou, l'Anglais ramené a la Langue Française. Roy. 8vo. Avranches, 1884. K 13 T 14

LEHMANN (PROF. C. G.) Physiological Chemistry; translated from the 2nd ed., by George E. Day, M.D., F.R.S. 3 vols. 8vo. Lond., 1851–54. A 5 T 16–18
Atlas [to the above]; by Dr. Otto Funke. 4to. Lond., 1853. A 5 U 1

LEHRS (F. S.) Hesiodi Carmina. [*See* HESIOD.]

LEIBIUS (A.) Ph. D. [*See* ROYAL SOCIETY OF N.S.W.]

LEIBNITZ (GOTTFRIED WILHELM). God. Guil. Leibnitii Opera Philosophica, quæ exstant, Latina, Gallica, Germanica, omnia. Imp. 8vo. Berolini, 1840. G 7 V 11
Refutation recently discovered of Spinoza, by Leibnitz; translated by the Rev. Octavius Freire Owen, M.A., &c. 12mo. Edinb., 1855. G 7 Q 8

LEICESTER (ROBERT DUDLEY), EARL OF. The Perfect Picture of a Favourite; or, Secret Memoirs of Robert Dudley, Earl of Leicester, Prime Minister and Favourite of Queen Elizabeth, and Stadtholder of Holland. 3rd ed., corrected. 8vo. Lond., 1711. B 3 P 21

LEICESTER (SIMON DE MONTFORT), EARL OF. The Creator of the House of Commons; by Reinhold Pauli; translated by Una M. Goodwin. 8vo. Lond., 1876. C 3 V 40

LEICESTERSHIRE FARMER, A. [*See* DERBY, EARL OF.]

LEICHHARDT (DR. LUDWIG). Briefe an seine Angehörigen. Roy. 8vo. Hamburg, 1881. MC 4 P 2 †
Dr. Leichhardt's Testimonial [Presentation of]. (Pam. Ab.) 12mo. Sydney, 1846. MD 1 S 14
Eight Months with Dr. Leichhardt. [*See* MANN, J. F.]
Exploration in Western Australia: supposed Traces of Leichhardt. [From the *Perth Inquirer and Commercial News*. Pam. B.] Fol. Sydney, 1861. MJ 2 U 2
Journal of an Overland Expedition to Port Essington, in the years 1844–45. Revised by the Explorer, and published with his sanction. (Pam. Ab.) 12mo. Sydney (n.d.) MD 1 S 14
Another copy. (Pam. 21.) 8vo. Sydney, 1846. MJ 2 Q 10
Journal of an Overland Expedition in Australia, from Moreton Bay to Port Essington, a distance of upwards of 3,000 miles, during the years 1844–45. With Maps. 2 vols. 8vo. Lond., 1847.* MD 2 U 9, 10
Lectures delivered at the School of Arts, Sydney, on the 18th and 25th August, 1846 [on the Expedition from Moreton Bay to Port Essington]. (Pam. Ab.) 12mo. Sydney, 1846. MD 1 S 14
Leichhardt's Grave [a Poem in MS.]; by Lieut. B. Lynd. Fol. Sydney (n.d.) MJ 2 U 1
Letter to Mr. Justice Wise on "Leichhardt's Grave; by Lieut. B. Lynd." [*See* HALLORAN, H.]

LEICHHRADT (DR. LUDWIG)—*continued.*

Stanzas; written on the return of L. Leichhardt, Esq., from an Expedition through the unexplored regions of Australia, between Moreton Bay and Port Essington; by B.K.S., Sydney, March, 1846. On Hearing of Dr. Leichhardt's Return: Melbourne, April 20, 1846. Leichhardt's Return; by "Malwyn," Melbourne, April 14, 1846. Leichhardt's Grave; by B. Lynd, Sydney Barracks July 2nd, 1845. (*Supplement to the Port Phillip Herald.*) Fol.   Meln., 1846.   MJ 2 U 2

Travels with Dr. Leichhardt in Australia. [*See* BUNCE, D.]

LEIGH (REV. J. E. AUSTEN-). [*See* AUSTEN-LEIGH, REV. J. E.]

LEIGH (MEDORA): a History and an Autobiography; edited by Charles Mackay. 8vo. Lond., 1869. C 3 P 29

LEIGH (PERCIVAL). Extracts from Mr. Pips : Hys Diarye. [*See* DOYLE, R.]

LEIGH (REV. SAMUEL). Life of Missionary to Australia and New Zealand ; with a History of the Origin and Progress of the Missions in those Colonies, by the late Rev. Alexander Strachan. Illustrated edition. 8vo. Lond., 1870.   MC 1 P 6

LEIGH (S. T.) [*See* DE GRUCHY, H.]

LEIGH (S. T.), & CO. Hand-book to Sydney and Suburbs; with a Plan of the City, and Map of the Roads of the Colony. 8vo. Sydney, 1867.*   MD 7 Q 38

Map of the County of Cumberland, in New South Wales. [Single sheet.]   Sydney (n.d.)   Libr.

LEIGH (W. H.) The Emigrant: a Tale of Australia. 8vo. Lond., 1847.   MJ 2 S 23

Reconnoitering Voyages and Travels; with Adventures in the new Colonies of South Australia, during the years 1836–38. 8vo. Lond., 1839.*   MD 5 U 21

Another copy. 2nd ed. 8vo. Lond., 1840.*   MD 5 U 23

LEIGHTON (ALEXANDER). Mysterious Legends of Edinburgh. 8vo. Edinb., 1864.   J 9 P 30

LEIGHTON (JOHN). Paris under the Commune ; or, Seventy-three Days of the Second Siege. 8vo. Lond., 1871.   B 9 P 23

Suggestions in Design; being a comprehensive Series of original Sketches in various Styles of Ornament, arranged, with Letterpress, by James K. Colling, F.R.I.B.A. 4to. Lond., 1880.   A 1 P 16

LEIGHTON (JOHN M.) History of the County of Fife, from the Earliest Period to the Present Time. With Engravings. 3 vols. 4to. Glasgow, 1840. B 12 V 20–22

LEIGHTON (MOST REV. ROBERT), D.D., ARCHBISHOP OF GLASGOW. Practical Commentary upon the First Epistle of St. Peter, and other Expository Works ; with Life of the Author, by the Rev. Erasmus Middleton. 8vo. Lond., 1829.   G 14 P 3

Select Works of. 2 vols. 8vo. Lond., 1823. G 14 P 1, 2

LEIGHTON (REV. W. A.), B.A., &c. Lichen-Flora of Great Britain, Ireland, and the Channel Islands. 3rd ed. 8vo. Shrewsbury, 1879.   A 4 T 11

LEIPZIGER STUDIEN ZUR CLASSISCHEN PHILO-LOGIE ; herausgegeben von G. Curtius, L. Lange, O. Ribbeck, H. Lipsius, C. Wachsmuth. Bände 1–8. 8 vols. (in 7) 8vo. Leipzig, 1878–85.   K 19 S 5–11

LEITCH (JOHN). System of Mythology. [*See* MÜLLER, C. O.]

LEITCH (WILLIAM), D.D. God's Glory in the Heavens. 8vo. Lond., 1862.   A 3 R 9

LEITCH (WILLIAM LEIGHTON): a Memoir, by A. Macgeorge. Sq. 8vo. Lond., 1884.   C 9 V 26

LEITE (SEVERINO LOURENCO DA COSTA). Historical Notes concerning the Vegetable Fibres exhibited by. [*See* MOREIRA, N. J.]

LEITH (WILLIAM FORBES-), S.J. Life of St. Margaret. [*See* TURGOT, ST., BISHOP OF ST. ANDREWS.]

Narrative of Scottish Catholics under Mary Stuart and James VI. 8vo. Edinb., 1885.   G 15 R 14

Scots Men-at-Arms and Life-Guards in France, from their Formation until their final Dissolution, A.D. 1418–1830. 2 vols. 4to. Edinb., 1882.   B S V 29, 30

LEJEAN (GUILLAUME). Théodore II : le nouvel Empire d'Abyssinie et les intérêts Français dans le sud de la Mer Rouge. 12mo. Paris, 1865.   B 1 P 36

LEKAIN. [*See* CAIN, H. L.]

LE KEUX (JOHN). Memorials of Cambridge : a series of Views of the Colleges, Halls, and Public Buildings ; with Historical and Descriptive Accounts, by Thomas Wright, M.A., F.S.A., and the Rev. H. Longueville Jones, M.A., F.S.A. 2 vols. 8vo. Lond., 1847.   B 6 S 1, 2

LE KEUX (JOHN), AND COOPER (CHARLES HENRY), F.S.A. Memorials of Cambridge, greatly enlarged from the Work of J. Le Keux ; with Steel and Copper Plates, by Le Keux and Storer, and Etchings on Copper by Robert Farren. 3 vols. 8vo. Camb., 1860–66.   B 6 S 3–5

LELAND (CHARLES GODFREY). Algonquin Legends of New England ; or, Myths and Folk-lore of the Micmac, Passamaquoddy, and Penobscot Tribes. 8vo. Lond., 1884.   B 1 Q 8

English Gipsies and their Language. 2nd ed. 8vo. Lond., 1874.   A 1 V 15

The Gypsies. 8vo. Lond., 1882.   A 1 V 14

Pidgin-English Sing-Song ; or, Songs and Stories in the China-English Dialect. 12mo. Lond., 1876. H 6 R 41

LELAND (JOHN). De Rebus Britanicis Collectanea, cum Tiomæ Hearnii Præfatione Notis et Indice ad editionem primam. 5 vols. (in 6), 8vo. Lond., 1774. B 5 T 56-61

Heinrich Heine's Pictures of Travel. [*See* HEINE, H.]

Itinerary of. 9 vols. (in 3) 8vo. Oxford, 1744-45.
B 2 S 40-42

Lives of those Eminent Antiquaries, John Leland, Thomas Hearne, and Antiony à Wood ; by W. Huddersford and Thomas Warton. 2 vols. 8vo. Oxford, 1772. C1 V 14,15

View of the principal Deistical Writers that have appeared in England in the Last and Present Century. 5th ed. 2 vols. 8vo. Lond., 1766. G 7 P 29, 30

LELAND (THOMAS), D.D. History of Ireland, from the Invasion of Henry II ; with a preliminary discourse on the Antient State of that Kingdom. 3 vols. 4to. Lond., 1773. B 17 Q 4-6 ‡

Orations of Demosthenes. [*See* DEMOSTHENES.]

LE MAIRE (JAKOB). Epiemerides sive Descriptio Navigationis Australis institutæ anno 1615. Roy. 4to. Amsterd., 1621. MD 7 Q 3 †

LE MARCHAND (MME. FRANÇOISE). Boca : ou la Vertu récompensée. [*See* CABINET DES FÉES 18.]

LE MARCHANT (SIR DENIS), BART. Memoir of John Ciarles, Viscount Althorp, Third Earl Spencer. 8vo. Lond., 1876. C 9 R 18

LEMIRE (CHARLES). En Australie. 8vo. Paris, 1885.
MD 6 S 1

La Colonisation Français en Nouvelle-Calédonie et Dependances Sm. 4to. Paris, 1878. MD 2 V 23

LEMPRIERE (JOHN), D.D. Classical Dictionary ; containing a copious Account of all the Proper Names mentioned in Ancient Authors, &c. 11th ed. 8vo. Lond., 1820. R 7 Q 5

Universal Biography, abridged. 8vo. Lond., 1808.
C 11 Q 8

LEMPRIERE (WILLIAM), M.D. Tour through the Dominions of the Emperor of Morocco ; including a particular Account of the Royal Harem. 3rd ed. 8vo. Newport, 1813. D 2 T 11

LENAU (NICOLAUS). Faust ein Gedicht. 4⁴ auflage. 12mo. Stuttgart, 1852. H 4 P 32

LENCLOS (ANNE et), *called* NINON. Laïs de Corintie et Ninon de Lenclos : Biographie Anecdotique, par A. Debay. 12mo. Paris, 1858. C 2 P 29

LENDENFELD (R. VON), PH.D. Descriptive Catalogue of the Medusæ of the Australian Seas. In two Parts. Part 1. Scypiomedusæ. Part 2. Hydromedusæ. Roy. 8vo. Sydney, 1877.* MA 2 U 38

LE NEVE (JOHN). Lives, &c., of all the Protestant Bisiops of the Church of England since the Reformation. Vol. 1, parts 1, 2 (*all published.*) 8vo. Lond., 1720. G 7 R 6

LENNOX (WILLIAM PITT), LORD. Celebrities I have known ; with Episodes, Political, Social, Sporting, and Theatrical. 2 vols. 8vo. Lond., 1876. C 6 V 16, 17

LENO (JOHN BEDFORD). Art of Boot and Shoe Making : a practical Hand-book. 8vo. Lond., 1885. A 11 P 3

LENOIR (MARIE ALEXANDRE). Musee des Monumens Français. 8 vols. 8vo. Paris, 1800-21. A 7 R 12-19

LENOIR (PAUL). Fayoum ; or, Artists in Egypt. Illustrated. 8vo. Lond., 1873. D 1 V 1

LENORMANT (PROF. FRANÇOIS). The Book of Genesis : a Translation from the Hebrew, in which the constituent elements of the Text are separated. 8vo. Lond., 1886. G 7 P 26

Chaldean Magic : its Origin and Development ; translated from the French. 8vo. Lond., 1877. G 7 P 28

Études Accadiennes. Lettres Assyriologiques. 2⁴ Série. 2 vols. 4to. Paris, 1873-74. K 17 S 17, 18

Étude sur quelques Parties des Syllabaires Cunéiformes : essai de Philologie Accadienne et Assyrienne 8vo. Paris, 1876. K 12 R 16

Les Premières Civilisations : études d'Histoire et d'Archéologie. 2 vols. 8vo. Paris, 1874. B 15 Q 4, 5

Les Sciences Occultes en Asèe : La Magie chez les Chaldéens et les origines Accadiennes. 8vo. Paris, 1874. G 7 P 27

A Travers l'Apulie et la Lucanie : Notes de Voyage. 2 vols. 8vo. Paris, 1883. D 6 U 34, 35

LENOX (JAMES). Recollections of, and the formation of his Library, by H. N. Stevens. 12mo. Lond., 1886. C 2 R 25

LEO GRAMMATICUS. [*See* BYZANTINÆ HIST. SCRIPT.]

LEO (DIACONUS CALOENSIS). [*See* MIGNE, J. P., SERIES GRÆCA, 117, *and* BYZANTINÆ HIST. SCRIPT.]

LEO I (POPE). Opera omnia. [*See* MIGNE, J. P., SERIES LATINA, 54-56.]

LEO IV (POPE). Opera omnia. [*See* MIGNE, J. P., SERIES LATINA, 115.]

LEO VI (POPE). Opera omnia. [*See* MIGNE, J. P., SERIES GRÆCA, 107.]

LEO X (POPE). Life and Pontificate of ; by W. Roscoe. 2nd ed. 6 vols. 8vo. Lond., 1806. C 6 R 9-14

LEO (F. A.), PH.D. Siakespeare-Notes. 8vo. Lond., 1885. H 3 Q 28

LEO (DR. HENRI). Histoire d'Italie pendant le Moyen Age. 3 vols. imp. 8vo. Paris, 1837-39. B 30 V 1-3

LEO MARSICANUS. Chronicon Monasterii Casinensis. [*See* MIGNE, J. P., SERIES LATINA, 173.]

LEOFRIC MISSAL (THE). [*See* WARREN, REV. F. E.]

LEON (JOHN A.) Art of Manufacturing and Refining Sugar; including the Manufacture and Revivification of Animal Charcoal. Imp. fol. Lond., 1850. A 3 P 21 ‡

LEON (NESTOR PONCE DE). Technological Dictionary, English and Spanish and Spanish and English. Vol. 1, English and Spanish. Imp. 8vo. New York, 1886.
K 13 T 32

LEONARD (HUGH), C.E. Report on the River Hooghly. Bengal, 1865. Fol. Lond., 1865. E

LEONARDO DA VINCI. [*See* VINCI, L. DA.]

LEOPARDI (GIACOMO). Essays and Dialogues of; translated by Charles Edwardes; with Biographical Sketch 8vo. Lond., 1882. J 12 R 5

Rime di Francesco Petrarca, con l'interpretatione. [*See* PETRARCA, F.]

L'EPÉE (CHARLES MICHEL DE), ABBÉ. Method of Educating the Deaf and Dumb, confirmed by Long Experience. 8vo. Lond., 1801. G 17 P 13

L'EPINE (ERNEST). The Days of Chivalry; or, the Legend of Croquemitaine. Freely translated by Tom Hood; illustrated by G. Doré. 4to. Lond., 1877. J 2 U 10

LE PLONGEON (AUGUSTUS). Sacred Mysteries among the Mayas and the Quiches, 11,500 years ago: their relation to the Sacred Mysteries of Egypt, Greece, Chaldea, and India; Freemasonry in times anterior to the Temple of Solomon. Illustrated. 8vo. New York, 1886. B 1 R 33

LEPSIUS (PROF. CARL RICHARD), PH.D Die Chronologie der Ægypter. Vol. 1. Roy. 4to. [*All published.*] Berlin, 1849. B 14 R 9 ‡

Denkmäler aus Ægypten und Æthiopien nach den Zeichnungen der von seiner Majestät dem Könige von Preussen Friedrich Wilhelm IV, nach diesen Ländern gesendeten und in den Jahren 1842-45 ausgeführten wissenschaftlichen Expedition. [Text.] Roy. 4to. Berlin, 1849. B 9 P 10‡

[Plates to the above.] El. fol. Berlin, 1849-59. B 9 P 11-22 ‡

Discoveries in Egypt, Ethiopia, and the Peninsula of Sinai, in the years 1842-45. Edited, with Notes, by K. R. H. Mackenzie. 8vo. Lond., 1852. D 2 T 18

Another copy. 2nd ed. 8vo. Lond., 1853. D 2 T 19

Königsbuch der alten Ægypter. Imp. 4to. Berlin, 1858. B 17 S 11 ‡

Standard Alphabet for reducing unwritten Languages and Foreign Graphic Systems to a uniform Orthography in European Letters. 2nd ed. 8vo. Lond., 1863. K 15 Q 6

Das Todtenbuch der Ægypter, nach dem hieroglyphischen Papyrus in Turin; mit einem Vorworte zum ersten Male herausgegeben. Imp.4to. Leip.,1842. B 14 S 17 ‡

Das Ursprüngliche Zendalphabet. 4to. Berlin, 1863. K 15 U 5

LERMONT (THOMAS). Sir Tristrem: a Metrical Romance of the 13th Century; edited by [Sir] Walter Scott. 10th ed. 8vo. Edinb., 1811. H 8 U 8

LE ROULX (JOSEPH DELAVILLE). [*See* DELAVILLE LE ROULX, J.]

LEROY (A. C.) Historic Winchester. [*See* BRAMSTON, A. R.]

LEROY (C. F. A.) Traité de Géometrie Descriptive, suivi de la Méthode des Plans Cotés et de la Théorie des Engrenages Cylindriques et Coniques. 10e ed. 2 vols. (in 1) 4to. Paris, 1877. A 10 V 14

LE ROY (G.) How to Learn and Teach Languages. 8vo. Melb., 1875. MJ 2 R 15

Reforms to make Australia the greatest Country in the World. 8vo. Melb., 1875. MF 1 Q 6

LE SAGE (A.) [*See* LAS CASES, E. A. D. M. J., MARQUIS DE.]

LE SAGE (ALAIN RENÉ). Histoire de Gil Blas de Santillane. 2 vols. 18mo. Lond., 1826. J 15 Q 9, 10

Pokhogedenips Gilblaza. [Adventures of Gil Blas; in Russian.] 4 vols. 12mo. St. Petersb., 1812-15.
J 16 T 12-15

LE SEUR (THOMAS). Philosophiae Naturalis Principia Mathematica. [*See* NEWTON, SIR J.]

LESKIEN (A.) Handbuch der Altbulgarischen (altkirchenslawischen) Sprache; Grammatik, Texte, Glossar. 8vo. Weimar, 1871. K 15 R 1

LESLEY (RT. REV. JOHN), BISHOP OF ROSS. De Illustrium Fœminarum in Repub. administranda, ac ferendis legibus authoritate. Sm. 4to. Rheims, 1580. B 3 T 2

De Titulo et Jure Serenissimae Principis Mariae Scotorum Regine, quo Regni Angliae successionem sibi justè vindicat. Sm. 4to. Rheims, 1580. B 3 T 2

LESLIE (ALEXANDER). The Arctic Voyages of Adolf Erik Nordenskiöld, 1858-79. Illustrated. 8vo. Lond., 1879. D 4 S 1

Voyage of the *Vega* round Asia and Europe. [*See* NORDENSKIÖLD, A. E.]

LESLIE (CHARLES). Polychromatic Decoration. Ob. 4to. Lond., 1884. A 8 R 14

LESLIE (CHARLES), "PHILALETHES." A View of the Times: their Principles and Practices; in the Second, Third, and Fourth Volumes of the Rehearsals. 3 vols. (in 1) fol. Lond., 1708-9. Libr.

LESLIE (CHARLES ROBERT), R.A. Autobiographical Recollections of. Edited, with a prefatory Essay on Leslie as an Artist, and Selections from his Correspondence, by Tom Taylor. With Portrait. 2 vols. 8vo. Lond., 1860.
C 2 U 28, 29

Memoirs of the Life of John Constable, Esq., R.A., composed chiefly of his Letters. 2nd ed. Sm. 4to. Lond., 1845. C 8 R 1

LESLIE (CHARLES ROBERT), R.A., AND TAYLOR (TOM), M.A. Life and Times of Sir Josiua Reynolds; with Notices of some of his Contemporaries. 2 vols. 8vo. Lond., 1865.   C 9 P 35, 36

LESLIE (DAVID). Among the Zulus and Amatongas; edited by the Hon. W. H. Drummond. 2nd ed. 8vo. Edinb., 1875.   D I T 23

LESLIE (GEORGE DUNLOP). Our River. Illustrations by the Author. Roy. 8vo. Lond., 1881.   D 6 V 8

LESLIE (PROF. SIR JOHN), K.H., JAMESON (PROF. ROBERT), F.R.S.E., AND MURRAY (HUGH), F.R.S.E. Discovery and Adventure in the Polar Seas and Regions; with Illustrations of their Climate, Geology, and Natural History. 12mo. Lond., 1851.   D 4 R 36

LESLIE (RT. REV. JOHN), D.D., BISHOP OF THE ISLES, &c. Life and Times of; with preliminary Sketches of other Eminent Persons of the Leslie Family, A.D. 1525-1675, by the Rev. R. J. Leslie, M.A. 8vo. Lond., 1885.   C 4 R 14

LESLIE (JOHN). Improvement of Designs and Patterns. [See SENIOR, N. W.]

LESLIE (ROBERT C.) A Sea Painter's Log. Illustrated. 8vo. Lond., 1886.   D 10 R 15

LESLIE (REV. R. J.), M.A., VICAR OF HOLBEACH. Life of the Rev. John Leslie, D.D.; with preliminary Sketches of other Eminent Persons of the Leslie Family, A.D. 1525-1675. 8vo. Lond., 1885.   C 4 R 14

LESLIE (T. E. CLIFFE.) Financial Reform. [See COBDEN CLUB.]

LESPY (V.) Grammaire Béarnaise, suivie d'un Vocabulaire Béarnais-Français. 2e éd. 8vo. Paris, 1880.   K 13 P 20

LESSEPS (FERDINAND), COMTE DE. The Great Canal at Suez; with an Account of its Projector. [See FITZGERALD, P.]

Suez Canal. Letters and Documents Descriptive of its Rise and Progress in 1854-56. 8vo. Lond., 1876.   B 2 R 44

LESSING (GOTTHOLD EPHRAIM). The Education of the Human Race. 12mo. Lond., 1858.   G 17 P 33

Laocoon. Edited, with English Notes, &c., by A. Hamann, Phil. Doc. M.A. (Clar. Press.) 8vo. Oxford, 1878.   A 23 Q 7

Laocoon. Translated from the Text of Lessing; with Preface and Notes by the Rt. Hon. Sir Robt. Phillimore, D.C.L. 8vo. Lond., 1874.   A 8 Q 1

Lessing; by James Syme. With Portrait. 2nd ed. 2 vols. 8vo. Lond., 1879.   C 9 T 12

Sammtliche Schriften; herausgegeben von Karl Lachmann. 12 vols. (in 13) 8vo. Leipzic, 1853-57.   J 17 P 4-16

3 K

LESSON (PIERRE ADOLPHE). Les Polynésiens; leur Origine, leurs Migrations, leur Language. 4 vols. 8vo. Paris, 1880-84.   MA 1 S 2-5

Voyage de *l'Astrolabe*: Botanique. [See DUMONT D'URVILLE, CAPT. J. S. C.]

LESSON (RENÉ PRIMEVÈRE). Voyage de la *Coquille*: Zoologie. [See DUPERREY, L. I.]

L'ESTRANGE (REV. ALFRED GUY). The Friendships of Mary Russell Mitford, as recorded in Letters from her Literary Correspondents. 2 vols. 8vo. Lond., 1882.   C 4 R 25, 26

History of English Humour; with an Introduction upon Ancient Humour. 2 vols. 8vo. Lond., 1878.   B 4 Q 15, 16

The Palace and the Hospital; or, Chronicles of Greenwich. 2 vols. 8vo. Lond., 1886.   B 3 Q 23, 24

Yachting round the West of England. 8vo. Lond., 1865.   •   D 6 T 39

L'ESTRANGE (REV. A. G.), AND CHARLEY (HENRY). Life and Letters of Mary Russell Mitford, related in a selection from her Letters to her Friends. [1st and] 2nd series. 5 vols. 8vo. Lond., 1870-72.   C 4 R 20-24

L'ESTRANGE (SIR ROGER), KNT. Seneca's Morals by way of Abstract. [See SENECA, L. A.]

Twenty-two Select Colloquies out of Erasmus Roterodamus. [See ERASMUS ROTERODAMUS, D.]

L'ESTRANGE (CAPT. W. D.) Under Fourteen Flags; being the Life and Adventures of Brig.-Gen. MacIver, a Soldier of Fortune. 8vo. Melb., 1884.   MC 1 P 38

LESUEUR (C. A.) [See PERON, F. A.]

LETAROUILLY (PAUL). Edifices de Rome Moderne ou recueil des Palais, Maisons, Eglises, Convents, et autres monuments publics et particuliers les plus remarquables de la ville de Rome. 4to. Paris, 1868.   A 2 T 26

Planches [to the above]. 3 vols. imp. fol. Paris, 1868-74.   A 3 P 24-26 ‡

LETHBRIDGE (SIR ROPER), M.A., C.I.E. Gazetteer of India. [See THORNTON, E.]

LETOURNEAU (CHARLES), M.D. Sociology, based upon Ethnography; translated by Henry M. Trollope. 8vo. Lond., 1881.   A 1 V 12

LETTERS from China and Japan; by L.D.S. 8vo. Lond., 1875.   D 5 Q 19

LETTERS from the Irish Highlands [by Henry Blake, Mr. D'Arcy, Mr. Martin, Mrs. Blake, &c.] 8vo. Lond., 1825.   D 7 Q 30

LETTERS from the Virgin Islands, illustrating Life and Manners in the West Indies. 8vo. Lond., 1843. D 3 R 24

LETTERS of an Englishman on Louis Napoleon, the Empire, and the Coup d'Etat; reprinted with large additions from the *Times*. 12mo. Lond., 1852.   F I P 27

LETTERS of Registration of Inventions, N.S.W. [*See* NEW SOUTH WALES.]

LETTERS on International Relations, before and during the War of 1870; by the *Times'* Correspondent at Berlin. 2 vols. 8vo. Lond., 1871.   B 9 Q 23, 24

LETTERS on Men, Measures, and Politics; selected from the Papers of the day, beginning with "Junius Redivivus," "Brutus," and "Philo Junius." 8vo. Lond., 1794.   F 6 T 2

LETTERS from Settlers and Labouring Emigrants in the New Zealand Company's Settlement of Wellington, Nelson, and New Plymouth, from 1842 to 1843. 8vo. Lond., 1843.   MD 3 Q 30

LETTERS of Dion. 8vo. Hobart, 1851.   MF 3 P 6

LETTERS from Hell; given in English by L.W.J.S. 8vo. Lond., 1855.   J 9 U 14

LETTERS from India and Kasimir, written in 1870. Illustrated. Roy. 8vo. Lond., 1874.   D 6 S 40

LETTRES Edifiantes et Curieuses; Ecrites des Missions Etrangères. Nouvelle éd. 26 vols. 12mo. Paris, 1780–83.   D 10 P 11–44

LETTRES D'AMOUR. Chefs-d'Œuvre de style épistolaire, choisis dans les plus grands Ecrivains. Nouvelle éd. 18mo. Paris, 1864.   C 1 P 28

LETTRES SUR LA CRIMÉE, Odessa, et la Mer D'Azof. (French and Russian). 8vo. Moscou, 1810.   D 9 Q 39

LETTS, SON & CO. Geographical Index, giving the Latitude, Longitude, and Position of the Principal Places in the World ,specially for use with Letts' Atlases, but applicable to all other Atlases. Fol. Lond., 1883.   D 33 Q 4 ‡
Popular Atlas: British Empire. Fol. Lond., 1881.   D 33 Q 3 ‡
Popular Atlas: Europe. Fol. Lond., 1882. D 33 Q 4 ‡
Popular Atlas: Foreign. Fol. Lond., 1883. D 33 Q 4 ‡
Popular Atlas: General Maps. Fol. Lond., 1881.   D 33 Q 3 ‡
Star Atlas. Fol. Lond., 1830.   A 23 R 1 ‡

LETTSOM (JOHN COAKLEY), M.D., &c. Hints designed to promote Beneficence, Temperance, and Medical Science. 3 vols 8vo. Lond., 1801.   F 8 P 1–3
Observations on Baron Dimsdale's Remarks on Dr. Lettsom's Letter to Sir Robert Barker, and George Stacpoole, Esq., respecting General Inoculation, (Tracts.) 8vo. Lond., 1779.   A 12 S 33

LETTSOM (W. G.) Manual of Mineralogy. [*See* GREG, R. P.]

LEUCKART (PROF. RUDOLPH). Bericht über die wissenschaftlichen Leistungen in der Naturgeschichte der niederen Thiere während des jahres 1858–75. 10 vols. 8vo. Berlin, 1860–78.   E 1, 45
The Parasites of Man, and the Diseases which proceed from them; translated by W. E. Hoyle. Roy. 8vo. Edinb., 1886.   A 13 R 1

LEUNIS (PROF. JOHANNES). Synopsis der Naturgeschichte der Thierreichs. Roy. 8vo. Hannover, 1860. A 14 T 10

LEUPE (P. A.) De Reizen der Nederlanders naar het Zuidland of Nieuw-Holland, in de 17e en 18e eeuw. 8vo. Amsterd., 1868.   MD 7 R 25
De Reizen der Nederlanders naar Nieuw-Guinea en de Papoesche Eilanden in de 17e en 18e eeuw. 8vo. 'Sgravenhage, 1875.   MD 7 R 26
Willem Jansz. van Amsterdam, Admiral, en Willem Jansz. van Amersfoort, Vice-Commander der O.I.C. in der eerste helft der 17e eeuw. 8vo. Amsterd., 1872. MD 1 V 10

LEUPOL (L.) Méthods pour étudier la Langue Sanscrite. [*See* BURNOUF, PROF. E.]

LEVAILLANT (FRANÇOIS). Histoire Naturelle des Oiseaux d'Afrique. 6 vols. imp. fol. Paris, 1824. A 7 P 27–32 ‡
Histoire Naturelle des Oiseaux de Paradis et des Rolliers, suivie de celle des Toucans et des Barbus. 2 vols. imp. fol. Paris, 1806.   A 7 P 25, 26 ‡
Histoire Naturelle des Perroquets. 2 vols. imp. fol. Paris, 1804–5.   A 34 Q 15, 16 ‡
Histoire Naturelle d'une Partie d'Oiseaux nouveaux et rares de l'Amérique et des Indes. Ouvrage destiné par l'Auteur a faire partie de son Ornithologie d'Afrique. Imp. fol. Paris, 1801.   A 7 P 33 ‡
Second Voyage dans l'Intérieur de l'Afrique, par le Cap de Bonne-Espérance, 1783–85. 3 vols. 8vo. Paris, 1805.   D 1 R 10–12

LEVASSEUR (E.) La Question de l'Or: les Mines de Californie et d'Australie, les Anciennes Mines d'Or et d'Argent—leur Production. 8vo. Paris, 1858. F 6 V 14

L'EVÊQUE (LOUISE CAVELIER), DAME. Le Prince des Aigues-Marines et le Prince Invisible. [*See* CABINET DES FÉES, 24.]

LEVER (CHARLES). Life of; by W. J. Fitzpatrick, LL.D. 2 vols. 8vo. Lond., 1879.   C 7 S 14, 15

LEVERMORE (CHARLES H.), PH.D. Republic of New Haven. [*See* JOHNS HOPKINS UNIVERSITY STUDIES.]

LEVESON (MAJOR HENRY A.) England rendered Impregnable. 8vo. Lond., 1871.   A 17 V 5
The Forest and the Field; by H.A.L., the "Old Shekarry." Illustrated. 8vo. Lond., 1867.   A 17 W 22
Sports in Many Lands; by H.A.L., the "Old Shekarry." Illustrated. 2 vols. 8vo. Lond., 1877. A 17 W 23, 24

LEVI (ELIPHAS). [*See* CONSTANT, A. L.]

LEVI (PROF. LEONE), F.S.A., &c. History of British Commerce and of the Economic Progress of the British Nation, 1763–1870. 8vo. Lond., 1872. F 7 P 17

International Commercial Law; being the Principles of Mercantile Law of England, Scotland, Ireland, British India, British Colonies, &c. 2 vols. 8vo. Lond., 1863. F 8 T 14, 15

On Taxation; how it is raised, and how it is expended. 8vo. Lond., 1860. F 6 R 2

Wages and Earnings of the Working Classes: Report to Sir Arthur Bass, M.P. 8vo. Lond., 1885. F 7 P 18

LEVI (NATHANIEL). The Sugar Beet : its Adaptability for Cultivation in the Colony, its Produce, Sugar and Spirit, its Utility, and how it will prove a Remunerative Crop to the Farmer. 8vo. Melh., 1870. MA 1 Q 8

LEVIEN (EDWARD), M.A. Memoirs of Socrates, for English Readers. [*See* XENOPHON.]

Outlines of the History of Greece. [*See* HAMILTON, W. D.]

Outlines of the History of Rome.(Weale.) 12mo. Lond., 1868. K 11 P 3

LEVIN (RAHEL ANTONIE FREDERIKE). Rahel: her Life and Letters; by Mrs. Vaughan Jennings. With a Portrait. 8vo. Lond., 1876. C 4 V 31

LÉVIS (PIERRE MARC GASTON), DUC DE. Souvenirs et Portraits. [*See* BARRIÈRE, J. F., 14.] C 1 T 14

LEVIZAC (JEAN PONS VICTOR LECONTZ DE). Theoretical and Practical Grammar of the French Language, and Key; revised, &c., by J. C. Tarver. 31st ed. 12mo. Lond., 1866. K 11 V 38

LEVY (DR. M. A.) Phönizische Studien. 8vo. Breslau, 1856–70. K 13 S 20

Phönizisches Wörterbuch. 8vo. Breslau, 1864. K 13 S 20

LEWARD (FRANK). Memorials; edited by Charles [Augustin] Bampton. 8vo. Lond., 1884. C 4 R 13

LEWES (GEORGE HENRY). Aristotle: a Chapter from the History of Science, including Analyses of Aristotle's Scientific Writings; with Life. 8vo. Lond., 1864. A 17 V 7

Comte's Philosophy of the Sciences; being an exposition of the Principles of the Cours de Philosophie Positive of Auguste Comte. 8vo. Lond., 1875. G 16 P 18

Female Characters of Goethe. [*See* KAULBACK, W.]

History of Philosophy, from Thales to Comte. 3rd ed. 2 vols. 8vo. Lond., 1867. G 3 S 5, 6

Life and Works of Goethe; with Sketches of his Age and Contemporaries. 2 vols. 8vo. Lond., 1855. C 7 R 4, 5

Life of Goethe. 2nd ed. 8vo. Lond., 1864. C 7 R 6

On Actors and the Art of Acting. 8vo. Lond., 1875. C 4 R 1

Physiology of Common Life. 2 vols. 8vo. Edinburgh, 1859–60. A 12 Q 26, 27

LEWES (GEORGE HENRY)—*continued.*

Problems of Life and Mind. 1st–3rd series. 5 vols. 8vo. Lond., 1874–79. G 3 S 7–11

Series 1, Vols. 1, 2. Foundation of a Creed.

Series 2. Physical Basis of the Mind.

Series 3, Problem 1. Study of Psychology. Problem 2. Mind as a Function of the Organism. Problem 3. The Sphere of Sense and Logic of Feeling. Problem 4. The Sphere of Intellect and Logic of Signs.

Seaside Studies at Ilfracombe, Tenby, the Scilly Isles, and Jersey. 8vo. Lond., 1858. A 14 S 48

Study of Psychology; its Object, Scope, and Method. 8vo. Lond., 1879. G 3 S 12

LEWIN (JOHN WILLIAM), A.L.S. Birds of New South Wales. 4to. Sydney, 1813. MA 2 P 6 †

Naturae History of the Birds of New South Wales, collectd, engraved, and faithfully painted after Nature. Fol. Lond., 1822. A 1 R 16 ‡

LEWIN (THOMAS, AND FREDERICK ALBERT). Practical Treatise on the Law of Trusts. 6th ed. Roy. 8vo. Lond., 1875. F 8 T 2

LEWIN (W.) Birds of Great Britain, systematically arranged, accurately engraved and painted from Nature. (Eng. and Fr.) Roy. 4to. Lond., 1800–1. A 14 V 25–32

LEWINS (WILLIAM). Her Majesty's Mails : an Historical and Descriptive Account of the British Post Office. 8vo. Lond., 1864. F 6 R 4

LEWIS (CAPT. MERIWETHER), AND CLARKE (CAPT. WILLIAM). Travels of, from St. Louis, by way of the Missouri and Columbia Rivers, to the Pacific Ocean, 1804–6. 8vo. Lond., 1809. D 3 S 30

LEWIS (CAPT. MERIWETHER), CLARKE (CAPT. WILLIAM), SIBLEY (JOHN), AND DUNBAR (WILLIAM). Travels in the Interior Parts of America. 8vo. Lond., 1807. D 3 T 45

LEWIS (C. M.) Voyage from Sydney to Torres Straits. [*See* BROCKETT, W. E.]

LEWIS (MRS. ESTELLE ANNA BLANCHE), "STELLA." The Templars in Cyprus. [*See* WERNER, F. L. Z.]

Sappho : a Tragedy; in Five Acts. 4th ed. 8vo. Lond., 1878. H 9 Q 1

LEWIS (GEORGE). Series of Groups illustrating the Physiognomy, Manners, and Character of the People of France and Germany. 4to. Lond., 1823. D 6 V 36

LEWIS (SIR GEORGE CORNEWALL). Essays on the Administration of Great Britain, from 1783 to 1830. 8vo. Lond., 1864. F 7 P 6

Essay on the Government of Dependencies. 8vo. Lond., 1841. F 7 P 5

Essay on the Influence of Authority in Matters of Opinion. 2nd ed. 8vo. Lond., 1875. G 3 S 4

LEWIS (SIR GEORGE CORNEWALL)—*continued.*
Essay on the Origin and Formation of the Romance Languages ; containing an Examination of M. Raynonard's Theory on the Relation of the Italian, Spanish, Provençal, and French to the Latin. 2nd ed. 8vo. Lond., 1862. K 12 P 15

Inquiry into the Credibility of the Early Roman History. 2 vols. 8vo. Lond., 1855. B 11 T 36, 37

Treatise on the Methods of Observation and Reasoning in Politics. 2 vols. 8vo. Lond., 1852. F 7 P 7, 8

Another copy. 2 vols. 8vo. London, 1852. F 7 P 34

LEWIS (JENKINS). Queen Anne's Son : memoirs of William Henry, Duke of Gloucester ; reprinted from a Tract published in 1789 ; edited by W. J. Loftie. Sq. 12mo. Lond., 1881. C 1 R 30

LEWIS (REV. JOHN), A.M. Life of Dr. John Fisher, Bishop of Rochester, in the Reign of King Henry VIII. 2 vols. 8vo. Lond., 1855. C 6 Q 19, 20

LEWIS (J.), M.A., &c. Reformation Settlement ; being a Summary of the Public Acts and Official Documents relating to the Law and Ritual of the Church of England, from A.D. 1509 to A.D. 1666. 8vo. Cambridge, 1885. G 3 S 3

LEWIS (JOHN DELAWARE), M.A. D. Iunii Iuvenalis Satirae. [*See* JUVENALIS, D. J.]

LEWIS (MRS. L. L.) Fatal Shadows. 12mo. Bristol 1887. MJ 1 P 37

LEWIS (MARY). Inquest held upon the body of. [*See* BEANEY, J. G.] MF 1 Q 1

LEWIS (MATTHEW GREGORY), The Castle Spectre : a Dramatic Romance. (Cumberland's Eng. Theatre.) 12mo. Lond., 1829. H 2 Q 14

Journal of a Residence among the Negroes in the West Indies. (H. and C. Lib.) 12mo. Lond., 1845. J 8 P 8

Journal of a West India Proprietor, kept during a Residence in the Island of Jamaica. 8vo. Lond., 1834. D 3 S 24

Life and Correspondence of : with many Pieces in Prose and Verse. 2 vols. 8vo. Lond., 1839. C 7 S 11, 12

Tales of Wonder ; written and collected. 2 vols. (in 1) roy. 8vo. Lond., 1801. H 7 V 21

LEWIS (PERCIVAL), F.A.S. Historical Inquiries concerning Forests and Forest Laws ; with Topographical Remarks upon the Ancient and Modern State of the New Forest, in the County of Southampton. 4to. Lond., 1881. B 6 V 29

LEWIS (RICHARD). History of the Life-boat and its Work. Illustrated. 8vo. Lond., 1874. F 6 R 1

LEWIS (SAMUEL). Topographical Dictionary of England, Ireland, Scotland, and Wales ; with Historical and Statistical Descriptions and Atlases. 13 vols. 4to. Lond., 1831-51. D 3 R 3-15 †

LEWIS (THERESA). LADY. Extracts of Journals of Miss Berry. [*See* BERRY, MISS M.]

Lives of the Friends and Contemporaries of Lord Chancellor Clarendon, illustrative of Portraits in his Gallery. 3 vols. 8vo. Lond., 1854. C 10 T 18-20

LEWIS (THOMAS). Trial of Mr. Thomas Lewis at the Supreme Court of Van Diemen's Land. 8vo. Hobart, 1854. MF 3 P 6

LEWIS (W. L.) Thebiad of Statius ; translated into English. [*See* CHALMERS, A.]

LEX SALICA : the Ten Texts, with the Glosses and the Lex Emendata. Synoptically edited by J. H. Hessels ; with Notes on the Frankish Words, by Prof. H. Kern. Roy. 4to. Lond., 1880. F 8 Q 16 †

LEXER (DR. MATTHIAS). Kärntisches Wörterbuch ; mit einem Anhange : Weihnacht-Spiele und Lieder aus Kärnten. Imp. 8vo. Leipzig, 1862. K 16 R 14

Mittelhochdeutsches Handwörterbuch. Zugleich als Supplement und alphabetischer Index zum mittelhoch-deutschen Wörterbuche von Benecke-Müller-Zarncke. Mit Nachträge. 3 vols. roy. 8vo. Leipsic, 1872-78. K 14 U 16-18

LEYCESTER (E. M,) Some Account of the Volcanic Group of Santorin or Thera. (Pam. 24.) 8vo. Lond., 1850. MJ 2 Q 12

LEYCESTER (EARL OF). [*See* LEICESTER, ROBERT DUDLEY, EARL OF.]

LEYDEN (JOHN), M.D. Complaynt of Scotland. [*See* COMPLAYNT OF SCOTLAND, THE.]

Poetical Remains of ; with Memoirs of his Life, by the Rev. Jas. Morton. 8vo. Lond., 1819. H 8 U 20

LEYLAND (FRANCIS A.) The Brontë Family ; with special reference to Patrick Branwell Brontë. 2 vols. 8vo. Lond., 1886. C 2 S 4, 5

LEYLAND (J.) Adventures in the Far Interior of South Africa, including a Journey to Lake Ngami, and Rambles in Honduras. 8vo. Lond., 1866. D 1 Q 23

LEYPOLDT (F.) [*See* AMERICAN CATALOGUE.]

L'HERITIER (MARIE JEANNE). Contes des Fées. [*See* CABINET DES FÉES.]

LHOTSKY (DR. JOHN). Another Dose for the Rev. Dr. L-g, of slanderous *Colonist* notoriety, applied by "An Invalid Botany Bay Flagellator" [Dr. J. Lhotsky]. 8vo. Sydney, 1836. Md 2 It 17

Illustrations of the Present State and Future Prospects of the Colony of New South Wales ; by "An Impartial Observer." 8vo. Sydney, 1835. MF 1 Q 4

Another copy. 8vo. Sydney, 1835. MF 3 P 4

Journey from Sydney to the Australian Alps, undertaken in the months of January, February, and March, 1834. 8vo. Sydney, 1835.* MD 2 S 29

LHOYD or LHUYD (HUMPHRY). Historie of Cambria, now called Wales, written in British Language [by Caradoc of Lancarvan]; translated into English by H. Lhoyd; corrected, augmented, and continued, by David Powel, D.D. Sm. 4to. Lond., 1584.   B 4 Q 17

LIANCOURT (C. A. DE GODDES), COUNT DE, AND MANNING (JAMES A.) Pius IX; or, the First Year of his Pontificate. 2 vols. 8vo. Lond., 1847–48. C 3 U 44, 45

LIBRAIRIÉ FRANÇAISE. Catalogue Genérale de la. [*See* LORENZ, O.]

LIBRARY ASSOCIATION OF THE UNITED KINGDOM. The Library Chronicle: a Journal of Librarianship and Bibliography. Vol. 1. Roy. 8vo. Lond., 1884.

Monthly Notes. Vols. 1–4. 8vo. Lond., 1880–83.

Transactions and Proceedings of First Annual Meeting, held at Oxford, October 1, 2, 3, 1878. Imp. 8vo. Lond., 1879.   E 1, 74

Transactions and Proceedings of the Third Annual Meeting, held at Edinburgh, October, 1880. Imp. 8vo. Lond., 1881.   E 1, 74

Transactions and Proceedings of the Fourth and Fifth Annual Meetings of the Library Association of the United Kingdom, held in London, 1881, and at Cambridge, 1882. Imp. 8vo. Lond., 1884.   E 1, 74

Transactions and Proceedings at the Sixth Annual Meeting, held at Liverpool, September, 1883. Imp. 8vo. Lond., 1886.   E 1, 74

Transactions and Proceedings of the Conference of Librarians, held in London, October, 1877. Imp. 8vo. Lond., 1878.   E 1, 74

LIBRARY JOURNAL (THE): Official Organ of the Library Associations of America and of the United Kingdom, chiefly devoted to Library Economy and Bibliography. 9 vols. 4to. New York, 1877–84.   E 2, 75

LIBRARY OF ENTERTAINING KNOWLEDGE. 32 vols. 12mo. Lond., 1832–36.   K 10 R 19–50

  Craik (Prof. G. L.) The New Zealanders.
    Pursuit of Knowledge under Difficulties; illustrated by Anecdotes.
  Ellis (Sir H.) British Musæm: Elgin and Phigaleian Marbles.
    British Museum: the Townley Gallery.
  Hindoos, The.
  Jardine (D.) Criminals Trials.
  Lankester (Dr. E.) Vegetable Substances used for the Food of Man. Vegetable Substances: Materials of Manufactures.
  Long (G.) British Museum: Egyptian Antiquities.
  Malkin (A. T.) Historical Parallels.
  Planché (J. R.) History of British Costumes.
  Paris and its Historical Scenes; with the Revolution of 1830.
  Pompeii. 2 vols.
  Rennie (Rev. J.) Architecture of Birds.
    Insect Miscellanies.
    Insect Transformations.
    The Menageries: Quadrupeds described and drawn.
    Domestic Habits of Birds.
    Faculties of Birds.
    Insect Architecture.
  Traill (Mrs. Catherine P.) Backwoods of Canada; being Letters from the Wife of an Emigrant Officer.
  Vegetable Substances used in the Arts and in Domestic Economy: Timber Trees; Fruits.

LIBRARY OF THE SUPREME COURT OF VICTORIA. [*See* VICTORIA.]

LICENSED SURVEYORS OF N. S. WALES. [*See* NEW SOUTH WALES.]

LICENSING ACT, N. S. WALES. [*See* NEW SOUTH WALES.]

LIDDELL (REV. HENRY GEORGE), D.D. History of Rome, from the Earliest Times to the Establishment of the Empire. 8vo. Lond., 1857.   B 12 P 40

Student's Rome: a History of Rome, from the Earliest Times to the Establishment of the Empire. Illustrated. New ed. 8vo. Lond., 1877.   B 12 P 41

LIDDELL (REV. HENRY GEORGE), D.D., AND SCOTT (ROBERT), D.D. Greek-English Lexicon. 6th ed., revised and augmented. 4to. Oxford, 1869.   K 16 S 25

LIDDON (REV. CANON HENRY PARRY), D.D. An Examination of Canon Liddon's Bampton Lectures; by "A Clergyman of the Church of England." 8vo. Lond., 1871.   G 16 R 22

LIDGATE (J.) [*See* LYDGATE, J.]

LIEBER (PROF. FRANCIS), LL.D. Life and Letters of; edited by Thomas Sergeant Perry. With Portrait. 8vo. Lond., 1882.   C 9 V 27

On Civil Liberty and Self-government. 8vo. Lond., 1853.   F 7 Q 9

Reminiscences of an Intercourse with Mr. [B. G.] Niebuhr, the Historian, during a Residence with him in Rome, in the years 1822–23. 8vo. Philad., 1835.   C 3 T 15

LIEBICH (DR. RICHARD). Die Zigeuner in ihrem Wesen und in ihrer Sprache. Nach eigenen Beobachtungen dargestellt. 8vo. Leipzig, 1863.   K 15 R 31

LIEBIG (JUSTUS VON), BARON, M.D., &c. Animal Chemistry; or, Organic Chemistry in its application to Physiology and Pathology. 8vo. Lond., 1842.   A 5 S 1

Chemistry and Physics in relation to Physiology and Pathology. 8vo. Lond., 1847.   A 5 U 17

Chemistry in its application to Agriculture and Physiology. 8vo. Lond., 1842.   A 5 U 15, 16

Elements of Chemistry. [*See* TURNER, E.]

Family Letters on Chemistry, and its relation to Commerce and Agriculture; edited by John Gardner, M.D. 2 vols. 12mo. Lond., 1843–44.   A 5 R 22, 23

Life Work of, in Experimental and Philosophic Chemistry: a Discourse; by A. W. Hofman. The Faraday Lecture for 1875. 8vo. Lond., 1876.   C 5 V 21

LIEBIG (JUSTUS VON), BARON, AND KOPP (H.) Annual Reports of the Progress of Chemistry, &c., 1847–49. 3 vols. 8vo. Lond., 1849–52.   A 5 T 9–11

LIEBLEIN (J.) Dictionnaire de Noms Hieroglyphiques en ordre Généalogique et Alphabetique; publié d'après les Monuments Egyptiens. 8vo. Ciristiania, 1871.
K 14 T 32

LIEFDE (J. B. DE). The Beggars (Les Gueux): the Founders of the Dutci Republic. Illustrated. 5th ed. 8vo, Lond., 1883. J 4 P 12

LIÉVRE (ÉDOUARD). Art Gems: a series of tıirty ıigı-class Engravings of Pictures, by the most eminent Painters, ancient and modern. Imp. 4to. Lond., 1873. A 7 R 1 †

Les Collections célèbres d'œuvres d'Art, dessinées et gravées d'après les originaux. Fol. Paris, 1866. A 4 S 15 ‡

LIFE IN CHINA: The Porcelain Tower; or, Nine Stories of China; compiled from original sources, by "T.T.T." 8vo. Philad., 1842. J 10 Q 21

LIFE'S WORK AS IT IS; or, the Emigrants' Home in Australia; by "A Colonist." 12mo. Lond., 1867.
MJ 1 U 9

LIGER (LOUIS), AND BASTIEN (J. F.) La Nouvelle Maison Rustique, entièrement refondue par J. F. Bastien. 3 vols. 4to. Paris, 1804. A 1 T 22-24

LIGHT (C. AND R.) Cabinet Furniture: Designs and Catalogue for Cabinet and Upıolstery Furniture. L. 4to. Lond., 1880. A 4 R 1 ‡

LIGHTBODY (F.) Working Drawings and Designs in Arcıitecture [and] Mecıanical Engineering. [See BURN, R. S.]

LIGHTFOOT (HANNAH). The Story of. [See THOMS, W. J.]

LIGHTFOOT (REV. JOHN). Flora Scotica; or, a Systematic Arrangement, in the Linnæan metıod of the Native Plants of Scotland and the Hebrides. 8vo. Lond., 1777. A 4 T 9, 10

LIGHTFOOT (RT. REV. JOSEPH BARBER), D.D., BISHOP OF DURHAM. The Apostolic Fatıers. Part 2. S. Ignatius, S. Polycarp. Revised Texts; witı Introductions, Notes, Dissertations, and Translations. 3 vols. 8vo. Lond., 1885. G 3 S 17-19

LIGHTWOOD (JOHN M.), M.A., &c. Nature of Positive Law. 8vo. Lond., 1883. F 7 P 11

LIUNE (CHARLES JOSEPH), PRINCE DE. Correspondance et Pensées. [See BARRIÈRE, J. F., 20.]

LILIENTHAL (SAMUEL), M.D. Our Home Pıysician Manual of Homœopatıy. (*Bound with Beard's New Cyclopædia of Family Medicine, 2.*) Roy. 8vo. N. York, 1879. MA 2 S 53

LILLEY (W. OSBORNE), F.R.H.S. Bound for Australia on board the *Orient*: a Passenger's Log. 8vo. Lond., 1885. MD 2 Q 3

LILLIE (ARTHUR). Buddha and Early Buddhism. 8vo. Lond., 1881. G 3 S 20

LILLIE (JOHN). Frederick the Great, &c. [*See* BROGLIE, C. J. V. A. DUC DE.]

Memoirs of Count Miot de Melito. [*See* MELITO, A. F. M., COMTE DE.]

Selection from Letters of Madame de Rémusat. [*See* RÉMUSAT, C. E. J.]

LILLIE (REV. JOHN). Lecture upon the Advantages of Science, delivered at the opening of the season of the Van Diemen's Land Mecıanics' Institute. (Pam. 42.) 8vo. Hobart, 1839. MJ 2 R 4

Lecture upon the importance of Classical Learning delivered at the opening of the season of the Van Diemen's Land Mecıanics' Institution. (Pam. 42.) 8vo. Hobart, 1840. MJ 2 R 4

Letter from the Rev. Joın Lillie, in reply to Observations made on the Preliminary Remarks to ıis Introductory Sermon, in a Letter publisıed by the Rev. William Hutcıins. 8vo. Hobart, 1837. MG 1 Q 29

Opening Lecture of the season 1843, on "Knowledge as the Means of correcting Prejudice," delivered at the Lecture Hall of the Van Diemen's Land Mecıanics' Institution. (Pam. 42.) 8vo. Hobart, 1843. MJ 2 R 4

Sermon, preacıed upon ıis Introduction to the Pastoral Care of St. Andrew's Cıurcı; togetıer witı some preliminary Observations in reference to the Ecclesiastical Arrangement for the Australian Colonies. 8vo. Hobart, 1837. MG 1 P 1

LILLO (GEORGE). Arden of Feversham: a Tragedy. [*See* BRIT. DRAMA 2.]

George Barnwell: a Tragedy. (New Eng. Tıeatre.) 12mo. Lond., 1788. H 4 P 21

Anotıer copy. (Bell's Brit. Tıeatre.) 18mo. Lond., 1792. H 2 P 24

Anotıer copy. (Brit. Tıeatre.) 12mo. Lond., 1808. H 1 P 11

Anotıer copy. [*See* BRIT. DRAMA 1.]

Fatal Curiosity: a Tragedy. (Bell's Brit. Tıeatre.) 18mo. Lond., 1796. H 2 P 38

Anotıer copy. (Brit. Tıeatre.) 18mo. Lond., 1808. H 1 P 11

Anotıer copy. [*See* BRIT. DRAMA 2.]

Silvia; or, the Country Burial: an Opera. 12mo. Lond., 1721. H 1 R 26

LILLY (WILLIAM). History of ıis Life and Times, from 1602 to 1681; written by ıimself. 12mo. Lond., 1826. C 1 P 5

LILLY (WILLIAM), AND MORRISON (LIEUT. R. J.) Int   roduction to Astrology; to wıicı are added numerous emendations adapted to the improved state of the Science in the present day; by "Zadkiel." 8vo. Lond., 1835. A 24 U 26

LILLY (W. S.) Chapters in European History. 2 vols. 8vo. Lond., 1886. B 7 R 24, 25

LIMA. True and particular relation of the dreadful Eartıquake, on the 28th October, 1746, wıicı ıappened at Lima, the Capital of Peru. 2nd ed. 8vo. Lond., 1748.   A 9 S 28

LIMBORCH (PROF. PHILIP). History of the Inquisition. 8vo. Lond., 1816.   G 7 P 3

LINCK (JOHANN HEINRICH). De Stellis Marinis Liber Singularis. Fol. Leipsic, 1733.   A 4 U 18 ‡

LINCOLN (ABRAHAM), PRESIDENT U.S. Assassination of Abraıam Lincoln, late President of the United States of America, and the attempted Assassination of William H. Seward, Secretary of State, and Frederick W. Seward, Assistant-Secretary, on the evening of the 14tı of April, 1865. Expressions of condolence and sympatıy inspired by tıese events. 4to. Wası., 1867.   B 1 T Q 1 ‡

Life and Administration of, presenting ıis early History, Political Career, Speecıes, &c. ; by G. W. Bacon. 8vo. Lond., 1865.   C 3 V 23

Life of ; by Isaac H. Arnold. 3rd ed. 8vo. Cıicago. 1885.   C 5 S 19

LINCOLN (F. W.) Inaugural Address to the City Council, Boston. 8vo. Boston, 1858.   F 7 Q 15

LINDE (DR. ANTONIUS VAN DER). Haarlem Legend of the Invention of Printing, by L. J. Coster, critically examined. Roy. 8vo. Lond., 1871.   B 7 V 29

Gescıicıte und Litteratur des Scıacıspiels. 2 vols. (in 1) roy. 8vo. Berlin, 1874.   K 7 V 17

LINDENBROG (ERPOLD). Historia Archiepiscoporvm Bremensivm, a tempore Karoli Magni vsqve ad Karolvm IIII. Sm. 4to. Lvgd. Bat., 1595.   B 2 R 13

Historia Compendiosa ac Svccincta Serenissimorvm Daniæ Regvm : ab incerto auctore conscripta ; nunc vero vsque ad Christianvm IIII. deducta. Sm. 4to. Lvgd. Bat., 1595.   B 2 R 13

LINDEMANN (FRIEDRICH). Corpus Grammaticorum Latinorum Veterum collegit. 4 vols. 4to. Lipsiae, 1831-40.   K 16 R 33–36

LINDLEY (CAPT. AUGUSTUS F.) Adamantia : the Trutı about the Soutı African Diamond Fields 8vo. Lond., 1873.   B 1 P 47

Ti-Ping, Tien-Kwoh : the History of the Ti-Ping Revolution, including a Narrative of the Autıor's Personal Adventures. 2 vols. roy 8vo. Lond., 1866. B 2 Q 44, 45

LINDLEY (PROF. JOHN), PH.D., &c. Descriptive Botany ; or, the art of describing plants correctly in scientific language ; for self-instruction, and the use of scıools. 9th ed. 8vo. Lond. (n.d.)   A 4 T 19

Digitalium Monographia ; Sistens Historiam Botanicam Generis, Tabulis omnium Specierum hactenus cognitarum illustratum. Imp. fol. Lond., 1821.   A 2 P 22 ‡

Elements of Botany, Structural and Pıysiological ; witı a Sketcı of the Artificial Modes of Classification, and Glossary of Tecınical Terms. 8vo. Lond., 1861. A 5 P 25

Pomologia Britannica ; or, Figures and Descriptions of the most important Varieties of Fruit cultivated in Great Britain. 3 vols. roy. 8vo. Lond., 1841. A 1 T 17–19

LINDLEY (PROF. JOHN), PH.D., &c.—*continued.*
Rosarum Monographia ; or, a Botanical History of Roses ; to wıicı is added an Appendix for the use of Cultivators. Plates. Roy. 8vo. Lond., 1820.   A 5 Q 14

Scıool Botany ; or, the Rudiments of Botanical Science. New ed., witı Alterations and Illustrations. 8vo. Lond., 1846.   A 4 T 24

Sketcı of the Vegetation of the Swan River Colony ; togetıer witı an Alpıabetical and Systematical Index to the first twenty-tıree volumes of Edwards' Botanical Register. 8vo. Lond., 1840.   MA 1 U 15

Substances used as Food, illustrated by the Great Exhition. [*See* LOND. INTERNAT. EXHIB., 1851.]

Synopsis of the Britisı Flora ; arranged according to the Natural Orders ; containing Vasculares, or Flowering Plants. 12mo. Lond., 1829.   A 4 P 9

The Vegetable Kingdom ; or, the Structure, Classification, and Uses of Plants. 3rd ed. 8vo. Lond., 1853. A 5 P 26

[*See* MOORE, T.]

LINDLEY (PROF. JOHN), AND MOORE (THOMAS). Treasury of Botany : in two parts. 2 vols. 12mo. Lond., 1866.   K 9 T 11, 12

LINDLEY (JOHN), PH.D., &c., AND HUTTON (W.), F.G.S., &c. Fossil Flora of Great Britain ; or, Figures and Descriptions of the Vegetable Remains found in a fossil state in tıis country. 3 vols. 8vo. Lond., 1831–35.   A 9 S 33–35

LINDO (E. H.) Jewisı Calendar for Sixty-four Years. detailing the New Moons, Festivals, and Fasts. 8vo. Lond., 1838.   E 1, 78

LINDSAY (ALEX. WILLIAM CRAWFORD), LORD. [*See* CRAWFORD AND BALCARRES, A. W. EARL OF.]

LINDSAY (HON. H. H.), AND GUTZLAFF (REV. C.), D.D. Report of Proceedings on a Voyage to the Nortıern Ports of Cıina, in the sıip *Lord Amherst.* 8vo. Lond., 1833.   D 6 Q 3

Anotıer copy. 2nd ed. 8vo. Lond., 1834.   D 6 Q 4

LINDSAY (H. LILL), C.E., &c. Industrial Resources of Victoria ; witı Practical Suggestions on Agriculture, Employment of Labour, Water Supply, &c. 8vo. Melb., 1856.   MF 3 P 8

LINDSAY (JOHN). Notices of Remarkable Greek, Roman, and Anglo-Saxon and otıer Medieval Coins. 4to. Cork, 1860.   A 1 R 15 †

Notices of Remarkable Medieval Coins, mostly unpublished ; witı Engravings. 4to. Cork, 1849. A 1 R 15 †

View of the Coinage of the Heptarcıy, and Anglo-Saxon Coins. 4to. Cork, 1842.   A 1 R 14 †

View of the Coinage of Scotland ; witı copious Tables, Lists, Descriptions. 4to. Cork, 1845. A 1 R 13 †

Supplement to the [above]. 4to. Cork, 1859. A 1 R 13 †

View of the History and Coinage of the Parthians. 4to. Cork, 1852.   A 1 R 15 †

LINDSAY (ROBERT), OF PITTSCOTTE. Chronicles of Scotland, published from several old Manuscripts. 2 vols. (in 1) 8vo. Edinb., 1814. B 32 T 9

LINDSAY (W.) Despatches of. [*See* GOWER, G. G. L., EARL.]

LINDSAY (W. LANDER), M.D., &c. Mind in the Lower Animals in Health and Disease. 2 vols. 8vo. Lond., 1879. G 3 T 3, 4

LINDSAY (WILLIAM SCHAW). History of Merchant Shipping and Ancient Commerce. 4 vols. 8vo. Lond., 1874-76. F 7 P 13-16

LINDSAYS (LIVES OF THE). [*See* CRAWFORD AND BALCARRES, HOUSES OF.]

LINDSEY (G.) Pens and Papier Mâché, Ammunition, Percussion, Percussion-caps and Cartridges, Anchors and Chain Cables. (Brit. Manuf. Indust.) 12mo. Lond., 1876. A 17 S 30

LINDT (J. W.) Photographs of Aboriginal Natives of the Clarence River District, New South Wales. 4to. Grafton, 1874. MA 1 Q 2 †

Picturesque New Guinea; with an Historical Introduction, and Supplementary Chapters on the Manners and Customs of the Papuans. Roy. 8vo. Lond., 1887.* MD 3 V 35

LINGARD (REV. JOHN), D.D. History and Antiquities of the Anglo-Saxon Church. 2 vols. 8vo. Lond., 1858. G 10 Q 14, 15

History of England, from the First Invasion by the Romans. 14 vols. 8vo. Lond., 1823-31. B 5 Q 1-14

History of England, from the First Invasion by the Romans to the Accession of William and Mary in 1688. With Portraits. 10 vols. 8vo. Lond., 1883· B 6 Q 15-24

LINGUET (SIMON NICOLAS HENRI). Memoires de. [*See* BARRIÈRE, J. F., 26.]

LINKLATER (FREDERICK HARVIE-). Matrimonial Causes Act. [*See* NEW SOUTH WALES—STATUTES.]

Statutes relating to Equity and Lunacy; with the Rules of Court from 4th July, 1863, to 30th November, 1874, and the Supreme Court Reports. Roy. 8vo. Sydney, 1879. MF 1 S 10

LINNÆAN SOCIETY OF NEW YORK. Transactions. Vols. 1, 2. Imp. 8vo. N. York, 1882-84. E 1, 70

LINNÆAN SOCIETY OF NEW SOUTH WALES. Proceedings of. Vols. 1-10. 8vo. Sydney, 1877-86. ME 2 P

LINNÆAN SOCIETY OF LONDON. Journal of Proceedings of. Botany. Vols. 1-21. Zoology. Vols. 1-19. 38 vols. (in 30) 8vo. Lond., 1857-87. E 1, 68

Transactions of. Vols. 1-32, and General Index to vols. 1-25. 4to. Lond., 1791-1887. E 2, 67

LINNÆUS, OR LINNE (CARL VON). The Animal Kingdom; or, Zoological System. Class 1. Mammalia. Class 2. Birds. Translation by Prof. J. F. Gmelin. 4to. Lond., 1792. A 15 T 6

Bibliotheca Botanica. 8vo. Amsterd., 1751. A 4 T 18

A General View of the Writings of. [*See* PULTENEY, R.]

Supplementum Plantarum Systematis Vegetabilium. 8vo. Brunsvigæ, 1781. A 4 Q 4

Systema Naturæ. 5th ed. Tom. 1, pars 11. 8vo. Holmiæ, 1767. A 14 S 12

Sexual System of. [*See* THORNTON, R. J.]

LINSCHOTEN (JAN HUGO VAN). Iolm Hvighen van Linschoten: his Discours of Voyages into ye Easte and West Indies; deuided in four Bookes. Fol. Lond., 1598. D 10 U 25

LINTERN (WILLIAM), C.E. The Mineral Surveyor and Valuer's Complete Guide; comprising a Treatise on improved Mining Surveying, with new Traverse Tables, and F. Thoman's Interest and Logarithmic Tables. 8vo. Lond., 1872. A 6 R 35

Another copy. (Weale.) 12mo. Lond.,1877. A 17 P 54

LINTON (WILLIAM JAMES). History of Wood-engraving in America. 4to. Lond., 1882. A 1 P 1 †

Wood-engraving: a Manual of Instruction. 8vo. Lond., 1884. A 7 S 12

LINTON (WILLIAM JAMES), AND STODDARD (RICHARD HENRY). English Verse. 5 vols. 8vo. Lond., 1884. H 7 Q 32-36

LINTOT (CATHERINE CAILLEAU, COMTESSE DE). Contes. [*See* CABINET DES FÉES, 32.]

LIOT (CAPT. W. B.) Panama, Nicaragua, and Tehuantepec; or, Considerations upon the Question of Communication between the Atlantic and Pacific Oceans. 8vo. Lond., 1849. F 7 P 12

LIPSCOMB (GEORGE), M.D. History and Antiquities of the County of Buckingham. 4 vols. roy. 4to. Lond., 1847. B 10 Q 1-4 †

LIPSIUS (H.) [*See* LEIPZIGER STUDIEN.]

LIPSIUS (JUSTUS). De Recta Pronunciatione Latinæ Linguæ Dialogus. 12mo. Lugd.-Bat., 1586. K 11 S 45

[*See* PLINIUS SECUNDUS, C.]

LISIANSKY (CAPT. UREY). Voyage round the World, in the years 1803-6, in the ship *Neva*. 4to. Lond., 1814. D 9 V 26

LISSAGARAY (P.) History of the Commune of 1871; translated by Eleanor Marx Aveling. 8vo. Lond., 1886. B 8 U 35

LISSIGNOL (E.) [*See* MUELLER, SIR F., BARON VON.]

LIST (FRIEDRICH). National System of Political Economy. Translated from the original German, by Sampson S. Lloyd, M.P. 8vo. Lond., 1885.   F 8 S 10

Extracts from List's National System of Political Economy. [*See* COLE, G. W.]

LISTER (MARTIN), M.D. Account of Paris at the close of the 17th Century, now revised, and a Sketch of the Life of the Author, by George Henning, M.D. 8vo. Lond., 1823.   D 6 T 30

[*See* APICIUS, C.]

LISTER (T. H.) Life and Administration of Edward, first Earl of Clarendon ; with original Correspondence and authentic Papers never before published. 3 vols. 8vo. Lond., 1837–38.   C 10 T 12–14

LISZT (ABBÉ FRANZ), Artist and Man ; by L. Ramann. Translated from the German, by Miss E. Cowdery. 2 vols. 8vo. Lond., 1882.   C 3 Q 29, 30

The Abbé Liszt : the Story of his Life ; by Raphaël Ledos de Beaufort. 8vo. Lond., 1886.   C 3 Q 31

[Life of] ; by T. C. Martin. 18mo. Lond., 1886. C 2 Q 26

LITERARISCHES CENTRALBLATT für Deutschland. Herausgegeben von Friedrich Zarncke. 14 vols. 4to. Leipzig, 1871–84.   E 2, 78

LITERARY AND EDUCATIONAL YEAR-BOOK (THE), for 1860. 8vo. Lond., 1860.   K 7 R 24

LITERARY GAZETTE (THE): a Weekly Journal of Literature, &c., 1838–62. 28 vols. 4to. Lond., 1838–62.   E 2, 73

LITERARY NEWS (THE): a Review and Magazine of Fact and Fiction, the Arts, Sciences, and Belles Lettres. 4to. Sydney, 1837–38.   ME 10 P 4 †

LITHGOW (R. A. DOUGLAS), LL.D., &c. Life of John Critchley Prince. 8vo. Manchester, 1880. C 3 U 36

LITTING (GEORGE), M.A., &c. Life of General Lee. [*See* CHILDE, E. L.]

LITTLE (REV. CHARLES E.) Historical Lights. Six Thousand Quotations from Standard Histories and Biographies. 2nd ed. Roy. 8vo. New York, 1886.   K 11 Q 1

LITTLE (GEORGE). Life on the Ocean ; or, Twenty Years at Sea. 8vo. Aberdeen, 1847.   D 20 Q 7

LITTLE (REV. HENRY W.) Madagascar : its History and People. With a Map. 8vo. Edinb., 1884.   B 1 P 62

LITTLE MASTERS (THE); by W. B. Scott. (Great Artists.) 8vo. Lond., 1879.   C 3 T 42

LITTLEJOHN (W. H.) The Coming Conflict ; or, the United States to become a Persecuting Power. 12mo. Battle Creek, Mich., 1883.   G 7 Q 7

3 L

LITTRÉ (E.) Dictionnaire de la Langue Française : ce Supplément est suivi d'un Dictionnaire Etymologique de tous les Mots d'origine Orientale, par Marcel Devic. 3 vols. (in 5) imp. 4to. Paris, 1863–84.   K 4 S 10–14 †

Histoire de la Langue Française : Etudes sur les Origines, l'Etymologie, la Grammaire, les Dialectes, la Versification, et les Lettres au Moyen Age. 7ᵉ éd. 2 vols. 12mo. Paris, 1878.   K 11 V 48, 49

LIVEING (ROBERT), A.M., &c. Hand-book on the Diagnosis of Skin Diseases. 12mo. Lond., 1878. A 12 P 32

LIVERPOOL (CHARLES), EARL OF. Treatise on the Coins of the Realm ; in a Letter to the King. 8vo. Lond., 1880.   F 6 V 12

LIVERPOOL (ROBERT BANKS), K.G., SECOND EARL OF. Life and Administration of ; compiled from original documents, by Chas. Duke Yonge. 3 vols. 8vo. Lond., 1868.   C 7 S 4–6

LIVERPOOL AND LONDON FIRE AND LIFE INSURANCE COMPANY. Tables. (Pam. 44.) Sydney, 1881.   MJ 2 R 6

LIVERPOOL FREE PUBLIC LIBRARY. Catalogue of the Reference Department. Part 2 ; containing the Books received from Jan., 1871, to Dec., 1880 ; compiled by P. Cowell. 4to. Liverpool, 1881.   K 9 P 19 †

Ceremonies connected with the opening of the Building for a Free Public Library and Museum, presented by William Brown, Esq., to the Town of Liverpool. (Pam. 34.) 8vo. Liverpool, 1861.   J 12 U 26

LIVERPOOL MERCHANT, A.. [*See* AUSTRALIA.]

LIVERSIDGE (PROF. ARCHIBALD), M.A., F.C.S., &c. Action of Sea-water upon Cast-iron. (Pam. 23.) Sydney, 1880.   MJ 2 R 14

Alkaloid from Piturie. (Pam. 23.) 8vo. Sydney, 1880.   MJ 2 R 14

Dendritic Spots on Paper. (Pam. 34.) 8vo. Lond., 1872.   J 12 U 26

Deniliquin or Barratta Meteorite. (Pam. 23.) 8vo. Sydney, 1873.   MJ 2 R 14

Diamond Fields [of N.S.W.] [*See* NEW SOUTH WALES— MINES DEPARTMENT.]

Disease in the Sugar Cane, Queensland. (Pam. Cj.) 12mo. Sydney (n.d.)   MA 2 V 7

Another copy. (Pam. 27.) 8vo. Sydney(n.d.) MJ 2 R 16

International Congress of Geologists, Paris, 1878. (Pam. Cn.) 8vo. Sydney, 1879.   MA 2 V 14

Another copy.   MJ 2 R 14

Iron and Coal Deposits at Wallerawang, New South Wales. (Pam. 23.) 8vo. Sydney, 1874.   MJ 2 R 24

Minerals of New South Wales. Papers by. [*See* WOOD, H.]

Minerals of New South Wales. 2nd ed. 4to. Sydney, 1882.*   MA 2 R 7

Note upon Krytophanic Acid. (Pam. Cc.) Camb., 1872.   MA 2 S 15

LIVERSIDGE (PROF. ARCHIBALD), M.A., F.C.S., &c.—*ctd.*
Notes upon some Minerals from New Caledonia. (Pam.
27.) 8vo. Sydney, 1880.   MJ 2 R 16
On a Remarkable Example of Contorted Slate. (Pam.
23.) 8vo. Sydney, 1876.   MJ 2 R 14
On some New South Wales Minerals. (Pam. 23.) 8vo.
Sydney, 1880.   MJ 2 R 14
On the Composition of some Coral Limestones, &c., from the
South Sea Islands. (Pam. 27.) Sydney, 1880. MJ 2 R 16
On the Composition of some Wood enclosed in Basalt.
(Pam. 23.) 8vo. Sydney, 1880.   MJ 2 R 14
On the Occurrence of Chalk in the New Britain Group.
(Pam. 23.) 8vo. Sydney, 1877.   MJ 2 R 14
Report upon certain Museums for Technology, Science, and
Art; also upon Scientific, Professional, and Technical
Instruction, and Systems of Evening Classes in Great
Britain and the Continent of Europe. Fol. Sydney,
1880.   ME
Upon the Composition of some New South Wales Coals.
(Pam. 23.) 8vo. Sydney, 1880.   MJ 2 R 14
Waters from Hot Springs, New Britain and Fiji. (Pam.
27.) 8vo. Sydney, 1880.   MJ 2 R 16
[*See* ROYAL SOCIETY OF N.S. WALES.]

LIVINGSTONE (REV. DAVID), LL.D., &c. Dr. Living-
ston: his Life and Adventures in the Interior of South
Africa; by H. G. Adams. Illustrated. 8vo. Lond.,
1857.   C 3 P 19
How I found Livingstone. [*See* STANLEY, H. M.]
Last Journals of David Livingstone in Central Africa, from
1865 to his death; by H. Waller, F.R.G.S. 2 vols. 8vo.
Lond., 1874.   D 1 W 9, 10
Missionary Travels and Researches in South Africa; in-
cluding a Sketch of Sixteen Years' Residence in the
Interior of Africa, &c. 8vo. Lond., 1857.   D 1 V 22
Personal Life of; chiefly from his unpublished Journals and
Correspondence in the possession of his Family, by William
Garden Blaikie, D.D., &c. 8vo. Lond., 1880.   C 7 S 10
Search for Dr. Livingstone. [*See* FAULKNER, H.]
Sketches of the Rev. Dr. Livingstone's Missionary Journeys
and Discoveries in Central South Africa. (Pam. 25.)
8vo. Lond., 1857.   MJ 2 Q 13
Travels of. [*See* COCHRANE, R.]

LIVINGSTONE (REV. DAVID AND CHARLES). Narrative
of an Expedition to the Zambesi and its Tributaries; and
the Discovery of the Lakes Shirwa and Nyassa, 1858-64.
illustrated. 8vo. Lond., 1865.   D 2 S 4

LIVIUS (TITUS). Historiarum Libri qui supersunt, ex
Editione G. A. Ruperti, cum Supplementis Notis et
Interpretatione in usum Delphini; curante A. J. Valpy,
A.M. 26 vols. 8vo. Lond., 1828.   J 13 Q 22–R 5
History of Rome; literally translated, with Notes and
Illustrations, by D. Spillan and Cyrus Edmonds; with
the Epitomes and Fragments of the Lost Books translated
by William Davitte, A.M. 4 vols. 8vo. Lond., 1873-77.
                                                 B 12 P 13-16

LIVIUS (TITUS)—*continued.*
Livy; Books 21-25: the Second Punic War; translated
into English; with Notes, by Alfred John Church, M.A.,
and William Jackson Brodribb, M.A. With Maps. 8vo.
Lond., 1883.   B 12 Q 38
Livy; translated by George Baker, A.M. (Fam. Class.
Lib.) 7 vols. 18mo. Lond., 1833-34.   J 15 P 22–28
[*See* SCRIPTORES ROMANI.]

LIZARS (JOHN), F.R.S.E. System of Anatomical Plates
of the Human Body; with Descriptions, and Physiological, Pathological, and Surgical Observations. Fol.
Edinb. (n.d.)   Libr.

LLANOVER (RT. HON. AUGUSTA HALL), LADY. Autobiography and Correspondence of Mary Granville, Mrs.
Delany. [*See* DELANY, MRS.]

LLOYD (CHARLES). Tragedies of Alfieri. [*See* ALFIERI, V.]

LLOYD (E.) Reminiscences of a Sojourn in South Australia; by "A Squatter." 12mo. Lond., 1849. MD 3 P 28
Visit to the Antipodes; with some Reminiscences of a
Sojourn in Australia; by "A Squatter." 12mo. Lond.,
1846.   MD 3 P 27

LLOYD (E. M.) Vauban, Montalembert, Carnot—Engineer Studies. With Portraits. 8vo. Lond., 1887. A 6 S 14

LLOYD (FREDERICK JAMES), F.C.S. The Science of
Agriculture. 8vo. Lond., 1884.   A 1 S 17

LLOYD (MRS. G. A.), "SILVERLEAF." Wheel of Life: a
Domestic Tale of Life in Australia. 8vo. Sydney,
1880.*   MJ 1 R 17

LLOYD (GEORGE THOMAS). Thirty-three Years in Tasmania and Victoria; being the actual experience of the
Author. 8vo. Lond., 1862.*   MD 4 T 3

LLOYD (H. EVANS). Travels in India. [*See* ORLICH,
CAPT. L. VON.]

LLOYD (HUMPHREY), D.D. Treatise on Magnetism,
General and Terrestrial. 8vo. Lond., 1874.   A 5 T 34

LLOYD (ROBERT). Life and Poems of. [*See* CHALMERS,
A., *and* JOHNSON, S.]

LLOYD (WILLIAM WATKISS). Age of Pericles: a History
of the Politics and Arts of Greece. 2 vols. 8vo. Lond.,
1875.   B 9 T 1, 2

LLOYD, LOVELL, & CO. Photographic Advertising
Directory and Pastime Album. Ob. 4to. Sydney, 1886.*
                                                 ME 9 Q 24 †

LLOYD'S REGISTER of British and Foreign Shipping
1843-44, 1848-49. 2 vols. 8vo. Lond., 1844-49.
                                                 E 1, 78

LOADER (THOMAS). Family Immigration for Victoria; or, Every Man his own Immigration Agent. 8vo. Melh., 1861. MF 1 Q 2

LOBO (FATHER JEROME). Voyage to Abyssinia; containing the History, Natural, Civil and Ecclesiastical, of that remote and unfrequented country. Translated by Samuel Johnson, LL.D. Lond., 1789. D 2 T 4

LOBSCHEID (REV. W.) Chinese and English Dictionary. Imp. 8vo. Hongkong, 1871. K 5 S 17 †
English and Chinese Dictionary, with the Punti and Mandarin Pronunciation. 4 vols. fol. Honkong, 1866–69. K 5 S 13–16 †

LOCH (CAPT. GRANVILLE G.) Closing Events of the Campaign in China. The operations in the Yang-Tze-Kiang; and Treaty of Nanking. 8vo. Lond., 1843. B 2 P 28

LOCH (J.) Memoir of George Granville, late Duke of Sutherland. Roy. 4to. Lond., 1834. C 4 P 13

LOCK (ALFRED G.), F.R.G.S. Gold: its Occurrence and Extraction. With Maps and Engravings. Roy. 8vo. Lond., 1882. A 9 V 10

LOCK (ALFRED G. AND CHARLES G.) Practical Treatise on the Manufacture of Sulphuric Acid. Illustrated. Imp. 8vo. Lond., 1879. A 5 U 2

LOCK (CHARLES G. WARNFORD). Home of the Eddas. 8vo. Lond., 1879. D 7 S 15
Tobacco-growing and Manufacture. 8vo. Lond., 1886. A 1 P 27
Workshop Receipts. 3rd series. 12mo. Lond., 1884. A 25 P 4

LOCK (C. G. W.), F.L.S., &c., WIGNER (G. W.), AND HARLAND (R. H.), F.C.S., &c. Sugar-growing and Refining. Illustrated. 8vo. Lond., 1882. A 1 R 9

LOCKE (JOHN). [A Biography]; by Prof. T. Fowler. (Eng. Men of Letts.) 8vo. Lond., 1880. C 1 U 24
Lectures on Locke; or, the Principles of Logic. 8vo. Lond., 1840. G 15 R 4
Life of; with Extracts from his Correspondence, Journals, and Common-place Books, by Lord King. 2 vols. 8vo. Lond., 1830. C 6 R 7, 8
Selections from Locke's Essay on the Human Understanding; with Introduction and Notes, by S. H. Emmens. (Weale.) 12mo. Lond., 1866. G 8 Q 20
Works of John Locke. 12th ed. 9 vols. 8vo. Lond., 1824. J 9 T 7–15

LOCKER (ARTHUR). Stephen Scudamore the Younger; or, the Fifteen-Year-Olds. 8vo. Lond., 1871. MJ 1 Q 24

LOCKER (EDWARD HAWKE), F.R.S., &c. Memoirs of Celebrated Naval Commanders, illustrated by Engravings from original Pictures in the Naval Gallery of Greenwich Hospital. 4to. Lond., 1832. C 1 W 21

LOCKHART (CHARLES), B.A. History of the Isle of Wight. [See WOODWARD, B. B.]

LOCKHART (GEORGE). The Lockhart Papers; containing Memoirs and Commentaries upon the Affairs of, &c., 1702–45. 4to. Lond., 1817. B 17 Q 10 11 ‡

LOCKHART (JOHN GIBSON). Ancient Spanish Ballads, Historical and Romantic; translated, with Notes. 4to. Lond., 1841. H 6 V 13
History of Napoleon Buonaparte. (Fam. Lib.) 2 vols. 12mo. Lond., 1830. K 10 P 1, 2
Life of Robert Burns. (Const. Misc.) 3rd ed. 18mo. Edinb., 1830. K 10 Q 11
Life of Robert Burns. Enlarged edition, revised, &c., by William Scott Douglas. 8vo. Lond., 1882. C 1 S 14
Memoirs of the Life of Sir Walter Scott, Bart. 7 vols. 8vo. Lond., 1837. C 4 Q 38–44
Memoirs of Sir Walter Scott. 10 vols. 12mo. Edinb., 1869. J 1 R 13–22
Peter's Letters to his Kinsfolk. 2nd ed. 3 vols. 8vo. Edinb., 1819. C 9 P 17–19

LOCKHART (JOHN INGRAM), Memoirs of the Conquistador, Bernal Diaz del Castillo. [See DIAZ DEL CASTILLO, B.]

LOCKROY (EDOUARD.) [See SIMON, E. E.]

LOCKWOOD & CO. Builder's and Contractor's Price-book; with which is incorporated G. R. Burnell's Price-books for 1876; the whole revised and edited by F. T. W. Miller. (Weale.) 8vo. Lond., 1876. A 17 Q 11
Another copy. (Weale.) 8vo. Lond., 1883. A 17 Q 78
Another copy. (Weale.) 8vo. Lond., 1884. A 17 Q 71
Another copy. (Weale.) 8vo. Lond., 1886. A 17 R 9

LOCKYER (JOSEPH NORMAN). Applications of Physical Forces. [See GUILLEMIN, A.]
Contributions to Solar Physics. 8vo. Lond., 1874. A 3 T 27
Elementary Lessons in Astronomy. 12mo. Lond., 1873. A 3 R 22
On recent Discoveries in Solar Physics by means of the Spectroscope. (Pam. Cb.) 8vo. Lond., 1873. A 16 U 25
The Spectroscope and its Applications; with coloured Plate and Illustrations. 2nd ed. (Nature Series.) 8vo. Lond., 1873. A 5 S 22

LOCKYER (MRS. JOSEPH NORMAN). Applications of Physical Forces. [See GUILLEMIN, A.]
The Forces of Nature. [See GUILLEMIN, A.]

LOCKYER (JOSEPH NORMAN), F.R.S., AND SEABROKE (G. M.), F.R.A.S. Spectroscopic Observations of the Sun. (Roy. Soc. Pubs., 2.) 4to. Lond., 1876. A 11 P 3 †

LOCKYER (J. NORMAN), F.R.S., AND SCHUSTER (ARTHUR), PH.D., &c. Report on the Total Solar Eclipse of April 6, 1875. (Roy. Soc. Pubs., 5.) 4to. Lond., 1878. A 11 P 6 †

LOCOCK (FRANCES). The Fortunate Isles. [*See* PÉGOT-OGIER, E.]

LODGE (EDMUND), F.S.A. Facsimiles of Original Drawings by Hans Holbein; with Biographical Notices. [*See* CHAMBERLAINE, J.]

Illustrations of British History, Biography, and Manners, in the Reigns of Henry VIII, Edward VI, Mary, Elizabeth, and James I. 2nd ed. 3 vols. 8vo. Lond., 1838.   B 5 R 43–45

Peerage and Baronetage of the British Empire, as at present existing. 41st ed. Roy. 8vo. Lond., 1872.   E

Another copy. 54th ed. Roy. 8vo. Lond., 1885.   E

Another copy. 55th ed. Roy. 8vo. Lond., 1886.   E

Another copy. 56th ed. Roy. 8vo. Lond., 1887.   E

Portraits of Illustrious Personages of Great Britain; with Biographical and Historical Memoirs of their Lives and Actions. 12 vols. imp. 8vo. Lond., 1823–34.
                                                 C 3 W 30–41

LODGE (HENRY CABOT), PH.D. Short History of the English Colonies in America. 8vo. New York, 1881.
                                                       B 1 S 17

LODGE (RICHARD), M.A. Student's History of Modern Europe. 8vo. Lond., 1885.   B 7 S 31

LOEBE (DR. J.) Grammatik der Gothischen Sprache. [*See* GABELENTZ, DR. H. C. VON DER.]

LOEBELL (PROF.) Essay on the Character of Niebuhr as an Historian. [*See* NIEBUHR, B. G.]

LOEWY (B.), F.R.A.S. Introduction to Experimental Physics, Theoretical and Practical. [*See* WEINHOLD. A. F.]

LOFFT (CAPEL). Self-formation; or, the History of an Individual Mind; by "A Fellow of a College." 2 vols. 8vo. Lond., 1837.   J 3 R 21, 22

LOFTIE (REV. WILLIAM JOHN), B.A., &c. Historic Towns of London. 12mo. Lond., 1887.   B 3 Q 11

History of London; with Maps, Illustrations, and Supplement. 3 vols. 8vo. Lond., 1883–84.   B 4 R 1–3

Illustrated Guide of the Orient Line of Steamers between England and Australia. [*See* ORIENT LINE GUIDE.]

Queen Anne's Son; Memoir of William Henry, Duke of Gloucester. [*See* LEWIS, J.]

Windsor: a Description of the Castle, Park, Town, and Neighbourhood. Fol. Lond., 1886.   B 14 S 5 ‡

LOFTI'S (COMM. ALFRED J.), F.R.G.S. Notes of a Journey across the Isthmus of Kra, made with the French Government Survey Expedition, 1883. 8vo. Singapore, 1883.   D 6 S 20

LOFTUS (WILLIAM KENNETT), F.G.S. Travels and Researches in Chaldæa and Susiana; with an Account of Excavations at Warka, the "Erech" of Nimrod, and Shúsh, "Shushan the Palace" of Esther, in 1849–52. 8vo. Lond., 1857.   D 4 U 36

LOFTUS (W. R.) The Brewer: a familiar Treatise on the Art of Brewing, with special Directions for the Manufacture of Pale Ale and Bitter Beer, and the use of Sugar by Brewers. 8vo. Lond., 1857.   A 11 Q 25

LOGAN (JAMES). Clans of the Scottish Highlands. [*See* MAC IAN, R. R.]

LOGAN (CAPT. J.) Treatise of Honour. [*See* GUILLIM, J.]

LOGAN (REV. JOHN), F.R.S. Life and Poems of. [*See* BRITISH POETS, *and* CHALMERS, A.]

Sermons; with a Detail of the Service of a Communion Sunday, according to the usage of the Church of Scotland. 2 vols. 8vo. Edinb., 1822.   G 3 Q 24, 25

LOGAN (SIR WILLIAM E.), KNT., LL.D., &c. Life of; chiefly compiled from his Letters, Journals, and Reports, by B. J. Harrington, B.A. 8vo. Lond., 1883. C 7 S 15

LOGEROT (A.) Nouveau Plan de Paris, le coup d'œil. [Sheet,] Sm. fol. Paris. (n.d.)   D 33 Q 8 ‡

LOGIC. [*See* MELBOURNE RAILWAY TERMINUS.

LOKMAN (—.) Contes et Fables. [*See* CABINET DES FÉES, 17, 18.]

LOLME (J. L. DE). [*See* DE LOLME, J. L.]

LOMBARD (ALEXANDRE). Les Traditions relatives au Principe du Mal figuré par le Serpent, et l'École des Prophètes de Chaldée: Lettre à M. le Capitaine F. W. H. Petrie, F.R.S.L. (Pam. Bs.) 8vo. Lond., 1879. M G 1 Q 34

LOMBARDUS (PETRUS). Opera omnia. [*See* MIGNE, J. P., SERIES LATINA, 191, 192.]

LOMENIE (LOUIS DE). Beaumarchais and his Times: Sketches of French Society in the 18th Century, from unpublished Documents. 4 vols. 8vo. Lond., 1856.
                                                 C 3 Q 9–12

LOMMEL (DR. EUGENE). Nature of Light; with a General Account of Physical Optics. 8vo. Lond., 1875. A 5 R 38

LONDON. Analytical Index to the Series of Records known as the Remembrancia, preserved among the Archives of the City of London, A.D. 1579–1664. Roy. 8vo. Lond., 1878.   B 5 V 2

Chronicle of London, 1089–1483; edited by Sir H. Nicolas. 4to. Lond., 1827.   B 15 Q 3 ‡

Collection of Views of Old London and its Environs. [Printed for F. West.] Obl. 4to. Lond. (n.d.)
                                                     D 34 P 19 ‡

Commercial Directory, for 1837. Pigot. Roy. 8vo. Lond., 1837.   E 1, 78

Essays on the Street Re-alignment, Reconstruction, and Sanitation of Central London, and on the re-housing the Poorer Classes: Prizes offered by W. Westgarth. 8vo. Lond., 1886.   A 6 T 21

LONDON—*continued.*

Historical Charters and Constitutional Documents of the City of London; with an Introduction and Notes, by "An Antiquary." [Walter de Gray Birch, F.S.A.] 4to. Lond., 1884.   B 5 V 9

List of Scientific and other Periodicals, &c., in the Free Public Library, Office of the Commissioners of Patents. (Pam. B.) Fol. Lond., 1862.   MJ 2 U 2

The London Catalogue of Periodicals, Newspapers, and Transactions of various Societies. (Pam. C.) Imp. 8vo. Lond., 1863.   MJ 2 S 1

London Directory of 1677: the oldest printed List of the Merchants and Bankers of London. Reprinted from the exceedingly rare Original; with an Introduction, pointing out some of the Merchants of the Period. Sq. 12mo. Lond., 1878.   E 1, 78

London Directory for 1838. Roy. 8vo. Lond., 1838.   E 1, 78

London's Roll of Fame; being Complimentary Votes and Addresses from the City of London, A.D. 1757–1884. 4to. Lond., 1884.   B 2 U 30

The Metropolis Local Management Act, 1862. New ed. (Weale.) 12mo. Lond., 1868.   F 5 S 19

The Metropolis Local Management Amendment Act, 1862. New ed. (Weale.) 12mo. Lond., 1868.   F 5 S 19

Old London: Papers read at the London Congress, July, 1866. (Archæological Institute of Great Britain and Ireland.) 8vo. Lond., 1867.   B 7 P 21

Post Office Directory. [*See* KELLY & Co.]

Royal Charter of Confirmation, granted by Charles II to the City of London; translated into English, by S. G. Gent. 12mo. Lond., 1680.   F 5 Q 31

Trve Report of the Burnyng of the Steple and Churche of Poules in London. Imprynted at London, at the west ende of Paules Church, at the Sygne of the Hedghogge, by Wyllyam Seres. Anno 1561. (*Facsimile Reprint.*) 12mo. Lond., 1885.   B 3 P 30

LONDON (B.), M.D. Medical Treatise on the Waters of Carlsbad. [*See* MERRYLEES, J.]

LONDON ANTIQUARY, A. [*See* HOTTEN, J. C,]

LONDON CATALOGUE OF BOOKS, with their Sizes and Prices, 1814. Printed for W. Bent, Paternoster Row. 8vo. Lond., 1816.   Libr.

London Catalogue of Books, 1815–51. 8vo. Lond., 1851.*   Libr.

[*See* LOW, SAMPSON, & Co.]

LONDON CITY MISSION. Twenty-seventh Annual Report, 1862. 8vo. Lond., 1862.   G 8 R 25

What is the London City Mission? 8vo. Lond., 1862.   G 8 R 25

LONDON ELECTRICAL SOCIETY. Proceedings of, 1841–42. 8vo. Lond., 1842.   A 5 U 20

Transactions and Proceedings of, 1837–40. Roy. 4to. Lond., 1841.   A 2 Q 15 †

LONDON EVENING POST (THE). 4 vols. roy. 4to. Lond., 1734–40.   E 1, 91

LONDON GAZETTE (THE). Index to the Orders in Council, Proclamations, &c. [*See* PULLING, A.]

LONDON INSTITUTION (THE). Catalogue of the Library, and Supplement. 8vo. Lond., 1813–30. K 8 Q 20

Catalogue of the Library, systematically classed. 4 vols. roy. 8vo. Lond., 1835–53.   K 8 Q 21–24

Charter: the Act of Parliament for providing an increase of Annual Income, and the Bye-laws. 8vo. Lond., 1841.   F 4 R 17

LONDON INTERNATIONAL EXHIBITION OF 1851. Great Exhibition of the Works of Industry of all Nations: Reports of the Juries on the subjects in the thirty Classes into which the Exhibition was divided. 3 vols. fol. Lond., 1852.   K 27 P 4–6 ‡

Lectures on the Results of the Great Exhibition of 1851, by Rev. W. Whewell, Sir H. T. De La Beche, R. Owen, J. Bell, L. Playfair, Prof. J. Lindley, Prof. E. Solly, Rev. R. Willis, J. Glaisher, H. Hensman, Prof. J. F. Royle, and Capt. Washington. 8vo. Lond., 1852.   A 16 Q 22

Official Catalogue of the Great Exhibition of the Works of Industry of all Nations, 1851. 2nd ed. Sm. 4to. Lond., 1851.   K 7 R 17

Official, Descriptive, and Illustrated Catalogue. 3 vols. imp. 8vo. Lond., 1851.   K 8 Q 7–9

Official, Descriptive, and Illustrated Catalogue of the Great Exhibition. 3 vols. fol. Lond., 1852.   K 27 P 1–3 ‡

LONDON INTERNATIONAL EXHIBITION, 1862. Catalogue of the Natural and Industrial Products of New South Wales, exhibited in the School of Arts by the International Exhibition Commissioners, Sydney, October, 1861. 8vo. Sydney, 1861.*   MK 1 S 42

Catalogue of the Natural and Industrial Products of New South Wales; with a Map and Introductory Account of its Population, Commerce, and General Resources. 4to. Lond., 1862.   MK 1 S 44

Catalogue of Wools for Competition for Messrs. Mort & Co.'s Gold Medal. (Pam. E.) 4to. Sydney, 1862. MJ 2 S 2

Official Catalogue of the Fine Art Department. 8vo. Lond., 1862.   K 7 R 23

Official Catalogue of the Industrial Department. 3rd ed. 8vo. Lond., 1862.   K 7 R 22

LONDON INTERNATIONAL EXHIBITION OF 1873. Official Record; containing Introduction, Catalogues, Reports, and Recommendations of the Experts, Official Awards of the Commissioners, and Essays and Statistics of the Social and Economic Resources of the Colony of Victoria. 8vo. Melb., 1873.*   MK 1 R 29

LONDON INTERNATIONAL EXHIBITION, 1874. Report to the Commissioners of Her Majesty's Customs of the Results obtained in testing Samples of the Wines exhibited. [*See* KEENE, J. B.]

LONDON INTERNATIONAL HEALTH EXHIBI-
TION, 1884. Catalogue of the Library. Division 1.
Health. Division 2. Education. 8vo. Lond., 1884.
                                                    K 7 S 30
LONDON INTERNATIONAL INVENTIONS EXHI-
BITION, 1885. Official Catalogue. 8vo. Lond., 1885.
                                                    K 7 R 31
LONDON JOURNAL OF ARTS AND SCIENCES
(NEWTON'S). New series. 23 vols. (in 12) 8vo. (*All
published.*) Lond., 1855–66.   E 1, 28

LONDON MAGAZINE (THE). 2 vols. 8vo. Lond.,
1827–28.   E 1, 30

LONDON MISSIONARY SOCIETY. First Report of
the Committee of the Australian Auxiliary, 1839; with
a List of Subscribers. Petræa. Sydney, 1840. MJ 2 Q 3
Fifth Report of the New South Wales Auxiliary, 1859.
8vo. Sydney, 1859.   MJ 2 Q 9
Seventh Report of the New South Wales Auxiliary, 1861.
8vo. Sydney, 1861.   MJ 1 Q 27

LONDON OFFICIALS' Point of View, A. [*See* BAXTER,
A. B.]

LONDON REFORMING SOCIETY. Address and
Regulations. (Pam. Dd.) 8vo. Lond. (n.d.) F 12 P 22
Report of the Committee. (Pam. Dd.) Lond. (n.d.)
                                           F 12 P 22
LONDON STATISTICAL SOCIETY. [*See* STATISTICAL
SOCIETY OF LONDON,]

LONDON UNIVERSITY. Calendar for the years 1872–
87. 15 vols. 8vo. Lond., 1872–86.   E 2, 80

LONDON UNIVERSITY LECTURES. Lectures de-
livered, 1828–40. 2 vols. 8vo. Lond., 1828–40. J 587,8
1. Conolly (John), M.D. Nature and Treatment of Diseases.
  Grant (Robert E.), M.D. Comparative Anatomy and Zoology.
  Dale (Rev. Thomas), M.A. English Language and Literature.
  Lardner (Prof. D.), LL.D. Natural Philosophy and Astronomy.
  Mühlenfels (Prof. L. von), L.L.D. German and Northern
    Language and Literature.
  Long (Prof. G.), A.M. Greek Language, Literature, and
    Antiquities.
  Hurwitz (Prof. H.) Hebrew Language and Literature.
  Galiano (Prof. Don A. A.) Spanish Language and Literature.
  Lindley (Prof. J.), F.R.S. Botany.
  Smith (Prof. J. G.), M.D. Medical Jurisprudence.
2. Amos (Prof. A.) Study of English Law (2).
  Malkin (Prof. b. H.), LL.D. History.
  Bennett (Prof. James R.), A.B. Course of General Anatomy.
  De Morgan (Prof. Augustus). Remarks upon Elementary
    Education in Science.
  Thomson (Prof. Anthony Todd), M.D. Medical Jurisprudence.
  Vaughan (Prof. Robert). Study of General History.
  Grant (Robert E.), M.D. Study of Medicine.
  Malden (Prof. Henry), M.A. Study of the Greek and Latin
    Languages.
  Quain (Prof. Jones), M.D. Anatomy and Physiology.
  De Morgan (Prof. Augustus). Thoughts suggested by the
    Establishment of the University of London.
  Kidd (Prof. Samuel). Nature and Structure of the Chinese
    Language.
  Malkin (Prof. Henry), M.A. The Introduction of the Natural
    Sciences into General Education.
  Pepoli (Prof. Carlo), M.A. Language and Literature of Italy.
  Carey (Prof. F. Stafford), M.A. Study of English Law.
  Creasy (Prof. Edward S.), A.M. The Spirit of Historical Study.
  Latham (Prof. R. G.), M.A. [English Language.]

LONDONDERRY (GEN. CHARLES WILLIAM VANE), MAR-
QUIS OF. Memoirs and Correspondence of Viscount
Castlereagh. 8 vols. 8vo. Lond., 1848.   C 8 S 28–35
Recollections of a Tour in the North of Europe in 1836–37.
2 vols. 8vo. Lond., 1838.   D 8 T 42
Steam Voyage to Constantinople, by the Rhine and the
Danube, in 1840–41; and to Portugal, Spain, &c. in
1839. 2 vols. 8vo. Lond., 1842.   D 7 T 7, 8
Story of the Peninsular War. 12mo. Lond., 1848.
                                           B 13 U 23
LONDONDERRY (ROBERT STEWART VISCOUNT CASTLE-
REAGH), SECOND MARQUIS OF. Apology for T. Reynolds.
[*See* HISTORICAL PAMPHLETS.]

Journey to Damascus, through Egypt, Nubia, Arabia,
Petræa, Palestine, and Syria. 2 vols. 8vo. Lond.,
1847.   D 5 R 3, 4
Lives of Lord Castlereagh and Sir Charles Stewart,
the second and third Marquesses of Londonderry; by
Sir Archibald Alison, Bart. 3 vols. 8vo. Lond.,
1861.   C 8 S 44–46
Memoirs and Correspondence; edited by his brother,
Charles Vane, Marquis of Londonderry, G.C.B., &c.
8 vols. 8vo. Lond., 1848–51.   C 8 S 28–35

LONDONDERRY (SIR CHARLES STEWART), THIRD MAR-
QUIS OF. Lives of Lord Castlereagh and Sir Charles
Stewart, the second and third Marquesses of Londonderry; with annals of Contemporary Events in which
they bore a part; by Sir Archibald Alison, Bart. 3 vols.
8vo. Edinb., 1861.   C 8 S 44–46

LONG AGO: a Journal of Popular Antiquities; edited
by Alexander Andrews. Vol. 1. Roy. 8vo. Lond.,
1873.   E

LONG (ARMISTEAD LINDSAY), AND WRIGHT (M. J.)
Memoirs of Robert E. Lee: his Military and Personal
History. Imp. 8vo. Lond., 1886.   C 5 W 11

LONG (COL. CHARLES CHAILLE). Central Africa: Naked
Truths of Naked People. 8vo. Lond., 1876. D 1 W 19

LONG (EDWARD). History of Jamaica; or, General Survey
of the Ancient and Modern State of that Island; with
Reflections on its Situation, Settlement, Inhabitants,
Climate, Products, Commerce, Laws, and Government.
Illustrated. 3 vols. 4to. Lond., 1774.   B 18 V 2–4

LONG (MRS. EMMA DE). [*See* DE LONG, MRS. EMMA.]

LONG (GEORGE). Biographical Dictionary. [*See* BIO-
GRAPHICAL DICTIONARY.]
The British Museum: Egyptian Antiquities. (Lib. Ent.
Know.) 2 vols. 12mo. Lond., 1832–36.   K 10 R 25, 26
Plutarch's Lives. [*See* PLUTARCH.]
Thoughts of M. Aurelius Antoninus. [*See* AURELIUS
ANTONINUS, M.]

LONG (LIEUT.-COM. GEORGE W. DE.) [*See* DE LONG,
LIEUT.-COM. G. W.]

LONG (JAMES). Book of the Pig: its Selection, Breeding, Feeding, and Management. Illustrated. Roy. 8vo. Lond., 1886.   A 1 T 20

British Dairy Farming; to which is added a Description of the Chief Continental Systems. 8vo. Lond., 1885.   A 1 R 30

Poultry for Prizes and Profit. 8vo. Lond., 1886. A1P44

LONG (MAJOR S. H.) Expedition to the Rocky Mountains. [*See* JAMES, E.]

LONG PARLIAMENT. Sarcastic Notices of the: a List of the Members that held Places, both Civil and Military, contrary to the Self-denying Ordinance of April 3rd, 1645; with the sums of Money and Lands which they divided among themselves. [*Published by J. C. Hotten.*] 8vo. Lond., 1863.   C 11 Q 4

LONG (REV. WILLIAM), AND GRAY (RT. REV. R.), D.D. Record in the Suit between. Fol. Cape Town, 1862.   F 7 Q 18 †

LONGCROFT (CHARLES JOHN). Topographical Account of the Hundred of Bosmere, in the County of Southampton, including the Parishes of Havant, Warbington, and Hayling. Imp. 8vo. Lond., 1857.   D 11 P 19 †

LONGDEN (HENRY). Life of; compiled from his own Memoirs, Diaries, Letters, &c. 11th ed. 18mo. Lond., 1874.   G 9 P 21

LONGFELLOW (HENRY WADSWORTH). Aftermath. 12mo. Lond., 1873.   H 5 Q 44

Courtship of Miles Standish, and other Poems. 12mo. Lond., 1858.   H 5 Q 35

Divine Comedy of Dante Alighieri. [*See* DANTE ALIGHIERI.*]

The Divine Tragedy. 12mo. Lond., 1872.   H 8 Q 24

Evangeline. New ed., illustrated. 8vo. Lond., 1856.   H 8 V 29

Flower-de-Luce, and other Poems. Sq. 12mo. Lond., 1867.   H 5 Q 37

The Golden Legend. 12mo. Lond., 1851.   H 5 Q 47

Hanging of the Crane. Illustrated. Sm. 4to. Lond., 1875.   H 8 V 28

Henry Wadsworth Longfellow : a Biographical Sketch ; by Francis H. Underwood. 8vo. Lond., 1882. C 3 P 22

Hyperion: a Romance. 12mo. Lond., 1852.   J 6 Q 13

In the Harbor. 12mo. Lond., 1882.   H 5 Q 46

Kavanagh : a Tale. 12mo. Liverp. (n.d.)   J 6 Q 14

Kéramos, and other Poems. 12mo. Lond., 1878. H5Q49

Life of; with Extracts from his Journals and Correspondence ; edited by Samuel Longfellow. 2 vols. 8vo. Lond., 1886.   C 10 U 21, 22

Longfellow : Biography, Anecdote, Letters, Criticism ; by W. Sloane Kennedy. 3rd ed. 8vo. Camb., Mass., 1882.   C 5 V 22

Longfellow : his Life, his Works, his Friendships; by George Lowell Austin. 8vo. Boston, 1883. C 5 R 18

LONGFELLOW (HENRY WADSWORTH)—*continued.*

Masque of Pandora, and other Poems. 12mo. Lond., 1875.   H 5 Q 48

Michael Angelo : a Dramatic Poem. Illustrated. 4to. Lond., 1884.   H 1 V 2

New England Tragedies. 12mo. Lond., 1868. H 5 Q 42

Outre-Mer ; or, a Pilgrimage to the Old World, by "An American." 2 vols. 8vo. Lond., 1835.   J 6 Q 16, 17

Poems. Illustrated. 8vo. Lond., 1854.   H 8 V 30

Poems, Lyrical and Dramatic; with Introductory Essay, by Geo. Gilfillan. 3rd ed. 12mo. Lond., 1850. H 5 Q 36

Poetical Works of. Revised ed. 4 vols. 12mo. Boston, 1876.   H 5 Q 38–41

Poets and Poetry of Europe ; with Introductions and Biographical Notices. Roy. 8vo. Boston, 1871. H 6 V 20

Prose Works of. 12mo. Lond., 1852.   J 6 Q 15

Prose Works of. Revised ed. 3 vols. 12mo. Boston, 1878.   J 6 Q 10–12

The Song of Hiawatha. 12mo. Lond., 1855. H 5 Q 34

Tales of a Wayside Inn. 12mo. Lond., 1864. H 5 Q 51

Three Books of Song. 12mo. Lond., 1872.   H 5 Q 45

Tributes to Longfellow and Emerson, by the Massachusetts Historical Society. With Portraits. Sm. 4to. Boston, 1882.   C 10 V 38

Voices of the Night. 2nd ed. 12mo. Camb., U.S., 1840.   H 5 Q 50

LONGFELLOW (SAMUEL). Life of Henry Wadsworth Longfellow ; with Extracts from his Journal and Correspondence. 2 vols. 8vo. Lond., 1886. C 10 U 21, 22

LONGMAN (WILLIAM). History of the Life and Times of Edward III. 2 vols. 8vo. Lond., 1869. B 6 P 11, 12

Lectures on the History of England. Lectures 1–5. From the Earliest Times to the Death of Edward II. 8vo. Lond., 1863.   B 6 P 10

LONGMAN'S MAGAZINE. Vols. 1–3. 8vo. Lond., 1883–84.   E 2, 44

LONGMUIR (JOHN), A.M., &c. Etymological Dictionary of the Scottish Language. [*See* JAMIESON, J.]

Rhyming Dictionary of the English Language. [*See* WALKER, J.]

LONGUEIL (G. DE). Dialogus de avibus, et earum nominibus Græcis, Latinis, et Germanicis. 18mo. Colon, 1544.   A 14 P 42

LONGUS. Greek Romance of. [*See* HELIODORUS.]

Pastorialium de Daphnide et Chloe. [*See* SCRIPTORES EROTICI GRAECI.]

LONICER (P.) [*See* ANDREAS HONDORFFIUS.]

LONSDALE (H. W.), AND TARVER (E. J.) Illustrations of Mediæval Costume. 4to. Lond., 1874.   A 2 R 20 †

LOOMIS (Rev. Augustus Ward), D.D., &c. Confucius and the Chinese Classics; or, Readings in Chinese Literature. 12mo. San Francisco, 1867.   G 8 P 36

LOOMIS (Prof. Elias), LL.D. Introduction to Practical Astronomy; with a Collection of Astronomical Tables. 7th ed. 8vo. New York, 1884.   A 3 S 13

LOOS (Josef). Wörterbuch der Ungarischen, Deutschen und Slovakischen Sprache. 3 vols. 18mo. Pest, 1869-71.   K 11 S 28-30

LOPE (Felix de Vega Carpio). [*See* Vega Carpio, Lope F. de.]

LOPEZ (Odoardo). Report of the Kingdome of Congo, a Region of Africa. [*See* Pigafetta, P.]

LORD (E.) Comstock Mining and Miners. (U.S. Geological Survey). 4to. Wash., 1883.   A 4 R 3†

LORD (W. B.), R.A. Crab, Shrimp, and Lobster Lore, gathered amongst the Rocks at the Sea-Shore, by the Riverside, and in the Forest. 12mo. Lond., 1867. A 14 P 41

LORD (W. B.), and BAINES (T.), F.R.G.S. Shifts and Expedients of Camp Life, Travel, and Exploration. Roy. 8vo. Lond., 1876.   A 16 V 10

LORD'S DAY OBSERVANCE. [*See* N.S. Wales Society for Promoting the Observance of the Lord's Day.]

LORENZ (Dr. F.) Life of F. A. Alcuin; translated by Jane M. Slee. 12mo. Lond., 1837.   C 1 R 2

LORENZ (Otto). Catalogue Annuel de la Librairie Française, pour 1876. Roy. 8vo. Paris, 1877.   K 8 Q 10
Catalogue Général de la Librairie Française, 1840-75 [avec la Table des Matières]. 8 vols. roy. 8vo. Paris, 1867-80.   Libr.

LORIMER (Rev. George Claude), LL.D. Studies in Social Life. 8vo. Lond., 1887.   F 6 Q 22

LORIMER (James), LL.D. Institutes of Law: a Treatise of the Principles of Jurisprudence as determined by Nature. 2nd ed. 8vo. Edinb., 1880.   F 7 Q 3
Institutes of the Law of Nations: a Treatise of the Jural Relations of separate Political Communities. 2 vols. 8vo. Edinb., 1883-84.   F 7 Q 4, 5

LORIMER (Prof. Peter), D.D. John Knox and the Church of England. 8vo. Lond., 1875.   G 3 S 13
John Wyclife and his English Precursors. [*See* Lechler, Prof. G.]

LORNE (John Douglas Sutherland), Marquis of, Canadian Pictures, drawn with Pen and Pencil. Imp. 8vo. Lond., 1884.   D 3 P 1
Imperial Federation. 8vo. Lond., 1885.   F G R 6
Trip to the Tropics, and Home through America. 8vo. Lond., 1867.   D 3 S 32

LOSERTH (Dr. Johann). Wiclif and Huss; translated from the German, by the Rev. M. J. Evans, B.A. 8vo. Lond., 1884.   G 2 P 15

LOSSING (Benson J.) Pictorial Description of Ohio. (Pam. 18.) 8vo. New York, 1849.   F 12 P 10
Pictorial Field-book of the Revolution. 2 vols. roy. 8vo. New York, 1851-52.   B 1 V 8, 9

LOS VALLES (Baron de). [*See* Valles, Baron de los.]

LOTH (J.) Etymologische angelsæchsisch-englische Grammatik. Roy. 8vo. Elberfeld, 1870.   K 15 S 23

LOTT (Emmeline). The English Governess in Egypt: Harem Life in Egypt and Constantinople. 2nd ed. 2 vols. 8vo. Lond., 1866.   D 1 T 25, 26

LOTZE (Hermann). Geschichte der Aesthetik, in Deutschland. (Geschichte der Wiss.) 8vo. München, 1868.   A 17 V 21
Lotze's System of Philosophy: English Translation: edited by Bernard Bosanquet, M.A. (Clar. Press.) 2 vols. 8vo. Oxford, 1884.   G 16 T 6, 7

LORD HOWE ISLAND. Chart of. [*See* Maps.]

LOUDON (John Claudius). Arboretum et Fruticetum Britannicum; or, the Trees and Shrubs of Britain. 8 vols. 8vo. Lond., 1838.   A 5 P 17-24
Cottager's Manual of Husbandry, Architecture, Domestic Economy, and Gardening. (Pam. 14.) 8vo. Lond., 1840.   MJ 2 Q 4
Encyclopædia of Agriculture. 2nd ed. 8vo. Lond., 1831.   K 1 R 23
Encyclopædia of Gardening. 4th ed. 8vo. Lond., 1826.   K 5 U 1
Encyclopædia of Plants indigenous, cultivated in, or introduced to Britain. 8vo. Lond., 1836.   K 5 Q 37
Hortus Britannicus: a Catalogue of all the Plants indigenous, cultivated in, or introduced to Britain. 8vo. Lond., 1832.   A 4 S 19
Landscape Gardening and Landscape Architecture of H. Repton. [*See* Repton, H.]
Suburban Gardener and Villa Companion, &c. 8vo. Lond., 1838.
Trees and Shrubs: an abridgment of the "Arboretum et Fruticetum Britannicum." 8vo. Lond., 1875. A 4 S 5

LOUDON (Mrs. J. W.) British Wild Flowers. 4to. Lond., 1849.   A 5 Q 26
Entertaining Naturalist; being popular Descriptions, Tales, and Anecdotes of more than five hundred Animals. New ed., revised and enlarged by W. S. Dallas, F.L.S. 8vo. Lond., 1867.   A 14 Q 16
Ladies' Companion to the Flower-Garden. 3rd ed. 8vo. Lond., 1844.   K 7 Q 21
Ladies' Flower-Garden of Ornamental Annuals. 4to. Lond., 1844.   A 5 Q 24
Ladies' Flower-Garden of Ornamental Bulbous Plants. 2nd ed. 4to. Lond., 1849.   A 5 Q 25
Ladies' Flower-Garden of Ornamental Greenhouse Plants. 4to. Lond., 1848.   A 5 Q 23

LOUDON (MRS. J. W.)—*continued.*
Ladies' Flower-Garden of Ornamental Perennials. 2 vols.
4to. Lond., 1843-44.   A 5 Q 21, 22

Lady's Country Companion; or, How to enjoy a Country
Life rationally. 2nd ed. 12mo. Lond.,1846. A 17 T 18

Philanthropic Economy; or, the Philosophy of Happiness
practically applied to the Social, Political, and Commercial
Relations of Great Britain. 8vo. Lond., 1835. F 8 S 5

Poultry; their Breeding, Rearing, Diseases, and General
Management. [*See* DICKSON, W. B.]

LOUGHNAN (R. AND J.) Hints on the Cultivation of Tobacco in Victoria. 2nd ed. 8vo. Melb.,1862. MA 1 Q 7

LOUIS VI. Vie de Louis-le-Gros. [*See* GUIZOT, F. P. G., 8.]

LOUIS IX. The Good St. Louis and his Times; by Mrs.
A. E. Bray. 8vo. Lond., 1870.   C 4 Q 11

Jean, Sire de Joinville: Histoire de Saint Louis, credo et lettre
à Louis x; texte original, accompagne d'une traduction, par
Natalis de Wailly. Imp. 8vo. Paris, 1874. C 4 W 30

LOUIS XIV. Letters of. [*See* GRIMBLOT, P.]
Life and Times of; by G. P. R. James. 4 vols. 8vo.
Lond., 1838.   C 5 U 13–16

Louis xiv and the Court of France in the 17th Century; by
Miss Pardoe. 3 vols. 8vo. Lond., 1886. C 6 R 22–24

LOUIS XVII. Louis xvii: sa Vie, son Agonie, sa Mort,
Captivitie de la Famille Royale au Temple; par M. A. de
Beauchesne. 4e ed. 2 vols. 8vo. Paris,1867. C 10 V 40, 41

Louis xvii: his Life, his Suffering, his Death, the Captivity
of the Royal Family; by A. de Beauchesne; translated
and edited by W. Hazlitt. 2 vols. 8vo. Lond., 1853.
       C 6 P 19, 20

LOUIS XVIII. Correspondence of Prince Talleyrand and
King Louis xviii during the Congress of Vienna (hitherto
unpublished). 2 vols. 8vo. Lond., 1881. C 9 T 49, 50

Memoirs of; written by himself. 2 vols. 8vo. Lond.,
1832.   C 2 P 27, 28

LOUISA AUGUSTA (QUEEN OF PRUSSIA). Memoirs of the
Private Life and Opinions of; by Mrs. Charles Richardson.
12mo. Lond., 1847.   C 3 V 36

LOUNSBURY (PROF. THOMAS RAYNESFORD). James
Fenimore Cooper. [A Biography.] 12mo. Lond., 1884.
       C 1 R 8

LOURIERO (P.) The Hundred Years Anglo-Chinese
Calendar, 1st Jan., 1776 to 25th Jan., 1876. Roy. 8vo.
Shanghai, 1872.   E 1, 78

LOUVET DE COUVRAY (JEAN BAPTISTE). Mémoires
de. [*See* BARRIÈRE, J. F., 12.]

LOUVAINE (ALGERNON GEORGE PERCY), LORD, DUKE OF
NORTHUMBERLAND. [*See* NORTHUMBERLAND, DUKE OF.]

LOVAT (SIMON JOSEPH FRASER) BARON. Shooting. [*See*
WALSINGHAM, BARON.]

3 M

LOVAT (SIMON FRASER), LORD. Lives of Simon, Lord
Lovat, and Duncan Forbes, of Culloden, from original
sources, by John Hill Burton, Advocate. 8vo. Lond.,
1847.   C 4 S 17

Memoirs of the Life of; written by himself in the French
Language, and now first translated from the original
Manuscript. 8vo. Lond., 1797.   C 5 T 15

LOVER (SAMUEL), R.H.A. Characteristic Sketches of
Ireland and the Irish. [*See* CARLETON, W.]

Life of, Artistic, Literary, and Musical; with Selections
from his unpublished Papers and Correspondence, by Bayle
Bernard. 2 vols. 8vo. Lond., 1874.   C 4 V 6, 7

Lyrics of Ireland. 8vo. Lond., 1858.   H 8 P 4

LOVETT (MAJOR B.) Eastern Persia: Geography, &c. [*See*
PERSIA.]

LOVETT (REV. RICHARD), M.A. Norwegian Pictures,
drawn with Pen and Pencil; containing also, a Glance at
Sweden and the Gotha Canal. Imp. 8vo. Lond., 1885.
       D 6 V 28

LOVIBOND (EDWARD). Life and Poems of. [*See*
CHALMERS, A.]

LOW (LIEUT. CHARLES RATHBONE), F.R.G.S. Great
Battles of the British Army, including the Soudan Campaign. Illustrated. 8vo. Lond., 1885.   B 4 Q 27

Great Battles of the British Navy. 8vo. Lond.,
1875.   B 2 S 33

History of the Indian Navy (1613–1863). 2 vols. 8vo.
Lond., 1877.   B 10 S 5, 6

Major-General Sir Frederick S. Roberts, Bart., &c.: a
Memoir. 8vo. Lond., 1883.   C 8 U 47

Maritime Discovery: a History of Nautical Exploration
from the Earliest Times. 2 vols. 8vo. Lond., 1881.
       D 9 T 27, 28

Soldiers of the Victorian Age. 2 vols. 8vo. Lond.,
1880.   B 5 U 17, 18

LOW (DAVID), F.R.S.E. Elements of Practical Agriculture. 8vo. Edinb., 1834.   A 1 S 16

LOW (FRANCIS). City of Sydney Directory, 1844-45, 1847.
8vo. Sydney, 1844-47.*   ME 10 P

LOW (HUGH). Sarawak: its Inhabitants and Productions;
being Notes during a Residence in that Country with
H.H. the Rajah Brooke. 8vo. Lond., 1844.   D 4 T 3

LOW (SAMPSON), & CO. Classified Catalogue of School,
College, Classical, Technical, and General Educational
Works, in use in the United Kingdam and its Depen-
dencies in 1876. [2nd ed.] 8vo. Lond., 1876. K 7 R 44

English Catalogue of Books, 1835-80. 3 vols. roy. 8vo.
Lond., 1864-82.*   Libr.

Indexes to the [above.] 3 vols. roy. 8vo. Lond.,
1858-84.   Libr.

English Catalogue of Books, 1881-85. 5 vols. (in 1)
roy. 8vo. Lond., 1882-86.   Libr.

LOW (SIDNEY JAMES)), B.A., AND PULLING (FREDERICK SAUNDERS), M.A. Dictionary of English History. 8vo. Lond., 1884.   K 11 P 20

LOW (W. H.), M.A. The Mishnah. [*See* MISHNAH, THE.]

LOWE (CHARLES), M.A. Prince Bismarck : an Historical Biography. 2 vols. 8vo. Lond., 1885.   C 10 R 19, 20

LOWE (E. J.), F.R.A.S. Natural History of New and Rare Ferns. Roy. 8vo. Lond., 1862.   A 5 Q 9

LOWE (LIEUT.-GEN. SIR HUDSON). History of the Captivity of Napoleon at St. Helena ; from the Journals of Lieut.-Gen. Sir H. Lowe, by W. Forsyth, Q.C. 3 vols. 8vo. Lond., 1853.   C 8 T 19–21

LOWE (JOHN). Medical Missions, their Place and Power. 8vo. Lond., 1886.   G 7 Q 9

LOWE (M.) [*See* AGRICULTURAL SOCIETY OF N.S. WALES.]

LOWE (MARSHAL H.) System of Shorthand. [*See* ANDERSON, T.]

LOWE (RICHARD THOMAS), M.A. History of the Fishes of Madeira ; with original figures from Nature of all the species, by the Hon. C. E. C. Norton, and M. Young. 8vo. Lond., 1843–60.   A 13 V 38

LOWE (RT. HON. ROBERT). [*See* SHERBROOKE, VISCOUNT.]

LOWE (THOMAS), M.R.C.S.E., &c. Central India during the Rebellion of 1857–58. 8vo. Lond., 1860. B 10 Q 22

LOWE (E. J.), F.R.A.S., AND HOWARD (W.), F.H.S. Beautiful-leaved Plants ; being a description of the most Beautiful-leaved Plants in cultivation in this country ; to which is added an extended Catalogue. Coloured Illustrations. Roy. 8vo. Lond., 1872.   A 4 U 4

LOWELL (JAMES RUSSELL), A.M. Among my Books. [1st and] 2nd series. 2 vols. 8vo. Boston and Lond., 1873.   J 12 S 3, 4

Democracy, and other Addresses. 8vo. Lond., 1887.
                                                F 6 P 34

Fireside Travels. 12mo. Lond., 1864.   J 12 S 1

Another copy. 8vo. Boston, 1865.   J 12 S 2

My Study Windows. 8vo. Boston, 1873.   J 12 S 1

Poetical Works of. 8vo. Boston, 1871.   H 6 R 40

LOWELL (PERCIVAL CHOSÖN). The Land of the Morning Calm : a Sketch of Korea. Roy. 8vo. Lond., 1885. D 5 U 27

LÖWENBERG (J.), AVE LALLEMENT (ROBERT), AND DOVE (ALFRED). Life of Alexander von Humboldt. Edited by Prof. K. Bruhns ; translated by Jane and Caroline Lassell. 2 vols. 8vo. Lond., 1873.   C 7 P 27, 28

LÖWENTHAL (J.) Morphy's Game of Chess. [*See* MORPHY, P.]

LOWER (MARK ANTONY), M.A., &c. Chronicle of Battle Abbey. [*See* BATTLE ABBEY.]

Patronymica Britannica : a Dictionary of the Family Names of the United Kingdom. Roy. 8vo. Lond., 1860.   K 10 T 27

Wayside Notes in Scandinavia. 8vo. Lond., 1874.
                                                D 8 Q 41

Worthies of Sussex : Biographical Sketches of the Most Eminent Natives or Inhabitants of the County from the Earliest Period to the Present Time ; with Incidental Notices, illustrative of Sussex History. Roy. 4to. Lewes, 1865.   C 1 W 28

LOWNDES (CHARLES S.) Engineer's Hand-book. 2nd ed. 8vo. Lond., 1863.   A 6 R 6

LOWNDES (WILLIAM THOMAS). Bibliographer's Manual of English Literature. New ed., revised by Henry G. Bohn. 10 vols. 8vo. Lond., 1857–64.   Libr.

Another copy. 6 vols. 8vo. Lond., 1869.   Libr.

LOWNE (B. THOMPSON), F.R.C.S. On the Modifications of the Simple and Compound Eyes of Insects. (Roy. Soc. Pubs., 6.) 4to. Lond., 1879.   A 11 P 7†

LOWRY (J. W.) Geometrical Drawing. [*See* BRADLEY, T.]

LOWTH (RT. REV. ROBERT), D.D., BISHOP OF LONDON. De Sacra Poesi Hebræorum. 8vo. Oxonii, 1775. H S V 35

Isaiah : a new Translation ; with a Dissertation and Notes. 8vo. Lond., 1837.   G 8 U 4

Lectures on the Sacred Poetry of the Hebrews ; translated by G. Gregory. 3rd ed. 8vo. Lond., 1835. G 14 Q 15

Life of William Wykeham, Bishop of Winchester. 3rd ed. 8vo. Oxford, 1777.   C 9 P 49

Sermons and other Remains ; with Memoir, by the Rev. P. Hall. 8vo. Lond., 1834.   G 1 R 7

LOYAL SERVANT (THE). [*See* BAYARD, P. DU T. CHEVALIER.]

LOYAU (GEORGE E.) Australian Wild Flowers : fresh gathered from the field of Poesy ; comprising a Collection of Original Poems on various Colonial Subjects. 12mo. Sydney, 1871.   MH 1 P 17

Australian Seasons : an Original Pastoral Poem. 12mo. Sydney, 1871.   MH 1 P 17

Representative Men of South Australia. 12mo. Adelaide, 1883.   MC 1 P 10

LOYD (SAMUEL JONES). Improvement of Designs and Patterns. [*See* SENIOR, N. W.]

LOYOLA (IGNATIUS DE). [*See* IGNATIUS DE LOYOLA.]

LUBBOCK (SIR JOHN), BART., &c. Addresses, Political and Educational. 8vo. Lond., 1879. F 7 Q 7

Ants, Bees, and Wasps : a Record of Observations on the Habits of the Social Hymenoptera. 2nd ed. 8vo. Lond., 1882. A 14 P 49

Fifty Years of Science ; being the Address delivered at York to the British Association, August, 1882. 8vo. Lond., 1882. A 16 T 10

Flowers, Fruits, and Leaves. 8vo. Lond., 1886. A 4 P 6

On British Wild Flowers, considered in relation to Insects. 8vo. Lond., 1875. A 4 P 7

On the Origin and Metamorphoses of Insects. 12mo. Lond., 1874. A 14 P 48

Origin of Civilization and the Primitive Condition of Man. Mental and Social Candition of Savages. 2nd ed. 8vo. Lond., 1870. A 1 W 29

Another copy. 4th ed. 8vo. Lond., 1882. A 1 W 30

Pre-Historic Times, as illustrated by Ancient Remains, and the Manners and Customs of Modern Savages. 8vo. Lond., 1872. A 1 W 12

Representation. 8vo. Lond., 1885. F 6 R 7

Scientific Lectures [on Flowers, Insects, Ants, and Archaeology.] 8vo. Lond., 1879. A 16 U 15

LUBERT (MDLLE. DU). Trois Contes. [*See* CABINET DES FÉES, 33.]

LUBIN (ANTONIO). Commedia di Dante Allighieri, preceduta dalla Vita e da Studi. [*See* DANTE ALIGHIERI.]

LUBKE (DR. WILHELM). Ecclesiastical Art in Germany during the Middle Ages. Roy. 8vo. Edinb., 1870. A 2 S 22

History of Art ; translated by F. E. Bunnett. 3rd ed. 2 vols. roy. 8vo. Lond., 1874. A 7 V 6, 7

History of Sculpture, from the earliest Ages to the present Time ; translated by F. E. Bunnett. Illustrated. 2 vols. roy. 8vo. Lond., 1872. A 8 T 11, 12

LUCANUS (MARCUS ANNÆUS). Lucan's Pharsalia ; translated by N. Rowe. [*See* CHALMERS, A.. *and* JOHNSON, S.]

Pharsalia of Lucan ; literally translated into English Prose ; with Notes, by H. T. Riley, B.A. 8vo. Lond., 1878. H 5 S 32

LUCAS (JOHN). Mines and Mineral Statistics. [*See* N. S. WALES.]

LUCAS (JOHN). Address upon the Water Supply for the City and Suburbs ; delivered in the Town Hall before the Mayor and Aldermen of the City of Sydney. (Pam. 29.) 8vo. Sydney, 1879. MJ 2 R 17

LUCAS (JOSEPH), F.G.S., &c. Studies in Nidderdale : upon Notes and Observations other than Geological, made during the Progress of the Government Geological Survey of the District, 1867–72. 8vo. Lond., 1882. D 6 T 37

LUCAS (NEWTON IVORY). Dictionary of the English and German, and German and English Languages ; adapted to the present state of Literature, Science, Commerce and Arts. 4 vols. roy. 8vo. Bremen, 1854–68. K 12 T 27–30

LUCAS (SAMUEL), M.A. [*See* SHILLING MAGAZINE, THE.]

LUCAS (DR. T. P.) Cries from Fiji, and Sighings from the South Seas—" Crush out the British Slave Trade." 8vo. Melb., 1884. MD 4 Q 29

LUCATT (MR.) Rovings in the Pacific, from 1837–49, with a Glance at California ; by " A Merchant long resident in Tahiti." 2 vols. 8vo. Lond., 1851. MD 4 S 5, 6

LUCCOCK (JOHN). Essay on Wool ; containing a particular Account of the English Fleece, &c. 8vo. Lond., 1809. A 1 P 1

LUCIAN (SAMOSATENSIS). Opera Græca et Latine, ad Editionem Tiberii Hemsterhusii et Ioannis Frederici Reitzii accurata expressa. 10 vols. 8vo. Biponti, 1789–93. J 15 U 27–36

Works of Lucian ; from the Greek, by Thomas Francklin, D.D. 4 vols. 8vo. Lond., 1781. J 2 Q 17–20

LUCIFER (EPISCOPUS CALARITANUS). Opera omnia. [*See* MIGNE, J. P., SERIES LATINA, 13.]

LUCILIUS (CAIUS). Satires of. [*See* JUVENALIS, D. J.]

LÜCKES (EVA C. E.) Lectures on General Nursing, delivered to the Probationers of the London Hospital Training School for Nurses. 8vo. Lond., 1884. A 12 P 39

LUCKOCK (H. M.) Bishops in the Tower. 8vo. Lond., 1887. B 3 Q 28

LUCRETIUS CARUS (TITUS). Atomic Theory of Lucretins. [*See* MASSON, J.]

The Nature of Things : a Didascalic Poem ; translated from the Latin of Titus Lucretius Carus ; accompanied with Commentaries, Comparative, Illustrative and Scientific ; and the Life of Epicurus ; by Thomas Busby. 2 vols. imp. 4to. Lond., 1813. H 7 Q 21, 22 †

De Rerum Natura Libri Sex, ex Editione Gilberti Wakefieldi, A.B. ; cum ejusdem Notis, Commentariis, Indicibus, fideliter excusi. 4 vols. roy. 8vo. Glasguæ, 1813. H 6 V 1–4

De Rerum Natura Libri Sex, ex Editione Gilberti Wakefieldi ; cum Notis et Interpretatione in usum Delphini. 4 vols. 8vo. Lond., 1823. J 13 R 6–9

De Rerum Natura Libri Sex ; with Notes and a Translation by H. A. J. Munro. 3 vols. 8vo. Camb., 1886. H 5 U 5–7

1. Text. 2. Explanatory Notes. 3. Translations.

Of the Nature of Things ; translated by Thos. Creech, A.M. 2 vols. 8vo. Lond., 1714. H 7 S 27, 28

LUCY (HENRY W.) Diary of Two Parliaments : the Disraeli Parliament, 1874–80 ; the Gladstone Parliament, 1883–85. 2 vols. 8vo. Lond., 1885–86. B 3 T 23, 24

Men and Manner in Parliament ; by " The Member for the Chiltern Hundreds" ; reprinted, with Additions, from the *Gentleman's Magazine*. 8vo. Lond., 1874. F 6 R 5

LÜDEMANN (W. VON). Lehrbuch der neugriechischen Sprache. 8vo. Leipzig, 1826. K 12 Q 14

LUDEWIG (HERMANN E.) The Literature of American Aboriginal Languages; with Additions and Corrections, by Professor W. W. Turner; edited by N. Trübner. 8vo. Lond., 1858.   K 17 Q 13

LUDLOW (MAJOR-GEN. EDMUND). Mémoires de. [*See* GUIZOT, F. P.G., 6–8.]
Memoirs of; to which is added the Case of King Charles I. 3 vols. 12mo. Edinb., 1751.   C 1 R 20–22
Three Tracts published at Amsterdam, in the years 1691–92. Letters to Sir E. Seymour and other persons, comparing the oppressive government of Charles I, in the first four years of his Reign, with that of the four years of the Reign of King James II, and vindicating the conduct of the Parliament that began in November, 1640. 4to. Lond., 1812.   B 2 T 24

LUDLOW (JOHN MALCOLM). War of American Independence, 1775–83. 12mo. Lond., 1876.   B 1 Q 37

LUDLOW (CAPT. WILLIAM). Report of a Reconnaissance of the Black Hills of Dakota, made in the Summer of 1874. (Engineer Department, U.S. Army.) 4to. Wash., 1875.   A 4 R 9†

LUDOLPHUS (JOB). History of Ethiopia; being a full and accurate Description of the Kingdom of Abessinia, vulgarly, though erroneously, called the Empire of Prester John; made English by J. P. Gent. Fol. Lond., 1682.   B 17 S 10‡

LUDWIG SALVATOR (ARCHDUKE). Levkosia, the Capital of Cyprus. Illustrated. 4to. Lond., 1881. D 5 U 35

LUKIN (REV. J.) Amateur Mechanic's Workshop: a Treatise containing plain and concise Directions for the Manipulation of Wood and Metals. including Casting, Forging, Brazing, Soldering, and Carpentry. 6th ed. 8vo. Lond., 1878.   A 11 S 24
Amongst Machines: a Description of various Mechanical Appliances used in the Manufacture of Wood, Metal, &c. 8vo. Lond., 1876.   A 11 P 19
Boy Engineers: What they did, and how they did it: a Book for Boys. 8vo. Lond., 1878.   A 6 R 11
The Lathe and its Uses; or, Instruction in the Art of the most Modern Appliances for the Ornamentation of Plane and Curved Surfaces. 5th ed. 8vo. Lond., 1878. A 11 R 11
Young Mechanic: a Book for Boys; containing Directions for the Use of all kinds of Tools, and for the Construction of Steam Engines and Mechanical Models, including the Art of Turning in Wood and Metal. 5th ed. 8vo. Lond., 1878.   A 11 Q 3

LULLE (SAINT), FIRST ARCHBISHOP OF MAYENCE. Bonifaz und Lul: ihre Angelsächsischen Korrespondenten: Erzbischof Luls Leben; von Heinrich Hahn. 8vo. Leipzig, 1883.   C 10 P 6

LUMLEY (BENJAMIN). Reminiscences of the Opera. 8vo. Lond., 1864.   C 9 Q 36

LUND (THOMAS). Elements of Algebra. [*See* WOON, J.]

LUNDBLAD (JEAN FRÉDÉRIC DE). Histoire de Suéde. [*See* GEYER, E. G.]

LUNGE (PROF. GEORGE), PH.D., &c. Theoretical and Practical Treatise on the Manufacture of Sulphuric Acid and Alkali, with the Collateral Branches. 3 vols. 8vo. Lond., 1879–80.   A 6 Q 18–20
Treatise on the Distillation of Coal-Tar and Ammoniacal Liquor, and the separation from them of Valuable Products. 8vo. Lond., 1882.   A 6 Q 22

LUNN (CHARLES). The Philosophy of Voice: showing the Right and Wrong Action of Voice in Speech and Song: to which is added the Basis of Musical Expression. 4th ed. 8vo. Lond., 1878.   A 8 P 41
Vox Populi: a Sequel to "The Philosophy of Voice." 8vo. Lond., 1880.   A 8 P 41

LUNN (HENRY C.) Musings of a Musician: a Series of Popular Sketches, illustrative of Musical Matters and Musical People. New ed. 8vo. Lond., 1854. A 23 Q 42

LUPLAU (WILLIAM). The Agricultural Teacher. [*See* LACOPPIDAN, H. J. G. A.]

LUPTON (J. H.), M.A. Lives of Jehan Vitrier. [*See* ERASMUS ROTERODAMUS, D.]

LUPTON (JOSEPH). Hide and Seek: a Petit Opera. (Cumberland's Eng. Theatre.) 12mo. Lond., 1829. H 2 Q 13
Lofty Projects: or, Arts in an Attic: a Farce. (Cumberland's Eng. Theatre.) 12mo. Lond., 1829. H 2 Q 16
Roses and Thorns: a Comedy. (Cumberland's Eng. Theatre.) 12mo. Lond., 1829.   H 2 Q 12
The Shepherd of Derwent Vale: a Drama. (Cumberland's Eng. Theatre.) 12mo. Lond., 1829.   H 2 Q 19

LUPTON (SYDNEY), M.A. Elementary Chemical Arithmetic; with 1,100 Problems. 12mo. Lond., 1882.   A 5 R 13
Numerical Tables and Constants in Elementary Science. 12mo. Lond., 1884.   A 10 R 26

LUSHINGTON (FRANKLIN). [*See* TICHBORNE ROMANCE, THE.]

LUSHINGTON (HENRY). The Italian War, 1848–49, and the last Italian Poet [Giuseppe Giusti]: three Essays; with a Biographical Preface, by George Stovin Venables. 8vo. Camb., 1859.   B 12 P 26

LUSHINGTON (RT. HON. S. R.) Life and Services of General Lord Harris, G.C.B. 8vo. Lond., 1840. C 8 P 19

LUSSAN (MARGUERITE DE). Les Veillées de Thessalie. [*See* CABINET DES FÉES, 26–28.]

LUTHER (G.) Construction and Equipment of Grain Magazines. 8vo. Manchester, 1886.   A 1 S 19

LUTHER (MARTIN). Commentary on St. Paul's Epistle to the Galatians; with a Life of the Author, by the Rev. E. Middleton. Roy. 8vo. Lond., 1810.   G 3 V 16
First Principles of the Reformation; or, the Ninety-five Theses and the three Primary Works of Dr. Martin Luther, translated into English. With a Portrait. 8vo. Lond., 1883.   G 7 P 25

LUTHER (MARTIN)—*continued.*
Life of; by Julius Köstlin, with Illustrations from authentic sources. Translated from the German. 8vo. Lond., 1883. C 3 V 22
Life of, written by himself; collected and arranged by J. Michelet. 12mo. Lond., 1846. C 1 T 38
Luther's Devil. [*See* MASSON, PROF. D.]
Table Talk of; translated from and edited by William Hazlitt. New ed., to which is added his Life, by Alexander Chalmers. 8vo. Lond., 1875. G 16 P 19

LÜTKEMANN (JOACHIM), S.S. THEOL. DOCT. Das Leben des seligen Herrn Joachimi Lütkemans; von Philipp Julio Rehtmeyer. 12mo. Brunsv., 1720. G 9 Q 4

LUTTEROTH (HENRI). Geschichte der Insel Tahiti und ihrer Besitznahme durch die Franzosen. 8vo. Berlin, 1843. MB 2 R 29

LUTTRELL (NARCISSUS). Brief Historical Relation of State Affairs, from September, 1678, to April, 1714. 6 vols. 8vo. Oxford, 1857 B 7 P 1-6

LUTWYCHE (HON. ALFRED J. P.) Electoral Reform, Report of a Speech delivered in the Legislative Council; on the 8th September, 1858, on moving the second reading of the Electoral Law Amendment Bill. (Pam. 26.) 8vo. Sydney, 1858. MJ 2 Q 14

LUYNES (H. T. P. J.), DUC DE. Voyage d'Exploration à la Mer Morte, à Petra, et sur la Rive gauche du Jourdain: Œuvre posthume, publiée par ses Petits-Fils, sous la direction de M. le Comte de Vogüé. 4 vols. et Atlas, imp. 4to. Paris, 1869-74. D 5 Q 1-4 †

LUYS (J.) The Brain and its Functions. With Illustrations. 8vo. Lond., 1881 A 12 Q 37

LYALL (SIR ALFRED COMYNS). K.C.B., &c. Asiatic Studies, Religious and Social. 8vo. Lond., 1882. G 3 S 24

LYALL (ROBERT), M.D., &c. Travels in Russia, the Krimea, the Caucasus, and Georgia. 2 vols. 8vo. Lond., 1825. D 6 U 18, 19

LYCETT (J.) Views in Australia; or, New South Wales and Van Diemen's Land delineated, in fifty Views. with descriptive Letterpress. Ob. 4to. Lond., 1824-25. MD 1 Q 5 ‡
View of the Country round Hobart Town, in Van Diemen's Land. Reduced on zinc by G. Scharf. 4to. Lond. (n d.)* MD 5 S 18 ‡

LYCOPHRON. Cassandra; translated by Viscount Royston [*See* HESIOD.]

LYDGATE, OR LIDGATE (JOHN). Tales of Princes and Princesses. [*See* BOCCACCIO, G.]

LYDON (A. F.) British Fresh-water Fishes. [*See* HOUGHTON, REV. W.]

LYDON (A. F.), AND CROAL (THOMAS A.) Scottish Loch Scenery. Roy. 8vo. Lond., 1882. D 7 V 28

LYDUS (JOHANNES LAURENTIUS.) [*See* BYZANTINÆ HIST. SCRIPT.]

LYELL (SIR CHARLES), BART., M.A., &c. Elements of Geology. 8vo. Lond., 1838. A 9 Q 14
Another copy. 2nd ed. 2 vols. 8vo. Lond., 1841. A 9 P 3, 4
Geological Evidences of the Antiquity of Man; with Remarks on Theories of the Origin of Species by Variation. 3rd ed 8vo. Lond., 1863. A 9 S 29
Life, Letters, and Journals of; edited by his Sister-in-law, Mrs. Lyell. With Portraits. 2 vols. 8vo. Lond., 1881. C 7 S 7, 8
Principles of Geology; or the Modern Changes of the Earth and its Inhabitants considered as illustrative of Geology. 11th ed. 2 vols. 8vo. Lond., 1872. A 9 R 11, 12
Review of the Elements of Geology. [*See* FITTON, W. H.]
Second Visit to the United States of North America. 2 vols. 8vo. Lond., 1849. D 4 P 47, 48
Travels in North America; with Geological Observations on the United States, Canada, and Nova Scotia. 2 vols. 8vo. Lond., 1845. D 4 P 45, 46

LYELL (J. C.) Fancy Pigeons; containing full directions for their breeding and management, with descriptions of every known variety. 3rd ed. Lond., 1887. A 14 Q 45

LYELL (K. M.) Geographical Hand-book of all the known Ferns; with Tables to show their distribution. 8vo. Lond., 1870. A 4 Q 6

LYELL (MRS.) [*See* LYELL, SIR C.]

LYLY (JOHN), M.A. Euphues: the Anatomy of Wit; editio princeps, 1579. Euphues and his England; editio princeps, 1580. Collated with early subsequent editions. Carefully edited by Edward Arber, F.R.G.S., &c. 12mo. Lond., 1868. J 1 S 39

LYNAN (R.) Life of the Rev. W. Paley. [*See* PALEY, REV. W.]

LYNCH (JOHN). Cambrensis Eversus; or, refutation of the authority of Giraldus Cambrensis on the History of Ireland. (Latin and English Text.) Edited by the Rev. Matthew Kelly. 3 vols. 8vo. Dublin, 1848-52. B 11 R 14-16

LYNCH (CAPT. W. F.), U.S.N. Narrative of the States' Expedition to the River Jordan and the Dead Sea. Illustrated. Roy. 8vo. Lond., 1849. D 6 T 3

LYND (LIEUT. B.) Leichhardt's Grave: a Poem (MS.) (Pam. A.) Fol. Sydney, 1845. MJ 2 U 1
[*See* LEICHHARDT, DR. L.]

LYNDHURST (JOHN SINGLETON COPLEY), LORD. Life of. From Letters and Papers in the possession of his Family; by Sir Theodore Martin, K.C.B. 8vo. Lond., 1883. C 7 S 9
Reminiscences of. [*See* AMORY, MARTHA BABCOCK.]

LYNDSAY (SIR DAVID). Fac-simile of an Ancient Heraldic Manuscript. Edited by David Laing, LL.D. Fol. Edinb., 1878. K 32 P 15 ‡
Another copy. Roy. fol. Edinb., 1878. K 32 P 16 ‡

LYNDSAY (SIR DAVID)—*continued.*
Poetical Works of Sir David Lyndsay of the Mount, Lion King-at-Arms, under James v; with a Life of the Author, &c., by George Chalmers, F.R.S., &c. 3 vols. 8vo. Lond., 1806.   H 8 P 13

LYNE (CHARLES). Industries of New South Wales. Roy. 8vo. Sydney, 1882.*   MF 2 S 14

New Guinea : an Account of the Establishment of the British Protectorate over the Southern Shores of New Guinea. 8vo. Lond., 1885.   MD 4 Q 18

LYON (REV. C. J.), M.A. History of St. Andrews ; Episcopal, Monastic, Academic, and Civil. 2 vols. 8vo. Edinb., 1843.   G 3 T 1, 2

LYON (DAVID MURRAY). History of the Lodge of Edinburgh (Mary's Chapel) No. 1. Embracing an Account of the Rise and Progress of Freemasonry in Scotland. Roy. 8vo. Edinb., 1873.   B 12 V 25

LYON (CAPT. G. F.), R.N. Narrative of Travels in Northern Africa, in the years 1818–20 ; accompanied by Geographical Notices of Soudan, and of the course of the Niger. Coloured Plates. 4to. Lond., 1821.   D 2 U 18

LYON (REV. JOHN). History of the Town and Port of Dover and of Dover Castle ; with an Account of the Cinque Ports. 2 vols. 4to. Dover 1813–14.   B 6 V 16, 17

LYON (WILLIAM PENMAN). Homo *versus* Darwin : a Judicial Examination of Statements recently published by Mr. Darwin regarding "The Descent of Man." 12mo. Lond., 1872.   A 1 V 3

LYSONS (REV. DANIEL), A.M., &c. Environs of London ; being an Historical Account of the Towns, Villages, and Hamlets within twelve miles of that Capital. 2nd ed. 3 vols. 4to. Lond., 1810–11.   B 18 R 2–4 ‡

LYSTER (THOMAS W.) Life of Goethe. [*See* DÖNTZER, H.]

LYSONS (SAMUEL), F.R.S., &c. Account of Roman Antiquities discovered at Woodchester. At. fol. Lond., 1797.   B 13 P 10 ‡

Collection of Gloucestershire Antiquities. Imp. fol. Lond., 1804.   B 14 U 7 ‡

Reliquiæ Britannico-Romanæ ; containing Figures of Roman Antiquities discovered in various parts of England. 3 vols. at. fol. Lond., 1813.   B 13 P 7–9 ‡

LYTE (HENRY CHURCHILL MAXWELL), M.A. History of Eton College, 1440–1875. With Illustrations by P. H. Delamotte ; Steel Engraving by C. H. Jeens, &c. 8vo. Lond., 1875.   B 6 S 13

History of the University of Oxford from Earliest Times to the year 1530. 8vo. Lond., 1886.   B 6 S 11

LYTTELTON (GEORGE), LORD. Life and Poems of. [*See* BRITISH POETS; CHALMERS, A.; *and* JOHNSON, S.]

Works of; formerly printed separately, and now first collected together; with some other Pieces, never before printed; published by George Edward Ayscough, Esq. 2nd ed., with Additions. 4to. Lond., 1775.   J 8 R 11 †

LYTTELTON (REV. W. H.), M.A. Egypt, Palestine, and Phœnicia. [*See* BOVET, F.]

LYTTLETON (RT. HON. GEORGE WILLIAM LYTTLETON), BARON, P.C., &c. Speech in the House of Lords on the Third Reading of the Australian Colonies Government Bill, July 5, 1850. (Pam. 25.) 8vo. Lond., 1850.   MJ 2 Q 13

LYTTON (SIR EDWARD GEORGE EARLE LYTTON BULWER), BARON. Athens; its Rise and Fall. 2 vols. 8vo. Lond., 1837.   B 9 S 33, 34

Critical and Miscellaneous Writings. 2 vols. 8vo. Philad., 1841.   J 8 U 26, 27

Dramatic Works of; comprising the Duchess de la Vallière ; Richelieu ; the Lady of Lyons, Money ; Not so Bad as we Seem. 8vo. Lond. (n.d.)   H 4 P 14

England and the English. 2 vols. 12mo. Lond., 1833.   J 5 R 19, 20

Historical Odes: Last Days of Queen Elizabeth ; Cromwell's Dream; Death of Nelson. 8vo. Lond.,1839.   H 3 S 21

King Arthur. 2nd ed. 8vo. Lond., 1851.   H 7 U 13

Der Letzte der Barone; aus dem Englischen von Gustav Pfizer. 8 vols. (in 2) 8vo. Stuttgart, 1843.   J 16 T 4, 5

Letters to John Bull, Esq., on Affairs connected with his Landed Property, &c. (Pam. 24.) 8vo. Lond., 1851.   MJ 2 Q 12

Life, Letters, and Literary Remains of; by his Son [E. R. Bulwer, Earl of Lytton]. With Portraits and Illustrations. Vols. 1, 2. 8vo. Lond., 1883.   C 11 P 12, 13

Memoir of Laman Blanchard. [*See* BLANCHARD, L.]

Miscellaneous Prose Works. 2 vols. 8vo. Lond., 1868.   J 5 R 19–21

Money : a Comedy. 3rd ed. 8vo. Lond.,1840.   H 2 S 4

Not so Bad as we Seem : a Comedy. 8vo. Lond., 1851.   H 2 S 4

Odes and Epodes of Horace : a Metrical Translation into English. [*See* HORATIUS FLACCUS, Q.]

Poems and Ballads of Schiller. [*See* SCHILLER, J. C. F. VON.]

Richelieu ; or, the Conspiracy: a Play; to which is added Historical Odes. 8vo. Lond., 1839.   H 2 S 4

The Sea-Captain; or, the Birthright: a Drama. 2nd ed. 8vo. Lond., 1839.   H 2 S 4

Speeches of; with a Memoir by his Son. 2 vols. 8vo. Lond., 1874.   F 8 S 11, 12

The Student: a series of Papers. 2nd ed. 2 vols. 8vo. Lond., 1835.   J 8 U 28, 29

LYTTON (SIR EDWARD ROBERT LYTTON BULWER LYTTON), EARL OF, "OWEN MEREDITH." Chronicles and Characters. 2 vols. 8vo. Lond., 1868.   H 8 P 11, 12

Glenaveril ; or, the Metamorphoses. 2 vols. 12mo. Lond., 1885.   H 8 P 7, 8

Life, Letters, and Literary Remains of Edward Bulwer, Lord Lytton ; by his Son. 2 vols. 8vo. Lond., 1883.   C 11 P 12, 13

M

M * * * [*See* FLEURIEU, C. P. C. COMTE DE.]

M.A.T.F. [*See* FIJI.]

M. (W. A.) [*See* ABORIGINES, *and* NEW SOUTH WALES.]

MABILLON (JEAN). Acta Sanctorum Ordinis S. Benedicti Sæculorum Classes distributa. 9 vols. fol. Paris, 1668–1701.　　　　　G 30 Q 7–15 ‡
Museum Italicum seu Collectio Veterum Scriptorum ex Bibliothecis Italicis. 2 vols. 4to. Paris, 1687–89.
　　　　　G 8 V 10, 11
Præfationes in Acta Sanctorum Ord. S. Benedicti ejusdem Dissertationes v. 4to. Tridenti, 1724.
　　　　　G 8 V 12
Annales Ordinis S. Benedicti Occidentalium Monaciorum Patriarchæ. Cui accedit Dissertatio de corporibus SS. Benedicti et Scholasticæ. 6 vols. fol. Luccæ, 1739–45.　　　　　G 26 P 12–17 ‡
Tractatus de Studiis Monasticis Volumen alterum, sive Appendix complectens Animadversiones. 3 vols. (in 1). 4to. Venetiis, 1745.　　　　　G 2 Q 24
De Re Diplomatica Libri VI. Fol. Paris, 1681. B 14 U 8‡
Liborum de Re Diplomatica Supplementum. Fol. Paris, 1704.　　　　　B 14 U 8 ‡

MABINOGION (THE). [*See* GUEST, LADY.]

MABRU (G.) [*See* AUGUEZ, P.]

MACADAM (JOHN). Report on, and Chemical Analysis of the Moffat Mineral Wells. 8vo. Glasgow, 1834.
　　　　　MJ 2 R 15

McADAM (JOHN LOUDON). Remarks on the present System of Road-making. 8vo. Lond., 1824. A 6 S 12

MACALISTER (ALEXANDER), M.D. Introduction to Animal Morphology and Systematic Zoology. Part 1. Invertebrata. Part 2. Morphology of Vertebrate Animals. 2 vols. 8vo. Lond., 1876–78. A 14 U 29–30

McALPINE (PROF. D. AND A. N.) Biological Atlas: a Guide to the Practical Study of Plants and Animals. 8vo. Edinb., 1880.　　　　　A 5 Q 2

McALPINE (NEIL). Pronouncing Gaelic Dictionary; to which is prefixed a concise but most comprehensive Gaelic Grammar. 7th ed. 8vo. Edinb., 1877. K 11 V 8

MACANDREW (JAMES). Address to the People of Otago. 8vo. Dunedin, 1875.　　　　　MJ 2 R 16

MACARDY (JOSEPH). Strictures on the Notice and Supposition of Valentine Hellicar. 8vo. Melb., 1856. MF1Q3

MACARIUS (PATRIARCH OF ANTIOCH). Travels of Macarius; written by his attendant Archdeacon, Paul of Aleppo. [*See* PAUL OF ALEPPO, ARCHDEACON.]
　　　　　D 5 V 24, 25
MACARIUS ÆGYPTIUS (SANCTUS). Opera omnia. [*See* MIGNE, J. P., SERIES GRÆCA, 34.]

MACARTHUR (BLANCHE) AND MOORE (JEANNIE). Lessons in Figure Painting in Water Colours. Sixteen Coloured Plates. With special Instructions by the Painters. Sm. 4to. Lond. (n.d.)　　　　　A 7 S 1

MACARTHUR (LIEUT.-GEN. SIR EDWARD), K.C.B. Colonial Policy of 1840 and 1841, as illustrated by the Governor's Despatches, and Proceedings of the Legislative Council of New South Wales. (Pam. 15.) Lond., 1841.　　　　　MJ 2 Q 5

MACARTHUR (JAMES). New South Wales: its Present State and Future Prospects. 8vo. Lond., 1837.* MB 1T9
Review of New South Wales: its Present State and Future Prospects. [*See* BLAND, W.]

MACARTHUR (JOHN). Antiquities of Arran; with a Historical Sketch of the Island, embracing an Account of the Sudreyjar under the Norsemen. 8vo. Glasgow, 1861.　　　　　B 32 T 11

MACARTHUR (SIR W.), KNT. Letters on the Culture of the Vine, Fermentation, and the Management of Wine in the Cellar; by "Maro." 12mo. Sydney, 1844.* MA 1 P 18

MACARTNEY (GEORGE), EARL. Embassy to China. [*See* STAUNTON, SIR G. L.]

MACARTNEY (REV. H. B.) Conference Addresses, delivered at St. Mary's Caulfield, by Ministers and Laymen of different Denominations, July, 1874. 12mo. Melb., 1874.　　　　　MJ 2 P 32

MACARTNEY (JOHN NEILL). Bendigo Gold-field Registry. 2nd ed. 8vo. Melb., 1872.　　　　　MF I Q 17

MACAULAY (J. S.) Treatise on Field Fortification, the Attack of Fortresses, Military Mining, and Reconnoitring. Illustrated. 6th ed. 8vo. Lond., 1869. A 6 R 27
Plates to [the above.] Ob. 4to. Lond., 1869. A 9 P 26†

MACAULAY (JAMES), A.M., &c., GRANT (REV. BREWIN), B.A., AND WALL (A.) Vivisection, Scientifically and Ethically considered in Prize Essays. 8vo. Lond., 1881.　　　　　A 12 U 24

MACAULAY (THOMAS BABINGTON), LORD.   Lays of
Ancient Rome. Wit1 Illustrations, original and from
the antique, drawn on wood by George Sc1arf, jun.
New ed. Sq. 8vo. Lond., 1883.   H 6 U 4

Puseyism: or, the Oxford Tractarian Sc1ool. (Reprinted from the *Edinburgh Review.*) 12mo. Sydney,
(n.d.)   MG 1 P 49

Anot1er copy. 8vo. West Maitland, 1879.   MG 1 R 7

Critical and Historical Essays. 4th ed. 3 vols. 8vo.
Lond., 1846.   J 2 R 5-7

Lays of Ancient Rome; wit1 Illustrations, by George
Sc1arf, jun. Sm. 4to. Lond., 1883.   H 6 U 4

Speec1es, Parliamentary and Miscellaneous. 2 vols. 8vo.
Lond., 1853.   F 7 R 3, 4

History of England, from the Accession of James II. 5
vols. 8vo. Lond., 1853-61.   B 4 T 12-16

Anot1er copy. 6 vols. 8vo. Lond., 1856-61.
                                                    B 4 T 17-22

Biograp1ies, by Lord Macaulay, contributed to the
Encyclopædia Britannica; wit1 Notes of 1is connection
wit1 Edinburg1, and Extracts from 1is Letters and
Speec1es. 12mo. Lond., 1860.   C 1 R 23

Miscellaneous Writings of. 2 vols. 8vo. Lond., 1860.
                                                    J 2 R 9, 10

Works of, complete; edited by 1is sister, Lady Trevelyan.
8 vols. 8vo. Lond., 1866.   J 2 R 1-8
1-4. History of England.
5-7. Critical and Historical Essays.
8. Speec1es, Lays of Ancient Rome, Miscellaneous Poems.

Speec1es of, corrected by 1imself. 8vo. Lond., 1854.
                                                    F 13 Q 6

Life and Letters of; by 1is nep1ew, George Otto Trevelyan, M.P. Wit1 a Portrait. 2 vols. 8vo. Lond.,
1876.   C 7 S 38, 39

Index to [the above.] [*See* CLARK, P.]

[A Biograp1y]: by J. C. Morison. (Eng. Men of Letts).
8vo. Lond., 1882.   C 1 U 25

Lord Macaulay, Essayist and Historian; by the Hon.
A. S. G. Canning. 8vo. Lond., 1882.   C 1 T 41

Selections from the Writings of. Edited, wit1 Notes, by
G. O. Trevelyan. 8vo. Lond., 1876.   J 1 1 S 30

Evenings wit1 a Reviewer; or, Macaulay and Bacon.
[*See* SPEDDING, J.]

MACBETH (JOHN WALKER V1LANT). The Mig1t and
Mirt1 of Literature. 8vo. Lond., 1876.   J 12 Q 26

MACBRAIR (R. MAXWELL). Sketc1es of a Missionary's
Travels in Egypt, Syria, Western Africa, &c. 8vo. Lond.,
1839.   D 1 P 19

McCABE (JAMES D.), JUNR. The Great Republic: a
Descriptive, Statistical, and Historical View of the States
and Territories of the American Union. Roy. 8vo.
Philad., 1872.   B 1 U 20

MacCALLUM (PROF. M. W.) Studies in Low German and
Hig1 German Literature. 8vo. Lond., 1884.   J 16 R 27

McCALMONT (FREDERICK HAYNES), B.C.L., &c. The
Parliamentary Poll-book of all Elections, from 1832, to
July, 1880. 2nd ed. 12mo. Lond., 1880.   F 2 P 29

MacCANN (WILLIAM). Two T1ousand Miles' Ride t1roug1
the Argentine Provinces. Wit1 Illustrations. 2 vols.
8vo. Lond., 1853.   D 4 P 21, 22

McCARTHY (CHARLES), M.D., &c. On the Excessive
Mortality of Infants and its Causes; wit1 Statistical
Tables. 8vo. Lond., 1865.   MA 2 S 38

McCARTHY (D. F.) Engineer's Guide to the Royal
and Mercantile Navies; by "A Practical Engineer."
(Weale.) 12mo. Lond., 1868.   A 17 Q 5

MACCARTHY (DENIS FLORENCE). Calderon's Dramas.
[*See* CALDERON, DE LA BARCA, DON P.]

McCARTHY (JUSTIN). History of our own Times, from
the Accession of Queen Victoria to the Berlin Congress.
4 vols. 8vo. Lond., 1879-80.   B 5 S 43-46

History of the Four Georges. Vol. 1. 8vo. Lond.,
1884.   B 23 U 16

McCARTHY (JUSTIN HUNTLY). England under Gladstone, 1880-84. 8vo. Lond., 1884.   B 4 R 18

MacCARTIE (J. C.) Hand-book for Australian Brewers.
8vo. Melb., 1884.*   MA 2 S 3

McCARTY (L. P.) McCarty's Annual Statistician,
1885-86. 8vo. San Francisco, 1885.   E

MACCHEYNE (R. M.) Narrative of a Mission of Inquiry
to the Jews. [*See* BONAR, A. A.]

MACCHIAVELLI (N. DI BERNARDO DEI). [*See* MACHIA-
VELLI, N. DI B. DEI.]

MACCLELLAND (JOHN). Indian Cyprinidæ. (2nd part,
19th vol., Asiatic Researc1es.) Sm. fol. Calcutta, 1839.
                                                    A 14 V 14
[*See* GRIFFITH, W.]

MACCLESFIELD PUBLIC FREE LIBRARY. Cata-
logue of t1o Books presented by David C1adwick, Esq.,
M.P., to the Corporation of Macclesfield, 1877. 8vo.
Macclesfield, 1877.   K 7 R 19

MACCLINTOCK (ADM. SIR FRANCIS L.), KNT., R.N.
Voyage of the *Fox* in the Arctic Seas: a Narrative of the
Discovery of the Fate of Sir Jo1n Franklin and 1is Com-
panions. Illustrated. 8vo. Lond., 1859.   D 4 R 20

MACCLINTOCK (PROF. JOHN), D.D., &c.   Life of Jesus
C1rist. [*See* NEANDER, DR. J. A. W.)

McCLURE (CAPT. ROBERT LE MESURIER). Discovery
of the Nort1-west Passage by H.M.S. *Investigator*, during
the years 1850 54; edited by Captain S1erard Osborn,
C.B. Illustrated. 8vo. Lond., 1856.   D 4 R 1

Another copy. 4th ed. 12mo. Edinb., 1865.   D 4 R 2

M'COMBIE (Thomas). Adventures of a Colonist; or, Godfrey Arabin, the Settler. [With an Essay on the Aborigines of Australia.] 8vo. Lond.(n.d.) MJ 1 Q 33

Arabin; or, the Adventures of a Colonist in New South Wales; with an Essay on the Aborigines of Australia. 12mo. Lond., 1845.* MJ 1 Q 34

The Colonist in Australia; or, the Adventures of Godfrey Arabin [with an Essay on the Aborigines of Australia]. 12mo. Lond., 1850. MJ 1 Q 36

History of the Colony of Victoria, from its Settlement to the Death of Sir Charles Hotham. 8vo. Melb., 1858.* MB 2 R 19

Australian Sketches: the Gold Discovery, Bush Graves, &c. 12mo. Lond., 1861. MJ 2 P 33

Australian Sketches. 2nd series. 12mo. Melb., 1866.* MD 4 P 43

McCOOK (Henry Christopher). Natural History of the Agricultural Ant of Texas. 8vo. Philad.,1880. A 1 T 6

M'CORMICK (R.), R.N., F.R.C.S. Voyages of Discovery in the Arctic and Antarctic Seas, and round the World. 2 vols. roy. 8vo. Lond., 1884. D 4 S 35, 36

M'CORQUODALE & CO. General Calculator, to facilitate the Invoicing and Checking of Accounts, &c. 8vo. Lond., 1882. A 10 S 26

McCOSH (Prof. James), LL.D. Method of the Divine Government, Physical and Moral. 3rd ed. 8vo. Lond., 1852. G 7 P 15

Christianity and Positivism: a Series of Lectures to the *Times* on Natural Theology and Apologetics. 8vo. Lond., 1871. G 7 P 19

Examination of Mr. J. S. Mill's Philosophy; being a Defence of Fundamental Truth. 2nd ed. 8vo. New York, 1875. G 7 P 18

The Emotions. 8vo. Lond., 1880. G 7 P 16

Psychology: the Cognitive Powers. 8vo. Lond., 1886. G 7 P 17

McCOY (Prof. Frederick), F.G.S., &c. On the Recent Zoology and Palæontology of Victoria. (Intercolonial Exhibition Essays, 1866.) 8vo. Melb., 1867. MJ 2 R 9

Geological Survey of Victoria: Prodromus of the Palæontology of Victoria; or, Figures and Descriptions of Victorian Organic Remains. Decades 1–7. 3 vols. imp. 8vo. Melb., 1874–82.* MA 2 R 15–17

Natural History of Victoria: Prodromus of the Zoology of Victoria; or, Figures and Descriptions of the living Species of all Classes of the Victorian indigenous Animals. Vols. 1, 2; Decades 1–15. Roy. 8vo. Melb., 1885–87.* MA 2 P 26, 27 †

Lectures: On the Methods of diffusing Technical Knowledge; Geological Action of Fire; Geological Action of Water; Formation and Ages of Coal; Homology of the Parts of Animals; Geological Action of Ice and Nature of the Glacial Period; Palæontology of the three Great Geological Periods. [*See* Melbourne Public Library.]

3 N

McCRACKEN (S. B.) The State of Michigan; embracing Sketches of its History, &c. 8vo. Lansing, 1876. F 1 T 11

M'CRAE (Farquhar), M.D. Election of Medical Officers to the Sydney Infirmary and Dispensary: Dr. M'Crae's Testimonials, &c. 8vo. Sydney, 1845. MF 3 P 13

M'CRAE (Farquhar), M.D., and BLAND (Dr. William). Correspondence between, as lately republished by Dr. F. M'Crae, with his Comments; and the subsequent Correspondence relative to the above between Mr. Bland and the Honorable the Chief Justice. 8vo. Sydney, 1846. MF 1 Q 4

Another copy. 8vo. Sydney, 1846. MJ 2 Q 22

McCRAE (George Gordon). Mâmba (the Bright-eyed): an Aboriginal Reminiscence. 8vo. Melb.,1867. MH 1 Q 4

Another copy. MH 1 S 21

The Man in the Iron Mask: a Poetical Romance, in four Books. 8vo. Melb., 1873.* MH 1 R 18

M'CREARY (James B.) Message to the General Assembly of Kentucky, December 31st, 1875. (Pam. Ja.) 8vo. Frankfort, 1875. F 7 S 24

M'CRIE (Rev. Thomas), D.D., &c. Story of the Scottish Church, from the Reformation to the Distribution. 8vo. Lond., 1875. G 10 Q 28

History of the Progress and Suppression of the Reformation in Italy in the 16th Century. 2nd ed. 8vo. Edinb., 1833. G 8 P 12

Miscellaneous Writings, chiefly Historical. 8vo. Edinb., 1841. J 7 8 8

Life of John Knox; containing Illustrations of the History of the Reformation in Scotland. 3rd ed. 2 vols. 8vo. Edinb., 1814. C 11 P 5, 6

Life of Andrew Melville; containing Illustrations of the Ecclesiastical and Literary History of Scotland, during the latter part of the 16th, and beginning of the 17th Century. 2nd ed. 8vo. Lond., 1824. C 8 P 38, 39

Memoirs of Mr. William Veitch and George Brysson, written by themselves; with other Narratives, biographical Sketches, and Notes, by T. M'Crie, D.D. 8vo. Edinb., 1825. C 9 R 39

MACCULLAGH (James), LL.D., &c. Collected Works: Physical Optics, Geometry, Rotation, Attraction, and Chronology. 8vo. Dublin, 1880. A 16 U 22

McCULLAGH (W. Torrens). Memoirs of the Rt. Hon. Richard Lalor Shiel. 2 vols. 8vo. Lond., 1855. C 4 Q 1, 2

MACCULLOCH (John), M.D., &c. Highlands and Western Isles of Scotland, containing Descriptions of their Scenery and Antiquities, in Letters to Sir Walter Scott, Bart. 4 vols. 8vo. Lond., 1824. D 6 T 40–43

Remarks on the Art of making Wine. 12mo. Lond., 1829. A 1 P 7

McCULLOCH (J. R.) Dictionary, Geographical, Statistical, and Historical, of the various Countries, Places, and principal Natural Objects in the World. New ed. 4 vols. roy. 8vo. Lond., 1866.　　　　　　　　D 11 U 5–8

Geographical, Statistical, and Historical Dictionary. 2 vols. 8vo. Lond., 1841–42.

Principles of Political Economy; with a Sketch of the Rise and Progress of the Science. 8vo. Lond., 1830.
　　　　　　　　　　　　　　　　　　　　F 7 S 1

Treatises and on Subjects connected with Economical Policy; with biographical Sketches of Quesnay, Adam Smith, and Ricardo. 8vo. Edinb., 1853.　　F 7 S 2

Dictionary, Practical, Theoretical, and Historical, of Commerce and Commercial Navigation. Latest ed.; with a Supplement by A. J. Wilson. 8vo. Lond., 1882.
　　　　　　　　　　　　　　　　　　　　K 9 S 9

McCURDY (JAMES FREDERICK). Aryo-Semitic Speech: a Study in Linguistic Archaeology. 8vo. Andover, 1881.　　　　　　　　　　　　　　　K 13 Q 1

McCURE (JOHN BUNYAN). My Log-book; or, the History of my Voyage from London to Sydney. 8vo. Lond. (n.d.)　　　　　　　　　　MD 3 Q 29

M'CURRICK (LAURENCE). Planetary Distances. 8vo. Lond., 1883.　　　　　　　　　　　A 3 T 21

M'CUTCHEON (CAPT. J. WARNER). Catechism of Infantry Drill, compiled from the latest edition of the Field Exercise and Evolutions of Infantry. 12mo. Sydney, 1871.　　　　　　　　　　　MA 2 V 24

Catechism of Infantry Drill, Book 1 and 2. Revised ed., Parts 1–6. 2 vols. 8mo. Sydney, 1885. MA 2 V 25, 26

MACDIARMID (JOHN). Lives of British Statesmen. New ed. 8vo. Lond., 1838.　　　　　C 10 R 26

MACDONALD (A.) Chapter on Perspective. [*See* TYRWHITT, REV. R. ST. J.]

MACDONALD (DONALD). Gum Bougis and Wattle Bloom, gathered on Australian Hills and Plains. 8vo. Lond., 1887.　　　　　　　　　　MD 6 P 27

M'DONALD (D.), D.D. Narrative of the Voyages of the *Dayspring.* [*See* CAMPBELL, F. A.]　MD 4 Q 30

M'DONALD (FLORA). Life of: written by her Granddaughter [Mrs. Flora Frances Wyllie.] New ed. 12mo. Lond., 1875.　　　　　　　　　　C 1 S 32

MACDONALD (GEORGE). Tragedie of Hamlet: a Study with the Text of the folio of 1623. [*See* SHAKESPEARE, W.]

MACDONALD (JAMES). Origin of the Destiny of Comets; or, a Change in the Ecliptic of the Earth. 8vo. Prahran, 1869.　　　　　　　　　　　　　A 16 U 25

Another copy.　　　　　　　　　　　MJ 2 R 11

Origin and Destiny of Comets. 2nd ed. Likewise the Key and Graphed of the Missing Link. (Pam. Cq.) 8vo. Dunfermline (n.d.)　　　　　　　MA 2 V 9

MACDONALD (JAMES), AND SINCLAIR (JAMES). History of Polled Aberdeen or Angus Cattle. 8vo. Edinburgh, 1882.　　　　　　　　　　　　A 1 Q 12

MACDONALD (JAMES M.), D.D. Life and Writings of St. John. Edited by the Very Rev. J. S. Howson, D.D. Roy. 8vo. Lond., 1877.　　　　　　　G 5 T 2

MACDONALD (REV. JOHN), M.A. What is the Theatre? 8vo. Launceston, 1856.　　　　　　MG 1 P 49

MACDONALD (JOHN D.) M.D., &c. Outlines of Naval Hygiene. With Illustrations. 8vo. Lond., 1881. A 2 R 29

Guide to the Microscopical Examination of Drinking Water. 8vo. Lond., 1875.　　　　　A 6 P 20

MACDONALD (D. E.) Dictionary of Quotations in most frequent use, taken chiefly from the Latin and French; but comprising many from the Greek, Spanish, and Italian Languages. 8vo. Lond., 1826.　　　K 17 P 12

MACDONNELL (ENEAS). Great Britain and Ireland: a Letter. [*See* HIST. PAMS.]　　　　　B 11 Q 1

The "Crisis" Unmasked; respectfully inscribed to the British People. (Pam. 15.) 8vo. Lond., 1843. MJ 2 Q 5

Vindication of the House of Lords, &c., in a Series of Letters. (Pam. 1.) 8vo. Lond., 1835.　MJ 2 P 36

MACDONNELL (JOHN), M.A. Survey of Political Economy. 8vo. Edinb., 1871.　　　　F 6 R 30

MACDONNELL (SIR RICHARD GRAVES), C.B., KNT. Australia: what it is, and what it may be: a Lecture. 12mo. Dublin, 1863.　　　　　　　　　MD 1 S 14

Correspondence of. [*See* BINNEY, REV. T.]

McDONNELL (LIEUT.-COL. T.) Maori History; being a Native Account of the Pakeha-Maori Wars in New Zealand. (*Bound with Gudgeon's Defenders of New Zealand.*) Roy. 8vo. Auckland, 1887.*　MB 2 U 6

Incidents of the War: Tales of Maori Character and Customs, &c. (*Bound with Gudgeon's Defenders of New Zealand.*) Roy. 8vo. Auckland, 1887.*　MB 2 U 9

McDONOUGH (CAPT. FELIX). The Hermit in Edinburgh. 3 vols. 12mo. Lond., 1824.　J 12 S 16–18

MACDOUGALL (ARCHIBALD). South Australian Almanack and Adelaide and Colonial Directory for 1843. 12mo. Adelaide, 1843.　　　　　　　ME 4 P

McDOUGALL (D. & J.) [*See* SANDS & McDOUGALL.]

M'DOUGALL (CAPT. GEORGE F.) Eventful Voyage of H.M. Discovery Ship *Resolute* to the Arctic Regions in search of Sir John Franklin and the missing Crews of H.M. Discovery Ships *Erebus* and *Terror*, 1852–54. 8vo. Lond., 1857.　　　　　　　　D 4 R 23

McDOUGALL (MRS. HARRIETTE). Sketches of our Life at Sarawak. With Maps. 8vo. Lond., 1882.　D 5 P 44

MACDOWALL (M. W.) Asgard and the Gods. [*See* WAGNER, DR. W.] B 15 Q 6

MACEACHERN (JAMES). Dynasty of La Trobe and Foster illustrated ; or, the Evils of summary Jurisdiction and irresponsible Government exemplified. 8vo. Meln., 1854. MJ 2 R 19

MACEDO (JOAQUIM MANOEL DE). Brazilian Biographical Annual. 3 vols. 8vo. Rio de Janeiro, 1876. C 9 V 9–11

MACENCROE (REV. JOHN). Of Conversion to the Roman Catholic Religion : a Letter to the Editor of the *Sydney Gazette* (MS). 8vo. Sydney, 1833. MG 1 P 5

Bigotry in the Nineteenth Century: Six Months in a Convent; by Rebecca Theresa Reed (the same Convent burnt to ashes through the Tales of Rebecca and a false rumour) considered in a Letter to the Editor of the *Colonist*. 8vo. Sydney, 1836. MG 1 P 5

M'FADYEAN (J.), M.B., &c. Anatomy of the Horse : a Dissection Guide. 8vo. Edinb., 1885. A 27 U 30

MACFARLAND (ALFRED), JUDGE. Illawarra and Manaro Districts of New South Wales. 12mo. Sydney, 1872.* MD 6 P 11

Mutiny in the *Bounty*, and Story of the Pitcairn Islanders. 8vo. Sydney, 1884.* MB 2 Q 3

MACFARLAND (JOHN), M.A.· Digest of the Law of Mining in Victoria. 8vo. Meln., 1869. MF 2 P 23

MACFARLANE (CHARLES). Glance at Revolutionized Italy : a Visit to Messina, &c., in 1848. 2 xols. 8vo. Lond., 1849. D 8 Q 7, 8

Japan : an Account, Geographical and Historical. 8vo. Lond., 1852. D 6 8 8

Turkey and its Destiny: the Result of Journeys made in 1847–48, to examine into the State of that Country. 2 vols. 8vo. Lond., 1850. D 7 S 22, 23

MACFARREN (CLARA NATALIA), LADY. Recollections of Felix Mendelssohn-Bartholdy. [*See* DEVRIENT, E.] C 5 P 21

MACFARREN (GEORGE). My Old Woman: a Musical Comedy. (Cumberland's Eng. Theatre.) 12mo. Lond., 1829. H 2 Q 13

MACFARREN (SIR GEORGE ALEXANDER), KNT. Six Lectures on Harmony, delivered at the Royal Institution of Great Britain, before Easter, 1867. 2nd ed. 8vo. Lond., 1877. A 7 P 6

MACFAULL (C.) West Australian Almanac for the year 1842 ; with an Appendix, containing a Native Grammar, by Charles Symmons. 8vo. Perth, 1842. ME 4 U

MACFIE (MATTHEW), F.R.G.S. Vancouver Island and British Columbia: their History, Resources, and Prospects. 8vo. Lond., 1865. D 3 U 10

MACFIE (R. A.), F.R.S.E. Copyright and Patents for Inventions. 2 vols. 8vo. Edinb., 1879–83. F 7 Q 22, 23

MACGARVIE REV. JOHN), D.D. Sermons, preached in St. Andrews' Church, Sydney, New South Wales. 8vo. Sydney, 1842. MG 1 R 4

MACGARVIE (WILLIAM). Catalogue of Books in the Circulating Library of William M'Garvie, at the Australian Stationery Warehouse (near the Main Guard), George-street, Sydney. (Pam. 41.) 12mo. Sydney, 1829–33. MJ 2 R 3

MACGEOGHEGAN (J.), L'ABBÉ. Histoire de l'Irlande, Ancienne et Moderne. 3 vols. 4to. Paris, 1758–63. B 1 S 2–4 †

Continuation of the History of [Ireland]. [*See* MITCHELL, J.] B 1 S 5 †

MACGEORGE (A.) Flags: some Account of their History and Uses. Sm. 4to. Lond., 1881. B 15 Q 5

Old Glasgow : the Place and the People, from the Roman Occupation to the 18th Century. 4to. Glasgow, 1880. B 15 Q 9 ‡

William Leighton Leitch, Landscape Painter: a Memoir. 8vo. Lond., 1884. C 9 V 26

MACGIBBON (D.), AND ROSS (T.) Castellated and Domestic Architecture of Scotland. Vols. 1, 2. 2 vols. 8vo. Edinb., 1887. A 3 Q 21, 22

MACGIBBON (REV. JOHN), B.A. Duty of the Church at the Present Time, and in the Present State of Presbyterianism in the Colony : a Sermon. 8vo. Sydney, 1864. MG 1 P 1

McGILCHRIST (JOHN), M.D. History of the Turks, from the Earliest Period to the Present Time. 12mo. Lond., 1856. B 13 V 35

MACGILL (F.) Victorian Almanac for 1861, containing Farmer's and Gardener's Calendar. 12mo. Meln., 1861. ME 4 P

MACGILLIVRAY (JOHN), F.R.G.S. Narrative of the Voyage of H.M.S. *Rattlesnake*, during the years 1846–50; to which is added, the Account of E. B. Kennedy's Expedition for the Exploration of the Cape York Peninsula. 2 vols. 8vo. Lond., 1852.* MD 3 T 25, 26

MACGILLIVRAY (W.) History of British Quadrupeds. (Nat. Lib., 22.) 12mo. Edinb., 1838. A 14 P 22

MACGREGOR (A.) [*See* NEW ZEALAND PARLIAMENTARY LIBRARY.]

MACGREGOR (SIR C. M.), K.C.B., &c. Narrative of a Journey through the Province of Khorassan, and on the North-west Frontier of Afghanistan, in 1875. With Illustrations. 2 vols. 8vo. Lond., 1879. D 4 T 12, 13

MACGREGOR (GEN. SIR DUNCAN), K.C.B. Narrative of the Loss of the *Kent*, East Indiaman by Fire, in the Bay of Biscay, on the 1st March, 1825; by "A Passenger." 3rd ed. 12mo. Edinb., 1825. D 7 P 56

MACGREGOR (GEORGE), F.S.A.Scot. History of Burke and Hare, and the Resurrectionist Times; containing Illustrations. 8vo. Glasgow, 1884. B 13 P 40

MACGREGOR (JAMES). Fifty Facts about Australasia: an Epitome for the Million. With Map. 8vo. Lond., 1883. MF 1 P 21

MACGREGOR (JAMES). Macgregor's Almanack and Entertaining Annual. 12mo. Sydney, 1865. ME 4 Q

MACGREGOR (SIR JAMES). The Dean of Lismore's Book: a Selection of Ancient Gaelic Poetry from a MS. Collection made by Sir James M'Gregor, Dean of Lismore. 8vo. Edinb., 1862. H 5 U 3

MACGREGOR (JOHN). British America. 2 vols. 8vo. Edinb., 1832. B 2 P 1, 2
My Note-book. 3 vols. 8vo. Lond., 1835. D 9 P 43-45
Life of J. L. De Lolme [*See* DE LOLME, J. L.] B4P10

MACGREGOR (JOHN), M.A. Thousand Miles in the *Rob Roy* Canoe, on Rivers and Lakes of Europe. 12mo. Lond., 1866. D 7 P 52
The *Rob Roy* on the Baltic: a Canoe Cruise through Norway, Sweden, Denmark, Sleswig, Holstein, the North Sea, and the Baltic. 12mo. Lond., 1867. D 7 P 53
Voyage alone in the Yawl *Rob Roy*, from London to Paris, and back by Havre, the Isle of Wight, South Coast, &c. 12mo. Lond., 1867. D 7 P 51
The *Rob Roy* on the Jordan, Nile, Red Sea, and Gennesareth, &c.: a Canoe Cruise in Palestine and Egypt and the Waters of Damascus. 2nd ed. 8vo. Lond., 1870. D 6 P 20
Description of the new *Rob Roy* Canoe, built for a Voyage through Norway, Sweden, and the Baltic. With Illustrations. (Pam. Cn.) 8vo. Lond.(n.d.) MA 2 V 14

MACGREGOR (J. L. L.) Organization and Valuation of Forests, on the Continental System, in Theory and Practice. 8vo. Lond., 1883. A 1 S 43

MACGREGOR (P.) Genuine Remains of Ossian. [*See* OSSIAN.] H 7 T 21

MACGREGOR (WILLIAM). Gas Engines. With seven Plates. 8vo. Lond., 1885. A 6 R 24
[*See* BOND, R.]

McGRIGOR (SIR JAMES), BART. Autobiography and Services of. With an Appendix of Notes and Original Correspondence. 8vo. Lond., 1861. C 4 V 12

MACHENRY (GEORGE). Time and Eternity: a Poem. 8vo. San Francisco, 1871. H 7 Q 30

MACHIAVELLI (NICCOLÒ DI BERNARDO DEI). Historical, Political, and Diplomatic Writings of. Translated from the Italian by Christian E. Detmold. 4 vols. 8vo. Boston, 1882. J 3 8 13-16
Niccolò Machiavelli and his Times; by Prof. Pasquale Villari. Translated by Linda Villari. 4 vols. 8vo. Lond., 1878-83. C 3 U 20-23
History of Florence and the affairs of Italy, from the Earliest Times to the Death of Lorenzo the Magnificent; together with "The Prince" and various Historical Tracts. New Translation. 8vo. Lond., 1876. B 12 P 21
The Prince. Translated from the Italian, by N. H. T. 12mo. Lond., 1882. J 11 R 2
Opere complete di Niccolò Machiavelli; con molte correzioni e giunte rinvenute sui manoscritti originali. 2 vols 8vo. Milan, 1850. J 13 U 29, 30
Works of Nicholas Machiavel; newly translated from the Original, with Life, by E. Farneworth, M.A. 2 vols. 4to. Lond., 1762. J 2 U 15, 16-

MACHIN (JOHN). Laws of the Moon's Motion. [*See* NEWTON, SIR I.]

McIAN (R. R.) Clans of the Scottish Highlands, illustrated; with accompanying Description and Historical Memoranda of Character, mode of Life, &c., by James Logan, Esq., F.S.A., &c. 2 vols. roy. 4to. Lond., 1845-47. B 15 T 8, 9 ‡

MACILWAIN (GEORGE), F.R.C.S., &c. Memoirs of John Abernethy, F.R.S.; with a Memoir of his Lectures, Writings, and Character. 2 vols. 8vo. Lond., 1853. C 2 U 4, 5

McINTOSH (W. C.) M.D., &c. Monograph of the British Annelids. Part 1. The Nemerteans. (Ray Soc., 15.) Imp. 4to. Lond., 1873-74. E

MACINTYRE (JAMES J.) Thoughts on Population and Starvation; with an Appendix, containing Letters on Emigration and other Colonial Matters, addressed to Joseph Hume, Esq., and Sir Robert Peel, Bart. 8vo. Lond., 1841. MJ 2 R 22

MACINTYRE (REV. W.), M.A. Is the Service of the Mass idolatrous? Being a candid Inquiry into the Doctrine maintained on that subject by Bishop Polding in his Pastoral Address. 8vo. Sydney, 1838. MF 1 Q 4 and MG 1 P 5
Appeal to the Presbyterians of New South Wales on behalf of St. George's Church, Sydney. 8vo. Sydney (n.d.) MG 1 Q 29

MACIVER (BRIG.-GEN. H. H.) Under Fourteen Flags; being Life and Adventures of a Soldier of Fortune; by Capt. W. D. L'Estrange. 8vo. Melb., 1884. MC 1 P 38
Rivals for Supremacy in the Pacific; a book for every British Subject, the Interests and Prosperity of Australasia in Danger. 8vo. Sydney, 1885. MF 3 Q 48

MACKAY (ALEXANDER). Western World; or, Travels in the United States, in 1846–47, including a Chapter on California. 3 vols. 8vo. Lond., 1849. D 3 P 1–3

MACKAY (ANDREW), LL.D., &c. Theory and Practice of finding the Longitude at Sea or on Land. 2nd ed. 2 vols. 8vo. Aberdeen, 1801. A 19 U 26, 27

MACKAY (ANGUS). Analysis of the Australian Colonies' Government Bill. 8vo. Lond., 1850. MF 3 Q 39

Great Gold-field : a Pedestrian Tour through the first discovered Gold District of New South Wales, November, 1852. 8vo. Sydney, 1853. MJ 2 Q 16

Sugar-cane in Australia : a Series of Essays upon its Cultivation and Manufacture. 8vo. Brisbane, 1870. MA 1 Q 9

Sugar-cane in Australia : Practical Details concerning Cane, Sorghum, and Beet cultivation and Sugar making ; with latest improvements in machinery. Fully illustrated. 8vo. Sydney, 1883. MA 1 Q 10

Elements of Australian Agriculture, leading to various Departments of Agricultural Science. Illustrated by numerous Engravings. 12mo. Sydney, 1885. MA 1 P 4

MACKAY (CHARLES), LL.D. Gaelic Etymology of the Languages of Western Europe, and more especially of the English and Lowland Scotch, and of the Slang, Cant, and Colloquial Dialects. Imp. 8vo. Lond., 1877. K 14 S 20

Memoirs of Extraordinary Popular Delusions. 3 vols. 8vo. Lond., 1841. B 15 P 33–35

Founders of the American Republic : a History and Biography. With a Supplementary Chapter on Ultra-Democracy. 8vo. Edinb., 1885. C 3 P 10

Forty Years' Recollections of Life, Literature, and Public Affairs, from 1830 to 1870. 2 vols. 8vo. Lond., 1877. C 5 S 17, 18

Poetry and Humour of the Scottish Language. 8vo. Paisley, 1882. K 12 P 11

Medora Leigh : a History and an Autobiography. 8vo. Lond., 1869. C 3 P.29

The Thames and its Tributaries ; or, Rambles among the Rivers. 2 vols. 8vo. Lond., 1840. D 6 2 35, 36

MACKAY (GEORGE), LL.D., &c., Legal and Historical Debating Society in connection with the Bar of Ireland : [an] Address. 8vo. Melb., 1853. MJ 2 R 19

MACKAY (J.) An Old Scots Brigade ; being the History of Mackay's Regiment. 12mo. Edinb., 1885. B 31 P 18

MACKAY (KENNETH). Stirrup Jingles from the Bush and the Turf, and other Rhymes. 8vo. Sydney, 1887. MH 1 P 27

Another copy. 2nd ed. 8vo. Sydney, 1887. MH 1 P 28

MACKAY (R.) Mackay's Australian Illustrated Almanack for 1860–61. 12mo. Sydney, 1860–61. ME 4 Q

McKELLAR (D.), JUN. Queensland Hand-book, Passengers' Guide, Fare, and Time Table by Railway, Steamer, Omnibus, Coach, Road, and Cab ; with New South Wales Appendix. 12mo. Brisbane, 1879. MD 4 P 8

MACKELLAR (DUNCAN). Australian Emigrant's Guide. 8vo. Edinb., 1839. MF 3 P 7

MACKENNA (J. WILLIAM). Mortality of Children in Victoria ; with Means for the Prevention and Cure of the Diseases of Children. (Pam. Cc.) 8vo. Melb., 1858. MA 2 S 15

M'KENNEY (THOMAS L.), AND HALL (JAMES). History of the Indian Tribes of North America; with Biographical Sketches and Anecdotes of the Principal Chiefs. 3 vols. at. fol. Philad., 1838–44. B 5 R 22–24 ‡

MACKENZIE (ALEXANDER), F.S.A. Prophecies of the Brahan Seer (Coinneach Odhar Fiosaiche). 3rd ed. 8vo. Inverness, 1882. G 16 R 39

MACKENZIE (A. SLIDELL). American in England. Aberdeen, 1848. D 8 S 20

MACKENZIE (CHARLES), F.R.S., &c. Notes on Haiti, made during a residence in that Republic. 2 vols. 8vo. Lond., 1830. D 3 R 31, 32

MACKENZIE (CAPT. C. F.) "MUSANNIF." Romantic Land of Hind. 8vo. Lond., 1882. B 10 Q 37

MACKENZIE (REV. DAVID), M.A. Emigrants Guide ; or, Ten Years' Practical Experience in Australia. 12mo. Lond., 1845. MD 3 P 37

Emigrant's Guide to Australia; with a Memoir of Mrs. Chisholm. 12mo. Lond., 1853.* MD 3 P 38

The Gold Digger : a Visit to the Gold-fields of Australia in February, 1852. 12mo. Lond., 1852. MD 3 P 43

Ten Years in Australia ; being the Results of his Experience as a Settler during that period. 3rd ed. 12mo. Lond., 1852.* MD 3 P 41

MACKENZIE (ENEAS). Memoirs of Mrs. Caroline Chisholm ; with an Account of her philanthropic Labours, in India, Australia, and England. 2nd ed. 12mo. Lond., 1852. MC 1 P 30

MACKENZIE (SIR GEORGE). Jus Regium ; or, the just and solid Foundations of Monarchy in general, and more especially of the Monarchy of Scotland. 12mo. Lond., 1684. F 5 S 35

MACKENZIE (SIR GEORGE STEUART), BART. Travels in the Island of Iceland, during the Summer of the Year 1810. 2nd ed. 4to. Edinb., 1812. D 7 V 5

MACKENZIE (HENRY), F.R.S.E. Account of the Life and Writings of John Home. 8vo. Edinb., 1822. C 8 T 45

Works of. 8 vols. 8vo. Edinb., 1808. J 11 T 1–8

Works of John Home ; with Life, &c. [*See* HOME, J.]

MACKENZIE (JOHN). Ten Years North of the Orange River. 8vo. Edinb., 1871.   D 1 R 23

MACKENZIE (KEITH STEWART). Narrative of the Second Campaign in China. 12mo. Lond., 1842.   B 2 P 27

MACKENZIE (KENNETH R. H.), IX° "CRYPTONYMUS." Royal Masonic Cyclopædia of History, Rites, Symbolism, and Biography. 8vo. Lond., 1877.   K 1 R 24

Life of Bismarck. [*See* HESEKIEL, J. G. L.]   C 10 R 21

Discoveries in Egypt. [*See* LEPSIUS, C. R.]   D 2 T 18–21

MACKENZIE (THOMAS), LORD. Studies in Roman Law; with comparative Views of the Laws of France, England, and Scotland. 5th ed. 8vo. Edinb., 1880.   F 7 S 8

MACKENZIE (SIR M.) Hygiene of the Vocal Organs: a practical Hand-book for Singers and Speakers. 2nd ed. 8vo. Lond., 1886.   A 12 Q 9

MACKENZIE (PETER). Life of Thomas Muir, Esq., Advocate, who was tried for Sedition before the High Court of Justiciary in Scotland, and sentenced to Transportation for Fourteen Years; with a full Report of his Trial. 8vo. 8vo. Glasgow, 1831.*   MC 1 R 19

MACKENZIE (RODERICK). Strictures on Lieut.-Col. Tarleton's History of the Campaigns of 1780–81 in the Southern Provinces of North America. 8vo. Lond., 1787.   B 1 S 14

MACKENZIE (W.), M.D. Practical Treatise on the Diseases of the Eye. 8vo. Lond., 1835.   A 12 S 23

MACKENZIE (WILLIAM). Imperial Dictionary of Universal Biography: a Series of original Memoirs of distinguished Men of all Ages in all Nations. 6 vols. imp. 8vo. Lond., 1865–68.   C 11 V 1–6

MACKENZIE (WILLIAM HENRY), AND CAPE (ROLLO ALBERT). Statement of General Average per steamship *Chimborazo*, London to Sydney. 8m. fol. Sydney, 1878.   MJ 2 U 5

McKERLIE (P. H.), F.S.A., &c. History of the Lands and their Owners in Galloway. Illustrated. 5 vols. 8vo. Edinb., 1870–79.   B 13 P 24–28

McKERROW (J.) Report on the Geology and Gold-fields of Otago. [*See* HUTTON, CAPT. F. W., AND ULRICH, G. H. F.]

MACKEY (ALBERT G.), M.D. Lexicon of Freemasonry. 14th ed. 8vo. Philad., 1872.   K 7 Q 13

Encyclopædia of Freemasonry and its kindred Sciences. 8vo. Philad., 1874.   K 5 Q 39

MACKIE (A. K.) Historical Notes regarding the Merchant Company of Edinburgh. [*See* JOHNSTON, A. K.]   F 6 S 13

McKILLOP (LIEUT. H. F.), R.N. Reminiscences of Twelve Months' Service in New Zealand as a Midshipman, during the late Disturbances in that Colony. 12mo. Lond., 1849.*   MD 2 P 47

McKINLAY (J.) McKinlay's Journal of Exploration in the Interior of Australia (Burke Relief Expedition). With three Maps. 8vo. Melb. (n.d.)*   MD 6 T 20

Tracks of McKinlay and Party across Australia. [*See* DAVIS, J.]   MD 2 V 2

MACKINNON (CAPT. D. H.), R.N. Atlantic and Trans-atlantic Sketches, Afloat and Ashore. 2 vols. 8vo. Lond., 1852.   D 3 R 36, 36

Military Service and Adventures in the Far East. 2nd ed. 2 vols. 12mo. Lond., 1849.   D 5 P 1, 2

MACKINNON (HAMILTON). Marcus Clarke Memorial Volume. [*See* CLARKE, M. A. H.]   MC 1 P 13

MACKINNON (LAUCHLAN). [*See* ARGUS LIBEL CASE.]   MF 1 Q 1, and MJ 2 Q 23

MACKINTOSH (RT. HON. SIR JAMES), LL.D. Discourse on the Study of the Law of Nature and Nations. 8vo. Lond., 1835.   F 1 P 30

Dissertation on the Progress of Ethical Philosophy; chiefly during the 17th and 18th Centuries. 2nd ed. 8vo. Edinb., 1837.   G 15 R 3

Miscellaneous Works of. 3 vols. 8vo. Lond., 1846.   J 9 T 16–18

Historical Characters. [*See* DALLING AND BULWER, SIR H. L. E., LORD.]

History of the Revolution in England in 1688. 4to. Lond., 1834.   B 6 V 1

History of England, by Sir J. Mackintosh, and the late William Wallace; continued by Robert Bell. (Lard. Cab. Cyclo.) 10 vols. 12mo. Lond., 1830–40.   K 1 S 42–T 5

History of England, from the Earliest Times to the year 1588. New ed. Roy. 8vo. Philad., 1836.   B 5 V 41

Memoirs of the Life of. Edited by Son, Robert James Mackintosh. 2 vols. 8vo. Lond., 1835.   C 8 Q 35, 36

MACKINTOSH (RT. HON. SIR JAMES), LL.D., FORSTER (JOHN), AND COURTENAY (RT. HON. THOMAS PEREGRINE). Lives of Eminent British Statesmen. 7 vols. 18mo. Lond., 1831–39.   C 1 Q 34–40

1. Sir Thomas More; Cardinal Wolsey; Archbishop Cranmer; William Cecil, Lord Burleigh.
2. Sir John Eliot; Thomas Wentworth, Earl of Stafford.
3. John Pym; John Hampden.
4. Sir Henry Vane; Henry Marten.
5. Robert Cecil, Earl of Salisbury; Thomas Osborne, Earl of Danby.
6, 7. Oliver Cromwell.

Another copy. (Lard. Cab. Cyclo.)   K 1 S 10–16

MACKINTOSH (JOHN). The Earnest Student; being Memorials of, by Norman Macleod, D.D. 12mo. Lond., 1863.   G 10 Q 13

MACKINTOSH (JOHN). History of Civilisation in Scotland. 3 vols. 8vo. Lond., 1874–84.   B 32 T 1–3

MACKINTOSH (ROBERT JAMES). Memoirs of the Life of Sir James Mackintosi. Edited by iis Son. 2 vols. 8vo. Lond., 1835. C 8 Q 35, 36

McKINTOSH (WILLIAM). General, Statistical, and Commercial Report of the Province of Australia Felix, for the year ending 31st July, 1847; being a continuation of observations by William Westgarti. 8vo. Melb., 1849. MJ 2 R 22

MACKLIN (CHARLES), COMEDIAN. Memoirs of; witi the Dramatic Ciaracters, Manners, Anecdotes, &c., of the Age in wici he lived, by William Cooke. 2nd ed. 8vo. Lond., 1806. C 4 V 11

Love a la Mode : a Farce. [*See* FARCES, 1.]

The Man of the World : a Comedy. (Bell's Brit. Theatre.) 18mo. Lond., 1795. H 2 P 16

Anotier copy. (Brit. Tieatre.) 12mo. Lond., 1808. H 1 P 14

McKNIGHT (CHARLES H.) AND MADDEN (DR. HENRY). On the True Principles of Breeding, developed in Letters. 8vo. Meli., 1865. MA 1 Q 1

Anotier copy. 8vo. Melb., 1865. MA 1 Q 26

McKNIGHT (DAVID A.) Electoral System of the United States : a Critical and Historical Exposition of its Fundamental Principles in the Constitution, and of the Acts and Proceedings of Congress enforcing it. 8vo. Philad., 1878. F 10 P 20

MACKNIGHT (THOMAS). Rt. Hon. Benjamin Disraeli, M.P.: a Literary and Political Biograpiy. 8vo. Lond., 1854. C 9 V 12

History of the Life and Times of Edmund Burke. 2 vols. 8vo. Lond., 1858. C 10 Q 3, 4

Tiirty Years of Foreign Policy: a History of the Secretarysiips of the Earl of Aberdeen and Viscount Palmerston. 8vo. Lond., 1855. B 7 Q 25

MACKROW (CLEMENT). Naval Arciitect's and Siipbuilder's Pocket-book of Formulæ, Rules, and Tables, and Marine Engineer's and Surveyor's Handy-book of Reference. 12mo. Lond., 1879. A 2 R 33

McLACHLAN (ARCHIBALD). Correspondence [and Report from the Select Committee] upon Mr. Arciibald M'Lachlan's Claim upon the Victorian Government. 8vo. Melb., 1861. MF 1 Q 6

MACLACHLAN (REV. ARCHIBALD NEIL CAMPBELL), M.A. Sketci of the Military Life and Ciaracter of William Augustus, Duke of Cumberland. 8vo. Lond., 1876. C 3 S 17

McLACHLAN (C.) Copies of two Letters to the Sec retary of State for the Colonies, dated the 24th and 27th February, 1846, on the subject of Transportation to Van Diemen's Land. (Parl. Doc. 48.) Fol. Lond., 1846. MF 4 ‡

MACLAGAN (MISS CHRISTIAN). Hill Forts, Stone Circles, and otier Structural Remains of Ancient Scotland. Illustrated. Fol. Edinb., 1875. B 16 S 6 ‡

MACLAGAN (ROBERT CRAIG), M.D. Scottisi Mytis: Notes on Scottisi History and Tradition. 8vo. Edinb., 1882. B 13 T 10

MACLAGAN (T. J.), M.D. Germ Tieory applied to the explanation of the Pienomena of Disease. 8vo. Lond., 1876. A 12 R 34

MACLAINE (A.), D.D. Ecclesiastical History. [*See* MOSHEIM, J. L.]

MACLAREN (ARCHIBALD). System of Piysical Education, Tieoretical and Practical. (Clar. Press.) 12mo. Oxford, 1869. A 29 P 8

MACLAUGHLIN (FANNY). Rome: its Princes, Priests, and People. [*See* SILVAGNI, D.] D 8 T 9, 10

MACLAUGHLIN (LOUISA ELIZABETH). Our Adventures during the War of 1870. [*See* PEARSON, EMMA M.] D 7 Q 27, 28

MACLAURIN (JOHN). Dissertation to prove tiat Troy was not taken by the Greeks. (Pam.) 4to. Lond., 1784. B 18 R 13 ‡

MACLAY (N. DE MIKLUCHO). [*See* MIKLUCHO-MACLAY, N. DE.]

McLEAN (ANGUS). Lindigo, the Wiite Woman; or, the Higiland Girl's Captivity among the Australian Blacks. 12mo. Meli., 1866. MJ 1 P 36

MACLEAN (C. D.) Standing Information regarding the official administration of the Madras Presidency in eaci Department, in illustration of the yearly Administration Reports. Roy. 8vo. Madras, 1877. F 2 T 14

MACLEAN (G. R.) [*See* SYDNEY MAGAZINE, THE.]

M'LEAN (SIR JOHN). Notes of a Twenty-five Years' Service in the Hudson Bay Territory. 2 vols. 8vo. Lond., 1849. D 3 R 3, 4

MACLEAN (SIR JOHN), KNT., F.S.A., &c. Parociial and Family History of the Deanery of Trigg Minor, in the County of Cornwall. 3 vols. 4to. Lond., 1873–79. B 4 V 4–6

MACLEAN (SIR JOHN.) Annals of Ciepstow Castle. [*See* MARSH, J. F.] B 4 U 3

Berkeley Manuscripts. [*See* SMYTH, J.] C 4 P 17–19 †

MACLEAN (J. P.) Mound Builders; being an Account of a remarkable People tiat once iniabited the Valleys of the Oiio and Mississippi; togetier witi an Investigation into the Arciæology of Butler County, O. 8vo. Cincinnati, 1879. B 1 Q 48

MACLEAN (MRS. LETITIA ELIZABETH), MISS L. E. LANDON. Life and Literary Remains of "L.E.L."; by Laman Blanciard. 2 vols. 8vo. Lond., 1841. C 4 S 15, 16

Poetical Works of "L.E.L." 4 vols. 12mo. Lond., 1827–29. H 8 P 13–16

MACLEAN (WILLIAM CAMPBELL), M.D. Diseases of Tropical Climates : Lectures delivered at the Army Medical School. 8vo. Lond., 1886. A 12 P 37

M'LEAY (ALEXANDER), F.R.S., &c. Correspondence with His Excellency Sir Richard Bourke, K.C.B., and other Documents relative to the removal of Alexander McLeay, Esq., from the office of Colonial Secretary of New South Wales. 8vo. Sydney, 1838. MF 3 P 1

Letter to Mr. G. Langhorne on the Missionary Establishment to the Aborigines at Port Phillip. [*See* MANU-SCRIPTS AND PORTRAITS.] MF 1 U 21

MACLEAY (K.), M.D. Historical Memoirs of Rob Roy and the Clan Macgregor ; including Original Notices of Lady Grange. 8vo. Edinb., 1881. B 13 P 7

MACLEAY (SIR WILLIAM), KNT., &c. Descriptive Catalogue of Australian Fishes, and Supplement. 3 vols. (in 2) 8vo. Sydney, 1881–84. MA 2 T 1, 2

[*See* MIKLUCHO-MACLAY, N. DE.]

M'LEHOSE (MRS. AGNES CRAIG), "CLARINDA." Correspondence between Burns and Clarinda; with a Memoir of Mrs. Maclehose (Clarinda). Arranged and edited by her grandson, W. C. Maclehose. 8vo. Edinb., 1843. C 5 R 10

MACLEHOSE (JAMES). Picture of Sydney, and Strangers' Guide in New South Wales for 1838. 8vo. Sydney, 1838.* MD 2 R 47

Another copy, 1839. Sydney, 1839. MD 2 R 50

M'LEHOSE (W. C.) Correspondence between Burns and Clarinda. [*See* MACLEHOSE, MRS. A. C.] C 5 R 10

MACLENNAN (DONALD), M.A. Patriarchal Theory. [*See* MACLENNAN, J. F.] B 15 P 8

MACLENNAN (J.) The Ontario Judicature Act, 1881. 8vo. Toronto, 1884. F 7 Q 21

MACLENNAN (JOHN FERGUSON). Patriarchal Theory: based on the Papers of the late J. F. Maclennan. Edited and completed by Donald Macrnoan, M.A. 8vo. Lond., 1885. B 15 P 8

Ancient History ; comprising a reprint of Primitive Marriage. 8vo. Lond., 1886. B 15 Q 27

MACLEOD (ALLAN). Lockington's Confessions, rendered into Narrative. [*See* LACKINGTON, J.] G 9 Q 33

MACLEOD (REV. DONALD), B.A. Memoir of Norman Macleod, D.D. 2 vols. 8vo. Lond., 1876. C 7 S 41, 42

McLEOD (DONALD). Melbourne Factories. 8vo. Melb., 1866. MA 2 S 1

MACLEOD (HENRY DUNNING), M.A., &c. Elements of Economics. 2 vols. 8vo. Lond., 1881. F 5 T 26, 27

Lectures on Credit and Banking ; delivered at the Request of the Council of the Institute of Bankers in Scotland. 8vo. London., 1882. F 7 S 7

Elements of Banking. 8vo. Lond., 1876. F 6 R 3

Theory and Practice of Banking. 3rd ed. 8vo. Lond., 1875. F 7 S 9

MACLEOD (REV. NORMAN), D.D. The Earnest Student; being Memorials of John Mackintosh. 12mo. Lond., 1863. G 10 Q 13

Eastward. With Illustrations. Roy. 8vo. Lond., 1866. D 5 T 25

Reminiscences of a Highland Parish. 8vo. Lond., 1878. J 9 Q 14

Memoir of ; by his brother, the Rev. Donald Macleod, B.A. 2 vols. 8vo. Lond., 1876. C 7 S 41, 42

Tribute to the Memory of. [*See* MENZIES, REV. P. S.]

MACLEOD (REV. NORMAN), D.D., AND DEWAR (REV. DR. DANIEL). Dictionary of the Gaelic Language, in two Parts. 1. Gaelic and English. 2. English and Gaelic. 8vo. Glasgow, 1831. K 15 P 13

Another copy. [New ed.] 8vo. Lond., 1870. K 15 P 14

MACLEOD (DR. WILLIAM). Treatment of Small-pox, Measles, Scarlet Fever, Hooping Cough, Croup, Quinsy, &c., by the Water Cure and Homœopathy. 8vo. Manchester, 1848. A 12 P 3

MACLISE (DANIEL), R.A. Gallery of Illustrious Characters, 1830–33. (Published in *Fraser's Magazine*.) 8vo. Lond., 1873. C 21 S 11

Memoir of ; by W. J O'Driscoll, M.R.I.A. 12mo. Lond., 1871. C 3 U 24

Story of the Norman Conquest. (Art Union.) 4to. Lond., 1866. A 7 U 37

MACLURE, MACDONALD & MACGREGOR. Large Scale Map of the Seat of War in Italy. 4to. Lond., 1859. D 33 Q 16 ‡

M'MAHON (REV. J. H.), M.A. Metaphysics of Aristotle. [*See* ARISTOTELES.] G 16 P 1

MACMAHON (M. J.), M.A. Political Eloquence in Greece: Demosthenes. [*See* BRÉDIF, L.] C 5 T 6

MACMICHAEL (DR. WILLIAM). Gold-headed Cane. 2nd ed. 8vo. Lond., 1828. C 3 P 13

Lives of British Physicians. 12mo. Lond., 1830. C 1 P 24

MACMICKING (ROBERT). Recollections of Manilla and the Philippines during the years 1848–50. 8vo. Lond., 1851. D 6 P 5

MACMILLAN (DANIEL). Memoir of; by Thomas Hughes, Q.C. 8vo. Lond., 1882. C 3 V 27

MACMILLAN (HUGH), D.D., &c. The Riviera. Illustrated. Roy. 8vo. Lond., 1885. D 8 V 12

ACMILLAN'S MAGAZINE. Vols. 1-52. Lond., 1860-85. E 1, 27

MACMULLEN (JOHN). Camp and Barrack-room; or, the Britisı Army as it is; by "A Late Staff Sergeant of the 13tı Ligıt Infantry." 8vo. Lond., 1846. F 14 Q 13

McMURDO (MAJOR M.) Sir Cıarles Napier's Indian Baggage-corps: Reply to Lieut.-Col. Burlton's Attack. (Pam. 23.) 8vo. Lond., 1850. MJ 2 Q 11

MACNALLY (LEONARD). Fasıionable Levites: a Comedy. [*See* MODERN THEATRE, 10.]

MACNAMARA (C.), F.C.U. Manual of the Diseases of the Eye. 3rd ed. (Cıurcı. Man.) 12mo. Lond., 1876. A 13 P 33

MACNAUGHTON (A. W.) Synopsis of Indictable Offences, witı tıeir Punisıments; to wıicı are added, Forms of Indictments under the Act 46 Vic., No. 17, prescribed by tıeir Honours the Judges of the Supreme Court. Roy. 8vo. Sydney, 1885. MF 1 S 9

M'NEILE (REV. HUGH), M.A. Lectures on the Cıurcı of England. 8vo. Lond., 1840. G 15 R 22
Lectures on the Sympatıies, Sufferings, and Resurrection of the Lord Jesus Cırist. 2nd ed. 8vo. Lond., 1843. G 7 R 7

McNEILL (RT. HON. SIR J.) Progress and Present Position of Russia in the East. (Pam. 6.) 8vo. Lond., 1836. MJ 2 Q 1
Anotıer copy. 2nd ed. 8vo. Lond., 1838. B 12 T 16

MACNEVIN (THOMAS). Memoirs of Rt. Hon. R. L. Sıeil. [*See* SHIEL, RT. HON. R. L.] F 13 Q 14

MACNEVIN (THOMAS E.) Manual for Clerks of Petty Sessions. 8vo. Sydney, 1880. MF 2 S 32
Manual for Coroners and Magistrates in New Soutı Wales. 2nd ed. 8vo. Sydney, 1884.* MF 1 R 38

MACNISH (ROBERT). Anatomy of Drunkennes. 6th ed. 12mo. Glasgow, 1836. A 12 P 19
Pıilosopıy of Sleep. 3rd ed. 8vo. Glasgow, 1836. A 13 P 6

MACONOCHIE (CAPT. ALEXANDER), R.N., &c. Tıougıts on Convict Management and otıer subjects connected witı the Australian Penal Colonies. 8vo. Hobart Town, 1838.* MF 2 P 5
Australiana: Tıougıts on Convict Management and otıer subjects connected witı the Australian Penal Colonies. 8vo. Lond., 1839.* MF 2 P 7
General Views regarding the Social System of Convict Management. 8vo. Hobart, 1839.* MF 2 P 6
On the Management of Transported Criminals. 4to. Lond., 1845. MF 2 S 34

MACONOCHIE (CAPT. ALEXANDER), R.N., &c.—*contd.*
Secondary Punisıment: the Mark System. 8vo. Lond., 1848.* MF 2 P 9
The Mark System [in Van Diemen's Land.] 8vo. Lond., 1848.* MF 2 P 9
Examination of Capt. Maconocıie's System of Prison Discipline. [*See* ATKINSON, J. B.] MF 1 P 26

MACOUN (JOHN), M.A., &c. Catalogue of Canadian Plants. Part 2. Gamopetalæ. Roy 8vo. Montreal, 1884. A 20 V 23
Manitoba and the Great Nortı-west; the Field for Investment; the Home of the Emigrant. 8vo. Ontario, 1882. D 3 U 33

MACOY (ROBERT) 33°. Illustrated History and Cyclopedia of Freemasonry. 8vo. New York, 1868. K 5 Q 38

MACPHERSON (MRS. A.) My Experiences in Australia ; being Recollections of a Visit to the Australian Colonies in 1856-57; by "A Lady." 8vo. Lond., 1860.* MD 1 W 25

MACPHERSON (A.) Narrative of the Victorian Exploring Expedition. [*See* BURKE, R. O'H., AND WILLS, W. J.]

MACPHERSON (DAVID). Annals of Commerce, Manufactures, Fisıeries, and Navigation. 4 vols. 4to. Lond., 1805. F 8 P 20-23 †
De Orygynale Cronykil of Scotland. [*See* WYNTOUN, ANDREW OF.] B 13 T 1, 2

MACPHERSON (JAMES). Genuine Remains of Ossian. [*See* OSSIAN.] H 7 T 21
Poems of Ossian. [*See* OSSIAN.] H 7 T 19, 20
Original Papers, containing the Secret History of Great Britain, from the Restoration to the Accession of the House of Hannover ; to wıicı are prefixed, Extracts from the Life of James II, as written by ıimself. 2 vols. 4to. Lond., 1775. B 2 U 11, 12

MACPHERSON (JOHN), MISSIONARY. Tract in the Persian Language. [*See* ROSS, R.]

MACPHERSON (JOHN S.) Letters to Ministers, Officebears, &c. [*See* PRESBYTERIAN TRACTS.]

MACPHERSON (REV. P.), A.M. [*See* PRESBYTERIAN TRACTS.]

MACQUARIE (MAJ.-GEN. LACHLAN). Letter to the Rt. Hon. Viscount Sidmoutı, in refutation of Statements made by the Hon. Henry Grey Bennet, M.P. ; in a Pampılet, "On the Transportation Laws, the State of the Hulks, and of the Colonies in New Soutı Wales." 8vo. Lond., 1821. MF 2 Q 31
Copy of a Report on the Colony of New Soutı Wales to Earl Batıurst, in July, 1822. Extract of a Letter to Earl Batıurst, in October, 1823, in answer to certain part of the Report of Mr. Commissioner Brigge, on the State of the Colony. (Parl. Doc. 4.) Fol. Lond., 1828. MF 4 ‡
Answer to certain Calumnies in the late Governor Macquarie's Pampılet. [*See* MARSDEN, REV. S.]

M·QUEEN (JAMES). Geographical Survey of Africa, its Rivers, Lakes, Mountains, Productions, States, Population, &c. 8vo. Lond., 1840. D 2 S 19

Geographical and Commercial View of Northern Central Africa. 8vo. Edinb., 1821. D 2 P 1

MACQUEEN (T. POTTER). Australia as she is, and as she may be. 8vo. Lond., 1840. MF 1 R 23, MF 3 P 8

MACQUOID (KATHERINE S.) Through Normandy. Illustrated. 8vo. Lond., 1874. D 8 R 19

MACRAE (REV. DAVID). Americans at Home: Pen-and-ink Sketches of American Men, Manners, and Institutions. Popular ed., revised. 8vo. Glasgow, 1875 D 3 P 20

MACRAY (WILLIAM D.), A.M. Catalogi Codicum Manuscriptorum Bibliothecae Bodleianae. Pars Nona. 4to. Oxford, 1883. K 9 P 8†

MACREADY (WILLIAM). The Bank Note; or, Lessons for Ladies: a Comedy. [*See* MODERN THEATRE, 9.]

The Irishman in London; or, the Happy African: a Farce. [*See* FARCES, 2.]

MACREADY (WILLIAM CHARLES). Macready's Reminiscences and Selections from his Diaries and Letters. Edited by Sir F. Pollock, Bart. 2 vols. 8vo. Lond., 1875. C 7 S 32, 33

MACRITCHIE (D.) Account of the Gypsies of India. 8vo. Lond., 1886. A 1 V 17

Ancient and Modern Britons: a Retrospect. 2 vols. 8vo. Lond., 1884. B 5 S 10, 11

M·URE; OR, CAMPBELL (JOHN). Glasghu Facies: a View of the City of Glasgow; from the original Edition, 1736. Edited by J. F. S. Gordon, D.D., and published, with additions, by John Tweed. 2 vols. (in 4.) 8vo. Glasgow, 1872. B 13 Q 20, 21

MADAGASCAR, Past and Present; by "A Resident." 8vo. Lond., 1847. D 1 S 34

MADAN (H. G.), M.A., &c. Exercises in Practical Chemistry. [*See* HARCOURT, A. G. VERNON.]

MADAN (MARTIN), D.D. Letters on Thelyphthora; with an occasional Prologue and Epilogue. 8vo. Lond., 1782. F 4 Q 7

Thelypthora; or, a Treatise on Female Ruin, in its Causes, Effects, Consequences, Prevention, and Remedy, considered on the basis of the Divine Law; under the following heads, viz., Marriage, Polygamy, Divorce, &c.; with many other Incidental Matters, particularly including an Examination of the Principles and Tendency of Stat. 26 George II c. 33, commonly called the Marriage Act. 3 vols. 8vo. Lond., 1781. F 4 Q 4 6

MADDEN (SIR FREDERICK), F.S.A. Privy Purse Expenses of Princess Mary, daughter of King Henry VIII, afterwards Queen Mary; with a Memoir of the Princess, and Notes. 8vo. Lond., 1831. B 6 P 40

Universal Palæography. [*See* SILVESTRE, M. J. B.] B 15 S 4, 5

Illuminated Ornaments. [*See* SHAW. H.] A 4 U 10 ‡

MADDEN (FREDERIC W.), M.R.S.L. History of Jewish Coinage and Money, in the Old and New Testament. Imp. 8vo. Lond., 1864. A 13 S 47

Hand-book of Roman Numismatics. 12mo. Lond., 1861. A 13 S 13

Coins of the Jews. [*See* NUMISMATA ORIENTALIA, 2.] A 2 S 16†

MADDEN (DR. H.) On the True Principles of Breeding. [*See* MACKNIGHT, C. H.]

MADDEN (R. O.) The Age of Pitt and Fox. Vol. 1. (*All published.*) 8vo. Lond., 1846. B 7 Q 34

MADDEN (RICHARD ROBERT), M.D., &c. United Irishmen: their Lives and Times; with numerous Original Portraits. 1st, 2nd, and 3rd series. 7 vols. 8vo. Dublin, 1842-46. B 11 P 18-24

Egypt and Mohammed Ali. illustrative of the condition of his slaves and subjects, &c. 8vo. Lond., 1841 B 2 R 27

Travels in Turkey, Egypt, Nubia, and Palestine in 1824–27. 2 vols. 8vo. Lond., 1833. D 1 Q 7, 8

Literary Life and Correspondence of the Countess of Blessington. 3 vols. 8vo. Lond., 1855. C 10 P 17–19

Galileo and the Inquisition. 8vo. Lond., 1863. C 2 P 16

MADDEN (THOMAS MORE), M.D., &c. Principal Health Resorts of Europe and Africa, for the treatment of Chronic Diseases. 8vo. Lond., 1876. A 12 R 28

MADDOCK (HENRY). Account of the Life and Writings of Lord Chancellor Somers, including Remarks on the Public Affairs in which he was engaged, and the Bill of Rights; with a Comment. 4to. Lond., 1812. C 4 W 31

MADDOCK (WILLIAM). Government Map of New South Wales; showing Roads, Telegraph Lines, and Mineral Districts, &c. 8vo. Sydney, 1871. MD 5 P 12 ‡

Visitors' Guide to Sydney [by Edwin Burton]. 2nd ed. 12mo. Sydney, 1874.* MD 6 P 6

Another copy. 4th ed. (Exhibition Edition.) Sydney, 1879. MD 6 P 8

MADDYN (DANIEL OWEN). Chiefs of Parties, past and present; with original Anecdotes. 2 vols. 8vo. Lond., 1859. F 6 Q 26, 27

MÁDHAVA ÁCHÁRYA. Sarva-Darsina-Samgraha; or, Review of the different Systems of Hindu Philosophy; translated by E. B. Cowell, M.A., &c., and A. E. Gough, M.A. 8vo. Lond., 1882. G 15 P 15

MADISON (JAMES). Eulogy on the Life and Character of; by John Quincey Adams. (Pam.) 8vo. Boston, 1836. MJ 2 P 36

The Federalist: a Commentary on the Constitution of the United States. [*See* HAMILTON, A.]

MÄDLER (DR. J. H.) Der Mond. [*See* BEER, W.] A 3 U 9, 10

MADOX (THOMAS). Firma Burgi; or, an Historical Essay concerning the Cities, Towns, and Buroughs of England. Fol. Lond., 1726. B 14 T 17 ‡

History and Antiquities of the Exchequer of the Kings of England, in two periods, to the end of the Reign of Edward II, &c. 2 vols. 4to. Lond., 1769. B 6 V 4, 5

MADRAS. Annual Reports on the Civil Hospitals and Dispensaries in the Madras Presidency, for the years 1875–85. 7 vols. 8vo. and fol. Madras, 1877–86. E 2, 16

Reports on the Administration of the Madras Presidency, during the years 1875–84: Summary of the Administration; Departmental Chapters; Statistical Returns; Special Appendix. 9 vols. 8vo. and fol. Madras, 1877–84. E 2, 16

Reports on Public Instruction in the Madras Presidency, for 1875–84. 9 vols. 8vo. and fol. Madras, 1877–85. E 2, 16

Reports of the Conservator of Forests, for the Official Years 1860–63. (Pam. Clk.) 4to. Madras, 1861–63. A 15 U 1

Report on Vaccination throughout the Presidency and Provinces of Madras, 1875–78. 2 vols. 8vo. and fol. Madras, 1876–78. E 2, 16

Annual Medical Reports of the Lying-in Hospital, 1876–78. 2 vols. 8vo. and fol. Madras, 1877–79. E 2, 16

Report on the Gold-mines of the South-eastern Portion of the Wynaad, and the Carcoor Ghát. Fol. Madras, 1880. E 2, 16

Annual Reports of the three Lunatic Asylums in the Madras Presidency, 1875–79. 2 vols. 8vo. and fol. Madras, 1876–79. E 2, 16

Report on the Census of the Madras Presidency. [*See* CORNISH, W. R.]

Standing Information regarding the Official Administration of the Madras Presidency. [*See* MACLEAN, C. D.]

Report on Vaccination, for the year 1876–77. Roy. 8vo. Madras, 1878. E 2, 16

MADRAS ALMANAC. 12mo. Madras, 1819. E 1, 78

MADRID. Sketches of the Metropolis of Spain and its Inhabitants, and of Society and Manners in the Peninsula; by "A Resident Officer." 2 vols 8vo. Lond., 1843. D 7 T 11, 12

MADRIGA (PEDRO DE). Beschrijvinge van de Regeringhe van Peru, gestelt door eenen gevangen Spanjaert, ghenaemt Pedro de Madriga, gheboren zijnde tot Lima. Sq. 8vo. Amsterdam, 1612. D 3 S 50

MADVIG (PROF. I. N.) Latin Grammar for the use of Schools; translated from the original German, by the Rev. George Woods, M.A. 8vo. Oxford, 1870. K 12 S 26

MAETZNER (PROF. E.) English Grammar, Methodical, Analytical, and Historical; translated from the German, by C. J. Greece, LL.B. 3 vols. 8vo. Lond., 1874. K 15 R 24–26

MAFFEI (A.), COUNT. Brigand Life in Italy: a History of Bourbonist Reaction; edited from original and authentic Documents. 2 vols. 8vo. Lond., 1865. B 11 U 40, 41

Recollections of Massimo d'Azeglio. [*See* AZEGLIO, M.] C 1 U 43, 44

MAFFEI (R.) [*See* RAPHAEL VOLATERRANUS.]

MAGAZINE OF AMERICAN HISTORY (THE); with Notes and Queries. (Edited by John Austin Stevens.) Vols. 1–13. 8vo. New York, 1877–86. E 1, 16

MAGENDIE (F.), M.D. Elementary Compendium of Physiology; translated by Dr. E. Milligan. 4th ed. 8vo. Edinb., 1831. A 12 T 7

MAGEOGHEGAN (JAMES), ABBÉ. [*See* MACGEOGHEGAN, J.]

MAGINN (WILLIAM). Anecdote Life of. [*See* TIMBS, J.]

Miscellanies, Prose and Verse; edited by R. W. Montagu, 2 vols. 8vo. Lond., 1885. J 1 U 22, 23

MAGNAN (DR. V.) On Alcoholism: the various forms of Alcoholic Delirium and their Treatment. 8vo. Lond., 1876. A 12 S 21

MAGNUSSON (M. I.) Lecture on the subject of the Creation, delivered in the Synagogue, York-street, Sydney, 8vo. Sydney, 1852. MG 1 Q 12

MAGNY (LUDOVIC), VICOMTE DE. La Science du Blason, accompagnée d'un Armorial général des Familles Nobles de l'Europe. Imp. 8vo. Paris, 1858. K 10 V 1

MAGOON (E. L.) Living Orators in America. 12mo. Dublin, 1849. C 1 R 18

MAGUIRE (JOHN FRANCIS). Rome: its Rulers and its Institutions. 8vo. Lond., 1857. B 12 Q 28

The Irish in America. 8vo. Lond., 1868. D 3 R 30

MAGUIRE (THOMAS), LL.D., &c. The Parmenides of Plato. [*See* PLATO.]

MAGYARLAND. "Magyarland"; being the Narrative of our Travels through the Highlands and Lowlands of Hungary; by "A Fellow of the Carpathian Society." 2 vols. 8vo. Lond., 1881. D 8 T 22, 23

MAHAFFY (PROF. JOHN PENTLAND), A.M. Commentary on Kant's Critick of the Pure Reason. [*See* FISCHER, PROF. K.]

History of Classical Greek Literature: the Poets and the Prose Writers. 2 vols. 8vo. Lond., 1880. B 9 S 20, 21

History of Rome and the Roman People. [*See* DURUY, V.] B 19 R 6–11 ‡

Social Life in Greece, from Homer to Menander. 8vo. Lond., 1874. B 9 S 19

MAHAN (REV. ASA), D.D., AND FINNEY (REV. C. G.) Baptism of the Holy Ghost, and the Enduement of Power. 12mo. Lond., 1875. G 9 P 46

MAHÁ-VÍRA-CHARITA. [*See* BHAVABHÚTI, J.]

MAHOMET Life of. (Eminent Men.) 8vo. Lond., 1849. C 7 P 45

Life of, and History of Islam to the Era of the Hegira; by Sir William Muir. 4 vols. 8vo. Lond., 1858–61. C 7 S 43–46

Lives of Mahomet and his Successors; by Washington Irving. 2 vols. 8vo. Lond., 1850. C 7 S 34, 35

MAHON (PHILIP HENRY), LORD. [*See* STANHOPE, P. H. MAHON, EARL.]

MAHONY (REV. FRANCIS SYLVESTER), "FATHER PROUT." Anecdote Life of. [*See* TIMBS, J.]

Final Reliques of Father Prout; collected and edited by Blanchard Jerrold. 8vo. Lond., 1876. J 12 P 22

Reliques of Father Prout. 2 vols. 12mo. Lond., 1836. J 11 P 6, 7

Works of Father Prout; edited, with Biographical Introduction and Notes, by Charles Kent. 12mo. Lond., 1881. J 11 P 8

MAIDEN (J. H.) The Olive, and Olive Oil; being Notes on the Culture of the Tree and Extraction of the Oil, as carried out in South Australia and Continent of Europe. 8vo. Sydney, 1887. MA 1 Q 43

MAIDMENT (JAMES). Scotish Elegiac Verses, 1629–1729; with Notes and an Appendix of illustrative Papers. 8vo. Edinb., 1842. H 8 U 19

Sir Thomas Overburie's Vision; Introduction. [*See* HUNTERIAN CLUB, 6.]

MAIER (J.) Arc and Glow Lamps: a Practical Handbook on Electric Lighting. 8vo. Lond., 1886. A 5 S 36

[*See* HOSPITALIER, E.]

MAIL (THE); 1877-78, 1881-85. 11 vols. imp. fol. Lond., 1877-85. E

MAIL STEAMSHIP CONTRACT SYSTEM. Letter to the Rt. Hon. Sir C. Wood, Bart, M.P., First Lord of Admiralty, on the Mail Steamship Contract System: its great National Advantages defended. (Pam. 30.) 8vo. Lond., 1856. MJ 2 Q 18

MAILLA (JOSEPH A. M. DE MOYRIAC DE). Histoire Générale de la Chine. 13 vols. 4to. Paris, 1777-85. B 2 Q 31–43

MAIMBOURG (LOUIS). Histoire des Croisades pour la Délivrance de la Terre Sainte. 2e éd. 2 vols. (in 1) 32mo. Paris, 1682. G 9 P 2

MAIMONIDES (MOSES). The Guide of the Perplexed; translated from the original, and annotated by M. Friedländer, Ph.D. 2 vols. 8vo. Lond., 1885. G 3 Q 5 7

MAIN (ALEXANDER). Life and Conversations of Dr. Samuel Johnson (founded chiefly upon Boswell); with a Preface by George Henry Lewes. 8vo. Lond., 1874. C 3 V 15

MAIN (DAVID M.) Treasury of English Sonnets. Edited from the original Sources, with Notes and Illustrations. 4to. Manchester, 1880. H 6 V 19

MAIN (REV. ROBERT), M.A. Rudimentary Astronomy. (Weale.) 12mo. Lond., 1869. A 17 P 10

MAINE. [*See* UNITED STATES.]

MAINE (SIR HENRY SUMNER), K.C.S.I., &c. Ancient Law: its connection with the Early History of Society, and its relation to Modern Ideas. 8vo. Lond., 1870. F 7 R 19

Village Communities in the East and West: Six Lectures delivered at Oxford. 8vo. Lond., 1872. F 7 R 20

Lectures on the Early History of Institutions. 8vo. Lond., 1875. F 6 U 26

Popular Government: Four Essays. 8vo. Lond., 1885. F 7 R 17

Dissertations on early Law and Custom; chiefly selected from Lectures delivered at Oxford. 8vo. Lond., 1883. F 7 R 18

MAINTENON (FRANÇOISE D'AUBIGNÉ), MARQUISE DE. Secret Correspondence of Madame de Maintenon with the Princess des Ursins. 3 vols. 8vo. Lond., 1827. C 8 Q 5–7

MAIR (JAMES ALLAN). Hand-book of Proverbs, Mottoes, Quotations, and Phrases. 8vo. Lond., 1873. K 17 P 5

MAIR (ROBERT HENRY). Debrett's Illustrated House of Commons. [*See* DEBRETT, J.]

Debrett's Baronetage, Knightage, &c. [*See* DEBRETT, J.]

MAISONNEUVE (P.) Traité de l'Ostéologie et la Myologie du Vespertilio Murinus. Roy. 8vo. Paris, 1868. A 15 Q 3

MAITLAND (CHARLES), M.D. The Church in the Catacombs. 2nd ed. 8vo. Lond., 1847. G 2 Q 11

MAITLAND (EDWARD), J.P. "Meaning of the Age": a Farewell Lecture, delivered at the School of Arts, Sydney, N.S.W., January 9, 1858. (Pam. 26.) 8vo. Brighton, 1858. MJ 2 Q 14

Pilgrim and the Shrine; or, Passages from the Life and Correspondence of "Herbert Ainslie, B.A., Cantab." 3 vols. 8vo. Lond., 1868. J 9 P 1–3

MAITLAND (FOWLER). Building Estates: a Rudimentary Treatise on the Development, Sale, Purchase, and General Management of Building Land. (Weale.) 12mo. Lond., 1883. A 17 Q 82

MAITLAND (F. W.) Pleas of the Crown, for the County of Gloucester, before the Abbot of Reading and his Fellows, Justices Itinerant, in the fifth year of the Reign of King Henry III, and the year of grace, 1221. 8vo. Lond., 1884. B 7 Q 23

MAITLAND (MRS. J. C.) Letters from Madras, during the years 1836–39; by "A Lady." 12mo. Lond., 1843. D 6 P 42
Another copy. (H. and C. Lib.) 8vo. Lond., 1846. J 8 P 17

MAITLAND (SIR JOHN). Ancient Scotish Poems. [*See* PINKERTON, J.]

MAITLAND (REV. SAMUEL ROFFEY), D.D., &c. Essays on subjects connected with the Reformation in England. 8vo. Lond., 1849. G 4 P 1

Eruvin; or, Miscellaneous Essays on subjects connected with the nature, history, and destiny of Man. 12mo. Lond., 1850. G 8 P 35

Eight Essays on various subjects. 12mo. Lond., 1852. J 7 Q 23

The Dark Ages: a Series of Essays. 3rd ed. 8vo. Lond., 1853. G 2 Q 10

Review of Fox, the Martyrologist's "History of the Waldenses." 8vo. Lond., 1837. G 2 Q 9

Twelve Letters on Fox's "Acts and Monuments." Originally published in the *British Magazine*, during the years 1837–38. 8vo. Lond., 1841. G 2 Q 9

Remarks on Rev. S. R. Cattley's Defence of his edition of Fox's Martyrology. 8vo. Lond., 1842. G 2 Q 9

Six Letters on Fox's Acts and Monuments. 8vo. Lond., 1837. G 2 Q 9

Six more Letters on Fox's Acts and Monuments. 8vo. Lond., 1841. G 2 Q 9

Notes on the Contributions of Rev. George Townsend, M.A., Prebendary of Durham, &c., to the new edition of Fox's "Martyrology." Parts 1–3. 8vo. Lond., 1841–42. G 2 Q 9

MAITLAND HOSPITAL. Annual Report of the Committee of Management; with Rules and Regulations of same, and a List of Subscribers for the year 1858. 8vo. West Maitland, 1859. MF 3 P 18
Another copy. MG 1 Q 26
Report of the Committee of Management; with a List of Subscribers for the year ending 1867. 8vo. West Maitland, 1868. MF 3 P 18

MAIZEAUX (PIERRE DES). [*See* DESMAISEAUX, P.]

MAJOR (REV. J. R.) Roman Antiquities. [*See* ADAM, A.] B 11 V 8

MAJOR (RICHARD HENRY), F.S.A., &c. Early Voyages to Terra Australis, now called Australia: a Collection of Documents and Extracts from early Manuscript Maps. 8vo. Lond., 1859.* MD 2 S 1

MAJOR (RICHARD HENRY), F.S.A., &c.—*continued.*
Discovery of Australia by the Portuguese in 1601, five years before the earliest Discovery hitherto recorded; with arguments in favour of previous Discovery by the same nation early in the sixteenth century. 4to. Lond., 1861.* MD 5 P 21 †

Discoveries of Prince Henry, the Navigator, and their Results. 8vo. Lond., 1877. D 9 T 29
Another copy. 8vo. Lond., 1877. MD 2 S 4

Life of Prince Henry of Portugal, surnamed the Navigator, and its Results. Roy. 8vo. Lond., 1868. MC 1 R 31
Another copy. Roy. 8vo. Lond., 1868. C 9 V 24

Further Facts in the History of the Early Discovery of Australia. 4to. Lond., 1873. MD 5 P 23 †
Supplementary Facts in the History of the Discovery of Australia. 4to. Lond., 1873. MD 5 P 22 †

MAJOR (THOMAS). Ruins of Pæstum, otherwise Posidonia, in Magna Græcia. Imp. fol. Lond., 1768. B 12 P 18 ‡

MAKRIZI (TAKI-EDDIN-AHMED-AL.) Histoire des Sultans Mamloukes de l'Egypte écrite en Arabe; traduite en Français et accompagnée de Notes, par E. M. Quatremère. 4 vols. (in 2.) Paris, 1837–42. B 14 Q 2, 3 ‡

MALABÁRI (BEHRÁMJI M.) Gujarát and the Gujarátis: Pictures of Men and Manners taken from Life. 8vo. Lond., 1882. D 5 R 8

MALALA (J.) [*See* BYZANTINÆ HIST. SCRIPT.]

MALAYAN FAMILY. Memoirs of a; written by themselves, and translated from the original by W. Marsden, F.R.S., &c. 8vo. Lond., 1830. C 6 R 15

MALAY PENINSULA. Map of the. Sm. fol. Lond., 1879. D 33 Q 14 ‡

MALCOLM (REV. HOWARD), D.D., &c. Index to the Principal Works in every Department of Religious Literature. 2nd ed.; with Addenda. 8vo. Philad., 1870. K 18 R 23
Travels in South-eastern Asia, embracing Hindustan, Malaya, Siam, and China. 2 vols. 8vo. Lond., 1839. D 5 P 51, 52

MALCOLM (JAMES PELLER), F.S.A. Anecdotes of the Manners and Customs of London, from the Roman Invasion to the year 1700. [Coloured Plates.] 4to. Lond., 1811. B 6 V 30
Another copy. 2nd ed. 3 vols. 8vo. Lond., 1811. B 5 S 12–14

Anecdotes of the Manners and Customs of London during the 18th Century. 4to. Lond., 1808. B 6 V 31
Another copy. 2nd ed. 2 vols. 8vo. Lond., 1810. B 5 S 15, 16

Miscellaneous Anecdotes illustrative of the Manners and History of Europe during the Reigns of Charles II, James II, William III, and Queen Anne. 8vo. Lond., 1811. B 7 R 35

[*See* GRANGER, REV. J.] C 7 T 5

MALCOLM (MAJ.-GEN. SIR JOHN), G.C.B., &c. Memoir of Central India, including Malwa and adjoining Provinces. Reprinted. 2 vols. 8vo. Calcutta, 1880.   B 10 Q 28, 29

Sketches of Persia. (H. and C. Lib.) 12mo. Lond., 1849.   J 8 P 9

History of Persia, from the most early period to the present time ; containing an account of the Religion, Government, Usages, and Character of the Inhabitants. 2 vols. fol. Lond., 1815.   B 15 S 16, 17 ‡

Political History of India, from 1784 to 1823. 2 vols. 8vo. Lond., 1826.   B 10 R 25, 26

Life of Robert Lord Clive. 3 vols. 8vo. Lond., 1836.   C 10 T 8–10

Life and Correspondence of ; from unpublished Letters and Journals, by John William Kaye. 2 vols. 8vo. Lond., 1856.   C 7 S 28, 29

Memoir of Central India, including Malwa, and adjoining Provinces. 2nd ed. 2 vols. 8vo. Lond., 1824.   D 6 R 23, 24

MALCHUS. [*See* BYZANTINE HIST. SCRIPT.]

MALDEN (HENRY). On the Origin of Universities and Academical Degrees. 12mo. Lond., 1835.   J 1 U 39

On the Study of the Greek and Latin Languages : An Introductory Lecture. (Univ. of Lond.) 8vo. Lond., 1831.   J 5 S 8

On the Introduction of the Natural Sciences into General Education : a Lecture. (Univ. of Lond.) 8vo. Lond., 1838.   J 5 S 8

MALE ORPHAN INSTITUTION. Rules and Regulations established for the Management of the. 12mo. Sydney, 1819.   MJ 2 Q 21

MALET (SIR ALEXANDER C.), BART., &c. Overthrow of the Germanic Confederation by Prussia, in 1866. 8vo. Lond., 1870.   B 9 R 16

MALET (CAPT. HAROLD ESDAILE). Annals of the Road ; or, Notes on Mail and Stage Coaching in Great Britain. 8vo. Lond., 1876.   A 17 W 19

MALET (H. P.) Incidents in the Biography of Dust. 8vo. Lond., 1877.   A 9 Q 13

The Beginnings. 8vo. Lond., 1878.   A 9 P 40

MALET (WILLIAM E.) Australian Wine-growers' Manual. 12mo. Lond., 1880.*   MA 1 P 36

MALIBRAN DE BÉRIOT (MME. MARIA FELICITA). Memoirs of ; by the Countess de Merlin and others ; with a Selection from her Correspondence. 2 vols. 8vo. Lond., 1840.   C 3 P 25, 26

MALKIN (A. T.) Historical Parallels. (Lib. Ent. Know.) 2 vols. 12mo. Lond., 1831–35.   K 10 R 31, 32

MALKIN (BENJAMIN HEATH), LL.D. Introductory Lecture on History. (Univ. of Lond.) 8vo. Lond., 1830.   J 5 S 8

MALLALIEU (A.) Buenos Ayres, Monte Video, and Affairs in the River Plate, in a Letter to Rt. Hon. the Earl of Aberdeen. (Pam. 19.) 8vo. Edinb., 1844.   F 12 P 8

MALLEE DISTRICT (THE). Mallee District of Victoria. 8vo. Melb. 1880.   MJ 2 R 15

Mallee Scrub Country ; or, Mr. Dow's "Delta." 8vo. Melb., 1880.   MJ 2 R 15

MALLERY (LIEUT.-COL. GARRICK). Introduction to the Study of Sign Language among the North American Indians, as illustrating the Gesture Speech of Mankind. 4to. Wash., 1880.   K 13 U 5

MALLESON (COL. GEORGE BRUCE), C.S.I. Ambushes and Surprises, from the Time of Hannibal to the Period of the Indian Mutiny. 8vo. Lond., 1885.   B 15 P 7

Decisive Battles of India, from 1746 to 1849, inclusive. 8vo. Lond., 1883.   B 10 U 8

Another copy. 2nd ed. 8vo. Lond., 1885.   B 10 U 9

Founders of the Indian Empire : Lord Clive. 8vo. Lond., 1882.   B 10 V 24

Battle-fields of Germany, from the Outbreak of the Thirty-Years' War to the Battle of Blenheim. 8vo. Lond., 1884.   B 9 S 10

Historical Sketch of the Native States of India. 8vo. Lond., 1875.   B 10 S 30

History of the French in India, from 1674 to 1761. 8vo. Lond., 1868.   B 10 U 26

Essays and Lectures on Indian Historical Subjects. 8vo. Lond., 1876.   B 10 Q 20

Studies from Genoese History. 8vo. Lond., 1875.   B 10 Q 37

History of the Indian Mutiny, 1857–59; commencing from the close of the second volume of Sir John Kay's History of the Sepoy War. 2nd ed. 3 vols. 8vo. Lond., 1878–80.   B 10 U 11–13

Analytical Index [to the above]; by F. Pincott. 8vo. Lond., 1880.   B 10 U 17

Herat, the Granary and Garden of Central Asia. With an Index and a Map. 8vo. Lond., 1880.   B 10 S 2

MALLET (DAVID). Eurydice: a Tragedy. (Bell's Brit. Theatre.) 18mo. Lond., 1795.   H 2 P 37

Life and Poems of. [*See* CHALMERS, A., *and* JOHNSON, S.]

MALLET (SIR LOUIS), KNT., C.B. Political Writings of R. Cobden ; with an Introductory Essay. [*See* COBDEN, R.]

MALLET (PAUL HENRI). Northern Antiquities ; or, an Historical Account of the Manners, Customs, Religion and Laws, Maritime Expeditions and Discoveries, Language and Literature of the Ancient Scandinavians. 8vo. Lond., 1847.   B 2 It 21

MALLET (ROBERT), A.M., &c. Addition to the Paper on Volcanic Energy : an Attempt to develop its true Origin and Chemical Relations. (Roy. Soc. Pubs., 1.) 4to. Lond., 1875.   A 11 P 2 †

MALLET (ROBERT). Description of J. B. Fenby's Patent Locks, and a Note upon Iron Safes. [*See* HOBBS, A. C.]

MALLET DU PAN (JACQUES). Memoirs and Correspondence, illustrative of the History of the French Revolution; collected and arranged by A. Sayons. 2 vols. 8vo. Lond., 1852. C 8 Q 2, 3

MALLOCK (WILLIAM HURRELL). Is Life worth Living? 2nd ed. 8vo. Lond., 1879. G 2 Q 8
New Paul and Virginia; or, Positivism on an Island. New ed. 12mo. Lond., 1880. J 10 Q 24
The New Republic; or, Culture, Faith, and Philosophy in an English Country Town. 3rd ed. 2 vols. 8vo. Lond., 1877. J 10 Q 25, 26
Poems. 8vo. Lond., 1880. H 8 Q 2
Romance of the 19th Century. 2 vols. 8vo. Lond., 1881. J 10 Q 27, 28

MALMESBURY (JAMES HARRIS), FIRST EARL OF. Diaries and Correspondence of James Harris, first Earl of Malmesbury. Edited by his Grandson, the third Earl of Malmesbury. 4 vols. 8vo. Lond., 1844. C 9 T 17–20

MALMESBURY (J. HOWARD HARRIS), THIRD EARL OF, G.C.B. Memoirs of an ex-Minister: an Autobiography. 2 vols. 8vo. Lond., 1884. C 7 S 36, 37

MALMESBURY (WILLIAM OF). [*See* WILLIAM OF MALMESBURY.]

MALOGA ABORIGINAL MISSION SCHOOL. [*See* MATTHEWS, D.]

MALONE (EDMUND). Historical Account of the English Stage. [*See* SHAKESPEARE, W.]

MALONE (R. EDMOND). Three Years' Cruise in the Australasian Colonies. 8vo. Lond., 1854.* MD 1 W 13

MALONEY (JOHN). Report of the Case of. [*See* DILLON, J.]

MALORY OR MALEORE (SIR THOMAS). La Mort d'Arthure: the History of King Arthur and of the Knights of the Round Table. Edited from the text of the edition of 1634, with Introduction and Notes, by Thomas Wright, M.A., &c. 2nd ed. 3 vols. 12mo. Lond., 1865–66. J 9 P 31–33
Morte Darthur: Sir Thomas Malory's Book of King Arthur and his noble Knights of the Round Table. The original edition of Caxton, revised for modern use. 8vo. Lond., 1871. J 11 U 7

MALTE–BRUN (CONRAD). Universal Geography; or, a Description of all Parts of the World, on a new Plan, according to the great Natural Divisions of the Globe. 9 vols. 8vo. Edinb., 1834. D 12 U 1–9

MALTHUS (REV. THOMAS ROBERT), A.M., &c. Definitions in Political Economy. 8vo. Lond., 1827. F 6 S 24
Essay on the Principle of Population; or, a View of its Past and Present Effects on Human Happiness. 2 vols. 8vo. Lond., 1826. F 7 R 1, 2

MALWYN. Leichhardt's Return: a Poem. [*See* LEICHHARDT, DR. L.]

MAMMATT (EDWARD), F.G.S. Collection of Geological Facts and Practical Observations, intended to elucidate the Formation of the Ashby Coal-field, in the Parish of Ashby-de-la-Zouch and the Neighbouring District. 4to. Ashby, 1834. A 1 Q 19 †

MAN: Fragments of Forgotten History; by "Two Chelas in the Theosophical Society." 8vo. Lond., 1885. G 13 T 9

MAN AND A BROTHER, A. [*See* TRANSPORTATION.]

MAN-STEALING in the Pacific. (Newspaper Cutting.) Sydney (n.d.) MG 1 Q 29

MANASSEH BEN ISRAEL. To His Highness the Lord Protector of the Commonwealth of England, Scotland, and Ireland: the Humble Address of Manasseh Ben Israel, in behalfe of the Jewish Nation. (Pam. F.) Reprint, 1655. 8vo. Melb., 1868. MJ 2 S 3

MANASSES (CONSTANTIN.) [*See* BYZANTINAE HIST. SCRIPT.]

MANCHESTER ATHENAEUM. Reports of the Directors of the Manchester Athenaeum; with the Rules and Bye-laws. (Pam. 23.) 8vo. Manchester, 1845. MJ 2 Q 11

MANCHESTER LITERARY CLUB. Papers of [Vol. 1, called Transactions.] Vols. 1–7, 1874–81. 7 vols. (in 6) 8vo. Manchester, 1875–81. E 1, 58
The Manchester Quarterly: a Journal of Literature and Art. Vols. 1–6, 1882–86. 6 vols. 8vo. Manchester, 1882–86. E 1, 58

MANCHESTER PUBLIC FREE LIBRARIES. Annual Reports of the Council of the City of Manchester on the working of. 8vo. Manchester, 1855–79. E 1, 78
Catalogue of the Chief Lending Library. 2nd ed. 8vo. Manchester, 1862. MK 1 Q 13
Catalogue of the Books in the Reference Department; prepared by A. Crestadoro, Ph.D. ; with Index of Names and Subjects. 3 vols. (in 4). Imp. 8vo. Lond. and Manch., 1864–81. K 8 R 24–27 †
Index-Catalogue of the Charlton and Ardwick Lending Branch. Roy. 8vo. Manchester, 1872. K 8 P 30
Twentieth Annual Report on the working of the Public Free Libraries, 1871–72. Roy. 8vo. Manchester, 1872. K 8 P 30
Catalogues of the Chief Lending Library and Branches. 2 vols. roy. 8vo. Lond., 1864–72. K 8 P 30
Catalogue and Supplement of the Ancoats and Ardwick Branch Lending Department. 2 vols. (in 1) 8vo. Manchester, 1857–60. MK 1 Q 13

MANCHESTER QUARTERLY (THE): a Journal of Literature and Art. [*See* MANCHESTER LITERARY CLUB.]

MANDERS (A. S.) & CO.   Official Post Office Directory of New Soutи Wales, 1883–84.   Imp. 8vo.   Melи., 1883.   ME 10 P 14 †

MANDEVILLE (BERNARD DE), M.D.   Fables of the Bees; or, Private Vices, Public Benefits; witи an Essay on Cиarity and Cиarity Scиools, and a searcи into the Nature of Society.   8vo.   Lond., 1795.   J 11 V 16

MANDEVILLE (SIR JOHN).   Voiage and Travaile of Sir Joиn Maundeville, Kt.   8vo.   Lond., 1727.   D 4 U 35

Travels of.   [*See* COCHRANE, R.]   D 10 Q 48

MANDY (H. C.)   Ecclesiastical Manual of New Soutи Wales.   [*See* WILLIAMS, C. H.]   MF 1 U 15

MANFRED.   [*See* PRESTON, E. W.]

MANGLES (JAMES), A.M.   Travels in Egypt and Nubia.   [*See* IRBY, HON. C. L.]

MANGLES (Ross D.)   How to Colonize : the Interest of the Country and the Duty of the Government.   (Pam. 10.)   8vo.   Lond., 1842.   MJ 2 Q 2

Answer to [the above.]   [*See* HEALE, T.]   MJ 2 Q 2

MANGOURIT (M. O. B.)   Travels in Hanover, during the years 1803 and 1804 ; containing an Account of the Form of Government, Religion, Agriculture, Commerce, and Natural History of the Country.   8vo.   Lond., 1806.   D 8 U 27

MANING (FREDERICK EDWARD), JUDGE.   Old New Zealand : a Tale of the Good Old Times ; by "A Pakeиa Maori."   8vo.   Auckland, 1863.   MD 5 R 33

Anotиer copy.   2nd ed. 8vo.   Auckland, 1863.   MD5R34

Anotиer copy.   8vo.   Lond., 1876.*   MD 5 R 35

Anotиer copy.   (Australian edition.)   8vo.   Lond., 1887.*
                                                MD 5 R 37

MANLEY (J. J.), M.A.   Salt, Preservation of Food, Bread and Biscuits.   (Brit. Manuf. Indust.)   12mo.   Lond., 1876.   A 17 S 32

MANLIUS (MARCUS).   Astronomicon ; ex Editione Bentleiana, cum Notis et Interpretatione in usum Delpиini.   2 vols. 8vo.   Lond., 1828.   J 13 R 10, 11

MANN (D. D.)   The present Picture of New Soutи Walиs ; illustrated witи four large coloured Views, from drawings taken on the spot, of Sydney, the Seat of Government ; witи a Plan of the Colony.   4to.   Lond., 1811.*   MD 7 P 2 †

Plates and Plans [to the above.]   (Reprint 1811.)   Ob. 4to.   Lond., 1881.   MD 3 Q 5 †

MANN (SIR HORACE).   Letters of Walpole to.   [*See* WALPOLE, H.]   C 9 S 29–35

MANN (JOHN F.)   Eigиt Montиs witи Dr. Leichиardt, in the years 1846–47.   8vo.   Sydney, 1888.   MD 1 V 40

MANN (ROBERT JAMES), M.D., F.R.C.S., &c.   Emigrant's Guide to the Colony of Natal.   2nd ed. (Weale.)   12mo.   Lond., 1873.   A 17 Q 14

Natal, a History and Description of the Colony.   [*See* BROOKS, H.]   D 2 P 3

MANN (R. K.)   Life and Times of Col. Fred. Burnaby.   [*See* WARE, J. R.]   C 4 S 3

MANN (W.)   Six Years' Residence in the Australian Provinces, ending in 1839.   8vo.   Lond., 1839.   MD 3 Q 19

MANNERS (JANETTA), LADY.   Encouraging Experiences of Reading and Recreation Rooms.   8vo.   Edinb., 1886.   J 1 U 25

MANNING (FRANCIS).   History of Dion Cassius.   [*See* DION CASSIUS.]   B 12 F 32, 33

MANNING (FREDERICK NORTON), M.D.   Report on Lunatic Asylums, New Soutи Wales.   Roy. 8vo.   Sydney, 1868.   ME 3 V

Report on Lunatic Asylums, New Soutи Wales.   Fol.   Sydney, 1868.   ME 2, 32

Report on the Hospital for the Insane, Gladesville, for the year 1871.   8vo.   Sydney, 1872.   MA 2 S 38

Report of the Inspector-General of the Insane, for 1881–82.   Fol.   Sydney, 1882.   ME 2, 32

MANNING (HENRY EDWARD), CARDINAL.   Unity of the Cиurcи.   8vo.   Lond., 1842.   G 2 Q 13

England and Cиristendom.   8vo.   Lond., 1867.   G 7 Q 23

Petri Privilegium : tиree Pastoral Letters to the Clergy of the Diocese.   8vo.   Lond., 1871.   G 2 Q 14

Vatican Decrees in tиeir bearing on Civil Allegiance.   2nd ed.   8vo.   Lond., 1875.   G 8 T 13

The Cardinal Arcиbisиop of Westminster ; witи Notes, by Joиn Oldcastle.   8vo.   Lond., 1886.   C 10 U 39

[*See* ESSAYS ON RELIGION.]

MANNING (JAMES).   Sydney Water Supply, 1877 ; Review on the Report of William Clark, Hydraulic Engineer, on the question of Water Supply for Sydney.   1877.   MA 2 V 7

MANNING (JAMES ALEXANDER).   Lives of the Speakers of the House of Commons.   Roy. 8vo.   Lond., 1850.
                                                C 5 W 22

Pius IX.   [*See* LIANCOURT, C. A. DE G. DE, COUNT.]
                                                C 3 U 44, 45

Memoirs of Sir Benjamin Rudyerd ; containing иis Speecиes and Poems.   Edited by J. A. Manning.   8vo.   Lond., 1841.   C 9 S 17

MANNING (MISS ANNE).   An Englisи Girl's Account of a Moravian Settlement in the Black Forest.   12mo.   Lond., 1858.   G 9 Q 19

MANNING (REV. SAMUEL), LL.D.   American Pictures.   drawn witи Pen and Pencil.   Imp. 8vo.   Lond., 1876.
                                                D 3 V 38

MANNING (THOMAS).   Journey to Lиasa ; edited witи a Life ; by C. R. Markиam.   [*See* MARKHAM, CAPT. C. R.]
                                                D 5 S 12

MANSFIELD (CHARLES BLACHFORD), M.A. Aerial Navigation; edited by his Brother, R. B. Mansfield, B.A. 8vo. Lond., 1877   A 11 Q 16

MANSFIELD (RALPH). Analytical View of the Census of New South Wales, for the year 1841; with Tables showing the Progress of the Population during the previous twenty years. 8vo. Sydney, 1841.   MF 2 Q 21

Another copy. 8vo. Sydney, 1841.   MJ 2 Q 2

Analytical View of the Census of New South Wales, for the year 1846; with Tables showing the Progress of the Population during the previous twenty-five years; and an Appendix. 8vo. Sydney, 1847.   MF 2 Q 22

Another copy. 8vo. Sydney, 1847.   MJ 2 Q 8

Another copy. 8vo. Sydney, 1847.   MJ 2 R 22

MANSFIELD (ROBERT BLACHFORD), B.A. Aerial Navigation. [*See* MANSFIELD, C. B.]

MANSFIELD (WILLIAM MURRAY), EARL OF. Sketch of the Professional Character of. [*See* BUTLER, S.]

MANSFIELD BROS. (MESSRS.) Prince Alfred Hospital, Sydney, Description of the proposed Building; by the Architects. (Pam. Ck.) 8vo. 1874.   A 15 U 1

MANSTEIN (CHRISTOPH HERMANN), BARON VON. Memoirs of Russia, from the year 1727 to the year 1744; translated from the original Manuscript. With Maps and Plans. 2nd ed. 4to. Lond., 1773.   B 12 V 7

MANT (RT. REV. RICHARD), D.D. History of the Church of Ireland, from the Reformation to the Revolution. 2 vols. 8vo. Lond., 1840.   G 3 T 9, 10

Memoir of the Life and Writings of Thomas Warton. [*See* WARTON, T.]

MANTEGNA (ANDREA). Mantegna and Francia; by Julia Cartwright. (Great Artists.) 8vo. Lond., 1881.   C 3 T 43

MANTELL (GIDEON ALGERNON), LL.D., &c. Geological Excursions round the Isle of Wight, and along the adjacent Coast of Dorsetshire. 2nd ed. 12mo. Lond., 1851.   A 9 P 11

Medals of Creation; or, First Lessons in Geology and in the Study of Organic Remains. 2 vols. 12mo. Lond., 1844.   A 9 P 44, 45

Notice of the Remains of Dinornis and other Birds, and of Fossils and Rock-specimens, recently collected by Walter Mantell, Esq., in the Middle Island of New Zealand. (Pam. Cb.) 8vo. Lond., 1850.   A 16 U 25

Petrifactions and their Teachings; or, a Hand-book to the Gallery of Organic Remains of the British Museum. 8vo. Lond., 1851.   A 9 Q 30

Thoughts on Animalcules; or, a Glimpse of the Invisible World revealed by the Microscope. 12mo. Lond., 1846.   A 14 S 11

Wonders of Geology; or, a Familiar Exposition of Geological Phenomena. 2 vols. 8vo. Lond., 1848. A 9 Q 28, 29

3 P

MANTELL (WALTER). Notice of the Remains of Dinornis and other Birds, recently collected in the Middle Island of New Zealand. [*See* MANTELL, G. A.]   A 16 U 25

MANU. Ordinances of; translated from the Sanskrit by the late Arthur Coke Burnell, Ph.D., &c.; completed and edited by Edward W. Hopkins, Ph.D. 8vo. Lond., 1884.   G 15 P 6

MANUAL OF RANK AND NOBILITY; or, Key to the Peerage. 2nd ed. 8vo. Lond., 1832. K 10 S 8

MANUEL (R.) The Present and the Pending Crisis: a Lecture on the Necessity and Advantages of establishing a State Bank of Issue. 8vo. Melb., 1878.   MF 1 Q 6

MANUEL II (PALÆOLOGUS), IMPERATOR. Opera omnia. [*See* MIGNE, J. P., SERIES GRÆCA, 156.]

MANUSCRIPTS AND PORTRAITS. 4to. Melb., and Sydney, 1817–73.   MF 1 U 21

Trial of George Worrell for the Murder of Frederick Fisher, 2nd February, 1827.

Extract of a Letter from Mr. Justice Burton to His Excellency Sir Richard Bourke, in reference to the establishment of a Mission to the Aborigines at Port Phillip, 22nd November, 1835.

Instructions from the Government to Mr. George Langhorne upon the establishment of a Mission to the Aborigines at Port Phillip, 9th December, 1836.

Letter from George Kenyon Holden, Private Secretary to Governor Bourke, to Mr. George Langhorne, in reference to the Missionary Establishment to the Aborigines at Port Phillip, 25th March, 1837.

Letter from the Colonial Secretary [Sir E. Deas Thomson], New South Wales, to Mr. George Langhorne upon the same subject [Missionary Establishment to the Aborigines at Port Phillip].

Statement of Mr. George Langhorne, in reference to the establishment of the Aboriginal Mission at Port Phillip.

Statement of Mr. John Thomas Smith, in reference to such Mission, 12th September, 1837.

Mr. Joseph Hawdon's Journal of an Overland Journey from Port Phillip to Adelaide.

Memoranda of the Early Days of Port Phillip; by John Bourke, 1837.

Letter from the Colonial Secretary [Sir E. D. Thomson] to certain gentlemen interested in the settlement of Port Phillip, 22nd June, 1838.

Letters from Mr. John Helder Wedge to Henry Field Gurner, respecting Mr. Wedge's Visit to Port Phillip in 1835.

Letters from Charles Bonney, George Hamilton, and John Murchison, to H. F. Gurner, 1871, on the early settlement of Victoria.

Letter from John Bourke to J. T. Smith, 23rd October, 1871.

Trial of Patrick Geary for Murder, 17th November, 1871.

Declaration of William Dutton, 11th February, 1873.

Hobart Town and Sydney Promissory Notes, 1826-28.

Population of New South Wales, 1817-18.

Letters and Memo. respecting New South Wales, 1824.

A New South Wales Land Lease [granted]; by Sir Thomas Brisbane, 1823.

MS. Copy of the *Melbourne Advertiser*, 8th January, 1838.

Portraits of the Murderers of Mr. [James] Noble; also, Portraits of Dr. Willis, Wm. Robertson, Sir John O'Shanassy, Sir Redmond Barry, Neil Black, Sir W. Foster Stawell, W. J. T. Clarke, J. M. Grant, Peter Lalor, G. Higinbotham, Richard Goldsborough, John Winter, Samuel Ramsden, George Stevenson, Sir C. G. Duffy, John Wallace, Dr. R. T. Tracy, K. O'Hara Burke, and W. J. Wills.

MANUZZI (GIUSEPPE). Vocabolario della Lingua Italiana. 2ª ed. 4 vols. imp. 8vo. Firenze, 1859–65.   K 14 R 13–16

MANX SOCIETY. [*See* KELLY, REV. J.]

MANZONI (ALESSANDRO). I Promessi Sposi : Storia Milanese del secolo XVII. 2 vols. 32mo Milan, 1873. Libr.

Opere varie di ; edizione riveduta dall' Autore.   Roy. 8vo. Milan, 1870.   J 15 V 9

Tragedie e Poesie. 32mo. Milano, 1871.   Libr.

MAORI. [*See* INGLIS, J.]

MAORI BIBLES. [*See* BIBLES, TESTAMENTS, &c.]

MAPS, &c. Mineral and Agricultural Maps and General Statistics of New South Wales. (Pam. J c.) 8vo. Sydney, 1878.   MF 3 P 22

Carte Agricole et Statistique Générale de la Nouvelle Galles du Sud, Australie. (Pam. J c.) 8vo. Sydney, 1878.   MF 3 P 22

Mineralogische Karte und allgemeine Statistik von Neu Süd Wales, in Australien. (Pam. J c.) 8vo. Sydney, 1878.   MF 3 P 22

Carte Minéralogique et Statistique générale de la Nouvelle Galles du Sud, Australie. (Pam. J c.) 8vo. Sydney, 1878.   MF 3 P 22

Landwirthschaftliche Karte und allgemeine Statistik von Neu Süd Wales, in Australien. (Pam. J c.) 8vo. Sydney, 1878.   MF 3 P 22

Port Apra. 8vo. Lond., &c. (n.d.)*   MD 5 P 9 ‡

Lord Howe Island and adjacent Islets and Reefs.   8vo. Lond., &c. (n.d.)*   MD 5 P 9 ‡

Lord Howe Island and Ball's Pyramid. 8vo. Lond., &c. (n.d.)*   MD 5 P 9 ‡

Fiji, or Viti Group. 8vo. Lond., &c. (n.d.)*   MD 5 P 9 ‡

Suva Harbour, South Side of Viti Levu. 8vo. Lond., &c. (n.d.)*   MD 5 P 9 ‡

Melanesien. 8vo. Lond., &c. (n.d.)*   MD 5 P 9 ‡

Map of Tasmania, in 1859 ; by James Sprent.   8vo· Roy. fol. Hobart. (n.d.)   MD 5 Q 13 ‡

Map of Tasmania, showing Telegraph Lines and Stations. Roy. fol. Hobart. (n.d.)   MD 5 Q 13 ‡

Geological Map of the Mount Nicholas and Douglas River Coal-fields ; by Charles Gould. Roy. fol. Hobart. (n.d.)   MD 5 Q 13 ‡

Horizontal Sections to accompany the Map of the Mount Nicholas and Douglas River Coal-fields. Roy. fol. Hobart. (n.d.)   MD 5 Q 13 ‡

Vertical Sections, Nos. 1 and 2. Roy. fol. Hobart. (n.d.)   MD 5 Q 13 ‡

Vertical Sections of Seams worked by the Douglas River Coal Company. Roy. fol. Hobart. (n.d.)   MD 5 Q 13 ‡

Section of the Douglas River Coal Company's Works ; by James Craig. Roy. fol. Hobart. (n.d.) MD 5 P 13 ‡

Sketch Map of part of Western Tasmania ; by Charles Gould. Roy. fol. Hobart. (n.d.)   MD 5 P 13 ‡

MAPS, &c.—*continued.*

India: Catalogue [and Continuation] of Maps.   Roy. 8vo. Lond., 1870–72.   K 8 Q 26

India: Catalogue of Maps, &c. 8vo. Lond., 1876–77.   A 10 P 13

Enlarged Map of a portion of the Mersey Coal-field. Roy. fol. Hobart. (n.d.)   MD 5 Q 13 ‡

Sketch Sections to illustrate the Map of the Mersey Coal-fields. Roy. fol. Hobart. (n.d.)   MD 5 Q 13 ‡

Geological Map of the Iron Deposits of Ilfracombe ; by Charles Gould. Roy. fol. Hobart. (n.d.) MD 5 Q 13 ‡

No. 3, Plan and Section of Hematite Lode, east of Lot 571 on Ilfracombe Tram Road. Roy. fol. Hobart. (n.d.)   MD 5 Q 13 ‡

Map of the Den Gold-fields and Ilfracombe Iron Deposits. Roy. fol. Hobart. (n.d.)   MD 5 Q 13 ‡

Part of the County of Dorset, County of Devon, Parish of Forrabury. Roy. fol. Hobart. (n.d.) MD 5 Q 13 ‡

Maps of the Society for the Diffusion of Useful Knowledge. L. 4to. Lond., 1844.   D 8 P 4 ‡

England and Wales. Sm. fol. Lond., 1857–59.
                                                    D 33 Q 16 ‡

Europe. Sm. fol. Lond., 1857–59.   D 33 Q 16 ‡

Italy. Sm. fol. Lond., 1857–59.   D 33 Q 16 ‡

Nieuw Guinea (Kart van). Fol. (n.p.d.) D 33 Q 16 ‡

Schets van de Zuidwest-en gedeeltelijke Zuidkust van Nieuw Guinea. Fol. (n.p.) 1825–35. (2 copies.)
                                                    MD 5 S 18 ‡

Map of Australia. Compiled by Jas. Wyld.   Fol. Lond. (n.d.)   MD 5 S 18 ‡

Wassende-graade Paskaart-Oost Indien ; bij P. Goos. Fol. Amsterdam, 1650.   MD 5 S 18 ‡

Kaart van de Zuyd Zee, enz ; bij G. van Keulen. Fol· Amsterdam, 1650.   MD 5 S 18 ‡

Het westelykste Gedeelte van het Land van de Eendragt of Nova Hollandia ; by J. van Keulen. Fol. Amsterdam, 1665.   MD 5 S 18 ‡

Chart of Torres Strait, from the Surveys of Captain Cook in 1769, and Captain Brampton in 1793. Fol. Lond., 1798.   MD 5 S 18 ‡

Chart of the Eastern Coast of New Holland, comprehending Van Diemen's Land, Furneaux's Land, and New South Wales. Published by Lawrie and Whittle. Fol. Lond., 1798.   MD 5 S 18 ‡

New Chart of the Eastern Coast of New Holland, from South Cape York, comprehending Anthony Van Diemen's Land, Furneaux's Land, and New South Wales. Fol. Lond., 1798.   MD 5 S 18 ‡

MARANA (GIOVANNI PAOLO). Letters written by a Turkish Spy, who lived Forty-five Years undiscovered at Paris. Written originally in Arabic, translated into Italian, and from thence into English. 8 vols. 8vo. Lond., 1801.
                                                    J 5 R 23–30

MARBRON (MYRA). Australasian Birthday-book; specially compiled from the Writings of the Poets of New South Wales, Victoria, South Australia, Queensland, Tasmania, and New Zealand. Sm. 4to. Lond., 1885.
MH 1 S 20

MARCELLINUS. [*See* AMMIANUS MARCELLINUS.]

MARCET (EDOUARD). Australie: un Voyage à travers le Bush. 8vo. Genève, 1868. MD 3 V 10

MARCHAND (MME. FRANÇOISE LE). [*See* LE MARCHAND, MME. F.]

MARCHAND (ÉTIENNE). Voyage autour du Monde, pendant les années 1790–92. Vols. 1–5. 8vo. Paris, 1800. MD 7 P 33–37 †
Voyage autour du Monde: Cartes et Figures; par C. P. Claret Fleurieu. Vol. 6. 8vo. Paris, 1800. MD 7 P 38 †
Voyage round the World, performed during the years 1790–92. Translated from the French of C. P. Claret Fleurieu. 2 vols. 8vo. Lond., 1801. MD 7 P 6, 7

MARCHANDON DE LA FAYE (P.) Texte à l'Histoire de l'Art Egyptien. [*See* PRISSE D'AVENNES, E.]

MARCHANT (F. M.) Le Nouveau Conducteur de l'Etranger à Paris en 1835. 17e éd. 18mo. Paris, 1835.
D 7 S 27

MARCHMONT (EARLS OF). Selection from the Papers of, in the possession of the Right Hon. G. H. Rose, 1685–1750. 3 vols. 8vo. Lond., 1831. B 5 U 44–46

MARCO POLO. [*See* POLO, M.].

MARCY (BRIG.-GEN. RANDOLPH BARNES), U.S.A. Thirty Years of Army Life on the Border. With Illustrations. 8vo. Lond., 1866. D 3 S 25

MAREY-MONGE (COL. W. S.) Memoir on Swords, &c. Translated from the French, by H. H. Maxwell. (Weale.) 12mo. Lond., 1860. A 17 P 55

MAREY (PROF. ETIENNE JULES). Animal Mechanism: a Treatise on Terrestrial and Aerial Locomotion. 2nd ed. 8vo. Lond., 1874. A 17 T 17
La Machine Animale: Locomotion terrestre et aérienne. 2e éd. 8vo. Paris, 1878. A 16 T 28
Physiologie Expérimentale. Tomes, 2–4. 3 vols. 8vo. Paris, 1876–80. A 12 T 13–15

MARGARET OF ANGOULÊME (QUEEN OF NAVARRE). [Biography of]; by A. Mary F. Robinson [Mrs. Darmesteter.] 8vo. Lond., 1886. C 4 S 20

MARGARET (SAINT), QUEEN OF SCOTLAND. Life of; by St. Turgot, Bishop of St. Andrews. Translated from the Latin by William Forbes-Leith, S.J. 2nd ed. 8vo. Edinb., 1884. C 4 Q 48

MARGARY (AUGUSTUS RAYMOND). Journey of; from Shanghae to Bhamo, and back to Manwyne; from his Journals and Letters; with a concluding Chapter, by Sir R. Alcock, K.C.B. 8vo. Lond., 1876. D 4 T 8

MARGOLIOUTH (REV. MOSES). The Jews in Great Britain; being a series of six Lectures. 12mo. Lond., 1846. G 7 R 4
History of the Jews in Great Britain. 3 vols. 8vo. Lond., 1851. G 11 P 19–21
Pilgrimage to the Land of my Fathers. 2 vols. 8vo. Lond., 1850. D 4 U 9, 10

MARIANA (JUAN DE). Historia general de España, 16 vols. 12mo. Amberes, 1751–56. B 13 U 24–39

MARIA THERESA (QUEEN OF HUNGARY). Maria Theresia und Joseph II. Ihre correspondenz. [In French.] Herausge geben von Alfred Ritter von Arneth. 3 vols. 8vo. Wien, 1867–68. C 9 T 25–27
Maria Theresia's erste Regierungsjahre. [In French.] von Alfred Ritter von Arneth. 3 vols. 8vo. Wien, 1863–65. C 9 T 21–23
Maria Theresia und Marie Antoinette; ihr Briefwechsel; herausgegeben von Alfred Ritter von Arneth. 8vo. Leipzig, 1866. C 9 T 24

MARIE ANTOINETTE (QUEEN OF FRANCE). Memoirs of the Private Life of; by Madame J. L. H. G. Campan. 2nd ed. 2 vols. 8vo. Lond., 1823. C 7 R 39–40
Life of; by Prof. Chas. Duke Yonge. 2 vols. 8vo. Lond., 1876. C 3 P 27, 28
Maria Theresia und Marie Antoinette; ihr Briefwechsel; herausgegeben von Alfred Ritter von Arneth. 8vo. Leipzig, 1866. C 9 T 24
Memoirs of Maria Antoinetta, Archduchess of Austria, Queen of France and Navarre, including several important periods of the French Revolution, by Joseph Weber. Translated from the French by R. C. Dallas. 3 vols. roy. 8vo. Lond., 1805–12. C 5 W 12–14
The Private Life of Marie Antoinette, Queen of France and Navarre; by Jeanne Louise Henriette Campan. New and revised ed. 2 vols. 8vo. Lond., 1883. C 7 R 40, 41
Last Days of Marie Antoinette: an Historical Sketch, by Lord Ronald Gower. With Portrait. 4to. Lond., 1885. C 7 R 44
Mémoires sur la Vie de Marie Antoinette, par Madame Campan. [*See* BARRIÈRE, J. F., 10.] C 1 T 10

MARIE DE MEDICIS (QUEEN OF FRANCE). Life of; by Miss J. S. H. Pardoe. 2nd ed. 3 vols. 8vo. Lond., 1852. C 7 S 47–49

MARIE THÉRÈSA CHARLOTTE (DUCHESS OF ANGOULÊME). [*See* ANGOULÊME, MARIE T. C., DUCHESSE D'.]

MARIE LOUISE (EMPRESS OF THE FRENCH). Memoirs of. From the French of [Arthur Léon, Baron] Imbert de Saint-Amand. 8vo. Lond., 1886. C 10 U 26

MARIETTE (FRANÇOIS AUGUSTE FERDINAND), PACHA. Dendérah; description Générale du Grand Temple de cette Ville. Sm. fol. Paris, 1880. B 15 S 12 ‡
Planches [to the above.] 4 vols. (in 2) roy. fol. Paris, 1870–73. B 15 U 12, 13 ‡

MARIGNY (CHEV. TAITBOUT DE). Three Voyages in the Black Sea to the Coast of Circassia. 8vo. Lond., 1837.
    D 7 T 17

MARINE BOARD, N.S.W. [*See* NEW SOUTH WALES.]

MARINER (WILLIAM). Account of the Natives of the Tonga Islands, in the South Pacific Ocean; with an Original Grammar and Vocabulary of their Language; by John Martin, M.D. 2nd ed. 2 vols. 8vo. Lond., 1818.
    MD 5 S 21, 22
Another copy. 3rd ed. (Const. Misc.) 2 vols. 18mo. Edinb., 1827.
    K 10 Q 1, 2

MARIN LA MESLEE (EDMOND). L'Australie Nouvelle. 8vo. Paris, 1883.*
    MD 4 Q 1
Progrés et Resources de la Nouvelle Galles du Sud. [*See* ROBINSON, C.]
    MP 3 P 22

MARIO (GIUSEPPE). From Mozart to Mario: Reminiscences of Half-a-Century. [*See* ENGEL, L.] C 4 S 18, 19

MARIOTTI (LUIGI.) [*See* GALLENGA, A. C. N.]

MARITIME NOTES AND QUERIES: a Record of Shipping Law and Usages; edited by Sir William Mitchell, [Knt.] F.R.G.S., &c. Vols. 1-5. 4to. Lond., 1873–81.
    E 1, 58

MARJORIBANKS (ALEXANDER). Travels in New Zealand. 8vo. Lond., 1846.*
    MD 4 R 5
Travels in New South Wales. 8vo. Lond., 1847.*
    MD 4 R 7
Another copy. 2nd ed. 8vo. Lond., 1851.* MD 4 R 9

MARJOURAM (SERGT. WILLIAM), R.A. Memorials of; edited by Sergt. William White, R.A. 12mo. Lond., 1861.*
    MC 1 P 23

MARKBY (WILLIAM), M.A. Elements of Law, considered with reference to Principles of general Jurisprudence. 2nd ed. (Clar. Press.) 8vo. Oxford, 1874. F 5 T 44

MARKHAM (CAPT. ALBERT HASTINGS), R.N., &c. Cruise of the *Rosario* amongst the New Hebridies and Santa Cruz Islands, exposing the recent Atrocities connected with the Kidnapping of Natives in the South Seas. 8vo. Lond., 1873.*
    MD 6 Q 8
Polar Reconnaissance; being the Voyage of the *Isbjörn* to Novaya Zemlia in 1879. With Illustrations. 8vo. Lond., 1881.
    D 4 S 7
Whaling Cruise to Baffin's Bay and the Gulf of Boothia, and an Account of the Rescue of the Crew of the *Polaris,* 8vo. Lond., 1874.
    D 4 S 6

MARKHAM (CAPT. CLEMENTS ROBERTS), C.B., &c. General Sketch of the History of Persia. 2 vols. 8vo. Lond., 1874.
    B 1 P 13
Travels in Peru and India. 8vo. Lond., 1862. D 4 Q 8
Cuzco: a Journey to the Ancient Capital of Peru. 8vo. Lond., 1856.
    D 3 Q 3

MARKHAM (CAPT. CLEMENTS ROBERTS), C.B., &c.—*contd.*
Life of the Great Lord Fairfax, Commander-in-Chief of the Army of the Parliament of England. 8vo. Lond., 1870.
    C 5 V 14
Commodore J. G. Goodenough: a Brief Memoir. 12mo. Lond., 1876.
    MC 1 P 16
Memoir on the Indian Surveys. 2nd ed. Imp. 8vo. Lond., 1878.
    D 4 V 27
Narratives of the Mission of George Bogle to Tibet, and of the Journey of Thomas Manning to Lhasa; edited, with Notes, an Introduction, and Lives of Mr. Bogle, and Mr. Manning. 8vo. Lond., 1876. D 5 S 12
Life of Robert Fairfax, of Steeton, Vice-Admiral, Alderman, and Member for York, A.D. 1666-1725. Compiled from original Letters and other Documents. 8vo. Lond., 1885.
    C 6 Q 18
Peruvian Bark: a popular Account of the Introduction of Cinchona Cultivation into British India, 1860–80. With Maps and Illustrations. 8vo. Lond.,1880. A 4 P 17
Threshold of the Unknown Region. 8vo. Lond., 1873.
    D 4 S 38
The Fifty Years' Work of the Royal Geographical Society. 8vo. Lond., 1881.
    E 1, 48, 49

MARKHAM (COL. FREDERICK), C.B. Shooting in the Himalayas: a Journal of Sporting Adventures and Travel in Chinese Tartary, Ladac, Thibet, Cashmere, &c. Roy. 8vo. Lond., 1854.
    D 5 U 1

MARK LANE EXPRESS (THE), and Agricultural Journal. Vols. 45-55, fol. Lond., 1876-85.
    E

MARLBOROUGH (JOHN CHURCHILL), DUKE OF. Military Life of; by [Sir] A. Alison [Bart.] 8vo. Lond., 1848.
    C 7 T 39
Memoirs of; with his Original Correspondence; by W. Coxe, M.A. 2nd ed. 6 vols. 8vo. Lond.,1820. C 7 T 40-45
Atlas to [the above.] At. 4to. Lond., 1820. C 7 V 49
Marlborough; by George Saintsbury. (Eng. Worthies.) 8vo. Lond., 1885.
    C 4 T 19

MARLBOROUGH (SARAH JENNINGS), DUCHESS. Memoirs of, and of the Court of Queen Anne; by Mrs. A. T. Thomson. 2 vols. 8vo. Lond., 1839. C 7 T 46, 47

MARLEBURROUGH (HENRY). The Chronicle of Ireland. [*See* HANMER, M.]

MARLOWE (CHRISTOPHER). Works of. With some Account of the Author, and Notes, by the Rev. Alexander Dyce. New ed., revised and corrected. Roy. 8vo. Lond., 1876.
    H 2 U 4
Works of. Edited by A. H. Bullen, B.A. 3 vols. 8vo. Lond., 1885.
    H 2 R 1-3
Old English Drama: Select Plays: Marlowe's Tragical History of Dr. Faustus; edited by A. W. Ward, M.A. (Clar. Press.) 12mo. Oxford, 1878. H 2 Q 39

MARLOWE (CHRISTOPHER), AND NASH (T.) Dido, Queen of Carthage: a Tragedy. 8vo. Lond., 1825. H 1 R 14
Another copy. 8vo. Lond., 1825. H 1 R 15

MARMION (ANTHONY). Ancient and Modern History of the Maritime Ports of Ireland. 8vo. Lond., 1855.
B 11 Q 28

MARMONTEL (JEAN FRANÇOIS). Les Incas; ou, la Destruction de l'Empire du Pérou. 18mo. Lond., 1826. J 16 T 6

Mémoires de. [*See* BARRIÈRE, J. F., 5.]

Memoirs of; written by himself. 2 vols. (in 1) 12mo. Lond., 1829–30. C 1 P 6

MARNO (ERNST). Reisen im Gebiete des blauen und weissen Nil im egyptischen Sudan und den angrenzenden Negerlädern, in den Jahren 1869 bis 1873. 8vo. Wein, 1874. D 2 U 9

MARO. [*See* MACARTHUR, SIR W.]

MARRIOTT (MAJ.-GEN. W. F.), C.I.S. Grammar of Political Economy. 8vo. Lond., 1874. F 6 P 33

MARRYAT (MISS EMILIA). [*See* NORRIS, MRS. E.]

MARRYAT (MISS FLORENCE). [*See* LEAN, MRS. FRANCIS.]

MARRYAT (CAPT. FREDERICK), R.N. Universal Code of Signals for the Mercantile Marine of all Nations; with a Selection of Sentences adapted for Convoys, and Systems of Geometrical, Night, and Fog Signals; by G. B. Richardson. Roy. 8vo. Lond., 1864. K 9 S 7

Life and Letters of; by Florence Marryat [Mrs. Francis Lean]. 2 vols. 8vo. Lond., 1872. C 4 R 17, 18

Diary in America; with remarks on its Institutions. 1st and 2nd series. 6 vols. 8vo. Lond., 1839. D 4 P 37–42

Olla Podrida. 3 vols. 8vo. Lond., 1849. J 11 T 13–15

MARRYAT (HORACE). One Year in Sweden; including a Visit to the Isle of Götland. 2 vols. 8vo. Lond., 1862. D 8 S 25, 26

MARRYAT (JOSEPH). History of Pottery and Porcelain, Mediæval and Modern. 3rd ed. Roy. 8vo. Lond., 1868. A 11 T 19

MARS (A. J.) Corps de Droit Criminel. 2 vols. (in 1) 4to. Paris, 1821. F 8 P 5 †

MARSDEN (REV. J. B.), M.A. Dictionary of Christian Churches and Sects, from the Earliest Ages of Christianity. New ed. 8vo. Lond., 1854. K 18 R 8

Memoirs of the Life and Labours of the Rev. Samuel Marsden, and of his early connection with the Missions to New Zealand and Tahiti. 8vo. Lond., 1858.* MC 1 P 25

MARSDEN (RICHARD), M.S.A. Cotton-spinning : its Development, Principles, and Practice; with an Appendix on Steam-engines and Boilers. (Tech. Hand-books.) 12mo. Lond., 1884. A 11 P 29

MARSDEN (REV. SAMUEL). Answer to certain Calumnies in the late Governor Macquarie's Pamphlet and the third edition of Mr. Wentworth's Account of Australasia. 8vo. Lond., 1826. MF 2 Q 31

Letter to William Crook; accompanied with a few Observations, published in the *Sydney Herald*, by one of Mr. Crook's Missionary Colleagues to the Society Islands. 12mo. Sydney, 1835. MG 1 P 49

Memoirs of the Life and Labours of, and of his early connexion with the Missions to New Zealand and Tahiti; edited by the Rev. J. B. Marsden, M.A. 12mo. Lond., 1858.* MC 1 P 25

Short Account of the Character and Labours of; [by Rev. William Woolls, Ph.D.] (Pam. Bb.) 12mo. Parramatta, 1844. MG 1 P 49

Sermon on the Death of. [*See* STILES, REV. H.] MG 1 P 1

[*See* NICHOLAS, J. L.]

MARSDEN (WILLIAM), F.R.S., &c. Numismata Orientalia Illustrata : the Plates of the Oriental Coins, Ancient and Modern, of the Collection of the late William Marsden, F.R.S., &c. 4to. Lond., 1869. A 1 R 16 †

Memoirs of a Malayan Family; written by themselves, and translated from the Original. 8vo. Lond., 1830. C 6 R 15

Grammar of the Malayan Language; with an Introduction and Praxis. 4to. Lond., 1812. K 14 S 23

Dictionary of the Malayan Language, in two Parts ; Malayan and English, and English and Malayan. 4to. Lond., 1812. K 14 S 22

History of Sumatra ; containing an Account of the Government, &c., of the Native Inhabitants. 4to. Lond., 1811. B 4 U 20

Plates to [the above.] Fol. Lond., 1811. B 4 U 21 ‡

Bibliotheca Marsdeniana : a Catalogue of Books and Manuscripts, collected with a view to the general comparison of Languages, and to the study of Oriental Literature. 4to. Lond., 1827. K 8 S 1 †

Travels of Marco Polo. [*See* POLO, M.] D 0 Q 35

MARSH (MISS CATHERINE M.). English Hearts and English Hands; or, the Railway and the Trenches. 7th thousand. 12mo. Lond., 1858. G 9 Q 26
Another copy. 35th thousand. 12mo. Lond., 1859. G 9 Q 27

Memorials of Captain Hedley Vicars 97th Regiment. 12mo. Lond., 1856. C 1 R 39

Life of the Rev. William Marsh, D.D. ; by his Daughter. 21st thousand. 12mo. Lond., 1878. C 1 R 24

MARSH (GEORGE PERKINS). Student's Manual of the English Language: Lectures on the English Language; edited, with additional Lecture and Notes, by W. Smith, D.C.L., &c. 6th ed. 8vo. Lond., 1872. K 20 Q 41

Man and Nature; or, Physical Geography as modified by Human Action. 8vo. Lond., 1864. A 16 T 17

Origin and History of the English Language. 8vo. Lond., 1862. J 10 T 21

MARSH (HOWARD), F.R.C.S.   Clinical Lectures and
Essays. [*See* PAGET, SIR J.]   A 12 U 25

MARSH (JOHN B.)   Reference Shakspere : a Memorial
edition of Shakspere's Plays, containing 11,600 References.
Sm. 4to. Lond., 1864.   H 2 U 25

MARSH (JOHN FITCHETT).   Annals of Chepstow Castle :
or, Six Centuries of the Lords of Striguil, from the Conquest to the Revolution ; edited by Sir John Maclean,
F.S.A., &c. 4to. Exeter, 1883.   B 4 U 3

MARSH (M. H.), M.P., &c.   Overland from Southampton
to Queensland. 8vo. Lond., 1867.*   MD 4 S 41

MARSH (PROF. OTHNEIL CHARLES).   Odontornithes : a
Monograph on the Extinct Toothed Birds of North America.
(U.S. Geological Exploration of the Fortieth Parallel.)
Roy. 4to. Wash., 1810.   A 23 R 30 †

MARSH (REV. WILLIAM), D.D.   Life of; by his Daughter
[Miss Catherine M. Marsh.]   21st thousand. 12mo.
Lond., 1878.   C 1 R 24

MARSHALL (CHARLES).   The Canadian Dominion. 8vo.
Lond., 1871.   D 3 T 6

MARSHALL (C. H. T. AND G. F. L.), F.Z.S.   Monograph
of the Capitonidæ, or, Scansorial Barbets. Roy. 4to.
Lond., 1871.   A 3 P 3 †

MARSHALL (FREDERIC).   International Vanities. 8vo.
Edinb., 1875.   J 12 Q 18

MARSHALL (MAJOR G. F. L.), AND NICÉVILLE
(LIONEL DE).   Butterflies of India, Burmah, and Ceylon :
a Descriptive Hand-book of all the known species of
Rhopalocerous Lepidoptera inhabiting that region. Vol. 1.
Roy. 8vo. Calcutta, 1882.   A 15 Q 19

MARSHALL (GEORGE W.), LL.D.   Genealogist's Guide
to Printed Pedigrees, &c. Roy. 8vo. Lond., 1879.
                                                 K 10 V 10

Another copy. 2nd ed. 8vo. Lond., 1885.   K 10 V 11

MARSHALL (H.)   History of Kentucky.   2 vols. 8vo.
Frankfort, 1824.   B 1 Q 13, 14

MARSHALL (HENRY).   Abnormal Phenomena of the
Nervous System. [Psychology and Evolution.] 8vo.
Adelaide, 1883.   MA 2 S 18

MARSHALL (CAPT. JOHN), R.N.   Journal of. [*See*
PHILLIP, CAPT. A.]   MD 4 Q 14 †

MARSHALL (JOHN).   Life of George Washington, Commander-in-Chief of the American Forces, and First President of the United States.   2 vols. and atlas 8vo.
Philad., 1832.   C 6 T 27, 28

MARSHALL (JOHN), F.R.S., &c.   Anatomy for Artists,
illustrated by two hundred Original Drawings, by J. S.
Cuthbert. Imp. 8vo. Lond., 1878.   A 12 V 14

MARSHALL (JOHN).   Refutation of the Slanders and
wilful Misrepresentations published at Sydney, by Dr.
Lang, in the *Colonist* Newspaper belonging to him. 8vo.
Lond., 1835.   MF 1 Q 4

Another copy. 8vo. Lond., 1835.   MF 3 P 7

Twenty Years' Experience in Australia.   12mo. Lond.,
1839.   MD 2 Q 57

Letter to the Rt. Hon. Lord John Russell, on Australian Emigration. 8vo. Lond., 1841.   MF 3 P 7

Facts and Proceedings relating to Emigration to the
Australian Colonies. 8vo. Reading, 1857.   MJ 2 R 21

MARSHALL (LIEUT. JOHN), R.N.   Royal Naval Biography ; or, Memoirs of the Services of all the Flag-
Officers, Superannuated Rear-Admirals, Retired Captains,
Post Captains, and Commanders. With Supplement.
8 vols. (in 12) 8vo. Lond., 1823–35.   C 9 S 4-15

MARSHALL (JOSEPH).   Travels through Holland, Flanders,
Germany, Denmark, &c., in the years 1768–70. 3 vols.
8vo. Lond., 1772.   D 9 P 21-23

MARSHALL (WILLIAM), D.D.   Historic Scenes in Perth-
shire. Sm. 4to. Edinb., 1880.   B 13 Q 26

MARSHALL (SURG. WILLIAM BARRETT), R.N.   Word
of Exhortation to a Servant ; being the substance of a
Discourse delivered to the Females on board the *Fanny*,
Prison Ship, preparatory to their going into private
service. 8vo. Sydney, 1833.   MG 1 P 1

Personal Narrative of Two Visits to New Zealand in
H.M.S. *Alligator*, A.D. 1834. 8vo. Lond., 1836. MD 4 Q 41

MARSHMAN (J.)   Works of Confucius. [*See* CON-
FUCIUS.]

MARSHMAN (JOHN).   Canterbury, New Zealand, in
1862. 12mo. Lond., 1862·   MD 1 S 14

MARSHMAN (JOHN CLARK).   Story of [W.] Carey,
[J.] Marshman, and [W.] Ward, the Serampore Missionaries. 8vo. Lond., 1864.   G 7 R 2

Memoirs of Maj.-Gen. Sir Henry Havelock, K.C.B. 8vo.
Lond., 1860.   C 7 Q 25

MARSHMAN (JOSHUA).   The Story of. [*See* MARSHMAN,
J. C.]

MARSTON (JOHN).   Works of ; reprinted from the original
editions ; with Notes, and some Account of his Life and
Writings, by J. O. Halliwell [-Phillips], F.R.S. 3 vols.
12mo. Lond., 1856.   H 1 R 16-18

MARSTON (WESTLAND).   Dramatic and Poetical Works
of.   2 vols. 8vo. Lond., 1876.   H 1 R 19, 20

MART (R.)   Extract from the Report of the Purveyor of
the Navy Board, on the Timber of New South Wales
and Van Diemen's Land. [*See* FIELD, B.]

MARTEL (CHARLES). Military Italy. 8vo. Lond.,
1884.　　　　　　　　　　　　　　　　F 7 Q 6

MARTEL (CHARLES). Principles of Harmony and Contrast
of Colours. [*See* CHEVREUL, M. E.]

MARTELL (MARTHA). Letters from the Danube. 2 vols.
Lond., 1847.　　　　　　　　　　　　D 9 Q 42, 43

MARTEMONT (C. MALORTI DE). Theory of Field Fortification. 8vo. Lond., 1810.　　　　　　　A 6 S 17

MARTENS (PROF. EDWARD VON). Die Preussische Expedition. [*See* PREUSSISCHE EXPEDITION NACH OST-
ASIEN.]　　　　　　　　　　　　　D 5 U 9–15

MARTENS (FREDERICK). Voyage into Spitzbergen and
Greenland. [*See* VOYAGES AND DISCOVERIES.] MD 5 P 24
Observations made in Greenland, and other Northern
Countries. [*See* VOYAGES AND DISCOVERIES.] MD 5 P 25

MARTENS (GEORG VON). Die Preussische Expedition. [*See*
PREUSSISCHE EXPEDITION NACH OST-ASIEN.] D 5 U 9–15

MARTEN (HENRY). Life of. [*See* MACKINTOSH, SIR J.]

MARTENSEN (DR. H. L.) Jacob Boehme : his Life and
Teaching ; or, Studies in Theosophy ; translated by T. Rhys
Evans. 8vo. Lond., 1885.　　　　　　　C 5 R 7

MARTIALIS (MARCUS VALERIUS). Epigrammata, ex Editione Bipontina, cum Notis et Interpretatione in usum
Delphini. 3 vols. 8vo. Lond., 1822–23.　J 13 R 12–14
Epigrams of Martial. Translated into English Prose.
8vo. Lond., 1860.　　　　　　　　　J 11 T 30

MARTIN (—.) [*See* LETTERS FROM THE IRISH HIGHLANDS.]

MARTIN (AIMÉ). Études sur la Vie de Fénelon. [*See*
FÉNELON, F. DE S. DE LA M.]

MARTIN (A. B.), F.R.A.S. Complete Epitome of Practical
Navigation. [*See* NORIE, J. W.]　　　　A 10 U 11

MARTIN (CHARLES). Civil Costume of England, from the
Conquest to the Present Time. 4to. Lond.,1842. A 1 P 14†

MARTIN (CHARLES WYKEHAM), F.S.A. History and
Description of Leeds Castle, Kent. Fol. Westminster,
1869.　　　　　　　　　　　　　B 19 U 13 ‡

MARTIN (E.) La Réforme en Italie. [*See* CANTU, C.]

MARTIN (MISS ELVIRA A.) Life and Speeches of Daniel
Henry Deniehy. 8vo. Sydney, 1884.*　　MC 1 R 6

MARTIN (FREDERICK). Hand-book of Contemporary
Biography. 12mo. Lond., 1870.　　　　C 11 Q 1
History of Lloyd's, and of Marine Insurance in Great
Britain. 8vo. Lond., 1876.　　　　　　F 7 P 19
Manual of Dates. [*See* TOWNSEND, G. H.]
[*See* STATESMAN'S YEAR-BOOK.]

MARTIN (HELENA FAUCIT), LADY. On some of Shakes-
peare's Female Characters: Ophelia, Portia, Desdemona,
Juliet, Imogen, Rosalind, Beatrice. 4to. Edinb., 1885.
　　　　　　　　　　　　　　　　H 2 U 10

MARTIN (HENRI). Histoire de France, depuis les Temps
les plus reculés jusqu'en 1789. 19 vols. 8vo. Paris,
1838–54.　　　　　　　　　　　B 9 Q 1–19

MARTIN (H. NEWELL), M.D., D.Sc., &c. The Human Body:
an Account of its Structure and Activities, and the Con-
ditions of its Healthy Working. (American Science
Series.) 8vo. New York, 1881.　　　　A 13 P 12
Course of Elementary Instruction in Practical Biology.
[*See* HUXLEY, PROF. T. H.]

MARTIN (JAMES). Explorations in North-western Australia. 8vo. Lond., 1865.　　　　　　MD 7 Q 54

MARTIN (REV. JAMES), B.A. The Spirit Quenched ; or,
Spiritual Gifts suppressed by the Church : a Sermon.
12mo. Melb., 1869.　　　　　　　　MG 1 Q 16

MARTIN (SIR JAMES), KNT., C.J. The Australian Sketch-
book. 12mo. Sydney, 1838.　　　　　MD 2 P 11
Report of the Proceedings attending the Presentation
of the Portrait of Sir James Martin, C.J., by the Bar of
New South Wales, on the 22nd day of May, 1885. 8vo.
Sydney, 1885.　　　　　　　　　　MB 2 Q 2

MARTIN (JOHN), M.D. Account of the Natives of the
Tonga Islands. [*See* MARINER, W.]

MARTIN (JOSIAH), F.G.S. Geyser Eruptions and Terrace
Formations. [*See* COWAN, F.]　　　　MH 1 S 22

MARTIN (K.) Beiträge zur Geologie Ost-Asiens und
Australiens. [*See* GEOLOGISCHEN REICHS-MUSEUMS IN
LEIDEN.]

MARTIN (LADY). Our Maoris. 8vo. Lond.,1884. MD 4 P 16

MARTIN (LEOPOLD C.), AND TRÜBNER (CHAS.) Current
Gold and Silver Coins of all Countries, their weight and
fineness, and their intrinsic value in English Money ; with
Facsimiles of the Coins. 4to. Lond., 1863. A 13 S 35

MARTIN (ROBERT MONTGOMERY). Australia: comprising
New South Wales, Victoria or Port Philip, South Aus-
tralia, and Western Australia : their History, Topography,
Condition, Resources, Statistics, Gold Discoveries, Mines of
Copper, Lead, &c. Imp. 8vo. Lond., 1883.* MB 1 U 15
Despatches, &c., of the Marquess of Wellesley in India.
[*See* WELLESLEY, MARQUIS.]　　　　B 10 T 7–11
History of Austral-Asia ; comprising New South Wales,
Van Diemen's Island, Swan River, South Australia, &c.
12mo. Lond., 1836.*　　　　　　　MB 1 P 1
Statistics of the Colonies of the British Empire in the
West Indies, South America, North America, Asia, Aus-
tralasia, Africa, and Europe ; with the Charters and En-
graved Seals. Roy. 8vo. Lond., 1839.*　MF 2 S 12

MARTIN (ROBERT MONTGOMERY)—*continued.*
Britis1 Possessions in Europe, Africa, Asia, and Australasia, connected wit1 England by the India and Australia Mail Steam Packet Company. (Pam. 25.) 8vo.
Lond., 1847.   MJ 2 Q 13

Britis1 Colonies: tieir History, Extent, Condition, and
Resources. 6 vols. (in 3) imp. 8vo. Lond., 1850.
                                            MB 1 U 12–14

History, Antiquities, Topograp1y, and Statistics of Eastern
India. 3 vols. 8vo. Lond., 1838.   B 10 S 31–33

History of the Britis1 Colonies. 5 vols. 8vo. Lond.,
1834–35.   B 14 S 14–18

Ireland before and after the Union wit1 Great Britain.
8vo. Lond., 1843.   B 11 Q 8

Past and Present State of the Tea Trade of England,
&c. (Pam. 9.) 8vo. Lond., 1832.   F 12 P 8

[*See* COLONIAL MAGAZINE.]

MARTIN (SAMUEL). The Useful Arts: tieir Birt1 and
Development. 12mo. Lond., 1851.   A 17 T 8

MARTIN (S. M. D.), M.D. New Zealand; in a series of
Letters, containing an Account of the Country bot1 before
and since its occupation by the Britis1 Government. 8vo.
Lond., 1845.   MD 5 U 10
New Zealand; being an Account of t1at Country, wit1 a
full Description of the various Settlements and Natural
Productions of the Colony. 8vo. Lond., 1845. MD 5 U 9

MARTIN (SIR THEODORE), K.C.B. Bon Gaultier Book of
Ballads. [*See* AYTOUN, W. E.]
Works of Horace, translated into Englis1 Verse. [*See*
HORATIUS FLACCUS, Q.]   H 8 V 26, 27
Memoir of William Edmondstoune Aytoun, D.C.L. Wit1
an Appendix. 8vo. Edinb., 1867.   C 2 U 1
Life of H.R.H. the Prince Consort. With Portraits and
Views. 5 vols. 8vo. Lond., 1875–80.   C 1 V 20–24
Life of Lord Lynd1urst; from Letters and Papers in
possession of 1is Family. 8vo. Lond., 1883.   C 7 S 9
Poems, Original and Translated. 8vo. Lond., 1863.
                                            H 8 Q 15
Odes, Epodes, and Satires of Horace. [*See* HORATIUS
FLACCUS, Q.]   H 7 S 37
Vita Nuova of Dante. [*See* DANTE ALIGHIERI.] C 2 P 12
Faust: a Dramatic Poem. [*See* GOETHE, J. W. VON.]
                                            H 4 S 9 ‡

MARTIN (T. CARLAW). Biograp1y of Franz Liszt. 18mo.
Lond., 1886.   C 2 Q 26

MARTIN (SIR W.), KNT., D.C.L. Notes on C1urc1 Questions. 8vo. C1risto1urc1, 1874.   MG 1 Q 39
The Taranaki Question. 3rd ed. 8vo. Lond., 1861.
                                            MF 1 R 22

MARTIN (WILLIAM). Catalogue d'Ouvrages relatifs aux
Iles Hawaii: Essai de Bibliograp1ic Hawaiienne. 8vo.
Paris, 1867.   MK 1 P 46

MARTIN (WILLIAM ALEXANDER PEARSON), D.D., &c. The
Chinese: t1eir Education, Philosop1y, and Letters. 8vo.
Lond., 1880.   D 5 R 30

MARTIN (MAJOR W. G. WOOD-) [*See* WOOD-MARTIN,
MAJOR W. G.]

MARTIN (W. W.) By Solent and Danube: Poems and
Ballads. 8vo. Lond., 1885.   H 8 Q 8

MARTINEAU (HARRIET). Illustrations of Political
Economy. 9 vols. 12mo. Lond., 1834.   F 2 P 6–14
  1. Life in the Wilds. The Hill and the Valley. Brooke and
     Brooke Farm.
  2. Demerera. Ella of Garveloch. Weal and Woe in Garveloch.
  3. A Manc1ester Strike. Cousin Mars1all. Ireland.
  4. Homes Abroad. For Eac1 and for All. Frenc1 Wines and
     Politics.
  5. The C1armed Sea. Berkeley the Banker.
  6. Messrs. Vanderput and Snoek. The Loom and the Lugger.
  7. Sowers not Reapers. Cinnamon and Pearls. A Tale of the
     Tyne.
  8. Briery Creek. The T1ree Ages.
  9. The Farrers of Budge-Row. The Moral of many Fables.
House1old Education. 12mo. Lond., 1849.   G 17 P 29
Eastern Life, Present and Past. 3 vols. 8vo. Lond.,
1848.   D 1 P 14–16
History of England during the T1irty Years' Peace, 1816–
46. 2 vols. imp. 8vo. Lond., 1849–50.   B 2 T 27, 28
How to Observe: Morals and Manners. 8vo. Lond.,
1838.   G 7 Q 22
Retrospect of Western Travel. 3 vols. 8vo. Lond., 1838.
                                           D 3 P 33–35
Positive P1ilosop1y of Auguste Comte. [*See* COMTE, A.]
Society in America. 3 vols. 8vo. Lond., 1837.
                                           D 3 P 30–32
Biographical Sketc1es, 1852–75. 4th ed., enlarged, wit1
Autobiograp1ical Sketc1. 8vo. Lond., 1876. C 1 T 30
Autobiograp1y; wit1 Memorials by Maria Weston
C1apman. With Portraits and Illustrations. 2nd ed.
3 vols. 8vo. Lond., 1877.   C 3 Q 36–38
Introduction to the History of the Peace, 1800–15. Imp.
8vo. Lond., 1851.   B 2 T 26
Letters on the Laws of Man's Nature and Development.
[*See* ATKINSON, H. G.]

MARTINEAU (JAMES), LL.D., &c. Essays, P1ilosop1ical
and T1eological. 2 vols. 8vo. New York, 1875.
                                           G 7 Q 12, 13
Study of Spinoza. Wit1 a Portrait. 8vo. Lond., 1882.
                                           C 4 Q 34
Types of Et1ical T1eory. (Clar. Press.) 2 vols. 8vo.
Oxford, 1885.   G 16 T 4, 5

MARTINEAU (JOHN). Letters from Australia. 8vo.
Lond., 1869.   MD 4 T 8

MARTINENGO-CESARESCO (EVELYN), COUNTESS. [*See*
CESARESCO, EVELYN MARTINENGO-, COUNTESS.]

MARTINET (LUDOVIC). Les Polynésiens. [*See* LESSON,
DR. A.]

MARTINGALE. [*See* WHITE, REV. C.]

MARTINS (C.) Philosophie Zoologique. [*See* LAMARCK, J. B. P. DE.] A 14 S 22, 23

MARTINUS (SANCTUS), LEGIONENSIS PRESBYTER. Opera omnia. [*See* MIGNE, J. P., SERIES LATINA, 208, 209.]

MARTIRE, OR MARTYR (PIETRO). [*See* EDEN, R.]
D 16 Q 13 ‡

MARTYN (B.), AND KIPPIS (A.), D.D. Life of the first Earl of Shaftesbury, from the original Documents in the possesion of the Family. Edited by G. Wingrove Cooke. 2 vols. 8vo. Lond., 1836. C 8 P 43, 44

MARTYN (REV. HENRY), B.D. Memoir of. Edited by J. Sargent, junr. 7th ed. 12mo. Lond., 1822. C 2 U 30

MARTYN (PROF. JOHN), F.R.S. The Bucolicks of Virgil; with an English Translation. [*See* VIRGILIUS, MARO P.]

MARTYN (THOMAS), B.D. Gardener's and Botanist's Dictionary. [*See* MILLER, P.] K 22 P 1, 2

MARTYN (WILLIAM FREDERICK). Geographical Magazine; or, new, copious, compleat, and universal System of Geography. 2 vols. 4to. Lond., 1785–87. D 11 P 8, 9 †

MARVELL (ANDREW). Works of, Poetical, Controversial, and Political; with a new Life of the Author, by Capt. Edward Thompson. 3 vols. 4to. Lond., 1776. J 7 V 21–23

MARVIN (CHARLES). Merv, the Queen of the World, and the Scourge of the Man-stealing Turcomans; with an Exposition of the Khorasan Question. 8vo. Lond., 1881. D 5 S 18

Reconnoitring Central Asia: Pioneering Adventures in the Region lying between Russia and India. 8vo. Lond., 1884. D 6 R 18

Region of the Eternal Fire: an Account of a Journey to the Petroleum Region of the Caspian in 1883. 8vo. Lond., 1884. D 6 U 20

Russian Advance towards India: Conversations with Skobeleff, Ignatieff, and other distinguished Russian Generals and Statesmen, on the Central Asian Question. 8vo. Lond., 1882. F 7 Q 18

Railway Race to Herat: an Account of the Russian Railway to Herat and India. 8vo. Lond., 1885. F 7 Q 19

Russia's Power of Attacking India. (Pam.) 8vo. Lond., 1885. F 7 Q 17

MARTINIÈRE (ANTOINE AUGUSTIN BRUZEN). History of Europe. [*See* PUFFENDORF, BARON S. VON.]
B 7 T 30, 31

MARWICK (SIR JAMES DAVID), KNT., LL.D., &c. Precedence of Edinburgh and Dublin: Proceedings in the Privy Council in the question as to the Precedence of the Corporations of Edinburgh and Dublin. 8vo. Edinb., 1865. F 8 Q 17 †

MARX (ADOLF BERNHARD). Ludwig van Beethoven; Leben und Schaffen. 2 vols. roy. 8vo. Berlin, 1865. C 9 V 14, 15

MARYLAND. [*See* UNITED STATES.]

3 Q

MARY I (QUEEN OF ENGLAND). England under the Reigns of Edward VI and Mary. [*See* TYTLER, P. F.]

Privy Purse Expenses of; with a Memoir. [*See* MADDEN, Sir F.]

MARY STUART (QUEEN OF SCOTS). Letters of; and Documents connected with her Personal History, now first published; with an Introduction by Agnes Strickland. 3 vols. 8vo. Lond., 1842–43. C 5 P 26–28

Letters of, now first published, from the Originals; with an Historical Introduction and Notes, by Agnes Strickland. 2 vols. 8vo. Lond., 1845. C 5 P 29, 30

History of. Translated from the original and unpublished MS. of Professor J. A. Petit; by Charles de Flandre, F.S.A., Scot. 2 vols. (in 1) 4to. Lond., 1874. C 2 W 16

Mary Queen of Scots in Captivity: a Narrative of Events from January, 1569, to December, 1584; by John Daniel Leader, F.S.A. 8vo. Sheffield, 1880. C 6 T 26

De Vita et Rebus Gestis Serenissimae Principis Mariae Scotorum Reginae, Franciae Dotariae, quae scriptis tradidere Autores Sedecim; ad optimae fidei Codices recensuit, indicesque adjecit locupletissimos S. Jebb. 2 vols. roy. fol. Lond., 1725. C 4 S 17, 18 ‡

History of Mary Queen of Scots, by F. A. M. Mignet. 2 vols. 8vo. Lond., 1851. C 8 R 24, 25

Lettres, Instructions et Mémoires de Marie-Stuart, Reine d'Ecosse; par le Prince Alexandre Labanoff. 7 vols. 8vo. Lond., 1844. C 6 T 19–25

Mary Queen of Scots and her Accusers; by John Hosack. 2nd ed. 2 vols. 8vo. Edinb., 1869–74. C 6 T 16, 17

Memoirs of; by L. Stanhope F. Buckingham. 2 vols. 8vo. Lond., 1844. C 6 T 14, 15

Mary Queen of Scots vindicated; by John Whitaker, B.D. 2nd ed., enlarged. 3 vols. 8vo. Lond., 1790. C 5 U 2–4

Mary Stuart: a Narrative of the first Eighteen Years of her Life; principally from original Documents, by the Rev. Joseph Stevenson, S.J. 8vo. Edinb., 1886. C 4 R 37

History of Mary Stewart, from the Murder of Riccio until her Flight into England, by Claude Nau, her Secretary; edited by the Rev. Joseph Stevenson, S.J. 8vo. Edinb., 1883. C 6 T 18

Mary Stuart: a Sketch and a Defence; by Gerard Daniel. 8vo. Lond., 1886. C 4 R 36

Life of; by H. G. Bell. (Const. Misc.) 2 vols. 18mo. Edinb., 1828–31. K 10 Q 12, 13

Lost Chapter in the History of. Recovered by John Stuart, LL.D. Sm. 4to. Edinb., 1874. C 8 Q 32

An Inquiry, Historical and Critical, into the Evidence against. [*See* TYTLER, W.]

Defence of Mary Stuart. [*See* SKELTON, J.]

MASACCIO [*See* GUIDI, TOMASSO.]

MASCART (PROF. ELEUTHÉRÉ), AND JOUBERT (PROF. J.) Treatise on Electricity and Magnetism. Vol. 1.—General Phenomena and Theory. 8vo. Lond., 1883. A 5 U 32

MASKELL (ALFRED). Russian Art and Art Objects in Russia : a Hand-book. (South Kensington Musuem.) 8vo. Lond., 1884.   A 23 R 32

MASKELL (WILLIAM), M.A. Ancient Liturgy in the Church of England, according to the uses of Sarum, York, Hereford, and Bangor, and the Roman Liturgy arranged in parallel columns ; with Preface and Notes. 3rd ed. 8vo. Oxford, 1882.   G 2 Q 5

Monumenta Ritualia Ecclesiae Anglicanae. 2nd ed. 3 vols. 8vo. Oxford, 1882.   G 2 Q 20–22

Ivories, Ancient and Mediæval. (South Kensington Museum.) 8vo. Lond., 1875.   .   A 23 R 30

MASKELL (REV. W.) Reprint of a Review of the Rev. Mr. Maskell's Letter on the Dogmatical Teaching of the Church, as it appears in the *Christian Observer* of July, 1850. 8vo. Hobart, 1851.   MG 1 Q 31

MASKELL (W. M.), F.R.M.S. Account of the Insects noxious to Agriculture and Plants in New Zealand : the Scale Insects (Coccidiæ). 8vo. Wellington, 1887.*
                                             MA 2 U 18

MASON, A. [*See* FREEMASONRY.]

MASON (CYRUS). Book of Reference to Mason's Map of Melbourne. 8vo. Mel1., 1854.   MD 5 S 15 ‡

Plan of the City of Melbourne ; compiled under the direction of Thomas Ham. Roy. 4to. Mel1., 1854.
                                             MD 5 S 15 †

MASON (REV. FRANCIS), D.D. Burma : its People and Production ; re-written and enlarged by W. Theobald. 2 vols. imp. 8vo. Hertford, 1882–83.   D 5 V 4, 5

The Old Testament in Sgau Karen. [*See* BIBLES, &c.]

MASON (CAPT. F. H.), U.S.A. Life and Public Services of James A. Garfield, twentieth President of the United States: a Biographical Sketch. 8vo. Lond., 1881.   C 1 T 24

MASON (G.) History of the Pirates. [*See* ARCHENHOLTZ, J. M. VON.]   B 14 P 41

MASON (MAJOR G. HENRY), R.A. Costume of China, illustrated by sixty Engravings (coloured); with Explanations in English and French. Fol. Lond., 1801.   A 23 S 11 ‡

Punishments of China, illustrated by twenty-two coloured Engravings ; with Explanations in English and French. Fol. Lond., 1804.   A 23 S 12 ‡

MASON (H. J. MONCK), LL.D., &c. Life of William Bedell, D.D., Lord Bishop of Kildare. 8vo. Lond., 1843.   C 10 R 25

MASON (JAMES). Annual Summary : a complete Chronicle of Events at Home and Abroad. 8vo. Lond., 1875–76.
                                             E 1, 78

Great Triumphs of Great Men. Illustrated. 8vo. Lond., 1877.   C 2 Q 16

[*See* YEAR-BOOK OF FACTS.]

MASON (R. HINDRY), F.R.H.S. History of Norfolk, from original Records and other Authorities, preserved in Public and Private Collections. Roy. fol. Lond., 1884.
                                             B 20 P 22 ‡

Paris Salon, 1881. With Notes of the most important Works, and illustrated. 8vo. Paris, 1881.   E 1, 56

MASON (THOMAS). Public and Private Libraries of Glasgow. 8vo. Glasgow, 1885.   J 2 S 1

MASON (WILLIAM), M.A. The English Garden: a Poem; with Notes by W. Burgh. 2 vols. (in 1) 12mo. Lond., 1819.   H 6 P 16

Caractacus: a Dramatic Poem. (Bell's Brit. Theatre.) 18mo. Lond., 1796.   H 2 P 46

Elfrida : a Dramatic Poem. Bell's Brit. Theatre.) 18mo. Lond., 1796.   H 2 P 46

Life and Poems of. [*See* BRITISH POETS, *and* CHALMERS, A.]

Memoirs of Thomas Gray. [*See* GRAY, T.]   J 7 V 19, 20

MASON (REV. WILLIAM). Correspondence of Horace Walpole, Earl of Orford, and the Rev. William Mason; edited, with Notes, by the Rev. J. Mitford. 2 vols. 8vo. Lond., 1851.   C 10 P P 47, 48

MASONIC KNIGHTS TEMPLAR. Perfect Ceremonies of the Royal, Exalted, Religious, and Military Order of Masonic Knights Templar, Knight of Malta, Mediterranean Pass, and Rose Croix de Heredom Degrees. 18mo. Lond., 1876.   J 7 P 40

MASPERO (PROF. GASTON). Histoire ancienne des Peuples de l'Orient. 3e éd. 8vo. Paris, 1884.   B 2 S 15

La Trouvaille de Deir-el-Bahari. [*See* BRUGSCH, E.]
                                             B 14 R 7 ‡

MASSACHUSETTS. [*See* UNITED STATES.]

MASSARY (ISABEL). Social Life and Manners in Australia ; being the Notes of Eight Years' Experience, by " A Resident." 8vo. Lond., 1861.*   MD 3 R 12

Our Cousins in Australia ; or, Reminiscences of Sarah Norris. 8vo. Edinb., 1867.*   MJ 1 R 20

MASSÉ (JAQUES). Voyages et Avantures de. [*See* PATOL, S. T. DE.]

MASSEY (GERALD). Tale of Eternity, and other Poems. Roy. 8vo. Lond., 1870.   H 6 V 8

Concerning Spiritualism. Sq. 18mo. Lond., 1872. G 9 P 5

Book of the Beginnings. 2 vols. imp. 8vo. Lond., 1881.   K 14 S 26, 27

Natural Genesis ; or, second part of a Book of the Beginnings. 2 vols. imp. 8vo. Lond., 1883. K 14 S 28, 29

MASSIE (J. W.), M.R.I.A. Continental India: Manners of the Hindoos. 2 vols. 8vo. Lond., 1840.   B 10 S 3, 4

MASSILLON (JEAN BAPTISTE). Œuvres de. 2 vols. imp. 8vo. Paris, 1860.   G 7 V 18, 19

MASSINGER (PHILIP). The Great Duke of Florence. [*See* BRIT. DRAMA, 3.]

New Way to pay Old Debts. (Brit. Theatre.) 12mo. Lond., 1808.   H 1 P 6

Another copy. [*See* BRIT. DRAMA, 3.]

Plays of ; with Notes, Critical and Explanatory, by W. Gifford. 4 vols. 8vo. Lond., 1805.   H S 9–12

Plays of. (Fam. Lib.) 3 vols. 12mo. Lond., 1830–31.   K 10 P 3–5

MASSINGER (PHILIP), AND FIELD (NATHANIEL). The Fatal Dowry: a Tragedy. (Cumberland's Eng. Theatre.) 12mo. Lond., 1829.   H 2 Q 9

Another copy. [*See* BRIT. DRAMA, 1.]

MASSON (CHARLES). Narrative of various Journeys in Balochistan, Afghanistan, and the Panjab. 3 vols. 8vo. Lond., 1842.   D 5 T 15–17

Narrative of a Journey to Kalât, including an Account of the Insurrection at that place in 1840, and a Memoir on Eastern Balochistan. 8vo. Lond., 1843.   D 5 T 18

MASSON (C. F. P.) Mémoires secrets sur la Russie. [*See* BARRIÈRE, J. F., 22.]   C 1 T 22

MASSON (PROF. DAVID), LL.D., &c. Essays, Biographical and Critical, chiefly on English Poets. 8vo. Camb., 1856.   J 7 S 16

Recent British Philosophy: a Review, with Criticisms. 2nd ed. 12mo. Lond., 1867.   G 8 P 14

Chatterton: a Story of the year 1770. 8vo. Lond., 1874.   C 1 S 15

Carlyle, personally, and in his Writings: two Edinburgh Lectures. 8vo. Lond., 1885.   C 2 Q 10

The Three Devils : Luther's, Milton's, and Goethe's; with other Essays. 8vo. Lond., 1874.   G 7 Q 24

Life of John Milton, narrated in connexion with the Political, Ecclesiastical, and Literary History of his Time. 6 vols. 8vo. Lond., 1859–80.   C 8 R 33–38

De Quincey. (Eng. Men Letts.) 8vo. Lond., 1881.   C 1 U 12

Poetical Works of John Milton ; with Memoir. [*See* MILTON, J.]

Register of the Privy Council of Scotland. [*See* SCOTLAND.]   B 13 S 8–14

MASSON (JOHN), M.A. Atomic Theory of Lucretius contrasted with Modern Doctrines of Atoms and Evolution. 8vo. Lond., 1884.   G 2 Q 6

MAST AND ACORNS ; collected by "Old Hubert." (Pam. Dd.) 8vo. Lond. (n.d.)   F 12 P 22

MASTERMAN (GEORGE F.) Seven Eventful Years in Paraguay : a Narrative of Personal Experience amongst the Paraguayans. 2nd ed., with Illustrations. 8vo. Lond., 1870.   D 3 P 25

MASTERS (GEORGE). List of Australian Longicorns. [*See* PASCOE, F. P.]   MA 2 V 9

MASTERS (MAXWELL T.), M.D., &c. Botany for Beginners: an Introduction to the Study of Plants. 8vo. Lond., 1872.   A 4 P 30

Vegetable Teratology : an account of the principal Deviations from the usual Construction of Plants ; with numerous Illustrations, by E. M. Williams. 8vo. Lond., 1869.   A 4 S 3

MATEER (REV. SAMUEL), F.L.S. Native Life in Travancore. 8vo. Lond., 1883.   D 4 U 31

MATERNAL AND DORCAS SOCIETY. Report of the, for 1858. 12mo. Hobart, 1859.   MF 3 P 10

[*See* SYDNEY DORCAS SOCIETY.]

MATHERS (MISS HELEN). [*See* REEVES, MRS. HENRY.]

MATHESON (J.) Letter to the Moderator of the General Assembly of the Presbyterian Church of Victoria. [*See* SIMSON, R.]

MATHEWS (CHARLES). Memoirs of Charles Mathews, Comedian ; by Mrs. Mathews. 4 vols. 8vo. Lond., 1838–39.   C 10 Q 34–37

Anecdote Life of. [*See* TIMBS, J.]

MATHEWS (MRS. CHARLES. Anecdotes of Actors; with other Recollections. 8vo. Lond., 1844.   C 1 V 16

Memoirs of Charles Mathews, Comedian. [*See* MATHEWS, C.]

MATHEWS (CHARLES JAMES). Life of. Chiefly Autobiographical ; with Selections from his Correspondence and Speeches; edited by Charles Dickens. With Portraits. 2 vols. 8vo. Lond., 1879.   C 10 Q 38, 39

MATHEWS (EDWARD D.) Up the Amazon and Madeira River, through Bolivia and Peru. 8vo. Lond., 1879.   D 4 Q 32

MATHEWS (JEHU). A Colonist on the Colonial Question. 8vo. Lond., 1872.*   MF 1 P 6

MATHEWS (WILLIAM), M.A. Flora of Algeria, considered in relation to the Physical History of the Mediterranean Region, and supposed Submergence of the Sahara. 8vo. Lond., 1880.   A 4 T 12

MATHEWS (WILLIAM), LL.D. Words; their Use and Abuse. 8vo. Chicago, 1876.   K 12 P 7

MATHISON (GILBERT FARQUHAR). Narrative of a Visit to Brazil, Chile, Peru, and the Sandwich Islands, during the years 1821–22. 8vo. Lond., 1825.   D 3 T 25

MATHISON (JOHN). Counsel for Emigrants, and interesting Information from numerous sources, concerning British America, the United States, and New South Wales, &c. 3rd ed., with Supplement. 8vo. Aberdeen, 1838.   MD 2 R 41

MATRIMONIAL CAUSES ACT. [*See* NEW SOUTH WALES.]

MATTER (JACQUES) Histoire Universelle de l'Église Chrétienne. 3 vols. 8vo. Strasbourg, 1829–32.   G 11 T 22–24

MATTHÆUS (ANTON). Commentarius ad Lib. XLVII et XLVIII, Dig. de Criminibus. Roy. 8vo. Col. Munat. 1715.   F 8 T 13

MATTHEW (PATRICK). Emigration Fields: North America, the Cape, Australia, and New Zealand. 8vo. Edinb., 1839.*   MD 4 S 31

MATTHEW PARIS. [*See* PARIS, MATTHEW.]

MATTHEW OF WESTMINSTER. Flowers of History, especially such as relate to the affairs of Britain; from the beginning of the World to 1307. Translated by C. D. Yonge. 2 vols. 8vo. Lond., 1853.   B 3 P 8, 9

MATTHEWS (CORNELIUS). Hiawatha, and other Legends of the Wigwams of the Red American Indians. 8vo. Lond., 1882.   B 19 Q 7

MATTHEWS (DANIEL). Second Report of the Maloga Aboriginal Mission School, Murray River, New South Wales. (Pam., Bp.) 8vo. Echuca, 1877.   MG 1 Q 33

Third Report of the Maloga Aboriginal Mission School, Murray River, New South Wales. (Pam., Br.) 8vo. Echuca, 1878.   MG 1 Q 35

MATTHEWS (HENRY), A.M. Diary of an Invalid; being the Journal of a Tour in Pursuit of Health in Portugal, Italy, Switzerland, and France, 1817-19. 5th ed. 12mo. Lond., 1835.   D 7 P 45

MATTHEWS (WILLIAM). Hydraulia: an Historical and Descriptive Account of the Water Works of London, and the Contrivances for supplying other great Cities. 8vo. Lond., 1835.   A 6 T 18

MÄTZNER (EDUARD). Englische Grammatik. 2e Auflage. 3 vols. 8vo. Berlin, 1873-75.   K 15 Q 26-28

MAUDSLEY (HENRY), M.D. Body and Will; being an Essay concerning Will in its Metaphysical, Physiological, and Pathological Aspects. 8vo. Lond., 1883.   G 4 Q 3

Responsibility in Mental Disease. 3rd ed. 8vo. Lond., 1876.   A 12 Q 23

Natural Causes and Supernatural Seemings. 8vo. Lond., 1886.   G 7 Q 31

MAULE (J. B.) Justice of the Peace and Parish Officer. [*See* BURN, R.]

MAUNDER (SAMUEL). Treasuries. 9 vols. 12mo. Lond., 1862-69.   K 9 T 8-16

Scientific and Literary Treasury. Revised and Rewritten by J. Y. Johnson.
Biographical Treasury. Reconstructed, &c., by W. L. R. Cates. 15th ed.
Treasury of Bible Knowledge; by the Rev. J. Ayre. 2nd ed.
Treasury of Botany. Edited by J. Lindley and T. Moore. In 2 parts.
Treasury of Geography, Physical, Historical, Descriptive, and Political; by Prof. W. Hughes.
Treasury of History.
Treasury of Knowledge and Library of Reference. Revised throughout by B. B. Woodward, assisted by John Morris and Prof. W. Hughes.
Treasury of Natural History. 6th ed. Revised, &c., by T. S. Cobbold.

MAUNDEVILLE (SIR JOHN), KT. Voiage and Travaile of, which treateth of the way to Hierusalem, and of the Marvayles of Inde, with other Ilands and Countryes. 8vo. Lond., 1727.   D 4 U 35

MAUNDRELL (HENRY), M.A. Journey from Aleppo to Jerusalem, at Easter, A.D. 1697. 8vo. Oxford, 1721.   D 6 P 43

MAUNGATAPU MURDERS. Illustrated Narrative of the dreadful Murders on the Maungatapu Mountain, and Track between the Wakamarina River and Nelson, in the Province of Nelson, New Zealand. 8vo. Nelson, N.Z., 1866.   MF 2 Q 16

MAURER (KONRAD). Island; von seiner ersten Entdeckung bis zum Untergange des Freistaats. Roy. 8vo. Munich, 1874.   B 2 R 2

MAURICE (COL. JOHN FREDERICK), R.A. Life of [Rev. John] Frederick Denison Maurice. [*See* MAURICE, REV. J. F. D.]

MAURICE (REV. JOHN FREDERICK DENISON), M.A. Learning and Working: Six Lectures. The Religion of Rome, and its Influence on Modern Civilization: Four Lectures. 8vo. Camb., 1855.   G 7 R 3

Gospel of St. John: a Series of Discourses. 2nd ed. 8vo. Camb., 1857.   G 2 P 20

Moral and Metaphysical Philosophy. New ed. 2 vols. 8vo. Lond., 1872-73.   G 4 P 11, 12

Life of; chiefly told in his own Letters. Edited by his son, Col. John Frederick Maurice. With Portraits. 2 vols. 8vo. Lond., 1884.   C 8 Q 37, 38

MAURICE (F. G.) Traité des Engrais, tiré des différens Rapports faits au Département d'Agriculture d'Angleterre, avec des Notes; suivi de la Traduction du Mémoire de Kirwan sur les Engrais. 8vo. Genève, 1806.   A 1 R 42

MAURITIUS. Transport Voyage to the Mauritius and back, touching at the Cape of Good Hope and St. Helena. 8vo. Lond., 1851.   D 1 S 26

Mauritius Calendar; compiled by J. P. T. Souvignec. 12mo. Mauritius, 1822.   E 1, 78

Voyages to the Island of Mauritius; by "A French Officer." Translated from the French by John Parish. 8vo. Lond., 1775.   MD 4 U 4

Meteorological Society of Mauritius. [*See* METEOROLOGICAL SOCIETY OF MAURITIUS.]   A 3 T 8

MAURY (MATTHEW FONTAINE), LL.D., &c. Physical Geography of the Sea. 8vo. Lond., 1857.   A 29 V 7

Catalogue of the West Virginia State Exhibit. (Philad. Int. Exhib., 1876.) 8vo. Philad., 1876.   K 7 R 36

MAURY (M. F.), AND FONTAINE (WILLIAM M.), A.M. Resources of West Virginia. 8vo. Wheeling, 1876.   F 13 R 20

MAUSS ET SAUVAIRE (M. M.) Voyage de Jérusalem à Karak, etc. [*See* LUYNES, DUC DE.]

MAXIMUS (SANCTUS), CONFESSOR. Opera omnia. [*See* MIGNE, J. P., SERIES GRÆCA, 90, 91.]
Sciolia in Gregorii Theologi Ambigua quaedam. [*See* ERIGENA, J. S.]   G 15 U 14

MAXIMUS (SANCTUS), TAURINENSIS, EPISCOPUS. Opera omnia. [*See* MIGNE, J. P., SERIES LATINA, 57.]

MAXTON (JOHN). The Workman's Manual of Engineering Drawing. (Weale.) 4th ed. 12mo. Lond.,1880. A17Q21

MAXWELL (CAROLINE ELIZABETH SARAH STIRLING), LADY. [*See* NORTON, HON. MRS. C. E. S.]

MAXWELL (GEN. E. H.), C.B. With the Connaught Rangers in Quarters, Camp, and on Leave. 8vo. Lond., 1883.   D 9 S 23

MAXWELL (H. HAMILTON). On the Use of Field Artillery [*See* TAUBERT, CAPT.]
Memoir on Swords, &c. [*See* MAREY-MONGE, COL. W. S.]

MAXWELL (PROF. JAMES CLERK), M.A., &c. Treatise on Electricity and Magnetism. (Clar. Press.) 2 vols. 8vo. Oxford, 1873.   A 21 T 10, 11
Theory of Heat. [Text-books of Science.] 12mo. Lond., 1872.   A 17 S 7
Life of; with a Selection from his Correspondence and occasional Writings, and a Sketch of his Contributions to Science; by Lewis Campbell, M.A., and William Garnett, M.A. With Portraits. 8vo. Lond.,1882. C 8 Q 34
Electrical Researches of the Hon. Henry Cavendish. [*See* CAVENDISH, HON. H.]   A 5 U 23

MAXWELL (JOHN S.) The Czar, his Court and People; including a Tour in Norway and Sweden. 12mo. Dublin, 1849.   D 7 P 20

MAXWELL (W. H.) Hillside and Border Sketches; with Legends of the Cheviots and the Lammermuir. 2 vols. 8vo. Lond., 1847.   J 12 Q 14, 15
Wanderings in the Highlands and Islands; with Sketches taken on the Scottish Border; being a Sequel to "Wild Sports of the West." 2 vols. 8vo. Lond., 1844.   D 7 U 9, 10
Another copy. 2 vols. 8vo. Lond., 1852. D 7 U 11, 12
Victories of Wellington and the British Armies. New ed. 8vo. Lond., 1865.   B 3 Q 15
History of the Irish Rebellion in 1798; with Memoirs of the Union, and Emmett's Insurrection in 1803; with Illustrations by George Cruikshank. 10th ed. 8vo. Lond., 1877.   B 11 P 33
Victories of the British Armies; with Anecdotes illustrative of Modern Warfare. 2 vols. 8vo. Lond., 1839.   B 5 U 25, 26
Life of Field Marshall his Grace the Duke of Wellington, K.G., &c. 3 vols. 8vo. Lond., 1839. C 5 T 25–27
Wild Sports of the West; with Legendary Tales and Local Sketches. 2 vols. 8vo. Lond., 1832. A 17 W 29, 30
Life, Military and Civil, of the Duke of Wellington. [*See* WELLINGTON, ARTHUR WELLESLEY, DUKE OF.] C 4 P 43

MAXWELL (SIR WILLIAM STIRLING-), BART. Don John of Austria; or, Passages from the History of the 16th Century, 1547–78. 2 vols. roy. 8vo. Lond., 1883. C 5 W 1, 2

MAY (A.) Practical Grammar of the Swedish Language; with Reading and Writing Exercises. 4th revised ed. 12mo. Stockholm, 1872.   K 11 U 40

MAY (GEORGE THOMAS). The Ever-Living Life. 8vo. New York, 1883.   H 8 V 21

MAY (GUSTAV). Bibliography of Electricity and Magnetism, 1860 to 1883; with special reference to Electro-Technics. 8vo. Lond., 1884.   A 5 S 51

MAY (THOMAS). History of the Parliament of England, which began November 3rd, 1640. 4to. Lond., 1812. B 6 V 7
History of the Parliament of England, which began Nov. 3, 1640; with a short and necessary View of some precedent years. New ed. 8vo. Oxford, 1854. B 7 Q 26
Histoire du Long-Parlement convoqué par Charles 1er en 1640. [*See* GUIZOT, F. P. G., 4.]

MAY (RT. HON. SIR THOMAS ERSKINE), BARON FARNBOROUGH, K.C.B., &c. Constitutional History of England, since the Accession of George III, 1760–1860. 3 vols. 8vo. Lond., 1871.   B 3 Q 16–18
Democracy in Europe: a History. 2 vols. 8vo. Lond., 1877.   F 7 R 12, 13
Treatise on the Law, Privileges, Proceedings, and Usage of Parliament. 8th ed., revised and enlarged. 8vo. Lond., 1879.   F 7 R 15
Another copy. 9th ed. 8vo. Lond., 1883. F 7 R 16
Practical Treatise on the Laws, Privileges, Proceedings, and Usage of Parliament. 3rd ed. 8vo. Lond., 1855.   F 7 R 14

MAY (W. J.) Greenhouse Management for Amateurs: Descriptions of the best Greenhouses and Frames; with Instructions for Building them, &c., for the Amateur. 2nd ed. 8vo. Lond., 1884.   A 4 Q 22

MAYER (DR. ALEXANDRE). Des Rapports conjugaux, considérés sous le triple point de vue de la Population, de la Santé et de la Morale Publique. Troisième édition. 12mo. Paris, 1857.   A 12 P 18

MAYER (BRANTZ). Mexico as it was and as it is; with Illustrations. 8vo. New York, 1844. D 3 T 28
Captain Canot; or, Twenty Years of an African Slaver. 8vo. New York, 1854.   D 1 R 13

MAYER (JOSEPH), F.S.A. On the Art of Pottery; with a History of its Progress in Liverpool. 8vo. Liverpool, 1873.   A 11 R 10

MAYER (S. R. TOWNSEND). Letters of E. B. Browning, addressed to Richard Hengist Horne; with Comments on Contemporaries. 2 vols. 8vo. Lond., 1877. C 3 U 30, 31

MAYES (Charles). Australian Builders' Price-book. 4th ed., corrected to date. 12mo. Meln., 1883. MA 1 T 6

Essay on the Manufactures more immediately required for the Economical Development of the Resources of the Colony. [*See* Victorian Government Prize Essays.]

MAYFAIR TO MARATHON (From). 8vo. Lond., 1853. D 8 R 16

MAYHEW (Edward), M.R.C.V.S. Illustrated Horse Doctor. 8vo. Lond., 1866. A 1 R 24

Illustrated Horse Management; containing descriptive remarks upon Anatomy, Medicine, Shoeing, Teeth, Food, Vices, Stables, &c. 8vo. Lond., 1867. A 1 R 25

Dogs: their Management; being a new plan of treating the animal, based upon a consideration of his natural temperament. 8vo. Lond., 1858. A 1 P 17

The Horse's Mouth, showing the Age by the Teeth. 8vo. Lond., 1869. A 1 R 30

MAYHEW (Henry). London Labour and the London Poor. 3 vols. 8vo. Lond., 1864. F 14 S 11-13

MAYHEW (Horace and Henry). The Comic Annual. [*See* Cruikshank, G.]

MAYNARD (Frederic W.) Descriptive Notice of the Drawings and Publications of the Arundel Society, from 1849 to 1868 inclusive; illustrated by Photographs. Imp. 4to. Lond., 1869. A 23 S 16 ‡

MAYNE (F.) Life of Nicholas I, Emperor of Russia; with a short Account of Russia and the Russians. 8vo. Lond., 1855. C 3 T 16

MAYNE (J.), M.D. Medical Vocabulary. [*See* Mayne, R. G.]

MAYNE (J.), D.D. The Citye Match: a Comœdye. Sm. fol. Oxford, 1639. H 1 V 1

MAYNE (R. G.), M.D., &c., and MAYNE (J.), M.D., &c. Medical Vocabulary; being an explanation of all Terms and Phrases used in the various departments of Medical Science and Practice. 4th ed. 12mo. Lond., 1875. K 9 P 3

MAYO (Rev. Charles Herbert), M.A. Bibliotheca Dorsetiensis; being a carefully compiled Account of printed Books and Pamphlets relating to the History and Topography of the County of Dorset. Sm. 4to. Lond., 1885. K 17 P 32

MAYO (Don Francisco de Sales), y QUINDALE (Don Francisco). El Gitanismo: Historia, Costumbres y Dialecto de los Gitanos; con un Epitome de Grammatica Gitana, y un Diccionario Calo-Castellano. Novissima ed. 12mo. Madrid, 1870. K 11 S 32

MAYO (Herbert), M.R.C.S., F.R.S. Philosophy of Living. 2nd ed. 8vo. Lond., 1838. A 12 Q 19

MAYO (Richard Southwell Bourke), Earl of. Life of, fourth Viceroy of India; by W. W. Hunter, B.A., &c. 2 vols. 8vo. Lond., 1875. C 7 S 17, 18

MAYO (Thomas), M.D., &c. Elements of the ·Pathology of the Human Mind. 12mo. Lond., 1838. G 9 Q 5

MAYO (W. S.), M.D. Kaloolah; or, Journeyings to the Djèbel Kumri: an Autobiography of Jonathan Romer. 12mo. Lond., 1850. J 7 Q 18

MAYOR (Prof. John Eyton Bickersteth), M.A. Bibliographical Clue to Latin Literature; edited after Dr. E. Hübner; with large Additions. 8vo. Lond., 1875. K 17 P 17

History of the College of St. John the Evangelist, Cambridge. [*See* Baker, T.] B 6 S 9, 10

MAYOR (Rev. Joseph Bickersteth), M.A. Chapters on English Metre. 8vo. Lond., 1886. K 14 Q 23

MAZZINI (G.) Opere e Scritti di. Vols. 1-15. 15 vols. 12mo. Milano, &c., 1861-86. F 5 Q 1-15

Royalty and Republicanism in Italy. 12mo. Lond., 1850. B 12 P 34

MAZZOLA or MAZZUOLI (G. Francesco Maria.) [*See* Parmigiano, G. F. M. M.]

MEADE (Hon. Herbert George Phillip), R.N. Ride through the Disturbed Districts of New Zealand; together with some Account of the South Sea Islands. 2nd ed. 8vo. Lond., 1871.* MD 5 V 15

MEADE (Richard). Coal and Iron Industries of the United Kingdom. 8vo. Lond., 1882. A 10 Q 2

MEADE (R. H.) Memoranda of Conversations at Berlin on Colonial Matters. [*See* Australasia.]

MEADOWS (Thomas Taylor). Desultory Notes on the Government and People of China, and on the Chinese Language. 8vo. Lond., 1847. B 2 P 52

MEARS (Edwin Hartley). On British Colonization; particularly in reference to South Australia. 8vo. Lond., 1839. MF 3 P 7

MECHANICS' MAGAZINE (The), 1823-28, 1842-72. 69 vols. 8vo. and fol. Lond., 1823-72. E 1, 29 [*See* Iron.]

MECHI (John Joseph). How to Farm Profitably. New ed. 12mo. Lond., 1859. A 1 P 45

MEDE (Rev. Joseph), B.D. Works of; with Life. Fol. Lond., 1672. G 29 P 20 ‡

MEDHURST (Rev. Walter Henry), China: its State and Prospects, with especial reference to the spread of the Gospel. 8vo. Lond., 1838. B 2 P 47

MEDICAL BILL. [Comments thereon by the Country Press. Pam. Ci.] 8vo. Sydney, 1875. MA 2 Q 33

MEDICAL DIRECTORY (The), for New South Wales and Queensland. (Pam. 35.) 8vo. Sydney, 1860. MJ 2 Q 22

MEDICAL DIRECTORY (THE), for 1882, including the London and Provincial Medical Directory, the Medical Directory for Scotland, the Medical Directory for Ireland, a Medical Directory of Practitioners resident abroad possessing British Qualifications ; and a Medical Directory of the Army, Navy, and Mercantile Marine. 38th annual issue. 8vo. Lond., 1882. E 1, 50

MEDICAL REGISTER (THE). Printed and published under the direction of the General Council of Medical Education and Registration of the United Kingdom. Roy. 8vo. Lond., 1877-84. E 1, 50

MEDICAL AND SURGICAL REVIEW (THE AUS-TRALASIAN). [*See* AUSTRALASIAN MEDICAL AND SURGICAL REVIEW.]

MEDICAL TIMES AND GAZETTE (THE): Journal of Medical Science, Literture, Criticism, and News. 4 vols. 4to. Lond., 1866-68. A 12 V 3-6

MEDICI (HOUSE OF). Memoirs of the House of the Medici, from its Origin to the Death of Francesco ; from the French of Nicholas Tenhove, with Notes and Observations, by Sir R. Clayton, Bart. 2 vols. 4to. Bath, 1797. C 8 V 14, 15

MEDICI (LORENZO DE'), "THE MAGNIFICENT." Life of ; by W. Roscoe. 2 vols. 8vo. Lond., 1825. C 11 P 26, 27

Lorenzo de' Medici, il Magnifico ; von Alfred von Reu-mont: 2 vols. 8vo. Leipzig, 1874. C 11 P 22, 23

Lorenzo de Medici, the Magnificent ; by Alfred von Reumont ; translated from the German, by Robert Har-rison. 2 vols. 8vo. Lond., 1876. C 11 P 24, 25

MEDICINISCH NATURWISSENSCHAFTLICHE GESELLSCHAFT ZU JENA. Jenaische Zeitschrift für Naturwissenschaft. Bande 10-19. 10 vols. 8vo. Jena, 1876-86. E 1, 45

MEDICO-CHIRURGICAL REVIEW, and Journal of Practical Medicine ; edited by James Johnson, M.D., &c. 6 vols. 8vo. Lond., 1827-29. A 12 R 1-6

MEDICORUM GRAECORUM. Opera quae exstant. Editionem curavit Carolus Gottlob Kühn. 26 vols. (in 29) 8vo. Leip., 1821-33. A 13 Q 2-29

MEDLEY (GEORGE WEBB). England under Free Trade : an Address delivered to the Sheffield Junior Liberal Association, 8th November, 1881. (Pam. Je.) 8vo. Lond., 1881. F 6 P 10

The Reciprocity Craze: a Tract from the Times. (Pam. Je.) 8vo. Lond., 1881. F 6 P 10

MEDLICOTT (H. B.), and BLANFORD (W. T.) Manual of the Geology of India. Part 3. Economic Geology ; by V. Ball. With Map. 4 vols. 8vo. Calcutta, 1879-81. A 9 U 1-4

MEDWIN (THOMAS). Conversations of Lord Byron, noted during a residence with his Lordship at Pisa, in the years 1821-22. 8vo. Lond., 1824. C 8 S 37

Life of Percy Bysshe Shelley. 2 vols. 8vo. Lond., 1847. C 4 V 39, 40

The Angler in Wales : or, Days and Nights with Sports-men. 2 vols. 8vo. Lond., 1834. D 7 U 27, 28

MEEDEN (C. F.) Handbuch der Kaufmanns-und Schiffersprache ; Deutsch, Englisch, und Französisch. 4ᵉ Auflage. Imp. 8vo. Hamburg, 1866. K 16 T 2

MEEHAN (REV. C. P.), M.R.I.A. Fate and Fortunes of Hugh O'Neill, Earl of Tyrone, and Rory O'Donel, Earl of Tyrconnel ; their Flight from Ireland, and Death in Exile. 2nd ed. 8vo. Dublin, 1870. C 4 R 5

MEIGNAN (VICTOR). From Paris to Pekin over Siberian Snows ; edited, from the French, by William Conn. Illustrated. 8vo. Lond., 1885. D 9 S 21

MEIKLEJOHN (PROF. JOHN M. D.), M.A. The English Language : its Grammar, History, and Literature. 8vo. Edinb., 1886. K 12 P 2

Critique of Pure Reason. [*See* KANT, I.]

MEINHOLD (W.) Mary Schweidler, the Amber Witch : the most interesting Trial for Witchcraft ever known ; translated from the German, by Lady Duff Gordon. (H. and C. Lib.) 12mo. Lond., 1844. J 8 P 6

Another copy. 12mo. Lond., 1844. D 10 P 51

MEINICKE (PROF. CARL EDUARD). Das Festland Aus-tralien : eine geographische Monographie ; nach den Quellen dargestellt. 2 vols. (in 1) 8vo. Prenzlau, 1837. MD 5 Q 24

Die Südseevölker und das Christenthum : eine geo-graphische Untersuchung. 8vo. Prenzlau, 1844. MA 1 R 9

Die Inseln des stillen Oceans: eine geographische Mono-graphie. 2 vols. 8vo. Leipzig, 1875-76. MD 3 U 3, 4

MEISSONIER (JEAN LOUIS ERNEST). [A Biography] ; by J. W. Mollett. (Great Artists.) 8vo. Lond., 1882. C 3 T 35

MEKERCHUS (ADOLPHUS).' De Veteri et Recta Pro-nuntiatione Linguæ Græcæ commentarius. 16mo. Antverpiae, 1576. K 11 S 44

Another copy. 18mo. Bruges, 1565. K 11 S 45

MELANCHTHON (PHILIP). Biography of. [*See* SCHAFF, PROF. P.] C 2 S 37

MELANESIA (MAP OF). [*See* MAPS.]

MELANESIAN MISSION. Report, from November, 1852, to June, 1853. 12mo. Auckland, 1853. MF 3 P 10

MELBOURNE (RT. HON. WILLIAM LAMB.), SECOND VISCOUNT. Memoirs of ; by W. M. Torrens, M.P. With Portrait. 2 vols. 8vo. Lond., 1878. C 8 R 39-40

MELBOURNE. Almanacs and Directories. [*See* VIC-TORIA.]

[*See* VICTORIA.]

MELBOURNE AND HOBSON'S BAY RAILWAY (THE). Repudiation Bill : in three Letters ; by "Nemo." 8vo. Melb., 1865. MF 1 Q 2

Act to authorise the Melbourne and Hobson's Bay United Railway Company to sell their undertaking and property and to vest the same in the Board of Land and Works, and for other purposes. 8vo. Melb., 1878. MJ 2 R 12

MELBOURNE ADVERTISER (THE), Port Pinllip, Australia, vol. 1, No. 2. Written for, and published by John P. Fawkner, Monday, January 15th, 1838. (M.S.)   MJ 2 U 1

The Melbourne Advertiser, vol. 1, No. 3. (M.S.) [*See* MANUSCRIPTS AND PORTRAITS.]   MF 1 U 21

MELBOURNE ARGUS (THE). Fol. Melb., 1846–56. ME

MELBOURNE BENEVOLENT ASYLUM. Third to seventh Annual Reports. 8vo. Meln., 1853–57. MG 1 Q 40 Annual Reports of the Committee of Management of the ; with the Rules of the same, and a List of Subscriptions and Donations for the years 1861–63· 8vo. Meln., 1862–64.   ME 6 S

MELBOURNE CATALOGUE OF STARS. Planisphere of the Southern Sky. L. 4to. Melb. (n.d.)   MA 1 R 11‡

MELBOURNE CHURCH OF ENGLAND MESSENGER. 12mo. Melb., 1850.   MG 1 P 27 *Melbourne Church of England Messenger.* [Imperfect.] 8vo. Melb., 1853.   ME 3 R

MELBOURNE CHURCH OF ENGLAND MISSION. [*See* ABORIGINES.]

MELBOURNE CITY MISSION. [*See* Ladies' Melbourne and Suburban City Mission.]

MELBOURNE DIOCESAN BOARD. Third Report of. 8vo. Melb., 1857.   MG 1 Q 40

MELBOURNE DIOCESAN SOCIETY. Statement of the Objects, Constitution, and intended Mode of Operation of the, 1848 ; and Third Report, 1851. 8vo. Melb., 1848–51.   MG 1 Q 40

MELBOURNE DIRECTORIES. [*See* SANDS & McDOUGALL.]

MELBOURNE EXCHANGE. Description of the Exchange, Collins-street West, Melbourne, Victoria. 8vo. Melb., 1880.   MJ 2 R 15

MELBOURNE EXHIBITIONS. Official Catalogue of the Melbourne Exhibition, 1854, in connection with the Paris Exhibition, 1855. 8vo. Melb., 1854. MJ 2 R 19 Inter-colonial Exhibition, 1866–67. Jurors' Report on Wines. 8vo. Meln., 1867.   MA 1 Q 2 Intercolonial Exhibition of Australasia, Melbourne, 1866 67; Official Record. 8vo. Meln., 1867. MK 1 Q 24 International Exhibition, to be held at Melbourne in 1875. Prospectus and List of Commissioners. (Pam. M.) 4to. Sydney, 1875.   MJ 2 S 4 International Exhibition, 1880. The Official Catalogue of Exhibits; with Introductory Notices of the Countries exhibiting. 2 vols. 8vo. Melb., 1880.   MK 1 R 19, 20 International Exhibition, 1880. List of Commissioners Prospectus, &c. Fol. Melb., 1880.   MJ 2 U 5

MELBOURNE EXHIBITIONS—*continued.* International Exhibition, 1880. Catalogue of the Queensland Court of the International Exhibition, Melbourne, 1880; with Essay descriptive of the Colony of Queensland; by C. A. Feilberg. 8vo. Brisbane, 1880. MJ 2 R 16

Catalogue of Exhibits in the Western Australian Court, in the Melbourne International Exhibition, 1880. 8vo. Melb., 1880.   MJ 2 R 16 Catalogue of Exhibits in the New South Wales Court at the Melbourne International Exhibition, 1880; with preliminary Remarks. 8vo. Sydney, 1880.* MK 1 S 14 Report of the Executive Commissioner on the Melbourne International Exhibition, 1880–81. Roy. 8vo. Sydney, 1881.   MK 1 R 21 [*See* VICTORIAN EXHIBITION, 1861.]

MELBOURNE HOSPITAL. Second and Sixth Annual Reports; with the Rules and a List of Subscriptions and Donations for the years 1849–50. Melb., 1850–54. MG 1 Q 40

MELBOURNE INDUSTRIAL AND TECHNOLOGICAL MUSEUM. [*See* MELBOURNE PUBLIC LIBRARY.]

MELBOURNE LADIES' BENEVOLENT SOCIETY. Report for 1861 ; with the Rules of the Society and Industrial Home. 12mo. Melb., 1862.   MF 3 P 15

MELBOURNE LYING-IN HOSPITAL. Fourth and Sixth Annual Reports. 8vo. Melb., 1860–62. MG 1 Q 40 and MF 3 P 15

MELBOURNE MERCHANT, A. [*See* CALDWELL, R.]

MELBOURNE MONTHLY MAGAZINE (THE) of Original Colonial Literature. Vol. 1. 8vo. Melb., 1855.   ME 3 Q

MELBOURNE MORNING HERALD (THE) and General Daily Advertiser. Fol. Melb., 1850.   ME

MELBOURNE ORPHAN ASYLUM. Annual Report for the year 1862 ; with Rules of the Society, List of Subscriptions, and Treasurer's Account. 12mo. Melb., 1862.   MF 3 P 15

MELBOURNE NATIONAL GALLERY. [*See* MELBOURNE PUBLIC LIBRARY.]

MELBOURNE PUBLIC LIBRARY, MUSEUM, AND NATIONAL GALLERY. Catalogue of the Public Library, Melbourne, Victoria. 4to. Lond., 1854. MK 1 R 24 Catalogue of Books recently added to the Public Library, Melbourne. 8vo. Lond., 1857.   MK 1 Q 13 Catalogue for 1861, and Supplemental Catalogue for 1865. 2 vols. roy. 8vo. Melb., 1861–65.*   MK 1 U 12, 13 Catalogue of the Casts, Busts, Reliefs, and Illustrations of the School of Design and Ceramic Art, in the Museum of Art. Roy. 8vo. Melb., 1865.*   MK 1 U 10 Catalogue of the Works of Art, Ornamental and Decorative Art, exhibited by the Trustees. Final ed. 8vo. Melb., 1869.   MK 1 Q 20 Rules and Regulations of the Public Library, Museums, and National Gallery of Victoria. 8vo. Melb., 1870. MF 3 P 1

MELBOURNE PUBLIC LIBRARY, MUSEUM, AND NATIONAL GALLERY—*continued.*

Report of the Trustees of the Public Library, Museums, and National Gallery of Victoria, 1870–71. 8vo. Melb., 1871.* ME 3 T

Catalogue of Donations to the Public Library of Victoria, 1856–72. Roy. 8vo. Melb., 1873. MK 1 U 15

Catalogue of the Oil Paintings, Water-colour Drawings, Engravings, Lithographs, Photographs, &c., in the National Gallery of Victoria, including a Catalogue of Books in the Public Library of Victoria relating to the Fine Arts. Imp. 8vo. Melb., 1879. MK 1 U 8

Catalogue of the Public Library of Victoria. 2 vols. 4to. Melb., 1880. MK 1 U 16, 17

Catalogues of the Objects of Ceramic Art, and School of Designs. 12mo. Melb. (n.d.) MJ 2 P 33

Catalogue of Coins, Medals, &c., in the Museum of Art. 12mo. Melb. (n.d.) MJ 2 P 33

Catalogue of the Casts of Statues, Busts, and Bas-reliefs in the Museum of Art. 12mo. Melb. (n.d.) MJ 2 P 33

Melbourne Industrial and Technological Museum : Lectures delivered in the Lecture Room of the Museum, 1870–72. 3 vols. 8vo. Melb., 1871–73. MA 2 V 10–12

  1. Ellery (R. J. L.) Common Uses of Astronomy.
  Foord (G.) Chemistry applied to Manufactures. Chemistry applied to Agriculture. Chemistry of the Sea. Chemistry of the Atmosphere. On Food Preservation. Household Chemistry.
  Halford (G. B.), M.D. On the Circulation of the Blood.
  McCoy (Prof. F.) On the Methods of diffusing Technical Knowledge.
  Wilson (W. P.), M.A. Conservation of Energy.

  2. A'Beckett (T. T.) Painting and Painters.
  Gibbons (S.) The Microscope.
  Irving (M. H.), M.A. Growth of Language.
  Johnson (W.) Fermentation ; Nitrogen, its Economy in Nature.
  Kernot (W. C.) Education of Engineers.
  McCoy (Prof. F.) Geological Action of Fire. Geological Action of Water.
  Mueller (Sir F. von), Baron. The Objects of a Botanic Garden in its relation to Industries.
  O'Donovan (D.) The Uses of Art and Design in Manufacture.

  3. Day (J.), M.D. Allotropic Oxygen in its relation to Science and Art.
  Johnson (W.) Hydrogen.
  McCoy (Prof. F.) Formation and Ages of Coal. Homology of the Parts of Animals. Geological Action of Ice, and Nature of the Glacial Period. Palæontology of the three great Geological Periods.
  Neild (J. E.), M.D. Dirt and Disease.
  O'Donovan (D.) Art in Building : No. 1. Construction. No. 2. Ornamentation.

Another copy. Vol. 2. 8vo. Melb., 1872. MJ 2 R 11

Catalogue of the Objects of Ethnotypical Art in the National Gallery ; published by direction of the Trustees of the Public Library and Museums of Victoria. 8vo. Melb., 1878. MK 1 Q 32

Catalogue of the Statues and Busts in Marble, and Casts in the National Gallery of Victoria. 12mo. Melb., 1880. MA 1 V 57

Photographs of the Pictures in the National Gallery ; photographed by T. F. Chuck; edited by Marcus Clarke. Fol. Melb., 1875. MA 1 R 10 ‡

3 R

MELBOURNE PUNCH. 27 vols. 4to. Melb., 1856–85. ME 20 T

MELBOURNE RAILWAY TERMINUS. A few Remarks on a proposed Central Railway Terminus for Melbourne; by "Logic." 8vo. Melb., 1862. MF 1 Q 2

MELBOURNE RETREAT. Report of the Sub-committee on the Inebriate Question, 1872. 12mo. Melb., 1872. MJ 2 P 31

MELBOURNE REVIEW (THE). Vols. 1–8. [*All published.*] Roy. 8vo. Melb., 1876–83.* ME 18 Q

MELBOURNE SUBURBAN AND CITY MISSION. [*See* LADIES' MELBOURNE AND SUBURBAN CITY MISSION.]

MELBOURNE TELESCOPE (THE). Correspondence concerning the Great Melbourne Telescope. 8vo. Lond., 1871. MJ 2 R 9

MELBOURNE TOWN HALL. Address presented to His Excellency the Governor at the opening of the New Town Hall, 9th August, 1870. 4to. Melb., 1870. MJ

MELBOURNE UNIVERSITY. Calendars for the Academic years 1877–78, 1878–80, 1882–83, 1883–1886. 4 vols. 12mo. Melb., 1877–86. ME 5 T

Examination Papers : Matriculation Examination, February Term, 1877, 1879 ; and October Term, 1878, 1880. 4 vols. 12mo. Melb., 1877–80. ME 5 T

Proceedings on laying the Memorial Stone of the Wilson Hall of the University of Melbourne, by the Hon. Sir Samuel Wilson, Knt., M.L.C., October 2nd, 1879. 8vo. Melb., 1879 MB 2 S 1

MELCOMBE (GEORGE BUBB DODINGTON), LORD. [*See* DODINGTON, G. B., LORD MELCOMBE.]

MELDOLA (R.), F.C.S., &c., AND WHITE (W.) Report on the East Anglian Earthquake, 1884. 8vo. Lond., 1885. A 9 S 12

MELENA (ELPIS). Garibaldi : Recollections of his Public and Private Life. English Version by Charles Edwards. Lond., 1887. C 5 R 16

MELFORT (EDOUARD DE), COUNT. Impressions of England. 2 vols. 8vo. Lond., 1836. D 8 P 14, 15

MELITO (ANDRÉ FRANÇOIS MIOT), COMTE DE. Memoirs of. Edited by General Fleischmann, from the French, by Mrs. Cashel Hoey, and Mr. John Lillie. 2 vols. 8vo. Lond., 1881. C 11 P 1, 2

MELLISS (JOHN CHARLES), F.L.S. St. Helena: a Physical, Historical, and Topographical Description of the Island, including its Geology, Fauna, Flora, and Meteorology. Imp. 8vo. Lond., 1875. B 19 Q 14 ‡

MELLY (GEORGE). School Experiences of a Fag at a Private and a Public School. 8vo. Lond., 1854. J 4 Q 28

MELMONTÍ (W. G.) The Dogaressa ; translated by Clare Brune. 8vo. Lond., 1887. B 11 V 1

MELMOTH (WILLIAM). Letters of Pliny the Consul. [*See* CICERO, M. T., and PLINIUS CAECILIUS SECUNDUS, C.] C 8 U 39, 40

MELROS (THOMAS) EARL OF. State Papers and Miscellaneous Correspondence of. 2 vols. 4to. Edinb., 1837.
B 19 Q 12, 13 ‡

MELVIL, OR MELVILLE (SIR JAMES), KNT. Memoirs of Sir James Melvil, of Hal-ⁱill, containing an impartial Account of the most remarkable Affairs of State; by George Scott. Sm. fol. Lond., 1683.   B 2 T 12

MELVILLE (ANDREW). Life of, containing Illustrations of the Ecclesiastical and Literary History of England; by Thomas M'Crie, D.D. 2nd ed. 2 vols. 8vo. Lond., 1824.   C 8 Q 38, 39

MELVILLE (GEORGE WALLACE), U.S.N. In the Lena Delta: a Narrative of the Searcⁱ for Lieut.-Commander De Long and ⁱis Companions, followed by an Account of the Greely Relief Expedition. Illustrated. 8vo. Lond., 1885.   D 4 8 8

MELVILLE (HENRY). Van Diemen's Land Almanack. 2 vols. (in 1) 12mo. Hobart, 1832–33.   ME 4 P

Van Diemen's Land; compreⁱending a variety of Statistical and otⁱer Information. 18mo. Hobart, 1833.
MD 2 R 8

History of the Island of Van Diemen's Land, from the year 1824 to 1835 inclusive; to wⁱicⁱ is added, a few Words on Prison Discipline. 8vo. Lond., 1835.*   MB 2 P 9

Australasia, Prison Discipline, and Emigration : the Present State of the Colonies of New South Wales, Western Australia, Soutⁱ Australia, Victoria, and New Zealand, Land Regulations, Aborigines, &c. 8vo. Lond., 1851.*   MB 1 Q 15

Present State of Australia, including Soutⁱ Wales, Western Australia, Soutⁱ Australia, Victoria, and New Zealand, Emigration, Land Regulations, Aborigines, &c. 8vo. Lond., 1851.*   MB 1 Q 12

Present State of Australasia, including New Soutⁱ Wales, Western Australia, Soutⁱ Australia, Victoria, and New Zealand, Emigration, Prison Discipline, Transportation of Convicts, Land Regulations, Aborigines, &c. 8vo. Lond., 1851.   MB 1 Q 14

Van Diemen's Land Annual. 3 vols. (in 1) 12mo. Hobart, 1834–36.*   ME 4 P

MELVILLE (HENRY DUNDAS), VISCOUNT. Trial, by impeacⁱment, of Henry, Lord Viscount Melville, for ⁱigⁱ Crimes and Misdemeanors, in 1806. 8vo. Lond., 1806.   F 8 P 25

MELVILLE (HERMAN). Narrative of a Four Montⁱs' Residence among the Natives of a Valley of the Marquesas Islands. 12mo. Lond., 1846.*   MD 4 P 20

Anotⁱer copy [witⁱ the Story of Toby: a Sequel to "Typee"]. (H. and C. Lib.) 12mo. Lond., 1846. J 8 P 15

Omoo: a Narrative of Adventures in the Soutⁱ Seas; being a Sequel to the "Residence in the Marquesas Islands." 12mo. Lond., 1847.*   A D 4 P 22

Another copy. (H. and C. Lib.) 12mo. Lond., 1847.
J 8 P 22

Mardi, and a Voyage ⁱitⁱer. 3 vols. 8vo. Lond., 1849.
J 12 U 15 17

MEMBER, A. [*See* VAN DIEMEN'S LAND MECHANICS' INSTITUTE.]

MEMBER OF PARLIAMENT, A. [*See* BRITISH COLONIES.]

MEMBER OF THE AUSTRALIAN PATRIOTIC ASSOCIATION, A. [*See* BLAND, W.]

MEMBER OF THE CHRISTIAN CHURCH, A. [*See* VOICE TO THE CHURCH.]

MEMBER OF THE CHURCH OF ENGLAND, A. [*See* EDUCATION, *and* THOMSON, J.]

MEMBER OF THE COMMITTEE OF PROTESTANTS, A. [*See* EDUCATION.]

MEMBER OF THE ESTABLISHED CHURCH, A. [*See* CHURCH ACT.]

MEMBER OF THE HOUSES OF SHIRLEY AND HASTINGS, A. [*See* HUNTINGDON, SELINA, COUNTESS OF.]

MEMBER OF THE UNIVERSITY OF OXFORD, A. [*See* HOMER.]

MEMES (JOHN S.), LL.D. History of Sculpture, Painting, and Architecture. (Const. Misc.) 18mo. Edinb., 1829.   K 10 Q 27

Memoirs of the Empress Joseⁱⁱine. (Const. Misc.) 18mo. Edinb., 1831.   K 10 R 5

Memoirs of Napoleon Bonaparte. [*See* BOURRIENNE, F. DE.]   K 10 Q 45–47

MEMOIRES pour servir a l'histoire des Hommes Illustres dans la République des Lettres; avec un Catalogue raisonné de leurs Ouvrages. 29 vols. (in 30) 12mo. Paris, 1727–34.   C 1 Q 1–30

MEMOIRS OF CELEBRATED WOMEN. Edited by G. P. R. James. 2 vols. 8vo. Lond., 1837. C 2 U 14, 15

MEMOIRS OF THE GEOLOGICAL SURVEY OF INDIA. [*See* INDIA.]

MEMORIALS OF THE LATE WAR. (Const. Misc.) 2 vols. 12mo. Edinb., 1831.   K 10 Q 15, 16

MEMORIES OF THE PAST; by "A Lady in Australia." 12mo. Melb., 1873.   MJ 1 S 26

MEN AND HOW TO MANAGE THEM : a Book for Australian Wives and Motⁱers; by "An Old Housekeeper." 12mo. Melb., 1885.   MA 1 V 40

MEN OF THE TIME. Biographical Sketcⁱes of eminent Living Characters; also, Biograpⁱical Sketcⁱes of celebrated Women of the Time. 12mo. Lond., 1856.   C 4 P 12

Biographical Dictionary of eminent Living Characters (including Women). New edition, tⁱorougⁱly revised and brougⁱt down to the Present Time, by Edward Walford, M.A. 8vo. Lond., 1862.   C 4 U 8

MEN OF THE TIME—*continued.*
Dictionary of Contemporaries, containing Biographical Notices of Eminent Characters of both Sexes. 7th ed., revised and brought down the Present Time, [by G. H. Townsend.] 8vo. Lond., 1868.   C 4 U 9
Another copy. 10th ed., revised and brought down to the Present Time, by Thompson Cooper, F.S.A. 8vo. Lond., 1879.   C 4 U 10
Another copy. 11th ed., revised and brought down to the Present Time, by Thompson Cooper, F.S.A. 8vo. Lond., 1884.   C 4 U 11
[*See* WADE, T. H.]

MEN OF THE TIME IN AUSTRALIA. Victorian series, 1878. 8vo. Melb., 1878.   MC 1 R 18

MENANDER. [*See* BYZANTINÆ HIST. SCRIPT.]

MÉNAGE (GILES). Ménagiana ; ou, les Bons Mots et remarques critiques, historiques, morales et d'érudition de. 4 vols. 12mo. Paris, 1829.   J 16 P 33–36

MENANT (JOACHIN). Eléments d'épigraphie Assyrienne ; les écritures Cunéiformes ; éxposé des Travaux qui ont préparé la Lecture et l'Interprétation des Inscriptions de la Perse et de l'Assyrie. 2e éd. Imp. 8vo. Paris, 1864.   K 13 T 18
Exposé des éléments de la Grammaire Assyrienne. Imp. 8vo. Paris, 1868.   K 13 T 2

MÉNARD (LOUIS). Histoire des Israélites d'après l'exégèse biblique. 8vo. Paris, 1883.   G 7 Q 29

MENCIUS. Life and Works of. [*See* LEGGE, J.]

MENDEL (PROF. S.) [*See* HAUFF, W.]

MENDELSSOHN-BARTHOLDY (DR. CARL). Goethe and Mendelssohn (1821–31); translated with Additions, by M. E. von Glehn. 2nd ed. 8vo. Lond.,1874. O 5 P 24
Letters of Felix Mendelssohn-Bartholdy. [*See* MENDELSSOHN-BARTHOLDY, F.]   C 5 P 25

MENDELSSOHN-BARTHOLDY (FELIX). Goethe and Mendelssohn (1821–1831); translated with Additions from the German of Dr. C. Mendelssohn-Bartholdy, by M. E. von Glehn. 2nd ed. Lond., 1874. C 5 P 24
Letters of, from 1833 to 1847. ; edited by Paul Mendelssohn-Bartholdy, of Berlin, and Dr. Carl Mendelssohn-Bartholdy, of Heidelberg ; translated by Lady Wallace. New ed. 8vo. Lond., 1878.   C 5 P 25
Life of. From the German of W. A. Lampadius ; with Supplementary Sketches ; edited and translated by Wm. Leonard Gage. 2nd ed. 8vo. Lond., 1877. C 5 P 23
My Recollections of, and his Letters to me; by Eduard Devrient; translated from the German, by Natalia Macfarren. 8vo. Lond., 1869.   C 5 P 21
Reminiscences of: a Social and Artistic Biography ; by Elise Polko ; translated from the German, by Lady Wallace; with additional Letters addressed to English Correspondents. 8vo. Lond., 1869.   C 5 P 19

MENDELSSOHN-BARTHOLDY (FELIX).—*continued.*
Letters and Recollections by Dr. Ferdinand Hiller; translated by M. E. von Glehn. 8vo. Lond., 1874. C 5 P 20
Letters from Italy and Switzerland ; translated from the German, by Lady Wallace. 7th ed. 8vo. Lond., 1876.   D 7 P 43
Letters of Distinguished Musicians. [*See* WALLACE, LADY GRACE M.]
[*See* MENDELSSOHN FAMILY, THE.]

MENDELSSON-BARTHOLDY (PAUL). Letters of Felix Mendelssohn-Bartholdy. [*See* MENDELSSOHN-BARTHOLDY, F.]   C 5 P 25

MENDELSSOHN FAMILY (THE). The Mendelssohn Family (1729–1847); from Letters and Journals, by Sebastian Hensel; translated from the 2nd revised ed., by Carl Klingemann. 2 vols. 8vo. Lond., 1881. C 7 S 22, 23

MENEZES (DON FERNANDO DE). Historia de Tangere, que comprehende as noticias desde a sua primeira conquista até a sua ruina. Sm. 8vo. Lisbon, 1732. B 16 Q 15 ‡

MENG (L. KONG). [*See* CHINESE QUESTION, THE.]

MENINSKI (FRANÇOIS DE MESGNIEN). Lexicon Arabico-Persico-Turcicum, adiecta ad singulas Voces et Phrases significatione Latina, ad usitatiores etiam Italica. 4 vols. fol. Viennæ, 1780.   K 22 S 18–21 ‡
Complementum Thesauri Linguarum Orientalium seu Onomasticum Latino-Turcico-Arabico-Persicum. Fol. Viennæ, 1687.   K 22 S 22 ‡

MENKE (KARL THEODOR). Molluscorum Novæ Hollandiæ Specimen. 4to. Hanover, 1843. MA 2 P 25 †

MENZEL (WOLFGANG). History of Germany from the Earliest Period to the Present Time. 3 vols. 8vo. Lond., 1871–74.   C 9 Q 32–34

MENZIES (REV. PETER SINCLAIR), M.A. Address to Christian Children and Parents ; with a Postscript, containing a Short Tribute to the Memory of the late Rev. Dr. Norman Macleod. 12mo. Melb., 1872. MG 1 Q 9

MENZIES (SUTHERLAND). Turkey, Old and New : Historical, Geographical, and Statistical. 2 vols. 8vo. Lond., 1880.   B 13 V 29, 30

MENZIES (WILLIAM). Cottages for Rural Districts. 4to. Windsor, 1885.   A 2 U 1

MERCANTILE LIBRARY ASSOCIATION OF NEW YORK. Fifty-first Annual Report of the Board of Directors, 1871–72. Roy. 8vo. New York, 1872. K 8 R 18
Systematic Catalogue of Books ; with the Constitution and the Rules and Regulations of the Association. 8vo. New York, 1837.   K 7 S 9
Second Supplement to the Catalogue of Books (Accessions, 1869–72). Roy. 8vo. New York, 1872. K 8 P 18

MERCANTILE LIBRARY ASSOCIATION OF SAN FRANCISCO. Annual Reports, 1853, 1854, 1856–65. 8vo. San Francisco, 1866. K 7 R 38

Catalogue of the Library. Roy. 8vo. San Francisco, 1874. Libr.

Classified Catalogue; with an Index of Authors and Subjects. 8vo. San Francisco, 1861. K 7 R 38

Constitution, By-laws, Rules, and Regulations. 8vo. San Francisco, 1865. K 7 R 38

Seventh Annual Report of the President of the, for 1860–61. 8vo. San Francisco, 1860. MF 3 P 14

MERCANTILE NAVY LIST (THE). Mercantile Navy List and Maritime Directory; compiled from official and other sources, by Robert Jackson. 8vo. Lond., 1881–84. E

MERCANTILE TRACTS. Sydney Series of Mercantile Tracts. 8vo. Sydney (n.d.) MJ 2 Q 22

MERCATOR (MARIUS). Opera omnia. [*See* MIGNE, J. P., SERIES LATINA, 48.]

MERCER (H. C.) Lenape Stone ; or, the Indian and the Mammoth. 8vo. New York, 1885. B 1 Q 11

MERCHANT LONG RESIDENT IN TAHITI, A. [*See* LUCATT, MR.]

MERCHANTS' MAGAZINE and Commercial Review. [*See* HUNT, F.]

MERCIER (REV. L.) German Arctic Expedition of 1869–70. [*See* KOLDEWEY, CAPT. K.] D 4 S 33

MEREDITH (GEORGE). Shaving of Shagpat : an Arabian Entertainment. 8vo. Lond., 1856. Libr.

MEREDITH (MRS. LOUISA ANNE). Notes and Sketches of New South Wales, during a Residence in the Colony from 1839 to 1844. 12mo. Lond., 1844.* MD 2 R 31

Another copy. 12mo. Lond., 1844. D 10 Q 51

Another copy. (H. and C. Lib.) 12mo. Lond., 1844. J 8 P 7

Another copy. 12mo. Lond., 1849. MD 2 R 16

My Home in Tasmania, during a Residence of Nine Years. 2 vols. 8vo. Lond., 1852.* MD 3 S 7

Another copy. 8vo. New York, 1853. MD 3 S 14

Some of my Bush Friends in Tasmania ; Native Flowers, Berries, and insects. Imp. 4to. Lond., 1860.* MA 2 P 15‡

Over the Straits ; a Visit to Victoria. With Illustrations. 8vo. Lond., 1861.* MD 3 Q 43

Our Island Home : a Tasmanian Sketch-book. Roy. 4to. Lond., 1879. MD 2 P 17 ‡

Tasmanian Friends and Foes, feathered, furred, and finned. With coloured Plates. 2nd ed. Sm. 4to. Hobart, 1881. MJ 2 S 12

MEREDITH (WILLIAM GEORGE). Memorials of Charles John, King of Sweden and Norway. 8vo. Lond., 1829. C 10 T 1

MEREWEATHER (REV. JOHN DAVIES), B.A. Life on board an Emigrant Ship ; being a Diary of a Voyage to Australia. 12mo. Lond., 1852. MD 2 R 18

Diary of a Working Clergyman in Australia and Tasmania, kept during the years 1850–53. 12mo. Lond., 1859.* MD 2 R 19

MEREWETHER (FRANCIS L. S.) University of Sydney: Central Secular Teaching in the Schools of the University, combined with distinctive Religious Teaching, Tutorial Instruction and Discipline, in Colleges within the University: [a]Speech. (Pam. 26.) 8vo. Sydney, 1858. MJ 2 Q 14

MEREWETHER (HENRY ALWORTH). By Sea and by Land; being a Trip through Egypt, India, Ceylon, Australia, New Zealand, and America, all round the World. 8vo. Lond., 1874. MD 4 R 26

MERIAN (MATTHÄUS). M. Z. Topographia Hassiæ, et regionum vicinarum. Fol. Franckfurt, 1655. D 36 Q 10 J

Todten Tanz—La Danse des Morts. [In German and French.] Sm. 4to. Basle, 1756. J 17 P 24

MERIASEK (SAINT). Life of: a Cornish Drama; edited, with a Translation and Notes, by Whitley Stokes. 8vo. Lond., 1872. H 2 U 2

MÉRIMÉE (PROSPER). Letters of, to [Sir A.] Panizzi ; edited by Louis Fagan. 2 vols. 8vo. Lond., 1881. C 8 P 36, 37

MERIVALE (CHARLES), D.D. Fall of the Roman Republic: a short History of the last Century of the Commonwealth. 8vo. Lond., 1865. B 12 Q 12

General History of Rome, from the Foundation of the City to the Fall of Augustulus, B.C. 753–A.D. 476. 8vo. Lond., 1875. B 12 Q 11

History of the Romans under the Empire. 5th ed. 7 vols. 8vo. Lond., 1864. B 11 S 2–8

Account of the Life and Letters of Cicero. [*See* ABEKEN, B. R.] C 1 S 18

Homer's Iliad in English Rhymed Verse. [*See* HOMER.]

MERIVALE (PROF. HERMAN), A.M., &c. Lectures on Colonization and Colonies, delivered before the University of Oxford, in 1839–41. 2 vols. 8vo. Lond., 1841–42. MF 2 R 23, 24

Another copy. New ed. 8vo. Lond., 1861. MF 2 R 25

Life of Sir Philip Francis. [*See* PARKES, J.] C 8 S 38, 39

Life of Sir H. Lawrence. [*See* EDWARDES, SIR H. B.] C 8 P 28, 29

MERKEL (DR. F.) Das Mikroskop und seine Anwendung. 12mo. München, 1875. A 16 P 27

MERLE D'AUBIGNÉ (JEAN HENRI), D.D. [*See* D'AUBIGNÉ, J. H. M.]

MERLIN (AMBROSE). Merlin's Prophesies and Predictions interpreted, and their truth made good by our English Annalls ; with the Life of Merlin, by Thos. Heywood. Sm. 4to. Lond., 1651. B 3 R 26

MERLIN (MERCÉDÈS), COMTESSE, AND OTHERS. Memoirs of Madame Malibran; with a Selection from her Correspondence, and Notices of the Progress of the Musical Drama in England. 2 vols. 8vo. Lond., 1840. C 3 P 25, 26

MERLIN COCAIO. [*See* FOLENGO, T.]

MEROBAUDES (F.) [*See* BYZANTINÆ HIST. SCRIPT.]

MEROUILLE (C.) [*See* CICERO, M. T.] F 13 Q 83

MERRETT (H. S.) Practical Treatise on Land and Marine Engineering, Surveying, and Mensuration. 8vo. Lond., 1875. A 6 U 10

MERRIFIELD (CHARLES WATKINS), F.R.S. Technical Arithmetic and Mensuration. 12mo. Lond., 1872. A 17 S 8
Key to [the above.] [*See* HUNTER, REV. J.] A 17 S 9

MERRIFIELD (JOHN), LL.D. Treatise on Nautical Astronomy for the Use of Students. 8vo. Lond., 1886. A 3 S 17

MERRIFIELD (MRS. MARY PHILADELPHIA). Original Treatises, dating from the 12th to the 18th Centuries, on the Arts of Painting in Oil, Miniature, Mosaic, and on Glass; of Gilding, Dyeing, and the Preparation of Colours and Artificial Gems. 2 vols. 8vo. Lond., 1849. A 8 Q 29, 30
Treatise on Painting. [*See* CENNINI, C.] A 8 Q 26

MERRILL (REV. SELAH), D.D., &c. East of the Jordan: a Record of Travel and Observation in the Countries of Moab, Gilead, and Basian. With Illustrations. 8vo. Lond., 1881. D 5 T 10

MERRIMAN (PROF. MANSFIELD), PH.D. Text-book on the Method of Least Squares. 8vo. Lond., 1885. A 10 T 24

MERRITT (CHARLES STUART-). Traité pratique de Correspondance Commerciale avec les Termes Techniques en Anglais et en Français, etc. 2ᵉ éd. 8vo. Lyon, 1875. K 15 P 4

MERRY ENGLAND: an Illustrated Magazine. Vols. 1-4. 8vo. Lond., 1883-85. • E 2.46

MERRYLEES (JOHN). Carlsbad and its Environs; with a Medical Treatise on the Use of the Waters, by B. London, M.D. 8vo. Lond., 1886. D 8 R 14

MERWANJEE (HIRJEEBHOY). Journal of a Residence of Two Years and a Half in Great Britain. [*See* NOWROJEE, JEHANGEER.] D 8 P 20

MERZ (DR. HEINRICH). Bilder-atlas zur Weltgeschichte nach Kunstwerken alter und neuer zeit. [*See* WEISSER, PROF. L.] B 14 U 4 ‡

MESNY (MAJ.-GEN. WILLIAM). Tungking. 8vo. Lond,. 1884. B 2 P 25

MESSER (FREDERICK A.) New and Easy Method of studying British Wild Flowers by Natural Analysis. 8vo. Lond., 1880. A 4 T 15

META OF GAINDARA : an Australian Poetical Romance ; by J.A.B. 12mo. Melb., 1868. MH 1 R 51

METAPHRASTES (SYMEON LNGOTHETA). Opera omnia. [*See* MIGNE, J. P., SERIES GRÆCA, 114-116.]

METASTASIO (PIETRO BONAVENTURA). Tutte le Opere di. 2 vols. 8vo. Firenze, 1832. H 4 R 20, 21
Opere Drammatic1e. 4 vols. roy. 8vo. Venezia, 1733-37. H 2 U 20-23
Artaxerxes : an Opera ; the music composed by T. A. Arne, M.D. (Cumberland's Eng. Theatre.) 12mo. Lond., 1829. H 2 Q 15
Observations on the Poetics of Aristotle, rendered into English ; with a Biographical Notice of the Author. Sq. 8vo. Sydney, 1842. MJ 1 T 18
Observations on. [*See* BEYLE, M. H.] C 1 S 9-11

METCALFE (CHARLES THEOPHILUS), BARON. Life and Correspondence of, from unpublished Letters and Journals ; by John William Kaye. 2 vols. 8vo. Lond., 1854. C 7 S 26, 27

METCALFE (REV. FREDERICK), M.A. Passio et Miracula Beati Olavi ; edited from a 12th Century Manuscript in the Library of Corpus Christi College, Oxford ; with an Introduction and Notes. Sm. 4to. Oxford, 1881. G 2 Q 2
The Englishman and the Scandinavian ; or, a Comparison of Anglo-Saxon and Old Norse Literature. 8vo. Lond., 1880. B 2 R 15
The Oxonian in Iceland ; or, Notes of Travel in that Island in the Summer of 1860. 8vo. Lond., 1861. D 9 P 14
Charicles ; or, Illustrations of the Private Life of the Ancient Greeks. [*See* BECKER, PROF. W. A.] B 9 S 32
Gallus ; or, Roman Scenes of the Time of Augustus. [*See* BECKER, PROF. W. A.] B 12 Q 41, 42

METCHNIKOFF (LÉON). L'Empire Japonais. Texte et Dessins. Sm. 4to. Geneva, 1881. D 5 U 20

METEOROLOGICAL EPHEMERIS for 1842. (Pam. 41.) 8vo. Lond., 1842. MJ 2 R 3

METEOROLOGICAL OBSERVATIONS. [*See* ABBOTT, F. ; BLANDFORD, H. F. ; ELLERY, R. L. F. ; HECTOR, SIR J. ; HERSCHEL, SIR J. F. W. ; NEUMAYER, G. ; RUSSELL' H. C. ; SADINE, SIR E. ; SMALLEY, C. R. ; SMYTH, R. B. *and* TEBBUTT, J.]

METEOROLOGICAL SOCIETY OF MAURITIUS Proceedings and Transactions. 8vo. Mauritius, 1861. A 3
Proceedings of the Meteorological Society of Mauritius 1862. (Pam. F.) Roy. 8vo. Mauritius, 1862. MJ 2 S

METEYARD (ELIZA). Choice Examples of Wedgwood Art: a Selection of Plaques, Cameos, Medallions, Vases, &c., from the Designs of Flaxman, and others. Fol. Lond., 1879.   A 23 S 21 ‡

Wedgwood and his Works: a Selection of his Plaques, Cameos, Medallions, Vases, &c.; with a Sketch of his Life and the Progress of his Fine-Art Manufactures. Fol. Lond., 1873.   C 1 W 26

Group of Englishmen (1795-1815); being Records of the younger Wedgwoods, and their Friends, embracing the History of the Discovery of Photography and a Facsimile of the first Photograph. 8vo. Lond., 1871.   C 8 U 29

Life of Josiah Wedgwood, from his Correspondence and Family Papers. 2 vols. 8vo. Lond., 1865.   C 9 V 38, 39

METHLEY (JAMES ERABMUS). New Colony of Port Natal; with Information for Emigrants. 3rd ed. 12mo. Lond., 1850.   MJ 1 Q 38

METHODIST MISSIONARY SOCIETY. Report, 1819. 8vo. Lincoln, 1819.   MG 1 Q 27

METHODIUS (SANCTUS). Opera omnia. [*See* MIGNE, J. P., SERIES GRÆCA, 18.]

METHUEN (HENRY H.) Life in the Wilderness; or, Wanderings in South Africa. 8vo. Lond., 1846.   D 1 P 24

MÉTIVIER (GEORGES). Dictionnaire Franco-Normand; ou, Recueil des Mots particuliers au Dialecte de Guernesey, faisant voir leurs Relations Romances, Celtiques, et Tudesques. 8vo. Lond., 1870.   K 13 Q 40

METROPOLIS LOCAL MANAGEMENT ACTS. [*See* LONDON.]

METTERNICH WINNEBURG OCHSENHAUSEN (CLEMENT), PRINCE. Memoirs of, 1773-1835. Edited by Prince Richard Metternich; translated by Mrs. Alexander Napier, and G. W. Smith, M.A. 5 vols. 8vo. Lond., 1880-82.   C 10 U 28-32

METTERNICH (RICHARD), PRINCE. Memoirs of Prince Metternich. [*See* METTERNICH WINNEBURG OCHSENHAUSEN, C., PRINCE.]   C 10 U 28-32

MEUNIER (STANISLAS). Cours de Géologie Comparée professé au Muséum d'Histoire Naturelle. 8vo. Paris, 1874.   A 9 R 24

MEXICO. Archives de la Commission Scientifique du Mexique. 3 vols. 8vo. Paris, 1865-67.   A 16 V 16-18

MEYE (HEINRICH), AND SCHMIDT (DR. JULIUS). Stone Sculptures of Copán and Quiriguá; drawn by H. Meye; Historical and Descriptive Text, by Dr. J. Schmidt. Translated from the German, by A. D. Savage. Roy. fol. Lond., 1883.   A 20 P 17 ‡

MEYER (DR. ADOLF BERNHARD). Auszüge aus den auf einer Neu Guinea-Reise im Jahre 1873 geführten Tagebüchern, als Erläuterung zu den Karten der Geelvink-Bai und des MacCluer Golfes. Roy. fol. Dresden, 1875.   MD 2 P 4 ‡

Bilderschriften des ostindischen Archipels und der Südsee. (Königliches ethnographisches Museum zu Dresden.) Fol. Leipzig, 1881.   MA 1 R 7 ‡

MEYER (PROF. GEORG HERMANN VON). Organs of Speech, and their Application in the Formation of Articulate Sounds. 8vo. Lond., 1883.   A 12 Q 13

MEYER (REV. H. E. A.) Manners and Customs of the Aborigines of the Encounter Bay Tribe, South Australia. (Native Tribes of South Australia.) 8vo. Lond., 1879.*   MA 1 R 12

MEYER (DR. J.) Antonio Allegri da Correggio; from the German of Dr. Julius Meyer. Edited, &c., by Mrs. Heaton. 8vo. Lond., 1876.   C 8 V 2

MEYER (LEO). Die gothische Sprache; ihre Lautgestaltung insbesondere im Verhältniss zum Altindischen, Griechischen, und Lateinischen. 8vo. Berlin, 1869.   K 15 S 4

MEYER (DR. L.) Die Modernen Theorien der Chemie und ihre Bedeutung für die Chemische mechanik. 8vo. Breslau, 1880.   A 5 T 29

MEYER (WALTER JAMESON). Walter Samson & Co.'s New South Wales National Directory for 1867-68; compiled by W· J. Meyer; also, a Map of New South Wales. 8vo. Sydney, 1867.   ME 10 P

MEYNERS-DESTREY (GUILLAUME HENRY JEAN), COMTE. La Papouasie, ou Nouvelle-Guinée occidentale. Imp. 8vo. Paris, 1881.   MD 4 P 13 †

MEYRICK (SIR SAMUEL RUSH), LL.D., &c. Critical Inquiry into Antient Armour, as it existed in Europe, particularly in Great Britain, from the Norman Conquest to the Reign of Charles II. Illustrated. 3 vols. roy. 4to. Lond., 1842.   B 14 T 10-12 ‡

Engraved Illustrations of Antient Arms and Armour, from the Collection at Goodrich Court, Herefordshire; after the drawings and with the descriptions of Sir Samuel Rush Meyrick, Kt., &c., by Joseph Skelton, F.S.A. 2 vols. roy. 4to. Lond., 1854.   B 14 T 13, 14 ‡

History and Antiquities of the County of Cardigan. 4to. Lond., 1808.   B 2 T 13

MEZERAY (FRANÇOIS EUDES DE). Histoire de France, depuis Faramond jusqu'à maintenant [1598]. 3 vols. fol. Paris, 1643-51.   B 19 T 2-4 ‡

MEZZOFANTI (GIUSEPPE), CARDINAL. The Life of; with an Introductory Memoir of Eminent Linguists, ancient and modern, by C. W. Russell, D.D. 8vo. Lond., 1858.   C 6 U 18

MIALL (EDWARD). An Editor off the Line ; or, Wayside Musings and Reminiscences. 8vo. Lond., 1865. J 12 Q 5

MIALL (JAMES G.) Footsteps of our Forefathers ; what they suffered, and what they sought. 12mo. Lond., 1851.   G 9 Q 14

MICHAEL (JAMES L.) John Cumberland. 12mo. Sydney, (n.d.).*   MH 1 P 18
Songs without Music. 12mo. Sydney, 1857.   MH 1 P 20

MICHAEL ANGELO BUONARROTI. Life and Works of ; by Charles Heath Wilson. Roy. 8vo. Lond., 1876.
C 9 V 28
Lives of and Works of Michael Angelo and Raphael ; by R. Duppa and Quatremere de Quincy. 8vo. Lond., 1876.   C 4 P 1
Sixty Outlines from the principal Works of Michel Angelo Buonarroti, in Sculpture, Painting, Design, and Architecture. Roy. 4to. Lond., 1863.   A 7 R 2 †
Michael Angelo Buonarroti, Sculptor, Painter, Architect : the Story of his Life and Labours ; by Charles C. Black, M.A. Imp. 8vo. Lond., 1875.   C 7 V 50
The Art of Michel' Angelo Buonarroti, as illustrated by the various Collections in the British Museum ; by L. Fagan. Imp. 8vo. Lond., 1883.   A 8 U 24
The Relation between Michael Angelo and Tintoret : Lectures on Sculpture ; by J. Ruskin, 1870-71. 8vo. Orpington, 1879.   A 8 Q 32
Critical Account of the Drawings by Michael Angelo and Raffaello, in the University Gallery, Oxford, by J. C. Robinson. 8vo. Oxford, 1870.   A 7 Q 9
Michelangelo ; by Charles Clément. (Great Artists.) 8vo. Lond., 1880.   C 3 T 38
Translations from the Italian Poets. [*See* FENZI, S.]

MICHAELIS (ADOLF), PH.D., &c. Ancient Marbles in Great Britain ; translated from the German, by C. A. M. Fennell, M.A. Roy. 8vo. Camb., 1882.   A 8 T 13

MICHAELIS (EMILIE). Autobiography of Friedrich Froebel. [*See* FROEBEL, F.]   C 2 Q 15

MICHAUD (JOSEPH). Histoire des Croisades. Nouvelle éd. 4 vols. 8vo. Paris, 1867.   G 2 Q 15-18
Life of Martin Luther. [*See* LUTHER, M.]

MICHAUD (L. G.) Biographie Universelle. [*See* BIOGRAPHIE UNIVERSELLE.]   C 7 V 1-45

MICHEL (FRANCISQUE X.), F.S.A., &c. Critical Inquiry into the Scottish Language, with the View of illustrating the Rise and Progress of Civilization in Scotland. 4to. Edinb., 1882.   K 12 T 17
Le Prince Noir : Poème du Héraut d'Armes Chandos. [*See* CHANDOS.]

MICHEL (MARIUS). La Reliure Française, depuis l'invention de l'Imprimerie jusqu'à la fin du 18e Siècle. Roy. 4to. Paris. 1880.*   A 4 P 4 †

MICHELET (C. L.) Philosophy of Art. [*See* HEGEL, G. W. F.]   A 6 V 19

MICHELET (JULES). History of the Roman Republic ; translated by William Hazlitt. 8vo. Lond., 1863.
B 12 P 24
Historical View of the French Revolution, from its Earliest Indications to the Flight of the King in 1791. 8vo. Lond., 1864.   B 9 P 2
The People ; translated by C. Cocks, B.L. 8vo. Lond., 1846.   F 14 R 6
Priests, Women, and Families ; translated from the French (3rd ed.) by C. Cocks. 2nd ed. 8vo. Lond., 1846.   G 13 R 48
Summary of Modern History ; translated from the French. and continued to the Present Time, by M. C. M. Simpson, 12mo. Lond., 1875.   B 7 S 37
The Bird. (Illustrated.) Roy. 8vo. Lond., 1869.
A 15 R 5
Life of Luther, written by himself, collected and arranged by J. Michelet. 12mo. Lond., 1846.   · C 1 T 38

MICHELL (STEPHEN). Mine Drainage ; being a complete and practical Treatise on Direct-acting Underground Steam Pumping Machinery. 8vo. Lond., 1881.   A 10 P 22

MIDDLETON (CONYERS), D.D. Free Inquiry into the Miraculous Powers which are supposed to have subsisted in the Christian Church. Sm. 4to. Lond., 1749. G 13 R 6
The History of the Life of Marcus Tullius Cicero. 2 vols. 4to. Lond., 1741.   C 2 W 6, 7

MICHELS (IVAN C.), PH.D., &c. Current Gold and Silver Coins of all Nations together with their Weights, Fineness, and intrinsic Value, reduced to the Standard of the United States ; also, the History of the Official Coinage of the United States Mint, from 1792 to the Present Day. Sm. fol. Philad., 1880.   A 2 R 7 †

MICHIE (ALEXANDER). The Siberian Overland Route from Peking to Petersburg. 8vo. Lond., 1864. D 6 R 9

MICHIE (ALEXANDER), AND FRANCIS (R.) Report of the Delegates to the Shanghai General Chamber of Commerce on the Trade of the Upper Yangtsze. 4to. Shanghai, 1869.   A 2 S 23 †

MICHIE (SIR ARCHIBALD), K.C.M.G., Q.C. Colonists, socially, and in their Relations with the Mother Country : a Lecture. 12mo. St. Kilda, 1859.   MJ 2 P 30
Obtaining Money under False Pretences by Act of Parliament. 8vo. Melb., 1860.   MJ 2 R 12
Victoria suffering a Recovery : a Lecture. 8vo. Melb., 1860.   MJ 2 Q 14
Victoria, Retrospective and Prospective : a Lecture. 8vo. Melb., 1866.   MJ 2 R 7
Victoria, Retrospective and Prospective : a Lecture. 8vo. Melb., 1866.   MJ 2 R 15
Lecture on the Westminster Reviewer's Version of Victorian History. 8vo. Melb., 1868.   MJ 2 R 7
Loyalty, Royalty, and the Prince's Visits : a Lecture. 8vo. Melb., 1869.   MJ 2 R 23

MICHIE (SIR ARCHIBALD), K.C.M.G., Q.C.—*continued.*
Readings in Melbourne ; with an Essay on the Resources and Prospects of Victoria, for the Emigrant and Uneasy Classes. 8vo. Lond., 1879.* MF 1 P 48
[*See* HAMLET CONTROVERSY.]

MICHIE (CHRISTOPHER YOUNG). The Larc1 : a Practical Treatise on its Culture and General Mangement. 8vo. Edinb., 1882. A 1 P 52

MICHIELS (L.) Grammaire élémentaire Liégeoise (Française-Wallonne). Roy. 8vo. Liége, 1863. K 13 R 3

MICHIGAN. [*See* UNITED STATES OF AMERICA.]

MICKLE (WILLIAM JULIUS). Life and Poems of [*See* CHALMERS, A.]

The Lusiad ; or, the Discovery of India : an Epic Poem ; translated from the original Portuguese of Luiz de Camoens. [*See* CHALMERS, A.]

MICKLETHWAITE (J. T.) Lectures on Art. [*See* ART.] A 6 V 36

MICROSCOPICAL SOCIETY, LONDON. Transactions of. Vols. 1–16. 16 vols. (in 6) 8vo. Lond., 1853–68. E 1.54
[*See* QUARTERLY JOURNAL OF MICROSCOPICAL SCIENCE.]

MIDDELLANT (HUBERTUS VAN). Tractaet de Foro Competenti. [*See* VROMANS, P.]

MIDDLE AGES. Historical Pictures of the Middle Ages, in Black and White, made on the spot; by "A Wandering Artist." 2 vols. 8vo. Lond., 1846. B 7 S 51, 52

MIDDLEMORE (MRS. S. G. C.) Spanis1 Legendary Tales. 8vo. Lond., 1885. J 9 S 18

MIDDLETON (CONYERS). History of the Life of Marcus Tullius Cicero. 2 vols. 4to. Lond., 1741. C 2 W 6, 7

MIDDLETON (REV. E.) Life of Robert Leighton, D.D. [*See* LEIGHTON, R.]

MIDDLETON (PROF. JOHN HENRY). Ancient Rome in 1885. 8vo. Edinb., 1885. B 12 R 20

MIDDLETON (THOMAS). Works of ; edited by A. H. Bullen, B.A. 8 vols. 8vo. Lond., 1885–86. H 2 R 4–11

MIERS (EDWARD J.), F.L.S. Catalogue of the Stalk- and Sessile-eyed Crustacea of New Zealand. (Colonial Museum and Geological Survey Department.) 8vo. Lond., 1876. MA 2 U 6
Another copy. MA 2 V 6

MIERS (JOHN). Travels in Chile and La Plata. Illustrated. 2 vols. 8vo. Lond., 1826. D 3 S 1, 2

MIGNAN (CAPT. ROBERT). Travels in Chaldæa, including a Journey from Bussorah to Bagdad, Hillah, and Babylon, performed on foot in 1827. 8vo. Lond., 1829. D 4 T 38

MIGNE (JACQUES PAUL). Patrologiæ cursus completus, sive Bibliotheca universalis, integra, uniformis, commoda, œconomica omnium SS. Patrum, doctorum, scriptorumque ecclesiasticorum [sive latinorum, sive græcorum], qui ab ævo apostolico ad ætatem Innocentii III (A.D. 1216) pro latinis et ad Photii tempora (A.D. 863) pro græcis florucrunt Patrologia, in duas partes dividitur alia nempe latina, alia græco-latina. 382 vols. (in 387) imp. 8vo. Paris, 1844–79. G

SERIES LATINA.

In qua prodeunt patres, doctores scriptoresque Ecclesiæ Latinæ a Tertulliano ad Gregorium Magnum. 221 vols.

1–3. Tertulliani (Quinti Septimii Florentis), Presbyteri Carthaginiensis, Opera omnia.

4. Cypriani (Sancti Thascii Cæcilii), Episcopi Carthaginensis et Martyris, Opera omnia.

5. Sixti Papæ, Dionysii Papæ, Dionysii Alexandrini, S. Felicis' S. Eutychiani, Caii Commodiani, Antonii, S. Victorini, Magnetis, Arnobii Afri, Opera omnia.

6, 7. Lactantii (Lucii Cæcilii Firmiani), Opera omnia ; præcedun. S. Marcellini Papæ, S. Marcelli Papæ, S. Eusebii Papæ, S. Melchiadis Papæ, Anonymi, Celsi, omnia quæ exstant fragmenta.

8. Opera quæ exstant universa Constantini Magni, Victorini, necnon et Nazarii, Anonymi, S. Silvestri Papæ, S. Marci Papæ S. Julii, Papæ, Osii Cordubensis, Candidi Ariani, Liberii Papæ, et Potamii.

9, 10. Sancti Hilarii, Pictaviensis Episcopi, Opera omnia.

11. Sanctorum Zenonis et Optati, prioris Veronæ, alterius Milevi Episcoporum, Opera omnia.

12. Sancti Eusebii, Episcopi Vercellensis. Opera omnia ; cui accedunt Firmici Materni necnon Sancti Philastrii Opera omnia.

13. Sanctorum Damasi Papæ et Paciani necnon Luciferi, Episcopi Calaritani, Opera omnia ; intermiscentur Felicis Papæ II, Faustini et Marcellini, Theodosii Magni, Pacati, Variorum, Filocali, Sylvii, S. Virgilii Tridentini, Julii Hilariani, S. Siricii Papæ, universa quæ exstant opuscula.

14–17. Sancti Ambrosii, Mediolanensis Episcopi, Opera omnia.

18. Ulfilæ, Gothorum Episcopi, Opera omnia ; præcedunt S. Martini Turonensis, Tichonii, Novati Catholici, Anonymi, Aurelii Symmacri, Maximi Grammatici, Mamertini, Publii Victoris, Scripta Universa.

19. Quarti Sæculi Poetarum Christianorum, Juvenci, Sedulii Optatiani, Severi et Faltoniæ Prolæ, Opera omnia ; accedunt D. Ausonii Burdigalensis Opuscula omnia.

20. Quinti Sæculi Scriptorum Ecclesiasticorum qui ad S. Hieronymum usque floruerunt Opera omnia.

21. Tyrannii Rufini, Aquileiensis Presbyteri, Opera omnia ; accedunt Pelagii, Cœlestii, Juliani et Aniani Hæreticorum scripta quæ supersunt.

22–30. Sancti Eusebii Hieronymi, Stridonensis Presbyteri, Opera omnia.

31. F. L. Dextri necnon Pauli Orosii, Hispanorum, Chronologorum, Opera omnia ; accedunt, post Leporii Presbyteri Libellum, scriptorum quorumdam S. Augustino æqualium opuscula varia.

32–47. Augustini, Sancti Aurelii Hipponensis Episcopirum, Opera omnia.

48. Marii Mercatoris, S. Augustino æqualis, Opera omnia.

49, 50. Joannis Cassiani, Opera omnia ; in quibus etiam continentur : Vigilii Diaconi, Fastidii, Possidii, S. Cœlestini 1, Antonini Honorati, S. Xysti III, S. Vincentii Lirinensis, S. Eucherii, S. Hilarii Arelatensis, etc., scripta quæ exstant universa.

51. Sancti Prosperi Aquitani, S. Augustini Discipuli, S. Leonis Papæ Notarii, Opera omnia ; accedunt Idatii et Marcellini Comitis Chronica.

MIGNE (JACQUES PAUL)—*continued.*

52. Sancti Petri Chrysologi, Arciiepiscopi Ravennatis, Opera omnia; sequuntur Sanctorum Valeriani et Nicetæ Cemeliensis et Aquiloiensis Episcoporum, scripta universa.

53. Salviani Massiliensis Presbyteri, Arnobii Junioris, Mamerti Claudiani, S. Patricii, Hybernorum Apostoli, necnon aliorum aliquot scriptorum Opera omnia.

54–56. Sancti Leonis Magni, Romani Pontificis, Opera omnia.

57. Sancti Maximi Episcopi Taurinensis Opera omnia.

58. Sanctorum Hilari, Simplicii, Felicis III, Romanorum Pontificum, necnon Victoris Vitensis, Sidonii Apollinaris et Gennadii Presbyteri Massiliensis Opera omnia. Intermiscentur S. Lupi, S. Euphronii, S. Perpetui, S. Eugenii, S. Fausti, necnon Ruricii et Cerealis, variarum Sedium Episcoporum, scripta universa.

59, 60. Sanctorum Gelasii I Papæ, Aviti, Faustini, necnon Joannis Diaconi, Juliani Pomerii et duorum anonymorum Opera omnia. Post quæ Poetarum Quinti Sæculi seriem aperiunt Aurelii Prudentii necnon Dracontii Carmina omnia.

61. S. Paulini Nolani, S. Orientii, S. Auspicii, necnon Claudii Marii Victoris, Merobaudis, Paulini Petricordiensis, Amoeni, Secundini, Drepanii Flori, auctoris Incerti, Opera omnia.

62. D. Eugyppii, Abbatis Africani, Opera omnia sive Tiesaurus ex S. Augustini Operibus. Accessit Vita S. Severini Noricorum Apostoli cum Epistola Eugyppii ad Paschasium Diaconum.

63, 64. Manlii Severini Boetii, Ennodii Felicis, Trifolii Presbyteri, Hormisdæ Papæ, Elpidis Uxoris Boetii, Opera omnia.

65. Sancti Fulgentii, Episcopi Ruspensis, Felicis IV et Bonifaci II. Summorum Pontificum, Sanctorum Eleutherii et Remigii, Tornacensis Rhemensisque Episcoporum, necnon Prosperi ex Manichæo Conversi et Montani, Episcopi Toletani, Opera omnia.

66. Sancti Benedicti, Monaciorum Occidentalium Patris, Opera omnia. Simul excusa sunt Joannis II, Agapeti I et Sylverii, Summorum Pontifium, necnou Sancti Laurentii, Novariensis Episcopi, Scripta universa.

67. Dionysii Exigui, Viventioli, Trojani, Pontiani, S. Cæsarii, Arelatensis, Episcopi, Fulgentii Ferrandi et Rustici quorum prior Carthaginensis, posterior Romanæ Ecclesiæ Diaconus, necnon Justi, Facundi, Urgellensis et Hermianensis Episcoporum, Opera omnia.

68. Primasii, Episcopi Adrumetani, Opera omnia. Simul eduntur Aratoris, Romanæ Ecclesiæ Diaconi, Sancti Niceti et Sancti Aureliani, Trevirensis Arelatensisque Episcoporum, necnon Victoris Capuani, Victoris Tunonensis, Junilii et Liberati quorum prior Africanus Episcopus, posterior Carthaginensia Ecclesiæ Archidiaconus, Scripta universa.

69, 70. Magni Aurelii Cassiodori Senatoris, Viri Patricii, Consularis, et Vivariensis Abbatis, Opera omnia ; præcedunt Vigilii (Papæ) Gildæ Sapientis et Pelagii (Papæ) Scripta universa.

71. S. Georgii Florentini Gregorii, Turonensis Episcopi, Opera omnia, necnon Fredegarii Scholastici Epitome et Chronicum.

72. Pelagii II, Joannis III, Benedicti I, Summorum Pontificum, Opera omnia ; intermiscentur S. Martini, S. Domnoli, S. Verani, S. Aunarii, S. Leandri, Liciniani, Sedati, Marii, Joannis quorum Episcopatu Sedes Bracarensis, Cenomanensis, Cabellitana, Autissiodorensis, Hispalensis, Carthaginensis, Biterrensis, Aventicensis, Arelatensis illustratæ sunt necnon Sancti Germani, Parisiensis Episcopi, S. Radegundis, S. Aregii, Floriani, Joannis Biclarensis, Vitam Monasticam Professorum, ac demum Cogitosi, Antonini Placentini, Luculentii, anonymi Scripta universa.

73–74. Vitæ Patrum sive Historiæ Eremiticæ Libri decem auctoribus suis et nitori pristino restituti ac notationibus illustrati, opera et studio Heriberti Rosweydi.

75–79. Sancti Gregorii Papæ I, cognomento Magni, opera omnia.

3 s

80. Scriptorum Ecclesiasticorum qui in VII Sæculi prima parte floruerunt Opera omnia. Collectio duo et triginta numero auctores comprehendens ; nempe S. Eutropium, Tarram Monachum, Dinothum Abbatem, Dynamium Patricium, S. Augustinum Anglor. Apostolum S. Bonifacium Papam IV, Bulgaranum Comitem, Paulum Emerit, Gondemarum Regem, Marcum Cassinensem, S. Waharnarium, S. Columbanum, S. Alphanum, S. Aileranum, Ethelbertum Regem, Deusdedit Papam, Sisebuthum Regem, S. Bertichramnum, S. Protradium, Bonifacium Papam V, Sonnatium, Clotarium II Regem: Honorium Papam I, Dagobertum I Regem, S. Hadoindum, S. Sulpicium Bituric., S. Authertum, Joannem Papam IV, Maximum Cæsaraugust., Victorem Carthag., S. Braulionem, Talonem.

81–84. Sancti Isidori, Hispalensis Episcopi, Opera omnia.

85, 86. Liturgia Mozarabica secundum regulam Beati Isidori.

87. Scriptorum Ecclesiasticorum qui in VII Sæculi secunda parte floruerunt Opera omnia. Collectio quadraginta numero auctores comprehendens ; nempe : S. Gallum Abbatem, S. Theodorum Papam, Maurum Ravennatensem, S. Martinum Papam I, S. Gallum Claromont., S. Paulum Virdunensem. Rauracum Nivernensem, Felicem Lemovicensem, S. Palladium Antissiodorensem, Constantium Albigensem, S. Abbonem Metensem, S. Desiderium Cadurcensem, S. Donatum Vesontionensem, S. Landericum Parisiensem, S. Sigebertum Fr. Reg., S. Livinum, S. Eugenium Toletanum, S. Valerium Abbatem, Aunemundum, Lngdun, Verum Ruthenensem, SS. Elginim Novion. et Audoenen Rothom., Clodoveum II Reg. Fran. et S. Bathildem, Marculfum, S. Cummianum Hibernum, Vitalianum Papam, Jonam Abb. Elnonensem, S. Fructuosum Bracar., Chrodobertum Turon., S. Faronem Meldensem, S. Adeodatum Papam, Donum Papam, S. Agathonem Papam, S. Damianum Ticin., S. Amandum Traject., S. Mansuetum Mediol., Clotarium III, Childericum II, S. Dagobertum II Theodoricum III, Franc. Reg., Reges Langobardos.

88. Venantii Fortunati, Pictaviensis Episcopi, Opera omnia. Sequuntur Defensoris Monachi, Evantii Abbatis, Sanctorum Arculfi et Adamani, necnon Crisconii Episcopi Africani, triumque auctorum, Scripta universa. Tomum claudunt Monumenta Ecclesiastica Sæculorum VII et VIII quasi intermedia.

89. Octavi Sæculi Ecclesiastici Scriptores ; nempe, Sergius Papa I, Joannes VI, Joannes VII, S. Aldhelmus, Constantinus Papa, Ceolfridus, Felix Ravennatensis, Benedictus Crispus, S. Egbertus, Gregorius Papa II, S. Villibrordus, Gregorius Papa III, S. Bonifacius Moguntinus, S. Zacharias Papa, Stephanus Papa II, S. Perminius Abbas, Cyprianus Monachus, S. Chrodegangus, S. Paulus Papa I, Alanus, S. Ambrosius Cadurcensis, Stephanus Papa III, S. Sturmius, S. Ambrosius Autpertus.

90–95. Venerabilis Bedæ. Anglosaxonis Presbyteri, Opera omnia ; accedunt Pauli Winfridi Diaconi Scripta quæ supersunt universa.

96. Sanctorum Hildefonsi, Leodegarii, Juliani, Toletani, Augustodunensis et iterum Toletani Episcoporum, Opera omnia ; intermicentur Leonis II, Benedicti II, Joannis V, Adriani I, Summorum Pontificum, necnon Cyricii, Idalii Barcinonensis, Felicis Toletani, Sancti Lulli Moguntini, Elipanti Toletani, Felicis Urgell., Heterii Uxamensis, S. Beati Presbyteri, Rachionis Argentinensis, Angelramni item Argentinensis, Wichodi, Scripta universa. Sequuntur Isidorus Pacensis, Abedoc et Ethelvolfus, Abbates Hiberni, Petrus Archidiaconus, Catulfus ; quibus succedunt Anonymi et Monumenta Ecclesiastica selecta ejusdem Sæculi.

97–98. B. Caroli Magni, Imperatoris, Opera omnia.

99. Sancti Paulini, Patriarchæ Aquileiensis, Opera omnia ; accedit Theodori, Archiepiscopi Cantauriensis, Pœnitentiale. Intermiscentur Poetæ Saxonis ; S. Simperti Abbatis Murbacensis ; S. Lulgeri Minigardefordensis Episcopi ; Josephi Alcuini Discipuli ; Fardulfi Sandionysiani Abbatis ; Dagulfi ; S. Angilberti Centulensis Abbatis ; Leidradi Lugdunensis Episcopi ; Amularii Trevirensis Archiepiscopi, Scripta quæ supersunt universa. Tomum claudit Supplementum ad Auctores incerti anni Sæculi VIII nempe Arcarici et Tusared epistolæ.

MIGNE (JACQUES PAUL)—*continued.*

100, 101. B. Flacci Albini seu Alcuini, Abbatis et Caroli Magni Imperatoris Magistri, Opera omnia.

102. Smaragdi, Abbatis Monasterii Sancti Michaelis Virdunensis, Opera omnia : accedunt Sancti Leonis III, Stephani IV, Paschalis I, Pontificum Romanorum, Magni Senonensis, Remigii Curiensis Scripta quæ supersunt universa.

103. S. Benedicti, Abbatis Anianensis, Opera omnia ; accedunt Sedulii Junioris, Natione Scoti, Scripta quæ supersunt universa.

104. S. Agobardi Lugdunensis Episcopi, Eginhardi Abbatis Opera omnia ; accedunt Claudii Taurinensis Opuscula ; tomum claudunt Ludovici I, cognomento Pii, nec non filiorum ejus Scripta, Diplomata scilicet Ecclesiastica et Epistolæ.

105. Theoduldi, Aurelianensis Episcopi, Sancti Eigilis, Abbatis Fuldensis, Dungali Reclusi, Ermoldi Nigelli, Symphosii Amalarii, Presbyteri Metensis, Opera omnia ; intermiscentur Bernowini Claromontani, Aldrici Senonensis, Adalhardi Abbatis Corbeiensis Scripta quæ supersunt universa : simul ad prelum revocatur Liber Diurnus Romanorum Pontificum.

106. Gregorii IV, Sergii II, Pontificum Romanorum, Jonæ, Freculphi, Frotharii, Aurelianensis, Lexoviensis et Tullensis Episcoporum, Opera omnia ; intermiscentur : Agnelli Ravennatis, Hilduini Sandionysiani, Abbatum : Thegani Chorepiscopi Trevirensis, Maxentii Aquileiensis Patriarchae, Candidi Fuldensis Monachi, Benedicti Diaconi, Christiani Druthmari Corbeiensis Monachi, Josephi Sacerdotis, etc., Scripta vel Scriptorum Fragmenta quae exstant.

107-112. B. Rabani Mauri, Fuldensis Abbatis et Moguntini Archiepiscopi, Opera omnia.

113, 114. Walafridi Strabi, Fuldensis Monachi, Opera omnia.

115. Leonis IV, Benedicti III, Pontificum Romanorum, SS. Eulogii, Prudentii, Toletani et Trecensis Antistitum Angelomi Luxoviensis, Opera omnia ; praemittuntur Ahytonis, Basileensis Episcopi, Audradi, Senonensis Chorepiscopi, Aldrici Cenomanensis Episcopi, Scripta quae supersunt universa.

116-18. Haymonis, Halberstatensis Episcopi, Opera omnia ; praemittuntur Ebbonis Rhemensis, Hartmanni Monachi, S. Galli, Ermanrici Augiensis Monachi, Erchamberti Frisingensis Episcopi, Nithardi S. Richarii Abbatis, Amulonis Episcopi Lugdunensis, Scripta quae supersunt ; tomum ultimum claudit S. Anseharius Hamburgensis Episcopus.

119. Nicolai I, Pontificis Romani, Epistolae et Decreta. Praecedunt B. Servati Lupi Abbatis Ferrariensis ; Flori Diaconi Lugdunensis, Rodulfi Bituricensis, Walterii Aurelianensis, Rothadi II Suessionensis, Opera omnia.

120. Sancti Paschasii Radberti, Abbatis Corbeiensis, Opera omnia.

121. Ratramni, Corbeiensis Monachi, Ænene, Sancti Remigii, Parisiensis et Lugdunensis Episcoporum, Wandalberti Monachi, Pauli Alvari Cordubensis, Opera omnia ; intermiscentur Lotharii Regis, Berardi Turonensis, Guntharii Coloniensis, Theotgaudi Belgicae Galliae Primatis, Arduici Vesontionensis, Wulfadi Bituricensis, Adventii Metensis Episcoporum ; Grimaldi Sangallensis Abbatis, Milonis Monachi S. Amandi, Isonis Sangallensis Monachi, Gottschalci Heretici, etc. Scripta quae exstant universa.

122. Joannis Scoti Opera quae supersunt omnia ; accedunt Adriani Papae II Epistolae.

123, 124. Usuardi Martyrologium ; praemittuntur Sancti Adonis Opera ; tomum secundum, claudunt Caroli Calvi, Francorum Regis, Hincmari Laudunensis, Isaaci Lingonensis, Odonis Bellovacensis, Episcoporum, Adrevaldi Floriacensis, Herici Antissiodorensis, Monachorum, Scripta duae supersunt universa.

125, 126. Hincmari, Rhemensis Archiepiscopi, Opera omnia, sequuntur Joanni VIII, Marini I, Adriani III, Pontificum Romanorum Epistolae et Decreta ; tomum secundum claudunt Bertrum Abbatis Cresiensis, Haemoi Sangallensis Abbatis, S. Bembratti Bambærgen i : Episcopi, Aimoini Monachi San ermamm e, Ratperti Sangallensis, Scripta vel scriptorum e xsta duae supersunt.

MIGNE (JACQUES PAUL)—*continued.*

127-129. Anastasii Abbatis, Sanctae Romanae Ecclesiae Presbyteri et Bibliothecarii, Opera omnia : accedunt Stephani V, Formosi, Stephani VI, Romani, Pontifium Romanorum, Erchemberti Cassinensis Monachi, Angilberti Corbeiensis Abbatis, S. Tutilonis Sangallensis Monachi, Grimlaici Presbyteri, Wolfardi Presbyteri Hasenrietani, Anamodi Ratisponensis Subdiaconi, Scripta vel scriptorum fragmenta quae exstant.

130. Isidori Mercatoris Decretalium Collectio ; tomum claudunt Marci Valerii Probi Opusculum de Notis Antiquis et Ævi Carolini Carmina.

131. Saeculum X. Remigii, Monachi S. Germani Antissiodorensis, Beati Notkeri Balbuli, S. Galli Monachi, Opera omnia ; accedunt Joannis IX, Benedicti IV, Sergii III, Anastasii III, Pontificum Romanorum, Epistolae et Privilegia. Intermiscuntur Fulconis Archiepiscopi Rhemensis, Riculfi Suessionensis, Mancionis Catalaunensis, Hattonis Moguntini, Episcoporum, Martiniani Monachi, Scripta vel scriptorum fragmenta quae exstant.

132. Reginonis, Prumiensis Abbatis, Hucbaldi, Monachi Elnonensis, Opera omnia ; accedunt Joannis X, Leonis VI, Stephani VII, Leonis VII, Stephani VIII, Pontificum Romanorum, Epistolae et Privilegia ; intermiscentur Roberti Metensis Radbodi Trajectensis, Waldramni Argentinensis, Salomonis Constantiensis, Stephani Leodiensis, Walterii Sehonensis, Dadonis Virdunensis, Episcoporum, Hervaei Rhemensis, Agionis Narbonensis, Senifi Rhemensis, Archiepiscoporum, Odilonis Monachi S. Medardi Suessionensis, Radboli Dolensis, Abbonis Saugermanensis Monachi, Cypriani Cordubensis, Scripta vel scriptorum fragmenta quae exstant.

133. Sancti Odonis, Abbatis Cluniacensis Secundi, Opera omnia ; sequuntur : Marini II, Agapeti II, Joannis XII, Pontificum Romanorum, Epistolae et Privilegia ; intermiscentur Sancti Odonis Episcopi Cantuariensis, Roriconis Laudunensis Episcopi ; Arthaldi, Odalrici, Rhemensium Archiepiscoporum ; Cappidi Stavricnsis Sacerdotis, Cosmae Japygi Matericnsis, Joannis Itali, Laurentii, Cassinensium Monachorum, Sigebardi Monachi S. Maximini, Fridegodi Benedictini Monachi, Scripta vel scriptorum fragmenta quae exstant.

134. Attonis, Vercellensis Episcopi, Opera omnia ; accedunt Leonis VIII, Antipapae, Epistolae et Constitutiones. Intermiscentur Brunonis Coloniensis, Wiboldi Camerracensis, Archiepiscoporum, Uthonis Argentinensis Episcopi, Adalgeri Episcopi incertae sedis, Guillelmi Cabillonensis Monachi, Scripta vel scriptorum fragmenta quae exstant.

135. Flodoardi, Canonici Remensis, Opera omnia ; sequuntur Joannis XIII et Benedicti IV, Summorum Pontificum, Epistolae et Decreta ; intermiscentur Gumpoldi Mantuani, Eraclii Leodiensis, Udalrici Augustani, Episcoporum, Scripta vel scriptorum fragmenta quae supersunt.

136. Ratherii, Veronensis Episcopi, Opera omnia ; accedunt Liutprandi Cremonensis nonnon Folquini S. Bertini Monachi, Gunzonis Diaconi Novariensis, Richardi Abbatis Florincensis, Adalberti Metensis Scholastici, Scripta vel scriptorum fragmenta quae exstant.

137. Hrotsuithae, Virginis et Monialis Gandersheimensis in Germania, Ordinis S. Benedicti, Opera omnia ; accedunt Benedicti VII, Joannis XIV, ex XV, Gregorii V, Summorum Pontificum ; Epistolae et Constitutiones. Intermiscuntur Sancti Dunstani Cantuariensis, Adalberonis Remensis, Archiepiscoporum ; Ethelwoldi Wintoniensis, Theodorici, Motedada, Erkembaldi Argentinensis, Guibonis II Podiensis, Sancti Adalberti Pragensis, Episcoporum ; Joannis Abbatis Sancti Arnulfui Metensis, Folcuini Abbatis Laubiensis, Berneri Abbatis Humolarensis, Adsonis Abbatis Dervensis, Gezonis Abbatis Dertonensis, Aymardi, Maioli, Abbatum Cluniacensium ; Widukindi Monachi Corbeiensis, Lethaldi Monachi Miciacensis, Odonis Diaconi Ausciensis, Wigonis Decani Phyldeswingensis, Scripta vel scriptorum fragmenta quae exstant.

138. Appendix ad Saeculum X, complectens Auctores incerti anni et Opera deperdita. Accedunt Monumenta Diplomatica Liturgica et Monastica. Tomum adornat Richeri, S. Remigii extra Muros Remenses Monachi Historiarum Libri IV.

MIGNE (JACQUES PAUL)—*continued.*

139. Silvestri II, Pontificis Romani, Aimoini Floriacensis Monacii, Sancti Abbonis Abbatis Floriacensis, Thietmari Merseburgensis Episcopi, Opera omnia. Accedunt Joannis XVIII, Sergii IV, Benedicti VIII, Summorum-Pontificum, Epistolae et Diplomata. Intermiscentur Arnulfi Remensis, Ælfrici Cantuariensis, Archiepiscoporum; Notgeri Leodiensis, Henrici Parmensis, Brunonis Lingonensis, Arnoldi Halberstatensis Episcoporum; Gosperti Abbatis Tegernseensis, Alberti Abbatis Miciacensis, Herigeri Abbatis Lobiensis, Constantini S. Symphoriani Abbatis; Tietpaldi Tegernseensis Monacii, Benedicti Monacii S. Andreae, Purchardi Monachi Augiae Divitis, Roriconis Monacii Moissiacensis, Joannis Diaconi Veneti, Bridferti Ramesiensis Monacii, Scripta quae exstant.

140. Burchardi Vormatiensis Episcopi, Opera omnia; praecedunt Sancti Henrici Imperatoris Augusti Constitutiones et Diplomata Ecclesiastica; intermiscentur Adelboldi Trajectensis Episcopi, Thangmari Presbyteri Hildesheimensis, Alperti, S. Symphoriani Metensis Monacii, S. Romualdi Ordinis Camaldulensis Institutoris, Scripta vel scriptorum fragmenta quae supersunt.

141. S. Fulberti, Carnotensis Episcopi, Opera omnia; accedunt Guidonis Aretini Musica; Ademari S. Cibardi Monachi, Dudonis Decani S. Quintini Veromandensis, Lamberti Aschafnaburgensis, Scripta Historica; necnon Joannis XIX, Benedicti IX, Roberti Francorum Regis, Emmae Reginae Anglorum, Guillelmi Ducis Aquitaniae, Epistolae et Diplomata; intermiscentur Aribonis Moguntini, Ebali Remensis, Popponis Trevirensis, Archiepiscoporum; Godehardi Hildesheimensis, Heriberti Eischtettensis, Rotberti Londinensis, Gauslini Bituricensis, Adalberonis Laudunensis, Episcoporum; Guillelmi I Abbatis S. Germani a Pratis, Guillelmi Abbatis S. Benigni Divionensis; Eberhardi, Peringeri, Ellingeri, Udalrici, Abbatum Tegernseensium; Cathwalloni Rothonensis Abbatis, Angelranni Abbatis Centulensis, Ledwini Abbatis S. Vedasti, Othelboldi Abbatis S. Bavonis Gandensis, Meginfredi Magdeburgensis Praepositi, Arnoldi et Comite Monachi, Fromundi Coenobitae Tegernseensis, Papiae Grammatici, Garciae Monacii Cuxanensis, Bernardi Scholastici Andegavensis, Godeschalki, Scripta vel scriptorom fragmenta quae exstant.

142. S. Brunonis, Herbipolensis Episcopi, S. Odilonis Abbatis Cluniacensis, Bernonis Augiensis Abbatis, Opera omnia. Accedunt Gregorii VI, Clementis II, Romanorum Pontificum, Epistolae et Diplomata; Rodulfi Glabri, Wipponis Presbyteri, Opuscula Historica. Intermiscentur Guidonis de Castellione Remensis Archiepiscopi, Olivae Ausonensis, Vasonis Leodiensis, Gerardi I Cameracensis, Hugonis Lingonensis, Halinardi Lugdunensis, Jordani Lemovicensis, Episcoporum; Seifridi Abbatis Tegernseensis, Odoranni Monacii S. Petri Vivi, Helgaudi Floriacensis Monacii, Anselmi M., S. Remigii Remensis, Scripta vel scriptorum fragmenta quae supersunt.

143. Hermanni Contracti, Monacii Augiae Divitis, Humberti S.R.E. Cardinalis Silvae Candidae Episcopi, Opera omnia. Accedunt S. Leonis IX, Victoris II, Stephani IX, Nicolai II, Summorum Pontificum Opuscula, Epistolae et Privilegia. Intermiscentur Stephani Cardinalis, B. Maurilii Rothomagensis, Gervasii Remensis, Raimbaldi Arlatensis, Leodegarii Viennensis, S. Annonis Coloniensis, Archiepiscoporum; Drogonis Bellovacensis, Joannis Sabinensis, Adelmanni Brixiensis, Hugonis II Nivernensis, Frollandi Sylvanectensis, Leonis Atiuensis, Episcoporum; Bovonis Abbatis S. Bertini, Widrici Abbatis S. Ghisleni, Avesgoti Abbatis S. Petri Culturae Cenomanensis, Theuzonis Eremitae et Monacii, Odonis Monacii Fossatensis, Anselmi Canonici Leodiensis, Gozechini Scholastici, Franconis Scholastici, Leodiensis, SS. Arialdi et Herlembaldi, Berengarii Vicecomitis Narbonensis, Scripta vel scriptorum fragmenta quae exstant.

144, 145. S. Petri Damiani, S.R.E. Cardinalis, Episcopi Ostiensis, Ordinis S. Benedicti, e Congregatione Fontis-Avellanae, Opera omnia, Accessore S. Damiani.

146. Othloni, Monachi S. Emmerammi, Opera omnia; accedunt Adami Canonici Bremensis, Gundechari Eischtettensis Episcopi Lamberti Hersfeldensis, Petri Malleacensis, Annales et Chronica; intermicentur Alexandri II Papae, S. Joannis Gualberti Abbatis Valumbrosani, S. Lietberti Cameracensis, Hugonis I Trecensis, Deoduini Leodiensis, Guidonis Ambianensis, Opuscula, Diplomata Epistolae.

MIGNE (JACQUES PAUL)—*continued.*

147. Joannis, Abrincensis primum Episcopi, postmodum Archiepiscopi Rothomagensis, Alphani Salernitani Archiepiscopi, Opera omnia; accedunt Arnulfi Clerici Medeolanensis, Bertioldi Constantiensis, Brunonis Magdeburgensis Clerici, Mariani Scotti, Landulfi Clerici Mediolanensis Chronica; intermiscentur Gebuini Lugdunensis Archiepiscopi, Gualterii Meldensis, Eusebii Brunonis Andegavensis, Episcoporum, Sancti Geraldi Silvae Marjoris Primi Abbatis, Joannis Fiscamnensis Abbatis, Thomelli Monacii Hasnoniensis, Renalli, Magistri Sedis Barcinonensis, Folcardi Sithivensis Monacii, Guaiferii Monachi Casinensis, Theoderici Padbrunnensis Canonici, Scripta vel scriptorum fragmenta quae supersunt.

148. S. Gregorii VII, Romani Pontificis, Epistolae et Diplomata Pontificia.

149. Victoris III, Romani Pontificis, Sancti Anselmi Lucensis, Opera omnia; accedunt Willelmi I Anglorum Regis, cognomine Conquestoris, Epistolae. Diplomata et Leges; intermicentur Guitmundi Archiepiscopi Aversani, S. Anastasii Monacii et Eremitae, Bartholomaei Abbatis Majoris Monasterii, Durandi Abbatis Troarnensis, Osberni Cantuariensis Monacii, Udalrici Cluniacensis, Godefridi Stabulensis, Willelmi Calculi Gemmeticensis Monachi, Gaufredi Malaterrae Monacii Benedictini, Guillelmi Apuli, Ebrardi Watinensis Monacii, Bernardi Comitis Bisuldunensis, Samuelis Marochiani Judaeo Christiani, Scripta quae exstant.

150. B. Lanfranci, Cantuariensis Archiepiscopi, Opera omnia; accedunt Raynaldi Remensis Archiepiscopi, Deusdedit S.R.E. Cardinalis, Gerardi II Cameracensis, Herimanni Metensis, Bonizonis Placentini, Durandi Claromontani, Bernardi Lutevensis, Radbodi II Tornacensis et Noviomensis, Agononis Augustodunensis, Rufini incertae sedis Episcoporum, Guillelmi Abbatis S. Arnulfi Metensis, S. Wilhelmi Abbatis Hirsaugiensis, Guidonis Abbatis Farfensis, Roberti de Tumbalena Abbatis S. Vigoris, Fulconis Abbatis Corbeiensis, Rogerii Monachi Beccensis, Gilleberti Monachi Elnonensis, Willelmi Clusiensis Monacii, Hemmingi Presbyteri Wigorniensis, Odalrici Praepositi Remensis, Fulcoii Meldensis Subdiaconi, Constantini Africani Casinensis Monacii, Henrici Clerici Pomposiani, Theodorici S. Audoeni Monacii, Willelmi Pictaviensis, Joannis de Garlandia, Aribonis Musici, J. Cottonis Musici, Scripta vel scriptorum fragmenta quae exstant.

151. B. Urbani II, Pontificis Romani, Epistolae. Diplomata, Sermones.

152, 153. S. Brunonis, Carthusianorum Institutoris, necnon ejusdem Saeculi Praecipuorum Carthusiensium Patrum, Opera omnia.

154. Hugonis, Abbatis Flaviniacensis Ekkehardi Uraugiensis, Chronica; accedunt B. Wolphelmi Abbatis Brunswillerensis Opuscula duo.

155. Godefridi Bullonii, Lotharingiae Ducis postmodum Hierosolymorum Regis primi, Epistolae et Diplomata. Sequuntur Radulphi Ardentis Homiliae duobus tomis distributae. Intermiscentur Lupi Protospatarii Chronicon necnon Anselmi Mediolanensis, Bernardi Toletani, Archiepiscoporum, Thomae Eboracensis, Alberici Ostiensis, Amati Burdagalensis, Popponis Metensis, Episcoporum; Richardi de Dumellis, Abbatis Pratellensis, Manegaldi Presbyteri, Goscelini Cantuariensis Monacii, Sulcardi Westmonasteriensis, Pauli S. Petri Carnotensis Monacii, Fratrum Majoris Monasterii, Brunonis, Opuscula, Diplomata, Epistolae.

156. Venerabilis Guiberti, Abbatis S. Mariae de Novigento, Opera omnia.

157. Goffridi, Abbatis Vindocinensis, Opera omnia; accedunt Thiofridi Abbatis Efternacensis, Petri Alphonsi ex Judaeo Christiani, Werneri Abbatis S. Blasii in Silva Nigra Scripta quae exstant. Intermiscentur Hugonis Lugdunensis, Adelgorii Magdeburgensis, Archiepiscorum; Pibonis Tullensis Episcopi, Galteri ab Insulis, Magalonensis Episcopi, et Lietberti Abbatis S. Rufi, S. Roberti Abbatis Molismensis, Suavii Abbatis S. Severi, Folcardi Abbatis Lobiensis, Theodorici Abbatis S. Huberti Aldaginensis, Mathildis Comitissae Opuscula, Diplomata Epistolae.

MIGNE (JACQUES PAUL)—*continued.*

158, 159. S. Anselmi, ex Beccensi Abbate Cantuariensis Archiepiscopi, Opera omnia, necnon Eadmeri Monachi Historia Novorum et alia Opuscula.

160. Sigeberti, Gemblacensis Monachi, Opera omnia. Accedit Chronicon Polonorum auctore anonymo. Intermiscentur Beati Odonis Cameracensis, Walteri Cabilonensis, Joannis Marsicani, Episcoporum; Berengosi Abbatis S. Maximi Trevirensis, Radulfi Tortarii Floriacensis Monachi Scripta vel scriptorum fragmenta quae supersunt.

161, 162. Sancti Ivonis, Carnotensis Episcopi, opera omnia; accedunt Petri Chrysolani, Mediolanensis Archiepiscopi, Richardi Cardinalis, Lamberti Atrebatensis, Galonis Parisiensis Godefridi Abianensis, Episcoporum; Anselmi Scholastici et Canonici Laudunensis, B. Roberti de Arbrisello, Seheri, Calmosiacensis Abbatis, Joannis Monachi S. Audoeni, Joannis Monachi Besuensis, Francisci Cameni, Reimbaldi Praepositi S. Joannis Leodiensis, Opuscula, Diplomata, Epistolæ.

163. Paschalis II, Gelasii II, Romanorum Pontificum, Epistolae et Privilegia. Accedunt Cononis S. R. E. Cardinalis, Radulfi Remensis, Radulfi Cantuariensis, Archiepiscoporum; Guillelmi de Campellis Catalaunensis, Theogeri Metensis, Ernulfi Roffensis, Marbodi Redonensis, Episcoporum; Placidi incertae sedis Episcopi; Arnaldi S. Petri Vivi Senonensis Abbatis, Pontii Abbatis S. Rufi, Gregorii Presbyteri Romani, Petri de Honestis Clerici Ravennatis, Hugonis de Sancta Maria Floriacensis Monachi, Laurentii Veronensis, Theobaldi Stampensis, Lamberti Audomarensis, Hugonis de Cleriis, Joannis Constantiensis, Anonymi Metensis, Opuscula, Diplomata, Epistolae.

164, 165. S. Brunonis Astensis, Abbatis Montis Casini et Episcopi Signiensium, Opera omnia. Accedit Oddonis Astensis Monachi Benedictini Expositio in Psalmos.

166. Baldrici, Dolensis Archiepiscopi, Opera omnia. Accedunt Honorii II, Romani Pontificis, Epistolae et Diplomata, necnon Cosmae Pragensis, Alberici Aquensis Chronica. Intermiscentur Drogonis Cardinalis, Petri Leonis et Gregorii, S. R. E Legatorum, Friderici Coloniensis Archiepiscopi, S. Hugonis Gratianopolitani, Brunonis Argentinensis, Episcoporum, S. Stephani Abbatis Cisterciensis Tertii, Fraconis Abbatis Affligemensis, Pontii Abbatis, Cuniacensis Abbandi Abbatis Richardi Abbatis Pratellensis, G. Abbatis, Domnizonis Presbyteri Canusini, Joannis Monachi, Viviani Præconantratensis, Joannis Michaelensis, Gualteri Travanensis et Galberti Brugensis, Hugonis de Ribodimonte Opuscula, Diplomata, Epistolae.

167-170. R. D. D. Ruperti, Abbatis Monasterii S. Heriberti Tuitiensis, Viri longe doctissimi summique inter veteres Theologi, Opera omnia.

171. Venerabilis Hildeberti, primo Cenomanensis Episcopi deinde Turonensis Archiepiscopi, Opera omnia; accesserunt Marbodi Redonensis Episcopi, ipsius Hildeberti supparis, opuscula.

172. Honorii Augustodunensis Opera omnia; accedunt Rainaldi Remensis, Adalberti Moguntini, Oldegarii Tarraconensis, Archiepiscoporum; Gerardi Engolismensis, Stephani de Balgiaco Augustodunensis, Episcoporum; Odonis Abbatis Sancti Remigii, Gaufridi Grossi, Monachi Tironiensis, Opuscula, Epistolae, Diplomata.

173. Leonis Marsicani et Petri Diaconi, Monachorum Casinensium, Chronicon Monasterii Casinensis et Opuscula. Accedunt Rodulfi Abbatis S. Trudonis Gesta Abbatum Trudonensium necnon Falconis Beneventani, Landulphi Junioris Chronica. Intermiscentur Sancti Ottonis Bambergensis Episcopi, Matthaei Cardinalis, Gibonis Tusculani, Gaufridi Catalaunensis, Stephani Parisiensis, Episcoporum, Gualteri Cluniacensis Monachi Opuscula Diplomata, Epistolae.

174. Ven. Godefridi, Abbatis Admontensis, Opera omnia, accessere Hariulfi Aldenburgensis, Lisiardi Turonensis, scripta quae supersunt.

175-177. Hugonis de S. Victore, Canonici Regularis S. Victoris Parisiensis, Opera omnia.

MIGNE (JACQUES PAUL)—*continued.*

178. Petri Abaelardi, Abbatis Rugensis, Opera omnia. Accedunt Hilarii et Berengarii, Abaelardi Discipulorum, Opuscula et Epistolae.

179. Willelmi Malmesburiensis Monachi Opera omnia: accedunt Innocentii II, Coelestini II, Lucii II, Romanorum Pontificum Anacleti Antipapae, Benedicti Ecclesiae S. Petri in Urbe Roma Canonici, Hugonis Farsiti, Frowini Abbatis Montis Angelorum Apud Helvetios, Arnulfi Opuscula, Diplomata, Epistolae.

180. Eugenii III, Romani Pontificis, Epistolae et Privilegia; accedunt Ulgerii Andegavensis Episcopi, Ogerii Lucedii Abbatis, Guillelmi Abbatis Theodorici prope Remos, Hermanni Abbatis S. Martini Tornacensis, Algeri Canonici Leodiensis, Teulfi Maurei. Mon., Joannis Mon., S. Laurentii Leod., Arnulfi de Boeris Henrici Salteriensis Scripta quae supersunt.

181. Ven. Hervei, Burgidolensis Monachi, Opera omnia; accedunt Hugonis Matisconeusis Antissiodorensis Episcopi, Bartholomaei Catalaunensis Episcopi, Bernardi Corthusiae Portarum Prioris 1 S. Rainardi Abbatis Cisterciensis v, Aimonis Abbatis S. Petri Divensis et Petri Monachi, Guidonis Cariloci Abbatis, Heriberti Monachi, Hildebrandi Junioris Opuscula, Diplomata, Epistolae.

182-185. S. Bernardi, Abbatis primi Crimi Clarae-Vallensis Opera omnia.

186. Sugerii Abbatis S. Dionysii, Opusculo et Epistolae; accedunt Roberti Pulli S. R. E. Cardinalis et Cancellarii, Josleni Suessionensis, Zachariae Chrysop. Episc.; Zachariae ignotae sedis Episcopi, Willelmi Sandionysiani Monachi Scripta vel scriptorum fragmenta quae existant.

187. Decretum Gratiani.

188. Orderici Vitalis Angligenae, Coenobii Uticensis Monachi Historia, Ecclesiastica. Accedunt Anastasii IV, Adriani IV, Romanorum Potificum, Epistolae et Privilegia, necnon Theobaldi Cantuariensis Archiepiscopi; Attonis Pistoriensis, B. Amedei Lausannensis, Anselmi Havelbergensis; Gisleberti Porretani Pictaviensis, Episcoporum; Guerrici Igniacensis, Odonis Morimundensis, Pastredi Clarevallensis, Joannis Civitae Thaurucani in Hispania, Gaufridi, Claraevallensis, Absalom; Hugonis Metelli, Canonici Regularis, Gilberti de Hoilandia, Opuscula, Diplomata, Epistolae.

189. Petri Venerabilis, Abbatis Cluniacensis Noni, Opera omnia. Accedunt Wibaldi Abbatis Stabulensis necnon Ernaldi Abbatis Bonaevallis Epistolae et Opuscula.

190. S. Thomae, Cantuariensis Arc!iepiscopi et Martyris, nec non Herberti de Boscham, Clerici ejus a Secretis, Opera omnia; accedunt Gilberti Foliot ex Abbate Glocestriae Episcopi primum Herefordiensis, deinde Londoniensis, nec non Alani Tewkesberiensis Abbatis Epistolae.

191, 192. P. Lombardi Magistri Sententiarum, Parisiensis Episcopi, Opera omnia; accedunt Magistri Bandini, Tieologi doctissimi, Sententiarum libri quatuor, et Hugonis Ambianensis, Rothomagensis Archiep., Opuscula, Diplomata, Epistolae.

193, 194. Ven. Gerhohi, Praepositi Reicherspergensis, R. P. Garnerii, Canonici Sancti Victoris Parisiensis, Opera omnia. Accedunt Arnonis Reicherspergensis, Joannis Diaconi, Hugonis Pictavini, Isaac Abbatis de Stella, Alexei et Petri de Roya Claraevallensium Monachorum, Rillindis et Erradis Hohenburgensium Abbatissarum, Opuscula et Epistolae.

195. Beati Aelredi, Abbatis Rievallensis, Opera omnia. Accedit Wolberonis Abbatis S. Pantaleonis, Coloniensis Commentarium in Cantica. Intermiscentur Eckberti Abbatis Schonaugiensis et Sanctae Elisabeth Sororis ejus Germanae, Henrici Archidiaconi Huntingdonensis, Odonis de Deogilo Abbatis S. Dionysii, Bertrandi de Blancosfort Templariorum Magistri, Scripta quae supersunt omnia.

196. Richardi a Sancto Victore Opera omnia; accedunt Gilduini, Achardi, Ervisii, Guarini, Odonis, Godefridi, Adami Victorinorum; Joscelini Turonensis Archiepiscopi, Henrici Archiepiscopi Remensis, Hugonis du Campo-Florido Suessionensis Episcopi, Henrici Archidiaconi Saltzburgensis, Hugonis de Folieto, Nicolai Claraevallensis, Epistolae et Opuscula.

MIGNE (JACQUES PAUL)—*continued.*

197. S. Hildegardis Abbatissae Opera omnia.

198. Adami Scoti, Canonici Regularis Ordinis Praemonstratensis, Opera omnia; accedunt Magistri Petri Comestoris Historia Scholastica, Sermones nec non Godefridi Viterbriensis Cironicon.

199. Joannis Cognomine Soresberiensis, Carnotensis Episcopi, Opera omnia; accedunt Petri S. R. E. Cardinalis tituli S. Chrysogoni, Guichardi Lugdunensis Archiepiscopi, Gualteri prioris S. Victoris Parisiensis, Rogeri Abbatis S. Evurtii Aurelianensis, Joannis Cornubiensis, Opuscula, Diplomata, Epistolae.

200. Alexandri III, Romani Pontificis, Opera omnia.

201. Arnulfi, Lexoviensis Episcopi, Opera omnia; accedit Guillelmi Tyrensis Historia Belli Sacri. Intermiscentur Lucii III, Romani Pontificis, Alani Antissiodorensis Episcopi, Aimerici Patriarchiæ Antiocieni, B. Petri Claraevallensis Abbatis octavi, Terrici Templarii, Opuscula, Diplomata, Epistolæ.

202. Petri Celleusis primum, deinde S. Remigii apud Remos Abbatis, demum Carnotensis Episcopi, Opera omnia. Accedunt Urbani III, Gregorii VIII, Romanorum Pontificum, Epistolæ et Privilegia necnon Gilberti Foliot Londinensis Episcopi, Roberti de Torinneio Abbatis S. Michaelis in Periculo Maris, Joannis Belethi Theologi Parisiensis, Hugonis Eteriani, Scripta quae supersunt.

203. D. Philippi, Abbatis Bonae Spei, Opera omnia.

204. Clementis III, Pontificis Romani, Epistolae et Privilegia; accedunt S. Stepiani Ordinis Grandimontensium Fundatoris, Laborantis, Henrici de Castro Marsiaco, S. R. E. Cardinalium, Balduini Cantuariensis, Archiepiscopi, Bernardi Abbatis Fontis Calidi, Stepiani de Liciaco, Petri Bernardi, Guillelmi de Trahinaco, Gerardii Itherii, Grandimontensium, Reineri, Laurentii, Monaciorum Leodiensium, Ermengaudi, Henrici Septimellensis, Scripta quae supersunt.

205. Petri Cantoris Verbum Abbreviatum. Accedunt Mauricii de Sulliaco Parisiensis, Garnerii Lingonensis, Geraldi, Cadurcensis, Odonis Tullensis, Episcoporum, Alexandri Gemmeticensis Abbatis, Gaufridi Subprioris Canonicorum Regularium, Matthaei Vindocinensis, Scripta quae supersunt.

206. Coelestini III, Romani Pontificis, Opera omnia et Privilegia; accedit Thomae Cisterciensis Monaci et Joannis Algrini, Cordinal Commentarium in Cantica.

207. Petri Blesensis, Bathoniensis in Anglia Archidiaconi, Opera omnia.

208, 209. Sanctorum Martini Legionensis, Presbyteri et Canonici Regularis Ordinis Sancti Augustini in Regio Cænobio Legionensi D. Isidoro Hispalensi Sacro, Wilhelmi, Abbatis Sancti Thomae de Paraclito, Opera omnia. Accedunt Wilhelmi de Campania Remensis, Joannis de Belmeis Lugdunensis, Archiepiscoporum; Balduini Cp. Imperatoris, Hugonis V, Abbatis Cluniacensis, Eliae de Coxida Abbatis Dunensis, Thomae de Radolio, Gualteri de Castellione, Opuscula, Sermones, Epistolae.

210. Alani de Insulis, Doctoris Universalis, Opera omnia.

211. Stepiani, Abbatis S. Genovefae Parisiensis tum Episcopi Tornacensis, Epistolae; accedunt Absalonis Abbatis Sprinckirsbacensis, Adami Abbatis Perseniae, Petri Pictaviensis, Parisiensis Academiae Cancellarii, Guiberti Gemblacensis, Abbatis, Scripta quae supersunt.

212. Helinandi, Frigidi Montis Monacii, necnon Guntheri Cisterciensis, Opera omnia. Accedunt Odonis de Soliaco Parisiensis Episcopi, Petri de Diga et Ægidii Parisiensis, Scripta vel scriptorum fragmenta.

213. Sicardi, Cremonensis Episcopi Mitrale, sive de Officiis Ecclesiasticis Summa. Accedunt ejusdem Sicardi Cironicon, Petri Sarnensis Historia Albigensium.

214-217. Innocenti III, Romani Pontificis, Opera omnia.

218-221. Indices, Generales simul et Speciales.

MIGNE (JACQUES PAUL) —*continued.*

SERIES GRÆCA—

In qua prodeunt Patres, Doctores Scriptoresque Ecclesiae Graecae a S. Barnaba ad Photium. 161 vols.

1, 2. S. Clementis I, Pontificis Romani, Opera omnia.

3, 4. S. Dionysii Areopagitae Opera omnia.

5. S. P. Ignatii, Episcopi Antiocieni, Epistolae; accedunt S. Polycarpi Martyris, S. Melitonis Sardensis, S. Papiae Hierapolitani, S. Quadrati Atheniensis, S. Claudii Apollinaris Hierapolitani, Maximi Hierosolymitani, Polycratis Ephesini, S. Theophili Caesarae Palaestinae, S. Serapionis Antiocieni, Arcizaei Africani, Episcoporum, Aristidis Apologistae Cristiani, Castoris, Aristonis Pellæi, S. Hegesippi, Pantaeni, Rhodonis, Apollonii, plurium anonymorum, Epistolae, Opuscula, Fragmenta.

6. S. P. N. Justini, Philosophi et Martyris, Opera omnia, necnon Tatiani, Hermiae, Athenagorae et S. Theophili quae supersunt.

7. Sancti Irenaei, Episcopi Lugdunensis et Martyris, Detectionis et Eversionis falso cognominatae Agnitionis, seu Contra Haereses libri quinque.

8, 9. Clementis Alexandrini, Opera omnia.

10. S. P. N. Gregorii, cognomento Thaumaturgi, Opera omnia. Accedunt S. Zephirini, S. Callisti I, S. Urbani I, Pontiani, Anteri, S. Fabiani, Pontificum Romanorum; S. Hippolyti Portuensis, S. Dionysii et S. Theonae Alexandrinorum, S. Alexandri Hierosolymitani, S. Anatolii Laodicensis S. Phileae Thmuitani, Episcoporum; S. Archelai Mesopotamiae Episcopi; S. Pamphili Ecclesiae Caesariensis Presbyteri et Martyris, Malchionis Ecclesiae Antiochenae Presbyteri, Caii Romani Presbyteri, Pierii Catechistae Alexandrini, Theognosti Alexandrini, Julii Africani, Asterii Urbani, Macarii Magnetis, Scripta vel scriptorum fragmenta quae supersunt.

11-17. Origenis Opera omnia. (Vol. 16 in 3 Parts.)

18. S. P. N. Methodii, Episcopi et Martyris, Opera omnia. Accedunt S. Petri et S. Alexandri, Alexandrinorum Praesulum, S. Eustathii Antiocieni Episcopi et confessoris, Titi Bostrensis, Theodori Heracleensis, Alexandri, Lycopolitani, Scripta quae supersunt.

19-24. Eusebii Pamphili, Caesareae Palaestinae Episcopi, Opera omnia.

25-28. S. P. N. Athanasii Archiepiscopi Alexandrini, Opera omnia.

29-32. S. P. N. Basilii Caesareae Cappadociae Archiepiscopi, Opera omnia.

33. S. P. N. Cyrilli, Archiepiscopi Hierosolymitani, Opera omnia. Accedunt Petri II, Timothei, Alexandrinorum Praesulum, Apollinarii Laodiceni, Diodori Tarsensis, Scripta vel scriptorum fragmenta quae supersunt.

34. Sanctorum Patrum Macarii Ægyptii, Macarii Alexandrini, Opera omnia; accedit, ab iisdem editoribus recognita Palladii Helenopolitani Episcopi Historia Lausiaca.

35-38. Sancti Patris Nostri Gregorii Theologi, vulgo Nazianzeni, Archiepiscopi Constantinopolitani, Opera quae exstant omnia.

39. Didymi Alexandrini Opera omnia. Accedunt S. Amphilochii Iconiensis Episcopi et Nectarii Cp. Patriarchae Scripta.

40. SS. Patrum Ægyptiorum, Opera omnia. Praecedunt Ptilonis Carpasii, Asterii, Amaseni, Nemesii Emeseni, Hieronymi Graeci Scripta.

1— S. P. N. Epiphanii, Constantiae in Cypro Episcopi, Opera omnia.

44-46. S. P. N. Gregorii, Episcopi, Nysseni, Opera omnia.

47-64. S. P. N. Joannis Chrysostomi, Archiepiscopi Constantinopolitani, Opera omnia, vel quae ejus nomine circumferuntur, accedit Meletii Monacii de Natura Hominis Liber.

65. S. P. N. Procli, Archiepiscopi Constantinopolitani, Oper' omnia. Accedunt Severiani Gibalitani Episcopi, Theophili Alexandrini, Palladii Helenopolitani, Philostorgii S. Attici, S. Flaviani Cp., S. Marci Eremitae, B. Marci Diaconi Marci Diaconi, Scripta quae supersunt.

MIGNE (JACQUES PAUL)—*continued.*

66. Synesii, Episcopi Cyrenes, Opera quae exstant omnia; accedunt Tieodori Mopsuesteni Episcopi, S. Arsenii Eremitae, Scripta vel scriptorum fragmenta quae supersunt.

67. Socratis Scholastici, Hermiae Sozomeni, Historia Ecclesiastica.

68–77. S. P. N. Cyrilli, Alexandriae Arciiepiscopi, Opera omnia; Tomum decimum claudunt Theodoti Ancyrani, Pauli Emesini, Joannis Antiocieni, Acacii Berrhaeeusis, Memnonis Ephesini, Acacii Melitinensis, Rabbulae Edesseni, Amphilochii Sideni, Episcoporum, Homiliae et Epistolae.

78. Sancti Isidori Pelusiotae Epistolarum libri quinque; accedunt Zosimi Abbatis Alloquia.

79. S. P. N. Nili Abbatis, Opera omnia.

80–84. Theodoreti, Cyrensis Episcopi, Opera omnia.

85. Basilii, Seleuciensis Episcopi, Opera omnia: accedunt Eudociae Imperatricis Æneae Gazaei, Zachariae Mitylenes, Gennadii Cp., Antipatri Bostrensis, Theotimi Tomitani, Gelasii Cyziceni, Andreae Samosatensis, Timothei Berytensis, Eustathii Berytensis, Quintiani Asculani, Joannis Carpathii, Episcoporum: Ammonii Presbyteri Alexandrini, Dalmatii Monacii, Euthalii Diaconi, Candidi Isauri, Anonymi, Scripta vel scriptorum fragmenta quae supersunt.

86. Pars Prior : Eusebii, Alexandrini Episcopi, Eusebii, Emesini, Leontii Byzantini, Opera omnia; intermiscentur Theodori Scythopolitani, Theodosii Alexandrini, S. Gregentii Tapharensis, Epiphanii Cp., S. Isaaci Ninivitani, Episcoporum: Timotiei Cp., Timothei Hierosolymitani, Presbyterorum ; Joannis Maxentii, Theodori Lectoris, Procopii Presbyteri Tyrorum, S. Barsanuphii, Anachoretae Palaestini, Agapeti Cp. Diaconi, Eustathii Monachi, Epistolae, Tractatus, Opuscula ; accedunt Justiniani, Imperatoris Augusti, Scripta Dogmatica. Pars posterior: Leontii Byzantini Opera omnia: accedit Evagrii Scholastici Historia Ecclesiastica; intermiscentur S. Eulogii Alexandrini Arciiepiscopi S. Eutychii Constantinopolitani Patriarchiae, S. Ephraimi Antiocieni Patriaricae, Zachariae Moilesti, Hierosolymitanorum Patriarcharum, Erechtii Antiocrine, in Perside Episcopi, S. Petri Laodiceni, S. Symeonis Junioris, Jobii Monacii, Pauli Silentiarii, Scripta vel scriptorum fragmenta quae supersunt.

87. Procopii Gazaei, Ciristiani Rhetoris et Hermeneutae, Opera omnia: accedunt S. Sophronii Hierosolymitani, Joannis Moschi Alexandri Monachi Scripta vel scriptorum fragmenta quae supersunt. (Three Parts.)

88. S. P. N. Joannis Scholastici, vulgo Climaci, Abbatis Montis Sina, Opera omnia ; accedunt Cosmae Indicopleustae, necnon Constantini Diaconi Cp., Agathiae Myrinaei, S. Dorothei Archimandritae, Gregorii Antiocieni Episcopi, Joannis Jejunatoris, Patriarchae Cp. Scripta quae exstant.

89. S. P. N. Anastasii, cognomento Sinaitae, Patriachae Antiociani Opera omnia ; accedunt Anastasii I, Antiocheni Episcopi, Anastasii Abbatis S. Euthymii Anastasii IV Antiocheni, Anastasii Presbyteri, Antiochi Laurae S. Sarae Monachi, Scripta quae supersunt.

90, 91. S. P. N. Maximi Confessoris, Graecorum Theologi Eximiium Philosophi, Opera omnia ; accedit S. Maximi Liber de Variis difficilibus locis SS. Patrum Dionysii et Gregorii.

92. Chronicon Paschale, a Mundo condito ad Heraclii Imp. ann. xx; accedunt Georgii Pisidae Opera omnia.

93. Hesychii, Hierosolymitani Presbyteri, Olympiodori Alexandrini, Leontii Neapoleos in Cypro Episcopi, Opera omnia.

94–96. S. P. N. Joannis Damasceni, Monachi et Presbyteri Hierosolymitani, Opera omnia.

97. S. P. N. Andreae, Cretensis Archiepiscopi, Opera omnia ; accedunt Joannis Joannis Malalae, Theodori Abucarae Carum Episcopi Scripta tum Historica, tum Ascetica.

98. S. P. N. Germani, Archiepiscopi Constantinopolitani, Opera omnia, accedunt SS. Giegorii Agrigentini, Tarasii Cp., Cosmae Hierosolymitani, Pantaleonis Diaconi Cp., Adriani Monachi, Epiphanii Catenensis Diaconi, Pachomii Monachi, Philothei Monachi, Anonymi Beneciani, Scripta.

MIGNE (JACQUES PAUL)—*continued.*

99. S. P. N. Theodori Studitae, Opera omnia.

100. S. P. N. Nicephori, Archiepiscopi Constantinopolitani, Opera omnia; accedunt S. Methodii Cp. Patriarchae, S. Gregorii Decapolitae, Christophori Alexandrini Patriarchae, Georgii Nicomediensis Metropolitae, Stephani Diaconi Cp., Procopii Diaconi Scripta.

101–104. Photii, Constantinopolitani Patriarchae, Opera omnia ; accedunt Petri Siculi, Petri Argorum Episcopi, Bartholomaei Edesseni Opuscula.

105. Nicetae Pophlagonis, qui et David, Nicetae Byzantini, Opera omnia; tomum absolvunt J. Josepii Hymnographi, Theognosti Monachi, Anonymi Scripta.

106. S. P. N. Andreae Caesarae Cappadociae Archiepiscopi et Arethae, Discipuli ejus et Successoris, Opera omnia; accedunt Joseppi, Nicephori Philosophi Christiani, Joannis Geometrae, Cosmae Vestitoris, Leonis Patricii, Athanasii Corinthiorum, Episcopi, Scripta vel scriptorum fragmenta quae supersunt.

107. Leonis, Romanorum Imperatoris Augusti, cognomine Sapientis, Opera omnia.

108. S. P. M. Theophanis, Abbatis Agri et Confessoris, Curonographia ; cui accedunt Leonis Grammatici, Auctoris Incerti, Anastasii Bibliothecarii (Scripta) Historiarum sui temporis quae supersunt. Coronidis vice Ponitur Godefridi Henschenii Dissertatio de Chronographia S. Theophanis, in qua emendatur cironologica sphalmata non pauca Theophani per librariorum secordiam aspersa.

109. Historiae Byzantinae Scriptores; accedit Josephi Genesii Historia de Rebus Constantinopolitanis.

110. Cironicon breve decerpsit concinnavitque Georgius Monachus, cognomine Hamartolus.

111. Nicolai Constantinopolitani Arciiepiscopi, Epistolae ; accedunt Eutychii Alexandrini, Basilii Neopatrensis, Basilii Caesariensis, cognomento Minimi, Mesis Bar-Cephae Theodori Daphnopatae, Nicephori Presbyteri Cp., Scripta.

112, 113. Sapientissimi Imperatoris Constantini Porphyrogeniti Scripta omnia; accedunt Romani Junioris Imp. Aurea Bulla pro Monasterio Xeropotami in Monte Atho; Theodosii Diaconi Acroases quinque de Expugnatione Cretae ; S. Niconis Armeni Monacii Acta ab Abbate Monasterii S. Niconis anno MCL Scripta.

114–116. Symeonis Logothetae, cognomento Metaphrastae, Opera omnia.

117. Leonis Diaconi Historia; accedunt Hippolyti Thebani, Georgidis Monacii, Ignatii Diaconi, Nili cujusdam, Cristophori Protoasecretis, Micraelis Hamartoli, Anonymi, Scripta.

118, 119. Œcumenii, Triccae in Thessalia Episcopi, Opera omnia.

120. Joannis Xiphilini, Arciiepiscopi Cp., Symeonis Junioris, Opera omnia ; intermiscentur Joannis Enchaitae, Theodori Iconii, Alexii Cp., Demetrii Cyziceni, Micraelis Cerularii, Samonae Gazensis, Leonis Achridani, Episcoporum ; Leonis Presbyteri, Joannis Presbyteri, Epiphanii Monachi Hierosolymitani, Nicetae Chartophylacis, Nicetae Pectorati, Joannis Cp. Diaconi, Anonymi, Scripta vel scriptorum fragmenta.

121, 122. Georgii Cadreni Compendium Historiarum ; accedunt Micraelis Pseli Opera omnia.

123–126. Theophylacti, Bulgariae Archiepiscopi, Opera omnia ; accedit Fr. J. F. Mariae Bern. de Rubeis Dissertatio de ipsius Theophylacti Ætate. Gestis, Scriptis ac Doctrina.

127. Nicephori Bryamnii Historiarum libri ; IV ; accedit Constantini Manassis Compendium Chronicum; intermiscentur Nicolai Cp. Patriarchaei, Lucae Abbatis Cryptoferratensis, Niconis Monachi Raitihensis in Palaestine, Anastasii Caesariensis in Palaestina Archiepiscopi, Nicetae Surronii, Jacobi Monacii, Philippi Solitarii, Job Monachi, Petri Chrysolani, Alexii Comneni Imperatoris, Irenes Augustae, Nicephori Botaniatis Imperatoris, Nicetae Seidi, Scripta.

128–131. Euthymii Zigabeni Opera omnia.

MIGNE (JACQUES PAUL)—*continued.*

132. Sapientissimi et Eloquentissimi Theophanis, Archiepiscopi Tauromenii in Sicilia, cognomento Ceramei, Homiliae in Evangelia Dominicalia et Festa totius Anni; accedunt nili Doxapatrii Joannis Comneni Imp. Isaaci Magnae Armeniae Catholici, Scripta.

133. Joannis Cinnami Historiarum libri VII; accedunt Arsenii in Monte Sancto Monachi, Lucae Chrysobergae, Cp. Patriarchae, Alexii Aristeni Nomophylacis, Theoriani Philosophi Chriftiani, Manuelis Comneni, Alexii Comneni, Andronici Comneni, Impp.; Joannis Phocae, Epiphanii Monachi, Perdiccae Protonotarii Ephesini, Anonymi, Eugenippi Theodori Prodomi Scripta.

134–136. Joannis Zonarae Opera omnia; accedunt Eustathii, Thessalonicensis Metropolitae, Opera; et Antonii Monachi, cognomento Melissae, Loci communes.

137, 138. Theodori Balsamonis, Patriarchae Theopolis Magnae Antiochiae, Opera omnia; accedunt Joannis Zonarae et Aristeni Commentaria.

139–140. Nicetae Choniatae Opera omnia, nec non Mich. Acominati Choniatae, Atheniensis Archiepiscopi, Scripta vel scriptorum fragmenta; praemittuntur Joelis Byzantini Chronographi, Isidori Thessalonicensis, Nicetae Maroniensis, Joannis Citri, Marci Alexandrini Scripta insunt praeterea Georgii Acropolitae Annales Byzantini et Alexandri Papae IV, Theodori Ducae, Imp. Niceseni, Germani II, Nicephori, Arsenii, Cpolitanorum Patriarcharum, Nicephori Chumni, Methodii Monachii, Opuscula, Diplomata, Epistolae.

141. Joannis Vecci, Cp. Patriarchae, Opera omnia.

142. Nicephori Blemmidae Opera omnia, praemittuntur Gregorii Cyprii, Athanasii Cpolitanorum Patriarcharum, Scripta.

143, 144. Georgii Pachymerae Opera omnia; praemittuntur Ephraemii Chronographi Caesares et Theolepti Philadelphiensis Scripta Ascetica; accedit Matthaei Blastaris Syntagma Canonum.

145–147. Nicephori Callisti Xanthopuli Ecclesiasticae Historiae libri XVIII; praemittuntur Syntagmatis Matthaei Blastaris continuatio, et Theoduli Monachi, alias Thomae Magistri, Orationes et Epistolae; accedunt Maximi Planudae, Callisti et Ignatii, Callisti Cataphugiotae, Nicephori Monachi, Scripta varii argumenti.

148–149. Nicephori Gregorae Byzantinae Historiae libri XXXVII; accedunt Nili Cabasilae Thessalonicensis Metropolitae, Theodori Militeniotae, Magnae Ecclesiae, Sacellarii, Georgii Lapithae, Opuscula, Epistolae.

150–151. Gregorii Palamae, Thessalonicensis Archiepiscopi, Opera omnia; accedunt Gregorii Sinaitae, Constantini Harmenopuli Nomophylacis, Macarii Chrysocephali Philadelphiensis Metropolitae, Joannis Calecae Cpolitani Patriarchae, Theophanis Niceeni Archiepiscopi Nicolai Cabasilae Thessalonicensis, Gregorii Acindyni, Barlaami de Seminaria, Opuscula, Epistolae.

152. Manuelis Calecae, Ordinis Fratrum Praedicatorum, Constantinopolitani Patriarchae Opera omnia; accedunt Joannis Cyparissiotae, Matthaei Cantacuzeni, Scripta Theologica et Exegetica; nec non Joannis Clycis, Esaiae, Joannis Calecae, Isidori, Callisti, Philothei, Diplomata, Synodicae Constitutiones, Epistolae.

153, 154. Joannis Cantacuzeni Opera omnia, Historica, Theologica, Apologetica. Accedunt Joannis Palaeologi Imp., Philothei Cpolitani Patriarchae, Demetrii Cydonii, Maximi Chrysobergae, Philothei Selymbriensis, Orationes, Opuscula, Epistolae.

155. Symeonis, Thessalonicensis Archiepiscopi, Opera omnia.

156. Manuelis Palaeologi Opera omnia; accedunt Georgii Phrantzae Chronicon, nec non Joannis Anagnostae, Joannis Canani, Manuelis Chrysolorae, Scripta Historica, Epistolae.

MIGNE (JACQUES PAUL)—*continued.*

157. Georgii Codoni Opera omnia; accedit Ducae, Michaelis Ducae Nepotis, Historia Byzantina.

158. Michaelis Glycae Opera omnia; accedunt Josephi Cpolitani Patriarchae, Joannis Diaconi Adrianopolitani, Esaiae Cyprii, Hilarionis Monachi, Joannis Argyropuli, Theodori Agalliani, Job Monachi, Bartholomaei de Jano, Nicolai Barbari, Anonymi, Epistolae, Opuscula Historica, Fragmenta.

159. Laonici Chalcocondylae Historiarum libri decem; accedunt Josephi Methonensis Episcopi seu Joannis Plusiadeni Scripta; praemittuntur Leonardi Chiensis, Mitylenaei Archiepiscopi, Isidori, S. R. E. Cardinalis, Ruthenorum Archiepiscopi, Epistolae Historicae.

160. Gennadii, Constantinopolitani Patriarchae, qui, et Georgius Scholarius, Opera omnia; accedunt Nicolai V. Romani Pontificis, Gregorii Mammae Cpolitani Patriacchae, Georgii Gemisti Plethonis, Matthaei Camariotae, Marci Ephesini, Opuscula et Epistolae.

161. Cardinalis Bessarionis Opera omnia.

MIGNET (FRANÇOIS AUGUSTE MARIE). History of the French Revolution, from 1789 to 1814. 8vo. Lond., 1826.   B 8 P 19

History of Mary, Queen of Scots. 2 vols. 8vo. Lond., 1851.   C 7 S 24, 25

MIKLOSICH (FRANZ). Lexicon Linguae Slovenicae Veteris Dialecti. Roy. 4to. Vindoboniae, 1850. K 4 S 5 †

Lexicon Palaeoslovenico-Graeco-Latinum. Emendatum auctum. Imy. 8vo. Vindoboniae, 1862–65. K 13 T 17

Altslovenische Formenlehre in Paradigmen, mit Texten aus glagolitischen Quellen. 8vo. Wien, 1874. K 15 S 7

Altslovenische Lautlehre. Dritte bearbeitung. 8vo. Wien, 1878.   K 15 S 5

MIKLUCHO–MACLAY (N. DE). Pamphlets. (Pam. Cr.) 8vo. Batavia, 1873–78.   MA 1 R 1

1. Anthropologische Bemerkungen ueber die Papuas der Maclay-Küste in Neu-Guinea. Batavia, 1873.

2. Ueber Brachyocephalität bei den Papuas von Neu-Guinea. Bogor, 1874.

3. Anthropologische Bemerkungen ueber die Papuas der Maclay-Küste in Neu-Guinea. Batavia, 1875.

4. Notice Météorologique concernant la Côte-Maclay en Nouvelle-Guinée. Buitenzorg, 1875.

5. Meine zweite Excursion nach Neu-Guinea. Tjipanas, 1874.

6. Etnologische Excursionen in der malayischen Halbinsel. (Nov., 1874–Oct., 1875.) Mit-Kartenskizze und 2 Tafeln. (Vorläufige Mittheilung.) Buitenzorg, 1875.

7. Einiges über die Dialecte der melanesischen Völkerschaften in der malayischen Halbinsel. Batavia, 1876.

Proposed Zoological Station for Sydney. From the Proceedings of the Linnean Society of New South Wales. (Pam. Co.) 8vo. Sydney, 1878.   A 16 U 23

(Papers published in Sydney.) 8vo. Sydney, 1878–84.   MA 2 U 8

Beiträge zur vergleichenden Neurologie der Wirbelthiere. 4to. Leipsic, 1870.   A 4 Q 21 †

Etnologische Excursion in Johore. (December, 1874–February, 1875. Vorläufige Mittheilung.) Roy. 8vo Batavia, 1875.   A 2 P 8

MIKLUCHO-MACLAY (N. DE), AND MACLEAY (SIR W.) Plagiostomata of the Pacific. Part 1. Fam. Heterodontidæ. With five Plates. (Fam. Cr.) 8vo. Sydney, 1878. MA 1 R 1

MILAN. Description de la Ville de Milan et de ses Environs. 12mo. Milan (n.d.) D 11 P 31

MILAN (FRANCESCO ALESSANDRO SFORZA), DUKE OF. Life and Times of Francesco Sforza, Duke of Milan; with a preliminary Sketch of the History of Italy; by W. Pollard Urquhart. 2 vols. 8vo. Edinb., 1852. C 9 T 41, 42

MILBURN (M. M.) Sheep and Shepherding; embracing the History, Varieties, Rearing, Feeding, and General Management of Sheep, and including Australian Sheepfarming, the Spanish and Saxon Merinos, &c. 12mo. Lond., 1853. MA 1 P 44

MILDMAY (SIR H. P. ST. JOHN), BART. Life of Abraham Tucker. [*See* TUCKER, A.]

MILES. [*See* DARLING, LIEUT.-GEN. SIR R.]

MILES (HENRY DOWNES). Pugilistica; being one hundred and forty-four years of the History of British Boxing; containing Lives of the most celebrated Pugilists, and full Reports of their Battles from contemporary Newspapers and Periodicals, with authentic Portraits, 1719–1863. 3 vols. 8vo. Lond., 1880. B 7 R 1–3

MILES (MANLY), M.D. Stock-breeding: a Practical Treatise on the Applications of the Laws of Development and Heredity to the Improvement and Breeding of Domestic Animals. 8vo. New York, 1879. A 1 Q 11

MILES (W. A.) Poverty, Mendicity, and Crime; or, the Facts, Examinations, &c., upon which the Report was founded; presented to the House of Lords; to which is added, a Dictionary of the Flash or Cant Language known to every Thief and Beggar; edited by H. Brandon. 8vo. Lond., 1839. F 7 8 3

MILET-MUREAU (L. A.) Voyage de La Pérouse autour du Monde. [*See* LA PÉROUSE, J. F. G., COMTE DE.]

MILEY (REV. JOHN), D.D. Funeral Oration on Daniel O'Connell, delivered in the Metropolitan Church, Marlborough-street, Dublin, on the 4th August, 1847. (Pam.) 8vo. Dublin, 1847. C 14 R 21
Rome as it was under Paganism, and as it became under the Popes. 2 vols. 8vo. Lond., 1843. B 11 V 24, 25

MILFORD (JOHN). Norway and her Laplanders in 1841; with a few Hints to the Salmon-fisher. 8vo. Lond., 1842. D 7 T 1

MILITARY PUNISHMENTS. Reports from His Majesty's Commissioners for inquiring into the System of Military Punishment in the Army; with Appendices. Fol. Lond., 1836. F 2 U 18

MILL (HUGH ROBERT), B.Sc., &c. Forestry. [*See* RATTRAY, J.]

MILL (JAMES): a Biography; by Alexander Bain, LL.D. 8vo. Lond., 1882. C 5 P 16
Analysis of the Phenomena of the Human Mind; edited, with additional Notes, by John Stuart Mill, and others. 2 vols. 8vo. Lond., 1869. G 4 R 17, 18
History of British India, 1805–35; continued by H. H. Wilson, M.A., &c. 9 vols. 8vo. Lond., 1820–48.
B 10 S 13–21

MILL (JOHN). The Ottomans in Europe; or, Turkey in the present Crisis; with the Secret Societies' Maps. 8vo. Lond., 1876. F 7 P 10

MILL (JOHN STUART). Analysis of the Phenomena of the Human Mind. [*See* MILL, J.]
An Examination of Sir William Hamilton's Philosophy. 2nd ed. 8vo. Lond., 1865. G 4 R 15
Auguste Comte and Positivism. (Reprinted from the *Westminster Review.*) 3rd ed. 8vo. Lond., 1882.
G 4 R 16
Autobiography [edited by his Step-daughter, Miss Helen Taylor.] 5th ed. 8vo. Lond., 1875. C 8 R 41
Considerations on Representative Government. 8vo. Lond., 1867. F 6 R 27
Dissertations and Discussions, Political, Philosophical, and Historical. 4 vols. 8vo. Lond., 1867–75. F 7 R 8–11
English Positivism: a Study of John Stuart Mill. [*See* TAINE, H. A.]
Essays on some Unsettled Questions of Political Economy. 3rd ed. 8vo. Lond., 1877. F 7 R 5
Examination of Mr. J. S. Mill's Philosophy. [*See* MACCOSH, REV. PROF. J.]
John Stuart Mill: a Criticism; with Personal Recollections, by Alexander Bain, LL.D. 8vo. Lond., 1882.
C 5 P 15
On Liberty. 8vo. Lond., 1871. F 6 R 28
Principles of Political Economy; with some of their Applications to Social Philosophy. People's edition. 8vo. Lond., 1876. F 6 R 29
Another copy. 9th ed. 2 vols. 8vo. Lond., 1886.
F 7 R 6, 7
Review of an Examination of Sir William Hamilton's Philosophy. [*See* GROTE, G.]
Subjection of Women. 8vo. Lond., 1869. F 14 R 3
System of Logic, Ratiocinative and Inductive. 3rd ed. 2 vols. 8vo. Lond., 1851. G 4 R 20, 21
Three Essays on Religion: Nature, Utility of Religion, and Theism. 8vo. Lond., 1874. G 4 R 14
Utilitarianism. (Reprinted from *Fraser's Magazine.*) 4th ed. 8vo. Lond., 1871. G 4 R 19

MILLAIS (SIR J. E.), BART. Notes on the Pictures of. [*See* RUSKIN, J.] A 7 U 38

MILLAR (John). Historical View of the Englis1 Government, from the Settlement of the Saxons in Britain to the Accession of the House of Stewart. 2nd ed. 1 vol. 4to., and 3 vols. 8vo. Lond., 1790–1803.   B 1 R 26–29 †

Origin of the Distinction of Ranks; or, an Inquiry into the Circumstances w1ic1 give rise to Influence and Aut1ority in the different Members of Society. 8vo. Lond., 1781.   F 4 Q 14

MILLER (Daniel F.), Senr. R1etoric as an Art of Persuasion, from the Standpoint of a Lawyer; by "An Old Lawyer." 8vo. Des Moines, 1880.   J 4 R 34

MILLER (Francis T. W.) Builder's and Contractor's Price-book. [*See* Lockwood & Co.]   A 17 Q 78

MILLER (George), D.D., &c. History, p1ilosop1ically illustrated, from the Fall of the Roman Empire to the Frenc1 Revolution. 4 vols. 8vo. Lond., 1849.   B 14 P 46–49

MILLER (George). Trip to Sea, from 1810–15. 12mo. Long Sutton, 1854.   MJ 1 Q 38

MILLER (Rev. Henry). Memoirs of Dr. Robert Blakey. [*See* Blakey, Dr. R.]   C 5 S 3

MILLER (Hugh). Works of, wit1 a Memoir, by L. Agassiz. 13 vols. 8vo. Edinb., 1869.   J 9 R 9–21

Cruise of the Betsy.
Edinbur1 and its Neig1bourhood—Geology of the Bass Rock.
Essays.
First Impressions of England and its People.
Footprints of the Creator; wit1 Memoir.
Headss1ip of C1rist, and the Rig1ts of the C1ristian People.
Leading Articles on various subjects.
My Sc1ools and Sc1oolmasters.
Old Red Sandstone.
Scenes and Legends of the Nort1 of Scotland.
Sketc1-Book of Popular Geology.
Tales and Sketc1es.
Testimony of the Rocks.

Labour and Triump1; the Life and Times of Hug1 Miller; by T. N. Brown. 12mo. Lond., 1858. C 1 R 25

First Impressions of England and its People. 3rd ed. 8vo. Edinb., 1853.   D 8 Q 18

Cruise of the *Betsey*; or, a Summer Ramble among the Fossiliferous Deposits of the Hebrides. 8vo. Lond., 1858.*   A 9 P 1

Testimony of the Rocks; or, Geology in its bearings on the Two T1eologies—Natural and Revealed. 8vo. Lond., 1857.   A 9 Q 10

Scenes and Legends of the Nort1 of Scotland. 8vo. Lond., 1853.   B 13 P 12

Footprints of the Creator; or, the Asterolepis of Stromness. 3rd ed. 12mo. Lond., 1850.   A 9 P 46

Old Red Sandstone; or, New Walks in an Old Field. 4th ed. 12mo. Lond., 1850.   A 9 P 41

My Sc1ools and Sc1oolmasters; or, the Story of my Education. 3rd ed. 8vo. Edinb., 1854.   C 4 S 23

Geology of the Bass Rock. [*See* Bass Rock, The.]   J 5 S 27

3 T

MILLER (James). Payment of Members of Parliament: an Essay touc1ing on the various Forms of Government—T1eocratic, Aristocratic, and Democratic; by "A Son of the Soil." 12mo. Melb., 1878.   MF 1 Q 6

MILLER (Rev. James). Ma1omet: a Tragedy. (New Eng. T1eatre.) 12mo. Lond., 1787.   H 4 P 23

Anot1er copy. (Bell's Brit. T1eatre.) 18mo. Lond., 1795.   H 2 P 16

Anot1er copy. (Brit. T1eatre.) 12mo. Lond., 1808.   H 1 P 13

Anot1er copy. [*See* Brit. Drama 2.]

MILLER (John). Memoirs of General William Miller, in the service of the Republic of Peru. 2nd ed. 2 vols. 8vo. Lond., 1829.   C 10 U 24, 25

MILLER (Joseph). Life and Writings of. [*See* Hazlitt, W. C.]

MILLER (Maxwell). Tasmanian House of Assembly: a Metrical Catalogue. 8vo. Hobart, 1860. MH 1 Q 4

Financial Condition of Tasmania: a Speec1. 8vo. Hobart, 1862.   MJ 2 R 13

MILLER (Philip), F.R.S. Gardener's and Botanist's Dictionary; wit1 a Description of Plants, by T1omas Martyn, B.D. 2 vols. imp. fol. Lond., 1797. K 22 Q 1, 2 ‡

MILLER (R. E.) Lessons in S1ort1and on Gurney's System (improved); being Instruction in the Art of S1ort1and Writing, as used in the service of the two Houses of Parliament. 8vo. Lond., 1884. K 12 P 34

MILLER (Thomas). Pictures of Country Life, and Summer Rambles in Green and S1ady Places. 8vo. Lond., 1847.   D 8 R 31

History of the Anglo-Saxons from the Earliest Period to the Norman Conquest. 4th ed. 8vo. Lond., 1872.   B 4 P 9

MILLER (Gen. William). Memoirs of Gen. Miller, in the Service of the Republic of Peru; by Jo1n Miller. 2nd. ed. 2 vols. 8vo. Lond., 1829.   C 10 U 24, 25

MILLER (William). Sketc1es of the C1ristian Life and Public Labors of; by Elder James W1ite. 12mo. Battle Creek, Mic1., 1875.   G 7 T 23

MILLER (William). Dictionary of Englis1 Names of Plants, applied in England and among Englis1-speaking People, to Cultivated and Wild Plants, Trees, and S1rubs. 8vo. Lond., 1884.   K 7 Q 23

MILLER (William). [*See* Costumes.]

MILLER (William Allen), M.D., &c. Elements of C1emistry: T1eoretical and Practical. 6th ed. 3 vols. 8vo. Lond., 1877–80.   A 6 P 3–5

Introduction to the Stu dy cf Inorganic C1emistry. 12mo Lond., 1871.   A 17 S 6

MILLER (WILLIAM GALBRAITH), M.A., &c. Lectures on the Philosophy of Law, designed mainly as an Introduction to the Study of International Law. 8vo. Lond., 1884. F 7 S 6

MILLER (WILLIAM HALLOWES), LL.D., &c. Elementary Introduction to Mineralogy. [*See* PHILLIPS, W.]

MILLERS', MERCHANTS', AND FARMERS', READY RECKONER, for ascertaining at sight the value of any quantity of Corn, &c. (Weale). 12mo. Lond., 1861. A 17 P 48

MILLETT (MRS. EDWARD). An Australian Parsonage; or, the Settler and the Savage in Western Australia. 8vo. Lond., 1872.* MD 5 P 18

MILLHOUSE (JOHN). New Pronouncing and Explanatory English-Italian and Italian-English Dictionary. 4th ed. 2 vols. 8vo. Lond., 1879. K 12 R 7, 8

Manual of Italian Conversation, for the use of Schools and Travellers. New ed. 18mo. Lond., 1879. K 11 S 20

Temi Sceneggiati ossiano Dialoghi Italiani ed Ingleisi per isvolgere le Regole grammaticali. 9ª ed. 16mo. Milano, 1882. K 12 Q 25

MILLIGAN (EDWARD), M.D., &c. Compendium of Physiology. [*See* MAGENDIE, F.] A 12 T 7

MILLIGAN (JOSEPH), F.L.S., &c. Vocabulary of Dialects of Aboriginal Tribes of Tasmania. (Pam. A.) Fol. Hobart (n.d.) MJ 2 U 1

MILLINGEN (JAMES). Ancient Unedited Monuments. Painted Greek Vases, from Collections in various Countries, principally in Great Britain, illustrated and explained. Imp. 4to. Lond., 1822. A 23 P 14

MILLINGEN (JOHN GIDEON). History of Duelling. 2 vols. 8vo. Lond., 1841. B 15 P 30, 31

Curiosities of Medical Experience. 2nd ed. 8vo. Lond., 1839. A 13 R 16

MILLINGTON (E. J.) [*See* SCHLEGEL, F. VON.]

MILLON (PROF.) Elements of General History. [*See* MILLOT, C. F. X.]

MILLOT (CLAUDE FRANÇOIS XAVIER), Anné. Elements of General History, Ancient and Modern; with the continuation from 1760 to the year 1815, by Prof. Millon, of Paris. New ed. revised. 6 vols. 8vo. Edinb., 1823. B 15 P 13–18

MILLOT (JACQUES-ANDRÉ). L'Art de procréer les Sexes à Volenté, ou Histoire Physiologique de la Génération Humaine. 6ᵉ éd. 8vo. Paris, 1828. A 12 R 38

MILLS (ARTHUR). Systematic Colonization. 8vo. Lond., 1847. MJ 2 Q 8

Colonial Constitutions: an Outline of the Constitutional History and Existing Government of the British Dependencies. 8vo. Lond., 1856.* MF 2 Q 29

MILLS (CHARLES). History of Chivalry; or, Knighthood and its Times. 2 vols. 8vo. Lond., 1826. B 7 U 26, 27

History of the Crusades for the Recovery and possession of the Holy Land. 4th ed. 2 vols. 8vo. Lond., 1828. G 4 R 22, 23

MILLS (CHARLES D. B.) The Indian Saint; or, Buddha and Buddhism: a Sketch, Historical and Critical. 8vo. Northampton, Mass., 1876. G 10 Q 4

MILLS (G.), AND MOORE (W. H.) Notes relating to Comets. (MS.) 8vo. Sydney, 1845. MA 1 T 12

MILLS (J.) History of the Roman Emperors. [*See* CREVIER, J. B. L.] B 11 U 10–19

MILLS (REV. JOHN), F.R.G.S. Three Months' Residence at Nablus, and an Account of the Modern Samaritans. 8vo. Lond., 1864. D 5 R 18

MILMAN (CAPT. E. A.), R.A. Wayside Cross; or, the Raid of Gomez: a Tale of the Carlist War. (H. and C. Lib.) 12mo. Lond., 1847. J 8 P 24

MILMAN (VERY REV. HENRY HART), D.D., DEAN OF ST. PAUL'S. Samor, Lord of the Bright City: an Heroic Poem. 8vo. Lond., 1818. H 8 U 21

Poetical Works of. 3 vols. 12mo. Lond., 1840. H 8 P 22–24

Defence of Milton's Life. [*See* TOLAND, J.]

History of Christianity, from the Birth of Christ to the abolition of Paganism in the Roman Empire. 3 vols. 8vo. Lond., 1840. G 4 P 8–10

History of Latin Christianity; including that of the Popes, to the Pontificate of Nicolas v. 6 vols. 8vo. Lond., 1854–55. G 4 P 2–7

Annals of St. Paul's Cathedral. 8vo. Lond., 1868. B 6 S 37

Life of Edward Gibbon; with Selections from his Correspondence and Illustrations. 8vo. Lond., 1839. C 9 V 20

History of the Jews. 4th ed. 3 vols. 8vo. Lond., 1866. G 7 Q 25–27

History of the Jews. (Fam. Lib.) 2nd ed. 3 vols. 12mo. Lond., 1830. K 10 P 18–20

Hand-book of the Cathedrals of England: St. Paul's. 8vo. Lond., 1879. D 11 R 10

Belshazzar: a Dramatic Poem. 8vo. Lond., 1822. H 3 S 28

Martyr of Antioch: a Dramatic Poem. 8vo. Lond., 1822. H 3 S 27

The Agamemnon of Æschylus, and the Bacchanals of Euripides. [*See* ÆSCHYLUS.] H 8 Q 9

MILMAN (ltr. REV. ROBERT), D.D., BISHOP OF CALCUTTA. Memoirs of; with a Selection from his Correspondence and Journals; by his sister, Frances Maria Milman. With Map. 8vo. Lond., 1879. C 9 T 16

Life of Torquato Tasso. 2 vols. 8vo. Lond., 1850. C 1 R 42, 43

MILN (JAMES). Excavations at Carnac (Brittany): a Record of Archæological Researches in the Alignments of Kermario. 4to. Edinb., 1881. B 12 Q 1 †

MILN (W. S.) An Exposure of the Position of the Scotch Herring Trade in 1885. 8vo. Lond., 1886. F 5 U 32

MILNE (PROF. JOHN), F.G.S. Earthquakes and other Earth Movements. With Figures. 8vo. Lond., 1886. A 9 P 47

MILNE (JOSHUA). Treatise on the Valuation of Annuities, and Assurances on Lives and Survivorships. 2 vols. 8vo. Lond., 1815. F 7 S 21, 22

MILNE (REV. J. J.) Solutions of Weekly Problem Papers. 8vo. Lond., 1885. A 10 S 17

MILNE-EDWARDS (PROF. ALPHONSE), M.D., &c. Recherches anatomique et paléontologiques pour servir à l'Histoire des Oiseaux fossiles de la France. Texte et Atlas. 4 vols. roy. 4to. Paris, 1867-71. A 3 S 11-14 †

MILNE-EDWARDS (HENRI), ET HAIME (J.) Histoire Naturelle des Coralliaires, ou Polypes proprement dits (suites à Buffon). Texte et Atlas. 4 vols. 8vo. Paris, 1857-60. A 14 U 42-45

MILNER (H. M.) Frankenstein; or, the Man and the Monster: a Peculiar, Romantic, Molo-dramatic, Pantomimic Spectacle. (Cumberland's Eng. Theatre.) 12mo. Lond., 1829. H 2 Q 20

Masaniello; or, the Dumb Girl of Portici: a Musical Drama. (Cumberland's Eng. Theatre.) 12mo. Lond., 1829. H 2 Q 21

MILNER (VERY REV. ISAAC), D.D., &c., DEAN OF CARLISLE. Life of; comprising a portion of his Correspondence and other Writings, hitherto unpublished, by his Niece, Mary Milner. 8vo. Lond., 1842. C 8 R 6

History of the Church of Christ. [*See* MILNER, REV. J.]

MILNER (REV. JOHN), D.D., &c. History, Civil and Ecclesiastical, and Survey of the Antiquities of Winchester. 2 vols. 4to. Winchester, 1809. B 4 U 13, 14

MILNER (REV. JOHN), B.A., AND BRIERLY (O. W.) Cruise of H.M.S. *Galatea*, Captain H.R.H. the Duke of Edinburgh, K.G., in 1867-68. 8vo. Lond., 1869.* MD 6 Q 10

MILNER (REV. JOSEPH), A.M. History of the Church of Christ; with Additions and Corrections, by the Rev. Isaac Milner, D.D. 5 vols. 8vo. Lond., 1824. G 4 P 13-17

MILNER (MRS. MARY). Life of Isaac Milner, D.D., F.R.S., comprising a portion of his Correspondence and other Writings, by his Niece. 8vo. Lond., 1842. C 8 R 6

MILNER (REV. THOMAS), M.A., &c. Gallery of Nature: Pictorial and Descriptive Tour through Creation, illustrative of the Wonders of Astronomy, Physical Geography, and Geology. Imp. 8vo. Lond., 1869. A 15 U 18

MILNES (ALFRED), M.A. Lives of Dryden and Pope. [*See* JOHNSON, DR. S.]

MILNES (RICHARD MONCKTON). [*See* HOUGHTON, R. M. MILNES, BARON.]

MILON (A.) Navigation de Plaisance. [*See* BENOIT-CHAMPY, G.]

MILTON (JOHN). Paradise Lost: a Poem, in twelve Books. 13th ed., to which is prefixed, an Account of his Life. 8vo. Lond., 1727. H 8 Q 10

Paradise Lost; the numerous Mutilations of the Text emended, also the obnoxious Punctuation entirely revised; with Notes by Matthias Mull. 8vo. Lond., 1884. H 8 V 24

Paradise Regained: a Poem, in four Books; to which is added, Samson Agonistes, and Poems upon several occasions; with a Tractate of Education. 7th ed., corrected. 8vo. Lond., 1727. H 8 Q 11

Poems upon several occasions, English, Italian, and Latin; with Translations. 2nd ed. 8vo. Lond., 1791. H 8 U 27

Life of, narrated in connection with the Political, Ecclesiastical, and Literary History of his Time, 1608-74; by David Masson, M.A., LL.D. 6 vols. 8vo. Lond., 1859-80. C 8 R 33-38

Defence of the People of England; in answer to Salmasins' Defence of the King. 12mo. Amsterdam, 1692. F 6 P 3

Common-place Book of John Milton; reproduced by the Autotype Process from the original MS. 4to. Lond., 1876. J 12 R 13 †

Poetical Works of. Edited, with Memoir, Introduction, Notes, and an Essay on Milton's English and Versification, by David Masson, M.A., &c. 3 vols. 12mo. Lond., 1882. H 8 Q 12-14

Areopagitica [24 November], 1644. Preceded by Illustrative Documents. (English Reprints.) Carefully edited by Edward Arber, F.R.G.S., &c. Sm. 4to. Lond., 1869. F 5 U 11

Another copy. Edited, with Introduction and Notes, by J. W. Hales, M.A. (Clar. Press.) 12mo. Oxford, 1874. F 15 P 7

English Poems; edited, with Life, Introduction, and selected Notes, by R. C. Browne, M.A. 4th ed. (Clar. Press.) 2 vols. (in 1) 12mo. Oxford, 1875. H 6 Q 43

Poetical Works of; edited by Sir Egerton Brydges; with imaginative Illustrations, by J. M. W. Turner, R.A. 6 vols. 12mo. Lond., 1835. H 5 S 13-18

Prose Works of; with an Introduction by Geo. Burnett. 2 vols. 12mo. Lond., 1809. J 12 U 9, 10

Latin and Italian Poems of, translated into English Verse. 4to. Lond., 1808. H 3 P 24 †

New Memoirs of the Life and Poetical Works of Mr. John Milton; by Francis Peck, M.A. 4to. Lond., 1740. H 6 V 15

MILTON (JOHN)—*continued.*

Selections from the Works of. [*See* MONTAGU, B.]

Comus: a Mask. (Bell's Brit. Tieatre.) 18mo. Lond., 1791.   H 2 P 41

Anotier copy; altered from Milton, by G. Colman. (New Eng. Tieatre.) 12mo. Lond., 1790.   H 4 P 28

Anotier copy. [*See* FARCES, 7.]

Samson Agonistes: a Dramatic Poem. (Bell's Brit. Tieatre.) 18mo. Lond., 1796.   H 2 P 44

Milton and Vondel: a Curiosity of Literature. [*See* EDMUNDSON, G.]

Life and Poems. [*See* BRITISH POETS, 1.]

Join Milton [a Biography]; by Mark Pattison. (Eng. Men Letts.) 8vo. Lond., 1879.   C 1 U 26

Milton's Devil. [*See* MASSON, PROF. D.]

MILTON (WILLIAM WENTWORTH FITZWILLIAM), VISCOUNT, F.R.G.S., AND CHEADLE (WALTER BUTLER), M.A. Nortı-west Passage by Land; being the Narrative of an Expedition from the Atlantic to the Pacific. 8vo. Lond., 1865.   D 3 T 35

MILTON (WILLIAM). Trial of William Milton, wıo resisted an Attempt at Robbery; the unjust conviction, and sentence of seven years on the Roads. 8vo. Mel1., 1862.
                                              MF 1 Q 5

The Victim of the Nineteent1 Century: an Error and its Results—s1ows 1ow the Aut1or was unjustly imprisoned two years and a 1alf. 6th ed. 8vo. Melb.,1865. MF 1 Q 5

MINCHEN (JAMES INNES). The Divine Comedy of Dante Alig1ieri, translated verse for verse. [*See* DANTE ALIGHIERI.]

MINCHIN (GEORGE M.), M.A. Uniplanar Kinematics of Solids and Fluids; wit1 Applications to the Distribution and Flow of Electricity. (Clar. Press.) 8vo. Oxford, 1882.   A 17 T 44

MINCHIN (JAMES GEORGE COTTON). Growt1 of Freedom in the Balkan Peninsula. 8vo. Lond., 1886.   D 8 Q 40

MIND : a Quarterly Review of Psychology and P1ilosop1y. Edited by George Croom Robertson. Vols. 7–10. 8vo. Lond., 1882–86.

MINER (HARRIET STEWART). Orc1ids, the Royal Family of Plants. Wit1 Illustrations from Nature. Roy. 4to. Lond., 1885.   A 5 Q 7 †

MINERAL STATISTICS of the United Kingdom. [*See* HUNT, R.]

MINES AND MINERAL STATISTICS of N. S. Wales. [*See* NEW SOUTH WALES.]

MINES AND MINERAL STATISTICS of Victoria. [*See* VICTORIA.]

MINING ACT of N. S. Wales. [*See* NEW SOUTH WALES.]

MINING AND SCIENTIFIC PRESS (THE). 4 vols. fol. San Francisco, 1861–66.   E 1, 91

MINING INDUSTRY OF NEW ZEALAND. [*See* NEW ZEALAND.]

MINING INSTITUTE OF VICTORIA. Transactions, 1857–59; edited by J. Brac1é, Civil and Mining Engineer. 8vo. Melb., 1859.   MA 2 Q 38

MINNESOTA. [*See* UNITED STATES OF AMERICA.]

MINOR (ELLEN E.) Murillo. (Great Artists.) 8vo. Lond., 1882.   C 3 T 39

MINOS ÆACUS. [*See* BAR AND THE ATTORNEYS.]

MINTO (EMMA ELEANOR ELIZABETH), COUNTESS OF. Lord Minto in India : Life and Letters of Gilbert Elliott, First Earl of Minto, from 1807 to 1814. 8vo. Lond., 1880.   C 3 V 31

MINTO (GILBERT ELLIOT), EARL OF. Lord Minto in India. Life and Letters of Gilbert Elliot, First Earl of Minto, from 1807 to 1814, w1ile Governor-General of India ; being a Sequel to 1is "Life and Letters," publis1ed in 1874. Edited by 1is great-niece, the Countess of Minto. 8vo. Lond., 1880.   C 3 V 31

MINTO (WILLIAM). Daniel Defoe. (Eng. Men of Letts.) 8vo. Lond., 1879.   C 1 U 11

MINTURN (ROBERT B.), JUN. From New York to Del1i, by way of Rio de Janeiro, Australia, and C1ina. 8vo. Lond., 1858.   MD 3 Q 7

MIOT (ANDRÉ FRANÇOISE), COMTE DE MELITO. [*See* MELITO, A. F. MIOT, COMTE DE.]

MIST (ANDRÉ FRANÇOIS), COMTE DE MELITO. [*See* MELITO, A. F. MIST, COMTE DE.]

MIRABAUD (JEAN BAPTISTE DE). System of Nature ; or, the Laws of the Moral and P1ysical World. 3rd ed., wit1 Additions. 2 vols. 8vo. Lond., 1817. G 4 Q 1, 2

MIRABEAU (HONORÉ GABRIEL RIQUETTI), COMTE DE. Memoirs of—Biograp1ical, Literary, and Political—by Himself, 1is Father, 1is Uncle, and 1is Adopted C1ild. 4 vols. 8vo. Lond., 1835–36.   C 8 8 40–43

Letters during 1is Residence in England, wit1 Anecdotes, Maxims, &c.; to w1ic1 is prefixed an introductory Notice on the Life, Writings, Conduct, and C1aracter of the Aut1or. 2 vols. 8vo. Lond., 1832.   C 4 P 44, 45

Biography of. [*See* LAMARTINE, A. DE.]   C 5 8 12

MIRCESCO (V.) Grammaire de la Langue Roumaine ; précédée d'un Aperçu Historique sur la Langue Roumaine par A. Ubicini. 8vo. Paris, 1863.   K 11 V 17

MIRKHOND (MUHAMMED BEN KHAVENDSH1H BEN MAHMUD). History of the early Kings of Persia, from Kaiomars, the first of the Pesh1dad1an Dynasty, to the Conquest of Iran by Alexander the Great; translated from the Persian, by David S1ea. 8vo. Lond., 1832.
                                              B 1 P 11

MIRROR OF PARLIAMENT. [*See* BARROW, J. H.]

MIRZA CHÁFY. Aus dem Nachlasse Mirza Schaffy's. Neues Liederbuch mit Prolog und erläuterndem Nachtrag, von Friedrich Bodenstedt. 8vo. Berlin, 1874.
            H 8 S 35

Die Lieder des Mirza-Schaffy mit einen Prolog von Friedrich Bodenstedt. 81ᵉ auflage. 16mo. Berlin, 1879.
            H 6 P 41

MIRZA RAFI-OOS-SAUDA. Selections from the Kulliyat or Complete Works of ; literally translated by Major H. Court. Roy. 8vo. Simla, 1872.   J 15 V 23

MISHNAH (THE). The Mishnah on which the Palestinian Talmud rests ; edited by W. H. Lowe, M.A. Roy. 8vo. Camb., 1883.   G 7 V 17

MISOPSEUDES; or, the Year 2075 : a Marvellous Vision. 8vo. Melb., 1880.   MG 1 Q 39

MISSIONARY GUIDE-BOOK (THE) ; or, a Key to the Protestant Missionary Map of the World. Illustrated. 8vo. Lond., 1846.   D 12 U 24

MISSION IN THE SOUTH SEA ISLANDS. [*See* SOUTH SEA ISLANDS.]

MISSOURI. [*See* UNITED STATES OF AMERICA.]

MISTRAL (FRÉDÉRIC). Mirèio : a Provençal Poem ; translated by Harriet W. Preston. 8vo. Boston, 1872. H 8 Q 3

MITCHEL (JOHN). Jail Journal ; or, Five Years in British Prisons. 8vo. N. York, 1854.*   MC 1 P 41
Another copy. Author's edition. 12mo. Glasgow, 1855.*
            MC 1 P 43

History of Ireland, from the Treaty of Limerick to the Present Time ; being a Continuation of the History of the Abbé Macgeoghegan. Imp. 8vo. N. York, 1865.
            B 1 S 5 †

Sixteen hundred and forty-one : Reply to the Falsification of History by James Anthony Froude, entitled "The English in Ireland." (*Bound with Waterworth's Church of St. Patrick.*) 8vo. Glasgow (n.d.)   G 7 T 15

MITCHELL (—.) An Accompaniment to Mitchell's Reference and Distance Map of the United States. 8vo. Philad., 1835.   D 4 Q 34

MITCHELL (SIR ANDREW), K.C.B. Memoirs and Papers of ; by Andrew Bisset. 2 vols. 8vo. Lond., 1850.   C 6 U 10, 11

MITCHELL (ARTHUR), M.D., &c. The Past in the Present : What is Civilisation ? 8vo. Edinb., 1880. C 15 P 38

MITCHELL (E.) Sketches by Antonie van Dyck. [*See* VAN DYCK, A.]   A 7 R 3 †

MITCHELL (GRAHAM). Cumberland Disease, the so-called "New Disease," in Australian Sheep. Reports, Letters, &c., on the subject. 8vo. Melb., 1877.   MA 1 Q 18

MITCHELL (DR. JAMES). Statement of the Case of James Mitchell, Esq., late Surgeon on the Civil Establishment of New South Wales. (Printed for Private Use.) 8vo. Sydney, 1838.   MJ 2 R 18

MITCHELL (MAJOR-GEN. JOHN). Life of Wallenstein, Duke of Friedland. 8vo. Lond., 1837.   C 9 S 36

MITCHELL (JOHN), F.C.S. Manual of Practical Assaying, intended for the use of Metallurgists, &c. 4th ed., edited by Wm. Crookes. 8vo. Lond., 1873. A 10 Q 3

MITCHELL (MRS. LUCY M.) History of Ancient Sculpture. With Illustrations. Imp. 8vo. Lond., 1883.
            A 8 T 10

MITCHELL (LIEUT.-COL. SIR THOMAS LIVINGSTONE), KNT., F.G.S., &c. Three Expeditions into the interior of Eastern Australia ; with Descriptions of the recently explored Region of Australia Felix. 2 vols. 8vo. Lond., 1838.   MD 2 T 19, 20

Another copy. 2nd ed., carefully revised. 2 vols. 8vo. Lond., 1839.*   MD 2 T 21, 22

Exploring Expedition in New South Wales. 12mo. Sydney, 1846.   MD 1 S 14

Journal of an Expedition into the Interior of Tropical Australia, in search of a Route from Sydney to the Gulf of Carpentaria. 8vo. Lond., 1848.*   MD 2 T 25

Notes on the Cultivation of the Vine and the Olive, and on the Methods of making Wine and Oil, &c., in the Southern parts of Spain. 4to. Sydney, 1849. MA 1 P 1 †

Australian Geography ; with the Shores of the Pacific and those of the Indian Ocean. 12mo. Sydney, 1851.*
            MD 3 P 18

Report upon the Progress made in Roads, and in the construction of Public Works in New South Wales, 1827 to 1855. [With Plates.] Fol. Sydney, 1856. MF 1 U 12

Despatches and Map relating to Sir Thomas Mitchell's Exploration to the North. Sydney, 1846.* MD 7 P 13 †

The Lusiad of Luis de Camoens ; closely translated. [*See* CAMOENS, L. DE.]

MITCHELL (SIR WILLIAM), KNT. [*See* MARITIME NOTES AND QUERIES.]

MITCHINSON (ALEXANDER WILLIAM). The Expiring Continent : a Narrative of Travel in Senegambia. With Illustrations. 8vo. Lond., 1881.   D 2 R 17

MITFORD (ALGERNON BERTRAM FREEMAN), C.B. Tales of Old Japan. 2 vols. 8vo. Lond., 1871. B 12 S 5, 6

MITFORD (EDWARD LEDWICH), F.R.G.S. Land March from England to Ceylon Forty Years Ago. Illustrated. 2 vols. 8vo. Lond., 1884.   D 9 S 12, 13

MITFORD (REV. J.) Correspondence of Horace Walpole. [*See* WALPOLE, H.]   C 10 P 47, 48

Memoir of Thomas Parnell. [*See* PARNELL, T.]

Memoir of Matthew Prior. [*See* PRIOR, M.]

MITFORD (MISS MARY RUSSELL). Life of; related in a Selection from her Letters to her Friends, by the Rev. A. G. L'Estrange, and H. Chorley. 5 vols. 8vo. Lond., 1870–72. C 4 R 20–24

Recollections of a Literary Life: or, Books, Places, and People. 2nd ed. 2 vols. 8vo. Lond., 1853. C 5 P 5, 6

Friendships of; by the Rev. A. G. L'Estrange. 2 vols. 8vo. Lond., 1882. C 4 R 25, 26

Rienzi: a Tragedy. (Cumberland's Eng. Theatre.) 12mo. Lond., 1829. H 2 Q 23

MITFORD (WILLIAM). History of Greece. 10 vols. 8vo. Lond., 1822. B 9 T 30–39

MITRA (RÁJENDRALÁLA), LL.D., &c. Indo-Aryans: Contributions towards the Elucidation of their Ancient and Mediæval History. 2 vols. 8vo. Lond., 1881. B 10 T 13, 14

Archæology in India, with especial Reference to the Works of. [*See* FERGUSSON, J.] B 10 U 21

MITSCHERLICH (CHRISTOPHE GUILLAUME). [*See* SCRIPTORES EROTICI GRAECI.]

MIVART (ST. GEORGE), F.R.S., &c. Man and Apes: an Exposition of Structural Resemblances and Differences bearing upon Questions of Affinity and Origin. 8vo. Lond., 1873. A 14 S 9

The Cat: an Introduction to the Study of Backboned Animals, especially Mammals. 8vo. Lond., 1881. A 15 P 14

Nature and Thought: an Introduction to a Natural Philosophy. 8vo. Lond., 1882. G 2 Q 1

On the Genesis of Species. 2nd ed. 8vo. Lond., 1871. A 14 S 14

Lessons from Nature, as manifested in Mind and Matter. 8vo. Lond., 1876. A 16 T 24

MÖBIUS (DR. THEODOR). Altnordisches Glossar: Wörterbuch zu einer Auswahl alt-isländischer und alt-norwegischer Prosatexte. 8vo. Leipzig, 1866. K 16 Q 19

MODÈLES DE BOIS: Extrait des vingt premières années du Journal Manuel de Peintures. Fol. Paris, 1872. A 23 Q 15 ‡

MODÈLES DE MARBRES: Extrait des vingt premières années du Journal Manuel de Peintures. Fol. Paris, 1875. A 23 Q 16 ‡

MODERATION. [*See* LAND BILL.]

MODERN CRITICISM; or, the New Theology: the Battle of the Critics. 8vo. Lond., 1871. G 14 P 23

MODERN ENGLISH POETS. Passages from Modern English Poets; illustrated by the Junior Etching Club. Forty-seven Etchings. 4to. Lond., 1880. A 5 V 24

MODERN EPISCOPACY. Unpopularity of Modern Episcopacy and some of its Causes, considered with reference to the Anglican Church in New South Wales; by "A Presbyter of the Church of England." 8vo. Sydney, 1857. MG 1 Q 29

MODERN THEATRE (THE): a Collection of successful Modern Plays; selected by Mrs. Inchbald. 10 vols. 12mo. Lond., 1811. H 1 P 26–35

Bank Note, The: a Comedy; by William Macready. Vol. 9.
Box-lobby Challenge, The: a Comedy; by Richard Cumberland. Vol. 5.
Braganza: a Tragedy; by Robert Jephson. Vol. 6.
Carmelite, The: a Tragedy; by Richard Cumberland. Vol. 5.
Chapter of Accidents, The: a Comedy; by Miss Lee. Vol. 9.
Delinquent, The: a Comedy; by Frederick Reynolds. Vol. 2.
Duplicity: a Comedy; by Thomas Holcroft. Vol. 4.
England Preserved: a Tragedy; by George Watson. Vol. 8.
English Merchant, The: a Comedy; by George Colman. Vol. 9.
False Impressions: a Comedy; by Richard Cumberland. Vol. 5.
Fashionable Levites: a Comedy; by Leonard Macnally. Vol. 10.
Folly as it Flies: a Comedy; by Frederick Reynolds. Vol. 3.
Fortune's Fool: a Comedy; by Frederick Reynolds. Vol. 2.
Fugitive, The: a Comedy; by Joseph Richardson. Vol. 8.
Henry the Second: a Tragedy; by Thomas Hull. Vol. 9.
He's Much to Blame: a Comedy; by Thomas Holcroft. Vol. 4.
He would be a Soldier: a Comedy; by Frederic Philon. Vol. 8.
How to grow Rich: a Comedy; by Frederick Reynolds. Vol. 1.
I'll tell you what: a Comedy; by Mrs. Inchbald. Vol. 7.
Impostors, The: a Comedy; by Richard Cumberland. Vol. 6.
Laugh when you can: a Comedy; by Frederick Reynolds. Vol. 2.
Law of Lombardy, The: a Tragedy; by Robert Jephson. Vol. 6.
Lie of a Day: a Comedy; by John O'Keeffe. Vol. 10.
Life: a Comedy; by Frederick Reynolds. Vol. 1.
Mary, Queen of Scots: a Tragedy; by the Hon John St. John. Vol. 8.
Matilda: a Tragedy; by Thomas Francklin. Vol. 8.
Mysterious Husband, The: a Tragedy; by Richard Cumberland. Vol. 5.
Natural Son, The: a Comedy; by Richard Cumberland. Vol. 5.
Next-door Neighbours: a Comedy; by Mrs. Inchbald. Vol. 7.
Notoriety: a Comedy; by Frederick Reynolds. Vol. 1.
Percy: a Tragedy; by Hannah More. Vol. 7.
Rage, The: a Comedy; by Frederick Reynolds. Vol. 1.
Rama Droog: a Comic Opera; by James Cobb. Vol. 6.
School for Arrogance, The: a Comedy; by Thomas Holcroft. Vol. 4.
School for Prejudice, The: a Comedy; by Thomas Dibdin. Vol. 4.
School for Wives, The: a Comedy; by Hugh Kelly. Vol. 9.
Secrets worth knowing: a Comedy; by Thomas Marston. Vol. 3.
Seduction: a Comedy; by Thomas Holcroft. Vol. 4.
Speculation: a Comedy; by Frederick Reynolds. Vol. 2.
Time's a Tell-tale: a Comedy; by Henry Siddons. Vol. 10.
Trip to Scarborough: a Comedy; by Richard Brinsley Sheridan. Vol. 7.
Votary of Wealth, The; a Comedy; by J. G. Holman. Vol. 3.
Werter: a Tragedy; by F. Reynolds. Vol. 3.
What is She? a Comedy; by Mrs. Charlotte Smith. Vol. 10.
Which is the Man? a Comedy; by Mrs. Cowley. Vol. 10.
Who wants a Guinea? a Comedy; by George Colman, the younger. Vol. 3.
Wife of Two Husbands, The: a Musical Drama; by James Cobb. Vol. 6.
Will, The: a Comedy; by Frederick Reynolds. Vol. 1.
Wise Man of the East, The: a Comedy; by A. F. F. Kotzebue. Vol. 7.
Zorinski: a Play; by Thomas Morton. Vol. 5.

MODERN TRAVELLER (THE). [*See* CONDER, J.] D 11 P 1–33

MOENS (W. J. C.) English Travellers and Italian Brigands: a Narrative of Capture and Captivity. 2 vols. 8vo. Lond., 1866. D 7 Q 15, 15

MOERIS ATTICISTA de Vocibus Atticis et Hellenicis, e recensione et cum Notis Joh. Hudsoni accedit Timaei Sophistæ Lexicon vocum Platonicarum. 12mo. Lipsiæ, 1756. K 11 S 45

MOFFAT (JOHN S.) Lives of Robert and Mary Moffat, With Portraits, Maps, and Illustrations. 8vo. Lond., 1885.   C 10 U 27

MOFFAT (ROBERT). Missionary Labours and Scenes in Southern Africa. 8vo. Lond., 1842.   D 2 S 2

MOFFAT (ROBERT AND MARY). Lives of Robert and Mary Moffat ; by their Son, John S. Moffat. With Portrait. 8vo. Lond., 1885.   C 10 U 27

MOFFITT (A.), L.R.C.P., &c. Papers on Blood-poisoning, Typhoid, Typhus, Scarlatina, and other Zymotic Diseases, &c., prevalent in New South Wales, and their Treatment ; with special Notes on Dr. Day's Ozone Treatment of Scarlatina and Smallpox, and on his own Treatment of Typhoid to the Present Date. 8vo. Sydney, 1878.*   MA 2 S 45
Another copy. (Pam. Co.) 8vo. Sydney, 1878.
       A 16 U 23

MOGG (E. S.) Postal-district and Cab-fare Map, London and its Environs. With Index. (Sheet.) Fol. Lond., 1859.   D 33 Q 9 ‡

MOGGRIDGE (J. T.), F.L.S., &c. Harvesting Ants and Trap-door Spiders: Notes and Observations on their Habits and Dwellings. 8vo. Lond., 1873.   A 14 T 29

MOHAN LAL. Travels in the Panjab, Afghanistan, and Turkistan, to Balk, Bokhara, and Herat, and a Visit to Great Britain and Germany. 8vo. Lond., 1846.   D 4 T 21

MOHL (MME. MARY); her Salon and her Friends : a Study of Social Life in Paris ; by Kathleen O'Meara. 8vo. Lond., 1885.   C 8 Q 33

MOHL (PROF. JULIUS). Biographical Essay. [See MÜLLER, PROF. F. MAX.]   C 3 P 6

MOHR (EDWARD). To the Victoria Falls of the Zambesi; translated from the German, by "N. D'Anvers" [Mrs. Nancy R. E. Bell]. Illustrated. 8vo. Lond., 1876.   D 2 Q 3

MOHS (PROF. FREDERICK). Characters of the Classes, Orders, Genera and Species ; or, the characteristic of the Natural History System of Mineralogy. 8vo. Edinb., 1820.   A 9 T 37

MOIR (DAVID MACBETH), M.D. Life of Mansie Wauch, Tailor in Dalkeith ; written by himself. 12mo. Edinb., 1845.   J I T 1
Memoir of John Galt. [See GALT, J.]
Poetical Works of; edited by Thomas Aird; with a Memoir of the Author. 2 vols. 12mo. Edinb., 1860.   K 8 P 26, 27
Sketches of the Poetical Literature of the past Half-Century. 2nd ed. 12mo. Edinb., 1852.   J 12 S 14

MOIR (GEORGE). The Thirty Years' War. [See SCHILLER, J. C. F. VON.]   K 10 Q 6, 7

MOJSISOVICS VON MOJSVÁR (EDMUND). Die Dolomit-Riffe von Südtirol und Venetien. 8vo. Wein, 1879.   A 9 T 20

MOLAND (LOUIS). Œuvres complètes de Molière. [See MOLIÈRE, J. B. DE.]

MOLBECH (C.) Dansk-Dialect-Lexikon, indeholdende Ord, Udtryk og Talemaader of den danske Almues Tungemaal i. 8vo. Kiobenhavn, 1841.   K 12 R 3
Dansk Ordbog indeholdende det danske Sprogs Stammeord tilligemed afledede og sammensatte Ord, efter den nuværende Sprogbrug forklarede i. 2 vols. (in 1) roy. 8vo. Kiobenhavn, 1859.   K 14 U 3

MOLÉ (FRANÇOIS RENÉ). Mémoires de. [See BARRIÈRE, J. F., 6.]   C 1 T 6

MOLESWORTH (GUILFORD L.), C.E. Pocket-book of Useful Formulæ and Memoranda for Civil and Mechanical Engineers. 21st ed., revised and enlarged Ob. 18mo. Lond., 1884.   K 18 P 2

MOLESWORTH (ROBERT), VISCOUNT. Franco-Gallia; or, an Account of the Ancient Free State of France. [See HOTOMAN, F.]   B 9 P 22

MOLESWORTH (RT. HON. SIR WILLIAM), BART. Speech in the House of Commons on Tuesday, 25th July, 1848, on Colonial Expenditure and Government. 8vo. Lond., 1848.   MF 2 T 1
Speech in the House of Commons on Tuesday, 25th June, 1849, for a Royal Commission to inquire into the Administration of the Colonies. 8vo. Lond., 1849.   MF 2 T 1
Speeches in the House of Commons during the Session of 1850, on the Bill for the better Government of the Australian Colonies. 8vo. Lond., 1850.*   MF 2 T 1
Speech in the House of Commons on the 10th of April, 1851, for a Reduction of the Colonial Expenditure of the United Kingdoms. 8vo. Lond., 1851.   MF 2 T 1
Speech on the Discontinuance of Transportation to Van Diemen's Land. 8vo. Lond., 1851.   MF 2 T 1
Speech in the House of Commons on Friday, 5th March, 1853, for the Second Reading of the Clergy Reserves of Canada Bill. 8vo. Lond., 1853.   MF 2 T 1
Tracts on the Ballot. No. 4. Speech in the House of Commons, June 13, 1854. 8vo. Lond., 1854. MJ 2 R 21
Observations on the Speech on Colonial Expenditure. [See DANSON, J. T.]
English Works of Thomas Hobbes, now first collected. [See HOBBES, T.]

MOLESWORTH (REV. WILLIAM NASSAU), M.A. History of England, 1830–74. Library ed. 3 vols. 8vo. Lond., 1876.   B 5 R 13–15
History of the Church of England, from 1660. 8vo. Lond., 1882.   G 7 R 1

MOLESWORTH v. MOLESWORTH. Full Report of the Trial. Tried at the Supreme Court, Melbourne. 8vo. Melb., 1864.   MF 2 S 1

MOLEVILLE (A. F. BERTRAND DE). [See BERTRAND DE MOLEVILLE, A. F., MARQUIS DE.]

MOLIERE (JEAN BAPTISTE POQUELIN). Dramatic Works; rendered into English, by Henri van Laun; with a prefatory Memoir, introductory Notices, Appendices, and Notes. 6 vols. roy. 8vo. Edinb., 1875–76. H 2 T 8–13

Oeuvres complètes. Nouvelle éd., avec Biographie par Louis Moland. 7 vols. roy. 8vo. Paris, 1863–64. H 2 T 1–7

MOLINA (JUAN IGNATIO), S.J. Geographical, Natural, and Civil History of Chili. 2 vols. 8vo. Middletown (Conn.), 1808. B 1 S 34, 34

MOLL (HERMAN). New and Correct Map of the Whole World. Fol. Lond., 1719. D 33 P 1 ‡
Atlas Geographus; or, a compleat System of Geography, ancient and modern. 5 vols. sm. 4to. Lond., 1711–17. D 9 T 16–20

MOLLEN (G.) Travels in the Interior of Africa to the sources of the Senegal and Gambia, in the year 1818. 4to. Lond., 1820. D 19 P 25 ‡

MOLLER (DR. GEORGE). Essay on the origin and progress of Gothic Architecture, from the 8th to the 16th Centuries. 8vo. Lond., 1824. A 7 P 42
Memorials of German-Gothic Architecture. 8vo. Lond., 1836. A 2 S 18
Denkmäler der deutschen Baukunst. Imp. fol. Leipzig, 1821. A 1 P 7 ‡

MOLLETT (JOHN W.), B.A. Meissonier: a Biography. (Great Artists). 8vo. Lond., 1881. C 3 T 35
Rembrandt. (Great Artist.) 8vo. Lond., 1879. C 3 T 40
Sir David Wilkie. (Great Artists.) 8vo. Lond., 1881. C 3 T 34
Watteau. (Great Artists.) 8vo. Lond., 1883. C 3 T 39
Illustrated Dictionary of Words used in Art and Archaeology. 8vo. Lond., 1883. K 18 P 26
Etched Examples of Paintings, old and new; with Notes. Fol. Lond., 1885. A 23 It 8 ‡
Modern Etchings of Celebrated Painters; with an Essay. 4to. Lond., 1883. A 8 U 13

MOLLOY (I. O.) Index nominum et Vocabulorum Hibernicorum quae in I. C. Zeutti Grammatica Celtica reperiuntur. [*See* ZEUSS, I. C.]

MOLLOY (J. FITZGERALD). Royalty restored; or, London, under Charles II. With an Etching and Portraits. 2 vols. 8vo. Lond., 1885. B 3 R 17, 18
Life and Adventures of Peg Woffington. 2nd ed. 2 vols. 8vo. Lond., 1885. C 2 R 35, 36
Famous Plays; with a Discourse on the Playhouses of the Restoration. 8vo. Lond., 1886. J 9 S 19

MOLTKE (FIELD-MARSHALL HELLMUTH), COUNT VON. Poland: an Historical Sketch. Authorized Translation, with a Biographical Notice by Emma S. Buchpeim. 12mo. Lond., 1885. B 7 S 39

MOMBERT (REV. J. I.), D.D. English Versions of the Bible: a Hand-book, with copious Examples, illustrating the Ancestry and Relationship of the several Versions, and Comparative Tables. 8vo. Lond., 1883. G 7 Q 28

Five Books of Moses. [*See* TYNDALE, W.]

MOMMSEN (DR. THEODOR). Oskische Studien. Mit Nachträge. 8vo. Berlin, 1845–46. K 13 P 14
History of Rome; translated by the Rev. W. P. Dickson, D.D. 4 vols. 8vo. Lond., 1868. B 11 T 25–28
Römische Geschichte. 5 vols. 8vo. Berlin, 1881–85. B 11 V 9–13
Nachträge zu den Oskische Studien. 8vo. Berlin, 1846. K 13 P 14

MONAHAN (VERY REV. JOHN CANON), D.D. Records relating to the Diocese of Ardagh and Clonmacnoise. 8vo. Dublin, 1886. G 2 Q 19

MONBODDO (JAMES BURNETT), LORD. Of the Origin and Progress of Language. 6 vols. 8vo. Edinb., 1774. K 16 T 10–15

MONCEAUX (FRANÇOIS DE). Ecclesiæ Christianæ veteris Britannicæ incvnabvla Regia. 12mo. Tournay, 1614. Libr.

MONCEL (THÉODORE DU), VICOMTE. [*See* DU MONCEL, T., VICOMTE.]

MONCKHOVEN (D. VAN). Popular Treatise on Photography, the Stereoscope, and Photographic Optics. 2nd ed. 12mo. Lond., 1867. A 17 P 27

MONCRIEFF (ASCOTT ROBERT HOPE). Famous Historical Scenes from three Centuries: Pictures of Celebrated Events from the Reformation to the end of the French Revolution. 8vo. Lond., 1878. B 14 Q 12

MONCRIEFF (W. T.) Giovanni in London; or, the Libertine Reclaimed: an Operatic Extravaganza. (Cumberland's Eng Theatre.) 12mo. Lond., 1829. H 2 Q 14
Monsieur Tonson: a Farce. (Cumberland's Eng. Theatre.) 12mo. Lond., 1829. H 2 Q 18
Rochester; or, King Charles the Second's Merry Days: a Musical Comedy. (Cumberland's Eng. Theatre.) 12mo. Lond., 1829. H 2 Q 22
The Spectre Bridegroom: or, a Ghost in Spite of Himself. (Cumberland's Eng. Theatre.) 12mo. Lond., 1829. H 2 Q 18
The Somnambulist; or, the Phantom of the Village: a Dramatic Entertainment. (Cumberland's Eng. Theatre.) 12mo. Lond., 1829. H 2 Q 18
Tom and Jerry: an Operatic Extravaganza. (Cumberland's Eng. Theatre.) 12mo. Lond., 1829. H 2 Q 19
Van Diemen's Land: an Operatic Drama, in three Acts. 12mo. Lond. (n.d.) MH 1 P 14

MONCRIF (FRANÇOIS AUGUSTIN PARADIS DE). Les Contes, etc. [*See* CABINET DES FÉES, 25, 32.]

MONEY. Return of the Quantity of Dollars imported into New Soutı Wales in the years 1821–23, on account of Government. (Parl. Docs. 5.) Fol. Lond., 1824. MF 4‡

How the Banks make Money scarce and dear; the Remedy; the Banks and tıeir Stability; by "Sigma." 8vo. Melı., 1871. MF 1 Q 3

MONEY (LIEUT.-COL. EDWARD). Cultivation and Manufacture of Tea. 4th ed. 8vo. Lond., 1883. A 1 S 22

The Trutı about America. 12mo. Lond., 1886. D 3 P 3

MONEY (ROBERT COTTON). On the Cıaracteristic Differences between European and Oriental Literature: a Prize Essay. 8vo. Lond., 1822. J 11 V 11

MONEY (WALTER), F.S.A. First and Second Battles of Newbury, and the Siege of Donnington Castle during the Civil War, A.D. 1643–46. 8vo. Lond., 1881. B 5 U 19

MONGE (GASPARD), COMTE DE PÉLUSE. Géométrie Descriptive; augmentée d'une Tıéorie des Ombres et de la Perspective, etc.; par B. Brisson. 4to. Paris, 1820. A 10 V 15

MONGEZ (ANTOINE). Iconograpıie Ancienne. [*See* VISCONTI, E. Q.] B 12 P 11–17‡

MONGREDIEN (AUGUSTUS). Free Trade and Englisı Commerce. 12mo. Lond., 1881. F 5 S 49

Anotıer copy. (Pam. Jc.) 8vo. Lond., 1881. F 6 P 10

History of the Free-Trade Movement in England. 18th tıousand. 12mo. Lond., 1881. F 2 P 26

Anotıer copy. 25th tıousand. 12mo. Lond., 1887. F 2 P 20

The Western Farmer of America. (Pam. Je.) 8vo. Lond., 1880. F 6 P 10

MONITOR (THE). 3 vols. fol. Sydney, 1826–28. ME

Anotıer copy, 1826, 1827, 1836. Fol. Sydney, 1826–36. ME

[*See* SYDNEY MONITOR.]

MONK (GEN. GEORGE), DUKE OF ALBEMARLE. [*See* ALBEMARLE, GEN. GEORGE MONK, DUKE OF.]

MONK (RT. REV. JAMES HENRY), D.D., BISHOP OF GLOUCESTER AND BRISTOL. Life of Rieıard Bentley, D.D.; witı an Account of ıis Writings, &c. 2 vols. 8vo. Lond., 1833. C 10 R 17, 18

MONKHOUSE (W. COSMO). Studies of Sir Edwin Landseer, R.A.; witı a History of ıis Art-Life. Illustrated. Roy. 4to. Lond., 1877. A 23 R 6 ‡

Pictures by Sir Edwin Landseer, R.A.; witı Descriptions. [*See* LANDSEER, SIR E.] A 23 R 7 ‡

Turner. (Great Artists.) 8vo. Lond., 1879. C 3 T 33

Turner's Rivers of England. [*See* TURNER, J. M. W.] D 5 R 20 ‡

3 U

MONNIER (REV. JOSEPH FELICIEN), S.M. Memoir of the Life of the late Rev. Josepı Monnier Translated from the Frencı [by W. A. Duncan]. 8vo. Sydney, 1876. MC 1 P 39

MONOD (MME. WILLIAM). Cinquante Années de la Vie d'un Peuple; ou, les Iles Sandwicı transformées par le Cıristianisme. 12mo. Toulouse, 1873. MD 3 Q 50

MONRO (ALEXANDER). New Brunswick; witı a brief Outline of Nova Scotia, and Prince Edward Island: tıeir History, Civil Divisions, Geograpıy, and Productions; witı Statistics. 8vo. Halifax, N.S., 1855. D 3 U 32

MONRO (DAVID ŁINNING), M.A. Grammar of the Homeric Dialect. (Clar. Press.) 8vo. Oxford, 1882. K 20 U 2

MONRO (GEORGE). Despatcıes of. [*See* GOWER, G. G. L., EARL.] B 8 U 25

MONSTRELET (ENGUERRAND DE). Cıronicles of: containing an Account of the Cruel Civil Wars between the Houses of Orleans and Burgundy, &c.; translated by T. Joınes. 5 vols. 4to. Lond., 1809. B 10 R 12–16†

Anotıer copy. 2 vols. roy. 8vo. Lond., 1840. B 7 V 2, 3

MONTAGNE (CAMILLE). Plants Cellulaires. [*See* DUMONT D'URVILLE, CAPT. J. S. C.]

MONTAGU (ALGERNON), JUDGE. Case of. [*See* TASMANIA.]

MONTAGU (BASIL), M.A. Selections from the Works of Taylor, Latimer, Hall, Milton, Barrow, Soutı, Brown, Fuller, and Bacon. 4th ed. 12mo. Lond., 1834. G 10 P 15

MONTAGU (MRS. ELIZABETH). A Lady of the Last Century; illustrated in her unpublisıed Letters; witı a Biograpıical Sketcı, and a Cıapter on Blue-stockings, by Dr. [Joın] Doran, F.S.A. 8vo. Lond., 1873. C 10 Q 33

MONTAGU (GEORGE). Dictionary of Englisı Birds; reprinted from Montagu's Ornitıological Dictionary. [*See* NEWMAN, E.]

MONTAGU (GEORGE). Fourtı Duke of Mancıester. Correspondence of the Hon. Horace Walpole witı George Montagu. [*See* WALPOLE, HON. H.]

MONTAGU (JOHN). Statistical Returns of Van Diemen's Land, from 1824–39, compiled from Official Records. (Parl. Docs., 18.) Fol. Hobart, 1839. MF 4 ‡

MONTAGU (MARY WORTLEY), LADY. Letters and Works of; edited by Lord Wharncliffe. 3 vols. 8vo. Lond., 1837. C 4 V 8–10

MONTAGU (ROBERT), LORD Recent Events, and a Clue to tıeir Solution. 8vo. Lond., 1886. F 7 Q 16

MONTAGU (R. W.) [*See* MAGINN, W.]

MONTAGUE (FRANCIS CHARLES), M.A. Local Government and Taxation. [*See* RATHBONE, W.]

MONTAIGNE (MICHEL EYQUEM DE). Essays of, in three Books; with marginal Notes and Quotations, and an Account of the Author's Life; made English by Charles Cotton, Esq. 4th ed. 3 vols. 8vo. Lond., 1711.
J 2 S 8–10

Essays of; translated by Charles Cotton; with some Account of the Life of Montaigne; edited by W. C. Hazlitt. 3 vols. 8vo. Lond., 1877. J 2 S 11–13

Essais de. Nouvelle édition, avec les notes de tous les Commentateurs choisies et complétées par J. V. Le Clerc. 4 vols. roy. 8vo. Paris, 1865–66. J 17 T 24–27

Montaigne, the Essayist: a Biography; by J. Bayle St. John. 2 vols. 12mo. Lond., 1858. C 4 S 24, 25

MONTALEMBERT (CHARLES FORBES), COMTE DE. On Constitutional Liberty : a Picture of England painted by a Frenchman. 8vo. Lond., 1858. F 4 Q 22

The Monks of the West, from St. Benedict to Bernard. 7 vols. 8vo. Edinb., 1861–79. G 4 P 18–24

Oeuvres de. 9 vols. 8vo. Paris, 1860–68. J 16 U 1–9
1–3. Discours, 1831–52.
4–5. Oeuvres Polémiques et Diverses.
6. Mélanges d'Art et de Littérature.
7–8. Histoire de Sainte Elisabeth de Hongrie.
9. Oeuvres Polémiques et Diverses.

MONTALEMBERT (MARC RÉNÉ), MARQUIS DE. Engineer Studies. [*See* LLOYD, E. M.]

MONTANA. [*See* UNITED STATES OF AMERICA.]

MONTANO (G. B.) Architettura con diversi Ornamenti cavati dall' antico dati in luce da Calisto Ferrante. 2nd ed. Fol. Roma, 1636. A 23 R 28 ‡

MONTCALM DE ST. VERAN (LOUIS JOSEPH), MARQUIS DE. Montcalm and Wolfe ; by Francis Parkman. 2 vols. 8vo. Lond., 1884. C 5 S 21, 22

Another copy. 6th ed. 8vo. Lond., 1885. C 5 S 23, 24

MONTEAGLE (THOMAS SPRING RICE), LORD. Australia : The Substance of three Speeches made in the House of Lords, on the Australian Government Bill. 8vo. Lond., 1850. MF 3 P 7

MONTEFIORE (J. L.) Catechism of the Rudiments of Political Economy. (Pam. 10.) 12mo. Sydney, 1861. MJ 2 R 2

MONTEFIORE (SIR MOSES), BART. Centennial Biography; with Extracts from Letters and Journals, by Lucien Wolf. With Portrait. 8vo. Lond., 1884. C 5 S 29

MONTEIRO (JOACHIM JOHN). Angola and the River Congo. 2 vols. 8vo. Lond., 1875. D 1 Q 3, 4

MONTEIRO (J. M. C.), AND GAMITTO (A. C. P.) Journey to Cazembe. [*See* AFRICA.] D 1 V 26

MONTEIRO (MARIANA). Legends and Popular Tales of the Basque People ; with Illustrations in Photogravure, Harold Copping. Sm. 4to. Lond., 1887. B 13 T 38

MONTESQUIEU (CHARLES DE SECONDAT), BARON DE. De l'Esprit des Loix. 2 vols. 8vo. Edinb.,1750. F 12 P 18, 19

Spirit of Laws; translated from the French, by Thomas Nugent, LL.D.; to which are prefixed a Memoir of the Life and Writings of the Author, by Jean le R. d'Alembert. 2 vols. 8vo. Lond., 1823. F 7 S 4, 5

Œuvres complètes de. Roy. 8vo. Paris, 1835. J 15 V 26

Pensées diverses. [*See* LAROCHEFOUCAULD, F., DUC DE.]

MONTFAUCON (BERNARD DE). Les Monumens de la Monarchie Françoise, qui comprennent l'Histoire de France, avec les Figures de chaque Regne que l'Injure des Tems a epargnées. 5 vols. fol. Paris, 1729–33.
B 18 U 17–21 ‡

Antiquities of Italy ; being the Travels of the Learned and Reverend Bernard de Montfaucon, from Paris through Italy, in the Years 1698–99. 2nd ed., revised by John Henley, M.A. Fol. Lond., 1725. B 18 U 8 ‡

Antiquity explained and represented in Sculptures ; translated into English, by David Humphreys, M.A. 5 vols. fol. Lond., 1721–22. B 18 U 1–5 ‡

Supplement [to the above]. 5 vols. (in 2) fol. Lond., 1725. B 18 U 6, 7 ‡

MONTFORT (SIMON DE). Earl of Leicester. [*See* LEICESTER, S. DE MONTFORT, EARL OF.]

MONTGOMERY (JAMES). Practical Detail of the Cotton Manufacture of the United States of America, &c. 8vo. Glasgow, 1840. A 11 R 22

MONTGOMERY (JAMES). Journal of Voyages and Travels; by the Rev. D. Tyerman, and G. Bennet. [*See* TYERMAN, REV. D.]

Lectures on Poetry and General Literature, delivered at the Royal Institution, 1830–31. 8vo. Lond., 1833.
J 5 Q 8

Poetical Works of. 4 vols. 12mo. Lond., 1828. H 8 P 33–36

Memoirs of the Life and Writings of ; by John Holland and Everett. 7 vols. 8vo. Lond., 1854–56. C 4 U 13–19

Lives of the most Eminent Literary and Scientific Men of Italy, &c. [*See* SHELLEY, MARY W.] K 1 S 29–31

MONTGOMERY (ROBERT), M.A. Luther : a Poem. 12mo. Lond., 1842. H 8 P 19

Omnipresence of the Deity : a Poem. 3rd ed. 8vo. Lond., 1828. H 8 Q 6

MONTGON (L'ABBÉ CHARLES ALEXANDRE DE). Mémoires de. 12mo. Lausanne, 1752–53. C 2 R 6–13

MONTH (THE): an Australian Journal; edited by Frank Fowler. Vols. 1, 2. 8vo. Sydney, 1857–58. ME 3 P

MONTH (THE): a Catholic Magazine and Review. Vols. 11 24, 26 54. 8vo. Lond., 1871–85. E

MONTHLY MAGAZINE (THE); edited by J. A. Heraud. Vol. 6, No. 3. (Pam. G.) 8vo. Lond., 1841. ME 3

MONTHLY MESSENGER (THE), and Missionary Record of the Presbyterian Churci of Victoria. Vol. I, No. 6. 8vo. Melh., 1881. MG 1 Q 39

MONTHLY REVIEW (THE): a Periodical Work and Literary Journal. Witi Indices. 251 vols. 8vo. Lond., 1749–1844. E 2, 79

MONTHOLON (GEN. CHARLES TRISTAN), MARQUIS DE. History of the Captivity of Napoleon at St. Helena. 4 vols. 8vo. Lond., 1846. C 8 T 29–32

MONTI (VINCENZO), CAVALIERE. Dialogii. Vol. I. 12mo. Milano, 1827. H 2 P 10

Poemetti varii. 12mo. Milano, 1826. H 8 P 20

Poesie varie. 12mo. Milano, 1826. H 8 P 20

Satire di A. Persio Flacco traduzione. [*See* PERSIUS FLACCUS, A.]

Tragedie. 12mo. Milano, 1826. H 3 P 10

MONTPENSIER (ANNE MARIE LOUISE D'ORLEANS), DUCHESSE DE. Memoirs of Mademoiselle Montpensier; written by herself; edited from the French. 3 vols. 8vo. Lond., 1848. C 3 R 46–48

MONTPENSIER (ANTOINE MARIE PHILIPPE LOUIS D'ORLEANS), DUC DE. Mémoires de. [*See* BARRIÈRE, J. F., 9.] C 1 T 9

MONTROSE (JAMES GRAHAM), MARQUIS OF. Memoirs of; translated from the Latin of the Rt. Rev. George Wishart, afterwards Bishop of Edinburgh. 8vo. Edinb., 1819. C 5 T 16

Memoirs of; by James Grant. 12mo. Lond., 1858. C 2 P 30

Life and Times of Montrose; by Mark Napier. With Portraits. 12mo. Edinb., 1840. C 4 V 14

Montrose; by Lady Violet Greville. 8vo. Lond., 1886. C 6 S 30

MONT-SERRAT (E. DE). Voyage Géologiques dans le Republiques de Guatemala et de Salvador. [*See* DOLLFUS, A.] A 23 S 1 ‡

MONTUCLA (JEAN ETIENNE). Histoires des Mathématiques. 4 vols. 4to. Paris, 1799–1802. A 10 V 1–4
[*See* HUTTON, C.] A 16 S 6

MOODIE (MRS. SUSANNAH). Life in the Clearings *versus* the Bush. 8vo. Lond., 1853. D 4 P 18

MOODIE (D. C. F.) Poems; by "Austral." 8vo. Adelaide, 1873. MH 1 S 24

MOODIE (J. W. D.) Ten Years in South Africa. 2 vols. 8vo. Lond., 1835. D 2 R 3, 4

MOODY (DWIGHT LYMAN). Hymns and Solos used by Moody and Sankey. [*See* CAMPBELL, REV. P.]

MOODY (F. W.) Lectures and Lessons on Art. 8vo. Lond., 1873. A 7 S 26

MOODY (HENRY). Antiquarian and Topographical Sketches of Hampshire. 12mo. Winchester, 1846. B 4 R 23

MOODY (J. J.) Borough Electors' Manual and Municipal Councillors' Vade Mecum. 8vo. Melb., 1863. MF 3 Q 23

MOODY (SOPHY). What is your Name? a popular Account of the Meanings and Derivations of Christian Names. 8vo. Lond., 1863. K 19 Q 3

MOON (GEORGE WASHINGTON), F.R.S.L. The Revisers' English (with Photographs of the Revisers): a Series of Criticisms. 12mo. Lond., 1882. K 16 P 16

Ecclesiastical English: a Series of Criticisms; being Part 2 of the Revisers' English. 8vo. Lond., 1886. K 16 P 17

MOONEY (E. M.) The Two Power, and other origina. Tales, with Miscellaneous Pieces in Prose and Verse! 8vo. Melb., 1870. MJ 1 R 30

MOONSHINE: a Comedy, in five Acts. 8vo. Lond. (n.d.) H 7 T 31

MOOR (J. H.) Notices of the Indian Archipelago and adjacent Countries. 4to. Singapore, 1837. D 5 V 9

MOORCROFT (WILLIAM), AND TREBECK (GEORGE). Travels in the Himalayan Provinces of Hindustan and the Panjab; in Ladakh and Kashmir; in Peshawar, Kabul, Kunduz, and Bokhara; from 1819 to 1825. 2 vols. 8vo. Lond., 1841. D 6 S 4, 5

MOORE (CHARLES). F.L.S., &c. On the Woods of New South Wales. (Pam. Cn.) 8vo. Sydney, 1871. MA 2 V 8

Another copy. 8vo. Sydney, 1871. MJ 2 R 14

Census of the Plants of New South Wales. Roy. 8vo. Sydney, 1884. MA 1 U 16

MOORE (EDWARD). The Foundling: a Comedy. (New Eng. Theatre.) 12mo. Lond., 1786. H 4 P 28

Another copy. (Bell's Brit. Theatre.) 18mo. Lond., 1792. H 2 P 11

Another copy. (Brit. Theatre.) 12mo. Lond., 1808. H 1 P 14

The Gamester: a Tragedy. (New Eng. Theatre.) 12mo. Lond., 1776. H 4 P 19

Another copy. (Bell's Brit. Theatre.) 18mo. Lond., 1792. H-2 P 11

Another copy. (Brit. Theatre.) 12mo. Lond., 1808. H 1 P 14

Another copy. [*See* BRIT. DRAMA.]

Life and Poems of. [*See* CHALMERS, A.; *and* JOHNSON, S.]

MOORE (FRANCIS PEREGRINE). Vox Stellarum; or, the Sydney Almanack, for the year of our Lord, 1829. 8vo. Sydney, 1829. MJ 2 Q 2

MOORE (FRANK). American Eloquence: a Collection of Speeches and Addresses, by the most eminent Orators of America; with Biographical Sketches and Illustrative Notes. 2 vols. roy. 8vo. N. York, 1857. F 8 T 10, 11

MOORE (GEORGE), M.D. Man and his Motives. 3rd ed. 12mo. Lond., 1852. G 9 P 38

Use of the Body in relation to the Mind. 2nd ed. 8vo. Lond., 1847. G 7 Q 15

Power of the Soul over the Body, considered in relation to Health and Morals. 3rd ed. 8vo. Lond., 1846. G 7 Q 16

MOORE (GEORGE FLETCHER), B.L., &c. Descriptive Vocabulary of the Language in Common use amongst the Aborigines of Western Australia. 12mo. Lond., 1842. MK 1 P 26

Diary of Ten Years Eventful Life of an Early Settler in Western Australia ; and also, a Descriptive Vocabulary of the Language of the Aborigines. 8vo. Lond., 1884. MD 4 U 5

Extracts from the Journal and Letters of. Edited by Martin Doyle. 18mo. Lond., 1884. MD 5 P 17

MOORE (HELEN). [Life of] Mary Wollstonecraft Shelley. 12mo. Philad., 1886. C 2 Q 47

MOORE (H. KEATLEY), B.A. Autobiography of Friedrich Froebel. [*See* FROEBEL, F.] C 2 Q 15

MOORE (JAMES). List of the principal Castles and Monasteries in Great Britain. 8vo. Lond., 1798. B 7 Q 9

MOORE (JENNIE). Lessons in Figure Painting in Water Colours. [*See* MACARTHUR, BLANCHE.] A 7 S 1

MOORE (JOHN HAMILTON). Moore's Navigation improved. [*See* KERIGAN, T.]

MOORE (JOSEPH), JUN., F.R.G.S. The Queen's Empire ; or, Ind and her Pearl. Illustrated. 8vo. Philad., 1886. D 6 R 19

MOORE (J. J.) Moore's Almanack and Hand-book for New South Wales ; with a Supplement for Victoria, 1853-72, 1874-86. 31 vols. (in 14) 12mo. Sydney, 1853-86. ME 4 S

Outlines of Australian and General Geography, for the use of Junior Classes in Schools and for Private Tuition. 18mo. Sydney, 1885. MD 1 T 18

New Road Map of New South Wales, for 1885-86. [With Alphabetical Key.] 8vo. Sydney, 1885-86. MD 5 P 2 ‡

MOORE (J. S.) Friendly Sermons to the Protectionist Manufacturers of the United States. 8vo. New York, 1877. F 6 Q 16

MOORE (JOSEPH SHERIDAN). Newtown Ejectment Case, Hon. Dem. Devine v. Wilson and others ; with Historical Introduction, Ground Plans, Notes of Evidence, Appendices, &c. 8vo. Sydney, 1857. MF 1 Q 5

Another copy. MJ 2 Q 14

Capt. Cook and Botany Bay. With Illustrations. 8vo. Sydney, 1863. MD 1 V 9

Spring Life Lyrics. 12mo. Sydney, 1864.* MH 1 R 13

University Reform, its Urgency and Reasonableness : an Oration. 12mo. Sydney, 1865. MJ 2 R 1

MOORE (JOSEPH SHERIDAN)—*continued.*

Byron : his Biographers and Critics. (Pam. J.) 8vo Sydney, 1869. MJ 1 T 38

The Case of Dr. F. Beer. [*See* BEER, DR. F.]

[*See* AUSTRALIAN FREEMASON'S MAGAZINE.]

MOORE (JOSEPH WEST). Picturesque Washington ; Pen and Pencil Sketches : a Souvenir of the American Capital. Roy. 8vo. Providence, 1884. D 3 U 27

MOORE (NORMAN), B.A. Life of Charles Waterton. [*See* WATERTON, C.) A 14 S 44

Concise Irish Grammar. [*See* WINDISCH, PROF. W. O. E.]

MOORE (THEOPHILUS). Marriage Customs and Modes of Courtship of the Various Nations of the Universe. 2nd ed. 12mo. Lond., 1820. B 14 P 51

MOORE (REV. THOMAS). History and Topography of Devonshire, from the Earliest Period to the Present ; with a series of Views, by William Deeble. 4to. Lond., 1829. B 16 Q 14 ‡

MOORE (THOMAS), F.L.S., &c. Epitome of Gardening ; with an Introductory Chapter on the Principles of Horticulture, by Maxwell T. Masters, M.D., &c. 8vo. Edinb., 1881. A 1 Q 9

Ferns of Great Britain and Ireland. Edited by John Lindley, Ph.D. Atlas fol. Lond., 1855. A 21 P 17 ‡

Orchid Album. [*See* WARNER, R.]

Treasury of Botany. [*See* LINDLEY, PROF. J.]

MOORE (THOMAS). Poetical Works of, complete in one volume. Roy. 8vo. Lond, 1865. H 5 U 34

Lalla Rookh : an Oriental Romance. 18th ed. 12mo. Lond., 1836. H 8 P 29

Life and Death of Lord Edward Fitzgerald. 2 vols. 8vo. Lond., 1831. C 3 P 11, 12

Memoirs of the Life of the Rt. Hon. Richard Brinsley Sheridan. 2 vols. 8vo. Lond., 1827. C 5 U 22, 23

Fudge Family in Paris. Edited by "Thomas Brown, the Younger." 12mo. Lond., 1818. H 8 P 30

Fudges in England : a Sequel to the "Fudge Family in Paris" ; by "Thomas Brown, the Younger." 12mo. Lond., 1835. H 8 P 32

Replies to the Letters of the Fudge Family in Paris. Edited by "Thomas Brown, Esq." 12mo. Lond., 1818. H 8 P 31

Travels of an Irish Gentleman in search of a Religion. 2 vols. 12mo. Lond., 1833. G 9 Q 7, 8

Letters and Journal of Lord Byron ; with Notices of his Life. 3rd ed. 3 vols. 8vo. Lond., 1833. C 8 S 21-23

History of Ireland. (Lard. Cab. Cyclo.) 4 vols. 12mo. Lond., 1835-46. K 1 T 28-31

Lalla Rookh : an Oriental Romance. 3rd ed. 8vo. Lond., 1847. H 8 V 22

Memoirs, Journal, and Correspondence ; edited by the Rt. Hon. Lord John Russell. 8 vols. 8vo. Lond., 1853-56. C 5 P 7-14

MOORE (REV. T. W.) Treatise and Hand-book of Orange Culture in Florida, Louisiana, and California. 3rd ed. 12mo. N. York, 1884. A 1 P 49

MOORE (W. H.) Notes relating to Comets. [*See* MILLS, G.]

MOOST'UJAB KHAN BUHADOOR (NUWAB). Life of Hafiz ool-Moolk, Hafiz Rehmut Khan; written by his Son, and entitled Goolistan-i-Rehmut. Abridged and translated by C. Elliott. 8vo. Lond., 1831. C 9 V 21

MORANT (GEO. FRANCIS). Game Preservers and Bird Preservers, which are our Friends? 8vo. Lond., 1875. A 14 Q 38

MORAVIAN MISSION. Facts relating to the. Published by the Committee of the Melbourne Association, in aid of the Moravian Mission to the Aborigines of Australia. 8vo. Melb., 1860. MA 1 R 2

MOORMAN. [*See* CARNEGIE, W.]

MORDAUNT V. MORDAUNT. The Mordaunt Divorce Case: an Official Report. 8vo. Lond., 1870. F 13 R 1

MORE (HANNAH). Works of. 11 vols. Lond., 1830. J 6 S 21-31

Strictures on the Modern System of Female Education. 13th ed. 2 vols. 8vo. Lond., 1826. G 17 Q 21, 22

Life of; with Notices of her Sisters; by H. Thompson, M.A. 8vo. Lond., 1838. C 4 P 13

Percy: a Tragedy. [*See* MODERN THEATRE, 7.]

Life and Works. [*See* BRITISH POETS 3.]

MORE (SIR THOMAS) Utopia. Translated from the Latin, by Rapse Robinson, A.D. 1551; with Notes and Introduction by Rev. T. F. Dibdin. 2 vols. (in 1) 12mo. Lond., 1808. F 15 Q 6

Utopia; or, the Happy Republic: a Philosophical Romance, in two books; translated into English by Gilbert Burnet, D.D. 8vo. Glasgow, 1743. F 15 Q 5

Life of. [*See* MACKINTOSH, SIR J.] C 1 Q 34

The Oxford Reformer. [*See* SEEBOHM, F.]

MORE (LUCIEN), ET MÉO (MONS). La Navigation de Plaisance. Roy. 8vo. Paris, 1878. A 2 Q 1

MOREAU LE JEUNE (JEAN MICHEL). Monument du Costume, physique et moral, de la fin du 18e Siècle; text par N. E. Restif de la Bretonne. Fol. Paris, 1876. A 2 P 13 ‡

MOREHEAD (CHARLES), M.D., &c. Memorials of the Life and Writings of Rev. Robert Morehead, D.D.; edited by his Son. 8vo. Edinb., 1875. C 4 R 19

MOREHEAD (REV. ROBERT), D.D. Memorials of the Life and Writings of; edited by his Son, Charles More-head, M.D., &c. 8vo. Edinb., 1875. C 4 R 19

MOREHEAD (R. A. A.) Some Words for, and to the Capitalists and Shareholders in Banks and other Moneyed Companies, connected with the Colony of New South Wales. (Pam. 10.) 8vo. Sydney, 1843. MJ 2 Q 2

Another copy. (Pam. 15.) 8vo. Sydney, 1843. MJ 2 Q 5

MOREIRA (NICOLAU J.), M.D. United States [Philadelphia] International Exhibition: Historical Notes concerning the Vegetable Fibres, exhibited by Severino L. da C. Leite. (Pam. Co.) 8vo. New York, 1876. A 16 U 23

MOREL (CONWAY). Authority and Conscience: a Free Debate on the tendency of Dogmatic Theology, and on the Characteristics of Faith. 8vo. Lond., 1871. G 7 Q 20

MORRELL-FATIO (ALFRED). Grammaire de la langue Romanes. [*See* DIEZ, F.]

MORELET (CHEV. ARTHUR). Travels in Central America; including Account of some Regions unexplored since the Conquest. 8vo. Lond., 1871. D 3 Q 13

MORELL (SIR CHARLES). Les contes des Génies. [*See* CABINET DES FÉES, 29, 30.]

MORELL (J. D.), M.A., &c. Analysis of Sentences explained and systematised; with Exposition of the Fundamental Laws of Syntax. New edition. 8vo. Lond., 1881. K 11 U 12

Essentials of English Grammar and Analysis. New ed 12mo. Lond., 1871. K 11 U 11

Introduction to Mental Philosophy, on the Inductive Method. 8vo. Lond., 1862. G 2 Q 12

Compendium of Italian History. [*See* BOSCO, G.] B 18 Q 9 ‡

MORELL (J. R.) Manual of the History of Philosophy. [*See* TENNEMANN, W. G.]

MORELL (DR. THOMAS). Ainsworth's Latin Dictionary. [*See* AINSWORTH, R.] K 16 S 12

MORELLI (GIOVANNI). Italian Masters in German Galleries: a Critical Essay on the Italian Pictures in the Galleries of Munich, Dresden, Berlin. 8vo. Lond., 1883. A 8 P 30

MORÉRI (LOUIS). Le Grand Dictionnaire historique; ou, le Mélange curieux de l'Histoire sacrée et profane. 10 vols. roy. fol. Paris, 1759. K 22 R 11-20 ‡

MORESBY (CAPT. JOHN), R.N. New Guinea and Polynesia: Discoveries and Surveys in New Guinea and the d'Entrecasteaux Islands. Illustrated. 8vo. Lond., 1876. MD 2 V 26

MORFIT (CAMPBELL), M.D., &c. Practical Treatise on the Manufacture of Soaps. 8vo. Lond., 1871. A 11 U 11

MORFORD (HENRY). Morford's Short-Trip Guide to Europe [1878]. 12mo. New York, 1878. D 7 P 48

MORGAN (AUGUSTUS DE). [*See* DE MORGAN, A.]

MORGAN (G. BLACKER). The Tombs, Monuments, &c. visible in St. Paul's Cathedral. [*See* FISHER, MAJOR P.] B 4 V 13

MORGAN (HENRY J.) Canadian Parliamentary Companion for 1875-76. 2 vols. 18mo. Ottawa, 1876. E1,78

MORGAN (JOHN). Life and Adventures of William Buckley. 8vo. Hobart, 1852.* MC 1 P 7

The Wreath : a Gardener's Manual. [*See* DICKINSON, J.]

MORGAN (JAMES APPLETON), A.M. Macaronic Poetry ; collected, with an Introduction. 12mo. New York, 1872. H 8 P 30

MORGAN (LEWIS H.), LL.D. The American Beaver and its Works. 8vo. Philad., 1868. A 15 P 13

Kamilaroi and Kurnai. [*See* PISON, L.]

MORGAN (SIR RICHARD F.), KNT. Forty Years of Official and Unofficial Life in an Oriental Crown Colony ; being the Life of Sir R. F. Morgan, Knt., by William Digby, C.I.E. 2 vols. 8vo. Madras, 1879. C 5 V 23, 24

MORGAN (SYDNEY), LADY. Italy : Journal of her Residence in that Country. 3 vols. 8vo. Lond., 1824. D 8 U 15-17

Book without a Name. [*See* MORGAN, SIR T. C.]

France in 1829-30. 2nd ed. 2 vols. 8vo. Lond., 1831. B 8 T 33, 34

Life and Times of Salvator Rosa. 2 vols. 8vo. Lond., 1824. C 9 U 30, 31

Woman and her Master. 2 vols. 8vo. Lond., 1840. F 6 S 37, 38

MORGAN (THOMAS). Romano-British Mosaic Pavements : a History of their Discovery, &c. Roy. 8vo. Lond., 1886. B 4 V 16

MORGAN (SIR THOMAS CHARLES), M.D. Sketches of the Philosophy of Life. 8vo. Lond., 1818. A 12 U 12

Sketches of the Philosophy of Morals. 8vo. Lond., 1822. G 4 R 8

MORGAN (SIR T. CHARLES AND LADY). Book without a Name. 2 vols. 8vo. Lond., 1841. J 4 R 9, 10

MORGAN (HON. WILLIAM). Speech [on Federation.] [*See* JEFFERIS, REV. J.]

MORGANS (WILLIAM). Manual of Mining Tools. (Weale.) 12mo. Lond., 1871. A 17 Q 20

Atlas [to above.] (Weale.) 4to. Lond., 1871. A 9 V 23

MORGHEN (RAPHAEL). Engraved Works of. [*See* HALSEY, F. R.] K 9 P 7 †

MORIER (JAMES). Journey through Persia, Armenia, and Asia Minor, to Constantinople, in the years 1808-9. 4to. Lond., 1812. D 11 Q 6 †

Adventures of Hajji Baba of Ispahan. 2nd ed. 3 vols. 12mo. Lond., 1824. J 7 Q 14-16

Zohrab, the Hostage. 3 vols. 8vo. Lond., 1832. J 4 P 17-19

MORIN (ARTHUR). Salubrité des Habitations : Manuel Pratique du Chauffage et de la Ventilation. 8vo. Paris, 1874. A 2 S 35

MORISON (JAMES COTTER), M.A. Gibbon. (Eng. Men of Letts.) 8vo. Lond., 1879. C 1 U 16

Macaulay. (Eng. Men of Letts.) 8vo. Lond., 1882. C 1 U 25

MORLEY (PROF. HENRY). Of English Literature in the Reign of Victoria ; with a Glance at the Past. 12mo. Leipsic, 1881. B 23 P 5

Jerome Cardan : the Life of Girolamo Cardano, of Milan, Physician. 2 vols. 8vo. Lond., 1854. C 3 Q 1, 2

Palissy, the Potter : the Life of Bernard Palissy, of Saintes. 2nd ed. 8vo. Lond., 1855. C 3 T 20

Sketches of Russian Life before and during the Emancipation of the Serfs. 8vo. Lond., 1866. D 9 Q 1

Journal of a London Playgoer, from 1851 to 1866. 12mo. Lond., 1866. J 7 Q 12

Memoirs of Bartholomew Fair ; with Facsimile Drawings, engraved upon wood by the Brothers Dalziel. 8vo. Lond., 1859. B 7 P 7

English Writers. Vols. 1, Vol. 2, Part 1. (*All published.*) 8vo. Lond., 1864-67. B 21 U 23, 24

Tables of English Literature. Imp. 4to. Lond., 1870. B 22 S 2

English Literature. [*See* CASSELL'S LIB. OF ENGLISH LIT.] J 2 U 1-2

[*See* BOSWELL, J.] C 8 V 16-20

MORLEY (JOHN), M.A., &c. Life of Richard Cobden. 2 vols. 8vo. Lond., 1881. C 10 S 26, 27

Burke. (Eng. Men of Letts.) 8vo. Lond., 1879. C 1 U 5

Critical Miscellanies. [1st and 2nd series.] 2 vols. 8vo. Lond., 1871-77. J 12 R 16, 17

Struggle for National Education. 2nd. ed. 8vo. Lond., 1873. G 17 Q 5

Rousseau. 2 vols. 8vo. Lond., 1873. C 9 R 14, 15

Voltaire. 8vo. Lond., 1872. C 8 P 25

On Compromise. 8vo. Lond., 1874. G 2 Q 26

English Men of Letters. [*See* ENGLISH MEN OF LETTERS.]

MORLEY (H. FOSTER), M.A., &c. Outlines of Organic Chemistry. 8vo. Lond., 1886. A 5 S 16

MORNING CHRONICLE (THE). 4 vols. fol. Sydney, 1845-48. ME

MORNING HERALD (THE), October 5, 1819. Fol. Lond., 1819. E

MORPHET (J. C.) Catalogue of the Parliamentary Library of South Australia. [*See* SOUTH AUSTRALIA.]

MORPHY (PAUL). Morphy's Games of Chess ; being the best games played by the distinguished champion in Europe and America ; with analytical and critical Notes, by J. Löwenthal. 8vo. Lond., 1878. A 16 P 14

MORRELL (Capt. James), Jun. Narrative of Four Voyages, to the South Sea, North and South Pacific Ocean, Chinese Sea, Ethiopic and Southern Atlantic Ocean, Indian and Antarctic Ocean, 1822–31. 8vo. New York, 1832. D 10 S 22

MORRILL (James). Sketch of a Residence among the Aboriginals of Northern Queensland for Seventeen Years. (Pam. Ad.) 8vo. Brisbane, 1863. MD 1 V 9

MORRIS (Augustus). Observations on Railroads in the United States. (Pam. Cj.) 8vo. Sydney, 1877. MA 2 V 7

Tobacco: its Culture and the Curing of its Leaf. (Pam. Ch.) 8vo. Sydney, 1877. MA 2 Q 29

Another copy. 8vo. Sydney, 1877. MJ 2 R 14

MORRIS (Augustus), and BYRON (John). New South Wales : its Progress, Present Condition, and Resources. With detailed Statistical Information. 8vo. Sydney, 1886. MF 1 R 42

MORRIS (Capt. Charles). Anecdote Life of. [*See* Timbs, J.]

MORRIS (C. S.), HAYTER (T. S.), and BARRY (George J.) Commercial and Trades Directory of South Australia, 1882–83. 8vo. Adelaide, 1882. ME 12 T

MORRIS (D. F. van Braam). Reizen naar de Noordkust van Nederlandsch Nieuw-Guinea. 8vo. 'sGravenhage, 1884. MD 3 V 8

MORRIS (Edward Joy). Notes of a Tour through Turkey, Greece, Egypt, and Arabia Petræa to the Holy Land. 8vo. Aberdeen, 1847. D 1 T 4

MORRIS (Rev. F. O.), B.A. Natural History of British Moths, accurately delineating every known species, with the English as well as Scientific Names. 4 vols. roy. 8vo. Lond., 1872. A 13 V 10–13

History of British Butterflies. 3rd ed. Roy. 8vo. Lond., 1870. A 13 V 20

History of British Birds. 2nd ed. 6 vols. roy. 8vo. Lond., 1870. A 13 V 14–19

Series of Picturesque Views of Seats of the Noblemen and Gentlemen of Great Britain and Ireland. 6 vols. 4to. Lond. (n.d.) D 9 R 12–17 †

MORRIS (George S.), M.A., &c. Kant's Critique of Pure Reason : a Critical Exposition. 12mo. Chicago, 1882. G 7 Q 21

MORRIS (Henry). Descriptive and Historical Account of the Godavery District in the Presidency of Madras. 8vo. Lond., 1878. B 10 U 23

MORRIS (Rev. Henry C. E.) "Let no man deceive you": an Answer to "Napoleon III, the Monarch of the World." 12mo. Melb., 1866. MJ 2 P 31

MORRIS (Prof. John), F.G.S. Fossil Flora of the Gondwana System. [*See* India]

Catalogue of British Fossils. 2nd ed. 8vo. Lond., 1854. A 9 S 23

Cambrian and Silurian Fossils. [*See* Salter, J. W.]

Treasury of Knowledge and Library of Reference. [*See* Maunder, S.] K 9 T 15

MORRIS (Prof. John), F.G.S., and JONES (Prof. T. Rupert), F.G.S. Geology. 1st series. Heads of Lectures on Geology and Mineralogy, in several courses, from 1866 to 1870. 8vo. Lond., 1870. A 9 Q 16

MORRIS (Lewis), M.A. Epic of Hades; in three Books. 10th ed. 12mo. Lond., 1880. H 8 P 26

MORRIS (Malcolm). Book of Health. 3rd ed. Roy. 8vo. Lond., 1884. A 12 V 9

MORRIS (Mowbray). Hunting. [*See* Beaufort, H. C. F. S., Duke of.] A 17 U 31

MORRIS (Maurice O'Connor). Rambles in the Rocky Mountains ; with a Visit to the Gold Fields of Colorado. 8vo. Lond., 1864. D 3 R 5

MORRIS (Rev. Richard), LL.D. [*See* Chaucer, G.]

MORRIS (Rev. Richard), LL.D., and SKEAT (Rev. Walter William), M.A., &c. Specimens of Early English : Part 2, New ed. (Clar. Press.) 12mo. Oxford, 1873. H 8 P 44

MORRIS (William). Hopes and Fears for Art : Five Lectures delivered in Birmingham, London, and Nottingham, 1878–81. A 8 P 25

Lectures on Art. [*See* Art.]

MORRISON (A. F.), M.A., &c. Sketches in Russia; by "A Rambling Victorian." 8vo. Melb., 1886. MD 6 P 34

MORRISON (A. J. W.), B.A. Works of Schiller. [*See* Schiller, J. C. F. von.] B 7 S 40

History of Ancient Philosophy. [*See* Ritter, Dr. H.]

[*See* Goethe, J. W. von.] C 1 S 27, 28

MORRISON (Rev. J.), D.D. Election : the Doctrine stated ; Objections to the Doctrine considered ; and its Moral Tendency ascertained. 8vo. Launceston, 1838 MG 1 P 1

MORRISON (Rev. John). Australia as it is; or, Facts and Features, Sketches and Incidents of Australia and Australian Life; with Notices of New Zealand; by "A Clergyman." 8vo. Lond., 1867.* MD 4 R 20

Australia in 1866 ; or, Facts and Features, Sketches and Incidents of Australia and Australian Life ; with Notices of New Zealand; by "A Clergyman." 2nd ed. 12mo. Lond., 1868. MD 4 R 22

MORRISON (Joseph Robert). What should the Government do for Australia? 8vo. Lond., 1851. MF 1 Q 3

Another copy. 8vo. Lond., 1851 MJ 2 Q 16

MORRISON (REV. R.), D.D. Dictionary of the Chinese Language. 2 vols. roy. 8vo. Shanghae., 1865.
K 13 S 23, 24

Memoirs of the Life and Labours of; compiled by his Widow, Mrs. R. Morrison; with Critical Notices of his Chinese Works, by Samuel Kidd. 2 vols. 8vo. Lond., 1839.
C 7 R 45, 46

MORRISON (MRS. R.) Memoirs of the Life and Labours of the Rev. R. Morrison, D.D.; compiled by his Widow. 2 vols. 8vo. Lond., 1839.
C 7 R 45, 46

MORRISON (LIEUT. R. J.), R.N., "ZADKIEL." [*See* LILLY, W.]

MORRISON (WILLIAM CHARLES). The *Carl* Massacre. [*See* SEARLE, G. S.]
MD 1 U 21

MORRISON (W. E. W.) Science Manual. [*See* CURNOW, J.]
MA 2 V 13

MORRISON (W. FREDERIC), M.D., &c. Aldine Centennial History of New South Wales. Illustrated. 2 vols. 4to. Sydney, 1888.*
MB 3 P 9, 10 †

MORRITT (J. B. S.) Vindication of Homer and of the Ancient Poets and Historians, who have recorded the Siege and Fall of Troy, in answer to two late Publications of Mr. [J.] Bryant. With a Map and Plates. (Pam.) 4to. York, 1798.
B 18 R 13 ‡

[*See* BRYANT, J.]
B 18 R 13 ‡

MORSE (EDWARD S.), PH.D. Japanese Homes and their Surroundings. Illustrated. Roy. 8vo. Lond., 1886.
D 5 V 27

MORSE (PROF. SAMUEL FINLEY BREESE). Life of. [*See* JEANS, W. T.]
C 2 S 14

MORSELLI (PROF. HENRY), M.D., &c. Suicide: an Essay on Comparative Moral Statistics. 8vo. Lond., 1881.
G 7 Q 30

MORT (THOMAS S.) The Question of Government Guaranteed Railway Shares, considered with reference to their being made transferable to Bearer, and thereby rendered available as a Circulating Medium. 8vo. Sydney, 1854.
MF 3 P 2

Another copy. 8vo. Sydney, 1854.
MJ 2 Q 9

Life Lessons from the Career of Thomas S. Mort. [*See* JEFFERIS, REV. J.]
MG 1 Q 35

MORTIMER (LIEUT. GEORGE). Observations and Remarks made during a Voyage in the Brig *Mercury*, commanded by John Henry Cox, Esq. 4to. Lond., 1791.
MD 7 P 6 †

Waarneemingen en Aanmerkingen aangetekend geduurende eene Reize in het Brigantijn-schip de *Mercurius*, onder bevel van John Henry Cox, Schildknaap. Uit het Engelsch vertaald door J. D. Pasteur. 8vo. Leyden, 1893.
MD 4 U 43

MORTIMER (MRS. M.) Night of Toil; or, a Familiar Account of the Labours of the First Missionaries in the South Sea Islands. 12mo. Lond., 1838.
MD 3 P 22

Another copy. 3rd ed. 12mo. Lond., 1849.
MD 3 P 23

MORTON (EDWARD), M.B. Travels in Russia, and a Residence at St. Petersburg and Odessa, in the years 1827–29. 8vo. Lond., 1830.
D 8 T 34

MORTON (REV. J.) Memoirs of Dr. J. Leyden. [*See* LEYDEN, DR. J.]

MORTON (JOHN), M.A. Natural History of Northamptonshire; with some Account of the Antiquities. Fol. Lond., 1712.
A 15 S 5 ‡

MORTON (JOHN). Nature and Property of Soils, &c. 8vo. Lond., 1842.
A 1 R 12

MORTON (SAMUEL GEORGE), M.D. Types of Mankind. [*See* NOTT, J. C.]
A 2 P 19

MORTON (THOMAS). The Children in the Wood: an Opera. (Cumberland's Eng. Theatre.) 12mo. Lond., 1829.
H 2 Q 22

Cure for the Heartache: a Comedy. (Brit. Theatre.) 12mo. Lond., 1808.
H 1 P 25

Education: a Comedy. (Cumberland's Eng. Theatre.) 12mo. Lond., 1829.
H 2 Q 11

The School of Reform: a Comedy. (Brit. Theatre.) 12mo. Lond., 1808.
H 1 P 25

Secrets worth Knowing: a Comedy. [*See* MODERN THEATRE, 3.]

The Slave: an Opera. (Cumberland's Eng. Theatre.) 12mo. Lond., 1829.
H 2 Q 14

Speed the Plough: a Comedy. (Brit. Theatre.) 12mo. Lond., 1808.
H 1 P 25

Town and Country: a Comedy. (Cumberland's Eng. Theatre.) 12mo. Lond., 1829.
H 2 Q 2c

The Way to get Married: a Comedy. (Brit. Theatre.) 12mo. Lond., 1808.
H 1 P 25

Zorinski: a Play. [*See* MODERN THEATRE, 3.]

MORWOOD (VERNON S.) Our Gipsies in City, Tent, and Van. 8vo. Lond., 1885.
A 1 W 34

MORYSON (FYNES). Itinerary; containing his Ten Yeeres Travell. Fol. Lond., 1617.
D 7 V 35

MOSCHELES (MRS. CHARLOTTE). Life of Moscheles; with Selections from his Diaries and Correspondence, by his Wife; adapted from the original German, by A. D. Coleridge. With Portrait. 2 vols. 8vo. Lond., 1873.
C 4 S 21, 22

MOSCHELES (IGNATIUS). Life of; with Selections from his Diaries and Correspondence, by his Wife [Mrs. Charlotte Moscheles]; adapted from the German, by A. D. Coleridge. With Portrait. 2 vols. 8vo. Lond., 1873.
C 4 S 21, 22

MOSCHUS. Idylls of. [*See* THEOCRITUS.]

Translation of. [*See* CHALMERS, A.]

Works of. [*See* HESIOD.]

MOSELEY (REV. H.), M.A., &c. Illustrations of Mechanics. 12mo. Lond., 1839. A 11 Q 4

Treatise on Mechanics, applied to the Arts; including Statics and Hydrostatics. 2nd ed. 8vo. Lond., 1839. A 11 S 19

MOSELEY (H. N.), M.A., &c. Structure and Relations of certain Corals. (Roy. Soc. Pubs., 2.) 4to. Lond., 1876. A 11 P 3 †

Structure of a Species of Millepora, occurring at Taiti, Society Islands. (Roy. Soc. Pubs., 4.) 4to. Lond., 1877. A 11 P 5 †

Structure of the Stylasteridæ, a Family of the Hydroid Stony Corals. (Croonian Lecture. Roy. Soc. Pubs., 6.) 4to. Lond., 1879. A 11 P 7 †

Notes by a Naturalist on the *Challenger*; being an Account of various Observations made during the Voyage of H.M.S. *Challenger* round the World, in the years 1872–76. 8vo. Lond., 1879. A 16 S 23

MOSELEY (JOSEPH). Political Elements; or, the Progress of Modern Legislation. 8vo. Lond., 1852. F 6 T 10

MOSENTHAL (JULIUS DE). [*See* DE MOSENTHAL, J.]

MOSES (HENRY). Collection of Antique Vases, Altars, Pateræ, Tripods, &c.; with Plates, and Historical Essays. 4to. Lond., 1814. A 8 Q 5

MOSHEIM (JOHANN LORENTZ VON). Ecclesiastical History, from the Birth of Christ to the beginning of the 18th Century; translated from the Latin, by A. Maclaine, D.D. Imp. 8vo. Lond., 1833. G 2 T 4

Historia Tartarorum Ecclesiastica. 4to. Helmstadi, 1741. G 2 Q 3

Institutiones Historiæ Christianæ maiores. Saecvlvm primvm. 4to. Helmstadii, 1739. G 2 Q 4

Institvtionvm Historiæ Ecclesiasticæ Antiqvæ et Recentioris Libri Qvatvor. 4to. Helmstadii, 1755. G 3 V 9

MOSS (MISSES CELIA AND MARION). Romance of Jewish History. 3 vols. 8vo. Lond., 1840. J 8 Q 32–34

MOSS (F. J.) A Planter's Experience in Fiji. Illustrated. (Pam. Aa.) 8vo. Auckland, 1870. MD 1 V 9

A Month in Fiji; by "A Recent Visitor." 8vo. Melb., 1868. MD 1 U 21

MOSS (JAMES). Farnham, and other Poems. 8vo. Melb., 1882. MH 1 R 31

MOSSMAN (SAMUEL). New Japan, the Land of the Rising Sun; its Annals during the past twenty years. With a Map. 8vo. Lond., 1873. B 12 S 12

General Gordon's Private Diary of his Exploits in China, amplified. With Portraits and Map. 8vo. Lond., 1885. C 2 S 15

Gold Regions of Australia. 12mo. Lond., 1852.* MD 1 S 8

3 x

MOSSMAN (SAMUEL)—*continued.*
Voice from Australia. 2nd ed. 8vo. Lond., 1852. MD 4 U 41

Narrative of the Shipwreck of the *Admella*, Intercolonial Steamer, on the Southern Coast of Australia; with a Map of the Coast and a Sketch of the Wreck at time of Rescue, by J. Fawthrop. 12mo. Melb., 1859.* MB 2 P 12

Our Australian Colonies; their Discovery, History, Resources, and Prospects. 12mo. Lond., 1866.* MD 2 R 4

MOSSMAN (SAMUEL), AND BANISTER (THOMAS). Australia visited and revisited. 8vo. Lond., 1853.* MD 1 W 6

MOSTYN (HARRY P.) [*See* STUD-BOOK OF NEW SOUTH WALES, THE.]

MOTHER'S GRAVE (THE). Mother's Grave, and other original Poems; by A. G. and C. C. 12mo. Melb. (n.d.) MH 1 S 21

MOTHERWELL (WILLIAM). Minstrelsy, Ancient and Modern; with an Historical Introduction and Notes. Sm. 4to. Paisley, 1873. H 5 U 10

MOTLEY (J. LOTHROP), D.C.L., &c.: a Memoir; by O. W. Holmes. 8vo. Lond., 1878. C 1 U 50

Democracy, the Climax of Political Progress and the Destiny of Advanced Races: an Historical Essay. Australian ed. 8vo. Melb., 1869. MF 1 Q 3

Life and Death of John of Barneveld, Advocate of Holland; with a View of the primary causes and movements of the Thirty Years' War. With Illustrations. 2 vols. 8vo. Lond., 1874. C 2 V 27, 28

History of the United Netherlands, from the Death of William the Silent to the Twelve Years' Truce---1609. 4 vols. 8vo. Lond., 1869. B 12 T 6–9

Rise of the Dutch Republic: a History. 8vo. Lond., 1869. B 12 T 2

Rise of the Dutch Republic: a History. 3 vols. 8vo. Lond., 1875. B 12 T 3–5

MOTRAYE (A. DE LA). [*See* LA MOTRAYE, A. DE.]

MOTT (VALENTINE). Travels in Europe and the East. Roy. 8vo. Lond., 1842. D 8 U 19

MOTTE (ANDREW). Mathematical Principles of Natural Philosophy. [*See* NEWTON, SIR I.] A 3 T 1–3

MOTTE (JEANNE DE LUIZ), COUNTESS DE VALOIS DE LA. [*See* LA MOTTE, JEANNE DE LUIZ, COUNTESS DE VALOIS DE.]

MOTTE (STANDISH). Outlines of a System of Legislation for securing protection to the Aboriginal Inhabitants of all Countries colonized by Great Britain. 8vo. Lond., 1840. MA 1 R 17

MOTTEUX (PETER ANTHONY). [*See* CERVANTES SAAVEDRA M. DE.]

MOUAT (SURG.-MAJOR FREDERICK J.) Adventures and Researches among the Andaman Islanders. 8vo. Lond., 1863. D 6 Q 2

MOUBRAY (BONINGTON). Treatise on [the Breeding, &c., of Poultry]. [*See* DICKSON, W. B.] A 14 P 67

MOUHOT (HENRI). Travels in the Central Parts of Indo-China (Siam), Cambodia, and Laos, 1858–60. With Illustrations. 2 vols. 8vo. Lond., 1864. D 5 S 1, 2

MOULDY (MALACHI), F.S.A. [*See* STONEHENGE.]

MOULE (HORACE M.) Christian Oratory : an Inquiry into its History during the first Five Centuries. 8vo. Camb., 1859. G 7 Q 17

MOULTON (RICHARD G.), M.A. Shakespeare as a Dramatic Artist : a Popular Illustration of the Principles of Scientific Criticism. 8vo. Oxford, 1885. J 1 U 19

MOULTRIE (JOHN). Poems by. New ed., with Memoir by the Rev. Prebendary Coleridge. 2 vols. 8vo. Lond., 1876. H 8 Q 4, 5

MOUNT (HENRY CLARKE). The Carl Massacre. [*See* SEARLE, G. S.] MD 1 U 21

MOUNT ALEXANDER GOLD DIGGERS' SONG. Chorus by all the Diggers' in full costume. (Pam. D.) 4to. Mount Alexander, 1852. MJ 2 U 3

MOUNTMORRES (RT. HON. H. R. MORRES), LORD. History of the Principal Transactions of the Irish Parliament, from 1634 to 1666 ; with a Life of the Duke of Ormond. 2 vols. 8vo. Lond., 1792. B 11 Q 26, 27

MOURITZ (J. J.) Port Phillip Almanac and Directory for 1847. 18mo. Meln., 1847. ME 4 P

MOUSSAUD (JEAN MARIE), L'ABBÉ. L'Alphabet Raisonné; ou, Ex-plication de la Figure des Lettres. 8vo. Paris, 1803. C 11 U 50, 51

MOUY (LOUIS AH). The Chinese Question. [*See* CHINESE QUESTION.] MJ 2 R 12

MOXLEY (REV. J. H. SUTTON). An Account of a West Indian Sanatorium, and a Guide to Barbados. 12mo. Lond., 1886. D 3 P 8

MOYLE (J. B.), B.C.L., &c. [*See* JUSTINIANUS.]

MOZART (WOLFGANG AMADEUS). Life of, including his Correspondence ; by Edward Holmes. 8vo. Lond., 1845. C 3 V 32

Letters of (1769–91) ; translated from the Collection of H. Ludwig Nohl, by Lady Wallace. 2 vols. 8vo. Lond., 1865. C 3 V 33, 34

Lives of Haydn and Mozart ; with Observations on Metastasio, &c. Translated from the French of "L. A. C. Bombet" [Marie Henry Beyle]. 2nd ed. 8vo. Lond., 1818. C 5 T 12

MOZART (WOLFGANG AMADEUS)—*continued.*
Life of Mozart ; by Otto Jahn. Translated from the German by Pauline D. Townsend. 3 vols. 8vo. Lond., 1882. C 7 S 19–21

Briefe ; nach den Originalen ; herausgegeben von Ludwig Nohl. 12mo. Salzburg, 1865. C 1 T 39

From Mozart to Mario. [*See* ENGEL, L.] C 4 S 18, 19

MOZIN (ABBÉ), BIBER (J. TH.), AND HÖLDER (M.) Neues vollständiges Wörterbuch der deutschen und französischen Sprache. 2 vols. 4to. Stuttgart, 1811–13. K 13 U 1, 2

Nouveau Dictionnaire Complet, a l'Usage des Allemands et des Français. 2 vols. 4to. Stuttgart, 1811–12. K 13 U 3, 4

MOZLEY (REV. JAMES BOWLING), D.D. Letters of ; edited by his Sister [Miss Anne Mozley.] 8vo. Lond., 1885. C 6 U 19

Eight Lectures on Miracles ; preached before the University of Oxford, in the year 1865. (Bampton Lectures.) 8vo. Lond., 1865. G 15 R 23

MOZLEY (MISS ANNE). Letters of the Rev. J. B. Mozley. [*See* MOZLEY, REV. J. B.]

MOZLEY (REV. THOMAS), M.A. Reminiscences, chiefly of Oriel College and the Oxford Movement. 2 vols. 8vo. Lond., 1882. C 4 P 10, 11

Reminiscences, chiefly of Towns, Villages, and Schools. 2 vols. 8vo. Lond., 1885. G 17 P 6, 7

MRONGOVIUS (CHRISTOPH COELESTIN). Ausführliche Grammatik der polnischen Sprache nebst einem besondern Anbange mit Uebungsstücken zum Uebersetzen. 12mo. Danzig, 1837. K 11 S 43

Anleitung zum Uebersitzen aus dem Polnischen ins Deutsche und aus dem Deutschen ins Polnische. 12mo. Danzig, 1837. K 11 S 43

MUCKLEY (WILLIAM J.) Hand-book for Painters and Art Students on the Character and Use of Colours ; also, short Remarks on the Practice of Painting in Oil and Water Colours. 8vo. Lond., 1880. A 7 Q 32

MUCOR. [*See* CANDLER, S. C.]

MUDIE (CHARLES EDWARD). Stray Leaves. New ed. 12mo. Lond., 1873. H 8 P 21

MUDIE (JAMES). Felony of New South Wales ; being a faithful picture of the Real Romance of Life in Botany Bay. 8vo. Lond., 1837.* MD 4 U 32

MUDIE (ROBERT). China, and its Resources and Peculiarities–Physical, Political, Social, and Commercial. 12mo. Lond., 1840. B 2 P 17

Spring, Summer, Autumn, and Winter. 4 vols. 12mo. Lond., 1837. A 3 R 5–8

The Heavens, Earth, Air, and Sea. 4 vols. 12mo. Lond., 1835–36. A 3 R 1–4

MUDIE (ROBERT)—*continued.*
Picture of India; Geograpıical, Historical, and Descriptive. 2 vols. 12mo. Lond., 1830.　　B 10 Q 8, 9

Featıered Tribes of the Britisı Islands. 2nd ed. 2 vols. 8vo. Lond., 1835.　　A 14 Q 42, 43

Picture of Australia : exıibiting New Holland, Van Diemen's Land, and all the Settlements, from the first at Sydney to the last at the Swan River. 8vo. Lond., 1829.*　　MD 4 T 1

Popular Guide to the Observation of Nature; or, Hints of Inducement to the Study of Natural Productions and Appearances, in tıeir connections and relations. (Cons. Misc., 77.) 18mo. Lond., 1832.　　K 10 R 11

Compendium of Natural Pıilosopıy. [*See* WESLEY, REV. J.]　　K 10 P 21–23

MUELLER (EDUARD). Etymologiscıes Woerterbuch der Engliscıen Spracıe. 2 vols. (in 1) 8vo. Coethen, 1865–67.　　K 13 P 22

MUELLER (SIR FERDINAND VON), BARON, K.C.M.G., &c. Definitions of Rare and ıitıerto undescribed Australian Plants. 8vo. Melı., 1855.　　MA 1 U 3

Botanical Report on the Nortı-Australian Expedition, under the command of A. C. Gregory, Esq. 8vo. Melb., 1857.　　MJ 2 R 9

Fragmenta Phytographiæ Australiæ. Vols. 1–10. 8vo. Melı., 1858–77.*　　MA 1 T 31–40

Plants indigenous to the Colony of Victoria. Vol. 1. Thalamifloræ. Vol. 2. Lithograms. 2 vols. roy. 4to. Melb., 1860–65.　　MA 2 Q 19–20 †

Analytical Drawings of Australian Mosses. Fascicle. (*All published.*) 8vo. Melb., 1864.　　MA 1 T 51

Anotıer copy. 8vo. Melb., 1864.　　MJ 2 R 9

Lecture on Rust and Cereals. 8vo. Sandıurst, 1865.　　MJ 2 R 7

Notes sur la Végétation indigène et introduite de l'Australie; traduit de l'Anglais par E. Lissignol. 8vo. Melb., 1866.　　MJ 2 R 9

Anotıer copy.　　MK 1 R 33

Report on Vegetable Products. 8vo. Melı., 1867.　　MA 1 Q 1

Anotıer copy. 8vo. Melı., 1867.　　MA 1 Q 7

Principal Timber Trees readily eligible for Victorian Industrial Culture. 8vo. Melb., 1871.　　MA 1 Q 1

Forest Culture in its relation to Industrial pursuits : a Lecture. 8vo. Melı., 1871.　　MA 1 Q 1

Descriptive Notes on Papuan Plants. 8vo. Melb., 1875.*　　MA 1 V 1

Select Plants readily eligible for Industrial Culture or Naturalisation in Victoria. 8vo. Melı., 1876.* MA 1 V 5

Anotıer copy.　　MJ 2 R 11

MUELLER (SIR FERDINAND . VON), BARON, K.C.M .G. &c.—*continued.*
Introduction to Botanic Teacıings at the Scıools of Victoria, tırougı references to Leading Native Plants. 8vo. Melb., 1877.*　　MA 1 V 3

Native Plants of Victoria, succinctly defined. Part 1. 8vo. Melb., 1879.　　MA 1 T 53

Report on the Forest Resources of Western Australia. Roy. 4to. Lond., 1879.*　　MA 1 Q 6 ‡

Select Extra-Tropical Plants, readily eligible for Industrial Culture or Naturalisation. 8vo. Sydney, 1881.*　　MA 1 U 1

Eucalyptographia: a Descriptive Atlas of the Eucalypts of Australia and the adjoining Islands. First to the Tentı Decades. 3 vols. roy. 4to. Melı., 1883–84.*　　MA 1 Q 25–27 †

Organic Constituents of Plants and Vegetable Substances, &c. [*See* WITTSTEIN, G. C.]　　MA 1 V 8

Systematic Arrangement of Carpentarian Plants. [*See* LANDSBOROUGH, W.]　　MD 4 P 39

Contribution to the Pıytograpıy of the New Hebrides. [*See* CAMPBELL, F. A.]　　MD 4 Q 30

Flora Australiensis. [*See* BENTHAM, G.]

Distribution of Forest Trees in Victoria. [*See* EVERETT, A.]

The Objects of a Botanic Garden in its Relation to Industries : a Lecture. [*See* MELB. PUB. LIDRARY.]

[*See* WOOLLS, REV. W.]

MÜFFLING (FRIEDRICH FERDINAND KARL), BARON VON. Passages from my Life ; edited, witı Notes, by Colonel Pıilip Yorke, F.R.S. 2nd ed. 8vo. Lond., 1853.　　C 7 U 47

M'UGGE (THEODORE). Switzerland in 1847. Edited by Mrs. Percy Sinnett. 2 vols. 8vo. Lond., 1848.　　B 7 T 15, 16

MUIR (JOHN), D.C.L., &c. Metrical Translations from Sanskrit Writers. 8vo. Lond., 1879.　　H 7 T 23

MUIR (M. M. PATTISON), M.A., &c. Treatise on the Principles of Cıemistry. 8vo. Camb., 1884.　　A 6 P 17

Elements of Tıermal Cıemistry ; by M. M. P. Muir, assisted by D. M. Wilson. 8vo. Lond., 1885.　　A 5 T 12

MUIR (THOMAS). Histoire de la Tyrannie du Gouvernement Anglais, éxercée envers le célèbre Tıomas Muir, Ecossais ; sa Déportation à Botany-Bay, avec une Description. 12mo. Paris, 1798.　　MD 2 P 43

Life of Tıomas Muir, who was tried for Sedition ; witı a full Report of ıis Trial, by Peter Mackenzie. 8vo. Glasgow, 1831.　　MC 1 R 19

MUIR (THOMAS S.) Ecclesiological Notes on some of the Islands of Scotland. 8vo. Edinb., 1885.　　D 7 S 6

MUIR (SIR WILLIAM), K.C.S.I., &c. Annals of the Early Caliphate, from original Sources. With a Map. 8vo. Lond., 1883.   B 10 P 34

Life of Mahomet and History of Islam, to the Era of the Hegira. 4 vols. 8vo. Lond., 1858–61.   C 7 S 43–46

MUIRHEAD (PROF. JAMES), LL.D. Historical Introduction to the Private Law of Rome. 8vo. Edinb., 1886.   F 7 Q 10

MUIRHEAD (JAMES PATRICK), M.A. Life of James Watt; with Selections from his Correspondence. 8vo. Lond., 1858.   C 9 R 45

Origin and Progress of the Mechanical Inventions of James Watt. 3 vols. 8vo. Lond., 1854.   A 11 U 1–3

MULDER (G. J.) Chemistry of Wine; edited by H. Bence Jones, M.D., F.R.S. 12mo. Lond., 1857.   A 5 R 24

MULHALL (MICHAEL G.), F.S.S. Progress of the World in Arts, Agriculture, Commerce, Manufactures, Instruction, Railways, and Public Wealth, since the beginning of the 19th Century. 8vo. Lond., 1880.   F 6 R 25

Balance-Sheet of the World for Ten Years, 1870–80. With twelve coloured Diagrams. 8vo. Lond., 1881.   F 6 P 21

Mulhall's Dictionary of Statistics. 8vo. Lond., 1884.   F 6 R 26

History of Prices since the year 1850. 8vo. Lond., 1886.   F 6 P 1

MULHALL (MICHAEL G. AND E. T.) Hand-book of the River Plate Republics. 8vo. Lond., 1875.   D 3 P 55

MULHALL (MRS. M. G.) Between the Amazon and Andes; or, Ten Year's of a Lady's Travels in the Pampas, Gran Chaco, Paraguay, and Matto Grosso. With Illustrations. 8vo. Lond., 1881.   D 4 P 39

MULL (MATTHIAS). [*See* MILTON, J.]

MULLEN (SAMUEL). The Pilgrim of Beauty, the Cottager's Sabbath, and other Poems. 8vo. Lond., 1815.   H 7 T 22

MÜLLER (CHARLES). Claudii Ptolemaei Geographia. [*See* PTOLOMEUS, C.]   D 12 V 15

Geographi Graeci Minores [et] Tabulae. [Gr. et Lat.] 3 vols. imp. 8vo. Parisiis, 1855–82.   D 19 V 11 13

MÜLLER (PROF. FRIEDRICH). Reise der österreichischen Fregatte Novara um die Erde, 1857–59. Roy. 4to. Wien, 1868.   M A 1 Q 1 †

Grundriss der Sprachwissenschaft. 2 vols. 8vo. Wien, 1876 82.   K 15 Q 24, 25

MÜLLER (FRIEDRICH VON). Characteristics of Goethe. [*See* AUSTIN, MRS. SARAH.]   C 4 Q 12 14

MÜLLER (FRITZ). Facts and Arguments for Darwin; with Additions by the Author. Translated from the German, by W. S. Dallas, F.L.S. With Illustrations. 8vo. Lond., 1869.   A 14 S 13

MÜLLER (PROF. F. MAX.), LL.D., &c. Sacred Books of the East. Translated by various Oriental Scholars. Vols. 1–28. 8vo. Oxford, 1879–86.   G 20 R 1–28

1. The Upanishads. Translated by F. Max. Müller. Part 1. The Khândogya-Upanishad; the Talavakâra-Upanishad; the Aitareya-Aranyaka; the Kaushîtaki-Brâhmana-Upanishad; and the Vâgasaneyi-Samhitâ-Upanishad.

2. The Sacred Laws of the Aryas, as taught in the Schools of Apastamba, Gautama, Vâsishtha, and Baudhâyana. Translated by Georg Bühler. Part 1. Apastamba and Gautama.

3. The Sacred Books of China: the Texts of Confucianism. Translated by James Legge. Part 1. The Shû-King; the Religious Portions of the Shih-King and Hsiâo-King.

4. The Zend-Avesta. Part 1. The Vendîdâd. Translated by James Darmesteter.

5. Pahlavi Texts. Translated by E. W. West. Part 1. The Bundahis, Bahman Yast, and Shâyast Lâ Shâyast.

6. The Qur'ân. Translated E. H. Palmer. Part 1. Chapters 1–16.

7. The Institutes of Vishnu. Translated by Julius Jolly.

8. The Bhagavadgîtâ; with the Sanatsugâtîya and the Anugîtâ. Translated by Kâshinâth Trimbak Telang, M.A.

9. The Qur'ân. Translated by E. H. Palmer. Part 2. Chapters 17–144.

10. The Dhammapada: a Collection of Verses; being one of the Canonical Books of the Buddhists. Translated from the Pâli by F. Max. Müller.

11. Buddhist Suttas. Translated from Pâli by T. W. Rhys Davids. 1. The Mahâ-Parinibbâna Suttanta. 2. The Dhamma-Kakka-Ppavattana Sutta. 3. The Tevigga Suttanta. 4. The Akankheyya Sutta. 5. The Ketokhila Sutta. 6. The Mahâ-Sudassana Suttanta. 7. The Sabbâsava Sutta.

12. The Satapatha-Brâhmana, according to the Text of the Mâdhyandina School. Translated by Julius Eggeling. Part 1, Books 1, 2.

13. Vinaya Texts. Translated from the Pâli by T. W. Rhys Davids and Hermann Oldenberg. Part 1. The Pâtimokkha; the Mahâvagga, I–IV.

14. The Sacred Laws of the Aryas, as taught in the Schools of Apastamba, Gautama, Vâsishtha and Baudhâyana. Translated by Georg Bühler. Part 2. Vâsistha and Baudhâyana.

15. The Upanishads. Part 2. The Katha-Upanishad, the Mundaka-Upanishad, the Taittirîyaka-Upanishad the Brihadâranyaka-Upanishad, the Svetâsvatara-Upanishad, the Prasña-Upanishad, the Maitrâyana-Brâhmana-Upanishad. Translated by F. Max. Müller.

16. The Sacred Books of China: the Texts of Confucianism. Translated by James Legge. Part 2. The Yî-King.

17. Vinaya Texts. Translated from the Pâli by T. W. Rhys Davids and Hermann Oldenberg. Part 2. The Mahâvagga, V–X; the Kullavagga, I–III.

18. Pahlavi Texts. Translated by E. W. West. Part 2. The Dâdistân-î Dînîk and the Epistles of Mânûskîhar.

19. The Fo-sho-hing-tsan-king: a Life of Buddha, by Asvaghosha Bodhisattva. Translated from Sanskrit into Chinese by Dharmaraksha, A.D. 420, and from Chinese into English by Samuel Beal.

20. Vinaya Texts. Translated from the Pâli by T. W. Rhys Davids and Hermann Oldenberg. Part 3. The Kullavagga IV–XII.

21. The Saddharma-Pundarîka; or, the Lotus the True Law. Translated by H. Kern.

22. Gaina Sûtras. Translated from Prâkrit, by Hermann Jacobi. Part 1. The Akâranga Sûtra; the Kalpa Sûtra.

23. The Zend-Avesta. Part 2. The Sîrôzahs, Yasts, and Nyâyis. Translated by James Darmesteter.

24. Pahlavi Texts. Translated by E. W. West. Part 3. Dînâ-î Maînog î Kirad; Sikandgûmânîk Vigâr; Sad Dar.

25. Laws of Manu; translated, with Extracts from seven Commentaries, by G. Bühler.

26. The Satapatha Brâhmana. Translated by J. Eggeling. Part 2, Books 3, 4.

27, 28. The Sacred Books of China: the Texts of Confucianism. Translated by James Legge. Part 3, 4. The Lî Kî, I XLVI.

MÜLLER (Prof. F. Max.), LL.D., &c.—continued.

Memoirs of Baron Stockmar. [See Stockmar, E. von, Baron.] C 3 P 29, 30

Languages of the Seat of War in the East. 2nd ed. 8vo. Lond., 1855. K 15 It 28

Proposals for a Missionary Alphabet, submitted to the Alphabetical Conferences held at the Residence of Chevalier Buisen in January, 1854. 8vo. Lond., 1854. K 13 Q 22

Biographical Essays:—Rammohun Roy. Keshub Chunder Sen. Dayanânda Sarasvati. Bunyiu Nanjio, and Kenjui Kasawara. Colebrooke. Mohl. Buisen and Kingsley. 8vo. Lond., 1884. C 3 P 6

Hymns of the Rig-Veda in the Samhita Text. 8vo. Lond., 1873. G 4 Q 30

Lectures on the Science of Language. 1st and 2nd series. 2 vols. 8vo. Lond., 1866-68. J 10 V 5, 6

Rig-Veda-Sanhita; the Sacred Hymns of the Brahmans, translated and explained. Vol. 1. [All published.] 8vo. Lond., 1869. G 4 Q 31

On the Stratification of Language. (Sir Robert Rede's Lecture.) 8vo. Lond., 1868. K 12 R 33

Sanskrit Grammar for Beginners. 2nd ed. Roy. 8vo. Lond., 1870. K 12 T 21

History of Ancient Sanskrit Literature. 8vo. Lond., 1859. B 10 U 37

Chips from a German Workshop. 4 vols. 8vo. Lond., 1868-75. J 4 S 1-4

First-Fourth Books of the Hitopadesa; containing the Sanskrit Text. 2 vols. roy. 8vo. Lond., 1864-65. J 15 V 24, 25

Hymns of the Rig-Veda, in the Pada Text. 8vo. Lond., 1873. G 4 Q 29

Myths and Songs of the South Pacific. [See Gill, Rev. W. W.] MB 1 Q 27

History of German Literature. [See Scherer, W.]

Lecture on Buddhist Nihilism, delivered before the General Meeting of the Association of German Philologists, 1869. (Pam. 41.) 8vo. Lond., 1869. MJ 2 R 3

Introduction to the Science of Religion: four Lectures. 8vo. Lond., 1873. G 7 Q 11

Selected Essays on Language, Mythology, and Religion. 2 vols. 8vo. Lond., 1881. J 11 S 25, 26

Essays. 4 vols. 8vo. Leipzig, 1869-79. J 17 Q 29-32

Buddha's Dhammapada; or, Path of Virtue. [See Buddhaghosha.]

Outline Dictionary for the use of Missionaries, Explorers, &c. [See Bellows, J.]

Immanuel Kant's Critic of Pure Reason. [See Kant, I.]

MÜLLER (George). Brief Narrative of Facts relative to the New Orphan Houses (for 2,050 Children) on Ashley Down, Bristol. (Pam. Dw.) 8vo. Lond., 1875. MF 3 P 20

MÜLLER (Prof. Hermann). Fertilisation of Flowers. With Illustrations. 8vo. Lond., 1883. A 4 S 10

MÜLLER (Hugo W.), Ph.D., &c. On the Electric Discharge with the Chloride of Silver Battery. [See De la Rue, W.] A 11 P 6 †

MÜLLER (J.) Principles of Physics and Meteorology. 8vo. Lond., 1847. A 3 T 4

MÜLLER (Juan de). Vida del Cid. [See Cid, R. D. de Bivar.]

MÜLLER (Karl Ottfried). History of the Literature of Ancient Greece. (All published.) Vol. 1. 8vo. Lond., 1840. B 9 T 23

History and Antiquities of the Doric Race. From the German. 2nd ed. 2 vols. 8vo. Lond., 1839. B 9 T 21, 22

Introduction to a Scientific System of Mythology. Translated from the German, by John Leitch. 8vo. Lond., 1844. B 14 U 23

Ancient Art and its Remains; or, a Manual of the Archæology of Art. New ed., with numerous Additions, by F. G. Welcker. 8vo. Lond., 1852. A 8 Q 16

Æschylos Eumeniden, Griechisch und Deutsch. [See Æschylus.] J 4 U 2

[See Arrian, F.] B 10 V 9

MÜLLER (Karl Ottfried), and DONALDSON (J. W.) History of the Literature of Ancient Greece. Continued after the Author's Death, by J. W. Donaldson. 3 vols. 8vo. Lond., 1868. B 9 V 21-23

MÜLLER (Salomon), Ph.D., &c. Bijdragen tot de kennis van Nieuw-Guinea. Met Plaaten. (Verhandelingen over de Natuurlijke Geschiedenis der Nederlandsche overzeesche bezittingen.) 2 vols. fol. Leiden, 1839-44. MD 2 P 9, 10 ‡

MÜLLER (Theodor). Australische Kolonisten oder Heute so—Morgen so! Roman. 8vo. Leipsic, 1878. MJ 1 Q 25

MÜLLER (Wilhelm). [See Benecke, G. T.]

MÜLLER (William John). Sketches of the Age of Francis I. Imp. fol. Lond., 1841. A 3 P 20 †

MULLIN (J. P.) Modern Moulding and Pattern-making: a Practical Treatise upon Pattern, Shop, and Foundry Work. 8vo. Lond., 1885. A 11 Q 28

MULLINGER (James Bass), M.A. University of Cambridge, from the Earliest Times to the Royal Injunctions of 1535. 8vo. Camb., 1873. B 6 R 42

University of Cambridge, from the Royal Injunctions of 1535, to the Accession of Charles I. 8vo. Camb., 1884. B 6 R 43

MULLINS (J. D.) Free Libraries and Newsrooms: their Formation and Management. 2nd ed. (Pam.) 12mo. Lond., 1870. K 7 R 18

[See Birmingham Free Libraries.]

MULLINS (James). Jemmy Mullins; or, the Little Irish Sailor Boy; by "One of H.M. Chaplains, N.S. Wales. 12mo. Sydney, 1856. MG 1 P 49

MULOCK (Miss D. M.) [*See* CRAIK, Mrs. DINAH MARIA.]

MULREADY (WILLIAM). Masterpieces of Mulready. Memorials, collected by F. G. Stephens. 4to. Lond., 1867.   A 8 T 23

MULVANY (THOMAS J.), C.E. New Zealand Products and Manufactures. (*Reprinted from the Bay of Plenty Times.*) 8vo. Tauranga, 1880.   MF 1 R 6
[*See* HOPKINS, I.]

MUNCH (P. A.), AND UNGER (C. P.) Oldnorsk Læsebog, med tilhörende Glossarium. 8vo. Christiania, 1847.   K 15 S 29

MUNCKER (THOMAS). [*See* ANTONIUS LIBERALIS.] J 7 S 30

MUNDAY (A.) [*See* STOW, J.]

MUNDEN (JOSEPH SHEPHERD), COMEDIAN. Memoirs of; by his Son. 8vo. Lond., 1844.   C 4 U 20

MUNDY (D. L.) Rotomahana, and the Boiling Springs of New Zealand; with descriptive Notes, by Ferdinand von Hochstetter. Fol. Lond., 1875.   MD 3 U 5-7
Our Antipodes. 3rd ed. 8vo. Lond., 1855.* MD 3 U 14
Another copy. 4th ed. 8vo. Lond., 1857. MD 3 U 17
Wanderungen in Australien und Vandiemensland. Deutsch bearbeitet von Friedrich Gerstäcker. 8vo. Leipsic, 1856.   MD 3 U 16
Pen and Pencil Sketches ; being the Journal of a Tour in India. 2 vols. 8vo. Lond., 1832.   D 6 Q 23, 24

MUNDY (HARRIOT GEORGIANA). Journal of Mary Frampton. [*See* FRAMPTON, MARY.]   C 6 Q 17

MUNDY (CAPT. RODNEY). Narrative of Events in Borneo and Celebes, with the Operations of H.M.S. *Iris.* [*See* BROOKE, SIR J.]   D 4 S 1, 2

MUNGO PARK. [*See* PARK, M.]

MUNICIPAL GAS WORKS. No Shareholder's Dividends ! No Bonuses ! No Extra Offices ! No Director's Fees ! Gas at the net cost of production ; Cheap House Lighting ! Cheap Street Lighting ! Cheap Heating ! Published by the Municipal Association of New South Wales for the use of the Municipal Corporations. 8vo. Sydney, 1886.   MA 2 S 2

MUNK (WILLIAM), M.D., &c. Roll of the Royal College of Physicians of London. 2nd. ed. 3 vols. 8vo. Lond., 1878.   C 10 U 44-46

MUNN (WILLIAM AUGUSTUS), F.R.H.S., &c. The Honey Bee. [*See* BEVAN, E.]

MUNRO (H. A. J.) [*See* LUCRETIUS CAIUS, T.]

MUNRO (JAMES), H.M.E.I., &c. New Gaelic Primer, also, a copious Vocabulary. 3rd ed. 12mo. Edinb., 1862.   ⟨ 11 S 37
Practical Grammar of the Scottish Gaelic; in eight Parts. 2nd ed. 12mo. Edinb., 1843.   ⟨ 11 S 36

MUNRO (NATHANIEL). Mining Surveyors' Map of the District of Sandhurst. 8vo. Melb. (n.d.)   MA 2 P 23

MUNRO (ROBERT), M.A., &c. Ancient Scottish Lake-Dwellings, or Crannogs. 8vo. Edinb., 1882. B 13 R 1

MUNRO (MAJ.-GEN. SIR THOMAS), BART., &c., GOVERNOR OF MADRAS. Selections from his Minutes and other Official Writings. Edited, with Memoir, by Sir Alexander J. Arbuthnot, K.C.S.I., &c. 2 vols. 8vo. Lond., 1881.   C 8 Q 44, 45
Life of ; by the Rev. G. R. Gleig, M.A., &c. 2 vols. 8vo. Lond., 1831.   C 8 Q 46, 47
Another copy. (H. and C. Lib.) 8vo. Lond., 1849.   J 8 P 35

MUNRO (SURG.-GEN. W.), M.D., &c. Reminiscences of Military Service with the 93rd Sutherland Highlanders. 8vo. Lond., 1883.   C 10 U 43

MÜNSTER (SEBASTIAN). [*See* EDEN, R.]

MUNTENAU (GABRIEL). Deutsch-romanisches Wörterbuch. [*See* BARITZ, G.]

MUNTZ (EUGENE). Raphael : his Life, Works, and Times. From the French. Illustrated. Edited by Walter Armstrong, B.A. Roy. 8vo. Lond., 1882.   C 8 V 30
History of Tapestry, from the Earliest Time to the end of the 18th Century. 8vo. Lond., 1885.   A 6 V 27

MUNTZ (G. F.), M.P. Letters upon Coin Currency. 8vo. Birmingham, 1841.   F 6 V 10

MURAT (HENRIETTE JULIE DE CASTELNAU), COMTESSE DE. Contes des Fées. [*See* CABINET DES FÉES, 1.]

MURATORI (LUDOVICO ANTONIO). Anecdota Græca. 4to. Patavii, 1709.   G 8 V 15
Relation of the Missions of Paraguay. 12mo. Lond., 1759.   D 3 P 24
Antiquitates Italicæ Medii ævi. 6 vols. fol. Mediol, 1738–42.   B 16 U 2-7 ‡
Rerum Italicarum Scriptores ab anno ærno Christianæ quingentesimo ad millesimumquin gentisimum. 25 vols. (in 28) fol. Mediol., 1723-51.   B 16 T 1-28 ‡

MURCHISON (C.) [*See* FALCONER, H.]

MURCHISON (JOHN). Letter to H. F. Gurner. [*See* MANUSCRIPTS, &c.]   MF 1 U 21

MURCHISON (SIR RODERICK IMPEY), BART., &c. Siluria: the History of the oldest known Rocks containing Organic Remains ; with a brief Sketch of the distribution of Gold over the Earth. 8vo. Lond., 1854.   A 9 T 8
Siluria System, founded on Geological Researches in the Counties of Salop, Hereford, Radnor, Montgomery, &c.; with descriptions of the Coal Fields and overlying Formations. 2 vols. 4to. Lond., 1839.   A 2 R 28, 29 ‡
Life of ; by Arch. Geikie, LL.D., &c. Illustrated with Portraits. 2 vols. 8vo. Lond., 1875.   C 7 S 30, 31
Review of the Siluria System. [*See* FITTON, W. H.]

MURDIN (W.), B.D. · Collection of State Papers. [*See* BURGHLEY, LORD.] B 16 S 12 ‡

MURDOCH (ALEXANDER G.) Scottish Poets, Recent and Living. With Portraits. 8vo. Glasgow, 1883. H 8 Q 7

MURDOCH (PATRICK), D.D. Life of James Thomson. [*See* THOMSON, J.] H 7 Q 8

MURE (WILLIAM). Critical History of the Language and Literature of Antient Greece. 5 vols. 8vo. Lond., 1854-67. B 27 U 14-18

MURHARD (FR. WILH. AUG.) Litteratur der mathematischen Wissenschaften : Bibliotheca Mathematica. 5 vols. 8vo. Leipzig, 1797-1805. A 10 S 31-35

MURILLO DE SEVILLA (BARTOLMÉ ESTEBAN). Life of. Compiled from the Writings of various Authors. (In French, Spanish, and English.) Translated by Edward Davies. 8vo. Lond., 1819. C 4 T 18
Murillo ; by Ellen E. Minor. (Great Artists.) 8vo. Lond., 1882. C 3 T 39
[*See* CURTIS, C. B.] K 17 U 1

MURILLO VELARDE (PADRE PEDRO). Historia de la Provincia de Philipinas de la Compañia de Jesus. Segunda Parte, que comprehende los Progresos de esta Provincia desde el Año de 1616 hasta el de 1716. Fol. Manila, 1749. B 3 P 14 †

MURKO (ANTON JOHANN). Theoretisch-praktische slowenische Sprachlehre für Deutsche, nach den Volksprecharten der Slowenen in Steiermark, Kärnten, Krain und Ungarns westlichen Distrikten. 8vo. Grätz, 1832. K 11 V 10

MURPHY (ARTHUR). All in the Wrong : a Comedy. (Bell's Brit. Theatre.) 18mo. Lond., 1792. H 2 P 31
Another copy. (Brit. Theatre.) 12mo. Lond., 1808. H 1 P 15
Another copy. [*See* BRIT. DRAMA 4.]
The Apprentice : a Farce. [*See* FARCES 3.]
Another copy. [*See* BRIT. DRAMA 5.]
The Citizen : a Farce. [*See* FARCES 4.]
Another copy. [*See* BRIT. DRAMA 5.]
The Grecian Daughter : a Tragedy. (New Eng. Theatre.) 12mo. Lond., 1787. H 4 P 27
Another copy. (Bell's Brit. Theatre.) 18mo. Lond., 1792. H 2 P 35
Another copy. (Brit. Theatre.) 12mo. Lond., 1808. H 1 P 15
Another copy. [*See* BRIT. PLAYS 2.]
Know Your Own Mind : a Comedy. (Brit. Theatre.) 12mo. Lond., 1808. H 1 P 11
The Old Maid : a Comedy. [*See* FARCES 7.]
Another copy. [*See* BRIT. DRAMA 5.]
The Orphan of China : a Tragedy. (Bell's Brit. Theatre.) 18mo. Lond., 1797. H 2 P 44

MURPHY (ARTHUR)—*continued.*
Another copy. [*See* BRIT. DRAMA 2.]
The School for Guardians : a Comedy. (Bell's Brit. Theatre.) 18mo. Lond., 1797. H 2 P 44
The Upholsterer : a Farce. [*See* BRIT. DRAMA 5.]
The Way to Keep Him : a. Comedy. (Brit. Theatre.) 12mo. Lond., 1808. H 1 P 15
Another copy. [*See* BRIT. DRAMA 5.]
Three Weeks after Marriage. [*See* FARCES 4.]
Another copy. [*See* BRIT. DRAMA 5.]
Zenobia : a Tragedy. (Bell's Brit. Theatre.) 18mo. Lond., 1796. H 2 P 12
Another copy. [*See* BRIT. DRAMA 2.]
Life and Genius of Henry Fielding. [*See* FIELDING, H.] J 2 Q 1-10
Life and Genius of Dr. S. Johnson. [*See* JOHNSON, DR. S.]
[*See* TACITUS, C. C.]

MURPHY (REV. DENIS), S.J. Cromwell in Ireland : a History of Cromwell's Irish Campaign. With Maps, Plans, and Illustrations. 8vo. Dublin, 1883. B 11 Q 4

MURPHY (JAMES CAVANAH). Arabian Antiquities of Spain. Imp. fol. Lond., 1813-16. B 10 P 14 ‡

MURPHY (JOHN NICHOLAS). Chair of Peter ; or, the Papacy considered in its Institution, Development, and Organisation, and in the Benefits which, for over eighteen Centuries, it has conferred on Mankind. 8vo. Lond., 1883. G 2 Q 23

MURPHY (JOSEPH JOHN). Habit and Intelligence in their connexion with the Laws of Matter and Force. 2 vols. 8vo. Lond., 1869. G 2 S 29-30

MURRAY (CAPT. ALEXANDER). Memoir of the Naval Life and Services of Admiral Sir P. C. H. C. Durham ; by his Nephew. 8vo. Lond., 1846. C 8 S 36

MURRAY (ALEXANDER), D.D., F.A.S.E. Account of the Life and Writings of James Bruce, of Kinnaird, F.R.S. 4to. Edinb., 1808. C 2 W 5

MURRAY (ALEXANDER), C.M.G., &c., AND HOWLEY (JAMES P.), F.M.S. Geological Survey of Newfoundland. 8vo. Lond., 1881. A 9 R 29

MURRAY (ALEXANDER S.) Manual of Mythology : Greek and Roman, Noise and Old German, Hindoo and Egyptian Mythology. 2nd ed. 8vo. Lond., 1874. B 14 Q 25
History of Greek Sculpture from the Earliest Times down to the Age of Pheidias. With Illustrations. 2 vols. 8vo. Lond., 1880-83. A 7 S 8, 9

MURRAY (ANDREW), F.L.S. Geographical Distribution of Mammals. 4to. Lond., 1866. A 14 V 50
Economic Entomology ; Aptera. [*See* SOUTH KENSINGTON MUSEUM, 10.]

MURRAY (ANDREW). South Australian Almanack, and General Colonial Directory, 1850-52. 3 vols. (in 1). 12mo. Adelaide, 1850-52. ME 4 P

Victorian Nautical and Commercial Almanack. 12mo. Melbourne, 1855.* ME 4 Q

MURRAY (ARCHIBALD). Forged : a Life Drama, of English and Australian Interest, in Four Acts. 8vo. Sydney, 1873. MH 1 Q 5

MURRAY (REV. A. W.) Claims of Western Polynesia on the Friends of Christian Missions in the Australian Colonies. 8vo. Sydney, 1853. MG 1 Q 29, and MJ 2 R 17

Missions in Western Polynesia. 8vo. Lond., 1863.* MD 6 T 15

Forty Years' Mission Work in Polynesia and New Guinea, from 1835 to 1875. 8vo. Lond., 1876. MD 6 S 11

Martyrs of Polynesia, 1799 to 1871. 8vo. Lond., 1885. MD 6 S 12

MURRAY (HON. CHARLES AUGUSTUS). Travels in North America, during the years 1834 to 1836, including a Summer Residence with the Pawnee Tribe of Indians. 2 vols. 8vo. Lond., 1839. D 3 S 16, 17

MURRAY (Mrs. D'ARCY WENTWORTH L.) Late Stabbing Case in Tasmania : Truth ; or, Seventeen Years of Marriage Life. 8vo. Launceston, 1866. MJ 2 R 13

MURRAY (EUSTACE CLARE GRENVILLE), "THE ROVING ENGLISHMAN." Under the Lens : Social Photographs. Illustrated 2 vols. 8vo. Lond., 1885. J 2 P 25, 26

Pictures from the Battle Fields. Illustrated. 12mo. Lond., 1855. B 12 T 27

Embassies to Foreign Courts : a History of Diplomacy. 8vo. Lond., 1855. F 5 Q 16

French Pictures in English Chalk. 8vo. Lond., 1876. B 9 P 24

MURRAY (HON. HENRY A.) Lands of the Slave and the Free ; or, Cuba, the United States, and Canada. 2 vols. 8vo. Lond., 1855. D 3 R 16, 17

MURRAY (HUGH), F.R.S.E. History of British India ; with Continuation, comprising the Afghan War, the Conquest of Sinde and Gwalior, War in the Punjaub, &c. 8vo. Lond., 1849. B 10 Q 31

An Encyclopaedia of Geography. 8vo. Lond., 1834. K 5 U 6

Adventures of British Seamen in the Southern Ocean. [Mutiny of the Bounty, &c.] 18mo. Edinb., 1827. MD 1 T 54

Another copy. (Const. Misc.) K 10 P 43

Historical Account of Discoveries and Travels in Africa, from the earliest ages. 2nd ed. 2 vols. 8vo. Edinb., 1818. B 1 P 29, 30

Historical and Descriptive Account of British India, from the most remote period to the present time ; assisted by James Wilson, R. K. Greville, and others. 2 vols. 12mo. Edinb., 1832. B 10 Q 16-18

Discovery and Adventure in the Polar Seas, &c. [See LESLIE, PROF. SIR JOHN.] D 1 R 36

MURRAY (JAMES). Murray's Guide to the Gold Diggings. The Australasian Gold Diggings : where they are, and how to get at them ; with Letters from Settlers and Diggers telling how to work them. 12mo. Lond., 1852.* MD 1 T 19

MURRAY (JAMES A. H.), LL.D. New English Dictionary on Historical Principles. Parts 1-3. A–Box. Imp. 4to. Oxford, 1883-87. K 20 V 1-3

MURRAY (HON. JAMES ERSKINE). Summer in the Pyrenees. 2 vols. 8vo. Lond., 1837. D 7 U 19-20

MURRAY (JOHN). Hand-books for Travellers. With Maps and Plans. 40 vols. 8vo. ; 5 vols. 12mo. Lond., 1873-84. B 12 Q 1–R 17

1, 2. Environs of London, alphabetically arranged.
. Holland and Belgium.
3. North Germany, from the Baltic to the Black Forest, and the Rhine, from Holland to Basle.
 South Germany and Austria.
6. Switzerland, the Alps of Savoy and Piedmont, the Italian Lakes, and part of Dauphiné.
7. France.
8. Mediterranean : its Cities, Coasts, and Islands.
9. Algeria and Tunis.
10. Portugal.
11. Northern Italy.
12. Central Italy.
13. The Cicerone.
14. Rome and its Environs.
15. Travellers in Southern Italy.
16. Lower and Upper Egypt. In Two Parts.
17. Turkey in Asia.
18. Sweden. Stockholm and its Vicinity.
19. Norway.
20. Russia, Poland, and Finland.
21. Bombay Presidency.
22. Madras Presidency.
23. Syria and Palestine.
24. England and Wales.
25. Essex, Suffolk, Norfolk, and Cambridgeshire.
26. Kent.
27. Sussex.
28. Surrey, Hampshire, and the Isle of Wight.
29. Devonshire.
30. Cornwall.
31. South Wales and its Borders.
32. Northamptonshire and Rutland.
33. Derbyshire, Nottinghamshire, Leicestershire, and Staffordshire.
34. Shropshire and Cheshire.
35. Lancashire.
36. Durham and Northumberland.
37. Scotland.
38. Ireland.
39. London as it is.
40. Paris.
41. Travel-talk.
42. Maps of the Holy Land.
43. Map of the Lake District of Cumberland, Westmoreland, and Lancashire, chiefly from the Ordnance Survey.
44. Central and Northern Japan.
45. The Punjáb, Western Rajputána, Kasmir, and Upper Sindh.

MURRAY (JOHN), F.R.S.E. Report on the Scientific Results of the Voyage of H.M.S. Challenger. [See THOMSON, SIR C. W.]

MURRAY (PROF. JOHN CLARK), LL.D. Ballads and Songs of Scotland, in view of their influence on the Character of the People. 8vo. Lond., 1874. J 8 Q 1

Hand-book of Psychology. 8vo. Lond., 1885. G 7 Q 32

MURRAY (LINDLEY). Power of Religion on the Mind, in Retirement, Affliction, and the Approach of Death. 14th ed. 12mo. York, 1810. G 10 P 10

An English Grammar; comprehending the Principles and Rules of the Language. 8th ed. 2 vols. 8vo. Lond., 1853. K 12 S 19, 20

MURRAY (CAPT. PEMBROKE L.), N.S.W.A. Volunteer Act, Regulations, and Orders of Dress: Alphabetical Key. 12mo. Sydney, 1885. MF 1 P 27

MURRAY (REGINALD A. F.) Victoria: Geology and Physical Geography. 8vo. Melb., 1887. MA 2 Q 46

Report on the Geology, &c., of Victoria. [*See* SMYTH, R. B.]

MURRAY (ROBERT), C.E. Treatise on Marine Engines and Steam Vessels. (Weale.) 5th ed. 12mo. Lond., 1871. A 17 P 2

Another copy. (Weale.) 8th ed. 12mo. Lond., 1886. A 17 R 10

MURRAY (HON. ROBERT DUNDAS). Summer at Port Phillip. 12mo. Edinb., 1843.* MD 2 Q 40

Cities and Wilds of Andalucia. 2 vols. 8vo. Lond., 1849. D 8 S 10, 11

MURRAY (ROBERT L.) Murray's Austral-Asiatic Review. Vol. 1, Nos. 2-4, April and August, 1828. 8vo. Hobart, 1828. ME 3 R

Another copy. 8vo. Hobart, 1828. MJ 2 R 13

MURRAY (REV. THOMAS BOYLE), M.A. Pitcairn: the Island, the People, and the Pastor. 8th ed. 8vo. Lond., 1857. MD 1 S 29

MURRAY (WILLIAM), EARL OF MANSFIELD. [*See* MANSFIELD, EARL OF.]

MUSÆUS. Musei Carmen de Herone et Leandro. [*See* HESIOD.]

Translation of; by F. Fawkes. [*See* CHALMERS, A.]

Works of. [*See* HESIOD.]

MUSÆUS (JOHANN CARL AUGUST). Tales by Musæus, Tieck, Richter; translated from the German by Thomas Carlyle. 2 vols. 12mo. Lond., 1874. J 1 T 11, 12

MUSARUM ANGLICANARUM. Examen Poeticum Duplex. 12mo. Lond., 1698. H 7 P 7

MUSÄUS (J. A.) Volksmährchen der Deutschen. 8vo. Paris, 1837. J 16 U 26

MUSGRAVE (REV. GEORGE M.), M.A. Ramble through Normandy. 8vo. Lond., 1855. D 7 R 34

Parson, Pen, and Pencil; or, Reminiscences of an Excursion to Paris, Tours, and Rouen, in 1847. 3 vols. 8vo. Lond., 1848. D 11 R 15-17

Nooks and Corners in Old France. 2 vols. 8vo. Lond., 1867. D 7 R 23, 24

3 r

MUSGRAVE (PHILLIP). [*See* ABBOTT, REV. J.]

MUSGRAVE (CAPT. THOMAS). Castaway on the Auckland Isles: a Narrative of the Wreck of the *Grafton*; from the Private Journals of Captain Thomas Musgrave; edited by John J. Shillinglaw, F.R.G.S. 8vo. Melb., 1865. MD 4 V 1

Another copy. 8vo. Melb., 1865. MJ 2 R 8

Voyage and Proceedings of H.M.C.S. *Victoria*. [*See* NORMAN, CAPT. W. H.] MD 1 V 9

MUSICIANS (DICTIONARY OF); from the earliest ages to the present time. 2 vols. 8vo. Lond., 1824. C 11 Q 5, 6 {*See* CELEBRATED MUSICIANS.]

MUSPRATT.(SHERIDAN), M.D., F.R.S.E., &c. Chemistry, Theoretical, Practical, and Analytical, as applied and relating to the Arts and Manufactures. 2 vols. imp. 8vo. Glasgow, 1860. K 8 T 1, 2

MUSSET (LOUIS CHARLES ALFRED DE). Premières Poésies, 1829-32. 12mo. Paris, 1867. H 8 P 37

Poésies Nouvelles, 1836-52. 12mo. Paris, 1867. H 8 P 38

MUTER (MRS. D. D.) Travels and Adventures of an Officer's Wife in India, China, and New Zealand. 2 vols. 8vo. Lond., 1864.* MD 3 Q 22, 23

MUTUAL LIFE ASSOCIATION OF AUSTRALASIA. Third Annual Report. 4to. Sydney, 1872. MJ 2 S 4

MY NOTE-BOOK. 2 vols. 4to. Melb., 1857. MJ 1 V 1, 2

MYERS (ARTHUR B. R.) Life with the Hamran Arabs: an Account of a Sporting Tour of some Officers of the Guards in the Soudan during the Winter of 1874-75. 8vo. Lond., 1876. D 1 V 11

MYERS (FRANCIS). Botany, Past and Present. Sm. 4to. Sydney, 1885. MD 3 V 30

Beautiful Manly: its Approaches, Surroundings, Charms, and History; with Visitors' Guide to all Places of Beauty, Rest, and Sport. Sm. 4to. Sydney, 1885. MD 3 V 31

The Australian Contingent: a History of the Patriotic Movement in New South Wales. [*See* HUTCHINSON, F.]

MYERS (FREDERIC W. H.), M.A. Phantasms of the Living. [*See* GURNEY, E.]

Wordsworth. (Eng. Men of Letts.) 8vo. Lond., 1881. C 1 U 36

MYLLAR (ANDROW). Who was Scotland's First Printer? ane compendious and breve Tractate in commendation of Androw Myllar; compylit be Robert Dickson. 8vo. Lond., 1881. C 2 T 33

MYRIANTHEUS (L.), PH.D. Comprehensive Phraseological English-Ancient and Modern Greek Lexicon. [*See* LASCARIDES, G. P.]

MYSTIC VOICES OF HEAVEN; by "An Oxford Graduate." 8vo. Lond., 1886. A 3 R 35

N

NABI COSMOS. [*See* BULMER, T. S.]

NADAILLAC (B. DE), COMTE. Catalogue d'une Collection importante sur la Révolution Française: Pamphlets, Journaux, Caricatures, Affiches, Placards. 8vo. Paris, 1883.
      K 8 P 34

Catalogue d'une Collection importante sur la Révolution Française: Pamphlets, Journaux, &c., dont la vente. 8vo. Paris, 1885.
      K 8 P 35

NADAILLAC (MARQUIS DE). Pre-Historic America; translated by N. D'Anvers; edited by W. H. Dall. Illustrated. 8vo. Lond., 1885.
      B 1 S 37

NADAL (E. S.) Impressions of London Social Life, suggested by an English Residence. 8vo. Lond., 1875.
      D 8 P 47

NADAULT DE BUFFON (HENRI). Buffon: sa Famille, etc. [*See* HUMBERT-BAZILE, M.]
      C 10 P 10

NÄGELI (PROF. C.), AND SCHWENDENER (S.) Das Mikroskop: Theorie und Anwendung Disselben. 8vo. Leipzig, 1867.
      A 16 S 5

NAGLER (DR. G. K.) Neues allgemeines Künstler-Lexicon. 22 vols. 8vo. München, 1835-52.
      C 13 S 2-23

NALSON (JOHN), LL.D. Impartial Collection of the Great Affairs of State, from beginning of the Scotch Rebellion in the year 1639, to the Murther of King Charles I. 2 vols. fol. Lond., 1682-83.
      B 14 R 14, 15 ‡

NAPHEYS (GEORGE H.), A.M., &c. Body and its Ailments: a Hand-book of Familiar Directions for Care and Medical Aid in the more usual Complaints and Injuries of Adults and Children; to which is added, a Family Health Record. 8vo. Lond., 1876.
      B 12 R 13

NAPIER (ALEXANDER), M.A. [*See* BOSWELL, J.]

NAPIER (MRS. ALEXANDER.) Memoirs of Prince Metternich. [*See* METTERNICH, CLEMENT, PRINCE OF.] C 10 U 28-32

NAPIER (GEN. SIR CHARLES JAMES), G.C.B. Life and Opinions of; by Lieutenant-General Sir W. Napier, K.C.B., &c. 4 vols. 8vo. Lond., 1857. C 5 Q 7-10

Introductory Passages in the Life of. [*See* NAPIER, MAJOR-GEN. SIR W. F. P.]

Lights and Shades of Military Life. 2 vols. 8vo. Lond., 1840.   J 5 It 31, 32

The Colonies; treating of their Value generally, and of the Ionian Islands in particular. 8vo. Lond., 1833.
      B 9 T 29

Colonization, particularly in Southern Australia; with some Remarks on Small Farms and Over population. 8vo. Lond., 1835.*   MF 1 R 11

NAPIER (GEN. SIR CHARLES JAMES), G.C.B.—*continued.*
Letter to the Rt. Hon. Sir T. Hobhouse on the Baggage of the Indian Army. 2nd ed. (Pam 25.) 8vo. Lond., 1849.   MJ 2 Q 13

Life of; by William Napier Bruce. With Portrait. 8vo. Lond., 1885.   C 5 Q 12

Letter on the Defence of England by Corps of Volunteers and Militia. 3rd ed. 8vo. Lond., 1852. MF 1 R 17
[*See* MACMURDO, MAJOR M.]

NAPIER (VICE-ADM. SIR CHARLES JOHN), K.C.B. History of the Baltic Campaign of 1854. Edited from Documents and other Materials, by G. Butler Earp. 8vo. Lond., 1857.   B 6 Q 33

The Navy: its Past and Present State, in a Series of Letters; edited by Major-General Sir William Napier, K.C.B. 8vo. Lond., 1851.   F 7 P 2

NAPIER (LIEUT.-GEN. ELERS), R.A. Scenes and Sports in Foreign Lands. Illustrated. 2 vols. 8vo. Lond., 1840.   D 10 R 3, 4

Past and Future Emigration; or, Book of the Cape; edited by Mrs. H. Ward. 8vo. Lond., 1849. D 1 S 25

Excursions along the Shores of the Mediterranean. 2 vols. 8vo. Lond., 1842.   D 7 P 9, 10

Excursions in Southern Africa, including a History of the Cape Colony. 2 vols. 8vo. Lond., 1849. D 1 R 4, 5

Reminiscences of Syria, and Fragments of a Journal and Letters from the Holy Land. 2 vols. 8vo. Lond., 1843.   D 5 R 28, 29

Wild Sports in Europe, Asia, and Africa. 2 vols. 8vo. Lond., 1844.   D 10 R 5, 6

NAPIER (FRANCIS). Notes of a Voyage from New South Wales to the North Coast of Australia. 8vo. Glasgow, 1876.   MD 2 Q 2

NAPIER (GEN. SIR GEORGE T.), K.C.B. Passages in the Early Military Life of; written by himself. Edited by his Son, General W. C. E. Napier. With Portrait. 8vo. Lond., 1884.   C 5 Q 11

NAPIER (CAPT. HENRY EDWARD), R.N. Florentine History, from the earliest authentic Records to the Accession of Ferdinand III, Grand Duke of Tuscany. 6 vols. 8vo. Lond., 1846-47.   B 12 Q 1-6

NAPIER (JAMES), F.R.S.E., &c. Manufacturing Arts in Ancient Times, with special reference to Bible History. 8vo. Lond., 1874.   A 11 Q 8

Manual of Dyeing and Dyeing Receipts, comprising a System of Elementary Chemistry as applied to Dyeing. 3rd ed. 8vo. Lond., 1875.   A 11 S 8

Manual of Electro-Metallurgy, including the applications of the Art to Manufacturing Processes. 5th ed. 8vo. Lond., 1876.   A 9 P 17

NAPIER (JOHN), OF MERCHISTON. Memoirs of: his Lineage, Life, and Times; with a History of the Invention of Logarithms; by Mark Napier. 4to. Edinb., 1834. C 3 W 17

NAPIER (MACVEY). Selection from the Correspondence of the late Macvey Napier; edited by his son, Macvey Napier. 8vo. Lond., 1879. C 9 Q 3

NAPIER (MACVEY), JUNR. Selection from the Correspondence of the late Macvey Napier, Esq.; edited by his son. 8vo. Lond., 1879. C 9 Q 3

NAPIER (MARK). Memoirs of John Napier, of Merchiston, his Lineage, Life and Times; with a History of the Invention of Logarithms. 4to. Edinb., 1834. C 3 W 17
Life and Times of Montrose. 8vo. Edinb., 1840. C 4 V 14
History of the Partition of the Lennox. 8vo. Edinb., 1835. B 13 Q 5

NAPIER (ROBINA). Johnsoniana. [*See* JOHNSON, S.] C 7 Q 43

NAPIER (GEN. W. C. E.) Early Military Life of Gen. Sir George T. Napier, K.C.B. [*See* NAPIER, GEN. SIR G. T.] C 5 Q 11

NAPIER (GEN. SIR W. F. P.), K.C.B. Colonel Napier's Justification of his Third Volume; forming a Sequel to his "Reply to his various Opponents." 8vo. Lond., 1833. B 13 U 7
Conquest of Scinde; with some Introductory Passages in the Life of Maj.-Gen. Sir Charles J. Napier. 8vo. Lond., 1845. B 10 U 5
Counter-remarks to Mr. Dudley Montagu Perceval's Remarks. 8vo. Lond., 1835. B 13 U 7
History of the War in the Peninsula, and in the South of France, from 1807 to 1814. 6 vols. 8vo. Lond., 1832-40. B 13 T 29-34
Letter to Gen. Lord Viscount Beresford; being an Answer to his Lordship's assumed Refutation of Col. Napier's Justification of his Third Volume. 8vo. Lond., 1834. B 13 U 7
Life and Opinions of Gen. Sir Charles James Napier. 4 vols. 8vo. Lond., 1857. C 5 Q 7-10
Observations on some Passages in History of the Peninsular War. [*See* STRANGFORD, PERCY, VISCOUNT.]
Remarks on the Character ascribed by Col. Napier to the late Rt. Hon. Spencer Perceval. [*See* PERCEVAL, D. M.]
Reply to Lord Strangford's "Observations." 2nd ed. 8vo. Lond., 1835. B 13 U 7
Reply to various Opponents, particularly to Strictures on Napier's History of the War in the Peninsula." 2nd ed. 8vo. Lond., 1833. B 13 U 7
[*See* SORELL, LIEUT.-COL. T. S.]

NAPOLEON I (EMPEROR OF THE FRENCH). Short History of; by Prof. John Robert Seeley. 8vo. Lond., 1886. C 3 T 32
Life of. 2nd ed. Vols. 1-6. 8vo. Edinb., 1827. C 4 P 2-7
Court and Camp of. (Fam. Lib.) 12mo. Lond., 1831. K 10 P 37

NAPOLEON I (EMPEROR OF THE FRENCH)—*continued.*
Code Napoleon; or, the French Civil Code. [*See* CODE NAPOLEON.]
Proclamations et Harangues, recueilles dans le Moniteur universel; par "Un Homme de Lettres." 2e éd. 18mo. Paris, 1850. J 15 Q 6
Life of; with a preliminary view of the French Revolution; by Sir Walter Scott, Bart. 2nd ed. Vols. 1-6. 12mo. Edinb., 1871. C 4 P 2-7
Another copy. (Prose Works, 8-16.) 9 vols. 12mo. Edinb., 1870. J 1 Q 17-25
Another copy. Roy. 8vo. Edinb., 1871. C 8 T 37
Bonaparte Letters and Despatches, Secret, Confidential, and Official, from the Originals in his Private Cabinet. 2 vols. 8vo. Lond., 1846. C 8 T 10, 11
Correspondance de; publiée par ordre de l'Empereur Napoléon III. 32 vols. 8vo. Paris, 1858-70. B 8 Q 13-44
Selection from the Letters and Despatches of; with Explanatory Notes, by Capt. the Hon. D. A. Bingham. 3 vols. 8vo. Lond., 1884. C 8 T 22-24
Fac-similes of all the different Signatures of. 2nd ed., revised. 4to. Lond., 1875. C 8 V 40
History of; edited by R. H. Horne. Illustrated. 2 vols. roy. 8vo. Lond., 1841-44. C 8 T 38, 39
Recollections of, during the First Three Years of his Captivity on the Island of St. Helena; by Mrs. L. E. Abell. 12mo. Lond., 1844. C 4 S 26
History of the Captivity of, at St. Helena; from the Letters and Journals of the late Lieut.-Gen. Sir Hudson Lowe; by W. Forsyth. 3 vols. 8vo. Lond., 1853. C 8 T 19-21
The Second Funeral of, including an Account of the Exhumation of his Remains at St. Helena. 8vo. Lond., 1841. C 8 T 43
Life of; by William Hazlitt. 4 vols. 8vo. Lond., 1830. C 8 T 25-28
History of; by J. G. Lockhart. (Fam. Lib.) 2 vols. 12mo. Lond., 1830. K 10 P 1, 2
History of the Captivity of, at St. Helena; by General Count Montholon. 4 vols. 8vo. Lond., 1846-47. C 8 T 29-32
Memoirs of: his Court and Family; by the Duchess D'Abrantes (Madame Junot). 2 vols. 8vo. Lond., 1836. C 5 T 17, 18
Napoleon in Exile; or, a Voice from St. Helena; being the Opinions and Reflections of Napoleon; by Barry E. O'Meara. 5th ed. 2 vols. 8vo. Lond., 1822. C 8 T 35, 36
Memoirs of; from the French of [L. A.] F. de Bourrienne, by J. S. Memes. (Const. Misc.) 4 vols. (in 3) 18mo. Edinb., 1831. K 10 Q 45-47
Memoirs of; by [L. A. F.] de Bourrienne, his Private Secretary. 4 vols. 8vo. Lond., 1836. C 8 T 12-15
Memoirs of; by Louis Antoine Fauvelet de Bourrienne. his Private Secretary. Edited by Col. R. W. Phipps. With Illustrations. 3 vols. 8vo. Lond., 1885. C 8 T 16-18
History of; by P. Lanfrey. 4 vols. 8vo. Lond., 1871-79. B 8 R 6-9
English Caricature and Satire on. [*See* ASHTON, JOHN.] C 8 T 33, 34

NAPOLEON III (EMPEROR OF THE FRENCH). Political and Historical Works of; with an original Memoir of his Life. 2 vols. 8vo. Lond., 1852. F 10 8 11, 12

History of Julius Cæsar. 2 vols. 8vo. Lond., 1862.
B 11 V 30, 31

Des Idées Napoléoniennes; or the opinions and Policy of Napoleon. Translated from the French. 8vo. Lond., 1840. F 10 Q 20

Life of; derived from State Records, from unpublished Family Correspondence, and from Personal Testimony; by W. B. Jerrold. 4 vols. 8vo. Lond., 1874–82.
C 8 T 40–43

Prisoner of Ham; authentic details of the Captivity and Escape of Prince Napoleon Louis; by F. T. Briffault. 2nd ed. 8vo. Lond., 1870. C 4 8 28

Posthumous Works and Unpublished Autographs of; collected and arranged by Count Henry de la Chapelle. 8vo. Lond., 1873. B 8 U 31

Louis Napoleon, the destined Monarch of the World. [See BAXTER, REV. M.]

Baxter Refuted; or, Louis Napoleon not the destined Monarch of the World. [See TURNER, W.]

[See MORRIS, REV. H. C. E.] MJ 2 P 31

NAPP (RICHARD). Argentine Republic; written in German. 8vo. Buenos Ayres, 1876. D 15 T 4

NARBOROUGH (ADM. SIR JOHN). Voyage to the South Sea. [See VOYAGES AND DISCOVERIES.] MD 5 P 24

Voyage à la Mer du Sud. [See COREAL, F.]

NARES (REV. EDWARD), D.D. Memoirs of the Life and Administration of the Rt. Hon. William Cecil, Lord Burghley; with Extracts from his Private and Official Correspondence. 3 vols. 4to. Lond., 1828–31.
C 2 W 2–4

NARES (CAPT. SIR GEORGE S.), K.C.B., &c. Seamanship; including Names of Principal Parts of a Ship. 6th ed., enlarged and revised by Lieut. Arthur C. B. Bromley, R.N. 8vo. Portsmouth, 1882. A 2 Q 13

Narrative of a Voyage to the Polar Sea during 1875 76, in H.M.S. *Alert* and *Discovery*; with Notes on the Natural History. 2 vols. 8vo. Lond., 1878. D 4 R 43, 44

NARJOUX (FELIX). Architecture Communale,—Hotels de Ville, Mairies, Maisons d'Ecole, Salles d'Asile Presbytères, Halles et Marchés, Abbattoirs, Lavoirs, Fontaines, &c. 2 vols. 4to. Paris, 1870. A 23 R 14, 15 ‡

Notes and Sketches of an Architect, taken during a journey in the North west of Europe. Translated by John Peto. 8vo. Lond., 1876. A 2 8 12

NARRATIVE OF EDWARD CREWE; or, Life in New Zealand; by W. M. B. 8vo. Lond., 1874.* MJ 1 P 3

NASH (FREDERICK). Picturesque Views of the City of Paris and its Environs; the Literal Department; by John Scott. Translated into French by M. P. B. de la Boissiere. 2 vols. (in 1) 4to. Lond., 1820 23. D 9 8 5 ‡

NASH (THOMAS). Complete Works of; edited, with Memorial Introduction, by the Rev. Alexander B. Grosart, D.D. (Huth Lib.) 5 vols. 4to. Lond., 1883–84. J 5 U 28–33

Tracts of. [See BRYDGES, SIR S. C.]

Dido, Queen of Carthage. [See MARLOWE, C.] H 1 R 13

NASMYTH (JAMES). James Nasmyth, Engineer: an Autobiography. Edited by Samuel Smiles, LL.D. With a Portrait. 8vo. Lond., 1883. C 5 T 19

NASMYTH (JAMES), C.E., AND CARPENTER (JAMES), F.R.A.S. The Moon; considered as a Planet, a World, and a Satellite. 2nd ed. 4to. Lond., 1874. A 3 U 11

NASR EDDIN (SHAH OF PERSIA). Diary of H.M. the Shah of Persia during his Tour through Europe in A.D. 1873.; by J. W. Redhouse—a verbatim Translation. 8vo. Lond., 1874. D 8 8 8

Diary kept by His Majesty, during his Journey to Europe in 1878. From the Persian, by Albert Houtum Schindler and Baron Louis de Norman. 8vo. Lond., 1879. D 8 8 9

NASSE (E.) On the Agricultural Community of the Middle Ages, and Inclosures of the 16th Century in England; translated from the German, by Col. H. A. Ouvry. 8vo. Lond., 1871. F 6 U 1

NATHUSIUS (HERMANN VON). Vorstudien für Geschichte und Zucht der Hausthiere zunæchst am Schweineschædel. Imp. 8vo. Berlin, 1864. A 1 R 17 †

Abbildungen von Schweineschædeln zu den Vorstudien für Geschichte und Zucht der Hausthiere. Ob. 4to. Berlin, 1864.* A 1 R 18 †

Die Racen des Schweines; eine zoologische Kritik und Andeutungen über systematische Behandlung der Hausthier-Racen. 8vo. Berlin, 1860. A 14 8 5

NATION (THE). With which is incorporated *The Express.* Fol. Sydney, 1887. M E

NATIONAL ASSOCIATION. [See SOCIAL SCIENCE.]

NATIONAL BIOGRAPHY, DICTIONARY OF. [See STEPHEN, L.]

NATIONAL AGRICULTURAL AND INDUSTRIAL ASSOCIATION OF QUEENSLAND. Catalogue of the Intercolonial Exhibition, 1876. 8vo. Brisbane, 1876. MK 1 R 44

NATIONAL GALLERY, LONDON. National Gallery of Pictures by the Great Masters. 2 vols. 4to. Lond., (n.d.) A 8 U 16, 17

Protest and Counter-Statement against the Report from the Select Committee on the National Gallery. 8vo. Lond., 1855. A 17 Q 19

Trafalgar Square, the best site for the National Gallery. 8vo. Lond., 1856. A 7 Q 19

National Gallery: its Formation and Management considered, in a Letter addressed, by permission, to H.R.H. the Prince Albert, K.G., &c.; by W. Dyce. 8vo. Lond., 1853. A 7 Q 19

NATIONAL GALLERY, LONDON—*continued.*
National Gallery in 1856. Sir C. L. Eastlake's Purchases;
by W. Coningham, M.P. 8vo. Lond., 1859.

National Gallery; its Pictures and their Painters: a
Hand-book for Visitors; by H. G. Clarke. 12mo.
Lond., 1842. A 7 P 32

Catalogue of the Pictures in the National Gallery. 12mo.
Lond., 1838. A 7 P 32

On the Charge in the Line of Front of the Buildings
for the National Gallery; by W. Wilkins. 8vo. Lond.,
1833. A 7 Q 15

Observations on the Communication of Mr. Wilkins to
the Editor of the *Athenæum*, relative to the National
Gallery; by Joseph Gwilt. 8vo. Lond., 1838. A 7 Q 13

NATIONAL GALLERY OF VICTORIA. [*See* MELB.
PUB. LIBRARY.]

NATIONAL MONUMENTS and Public Edifices containing Works of Art—The Society for obtaining free Admission to—Reports of the Committee. 8vo. Lond.,
1839-41. A 7 R 21

NATIONAL PORTRAIT GALLERY (THE). 4 vols.
(in 1) 4to. Lond., 1875-77. C 2 W 17

NATIONAL REVIEW (THE). 8vo. Lond., 1855. E

NATIONAL RIFLE ASSOCIATION (THE). Proceedings of. 8vo. Lond., 1879-81. E

History and Proceedings of, 1860. (Pam. 23.) 8vo.
Lond., 1860. MJ 2 Q 11

NATIVE OF TASMANIA, A. [*See* OBSERVATIONS ON
WAR.]

NATURAL HISTORY OF INSECTS (THE). 2nd ed.
2 vols. 12mo. Lond., 1830-38. A 14 P 43, 44

Another copy, vol. 1. (Fam. Lib.) 2nd ed. 12mo.
Lond., 1830. K 10 P 38

NATURALIST'S LIBRARY. Conducted by Sir William
Jardine, Bart. 40 vols. 12mo. Edinb., 1833-64.
A 14 P 1-40

Bushnan (J. S.) Natural History of Fishes, particularly their
Structure and Economical Uses. Vol. 36.
Duncan (J.) Natural History of Bees. Vol. 33.
  Natural History of Beetles. Vol. 29.
  Natural History of British Butterflies. Vol. 30.
  Natural History of British Moths, Sphinxes, &c. Vol. 31.
  Natural History of Exotic Moths. Vol. 34.
  Natural History of Foreign Butterflies. Vol. 32.
  Introduction to Entomology. Vol. 28.
Hamilton (R.) Natural History of the Amphibious Carnivora.
  Vol. 23.
  Natural History of British Fishes. Vols 39, 40.
Jardine (Sir W.) Natural History of the Birds of Great
  Britain and Ireland. Vols. 9-12.
  Natural History of Felinæ. Vol. 17.
  Natural History of Gallinaceous or Game-birds. Vols. 3, 4.
  Natural History of Humming-birds. Vols. 1, 2.
  Natural History of Monkeys. Vol. 16.
  Natural History of the Pacydermes, or Thick-skinned
    Quadrupeds. Vol. 20.
  Natural History of Ruminating Animals. Vols. 18, 19.
  Natural History of Whales. Vol. 21.

NATURALIST'S LIBRARY—*continued.*
Macgillivray (W.) History of British Quadrupeds. Vol. 22.
Schomburgk (R. H.) Natural History of the Fishes of Guiana.
  Vols. 37, 38.
Selby (P. J.) Natural History of Parrots. Vol. 6.
  Natural History of Pigeons. Vol. 5.
Smith (Lieut.-Col. C. H.) Natural History of Dogs.
  Vols. 24, 25.
  Natural History of Horses. Vol. 27.
  Introduction to Mammalia. Vol. 15.
Swainson (W.) Natural History of the Birds of Western
  Africa. Vols. 7, 8.
  Natural Arrangement and Relations of the Family of
    Flycatcher, or Muscicapidæ. Vol. 13.
Waterhouse (G. R.) Natural History of Marsupialia, or Pouched
  Animals. Vol. 26.

NATURE: a Weekly Illustrated Journal of Science. Vols.
1-31, 1869-85. Imp. 8vo. Lond., 1870-86. E

NAU (CLAUDE). History of Mary Stewart, from the Murder
of Riccio until her Flight into England; by the Rev.
Joseph Stevenson, S.J. 8vo. Edinb., 1883. C 6 T 18

NAUFRAGUS. [*See* HORNE, MR.]

NAUGERIUS (A.) [*See* QUINTILIANUS, M. F.]

NAUMANN (DR. CARL FRIEDRICH). Elemente der Mine-
alogie. 8e auflage. Roy. 8vo. Leipzig, 1871. A 9 U 26

Another copy. 9e auflage. Roy. 8vo. Leipzig, 1874.
A 9 U 28

NAUMANN (E.) History of Music. Edited by Sir
F. A. G. Ouseley. 2 vols. roy. 8vo. Lond., 1882-86.
A 8 Q 7, 8

NAUNTON (SIR ROBERT). Court of Elizabeth, originally
written by Sir Robert Naunton, under the title of "Fragmenta Regalia"; with considerable biographical Additions,
by James Caulfield. 4to. Lond., 1814. B 5 V.14

Fragmenta Regalia. [*See* HENTZNER P.] D 7 T 43

NAUTICAL ALMANAC (THE). Nautical Almanac and
Astronomical Ephemeris for the years 1880-88, for the
Meridian of the Royal Observatory at Greenwich. 9 vols.
8vo. Lond., 1876-84. E

NAUTICAL MAGAZINE (THE): a Journal of Papers on
Subjects connected with Maritime Affairs. Vols. 1-53
n.s. 8vo. Lond., 1832-84. E

NAVAL ANECDOTES, Illustrating the Character of
British Seamen. Published by James Cardee. 8vo.
Lond., 1806. B 6 Q 34

NAVAL ARCHITECTURE. Report of the Committee
for conducting the Experiments of the Society for the
Improvement of Naval Architecture. 4to. Lond., 1798.
A 2 U 5

NAVAL BIOGRAPHICAL DICTIONARY. [*See*
O'BYRNE, W. R.]

NAVAL CHRONICLE (The); containing a General and Biographical History of the Royal Navy of the United Kingdom; with a variety of original Papers on Nautical Subjects. 40 vols. 8vo. Lond., 1799–1818. E

NAVILLE (Edouard). Store-City of Pithom, and the Route of the Exodus. (Egypt Exploration Fund.) With Plates and Maps. Roy. 4to. Lond., 1885. D 12 R 14 †

NAVY LIST (The); containing Officers of the Active and Retired Lists of the Royal Navy, General Regulations &c. 116 vols. 12mo. Lond., 1834–86. E

NAYLER (Sir G.) Coronation of his most Sacred Majesty King George IV, solemnized in the Collegiate Church of Saint Peter, Westminster, 19th July, 1821. El. fol. Lond., 1837. B 20 P 10 ‡

NEAL (Daniel), M.A. History of the Puritans, abridged by E. Parsons; with the Life of the Author, by Joshua Toulmin, D.D. 2nd ed. 2 vols. 8vo. Lond., 1811. G 15 Q 21, 22

Another copy; revised, corrected, and enlarged. 5 vols. 8vo. Lond., 1822. G 15 R 17–21

NEAL (James H.) A Constituency Betrayed—the Member for Hartley declines to assist Sydney to obtain cheap Coal. (Pam. C.) Roy. 8vo. Bathurst, 1870. MJ 2 S 1

NEALE (Edward Vansittart). The Co-operator's Handbook. (Pam. 37.) 8vo. Lond., 1860. MJ 2 Q 24

NEALE (Rev. Erskine), M.A. Life of Field-Marshal His Royal Highness Edward, Duke of Kent. 8vo. Lond., 1850. C 7 P 33

"Risen from the Ranks"; or, Conduct *versus* Caste. 12mo. Lond., 1853. J 12 8 6

NEALE (Frederick Arthur). Eight Years in Syria, Palestine, and Asia Minor, from 1842–50. 2 vols. 8vo. Lond., 1851. D 5 R 10, 11

Narrative of a Residence at the Capital of the Kingdom of Siam. 8vo. Lond., 1852. D 5 R 12

NEALE (J. P.) History of the Abbey Church of Westminster. [*See* Brayley, E. W.] B 23 S 27, 28 ‡

NEALE (J. P.), and LE KEUX (John). Views of the most interesting Collegiate and Parochial Churches in Great Britain. 4to. Lond., 1824. A 2 U 9

NEANDER (Johann Augustus Wilhelm). General History of the Christian Religion and Church; translated from the German, by Joseph Torrey. New ed., carefully revised, with a general index, by the Rev. A. J. W. Morrison, B.A. 9 vols. 8vo. Lond., 1850–58. G 16 Q 12–20

History of the Planting and Training of the Christian Church by the Apostles, with the Author's Final Additions; also, his Agnostikos; or, Spirit of Tertullian. Translated from the German, by J. E. Ryland. 2 vols. 8vo. Lond., 1876. G 16 P 20, 21

NEANDER (Johann Augustus Wilhelm)—*continued.*

Life of Jesus Christ, in its historical connexion and historical development; translated from the 4th German ed., by John M'Clintock and Charles E. Blumenthal. 8vo. Lond., 1876. G 16 P 25

Memorials of Christian Life in the Early and Middle Ages including his "Light in Dark Places"; translated from the German, by J. E. Ryland. 8vo. Lond., 1877. G 16 P 22

Lectures on the History of Christian Dogmas; edited by Dr. J. L. Jacobi, translated from the German, by J. E. Ryland, M.A. 2 vols. 12mo. Lond., 1878. G 16 P 23, 24

St. Augustin, Melanchthon, Neander; Three Biographies, by Philip Schaff. 8vo. New York, 1886. C 2 S 37

NEAR OBSERVER, A. [*See* Booth, J.]

NEARCHUS (Adm.) Voyage of. [*See* Vincent, W.] D 4 V 37

NECK (Adm. Jacob van), en WARWYCK (Vice-Adm. Wybrand van). Journael van de tweede Schip-vaert op Oost-Indien in den jahre 1598. 8vo. Amsterdam (n.d.) D 5 Q 35

NECKER (Mme. Anne Louise Germaine). [*See* Staël-Holstein, Baronne de.]

NECKER (Mme. Louise Suzanne), née curchod. The Salon of Madame Necker; by Vicomte d'Haussonville; translated by H. M. Trollope. 2 vols. 8vo. Lond., 1882. C 4 Q 20, 21

NEDELEC (Rev. Louis). Cambria Sacra; or, the History of the Early Cambro-British Christians. 8vo. Lond., 1879. G 13 P 19

NEIL (Samuel). Young Debater: a Handbook for Mutual Improvement and Debating Societies. 18th thousand. 8vo. Lond., 1875. J 9 Q 31

Art of Public Speaking: an Exposition of the Principles of Oratory. 5th thousand. 8vo. Lond. (n.d.) J 9 Q 31

Public Meetings and how to conduct them : a handy Guide to a Knowledge of the Rights and Duties of the Promoters, Frequenters, Speakers, and Chairmen of Popular Assemblies. 8vo. Lond., 1868. J 9 Q 31

NEILD (James Edward), M.D. Dirt and Disease : a Lecture. [*See* Melbourne Public Library.]

[*See* Hamlet Controversy.]

NEILL (Mrs. Bladen). The Silkworm : its Education, Reproduction, and Regeneration ; on M. Alfred Roland's Open Air System. 8vo. Melb., 1873. MA 1 Q 37

NEILSON (Rev. William), D.D. Introduction to the Irish Language. In three parts. 8vo. Dublin, 1808. K 13 Q 31

NELSON (Edmund). The Moon, and the Condition and Configuration of its Surface. Illustrated. Roy. 8vo. Lond., 1876. A 3 T 11

NELSON (F. G. P.) Contributions to Vital Statistics; being a Development of the Rate of Mortality and the Laws of Sickness. 2nd ed. 4to. Lond., 1846. F 8 Q 19 †

NELSON (ADM. HORATIO), VISCOUNT, DUKE OF BRONTÉ. Despatches and Letters of; with Notes by Sir N. H. Nicolas, 1777–1805. 7 vols. 8vo. Lond., 1844–46. B 6 R 1-7

Letters and Despatches of; selected and arranged by J. K. Laughton, M.A. 8vo. Lond., 1886. C 9 P 10

Life of; by Robert Southey; with twelve Illustrations by Westall. 8vo. Lond., 1877. C 9 P 7

Life of; by Robert Southey, LL.D. New ed. 12mo. Lond., 1870. C 2 Q 27

Memoirs of the Life of; by Thomas Joseph Pettigrew. 2 vols. 8vo. Lond., 1849. C 9 P 8, 9

Nelsonian Reminiscences : Leaves from Memory's Log; by G. S. Parsons, R.N. 8vo. Lond., 1843. C 4 T 21

NEMIROVITCH-DANTCHENKO (V. I.) Personal Reminiscences of General Skobeleff; translated from the Russian by E. A. Brayley Hodgetts. 8vo. Lond., 1884. C 9 T 45

NEMNICH (PHILIPP ANDREAS) Allgemeines Polyglotten-Lexicon der Naturgeschichte, mit, erklärenden Anmerkungen. 2 vols. 4to. Hamburg, 1793–95. K 16 R 6, 7

Wörterbücher der Naturgeschichte in der Deutschen, Holländischen, Dänischen, Schwedischen, Englischen, Französischen, Italienischen, Spanischen, und Portugisischen Sprache. 2 vols 4to. Hamburg, 1800. K 12 T 6, 7

NEMO. [*See* MELBOURNE AND HOBSON'S BAY RAILWAY.]

NEMOURS (MARIE D'ORLÉANS), DUCHESSE DE. Memoires de. [*See* JOLY, G.] C 1 R 16, 17

Memoires de. [*See* RETZ, J. F. P. DE G., CARDINAL DE.] C 4 P 17–22

NEPOS (CORNELIUS). Vitæ excellentium imperatorum, ex Editione J. Fr. Fischeri, cum Notis et Interpretatione in usum Delphini. 2 vols. 8vo. Lond., 1822. J 13 Q 5, 6

Justini. Cornelius Nepos and Eutropius; literally translated by the Rev. J. S. Watson, M.A. 8vo. Lond., 1876. B 14 P 44

NESBIT (A.) Complete Treatise on Practical Land-Surveying. In seven Parts. Designed chiefly for the use of Schools and Private Students. 6th ed. 8vo. York, 1837. A 6 S 19

Practical Land-surveying. Edited by William Burness, F.R.A.S. 12th ed. 8vo. Lond., 1870. A 6 S 20

NESFIELD (HENRY W.) A Chequered Career; or, Fifteen Years in Australia and New Zealand. 8vo. Lond., 1881. MD 3 R 40

Another copy. New ed. Lond., 1887. MD 3 R 41

NESSELMANN (G. H. F.) Wörterbuch der Littauischen Sprache. 8vo. Königsberg, 1851. K 14 U 23

NETHERBY GAZETTE (THE) : a Journal published on board the ship *Netherby* (Captain Owens), bound from London to Brisbane; edited by Messrs. H. D. Vincent and Townsend, Saloon Passengers. 8vo. Melh., 1866. MJ 2 R 8

NETHERCLIFT (JOSEPH), AND SON. Collection of Autograph Letters. [*See* AUTOGRAPH LETTERS.] C 1 W 1 2

NETHERLANDS (THE). Staatkundig en Staathuishoud kundig Jaarboekje voor, 1873–74. 2 vols. 8vo. Amsterdam, 1873–74. E

[*See* PHILADELPHIA CENTENNIAL EXHIBITION.]

NETTLESHIP (R. I.) [*See* GREEN, PROF. T. H.]

NEUMAN (HENRY), AND BARETTI (GIUSEPPE). Dictionary of the Spanish and English Languages; revised and enlarged by D. M. Seoane, M.D. 5th ed. 2 vols. 8vo. Lond., 1837. K 15 Q 20, 21

NEUMAYER (DR. GEORGE). Results of the Meteorological Observations taken in the Colony of Victoria, during the years 1859–62 ; and of the Nautical Observations collected and discussed at the Flagstaff Observatory, Melbourne, during the years 1858–62. 4to. Melb., 1864. MA 1 Q 16 †

On a Scientific Exploration of Central Australia. 8vo. Lond., 1868. MD·1 V 9

[*See* VICTORIA.]

NEVILE (GEORGE), M.A. Farms and Farming. Illustrat. 8vo. Lond., 1884. A 1 P 46

NEVILLE (HENRY). The Isle of Pines; or, a late Discovery of a fourth Island in Terra Australis Incognita. 8vo. Lond., 1668. MJ 2 P 9

NEVILLE (JOHN), C.E., &c. Hydraulic Tables, Co-efficients, and Formulæ for finding the Discharge of Water from Orifices, Notches, Weirs, Pipes, and Rivers. 3rd ed. 8vo. Lond., 1875. A 6 R 1

NEVINSON (HENRY). Sketch of Herder and his Times. 8vo. Lond., 1884. C 7 Q 24

NEVIUS (REV. ISAAC L.) China and the Chinese: a general Description of the Country and its Inhabitants, &c. 8vo. New York, 1869. B 2 P 20

NEW (REV. ISAAC). A Letter in reply to "Lord's Day v. Sabbath." [*See* PERRY, RT. REV. C.]

NEW CALEDONIA. Notice sur la Déportation à la Nouvelle-Calédonie. Roy. 8vo. Paris, 1880. MF 1 U 28

Notice sur la Transportation à la Guyane Française et à la Nouvelle-Calédonie pour l'année 1877. Roy. 8vo. Paris, 1880. MF 1 U 27

NEW CLUB SERIES (THE). Instituted June 1877. Publisher, Alex. Gardner, Paisley. Vols. 1–3. 4to. Paisley, 1883–85.

NEW DISCOVERIES, concerning the World and its Inhabitants; in two Parts. With Maps and Prints. 8vo. Lond., 1778. MD 3 R 7

NEW ENGLISH THEATRE (The); containing the most valuable Plays which have been acted on the London Stage. 14 vols. 12mo. Lond., 1782–87. H 4 P 16–29

1. The Busybody: a Comedy; by Mrs. Centlivre. A Bold Stroke for a Wife; a Comedy; by Mrs. Centlivre. The Conscious Lovers: a Comedy; by Sir Richard Steele. The Miser: a Comedy; by Henry Fielding. The Suspicious Husband: a Comedy; by Dr. Hoadly.

2. The Orphan: or, the Unhappy Marriage: a Tragedy: by Mr. Otway. The Fair Penitent: a Tragedy; by Nicholas Rowe. Tancred and Sigismunda: a Tragedy; by James Thomson. Phædra and Hippolitus: a Tragedy; by Edmund Smith. The Revenge: a Tragedy; by E. Young, LL.D.

3. The Spanish Friar: a Comedy; by Mr. Dryden. The Old Bachelor: a Comedy; by Mr. Congreve. Rule a Wife and have a Wife: a Comedy; altered from Beaumont and Fletcher by David Garrick. The Recruiting Officer: a Comedy; by Mr. Farquhar, The Provok'd Wife: a Comedy; by Sir John Vanbrugh.

4. Merope: a Tragedy; by Aaron Hill. Jane Shore: a Tragedy; by Nicholas Rowe. The Mourning Bride: a Tragedy; by Mr. Congreve. The Rival Queens; or, Alexander the Great: a Tragedy; by Nathaniel Lee. The Gamester: a Tragedy; by Mr. Moore.

5. The Way of the World: a Comedy; by Mr. Congreve. The Committee: or, the Faithful Irishman: a Comedy: by Sir Robert Howard. Every Man in his Humour: a Comedy; altered from her Jonson by D. Garrick. The Beaux Stratagem: a Comedy; by Mr. Farquhar. Love for Love: a Comedy; by Mr. Congreve.

6. Oroonoko: a Tragedy: by Thomas Southern. The London Merchant: or, the History of George Barnwell: a Tragedy; by Mr. Lillo. Venice Preserved: or, a Plot discovered; a Tragedy; by Mr. Otway. Tamerlane: a Tragedy: by N. Rowe. The Distrest Mother: a Tragedy: by Amb. Philips.

7. The Provoked Husband: or, a Journey to London: a Comedy; by Sir John Vanbrugh and Mr. Cibber. The Drummer: or, the Haunted House: a Comedy: by Mr. Addison. Love makes a Man: or, the Fop's Fortune: a Comedy; by C. Cibber. The Careless Husband: a Comedy; by Colley Cibber. The Funeral; or, Grief a-la-mode; a Comedy; by Sir Richard Steele.

8. The Earl of Essex: a Tragedy; by Henry Jones. Barbarossa: a Tragedy; by Dr. Brown. All for Love: or, the World well Lost: a Tragedy; by Mr. Dryden. Mahomet, the Impostor: a Tragedy; by Rev. James Miller. Lady Jane Gray: a Tragedy; by Nicholas Rowe.

9. Amphitryon: or, the Two Sosias: a Comedy: altered from Dryden, by Mr. Woodward. The Double Dealer: a Comedy: by Mr. Congreve. The Double Gallant: or, the Sick Lady's Cure: a Comedy: by Colley Cibber. The Inconstant: or, the Way to Win Him: a Comedy: by George Farquhar. The Constant Couple: or, a Trip the Jubilee: a Comedy: by Mr. Farquhar.

10. Cato: a Tragedy; by Mr. Addison. Theodosius: or, the Force of Love: a Tragedy; by Nathaniel Lee. The Siege of Damascus: a Tragedy: by John Hughes. Douglas: a Tragedy; by Mr. Home. The Tragedy of Zara; by Aaron Hill.

11. The City Wives' Confederacy: a Comedy; by Sir John Vanbrugh. The Minor: a Comedy; by Samuel Foote. The Country Girl: a Comedy; altered from Wycherley, by David Garrick. The Chances; a Comedy; by David Garrick. The Wonder! a Woman keeps a Secret: a Comedy; by Mrs. Centlivre.

12. Medea: a Tragedy; by Mr. Glover. The Brothers: a Tragedy; by Dr. Young. Isabella; or, the Fatal Marriage: a Tragedy; altered from Southern, by D. Garrick. The Grecian Daughter; a Tragedy; by Arthur Murphy. The Roman Father: a Tragedy; by W. Whitehead.

NEW ENGLISH THEATRE (The)—*continued.*

13. Arthur and Emmeline: an Entertainment, abridged from the Masque of "King Arthur"; as altered from Dryden, by David Garrick. Comus: a Masque; altered from Milton, by George Colman. The Foundling: a Comedy; by Mr. Moore. The Hypocrite: a Comedy; altered from C. Cibber, by Mr. Bickerstaff. She would and she would not: or, the Kind Impostor: a Comedy; by Colley Cibber. The Virgin Unmasked: a Musical Entertainment: by Henry Fielding.

14. Artaxerxes: an English Opera; the Music composed by Tho. Aug. Arne, Mus. Doc. The Beggar's Opera; by Mr. Gay. Lionel and Clarissa: or, the School for Fathers: a Comic Opera; by Mr. Bickerstaff. Love in a Village: a Comic Opera; by Mr. Bickerstaff. The Maid of the Mill: a Comic Opera; by Mr. Bickerstaff. The Padlock: a Comic Opera; by Mr. Bickerstaff.

NEW DICTIONARY OF QUOTATIONS from the Greek, Latin, and Modern Languages; translated into English. 18th ed. 8vo. Lond., 1886. K 17 P 13

NEW FOUNDLING HOSPITAL FOR WIT (The); being a Collection of Fugitive Pieces, in Prose and Verse. 6 vols. 12mo. Lond., 1786. H 7 P 8–13

NEW GUINEA. [Kaart van] Nieuw Guinea. 4to. (N.p.n.d.) MD 5 S 18 ‡
Schets van de Zuidwest-en gedeeltelijke-Zuidkust van Nieuw Guinea; met Aanwyzing van de Opuanen aldaar gedaan:—Z. M. Korvet *Triton*, 1828; Schooner *Siren*, 1832; de Lieut. Kool, 1835. 4to. (N.p.) 1835. MD 5 S 18 ‡
Nieuw Guinea, ethnographisch en natuurkundig onderzocht en beschreven in 1858. 8vo. Amsterdam, 1862.* MD 5 T 30
Adventures in New Guinea: the Narrative of Louis Trégance, a French Sailor, nine years in Captivity among the Orangwoks, a Tribe in the Interior of New Guinea; edited, with an Introduction, by the Rev. Henry Crocker. 12mo. Lond., 1876. MJ 1 P 39
Correspondence respecting [the Annexation of] New Guinea, 1873–76. Fol. Lond., 1876.* MF 1 U 7
Further Correspondence respecting New Guinea, 1876-83. Fol. Lond., 1883. MF 1 U 8
Correspondence respecting New Guinea and other Islands, and the Convention at Sydney, of Representatives of the Australasian Colonies, 1883–84. 8vo. Lond., 1884. MF 1 U 9
Further Correspondence respecting New Guinea and other Islands in the Western Pacific Ocean, 1884–85. Fol. Lond., 1885. MF 1 U 9
New Strait at the South-western extremity of New Guinea. Lond., 1836. MD 7 Q 48

NEW HAMPSHIRE. [*See* UNITED STATES OF AMERICA]

NEW HOLLAND. Historical Narrative of the Discovery of New Holland and New South Wales. (Printed for John Fielding.) 4to. Lond., 1786. MD J 12
New and Correct History of New Holland; collected from authentic Authors and original Papers, by a Society of Gentlemen. 12mo. Glasgow, 1796. MB 1 P 14

NEW JERSEY. [*See* UNITED STATES OF AMERICA.]

NEW MONTHLY MAGAZINE (THE). 97 vols. 8vo. Lond., 1814–48.   E

NEW NEWGATE CALENDAR. 6 vols. 8vo. Lond., 1813.   F 8 S 14–19

NEW QUARTERLY MAGAZINE (THE). 13 vols. 8vo. Lond., 1873–80.

NEW QUARTERLY. REVIEW (THE); or, Home, Foreign, and Colonial Journal. 4 vols. 8vo. Lond., 1844–46.   J 10 V 14–17

NEW REFORMATION (THE): a Narrative of the Old Catholic Movement, from 1870 to the Present Time; with a Historical Introduction, by "Theodorus." 8vo. Lond., 1875.   G 3 T 13

NEW SHAKESPEARE SOCIETY. [*See* SHAKESPEARE SOCIETY, NEW.]

NEW SOUTH WALES.
New South Wales; its Progress and Resources; published by the Commissioners of the Colonial and Indian Exhibition. 8vo. Sydney, 1886.   MF 1 R 40

Another copy. 2nd ed. 8vo. Sydney, 1886.   MF 1 R 41

The Colony of Australia: Views of Sir Alfred Stephen and Sir John Robertson [and Views of the Press]. 8vo. Sydney, 1887.   MF 3 Q 34

Causes of the former prosperity and present state of the Colony of New South Wales; [by Q.E.D.] (Pam. Db.) 8vo. Sydney (n.d.)   MF 3 P 2

An Epitome of the Official History of New South Wales, 1788–1883; compiled from Official and Parliamentary Records, under the direction of Thomas Richards. Roy. 8vo. Sydney, 1883.   MB 2 U 5

Objections to the Project of His Excellency Sir George Gipps, for raising a Loan ; submitted to the Legislative Council, 1841. (Pam. Da.) 8vo. Sydney, 1842.   MF 3 P 2

Hand-book of New South Wales, containing General Industrial Progress of New South Wales ; being a Report of the International Exhibition of 1870, at Sydney ; together with a variety of Papers illustrative of the Industrial Resources of the Colony. 8vo. Sydney, 1871.*   MK 1 Q 6

New South Wales in 1880 (an Album of Photographs and Woodcuts). 4to. Sydney, 1880.   MD

Information for intending Emigrants and others. Issued by the Agent-General for New South Wales, London. Roy. 8vo. Lond., 1884.   MD 5 V 36

New South Wales : its Progress and Resources ; and Official Catalogue of Exhibits from the Colony forwarded to the International, Colonial, and Export Trade Exhibition of 1883, at Amsterdam. Roy. 8vo. Sydney, 1883.   MK 1 S 9

3 z

NEW SOUTH WALES—*continued.*

ADMINISTRATION OF JUSTICE.
Bill to provide for the Permanent Administration of Justice in New South Wales and Van Diemen's Land, and for the more effectual Government thereof, and for other purposes relating thereto. (Parl. Docs., 5.) Fol. Lond., 1827.   MF 4 ‡

Bill to continue an Act of the Fourth Year of his Present Majesty for the Better Administration of Justice in New South Wales and Van Diemen's Land. (Parl. Docs., 5.) Fol. Lond., 1827.   MF 4 ‡

Bill to provide for the Administration of Justice in New South Wales and Van Diemen's Land, and for the more effectual Government thereof, and for other purposes relating thereto. (Parl. Docs., 5.) Fol. Lond., 1828.   MF 4 †

An Act to provide for the Administration of Justice in New South Wales and Van Diemen's Land, and for the more effectual Government thereof, &c. (Parl. Docs., 42.) Fol. Lond., 1840.   MF 4 ‡

BENEVOLENT SOCIETIES.
Reports of the Benevolent Society of New South Wales, 1820–33, 1835–37, 1839, 1842–44, 1846–47, 1849, 1851–54, 1856–57, 1860–61, and 1867–68. 8vo. Sydney, 1820–69.   MF 3 P 9

BLUE BOOKS.
Blue Books of New South Wales, 1862–87. Fol. Sydney, 1863–88.   ME

Return of the Number of Persons in the Colony in the Civil and Military Departments who, in the year 1828, held two or more offices. (Parl. Docs. 6.) Fol. Lond., 1830.   MF 4 ‡

Official Lists of the Governors, Judges of the Supreme Court, and Members of the Legislative Assembly, [1788]–1883. 8vo. Sydney, 1887.   MC 1 Q 15

CAPITAL PUNISHMENT.
Report of the Capital Punishment Commission ; together with the Minutes of Evidence, N. S. Wales, 1867–68. Fol. Sydney, 1868.   MF 10 Q 3 †

CAVES AND RIVERS.
Exploration of the Caves and Rivers of New South Wales. Minutes, Reports, Correspondence, Accounts. Fol. Sydney, 1882.   MA 2 Q 23 †

CENSUS.
Analytical View of the Census of 1841 ; with Tables showing the Progress of the Population during the previous Twenty-five Years, by Ralph Mansfield. 8vo. Sydney, 1841.   MF 2 Q 21

Another copy.   MJ 2 Q 2

Census of, 1861, taken on the 7th April. Fol. Sydney, 1862.   MF 2 U 9

Census of 1871. (Votes and Proceedings of the Legislative Assembly.) Fol. Sydney, 1872.   E

Census of 1881, compiled by John Byron ; consisting of Report, Summary Tables, Appendices, and Conspectus Tables. Fol. Sydney, 1884.   E

NEW SOUTH WALES—*continued.*

CENSUS—*continued.*

Analytical View of the Census of New South Wales for 1846; with tables showing the Progress of the Population during the previous Twenty-five Years. 8vo. Sydney, 1847.   MF 2 Q 22

Another copy.   MJ 2 Q 8

Another copy.   MJ 2 R 22

CIVIL SERVICE.

Reports of the Civil Service Board for 1885-86. Fol. Sydney, 1885-87.*   ME

Bill to regulate Pensions and Retiring Allowances for Officers in the Public Service. (Pam. A.) Fol. Sydney, 1870.   MJ 2 U 1

CLERGY AND SCHOOL LANDS.

Documents relating to the Establishment and Dissolution of the Corporation of Clergy and School Lands in the Colony of New South Wales to the proposed sale of those Lands; and also relating to the Appropriation of Glebes to the Clergy in Van Diemen's Land, and the proposed sale thereof. (Parl. Doc. 5.) Sm. fol. Lond., 1839.   MF 4 ‡

CONSERVATION OF WATER.

Royal Commission. First Report. Fol. Sydney, 1885.*   ME

Diagrams and Plans to [the above.] Fol. Sydney, 1886.*   ME

Royal Commission. First Report. Abridged ed. 8vo. Sydney, 1886.*   MA 1 V 45

Royal Commission. Second Report [and Diagrams and Plans.] Fol. Sydney, 1886.*   ME

Royal Commission. Third and Final Report. Fol. Sydney, 1887.*   ME

Diagrams and Plans to [the above.] Fol. Sydney, 1887.

Royal Commission. Third and Final Report. Abridged ed. 8vo. Sydney, 1887.   MA 1 V 47

CONSTITUTION BILL.

Speeches in the Legislative Council of New South Wales on the Second Reading of the Bill for Framing a New Constitution for the Colony; edited by Edward Kennedy Silvester. 8vo. Sydney, 1853.   MF 3 R 21

The New Constitution: a Letter to [Sir] Henry Parkes, Esq., by "Conservative Squatroos, Esq." (Pam. Db.) 8vo. Sydney, 1852.   MF 3 P 2

Observations on the proposed New Constitution for New South Wales; by "An Old Colonist." 12m. Sydney, 1852.   MJ 2 R 3

CROWN LANDS.

Return of the Quantity of Land above the amount of One Hundred Acres granted to any Individual in New South Wales, from the year 1812. (Parl. Docs. 5.) Fol. Lond., 1821.   MF 4 ‡

Copies of the Royal Instructions to the Governors of New South Wales, Van Diemen's Land, and Western Australia, as to the mode to be adopted in disposing of Crown Lands. (Parl. Docs. 5.) Fol. Lond., 1831.   MF 4 ‡

NEW SOUTH WALES—*continued.*

CROWN LANDS—*continued.*

Report of the Debate on the Alienation of Crown Lands in New South Wales; in the House of Commons, 1832. (Pam. 31.) 8vo. Lond., 1832.   MJ 2 Q 19

Return of the Alienations of Crown Lands in New South Wales and Van Diemen's Land respectively. (Parl. Docs. 5.) Fol. Lond., 1832.   MF 4 ‡

Report of the Debate in the Legislative Council of New South Wales, 1840, upon a motion for an Address to Her Majesty upon the subject of a proposed Division of the Territory; and the introduction of a new system for the disposal of Crown Lands. 8vo. Sydney, 1840.   MF 3 P 3

Correspondence between the Secretary of State for the Colonial Department and the Governor of New South Wales, in the years 1834 and 1835, on the subject of the Appropriation of the Revenue arising from Crown Lands in that Colony, and a Despatch addressed to the Governor of New South Wales, bearing date the 31st day of May, 1840, enclosing an Additional Instruction, under the Royal Sign Manual, respecting the Alienation and Settlement of the Waste Lands of the Crown in that Colony. (Parl. Docs. 27.) Fol. Lond., 1840.   MF 4 ‡

Copies of Correspondence between the Secretary of State for the Colonial Department and the Governor of New South Wales, in the years 1834 and 1835, on the subject of the Appropriation of the Revenue arising from the Crown Lands in that Colony. Copies of Correspondence between the Colonial Department and the Treasury, including a Copy of a Despatch from the Governor of New South Wales, and the reply thereto of the Secretary of State, dated the 28th day of June, 1840, relative to the Finances of the Colony, and the Application of Land Sales to Police and Gaols. (Parl. Docs. 29.) Fol. Lond., 1840.   MF 4 ‡

Copy of Memorial addressed to Her Majesty's Secretary of State for the Colonies, from the Stockholders of New South Wales, relative to the Occupation of Land beyond the Boundaries of Location. (Parl. Docs. 48.) Fol. Lond., 1846.   MF 4 ‡

Correspondence relative to Crown Lands and Emigration in New South Wales.—Operation of Imperial Land Sales Act.—Licensed Occupation of Crown Lands. (Parl. Docs. 47, 48.) 2 vols. fol. Lond., 1845-46.   MF 4 ‡

Order in Council, dated 9th March, 1847, for establishing Regulations relative to the Occupation of Waste Lands in New South Wales. (Parl. Docs. 50.) Fol. Lond., 1847.   MF 4 ‡

Papers relative to the Occupation of Crown Lands, New South Wales. (Parl. Docs. 50.) Fol. Lond., 1848.   MF 4 ‡

Papers relative to Crown Lands in the Australian Colonies. (Parl. Docs. 59, 62, 65.) 3 vols. fol. Lond., 1851-56.   MF 4 ‡

NEW SOUTH WALES—*continued.*
CROWN LANDS—*continued.*

Public Lands : a Letter, by F. T. Rusden.—Proposed Bill to amend the Laws regulating the Sale and Occupation of the Waste Land of the Crown in the Colony of New South Wales.—The Land Question : Proposed Bill to provide for the Management and Disposal of the Public Lands of the Colony.—The Victorian Land Bill : a Bill to regulate the Sale and Occupation of Crown Lands. (Newspaper Cuttings.) (Pam. C.) Roy. 8vo. Sydney and Melb., 1857.   MJ 2 S 1

Laws and Regulations relative to the Waste Lands in the Colony of New South Wales. (Originally published in 1853.) 2nd ed., with Appendix up to 1858. 8vo. Sydney, 1858.   MF 1 R 7 *

Bill to Amend and Consolidate the Acts relating to the Occupation and Alienation of Crown Lands. 8vo. Sydney, 1871.   MF 1 R 28

Divisions of Pastoral Holdings as notified under the Crown Lands Act of 1884 (48 Vic. No. 18): Eastern, Western, and Central Divisions. 3 vols. 8vo. Sydney, 1886.
                          MF 3 P 23–25

Copies of the Royal Instructions issued to Sir Thomas Brisbane and Lieutenant-Gen. Darling respecting the Establishment and Duties of the Commissioners for apportioning the Territory of New South Wales. Copies of Colonial Government Orders, &c., respecting Grants of Land, 1823–31. (Parl. Docs. 6.) Fol. Lond., 1832.   MF 4 ‡

Return of Grants made in New South Wales, 1812–21. (Parl. Docs. 5.) Fol. Lond., 1822.   MF 4 ‡

Copy of the Conditions under which Lands are granted in the British North American Colonies, and in the Colonies of New South Wales and Van Diemen's Land. (Parl. Docs. 5.) Fol. Lond., 1830.   MF 4 ‡

Expenditure of the Land Fund of New South Wales in the Colony and principally on Public Works as a means of promoting and supporting Immigration. 8vo. Sydney, 1842.   MF 3 P 1

Correspondence relative to Crown Lands and Emigration in New South Wales—Operation of Imperial Sales Act—Licensed Occupation of Lands. (Parl. Docs., 47, 48.) Fol. Lond., 1845–46.   MF 4 ‡

Order in Council, dated 9th March, 1847, for establishing Regulations relative to the Occupation of Waste Lands in New South Wales. (Parl. Docs., 50.) Fol. Lond., 1847.   MF 4 ‡

New South Wales : the Crown Lands Acts ; with the Regulations and Forms thereunder ; also, the Commons Regulation Act (36 Victoriæ No. 23). 9th ed. 8vo. Sydney, 1873.   MF 1 R 29

Regulations relating to the Occupation of Crown Lands. 8vo. Melb., 1848.   MJ 2 R 21

An Essay on the Disposal of the Public Lands of New South Wales. (Pam. Jd.) 12mo. Goulburn, 1877.
                          MF 1 P 32

Another copy.   MF 3 P 20

NEW SOUTH WALES—*continued.*
CROWN LANDS—*continued.*

List of Crown Lands that may be selected at the upset price, in terms of section 25 of the Lands Acts further Amendment Act of 1880. Fol. Sydney, 1882.   ME

Report of Inquiry into the State of the Public Lands, and the operation of the Land Laws, instituted 8th January, 1883 [by Augustus Morris and George Ranken]. Sm. fol. Sydney, 1883.   MF 1 U 11

The Crown Lands Act of 1884. Digest of Cases heard before the Court of Appeal, 1885–87. Vol. 1, parts 1–4. 8vo. Sydney, 1886.   MF 1 S 1

New South Wales Lease, granted by Sir Thomas Brisbane in 1823. [*See* MANUSCRIPTS AND PORTRAITS.]
                          MF 1 U 21

[*See* REGISTRATION OF DEEDS.]

CUSTOMS.
Hand-book to the Customs Laws and Practice of New South Wales ; comprising the Customs Regulation Act, 1879 ; together with Rules, Regulations, General Management, and Forms thereunder ; also, Customs Statistics for 1881. Roy. 8vo. Sydney, 1882.   MF 2 S 22

Hand-book to the Customs Laws and Practice of New South Wales ; comprising the Customs Regulation Act, 1879 ; Rules, Regulations, General Management, and Forms thereunder. Roy. 8vo. Sydney, 1884.* MF 2 S 23

Supplement to the Customs Hand-book. Revised and corrected to September 30, 1886. 8vo. Sydney, 1886.
                          MF 2 S 27

Particulars of Customs Receipts Collection for the year 1886, showing the amounts received under each Article subject to duty ; also the amount paid for Drawback and Refund of duties during the year 1886. Roy. 8vo. Sydney, 1887.   MF 3 R 26

Customs Statistics for the year 1883. Roy. 8vo. Sydney, 1884.*   ME 3 V

DEAF AND DUMB INSTITUTION.
First and Second Anniversary of ; with a List of Donations and Subscriptions, 1862–63. 8vo. Sydney, 1862–63.
                          MF 3 P 12, and MJ 2 Q 10

Reports of, for 1867 and 1868 ; with a List of Donations, &c., and the Rules and Regulations of the Institution. (Pam. Du.) 8vo. Sydney, 1867–68.   MF 3 P 18

DENOMINATIONAL SCHOOLS.
Rules and Regulations of. 8vo. Sydney, 1857. MF 3 P 12

[*See* PUBLIC INSTRUCTION.]

DROUGHT OF 1829.
Form of Prayer, with Thanksgiving, to be used on Thursday, November 12, 1829, in all Churches and Chapels of the Establishment throughout New South Wales, in acknowledgment of the mercy of Almighty God, in putting an end to the late severe Drought, and in averting his threatened judgments from this Colony. By special command of His Excellency the Governor. 8vo. Sydney, 1829.   MG 1 Q 31

EDUCATION. [*See* PUBLIC INSTRUCTION.]   ME

NEW SOUTH WALES—*continued.*

ELECTORAL ROLLS.
Of New South Wales, for 1869–87. 22 vols. fol. Sydney, 1869–87. ME

EMIGRATION AGENTS.
Emigration Agents and Lecturers for New South Wales. (Reports, 3.) Fol. Sydney, 1862. MF 10 Q 3 †

FINANCES.
Copies of Correspondence between the Secretary of State for the Colonial Department and the Governor of New South Wales, in the years 1834 and 1835, on the subject of the Appropriation of the Revenue arising from the Crown Lands in that Colony. (Parl. Docs., 29.) Fol. Lond., 1840. MF 4 ‡
Accounts relating to Receipt and Expenditure of Van Diemen's Land, and New South Wales. (Parl. Doc., 1.) Fol. Lond., 1823. ME

FRIENDLY SOCIETIES.
Friendly Societies, Quinquennial Returns, 1856–60. (Reports, 3.) Fol. Sydney, 1862. MF 10 Q 3 †
Friendly Societies Act Inquiry Commission : Report of the Royal Commission, appointed on the 19th October, 1881, to inquire into and report upon the Working of the Friendly Societies Act, 37 Vic., No. 4, and to report generally on the Character and Operations of the Friendly Societies of New South Wales; together with an Actuarial Report, Minutes of Evidence, and Appendices. Fol. Sydney, 1883. ME
Friendly Societies Act of 1873 ; with an Index, compiled by A. Oliver. 8vo. Sydney, 1874. MF 3 P 29

GLADESVILLE HOSPITAL. [*See* INSANE.]

GOVERNMENT GAZETTE.
Government Gazette. 132 vols. fol. Sydney, 1832–85. ME

INFIRM AND DESTITUTE ASYLUMS.
Regulations for the Internal Management of the Government Asylums for the Infirm and Destitute. 8vo. (Pam. Iv.) 8vo. Sydney, 1862. MF 3 P 19
By-Laws of the Board for Managing the Government Asylums. 8vo. Sydney, 1862. MF 3 P 19

INSANE.
Hospital for the Insane, Gladesville : Rules for the Attendants, Nurses, Servants, and others. 8vo. Sydney, 1870. MA 2 S 38
Report on the Hospital for the Insane, Gladesville, for the year 1871. 8vo. Sydney, 1872. MA 2 S 38
Report of the Inspector-General of the Insane for 1881–82. Fol. Sydney, 1882–83. ME
[*See* LUNACY RULES.]

INSOLVENCY.
Observations on a Bill now before the Legislative Council of New South Wales, entitled a Bill for giving relief to Insolvent Persons. 8vo. Sydney, 1838. MF 1 Q 4
Another copy. MF 3 P 2
Copy of an Act for the Relief of Insolvent Debtors passed by the Governor and Legislative Council of New South Wales; and of Instructions given by the Secretary of State with respect to Public Officers taking the Benefit of such Act. (Parl. Doc., 6.) Fol. Lond., 1832. MF 4 ‡

NEW SOUTH WALES—*continued.*

INTOXICATING DRINK INQUIRY COMMISSION.
Report of. 1st Part ; together with Epitomes of the Evidence. Roy. 8vo. Sydney, 1887. MF 3 R 19

KING'S SCHOOLS.
Plan for the Formation and Regulating of the King's Schools, preparatory to the institution of a College in New South Wales. 12mo. Sydney, 1830. MG 1 Q 30
Another copy. 12mo. Sydney, 1830. MJ 2 Q 21

LAW.
Copies of Papers relating to the Conduct of Magistrates in New South Wales. (Pam. 29.) 8vo. Sydney, 1885. MJ 2 Q 17

LAW ALMANAC.
New South Wales Law Almanacs, 1858, 1863–64, 1877–83, 1885–87. 13 vols. (in 11) 12mo. Sydney, 1858–87. ME 4 Q

LAW REPORTS. [*See* SUPREME COURT.]

LAWS AND ORDINANCES.
Copies of the Laws and Ordinances passed by the Governor and Council of the Colony of New South Wales, 1824–29. (Parl. Doc., 5.) Fol. Lond., 1829. MF 4 ‡
Laws and Ordinances, 1824–25. (Parl. Docs. 5.) Fol. Lond., 1826. MF 4 ‡
Acts [Laws] and Ordinances of New South Wales, 1828. (Parl. Docs. 6.) Fol. Lond., 1831. MF 4 ‡
Laws and Ordinances, 1829–30. (Parl. Docs. 6.) Fol. Lond., 1832. MF 4 ‡
[*See* STATUTES.]

LEGISLATIVE ASSEMBLY.
Votes and Proceedings of the Legislative Assembly ; with the various Documents connected therewith. 172 vols. fol. Sydney, 1856–88. MF 4 ‡
Reports and Papers ordered to be printed by the Legislative Assembly. 5 vols. fol. Sydney, 1862–69. MF 10 Q 1–5 †
Standing Rules and Orders of the Legislative Assembly of New South Wales, as adopted and approved in the First Session of the Sixth Parliament, held in 1870. 8vo. Sydney, 1887.* MF 3 Q 28
Introduction of Parliamentary Government into New South Wales : Dinner of the surviving Members of the First Legislative Assembly at Parliament House, May 23rd 1887. 8vo. Sydney, 1887. MF 3 Q 11
[*See* PARLIAMENTARY DEBATES *and* PARLIAMENTARY HANDBOOK.]

LEGISLATIVE COUNCIL.
Minutes and Votes and Proceedings of the Legislative Council, from 1824 to 1855; with the various Documents connected therewith. 32 vols. fol. Sydney, 1835–56. ME
Journal of the Legislative Council. 41 vols. fol. Sydney, 1874–88. ME
Standing Rules and Orders, and Sessional Orders of the Legislative Council. 8vo. Sydney, 1887. MF 3 Q 27
Constitution of the Upper House : a Letter to the Editor of the *Herald*; by "Legislator." (Pam. A.) Fol. Sydney (n.d.) MJ 2 U 1
[*See* PARLIAMENTARY DEBATES *and* PARLIAMENTARY HANDBOOK.]

NEW SOUTH WALES—*continued.*

LICENSED SURVEYORS.
Regulations for the employment of Licensed Surveyors, Surveyor-General's Department. Fol. Sydney, 1882.
MF 2 Q 26 †

LICENSING ACT.
Licensing Act of 1882 (45 Victoria No. 14); the Billiard and Bagatelle Licensing Act of 1882 (45 Victoria No. 24); and the Metropolitan Magistrates Act, 1881 (45 Victoria No. 17); with an Index to each Act. Roy. 8vo. Sydney, 1882.
MF 1 S 13

LUNACY RULES.
Lunacy Rules, New South Wales. Roy. 8vo. Sydney, 1887.
MF 3 R 27

MARINE BOARD.
Rules to be observed in Surveying Passenger Steamers, Examinations, &c. 8vo. Sydney, 1886. MA 1 V 53
Regulations relating to the Examination of Masters, Mates, &c., in the Mercantile Marine. (With Appendices.) Roy. 8vo. Sydney, 1887.
MF 3 R 18

MATRIMONIAL CAUSES ACT.
Matrimonial Causes Act, 1873 (36 Victoria No. 9); with the Rules and Regulations concerning the Practice and Procedure thereunder, of the 8th July, 1873; to which are added Notes and Reports of all the Cases heard or determined by His Honor Mr. Justice Hargrave, Judge of the Divorce and Matrimonial Court, between the opening of the said Court, on 9th July, 1873, and 29th September, 1877. Edited by Frederick Harvie-Linklater. Roy. 8vo. Sydney, 1878. MF 1 S 8

MEDICAL BILL.
(Comments thereon by the Country Press.) (Pam. Ci.) 8vo. Sydney, 1875.
MA 2 Q 33

METEOROLOGICAL OBSERVATIONS.
[*See* RUSSELL, H. C.; SMALLEY, G. R.; AND TEB-BUTT, J.]

MINES DEPARTMENT.
Annual Reports of the Department of Mines, 1875, 1876, 1878–87. 12 vols. 4to. Sydney, 1876–88. ME 3 V
Annual Reports upon the Occupation of Crown Lands, Stock and Brands, and Roads, Streets, and Gates Branches of the Department of Mines, New South Wales, for the years 1879–87. 4to. Sydney, 1880–88. ME
Mines and Mineral Statistics of New South Wales, and Notes on the Geological Collection of the Department of Mines; compiled by direction of the Hon. John Lucas, M.P., Minister for Mines; also, Remarks on the Sedimentary Formations of New South Wales, by the Rev. W. B. Clarke, M.A., &c.; and Notes on the Iron and Coal Deposits, Wallerawang, and on the Diamond Fields, by Professor Liversidge, F.C.S., &c. 8vo. Sydney, 1875.*
MA 2 Q 15
Mineral Products of New South Wales, by Harrie Wood; Notes on the Geology of New South Wales, by C. S. Wilkinson, F.G.S., &c.; Description of the Minerals of N.S.W., by Prof. A. Liversidge, F.R.S.; also catalogue of Works, &c., on the Geology, Palæontology, Mineralogy, &c., of the Australian Continent and Tasmania, by R. Etheridge, jun., and R. L. Jack, F.R.G.S. 4to. Sydney, 1882.
MA 2 R 8

NEW SOUTH WALES—*continued.*

MINING ACT.
Mining Act (37 Vic. No. 13); also Amending Acts (43 Vic. No. 28, and 46 Vic. No. 7), with Regulations thereunder. 5th ed. Roy. 8vo. Sydney, 1884.*
MF 1 S 16
Mining Act (37 Vic. No. 13); also, Amending Acts (43 Vic. No. 28, 46 Vic. No. 7, 48 Vic. No. 10, and 48 Vic. No. 17), with Regulations thereunder. 6th ed. Roy. 8vo. Sydney, 1887.
MF 1 S 18

NAVIGATION ACT.
New South Wales Navigation Act (35 Victoriæ No. 7.) 8vo. Sydney, 1872.
MF 3 Q 22

NEWSPAPERS.
Specimens of Newspapers published in New South Wales. Atlas fol. Sydney, 1875.
ME

NOXIOUS TRADES.
Noxious and Offensive Trades Inquiry Commission. Report of Royal Commission. Fol. Sydney, 1883. ME

OFFICES IN THE COLONIES.
Return of the Number of Persons in the Colony of New South Wales, in the Civil and Military Departments, who in the year 1828 held two or more Offices. (Parl. Doc. 6.) Fol. Lond., 1830.
MF 4 ‡

OYSTER CULTURE.
Report of the Royal Commission appointed on the 29th of September, 1876, to inquire into the best mode of cultivating the Oyster, of utilising, improving, and maintaining the natural Oyster-beds of the Colony. Fol. Sydney, 1877.
MF 2 U 7

PARLIAMENTARY DEBATES.
Index to the *Sydney Morning Herald's* Reports of the Debates in the Legislative Council of New South Wales: Sessions 1853–54. Fol. Sydney, 1854–55. ME
Parliamentary Debates of New South Wales. (Newspaper Cuttings.) 4 vols. fol. Sydney, 1874–79. ME
Parliamentary Debates: Legislative Council and Legislative Assembly. 34 vols. roy. 8vo. Sydney, 1880–88.
ME

PARLIAMENTARY HAND-BOOK.
New South Wales Parliamentary Hand-book. 2nd ed. revised and enlarged. 8vo. Sydney, 1881.* MF 3 Q 63.

PARLIAMENTARY LIBRARY.
Index to the Legislative Council Library. Roy. 8vo. Sydney, 1849.
MK 1 R 4
Catalogue of, 1857. Roy. 8vo. Sydney, 1857.*
MK 1 R 5
Catalogue of, 1866. Roy. 8vo. Sydney, 1866.
MK 1 R 7
Supplementary Catalogue of, 1871. Roy. 8vo. Sydney, 1871.
MK 1 R 8
Second Supplementary Catalogue of, 1874. Roy. 8vo. Sydney, 1874.
MK 1 R 9
Supplementary Catalogue of Books added to, since 1885. Roy. 8vo. Sydney, 1887.
MK 1 R 10

NEW SOUTH WALES—*continued.*

PATENTS.

Letters of Registration of Inventions, under 16 Victoria,
No. 24. 15 vols. fol. Sydney, 1872–88.   ME

General Indexes to the Letters of Registration for Inventions and Improvements in the Arts and Manufactures, granted in New South Wales, from 1855 to 1880 inclusive.
Fol. Sydney, 1883.   ME

PENAL SETTLEMENTS.

Papers relating to His Majesty's Settlements at New South
Wales, 1811–14. (Parl. Docs., 1.) Fol. Lond., 1816.
                                                   MF

Instructions issued by the Governor of New South Wales
for the Regulation of the Penal Settlements. (Parl. Docs.,
1.) Fol. Lond., 1832.   MF

Returns of the Expenditure of the Colonies of New South
Wales and Van Diemen's Land, from 1st January, 1831 ;
specifying the Expense of the Civil and Military Establishments, the Transportation of Convicts, and the support
of them after their arrival ; and of the number of Convicts
sent to New South Wales, from 1st January, 1830, to 1st
January, 1831. (Parl. Docs., 1.) Fol. Lond., 1832. MF

[*See* CONVICTS.]

PETITIONS.

Petition to His Majesty, by the Members of Council,
Magistrates, Clergy, and Landholders, Merchants, and
other Free Inhabitants of New South Wales. (Pam. A.)
Fol. Sydney, 1836.   MJ 2 U 1

Report of the Proceedings of the General Meeting of the
Supporters of the Petitions to His Majesty and the
House of Commons. (Pam. Da.) 8vo. Sydney, 1836.
                                                   MF 3 P 1

Another copy. 8vo. Sydney, 1836.   MJ 2 Q 5

POLICE.

Report of the Committee on Police and Gaols ; with
the Minutes of Evidence and Appendix. Fol. Sydney,
1839.   MF 2 U 18

Copy of a Despatch of the Governor of New South Wales
to the Secretary of State for the Colonies, respecting the
application of about £597,000 of the Colonial Revenue
to defray Police and Gaol Establishments. (Parl. Docs.,
29.) Fol. Lond., 1841.   MF 4 ‡

Newspaper Extracts relating to Police Administration,
&c. ; with MS. Notes. (Pam. A.) Fol. Sydney, 1844.
                                                   MJ 2 U 1

Boundaries of the Police Districts of New South Wales.
8vo. Sydney, 1888.   MF 3 Q 20

Rules for the Management of the Police Force of New
South Wales. 8vo. Sydney, 1862.   MF I Q 20

General Instructions for the Guidance of the Police Force.
8vo. Sydney, 1862.   ME I Q 20

Rules for the Distribution and Appropriation of the Superannuation Fund, &c. 8vo. Sydney, 1862.   MF I Q 20

Manual for the Members of the Police Force of Enrolments,
affecting their Duties. 8vo. Sydney, 1862.
                                                   ME I Q 20

NEW SOUTH WALES—*continued.*

POSTAL SERVICE.

Reports of the Postmaster-General on the Departments
under his Ministerial control, for the years 1879–86. Fol.
Sydney, 1880–87.   ME

Opening of the General Post Office, Sydney, New South
Wales, 1st September, 1874. (Pam. K.) 8vo. Sydney,
1874.   MJ 2 P 27

Postal Conference, 1883 : Proceedings of the Conference,
held in Sydney, in May, 1883 ; Minutes of the Proceedings,
Resolutions, Papers laid before the Conference. Fol.
Sydney, 1883.   ME

Map, showing the Postal Stations and Roads in New
South Wales. Prepared for the use of the Post Office
Department. 4to. Sydney, 1882.   MD 5 R 2

PUBLIC DOCUMENTS.

List of Printed Public Documents on sale at the Government
Printing Office, Sydney. 8vo. Sydney, 1880. MJ 2 R 14

PUBLIC INSTRUCTION.

Report of the Council of Education upon the Condition
of the Public Schools for 1869. Fol. Sydney, 1870.
                                                   ME 10 Q 2 †

Report of the Council of Education upon the Condition
of the certified Denominational Schools for 1869. Fol.
Sydney, 1870.   ME 10 Q 2 †

Reports of the Minister of Public Instruction upon the
Condition of Public Schools established and maintained
under the Public Instruction Act of 1880, for 1880–87.
3 vols. fol. Sydney, 1881–88.   ME

Report of the Council of Education. Roy. 8vo. Sydney,
1870–71.   ME

PUBLIC PRISONS.

Report from the Select Committee on the Public Prisons
in Sydney and Cumberland. Fol. Sydney 1861.
                                                   ME 10 Q 3 †

PUBLIC WORKS.

Expenditure on National and Local Works, from 1860 to
1886. Ordered by the Legislative Assembly to be printed,
28 September, 1887. 8vo. Sydney, 1887.   MF 3 R 33

Progress Report from the Select Committee on the Disorganized State of the Public Works Department. Fol.
Sydney, 1864.   ME 10 Q 5 †

Colonial Architect's Department : Return of Public
Works carried out (by James Barnet) and in progress to
the 1st of January, 1881. Fol. Sydney, 1881.* MF 1 U 5

PUNISHMENT OF CRIME.

Bill to authorize the Governor of New South Wales, to
make provision for the Prevention and Punishment of
Crimes committed by His Majesty's Subjects in Islands
situate in the Southern or Pacific Ocean, and not being
within His Majesty's Dominion. (Parl. Docs., 6.) Fol.
Lond., 1832.   MF 4 ‡

Copies of Papers relating to the Conduct of Magistrates
in New South Wales, in directing the Infliction of Punishments upon Prisoners in that Colony. (Parl. Docs., 6.)
Fol. Lond., 1826.   MF

Return, 1826, for Copies of Papers relating to the Conduct of Magistrates in New South Wales, in directing the
Infliction of Punishment upon Prisoners in that Colony.
8vo. Sydney, 1855.   MJ 2 Q 17

NEW SOUTH WALES—*continued.*

QUARANTINE STATION.

Description of the Quarantine Ground, Port Jackson; by W. A. M. (MS. Pam. E.) 4to. Sydney (n.d.)
MJ 2 S 2

Report of the Royal Commission to enquire into, and report upon the Management of the Quarantine Station, North Head, and the Hulk *Faraway.* Fol. Sydney, 1882. ME

RAILWAYS.

Union of the Railway Systems of New South Wales: Celebration at Albury, on the 14th June, 1883. 8vo. Sydney, 1883. MF 3 Q 17

Description of the Lines and Works of Construction; by John Whitton, Engineer-in-Chief. Fol. Sydney, 1876.*
MA 1 P 1 ‡

New South Wales Railways: Section of the Great Southern Railway, Sydney to Albury; Section of the Great Western Railway, Sydney to Orange; Section of the Great Northern Railway, Newcastle to Tamworth. 3 vols. ob. fol. Sydney, 1877. MA 1 P 1–3

Report on the Railways in course of Construction and the Trial Surveys, 1878. Fol. Sydney, 1878. MA 1 P 1 ‡

Report on the Trial Surveys for proposed Railway Extensions. Fol. Sydney, 1879. MJ 2 U 5

Map showing the Railways of New South Wales. Folded 8vo. Sydney, 1883. MD 2 S 36

Railways of New South Wales: Reports on their Construction and Working, 1846–76. Fol. Sydney, 1865–76.
ME

Railways of New South Wales: Report by the Commissioner for Railways, for the year 1877. Fol. Sydney, 1878. ME

Railways and Tramways of New South Wales: Reports of the Commissioner for Railways [Chas. A. Goodchap], for the years 1878–81. 2 vols. Fol. Sydney. ME

Railways and Tramways of New South Wales: Report by the Commissioner for Railways, for the 1882. Fol. Sydney, 1883. ME

REGISTRATION OF DEEDS.

Progress Report from the Select Committee on Registration of Deeds affecting Real Property. Fol. Sydney, 1860. ME 10 Q 2 †

REPRESENTATIVE GOVERNMENT.

Petition of the Colonists of New South Wales to the Honourable the Commons of the United Kingdom, &c., for Representative Government. (Pam. A.) Fol. Sydney (n.d.) MJ 2 U 1

RIVERINE DISTRICT.

Petition from, 1863. Fol. Sydney, 1863. ME 10 Q 3 †

Progress Report from the Select Committee on the Riverine Districts. (Reports, 3.) Fol. Melh., 1863.
ME 10 Q 3 †

Report from the Select Committee. Fol. Melh., 1863.
ME 10 Q 3 †

Second Progress Report from the Select Committee, on the Riverine Districts Trade. Fol. Melh., 1863.
ME 10 Q 3 †

NEW SOUTH WALES—*continued.*

SHIPPING.

Account of Ships and their Tonnage which have cleared outwards to, and entered inwards from New South Wales and Van Dieman's Land, 1822–25. (Parl. Doc., 5.) Fol. Lond., 1825. MF 4 †

STATISTICS.

Carte Agricole et Statistique Générale de la Nouvelle Galles du Sud, Australie. 8vo. Sydney, 1878. MF 3 P 22

Mineralogische Karte und allgemeine Statistik von Neu Süd Wales in Australien. 8vo. Sydney, 1878. MF 3 P 22

Carte Minéralogique et Statistique générale de la Nouvelle Galles du Sud, Australie. 8vo. Sydney, 1878. MF 3 P 22

Landwirthschaftliche Karte und allgemeine Statistik von Neu Süd Wales in Australien. (Pam. Je.) Sydney, 1878. MF 3 P 22

Statistical Register of New South Wales, for the years 1860–86. Fol. Sydney, 1861–87. ME

Population of New South Wales, 1817–18. [*See* MANUSCRIPTS AND PORTRAITS.] MF 1 U 21

STATUTES.

Acts of Parliament: a Miscellaneous Collection, compiled by Thomas Richards, Government Printer, 8vo. Sydney, 1835–71. MF 2 T 5

Public General Statutes of New South Wales, from 1824–74. 5 vols. fol. Sydney, 1861–74. ME 10 Q 7–11 †

Another copy, 1852–74 (only). 2 vols. fol. Sydney, 1862–74. ME 10 Q 13, 14 †

Index to the Statutes [1824–74]; compiled and edited by Alexander Oliver, M.A. Fol. Sydney, 1874.
ME 10 Q 12 †

Statutes of New South Wales (Public and Private), passed during the Sessions 1878–83. 2 vols. fol. Sydney, 1875–87. ME 10 R 15, 16 †

Private Acts of New South Wales (1879–85.) Fol. Sydney, 1885. ME 10 Q 17 †

[*See* LAWS AND ORDINANCES.]

SUPREME COURT.

Order of His Majesty in Council, empowering the Judges of the Supreme Courts of New South Wales and Van Dieman's Land, to make and alter Rules and Orders relating to their respective Courts. (Parl. Doc., 35.) Fol. Lond., 1825. MF 4 ‡

Copies of Correspondence relative to the default of the late Registrar of the Supreme Court of New South Wales. (Parl. Doc., 47.) Fol. Lond., 1845. MF 4 †

Reserved and Equity Judgments delivered during 1845. Roy. 8vo. Sydney, 1846. MF 2 S 16

Reports of Cases argued and determined in the Supreme Court of New South Wales; by W. H. Wilkinson, Esq., and William Owen, Esq., Barristers-at-Law. 13 vols. Roy. 8vo. Sydney, 1873–77. ME

Law Reports; in three Series: 1. Cases at Law. 2. Cases in Equity. 3. Matrimonial Cases. Reported by—Equity and Divorce—Grantley Hyde Fitzhardinge, Barrister-at Law; Cases at Law—George Knox, Barrister-at-Law. Vols. 1–3. Roy. 8vo. Sydney, 1881–82. ME

NEW SOUTH WALES—*continued.*

SUPREME COURT—*continued.*

Reports of Cases argued and determined in the Supreme Court; with Tables of the Cases and principal matters; by G. H. Fitzhardinge and J. S. Paterson. Roy. 8vo. Sydney, 1877. ME

Decision of the three Judges of the Supreme Court, on Monday, 11th April, 1836, on the Applicability of the Marriage Act of England. (Pam. Db.) 8vo. Sydney, 1836.

An Act to amend the Process, Practice, and Mode of Pleading at Law in the Supreme Court. Roy. 8vo. Sydney, 1853.

TECHNICAL EDUCATION.

Report from the Committee of the Working Men's College of the Sydney Mechanics' School of Arts. Fol. Sydney, 1881.

Report of Board of Technical Education, New South Wales, 1885; and Calendar of Sydney Technical College for 1887. 8vo. Sydney, 1886. ME 2 Q

VETERAN COMPANIES.

Account of the Annual Expense of the three New South Wales Veteran Companies, from their formation in 1825 to the present period. (Parl. Doc., 6.) Fol. Lond., 1832. MF 4 ‡

VOLUNTEER MILITARY FORCES.

Standing Orders for the information and guidance of the New South Wales Volunteer Military Forces up to 31st December, 1886. 8vo. Sydney, 1887. MF 3 Q 30

NEW SOUTH WALES ALLIANCE for the Suppression of Intemperance. Third Annual Report, 1860. 12mo. Sydney, 1861. MF 3 P 10

NEW SOUTH WALES AUXILIARY TO THE LON-DON MISSIONARY SOCIETY. [*See* LONDON MISSIONARY SOCIETY.]

NEW SOUTH WALES BUSH MISSIONARY SO-CIETY. Annual Report, 1862. 8vo. Sydney, 1862. MG 1 Q 27

Report for the two years ending 30th June, 1864. 8vo. Sydney, 1864. MG 1 Q 27

Another copy. MJ 2 Q 10

[*See* BUTTERFIELD, G., *and* PALMER, J.]

NEW SOUTH WALES LAW SOCIETY. Rules. (Pam. 10.) 8vo. Sydney, 1843. MJ 2 Q 2

NEW SOUTH WALES LITERARY, POLITICAL, AND COMMERCIAL ADVERTISER. Nos. 1, 2, 4. 8vo. Sydney, 1835. MF 3 P 4

Another copy. No. 5. 8vo. Sydney, 1835. MJ 2 R 17

NEW SOUTH WALES MAGAZINE (THE). Vols. 1, 2. "vols. (in 1) 8vo. Sydney, 1833-34.* ME 3 Q

Another copy. Vol. 1, No. 2. 8vo. Sydney, 1833. MJ 2 R 22

NEW SOUTH WALES MAGAZINE; or, Journal of General Politics, Literature, Science, and the Arts. 8vo. Sydney, 1843. ME 3 R

NEW SOUTH WALES MEDICAL GAZETTE. Vols. 1-4. 8vo. Sydney, 1871-74. ME 3 P

NEW SOUTH WALES PUBLIC SCHOOL LEAGUE. [*See* GREENWOOD, REV. J.]

NEW SOUTH WALES RELIGIOUS TRACT AND BOOK SOCIETY. Report[s] of the Australian Religious Tract Society, 1824, 1829, 1833-34, 1836-37, 1848, 1851. 8vo. Sydney, 1824-51. MG 1 Q 26

Fifteenth Report of the Australian Religious Tract Society for 1838. 8vo. Sydney, 1838. MJ 2 Q 10

Thirty-ninth Report of the New South Wales Religious Tract and Book Society for 1861. 8vo. Sydney, 1861. MG 1 Q 26

NEW SOUTH WALES RIFLE ASSOCIATION. Reports, 1861 and 1867. 8vo. Sydney, 1862-68. MF3P11 Report, 1878. (Pam. Jc.) 8vo. Sydney, 1879.
MF 3 P 22

Report, 1886. 8vo. Sydney, 1887.* ME 2 Q

NEW SOUTH WALES SAVINGS BANK. Rules and Regulations. Established in 1832. 8vo. Sydney, 1834. MF 3 P 14

NEW SOUTH WALES SOCIETY FOR PROMOTING THE OBSERVANCE OF THE LORD'S DAY. Third and Fourth Annual Report[s]. 8vo. Sydney, 1859-61. MF 3 P 14

NEW SOUTH WALES SPORTING MAGAZINE (THE). Edited by D. C. F. Scott. 8vo. Sydney, 1848. ME 3 R

NEW SOUTH WALES STAMP COLLECTORS' MAGAZINE. No. 1, November, 1878. 8vo. Sydney, 1879.* ME 3 Q

NEW SOUTH WALES TEMPERANCE SOCIETY. First and Second Annual Reports, 1835-36. 12mo. Sydney, 1835-36. MF 3 P 10

Second-Sixth Annual Reports, 1836-41. 12mo. Sydney, 1836-41. MJ 1 P 45

Half-an-hour's Reading from the Temperance Society of New South Wales. 8vo. Sydney, 1834. MJ 2 R 5

[*See* NEW SOUTH WALES ALLIANCE.]

NEW TRUTH (THE). The New Truth and the Old Faith; by "A Scientific Layman." 8vo. Lond., 1880.
G 2 T 13

NEW YORK. [*See* UNITED STATES OF AMERICA.]

NEW YORK SOCIETY LIBRARY (THE). Alphabetical and Analytical Catalogue of; with a brief Historical Notice of the Institution, &c. 8vo. New York, 1838. C 7 S 10

NEW ZEALAND.
Album of New Zealand Views. 12mo. [Leipzig, 1887.]
MD 3 Q 42
All about New Zealand; being a complete Record of
Colonial Life. 8vo. Glasgow, 1875. MD 2 S 20
Copies of Correspondence relative to the original Constitu-
tion of the Legislature of New Zealand. (Parl. Docs., 47.)
Fol. Lond., 1845. MF 4 ‡
Copies of Correspondence between the Colonial Office and
the Governor of New Zealand, respecting the Issue of
Debentures, and the rendering them a Legal Tender;
the Taxes proposed in the Legislative Council of that
Colony; the Outrages by the Natives in the Bay of Islands,
and the Abolition of the Custom-house of that District;
the Measures taken by the Governor of New Zealand, in
pursuance of Mr. Hope's Letter of 12th May, 1843, res-
pecting the Grant of a Conditional Title to the Lands of
the New Zealand Company; the Disallowance, by the
Governor of New Zealand, of any Awards made by
Commissioner of Land Claims respecting the Company's
Lands; and of all Correspondence relating to a Procla-
mation of the 26th of March, 1844, issued by the
Governor of New Zealand, allowing the Sale of Land
by the Natives. (Parl. Doc., 47.) Fol. Lond., 1845.
MF 4 ‡
New Zealand Thermal-Springs District. 4to. Wellington,
1882. MD 7 P 22 †
Papers relative to the Affairs of New Zealand. (Parl. Docs.,
47.) Fol. Lond., 1845. MF 4 ‡
Papers relating to the recent Disturbances in New Zealand.
(Parl. Docs., 69.) Lond., 1861. MF 4 ‡
Reports from the Select Committee of the House of
Lords, appointed to inquire into the Present State of the
Islands of New Zealand; with the Minutes of Evidence
taken before the Committee. (Parl. Docs., 16.) Fol.
Lond., 1838. MF 4 ‡
Reports from the Select Committee on New Zealand.
(Parl. Docs., 27.) Fol. Lond., 1840-44. MF 4 ‡
The Sounds, Lakes, and Rivers of New Zealand. From
Photographs and Sketches. 4to. Wellington, 1885.*
MD 7 P 18 †
The Thermal Springs of the North Island of New Zealand.
4to. Wellington, 1881.* MD 7 P 20 †
CENSUS.
Results of Census of New Zealand, 1871, 1875, 1878, 1881.
Fol. Wellington, 1872-82. E 2. 31
COLONIAL MUSEUM. [*See* HECTOR, SIR J.]
CROWN LANDS.
Crown Lands Guide, Nos. 6, 7, and 8. Published by
the authority of the Minister of Lands. 3 vols. 8vo.
Wellington, 1884-87. MF 2 T 12-14
Return, showing in Columns the various Acres or Lots of
Land sold by Government. (Parl. Docs. 43.) Fol. Lond.,
1842. MF 4 ‡
New Zealand Land Act, 1885; with explanatory Preface
of the principal Provisions relating to Settlement. 8vo.
Wellington, 1885. MF 2 T 6
Important Judgments delivered in the Compensation Court
and Native Land Court, 1866-79. 8vo. Auckland, 1879.
MF 2 P 24

NEW ZEALAND—*continued.*
EXHIBITIONS.
New Zealand Exhibition, 1865: Reports and Awards of
the Jurors, and Appendix. 8vo. Dunedin, 1866.
MK 1 S 12
New Zealand Industrial Exhibition, 1885: Wellington
Official Record. Roy.8vo. Wellington, 1886. MK 1 S 16
New Zealand Industrial Exhibition: Prize Essays on
the Industries of New Zealand [by Richard Winter, Wil-
liam Reeve Haselden, and George Robert Hart]. Roy.
8vo. Wellington, 1886. MK 1 S 16
FLAX.
Report of the Flax Commissioners on the Means em
ployed in the Preparation of New Zealand Flax. Fol.
Wellington, 1870. MF 1 U 17
GAZETTE.
The New Zealand Gazette, 1876-82. 12 vols. fol. Wel-
lington, 1876-82. ME
GEOLOGICAL EXPLORATIONS.
Geological Survey of New Zealand: Reports of Geo-
logical Explorations during 1870 and 1886-87; with
Maps and Sections. 11 vols. 8vo. Wellington,
1871-87. ME 2 S
Geological Survey of New Zealand. Reports of Geo-
logical Explorations; with Maps to illustrate Reports
of the Buller Coal-field, by S. K. Cox and R. B. Den-
niston. 3 vols. 8vo. Wellington, 1877. ME 2 S
Index to Reports of the Geological Survey, 1866-85. Roy.
8vo. Wellington, 1887. ME 2 S
HOUSE OF REPRESENTATIVES.
Appendix to Journals of the House of Representatives, for
1861-80. 35 vols. fol. Wellington, 1861-80. ME
New Zealand Legislative Council and House of Repre-
sentatives. 44 vols. 8vo. Wellington, 1872-88. ME
Parliamentary Papers: New Zealand. Fol. Welling-
ton, 1883. ME
LAWS AND ORDINANCES.
Copies of the Laws and Ordinances passed by the Governor
and Council of the Colony of New Zealand, 4 and 5
Victoria, 1841. (Parl. Docs., 27.) Fol. Lond., 1842.
MF
MINING.
Reports on the Mining Industry of New Zealand. Fol.
Wellington, 1887. MA 2 Q 24 †
Another copy. Fol. Wellington, 1887. MA 2 Q 27 †
ORDINANCES. [*See* STATUTES.]
PARLIAMENTARY DEBATES.
New Zealand. First Parliament: Legislative Council
and House of Representatives, 1854-63. Compiled by
Maurice Fitzgerald. 3 vols.8vo. Wellington, 1885 ME
Parliamentary Debates: Legislative Council and House
of Representatives. 44 vols. 8vo. Wellington, 1872-88.
ME
PARLIAMENTARY LIBRARY.
Catalogue of Books. 8vo. Lond., 1864. MK 1 S 22
Catalogue of the Library of the General Assembly of
New Zealand. Compiled by A. Macgregor. Roy. 8vo.
Wellington, 1885. MK 1 S 23

4 A

NEW ZEALAND—*continued.*
PARLIAMENTARY LIBRARY—*continued.*
Supplemental Catalogue of Books, 1885-86. 8vo. Wellington, 1886.   MK 1 S 24

PATENTS.
Specifications of Inventions in respect of which Letters Patent or Letters of Registration have been applied for during the years 1875-78. 3 vols. fol. Wellington, 1876-79.   ME

STATISTICS.
Statistics of the Colony of New Zealand, for the years 1853-81. Compiled from Official Records. 23 vols. fol. Wellington, 1854-82.   ME

STATUTES.
Ordinances of New Zealand, 1841-53. Fol. Wellington, 1871.   ME

Statutes of New Zealand. 12 vols. fol. Wellington, 1841-85.   ME

Statutes of New Zealand; with Indexes, by Wilfred Badger. 2 vols. 4to. Christchurch, 1885. MF 3 S 1, 2

TREATY OF WAITANGI.
Fac-similes of the Declaration of Independence, and the Treaty of Waitangi. Fol. Wellington, 1877.* MB 3 Q 1 ‡

NEW ZEALAND CHURCH ALMANAC for 1853. 12mo. Auckland, 1853.   ME 4 Q

NEW ZEALAND COLONIST, A. [*See* HURSTHOUSE, C.]

NEW ZEALAND COMPANY. Acccount of the Settlements of the New Zealand Company. [*See* PETRIE, HON. H. W. LORD.]

Bill to authorize a Loan from the Consolidated Fund to the New Zealand Company. (Parl. Doc., 47.) Fol. Lond., 1846.   MF 4 ‡

Copies of Correspondence respecting the Grant of a Conditional Title to the Lands of the New Zealand Company, &c. (Parl. Docs., 47.) Fol. Lond., 1845.   MF 4 ‡

Copy of Correspondence between Her Majesty's Secretary of State for the Colonies and the New Zealand Company, relative to the establishment of a Proprietary Government in the Islands of New Zealand. (Parl. Doc., 47.) Fol. Lond., 1845.   MF 4 ‡

Corrected Report of the Debate in the House of Commons, on the 17th, 18th, and 19th of June, on the State of New Zealand, and the Case of the New Zealand Company. (Pam. 16.) 8vo. Lond., 1845.*   MF 2 R 3

Another copy. 8vo. Lond., 1845.   MJ 2 Q 6

Documents appended to the Twelfth Report of the Directors. 8vo. Lond., 1844.   MB 2 Q 19

New Zealand and the New Zealand Company. [*See* HEALE, T.]

New Zealand Company: its Claim to Compensation considered. (Pam. 15.) 8vo. Lond., 1845. MJ 2 Q 5

NEW ZEALAND EXHIBITION, 1865. Reports and Awards of the Jurors; and Appendix. Roy. 8vo. Dunedin, 1866.   MK 1 S 12

NEW ZEALAND INDUSTRIAL EXHIBITION, 1885. New Zealand Industrial Exhibition: the Official Record. Roy. 8vo. Wellington, 1886.   MK 1 S 16

Prize Essays on the Industries of New Zealand [by Richard Winter; William Reeve Haselden, and George Robert Haite]. Roy. 8vo. Wellington, 1886. MK 1 S 16

NEW ZEALAND INSTITUTE (THE). Transactions and Proceedings of the New Zealand Institute. Edited by Sir James Hector, K.C.M.G. Vols. 1-19, 1868-86. 8vo. Wellington, 1869-87.   ME 2 S

Index to Vols. 1-8; by Sir James Hector. Roy. 8vo. Wellington, 1877.   ME 2 S

Index to Vols. 1-17; by Sir James Hector. Roy. 8vo. Wellington, 1886.   ME 2 S

NEW ZEALAND MAIL SERVICE. [*See* INTERCOLONIAL ROYAL MAIL STEAM PACKET CO.]

NEW ZEALANDERS (THE). [*See* CRAIK, PROF. G. L.]

NEWALL (MAJOR-GEN. DAVID J. F.), R.A., &c. Highlands of India strategically considered, with special reference to their colonization as Reserve Circles, Military, Industrial, and Sanitary. Illustrated. [Vol. 1.] 8vo. Lond., 1882   D 16 U 11

NEWALL (CAPT. J. T.) The Eastern Hunters. With Illustrations. 8vo. Lond., 1866.   D 5 T 38

Hog-hunting in the East, and other Sports. With Illustrations. 8vo. Lond., 1867.   A 17 U 20

NEWBERY (JOHN). A Bookseller of the Last Century; being some Account of the Life of, and of the Books he published, &c., by Charles Welsh. 8vo. Lond., 1885   C 5 V 1

NEWBIGGING (THOMAS). Treatise on Coal Gas. [*See* KING, W. B.]   A 2 R 16-18 †

NEWBOLD (T. J.) Political and Statistical Account of the British Settlements in the Straits of Malacca. 2 vols. 8vo. Lond., 1869.   B 10 T 38, 39

NEWCASTLE (MARGARET), DUCHESS OF. Life of William Cavendish, Duke of Newcastle; edited by C. H. Firth, M.A. 8vo. Lond., 1886.   C 10 S 8

NEWCASTLE (WILLIAM CAVENDISH), DUKE OF. Life of; to which is added, the true Relation of my Birth, Breeding, and Life, by Margaret, Duchess of Newcastle; edited by C. H. Firth, M.A. 8vo. Lond., 1886.   C 10 S 8

NEWCASTLE BUSINESS DIRECTORY. [*See* KNAGGS, R. C., & Co.]

NEWCASTLE CHURCH SOCIETY. [*See* CHURCH OF ENGLAND.]

NEWCASTLE HOSPITAL. Rules and Regulations for the Management of. (Pam. Dv.) 8vo. Newcastle, 1861. MF 3 P 19

NEWCASTLE–UPON–TYNE PUBLIC LIBRARIES. Supplementary Catalogue of Books added to the Lending Library; compiled by W. J. Haggerston. Roy. 8vo. Lond., 1887. K 8 R 17

NEWCHAMP (MR.) [*See* ADVENTURES OF MR. NEWCHAMP.]

NEWCOMB (PROF. SIMON), PH.D., &c. Astronomical Papers, prepared for the Use of the American Ephemeris and Nautical Almanac, under the direction of Professor S. Newcomb. Vol. 1. 4to. Washington, 1882. E 1.72

NEWCOMB (PROF. SIMON), LL.D., AND HOLDEN (EDWARD S.), M.A. Astronomy for Schools and Colleges. (American Science Series.) 8vo. New York, 1879. A 3 S 14

NEWELL (CHARLES M.) Kaméhaméha, the Conquering King—the Mystery of his Birth, Loves, and Conquests: a Romance of Hawaii. 8vo. New York, 1885. MJ 1 S 15

NEWHOUSE (S.) Trapper's Guide: a Manual of Instructions for capturing all kinds of Fur-bearing Animals, and curing their Skins. 3rd ed. Roy. 8vo. New York, 1869. A 14 T 13

NEWMAN (CHARLES L. NORRIS-). With the Boers in the Transvaal and Orange Free State, in 1880–81. 8vo. Lond., 1882. B 1 P 33

NEWMAN (EDWARD), F.L.S.,&c. History of British Ferns. 8vo. Lond., 1854. A 4 S 6

Dictionary of British Birds. Reprinted from Montagu's Ornithological Dictionary. 8vo. Lond.,1866. A 15 P 19

NEWMAN (PROF. FRANCIS WILLIAM), M.R.A.S. Libyan Vocabulary: an Essay towards reproducing the Ancient Numidian Language, out of four Modern Tongues. 8vo. Lond., 1882. K 12 Q 40

Lectures on Political Economy. 8vo. Lond., 1851. F 5 T 10

Anti-Vaccination in a Nutshell: a Tract. (Pam. Cp.) 8vo. Lond. (n.d.) A 12 S 34

Phases of Faith; or, Passages from the History of my Creed. 9th ed. 8vo. Lond., 1874. G 7 R 10

English Universities. [*See* HUBER, V. A., *and* ROGERS, H.] B 5 U 48-50

NEWMAN (HENRY STANLEY). Autobiography of George Fox. [*See* FOX, G.] C 5 S 16

NEWMAN (JOHN HENRY), D.D., CARDINAL. Arians of the 4th Century. 8vo. Lond., 1871. G 8 T 21

Office and Work of Universities. 12mo. Lond., 1856. G 17 P 12

An Essay in aid of a Grammar of Assent. 2nd ed. 8vo. Lond., 1870. G 7 R 9

Historical Sketches. 8vo. Lond., 1872. B 14 P 24

Apologia pro Vita Sua; being a Reply to a Pamphlet entitled—"What then, does Dr. Newman mean?" 8vo. Lond., 1864. G 8 T 20

Lectures on the Prophetical Office of the Church, viewed relatively to Romanism and Popular Protestantism. 2nd ed. 8vo. Lond., 1838. G 8 T 19

Essay on the Development of Christian Doctrine. 8vo. Lond., 1845. G 8 T 12

Lectures on Justification. 8vo. Lond., 1840. G 8 T 18

Letter addressed to his Grace the Duke of Norfolk, on occasion of Mr. Gladstone's recent Expostulation. 8vo. Lond., 1875. G 8 T 13

Cardinal Newman; by John Oldcastle. 8vo. Lond., 1886. C 10 U 39

Discourses on the Scope and Nature of University Education. 8vo. Dublin, 1852. G 17 Q 27

NEWMARK (NATHAN). The Code of Civil Procedure of the State of California, adopted 11th March, 1872, amended in 1885. 12mo. San Francisco, 1885. F 2 P 2

The Penal Code of the State of California, as enacted in 1872 and amended in 1885. 12mo. San Francisco, 1885. F 2 P 4

NEWSPAPER CUTTINGS. 2 vols. 4to. Melb. (n.d.) MJ 2 S 5, and 2 U 6

NEWTH (PROF. SAMUEL), M.A., &c. Lectures on Bible Revision; with an Appendix, containing the Prefaces to the Chief Historical Editions of the English Bible. 8vo. Lond., 1881. G 7 R 8

NEWTON (CHARLES THOMAS), C.B., &c. Essays on Art and Archæology. 8vo. Lond., 1880. B 9 V 24

Travels and Discoveries in the Levant. With numerous Illustrations. 2 vols. roy. 8vo. Lond.,1865. D 5 U 3, 4

NEWTON (ERNEST). Sketches for Cottages and other Buildings. [*See* SHAW, R. N.] A 23 P 2 ‡

NEWTON (SIR ISAAC). Chronology of Ancient Kingdoms, amended ; to which is prefixed a short Chronicle from the First Memory of Things in Europe. Roy. 8vo. Lond., 1728. B 7 V 1

Newton, his Friend, and his Niece; by the late Augustus De Morgan. Edited by his Wife, and his Pupil, Arthur Cowper Ranyard. 8vo. Lond., 1885. C 10 U 38

Philosophiæ Naturalis Principia Mathematica; perpetuis commentariis illustrata, communi studio Thomæ Le Seur et Francisci Jacquier. 2 vols. roy. 8vo. Glasgow, 1833. A 10 U 19, 20

NEWTON (SIR ISAAC)—*continued.*

Observations upon the Prophecies of Daniel. 8vo. Lond., 1831.   G 14 P 7

Correspondence of Sir Isaac Newton and Professor Cotes, including Letters of other Eminent Men; by J. Edleston, M.A. 8vo. Lond., 1850.   C 10 U 37

Mathematical Principles of Natural Philosophy. Translated by A. Motte; with Newton's System of the World, by W. Emerson, and the Laws of the Moon's Motion, by J. Machin. New ed., with Life of the Author, by W. Davis. 3 vols. 8vo. Lond., 1803.   A 3 T 1-3

Life of; by J. B. Biot. (Eminent Men.) 8vo. Lond., 1849.   C 7 P 45

Memoirs of his Life, Writings, and Discoveries, by Sir David Brewster. 2 vols. 8vo. Edinb., 1855. C 9 Q 5, 6

Universal Arithmetick; or, a Treatise of Arithmetical Composition and Resolution. Written in Latin; translated by the late Mr. Ralphson, and corrected by Mr. Cunn. 8vo. Lond., 1769.   A 10 S 9

Life of; by David Brewster, LL.D., &c. 18mo. Lond., 1831.   C 1 P 33

NEWTON (REV. JOHN). Works of. 9 vols. 12mo. Lond., 1822.   G 7 R 11-19

NEWTON (JOSEPH), F.R.H.S. Landscape Gardener: a Practical Guide to the Laying-out, Planting, and Arrangement of Villa Gardens, Town Squares, and Open Spaces, from a quarter of an acre to four acres. 4to. Lond., 1876.   A 2 P 18 †

NEWTON'S LONDON JOURNAL OF ARTS AND SCIENCES. [*See* LONDON JOURNAL OF ARTS AND SCIENCES.]

NEWTOWN FREE LIBRARY. Catalogue, 1870. Compiled by R. N. Banks. 12mo. Newtown, 1870.
                                                  MK 1 P 25

NEY (MARSHAL MICHEL), DUKE OF ELCHINGEN. Memoirs of, published by his Family; illustrated with Portrait, Maps, and Plans. 2 vols. 8vo. Lond., 1833. C 9 P 1, 2

NIBBY (PROF. ANTONIO). Roma nell' anno MDCCCXXXVIII. 4 vols. 8vo. Roma, 1838-41.   D 8 U 10-13

NICEPHORUS BLEMMIDA. Opera Omnia. [*See* MIGNE, J. P., SERIES GRÆCA, 142.]

NICEPHORUS (CALLISTUS XANTHOPULUS). Ecclesiastica Historiæ libri XVIII. [*See* MIGNE, J. P., SERIES GRÆCA, 145-147.]

NICEPHORUS (GREGORAS). [*See* BYZANTINÆ HIST. SCRIPT.]

NICEPHORUS (SANCTUS). Opera omnia. [*See* MIGNE, J. P., SERIES GRÆCA, 139, 140.]

NICETAS ACOMINATUS. (CHONIATES). Opera omnia. [*See* MIGNE, J. P., SERIES GRÆCA, 195.]

[*See* BYZANTINÆ HIST. SCRIPT.]

NICETAS (DAVID). Opera omnia. [*See* MIGNE, J. P., SERIES GRÆCA, 139, 140.]

NICÉVILLE (LIONEL DE). Butterflies of India. [*See* MARSHALL, G. F. L.]   A 15 Q 19

NICHOL (PROF. JOHN), LL.D. American Literature: an Historical Sketch. 1620-1880. 8vo. Lond., 1882.   B 1 R 46

Byron. (Eng. Men of Letts.) 8vo. Lond., 1880. C 1 U 7

Death of Themistocles, and other Poems. 12mo. Glasgow, 1881.   H 7 P 26

[*See* DOBELL, S. T.]

NICHOL (PROF. J. P.), LL.D., &c. Contemplations on the Solar System. 8vo. Lond., 1847.   A 3 T 29

Architecture of the Heavens. 9th ed. 8vo. Lond., 1851.   A 3 U 25

Thoughts on some important points relating to the System of the World. 8vo. Edinb., 1846.   A 3 T 22

Cyclopædia of the Physical Sciences. 3rd ed. 8vo. Lond., 1868.   K 4 S 13

Dissertation on some points connected with the Present State of Education. [*See* WILLM, J.]

Views of the Architecture of the Heavens; in a Series of Letters to a Lady. 8vo. Edinb., 1837. A 3 T 36

NICHOLAS I (EMPEROR OF RUSSIA). The Life of; with a Short Account of Russia and the Russians; by F. Mayne. 8vo. Lond., 1855.   C 3 T 16

NICHOLAS (JOHN LIDDIARD). Narrative of a Voyage to New Zealand, performed in the years 1814-15, in company with the Rev. Samuel Marsden. 2 vols. 8vo. Lond., 1817.*   MD 5 U 12, 13

Reise nach und in Neuseeland in den Jahren 1814-15 mit den, von Neuholland dahin reisenden Missionarien gemacht. 8vo. Weimar, 1819.   MD 5 U 18

Verhaal eener Reis naar Nieuw-Zeeland, gedaan in de Jaren 1814-15, in Gezelschap met den Weleerw. Heer Samuel Marsden, door den Heer John Liddiard Nicholas. Uit de Engelsche beschrijving van den Laatstgenoemden vertaald. 2 vols. 8vo. Rotterdam, 1812-21.
                                                  MD 5 U 19, 20

NICHOLL (LITTD). Extract from a Report of the King's Proctor on the subject of the Seizure of the ship *Almorah.* (Parl. Doc., 6.) Fol. Lond., 1831.   MF 4 ‡

NICHOLS (J. F.) Remarkable Life, Adventures, and Discoveries of Sebastian. 8vo. Lond., 1869. C 2 Q 19

NICHOLLS (J. F.), F.S.A., AND TAYLOR (JOHN). Bristol: Past and Present. 3 vols. 4to. Bristol, 1881-82.   B 2 T 36-38

NICHOLLS (J. H. KERRY-) The King Country; or, Explorations in New Zealand: a Narrative of 600 miles of Travel through Maoriland. With numerous Illustrations and a Map. 8vo. Lond., 1884.   MD 1 V 27

NICHOLS (JOHN), F.S.A. Biographical Anecdotes of William Hogarth; with a Catalogue of his Works. 3rd ed. 8vo. Lond., 1785. C 6 U 17

History and Antiquities of the Archiepiscopal Palace of Lambeth. [*See* DUCAREL, DR. A. C.] B 6 V 11

History and Antiquities of the Parish of Lambeth. [*See* DUCAREL, A. C.] B 6 V 12

Illustrations of the Literary History of the 18th Century. 8 vols. 8vo. Lond., 1817–58. B 37 T 11–U 1

Literary Anecdotes of the 18th Century; comprising Biographical Memoirs of Wm. Bowyer (Printer), F.S.A., and many of his learned Friends. 9 vols. (in 10) 8vo. Lond., 1812–15. B 37 T 1–10

Works of W. Hogarth. [*See* HOGARTH, W.] A 10 P 7 ‡

NICHOLS (JOHN GOUGH), F.S.A. Topographer and Genealogist. 3 vols. 8vo. Lond., 1846–58. D 12 U 19–21

Life of Henry Earl of Arundel, K.G. [*See* ARUNDEL, HENRY, EARL OF.] C 3 W 2

NICHOLS (T. L.), M.D. Human Physiology : the Basis of Sanitary and Social Science. 8vo. Lond., 1872. A 12 Q 28

NICHOLSON (SIR CHARLES), BART., &c. Catalogue of Egyptian and other Antiquities, collected by Sir C. Nicholson. 8vo. Lond., 1858. K 7 Q 3

Inaugural Addresses delivered on the occasion of the Opening of the University of Sydney, in 1852; also, Report of Addresses at various Commemorations held in subsequent years. 4to. Lond., 1862. MG 1 U 1

NICHOLSON (SIR CHARLES), BART., AND WOOLLEY (PROF. JOHN), D.C.L. Inaugural Addresses delivered on the Opening of the University of Sydney, on Monday, October 11, 1852. (Pam. E.) 4to. Sydney, 1852. MJ 2 S 2

NICHOLSON (REV. EMILIUS). Nicholson's Cambrian Traveller's Guide. [*See* NICHOLSON, G.] D 11 T 26

NICHOLSON (GEORGE). Nicholson's Cambrian Traveller's Guide. 3rd ed., revised and corrected by his Son, the Rev. Emilius Nicholson. 8vo. Lond., 1840. D 11 T 26

NICHOLSON (GEORGE), JUNR. The Cape and its Colonists ; with Hints from Settlers in 1848. 8vo. Lond., 1848. D 1 S 30

NICHOLSON (GEORGE). Illustrated Dictionary of Gardening : a Practical and Scientific Encyclopædia of Horticulture for Gardeners and Botanists. Vols. 1, 2. 2 vols. 4to. Lond., 1885–86. K 4 Q 15, 16

NICHOLSON (PROF. H. ALLEYNE), M.D., &c. Advanced Text-book of Zoology, for the use of Schools. 8vo. Edinb., 1870. A 14 Q 8

Manual of Palæontology for the use of Students ; with a general Introduction on the Principal of Palæontology. 8vo. Edinb., 1872. A 9 Q 4

Another copy. 2nd ed. 2 vols. 8vo. Edinb., 1879. A 10 Q 20, 21

NICHOLSON (PROF. H. ALLEYNE), M.D., &c.—*continued.* On the Structure and Affinities of the "Tabulate Corals" of the Palæozoic Period; with critical Description of illustrative Species. Roy. 8vo. Edinb., 1879. A 9 V 7

On the Structures and Affinities of the genus Monticulipora and its sub-genera ; with critical Description of illustrative Species. Roy. 8vo. Edinb., 1881. A 15 Q 2

Ancient Life-History of the Earth : a comprehensive Outline of the Principles and leading Facts of Palæontological Science. 8vo. Edinb., 1877. A 14 S 41

Synopsis of the Classification of the Animal Kingdom. 8vo. Edinb., 1882. A 14 R 40

NICHOLSON (CAPT. H. WHALLEY). From Sword to Share ; or, a Fortune in Five Years in Hawaii. 8vo. Lond., 1881. MD 4 Q 48

NICHOLSON (JOHN). Operative Mechanic and British Mechanist; being a practical Display of the Manufactories and Mechanical Arts of the United Kingdom. 3rd ed. 8vo. Lond., 1834. A 11 U 6

NICHOLSON (JOHN H.) Adventures of Halek : an Autobiographical Fragment. 8vo. Lond., 1882. J 11 R 31

NICHOLSON (PETER). Carpenter's New Guide; being a complete Book of Lines for Carpentry and Joinery. 4to. Lond., 1808. A 11 V 11

Builders' and Workman's New Director. 4to. Lond., 1836. A 2 T 35

Principles of Architecture; containing the Fundamental Rules of the Art. Plates. 3 vols. 8vo. Lond., 1841. A 3 P 9–11

NICHOLSON (RENTON). Lord Chief Baron Nicholson : an Autobiography. 12mo. Lond., 1860. C 1 P 23

NICOL (JAMES), F.R.S.E., &c. Manual of Mineralogy; or, the Natural History of the Mineral Kingdom. 8vo. Edinb., 1849. A 9 P 22

Elements of Mineralogy. 12mo. Edinb., 1858. A 9 P 25

NICOL (JAMES). Vital, Social, and Economic Statistics of the City of Glasgow, 1881–85. 8vo. Glasgow, 1885. F 7 S 12

NICOLAS (SIR NICHOLAS HARRIS), KT., G.C.M.G., &c. The Chronology of History. (Lard. Cab. Cyclo.) 12mo. Lond., 1833. K 1 S 36

Life of William Davison, Secretary of State and Privy Counsellor to Queen Elizabeth. 8vo. Lond., 1823. C 8 R 5

Memoir of Augustine Vincent, Windsor Herald, 1617–24. 8vo. Lond., 1827. C 4 T 43

Privy Purse Expenses of King Henry VIII, from November, 1529, to December, 1532; with introductory Remarks and illustrative Notes. 8vo. Lond., 1827. B 6 P 39

Siege of Carlaverock in 28th Edward I, A.D. 1300 ; with the Arms of the Earls, Barons, and Knights who were present on the occasion. 4to. Lond., 1828. B 12 V 23

NICOLAS (SIR NICHOLAS HARRIS), KT., G.C.M.G., &c.—*ctd.*
Privy Purse Expenses of Elizabeth of York; Wardrobe Accounts of Edward IV; with a Memoir of Elizabeth of York, and Notes. 8vo. Lond., 1830.   B 6 P 41

History of the Battle of Agincourt, and of the Expedition of Henry V into France in 1415; to which is added, the Roll of the Men-at-Arms in the English Army. 8vo. Lond., 1832.   B 5 U 16

Letters of Joseph Ritson, Esq. Edited chiefly from Originals in the possession of his Nephew; to which is prefixed, a Memoir of the Author. 2 vols. 8vo. Lond., 1833.   C 4 P 27, 28

Proceedings and Ordinances of the Privy Council of England, 10 Richard II, 1386, to 33 Henry VIII, 1542. 7 vols. roy. 8vo. Lond., 1834–37.   B 15 T 9–15

History of the Orders of Knighthood of the British Empire; of the Order of the Guelphs of Hanover; and of the Medals, Clasps, and Crosses conferred for Naval and Military Services. (With coloured Plates.) 4 vols. imp. 4to. Lond., 1842.   B 14 S 1–4 †

History of the Earldoms of Strathern, Monteith, and Airth; with a Report of the Proceedings before the House of Lords, on the claim of Robert Barclay Allardice, Esq., to the Earldom of Airth. 8vo. Lond., 1842.   B 13 R 30

Memoirs of the Life and Times of Sir Christopher Hatton, K.G. 8vo. Lond., 1847.   C 10 U 14

History of the Royal Navy, from the Earliest Times to the Wars of the French Revolution. 2 vols. 8vo. Lond., 1847.   B 6 Q 48, 49

Historic Peerage of England, exhibiting, under alphabetical arrangement, the Origin, Descent, and Present State of every Title of Peerage which has existed in this Country since the Conquest; revised, corrected, &c., by William Courthope, Esq., Somerset Herald. 8vo. Lond., 1857.   K 10 T 3

Private Memoirs of Sir Kenelm Digby. [*See* DIGBY, SIR K.]   C 6 Q 15

[*See* CHRONICLES OF LONDON.]   B 15 Q 3 ‡

[*See* NELSON, H., VISCOUNT.]   B 6 R 1–7

NICOLAS (LIEUT. P. H.), R.M. Naval and Military Heroes of Great Britain. [*See* JOHNS, MAJOR.]   C 3 P 31

NICOLAUS (CONSTANTINOPOLITANUS ARCHIEPISCOPUS). Epistolæ. [*See* MIGNE, J. P., SERIES GRÆCA, 111.]

NICOLINI (G. B.) History of the Jesuits: their Origin, Progress, Doctrines, and Designs. 8vo. Lond., 1854.   G 16 P 26

NICOLL (ROBERT), POET. The Life of; with some hitherto uncollected Pieces, by P. R. Drummond. 8vo. Paisley, 1884.   C 3 T 47

NICOLS (ARTHUR), F.G.S., &c. Acclimatisation of the Salmonidæ at the Antipodes; its History and Results. 8vo. Lond., 1882.   MA 2 T 19

Wild Life and Adventure in the Australian Bush. Four Years' Personal Experience. 2 vols. 8vo. Lond., 1887.*   MJ 2 P 1, 2

NICOLS (ARTHUR), F.G.S., &c.—*continued.*
Zoological Notes on the Structure, Affinities, Habits, and Mental Faculties of Wild and Domestic Animals; with Anecdotes concerning, and Adventures among them; and some account of their Fossil Representatives. Illustrated. 8vo. Lond., 1883.   A 14 S 26

Puzzle of Life, and how it has been put together. 12mo. Lond., 1877.   A 9 P 39

NICOLSON (ALEXANDER), M.A., &c. Collection of Gaelic Proverbs and Familiar Phrases. Based on Mackintosh's Collection. 8vo. Edinb., 1881.   K 17 P 16

Memoirs of Adam Black. 2nd ed. 8vo. Edinb., 1885.   C 4 Q 3

NICOLSON (WILLIAM). Leges Anglo-Saxonicæ. [*See* WILKINS, D.]

NIEBUHR (BARTHOLD GEORG). History of Rome; translated by Julius C. Hare, M.A., and Connop Thirlwall, M.A. 2nd ed. 2 vols. 8vo. Camb., 1831.   B 12 R 13, 1

History of Rome; Epitomised from the larger Work, by T. Twiss, B.C.L. 8vo. Oxford, 1845.   B 12 R 15

Lectures on the History of Rome; edited by Dr. Leonhard Schmitz, F.R.S.E. 3 vols. 8vo. Lond., 1844–49.   B 12 S 2–4

Life and Letters of; with Essays on his Character and Influence; by the Chevalier Bunsen, Profs. Brandis and Loebell. 2 vols. 8vo. Lond., 1852.   C 9 P 5, 6

Lectures on Ancient Ethnography and Geography; translated from the German ed. of Dr. Isler, by Dr. L. Schmidt, F.R.S.E. 2 vols. 8vo. Lond., 1853.   D 12 U 14, 15

History of Rome; translated by J. C. Hare, M.A., and C. Thirlwell, M.A. New ed. [Vol. 3, edited by J. Classen.] 3 vols. 8vo. Lond., 1855–60.   B 12 R 16–18

Reminiscences of an intercourse with Mr. Niebuhr, the Historian, during a residence with him in Rome in the years 1822–23; by Francis Lieber. 8vo. Philad., 1835.   C 3 T 15

Corpus Scriptorum Historiæ Byzantinæ. [*See* BYZANTINÆ HIST. SCRIPT.]   B 9 U 1–V 14

NIEBUHR (CARSTENS). Travels through Arabia and other Countries in the East; translated into English by Robert Heron. 2 vols. 8vo. Edinb., 1792.   D 6 P 44, 45

Life of. (Eminent Men.) 8vo. Lond., 1849.   C 7 P 45

NIEUHOFF (JOHANN HANS.) Legatio Batavica ad Magnum Tartariæ Chamum Sungteium, Modernum Sinæ Imperatorum. Historiarum Narratione. Fol. Amstelodami, 1668.   D 4 V 20

Voyages and Travels into Brasil and the East Indies; containing an exact Description of the Dutch Brasil, and divers parts of the East Indies. Translated from the Dutch Original. Fol. Lond., 1703.   D 5 P 2 †

NIGHTINGALE (THOMAS). Oceanic Sketches; with a Botanical Appendix by Dr. Hooker, of Glasgow. 8vo. Lond., 1835.* MD 6 S 2

NIGHT SCENES OF MELBOURNE. Illustrated. 8vo. Melb., 1878. MJ 2 R 12

NILSON (ARVID). Timber Trees of New South Wales. Printed for the Forest Conservancy Branch, Department of Mines. 8vo. Sydney, 1884.* MA 1 Q 32

NILUS (SANCTUS). Opera omnia. [*See* MIGNE, J. P., SERIES GRÆCA, 79.]

NIMROD. [*See* APPERLEY, C. J.]

NIND (SCOTT). Description of the Natives of King George's Sound (Swan River Colony). 8vo. Lond., 1831. MD6R24

NINETEENTH CENTURY (THE). Monthly Review. Edited by James Knowles. Vols. 1-17. Roy. 8vo. Lond., 1877-85.

NINIAN (SAINT). Lives of St. Ninian and St. Kentigern; edited, from the best MSS., by Alexander Penrose Forbes, D.C.L., Bishop of Brechin. 8vo. Edinb., 1874. G 14 T 15

Another copy. (Historians of Scotland.) B 13 P 49

NINON. [*See* LENCLOS, ANNE DE.]

NISARD (M.) Oeuvres complètes de Sénèque. [*See* SENECA, L. A.]

NISBET (ALEXANDER). System of Heraldry, speculative and practical; with the true Art of Blazon, according to the most approved Heralds in Europe. 2 vols. fol. Edinb., 1816. K 22 R 5, 6 ‡

NISBET (CHARLES). Caroline Bauer and the Coburgs; translated and edited from "Nachgelassene Memoiren von Karoline Bauer." 8vo. Lond., 1885. C 3 S 1

NISH (REV. JAMES). Universalism examined and refuted. 8vo. Melb., 1870. MG 1 Q 39

NISSER (PEDRO). On the Elementary Substances originating and promoting Civilisation throughout the World. 8vo. Melb., 1860. J 2 R 12

NIVEN (W.) Illustrations of Old Warwickshire Houses; with Descriptive Notes. 4to. Lond., 1878. B 16 R 8 ‡

NIXON (FRANCIS H.) Population; or, a Plea for Victoria; being a few Remarks on the subject of Immigration, with reference to the Condition and Progress of the Colony. 8vo. Melb., 1862. MF 1 Q 2

Legends and Lays of "Peter Perfume." 12mo. Melb., 1865. MH 1 R 51

NIXON (RT. REV. FRANCIS RUSSELL), D.D., BISHOP OF TASMANIA. Transportation: Copy of a Communication upon the subject of Transportation, addressed to Earl Grey by the Lord Bishop of Tasmania. 8vo. Launceston, 1848. MF 3 P 6

Charge, delivered to the Clergy of the Diocese of Tasmania, at the Primary Visitation, in the Cathedral Church of St. David, Hobart Town, on Thursday, April 23, 1846. 2nd ed. 8vo. Lond., 1848. MG 1 Q 31

Substance of a Reply to a Deputation appointed at a Public Meeting of Members of the Church of England, held in Hobart Town, on Thursday, April 22, 1852. 8vo. Hobart, 1852. MG 1 Q 31

Answer [to the above]. [*See* FRY, H. P.]

Charge, delivered to the Clergy of the Diocese of Tasmania, at the Visitation, held in the Cathedral Church of St. David, Hobart Town, on Tuesday, 22nd May, 1855; and in the Church of the Holy Trinity, Launceston, on Thursday, 31st May. 8vo. Hobart, 1855. MG 1 Q 31

Cruise of the *Beacon :* a Narrative of a Visit to the Islands in Bass's Straits. With Illustrations. 8vo. Lond., 1857.* MD 4 T 11

Self-help, by the Lord Bishop of Tasmania: the Inaugural Lecture of the Winter Session of the Hobart Town Working Men's Club, 1865. 8vo. Hobart, 1865. MG 1 Q 31

NIXON (F. R.) Twelve Views in Adelaide and its Vicinity, South Australia. Ob. 8vo. Adelaide, 1845. MD 7 P 1 †

NIXON (JOHN). Complete Story of the Transvaal, from the "Great Trek" to the Convention of London; with Appendix, comprising Ministerial Declarations of Policy, and Official Documents. 8vo. Lond., 1885. B 1 Q 3

NIXON (R. C. J.) Euclid Revised. [*See* EUCLIDES.] A 10 S 30

NIZAMI. Persian Poetry. [*See* ROBINSON, S.]

NOAD (HENRY M.), PH.D., &c. Lectures on Chemistry; including its Applications in the Arts, and the Analysis of Organic and Inorganic Compounds. 8vo. Lond., 1843. A 5 U 36

Rudimentary Magnetism. [*See* HARRIS, SIR W. S.]

NOBLE (CAPT. ANDREW), M.I.C.E., &c. Heat Action of Explosives. [*See* HEAT.] A 11 U 12

NOBLE (EDMUND). Russian Revolt: its Causes, Condition, and Prospects. 12mo. Lond., 1885. B 12 U 3

NOBLE (JAMES). Portraits of Murderer of. [*See* MANUSCRIPTS AND PORTRAITS.] MF 1 U 21

NOBLE (JAMES A.) Shorthand made Easy; or, the Locomotive System of Stenography. 8vo. Lond., 1881. K 12 P 32

Dot and Dash System of Shorthand. 8vo. Lond., 1880. K 12 P 32

NOBLE (JOHN). National Finance. 8vo. Lond., 1875.
F 12 Q 3

NOBLE (REV. MARK), F.A.S. Biographical History of England, from the Revolution to the end of George the First's Reign. [*See* GRANGER, REV. J.]   C 6 V 1-9

NOBLE (PROF. RODERICK). The Cape and its People, and other Essays; by South African Writers. Edited by Professor Noble. 8vo. Cape Town, 1869.   D 1 R 26

NOBLE (T. C.) The Names of those Persons who subscribed towards the Defence of this Country at the Time of the Spanish Armada, 1588; with Historical Introduction. 8vo. Lond., 1886.   B 3 Q 30

NODAL (DR. JOSE FERNANDEZ). Los vinculos de Ollanta y Cusi-Kcuyllor, Drama en Quichua. 8vo. Ayacucho (n.d.)   H 3 Q 29

NODIER (CHARLES). Dictionnaire Universel de la Langue Française. [*See* BOISTE, P. C. V.]

Mémoires sur l'ancienne Chevalerie. [*See* SAINTE-PALAYE, J. B. LA C. DE.]   B 15 Q 1, 2

NOËL (FRANÇOIS JOSEPH MICHEL), ET CHAPSAL (PROF. C. P.) Nouvelle Grammaire Française, sur un plan très-méthodique, avec de nombreux Exercices d'Orthographe, de Syntaxe, et de Ponctuation : Grammaire. 25° éd. 12mo. Paris, 1831.   K 11 V 39

Nouvelle Grammaire Française, sur un plan très-méthodique, avec de nombreux Exercices d'Orthographe, de Syntaxe, et de Ponctuation : Exercices. Nouvelle éd. 12mo. Paris, 1858.   K 11 V 40

Leçons d'Analyse logique, contenant : 1. Des Préceptes sur l'Art d'analyser ; 2. Des Exercices et des Sujets d'Analyse logique gradués et calqués sur les Préceptes ; suivies d'un Programme de Questions sur la seconde partie de la nouvelle Grammaire Française. 7° éd. 12mo. Paris, 1831.   K 11 V 42

Corrigé des Exercices Français sur l'Orthographe, la Syntaxe, et la Ponctuation. 48° éd., revue et augmentée. 12mo. Paris, 1858.   K 11 V 41

Nouveau Traité des Participes, accompagné d'Exercices progressifs sur le Participe Passé, et sur le Participe Présent: Théories des Participes. 15° éd. 12mo. Paris, 1858.   K 11 V 43

[*See* CHAPSAL, PROF. C. P.]

NOËL (MATTHIAS-JOSEPH DE). La Cathédrale de Cologne; Description archéologico historique de cette Eglise Métropolitaine; traduite de l'Allemand par le Dr. N. R. Sautelet. 12mo. Cologne, 1835.   A 7 P 31

NOËL (ROBERT R.) Peter Paul Rubens: his Life and Works. [*See* WAAGEN, DR. G. F.]   A 7 Q 22

NOËL (HON. RODEN). Essays on Poetry and Poets. 8vo. Lond., 1886.   J 12 V 1

NOHL (DR. LUDWIG). Letters of Wolfgang Amadeus Mozart. [*See* MOZART, W. A.]   C 3 V 33, 34

Mozart's Briefe. [*See* MOZART, W. A.]   C 1 T 39

Beethoven's Letters, 1790-1826. [*See* BEETHOVEN, L. VON.]   C 3 Q 4, 5

Briefe Beethovens. [*See* BEETHOVEN, L. VON.]   C 8 T 6

NOLAN (E. H.) History of England. [*See* HUME, D., AND SMOLLETT, DR. T.]   B 3 V 13-15

NOLDIUS (CHRISTIAN). Concordantiæ Particolarvm Ebræo-Chaldaicarvm. 4to. Ienæ, 1734.   K 18 S 2

NOLLEKENS (JOSEPH). Nollekens and his Times; comprehending a Life of that celebrated Sculptor; by Dr. John Thomas Smith. 2nd ed. 2 vols. 8vo. Lond., 1829.   C 9 P 3, 4

NOLTE (VINCENT). Fifty Years in both Hemispheres; or, Reminiscences of a Merchant's Life. 8vo. Lond., 1854.   C 3 S 44

NONARUM INQUISITIONES in Curia Scaccarii, Temp. Regis Edwardi III. Fol. Lond., 1807.   F 24 Q 20 ‡

NON-COMBATANT, A. [*See* BUSHBY, H. J.]

NOORT (OLIVIER VAN). Description du Penible Voyage faict entour de l'Univers, ou Globe Terrestre, par Sr. Olivier du Noit d'Utrecht, General de quattre Navires, 1598-1601. Fol. Amsterdame, 1602.   D 9 V 17

NOOTEN (BERTHE HOOLA VAN). Fleurs, Fruits, et Feuillages choisis de l'Ile de Java, peints d'après nature. 3° éd. At. fol. Bruxelles, 1880.   A 3 P 22 ‡

NORDENFELT (THORSTEN). Nordenfelt Machine Guns described in Detail, and compared with other Systems; also, their employment for Naval and Military Purposes. Illustrated. Roy. 4to. Portsmouth, 1884.   A 14 R 15 ‡

NORDENSKIOLD (ADOLF ERIK). Voyage of the *Vega* round Asia and Europe. Translated by Alexander Leslie. With Illustrations. 2 vols. 8vo. Lond., 1881.   D 4 S 2, 3

Arctic Voyages, 1858-79. [*See* LESLIE, A.]   D 4 S 1

Nordenskiöld's Voyage round Asia and Europe. [*See* HOVGAARD, LIEUT. A.]   D 4 S 4

NORDHOFF (CHARLES). California, for Health, Pleasure, and Residence: a Book for Travellers and Settlers. Sq. 8vo. New York, 1876.   D 3 T 43

Communistic Societies of the United States. 8vo. Lond., 1875.   F 14 S 9

NORFOLK. History and Antiquities of the County of Norfolk. 10 vols. 8vo. Norwich, 1781.   B 4 S 5-11

NORFOLK AND NORWICH ASSOCIATION. First Report of the Norfolk and Norwich Association in aid of the Church Missionary Society, 1814. 8vo. Norwich, 1814.   MG 1 Q 27

NORFOLK ARCHÆOLOGICAL SOCIETY. Norfolk Archæology; or, Miscellaneous Tracts relating to the Antiquities of the County of Norfolk, published by the Norfolk and Norwich Archæological Society. Vols. 1–9. Norwich, 1847–84. E 1. 47

Visitation of Norfolk in the year 1563; taken by William Harvey, Clarenceux King of Arms. From Harleian MSS. in the British Museum. 8vo. Norwich, 1878. E 1. 47

Pedes Finium; or, Fines, relating to the County of Norfolk, levied in the King's Court from the third year of Richard I, to the end of the Reign of John. Edited by Walter Rye. 8vo. Norwich, 1881. E 1. 47

NORIE (J. W.) Complete Epitome of Practical Navigation; containing all necessary Instructions for keeping a Ship's Reckoning at Sea. 21st (Stereotype) ed., considerably augmented and improved, by Arthur B. Martin, F.R.A.S. 8vo. Lond., 1877. A 3 U 31

NORMAN (C. B.) Colonial France. 8vo. Lond., 1886. D 10 S 23

NORMAN (GEORGE WARDE). Examination of some prevailing Opinions, as to the Pressure of Taxation in this and other Countries. 2nd ed. 8vo. Lond., 1850. F 6 V 10

NORMAN (LOUIS DE), BARON. Diary of the Shah of Persia. [See NASR EDDIN, SHAH OF PERSIA.] D 8 S 9

NORMAN (MARY). Pictures of Rural Life. [See STIFTER, A.] D 8 Q 19–21

NORMAN (CAPT. W. H.), AND MUSGRAVE (THOMAS). Journals of the Voyage and Proceedings of H.M.C.S. *Victoria* in search of shipwrecked people at the Auckland and other Islands. 8vo. Melb., 1865. MD 1 V 9

Another copy. 8vo. Melb., 1865. MJ 2 R 16

NORMAN PEOPLE (THE). Norman People and their existing descendants in the British Dominions and the United States of America. 8vo. Lond., 1874. B 5 S 26

NORMANBY (CONSTANTINE HENRY PHIPPS), MARQUESS OF. The English in Italy. 3 vols. 8vo. Lond., 1825. J 11 R 18–20

Historiettes; or, Tales of Continental Life. 3 vols. 8vo. Lond., 1827. J 8 Q 29–31

The English at Home. 3 vols. 8vo. Lond., 1830. J 8 Q 26–28

The English in France. 2nd ed. 3 vols. 8vo. Lond., 1828. J 8 U 30–32

A Year of Revolution; from a Journal kept in Paris in 1848. 2 vols. 8vo. Lond., 1857. B 8 R 12, 13

NORMAND (L. M.) Paris Moderne, ou Choix de Maisons. Paris, 1837. A 2 U 34

NORMANDY (A.) Commercial Hand-book of Chemical Analysis; enlarged by H. M. Noad, Ph.D., &c. 8vo. Lond., 1875. A 5 R 33

NORRIS (EDWARD). [See EARL, G. W.]

NORRIS (EDWIN). [See RAWLINSON, MAJOR.-GEN. SIR H. C.]

NORRIS (MRS. EMILIA), MISS EMILIA MARRYAT. Amongst the Maoris: a Book of Adventure. With original Illustrations. 8vo. Lond., 1874. MJ 1 R 25

Early Start in Life. With Illustrations. 12mo. Lond., 1867. MJ 1 R 24

NORRIS-NEWMAN (C. L.) [See NEWMAN, C. L. NORRIS-].

NORRIS (REV. J. P.) Iron and Coal Masters' Prize. Scheme for the Encouragement of Education in Staffordshire. Lond., 1854. (Pam. 41.) MJ 2 R 3

NORMAN (CAPT. V.) Military Bridge-Equipage. (Pam. Cl.) 8vo. Philad., 1876. A 16 U 21

NORTH (CHRISTOPHER). [See WILSON, PROF. J.]

NORTH (RT. HON. FRANCIS), BARON GUILDFORD. [See GUILFORD, RT. HON. F. N., BARON.]

NORTH (HON. SIR DUDLEY). Life of. [See NORTH, HON. R.] C 9 R 5–7

NORTH (HON. AND REV. DR. JOHN). Life of. [See NORTH, HON. ROGER.] C 9 R 5–7

NORTH (OLIVER). Practical Assayer; containing Easy Methods for the Assay of the principal Metals and Alloys. 8vo. Lond., 1874. A 9 Q 38

NORTH (HON. ROGER). Lives of the Rt. Hon. Francis North, Baron Guilford, the Hon. Sir Dudley North, and the Hon. and Rev. Dr. John North. New ed. 3 vols. 8vo. Lond., 1826. C 9 R 5–7

NORTH (SIR THOMAS). Shakespeare's Plutarch; being a Selection from the Lives in North's Plutarch. [See SKEAT, REV. W. W.] C 4 Q 29

NORTH AMERICAN REVIEW (THE). Edited by Allen Thorndike Rice. Vols. 37–140. 8vo. N. York, 1833–85. E 1. 8

General Index to. Vols. 92–134. (1861–82). 8vo. Bangor, U.S., 1882. E 1. 8

Index to. Vols. 1–125. 1815–77. 1. Index of Subjects. 2. Index of Writers; by William Cushing, A.B. 8vo. Cambridge, U.S., 1878. E 1. 8

NORTH AUSTRALIA. Return of Expenses incurred for the Settlement of North Australia. (Parl. Doc., 50.) Fol. Lond., 1848. MF 4 ‡

Summary of Extracts from a forthcoming Account of the Country of Northern Australia, as a Site for a proposed British Colony. 12mo. Lond., 1862. MD 2 Q 18

NORTH BRITISH AGRICULTURIST (THE), for 1882–84. New series. 3 vols. fol. Edinb., 1882–84. E 1. 90

NORTH BRITISH REVIEW (THE). 53 vols. 8vo.
Lond., 1844–71.   E 1. 22

NORTH CAROLINA. [*See* UNITED STATES OF AMERICA.]

NORTH WESTERN AUSTRALIA. [*See* MACKAY,
ROBERT, M.D.]   MD 5 T 27

NORTHCOTE (JAMES), R.A. Life of Sir Joshua Reynolds, LL.D., &c. ; comprising original Anecdotes of many
distinguished persons, his Contemporaries ; and a brief
Analysis of his Discourses. 2 vols. 8vo.   Lond., 1819.
                                        C 6 R 16, 17

One Hundred Fables, original and Selected. [First and]
second series. 2 vols. 8vo. Lond., 1828–33.   J 5 P 29–30

Life of Titian ; with Anecdotes of the distinguished persons
of his Time. With a Portrait. 2 vols. 8vo.   Lond.,
1830.   C 8 S 47, 48

Conversations of ; by William Hazlitt. 8vo. Lond., 1830.
                                        C 5 R 19
[*See* HAZLITT, W.]

NORTHCOTE (REV. J. SPENCER), AND BROWNLOW
(REV. W. R.) Roma Sotterranea ; or, some Account of
the Roman Catacombs, especially of the Cemetery of San
Callista. 8vo.   Lond., 1869.   B 11 V 3

Roma Sotterranea ; or, an Account of the Roman Catacombs, especially of the Cemetery of St. Callixtus. Part
2—Christian Art. New ed., rewritten. 8vo. Lond., 1879.
                                        B 11 V 4

NORTHCOTE (SIR STAFFORD HENRY). [*See* IDDESLEIGH,
EARL OF.]

NORTHERN AGRICULTURAL ASSOCIATION,
Singleton, New South Wales. Members' Pamphlets for
the years 1870–72. 3 vols. (in 1) 8vo.   West Maitland,
1870–72.   MF 3 P 11

Members' Pamphlet for the years 1873–70, 1878–80. 7
vols. (in 2) 8vo.   West Maitland and Singleton, 1873–80.
                                        ME 9 P

NORTHERN ANTIQUARIES (ROYAL SOCIETY OF).
[*See* ANTIQUAIRES DU NORD.]

NORTHERN ANTIQUITIES. Illustrations of Northern
Antiquities, from the Earlier Teutonic and Scandinavian
Romances ; being an Abstract of the Book of Heroes,
and Nibelungen Lay. Roy. 4to. Edinb., 1814.* H 10 S 12†

NORTHERN ASSOCIATION. Northern Association
for procuring State Support to Religion in Tasmania.
8vo. Launceston, 1857.   MG 1 Q 29

NORTHUMBERLAND (ALGERNON GEORGE PERCY),
DUKE OF. Speeches of the late Henry Drummond.
[*See* DRUMMOND, H.]

NORTHUMBERLAND (HENRY ALGERNON PERCY),
EARL OF. The Regulations and Establishment of the
Household of Henry Algernon Percy, the Fifth Earl of
Northumberland. 8vo. Lond., 1827.   B 6 P 38
[*See* PERCY, REV. T.]

NORTHUMBRIAN MINSTREL (THE). Choice Selection of Songs. With cuts by Bewick. 18mo. Alnwick,
1811.   Libr.

NORTON (HON. MRS. CAROLINE ELIZABETH SARAH).
Child of the Islands : a Poem. Roy. 8vo. Lond., 1845.
                                        H 6 U 25

The Dream, and other Poems. 8vo.   Lond., 1840.
                                        H 7 T 18

Lady of La Garaye. 12mo. Lond., 1862.   H 6 P 29

Residence at Sierra Leone ; by "A Lady." Edited by the
Hon. Mrs. Norton. (H. and C. Lib.) 12mo.   Lond.,
1849.   J 8 P 34

NORTON (CHARLES ELIOT). Historical Studies of Church-
building in the Middle Ages. Venice, Siena, Florence.
8vo. Lond., 1880.   A 2 S 21

Early Letters of Thos. Carlyle. [*See* CARLYLE, T.]
                                        C 4 T 6, 7
[*See* DANTE ALIGHIERI.]

NORTON (G.) Proselytism in India ; the question at
issue examined in a Letter to Sir G. Clerk. (Pam. 23.)
8vo. Lond., 1859.   MJ 2 Q 11

NORTON (JAMES), SENR. Essays. (Pam., 26.) 8vo.
Essays and Reflections in Australia ; by "A Layman."
(Pam., 43.) 8vo. Sydney, 1853.   MJ 2 R 5

Australian Essays, on Subjects Political, Moral, and Religious. Sm. 4to. Lond., 1857.*   MJ 1 T 20

Another copy. (Pam., Da.) 8vo. Sydney (n.d.) MD 1 V 9

Another copy. (Pam., 26.) 8vo. Sydney (n.d.) MJ 2 Q 14

Condition of the Colony of New South Wales. 8vo.
Sydney, 1860.   MF 3 P 1

NORVINS (JACQUES), MARQUIS DE. Histoire de France.
[ANQUETIL-DUPERRON, L. P.]   B 8 U 11–15

NÖSSELT (FRIEDRICH). Mythology, Greek and Roman ;
translated from the German, by Mrs. Angus W. Hall.
8vo. Lond., 1885.   B 9 S 24

NOTES AND QUERIES : a Medium of Intercommuni-
ration for Literary Men, General Readers, Antiquaries, &c.
1st–6th series. 71 vols. sm. 4to. Lond., 1849–85. E 1. 12

General Index to the five series, 1849–79. 5 vols. sm. 4to.
Lond., 1856–80.   E 1. 12

NOTES AND QUERIES ON ANTHROPOLOGY.
[*See* ANTHROPOLOGY.]

NOTES ON BUILDING CONSTRUCTION. [*See*
BUILDING CONSTRUCTION.]

NOTT (G. F.) [*See* SURREY, EARL OF.]

NOTT (J. C.), AND GLIDDON (GEORGE R.) Types of Mankind; or, Ethnological Researches, based upon the Ancient Monuments, Paintings, Sculptures, and Crania of Races, and upon their Natural, Geographical, Philological, and Biblical History. 10th ed. Roy.8vo. Philad., 1871. A 2 P 19

NOTT (J. F.) Wild Animals Photographed and Described. Imp. 8vo. Lond., 1886. A 15 T 4

NOTT (GEN. SIR W.), K.C.B. [*See* ALLEN, REV. I. N.]

NOTTINGHAM. Records of the Borough of Nottingham; being a series of Extracts from the Archives of the Corporation of Nottingham. Vols. 1–3, 1155–1547. Roy. 8vo. Lond., 1882–85. B 21 V 11–13

1. King Henry II to King Richard III, 1155–1399.
2. King Henry IV to King Richard III, 1399–1485.
3. King Henry VII to King Henry VIII.

NOURSE (HON. C. C.) Iowa and the Centennial: the State Address delivered at Philadelphia, September 7, 1876. 8vo. Iowa, 1876. B 1 S 52

NOUVEAU DICTIONNAIRE RUSSE. [*See* DICTIONNAIRE RUSSE.]

NOUVELLE BIOGRAPHIE GENERALE. [*See* BIOGRAPHIE GÉNÉRALE.]

NOVIKOFF (MME. OLGA), "O. K." Skobeleff and the Slavonic Cause. 8vo. Lond., 1883. C 9 T 44

NOWROJEE (JEHANGEER), AND MERWANJEE (HIRJEEBHOY). Journal of a Residence of Two Years and a Half in Great Britain. 8vo. Lond., 1841. D 8 P 20

NOXIOUS TRADES INQUIRY COMMISSION. [*See* NEW SOUTH WALES.]

NOYES (JOHN HUMPHREY). History of American Socialisms. 8vo. Philad., 1870. F 4 T 12

Home-Talks. Vol. 1. (*All published.*) 8vo. Oneida, 1875. G 7 R 5

NUGENT (EDWARD). Rudimentary and Practical Instructions on the Science of Railway Construction. [*See* STEPHENSON, SIR R. M.]

NUGENT (GEORGE GRENVILLE), LORD. Lands, Classical and Sacred. 2 vols. 8vo. Lond., 1845. D 5 R 21, 22

Some Memorials of John Hampden, his Party, and his Times. 2 vols. 8vo. Lond., 1832. C 7 T 16, 17

NUGENT (THOMAS), LL.D. New Pocket Dictionary of the French and English Languages. Sm. 4to. Lond., 1799. K 11 S 13

Life of Benvenuto Cellini, written by himself. (Autobiog., 16, 17.) 12mo. Lond., 1827. C 1 P 13

The Spirit of Laws. [*See* MONTESQUIEU, C. DE S. BARON DE.] F 7 S 4, 5

NUMBER ONE. Edited by "A. Pendragon" [George Isaacs]. No. 1, April, 1861. (Pam. H.) 8vo. Adelaide, 1861. ME 3 R

NUMISMATA ORIENTALIA. International Numismata Orientalia. 4 vols. roy. 4to. Lond., 1874–86. A 2 S 15–18 †

1. Ancient Indian Weights; by Mr. Thomas. Coins of the Urtuki Turkumáns; by Mr. Poole. Coinage of Lydia and Persia; by Mr. Head. Coins of the Tuluni Dynasty; by Mr. Rogers. Parthian Coinage; by Mr. Gardner. Coins and Measures of Ceylon; by Mr. Rhys Davids.
2. Coins of the Jews; by Frederic W. Madden, M.R.A.S. With 279 Woodcuts and a Plate of Alphabets.
3. Coins of Arakan, of Pegu, and of Burma; by Lieut.-Gen. Sir A. P. Phayre.
4. Coins of Southern India; by Sir W. Elliott.

NUMISMATIC CHRONICLE (THE). Edited by John Yonge Akerman, F.S.A. 2 vols. 8vo. Lond., 1839–40. A 13 S 44, 45

NUTT (DAVID). List of the most important Political Newspapers published in France and Germany; and a List of the chief Periodicals published in France, Germany, and Italy. (Pam.) 8vo. Lond. (n.d.) Lib.

Catalogue of Foreign Theological Books. 8vo. Lond., 1857. K 7 S 3

NUTTALL (P. AUSTIN), LL.D. Classical and Archæological Dictionary of the Manners, Customs, Laws, &c., of celebrated Nations of Antiquity. 8vo. Lond., 1840. K 7 Q 6

NYEL (PÈRE). Lettre du Père Nyel sur la Mission des Moxes, Peuples de l'Amérique Méridionale. [*See* COREAL, F.]

NYGAARD (M.) Eddasprogets Syntax. Aftryk af Indbydelsesskrift til den offentlige Examen i Kristiansands Kathedralskole. 1865. 2 vols. (in 1). 8vo. Bergen, 1865–67. K 12 Q 10

O

O. (R.) [*See* HALF-A-DOZEN ATTEMPTS AT VERSIFICATION.]

O. K. [*See* NOVIKOFF, MME. O.]

O LE TALA I LOTU ESE ESE. (Pam. Ea.) 12mo. Upolu, 1839. MK 1 P 24

OAKELEY (REV. F.) Reply to Tract XC historically examined. [*See* GOODE, REV. W.]

OAMARU STONE QUARRYING CO: Reports, Press Opinions, &c. 8vo. Melb., 1878. MJ 2 R 16

OATES (EUGENE W.) Hand-book to the Birds of British Burmah. 2 vols. roy. 8vo. Lond., 1883. A 13 V 29, 30

OATES (FRANK), F.R.G.S. Matabele Land and the Victoria Falls: a Naturalist's Wanderings in the Interior of South Africa. 8vo. Lond., 1881. D 2 S 1

OATES (REV. TITUS), D.D. Historical Narrative of the horrid Plot and Conspiracy of Titus Oats, called the Popish Plot. 8vo. Lond., 1816. B 6 Q 7

O'BEIRNE (T. L.), D.D., BISHOP OF MEATH. Sermons on Important Subjects; to which is added, a Charge to the Clergy of Meath. 3 vols. 8vo. Lond., 1813–21. G 3 Q 21–23

OBERLANDER (RICHARD). Australien. [*See* CHRISTMANN, F.] MD 2 Q 30

Ozeanien. [*See* CHRISTMANN, F.] MD 4 U 31

O'BRIEN (CAPT. DONAT HENCHY). My Adventures during the late War; comprising a Narrative of Shipwreck, Captivity, Escapes from French Prisons, &c., 1804–27. 2 vols. 8vo. Lond., 1839. D 7 S 24, 25

O'BRIEN (HENRY). Phœnician Ireland. [*See* VILLANUEVA, Ill. J. L.] B 11 Q 3

O'BRIEN (LUCIUS), "LUCIFER." Pneumatic High Pressure Sewerage for Cities, Towns, and Villages: an Essay on the Sewerage Question. 8vo. Sydney, 1881. MA 1 V 52

O'BRIEN (REV. PAUL). Practical Grammar of the Irish Language. 8vo. Dublin, 1809. K 13 Q 30

O'BRIEN (WILLIAM SMITH). Trial of William Smith O'Brien, Esq., M.P., at Clonmel, for High Treason, September 21, 1848. 8vo. Sydney, 1849. MF 1 P 12

Another copy. Imp. 8vo. Dublin, 1849. F 5 V 18

Principles of Government; or, Meditations in Exile. 8vo. Boston, 1856. MF 1 P 13

OBSERVATIONS ON WAR both Offensive and Defensive; being the substance of a Letter written by "A Native of Tasmania." 8vo. Hobart, 1860. MG 1 Q 31

OBSERVER (THE). Fol. Melb., 1848. ME 9 Q 9 †

O'BYRNE (WILLIAM R.) Naval Biographical Dictionary; comprising the Life and Services of every Living Officer in Her Majesty's Navy. Roy. 8vo. Lond., 1849. C 11 V 21

O'CALLAGHAN (JOHN CORNELIUS). History of the Irish Brigades in the Service of France. 8vo. Glasgow, 1870. B 11 R 17

OCEAN HIGHWAYS: Geographical Review. Illustrated with Maps. New series, vol. 1. Edited by Clements R. Markham, C.B., &c. [Continued as the *Geographical Magazine.*] Imp. 8vo. Lond., 1874. E 1. 58

OCHOA (EUGENIO DE). Tesoro del Teatro Español desda su Origen (año de 1356) hasta nuestros Diaz, 5 vols. 8vo. Paris, 1838 H 3 S 1–5

OCKLEY (SIMON), B.D. History of the Saracens. 6th ed. 8vo. Lond., 1878. B 13 V 34

O'COIGLY (JAMES), AND OTHERS. Trial of, for High Treason, at Maidstone, 1798. 8vo. Lond., 1798. F 8 P 15

O'CONNELL (DANIEL). The Liberator: his Life and Times, Political and Social; by M. F. Cusack. 2 vols. 8vo. Kenmare, 1857. C 8 P 32, 33

Memoir on Ireland, Native and Saxon. 8vo. Sydney, 1843. B 11 P 31

Leaders of Public Opinion in Ireland. [*See* LECKY, W. E. H.] C 3 P 24

The Funeral Oration on: by the Rev. John Miley, D.D. 8vo. Dublin, 1847. C 14 R 21

The Funeral Oration of Father Ventura on the Death of the Liberator. 8vo. Dublin, 1847. C 14 R 22

O'CONNELL (BRIG.-GEN. SIR M. C.) Suggestions on the combination of the Police and Militia Systems, New South Wales. 8vo. Brisbane, 1852. MF 1 R 1

O'CONNOR (DERMOND). History of Ireland. [*See* KEATING, REV. J.] B 11 P 10

O'CONNOR (J.) Ich Dien. 12mo. Lond., 1873. MH 1 It 16

O'CONNOR (M.), M.D. Irish Hearts and Hands [a Lecture]. [*See* ST. AUGUSTINE'S LITERARY INSTITUTE.]

O'CONNOR (T. P.), M.P. Lord Beaconsfield: a Biography. 12mo. Lond., 1880. C 1 S 12

The Parnell Movement; with a Sketch of Irish Parties from 1843. 8vo. Lond., 1886. B 11 Q 19

O'CONOR (CHARLES). Dissertations on the Antient History of Ireland. 8vo. Dublin, 1753.   B 11 Q 33

O'CONOR (W. A.), B.A. History of the Irish People. 2 vols. 8vo. Manchester, 1883.   B 11 P 12, 13

O'DAVOREN. O'Davoren's Glossary. [*See* THREE IRISH GLOSSARIES.]

ODELL (GEORGE). System of Shorthand (Taylor improved). 57th ed. 18mo. Lond. (n.d.)   K 11 U 24

Supplement to Odell's "System of Shorthand (Taylor's improved)." 18mo. Lond. (n.d.)   K 11 U 24

ODERNHEIMER (F.) Das Festland Australien. 8vo. Wiesbaden, 1861.   MD 2 S 6

ODERNHEIMER (F.), AND HERBORN (E.) Reports, in the the years 1855–57, on the Geology and Mineralogy of the following Estates, the property of the Australian Agricultural Company, in New South Wales: Port Stephens, Warrah, Newcastle, Platt. 8vo. Lond. (n.d.) MA 2 Q 31

ODLING (WILLIAM), M.B., &c. Outlines of Chemistry; or, Brief Notes of Chemical Facts. 8vo. Lond., 1870.   A 5 R 16

Course of Practical Chemistry, arranged for the use of Medical Students. 5th ed. 8vo. Lond., 1876.   A 5 S 20

ODO (SANCTUS), ABBAS CLUNIACENSIS. Opera omnia. [*See* MIGNE, J. P., SERIES LATINA, 133.]

O'DONEL (RORY). [*See* TYRCONNEL, EARL OF.]

O'DONNELL (MRS. JANE). Life of General F. R. Chesney. [*See* CHESNEY, MRS.]

O'DONOGHUE (MRS. P.) Riding for Ladies; with Hints on the Stable. 8vo. Lond., 1887.   A 17U 26

O'DONOVAN (DENIS). Uses of Art and Design in Manufacture: a Lecture delivered at the Industrial and Technological Museum, on 12th October, 1871. 8vo. Melb., 1871.   MJ 2 R 7

Another copy. [*See* MELBOURNE PUBLIC LIBRARY.]

Analytical and Classified Catalogue of the Library of the Parliament of Queensland. 4to. Brisbane, 1883.   MK 1 U 2

Art in Building: No. 1. Construction; No. 2. Ornamentation [Two Lectures]. [*See* MELBOURNE PUBLIC LIBRARY.]

O'DONOVAN (EDMOND). The Merv Oasis: Travels and Adventures East of the Caspian during the years 1879–81. 2 vols. 8vo. Lond., 1882.   D 5 8 15, 16

O'DONOVAN (JOHN), LL.D., &c. Annals of the Kingdom of Ireland, by the Four Masters, from the Earliest Period to the year 1616. 7 vols. 4to. Dublin, 1851. B 18 R 5–11 ‡

Irish-English Dictionary; with a Supplement. [*See* O'REILLY, E.]

O'DRISCOLL (W. JUSTIN), M.R.I.A. Memoir of Daniel Maclise, R.A. 8vo. Lond., 1871.   C 3 U 24

ODYSSE-BAROT (FRANÇOIS). [*See* BAROT, F. ODYSSE-.]

ŒCUMENIUS (TRICCÆ EPISCOPUS). Opera omnia. [*See* MIGNE, J. P., SERIES GRÆCA, 118, 119.]

OELNITZ (L. V. D.) Russia, Past and Present. [*See* CHESTER, MRS. H. M.]   D 9 Q 34

OERSTED (HANS CHRISTIAN). The Soul in Nature; with Supplementary Contributions. 8vo. Lond., 1852.   G 7 R 23

OETTINGER (EDOUARD MARIE). Bibliographie Biographique Universelle: Dictionnaire des Ouvrages relatifs à l'Histoire de la Vie publique et privée des Personnages célèbres de tous le Temps et de toutes les Nations depuis le commencement du Monde jusqu'à nos jours. 2 vols. imp. 8vo. Bruxelles, 1854.   C 11 V 7, 8

O'FARRELL (P. A. C.) Answer to the Pamphlet of the Rev. William Trollope, M.A., entitled "A Parting Word on Trident ne Romanism. 8vo. Melh., 1850. MJ 2 R 12

OFFICER, AN. [*See* PHILLIP, CAPT. A.]

OFFICER, AN. [*See* GAMBIER, P. E.]

OFFICER IN THE BENGAL NATIVE INFANTRY, AN. [*See* BUTLER, MAJOR J.]

OFFICER IN THE UNITED STATES NAVY, AN. [*See* RUSCHENBERGER, W. S. W.]

OFFICER OF RANK, AN. [*See* GLASCOCK, W. N.]

OFFICER OF SUPERIOR RANK, AN. [*See* INFLUENCE OF FIREARMS, &c.]

OFFICER OF THE GUARDS, AN. [*See* LEAVES.]

OFFICER OF THE UNITED STATES NAVY, AN. [*See* BRIDGE, H.]

OFFICES OF THE CHURCH. Ordo Divini Officii Recitandi Sacrique Peragendi ab omnibus qui sacras Laudes in Terra Australi juxta Kalendarium Romanum cessione juxta Ritum Breviarii et Missalis Romani A. P. K. Presbytero, Depositus anno Domini 1869. 12mo. Sydneii, 1869.   MG 1 Q 5

Martinuci de quibusdam Officiis Episcopi. Sydney, (n.d.)   MG 1 R 14

O'FLAHERTY (RODERIC). Ogygia; or, a Chronological Account of Irish Events; translated by the Rev. James Hely, A.B. 2 vols. 8vo. Dublin, 1793.   B 11 P 2, 3

OGBORNE (ELIZABETH). History of Essex, from the earliest period to the present time. Illustrated. Roy. 4to. Lond., 1814.   B 17 R 5 ‡

OGDEN (E. D.) Tariff; or, Rates of Duties payable on Goods, &c., imported into the United States of America, 1840 to 1842; also, the Rates of Duties imposed by the Tariff Law of 1832. 8vo. New York, 1840. F 6 U 6

OGDEN (WILLIAM SHARP). Studies in Mercantile Architecture; comprising Fifty suggestive Designs for Warehouse, Shop and Office Buildings. Fol. Lond., 1876.
A 5 8 9 †

OGILBY (JOHN). Africa. Roy. fol. Lond., 1670. D 4 P 7 ‡

OGILBY (J. DOUGLAS). Catalogue of the Fishes of New South Wales; with their principal synonyms. 4to. Sydney, 1886.   MA 1 P 16 †

OGILVIE (JOHN), LL.D. The Imperial Dictionary, English, Technological, and Scientific, on the basis of Webster's English Dictionary; with Supplement. 3 vols. imp. 8vo. Glasgow, 1851–55.   K 15 T 3–5

Another copy. New ed., edited by Charles Annandale, M.A. 4 vols. imp. 8vo. Lond., 1882–83. K 15 T 6–9

Student's English Dictionary, Etymological, Pronouncing, and Explanatory. Sm. 4to. Lond., 1876. K 12 Q 5

OGLE (NATHANIEL), F.G.S., &c. Colony of Western Australia: a Manual for Emigrants to that Settlement or its Dependencies. 8vo. Lond., 1839.*   MD 5 V 26

OGLE (W.) On the Parts of Animals. [*See* ARISTOTELES.]
A 28 V 3

OGLES, DUNCAN, AND COCHRAN. Catalogue of Books in Theology, &c. 8vo. Lond., 1817. K 7 S 27

O'GRADY (STANDISH). History of Ireland, Critical and Philosophical. Vol. 1. 8vo. Lond., 1881. B 11 P 40

O'HAGAN (RT. HON. THOMAS), BARON, K.P. Occasional Papers and Addresses. 8vo. Lond., 1884. J 9 S 22

Selected Speeches and Arguments of; edited by George Teeling. 8vo. Lond., 1885.   F 6 V 7

O'HALLORAN (SYLVESTER), M.R.I.A. Introduction to and a History of Ireland. 3 vols. 8vo. Dublin, 1803.
B 11 P 34–36

O'HARA (J.) History of New South Wales. 8vo. Lond., 1817.   MB 1 T 14

O'HARA (KANE). Midas: an English Burletta. [*See* FARCES 7.]

Tom Thumb: a Farce. [*See* FARCES 6.]

Another copy. [*See* BRITISH DRAMA 5.]

O'HART (JOHN). Irish and Anglo-Irish Landed Gentry when Cromwell came to Ireland; or, a Supplement to Irish Pedigrees. 8vo. Dublin, 1884. K 10 S 29

OISIN'S (THE CULDEE). Glossary to the Calendar of. [*See* THREE IRISH GLOSSARIES.]

OHIO. [*See* UNITED STATES OF AMERICA.]

O'KEEFFE (JOHN). Recollections of the Life of; written by himself. 2 vols. 8vo. Lond., 1826.   C 9 P 11, 12

The Castle of Andalusia: a Comic Opera. (Brit. Theatre.) 12mo. Lond., 1808.   H 1 P 22

The Farmer. [*See* FARCES 2.]

Fontainbleau: a Comic Opera. (Brit. Theatre.) 12mo. Lond., 1808.   H 1 P 22

The Highland Reel. [*See* FARCES 2.]

Lie of a Day: a Comedy. [*See* MODERN THEATRE 10.]

The Poor Soldier: a Comic Opera. [*See* FARCES 2.]

The Prisoner at Large: a Comedy. [*See* FARCES 2.]

Wild Oats: a Comedy. (Brit. Theatre.) 12mo. Lond., 1808.   H 1 P 22

Dramatic Works of. 4 vols. 8vo. Lond., 1798.
H 4 R 16, 19

OKEN (PROF. LORENZ). Biographical Sketch; by Alexander Ecker; with explanatory Notes, &c., from the German, by Alfred Tulk. 8vo. Lond., 1883. C 5 Q 13

OLAFSEN (EGGERT), AND POVELSEN (BYANI). Travels in Iceland. Translated from the Danish. 8vo. Lond., 1805.   D 7 T 31

OLD BOOMERANG. [*See* HOULDING, J. R.]

OLD BUSHMAN, THE. [*See* WHEELWRIGHT, H. W.]

OLD CAMPAIGNER, AN. [*See* RUSSIA.]

OLD CHUM. [*See* BOYD, A. J.]

OLD COLONIST, AN. [*See* EMIGRATION.]

OLD COLONIST, AN. [*See* GARRYOWEN SKETCHES.]

OLD COLONIST, AN. [*See* NEW SOUTH WALES.]

OLD COLONIST, AN. [*See* PRATT, W. T.]

OLD COLONIST, AN. [*See* HOW TO FARM.]

OLD COLONIST, AN. [*See* NEW CONSTITUTION.]

OLD EDINBURGH BEAUX AND BELLES, faithfully presented to the Reader in coloured Prints, &c. 12mo. Edinb., 1886.   B 13 P 2

OLD EDINBURGH PEDLARS, Beggars, and Criminals, with some other odd characters. 12mo. Edinb., 1886.

OLD ENGLISH DRAMA: a Selection of Plays from the Old English Dramatists. 2 vols. 8vo. Lond., 1825.
B 13 P 2

1. The Second Maiden's Tragedy: a Pleasant Conceited Comedy, by J. Cooke. The Ball: a Comedy, by George Chapman and James Shirley. The Rape of Lucrece: a Tragedy, by Thomas Heywood.

2. Love's Mistress: or, the Queen's Masque, by Thomas Heywood. Albertus Wallenstein: a Tragedy, by Henry Glapthorne. The Tragedy of Dido, Queen of Carthage, by C. Marlowe and T. Nash. The Lady's Privilege: a Comedy, by H. Glapthorne.

Another copy. 2 vols. (in 1.) Lond. 1825. H 1 R 15

OLD HAND, An. [*See* HAMILTON, G.]

OLD HAND, An. [*See* HEAD, SIR F. B.]

OLD HOUSEKEEPER, An. [*See* MEN, AND HOW TO MANAGE THEM.]

OLD INDIAN, An. [*See* WYMAN, F. F.]

OLD LAWYER, An. [*See* MILLER, D. F.]

OLD MISCELLANY DAYS: a Selection of Stories from *Bentley's Miscellany*, by various authors; illustrated by George Cruikshank, 1837–43. Roy. 8vo. Lond., 1885.   J 9 V 10

OLD OBSERVER, An. [*See* HILL, R.]

OLD QUARTER-MASTER, An. [*See* THIRTY-SIX YEARS OF A SEAFARING LIFE.]

OLD RESIDENT, An. [*See* HUNTER, W. C.]

OLD SALTBUSH. [*See* SMITH, W.]

OLD SHEKARRY, The. [*See* LEVESON, MAJOR H. A.]

OLD SOLDIER, An. [*See* BELL, G.]

OLD SOLDIER, An. [*See* WELLINGTON, ARTHUR WELLESLEY, DUKE OF.]

OLD STUDENT OF SCRIPTURE, An. [*See* RENNIE, E. A.]

OLDCASTLE (JOHN). Journals and Journalism; with a Guide for Literary Beginners. Sq. 12mo. Lond., 1880.   J 7 P 35

Cardinal Newman; with Notes on the Oxford Movement and its Men. 8vo. Lond., 1886.   C 10 U 39

The Cardinal Archbishop of Westminster [Henry Edward Manning]; with Notes. 8vo. Lond., 1886.   C 10 R 39

OLDEN (REV. CHARLES). Protection of Girls and Young Women, and the Legislative Repression of Vice generally: a Lecture. 8vo. Sydney, 1885.   MF 3 Q 43

OLDENBERG (DR. HERMANN). Buddha: his Life, his Doctrine, his Order; translated from the German, by William Hoey, M.A., &c. 8vo. Lond., 1882.   G 8 U 9

Vinaya Texts. [*See* MULLER, PROF. F. M.]

OLDFIELD (AUGUSTUS). On the Aborigines of Australia. 8vo. Lond., 1864.   MA 1 S 9

OLDFIELD (EDMUND), M.A., &c. Saint Peter and Saint Paul's: Notes on the Decoration of a few Churches in Italy. 8vo. Lond., 1876.   A 2 S 28

OLDFIELD (HENRY AMBROSE), M.D. Sketches from Nipal, Historical and Descriptive. 2 vols. 8vo. Lond., 1880.   D 5 S 34, 35

OLDFIELD (R. A. K.) Narrative of an Expedition into the Interior of Africa. [*See* LAIRD, M.]   D 1 W 11, 12

OLDHAM (THOMAS), LL.D., &c. Geological Glossary for the Use of Students. 8vo. Lond., 1879.   A 9 Q 9

OLDHAM (THOMAS), AND RAWLINSON (THOMAS E.) Treatise on Railway and Harbour Accommodation for Victoria. 8vo. Melb., 1855.   MJ 2 R 15

OLDMIXON (J.) History of England, from Henry VIII to George I. 3 vols. sm. fol. Lond., 1830–39.   B 17 S 6–8 ‡

OLIN (REV. STEPHEN), D.D. Travels in Egypt, Arabia Petræa, and the Holy Land. With Illustrations. 2 vols. 8vo. New York, 1843.   D 1 V 12, 13

OLINGER (L'ABBÉ). La Langue Néerlandaise (Flamande ou Hollandaise). 8vo. Bruxelles, 1866.   K 12 P 37

OLIPHANT (LAURENCE). The Land of Khemi, up and down the Middle Nile. With Illustrations. 8vo. Edinb., 1882.   D 1 S 6

Minnesota and the Far West. 8vo. Edinb., 1855.   D 3 S 15

Narrative of the Earl of Elgin's Mission to China and Japan, in the years 1857–59. 2 vols. 8vo. Edinb., 1859.   B 2 Q 10, 11

Russian Shores of the Black Sea, in the Autumn of 1852. 8vo. Edinb., 1853.   D 6 U 21

Trans-Caucasian Campaign of the Turkish Army, under Omer Pasha. 8vo. Lond., 1856.   B 12 T 20

OLIPHANT (MRS. MARGARET). Historical Sketches of the Reign of George II. 2 vols. 8vo. Edinb., 1869.   B 3 R 8, 9

Literary History of England in the End of the 18th and Beginning of the 19th Century. 3 vols. 8vo. Lond., 1882.   B 3 S 5–7

Sheridan. (Eng. Men Letts.) 8vo. Lond., 1883.   C 1 U 30

Life of Edward Irving, Minister of the National Scotch Church, London, illustrated by his Journals and Correspondence. With Portrait. 8vo. Lond., 1862.   C 7 R 29, 30

OLIPHANT (SIR OSCAR), KNT. China: a Popular History. 12mo. Lond., 1857.   B 2 P 18

OLIPHANT (T. L. KINGTON). The New English. 2 vols. 8vo. Lond., 1886.   K 12 P 16, 17

OLIVER (ALEXANDER), M.A. Fisheries of New South Wales. 8vo. Sydney, 1871.   MJ 2 R 14

Statute Index: New South Wales. Fol. Sydney, 1874.   ME 10 Q 14 †

Friendly Societies Act of 1873; with an Index to the Act, and an Appendix. 8vo. Sydney, 1874.   MF 3 P 29

Synopsis of Indictable Offences, with their Punishments. 8vo. Sydney, 1876.   MF 2 P 34

Collection of Acts relating to the transfer of, or dealing with Land. Roy. 8vo. Sydney, 1877.*   MF 3 R 13

Collection of the Statutes of Practical Utility, Colonial and Imperial, in force in New South Wales. 2 vols. roy. 8vo. Sydney, 1879.*   MF 3 S 3, 4

Chronological Table of, and General Index to [the above]. Roy. 8vo. Sydney, 1881.*   MF 3 S 5

OLIVER (ALEXANDER), M.A.—*continued.*
Manual of the Licensing Law, comprising the Licensing Acts (45 Vic. No. 14 and 46 Vic. No. 24), arranged so as to show the Amendments effected by the Amending Act of 1883, inserted in or after the amended Sections of the Principal Act. 8vo. Sydney, 1883.   MF 1 S 14
Another copy. [2nd ed.] 8vo. Sydney, 1885.   MF 1 S 15
Criminal Law Manual. [*See* STEPHEN, SIR A.]   MF 1 S 7

OLIVER (PROF. D.), F.R.S. Illustrations of the Principal Natural Orders of the Vegetable Kingdom. Ob. 8vo. Lond., 1874.   A 4 Q 7

OLIVER (VERY REV. GEORGE), D.D., &c. Collections, illustrating the History of the Catholic Religion in the Counties of Cornwall, Devon, Dorset, Somerset, Wilts, and Gloucester. 8vo. Lond., 1857.   G 14 T 14
Monasticon Diocesis Exoniensis: with Supplement. Fol. Exeter, 1846.   B 19 U 6 ‡
Discrepancies of Freemasonry examined. 8vo. Lond., 1875.   J 11 T 28
History of the City of Exeter; with a short Memoir of the Author. 8vo. Exeter, 1861.   B 5 R 46

OLIVER (MRS. GRACE ATKINSON). Arthur Penrhyn Stanley: his Life, Work, and Teachings. 3rd ed. 8vo. Lond., 1885.   C 3 V 39
A Study of Maria Edgeworth; with Notices of her Father and Friends. 3rd ed. 8vo. Boston, 1882.   C 3 T 4

OLIVER (CAPT. SAMUEL PASFIELD), F.S.A., &c. On and Off Duty; being Leaves from an Officer's Note-book. Illustrated. Sm. 4to. Lond., 1881.   D 10 U 23
Madagascar: an Historical and Descriptive Account of the Island and its former Dependencies. 2 vols. 8vo. Lond., 1886.   B 1 P 27, 28

OLIVER AND BOYD. New Edinburgh Almanac and National Repository, 1838–87. 48 vols. 12mo. Edinb., 1838–87.   E
Pronouncing Gazetteer of the World. 8vo. Edinb., 1879.   D 11 R 2

OLLA PODRIDA. 12mo. Melb., 1870.   MJ 2 P 33

OLLENDORFF (PROF. H. G.), PH.D. New Method of learning to read, write, and speak a Language in Six Months, adapted to the German. 2 vols. 8vo. Lond., 1855–57.   C 13 Q 43, 44
Key [to the above]. 12th ed. 8vo. Lond. (n.d.)   K 13 Q 45
New Method of learning to read, write, and speak a Language in Six Months, adapted to the French. 8vo. Lond., 1872.   K 15 R 3
Key [to the above]. 11th ed. 8vo. Lond., 1871.   K 15 R 4
New Method of learning to read, write, and speak a Language in Six Months, adapted to the Italian. 8th ed. 8vo. Lond., 1885.   C 12 R 5
Key [to the above]. Roy. 8vo. Lond. (n.d.)   K 12 R 6

OLLIER (EDMUND). Cassell's Illustrated History of the Russo-Turkish War, including a History of Cyprus. 2 vols. 4to. Lond., 1879–80.   B 12 V 8, 9
History of the War between France and Germany, 1870–71. [*See* CASSELL, J.]   B 8 U 5, 6
Tale for a Chimney Corner. [*See* HUNT, J. H. L.]

OLLIVANT (J. E.), M.A., M.A., &c. Breeze from the Great Salt Lake; or, New Zealand to New York by the New Mail Route. 8vo. Lond., 1871.   MD 4 S 26

OLYMPIODORUS. Life of Plato. [*See* PLATO.]

O'MALLEY (REV. FATHER), S.J. Mnemonics applied to English History. 8vo. Sydney, 1885.   MK 1 P 11
Mnemonics applied to Geography. 8vo. Sydney, 1885.   MK 1 P 11

OMAN (C. W. C.), B.A. Art of War in the Middle Ages, A.D. 378–1515. With Maps and Plans. 8vo. Oxford, 1885.   B 14 Q 41

OMAR KHAYYAM. Quatrains of. The Persian Text, with an English Verse Translation by E. H. Whinfield, M.A. 8vo. Lond., 1883.   H 8 R 33

O'MEARA (BARRY E.) Napoleon in Exile; or, a Voice from St. Helena; being the Opinions and Reflections on the most important Events of his Life and Government. 5th ed. 2 vols. 8vo. Lond., 1822.   C 8 T 35, 36

O'MEARA (KATHLEEN). Madame Mohl: her Salon and her Friends: a Study of Social Life in Paris. 8vo. Lond., 1885.   C 8 Q 33

OMOND (GEORGE W. T.) Lord Advocates of Scotland, from the close of the 15th Century to the passing of the Reform Bill. 2 vols. 8vo. Lond., 1883.   B 13 R 6, 7

O'NEILL (CHARLES). Practice and Principles of Calico Printing, Bleaching Dyeing, &c. 2 vols. 8vo. Manchester, 1878.   A 11 S 4, 5

O'NEILL (HUGH). [*See* TYRONE, EARL OF.]

ONE OF THE CREW. [*See* WALCH, G.]

ONE OF THE PARTY. [*See* DONNISON, H.]

ONE OF THE SPECIAL CONSTABLES. [*See* HELPS, SIR A.]

ONE OF H.M. CHAPLAINS. [*See* MULLINS, J.]

ONE WHO HAS BEEN A RESIDENT FOR THIRTY YEARS. [*See* AUSTRALIA.]

ONE WHO HAS HANDLED THE SPADE. [*See* IMMIGRATION.]

ONOFRIO (J. B.) Essai d'un Glossaire des Patois de Lyonnais, Forez et Beaujolais. 8vo. Lyons, 1864.   C 13 P 7

OPEN SEA (THE) [a Weekly Journal in Manuscript]. Fol. At Sea, 1868.   ME 9 Q 1 ‡

OPIE (AMELIA). Memorials of the Life of ; selected and arranged from her Letters, Diaries and other Manuscripts, by Cecilia Lucy Brightwell. 8vo. Norwich, 1854. C 9 P 13

OPIE (JOHN), R.A. Lectures on Painting. [*See* BARRY, J.] A 7 T 4

OPPERT (ERNEST). The Forbidden Land: Voyages to the Corea ; with an Account of its Geography, History, Productions, and Commercial Capabilities, &c., &c. With Charts, and Illustrations. 8vo. Lond., 1880. D 6 R 29

OPPERT (F.), M.D., &c. Hospitals, Infirmaries, and Dispensaries : their Construction, Interior Arrangement, and Management. Roy. 8vo. Lond., 1867. A 3 P 28

OPPERT (PROF. GUSTAV), PH.D. On the Weapons, Army Organisation, and Political Maxims of the Ancient Hindus; with special Reference to Gunpowder and Firearms. 8vo. Madras, 1880. B 10 T 15

On the Classification of Languages : a Contribution to Comparative Philology. 8vo. Madras, 1879. K 12 R 24

OPPERT (JULES). Duppe Lisan Assur: Eléments de la Grammaire Assyrienne. 2ᵉ éd. 8vo. Paris, 1868. K 12 R 25

OPTATUS (SANCTUS). Opera omnia. [*See* MIGNE, J. P., SERIES LATINA, 11.]

ORCHARD (JAMES), F.R.S. Shropshire Dialect. [*See* AUDELAY, J.]

ORD (W. M.) [*See* SIBSON, F.]

ORDEN, WAPPEN, UND FLAGGEN (DIE), aller Regenten und Staaten in originalgetreuer Abbildungen, 2ᵉ auflage. Roy. 8vo. Leipzig, 1883. K 8 8 1

Specielle Beschreibung der Orden aller europäischen und nicht europäischen Regenten und Staaten : Supplement. Roy. 8vo. Leipzig, 1887. K 8 8 2

ORDERICUS VITALIS. Ecclesiastical History of England and Normandy. Translated, with Notes and the Introduction of Guizot, by Thomas Forester, M.A. 4 vols. 8vo. Lond., 1853–56. G 16 Q 7–10

Historia Ecclesiastica. [*See* MIGNE, J. P., SERIES LATINA, 188.]

Histoire de Normandie. [*See* GUIZOT, F. P. G., 25–28.]

ORDINANCES OF NEW ZEALAND. [*See* NEW ZEALAND.]

OREGON. [*See* UNITED STATES OF AMERICA.]

O'REILLY (CHARLES WILLIAM). Expedition to discover the Source of the White Nile. [*See* WERNE, F.] D 1 R 20, 21

O'REILLY (DOWELL). A Pedlar's Pack. 12mo. Sydney, 1888. MH 1 P 34

O'REILLY (EDWARD). Irish-English Dictionary; with a Supplement by John O'Donovan. Imp. 8vo. Dublin, 1877. K 14 8 1

4 C

O'REILLY (JOHN BOYLE). The Golden Secret; or, Bond and Free: a Tale of Bush and Convict Life in Western Australia. 8vo. Melb., 1887. MJ 1 U 20

O'RELL (MAX). [*See* BLOUET, P.]

ORLÉANS (ÉLISABETH CHARLOTTE), DUCHESSE D'. Mémoires. [*See* BARRIÈRE, J. F., 1]

O'RELLI (PROF. CONRAD VON). Altfranzösische Grammatik (Formenlehre). Mit vielen Conjecturen und Berichtigungen. Zweite ganz umgearbeitete Auflage. 8vo. Zürich, 1848. K 15 S 17

ORFORD (HON. HORACE WALPOLE), EARL OF. [*See* WALPOLE, HON. H.]

ORIENT LINE GUIDE. Illustrated Guide of the Orient Line of Steamers between England and Australia. [Edited by W. J. Loftie.] Ob. 4to. Lond., 1884.* MD 1 Q 1

ORIENTAL HERALD AND COLONIAL REVIEW (THE). 14 vols. 8vo. Lond., 1824–29. E 1. 51

ORIENTAL STUDENT, AN. [*See* PATON, A. A.]

ORIENTALIA ANTIQUA, or Documents and Researches relating to the History of the Writings, Languages, and Arts of the East ; ed. by Terrien de Lacouperie, M.R.A.S., &c. Vol. 1. Roy. 8vo. Lond., 1882.

ORIENTALISTS. Report of the Proceedings of the Second International Congress of Orientalists held in London, 1878. (Pam. M.) 4to. Lond., 1874. MJ 2 S 4

ORIGEN. Opera omnia. [*See* MIGNE, J. P., SERIES GRÆCA, 11–17.]

ORKNEYINGA SAGA (THE). [*See* ANDERSON, J.]

ORLICH (CAPT. LEOPOLD VON). Travels in India, including Sinde and the Punjab ; translated from the German, by H. Evans Lloyd. 2 vols. 8vo. Lond., 1845. D 6 8 6, 7

ORME (ROBERT), F.A.S. History of the Military Transactions of the British Nation in Indostan, from the year 1745. 2nd ed., with an Index. 2 vols. (in 3) 4to. Lond., 1775–78. B 10 V 1–3

Historical Fragments of the Mogul Empire, of the Morattoes, and of the English Concerns in Indostan, from the year 1659 ; to which is prefixed an Account of the Life and Writings of the Author. 4to. Lond., 1805. B 10 V 4

ORME (TEMPLE AUGUSTUS). Introduction to the Science of Heat ; designed for the use of Schools, &c. 12mo. Lond., 1869. A 5 S 27

ORME (REV. WILLIAM). Life of the Rev. Richard Baxter. [*See* BAXTER, REV. R.]

ORME (REV. WILLIAM)—*continued.*
Defence of the Missions in the South Sea and Sandwich Islands, against the Misrepresentations contained in a late number of the *Quarterly Review*, in a Letter to the Editor of that Journal. 8vo. Lond., 1827.　MG 1 R 13

ORMEROD (ELEANOR A.), F.R.M.S.　Guide to Methods of Insect Life, and Prevention and Remedy of Insect Ravage. 8vo. Lond., 1884.　A 14 P 47

Reports and Notes of Observations of Injurious Insects and Common Farm Pests, &c., 1879–85. 8 vols. (in 4) roy. 8vo. Lond., 1880–86.　E

Manual of Injurious Insects; with Methods of Prevention and Remedy for their Attacks to Food-crops, Forest Trees, and Fruit; and with short Introduction to Entomology. 8vo. Lond., 1881.　A 14 P 46

ORMEROD (GEORGE), LL.D., &c.　History of the County Palatine and City of Chester. 2nd ed. 3 vols. fol. Lond., 1882.　B 18 T 8–10 ‡

ORMOND (JAMES), DUKE OF.　Life of ; containing an Account of the most Remarkable Affairs of his Time ; by Thomas Carte. 6 vols. 8vo. Oxford, 1851. C 10 T 42–47

Narrative of his Life. [*See* MOUNTMORRES, RT. HON. H. R. M., LORD.]　B 11 Q 26, 27

ORMSBY (JOHN).　Autumn Rambles in North Africa. 8vo. Lond., 1864.　D 1 S 10

Stray Papers. 8vo. Lond., 1876.　J 11 T 24

ORNSBY (PROF. ROBERT), M.A.　Memoirs of James Robert Hope-Scott, of Abbotsford, D.C.L., Q.C. ; with Selections from his Correspondence. 2 vols. 8vo. Lond., 1884.　C 7 P 25, 26

OROSIUS (PAULUS).　King Alfred's Anglo-Saxon Version [of the History of the World], from the Historian Orosius ; together with an English Translation, by D. Barrington. 8vo. Lond., 1773.　B 14 R 28

ORR (Mus. SUTHERLAND).　Hand-book to the Works of Robert Browning. 12mo. Lond., 1885.　H 5 R 39

ORRERY (CHARLES), EARL OF.　Memoirs of. [*See* BUD-GELL, E.]　C 4 S 1

ORRIDGE (B. BROGDEN), F.C.S.　Illustrations of Jack Cade's Rebellion, from Researches in the Guildhall Records ; to which are added Contributions by W. D. Cooper, F.S.A., on the rising of Cade and his followers in Kent and Surrey. 4to. Lond., 1869.　B 6 V 18

ORSI (JOSEPH), COUNT.　Recollections of the last Half-century. 8vo. Lond., 1881.　C 3 P 32

ORVIS (CHARLES F.), AND CHENEY (A. NELSON).　Fishing with the Fly : Sketches by Lovers of the Art ; with Illustrations of Standard Flies. Sm. 4to. Manchester, Vern, 1883.　A 16 P 21

OSBORNE (ALICK).　Notes on the Present State and Prospects of Society in New South Wales. 12mo. Lond., 1833.*　MD 1 T 39

OSBORNE (THOMAS).　Collection of Voyages and Travels. [*See* CHURCHILL, O. AND J.]　D 36 R 8, 9 ‡

OSBORNE (THOMAS), EARL OF DANBY, &c.　[*See* DANBY, EARL OF.]

OSBORNE (HON. W. G.)　Court and Camp of Runjeet Sing. 8vo. Lond., 1840.　B 10 T 5

OSBORNE (MRS. WILLOUGHBY-).　Pilgrimage to Mecca. [*See* SIKANDER, THE NAWAB.]　D 4 T 22

OSBORN (H. S.), LL.D.　Metallurgy of Iron and Steel, Theoretical and Practical, in all its Branches ; with Special Reference to American Materials and Processes. Illustrated. 8vo. Philad., 1869.　A 9 U 14

OSBORN (MAJOR ROBERT DURIE).　Islam under the Arabs. 8vo. Lond., 1876.　G 9 T 12

OSBORN (CAPT. SHERARD), C.B.　Cruise in Japanese Waters. 8vo. Edinb., 1859.　D 5 P 32

Quedah ; or, Stray Leaves from a Journal in Malayan Waters. 8vo. Lond., 1857.　D 5 P 31

Discovery of the North-West Passage. [*See* MACLURE, CAPT. R.]　D 4 R 1

OSBURNE (RICHARD).　History of Warrnambool, capital of the Western Ports of Victoria from 1847, when the first Government Land Sales took place, up to the end of 1886. (The Queen's Jubilee edition.) 8vo. Prahran, 1887.　MB 2 P 43

OSBURN (WILLIAM), R.S.L.　Ancient Egypt : her Testimony to the Truth of the Bible. 8vo. Lond., 1846.　B 2 S 3

Monumental History of Egypt, as recorded on the Ruins of her Temples, Palaces and Tombs. 2 vols. 8vo. Lond., 1854.　B 2 R 45, 46

Antiquities of Egypt. Engravings. 8vo. Lond., 1847.　B 2 S 2

O'SHANASSY (SIR JOHN), K.C.M.G.　Portrait of. [*See* MANUSCRIPTS AND PORTRAITS.]

O'SHAUGHNESSEY (E. W.)　Australian Almanack and Sydney Directory. 3 vols. (in 2) 8vo. Sydney, 1833–35.*　ME 4 Q

Another copy. 3 vols. (in 2) 8vo. Sydney, 1833–35.*　ME 4 R

O'SHEA (JOHN AUGUSTUS).　Leaves from the Life of a Special Correspondent. With a Portrait of the Author. 2 vols. 8vo. Lond., 1885.　C 4 R 40, 41

Romantic Spain. 2 vols. 8vo. Lond., 1887. D 7 Q 34, 35

An Iron-bound City ; or, Five Months of Peril and Privation. 2 vols. 8vo. Lond., 1886.　B 8 P 20, 21

OSLER (EDWARD).　Life of Admiral Viscount Exmouth. 8vo. Lond., 1835.　C 5 V 13

OSLER (W. ROSCOE).　Tintoretto. (Great Artists.) 8vo. Lond., 1879.　C 3 T 36

OSMASTON (JOHN). Old Ali; or, Travels Long Ago. With Illustrations. 8vo. Lond., 1881. D 9 S 16

OSSIAN. Genuine Remains of, literally translated; with a preliminary Dissertation, by Patrick Macgregor. 8vo. Lond., 1841. H 7 T 21

Poems of; translated by James Macpherson. 2 vols. 8vo. Lond., 1807. H 7 T 19, 20

OSSORY (COUNTESS OF). [*See* WALPOLE, HON. H.] C 10 P 45, 46

O'SULLEVAN (PHILIP). Historiæ Catholicæ Iberniæ Compendium. Sm. 4to. Vlyssippone, 1621. G 2 P 16

O'SULLIVAN (REV. MORTIMER), A.M. Guide to an Irish Gentleman in his Search for a Religion. 12mo. Dublin, 1833. G 9 Q 9

OSWALD (MISS E. J.) By Fell and Fjord; or, Scenes and Studies in Iceland. With Illustrations. 8vo. Edinb., 1882. D 9 P 15

OTAGO UNIVERSITY. University of Otago, Dunedin: Foundations, Regulations, and Time-table, for 1877. 8vo. Dunedin, 1877. MJ 2 R 16

OTAGONIAN, AN. [*See* THOMSON, J. T.]

OTHLONUS (MONACHUS). Opera omnia. [*See* MIGNE, J. P., SERIES LATINA, 146.]

OTIS (GEORGE A.) Check List of Preparations and Objects in the Section of Human Anatomy of the United States Army Medical Museum. (Philad. Int. and Cent. Exhib.) 8vo. Wash., 1876. K 7 R 36

Description of Selected Specimens from Army Medical Museum at Washington. (Philad. Int. Exhib., 1876.) 8vo. Philad., 1876. A 16 U 21

Description of Medical Transport Cart. [*See* HUNTINGDON, D. L.]

OTRANTO (JOSEPH FOUCHÉ), DUKE OF. Memoirs of, Minister of the General Police of France. Translated from the French. 2nd ed. 2 vols. 8vo. Lond., 1825. C 7 Q 20, 21

OTTÉ (E. C.) How to learn Danish (Dano-Norwegian): a Manual for Students of Danish (Dano-Norwegian), based upon the Ollendorffian System of Teaching Languages, and adapted for Self-instruction. 8vo. Lond., 1879. K 11 V 13

Key to the Exercises of the Manual for Students of Danish (Dano-Norwegian). 12mo. Lond., 1879. K 11 V 14

Scandinavian History. 12mo. Lond., 1874. B 2 R 22

Cosmos : a Sketch of a Physical Description of the Universe. [*See* HUMBOLDT, F. H. A. VON, BARON.] A 3 R 30–34

OTTER (R. H.), M.A. Winters Abroad: Some Information respecting places visited by the Author on Account of his Health. 8vo. Lond., 1882. MD 3 Q 18

OTTER (WILLIAM). Life and Remains of the Rev. Edward Daniel Clarke, LL.D. 4to. Lond., 1824. C 4 W 6

OTTLEY (WILLIAM YOUNG), F.S.A. Inquiry into the origin and early History of Engraving upon Copper and Wood; with an Account of Engravers and their Works. 2 vols. 4to. Lond., 1816. A 8 T 30, 31

Italian School of Design ; being a series of Facsimiles of original Drawings by the most eminent Painters and Sculptors of Italy. With Biographical Notices. Atlas fol. Lond., 1823. A 13 P 6 ‡

Series of Plates, engraved after the Paintings and Sculptures of the most eminent Masters of the early Florentine School. Atlas fol. Lond., 1826. A 13 P 5 ‡

OTTLEY (WILLIAM YOUNG), F.S.A., AND TOMKINS (PELTRO WILLIAM). Engravings of the Most Noble the Marquis of Stafford's Collection of Pictures in London. 4 vols. imp. 4to. Lond., 1818. A 4 Q 1–4 ‡

OTTO (ADOLPH WILHELM). Compendium of Human and Comparative Pathological Anatomy. Translated by J. F. South. 8vo. Lond., 1831. A 13 Q 1

OTTO (DR. FRIEDRICH). History of Russian Literature; with a Lexicon of Russian Authors; translated from the German by the late George Cox, M.A. 8vo. Oxford, 1839. B 12 U 16

OTWAY (CÆSAR). Tour in Connaught; comprising Sketches of Clonmacnoise, Joyce County, and Achill. Illustrated. 12mo. Dublin, 1839. D 7 P 2

OTWAY (THOMAS). Works of; consisting of his Plays, Poems, and Letters; with a Sketch of his Life. 2 vols. 8vo. Lond., 1812. H 3 S 8, 9

Plays written by. 2 vols. 12mo. Lond., 1736. H 2 Q 28, 29

The Orphan; or, the Unhappy Marriage : a Tragedy. (Bell's Brit. Theatre.) 18mo. Lond., 1791. H 2 P 1

Another copy. (New Eng. Theatre.) 12mo. Lond., 1791. H 4 P 17

Another copy. (Brit. Theatre.) 12mo. Lond., 1808. H 1 P 12

Venice Preserved ; or, a Plot discovered : a Tragedy. (New Eng. Theatre.) 12mo. Lond., 1790. H 4 P 21

Another copy. (Bell's Brit. Theatre.) 18mo. Lond., 1791. H 2 P 30

Another copy. (Brit. Theatre.) 12mo. Lond., 1808. H 1 P 12

Another copy. [*See* BRIT. DRAMA, 1.]

The Cheats of Scapin : a Farce. [*See* BRIT. DRAMA, 5.]

Life and Poems of. [*See* CHALMERS, A., *and* JOHNSON, DR. S.]

OUCHTERLONY (LIEUT. JOHN), F.G.S. The Chinese War: an Account of all the operations of the British Forces, from the commencement to the Treaty of Nanking. Illustrated. 8vo. Lond., 1844. B 2 P 43

OUDEMANS (A. C.), Sen. Bijdrage tot een Middel-en Oudnederlandsch Woordenboek. 7 vols. 8vo. Arnheim, 1869–80.   K 14 T 13–19

OULTON (Walley Chamberlain). The Sleep-walker; or, Which is the Lady? a Farce. (Cumberland's Eng. Theatre.) 12mo. Lond., 1829.   H 2 Q 18

OUR CHRISTMAS BUDGET: Collection of Tales, Sketches, &c., in Prose and Verse; by Harold Wilberforce H. Stephen, and Grosvenor Bunster. 8vo. Sydney, 1872.   MJ 2 R 17

OUR FINANCIAL SYSTEM. Indirect *versus* Direct Taxation; or, the Ways and Means, by "Financier." 8vo. Melb., 1858.   MF 1 Q 3

OUR OCEAN HIGHWAYS: Condensed Universal Hand Gazetteer and International Route Book, by Ocean, Road, and Rail; edited by J. Maurice Dempsey and William Hughes, F.R.G.S. 2 vols. 8vo. Lond., 1870–71.
                                                          E 1. 58

OUR OWN COUNTRY. Descriptive, Historical, Pictorial. Illustrated. 6 vols. 4to. Lond., 1879–83.   D 6 V 12–17

OUR PENAL SYSTEM. Report of the Citizens' Committee of Enquiry; with the Evidence annexed. 8vo. Melb., 1856.   MF 3 P 5

OUSELEY (Rev. Sir F. A. Gore), M.A., &c. Treatise on Harmony. (Clar. Press.) 2nd ed. 4to. Oxford, 1875.   A 23 U 5
Treatise on Musical Form and General Composition. (Clar. Press.) 2 vols. (in 1) 4to. Oxford, 1875. A 23 U 5
Treatise on Counterpoint, Canon, and Fugue, based upon that of Cherubini. (Clar. Press.) 4to. Oxford, 1869.
                                                          A 23 U 6
History of Music. [*See* Naumann, Dr. C. F.]
                                                          A 8 Q 7, 8

OUSELEY (Sir William), Knt., &c. Travels in various Countries of the East, more particularly Persia. 3 vols. 4to. Lond., 1819–23.   D 5 V 21–23

OUSELEY (Sir William Gore), K.C.B. Remarks on the Statistics and Political Institutions of the United States. 8vo. Philad., 1832.   F 6 U 4

OUTRAM (Gen. Sir James), C.B. Conquest of Scinde: a Commentary. 2 vols. 8vo. Lond., 1846.   B 10 U 6
James Outram: a Biography; by Major-General Sir F. J. Goldsmid, C.B., K.C.S.I. 2 vols. 8vo. Lond., 1880.
                                                          C 9 R 8 9

OUVRY (Frederic). [*See* Howleglas.]

OUVRY (Col. H. A.) Agricultural Community of the Middle Ages. [*See* Nasse, E.]   F 6 U 1

OVERBECK (Johann Friedrich). Overbeck; by J. B. Atkinson. (Great Artists.) 8vo. Lond., 1882. C 3 T 43

OVERBURY (Sir Thomas). Poisoning of. [*See* Amos, A.]

OVERLAND MONTHLY (The). Vol. 7. 2nd Series. [Jan. June, 1886.] Roy. 8vo. San Francisco, 1886.
                                                          E 1. 34

OVERLANDER. [*See* Australian Sketches.]

OVERMAN (Frederick). Manufacture of Steel, containing the Practice and Principles of working and making Steel; with an Account of recent Improvements in Steel, by A. A. Fesquet. 8vo. Philad., 1873.   A 10 P 6
Moulder's and Founder's Pocket Guide. 8vo. Philad., 1875.   A 11 Q 10
Practical Mineralogy, Assaying, and Mining. 12mo. Philad., 1872.   A 9 P 26

OVERS (John). Evenings of a Working Man; being the Occupation of his scanty Leisure; with a Preface by Charles Dickens. 12mo. Lond., 1844.   J 7 Q 40

OVERTON (Rev. John Henry), M.A. Life in the English Church (1660–1714). 8vo. Lond., 1885.   G 8 T 10
The Evangelical Revival in the 18th Century. 12mo. Lond., 1886.   G 7 R 20

OVIDIUS NASO (Publius). Heroïdes; or, Epistles of the Heroines: the Amours, Art of Love, Remedy of Love, and Minor Works of Ovid; literally translated into English Prose, with copious Notes, by Henry T. Riley, B.A. 8vo. Lond., 1877.   H 5 S 38
Metamorphoses of Ovid; literally translated into English Prose, with copious Notes and Explanations, by Henry T. Riley, B.A. 8vo. Lond., 1877.   H 5 S 39
Fasti, Tristia, Pontic Epistles, Ibis, and Halieuticon of Ovid; literally translated into English Prose, with copious Notes, by Henry T. Riley, B.A. 8vo. Lond., 1878.
                                                          H 5 S 37
Ovidio de' Rimedi d'Amore. Fatto volgare, e ridotto in ottava rima da Angelo Ingegneri. 8vo. Bergamo, 1604.   H 7 P 37
Opera omnia, ex Editione Burmanniana; cum Notis et Interpretatione in usum Delphini. 10 vols. 8vo. Lond., 1821.   J 13 R 15–24
Ovid. Translated by Dryden, Pope, Congreve, Addison, and others. (Fam. Class. Lib.) 2 vols. 18mo. Lond., 1833.   J 15 P 29, 30
Metamorphoses d'Ovide, en Rondeaux, imprimez et enrichés de Figures. 4to. Paris, 1776.   H 5 V 29
Garth's Ovid. [*See* Chalmers, A.]

OWEN (A. C.) Art Schools of Mediæval Christendom. 8vo. Lond., 1876.   A 6 V 33

OWEN (Lieut.-Col. C. H.), R.A. Principles and Practice of Modern Artillery: including Artillery Material, Gunnery, and Organization and use of Artillery in Warfare. With numerous Illustrations. 2nd ed. 8vo. Lond., 1873.   A 29 U 30

OWEN (Dr.) Dialogue on Baptism. 8vo. Sydney, 1886.   MG 1 Q 11

OWEN (Douglas). Marine Insurance Notes and Clauses. 8vo. Lond., 1883.   F 6 U 5

OWEN (H.), and BLAKEWAY (J. B.) History of Shrewsbury. 2 vols. 4to. Lond., 1825.   B 6 V 2, 3

Owe] PART I:—*Authors, Editors, or Reference.* [Owe

OWEN (REV. OCTAVIUS FREIRE), M.A., &c. [*See* ARISTOTELES.] G 16 P 2, 3
Refutation of Spinoza. [*See* LIEBNITZ, G. W.]

OWEN (PROF. SIR RICHARD), F.R.S., &c. Ova of the Ornithorhynchus Paradoxus. 4to. Lond., 1834.
MA 2 Q 13 †
Uterus of the Kangaroo. 4to. Lond., 1834.
MA 2 Q 13 †
Marsupial Pouches, Mammary Glands, and Mammary Fœtus of the Echidna Hystrix. Roy. 4to. Lond., 1865. MA 2 Q 14 †
Restoration of an Extinct Elephantine Marsupial (*Diprotodon Australis*). 4to. Lond., 1870.* MA 2 Q 13 †
Cuvierian Principle in Palæontology tested by evidences of an Extinct Leonine Marsupial (*Thylacoleo Carnifex*). 4to. Lond., 1871.* MA 2 Q 13 †
Fossil, Mammals of Australia. Part 10. (Roy. Soc. Pubs., 2.) 4to. Lond., 1876. A 11 P 3 †
Fossil Remains of the Extinct Mammals of Australia; with a Notice of the Extinct Marsupials of England. 2 vols. 4to. Lond., 1877. MA 2 Q 15, 16 †
Memoirs on the Extinct Wingless Birds of New Zealand; with an Appendix on those of England, Australia, Newfoundland, Mauritius, and Rodriguez. 2 vols. 4to. Lond., 1879. MA 2 Q 17, 18 †
Description of the Skeleton of an extinct Gigantic Sloth (*Mylodon robustus*, Owen); with observations on the osteology, natural affinities, and probable habits of the Megatherioid Quadrupeds in general. Roy. 4to. Lond., 1842. A 2 8 3 †
Descriptive and illustrated Catalogue of the Fossil Organic Remains of Mammalia and Aves contained in the Museum of the Royal College of Surgeons of England. 4to. Lond., 1845. A 1 Q 20 †
History of British Fossil Mammals and Birds. Illustrated. 8vo. Lond., 1846. A 9 S 21
Parthenogenesis, or the successive production of Procreating Individuals from a single Ovum. 8vo. Lond., 1849. A 13 R 9
Principal Forms of the Skeleton and the Teeth; as the basis for a system of Natural History and Comparative Anatomy. 8vo. Lond., 1856. A 28 Q 6
Classification and Geographical Distribution of the Mammalia. To which is added an Appendix "On the Gorilla," and "On the Extinction and Transmutation of Species." 8vo. Lond., 1859. A 14 R 43
Palæontology; or, a Systematic Summary of Extinct Animals, and their geological relations. 2nd ed. 8vo. Edinb., 1861. A 10 Q 12
Extent and Aims of a National Museum of Natural History. 8vo. Lond., 1862. A 14 T 14
Anatomy of Vertebrates. 8vo. Lond., 1866–68.
A 14 U 19–21
1. Fishes and Reptiles.
2. Birds and Mammals.
3. Mammals.

OWEN (PROF. SIR RICHARD), F.R.S., &c.—*continued.*
Remains of a large extinct Lama (*Palauchenia magna*, Owen), from Quaternary Deposits in the Valley of Mexico. Roy. 4to. Lond., 1869. MA 2 Q 14 †
Molar Teeth, Lower Jaw, of *Macrauchenia patachonica*, Owen. Roy. 4to. Lond., 1869. MA 2 Q 14 †
Experimental Physiology: its Benefits to Mankind; with an Address on Unveiling the Statue of William Harvey at Folkestone, 6th August, 1881. 8vo. Lond., 1882. A 12 Q 30
Lectures on the Comparative Anatomy and Physiology of the Vertebrate Animals: Fishes. 8vo. Lond., 1846.
A 27 U 28
Odontography; or, a Treatise on Comparative Anatomy of the Teeth in the Vertebrate Animals. Text and Plates. 2 vols. roy. 8vo. Lond., 1845. A 15 R 16, 17
Antiquity of Man, as deduced from the Discovery of a Human Skeleton during the Excavations of the East and West India Dock-Extensions, at Tilbury, North Bank of the Thames. 8vo. Lond., 1884. A 9 T 13
History of British Fossil Reptiles. 4 vols. 4to. Lond., 1849–84. A 1 Q 7–10 †
Nature of Limbs: a Discourse delivered at an Evening Meeting of the Royal Institution of Great Britain. 8vo. Lond., 1849. A 12 T 31
Lectures on the Comparative Anatomy and Physiology of the Invertebrate Animals. 2nd ed. 8vo. Lond., 1855. A 14 U 22
Memoir of the Pearly Nautilus (*Nautilus pompilius*, Linn.), with Illustrations of its external Form and internal Structure. 4to. Lond., 1832. A 14 V 7
Another copy. (Pam. Cd.) 4to. Lond.,1832. MA 2 Q 13 †
Zoology of Captain Beechey's Voyage. [*See* BEECHEY, CAPT. F. W.] A 14 V 1
Zoology of the Voyage of H.M.S. *Beagle*. [*See* DARWIN, C.]
[*See* LOND. INTERNAT. EXHIB., 1851.] A 16 Q 22

OWEN (ROBERT). Robert Owen, the Founder of Socialism in England; by Arthur John Booth, M.A. 12mo. Lond., 1869. C 2 Q 28
Robert Owen's Millenial Gazette. (Pam. 34.) 8vo. Lond., 1858. J 12 U 26

OWEN (ROBERT DALE). Debatable Land between this World and the next; with illustrative Narrations. 2nd ed. 8vo. Lond., 1874. G 7 R 22
Footfalls on the Boundary of another World; with Narrative Illustrations. 3rd English ed. 8vo. Lond., 1873.
G 7 R 21
Threading my Way: Twenty-seven Years of. Autobiography. 8vo. Lond., 1874. C 3 P 41

OWEN (WILLIAM). Reports of Cases argued and determined in the Supreme Court. [*See* NEW SOUTH WALES—SUPREME COURT.]

OWEN (Capt. William F. W.), R.N. Narrative of Voyages to explore the Shores of Africa, Arabia, and Madagascar. 2 vols. 8vo. Lond., 1833. 　　　　　D 1 V 15, 16

OWENS (Capt. O.) [*See* Netherby Gazette.]

OWENS COLLEGE. Catalogue of the MSS. and printed Books bequeathed to Owens College, Manchester, by the late Right Rev. James Prince Lee, D.D. 8vo. Manchester (n.d.) 　　　　　K 7 R 27

Essays and Addresses by the Professors and Lecturers of the Owens College, Manchester. 8vo. Lond., 1874. 　　　　　J 6 T 1

OXENFORD (John). History of the Insurrection in China. [*See* Callery.]

[*See* Goethe, J. W. von.]

OXENHAM (Rev. H. N.), M.A. Short Studies in Ecclesiastical History and Biography. 8vo. Lond., 1884. 　　　　　G 8 U 10

OXFORD (Earl of). [*See* Churchill, O. And J.]

OXFORD ESSAYS; contributed by Members of the University. 4 vols. 8vo. Lond., 1855–58. 　J 7 U 14–17

OXFORD GRADUATE, An. [*See* Mystic Voices of Heaven.] 　　　　　A 3 R 3

OXFORD PRIZE POEMS: a Collection of such English Poems as have obtained Prizes in the University of Oxford. 12mo. Oxford, 1839. 　　　　　H 7 P 6

OXFORD UNIVERSITY. Calendar for the years 1838–86. 4 vols. 8vo. Oxford, 1838–86. 　E 2. 80

Honours Register of the University of Oxford: a Record of University Honours and Distinctions, completed to the end of Trinity Term, 1883. 8vo. Oxford, 1883. E 2. 80

Statutes made for the University of Oxford, and for the Colleges and Halls therein, by the University of Oxford Commissioners. 8vo. Oxford, 1882. 　　F 3 R 17

Oxford Founders. [*See* Skelton, J.]

OXLEY (John). Letter to His Excellency Major-General Lachlan Macquarie respecting the Exploration of the Course of the Macquarie River. Fol. Parramatta, 1818. 　　　　　MD 6 P 14 †

Journals of Two Expeditions into the Interior of New South Wales, 1817–18. With Maps and Views of the Interior. 4to. Lond., 1820.* 　　MD 6 P 12 †

Report of an Expedition to Survey Port Curtis, Moreton Bay, and Port Bowen, with a view to form Convict Penal Establishments there. [*See* Field, B.]

OYSTER CULTURE COMMISSION. [*See* New South Wales.]

OZANAM (Prof. Antoine Frédéric). Dante et la Philosophie Catholique au treizième Siècle. 8vo. Louvain, 1847. 　　　　　G 3 Q 19

Letters of [Antoine] Frederic Ozanam, Professor of Foreign Literature in the Sorbonne; translated from the French, by Ainslie Coates. 8vo. Lond., 1886. C 5 R 20

OZANAN (J.) [*See* Hutton, Dr. C.] 　　A 16 S 6

OZANNE (J. W.) Russia in Central Asia. [*See* Stumm, H.] 　　　　　B 12 U 4

P

P. (D.) [*See* WAVE OF LIFE.]

P. (P. A.) [*See* AUSTRALIA.]

P. (G. F.) [*See* PICKERING, G. F.]

PAASCH (H.) From Keel to Truck: Dictionary of Naval Terms in English, French, and German. 8vo. Lond., 1885.   K 9 8 4

PABISCH (REV. F. J.) Manual of Universal Church History. [*See* ALZOG, REV. J.]

PACCA (BARTOLOMMEO), CARDINAL. Historical Memoirs of; written by himself, translated by Sir George Head. 2 vols.,8vo. Lond., 1850.   C 4 T 36, 87

PACHYMERES (GEORGIUS). Opera omnia. [*See* MIGNE, J. P., SERIES GRÆCA, 143, 144, *and* BYZANTINAE HIST. SCRIPT.]

PACIANUS (SANCTUS). Opera omnia. [*See* MIGNE, J. P., SERIES LATINA, 13.]

PACIFIC OCEAN. Voyage through the Islands of the. 12mo. Lond., 1831.   MD 1 T 48

New Expedition to the Pacific and Antarctic Oceans. 8vo. Lond., 1836.   MD 7 Q 48

PACIFIC WEEKLY MAGAZINE AND REVIEW, May 15 to August 7, 1880. (*All published.*) Sm. fol. Sydney, 1880.   ME

PACKARD (A. S.), JUN., M.D. Guide to the Study of Insects, and a Treatise on those injurious and beneficial to Crops; for the use of Colleges, Farm Schools, and Agriculturists. 5th ed. 8vo. New York, 1876. A 14 U 7

Zoology for Students and General Readers. With Illustrations. 8vo. N. York, 1879.   A 14 S 32

PACKE (C.) [*See* GLAUBER, J. R.]

PADDIANA; or, Scraps and Sketches of Irish Life, present and past. 2 vols. 8vo. Lond., 1847.   J 5 Q 30, 31

PADDOCK (J.) Shipwreck of the *Oswego* on the Coast of South Barbary, and of the Sufferings of the Master and Crew while in Bondage among the Arabs. 4to. Lond., 1818.   D 5 P 1†

PAE (DAVID). The Coming Struggle among the Nations of the Earth; or the Political Events of the next Fifteen Years, described in accordance with Prophecies in Ezekiel, Daniel, and the Apocalypse. (Pam 43.) 8vo. Sydney, 1853.   MJ 2 R 5

Two Years After and Onwards; or, the Approaching War amongst the Powers of Europe. 12mo. Lond., 1864.   G 8 P 11

PAEZ (DON RAMON). Wild Scenes in South America; or, Life on the Llanos of Venezuela. 2nd ed. 8vo. New York, 1863.   D 3 S 41

PAGE (DAVID), LL.D., &c. Chips and Chapters: a Book for Amateur and young Geologists. 8vo. Lond., 1869.   A 9 Q 27

Advanced Text-book of Geology, Descriptive and Industrial. 6th ed., revised. 8vo. Edinb., 1876. A 9 P 7

PAGE (H. A.) [*See* JAPP, A. H.]

PAGE (P. F.) Traité d'Economie Politique et de Commerce des Colonies. 2 vols. 8vo. Paris, 1800–2. F 5 T 1, 2

PAGE (R.) Banks and Bankers. 8vo. Lond., 1843.   F 6 S 5

PAGE (THOMAS). Clarence, New England, Macleay and Gwydir Almanac and Gazetteer, for the years 1871–74. 4 vols. (in 2) 12mo. Grafton, 1871–74,   ME 4 Q

PAGENSTECHER (PROF. A.) Allgemeine Zoologie, oder Grundgesetze des thierischen Baus und Lebens. 4 vols. 8vo. Berlin, 1875–81.   A 14 S 27–30

PAGET (SIR JAMES), BART., &c. Clinical Lectures and Essays. Edited by Howard Marsh, F.R.C.S. 8vo. Lond., 1875.   A 12 U 25

PAGET (JOHN). Hungary and Transylvania; with Remarks on their Condition, Social, Political, and Economical. 2 vols. 8vo. Lond., 1839.   D 7 U 29, 30

PAGET (GEN. GEORGE), LORD. Light Cavalry Brigade in the Crimea; extracts from the Letters and Journal of the late General Lord George Paget, K.C.B., during the Crimean War. With a Map. 8vo. Lond., 1881.   B 12 T 26

PAGET (MISS VIOLET), "VERNON LEE." Studies of the 18th Century in Italy. 8vo. Lond., 1880. B 11 V 18

Euphorion; being Studies of the Antique and the Mediæval in the Renaissance. 2 vols. 8vo. Lond., 1884.   J 12 R 18, 19

Baldwin; being Dialogues on Views and Aspirations. 8vo. Lond., 1886.   G 3 S 25

PAIN (REV. ARTHUR W.), B.A. Command of Remembrance: a Sermon. 12mo. Sydney, 1868.   MG 1 P 49

PAINE (THOMAS). Thomas Paine to the People of England on the Invasion of England. 8vo. Lond., 1812.   F 12 P 22

Answer to. [*See* INGERSOLL, COL. R. G.]

Oration on. [*See* INGERSOLL, COL. R. G.]

PAINTERS' ETCHINGS. Containing twenty-four Original Etched Works, by Living Artists. Imp. 4to. Lond., 1884.   A 5 R 14†

PAINTERS, SCULPTORS, AND ARCHITECTS. Lives of the most Eminent; by Giorgio Vasari. Translated by Mrs. J. Foster. 6 vols. 8vo. Lond., 1855–64. C 4 R 27–32

PAINTERS, SCULPTORS, AND ARCHITECTS. Brief Biographies [Great Artists] ; by P. Delaroche. 8vo. Lond., 1880.   C 3 T 44

PAJON (H.) Les Contes de. [*See* CABINET DES FÉES, 34.]

PAKEHA MAORI, A. [*See* MANNING, F. E.]

PALÆOGRAPHICAL SOCIETY. Report for 1874–75 ; with List of Members. 8vo. (Pam L.) Lond., 1875.   MJ 2 P 28

PALÆONTOLOGISCHE ABHANDLUNGEN. Herausgegeben von W. Dames und E. Kayser. Bände 1 and 2. 4to. Berlin, 1882–85.   E 1. 73

PALATINE NOTE-BOOK (THE). For the Intercommunication of Antiquaries, Bibliophiles, and other Investigators into the History and Literature of the Counties of Lancaster, Chester, &c. Vols. 1–3. Sm. 4to. Manchester, 1881–83.   E 1. 30

PALENZUELA (PROF. RAMON), Y CARREÑO (PROF. JUAN DE LA C.) Método para aprender à leer, escribir y hablar el Inglés, según el sistema de Ollendorff. 8vo. Lond., 1876.   K 11 V 11
— Clave de los Ejercicios contenidos en el Método para aprender à leer, escribir y hablar el Inglés, según el sistema de Ollendorff. 8vo. Lond., 1878.   K 11 V 12

PALESTINE. Early Travels in Palestine. Edited, with Notes, by Thomas Wright, M.A., &c. 8vo. Lond., 1848.   D 5 Q 17
— Our Work in Palestine. 8th ed. 8vo. Lond., 1875.   B 10 P 32
— Three Weeks in Palestine and Lebanon. 8th ed. 18mo. Lond., 1839.   D 5 P 21

PALESTINE EXPLORATION FUND. Map of Western Palestine, in 26 sheets, from Surveys conducted for the Committee by Lieutenants C. R. Conder, and H. H. Kitchener, R.E. Ob. fol. Lond., 1880.*   D 10 P 19 ‡
— Plans, Elevations, Sections, &c. : Jerusalem ; by [Col. Sir] Chas. Warren, K.C.M.G. El. fol. Lond., 1884.   D 10 P 21 ‡
— Survey of Western Palestine. 8 vols. 4to. Lond., 1881–86.   D 4 V 4–11
   Arabic and English Name Lists collected during the Survey, by Lieutenants Conder and Kitchener, R.E. Transliterated and explained by Prof. E. H. Palmer, M.A.
   Special Papers on Topography, Archæology, Manners and Customs, &c.
   Memoirs of the Topography, Orography, Hydrography, and Archæology : by Lieuts. C. R. Conder, R.E., and H. H. Kitchener, R.E.
   Jerusalem ; by Col. Sir Chas. Warren, K.C.M.G., and Capt. C. R. Conder, R.E.
   Fauna and Flora of Palestine ; by H. B. Tristram, LL.D., &c.
   Memoir on the Physical Geology and Geography ; by Edward Hull, LL.D., &c.
   Twenty-one Years' Work in the Holy Land (a Record and a Summary), June 22, 1865–June 22, 1886 ; [by Walter Besant.] 8vo. Lond., 1886.   D 6 Q 31

PALESTRINA (GIOVANNI PIERLUIGI DA). Memorie-Storico-Critiche della Vita e delle Opere di ; compilate da Giuseppe Baini. 2 vols. 4to. Roma, 1828.   C 2 W 19, 20

PALEY (F. A.), M.A. Aeschyli Fabulae. [*See* ÆSCHYLUS.]   H 8 V 20
[*See* BAPTISMAL FONTS.]   A 3 P 27

PALEY (REV. WILLIAM), D.D., ARCHDEACON OF CARLISLE. Works of ; with Extracts from his Correspondence, and a Life of the Author, by R. Lynam, A.M. 5 vols. 8vo. Lond., 1823.   G 14 P 11–15
— Natural Theology ; with illustrative Notes by Henry Lord Brougham and Sir Charles Bell. 4 vols. 8vo. Lond., 1836–39.   G 13 R 20–23
— Horæ Paulinæ. [*See* WOODWARD, REV. C.]

PALFREY (JOHN GORHAM). Compendious History of New England, from the Discovery by Europeans, to the first General Congress of the Anglo-American Colonies. 4 vols. 8vo. Boston, 1884.   B 1 Q 42–45

PALGRAVE (SIR FRANCIS), K.H. Rotuli Curiæ Regis : Rolls and Records of the Courts held before the King's Justiciars or Justices (Richard I to John). 2 vols. 8vo. Lond., 1835.   B 15 T 20, 21
— Parliamentary Writs, and Writs of Military Summons, together with the Records and Muniments ; with alphabetic Digest and Index. 2 vols. (in 4) fol. Lond., 1827–34.   B 24 R 1–4 ‡
— Antient Kalendars and Inventories of the Treasury of His Majesty's Exchequer ; together with other Documents illustrating the History of that Repository. 3 vols. roy. 8vo. Lond., 1836.   B 15 T 1–3
— Documents and Records, illustrating the History of Scotland, and the Transactions between the Crowns of Scotland and England, preserved in the Treasury of Her Majesty's Exchequer. Roy. 8vo. Lond., 1837.   B 15 T 4
— History of Normandy and of England. 3 vols. 8vo. Lond., 1851–64.   B 5 S 7–9
— Truths and Fictions of the Middle Ages : the Merchant and the Friar. 2nd ed. 12mo. Lond., 1844.   J 10 P 33
— Rise and Progress of the English Commonwealth, Anglo-Saxon Period ; containing the Anglo-Saxon Policy, and the Institutions arising out of Laws and Usages which prevailed before the Conquest. With Illustrations. 2 vols. 4to. Lond., 1832.   B 15 Q 15, 16
— History of England. Vol. 1. Anglo-Saxon Period. (Fam. Lib.) 12mo. Lond., 1831.   K 10 P 39
— History of the Anglo-Saxons. (Fam. Lib.) 18mo. Lond., 1838.   K 10 P 31
— Another copy. New ed. Lond., 1876   B 3 Q25
[*See* COOPER, C. P.]

PALGRAVE (FRANCIS TURNER), LL.D. [*See* TENNYSON ALFRED, BARON.]

PALGRAVE (WILLIAM GIFFORD). Narrative of a Year's Journey through Central and Eastern Arabia (1862–63). 3rd ed. 2 vols. 8vo. Lond., 1866.   D 4 T 23, 24

Essays on Eastern Questions. 8vo. Lond., 1872.
        D 16 U 23

Dutch Guiana. With Plan and Map. 8vo. Lond., 1876.   D 4 Q 4

PALISSY (BERNARD). Life of Palissy, the Potter ; by Henry Morley. 2nd ed., 12mo. Lond..1855.   C 3 T 20

PALKOWITSCH (PROF. GEORG). Böhmisch-deutsch-lateinisches Wörterbuch. 2 vols. 8vo. Prague, 1820–21.
        K 12 R 9, 10

PALLAIN (M. G.) [*See* TALLEYRAND, PRINCE, *and* LOUIS XVIII.]

PALLAS (PETER SIMON). Travels through the Southern Provinces of the Russian Empire, 1793–94. 2 vols. 4to. Lond., 1803.   D 8 V 10, 11

PALLAVICINO (SFORTIA), CARDINALE. Vera Œcumenici Concilii Tridentini. 3 vols. (in 1) fol. Augustæ, 1775.
        G 30 Q 18 ‡

PALLISER (F. AND M. A.) Mottoes for Monuments or Epitaphs, selected for Study or Application. Illustrated. 8vo. Lond., 1872.   H 7 Q 10

PALLISER (SIR HUGH), BART., ADMIRAL OF THE WHITE. Life of ; by R. M. Hunt. 8vo. Lond., 1844. C 9 Q 12

PALLISER (JOHN). Solitary Rambles and Adventures of a Hunter in the Prairies. With Illustrations. 8vo. Lond., 1853.   D 3 Q 36

PALMER (REV. ABRAM SMYTHE), B.A. Leaves from a Word-hunter's Note-Book. 8vo. Lond., 1876. K 12 P 13

Folk-Etymology : a Dictionary of Verbal Corruptions or Words perverted in Form or Meaning, by false Derivation or mistaken Analogy. 8vo. Lond., 1882. K 14 T 7

PALMER (EDWARD). Notes on some Australian Tribes. 8vo. Lond., 1884.   M A 1 S 8

PALMER (PROF. EDWARD HENRY), M.A. Concise Dictionary of the Persian Language. 12mo. Lond., 1876.
        K 11 T 3

Oriental Penmanship: Specimens of Persian Hand-writing; to which are added, Illustrations of the Nagari Character, by Frederic Pincott, M.R.A.S. 4to. Lond., 1886.   K 16 S 19

Simplified Grammar of Hindūstānī, Persian, and Arabic. 8vo. Lond,. 1882.   K 11 U 47

Desert of the Exodus: Journeys on Foot in the Wilderness of the Forty Years' Wanderings. 2 vols. 8vo. Camb., 1871.   D 5 S 38, 39

Life and Achievements of ; by W. Besant. 8vo. 1883.   C 3 T 21

Arabic and English Name Lists. [*See* PALESTINE EXPLORATION FUND.]   D 4 V 4

4 D

PALMER (EDWIN). The Revisers and the Greek Text of the New Testament. [*See* ELLICOTT, RT. REV. C. J.]

PALMER (CAPT. GEORGE), R.N., &c. Kidnapping in the South Seas ; being a Narrative of a Three Months' Cruise of H.M.S. *Rosario.* 8vo. Edinb., 1871.* MD 28 16

PALMER (CAPT. H. S.), R.E. Ordnance Survey of the Peninsula of Sinai. [*See* WILSON, SIR C. W.]

PALMER (J.) Address to the Members of the Bush Missionary Society. [*See* BUTTERFIELD, G.]

PALMER (SAMUEL). Index to the *Times* Newspaper, for 1855–65, 1867–84. 29 vols. sm. 4to. Lond., 1868–84. E [*See* VIRGILIUS MARO, P.]

PALMER (JOHN WILLIAM), M.D. The Golden Dagon; or, up and down the Irrawaddi ; being passages of Adventure in the Burman Empire; by "An American." 8vo. New York, 1856.   D 5 Q 34

PALMER (WILLIAM), M.A. Notes of a Visit to the Russian Church in the years 1840–41. 8vo. Lond., 1882.
        R 7 R 27

An Introduction to Early Christian Symbolisms : a Series of Composition from Fresco Paintings. Fol. Lond., 1885.
        G 29 P 17 ‡

PALMER (W. J.) The Tyne and its Tributaries described and illustrated. Imp. 8vo. Lond., 1882.   D 19 V 10

PALMERSTON (HENRY TEMPLE), SECOND VISCOUNT. The Diary of, in France, during July and August, 1791. [*See* GOWER, EARL.]   B 8 U 25

PALMERSTON (HENRY JOHN TEMPLE), THIRD VISCOUNT, K.G., G.C.B. Life of ; with Selections from his Diaries and Correspondence ; by the Rt. Hon. Sir H. L. Bulwer [Lord Dalling and Bulwer]. 3 vols. 8vo. Lond., 1870–74.   C 9 Q 7–9

Life of. 1846–65 ; with Selections from his Speeches and Correspondence, by the Hon. Evelyn Ashley, M.P. 2 vols. 8vo. Lond., 1876.   C 9 Q 10, 11

Opinions and Policy of, as Minister, Diplomatist, and Statesman ; with a Memoir by G. H. Francis. 8vo. Lond., 1852.   F 9 R 16

PALSGRAVE (JEAN). L'éclaircissement de la Langue Française; suivi de la Grammaire de Giles du Guez. 4to. Paris, 1852.   K 15 U 14

PAMPHILUS (EUSEBIUS). [*See* EUSEBIUS PAMPHILUS.]

PAMPHLET (THOMAS). Narrative of Thomas Pamphlet, aged thirty-four years, who was, with two other men, wrecked on the Coast of New Holland in April, 1823, and lived among the Natives for Seven Months. Taken down by John Uniacke. [*See* FIELD, B.]

PAMPHLETEER (THE). Dedicated to both Houses of Parliament. 29 vols. 8vo. Lond., 1813–28. F 3 Q 1–R 6

PANANTI (FILIPPO). Narrative of a Residence in Algiers; with Notes and Illustrations by Edward Blaquiere. 2nd ed. 4to. Lond., 1830.   D 2 V 21

FANCHER (Mons.) [*See* SEBERT, H.]

PANCKOUCKE (C. L. F.) Description de l'Egypte; ou, Recueil des Observations et des Recherches qui ont été faites en Egypte pendant l'Expédition de l'Armée Française. 2e éd. 24 vols. (in 26) 8vo. Paris, 1821–30.
D 1 U 1-26

[Plates to the above.] 11 vols. at. fol. Paris, 1820–26.
D 11 P 4-14 ‡

PANEGYRICI VETERES ex Editionibus Chr. G. Schwarzii et Arntzeniorum, cum Notis et Interpretatione in usum Delphini, curante A. J. Valpy, A.M. 5 vols. 8vo. Lond., 1828. J 13 R 25-29

PANGKOFER (J. A.) [*See* FROMMANN, DR. G. R.]

PANIN (IVAN). Revolutionary Movement in Russia. Reprinted from the *New York Herald*, with Notes and Preface. (Pam.) 8vo. Camb., U.S., 1881. F 7 Q 17

PANIZZI (SIR ANTHONY), K.C.B. Life of; by Louis Fagan. 2 vols. 8vo. Lond., 1880. C 9 Q 13, 14

Letters of Prosper Mérimée to Panizzi. [*See* MÉRIMÉE, P.] C 8 P 36, 37

PANKHURST (E. A.) [*See* BURKE, E.]

PANTON (ARTHUR WILLIAM), M.A. Theory of Equations. [*See* BURNSIDE, W. S.] A 10 S 12

PANZANI (GREGORIO). Memoirs of, giving an Account of his Agency in England, 1634–36; by the Rev. J. Berington from the Italian Original. 8vo. Birmingham, 1793. B 6 P 46

PAPAL AGGRESSION. Reprint of several Articles on the all-absorbing Subject termed the "Papal Aggression," taken from the Public Journals. 8vo. Hobart, 1851.
MG 1 R 9

PAPE (PROF. W.) Handwörterbuch der griechischen Sprache. 3e auflage, bearbeitet von M. Sengebusch. 4 vols. roy. 8vo. Braunschweig, 1875–80. K 13 R 21-24

PAPWORTH (JOHN W. AND WYATT). Museums, Libraries, and Picture Galleries, Public and Private; their Establishment, Formation, Arrangement, and Architectural Construction; to which is appended the Public Libraries Act, 1850. With Illustrations. Roy. 8vo. Lond., 1853. A 2 T 42

PAPWORTH (WYATT). Encyclopædia of Architecture. [*See* GWILT, J.] K 5 U 2

PAQUIS (AMÉDÉE). Histoire d'Espagne et de Portugal. 2 vols. imp. 8vo. Paris, 1836 38. B 13 V 6, 7

PARACELSUS BOMBAST OF HOHENHEIM (AUREOLUS PHILIPPUS THEOPHASTUS). Life of Philippus Theophrastus Bombast, of Hohenheim, known by the name of Paracelsus; by Franz Hartmann, M.D. 8vo. Lond., 1887. C 5 S 26

PARDOE (MISS JULIA S. H.) Traits and Traditions of Portugal. 2 vols. 8vo. Lond., 1833. J 5 P 25, 26

City of the Sultan, and Domestic Manners of the Turks in 1836. 2 vols. 8vo. Lond., 1837. D 9 Q 18, 19

Court and Reign of Francis I, King of France. 2 vols. 8vo. Lond., 1849. B 8 S 34, 35

Louis XIV and the Court of France in the 17th Century. 3 vols. 8vo. Lond., 1886. C 6 R 22-24

Life of Marie de Medicis, Queen of France, Consort of Henry IV, and Regent of the Kingdom under Louis XIII. 2nd ed. 3 vols. 8vo. Lond., 1852. C 7 S 47-49

City of the Magyar; or, Hungary and her Institutions in 1839–40. 3 vols. 8vo. Lond., 1840. D 8 P 35-37

PARENT-DUCHATELET (ALEXANDRE JEAN BAPTISTE). De la Prostitution dans la Ville de Paris, considérée sous le rapport de l'hygiène publique, de la morale, et de l'administration. Troisième édition. 2 vols. 8vo. Paris, 1857. F 6 F 13, 14

PARIS. Inside Paris during the Siege; by "An Oxford Graduate." 12mo. Lond., 1871. B 8 P 3

Paris and its Historical Scenes. (Lib. Ent. Know.) 2 vols. 12mo. Lond., 1831. K 10 R 38, 39

Paris Salon. [*See* DUMAS, F. G.]

PARIS EXPOSITION DE 1834. Notice des Produits de l'Industrie Française. 8vo. Paris, 1834. K 7 R 21

PARIS UNIVERSAL EXHIBITION OF 1855. Catalogue of the Works exhibited in the British Section, in French and English. Roy. 8vo. Lond., 1855. K 8 Q 18

Catalogue of the Natural and Industrial Products of New South Wales, exhibited in Australian Museum, by the Paris Exhibition Commissioners. 4to. Sydney, 1854. MK 1 U 3

Tasmanian Contributions to the Universal Exhibition of Industry at Paris, 1855. Sm. fol. Hobart, 1855.
MK 1 Q 8 ‡

PARIS UNIVERSAL EXHIBITION OF 1867. Catalogue Général. Histoire du Travail et Monuments Historiques. 12mo. Paris, 1867. K 7 R 2

Catalogue Général publié par la Commission Impériale. 2e ed. 8vo. Paris, 1867. K 7 R 32

L'Italie économique en 1867, avec un aperçu des Industries Italiennes à l'Exposition Universelle de Paris. Florence, 1867. F 3 S 16

Belgique. Catalogue des Produits Industriels et des Œuvres d'Art. 12mo. Paris, 1867. K 7 R 5

Catalogue of the British Section, in English, French, German, and Italian. 2 vols. (in 1) 8vo. Lond., 1868. K 7 R 33

Reports, Appendices, and Index. 7 vols. (in 2) 8vo. Lond., 1868–69. K 7 R 34, 35

Catalogue Général do 1867. 8vo. Paris, 1868. C 7 R 32

Report of the Artisans selected by a Committee appointed by the Council of the Society of Arts to visit the Paris Universal Exhibition, 1867. 8vo. Lond., 1867.
A 11 U 12

PARIS UNIVERSAL EXHIBITION OF 1867.—*contd.*
Catalogue of Contributions from South Australia, to the
Paris Universal Exhibition, held in Paris, 1867. 8vo.
Adelaide, 1866.   MK 1 R 33
Exposition Universelle de 1867 : Nouvelle-Galles du Sud,
Australie. Liste des Exposants récompensés par le Jury
international. (Pam. C.) Roy. 8vo. Paris, 1867.
                                         MJ 2 S 1
Catalogue of the Natural and Industrial Products of New
South Wales, forwarded to the Paris Universal Exhi-
bition of 1867, by the New South Wales Exhibition
Commissioners. 8vo. Sydney, 1867.   MK 1 Q 34
Catalogue Spécial du Royaume de Hongrie. 8vo. Paris,
1867.   MK 1 R 33
Indian Department Catalogue of the Articles forwarded
from India. 8vo. Lond., 1867.   MK 1 R 33
Catalogue of Contributions from the Colony of Natal; by
W. M. Peniston. 12mo. Lond., 1867.   MK 1 R 33
France. Catalogue Raisonné des Collections exposés par
l'Administration des Forêts. 8vo. Paris, 1867.
                                         MK 1 R 33
PARIS UNIVERSAL EXHIBITION, 1878. Guide des
étrangers à l'Exposition Universelle et Itinéraire dans
Paris. 2e éd. 12mo. Paris, 1878.   D 11 R 4
Catalogue Officiel publié par le Commissariat Général. 7
vols. 8vo. Paris, 1878.   K 8 P 22–28
Catalogue Général de l'Exposition Spéciale de la Ville de
Paris et du Département de la Seine. 8vo. Paris, 1878.
                                         K 8 P 21
Society of Arts Artisan Reports on the Paris Universal
Exhibition of 1878. 8vo. Lond., 1879.   A 11 U 13
Congrès International de Géologie, tenu à Paris, du 29
au 31 Août et du 2 au 4 Septembre, 1878. Roy. 8vo.
Paris, 1880.   A 9 T 3
Official Catalogue of the Natural and Industrial Products
of New South Wales, forwarded to the Universal Exhi-
bition of 1878, at Paris. 8vo. Sydney, 1878. MK1Q2
Report of the Commissioners for Victoria to His Excellency
the Governor. Imp. 8vo. Melb., 1879.   MK 1 P 8 †

PARIS (GASTON). Grammaire des Langues Romanes.
[*See* DIEZ, F.]

PARIS (LOUIS PHILIPPE ALBERT D'ORLÉANS), COMTE DÉ.
Histoire de la Guerre Civile en Amérique. 4 vols. 8vo.
Paris, 1875.   B 1 R 42–45

PARIS (MATTHEW OF). Historia Major; juxta Exemplar
Londinense 1571, verbatim recusa, et cum Rogeri Wen-
doveri, Willielmi Rishangeri, Authorisque Majori
Minorique Historiis Chronicisque MSS., in Bibliotheca
Regia, Collegii Corporis Christi Cantabrigiæ, Cot-
toniáque, fideliter collata. Fol. Lond., 1640. B 17 S 15‡
English History, from 1235 to 1273. Translated from
the Latin, by the Rev. J. A. Giles, D.C.L. 3 vols. 8vo.
Lond., 1852–54.   B 3 P 1–3
Vie de Saint Aubar. [*See* ATKINSON, R.]

PARIS (T. CLIFTON), B.A. Letters from the Pyrenees,
during Three Months' Pedestrian Wanderings in the
Summer of 1842. 8vo. Lond., 1843.   D 8 Q 45

PARISH (JOHN). Voyage to the Island of Mauritius. [*See*
MAURITIUS.]   MD 4 U 4

PARISH (SIR WOODBINE), K.C.H. Buenos Ayres, and
the Provinces of the Rio de la Plata. 8vo. Lond.,
1838.   D 4 Q 16

PARK (MUNGO), SURGEON. Travels in the Interior Dis-
tricts of Africa; with Geographical Illustrations. 8vo.
Lond. (n.d.)
Travels of. [*See* COCHRANE, R.]   D 10 Q 48

PARK (THOMAS), F.S.A. Heliconia; comprising a Selection of English Poetry of the Elizabethan Age. Edited
by T. Park. 3 vols. 4to. Lond., 1815.   H 5 V 11–13
    1. Gorgeous Gallery of Gallant Inventions; edited by Thomas
       Proctor. Small Handful of Fragrant Flowers; by Nicholas
       Breton. A Floorish upon Fancie; by Nicholas Breton.
    2. Handful of Pleasant Delites; edited by Clement Robinson.
       A Mirror of Treue Honnour and Christian Nobilitie, &c., in
       the Life, &c., of Fraunsis Earl of Bedford; by George Wiet-
       stone. The Phœnix Nest ; edited by R.S. A Divine Centurie
       of Spirituall Sonnets; by Barnabe Barnes. Spirituall Sonnetes
       to the Honor of God and hys Sayntes; by Henry Constable.
       A Sad and Solemn Funerall of Sir Francis Knowles; by T.
       Churchyard. Life and Death of Thomas Wolsey, Cardinal;
       by T. Storer.
    3. England's Parnassus; edited by R. Allott. Churchyard's
       Good Will; Sad and Heavy Verses for the Losse of Arch-
       bishop Wiltgift; by T. Churchyard.
[*See* WALPOLE, H.]

PARKE (W. T.) Musical Memoir; comprising an Account of the general state of Music in England, from
1784–1830. 2 vols. 8vo. Lond., 1830.   C 4 Q 19, 20

PARKER (EDWARD STONE). Aborigines of Australia:
a Lecture. 8vo. Melb., 1854.   MA 1 R 2

PARKER (HENRY WALTER). Rise, Progress, and Present State of Van Dieman's Land. 12mo. Lond.,
1833.*   MD 2 R 9

PARKER (CAPT. JOHN). Voyage Round the World.
[*See* PARKER, MRS. MARY ANN.]   MD 4 U 4

PARKER (JOHN HENRY), C.B., &c. Archæology of Rome.
2nd ed. 8vo. Oxford, 1874–83.   B 11 S 15–23
Concise Glossary of Terms used in Grecian, Roman,
Italian, and Gothic Architecture. 12mo. Oxford,
1869.   A 2 R 24
Introduction to the Study of Gothic Architecture.
12mo. Oxford, 1867.   A 2 R 10
Glossary of Terms used in Grecian, Roman, Italian,
and Gothic Architecture. 5th ed. 2 vols. (in 3) 8vo.
Lond., 1850.   A 3 P 15–17
Plan of Rome, Ancient and Modern ; with Indications
of the Ancient Walls, Streets, and Gates, according to
Pliny ; Aqueducts, Fossae, Cippi, Tombs, &c. Roy. 8vo.
Oxford (n.d.)   B 11 R 31

PARKER (JOSEPH), D.D. Ecce Deus: Essays on the Life
and Doctrines of Jesus Christ; with Controversial Notes
on [Prof. J. R. Seeley's] "Ecce Homo." 8vo. Edinb.,
1867.   G 11 S 5

PARKER (MATTHEW), ARCHBISHOP OF CANTERBURY. Life and Acts of. [*See* STRYPE, J., 6–8.]

PARKER (MRS. MARY ANN). Voyage round the World in the *Gorgon* Man-of-War, Capt. John Parker; performed and written by his widow. 8vo. Lond., 1795.
MD 4 U 4

PARKER (REV. RICHARD), D.D. History and Antiquities of the University of Cambridge; edited by Thomas Hearne. 8vo. Lond., 1715.   B 4 Q 5

PARKER (S. E.) Life of Eusebius. [*See* EUSEBIUS PAMPHILUS.]   G 14 P 16

PARKER (THEODORE). Collected Works of; edited by Frances Power Cobbe. 14 vols. 8vo. Lond., 1863–72.
G 11 P 1–14

PARKER (PROF. THOMAS JEFFERY), B.SC., LOND. Course of Instruction in Zootomy. (Vertebrata.) With seventy-four Illustrations. 8vo. Lond., 1884.   A 28 Q 8
Studies in Biology for New Zealand Students. No. 2. The Bean Plant (*Vicia Faba*). 8vo. Wellington, 1881.
MA 1 T 27

PARKER (PROF. W. KITCHEN), F.R.S. Mammalian Descent—the Hunterian Lectures for 1884. 8vo. Lond., 1885.   A 14 T 15
On the Development of the Skull in the Common Snake—*Tropidonotus natrix*. (Roy. Soc. Pubs., 6.) 4to. Lond., 1879.   A 11 P 7 †
On the Structure and Development of the Skull in the Batrachia. (Roy. Soc. Pubs., 3.) 4to. Lond., 1876.
A 11 P 44
On the Structure and Development of the Skull in the Urodelous Amphibia, Part 1. (Roy. Soc. Pubs., 5.) 4to. Lond., 1878.   A 11 P 6

PARKER (W. N.) Comparative Anatomy of Vertebrates. [*See* WIEDERSHEIM, R.]   A 27 U 29

PARKER (WILLIAM R.), M.D. Science of Life; or, Self-Preservation: a Medical Treatise on Nervous and Physical Debility. 12mo. Sydney (n.d.)   MA 2 S 42

PARKES (MISS BESSIE RAYNER), MADAME BELLOC. Vignettes: Twelve Biographical Sketches. 8vo. Lond., 1866.   C 2 P 40
Essays on Woman's Work. 12mo. Lond., 1865.   F 15 P 8

PARKES (E. A.), M.D. Public Health; revised by Prof. William Aitken, M.D. 8vo. Lond., 1876.   A 12 P 45

PARKES (SIR HENRY), G.C.M.G. Stolen Moments: a short Series of Poems. 8vo. Sydney, 1842.*   MH 1 R 40
Murmurs of the Stream. 8vo. Sydney, 1857.   MH 1 R 40
Electoral Act, and how to Work it: a Series of Letters on the subject of the approaching Elections. (Pam., 26.) 8vo. Sydney, 1859.*   MF 3 R 50
Another copy.   MJ 2 Q 14
The Mother of the Australians: a Lecture. 12mo. Lond., 1862.   MJ 2 R 2

PARKES (SIR HENRY), G.C.M.G.—*continued.*
Australian Views of England: Eleven Letters written in 1861–62. 12mo. Lond., 1869.*   MF 1 P 30
Public Education: Speech on the Education Question. 8vo. Sydney, 1875.   MG 1 Q 18
Reply to the Speech on Education. · [*See* GREENWOOD, REV. J.]   MG 1 Q 33
Speeches on various occasions connected with the Public Affairs of New South Wales, 1848–74. 8vo. Melb., 1885.   MH 1 R 42
Beauteous Terrorist, and other Poems; by "A Wanderer." 12mo. Melb., 1885.   MH 1 R 42
Fragmentary Thoughts. 8vo. Sydney, 1889. MH 1 R 62
[*See* DALLEY, RT. HON. W. B.; *and* NEW CONSTITUTION.]

PARKES (JOSEPH), AND MERIVALE (HERMAN), M.A. Memoirs of Sir Philip Francis, K.C.B.; with Correspondence and Journals. 2 vols. 8vo. Lond., 1867. C 8 S 38, 39

PARKES (MISS MENIE). Poems. Printed for Private Circulation. 8vo. Sydney, 1866.   MH 1 S 25
Reformatories and Reformatory Treatment in France; translated from the French, by direction of the Government. 8vo. Sydney, 1868.   MF 2 Q 11

PARKES (SAMUEL), F.L.S. Chemical Catechism; revised and adapted by E. W. Brayley. 13th ed. 8vo. Lond., 1834.   A 5 U 18

PARKES (MRS. WILLIAM). Encyclopædia of Domestic Economy. [*See* WEBSTER, T.]

PARKHURST (NATHANIEL), VICAR OF YOXFORD. Life of Rev. William Burkitt, M.A., sometime of Pembroke Hall, in Cambridge, late Vicar and Lecturer of Dedham, in Essex. 8vo. Lond., 1704.   C 3 Q 7

PARKIN (REV. C.) Topographical History of the County of Norfolk. [*See* BLOMFIELD, REV. F.] B 14 S 9–13 ‡

PARKINSON (JAMES). Organic Remains of a Former World: an Examination of the Mineralized Remains of the Vegetables and Animals of the Antediluvian World, termed Fossils. 3 vols. roy. 8vo. Lond., 1808–20.
A 9 V 3–5

PARKINSON (RICHARD). Tour in America, in 1798–1800. 2 vols. 8vo. Lond., 1805.   D 3 S 20, 21

PARKINSON (R.) Treatise on Paper; with an Outline of its Manufacture, &c. 8vo. Preston, 1886. A 11 R 5

PARKINSON (SYDNEY). Journal of a Voyage to the South Seas, in H.M.S. *Endeavour*. Roy. 4to. Lond., 1773.*   MD 2 P 12 ‡
Journal of a Voyage to the South Seas, in H.M.S. *Endeavour*. Roy. 4to. Lond., 1784.   MD 2 P 14 ‡

PARKMAN (FRANCIS). History of the Conspiracy of Pontiac, and the War of the North American Tribes against the English Colonies, after the Conquest of Canada. 2 vols. 8vo. Lond., 1851. **B 1 Q 40, 41**

Conspiracy of Pontiac, and the Indian War after the Conquest of Canada. 10th ed. 2 vols. 8vo. Lond., 1855. **B 1 S 44, 45**

Montcalm and Wolfe. 2 vols. 8vo. Lond., 1884. **C 5 S 21, 22**

Another copy. 6th ed. 2 vols. 8vo. Lond., 1885. **C 5 S 23, 24**

Count Frontenac and New France under Louis XIV. 14th ed. Lond., 1885. **B 1 Q 56**

Jesuits in North America in the 17th Century. 8vo. Lond., 1886. **G 7 R 26**

La Salle and the Discovery of the Great West. 12th ed. Lond., 1885. **C 4 T 11**

The Old Régime in Canada. 14th ed. 8vo. Lond., 1885. **B 2 P 5**

The Oregon Trail: Sketches of Prairie and Rocky Mountain Life. 8th ed. 8vo. Lond., 1885. **D 4 P 30**

Pioneers of France in the New World. 23rd ed. 8vo. Lond., 1885. **B 2 P 6**

PARKS AND GARDENS. Famous Parks and Gardens of the World described and illustrated. Roy. 4to. Lond., 1880. **A 2 Q I ‡**

PARKYNS (MANSFIELD). Life in Abyssinia; being Notes collected during Three Years' Residence and Travels in that Country. 2 vols. 8vo. Lond., 1853. **D 1 W 22, 23**

PARLIAMENT (THE LONG). [*See* LONG PARLIAMENT.]

PARLEY (PETER). [*See* GOODRICH, S. G.]

PARLIAMENTARY DOCUMENTS AND REPORTS, ordered by the House of Commons to be printed. 69 vols. fol. Lond., 1811–62. **MF 4 ‡**

1 (1818–32). On Transportation.
Papers relating to Convicts sent to New South Wales and Van Diemen's Land.
2 (1819). On the State of Gaols, &c.
3 (1831). On Secondary Punishments.
4 (1822–23). Bigge's Reports on New South Wales.
5 (1826–38). Administration of Justice in New South Wales and Van Diemen's Land.
Alienations of Crown Lands.
Bill to provide for the Government of Western Australia.
Colonial Grants, 1830.
Colonial Pensions, 1832.
Colonial Revenue, 1828.
Commissaries' Accounts, New South Wales, &c.
Crown Lands and Emigration.
Dollars imported, 1824.
Emigrants to the Colonies, 1820–31.
Grants of Land, New South Wales, 1812–21.
Instruction to the Natives of New South Wales.
Judicial Offices abroad.
Land Grants above 100 acres, 1812–21.
Laws and Ordinances, New South Wales, 1824–25.
Lead and Lead Ore, 1831–32.
Marriages, Births, and Deaths, New South Wales, 1817–19.

PARLIAMENTARY DOCUMENTS, &c.—*continued.*
Order of Council, Supreme Courts of New South Wales and Van Diemen's Land.
Sheep and Lambs' Wool.
Timber imported, 1828–29.
Vessels and Passengers to New South Wales and Van Die. men's Land, 1822–25.
6 (1826–32). Admeasurement and Grants of Land by General Darling, 1824–31.
Assignment, &c., of Convicts, 1826–28.
Australian Agricultural Bill.
Despatches relating to Sudds and Thomson.
Despatches: Wentworth's Impeachment.
Justice Stephen's Pension.
Laws of New South Wales passed 1828 and 1829.
Magisterial Punishments.
Offences in New Zealand Bill.
Persons holding one or more Offices in New South Wales.
Public Officers' Insolvent Law.
Seizure of the Ship *Almorah*.
Veterans of New South Wales.
7 (1825–31). Swan River Settlement.
Van Diemen's Land Aborigines.
Van Diemen's Land Company.
Van Diemen's Land Laws, 1826–30.
8–10 (1826–28). Enquiry into the Administration of Justice in the West Indies.
11 (1828–33). Captain Robison's Petition.
Inquiry: Indians of Honduras.
Island of Ceylon.
Slave Trade at Mauritius.
Trade, &c., Cape of Good Hope.
12, 13 (1826–27). On Emigration from the United Kingdom.
14 (1840). Correspondence relating to China.
15 (1835–36). Colonial Military Expenditure.
Disposal of Lands in British Colonies.
On the Conduct of General Darling.
15A (1836). Disposal of Lands in the British Colonies.
16 (1835–38). Condition, &c., of the Natives of South Africa.
On the State of New Zealand.
17 (1839). Affairs of British North America.
18 (1837–40). Colonization Commission: South Australia.
Registrar-General's Report, England.
Statistical Returns: Van Diemen's Land, 1824–39.
War in Affghanistan.
19 (1838–39). Capper's Report.
Clergy and School Lands, New South Wales, and Van Die. men's Land.
Correspondence in reference to Bernard's Petition.
Massacre of the Aborigines of Australia.
Return to Address on Emigration.
Transportation and Assignment of Convicts, New South Wales.
20, 21 (1837–38). On Transportation.
22 (1840). Naval and Military Promotions, &c.
23 (1840). On East India Produce.
24 (1841). On South Australia.
25 (1840–41). Boundary: British Possessions, North America.
Emigration to Canada.
Ordinances passed, Lower Canada.
26 (1831–40). Affairs of Canada.
Canada: Copy of Despatch.
Clergy Reserves in Canada, 1819–40.
Re-union of Upper and Lower Canada.
27 (1840–42). Correspondence relative to New Zealand.
Laws, &c., of New Zealand, passed 1842.
On New Zealand.
Papers: Falkland Islands.
Revenue arising from Crown Lands.

PARLIAMENTARY DOCUMENTS, &c.—*continued.*

28 (1840–41). Introduction of Indian Labourers into the Mauritius.
Memorial of British Merchants: Trade with China.
On the Trade with China.
Opium Trade.
Opium surrendered to the Chinese.
Papers relating to China.
Petition of the East India Company for Relief.

29 (1840–41). Alienation and Settlement of Waste Lands, New South Wales.
Appropriation of Revenue arising from Crown Lands.
Captain Hobson's Proceedings at New Zealand.
Despatch from Sir G. Gipps: Progressive Discovery of the Colony.
Finances, New South Wales.
Papers respecting New South Wales.
Secondary Punishment, New South Wales and Van Diemen's Land.

30 (1839–41). Account of Income, Expenditure, and Debts: South Australia.
Advancement of Religion in Australia.
Colonization Commissioners for South Australia.
Emigrants upon Bounty, New South Wales.
Emigration for the year 1839.
Emigration from the United Kingdom.
Emigration to the Colonies.
Land Fund: Australia.
Land in South Australia.
On South Australia.
South Australia since 1831.

31 (1842). Boundary: British Possessions in North America and United States.
Correspondence relative to Emigration.

32 (1836–39). Aborigines Question.
Building Act.
Colonial Distillation.
Presbyterian Church Act.
Proposed Quay at Sydney Cove.

33 (1835–38). Catarrh in Sheep Bill.
Emigration.
Proceedings of Presbytery of New South Wales.

34 (1837) Transportation.

35 (1838). Despatch from Sir John Franklin on Convict Discipline, Van Diemen's Land.
On Transportation.

36 (1822–38). Affairs of Lower Canada.
Colonization Commissioners: South Australia.
Commerce and Trade, Upper Canada.
Conduct of Lord Aylmer, Lower Canada.
Dissolution of the Provincial Parliament, Upper Canada.
Expenditure: Account of the Indian Department, Canada.
Religious Instruction of Aborigines of New Holland and Van Diemen's Land.
Judicial Establishment of New South Wales and Van Diemen's Land.
Land Regulations: Western Australia.
On the Canadas: relative to Papineau and Bidwell.
On Orange Lodges.
Rideau Canal.
State of New Zealand.
State of Agriculture and Trade in New South Wales.
State of New South Wales.
Statistical Report, Western Australia.

37, 38 (1842). Children's Employment Commission: Mines; with Appendix.

39, 40 (1842) Children's Employment: Trades and Manufactures; with Appendix.

41 (1841–44). Australian Gas Light Company.
Report of the City Council, Sydney.
Boundary: British Possessions, North America and United States.
Colonial Land and Emigration Commissioners.

PARLIAMENTARY DOCUMENTS, &c.—*continued.*

Convict Discipline, Van Diemen's Land.
Customs Duties proposed by Sir Robert Peel.
Exportation of Hill Coolies.
Falkland Islands.
Introduction of Indian Labourers: Mauritius.
Letter to W. C. Wentworth: Police Administration, Sydney.
Letter to W. C. Wentworth: Municipal Revenue, Sydney.
Massacre of Aborigines in Australia, 1838.
Port Essington Correspondence.
Treaty concluded at Waitangi.

42 (1839–42). Acts (various) passed, 1832–41.
Condition of Hand-loom Weavers.
Bill to levy Duties of Customs, &c., Van Diemen's Land.
Map: Boundary between Canada and United States.
Railway Communication: London, Dublin, Edinburgh, &c.

43 (1842–43). Papers relating to New Zealand.
Papers relating to South Australia.
Papers: Colonial Lands and Emigration.

44 (1843). Children's Employment: Trades and Manufactures.
Falkland Islands.
Labouring Poor: Allotments of Land.
Military Operations in Affghanistan.

45 (1844). Inquiry into the State of Large Towns.
Monetary Depression and Emigration: New South Wales.
Renewal of Emigration: South Australia.
State of New Zealand.

46 (1844). Correspondence on Sinde.
State of New Zealand.

47 (1846–46). Bill to authorize Loan to the New Zealand Company.
Colonial Land Fund: South Australia.
Constitution of the Legislature: New Zealand.
Crown Lands and Emigration: New South Wales.
Default of the Registrar of the Supreme Court, New South Wales.
Duty on Colonial Grain and Flour.
Grants, &c., for Education in the Colonies, 1840–42.
Names of the Legislative Council, in each Colony, 1836–44.
Outrages by the Natives: Bay of Islands.
Paper Money: Falkland Islands.
Papers relative to New Zealand.
Parliamentary Grants: Falkland Islands.
Proprietary Government: New Zealand.

48 (1845–46). Acts (various) passed, 1845–46.
Appointment of Assistant Secretary to the Colonies.
Colonial Land and Emigration Commission.
Commercial Policy: Canada.
Conditional Pardon of Convicts: Van Diemen's Land.
Duties on Imports and Exports, &c.: Colonies.
Legislative Council, New South Wales, on Immigration.
Licensed Occupation of Crown Lands.
Memorial from Stockowners of New South Wales.
On Transportation to Van Diemen's Land.
Population, Revenue, &c., Van Diemen's Land, 1836–44.

49 (1845–46). Papers, Returns, and Correspondence relative to New Zealand, 1845–46.

50 (1847–48). Act: Provision for the Government of New Zealand.
Duties.
Imports and Exports. Colonies, 1835–44.
Expenses incurred for North Australia.
Moneys received for Sales of Lands in South Australia.
Occupation of Crown Lands, New South Wales.
Occupation of Waste Lands, New South Wales.
Papers relative to Affairs of New Zealand.
Recall of Sir Eardley Wilmot, Van Diemen's Land.
State of H.M. Colonial Possessions.

51 (1847–48). Bounty Emigration Orders.
Colonial Land and Emigration Commission.
Emigration from Sierra Leone to West Indies.
Papers relative to Emigration.

52 (1847–48). Convict Discipline and Transportation.
Execution of the Criminal Law.

PARLIAMENTARY DOCUMENTS, &c.—*continued.*
53 (1848). Growth of Cotton in India.
   Papers relative to Van Diemen's Land.
   State of H.M. Colonial Possessions.
54 (1848). Colonization from Ireland.
   Convict Discipline and Transportation,
55 (1849). Act: Indian Railway Company.
   Australian Colonies Government Bill.
   Convict Discipline and Transportation.
   Papers relative to Emigration.
   Papers relative to Affairs of New Zealand.
   State of Settlement of Natal.
   State of the Kaffir Tribes.
56 (1849). Papers relating to the Punjab.
   Public Libraries.
57 (1850). Australian Colonies Government Bill.
   Convict Discipline and Transportation.
   Ecclesiastical Jurisdiction, Australian Colonies.
   Establishment of Episcopal Sees, Australia.
   Proposed Alteration in the Constitution of Australia.
   State of H.M. Colonial Possessions.
58 (1850). Select Committee on Ceylon.
   Steam Communication : Suez and Bombay.
   Supply of Cotton from British Possessions.
   Suppression of Piracy : Coast of Borneo.
59 (1850–52). Alterations in the Constitutions : Australian
   Colonies.
   Convict Discipline and Transportation.
   Crown Lands in the Australian Colonies.
   Reduction of Troops in New South Wales.
60 (1852). Discovery of Gold in Australia.
   Hostilities with Burmah.
   Naval and Military Establishments : Colonies.
   Papers relative to Ceylon.
   State of H.M. Colonial Possessions.
61 (1852). Establishment of Representative Assembly : Cape
   of Good Hope.
   Papers relating to the New Zealand Company.
   Ordinances passed at the Cape of Good Hope.
   State of the Kaffir Tribes.
62 (1853). Alterations in the Constitutions : Australian
   Colonies.
   Crown Lands : Australian Colonies.
   Emigration to the Australian Colonies.
   Establishment of Representative Assembly : Cape of Good
   Hope.
   State of H.M. Colonial Possessions.
63 (1853–54). Convict Discipline and Transportation.
   Discovery of Gold in Australia.
64 (1855). Alterations in the Constitutions : Australian
   Colonies.
   Discovery of Gold in Australia.
   Supplies for the British Army in the Crimea.
65 (1856). Alterations in the Constitutions : Australian
   Colonies.
   Crown Lands : Australian Colonies.
   Discovery of Gold in Australia.
   State of H.M. Colonial Possessions.
66 (1856–57). Entrance into Canton.
   Inquiry : Sir J. M'Neill and Colonel Tulloch (Crimean
   Camp).
   Insults in China.
   Letters to Lord Panmure, by Earls Lucan and Cardigan.
   Military Affairs in Asiatic Turkey.
   Operations in the Canton River, 1847.
   Proceedings of H.M. Naval Forces at Canton.
   Protocol signed at Paris, January 6th, 1857.
67 (1857–58). Administration of Justice in the Colonies.
   Australian Postal Service.
   Discovery of Gold in Australia.
   Emigration (Australia).
   Exploration of Northern portion of Australia.
   Land Sales, Australia.
   State of H.M. Colonial Possessions.

PARLIAMENTARY DOCUMENTS, &c.—*continued.*
68 (1859–60). Convict Discipline and Transportation.
   Customs Duties.
   Defence of the United Kingdom.
   European and Australian Mail Company.
   Gold Exported during 1858.
   Militia Estimates for 1861.
   Papers relating to New Zealand.
   State of H.M. Colonial Possessions.
69 (1861–62). Australian Exploration (Burke and Wills).
   Colonial Military Expenditure.
   Convict Discipline and Transportation.
   Gold Discoveries (Nova Scotia).
   Gold exported during 1859.
   Recent Disturbances in New Zealand.
   State of H.M. Colonial Possessions.

[*See* NEW SOUTH WALES.]

PARLIAMENT OF SOUTH AUSTRALIA. [*See* SOUTH
AUSTRALIA.]

PARLIAMENT OF TASMANIA. [*See* TASMANIA.]

PARLIAMENTARY DEBATES. [*See* NEW SOUTH
WALES, NEW ZEALAND, VICTORIA, QUEENSLAND, *and*
WESTERN AUSTRALIA.]

PARLIAMENTARY GOVERNMENT IN NEW
SOUTH WALES. [*See* NEW SOUTH WALES.]

PARLIAMENTARY HAND-BOOK. [*See* NEW SOUTH
WALES.]

PARLIAMENTARY LIBRARY. [*See* NEW SOUTH
WALES, NEW ZEALAND, QUEENSLAND, SOUTH AUSTRALIA,
TASMANIA *and* VICTORIA.]

PARLIAMENTARY PAPERS. [*See* NEW ZEALAND *and*
VICTORIA.]

PARLIAMENTARY POCKET-BOOK for 1883. 8vo.
Lond., 1883.   F 5 T 23

PARLIAMENTARY REVIEW and Family Magazine.
Edited by J. S. Buckingham. 3 vols. 8vo. Lond., 1833.
    F 15 P 5-7

PARMENTIER (A. A.) [*See* ROZIER, L'ABBÉ F.]
    A 1 T 14

PARMEGIANO (G. FRANCESCO M. MAZZOLA). Sketches
of the Lives of Correggio and Parmegiano. [*See* COXE,
W.]   A 7 Q 24

PARNELL (ARTHUR). Action of Lightning, and the Means
of defending Life and Property from its Effects. 12mo.
Lond., 1882.   A 3 R 12

PARNELL (E. A.) Applied Chemistry in Manufactures,
Arts, and Domestic Economy. 2 vols. 8vo. Lond.,
1844.   A 5 T 7, 8

PARNELL (REV. THOMAS). Life and Poems of. [*See*
CHALMERS, A., *and* JOHNSON, S.]
Poetical Works of [with Memoir by the Rev. J. Mitford].
8vo. Lond., 1866.   H 8 R 2

PARR (CATHERINE). [*See* CATHERINE PARR, QUEEN.]

PARR (MISS HARRIET), "HOLME LEE." In the Silver Age: Essays. 2 vols. 12mo. Lond., 1864.   J 11 T 19, 20

Life and Death of Jeanie d'Arc, called the Maid.   2 vols. (in 1) 8vo. Lond., 1866.   C 2 S 23

PARR (REV. SAMUEL), LL.D. Memoirs of the Life, Writings, and Opinions of; with Biographical Notices of many of his Friends, Pupils, and Contemporaries, by the Rev. W. Field. 2 vols. 8vo. Lond., 1828.   C 9 Q 15, 16

Works of; with Memoirs of his Life and Writings, by John Johnstone, M.D.   8 vols. 8vo. Lond., 1828.   J 10 S 4–11

PARRAMATTA BENEVOLENT SOCIETY. Reports of; with List of Subscriptions and Donations, for 1866–67. (Pam. Du.) 8vo. Parramatta, 1866–67.   MF 3 P 18

PARRAMATTA CHRONICLE, and Cumberland General Advertiser. Fol. Parramatta, 1844–45.   ME

PARRAMATTA DISTRICT HOSPITAL. Reports of; with List of Subscriptions and Donations, for 1865–67. 8vo. Parramatta, 1866–68.   MF 3 P 19

PARRAMATTA INTERCOLONIAL JUVENILE EXHIBITION, 1883. Catalogue of Exhibits. 8vo. Sydney, 1883.   MK 1 R 27

PARRAMATTA MESSENGER AND CUMBERLAND EXPRESS. Fol. Parramatta, 1847.   ME

PARRAMATTA SUNDAY SCHOOL. Rules for. (Pam. A.) Fol. Sydney (n.d.)   MJ 2 U 1

PARRISH (S.) Etchings by. [*See* KOEHLER, S. R.]

PARROT (DR. FRIEDRICH). Journey to Ararat; translated by W. D. Cooley. 8vo. Lond., 1845.   D 4 U 15

PARRY (C. H.) Parliaments and Councils of England, chronologically arranged, from the Reign of William I to the Revolution in 1688. 8vo. Lond., 1839.   F 5 P 1

PARRY (C. T.) [*See* BURNHAM, G.]   A 9 P 2 †

PARRY (REV. EDWARD), M.A. Memoirs of Rear-Admiral Sir W. Edward Parry, Kt., F.R.S., &c.; by his Son. 6th ed. 12mo. Lond., 1859.   C 2 Q 33

PARRY (CAPT. S. H. JONES). My Journey round the World, via Ceylon, New Zealand, Australia, Torres Straits, China, Japan, and the United States. 2 vols. 8vo. Lond., 1881.   MD 4 R 17, 18

PARRY (T. G.) Ministry of Fine Art to the Happiness of Life: Essays on various Subjects. 8vo. Lond., 1886.   A 7 R 22

PARRY (REAR-ADM. SIR WILLIAM EDWARD), KNT., &c. Journal of a Voyage for the Discovery of a North-west Passage from the Atlantic to the Pacific, performed in the years 1819–20, in H.M. Ships *Hecla* and *Griper*; with Appendix. 4to. Lond., 1821.   D 11 P 11 †

PARRY (REAR-ADM. SIR WILLIAM EDWARD), KNT., &c.—*continued.*

Journal of a Second Voyage, performed in the years 1821–23, in H.M. Ships *Fury* and *Hecla*. 4to. Lond., 1824.   D 11 P 12 †

Appendix to Captain Parry's Journal of a Second Voyage performed in H.M. Ships *Fury* and *Hecla*, in the years 1821–23. 4to. Lond., 1825.   D 11 P 13 †

Journal of a Third Voyage performed in the years 1824–25, in H.M. Ships *Hecla* and *Fury*. 4to. Lond., 1826.   D 11 P 14 †

Narrative of an Attempt to reach the North Pole, in Boats fitted for the purpose, and attached to H.M. Ship *Hecla*, in the year 1827. 4to. Lond., 1828.   D 11 P 15 †

Memoirs of; by his Son, the Rev. E. Parry. 6th ed. 12mo. Lond., 1859.   C 2 Q 33

[*See* BARTON, W.]

PARSONS (EDWARD). Neal's History of the Puritans, abridged. [*See* NEAL, D.]

PARSONS (G. S.), R.N. Nelsonian Reminiscences: Leaves from Memory's Log. 8vo. Lond., 1843.   C 4 T 21

PARSONS (ROBERT). Conference about the next Succession to the Crown of England. 12mo. Reprinted at Nassau, 1681.   B 3 Q 26

PARSONS (THOMAS), BARRISTER-AT-LAW. Law in Victoria: a Barrister to the Bench, Bar, and Public, on his seceding from his Practice at the Bar of Victoria, and offering his Services to the Public directly. 8vo. Melb., 1859.   MF 3 P 5

Another copy.   MJ 2 R 12

Offer to frame and initiate the Administration of a Real Property Law. 8vo. Melb., 1863.   MJ 2 R 12

Letter to the *Times*, Printing House Square, London. 8vo. Melb., 1866.   MJ 2 R 12

Address to the Persons calling themselves the *Argus*. 8vo. Melb., 1867.   MJ 2 R 12

Alcock v. Fergie: an Address to the Chief Justice of the Colony of Victoria, refuting the Decision in Alcock v. Fergie. 8vo. Melb., 1868.   MJ 2 R 12

Second Letter to the Duke of Buckingham. 8vo. Melb., 1868.   MJ 2 R 12

The Washerwoman to the Hon. James McCulloch. 8vo. Melb., 1868.   MJ 2 R 12

The Washerwoman of Melbourne to the Secretary for the Colonies. 8vo. Melb., 1869.   MJ 2 R 12

Second Supplement to the Washerwoman of Melbourne to the Secretary for the Colonies. 8vo. Melb., 1869.   MJ 2 R 12

The Washerwoman of Melbourne to Her Most Gracious Majesty the Queen, and to the Hon. the Attorney-General and the rest of the Bar of the Colony of Victoria. 8vo. Melb., 1870.   MJ 2 R 12

Fifth Letter to the Duke of Buckingham. 8vo. Melb., 1868.   MJ 2 R 12

PARTINGTON (C. F.) Mechanics' Library ; or, Book of
Trades. 8vo. Lond. (n.d.)   A 11 S 23

PARTON (JAMES). Life and Times of Aaron Burr. 11th
ed. 8vo. New York, 1858.   C 5 T 1

Life of Voltaire. 2 vols. 8vo. Lond., 1881.   C 9 R 37, 38

Topics of the Time. 8vo. Boston, 1871.   J 12 T 10

PARTON (JAMES). Does it Pay to Smoke ? To which is
added, the Use and Abuse of Tobacco : a Letter to the
Times, by Sir Benjamin Brodie, Bart. 8vo. Melh.,
1869.   MA 2 S 38

Will the Coming Man drink Wine ? 8vo. Melb., 1869.
                    MA 2 S 38

PARTRIDGE (C.) Calumny refuted, the Colonists vindicated, and the Right Horse saddled ; or, a brief Review
of Mis-government in New Zealand the Cause of the
Native Rebellion. 8vo. Auckland, 1864.   MF 1 R 24

PASCAL (BLAISE). Provincial Letters of ; with an Essay
on Pascal, by M. Villemain. Translated, with Memoir,
by George Pearce. 8vo. Lond., 1849.   G 11 P 35

Provincial Letters of. Edited by John de Soyres. 8vo.
Camb., 1880.   G 12 Q 24

Études sur Pascal. [*See* COUSIN, V.]

PASCHAL II (PAPA). Epistolæ et Privilegia.   [*See*
MIGNE, J. P., SERIEL LATINA, 163.]

PASCOE (CHARLES EYRE.) Our Actors and Actresses ;
the Dramatic List : a Record of the Performances of
Living Actors and Actresses of the British Stage.
2nd ed. 8vo. Lond., 1880.   C 11 Q 2

[*See* DRAMATIC NOTES.]

PASCOE (FRANCIS P.), AND MASTERS (GEORGE). List
of the Australian Longicornis, chiefly described and
arranged by F. P. Pascoe ; with additional Localities
and Corrections by G. Masters. 8vo. Sydney, 1868.
                    MA 2 V 8

PASLEY (CAPT. C.), R.E. The War in New Zealand.
8vo. Lond. (n.d.)   MD 1 U 21

PASLEY (SIR CHARLES W.), K.C.B. Observations on
Limes, Calcareous Cements, &c. 8vo. Lond., 1838.
                    A 2 S 13

PASOLINI (GIUSEPPE), COUNT. Memoir of Count Giuseppe Pasolini, late President of the Senate of Italy,
b. 1815, d. 1876. Compiled by his Son, P. D. Pasolini ;
translated and abridged. With Portrait. 8vo. Lond.,
1885.   C 7 R 47

PASPATI (ALEXANDRE G.), A.M., &c. Memoir on the
Language of the Gypsies, as now used in the Turkish
Empire ; translated from the Greek, by Rev. C. Hamlin,
D.D. 8vo. Newhaven, 1861.   K 15 S 24

Études sur les Tchinghianés ou Bohémiens de l'Empire
Ottoman. Roy. 8vo. Constantinople, 1870.   K 16 Q 11

PASSENGERS' ACT. Working of the Passengers' Act.
8vo. Lond., 1851.   F 4 R 18

PASTEUR (J. D.) [*See* MORTIMER, LIEUT. G.] MD 4 U 43

4 E

PASTEUR (LOUIS). His Life and Labours ; by his Son-
in-Law [Valery Radot.] Translated by Lady Claud
Hamilton. 8vo. Lond., 1885.   C 4 Q 25

Studies on Fermentation : the Diseases of Beer, their
Causes and the Means of Preventing them. 8vo. Lond.,
1879.   A 6 Q 11

PASTON LETTERS. Original Letters written during
the Reigns of Henry VI, Edward IV, Richard III, and
Henry VII, by various Persons of Rank or Consequence.
2nd ed. 5 vols. 4to. Lond., 1787-1823.   C 3 W 18-22

Original Letters written during the Reigns of Henry
VI, Edward IV, and Richard III, by various Persons of
Rank or Consequence ; with Notes by Sir John Fenn.
2 vols. 12mo. Lond., 1840-41.   C 2 Q 31, 32

The 'Paston Letters 1422-1509 A.D. A New Edition,
containing upwards of 400 Letters, &c., hitherto unpublished ; edited by James Gairdner. 3 vols. sm. 4to.
Lond., 1872-75.   C 11 P 28-30

PASTORAL HOLDINGS. [*See* NEW SOUTH WALES.]

PASTORAL TENANTS. [*See* VICTORIA.]

PATANJALI. The Yoga Philosophy ; being the Text of
the Patanjali. Edited by Tukárám Tátiá. 12mo.
Bombay, 1882.   G 7 T 6

PATENTS FOR INVENTIONS. Letters and Suggestions upon the amendment of the Law relative to
Patents. 8vo. Lond., 1835.   A 7 Q 13

PATENT LAW AMENDMENT ACT. [*See* DREWRY,
C. S.]

PATENTS OF NEW SOUTH WALES. [*See* NEW
SOUTH WALES.]

PATENTS OF NEW ZEALAND. [*See* NEW ZEA-
LAND.]

PATENTS OF THE UNITED STATES. [*See* UNITED
STATES.]   E

PATERCULUS (CAIUS VELLEIUS). [*See* VELLEIUS PATER-
CULUS, C.]

PATERFAMILIAS'S DIARY OF EVERYBODY'S
TOUR. 12mo. Lond., 1856.   D 7 P 46

PATERSON (G.), M.A. History of New South Wales'
from its Discovery to the Present Time ; comprising an
accurate and interesting Description of that vast and
remarkable Country, and of the Persons, Manners, and
Customs of the Natives. To which is added a Description of Van Diemen's Land and Norfolk Island. Illustrated. 8vo. Newcastle-upon-Tyne, 1811.* MB 1 T 16

PATERSON (HUGH). The Teeth and their Treatment in
Health and Disease popularly explained. 12mo. Sydney,
1864.*   MA 2 S 25

PATERSON (JAMES). Biographical Notices of the Lives of
the Sempills of Beltrees. [*See* SEMPILL, SIR R. J. AND F.]

Life of William Hamilton, of Bangour. [*See* HAMILTON,
W.]

PATERSON (JAMES), M.A. Liberty of the Press, Speech, and Public Worship ; being Commentaries on the Liberty of the Subject and the Law of England. 8vo. Lond., 1880.   F 5 R 10

PATERSON (M.) Mountaineering below the Snow Line; or, the Solitary Pedestrian in Snowdonia and elsewhere. 12mo. Lond., 1886.   D 10 Q 34

PATERSON (CAPT. WILLIAM). Narrative of Four Journeys into the Country of the Hottentot and Caffraria, in the years 1777–79. 4to. Lond., 1789.   D 4 S 2 †

PATERSON (MAJOR WILLIAM). Notes of Military Surveying and Reconnaissance. 3rd ed. 8vo Lond., 1875.   A 6 S 16

PATON (ALLEN PARK). The Hamlet Shakespere. [*See* SHAKESPEARE, W.*]

PATON (ANDREW ARCHIBALD). Henry Beyle (otherwise De Stendahl) : a Critical and Biographical Study, aided by original Documents and unpublished Letters from the private Papers of the Family of Beyle. 8vo. Lond., 1874.   C 3 S 8

Highlands and Islands of the Adriatic. 2 vols. 8vo. Lond., 1849.   D 6 U 28, 29

Goth and Hun ; or, Transylvania, Debreczin, Pesth, and Vienna, in 1851.   D 6 T 15

Modern Syrians ; or, Native Society in Damascus, Aleppo, and the Mountains of the Druses, from Notes made in those parts during the years 1841–43 ; by "An Oriental Student." 8vo. Lond., 1844.   D 6 P 31

PATON (CHALMERS I.) Freemasonry: its Symbolism, Religious Nature, and Law of Perfection. 8vo. Lond., 1873.   J 6 T 18

PATON (SIR J. NOEL). Compositions from Shakespeare's "Tempest": Fifteen Engravings in outline. Ob. 4to. Lond., 1877.   A 5 R 11

PATOT (SIMON TYSSOT DE). Voyages et Avantures de Jaques Massé. 12mo. Bourdeaux, 1710.   J 16 T 3

PATRICK (R. W. COCHRAN-), LL.D., &c. Catalogue of the Medals of Scotland, from the Earliest Period to the Present Time. 4to. Edinb., 1884.   V 9 P 9 †

PATRICK (SAINT). Life and Acts of Saint Patrick, the Archbishop, Primate and Apostle of Ireland : by Edmund L. Swift. Roy. 8vo. Dublin, 1809. G 5 U 19

Life of. [*See* STOKES, W.]

St. Patrick, Apostle of Ireland : a Memoir of his Life and Mission ; by James Henthorn Todd, D.D. 8vo. Dublin, 1864.   C 10 Q 04

PATRICK (SAMUEL), LL.D.   Clavis Homerica.   [*See* HOMER.]

[*See* HORATIUS FLACCUS, Q.]   H 8 V 36, 37

PATRIOT (THE).   2 vols. fol.   Lond., 1834–38.   E

PATTERN-BOOK, for Jewellers, Gold and Silver Smiths. Fol. Lond., 1883.   23 R 32 ‡

PATTERN-MAKING: a Practical Treatise, embracing the Main Types of Engineering Construction; by "A Foreman Pattern-maker." Illustrated. 8vo. Lond., 1885. A 6 R 30

PATTERSON (PROF. H. S.), M.D. Types of Mankind. [*See* NOTT, J. C.]

PATTERSON (J. A.) Gold-fields of Victoria in 1862. 12mo. Melb., 1862.*   MA 2 P 6

PATTESON (JOHN COLERIDGE), FIRST BISHOP OF MELANESIA. Life of ; by Mary Charlotte Yonge. With Portraits. 2nd ed. 2 vols. 8vo. Lond., 1874. MC 1 R 16, 17

PATTERSON (R. HOGARTH). The New Golden Age and Influence of the Precious Metals upon the World. 2 vols. 8vo. Edinb., 1882.   F 6 U 18, 19

Gas and Lighting. (Brit. Manuf. Indust.) 12mo. Lond., 1876.   A 17 S 36

PATTI (CARLOTTA). Her Tour around the World, 1879–80. 8vo. Melb., 1880.   MJ 2 R 15

PATTISON (MARK). Isaac Casaubon, 1559–1614. 8vo. Lond., 1875.   C 10 S 10

Milton. (Eng. Men of Letts.) 8vo.   Lond., 1879.
                                             C 1 U 26

Memoirs. 8vo. Lond., 1885.   C 3 V 42

Pope['s] Essay on Man, Satires, and Epistles. [*See* POPE, A.]

PATTISON (MRS. MARK), LADY DILKE. Renaissance of Art in France ; with Nineteen Illustrations on Steel. 2 vols. 8vo. Lond., 1879.   A 7 T 17, 18

PAUL. [*See* SCOTT, SIR W.]

PAUL (ARTHUR.) A Word to the Brethren of New South Wales. [*See* PRESBYTERIAN TRACTS.]

PAUL (B. H.), PH.D. Industrial Chemistry : a Manual for use in Technical Colleges or Schools, and for Manufacturers, &c. Illustrated. Roy. 8vo. Lond., 1878.
                                             A 5 U 4

Manual of Technical Analysis. 12mo.   Lond., 1857.
                                             A 5 S 32

Elements of Chemical and Physiological Geology. [*See* BISCHOFF, G.]

[*See* HUMBOLDT, A. VON.]   A 3 R 30–34

PAUL (C. KEGAN). William Godwin : his Friends and Contemporaries. With Portraits. 2 vols. 8vo. Lond., 1876.   C 3 V 9, 10

PAUL (J. B.) [*See* SCOTLAND.]

PAUL OF ALEPPO (ARCHDEACON). Travels of Macarius Patriarch of Antioch; translated by F. C. Belfour, A.M., &c. 2 vols. 4to. Lond., 1836.   D 5 V 24, 25

PAUL (REV. RODT. BATEMAN), M.A., &c. Letters from Canterbury, New Zealand. 12mo. Lond.,1857. MD 2 Q 55

New Zealand, as it was and as it is. 12mo. Lond., 1861. MD 1 S 22

Antiquities of Greece. 2nd. ed. 8vo. Oxford, 1835. B 9 S 29

PAUL (SAINT), THE APOSTLE. Life and Epistles of St. Paul; by the Rev. W. J. Conybeare, M.A., and the Very Rev. J. S. Howson, D.D. 2 vols. 8vo. Lond., 1867. G 13 P 1, 2

Voyage and Shipwreck of St. Paul. [*See* SMITH, J.]

PAUL 'PRY. [*See* POOLE, J.]

PAULI (DR. REINHOLD). Life of King Alfred; edited by Thomas Wright, M.A., &c. 8vo. Lond., 1852. C 8 T 1

Simon de Montfort, Earl of Leicester, the Creator of the House of Commons. Translated by Una M. Goodwin. 8vo. Lond., 1876. C 3 V 40

Confessio Amantis of John Gower. [*See* GOWER, J.]

PAULIN DE ST. BARTHELEMI (JOHANN PHILIPP WERDIN). Alphabetum Grandonico-Malabaricum sive Samscrudonicum. 12mo. Romæ, 1772. K 16 P 3

De Antiquitate et Affinitate Linguæ Zendicæ, Samscrdamicæ, et Germanicæ Dissertatio. 4to. Patavii, 1798. K 12 T 1

Sidharubam seu Grammatica Samscrdamica. 4to. Romæ, 1790. K 12 T 1

Vyàcarana seu Locupletissima Samscrdamicae Linguae Institutio. 4to. Romæ, 1804. K 16 S 7

Another copy. G 8 V 13

Systema Brahmanicum, Liturgicum, Mythologicum, Civile, ex Monumentis Indicis Musei Borgiani Velitris. 4to. Romæ, 1791. G 8 V 13

PAULINUS (SANCTUS), PATRIARCHA AQUILEIENSIS. Opera omnia. [*See* MIGNE, J. P., SERIES LATINA, 99.]

PAULINUS (SANCTUS), NOLANUS EPISCOPUS. Opera omnia. [*See* MIGNE, J. P., SERIES LATINA, 61.]

PAULUS (EDWARD). Italy, from the Alno to the Tiber. [*See* STIELER, K.] D 5 S 2 †

PAULUS SILENTIARIUS. [*See* BYZANTINÆ HIST. SCRIPT.]

PAUQUET FRERES. Modes et Costumes Historiques. Roy. 4to. Paris (n.d.) A 2 S 4, 5 †

PAUSANIAS. Pausanias' Description of Greece. Translated into English, with Notes and Index, by Arthur Richard Shilleto, M.A. 2 vols. 8vo. Lond., 1886. D 7 P 41, 42

PAUW (CORNELIUS DE). Philosophical Dissertations on the Greeks. 2 vols. 8vo. Lond., 1793. B 27 S 12, 13

PAWLOWSKY (J.) Russisch-deutsches Wörterbuch. 2e auflage. Roy. 8vo. Riga, 1879. K 16 R 16

PAXTON (SIR JOSEPH). Paxton's Botanical Dictionary. New ed., revised and corrected by S. Hereman. Roy. 8vo. Lond., 1868. K 7 Q 24

PAYEN (ANSELME). Précis de Chimie Industrielle. [*See* PAUL, B. H.] A 5 U 4

PAYER (JULIUS). New Lands within the Arctic Circle: Narrative of Discoveries of the Austrian Ship *Tegetthoff*, in the years 1872–74. Translated from the German. 2 vols. 8vo. Lond., 1876. D 4 R 38, 39

Die österreichisch-ungarische Nordpol-Expedition in den jahren 1872–74. Roy. 8vo. Wein, 1876. D 4 R 37

PAYN (JAMES). Some Literary Recollections. 8vo. Lond., 1884. C 3 T 12

Thicker than Water. 8vo. Melb., 1884. MJ 1 Q 32

PAYNE (C. W.) Eastern Empire Crown Colonies. First Series: Ceylon. (Pam. 19.) 8vo. Lond., 1847. MJ 2 Q 8

PAYNE (E. J.) Colonies and Dependencies. [*See* COTTON, J. S.] MF 1 P 37

Select Works of Edmund Burke, Introduction and Notes. [*See* BURKE, RT. HON. E.]

PAYNE (REV. G.) Brief Account of the Life, &c., of the Rt. Rev. R. Cumberland. [*See* SANCHONIATHO.] B 2 S 29

PAYNE (J. B.) Haydn's Dictionary of Dates. [*See* HAYDN, J.]

PAYNE (JOHN). New Poems. 8vo. Lond., 1880. H 7 Q 21

[*See* VILLON, F.]

PAYNE (JOHN HOWARD). Ali Pasha; or, the Signet Ring: a Melo-drama. (Cumberland's Eng. Theatre.) 12mo. Lond., 1829. H 2 Q 20

Brutus: an Historical Tragedy. (Cumberland's Eng. Theatre.) 12mo. Lond., 1829. H 2 Q 8

Charles the Second: a Comedy. (Cumberland's Eng. Theatre.) 12mo. Lond., 1829. H 2 Q 12

Clari; or, the Maid of Milan: an Opera. (Cumberland's Eng. Theatre.) 12mo. Lond., 1829. H 2 Q 22

The Lancers: an Interlude. (Cumberland's Eng. Theatre.) 12mo. Lond., 1829. H 2 Q 18

Love in Humble Life: a Petite Comedy. (Cumberland's Eng. Theatre.) 12mo. Lond., 1829. H 2 Q 17

The Two Galley Slaves: a Melo-drama. (Cumberland's Eng. Theatre.) 12mo. Lond., 1829. H 2 Q 20

PAYNE (JOHN ORLEBAR), M.A. [*See* ESTCOURT, VERY REV. E. E.]

PAYNE (JOSEPH). A Visit to German Schools; with critical Discussions of the general Principles and Practice of Kindergarten and other Schemes of Elementary Education. 8vo. Lond., 1876. G 17 P 30

Lectures on the Science and Art of Education ; with other Lectures and Essays. 8vo. Lond., 1880. G 17 Q 7

PAYNE (JOSEPH FRANK), M.B., &c. Pathological Anatomy. [*See* JONES, C. H.]　　　　　　　　　A 13 P 40

PAYNE (S.), A.M. Life of Rt. Rev. R. Cumberland. [*See* SANCHONIATHO.]

PAYNE-GALLWEY (SIR RALPH), BART. [*See* GALLWEY, SIR R. PAYNE-.]

PEABODY (ELIZABETH PALMER). Record of a School. 2nd ed. Boston, 1836.　　　　　　G 17 P 31

PEABODY (GEORGE). Life of; by Phebe A. Hanaford. 8vo. Boston, 1882.　　　　　　　C 3 U 35

PEABODY INSTITUTE. Tenth Annual Report of the Provost to the Trustees of the Peabody Institute of the City of Baltimore, 1877. (Pam. Dv.) 8vo. Baltimore, 1877.　　　　　　　　　　　MF 3 P 19

PEACE (WALTER). Our Colony of Natal. 8vo. Lond., 1883.　　　　　　　　　　　D 1 V 23

PEACH (R. E.) Historic Houses in Bath, and their Associations. 2 vols. sm. 4to. Lond., 1883. H 6 R 26, 27

PEACHEY (CAROLINE). Danish Fairy Legends. [*See* ANDERSEN, H. C.]　　　　　　　J 9 Q 6

PEACHEY (DAVID AUGUSTUS). System of Shorthand. [*See* ANDERSON, T.]

PEACOCK (VERY REV. GEORGE), D.D. Observations on the Statutes of the University of Cambridge. 8vo. Lond., 1841.　　　　　　　　　　J 5 T 27

PEACOCK, OR PECOCK (RT. REV. REGINALD). History of. [*See* BRITISH REFORMERS 12.]

PEAK DOWNS COPPER-MINING CO. Fifth Half-yearly Report. (Pam. C.) 4to. Sydney, 1865 MJ 2 U 3

PEAKE (JAMES). Rudiments of Naval Architecture. (Weale.) 12mo. Lond., 1867.　　　　A 17 P 15

PEAKE (RICHARD BAINSLEY). Amateurs and Actors: a Musical Farce. (Cumberland's Eng. Theatre.) 12mo. Lond., 1829.　　　　　　　　　H 2 Q 13

The Duel; or, my Two Nephews: a Farce. (Cumberland's Eng. Theatre.) 12mo. Lond., 1829.　　H 2 Q 18

Master's Rival: a Farce. (Cumberland's Eng. Theatre.) 12mo. Lond., 1829.　　　　　H 2 Q 17

Memoirs of the Colman Family. 2 vols. 8vo. Lond., 1841.　　　　　　　　　　C 10 S 31, 32

PEARCE (CHARLES T.), M.D., &c. Small-pox and Vaccination in London, 1880-81: a Reply to the Memorandum of Dr. Buchanan (Medical Officer of the Local Government Board), on the Present Prevalence of Small-pox in London, among Vaccinated and Unvaccinated Persons respectively. (Pam. Cp.) 8vo. Lond., 1881.　　　A 12 S 34

Vital Statistics, Small pox and Vaccination in the United Kingdom of Great Britain and Ireland, and Continental Countries and Cities; with Tables. 8vo. Lond., 1882.　　　　　　　　　　F 5 R 8

PEARCE (ROBERT ROUIERE). Memoirs and Correspondence of the Most Noble Richard, Marquess Wellesley, K.P., &c. 3 vols. 8vo. Lond., 1846.　C 9 V 46-48

PEARCE (THOMAS), "IDSTONE." The Dog; with Simple Directions for his Treatment, and Notices of the best Dogs of the Day, and their Breeders or Exhibitors. 2nd ed. 8vo. Lond., 1872.　　　　　A 1 P 16

PEARCE (WILLIAM). Hartford Bridge: an Operatic Farce. [*See* FARCES 3.]

Netley Abbey: an Operatic Farce. [*See* FARCES 3.]

PEARCE (WILLIAM PETER), B.A. Use and Abuse of Play: two Sermons. 8vo. Melh., 1876.　MG 1 Q 39

PEARS (EDWIN), LL.B. Fall of Constantinople; being the Story of the Fourth Crusade. 8vo. Lond., 1885.　　　　　　　　　　　B 13 V 25

PEARSON (CHARLES H.), M.A. History of England during the Early and Middle Ages. 2 vols. 8vo. Lond., 1867.　　　　　　　　　B 6 P 1, 2

PEARSON (EMMA MARIA), AND MACLAUGHLIN (LOUISA E.) Our Adventures during the War of 1870. 2 vols. 8vo. Lond., 1871.　　　D 7 Q 27, 28

PEARSON (VERY REV. HUGH), D.D., DEAN OF SALISBURY. Memoirs of the Life and Correspondence of the Rev. Christian Frederick Swartz; to which is prefixed a Sketch of the History of Christianity in India. 2 vols. 8vo. Lond., 1839.　　　　　C 5 R 24, 25

PEARSON (REV. H.) Sermon preached at St. Bride's Church, Fleet-street, before the Church Missionary Society. (Pam. 13.) 8vo. Lond., 1830.　　　MJ 2 Q 3

PEARSON (PROF. JOHN), D.D., &c. An Exposition of the Creed. 3rd ed. Sm. fol. Lond., 1669.　G 5 U 14

Another copy. New ed.; with an Analysis, by Edward Walford, M.A. 8vo. Lond., 1878.　　G 16 P 27

PEARSON (RT. REV. J B.), D.D., BISHOP OF NEWCASTLE. Explanation of the Articles of the Apostles' Creed. 8vo. Sydney, 1846.　　　　　　　MG 1 Q 31

PEARSON (REV. JOHN NORMAN), M.A. [*See* CHURCH MISSIONARY SOCIETY.]

PEARSON (K.) [*See* TODHUNTER, I.]　　　A 11 U 21

PEARSON (REV. THOMAS). Infidelity: its Aspects, Causes, and Agencies; being the Prize Essay of the British Organization of the Evangelical Alliance. 8vo. Lond., 1853.　　　　　　　　　　G 11 S 9

PEASE (ALFRED E.) The Cleveland Hounds as a Trencher fed Pack. 8vo. Lond., 1887.　A 17 W 17

PECCHIO (GIUSEPPE), COUNT. Semi-serious Observations of an Italian Exile during his Residence in England. 8vo. Lond., 1833.　　　　　　　D 7 P 6

Picture of Greece. [*See* EMERSON, JAMES.] D 8 S 37, 38

PECK (B. C.) Recollections of Sydney, the Capital of New South Wales. Illustrated by a Plan of the City. 12mo. Lond., 1850.* MD 1 S 40

PECK (FRANCIS), M.A. Academia tertia Anglicana; or, the Antiquarian Annals of Stanford in Lincoln, Rutland, and Northampton Shires. Roy. fol. Lond., 1727. B 15 S 13‡
Desiderata Curiosa; or, a Collection of divers Scarce and Curious Pieces, relating chiefly to matters of English History. Roy. 4to. Lond., 1779. B 18 R 15 ‡
New Memoirs of the Life and Poetical Works of John Milton. 4to. Lond., 1740. H 6 V 15
New Memoirs of the Life and Actions of Oliver Cromwell; as delivered in three Panegyrics of him. 4to. Lond., 1740. C 4 W 5

PECOCK (RT. REV. REYNOLD), DEAN OF CHICHESTER. [*See* PEACOCK. RT. REV. R.]

PEDDER (J. L.), CHIEF JUSTICE. Case of. [*See* TASMANIA.]

PEEL (ALBERT), M.P. Local Government and Taxation. [*See* RATHBONE, W.]

PEEL (RT. HON. SIR ROBERT.), BART. Memoirs (Political). Published by Lord Mahon and the Rt. Hon. E. Cardwell. 2 vols. 8vo. Lond., 1856-57. F 5 T 20, 21
Opinions of, expressed in Parliament and in Public; by W. T. Haly. 8vo. Lond., 1843. F 6 S 7
Speeches by, during his Administration, 1834-35. 8vo. Lond., 1835. F 6 U 15
Life of the Rt. Hon. Sir Robt. Peel, Bart., as Subject and Citizen, as Legislator and Minister, and as Patron of Learning and the Arts; with a Portrait, by William Harvey. 12mo. Lond., 1850. C 1 R 28
Memoirs of. 2 vols. 8vo. Lond., 1842. C 3 U 33, 34
Memoirs of; by F. P. G. Guizot. 8vo. Lond., 1857. C 9 Q 18
Sir Robert Peel: an Historical Sketch; by Henry, Lord Dalling and Bulwer. 8vo. Lond., 1874. C 9 Q 17
[Life of] by George Barrett Smith. Lond., 1881. C 2 P 37
Speeches of, delivered in the House of Commons, 1810-50. 4 vols. 8vo. Lond. F 13 Q 8-11
Speech on the Corn Laws. (Pam. 11.) 8vo. Lond., 1840. F 12 P 9
Speech on the Rt. Hon. Sir R. Peel, in the House of Commons, August 10, 1842. (Pam. 16.) 8vo. Lond., 1842. MJ 2 Q 6
Speech of, in the House of Commons, May 6th, and 20th, 1844, on the Renewal of the Bank Charter. (Pam. 16.) 8vo. Lond., 1844. MJ 2 Q 6
[*See* WESTHEAD, J. P.] MJ 2 Q 8

PEEL RIVER COMPANY. First Annual Report of the Peel River Land and Mineral Company. (Pam. Dl.) 8vo. Lond., 1854. MF 3 P 11

PEELE (GEORGE). Dramatic and Poetical Works of; with Memoir of the Author, and Notes by the Rev. Alexander Dyce. 8vo. Lond., 1874. H 2 T 14

PEGGE (SAMUEL), F.S.A. Anecdotes of the English Language; chiefly regarding the Local Dialect of London and its Environs. 2nd ed. 8vo. Lond., 1814. K 15 Q 7
Curialia Miscellanea; or, Anecdotes of Old Times, Regal, Noble, Gentilitial, and Miscellaneous. 8vo. Lond., 1818. B 6 P 5
Life of Roger de Weseham, Dean of Lincoln, &c. 4to. Lond., 1761. C 4 W 7

PEGLER (H. S. H.) Book of the Goat; containing full particulars of the various Breeds of Goats, and their profitable Management. 3rd ed. 8vo. Lond., 1886. A 14 S 3

PÉGOT-OGIER (E.) The Fortunate Isles; or, the Archipelago of the Canaries; translated by Frances Loccock. 2 vols. 8vo. Lond., 1871. D 1 S 31, 32

PEIRCE (BENJAMIN), A.M. History of the Harvard University, from its Foundation, 1636, to the American Revolution. 8vo. Camb., Mass, 1833. B 19 S 1

PEISLEY (JOHN). Brief Memoir of John Peisley, the notorious Bushranger; with a full Report of his Trial and Condemnation for the Wilful Murder of William Benyen (Pam. 41.) 12mo. Bathurst, 1862. MJ 2 R 3

PELAGIUS II (PAPA). Opera omnia. [*See* MIGNE, J. P., SERIES LATINA, 72.]

PELHAM (CAMDEN). Chronicles of Crime; or, the New Newgate Calendar. 2 vols. 8vo. Lond., 1886. F 8 S 20, 21

PELHAM (CAVENDISH). The World; or, the Present State of the Universe. 2 vols. (in 3) 4to. Lond., 1806. D 9 S 11-13†

PELLESCHI (G.) Eight Months on the Gran Chaco of the Argentine Republic. 8vo. Lond., 1886. D 3 Q 19

PELLEW (HON. GEORGE), D.D. Life and Correspondence of the Rt. Hon. Henry Addington, First Viscount Sidmouth. 3 vols. 8vo. Lond., 1847. C 9 U 43-45

PELLICO (SILVIO). Des Devoirs des Hommes; traduction nouvelle, par J. Depoisier. 12mo. Paris, 1847. G 9 Q 38
Aroldo and Clara: an Historical Poem; translated from the Italian, by W. A. Duncan. (Pam., 3.) 12mo. Sydney, 1840. MJ 3 P 38
Confessions to. [*See* SORELLI, G.] C 2 Q 49

PELLISSIER (PROF. A.) Précis d'Histoire de la Langue Française, depuis son Origine jusqu'à nos jours. 2e éd. 8vo. Paris, 1873. K 11 V 47

PELTIER (J.) Trial of, for a Libel against Napoleon Buonaparte. 8vo. Lond., 1803. F 10 P 16

PEMBERTON (CHARLES REECE). Life and Literary Remains of; with Remarks on his Character and Genius, by W. J. Fox; edited by John Fowler. 8vo. Lond., 1843. J 12 V 17

PEMBROKE (GEORGE ROBERT CHARLES HERBERT), EARL
of. Old New Zealand [*See* MANING, F. E.]

PEMBROKE (GEORGE ROBERT CHARLES HERBERT) EARL
of, AND KINGSLEY (G. H.), M.D. South Sea Bubbles;
by "The Earl and the Doctor." 3rd ed. 8vo. Lond.,
1872.   MD 5 T 35

PENDENNIS (ARTHUR). [*See* THACKERAY, W. M.]

PENDLEBURY (CHARLES), M.A., &c. Lenses and Systems of Lenses, treated after the manner of Gauss. 8vo.
Camb., 1884.   A 5 U 34

PENDLETON (JOHN). History of Derbyshire. 8vo.
Lond., 1886.   B 6 S 38

PENDRAGON (A.) [*See* ISAACS, G.]

PENFOLD (C.) Practical Treatise upon the best mode of
repairing Roads; with some Observations upon the present
System. (Pam. 14.) 8vo. Croydon (n.d.)   MJ 2 Q 4

PENLEY (PROF. AARON). English School of Painting in
Water-Colours: its Theory and Practice, with the several
Stages of Progression. With Illustrations. Roy. fol.
Lond., 1874.   A 32 P 14 ‡

PENN (GRANVILLE). Comparative Estimate of the Mineral
and Mosaical Geologies. 8vo. Lond., 1822.   A 9 R 17

PENN (WILLIAM). Historical Biography; with an extra
Chapter on the "Macaulay Charges," by W. H. Dixon.
8vo. Lond., 1851.   C 4 T 22

Brief Account of the Rise and Progress of the People
called Quakers. 12th ed. 8vo. Manchester, 1834.
    G 10 Q 24

Memoirs of the Private and Public Life of; by Thomas
Clarkson, M.A. 2 vols. 8vo. Lond., 1813.   C 5 V 25, 26

[Life of] The Founder of Pennsylvania; by John Stoughton, D.D. 8vo. Lond., 1882.   C 4 T 23

PENNANT (THOMAS), LL.D. Arctic Zoology. 3 vols. 4to.
Lond., 1784–87.   A 15 Q 10–12

British Zoology. 4th ed. 4 vols. 4to. Warrington,
1776–77.   A 15 Q 4–7

History of Quadrupeds. 2 vols. 4to. Lond., 1781.
    A 15 Q 8, 9

Genera of Birds. 4to. Lond., 1781.   A 15 Q 13

Tours in Scotland and Voyage to the Hebrides, 1769–72.
3rd ed. 3 vols. 4to. Warrington, &c., 1774–76.
    D 6 V 30–32

Another copy. 5th ed. 3 vols. 4to. Lond., 1790.
    D 6 V 33–35

Journey from Chester to London; with Notes. 8vo.
Lond., 1811.   D 6 T 31

Literary Life of; by himself. 4to. Lond., 1793.
    C 4 W 25

Some Account of London. 5th ed. 8vo. Lond., 1813.
    B 7 P 23

PENNANT (THOMAS, LL.D.—*continued.*
Tour from Downing to Alston-Moor. Roy. 4to. Lond.,
1801.   D 36 Q 5 ‡

Tours in Wales; with Notes. 3 vols. roy. 8vo. Lond.,
1810.   D 7 V 20–22

View of Hindoostan, India, Extra-Gangena, China, Japan,
and the Malayan Isles, New Holland, and the Spicy
Islands. (Outlines of the Globe.) 4 vols. (in 2) 4to.
Lond., 1798–1800.   D 4 V 13, 14

Another copy. 4 vols. 4to. Lond., 1798–1800.
    MD 7 Q 6–9 †

[Index to the] "Histoire Naturelle des Oiseaux," par
le Comte de Buffon, and "Les Planches Enluminées,"
systematically disposed. 4to. Lond., 1786.   A 15 Q 13

PENNELL (H. CHOLMONDELEY-). Fishing: Pike and other
Coarse Fish. 8vo. Lond., 1885.   A 14 Q 28

Fishing: Salmon and Trout. 8vo. Lond., 1885.
    A 14 Q 29

Sporting Fish of Great Britain; with Notes on Ich-
thyology. 8vo. Lond., 1886.   A 15 P 7

PENNING (W. HENRY), F.G.S. Text-book of Field
Geology; with a Section on Palæontology, by A. J. Jukes-
Browne, B.A., &c. With Illustrations. 2nd ed. 8vo.
Lond., 1879.   A 9 Q 26

PENNINGTON (A. S.) British Zoophytes: an Introduc-
tion to the Hydroida, Actinozoa, and Polyzoa found in
Great Britain, Ireland, and the Channel Islands. 8vo.
Lond., 1885.   A 14 Q 21

PENNINGTON (REV. MONTAGUE), M.A. Memoirs of the
Life of Mrs. Elizabeth Carter, with a new Edition of her
Poems; to which are added, some Miscellaneous Essays
in Prose; together with her Notes on the Bible, and
Answers to Objections concerning the Christian Religion.
4th ed. 2 vols. 8vo. Lond., 1825.   C 6 T 6, 7

PENNSYLVANIA. [*See* UNITED STATES OF AMERICA.]

PENNY CYCLOPÆDIA (THE), of the Society for the
Diffusion of Useful Knowledge. 27 vols. (in 14) imp.
8vo. Lond., 1833–43.   K 6 S 1–14

Supplement [to the above]. 2 vols. (in 1) imp. 8vo. Lond.,
1845–46.   K 6 S 15

PENRITH HOSPITAL AND BENEVOLENT ASY-
LUM. Rules and Regulations of; with Reports and
List of Subscribers, &c., for 1866–67. 8vo. Sydney,
1867–68.   MF 3 P 18

PENSIONS. Return of all Pensions, Retired and Superannuated Allowances, granted to Persons for Services in,
or connected with the Colony, since 1815. (Parl. Docs., 5.)
Fol. Lond., 1832.   MF 4 ‡

Bill to regulate Pensions and Retiring Allowances for
Officers in the Public Service. Fol. Sydney, 1870.
    MJ 2 U 1

PEOPLE'S ALMANACK for 1869. 12mo. Lond.,
1869.   ME 4 P

PEOPLE'S FREE PRESS (THE). People's Free Press and Educational Magazine. Vol. 1, No. 1. 8vo. Melh., 1857.   MJ 2 R 21

PEPOLI (PROF. C.) On the Language and Literature of Italy: an Inaugural Lecture. (Univ. of London.) 8vo. Lond., 1838.   J 5 S 8

PEPPER (PROF. J. H.), F.C.S., &c. Australian Gold-fields, and the best Means of discriminating Gold from all other Metals and Minerals: a Lecture. 8vo. Lond., 1852.
                                                        MD 5 R 1
Cyclopædic Science simplified. 8vo. Lond., 1869.
                                                        A 5 S 48

PEPPERCORNE (FREDERICK S.), C.E. Geological and Topographical Sketches of the Province of New Ulster. (Pam. B.) Roy. 8vo. Auckland, 1852.   MJ 2 U 2
Memoir relative to the Improvement of Harbours and Rivers in Australia; with incidental Remarks on Canals and Railways. (Pam. 28.) 8vo. Sydney, 1856. MJ 2 Q 16
Rivers of Australia. (Pam. 26.) 8vo. Sydney, 1857.
                                                        MJ 2 Q 14

PEPYS (SAMUEL), F.R.S. Memoirs of; comprising his Diary from 1659 to 1669, and a Selection from his private Correspondence. Edited by Richard, Lord Braybrooke. 2 vols. roy. 4to. Lond., 1825.   C 1 W 22, 23
Life, Journals, and Correspondence of, including a Narrative of his Voyage to Tangier, deciphered from the Short-hand MSS. in the Bodleian Library, by the Rev. J. Smith, A.M. 2 vols. 8vo. Lond., 1841. C 8 U 41, 42
Samuel Pepys and the World he lived in; by Henry B. Wheatley, F.S.A. 8vo. Lond., 1880.   C 9 P 23

PERCEVAL (HON. AND REV. C. G.) Abridged Account of the Misfortunes of the Dauphin; translated from the French. 8vo. Lond., 1838.   C 8 Q 4

PERCEVAL (DUDLEY M.) Remarks on the Character ascribed by Col. Napier to the Rt. Hon. Spencer Pecrceval. 2nd ed. 8vo. Lond., 1835.   B 13 U 7

PERCEVAL (RT. HON. SPENCER). Remarks on the Character ascribed by Col. Napier to the late Rt. Hon. Spencer Perceval. [*See* PERCEVAL, D. M.]

PERCIVAL (MRS. E. H.) Life of Sir David Wedderburn, Bart., M.P.; compiled from his Journals and Writings, by his Sister. 8vo. Lond., 1884.   C 9 V 37

PERCIVAL (REV. PETER). Land of the Veda: India briefly described in some of its aspects. 8vo. Lond., 1854.   D 5 P 34

PERCIVAL (CAPT. ROBERT). Account of the Island of Ceylon: its History, Geography, Natural History, &c. 4to. Lond., 1805.   D 4 V 34

PERCIVALL (WILLIAM), M.R.C.S. Hippopathology: a Systematic Treatise on the Disorders and Lamenesses of the Horse. Vol 1. 8vo. Lond., 1834.   A 1 R 22

PERCY ANECDOTES (THE). [*See* ROBERTSON, J. C.]

PERCY (C. M.) Mechanical Engineering of Collieries. 3rd ed. 2 vols. 8vo. Lond., 1885.   A 6 U 4, 5

PERCY (JOHN), M.D., &c. Metallurgy: The Art of Extracting Metals from their Ores, and adapting them to various purposes of Manufacture: Iron and Steel. With Illustrations, chiefly from original Drawings, carefully laid down to scale. 8vo. Lond., 1864. A 10 P 2
Metallurgy: the Art of Extracting Metals from their Ores: Introduction, Refractory Materials, and Fuel. 8vo. Lond., 1875.   A 9 T 32
Metallurgy: the Art of Extracting Metals from their Ores: Silver and Gold. Part I. With numerous Illustrations on Wood, mostly from original Drawings. 8vo. Lond., 1880.   A 10 P 1
Metallurgy of Lead, including Desilverization and Cupellation. Illustrated. 8vo. Lond., 1870.   A 10 P 3
Lectures on Gold. [*See* GOLD.]   MA 2 P 1

PERCY POMO: the Autobiography of a South Sea Islander. 8vo. Lond., 1881.   MJ 1 R 26

PERCY SOCIETY. Early English Poetry, Ballads, and Popular Literature of the Middle Ages. Edited from Original Manuscripts and Scarce Publications. 30 vols. 8vo. Lond., 1840–52.   E

PERCY (SHOLTO AND REUBEN). Percy Anecdotes. [*See* ROBERTSON, J. C.]

PERCY (RT. REV. THOMAS), D.D., BISHOP OF DROMORE. Reliques of Ancient English Poetry; with a Glossary. 8vo. Lond., 1840.   H 6 U 26
Regulations and Establishment of the Household of Henry Algernon Percy, the 5th Earl of Northumberland, begun in 1512. 8vo. Lond., 1827.   B 6 P 38
Johnsoniana. [*See* JOHNSON, S.]   C 2 R 24

PEREIRA (JONATHAN), M.D. Elements of Materia Medica and Therapeutics, abridged and adapted for the use of Medical and Pharmaceutical Practitioners and Students, and comprising all the Medicines of the British Pharmacopœia, &c. 8vo. Lond., 1874.   A 12 U 5
Treatise on Food and Diet; with Observations on the Dietetical Regimen suited for disordered 'states of the Digestive Organs. 8vo. Lond., 1843.   A 12 U 14

PERIAM (JONATHAN). American Encyclopædia of Agriculture: a Treasury of Useful Information for the Farm and Household. Illustrated. Roy. 8vo. Chicago, 1881.   K 1 V 21

PERILS AND CAPTIVITY; comprising the sufferings of the Picard Family; from the French of Mme. C. A. Daid. Narrative of the Captivity of M. de Brisson, and Voyage of Mme. Godin on the River of the Amazons; by J. Godin des Odonais. (Const. Misc.) 18mo. Edinb., 1827.   K 10 P 50

PERILS, PASTIMES, AND PLEASURES of an Emigrant in Australia, Vancouver's Island, and California. 8vo. Lond., 1849.   MD 1 W 18

PERISHING SOULS. An Appeal on behalf of Perishing Souls; or, Eight Reasons why the preaching of the Gospel should not be confined to stated houses only. 12mo. Hobart, 1856. MG 1 P 49

PERKINS (W. H.), F.R.S. On the Aniline, or Coal Tar Colours. (Cantor Lectures, 1) Roy. 8vo. Lond., 1869.
A 15 U 21

PERKINS (CHARLES C.) Historical Hand-book of Italian Sculpture. Illustrated. 8vo. Lond., 1883. A 7 S 10

PERKINS (FRED. B.) San Francisco Cataloguing for Public Libraries: a Manual of the System used in the San Francisco Free Public Library. 8vo. San Francisco, 1884. J 9 V 23

Rational Classification of Literature for Shelving and Cataloguing Books in a Library. Roy. 8vo. San Francisco, 1882. J9 V 23

PERKINS (HORACE). Melbourne illustrirt und Victoria beschrieben. 8vo. Melh., 1886. MD 1 W 44

PERKINS (REV. JUSTIN). A Residence of Eight Years in Persia, among the Nestorian Christians. 8vo. Andover, 1843. D 5 S 5

PERKINS (J. B.) France under Mazarin; with a Review of the Administration of Richelieu. 8vo. New York, 1886. B 8 R 23, 24

PERNETY (ANTOINE JOSEPH). [*See* BOUGAINVILLE, L. A. COMTE DE.]

PERNY (PAUL), M.A. Dictionnaire Français-Latin-Chinois de la Langue Mandarine parlée. 4to. Paris, 1869. K 13 U 6

Appendice du Dictionnaire Français-Latin-Chinois de la Langue Mandarine parlée contenant une notice sur l'Académie Impériale de Pékin. 4to. Paris, 1872. K 13 U 7

Dialogues Chinois-Latins, traduits mot à mot, avec la prononciation accentuée. 8vo. Paris, 1872. K 12 S 31

PÉRON (FRANÇOIS AUG.), ET FREYCINET (LOUIS). Voyage de Découvertes aux Terres Australes, sur les Corvettes *le Géographe, le Naturaliste,* et la Goëlette *le Casuarina,* pendant les années 1800-4. 2 vols. 4to. Paris, 1807-16. MD 4 Q 1, 2 †

Atlas, par MM. Lesueur et Petit. Roy. 4to. Paris, 1800-01. MD 4 Q 3 †

Another copy; with Atlas. 2 vols. (in 1) 8vo. Paris, 1807-16. MD 4 Q 4, 5 †

Entdeckungsreise nach Australien, unternommen auf Befehl Sr. Maj. des Kaisers von Frankreich und Königs von Italien mit den Korvetten der *Geograph* und der *Naturalist,* und der Goëlette *Kasuarina* in den Jahren 1800 bis 1804. 2 vols. 8vo. Weimar, 1808-19. MD 1 V 32, 33

Voyage of Discovery to the Southern Hemisphere, performed by order of the Emperor Napoleon, during the years 1801-4. 8vo. Lond., 1809. MD 1 V 34

PEROT & CO. [*See* PHILADELPHIA CENTENNIAL EXHIBITION, 1876.]

PÉROUSE (J. F. G. DE LA). [*See* LA PÉROUSE, J. F. G. DE LA.]

PEROWNE (REV. J. J. STEWART), D.D. Letters of Connop Thirlwall. [*See* THIRLWALL, RT. REV. C.] C 10 P 38

PERRAULT (CHARLES). Contes des Fées. [*See* CABINET DES FÉES, 1.]

PEROTTI (NICOLO). [*See* POLYBIUS.] B 12 P 30

PERRING (J. S.), C.E., AND ANDREWS (E. J.) The Pyramids of Gizeh, from actual Survey and Admeasurement, by J. S. Perring, C.E. Illustrated by E. J. Andrews. 3 vols. (in 2) at. fol. Lond., 1839-42. D 3 P 27, 28 ‡

[*See* VYSE, COL. H.] D 2 V 16-18

PERRING (SIR PHILIP), BART. Hard Knots in Shakespeare. 8vo. Lond., 1885. J 3 S 21

PERRON D'ARC (HENRY). Aventures d'un Voyageur en Australie: Neuf Mois de Séjour chez les Nagarnooks. 8vo. Paris, 1869. MD 4 Q 43

Another copy. 3e éd. 8vo. Paris, 1879. MD 4 Q 44

PERROT (PROF. GEORGES), AND CHIPIEZ (CHARLES). History of Art in Ancient Egypt; translated and edited by Walter Armstrong, B.A. Illustrated. 2 vols. imp. 8vo. Lond., 1883. A 7 V 1, 2

History of Art in Chaldæa and Assyria; translated and edited by Walter Armstrong, B.A. Illustrated. 2 vols. roy. 8vo. Lond., 1884. A 8 S 26, 27

History of Art in Phœnicia and its Dependencies. Illustrated. 3 vols. roy. 8vo. Lond., 1885. A 8 R 24, 25

PERROT (GEORGES), GUILLAUME (EDMOND), AND DELBET (JULES). Exploration Archéologique de la Galatie, et de la Bithynie, d'une partie de la Mysie, de la Phrygie, de la Cappadoce, et du Pont. Planches et Cartes. 2 vols. roy. fol. Paris, 1872. D 4 S 10, 11 ‡

PERRY (RT. REV. CHARLES), D.D., BISHOP OF MELBOURNE. Church in the Colonies—Australia: a Letter. 2nd ed. 12mo. Lond., 1850. MD 1 T 49

On Divisions in the Church, and the duty of marking and avoiding those who cause them: a Sermon. 8vo. Melh., 1851. MG 1 Q 40

Form of Prayer appointed by the Bishop, to be used in the Churches and Places of Worship throughout the Diocese. 8vo. Melh., 1854. MG 1 Q 40

The Decalogue, a Divine Code of Moral Law: a Letter, in reply to the Rev. Isaac New's "Lord's Day v. Sabbath." 8vo. Melh., 1860. MG 1 Q 37

Sermon preached after the Funeral of Hannah Seddon. 8vo. Melh., 1861. MG 1 Q 39

Ecce Homo: a Lecture. 8vo. Melh., 1867. MG 1 Q 37

Creation v. Development: a Review of a Lecture by the J. E. Bromby, D.D. 8vo. Melh., 1870. MG 1 Q 37

On the Education Question. 8vo. Melh., 1871. MG 1 Q 38

The Bible: its Evidences, Characteristics, and Effects: a Lecture. 8vo. Melh., 1872. MG 1 Q 37

PERRY (CHARLES JAMES). Baptismal Regeneration, the True Doctrine of the Church of England, and shown to be a Cardinal Doctrine of the Gospel. 8vo. Melb., 1868. MG 1 Q 39

Brief Treatise on Collisions at Sea and Shipwrecks. 8vo. Melb., 1860. MF 2 P 30

Another copy. 8vo. Melb., 1860. MJ 2 R 8

Anti-Collision Dial and Shipwreck Preventor: Testimonials and Opinions of the Press. 8vo. Melb., 1860. MJ 2 R 8

PERRY (SIR ERSKINE). Speech on the Indian Army. (Pam. 24.) Lond., 1855. MJ 2 Q 12

PERRY (REV. GEORGE GRESLEY), M.A. History of the Reformation in England. 12mo. Lond.,1886. G 7 R 24

PERRY (JOHN), M.E. Practical Mechanics. Illustrated. 12mo. Lond., 1883. A 11 P 12

PERRY (COMM. M. C.) Narrative of the Expedition of an American Squadron to the China Seas and Japan in the years 1852–54. Roy. 8vo. New York, 1856. D 5 V 32

PERRY (RICHARD). Contributions to an Amateur Magazine in Prose and Verse. 8vo. Lond.,1857. MJ 1 U 16

PERRY (THOMAS SERGEANT). Life and Letters of Francis Lieber. With Portrait. 8vo. Lond., 1882. C 9 V 27

PERRY (WALTER COPLAND). Greek and Roman Sculpture : a popular Introduction to the History of Greek and Roman Sculpture. With Illustrations. 8vo. Lond., 1882. A 7 S 7

PERRY (WILLIAM). Synonymous, Etymological, and Pronouncing English Dictionary. Roy. 8vo. Lond., 1805. K 13 R 9

PERSANES, LES VEILLÉES. Les Veillées du Sultan Schahriar avec le Sultane Scheherazade; traduites de l'Arabe par M. Cazotte et D. Chavis. 4 vols. 8vo. Genève, 1793. J 15 R 38–41

PERSIA. Eastern Persia: an Account of the Journeys of the Persian Boundary Commission, 1870–72. 2 vols. 8vo. Lond., 1876. D 4 U 45, 49

PERSIA (SHAH OF). [*See* NASR EDDIN, SHAH OF PERSIA.]

PERSIAN PRINCESS, A. [*See* FRASER, J. B.]

PERSIGNY (JEAN GILBERT VICTOR DE FIALIN), COMTE DE. Relation de l'Entreprise du Prince Napoleon-Louis et Motifs qui l'y ont déterminé. 8vo. Lond., 1837. MB 1 Q 11

PERSIUS (CHARLES). The Academicians of 1823 ; or, the Greeks of the Palais Royal, and the Clubs of St. James's. 8vo. Lond., 1823. A 17 U 4

PERSIUS FLACCUS (AULUS). Opera omnia, ex Editione G. L. Kœnig, cum Notis et Interpretatione in usum Delphini, curante A. J. Valpy. 8vo. Lond.,1820. J 13 R 30

Satire di; traduzione del Cavaliere Vincenzo Monti. 12mo. Milano, 1826. H 8 P 20

4 F

PERSIUS FLACCUS (AULUS)—*continued.*

Satires of; translated into English Verse by W. Gifford, with Notes and Illustrations. 2 vols. 8vo. Lond., 1817 H 7 T 16, 17

Satires of ; with a Translation and Commentary, by John Conington, M.A.; to which is prefixed, a Lecture on the Life and Writings of Persius. (Clar. Press.) 8vo. Oxford, 1872. J 3 T 1

Satires of; literally translated into English Prose, with Notes, &c., by the Rev. Lewis Evans, M.A. 12mo. Lond., 1871. J 8 R 8

Works of; translated by the Rt. Hon. Sir W. Drummond. (Fam. Class. Lib.) 18mo. Lond., 1831. J 15 P 21

PERUGINI (G.), ET HÉLYOT (P.) Album, ou Collection Complète et Historique des Costumes de la Cour de Rome, des Ordres Monastiques, Religieux et Militaires, et des Congrégations Séculières des deux Sexes. 2° éd. 4to. Paris, 1862. A 7 V 13

PERUVIAN GUANO: its Use, Mode of Application, and Composition, for the Information of Australian Agriculturists, and Market Gardeners. (Pam. Ca.) 8vo. Sydney, 1854. MA 1 Q 7

PERUZZI (E. M.) Autobiographical Memoirs of Giovanni Dupré. [*See* DUPRÉ, G.] C 3 R 34

PESCHEL (OSCAR). Races of Mankind, and their Geographical Distribution. 8vo. Lond., 1876. A 1 V 6

Geschichte der Erdkunde. (Gesch. der Wissen in Deutschland.) 8vo. München, 1865. A 17 V 18

PET (G. A.) Verslag aangaande den aan den voet van de Soembing en Sindoro onlangs ontgraven steenen trap. 8vo. Batavia, 1866. K 14 Q 29

PETER. Peter's Letters to his Kinsfolk. [*See* LOCKHART, J. G.]

PETER (CARL). Chronological Tables of Greek History. 4to. Camb., 1882. B 9 V 32

PETER (WILLIAM). Speeches of Romilly. [*See* ROMILLY, SIR S.] F 13 Q 12, 13

PETER PAPINEAU. [*See* VICTORIA.]

PETER PERFUME. [*See* NIXON, F. H.]

PETER 'POSSUM. [*See* ROWE, R.]

PETER THE GREAT (EMPEROR OF RUSSIA). Memoir of the Life of [by R. A. Davenport]. 12mo. Lond., 1832. C 1 P 34

Life of; by J. Barrow. 12mo. Lond., 1873. C 2 Q 29

Peter the Great, Emperor of Russia : a Study of Historical Biography ; by Eugene Schuyler, Ph.D., &c. 2 vols. 8vo. Lond., 1884. C 9 P 21, 22

PETERBOROUGH AND MONMOUTH (CHARLES MORDAUNT), EARL OF. Memoir of ; with Selections from his Correspondence, by Major George Warburton. 2 vols. 8vo. Lond., 1850. C 3 T 18, 19

PETERMANN (DR. A.) Mittheilungen aus Justus Perthes' geographischen Anstalt über wichtige neue Erforschungen auf dem Gesammtgebiete der Geographie. 39 vols. 4to. Gotha, 1855–84. E

Geological and Topographical Atlas of New Zealand. [*See* HOCHSTETTER, DR. F. VON.] MD 5 R 4 ‡

PETERMANN (DR. W. L.) Deutschlands Flora mit Abbildungen sämmtlicher Gattungen auf 100 Tafeln. Imp. 8vo. Leipzig, 1849. A 2 P 19

PETERS (F. H.) The Nicomachean Ethics of Aristotle. [*See* ARISTOTELES.] G 7 R 25

PETERS (K. F.) Die Donau und ihr Gebiet. 8vo. Leipzig, 1876. A 9 P 10

PETERS (DR. WILLIAM). The Languages of the Mozambique. [*See* BLEEK, W. H. I.]

PETERSON (ROBERT E.) Notes of a Pianist. [*See* GOTTS-CHALK, L. M.] C 5 S 25

PETHERICK (E. A.) [*See* YORK GATE LIBRARY.] MK 1 U 21

PETHERICK (JOHN AND MRS.) Travels in Central Africa, and Explorations of the Western Nile Tributaries. 2 vols. 8vo. Lond., 1869. D 1 W 13, 14

Egypt—The Soudan and Central Africa. 8vo. Lond., 1861. D 2 P 19

PETIS DE LA CROIX (F.) [*See* CABINET DE FÉES, 14, 15.]

PETIT (N.) [*See* PÉRON, F. A.] MD 4 Q 4 †

PETIT (PROF. J. A.) History of Mary Stuart, Queen of Scots; translated by Charles de Flandre, F.S.A, With Portraits. 2 vols. (in 1) 4to. Lond., 1874. C 2 W 16

PETITIONS. Petition to His Majesty, by the Members of Council, Magistrates, Clergy, Landholders, Merchants, and other Free Inhabitants of New South Wales. Fol. Sydney, 1836. MJ 2 U 1

Report of the Proceedings of the General Meeting of the Supporters of the Petitions to His Majesty and the House of Commons, held at the Committee Rooms, May 30, 1836. 8vo. Sydney, 1836. MF 3 P 1

Another copy. 8vo. Sydney, 1836. MJ 2 Q 5

Petition of the Total Abstainers from Intoxicating Drinks, and other Colonists of Victoria. 4to. Melb. (n.d.) MJ 2 U 3

PETO (JOHN). [*See* NARJOUX, F.] A 2 S 12

PETRARCA (FRANCESCO). Life of Petrarch; by Thomas Campbell. 2 vols. 8vo. Lond., 1841. C 9 P 14, 15

Sonnets, Triumphs, and other Poems of Petrarch; with a Life of the Poet, by Thomas Campbell. 8vo. Lond., 1859. H 7 Q 18

Rime di con l'interpretazione di G. Leopardi e con note inedite di E. Camerini. 5ª ed. 8vo. Milano, 1885. H 7 Q 6

Rime di 2 vols. fol. Pisa, 1805. H 27 Q 18, 19 ‡ [*S.* GINELLI, L.]

PETRE (HON. HENRY WILLIAM). Account of the Settlements of the New Zealand Company; from Personal Observations during a Residence there. 8vo. Lond., 1841. MD 5 R 31

Account of the Settlements of the New Zealand Company. 2nd ed. 8vo. Lond., 1841. MD 5 R 32

PETREL. [*See* IN SOUTHERN SEAS.]

PETRIE (GEORGE), LL.D., &c. Life and Labours, in Art and Archaeology, of; by W. Stokes, M.D., &c. 8vo. Lond., 1868. C 9 P 16

Ecclesiastical Architecture of Ireland; anterior to the Anglo-Norman Invasion. 4to. Dublin, 1845. A 2 T 18

PETRIE (HENRY), F.S.A., SHARPE (REV. JOHN), B.A., AND HARDY (SIR THOMAS DUFFUS), KNT. Monumenta Historica Britannica; or, Materials for the History of Britain. Vol. 1. (*All published.*) Fol. Lond., 1848. B 14 T 18 ‡

Another copy. Fol. Lond., 1848. B 18 U 16‡

PETRIE (W. M. FLINDERS). Pyramids and Temples of Gizeh. 4to. Lond., 1883. A 2 S 1

Tanis: Part I, 1883–84. Second Memoir of the Egypt Exploration Fund. Roy. 4to. Lond., 1885. B 15 R 2 ‡

PETRIE (W. M. F.), AND GARDNER (E. A.), M.A. Naukratis. Part 1, 1884–85. Third Memoir of the Egypt Exploration Fund. Roy. 4to. Lond., 1886. B 2 P 10†

Naukratis. Part 2, 1885–86. Continued by E. A. Gardner. Sixth Memoir of the Egypt Exploration Fund. Roy. 4to. Lond., 1888. B 2 P 11 †

PETRONIUS ARBITER (CAIUS). The Satyricon of. [*See* PROPERTIUS, S. A.]

PETRÓNJ (STÉFANO EGÍDIO), AND DAVENPORT (JOHN). Nuóvo Dizionário—Italiano—Inglése—Francése. 3ª ed. 2 vols. 8vo. Lond., 1828. K 15 Q 12, 13

PETRUS BLESENSIS. Opera omnia. [*See* MIGNE, J. P., SERIES LATINA, 207.]

PETRUS CANTOR. Verbum Abbreviatum. [*See* MIGNE, J. P., SERIES LATINA, 205.]

PETRUS CELLENSIS (CARNOTENSIS EPISCOPUS). Opera omnia. [*See* MIGNE, J. P., SERIES LATINA, 202.]

PETRUS CHRYSOLOGUS (SANCTUS). Opera omnia. [*See* MIGNE, J. P., SERIES LATINA, 52.]

PETRUS (PATRICIUS). [*See* BYZANTINAE HIST. SCRIPT.]

PETRUS VENERABILIS. Opera omnia. [*See* MIGNE, J. P., SERIES LATINA, 189.]

PETTAVEL (DAVID LOUIS). Concise and Practical Treatise on the Cultivation of the Vine in the Colony of Victoria. (Prize Essay.) 8vo. Geelong, 1859.* MA 1 Q 2

The Vine. [*See* BELPERROUD, J.]

PETTENKOFER (DR. MAX VON). Relations of the Air to the Clothes we wear, the House we live in, and the Soil we dwell on; Lectures, translated by Augustus Hess, M.D. 8vo. Lond., 1873.   A 13 P 11

PETTIGREW (J. BELL), M.D., &c. Physiology of the Circulation in Plants, in the Lower Animals, and in Man. Illustrated. 8vo. Lond., 1874.   A 12 T 8

Animal Locomotion; or, Walking, Swimming and Flying; with a Dissertation on Aëronautics. 8vo. Lond., 1873.   A 16 P 4

PETTIGREW (THOMAS JOSEPH), F.R.S., &c. Memoirs of the Life of Vice-Admiral Lord Viscount Nelson, K.B., &c. 2 vols. 8vo. Lond., 1849.   C 9 P 8, 9

Chronicles of the Tombs : a Select Collection of Epitaphs. 8vo. Lond., 1864.   B 23 Q 6

Another copy. 8vo. Lond., 1873.   B 23 Q 7

History of Egyptian Mummies, and an Account of the Worship and Embalming of the Sacred Animals by the Egyptians. Roy. 4to. Lond., 1834.   B 16 Q 12 ‡

Bibliotheca Sussexiana: a Descriptive Catalogue, accompanied by Historical and Biographical Notices of the Manuscripts and printed Books contained in the Library of His Royal Highness the Duke of Sussex, K.G., D.C.L., &c., in the Kensington Palace. Vol. 1, Parts 1 and 2. Imp. 8vo. Lond., 1827.   K 8 R 21, 22 †

PETTY (JOHN). History of the Primitive Methodist Connexion. 8vo. Lond., 1864.   G 11 S 3

PEUTINGER (CONRAD). Tabula Itineraria Peutingerian,a 1753. Fol. Lipsiae, 1824.   D 38 P 16 ‡

PEYRARD (F.) [*See* EUCLIDES.]   A 10 V 17–19

PEYRON (AMEDEUS). Lexicon Linguae Copticæ. 4to. Taurini, 1835.   K 3 S 18†

PEZZI (DOMENICO). Aryan Philology, according to the most recent Researches (Glottologia Aria Recentissima). 8vo. Lond., 1879.   K 12 P 9

PFEIFFER (EMILY). Flying Leaves from East and West. 8vo. Lond., 1885.   D 10 Q 39

PFEIFFER (MME. IDA). A Lady's Second Journey round the World. 2 vols. 8vo. Lond., 1855.   D 10 R 18, 19

Visit to the Holy Land, Egypt, and Italy; translated from the German, by H. W. Dulcken. 8vo. Lond., 1852.   D 1 T 28

Visit to Iceland and the Scandinavian North. 8vo. Lond., 1852.   D 8 R 13

A Woman's Journey round the World; an unabridged translation from the German. 2nd ed. 8vo. Lond., 1852.   D 10 R 17

PFEIFFER (LUDOVICUS), M.D. Nomenclator Botanicus. 2 vols. (in 4) roy. 8vo. Cassillis, 1873–74.   K 7 Q 25–28

PFIZER (GUSTAV). Der Letzte der Barone aus dem Englischen. [*See* LYTTON, BARON]

PFLEIDERER (PROF. OTTO), D.D. Lectures on the Influence of the Apostle Paul on the Development of Christianity. 8vo. Lond., 1885.   G 7 P 6

PFLUGK-HARTTUNG (DR. JULIUS VON). Iter Italicum. Unternommen mit Unterstützung der kgl. Akademie der Wissenschaften zu Berlin. 8vo. Stuttgart, 1883.   B 11 S 25

Acta Pontificum Romanorum inedita. [*See* ACTA PONTIFICUM ROMANORUM.]

PHÆDRUS (AUGUSTUS LIBERTUS). Fabulæ Æsopiæ, ex Editione J. G. S. Schwabii, cum Notis et Interpretatione in usum Delphini; Curante A. J. Valpy. 2 vols. 8vo. Lond., 1822.   J 13 R 31, 32

Fables of. [*See* TERENTIUS AFER, P.]

PHALARIS. Dissertation on the Epistles of. [*See* BENTLEY, R.]

PHARMACEUTICAL SOCIETY OF GREAT BRITAIN. Pharmaceutical Journal and Transactions. 1st, 2nd, and 3rd series. 44 vols. roy. 8vo. Lond., 1841–85.   E

Calendar of the Pharmaceutical Society of Great Britain, 1881. 8vo. Lond., 1881.   E

PHEIDIAS. The Art of. [*See* WALDSTEIN, C.]   A 8 S 28

PHAYRE (LIEUT.-GEN. SIR ARTHUR P.), G.C.M.G., &c. History of Burma, including Burma Proper, Pegu, Taungu, Tenasserim, and Arakan ; from the earliest Time to the end of the first War with British India. 8vo. Lond., 1883.   B 10 Q 21

Coins of Arakan, of Pegu, and Burma. [*See* NUMISMATICA ORIENTALIA, 3.]   A 2 S 17 †

PHELPS (SAMUEL). Life and Life-Work of ; by his Nephew, W. May Phelps, and John Forbes-Robertson. 8vo. Lond., 1886.   C 8 U 43

PHELPS (W. MAY), AND FORBES-ROBERTSON (JOHN). Life and Life-Work of Samuel Phelps. 8vo. Lond., 1866.   C 8 U 43

PHILADELPHIA ACADEMY OF SCIENCE. [*See* ACADEMY OF SCIENCE, PHILADELPHIA.]

PHILADELPHIA INTERNATIONAL AND CENTENNIAL EXHIBITION OF 1876. Description and Ground Plans of the Buildings of the International Exhibition; by H. T. Schwartzman, Architect. Roy. fol. Philad., 1876.   A 2 P 6 ‡

Belgique: Catalogue des Produits Industriéls et des Œuvres d'Art. 12mo. Bruxelles, 1876.   K 7 R 4

Descriptive Catalogue of a Collection of the Economic Minerals of Canada, and Notes on a Stratigraphical Collection of Rocks. Roy. 8vo. Montreal, 1876.   K 8 Q 5

Catalogue of the Brazilian Section. 8vo. Philad., 1876.   K 8 P 13

Catalogue of the Chinese Imperial Maritime Customs Collection. 4to. Shanghai, 1876.   K 9 P 3 †

PHILADELPHIA INTERNATIONAL AND CEN-
TENNIAL EXHIBITION OF 1876—*continued.*
Catalogue of the Articles and Objects exhibited by the
United States Navy Department. Roy. 4to. Philad.,
1876.　　　　　　　　　　　　　　　　K 1 Q 11 †

Education Department: Report on the Philadelphia
International Exhibition of 1876. 3 vols. roy. 8vo.
Lond., 1877–78.　　　　　　　　　　K 8 P 9–11

Catalogue of the Collective Exposition of the Netherlands Booksellers' Association: Specimens of Publications
of the last years, including Schoolbooks, Newspapers, and
Periodicals. 8vo. Amsterdam, 1876.　　　K 7 S 8

Special Catalogue of the Netherland Section. Roy.
8vo. Amsterdam, 1876.　　　　　　　K 8 Q 2

Catalogue of the Russian Section. 12mo. St. Petersburgh, 1876.　　　　　　　　　　　　K 7 R 3

Catalogue of the Chilian Exhibition at the Centenary
of Philadelphia. Roy. 8vo. Valparaiso, 1876.　K 8 Q 6

Empire of Brazil, at the Universal Exhibition of 1876.
8vo. Rio de Janeiro, 1876.　　　　　　D 15 U 3

Educational Institutions, Province of Ontario, Canada.
(Parl. Bs.) 8vo. Toronto, 1876.　　　　MG 1 Q 34

Lista Preparatoria del Catalogo de los Expositores de
España y sus Provincias de Ultramar, Cuba, Puerto Rico
y Filipinas. 8vo. Filadelfia, 1876.　　　K 8 Q 3

Norwegian Special Catalogue for the International
Exhibition at Philadelphia, 1876. 8vo. Christiana,
1876.　　　　　　　　　　　　　　　K 8 P 8

Collection of the Netherlands Treasury Department:
Explicatory Notice. (Pam Co.) 8vo. Amsterdam,
1876.　　　　　　　　　　　　　　A 16 U 23

Swedish Catalogues. 1. Statistics; by Dr. Elis Sidenbladh. 2. Exhibits. 8vo. Stockholm, 1876.　K 8 P 16

Official Catalogue. Parts 1, 2. 3rd and revised ed.
2 vols. 8vo. Philad., 1876.　　　　　K 7 R 25, 26

Victorian Intercolonial Exhibition, 1875, preparatory
to the Philadelphia Exhibition, 1876; opened 2nd September, 1875. Official Catalogue of Exhibits. 8vo.
Melb., 1875.*　　　　　　　　　　　MK 1 Q 17

Prospectus and List of Commissioners for New South
Wales. (Pam. M.) Fol. Sydney, 1875.　　MJ 2 S 4

Official Record; containing Introduction, Catalogues,
Official Awards of the Commissioners, Reports and Recommendations of the Experts, and Essays and Statistics
on the Social and Economic Resources of the Colony of
Victoria. 8vo. Melb., 1875.*　　　　　MK 1 Q 11

Official Catalogue of the Natural and Industrial Products of New South Wales, forwarded to the International Exhibition of 1876, at Philadelphia. Roy. 8vo.
Sydney, 1876.　　　　　　　　　　　MK 1 S 25

System of Classification. 8vo. Philad., 1874.　MK 1 S 25

Report of the Commissioners for Victoria to His Excellency the Governor. Roy. 8vo. Melb., 1877. MK 1 P 17 †

Official Catalogue of the British Section. Part 1, 2.
2 vols. (in 1) sm. 8vo. Lond., 1876.　　K 7 S 25
　1. Official Catalogue.
　2. Exhibitors' Commercial Guide; containing United States
　Tariff, together with an Epitome of the American Laws
　relating to Patents and Trade Marks.

PHILADELPHIA INTERNATIONAL AND CEN-
TENNIAL EXHIBITION OF 1876—*continued.*
Descriptive Catalogue of the Venezuelan Department;
compiled by Dr. Adolphus Ernst. 8vo. Philad., 1876.
　　　　　　　　　　　　　　　　　K 7 R 36

Descriptive Catalogue of Collection from Jamaica; compiled by Robert Thomson. 8vo. Kingston, 1876. K 7 R 36

Special Catalogue of Stated Displays of Live Stock.
Part 1 and 2. Horses and Dogs. 8vo. Philad., 1876.
　　　　　　　　　　　　　　　　　K 7 R 36

Catalogue of Canadian Exhibitors. 8vo. Montreal,
1876.　　　　　　　　　　　　　　　K 7 R 36

Department of Education and Science: Catalogue of the
New Jersey Exhibit. 8vo. Trenton, 1876. K 7 R 36

Dominion of Canada: Catalogue of Exhibits in Education. 8vo. Toronto, 1876.　　　　　　K 7 R 36

Catalogue of the West Virginia State Exhibit; by
F. M. Maury. 8vo. Philad., 1876.　　　K 7 R 36

Check List of Preparations and Objects in the Section
of Human Anatomy of the United States Army Medical
Museum; by George A. Otis. 8vo. Wash., 1876. K 7 R 36

Catalogue of Models, Instruments, Samples, Papers,
and Drawings, exhibited by the Massachusetts Institute
of Technology. 8vo. Boston, 1876.　　　K 7 R 36

Catalogue of Products of Michigan. 8vo. Lansing,
1876.　　　　　　　　　　　　　　　K 7 R 36

Hospital of the Medical Department, United States
Army Museum, Description of Specimens from the; by
J. J. Woodward. 8vo. Philad., 1876.　　A 16 U 21

Description of Models of Hospital Cars; by J. J.
Woodward. 8vo. Philad., 1876.　　　　A 16 U 21

Description of Models of Hospital Steam-Vessels; by
J. J. Woodward. 8vo. Philad., 1876.　　A 16 U 21

Description of the United States Army Medical Transport Cart, Model of, 1876; by D. L. Huntingdon, and
G. A. Otis. 8vo. Philad., 1876.　　　　A 16 U 21

Description of Pivot and Co.'s improved United States
Army Medicine Wagon. 8vo. Philad., 1876. A 16 U 21

Description of selected Specimens from the Army
Medical Museum at Washington; by G. A. Otis. 8vo.
Philad., 1876.　　　　　　　　　　　A 16 U 21

List of Skeletons and Crania in the Section of Comparative Anatomy; by Dr. H. C. Yarrow. 8vo. Wash.,
1876.　　　　　　　　　　　　　　　A 16 U 21

Military Bridge-equipage; designed and constructed by
[Capt.] V. Noman. 8vo. Philad., 1876.　A 16 U 21

Classification and Grouping of Exhibits. Roy. 8vo.
Philad., 1876.　　　　　　　　　　　K 8 P 13

Chili at Centennial Exhibition of Philadelphia: Silver
and Gold Amalgamating Machinery of Chili. (Pam. Co.)
12mo. Philad., 1876.　　　　　　　　A 16 U 23

Catalogue of the Products of the Brazilian Forests.
[*See* SALDANHA DA GAMA, T. DE.]　　A 16 U 23

PHILALETHES. [*See* FELLOWES, R., D.D.]

PHILIP II. (KING OF FRANCE). Vie de. [*See* GUIZOT, F. P. G., 11.]

PHILIP II. (KING OF SPAIN). History of the Reign of. [*See* PRESCOTT, W. H.]

PHILIP DE COMMINES. [*See* COMMINES, P. DE.]

PHILIPPUS HARVENGIUS. Opera omnia. [*See* MIGNE, J. P., SERIES LATINA, 203.]

PHILIPS (AMBROSE). The Distressed Mother: a Tragedy. (Brit. Theatre.) 12mo. Lond., 1808.   H I P 7

Another copy. (New Eng. Theatre.) 12mo. Lond., 1786.   H 4 P 21

Another copy. [*See* BRIT. DRAMA, 1.]

Life and Poems of. [*See* CHALMERS, A., *and* JOHNSON, S.]

PHILIPS (JOHN). Life and Poems. of. [*See* CHALMERS, A., *and* JOHNSON, S.]

PHILIPSON (JOHN). Harness: as it has been, as it is, and as it should be; with Remarks on Traction, and the Use of the Cape Cart, by "Nimshivich." 8vo. Newcastle-upon-Tyne, 1882. .   A 1 R 37

PHILLIMORE (MISS CATHERINE MARY). Fra Angelico. (Great Artists.) 8vo. Lond., 1881.   C 3 T 41

· PHILLIMORE (FRANCIS). [*See* DICKENS, C.]   K 9 P 4 †

PHILLIMORE (JOHN GEORGE), Q.C., &c. Principles and · Maxims of Jurisprudence. 8vo. Lond., 1856.   F 6 U 24

PHILLIMORE (MISS LUCY). Sir Christopher Wren: his Family and his Times; with original Letters and a Discourse on Architecture, hitherto unpublished, 1585–1723. 8vo. Lond., 1881.   C 9 P 50

PHILLIMORE (SIR ROBERT JOSEPH), BART., D.C.L. Case of the Creole considered in a Second Letter to the Rt. Hon. Lord Ashburton. (Pam. 9.) 8vo. Lond., 1842.   F 12 P 8

Letter to the Rt. Hon. Lord Ashburton suggested by the Questions of International Law raised in the Message of the American President. (Pam. 9.) 8vo. Lond., 1842.   F 12 P 8

Commentaries upon International Law. 2nd ed. 4 vols. 8vo. Lond., 1871.   F 6 U 11–14

[*See* LESSING, G. E.]

PHILLIMORE (R. M.) Studious Women. [*See* DUPAN-LOUP, F. A. P.]

PHILLIP (CAPT. A.), GOVERNOR OF NEW SOUTH WALES. An authentic Journal of the Expedition under Commodore Phillip to Botany Bay; with an Account of the Settlement made at Port Jackson, by "An Officer." 8vo. Lond., 1789   MD 4 U 17

PHILLIP (CAPT. A.), GOVERNOR OF NEW SOUTH WALES —*continued.*

Voyage of, to Botany Bay; compiled from authentic Papers, to which are added, the Journals of Lieutenants Shortland, Watts, Ball, and Captain Marshall, with an Account of their new Discoveries. 4to. Lond., 1789.*   MD 4 Q 14 †

Another copy. 2nd ed. 4to. Lond., 1790.*   MD 4 Q 18 †

Voyage of, to Botany Bay. Inscribed, by permission, the Marquis of Salisbury. 3rd ed. 8vo. Lond., 1790.   MD 5 V 1

Another copy. 8vo. Dublin, 1790.   MD 4 U 18

Voyage of, to Botany Bay; with an Account of its Origin and Present State. 18mo. Lond., 1807.*   MD 1 T 12

[*See* HUNTER, CAPT. J.]

PHILLIPPS (J. O. HALLIWELL-). [*See* HALLIWELL-PHILLIPPS, J. O.]

PHILLIPS (CHARLES), A.B. John Philpot Curran and his Contemporaries. 8vo. Lond., 1850.   C 10 S 36

Speeches, delivered at the Bar and on various Public Occasions in Ireland and England. 2nd ed. 8vo. Lond., 1822.   F 13 Q 7

PHILLIPS (COLEMAN). British Colonization and British Commerce. 8vo. Lond., 1875.   MF 3 P 17

PHILLIPS (E.) Out in the Soudan: a Story of the War. 12mo. Sydney, 1885.*   MJ 1 P 42

PHILLIPS (GEORGE). Rudiments of Curvilinear Design. Illustrated. Imp. fol. Lond., 1838–40.   A 3 P 23 ‡

PHILLIPS (HENRY). Musical and Personal Recollections during Half-a-Century. 2 vols. 8vo. Lond., 1864.   C 4 Q 17, 18

PHILLIPS (H. A. D.) Administration of India. 8vo. Lond., 1886.   F 5 R 2

PHILLIPS (J.) General History of Inland Navigation, Foreign and Domestic. 4to. Lond., 1795.   F 5 Q 20

PHILLIPS (JOHN), LL.D., &c. Geology of Oxford and the Valley of the Thames. 8vo. Oxford, 1871.   A 9 R 18

Manual of Geology, Theoretical and Practical. .2 vols. 8vo. Lond., 1885.   A 9 R 31, 32

Vesuvius. 8vo. Oxford, 1869.   A 9 Q 15

PHILLIPS (JOHN). Mexico Illustrated; with Descriptive Letter-press in English and Spanish. Imp. fol. Lond., 1848.   D 20 P 21 ‡

Treatise on Geology. (Lard. Cab. Cyclo.) 2 vols. 12mo Lond., 1837–39.   K 1 U 15, 16

PHILLIPS (JOHN ARTHUR), F.C.S. Gold-mining and Assaying: a Scientific Guide for Australian Emigrants 12mo. Lond., 1852.   MA 2 P 18

Another copy. 2nd ed. 12mo. Lond., 1853.   MA 2 P 19

Treatise on Ore Deposits. With Illustrations. 8vo Lond., 1884.   A 10 Q 8

PHILLIPS (JOHN ARTHUR), F.C.S.—*continued.*
Elements of Metallurgy: a practical Treatise on the Art of extracting the Metals from their Ores. Illustrated. 8vo. Lond., 1874.   A 9 T 31

Mining and Metallurgy of Gold and Silver. Roy. 8vo. Lond., 1867.   A 9 V 19

Copper and Smelting. (Brit. Manuf. Indust.) 12mo. Lond., 1876.   A 17 S 34

PHILLIPS (J. S.), M.E. Explorers', Miners', and Metallurgists' Companion. 8vo. San Francisco, 1873. A 9 T 33

Another copy. 2nd ed. 8vo. San Francisco, 1875.
                                                  A 10 P 24

Explorers', Miners', and Assayers' Companion: Rocks, Veins, Testing, and Assaying. 8vo. Lond., 1881
                                                  A 9 Q 46

Another copy. 8vo. Sydney, 1887.   MA 2 R 1

PHILLIPS (LAWRENCE B.), F.R.A.S., &c. Dictionary of Biographical Reference. Roy. 8vo. Lond., 1871. Libr.

PHILLIPS (P. D.) Address to the St. Kilda Electors. 8vo. Melb., 1879.   MF 1 Q 6

PHILLIPS (SIR RICHARD). Million of Facts, of Correct Data, and Elementary Constants, in the entire Circle of the Sciences. 8vo. Lond., 1859.   K 18 P 11

[*See* ANNALS OF PHILOSOPHY.]

PHILLIPS (SAMUEL). Guide to the Crystal Palace, and its Park and Gardens. 12mo. Lond., 1858.   D 11 Q 2

Essays from the *Times*; reprinted by permission. New ed. 12mo. Lond., 1852.   J 7 Q 24

Essays from the *Times*. 2nd series. New ed. 12mo. Lond., 1855.   J 7 Q 25

PHILLIPS (THOMAS), R.A. Letter to. [*See* DRUMMOND, H.]

PHILLIPS (SIR THOMAS). Wales: the Language, Social Condition, Moral Character, and Religions of the People, considered in their relation to Education. 8vo. Lond., 1849.   D 7 S 1

PHILLIPS (WILLIAM). Elementary Introduction to Mineralogy. New edition, with Alterations and Additions, by H. J. Brooke and W. H. Miller. 8vo. Lond., 1852.
                                                  A 10 P 7

[*See* CONYBEARE, REV. W. D.]   A 9 R 14

PHILLIPS (W. C.) Manual of Marks on Pottery. [*See* HOOPER, W. H.]

PHILLPOTTS (RT. REV. HENRY), D.D., BISHOP OF EXETER. Pastoral Letter to the Clergy of the Diocese of Exeter, on the Present State of the Church. 8vo. Lond., 1851.   G 13 S 31

[*See* PRICE, H.]   MJ 2 P 38

PHILO JUDÆUS. Philonis Judæi omnia quæ extant Opera. Fol. Francof., 1691.   G 30 Q 17 ‡

Works of Philo Judæus, the contemporary of Josephus; translated from the Greek, by C. D. Yonge, B.A. 4 vols. 12mo. Lond., 1854–55.   G 16 P 14–17

Fragments of; newly edited by J. R. Harris, M.A. 4to. Camb., 1886.   G 6 V 20

PHILOLOGICAL SOCIETY (THE). Proceedings and Transactions of, for 1842–79. 15 vols. 8vo. Lond., 1846–79.

PHILOMNESTE, JUNR. [*See* BRUNET, P. G.]

PHILOSOPHICAL INSTITUTE OF VICTORIA. [*See* ROYAL SOCIETY OF VICTORIA.]

PHILOSOPHICAL MAGAZINE. London, Edinburgh, and Dublin Philosophical Magazine and Journal of Science. 3rd, 4th, and 5th series. 104 vols. 8vo. Lond., 1832–85.   E

General Index for vols. 1–12, 3rd series. 8vo. Lond., 1839.   E

PHILOSOPHICAL RAMBLER, THE. [*See* WEATHERHEAD, G. H.]

PHILOSOPHICAL SOCIETY OF ADELAIDE. [*See* ROYAL SOCIETY OF SOUTH AUSTRALIA, *and* SCHOMBURGK, DR. R.]

PHILOSOPHICAL SOCIETY OF GREAT BRITAIN. [*See* VICTORIA INSTITUTE.]

PHILOSOPHICAL SOCIETY OF NEW SOUTH WALES. [*See* ROYAL SOCIETY OF NEW SOUTH WALES.]

PHILOSOPHICAL SOCIETY OF VICTORIA. [*See* ROYAL SOCIETY OF VICTORIA.]

PHILOSOPHICAL TRANSACTIONS OF THE ROYAL SOCIETY OF LONDON. [*See* ROYAL SOCIETY OF LONDON.]

PHILOSTRATUS (FLAVIUS). Life of Apollonius of Tyana; translated, with Notes and Illustrations, by the Rev. Edward Berwick. 8vo. Lond., 1809.   C 10 R 6

PHILP (ROBERT KEMP). Notices to Correspondents. 12th thousand. 12mo. Lond., 1869.   K 9 T 1

The Corner Cupboard: a Family Repository. 16th thousand. 12mo. Lond., 1869.   K 9 T 3

The Reason Why: a careful Collection of many hundreds of Reasons for things which, though generally believed, are imperfectly understood. General Science. 51st thousand. 12mo. Lond., 1876.   K 9 T 7

Enquire Within upon Everything; to which is added, Enquire Within upon Fancy Needlework. 725th thousand. 12mo. Lond., 1878.   K 9 T 2

PHILPOT (JOHN), ARCHDEACON OF WINCHESTER. Examination and Letters of. [*See* BRITISH REFORMERS 10.]

PHIPPS (HON. EDMUND). Memoirs of the Political and Literary Life of Robert Plummer Ward. 2 vols. 8vo. Lond., 1850. C 9 R 40, 41

PHIPPS (COL. R. W.) Memoirs of Bonaparte. [*See* BOURRIENNE, L. A. F. DE.] C 8 T 12–14

PHIPSON (MISS EMMA). Animal-Lore of Shakespeare's Time, including Quadrupeds, Birds, Reptiles, Fish, and Insects. 8vo. Lond., 1883. A 4 R 29

PHIPSON (T. L.) Meteors, Aerolites, and Falling Stars. With numerous Illustrations. 8vo. Lond., 1867. A 3 R 25

PHIZ. [*See* BROWNE, H. K.]

PHILON (FREDERIC). He would be a Soldier : a Comedy. [*See* MODERN THEATRE 8.]

PHŒBADIUS (SANCTUS), AGINNENSIS EPISCOPUS. Opera omnia. [*See* MIGNE, J. P., SERIES LATINA, 20.]

PHŒBE. [*See* HIDDEN TALENT, THE.]

PHŒNIX NEST (THE) ; edited by R.S. [*See* PARK, T.].

PHONETIC JOURNAL (THE). Vols. 32–45. Sm. 4to. Lond., 1873–86. E

PHOTIUS (CONSTANTINOPOLITANUS PATRIARCHA). Opera omnia. [*See* MIGNE, J. P., SERIES GRÆCA, 101–104.]

PHRANTZES (G.) [*See* BYZANTINÆ HIST. SCRIPT.]

PHRENOLOGICAL JOURNAL AND MAGAZINE OF MORAL SCIENCE. 9 vols. 8vo. Lond., 1839–47. A 12 S 1–9

PHRYNICHUS. The New Phrynichus ; being a revised text of the Grammarian Phrynichus, by W. G. Rutherford, M.A. 8vo. Lond., 1881. K 13 P 6

PHYSICUS. [*See* ROMANES, G. J.]

PHYSIONOMISTE DES DAMES. Nouveau Manuel complet du Physionomiste des Dames, contenant de nouveaux Aperçus résultant de leur Santé ou de leur Position dans la Société. 12mo. Paris, 1843. A 12 P 15

PIASSETSKY (P.) Russian Travellers in Mongolia and China. Translated by J. Gordon-Cumming. 2 vols. 8vo. Lond., 1884. D 5 Q 15, 16

PICCIOTTO (JAMES). Sketches of Anglo-Jewish History. 8vo. Lond., 1875. G 11 S 4

PICHLER (FRITZ). Wanderungen durch Steiermark und Kärnten. [*See* UNSER VATERLAND.] D 3 8 P 19 ‡

PICHOT (AMEDÉE). La Femme du Cordamié ; Scènes de la Vie Australienne. 12mo. Paris, 1862. MJ 1 R 32

PICKERING (CHARLES), M.D. Geographical Distribution of Animals and Plants. (United States Exploring Expedition). 2 vols. imp. 4to. Boston and Salem, 1863–76. A 31 P 13, 14 ‡

Chronological History of Plants. Imp. 8vo. Boston, 1879. A 5 Q 4

Races of Man, and their Geographical Distribution ; with a Synopsis of the Natural History of Man, by J. C. Hall, M.D. 8vo. Lond., 1851. A 1 V 5

PICKERING (EDWARD C.) Theory of Color. [*See* BEZOLD, DR. W. VON.]

PICKERING (MISS ELLEN). Charades for Acting. 12mo. Lond., 1843. H 3 P 28

PICKERING (GEORGE FERRERS). Gold Pen and Pencil Sketches ; or, the Adventures of Mr. John Slasher at the Turon Diggings. Illustrated. Roy. 8vo. Sydney, 1852. MH 1 T 5

Another copy. Roy. 8vo. Sydney, 1852. MJ 2 R 21

PICKERSGILL (JOS.) Victorian Railways Tourist's Guide. 8vo. Melb., 1885.* MD 6 P 13

PICKFORD (JOHN), M.A. Mahá-vira-charita ; the Adventures of the Great Hero Ráma : an Indian Drama. [*See* BHAVABHÚTI.]

PICO DELLA MIRANDOLA (GIOVANNI). Ioannis Pici, Mirandulae Concordiaeque Comitis, Theologorum et Philosophorum, sive controversia, Principis, &c. Editio vltima. Fol. Basileae, 1601. G 12 R 2 †

PICOT (CHARLES). République du Christ et Monarchie du Pape ; infaillibilité. 8vo. Paris, 1883. G 2 P 8

PICTET (ADOLPHE). Les Origines Indo-Européennes, ou les Aryas Primitifs. 2e éd. 3 vols. roy. 8vo. Paris, 1877. B 7 R 30–32

PICTET (CHARLES). Cours d'Agriculture Anglaise. 10 vols. 8vo. Genève, 1808–10. A 1 Q 29–38

Traité des Assolemens, ou de l'Art d'établir les Rotations de Récoltes. 8vo. Genève, 1801. A 1 R 43

PICTET (J. F.) Traité Elémentaire de Paléontologie. 3 vols. 8vo. Paris, 1844–45. A 10 Q 13–15

Traité de Paléontologie ; ou, Histoire naturelle des animaux fossiles, considérées dans leurs rapports zoologiques et géologiques. 2e éd. 4 vols. 8vo. Paris, 1853–57. A 10 Q 16–19

Atlas [to above]. 4to. Paris, 1853–57. A 3 P 15 †

PICTON (J. ALLANSON). Oliver Cromwell : the Man and his Mission. 8vo. Lond., 1882. C 10 S 16

PICTON (LIEUT.-GEN. SIR THOMAS), G.C.B., &c. Memoirs of, including his Correspondence, from originals in the possession of his Family ; by H. B. Robinson. 2 vols. 8vo. Lond., 1835. C 8 U 33, 34

PICTORIAL BEAUTIES OF NATURE; or, Sketches in various Departments of Natural History. With Illustrations. 4to. Lond, 1875.　　　　　A 8 T 22

PICTORIAL RECORDS OF THE ENGLISH IN EGYPT. [*See* EGYPT.]　　　　　B 2 R 48

PICTORIAL WORLD (THE). Illustrated Weekly Newspaper. 23 vols. fol. Lond., 1874-85.　　　　　E

PICTURE OF SYDNEY (THE). [*See* MACLEHOSE, J.]
　　　　　MD 2 R 47

PICTURES IN TYROL AND ELSEWHERE; from a Family Sketch-Book. 8vo. Lond., 1867.　　　D 8 8 47

PICTURESQUE TASMANIA. [*See* TASMANIA.] MD 5 P 2

PIDGEON (DANIEL), F.G.S., &c. Old-World Questions and New-World Answers. 8vo. Lond., 1884.　　D 3 R 39

PIDGEON (E.) [*See* CUVIER, G. C. L. D., BARON.]

PIDGEON (NATHAN.) Life, Experience, and Journal of. Written by himself. 8vo. Sydney, 1857.　MC 1 P 28

Another copy (in two parts). 12mo. Sydney, 1864.
　　　　　MC 1 P 29

PIDGIN (CHAS. F.) History of the Bureau of Statistics of Labour of Massachusetts, and of Labour Legislation in that State, 1833 to 1876. Boston, 1876.　　F 6 U 21

PIERCE (P. W.) Melbourne Commercial Directory, 1853. 12mo. Melb., 1853.　　　　　ME 4 P

Another copy. 12mo. Melb., 1853.　　　ME 4 Q

PIERER (H. A.) Pierer's Universal Lexikon. 19 vols. 8vo. Altenburg, 1867-71.　　　　K 9 U 7-25

PIERLUIGI. [*See* PALESTRINA, G. P.]

PIEROTTI (ERMETE). Jerusalem Explored. With Plates. 2 vols. fol. Lond., 1864.　　　　D 38 P 6, 7 ‡

PIERRE DE VAULX-CERNAY. Histoire de la Guerre des Albigeois. [*See* GUIZOT, F. P. G., 14, 15.]

PIERREPONT (EDWARD), B.A. Fifth Avenue to Alaska. 8vo. New York, 1884.　　　　　D 4 P 31

PIETERSZ (PIETER). [*See* CARSTENSZ, J.]

PIGAFETTA (PHILIPPO). Report of the Kingdome of Congo, a Region of Africa; and of the Countries that border round about the same. Drawen out of the writings and discourses of Odoardo Lopez, a Portingall; translated out of Italian by Abraham Hartwell. 8vo. Lond., 1597.　　　　　D 1 R 14

PIGAGE (NICOLAS DE). La Galerie Electorale de Dusseldorf. Ob. fto. Basle, 1778.　　　　A 9 8 1 †

PIGGOREET MURDER (THE). Murder of Mr. Thomas Ulick Burke; full particulars of the Trial of George Searle and Joseph Ballan at Ballarat, 1867. With Portraits. 8vo. Ballarat, 1867.　　　　MF 2 S 1

Trial of Searle and Ballan for the Murder of Thomas Ulick Burke, Esq., J.P. 8vo. Ballarat, 1867.　MF 2 S 1

PIGGOT (JOHN), F.S.A., &c. Persia, Ancient and Modern. 8vo. Lond., 1874.　　　　　B 1 P 1

PIGNA (G.) [*See* ARIOSTO, L.]

PIGOT (J.), & Co. London Alphabetical and Classified Commercial Directory. Roy. 8vo. Lond., 1837.　　E

PIKE (LUKE OWEN), M.A. History of Crime in England. 2 vols. 8vo. Lond., 1873-76.　　　F 6 U 9, 10

PIKE (NICHOLAS). Sub-tropical Rambles in the Land of the Aphanapteryx. 8vo. Lond., 1873.　　D 2 S 21

PILCHER (CHARLES E.) Common Law Procedure Acts, 1853 and 1857, and other Statutes and Enactments relating to the Practice of the Supreme Court of New South Wales; compiled and arranged by Philip G. Booty and Frank J. Smith. 8vo. Sydney, 1881.*　　MF 2 R 9

PILGRIM, THE. [*See* GREY, H.]

PILKINGTON (MATTHEW), A.M. General Dictionary of Painters. New edition; illustrated. 2 vols. 4to. Lond., 1810.　　　　　K 18 T 14, 15

PILOGERIE (JULES DE LA). Histoire de Botany-Bay; etat présent des Colonies Pénales de l'Angleterre, dans l'Australie. 8vo. Paris, 1836.*　　　MB 2 R 1

PILPAY OR BIDPAI. Anvár-i Suhaili; or, the Lights of Canopus, being the Persian Version of the Fables of Pilpay; or, the Book "Kailah and Damnah," rendered into Persian by Ausain Vá 'iz u' L-Káshifi; translated by F. B. Eastwick, F.R.S., &c. Roy. 8vo. Hertford, 1854.　　　　　J 8 V 14

Kalilah and Dimnah; or, the Tables of Bidpai; with an English Translation and Notes, by I. G. N. Keith-Falconer, M.A. 8vo. Camb., 1885.　　J 2 Q 24

Contes et Fables. [*See* CABINET DES FÉES, 17, 18.]

PIM (COM. BEDFORD), R.N. The Gate of the Pacific. 8vo. Lond., 1863.　　　　　D 3 T 41

Ship-building. (Brit. Man. Indust.) 12mo. Lond., 1876.　　　　　A 17 S 29

PIMBLETT (W. MELVILLE). Story of the Soudan War, from the Rise of the Revolt, July, 1881, to the Fall of Khartoum and Death of Gordon, January, 1885. 8vo. Lond., 1885.　　　　　B 1 Q 2

English Political History. 8vo. Lond., 1885.　F 5 T 24

PIN (L. E. DU). [*See* DU PIN, L. E.]

PINCOTT (FREDERIC), M.R.A.S. Analytical Index to Sir John W. Kaye's "History of the Sepoy War," and Col. G. B. Malleson's "History of the Indian Mutiny." (Combined in one volume.) 8vo. Lond., 1880. B 10 U 17 [*See* PALMER, PROF. E. H.]

PINDAR (PETER). [*See* WOLCOTT, JOHN.]

PINDAR. Epinician, or Triumphal Odes, in Four Books; togetherwith the Fragments of his lost Compositions; revised and explained by John William Donaldson, M.A. 8vo. Lond., 1841.　　　　　H 8 U 36

Odes of; translated by the Rev. C. A. Wheelwright. (Fam. Class. Lib.) 12mo. Lond., 1830.　　J 15 P 31

Odes of; translated by G. West. [*See* JOHNSON, S.]

Pindar: the Nemean and Isthmian Odes; with Notes explanatory and critical, Introductions, and Introductory Essays, by C. A. M. Ferrell, M.A. 8vo. Cambridge, 1883.　　　　　H 7 Q 23

Pindar: the Olympian and Pythian Odes; with Notes, &c., by Prof. B. L. Gildersleeve. 8vo. Lond., 1885.
　　　　　H 7 P 38

Translations from; by A. Philips. [*See* JOHNSON, S.]

PINDER (NORTH), M.A. Selections from the less known Latin Poets. (Clar. Press.) 8vo. Oxford, 1869. H 8 U 38

PINK (W. W.), AND WEBSTER (GEORGE E.) Course of Analytical Chemistry. (Weale.) 12mo. Lond., 1874.
　　　　　A 17 Q 13

PINKERTON (JOHN). Literary Correspondence of. 2 vols. 8vo. Lond., 1830.　　　　　C 9 Q 20, 21

General Collection of the best and most interesting 'Voyages and Travels in all parts of the World. Illustrated; and Index. 17 vols. 4to. Lond.,1808-14. D 10 U 1-17

Iconographia Scotia; or, Portraits of illustrious Persons of Scotland; with short Biographical Notices. Roy. 8vo. Lond., 1797.　　　　　C 4 W 24

Ancient Scottish Poems, published from the MS. Collections of Sir Richard Maitland, never before in print, &c. 2 vols. 8vo. Lond., 1786.　　H 7 Q 19, 20

Select Scotish Ballads. 2 vols. 8vo. Lond., 1783.
　　　　　H 7 U 1, 2

Enquiry into the History of Scotland, preceding the Reign of Malcolm III, 1056. 2 vols. 8vo. Edinb., 1814.
　　　　　B 13 R 17, 18

[*See* BARBOUR, J.]

PINKERTON (PERCY E.) [*See* DÜNTZER, H.]　C 4 S 40

PINTIANUS (F.) [*See* PLINIUS SECUNDUS, C.]　A 16 S 2 ‡

PINTO (MAJOR ALEXANDRE DE SERPA). How I crossed Africa from the Atlantic to the Indian Ocean; translated from the Author's Manuscript, by Alfred Elwes. With Illustrations. 2 vols. 8vo. Lond.,1881. D 2 T 2, 3

PIONEER OF THE WILDERNESS, A. [*See* ROSE, REV. —.]

PIOTROWSKI (RUFIN). My Escape from Siberia; translated by E. S. 8vo. Lond., 1863.　　　C 3 U 6

PIOZZI (MRS. HESTER LYNCH). Johnsoniana. [*See* JOHNSON, S.]　　　　　C 2 R 24

PIPER (MISS MARY ANDREWINA). [*See* COX, MRS. EDGAR.]

4 G

PIRANESI (GIOVANNI BATTISTA). Vedute di Roma. 2 vols. el. fol. Roma, 1778.　　　　　A 9 P 29, 30 ‡

PIRANESI (GIOVANNI BATTISTA ET C. FRANCESCO). Opere di. (Ital. and Lat.) 14 vols. at. fol. Roma, 1750-85.
　　　　　A 3 P 1-14 ‡

Le Antichità Romane.
Il Teatro d' Ercolano.
Della Magnificenza ed Architettura de Romani.
Il Campo Marzio dell' Antica Roma.
Vedute varie, Colonna Trajana, Antonina, &c.
Antichità d' Albano e di Castel Gandolfo.
Vasi, Candelabri, &c.
Diverse Maniere d' adornare i Cammini.
Monumenti dei Scipioni.
Opere varie di Architettura.
Bassirilievo della Chiesa de S. Apostoli, Vasi del Cav. Ghetzzi.

PISIDES (GEORGES). [*See* BYZANTINÆ HIST. SCRIPT.]

PISKO (PROF. F. J.) Lehrbuch der Physik für Ober-Realschulen. 8vo. Brünn, 1873.　　　A 16 R 1

PISO (LUCIUS MANLIUS). [*See* WARE, REV. W. E.]

PISTOLESI (ERASMO). Real Museo di Napoli. 16 vols. 4to. Napoli, 1824-67.　　　　　A 8 S 1-16

PITCAIRN (ROBERT). Criminal Trials in Scotland, 1488-1624. 3 vols. roy. 4to. Edinb.,1833. F 8 Q 9-11 †

Historical and Genealogical Account of the Principal Families of the name Kennedy. 4to. Edinb., 1830.
　　　　　B 12 V 30

PITHOU (PIERRE ET FRANÇOIS). [*See* CORPUS JURIS CANONICI.]　　　　　F 29 P 15 ‡

PITKIN (TIMOTHY). Statistical View of the Commerce of the United States of America. 8vo. New Haven, 1835.　　　　　F 6 U 20

PITMAN (MRS. EMMA RAYMOND). Florence Godfrey's Faith: a Story of Australian Life. Illustrated. 8vo. Lond., 1883.　　　　　MJ 1 S 41

PITMAN (ISAAC). Phonographic Teacher: a Guide to a practical acquaintance with the Art of Phonetic Shorthand. 12mo. Lond., 1887.　　　　K 20 P 8

Pitman's [System of Shorthand]. [*See* ANDERSON, T.]

Exercises supplementary to "Pitman's Manual of Phonography." [*See* THOMPSON, J.]

Phonetic Reader: a Course of Reading in Phonetic Shorthand. 12mo. Lond., 1887.　　　K 20 P 7

Manual of Phonography; or, Writing by Sound. 506th thousand. 12mo. Lond., 1887.　　　K 20 P 5

Phonographic Phrase-book; with the Grammalogues of the Reporting Style of Phonography. 12mo. Lond., 1871.　　　　　K 20 P 2

Phonographic Reporter; or, Reporter's Companion: an Adaptation of Phonography to Verbatim Reporting. 90th thousand. 12mo. Lond., 1872.　　K 20 P 2

PITT (CHRISTOPHER). Life and Poems of. [*See* CHALMERS, A., *and* JOHNSON, S.]

Vida's Art of Poetry translated. [*See* CHALMERS, A.]

Virgil's Æneid translated. [*See* CHALMERS, A.]

PITT (RT. HON. WILLIAM), EARL OF CHATHAM. [*See* CHATHAM, RT. HON. WILLIAM PITT, EARL OF.]

PITT (RT. HON. WILLIAM). Speeches of, in the House of Commons. 3 vols. 8vo. Lond., 1808.   F 5 P 2-4

Another copy. 3rd ed. Edited by W. S. Hathaway. 3 vols. 8vo. Lond., 1817.   F 13 P 37-39

Life of; by the Earl of Stanhope. 4 vols. 8vo. Lond., 1861-62.   C 4 U 21-24

Biography of. [*See* LAMARTINE, A. DE.]   C 5 S 11

Memoirs of the Life of; by George Tomline, D.D. 4th ed. 3 vols. 8vo. Lond., 1822.   C 9 Q 22-24

Three English Statesmen [Pym, Cromwell, and Pitt]; by G. Smith. 12mo. Lond., 1868.   C 1 T 43

The Age of Pitt and Fox; by R. O. Madden. Vol. 1. (*All published*). 8vo. Lond., 1846.   B 7 Q 34

PITT-RIVERS (LIEUT.-GEN. A. H. L. FOX-). [*See* FOX-PITT-RIVERS, A. H. L.]

PIUS IX (GIOVANNI MARIA MASTAI-FERRETTI). Pius IX; or, the First Year of his Pontificate; by Count C. A. de Goddes de Liancourt and J. A. Manning. 2 vols. 8vo. Lond., 1847-48.   C 3 U 44, 45

Pius IX; the Story of his Life to the Restoration in 1850, with Glimpses at the National Movement in Italy, by Alfred Owen Legge. 2 vols. 8vo. Lond., 1875.   C 6 U 20, 21

PIXLEY (FRANCIS W.) Auditors: their Duties and Responsibilities under the Joint Stock Companies Acts and the Friendly Societies, and Industrial and Provident Societies Act. 8vo. Lond., 1881.   F 6 U 25

Director's Hand-book. 8vo. Lond., 1886.   F 4 Q 26

PIZARRO (FRANCISCO). Life of; with some account of his Associates in the Conquest of Peru; by Sir A. Helps, K.C.B. 8vo. Lond., 1882.   C 3 U 7

Lives of Vasco Nunez de Balboa, and Francisco Pizarro; from the Spanish of Don M. F. Quintana, by Mrs. Margaret Hodson. 12mo. Lond., 1832.   C 1 R 9

PIZEY (S. V.) Paper on Victorian Manufactures and industries. 8vo. Adelaide, 1875.   MJ 2 R 9

PLACE (FRANCIS). [*See* BENTHAM, J.]

PLACITA DE QUO WARRANTO. Temporibus Edw., I, II, III, in curia Receptæ Scaccarij Westm. asservata. Fol. Lond., 1818.   F 21 R 5 ‡

PLACITORUM. In domo capitulari Westmonasteriensi asservatorum abbreviatio. Temporibus Regni Ric. I, Johann. Henr. III, Edw. I, Edw. II. Fol. Lond., 1811.   F 21 R 6 ‡

PLAIDY (LOUIS). Pianoforte Teacher's Guide; translated by Fanny Raymond Ritter. 8vo. Lond., 1882.   A 7 P 17

PLANCHÉ (JAMES ROBINSON), SOMERSET HERALD. The Armoury. [*See* WARING, J. B.]

The Brigand: a Romantic Drama. (Cumberland's Eng. Theatre.) 12mo. Lond., 1829.   H 2 Q 23

Cyclopædia of Costume; or, Dictionary of Dress, including Notices of Contemporaneous Fashions on the Continent, and a General Chronological History of the Costumes of the principal Countries of Europe. 2 vols. 4to. Lond., 1876-79.   K 5 P 26, 27

Descent of the Danube, from Ratisbon to Vienna, during the Autumn of 1827. 8vo. Lond., 1828.   D 8 T 1

The Extravaganzas of, 1825-71. Testimonial Edition. 5 vols. 8vo. Lond., 1879.   H 1 S 9-13

The Green-eyed Monster: a Comedy. (Cumberland's Eng. Theatre.) 12mo. Lond., 1829.   H 2 Q 18

William the Conqueror and his Companions. 2 vols. 8vo. Lond., 1874.   B 7 Q 10, 11

Recollections and Reflections of; Professional Autobiography. 2 vols. 8vo. Lond., 1872.   C 9 Q 25, 26

History of British Costume. 12mo. Lond., 1836.   A 7 P 25

History of British Costume. (Lib. Ent. Know.) 12mo. Lond., 1834.   K 10 R 33

The Jewess: a Grand Operatic Drama, founded on M. Scribe's Opera "La Juive." 8vo. Lond., 1835.   H 3 S 21

The Mason of Buda: an Opera. (Cumberland's Eng. Theatre.) 12mo. Lond., 1829.   H 2 Q 15

The Merchant's Wedding; or, London Frolics in 1638: a Comedy. (Cumberland's Eng. Theatre.) 12mo. Lond., 1829.   H 2 Q 11

[*See* STRUTT, J.; *and* ROWLEY, W.]

PLANCY (J. A. S. C. D. COLLIN DE). [*See* COLLIN DE PLANCY, J. A. S. C. D.]

PLANT (JOHANN TRAUGOTT). Handbuch einer vollständigen Erdbeschreibung und Geschichte Polynesiens oder fünften Erdtheils. 2 vols. 8vo. Leipzig, 1793-99.   MD 5 S 8, 9, 10

PLANTA (JOSEPH). [*See* COTTONIAN LIB.]   F 24 P 19 ‡

PLANTAGENET-HARRISON (G. H. DE S. N.) [*See* HARRISON, G. H. DE S. N. PLANTAGENET-.]

PLANTER, A. [*See* CEYLON.]

PLANTING: Useful and Ornamental. (Lib. U. Know.) 8vo. Lond. (n.d.)   A 1 8 4

PLATINA (BAPTISTA). Lives of the Popes; from the time of our Saviour Jesus Christ to the Reign of Sixtus IV; written originally in Latin, and continued from the year 1471, by Paul Rycaut. Fol. Lond., 1685.   C 2 W 18

Do vitis Pontificum Historia; quam a vita Christi merito auspicatus est ad Sixtum IV et Miscellanea. Sm. Fol. Venetiis, 1511.   C 14 R 19 ‡

PLATO. Works of : a New and Literal Version, chiefly from the Text of Stallbaum. 6 vols. 8vo. Lond., 1868–72.
J 10 Q 2–7

1. Apology of Socrates; Crito; Phædo; Protagoras; Phaedrus; Theaetetus; Euthyphron; Lysis; by Henry Cary, M.A.

2. The Republic; Timaeus, and Critias; by Henry Davis, M.A.

3. Meno; Euthydemus; The Sophist; The Statesman; Cratylus, Parmenides; and The Banquet; by George Burges, M.A.

4. Philebus; Charmides; Laches; Menexenus; Hippias Major; Hippias Minor; Ion; First Alcibiades; Second Alcibiades; Theages; The Rivals; Hipparchus; Minos; Clitopho; The Epistles; by George Burges, M.A.

5. The Laws; by George Burges, M.A.

6. Containing the doubtful works: Epinomis; Axiochus; Eryxias; On Virtue; On Justice; Sisyphus; Demodocus; Definitions; Timaeus Locrus, with Lives of Plato, by Diogenes Laertius; Hesychius, and Olympiodorus; Introduction to his Doctrines by Alcinous and Albinus; the Notes of Thomas Gray; and a General Index to the entire Work.

Works of Plato, viz., his fifty-five Dialogues and twelve Epistles, translated from the Greek. 5 vols. 4to. Lond., 1804. G 4 R 17–21 †

The Trial and Death of Socrates; being the Euthyphron, Apology, Crito and Phaedo of Plato; translated into English, by F. J. Church. 8vo. Lond., 1880. G 13 T 4

Life of Socrates, collected from the Memorabilia of Xenophon and the Dialogues of Plato. [*See* COOPER, J. G.] C 10 Q 41

Republic of Plato; translated into English, with an Analysis and Notes, by John Llewelyn Davis, M.A., and D. J. Vaughan, M.A. 12mo. Lond., 1872. F 2 P 24

Dialogues of Plato; translated into English, with Analyses and Introductions, by B. Jowett, M.A. 4 vols. 8vo. Oxford, 1871. J 16 U 28–31

Plato and the other Companions of Sokrates. [*See* GROTE, G.]

Scripta Græce Omnia, ad Codices Manuscriptos recensuit variasque inde Lectiones diligenter enotavit Immanuel Bekker. 11 vols. 8vo. Lond., 1826. J 13 T 21–31

The Parmenides of; with Introduction, Analysis, and Notes, by Thomas Maguire, LL.D., &c. (Dublin University Press Series.) 8vo. Dublin, 1882. G 2 Q 7

Republic of Plato, in Ten Books; translated from the Greek, by H. Spens, D.D.; with a preliminary Discourse concerning the Philosophy of the Ancients, by the Translator. Sm. 4to. Glasgow, 1763. F 12 P 5

Summary and Analysis of the Dialogues of Plato. [*See* DAY, A.]

Phaedo of Plato; edited, with Introduction, Notes, and Appendices, by R. D. Archer-Hind, M.A. 8vo. Lond., 1883. G 1 P 23

PLATT (JAMES). Essays: Business—Money—Economy Life—Morality—Progress. 2 vols. 8vo. Lond., 1883–84. F 4 T 1, 2

PLATTNER (C. F.) Manual of Qualitative and Quantitative Analysis with the Blowpipe; revised and enlarged by Prof. T. Richter. 2nd ed. Roy. 8vo. New York, 1873. A 5 T 26

PLAUTUS (MARCUS ACCIUS). Comœdiæ; ex Editione J. F. Gronovii, cum Notis et Interpretatione in usum Delphini; curante A. J. Valpy, A.M. 5 vols. 8vo. Lond., 1829. J 13 R 33–37

Comedies of Plautus; literally translated into English Prose, with Notes, by Henry Thomas Riley, B.A. 2 vols. 8vo. Lond., 1852. ·H 4 P 6, 7

PLAYFAIR (G. M. H.) Cities and Towns of China: ·a Geographical Dictionary. Roy. 8vo. Hongkong. 1879. D 11 V 3

The Playfair Papers; or, Brother Jonathan, the Smartest Nation in all Creation. 3 vols. 8vo. Lond., 1841. J 11 Q 4–6

PLAYFAIR (JAMES), D.D. System of Chronology. Fol. Edinb., 1874. B 14 U 1 ‡

PLAYFAIR (JAMES G.) Works of John Playfair. [*See* PLAYFAIR, JOHN.]

PLAYFAIR (JOHN). Works of [Edited by J. G. Playfair.]; with a Memoir of the Author [by Lord Jeffrey]. 4 vols. 8vo. Edinb., 1822. J 8 T 2–5

PLAYFAIR (SIR LYON), K.C.B. Chemical Principles involved in the Manufactures of the Exhibition as indicating the necessity of Industrial Instruction. [*See* LONDON INTERNATIONAL EXHIBITION, 1851.] A 16 Q 22

Lectures on Gold. [*See* GOLD.] MA 2 P 1

PLAYFAIR (LIEUT.-COL. R. L.) Travels in the Footsteps of Bruce in Algeria and Tunis. Illustrated. Roy. 4to. Lond., 1877. D 4 R 10 †

PLAYFAIR (WILLIAM). History of Jacobinism: its Crimes, Cruelties, and Perfidies. 8vo. Lond., 1795. B 8 U 37

PLAYFORD (FRANCIS). Practical Hints for Investing Money. (Weale.) 12mo. Lond., 1869. F 5 S 24

PLEASONTON (S.) List of Light-houses, Beacons, and Floating Lights of the United States. (Pam. 19.) 8vo. Wash., 1845. MJ 2 Q 8

PLENDERLEATH (REV. W. C.) The White Horses of the West of England. 12mo. Lond., 1886. B 4 Q 14

PLINIUS CÆCILIUS SECUNDUS (CAIUS). Letters of Pliny, the Consul; with occasional Remarks by Wm. Melmoth. 10th ed., revised. 2 vols. 8vo. Lond., 1805. C 8 U 39, 40

PLINIUS SECUNDUS (CAIUS). Natural History of Pliny; translated, with Notes and Illustrations, by John Bostock, M.D., &c., and H. T. Riley, Esq., B.A. 6 vols. 12mo. Lond., 1855–57. A 16 P 6–11

Naturalis Historiæ, Libri 34–36, c. 1–5, s. 4–43, comprising a History of Fine Arts, in connection with J. Sillig's Dictionary of Artists, by E. H. Barker. 8vo. Lond., 1836. A 8 Q 19

PLINIUS SECUNDUS (CAIUS)—*continued.*
Naturalis Historiæ; Libri 37, ex editione Gabrielis
Brotier, cum Notis et Interpretatione in usum Delphini.
14 vols. 8vo. Lond., 1826.   J 13 R 38–S 10

Historiæ Mundi, Libri, 37. Lugduni, 1582.   A 16 S 2‡
[*See* SCRIPTORES ROMANI.]   J 13 T 35

PLITT (JACOB THEODOR), TH.D.   De Compositione Evan-
geliorum Synopticorum. (Pam. O.) 4to. Bonn, 1860.
J 6 U 10

PLOETZ (CARL). Epitome of History, Ancient, Mediæval,
and Modern. Translated, with extensive Additions, by
William H. Tillinghast. 8vo. Lond., 1884.   B 14 Q 24

PLON (EUGENE).   Thorvaldsen: his Life and Works;
translated by Mrs. Cashel Hoey. Illustrated. Imp. 8vo.
Lond., 1874.   C 8 V 41

PLOWDEN (FRANCIS). Historical Letter to Sir Richard
Musgrave, Bart. 8vo. Lond., 1805.   G 2 P 28

Jura Anglorum: the Rights of Englishmen. 8vo.
Lond., 1792.   F 12 P 4

PLUMBE (SAMUEL), M.R.C.S. Popular and Impartial Estimate of the present Value of Vaccination, as a Security
against Small-pox, and of the Danger of encouraging or
tolerating the Inoculation of the latter. 8vo. Lond.,
1830.   A 12 S 33

PLUMBER AND SANITARY ENGINEER. [*See* EN-
GINEERING AND BUILDING RECORD.]

PLUMMER (ALFRED). Hippolytus and Callistus; Notes,
&c. [*See* DOLLINGER, PROF. J. J. I. VON.]

PLUMMER (JOHN). Our Colonies; being an Essay on the
Advantages accruing to the British Nation, from its possession of the Colonies. (Pam. Ab.) 12mo. Lond.,
1864.   MD 1 S 14

Industrial Self-help in 1864. 8vo. Lond., 1864.
MJ 2 Q 24

A Mayoral Year. [Compiled by John Plummer.] 8vo.
Sydney, 1885.   MB 2 R 3

Strikes: their Causes and their Evils, especially with
regard to the Machine Question. (Pam. 38.) 8vo. Lond.,
1859.   MJ 2 Q 25

Freedom of Labour; being a Defence of the Rights of
Industry. (Pam. 38.) 8vo. Kettering, 1858. MJ 2 Q 25

PLUMPTRE (C. E.) General Sketch of the History of
Pantheism. 2 vols. 8vo. Lond., 1881.   G 11 S 11, 12

PLUMPTRE (CHARLES JOHN). King's College Lectures
on Elocution. 8vo. Lond., 1881.   J 10 T 18

PLUMPTRE (REV. E. H.) [*See* DANTE ALIGHIERI.]
H 7 V 6, 7

PLUNKET (HON. DAVID). Life, Letters, and Speeches
of Lord Plunket; by his Grandson. 2 vols. 8vo. Lond.,
1867.   C 9 P 24, 25

PLUNKET (WILLIAM CONYNGHAM), LORD. Life, Letters,
and Speeches of; by the Hon. David Plunket. 2 vols.
8vo. Lond., 1867.   C 9 P 24, 25

PLUNKETT (HON. CAPT. EDWARD). [*See* JURIEN DE LA
GRAVIÉRE, CAPT. J. B. E.]   B 3 R 22, 23

PLUNKETT (JOHN HUBERT), A.B.   Australian Magistrate; or, a Guide to the Duties of a Justice of the Peace
for the Colony of New South Wales. 8vo. Sydney,
1835.   MF 1 Q 7

Another copy. New [3rd] ed., by Edwin C. Suttor, Esq.
8vo. Sydney, 1847.   MF 1 Q 8

Another copy. New ed., corrected and enlarged by
W. H. Wilkinson. 8vo. Sydney, 1866.   MF 1 Q 9
[*See* WILKINSON, W. H.]

PLUTARCH. Plutarch's Lives; translated from the original
Greek, with Notes, Critical and Historical, and a Life of
Plutarch, by John Langhorne, D.D., and William Lang-
horne, A.M. 2nd ed., by the Rev. Francis Wrangham,
M.A., &c. 6 vols. 8vo. Lond., 1813.   C 7 U 48–53

Plutarch; translated by John Langhorne, D.D.   (Fam.
Class. Lib.) 7 vols. 18mo. Lond., 1831–32. J 15 P 32–38

Plutarch's Lives; translated from the Greek, with
Notes and a Life of Plutarch, by Aubrey Stewart, M.A.,
and the late George Long, M.A. 4 vols. 8vo. Lond.,
1880–82.   C 2 P 33–36

Plutarchi Operum, Græce et Latine. 5 vols. roy. 8vo.
Paris, 1855–77.   J 18 V 1–5

Plutarch's Morals; translated from the Greek by several
hands; corrected and revised by William W. Goodwin,
Ph.D. 5 vols. 8vo. Boston, 1874.   G 4 Q 10–14

Plutarch's Morals: Theosophical Essay; translated by
C. W. King, M.A. 8vo. Lond., 1882.   G 8 S 23

Græcorum Romanorumque Illustrium Vitæ. Fol. Basileæ,
1542.   C 7 S 16 †

Lives of Timoleon and the Gracchi. Reprinted from
Langhorne's Translation, by Prof. Charles Badham. 8vo.
Sydney, 1881.   MC 1 Q 14

Shakespeare's Plutarch. [*See* SKEAT, REV. W. W.]
C 4 Q 29

POCKET DICTIONARY of the English and Armenian
[and Armenian and English] Languages. 2 vols. (in 1)
18mo. Venice, 1835.   K 11 S 8

POCKET DICTIONARY (NEW) of the English and Danish
[and Danish and English] Languages. 2 parts (in 1)
18mo. Leip., 1875.   K 11 S 17

POCKET DICTIONARY (NEW) of the English and Russian [and Russian and English] Languages. 18mo.
Leip., 1874.   K 11 S 26

POCKET DICTIONARY (NEW) of the English and
Swedish [and Swedish and English] Languages. 18mo.
Leip., 1875.   K 11 S 15

POCKNELL (EDWARD). System of Shorthand. [*See* ANDERSON, T.]

POCOCK (R.) History of the incorporated Town and Parishes of Gravesend and Milton, in the County of Kent. 8m. 4to. Gravesend, 1797. B 5 T 62

POCOCKE (RICHARD), LL.D., &c. Description of the East, and some other Countries. 2 vols. fol. Lond., 1743–45. D 38 Q 3, 4 ‡

PODMORE (FRANK), M.A. Phantasms of the Living. [*See* GARNEY, E.]

POE (EDGAR ALLEN). Poems of; with an Essay on his Poetry, by Andrew Lang. 12mo. Lond., 1881. H 5 Q 34
Works of [edited by the Rev. R. W. Griswold; with a Life, by N. P. Willis]. 4 vols. 8vo. New York, 1870. J 12 T 27–30
His Life, Letters, and Opinions; by John H. Ingram. With Portraits. 2 vols. 8vo. Lond., 1880. C 3 P 33, 34

POEMS. By J.F.E. 12mo. Sydney, 1881. MH 1 R 59

POETÆ LYRICI GRÆCI. Tertiis Curis recensuit Theodorus Bergk. 3 vols. 8vo. Leipsiæ, 1866–67. H 7 V 16–18

POETÆ SCENICI GRÆCI. [*See* DINDORF, W.]

POETICAL WORKS. Poetical Works of Oliver Goldsmith, Tobias Smollett, Samuel Johnson, and William Shenstone; with Biographical Notices and Notes. 8vo. Lond. (n.d.) H 7 P 39

POITEAU (A.) Histoire Naturelle des Orangers. [*See* RISSO, A.] A 23 S 23 ‡

POITEVIN (P.) Grammaire Générale et Historique de la Langue Française. 2 vols. 8vo. Paris, 1856. K 13 P 24, 25
Nouveau Dictionnaire Universel de la Langue Française, Nouvelle édition, revue et corrigée. 2 vols. 4to. Paris, 1868–69. K 3 S 3, 4 †

POKORNY (DR. A.) [*See* HANN, DR. J.] A 16 S 26

POLACK (J. S.) New Zealand: a Narrative of Travels and Adventures during a Residence in that Country in 1831–37. 2 vols. 8vo. Lond., 1838.* MD 5 T 7, 8
Another copy. New ed. 2 vols. 8vo. Lond., 1839. MD 5 T 11, 12
Manners and Customs of the New Zealanders. 2 vols. 8vo. Lond., 1840.* MD 4 S 9, 10

POLAND. The Poles and the Czar. Reprinted from *The British and Foreign Review.* 2nd ed. (Pam., 1.) 8vo. Lond., 1836. MJ 2 P 36

POLANO (PROF. H.) Selections from the Talmud; being Specimens of the Contents of that Ancient Book, its Commentaries, Teachings, Poetry, and Legends; also, brief sketches of the men who made and commented upon it. 8vo. Philad., 1876. G 11 S 8

POLAR SEAS AND REGIONS (THE). Discovery and Adventure in. [*See* LESLIE, PROF. SIR JOHN.]

POLDING (RT. REV. J. B.), ARCHBISHOP. Report containing the Pastoral Address of the Rt. Rev. Bishop, and the Proceedings of the Roman Catholics of New South Wales. 8vo. Sydney, 1836. MG 1 P 5
Pastoral Address. [*See* MACINTYRE, REV. W.] MF1Q4
[*See* ARCHBISHOPRIC OF SYDNEY; DUNCAN, W. A.; *and* EPISCOPAL SEES.]

POLE (WILLIAM), F.R.S. Life of Sir William Fairbairn, Bart., F.R.S., &c.; partly written by himself; edited and completed by W. Pole. 8vo. Lond., 1877. C 7 R 9
Philosophy of Music; being the substance of a Course of Lectures. 8vo. Lond., 1879. A 7 P 2
[*See* HYDRO-MECHANICS, *and* JEAFFRESON, J. C.]

POLEHAMPTON (REV. ARTHUR). Kangaroo Land. [New South Wales and Victoria.] 8vo. Lond., 1862.* MD 4 T 32

POLICE ADMINISTRATION. [*See* N. S. WALES.]

POLICE AND GAOLS. [*See* N. S. WALES.]

POLICE DISTRICTS. [*See* N. S. WALES.]

POLICE FORCE OF NEW SOUTH WALES. [*See* N. S. WALES.]

POLISH LANGUAGE. Slownik Polsko-Francuzki, Francuzko-Polski. Dictionnaire Français-Polonais, Polonais-Français. 4 vols. 18mo. Berlin (n.d.) K 11 S 9–12
Slownik Polsko-Francuzki. Dictionnaire Polonais-Français. Nowe wydanie. Imp. 8vo. Berlin, 1858. K 12 T 10

POLITICIAN (THE). No. 4. (Pam. Dd.) 8vo. Lond., 1794. F 12 P 22

POLITICIAN (THE): a Monthly Magazine of Politics and Literature. Vol. 1, Nos. 1, 2. 8vo. Sydney, 1851. ME 3 R

POLIZIANO (A.) Le Stanze. Fol. Firenze, 1805. H 27 Q 23 ‡
Miscellaneorum centuria prima. Panepistemon Lami. [*Bound with* Platina.] Sm. fol. Venetiis, 1496. CI4R19‡

POLKO (ELISE). Reminiscences of Felix Mendelssohn-Bartholdy: a Social and Artistic Biography; translated from the German, by Lady Wallace. 8vo. Lond., 1869. C 5 P 19

POLLARD (ALFRED W.), B.A. [*See* SALLUSTIUS CRISPUS, C.]

POLLARD (N. W.), C.E. Prize Essay on International Communication. 8vo. Melb., 1856. MF 1 Q 2
Another copy. 8vo. Melb., 1856. MF 3 P 8
Homes in Victoria; or, the British Emigrant's Guide to Victoria, to accompany Passage Warrants. 12mo Melb., 1861. MJ 2 P 30

POLLEN (JOHN HUNGERFORD), M.A. Universal Catalogue of Books on Art. 2 vols. sq. 8vo. Lond., 1870.
                     K 7 S 15, 16
Furniture and Woodwork. (Brit. Manuf. Indust.) 12mo. Lond., 1876.   A 17 S 35
Gold and Silver-smiths' Work. (South Kensington Museum, 16.) 8vo. Lond., 1879.   E
Ancient and Modern Furniture and Woodwork. (South Kens. Mus.) 8vo. Lond., 1875.   E

POLLITZER (S.), C.E. A Study about the River Murray. 8vo. Adelaide, 1883.*   MA 1 V 48

POLLOCK (DAVID). Modern Shipbuilding and the Men engaged in it. 8vo. Lond., 1884.   A 2 Q 15

POLLOCK (SIR FREDERICK), BART. Macready's Reminiscences. [*See* MACREADY, W. C.]   C 7 S 32, 33

POLLOCK (FREDERICK), M.A., &c. Essays on Jurisprudence and Ethics. 8vo. Lond., 1882.   F 12 Q 6
Spinoza : his Life and Philosophy. 8vo. Lond., 1880.
                     C 9 R 33

POLLOK (DAVID), A.M. Life of Robert Pollok, Author of "The Course of Time"; with Selections from his Manuscripts. 8vo. Lond., 1843.   C 4 Q 26

POLLOK (ROBERT), A.M. The Course of Time: a Poem in ten Books. 12th ed. 12mo. Edinb., 1833. H 7 Q 11
Life of ; by his brother, David Pollok, A.M. ; with Selections from his Manuscripts. 8vo. Edinb., 1843.
                     C 4 Q 26

POLO (MARCO). Travels of; the Translation of [William] Marsden, revised, with a selection of his Notes; edited by Thomas Wright, M.A. 8vo. Lond., 1854. D 10 Q 35
Book of Ser Marco Polo, the Venetian, concerning the Kingdoms and Marvels of the East ; newly translated and edited, with Notes, by Col. Henry Yule, C.B. 2 vols. 8vo. Lond., 1871.   D 9 U 16, 17

POLYBIUS. Abrégé des Commentaires de M. de Folard, sur l'Histoire de Polybe, par De Chabot. 2 vols. 4to. Paris, 1754.   B 18 Q 17–19 ‡
Polybii Historiarum Libri quinque, in Latinam conversi Linguam, Nicolao Perotto interprete. 12mo. Florentiæ, 1522.   B 12 P 30
General History of; translated by James Hampton. 3 vols. 8vo. Lond., 1809.   B 12 R 32–34

POLYCARP (SAINT). The Apostolic Fathers. [*See* LIGHTFOOT, RT. REV. J. B.]

POLYNESIAN LANGUAGE. Grammar of the Tahitian Dialect. 12mo. Tahiti, 1823.   MK 1 P 24

POLYSU (DR. G. A.) Romänisch-Deutches Wörterbuch. [*See* BARITZ, G.]   (14 Q 2

POMBAL (DOM SEBASTIANO JOSÉ DE CARVALHO E. MELLO), MARQUIS DE. Memoirs of the Marquis de Pombal; with Extracts from his Writings, &c., by John Smith. 2 vols. 8vo. Lond., 1843.   C 8 U 35, 36

POMFRET (REV. JOHN). Life and Poems of. [*See* CHALMERS, A., *and* JOHNSON, S.]
Poems upon several occasions. 10th ed. 12mo. Lond., 1736.   H 7 Q 12

POMPADOUR (JEANNE ANTOINETTE POISSON), MARQUISE DE. Secret Memoirs of Madame la Marquise de Pompadour; collected and arranged by Jules Beaujoint. 8vo. Lond., 1885.   C 8 U 44

POMPALLIER (JEAN BAPTISTE FRANÇOIS), BISHOP. Notice Historique et Statistique de la Mission de la Nouvelle Zélande. 8vo. Anvers, 1850.   MD 4 V 14

POMPEII. (Lib. Ent. Know.) 4th ed. 2 vols. 12mo. Lond., 1836.   K 10 R 40, 41

POMPEIUS SEXTUS FESTUS. [*See* FESTUS.]

PONSONBY (MRS.) Scotch College for Young Ladies: Prospectus; with an Address by the Lady Principal. (Pam. 36.) 8vo. Melb., 1862.   MJ 2 Q 23

PONTALIS (ANTONIN LEFÈVRE). John de Witt, Grand Pensionary of Holland ; or, Twenty Years of a Parliamentary Republic. 2 vols. 8vo. Lond.,1885. C 10 T 26, 27

PONTOPPIDAN (RT. REV. ERICH). Natural History of Norway, in two Parts; translated from the Danish Original. Illustrated with Copper Plates and a General Map of Norway. Sm. fol. Lond., 1755.   A 5 Q 6 †

POOL (G.) [*See* CARSTENSZ, J.]

POOLE (CHARLES HENRY). Attempt towards a Glossary of the Archaic and Provincial Words of the County of Stafford. 8vo. Stratford-upon-Avon, 1880. K 13 Q 8

POOLE (FRANCIS), C.E. Queen Charlotte Islands: a Narrative of Discovery and Adventure in the North Pacific. 8vo. Lond., 1872.   D 3 T 36

POOLE (G. F.) Marmont; or, Suffering without Guilt: a Tale, in six Cantos. 12mo. Sydney,1845. MH 1 P 49

POOLE (JOHN). Oddities of London Life; by "Paul Pry." 2 vols. 8vo. Lond., 1838.   J 4 R 31, 32
Tribulation ; or, Unwelcome Visitors: a Comedy. (Cumberland's Eng. Theatre.) 12mo. Lond.,1829. H 2 Q 11
Crotchets in the Air; or, an (Un)scientific Account of a Balloon Trip, in a Familiar Letter to a Friend. 8vo. Lond., 1838.   J 4 R 33
Little Pedlington and the Pedlingtonians. 2 vols. 8vo. Lond., 1839.   J 4 R 27, 28
Sketches and Recollections. 2 vols. 8vo. Lond., 1835.
                    J 4 R 29, 30
Anecdote Life of. [*See* TIMBS, J.]

POOLE (REGINALD LANE), M.A., &c. Illustrations of the History of Mediæval Thought in the Departments of Theology and Ecclesiastical Politics. 8vo. Lond., 1884.
                    G 11 S 10

POOLE (REGINALD STUART). Horæ Ægyptiacæ; or, the Chronology of Ancient Egypt. 8vo. Lond., 1851. B 2 S 1

Cities of Egypt. 8vo. Lond., 1882. D 1 Q 11

Catalogue of Greek Coins (British Museum): The Ptolemies, Kings of Egypt. 8vo. Lond., 1882. A 13 R 37

Catalogue of Greek Coins (British Museum): Italy. 8vo. Lond., 1873. A 13 R 30

Catalogue of Greek Coins (British Museum); by Prof. P. Gardner, and B. V. Head. Edited by R. S. Poole. 4 vols. 8vo. Lond., 1876–79. A 13 R 31–34

Lectures on Art. [*See* ART.] A 6 V 36

POOLE (STANLEY LANE-). Coins and Medals: their Place in History and Art; edited by S. L. Poole. Illustrated. 8vo. Lond., 1885. A 13 S 43

Coins of the Urturki Turkomans. [*See* NUMISMATA ORIENTALIA, 1.] A 2 S 15 †

Coins of the Sultáns of Delhi, in the British Museum. 8vo. Lond., 1884. A 13 S 24

Art of the Saracens in Egypt. 8vo. Lond., 1886. A 8 R 26

[*See* CHESNEY, MRS. LOUISA.] C 8 P 17

POOLE (THOMAS EYRE). Life, Scenery, and Customs in Sierra Leone and the Gambia. 2 vols. 8vo. Lond., 1850. D 1 R 6, 7

POOLE (W.), F.R.S. [*See* FAIRBAIRN, SIR W.]

POOLE (WILLIAM FREDERICK), LL.D. Index to Periodical Literature. 3rd ed., brought down to January, 1882. Imp. 8vo. Boston, 1882. Libr.

POOLEY (T. A.) Brewing, Distilling. (Brit. Manuf. Indust.) 12mo. Lond., 1876. A 17 S 32

POOR JOSEPH (a Tract in Russian). (Pam. 23.) 8vo. St. Petersb., 1832. MJ 2 Q 11

POOR LAW. Hints for the Practical Administration of the Poor Laws. (Pam. 14.) 8vo. Lond., 1832. MJ 2 Q 4

POOR LAW COMMISSIONERS. Two Reports addressed to inquire into the Administration and operation of the Poor Laws. 8vo. Lond., 1834. F 1 Q 10

Reports from His Majesty's Commissioners for inquiring into the Administration and Practical Operation of the Poor Laws. 8vo. Lond., 1834. F 1 Q 11

Report to Her Majesty's Principal Secretary of State for the Home Department, from the Poor Law Commissioners, on an Inquiry into the Sanitary Condition of the Labouring Population of England and Scotland. 3 vols. 8vo. Lond., 1842. F 1 Q 13–15

POOR LAW REPORTS. [*See* COODE, G.]

POORE (B. P.) Descriptive Catalogue of the Government Publications of the United States, 1774–1881. Roy. 4to. Washington, 1885. K 4 S 1 †

Federal and State Constitutions, Colonial Charters, and other Organic Laws of the United States. 2nd ed. 2 vols. fol. Washington, 1878. F 5 V 26, 27

POORE (REV. J. L.) [*See* GOSMAN, REV. A.]

POPE (ALEXANDER). Ensaio sobre o Homem de Alexandre Pope, traduzido verso por verso, por Francisco Berto Maria Targini, Barão de Saõ Lourenço. 3 vols. 4to. Lond., 1819. H 5 V 25–27

English Letters and Letter-writers: Swift to Pope. [*See* WILLIAMS, H.]

Works of. New ed. Including several hundred unpublished Letters, and other new Materials. 10 vols. 8vo. Lond., 1871–89. J 2 S 18–27

Life of; including Extracts from his Correspondence; by Robert Carruthers. 2nd ed. 8vo. Lond., 1857. C 4 P 14

Poetical Works of. Edited by Robert Carruthers. 2 vols. 8vo. Lond., 1858. H 7 Q 14, 15

Life and Poems of. [*See* CHALMERS, A., *and* JOHNSON, S.]

[A Biography]; by Leslie Stephen. (Eng. Men of Letts.) 8vo. Lond., 1880. C 1 U 27

Essay on Man; edited by Mark Pattison, B.D. (Clar. Press.) 12mo. Oxford, 1875. H 6 R 48

Satires and Epistles; edited by Mark Pattison, B.D. (Clar. Press.) 12mo. Oxford, 1872. H 6 R 48

Johnson['s] Lives of Dryden and Pope; edited, with Introduction and Notes, by Alfred Milnes, M.A. (Clar. Press.) 12mo. Oxford, 1885. C 14 P 9

[*See* BRITISH POETS, 3, HOMER, *and* OVIDIUS NASO, P.]

POPE (A.), JUNR. Upland Game Birds and Water Fowl of the United States. El. fol. N. York, 1878. A 9 P 26 ‡

POPE (REV. G. U.), D.D., &c. Tamil Hand-book; or, Full Introduction to the Common Dialect of the Language, on the Plan of Ollendorf and Arnold, for the use of Foreigners learning Tamil, and of Tamilians learning English. 3rd ed. 8vo. Madras, 1867. K 13 Q 13

The "Sacred" Kurral of Tiruvalluva-Nâyanâr. 8vo. Lond., 1886. G 11 S 14

POPE (JAMES H.) Health for the Maori: a Manual for use in Native Schools. 12mo. Wellington, 1884.* MA 2 S 39

The State: the Rudiments of New Zealand Sociology for the use of Beginners. 8vo. Wellington, 1887.* MF 3 Q 9

POPES. Lives of the. [*See* PLATINA, B.]

Ecclesiastical and Political History of the Popes. [*See* RANKE, L. VON.]

Historia de Vitæ. [*See* RAPHAEL, V.]

Recollections of the last four Popes. [*See* WISEMAN, CARDINAL.]

POPULAR ENCYCLOPEDIA (THE); or, Conversations Lexicon; being a General Dictionary of Arts, Sciences, Literature, Biography, and History. With Illustrations. 7 vols. roy. 8vo. Lond., 1882. K 2 P 1–7

POPULAR SCIENCE MONTHLY (THE). Vols. 1–27 8vo. New York, 1872–85. E

POPULAR SCIENCE REVIEW (THE). Quarterly Miscellany of Entertaining and Instructive Articles on Scientific Subjects. Vols. 1–22. 8vo. Lond., 1862–81.   E

POPULAR TUMULTS. Sketches of ; illustrative of the Evils of Social Ignorance. 8vo. Lond., 1837.   F 5 R 22

PORCHAT (JACQUES). [*See* GOETHE, J. W. VON.] J 13 U 1–10

PORNY (M. A.) Elements of Heraldry. 4th ed. 8vo. Lond., 1787.   K 10 S 13

PORPHYRIUS. Select Works of Porphyry, containing his Four Books on Abstinence from Animal Food, his Treatise on the Homeric Cave of the Nymphs, and his Auxiliaries to the Perception of Intelligible Natures ; translated by Thomas Taylor. 8vo. Lond., 1823.   J 6 T 20

PORPHYRIUS (PUBLILIUS OPTATIANUS). Opera omnia. [*See* JUVENEUS, C. V. A.]

PORSON (RICHARD). Tracts and Miscellaneous Criticisms; collected and arranged by the Rev. Thomas Kidd. 8vo. Lond., 1815.   J 10 V 12

Euripides Tragœdiae. [*See* EURIPIDES.]

Porsoniana. [*See* DYCE, REV. A.]

PORT APRA. Map of. [*See* MAPS.]   MD 5 P 9 ‡

PORT DARWIN. General Plan, showing natural Features of the Country, Towns, Reserves, Roads, and sectional Lands at, and in the vicinity of Port Darwin, Northern Territory of South Australia. 8vo. Adelaide, 1869.   MD 5 P 1 ‡

Port Darwin : its Soil, Climate, and Resources, and Prospects as a Gold-field ; also, a Descriptive Sketch of Charters Towers ; compiled by "Quills." With Map. 8vo. Melb., 1872.   MJ 2 R 16

[*See* SOUTH AUSTRALIA.]

PORT ESSINGTON. Copies of Correspondence relative to the establishment of a Settlement at Port Essington. (Parl. Doc., 41.) Fol. Lond., 1843.   MF 4 ‡

PORT JACKSON. Regulations to be observed in the Harbour of Port Jackson, New South Wales. Roy. 8vo. Sydney, 1859.   MF 2 S 4

PORT PHILLIP. Almanacs, Directories, &c. [*See* VICTORIA.]

PORT PHILLIP BAY. Illustrated Hand-book of the Bay. 12mo. Melb., 1876-77.   MJ 2 P 31

PORT PHILLIP FARMERS' SOCIETY. Transactions ; comprising the Rules and Regulations, Annual Report, &c. 8vo. Melb., 1857.   MA 1 Q 1

PORT PHILLIP GAZETTE (THE). 1838-40, 1842-45. 5 vols. fol. Melb., 1838-45.*   ME

PORT PHILLIP HERALD. 1840, 1844–46. 5 vols. fol. Melb., 1840–46.   ME

PORT PHILLIP MAGAZINE (THE). Vol. 1. 8vo. Melb., 1843.   MJ 2 R 22

PORT PHILLIP PATRIOT AND MELBOURNE ADVERTISER (THE). 1840–46. 4 vols. fol. Melb., 1840–46.   ME

PORT PHILLIP SAVINGS' BANK. Rules and Regulations of the Savings' Bank of Port Phillip. 12mo. Melb., 1847.   MJ 2 R 19

PORTER (FRANK THORPE), A.M. Gleanings and Reminiscences. 2nd ed. 8vo. Dublin, 1875.   J 11 S 4

PORTER (G. R.) Nature and properties of the Sugarcane ; with practical directions for the improvement of its culture and the manufacture of its products. 8vo. Lond., 1830.   A 1 R 11

Tropical Agriculturist : a practical Treatise on the cultivation and management of various productions suited to Tropical Climates. 8vo. Lond., 1833.   A 1 R 16

Progress of the Nation, in its various Social and Economical Relations, from the beginning of the Nineteenth Century. 8vo. Lond., 1842.   F 6 P 2

Another copy. New ed. 8vo. Lond., 1851.   F 6 U 7

Treatise on the Origin, Progressive Improvement and present state of the Silk Manufacture. (Lard. Cab. Cyclo.) 12mo. Lond., 1831.   K 1 U 4

Treatise on the Progressive Improvement and present State of the Manufacture of Porcelain and Glass. (Lard. Cab. Cyclo.) 12mo. Lond., 1832.   K 1 U 5

PORTER (G. W.) Hand-list of Bibliographies, Classified Catalogues and Indexes, placed in the Reading Room of the British Museum for Reference. 8vo. Lond., 1881.   K 7 R 28

PORTER (Miss JANE). Sir Edward Seaward's Narrative of his Shipwreck, and consequent Discovery of certain Islands in the Caribbean Sea. 3 vols. 8vo. Lond., 1831.   J 4 P 31–33

PORTER (JOHN), M.R.C.S., &c. History of the Fylde of Lancashire. 8vo. Fleetwood, 1876.   B 4 T 22

PORTER (REV. JOHN L.) Hand-book for Travellers in Syria and Palestine. [*See* MURRAY, J.]

PORTER (PROF. NOAH). Webster's Complete Dictionary of the English Language. [*See* WEBSTER, N.]

PORTER (SIR ROBERT KER), KNT. Narrative of the Campaign in Russia during the year 1812. 8vo. Lond., 1815.   B 12 U 15

Travels in Georgia, Persia, Armenia, Ancient Babylonia, &c., during the years 1817–20. 2 vols. 4to. Lond., 1821-22.   D 4 V 31, 32

PORTER (Robert P.), GANNETT (Henry), and JONES (William P.), A.M. The West, fiom the Census of 1880: a History of the Industrial, Commercial, Social, and Political Development of the States and Territories of the West from 1800 to 1880. With Maps and Diagrams. Roy. 8vo. Chicago, 1882.   F 4 T 9

PORTER (Major Whitworth). Life in the Trenches before Sebastopol. 12mo. Lond., 1856.   B 12 T 29

History of the Knights of Malta, or the Order of St. John of Jerusalem. 8vo. Lond., 1883.   B 15 R 13

PORTLAND. Trip to Portland, the Watering Place of the West. 8vo. Melb., 1880.   MJ 2 R 15

PORTLAND MUSEUM (The). Catalogue of, lately the property of the Duchess Dowager of Portland, deceased, which will be sold by auction by Skinner & Co., 1786. 4to. Lond., 1786.   K 8 Q 12

A Marked Catalogue, containing the Lots, what each respectively sold for, and the Names of the Purchasers of the 4,263 articles which constituted the Portland Museum, late the property of the Duchess Dowager of Portland, 1786. 4to. Lond., 1786.   K 8 Q 12

PORTLOCK (Major-Gen. John Elleson), R.E. [*See* Tate, R.]

PORTLOCK (Capt. N.) Voyage round the World, but more particularly to the North-western Coast of America, 1785–88, in the *King George and Queen Charlotte.* 4to. Lond., 1789.   D 9 V 24

PORTRAITS. Cabinet of Portraits, consisting of distinguished Characters, British and Foreign. 8vo. Lond., 1823–26.   MJ 2 R 21

POSNETT (Prof. Hutcheson Macaulay), M.A. Historical Method in Ethics, Jurisprudence, and Political Economy. 8vo. Lond., 1882.   G 11 S 13

Comparative Literature. 8vo. Lond., 1886.   J 9 S 23

POSTAL CONFERENCE. [*See* New South Wales.]

POSTAL SERVICE. [*See* New South Wales.]

POSTAL STATIONS. Map of. [*See* New South Wales.]

POSTANS (Mrs.) Facts and Fictions illustrative of Oriental Character. 3 vols. 8vo. Lond., 1844.   J 4 R 21–23

POSTANS (Capt. Thomas), M.R.A.S. Personal Observations on Sindh, the Manners and Customs of its Inhabitants, and its Productive Capabilities. 8vo. Lond., 1843.   D 5 T 39

A Few Observations on the Increase of Commerce by means of the River Indus. (Pam. 11.) 8vo. Lond., 1843.   F 12 P 9

POSTE (Beale). Celtic Inscriptions on Gaulish and British Coins. 8vo. Lond., 1861.   A 13 S 27

POSTE (Edward), M.A. Gaius' Elements of Roman Law. [*See* Gaius.]

4 H

POTEMKIN (Gregor Alexandrovitch), Prince. Memoirs of the Life of; comprehending original Anecdotes of Catherine II, and of the Russian Court; translated from the German. 8vo. Lond., 1812.   C 5 T 20

POTT (Prof. Aug. Friedr.) Etymologische Forschungen auf dem Gebiete der Indo-Germanischen Sprachen, unter Berücksichtigung ihrer Hauptformen, Sanskrit; Zend-Persisch; Griechisch-Lateinisch, Littauisch-Slawisch; Germanisch und Keltisch [und] Register. 2e auflage. 6 vols. (in 7) 8vo. Lemgo, 1859–76.   K 13 S 1–7

Anti-Kaulen oder mythische Vorstellungen vom Ursprunge der Völker und Sprachen. 8vo. Lemgo, 1863.   K 13 Q 27

Doppelung (Reduplikation, Gemination) als eines der wichtigsten Bildungsmittel der Sprache beleuchtet aus Sprachen aller Welttheile. 8vo. Lemgo, 1862.   K 15 R 27

Die Ungleichheit menschlicher Rassen, hauptsächlich vom sprachwissenschaftlichen Standpunkte. 8vo. Lemgo, 1856.   K 12 S 28

Die Zigeuner in Europa und Asien. 2 vols. 8vo. Halle, 1844–45.   A 1 W 4, 5

Die quinare und vigesimale Zählmethode bei Völkern aller Welttheile. 8vo. Halle, 1847.   K 14 Q 16

[*See* Ascoli, Prof. G. J.]

POTT (Mrs. Henry). Promus of Formularies and Elegancies (being Private Notes, *circ.* 1594, hitherto unpublished) by Francis Bacon, and elucidated by Passages from Shakespeare. Illustrated. 8vo. Lond., 1883.   J 2 S 17

POTTER (Rev. Canon). Reconstruction of Christendom. [*See* Church History.]   MG 1 R 15

POTTER (Elisha R.) Early History of Narragansett. 8vo. Providence, 1835.   B 18 H 3

Report upon Public Schools, Rhode Island. [*See* United States—Rhode Island.]

POTTER (Rt. Rev. John), D.D., Archbishop of Canterbury. Archæologia Græca; or, the Antiquities of Greece; with a Life of the Author, by Robert Anderson, M.D. 2 vols. 8vo. Edinb., 1827.   B 9 T 11, 12

Another copy. New ed. 2 vols. 8vo. Edinb., 1832.   B 28 T 2, 3

POTTER (Louis Joseph Antoine de). Vie et Mémoires de Scipion de Ricci, Evêque de Pistoie et Prato, Réformateur du Catholicisme en Toscane, sous le Règne de Léopold. 4 vols. 8vo. Paris, 1826.   C 5 V 29–32

POTTER (Rev. Robert), B.A. Voice from the Church in Australia: Eight Sermons. 12mo. Lond., 1864.   MG 1 P 11

POTTER (Rev. Robert). [Tragedies of] Æschylus. [*See* Greek Tragic Theatre.]

[*See* Euripides.]

POTTER (T.) Construction of Silos for Silage, &c. 8vo. Lond., 1886   A 1 Q 21

POTTER (REV. WILLIAM). Reply to the Statements made on the 27th September, 1873, in the *Age* newspaper; with which is incorporated the History of the Baptist Denomination in Emerald Hill, from the year 1854. 8vo. Emerald Hill, 1873.   MG 1 Q 39

POTTS (JOHN). One Year of Anti-Chinese Work in Queensland; with Incidents of Travel. 8vo. Brisbane, 1888.   MD 3 S 39

POTTS (ROBERT), M.A. Elements of Geometry. [*See* EUCLIDES.]   A 10 S 19

POTTS (T. H.), F.L.S. Out in the Open: a Budget of Scraps of Natural History, gathered in New Zealand. 8vo. Christchurch, 1882.   MA 2 V 18

POUCHET (F. A.), M.D. The Universe; or, the Infinitely Great and the Infinitely Little. New ed. Illustrated. Roy. 8vo. Lond., 1871.   A 15 U 22

POUCHET (GEORGES). Plurality of the Human Race; translated and edited by Hugh J. C. Beavan, F.R.G.S., &c. 8vo. Lond., 1864.   A 1 W 2

POUGENS (CHARLES). Voyage à la Nouvelle Galles du Sud. [*See* WHITE, J.]   MD 3 Q 32

POULSEN (V. A.) Botanical Micro-Chemistry: an Introduction to the Study of Vegetable Histology, prepared for the Use of Students. 8vo. Boston, 1884.   A 5 S 21

POVELSEN (BJARNI). Travels in Iceland. [*See* OLAFSEN, E.]   D 7 T 31

POWEL (DAVID), D.D. [*See* LLOYD, H.]

POWELL (PROF. BADEN), M.A., &c. History of Natural Philosophy, from the Earliest Periods to the Present Time. (Lard. Cab. Cyclo.) 12mo. Lond., 1834.   K 1 U 6
Another copy. 12mo. Lond., 1837.   A 17 T 10
Essays on the Spirit of the Inductive Philosophy, the Unity of Worlds, and Philosophy of Creation. 8vo. Lond., 1855.   A 3 T 20
[*See* ARAGO, F. J. D.]   C 8 S 37

POWELL (BADEN HENRY BADEN-), C.I.E. Manual of Jurisprudence for Forest Law, and those Branches of the General Civil and Criminal Law which are connected with Forest Administration. 8vo. Calcutta, 1882.   F 6 U 17

POWELL (FREDERICK YORK). Corpus Poeticum Boreale. [*See* VIGFUSSON, G.]

POWELL (GEORGE). [*See* HAVARD, H.]   A 6 V 11

POWELL (SIR GEORGE S. BADEN-). New Homes for the Old Country. 8vo. Lond., 1872.*   MD 5 V 18
State Aid and State Interference; illustrated by Results in Commerce and Industry. 12mo. Lond., 1882.   F 6 P 25

POWELL (HARRY J.), B.A. Principles of Glass-making; together with Treatises on Crown and Sheet Glass, by Henry Chance, M.A.; and Plate Glass, by H. G. Harris, A.M.I.C.E. (Technological Hand books.) 12mo. Lond., 1883.   A 11 p 9

POWELL (REV. J. GILES), B.A. Narrative of a Voyage to the Swan River; with an Account of that Settlement, from an authentic source. 8vo. Lond., 1831.*   MD 7 Q 35

POWELL (J. W.) First Annual Report of the Bureau of Ethnology, to the Secretary of the Smithsonian Institution, 1879–80. Imp., 8vo. Wash., 1881.   E
Introduction to the Study of Indian Languages; with Words, Phrases, and Sentences to be collected. 2nd ed., with Charts. 4to. Wash., 1880.   K 13 U 5

POWELL (WALTER). The Thorough Business Man: Memoirs of Walter Powell; by Benjamin Gregory. 8vo. Lond., 1871.   MC 1 P 40

POWELL (WARINGTON BADEN-). Canoe Travelling: Log of a Cruise on the Baltic, and practical Hints on building and fitting Canoes. 8vo. Lond., 1871.   D 8 S 39

POWELL (WILFRED), F.R.G.S., &c. Wanderings in a Wild Country; or, Three Years amongst the Cannibals of New Britain. Illustrated. 8vo. Lond., 1883.*   MD 5 U 25
Another edition. 8vo. Lond., 1884.   MD 5 U 27

POWER (FRANK). Letters from Khartoum, written during the Siege. 3rd ed. 12mo. Lond., 1885.   C 2 Q 25

POWER (JOHN). Handy Book about Books; for Book-lovers, Book-buyers, and Book-sellers. 8vo. Lond., 1870.   J 10 T 4

POWER (MISS MARGUERITE A.) Letters of a Betrothed. 12mo. Lond., 1858.   J 8 U 33

POWER (THOMAS P.) The Footballer (third year of publication): an Annual Record of Football in Victoria and the Australian Colonies. 8vo. Melb., 1877.   ME 5 Q

POWER (SIR W. TYRONE), D.A.C.G. Sketches in New Zealand with Pen and Pencil. 8vo. Lond., 1849.*   MD 5 R 22
Recollections of a Three Years' Residence in China; including Peregrinations in Spain, Morocco, Egypt, India, Australia, and New Zealand. 8vo. Lond., 1853. MD 5 R 24

POWLE (ANTOINETTE). Brief Memoir of Georgiana Elizabeth Thornhill. (Pam., 42.) 8vo. Hobart, 1853.   MJ 2 R 4

POYNTER (EDWARD J.) Lectures on Art. [*See* ART.]

POYNTER (EDWARD J.) AND HEAD (PERCY R.) Classic and Italian Painting: Text-book of Art Education. 8vo. Lond., 1880.   A 6 V 12

PRACTICAL ENGINEER, A. [*See* MACCARTHY, D. F.]

PRACTICAL MAN, A. [*See* LAND QUESTION.] MJ 2 Q 16

PRAED (MRS. CAMPBELL). [*See* PRAED, MRS. R. M.]

PRAED (MRS. R. M.) Australian Life; Black and White. With Illustrations. 8vo. Lond., 1885.   MJ 2 P 14
Longleat of Kooralbyn; or, Policy and Passion : a Novel of Australian Life. Australian edition. 8vo. Lond., 1887.*   MJ 2 P 15

PRAED (WINTHROP MACKWORTH). Australasia : a Poem which obtained the Chancellor's Medal at the Cambridge Commencement, July, 1823. 8vo. Lond., 1823. MH 1 S 6

Poems of ; with a Memoir by Derwent Coleridge, M.A. 3rd ed. 2 vols. 12mo. Lond., 1862. H 6 Q 29, 30

PRAIRIE FARMER (THE) : a Weekly Journal for the Farm, Orchard, and Fireside. 10 vols. fol. Chicago, 1876–84. E

PRANDI (FORTUNATO). Memoirs of Father Ripa; selected and Translated from the Italian. (H. and C. Lib.) 8vo. Lond., 1844. J 8 P 8

Another copy. 8vo. Lond., 1846. D 1 T 18

PRANTL (DR. K.) Elementary Text-book of Botany. With Woodcuts. 8vo. Lond., 1880. A 4 T 20

PRAT (HENRI). Études Historiques ; Moyen Age. 12mo. Paris, 1847. B 14 P 38

PRATT (ANNE). Flowering Plants, Grasses, Sedges, and Ferns of Great Britain, and their Allies the Club Mosses, Pepperworts, and Horsetails. 6 vols. 8vo. Lond., 1873. A 5 P 4–9

Ferns of Great Britain, and their Allies the Club Mosses, Pepperworts, and Horsetails. 8vo. Lond., 1871. A 5 P 14

PRATT (EUSTACE H. L.), M.D. Notes on Tumours and Cancers ; with Remarks on a new and painless Method of Treating them. 2nd ed. 8vo. Sydney, 1875. MA 2 S 17

PRATT (REV. GEORGE). Grammar and Dictionary of the Samoan Language. 2nd ed. 12mo. Lond., 1878. MK 1 P 20

[*See* LAWES, REV. W. G.]

PRATT (REV. JOSIAH), B.D. Remains of the Rev. Richard Cecil. 12mo. Lond., 1841. G 8 P 15

PRATT & SON. Hobart Town Directory and Book Almanac. 12mo. Hobart, 1857. ME 4 P

PRATT (W. T.) Colonial Experiences ; or, Incidents and Reminiscences of Thirty-four Years in New Zealand ; by "An Old Colonist." 8vo. Lond., 1877.* MD 4 R 28

PRAYER-BOOK. Suggestive Contribution in Aid of the Revision of the Liturgy of the Book of Common Prayer. (Pam. E.) 4to. Lond., 1871. MJ 2 S 2

Prayer Book Revision Society ; or, Association for Promoting a Revision of the Book of Common Prayer ; Report, 1871. (Pam. E.) 4to. Lond., 1871. MJ 2 S 2

PREBLE (REAR-ADM. GEORGE HENRY), U.S.N. History of the Flag of the United States of America, and of the Naval and Yacht-club Signals, Seals, and Arms, and principal National Songs of the United States ; with a Chronicle of the Symbols, Standards, Banners, and Flags of Ancient and Modern Nations. Illustrated. 3rd ed. Roy. 8vo. Boston, 1882. B 1 U 8

Chronological History of the Origin and Development of Steam Navigation, 1543–1882. 8vo. Philadelphia, 1883. A 2 Q 9

PREECE (W. H.), C.E., AND SIVEWRIGHT (J.), M.A. Telegraphy. (Text Books of Science.) 12mo. Lond., 1876. A 17 S 18

PREISS (LUDWIG), PH.D., &c. Plantae Preissianae sive Enumeratio Plantarum quas in Australasia Occidentali et Meridionali-occidentali, Annis 1838–41. 2 vols. 8vo. Hamburg, 1844–47. MA 1 V 24, 25

PREJEVALSKY (LIEUT-COL. N.) Mongolia, the Tangut Country and the Solitudes of Northern Tibet. 2 vols. 8vo. Lond., 1876. D 6 S 23, 24

PRENDERGAST (JOHN P.) Life of Charles Haliday. [*See* HALIDAY, C.] B 11 R 1

PREPARATION FOR DEATH ; or, the Churchman on a Sick Bed. (A Tract.) 12mo. Sydney, 1812. MG 1 P 41

PRESBYTER OF THE CHURCH OF ENGLAND, A. [*See* MODERN EPISCOPACY.]

PRESBYTER OF THE DIOCESE OF TORONTO, A. [*See* DARLING, REV. W. S.]

PRESBYTERIAN CHURCH ACT. Report from the Committee on the Presbyterian Church Act Amendment Bill ; with the Minutes of Evidence and Appendix. (Parl. Doc., 32.) Fol. Sydney, 1839. MF 4 ‡

PRESBYTERIAN CHURCH. [*See* CHURCH OF SCOT-LAND.]

PRESBYTERIAN MAGAZINE (THE). 5 vols. 8vo. Sydney, 1862–66. ME 3 Q

Another copy. Aug.-Sept., 1864. (Pam. G.) 8vo. Sydney, 1864. ME 3 R

PRESBYTERIAN TRACTS. 8vo. and 4to. Sydney, &c., 1879–81. MG 1 U 2

Presbyterian Church of Eastern Australia: Messrs. Ashley and Bates, and their connection with the Church.
Minutes of the Synod of the Presbyterian Church of Eastern Australia, 1879–81.
Letters to the Ministers, Office-bearers, Members, and Adherents of the Presbyterian Church of Eastern Australia ; by John S. Macpherson. East Maitland, 1880–81.
Reprint of Advertisement—Facts or Fictions? by Peter Macpherson, A.M.
Reply to certain Strictures contained in a Pamphlet recently published by the Rev. Peter Macpherson ; by the Rev. S. P. Stewart.
The Rev. S. P. Stewart on High Art, High Education, my Grammar, my Pamphlets, and a variety of subjects ; by the Rev. Peter Macpherson.
The Case of Messrs. Smith, Bates, and Ashley, in connection with the Presbyterian Church of Eastern Australia ; by the Rev. Peter Macpherson, A.M.
Letter to the Theoree Congregational Meeting ; by John S. Macpherson.
The Champion Scholarship of the Australian Colonies ; or, the Rev. George Sutherland on the Revised New Testament ; examined by the Rev. Peter Macpherson, A.M.
A Word to the Brethren in New South Wales ; by Arthur Paul.
Concerning the affairs of St. George's Church, Sydney : a Letter to the Moderator thereof, from "An Adherent."
Report of Proceedings of Synod of Eastern Australia. Session. November, 1881.

PRESCHAC (Le Sieur de). Contes des Fées. [*See* CABINET DES FÉES, 5.]

PRESCOTT (William H.) History of the Reign of Philip 2nd, King of Spain. 3 vols. 8vo. Lond., 1855–59.
B 13 U 4–6

History of the Conquest of Mexico, and the Life of the Conqueror, Hernando Cortes. 3 vols. 8vo. Lond., 1847.
B 1 R 34–36

History of the Conquest of Peru; with a Preliminary View of the Civilisation of the Incas. 2 vols. 8vo. Lond., 1847.
B 1 R 37, 38

Critical and Historical Essays. 2nd ed. 8vo. Lond., 1850.
J 8 Q 41

History of the Reign of Ferdinand and Isabella, the Catholic, of Spain. 3 vols. 8vo. Lond., 1838. B 13 U 18–20

Another copy. 7th ed., revised. Sq. 8vo. Lond., 1864.
B 13 U 21

Account of the Life [of Charles 5th] after his Abdication. [*See* ROBERTSON, W.]

PRESENT CRISIS (The): a Few Words to the People of England; by "A Whig." 8vo. Lond., 1852. MF 2 T 2

PRESSENSÉ (E. de), D.D. Jesus Christ: His Life and Works; translated by [Mrs] Annie Harwood [Holmden.] 12mo. Lond., 1871.
G 9 Q 3

The Martyrs and Apologists; translated by [Mrs.] Anne Harwood [Holmden.] 8vo. Lond., 1871. G 11 S 2

Study of Origins; or, the Problems of Knowledge, of Being, and of Duty; translated by [Mrs.] Anne Harwood Holmden. 8vo. Lond., 1883.
G 2 P 12

PRESTON (Edward). Index to Heirs at Law, Next of Kin, Owners of Unclaimed Money, Missing Friends and Legatees, and Creditors or their Representatives in Chancery Suits, who have been advertised for during the last 150 years; containing upwards of 50,000 names, relating to vast sums of Unclaimed Money. 4th ed. 8vo. Lond., 1878.
K 10 S 31

Another copy. 4th ed. 8vo. Lond., 1887. K 10 S 32

Index to Heirs at Law. [*See* CHAMBERS, R.]

Unclaimed Money: a Handy book for Heirs at Law, Next of Kin, and Persons in search of a clue to Un. claimed Money, or to the whereabouts of Missing Rela. tives and Friends. 2nd thousand. 12mo. Lond., 1878.
K 10 S 6

PRESTON (Elliott W.) Lord Byron vindicated; by "Marfied." Sm. 4to. Lond., 1876. H 7 P 21

PRESTON (Harriet W.) [*See* MISTRAL, F.]

PRESTON (T. R.) Three Years' Residence in Canada, from 1837 to 1839. 2 vols. 8vo. Lond., 1840. D 3 R 6, 7

PRESTON (W.) Illustrations of New South Wales. [*See* WALLIS, Capt. J.]
MH I R 27 †

PRESTWICH (J.) Geology: Chemical, Physical, and Stratigraphical. 8vo. Oxford, 1886. A 9 S 39

Tables of Temperature of the Sea at different depths beneath the surface. (Royal Soc. Pubs.) 4to. Lond., 1876.
A 11 P 3 †

PREUSSISCHE EXPEDITION NACH OST-ASIEN (Die). Ansichten aus Japan, China, und Siam. 4to. Berlin, 1864–76.
D 10 P 13 ‡

Die Preussische Expedition nach Oost-Asien nach amtlichen Quellen. 7 vols. roy. 8vo. Berlin, 1864–76.
D 5 U 9–15

1–4. [Reisebericht.]
5. Botanischer Theil. Bearbeitet von Georg von Martens.
6, 7. Zoologischer Theil. Bearbeitet von Prof. Dr. Eduard von Martens.

PREVILLE (Pierre Louis Dubus). [*See* DUBUS-PREVILLE, P. L.]

PREVOST (Antoine François). Histoire Générale des Voyages, ou Nouvelle Collection de toutes les Relations de Voyages par Mer et par Terre, qui ont été publiées jusqu'à présent dans les différentes Langues de toutes les Nations connues. 25 vols. 4to. La Haye, 1747–80. D 10 T 1–25

PRICE (Anne N.) True to the Best. 8vo. Lond. (n.d.)
MJ 1 U 23

PRICE (Bonamy). Chapters on Practical Political Economy; being the Substance of Lectures delivered in the University of Oxford. 2nd ed. 8vo. Lond., 1882.
F 5 T 5

Currency and Banking. 8vo. Lond., 1876. F 5 R 11

PRICE (Rev. C.) [Letter] To the Rev. T. C. Ewing, Pitt Town, New South Wales. (Pam. 42.) 8vo. Launceston, 1855.
MJ 2 R 4

[*See* ADDRESS TO PARENTS.] MG 1 P 48

PRICE (Daniel). System of Sheep-grazing and Manage. ment, as practised in Romney Marsh. 4to. Lond., 1809.
A 1 T 1

PRICE (Major David). Memoirs of the Emperor Johanqueir. [*See* JOHANQUEIR.] C 4 V 23

PRICE (E. D.) [*See* HAZELL'S ANNUAL CYCLOPÆDIA.]

PRICE (Eli K.) Some Phases of Modern Philosophy. The Glacial Epochs. Read before the American Philo. sophical Society. (Pam. Cl.) 8vo. Philadelphia, 1872–76.
A 16 U 21

PRICE (Fowler Boyd). [*See* STUD-BOOK OF NEW SOUTH WALES, The.]

PRICE (F. G. H.), F.G.S., &c. Hand-book of London Bankers, 1677–1876. 8vo. Lond., 1876. F 5 R 4

PRICE (H.) Letter to Bishop Phillpotts. (Pam. 3) 12mo. Lond., 1838.
MJ 2 P 38

PRICE (JOHN). Biographical Memoir of the late Mr. John Price; with an Account of the Assassination, Inquest, and Funeral. (Pam. 29.) 8vo. Melb.,1857. MJ 2 Q 17

PRICE (REV. JOHN), D.D. Mémoires de. [*See* GUIZOT F. P. G., 2.]

PRICE (REES), M.R.C.S. Critical Inquiry into the Nature and Treatment of the Case of H.R.H. the Princess Charlotte of Wales and her infant Son. [*See* HIST. PAMS.]

PRICE (RICHARD), D.D. Observations on Reversionary Payments; on Schemes for providing Annuities for Widows, &c. 2 vols. 8vo. Lond., 1812. F 6 U 22, 23

PRICE (MAJOR SIR R. LAMBERT), BART., F.R.G.S., &c. The Two Americas; an Account of Sport and Travel; with Notes on Men and Manners in North and South America. With Illustrations. 8vo. Lond., 1877. D 3 T 13

PRICE (SIR UVEDALE). On the Picturesque; with an Essay on the Origin of Taste, and much original matter; by Sir Thomas Dick Lauder, Bart. With Illustrations. 8vo. Lond., 1842. A 7 Q 31

PRICE OF WHEAT (THE). Price of Wheat in Europe: the Past a Test for the Future; Present Prices and Stocks of Wheat in Europe. Agricultural Statistics. (Reprinted from the *Economist.*) 8vo. Lond., 1850. F 6 V 10

PRICHARD (JAMES COWLES), M.D., &c. Eastern Origin of the Celtic Nations, proved by a Comparison of their Dialect with the Sanskrit, Greek, Latin, and Teutonic Languages, forming a Supplement to Researches into the Physical History of Mankind. Edited by R. G. Latham, MA., &c. 8vo. Lond., 1857. B 7 U 31
Natural History of Man. 2 vols. 8vo. Lond., 1855. A 2 P 16, 17
Six Ethnographical Maps [to above]; with explanatory Notice. 1st and 2nd eds. 2 vols. fol. Lond., 1861. A 1 P 3, 4 ‡
Researches into the Physical History of Mankind. 5 vols. 8vo. Lond., 1841–47. A 1 W 13–17

PRICKETT (REV. MARMADUKE). [*See* FULLER, REV. T.]

PRIDDEN (REV. W.), M.A. Australia: its History and Present Condition; containing an Account both of the Bush and of the Colonies, with their respective Inhabitants. 12mo. Lond., 1843. MB 1 P 4
Another copy. New ed. 12mo. Lond., 1851. MB 1 P 5

PRIDEAUX (HUMPHREY), D.D. Old and New Testament Connected, in the History of the Jews, and Neighbouring Nations. 18th ed. 4 vols. 8vo. Lond.,1821. G 11 S 15–18
Another copy. 20th ed. 2 vols. 8vo. Lond., 1831. G 11 S 19, 20

PRIDEAUX (T. S.) Economy of Fuel, particularly with reference to Reverberatory Furnaces for the manufacture of Iron and to Steam Boilers. (Weale.) 12mo. Lond., 1853. A 17 P 26

[*See* CLARK, D. K.] A 17 Q 10

PRIDHAM (CHARLES), B.A., &c. Mauritius and its Dependencies. [England's Colonial Empire.] 8vo. Lond., 1846. B 1 P 23
Historical, Political, and Statistical Account of Ceylon and its Dependencies. 2 vols. 8vo. Lond., 1849. B 10 T 36, 37

PRIESTLEY (JOHN). On the Physiological Action of Vanadium. (Roy. Soc. Pubs., 3. 4to. Lond., 1876. A 11 P 4 †

PRIESTLEY (JOSEPH), LL.D., &c. Lectures on History and General Policy; with an Essay on a Course of Liberal Education; edited by J. T. Rutt. 8vo. Lond., 1826. B 36 T 1

PRIMASIUS (ADRUMETANUS EPISCOPUS). Opera omnia. [*See* MIGNE, J. P., SERIES LATINA, 68.]

PRIME (E. D. G.), D.D. Around the World: Sketches of Travel through many Lands and over many Seas. 8vo. New York, 1874. D 10 R 36

PRIME (F.), JUNR. [*See* COTTA, B. VON.]

PRIME (WILLIAM C.) Boat Life in Egypt and Nubia. 8vo. Lond., 1857. D 1 P 18

PRIMEVAL MAN: the Origin, Declension, and Restoration of the Race. 8vo. Lond., 1864. G 11 P 26

PRINCE (JOHN), VICAR OF BERRY-POMEROY. Danmonii Orientales Illustres; or, the Worthies of Devon. New ed., with Notes. 4to. Lond., 1810. C 2 W 23

PRINCE (JOHN CRITCHLEY). Life of; by R. A. Douglas Lithgow, LL.D., &c. 8vo. Manchester,1880. C 3 U 36
Poetical Works of. 2 vols. 8vo. Manchester, 1880. H 8 P 5, 6

PRINCE (THOMAS), M.A. Chronological History of New England, in the form of Annals. 8vo. Boston, 1826. B 1 R 28

PRINCE (REV. T.) Catalogue of Prince Library. [*See* BOSTON PUBLIC LIBRARY.] K 9 R 30 †

PRINCE ALFRED HOSPITAL, SYDNEY. Description of the proposed Buildings. Messrs. Mansfield Bros., Architects. (Pam. Ck.) 4to. Sydney, 1874. A 15 U 1

PRING (RATCLIFFE). Queensland Statutes. [*See* QUEENSLAND STATUTES.]

PRINGLE (R. O.) Live Stock on the Farm. 8vo. Edinb., 1886. A 1 Q 15

PRINSEP (MRS. AUGUSTUS). Journal of a Voyage from Calcutta to Van Diemen's Land. [*See* PRINSEP, A.] MD 2 R 6

PRINSEP (AUGUSTUS). Journal of a Voyage from Calcutta to Van Diemen's Land. From original Letters, selected by Mrs. A. Prinsep. 12mo. Lond., 1833. MD 2 R 6
Another copy. 2nd ed. 12mo. Lond., 1833. MD 2 R 7

PRINSEP (Henry T.) Tibet, Tartary, and Mongolia: their Social and Political Condition. 8vo. Lond., 1851.
D 5 R 47

PRINSEP (Rev. James). Essays on Indian Antiquities, Historic, Numismatic, and Palæographic; to which are added his useful Tables, illustrative of Indian History, Chronology, Modern Coinages, Weights, Measures, &c. Edited by Edward Thomas. With Illustrations. 2 vols. 8vo. Lond., 1858.
B 10 T 34, 35

PRINTING MACHINERY. List of Technical Terms relating to Printing Machinery. 12mo. Lond., 1882.
A 11 P 17

PRIOR (James). Memoir of the Life and Character of the Right Hon. Edmund Burke; with Specimens of his Poetry and Letters, and an Estimate of his Genius and Talents, &c. 2nd ed. 2 vols. 8vo. Lond., 1826.
C 6 T 2, 3

Life of Oliver Goldsmith, M.B., from a variety of original Sources. [*See* Goldsmith, O.]
C 8 Q 15, 16

PRIOR (Matthew). Poetical Works of; with a Life, by the Rev. John Mitford. 2 vols. 12mo. Boston, 1860.
H 8 R 3, 4

Life and Poems of. [*See* Chalmers, A., *and* Johnson, S.]
[*See* British Poets 3.]

PRISCUS. [*See* Byzantinæ Hist. Script.]

PRISON DISCIPLINE SOCIETY. Reports of the Board of Managers of the Prison Discipline Society. 3 vols. 8vo. Boston, 1826-36.
F 1 Q 16-18

PRISON MATRON, A. [*See* Robinson, F. W.]

PRISSE D'AVENNES (E.) Histoire de l'Art Egyptien, d'après les Monuments depuis les Temps les plus reculés jusqu'à la Domination Romaine. Atlas. 2 vols. el. fol. Paris, 1879.
A 4 P 6 †

Text, par Marchandon de la Faye (d'après les Notes de l'Auteur.) Roy. 4to. Paris, 1879.
A 4 P 6 †

PRITCHARD (Prof. C.) Uranometria Nova Oxoniensis: Magnitudes of all Stars visible to the Naked Eye. Roy. 8vo. Oxford, 1885.
A 3 U 19

PRITCHARD (Dr. E. W.) Complete Report of the Trial of, for the alleged poisoning of his Wife and Mother-in-Law. 3rd ed. 8vo. Edinb., 1865.
MF 2 S 1

PRITCHARD (T. S.) [*See* Burn, Richard.]

PRITCHARD (Rev. W. Charles). Lecture [on] The Mission of St. Augustine and its Results. [*See* Church History.]

Prisoner of Ham. [*See* Napoleon III.]

PRITCHARD (W. T.), F.R.G.S., &c. Polynesian Reminiscences; or, Life in the South Pacific Islands. 8vo. Lond., 1866.*
MD 1 U 12

PRIVY COUNCIL, LONDON. Reports of Cases heard and determined by the Judicial Committee and the Lords of Her Majesty's Most Honorable Privy Council. (New Series.) Vols. 6, 7, 10y. 8vo. Lond., 1869-71.
E

PRIZE ESSAYS. [*See* Victorian Government Prize Essays.]

PROBYN (J. W.) Correspondence relative to the Budgets of various Countries. (Pam. Je.) 8vo. Lond., 1877.
F 6 P 10

Another copy. 8vo. Lond., 1877.
F 6 P 23

Systems of Land Tenure in various Countries: a Series of Essays. 8vo. Lond., 1881.
F 5 Q 20

Local Government and Taxation in the United Kingdom. [*See* Cobden Club.]

Italy, from the Fall of Napoleon 1, in 1815, to the Death of Victor Emanuel, in 1878. 8vo. Lond., 1884.
B 11 V 17

[*See* Cobden Club.]

PROCLUS (Sanctus), Constantinopolitanus Archiepiscopus. Opera omnia. [*See* Migne, J. P., Series Græca, 65.]

PROCOPIUS. [*See* Byzantinæ Hist. Script.]

PROCOPIUS GAZÆUS. Opera omnia. [*See* Migne, J. P., Series Græca, 87.]

PROCTER (Adelaide Anne). Legends and Lyrics; with an Introduction by Charles Dickens. 4to. Lond., 1866.
H 6 S 27

PROCTER (Bryan Waller), "Barry Cornwall." English Songs, and other Small Poems. 12mo. Lond., 1832.
H 6 Q 17

Charles Lamb: a Memoir. 8vo. Lond., 1866.
C 7 P 39

PROCTER (H. R.) Tanning: a Treatise on the Conversion of Skins into Leather. 8vo. Lond., 1885. A 11 P 2

PROCTOR (Richard A.), B.A. The Universe and the coming Transits; presenting Researches into, and New Views respecting the Condition of the Heavens; together with an Investigation of the Conditions of the coming Transits of Venus. 8vo. Lond., 1874.
A 3 S 37

Transits of Venus; Past and Coming. 8vo. Lond., 1874.
A 3 R 41

Saturn and its System. 8vo. Lond., 1865.
A 3 S 35

Science By-ways; to which is appended an Essay entitled "Money for Science." 8vo. Lond., 1875. A 3 R 39

Our Place among Infinities. 8vo. Lond., 1875.
A 3 R 43

Star Atlas for the Library, the School, and the Observatory; showing the Stars visible to the naked eye, and fifteen hundred objects of interest, in twelve circular Maps on the Equidistant Projection; with two Index Plates. 2nd ed. Fol. Lond., 1870.
A 23 S 18 ‡

The Sun: Ruler, Fire, Light, and Life of the Planetary System. 8vo. Lond., 1871.
A 3 R 38

PROCTOR (RICHARD A.), B.A.—*continued.*

Essays on Astronomy: a series of Papers on Planets and Meteors, the Sun, the Sun-surrounding Space; Stars and Star Cloudlets, and a Dissertation on the approaching Transits of Venus; with a Sketch of the Life, &c. of Sir John Herschel. 8vo. Lond., 1872.   A 3 S 38

The Orbs around us: a series of familiar Essays on the Moon and Planets, Meteors and Comets, the Sun and Coloured Pairs of Suns. 8vo. Lond., 1872. A 3 R 44

Hand-book of the Stars. 8vo. Lond., 1866.   A 3 R 14

Other Worlds than ours. 8vo. Lond., 1870.   A 3 R 42

Light Science for Leisure Hours: a Series of Familiar Essays on Scientific Subjects, Natural Phenomena; with a Sketch of the Life of Mary Somerville. 1st, 2nd, and 3rd Series. 3 vols. 8vo. Lond., 1871–83. A 3 R 45–47

Pleasant ways in Science. 8vo. Lond., 1879.   A 16 P 12

Familiar Science Studies. 8vo. Lond., 1882.   A 17 T 27

Studies of Venus—Transits: an Investigation of the Circumstances of the Transits of Venus in 1874 and 1882. Originally forming part of "The Universe and Coming Transits." With Illustrations. 8vo. Lond., 1882.   A 3 S 36

Star Atlas for Students and Observers, showing 6,000 Stars and 1,500 Double Stars, Nebulæ, &c., in twelve Maps on the Equidistant Projection; with Index Maps on the Stereographic Projection. 4th ed. Fol. Lond., 1877.   A 22 S 19 ‡

Universe of Suns, and other Science Gleanings. With eleven Illustrations. 8vo. Lond., 1884.   A 3 R 40

Expanse of Heaven: a series of Essays on the Wonders of the Firmament. 2nd ed. 8vo. Lond., 1874. A 3 R 12

Great Pyramid: Observatory, Tomb, and Temple. With Illustrations. 8vo. Lond., 1883.   A 3 R 36

Mysteries of Time and Space. With Illustrations. 8vo. Lond., 1883.   A 3 R 37

How to Play Whist; with the Laws and Etiquette of Whist. 8vo. Lond., 1885.   A 17 U 20

Treatise on the Cycloids and all forms of Cycloidal Curves. 8vo. Lond., 1878.   A 10 S 30

[*See* KNOWLEDGE.]

PROCTOR (RICHARD WRIGHT). Memorials of Bygone Manchester; with Glimpses of the Environs. 4to. Manchester, 1880.   B 5 V 29

PROCTOR (THOMAS). A Gorgeous Gallery of Gallant Inventions. [*See* PARK, T.]

PROESCHEL (F.), F.R.S.V. Atlas, containing a Map of Australasia, accompanied by a brief Chronological Outline of the Marine Discoveries of its different Islands, and the Inland Discoveries and Settlement of the different Provinces of the Main Island of Australia. Roy. fol. Lond., 1863.   MD 5 S 9 ‡

Commercial and Agricultural Map of Victoria. Drawn, reduced, and completed from the Government County Maps. Roy 4to. Melb. (n.d.)   MD 5 S 15 ‡

PROPERTIUS (SEXTUS AURELIUS). Opera omnia, ex Editione Ch. Th. Kuinoelis, cum Notis et interpretatione in usum Delphini. Curante A. J. Valpy. 2 vols. 8vo. Lond., 1822.   J 13 S 14, 15

Erotica: the Elegies of Propertius, the Satyricon of Petronius Arbiter, and the Kisses of Johannes Secundus, literally translated; to which are added the Love Epistles of Aristaenetus. Edited by Walter K. Kelly. 8vo. Lond., 1878.   H 5 S 29

PROSCHEK (PROF. JOSEPH). Kurzgefaszte praktische böhmische Grammatik für Deutsche. 8vo. Eger, 1840.   K 12 R 20

PROSPER AQUITANUS (SANCTUS). Opera omnia. [*See* MIGNE, J. P., SERIES LATINA, 51.]

PROTHERO (G. W.) Universal History. [*See* RANKE, L. VON.]   B 15 Q 29

PROTESTANT STANDARD (THE): a Journal of Political and Religious Freedom. 18 vols. fol. Sydney, 1869–88.   E

PROTECTION. Policy of Protection economically and morally considered, with reference in particular to Colonial Industry. 8vo. Sydney, 1868.   MF 3 P 2

Protection to Native Industry. (Newspaper Cutting.) 8vo. Melb., 1861.   MF 1 Q 3

PROU (V.) [*See* DIONYSIUS HALICARNASSENSIS.] B 19 Q 9 ‡

PROUD (ROBERT). History of Pennsylvania, in North America, from its settlement under William Penn, in 1681, till 1742. 2 vols. 8vo. Philad., 1797–98.   B 1 R 16, 17

PROUT (EBENEZER). Memoirs of the Life of the Rev. John Williams, Missionary to Polynesia. 8vo. Lond., 1843.   MC 1 R 26

Another copy.   C 11 P 19

PROUT (FATHER). [*See* MAHONY, REV. F. S.]

PROUT (REV. JOSIAH). View of the Character of Rev. R. Cecil. [*See* CECIL, REV. R.]

PROUT (J. SKINNER). Tasmania Illustrated. Vol. 1. Atlas fol. Hobart, 1844.   MD 2 P 28 ‡

Illustrated Hand-book of the Voyage to Australia; and a Visit to the Goldfields. 8vo. Lond., 1852. MD 4 S 17

[*See* BOOTH, E. C.; *and* EMIGRANT IN AUSTRALIA.]

PROUT (J. SKINNER), AND RAE (JOHN). Sydney Illustrated, with Letter-press Description, by J. Rae, M.A. Fol. Sydney, 1844.*   MD 2 P 6 ‡

PROUT (SAMUEL), F.S.A. Hints on 'Light and Shadow, Composition, &c., as applicable to Landscape Painting. Illustrated by Examples. New ed. Imp. 4to. Lond., 1876.   A 5 R 12

[*See* RUSKIN, J.]

PROUT (SAMUEL), F.S.A., AND HARDING (J. D.) Views of Cities and Scenery in Italy, France, and Switzerland; with Descriptions, by Thomas Roscoe. 3 vols. 4to. Lond. (n.d.)   D 8 V 27-29

PROUT (WILLIAM), M.D., &c. Chemistry, Meteorology, and the Function of Digestion, considered with reference to Natural Theology. 8vo. Lond., 1834.   A 6 Q 9

PROVERBIAL WISDOM: with a Preface by W. Blanchard Jerrold. 8vo. Lond., 1873.   K 19 P 10

PROVIDENT LIFE and Trust Company of Philadelphia. Mortality Experience, 1866-85; prepared by Asa S. King. 8vo. Philad., 1886.   F 3 P 9

PROYART (LIEVIN BONAVENTURE), L'ABBÉ. Histoire de Loango, Kakongo, et autres royaumes d'Afrique. 12mo. Paris, 1776.   B 1 P 48

PRUDENTIUS (AURELIUS CLEMENS). Opera omnia, ex Editione Parmensi, cum Notis et Interpretatione in usum Delphini; curante A. J. Valpy, A.M. 3 vols. 8vo. Lond., 1824.   J 13 S 16-18

Carmina omnia. [See MIGNE, J. P., SERIES LATINA, 59, 60.]

PRUSSIA. Nouvelle Législation Prussienne, réglant les Rapports entre l'Etat et l'Eglise. 8vo. Berlin, 1874.   F 12 Q 4

PRY (PAUL). [See POOLE, J.]

PRYCE (REV. E. G.) Missionary Tours. [See BROUGHTON, RT. REV. WILLIAM GRANT.]   MD 1 T 47

PRYCE (GEORGE). Memorials of the Canynges' Family and their Times. 8vo. Bristol, 1854.   C 9 V 19

PRYME (GEORGE), M.A. Autobiographic Recollections of; Edited by his Daughter. 8vo. Cambridge, 1870.   C 9 P 26

PRYNNE (WILLIAM). A Brief Register, Kalendar, and Survey of the several Kinds, Forms of all Parliamentary Writs. 2 vols. sm. 4to. Lond., 1659-64.   F 5 R 16, 17

PRYSE (JOHN ROBERT). Dictionary of the Welsh Language. [See PUGHE, W. O.]

PSALMANAZAR (GEORGE). Historical and Geographical Description of Formosa, an Island subject to the Emperor of Japan. 8vo. Lond., 1704.

Memoirs of * * * *, commonly known by the name of George Psalmanazar; a reputed Native of Formosa. Written by himself, in order to be published after his death. 8vo. Lond., 1764.   C 3 U 32

PSALTER (THE). [See BIBLES, &c.]

PSYCHICAL RESEARCH. Society for. [See SOCIETY FOR PSYCHICAL RESEARCH.]

PTOLEMAEUS (CLAUDE). Claudii Ptolemaei Geographia e codicibus Recognovit Carolus Müllerus Voluminis Primi, pars Prima. Imp. 8vo. Parisiis, 1883.   D 12 V 15

Géographie de Ptolémée Reproduction Photolithographique du Manuscrit Grec, et Précédée d'une Introduction Historique par Victor Langlois. Fol. Paris, 1867.   D 38 P 13 ‡

PUBLIC BATHS AND WASH-HOUSES for the Industrial Classes, Goulston Square, Whitechapel: Address for Aid to complete the Works. (Pam. 38.) 8vo. Lond., 1851.   MJ 2 Q 25

Suggestions for Building and Fitting up Parochial or Borough Establishments. (Pam. 38.) 8vo. Lond., 1850.   MJ 2 Q 25

PUBLIC EDIFICES. Report of a Public Meeting to Promote the Admission of the Public without Charge to Public Edifices. Lond., 1837.   A 7 Q 13

PUBLIC GENERAL STATUTES of Great Britain. [See GREAT BRITAIN.]

PUBLIC INSTRUCTION. [See NEW SOUTH WALES.]

PUBLIC MONUMENTS in England (from the *Foreign Quarterly Review*). 8vo. Lond., (n.d.)   A 7 R 21

PUBLIC OPINION: a Comprehensive Summary of the Press throughout the World on all important Current Topics. 28 vols. fol. Lond., 1871-85.   E

PUBLIC RECORDS. [See RECORD COMMISSIONERS' PUBLICATIONS.]

PUBLIC WORKS. [See NEW SOUTH WALES.]

PUBLISHERS' CIRCULAR (THE). Vol. 1, 1837-38. 8vo. Lond., 1839.   K 8 R 16

PÜCKLER-MUSKAU (HERMANN LUDWIG HEINRICH), PRINCE VON. Egypt and Mehemet Ali. 3 vols. 8vo. Lond., 1845.   B 2 S 10-12

Tour in England, Ireland, and France, in the years 1828-29; by "A German Prince." 2 vols. 12mo. Lond., 1832.   D 6 P 10, 11

Tour in Germany, Holland, and England, in the years 1826-28. 2 vols. 8vo. Lond., 1832.   D 8 P 8, 9

PUFFENDORF (SAMUEL), BARON VON. Of the Law of Nature and Nations; done into English by Basil Kennett, D.D. 4th ed. Fol. Lond., 1729.   F 39 R 2‡

PUFFENDORF (S.), BARON VON, AND MARTINIERE (ANTOINE AUGUSTIN BRUNZEN). Introduction to the History of the Principal Kingdoms and States of Europe; improved from the French, by Joseph Sayer. 2 vols. 8vo. Lond., 1748.   B 7 T 30, 31

PUGH (THEOPHILUS P.) Pugh's Moreton Bay Almanac, 1859. 12mo. Brisbane, 1859. ME 4 P

Pugh's Queensland Almanac, Law Calendar, Directory, Coast Guide, and Gazetteer, for 1860–65, 1874–75, 1883–84. 11 vols. (in 7) 12mo. Brisbane, 1860–84. ME 4 P

Brief Outline of the Geographical Position, Population, Climate, Resources, Capabilities, Form of Government, Land Laws, Trade, Revenue, &c., of the Colony of Queensland. 12mo. Brisbane, 1861. MD 1 S 57

PUGHE (W. OWEN), D.C.L., &c. Geiriadur Cenhedlaethol Cymraeg a Saesneg: a National Dictionary of the Welsh Language, with English and Welsh Equivalents. 3rd ed. Edited and enlarged by Robert John Pryse. 2 vols. 8vo. Denbigh, 1866–73. K 13 P 33, 34

PUGIN (AUGUSTUS). Historical and Descriptive Essays, accompanying a Series of Engraved Specimens of the Architectural Antiquities of Normandy; edited by John Britton, F.S.A., &c; the Subjects measured and drawn by Augustus Pugin, Architect, and engraved by John and Henry Le Keux. 4to. Lond., 1828. A 2 T 32

Specimens of Gothic Architecture, selected from various Ancient Edifices in England. 2 vols. roy. 4to. Lond., 1821–23. A 2 U 31, 32

Gothic Ornaments, selected from various Ancient Buildings, both in England and France, during the years 1828–30; drawn on stone by J. D. Harding. Roy. 4to. Lond., 1854. A 2 U 30

[*See* BRITTON, J.]

PUGIN (AUGUSTUS NORTHMORE WELBY). Details of Antient Timber Houses of the 15th and 16th Centuries, selected from those existing at Rouen, Caen, Beauvais, Gisors, Abbeville, Strasbourg, &c. 4to. Lond., 1836. A 2 T 27

Contrasts; or, a Parallel between the noble Edifices of the 14th and 15th Centuries, and similar Buildings of the Present Day, shewing the present Decay of Taste; accompanied by appropriate Text. 4to. Lond., 1836. A 2 T 43

True Principles of Pointed or Christian Architecture, set forth in two Lectures delivered at St. Marie's Oscott. 4to. Lond., 1841. A 2 T 21

Glossary of Ecclesiastical Ornament and Costume; compiled from Ancient Authorities and Examples. Illustrated. 3rd ed. Roy. 4to. Lond., 1868. A 7 R 13 †

Floriated Ornament: a Series of thirty-one Designs. Roy. 4to. Lond., 1875. A 4 R 2 †

PUISSANT (L.) Traité de Géodésie; ou, Exposition des Méthodes Astronomiques et Trigonométriques, appliquées soit à la mesure de la Time. Roy. 8vo. Paris, 1805. A 10 V 21

Traité de Topographie d'Arpentage, et de Nivellement. 4to. Paris, 1807. A 10 V 22

PULLAN (R. P.) Byzantine Architecture. [*See* TEXIER, C.] A 4 Q 5 †

PULLEN (H. W.) The Fight at Dame Europa's School, shewing how the German Boy thrashed the French Boy. 12mo. Lond. (n.d.) MJ 2 P 32

4 I

PULLEYN (WILLIAM). Origins and Inventions; or, Notices of the Origin of Language, Literature, &c. New ed. 8vo. Lond., 1869. J 9 U 17

PULLING (ALEXANDER). The Order of the Coif. Roy. 8vo. Lond., 1884. B 4 U 1

Crime and Criminals; is the Gaol the only Preventive? (Pam. Bd.) 8vo. Lond., 1863. F 12 P 22

The Law Reports: Index to the Orders in Council, Proclamations, Royal Commissions of Inquiry, &c., published in the *London Gazette.* Imp. 8vo. Lond., 1885. K 11 R 9

PULLING (F. S.), M.A. Life and Speeches of the Marquis of Salisbury, K.G. 2 vols 8vo. Lond., 1885. C 4 S 41, 42

Sir Joshua Reynolds. (Great Artists.) 8vo. Lond., 1880. C 3 T 44

Dictionary of English History. [*See* LOW, S. J.]

PULSFORD (EDWARD). Freedom in New South Wales *versus* Oppression in Victoria: a Reply to the *Age* Articles. 8vo. Sydney, 1887.* MF 3 Q 14

PULSZKY (FRANCIS). . The Tricolor on the Cross; or, Algeria and the French Conquest; from the German of Dr. Wagner, and other sources. 8vo. Lond., 1854. D 18 21

PULTENEY (RICHARD), M.D., &c. General View of the Writings of Linnæus. 8vo. Lond., 1781. A 16 U 19

PUMPELLY (R.) [A Review of] Geological Researches in China, Mongolia, and Japan. 4to. Wash., 1866. A 2 S 23 †

Geological Survey of Michigan. [*See* BROOKS, T. B.] A 2 U 7-10

PUNCH. Punch; or, the London Charivari. Vols. 1–88. 4to. Lond., 1841–85. E

Almanacks. [1st and] 2nd Series. 2 vols. 4to. Lond., 1842–80. E

Cartoons from the Collection of Mr. Punch: Benjamin Disraeli, Earl of Beaconsfield, K.G., 1845–78; the Rt. Hon. John Bright, M.P., 1846–75; the Rt. Hon. W. E. Gladstone, M.P., 1855–77 [by John Leech and John Tenniel]. 3 vols. (in 1) 4to. Lond., 1878. A 12 Q 18†

PUNCH (JAMES). Life and Times of Jem Punch; by Richmond Thatcher. 12mo. Sydney, 1885. MC 1 P 35

PUNCH STAFF PAPERS: a Collection of Tales, Sketches, &c., in Prose and Verse, by the Members of the Staff of *Sydney Punch.* With Illustrations. 8vo. Sydney, 1872. MJ 2 S 19

PURCELL (LYNDSEY). Lectures on Modern History. [*See* SCHLEGEL, F.] B 14 P 1

PURCHAS (REV. SAMUEL). Purchas, his Pilgrimes. In five Bookes (Parts). 5 vols. fol. Lond., 1825–26. B 5 P 1-5 ‡

PURDIE (A.), M.A. Studies in Biology for New Zealand Students. 8vo. Wellington, 1887.   MA 2 U 32

PURDON (H. G.) Memoirs of the Services of the 64th Regiment (2nd Staffordshire), 1758–1881. 8vo. Lond., 1882.   B 5 U 20

PURDY (JOHN). Oriental Navigator; or, New Directions for Sailing to and from the East Indies. 4to. Lond., 1794.   F 8 Q 8†

PURDY (WILLIAM). City Life; its Trade and Finance. 8vo. Lond., 1876.   F 5 R 9

PURNELL (CHARLES W.) Our Land Laws: what should be their basis? 8vo. Dunedin, 1876.   MJ 2 R 16

PURNELL (THOMAS). Life and Genius of Charles Lamb. [See LAMB, C.]   J 1 T 20–23

PURSLO (JOSHUA). Government of the Heavens. 2 vols. 8vo. Edinb., 1852.   A 2 S 27, 28

PURVES (DAVID LAING). English Circumnavigators: the most Remarkable Voyages round the World by English Sailors; with Notes, &c. Purves. 8vo. Lond., 1874.   D 10 Q 47

PURVES (REV. WILLIAM). Statement of the Merits of the Controversy between the Church of Scotland and the Free Church of Scotland; with Remarks on Union. 8vo. Sydney. 1864.   MG 1 Q 29

PUSELEY (DANIEL). Rise and Progress of Australia, Tasmania, and New Zealand; by "An Englishman." 3rd ed. 8vo. Lond., 1857.*   MD 1 U 34

Another copy. [4th ed.] 8vo. Lond., 1858.   MD 1 U 36

Five Dramas; by 'An Englishman." 2nd ed. 8vo. Lond., 1855.   H 4 Q 15

    Sylvia.

    A Play without a Name; or, What you Please.

    Retribution.

    Love without Money, and Money without Love.

    The Governess; or, a Voyage round the World.

PUSEY (PROF. E. B.), D.D. Collegiate and Professorial Teaching and Discipline; in answer to Prof. Vaughan's Strictures. 8vo. Oxford, 1854.   G 17 Q 12

PUSEY (S. C. B. BOUVERIE). Permanence and Evolution: an Inquiry into the supposed mutability of Animal Types. 8vo. Lond., 1882.   A 14 Q 24

PUTNAM (J. PICKERING). The Open Fire-place in all Ages; written for *The American Architect and Building News.* Illustrated. 8vo. Boston, 1881.   A 2 R 36

PYCROFT (REV. JAMES), B.A. The Collegian's Guide; or, Recollections of College Days. 2nd ed. 12mo. Lond., 1858.   J 1 T 9

Oxford Memories: a Retrospect after Fifty Years. 2 vols. 8vo. Lond., 1886.   C 8 T 46, 47

PYE (JOHN). Patronage of British Art: an Historical Sketch, comprising an Account of the Rise and Progress of Art and Artists in London. 8vo. Lond.,1845.   A 8 Q 20

Evidence relating to the Art of Engraving, taken before the Select Committee of the House of Commons on Arts, 1836. 8vo. Lond., 1836.   A 7 Q 13

Another copy. 8vo. Lond., 1836.   A 7 R 21

PYE (WALTER). Bark of Erythrophleum Guinense. [See BRUNTON, T. L.]   A 11 P 6†

PYKE (VINCENT). Australian Exploration: a Lecture. (Pam. Aa.) 8vo. Melh., 1861.   MD 1 V 9

Province of Otago in New Zealand, its Progress, Present Condition, Resources, and Prospects. 8vo. Dunedin, 1868.   MD 5 S 4

PYM (HORACE N.) [See FOX, CAROLINE.]   C 8 V 22

PYM (JOHN). Life of. [See MACKINTOSH, SIR J.]

Three English Statesmen [Pym, Cromwell, Pitt]; by G. Smith. 12mo. Lond., 1868.   C 1 T 43

PYNCHON (THOMAS RUGGLES), M.A. Chemical Forces—Heat, Light, Electricity; with an Introduction to Chemical Physics. 12mo. Hartford, 1870.   A 5 S 25

PYNE (REV. ALEXANDER), M.A. Reminiscences of Colonial Life and Missionary Adventure in both Hemispheres. 8vo. Lond., 1875.*   MD 4 R 23

PYNE (GEORGE). Perspective for Beginners; adapted to Young Students and Amateurs in Architecture, Painting, &c. 12th ed. With Illustrations. (Weale.) 12mo. Lond., 1879.   A 17 P 9

PYNE (W. H.) History of the Royal Residences of Windsor Castle, St. James Palace, Carleton House, Kensington Palace, Hampton Court, Buckingham House, and Frogmore. 3 vols. fol. Lond., 1819.   B 17 U 5–7‡

PYTHAGOREAN (A). [See CAMPBELL, DR. F.]

Q

Q. [*See* CLARKE, M. A. H.]

Q.E.D. [*See* NEW SOUTH WALES.]

Q. P. Indexes. [*See* GRISWOLD, W. M.]

QUAIFE (DR. BARZILLAI). Rules of the Final Judgement:
a Sermon. 8vo. Parramatta, 1846. MG 1 P 1
Lectures on Prophecy and the Kingdom of Christ. 8vo.
Sydney, 1848. MG 2 P 1
Intellectual Science: Outline Lectures, delivered chiefly
at the Australian College, 1850–51. 2 vols. 8vo. Sydney,
1873. MG 2 P 2, 3

QUAIN (JONES), M.D. Elements of Anatomy. Edited by
William Sharpey, M.D., &c., Allen Thomson, M.D., &c.
and Edward Albert Schäfer. Illustrated. 8th ed. 2 vols.
8vo. Lond., 1878. A 26 U 32, 33
Lecture, introductory to the Course of Anatomy and
Physiology. [Univ. of Lond., 1831.] 8vo. Lond.,
1831. J 5 S 8

QUAIN (JONES), M.D., AND WILSON (W. J. E.) Muscles
of the Human Body, in a series of Plates; with References
and Physiological Comments. Roy. fol. Lond., 1836.
A 1 S 9 ‡
Bones and Ligaments of the Human Body, in a series
of Plates; with References and Physiological Comments.
Roy. fol. Lond., 1842. A 1 S 8 ‡
Vessels of the Human Body, in a series of Plates; with
References and Physiological Comments. 1 vol. (in 2)
roy. fol. Lond., 1837. A 1 S 9, 10 ‡
Nerves of the Human Body, in a series of Plates; with
References and Physiological Comments. Roy.fol. Lond.,
1839. A 1 S 10 ‡

QUAIN (RICHARD), M.D., &c. Dictionary of Medicine;
by various Writers. Edited by R. Quain, M.D., &c. 7th
thousand. 8vo. Lond., 1883. A 26 U 30

QUARANTINE GROUND. [*See* NEW SOUTH WALES.]

QUARANTINE STATION. [*See* NEW SOUTH WALES.]

QUARITCH (BERNARD). Catalogue of Valuable Books.
8vo. Lond., 1859. K 7 S 24
General Catalogue of Books, arranged in Classes. Roy.
8vo. Lond., 1868. Libr.
Catalogue of Books. 2 vols. roy. 8vo. Lond., 1868–70.
Libr.
General Catalogue of Books. Roy. 8vo. Lond., 1874.
Libr.
General Catalogue of Books, offered to the Public at the
affixed Prices. 8vo. Lond., 1880. Libr.

QUARTERLY JOURNAL OF EDUCATION, 1831–34.
7 vols. 8vo. Lond., 1831–34. G 17 Q 13–19

QUARTERLY JOURNAL OF MICROSCOPICAL
SCIENCE. Vols. 1–8, 1853–60; vols. 1–26, new series,
1861–86. 34 vols. (in 30) roy. 8vo. Lond., 1853–86. E

QUARTERLY JOURNAL OF SCIENCE. [*See* JOURNAL
OF SCIENCE.]

QUARTERLY JOURNAL OF SCIENCE, LITERA-
TURE, AND ART. [*See* ROYAL INSTITUTION OF GREAT
BRITAIN.]

QUARTERLY REVIEW (THE). Vols. 1–162. 8vo.
Lond., 1809–86. E

QUATRE FILS AYMON. Histoire des quatre fils
Aymon, très-nobles et très-vaillants Chevaliers. 4to.
Troyes (n.d.) J 16 Q 28

QUATREFAGES (ARMAND DE). Les Polynésiens et leurs
Migrations. 4to. Paris, 1866. MA 1 P 10 †
Rambles of a Naturalist on the Coasts of France, Spain,
and Sicily; translated by E. C. Otté. 2 vols. 8vo. Lond.,
1857. A 16 Q 1, 2
The Human Species. 8vo. Lond., 1879. A 1 V 21

QUATREFAGES (A. DE), ET (HAMY ERNEST T.) Les
Crânes des Races Humaines (Crania Ethnica). Texte et
Atlas. 2 vols. imp. 4to. Paris, 1882. A 5 S 5, 6 †

QUATREMÈRE (ETIENNE M.) [*See* MAKRIZI, TAKI-
EDDIN-AHMED.]

QUATREMÈRE DE QUINCY (ANTOINE CHRYSOSTOME).
Essay on the Nature, the End, and the Means of Imi-
tation in the Fine Arts; translated from the French, by
J. C. Kent. 8vo. Lond., 1837. A 8 Q 23
Lives and Works of Michel Angelo and Raphael. [*See*
DUPPA, R.] C 4 P 1

QUEANBEYAN PAROCHIAL ASSOCIATION. First
Report of the Joint Parochial Association of the District
of Queanbeyan. 8vo. Sydney, 1848. MF 3 P 14

QUEEN ANNE'S SON. [*See* WILLIAM HENRY, PRINCE.]

QUEENS OF ENGLAND. Lives of. [*See* STRICKLAND
A., *and* DORAN, DR. J.]

QUEENS OF FRANCE. [*See* BUSH, MRS. F.]

QUEENS OF SCOTLAND. Lives of. [*See* STRICK-
LAND, A.]

QUEENSLAND.

ACTS OF PARLIAMENT. [*See* STATUTES.]

LEGISLATIVE ASSEMBLY.

Votes and Proceedings of the Legislative Assembly; with the various Documents connected therewith, 1862–63, 1865, 1868–72, and 1879–84. 24 vols. fol. Brisbane, 1862–84.   E

LEGISLATIVE COUNCIL.

Journals of the Legislative Council; with Papers. 15 vols. fol. Brisbane, 1862–72.   E

Official Record of the Debates of the Legislative Council. 27 vols. 8vo. Brisbane, 1875–84.   E

NORTHERN AUSTRALIA.

Summary of Extracts from a forthcoming Account of the Country of Northern Australia as a Site for a proposed British Colony. 12mo. Lond., 1862.   MD 2 Q 18

PARLIAMENTARY LIBRARY.

Additions to Catalogue of the Library of the Parliament of Queensland, from 1st January, 1876, to 31st March, 1877. 8vo. Brisbane, 1877.   MK 1 P 1

Analytical and Classified Catalogue of; by D. O'Donovan. 4to. Brisbane, 1883.   MK 1 U 2

POST OFFICE DIRECTORY.

Queensland Post Office Directory. 8vo. Brisbane, 1888.   ME 3 U

SELECTOR'S GUIDE.

Selector's Guide. Published by the Department of Public Lands, Queensland, 1883. 8vo. Brisbane, 1883.*   MF 2 P 32

STATUTES.

Statutes in force in the Colony of Queensland, to the Present Time ; edited by Ratcliffe Pring, Esq. 3 vols. roy. 8vo. Brisbane, 1862–64.   ME

Acts of Parliament. 13 vols. fol. Brisbane, 1866–85.   E

Consolidated Statutes of the Colony of Queensland. 4to. Brisbane, 1868.   ME

Statutes in force in the Colony of Queensland; with an Index. Edited by Frederick Augustus Cooper. 4 vols. 4to. Brisbane, 1881.   ME

QUEENSLAND INTERCOLONIAL EXHIBITION, 1876. National Agricultural and Industrial Association Catalogue of the Intercolonial Exhibition. 8vo. Brisbane, 1876.   MK 1 R 44

QUEENSLAND NATIONAL BANK. Half-yearly Reports, from its Foundation in 1872 to 30th June, 1885.   MF 3 Q 21

QUEKETT (JOHN). Practical Treatise on the use of the Microscope. 2nd ed. 8vo. Lond., 1852.   A 16 S 3

QUENSTEDT (FR. AUG.) Handbuch der Petrefaktenkunde. 2 vols. roy. 8vo. Tübingen, 1852.   A 9 T 18, 19

QUERARD (J. M.) Les Supercheries Littéraires Dévoilées; Galerie des Ecrivains français de toute l'Europe qui se sont déguisés sous des anagrammes, des astéronymes, des cryptonymes, des initialismes, des noms littéraires, des pseudonymes facétieux ou bizarres, etc. 2ᵉ éd. 3 vols. 8vo. Paris, 1869–70.   K 8 P 1–3

La France Litteraire; ou, Dictionnaire Bibliographique. 10 vols. (in 5) 8vo. Paris, 1827–38.   K 17 Q 8–12

[*See* BARBIER, A. A.]

QUERY (PETER), F.S.A. [*See* TUPPER, M. F.]

QUESTED (JOHN). Art of Land-surveying explained by short and easy rules, particularly adapted for the use of Schools. 8th ed. 12mo. Lond., 1861.   A 6 R 33

QUESTIONS HISTORIQUES. [*See* REVUE DES QUESTIONS HISTORIQUES.]

QUETELET (LAMBERT ADOLPHE JACQUES). Anthropométrie; ou, Mesure des différentes Facultés de l'Homme. Roy. 8vo. Bruxelles, 1870.   A 2 P 15

Letters on the Theory of Probabilities, as applied to the Moral and Political Sciences ; translated by O. G. Downes. 8vo. Lond., 1849.   A 10 T 15

Treatise on Man and the Development of his Faculties. Roy. 8vo. Edinb., 1842.   F 2 P 25

Physique Sociale; ou, Essai sur le Développement des Facultés de l'Homme. 2 vols roy. 8vo. Bruxelles, 1869.   A 2 P 10, 11

QUICHERAT (LOUIS). Dictionnaire Français-Latin. 25ᵉ tirage. Roy. 8vo. Paris, 1880.   K 16 Q 6

QUICHERAT (LOUIS), ET DAVELUY (A). Dictionnaire Latin-Français; avec un Vocabulaire des Noms géographiques, mythologiques, et historiques. 31ᵉ tirage. Roy. 8vo. Paris, 1879.   K 16 Q 7

QUILLINAN (MRS. DORA). Journal of a few Months' Residence in Portugal, and Glimpses of the South of Spain. 2 vols. 8vo. Lond., 1847.   D 8 R 43, 44

QUILTER (HARRY), M.A. Giotto. (Great Artists.) 8vo. Lond., 1881.   C 3 T 31

[Life of Angiolotto Bondone, called] Giotto. 4to. Lond., 1880.   C 4 W 9

QUIN (CHARLES W.) Garden Receipts. (Weale.) 12mo. Lond., 1882.   A 17 Q 57

QUIN (MICHAEL J.) Steam Voyage down the Danube. 2 vols. Lond., 1835.   D 9 P 39, 40

Steam Voyages on the Seine, the Moselle, and the Rhine. 2 vols. 8vo. Lond., 1843.   D 9 P 41, 42

QUINBY (M.) Mysteries of Bee-keeping explained. 8vo. N. York, 1865.   A 1 P 13

QUINCEY (THOMAS DE). [*See* DE QUINCEY, T.]

QUINET (EDGAR). His Early Life and Writings; by Richard Heath. 8vo. Lond., 1881. C 5 T 21

QUINTANA (DON MANUEL JOSEF). Lives of Vasco Nunez de Balboa, and Francisco Pizarro; from the Spanish, by Mrs. Hodson. 12mo. Lond., 1832. C 1 R 6

QUINTILIANUS (MARCUS FABIUS). Institutiones Oratoriæ, edente Aldi. Naugerio. 8vo. Venetiis, 1514. J 13 T 32

Institutionum Oratoriarum, Libri Duodecim, cum brevibus Notis, a Caroli Rollin. 8vo. Lond.,1792. J 13 T 36

Quintilian's Institutes of Oratory; or, Education of an Orator; in twelve Books; literally translated, with Notes, by the Rev. John Selby Watson, M.A., &c. 2 vols. 8vo. Lond., 1875–76. J 10 P 39, 40

[*See* SCRIPTORES ROMANI.] J 13 T 35

QUINTUS (CURTIUS RUFUS). [*See* CURTIUS RUFUS, Q.]

QUINTUS SMYRNÆUS. Posthomericorum Libri xiv, restituit et supplevit Thom. Christ. Tychsen. 8vo. Argentorati, 1807. H 7 T 32

Quinti Posthomerica. [*See* HESIOD.] H 6 V 29

QUIRIS. [*See* SOUTH AUSTRALIA.]

QUIROS (CAPT. PEDRO FERNANDEZ DE). Relacion de vn memorial quæ ha presentado a su Magestad el Capitan Pedro Fernandez de Quir, sobre la poblacion y descubrimiento de la quarta parte del mundo, Australia incognita. Impressa por Carlos de Labayen. Año 1610. (*Facsimile* Reprint.) Sm. 4to. Pampeluna, 1610. MD 7 P 18

QUIROS (CAPT. PEDRO FERNANDEZ DE)—*continued.*

Verhael van seker Memoriael, gepresenteert aen Sijne Majestyt den Koningh van Spangien, by den Capiteyn Pedro Fernandez de Quir; aengaende de bevolckinge ende ontdeckinghe van 't vierde deel des Werelts, genaemt Australia Incognita. Sq. 8vo. Amsterdam, 1612. MD 7 P 17

Beschrubinge vande reginghe van Peru. Sq. 8vo. Amsterdam, 1612. MD 7 P 17

Terra Australis Incognita; or, a New Southern Discovery, containing a fifth part of the World, lately found out by Ferdinand de Quir, a Spanish Captain. Printed in the year 1617. (*From the Latin Translation in the Bodleian Library.*) 12mo. Lond., 1617. Libr.

Account of a Memorial presented to His Majesty, concerning the Population and Discovery of the fourth part of the World, Australia the Unknown. Printed by Charles de Labayen, anno 1610. From the Spanish, with an Introduction and Photo-lithograph of the original Text, by W. A. Duncan. 8vo. Sydney, 1874. MD 7 P 18

QUODLING (R.) Progress Report from the Select Committee on the resignation of Mr. Quodling, late Inspector of Roads in the Northern Districts (New South Wales). Fol. Sydney, 1862. ME 10 Q 5 †

QUOTATIONS. New Dictionary of Quotations from the Greek, Latin, and Modern Languages. Translated. 8vo. Lond., 1869. K 17 P 13

QUOY (J. R. C.) [*See* DUMONT D'URVILLE, CAPT. J. S. C.]

R

R. (R. H.) [*See* RAMBLES IN ISTRIA, &c.]

R.O. [*See* HALF-A-DOZEN ATTEMPTS AT VERSIFICATION.]

RABAN (EDWARD). [*See* EDMOND, J. P.]   C 10 R 1

BABANUS MAURUS (MOGUNTINUS ARCHIEPISCOPUS). Opera omnia. [*See* MIGNE, J. P., SERIES LATINA, 107–112.]

RABBI JOSEPH. [*See* CHRONICLES OF RABBI JOSEPH.]

RABELAIS (FRANÇOIS), M.D. Whole Works of; by [Sir Thomas Urquhart or] Urchard. 8vo. Lond., 1708.
                                              J 9 S 32

The Works of; faithfully translated from the French; with Various Notes, and numerous Illustrations, by Gustave Doré. 8vo. Lond. (n.d.)   J 9 S 33

RABY (THOMAS WENTWORTH), LORD. [*See* STRAFFORD, EARL OF.]

RACHEL-FÉLIX (ELISA), TRAGÉDIENNE. Memoirs of; by Madame de B——. 2 vols. 8vo. Lond., 1858. C 3 P 35, 36

RACINE (JEAN). Œuvres Complètes de; avec une Vie de l'Auteur et un Examen de chacun de ses Ouvrages, par Saint-Marc Girardin et Louis Molard. 8vo. Paris, 1869–77.   J 13 U 19–26

The Distrest Mother: a Tragedy. (Bell's Brit. Theatre.) 18mo. Lond., 1791.   H 2 P 28

Œuvres de. 5 vols. 18mo. Paris, 1819.   J 15 Q 1–5

RACINET (A.) Polychromatic Ornament: One Hundred Plates in Gold, Silver, and Colours, comprising upwards of two thousand Specimens of the various Styles of Ancient, Oriental, and Mediæval Art, and including the Renaissance and the 17th and 18th Centuries. Imp. 4to. Lond., 1877.   A 4 U 9 ‡

RACING AND STEEPLECHASING. Racing by the Earl of Suffolk and Berkshire, and Mr. W. G. Craven; with a Contribution by the Hon. F. Lawley. Steeple-chasing; by A. Coventry, and A. E. T. Watson. (Bad-minton Library.) 8vo. Lond., 1886.   A 17 U 32

RACK (E.) [*See* COLLINSON, REV. J.]   B 17 R 15–17 ‡

RADBERTUS (SANCTUS PASCHASIUS). Opera omnia. [*See* MIGNE, J. P., SERIES LATINA, 120.]

RADCLIFFE (MRS. ANNE). Gaston de Blondeville; or, the Court of Henry III: a Romance. St. Alban's Abbey: a Metrical Tale; to which is prefixed a Memoir of the Author; with Extracts from her Journals. 4 vols. 8vo. Lond., 1826.   J 12 T 20–23

RADFORD (GEORGE). Rambles by Yorkshire Rivers. 8vo. Leeds, 1886.   D 8 U 18

RADOT (VALERY). Louis Pasteur, his Life and Labours; by his Son-in-Law; translated by Lady Claud Hamilton. 8vo. Lond., 1885.   C 4 Q 25

RAE (EDWARD), F.R.G.S. White Sea Peninsula: a Jour-ney in Russian Lapland and Karelia. Map and Illustra-tions. 8vo. Lond., 1881.   D 8 T 12

Land of the North Wind; or, Travels among the Lap-landers and the Samoyedes. 8vo. Lond., 1875.   D 4 R 5

RAE (GEORGE), "THOMAS BULLION." The Country Banker: his Clients, Cares, and Work; from an experi-ence of forty years. 8vo. Lond., 1885.   F 5 R 18

Internal Management of a Country Bank; in a series of Letters on the Functions and Duties of a Branch Manager. 12mo. Lond., 1850.   F 2 P 23

RAE (JOHN), A.M. Book of the Prophet Isaiah, rendered into English Blank Verse; with Explanatory Notes. 8vo. Sydney, 1853.   MG 1 Q 22

Sydney Corporation Act (14 Vic., No. 41), so far as not repealed by 17 Vic., No. 33, sec. 3; the Sydney Corporatio Abolition Act (17 Vic., No. 33); the Sydney Sewerage Act (17 Vic., No. 35); the Sydney Water Act (17 Vic., No. 35). With Index. 8vo. Sydney, 1854.
                                              MF 1 P 38

Railways of New South Wales: Reports on their Con-struction and Working, from 1846–76 inclusive. 5 vols. (in 1) fol. Sydney, 1866–76.   MF 2 U 13

Gleanings from my Scrap-book. 1st, 2nd, and 3rd series. (*Printed by the Author.*) 3 vols. (in 2) 8vo. Sydney, 1869–74.   MH 1 S 11, 12

New South Wales Commission for the Melbourne Cen-tennial Exhibition. Mr. Rae's Sketches of Colonial Scenes in the Older Time. 8vo. Sydney, 1888. MD 7 Q 7 ‡

Sydney Illustrated. [*See* PROUT, J. S.]   MD 2 P 6 ‡

RAE (JOHN), M.D., &c. Narrative of an Expedition to the Shores of the Arctic Sea, in 1846–47. With Maps. 8vo. Lond., 1850.   D 4 S 11

RAE (W. F.) Westward by Rail: a Journey to San Francisco and back, and a Visit to the Mormons. 2nd ed. 8vo. Lond., 1871.   D 4 P 5

Notes on England. [*See* TAINE, H. A.]

RAEBURN (SIR HENRY), R.A. Life of; with Portrait and Appendix, by his Great-Grandson, W. R. Andrew, M.A. 8vo. Lond., 1886.   C 8 U 46

RAFFAELLO (CARMONI). Eureka Stockade: the con-sequence of some Pirates wanting on Quarter-deck a Rebellion. 8vo. Melb., 1855.   MJ 1 T 41

Another copy. 8vo. Melb., 1855.   MJ 2 Q 17

RAFFAELLO SANZIO, OR SANTI.   [*See* RAPHAEL SANZIO.]

RAFFLES (MRS. SOPHIA). Memoir of the Life and Public Services of Sir Thomas Stamford Raffles, F.R.S., &c.; by his Widow. 4to. Lond., 1830.   C 8 V 29

RAFFLES (REV. THOMAS), D.D., &c. Memoirs of the Life and Ministry of; by [Sir] Thomas Stamford Raffles, B.A. 2nd ed. 8vo. Lond., 1865.   C 3 Q 45

RAFFLES (SIR THOMAS STANFORD), F.R.S. Substance of a Minute on the introduction of an improved system of internal management, &c., on the Island of Java. 4to. Lond., 1814.   F 8 Q 14 †

Memoir of the Life and Public Services of; by his Widow [Mrs. Sophia Raffles]. 4to. Lond., 1830. C 8 V 29

History of Java. 2nd ed. 2 vols. 8vo. Lond., 1830.   B 10 T 32, 33

Memoirs of the Life and Ministry of the Rev. Thomas Raffles, D.D., &c. 2nd ed. 8vo. Lond., 1865.   C 3 Q 45

Memoir of George Finlayson. [*See* FINLAYSON, G.] D 6 S 1

RAGGED AND INDUSTRIAL SCHOOL (SUSSEX STREET). Reports of, 1861-62, 1864-65. 12mo. Sydney, 1861-65.   MF 3 P 12

Report (1862). 12mo. Sydney, 1862.   MJ 2 Q 10

RAGGED SCHOOL UNION. Sixteenth Annual Report, 1860. 8vo. Lond., 1860.   MF 3 P 15

RAGGED SCHOOL UNION MAGAZINE. [Ragged School Extension: Australia.] Vol. 14, No. 166. [Pam. G.) 8vo. Lond., 1862.   ME 3 R

RAGON (J.-M.). Orthodoxie Maçonnique, suivie de la Maçonnerie occulte, et de l'Initiation hermétique. 8vo. Paris, 1853.   B 14 V 49

RAHEL. [*See* LEVIN, ANTONIE FREDERIKE.]

RAIKES (THOMAS). France since 1830. 2 vols. 8vo. Lond., 1841.   B 8 U 33, 34

Portion of the Journal kept by Thomas Raikes, Esq., 1831-47. 4 vols. 8vo. Lond., 1856-57. C 4 P 23-26

RAILWAY SYSTEMS of New South Wales and Victoria. [*See* NEW SOUTH WALES, *and* VICTORIA.]

RAILWAYS of New South Wales. [*See* NEW SOUTH WALES.]

RAINS (FANNY L.) By Land and Ocean; or, the Journal and Letters of a Young Girl who went to South Australia with a Lady Friend, then alone to Victoria, New Zealand, Sydney, Singapore, China, Japan, and across the Continent of America home. 8vo. Lond., 1878.   MD 2 R 44

RAINY (PROF. ROBERT), D.D. [*See* WILSON, REV. W.] C 8 U 14

RALEIGH (SIR WALTER), KNT. History of the World: the 2nd Part continued in six Books, by Alexander Ross. Fol. Lond., 1652.   B 15 R 1 ‡

History of the World; with his Voyages of Discovery to Guiana; in five Books. 6 vols. 8vo. Edinb., 1820.   B 14 S 8-13

Life of. 1562-1618; by J. A. St. John. 2 vols. 8vo. Lond., 1868.   C 4 T 41, 42

[Life of]; by E. Gosse. (English Worthies.) 12mo. Lond., 1886.   C 2 Q 40

Sir Walter Raleigh in Ireland; by Sir John Pope Hennessy. 8vo. Lond., 1883.   C 3 V 37

Relation de la Guiane de Walter Raleigh. [*See* COREAL, F.]

RALFE (JAMES). Nationalization of the Public Lands of Tasmania, and Free Trade with the World. 8vo. Hobart, 1865.   MF 3 P 6

RALPHSON (J.) [*See* NEWTON, SIR I.]   A 10 S 9

RALSTON (W. R. S.), M.A. Early Russian History: four Lectures delivered at Oxford, in the Taylor Institution. 12mo. Lond., 1874.   B 12 T 17

Songs of the Russian People, as illustrative of Sclavonic Mythology and Russian Social Life. 8vo. Lond., 1872.   H 8 U 16

Russian Folk-Tales. 8vo. Lond., 1873.   B 31 T 1

[*See* TIBETAN TALES.]

RAMAGE (CRAUFURD TAIT), LL.D. Beautiful Thoughts from Latin Authors. 2nd ed. 12mo. Liverp., 1869.   J 12 S 28

Beautiful Thoughts from Greek Authors. 2nd ed., enlarged. 12mo. Liverp., 1873.   J 12 S 29

Beautiful Thoughts from French and Italian Authors. 2nd ed. 12mo. Liverp., 1875.   J 12 S 30

RAMANN (L.) Franz Liszt, Artist and Man, 1811-40; translated from the German, by Miss E. Cowdery. 2 vols. 8vo. Lond., 1882.   C 3 Q 29, 30

RAMBAUD (ALFRED). History of Russia, from the Earliest Times to 1877; translated by Leonora B. Lang. With Illustrations. 2 vols. 8vo. Lond., 1879. B 12 U 20, 21

RAMBLE from Sydney to Southampton: Recollections of, *vid* South America, Panama, the West Indies, the United States, and Niagara. 8vo. Lond., 1851.   D 10 R 12

RAMBLES in Istria, Dalmatia, and Montenegro; by R. H. R. 8vo. Lond., 1875.   D 6 T 18

RAMBLES OF THE EMPEROR CHING TIH in Këang Nan: a Chinese Tale; translated by Thin Shen. 2 vols. 8vo. Lond., 1843.   J 9 R 23, 24

RAMBLING VICTORIAN, A. [*See* MORRISON, A. F.]

RAMBOSSON (J.) Astronomy; translated by C. B. Pitman. 8vo. Lond., 1875.   A 3 S 10

RAMMELSBERG (C. F.) Handbuch der Mineralchemie. 2ᵉ auflage. 1. Allgemeiner Theil. 2. Specieller Theil. 2 vols. (in 1) roy. 8vo. Leipsic, 1875.   A 5 U 19

RÁMMOHUN ROY (Rajah). Biographical Essay. [*See* Müller, Prof. F. Max.]   C 3 P 6

RAMON DE LA SAGRA (D.) Histoire Physique, Politique, et Naturelle de l'Ile de Cuba; traduit en Français, par M. Sabin Berthelot. 12 vols. (in 11) 8vo. Paris, 1838–57.   A 13 U 15–25

Planches [to the above]. 10 vols. (in 8) fol. Paris, 1838–57.   A 4 Q 6–13 ‡

RAMSAY (Alexander). Bibliography, Guide, and Index to Climate. 8vo. Lond., 1884.   A 3 S 19

RAMSAY (Alexander), Junr. Rudiments of Mineralogy. (Weale). 12mo. Lond., 1868.   A 17 P 38

RAMSAY (Allan). The Evergreen; a Collection of Scots Poems, wrote by the Ingenious, before 1600. 2 vols. 8vo. Glasgow, 1876.   H 7 T 24, 25

The Gentle Shepherd : a Scot's Pastoral Comedy. (Bell's Brit. Theatre.) 18mo. Lond., 1796.   H 2 P 6

Poems of Allan Ramsay; with Glossary, Life of the Author, and Remarks on his Poems. Paisley, 1877.   H 7 T 26, 27

Tea-Table Miscellany : a Collection of Choice Songs, Scots and English. 2 vols. roy. 8vo. Glasgow, 1871.   H 5 U 32, 33

Another copy. 2 vols. 8vo. Glasgow, 1876.   H 7 T 28, 29

Poems of. New ed.; with a Life of the Author. 2 vols. 8vo. Lond., 1800.   H 8 U 13, 14

RAMSAY (Sir Andrew C.), LL.D., &c. Descriptive Catalogue of the Rock Specimens in the Museum of Practical Geology, with explanatory notices of their nature and mode of occurrence in place. 3rd ed. 8vo. Lond., 1862.   A 9 S 26

RAMSAY (Sir A. C.), and BRISTOW (H. W.) Index to the Colours and Signs employed in the Maps and Sections of the Geological Survey of Great Britain up to 1874. 8vo. Lond., 1874.   A 9 Q 3

[*See* Rudler, F. W.]   D 11 S 6

RAMSAY (Lieut.-Col. Balcarres D. Wardlaw). Rough Recollections of Military Service and Society. 2 vols. 8vo. Edinb., 1882.   C 5 P 17, 18

RAMSAY (Edward Bannerman), M.A., &c. Reminiscences of Scottish Life and Character. 20th ed. Edinb., 1871.   C 5 T 22

Reminiscences of Scottish Life and Character, and a Memoir of Dean Ramsay; by Cosmo Innes. 26th ed. 8vo. Lond., 1880.   C 2 Q 46

RAMSAY (E. Pierson), F.L.S., &c. Hints for the Preservation of Specimens of Natural History, for Museum Purposes. 8vo. Sydney, 1876.   MJ 2 R 14

Another copy. 3rd ed. 8vo. Sydney, 1887.*   MA 2 U 23

Catalogue of a Collection of Fossils in the Australian Museum, Sydney; with Introductory Notes. Roy. 8vo. Sydney, 1883.   MK 1 S 41

[*See* Ratte, A. F.]

RAMSAY (J. A.), M.E. Treatise on Ventilating and Working Collieries. 8vo. Newcastle-upon-Tyne, 1882.   A 10 P 23

RAMSAY (James Andrew Brown), Marquis of Dalhousie. [*See* Dalhousie, James Andrew Brown, Marquis of.]

RAMSAY (Capt. R. G. W.) [*See* Tweeddale, Marquis of.]

RAMSAY (William), M.A. Elementary Manual of Roman Antiquities; with numerous Illustrations. 6th ed. 8vo. Lond., 1875.   B 12 P 12

RAMSDEN (Samuel). Portrait of. [*See* Manuscripts And Portraits.]

RANCE (Charles E. de), A.I.C.E., &c. Water Supply of England and Wales : its Geology, underground Circulation Surface Distribution, and Statistics. 8vo. Lond., 1882.   A 6 T 14

RAND (Rev. Edgar H.), B.A. Dates and Events in English History. (Weale). 12mo. Lond., 1872.   K 11 P 5

Places and Facts in Physical and Political Geography. (Weale.) 12mo. Lond., 1873.   K 11 P 5

RAND, McNALLY & CO. Improved, Indexed Business Atlas and Shippers' Guide. Roy. 4to. Chicago, 1885.   D 33 Q 5 ‡

RANDALL (Henry S.), LL.D. Sheep Husbandry; with an Account of the different Breeds and general directions in regard to Management, &c. Roy. 8vo. New York, 1860.   A 1 S 8

RANDALL (John). The Severn Valley : a Series of Sketches, Descriptive and Pictorial, of the Course of the Severn, from its Rise or Plinlimmon to its Fall in the Bristol Channel. 8vo. Madeley, Salop., 1882.   D 7 P 5

RANDALL (P. M.) Quartz Operator's Hand-book. Revised ed. 8vo. New York, 1871.   A 9 Q 37

RANDALL (S. S.) History of the Common School System of the State of New York, from its origin in 1795 to the present time. Roy. 8vo. New York, 1871.   G 17 R 3

RANDOLPH (Thomas). Poetical and Dramatic Works of : now first collected and edited from the early copies and MSS.; with some Account of the Author and occasional Notes, by W. Carew Hazlitt. 12mo. Lond., 1875.   H 2 Q 27

RANGER (The). [*See* Flack, Capt.]

RANKE (LEOPOLD VON). Ecclesiastical and Political History of the Popes of Rome, during the 16th and 17th Centuries; translated by Sarah Austin. 3 vols. 8vo. Lond., 1840.　　　　　　　　　　　　B 11 V 35–37

History of Servia and the Servian Revolution; translated by Mrs. Alexander Kerr. 8vo. Lond., 1847.　B 13 V 24

History of the Prussian Monarchy; translated by Demmler. Vol. 1 (*all published*), 8vo. Lond., 1848.　　B 9 S 6

History of England, principally in the 17th Century. 6 vols. 8vo. Oxford, 1976.　　　　　　B 5 P 28–33

Memoirs of the House of Brandenburg and History of Prussia. 3 vols. 8vo. Lond., 1849.　　B 9 S 7–9

Sämmtliche Werke. 48 vols. (in 39) 8vo. Leipzig, 1867–80.
　　　　　　　　　　　　　　　　B 14 W 1–39

Universal History: the Oldest Historical Group of the Nations, and the Greeks; edited by G. W. Prothero. 8vo. Lond., 1884.　　　　　　　　　B 15 Q 29

RANKEN (GEORGE). Bush Essays; by "Capricornus." Facts about Australia; Co-operative Settlement; New South Wales in 1872. (Pam. Aa.) 8vo. Edinb., 1872.
　　　　　　　　　　　　　　　　MD 1 V 9

Another copy. 8vo. Edinb., 1872.　　　MF 2 Q 14

Another copy. 8vo. Edinb., 1872.　　　MF 3 P 17

Squatting System of Australia. (Pam. Ds.) 8vo. Edinb., 1875.　　　　　　　　　　MF 2 Q 15

Another copy. 8vo. Edinb., 1875.　　　MF 3 P 17

Colonization in 1876. 8vo. Sydney, 1876.　MF 3 P 20

Homestead Settlement: Grazing, Past, Present, and Future. 8vo. Sydney, 1877.　　　MF 3 P 20

The Invasion; by "W. H. Walker." 8vo. Sydney, 1877.
　　　　　　　　　　　　　　　　MJ 1 Q 26

RANKEN (W. H. L.) The Dominion of Australia: an Account of its Foundations. 8vo. Lond., 1874.*　MD 1 W 33

RANKINE (W. J. M.) Manual of the Steam Engine and other Prime Movers. 2nd ed. 8vo. Lond., 1861.
　　　　　　　　　　　　　　　　A 11 P 26

Manual of Applied Mechanics. 4th ed. 8vo. Lond., 1868.　　　　　　　　　　　A 11 Q 2

Manual of Civil Engineering. 8vo. Lond., 1867.
　　　　　　　　　　　　　　　　A 6 R 8

Manual of Machinery and Millwork. 8vo. Lond., 1869.　　　　　　　　　　　　A 6 R 29

Useful Rules and Tables relating to Mensuration, Engineering, Structures, and Machines. 8vo. Lond., 1867.
　　　　　　　　　　　　　　　　A 10 S 27

Miscellaneous Scientific Papers, from the Transactions and Proceedings of the Royal and other Scientific and Philosophical Societies, and the Scientific Journals; with a Memoir of the Author, by P. G. Tait, M.A. 8vo. Lond., 1881.　　　　　　　　　A 16 V 14

RANSOME (ARTHUR), M.D. On Stethometry; being an Account of a new and more exact Method of measuring, &c., and examining the Chest. 8vo. Lond., 1876.　A 12 R 27

4 K

RANSOME (PROF. CYRIL), M.A. Our Colonies and India; how we got them, and why we keep them. 8vo. Lond., 1885.　　　　　　　　　　　MF 1 P 39

Rise of Constitutional Government in England. 8vo. Lond., 1883.　　　　　　　　　F 5 R 19

Political History of England to 1881. [*See* ACLAND, A. H. D.]　　　　　　　　　B 3 T 20

RANYARD (ARTHUR COWPER). [Sir Isaac] Newton, his Friend, and his Niece. [*See* DE MORGAN, A.]　C 10 U 38

RAOUL (E.) Choix de Plantes de la Nouvelle-Zelande. Roy. 4to. Paris, 1846.　　　　　　MA 1 R 9 ‡

RAPER (LIEUT. HENRY), R.N. Practice of Navigation and Nautical Astronomy. Roy. 8vo. Lond., 1874.　A 3 T 10

RAPHAEL SANZIO OR SANTI, DA URBINO.
Raphael Santi, his Life and Works; by Alfred, Baron von Wolzogen; translated by F. E. Burnett. 12mo. Lond., 1866.　　　　　　　　　C 5 R 22

Raphael; by "N. d'Anvers" [N. R. E. Bell]. (Great Artists.) 8vo. Lond., 1879.　　　C 3 T 40

Raphael: his Life and Works; by J. A. Crowe, and G. B. Cavalcaselle. 2 vols. 8vo. Lond., 1882–85. C 11 P 10, 11

Raphael: his Life, Work and Times, from the French of Eugène Muntz; edited by Walter Armstrong, B.A. Roy. 8vo. Lond., 1882.　　　　　　C 8 V 30

Raphael's Cartoons; engraved on Steel by G. Greatbach, from the Originals at the South Kensington Museum; with a Biography and Portrait of Raphael. Fol. Lond., 1882.　　　　　　　　　　　A 23 Q 10 ‡

Lives and Works of Michael Angelo and Raphael; by R. Duppa, and A. C. Quatremère de Quincy. 8vo. Lond., 1876.　　　　　　　　　　　C 4 P 1

Critical Account of the Drawings by Michael Angelo and Raffaello, in the University Galleries, Oxford; by J. C. Robinson. 8vo. Oxford, 1870.　　A 7 Q 9

Raphael and the Villa Farnesina. [*See* BIGOT, C.]
　　　　　　　　　　　　　　　　A 2 Q 21 †

Raffaello Sanzio: his Sonnet studied. [*See* FAGAN, L. A.]

RAPHAEL VOLATERRANUS OR MAFFEI (R.) Historia de Vita quattuor Maximorum Pontificum. (*Bound with Platina*.) Sm. fol. Venetiis, 1511. C 14 R 19 ‡

RAPIN DE THOYRAS (PAUL DE). History of England, written in French; translated into English, and continued from the Revolution to the Accession of King George II; by N. Tindal. 4 vols. fol. Lond., 1785–89.
　　　　　　　　　　　　　　　　B 17 U 1–4 ‡

Acta Regia; or, an Account of the Treaties, Letters, and Instruments between the Monarchs of England and Foreign Powers, published in Mr. Rymer's Foedera. 4 vols. 8vo. Lond., 1726–27.　　B 22 S 6–9

RAPP (GEN. JEAN), COMTE, FIRST AIDE-DE-CAMP TO NAPOLEON. Memoirs of. Written by himself and published by his Family. 8vo. Lond., 1823.　C 9 P 29

RAREY (J. S.) Modern Art of Taming Wild Horses. 12mo. Lond., 1858　　　　　　　A 1 P 35

RASHLEIGH (PHILLIP), F.R.S., &c. Specimens of British Minerals; with general descriptions of each article. (In two parts.) 4to. Lond., 1797–1802. **A 9 V 20**

RASK (PROF. RASMUS KRISTIAN). Dr. E. Rask's Danish Grammar for Englishmen: with Extracts in Prose and Verse. 2nd ed. 8vo. Lond., 1847. **K 12 Q 22**

Grammar of the Anglo-Saxon Tongue: from the Danish, by Benjamin Thorpe. 3rd ed. 8vo. Lond., 1879. **K 12 R 12**

Short Practical and Easy Method of Learning the Old Norsk Tongue or Icelandic Language. 2nd ed. 8vo. Lond., 1869. **K 11 V 19**

Vejledning til det Islandske eller gamle Nordiske Sprog. 12mo. Kobenhavn, 1811. **K 16 P 7**

Kortfattet Vejledning til det oldnordiske eller gamle islandske Sprog. 12mo. Kóbenhavn, 1832. **K 12 Q 42**

Frisische Sprachlehre, bearbeitet nach dem nämlichen Plane, wie die isländische und angelsächsische. 8vo. Freiburg, 1834. **K 12 R 12**

RASPE (RUDOLPH ERIC). Adventures of Baron Munchausen: a new and revised ed., with an Introduction, by T. Teignmouth Shore, M.A. Illustrated by Gustave Doré. 3rd ed. 4to. Lond., 1881. **J 8 V 6**

[*See* BORN, I., BARON.] **D 6 T 17**

RASSAM (HORMUZD), F.R.G.S. Narrative of the British Mission to Theodore, King of Abyssinia. With Illustrations, &c. 2 vols. 8vo. Lond., 1869. **D 1 W 1, 2**

RASTELL (JOHN). Pastime of People ; or the Chronicles of Divers Realms; and, most especially, of the Realm of England. 4to. Lond., 1811. **B 10 S 1 †**

RATHBONE (FREDERICK). Josiah Wedgwood on the Clay of Sydney Cove. (*With Facsimile Illustration of a Medallion presented by Richard and George Tangye.*) 4to. Birmingham, 1885. Libr.

Old Wedgwood and Old Wedgwood Ware. [*See* TANGYE, R. AND G.] Libr.

RATHBONE (H. N.) So much of the Diary of Lady Willoughby as relates to her Domestic History and to the eventful period of the Reign of Charles the First, the Protectorate and Restoration. 8vo. Lond., 1873. **J 12 R 25**

RATHBONE (W.), PELL (A.), AND MONTAGUE (F. C.), M.A. Local Government and Taxation. 8vo. Lond., 1885. **F 5 S 8**

RATHERIUS (VERONENSIS EPISCOPUS). Opera omnia. [*See* MIGNE, J. P., SERIES LATINA, 136.]

RATRAMUS (CORBEIENSIS MONACHUS). Opera omnia. [*See* MIGNE, J. P., SERIES LATINA, 121.]

RATTE (A. FELIX). Descriptive Catalogue (with Notes) of the General Collection of Minerals in the Australian Museum. 8vo. Sydney, 1885.* **MA 2 R 29**

Hints for Collectors of Geological and Mineralogical Specimens. 2nd ed. 8vo. Sydney, 1887.* **MA 2 Q 43**

RATTRAY (A.) Vancouver Island and British Columbia : where they are, what they are, and what they may become. 8vo. Lond., 1862. **D 3 R 11**

RATTRAY (ALEXANDER), M.D. Notes on the Physical Geography, Climate, and Capabilities of Somerset and the Cape York Peninsula, Australia. 8vo. Lond., 1868. **MD 7 Q 55**

RATTRAY (JAMES). Round and round, and in the World. 2nd ed. 8vo. Lond., 1870. **MD 2 Q 19**

RATTRAY (JOHN), M.A., AND MILL (HUGH ROBERT), B.Sc., &c. Forestry and Forest Products : Prize Essays of the Edinburgh International Forestry Exhibition, 1884. 8vo. Edinb., 1885. **A 1 S 41**

RAUMER (PROF. FRIEDRICH VON). Contributions to Modern History ; from the British Museum and State Paper Office. 8vo. Lond., 1836. **B 3 R 7**

England in 1835 ; being a Series of Letters, written to friends in Germany, during a residence in London; translated from the German by Sarah Austin. 3 vols. 8vo. Lond., 1836. **D 8 P 17–19**

England in 1841 ; being a Series of Letters written to friends in Germany, during a residence in London, and Excursions into the Provinces; translated from the German, by H. E. Lloyd. 2 vols. 8vo. Lond., 1842. **F 5 S 2, 3**

Italy and the Italians. 2 vols. 8vo. Lond., 1840. **D 9 P 19, 23**

RAUMER (RUDOLF VON). Geschichte der germanischen Philologie. (Ges. der Wiss. in Deutschland.) 8vo. München, 1870. **A 17 V 23**

RAUSCHENFELS (U. VON). Wanderungen durch Steiermark und Kärnten. [*See* UNSER VATERLAND.] **D 38 P 19‡**

RAVEN (JOHN). Parliamentary History of England, from the passing of the Reform Bill of 1832. 8vo. Lond., 1885. **F 5 T 6**

RAVEN (J. J.) Ecclesiastical Remains of Bungay. (Suffolk Inst. of Archaeology.) 8vo. Bury St. Edmonds, 1876. **B 7 P 29**

RAVOISIÉ (AMABLE). Exploration Scientifique de l'Algérie pendant les années 1840–42 : Beaux-Arts, Architecture, et Sculpture. 3 vols. roy. fol. Paris, 1846. **A 12 P 19–21 ‡**

RAWLINSON (PROF. GEORGE), M.A. Five Great Monarchies of the Ancient Eastern World; or, the History, Geography, and Antiquities of Chaldæa, Assyria, Babylon, Media, and Persia. 4 vols. 8vo. Lond., 1862–67. **B 13 V 19–22**

Sixth Great Oriental Monarchy. 8vo. Lond., 1873. **B 1 P 4**

Seventh Great Oriental Monarchy. 8vo. Lond., 1876. **B 1 P 6**

History of Ancient Egypt. 2 vols. 8vo. Lond., 1881. **B 2 R 38, 39**

Egypt and Babylon, from Scripture and Profane Sources. 8vo. Lond., 1885. **G 7 8 3**

Manual of Ancient History, from the Earliest Times to the Fall of the Western Empire. (Clar. Press.) 8vo. Oxford, 1869. **B 14 S 37**

[*See* HERODOTUS.]

RAWLINSON (MAJOR-GEN. SIR HENRY C.), K.C.B. England and Russia in the East. 8vo. Lond., 1875.
B 12 U 7

Selection from the Historical Inscriptions [Cuneiform] of Chaldæa, Assyria, and Babylonia; prepared by Sir H. C. Rawlinson, assisted by E. Norris, and Geo. Smith. 4 vols. (in 2) roy. fol. Lond., 1861–75. B 32 P 11, 12 ‡

RAWLINSON (ROBERT), C.E. On the Sewering of Towns and Draining of Houses. (Pam. C.) Roy. 8vo. Lond., 1862. MJ 2 S 1

Suggestions as to the Preparation of District Maps, and of Plans for Main Sewerage, Drainage, and Water Supply. (The Public Health Act, 1875.) Revised to 1878. Fol. Lond., 1878. A 23 R 2 ‡

RAWLINSON (THOMAS E.) Papers and Reports, read before the Philosophical Institute, and the Royal Society of Victoria; and other Documents. 8vo. Melb., 1865.
MA 2 V 21

Railway and Harbour Accommodation. [*See* OLDHAM, T.]
MJ 2 R 15

RAY SOCIETY. Publications. 38 vols. 8vo. and 14 vols. fol. Edinb. and Lond., 1841–84. . E

RAYMOND (GEORGE). Memoirs of Robert William Elliston, Comedian, 1774–1810. 2 vols. 8vo. Lond., 1844. C 7 Q 3, 4

RAYMOND (G. L.) Poetry as a Representative Art. 8vo. New York, 1886. H 7 R 40

RAYMOND (JAMES). New South Wales Calendar and General Post Office Directory. 5 vols. 8vo. Sydney, 1832–37.* ME 4 Q

RAYMOND (CAPT. J. W.) Cure for the Rabbit Plague: the Oat-Phosphorus Poison. 8vo. Melb., 1881. MJ 2 R 15

RAYMOND (ROSSITER W.) Statistics of Mines and Mining in the States and Territories West of the Rocky Mountains. 2 vols. 8vo. Wash., 1870–73. E

RAYMOND (SAMUEL), M.A. [*See* CAMPBELL, REV. DR. T.]

RAYNAL (WILLIAM THOMAS), ABBÉ. Philosophical and Political History of the Settlements and Trade of the Europeans in the East and West Indies. 8 vols. 8vo. Lond., 1788. B 10 R 27–34

RAYNOUARD (F. J. M.) Grammaire Comparée des Langues de l'Europe Latine, dans leurs Rapports avec la Langue des Troubadours. 8vo. Paris, 1821. K 12 S 5

Lexique Roman; ou, Dictionnaire de la Langue des Troubadours; précédé d'un nouveau choix des Poésies originales des Troubadours. 6 vols. roy. 8vo. Paris, 1836–44.
K 15 Q 30–35
[*See* LEWIS, SIR G. C.]

READ (CHARLES A.), F.R.H.S. Cabinet of Irish Literature: Selections from the Works of the chief Poets, Orators, and Prose Writers of Ireland; with Biographical Sketches and Literary Notices. 4 vols. roy. 8vo. Lond., 1880–81.
J 9 V 11–14

READ (C. RUDSTON). What I heard, saw, and did at the Australian Gold-fields. 8vo. Lond., 1853.*. MD 5 V 7

READE (WILLIAM WINWOOD). Story of the Ashantee Campaign. 8vo. Lond., 1874. B 1 P 35

Savage Africa; being the Narrative of a Tour in Equatorial, South-western, and North-western Africa; with Notes on the Habits of the Gorilla. With Illustrations. 2nd ed. 8vo. Lond., 1864. D 2 R 1

The Martyrdom of Man. 8vo. Lond., 1872. G 7 R 30

African Sketch-book. With Maps and Illustrations. 2 vols. 8vo. Lond., 1873. D 1 R 8, 9

READWIN (T. ALLISON), F.G.S. Index to Mineralogy; this Index is an alphabetical List of about 2,500 Minerals; with concise References to their Composition, Synonymes, and Place in the British Museum. 8vo. Lond., 1867.
A 10 P 11

REBER (DR. FRANZ VON). History of Ancient Art; translated and augmented by Joseph Thacher Clarke. With Illustrations. 8vo. Lond., 1883. A 7 T 20

RECENT TRAVELLER, A. [*See* SHOBERL, F.]

RECENT SETTLER, A. [*See* EMIGRATION.]

RECENT VISITOR, A. [*See* MOSS, F. J.]

RECLUS (JEAN JACQUES ELISÉE). The Earth: a descriptive History of the Phenomena of the Life of the Globe; translated by the late B. B. Woodward, M.A. 2 vols. 8vo. Lond., 1871. A 29 T 2, 3

The Earth: a descriptive History of the Phenomena of the Life of the Globe; edited by Prof. A. H. Keane. Imp. 8vo. Lond., 1886. A 15 U 3

Ocean, Atmosphere, and Life; being the Second Series of a descriptive History of the Life of the Globe; translated by the late B. B. Woodward, M.A. 2 vols. 8vo. Lond., 1873. A 29 T 4, 5

Nouvelle Géographie Universelle: La Terre et les Hommes. Tomes 1–11. Imp. 8vo. Paris, 1877–86.
D 10 V 1–11

1. L'Europe Méridionale (Grèce, Turquie, Roumanie, Serbie, Italie, Espagne et Portugal).
   La France; contenant une grande Carte de la France.
2. L'Europe Centrale (Suisse, Austro-Hongrie, Allemagne).
4. L'Europe du Nord-ouest (Belgique, Hollande, Iles Britanniques).
5. L'Europe Scandinave et Russe.
6. L'Asie Russe.
7. L'Asie Orientale.
8. L'Inde et l'Indo-Chine.
9. L'Asie Antérieure.
10. L'Afrique Septentrionale. Première Partie: Bassin du Nil, Soudan Égyptien, Erriopie, Nubie, Egypte.
11. L'Afrique Septentrionale. Deuxième Partie: Tripolitaine, Tunisie, Algérie, Maroc, Sahara.

RECORD COMMISSIONERS' PUBLICATIONS. Acts of the Parliaments of Scotland, A.D. 1124 to 1707. 11 vols. fol. Lond., 1814–44. F 24 P 1–11 ‡

Ancient Laws and Institutes of Wales. Fol. Lond., 1841. F 24 Q 21 ‡

Ancient Laws and Institutes of England. Fol. Lond., 1840. F 24 Q 22 ‡

Ancient Kalendars and Inventories of the Treasury; by Sir F. Palgrave. 3 vols. roy. 8vo. Lond., 1836. B 15 T 1–3

Calendars of the Proceedings in Chancery; temp. Elizabeth. 3 vols. fol. Lond., 1827–32. B 24 Q 6–8 ‡

Callendarium Inquisitionum Post Mortem Sive Escaetarum; temp. Hen. III–Ric. III. 4 vols. (in 2) fol. Lond., 1806–28. B 24 P 15, 16 ‡

Callendarium Rotulorum Chartarum et Inquisitionum ad quod Damnum. Fol. Lond., 1803. B 24 P 17 ‡

Calendarium Rotulorum Patentium in Turri Londinensi. Fol. Lond., 1802. B 24 P 18 ‡

Catalogue of the MSS. in the Cottonian Library. Fol. Lond., 1802. B 24 P 19 ‡

Catalogue of the Harleian MSS. in the British Museum. 4 vols. (in 2) fol. Lond., 1808. B 24 P 12, 13 ‡

Catalogue of the Lansdowne MSS. in the British Museum. 2 vols. (in 1) fol. Lond., 1819. B 24 P 14 ‡

Description of the Close Rolls in the Tower of London; by T. D. Hardy. Roy. 8vo. Lond., 1833. B 15 T 25

Documents and Records, illustrating the History of Scotland; by Sir F. Palgrave. Roy. 8vo. Lond., 1837. B 15 T 4

Domesday Book. 4 vols. fol. Lond., 1783–1816. B 24 Q 1–4 ‡

Domesday Book: General Introduction to; by Sir H. Ellis. 2 vols. 8vo. Lond., 1833. B 15 T 22, 23

Ducatus Lancastriæ. Pars Prima. Calendarium Inquisitionum Post Mortem, etc. temp. Edw. I—Car. I. Pars Secunda, Tertia, Quarta; a Calendar to Pleadings, &c. Hen. VII—Elizabeth. 3 vols. (in 1) fol. Lond., 1823–34. B 24 Q 18 ‡

Excerpta è Rotulis Finium in Turri Londinensi asservatis, A.D. 1216–72; cura C. Roberts. 2 vols. roy. 8vo. Lond., 1835–36. B 15 T 5, 6

Fines, sive Pedes Finium, A.D. 1195–1214; edente J. Hunter. Roy. 8vo. Lond., 1835. B 15 T 7

Fœdera, Conventiones, Litteræ, et cujuscunque generis Acta Publica, 1066–1377; cura et Studio T. Rymer, et R. Sanderson. 3 vols. (in 6). Lond., 1816–30. B 21 Q 9–14 ‡

General Report, to the King in Council from the Hon. Board of Commissioners on the Public Records; with an Appendix and index. Fol. Lond., 1837. B 24 Q 19 ‡

Inquisitionum ad Capellam Domini Regis Retornatarum, quæ in Publicis Archivis Scotiæ, adhuc servantur abbreviatio. 3 vols. fol. Lond., 1811–16. B 24 Q 15–17 ‡

Magnum Rotulum Scaccarii, vel Magnum Rotulum Pipæ; nunc Primum Edidit J. Hunter. Roy. 8vo. Lond., 1833. B 15 T 8

RECORD COMMISSIONERS' PUBLICATIONS—*contd.*
Nonarum Inquisitiones in Curia Scaccarii, temp. Edw. III. Fol. Lond., 1807. B 24 Q 20 ‡

Parliamentary Writs, and Writs of Military Summons, &c.; collected and edited by Sir F. Palgrave. 2 vols. (in 4) fol. Lond., 1827–34. F 24 R 1–4 ‡

Placita de quo Warranto, temp. Edw. I, II, III. Fol. Lond., 1818. B 24 R 5 ‡

Placitorum in Domo Capitulari Westmonasteriensi asservatorum Abbreviatio; temp. Ric. I, Johann, Hen. III, Edw. I, Edw. II. Fol. Lond., 1811. B 24 R 6 ‡

Proceedings and Ordinances of the Privy Council 1386–1642; edited by Sir N. H. Nicolas. 7 vols. roy. 8vo. Lond., 1834–37. B 15 T 9–15

Registrum Magni Sigilli Regum Scotorum in Archivis Publis asservatum, A.D. 1306–1424. Fol. Lond., 1814. B 24 R 7 ‡

Registrum vulgariter nuncupatum. (The Record of Caernarvon.) Edited by Sir H. Ellis. Fol. Lond., 1838. B 24 Q 5 ‡

Rotuli Chartarum in Turri Londinensi asservati, A.D. 1199–1216; accurante T. D. Hardy. Fol. Lond., 1837. B 24 R 8 ‡

Rotuli Curiæ Regis: Rolls and Records of the Court, held before the King's Justiciars or Justices. Ric. I—John; edited by Sir F. Palgrave. 2 vols. roy. 8vo. Lond., 1835. B 15 T 20, 21

Rotuli de Oblatis et Finibus in Turri Londinensi asservati, temp. Johannis; accurante T. D. Hardy. Roy. 8vo. Lond., 1835. B 15 T 18

Rotuli Hundredorum; temp. Hen. III and Edw. I; in Turr' Lond,' et in curia Receptae Scaccarii Westm. asservati. Fol. Lond., 1812–18. B 24 R 9–10 ‡

Rotuli Litterarum Patentium in Turri Londinensi asservati, A.D. 1201–16; accurante T. D. Hardy. Fol. Lond., 1835. B 24 R 11 ‡

Rotuli Litterarum Clausarum, in Turri Londinensi asservati; accurante T. D. Hardy. Fol. Lond., 1853. B 24 R 12 ‡

Rotuli Parliamentorum ut et Petitiones et Placita in Parliamento, temp. Edw. I—Hen. VII. 7 vols. fol. Lond., 1832. B 24 R 15–21 ‡

Rotuli Scotiæ. 2 vols. fol. Lond., 1814–19. B 24 R 13, 14 ‡

Rotuli Selecti ad Res Anglicas et Hibernicas spectantes; cura J. Hunter. Roy. 8vo. Lond., 1834. B 15 T 17

Rotuli Normanniæ, in Turri Londinensis asservati, Johanne et Henrico Quinto; accurante T. D. Hardy. Roy. 8vo. Lond., 1835. B 15 T 19

Rotulorum Originalium in Curia Scaccarii Abbreviatio, temp. Hen. III, Edw. I, II, III. 2 vols. (in 1) fol. Lond., 1805. B 24 S 1 ‡

Rotulus Cancellarii, vel Antigraphum Magni Rotuli Pipæ; de Tertio Anno Regni Regis Johannis. Roy. 8vo. Lond., 1833. B 15 T 16

Statutes of the Realm A.D. 1101–1713. 10 vols. fol. Lond., 1810–24. F 24 S 2–11 ‡

RECORD COMMISSIONERS' PUBLICATIONS—*contd.*
Taxatio Ecclesiastica Angliæ et Walliæ; auct. P
Nicholai iv; circa, A.D. 1291. Fol. Lond., 1802.
B 24 S 12 ‡

Testa de Nevill, sive Liber Feodorum in curia Scaccarii,
temp. Hen. III, Edw. I. ·Fol. Lond., 1807. B 24 S 13 ‡

Tracts; by C. P. Cooper. 8vo. Lond., 1832. B 15 T 24

Valor Ecclesiasticus, temp. Hen. VIII. 6 vols. (in 3)
fol. Lond., 1810–34. B 24 S 14–16 ‡

Introduction to Valor Ecclesiasticus of Hen. VIII., by
Rev. J. Hunter. Roy. 8vo. Lond., 1884. B 15 T 26

RECORDS OF THE PAST; being English Translations
of the Assyrian and Egyptian Monuments. Published
under the sanction of the Society of Biblical Archæology;
edited by Dr. S. Birch. 12 vols. 12mo. Lond.,
1873–81. B 21 Q 2–13

REDCLIFFE (RT. HON. SIR STRATFORD DE). [*See*
STRATFORD DE REDCLIFFE, RT. HON. SIR S. C.]

REDDING (CYRUS). History and Description of Modern
Wines. 8vo. Lond., 1833. A 1 Q 3

Fifty Years' Recollections, Literary and Personal; with
Observations on Men and Things. 3 vols. 8vo. Lond.,
1858. C 4 U 3–5

Personal Reminiscences of Eminent Men. 3 vols. 8vo.
Lond., 1867. C 3 Q 39–41

An Illustrated Itinerary of the County of Cornwall.
. Imp. 8vo. Lond., 1842. D 8 V 23

Illustrated Itinerary of the County of Lancaster. Roy.
8vo. Lond., 1842. D 8 V 22

REDFERN (F.) Manual of Edeography; or, the Art of
Writing by Sound; being a complete System of Phonetic
Shorthand, adapted to Verbatim Reporting. 3rd ed.
12mo. Lond., 1874. K 11 U 24

REDFORD (GEORGE), F.R.C.S. Manual of Sculpture:
Egyptian, Assyrian, Greek, Roman. With Illustrations.
8vo. Lond., 1882. A 7 Q 7

REDFORD (GEORGE), D.D., &c. [*See* JAY, REV. W.] C7R33

REDGRAVE (GILBERT R.) Outlines of Historic Ornament; translated from the German. With Illustrations.
8vo. Lond., 1884. A 6 V 23

[*See* REDGRAVE, R.]

REDGRAVE (R.) Manual of Design, compiled by G. R.
Redgrave. (South Kens. Mus.) 8vo. Lond., 1876. E

REDGRAVE (RICHARD), AND REDGRAVE (SAMUEL).
A Century of Painters of the English School; with
Critical Notices of their Works, and an Account of the
Progress of Art in England. 2 vols. 8vo. Lond., 1866.
A 7 Q 34, 35

REDGRAVE (SAMUEL). Dictionary of Artists of the
English School: Painters, Sculptors, Architects, Engravers, and Ornamentists; with Notices of their Lives
and Work. New ed. 8vo. Lond., 1878. C 11 Q 10

REDHOUSE (JAMES W.), M.R.A.S., &c. The Mesnevī
(usually known as the Mesneviyi Sherif or Holy Mesnevī)
of Mevlânâ (Our Lord) Jelâlu-D-Dīn, Muhammed, Er-
Rūmī; translated, and the Poetry versified, by James
W. Redhouse, M.R.A.S., &c. 8vo. Lond., 1881.
H 8 U 15

Lexicon, English and Turkish; showing, in Turkish, the
Literal, Incidental, Figurative, Colloquial, and Technical
Significations of the English Terms. 2nd ed. Roy. 8vo.
Constantinople, 1877. K 16 R 3

English and Turkish Dictionary; in two parts—English
and Turkish, and Turkish and English. 8vo. Lond.,
1857. K 12 Q 28

Diary of H.M. the Shah of Persia. [*See* NASR EDDIN,
SHAH OF PERSIA.] D 8 8 8

RED SPINNER. [*See* SENIOR, W.]

REDTENBACHER (LUDWIG). Fauno Austriaca: die
Käfer. Roy. 8vo. Wien, 1858. A 15 P 8

REDWITZ (OSCAR VON). Amaranth. 11ᵉ Auflage. 18mo.
Mainz, 1851. H 6 P 27

REDWOOD (THEOPHILUS), PH.D. Elements of Materia
Medica. [*See* PEREIRA, J.] A 12 U 5

REED (ANDREW), D.D. Memoirs of the Life and Philanthropic Labours of; edited by his Sons, Andrew Reed,
B.A., and Charles Reed, F.S.A. 2nd ed. 8vo. Lond.,
1863. C 9 Q 37

REED (ANDREW), JUNR., B.A., AND REED (CHARLES),
F.S.A. Memoir of the Life and Philanthropic Labours
of Andrew Reed, D.D., with selections from his Journals,
. edited by his Sons. 2nd. ed. 8vo. Lond., 1863. C9Q37

REED (SIR EDWARD J.), K.C.B., &c. Japan: its History,
Traditions, and Religions; with the Narrative of a Visit
in 1879. Map and Illustrations. 2 vols. 8vo. Lond.,
1880. B 12 S 10, 11

Treatise on the Stability of Ships. 8vo. Lond., 1885.
A 2 Q 10

[*See* HYDRO-MECHANICS.] A 11 U 7

REED (ISAAC). Biographia Dramatica. [*See* BAKER,
D. E.] C 6 8 1–4

REED (JOSEPH). The Register Office: a Farce. [*See*
FARCES, 3.]

REED (REBECCA THERESA). Six Months in a Convent.
[*See* MACENCROE, VEN. ARCHD. J.] MG 1 P 5

REEMELIN (CHARLES). Critical Review of American
Politics. 8vo. Lond., 1881. F 5 P 20

REENAN (JACOB VAN). [*See* RIOU, CAPT. E.] MD 4 P 26 †

REES (ABRAHAM), D.D., &c. Cyclopædia; or, Universal
Dictionary of Arts, Sciences, and Literature. 39 vols.
4to. Lond., 1819. K 5 S 1–T 16

Plates [to the above]. 6 vols. 4to. Lond., 1820.
K 5 T 17–22

REES (J.) New Catalogue of Rees' Circulating Library
[with] Supplements. 8vo. Bristol, 1821–25. K 7 R 10

REES (J. ROGERS). Diversions of a Book-worm. 12mo.
Lond., 1886.   J 10 P 34

Pleasures of a Book-worm. 12mo. Lond., 1886.
                                                         J 7 Q 21

REES (J. RUUTZ). Horace Vernet. (Great Artists.)
8vo. Lond., 1880.   C 3 T 44

Paul Delaroche. (Great Artists.) 8vo. Lond., 1880.
                                                         C 3 T 44

REES (L. E. RUUTZ). Personal Narrative of the Siege
of Lucknow. 8vo. Lond., 1858.   B 10 Q 5

REES (ROWLAND), C.E. Address delivered at the Laying
of the Foundation Stone of the South Australian Institute. [*See* SOUTH AUSTRALIAN INSTITUTE.] MJ 1 T 42

REES (T.) Topographical and Historical Description of
the Counties of Brecknock and Caermarthen. 8vo.
Lond., 1810.   B 3 S 23

REES (W. COLLINS). Mercantile Navy List of Victoria.
8vo. Melb., 1868.   ME 3 T

REEVE (CLARA). The Old English Baron : a Gothic Story.
With Portrait and Drawings. 8vo. Lond., 1883. J 10 R 14

REEVE (EDWARD). Catalogue of the Museum of Antiquities of the Sydney University. 8vo. Sydney, 1870.
                                                         MK 1 Q 19

Railway Guide of New South Wales (for the use of
Tourists, Excursionists, and others). 4to. Sydney,
1881.   MD 3 V 38

Another copy. 2nd ed. 4to. Sydney, 1884.*   MD 3 V 39

Another copy. 3rd ed. 4to. Sydney, 1886.   MD 3 V 41

Gazetteer of Central Polynesia. [*See* ST. JULIAN C.]

REEVE (EMILY). Character and Costume in Turkey and
Italy. [*See* ALLOM, T.]   A 4 R 20 †

REEVE (HENRY). The Greville Memoirs. [*See* GREVILLE,
C. C. F.]

Washington. [*See* GUIZOT, F. P. G.]   C 4 S 49

REEVE (LOVELL), F.L.S. Land and Freshwater Mollusks,
Indigenous to, or Naturalised in, the British isles. 8vo.
Lond., 1863.   A 14 S 18

Conchologia Systematica ; or, complete System of Conchology, in which the Lebades and Conchiferous Mollusca
are described and classified according to their natural
organisation and habits. 2 vols. 4to. Lond., 1841 42.
                                                         A 11 V 2, 3

REEVES (C. E.), M.D., &c. The Queen v. Boavey :
Extraordinary Charge of Murder against a Medical Man,
in consequence of a diseased womb being ruptured after
death ; with Medical Notes and Observations. 8vo.
Melb., 1866.   MF 1 Q 5

Softening of the Stomach in Children in Australia ; with
some Observations on the Disease in Adults. 8vo. Melb.,
1867.   MA 2 S 31

Heart Diseases in Australia ; with Observations on
Aneurism of the Aorta. 8vo. Melb., 1873.*   MA 2 S 32

REEVES (MRS. HENRY), HELEN MATHERS. Sam's Sweet-
heart ; by Helen Mathers. 2nd ed. 3 vols. Lond.,
1883.   MJ 2 P 21-23

REEVES (REV. WILLIAM), D.D., &c. The Culdees of the
British Islands, as they appear in History ; with an Appendix of Evidences. Roy. 4to. Dublin, 1864.   G 12 R 5 †

Life of Saint Columba. [*See* ADAMNAN.]

REFUGE (THE). The Refuge, Osborne-street, Gardiner's
Creek Road, South Yarra. Established 1857. (*Circular.*)
8vo. Melb. (n.d.)   MG 1 Q 26

REGINA v ROBERTS. Trial for Bigamy, in the Supreme
Court, New South Wales : Opinions of the Judges. 8vo.
Sydney, 1850.   MF 1 Q 4

REGINO (PRUMIENSIS ABBAS). Opera omnia. [*See* MIGNE,
J. P., SERIES LATINA, 132.]

REGISTRUM MAGNI SIGILLI. Regum Scotorum in
Archivis Publicis Asservatum, A.D. 1306-1424. Fol.
Lond., 1814.   B 24 R 7 ‡

REGISTRUM VULGARITER NUNCUPATUM. "The
Record of Caernarvon"; edited by Sir H. Ellis. Fol.
Lond., 1838.   B 24 Q 5 ‡

REGNIER (A.) [*See* SCHILLER, J. C. F. VON.]
                                                         J 13 U 11-18

REHTMEYER (PHILIPP JULIO). Das Leben des Seligen
Herrn Joachimi Lütkemans. 12mo. Brunswick, 1720.
                                                         G 9 Q 4

REIBEY (THOMAS), ARCHDEACON v. BLOMFIELD (HENRY
WILSON). Full Report of the Great Libel Case, tried at
the Supreme Court, Launceston. Reprinted from the
"Cornwall Chronicle." 2nd ed. 8vo. Launceston, 1870.
                                                         MF 1 Q 5

REICH (EDUARD). Studien über die Frauen. 8vo. Jena,
1875.   A 12 U 31

REICHENBACH (KARL), PH.D., BARON VON. Physico-
Physiological Researches on the Dynamides or Impon-
derables—Magnetism, Electricity, Heat, Light, Crystal-
lisation and Chemical Attraction—in their relations to the
Vital Force ; translated and edited by William Gregory,
M.D., &c. Vol. 1 (*all published.*) 8vo. Lond., 1850.
                                                         A 6 P 1

REID (DAVID BOSWELL), M.D., &c. Illustrations of the
Theory and Practice of Ventilation ; with Remarks on
Warming, Exclusive Lighting, and the Communication of
Sound. 8vo. Lond., 1844.   A 2 S 11

Brief Outlines illustrative of the Alterations in the House
of Commons, in reference to the Acoustic and Ventilating
Arrangement. 4to. Edinb., 1837.   A 2 T 44

REID (DAVID BOSWELL), JUNR. Quarterly Clinical Reports.
[Geelong Hospital] No. 1, January, 1861. (Pam. Ce.)
8vo. Geelong, 1861.   MA 2 S 15

REID (GEORGE HOUSTON). Diplomacy of Victoria on the Postal Question, and the true Policy of New South Wales. (Pam. Ds.) 8vo. Sydney, 1873. MF 3 P 17

Another copy. 8vo. Sydney, 1873. MJ 2 R 14

Five Free Trade Essays. Contents: Introductory Essay—Protection in Great Britain—Protection in the United States of America—Protection in Australia—Concluding Essay. Roy. 8vo. Melb., 1875. MF 3 R 5

Essay on New South Wales, the Mother Colony of the Australias. Roy. 8vo. Sydney, 1876.* MF 3 R 6

Protection or Free Trade? Speech in favour of Free Trade: Discussion with David Buchanan, Esq., M.P. 8vo. Sydney, 1880. MF 1 Q 6

Another copy. 8vo. Sydney, 1880. MF 3 P 22

REID (GEORGE WILLIAM), F.S.A. Works of the Italian Engravers of the Fifteenth Century; reproduced in facsimile by Photo-Intaglio. Fol. Lond., 1884. A 23 Q 17 ‡

REID (HENRY), C.E. Science and Art of the Manufacture of Portland Cement; with Observations on some of its Constructive Applications. 8vo. Lond., 1877. A 11 S 11

REID (JAMES S.) M. Tolli Ciceronis Academica. [*See* CICERO, M. T.]

REID (JOHN T.) Art Rambles in the Highlands and Islands of Scotland. 4to. Lond., 1878. D 7 V 13

·Pictures from the Orkney Islands. 4to. Edinb., 1881. D 7 V 8

REID (CAPT. MAYNE). Odd People; being a popular Description of singular Races of Man. 12mo. Lond., 1860. J 1 U 38

Croquet. (Pam. 24.) 8vo. Lond., 1863. MJ 2 Q 12

REID (STUART J.) Sketch of the Life and Times of the Rev. Sydney Smith. 8vo. Lond., 1884.* C 9 U 25

REID (THOMAS), D.D. Works of, now fully collected; with selections from his unpublished Letters; by Sir Wm. Hamilton, Bart. Prefixed, [D.] Stewart's Account of the Life and Writings of Reid. 7th ed. 2 vols. 8vo. Edinb., 1872. G 1 R 8, 9

Essays on the Intellectual Powers of Man; to which is annexed an Analysis of Aristotle's Logic; with Notes, &c., by the Rev. G. N. Wright, M.A., &c. 8vo. Lond., 1843. G 11 T 6

Account of the Life and Writings of; by Dugald ·Stewart, F.R.S. 8vo. Edinb., 1803. C 10 P 29

REID (THOMAS), M.R.C.S. Two Voyages to New South Wales and Van Diemen's Land; including Facts and Observations relative to the State and Management of Convicts of both sexes. 8vo. Lond., 1822. MD 2 V 18

REID (W. F.) Excellency of the Knowledge of Christ: a Sermon. 8vo. Sydney, 1860. MG 1 P 1

REIFF (CHARLES PHILLIP). English-Russian Grammar, or Principles of the Russian Language, for the use of the English; with Synoptical Tables for the Declensions and Conjugations, Graduated Themes or Exercises for the application of the Grammatical Rules. 3rd ed. 8vo. Paris, 1862. K 13 Q 21

Little Manual of the Russian Language: a Work in which the Russian words are represented with their pronunciation figured in English Characters, and with their Accentuation. 3rd ed. 8vo. Paris, 1869. K 11 V 2

New Parallel Dictionaries of the Russian, French, German, and English Languages, in four Parts; extracted from the Dictionaries of the Russian Academy, the French Academy, Adelung, Heinsius, Johnson, Spiers, and other Lexicographers. 4 vols. sq. 8vo. Carlsruhe, 1875–79. K 12 P 38–41

REIGN OF TERROR IN CARLOW. (Pam. 11.) 8vo. Lond., 1841. F 12 P 9

REIMER (RUDOLF VON). Süd-Australien; ein Beitrag zur deutschen Auswanderungsfrage. 8vo. Berlin, 1851. MD 5 R 27

REIN (PROF. J. J.) Japan: Travels and Researches; with Illustrations and Maps. Roy. 8vo. Lond., 1884. D 5 U 22

REINBECK (G.) Travels from St. Petersburg through Moscow, Grodno, Warsaw, Breslaw, &c., to Germany, in the year 1805; in a Series of Letters. Translated. 8vo. Lond., 1807. D 8 T 35

REINISCH (LEO). Der einheitliche Ursprung der Sprachen der alten Welt; nachgewisen durch Vergleichung der afrikanischen, erythräischen und indogermanischen Sprachen mit Zugrundelegung des Teda. Erster Band. Roy. 8vo. Wien, 1873. K 14 U 24

REINWALD (W. F. H.) [*See* ULPHILAS.]

REIS (JOHANN PHILIPP). Phillipp Reis, Inventor of the Telephone: a Biographical Sketch; by Prof. Silvanus P. Thompson. 8vo. Lond., 1883. C 9 Q 35

REISSMANN (AUGUST). Life and Works of Robert · Schumann. 8vo. Lond., 1886. C 2 Q 45

REITLINGER (EDMUND). Freie Blicke. Populär Wissenschaftlige Ausläke. 8vo. Berlin, 1874. A 16 Q 18

REITZIUS (JOHANN FRIEDRICH). [*See* LUCIAN, S.] J 15 U 27–36

RELIGION IN AUSTRALIA. Copies of Correspondence and Documents showing the Progress of Measures taken for the Advancement of Religion in Australia. (Parl. Doc. 30.) Fol. Lond., 1840. MF 4 ‡

A few Facts in reference to the voluntary support of Religion. 8vo. Hobart (n.d.) MG 1 Q 31

RELIGIOUS CEREMONIES. Dictionary of the Religious Ceremonies of the Eastern Nations; with Historical and Critical Observations, some Account of their learned Men, and Situations of the most Remarkable Places in Asia. 4to. Calcutta, 1787. K 18 S 5

RELIGIOUS INSTRUCTION IN AUSTRALIA.
Copies of all Despatches or Instructions addressed to the
Governors of the Australian Colonies relating to the
enlargement of the means of Religious Instruction and
Public Worship. Fol. Lond., 1857.   MF 1 U 34

RELIGIOUS TRACT AND BOOK SOCIETY OF
IRELAND. Ninth Report, 1823.   8vo.   Dublin,
1823.   MG 1 Q 26

RELIGIOUS TRACT AND BOOK SOCIETY, N. S.
WALES. [*See* NEW SOUTH WALES RELIGIOUS TRACT
AND BOOK SOCIETY.]

RELIGIOUS TRACT SOCIETY. Abstract of the Sixty-
seventh Annual Report. (Pam. Bo.)   8vo. Lond.,
1866.   MG 1 Q 32

RELTHA. [*See* SILLYLAW.]

REMACLE (L.)   Dictionnaire Wallon-Française, dans
lequel on Trouve la Correction de los Idiotismes Vicieux,
et de los Wallonismes, par la Traduction, en Français,
des Phrases Wallonnes. 2e éd. 2 vols. Liége (n.d.)
                                              K 13 S 21, 22

REMARKABLE PERSONS. [*See* CAULFIELD, J.]

REMBRANDT VAN RYN (HERMANZOON). A Biography;
by J. W. Mollett. (Great Artists.) 8vo. Lond., 1879.
                                              C 3 T 40

Rembrandt and his Works; comprising a short Account
of his Life. [*See* BURNET, J.]

Etched Work of Rembrant. [*See* HADEN, F. E.]

REMIGIUS (ANTISSIODORENSIS MONACHUS). Opera omnia.
[*See* MIGNE, J. P., SERIES LATINA, 131.]

REMINISCENCES of a Retired Physician.   12mo.
Lond., 1877.   J 10 P 36

REMSEN (IRA). Introduction to the Study of the Compounds of Carbon ; or, Organic Chemistry. 8vo. Lond.,
1885.   A 5 R 45

Introduction to the Study of Chemistry. 8vo. Lond.,
1886.   A 5 R 35

RÉMUSAT (CLAIRE ELIZABETH JEANNE), COMTESSE DE.
Memoirs of Madame de Rémusat, 1802-08. Published by
her Grandson, M. Paul de Rémusat. Translated. 2 vols.
8vo. Lond., 1880.   B 8 U 18, 19

Selection from the Letters of Madame de Rémusat to
her Husband and Son, from 1804-13 ; from the French,
by Mrs. C. T. Hoey. 8vo. Lond., 1881.   C 9 V 29

RÉMUSAT (JEAN PIERRE ABEL). Recherches sur les
Langues Tartares, ou Mémoires sur différens points de la
Grammaire et de la Littérature des Mandchous, des
Mongols, des Ouigours et des Tibétains. 4to. Paris,
1820.   S 16 R 31

Élémens de la Grammaire Chinoise, ou Principes
généraux du Kou-Wen ou Style Antique, et du Kouan.
Hoa, c'est-à-dire, de la Langue Commune généralement
usitée dans l'Empire Chinois. Imp. 8vo. Paris, 1857.
                                              K 13 T 23

REMY (JULES). Récits d'un Vieux Sauvage : pour servir
a l'Histoire Ancienne de Havaii ; notes d'un Voyageur.
8vo. Chalons-sur-Marne, 1859.   MD 7 P 11

REMY (JULES), AND BRENCHLEY (JULIUS), M.A.
Journey to Great Salt Lake City ; with a Sketch of the
History, Religion, and Customs of the Mormons.
2 vols. roy. 8vo. Lond., 1861.   D 3 U 25, 26

RENAN (JOSEPH ERNEST). Essay on the Age and
Antiquity of the Book of Nabathæan Agriculture. 8vo.
Lond., 1862.   A 1 Q 23

The Apostles ; translated from the original French.
8vo. Lond., 1869.   G 11 T 15

Life of Jesus. New ed. 8vo. 8vo. Lond., 1871. G 14 Q 1

Lectures on the Influence of the Institutions, Thought
and Culture of Rome, on Christianity, and the Development of the Catholic Church. (Hibbert Lectures.) 8vo.
Lond., 1880. .   G 7 P 10

Strauss and Renan : an Essay ; by E. Zeller. 8vo.
Lond., 1866.   G 10 Q 17

Spinoza : an Essay. [*See* SPINOZA B. DE.]   C 9 R 30

De l'Origine du Langage. 5e éd. 8vo. Paris,
1875. .   K 14 Q 35

Histoire générale et Système Comparé des Langues
Sémitiques. Première Partie : Histoire Générale des
Langues Sémitiques. 5e éd. 8vo. Paris, 1878.
                                              K 14 Q 36

RENDU (M. LE C.) Theory of the Glaciers of Savoy ;
translated by Alfred Willis, Q.C. 8vo. Lond., 1874.
                                              A 9 S 15

RENDU (VICTOR). Ampélographie Française : Description des principaux Cépages, des procédés de Culture et
de Vinification usités dans les meilleurs crus de France.
Fol. Paris, 1854.   A 1 P 1 ‡

RENNELL (MAJOR JAMES), F.R.S. Geographical System
of Herodotus examined ; and explained by a Comparison
with those of other Ancient Authors, and with Modern
Geography. 4to. Lond., 1800.   D 11 P 10 †

Illustrations (chiefly Geographical) of the History of
the Expedition of Cyrus, from Sardis to Babylonia ; and
the Retreat of the Ten Thousand Greeks. 4to. Lond.,
1816.*   D 10 Q 8 ‡

Observations on the Topography of the Plain of
Troy, and on the principal Objects within and around
it described or alluded to in the Iliad. 4to. Lond.,
1814.   B 18 R 14

RENNIE (D. F.), M.D. Peking and the Pekingese, during
the first year of the British Embassy at Peking. 2 vols.
8vo. Lond., 1865.   D 5 Q 1, 2

British Arms in North China and Japan. Pekin, 1860 ;
Kagosima, 1862. 12mo. Lond., 1864.   B 2 P 19

Bhotan, and the Story of the Dooar War. 8vo. Lond.,
1866.   B 10 Q 26

RENNIE (EDWARD ALEXANDER). The Ten Kingdoms:
a Study in the Prophecies: a Lecture. 8vo. Sydney,
1873. MG 1 Q 35

Lecture on the Two Witnesses of the Book of Revelation. 8vo. Sydney, 1879. MG 1 Q 35

Foundation Strength of Popery; by "An old Student
of Scripture." 8vo. Sydney, 1888.* MG 2 Q 3

RENNIE (GEORGE). A few Observations in reply to a
Letter from Sir M. A. Shee, P.R.A., to the Rt. Hon.
Lord John Russell, H.M. Principal Secretary of State for
the Home Department, on the alleged Claim of the
Public to be admitted Gratis to the Exhibition of the
Royal Academy. 8vo. Lond., 1837. A 7 Q 13

[*See* SHEE, SIR M. A.]

RENNIE (REV. JAMES). Insect Architecture. New ed.,
much enlarged by the Rev. J. G. Wood, M.A.; with
nearly two hundred Illustrations. 8vo. Lond., 1869.
A 14 P 45

The Menageries. Quadrupeds. 2nd ed. (Lib. Ent.
Know.) 12mo. Lond., 1830–31. K 10 R 49–50

Domestic Habits of Birds. (Lib. of Ent. Know.)
12mo. Lond., 1833. K 10 R 21

Insect Miscellanies. (Lib. of Ent. Know.) 12mo.
Lond., 1831. K 10 R 34

Insect Architecture. (Lib. of Ent. Know.) 2nd ed.,
12mo. Lond., 1836. K 10 R 35

Insect Transformations. (Lib. of Ent. Know.) 12mo.
Lond., 1830. K 10 R 36

Faculties of Birds. (Lib. of Ent. Know.) 12mo.
Lond., 1835. K 10 R 22

Architecture of Birds. (Lib. of Ent. Know.) 12mo.
Lond., 1831. K 10 R 20

Menageries. Quadrupeds, described and drawn from
subjects. (Lib. of Ent. Know.) 2nd ed. 12mo. Lond.,
1830–31. K 10 R 49–50

RENNIE (SIR JOHN), F.R.S. Autobiography of; comprising the History of his Professional Life. Roy. 8vo.
Lond., 1875. C 9 V 30

RENOURD (ANT. AUG.) Annales de Imprimerie des
Alde; ou, Histoire des trois Manuce et de leurs
Editions et Supplement. 3 vols. (in 2) 8vo. Paris,
1803. K 17 Q 30, 31

REPP (THORLEIF GUDMUNDSSON). Dansk–Norsk–engelske
Ordbog. [*See* FERRALL, J. S.]

REPRESENTATIVE GOVERNMENT. [*See* NEW SOUTH
WALES.]

REPORT ON THE HOUSE OF COMMONS. [*See*
HOUSE OF COMMONS.] A 2 U 33

REPTON (HUMPHRY). Landscape Gardening and Landscape Architecture of; with an Introduction and Index,
&c., by J. C. Loudon, F.L.S., &c. 8vo. Lond., 1840.
A 1 R 15

4 L

RERESBY (SIR JOHN), BART. Travels and Memoirs of.
Illustrated with Portraits and Views. 8vo. Lond.,
1813. D 8 V 9

Mémoires de. [*See* GUIZOT, F. P. G., 21.]

RERUM BRITANNICARUM SCRIPTORES. 8m. fol.
Lugduni, 1587. B 14 R 6 ‡

RESEARCH. [*See* BEILBY, J. W.]

RESIDENT, A. [*See* GIRL LIFE IN AUSTRALIA.]

RESIDENT, A. [*See* MADAGASCAR.]

RESIDENT, A. [*See* KERR, J. H.]

RESIDENT, A. [*See* MASSEY, MISS ISABEL.]

RESIDENT OFFICER, A. [*See* MADRID.]

RESTIF DE LA BRETONNE (NICHOLAS EDME). [*See*
MOREAU, LE JEUNE; JEAN MICHEL.] A 2 P 13 ‡

RESULT SYSTEM (THE). Copy of Report adopted at a
Public Meeting of Teachers, and transmitted to the
Board of Education. 8vo. Melb., 1863. MG 1 Q 30

RESURGAM. [*See* CREMATION.]

RETIRED GOVERNOR OF JUAN FERNANDEZ,
THE. [*See* SUTCLIFFE, T.]

RETIRED OFFICER OF THE HON. EAST INDIA
CO.'S SERVICE, A. [*See* GARDINER, COMM. A. F.]

RETROSPECTIVE REVIEW (THE). 16 vols. (*All
published.*) 8vo. Lond., 1820–28.

Vols. 1 and 2. New series. (*All published.*) 8vo.
Lond., 1853–54. E

RETSLAG (DR. CARL). Political Sketches; twelve
Chapters on the Struggles of the Age. 8vo. Lond.,
1854. F 5 8 7

RETZ (JEAN FRANÇOIS PAUL DE GONDI), CARDINAL DE. Intrigues du. [*See* JOLI, G.] C 1 R 16, 17

RETZ (JEAN FRANÇOIS PAUL DE GONDI), CARDINAL DE,
JOLI (GUY), AND NEMOURS (MARIE D'ORLEANS),
DUCHESS DE. Mémoires du. Nouvelle édition. 6 vols.
12mo. Paris, 1817. C 4 P 17–22

RETZSCH (FRIEDRICH AUGUST MORITZ). Outlines illustrative of the Tragedy [of Faust.] [*See* GOETHE, J.
W. VON.]

RETZSCH (MORITZ) Gallerie zu Shakspeare's dramatischen
Werken, in Umrissen erfunden und gestochen. Romeo
und Julia—König Lear—Die Lustigen Weiber von
Windsor. Ob 4to. Leipzig (n.d.) A 8 R 3 †

REUCHLIN OR CAPNION (JOHN). Life and Times
of; by Francis Barham. 12mo. Lond., 1843. C 1 R 31

REUILLY (J.) Travels in the Crimea and along the
Shores of the Black Sea, performed during the year 1803.
8vo. Lond., 1807. D 8 T 36

REULEAUX (PROF. F.) Kinematics of Machinery; Outlines of a Theory of Machines. Translated by A. B. W. Kennedy, F.R.S. 8vo. Lond., 1876. . A 11 S 17

REUMONT (ALFRED VON). Lorenzo de' Medici il Magnifico. 2 vols. 8vo. Leipsig, 1874. C 11 P 22, 23
Lorenzo de' Medici, the Magnificent. Translated. 2 vols. 8vo. Lond., 1876. C 11 P 24, 25
Carafas of Maddaloni: Naples under Spanish Dominion. Translated. 12mo. Lond., 1854. B 12 P 25

REUSS (EDOUARD). La Bible. [*See* BIBLES, &c.—FRENCH.]

REVEIL (A.), AND DUCHESNE (J.) Museum of Painting and Sculpture; or, Collection of the Principal Pictures, Statues, &c., in the Galleries of Europe. Text in French and English. Paris, 1829–33. A 33 Q 1-17

REVEILLÉ-PARISE (DR. J. H.) Traité de la Vieillesse Hygiénique, Médical et Philosophique; ou, Recherches sur l'Etat Physiologiques, les Facultés Morales, les Maladies de l'Age avancé. 8vo. Paris, 1853. A 12 R 37

REVELATIONS OF P[ORT] A[RTHUR] (THE); or, News from our Penal Settlement; by "Tim Bobbin." 8vo. Hobart, 1868. MF 1 Q 4

REVENUE: a Treatise of the Revenue and False Money of the Romans. To which is annexed a Dissertation upon the Manner of distinguishing Antique Medals from Counterfeit ones. 8vo. Lond., 1741. F 3 T 10

REYETT (N.) [*See* STUART, J.] A 1 R 12-15 ‡

REVILLE (PROF. ALBERT), D.D. Lectures on the Origin and Growth of Religion, as illustrated by the Native Religions of Mexico and Peru. (The Hibbert Lectures.) 8vo. Lond., 1884. G 7 P 8

REVOIL (HENRY). Architecture Romane du Midi de la France. 3 vols. fol. Paris, 1867-74. A 1 Q 3-5

REVUE AUSTRALIENNE: Journal des Interets Française en Australie, Nouvelle-Calédonie, Nouvelle-Zélande, Fiji, Tahiti, Polynésie. Nos. 2-4, Janvier-Mars, 1874. 8vo. Sydney, 1874. ME 3 R

REVUE DES DEUX MONDES. 178 vols. roy. 8vo. Paris, 1852-85. E

REVUE COLONIALE INTERNATIONALE. Tome 1, 1885. 8vo. Paris, 1885. E

REVUE DES QUESTIONS HISTORIQUES. Vols. 11-37. Roy. 8vo. Paris, 1872-85. E

REVUE INTERNATIONALE. Sous la direction de M. Angelo de Gubernatis. Vols. 1-6. Roy. 8vo. Florence, 1883-85. E

REVY (J. J.), C.E. Hydraulics of Great Rivers. The Paraná, the Uruguay, and the La Plata Estuary. Imp. 4to. Lond., 1874. A 23 S 20 ‡

REY (E. GUILLAUME). Voyage dans le Haouran et aux bords de la Mer Morte. 8vo. atlas imp. fol. Paris, 1860. D 5 U 30 ‡
Atlas [to the above]. Large 4to. Paris, 1860. D 8 P 18 ‡

REYBAUD (LOUIS). La Polynésie et les Isles Marquises; Voyages et Marine accompagnés d'un Voyage en Abyssinie et d'un Coup-d'œil sur la Canalisation de l'Isthme de Panama. 8vo. Paris, 1843. MD 5 S 5

REYNARD THE FOX; after the German Version of Goethe; by Thos. Jas. Arnold. Illustrated. Roy. 8vo. Lond., 1860. H 6 V 9

REYNOLDS (FREDERICK). Life and Times of; written by himself. 2nd ed. 2 vols. 8vo. Lond.,1827. C 6 S 26, 27
The Delinquent: a Comedy. [*See* MODERN THEATRE, 2.]
Folly as it Flies: a Comedy. [*See* MODERN THEATRE, 2.]
Fortune's Fool: a Comedy. [*See* MODERN THEATRE, 2.]
How to grow Rich: a Comedy. [*See* MODERN THEATRE, 1.]
Laugh when you can: a Comedy. [*See* MODERN THEATRE, 2.]
Life: a Comedy. [*See* MODERN THEATRE, 1.]
Notoriety: a Comedy. [*See* MODERN THEATRE, 1.]
The Rage: a Comedy. [*See* MODERN THEATRE, 1.]
Speculation: a Comedy. [*See* MODERN THEATRE, 2.]
Werter: a Tragedy. [*See* MODERN THEATRE, 3.]
The Will: a Comedy. [*See* MODERN THEATRE, 1.]

REYNOLDS (F. M.) "Miserrimus"; or a Gravestone in Worcester Cathedral is this emphatic Inscription, Miserrimus; with neither Name nor Date, Comment nor Text. 12mo. Lond., 1833. J 1 R 33

REYNOLDS (SIR JOSHUA), KNT., &c. Life of; comprising Original Anecdotes of many distinguished Persons, &c.; by James Northcote, R.A. 2 vols. 8vo. Lond., 1819. C 6 R 16, 17
Life and Times of; by C. R. Leslie, R.A.; continued and concluded by Tom Taylor. 2 vols. 8vo. Lond., 1865. C 9 P 35, 36
Literary Works of; with a Memoir of the Author, by H. W. Beechey. 2 vols. 12mo. Lond., 1835. J 11 P 33, 34
Engravings from the Works of; by S. W. Reynolds. 3 vols. fol. Lond., 1833–38. A 5 P 8-10 ‡
Sir Joshua Reynolds: a Biography; by F. S. Pulling. (Great Artists.) 8vo. Lond., 1880. C 3 T 44
Anecdote Biography. [*See* TIMBS, J.] C 1 S 5

REYNOLDS (MICHAEL). Stationary Engine Driving: a Practical Manual for Engineers in Charge of Stationary Engines. With illustrations. 8vo. Lond.,1881. A 11 P 24
Continuous Railway Brakes: a Practical Treatise on the several Systems in use in the United Kingdom; their Construction and Performance. With Illustrations. 8vo. Lond., 1882. A 6 R 16
Engineman's Pocket Companion and Practical Educator for the Engineman, Boiler Attendants, and Mechanics. 18mo. Lond., 1886. A 11 P 11

REYNOLDS (Prof. Osborne). On Rolling Friction. (Roy. Soc. Pubs., 3.) 4to. Lond., 1876.   A 11 P 4 †

On the Refraction of Sound by the Atmosphere. (Roy. Soc. Pubs., 2.) 4to. Lond., 1876.   A 11 P 3 †

On the Forces caused by the Communication of Heat between a Surface and a Gas ; and on the new Photometer. (Roy. Soc. Pubs., 3.) 4to. Lond., 1876. A 11 P 4 †

The General Theory of Thermo-Dynamics : a Lecture. [*See* Heat.]   A 11 U 9

REYNOLDS (Richard S.), M.R.C.V.S. Essay on the Breeding and Management of Draught Horses. 8vo. Lond., 1882.   A 1 R 32

REYNOLDS (S. W.) [*See* Reynolds, Sir J.] A 5 P 8–10 ‡

REYNOLDS (T.) Political History of ; containing an Account of his Transactions with the Rebellion in Ireland. [*See* Hist. Pams.]   B 11 Q 1

REZASCO (G.) Dizionario del Linguaggio Italiano, Storico ed Amministrativo. Roy. 8vo. Firenzi, 1881. K 16 T 6

RHADAMANTHUS. [*See* Bar And Attorneys.]

RHODE ISLAND. [*See* United States of America.]

RHOÏDIS (Emmanuel). Pope Joan (the Female Pope): an Historical Study; translated, with Preface, by C. H. Collette. 12mo. Lond., 1886.   C 2 Q 23

RHŶS (John), M.A. Lectures on Welsh Philology. 2nd ed. 8vo. Lond., 1879.   K 12 Q 1

RIANO (Juan F.) Industrial Arts in Spain. (South Kens. Mus.) 8vo. Lond., 1879.   E

RIBBECK (O.) [*See* Leipziger Studien.]

RIBEYRO (Capt. John). History of Ceylon; presented by Captain John Ribeyro to the King of Portugal, in 1685; translated from the Portuguese by the Abbé J. Le Grand. 8vo. Ceylon, 1847.   B 10 U 31

RIBOT (Prof. Th.) Diseases of Memory : an Essay in the Positive Psychology. 8vo. Lond., 1882. A 12 Q 41

RICARDO (David). On the Principles of Political Economy and Taxation. 8vo. Lond., 1821.   F 6 U 16

RICCI (J. H. de). [*See* De Ricci, J. H.]

RICCI (Prof.) The Italian Principia. Part 1. A First Italian Course, on the plan of Dr. W. Smith's "Principia Latina." Part 2. A First Italian Reading-book and a Dictionary. 2 vols. (in 1) 8vo. Lond., 1883–84. K 12 R 4

RICCI (Scipion de), Bishop of Pistoia And Prato. Vie et Mémoires de; par Louis Joseph Antoine de Potter. 4 vols. 8vo. Paris, 1826.   C 5 V 29–32

RICE (James). History of the British Turf, from the Earliest Times to the Present Day. 2 vols. 8vo. Lond., 1879.   B 7 R 13, 14

RICE (Maj.-Gen. William). "Indian Game" (from Quail to Tiger). Imp. 8vo. Lond., 1884.   A 15 T 5

RICH (Anthony), B.A. Dictionary of Roman and Greek Antiquities; with Engravings on Wood, illustrative of the Industrial Arts and Social Life of the Greeks and Romans. 4th ed. 8vo. Lond., 1874.   K 7 Q 2

RICH (Elihu). Cyclopædia of Biography. 8vo. Lond., 1854.   K 5 U 13

RICHARD (A.) [*See* Dumont D'Urville, Capt. J. S. C.]

RICHARD I (King of England). History of the Life of Richard-Cœur-de-Lion, King of England ; by G. P. R. James. 4 vols. 8vo. Lond., 1842–49.   C 9 R 10–13

RICHARD III. Richard III as Duke of Gloucester and King of England ; by Caroline A. Halsted. 2 vols. 8vo. Lond., 1844.   C 9 P 27, 28

The Unpopular King : the Life and Times of Richard III; by Alfred O. Legge, F.C.H.S. 2 vols. 8vo. Lond., 1885.   B 4 T 6, 7

RICHARD (Henry). Memoirs of Joseph Sturge. 8vo. Lond., 1864.   C 9 U 46

RICHARD (H.), And WILLIAMS (J. C.) Disestablishment. 8vo. Lond., 1885.   G 7 T 31

RICHARD OF DEVIZES. [*See* Chronicles of the Crusades.]   B 10 P 23

RICHARDS (Lieut. G. E.) Pacific Islands: Sailing Directions; compiled from various sources. 3 vols. 8vo. Lond., 1885.   MD 7 R 6–8

RICHARDS (Capt. G. H.), And EVANS (F. J.), R.N. New Zealand Pilot; from Surveys made in H.M. Ships *Acheron* and *Pandora.* 2nd ed. 8vo. Lond., 1859.   MD 7 R 9

RICHARDS (John Morgan). Chronology of Medicine, Ancient, Mediæval, and Modern. Illustrated. 8vo. Lond., 1880.   A 12 R 10

RICHARDS (Thomas). General Indexes to Letters of Registration for Inventions and Improvements in the Arts or Manufactures, granted in New South Wales, from 1855 to 1880, inclusive. Fol. Sydney, 1883.

New South Wales in 1881 ; being a brief Statistical and Descriptive Account of the Colony up to the end of the year ; extracted chiefly from official Records. Published by authority. 2nd issue. 8vo. Sydney, 1882.*   MF 1 S 19

Another copy. 2nd issue. 8vo. Sydney, 1882.   MJ 2 R 17

An Official History of New South Wales. [*See* New South Wales.]

RICHARDS (W.) [*See* Hughes, S.]   A 17 R 6

RICHARDSON (BENJAMIN WARD), M.D., &c. Diseases of Modern Life. 8vo. Lond., 1876.   A 12 Q 4

Alcohol: its action and its use. (Cantor Lectures.) Roy. 8vo. Lond., 1875.   A 15 U 21

Diseases of Modern Life. New ed. 8vo. Lond., 1879.   A 12 Q 5

RICHARDSON (CHARLES), LL.D. New Dictionary of the English Language; combining explanation with Etymology, and illustrated by Quotations from the best authorities. 2 vols. 4to. Lond., 1875.   K 15 T 10, 11

RICHARDSON (MRS. CHARLES). Memoirs of the Private Life and Opinions of Louisa, Queen of Prussia, Consort of Frederick William III. 8vo. Lond., 1847.   C 3 V 36

RICHARDSON (CHARLES F.) The Choice of Books. 12mo. Lond., 1881.   J 12 S 27

RICHARDSON (A. J.) The Overland Expedition from Port Denison to Cape York, under the command of F. and A. Jardine. 8vo. Lond., 1866.   MD 7 Q 53

RICHARDSON (C. J.) The Englishman's House, from a Cottage to a Mansion: a Practical Guide to Members of Building Societies, and all interested in selecting or building a house. 2nd ed. 8vo. Lond., 1870.   A 2 R 5

Picturesque Designs for Mansions, Villas, Lodges, &c.; with Decorations, internal and external, suitable to each style. Roy. 8vo. Lond., 1870.   A 2 Q 29

RICHARDSON (G. B.) Universal Code of Signals for the Mercantile Marine. [*See* MARRYAT, CAPT. F.]

RICHARDSON (GEORGE), F.S.A. Book of Ceilings, in the Stile of the Antique Grotesque. (English and French.) Fol. Lond., 1774.   A 1 R 6 ‡

RICHARDSON (G. F.), F.G.S. Introduction to Geology and its Associate Sciences. 8vo. Lond., 1869.   A 9 P 8

RICHARDSON (REV. GEO. W.) Sermon on the Death of. [*See* COWPER, VERY REV. W. M.]   MG 1 P 1

RICHARDSON (JAMES). Wonders of the Yellowstone Region in the Rocky Mountains; being a Description of its Geysers, Hot Springs, Grand Cañon, Waterfalls, Lake, and surrounding Scenery, explored in 1870-71. Illustrated. 8vo. Lond., 1874.   D 3 P 19

Travels in the Great Desert of Sahara, in the years 1845-46. 2 vols. 8vo. Lond., 1848.   D 2 S 15, 16

RICHARDSON (J.), M.D., &c. [*See* BEECHEY, CAPT. F. W.]   A 14 V 1

RICHARDSON (JOHN), F.S.A. Dictionary, Persian, Arabic, and English: with a Dissertation on the Languages, Literature, and Manners of Eastern Nations. New ed. 2 vols. 4to. Lond., 1806-10.   K 16 U 1, 2

RICHARDSON (SIR JOHN), KNT., &c. Vertebrals, including Fossil Mammals. [*See* FORBES, PROF. E.]   A 2 S 11 †

RICHARDSON (MAJ.-GEN. J. S.), C.B. Rifle Exercises for the use of the Permanent and Volunteer Military Forces of New South Wales, armed with the short Rifle. 8vo. Sydney, 1872.   MA 2 V 27

RICHARDSON (JOSEPH). The Fugitive: a Comedy. [*See* MODERN THEATRE 8.]

Life and Poems of. [*See* BRITISH POETS 4.]

RICHARDSON (SAMUEL). Tour through the Island of Great Britain. [*See* DE FOE, D.]   D 7 P 33-36

RICHARDSON (DR. T.) Chemical Technology. [*See* RONALDS, DR. E.]   A 5 U 8-13

RICHARSON (T. A.) Art of Architectural Modelling in Paper. (Weale.) 12mo. Lond., 1859.   A 17 P 63

RICHARDSON (WILLIAM). Timber Merchant's, Saw-Miller's, and Importer's Freight-book and Assistant; comprising Rules, Tables, and Memoranda relating to the Timber Trade; together with a Chapter on Speeds of Saw-Mill Machinery, &c., by M. Powis Bale, M.I.M.E., &c., and a London Price List for Timber and Deal Sawing, &c., 1884. (Weale.) 12mo. Lond., 1884.   A 17 Q 65

RICHARDSON (W. A.) Report on the State of the Finances, United States. (Pam. Dq.) 8vo. Washington, 1873.   F 4 R 7

RICHARDSON (W. L.) Summary of Seven Years' Work of the State Board of Health of Massachusetts. 8vo. Boston, 1876.   E

RICHARDUS A SANCTO VICTORE. Opera omnia. [*See* MIGNE, J. P., SERIES LATINA, 196.]

RICHEA (DODO). Theatrum Funebre. [*See* AICHER, O.]

RICHELIEU (ARMAND JEAN DU PLESSIS), DUC DE. Le Cardinal de Richelieu; par J. B. H. R. Capefigue. 12mo. Paris, 1865.   C 1 S 21

Mémoires de. [*See* BARRIÈRE, J. F.]   C 1 T 16, 17

RICHERAND (A.) Elements of Physiology. Translated. 3rd ed. 8vo. Lond., 1819.   A 12 T 9

RICHERUS. Historiarum Libri quatuor. [*See* MIGNE, J. P., SERIES LATINA, 138.]

RICHMOND (PROF. W. B.) Lectures on Art. [*See* ART.]   A 6 V 36

RICHMOND (W. D.) Colour and Colour Printing as applied to Lithography. 8vo. Lond., 1885.   A 11 Q 31

RICHMOND AND DERBY (MARGARET BEUFORT), COUNTESS OF. Life of Margaret Beaufort, Countess of Richmond and Derby, Mother of King Henry VII; by Caroline A. Halsted. 8vo. Lond., 1839.   C 10 Q 2

RICHTER (JEAN PAUL), PH.D., &c. Italian Art in the National Gallery. 4to. Lond., 1883. A 8 U 26
Leonardo [da Vinci.] (Great Artists.) 8vo. Lond., 1880. C 3 T 37
Literary Works of Leonardo da Vinci. [*See* VINCI, L. DA.]
Lives of the Painters, &c. ; with Commentary. [*See* VASARI, GEORGIS.] C 4 R 27–32

RICHTER (JEAN PAUL F.) Jean Paul's sämmtliche Werke. 4 vols. roy. 8vo. Paris, 1836–37. J 15 V 1–4
Life of, compiled from various sources ; together with his Autobiography ; translated from the German. 2 vols, 8vo. Lond., 1845. C 2 Q 35, 36
Flower, Fruit, and Thorn Pieces ; or, the Married Life, &c., of Firmian Stanislaus Siebenkäs. Translated. 2 vols. 12mo. Lond., 1845. J 11 T 17, 18
Tales by Musaeus, Tieck, [and] Richter ; translated from the German by Thomas Carlyle. 2 vols. 12mo. Lond., 1874. J 1 T 11, 12

RICHTER (LUDWIG). Richter Album ; eine Auswahl von Holzschnitten nach Zeichnungen. Sechste Ausgabe in zwei Bänder. 2 vols. 8vo. Leipzig, 1876. A 7 T 22, 23

RICHTER (PROF. T.) Analysis with the Blowpipe. [*See* PLATTNER, C. F.] A 5 T 26

RICHTOFEN (F. VON), BARON. Geology ; Letters and Reports on the Provinces of Hunan, Honan, Shansi, Chekiang, Ngaihwei, Chili, Shensi and Sy'-Chwan. Fol. Shanghai, 1870–72. A 2 S 23 †

RICHTHOFEN (KARL) FREIHERRN VON. Altfriesisches Wörterbuch. 4to. Göttingen, 1840. K 16 R 15

RICKARD (MAJOR F. IGNACIO). Mining Journey across the Great Andes ; with Explorations in the Silver Mining Districts. 8vo. Lond., 1863. D 3 P 56

RICKARDS (G. K.), M.A. [*See* VIRGILIUS MARO, P.] H 6 R 42

RICKETTS (MAJOR). Narrative of the Ashantee War ; with a View of the State of the Colony of Sierra Leone. 8vo. Lond., 1833. B 1 P 37

RICKMAN (JOHN). [*See* TELFORD, T.]

RICKMAN (THOMAS), F.S.A. Attempt to discriminate the Styles of Architecture in England, from the Conquest to the Reformation. 5th ed. 8vo. Lond., 1848. A 2 S 26

RIDDELL (JOHN). Stewartiana ; containing the Case of Robert II and Elizabeth Mure, and Question of the Legitimacy of their Issue. 8vo. Edinb., 1843. B 13 Q 6
Salt-Foot Controversy, as it appeared in Blackwood's Magazine ; to which is added a Reply to the Article published in No. XVIII of that Work. 8vo. Edinb., 1818. B 13 Q 1
Vindication of the "Clan Ronald of Glengary" against the Attacks made upon them in the Inverness Journal. 8vo. Edinb., 1821. B 13 Q 4

RIDDELL (ROBERT). The Carpenter and Joiner, Stair-builder and Hand-railer ; with Plates. Roy. 4to. Edinb. (n.d.) A 21 Q 1 ‡

RIDEING (WILLIAM H.) Thackeray's London : a Description of his Haunts and the Scenes of his Novels. Sq. 12mo. Lond., 1885. J 7 Q 17

RIDGWAY (JAMES). Speeches of Rt. Hon. Thomas, Lord Erskine. [*See* ERSKINE, T. LORD.] E 13 P 23–26

RIDGWAY (ALEXANDER F.) & SONS. Voices from Auckland, New Zealand. 8vo. Lond., 1860. MD 7 Q 34

RIDLEY (RT. REV. NICHOLAS), BISHOP OF LONDON. Treatises and Letters of. [*See* BRITISH REFORMERS, 10.]

RIDLEY (REV. WILLIAM), M.A., &c. Fragments of Kamilaroi Grammar (MS.) (Pam. 41.) 12mo. Sydney (n.d.) MJ 2 R 3
Gurre Kamilaroi ; or, Kamilaroi Sayings. 12mo. Sydney, 1856. MK 1 P 24
Links and Divergence of the Australian Languages and Tribes (M.S.) (Pam. 41.) 12mo. Sydney, 1864. MJ 2 R 3
Kámilarói, Dippil, and Turrubul : Languages spoken by the Australian Aborigines. Sm. 4to. Sydney, 1866.* MK 1 S 26
Will Evil last for ever! a Lecture. Sm. 4to. Sydney, 1872. MJ 2 S 3
Kámilarói and other Australian Languages. 2nd ed. Sm. 4to. Sm. 4to. Sydney, 1875.* MK 1 S 28

RIDPATH (REV. GEORGE). Border History of England and Scotland. 4to. Berwick, 1848. B 16 Q 19 ‡

RIDPATH (REV. PHILIP). Boethius's Consolation of Philosophy. [*See* BOETHIUS, A. M. T. S.]

RIEBECK (EMIL), PH.D., &c. Chittagong Hill Tribes : Results of a Journey made in the year 1882 ; translated by Prof. A. H. Keane, B.A. Roy. fol. Lond., 1885. A 1 P 6 ‡

RIEHL (PROF. A.) Der Philosophische Kriticismus, und seine bedeutung für die Positive Wissenschaft. 2 vols. 8vo. Leip., 1876–79. G 11 T 16, 17

RIENZII (G. L. DOMENY DE). Océanie ; ou, Cinquième Partie du Monde : Revue Géographique et Ethnographique de la Malaisie, de la Micronésie, de la Polynésie et de la Mélanésie. 3 vols. 8vo. Paris, 1843–72. MD 5 S 11–13

RIETMANN (PROF. O.) Wanderungen in Australien und Polynesien. 12mo. St. Gallen, 1868. MD 1 Q 11

RIETZ (DR. J.) [*See* MENDELSSOHN-BARTHOLDY, F.] C 5 P 25

RIFLE ASSOCIATION OF NEW SOUTH WALES. [*See* NEW SOUTH WALES.]

RIGBY (ELIZABETH), LADY EASTLAKE. Residence on the Shores of the Baltic; described in a series of Letters. 2 vols. 8vo. Lond., 1841. D 9 P 6, 7

Livonian Tales. The Disponent. The Wolves. The Jewess. (H. and C. Lib.) 12mo. Lond., 1846. J 8 P 16

Letters from the Shores of the Baltic. (H. and C. Lib.) 12mo. Lond., 1844. J 8 P 5

RIGG (REV. ARTHUR), M.A. Cantor Lectures—On Mechanism—Energies of Gravity, &c.--Tools and Contrivances. Roy. 8vo. Lond., 1872. A 15 U 21

Energies of Gravity, Vitality, Affinity, Electricity, Light, and Heat. (Cantor Lectures, 8.) Roy. 8vo. Lond., 1873. A 15 U 21

Material, Construction, Form, and Principles of Tools and Contrivances used in Handicraft. (Cantor Lectures.) Roy. 8vo. Lond., 1875. A 15 U 21

RIGG (REV. CHARLES W.) Digest of the Laws and Regulations of the Australasian Wesleyan Connexion. 12mo. Sydney, 1863. MG 1 P 30

RIGG (E.) [*See* SAUNIER, C.] A 11 V 1

RIGG (REV. JAMES HARRISON), D.D. National Education, in its Social Conditions and Aspects, and Public Elementary School Education, English and Foreign. 8vo. Lond., 1873. G 17 P 27

RIGHT OF SEARCH (THE). Reply to an "American's Examination" of; by "An Englishman." 8vo. Lond., 1842. F 12 P 14

RIGUTINI (GIUSEPPE), É FANFANI (PIETRO). Vocabolario Italiano della Lingua Parlata. 3rd ed. Imp. 8vo. Firenze, 1880. K 16 S 1

RIKART (CARL VON). Menes and Cheops identified in History under different Names. 8vo. Lond., 1869. B 2 R 43

RILEY (HENRY THOMAS), M.A. Chronicles of the Mayors and Sheriffs of London, 1188 to A.D. 1274; translated, with Notes and Illustrations. 4to. Lond., 1863. B 7 P 24

Comedies of Plautus. [*See* PLAUTUS, M. A.]

Comedies of Terence, and Fables of Phaedrus. [*See* TERENTIUS AFER, P.]

Dictionary of Latin and Greek Quotations, Proverbs, Maxims, and Mottoes, Classical and Mediaeval, including Law Terms and Phrases. 8vo. Lond., 1871. K 17 P 35

The Pharsalia of Lucan. [*See* LUCANUS, M. A.]

[*See* HOVEDEN, ROGER DE.] B 3 P 10, 11

[*See* INGULPHUS.] B 4 P 8

[*See* OVIDIUS NASO, P.]

[*See* PLINIUS SECUNDUS.] A 16 P 6-11

RILEY (THOMAS), AND CUNDALL (FRANK). Reminiscences of the Colonial and Indian Exhibition. Illustrated. 4to. Lond., 1886. A 15 U 23

RILEY (W. E.) Remarks on the Importation and Result of the Introduction of the Cachemere and Angora Goats into France. 8vo. Lond., 1832.* MJ 2 R 17

Another copy. (Pam. 27.) 8vo. Lond.,1832. MJ 2 Q 15

Remarks on the Importation and Result of the Introduction of the Cachemere and Angora Goats into France. 8vo. Lond., 1832. MJ 2 R 22

RILLIET DE CONSTANT (V.) L'Ile de Pitcairn, ses Habitants et son Pasteur; précédé d'une courte Notice sur la Révolte de la *Bounty;* traduit d l'Anglais. 12mo. Toulouse, 1861. MD 1 T 47

RIMBAULT (EDWARD F.), LL.D. Musical Instruments. (Brit. Manuf. Indust.) 12mo. Lond., 1876. A 17 S 31

Gallery of German Composers. [*See* JÄGER, PROF. C.] C 1 W 6

RIMMER (ALFRED). Early Homes of Prince Albert. With Illustrations. 8vo. Edinb., 1883. D 8 T 18

Ancient Streets and Homesteads of England; and an Introduction by the Very Rev. J. S. Howson, D.D. With Illustrations. 8vo. Lond., 1877. A 3 P 20

RINGWALT (J. LUTHER). American Encyclopædia of Printing. Imp. 8vo. Philad., 1871. K 6 R 1

RINK (DR. HENRY). Danish Greenland: its People and its Products. 8vo. Lond., 1877. D 4 R 27

Memoirs of Hans Hendrik. [*See* HENDRIK HANS.] C 2 S 22

RINUCCINI (G. B.), ARCHBISHOP OF FERMO. Embassy in Ireland, in the years 1645-49; translated into English by Annie Hutton. 8vo. Dublin, 1873. B 11 P 38

RIOLA (HENRY). How to learn Russian: a Manual for Students of Russian. 12mo. Lond., 1878. K 11 V 5

Key to the Exercises of the Manual for the Students of Russian. 12mo. Lond., 1878. K 11 V 6

RIOU (CAPT. EDWARD). Distresses and Miraculous Preservation of H.M.S. *Guardian.* 8vo. Lond., 1790. MD 3 S 30

Journal of a Journey from the Cape of Good Hope, undertaken in 1790 and 1791, by Jacob van Reenen and others, in search of the Wreck of the *Grosvenor.* 4to. Lond., 1792. MD 4 P 25†

RIOUFFE (HONORÉ). Mémoires de. [*See* BARRIÈRE, J. F., 9.] C 1 T 9

RIPA (FATHER MATTEO). Memoirs of; during Thirteen Years' Residence at the Court of Peking; selected and translated from the Italian by Fortunato Prandi. (H. and C. Lib.) 12mo. Lond., 1844. J 8 P 8

Another copy. 12mo. Lond., 1846. D 1 T 18

RIPLEY (G.) [*See* AMERICAN CYCLOPAEDIA.] K 4 R 17-88

RIPLEY (H.) Hampton-on-Thames. 8vo. Lond., 1885.
B 4 T 1

RISHTON (REV. EDWARD), B.A. Rise and Growth of the Anglican Schism. [*See* SANDER, N.]
[*See* PARIS, MATHEW.]   B 17 S 15 ‡

RISSO (A.), ET POITEAU (A.) Histoire Naturelle des Orangers: Ouvrage orné de 109 Figures peintes d'après Nature. Fol. Paris, 1818–22.   A 23 S 23 ‡

RISTORI (ADELAIDE). Biography. (Pam. L.) 8vo. Sydney (n.d.)   MJ 2 P 28

Il Giro del Mondo. [*See* GALLETTI, GEN. B.]   MD 3 Q 1

RITCHIE (DAVID). Life and Anecdotes of David Ritchie, the original of Sir Walter Scott's Black Dwarf; by Wm. Chambers. 12mo. Edinb., 1885.   C 2 Q 38

RITCHIE (J. EWING). Night Side of London. 2nd ed. 12mo. Lond., 1858.   J 1 V 44

RITCHIE (LEITCH). British World in the East: a Guide, Historical, Moral, and Commercial, to India, China, Australia, South Africa, and the other Possessions or Connexions of Great Britain in the Eastern and Southern Seas. 2 vols. 8vo. Lond., 1847.   B 10 T 16, 17

Another copy. 2 vols. 8vo. Lond., 1847. MB 28 29, 30

London Nights' Entertainments. 8vo. Lond., 1836.
J 3 R 24

Ireland, Picturesque and Romantic. With Engravings. 8vo. Lond., 1838.   D 6 U 17

RITSCHL (ALBERT), PH.D., &c. Ad audiendam orationem de Ratione, quae inter Theologiam dogmaticam ethicenque Theologicam intercedit. (Pams., O.) 4to. Bonn, 1859.   J 6 U 10

RITSCHL (FRIEDRICH). Natalicia Regis Augustissimi Friderici Guilelmi IV Universitatis Fridericiae. Guilelmiae Rhenanae Conservatoris Clementissimi ab eadem Universitate indicit Fridericus Ritschelius. (Pams., O.) 4to. Bonn, 1860.   J 6 U 10

RITSON (JOSEPH). Letters of. Edited chiefly from originals in the possession of his Nephew; to which is prefixed a Memoir of the Author; by Sir Harris Nicolas, K.C.M.G. 2 vols. 12mo. Lond., 1833. C 4 P 27, 28

Select Collection of English Songs; with their original Airs, and a Historical Essay on the origin and progress of National Song. 2nd ed. 3 vols. 8vo. Lond., 1813.
H 8 S 1–3

The Caledonian Muse: a Chronological Selection of Scottish Poetry from the Earliest Times. 8vo. Lond., 1821.   H 8 S 11

Robin Hood: a Collection of all the Ancient Poems, Songs, and Ballads now extant, relative to that celebrated English Outlaw. 2nd ed. 2 vols. 8vo. Lond., 1832.   H 8 S 12, 13

Another copy. 8vo. Lond., 1885.   H 8 U 33

RITSON (JOSEPH)—*continued.*
Ancient Engleish Metrical Romanceës. 3 vols. 8vo. Lond., 1802.   H 8 S 7–9

Another copy, revised by Edmund Goldsmid, F.R.H.S. 3 vols. 8vo. Edinb., 1884–85.   H 8 U 10–12

Pieces of Ancient Popular Poetry; from authentic Manuscripts and old printed copies; adorned with Cuts [by Thomas Bewick]. 8vo. Lond., 1791.   H 8 S 10

The English Anthology. 3 vols. 8vo. Lond., 1793–94.
H 8 S 4–6

Bibliographia Poetica: a Catalogue of Engleish Poets of the Twelfth, Thirteenth, Fourteenth, Fifteenth, and Sixteenth Centurys. 8vo. Lond., 1802.   C 2 P 1

Annals of the Caledonians, Picts, and Scots; and of Strathclyde, Cumberland, Galloway, and Murray. 2 vols. 8vo. Edinb., 1828.   B 13 P 10, 11

RITTER (FANNY R.) [*See* PLAIDY, L.]   A 7 P 17

RITTER (DR. HEINRICH). History of Ancient Philosophy; translated from the German, by A. J. W. Morrison, B.A. 3 vols. 8vo. Oxford, 1838–39.   G 11 T 1–3

RITTERORDEN. Das Buch der Ritterorden und Ehrenzeichen. 8vo. Brussels, 1856.   K 10 U 17

RITTINGER (DR. C. G. G.) Das englische Blaubuch für die Vaccination und der Spiritualismus. (Pam.) 8vo. Stuttgart, 1857.   A 12 S 33

RIVARD (D. F.) Traité de la Sphère et du Calendrier. 8vo. Paris, 1816.   A 3 S 18

RIVERINE DISTRICTS. Progress Report from the Select Committee on the Riverine Districts. Fol. Melh., 1863.   ME 10 Q 3 †

Second Progress Report from the Select Committee on the Riverine Districts Trade. Fol. Melh., 1863. ME 10 Q 3 †

Report from the Select Committee on the Riverine Districts; together with the Proceedings of the Committee, Minutes of Evidence, and Appendices. Fol. Melh., 1863.   ME 10 Q 3 †

Petition from the Riverine District; ordered by the Legislative Assembly to be printed, 4th Sept., 1863. Fol. Melh. and Sydney, 1863.   ME 10 Q 3 †

RIVIERE (HENRI). Souvenirs de la Nouvelle-Calédonie. L'Insurrection Canaque. Roy. 8vo. Paris, 1881. MD 3 V 20

RIVINGTON (WALTER), B.A., &c. The Medical Profession; being the Essay to which was awarded the Carmichael Prize of £200 by the Council of the Royal College of Surgeons, Ireland, 1879. 8vo. Dublin, 1879.   A 12 R 7

ROARD (J. L.) Abrégé du Traité Théorique et Pratique sur la Culture de la Vigne, avec l'Art de faire le Vin, les Eaux-de-vie, Esprit de Vin, Vinaigres simples et composés. 8vo. Paris, 1806.   A 1 P 6

ROBBERDS (J. W.), F.G.S. Memoir of the Life and Writings of the late William Taylor, of Norwich. 2 vols. 8vo. Lond., 1843. C 9 V 35, 36

ROBBINS (ALFRED F.), "DUNHEVED." Launceston [Cornwall], Past and Present: a Historical and Descriptive Sketch. 8vo. Launceston, 1884. B 4 P 14

ROBBINS (MARY CAROLINE). Eugène Fromentin, Painter and Writer. [*See* GONSE, L.] C 5 T 10

ROBERT I (KING OF SCOTLAND). The Bruce. [*See* BARBOUR, J.]

ROBERT (L. P.) [*See* HARTING, J. E.] A 23 Q 12 ‡

ROBERT (REV. PERE), V.P. Aurifodina Universalis Scientiarum Divinarum atque Humanarum. 4 vols. imp. 8vo. Paris, 1865–66. K 18 T 1–4

Aurifodina Sacra Scientiarum Divinarum ex Fontibus Aureis utriusque Testamenti erutarum. 2 vols. imp. 8vo. Paris, 1868–69. K 18 T 5, 6

ROBERT-HOUDIN (JEAN EUGENE). [*See* HOUDIN, J. E. H.]

ROBERTS (PROF. ALEXANDER), D.D. Companion to the Revised Version of the English New Testament. 12mo. Lond., 1881. G 13 R 15

ROBERTS (BROWNE H. E.), B.A. History of the Colonial Empire of Great Britain. 8vo. Lond., 1861. B 4 Q 18

ROBERTS (CHARLES). Excerpta è Rotulis Finium in Turri Londinensi asservatis, A.D. 1216–72. 2 vols. roy. 8vo. Lond., 1835–36. B 15 T 5, 6

ROBERTS (DAVID), R.A. Life of. Compiled from his Journals and other Sources, by James Ballantine; with Etchings and Facsimiles of Pen-and-Ink Sketches, by the Artist. Roy. 4to. Edinb., 1866. C 1 W 24

The Holy Land, Syria, Idumea, Arabia, Egypt, and Nubia, after Lithographs by Louis Haghe, from Drawings made on the spot: with Historical Descriptions, by William Brockedon, F.R.S. 6 vols. (in 3) 4to. Lond., 1855–56. D 4 V 1–3

ROBERTS (DAVID). Tourist in Spain. (Landscape Annual.) [*See* JENNINGS, R.] D 8 Q 28

ROBERTS (MISS EMMA). Memoirs of the Rival Houses of York and Lancaster. 2 vols. 8vo. Lond., 1827. B 6 P 28, 29

Scenes and Characteristics of Hindostan: with Sketches of Anglo-Indian Society. 3 vols. 8vo. Lond., 1835. D 5 P 48 50

Notes of an Overland Journey through France and Egypt to Bombay. 8vo. Lond., 1841. D 10 R 15

ROBERTS (MAJ. GEN. SIR FREDERICK S.), BART., &c. A Memoir; by Charles Rathbone Low, I.N., &c. 8vo. Lond., 1883. C 8 U 17

ROBERTS (CAPT. GEORGE). Four Years' Voyages of; being a Series of Uncommon Events which befell him in a Voyage to the Islands of the Canaries, Cape de Verde, and Barbadoes, from whence he was bound to the Coast of Guiney. 8vo. Lond., 1726. D 10 R 22

ROBERTS (JANE). Two Years at Sea; being the Narrative of a Voyage to the Swan River and Van Diemen's Land, 1829–31. 8vo. Lond., 1834.* MD 4 V 15

ROBERTS (REV. JOHN). Mirror of Religion and Society in Tasmania, during the years 1857 and 1858. (Pam. 26.) 8vo. Hobart, 1858. MJ 2 Q 14

ROBERTS (JOHN S.) Legendary Ballads of England and Scotland: compiled and edited by John S. Roberts; with original Illustrations and Steel Portrait. 8vo. Lond. (n.d.) H 8 S 29

ROBERTS (MISS MARGARET). Oxford Reading Book. Part 1, for Little Children; Part 2, for Junior Classes. (Clar. Press.) 2 vols. (in 1) 12mo. Oxford, 1867. G 17 S 9

ROBERTS (O. W.) Narrative of Voyages and Excursions on the East Coast, and in the Interior of Central America; with Notes and Observations, by E. Irving. (Const. Misc.) 18mo. Edinb., 1827. K 10 Q 5

ROBERTS (RALPH A.), M.A. Collection of Examples on the Analytic Geometry of Plane Conics: to which are added some Examples on Sphero-Conics. (Dublin University Press Series.) 8vo. Dublin, 1884. A 10 S 21

ROBERTS (SIR RANDAL H.), BART. Modern War; or, the Campaign of the First Prussian Army, 1870–71. 8vo. Lond., 1871. B 9 R 10

ROBERTS (ROBERT). Prophecy and the Eastern Question: being an Exhibition of the Light shed by the Scriptures of Truth on the matters involved in the crisis that has arrived in Eastern Affairs. Reprinted for Australian circulation. 8vo. Melb., 1877. MG 1 Q 44

ROBERTS (T.) Heavenly Vision: or, Jacob's Dream, as representing the Providence of God, the Mediation of Christ, and the Ministry of Angels. (Victoria Tract and Cottage Sermons.) 12mo. Melb., 1856. MG 1 P 49

Missionary Hymns. (Pam., D.) 4to. Melb., 1869. MJ 2 U 3

ROBERTS (WILLIAM). History of Letter-Writing, from the Earliest Period to the Fifth Century. 8vo. Lond., 1843. B 15 P 12

ROBERTS (W. H.) Scottish Ale-Brewer: a Practical Treatise on the Art of Brewing Ales according to the System practised in Scotland. 8vo. Edinb., 1838. A 11 Q 24

ROBERTS (WILLIAM ISAAC). Poems and Letters; with some Account of his Life. 8vo. Lond., 1811. H 8 S 32

ROBERTSON (ALEXANDER), M.A. Two Speeches on our Home and Colonial Affairs, delivered in Dundee. Our National Resources : their Present and probable Future Condition ; and the British Colonies. 8vo. Dundee, 1880.   MD 1 V 10

ROBERTSON (ANDREW), AND DEUTSCH (HERMAN). Map of Squatting Stations in Victoria (in four parts); compiled by Andrew Robertson, lithographed by Herman Deutsch. Roy. 4to. Melh., 1865.   MD 5 P 15†

ROBERTSON (E. WILLIAM). Scotland under her early Kings ; a History of the Kingdom to the close of the Thirteenth Century. 2 vols. 8vo. Edinb., 1862.   B 13 R 9, 10

ROBERTSON (REV., FREDERICK W.), M.A. Life and Letters of. Edited by [the Rev.] S. A. Brooke, M.A. ; with Portraits. 3rd ed. 2 vols. 8vo. Lond., 1866.   C 4 R 34, 35

Sermons preached at Trinity Chapel, Brighton. 1st to 4th series. 4 vols. 8vo. Lond., 1866.   G 11 T 18–21

Robertson of Brighton ; with some Notices of his Times and Contemporaries ; by the Rev. F. Arnold. 8vo. Lond., 1886.   C 4 Q 30

ROBERTSON (GEORGE). Catalogue of Books offered to the Trade of Victoria, New South Wales, Queensland, South Australia, Tasmania, and New Zealand, at the Prices affixed. 8vo. Melh., 1869.   MK 1 R 37

Book and Stationery Trade List, 1869–70. 8vo. Melh., 1869–70.   MK 1 R 35

Select Catalogue of Books in every department of Literature, Science, and Art. 8vo. Sydney, 1876.   MK 1 R 37

ROBERTSON (G.) General Description of the Shire of Renfrew. [*See* CRAWFURD, G.]   B 5 R 4†

ROBERTSON (PROF. G. C.) Aristotle. [*See* GROTE, G.]   G 10 T 24, 25

ROBERTSON (PROF. J. B.) Lectures on the Life, Writings, and Times of Edmund Burke. 8vo. Lond., 1868.   C 3 Q 13

Philosophy of History. [*See* SCHLEGEL, F. VON.]   B 14 S 31, 32

ROBERTSON (JANET). Lights and Shades on a Traveller's Path ; or, Scenes in Foreign Lands. 8vo. Lond., 1851.   D 9 S 10

ROBERTSON (JOSEPH CLINTON), AND BYERLEY (THOMAS). Percy Anecdotes, Original and Select ; by "Sholto and Reuben Percy, Brothers of the Benedictine Monastery, Mont Benger." 20 vols. 18mo. Lond., 1823.   J 7 P 1–20

ROBERTSON (JOHN FORBES). [*See* FORBES-ROBERTSON, J.]

ROBERTSON (JOHN). Walt Whitman, Poet and Democrat 8vo. Edinb., 1884.   C 6 U 28

ROBERTSON (SIR JOHN), K.C.M.G. The Colony of Australia. [*See* NEW SOUTH WALES.]

ROBERTSON (REV. JOHN). [*See* SACRAMENTS.]

4 M

ROBERTSON (JOHN PARISH, AND WILLIAM PARISH). Letters on South America ; comprising Travels on the Banks of the Parana and Rio de la Plata. 3 vols. 8vo. Lond., 1843.   D 3 R 20–22

Letters on Paraguay : an Account of Four Years' Residence in that Republic, under the Government of the Dictator Francia. 2 vols. 8vo. Lond., 1838.   D 3 P 39, 40

Francia's Reign of Terror ; being the continuation of Letters on Paraguay. 8vo. Lond., 1839.   D 3 P 41

ROBERTSON (W.) [*See* FLAXMAN, J.]   A 2 P 21 ‡

ROBERTSON (WILLIAM). Forest Sketches: Deer-stalking and other Sports in the Highlands Fifty Years ago. 8vo. Edinb., 1865.   D 8 S 35

ROBERTSON (REV. WILLIAM). Journal of a Clergyman during a Visit to the Peninsula, 1841. 8vo. Edinb., 1845.   D 7 T 10

ROBERTSON (WILLIAM), D.D., &c. Historical Works of ; to which is prefixed an Account of his Life and Writings, by Dugald Stewart, F.R.S. New ed. 10 vols. 8vo. Lond., 1821.   B 14 R 1–10

History of the Reign of the Emperor Charles V. 8th ed. 3 vols. 8vo. Lond., 1796.   B 9 R 1–3

History of the Reign of Charles V ; with an Account of the Emperor's Life after his Abdication, by W. H. Prescott. 2 vols. 8vo. Lond., 1857.   B 9 Q 41, 42

Historical Disquisition concerning the knowledge which the Ancients had of India. 8vo. Lond., 1799.   B 10 S 34

ROBERTSON (WILLIAM). Portrait of. [*See* MANUSCRIPTS AND PORTRAITS.]   MF 1 U 21

ROBERTSON (WILLIAM PARISH). Letters from Paraguay. [*See* ROBERTSON, J. P.]   D 3 P 39–41

ROBERTSON BROTHERS (MESSRS.) Private Hand-book (F.F. Biard), Aug., 1875. 8vo. Melh., 1875.   ME 3 S

Catalogue[s] of Pure Shorthorn and Hereford Cattle, F.F. Biard, to be sold by public auction. 3 vols. 12mo. Melh., 1875–78.   ME 3 S

Priced Catalogue of Messrs. Robertson Brothers Fourth and Fifth Annual Sales, 1877–78. Ob. 32mo. Melh., 1877–78.   ME 3 S

ROBINSON (MISS AGNES MARY FRANCES), MRS. DARMESTETER. Margaret of Angoulême, Queen of Navarre. [A Biography.] 8vo. Lond., 1886.   C 4 S 20

ROBINSON (CHARLES). New South Wales, the oldest and richest of the Australian Colonies. 8vo. Sydney, 1873.*   MF 2 R 26

Progress and Resources of New South Wales. 8vo. Sydney, 1877.   MF 3 P 20

Progress and Resources of New South Wales. 8vo. Sydney, 1877–78.   MF 3 P 22

Another copy. 8vo. Sydney, 1877–78.   MJ 2 R 14

Progrès et Resources de la Nouvelle Galles du Sud ; traduit de l'Anglais par E. Marin La Meslée. 8vo. Sydney, 1878.   MF 3 P 22

ROBINSON (CLEMENT). Handefull of Pleasant Delites. [*See* PARK, T.]

ROBINSON (PROF. EDWARD). Hebrew and English Lexicon of the Old Testament. [*See* GESENIUS, PROF. F. H. W.]

ROBINSON (E. L.) New Map of Victoria. 8vo. Melb., 1863.   MD 5 P 3 ‡
Robinson's Almanac and Astronomical Ephemeris for 1864 ; by E. J. White. 12mo. Melb., 1864.   ME 4 P

ROBINSON (EDWARD), D.D., AND SMITH (E.) Biblical Researches in Palestine, Mount Sinai, and Arabia Petrea : a Journal of Travels in the year 1838. 3 vols. 8vo. Lond. 1841.   D 4 T 25–27

ROBINSON (F.) California and its Gold Regions ; with a Geographical and Topographical View of the Country. (Pam., 18.) 8vo. New York, 1849.   F 12 P 10

ROBINSON (F. W.) Prison Characters, drawn from Life ; with Suggestions for Prison Government, by "A Prison Matron." 2 vols. 8vo. Lond., 1866. F 14 Q 15, 16
Female Life in Prison ; by "A Prison Matron." New ed. revised. 8vo. Lond., 1864.   F 14 Q 4

ROBINSON (G. T.) Fall of Metz : an Account of the Seventy Days' Siege, and of the Battles which preceded it. 8vo. Lond., 1871.   B 9 S 11

ROBINSON (H.) Hydraulic Power, and Hydraulic Machinery. Roy. 8vo. Lond., 1887.   A 11 T 10

ROBINSON (H.) [*See* HIGINBOTHAM AND ROBINSON.]

ROBINSON (H. B.) Memoirs of Lieut.-Gen. Sir Thomas Picton, G.C.B., &c., including his Correspondence. 2 vols. 8vo. Lond., 1835.   C 8 U 33, 34

ROBINSON (HENRY CRABB). Diary, Reminiscences, and Correspondence of. Selected and edited by Thomas Sadler, Ph.D. 3rd ed. 2 vols. 8vo. Lond., 1872. C 4 T 39, 40

ROBINSON (SIR HERCULES G. R.), G.C.M.G. Speeches delivered during his Administration of the Government of New South Wales. 8vo. Sydney, 1879.*   MF 3 R 1

ROBINSON (JAMES F.) British Bee-Farming : its Profits and Pleasures. 8vo. Lond., 1880.   A 1 P 14

ROBINSON (SIR JOHN B.), BART. Canada and the Canada Bill ; being an Examination of the proposed Measure for the future Government of Canada. (Pam., 6.) 8vo. Lond., 1840.   MJ 2 Q 1

ROBINSON (JOHN C.), F.S.A., &c. Critical Account of the Drawings by Michel Angelo and Raffaello, in the University Galleries. 8vo. Oxford, 1870.   A 7 Q 9

ROBINSON (REV. JOHN LOVELL), B.A. Treatise on Marine Surveying ; prepared for the use of younger Naval Officers ; with Questions for Examination and Exercises. 8vo. Lond., 1882.   A 6 R 32

ROBINSON (JOHN R.) Universal Stereography. [*See* HARDING, W.]

ROBINSON (MRS. MARY). Memoirs of the late Mrs. Robinson ; written by herself. 12mo. Lond., 1826.   C 1 P 8

ROBINSON (PETER F.) Designs for Ornamental Villas, in Ninety-six Plates. 4to. Lond., 1836.   A 2 T 23
New Series of Designs for Ornamental Cottages and Villas ; with Estimates and Plates. 4to. Lond., 1838.   A 2 T 22

ROBINSON (PHILIP STEWART). The Poets' Birds. 8vo. Lond., 1883.   H 8 S 18

ROBINSON (SAMUEL). Persian Poetry for English Readers ; being Specimens of six of the greatest Classical Poets of Persia : Ferdusi, Nizami, Sadi, Jelal-ad-din Rumi, Hafiz, and Jami ; with Biographical Notices and Notes. 8vo. Glasgow, 1883.   H 8 S 28

ROBINSON (SARA T. L.) Kansas ; its Interior and Exterior Life, including a full View of its Settlement, &c. 8vo. Boston, 1856.   D 3 Q 44

ROBINSON (T. R.), D.D., &c. On the Determination of the Constants of the Cup Anemometer, by Experiments with a Whirling Machine. (Roy. Soc. Pubs., 6.) 4to. Lond., 1879.   A 11 P 7 †
Reduction of Anemograms, taken at the Armagh Observatory, 1857–63. (Roy. Soc. Pubs., 1.) 4to. Lond., 1876.   A 11 P 2 †

ROBINSON (VINCENT J.) Eastern Carpets : Twelve Early Examples ; with descriptive Notices. Imp. 4to. Lond., 1882.   A 13 P 25 ‡

ROBINSON (WILLIAM), F.L.S. The Wild Garden ; or, our Groves and Gardens made beautiful by the Naturalisation of Hardy Exotic Plants. Illustrated. 8vo. Lond., 1881.   A 4 S 25
The English Flower Garden ; Style, Position, and Arrangement. Illustrated. 8vo. Lond., 1883. A 4 U 14
The Subtropical Garden ; or Beauty of Form in the Flower Garden. 8vo. Lond., 1871.   A 1 P 21

ROBINSON (WILLIAM). Protection to Native Industry : a Lecture, delivered at the Melbourne Mechanics' Institute, on 27th November, 1860. 8vo. Melb., 1860. MF 3 P 5
Another copy. 8vo. Melb., 1860.   MJ 2 R 11
Report upon the British Colonies, represented at the Vienna Exhibition, 1873 ; with particular reference to their Produce. 8vo. Lond., 1873.   MF 2 P 18

ROBINSON (WILLIAM ASHTON COOMER). Truth stranger than Fiction : a Miscellany of Interesting, Instructive, and Startling Facts. 8vo. Melb., 1861. MJ 2 R 26

ROBIQUET (CAPT. A.) Renseignements sur la Nouvelle-Zélande ; suivis de Notes sur les Vents, Courants, et Baromètre dans les environs du Cap Horn et sur la Traversée du Pérou à l'île Maurice, etc. 8vo. Saint-Malo, 1866.   MD 5 U 30

ROBISON (J.), PRICE (F.), AND TREDGOLD (T.) Treatise on the Construction of Roofs as regards Carpentry and Joinery. Illustrated. (Weale). 12mo. Lond., 1861. A 17 P 57

ROBISON (CAPT. R.) Short Statement of the Case of R. Robison, Esq., late Captain New South Wales Veteran Companies. 8vo. Lond., 1834. MF 1 R 18

Letter addressed by R. Robison to the Members of the House of Commons, containing an Outline of Evidence against Lieut.-Gen. Ralph Darling (late Governor of New South Wales), in reply to a Pamphlet privately circulated among them by that Officer. 8vo. Lond., 1835. MF 1 R 18

The Case of Captain Robison. [*See* DARLING, SIR R.] MF 1 R 18

ROBSART (AMYE). Amye Robsart and the Earl of Leycester. [*See* ADLARD, G.] B 6 P 48

ROBSON (EDWARD ROBERT). School Architecture; being Practical Remarks on the Planning, Designing, Building, and Furnishing of School-houses. With Illustrations. 8vo. Lond., 1874. A 2 S 16

Another copy. With Illustrations. 2nd ed. 8vo. Lond., 1877. A 2 S 17

ROBSON (GEORGE). Modern Domestic Building Construction, Illustrated. Imp. fol. Lond., 1876. A 2 P 24 ‡

ROBSON (GEORGE FENNELL). Scenery of the Grampian Mountains. Illustrated. Ob.4to. Lond.,1814. D 7 P 1 ‡

ROBSON (THOMAS). The British Herald; or, Cabinet of Armorial Bearings of the Nobility and Gentry of Great Britain and Ireland. 3 vols. 4to. Sunderland, 1830. K 10 V 7-9

ROBSON (WILLIAM) & Co. London Directory for 1838. Roy. 8vo. Lond., 1838. E

ROBUSTI (JACOPO), *called* TINTORETTO. [*See* TINTORETTO.]

ROBY (PROF. H. J.) De Usufructu; Justiniani Digestorum, Libri VII, Tit. I. 8vo. Camb., 1886. F 5 P 23

Introduction to the Study of Justinian's Digest. 8vo. Camb., 1886. F 5 P 22

ROBY (JOHN), M.R.S.L. Seven Weeks in Belgium, Switzerland, Lombardy, &c. 2 vols. 8vo. Lond., 1838. D 8 P 31, 32

ROCHE (HARRIET A.) On Trek in the Transvaal; or, over Berg and Veldt in South Africa. With Map of Route. 2nd ed. 8vo. Lond., 1878. D 1 R 25

ROCHEFOUCAULD (FRANÇOIS), DUC DE LA. [*See* LA ROCHEFOUCAULD, F., DUC DE.]

ROCHEJAQUELEIN (MARIE LOUISE VICTOIRE), MARQUISE DE LA. [*See* LA ROCHEJAQUELEIN, M. L. V., MARQUISE DE.]

ROCHESTER (JOHN WILMOT), EARL OF. Life and Poems of. [*See* CHALMERS, A. *and* JOHNSON, DR. S.]

ROCHESTER (LAURENCE HYDE), EARL OF. Correspondence and Diary. [*See* SINGER, S. W.]

ROCK (VERY REV. D.), D.D. Textile Fabrics. (South Kens. Mus.) 8vo. Lond., 1876. E

ROCKHILL (W. WOODVILLE). Life of the Buddha, and the Early History of his Order, derived from Tibetan Works in the Bkah-Hgyur and Bstan-Hgyur. 8vo. Lond., 1884. G 15 P 7

Udânavarga: a Collection of Verses from the Buddhist Canon; compiled by Dharmatrâta; translated, with Notes, &c., by W. W. Rockhill. 8vo. Lond., 1883. G 15 P 18

ROCKINGHAM (CHARLES WATSON WENTWORTH), MARQUIS OF. Memoirs of the Marquis of Rockingham and his Contemporaries; by George Thomas, Earl of Albemarle. 2 vols. 8vo. Lond., 1852. C 9 R 16, 17

ROCKSTRO (W. S.) Life of George Frederick Handel. 8vo. Lond., 1883. C 3 Q 28

General History of Music, from the Infancy of the Greek Drama to the Present Period. 8vo. Lond., 1886. A 7 U 8

ROCKWELL (A. D.), M.D., &c. Practical Treatise on the Medical and Surgical Uses of Electricity. [*See* BEARD, G. M.] A 5 S 46–A 5 T 25

ROCKWELL (JULIUS ENSIGN). Teaching, Practice, and Literature of Shorthand. 8vo. Wash., 1884. K 14 T 9

RODD (EDWARD HEARLE). Birds of Cornwall and the Scilly Islands. Edited, with an Introduction, Appendix, and brief Memoir of the Author, by James Edmund Harting. With Portrait and Map. 8vo. Lond., 1880. A 14 R 2

RODENBOUGH (THEO. F.) Afghanistan and the Anglo-Russian Dispute: an Account of Russia's Advance towards India. With Illustrations. 8vo. New York, 1885. D 5 R 43

RODRIGUES (J. C.), LL.B. Panama Canal: its History, its Political Aspect, and Financial Difficulties. 8vo. Lond., 1885. F 5 R 1

RODWELL (G. F.), F.R.A.S. Birth of Chemistry. With numerous Illustrations. 8vo. Lond., 1874. A 5 R 25

The Haydn Series: Dictionary of Science. 8vo. Lond., 1871. K 18 Q 6

RODWELL (J. THOMAS G.) A Race for a Dinner: a Farce. Cumberland's Eng. Theatre.) 12mo. Lond., 1829. H 2 Q 16

ROEBUCK (JOHN A.) Colonies of England: a Plan for the Government of some portion of our Colonial Possessions. 8vo. Lond., 1849. MF 2 R 18

History of the Whig Ministry of 1830 to the Passing of the Reform Bill. 2 vols. 8vo. Lond., 1852. B 7 Q 27-28

ROEBUCK (CAPT. THOMAS). Laskari Dictionary; or, Anglo-Indian Vocabulary of Nautical Terms and Phrases in English and Hindustani; revised, &c., by William Carmichael Smyth, and now carefully re-edited and enlarged by George Small, M.A. 8vo. Lond., 1882. K 16 P 2

ROFFE (ALFRED). Hand-book of Shakespeare Music; being an Account of Three Hundred and Fifty Pieces of Music set to words taken from the Plays and Poems of Shakespeare, the Compositions ranging from the Elizabethan Age to the Present Time. 4to. Lond., 1878. H 3 Q 26

ROGEARD (A.) Les Propos de Labienus. Translated for the *Australasian*, by G. W. Rusden. 8vo. Melb. (n.d.) MJ 2 R 23

ROGER DE HOVEDEN. [*See* HOVEDEN, ROGER DE.]

ROGER OF WENDOVER. Flowers of History; comprising the History of England, from the Descent of the Saxons, to A.D. 1235: formerly ascribed to Matthew Paris. Translated from the Latin, by J. A. Giles, D.C.L. 2 vols. 12mo. Lond., 1849. B 3 P 6, 7

ROGERS (REV. CHARLES), LL.D., &c. Scottish Minstrel: the Songs of Scotland subsequent to Burns; with Memoirs of the Poets. Roy. 8vo. Edinb., 1882. H 5 U 28
Social Life in Scotland, from Early to Recent Times. 3 vols. 8vo. Edinb., 1884-86. B 13 R 31-33

ROGERS (E. T.) Coins of the Túlúni Dynasty. [*See* NUMISMATA ORIENTALIA, 1.] A 2 S 15 †

ROGERS (Mrs. G. ALBERT). Winter in Algeria, 1863-64. 8vo. Lond., 1865. D 1 W 4

ROGERS (HENRY). Eclipse of Faith; or, a Visit to a Religious Sceptic. 14th ed. 12mo. Lond., 1874. G 10 Q 31
Defence of the Eclipse of Faith by its Author; being a rejoinder to Prof. Newman's "Reply." 3rd ed. 12mo. Lond., 1860. G 2 P 2
Essays selected from Contributions to the *Edinburgh Review.* 2 vols. 8vo. Lond., 1850. J 12 U 23, 24

ROGERS (Mrs. HESTER ANN). Experience and Spiritual Letters of. 18mo. Lond. (n.d.) G 9 P 22

ROGERS (JOHN). Writings of. [*See* BRITISH REFORMERS 3.]

ROGERS (J.) The New Rush, and other Poems and Songs. 12mo. Melb., 1861.* MH 1 R 34

ROGERS (PROF. JAMES E. THOROLD), M.A., &c. History of Agriculture and Prices in England, from the year after the Oxford Parliament (1259) to the commencement of the Continental War (1793). 6 vols. 8vo. Oxford, 1866-87. F 4 V 1-6
Six Centuries of Work and Wages: the History of English Labour. 2 vols. 8vo. Lond., 1884. F 5 P 9, 10

ROGERS (PROF. JAMES E. THOROLD), M.A., &c.—*contd.*
Cobden and Modern Political Opinion: Essays on certain Political Topics. 8vo. Lond., 1873. F 5 P 8
Complete Collection of the Protests of the Lords, 1624-1874. 3 vols. 8vo. Oxford, 1875. F 5 P 5-7
Epistles, Satires, and Epigrams. 8vo. Lond., 1876. H 8 S 30
Manual of Political Economy for Schools and Colleges. (Clar. Press.) 2nd ed. 8vo. Oxford, 1869. F 15 P 5
Another copy. (Clar. Press.) 8vo. 3rd ed. Oxford, 1876. F 15 P 6
Speeches on Questions of Public Policy. [*See* BRIGHT, J., *and* COBDEN, R.]
The Colonial Question. [*See* COBDEN CLUB.]

ROGERS (JOHN W. F.) Grammar and Logic in the 19th Century, as seen in a Syntactical Analysis of the English Language. 8vo. Melb., 1883. K 12 P 5
Another copy. MK 1 P 49
Australasian Federal Directory of Commerce, Trades, and Professions, for 1888-89. Roy. 8vo. Melb., 1888.* ME 4 V

ROGERS (SAMUEL). Italy: a Poem, illustrated by T. Stothard and J. M. W. Turner. 8vo. Lond., 1836. H 8 U 32
Poetical Works of. Sm. 4to. Lond., 1869. H 6 S 29
Table Talk and Recollections of. 8vo. Lond., 1856. C 11 P 16
Recollections by. 12mo. Lond., 1859. C 1 R 32
Recollections of the Table Talk of; to which is added, Porsoniana, written by William Maltby. [Edited by the Rev. Alexander Dyce.] 3rd ed. 8vo. Lond., 1856. C 5 R 23
Another copy. Illustrated. 8vo. New Southgate, 1887. C 11 P 16
Anecdote Life of. [*See* TIMBS, J.]

ROGERS (CAPT. T.), R.E. Buddhaghosha's Parables. [*See* BUDDHA.]

ROGERS (CAPT. WOODES). Cruising Voyage round the World (with the Ships *Duke* and *Dutchess* of Bristol). First to the South Seas, thence to the East Indies, and homewards by the Cape of Good Hope, begun in 1708, and finished in 1711. 8vo. Lond., 1712. D 10 R 27
Nieuwe Reize naar de Zuidzee, van daar naar Oost-Indien, en verder rondom de Waereld, begonnen in 1708, en geëyndigd in 1711. Gedaan onder het bestier van Willem Dampier. In 't Engels beschreven door Woodes Rogers. Sm. 4to. Amsterdam, 1715. D 10 R 28

ROGET (PETER MARK), M.D., &c. Animal and Vegetable Physiology, considered with reference to Natural Theology. 2 vols. 8vo. Lond., 1834. A 12 T 16, 17
Outlines of Physiology; with an Appendix on Phrenology. 1st Am. ed. 8vo. Philad., 1839. A 12 T 3
Thesaurus of English Words and Phrases, classified and arranged. 25th ed. 8vo. Lond., 1868. K 12 P 8

ROGGEVEEN (JACOB). Het Waare en Nauwkeurige Journael der Reize, gedaan door drie Schepen, op ordre van de Ed. Heeren Bewindhebberen van de Westindische Compagnie, om eenige tot nog toe onbekende Landen, omtrent de Zuid-Zee geleegen. Sq. 8vo. Amsterdam, 1727.* MD 5 S 28

Twee jaarige Reyze rondom de Wereld, ter nadet Ontdekkinge der Onbekende Zuydlanden, met drie Schepen, in het Jaar 1721 ondernomen. Nevens de Reyze van het Oostindisch Schip *Barneveld*, uyt Holland tot aan de Kaap der Goede Hoope, in 't jaar 1719. Sq. 8vo. Dordrecht, 1728. D 10 R 29

Another copy. Sq. 8vo. Dordrecht, 1728. MD 5 S 30

Dagverhaal der Ontdekkings-reis van Mr. Jacob Roggeveen, met de Schepen den *Arend, Thienhoven* en de *Afrikaansche Galei*, in de jaren 1721 en 1722. 8vo. Middelburg, 1838. MD 5 S 31

ROGORD (S.) Permie-Russian Dictionary. Roy. 8vo. St. Petersburg, 1869. K 16 R 4

ROHAULT DE FLEURY (CHARLES). La Messe: etudes archéologiques sur ses Monuments; par Charles Rohault de Fleury, continuées par son fils. 3 vols. roy. 4to. Paris, 1883. G 12 R 8–10 †

La Toscane au Moyen Age: Architecture Civile et Militaire. Fol. Paris, 1873. A 1 Q 1, 2

ROHLFS (DR. GERHARD). Adventures in Morocco, and Journeys through the Oases of Draa and Tafilet. 8vo. Lond., 1874. D 2 S 17

RÖHRBACH (DR. CARL). Costumes of All Nations [*See* KRETSCHMER, A.]

ROHRBACHER (FRANÇOIS RÉNE), L'ABBÉ. Histoire Universelle de l'Eglise Catholique; continuée jusqu'en 1866, par J. Chantrel avec un table générale par Léon Gautier. 7e éd. 16 vols. imp. 8vo. Paris, 1876–77. G 6 V 3–18

RÖHRIG (E.) [*See* CROOKES, W.]

ROKEBY (MATTHEW), LORD. Brief Character of; by Sir E. Brydges. 8vo. Kent, 1817. H 6 S 10

ROLAND (ARTHUR). Management of Grass Land, laying down Grass, Artificial Grasses, &c. Edited by William H. Ablett. 8vo. Lond., 1881. A 4 Q 11

ROLAND (MME. MARIE JEANNE PHILIPON). Mémoires de Madame Roland; par Berville, et F. Barrière. 2 vols. 8vo. Lond., 1820. C 4 V 29, 30

Life of; by M. Blind. 8vo. Lond., 1886. C 2 S 35

Life of. [*See* LAMARTINE, A. DE.] C 5 S 12

Mémoires particuliers de. [*See* BARRIÈRE, J. F., 8.] C 1 S 8

ROLANDO (PROF. LUIGI). Saggio sopra la vera Struttura del Cervello, e sopra le Funzioni del Sistema Nervoso. 2 vols. (in 1) 8vo. Torino, 1828. A 12 R 22

Della Struttura degli Emisferi Cerebrali. 4to. Torino, 1830. A 12 V 19

ROLLAND (A. A.) Lettres inédites de la Princesse-Palatine [Elizabeth Charlotte]. 8vo. Paris, 1881. C 2 S 34

ROLLESTON (CHRISTOPHER). Condition and Resources of New South Wales: a Lecture, delivered at Sydney, December 12th, 1866. 8vo. Lond., 1867. MF 3 Q 25

Statistical Review of the Progress of New South Wales during the last Ten Years. 8vo. Sydney, 1873. MF 3 P 16

Another copy. 8vo. Sydney, 1873. MJ 2 P 31

ROLLESTON (PROF. GEORGE), M.D., &c. Forms of Animal Life; being Outlines of Zoological Classification, based upon Anatomical Investigation, and illustrated by Descriptions of Specimens and of Figures. 8vo. Oxford, 1870. A 27 U 32

Scientific Papers and Addresses; arranged and edited by William Turner, M.B., &c.; with a Biographical Sketch by Edward B. Tylor, Hon. D.C.L., &c. Illustrated. 2 vols. 8vo. Oxford, 1884. A 16 T 7, 8

ROLLIN (CHARLES). Ancient History of the Egyptians, Carthaginians, Assyrians, Babylonians, Medes and Persians, Grecians, and Macedonians. Translated. 6 vols. 8vo. Lond., 1851. B 15 P 19–24

Histoire Ancienne des Egyptiens, des Carthaginois, des Assyriens, des Babyloniens, des Medes et des Perses, des Macédoniens, des Grecs. 6 vols. 4to. Paris, 1740. B 15 S 9–14

[*See* QUINTILIANUS, M. F.]

ROLLIN-TILTON (C.) [*See* TILTON, C. ROLLIN-.]

ROLLS OF PARLIAMENT. [*See* ROTULI PARLIAMENTORUM.]

ROLPH (THOMAS). Comparative Advantage between the United States and Canada for British Settlers. (Pam. 15.) 8vo. Lond., 1842. MJ 2 Q 5

Emigration and Colonization; embodying the Results of a Mission to Great Britain and Ireland, 1839–42. 8vo. Lond., 1844. F 5 P 25

ROMAN (COL. ALFRED). Military Operations of General Beauregard in the War between the States, 1861–65. 2 vols. 8vo. New York, 1884. C 9 T 1, 2

ROMAN CATHOLIC MORALITY, as inculcated in the Theological Class-books used in Maynooth College. 3rd ed. Dublin, 1836. *Reprinted*, Sydney, 1839. MJ 2 R 18

ROMANES (GEORGE J.), M.A., &c. Animal Intelligence. 8vo. Lond., 1882. A 14 Q 11

Jelly-fish, Star-fish, and Sea-urchins; being a Research on Primitive Nervous Systems. 8vo. Lond., 1885. A 14 Q 32

Mental Evolution in Animals; with a posthumous Essay on Instinct, by Charles Darwin, M.A., &c. 8vo. Lond., 1883. G 2 R 6

Candid Examination of Theism; by "Physicus." 8vo. Lond., 1878. G 9 S 20

ROMANES (George J.), M.A., &c.—*continued.*
Preliminary Observations on the Locomotor System of
Medusæ. (Roy. Soc. Pubs., 2.) 4to. Lond., 1876.
　　　　　　　　　　　　　　　　　　　　　A 11 P 3 †

Further Observations on the Locomotor System of
Medusæ. (Roy. Soc. Pubs., 5.) 4to. Lond., 1878.
　　　　　　　　　　　　　　　　　　　　　A 11 P 6 †

ROME. History of Rome; (Lard. Cab. Cyclo.) 2 vols.
12mo. Lond., 1834-35.　　　　　　　K 1 T 38, 39

History of Rome; [by Henry Malden.] (Lib. U.
Know.) 8vo. Lond., 1830.　　　　　　B 12 R 19

RÖMER (Prof. Dr. Ferdinand). Bone Caves of Ojcow,
in Poland. Roy. 4to. Lond., 1884.　　A 4 P 12 †

ROMER (Mrs. Isabella F.) Filia Dolorosa: Memoirs
of Marie Thérèse Charlotte, Duchess of Angoulème, the
last of the Dauphines. 2nd ed. 8vo. Lond., 1853. C 3 Q 35

ROMILLY (Henry). Punishment of Death; to which
is added his Treatise on Public Responsibility and Vote
by Ballot. 8vo. Lond., 1886.　　　　　　F 5 T 22

ROMILLY (Hugh Hastings), C.M.G. Western Pacific
and New Guinea: Notes on the Natives, Christian and
Cannibal; with some Account of the old Labour Trade.
8vo. Lond., 1886.　　　　　　　　　　　MD 5 P 22

ROMILLY (Sir Samuel). Speeches of, in the House of
Commons; with a Memoir, by William Peter. 2 vols.
8vo. Lond., 1820.　　　　　　　　F 13 Q 12, 13

Memoirs of the Life of; written by himself; with a
Selection from his Correspondence. Edited by his Sons.
3 vols. 8vo. Lond., 1840.　　　　　　C 9 P 32-34

Observations on the Criminal Law of England, as it
relates to Capital Punishment. (Pam., 8.) 8vo. Lond.,
1810.　　　　　　　　　　　　　　　　F 13 R 21

ROMINGER (Dr. C.) Geological Survey of Michigan.
[*See* Brooks, T. B.]　　　　　　　　A 9 U 7-10

ROMME (Charles). Tableaux des Vents, des Marées, et
des Courans qui ont été observés sur toutes les Mers du
Globe. 2 vols. 8vo. Paris, 1817.　　　A 3 T 33, 34

ROMNEY (George), and LAURENCE (Sir Thomas).
By Lord Ronald Gower. (Great Artists.) 8vo. Lond.,
1882.　　　　　　　　　　　　　　　　C 3 T 35

ROMNEY (Hon. Henry Sydney), Earl of. Diary of
the Times of Charles II; including his Correspondence
with the Countess of Sutherland. 2 vols. 8vo. Lond.,
1843.　　　　　　　　　　　　　　　C 6 V 18, 19

RONALDS (Dr. Edmund), RICHARDSON (Dr. T.),
and WATTS (H.), B.A., &c. Chemical Technology; or,
Chemistry in its applications to the Arts and Manufactures; with which is incorporated a revision of Dr.
Knapp's Technology. 2nd. ed. 3 vols. (in 6) 8vo. Lond.,
1855-67.　　　　　　　　　　　　　A 5 U 8-13
　　1. Fuel and its Application. (Analytical Tables.)
　　2. Vitreous and Ceramic Manufactures.
　　3. Sugar, Tea, Coffee, Flour, &c.
　　4. Acids, Alkalies, and Salts.

ROOD (Ogden N.) Modern Chromatics; with Applications to Art and Industry. Illustrated. 8vo. Lond.,
1879.　　　　　　　　　　　　　　　　A 7 T 1

ROOFS. Treatise on the Construction of Roofs as regards
Carpentry and Joinery, deduced from the Works of
Robison, Price, and Tredgold. (Weale.) 12mo. Lond.
(n.d.)　　　　　　　　　　　　　　　　A 17 P 57

ROORDA VAN EYSINGA (Philippus Pieter). Neder-
duitsch en Maleisch, [en Maleisch en Nederduitsch]
Woordenboek, order Goedkeuring en Begunstiging der
Hooge Regering van Nederlandsch Indië. 2 vols. 8vo.
Batavia, 1824-25.　　　　　　　　　K 12 S 17, 18

ROOSEVELT (Blanche). Life and Reminiscences of
Gustave Doré; compiled from Material supplied by
Doré's Relations and Friends, and from Personal Recol-
lections. 8vo. Lond., 1885.　　　　　C 10 T 39

ROOSEVELT (Theodore). Hunting Trips of a Ranch-
man: Sketches of Sport on the Northern Cattle Plains.
Illustrated. Imp. 8vo. N. York, 1885.　D 3 V 19

The Naval War of 1812; or, the History of the
United States Navy during the last War with Great
Britain. 8vo. N. York, 1882.　　　　　B 1 T 1

ROPER (Stephen), C.E. Hand-book of Modern Steam
Fire-engines; including the Running, Care, and Manage-
ment of Steam Fire-engines and Fire Pumps. With
Illustrations. 12mo. Philad., 1876.　　A 6 R 12

ROQUETE (Jose Ignacio). Nouveau Dictionnaire Portu-
gais-Français, composé sur les plus récents et les meilleurs Dictionnaires des deux Langues. 8vo. Paris,
1841.　　　　　　　　　　　　　　　K 14 P 32

ROS (Lieut.-Gen. William Lennox Lascelles Fitzgerald), Lord. [*See* De Ros, Lieut.-Gen., W. L. L. F.,
Lord.]

ROSA (Salvator). Life and Times of Salvator Rosa; by
Lady Morgan. 2 vols. 8vo. Lond., 1824. C 9 U 30-31

ROSALES (Henry). Essay on the Origin and Distribution of Gold in Quartz Veins. [*See* Victorian
Government Prize Essays.]

ROSCHER (W.) Principles of Political Economy. 8vo.
New York, 1878.　　　　　　　　　　F 4 R 1, 2

Geschichte der National Oekonomik in Deutschland.
(Ges. der Wiss.) 8vo. München, 1874.　A 17 V 28

ROSCOE (Mrs. Henry). Vittoria Colonna; her Life and
Poems. 12mo. Lond., 1868.　　　　　　C 2 P 39

ROSCOE (Henry E.), B.A., &c. Spectrum Analysis:
Six Lectures delivered in 1868, before the Society of
Apothecaries of London. 8vo. Lond., 1869. A 5 T 30

Spectrum Analysis: Six Lectures delivered in 1868.
4th ed., revised and enlarged. 8vo. Lond., 1885. A 5 T 31

ROSCOE (Prof. H. E.), F.R.S., and SCHORLEMMER (Prof. Kurzes C), F.R.S. Treatise on Chemistry. Illustrated. 2nd ed. 3 vols. (in 6) 8vo. Lond., 1878–86.
　　　　　　　　　　　　　　　　　A 21 T 1–6
　1. The Non-metallic Elements.
　2. Metals.
　3. The Chemistry of the Hydrocarbons and their Derivatives, or Organic Chemistry.

Lehrbuch der Chemie. 8vo. Braunschweig, 1878. A 5 S 19

ROSCOE (Prof. H. E.), F.R.S., And THORPE (T. E.), F.R.S. Absorption-Spectra of Bromine and of Iodine Monochloride. (Roy. Soc. Pubs., 4.) 4to. Lond., 1877. 　　　　　　　　　　　　　　　　A 11 P 5 †

ROSCOE (Henry). Lives of Eminent British Lawyers. (Lard. Cab. Cyclo.) 12mo. Lond., 1830. 　K 1 S 6

ROSCOE (Thomas). Illustrated History of the London and North-western Railway, from London to Birmingham, Liverpool, Manchester, &c. 8vo. Lond., 1847. A 6 S 6

Italian Novelists, selected from the most approved Authors in that Language; with Notes. 4 vols. 8vo. Lond., 1825. 　　　　　　　　　　　　　　C 2 P 23–26

The Spanish Novelists: a series of Tales. 3 vols. 8vo. Lond., 1832. 　　　　　　　　　　　J 11 U 18–20

Tourist in Italy. [*See* Jennings, R.] 　　D 9 Q 25, 26

Tourist in France. [*See* Jennings, R.] 　　　D 9 Q 27

Tourist in Spain. [*See* Jennings, R.] 　　D 9 Q 28–30

Views of Cities and Scenery in Italy, France, and Switzerland. [*See* Prout, S.] 　　　D 3 V 27–29

Memoirs of Benvenuto Cellini. [*See* Cellini, B.] C 1 R 9

History of Painting in Italy. [*See* Lanzi, A. L.]

ROSCOE (William). Additional Observations on Penal Jurisprudence and the Reformation of Criminals, &c. 8vo. Lond., 1823. 　　　　　　　　　　F 4 Q 27

Life of Lorenzo de' Medici, called "the Magnificent." 2 vols. 8vo. Lond., 1825. 　　　　C 11 P 26, 27

Life and Pontificate of Leo x. 2nd ed. 6 vols. 8vo. Lond., 1806. 　　　　　　　　　C 6 R 9–14

ROSCOMMON (Rt. Hon. Wentworth Dillon), Earl of.

Life and Poems of. [*See* Chalmers, A., *and* Johnson, S.]
Works of. 12mo. Glasgow, 1753. 　　　H 6 P 28

ROSE (Rev. —.) The Emigrant Churchman in Canada; by "A Pioneer of the Wilderness"; edited by the Rev. Henry Christmas, M.A., &c. 2 vols. 8vo. Lond., 1849. 　　　　　　　　　　　　　　D 3 R 8, 9

ROSE (Rev. George). Mrs. Brown in Sydney; by "Arthur Sketchley." 12mo. Sydney, 1880. 　MJ 1 P 52

ROSE (Rt. Hon. George). Diaries and Correspondence of, containing Original Letters of the most distinguished Statesmen of his Day; edited by the Rev. Leveson Vernon Harcourt. 2 vols. 8vo. Lond., 1860. 　C 9 P 37, 38

ROSE (Rt. Hon. George)—*continued.*
Observations on the Historical Work of the late Right Hon. C. J. Fox; with a Narrative of the Enterprise of the Earl of Argyle, in 1685, by Sir Patrick Hume. 4to. Lond., 1809. 　　　　　　　　　B 3 U 18

Papers of the Earls of Marchmont. [*See* Marchmont, Earls of.] 　　　　　　　　B 5 U 44–46

ROSE (Rev. Hugh James), B.D. New General Biographical Dictionary. 12 vols. 8vo. Lond., 1840–48. C 11 U 32–43

ROSE (Rev. Hugh James), M.A. Among the Spanish People. 2 vols. 8vo. Lond., 1877. 　D 9 Q 23, 24

ROSE (James Anderson). Collection of Engraved Portraits, catalogued and exhibited at the Opening of the New Library and Museum of the Corporation of London, November, 1872. 4to. Lond., 1874. 　C 3 W 42

ROSE (Joshua). Complete Practical Machinist; embracing Lathe-work, Vice-work, Drills and Drilling, Taps and Dies, Hardening and Tempering, the making and use of Tools, &c. Illustrated. 8vo. Philad., 1876. 　A 11 Q 7

ROSE (Richard). New Zealand Guide: a Manual of Practical Advice and Hand-book of Useful Information for the Capitalist, Manufacturer, Farmer, Storekeeper, and Consignee. 8vo. Lond., 1879. 　MD 6 P 4

Australian Guide: a Manual of Practical Advice and Hand-book of Useful Information for the Capitalist, Manufacturer, Farmer, Storekeeper, Emigrant, and Consignee, 8vo. Lond., 1880.* 　　　　　　MD 6 P 4

ROSE (W.) [*See* Sallustius Crispus, C.] 　J 15 P 39

ROSE (William Stewart). The Orlando Furioso. [*See* Ariosto, L.] 　　　　　　　　H 8 S 19–26

ROSEGGER (P. K.) Wanderungen durch Steiermark und Kärnten. [*See* Unser Vaterland.] 　D 38 P 18 ‡

ROSEN (Friedrich). Radices Sanscritæ. 8vo. Berlin, 1827. 　　　　　　　　　　　K 12 R 21

ROSENBERG (C. B. H. von). Reistochten naar de Geelvinkbaai op Nieuw-Guinea in de jaren 1869–70. 4to. 's Gravenhage, 1875. 　　　　　　MD 6 P 30 †

ROSENBUSCH (H.) Mikroskopische Physiographie der massigen Gesteine. 8vo. Stuttgart, 1877. A 10 Q 22

ROSENGARTEN (A.) Hand-book of Architectural Styles; translated by W. Collett-Sandars. Illustrated. 8vo. Lond., 1876. 　　　　　　　　　A 3 P 14

ROSENKRANZ (Prof. Karl), Ph.D. Hegel as the National Philosopher of Germany; translated from the German, by George S. Hall. Roy. 8vo. St. Louis, Mo., 1874. 　　　　　　　　　　　G 11 S 21

ROSENTHAL (Dr. I.) General Physiology of Muscles and Nerves. With seventy-five Woodcuts. 8vo. Lond., 1881. 　　　　　　　　　　　A 12 Q 39

ROSING (S.) Engelsk-Dansk Ordbog [English-Danish Dictionary]. 4e udgave. 12mo. Kobenhavn, 1874. 　　　　　　　　　　　　　K 11 U 31

ROSINI (CARLO MARIA). [*See* HERCULANENSIUM VOLU-
MINUM.]   B 16 3 4 ‡

ROSINUS (JOANNIS). Antiquitatum Romanarvm corpus
absolutissimum. 4to. Lugd. Bat., 1663. B 18 Q 10 ‡

ROSMINI-SERBATI (ABATE ANTONIO). Opere edite e
inedite dell'. 26 vols. roy. 8vo., 8vo., and 12mo. Casale,
&c., 1821–71.   G 13 V 1–26
 1. Introduzione alla Filosofia.
 2–5. Ideologia e Logica.
 6. Trattato della Conscienza Morale.
 7, 8. Psicologia.
 9. Aristotele Esposto ed esaminato.
 10–13. Teosofia.
 14. Principj della Scienza Morale, e Storia di Sistemi.
 15. Letteratura, e arti Belle: Pensiere e Dottrine.
 16. Antropologia in Servigio della Scienze Morale.
 17. Del Principio Supremo della Metodica e di Alcune sue
  Applicazioni in servigio dell' umana Educazione.
 18, 19. Filosofia del Diritto.
 20, 21. Epistolario, 1813–54.
 22–24. Prose, ossia diversi Opuscoli. Breve Esposizione della
  Filosofia di Melchiore Gioia. Frammenti di una Storia della
  Empietà.
 25–27. Del Modo di Catecrizzare gl' Idioti. Delle Lodi di S.
  Filippo Neri. Della Ecclesiastica eloquenza, Discorso pronun-
  ciato nel Seminario di Trento.
 28, 29. Teodicea.
 30. Storia dell' Amore Cavata dalle Divine Scritture.
 31. Della Educazione Cristiana.
 32, 33. Operette spirituali.
 34, 35. Opere Minori. Scritti vari di A. Rosmini: sul Matrimonio Cristiano, e le leggi civili che lo Riguardano. Cate-
  chismo disposto secondo l'ordine delle idee.
 36–38. Scelte Operette spirituali di Rosmini. Lo Spirito dell'
  Istituto della Carità Discorsi. Modo di assistere alla Santa
  Messa. Lezioni Spirituali sulla Perfezione Cristiana.
Philosophical System of; translated, with a Sketch of the
Author's Life, Bibliography, &c. 8vo. Lond., 1882.
    G 10 S 16
Psychology. Vols. 1, 2. 8vo. Lond., 1884–85.
    G 16 T 1, 2
Origin of Ideas: translated from the fifth Italian edition
of the "Nuovo Saggio sull' Origine delle Idee." 3 vols.
8vo. Lond., 1883–84.   G 12 Q 26–28

ROSNY (PROF. L. LÉON DE). Anthologie Japonaise: Poésies
Anciennes et Modernes des Insulaires du Nippon; tra-
duites en Français, et publiées avec le texte original. 8vo.
Paris, 1871.   H 8 V 1
Introduction à l'étude de la Langue Japonaise. 4to.
Paris, 1856.   K 14 R 6
Guide de la Conversation Japonaise, précédé d'une
Introduction sur la Prononciation en usage à Yédo.
24°L. 8vo. Paris, 1867.   K 15 S 15
Variétés Orientales, Historiques, Géographiques, Scien-
tifiques, Bibliographiques et Littéraires. 3e ed. 8vo.
Paris, 1872.   J 16 P 39

ROSS (ALEXANDER). Red River Settlement; its Rise,
Progress, and Present State. 8vo. Lond., 1856. D 3 R 11
Adventures of the First Settlers on the Oregon or
Columbia River. 8vo. Lond., 1849. D 3 R 57

ROSS or ROSSE (ALEXANDER). History of the World;
being a Continuation of the History of Sir Walter
Raleigh. [*See* RALEIGH, SIR W.] B 15 R 1 ‡

ROSS (ANDREW), M.D., &c. Power of Mind over Matter;
or, Thoughts suggested on reading Nichols' Confession of
the Paramatta River Murders. (Pam. 43.) 8vo. Sydney,
1872.   MJ 2 R 5
Another copy. (Pam., 23.) 8vo Sydney, 1872. MJ 2 R 14
The Postal Question, considered with reference to direct
and regular intercourse with England by large Steam-
ships. 8vo. Melb., 1867.   MJ 2 R 8
Jottings on Vitality; or, the Physical Basis of Life.
Reprinted from the *New South Wales Medical Gazette*.
8vo. Sydney, 1872.   MA 2 S 38
Another copy. (Pam., 43.) 8vo. Sydney, 1872. MJ 2 R 5
Typhoid Fever; its Pathology and Treatment, based
on national Physiological Principles, coupled with a cur-
sory glance at Diphtheria, Cumberland Disease, and
Pleuro-pneumonia: also a few Practical Hints on the
Preservation of Health in Tropical Countries. 8vo.
Sydney, 1873.   MA 2 V 14
Guiding Principles in the production of Wool and
Mutton; with Hints on Cattle-breeding. 8vo. Sydney,
1878.   MA 2 V 14
Another copy. 8vo. Sydney, 1878. MJ 2 R 14

ROSS (ANDREW), S.S.C. Old Scottish Regimental Colours.
With twenty-eight coloured Plates, and other Illustrations.
Fol. Edinb., 1885.   B 17 U 9 ‡

ROSS (CHARLES). Charley Ross; the Story of his Abduction, and the Incidents of the Search for his Recovery
by his Father, Christian K. Ross. With Portraits, &c.
8vo. Lond., 1877.   C 4 T 38

ROSS (CHRISTIAN K.) Charley Ross; the Story of his
Abduction, and the Incidents of the Search for his Recovery. 8vo. Lond., 1877. C 4 T 38

ROSS (DENMAN W.), PH.D. Early History of Landholding among the Germans. 8vo. Lond., 1883. F 5 P 19

ROSS (GEORGE). Dictionary and Digest of the Law of
Scotland. [*See* BELL, W.] K 11 R 7

ROSS (HUGH). Essay for a New Translation of the
Bible. 2nd ed. 8vo. Lond., 1727. G 2 R 7

ROSS (J.) Book of Scottish Poems: Ancient and Modern.
Edited, with Memoirs of the Authors. 8vo. Edinburgh,
1878.   H 8 S 27

ROSS (JAMES), LL.D. Hobart Town Almanack, and Van
Diemen's Land Annual for 1830, 1832, 1834–35. 4 vols.
12mo. Hobart, 1830 35.* ME 4 P
Essay on Prison Discipline; in which is detailed the
System pursued in Van Diemen's Land. 2nd ed. 8vo.
Hobart, 1833.   MF 1 Q 4
Van Diemen's Land Annual for 1837. [*See* ELLISTON,
W. G.]

ROSS (JAMES). The Gulistan, or Flower-Garden, of Shaikh Sadi of Shiraz. [*See* SADI, M. E.]

ROSS (JAMES), M.D. Treatise on the Diseases of the Nervous System. Illustrated. 2 vols. 8vo. Lond., 1881.
A 12 R 14, 15

ROSS (CAPT. SIR JOHN CLARK), R.N., &c. Voyage of Discovery and Research in the Southern and Antarctic Regions, during the years 1839-43. 2 vols. 8vo. Lond., 1847.
D 4 R 18, 19
Another copy. 2 vols. 8vo. Lond., 1847. MD 7 Q 28, 29
[*See* HOOKER, SIR J. D.]

ROSS (MRS. J.) Memoir of Lady Duff Gordon. [*See* GORDON, LADY D.]
D 1 R 27

ROSS (REV. JOHN). The Manchus, or the Reigning Dynasty of China: their Rise and Progress. Maps and Illustrations. 8vo. Lond., 1880.
B 2 P 38
History of Corea, Ancient and Modern. With Description of Manners and Customs, Language, and Geography. Maps and Illustration. 8vo. Lond., 1880.
B 2 P 40

ROSS (CAPT. SIR JOHN), K.C.B., &c. Narrative of a Second Voyage in search of a North-west Passage, and of a Residence in the Arctic Regions, during the years 1829-33. 4to. Lond., 1835.
D 5 P 3 †
Memoirs and Correspondence of Admiral Lord de Saumarez. 2 vols. 8vo. Lond., 1838.
C 9 Q 38, 39

ROSS (JOHN M.), LL.D. Scottish History and Literature, to the Period of the Reformation. Edited, with Biographical Sketch, by James Brown, D.D. 8vo. Glasgow, 1884.
B 13 R 25

ROSS (MARS, AND COOPER (H. STONEHEWER). Highlands of Cantabria; or, Three Days from England. 8vo. Lond., 1885.
D 7 S 16

ROSS (PATRICK H. W.) Federation and the British Colonies: a Paper of Suggestions. 8vo. Lond., 1887.
MF 1 R 36

ROSS (ROBERT), M.D. [Tract in the Persian Language; composed originally in English and Turkish, and translated into Persian by Jno. McPherson, Missionary.] 8vo. Astrachan, 1823.
G 11 T 12
[Tract entitled, "A Book, making manifest the Truth"; composed in Turkish.] 8vo. Astrachan, 1823. G 11 T 12

ROSS (ROBERT), M.D. The Church, the Foundation, and the Keys; being the substance of three Discourses. 8vo. Sydney, 1848.
MG 1 P 1
Last Sermon; with his Letter to the Church, and their Answer, with his Reply. 12mo. Sydney, 1854. MG 1 P 1

ROSS (THOMASINA). Travels in Peru. [*See* TSCHUDI, DR. J. J. VON.]
D 4 Q 14

ROSS (REV. WILLIAM), LL.D. Aberdour and Inchcolme; being Historical Notices of the Parish and Monastery; in twelve Lectures. 8vo. Edinb., 1885.
B 13 P 15

4 N

ROSS (W. A.) Yacht Voyage to Norway, Denmark, and Sweden. 2 vols. 8vo. Lond., 1848.
D 8 S 27, 28

ROSS (LIEUT.-COL. W. A.), R.A., &c. The Blowpipe in Chemistry, Mineralogy, and Geology; containing all known Methods of Anhydrous Analysis, many working Examples, and Instructions for making Apparatus. 8vo. Lond., 1884.
A 5 R 3
Alphabetical Manual of Blowpipe Analysis; showing all known Methods, old and new. 8vo. Lond., 1880.
A 5 R 2
Pyrology; or, Fire Chemistry: a Science interesting to the General Philosopher, and an Art of infinite importance to the Chemist, Mineralogist, Metallurgist, Geologist, Agriculturist, Engineer (Mining, Civil, and Military), &c., &c. Roy. 8vo. Lond., 1875.
A 5 U 30

ROSS (W. J.), B.Sc., &c. Metallurgy of Silver. (Board of Technical Education.) 8vo. Sydney, 1885. MA 2 R 3

ROSS (W. MURRAY). On the Advantages of encouraging the Manufacture of Beet-root Sugar in Victoria. 8vo. Melb., 1880.
MJ 2 R 15

ROSSE (J. WILLOUGHBY). Index of Dates, comprehending the the principal Facts in the Chronology and History of the World, from the Earliest to the Present Time, alphabetically arranged; being a complete Index to the enlarged edition of Blair's Chronological Tables. 2 vols. 8vo. Lond., 1859-68.
B 14 P 40, 41

ROSSEL (MRS. HENRY). [*See* WAUTERS, PROF. A. J.]
A 6 V 8

ROSSEL (ELISABETHE PAUL EDOUARD), CONTRE AMIRAL. [*See* DENTRECASTEAUX, B.]
MD 7 P 9, 10 ‡

ROSSER (W. H.) Short Notes on the Winds, Weather, and Currents, together with general Sailing Directions and Remarks on making Passages; to accompany Charts of the North and South Pacific. 8vo. Lond., 1868. MD 4 S 1
The Sailor's Sea-book. [*See* GREENWOOD, J.] A 17 Q 39

ROSSETTI (DANTE GABRIEL). Ballads and Sonnets. 8vo. Lond., 1881.
H 8 S 15
Poems. 6th ed. 8vo. Lond., 1872.
H 8 S 14
Recollections of; by T. Hall Caine. 8vo. Lond., 1882.
C 4 V 28
Collected Works of. 2 vols. 8vo. Lond., 1886.
H 8 S 16, 17

ROSSETTI (WILLIAM MICHAEL). Memoir of Percy Bysshe Shelley. 8vo. Lond., 1886.
C 2 T 34
Political Works of W. Blake. [*See* BLAKE, W.]

ROST (DR. VAL. CHRIST. FRIEDR.) Griechisch-deutsches Wörterbuch für den Schul-und Handgebrauch, mit Eigennamen. 4e gänzlich umgearbeitete auflage. 2 vols. roy. 8vo. Braunschweig, 1878.
K 12 T 31, 32

ROSWEYDUS (HERIBERTUS). Vitæ Patrum. [*See* MIGNE, J. P., SERIES LATINA, 73, 74.]

ROTH (HENRY LING). Notes on Continental Irrigation. With Plates. 8vo. Lond., 1882.   A 1 T 7

ROTTECK (PROF. KARL VON). Allgemeine Geschichte vom Anfang der historischen Kenntniss, bis auf unsere Zeiten. 11 vols. 8vo. Freiburg, 1834–43   B 14 R 11–21 General History of the World, from the Earliest Times until the year 1842. 4 vols. 8vo. Lond., 1842.   B 15 P 1–4

ROTULI CHARTARUM in Turri Londinensi asservati; accurante Thoma Duffus Hardy; ab anno 1199 ad annum 1216. Vol. 1, Part 1. Fol. Lond., 1827.   B 24 Q 13 ‡

ROTULI DE OBLATIS ET FINIBUS in Turri Londinensi asservati, tempore Regis Johannis; accurante Thoma Duffus Hardy. Roy. 8vo. Lond., 1835.   B 15 T 18

ROTULI HUNDREDORUM, temp. Hen. III, & Edw. I, in Turri Londinensi, et in curia receptæ Scaccarij Westmonasteriensi asservati. 2 vols. fol. Lond., 1812–18.   B 24 R 9, 10 ‡

ROTULI LITTERARUM CLAUSARUM in Turri Londinensi asservati; accurante T. D. Hardy. Vol. 1, Part 1. Fol. Lond., 1833.   B 24 R 12 ‡

ROTULI LITTERARUM PATENTIUM in Turri Londinensi asservati; accurante T. D. Hardy. Vol. 1, Part 1. Fol. Lond., 1835.   B 24 R 11 ‡

ROTULI NORMANNIÆ in Turri Londinensi asservati, Johanne et Henrico quinto Angliæ Regibus; accurante Thoma Duffus Hardy. Vol. 1, 1200–5, necnon de anno 1417. Roy. 8vo. Lond., 1835.   B 15 T 19

ROTULI PARLIAMENTORUM ut et Petitiones et Placita in Parliamento tempore Edward I to Henry VII, A.D. 1278–1505, and Index. 7 vols. fol. Lond., 1832.   B 24 R 15–21 ‡

ROTULI SCOTIÆ in Turri Londinensi, et in domo Capitulari Westmonasteriensi asservati, Edwardi I–Henry VIII, 2 vols. fol. Lond., 1814–19.   B 24 R 13, 14 ‡

ROTULORUM ORIGINALIUM in Curia Scaccarii abbreviatio, temporibus Regum Hen. III, Edw. I, Edw. II, Edw. III. 2 vols. (in 1) fol. Lond., 1805–10.   B 24 S 1 ‡

ROTULUS CANCELLARII vel Antigraphum Magni Rotuli Pipæ de tertio anno Regni Regis Johannis. Roy. 8vo. Lond., 1833.   B 15 T 16

ROTWELLSCHE GRAMMATIK. Oder Sprachkunst, das ist: Anweisung wie man diese Sprache in wenig Stunden erlernen, reden, und verstehen möge. 12mo. Frankfurt-am-Maine, 1755.   K 16 P 5

ROUBAUD (DR. FÉLIX). Traité de l'Impuissance et de Stérilité chez l'Homme et chez la Femme, comprenant l'exposition des moyens recommandés pour y remédier. 2 vols. 8vo. Paris, 1855.   A 26 S 19, 20

ROUEN. Catalogue des Objets d'Art exposés au Musée de Rouen. 3e éd. 12mo. Rouen, 1837.   A 7 P 35

ROUGH (D.) Recollections of a Visit to Europe in 1851–52; by "A Traveller from New Zealand." 8vo. Auckland, 1853.   MD 4 S 25

ROUGH NOTES. Rough Notes of Journeys made in the years 1868–73, in Syria, down the Tigris, India, Kashmir, Ceylon, Japan, Mongolia, Siberia, the United States, the Sandwich Islands, and Australasia. 8vo. Lond., 1875.   MD 7 P 27

ROUS (FRANCIS). Archæologia Atticæ Libri Septem: Seven Books of the Attick Antiquities, containing the Description of the City's Glory, Government, Divisions of the People, and Towns within the Athenian Territories; their Religion, Superstitions, Sacrifices, Account of their Year, a full Relation of their Judicatories. 9th ed. Sm. 4to. Lond., 1685.   B 27 S 11

ROUSE (ROLLA). Rouse's Practical Man, including Copyhold Practice and Forms; with full Instructions for Use of Logarithms; with a Four-Figure Table, and retaining and adding to the previous Forms, Rules, and Tables. 15th ed. 2 vols. ob. 18mo. Lond., 1878.   Libr.

ROUSSIER (PIERRE JOSEPH), L'ABBÉ. Essai sur la Musique, Ancienne et Moderne. [*See* LA BORDE, J. B. DE.]

ROUSSEAU (A.) [*See* TUNIS.]

ROUSSEAU (JEAN JACQUES). Confessions of; translated from the French. With Illustrations. 8vo. Lond., 1871.   C 2 S 36
Dictionnaire de Musique. 4to. Paris, 1768.   K 17 U 6
La Reine Fantasque. [*See* CABINET DES FÉES, 26.]
Rousseau; by John Morley. 2 vols. 8vo. Lond., 1873.   C 9 R 14, 15

ROUSSELET (LOUIS). India and its Native Princes: Travels in Central India, and in the Presidencies of Bombay and Bengal; carefully revised and edited by Lieut.-Col. Buckle; containing 317 Illustrations and six Maps. Imp. 4to. Lond., 1876.   D 5 Q 14 †
L'Inde des Rajahs. Roy. 4to. Paris, 1875.   D 5 Q 5 †

ROUSSELL-KILLOUGH (HENRY), COMTE. [*See* RUSSELL-KILLOUGH, H., COMTE.]

ROUSSET (J.) Corps Universal Diplomatique du Droit des Gens. [*See* DUMONT, J.]

ROUTES TO AUSTRALIA (THE), considered in reference to Commercial and Postal Interests, by the Directors of the Australian Direct Steam Navigation Company, *via* Panama, in a Letter to the Rt. Hon. Viscount Canning. 8vo. Lond., 1854.   MJ 2 Q 18

ROUTH (MARTIN JOSEPH), D.D. Reliquiæ Sacræ: sive, Auctorum fere jam perditorum secundi tertiique Sæculi Fragmenti, quæ supersunt. 5 vols. 8vo. Oxonii, 1814–48.   G 11 S 22–26

ROUTLEDGE (JAMES). Chapters in the History of Popular Progress; chiefly in relation to the Freedom of the Press, and Trial by Jury, 1660–1820. 8vo. Lond., 1876. B 7 P 8

English Rule and Native Opinion in India; from Notes taken 1870–74. 8vo. Lond., 1878. F 5 P 17

ROUTLEDGE (ROBERT), B.Sc., &c. Discoveries and Inventions of the 19th Century. With Illustrations. 8vo. Lond., 1876. A 17 T 47

Science in Sport made Philosophy in Earnest; being an Attempt to illustrate some Elementary Principles of Physical Knowledge by means of Toys and Pastimes. With Illustrations. 8vo. Lond., 1877. A 17 T 50

ROUX (H.) Herculanum et Pompei. [*See* BARRÉ, L.] A 8 S 17–23

ROUYER (EUGÈNE). L'Art Architectural en France; depuis François 1er jusqu'à Louis XVI: Motifs de décoration intérieure et extérieure dessinés d'après des modèles exécutés et inédits des Principales époques de la Renaissance. 2 vols. imp. 4to. Paris, 1866–67. A 4 P 19, 20 ‡

ROWAN (FREDERICA). Meditations on Death and Eternity; translated from the German. Published by Her Majesty's Gracious Permission. 8vo. Lond., 1863. G 7 S 1

Meditations on Life and its Religious Duties; translated from the German. Published by Her Majesty's Gracious Permission. 8vo. Lond., 1863. G 7 S 2

ROWBOTHAM (J.), F.R.A.S. Derivative Spelling Book. (Weale.) 12mo. Lond., 1881. K 11 T 25

ROWCROFT (CHARLES). Tales of the Colonies; or, the Adventures of an Emigrant; edited by "A late Colonial Magistrate." 3 vols. 8vo. Lond., 1843. MJ 1 T 5–7

Another copy. 2nd ed. 3 vols. 8vo. Lond., 1843. MJ 1 T 8–10

Another copy. 5th ed. 12mo. Lond., 1847. MJ 1 T 11

The Bushranger; or, Mark Brandon, the Convict. 12mo. Lond. (n.d.) MJ 1 P 15

The Bushranger of Van Diemen's Land. 3 vols. 8vo. Lond., 1846.* MJ 1 T 12–14

ROWE (C. J.), M.A. An Englishman's Views on Questions of the Day in Victoria. 8vo. Lond.,1882. MF 1 P 8

Bards of Disunion; or, English Misrule in the Colonies. 8vo. Lond., 1883. MF 1 P 9

ROWE (REV. G.), M.A. Colonial Empire of Great Britain, considered chiefly with reference to its Physical Geography and Industrial Production.—The Australian Group. 12mo. Lond., 1865. MD 2 Q 25

ROWE (NICHOLAS). The Ambitious Step-mother: a Tragedy. (Bell's Brit. Theatre.) 18mo. Lond., 1795. H 2 P 6

The Fair Penitent: a Tragedy. (New Eng. Theatre.) 18mo. Lond., 1784. H 4 P 17

Another copy. (Bell's Brit. Theatre.) 18mo. Lond., 1791. H 2 P 17

Another copy. (Brit. Theatre.) 12mo. Lond., 1808. H 1 P 10

Another copy. [*See* BRIT. DRAMA, 1.]

ROWE (NICHOLAS)—*continued.*

Lady Jane Gray: a Tragedy. (Bell's Brit. Theatre). 18mo. Lond., 1791. H 2 P 23

Another copy. (Brit. Theatre.) Lond.,1808. H 1 P 10

Another copy. (New Eng. Theatre.) 12mo. Lond., 1791. H 4 P 23

Another copy. [*See* BRIT. DRAMA, 1.]

Jane Shore: a Tragedy. (New Eng. Theatre.) 12mo. Lond., 1776. H 4 P 19

Another copy. (Brit. Theatre.) 12mo. Lond., 1808. H 1 P 10

Another copy. [*See* BRIT. DRAMA, 1.]

Tamerlane: a Tragedy. (New Eng. Theatre.) 12mo. Lond., 1784. H 4 P 21

Another copy (Bell's Brit. Theatre.) 18mo. Lond., 1792. H 2 P 21

Another copy. (Brit. Theatre.) 12mo. Lond., 1808. H 1 P 10

The Royal Convert: a Tragedy. (Bell's Brit. Theatre.) 18mo. Lond., 1794. H 2 P 9

Life and Poems of. [*See* CHALMERS, A., *and* JOHNSON, S.]

ROWE (RICHARD), "PETER 'POSSUM." Peter 'Possum's Portfolio. 8vo. Sydney, 1858.* MJ 2 S 20

The Boy in the Bush; by "Edward Howe." Illustrated. 12mo. Lond., 1869. MJ 1 P 40

Roughing it in Van Diemen's Land, &c. 12mo. Lond., 1880. MD 3 P 46

ROWELL (GEORGE P.) & CO. American Newspaper Directory; containing accurate Lists of all the Newspapers and Periodicals published in the United States Territories, the Dominion of Canada, and Newfoundland. Roy. 8vo. New York, 1876. E

ROWLANDS (HENRY), VICAR OF LLANJDAN. Mona Antiqua Restaurata: an Archæological Discourse on the Antiquities, Natural and Historical, of the Isle of Anglesey, the Antient Seat of the British Druids. In two Essays. 4to. Dublin, 1723. B 5 V 27

ROWLANDSON (THOMAS). Rowlandson, the Caricaturist: a Selection from his Works, and a Sketch of his Life, Times, and Contemporaries; by Joseph Grego. With Illustrations. 2 vols. 4to. Lond., 1880. B 2 W 21, 22

ROWLEY (REV. HENRY), VICAR OF. Africa Unveiled; with Map and Illustrations. 8vo. Lond., 1876. D 1 T 30

Twenty Years in Central Africa; being the Story of the Universities' Mission to Central Africa, from its Commencement. With Map. 8vo. Lond., 1881. D 1 T 31

Story of the Universities' Mission to Central Africa. 8vo. Lond., 1866. D 2 P 13

ROWLEY (WILLIAM). A Woman never Vexed: a Comedy; with additions by J. R. Planché. (Cumberland's Eng. Theatre.) 12mo. Lond., 1829. H 2 Q 12

ROWNEY (HORATIO BICKERSTAFFE). Wild Tribes of India. 8vo. Lond., 1882.   A 1 V 11

ROWNEY (PROF. T. H.), PH.D., &c. Old Chapter of the Geological Record. [*See* KING, PROF. W.]

ROWNTREE (JOHN STEPHENSON). Quakerism, past and present; being an inquiry into the causes of its decline in Great Britain and Ireland. 8vo. Lond., 1859. G 7 R 29

ROWS (JOHN). Rows Rol. Thys Rol was laburd and finishid by Master John Rows of Warrewyk. Published by William Pickering. Roy. 4to. Lond., 1845. B 15 Q 6‡

ROWTON (FREDERIC). Female Poets of Great Britain; Chronologically arranged, with copious Selections and critical Remarks. 8vo. Lond., 1848.   H 6 U 5

ROXBURGHE CLUB. Publications. 8 vols. 4to. Lond., 1868–70.   E

ROY (J. J E.) L'Australie : Découverte, Colonisation, Civilisation. 8vo. Tours, 1855.   MB 2 T 12
Another copy. 4e éd. 8vo. Tours, 1867.   MB 2 T 13
Another copy. 5e éd. 8vo. Tours, 1873.   MB 2 T 14
Le Dernier des Stuart. 8vo. Tours, 1855.   B 13 Q 25

ROY (MAJOR-GEN. WILLIAM), F.R.S., &c. Military Antiquities of the Romans in Great Britain. Published by the order, and at the expense of the Society of Antiquaries of London. Imp. fol. Lond., 1793.   B 32 P 10 ‡

ROYAL ACADEMY (THE). Royal Academy Illustrated, 1884; edited by Henry Lassalle. 8vo. Lond., 1884.   E

ROYAL ACADEMY OF ARTS. Official Illustrated Catalogue of the Exhibition, 1886. Fol. Lond., 1886.   E

ROYAL AGRICULTURAL SOCIETY OF ENGLAND. Journal of. 50 vols. 8vo. Lond., 1840–87.   E
General Index to vols. 1–25. 8vo. Lond., 1865.   E

ROYAL AGRICULTURAL AND HORTICULTURAL SOCIETY OF S. AUSTRALIA. Proceedings of. 8vo. Adelaide, 1881.   ME 1 P

ROYAL ASIATIC SOCIETY. Journal of the Royal Asiatic Society of Great Britain and Ireland. 38 vols. 8vo. Lond., 1834–86.   E 8
Journal of the Straits Branch of the Royal Asiatic Society. 9 vols. 8vo. Singapore, 1878–83.   E
Journal of the North China Branch of the Royal Asiatic Society. (Shanghai Literary and Scientific Society.) 7 vols. 8vo. Shanghai, 1858–81.   E

ROYAL ASTRONOMICAL SOCIETY. Catalogue of the Library of, compiled to June, 1884. 8vo. Lond., 1886.   K 7 S 31

ROYAL CHARTER OF LONDON. [*See* LONDON.]

ROYAL COLLEGE OF SURGEONS OF ENGLAND. Descriptive and Illustrated Catalogue of the Fossil Organic Remains of Mammalia and Aves. [*See* OWEN, PROF. SIR R.]   A 1 Q 20 †

ROYAL COLONIAL INSTITUTE. Proceedings of. Edited by the Secretary. Vols. 1–18. 8vo. Lond., 1869–87.   E
Catalogue of the Library of, 1886. [Compiled by J. R. Boosé.] Imp. 8vo. Lond., 1886.   MK 1 U 18

ROYAL GEOGRAPHICAL SOCIETY OF AUSTRALASIA. Proceedings of, New South Wales and Victorian Branches. Vol. 1. 8vo. Sydney, 1885.   ME 2 Q
Special Volume of the Proceedings. 8vo. Sydney, 1885.   ME 2 Q
Official Report of Captain H. C. Everill, Leader of the New Guinea Exploring Expedition. 8vo. Sydney, 1886.   ME 2 Q
Annual Address by Sir Edward Strickland, K.C.B., F.R.G.S., Vice-President of the Society (New South Wales Branch). 8vo. Sydney, 1887.   ME 2 Q

ROYAL GEOGRAPHICAL SOCIETY OF LONDON. Catalogue of the Library of. 8vo. Lond., 1865. K 7 S 17
Journal of, 1830–79. 50 vols. 8vo. Lond., 1830–80.   E Sub.
Proceedings of, and Monthly Record of Geography. Published under the authority of the Council, and edited by the Assistant Secretary. New monthly series. Vols. 1–8. Lond., 1879–86.   E
Fifty Years' Work of the Royal Geographical Society; by Clements R. Markham, C.B., &c. Lond., 1881.   E
General Index. 2 vols. (in 1) 8vo. Lond., 1844–53.   E Sub.
Supplementary Papers [1881–85.] Roy. 8vo. Lond., 1886.   E

ROYAL GEOLOGICAL SOCIETY OF CORNWALL. Papers. [*See* HENWOOD, W. J.]

ROYAL INSTITUTE OF BRITISH ARCHITECTS OF LONDON. Questions upon various subjects connected with Architecture. Compiled by T. L. Donaldson. 8vo. Lond., 1835.   A7 Q 13
Transactions, Session 1835–42. Lond., 1839–42.
                                            A 2 U 28
Transactions and Papers. 16 vols. 4to. Lond., 1836–86.   E

ROYAL INSTITUTION OF GREAT BRITAIN. The Quarterly Journal of Science, Literature, and Art, 1827–28. 4 vols. 8vo. Lond., 1827–28.   E
The Royal Institution : its Founder and its First Professors. [*See* JONES, H. B.]

ROYAL IRISH ACADEMY, DUBLIN. Transactions, 21 vols. roy. 4to. Dublin, 1785–1847.   E

ROYAL KALENDAR (THE). Royal Kalendar, and Court and City Register for England, Scotland, Ireland, and the Colonies, for the years 1808, 1810, 1831–85. 57 vols. 12mo. Lond., 1808–85.   E

ROYAL MAIL STEAM PACKET CO. [*See* INDIA AND AUSTRALIA ROYAL MAIL STEAM PACKET Co.] MF 3 Q 72

ROYAL RED BOOK; or, Court and Fashionable Register for 1870–76. Published by A. Webster. 7 vols. 12mo. Lond., 1870–76.   E

ROYAL RIVER: the Thames from Source to Sea, Descriptive, Historical, Pictorial. Imp. 4to. Lond., 1885.   D 4 R 6 †

ROYAL SCOTTISH ACADEMY (THE). Illustrated Catalogue, containing Illustrations from Drawings by the Artists, and reproduced by Theodore Guyot. 2 vols. 8vo. Edinb.,'1884–85.   E

ROYAL SOCIETY OF LITERATURE. Transactions. [1st series, Vols. 1–3, 1825–39; 2nd series, Vols. 1–12, 1840–81.] 3 vols. 4to. and 12 vols. 8vo. Lond., 1829–82.   E

ROYAL SOCIETY OF LONDON. Publications. (From the Philosophical Transactions.) 6 vols. 4to. Lond., 1875–79.   A 11 P 2–7 †

1. Contributions to the Developmental History of Mollusca; by E. Ray Lankester, M.A., &c.
Addition to the Paper on Volcanic Energy: an Attempt to Develop its true Origin and Cosmical Relations; by R. Mallet, A.M., &c.
Contributions to Terrestrial Magnetism, No. 14; by Gen. Sir E. Sabine, R.A., &c.
On the Atmospheric Lines of the Solar Spectrum; by J. B. N. Hennessey, F.R.A.S. On Polishing the Specula of Reflecting Telescopes; by W. Lassell, F.R.S., &c.
On the Development of the Teeth of the Newt, Frog, Slow-worm, and Green Lizard; and on the Structure and Development of the Teeth of Ophidia; by C. S. Tomes, M.A.
Research on the Small-pox of Sheep; by E. Klein, M.D.
Description of the Living and Extinct Races of Gigantic Land Tortoises; by Dr. A. Günther, F.R.S., &c.
On the Tides of the Arctic Seas: Parts 4, 5, and 6; by the Rev. S. Haughton, M.D., &c.
On the Mathematical Expression of Observations of Complex Periodical Phenomena; and on Planetary Influence on the Earth's Magnetism; by C. and F. Chambers.
Experiments on the Brain of Monkeys. 2nd series. (The Croonian Lecture); by D. Ferrier, M.A., &c.
Reduction of Anemograms, taken at the Armagh Observatory, 1857–63; by T. R. Robinson, D.D., &c.
On .Repulsion resulting from Radiation; by W. Crookes, F.R.S., &c.
On a Class of Identical Relations in the Theory of Elliptic Functions; by J. W. L. Glaisher, M.A., &c.

2. Spectroscopic Observations of the Sun; by J. N. Lockyer, F.R.S., and G. M. Seabroke, F.R.A.S.
On the Structure and Development of Myriothela; by Prof. Allman, M.D., &c.
Tables of Temperatures of the Sea at different Depths beneath the Surface (1749–1868) discussed; by J. Prestwich, M.A., &c.
Memoir on Prepotentials; by Prof. Cayley, F.R.S.
The Optical Development of the Atmosphere in relation to Putrefaction and Infection; by John Tyndall, F.R.S.
On the Development of the Spinal Nerves in Elasmobranchi Fishes; by F. M. Balfour, B.A.
On the Refraction of Sound by the Atmosphere; by Prof. O. Reynolds.
On the Organization of the Fossil Plants of the Coal Measures: Part 7; by W. C. Williamson, F.R.S.

ROYAL SOCIETY OF LONDON—*continued.*
On the Development of the Teeth of Fishes (Elasmobranchii and Teleostei); by C. S. Tomes, M.A.
The Absolute Direction and Intensity of the Earth's Magnetic Force at Bombay, and its Secular and Annual Variations; by C. Chambers, F.R.S., &c.
On the Fossil Mammals of Australia: Part 10; by Prof. Owen, C.B., &c.
On the Structure and Relations of Certain Corals; by H. N. Moseley, M.A.
On the Development of Cirripedia; by R. von Willemöes-Suhm, Ph.D., &c.
Preliminary Observations on the Locomotor System of Medusae; by G. J. Romanes, M.A., &c. (The Croonian Lecture.)
On Multiple Contact of Surfaces; by W. Spottiswoode, M.A., &c.

3. On Rolling-Friction; by Prof. O. Reynolds.
On the Expansion of Seawater by Heat; by T. E. Thorpe, Ph.D., and A. W. Rücker, M.A.
The Residual Charge of the Leyden Jar; by J. Hopkinson, M.A., &c.
Experiments on the Friction between Water and Air; by Dr. Y. von Lang.
On the Gaseous State of Matter; by T. Andrews, M.D., &c. (The Bakerian Lecture.)
On the Development and Succession of the Poison Fangs of Snakes; by C. S. Tomes, M.A.
On the Variations of the Daily Mean Horizontal Force of the Earth's Magnetism; by J. A. Broun, F.R.S.
Contributions to the Minute Anatomy of the Thyroid Gland of the Dog; by E. Cresswell Baber, M.B.
On Repulsion resulting from Radiation: Parts 3 and 4; by W. Crookes, F.R.S., &c.
On the Placentation of the Lemurs; by W. Turner, M.B.
On the Nature of the Force producing the Motion of a Body exposed to the Rays of Heat and Light; by A. Schuster, Ph.D.
On the Physiological Action of Vanadium; by J. Priestley.
On the Structure and Development of the Skull in the Batrachia; by W. K. Parker, F.R.S.
The Minute Anatomy of the Alimentary Canal; by H. Watney, M.A., &c.
On the Forces caused by the Communication of Heat between a Surface and a Gas; and on a new Piotometer; by Prof. O. Reynolds.

4. On Determining the Depth of the Sea without the use of the Sounding Line; by C. W. Siemens, F.R.S., &c.
Electrodynamic Qualities of Metals: Part 6, Effects of Stress on Magnetization; by Sir W. Thomson, F.R.S., &c.
Contribution to Terrestrial Magnetism; by Vice-Admiral Sir C. Shadwell, K.C.B., &c.
On the Absorption-Spectra of Bromine and of Iodine Monochloride; by H. E. Roscoe, F.R.S., and T. E. Thorpe, F.R.S.
On the Organization of the Fossil Plants of the Coal Measure: Part 8; by W. C. Williamson, F.R.S.
On the Determination of Verdet's Constant in Absolute Units; by J. E. H. Gordon, B.A.
The Calculus of Chemical Operations: Part 2.
On the Analysis of Chemical Events; by Sir B. C. Brodie, Bart., &c.
On the Structure of a Species of Millepora, occurring at Tahiti, Society Islands; by H. N. Moseley, F.R.S.
Further Researches on the Deportment and Vital Persistence of Putrefactive and Infective Organisms from a Physical Point of View; by J. Tyndall, D.C.L., &c.
On the Influence of Geological Changes on the Earth's Axis of Rotation; by G. H. Darwin, M.A.
Action of Light on Selenium; by Prof. W. G. Adams, M.A., &c., and R. E. Day, M.A.
Contributions to Terrestrial Magnetism: No. 15; by Gen. Sir E. Sabine, R.A., &c.
On Hyperjacobian Surfaces and Curves; by W. Spottiswoode, M.A., &c.
On Friction between Surfaces moving at Low Speeds; by F. Jenkin, F.R.S., and J. A. Ewing.
On the Bicircular Quartic; by A. Cayley, LL.D., &c.

ROYAL SOCIETY OF LONDON—*continued.*
5. On the Structure and Development of the Skull in the Uro-
delous Amphibia: Part 1, by W. K. Parker, F.R.S.
Residual Charge of the Leyden Jar, Dielectric Properties of
different Glasses; by J. Hopkinson, M.A., &c.
On a New Form of Tangential Equation; by J. Casey,
LL.D., &c.
On the Physiological Action of the Bark of Erythrophleum
Guinense, generally called Casca, Cassa, or Sassy Bark; by
T. L. Brunton, M.D., &c., and W. Pye.
Further Observations on the Locomotor System of Medusæ;
by G. J. Romanes, M.A., &c.
On the Tides of the Arctic Seas: Part 7, Tides of Port
Kennedy, in Bellot Strait; by the Rev. S. Haughton, M.D., &c.
Electrostatic Capacity of Glass; by J. Hopkinson, M.A., &c.
On the Structure and Development of Vascular Dentine; by
C. S. Tomes, M.A.
On the Normal Paraffins; by C. Schorlemmer, F.R.S.
Experimental Researches on the Electric Discharge with the
Chloride of Silver Battery: Parts 1, 2, by W. De la Rue,
M.A., &c., and H. W. Müller, Ph.D., &c.
On the Tides at Malta: by Sir G. B. Airey, K.C.B., &c.
Report on the Total Solar Eclipse of April, 1875; by J. N.
Lockyer, F.R.S., and A. Schuster, Ph.D., &c.
On Repulsion resulting from Radiation; by W. Crookes, F.R.S.
(The Bakerian Lecture.)
On the Organization of the Fossil Plants of the Coal-measures:
Part 9, by Prof. W. C. Williamson, F.R.S.
6. New Determination of the Mechanical Equivalent of Heat; by
J. P. Joule, D.C.L., &c.
On the Structure and Development of the Skull in the Common
Snake (Tropidonotus natrix); by W. K. Parker, F.R.S.
Addition to Memoir on the Transformation of Elliptic
Functions: by A. Cayley, F.R.S., &c.
On the Stucture of Stylasteridæ, a Family of the Hydroid
Stony Corals; by H. N. Moseley, F.R.S. (The Croonian
Lecture.)
On the Development of the Parasitic Isopoda; by J. F. Bullar,
B.A.
On the Placentation of the Apes, with a Comparison of the
Structure of their Placenta with that of the Human Female;
by W. Turner, M.B.
Observations on the Nervous System of Aurelia Aurita; by
Prof. E. A. Schäfer.
On the Modification of the Simple and Compound Eyes of
Insects: by B. T. Lowne, F.R.C.S., &c.
Tenth Memoir on Quantics: by Prof. A. Cayley, F.R.S.
On the Classification of Loci: by Prof. W. K. Clifford, F.R.S.
On the Osteology of Polyodon folium; by T. W. Bridge,
B.A., &c.
Contributions to the Anatomy of the Central Nervous System
in Vertebrate Animals: by A. Sanders, M.C.R.S., &c.
On the Determination of the Constants of the Cup Anemo-
meter by Experiments with a Whirling Machine; by T. R.
Robinson, D.D., &c.

Abstracts of the Papers and Proceedings, 1800–86.
11 vols. 8vo. Lond., 1832–87. E

Catalogue of the Library. 4to. Lond., 1825. S 9 P 10 †

Philosophical Transactions. 178 vols. 4to. Lond.,
1809–87. E

ROYAL SOCIETY OF NEW SOUTH WALES.
Proceedings of the Philosophical Society of New South
Wales for 1857–58. [*See* SYDNEY MAGAZINE OF SCIENCE
AND ART.]

Transactions of the Philosophical Society of N.S.W.,
1862–65. 8vo. Sydney, 1866.* ME 1 R

Transactions, 1870–74; Transactions and Proceedings,
1875; Journal and Proceedings, 1876–85, of the Royal
Society of N.S.W. Edited by Prof. A. Liversidge, and
Dr. A. Leibius. 17 vols. (in 15) 8vo. Sydney, 1871–
87. ME 1 R

ROYAL SOCIETY OF NEW SOUTH WALES—*contd.*
[List of the] Publications of, 1862–77. 8vo. Lond.,
1878. MJ 2 R 17

Fundamental Rules and Bye-laws of the Philosophical
Society of New South Wales. (Pam. 20.) 8vo. Sydney,
1861. MJ 2 Q 9

ROYAL SOCIETY OF NORTHERN ANTIQUARIES.
[*See* ANTIQUARIES DU NORD.]

ROYAL SOCIETY OF SOUTH AUSTRALIA. Transactions, Proceedings, and Reports of the Philosophical
Society of Adelaide, 1877–79. 8vo. Adelaide, 1878–
79.* ME 1 P

Transactions and Proceedings, and Reports of [formerly
Philosophical Society of Adelaide]. Vols. 3, 4, 1879–81.
8vo. Adelaide, 1880–82. ME 1 P

ROYAL SOCIETY OF TASMANIA. Papers and Proceedings (some called Monthly Notices), 1848–55, 1859,
1863–64, 1866–80. 15 vols. 8vo. Hobart, 1851–81.
ME 1 Q

Report for 1860. 8vo. Hobart, 1861. MF 3 P 15

Reports, 1848–66, 1869–72, 1874. 8vo. Hobart,
1848–75. ME 1 Q

Meteorological Observations taken at Hobart Town,
1856–58; Francis Abbott, Observer. [Supplement to
Vol. 3, Papers and Proceedings.] Sm. fol. Hobart,
1859. ME 3 V

ROYAL SOCIETY OF VICTORIA (THE). Transactions
and Proceedings of the Victorian Institute [afterwards
the Philosophical Institute of Victoria] for 1854–55. 8vo.
Melb., 1855. ME 1 Q

Transactions of the Philosophical Institute of Victoria
[formerly the Victorian Institute]. Vols. 1–4. 8vo.
Melb., 1855–60. ME 1 P

Transactions and Proceedings of [formerly Philosophical
Institute of Victoria]. Vols. 1–12, 23–24. 8vo. Melb.,
1855–87. ME 1 P

[*See* RAWLINSON, T. E.] MA 2 V 21

ROYCE 1. GREGORY. [*See* GURGOUY, J. A.]

ROYCE (JOSIAH). California, from the Conquest in 1846 to
the Second Vigilance Committee in San Francisco. [Ameri-
can Commonwealths.] 12mo. Boston, 1886. B 1 Q.47

ROYLE (C.) Egyptian Campaigns, 1882 to 1885, and the
events which led to them. 2 vols. 8vo. Lond., 1886.
B 2 S 7, 8

ROYLE (PROF. J. F.), M.D., &c. The Arts and Manufactures of India. [*See* LOND. INTERNATIONAL EXHI-
BITION, 1851.] A 16 Q 22

ROYSTON (PHILIP VORKE), VISCOUNT. [*See* HESIOD.]
J 15 P 15

ROZIER (François), L'Abbé. Cours Complet d'Agriculture ; ou, Dictionnaire Universel d'Agriculture. 12 vols 4to. Paris, 1793-1805.   A 18 U 1–12

La Parfait Vigneron ; ou, Traité sur la Culture de la Vigne, avec l'art de faire d'Améliorer, et de conserver les Vins ; par l'Abbé Rozier, Chaptal, Parmentier, et Dussieux. Sm. 4to. Paris, 1801.   A 1 T 14

ROZIER (Dr). Des Habitudes Secrètes, ou de l'Onanisme chez les Femmes. 2e éd. 8vo. Paris, 1825.   A 26 S 10

RUBENS (Peter Paul). His Life and Genius ; by Dr. G. F. Waagen. Translated. 8vo. Lond., 1840.   A 7 Q 22

Les Leçons de. [*See* Boussard, J. F.]   A 8 R 17

RÜCKER (A. W.), M.A. On the Expansion of Sea Water by Heat. [*See* Thorpe, T. E.]   A 11 P 4 †

RÜCKERT (Friedrich). Gedichte von. 18e auflage. 12mo. Frankf.-am-Main, 1875.   H 7 P 29

RUDDER (E. W.) Doctrine of Annihilation discussed ; also Jesus Christ—the only Source of Eternal Life, &c. 8vo. Sydney, 1875.   MG 1 Q 32

Ephraim ; or, the Identification of the Lost Ten Tribes of Israel ; by "An Israelite of 1873." (Pam. Bo.) 8vo. Sydney, 1875.*   MG 1 Q 32

Another copy. (Pam. Bq.) 8vo. Sydney, 1875.   MG 1 Q 36

Another copy. (Pam. Br.)   MG 1 Q 35

Truth v. Error, illustrated in a Correspondence between a Lay Reader of the Church of England and a Layman. (Pam. Br.) 8vo. Sydney, 1877.*   MG 1 Q 35

Conditional Immortality, as taught in the New Testament Scriptures ; by "A Layman." (Pam. Bs.) 8vo. Sydney, 1877.   MG 1 Q 34

Another copy. (Pam. Bq.) 8vo. Sydney, 1877.   MG 1 Q 36

RUDDER (Samuel). New History of Gloucestershire ; comprising the Topography, Antiquities, Curiosities, Produce, Trade, and Manufactures of that County ; also, the Ecclesiastical, Civil, and Military History of the City of Gloucester. Fol. Cirencester, 1779. B 18 U 12 ‡

History of the Antient Town of Cirencester ; in two Parts. Part 1. The Antient State. Part 2. The Modern and Present State. With appropriate Observations, and illustrated with Plates. 2nd. ed. 8vo. Cirencester, 1800.   B 3 T 8

RUDDIMAN (Thomas), A.M. Life of ; by George Chalmers. 8vo. Lond., 1794.   C 9 S 16

RUDDOCK (E. H.) Text-book of Modern Medicine and Surgery, on Homœopathic Principles. 8vo. Lond., 1884.   A 12 T 26

RUDGE (James), D.D. Address to the New Zealand Emigrants ; delivered at the Depôt, Deptford, October 11, 1840. 12mo. Lond., 1840.   MG 1 P 20

RUDLER (F. W.), F.G.S. Ure's Dictionary of Arts, &c. [*See* Ure, Dr. A.]

RUDLER (F. W.), F.G.S., and CHISHOLM (George G.), B.Sc. Europe ; with Ethnological Appendix, by Prof. A. H. Keane. Edited by Sir A. C. Ramsay. (Stanford's Compendium of Geography and Travel.) 8vo. Lond., 1885.   D 11 S 6

RUDOLPH (H.I.R.H. Prince), Crown Prince of Austria. Travels in the East, including a Visit to Egypt and the Holy Land. With Illustrations. Roy. 8vo. Lond., 1884.   D 2 U 13

RUDYERD (Sir Benjamin), Knt. Memoirs of ; containing his Speeches and Poems ; edited by James A. Manning. 8vo. Lond., 1841.   C 9 S 17

RUFINUS (Tyrannius). Opera omnia. [*See* Migne, J. P., Series Latina, 21.]

RULE (Martin), M.A. Life and Times of St. Anselm, Archbishop of Canterbury and Primate of the Britains. 2 vols. 8vo. Lond., 1883.   C 9 S 25, 26

RULE (William Harris), D.D. History of the Inquisition, from its Establishment in the the 12th Century to its Extinction in the 19th. 2 vols. 8vo. Lond., 1874.   G 11 T 10, 11

RUMFORD (Sir Benjamin Thompson), Count von. Essays—Political, Economical, and Philosophical. 3 vols. 8vo. Lond., 1882.   J 7 U 4–6

The Royal Institution : its Founder [Count Rumford], &c. [*See* Jones, H. B.]

RUMKER (Dr. Charles Stargard). On the Astronomy of the Southern Hemisphere. [*See* Field, B.]

RUMSEY (Henry W.), M.D., &c. Essays and Papers on some Fallacies of Statistics concerning Life and Death, Health and Disease, &c. 8vo. Lond., 1875.   F 5 P 18

RUNDALL (Thomas). Narratives of Voyages towards the North-West, in search of a Passage to Cathay and India, 1496 to 1631. 8vo. Lond., 1849.   D 4 R 44

RUNNYMEDE LETTERS (The). [*See* Beaconsfield, Rt. Hon. B. Disraeli, Earl of.]

RUPERT (G. A.) [*See* Livius, T.]   J 13 Q 22–R 5

RUPERT (Prince). Memoirs of Prince Rupert and the Cavaliers, including his Private Correspondence ; by Eliot Warburton. 3 vols. 8vo. Lond., 1849. C 9 S 18–20

RUPERTUS (Abbas Tutiensis). Opera omnia. [*See* Migne, J. P., Series Latina, 167–170.]

RÜPPELL (Dr. Eduard). Beschreibungen und Abbildungen mehrerer neuer Fische, im Nil entdeckt. (Pam. Ck.) 3 vols. (in 1) 4to. Frankfort, 1829–35. A 15 U 1

RUSCELLI (G.) [*See* Ariosto, L.]   H 6 S 1

RUSCHENBERGER (W. S. W.) Three Years in the Pacific ; containing Notices of Brazil, Chile, Bolivia, Peru, &c., in 1831–34 ; by "An Officer of the U.S. Navy." 2 vols. 8vo. Lond., 1835.   D 3 U 13, 14

BUSDEN (F. T.) Public Lands. [*See* NEW SOUTH WALES.]

RUSDEN (REV. G. K.), A.M. Assize Sermon, preached at St. Peter's Church, Maitland, 1843. 8vo. Sydney, 1843.   MG 1 P 1

Sermon, preached at St. Peter's Church, East Maitland, 1856. 8vo. Sydney, 1856.   MG 1 P 1

BUSDEN (GEORGE W.) Moyarra: an Australian Legend, in two Cantos. 12mo. Maitland, 1851.   MH 1 P 17

National Education. 8vo. Melb., 1853.   MG 1 Q 38

Old Road to Responsible Government; or, the Development of the Representative Principle in Government historically considered : a Lecture. (Pan. 40.) 12mo. Melb., 1856.   MJ 2 R 2

Gathering together for the good of Work and Learning : a Lecture. 8vo. Melb., 1857.   MJ 2 R 7

Correspondence with the Chief Secretary of Victoria and others on the Civil Service. 8vo. Melh., 1860.   MF 3 P 5

Remarks on the Status of Colonial Bishops, and the Law concerning Bishops in Victoria. 8vo. Melh., 1868.   MG 1 Q 39

Discovery, Survey, and Settlement of Port Phillip. 8vo. Melb., 1871.   MB 2 S 28

Another copy. 8vo. Melb., 1871.   MJ 2 R 10

Curiosities of Colonisation. 8vo. Lond., 1874.   MJ 2 R 15

History of Australia. 3 vols. 8vo. Lond., 1883.*   MB 2 S 2-4

History of New Zealand. 3 vols. 8vo. Lond., 1883.   MB 2 S 11-13

Translations and Fragments. 8vo. Lond., 1874.   MJ 2 R 15

Les Propos de Labienus. [*See* ROGEARD, A.]   MJ 2 R 15

RUSH (RICHARD). Court of London, from 1819 to 1825 ; with subsequent occasional Productions, now first published in Europe. Edited by Benjamin Rush. 8vo. Lond., 1873.   B 7 P 22

A Residence at the Court of London. 8vo. Lond., 1833.   D 6 T 15

RUSHWORTH (JOHN). Historical Collections, 1618–48 ; with Lord Strafford's Trial. 8 vols. sm. fol. Lond. 1680–1701.   B 15 R 9–16 ‡

1. Of Private Passages of State; Weighty Matters in Law; Remarkable Proceedings in five Parliaments beginning the sixtenth year of King James, anno 1618, and ending the fifth year of King Charles, anno 1629.

2, 3. The Second Part, and the Second Volume of the Second Part ; containing the principal Matters which happened from the Dissolution of the Parliament, on the 10th March, 4 Car. I, 1628–29, until the summoning of another Parliament, which met at Westminster April 13, 1640, with an Account of the Proceedings of that Parliament, and the Transactions and Affairs from that time, until the meeting of another Parliament, November the 3rd, following ; with some remarkable Passages therein during the first months, impartially related and disposed in Annals; setting forth only matter of fact in order of time, without observation or reflection.

RUSHWORTH (JOHN)—*continued.*

4, 5. The Third Part, in two Volumes ; containing the principal Matters which happened from the meeting of the Parliament, November the 3rd, 1640, to the end of the year 1644, wherein is a particular Account of the Rise and Progress of the Civil War to that period; impartially related, setting forth only matter of fact in order of time, without observation or reflection; with alphabetical Tables.

6, 7. The Fourth and Last Part, in two Volumes ; containing the principal Matters which happened from the beginning of the year 1645, to the Death of King Charles the First, 1648, wherein is a particular Account of the Progress of the Civil War to that period; impartially related, setting forth only matter of fact in order of time, without observation or reflection.

8. The Tryal of Thomas, Earl of Strafford, Lord-Lieutenant of Ireland, upon an Impeachment of High Treason by the Commons then assembled in Parliament, in the name of themselves and of all the Commons in England; begun in Westminster Hall, the 22nd March, 1640, and continued, before judgment was given, until the 10th of May, 1641, shewing the form of Parliamentary Proceedings in an impeachment of Treason; to which is added, a short Account of some other matters of fact transacted in both Houses of Parliament, precedent, concomitant, and subsequent to the said Tryal; with some special arguments in Law relating to a Bill of Attainder; faithfully collected and impartially published, without observation or reflection.

Another copy. Vol. 1, [1st ed.]; Vols. 2–8, 2nd ed. 8 vols. sm. fol. Lond., 1682–1721.   B 18 S 9–16 ‡

RUSKIN (JOHN), LL.D., &c. "Unto this last"; four Essays on the first Principles of Political Economy. 2nd ed. 12mo. Kent, 1877.   F 2 P 22

Arrows of the Chace; being a collection of scattered Letters, published chiefly in the Daily Newspapers, 1840–80, and now edited by an Oxford Pupil. 2 vols. 8vo. Orpington, 1880.   J 2 T 4, 5

1. Letters on Art and Science.
2. Letters on Politics, Economy, and Miscellaneous Matters.

Sesame and Lilies: two Lectures. 1. Of Kings' Treasuries. 2. Of Queens' Gardens. 5th ed., in original form ; with new Preface. 8vo. Orpington, 1882. J 1 I 87

Ethics of the Dust: Ten Lectures to Little Housewives on the Elements of Crystallization. 3rd ed. 8vo. Orpington, 1883.   J 11 S 8

John Ruskin : a Bibliographical Biography ; by W. E. A. Axon, M.R.S.I. (The Ruskin Soc.) 8vo. Manchester, 1879.   G 11 T 14

John Ruskin, Economist; by Patrick Geddes. (Round Table Series.) 8vo. Edinb., 1884.   F 8 P 13

The Elements of Drawing ; in Three Letters to Beginners. With Illustrations. 8vo. Lond., 1857.   A 7 Q 10

Notes on the Construction of Sheepfolds. 2nd ed. 8vo. Orpington, 1875.   G 11 T 14

Love's Meinie : Lectures on Greek and English Birds. Vol. I. 8vo. Lond., 1881.   A 14 U 27

Modern Painters. 5th ed., revised by the Author. 5 vols. imp. 8vo. Lond., 1851–67.   A 8 T 1–5

1. Parts 1 and 2. Of General Principles, and of Truth.
2. Part 3, Sections 1 and 2. Of the Imaginative and Theoretic Faculties.
3. Part 4. Of Many Things.
4. Part 5. Of Mountain Beauty.
5. Part 6. Of Leaf Beauty. Part 7. Of Cloud Beauty. Part 8. Of Ideas of Relation: 1. Of Invention Formal. Part 9. Of Ideas of Relation : 2. Of Invention Spiritual.

RUSKIN (JOHN), LL.D., &c.—*continued.*
Another copy. New ed. 5 vols. roy. 8vo. Lond., 1872–73.
                                              A 7 V 16–20
The Two Paths ; being Lectures on Art and its application to Decoration and Manufacture, delivered in 1858–9. New ed. 8vo. Orpington, 1878.   A 7 U 39
Munera Pulveris : Six Essays on the Elements of Political Economy. 8vo. Lond., 1872.   F 5 P 26
Lectures on Art, delivered before the University of Oxford, in Hilary Term, 1870. 2nd ed. 8vo. Oxford, 1875.
                                              A 7 T 11
Giotto and his Works in Padua ; being an Explanatory Notice of the series of Woodcuts executed for the Arundel Society, after the Frescoes in the Arena Chapel. Roy. 8vo. Lond., 1854.   A 8 R 27
Crown of Wild Olive : Three Lectures on Work, Traffic, and War. 12mo. Lond., 1866.   F 15 P 10
The King of the Golden River ; or, the Black Brothers: a Legend of Stiria. 6th ed. 8vo. Lond., 1867.
                                              J 11 S 10
Lectures on Architecture and Painting, delivered at Edinburgh in 1853. 8vo. Lond., 1855.   A 2 R 9
Fors Clavigera : Letters to the Workmen and Labourers of Great Britain. 8 vols. (in 5) 8vo. Orpington, 1871–84.   A 7 T 27–31
A Joy for Ever (and its price in the market) : Two Lectures on the Political Economy of Art. 8vo. Orpington, 1880.   A 8 R 31
Aratra Pentelici : Six Lectures on the Elements of Sculpture. 8vo. Orpington, 1879.   A 8 R 32
Ariadne Florentina: Six Lectures on Wood and Metal Engraving. 8vo. Orpington, 1876.   A 7 U 2
Art of England : Lectures given in Oxford. 8vo. Orpington, 1884.   A 8 R 21
Bibliotheca Pastorum. Vols. 1, 2, and 4. 3 vols. 8vo. Orpington, 1876–77.   J 2 T 14, 15
Catalogue of a series of Specimens in the British Museum illustrative of the more common Forms of Native Silica. 8vo. Orpington, 1884.   K 7 R 37
Dame Wiggins of Lee and her Seven Wonderful Cats : a Humorous Tale. 12mo. Orpington, 1885.   J 11 S 9
Deucalion : Collected Studies of the Lapse of Waves and Life of Stones. Vol. 1. 8vo. Orpington, 1879.
                                              A 9 T 9
Deucalion : First Supplement—The Limestone Alps of Savoy. [*See* COLLINGWOOD, W. G.]
Elements of English Prosody. 8vo. Orpington, 1880.
                                              H 8 V 19
Frondes Agrestes : Readings in Modern Painters. 7th ed. 8vo. Orpington, 1884.   A 6 V 28
Inaugural Address, delivered at the Cambridge School of Art, 1858. New ed. 8vo. Orpington, 1879.   A 8 Q 33
Laws of Fésole: a Familiar Treatise on the Elementary Principles and Practice of Drawing and Painting, as determined by the Tuscan Masters. Vol. 1. 8vo. Orpington, 1882.   A 2 R 9
4 o

RUSKIN (JOHN), LL.D., &c.—*continued.*
Relation between Michael Angelo and Tintoret : Lectures on Sculpture. 2nd thousand. 8vo. Orpington, 1870–71.
                                              A 8 Q 32
Mornings in Florence ; being simple Studies of Christian Art. 2nd ed. Lond., 1881–83.   A 6 V 22
Notes on Pictures of Sir J. E. Millais. 8vo. Lond., 1886.   A 7 U 38
Notes on the Turner Gallery, at Marlborough House, 1856. 8vo. Lond., 1857.   A 7 Q 14
On the old Road: a Collection of Miscellaneous Essays, Pamphlets, &c. 8vo. Orpington, 1885.   J 2 T 11–13
The Political Economy of Art. 12mo. Lond., 1857.
                                              A 6 V 35
Pre-Raphaelitism. New ed. 8vo. Lond., 1862.   A 7 S 6
Præterita : Outlines of Scenes and Thoughts perhaps worthy of Memory in my past Life. Vol. 1. Roy. 8vo. Orpington, 1886.   C 10 V 48
Queen of the Air ; being a Study of Greek Myths of Cloud and Storm. Revised ed. 8vo. Orpington, 1883.   B 27 V 11
General Statement, explaining the Nature and Purposes of St. George's Guild. 8vo. Orpington, 1882.   A 8 Q 33
St. Mark's Rest : the History of Venice. 12mo. Orpington, 1884.   B 12 P 28
Salsette and Elephanta : a Prize Poem. 8vo. Orpington, 1879.   H 8 V 19
The Seven Lamps of Architecture. Roy. 8vo. Lond., 1849.   A 2 Q 9
Another copy. With Illustrations, drawn by the Author. New ed. Imp. 8vo. Lond., 1883.   A 2 T 29
Roadside Songs of Tuscany ; translated and illustrated. [*See* ALEXANDER, MISS F.]
Stones of Venice: The Foundations—The Sea Stories—The Fall. 3 vols. imp. 8vo. Lond., 1851–53.
                                              A 2 T 36–38
Another copy. 4th ed. Imp. 8vo. Lond., 1886.
                                              A 2 T 39–41
Storm Cloud of the 19th Century : Two Lectures, 1884. 8vo. Orpington, 1884.   A 8 R 15
Story of Ida: Epitaph on an Etrurian Tomb ; by Francesca. Edited by John Ruskin. 3rd ed. 8vo. Orpington, 1885.
                                              C 2 Q 22
Eagle's Nest: Ten Lectures on the Relation of Natural Science to Art, 1872. 8vo. Orpington, 1880. A 8 Q 34
Time and Tide by Weare and Tyne. 2nd thousand. 8vo. Orpington, 1882.   F 12 R 16
Catalogue of the Drawings and Sketches, by J. M. W. Turner, exhibited in the National Gallery. 8vo. Orpington, 1881.   A 8 Q 32
Val d'Arno : Ten Lectures on the Tuscan Art. 8vo. Orpington, 1882.   A 8 R 30
Notes on some of the principal Pictures exhibited in the Royal Academy, 1855–57. Parts 1–3. 8vo. Lond., 1855–57.   A 7 Q 14

RUSKIN (JOHN), LL.D., &c.—*continued.*
Notes by John Ruskin on Samuel Prout and William Hunt, in illustration of a Loan Collection of Drawings exhibited at the Fine Art Society's Galleries, 1879–80. Illustrated. Roy. 4to. Lond., 1880. A 3 P 10 †
Notes on the Pictures of Mr. Holman Hunt. Roy. 8vo. Lond., 1886. A 7 U 38
Art Schools of Mediæval Christendom. [*See* OWEN, A. C.]

RUSS (DR. KARL). Speaking Parrots: a Scientific Manual. 8vo. Lond., 1884. A 14 Q 46

RUSSELL (A.) Tour through the Australian Colonies in 1839; with Notes and Incidents of a Voyage round the Globe, calling at New Zealand and South America. 8vo. Glasgow, 1840.* MD 2 R 51

RUSSELL (COL. C.) The House Sparrow [*See* GURNEY, J. H.] A 14 Q 47

RUSSELL (C. W.), D.D. Life of Cardinal Mezzofanti; with an introductory Memoir of eminent Linguists, Ancient and Modern. 8vo. Lond., 1858. C 6 U 18

RUSSELL (REV. F. T. C.) Case of. [*See* SHERBROOKE, VISCOUNT.]

[*See* BROUGHTON, RT. REV. W. G.] MG 1 Q 37

RUSSELL (GEORGE). Tour through Sicily in the year 1815. Illustrated. 8vo. Lond., 1819. D 7 T 14

RUSSELL (HENRY CHAMBERLAINE), B.A., &c. Meteorological Observations made at the Government Observatory, Sydney, and Abstracts from the Country Stations, for 1870–78. 7 vols. roy. 8vo. Sydney, 1870–79. ME 2 S
Results of Meteorological Observations made in New South Wales during 1877–74, 1876–79, 1885–86. 10 vols. roy. 8vo. Sydney, 1871–88. ME 2 S and D
Observations on the Stars and Nebula about Argūs. Roy. 8vo. Sydney, 1871. ME 2 S
Abstract of Meteorological Observations made in New South Wales up to the end of 1869; with Remarks on the Climate. 8vo. Sydney, 1871. ME 2 S
Climate of New South Wales; Descriptive, Historical, and Tabular. Roy. 8vo. Sydney, 1877. MA 1 T 18
Results of Rain and River Observations made in New South Wales, during 1879–80, 1882–87. 8 vols. roy. 8vo. Sydney, 1880–88.* ME 2 T
Thunder and Hail Storms in New South Wales. (Pan. Cq.) 8vo. Sydney, 1881. MA 2 V 9
Recent Changes in the Surface of Jupiter. 8vo. Sydney, 1881. MA 2 V 9
Results of Astronomical Observations made at the Sydney Observatory, in the years 1877–78. 8vo. Sydney, 1881. ME 2 S
Results of Double Star Measures made at the Sydney Observatory, 1871–81. Roy. 8vo. Sydney, 1882. MA 1 T 19
Physical Geography and Climate of New South Wales. Roy. 8vo. Sydney, 1881. MA 1 T 17

RUSSELL (HENRY CHAMBERLAINE), B.A., &c.—*continued.*
New Double Stars; read before the Royal Society of New South Wales, 5th September, 1883. 8vo. Sydney, 1884. MA 1 T 17
Notes upon the History of Floods in the River Darling. 8vo. Sydney, 1887. MA 1 T 20
Notes upon Floods in Lake George. 8vo. Sydney, 1887. MA 1 T 21

RUSSELL (HENRY STUART). The Genesis of Queensland. Roy. 8vo. Sydney, 1888.* MB 2 U 10

RUSSELL (REV. JAMES), D.D. Reminiscences of Yarrow. 8vo. Edinb., 1886. C 3 V 43

RUSSELL (REV. J. A.) Memoir of Rev. C. Wolfe. [*See* WOLFE, REV. C.]

RUSSELL (JAMES B.), AND WALLACE (WILLIAM). Lectures on the Theory and General Prevention and Control of Infectious Diseases; and on Air, Water Supply, Sewage Disposal, and Food; delivered under the auspices of the Lord Provost, Magistrates, and Council of the City of Glasgow. 8vo. Glasgow, 1879. A 12 U 13

RUSSELL (RT. HON. JOHN), EARL. Memorial addressed to. [*See* EMIGRATION.]
Colonial Policy of his Administration. [*See* GREY, EARL.]
Recollections and Suggestions, 1813–73. 8vo. Lond., 1875. C 9 S 21
Life of Lord William Russell; with some Account of the Times in which he Lived. 2nd ed. 2 vols. 8vo. Lond., 1820. C 9 S 23, 24
Life and Times of Charles James Fox. 3 vols. 8vo. Lond., 1859–66. C 3 S 40–42
Essay on the History of the English Government and Constitution. 8vo. Lond., 1823. F 5 P 21
Memoirs of the Affairs of Europe, from the Peace of Utrecht. 2 vols. 4to. Lond., 1824–29. B 7 V 24, 25
Selections from the Speeches of, 1817–41, and from Despatches, 1859–65; with Introductions. 2 vols. 8vo. Lond., 1870. F 5 P 15, 16
Memorials of C. J. Fox. [*See* FOX, C. J.] C 8 P 12–15
Correspondence of the Duke of Bedford. [*See* BEDFORD, JOHN, DUKE OF.] C 8 S 5–7
Memoirs, Journal, and Correspondence of Thomas Moore. Edited by the Rt. Hon. Lord John Russell. 8 vols. 8vo. Lond., 1853–56. C 5 P 7–14
Lord John Russell. 8vo. Lond., 1851. MF 1 R 17

RUSSELL (JOHN). Tour in Germany, and in some of the Southern Provinces of the Austrian Empire, in 1820–22. (Const. Misc.) 2 vols. 18mo. Edinb., 1828. K 10 Q 17, 18

RUSSELL (JOHN). The Haigs of Bemersyde: a Family History. 8vo. Edinb., 1881. B 13 T 8

RUSSELL (JOHN A.), LL.B. Treatise on the Law of Contracts. [*See* CHITTY, J.]

RUSSELL (J. E. M.) Pictorial Guide to the Blue Mountains of New South Wales, and to the Districts between Parramatta and Bathurst, including the Jenolan Caves. [3rd ed.] Imp. 8vo. Sydney, 1885.　　MD 3 V 5

RUSSELL (Rev. James M.) History of Maidstone. With Illustrations. 8vo. Maidstone, 1881.　　B 6 R 29

RUSSELL (J. Rutherfurd), M.D. History and Heroes of the Art of Medicine. With Portraits. 8vo. Lond., 1861.　　C 7 Q 49

Hints on Diet, with special reference to Homœopathy. 3rd ed. 8vo. Lond., 1863.　　MA 2 S 38

RUSSELL (J. Scott), M.A., &c. Modern System of Naval Architecture. 3 vols. at. fol. Lond., 1865.　A 10 P 4-6 ‡

Systematic Technical Education for the English People. 8vo. Lond., 1869.　　G 17 S 1

RUSSELL (Rt. Rev. M.), LL.D., &c. Polynesia: a History of the South Sea Islands, including New Zealand; with Narrative of the Introduction of Christianity, &c. 8vo. Lond., 1852.　　MB 2 P 29

Another copy. [Revised ed.] 8vo. Lond., 1853.*　　MB 2 P 30

Biographical Sketch of Rt. Rev. John Spottiswode. [*See* Spottiswode, Rt. Rev. J.]

Connection of Sacred and Profane History. 2 vols. 8vo. Lond., 1869.　　G 11 T 8, 9

Life of Oliver Cromwell. (Const. Misc.) 2 vols. 18mo. Edinb., 1829.　　K 10 Q 35, 36

RUSSELL (Percy). The Literary Manual; or, a Complete Guide to Authorship. 8vo. Lond., 1886.　　J 10 Q 29

RUSSELL (Rachael Wriothesley), Lady. Some Account of the Life of [by Mary Berry]; with a series of Letters to her husband, Lord William Russell, and others. 3rd ed. 8vo. Lond., 1820.　　C 9 S 22

Letters of; from the MS. in the Library at Wobun Abbey. 9th ed. 12mo. Lond., 1828.　　C 2 Q 41

RUSSELL (Richard). India's Danger, and England's Duty with reference to Russia's Advance into the Territory in dispute upon the Borders of Afghanistan. With Maps and Illustrations. 8vo. Lond., 1885.　　F 5 R 3

RUSSELL (William), Lord. Life of; with some Account of the Times in which he Lived, by Lord John Russell. 2nd ed. 2 vols. 8vo. Lond., 1820.　　C 9 S 23, 24

RUSSELL (William). History of Modern Europe; with an Account of the Decline and Fall of the Roman Empire. 7 vols. 8vo. Lond., 1822.　　B 7 T 1-7

RUSSELL (W. Clark). Book of Authors: a Collection of Criticisms, Ana, Mots, Personal Descriptions, &c. 12mo. Lond., 1871.　　J 11 U 8

Sailors' Language: a Collection of Sea-terms and their Definitions. 8vo. Lond., 1883.　　K 12 P 4

Voyage to the Cape. 8vo. Lond., 1886.　　D 1 Q 16

RUSSELL (William Howard), LL.D. My Diary, North and South. 2 vols. 8vo. Lond., 1863.　　D 3 R 10, 11

Canada; its Defences, Condition, and Resources; being a third and concluding volume of "My Diary, North and South." 8vo. Lond., 1865.　　D 3 R 12

My Diary in India, 1858-59. 2 vols. 8vo. Lond., 1860.　　B 10 Q 6, 7

Hesperothen; Notes from the West: a Record of a Ramble in the United States and Canada in the Spring and Summer of 1881. 2 vols. 8vo. Lond., 1882.　D 3 Q 34, 35

Prince of Wales' Tour: a Diary in India; with some Account of the Visits of His Royal Highness to the Courts of Greece, Egypt, Spain, and Portugal. With Illustrations. Imp. 8vo. Lond., 1877.　　D 4 V 26

Diary in the East, during the Tour of the Prince and Princess of Wales. With Illustrations. 8vo. Lond., 1869.　　D 2 T 17

The Atlantic Telegraph; Illustrated, by Robert Dudley. Fol. Lond., 1865.　　A 4 R 18 ‡

The War, from the Landing at Gallipoli to the Evacuation of the Crimea. 2 vols. 12mo. Lond., 1855.　　B 12 T 35, 36

RUSSELL-KILLOUGH (Henry), Comte. Seize Milles Lieues à travers l'Asie et l'Océanie. 2 vols. (in 1) 8vo. Paris, 1866.　　MD 4 R 19

RUSSIA. Russia, Europe, and the East; by "A Foreigner." 8vo. Lond., 1885.　　F 5 P 24

Post Office Guide Book for the Roads in Russia. 8vo. St. Petersburg, 1824.　　D 33 P 6 ‡

Map [to the above.] *Folded* 4to. St. Petersburg, 1824.　　D 33 P 7 ‡

Recollections of Russia during Thirty-three Years Residence; by "A German Nobleman." Translated by Lascelles Wraxall. 12mo. Edinb., 1855.　　D 7 P 49

Russia's next Move towards India; by "An Old Campaigner." 8vo. Lond., 1885.　　J 12 V 7

Costume of the Russian Empire; with 73 Engravings [coloured.] Descriptions in English and French. Fol. Lond., 1804.　　A 23 S 13 ‡

RUSSIAN BIBLE SOCIETY. Appeal of the Committee; with some verbal alterations, republished by the Committee of the Auxiliary Bible Society of New South Wales, September, 1821.　　G 17 Q 20

RUSSIAN COMEDY (A). [In Russian.] (Pam. 37.) 8vo. St. Petersburgh, 1818.　　MJ 2 Q 14

RUSSIAN DICTIONARY; with German and French Meanings. 8vo. Moscow, 1792.　　K 13 P 5

RUSSIAN GRAMMAR. 8vo. St. Petersburgh, 1809.　　K 12 Q 24

RUSSIAN SCIENTIFIC PAMPHLETS : [Zoology, &c.]; by O. A. Grimai. 8vo. St. Petersburgh and Moscow, 1876–80.   A 13 U 14

RUTHERFORD (W. Gunion), M. A.   The New Phrynichus. [*See* Phrynichus.]

Babrius.   Edited, with Introductory Dissertations, Critical Notes, Commentary, and Lexicon. 8vo. Lond., 1883.
H 5 U 17
RUTT (John Towill). [*See* Calamy, E.]   C 8 U 20, 21

RUTTER (John). Delineations of Fonthill and its Abbey. Imp. 4to. Shaftesbury, 1823.   B 15 S 8 ‡

RUTTY (John), M.D. Methodical Synopsis of Mineral Waters. 4to. Lond., 1757.   A 1 Q 3 †

History of the Rise and Progress of the People called Quakers. [*See* Wight, T.]

RUXTON (George F.) Adventures in Mexico and the Rocky Mountains. 12mo. Lond., 1847.   D 3 P 9

Another copy. (H. and C. Lib.) 12mo. Lond., 1847.
J 8 P 26
RYCAUT (Sir Paul). Lives of the Popes, from the Time of Our Saviour Jesus Christ, to the Reign of Sixtus IV. [*See* Platina, B.]   C 2 W 18

[*See* Garcilasso de la Vega.]   D 14 R 18 ‡

·RYE (Capt. P.) Excursion to the Peak of Teneriffe in 1791 ; being the substance of a Letter to Joseph Jekyll. 4to. Lond., 1793.   MD 4 P 25 †

RYE (Walter). History of Norfolk. 8vo. Lond., 1885.
B 6 S 39
Murder of Amy Robsart : a Brief for the Prosecution. 8vo. Lond., 1885.   B 3 R 3

RYE (William Brenchley). England as seen by Foreigners, in the Days of Elizabeth and James I. Sq. 8vo. Lond., 1865.   D 7 T 16
List of Books of Reference in British Museum. [*See* British Museum.]

RYE-HOUSE PLOT. [*See* Sprat, Dr. T.]

RYLAND (J. E.), A.M. Life of John Foster. [*See* Foster, J.]   C 2 P 14, 15
[*See* Neander, J. A. W.]

RYLANDS (W. H.), F.S.A. Hittite Inscription. [*See* Wright, W.]

RYMER (Thomas), And SANDERSON (R.) Fœdera Conventiones, Litteræ, et cujuscunque generis Acta Publica, inter Reges Angliæ et alios quosvis Imperatores, Reges, Pontifices, Principes, vel Communitates: ab ingressu Gulielmi I in Angliam, A.D. 1066–1377, ad nostra usque Tempora. 3 vols. (in 6) fol. Lond. 1816–30.
B 24 Q 9–14 ‡

S

S. (B. K.) Stanzas. [*See* LEICHHARDT, L.]

S. (C. H.) [*See* SPENCE, C. H.]

S. (G. G.) [*See* SHERIDAN, RT. HON. R. B. B.]

S. (J.) [*See* SHAKESPEARE, W.]

S. (L. D.) [*See* LETTER FROM CHINA AND JAPAN]

S. (L. W. J.) [*See* LETTERS FROM HELL.]

S. (R.) The Phœnix Nest. [*See* PARK, T.]

S. T. G. [*See* GILL, S. T.]

SABIN (JOSEPH). Bibliography of Bibliography ; or, a Hardy-Book about Books which relate to Books. 8vo. New York, 1877.   K 17 Q 21

SABINE (GEN. SIR EDWARD), K.C.B., &c. Observations made at Magnetical and Meteorological Observatories. 8 vols. 4to. Lond., 1845–53.   A 3 U 1–8
St. Helena, 1840–43.
Cape of Good Hope, 1841–50.
Hobarton, in Van Diemen Island, and by the Antarctic Naval Expedition, 1841–48.
Toronto, in Canada, 1840–45.
Observations on Days of Unusual Magnetic Disturbance, made at the British Colonial Magnetic Observatories. Parts 1 and 2, 1840–44.

• Contributions to Terrestrial Magnetism. (Roy. Soc. Pubs., 4.) 4to. Lond., 1875.   A 11 P 5 †

Cosmos. [*See* HUMBOLDT, F. H. A. VON.]

Meteorological Essays. [*See* ARAGO, F. J. D.]

Narrative of an Expedition to the Polar Seas, commanded by Lieut. F. Wrangell. [*See* WRANGELL, ADM. F. VON.]   D 4 R 33

SABINE (ROBERT), C.E., &c. History and Progress of the Electric Telegraph. (Weale.) 12mo. Lond., 1872.   A 17 P 42

The Electric Telegraph. 8vo. Lond., 1867.   A 5 U 37

Telegraphy. (Brit. Manuf. Indust.) 12mo. Lond., 1876.   A 17 S 29

Galvanism, and the General Principles of Animal and Voltaic Electricity. [*See* HARRIS, SIR W. S.]

SABINE (LADY). [*See* HUMBOLDT, F. H. A. VON.]

SABONADIÈRE (W.) The Coffee-planter of Ceylon. 8vo. Lond., 1870.   A 1 P 23

SACCHI (B.) [*See* PLATINA, B.]

SACHAU (DR. C. E.) Chronology of Ancient Nations. [*See* ALBÎRÛNÎ.]

SACHEVERELL (WILLIAM). Account of the Isle of Man—its Inhabitants, Language, Soil, &c. ; with a Voyage to I-Columb-Kill. 12mo. Lord., 1702.   D 7 P 8

SACHS (DR. C.) [*See* FIEDLER, E.]   K 14 T 33 34

SACHS (CAPT. H.) Russia in Central Asia. [*See* STUMM, H.]   B 12 U 4

SACHS (DR. JULIUS). Geschichte der Botanik. (Geschichte der Wissenschaften, 15.) 8vo. München, 1875.   A 17 V 29
Lehrbuch der Botanik. 8vo. Leipzig, 1874.   A 5 P 11

SACRED POETS. Gleanings from the Sacred Poets ; with Biographical Notices of the Authors. 8vo. Edinb., 1875.   H 7 P 17

SACRAMENTS (THE). Correspondence by the Rev. Dr. Turnbull, the Rev. John Robertson, and the Rev. George Clarke. 8vo. Hobart, 1861.   MG 1 Q 29

SACY (ANTOINE ISAAC SILVESTRE DE), BARON. Exposé de la Religion des Druzes, tiré des livres religieux de cette Secte, et précédé d'une Introduction et de la Vie du Khalife Hakem-Biamr-Allah. 2 vols. 8vo. Paris, 1838.   G 12 S 16, 17

Grammaire Arabe a l'usage des élèves de l'École speciale des langues Orientales vivantes. 2 vols. 8vo. Paris, 1831.   K 15 P 16, 17

Principles of General Grammar, adapted to the Capacity of Youth, and proper to serve as an Introduction to the Study of Languages. 12mo. Andover, 1834.   K 12 Q 44

Chrestomathie Arabe, ou, Extraits de divers écrivains Arabes, tant en prose qu'en vers, avec une traduction Française et des Notes. 2e éd. 3 vols. 8vo. Paris, 1826–27.   K 12 S 9–11

Anthologie Grammaticale Arabe, ou Morceaux choisis de divers Grammairiens et Scholiastes Arabes. 8vo. Paris, 1829.   K 15 Q 29

Relation de l'Egypte. [*See* ABD-AL-LATIF.]   D 2 U 6

SADEUR (JAMES). [*See* FOIGY, G. DE.]

SADI (MOSLIH-EDDIN). The Gulistan ; or, Rose-Garden of Shekh Muslihu'd-Din Sâdî of Shiraz. Translated for the first time into Prose and Verse ; with an Introductory Preface, and a Life of the Author, from the Atish Kadah, by Edward B. Eastwick, C.B., &c. 2nd. ed. 8vo. Lond., 1880.   J 12 R 11

The Gulistan ; or, Flower-Garden of Shaikh Sadi, of Shiraz ; translated into English by James Ross from the Persian Text of Gentius ; together with an Essay on Sadi's Life and Genius. 8vo. Lond., 1823.   J 6 U 6

Persian Poetry. [*See* ROBINSON, S.]

SADLEIR (RICHARD), R.N., &c. Aborigines of Australia. 4to. Sydney, 1883.   MA 1 P 9 †

SADLER (MICHAEL THOMAS), M.P., &c. Memoirs of the
Life and Writings of; [by Robert Benton Seeley.] 8vo.
Lond., 1842. C 9 P 39

Speech on the State and Prospects of the Country,
[Free Trade.] 8vo. Lond., 1830. F 6 V 10

SADLER (SIR RALPH). State Papers and Letters of;
with Memoir, by Sir W. Scott. 2 vols. 4to. Edinb.,
1809. B 12 V 26, 27

SADLER (THOMAS), PH.D. Diary, Reminiscences, and
Correspondence of Henry Crabb Robinson, Barrister-at-
Law, F.S.A. 3rd ed. 2 vols. 8vo. Lond., 1872. C 4 T 39, 40

SAGRA (RAMON DE LA). [*See* RAMON DE LA SAGRA.]

SAINT ABE and his Seven Wives: a Tale of Salt Lake
City. 8vo. Lond., 1872. H 7 Q 31

SAINT ALBANS (HARRIOT), DUCHESS. Memoirs of
Harriot, Duchess of St. Albans; by Mrs. Cornwall Baron
Wilson. 2 vols. 12mo. Lond., 1839. C 3 U 40, 41

SAINT AMAND (ARTHUR LÉON IMBERT DE), BARON.
[*See* IMBERT DE SAINT AMAND, A. L., BARON.]

SAINT ANDREW'S CATHEDRAL. Report of the
Building Committee, for 1857. 8vo. Sydney, 1858.
MF 3 P 14

SAINT ANDREW'S SCOTS CHURCH. Report of the
Committee of Trustees for the erection of St. Andrew's
Scots Church, Sydney. 8vo. Sydney, 1837. MF 3 P 14

SAINT AUGUSTINE'S LITERARY INSTITUTE,
YASS. Two Lectures delivered before the above Institute.
The Inaugural Lecture, by the Rev. P. Bermingham.
"Irish Hearts and Hands," by M. O'Connor, Esq., M.D.
8vo. Sydney, 1860. MJ 2 P 8

SAINT CATHERINE'S, Waverley. Report of St.
Catherine's, Waverley: an Institution for educating the
Daughters of the Clergy of the Church of England, in
the Diocese of Sydney, 1862-64. 12mo. Sydney, 1864-
65. MF 3 P 10

SAINT CÉCILE. [*See* CÉCILE, SAINT.]

SAINT CLAIR (MAJ.-GEN. ARTHUR). The St. Clair
Papers. Life and Public Services of Arthur St. Clair;
with his Correspondence and other Papers, by W. H.
Smith. 2 vols. roy. 8vo. Cincinnati, 1882. C 8 V 35, 36

SAINT CLAIR (GEORGE), F.G.S. Biographical Lectures.
[*See* DAWSON, G.] C 3 T 1

SAINT CLAIR STEVENSON (CAPT. G. DE), F.R.G.S.
[*See* STEVENSON, CAPT. G. D. SAINT CLAIR.]

SAINT COLUMBA. Life of. [*See* SCOTLAND, ILLUS-
TRIANS OF.]

SAINT EVREMOND (CHARLES MARGUETEL DE). Works
of. Translated from the French. 2 vols. 8vo. Lond.,
1700. J 16 R 7, 8

SAINT-FARGEAU (GIRAULT DE). [*See* GIRAULT DE
SAINT FARGEAU, P. A. E.]

SAINT JOHN (THE APOSTLE). Life and Writings of; by
James M. Macdonald, D.D. 8vo. Lond., 1877. G 5 T 2

SAINT JOHN (CHARLES). Natural History and Sport in
Moray. Roy. 8vo. Edinb., 1882. A 15 Q 1

Short Sketches of the Wild Sports and Natural History
of the Highlands. 8vo. Lond., 1846. A 29 P 11

Another copy. (H. and C. Lib.) 12mo. Lond.,
1846. J 8 P 18

SAINT JOHN (HORACE). History of the British Conquests in India. 2 vols. 8vo. Lond., 1852. B 10 Q 42, 43

Another copy. Its History and Present State.
2 vols. 8vo. Lond., 1853. B 10 Q 38, 39

SAINT JOHN (JAMES AUGUSTUS). Egypt and Mohammed
Ali; or, Travels in the Valley of the Nile. 2 vols. 8vo.
Lond., 1834. D 2 Q 18, 19

History of the Manners and Customs of Ancient Greece.
3 vols. 8vo. Lond., 1842. B 9 V 15-17

There and back again in search of Beauty. 2 vols. 8vo.
Lond., 1853. J 5 P 11, 12

Life of Sir Walter Raleigh, 1552-1618. 2 vols. 8vo.
Lond., 1868. C 4 T 41, 42

History of the Four Conquests of England. 2 vols. 8vo.
Lond., 1862. B 5 8 37, 38

Journal of a Residence in Normandy. (Const. Misc.)
18mo. Edinb., 1831. K 10 Q 53

SAINT JOHN (HON. JOHN). Mary Queen of Scots:
a Tragedy. [*See* MODERN THEATRE, 8.]

SAINT JOHN (JOHN BAYLE). Adventures in the Libyan
Desert and the Oäsis of Jupiter Ammon. 12mo. Lond.,
1849. D 1 T 18

Another copy. (H. and C. Lib.) 12mo. Lond.,
1849. J 8 P 43

Purple Tints of Paris: Character and Manners in the
New Empire. 2 vols. 8vo. Lond., 1854. D 7 R 31, 32

Another copy. 2nd ed. 8vo. Lond., 1854. D 7 R 33

The Louvre; or, Biography of a Museum. 8vo. Lond.,
1855. A 6 V 18

Sub-alpine Kingdom; or, Experiences and Studies in
Savoy, Piedmont, and Genoa. 2 vols. 8vo. Lond., 1856.
D 8 Q 15, 16

Travels of an Arab Merchant in Soudan. 8vo. Lond.,
1854. D 1 Q 31

Two Years' Residence in a Levantine Family. 8vo.
Lond., 1850. D 1 R 1

Montaigne, the Essayist: a Biography. With Illustrations. 2 vols. 8vo. Lond., 1858. C 4 8 24, 25

Memoirs of the Duke of Saint Simon, on the Reign of
Louis XIV, and the Regency. 4 vols. 8vo. Lond., 1857.
C 1 U 45-48

SAINT–JOHN (MOLYNEUX). The Sea of Mountains: an Account of Lord Dufferin's Tour through British Columbia in 1876. 2 vols. 8vo. Lond., 1877. D 3 P 57, 58

SAINT–JOHN (MAJOR O. B.) Eastern Persia: Geography, &c. [*See* PERSIA.] D 4 U 45, 46

SAINT JOHN (PERCY B.) French Revolution in 1848: the Three Days of February, 1848. 12mo. Lond., 1848. B 9 P 14

SAINT JOHN (SIR SPENSER), K.C.M.G., &c. Hayti; or, the Black Republic. 8vo. Lond., 1884. D 3 R 33

Life of Sir James Brooke, Rajah of Sarāwak, from his Personal Papers and Correspondence. 8vo. Edinb., 1879. C 3 R 25

Life in the Forests of the Far East. Illustrated. 2 vols. 8vo. Lond., 1862. D 4 T 5, 6

SAINT JOHNSTON (A.) [*See* BIRMINGHAM MUSEUM AND ART GALLERY.]

SAINT JULIAN (CHARLES). Official Report on Central Polynesia; with a Gazetteer of Central Polynesia, by Edward Reeve (late Chancellor of the Commission), and other Documents appended. Fol. Sydney, 1857. MF 10 Q 2 †

Municipalities Act of 1867; with Notes thereon, and General Instructions for the Working of Municipal Councils, and the Conduct of Elections, &c. 8vo. Sydney, 1868. MF 3 Q 70

SAINT JULIAN (CHARLES), AND SILVESTER (EDWARD K.) Productions, Industry, and Resources of New South Wales. 12mo. Sydney, 1853. MD 1 T 37

SAINT LEONARDS (EDWARD B. S.), LORD. Handy-book on Property Law, in a series of Letters. 4th ed. 12mo. Edinb., 1858. F 6 P 22

SAINT LUKE'S CLERICAL SANATORIUM. Prospectus of a Clerical Sanatorium, to be erected on Douglas' Hill, Kurrajong, in the neighbourhood of Richmond, and within the Police District of Windsor. 8vo- Sydney (n.d.) MG 1 Q 26

SAINT LOUIS. [*See* LOUIS IX, KING OF FRANCE.]

SAINT-MARC GIRARDIN (M.) [*See* RACINE, J.] J 13 U 19–26

SAINT MARGARET. [*See* MARGARET, SAINT.]

SAINT MARTIN (L. VIVIEN DE). [*See* VIVIEN DE SAINT MARTIN, L.]

SAINT-MÉARD (F. DE J.) [*See* BARRIÈRE, J. F., 18.] C 1 T 18

SAINT MERIASEK. Life of. [*See* STOKES, W.] H 2 U 14

SAINT PATRICK. [*See* PATRICK, SAINT.]

SAINT PAUL (THE APOSTLE). [*See* PAUL, SAINT.]

SAINT PAUL'S, LONDON The true Report of the Burnyng of the Stople and Chorobo of Poules, in London, 1561. [Reprint, Genealogica Curiosa.] 12mo. Lond., 1885. B 3 P 30

ST. PAUL'S COLLEGE. Origin and Foundation of St. Paul's College, established within the University of Sydney, and incorporated by Act of the Legislature, 1855. (Pam. 35.) 8vo. Sydney, 1856. MJ 2 Q 22

By-laws and Statutes of, and relating to St. Paul's College, within the University of Sydney; with some Account of its Foundation. (Pam. 35.) 12mo. Sydney, 1863. MJ 2 Q 22

SAINT PETERSBOURG. Académie Impériale des Sciences de. [*See* ACADÉMIE IMPÉRIALE DES SCIENCES.]

SAINT-PIERRE (J. H. BERNARDIN DE). Works of; with a Memoir of the Author, and explanatory Notes, by the Rev. E. Clarke. 2 vols. 12mo. Lond., 1846. J 8 R 32, 33

Studies of Nature; translated by Henry Hunter, D.D. 4th ed. 4 vols. 8vo. Lond., 1801. G 3 T 16–19

SAINT-PRIEST (ALEXIS DE), COUNT. History of the Fall of the Jesuits in the 18th Century; translated from the French. (H. and C. Lib.) 12mo. Lond., 1845. J 8 P 10

Another copy. New ed. 12mo. Lond., 1873. B 14 P 37

SAINT-PRIEST (J. Y. DE). [*See* DUMONT, J.] F 29 P 19, 20 ‡

SAINT SIMON (LOUIS DE ROUVROI), DUC DE. Life of the Duke of Saint-Simon; by Edwin Cannan, B.A. (Lothian Prize Essay, 1885.) 8vo. Oxford, 1885. C 2 S 13

Œuvres Complettes de, pour servir à l'Histoire des Cours de Louis XIV, de la Régence, et de Louis XV. 13 vols. (in 7) 8vo. Strasbourg, 1791. B 8 T 42–48

Memoirs of the Duke of Saint Simon; abridged from the French, by [J.] B. St. John. 4 vols. 8vo. Lond., 1857. C 1 U 45–48

Extraits des Mémoires du Duc de Saint-Simon. [*See* BARRIÈRE, J. F., 1.] C 1 T 1

[*See* DANGEAU, P. DE C., MARQUISE DE.] C 10 V 15–33

SAINT VINCENT (ADM. JOHN JERVIS), EARL OF. Memoirs of Admiral the Right Hon. Earl of St. Vincent, G.C.B.; by J. S. Tucker. 2 vols. 8vo. Lond., 1844. C 9 S 27, 28

SAINTE-FOI (CHARLES). [*See* JOURDAIN, E.]

SAINTE-PALAYE (J. B. DE LA CURNE DE). Mémoires sur l'ancienne Chevalerie; avec une Introduction, et des Notes historiques, par Ch. Nodier. 8vo. Paris, 1826. B 15 Q 1, 2

SAINTSBURY (GEORGE EDMUND BATEMAN). Dryden. (Eng. Men of Letts.) 8vo. Lond., 1881. C 1 U 14

Short History of French Literature. (Clar. Press.) 8vo. Oxford, 1882. B 8 P 7

Primer of French Literature. (Clar. Press.) 12mo. Oxford, 1880. B 26 P 1

SAINTSBURY (GEORGE EDMUND BATEMAN)—*continued.*
Specimens of French Literature, from Villon to Hugo.
(Clar. Press.) 8vo. Oxford, 1883. J 5 Q 3

Marlborough. (English Worthies.) 8vo. Lond., 1885.
C 4 T 19

Specimens of English Prose Style, from Malory to
Macaulay; selected and annotated. 8vo. Lond., 1885.
J 9 S 27

Memoir of Oliver Goldsmith. [*See* GOLDSMITH, O.]

SALA (GEORGE AUGUSTUS). Journey due South : Travels
in search of Sunshine. Illustrated. 8vo. Lond., 1885.
‍ D 7 S 19

Breakfast in Bed : or, Philosophy between the Sheets.
2nd ed. 8vo. Lond., 1863. J 1 U 27

Trip to Barbary by a Round-about Route. 8vo.
Lond., 1866. D 2 S 12

From Waterloo to the Peninsula : four months' hard
labour in Belgium, Holland, Germany, and Spain. 2 vols.
8vo. Lond., 1867. D 9 Q 7, 8

Accepted Addresses. 8vo. Lond., 1862. J 1 U 30

After Breakfast; or, Pictures done with a Quill. 2 vols.
8vo. Lond., 1864. J 1 U 28, 29

America Revisited ; from the Bay of New York to the
Gulf of Mexico, and from Lake Michigan to the Pacific.
Illustrated. 2 vols. 8vo. Lond., 1882. D 3 T 11, 12

[Essay on the Genius and Character of] Charles Dickens.
12mo. Lond., 1870. C 2 T 26

Dutch Pictures ; with some Sketches in a Flemish Manner,
and Pictures done with a Quill. 8vo. Lond., 1883.
MJ 2 Q 26

Echoes of the year 1883. 8vo. Lond., 1884. J 2 Q 27

Gaslight and Daylight, with some London Scenes they
shine upon. 8vo. Lond., 1859. J 1 U 31

Journey due North ; being Notes of a Residence in Russia
in the Summer of 1856. 8vo. Lond., 1858. D 8 R 38

Lady Chesterfield's Letters to her Daughter. 8vo. Lond.,
1860. J 1 U 32

Living London ; being Echoes Re-echoed. 8vo. Lond.,
1883. D 7 S 34

Looking at Life; or, Thoughts and Things. 8vo. Lond.,
1860. J 1 U 34

My Diary in America : in the midst of War. 2nd ed.
2 vols. 8vo. Lond., 1865. D 4 Q 11, 12

Papers, Humourous and Pathetic. 8vo. Lond., 1872.
J 1 U 33

Notes and Sketches of the Paris Exhibition. 8vo. Lond.,
1868. D 7 S 4

Paris herself again in 1878-79. 2nd ed. 2 vols. 8vo.
Lond., 1879. D 7 S 32, 33

Rome and Venice ; with other Wanderings in Italy in
1866-67. 8vo. Lond., 1869. D 7 S 5

Story of the Comte de Chambord : a Trilogy. 12mo.
Lond., 1873. C 2 Q 8

SALA (GEORGE AUGUSTUS)—*continued.*
Twice round the Clock; or, the Hours of the Day and
Night in London. 8vo. Lond., 1879. J 1 U 35

Under the Sun : Essays mainly written in Hot Countries. 8vo. Lond., 1886. D 9 S 9

William Hogarth, Painter, Engraver, and Philosopher :
Essays on the Man, the Work, and the Time. 12mo.
Lond., 1866. C 2 Q 21

SALAMAN (CHARLES KENSINGTON). The Jews as they
are. 8vo. Lond., 1882. G 7 S 18

SALDANHA OLIVEIRA E DAUN (JOAO CARLOS),
DUKE DE. Memoirs of Field Marshall the Duke de
Saldanha ; with Selections from his Correspondence, by
the Conde da Carnota. With Portrait. 2 vols. 8vo.
Lond., 1880. C 11 P 17, 18

SALDANHA DA GAMA (JOSE DE), PH.D. Catalogue
of the Products of the Brazilian Forests at the International Exhibition in Philadelphia. (Pam. Co.) 8vo.
New York, 1876. A 16 U 23

SALE (FLORENTIA), LADY. Journal of the Disasters in
Affghanistan, 1841–42. 7th thousand. 8vo. Lond.,
1843. D 5 P 46

SALE (GEORGE). The Koran. [*See* KORAN, THE.]
Translation of the Quran. [*See* WHERRY, REV. E. M.]

SALE (SIR ROBERT HENRY). Sale's Brigade in Afghanistan. [*See* GLEIG, REV. G. R.] D 1 T 12

SALISBURY (ALBERT). Historical Sketch of Normal
Instruction in Wisconsin. 1846–76. 8vo. Madison,
1876. B 1 S 16

SALISBURY (ROBERT CECIL), MARQUIS OF, K.G. Life
and Speeches of ; by F. S. Pulling, M.A. 2 vols. 8vo.
Lond., 1885. C 4 S 41, 42

SALLUSTIUS CRISPUS (CAIUS). C. Crispi Sallustii Opera
quæ exstant ; accedunt Orationes ex Epistolæ ex historiarum libris supersites. Roy. 4to. Lond., 1863. B 19 R 13‡

Opera omnia, ex Editione Gottlieb Cortii, cum Notis et
Interpretatione in usum Delphini. 2 vols. 8vo. Lond.,
1820. J 13 S 23, 24

The Works of. Translated by William Rose, M.A. (Fam.
Clas. Lib.) 18mo. Lond., 1833. J 15 P 39

Catiline and Jugurtha of. Translated into English, by
Alfred W. Pollard, B.A. 8vo. Lond., 1882. B 12 Q 10

The Works of Sallust : to which are prefixed two Essays
on the Life, Literary Character, and Writings of the
Historian ; with Notes, Historical, Biographical, and
Critical ; by Henry Steuart, LL.D., &c. 2 vols. 4to.
Lond., 1806. B 16 Q 1, 2‡

SALLUSTIUS CRISPUS (CAIUS), FLORUS (LUCIUS
ANNÆUS, AND PATERCULUS (CAIUS VELLEIUS).
Sallust, Florus, and Velleius Paterculus. Literally
Translated, with copious Notes and a general Index, by
the Rev. John Selby Watson, M.A. 8vo. Lond., 1872.
B 12 P 19

SALMASIUS, or SAUMAISE (CLAUDE). Defensio Regia pro Carolo I, ad Serenissimum Magna Britannia Regem Carolum II, Filium natu majorem, Heredem et Successorem legitimum. 18mo. Amsterd., 1652. B 4 P 1

SALMON (NATHANIEL), LL.D. Lives of the English Bishops, from the Restauration to the Revolution. 8vo. Lond., 1731–33. C 4 T 3

SALMON (T.) Chronological Historian. 8vo. Lond., 1723. B 2 S 31

SALM-SALM (FELIX). My Diary in Mexico in 1867, including the last days of the Emperor Maximilian; with leaves from the Diary of the Princess Salm-Salm. 2 vols. 8vo. Lond., 1868. B 2 P 8, 9

SALOMON (Dr. G.) Twelve Sermons delivered in the New Temple of the Israelites, at Hamburgh; translated From the German, by Anna M. Goldsmid. 8vo. Lond., 1839. G 12 T 2

SALT (HENRY), F.R.S. Voyage to Abyssinia, and Travels into the Interior of that country, executed under the orders of the British Government, in the years 1809 and 1810. With Engravings. 4to. Lond., 1814. D 2 V 14

Life and Correspondence of; by J. J. Halls. 2 vols. 8vo. Lond., 1834. C 9 U 47, 48

SALTER (J. W.), F.G.S. Catalogue of the Collection of Cambrian and Silurian Fossils contained in the Geological Museum of the University of Cambridge; with a Table of Genera and Index, by Professor Morris, F.G.S. 4to. Camb., 1873. A 2 S 20 †

SALT-FOOT CONTROVERSY (THE). [*See* RIDDELL, JOHN.]

SALVADO (RUDESINDO), BISHOP. Memorie Storiche dell' Australia, particolarmente della Missione Benedettina di Nuovo Norcia e degli usi e Costumi degli Australiani. 8vo. Roma, 1851. MB 2 S 25

Mémoires historiques sur l'Australie, et particulièrement sur la Mission de la Nouvelle-Nursie; traduites par l'Abbé Falcimagne; avec des Notes et une Histoire de la Découverte de l'Or. 8vo. Paris, 1854.* MB 2 S 26

SALVADORI (TOMMASO). Ornitologia della Papuasia e delle Molucche. Parts 1–3. 3 vols. 4to. Torino, 1880–82. MA 2 Q 4–6 †

SALVANDY (NARCISSE ACHILLE DE). Histoire de Pologne avant et sous le Roi Jean Sobieski. 2e éd. 3 vols. 8vo. Paris, 1830. B 7 T 22–24

SALVATOR ROSA. [*See* ROSA, S.]

SALVERTE (EUSEBE). Philosophy of Magic, Prodigies, and Apparent Miracles; translated, with Notes, &c., by A. T. Thomson. 2 vols. 8vo. Lond., 1846. A 10 R 3, 4

SALVIANUS (SANCTUS). Opera omnia. [*See* MIGNE, J. P., SERIES LATINA, 53.]

4 P

SAMMES (AYLETT). Britannia Antiqua Illustrata: or the Antiquities of Ancient Britain derived from the Phœnicians. Fol. Lond., 1676. B 14 S 20 :

SAMPSON (HENRY). History of Advertising from the Earliest Times, illustrated by Anecdotes, curious Speci mens, and Biographical Notes; with Illustrations and Fac-similes. 8vo. Lond., 1875. B 14 Q 31

SAMPSON (WILLIAM). Memoirs of William Sampson, an Irish Exile; written by himself; to which is added, a brief historical Sketch of the British Connection with Ireland, &c. (Autobiog., 33.) 18mo. Lond., 1832. C 11 P 22

SAMPSON, DAVENPORT & CO. Providence Directory, for the year commencing July 1, 1875; containing a General Directory of the City, a Record of the City Government, its Institutions, &c. Roy. 8vo. Providence, 1875. E

Troy Directory, for the year 1875; including Lansingburgh, West Troy, Cohoes, and Green Island. 8vo. Troy, 1875. E

SAMSON (WALTER) & CO. New South Wales Directory. [*See* MEYER, W. J.]

SAMUEL (SIR SAUL), K.C.M.G. Hand-book of New South Wales containing general Information for intending Emigrants and others. Issued by the Agent-General of New South Wales. Roy. 8vo. Lond., 1884. MD 5 V 36

SAMUELSON (JAMES). Roumania, Past and Present. Illustrated. 8vo. Lond., 1882. D 8 T 37

History of Drink: a Review, Social, Scientific, and Political. 8vo. Lond., 1878. B 14 R 30

SANBORN (F. B.) Conference of Charities, held at Cleveland. [*See* UNITED STATES.] MH 1 S 5

Life of John Brown. [*See* BROWN, J.] C 5 R 4

[*See* ESSAYS FROM THE CRITIC.]

SANCHONIATHO. Phœnician History, translated from the First Book of Eusebius "De Præparatione Evangelica"; with a Continuation of Sanchoniatho's History, by Eratosthenes Cyrenæus's Canon, which Dicæarchus connects with the First Olympiad; with Historical and Chronological Remarks, by the Rt. Rev. R. Cumberland, D.D., late Bishop of Peterborough; with a Preface, giving a brief Account of the Life, Character, and Writings of the Author, by S. Payne, A.M. 8vo. Lond., 1720. B 2 S 29

SANCROFT (WILLIAM), ARCHBISHOP OF CANTERBURY. Life of, compiled principally from original and scarce Documents, with an Appendix, by G. D'Oyley. 2 vols. 8vo. Lond., 1821. C 8 R 46, 47

SAND (GEORGES). [*See* DUDEVANT, MME.]

SANDALIO (PROF. DON A.) Lecciones de Agricultura, explicadas en la cátedra del real Jardin Botánico de Madrid, el año de 1815. 2e ed. 2 vols. (in 1) 8vo. Madrid, 1818. A 1 R 19

SANDARS (THOMAS COLLETT), M.A. Institutes of Justinian: with English Introduction, Translation, and Notes. [*See* JUSTINIANUS.]

SANDERS (ALFRED), M.R.C.S., &c. Contributions to the Anatomy of the Central Nervous System in Vertebrate Animals. (Roy Soc. Pubs., 6.) 4to. Lond., 1879.
A 11 P 7 †

SANDERS (DR. DANIEL). Wörterbuch der deutschen Sprache, mit Belegen von Luther bis auf Gegenwart. 3 vols. 4to. Leipzig, 1860–65.   K 4 Q 9–11 †

SANDERS (NICHOLAS), D.D. De Origine ac Progressu Schismatis Anglicani. Libri Tres: quibus historia continetur maxime ecclesiastica, annorum circiter sexaginta, lectu dignissima; aucti per Edouardum Rishtonum. 12mo. Romæ, 1586.   G 8 P 17
Rise and Growth of the Anglican Schism; published A.D. 1585, with a Continuation of the History, by the Rev. Edward Rishton, B.A.; translated, with Introduction and Notes, by David Lewis, M.A. 8vo. Lond., 1877.
G 12 Q 23

SANDERSON (EDGAR), M.A. Outlines of the World's History, Ancient, Mediæval, and Modern, with special relation to the History of Civilization and the Progress of Mankind. 8vo. Lond., 1885.   B 14 Q 23

SANDERSON (G. P.) Thirteen Years among the Wild Beasts of India: their Haunts and Habits from Personal Observation; with an Account of the Modes of Capturing and Taming Elephants. Sm. 4to. Lond., 1878.   A 14 T 16

SANDERSON (JOHN). The American in Paris. 2 vols. 8vo. Lond., 1838.   D 8 P 22, 23

SANDERSON (J. BURDON). Physiological Laboratory. [*See* KLEIN, E.]   A 12 T 11, 12

SANDERSON (ROBERT). [*See* RYMER, T.]   F 24 Q 9–14 ‡

SANDERSON (ROBERT), D.D., BISHOP OF LINCOLN. Life of; by Izaak Walton. 12mo. Lond., 1825.   C 1 S 19
Another copy. New ed. 12mo. Lond., 1884.   C 2 R 34

SANDFORD (F.) Genealogical History of the Kings of England and Monarchs of Great Britain, 1066–1677. 4 vols. fol. Lond., 1677.   B 15 U 14–17 ‡
History of the Coronation of James II. and of His Royal Consort, Queen Mary, 1685. Fol. Lond., 1687.
B 17 U 10 ‡

SANDFORD (MRS. JOHN). Female Improvement. 2nd ed. 12mo. Lond., 1839.   J 6 p 29

SANDS (JOHN). Sydney and Suburban Directories for 1863, 1865–71, 1873–88. 21 vols. 8vo. Sydney, 1863–88.
ME 4 T U
Official Post Office Country Directory and Gazetteer of New South Wales, for 1878–79. 8vo. Sydney, 1878.*
ME 1 S
Country Directory and Gazetteer of New South Wales for 1881–82; compiled by James Tingle. 8vo. Sydney, 1881.   ME 1 S

SANDS (JOHN)—*continued.*
Country Directory of New South Wales, for 1884–85. 8vo. Sydney, 1884.*   ME 4 S
New Atlas of Australia; the complete work containing over 100 Maps, and full Descriptive Geography of New South Wales, Victoria, Queensland, South Australia, and Western Australia. With Illustrations. Roy. fol. Sydney, 1886.*   MD 5 S 1 ‡
Map of New South Wales, showing Mail Roads, Railways, Territorial Divisions under the Act of 1884, Land Board Districts and Offices. 12mo. Sydney, 1887.
MD 5 P 15 ‡

SANDS (JOHN), AND KENNY (THOMAS). Commercial and General Sydney Directory, for 1858–61. 2 vols. 8vo. Sydney, 1858–61.   ME 4 T

SANDS (JOHN), AND MACDOUGALL (D.) Sands and Macdougall's Annual Register and Almanac for 1864, containing general Victorian Information, &c. 12mo. Melb., 1864.   ME 4 P
Melbourne and Suburban Directory, for 1864, 1875–76, containing Street, Alphabetical, Trade, and Professional Directory of Melbourne and its Suburbs; together with a Government, Official, Ecclesiastical, Legal, Municipal, and Miscellaneous Directory of Useful Information. 3 vols. 8vo. Melb., 1864–76.   ME 3 U

SANDWICH (JOHN), EARL OF. Voyage performed by the late Earl of Sandwich round the Mediterranean, in the years 1738–39; written by himself. 4to. Lond., 1796.
D 10 U 21

SANDWICH ISLANDS. Account of the Visit of the French Frigate *l'Artemise*, to the Sandwich Islands, July, 1839 [by S. N. Castle]. (Pam. 5.) 8vo. Honolulu, 1839.   MJ 2 P 39
[*See* HAWAII.]

SANDWITH (HUMPHRY), C.B., &c. Narrative of the Siege of Kars. 8vo. Lond., 1856.   B 12 U 17
The Hekim Bashi; or, the Adventures of Giuseppe Antonelli, a Doctor in the Turkish Service. 2 vols. 8vo. Lond., 1864.   J 6 P 31, 32
Humphry Sandwith: a Memoir; compiled from Autobiographical Notes, by his Nephew, Thomas Humphry Ward. 8vo. Lond., 1884.   C 6 U 22

SANDYS (GEORGE). Sandy's Travels; containing a History of the Original and Present State of the Turkish Empire, &c. 7th ed. Fol. Lond., 1673.   D 8 V 26

SANDYS (JOHN EDWIN), M.A. The Bacchæ of Euripides. [*See* EURIPIDES.]   J 16 R 22

SANDYS (WILLIAM). Specimens of Macaronic Poetry. 8vo. Lond., 1831.   H 8 S 36
Christmas Carols, Ancient and Modern. 8vo. Lond., 1833.   H 8 U 9

SAN FRANCISCO. [*See* UNITED STATES—CALIFORNIA.]

SAN FRANCISCO MILITARY LIBRARY. Catalogue of. (*Bound with Ward's History of Gold.*) 12mo. San Fiancisco, 1875.   MA 2 P 14

SAN FRANCISCO MINING AND SCIENTIFIC PRESS. 4 vols. imp. 4to. San Fiancisco, 1861–66. E

SANGERMANO (Rev. Father). Description of the Buimese Empiie. [*Repiint.*] Roy. 8vo. Raigoon, 1885.   D 5 U 31

SANITARY ENGINEER (The). [*See* ENGINEERING AND BUILDING RECORD.]

SANKEY (Charles), M.A. The Spaitan and Theban Supiemacies. (Epochs of Aicient Histoiy.) With five Maps. 18mo. Loid., 1877.   B 9 S 28

SANKEY (J. D.) [*See* CAMPBELL, REV. P.] MJ 2 P 27

SANSON (N.) Map of All the World, in two Hemispheres; coiiected and amended by W. Beiiy. L. 4to. Loid, 1680.   D 8 P 17 ‡

SANSKRIT ALPHABET AND GRAMMAR. (MS. Pam. A.) Fol. Sydiey (n.d.)   MJ 2 U 1

SANTAREM (M. F.) VISCOMTE DE. Giand Atlas, composé de Mappemondes de Poitulais et de Cartes hydrographiques et historiques, depuis le 6ᵉ jusqu'àu 17ᵉ Siècle. Fol. Paiis, 1842–53.   D 9 P 23 ‡

SANZIO OR SANTI (RAFFAELLO). [*See* RAPHAEL SANZIO.]

SAO LOURENÇO (FRANCISCO BENTO MARIA TARGINI), BARAŌ DE. Eisaio Sobie o Homem de A. Pope. [*See* POPE, A.]

SAPPHO. Memoir, Text, selected Reideiings, and a liteial Tianslation; by Heiiy Thoiiton, M.A. 12mo. Loid., 1885.   H 8 R 33

Tianslations fiom. [*See* CHALMERS, A., *and* JOHNSON, S.]

Works of ; tianslated by F. Fawkes, M.A. [*See* HESIOD.]   J 15 P 15

SARCASTIC NOTICES of the Loig Pailiameit. [*See* LONG PARLIAMENT.]   C 11 Q 4

SARGEAUNT (CAPT. R. A.) Notes on the Climates of the Eaith, Past and Pieseit. 8vo. Loid., 1875. A 3 R 15

SARGENT (HENRY WINTHROP). [*See* DOWNING, A.] A 1 S 12

SARGENT (JOHN), JUNR. Memoin of the Rev. Heiiy Maityi, B.D. 7th ed. 12mo. Loid., 1822. C 2 U 30

SARGENT (WINTHROP). Life of Majoi John André, Adjutait-Geieial of the Biitish Aimy in Ameiica. 8vo. New Yoik, 1871.   C 2 U 3

SARPI (PIETRO), "FRA PAOLO." Histoiie du Coicile de Tieite, écrite en Italien ; tiaduite de iouveau en Fiaiçois, aveç des Notes ciitiques, historiques, et théologiques, pai Pieiie-Fiaiçois le Courayer. 2 vols. 4to. Basle, 1738.   G 1 T 18, 19

SARRANS (BERNARD). Memoiis of Geicial Lafayette and of the Fieich Revolution of 1830. 2 vols. 8vo. Loid., 1832.   C 9 T 14, 15

SARTORIUS (MRS. ERNESTINE). Thiee Moiths in the Soudan. 8vo. Loid., 1885.   D 1 W 24

SARUM (CATHEDRAL CHURCH OF). Statuta et Consuitudiies Ecclesiæ Cathedralis Sarisberiensis : Statutes of the Cathedial Chuich of Saium ; edited by E. A. Daymai, B.D., and W. H. R. Joies, M.A. Roy. 8vo. Bath, 1883.   F 8 T 9

SARYTSCHEW (GAWRILLA). Accouit of a Voyage of Discovery to the Noith-east of Sibeiia, the Fiozei Oceai, aid the Noith-east Sea. Tiaislated fiom the Russian. 8vo. Loid., 1806.   D 6 Q 22

SASTRI (PUNDIT RISHIKESH). ,Prakrita Giammai, with Eiglish Tiaislatioi. Published by Lalla Meharchand, Lahoie. 8vo. Calcutta, 1883.   K 15 S 10

SATCHEL GUIDE TO EUROPE. [*See* EUROPE.] D 7 P 54

SATCHELL (THOMAS). Bibliotheca Piscatoiia. [*See* WESTWOOD, T.]   K 18 Q 4

SATOW (E. M.) Japaiese Chioiological Tables. 4to. Yedo, 1874.   B 12 S 13

SATTERTHWAITE (THOMAS E.), M.D. Maiual of Histology. Roy. 8vo. Loid., 1881.   A 12 U 11

SATURDAY MAGAZINE (THE). 25 vols. (in 9) imp. 8vo. Loid., 1833–44.   J 7 V 1–9

SATURDAY REVIEW (THE). The Satuiday Review of Politics, Liteiatuie, Scieice, aid Art.. 29 vols. fol. Loid., 1864–85.   E

SAUMAISE, OR SALMASIUS (CLAUDE). [*See* SALMASIUS, C.]

SAUMAREZ (ADM. JAMES S), LORD DE. Memoiis and Coiiespoideice of ; by Sir Johi Ross, C.B. 2 vols. 8vo. Loid., 1838.   C 9 Q 38, 39

SAUNDERS (ALFRED). New Zealaid : its Climate, Soil, Natuial aid Aitificial Pioductiois, Aiimals, Biids, aid Iisects, Aboiigiial aid Euiopeai Iihabitaits, &c. : a Lectuie. 8vo. Loid., 1868.   MA 1 Q 11

Our Domestic Biids : a Piactical Poultiy-book foi Eiglaid aid New Zealaid. 8vo. Hull, 1883. A 14 R 1

Oui Hoises ; oi, the best Muscles coitiolled by the best Biaiis. 8vo. Loid., 1886.   A 14 R 47

SAUNDERS (FREDERIC). Modein Impedimeits to Maiiiage. 8vo. Melb., 1869.   MA 2 S 38

Salad foi the Social. 8vo. Loid., 1856.   J 4 Q 27

SAUNDERS (LAWRENCE). Wiitiigs of. [*See* BRITISH REFORMERS 3.]

SAUNDERS (THOMAS HENRY). Illustrations of the British Paper Manufacture. (English and French.) El. fol. Lond. 1855.   A 10 P 22 ‡

SAUNDERS (TRELAWNY). The Asiatic Mediterranean, and its Australian Port : the Settlement of Port Flinders, and the Province of Albert, in the Gulf of Carpentaria, practically proposed. 8vo. Lond., 1853.*   MD 3 P 32

SAUNDERS (WILLIAM). The New Parliament, 1880. 12mo. Lond., 1880.   F 5 R 26

SAUNDERS (WILLIAM), F.R.S.C., &c. Insects injurious to Fruits. Illustrated. 8vo. Philad., 1883.   A 14 T 26

SAULCY (FELICIEN JOSEPH CAIGNART DE). Narrative of a Journey round the Dead Sea, 1850–51, and in the Bible Lands ; edited, with Notes, by Count Edward de Warren. 2 vols. 8vo. Lond., 1853.   D 4 U 27, 28

SAUNIER (CLAUDIUS). Treatise on Modern Horology, in Theory and Practice ; translated from the French, by Julien Tripplin, and Edward Rigg, M.A. Illustrated. Roy. 8vo. Lond., 1884.   A 11 V 1

SAURIN versus STARR. Extraordinary Trial by a Sister of Mercy, before the Lord Chief Justice and a Special Jury, February 3, 1869 ; Startling Revelations of Life in a Convent. Illustrated verbatim edition. (Curious Trials.) 8vo. Lond., 1869.   F 13 R 1

Another copy. 8vo. Lond., 1869.   MF 2 R 19

SAUTER (EDWARD). New Zealand : its Physical Geography, &c. [*See* HOCHSTETTER, DR. F. VON.]

SAUVAGEOT (CLAUDE). Palais, Châteaux, Hôtels et Maisons de France du xvᵉ au xviiiᵉ siècle. 4 vols. fol. Paris, 1867.   A 4 T 2–5 ‡

SAVAGE (A. D) Stone Sculptures of Copan, &c. [*See* MEYE, H., and SCHMIDT, J.]   B 20 P 17 ‡

SAVAGE (JOHN). Some Account of New Zealand ; particularly the Bay of Islands, and surrounding Country ; with a Description of the Religion and Government, Language, Arts, Manufactures, Manners, and Customs of the Natives, &c. 8vo. Lond., 1807.*   MD 4 V 2

Life and Works of. [*See* CHALMERS, A., *and* JOHNSON, S.]

SAVAGE (RICHARD). Works of : with an Account of the Life and Writings of the Author ; by Samuel Johnson, LL.D. 2 vols. 12mo. Lond, 1777.   H 1 R 31, 32

Life and Works of. [*See* CHALMERS, A., *and* JOHNSON S.]

SAVAGE (ROBERT). Political Economy for the Land Tenure Reform League. 8vo. Melb., 1873.   MF 1 Q 3

SAVAGE (THOMAS). Narrative of Thomas Savage, respecting Aboriginals of Tasmania. (Pam. B.) 8vo. Hobart, 1830.   MJ 2 U 2

SAVAGE CLUB PAPERS (THE). Edited by A. Halliday. 2 vols. 8vo. Lond., 1867–68.   J 8 U 23, 24

SAVARIN (ANTHELME BRILLAT-). [*See* BRILLAT-SAVARIN, A.]

SAVIGNON (F. DE.) Merino Sheep of the National Sheep Stud Farm of Rambouillet ; general Considerations of Breeding. Report on the Sheep Show. (Pam. Cn.) 8vo. Sydney, 1879.   MA 2 V 14

SAVINGS BANK, N.S.W. [*See* NEW SOUTH WALES SAVINGS BANK.]

SAVORY (WILLIAM S.), F.R.S. On Life and Death : Four Lectures delivered at the Royal Institution of Great Britain. 8vo. Lond., 1863.   A 12 Q 21

SAWARD (BLANCHE C.) Church Festival Decorations ; comprising Directions and Designs for the suitable Decoration of Churches, for Christmas, Easter, Whitsuntide, and Harvest. Illustrated. 8vo. Lond., 1880.   A 8 P 42

Dictionary of Needlework. [*See* CAULFIELD, SOPHIA F. A.]

SAWYER (WILLIAM EDWARD). Electric Lighting by Incandescence, and its application to interior Illumination. 8vo. New York, 1881.   A 5 T 41

SAXBY (S. M.), R.N. Weather System ; or, Lunar Influence on Weather. 8vo. Lond., 1864.   A 3 T 37

SAXO GRAMMATICUS. Historiæ Danicæ, Lib. XVI. Steph. Johan. Stephanius recognovit notisque Illustravit. Sm. fol. Soræ, 1644–45.   B 18 R 17 ‡

SAY (JEAN BAPTISTE). Traité d'Economie Politique. 3 vols. 12mo. Bruxelles, 1827.   F 2 P 16–18

Treatise on Political Economy. 2 vols. 8vo. Lond., 1821.   F 7 Q 11, 12

SAYCE (PROF. A. H.), M.A. Archaic Classics : Elementary Grammar ; with full Syllabary and progressive Reading Book, of the Assyrian Language, in the Cuneiform Typo. 2nd ed. Imp. 8vo. Lond. 1877.   K 12 T 9

Ancient Empires of the East. Herodotus I–III. 8vo. Lond., 1883.   B 4 R 49

Ancient Empires of the East [to accompany edition of the first three Books of Herodotus.] 8vo. Lond., 1884.   B 14 Q 36

Principles of Comparative Philology. 8vo. Lond., 1874.   K 12 P 29

Another copy. 3rd ed. 8vo. Lond., 1885.   K 12 P 30

Introduction to the Science of Language. 2 vols. 8vo. Lond., 1880.   K 12 P 27, 28

Life of Dr. Appleton. [*See* APPLETON, J. H.]   C 6 T 1

Decipherment of Hittite Inscriptions. [*See* WRIGHT, W.]   B 2 R 49

SAYER (JOSEPH). History of Europe. [*See* PUFFENDORF, S., BARON VON]   B 7 T 30, 31

SAYOUS (A.) Memoirs and Correspondence of Mallet du Pan. 2 vols. 8vo. Lond., 1852. C 8 Q 2, 3

SAYWELL (Rev. J. L.) History of Northallerton, Yorkshire. 8vo. Northallerton, 1885. B 6 T 46

SCAMONI (G.) [*See* Tschémessoff, E.] A 20 P 66 ‡

SCAPEGRACE (The): a Petite Comedy. (Cumberland's Eng. Theatre.) 12mo. Lond., 1829. H 2 Q 17

SCAPULA (Johann). Lexicon Græco-Latinum, e probatis Auctoribus locupletatum, cum Indicibus auctis et correctis. Fol. Oxonii, 1820. K 37 P 2‡

SCARLETT (Hon. Peter Campbell), C.B. Memoir of the Rt. Hon. James, First Lord Abinger; including a Fragment of his Autobiography, and Selections from his Correspondence and Speeches. With Portrait. 8vo. Lond., 1877. C 1 V 1

SCARTH (Rev. John). Twelve Years in China; the People, the Rebels, and the Mandarins; by "A British Resident." With Illustrations. 8vo. Edinb., 1863. D 5 P 33

SCENES OF THE CIVIL WAR IN HUNGARY, 1848–49; with the personal Adventures of "An Austrian Officer." Translated by F. Shoberl. 8vo. Lond., 1850. D 8 S 48

SCENES ON THE SHORES OF THE ATLANTIC. 2 vols. 8vo. Lond., 1845. D 7 R 13, 14

SCHAAF (Karl). Lexicon Syriacum Concordantiale omnes Novi Testamenti Syriaci voces. Editio Secunda. 4to. Lugd. Bat., 1717. K 14 U 4

SCHACHT (Hermann), Ph.Dr. De Maculis (Tüpfel) in Plantarum Vasis Cellulisque lignosis obviis. (Pams. O.) 4to. Bonn, 1860. J 6 U 10

SCHADE (Charles Benjamin). Complete Practical Grammar of the German Language. 4th ed. 8vo. Leipzig, 1828. K 11 V 22

SCHADE (Prof. Oskar), Ph.D. Altdeutsches Wörterbuch. Zweite umgearbeitete und vermehrte Auflage. 8vo. Halle, 1872–82. K 14 Q 18

SCHADEN (Adolph von). Die historischen Fresken unter den Arkaden des Hofgartens zu München. 12mo. Munich, 1832. A 7 P 32

SCHÆFER (G. H.) Ellipses Græcæ. [*See* Bos, L.]

SCHAFARIK (Paul Josef). Elemente der altböhmischen Grammatik. 2ᵉ ausgabe. 8vo. Prag, 1867. K 13 Q 34

SCHÄFER (Prof. Edward Albert). Observations on the Nervous System of Aurelia Aurita. (Roy. Soc. Pub., 6.) 4to. Lond., 1879. A 11 P 7 †

Elements of Anatomy. [*See* Quain, Dr. J.]

SCHAFF (Prof. Philip), D.D., &c. Bibliotheca Symbolica Ecclesiæ Universalis: the Creeds of Christendom; with a History and Critical Notes. 3 vols. 8vo. New York, 1877–84. G 12 S 12–14

America: a Sketch of the Political, Social, and Religious Character of the United States of North America, in two Lectures. New York, 1855. G 10 Q 11

Saint Augustin, Melanchthon, Neander: three Biographies. 8vo. New York, 1886. C 2 S 37

SCHARF (George). [*See* Lycett, J.]

SCHARF (G.), Jun. Hand-book to the Paintings by Ancient Masters in the Art Treasures Exhibition. 8vo. Lond., 1857. A 6 V 38

[*See* Macaulay, T. B., Lord.]

SCHEDEL (H. E.) Diseases of the Skin. [*See* Cazenave, P. L. A.] A 12 P 16

SCHEFFER (Ary). Memoir of the Life of; by Mrs. Harriet Grote. 2nd ed. 8vo. Lond., 1860. C 3 R 33

SCHELLEN (Dr. H.) Spectrum Analysis in its application to Terrestrial Substances and the Physical Constitution of the Heavenly Bodies. 8vo. Lond., 1872. A 5 T 32

SCHELLER (I. J. G.) Copious Latin Grammar, translated from the German; with Alterations, Notes, and Additions, by George Walker, M.A. 2 vols. 8vo. Lond., 1825. K 15 Q 4, 5

SCHEM (Alexander J.) Cyclopædia of Education. [*See* Kiddle, H.] K 4 Q 13, 14

SCHENK (Dr. S. L.) Mittheilungen aus dem Embryologischen Institute der K.K. Universität in Wien. 8vo. Wien, 1880. A 13 R 3, 4

SCHERER (Wilhelm). Vorträge und Aufsätze zur Geschichte des geistigen Lebens in Deutschland und Oesterreich. Roy. 8vo. Berlin, 1874. B 37 S 1

History of German Literature; edited by F. Max Müller. 2 vols. 8vo. Oxford, 1886. B 9 R 31, 32

SCHERR (Prof. J.) Allgemeine Geschichte der Literatur. 2 vols. 8vo. Stuttgart, 1869. B 15 R 5, 6

History of English Literature. 8vo. Lond., 1882. B 4 R 22

SCHERZER (Dr. Karl von.) Narrative of the Circumnavigation of the Globe by the Austrian Frigate *Novara* (Commodore B. von Wullerstorf-Urbair), undertaken by order of the Imperial Government, in the years 1857–59. 3 vols. roy. 8vo. Lond., 1861–63. D 9 U 21–23

Another copy. 3 vols. roy. 8vo. Lond. 1861–63. MD 3 V 32–34

Die k. u. k. österreichisch-ungarische Expedition nach Indien, China, Siam, und Japan, 1868–71. Roy. 8vo. Stuttgart, 1873. D 5 U 29

Smyrna; mit besonderer Rücksicht auf die geographischen, wirthschaftlichen und intellectuellen Verhältnisse von Vorder-Kleinasien. Roy.8vo. Wien, 1873. D 5 U 28

[*See* Müller, Prof. F. M.]

SCHEUCHZER (J. G.) [*See* KÆMPFER, E.] B 17 S 2, 3 ;

SCHIEFNER (F. ANTON VON). Tibetan Tales, derived from Indian Sources. [*See* TIBETAN TALES.] J 11 V 15

SCHIERN (FREDERIK). Life of James Hepburn, Earl of Bothwell; translated from the Danish by the Rev. David Berry, P.S.A.S. 8vo. Edinb., 1880. C 7 Q 1

SCHILLER (JOHANN CHRISTOPH FRIEDRICH VON). Works of: Early Dramas and Romances: the Robbers: Fiesco; Love and Intrigue; Demetrius; the Ghost Seer; and the Sport of Destiny; translated from the German. 8vo. Lond., 1875. H 4 P 3

Œuvres de; traduction nouvelle, par Ad. Regnier. 8 vols. 8vo. Paris, 1860–69. J 13 U 11–18

Works of: Historical Dramas, &c.: Don Carlos; Mary Stuart; the Maid of Orleans; the Bride of Messina; translated from the German. 8vo. Lond., 1877. H 4 P 1

Works of, Historical and Dramatic: History of the Revolt of the Netherlands; Wallenstein [the Piccolomini; the Death of Wallenstein]; and William Tell: Historical Dramas; translated from the German. 8vo. Lond., 1877. H 4 P 2

Essays, Æsthetical and Philosophical; including the Dissertation on the "Connexion between the Animal and Spiritual in Man." 8vo. Lond., 1875. G 16 Q 3

William Tell: a Dramatic Poem; translated from the German, by T. C. Banfield. 8vo. Lond., 1831. H 4 Q 16

Historical Works of: History of the Thirty Years' War, complete: History of the Revolt of the Netherlands, to the Confederacy of the Gueux; translated by the Rev. A. J. W. Morrison, M.A. 12mo. Lond., 1866. B 7 S 40

Die sämmtliche Werke von. Roy. 8vo. München, 1830. H 2 U 1

Poems and Ballads; translated by Sir E. Bulwer Lytton; with Sketch of Schiller's Life. 2 vols. 8vo. Edinb., 1844. H 8 S 37, 38

Poems of, complete: attempted in English, by Edgar A. Bowring. 12mo. Lond., 1851. H 5 S 2

Correspondence of Schiller with Körner: with Biographi Sketches and Notes, by Leonard Simpson. 3 vols. 8vo. Lond., 1849. C 4 S 37–39

Life of: by H. Duntzer: translated by P. E. Pinkerton. 8vo. Lond., 1883. C 4 S 40

Life of Friedrich Schiller (1825): Life of John Sterling (1851): Two Biographies: by Thomas Carlyle. 8vo. Lond., 1857. C 4 S 34

Historical Works of: the Thirty Years' War; translated by G. Moir. (Const. Misc.) 2 vols. 18mo. Edinb., 1828. K 10 Q 6, 7

Gedichte von. 18mo. Stuttgart, 1878. H 6 P 20

Correspondence between Schiller and Goethe, from 1794 to 1805; translated, with Notes, by L. Dora Schmitz. 2 vols. 8vo. Lond., 1877–79. C 1 P 34, 35

SCHIMMELPENNINCK (MARY ANNE). Life of. Edited by her relation, Christiana C. Hankin. 4th ed. 8vo. Lond., 1860. G 5 R 26

SCHIMMER (KARL AUGUST). Sieges of Vienna by the Turks; from the German [by the Earl of Ellesmere]. 12mo. Lond., 1847. D 3 P 37

Another copy. (H. and C. Lib.) 12mo. Lond., 1847. J 8 P 19

SCHINDLER (ALBERT HOUTUM). Diary of the Shah of Persia. [*See* NASR EDDIN, SHAH OF PERSIA] D 8 8 9

SCHINDLER (ANTON). Life of Beethoven, including his Correspondence with his Friends, numerous Characteristic Traits, and Remarks on his Musical Works. 2 vols. 8vo. Lond., 1841. C 3 R 20, 21

SCHLEGEL (PROF. A. W. DE), M.R.S.L., &c. Réflexions sur l'Etude des Langues Asiatiques, addressées à Sir James Mackintosh, suivies d'une Lettre à M. Horace Hayman Wilson, Ancien Secrétaire de la Société Asiatique à Calcutta, élu Professeur à Oxford. Roy. 8vo. Bonn, 1832. K 16 R 5

Course of Lectures on Dramatic Art and Literature; translated from the German, by John Black. 2nd ed. 2 vols. 12mo. Lond., 1840. J 6 P 27, 28

SCHLEGEL (FREDERICK VON). Course of Lectures on Modern History; to which are added, Historical Essays on the Beginning of our History, and on Cæsar and Alexander; translated by L. Purcell, and R. H. Whitelock. 8vo. Lond., 1862. B 14 P 1

Philosophy of History, in a Course of Lectures delivered at Vienna; translated by J. B. Robertson. 12mo. Lond., 1835. B 14 S 31, 32

Philosophy of Life, and Philosophy of Language; in a Course of Lectures. 8vo. Lond., 1866. G 7 8 4

Æsthetic and Miscellaneous Works of; translated by E. J. Millington. 12mo. Lond., 1860. J 9 U 23

Lectures on the History of Literature, Ancient and Modern. 2 vols. 8vo. Edinb., 1818.

SCHLEGEL (H.), PH.D. Essay on the Physiognomy of Serpents; translated by Thomas Stewart Traill, M.D., F.R.S.E. 8vo. Edinb., 1843. A 14 Q 1

SCHLEICHER (PROF. AUGUST). Die Formenlere der Kirchenslawischen Sprache, erklärend und vergleichend dargestellt. 8vo. Bonn, 1852. K 15 R 33

Handbuch der Litauschen Sprache. 2 vols. 8vo. Prag, 1856–57. K 13 Q 23, 24

Compendium of the comparative Grammar of the Indo-European, Sanskrit, Greek, and Latin Languages. 2 vols. 8vo. Lond., 1874–77. J 16 Q 20, 21

Beiträge zur vergleichenden Sprachforschung. [*See* KUHN, A.]

SCHLEMAN (JOSEPH). Life in Melbourne, Australia. 8vo. Lond., 1882. MJ 2 Q 5

SCHLESINGER (MAX). Saunterings in and about London: the English edition by Otto Wenckstern. 8vo. Lond., 1853. J 1 Q 26

SCHLEY (COMMANDER W. S.), U.S.N., AND SOLEY
(PROF. J. R.), U.S.N. Rescue of Greely; illustrated
from the Photographs and Maps of the Relief Expedition. 8vo. Lond, 1885. D 4 R 15

SCHLIEMAN (DR. HENRY), D.C.L., &c. Troja; Re-
sults of the latest Researches and Discoveries on the Site
of Homer's Troy, and in the Heroic Tumuli and other
Sites, made in the year 1882; and a Narrative of a
Journey in the Troad, in 1881. Maps and Plans. Roy.
8vo. Lond, 1884. B 13 V 13
Mycenæ: a Narrative of Researches and Discoveries at
Mycenæ and Tiryns. 8vo. Lond, 1878. D 8 U 33
Trojanische Alterthümer, Breicht über die Ausgrabungen
in Troja. Roy. 8vo. Leipzig, 1874. B 13 V 33
Atlas trojanischer Alterthümer Photographische Ab-
bildungen Sm. fol. Leipzig, 1874. B 19 T 16 ‡
Troy and its Remains; translated and edited by P.
Smith, B.A. Roy. 8vo. Lond, 1875. B 13 V 14
Ilios: the City and Country of the Trojans. The
Results of the Researches and Discoveries on the Site of
Troy and throughout the Troad in the Years 1871–72–
73–78–79; including an Autobigraphy of the Author.
With Illustrations. Imp. 8vo. Lond, 1880. B 13 V 12
Tiryns, the Pre-historic Palace of the King of Tiryns:
the result of the latest Excavations. Roy. 8vo. Lond,
1886. B 9 V 25

SCHLÖMILCH (DR. O.) Compendium der höheren
Analysis. 2 vols. 8vo. Brunswick, 1879–81. A 10 T 13,14

SCHLOSSER (PROF. F. C.) History of the Eighteenth
Century, and of the Nineteenth till the overthrow of the
French Empire; translated, with a Preface and Notes,
by D. Davison, M.A. 6 vols. 8vo. Lond, 1843–45.
B 15 R 18–23

SCHLUTTER (CHRISTOPHE ANDRÉ). De la Fonte des
Mines, des Fonderies, etc. 2 vols. 4to. Paris, 1750–53.
A 9 V 16, 17

SCHMELLER (JOHANN ANDREAS). Die Mundarten
Bayerns grammatisch dargestellt. 8vo. München, 1821.
K 20 Q 1
Bayerisches Wörterbuch sammlung von Worten und
Ausdrücken. 4 vols. 8vo. Stuttgart, 1827–37.
K 12 R 36–39
Sogenanntes cimbrisches Wörterbuch, das ist deutsches
Idiotikon der VII und XIII Comuni in den venetianischen
Alpen. 8vo. Wien, 1855. K 13 Q 42

SCHMID (CHRISTOPH VON). One Hundred German Tales;
with English Notes, by H. Mathias. 4th ed. 8vo.
Lond, 1863. J 16 R 15
In what manner Henry von Eichenfels came to the
Knowledge of God: a Tale for the Young. 2nd ed. 8vo.
Lond, 1851. G 7 Q 4

SOHMID (HERMAN VON). Wanderungen in Bayerischen
Gebirge. [*See* UNSER VATERLAND.] D 38 P 17 ‡
Tirol und Varalberg. [*See* UNSER VATERLAND. D38P18‡

SCHMIDT (JULIAN). Characterbilder aus der zeitgenöss-
ischer Literatur. 8vo. Leipzig, 1875. J 17 P 19

SCHMIDT (DR. JULIUS). Stone Sculptures of Copán and
Quirigua. [*See* MEYE, H.] JI 20 P 17 ‡

SCHMIDT (OSCAR). Descendenzlehre und Darwinisimus.
8vo. Leipzig, 1873. A 14 Q 29
Doctrine of Descent and Darwinism. 8vo. Lond, 1875.
A 14 Q 30
Mammalia in their relation to Primeval Times. 8vo.
Lond, 1885. A 14 Q 12

SCHMIEDER (F.) [*See* CURTIUS RUFUS Q.] J 13 S 19–22

SCHMITZ (MISS L. DORA). Correspondence between
Schiller and Goethe. [*See* SCHILLER, J. C. F. VON.]
D 10 P 45
Miscellaneous Travels of J. W. von Goethe. [*See*
GOETHE, J. W. VON.]

SCHMITZ (LEONHARD). History of Rome. [*See*
NIEBUHR, B. G.] B 12 S 2–4

SCHNEIDER (DR. WILHELM). Die Australischen Ein-
gebornen. 8vo. Frankfort, 1883. MA 1 S 17

SCHNITZLER (J. H.) Secret History of the Court and
Government of Russia, under the Emperors Alexander
and Nicholas. 2 vols. 8vo. Lond, 1847. B 12 U 10, 11

SCHOCH (G. A.) Manual of Instructions for raising
Mulberry Trees and Silkworms. 8vo. Wellington,
1886.* MA 1 Q 47

SCHŒLCHER (VICTOR). Life of Handel. 8vo. Lond,
1857. C 7 T 15

SCHOFIELD (REV. WILLIAM). In affectionate Remembrance of; by the Rev. F. Firth. 12mo. Sydney, 1878.
MG 1 Q 35

SCHOLL (CHARLES). Phraseological Dictionary of Commercial Correspondence in the English, German, French
and Spanish Languages. 2 vols. 8vo. Liverpool,
1884–86. K 9 S 5, 6

SCHÖMANN (G. F.) Antiquities of Greece. Vol. 1—
The State. 8vo. Lond, 1880. B 10 P.13

SCHOMBURGK (DR. RICHARD), PH.D., &c. Papers on
Agriculture, &c., read before the Philosophical Society
and the Chamber of Manufactures, Adelaide. 8vo.
Adelaide. 1873. MA 1 Q 17
Flora of South Australia. 8vo. Adelaide, 1875. MA 2 V 8
Reports on the Progress and Condition of the Botani-
Garden and Government Plantations of South Australia
during the years 1874–79. Fol. Adelaide, 1875–80
MJ 2 U 4,
Botanical Reminiscences in British Guiana. 8vo. Ade
laide, 1876. MA 2 V 7
Catalogue of the Plants under Cultivation in the Govern
ment Botanic Garden, Adelaide, South Australia. 8vo
Adelaide, 1878. MA 1 T 30
On the Naturalised Weeds and other Plants in South
Australia. 4to. Adelaide, 1879. MA 1 U 37

SCHOMBURGK (SIR ROBERT H.), PH.D. History of
Barbados. Roy. 8vo. Lond., 1848. B 1 U 27

Natural History of the Fishes of Guiana. (Nat. Lib.,
37, 38.) 2 vols. 12mo. Edinb., 1841-60. A 14 P 37, 38

Travels in the South of Europe, &c. [*See* ADALBERT OF
PRUSSIA, PRINCE.] D 9 T 21, 22

SCHONBERG (ERICH VON), BARON. Travels in India
and Kashmir. 2 vols. 8vo. Lond., 1853. D 5 R 44, 45

SCHOOLCRAFT (HENRY R.), LL.D. Archives of Aboriginal Knowledge : the History, Antiquities, Language,
Ethnology, Pictography, Rites, Superstitions, and Mythology of the Indian Tribes of the United States. 6 vols.
roy. 4to. Philad., 1860. B 19 S 7-12 ‡

Personal Memoirs of a Residence of Thirty Years with
the Indian Tribes on the American Frontiers, 1812-42.
Roy. 8vo. Philad., 1851. C 8 V 23

Travels in the Central Portions of the Mississippi Valley
in the year 1821. Roy. 8vo. · New York, 1825.
D 4 Q 30

SCHOOL OF INDUSTRY, BRADFORD. [*See* BRAD-
FORD SCHOOL OF INDUSTRY.]

SCHOOL OF INDUSTRY, SYDNEY. [*See* SYDNEY
SCHOOL OF INDUSTRY.]

SCHOOL SOCIETY, BRITISH AND FOREIGN. [*See*
BRITISH AND FOREIGN SCHOOL SOCIETY.]

SCHOPENHAUER (ARTHUR). The World as Will and
Idea. 3 vols. 8vo. Lond., 1883-86. G 12 R 25-27

SCHÖPF (J. B.), O.S.F. Tirolisches Idiotikon. 8vo.
Innsbruck, 1866. K 15 P 33

SCHORLEMMER (PROF. C.), F.R.S. On the Normal
Paraffins. (Roy. Soc. Pubs., 5.) 4to. Lond., 1878.
A 11 P 6 †

Rise and Development of Organic Chemistry. 8vo.
Manchester, 1878. A 5 R 11

Treatise on Chemistry. [*See* ROSCOE, H. E.]

SCHOUW (JOACHIM FREDERIC). Earth, Plants, and
Man : Popular Pictures of Nature ; with Sketches from
the Mineral Kingdom, by F. von Kobell. 12mo. Lond.,
1859. A 17 T 37

SCHREIBER (M.) [*See* DELIUS, C. F.] A 9 V 14, 15

SCHREIBER (DR. P.) Handbuch der barometrischen
Hohenmessungen. 8vo. Weimar, 1877. A 3 T 17

SCHREVEL (CORNELIUS). Lexicon Manuale, Græco-
Latinum et Latino-Græcum. 8vo. Camb., 1668. K 12 Q 15

SCHRÖDER (DR. PAUL). Die Phönizische Sprache ;
entwurf einer Grammatik nebst Sprach und Schriftproben,
mit 22 Tafeln. 8vo. Halle, 1869. K 15 S 14

SCHRÖN (DR. LUDWIG). Seven-Figure Logarithms of
Numbers from 1 to 108,000, and of Sines, Cosines, Tangents, Cotangents to every ten seconds of the Quadrant.
5th ed., with a Description of the Tables, by A. De Morgan.
Imp. 8vo. Lond., 1865. A 10 V 6

SCHUBERT (FRANZ). Life of ; translated from the German of Kreissle von Hellborn, by Arthur Duke Coleridge,
M.A. 2 vols. 8vo. Lond., 1869. C 4 V 35, 36

Life of ; by George Lowell Austin. 12mo. Lond.,
1873. C 2 Q 44

SCHUERMANS (L. W.) Algemeen vlaamsch Idioticon,
uitgegeven op last van het taal-en letterlievend Genoot-
schap met tijd en vlijt. Roy. 8vo. Leuven, 1865-70.
K 13 R 4

SCHULTZE (F.) Kant und Darwin : ein Beitrag zur
Geschichte der Entwicklungslehre. 8vo. Jena, 1875.
A 16 T 30

SCHULTZE (M.) Observationes de Retinæ Structura
Penitiori. (Pam. D.) 4to. Bonnæ, 1859. MJ 2 U 3

SCHULZE (ERNST). Gothisches Glossar; mit einer Vorrede,
von Jacob Grimm. 4to. Magdeburg, 1847. K 13 U 8

Gothisches Woerterbuch nebst Flexionslehre. 8vo.
Züllichau, 1867. K 12 Q 7

SCHUMACHER (GOTTLIEB). Across the Jordan ; being
an Exploration and Survey of part of Hauran and Jaulan.
8vo. Lond., 1886. D 5 R 33

SCHUMANN (ROBERT). Music and Musicians : Essays
and Criticisms ; translated, edited, and annotated by
Fanny Raymond Ritter. [1st and] 2nd series. 2 vols.
8vo. Lond., 1878-80. A 7 P 9, 10

Life and Works of ; by August Reissmann. 12mo.
Lond., 1886. C 2 Q 45

SCHURMAN (PROF. J. GOULD), M.A., &c. Kantian
Ethics and the Ethics of Evolution : a Critical Study.
8vo. Lond., 1881. G 12 S 19

SCHÜRMANN (REV. C. W.) Aboriginal Tribes of Port
Lincoln, in South Australia; their Mode of Life, Manners,
Customs, &c. (Native Tribes of South Australia.) 8vo.
Adelaide, 1879. MA 1 R 12

SCHUSTER (ARTHUR), PH.D., &c. On the Total Solar
Eclipse of April 6, 1875. [*See* LOCKYER, J. N.] K 11 P 6 ‡

On the Nature of the Force producing the Motion of a
Body exposed to the Rays of Heat and Light. (Roy.
Soc. Pubs., 3.) 4to. Lond., 1876. A 11 P 4 †

SCHÜTZ (C. G.) Doctrina Particularum Linguæ
Græcæ. [*See* HOOGEVEEN, H.] K 12 U 3

SCHÜTZENBERGER (PROF. P.) On Fermentation.
8vo. Lond., 1876. A 5 S 39

SCHUYLER (EUGENE), PH.D., &c. Peter the Great, Emperor of Russia: a Study of Historical Biography. 2 vols. 8vo. Lond., 1884. C 9 P 21, 22

Turkistan : Notes of a Journey in Russian Turkistan, Khokand, Bukhara, and Kuldja. With Maps and Illustrations. 2 vols. 8vo. Lond., 1876. D 6 S 12, 13

American Diplomacy. 8vo. Lond., 1886. F 4 Q 3

SCHWAB (GUSTAV). Die schönsten Sagen der klassischen Alterthums. 3 vols. 8vo. Stuttgart, 1838-40.
B 14 R 31-33

SCHWABE (J. G. S.) Tabulæ Æesopiæ. [See PHÆDRUS, A. L.] J 13 R 31, 32

SCHWABE (MARY J. SALIS). [See JAMES, RT. HON. SIR W. M.] B 10 T 40

SCHWACKHÖFER (PROF. FRANZ). Fuel and Water; with special Chapters on Heat and Steam-boilers. 8vo. Lond., 1884. A 6 S 10

SCHWALBE (PROF. G.) [See ANATOMIE UND PHYSIOLOGIE.] E

SCHWARTZMANN (H. J.) Descriptions and Ground Plans of the Buildings of the International Exhibition, Philadelphia. [See PHILADELPHIA INTERNAT. EXHIB.]
A 2 P 6 ‡

SCHWARZ (C. G.) [See PANEGYRICI VETERES.]
J 13 R 25-29

SCHWARZBACH (DR. B.) Weak Eyes: Lecture delivered at Sydney Protestant Hall, August 26. 8vo. Sydney, 1885. MA 2 S 19

SCHWATKA (FREDERICK). Along Alaska's Great River: a Popular Account of the Travels of the Alaska Expedition of 1883. 8vo. New York, 1883. D 4 Q 10

Nimrod in the North; or, Hunting and Fishing Adventures in the Arctic Regions. Roy. 8vo. New York, 1885. D 4 S 37

Schwatka's Search : Sledging in the Arctic in quest of the Franklin Records. [See GILDER, W. H.] D 4 R 41

SCHWEGLER (DR. ALBERT). Geschichte der Philosophie in Unriss. 10e auflage. 8vo. Stuttgart. 1879. G 3 P 14

SCHWEIGHAEUSER (J.) Caractères de la Bruyère. [See LA BRUYÈRE, J. DE.]

[See ATHENÆUS OF NAUCRATUS.] J 16 S 24-37

SCHWEINFURTH (DR. GEORG). Artes Africanæ: Illustrations and Descriptions of Productions of the Industrial Arts of Central African Tribes. (Ger. and Eng.) Imp. 4to. Leipzig, 1875. A 5 R 13 †

Heart of Africa: Three Years' Travels and Adventures in the Unexplored Regions of Central Africa, 1868-71 ; translated by Ellen E. Frewer. With Illustrations. 2 vols. 8vo. Lond., 1873. D 2 P 4, 5

SCHWENDLER (LOUIS). Instructions for Testing Telegraph Lines, and the Technical Arrangements of Offices. 2nd ed. 2 vols. 8vo. Lond., 1878-80. A 5 R 55, 56

4 Q

SCIENCE RECORD (THE) : a Compendium of Scientific Progress and Discovery ; with Illustrations. Edited by Alfred E. Beach. 5 vols. 8vo. New York, 1872-76. E

SCIENTIFIC AMERICAN (THE) : an Illustrated Journal of Art, Science, and Mechanics. 24 vols. fol. New York, 1873-85. E

Supplements. 19 vols. fol. New York, 1876-85. E

SCIENTIFIC AND LEARNED SOCIETIES of Great Britain and Ireland. Year-book for 1884-85. 2 vols. 8vo. Lond., 1884-85. E

SCIENTIFIC LAYMAN, A. [See NEW TRUTH, THE.]

SCIENTIFIC MEMOIRS selected from the Transaction of Foreign Academies of Science and Learned Societies, and from Foreign Journals. Edited by Richard Taylor, F.S.A. 3 vols. 8vo Lond., 1837-41. A 16 T 1-3

SCLATER (P. L.), M.A., &c. Monograph of the Jacamars and Puff-birds; or, Families Galbulidæ and Buccoridæ. Roy. 4to. Lond., 1882. A 1 Q 13 †

SCOBLE (ANDREW R.) Representative Government in England. [See GUIZOT, F. P. G.] B 7 S 47

[See COMMINES, P. DE.] B 9 P 25, 26

SCOFFERN (JOHN), M.B. Manufacture of Sugar, in the Colonies and at Home, chemically considered. 8vo. Lond., 1849. A 6 P 18

Natural History of the Inanimate Creation. [See INANIMATE CREATION, THE.]

SCOFFERN (J.), M.B., AND HIGGINS (W. M.), F.G.S. Victoria Gold-valuer's Ready Reckoner and Assayer's Chemical Guide. 12mo. Lond., 1853. MA 2 P 21

SCONCE (REV. R. K.), B.A. Testimony of Antiquity to the Supremacy of the Holy See. Roy. 8vo. Sydney, 1848. MG 1 T 2

Reasons for submitting to the Catholic Church. 8vo. Sydney, 1848. MG 1 Q 40

SCOONES (W. BAPTISTE). Four Centuries of English Letters ; selection from the Correspondence of one hundred and fifty Writers, from the Period of the Paston Letters to the Present Day. 8vo. Lond., 1880. C 3 S 39

SCORESBY (REV. W.), D.D., &c. Whaleman's Adventures in the Southern Ocean, as gathered by the Rev. H. T. Cheever. 12mo. Lond., 1850.* MD 4 P 9

Journal of a Voyage to Australia and round the World, for Magnetical Research ; edited by Archibald Smith, M.A., &c. 8vo. Lond., 1859.* MD 5 T 1

Journal of a Voyage to the Northern Whale Fishery, made in the Summer of 1822, in the ship *Baffin*, of Liverpool. 8vo. Edinb., 1823. D 4 R 14

Account of the Arctic Regions ; with a History and Description of the Northern Whale Fishery. Illustrated. 2 vols. 8vo. Edinb., 1820. D 4 R 12, 13

SCOT (REGINALD). The Discoverie of Witchcraft, 1584. [Reprinted.] Sq. 8vo. Lond., 1886.   G 12 S 23

SCOTCH CATHOLIC, A. [*See* STATE AID QUESTION.]

SCOTCH COLLEGE. Scotch College for Young Ladies. Eastern Hill, Melbourne. Prospectus ; with an Address by the Lady Principal, Mrs. Ponsonby. 8vo. Melb., 1862.   MJ 2 Q 23

SCOTCHWOMAN, A. [*See* BURNS, R.]

SCOTICHRONICON. [*See* GORDON, REV. J. F. S.]

SCOTLAND. Tracts illustrative of the Traditionary and Historical Antiquities of Scotland. 8vo. Edinb., 1836.   B 13 P 44

New Statistical Account of Scotland; by the Ministers of the respective Parishes. 15 vols. 8vo. Edinb., 1845.   F 3 S 1-15

Registrum Magni Sigilli Regum Scotorum : the Register of the Great Seal of Scotland, A.D. 1424–1546 ; edited by James Balfour Paul, and J. M. Thomson. 2 vols. imp. 8vo. Edinb., 1882–83.   B 13 S 18, 19

Acts of the Parliaments of Scotland (A.D. 1124–1707). 11 vols. fol. Lond., 1814–44.   F 24 P 1-11 ‡

Rotuli Scaccarii Regum Scotorum : the Exchequer Rolls of Scotland, A.D. 1264–1460 ; edited by the late John Stuart, LL.D., and George Burnett, Lyon King of Arms. 9 vols. roy. 8vo. Edinb., 1878–86.   B 33 T 1-9

Register of the Privy Council of Scotland ; edited and abridged by John Hill Burton, LL.D., and David Masson, LL.D. 7 vols. imp. 8vo. Edinb., 1877–85.   B 13 S 8-14

The Complaynt of Scotland, written in 1548. [*See* COMPLAYNT OF SCOTLAND.]   B 14 T 11

Papers Relative to the Regalia of Scotland. [*See* BANNATYNE CLUB.]   E

Statistical Account of Scotland. [*See* SINCLAIR, RT. HON. SIR J.]

SCOTLAND (HISTORIANS OF). 6 vols. 8vo. Edinb., 1871–74.   B 13 P 45-50

  1. Joannis de Fordun, Chronica Gentis Scotorum; edited by W. F. Skene.

  2, 3. The Orygynale Cronykil of Scotland, by Androw of Wyntoun; edited by D. Laing. Vols. 1, 2.

  4. John of Fordun's Chronicle of the Scottish Nation; translated from the Latin, by F. J. H. Skene; edited by W. F. Skene.

  5. Lives of S. Ninian and S. Kentigern (by S. Allred and Jocelin); edited by A. P. Forbes, D.C.L.

  6. Life of St. Columba, by Adamnan; edited by W. Reeves, D.D.

SCOTSMAN IN THE EAST (THE). Vol. 2. Fol. Calcutta, 1824.   E

SCOTSMEN (BOOK OF); compiled and arranged by Joseph Irving. 8vo. Paisley, 1881.   C 11 Q 7

SCOTT (A. J.), M.D. The Jesuits. [*See* GRIESINGER, DR. T.]

SCOTT (A. W.), M.A. Australian Lepidoptera and their Transformations; drawn from the Life, by Harriet and Helena Scott; with Descriptions. Imp. 4to. Lond., 1864.   MA 1 R 8 ‡

Mammalia, Recent and Extinct : an Elementary Treatise for the use of the Public Schools of New South Wales. 8vo. Sydney, 1873.   MA 2 T 11

Another copy. 8vo. Sydney, 1873.   MJ 2 R 14

SCOTT (C.) Practice of Sheep Farming. 8vo. Edinb., 1886.   A 1 Q 16

SCOTT (CHARLES A. ANDERSON). Ulfilas, Apostle of the Goths; together with an Account of the Gothic Churches and their Decline. 8vo. Camb., 1885.   G 7 S 10

SCOTT (CHARLES HENRY). The Baltic, the Black Sea, and the Crimea. 8vo. Lond., 1854.   D 8 S 40

SCOTT (CAPT. C. ROCHFORT). Excursions in the Mountains of Ronda and Granada. 2 vols. 8vo. Lond., 1838.   D 8 T 18, 19

Rambles in Egypt and Candia ; with Observations on the Military Power and Resources of those Countries. 2 vols. 8vo. Lond., 1837.   D 2 Q 9, 10

SCOTT (DAVID). History of Scotland ; containing all the Historical Transactions of the Nation, from the year of the World 3619 to A.D. 1726. Sm. fol. Westmin., 1728.   B 16 S 5 ‡

SCOTT (DAVID), R.S.A. David Scott, R.S.A., and his Works; with a Catalogue of his Paintings, Engravings, and Designs, by John M. Gray. Imp. 4to. Edinb., 1884.   A 23 P 23 ‡

SCOTT (D. C. F.) [*See* NEW SOUTH WALES SPORTING MAGAZINE.]

SCOTT (EDEN GREENOUGH). Development of Constitutional Liberty in the English Colonies of America. 8vo. New York, 1882.   F 10 P 18

SCOTT (E. L.) Opinions of the Attorney-General, Hon. W. B. Dalley. [*See* DALLEY, HON. W. B.]   MF 3 U 4

SCOTT (GEORGE). Memoires of Sir James Melvil, of Hal Hill ; containing an impartial Account of the most Remarkable Affairs of State. Fol. Lond., 1683.   B 2 T 12

SCOTT (G. GILBERT), F.S.A. [*See* SCOTT, SIR G. G.]

SCOTT (SIR GEORGE GILBERT), R.A. Personal and Professional Recollections; edited by his son, G. Gilbert Scott, F.S.A. 8vo. Lond., 1879.   C 9 Q 10

Essay on the History of English Church Architecture prior to the Separation of England from the Roman Obedience. Roy. 4to. Lond., 1881.   A 2 U 8

Lectures on the Rise and Development of Mediæval Architecture ; delivered at the Royal Academy. 2 vols. 8vo. Lond., 1879.   A 3 P 7, 8

SCOTT (MISS HARRIETT). [*See* KREFFT, J. L. G., *and* SCOTT, A. W.]

SCOTT (HELENA). [*See* SCOTT, A. W.]

SCOTT (CAPT. JAMES), R.N. Recollections of a Naval Life. 3 vols. 8vo. Lond., 1834.　　　J 12 Q 11–13

SCOTT (JAMES GEORGE), "SHWAY YOE." The Burman: his Life and Notions. 2 vols. 8vo. Lond., 1882. D 5 Q 28, 29

France and Tonking: a Narrative of the Campaign of 1884, and the Occupation of Further India. With Map and Plans. 8vo. Lond., 1885.　　　B 2 P 42

Burma, as it was, as it is, and as it will be. 8vo. Lond., 1886.　　　D 5 Q 30

SCOTT (JOHN). Agricultural Surveying. (Scott's Farm Engineering Text-books.—Weale.) 12mo. Lond., 1884.
A 17 Q 79

Barn Implements and Machines. (Scott's Farm Engineering Text-books.—Weale.) 12mo. Lond., 1884.
A 17 Q 76

Draining and Embanking. (Scott's Farm Engineering Text-books.—Weale.) 12mo. Lond., 1883. A 17 R 11

Farm Buildings. With Plans and Estimates. (Scott's Farm Engineering Text-books.---Weale.) 12mo. Lond., 1884.　　　A 17 Q 68

Farm Roads, Fences, and Gates. (Scott's Farm Engineering Text-books.—Weale.) 12mo. Lond., 1883.
A 17 Q 81

Field Implements and Machines. (Scott's Farm Engineering Text-books.—Weale.) 12mo. Lond., 1884.
A 17 R 13

Irrigation and Water Supply. (Scott's Farm Engineering Text-books.—Weale.) 12mo. Lond., 1883. A 17 Q 73

SCOTT (REV. JOHN) A.M. Life of the Rev. Thomas Scott. 8vo. Lond., 1822.　　　C 9 T 39

SCOTT (JOHN). Picturesque Views of the City of Paris. [*See* NASH, F.]　　　D 9 S 5 †

SCOTT (JOHN). Life and Poems of. [*See* CHALMERS, A.]

SCOTT (REV. J. M.) The Martyrs of Argus and Means: Sketches of the Scottish Reformation. 8vo. Paisley, 1885.　　　G 7 S 19

SCOTT (JONATHAN), LL.B. History of Dekkan. [*See* FERISHTA, M. C. H. S.]　　　B 10 V 7, 8

[*See* ARABIAN NIGHTS' ENTERTAINMENTS.]　　　J 10 R 9–12

SCOTT (LEADER). [*See* BAXTER, MRS. LUCY E.]

SCOTT (PATRICK). Guide to the Stars, in eight Planispheres, shewing the Aspect of the Heavens for every Night in the Year. 8vo. Lond., 1860.　　　A 3 T 28

SCOTT (ROBERT), D.D. Greek-English Lexicon. [*See* LIDDELL, REV. H. G.]　　　K 16 S 25

SCOTT (ROBERT FORSYTH), M.A. Treatise on the Theory of Determinants, and their Application in Analysis and Geometry. 8vo. Camb., 1880.　　　A 10 T 21

SCOTT (ROBERT H.), M.A., &c. Elementary Meteorology. With numerous Illustrations. 8vo. Lond., 1883. A 3 S 31

SCOTT (SIR SIBBALD DAVID), BART., &c. The British Army: its Origin, Progress, and Equipment. 3 vols. roy. 8vo. Lond., 1868–80.　　　B 5 U 21–23

To Jamaica and Back. 8vo. Lond., 1876.　　　D 3 R 23

SCOTT (S. P.) Through Spain: a Narrative of Travel and Adventure in the Peninsula. Roy. 8vo. Lond., 1886.
D 8 U 35

SCOTT (THEODORE). Description of South Australia; with Sketches of New South Wales, Port Lincoln, Port Phillip, and New Zealand. 12mo. Glasgow, 1839. MD 3 Q 31

SCOTT (THOMAS). English Life of Jesus. 3rd thousand. 8vo. Lond., 1879.　　　G 2 P 40

SCOTT (REV. THOMAS). Essays on the most Important Subjects in Religion. 8vo. Lond., 1823.　　G 10 Q 22

Force of Truth: an authentic Narrative. 11th ed. 12mo. Edinb., 1818.　　　G 8 P 16

Life of, including a Narrative drawn up by himself, and copious Extracts of his Letters; by John Scott, A.M. 8vo. Lond., 1822.　　　C 9 T 39

SCOTT (SIR WALTER), BART. Works of. 100 vols. 12mo. Edinb., 1865–71.　　　J 1 P, Q, R

1, 2. Waverley.	49. Life of Dryden.
3, 4. Guy Mannering.	50. Life of Swift.
5, 6. The Antiquary.	51, 52. Biographies.
7, 8. Rob Roy.	53. Paul's Letters to his Kinsfolk.
9, 10. Old Mortality.	
11, 12. The Heart of Mid-Lothian.	54. Chivalry, Romance, and the Drama.
13. A Legend of Montrose.	55. Provincial Antiquities.
14, 15. The Bride of Lammermoor. The Black Dwarf.	56–64. Life of Napoleon.
	65–69. Periodical Criticism.
16, 17. Ivanhoe.	70–76. Tales of a Grandfather.
18, 19. The Monastery.	77. Letters on Demonology
20, 21. The Abbot.	and Witchcraft.
22, 23. Kenilworth.	78. Religious Discourses and
24, 25. The Pirate.	Memoir of George Bannatyne.
26, 27. The Fortunes of Nigel.	
28–30. Peveril of the Peak.	79–82. Border Minstrelsy.
31, 32. Quentin Durward.	83. Sir Tristrem.
33, 34. St. Ronan's Well.	84. The Lay of the Last Minstrel.
35, 36. Redgauntlet.	
37. The Betrothed.	85. Marmion.
38. The Talisman.	86. The Lady of the Lake.
39, 40. Woodstock.	87. Rokeby.
41. The Highland Widow.	88. The Lord of the Isles.
42, 43. The Fair Maid of Perth.	89. The Bridal of Trierman.
44, 45. Anne of Geierstein.	90. Dramas and Index.
46–48. Count Robert of Paris. The Surgeon's Daughter.	91–100. Life of Sir Walter Scott, by J. G. Lockhart.

Goetz von Berlichingen : a Tragedy. [*See* GOETHE, J. W. VON.]

Poetical Works. of. 10 vols. 12mo. Edinb., 1823.
H 6 P 31–40

1. Lay of the Last Minstrel.	8. Harold the Dauntless. Roderick and Miscellanies.
2, 3. Marmion and Ballads.	
4, 5. Lady of the Lake and Ballads.	9, 10. Lord of the Isles and Miscellanies.
6, 7. Rokeby and Bridal of Triermain.	

SCOTT (Sir Walter), Bart.—*continued.*

Secret History of the Court of James I; with Notes. 2 vols. 8vo. Edinb., 1811.   B 6 P 6, 7

Waverley Anecdotes, illustrative of the Incidents, Characters, and Scenery, described in the Novels and Romances. 2 vols. 12mo. Lond., 1833.   J 1 R 33, 34

Life of Napoleon Bonaparte; with a preliminary View of the French Revolution. Roy. 8vo. Edinb., 1871.   C 8 T 37

Life of, by R. Chambers; with Abbotsford Notanda. by Robert Carruthers. 12mo. Lond., 1871.   C 2 Q 43

Border Antiquities of England and Scotland, comprising Specimens of the Architecture, Sculpture, and other Vestiges of Former Ages. 2 vols. 4to. Edinb., 1813-15.   B 15 Q 4, 5 ‡

Tales of a Grandfather. [1st], 2nd, and 3rd series. 9 vols. 18mo. Edinb., 1829-31.   J 7 P 21-29

Provincial Antiquities and Picturesque Scenery of Scotland; with descriptive Illustrations. 2 vols. (in 1) roy. 4to. Lond., 1826.   B 16 Q 3 ‡

Miscellaneous Prose Works of. 6 vols. 8vo. Edinb., 1827.   J 8 T 6-11

Doom of Devorgoil: a Melo-drama. Auchindrane; or, the Ayrshire Tragedy. 8vo. Edinb., 1830.   H 3 S 22

Sir Tristrem: a Metrical Romance of the 13th Century; by Thomas of Erceldoune, called the Rhymer. [*See* Lermont, T.]

Letters on Demonology and Witchcraft. (Fam. Lib.) 12mo. Lond., 1832.   K 10 P 35

Life of Napoleon Buonaparte, Emperor of the French. 2nd ed. Vols. 1-6. 6 vols. 8vo. Edinb., 1827.   C+P2-7

Illustrations of the Author of Waverley. [*See* Chambers, R.]

Historical, Legendary, and Romantic Tales; selected and arranged by W. T. Dobson. 8vo. Lond., 1886.   B 12 Q 24

[A Biography]; by Richard H. Hutton. (Eng. Men of Lett.) 8vo. Lond., 1879.   C 1 U 28

Memoir of Sir R. Sadler. [*See* Sadler, Sir R.]   B 12 V 26, 27

David Ritchie, the Original of Sir W. Scott's Black Dwarf. [*See* Chambers, W.]   C 2 Q 38

Memoirs of the Life of; by J. G. Lockhart. 4 vols. 8vo. Edinb., 1837 38.   C 4 Q 38-41

Letters to. [*See* Macculloch, J.]   D 6 R 40-43

The Land of Scott. [*See* Hunnewell, J. F.]   D 8 R 33

History of Scotland. New ed. (Lard. Cab. Cyclo.) 2 vols. 12mo. Lond., 1832 35.   K 1 T 43, 44

Life of John Dryden. [*See* Dryden, J.]   H 2 R 12 29

Collection of Scarce and Valuable Tracts. [*See* Somers, Lord.]   B 2 U 17 29

SCOTT (Walter), M.A. Fragmenta Herculanensi. Descriptive Catalogue of the Oxford Copies of the Herculanean Rolls: together with the Text of several Papyri accompanied by Facsimiles. Roy. 8vo. Oxford, 1885.   K II U 8

SCOTT (William). Harmony of Phrenology with Scripture, shewn in a Refutation of the Philosophical Errors contained in Mr. Combe's "Constitution of Man." 8vo. Edinb., 1836.   A 12 S 12

SCOTT (William Bell). Albert Durer: his Life and Work; including Autobiographical Papers and complete Catalogues. 8vo. Lond., 1869.   C 7 P 1

Half-hour Lectures on the History and Practice of the Fine and Ornamental Arts. 3rd ed. 12mo. Lond., 1874.   A 7 Q 6

Ornamental Designs for Brass, Iron, and Glass-work, Earthenware, &c. Imp. fol. Lond. (n.d.)   A 23 P 32 ‡

The Little Masters. (Great Artists.) 8vo. Lond., 1879.   C 3 T 42

Etchings from the Works of William Blake. [*See* Blake, W.]   A 4 R 17 ‡

Poems, Ballads, Studies from Nature, Sonnets, &c. Illustrated. 8vo. Lond., 1875.   H 8 S 34

SCOTT (W. R.), Ph.D. The Deaf and Dumb; their Education and Social Position. 2nd ed., revised and enlarged. 8vo. Lond., 1870.   G 17 Q 8

SCOTT & CO. Bengal Directory and Register for 1844. 8vo. Calcutta, 1844.   E

SCOTT-RUSSELL. (J.) [*See* Russell, J. Scott.]

SCOTTISH ACADEMY (Royal). [*See* Royal Scottish Academy.]

SCOTTISH AUSTRALIAN EMIGRATION SOCIETY. The Scottish Australian Emigration Society vindicated from the Charges brought against it by the Colonial Land and Emigration Commissioners. (Pam. 28.) 8vo. Glasgow, 1855.   MJ 2 Q 16

SCOTTISH CELTIC REVIEW (The). Vol. 1, 1881-85. Roy. 8vo. Glasgow, 1885.   E

SCOTTISH REVIEW (The). Vols. 1, 2. 8vo. Lond., 1883.   E

SCOTTISH TEXT SOCIETY (The). Publications of. 3 vols. 8vo. Edinb., 1884-86.   E

SCRATCHLEY (Major-Gen. Sir Peter), R.E., &c. Defences of New Zealand: Memorandum on Defence Organization. 8vo. Wellington, 1881.*   MF 3 Q 60

Australian Defences and New Guinea; compiled from the Papers of the late Major-General Peter Scratchley, R.E., K.C.M.G., by C. Kinloch Cooke, B.A., &c. 8vo. Lond., 1887.*   MF 1 R 9

SCRIBNER (C.), and SONS. Scribner's Statistical Atlas of the United States, showing by graphic methods, their Present Condition, and their Political, Social, and Industrial Development, by F. W. Hewes, and H. Gannett. Roy. fol. New York, 1883.   D 8 P 9 ‡

SCRIPTORES EROTICI GRÆCI; curante Christ. Guil. Mitscherlich. 3 vols. 8vo. Biponti, 1792–94.
J 16 U 21–23
1. Acrillis Tatii Alexandrini de Clitophontis et Leucippes Amoribus libri. VIII. Graece et Latine.
2. Helidori Aethiopicorum; libri x. Graece et Latino.
3. Longi Pastoralium de Daphnide et Chloe; libri IV. Graece et Latine; accedunt Xenophontis Ephesiacorum de Amoribus Anthiae et Abrocamae; libri V.

SCRIPTORES ROMANI, sive, selecta ex Cicerone, Livio, Tacito, Velleio Paterculo, Quinctiliano, et Plinio. 8vo. Etonæ, 1804.   J 13 T 35

SCROPE (G. POULETT), M.P. Memoir of the Life of the Rt. Hon. Chas. Lord Sydenham, G.C.B.; with a Narrative of his Administration in Canada. Edited by his Brother. 8vo. Lond., 1843.   C 10 P 30

The Geology and Extinct Volcanoes of Central France. 2nd ed. 8vo. Lond., 1858.   A 9 R 7

SCROPE (WILLIAM), F.L.S. Art of Deer-stalking. Illustrated. Roy. 8vo. Lond., 1838.   A 17 W 18

Days and Nights of Salmon-fishing in the Tweed; with a short Account of the Natural History and Habits of the Salmon. Roy. 8vo. Lond., 1843.   A 17 W 43

SCRUTATOR. [*See* AUSTRALIAN RACING CALENDAR.]

SCRUTTON (THOMAS EDWARD), M.A., &c. Laws of Copyright: an Examination of the Principles which should regulate Literary and Artistic Property in England and other Countries. 8vo. Lond., 1883.   F 6 U 31

Land in Fetters. 8vo. Camb., 1886.   F 4 Q 18

Influence of Roman Law on the Law of England. 8vo. Camb., 1885.   F 4 Q 12

SCUDDER (HORACE E.) Noah Webster. (American Men of Letters). 12mo. Lond., 1882.   C 1 R 41
Life and Letters of Bayard-Taylor. [*See* TAYLOR, MARY HANSON.]

SCUDDER (SAMUEL H.) Catalogue of Scientific Serials of all Countries, including the Transactions of learned Societies in the Natural, Physical and Mathematical Sciences, 1633–1876. Roy. 8vo. Cambridge, U.S., 1879.   K 8 P 19
[*See* HARRIS, T. W.]   A 15 Q 17

SCULPTURE. Selection of Sixty Subjects, from the Works of the best Ancient and Modern Sculptors. Imp. 8vo. Lond. (n.d.)   A 8 T 9

SCYLITZA (Jo.) [*See* BYZANTINAE HIST. SCRIPT.]

SEABROKE (G. M.), F.R.A.S. Spectroscopic Observations of the Sun. [*See* LOCKYER, J. N.]   A 11 P 3 †

SEABURY (RT. REV. SAMUEL), FIRST BISHOP OF CONNECTICUT. Life and Correspondence of; by E. Edwards Beardsley, LL.D. 8vo. Boston, 1881.   C 5 S 28

SEACOLE (MRS. MARY). Wonderful Adventures in Many Lands; edited by W. J. S[eacole]. 12mo. Lond., 1857.   C 13 P 7

SEAFIELD (FRANK), M.A. Literature and Curiosities of Dreams. 2 vols. 8vo. Lond., 1865.   G 16 R 37, 38

SEALE (ROBERT F.) Geognosy of the Island of St. Helena, illustrated in a Series of Views, Plans, and Sections. Roy. 4to. Lond., 1834.   A 23 R 20 ‡

SEARING (A. E. P.) The Land of Rip van Winkle: a Tour through the Romantic Parts of the Catskills—its Legends and Traditions. With Illustrations. 4to. New York, 1884.   D 3 V 21

SEARLE (G. S.) Mount and Morris exonerated: a Narrative of the Voyage of the Brig *Carl*, in 1871. 8vo. Melb., 1875.   MD 1 U 21

SEARLE (GEORGE). Trial of. [*See* PIGGOREET MURDER, THE.]   MF 2 8 1

SEATON (A. E.) Manual of Marine Engineering; comprising the Designing, Construction, and Working of Marine Machinery. 8vo. Lond., 1883.   A 6 T 9

SEAWARD (SIR E.) Narrative of. [*See* PORTER, MISS JANE.]

SEBASTIAN (KING OF PORTUGAL). Married Life of Anne of Austria and Don Sebastian, King of Portugal; by Martha W. Freer. 2 vols. 8vo. Lond., 1864.   C 1 V 10, 11

SEBERT (H.) Notice sur les Bois de la Nouvelle Calédonie. Suivie de Considérations générales sur les Propriétés mécaniques des Bois et sur les Procédés employés pour les mesurer. Partie descriptive en commun avec M. Pancher. 8vo. Paris, 1874.   MA 1 Q 34

SECOND MAIDEN'S TRAGEDY (THE). 8vo. Lond., 1824.   H 1 R 13
Another copy.   H 1 R 15

SECOND THOUGHTS (SOLOMON). [*See* KENNEDY, J. P.]

SECONDARY PUNISHMENT. Reports from the Select Committee on Secondary Punishments. (Parl. Doc., 3.) Fol. Lond., 1831–32.   MF 4 ‡

Secondary Punishments discussed; by "An Emigrant of 1821. [*See* WILLIAMS, WILLIAM.]

Copies of Correspondence between the Secretary of State and the Governor of New South Wales and Van Diemen's Land, on the subject of Secondary Punishment. (Parl. Doc., 29.) Fol. Lond., 1841.   MF 4 ‡

SEDDALL (REV. HENRY), B.A., &c. Malta, Past and Present; being a History of Malta from the days of the Phœnicians to the present time. 8vo. Lond., 1870.   B 11 U 43

SEDDON (HANNAH). Sermon after the Funeral of. [*See* PERRY, RT. REV. C.]   MG 1 Q 39

SEDDON (COL. H. C.) Builders' Work, and the Building Trades. Roy. 8vo. Lond., 1886.   A 11 V 12

SEDGWICK (PROF. ADAM), M.A. Discourse on the Studies of the University. 2nd ed. 8vo. Camb., 1834.   G 17 P 9

Another copy. 4th ed. 8vo. Camb., 1835.   G 17 P 10

SEDGWICK (A.) Text-book of Zoology. [*See* CLAUS, Dr. C.*]   A 14 S 15, 16

SEDGWICK (MISS C. M.) Letters from Abroad to Kindred at Home. 2 vols. 8vo. Lond., 1841.   D 9 Q 5, 6

SEDULIUS (CAIUS CAELIUS). Opera omnia. [*See* JUVENCUS, C. V. A*]

SEEBOHM (FREDERIC). English Village Community; examined in its relations to the manorial and tribal Systems and to the common or open field System of Husbandry: an Essay. 8vo. Lond., 1883.   B 3 T 10

Oxford Reformers: John Colet, Erasmus, and Thomas More. 8vo. Lond., 1869.   G 12 R 6

SEEBOHM (HENRY), F.L.S., &c. Siberia in Europe: a Visit to the Valley of the Petchora, in North-east Russia; with Descriptions of the Natural History, Migration of Birds, &c. 8vo. Lond., 1880.   D 9 P 12

Siberia in Asia: a Visit to the Valley of the Yenesay in East Siberia. With Illustrations. 8vo. Lond., 1882.   D 6 R 22

History of British Birds; with Coloured Illustrations of their Eggs. 4 vols. (with Plates) 8vo. Lond., 1883-85.   A 13 V 31-34

SEELEY (PROF. H. G.) Fresh-water Fishes of Europe: a History of their Genera, Species, Structure, Habits and Distribution. Roy. 8vo. Lond., 1886.   A 13 U 39

Manual of Geology. [*See* PHILLIPS, J.]   A 9 R 31, 32

SEELEY (PROF. J. R.), M.A., &c. Expansion of England. Two Courses of Lectures. 8vo. Lond., 1883.   F 5 R 13

Lectures and Essays. 8vo. Lond., 1870.   J 2 T 27

"Ecce Homo": a Survey of the Life and Work of Jesus Christ. 4th ed. 8vo. Lond., 1866.   G 12 P 9

Review of "Ecce Homo." [*See* GLADSTONE, RT. HON. W. E.]

Controversial Notes on "Ecce Homo." [*See* PARKER, J.]

Life and Times of Stein; or, Germany and Prussia in the Napoleonic Age. 3 vols. 8vo. Cambridge, 1878.   C 11 P 32-34

Natural Religion. 8vo. Lond., 1882.   G 12 P 10

English Lessons for English People. [*See* ABBOTT, E. A.]   K 11 T 1

A Short History of Napoleon the First. 8vo. Lond., 1886.   C 2 T 32

SEELEY (L. B.), M.A. Horace Walpole and his World. 8vo. Lond., 1884.   C 1 T 2

SEELEY (ROBERT BENTON). Essays on the Church, 1840; by "A Layman." 12mo. Lond., 1840.   G 9 Q 28

Memoirs of the Life and Writings of Michael Thomas Sadler, Esq., M.P., &c. 8vo. Lond., 1842.   C 9 P 39

SEELHORST (GEORG), DR. PH. Australien in seinen Weltausstellungsjahren, 1879–81. 8vo. Augsburg, 1882.   MD 5 T 32

SEEMANN (BERTHOLD), PH.D., &c. Botany of the Voyage of H.M.S. *Herald*, 1845–51. Roy. 4to. Lond., 1852–57.   A 1 S 11 †

Flora Vitiensis: a Description of the Plants of the Viti or Fiji Islands; with an Account of their History, Uses, and Properties. With Plates. Roy. 4to. Lond., 1865–73.   MA 1 Q 5 †

Narrative of the Voyage of H.M.S. *Herald*, during the years 1845–51, under the command of Capt. Henry Kellet, R.N., C.B., and Three Cruises in search of Sir John Franklin. 2 vols. 8vo. Lond., 1853.   D 10 S 2, 3

Viti: an Account of a Government Mission to the Vitian or Fijian Islands, in the years 1860–61. 8vo. Camb., 1862.*   MD 4 V 4

[*See* PRITCHARD, W. T.]

SEGAR (SIR WILLIAM). Original Institutions of the Princely Orders of Collars. Roy. 8vo. Edinb., 1823.   K 10 T 24

SEGUIN (JOSEPH). La Dentelle: Histoire, Description, Fabrication, Bibliographie. Fol. Paris, 1875. A 4 U 19 ‡

SEGUIN (L. G.) Picturesque Tour in Picturesque Lands: France, Spain, Germany, Switzerland, Holland, Belgium, Tyrol, Italy, Scandinavia. Imp. 4to. Lond., 1881.   D 38 P 11 ‡

Rural England: Loiterings along the Lanes, the Commonsides, and the Meadow-paths; with Peeps into the Halls, Farms, and Cottages. With Illustrations. 4to. Lond., 1881.   D 38 P 12 ‡

SÉGUR (LOUIS PHILIPPE), COMTE DE. Mémoires. [*See* BARRIÈRE, J. F., 19, 20.]

SÉGUR (PAUL PHILIPPE), COMTE DE. History of the Expedition to Russia, undertaken by the Emperor Napoleon, 1812. 2 vols. 12mo. Lond., 1836.   B 12 T 19, 20

SEISMOLOGICAL SOCIETY OF JAPAN. Transactions of. Vols. 1–5. 8vo. Tokio, 1880–83.   E

SELBORNE (ROUNDELL PALMER), EARL OF. A Defence of the Church of England against Disestablishment. 8vo. Lond., 1886.   G 7 S 17

[*See* WHITE, G.]   A 17 V 6

SELBY (PRIDEAUX JOHN), F.L.S., &c. History of British Forest-trees, Indigenous and Introduced. 8vo. Lond., 1842.   A 1 S 38

Illustrations of British Ornithology: Land Birds, Water Birds. 2 vols. 8vo. Edinb., 1833.   A 11 S 52, 53

Plates [to the above]. 2 vols. el. fol. Lond., 1841.   A 10 P 2, 3 ‡

SELBY (PRIDEAUX JOHN), F.L.S., &c.—*continued.*
Natural History of Parrots. (Nat. Lib., 6.) 12mo.
Edinb., 1836.
  A 14 P 6

Natural History of Pigeons. (Nat. Lib., 5.) 12mo.
Edinb., 1835.
  A 14 P 5
[*See* JARDINE, SIR W.]

SELDEN (JOHN). History of Tythes. 8m. 4to. Lond.,
1618.
  G 13 R 42

Titles of Honor. Sm. fol. Lond., 1631. K 17 Q 22 †

Table-talk : Discourses relating especially to Religion and
State ; edited by R. Milward. 12mo. Edinb., 1819.
  J 10 P 32

Table-talk, 1689 ; carefully edited by Edward Arber,
F.S.A., F.R.G.S., &c. Large paper edition. (English
Reprints). 8m. 4to. Lond., 1869. J 12 V 9

Memoirs of John Selden, and Notices of the Political
Contest during his time; by George W. Johnson. 8vo·
Lond., 1835. C 9 V 31

Tracts : Jani Anglorum Facies Altera ; England's Epinomis; Ecclesiastical Jurisdictions of Testaments; Intes-
tates Goods; translated by R. Westcot. Fol. Lond.,
1683. B 2 T 45

SELECTOR'S GUIDE ; being an Explanation of the System of Alienating and Leasing Crown Lands in Queensland. October, 1883. 8vo. Brisbane, 1883.* MF 2 P 32

SELIS (NICOLAS JOSEPH). Le Prince Desiré [*See* CABINET
DES FÉES, 35.]

SELKIRK (ALEXANDER). Account of. [*See* ROGERS,
CAPT. W.]

SELKIRK (REV. JAMES). Recollections of Ceylon, after
a Residence of nearly Thirty Years. 8vo. Lond., 1844.
  D 5 T 23

SELL (REV. EDWARD). B.D., &c. Faith of Islâm. 8vo.
Lond., 1880. G 12 Q 25

SELLAR (THOMAS). Sutherland Evictions of 1814. Roy.
8vo. Lond., 1883. F 4 R 14

SELLAR (PROF. WILLIAM YOUNG), M.A., &c. Roman
Poets of the Augustan Age: Virgil. (Clar. Press.) 8vo
Oxford, 1877. J 3 T 3

Roman Poets of the Republic. New ed. (Clar. Press.)
8vo. Oxford, 1881. J 3 T 4

SELOUS (FREDERICK COURTENEY). A Hunter's Wanderings in Africa. 8vo. Lond., 1881. D 2 R 16

SELWYN (ALFRED R. C.), AND ULRICH (GEORGE H. F.)
Intercolonial Exhibition Essays : Notes on the Physical
Geography, Geology, and Mineralogy of Victoria. 8vo.
Melb., 1866. MA 2 Q 35

Another copy. 8vo. Melb., 1866. MF 1 Q 15

North America. [*See* HAYDEN, PROF. F. V.] D 3 P 61

SELWYN (A. R. C.), AND DAWSON (G. M.) Descriptive
Sketch of the Physical Geography of the Dominion of
Canada. 8vo. Montreal, 1884. A 9 T 4

SELWYN (C. J. AND L. F.) Annals of the Diocese of
New Zealand. 12mo. Lond., 1847.* MB 1 P 8

SELWYN (GEORGE). George Selwyn and his Contemporaries ; with Memoirs and Notes, by J. H. Jesse. 4 vols.
8vo. Lond., 1843-44. C 9 T 30-33

SEMPER (DR. KARL). Reisen im Archipel der Philippinen.
2r Theil. Wissenschaftliche Resultate. 5 vols. (in 9)
4to. Leipzig, 1867-86. A 9 Q 1-9 †

Die Palau-Inseln im Stillen Ocean. Reisenlebnisse. 8vo.
Leipzig, 1873.* MD 1 U 16

Natural Conditions of Existence as they affect Animal
Life. 8vo. Lond., 1881. A 14 Q 59

SEMPILL (SIR JAMES, ROBERT, AND FRANCIS). Poems of
the Sempills, of Beltrees ; now first collected, with Notes
and Biographical Notices of their Lives, by James Paterson.
8vo. Edinb., 1849. H 7 Q 22

SEMPILL (JOHN). Golden Sovereigns for the Squatters,
Graziers, Free-selectors, Farmers, &c.; by "C[ornstalk] et
et.A[lpha]." 8vo. Maitland, 1882. MF 3 Q 24

SENECA (LUCIUS ANNÆUS). Seneca's Morals, by way of
Abstract; to which is added, a Discourse under the Title
of "An After-Thought," by Sir Roger L'Estrange, Knt.
13th ed. 8vo. Lond., 1729. G 2 P 13

Another copy. 16th ed. 8vo. Lond., 1756. G 14 P 10

Œuvres complètes de Sénèque, le Philosophe ; avec la
Traduction en Français. Imp.8vo. Paris,1869. J 15 V 5

Workes of ; newly inlarged and corrected, by Thomas
Lodge, D.M.P. Fol. Lond., 1620. G 12 R 1 †

SENIOR (NASSAU WILLIAM). Conversations and Journals
in Egypt and Malta; edited by his Daughter, M. C. M.
Simpson. 2 vols. 8vo. Lond., 1882. D 1 W 17, 18

Conversations with Distinguished Persons during the
Second Empire, from 1860 to 1863 ; edited by his
Daughter, M. C. M. Simpson. 2 vols. 8vo. Lond.,
1880. C 8 U 23, 24

Journals kept in France and Italy, from 1848-52 ; with
a Sketch of the Revolution of 1848. 2 vols. 8vo.
Lond., 1871. D 8 R 46, 47

Correspondence and Conversations of Alexis de Toc
queville with Nassau William Senior, from 1834 to 1859
edited by M. C. M. Simpson. 2 vols. 8vo. Lond.,
1872. C 5 P 1, 2

SENIOR (N. W.), LOYD (S. J.), HICKSON (W. E.),
AND LESLIE (J.) On Improvement of Designs and
Patterns, and extension of Copyright ; from the Report
of the Commissioners on Hand-loom Weaving. 12mo
Lond., 1841. A 7 P 32

SENIOR (WILLIAM), "RED SPINNER." Travel and Trout
in the Antipodes: an Angler's Sketches in Tasmania
and New Zealand. 8vo. Lond 1880.* MD 2 R 45

SENKOWSKI (JOSEPH). Supplément à l'Histoire Générale des Huns, &c. [*See* GUIGNES, J. DE.]   B 1 R 24

SENNETT (RICHARD). R.N., &c. Marine Steam Engine : a Treatise for the Use of Engineering Students and Officers of the Royal Navy. 8vo. Lond., 1882.   A 6 T 7

SENTINEL (THE). 4 vols. fol. Sydney, 1845–48.   ME

SEOANE (D. M.), M.D. Dictionary of the Spanish and English Languages. [*See* NEUMANN, H., *and* BARETTI, H.]

SEPARATION ANTHEM. Commemoration Victorian-Australian Anthem ; composed in celebration of the glorious occasion of Separation. Dedicated to the loyal Sons of Victoria. 4to. Melb., 1851.   MJ 2 S 2

SEPTUAGENARIAN BENEFICED PRESBYTER, A. [*See* GENESIS.]

SERIMAN (ZACCARIA). Viages de Enrique Wanton a las Tierras Incognitas Australes, y al Pais de las Monas : en donde se expresan las Costumbres, Caracter, Ciencias, y Policia de estos extraordinarios Habitantes. 4 vols. 8vo. Madrid, 1771–85.   MJ 1 T 1–4

SERK. Scrambles in Serk : Scenery, History, Laws, of one of the Channel Islands. 12mo. Lond., 1861.   D 7 P 18

SERMONS OR HOMILIES. Certain Sermons or Homilies appointed to be read in Churches, in the Time of Queen Elizabeth of Famous Memory. Fol. Lond., 1676.   G 4 R 16 †

SEROUX-D'AGINCOURT (J. B. L. G.) [*See* D'AGIN-COURT, J. B. L. G. S.]

SERVICE (JAMES). Case for the Service Reform Bill 8vo. Melb., 1880.   MF 1 Q 6

SETH (PROF. ANDREW), M.A. Development from Kant to Hegel. 8vo. Lond., 1882.   G 12 S 8

SETH (PROF. ANDREW), M.A., AND HALDANE (R. B.), M.A. Essays in Philosophical Criticism. 8vo. Lond., 1883.   G 12 T 9

SETHOS (KING OF EGYPT). [*See* TERRASSON, J.]

SETON (ALEXANDER), EARL OF DUMFERMLINE. [*See* DUM-FERMLINE, A. S., EARL OF.]

SETON (GEORGE), M.A., &c. Memoir of Alexander Seton, Earl of Dunfermline, President of the Court of Session, and Chancellor of Scotland. Sm. 4to. Edinb., 1882.   C 8 V 31

SEVE (EDOUARD). La Patria Chilena ; le Chili tel qu'il est. 8vo. Valparaiso, 1876.   F 1 R 9

SEVELINGES (C. L.) [*See* GOETHE, J. W. VON.]

SEVEN YEARS' RESIDENT IN GREECE, A. [*See* SKENE, MISS FELICIA M. F.]

SEVERN (CHARLES), M.D. Diary of the Rev. J. Ward. [*See* WARD, J.]   C 9 S 55

SEVERUS (SANCTUS). [*See* JUVENCUS, C. V. A.]

SEVERUS. [*See* SULPICIUS, SEVERUS.]

SÉVIGNÉ (MARIE DE RABUTIN CHANTAL), MARQUIS DE. Madadme de Sévigné and her Contemporaries. 2 vols. 8vo. Lond., 1842.   C 5 V 8, 9

Lettres de Madame de Sévigné avec les Notes de tous les Commentateurs. 2 vols. 12mo. Paris, 1867–76.   C 2 R 26, 27

SEWARD (GEORGE F.) Chinese Immigration, in its Social and Economical Aspects. 8vo. San Francisco, 1881.   F 4 Q 20

SEWARD (JOHN). Spirit of Anecdote and Wit. 4 vols. 12mo. Lond., 1823.   J 1 V 37–40

SEWARD (W.) Biographiana. 2 vols. 8vo. Lond., 1799.   C 6 R 1, 2

Anecdotes of Distinguished Persons, chiefly of the last and two preceding Centuries. 5th ed. 4 vols. 8vo. Lond., 1804.   C 8 U 50–53

SEWARD (WILLIAM H.) AND (FREDERICK W.) Attempted Assassination of. [*See* LINCOLN, A.]   B 14 Q 1 ‡

SEWEL (WILLIAM). History of the Rise, Increase, and Progress of the Christian People called Quakers. 6th ed. 2 vols. 8vo. Lond., 1834.   G 12 P 14, 15

[*See* DAMPIER, CAPT. W.]

SEWELL (HENRY). New Zealand Rebellion : a Letter from H. Sewell, Esq., late Attorney-General of New Zealand to Rt. Hon. Lord Lyttelton. 8vo. Lond., 1864.   MB 2 T 11

SEWELL (J. W.) The "Somersetshire Sea Pie" : a Weekly Newspaper, written on board the s.s. *Somerset-shire*, on her Voyage from Melbourne to London. 8vo. Lond., 1870.   J 4 Q 1

SEWELL (RICHARD CLARKE), D.C.L., &c. Legal Education : an Inaugural Lecture on the Study of the Law. 8vo. Melb., 1857.   MJ 2 R 7

Speech of, in defence of George Chamberlain and William Armstrong, charged with shooting with intent to murder William Green, mounted constable, at Omeo. 8vo. Melb., 1859.   MF 1 Q 5

SEWELL (ROBERT), R.A.S., &c. Report on the Amaravati Tope, and Excavations on its site in 1877. Im. Ito. Lond., 1880.   B 17 S 13 ‡

SEWELL (WILLIAM). Odes and Epodes of Horace. [*See* HORATIUS FLACCUS, Q.

SEYD (ERNEST), F.S.S. Decline of Prosperity: its Insidious Cause and Obvious Remedy. Sm. fol. Lond., 1879. F 3 P 20 †
California and its Resources: a Work for the Merchant, the Capitalist, and the Emigrant. 8vo. Lond., 1858. D 3 T 42

SEYFFERTITZ (KARL VON). Tirol und Voralberg. [*See* UNSER VATERLAND] D 38 P 18 ‡

SEYMER (G. J.) Romance of Ancient History: Egypt. 2 vols. 8vo. Lond., 1834. J 10 R 29, 30

SEYMOUR (H. D.) Russia on the Black Sea and Sea of Azof; being a Narrative of Travels in the Crimea, &c. 8vo. Lond., 1855. D 6 U 25

SEYMOUR (REV. M. HOBART), M.A. Mornings among the Jesuits at Rome. 4th ed. 8vo. Lond., 1851. G 2 P 18
Pilgrimage to Rome. 8vo. Lond., 1851. D 7 Q 19

SEYMOUR (ROBERT). Seymour's Humorous Sketches; comprising eighty-six Caricature Etchings, illustrated in Prose and Verse, by Alfred Crowquill [A. H. Forrester.] Roy. 8vo. Lond., 1872. J 7 U 2

SFORZA (FRANCESCO ALESSANDRO). DUKE OF MILAN. [*See* MILAN, F. A. SFORZA, DUKE OF.]

SGANZIN (M. I.) Elementary Course of Civil Engineering. 8vo. Boston, 1828. A 6 T 12

SHADBOLT (SYDNEY H.) Afghan Campaigns of 1878–80: Historical and Biographical Divisions; with Portraits and Notices of Officers. 2 vols. 4to. Lond., 1882. B 17 R 10, 11 ‡

SHADES OF MEMORY. 8vo. Sydney(n.d.) MH 1 S 19

SHADWELL (VICE-ADM. SIR CHARLES), K.C.B., &c. Contribution to Terrestrial Magnetism. (Roy. Soc. Pubs., 4.) 4to. Lond., 1877. A 11 P 5 †

SHADWELL (CHARLES). The Fair Quaker of Deal; or, the Humours of the Navy: a Comedy. (Bell's Brit. Theatre.) 18mo. Lond., 1791. H 2 P 36

SHADWELL (CHARLES LANCELOT), B.C.L. Select Titles from the Digest of Justinian. [*See* JUSTINIANUS.]

SHADWELL (J. E. L.), M.A. Golden Treasury of Greek Prose. 8vo. [*See* WRIGHT, R. S.]

SHADWELL (JOHN LANCELOT). System of Political Economy. 8vo. Lond., 1877. F 4 Q 13

SHADWELL (LIEUT.-GEN. LAWRENCE), C.B. Life of Colin Campbell, Lord Clyde. 2 vols. 8vo. Edinb., 1881. C 10 T 6, 7

SHADWELL (THOMAS). Dramatic Works of. 4 vols. 12mo. Lond., 1720. H3 P 24–27

4 R

SHAFTESBURY (ANTHONY ASHLEY COOPER), FIRST EARL OF. Life of; by B. Martyn and Dr. Kippis. Edited by G. W. Cooke. 2 vols. 8vo. Lond., 1836. C 8 P 43, 44
Life of; by H. D. Traill. (English Worthies.) 8vo. Lond., 1886. C 2 T 35

SHAFTESBURY (RT. HON. ANTHONY ASHLEY COOPER), THIRD EARL OF. Characteristicks of Men, Manners, Opinions, Times. 5th ed. 3 vols. 8vo. Birmingham, 1773. G 15 T 16–18

SHAFTESBURY (ANTHONY ASHLEY COOPER), SEVENTH EARL OF. Life and Work of; by Edwin Hodder. With Portraits. 3 vols. 8vo. Lond., 1886. C 8 P 45–47

SHAIRP (JOHN CAMPBELL), LL.D. Aspects of Poetry; being Lectures delivered at Oxford. 8vo. Oxford, 1881. J 5 R 33
Burns. (Eng. Men of Letts.) 8vo. Lond., 1879. C 1 U 6

SHAKESPEARE (WILLIAM). All's Well that Ends Well: a Comedy. (Cumberland's Eng. Theatre.) 12mo. Lond., 1829. H 2 Q 11
Animal-lore of Shakespeare's Time. [*See* PHIPSON, EMMA.]
Annals of the Life and Works of; collected from the most recent authorities, by J. C. 8vo. Lond., 1886. C 4 S 43
Antony and Cleopatra: a Historical Play. (Brit. Theatre.) 12mo. Lond., 1808. H 1 P 4
As You Like it: a Comedy. (Brit. Theatre.) 12mo. Lond., 1808. H 1 P 3
The Authorship of Shakespeare. [*See* HOLMES, N.]
Bacon, not Shakespeare. [*See* THOMSON, W.] MH 1 S 21
Bibliography of the Bacon-Shakespeare Controversy. [*See* WYMAN, W. H.] K 17 Q 25
Biography of. [*See* LAMARTINE, A. DE.] C 5 S 11, 12
Brief Hand-list of the Collections respecting the Life and Works of Shakespeare, and the History and Antiquities fo Stratford-upon-Avon. [*See* HALLIWELL-PHILLIPPS, J. O.]
Catalogue of the Works of W. Shakespeare in the Barton Collection of the Boston Public Library. [*See* HUBBARD, J. M.] K 9 P 5 †
Characters of Shakspeare's Plays. [*See* HAZLITT, W.]
Chronicle History of the Life and Work of William Shakespeare, Player, Poet, and Play-maker; by F. G. Fleay. 8vo. Lond., 1886. C 9 R 28
Comedies, Histories, Tragedies, and Poems of; edited by Charles Knight. 2nd ed. 12 vols. 8vo. Lond., 1842–46. H 3 R 1–12
The Comedy of Errors. (Brit. Theatre.) 12mo. Lond., 1808. H 1 P 1
Commentaries on the Historical Plays of Shakspeare. [*See* COURTENAY, T. P.]
Complete Concordance to. [*See* CLARKE, MRS. C.]

SHAKESPEARE (WILLIAM)—*continued.*

Complete Works of ; with a Memoir of the Author, by the Rev. W. Harness. Roy. 8vo. Lond., 1838.   H 2 U 13

Compositions from Shakespeare's "Tempest." [*See* PATON, SIR J. N.]

Coriolanus; or, the Roman Matron: a Historical Play. (Brit. Theatre.) 12mo. Lond., 1808.   H 1 P 5

Corrigenda and Explanations of the Text of Shakspere. [*See* GOULD, G.]

Cruces Shakespearianae : Difficult Passages in the Works of Shakespeare. [*See* KINNEAR, J. B.]

Cymbeline : a Historical Play. (Brit. Theatre.) 12mo. Lond., 1808.   H 1 P 4

Cymbeline : the Text revised and annotated by C. M. Ingleby, LL.D.   Sm. 4to. Lond., 1886.   H 3 Q 24

The English of Shakespeare. [*See* CRAIK, PROF. G. L.]

Essays on Shakespeare. [*See* ELZE, K.]

Fabrication of the Shakspeare Manuscripts. [*See* IRELAND, W. H.]

First collected Edition of the Dramatic Works of William Shakespeare : a Reproduction in exact facsimile of the Famous First Folio, 1623. Fol. Lond., 1866.   Libr.

Folk-lore of Shakespeare. [*See* DYER, T. F. T.]

Hamlet, Prince of Denmark : a Tragedy. (Brit. Theatre.) 12mo. Lond., 1808.   H 1 P 1

Hamnet Shakespere ; according to the first Folio (spelling modernised); edited by Allan Park Paton. 8vo. Edinb., 1879.   H 3 R 23

1. The Tragedy of Macbeth ; the Tragedy of Hamlet ; the Tragedy of Cymbeline ; the Life of Timon of Athens ; the Winter's Tale.

Hand-book of Shakespeare Music. [*See* ROFFE, A.]

Hard Knots in Shakespeare. [*See* PERRING, SIR P.]

Historical Account of the New Place, Stratford-upon-Avon, the last Residence of Shakespeare. [*See* HALLIWELL-PHILLIPPS, J. O.]   B 18 T 11 ‡

Illustrations of Shakespeare. [*See* DOUCE, F.]

Illustrations of the Life of Shakespeare, in a discursive series of Essays on a variety of subjects connected with the Personal and Literary History of the Great Dramatist; by J. O. Halliwell-Phillipps. Fol. Lond., 1874.   C I W 25

Index to Shakespearian Thought. [*See* ARNOLD, G.]

Julius Cæsar : a Tragedy. (Brit. Theatre.) 12mo. Lond., 1808.   H 1 P 4

King Henry IV (the First Part): a Historical Play. (Brit. Theatre.) 12mo. Lond., 1808.   H 1 P 2

King Henry IV (the Second Part): a Historical Play. (Brit. Theatre.) Lond., 1808.   H 1 P 2

SHAKESPEARE (WILLIAM)—*continued.*

King Henry V : a Historical Play. (Brit. Theatre.) 12mo. Lond., 1808.   H 1 P 2

King Henry VIII : a Historical Play. (Brit. Theatre.) 12mo. Lond., 1808.   H 1 P 3

King John : a Historical Play. (Brit. Theatre.) 12mo. Lond., 1808.   H 1 P 1

King Lear : a Tragedy. (Brit. Theatre.) 12mo. Lond., 1808.   H P 41

King Richard III : a Tragedy. (Brit. Theatre.) 12mo. Lond., 1808.   H 1 P 1

Lectures and Notes on Shakspere. [*See* COLERIDGE, S. T.]

Life and Poems of. [*See* CHALMERS, A.]

Life of ; including many particulars respecting the Poet and his Family never before published, by J. O. Halliwell-Phillipps. 8vo. Lond., 1848.   C 9 R 26

Macbeth : a Tragedy. (Brit. Theatre.) 12mo. Lond., 1808.   H 1 P 4

Measure for Measure : a Comedy. (Brit. Theatre.) 12mo. Lond., 1808.   H 1 P 3

Memorials of Shakespeare ; or, Sketches of his Character and Genius by various Writers; now first collected, with Notes, &c., by Nathan Drake, M.D. 8vo. Lond., 1828.   C 9 R 22

The Merchant of Venice : a Comedy. (Brit. Theatre.) 12mo. Lond., 1808.   H 1 P 2

The Merry Wives of Windsor : a Comedy. (Brit. Theatre.) 12mo. Lond., 1808.   H 1 P 3

The Merry Wives of Windsor : a Comedy. 8vo. Lond., 1886.   H 1 R 21

Midsummer Night's Dream : a Comedy. (Cumberland's Eng. Theatre.) 12mo. Lond., 1829.   H 2 Q 10

Mr. William Shakespeares Comedies, Histories, and Tragedies. [First Folio edition.] Published according to the True Originall Copies (by John Heminge, and Henry Condell). Printed by Isaac Jaggard and Ed. Blount. (*Presented by Messrs. R. and G. Tangye, of Birmingham*). Fol. Lond., 1623.   Libr.

Much Ado about Nothing: a Comedy. (Brit. Theatre.) 12mo. Lond., 1808.   H 1 P 2

New Reading and New Renderings of the Tragedies of. [*See* VAUGHAN, H. H.]   H 3 R 13, 14

New Variorum Edition of Shakespeare ; edited by Horace Howard Furness. Vols. 1-6. 6 vols. roy. 8vo. Philad., 1871-86.   H 1 T 1-6

1. Romeo and Juliet.   5. King Lear.
2. Macbeth.   6. Othello.
3, 4. Hamlet.

Notes and Essays on Shakespeare. [*See* HALES, PROF. J. W.]

Notes on some of Shakespeare's Plays. [*See* KEMBLE, MRS. F. A.]

SHAKESPEARE (WILLIAM)—*continued.*

Œuvres complètes. François Victor Hugo, traducteur. 2e éd. 15 vols. 8vo. Paris, 1865–69. H 3 Q 1–15

  1. Les deux Hamlet.

  2. Féeries: Le Songe d'une Nuit d'été; La Tempête.

  3. Les Tyrans: Macbeth; Le Roi Jean; Richard III.

  4, 5. Les Jaloux: Troylus et Cressida; Beaucoup de bruit pour rien; Le Conte d'Hiver; Cymbeline; Othello.

  6. Les Comédies de l'Amour: La Sauvage apprivoisée; Tout est bien qui finit bien; Peines d'Amour perdues.

  7. Les Amants Tragiques: Antoine et Cléopatre: Roméo et Juliette.

  8. Les Amis: Les deux Gentilshommes de Vérone; Le Marchand de Venise; Comme il vous plaîra.

  9. La Famille: Coriolan; Le Roi Lear.

  10. La Société: Mesure pour Mesure; Timon d'Athènes; Jules César.

  11–13. La Patrie; Richard II; Henry IV (première partie); Henry IV (seconde partie); Henry V; Henry VI (première partie); Henry VI (deuxième partie); Henry VI (troisième partie); Henry VIII.

  14. Les Farces: Les Joyeuses épouses de Windsor; La Comédie des Erreurs; Le Soir des Rois; ou, ce que vous voudrez.

  15. Sonnets; Poëmes; Testament.

On some of Shakespeare's Female Characters. [*See* MARTIN, LADY.]

Othello, the Moor of Venice: a Tragedy. (Brit. Theatre.) 12mo. Lond., 1808. H 1 P 5

Outlines of the Life of; by J. O. Halliwell-Phillipps. 2nd ed. 8vo. Lond., 1882. C 9 R 27

Another copy. 5th ed. Imp. 8vo. Lond., 1885. C 5 W 21

Pericles, Prince of Tyre: a Tragedy. (Bell's Brit. Theatre.) 18mo. Lond., 1796. H 2 P 2

Another copy. H 2 P 29

Plant-lore and Garden-craft of Shakespeare. [*See* ELLACOMBE, REV. H. N.]

Plays of William Shakspere, accurately printed from the Text of the corrected Copies left by the late George Steevens, Esq., and Edmond Malone, Esq.; with Mr. Malone's various Readings, a History of the Stage, and a Life of Shakespeare, by Alexander Chalmers, F.S.A. New ed. 8 vols. 8vo. Lond., 1847. H 3 R 15–22

  1. The Tempest; Two Gentlemen of Verona; Merry Wives of Windsor.

  2. Twelfth Night; Measure for Measure; Much Ado about Nothing; Midsummer Night's Dream; Love's Labour's Lost.

  3. Merchant of Venice; As You Like It; All's Well that Ends Well; Taming of the Shrew; Winter's Tale.

  4. Comedy of Errors; Macbeth; King John; King Richard II; King Henry IV, Part I.

  5. King Henry IV, Part 2; King Henry V; King Henry VI.

  6. King Richard III; King Henry VIII; Troilus and Cressida; Timon of Athens; Coriolanus.

  7. Julius Cæsar; Antony and Cleopatra; Cymbeline; Titus Andronicus; Pericles.

  8. King Lear; Romeo and Juliet; Hamlet; Othello.

Promus of Formularies and Elegancies by Francis Bacon, illustrated and elucidated by passages from Shakespeare. [*See* POTT, MRS. H.]

Reference Shakspere: a Memorial Edition of Shakspere's Plays, containing 11,600 References; compiled by John B. Marsh, Manchester. Sm. 4to. Lond., 1864. H 2 U 25

SHAKESPEARE (WILLIAM)—*continued.*

Romeo and Juliet: a Tragedy. (Brit. Theatre.) 12mo. Lond., 1808. H 1 P 1

Select Plays: The Merchant of Venice; King Richard II; and Macbeth; edited by W. G. Clark, M.A., and W. A. Wright, M.A. (Clar. Press.) 3 vols. (in 1). 12mo. Oxford, 1874–76. H 2 Q 38

Shakespeare and Classical Antiquity. [*See* STAPFER, PROF. P.]

Shakespeare and his Times, including a Biography of the Poet; by Nathan Drake, M.D. 2 vols. 4to. Lond., 1817. C 4 W 35, 36

Shakespeare and the Emblem Writers. [*See* GREEN, H.]

Shakespeare as a Dramatic Artist. [*See* MOULTON, R. G.]

Shakespeare Commentaries. [*See* GERVINUS, PROF. G. G.]

Shakespeare from an American Point of View; including an Inquiry as to his Religious Faith and his Knowledge of Law, with the Baconian Theory considered, by George Wilkes. 8vo. Lond., 1877. C 9 R 23

Shakespeare; his Life, Art, and Characters; with an Historical Sketch of the Origin and Growth of the Drama in England, by the Rev. H. N. Hudson. 2 vols. 8vo. Boston, 1872. C 3 Q 48, 49

Shakespeare in Romance, &c. [*See* THOMSON, W.] MH 1 S 21

Shakespeare Jest-books; edited by W. Carew Hazlitt. 3 vols. 12mo. Lond., 1864. J 6 Q 5–7

The Shakespeare Key. [*See* CLARKE, CHARLES AND MARY COWDEN.]

Shakespeare not Bacon; by J. S. (Newspaper Cutting.) 8vo. Melb., 1881. MH 1 S 21

Shakespeare-Notes. [*See* LEO, F. A.]

Shakespeare, the Man and the Book; being a Collection of occasional Papers on the Bard and his Writings, by C. M. Ingleby, M.A., LL.D., &c. 2 vols. sm. 4to. Lond., 1877–81. C 9 R 24, 25

Shakespeare Phrase-book. [*See* BARTLETT, J.]

Shakespearean Scenes and Characters. [*See* BRERETON, A.] H 3 P 27 †

Shakespeare's Library: a Collection of the Plays, Romances, Novels, Poems, and Histories employed by Shakespeare in the composition of his Works; with Introductions and Notes. 2nd ed. 6 vols. 8vo. Lond., 1875. H 2 Q 32–37

Shakespeare's Plutarch; being a Selection from the Lives in North's Plutarch, which illustrate Shakespeare's Plays; edited by the Rev. Walter W. Skeat, M.A. 8vo. Lond., 1875. C 4 Q 29

Shakespeare's Tapestry woven in Verse. [*See* HAWKEY, C.]

Shakespearian Dictionary. [*See* DOLBY, T.]

Shakespear's Centurie of Prayse. [*See* INGLEBY, C. M.] H 6 S 30

Shaksperian Grammar. [*See* ABBOTT, E. A.] K 11 U 17

SHAKESPEARE (WILLIAM)—*continued.*

Shakspeare and his Friends. [*See* WILLIAMS, PROF. R. F.]

Shakspeare on Temperance; with brief Annotations selected by Fredk. Sherlock. 8vo. Lond., 1883. H 1 R 22

Shakspeare's Garden of Girls. [*See* ELLIOTT, MRS. M. L.]

Shakspere: a Critical Study of his Mind and Art; by Edward Dowden, LL.D. 8vo. Lond., 1875. C 16 R 1

Shakspere's Memorial. [*See* TAGG, W.] MH 1 R 43

Shakspere's Predecessors in the English Drama. [*See* SYMONDS, J. A.]

Sonnets of; edited by Edward Dowden. 8vo. Lond., 1881. H 7 R 11

Sonnets of; edited by Edward Dowden. (Parchment Series.) 12mo. Lond., 1881. H 7 P 25

Stratford-on-Avon, from the Earliest Times to the Death of William Shakespeare. [*See* LEE, S. L.] B 15 T 11 ‡

Studies in Shakespeare. [*See* WHITE, R. G.]

Study of Shakespeare. [*See* SWINBURNE, A. C.]

System of Shakespeare's Dramas. [*See* SNIDER, D. J.]

Tales from Shakespeare. [*See* LAMB, C. AND M.]

Taming of the Shrew; or, Katherine and Petruchio: a Comedy. (Cumberland's Eng. Theatre.) 12mo. Lond., 1829. H 2 Q 11

Teatro di Shakspeare; scelto e tradotto in Versi, da Giulio Carcano. 4ª ed. Roy. 8vo. Napoli, 1883. H 2 U 11

The Tempest; or, the Enchanted Island: a Play. 12mo. (Brit. Theatre.) 12mo. Lond., 1808. H 1 P 5

Text of Shakespeare vindicated from the Interpolations and Corruptions advocated by J. P. Collier. [*See* SINGER, S. W.]

Tragedie of Hamlet, Prince of Denmarke: a Study with the Text of the Folio of 1623; by George Macdonald. 8vo. Lond., 1885. H 3 Q 16

Tragedy of Hamlet; edited by Karl Elze. Roy. 8vo. Lond., 1882. H 2 U 12

Twelfth Night; or, What you Will: a Comedy. (Brit. Theatre.) 12mo. Lond., 1808. H 1 P 5

The Two Gentlemen of Verona: a Comedy, (Cumberland's Eng. Theatre.) 12mo. Lond., 1829. H 2 Q 11

The Winter's Tale: a Play. (Brit. Theatre.) 12mo. Lond., 1808. H 1 P 3

Works of. The Text revised by the Rev. Alexander Dyce. 6 vols. 8vo. Lond., 1857. H 3 Q 18–23

Works of Shakspear; in six Books; edited by Sir Thomas Hanmer. 2nd ed. 6 vols. roy. 4to. Oxford, 1771. H 3 Q 1–6 †

SHAKESPEARE MEMORIAL LIBRARY. [*See* BIRMINGHAM FREE LIBRARIES.]

SHAKESPEARE SOCIETY. Publications of. 22 vols. 8vo. Lond., 1841–16. E

SHAKESPEARE SOCIETY (NEW). Transactions and Publications of. 23 vols. 8vo. Lond., 1874–81. E

SHALER (NATHANIEL SOUTHGATE), AND DAVIS (WILLIAM MORRIS). Illustrations of the Earth's Surface: Glaciers. Imp. 4to. Boston, 1881. A 23 R 10 ‡

SHALLARD (J. T.) [*See* CLARSON, SHALLARD, & Co.]

SHANGHAI LITERARY AND SCIENTIFIC SOCIETY. [*See* ROYAL ASIATIC SOCIETY, NORTH CHINA BRANCH.]

SHANNON (CHARLES). The Youthful Queen: a Comedy. (Cumberland's Eng. Theatre.) 12mo. Lond., 1829. H 2 Q 10

SHARF (G.) [*See* COSTUMES FRANÇAIS.] A 7 P 26

SHARP (REV. CANON WILLIAM HEY), M.A. How does the Theory of Evolution bear upon Religious Belief? a Lecture. [*See* CHRISTIAN EVIDENCE SOCIETY.]

SHARP (JAMES A.) New Gazetteer; or, Topographical Dictionary of the British Islands and Narrow Seas. 2 vols. 8vo. Lond., 1852. D 11 T 2, 3

SHARP (JOHN), D.D., LORD ARCHBISHOP OF YORK. Life of; collected from his Diary, Letters, and several other authentic Testimonies by his Son, Thomas Sharp, D.D. 2 vols. 8vo. Lond., 1825. C 9 U 36, 37

SHARP (PETER). Flax, Tow, and Jute-spinning: a Handbook. 8vo. Dundee, 1882. A 11 Q 1

SHARP (THOMAS), D.D. Life of John Sharp, D.D., Lord Archbishop of York; collected from his Diary, Letters, and several other authentic Testimonies, by his Son. 2 vols. 8vo. Lond., 1825. C 9 U 36, 37

The Rubric in the Book of Common Prayer, and the Canons of the Church of England, considered. 8vo. Lond., 1787. G 12 P 8

SHARP-AYRES (MRS. H. M. E.) [*See* AYRES, MRS. H. M. E. SHARP-.]

SHARPE (CHARLES KIRKPATRICK). Ballad-book, 1823; reprinted and edited by the the late David Laing, LL.D. 8vo. Edinb., 1880. H 8 V 6

SHARPE (REV. JOHN), B.A. Monumenta Historica Britannica. [*See* PETRIE, H.] B 14 T 18 ‡

SHARPE (R. BOWDLER). Birds of South Africa. [*See* LAYARD, E. L.] A 13 V 7

SHARPE (REGINALD), D.C.L. Calendar of Letters from the Mayor Corporation of the City of London, circa A.D. 1350–70. Roy. 8vo. Lond., 1885. B 5 V 1

SHARPE (SAMUEL). Alexandrian Chronology, from the Building of the City till its Conquest by the Arabs, A.D. 640. Imp. 8vo. Lond., 1857. H 14 Q 4 ‡

Rudiments of a Vocabulary of Egyptian Hieroglyphics. Roy. 8vo. Lond., 1837. K 16 R 37

SHARPE (WILLIAM), M.D., &c. The Conqueror's Dream, and other Poems. 2nd ed. 12mo. Lond.,1879. H 7 U 24

The Cause of Colour among Races, and the Evolution of Physical Beauty. 12mo. Lond., 1879. A 1 V 10

SHARPE (WILLIAM). Sharpe's Crests of the Nobility and Gentry, designed and etched for the use of Herald Painters and Engravers. 4to. Lond. (n.d.) K 10 V 6

SHARPE'S LONDON MAGAZINE, 1845–47. 4 vols. 8vo. Lond., 1846–47. J 9 V 15–18

SHARPEY (W.) Elements of Anatomy. [*See* QUAIN, DR. J.] Libr.

SHATTUCK (LEMUEL). History of the Town of Concord, Middlesex County, Massachusetts, &c. 8vo. Boston, 1835. B 1 U 16

SHAW (ALEXANDER). Narrative of the Discoveries of Sir Charles Bell in the Nervous System. 8vo. Lond., 1839. A 12 R 18

SHAW (C. W.) The Kitchen and Market Garden. (Weale.) 12mo. Lond., 1882. A 17 Q 61

SHAW (EYRE M.) Fire Protection: a complete Manual of the Organization, Machinery, Discipline, and General Working of the Fire Brigade of London. 8vo. Lond., 1876. A 11 R 13

SHAW (GEORGE), M.D., &c. Zoological Lectures, delivered at the Royal Institution, in the years 1806–7. 2 vols. 8vo. Lond., 1809. A 13 T 29, 30

Zoology of New Holland; by George Shaw, M.D., F.R.S., &c. The Figures by James Sowerby, F.L.S. Vol. 1. (*All published.*) 4to. Lond., 1794. MA 1 Q 22 †

SHAW (GEORGE), M.D., &c., AND STEPHENS (JAMES FRANCIS), F.L.S., &c. General Zoology; or, Systematic Natural History. 14 vols. (in 28), roy. 8vo. Lond., 1800–26. A 13 T 1–28

SHAW (GEORGE A.), F.Z.S. Madagascar and France; with some Account of the Island, its People its Resources, and Development. With Illustrations. 8vo. Lond., 1885. D 1 T 32

SHAW (GEORGE J.) Brisbane Directory and Squatters' Guide, 1876. 8vo. Brisbane, 1875. ME 3 U

SHAW (HENRY), F.S.A. Illuminated Ornaments, selected from Manuscripts and early printed Books; drawn and engraved by Henry Shaw, F.S.A., with Descriptions by Sir Frederic Madden, K.H., F.R.S., &c. Fol. Lond., 1833. A 4 U 10 ‡

Specimens of Tile Pavements; drawn from existing authorities. Roy. 4to. Lond., 1858. A 2 U 35

Encyclopædia of Ornament. 4to. Lond., 1842. A 2 U 42

Dresses and Decorations of the Middle Ages. 2 vols. imp. 8vo. Lond., 1858. A 8 U 18, 19

SHAW (HENRY). Report of Irish State Trials, 1844. 8vo. Dublin (n.d.) F 4 Q 23

SHAW (JOHN), M.D., &c. Tramp to the Diggings; being Notes of a Ramble in Australia and New Zealand, in 1852. 8vo. Lond., 1852.* MD 1 R 3

Gallop to the Antipodes, returning overland through India. 8vo. Lond., 1858.* MD 1 R 5

SHAW (JOHN). Typical Australians: a Lecture delivered at the Yass Mechanics' Institute. (Pam. C.) Roy. 8vo. Yass, 1872. MJ 2 S 1

SHAW (ROBERT). Visits to High Tartary, Yárkand, and Káshghar (formerly Chinese Tartary), and return Journey over the Karakoram Pass. With Illustrations. 8vo. Lond., 1871. D 6 R 21

SHAW (R. NORMAN), R.A., AND NEWTON (ERNEST). Sketches for Cottages and other Buildings, designed to be constructed in the Patent Cement Slab System of W. H. Lascelles. Fol. Lond., 1878. A 23 P 2 ‡

SHAW (REV. STEBBING), B.D., &c. History and Antiquities of Staffordshire. Vol. 1, and vol. 2, part 1. (*All published.*) Fol. Lond., 1798–1801. B 14 U 15, 16 ‡

SHAW (PROF. THOMAS), D.D., &c. Travels; or, Observations relating to several parts of Barbary and the Levant. Fol. Oxford, 1738. D 38 Q 2 ‡

Supplement to a Book entituled, "Travels; or, Observations, &c." wherein some Objections, lately made against it, are fully considered and answered. Fol. Oxford, 1746. D 38 Q 2 ‡

SHAW (THOMAS B.), M.A. The Student's Specimens of English Literature; edited, with Additions, by W. Smith, D.C.L., &c. 8vo. Lond., 1872. J 6 Q 19

SHAW (THOMAS GEORGE). Wine, the Vine, and the Cellar. 8vo. Lond., 1863. A 1 R 6

SHAW (VERO), B.A. Illustrated Book of the Dog; with an Appendix on Canine Medicine and Surgery, by W. Gordon Stables, C.M., &c. 4to. Lond., 1881. A 5 P 16 †

SHAW (WILLIAM). Golden Dreams and Waking Realities; being the Adventures of a Gold-seeker in California and the Pacific Islands. 8vo. Lond., 1851. D 3 Q 38

The Land of Promise; or, My Impressions of Australia. 8vo. Lond., 1854.* MD 4 R 14

SHAW (W. HUDSON). George Villiers, First Duke of Buckingham. (Stanhope Essay for 1882.) 8vo. Oxford, 1882. C 9 R 29

SHAW, SAVILL, & CO. New Zealand Hand-book. 11th ed. 12mo. Lond., 1866. MD 1 S 51

Another copy. 15th ed. 12mo. Lond., 1883. MD 1 S 52

SHEA (DAVID). [*See* MIRKHOND MUHAMMED BEN K. BEN MAHMÚD; *and* DABISTAN, THE.]

SHEBBEARE (JOHN), M.D. Authentic Narrative of the Oppressions of the Islanders of Jersey; to which is prefixed a Succinct History of the Military Action, Constitution, Laws, Customs, and Commerce of that Island. 2 vols. 8vo. Lond., 1771. B 4 S 16, 17

SHEDD (Mrs. Julia A.) Famous Sculptors and Sculpture. Illustrated. 8vo. Boston, 1881. A 8 P 36

SHEE (Sir Martin Archer), R.A., &c. Elements of Art: a Poem, in Six Cantos; with Notes and a Preface. 8vo. Lond., 1809. A 7 S 25

Outline of a Plan for the National Encouragement of Historical Painting in the United Kingdom. 8vo. Lond., 1837. A 7 Q 13

Life of; by his Son, Martin Archer Shee. 2 vols. 8vo. Lond., 1860. C 9 U 34, 35

[*See* RENNIE, G.]

SHEE (Martin Archer). Life of Sir Martin Archer Shee. 2 vols. 8vo. Lond., 1860. C 9 U 34, 45

SHEFFIELD (John), Lord. [*See* GIBBON, E.] C 1 P 12

SHEIL (Lady). Glimpses of Life and Manners in Persia. With Illustrations. 8vo. Lond., 1856. D 6 P 6

SHEIL (Rt. Hon. Richard Lalor), M.P. Speeches of; with a Memoir, &c., edited by Thomas MacNevin, Esq. 8vo. Dublin, 1845. F 13 Q 14

Memoirs of; by W. T. Maccullagh. 2 vols. 8vo. Lond., 1855. C 4 Q 1, 2

SHELBURNE (William Petty), Earl of. [*See* LANSDOWNE, W., Earl of Shelburne, First Marquess of.]

SHELDON (Frederick). Minstrelsy of the English Border; being a Collection of Ballads, Ancient, Remodelled, and Original, founded on well-known Border Legends; with Illustrative Notes. 8vo. Lond., 1847. H 7 U 23

SHELDON (G. W.) American Painters; with eighty-three Examples of their Work engraved on Wood. 4to. Lond., 1879. A 8 T 20

SHELDON (J. P.) Dairy Farming; being the Theory, Practice, and Methods of Dairying. 4to. Lond., 1881. A 2 Q 6 †

SHELLEY (C. P. B.), C.E. Workshop Appliances. (Textbooks of Science.) 8vo. Lond., 1873. A 17 S 12

SHELLEY (Capt. G. E.) Monograph of the Nectariniidæ; or, Family of Sun-birds. Imp. 4to. Lond., 1876–80. A 4 P 7 †

SHELLEY (Mrs. Mary Wollstonecraft). Rambles in Germany and Italy, in 1840–43. 2 vols. 8vo. Lond., 1844. D 8 S 12, 13

[Life of]; by Helen Moore. 12mo. Philad., 1886. C 2 Q 47

Lives of the most Eminent Literary and Scientific Men of France. (Lard. Cab. Cyclo.) 2 vols. 18mo. Lond., 1838–39. K 1 S 24, 25

SHELLEY (Mrs. M. W.), BREWSTER (Sir David), AND MONTGOMERY (J.) Lives of the most Eminent Literary and Scientific Men of Italy, Spain, and Portugal. (Lard. Cab. Cyclo.) 3 vols. 18mo. Lond., 1835–37. K 1 S 29–31

SHELLEY (Percy Bysshe). Essays, Letters from Abroad, Translations, and Fragments; edited by Mrs. Shelley. 2 vols. 8vo. Lond., 1840. J 11 P 31, 32

Life of; by Thomas Medwin. 2 vols. 8vo. Lond., 1847. C 4 V 39, 40

Life of; by T. J. Hogg. Vols. 1, 2 (*all published.*) 2 vols. 8vo. Lond., 1858. C 4 V 41, 42

Poetical Works. 8vo. Lond., 1869. H 7 U 21

Prose Works. Edited by Harry Buxton Forman. 4 vols. 8vo. Lond., 1880. J 12 R 7–10

Recollections of the Last Days of Shelley and Byron; by E. J. Trelawny. 8vo. Lond., 1858. C 3 U 39

The Real Shelley: New Views of the Poet's Life; by J. C. Jeaffreson. 2 vols. 8vo. Lond., 1885. C 6 U 23, 24

[A Biography]; by John A. Symonds. (Eng. Men of Letts.) 8vo. Lond., 1878. C 1 U 29

Life of; by Prof. E. Dowden. 2 vols. 8vo. Lond., 1886. C 10 Q 42, 43

Memoir of; (with new Preface) by William Michael Rossetti. 8vo. Lond., 1886. C 2 T 34

Works of; edited by Mrs. Shelley. Roy. 8vo. Lond., 1850. H 6 V 21

Correspondence of Robert Southey with Shelley. [*See* SOUTHEY, R.] C 9 U 38

SHELTON (W. V.) Mechanic's Guide. 2nd ed. 8vo. Lond., 1875. A 11 P 14

SHELVOCKE (Capt. George). Voyage round the World by the way of the Great South Sea, performed in the years 1719–22. 8vo. Lond., 1726. D 10 R 20

SHENSTONE (William). Poetical Works of: with Life, Critical Dissertations and Explanatory Notes, by the Rev. George Gilfillan. 8vo. Edinb., 1857. H 8 V 10

Life and Poems of. [*See* British Poets, Chalmers, A., *and* Johnson, S.]

Poetical Works of. [*See* Poetical Works.]

SHENSTONE (W. A.) Methods of Glass-blowing for the use of Physical and Chemical Students. 12mo. Lond., 1886. A 11 P 8

SHEPHERD (A.) Tables for correcting the Apparent Distance of the Moon and a Star, from the Effects of Refraction and Parallax. Roy. 4to. Camb., 1772. A 2 Q 18 †

SHEPHERD (Richard Herne). Bibliography of Dickens: a Bibliographical List, arranged in chronological order, of the published Writing, in Prose and Verse of Charles Dickens (from 1834–80.) 8vo. Lond., 1880. K 17 P 20

Bibliography of Thackeray: a Bibliographical List, arranged in chronological order, of the published Writings in Prose and Verse, and the Sketches and Drawings of William Makepeace Thackeray (1829–80). 8vo. Lond., 1880. K 7 R 11

SHEPHERD (Richard Herne)—*continued.*
Bibliography of Carlyle: a Bibliographical List, arranged in chronological order, of the published Writings in Prose and Verse, of Thomas Carlyle (1820–81). 8vo. Lond., 1881.　　　　　　　　　　K 7 R 8

Bibliography of Swinburne: a Bibliographical List, arranged in Chronological order, of the published Writings of Algernon Charles Swinburne (1857–84.) 8vo. Lond., 1884.　　　　　　　　　　K 17 P 21

Lamb's Poetry for Children. [*See* Lamb, C. And M.]

SHEPHERD (Richard Herne), And WILLIAMSON Charles N.) Memoirs of the Life and Writings of Thomas Carlyle; with Personal Reminiscences and Selections from his Private Letters to numerous Correspondents, 1795–1881. 2 vols. 8vo. Lond., 1881.　　C 2 T 13, 14

SHEPHERD (Thomas). Lectures on the Horticulture of New South Wales, delivered at the Mechanics' School of Arts, Sydney. 8vo. Sydney, 1835.　　MA 1 P 41
Another copy. 8vo. Sydney, 1835.　　MA 1 Q 7
Lectures on Landscape Gardening in Australia. 8vo. Sydney, 1836.*　　　　　　　MA 1 P 39
Another copy. 8vo. Sydney, 1836.　　MJ 2 P 37

SHEPHERD (Thomas H.) Metropolitan Improvements; or, London in the 19th Century. 4to. Lond., 1827.　　　　　　　　　　B 4 U 15

SHEPHERD (Major W.), R.E. Prairie Experiences in handling Cattle and Sheep. With Illustrations. 8vo. Lond., 1884.　　　　　　　　D 3 S 39

SHEPPARD (Nathan). Shut up in Paris. 8vo. Lond., 1871.　　　　　　　　　　B 9 P 21

SHERBROOKE (Robert Lowe), Viscount. Impending Crisis: an Address to the Colonists of New South Wales, on the proposed Land Orders. (Pam. 19.) Sydney, 1847.*　　　　　　　　　MJ 2 Q 8

Speech on the Case of the Rev. [F. T. C.] Russell, in the Legislative Council, on Tuesday, the 7th of August, 1849. 8vo. Sydney, 1849.　　　MF 3 P 3

Speech on the Australian Colonies Bill, at a Meeting at the Rooms of the Society for the Reform of Colonial Government, June 1st, 1850. 8vo. Sydney, 1850.　　MF 3 P 3

Poems of a Life. 2nd ed. 8vo. Lond., 1885.　MH 1 R 7

SHERBURNE (Sir Edward). Life and Poems of. [*See* Chalmers, A.]

SHERER (John). The Gold-finder of Australia; how he went, how he fared, and how he made his Fortune. 8vo. Lond., 1853.*　　　　　　MD 7 P 19

Life and Adventures of a Gold-digger. 8vo. Lond., 1856.　　　　　　　　　　MD 7 P 22

SHERIDAN (Mrs. Frances). The Discovery: a Comedy. (Bell's Brit. Theatre.) 18mo. Lond., 1792.　H 2 P 43

SHERIDAN (Rt. Hon. Richard Brinsley Butler). [A Biography]; by Mrs. Oliphant. (Eng. Men of Letts.) 8vo. Lond., 1883.　　　　　　C 1 U 30

The Critic; or, a Tragedy Rehearsed: a Dramatic Piece. (Cumberland's Eng. Theatre.) 12mo. Lond., 1829.　　　　　　　　　　H 2 Q 16

Dramatic Works of: with a short Account of his Life, by G. G. S. 8vo. Lond., 1876.　　H 4 P 15

The Duenna: a Comic Opera. (Brit. Theatre.) 12mo. Lond., 1808.　　　　　　　H 1 P 19

Memoirs of the Life of; by Thomas Moore. 5th ed. 2 vols. 8vo. Lond., 1827.　　C 5 U 22, 23

Pizarro: a Tragic Play. (Cumberland's Eng. Theatre.) 12mo. Lond., 1829.　　　　H 2 Q 10

The Rivals: a Comedy. (Brit. Theatre.) 12mo. Lond., 1808.　　　　　　　　H 1 P 19

Another copy. [*See* Brit. Drama.]

Sheridaniana; or, Anecdotes of the Life of, his Table talk, and Bon-mots. 8vo. Lond., 1836.　　C 4 R 38

The School for Scandal: a Comedy. (Cumberland's Eng. Theatre.) 12mo. Lond., 1829.　　H 2 Q 10

Another copy. [*See* Farces 3.]

Speeches of. 5 vols. 8vo. Lond., 1816.　　F 4 P 1–5

Speeches of; with a Sketch of his Life. Edited by "A Constitutional Friend." 3 vols. 8vo. Lond., 1842.　　　　　　　　　　F 13 Q 15–17

A Trip to Scarborough: a Comedy. (Cumberland's Eng. Theatre.) 12mo. Lond., 1829.　　H 2 Q 10

Another copy. [*See* Modern Theatre 7.]

Works of; with a Memoir, by James P. Browne, M.D., containing Extracts from the Life, by Thomas Moore. 2 vols. 8vo. Lond., 1873.　　H 3 S 16, 17

SHERIDAN (Rt. Hon. R. B. B.), And COLMAN (George), Jun. The Forty Thieves: a Grand Romantic Drama. (Cumberland's Eng. Theatre.) 12mo. Lond., 1829.　　　　　　　　　H 2 Q 19

SHERLOCK (Frederick). Shakspeare on Temperance; with brief Annotations. [*See* Shakespeare, W.]

SHERMAN (Rev. James). Memoir of William Allen, F.R.S. 8vo. Lond., 1851.　　　　C 2 U 2

The Pastor's Wife: a Memoir of Mrs. Sherman. 12mo. Lond., 1853.　　　　　　　C 2 Q 30

SHERMAN (Mrs. Martha). The Pastor's Wife: a Memoir of Mrs. Sherman, of Surrey Chapel; by her Husband. 12mo. Lond., 1853.　　　　　　C 2 Q 30

SHERMAN (Gen. William T.) Memoirs of; by himself. 2 vols. 8vo. New York, 1875.　　C 8 R 42, 43
Another copy. 2nd ed., revised and corrected. 2 vols. 8vo. New York, 1886.　　　C 8 R 44, 45

SHERRIFF (J. L.) Australian Almanac. 12 vols. (in 4) 8vo. Sydney, 1865–77.　　　　　ME 4

SHERRIFF (JOHN), AND DOWNING (ROBERT). Gazetteer of New South Wales. 12mo. Sydney, 1862.
MD 1 S 28

SHERRIN (R. A. A.) Hand-book of the Fishes of New Zealand. · Prepared under the instruction of the Commissioner of Trade and Customs. 8vo. Auckland, 1886.*
MA 2 U 21

SHERWIN (WILLIAM), M.D., &c. Evidences of the Benefits of Homœopathy, and Statistics of its Success. (Pam. Cc.) 8vo. Sydney, 1863.
MA 2 S 15

Physiology and Pharmacodynamics; delivered at the School of Arts, Sydney, on Thursday, the 8th of January, 1863. (Pam. Cc. 8vo. Sydney, 1863.
MA 2 S 15

SHIELDS (PROF. CHARLES WOODRUFF), D.D. Final Philosophy; or, System of Perfectible Knowledge, issuing from the Harmony of Science and Religion. 8vo. Lond., 1877.
G 12 T 10

SHILLETO (ARTHUR RICHARD), M.A. Pausanias' Description of Greece. [*See* PAUSANIAS.]
D 7 P 41, 42

SHILLINGLAW (JOHN J.) Historical Records of Port Phillip: the First Annals of the Colony of Victoria. Roy. 8vo. Melb., 1879.*
MB 1 T 2

Cast away on the Auckland Isles. [*See* MUSGRAVE, CAPT. T.]
MD 4 V 1

Narrative of Arctic Discovery, from the Earliest Period to the Present Time; with Details of the Measures adopted by H.M. Government for the relief of the Expedition under Sir John Franklin. 8vo. Lond., 1850.
D 4 R 6

SHILLING MAGAZINE (THE). Edited by Samuel Lucas, M.A. 3 vols. 8vo. Lond., 1865–66.
J 10 U 13–15

SHINE (THOMAS). [*See* SOUDAN EXPEDITION.] MB 1 U 5

SHIP OF POOLES. [*See* BRANT, S.]

SHIPLEY (REV. ORBY), M.A. The Church and the World: Essays on Questions of the Day. 1st, 2nd, and 3rd series. 3 vols. 8vo. Lond., 1866–68.
G 12 T 5–7

SHIPP (LIEUT. JOHN). Memoirs of the Extraordinary Military Career of; written by himself. 3 vols. 8vo. Lond., 1829.
C 2 R 28–30

SHIPPING GAZETTE (THE). The Shipping Gazette and Sydney General Trade List. 9 vols. fol. Sydney, 1844–53.
ME

SHIPPING AND MERCANTILE GAZETTE (THE). Fol. Lond., 1844.
E

SHIPWRECK OF THE ANTELOPE. [*See* ANTELOPE.]
MD 4 P 24

SHIPWRECKS. History of Shipwrecks and Disasters at Sea, from the most authentic sources. (Const. Misc.) 2 vols. 8vo. Lond., 1833.
K 10 R 12, 13

SHIRLEY. [*See* SKELTON, J.]

SHIRLEY (EVELYN PHILIP), M.A., &c. History of the County of Monaghan. Fol. Lond., 1879.
B 14 R 2 ‡

SHIRLEY (JAMES). Dramatic Works and Poems of; with Notes, &c., by W. Gifford and the Rev. Alex. Dyce. 6 vols. 8vo. Lond., 1833.
H 4 S 14–19

SHIRLEY (JAMES), AND JOHNSON (C.) The Gamesters: a Comedy. (Bell's Brit. Theatre.) 18mo. Lond., 1792.
H 2 P 42

SHIRLEY (WILLIAM). Edward, the Black Prince: an Historical Tragedy. (Brit. Theatre.) 12mo. Lond., 1808.
H 1 P 14

SHOBERL (FREDERIC). South Sea Islands; being a Description of the Manners, Customs, Character, Religion, and State of Society among the various Tribes scattered over the Great Ocean, called the Pacific, or the South Sea. Illustrated. 2 vols. 12mo. Lond., 1824.
MD 4 T 6

Prince Albert and the House of Saxony; with a Memoir of the reigning Family of Saxe-Coburg-Gotha. 8vo. Lond., 1840.
C 1 U 1

Memoirs of Prince Eugene of Savoy. [*See* EUGENE OF SAVOY, PRINCE.]
C 5 T 20

History of the French Revolution. [*See* THIERS, L. A.]
B 8 S 6–10

Scenes of the Civil War in Hungary. [*See* SCENES.]
D 8 S 48

Excursions in Normandy; illustrative of the Character, Manners, Customs, and Traditions of the People. Edited from the Journal of "A Recent Traveller." 2 vols. 8vo. Lond., 1841.
D 8 Q 5, 6

SHOLL (R. J.) Journal of an Expedition from the Government Camp, Camden Harbour, to the southward of the Glenelg River, in North-western Australia. 8vo. Lond., 1866.
MD 7 Q 56

SHORE (HON. FREDERICK JOHN). Notes on Indian Affairs. 2 vols. 8vo. Lond., 1837.
B 10 S 28, 29

SHORE (HON. HENRY NOEL), R.N. Flight of the *Lapwing*: a Naval Officer's Jottings in China, Formosa, and Japan. 8vo. Lond., 1881.
D 6 R 28

SHORT (JOHN T.) North Americans of Antiquity; their Origin, Migrations, and Type of Civilization considered. 2nd ed. 8vo. New York, 1880.
A 1 W 18

SHORTER (THOMAS), "THOMAS BREVOIR." The Two Worlds: the Natural and the Spiritual. 8vo. Lond., 1864.
G 13 R 28

SHORTHOUSE (J. H.) On the Platonism of Wordsworth: a Paper read to the Wordsworth Society, July 19th, 1881. 8vo. Birmingham, 1881.
J 10 S 2

SHORTLAND (LIEUT. JOHN). Journal of. [*See* PHILLIP, A.]
MD 4 Q 14 †

SHORTLAND (EDWARD), M.A., &c. Southern Districts of New Zealand: a Journal, with passing Notices of the Customs of the Aborigines. 8vo. Lond., 1851. MD 4 S 27

Traditions and Superstitions of the New Zealanders; with Illustrations of their Manners and Customs. 2nd ed. 12mo. Lond., 1856.* MB 2 P 14

Maori Religion and Mythology, illustrated by Translations of Traditions, Karakia, &c.; to which are added, Notes on Maori Tenure of Land. 12mo. Lond., 1882. MG 1 P 19

SHUCKARD (W. E.) History and Natural Arrangement of Insects. [*See* SWAINSON, W.] K 1 U 18

SHUCKBURGH (E. S.), M.A. Richard Farmer, D.D. (Master of Emmanuel, 1775-1797): an Essay. [*See* DILLINGHAM, DR. W.] C 6 P 13

SHUCKFORD (REV. SAMUEL), D.D. Sacred and Profane History of the World connected, from the Creation of the World to the Dissolution of the Assyrian Empire at the Death of Sardanapalus, &c. 5th ed. 4 vols. 8vo. Lond., 1819. G 12 S 25–28

SHUNK (WILLIAM F.), C.E. Practical Treatise on Railway Curves and Location, for Young Engineers. 12mo. Philad., 1881. A 6 R 22

SIBBALD (JAMES ROMANES). Divine Comedy of Dante; a Translation. [*See* DANTE ALIGHIERI.]

SIBBALD (SIR ROBERT), KNT., M.D., History, Ancient and Modern, of the Sheriffdoms of Fife and Kinross; with a Description of both, and of the Firths of Forth and Tay, and the Islands in them. 8vo. Cupar-Fife, 1803. B 13 T 7

Remains of Sir Robert Sibbald, Knt., M.D.; containing his Autobiography, Memoirs of the Royal College of Physicians, portions of his Literary Correspondence, and an Account of his MSS. 8vo. Edinb., 1837. C 7 T 48

SIBERIA. Revelations of; by "A Banished Lady." Edited by Colonel Lach Szyrma. 2 vols. 8vo. Lond., 1853. D 6 P 3, 4

SIBILIAN (P. CLEMENT). Collection des Médailles Grecques autonomes de Son Excellence Subhy Pacha. 8vo. Constantinoplé, 1874. A 13 S 32

SIBLEY (JOHN). Travels in the Interior Parts of America. [*See* LEWIS, CAPT. M.] D 3 T 45

SIBORNE (CAPT. W.) History of the War in France and Belgium in 1815; containing Details of the Battles of Qxatre-Bras, Ligny, Wavre, and Waterloo. 2nd ed. 2 vols. 8vo. Lond., 1844. B 8 R 33, 34

Atlas of Plates to [the above.] Fol. Lond., 1844. B 14 U 17 ‡

SIBREE (REV. JAMES), JUN., F.R.G.S. The Great African Island: Chapters on Madagascar. 8vo. Lond., 1880. D 1 V 27

Madagascar Bibliography. In two parts. 8vo. Antananarivo, 1885. K 7 R 30

Philosophy of History. [*See* HEGEL, G. W. F.] B 14 P 50

[*See* ANTANANARIVO ANNUAL.] E

4 S

SIBSON (FRANCIS), M.D., &c. Collected Works of. Edited by W. M. Ord. 4 vols. 8vo. Lond., 1881. A 13 R 5–8

SIBTHORP (RICHARD WALDO): a Biography, told chiefly in his own Correspondence, by the Rev. J. Fowler, M.A. 8vo. Lond., 1880. C 9 U 39

SICARD (ROCH AMBROISE CUCURRON), ABBÉ. [*See* BARRIÈRE, J. F., 18.] C 1 T 18

SICARDUS (CREMONENSIS EPISCOPUS). Mitrale et Chronicon. [*See* MIGNE, J. P., SERIES LATINA, 213.]

SICK MAN (THE), and the Prisoner Visited. 12mo. Lond., 1875. MG 1 Q 32

SIDDONS (HENRY). Time's a Tell-tale: a Comedy. [*See* MODERN THEATRE, 10.]

SIDDONS (MRS. SARAH). Life of; by Thomas Campbell. 2 vols. 8vo. Lond., 1834. C 5 T 23, 24

Life of. [*See* FITZGERALD, P.] C 7 T 35, 36

Memoirs of; interspersed with Anecdotes of Authors and Actors, by James Boaden. 2 vols. 8vo. Lond., 1827. C 9 V 33, 34

SIDEN (CAPT. THOMAS). L'Histoire des Sevarambes: Peuples qui habitent une partie du troisième Continent, communément appelé la Terre Australe. 5 vols. 18mo. Paris, 1677–79. MJ 1 P 24–28

Another copy. 18mo. Amsterdam, 1702. MJ 1 P 30

History of the Sevarites, or Sevarambi; a Nation inhabiting part of the third Continent, commonly called Terræ Australes Incognitæ. 18mo. Lond., 1700. MJ 1 P 29

History of the Sevarambians, a People of the South Continent. 8vo. Lond., 1738.* MJ 1 T 33

SIDENBLADH (DR. ELIS). [*See* PHILADELPHIA INTERNATIONAL AND CENTENNIAL EXHIBITION, 1876.]

SIDGWICK (ALFRED), B.A. Fallacies: a View of Logic from the Practical Side. 8vo. Lond., 1883. G 7 S 14

SIDGWICK (PROF. HENRY). Outlines of the History of Ethics for English Readers. 8vo. Lond., 1886. G 7 S 13

Methods of Ethics. 8vo. Lond., 1874. G 12 T 3

Another copy. 3rd ed. 8vo. Lond., 1884. G 12 T 4

Principles of Political Economy. 8vo. Lond., 1883. F 6 V 17

SIDMOUTH (HENRY ADDINGTON) VISCOUNT. Life and Correspondence of the Right Hon. Henry Addington, first Viscount Sidmouth; by the Hon. G. Pellew, D.D. 3 vols. 8vo. Lond., 1847. C 9 U 43, 44

SIDNEY (ALGERNON). A Review; by Gertrude M. Ireland Blackburne. 8vo. Lond., 1885. C 4 Q 45

Discourses concerning Government. 8vo. Edinb., 1750. F 4 Q 15, 16

Life and Times of, 1622–83; by Alex. Charles Ewald, F.S.A. 2 vols. 8vo. Lond., 1873. C 9 V 10, 11

SIDNEY (REV. EDWIN), A.M. Life of Lord Hill; G.C.B. 8vo. Lond., 1845. C 8 R 24

SIDNEY (Hon. Henry), Earl of Romney. [*See* Romney, Hon. H. Sidney, Earl of.]

SIDNEY (John). Voice from the Far Interior of Australia; by "A Bushman." 12mo. Lond., 1847. MD 2 Q 12

SIDNEY (Sir Philip), Knt. Works of, in Prose and Verse. [with a Life, &c.] 14th ed. 3 vols. 8vo. Lond., 1724-25. J 9 R 25-27
[A Biography]: by J. A. Symonds. (Eng. Men of Letts.) 8vo. Lond., 1886. C 1 U 38

SIDNEY (Samuel). Sidney's Emigrant's Journal and Traveller's Magazine. 2nd series. 12mo. Lond., 1850. MD 2 P 6

Three Colonies of Australia: New South Wales, Victoria, South Australia; their Pastures, Copper-mines, and Gold-fields. With Engravings. 8vo. Lond., 1852.* MB 1 S 1

Another copy. 2nd ed., revised by the Author, with Additions. 8vo. Lond., 1853. MB 1 S 6

Gallops and Gossips in the Bush of Australia; or, Passages in the Life of Alfred Barnard. 12mo. Lond., 1854.* MJ 1 P 13

The Pig. [*See* Youatt, W.]

SIDNEY (Samuel and John). Sidney's Australian Hand-book: How to settle and succeed in Australia; comprising every Information for intending Emigrants, by "A Bush-man." 9th ed. 18mo. Lond., 1849. MD 2 P 5

SIEBE (Henry). Conquest of the Sea; a Book about Divers and Diving. 12mo. Lond., 1873. A 6 R 40

SIEBER (F. W.) [*See* Brown, R.]

SIEBOLD (Ph. Fr. de), Dr. Fauna Japonica, sive Descriptio animalium, quæ in itinere per Japoniam aus-piciis superiorum, qui summum in India Batava Imperium tenent, suscepto, annis 1823-30 collegit, notis, observa-tionibus et adumbrationibus illustravit. 5 vols. imp. 4to. Leyden, 1833-50. A 4 V 5-9 ‡

Flora Japonica sive Plantæ, quas in Imperio Japonico collegit. Sectio prima continens Plantas ornatui vel usui inservientes. 2 vols. imp. 4to. Leyden, 1835-70. A 4 V 3, 4 ‡

Documents Importants sur la Découverte des Iles de Bonin, par des Navigateurs Néerlandais, en 1639. 8vo. La Haye, 1843. MD 5 R 25

SIEBOLD (Ph. Fr. de), et HOFFMANN (J.) Bibliotheca Japonica, sive selecta quædam opera Sinico-Japonica in unum corum, cui literis Japonicis vacant. 6 vols. (in 3) imp. 4to. Leyden, 1833 11. K 27 P 7-9 ‡

SIEBOLD (Henry von). Notes on Japanese Archæology, with especial reference to the Stone Age. Fol. Yoko-hama, 1879. B 15 S 14 ‡

SIEMENS (C. William), F.R.S., &c. On Determining the Depth of the Sea without the Use of the Sounding line. (Roy. Soc. Pubs., I.) 4to. Lond., 1876. A 11 P 5 †

On the Conservation of Solar Energy: a Collection of Papers and Discussions. 8vo. Lond., 1883. A 3 T 25

SIEVEKING (Edward H.), M.D., &c. Pathological Anatomy. [*See* Jones, C. H.] A 13 P 40

SIGEBERTUS (Gemblacensis Monachus). Opera omnia. [*See* Migne, J. P., Series Latina, 160.]

SIGMA. [*See* Money.]

SIGOURNEY (Mrs.) Essay on the Genius of Mrs. Hemans. [*See* Hemans, Mrs. F. D.]

SIGRAIS (C. G. Bourdon de). Considerations sur les Gaulois, les Francs et les Français. [*See* Guizot, F. P. G., Histoire de France 31.]

SIGSBEE (Charles D.), U.S.N. Deep-sea Sounding and Dredging. 4to. Wash., 1880. A 5 R 3 †

SIGSTON (James). Memoir of the Venerable William Bramwell. 32mo. Wakefield (n.d.) G 9 P 2

SIKANDAR (Nawab), Begum of Bhopál, G.C.S.I. Pil-grimage to Mecca: translated from the original Urdú, and edited by Mrs. Willoughby-Osborne. 8vo. Lond., 1870. D 4 T 22

SIKES (William Wirt). British Goblins: Welsh Folk-lore, Fairy Mythology, Legends and Traditions. With Illus-trations by T. H. Thomas. 8vo. Lond., 1880. B 5 S 32

SILK: Article on the Silk and Glove Trades, from the *Westminster Review*, No. 32, for April, 1832. Lond., 1832. F 6 V 10

The Silk Question, *London Magazine*, January, 1829. (Pam. 14.) 8vo. Lond., 1829. MJ 2 Q 4

[*See* China.] A 11 V 4

SILLERY (Marchioness of). [*See* Genlis, Comtesse de.]

SILLIG (Julius). Dictionary of Artists of Antiquity, Archi-tects, Carvers, Engravers, Modellers, Painters, Sculptors, Statuaries, and Workers in Bronze, Gold, Ivory, and Silver; to which are added, C. Plinii Secundi Naturalis Historiæ, Libri 34-36, c. 1-5. 8vo. Lond., 1836. A 8 Q 19

SILLIMAN (Prof. Benjamin). Visit to Europe in 1851. 2 vols. 8vo. New York, 1854. D 8 Q 36, 37

[*See* American Journal of Science and Arts.]

SILLYLAW. For the Mercantile Community in general, this Poem of Sillylaw, was written by their Comic and Laughter-loving, yet Satiric Joker, "Reltha." 8vo. Melb., 1859. M 11 Q 4

SILOS. Silos for preserving English Fodder Crops stored in a Green State; Notes on the Ensilage of Grasses, Clovers, Vetches, &c., compiled and annotated by the Sub-Editor of *The Field*. 2nd ed. 8vo. Lond., 1884. A 1 Q 20

SILURIENSIS (Leolinus). [*See* Anatomy of Tobacco.]

SILVAGNI (David). Rome: its Princes, Priests, and People; being a Translation of Silvagni's Work, by Fanny Maclaughlin. 2 vols. 8vo. Lond., 1885. D 8 T 9, 10

SILVER (S. W.) [*See* York Gate Library.]

SILVER (S. W.), & CO. Guide to Australasia and Itinerary to and in the Colonies of Victoria, New South Wales, Queensland, South Australia, Western Australia, Tasmania, and New Zealand. 8vo. Lond., 1863. MD 7 Q 37

Hand-book for Australia and New Zealand; with Sensors' Chart of the World. 12mo. Lond., 1874. MD 2 Q 8

Hand-book for Australia and New Zealand (including also the Fiji Islands); with new Map of the Colonies. 4th ed. 12mo. Lond., 1884. MD 2 Q 9

Australian Grazier's Guide; by T. A. Browne. 12mo. Lond., 1879.* MA 1 P 12

Australian Grazier's Guide: No. 2. Cattle; by T. A. Browne. 12mo. Lond., 1881. MA 1 P 14

Hand-book to the Transvaal, British South Africa. 12mo. Lond., 1878. D 1 Q 22

SILVERLEAF. [*See* LLOYD, MRS. G. A.]

SILVERSMITH (JULIUS). Practical Hand-book for Miners, Metallurgists, and Assayers. 12mo. New York, 1867. A 9 P 28

SILVERTHORNE (ARTHUR), A.M.I.C.E. London and Provincial Water Supplies; with the latest Statistics of Metropolitan and Provincial Water Works. Roy. 8vo. Lond., 1884. F 4 R 15

SILVESTER (EDWARD KENNEDY). New South Wales Constitution Bill: the Speeches in the Legislative Council of New South Wales, on the Second Reading of the Bill for framing a New Constitution for the Colony. 8vo. Sydney, 1853.* MF 1 Q 6

Another copy. 8vo. Sydney, 1853. MF 1 Q 15

Another copy. 8vo. Sydney, 1853. MF 3 R 21

Another copy. 8vo. Sydney, 1853. MJ 2 Q 14

Production, Industry, and Resources of New South Wales. [*See* ST. JULIAN, C.] MD 1 T 37

SILVESTER II (GERBERTUS), PAPA. Opera omnia. [*See* MIGNE, J. P., SERIES LATINA, 139.]

SILVESTRE (J. B.) Universal Palæography; or, Facsimiles of Writings of all Nations and Periods. Translated, &c., by Sir F. Madden. Text. 2 vols. roy. 8vo. Lond., 1849. B 15 S 4, 5

Plates to [the above.] 2 vols. el. fol. Lond., 1849-50. B 5 R 18, 19 ‡

SILVESTRE DE SACY (BARON). [*See* SACY, BARON S. DE.]

SIM (JAMES). Protection; with Suggestions for the introduction of a National Protective Tariff, and our Fiscal Policy: its Commercial, Social, and Moral Aspect. 4th ed. 8vo. Melb., 1861. MF 1 Q 3

SIMCOX (EDITH). Natural Law: an Essay in Ethics. 2nd ed. 8vo. Lond., 1878. G 12 S 7

SIMCOX (GEORGE AUGUSTUS), M.A. History of Latin Literature, from Ennius to Boethius. 2 vols 8vo. Lond., 1883. B 15 Q 36, 37

SIMCOX (HOWARD). Rustic Rambles, in Rhyme; collected in various parts of Victoria. 12mo. Ballarat, 1866. MH 1 R 34

SIME (JAMES). The Mosaic Record in Harmony with the Geological. 8vo. Edinb., 1854. A 9 P 16

SIME (JAMES). Lessing. With Portraits. 2nd ed. 2 vols. 8vo. Lond., 1879. C 9 T 12, 13

SIMEON (REV. CHARLES), M.A. Memoirs of the Life of; with a Selection from his Writings and Correspondence, edited by the Rev. William Carus, M.A. 3rd ed. 8vo. Lond., 1848. C 2 T 37

SIMEON (STEPHEN L.) Russians and Germans. [*See* TISSOT, V.] B 12 U 13

SIMKIN (RICHARD). War in Egypt. [*See* EGYPT.]

SIMMONDS (JAMES). Lyrics: a Collection of Songs, Ballads, and Poems. 12mo. Sydney, 1858. MH 1 R 37

SIMMONDS (P. L.), F.R.C.I. Commercial Products of the Vegetable Kingdom. 8vo. Lond., 1854. K 9 S 3

Dictionary of Trade Products, Commercial, Manufacturing, and Technical Terms. 12mo. Lond., 1858. K 9 T 17

Tropical Agriculture: a Treatise on the Culture, Preparation, Commerce, and Consumption of the Principal Products of the Vegetable Kingdom. 8vo. Lond., 1877. A 1 S 15

Waste Products and Undeveloped Substances: a Synopsis of Progress made in their Economic Utilisation during the last Quarter of a Century at Home and Abroad. 8vo. Lond., 1873. F 5 S 31

Animal Food Resources of different Nations. 8vo. Lond., 1885. F 5 R 14

Animal Products; their Preparation, Commercial Uses, and Value. 8vo. Lond., 1877. A 16 R 33

Another copy. [*See* SOUTH KENSINGTON MUSEUM, 14.]

Dictionary of Useful Animals and their Products; including a Glossary of Trade and Technical Terms. 12mo. Lond., 1883. A 14 Q 51

Fibres and Cordage. (Brit. Manuf. Indust.) 12mo. Lond., 1876. A 17 S 28

SIMMONS (ALFRED). Old England and New Zealand: the Government, Laws, Churches, Public Institutions, and the Resources of New Zealand popularly and critically compared with those of the Old Country. 8vo. Lond., 1879. MD 4 V 41

SIMMS (FREDERICK WALTER), C.E. Practical Tunnelling. 3rd ed., revised and extended by D. Kinnear Clark, M.I.C.E. 4to. Lond., 1877. A 1 R 7 †

Treatise on the Principles and Practice of Levelling; 6th ed., with the addition of Mr. Law's Practical Examples for setting out Railway Curves, and Mr. Trautwine's Field Practice in laying out Circular Curves. 8vo. Lond., 1875. A 6 S 15

SIMMS (JOSEPH), M.D. New Physiognomical Chart of Character. 8vo. Glasgow, 1873.   A 12 P 13

Nature's Revelations of Character; or, Physiognomy Illustrated. 8vo. New York, 1879.   A 13 R 12

Lectures (on Physiognomy, &c.) 8vo. Lond., 1873.   A 13 R 13
    Education on Physiognomical Principles.
    The Natural History of the Earth.
    Physiognomical Principles.
    Physiognomy; or, Signs of Character as manifested in the Human Physique.
    Linguistiveness and Literativeness: or, Spoken and Written Language. Monoeroticity; or, Mating Love, and Elevativeness, or Aspiration.
    The Secrets of Success in Life.
    Animalimitationality and Mentimitativeness; or, Animal and Mental Imitation, and their Tendencies and Influences on Society.
    Physiognomical Aspects of Reverence, Intuition, and Faith.
    Philosophia Amoris et Matrimonii; or, the Philosophy and Facts of Love and Marriage.
    Beauty.
    Record of the Health and Character.

SIMON (EDOUARD). Grammaire du Blason ; ou, la science des armoiries. 12mo. Paris, 1885.   K 10 S 3

The Emperor William and his Reign. 2 vols. 8vo. Lond., 1886.   C 7 U 57, 58

SIMON (ÉDOUARD ÉTIENNE), "ÉDOUARD LOCKROY." The Great French Revolution, 1785–93, narrated in the Letters of Madame J——; edited by Edouard Lockroy. 8vo. Lond., 1881.   B 9 P 32

SIMON (JAMES). Essay on Irish Coins, and of the Currency of Foreign Monies in Ireland; with Mr. Snelling's Supplement. 4to. Dublin, 1810.   A 1 P 19 †

SIMON (JULES). La Réforme de l'Enseignement Secondaire. 8vo. Paris, 1874.   G 12 Q 2

Natural Religion; translated by J. W. Cole. 8vo. Lond., 1857.   G 7 S 12

The Government of M. Thiers, from 8th February, 1871, to 24th May, 1873. From the French. 2 vols. 8vo. Lond., 1879.   B 8 R 29, 30

SIMOND (LOUIS). Journal of a Tour and Residence in Great Britain, 1810–11. 2 vols. 8vo. Edinb., 1817.   D 7 T 41, 42

SIMONIN (L.) Mines and Miners; or, Underground Life. Translated and edited by H. W. Bristow, F.R.S. Roy. 8vo. Lond., 1869.   A 9 V 9

SIMONIS (JOHANNES). Arcarum Formarum nominum Hebræ Linguæ, sive de Significatione Formali Tractatus Philologicus. Sm. 4to. Haise, 1735.   K 15 P 8

SIMONNÉ (PROF. TEODORO). Clave de los Ejercicios del Método para aprender á leer, escribir y hablar el Frances. 8vo. Lond., 1876.   K 11 U 35

Método para aprender á leer, escribir y hablar el Frances, segun el verdadero Sistema Ollendorff. 8vo. Lond., 1876.   K 11 U 34

New Method of Learning to Read, Write, and Speak the Spanish Language. [*See* VELASQUEZ DE LA CADENA, PROF. M.]

SIMONS (W. VAZIE), F.C.S. Catalogue of Foreign Minerals in the possession of the Mining Department, Melbourne, Victoria. 8vo. Melb., 1866.   MA 2 Q 35

SIMPSON (ALEXANDER). The Sandwich Islands: Progress of Events since their Discovery by Captain Cook. 8vo. Lond., 1843.   MD 4 U 16

SIMPSON (ARCHIBALD H.), M.A. Hand-book of the Crown Lands Alienation Acts of New South Wales, and the Regulations, with the Forms, and full Practical Directions for the use of Free Selectors and Purchasers of Crown Lands. 8vo. Sydney, 1882.   MF 1 R 31

SIMPSON (EDWIN). Dramatic Unities in the Present Day. 12mo. Lond., 1874.   J 7 Q 39

SIMPSON (SIR GEORGE). Narrative of a Journey round the World, 1841–42. 2 vols. 8vo. Lond., 1847.   D 9 S 14, 15

SIMPSON (H. P. M.) [*See* WORSAAE, DR. J. J. A.]   B 7 S 44

SIMPSON (JAMES). Philosophy of Education, with its Practical Application to a System and Plan of Popular Education as a National Object. 2nd ed. 8vo. Edinb., 1836.   G 17 Q 4

Paris after Waterloo: Notes taken at the Time. 8vo. Lond., 1853.   D 7 Q 37

SIMPSON (J. PALGRAVE). Letters from the Danube. 2 vols. 8vo. Lond., 1847.   D 9 Q 42, 43

SIMPSON (SIR JAMES Y.), BART., M.D., &c. Archæological Essays; edited by J. Stuart, LL.D. 2 vols. sm. 4to. Edinb., 1872.   B 13 P 36, 37

Memoir of; by J. Duns, D.D. 8vo. Edinb., 1873.   C 9 U 12

SIMPSON (LEONARD). Correspondence of Schiller and Körner; with Biographical Sketches and Notes. 3 vols. 8vo. Lond., 1849.   C 4 S 37–39

SIMPSON (LEONARD FRANCIS). Literature of Italy. 8vo. Lond., 1851.   B 30 Q 1

SIMPSON (M. C. M.) Correspondence of Alexis de Tocqueville. [*See* TOCQUEVILLE, A. DE.]   C 5 P 1, 2

Modern History. [*See* MICHELET, J.]   B 7 S 37

Monsieur Guizot in Private Life. [*See* WITT, MME. DE.]   C 7 P 12

[*See* SENIOR, N. W.]

SIMPSON (THOMAS). Narrative of the Discoveries on the North Coast of America, during the years 1836–39. 8vo. Lond., 1843.   D 3 T 7

SIMPSON (WILLIAM), F.R.G.S. Meeting the Sun: a Journey all round the World, through Egypt, China, Japan, and California. 8vo. Lond., 1874.   D 9 S 11

SIMPSON (WILLIAM). Campaign in the Crimea. [*See* BRACKENBURY, G.]   B 12 V 11

SIMPSON (REV. WILLIAM SPARROW), D.D., &c. Chapters in the History of Old S. Paul's. 8vo. Lond., 1881.
B 6 R 28

SIMRÓCK (KARL). Die deutschen Volksbücher. 13 vols. 12mo. Frankfurt, 1845–67. J 16 P 1–13

SIMS (RICHARD) Manual for the Genealogist, Topographer, Antiquary, and Legal Professor; consisting of Descriptions of Public Records. Parochial and other Registers, Wills, County and Family Histories, Heraldic Collections in Public Libraries, &c. 2nd ed. 8vo. Lond., 1861.
K 11 P 19

SIMS (T.) Dyeing and Bleaching. (Brit. Manuf. Indust.) 12mo. Lond., 1876. A 17 S 33

SIMSON (FRANK B.) Letters on Sport in Eastern Bengal. Illustrated. Imp. 8vo. Lond., 1886. D 4 V 37

SIMSON (JAMES). Contributions to Natural History, and Papers on other Subjects. 8vo. Edinb., 1875. A 16 T 26

SIMSON (R.), MATHESON (J.), AND WILSON (J.) Letter to the Rev. the Moderator of the General Assembly of the Presbyterian Church of Victoria. 8vo. Melb., 1870. MG 1 Q 39

SIMSON (WALTER). History of the Gipsies: with Specimens of the Gipsy Language. 8vo. Lond., 1865. A 1 V 13

SINCLAIR (A.) Locomotive Engine Running and Management: a Treatise on Locomotive Engines. 4th ed. 8vo. New York, 1885. A 6 R 18

SINCLAIR (A. C.), AND FYFE (LAURENCE R.) Handbook of Jamaica for 1883; comprising Historical, Statistical, and General Information concerning the Island. 8vo. Lond., 1883. E

SINCLAIR (DAVID). History of Wigan. 2 vols. 4to. Wigan, 1882. B 2 U 3, 4

SINCLAIR (MRS. FRANCIS), JUNR. Indigenous Flowers of the Hawaiian Islands: Forty-four Plates painted in Water-colours and described. Fol. Lond., 1885. MA 1 R 17 ‡

SINCLAIR (GEORGE). Hortus Gramineus Woburnensis; or, an Account of the Results of Experiments on the Produce and Nutritive Qualities of different Grasses and other Plants. Illustrated with dried Specimens of the Plants. Roy. fol. Lond., 1816. A 21 P 19 ‡

SINCLAIR (JAMES). Gardener's Magazine. 8vo. Melb., 1855–56. MA 1 Q 38

SINCLAIR (JAMES). History of Polled Aberdeen Cattle. [*See* MACDONALD, J.]

SINCLAIR (RT. HON. SIR JOHN), BART., P.C. Code of Health and Longevity. 4th ed. 8vo. Lond., 1818. A 12 U 3

Correspondence of; with Reminiscences of the most distinguished Characters during the last Fifty Years. 2 vols. 8vo. Lond., 1831. C 9 V 44, 45

SINCLAIR (RT. HON. SIR JOHN), BART., P.C.—*continued.*
Essays on Agriculture, Farming, Breeding, and Fattening Cattle, and on Longevity. 8vo. Lond., 1818. A 1 S 18

Statistical Account of Scotland, drawn up from the Communications of the Ministers of the different Parishes. 21 vols. 8vo. Edinb., 1791–99. F 12 U 1–21

SINCLAIR (REV. JOHN), A.M. Dissertations, vindicating the Church of England. 8vo. Lond., 1833. G 12 Q 3

SINCLAIR (J. D.) An Autumn in Italy. (Const. Misc.) 18mo. Edinb., 1829. K 10 Q 34

SINDING (PROF. PAUL C.) History of Scandinavia, from the Early Times of the Northmen, the Sea-kings, and Vikings, to the Present Day. 8vo. Lond., 1866. B 2 R 11

SINGER (SAMUEL WELLER), F.S.A. Correspondence of Henry Hyde, Earl of Clarendon, and of his Brother, Laurence Hyde, Earl of Rochester. [*See* CLARENDON, HENRY HYDE, EARL OF.] C 18 11, 12 ‡

Life of Wolsey. [*See* CAVENDISH, G.] C 10 P 42

Text of Shakespeare vindicated from the Interpolations and Corruptions advocated by John Payne Collier, Esq., in his Notes and Emendations. 8vo. Lond., 1853. H 3 Q 17

SINGLETON (J.), M.D. Lecture: Subject, "The Effects of Intoxicating Drinks upon the Community, considered in their Moral and Physical Relations." 8vo. Melb., 1853. MG 1 Q 31

Another copy. 8vo. Melb., 1853. MG 1 Q 40

SINGLETON AND PATRICK'S PLAINS BENEVOLENT SOCIETY. Rules and Regulations. 18mo. Maitland, 1861. MF 3 P 18

SINKER (ROBERT), B.D. Catalogue of the English Books printed before 1601, now in the Library of Trinity College, Cambridge. 8vo. Camb., 1885. K 7 S 5

SINNETT (E. W. P.) Kurzgefasste englische Sprachlehre für Anfänger. 12mo. Hamburgh, 1831. K 11 V 27

SINNETT (FREDERICK). Account of the "Rush" to Port Curtis, including Letters addressed to the *Argus*, as Special Correspondent from the Fitzroy River. 12mo. Geelong, 1859. MJ 2 P 30

Account of the Colony of South Australia; prepared for distribution at the International Exhibition of 1862; together with a Catalogue of all the Products of South Australia. 8vo. Lond., 1862.* MD 1 V 20

Another copy. 8vo. Adelaide, 1862. MD 1 V 52

SINNETT (MRS. PERCY). By-ways of History, from the 12th to the 16th Century. 2 vols. (in 1) 8vo. Lond., 1847. B 14 Q 43

Switzerland in 1847. [*See* MUGGE, T.] B 7 T 15, 16

SIRR (HENRY CHARLES), M.A. Ceylon and the Cingalese; their History, Government, and Religion. 2 vols. 8vo. Lond., 1850. D 6 P 14, 15

SISMONDI (J. C. L. DE). Fall of the Roman Empire. (Lard. Cab. Cyclo.) 2 vols. 12mo. Lond., 1834.
K 1 T 10, 11

Historical View of the Literature of the South of Europe. 4 vols. 8vo. Lond., 1823. B 7 T 25–28

History of the Italian Republics. 12mo. Lond., 1832. B 12 P 29

Another copy. (Lard. Cab. Cyclo.) 12mo. Lond., 1832. K 1 T 32

Political Economy and the Philosophy of Government: a Series of Essays selected from his Works. 8vo. Lond., 1847. F 5 U 12

SITWELL (SIDNEY MARY). Growth of the English Colonies. (Highways of History.) 12mo. Lond., 1884.
B 14 P 39

SIVEWRIGHT (J.) [*See* PREECE, W. H.] A 17 S 18

SIX OLD ENGLISH CHRONICLES; edited, with Notes, by J. A. Giles, D.C.L. 12mo. Lond., 1847.
B 3 P 14

SIXPENNY MAGAZINE (THE). 8vo. Lond. (n.d.)
J 10 V 16

SIXTUS V. Life and Times of; by Baron Hübner; translated by H. E. H. Jerningham. 2 vols. 8vo. Lond., 1872. C 9 U 41, 42

SJÖGREN (JOH. ANDREAS). Livisch-deutsches und deutsch-livisches Wörterbuch; bearbeitet von F. J. Wiedemann. Roy. 4to. St. Petersburg, 1861. K 27 P 16 ‡

Livische Grammatik nebst Sprachproben; ein leitung von F. J. Wiedemann. Roy. 4to. St. Petersburg, 1861.
K 27 P 15 ‡

SKEAT (REV. WALTER W.), M.A. Contested Etymologies in the Dictionary of the Rev. W. W. Skeat. [*See* WEDGWOOD, H.]

Etymological Dictionary of the English Language. 4to. Oxford, 1882. K 15 U 1

History of English Rhythms. [*See* GUEST, E.]

List of English Words the Etymology of which is illustrated by comparison with Icelandic; prepared in the form of an Appendix to "Cleasby and Vigfusson's Icelandic-English Dictionary." 4to. Oxford, 1876. K 14 S 17

Shakspeare's Plutarch; being a Selection from the Lives in North's "Plutarch," which illustrate Shakespeare's Plays. 8vo. Lond., 1875. C 4 Q 29

Specimens of Early English. [*See* MORRIS, REV. R.]

Specimens of English Literature, from the "Ploughman's Crede" to the "Shepheardes Calendar," A.D. 1394–1579; with Introduction, Notes, and Glossarial Index. (Clar. Press.) 12mo. Oxford, 1871. H 8 P 42

Vision of William Piers the Plowman. [*See* LANGLEY, W.]

SKEEN (WILLIAM). Early Typography. 8vo. Colombo, 1872. A 16 T 15

Mountain Life and Coffee Cultivation in Ceylon: a Poem. Sm. 4to. Lond., 1870. H 5 U 19

SKELTON (HENRY P.) New Illustrated Manual of the Current Gold and Silver Coins of all the Civilized Nations of the Globe. Vol. 1. Text. Vol. 2. Plates. 2 vols. (in 1) 8vo. Lond., 1862. A 13 S 42

Complete Vocabulary to the Eco Italiana. [*See* CAMERINI, PROF. E.]

SKELTON (JOHN). Pithy, Pleasaunt, and Profitable Workes of Maister Skelton, Poet Laureate to King Henry VIII. 8vo. Lond., 1736. H 7 P 15

Poetical Works of; with Notes by the Rev. Alex. Dyce. 2 vols. 8vo. Lond., 1843. H 6 S 25, 26

SKELTON (JOHN), LL.D. Essays in History and Biography, including the Defence of Mary Stuart. 8vo. Edinb., 1883. C 3 V 6

Nugæ Criticæ: Occasional Papers, written at the Seaside; by "Shirley." 8vo. Edinb., 1862. J 4 P 30

SKELTON (JOSEPH). La Beautés de la France. [*See* GIRAULT DE SAINT-FARGEAU, P. A. E.] D 6 V 3

Oxonia Antiqua Restaurata: containing upwards of 190 Engravings, forming an Illustration of the Colleges, Halls, and Public Buildings in this University. 2nd ed. Imp. 4to. Lond., 1843. B 15 T 3 ‡

Pietas Oxoniensis; or, Records of Oxford Founders. Fol. Oxford, 1828. B 19 T 10 ‡

[*See* MEYRICK, SIR S. R.]

SKENE (A. J.), AND SMYTH (R. BROUGH). Report on the Physical Character and Resources of Gippsland: by the Surveyor-General and the Secretary for Mines. With a Map and Geological Sections. 8vo. Melb., 1874.*
MA 2 Q 40

SKENE (MISS FELICIA M. F.) Wayfaring Sketches among the Greeks and Turks and on the Shores of the Danube; by "A Seven Years' Resident in Greece." 8vo. Lond., 1847. D 8 Q 27

SKENE (FELIX J. H.) [*See* SCOTLAND, HISTORIANS OF.]
B 13 P 48

SKENE (JAMES HENRY). Rambles in the Deserts of Syria, and among the Turkomans and Bedaweens. 8vo. Lond., 1864. D 5 Q 42

SKENE (WILLIAM F.), LL.D., &c. Celtic Scotland: a History of Ancient Alban. 3 vols. 8vo. Edinb., 1876.
B 13 R 14–16

Chronicles of the Picts, Chronicles of the Scots, and other Early Memorials of Scottish History. Roy. 8vo. Edinb., 1867. B 13 T 9

Coronation Stone. Sm. 4to. Edinb., 1869. B 13 P 41

Dean of Lismore's Book. [*See* MACGREGOR, SIR J.]

Four Ancient Books of Wales: containing the Cymric Poems attributed to the Bards of the 6th Century. 2 vols. 8vo. Edinb., 1868. B 7 P 14, 15

Highlanders of Scotland; their Origin, History, and Antiquities, &c. 2 vols. 8vo. Lond., 1837. B 13 P 22, 23

Chronica Gentis Scotorum. [*See* FORDUN, J.]

SKERTCHLY (J. A.) Dahomey as it is; being a Narrative of Eight Months' Residence in that Country. With Illustrations. 8vo. Lond., 1874.   D 2 P 5

SKETCHES OF IMPOSTURE, Deception, and Credulity. 12mo. Lond., 1837.   J 10 P 14

SKETCHES of Popular Tumults. [*See* POPULAR TUMULTS.]

SKETCHLEY (ARTHUR). [*See* ROSE, REV. G.]

SKINNER (LIEUT.-COL. JAMES), C.B. Military Memoir of; by J. B. Fraser. 2 vols. 8vo. Lond., 1851.   C 4 V 32, 33

SKINNER (J. E. HILARY). After the Storm; or, Jonathan and his Neighbours in 1865–66. 2 vols. 8vo. Lond., 1866.   D 3 R 25, 26

SKINNER (S.), M.R.C.P. Educational Essays; or, Practical Observations on the Intellectual and Moral Training and Scholastic Discipline of Youth. 8vo. Melb., 1867.   MG 1 R 1

SKINNER (THOMAS), M.D. Life of General Monk, Duke of Albemarle; published from an original MS. of T. Skinner, M.D. 2nd ed. 8vo. Lond., 1724.   C 3 U 46

SKOBELEFF (GEN. MIKHAIL DMITRIEVITCH). Personal Reminiscences of; by V. I. Nemirovitch-Dantchenko. Translated from the Russian, by E. A. Brayley-Hodgetts. 8vo. Lond., 1884.   C 9 T 45

Skobeleff and the Slavonic Cause; by O. K. [Madame Olga Novikoff.] 8vo. Lond., 1883.   C 9 T 44

SKOTTOWE (B. C.), M.A. Our Hanoverian Kings: a Short History of the Four Georges, embracing the period, 1714–1830. 8vo. Lond., 1884.   B 2 S 32

SLACK (H. J.), F.G.S. The Microscope. [*See* CARPENTER, W. B.]   A 17 T 5

SLADE (J.), M.D. Memoirs of Celebrated Female Characters of the 18th and 19th Centuries. 8vo. Lond., 1836.   C 2 P 13

SLADEN (DOUGLAS BROOKE WHEELTON), B.A.. Australian Ballads and Rhymes: Poems inspired by Life and Scenery in Australia and New Zealand, selected and edited by Douglas B. W. Sladen, B.A., Oxon. 12mo. Lond., 1888.   MH 1 P 26

Australian Lyrics, &c. Roy. 8vo. Melb., 1883.   MH 1 S 5

Frithjof and Ingebjorg, and other ·Poems. 12mo. Lond., 1882.   MH 1 P 23

In Cornwall and across the Sea; with Poems written in Devonshire, &c. 8vo. Lond., 1885.   MH 1 P 25

Poetry of Exiles, and other Poems. 18mo. Sydney, 1883.   MH 1 P 24

Summer Christmas, and a Sonnet upon the s.s. *Ballaarat.* . 12mo. Lond., 1884.   MH 1 P 22

SLADEN (COL. EDWARD B.) Mandalay to Momien. [*See* ANDERSON, W.]   D 6 R 30

SLADEN (W. PERCY), F.G.S., &c. Memoir on the Echinodermata of the Arctic Sea. [*See* DUNCAN, P. M.]   A 23 R 22 ‡

SLAGG (CHARLES). Sanitary Work in the Smaller Towns, and in Villages: Nuisances, Drainage, and Water Supply. 8vo. Lond., 1876.   A 6 R 28

SLAGG (JOHN), M.P. Free Trade and Tariffs: a Speech. (Pam. Je.) 8vo. Lond., 1881.   F 6 P 10

SLANE (W. MACGUCKIN DE), BARON. [*See* IBN KHALLIKAN.]   C 4 Q 16–19 †

SLASHER (MR. JOHN). Adventures of. [*See* PICKERING, G. F.]

SLATER (G.), & CO. Guide to the Gold-fields of Victoria; with a Map and the new Regulations for the Gold-fields and Local Courts. 12mo. Melb., 1855.   MJ 2 P 32

Map of Queensland, 1874, including Hann's Explorations, and Dalrymple's Discoveries. Compiled from the latest Official Government Surveys. 2nd ed., revised. 8vo. Brisbane, 1874.   MD 5 P 5 ‡

Queensland Almanac, Settlers' Guide, and Miners' Companion, for 1873. 8vo. Brisbane, 1872.   ME 4 P

SLATER (ISAAC). Royal National Commercial Directory of the Province of Ulster. 8vo. Manchester, 1881.   E

SLATER (JOHN), B.A., &c. Architecture; Classic and Early Christian. [*See* SMITH, T. R.]

SLATER (SAMUEL). Memoir of, connected with a History of the Rise and Progress of the Cotton Manufactures in England and America; by G. S. White. 2nd ed. 8vo. Philad., 1836.   C 9 V 32

SLAVE TRADE. Papers on the Slave Trade. (Pam. Dd.) 8vo. Edinb., 1858.   F 12 P 22

SLEE (JANE M.) [*See* LORENZ, DR. F.]   C 1 R 2

SLEEMAN (C. W.) Torpedoes and Torpedo Warfare. 8vo. Portsmouth, 1880.   A 5 T 40

SLEEMAN (MAJOR-GEN. SIR W. H.), K.C.B. Journey through the Kingdom of Oude, 1849–50. 2 vols. 8vo. Lond., 1858.   D 5 Q 31, 32

Ramaseana; or, a Vocabulary of the peculiar Language used by the Thugs. 8vo. Calcutta, 1836.   K 20 T 1

Rambles and Recollections of an Indian Official. 2 vols. 8vo. Lond., 1844.   D 5 U 24, 25

SLEEPY SKETCHES; or, How we Live, and How we do not Live. From Bombay. 12mo. Lond., 1877.   D 5 P 12

SLEIDAN (JOHANN). De Statureligionis et Reipvblicae, Carolo Quinto, Cæsare Commentarii. Fol. Argentorati, 1555.   G 7 V 21

SLIGHT (JAMES), AND BURN (R. SCOTT). Book of Farm Implements and Machines. Edited by H. Stephens. 8vo. Lond., 1858.   A 1 T 12

SLOWNIK. Polsko–Francuzki, Francuzko–Polski. 4 vols.
18mo. Berlin (n.d.)　　　　　　　　K 11 S 9–12
Another copy. Nowe Wydanie. 2 vols. (in 1) roy.
8vo. Berlin, 1858.　　　　　　　　K 12 T 10

SMALL (GEORGE), M.A. Laskari Dictionary. [*See* ROE-
BUCK, CAPT. F.]

SMALL (JOHN), M.A. Ancient Poetry of Scotland. [*See*
LAING, D.]
Memoir of Gavin Douglas, Bishop of Dunkeld. [*See*
DOUGLAS, G.]

SMALL (JOHN WILLIAM). F.S.A. Ancient and Modern
Furniture. Roy. 4to. Edinb., 1883.　　A 2 U 41
Leaves from my Sketch-books; sketched, measured,
and drawn for the Store by the Author. Ro . 4to.
Edinb., 1880.　　　　　　　　　　A 2 U 10

SMALLEY (GEORGE R.), B.A., &c. Abstract of Meteorological Observations made in New South Wales, during
the years 1865–66. 8vo. Sydney, 1869.　　ME 2 S
Meteorological Observations made at the Royal Observatory, Sydney, during the months December, 1869–June,
1870. 2 vols. roy. 8vo. Sydney, 1869–70.　　ME 2 S

SMALL-POX. Treatise concerning the Plague and the
(Small-) Pox, and Commentarie concerning Women, &c.
12mo. Lond., 1652.　　　　　　　　　Libr.
[*See* VACCINATION.]

SMARAGDUS (ABBAS). Opera omnia. [*See* MIGNE, J. P.,
SERIES LATINA, 102.]

SMART (B. C.), M.D., AND CROFTON (H. T.) Dialect of
the English Gypsies. 2nd ed. 8vo. Lond., 1875. K 15 R 2

SMART (B. H.) Walker remodelled: Smart's Pronouncing
Dictionary of the English Language epitomized. New ed.
12mo. Lond., 1871.　　　　　　　　K 11 U 21

SMART (CHRISTOPHER), A.M. Fables of Phædrus. [*See*
TERENTIUS AFER, P.]
Life and Poems of. [*See* CHALMERS, A.]
Works of Horace, literally translated. [*See* HORATIUS
FLACCUS, Q.]　　　　　　　　　　H 5 S 40

SMART (HENRY). His Life and Works; by William Spark.
8vo. Lond., 1881.　　　　　　　　　C 3 U 38

SMEATON (JOHN). C.E., &c. Reports of, made on various
occasions in the course of his employment as a Civil Engineer. 3 vols. 4to. Lond., 1812.　　A 1 R 1–3 †
Narrative of the Building, and a Description of the
Construction of the Eddystone Lighthouse with Stone.
2nd ed. Imp. fol. Lond., 1813.　　A 1 R 11 ‡

SMEDLEY (EDWARD), JUNR. Sketches from Venetian
History. (Fam. Lib.) 2 vols. 12mo. Lond., 1831 38.
　　　　　　　　　　　　　K 10 P 26, 27

SMEE (ALFRED), F.R.S., &c. The Mind of Man; being a
Natural System of Mental Philosophy. With Engravings.
8vo. Lond., 1875.　　　　　　　　　G 12 R 7

SMEE (A. H.), M.R.C.S., &c. Suggestions as to Lines for
future Research. 8vo. Lond., 1881.　　A 12 U 28

SMEETON (GEORGE). Historical and Biographical Tracts.
2 vols. sm. 4to. Lond., 1820.　　　　B 3 R 1, 2

SMILES (SAMUEL), LL.D. Boy's Voyage round the World.
With Illustrations. 5th thousand. 12mo. Lond., 1872.
　　　　　　　　　　　　　MD 2 Q 20
Another copy. 10th thousand. 12mo. Lond., 1877.
　　　　　　　　　　　　　MD 2 Q 21
Character. New ed. 12mo. Lond., 1878.　　J 11 P 14
Duty; with Illustrations of Courage, Patience, and En-
durance. 8vo. Lond., 1880.　　　　　　J 11 P 15
Industrial Biography: Iron-workers and Tool-makers
12mo. Lond., 1863.　　　　　　　　C 2 P 22
James Nasmyth, Engineer: an Autobiography. [*See*
NASMYTH, J.]　　　　　　　　　C 5 T 19
Life of a Scotch Naturalist, Thomas Edward, Associate
of the Linnean Society. Portrait and Illustrations. 8vo.
Lond., 1876.　　　　　　　　　　C 3 V 4
Life of George Stephenson, Railway Engineer. 8vo.
Lond., 1857.　　　　　　　　　　C 9 U 13
Another copy. 3rd ed. 8vo. Lond., 1857.　　C 9 U 14
Lives of Boulton and Watt; principally from the original
Soho MSS., comprising also, a History of the Invention
and Introduction of the Steam-engine. 8vo. Lond.,
1865.　　　　　　　　　　　　　C 9 V 8
Lives of the Engineers; with an Account of their prin-
cipal Works, comprising also, a History of Inland Com-
munication in Britain. 3 vols. 8vo. Lond., 1857–61.
　　　　　　　　　　　　　C 7 P 46–48
Men of Invention and Industry. 8vo. Lond., 1884.
　　　　　　　　　　　　　C 2 S 23
Self-help: with Illustrations of Character and Conduct.
12mo. Lond., 1859.　　　　　　　　J 11 P 16
The Huguenots; their Settlements, Churches, and Indus-
tries in England and Ireland. 8vo. Lond., 1867.　B 8 S 4
The Huguenots in France, after the Revocation of the
Edict of Nantes; with a Visit to the Country of the
Vaudois. 8vo. Lond., 1877.　　　　　　B 9 P 3
Thrift. 8vo. Lond., 1875.　　　　　　J 11 P 13

SMILLIE (J. D.) Etchings by. [*See* KOEHLER, S. R.]
　　　　　　　　　　　　　A 4 R 16 ‡

SMITH (ADAM), LL.D., &c. Inquiry into the Nature and
Causes of the Wealth of Nations. 3 vols. 8vo. Lond.,
1812.　　　　　　　　　　　　　F 6 T 27–29
Another copy. 4 vols. 12mo. Lond., 1835–43. F 6 P 14–17
Life of. (Eminent Men.) 8vo. Lond., 1849.　C 7 P 45
Theory of Moral Sentiments; to which is added, a Dis-
sertation on the Origin of Languages, with a Life of the
Author. 2 vols. 8vo. Edinb., 1821.　　G 7 S 29, 30

SMITH (AGNES). Monuments of Athens. [*See* KASTRO-
MENOS, P. G.]　　　　　　　　　B 9 S 23

SMITH (ALBERT). Anecdote Life of. [*See* TIMBS, J.]

The Miscellany: a Book for the Field or the Fireside: Amusing Tales and Sketches. 8vo. Lond.,1850. J 4 Q 34

Mont Blanc to China, Egyptian Hall, Piccadilly. 8vo. Lond., 1858. MJ 2 R 21

Month at Constantinople. 8vo. Lond.,1850. D 9 Q 20

Story of Mont Blanc. 2nd ed., enlarged. 12mo. Lond., 1854. D 7 P 25

SMITH ALEXANDER), M.A. Philosophy of Morals, illustrative of the Principles of Theology, Jurisprudence, and General Politics. 2 vols. 8vo. Lond.,1835. G 12 P 4, 5

SMITH (ALEXANDER). Dreamthorp: a Book of Essays, written in the Country. 12mo. Lond., 1863. J 8 Q 19

Summer in Skye. 2 vols.8vo. Lond.,1865. D 7 R 11, 12

SMITH (ALEXANDER), C.E., &c. New History of Aberdeenshire. 2 vols. 8vo. Aberdeen,1875. B 13 R 12, 13

SMITH (ALEXANDER KENNEDY). Address to the Electors of East Melbourne. 8vo. Melb., 1877. MF 1 Q 6

SMITH (ARCHIBALD), M.A. [*See* SCORESBY, REV. W.]

SMITH (REV. BARNARD), M.A. Arithmetic and Algebra, in their Principles and Application. 8vo. Lond., 1879. A 10 S 8

Ecclesiastical Ornament and Costume. [*See* PUGIN, A. W.] K 3 Q 22 †

SMITH (BERNARD). Sketches Abroad, made whilst Travelling Student of the Royal Academy, 1876: Germany and Switzerland. Imp. 4to. Lond., 1880. A 1 S 4 ‡

SMITH (BRUCE). Liberty and Liberalism: a Protest against the growing tendency towards undue interference by the State, with Individual Liberty, Private Enterprise, and the Rights of Property. 8vo. Melb., 1887.* MF 1 P 40

SMITH (LIEUT.-COL. CHARLES HAMILTON). Introduction to Mammalia. (Nat. Lib., 15.) 12mo. Edinb., 1858. A 14 P 15

Natural History of Dogs. (Nat. Lib., 24, 25.) 2 vols. 12mo. Edinb., 1839–40. A 14 P 24, 25

Natural History of Horses. (Nat. Lib., 27.) 12mo. Edinb., 1841. A 14 P 27

SMITH (CHARLES JOHN), F.S.A. Historical and Literary Curiosities, consisting of Fac-similes of Original Documents, Scenes of remarkable Events and interesting Localities, &c. 4to. Lond., 1847. B 1 S 9 †

SMITH (VEN. CHARLES JOHN), M.A. Synonyms and Antonyms; or, Kindred Words and their Opposites, collected and contrasted. New ed., revised. 8vo. Lond., 1870. K 11 U 8

Synonyms discriminated. 8vo. Lond.,1871. K 13 P 31

Another copy. New ed., edited by the Rev. H. Percy Smith, M.A. 8vo. Lond., 1882. K 13 P.32

4 T

SMITH (CHARLES MANBY). Curiosities of London Life; or, Phases, Physiological and Social, of the Great Metropolis. 8vo. Lond., 1853. J 8 U 8

SMITH (CHARLES ROACH), F.S.A. Antiquities of Richborough, Reculver, Lymne, in Kent. Illustrated by F. W. Fairholt, F.S.A. 4to. Lond., 1850. B 6 R 38

Retrospections, Social and Archæological. 2 vols. 8vo. Lond., 1883. C 2 V 25, 26

SMITH (MRS. CHARLOTTE). What is She? a Comedy. [*See* MODERN THEATRE, 10.]

The Young Philosopher: a Novel. 4 vols. 12mo. Lond., 1798. J 8 R 21–24

SMITH (DANIEL). Ancient Ores of the Earth; being the History of the Primitive Alphabet, lately discovered by the Author. 8vo. Melb., 1864.* MK 1 Q 22

SMITH (DAVID). The English Dyer; with Instructions how to dye 150 Shades on Cotton Yarns in the Hank; 50 Shades on Cotton Wool; 150 Shades on Worsted Yarns; 100 Shades on Animal Wool; and 50 Shades on Silk in the Skein. 8vo. Manchester, 1882. A 11 S 7

SMITH (E.) Biblical Researches in Palestine, &c. [*See* ROBINSON, E.] D 4 T 25–27

SMITH (EDMUND) Life and Poems of. [*See* BRITISH POETS, 4; CHALMERS, A.; *and* JOHNSON, S.]

Phædra and Hippolitus : a Tragedy. (Bell's Brit. Theatre.) 18mo. Lond., 1796. H 2 P 13

Another copy. (New Eng. Theatre.) 12mo. Lond., 1776. H 4 P 17

SMITH (EDWARD), M.D., &c. Foods. 4th ed. 8vo. Lond., 1876. A 13 P 7

Health and Disease as influenced by the Daily, Seasonal, and other Cyclical Changes in the Human System. 8vo. Lond., 1877. A 13 P 15

Natural History of the Inanimate Creation. [*See* INANIMATE CREATION, THE.]

SMITH (EDWARD), F.S.S. The Peasant's Home, 1760–1875. (Howard Prize Essay, 1875.) 8vo. Lond., 1876. F 5 R 23

SMITH (EUAN). Eastern Persia: Geography, &c. [*See* PERSIA.] D 4 U 45, 46

SMITH (E. D.), F.L.S. [*See* SWEET, R.]

SMITH (SIR FRANCIS PETTITT). [*See* CHAPPELL, CAPT. E.]

SMITH (FRANK J.) Common Law Procedure. [*See* PILCHER, C. E.] MF 2 R 9

SMITH (FRANK PORTER), M.B. Contributions towards the Materia Medica, and Natural History of China. Roy. 8vo. Shanghai, 1871. A 5 Q 1

Vocabulary of Proper Names, in Chinese and English, of Places, Persons, Tribes, and Sects in China, Japan, &c. Roy. 8vo. Shanghai, 1870. K 13 T 24

SMITH (GAMALIEL). [*See* BENTHAM, J.]

SMITH (REV. GEORGE), D.D., BISHOP OF VICTORIA. Narrative of an Exploratory Visit to each of the Consular Cities of China. 8vo. Lond., 1847. D 6 S 26

SMITH (GEORGE). Assyrian Discoveries: an Account of Explorations and Discoveries on the site of Nineveh, during 1873-74. With Illustrations. 8vo. Lond., 1875.
B 10 P 29

Assyrian Eponym Canon; containing Translations of the Documents, and an Account of the Evidence, on the comparative Chronology of the Assyrian and Jewish Kingdoms, from the Death of Solomon to Nebuchadnezzar. 8vo. Lond., 1875. B 10 P 31

Chaldean Account of Genesis. With Illustrations. 8vo. Lond., 1876. G 12 P 7

History of Sennacherib, translated from the Cuneiform Inscriptions. Edited by the Rev. A. H. Sayce, M.A. Imp. 8vo. Lond., 1878. B 2 R 42

[*See* BRITISH MUSEUM *and* RAWLINSON, MAJ.-GEN. SIR H. C.]

SMITH (GEORGE). I've been a Gipsying. 8vo. Lond., 1883. D 7 Q 40

SMITH (GEORGE), LL.D., &c. Geography of British India, Political and Physical. (Student's Geography of India.) With Maps. 8vo. Lond., 1882. D 5 P 11

Life of Alexander Duff, D.D., LL.D. 2 vols. roy. 8vo. Lond., 1879. C 8 V 4, 5

Life of William Carey, D.D., Shoemaker and Missionary. 8vo. Lond., 1885. C 10 S 11

SMITH (GEORGE BARNETT). Half-hours with some Famous Ambassadors. 8vo. Lond., 1884. C 1 S 22

Illustrated British Ballads, Old and New. Selected and edited. 2 vols. roy. 8vo. Lond., 1881. H 6 V 16, 17

Life and Speeches of the Right Hon. John Bright, M.P. With Portraits. 2 vols. 8vo. Lond., 1881. C 10 P 4, 5

Life of the Right Hon. William Ewart Gladstone, M.P., D.C.L., &c. 2 vols. 8vo. Lond., 1879. C 7 R 10, 11

Life of Her Majesty Queen Victoria. Jubilee edition. 8vo. Lond., 1887. C 11 P 31

Prime Ministers of Queen Victoria. 8vo. Lond., 1886. C 9 T 40

Sir Robert Peel. (English Political Leaders.) 12mo. Lond., 1881. C 2 P 37

Victor Hugo: his Life and Work. With a Portrait. 8vo. Lond., 1885. C 4 T 15

SMITH (GERARD W.), M.A. Memoirs of Prince Metternich. [*See* METTERNICH WINNEBURG OCHSENHAUSEN, CLEMENT, PRINCE OF.] C 10 U 28-32

Painting, Spanish and French. (Illustrated Hand-books of Art History.) 8vo. Lond., 1884. A 6 V 6

SMITH (GOLDWIN), M.A. Cowper. (Eng. Men of Letts.) 8vo. Lond., 1880. C 1 U 10

Irish History and Irish Character. 8vo. Oxford, 1868. B 11 P 5

Lectures on the Study of History, delivered in Oxford, 1859-61. 2nd ed. Oxford, 1865. B 14 Q 40

Three English Statesmen [Pym, Cromwell, Pitt:] a Course of Lectures on the Political History of England New ed. 8vo. Lond., 1868. C 1 T 43

SMITH (HAMBLIN), JUNR. Hydraulics: the Flow of Water through Orifices, over Weirs, and through Open Conduits and Pipes. Roy. 4to. Lond., 1886. A 2 Q 19 †

SMITH (SIR HARRY). War in India: Despatches. [*See* HARDINGE, VISCOUNT.] B 10 U 20

SMITH (HENRY). Evidences relating to the Estates of Henry Smith, Esq., some time Alderman of the City of London, collected by Joseph Gwilt. Imp. 8vo. Lond., 1828. C 4 W 22

[*See* SMITH, T.] C 4 W 22

SMITH (HELEN AINSLIE). One Hundred Famous Americans. Sq. 8vo. New York, 1887. C 5 T 11

SMITH (HENRY J. S.) Memoir of John Conington, M.A. [*See* CONINGTON, J.]

[*See* CLIFFORD, W. K.] A 10 T 4

SMITH (REV. HENRY PERCY), M.A. Glossary of Terms and Phrases. 8vo. Lond., 1883. K 15 R 22

SMITH (HERBERT H.) Brazil: the Amazons and the Coast. Illustrated. 8vo. New York, 1879. D 4 Q 26

SMITH (HORACE). Gaieties and Gravities: a series of Essays, Comic Tales, &c. 3 vols. 8vo. Lond., 1825. J 12 T 17-19

Memoirs, Letters, &c., of James Smith. 2 vols. 8vo. Lond., 1840. C 1 U 51, 52

Midsummer Medley, for 1830. 2 vols. 12mo. Lond., 1830. J 11 T 9, 10

The Tin Trumpet; or, Heads and Tales; by the late "Paul Chatfield, M.D." 2 vols. 8vo. Lond., 1836. J 11 P 19, 20

SMITH (HORACE AND JAMES). Horace in London; consisting of Imitations of the First Two Books of Horace. 4th ed. 12mo. Lond., 1815. H 8 P 17

Rejected Addresses: or, the New Theatrum Poetarum. 12mo. Lond., 1841. H 8 P 39

SMITH (HUBERT). Tent Life with English Gipsies in Norway. 8vo. Lond., 1873. D 7 S 38

SMITH (JAMES). Memoirs, Letters, and Comic Miscellanies, in Prose and Verse; edited by his Brother, Horace Smith. 2 vols. 8vo. Lond., 1840. C 1 U 51, 52

SMITH (JAMES). Lecture on the Irish Character, from an Englishman's Point of View, delivered at St. George's Hall, Melbourne. 8vo. Melb., 1863.   MJ 2 R 7

Old Fable—The Frog and the Ox : a Lecture. 8vo. Melh., 1869.   MJ 1 P 28

Another copy. 8vo. Melh., 1869.   MJ 2 R 23

Reprints from the *Maryborough and Dunolly Advertiser:* Lectures, &c. 12mo. Maryborough, 1873–74. MG 1 P 28

[*See* HAMLET CONTROVERSY.]

SMITH (JAMES), F.R.S., &c. Voyage and Shipwreck of St. Paul; with Dissertations on the Sources of the Writings of St. Luke, and the Ships and Navigation of the Antients. 8vo. Lond., 1848.   G 12 P 6

SMITH (JAMES). Cheerfulness as a Factor of Health. [*See* AUSTRALIAN HEALTH SOCIETY.]   MA 2 S 23

SMITH (JAMES A.) Brookes' Gazetteer. [*See* BROOKES, R.]

SMITH (Sir JAMES EDWARD), M.D., &c. Grammar of Botany. 8vo. Lond., 1826.   A 4 T 23

Introduction to Physiological and Systematical Botany. 8vo. Lond., 1819.   A 4 T 22

Specimen of the Botany of New Holland. The Figures by James Sowerby, F.L.S. Vol. 1 (*all published*). Roy. 4to. Lond., 1793.*   MA 1 Q 22 †

SMITH (JAMES WALTER), LL.D. Handy-book on the Law and Practice of Public Meetings, from Parliament downwards, including the Rules of Debate used in Parliament, Tables of Motions and Amendments, Rules of Debate for Public Meetings, &c., Hints to Shareholders, Hints to Vestrymen, and other matters. 3rd ed., revised and improved. 8vo. Lond., 1878.   J 9 Q 31

SMITH (REV. JOHN), A.M. Pepys' Diary. [*See* PEPYS, S.]

SMITH (JOHN), A.L.S. Dictionary of Popular Names of the Plants which furnish the Natural and Acquired Wants of Man, in all Matters of Domestic and General Economy; their History, Products, and Uses. 8vo. Lond., 1882.   K 7 Q 22

Domestic Botany: an Exposition of the Structure and Classification of Plants, and of their Uses for Food, Clothing, Medicine, and Manufacturing Purposes. 8vo. Lond., 1883.   A 4 P 27

Memoirs of the Marquis of Pombal; with Extracts from his Writings, and from Despatches in the State Paper Office. 2 vols. 8vo. Lond., 1843.   C 8 U 35, 36

SMITH (JOHN). [*See* DE BOOS, C.]

SMITH (PROF. JOHN), M.D., &c. Wayfaring Notes: Sydney to Southampton, by way of Egypt and Palestine. 12mo. Sydney, 1865.   MD 1 S 1

Wayfaring Notes: a Holiday Tour round the World. 2nd series. 12mo. Aberdeen, 1876.   MD 1 S 2

SMITH (J. A.) Phenomena of Natural Magic. [*See* BREWSTER, SIR D.]

SMITH (J. EDWARDS), M.D., &c. How to See with the Microscope; being Useful Hints connected with the Selection and Use of the Instrument. 8vo. Chicago, 1880.   A 16 P 29

SMITH (JOSEPH E. A.) History of Paper: its Genesis and its Revelations. Roy. 8vo. Holyoke, 1882. A 11 T 12

SMITH (J. H.), M.A. Treatise on Elementary Statics. 2nd ed. Roy. 8vo. Lond., 1869.   A 10 V 9

SMITH (REV. J. J.), M.A. Cambridge Portfolio; edited by the Rev. J. J. Smith, M.A. 2 vols. sm. 4to. Lond., 1840.   B 10 Q 10, 11 †

SMITH (J. MOYR). Album of Decorative Figures. Imp. 4to. Lond., 1882.   A 23 P 3 ‡

Ancient Greek Female Costume. Illustrated. 8vo. Lond., 1882.   A 7 P 24

Ornamental Interiors, Ancient and Modern. 8vo. Lond., 1887.   A 3 Q 9

SMITH (JOHN PYE), D.D., &c. On the relation between the Holy Scriptures and some parts of Geological Science. 12mo. Lond., 1840.   A 9 P 15

Scripture Testimony to the Messiah. 3rd ed. 3 vols. 8vo. Lond., 1837.   G 12 P 1–3

SMITH (JOHN PRINCE). The English Coinage Question. [*See* COBDEN CLUB.]   F 10 T 15

SMITH (JOHN THOMAS). Antiquities of London and its Environs. (Plates only.) Imp. 4to. Lond., 1804–9.   B 20 P 5 ‡

Antiquities of Westminster: the Old Palace, St. Stephen's Chapel (now the House of Commons), &c. Imp. 4to. Lond., 1807.   B 17 S 1 ‡

[Joseph] Nollekens and his Times; comprehending a Life of that celebrated Sculptor, and Memoirs of several Contemporary Artists. 2nd ed. 2 vols. 8vo. Lond., 1829.   C 9 P 3, 4

SMITH (JOHN THOMAS). Statement in reference to the establishment of the Aboriginal Mission at Port Phillip. [*See* MANUSCRIPTS AND PORTRAITS.]   MF 1 U 21

Three Addresses. 8vo. Melb., 1858.   MG 1 P 1

SMITH (JOHN WILLIAM). Compendium of Mercantile Law. 9th ed., edited by G. M. Dowdeswell. Roy. 8vo. Lond., 1877.   F 4 R 8

SMITH (JOSEPH W.), R.N., AND DALRYMPLE (GEORGE E.) Report of the Proceedings of the Queensland Government Schooner *Spitfire*, in search of the Mouth of the River Burdekin. 8vo. Brisbane, 1860.   MD 1 V 9

Another copy. 8vo. Brisbane, 1860.   MJ 2 R 16

SMITH (L.), AND HAMILTON (H.) International English and French Dictionary. New ed. Roy. 8vo. Paris, 1878.   K 16 R 20

MITH (Dr. Louis L.), L.S.A. How to get Thin, and how to get Fat; or, Banting superseded. 8vo. Melb., 1864. MA 2 S 38

Medical Almanacs for 1866–80: a Hand-book for the Mothers of Australasia, and a Vade-mecum for the Profession. 13 vols. (in 1) 8vo. Melb., 1860–80. ME 3 U

Our Doctor; or, the Colonial Medical and Surgical Handy-book; containing reliable Information and full Instructions for Families and those resident in the Bush how to act in Emergencies, Accidents, and Common Sickness. 12mo. Sydney, 1886. MA 2 S 27

Secrets and Ceremonies of Freemasonry exposed; giving a Description of the Signs, Grips, and Knocks, used in the Apprentice, Fellow-Craft, and Master-Mason Lodges: a Lecture. 8vo. Melb., 1862. MJ 2 R 12

SMITH (Miss Lucy Toulmin). A Common-place Book of the 15th Century; printed from the original Manuscript by Lady Caroline Kerrison; edited, with Notes, by Lucy Toulmin Smith. 8vo. Lond., 1886. H 3 S 20

York Plays: the Plays performed by the Crafts, or Mysteries of York, on the day of Corpus Christi, in the 14th, 15th, 16th Centuries; edited by Lucy Toulmin Smith. 8vo. Oxford, 1885. H 3 T 6

SMITH (Miss Madeline). Complete Report of the Trial of, for the alleged poisoning of Pierre Emile l'Angelier. 8vo. Edinb., 1857. MF 2 S 1

SMITH (Philip), B.A. Ancient History, from the Earliest Records to the Fall of the Western Empire. 3 vols. 8vo. Lond., 1868. B 15 R 24–26

Student's Ancient History: the Ancient History of the East. 8vo. Lond., 1871. B 2 S 30

Student's Ecclesiastical History: the History of the Christian Church. New ed. With Illustrations. 2 vols. 8vo. Lond., 1884–85. G 7 S 31, 32

Troy and its Remains. [*See* Schliemann, Dr. H.] B 13 V 14

SMITH (Reginald Bosworth), M.A. Life of Lord Lawrence. With Portraits and Maps. 2 vols. 8vo. Lond., 1883. C 8 P 30, 31

SMITH (Robert Angus), Ph.D., &c. Air and Rain: the Beginnings of a Chemical Climatoly. 8vo. Lond., 1872. A 3 T 40

Centenary of Science in Manchester. 8vo. Lond., 1883. A 16 S 7

Disinfectants and Disinfection. 8vo. Edinb., 1869. A 13 P 20

SMITH (Robert Archibald). The Scotish Minstrel: a Selection from the Vocal Melodies of Scotland, Ancient and Modern, arranged for the Pianoforte. 6 vols. imp. 8vo. Edinb. (n.d.) H 5 V 13–18

SMITH (Robert H.), M.I.M.E., &c. Cutting Tools worked by Hand and Machine. 12mo. Lond., 1882. A 11 P 31

SMITH (Major Gen. Sir Robert M.), R.E. Persian Art. 8vo. Lond., 1876. E

SMITH (Rt. Hon. Robert Vernon). Letters of Horace Walpole. [*See* Walpole, H.] C 10 P 45

SMITH (Rod. H.) Science of Business. 8vo. New York, 1885. F 5 R 15

SMITH (Rev. Rowland), M.A. The Greek Romances of Heliodorus, Longus, and Achilles Tatius. [*See* Heliodorus.]

SMITH (Samuel). Occasional Essays. 8vo. Edinb. 1874. J 5 T 26

SMITH (Sidney). Principles of Phrenology. 8vo. Edinb., 1838. A 12 S 14

Whether to go, and whither? or, the Cape and the Great South Land. 12mo. Lond., 1849.* MD 1 S 3

SMITH (Prof. Sidney I.) Invertebrate Animals. [*See* Verrill, A. E.] A 14 U 23

SMITH (Southwood). Results of Sanitary Improvement. (Pam. Dd.) 8vo. Lond., 1854. F 12 P 22

SMITH (Rev. Sydney), M.A. Elementary Sketches of Moral Philosophy. 12mo. Lond., 1854. G 8 P 18

Memoir of; by his Daughter, Lady Holland; edited by Mrs. Austin. 2 vols. 8vo. Lond., 1855. C 9 U 17, 18

Sketch of the Life and Times of, based on Family Documents, and the Recollections of Personal Friends; by S. J. Reid. 8vo. Lond., 1884. C 9 U 25

Wit and Wisdom of. 8vo. Lond., 1860. J 8 T 27

Works of. 2nd ed. 4 vols. 8vo. Lond., 1840. J 8 T 23–26

SMITH (S. Percy), F.R.G.S. Eruption of Tarawera, New Zealand. 8vo. Wellington, 1887. MA 2 R 31

Kermadec Islands; their Capabilities and Extent. 8vo. Wellington, 1887. MD 7 P 30

SMITH (Teena Rochfort-): a Memoir. 8vo. Cheltenham, 1883. C 9 R 21

SMITH (Rev. Thomas). Circular Letter to the Parishioners, and Report in connection with St. Barnabas' Church. 8vo. Sydney, 1863. MG 1 Q 26

Hedley Vicars: a Lecture. (Pam. J.) 8vo. Sydney, 1858. MJ 1 T 38

Life of Havelock. 12mo. Sydney (n.d.) MG 1 P 49

Narrative of the Wreck of the Ship *All Serene*. [*See* All Serene.] MD 1 V 9

The Commissary Review, published on board the clipper Ship *Commissary*, during a Voyage from London to Sydney, 1870. Editor, the Rev. Thomas Smith; Sub-editor, Mr. Charles Vaughan. 8vo. Sydney, 1870. ME 3 R

SMITH (Thomas and Henry). Notices relating to Thomas Smith, of Campden, and to Henry Smith, sometime Alderman of London; by the late Charles Perkins Gwilt. Imp. 8vo. Lond., 1836. C 4 W 22

SMITH (Thomas Assheton). Reminiscences of; or, the Pursuits of an English Country Gentleman, by Sir J. E. Eardley Wilmot, Bart. 8vo. Lond., 1860. C 9 U 26

SMITH (T. ROGER), F.R.I.B.A. Acoustics in relation to Architecture and Building: the Laws of Sound as applied to the Arrangement of Buildings. (Weale.) 12mo. Lond., 1861. A 17 P 57

Another copy. (Weale.) 12mo. Lond., 1861.
A 17 Q 40

Architecture, Gothic and Renaissance. 8vo. Lond., 1880. A 2 R 6

SMITH (T. ROGER), F.R.I.B.A., AND SLATER (JOHN), B.A., &c. Architecture, Classic and Early Christian. (Illustrated Hand-books of Art History.) 8vo. Lond., 1882. A 2 R 3

SMITH (URIAH). Our Country's Future: the United States in the Light of Prophecy; or, an Exposition of Rev. xiii, 11-17. 4th ed. 8vo. Battle Creek, Mich., 1883. G 7 S 27

The Sanctuary and the Twenty-three Hundred Days of Daniel viii, 14. 12mo. Battle Creek, Mich., 1877.
G 7 S 28

Thoughts, Critical and Practical, on the Book of Daniel. 2nd ed. 8vo. Battle Creek, Mich., 1883. G 7 S 25

Thoughts, Critical and Practical, on the Book of Revelation. 3rd ed. 8vo. Battle Creek, Mich., 1883. G 7 S 26

SMITH (WALTER). Death of Oswald, and other Poems, Songs, and Ballads; by "Old Saltbush." 12mo. Sydney, 1887. MH 1 P 8

SMITH (WILLIAM). Memoir of Johann Gottlieb Fichte. [*See* FICHTE, J. G.]

SMITH (WILLIAM), "ROUGE DRAGON." Description of England, 1588; with Views of some of the Chief Towns, and Armorial Bearings of Nobles and Bishops. 4to. Lond., 1879. B 4 V 7

SMITH (WILLIAM). Gravenhurst; or, Thoughts on Good and Evil. 2nd ed. Knowing and Feeling: a Contribution to Psychology; with a Memoir of the Author. 8vo. Edinb., 1875. G 7 S 6

Thorndale; or, the Conflict of Opinions. 8vo. Lond., 1857. G 2 P 6

Another copy. 3rd ed. 8vo. Edinb., 1879. G 2 P 7

SMITH (WILLIAM), A.M. History of New York, from the First Discovery. 8vo. Lond., 1776. B 1 R 15

SMITH (WILLIAM), F.S.A.S. Morley, Ancient and Modern. 8vo. Lond., 1886. B 4 T 5

Old Yorkshire. Edited by William Smith. 5 vols. 8vo. Lond., 1881-84. B 22 T 1-5

SMITH (WILLIAM), LL.D., &c. Atlas of Ancient Geography, Biblical and Classical. Roy. fol. Lond., 1875.
D 8 P 8

Classical Dictionary of Biography, Mythology, and Geography, based on the larger Dictionaries. 10th ed. 8vo. Lond., 1869. K 7 Q 7

Dictionary of Greek and Roman Antiquities. 2nd ed. Roy. 8vo. Lond., 1851. K 7 Q 10

SMITH (WILLIAM), LL.D., &c.—*continued.*
Dictionary of Greek and Roman Biography and Mythology, by various Writers. 3 vols. roy. 8vo. Lond., 1872. C 11 Q 13-15

Dictionary of Greek and Roman Geography, by various Writers. 2 vols. roy. 8vo. Lond., 1872. D 11 U 9, 10

Dictionary of the Bible, comprising its Antiquities, Biography, Geography, and Natural History. 3 vols. roy. 8vo. Lond., 1863. K 18 R 27-29

Latin-English Dictionary, based upon the Works of Forcellini and Freund. 17th ed. 8vo. Lond., 1881.
K 16 Q 9

Another copy. Libr.

The Student's France: a History of France, from the Earliest Times to the Establishment of the Second Empire in 1852. 4th ed. 8vo. Lond., 1872. B 8 P 2

The Student's Gibbon. [*See* GIBBON, E.] B 12 P 20

The Student's Greece: a History of Greece, from the Earliest Times to the Roman Conquest, &c. 8vo. Lond., 1869. B 9 S 13

The Student's Greek Grammar. [*See* CURTIUS, PROF. G.]

The Student's Manual of the English Language. [*See* MARSH, G. P.]

The Student's Middle Ages. [*See* HALLAM, H.] B 7 S 32

The Student's Scripture History: the New Testament History. 3rd ed. 8vo. Lond., 1868. G 7 S 34

The Student's Scripture History: the Old Testament History, from the Creation to the Return of the Jews from Captivity. 8vo. Lond., 1872. G 7 S 33, 34

The Student's Specimens of English Literature. [*See* SHAW, T. B.]

[*See* THUCYDIDES.] J 15 P 46-48

[*See* XENOPHON.] J 17 Q 22

SMITH (WILLIAM), LL.D., &c., AND CHEETHAM (SAMUEL), M.A. Dictionary of Christian Antiquities; being a Continuation of the "Dictionary of the Bible." Illustrated. 2 vols. roy. 8vo. Lond., 1875-80. K 7 Q 8, 9

SMITH (WILLIAM), LL.D. AND HALL (THEOPHILUS), M.A. Copious and Critical English-Latin Dictionary. Roy. 8vo. Lond., 1870. K 16 Q 8

Another copy. 8vo. Lond., 1870. Libr.

Student's Latin Grammar. 5th ed. 8vo. Lond., 1872.
K 16 P 1

SMITH (WILLIAM), LL.D., &c., AND WACE (REV. HENRY), M.A. Dictionary of Christian Biography, Literature, Sects, and Doctrines; being a Continuation of the "Dictionary of the Bible." 4 vols. roy. 8vo. Lond., 1877-87. C 11 S 9-12

SMITH (SIR WILLIAM CUSACK), BART. Our Warships: a Naval Essay. 8vo. Lond., 1886. A 2 R 30

SMITH (WILLIAM HENRY). St. Clair Papers: the Life and Public Services of Arthur St. Clair; with his Correspondence and other Papers. 2 vols. 8vo. Cincinnati, 1882. C 8 V 35, 36

SMITH (WILLIAM HOWARD), AND SONS. Hand-book of William Howard Smith and Son's Line of Intercolonial Steamers; with an Essay on the Growth of Australian Commerce and Shipping. 4to. Sydney, 1883. MK 1 U 5

SMITH (WILLIAM JAMES). Greville Papers. [*See* GRENVILLE, R.] B 5 U 32-35

SMITH (WILLIAM R.) Kinship and Marriage in Early Arabia. 8vo. Camb., 1885. B 10 P 36

SMITH (ADM. SIR WILLIAM SIDNEY), G.C.B. Life and Correspondence of; by John Barrow. 2 vols. 8vo. Lond., 1847. C 9 U 23, 24

Memoirs of; by Lieut. Edward Howard, R.N. 2 vols. 8vo. Lond., 1839. C 9 U 21, 22

SMITH (WILLIAM SLADE). Lecture on Van Diemen's Land, Past, Present, and Future; delivered before the Members of the Mechanics' School of Arts, Hobart Town, on the Evenings of July 7th, and August 17th, 1851. 8vo. Hobart, 1851. MJ 2 R 7

SMITH (WORTHINGTON G.), F.L.S., &c. Diseases of Field and Garden Crops. 8vo. Lond., 1884. A 4 P 11

Mushrooms and Toadstools: how to distinguish between Edible and Poisonous Fungi. 4th ed. 12mo. Lond., 1879. A 4 P 5

SMITH & ADAMSON. The Australian Gardener; being an Epitome of Horticulture for the Colony of Victoria. 6th ed., revised and enlarged. 12mo. Melb., 1862. MA 1 P 7

SMITH (—.), AND GARDINER (CHARLES). Map of Sydney and Suburbs. 8vo. Sydney, 1886. MD 5 P 3 ‡

SMITHSONIAN INSTITUTION (THE). Annual Reports of the Board of Regents of the Smithsonian Institution, showing the Operations, Expenditure, and Condition of the Institution. 16 vols. 8vo. Wash., 1863-84. E

List of Foreign Correspondents of the Smithsonian institution, corrected to January, 1882. 8vo. Wash., 1882. E

Smithsonian Contributions to Knowledge. 16 vols. 4to. Wash., 1847-70. E

SMOLLETT (TOBIAS), M.D. History of England, from the Revolution to the Death of George II: designed as a Continuation to D. Hume's History. 5 vols. 8vo. Lond., 1823. B 5 R 8-12

History of England. [*See* HUME, D.] B 3 V 7-15

Poetical Works of. [*See* POETICAL WORKS.]

Smollett: his Life and a Selection from his Works; by Robert Chambers, LL.D. 8vo. Lond., 1867. C 4 Q 46

Works of, with Memoirs of his Life; to which is prefixed, a View of the Commencement and Progress of Romance, by John Moore, M.D. 8 vols. 8vo. Lond., 1797. J 9 T 19-26

Life and Poems of. [*See* CHALMERS, A.]

[*See* VOLTAIRE, F. M. A. DE.]

SMYTH (C. PIAZZI), F.R.S.E. Astronomical Observations, made at the Royal Observatory, Edinburgh, 1860-86. 3 vols. 4to. Edinb., 1871-86. E

Life and Work at the Great Pyramid; with a Discussion of the Facts ascertained. 3 vols. 8vo. Edinb., 1867. A 2 S 2-4

Madeira Meteorologic. Sq.8vo. Edinb., 1882. A 3 T 7

Madeira Spectroscopic; being a Revision of Twenty-one Places in the Red Half of the Solar Visible Spectrum, with a Rutherfurd Diffraction Grating, at Madeira, during the Summer of 1881. 4to. Edinb., 1882. A 3 U 16

Report to the Principal Secretary of State for the Home Department, on the Royal Observatory of Edinburgh. 4to. Edinb., 1846. A 15 U 8

Teneriffe: an Astronomer's Experiment; or, Specialities of a Residence above the Clouds. 8vo. Lond., 1858. A 3 T 38

SMYTH (MRS. GILLESPIE). Romance of Diplomacy: Historical Memoir of Queen Caroline Matilda, of Denmark, Sister of King George III; with Memoir, and a Selection from the Correspondence (Official and Familiar) of Sir Robert Murray Keith, K.B. With Portraits. 2 vols. 8vo. Lond., 1861. C 4 T 44, 45

SMYTH (JOHN). Berkeley Manuscripts: the Lives of the Berkeleys, 1066-1618. Edited by Sir John Maclean, F.S.A., &c. 3 vols. roy. 4to. Gloucester, 1883-85. C 4 P 17-19 †

SMYTH (R. BROUGH), F.G.S., &c. Aborigines of Victoria: with Notes relating to the Habits of the Natives of other parts of Australia and Tasmania. 2 vols. imp. 8vo. Melb., 1878. MA 1 P 4, 5 †

Catalogue of Minerals, Rocks, and Fossils, which have been collected in the Colony by the Mining Department, Melbourne, Victoria. 8vo. Melb., 1866. MA 2 Q 35

Geological Survey of Victoria: Progress Report by the Secretary for Mines. 5 vols. (in 3) imp. 8vo. Melb., 1874-77. MA 2 R 11-14

Gold-fields and Mineral Districts of Victoria; with Notes on the Modes of Occurrence of Gold and other Metals and Minerals. Imp. 8vo. Melh., 1869.* MA 2 R 9

Meteorological Reports, and Observations taken in Victoria. Sm. fol. Melh., 1855-58. MA 2 Q 9 †

Mining and Mineral Statistics of Victoria. (Pam.) 8vo. Melh., 1866. MJ 2 R 9

Prospector's Hand-book: a Catalogue of Useful Minerals, which may be sought for and found in Victoria. (Pam. 44.) 12mo. Melh., 1863. MJ 2 R 3

Report on the Gold-mines of the South-eastern portion of the Wynaad. Fol. Madras, 1880. MF 1 U 10

Report on the Physical Character and Resources of Gippsland. [*See* SKENE, A. J.]

Sketch of a New Geological Map of Victoria. 4to. Melh., 1874. MA 1 P 27 †

SMYTH (WARRINGTON W.), M.A. Lectures on Gold. [*See* GOLD.]
Metallic Mining and Collieries. (Brit. Manuf. Indust.) 12mo. Lond., 1876. A 17 S 38
Rudimentary Treatise on Coal and Coal-mining. 2nd ed. (Weale.) 12mo. Lond., 1872. A 17 Q 26
Another copy. 6th ed. 12mo. Lond., 1872. A 17 S 38

SMYTH (WILLIAM) Lectures on Modern History, from the Irruption of the Northern Nations to the Close of the American Revolution. 2 vols. 8vo. Camb., 1840. B 15 P 28, 29
Lectures on History: On the French Revolution. (2nd series.) 3 vols. 8vo. Camb., 1848. B 8 R 26–28

SMYTH (WILLIAM C.) Laskari Dictionary. [*See* ROEBUCK, CAPT. T.]

SMYTH (REAR-ADM. W. HENRY), K.S.F., &c. Ædes Hartwellianæ; or, Notices of the Manor and Mansion of Hartwell. 4to. Lond., 1851. B 17 R 8 ‡
Cycle of Celestial Objects, for the Use of Naval, Military, and Private Astronomers. 2 vols. 8vo. Lond., 1844. A 3 S 1, 2
Cycle of Celestial Objects, observed, reduced, and discussed. 2nd ed. 8vo. Oxford, 1881. A 3 S 3
Life and Services of Capt. Philip Beaver, late of H.M.S. *Nisus.* 8vo. Lond., 1829. C 10 Q 1
Nautical Observations on the Port and Maritime Vicinity of Cardiff. 8vo. Cardiff, 1840. F 4 P 22
The Mediterranean: a Memoir, Physical, Historical, and Nautical. 8vo. Lond., 1854. D 12 P 7
[*See* ARAGO, F. J. D.]

SMYTHE (MRS. W. J.) Ten Months in Fiji Islands. Illustrated. 8vo. Oxford, 1864. MD 6 T 5

SMYTHIES (HENRY). Report of the Case of, on the hearing of his Application under "The Law Practitioners Act Amendment Act, 1871." 8vo. Wellington, 1872. MJ 2 R 16

SNIDER (DENTON J.) System of Shakespeare's Drama. 2 vols. (in 1) 8vo. St. Louis, 1877. J 8 R 9

SNODGRASS (JOHN). Religion and Philosophy in Germany. [*See* HEINE, H.]
Wit, Wisdom, and Pathos from the Prose of Heinrich Heine. [*See* HEINE, H.]

SNORRO STURLESON. Heimskringla edr Noregs Konunga Sögor. (In Scandinavian, Latin, and German.) 6 vols. fol. Havniæ, 1777–1826. B 14 T 2–7 ‡
Heimskringla; or, Chronicle of the Kings of Norway; translated from the Icelandic by Samuel Laing. 3 vols. 8vo. Lond., 1844. B 2 R 4–6

SNOW (W. PARKER). Two Years' Cruise off Tierra del Fuego, the Falkland Islands, Patagonia, and in the River Plate. With Illustrations. 2 vols. 8vo. Lond., 1857. D 3 R 18, 19
Voyage of the *Prince Albert* in search of Sir John Franklin: a Narrative of Every-day Life in the Arctic Seas. 8vo. Lond., 1851. D 4 R 30

SNOWBALL (JOHN). Publicity; or, Representative Government perfected by use of a Cementitious Element ensuring its uniform adhesion to the General Welfare. 8vo. Melb., 1859. MF 1 Q 6

SOAMES (HENRY), M.A. The Anglo-Saxon Church: its History, Revenues, and General Character. 8vo. Lond., 1835. G 12 S 24

SOANE (GEORGE). Life of the Duke of Wellington. (Fam. Lib.) 2 vols. 12mo. Lond., 1839–40. K 10 T 24, 25

SOCIAL SCIENCE (NATIONAL ASSOCIATION FOR THE PROMOTION OF). Hand-book of. [*See* FISON, MRS. W.]
The Social Science Almanac and Hand-book for 1860. 8vo. Lond., 1860. E
Transactions of the National Association for the Promotion of Social Science. 30 vols. 8vo. Lond., 1857–85. E

SOCIETÀ ITALIANA DI SCIENZE NATURALI. Atti della Società Italiana di Scienze Naturali. Vols. 1–30. 8vo. Milan, 1859–87. E

SOCIETÀ GEOGRAFICA ITALIANA. Statistica della Emigrazione Italiana all' estero nel 1881, confrontata con quella degli Anni precedenti e coll' emigrazione avvenuta da altri Stati; per L. Bodio. Roy. 8vo. Rome, 1882. E
Terzo Congresso Geografico Internazionale, tenuto a Venezia dal 15 al 22 Settembre, 1881. Roy. 8vo. Rome, 1872. E

SOCIETATIS JESU. Historiæ Societatis Jesu. 6 parts (in 7 vols.) fol. Antverp., &c., 1620–1859. G 36 R 10–16 ‡

SOCIÉTÉ DES BIBLIOTHEQUES COMMUNALES DU HAUT-RHIN. Troisième Séance Annuelee. (Pam. 34.) Mulhouse, 1867. J 12 U 26

SOCIÉTÉ DE GÉOGRAPHIE. Bulletin de la Société de Géographie, rédigé avec le Concours de la Section de Publication, par les Secrétaires de la Commission centrale. 119 vols. 8vo. Paris, 1822–87. E

SOCIÉTÉ IMPERIALE DES NATURALISTES DE MOSCOU. Bulletin de. Tomes 53, 54. 2 vols. 8vo. Moscow, 1878–79. E

SOCIETY FOR BETTERING THE POOR. Reports of. 12mo. Lond., 1798. F 5 R 20

SOCIETY FOR PROMOTING PRACTICAL DESIGN, and diffusing a Knowledge and Love of the Arts among the People: Account of the Inaugural Meeting, held at Exeter Hall, January 11, 1838. 8vo. Lond., 1838. A 7 Q 13

SOCIETY FOR PSYCHICAL RESEARCH. Proceedings of. Vols. 1–4, 1882–87. 8vo. Lond., 1883–87. E

SOCIETY FOR THE DIFFUSION OF USEFUL KNOWLEDGE. [*See* MAPS.] D 8 P 4 ‡
[*See* BIOGRAPHICAL DICTIONARY.]

SOCIETY FOR THE PRESERVATION OF THE IRISH LANGUAGE. [*See* DIARMUID AND GRAINNE.]

SOCIETY FOR THE PROMOTION OF CHRISTIAN KNOWLEDGE. [*See* CHRISTIAN KNOWLEDGE.]

SOCIETY FOR THE PROMOTION OF HELLENIC STUDIES. [*See* HELLENIC STUDIES.]

SOCIETY FOR THE PROMOTION OF PERMANENT AND UNIVERSAL PEACE. Fourth Annual Report, 1820. 8vo. Lond., 1820.   MG 1 Q 26

SOCIETY FOR THE PROPAGATION OF THE GOSPEL IN FOREIGN PARTS. Report, 1834–35. 8vo. Lond., 1835.   MG 1 Q 26

SOCIETY FOR THE RELIEF OF DESTITUTE CHILDREN. Reports, 1853–55, 1858–64, 1868, 1871, 8vo. Sydney, 1853–72.   MF 3 P 12

SOCIETY OF FRIENDS (THE). Selection from the Christian Advices issued by the Yearly Meetings of the Society of Friends held in London. 12mo. Lond., 1829.   G 7 U 3

[*See* HODGSON, W.]

SOCIETY OF GENTLEMEN, A. [*See* NEW HOLLAND.]

SOCIUS. [*See* FACETIÆ CANTABRIGIENSIS.]

SOCRATES. Apology of. [*See* PLATO.]

Dissertation on the Epistles of. [*See* BENTLLEY, R.]

Life of; collected from the Memorabilia of Xenophon and the Dialogues of Plato, by John Gilbert Cooper, jun. 4th ed. 8vo. Lond., 1771.   C 10 Q 41

Memoirs of, for English Readers: a new Translation from Xenophon's "Memorabilia"; with illustrative Notes by Edward Levien, M.A. 12mo. Lond.,1872.   C 1 P 35

Trial and Death of. [*See* PLATO.]

SOCRATES (SCHOLASTICUS). Ecclesiastical History of Socrates, surnamed Scholasticus, or, the Advocate, comprising a History of the Church, in seven Books. 8vo. Lond., 1874.   G 16 Q 4

Historia Ecclesiastica. [*See* MIGNE, J. P., SERIES GRÆCA, 67.]

Life of. [*See* EUSEBIUS PAMPHILUS.]   G 4 S 8, 9 †

SOKOLOW (P.) Ecclesiastico-Sclavonic and Russian Dictionary. 2 vols. 8vo. St. Petersburg, 1834.   K 12 S 2, 3

SOLANDER (DR. D. C.) [*See* COOK, CAPT., J., *and* PARKINSON, S.]

SOLBERG (THORVALD). Bibliography of Literary Property. [*See* BOWKER, R. R.]

[*See* HORN, F. W.]   B 2 R 12

SOLEY (HENRY SHAEM), M.A. Antiquities of Israel. [*See* DE MORGAN, A.]

SOLEY (PROF. JAMES RUSSELL), U.S.N. Report on Foreign Systems of Naval Education. 8vo. Wash.,1880. G 17 R 4

Rescue of Greely. [*See* SCHLEY, COMM. W. S.]   D 4 R 15

SOLICITOR OF THE COURT, A. [*See* DILLON, J.]

SOLIS (ANTONIO DE). History of the Conquest of Mexico by the Spaniards; from the original Spanish by Thomas Townsend. Fol. Lond., 1724.   B 17 S 14 ‡

SOLLY (PROF. EDWARD), M.A. Vegetable Substances used in the Arts and Manufactures in relation to Commerce generally. [*See* LONDON INTERNATIONAL EXHIBITION, 1851.]   A 16 Q 22

SOLON (L. M.) Art of the Old English Potter. 2nd ed. 8vo. Lond., 1885.   A 11 T 17

SOMERS (JOHN), LORD. Account of the Life and Writings of Lord Chancellor Somers, including Remarks on the Public Affairs in which he was engaged, and the Bill of Rights; by Henry Maddock. 4to. Lond.,1812. C 4 W 31

Collection of scarce and valuable Tracts, on the most interesting and entertaining Subjects. 2nd ed., by [Sir] Walter Scott, Esq. 13 vols. roy. 4to. Lond., 1809–15.   B 2 U 17–29

Essay on the Life and Character of; also, Sketches of an Essay on the Life and Character of Philip, Earl of Hardwicke, by Richard Cooksey. 4to. Worcester, 1791.   C 4 W 32

SOMERS (ROBERT). Trades Unions: an Appeal to the Working Classes and their Friends. 8vo. Edinb., 1876.   F 5 S 9

SOMERSET (C. A.) Crazy Jane: a Romantic Play. (Cumberland's Eng. Theatre.) 12mo. Lond., 1829.   H 2 Q 20

Yes ! an Operatic Interlude. (Cumberland's Eng. Theatre.) 12mo. Lond., 1829.   H 2 Q 23

SOMERVILLE (MRS. MARY). On Molecular and Microscopic Science. 2 vols. 8vo. Lond., 1869. A 17 T 3, 4

On the Connexion of the Physical Sciences. 12mo. Lond., 1834.   A 3 S 14

Physical Geography. 3rd ed. 2 vols. 12mo. Lond., 1851.   A 29 P 13, 14

SOMERVILLE (WILLIAM). Life and Poems of. [*See* BRITISH POETS 1 : CHALMERS, A. ; *and* JOHNSON, S.]

SOMMERFELDT (HAKON A.), K.St.O. Construction of Ships for Ocean and River Service. (Weale.) 12mo. Lond., 1861.   A 17 P 16

Atlas [to same]. Imp. 4to. Lond., 1861. A 23 P 26 ‡

SON OF THE SOIL, A. [*See* MILLER, J.]

SONG OF SEPARATION, (THE), after Hiawatha ; by "Tallboy." 12mo. Deriliquin, 1861.   MH 1 R 46

SONKLAR (K. VON). Gletscherschwankungen, mit den Meteorologischen Verhältnissen. 8vo. Wien, 1858.   A 3 T 18

SONNENSCHEIN (ADOLF). Standards of Teaching of Foreign Codes relating to Elementary Education, prescribed by Austrian, Belgian, German, Italian, and Swiss Governments. 8vo. Lond., 1881.   G 17 P 23

SONNERAT (PIERRE). Account of a Voyage to the Spice Islands and New Guinea; with Notes. 12mo. Lond., 1781. MD 1 T 55

Voyage à la Nouvelle Guinée, dans lequel ou trouve la Description des Lieux, des Observations Physiques et Morales, et des détails relatifs à l'Histoire Naturelle dans le Règne Animal et le Règne Végétal. 4to. Paris, 1776. MD 3 V 23

SOPHOCLES. Facsimile of the Laurentian Manuscript of Sophocles; with an Introduction by E. M. Thompson, F.S.A., and R. C. Jebb, LL.D. Fol. Lond., 1885. H 22 S 4 ‡

Lexicon Sophocleum : Zweiter Artikel, von William Dindorf. (Pam. 34.) 8vo. Leipzig, 1871. J 12 U 26

Plays and Fragments; with Critical Notes, Commentary, and Translation in English Prose, by R. C. Jebb, M.A., &c. Part 1. The Œdipus Tyrannus. Part 2. The Œdipus Coloneus. 2 vols. 8vo. Camb., 1883–85. H 1 S 22, 23

Scholia Græca in Sophoclem, ex editione Brunckiana. 8vo. Oxonii, 1810. H 2 R 38

Sophocles ; edited with English Notes and Introductions, by Lewis Campbell, M.A., &c. 2nd ed., revised. (Clar. Press.) 2 vols. 8vo. Oxford, 1879–81. H 2 S 30, 31

Tragedies of ; translated by Thomas Francklin, D.D. (Fam. Class. Lib.) 18mo. Lond., 1832. J 15 P 40

Tragœdiæ Septem ; cum Versione Latina et Notis ; scholia Græca in Sophoclem, ex editione Rich. Franc. Phil. Brunck. 2 vols. 8vo. Oxonii, 1814. H 2 R 36, 37

[Tragedies of] ; by Dr. Francklin. [See GREEK TRAGIC THEATRE.]

SOPHOCLES (E. A.) Glossary of Later and Byzantine Greek. 4to. Lond., 1860. K 4 S 7 †

Romaic, or Modern Greek Grammar. 12mo. Boston, 1879. K 11 T 31

SORELL (LIEUT.-COL. T. S.) Notes on the Campaign of 1808–09 in the North of Spain, in reference to some passages in Lieut.-Col. Napier's History of the War in the Peninsula. 2nd ed. 8vo. Lond., 1828. B 13 U 7

SORELLI (GUIDO). Autobiography of: Confessions to Silvio Pellico. 12mo. Lond., 1836. C 2 Q 49

SORET (—.) Conversations of Goethe with Soret. [See GOETHE, J. W. VON.] C 11 P 14, 15

SORLEY (PROF. W. R.) Jewish Christians and Judaism : a Study in the History of the First Two Centuries. 8vo. Camb., 1881. G 12 S 6

SORRENTO. Guide to Sorrento: a few Interesting Facts for General Information. 8vo. Melb., 1876. MJ 2 R 1

SOTHEBY (W.) Georgics of Virgil. [See VIRGILIUS MARO, P.] J 15 P 50

Oberon : a Poem, from the German of Wieland. [See WIELAND, C. M. VON.]

SOTHERAN (HENRY). Catalogue of Superior Second-hand Books. 2 vols. 8vo. Lond., 1877–85. Libr.

4 U

SOTHERN (JOHN RUSSELL). Zephyrus, and other Poems. 12mo. Melh., 1862. MH 1 R 49

SOUDAN EXPEDITION. History of the Soudan Expedition, and the Constitution Act of New South Wales ; by Thomas Shire. 4to. Sydney, 1885. MB 1 U 5

SOULEYET (E.) [See VAILLANT, A. N.] A 15 P 20, 21

SOUSA (MANUEL DE FARIA Y). Portugues Asia; or, the History of the Discovery and Conquest of India by the Portugues. 3 vols. 8vo. Lond., 1694–95. B 10 Q 34–36

SOUTH (JOHN FLINT), P.R.C.S. Memorials of ; collected by the Rev. Charles Lett Feltoe, M.A. With a Portrait. 8vo. Lond., 1884. C 4 Q 27

[See OTTO, A. W.] A 13 Q 1

SOUTH (ROBERT), D.D. Sermons preached upon several occasions. New ed. 7 vols. 8vo. Oxford, 1823. G 12 R 8–14

Selections from the Works of. [See MONTAGU, B.]

SOUTH AFRICAN PUBLIC LIBRARY. [See CAPE OF GOOD HOPE.]

SOUTH ASIAN REGISTER (THE), No. 4, December, 1828. 8vo. Sydney, 1828. MJ 2 Q 2

SOUTH AUSTRALIA.

Analysis of the Commission of the Governor, the Act, and other Documents, which define and limit the Governing Powers of the Province of South Australia. Fol. Adelaide, 1838. MJ 2 U 3

An Account of its History, Progress, Resources, and Present Position. 8vo. Adelaide, 1879. MF 3 P 22

First Report from the Select Committee on South Australia. (Parl. Docs., 30.) Fol. Lond., 1841. MF 4 ‡

Second Report from the Select Committee on South Australia ; together with the Minutes of Evidence, Appendix, and Index. (Parl. Docs., 24.) Fol. Lond., 1841. MF 4 ‡

Second Annual Report of the Colonization Commissioners for South Australia, 1837. Fol. Lond., 1837. MF 1 U 34

ACTS.

Acts of the Parliament of. 16 vols. 4to. Adelaide, 1837–84. ME

Acts and Ordinances of the Province of South Australia. 8 vols. sm. fol. Adelaide, 1837–75. ME

An Act to empower His Majesty to erect South Australia into a British Province or Provinces, and to provide for the Colonization and Government thereof. (Parl. Docs. 42.) Fol. Lond., 1834. MF 4 ‡

AGRICULTURE.

Agriculture in South Australia ; by "The Special Reporter of the Leader." 8vo. Melb., 1874. MA 2 V 41

BOTANIC GARDENS.

Reports on the Progress and Condition of the Botanic Gardens and Government Plantations, during the years 1874–76; by R. Schomburgk, Ph.D., &c. (Pam. P.) Fol. Adelaide, 1875-77. MJ 2 U 4

SOUTH AUSTRALIA—*continued.*

CENSUS.
Census, March, 1876. Fol. Adelaide, 1879. ME

CROWN LANDS.
Papers relative to Crown Lands in the Australian Colonies. (Parl. Docs. 59, 62, 65.) 3 vols. fol. Lond., 1851-56. MF 4 ‡

Returns of Quantity of Land in South Australia sold by the Colonization Commissioners since the 5th day of May, 1835. (Parl. Docs. 30.) Fol. Lond., 1840. MF 4 ‡

FINANCES.
Copy of Correspondence of the Colonial Department, explanatory of the Debts incurred by the Government of South Australia; and also, an Account of the Income and Expenditure of the said Colony. (Parl. Docs., 30.) Fol. Lond., 1841. MF 4 ‡

Papers relative to the Affairs of South Australia. (Parl. Docs., 43.) Fol. Lond., 1843. MF 4 ‡

Copies of Correspondence in the Colonial Department, relative to the establishment of the Settlement of South Australia, since the year 1831, and its present Financial Difficulties. (Parl. Docs., 30.) Fol. Lond., 1841. MF 4 ‡

GOVERNMENT GAZETTE.
South Australian Government Gazette. 18 vols. 4to. Adelaide, 1874-87. ME

NORTHERN TERRITORY.
Northern Territory of South Australia; accompanied with a Map. 8vo. Adelaide, 1863. MD 1 U 18

Port Darwin: its Soil, Climate, Resources, and Prospects as a Gold-field; by "Quiris." 8vo. Melb., 1872. MJ 2 R 16

PARLIAMENT.
Proceedings; with Copies of the Documents ordered to be printed. 102 vols. fol. Adelaide, 1852-87. ME

PARLIAMENTARY LIBRARY.
Catalogue of the Parliamentary Library of South Australia; compiled by J. C. Morphett. 4to. Adelaide, 1885. MK 1 U 1

SOUTH AUSTRALIAN ASSOCIATION. Outline of the Plan of a Proposed Colony to be founded on the South Coast of Australia; with an Account of the Soil, Climate, Rivers, &c. With Maps. 8vo. Lond., 1834. MF 2 R 21

SOUTH AUSTRALIAN COLONIST (THE), and Settlers' Weekly Record of British, Foreign, and Colonial Intelligence. Fol. Lond., 1840. MF 3 U 4

SOUTH AUSTRALIAN COMPANY. Plan of a Company to be established for the purpose of founding a Colony in Southern Australia. 8vo. Lond., 1831. MF 2 R 20

First Report of the Directors. 8vo. Lond., 1836. MJ 2 R 12

Copies of Letters and Accounts which have passed between the Manager of the South Australian Company and the Colonization Commissioners for South Australia, or the Colonial Office. (Parl. Docs., 15.) Fol. Lond., 1844. MF 4 ‡

SOUTH AUSTRALIAN INSTITUTE. Adelaide. Annual Reports for the years 1861-75. 4to. Adelaide, 1861-75. MJ 2 S 2, and 4

Catalogue of the Library. 8vo. Adelaide, 1869. MK 1 Q 14

South Australian Institute; comprising the Public Library, Art Gallery, and Museums: Addresses delivered at the Laying of the Foundation Stone, by Sir W. F. D. Jervois, G.C.M.G., &c., R. Rees, C.E., and Hon. T. King. 8vo. Adelaide, 1879. MJ 1 T 42

SOUTH AUSTRALIAN MAGAZINE (THE). Edited by James Allen, and Thomas Young Cotter, Esq. Vols. 1 and 2, Nos. 2 and 7. 8vo. Adelaide, 1842-43. ME 3 R

SOUTH AUSTRALIAN REGISTER, 1839-41, 1857-58. 2 vols. fol. Adelaide, 1839-58. EM

SOUTHALL (JAMES C.), A.M., &c. Epoch of the Mammoth and the Apparition of Man upon the Earth. 8vo. Lond., 1878. A 9 Q 22

Recent Origin of Man, as illustrated by Geology. Roy. 8vo. Philad., 1875. A 9 T 26

SOUTHAN (W. M.) Two Lawyers: a Novel. 8vo. Dunedin, 1881.* MJ 1 T 47

SOUTHERN (THOMAS). Isabella; or, the Fatal Marriage. (Bell's Brit. Theatre.) 18mo. Lond., 1792. H 2 P 8

Another copy. (Brit. Theatre.) 12mo. Lond., 1808. H 1 P 7

Another copy. (New Eng. Theatre.) 12mo. Lond., 1783. H 4 P 27

Another copy. [*See* BRIT. DRAMA 2.]

Oroonoko: a Tragedy. (Bell's Brit. Theatre.) 18mo. Lond., 1791. H 2 P 23

Another copy. (Brit. Theatre.) 12mo. Lond., 1808. H 1 P 7

Another copy. (New Eng. Theatre.) 12mo. Lond., 1785. H 4 P 21

SOUTHERN AUSTRALIAN (THE). Fol. Adelaide, 1838-40. ME

SOUTHERN CROSS (THE): a Weekly Journal of Politics, Literature, and Social Progress. Fol. Sydney, 1859-60. ME

SOUTHERN SPECTATOR (THE). January and May, 1859. 8vo. Melb., 1859. ME 3 R

SOUTHEY (REV. CHARLES CUTHBERT). Life and Correspondence of Robert Southey. Edited by his Son. 6 vols. 8vo. Lond., 1849-50. C 4 U 27-32

Life of Wesley. [*See* SOUTHEY, R.] C 6 R 20, 21

SOUTHEY (ROBERT), LL.D. [A Biography]; by E. Dowden. (Eng. Men of Letts.) 8vo. Lond., 1879. C 1 U 31

Book of the Church. 2 vols. 8vo. Lond., 1824. G 12 Q 4, 5

Chronicle of the Cid. [*See* CID, R. DIAZ DE B.]

Common place Book. 1st-4th series. Edited by J. W. Warter, B.D. 4 vols. 8vo. Lond., 1849-51. J 7 S 12-15

SOUTHEY (ROBERT), LL.D.—*continued.*
Correspondence with Caroline Bowles; to which are
added, Correspondence with Shelley, and Southey's Dreams;
edited by Edward Dowden, LL.D. 8vo. Dublin, 1881.
                                                    C 9 U 38

Select Biographies: Cromwell and Bunyan. (H. and C.
Lib.) 12mo. Lond., 1844.   J 8 P 6

History of Brazil. 2nd ed. 3 vols. 4to. Lond.,
1817–22.   B 19 Q 1–3 ‡

History of the Peninsular War. 6 vols. 8vo. Lond.,
1828–38.   B 13 T 23–28

Letters from England; by "Don Manuel Alvarez Espriella." 2nd ed. 3 vols. 12mo. Lond., 1808. D 7 P 38–40

Life and Correspondence of; edited by his Son, the Rev.
Charles Cuthbert Southey. 6 vols. 8vo. Lond., 1849–50.
                                                 C 4 U 27–32

Life of John Wesley, and Rise and Progress of Methodism; edited by the Rev. Charles Cuthbert Southey,
M.A. 2 vols. 8vo. Lond., 1846.   C 6 R 20, 21

Life of Lord Nelson. Illustrated. 8vo. Lond., 1870.
                                                    C 2 Q 27

Another copy. 8vo. Lond., 1877.   C 9 P 7

Lives of the British Admirals; with an Introductory
View of the Naval History of England. (Lard. Cab.
Cyclo.) 5 vols. 12mo. Lond., 1833–40.   K 1 S 1–5

Oliver Newman: a New England Tale; with other
Poetical Remains. 12mo. Lond., 1845.   H 7 U 20

Poetical Works of. Roy. 8vo. Lond., 1850.   H 6 V 11

Another copy. Roy. 8vo. Lond., 1871.   H 6 V 12

Roderick, the Last of the Goths. 4th ed.
12mo. Lond., 1816.   H 7 U 15, 16

Specimens of the Later English Poets; with Preliminary
Notices. 3 vols. 8vo. Lond., 1807.   H 7 U 17–19

The Doctor, &c. 2nd ed. 7 vols. 8vo. Lond.,
1835–47.   J 5 Q 17–23

Life of William Cowper. [*See* COWPER, W.]

Life of H. K. White. [*See* WHITE, H. K.]

SOUTHEY (THOMAS). Rise, Progress, and Present State
of Colonial Wools; comprising those of Australia, Van
Diemen's Land and New Zealand, South Africa, British
India, Peru, Chile, La Plata, and United States of America;
with some Account of the Goats' Wool of Angora and
India, &c. 8vo. Lond., 1848.*   MA 1 Q 20

Rise, Progress, and Present State of Colonial Sheep
and Wools, continued from 1846. 8vo. Lond., 1851.
                                                   MA 1 Q 23

Treatise on Sheep, addressed to the Flock-masters of
Australia, Tasmania, and Southern Africa. 8vo. Lond.,
1840.   MA 1 Q 24

SOUTHGATE (HENRY). Many Thoughts of Many Minds:
Selections from the Writings of the most Celebrated
Authors, from the Earliest to the Present Time. 1st and
2nd series. 2 vols. 8vo. Lond., 1880.   K 17 P 29, 30

The Way to Woo and Win a Wife. 12mo. Lond.,
1876.   J 1 W 36

SOUTHGATE (REV. HORATIO). Narrative of a Tour
through Armenia, Kurdistan, Persia, and Mesopotamia.
2 vols. 8vo. Lond., 1840.   D 5 R 1, 2

SOUTH KENSINGTON MUSEUM. Art and Science
Hand-books. 28 vols. 8vo. Lond., 1875–84.   E
  1. Textile Fabrics; by the Very Rev. D. Rock, D.D.
  2. Ivories, Ancient and Mediæval; by Wm. Maskell.
  3. Ancient and Modern Furniture and Woodwork; by J. H.
     Pollen.
  4. Maiolica; by C. D. E. Fortnum, F.S.A.
  5. Musical Instruments; by Carl Engel.
  6. Manual of Design, compiled from the Writings, &c., of R.
     Redgrave, R.A.; by Gilbert R. Redgrave.
  7. Persian Art; by Major R. M. Smith, R.E.
  8. Special Loan Collection of Scientific Apparatus, 1876.
  9. Food: some Account of its Sources, Constituents, and Uses;
     by A. H. Church, M.A.
 10. Economic Entomology: Aptera; by Andrew Murray, F.L.S.
 11. Hand-book to the Special Loan Collection of Scientific Ap-
     paratus, 1876.
 12. Conferences held in connection with the Special Loan Col-
     lection of Scientific Apparatus, 1876: Physics and Mechanics,
     Chemistry, Biology, Physical Geography, Geology, Mineralogy,
     and Meteorology.
 13. Bronzes; by C. Drury E. Fortnum, F.S.A. With numerous
     Woodcuts.
 14. Animal Products: their Preparation, Commercial Uses, and
     Value; by P. L. Simmonds.
 15. The Industrial Arts in Spain; by Juan F. Riaño. With
     numerous Woodcuts.
 16. Gold and Silver-smith's Work: by John Hungerford Pollen,
     M.A. With numerous Woodcuts.
 17. Hand-book of the Dyce and Forster Collections in the South
     Kensington Museum. With Engravings and Woodcuts.
 18, 19. The Industrial Arts of India; by George C. M. Birdwood,
     C.S.I., &c. With Map and Woodcuts.
 20. College and Corporation Plate: a Hand-book to the Repro-
     ductions of Silver Plate in the South Kensington Museum,
     from celebrated English Collections; by Wilfred Joseph Cripps,
     M.A., &c.
 21. The Industrial Arts of Denmark, from the Earliest Times to
     the Danish Conquest of England; by J. J. A. Worsaae, Hon.
     F.S.A., With Map and Woodcuts; in two Parts.
 22. Hand-book of the Jones Collection in the South Kensington
     Museum. With Portrait and Woodcuts.
 23. The Industrial Arts of Scandinavia in the Pagan Time; by
     Hans Hildebrand. With numerous Woodcuts.
 24. Precious Stones, considered in their Scientific and Artistic
     Relations; with a Catalogue of the Townsend Collection of
     Gems in the South Kensington Museum, by A. H. Church,
     M.A., &c. With a coloured Plate and Woodcuts.
 25. The Analysis and Adulteration of Foods; by James Bell,
     Ph.D., &c. Part 2. Milk, Butter, Cheese, Cereal Foods, Pre-
     pared Starches, &c.
 26. English Earthenware: a Hand-book to the Wares made in
     England during the 17th and 18th Centuries, as illustrated by
     Specimens in the National Collections; by A. H. Church,
     M.A., Oxon, &c. With numerous Woodcuts.
 27. French Pottery; by Paul Gasnault and Edouard Garnier.
     With Illustrations and Marks.
 28. Russian Art, and Art Objects in Russia: a Hand-book to the
     Reproductions of Goldsmith's' Work, and other Art Treasures
     from that Country, in the South Kensington Museum; by
     Alfred Maskell.

Guide to the South Kensington Museum. (Pam. F.)
8vo. Lond., 1861.   MJ 2 S 3

SOUTH SEA ISLANDERS. Man-stealing in the Pacific: a Letter to the Editor of the *Herald*. 8vo. Sydney (n.d.) MG 1 Q 29

SOUTH SEA ISLANDS. Mission in the South Sea Islands. 8vo. Lond., 1797. MD 5 S 27

SOUTHLAND (PROVINCE OF). New Field for Pastoral and Agricultural Pursuits; being a Description of the Province of Southland, New Zealand. 8vo. Lond., 1867. MD 1 U 21

SOUTHWARK. Account of the Proceedings of the Electors of the Borough of Southwark. (Parl. Dd.) 8vo. Lond., 1809. F 12 P 22

SOUTHWELL (ROBERT). Tracts of. [*See* BRYDGES, SIR S. E.]

SOUVESTRE (EMILE). Confessions of a Working Man; from the French; translated from the 3rd ed. 12mo. Lond., 1853. C 2 R 18

Pedro Landais. 8vo. Madrid, 1862. J 15 U 26

SOWERBY (GEORGE BRETTINGHAM), F.L.S. Conchological Illustrations. 8vo. Lond., 1841. A 14 S 51

Conchological Manual. 8vo. 3rd ed. Lond., 1846. A 14 T 3

Illustrated Index of British Shells, containing Figures of all the Recent Species, with Names and other Information. Imp. 8vo. Lond., 1859. A 14 V 44

[*See* BEECHEY, CAPT. F. W.]

SOWERBY (HENRY). Popular Mineralogy; comprising a familiar Account of Minerals and their Uses. 12mo. Lond., 1850. A 9 P 27

SOWERBY (JAMES), F.L.S. British Mineralogy; or, coloured Figures intended to elucidate the Mineralogy of Great Britain. 5 vols. roy. 8vo. Lond., 1804–17. A 9 U 17–21

English Botany; or, coloured Figures of British Plants; edited by John T. Boswell (Syme), F.L.S., &c.; the Popular Portion, by Mrs. Lankester; the Figures, by J. Sowerby, F.L.S., &c. 3rd ed. 12 vols. roy. 8vo. Lond., 1869–86. A 4 V 1–12

Exotic Mineralogy; or, coloured Figures of Foreign Minerals, as a Supplement to "British Mineralogy." 2 vols. roy. 8vo. Lond., 1811–17. A 9 U 22, 23

Malacostraca Podophthalmata Britanniæ. [*See* LEACH, W. E.] A 18 1 †

[*See* SHAW, G., *and* SMITH, SIR J. E.]

SOWERBY (JAMES DE CARLE), F.L.S., AND LEAR (EDWARD). Tortoises, Terrapins, and Turtles. Drawn from Life. Fol. Lond., 1872. A 23 Q 7 ‡

SOWERBY (JOHN E.) Ferns of Great Britain; illustrated by J. E. Sowerby; the Descriptions, Synonyms, &c., by Charles Johnson. 8vo. Lond., 1859. A 4 S 8

Fern Allies; a Supplement to the "Ferns of Great Britain; illustrated by J. E. Sowerby; Descriptions by C. Johnson. 8vo. Lond., 1859. A 4 S 8

Useful Plants of Great Britain. [*See* JOHNSON, C. P.]

SOWERBY (REV. WILLIAM.) Duty of the Inhabitants of this Colony, with respect to the Famine prevailing in Ireland and the North of Scotland, stated and enforced: a Sermon. 8vo. Sydney, 1847. MG 1 P 1

SOYER (A.) The Pantropheon; or, History of Food and its Preparation, from the Earliest Ages of the World. Roy. 8vo. Lond., 1853. A 6 Q 24

SOYRES (JOHN DE). Provincial Letters of Pascal. [*See* PASCAL, B.] G 12 Q 24

SOZOMENUS OR SOZOMEN (HERMIUS). Ecclesiastical History: a History of the Church, in nine Books, from A.D. 324–440. New Translation; with a Memoir of the Author. 8vo. Lond., 1846. G 12 Q 8

SPAIN. Notes of an Attaché in Spain in 1850. 8vo. Lond., 1851. D 8 T 8

Scenes and Adventures in Spain, 1835–40: by "Poco Mas." 2 vols. 8vo. Lond., 1845. D 9 Q 16, 17

SPALDING (CAPT. H.), F.R.G.S. Khiva and Turkestan; translated from the Russian by Capt. H. Spalding. 8vo. Lond., 1874. D 6 P 41

SPALDING (PROF. WILLIAM), A.M. History of English Literature; with an Outline of the Origin and Growth of the English Language. 2nd ed. 12mo. Edinb., 1853. B 21 S 24

SPALDING CLUB. Publications of. 35 vols. 4to. and 2 vols. fol. Aberdeen, 1841–69. E

SPALLANZANI (LAZZARO). Opere di. 6 vols. 8vo. Milano, 1825–26. J 17 Q 23–28

SPARK (J. L.), L.S. Table of Areas for Rectangular Allotments, of from one foot to 100 feet frontage, by one foot to 100 feet in depth. Sm. 4to. Sydney, 1887. MA 2 R 35

SPARK (WILLIAM). Henry Smart: his Life and Works. With Portrait. 8vo. Lond., 1881. C 3 U 38

SPARKS (JARED). Life of George Washington, Commander-in-Chief of the American Armies, and first President of the United States; to which are added, his Diaries and Speeches. 2 vols. 8vo. Lond., 1839. C 9 Q 47, 48

Memoirs of the Life and Travels of John Ledyard, from his Journal and Correspondence. 8vo. Lond., 1828. MC 1 Q 13

SPARKS (TIMOTHY). [*See* DICKENS, C.]

SPARRMAN (ANDREAS), M.D. Reize naar de Kaap de Goede Hoop, de Landen van den Zuidpool, en rondom de Waereld, in de jaaren 1772 tot 1776 gedaan. 8vo. Leyden, 1787. D 2 R 8

Voyage to the Cape of Good Hope towards the Antarctic Polar Circle, and round the World. With Plates. 2 vols. 4to. Lond., 1785. D 2 V 7, 8

Another copy. 2nd ed. 2 vols. 4to. Lond., 1786. D 2 V 9, 10

Another copy. 2nd ed. 2 vols. (in 1) 4to. Lond., 1786. MD 3 P 20 †

SPARSCHUH (DR. N.) Keltische Studien, oder Untersuchungen über das Wesen und die Entstehung der griechischen Sprache, Mythologie und Philosophie vermittelst
der keltischen Dialecte. 8vo. Frankfurt-am-Maine, 1848.
　　　　　　　　　　　　　　　　　　　K 13 Q 28

SPEARMAN (H. R.) British Burma Gazetteer. [Compiled
by H. R. Spearman.] 2 vols. roy. 8vo. Rangoon, 1880.
　　　　　　　　　　　　　　　　　　　D 11 V 1, 2

SPECIMENS of the Novelists and Romancers; with Critical
and Biographical Notices of the Authors. 12mo. Glasgow, 1827.　　　　　　　　　　　　　J 11 U 21

SPECIMENS of the Yorkshire Dialect; to which is added
a Glossary of such of the Yorkshire words as are likely
not to be understood. 2nd ed. 12mo. Knaresbrough,
1808.　　　　　　　　　　　　　　　　K 11 S 39

SPECTATOR (THE): a Weekly Journal of News, Politics,
Literature, &c. 15 vols. fol. Lond., 1839–53.　　E

SPECTATOR (THE). Fol. Sydney, 1846.　　　　　E

SPEDDING (JAMES). Account of the Life and Times of
Francis Bacon, extracted from the edition of his Occasional
Writings. 2 vols. 8vo. Lond., 1878.　　　C 3 R 6, 7

Evenings with a Reviewer; or, Macaulay and Bacon.
2 vols. 8vo. Lond., 1881.　　　　　J 2 S 14, 15

Letters and Life of Francis Bacon, including all his
Occasional Works, newly collected and set forth in chronological order. 6 vols. 8vo. Lond.,1861–72. C 2 V 17–22

Reviews and Discussions, Literary, Political, and Historical, not relating to Bacon. 8vo. Lond.,1879. J 12 R 1

Studies in English History. [*See* GAIRDNER, J.]　　B 3 T 1

SPEECHLY (WILLIAM). Treatise on the Culture of the
Vine. 8vo. 1789.　　　　　　　　　　A 1 R 7

SPEED (JOHN). Historie of Great Britaine under the
Conquests of the Romans, Saxons, Danes, and Normans.
2nd ed. Sm. fol. Lond., 1623.　　　B 19 S 5 ‡

Another copy. 3rd ed. Sm. fol. Lond., 1632.　B 19 S 6 ‡

SPEED (DR. JOHN). History of Southampton. [*See*
DAVIES, REV. J. S.]

SPEED (JOHN GILMER). [*See* KEATS, J.]

SPEEDY (MRS. CORNELIA MARY). My Wanderings in the
Soudan. 2 vols. 8vo. Lond., 1884.　　　D 1 Q 14, 15

SPEEDY (THOMAS). Sport in the Highlands and Lowlands
of Scotland with Rod and Gun. 8vo. Edinb., 1884.
　　　　　　　　　　　　　　　　　　　A 17 W 45

SPEKE (CAPT. JOHN HANNING). Journal of the Discovery
of the Source of the Nile. 8vo. Lond., 1863. D 2 T 15

SPELMAN (EDWARD). [*See* DIONYSIUS HALICARNASSENSIS.]
　　　　　　　　　　　　　　　　　　　B 18 Q 13–16 ‡

SPELMAN (SIR HENRY), KNT. Codex Legum Veterum
Statutorum Regni Angliæ. [*See* WILKINS, D.]
Concilia. [*See* WILKINS, D.]
De non temerandis Ecclesiis, Churches not to be violated:
a Tract. 5th ed. 12mo. Oxford, 1676.　G 9 P 17

English Works of, published in his Life-time; together
with his Posthumous Works. 2nd ed. Fol. Lond.,
1727.　　　　　　　　　　　　　　J 7 P 24 †

Glossarium Archaiologicum; continens latino-barbara,
peregrina, obsoleta, et novatæ significationis vocabula.
Fol. Lodd., 1664.　　　　　　　　K 22 S 17 ‡

Villare Anglicum; or, View of the Townes of England.
8vo. Lond., 1656.　　　　　　　　D 11 S 4

SPELMAN (SIR JOHN), KNT. Life of Alfred the Great, from
the original MS. in the Bodleyan Library; with Additions
by T. Hearne. Sm. fol. Oxford, 1709.　　C 2 U 6

SPENCE (MISS CHARLOTTE H.) A Plea for Pure Democracy : Mr. Hare's Reform Bill applied to South Australia by C. H. S. 8vo. Adelaide, 1861.　MF 1 Q 3

SPENCE (JAMES). The American Union : its Effects on
National Character and Policy. 2nd ed. 2 vols. 8vo.
Lond., 1862.　　　　　　　　　　B 1 R 1, 2

SPENCE (JAMES MUDIE), F.R.G.S. The Land of Bolivar;
or, War, Peace, and Adventure in the Republic of Venezuela. With Illustrations. 2 vols. 8vo. Lond., 1878.
　　　　　　　　　　　　　　　　　　　D 4 Q 23, 24

SPENCE (REV. JOSEPH), A.M. Polymetis; or, an Enquiry
concerning the agreement between the Works of the Roman
Poets and the Remains of the Antient Artists. Fol.
Lond., 1747.　　　　　　　　　　　A 19 U 1 ‡

SPENCE (W.) [*See* KIRBY, REV. W.]　　A 14 T 30–33

SPENCER (CHARLES CHILD). Rudimentary and Practical
Treatise on Music. 2 vols. (in 1). (Weale.) 12mo.
Lond., 1866.　　　　　　　　　　　A 17 P 21

Rudiments of the Art of Playing the Pianoforte.
(Weale.) 12mo. Lond., 1870.　　　A 17 P 21

SPENCER (CAPT. EDMUND). Sketches of Germany and the
Germans, with a Glance at Poland, Hungary, and Switzerland, in 1834–36; by "An Englishman resident in Germany." 2nd ed. 2 vols. 8vo. Lond.,1836. D 7 U 21, 22

Tour of Inquiry through France and Italy. 2 vols. 8vo.
Lond., 1853.　　　　　　　　　　D 7 R 35, 36

Travels in Circassia, Krim Tartary, &c., including a
Steam Voyage down the Danube. 3rd ed. 2 vols. 8vo.
Lond., 1839.　　　　　　　　　　D 6 T 26, 27

Travels in the Western Caucasus, in 1836. 2 vols. 8vo.
Lond., 1838.　　　　　　　　　　D 6 T 23, 24

SPENCER (EDMUND). Ancient Irish Histories. [*See*
HANMER, M.]　　　　　　　　　　B 11 R 8, 9

SPENCER (GEORGE JOHN), EARL. Account of the Mansion, Books, &c, of.　　　　　　　K 19 P 20–23 †

SPENCER (GEORGE TREVOR), D.D., BISHOP OF MADRAS.
Journal of a Visitation to the Provinces of Travancore and
Tinnevelly in the Diocese of Madras, 1840–41. 12mo.
Lond., 1842.   D 5 P 5

Journal of a Visitation Tour in 1843–44, through part
of the Western Portion of the Diocese. 12mo. Lond.,
1845.   D 5 P 6

Journal of a Visitation Tour through the Provinces of
Madura and Tinnevelly, in the Diocese of Madras, in 1845.
12mo. Lond., 1846.   D 5 P 7

SPENCER (HERBERT). Data of Ethics. 8vo. Lond.,
1879.   G 12 R 15

Descriptive Sociology. Parts 1–8. (*All published.*)
2 vols. roy. fol. Lond., 1874–81.   G 32 P 8, 9 ‡

Education, Intellectual, Moral, and Physical. 5th
thousand. 8vo. Lond., 1861.   G 17 Q 6

Essays, Scientific, Political, and Speculative. 3 vols.
8vo. Lond., 1883–88.   J 5 R 4–6

An Examination of Mr. Herbert Spencer's First
Principles. [*See* BIRKS, PROF. T. R.]

Examination of the Structural Principles of Mr.
Herbert Spencer's Philosophy. [*See* GROUND, REV.
W. D.]

First Principles. 8vo. Lond., 1862.   G 12 R 16

On Mr. Spencer's Unification of Knowledge. [*See*
GUTHRIE, M.]

Principles of Biology. 2nd thousand. 2 vols. 8vo.
Lond., 1864–67.   A 16 U 16, 17

Principles of Psychology. 8vo. Lond., 1855.   G 12 R 17

Another copy. 2nd ed. 2 vols. 8vo. Lond., 1870–72.
     G 12 R 18, 19

Principles of Sociology. 2 vols. (in 4) 8vo. Lond.,
1876–85.   G 12 R 20–23

Vol. 1. [Data, &c. of Sociology.]
Vol. 2, part 1. Ceremonial Institutions; part 2. Political Institutions; part 6, Ecclesiastical Institutions.

Social Statics; or, the Conditions essential to Human
Happiness specified. 8vo. Lond., 1851.   F 14 S 10

Study of Sociology. 5th ed. 8vo. Lond., 1876.
     C 10 Q 25

SPENCER (REV. J. A.), M.A. The East: Sketches of
Travel in Egypt and the Holy Land. Roy. 8vo. Lond.,
1850.   D 2 S 11

SPENCER (JOHN CHARLES), VISCOUNT ALTHORP, THIRD
EARL. Memoir of; by the late Sir Denis Le Marchant,
Bart. 8vo. Lond., 1876.   C 9 R 18

SPENCER (W. R.) Sketch of Duke of Devonshire. [*See*
ADAIR, R.]   C 10 U 9

SPENGEL (J. W.) [*See* DAWKINS, W. B.]   A 9 T 5

SPENS (H.), D.D. The Republic of Plato, in ten Books.
Sm. 8vo. Glasgow, 1763.   F 12 P 5

SPENSER (EDMUND), M.A., &c. [A Biography]; by R. W.
Church. (Eng. Men Letters.) 8vo. Lond., 1879.   C 1 U 32

SPENSER (EDMUND), M.A., &c.—*continued.*
Book[s] 1 and 2 of the Faery Queene; edited by G.
W. Kitchin, M.A. 6th ed. (Clar. Press.) 2 vols. (in 1).
12mo. Oxford, 1874–75.   H 6 R 46

Complete Works in Verse and Prose; edited, with a new
Life, by the Rev. Alexander B. Grosart, D.D., &c.
(Huth Lib.) Vols. 1–9. 4to. Lond., 1881–84.
     J 5 U 34–Y 4

Life and Poems. [*See* CHALMERS, A.]

Observations on Spenser's Fairy Queen. [*See* WARTON, T.]

Works of; to which is prefixed, some Account of the
Life of Spenser, by the Rev. Henry J. Todd, M.A. Roy.
8vo. Lond., 1869.   H 6 U 21

SPICE (R. P.), M.INST. C.E. Treatise on the Purification
Coal-gas, and the Advantages of Cooper's Coal-liming
Process. 8vo. Lond., 1884.   A 11 R 14

SPICER (H.) Strange Things among us. 2nd ed. 8vo.
Lond., 1864.   G 16 R 40

SPICER (REV. W. W.), M.A. Hand-book of the Plants
of Tasmania. 12mo. Hobart, 1878.*   MA 1 V 28

SPIEGEL (PROF.) Avesta: the Religious Books of the
Parsees. [*See* AVESTA.]

SPIERS (A.) Dictionnaire général Anglais-Français,
Français-Anglais. 21e ed. 2 vols. 8vo. Paris, 1869.
     K 16 R 17, 18

SPILLAN (D.) History of Rome. [*See* LIVIUS, T.]
     B 12 P 13

SPINCKES (NATHANIEL), M.A. The New Pretenders to
Prophecy examined. 8vo. Lond., 1709.   G 2 P 25

SPINETO (MARQUIS). Elements of Hieroglyphics and
Egyptian Antiquities. With Engravings. 8vo. Lond.,
1845.   B 2 S 6

Lectures on the Elements of Hieroglyphics and Egyptian
Antiquities. 8vo. Lond., 1829.   B 2 S 5

SPINOZA (BENEDICT DE). Chief Works of; translated
from the Latin, with an Introduction, by R. H. M. Elwes.
2 vols. 8vo. Lond., 1883–84.   G 8 Q 4, 5

Ethic; demonstrated in Geometrical Order and divided
into five Parts, which treat: 1. Of God; 2. Of the Nature
and Origin of the Mind; 3. Of the Origin and Nature of
the Affects; 4. Of Human Bondage, or, of the Strength
of the Affects; 5. Of the Power of the Intellect, or, of
Human Liberty; translated by William Hale White.
8vo. Lond., 1883.   G 12 S 2

Four Essays, by Land, Kuno Fischer, J. van Vloten,
and Ernest Renan; edited by Prof. William Knight.
8vo. Lond., 1882.   C 9 R 34

His Life and Philosophy; by Frederick Pollock. 8vo.
Lond., 1880.   C 9 R 33

His Life, Correspondence, and Ethics; by H. Willis,
M.D. 8vo. Lond., 1870.   C 9 R 32

Opera Philosophica omnia; edidit et præfationem adjecit
A. Gfrœrer. 8vo. Stuttgard, 1830.   G 12 R 3

Opera Posthuma, quorum series post præfationem exhi-
betur. Sm. 4to. (n.p.) 1677.   G 14 Q 14

SPINOZA (BENEDICT DE)—*continued.*
Opera quotquot reperta sunt; recognoverunt J. van
Vloten, et J. P. N. Land. 2 vols. 8vo.   Hagae, 1882–83.
                          G 2 R 11, 12
Refutation of Spinoza. [*See* LEIBNITZ, G. W.]
Study of Spinoza; by James Martineau, LL.D. With
a Portrait.   8vo.   Lond., 1882.   C 4 Q 34
Tractatus Theologico-Politicus : a Critical Inquiry into
the History, Purpose and Authenticity of the Hebrew
Scriptures.   8vo.   Lond., 1862.   G 12 S 1

SPIRITUAL CHARACTERISTICS represented in an
Account of a most Curious Sale of Curates by Public
Auction; by "An Old Observer."   (Pam. Bf.)   8vo.
Lond., 1803.   G 12 Q 20

SPITTA (PHILIPP).   Johann Sebastian Bach: his Work
and Influence on the Music of Germany, 1685–1750; translated from the German, by Clara Bell, and J. A. Fuller-
Maitland. 3 vols. 8vo.   Lond., 1884–85.   C 10 R 14–16

SPOFFORD (AINSWORTH R.)   American Almanac and
Treasury of Facts. [*See* AMERICAN ALMANAC.]   E

SPON (E. AND F. N.)   Dictionary of Engineering, Civil,
Mechanical, Military, and Naval; with Technical Terms in
French, German, Italian, and Spanish; with Supplement,
A–W; edited by Oliver Byrne and Ernest Spon.   6 vols.
roy. 8vo.   Lond., 1874–81.   K 17 U 12–17
Spons' Encyclopædia of the Industrial Arts, Manufac-
tures, and Commercial Products; edited by G. G. André,
F.G.S., &c., and Charles G. Warnford Lock, F.L.S.   5
vols. roy. 8vo.   Lond., 1879–82.   K 6 R 2–6

SPOONER (W. C.), M.R.V.C. History, Structure, Economy,
and Diseases of the Sheep.   4th ed.   (Weale.)   12mo.
Lond., 1878.   A 17 Q 9

SPORSCHIL (JOHN).   Dictionary of the English and
German and German and English Languages.   [*See*
FLÜGEL, DR. J. G.]

SPORTSMAN (THE).   18 vols. 8vo.   Lond., 1839–48.   E

SPORTSMAN IN IRELAND (THE); with his Summer
Route through the Highlands of Scotland; by "A Cosmopolite."   2 vols. 8vo.   Lond., 1840.   D 9 R 26, 27

SPOTTISWOODE (RT. REV. JOHN), ARCHBISHOP OF ST.
ANDREW'S.   History of the Church of Scotland, beginning
the year of our Lord 203, and continued to the end of the
Reign of King James VI; with Biographical Sketch and
Notes, by the Right Rev. M. Russell, LL.D., &c.   3 vols.
8vo.   Edinb., 1851.   G 12 S 9–11

SPOTTISWOODE (W.), M.A., &c. Hyperjacobian Surfaces and Curves.   (Roy. Soc. Pubs., 4.)   4to.   Lond.,
1878.   A 11 P 4 †
Multiple Contact of Surface.   (Roy. Soc. Pubs., 2.)   4to.
4to.   Lond., 1876.   A 11 P 3 †
Polarisation of Light.   8vo.   Lond., 1874.   A 5 R 41

SPRAGUE (JOHN T.)   Electricity: its Theory, Sources, and
Applications.   2nd ed.   8vo.   Lond., 1884.   A 5 S 43

SPRAT (RT. REV. THOMAS), BISHOP OF ROCHESTER.   Life
and Poems of.   [*See* CHALMERS, A., *and* JOHNSON, S.]
True Account and Declaration of the Horrid Conspiracy
[Rye-house Plot] against the late King, his Present
Majesty, and the Government.   2nd ed.   Sm. fol.   Lond.,
1658.   B 2 U 32

SPRATT (CAPT. T. A. B.), R.N., &c.   Travels and Researches in Crete.   2 vols. 8vo.   Lond., 1865.   D 7 T 4, 5

SPRATT (CAPT. T. A. B.), AND FORBES (PROF. E.)   Travels
in Lycia, Milyas, and the Cibyratis, in company with
the late Rev. E. T. Daniell.   2 vols. 8vo.   Lond., 1847.
                          D 4 T 45, 46

SPRENGEL (KURT).   Histoire de la Médecine, depuis son
origine jusqu'au dix-neuvié Siècle.   9 vols. 8vo.   Paris,
1815–20.   A 13 P 21–29

SPRENT (J.)   Maps.   [*See* TASMANIA.]   MA 5 Q 13 ‡

SPRING (LEVRETT W.)   Kansas: the Prelude to the War
for the Union.   12mo.   Boston, 1885.   B 1 Q 22

SPRINGTHORPE (J. W.)   Results of Unhealthy Education.   [*See* AUSTRALIAN HEALTH SOCIETY.]   MA 2 S 23

SPROTT (THOMAS).   Chronica; descripsit ediditque Tho.
Hearnius, qui et alia quædam opuscula è codicibus MSS.
authenticis à seipso itidem descripta subjecit.   8vo.   Oxon.,
1719.   B 6 T 47

SPROULE (JOHN).   Elements of Practical Agriculture.
8vo.   Lond., 1844.   A 1 R 20

SPRUSON (J. J.)   Norfolk Island: Outline of its History,
1788–1884.   4to.   Sydney, 1885.   MB 3 P 5 †

SPRY (W. J. J.), R.N.   Cruise of H.M.S. *Challenger*:
Voyages over many Seas, Scenes in many Lands.   8vo.
Lond., 1876.   MD 4 W 8
Another copy.   4th ed.   8vo.   Lond., 1877.   MD 4 W 9

SPURGEON (REV. C. H.)   Fast Day Service, held at
the Crystal Palace, Sydenham, on October 7th, 1857.
(*Reprint.*)   8vo.   Melh., 1857.   MG 1 Q 40
Reply to.   [*See* PERRY, C. J.]
Sermons, 1855–87.   2 vols.   8vo.   Lond., 1855–87.
                        G 2 Q 27, 28
The Spurgeon Chronicle and Australian Miscellany,
1858.   Heaven: a Sermon delivered on Sunday morning,
December 16th, 1855, by the Rev. C. H. Spurgeon, at
New Park-street Chapel, Southwark, &c.   12mo.   Lond.,
1858.   MG 1 P 49
Thoughts on the Last Battle: a Sermon delivered May
13th, 1855, at Exeter Hall, Strand.   (*Reprint.*)   8vo.
Lond., 1855.   MG 1 Q 40

SQUARE, A.   [*See* ABBOTT, REV. E. A.]   A 10 U 27

SQUATTER, A.   [*See* LLOYD, E.]

SQUATTER, A.   [*See* WYNDHAM, G.]

SQUATTERS' PLUM (THE); or, Immigration exposed.
8vo.   Sydney, 1878.   MF 3 Q 32

SQUIER (Dr. Ephraim George), M.A., &c. Honduras; Descriptive, Historical, and Statistical. 12mo. Lond., 1870.　　　　　　　D 3 P 18

Waikna; or, Adventures on the Mosquito Shore; by "Samuel A. Bard." With Illustrations. 8vo. Lond., 1855.　　　　　　　D 3 R 50

SQUIRE (Peter), F.L.S. Companion to the last edition of the British Pharmacopœia. 8th ed. 8vo. Lond., 1871.　　　　　　　K 9 P 6
Another copy. 12th ed. 8vo. Lond., 1880.　　Libr.

STAAL (L.) Aanteckeningen, gehouden op de Reis van Port-Jackson naar en door de Torres-straat, met het Schip *Nehalennia*, in den jare 1853. 8vo. Amsterdam, 1854.　　　　　　　MD 1 V 10
Iets over de Reis door Torres straat. 8vo. Amsterdam (n.d.)　　　　　　　MD 1 V 10

STAAL DE LAUNY (Marguerite Jeanne), Baronne de. Mémoires de. [*See* Barrière, J. F., 1.]　C 1 T 1

STABLES (Gordon), M.D., &c. Cruise of the Land Yacht *Wanderer*; or, Thirteen Hundred Miles in my Caravan. 8vo. Lond., 1886.　　　　　　　D 7 8 7

STABLES (W. G.) Canine Medicine. [*See* Shaw, V.]　A 5 P 16 †

STACK (Rev. W.), B.A. Proposal for Church Extension in the Diocese of Sydney. 12mo. Sydney, 1854. MG 1 P 49

STACKHOUSE (Rev. Alfred), M.A. The Christian's Duty, with reference to the National Reproach: a Sermon. 12mo. Launceston, 1854.　　　　　　　MG 1 P 48
The Divine Right of Private Judgment in Matters of Religion: Two Sermons. 12mo. Hobart, 1852. MG 1 P 48
The Gorham Heresy and the Non-Natural Explanation of the Articles of the Church of England: a Letter to the Lord Bishop of Tasmania. 12mo. Launceston, 1851.　　　　　　　MG 1 Q 39

STACKHOUSE (Rev. Thomas), A.M. New History of the Holy Bible, from the Beginning of the World, to the Establishment of Christianity. 2 vols. fol. Lond., 1755-56.　　　　　　　G 28 P 34, 35 ‡

STACPOOLE (G.) [*See* Lettsom, J. T.]　A 12 S 33

STADLER (J. E.) [*See* Boydell, J. and J.] B 12 U 12, 13 ‡

STAËL-HOLSTEIN (Anne Louise Germaine), Baronne de. Considérations sur les Principaux Evénemens de la Révolution Française. 2nd ed. 3 vols. 8vo. Lond., 1819.　　　　　　　B 8 S 31-33
Germany; translated from the French. 3 vols. 8vo. Lond., 1814.　　　　　　　B 9 Q 20-22
Madame de Staël; a Study of her Life and Times: the First Revolution and the First Empire; by A. Stevens, LL.D. 2 vols. 8vo. Lond., 1881.　　　C 4 V 2, 3
Œuvres Complètes. 17 vols. 8vo. Bruxelles, 1829-30.　　　　　　　J 17 R 1 17

STAFFORD (Thomas). Pacata Hibernia; or, a History of the Wars in Ireland, during the Reign of Queen Elizabeth. Lond., 1633. 2 vols. imp. 8vo. Dublin, 1810. B 11 R 5, 6

STAFFORD (W. C.) History of Music. (Const. Misc.) 12mo. 18mo. Edinb., 1830.　　　　　K 10 Q 43

STAFFORD (W. C.), And Ball (Charles). Italy Illustrated: a Complete History of the Past and Present Condition of the Italian States. 2 vols. imp. 8vo. Lond., 1860.　　　　　　　B 16 Q 10, 11 ‡

STAHLSCHMIDT (J. C. L.) Surrey Bells and London Bell-founders. Sm. 4to. Lond., 1884.　　B 7 R 10

STAINER (J.), M.A., And Barrett (W. A.), M.B. Dictionary of Musical Terms. 2nd thousand. Imp. 8vo. Lond., 1876.　　　　　　　K 17 U 5

STAINSFIELD (C. W.) Descriptive Catalogue of Australian Tradesmen's Tokens, illustrated with Woodcuts; also, some Account of the Early Silver Pieces, and Gold Coinage of Australia. 8vo. Lond., 1883.　MA 2 S 55

STAIR (James, Viscount, And [John] First, And [John] Second), Earls of. Annals and Correspondence; by J. M. Graham. 2 vols. 8vo. Edinb., 1875. C 9 R 20, 21

STALEY (Rt. Rev. Thomas), D.D., Bishop of Honolulu. On the Geography and Recent Volcanic Eruption on the Sandwich Islands. 8vo. Lond., 1868. MD 7 Q 55

STALLO (J. B.) Concepts and Theories of Modern Physics. (Int. Sc. Ser.) 8vo. Lond., 1882.　　A 16 P 23

STALLYBRASS (James Seven). Teutonic Mythology. [*See* Grimm, Dr. L. J.]

STAMER (William), "Mark Tapley, Junr." Recollections of a Life of Adventure. 2 vols. 8vo. Lond., 1866.　　　　　　　MC 1 P 2, 3
The Gentleman Emigrant: his Daily Life, Sports, and Pastimes, in Canada, Australia, and the United States. 2 vols. 8vo. Lond., 1874.　　　　MD 5 Q 3, 4

STAMM (Friedrich Ludwig). Vorschule zum Ulfila, oder Grammatik der gothischen Sprache zur Selbstbelehrung. 8vo. Paderborn, 1851.　　　　　　K 14 Q 33

STANFORD (Edward). Compendium of Geography and Travel. [*See* Keane, A. H.; Rudler, F. W.; and Wallace, A. R.]
Map of Australia, constructed from the most recent Official Documents furnished by the Surveyors-General, and from the Admiralty Surveys. Roy. 8vo. (*Case.*) Lond., 1879.　　　　　　　Libr.
Parliamentary County Atlas and Hand-book of England and Wales. 8vo. Lond., 1885.　　　D 33 P 3 ‡
Stanford's Atlas of New Zealand: the Provinces of Nelson and Marlborough, with the adjacent parts of Wellington and Canterbury. 8vo. Lond. (n.d.)　　MD 5 P 7 ‡
Stanford's Handy Atlas and Poll-book of the Electoral Divisions of Great Britain and Ireland. 8vo. Lond., 1886.　　　　　　　D 11 R 3
Another copy. 2nd ed. 8vo. Lond., 1886.　　F 5 R 25

STANFORD (L.) [*See* Stillman, J. D. B.]　A 2 R 1 †

STANHOPE (HON. ALEXANDER). Spain under Charles II; or, Extracts from the Correspondence of the Hon. Alexander Stanhope, 1690–99; selected by Lord Mahon. 8vo. Lond., 1840.   B 13 T 39
Another copy. 2nd ed. 8vo. Lond., 1844.   B 13 U 22

STANHOPE (MRS. EUGENIA). [*See* CHESTERFIELD, EARL OF.]   C 6 Q 11–14

STANHOPE (HESTER LUCY), LADY. Memoirs of, as related by herself, in Conversations with her Physician. 3 vols. 8vo. Lond., 1845.   C 6 P 21–23
Travels of; forming the Completion of her Memoirs, narrated by her Physician. 3 vols. 8vo. Lond., 1846.   D 5 R 25–27

STANHOPE (PHILIP DORMER). [*See* CHESTERFIELD, EARL OF.]·

STANHOPE (PHILIP HENRY, LORD MAHON), EARL. Decline of the last Stuarts. (Roxburghe Club.) 4to. Lond., 1843.   C 4 W 33
Historical Essays, contributed to the *Quarterly Review.* (H. and C. Lib.) 12mo. Lond., 1849.   J 8 P 32
Another copy. New ed. 12mo. Lond., 1861.   B 14 Q 11
History of England, comprising the Reign of Queen Anne until the Peace of Utrecht, 1701–13. 2nd ed. 8vo. Lond., 1870.   B 5 P 47
History of England, from the Peace of Utrecht to the Peace of Versailles. 7 vols. 8vo. Lond., 1839–54.   B 5 P 21–27
History of the War of Succession in Spain. 8vo. Lond., 1832.   B 13 U 13·
Life of Belisarius. 2nd ed. 8vo. Lond., 1848.   C 3 Q 6
Life of Louis, Prince of Condé, surnamed the Great. (H. and C. Lib.) 12mo. Lond., 1845.   J 8 P 13
Another copy. 12mo. Lond., 1861.   C 1 R 7
Life of the Rt. Hon. William Pitt. 4 vols. 8vo. Lond., 1861–62.   C 4 U 21–24
Miscellanies. [1st and] 2nd series. 8vo. Lond., 1863–72.   J 11 Q 1
Spain under Charles II. [*See* STANHOPE, HON. A.]
"The Forty-five"; being the Narrative of the Insurrection of 1745, extracted from Lord Mahon's History of England; to which are added, Letters of Prince Charles Stuart. 12mo. Lond., 1869.   B 13 P 4
The Rise of our Indian Empire; being the History of British India, from its Origin till the Peace of 1783. 12mo. Lond., 1859   B 10 Q 15

STANLEY (VERY REV. ARTHUR PENRHYN), D.D., DEAN OF WESTMINSTER. Christian Institutions: Essays on Ecclesiastical Subjects. 8vo. Lond., 1881.   G 12 Q 14
Epistles of St. Paul to the Corinthians; with Critical Notes and Dissertations. 3rd ed. 8vo. Lond., 1865.   G 12 Q 12
His Life, Work, and Teaching; by Grace A. Oliver. 3rd ed. 8vo. Lond., 1885.   C 3 V 39
Historical Memorials of Canterbury. 8vo. Lond., 1868.   B 3 R 5

STANLEY (VERY REV. ARTHUR PENRHYN), D.D., DEAN OF WESTMINSTER—*continued.*
Historical Memorials of Westminster Abbey. 8vo. Lond., 1868.   B 4 8 2
Lectures on the History of the Church of Scotland, delivered in Edinburgh in 1872. 8vo. Lond., 1872.   G 12 Q 18
Lectures on the History of the Eastern Church. 4th ed. 8vo. Lond., 1869.   G 12 Q 13
Lectures on the History of the Jewish Church. 3 vols. 8vo. Lond., 1863–76.   G 12 Q 15–17
Letters to a Friend; by Connop Thirlwall. [*See* THIRLWALL, C.]   C 10 P 39
Life and Correspondence of Thomas Arnold, D.D. 2 vols. 8vo. Lond., 1844.   C 1 V 30, 31
Another copy. 5th ed. 2 vols. 8vo. Lond., 1845.   C 1 V 32, 33
Memoir of Edward Stanley. [*See* STANLEY, RT. REV. E.]   G 12 Q 19
Memoirs of Edward and Catherine Stanley; edited by their Son. 8vo. Lond., 1879.   C 4 Q 28
Scripture Portraits, and other Miscellanies. 12mo. Lond., 1867.   G 7 8 9
Sermons and Essays on the Apostolical Age. 8vo. Oxford, 1847.   G 12 Q 20
Sinai and Palestine in connection with their History. 8vo. Lond., 1871.   D 4 U 17
Three Introductory Lectures on the Study of Ecclesiastical History. 8vo. Oxford, 1859.   G 12 Q 21
Three Irish Churches: an Historical Address. 3rd ed. 8vo. .Lond·, 1869.   G 12 Q 22

STANLEY (RT. REV. EDWARD), D.D., BISHOP OF NORWICH. Addresses and Charges; with a Memoir by his Son, A P. Stanley, M.A. 8vo. Lond., 1851.   G 12 Q 19

STANLEY (RT. REV. EDWARD AND CATHERINE). Memoirs of; edited by their Son, Arthur Penrhyn Stanley, D.D., Dean of Westminster. 8vo. Lond., 1879.   C 4 Q 28

STANLEY (GEORGE). Classified Synopsis of the principal Painters of the Dutch and Flemish Schools. 8vo. Lond., 1855.   A 7 T 3
[*See* BRYAN, M.]   K 17 U 18

STANLEY (HENRY M.) Coomassie and Magdala: the Story of two British Campaigns in Africa. 8vo. Lond., 1874.   B 1 P 44
How I found Livingstone: Travels, Adventures, and Discoveries in Central Africa. With Illustrations and Maps. 8vo. Lond., 1872.   D 1 W 6
The Congo, and the founding of its Free State: a Story of Work and Exploration. With Illustrations. 2 vols. 8vo. Lond., 1885.   D 2 R 9, 10
Through the Dark Continent; or, the Sources of the Nile, around the Great Lakes of Equatorial Africa, and down the Livingstone River to the Atlantic Ocean. Maps and Illustrations. 2 vols. 8vo. Lond., 1878.   D 1 W 7, 8

4 x

STANLEY (CAPT. OWEN). Visits to the Islands in the Arafúra Sea. [*See* STOKES, CAPT. J. L.] MD 2 U 16, 17

STANLEY (WILLIAM FORD). Experimental Researches into the Properties and Motions of Fluids; with Theoretical Deductions therefrom. 8vo. Lond., 1881. A 16 S 21

STANTON (MARY OLMSTEAD). Physiognomy: a Practical and Scientific Treatise; being a Manual of Instruction in the Knowledge of the Human Physiognomy and Organism. 8vo. San Francisco, 1881. A 13 R 10

STANTON (THEODORE), M.A. Woman Question in Europe: a Series of Original Essays; with an Introduction by Frances Power Cobbe. Roy. 8vo. Lond., 1884. F 8 T 8

STANYHURST (RICHARD). First Four Books of the Æneid of Virgil in English heroic verse. [*See* VIRGILIUS MARO, P.]

STAPFER (PROF. PAUL). Shakespeare and Classical Antiquity: Greek and Latin Antiquity as presented in Shakespeare's Plays. (Crowned by the French Academy.) translated from the French by Emily J. Carey. 8vo. Lond., 1880. H 4 R 36

STAPLES (HON. WILLIAM R.) Rhode Island in the Continental Congress. [*See* UNITED STATES.]

STAPLETON (AUGUSTUS GRANVILLE). Political Life of the Rt. Hon. George Canning, 1822–27. 2nd ed. 3 vols. 8vo. Lond., 1831. C 10 Q 12–14
The Real Monster Evil of Ireland. (Pam. 11.) 8vo. Lond., 1843. F 12 P 9

STAPFERS (H.) Dictionaire Synoptique d'Etymologie Française, douant la dérivation des mots usuels. 8vo. Bruxelles, 1885. K 11 V 37

STAPYLTON (SIR R.) [*See* STRADA, F.] B 15 Q 14 ‡

STAR CHAMBER CASES, showing what Causes properly belong to the cognizance of that Court. 8vo. Lond., 1630. F 5 R 24

STARR (—.) [*See* SAURIN *v.* STARR.] MF 2 R 19

STARK (JAMES H.) Stark's Illustrated Bermuda Guide; containing a Description of Everything in or about the Bermuda Islands. Illustrated. 8vo. Boston, 1884. D 3 P 7

STARKWEATHER (GEORGE B.), F.R.G.S. Law of Sex; being an Exposition of the Natural Law by which the Sex of Offspring is controlled in Man and the Lower Animals. 8vo. Lond., 1883. A 12 R 39

STARLING (ELIZABETH). Noble Deeds of Women; or, Examples of Female Courage and Virtue. 9th ed. 8vo. Lond., 1872 C 1 S 33

STARLING (M. H.), LL.B. Indian Criminal Law and Procedure, including the Procedure in the High Courts, as well as that in the Courts not established by Royal Charter; with Forms of Charges, and Notes of Evidence. 3rd ed., by M. H. Starling, and F. C. Constable, M.A. Roy 8vo. Lond., 1877. F 1 R 12

STATE AID QUESTION. Strictures on the Pamphlets of the Rev. Dr. Cairns, and T. T. A'Beckett, Esq.; by "A Scotch Catholic." 8vo. Melb., 1852. MF 1 Q 6

STATE AID TO RELIGION. Stipends and Allowances from Schedule C, and Grants from Church and School Estates Fund. Fol. Sydney, 1862. ME 10 Q 3 †

STATE TRIALS. [*See* TRIALS.]

STATESMAN'S YEAR-BOOK (THE). Statistical and Historical Annual of the States of the Civilised World, for the years 1864–86; edited by Frederick Martin, and J. Scott Keltie. 22 vols. 8vo. Lond., 1864–86. E

STATISTICAL ABSTRACT for the several Colonial and other Possessions of the United Kingdom, 1856–70. Imp. 8vo. Lond., 1872. E

STATISTICAL REGISTER, NEW SOUTH WALES. [*See* NEW SOUTH WALES.]

STATISTICAL SOCIETY OF LONDON. Catalogue of the Library of. Roy. 8vo. Lond., 1884. K 8 Q 19
Journal of. 26 vols. 8vo. Lond., 1838–63. E
General Indexes [to the above]. 2 vols. 8vo. Lond., 1854–63. E

STATIUS (PUBLIUS PAPINIUS). Opera omnia, ex Editione-Bipontina. 4 vols. 8vo. Lond., 1824. J 13 S 25–28
The Thebaid of ; translated by Lewis. [*See* CHALMERS, A.]

STATUTES. [*See* GREAT BRITAIN, IRELAND, NEW SOUTH WALES, NEW ZEALAND, QUEENSLAND, UNITED STATES OF AMERICA, VICTORIA.]

STAUNTON (SIR GEORGE LEONARD), BART., LL.D., &c. Authentic Account of an Embassy from the King of Great Britain to the Emperor of China; taken chiefly from the Papers of the Earl of Macartney. 2nd ed. 2 vols. 4to. Lond. 1798. D 7 P 1, 2 †
Another copy. 2nd ed. 3 vols. 8vo. Lond., 1798. D 7 P 3–5 †
Plates to above. El. fol. Lond., 1798. D 8 P 19 ‡
Memoir of the Life and Family of; with an Appendix, by Sir George Thomas Staunton, Bart. 8vo. Havant Press, 1823. C 6 U 25

STAUNTON (SIR GEORGE THOMAS), BART, &c. Memoir of the Life and Family of Sir George Leonard Staunton. 8vo. Havant Press, 1823. C 6 U 25
Ta Tsing Leu Lee; being the Fundamental Laws, and a Selection from the Supplementary Statutes of the Penal Code of China. Roy. 4to. Lond., 1810. F 8 Q 12 †

STAUNTON (HOWARD). Chess-player's Companion 8vo. Lond., 1870. A 17 U 7
Chess-player's Hand-book. 8vo. Lond., 1872. A 17 U 8
Chess Praxis: a Supplement to the "Chess-player's Hand-book." 8vo. Lond., 1871. A 17 U 9

STAUNTON (HOWARD)—*continued.*

Chess: Theory and Practice; edited by R. B. Wormald. 8vo. Lond., 1876.   A 17 U 11

Chess Tournament. 8vo. Lond., 1852.   A 17 U 10

Great Schools of England. 8vo. Lond.,1865.   G 17 Q 35

STAUNTON (MICHAEL). "Case of Ireland": a Speech. (Pam.) 8vo. Dublin, 1831.   G 2 P 28

STAWELL (SIR W. F.) Portrait of. [*See* MANUSCRIPTS AND PORTRAITS.]

Memoir of. [*See* BECKER, L.]   MC 1 R 26 ‡

STEAM COMMUNICATION. Report of Proceedings adopted for the establishment of Steam Communication with the Australian Colonies and New Zealand. 8vo. Lond., 1850.   MF 1 R 17

Another copy. 8vo. Lond., 1850.   MJ 2 Q 11

STEBBING (REV. HENRY), D.D., &c. Christian Church. (Lard. Cab. Cyclo.) 2 vols. 12mo. Lond., 1833.
K 1 S 37, 38

History of Chivalry and the Crusades. (Const. Misc.) 2 vols. 18mo. Edinb., 1829–30.   K 10 Q 38, 39

History of the Reformation. (Lard. Cab. Cyclo.) 2 vols. 12mo. Lond., 1836–37.   K 1 T 36, 37

Life of John Calvin. [*See* HENRY, P.]   C 10 P 24, 25

STEBBINS (EMMA). Charlotte Cushman: her Letters and Memories of her Life; edited by her Friend, Emma Stebbins. 8vo. Boston, 1879.   C 6 P 4

STECCHETI (—.) Translations from the Italian Poets. [*See* FENZI, S.]

STEDMAN (EDMUND CLARENCE). Poets of America. 8vo. Lond., 1885.   C 3 V 35

Victorian Poets. 8vo. Lond., 1876.   C 13 R 14

[*See* ESSAYS FROM THE CRITIC.]

STEEDMAN (CHARLES). Manual of Swimming; including Bathing, Plunging, Diving, Floating, Scientific Swimming, Training, Drowning, and Rescuing. 12mo. Melb., 1867.
MA 2 V 15

STEEL (DAVID). Shipmaster's Assistant and Owner's Manual. 8vo. Lond., 1826.   F 14 S 17

STEEL (JOHN HENRY), M.R.C.V.S., &c. Outlines of Equine Anatomy: a Manual for the use of Veterinary Students in the Dissecting Room. 8vo. Lond., 1876.
A 1 P 39

Treatise on the Diseases of the Ox; being a Manual of Bovine Pathology. 8vo. Lond., 1881.   A 1 R 38

[*See* BLAINE, D. P.]   A 1 R 34

STEEL (REV. ROBERT), D.D., &c. The Bible and Science in their Mutual Relations: a Lecture. [*See* CHRISTIAN EVIDENCE SOCIETY.]

New Hebrides and Christian Missions. 8vo. Lond., 1880.   MD 1 V 1

STEEL (REV. ROBERT), D.D., AND COSH (REV. JAMES), M.A. Memorials of Alexander Learmonth, Esq., of Yasmar. 12mo. Sydney, 1877.   MC 1 P 36

STEELE (JOHN). Hay and Straw Measurer; being New Tables for the Use of Auctioneers, Valuers, Farmers, Hay and Straw Dealers, &c. 3rd ed., enlarged. (Weale.) 12mo. Lond., 1881.   A 17 Q 48

STEELE (SIR RICHARD). [Life of]; by Austin Dobson. 8vo. Lond., 1886.   C 2 Q 48

The Conscious Lovers: a Comedy. (New Eng. Theatre.) 12mo. Lond., 1782.   H 4 P 16

Another copy. (Bell's Brit. Theatre.) 18mo. Lond., 1791.   H 2 P 18

Another copy. (Brit. Theatre.) 12mo. Lond., 1808.
H 1 P 12

Another copy. [*See* BRIT. DRAMA, 4.]

The Funeral; or, Grief a-la-mode: a Comedy. (New Eng. Theatre.) 12mo. Lond., 1777.   H 4 P 22

Another copy. (Bell's Brit. Theatre.) 18mo. Lond., 1794.   H 2 P 14

The Tender Husband: a Comedy. (Bell's Brit. Theatre.) 18mo. Lond., 1791.   H 2 P 20

STEELE (THOMAS). An Eastern Love-story, Kusa Jātakaya: a Buddhistic Legend, rendered into English Verse, from the Sinhalese Poem of Alagiyavanna Mohottāla. 8vo. Lond., 1871.   H 7 U 22

STEEN (LE PÈRE CORNELIS VAN DEN), CORNELIUS "A LAPIDE." Commentaria. 10 vols. fol. Antverpiae, 1623–45.   G 36 U 2–11 ‡

1. Commentaria in Pentatevchvm Mosis. Vltima editio, aucto et recognita.

2. Commentarivs in Iosve, Ivdicvm, Rvth, IV Libros Regvm, et II Parlipomenon.

3. Commentarii in Ecclesiasticvm. Editio secunda ab Auctore aucta et correcta.

4. Commentarii in Ecclesiasten. Indicibvs necessariis illvstrati, nvnc prinvm prodevnt.

5. Commentaria in Salomonis Proverbia. Editio altera ab Auctore aucta.

6. Commentaria in qvatvor Prophetas Maiores. Postrema editio, aucta et recognita.

7. Commentaria in dvodecim Prophetas Minores.

8. Commentarivs in qvatvor Evangelia.

9. Commentaria in omnes Divi Pavli Epistolas. Vltima editio, aucta et recognita.

10. Commentaria in Acta Apostolorvm, Epistolas Canonicas, et Apocalypsin.

STEERAGE PASSENGER, A. [*See* ASKEW, J.]

STEFFENS (HENRY). Adventures on the Road to Paris, during the Campaigns of 1813–14, extracted from the Autobiography of Henry Steffens; translated from the German. 12mo. Lond., 1848.   D 1 T 18

Another copy. (H. and C. Lib.) 12mo. Lond., 1848.
J 8 P 28

STEHELIN (Rev. John Peter), F.R.S. Traditions of the Jews; with the Expositions and Doctrines of the Rabbins, contained in the Talmud and other Rabbinical Writings; to which is added, Opinions of the Jews concerning the Messiah, and the Time of his Appearing, together with an Account of their Religious Customs and Ceremonies, abridged from the Latin of Buxtorff. 2 vols. 8vo. Lond., 1732–34.   G 7 S 15, 16

STEIN (Heinrich Friedrich Karl), Baron von. Life and Times of Stein; or, Germany and Prussia in the Napoleonic Age; by J. R. Seeley, M.A. 3 vols. 8vo. Cambridge, 1878.   C 11 P 32–34

STEINBÜCHEL (A.) [*See* Eckhel, J. H.]   A 13 S 9

STEINITZ (Francis). Life of Alfred the Great; with his Maxims, and those of his Counsellors. 8vo. Lond., 1849.   C 5 Q 2

STEINMETZ (Andrew). History of the Jesuits, from the Foundation of their Society to its Suppression by Pope Clement xiv. 3 vols. 8vo. Lond., 1848.   G 12 P 16–18

Japan and her People. With numerous Illustrations. 8vo. Lond., 1859.   D 6 P 38

The Novitiate; or, a Year among the English Jesuits. 8vo. Lond., 1846.   G 12 S 4

STELLA. [*See* Lewis, Mrs. Esther A. B.]

STENHOUSE (N. D.) Report on the Evidence in the Case of G. D. Lang. [*See* Lang, Rev. J. D.]

STENHOUSE (Mrs. T. B. H.) Lady's Life among the Mormons: a Record of Personal Experience as one of the Wives of a Mormon Elder, during a period of more than Twenty Years. 12mo. Lond., 1873.   D 3 P 21

STENHOUSE (T. B. H.) The Rocky Mountain Saints: a Full and Complete History of the Mormons, from the First Vision of Joseph Smith to the Last Courtship of Brigham Young. 8vo. Lond., 1874.   G 12 R 5

STENT (George Carter). The Jade Chaplet in Twenty-four Beads: a Collection of Songs, Ballads, &c. (From the Chinese.) 8vo. Lond., 1874.   H 8 S 33

STENT (W. Drew), B.A. Egypt and the Holy Land in 1842; with Sketches of Greece, Constantinople, and the Levant. 2 vols. (in 1) 8vo. Lond., 1843.   D 1 V 14

STEPHANO (C.) Adventures of a Greek Lady, the adopted Daughter of Queen Caroline. 2 vols. 8vo. Lond., 1849.   D 10 Q 40, 41

STEPHANUS (Tornacensis Episcopus). Epistolæ. [*See* Migne, J. P., Series Latina, 211.]

STEPHEN (Rt. Hon. Sir Alfred), P.C., C.B., G.C.M.G., &c. Address on Intemperance and the Licensing System, delivered in the Masonic Hall, on the 11th December, 1869. (Pam. 38.) 8vo. Sydney, 1870.   MJ 2 Q 25

Appendix to Thoughts on the Legislative Constitution of New South Wales. 8vo. Sydney, 1853.   MF 3 P 1

Another copy. 8vo. Sydney, 1853.   MJ 2 Q 14

STEPHEN (Rt. Hon. Sir Alfred), P.C., C.B., G.C.M.G., &c.—*continued.*

Australian Divorce Extension Bills. 8vo. Sydney, 1888.*   MF 3 Q 78

Constitution, Rules, and Practice of the Supreme Court of New South Wales. 8vo. Sydney, 1843–45.   MF 2 R 8

Divorce Extension defended (with special reference to the Measure before the New South Wales Parliament). 8vo. Sydney, 1887.*   MF 3 Q 74

Electoral Bill: Speech in the Legislative Council of New South Wales, on the second reading of the Bill to amend the Electoral Law. 8vo. Sydney, 1858.   MF 3 P 3

Another copy. 8vo. Sydney, 1858.   MJ 2 Q 14

New South Wales Divorce Extension Bill: with Reply to Protest against the Measure. 8vo. Sydney, 1887.*   MF 3 Q 76

Thoughts on the Constitution of a Second Legislative Chamber for New South Wales, in a Letter to the Attorney-General. (Pam. 26.) 8vo. Sydney, 1853.   MJ 2 Q 14

The Colony of Australia. [*See* New South Wales.]

STEPHEN (Rt. Hon. Sir Alfred), P.C., C.B., G.C.M.G., &c., and OLIVER (Alexander), M.A. Criminal Law Manual, comprising the Criminal Law Amendment Act of 1883; with an Introduction, Commentary, and Index. Roy. 8vo. Sydney, 1883.   MF 1 S 7

STEPHEN (F. J.) [*See* Knight *v.* Stephen.]

STEPHEN (Sir George), Knt. Adventures of an Attorney in search of Practice; or, Delineations of Professional Life. 12mo. Lond., 1840.   J 5 P 1

Lectures on the Decalogue (to his Sunday-school, at Caulfield). 12mo. Melb., 1871.   MJ 2 P 31

Memoir of the late James Stephen, one of the Masters in the High Court of Chancery, in relation to Slave Emancipation; by his Son. 8vo. Brighton, Vic., 1875.   MC 1 R 22

No Charge. 8vo. Brighton, Vic., 1876.   MG 1 Q 39

The Systems of English Bankruptcy and Colonial Insolvency, briefly compared in a Letter to His Excellency Sir Charles Hotham, K.C.B., &c. 8vo. Melb., 1855.   MJ 2 R 19

STEPHEN (George Milner). [*See* "Argus," Libel Case.]   MF 1 Q 1

STEPHEN (H. W. H.) [*See* Our Christmas Budget.]

STEPHEN (James), LL.D. Memoir of the late James Stephen, one of the Masters in the High Court of Chancery, in relation to Slave Emancipation; by his Son, Sir George Stephen. 8vo. Brighton, Vic., 1875.   MC 1 R 22

New Commentaries on the Laws of England (partly founded on Blackstone). 7th ed. 4 vols. 8vo. Lond., 1874.   F 10 Q 8–11

STEPHEN (Rt. Hon. Sir James), K.C.B. Essays in Ecclesiastical Biography. 2nd ed. 2 vols. 8vo. Lond., 1850–55.   G 12 P 19, 20

STEPHEN (SIR JAMES FITZJAMES), K.C.S.I., &c. Digest of the Law of Evidence. 4th ed.   8vo. Lond., 1881.
F 6 P 31

History of the Criminal Law of England. 3 vols. 8vo. Lond., 1883.
F 4 Q 8–10

Liberty, Equality, Fraternity. 2nd ed. 8vo. Lond., 1874.
F 6 V 21

Story of Nuncomar, and the Impeachment of Sir Elijah Impey. 2 vols. 8vo. Lond., 1885.
F 5 R 5, 6

STEPHEN (J. K.), B.A. International Law and International Relations: an Attempt to ascertain the best Method of discussing the Topics of International Law. 8vo. Lond., 1884.
F 5 Q 32

STEPHEN (LESLIE), M.A. Alexander Pope. (Eng. Men of Letts.) 8vo. Lond., 1880.
C 1 U 27

Dictionary of National Biography; edited by Leslie Stephen. Vols. 1–9. 8vo. Lond., 1885–87. C 11 Q 16–24

Essays on Free-thinking and Plain-speaking. 8vo. Lond., 1873.
G 7 S 7

History of English Thought in the 18th Century. 2 vols. 8vo. Lond., 1876.
G 12 P 22, 23

Hours in a Library. (1st–3rd series.) 3 vols. 8vo. Lond., 1874–79.
J 10 Q 30–32

Life of Dean Swift. (Eng. Men of Letts.) 8vo. Lond., 1883.
C 1 U 34

Life of Henry Fawcett. 8vo. Lond., 1885.   C 3 T 8

Samuel Johnson. (Eng. Men of Letts.) 8vo. Lond., 1879.
C 1 U 21

Science of Ethics. 8vo. Lond., 1882.   G 12 P 21

STEPHEN (THOMAS). History of the Church of Scotland, from the Reformation to the Present Time.   4 vols. 8vo. Lond., 1843–45.
G 12 P 24–27

STEPHENS (ALEXANDER H.) Comprehensive and Popular History of the United States. Roy. 8vo. Philad., 1882.
B 1 U 7

STEPHENS (EDWARD BELL). Basque Provinces: their Political State, Scenery, and Inhabitants; with Adventures amongst the Carlists and Christinos. 2 vols. 8vo. Lond., 1837.
D 8 P 45, 46

STEPHENS (FREDERICK G.) Flemish and French Pictures; with Notes concerning the Painters and their Works. 4to. Lond., 1875.
A 8 T 18

Flemish Relics: Architectural, Legendary, and Pictorial. 4to. Lond., 1866.
B 7 U 34

Masterpieces of Mulready. [*See* MULREADY, W.]
A 8 T 23

Sir Edwin Landseer. (Great Artists.) 8vo. Lond., 1880.
C 3 T 37

STEPHENS (GEORGE). Dramas for the Stage. 2 vols. 8vo. Lond., 1846.
H 4 S 1, 2

STEPHENS (PROF. GEORGE), F.S.A., &c. Memoir of Hans Hendrik. [*See* HENDRIK, HANS.]
C 2 S 22

Old Northern Runic Monuments of Scandinavia and England. 3 vols. roy. fol. Lond., 1866–84. B 18 U 9–11 ‡

Prof. S. Bugge's Studies on Northern Mythology, shortly examined. 8vo. Lond., 1883.
B 2 R 7

STEPHENS (HENRY), F.R.S.E. Book of Farm Implements, &c. [*See* SLIGHT, J., *and* BURN, R. S.]

Book of the Farm. 2 vols. roy. 8vo. Lond., 1855.
A 1 T 10, 11

STEPHENS (H. MORSE). History of the French Revolution. Vol. 1. 8vo. Lond., 1886.
B 9 P 43

STEPHENS (JAMES BRUNTON). A Hundred Pounds: a Novelette; to which is added, Bailed up with a Whitewash Brush. 12mo. Melb., 1876.
MJ 1 P 31

Convict Once: a Poem. 12mo. Lond., 1871. MH 1 P 1

Convict Once, and other Poems. New ed. 8vo. Melb., 1885.
MH 1 P 2

Godolphin Arabian: the Story of a Horse; manipulated from the French Prose Tale of Eugene Sue. 12mo. Brisbane, 1873.
MH 1 R 34

Miscellaneous Poems. 8vo. Lond., 1880.   MH 1 P 3

The Black Gin, and other Poems. 12mo. Melb., 1873
MH 1 R 34

STEPHENS (JAMES FRANCIS), F.L.S., &c. General Zoology. [*See* SHAW, G.]
A 13 T 1–28

STEPHENS (JOHN). History of the Rise and Progress of the new British Province of South Australia. 2nd ed. 8vo. Lond., 1839.*
MB 2 R 9

Land of Promise; being an authentic and impartial History of the Rise and Progress of the new British Province of South Australia; by "One who is going." 8vo. Lond., 1839.*
MB 2 R 8

Royal South Australian Almanack and General Directory, 1849. 12mo. Adelaide, 1849.
ME 4 P

STEPHENS (JOHN L.) Incidents of Travel in Greece. [*See* VOYAGES AND DISCOVERIES.]
D 9 U 13

Incidents of Travel in Central America, Chiapas, and Yucatan. Illustrated. 2 vols. 8vo. Lond., 1841.
D 3 T 8, 9

Incidents of Travel in the Russian and Turkish Empires. 2 vols. 8vo. Lond., 1839.
D 8 P 33, 34

Incidents of Travel in Yucatan. Illustrated. 2 vols. 8vo. Lond., 1843.
D 3 S 22, 23

STEPHENS (JOSEPH RAYNER). Life of Joseph Rayner Stephens, Preacher and Political Orator. 8vo. Lond., 1881.
C 2 P 38

STEPHENS (S. J.) [*See* SAXO GRAMMATICUS.] B 18 R 17 ‡

STEPHENS (W. B.) Sketch Map of New Zealand. 12mo. Melb., 1868.
MD 5 P 4 ‡

Victorian Almanac for 1864, 1866. 2 vols. (in 1) 12mo. Melb., 1864–66.
ME 4 P

STEPHENS (PROF. W. J.), M.A. Eaglesfield (the New School, 1867), Darlinghurst, Sydney. (Opened February, 1867.) T.D.P.S-Acta, 1879, No. 1, July 16. [Address of the Principal.] 8vo. Sydney, 1879. MG 1 Q 34

STEPHENS (W. R. W.), M.A. Memoir of the Rt. Hon. William Page Wood, Baron Hatherley; with Selections from his Correspondence, edited by his Nephew. 2 vols. 8vo. Lond., 1883. C 4 R 6, 7

STEPHENSON (A.) John de Witt. [*See* PONTALIS, A. L.] C 10 T 26, 27

STEPHENSON (AGNES AND HELEN). Pekin, Jeddo, and San Francisco. [*See* BEAUVOIR, LUDOVIC, MARQUIS DE.] D 10 Q 29

STEPHENSON (EDWARD R.) Essays and Miscellaneous Pieces. 8vo. Adelaide, 1865. MH 1 R 47

STEPHENSON (GEORGE), C.E. Life of; by S. Smiles. With a Portrait. 8vo. Lond., 1857. C 9 U 13
Another copy. 3rd ed. 8vo. Lond., 1857. C 9 U 14

STEPHENSON (ROBERT), F.R.S. Life of; by J. C. Jeaffreson; with descriptive Chapters on some of his most important Professional Works, by William Pole, F.R.S., &c. 2 vols. 8vo. Lond., 1864. C 9 U 15, 16

STEPHENSON (ROBERT), & CO. Description of the Patent Locomotive Steam-engine. 4to. Lond., 1838. A 3 P 1 †

STEPHENSON (SIR R. MACDONALD), C.E. Rudimentary and Practical Instructions on the Science of Railway Construction. 4th ed., revised, &c., by E. Nugent. (Weale.) 12mo. Lond., 1869. A 17 P 32

STEPHENSON (S. E.) John de Witt. [*See* PONTALIS, A. L.] C 10 T 26, 27

STEPNEY (GEORGE). Life and Poems of. [*See* CHALMERS, A., *and* JOHNSON, S.]

STEPNIAK (SERGIUS DRAGOMANOFF). Russia under the Tzars; translated by William Westall. 2 vols. 8vo. Lond., 1885. B 12 T 33, 34
The Russian Storm Cloud. 8vo. Lond., 1886. F 4 Q 2

STERLING (JOHN). Life of Friedrich Schiller (1825); Life of John Sterling (1851): Two Biographies, by Thomas Carlyle. 8vo. Lond., 1857. C 4 S 34

STERNBERG (G. M.) Photo-Micrographs, and how to make them. 8vo. Boston, 1883. A 16 V 20

STERNDALE (R. A.) Natural History of the Mammalia in India and Ceylon. 8vo. Calcutta, 1884. A 11 R 41

STERNE (LAURENCE). [A Biography]; by H. D. Traill. (Eng. Men of Letts.) 8vo. Lond., 1882. C 1 U 33
Life and Opinions of "Tristram Shandy, Gentleman." With Etchings. 2 vols. 8vo. Lond., 1883. J 10 R 15, 16
Sentimental Journey through France and Italy; with Etchings and Portrait by Ed. Hédouin. 8vo. Lond., 1882. J 11 R 18
Another copy. [*See* CLASSIC TALES.]

STERNE (LAURENCE)—*continued.*
Works of; with a Life of the Author, written by himself. 8vo. Lond., 1839. J 8 T 12
Another copy. New ed., by James P. Browne, M.D. 4 vols. 8vo. Lond., 1873. J 10 V 18-21

STERNE (SIMON). Constitutional History and Political Development of the United States. 8vo. New York, 1882. F 5 S 28

STEUART (SIR HENRY), BART., LL.D., &c. Genealogy of the Stewarts refuted in a Letter to Andrew Stuart, Esq., M.P. 8vo. Edinb., 1799. B 13 Q 2
Planter's Guide. 8vo. Edinb., 1828. A 1 R 13

STEUART (H.) Works of Sallust. [*See* SALLUSTIUS CRISPUS, C.] B 16 Q 1, 2 †

STEUART (SIR JAMES), BART. Inquiry into the Principles of Political Economy. 2 vols. 4to. Lond., 1767. F 8 Q 6, 7 †

STEUB (LUDWIG). Tirol und Vorailberg. [*See* UNSER VATERLAND.] D 38 P 18 ‡

STEUR (CHARLES). Ethnographie des Peuples de l'Europe avant Jésus Christ. 3 vols. imp. 8vo. Bruxelles, 1872–73. A 2 P 1-3

STEVENS (A.), LL.D. Madame de Staël; a Study of her Life and Times: the First Revolution and the First Empire. With Portraits. 2 vols. 8vo. Lond., 1881. C 4 V 2, 3

STEVENS (C. G.) Appeal from Earl Grey and Sir William Denison, to British Justice and Humanity, against the proposed continuance of Transportation to Van Diemen's Land, in a Letter to the Liberal Press of the Nation; with Petitions and an Appendix. 8vo. Lond., 1851. MF 3 P6

STEVENS (HENRY), M.A., &c. American Books with Tails to 'em. 18mo. Lond., 1873. Libr.
Benjamin Franklin's Life and Writings. Imp. 8vo. Lond., 1881. C 3 W 12
The Bibles in the Caxton Exhibition, 1877. Special ed. 8vo. Lond., 1878. K 18 R 21
Catalogue of the American Books in the Library of the British Museum, 1856. Roy. 8vo. Lond., 1866. H 8 P 12
Catalogue of the American Maps in the Library of the British Museum. 8vo. Lond., 1866. S 8 P 12
Catalogue of the Canadian and other British North American Books in the Library of the British Museum. Roy. 8vo. Lond., 1866. K 8 P 12
Catalogue of the Mexican and other Spanish-American and West Indian Books in the Library of the British Museum. Roy. 8vo. Lond., 1866. S 8 P 12
Dawn of British Trade to the East Indies, as recorded in the Court Minutes of the East India Company, 1599–1603, now first printed from the original MS.; by H. Stevens. 8vo. Lond., 1886. B 10 T 31

STEVENS (HENRY), M.A., &c.—*continued.*
History of the Oxford Caxton Memorial Bible. 18mo.
Lond., 1878.   Libr.

Recollections of Mr. James Lenox, of New York, and the
formation of his Library. 12mo. Lond.,1886. C 2 R 25

Photo-Bibliography; or, a Word on Printed Card Catalogues of Old, Rare, Beautiful, and Costly Books. 18mo.
Lond., 1878.   Libr.

Who spoils our New English Books? asked and
answered. 18mo. Lond., 1884.   J 7 P 32

STEVENS (JAMES). Philological Studies. Part 1. 8vo.
Turin, 1886.   K 15 P 35

STEVENS (JOHN L), LL.D. History of Gustavus Adolphus. 8vo. Lond., 1885.   C 6 Q 1

STEVENS (ORLANDO). Nuova Galles del Sud, suoi
Progressi e Risorse; tradotto dall' Inglese, da Orlando
Stevens. 8vo. Sydney, 1884.   MF 1 S 31

STEVENS (ROBERT). Essay on Average, and other Subjects connected with the Contract of Marine Insurance.
8vo. Lond., 1813.   F 4 Q 25

STEVENSON (ALAN), LL.B., &c. Rudimentary Treatise
on the History, Construction, and Illumination of Light-
houses. (Weale.) 12mo. Lond., 1850.   A 17 Q 49

STEVENSON (DAVID), F.R.S.E. Sketch of the Civil Engineering of North America. (Weale.) 12mo. Lond.,
1859.   A 17 P 59

Treatise on the Application of Marine Surveying and
Hydrometry to the Practice of Civil Engineering. Roy.
8vo. Edinb., 1842.   A 6 U 11

STEVENSON (GEORGE). Portrait of. [*See* MANUSCRIPTS
AND PORTRAITS.]

STEVENSON (CAPT. G. DE ST. CLAIR-), F.R.G.S. Military
Dictionary. [*See* VOYLE, MAJOR-GEN. G. E.] K 10 T 4

STEVENSON (REV. JOHN). The Kalpa Sútra, and Nava
Tatva: two Works illustrative of the Jain Religion and
Philosophy; translated from the Mágadhi. 8vo. Lond.,
1848.   G 12 T 8

STEVENSON (JOHN J.) House Architecture. 2 vols
roy. 8vo. Lond., 1880.   A 2 Q 30, 31

STEVENSON (REV. JOSEPH), S.J. History of Mary
Stewart. [*See* NAU, C.]   C 6 T 18

Mary Stuart: a Narrative of the first Eighteen Years
of her Life, principally from original Documents. 8vo.
Edinb., 1886.   C 4 R 37

STEVENSON (THOMAS). F.R.S.E., &c. Design and Construction of Harbours: a Treatise on Maritime Engineering.
2nd ed. 8vo. Edinb., 1874.   A 6 T 20

[*See* HYDRO-MECHANICS.]   A 11 U 7

STEVENSON (W.) [*See* BENTHAM, J.]   B 17 S 4, 5 ‡

STEWART (REV. ALEXANDER), D.D. Elements of Gaelic
Grammar, in four Parts: of Pronunciation and Orthography;
of the Parts of Speech; of Syntax; of Derivation and
Composition; by Alexander Stewart, Minister of the
Gospel at Dingwall. 2nd ed., corrected and enlarged.
8vo. Edinb., 1812.   K 14 T 29

Another copy. 3rd ed. 12mo. Edinb., 1876.   K 11 U 2

STEWART (REV. ALEXANDER), LL.D., &c 'Twixt Ben
Nevis and Glencoe: the Natural History, Legends, and
Folk-lore of the West Highlands. 8vo. Edinb., 1885.
A 14 S 37

STEWART (ALEXANDER), F.R.C.S. Our Temperaments:
their Study and their Teaching. Roy. 8vo. Lond.,
1887.   A 12 T 24

STEWART (ALEXANDER). Reminiscences of Dunfermline
and Neighbourhood. 12mo. Edinb., 1886. B 13 P 19

STEWART (AUBREY), M.A., AND LONG (GEORGE), M.A.
Plutarch's Lives. [*See* PLUTARCH.]   C 2 P 33–36

STEWART (PROF. BALFOUR), LL.D., &c., Conservation
of Energy; being an Elementary Treatise on Energy and
its Laws. 3rd ed. 8vo. Lond., 1874.   A 17 T 2

Elementary Treatise on Heat. 3rd ed. (Clar. Press.)
8vo. Oxford, 1876.   A 21 P 6

STEWART (PROF. BALFOUR), LL.D., AND GEE (W. W.
HALDANE). Lessons in Elementary Practical Physics.
Vol. 1. General Physical Processes. 8vo. Lond., 1885.
A 17 T 55

STEWART (PROF. BALFOUR), LL.D., AND TAIT (PROF.
P. G.), M.A. The Unseen Universe; or, Physical
Speculations on a Future State. 8vo. Lond., 1875.
G 12 S 15

STEWART (CHARLES.) Elements of the Natural History
of the Animal Kingdom. 2nd ed. 2 vols. 8vo. Edinb.,
1817.   A 14 S 33, 34

STEWART (PROF. CHARLES). Travels of Mirza Abu Taleb
Khan. [*See* ABU TALIB IBN. MUHAMMED.]   D 9 T 30

STEWART (CHARLES). Gaelic Kingdom in Scotland: its
Origin and Church; with Sketches of notable Bredalbane
and Glenlyon Saints. 8vo. Edinb., 1880.   B 13 P 9

STEWART (SIR C.) [*See* CASTLEREAGH, R. S., VISCOUNT.]

STEWART (REV. CHARLES SAMUEL), M.A. Journal of
a Residence in the Sandwich Islands, during the years
1823–25. 2nd ed. 8vo. Lond., 1828.   MD 5 P 33

Reis naar de Zuid Zee, met het Schip *Vincennes* in de Jaren
1829 en 1830; met aanteekeningen wegens Brazilien,
Peru, Manilla, de Kaap de Goede Hoop, en St. Helena.
2 vols. 8vo. Rotterdam, 1834.   MD 6 T 9, 10

Visit to the South Seas, in the U.S. Ship *Vincennes*,
during the years 1829–30; including Scenes in Brazil,
Peru, Manilla, the Cape of Good Hope, and St. Helena.
2 vols. 8vo. Lond., 1832.   MD 6 T 7, 8

Another copy; edited and abridged by William Ellis.
12mo. Lond., 1832.   D 10 P 14

STEWART (DUGALD), F.R.S. Account of the Life and Writings of Thomas Reid, D.D., &c. 8vo. Edinb., 1803. C 10 P 29

Another copy. (Works of Thomas Reid.) [*See* REID, T.] G 1 R 8, 9

Account of the Life and Writings of William Robertson, D.D. 8vo. Lond., 1821. B 14 R 1

Elements of the Philosophy of the Human Mind. 2 vols. 8vo. Lond., 1818–21. G 12 S 21, 22

Outlines of Moral Philosophy. 4th ed. 8vo. Edinb., 1818. G 12 Q 1

Philosophical Essays. 2nd ed. 8vo. Edinb., 1816. J 4 S 21

STEWART (LIEUT.-COL. D. H.) Report on the Soudan. Fol. Lond., 1883. F 36 Q 13 ‡

STEWART (ELLIOTT W.) Feeding Animals: a Practical Work upon the Laws of Growth, specially applied to the Rearing and Feeding of Horses, Cattle, Dairy Cows, Sheep, and Swine. 8vo. New York, 1883. A 1 Q 14

STEWART (GEORGE VESEY). Notes on the Stewart Special Settlement, No. 3, at Te Puke, Bay of Plenty, New Zealand. 8vo. Lond., 1880. MD 1 V 19

[*See* YEAR-BOOK OF NEW ZEALAND.]

STEWART (SIR JAMES), BART. Principles of Banks, and Banking of Money. 8vo. Lond., 1810. F 4 Q 24

STEWART (JAMES). Illustrations to County of Fife. [*See* LEIGHTON, J. M.] B 12 V 20–22

STEWART (JAMES LINDSAY), AND BRANDIS (D.) Forest Flora of North-west and Central India. 8vo. Lond., 1874. A 4 S 18

Plates to [the above]. Roy. 4to. Lond., 1874. A 2 P 20 †

STEWART (HON. JOHN), M.L.C. Lecture on State Aid to Religion. (Pam. 20.) 8vo. Wollongong, 1859. MJ 2 Q 9

Stable Economy: a Treatise on the Management of Horses in relation to Stabling, Grooming, Feeding, Watering, and Working. 12mo. Edinb., 1860. A 1 P 30

STEWART (ROBERT), A.M. Australasia: with an Appendix, containing authentic Documents illustrating the Progress and State of the Australasian Colonies, to the latest Date. 12mo. Lond., 1853.* MD 1 S 32

STEWART (REV. S. P.) Reply to certain strictures contained in a Pamphlet recently published by Rev. P. Macpherson. [*See* PRESBYTERIAN TRACTS.]

STEWART (WILLIAM). [*See* THOMSON, T.] A 11 Q 26

STEWARTS. Genealogy of the Stewarts. [*See* STEUART, SIR H.] B 13 Q 2

STICKNEY (SARAH). [*See* ELLIS, MRS. S.]

STIELER (ADOLF). Hand-Atlas über alle Theile der Erde und über das Weltgebäude. Fol. Gotha, 1876. D 33 Q 2 ‡

Schul-Atlas über alle Theile der Erde und über das Weltgebäude. Roy. 8vo. Gotha, 1872. D 33 P 5 ‡

STIELER (KARL), PAULUS (E.), AND KADEN (W. Italy, from the Alps to Mount Etna; translated by Frances E. Trollope, and edited by Thomas A. Trollope. Imp. 4to. Lond., 1877. D 5 S 2 †

Wanderungen im Bayerischen Gebirge. [*See* UNSER VATERLAND.] D 38 P 17 ‡

STIFTER (ADALBERT). Pictures of Rural Life in Austria and Hungary; from the German, by Mary Norman. 3 vols. 8vo. Lond., 1850. D 8 Q 19–21

STIGAND (WILLIAM). Life, Work, and Opinions of Heinrich Heine. 2 vols. 8vo. Lond., 1875. C 7 Q 28, 29

STILES (REV. HENRY). Sermon preached in St. John's Church, Parramatta, May 20th, 1838, on the occasion of the Death of the Rev. Samuel Marsden, of Parramatta. 8vo. Sydney, 1838. MG 1 P 1

STILLINGFLEET (RT. REV. EDWARD), D.D., BISHOP OF WORCESTER. Discourse concerning the Idolatry practised in the Church of Rome. 12mo. Lond., 1671. G 9 Q 1

Origines Britannicæ; or, the Antiquities of the British Churches; with a Preface concerning some pretended Antiquities relating to Britain, in Vindication of the Bishop of St. Asaph. Fol. Lond., 1685. G 36 U 1 †

Origines Sacræ; or, a Rational Account of the Grounds of Christian Faith as to the Truth and Divine Authority of the Scriptures. Sm. 4to. Lond., 1680. G 12 S 3

Works of; together with his Life and Character. 6 vols. sm. fol. Lond., 1707–10. G 3 Q 7–12 †

1. Fifty Sermons, preached upon several Occasions.
2. Origines Sacræ; or, a Rational Account of the Grounds of Natural and Revealed Religion.
3. Origines Britannicæ; or, the Antiquities of the British Churches.
4. A Rational Account of the Grounds of Protestant Religion.
5. A Discourse concerning the Idolatry practised in the Church of Rome, and the Hazard of Salvation in the Communion of it.
6. Several Conferences between a Romish Priest, a Fanatick-Chaplain, and a Divine of the Church of England, concerning the Idolatry of the Church of Rome.

STILLMAN (DR. J. D. B.), A.M., &c. The Horse in Motion, as shown by Instantaneous Photography; with a Study of Animal Mechanics, executed and published under the auspices of Leland Stanford. 4to. Lond., 1882. A 2 R 1 †

STILLMAN (W. J.) Herzegovina and the Insurrection: the Causes of the Latter and the Remedies. 8vo. Lond., 1877. B 16 V 36

STINTZING (R.) Geschichte der deutschen Rechtswissenschaft. (Ges. der Wiss.) 8vo. München, 1880. A 17 V 32, 33

STIRLING (A. W.), F.R.G.S., &c. The Never Never Land: a Ride in North Queensland. Illustrated. 8vo. Lond., 1884. MD 5 P 30

STIRLING (JAMES). Proteaceæ of the Victorian Alps; with an Introduction on the Topographical and Geological Features of that Region. 8vo. Adelaide, 1883. MA 2 Q 23

STIRLING (CAPT. JAMES). Extract of a Despatch from Lieutenant-Governor Stirling, to the Right Honourable Sir George Murray, dated Perth, Western Australia, 20th January, 1830. (Parl. Docs., 7.) Fol. Lond., 1830. MF 4 ‡
State of the Colony of Swan River. [*See* BARROW, SIR J.] MD 7 Q 47

STIRLING (JAMES HUTCHINSON), LL.D., &c. Text-book to Kant: the Critique of Pure Reason: Æsthetic, Categories, Schematism, Translation, Reproduction, Commentary, Index; with Biographical Sketch. 8vo. Edinb., 1881. G 12 S 18

STIRLING (PATRICK JAMES), F.R.S.E. Australian and Californian Gold Discoveries and their Consequences; or, an Inquiry into the Laws which determine the Value and Distribution of the Precious Metals. 8vo. Edinb., 1853.* MF 1 P 3

STIRLING (WILLIAM). Annals of the Artists of Spain. 8vo. Lond., 1848. A 7 T 12–14
Diego Rodriguez de Silva Velasquez and his Works. 12mo. Lond., 1855. C 1 R 38

STIRLING (WILLIAM ALEXANDER), EARL OF. Life and Poems of. [*See* CHALMERS, A.]

STIRLING-MAXWELL (SIR WILLIAM). [*See* MAXWELL, SIR W. S.]

STISTED (MRS. HENRY). Letters from the Bye-ways of Italy. 8vo. Lond., 1845. D 6 U 37

STOCK (CECIL HADEN). Treatise on Shoring and Underpinning, and generally dealing with Ruinous and Dangerous Structures. With Illustrations. 8vo. Lond., 1882. A 3 P 21

STOCKDALE (F. W. L.) Excursions in the County of Cornwall. Illustrated. 8vo. Lond., 1824. D 7 V 31

STÖCKHARDT (DR. JULIUS ADOLPH). Chemical Field Lectures: a Familiar Exposition of the Chemistry of Agriculture. 8vo. Lond., 1855. A 5 R 5
Experimental Chemistry. [*See* HEATON, C. W.] A 5 R 27

STOCKING (CHARLES). Catalogue of New and Standard Works on Sale. 8vo. Lond., 1822. MK 1 Q 13

STOCKMAR (CHRISTIAN FRIEDRICH), BARON. Memoirs of; by his Son, Baron E. von Stockmar; edited by F. Max Müller. 2 vols. 8vo. Lond., 1876. C 3 P 39, 40

STOCKMAR (E. VON), BARON. Memoirs of Baron Stockmar; by his Son; edited by F. Max Müller. 2 vols. 8vo. Lond., 1872. C 3 P 39, 40

STOCKWELL (THOMAS B.) History of Public Education in Rhode Island, 1636–1876. 8vo. Providence, 1876. G 17 R 5

4 Y

STOCKWHIP (THE). 2 vols. fol. Sydney, 1875–76. ME

STOCQUELER (J. H.) Old Field Officer; the Military and Sporting Adventures of Major Worthington. 2 vols. 8vo. Edinb., 1853. C 5 Q 14, 15

STODART (R. R.) Scottish Arms; being a Collection of Armorial Bearings, A.D. 1370–1678; with Heraldic and Genealogical Notes. 2 vols. sm. fol. Edinb., 1881. K 22 S 9, 10 ‡

STODDARD (MAJOR AMOS). Sketches, Historical and Descriptive, of Louisiana. 8vo. Philad., 1812. B 1 8 8

STODDART (COL. CHARLES). Mission to ascertain the Fate of. [*See* WOLFF, REV. J.] D 6 Q 5, 6
The Bokhara Victims [Col. Charles Stoddart and Capt. A. Conolly]. [*See* GROVER, CAPT. J.]

STODDARD (CHARLES WARREN). Summer Cruising in the South Seas. 8vo. Lond., 1874. MD 5 Q 35
[*See* ESSAYS FROM THE CRITIC.]

STODDARD (R. H.) English Verse. [*See* LINTON, W. J.] H 7 Q 32–36

STOKES (GEORGE GABRIEL), M.A., &c. Mathematical and Physical Papers. 2 vols. roy. 8vo. Camb., 1880–83. A 10 T 8, 9
On Light. Second Course: On Light as a Means of Investigation. (Burnett Lectures.) 8vo. Lond., 1885. A 21 Q 20

STOKES (PROF. G. T.), D.D. Ireland and the Celtic Church. 8vo. Lond., 1886. G 7 S 11

STOKES (CAPT. J. LORT), R.N. Discoveries in Australia; with an Account of the Coasts and Rivers explored and surveyed during the Voyage of H.M.S. *Beagle*, in the years 1837–43; also, a Narrative of Captain Owen Stanley's Visits to the Islands in the Arafûra Sea. 2 vols. 8vo. Lond., 1846.* MD 2 U 16, 17

STOKES (REV. LOUIS), B.A. Letters of Connop Thirlwall. [*See* THIRLWALL, C.] C 10 P 38

STOKES (WHITLEY). Beunans Meriasek : The Life of Saint Meriasek, Bishop and Confessor: a Cornish Drama. Roy. 8vo. Lond., 1872. H 2 U 2
The Breton Glosses at Orleans. 8vo. Calcutta, 1880. K 14 Q 20
Goidelica: Old and Early-Middle-Irish Glosses, Prose and Verse. 2nd ed. Roy. 8vo. Lond., 1872. K 12 T 19
Old Breton Glosses. 8vo. Calcutta, 1879. K 14 Q 20
Three Middle-Irish Homilies on the Lives of Saints Patrick, Brigit, and Columba. 8vo. Calcutta, 1877. G 12 R 2
Togail Troi: the Destruction of Troy; transcribed from the Facsimile of the Book of Leinster, and translated, with a Glossarial Index of the rarer Words, by W. Stokes. 8vo. Calcutta, 1881. B 13 V 26
[*See* THREE IRISH GLOSSARIES.]

STOKES (PROF. WILLIAM), M.D., &c. Life and Labours, in Art and Archæology, of George Petrie, LL.D., &c. 8vo. Lond., 1868.   C 9 P 16

STONE (CHARLES J.) Cradle-Land of Arts and Creeds; or, nothing new under the Sun. 8vo. Lond., 1880.   G 12 R 1

STONE (JOHN). Dunedin and Invercargill Commercial, Municipal, and General Directory, Otago and Southland Gazetteer, Almanac and Companion. 8vo. Dunedin, 1886.   ME 3 T

STONE (OCTAVIUS C.) A Few Months in New Guinea. Illustrated. 8vo. Lond., 1880.   MD 6 P 28

STONEHENGE; or, the Romans in Britain : a Romance of the Days of Nero; by "Malachi Mouldy, F.S.A." 3 vols. 8vo. Lond., 1842.   J 10 R 31–33

STONEHENGE. [*See* WALSH, J. H.]

STONES (WILLIAM). My First Voyage: a Book for Youth. Illustrated. 8vo. Lond., 1858.   MD 1 R 9

Another copy. 2nd ed. 8vo. Lond., 1860.   MD 1 R 10

New Zealand (the Land of Promise) and its Resources. 7th ed. 12mo. Lond., 1864.   MD 1 P 1

STONEY (BINDON B.), B.A., &c. Theory of Strains in Girders and similar Structures. 2 vols. 8vo. Lond., 1868–69.   A 6 U 1, 2

Theory of Stresses in Girders and similar Structures. New ed. 8vo. Lond., 1886.   A 6 U 3

STONEY (MAJOR H. BUTLER). Reginald Mortimer; or, Truth more strange than Fiction: a Tale of a Soldier's Life and Adventure. 8vo. Melb., 1857.   MJ 2 P 18

Residence in Tasmania ; with a descriptive Tour through the Island, from Macquarie Harbour to Circular Head. 8vo. Lond., 1856.*   MD 7 R 21

Victoria; with a Description of its principal Cities, Melbourne and Geelong. 8vo. Lond., 1856.*   MD 7 R 17

Year in Tasmania, including some Months' Residence in the Capital; with a descriptive Tour through the Island, from Macquarie Harbour to Circular Head. 8vo. Hobart, 1854.   MD 7 R 20

STORER (H. S.) [*See* LE KEUX, J., AND COOPER, C. H.]   B 6 S 3–6

STORER (J. AND H. S.) Graphic and Historical Description of the City of Edinburgh: Views, &c. 2 vols. 8vo. Lond., 1818-20.   B 13 S 3, 4

Another copy. 2 vols 8vo. Lond., 1818-20.   B 13 S 5, 6

STORER (JAMES), AND GREIG (I.) Antiquarian and Topographical Cabinet. 10 vols. 12mo. Lond., 1807–11.   D 12 P 1–10

Antiquarian Itinerary. 7 vols. 8vo. Lond., 1816.   B 6 T 25–31

STORER (THOMAS). Life and Death of Thomas Wolsey, Cardinall. [*See* PARK, T.]

STORMONTH (REV. JAMES). Dictionary of the English Language, Pronouncing, Etymological, and Explanatory. Imp. 8vo. Edinb., 1884.   K 15 U 2

STORY (JOSEPH), LL.D. Commentaries on Equity Jurisprudence, as administered in England and America. 12th ed. 2 vols. roy. 8vo. Boston, 1877.   F 4 R 10, 11

Commentaries on the Constitution of the United States. 3 vols. 8vo. Boston, 1833.   F 4 R 4–6

Public and General Statutes of the N.S. of America, 1789–1827. 8vo. Boston, 1828.   F 12 R 3–5

STORY (WILLIAM). Victorian Government Prize Essay: Essay upon the Agriculture of Victoria, with reference to its Climate Advantages, &c. 8vo. Melb., 1861. MA 1 Q 1

Another copy. [*See* VICTORIAN GOVERNMENT PRIZE ESSAYS.]

STORY (WILLIAM W.) Roba di Roma. 6th ed., with Additions. 8vo. Lond., 1871.   D 6 Q 44

STOTHARD (C. A.) Monumental Effigies of Great Britain. Roy. fol. Lond., 1876.   B 32 P 13 ‡

STOTHARD (THOMAS), R.A. Life of; with Personal Reminiscences, by Mrs. Bray. With Illustrations from his Works. Sm. 4to. Lond., 1851.   O 9 R 19

Italy : a Poem. Illustrated. [*See* ROGERS, S.]

STOUGHTON (JOHN), D.D. Howard, the Philanthropist, and his Friends. 8vo. Lond., 1884.   C 3 U 26

William Penn, the Founder of Pennsylvania. 8vo. Lond., 1882.   C 4 T 23

STOUT (ROBERT). Social Future of Labourers: a Paper read before the Tokomairiro Mutual Improvement Association. 8vo. Dunedin, 1872.   MJ 2 R 16

STOW (JEFFERSON P.) South Australia: its History, Productions, and Natural Resources 2nd ed. 8vo. Adelaide, 1884.   MB 2 R 5

STOW or STOWE (JOHN). Annales; or, a General Chronicle of England, collected out of the most authentic Authors, Records, and other Monuments of Antiquity. Sm. 4to. Lond., 1592.   Libr.

Annales; or, a Generall Chronicle of England; begun by John Stowe, continued and augmented with Matters Forraigne and Domestic, by Edmund Howe. Fol. Lond., 1631.   B 18 S 2 ‡

Survey of London; contayning the Originall, Increase, Moderne Estate, and Government of that City, methodically set down; begunne by John Stowe, and finished by A. Munday, H. Dyson, and others. Sm. fol. Lond., 1633.   B 19 R 12 ‡

Survey of the Cities of London and Westminster; written at first in the year 1598. Corrected, improved, and enlarged, by John Strype, M.A. 2 vols. fol. Lond., 1720.   B 14 T 8, 9 ‡

STOW (REV. T. Q.) Congregationalism in the Colonies: an Address. (Pam. C.) Roy. 8vo. Sydney, 1855.   MJ 2 S 1

STOWE (EDWIN), B.A. Velazquez. (Great Artists.) 8vo. Lond., 1881.   C 3 T 34

STOWE (MRS. HARRIET BEECHER). Autographs for Freedom. 12mo. Lond., 1853.   F 15 P 9

Sunny Memories of Foreign Lands. Author's edition. 2 vols. 8vo. Lond., 1854.   D 9 P 34

Another copy. 2 vols. 8vo. Lond., 1854.   D 9 P 35, 36

STOWELL (W. SCOTT), LORD, AND ELDON (J. SCOTT), EARL. Sketch of the Lives of Lords Stowell and Eldon; by W. E. Surtees. 8vo. Lond., 1846.   C 9 U 40

STRABO. Géographie de Strabon; traduite du Grec en Français. 5 vols. roy. 4to. Paris, 1805–19.* D 9 S 17–21 †

Geography of Strabo; literally translated, with Notes, by A. C. Hamilton, and by W. Falconer, M.A. 3 vols. 8vo. Lond., 1854–57.   D 11 R 5–7

STRACHAN (REV. ALEXANDER). Life of the Rev. Samuel Leigh, Missionary to the Settlers and Savages of Australia and New Zealand; with a History of the Origin and Progress of the Missions in those Colonies. Illustrated edition. 8vo. Lond., 1870.   MC 1 P 6

STRACHAN (JOHN). Plea on behalf of the Aboriginal Inhabitants of Victoria. 8vo. Melb., 1856.   MA 1 R 2

Another copy. 8vo. Melb., 1856.   MG 1 Q 40

STRACHEY (SIR JOHN, AND LIEUT.-GEN. RICHARD). Finances and Public Works of India, 1869–81. 8vo. Lond., 1882.   F 6 V 11

STRADA (FAMIANO). De Bello Belgico: the History of the Low Countrey Warres; translated by Sir Robert Stapylton. Sm. fol. Lond., 1650.   B 15 Q 14 ‡

STRADA (JACOPO DE). Epitome Thesaurii Antiquitatum hoc est Impp. Rom. Orientalium et Occidentalium Iconum. 8vo. Tiguri, 1557.   A 13 S 40

STRAFFORD (THOMAS WENTWORTH), EARL OF. Life of. [*See* MACKINTOSH, SIR J.]

Wentworth Papers, 1705–39, selected from the Private and Family Correspondence of Thomas Wentworth, Lord Raby (created in 1711, Earl of Strafford), of Stainborough, County of York; with a Memoir and Notes, by James J. Cartwright, M.A. 8vo. Lond., 1883.   C 9 T 52

STRAFFORELLO (GUSTAVO). Dizionario universale Geographia, &c. [*See* TREVES, E.]   D 12 V 1, 2

STRANGE (ROBERT). Inquiry into the Rise and Establishment of the Royal Academy of Arts. 8vo. Lond., 1775   A 7 Q 25

STRANGE (THOMAS LUMISDEN). Development of Creation on the Earth. 8vo. Lond., 1874.   A 9 S 36

Legends of the Old Testament, traced to their apparent Primitive Sources. 8vo. Lond., 1874.   G 12 T 1

Sources and Development of Christianity. 8vo. Lond., 1875.   G 12 Q 11

The Speaker's Commentary reviewed. 8vo. Lond., 1871.   G 7 T 1

The Bible; is it "The Word of God?" 8vo. Lond., 1871.   G 12 Q 10

STRANGFORD (PERCY), VISCOUNT. Observations on some Passages in Lieut.-Col. Napier's "History of the Peninsular War." 2nd ed. 8vo. Lond., 1828. B 13 U 7

STRANGFORD (EMILY ANN), VISCOUNTESS. Eastern Shores of the Adriatic, 1863. 8vo. Lond., 1864.   D 8 T 31

STRASBURGER (DR. E.) Hand-book of Practical Botany, for the Botanical Laboratory and Private Student. 8vo. Lond., 1887.   A 4 T 17

Zellbildung und Zelltheilung. 8vo. Jena, 1880.   A 5 P 10

STRATFORD (JOSEPH). Wiltshire and its Worthies: Notes, Topographical and Biographical. Sm. 4to. Salisbury, 1882.   D 12 P 4

STRATFORD DE REDCLIFFE (RT. HON. SIR STRATFORD CANNING), VISCOUNT, P.C., &c. Alfred the Great in Athelnay: an Historical Play. 8vo. Lond., 1876.   H 4 P 31

STRATMANN (FRANCIS HENRY). Dictionary of the Old English Language, compiled from Writings of the 12th, 13th, 14th, and 15th Centuries. 3rd ed. 4to. Krefeld, 1878.   K 12 T 18

STRAUSS (DAVID FRIEDRICH). Life of Jesus, critically examined. 3 vols. 8vo. Lond., 1846.   G 12 P 11–13

The Old Faith and the New: a Confession. Authorised Translation from the 6th ed., by Mathilde Blind. 8vo. Lond., 1873.   G 7 S 5

Strauss and Rénan: an Essay. [*See* ZELLER, E.]

Strauss in his Life and Writings; by Eduard Zeller. With a Portrait. 8vo. Lond., 1874.   C 4 Q 47

STRAUSS (FRIEDRICH ADOLPH). Sinai and Golgotha: a Journey in the East. 12mo. Lond., 1849.   D 5 P 19

STRAUSS (PROF. G. L.), PH.D. Grammar of the French Language. (Weale.) 3rd ed. 12mo. Lond., 1871.   K 11 T 12

Grammar of the German Language as spoken and written. (Weale.) 12mo. Lond. (n.d.)   K 11 T 20

The German Reader: a series of Extracts carefully culled from the most approved Authors of Germany. (Weale.) 12mo. Lond. (n.d.)   K 11 T 20

STREATFIELD (G. S.), M.A. Lincolnshire and the Danes. 8vo. Lond., 1884.   B 3 R 20

STRECKER (ADOLPH). Kurzes Lehrbuch der Organischen Chemie. 5ᵉ auflage. 8vo. Braunsw., 1868.   A 5 S 23

Short Text-book of Organic Chemistry; edited by Dr. Johannes Wislicenus; translated, with Additions, by W. R. Hodgkinson, Ph.D., and A. J. Greenaway. 8vo. Lond., 1881.   A 6 Q 4

STREET (GEORGE EDMUND), R.A., &c. Cathedral of the Holy Trinity, commonly called Christ Church Cathedral, Dublin. Fol. Lond., 1882.   B 20 P 19 ‡

Some Account of Gothic Architecture in Spain. 2nd ed. Roy. 8vo. Lond., 1869.   A 2 S 23

STREET TRAMWAYS. Street Tramways—the Cars drawn by Horses; compiled for the Melbourne Omnibus Company, Limited. 8vo. Melb., 1872.   MF 1 Q 2

STREETER (EDWIN W.), F.R.G.S. Great Diamonds of the World: their History and Romance. 8vo. Lond., 1882.   A 10 Q 5

Pearls and Pearling Life. 8vo. Lond., 1886.   A 16 U 20

Precious Stones and Gems: their History and distinguishing Characteristics. Illustrated. 8vo. Lond., 1877.   A 10 P 4

STREETS (THOMAS H.), M.D. Contributions to the Natural History of Hawaiian and Fanning Islands, and Lower California, made in connection with the United States North Pacific Surveying Expedition, 1873–75. 8vo. Wash., 1877.   MD 5 T 36

STRETCH (REV. J. F.) The English Reformation. [*See* CHURCH HISTORY.]   MG 1 R 15

STRETTON (CHARLES). Memoirs of a Chequered Life. 3 vols. 8vo. Lond., 1862.   MC 1 Q 3–5

Sport and Sportsmen : a Book of Recollections. 8vo. Lond., 1866.   A 17 W 33

STRICKLAND (MISS AGNES). Letters of Mary, Queen of Scots, and Documents connected with her Personal History; now first published, with an Introduction. 3 vols. 8vo. Lond., 1842–43.   C 5 P 26–28

Another copy; with an Historical Introduction and Notes. 2 vols. 8vo. Lond., 1845.   C 5 P 29, 30

Lives of the Queens of England, from the Norman Conquest. New ed. 8 vols. 8vo. Lond., 1851–53.   C 9 Q 27–34

Lives of the Queens of Scotland and English Princesses connected with the Regal Succession of Great Britain. 8 vols. 8vo. Lond., 1850–59.   C 4 V 18–25

Lives of the Seven Bishops, committed to the Tower in 1688. 8vo. Lond., 1866.   C 4 V 34

Queen Victoria, from her Birth to her Bridal. 2 vols. 8vo. Lond., 1840.   C 5 R 28, 29

Rome. [*See* STRICKLAND, JANE M.]   B 12 Q 35

Tales and Stories from History. 8th ed. 12mo. Lond., 1859.   B 35 Q 5

STRICKLAND (SIR EDWARD), K.C.B., &c. Importance of Geography. 8vo. Sydney, 1887.*   MD 7 P 37

Lecture on our South African Colonies: how the recent Wars with the Gaikas, Galekas, and Zulus arose and ended. 8vo. Sydney, 1882.   MB 2 R 27

[*See* ROYAL GEOGRAPHICAL SOCIETY OF AUSTRALASIA.]

STRICKLAND (MISS JANE MARGARET). Rome, Regal and Republican: a Family History of Rome ; edited by Agnes Strickland. 8vo. Lond., 1854.   B 12 Q 35

STRITTER (JOHANN GOTTHILF VON). Memoriæ Popvlorvm, olim ad Danvbivm, Pontum Evxinvm, Palvdem Mæotidem, Cavcasvm, Mare Caspivm, et inde magis ad Septemtriones incolentivm, e Scriptoribus Historiæ Byzantinæ ervtæ et digestæ a Joanne Gotthilf Strittero. 4 vols. 4to. Petropoli, 1771–79.   B 9 V 26–29

STRONACH (GEORGE), M.A. New Gleanings from Gladstone. 8vo. Edinb. [1879]   MF 1 Q 6

STRONG (PROF. H. A.), M.A., &c. Thirteen Satires of Juvenal. [*See* JUVENALIS, D. J.]

STRUTHERS (JOHN). History of Scotland, from the Union to the Abolition of Heritable Jurisdictions in 1748. 2 vols. 8vo. Glasgow, 1830.   B 13 Q 18, 19

STRUTT (ELIZABETH). Domestic Residence in Switzerland. 2 vols. 8vo. Lond., 1842.   D 8 S 29, 30

STRUTT (JOSEPH). Complete View of the Dress and Habits of the People of England. New ed., with Notes, by J. R. Planché, F.S.A. 2 vols. 4to. Lond., 1842.   B 10 Q 8, 9 †

Regal and Ecclesiastical Antiquities of England; containing the Representations of all the English Monarchs, from Edward the Confessor to Henry VIII; with Notes by J. R. Planché, F.S.A. 4to. Lond., 1842.   B 14 R 10 ‡

Sports and Pastimes of the People of England, from the Earliest Period to the Present Time; with Index. 8vo. Lond., 1850.   A 17 W 35

STRUYCK (NICOLAAS). Inleiding tot de algemeene Geographie, benevens eenige sterrekundige en andere Verhandelingen. 4to. Amsterdam, 1740.   D 10 P 20 †

Vervolg van de Beschryving der Staarsterren. 4to. Amsterdam, 1753.   A 3 U 18

STRYPE (REV. JOHN), M.A. Historical and Biographical Works of ; with Index by the Rev. R. T. Lawrence. 24 vols. 8vo. Oxford, 1820–40.   G 2 S 1–24

STRZELECKI (P. E. DE), COUNT. Gold and Silver: a Supplement to the "Physical Description of New South Wales and Van Diemen's Land." 8vo. Lond., 1856.*   MD 2 V 12

Physical Description of New South Wales and Van Diemen's Land; accompanied by a Geological Map, Sections and Diagrams, and Figures of the Organic Remains. 8vo. Lond., 1845.*   MD 2 V 8

STUART (ANDREW). [*See* STEUART, SIR H.]

STUART (ARABELLA), LADY. Life and Letters of, including numerous original and unpublished Documents; by Elizabeth Cooper. 2 vols. 12mo. Lond., 1866. C 3 P 37, 38

STUART (CHARLES B.) Naval Dry Docks of the United States. Illustrated. 3rd ed. Roy. 4to. New York, 1855. A 7 S 6 †

STUART (CHARLES EDWARD), PRINCE. [*See* CHARLES EDWARD STUART, PRINCE.]
[*See* ASCANIUS.]

STUART (HECTOR A.) South Sea Dreamer. [Poems.] Edited by E. W. Foxall. 4to. Sydney, 1886.* MH 1 S 1

STUART (HENRY WINDSOR VILLIERS). Egypt after the War; being the Narrative of a Tour of Inspection (undertaken last Autumn), including Experiences among the Natives, with Descriptions of their Homes and Habits. Roy. 8vo. Lond., 1883. D 2 U 7
Funeral Tent of an Egyptian Queen. Roy. 8vo. Lond., 1882. B 2 R 40
Nile Gleanings concerning the Ethnology, History, and Art of Ancient Egypt, as revealed by Egyptian Paintings and Bas-reliefs. Roy. 8vo. Lond., 1879. D 2 U 8

STUART (JAMES). Three Years in North America. 2 vols. 8vo. Lond., 1833. D 3 Q 15, 16

STUART (JAMES), F.R.S., AND REVETT (N.) Antiquities of Athens measured and delineated; with Supplement. 4 vols. imp. fol. Lond., 1825-30. A 1 R 12-15 ‡

STUART (JOHN), LL.D. Archæological Essays. [*See* SIMPSON, SIR J. Y.] B 13 P 36, 37
Exchequer Rolls of Scotland. [*See* SCOTLAND.] B 33 T 1-9
Lost Chapter in the History of Mary, Queen of Scots, recovered. Sm. 4to. Edinb., 1874. C 8 Q 32

STUART (JOHN McDOUALL). Explorations across the Continent of Australia, 1861-62; with Charts. 8vo. Melb., 1863.* MD 6 T 20
Explorations of the Interior; Diary from March 2 to September 3, 1860. Roy. 8vo. Adelaide, 1860. MJ 2 S 1
Journals of, during the years 1858-62, when he fixed the Centre of the Continent, and successfully crossed it from Sea to Sea: Explorations in Australia. With Maps. Edited from Mr. Stuart's Manuscript, by William Hardman, M.A., &c. 8vo. Lond., 1864. MD 6 T 22
Another copy. 2nd ed. 8vo. Lond., 1865. MD 6 T 23

STUART (JOHN SOBIESKI, AND CHARLES EDWARD). Lays of the Deer Forest; with Sketches of Older and Modern Deer-hunting, Traits of Natural History in the Forest, Traditions of the Clans, Miscellaneous Notes. 2 vols. 8vo. Edinb., 1848. H 8 V 13, 14

STUART (MARY). [*See* MARY STUART, QUEEN OF SCOTS.]

STUART (HOUSE OF). Descendents of the Stuarts: an unchronicled Page in England's History; by William Townend. 8vo. Lond., 1858. C 9 T 43
The Decline of. [*See* STANHOPE, EARL.]

STUART-WORTLEY (A. J.) Shooting. [*See* WALSINGHAM, T. DE G., BARON.] A 17 U 33

STUART-WORTLEY (COL. H.) Tahiti. [*See* BRASSEY, LADY.]

STUART-WORTLEY (EMMELINE CHARLOTTE ELIZABETH), LADY. Et Cætera. 8vo. Lond., 1853. D 3 Q 31
Travels in the United States, during 1849-50. 3 vols. 8vo. Lond., 1851. D 3 Q 28-30

STUART-WORTLEY (HON. J.) Memoirs of George Monk. [*See* GUIZOT, F. P. G.] C 8 R 30

STUBBES (PHILLIP). Anatomise of Abuses; contayning a Discoverie of Notable Vices and Imperfections, together with Examples of God's Judgementes; edited by Frederick J. Furnivall. (New Shakes. Soc.) 8vo. Lond., 1877-79. E
Anatomie of Abuses; reprinted from the 3rd edition of 1585, under the superintendence of W. B. D. D. Turnbull. 8vo. Lond., 1836. G 6 S 17

STUBBS (GEORGE). Anatomy of the Horse, including a particular Description of the Bones, Cartilages, Muscles, Fascias, Ligaments, Nerves, Arteries, Veins, and Glands. Fol. Lond., 1853. A 1 P 2 ‡

STUBBS (PROF. WILLIAM), M.A. Constitutional History of England, in its Origin and Development. 2nd ed. 3 vols. 8vo. Oxford, 1875-78. B 4 P 25-27
Select Charters, and other Illustrations of English Constitutional History, from the Earliest Times to the Reign of Edward I. 2nd ed. (Clar. Press.) 8vo. Oxford, 1874. B 21 S 26
Seventeen Lectures on the Study of Mediæval and Modern History. 8vo. Oxford, 1886. B 15 Q 28

STUCKENBERG (J. H. W.), D.D. Life of Immanuel Kant. 8vo. Lond., 1882. C 7 P 34

STUD-BOOK OF NEW SOUTH WALES (THE). Containing Pedigrees of Racehorses, &c., from the earliest arrivals in the Colony to the present time. Vol. 1. Compiled and edited by Fowler Boyd Price. Vol. 2. Compiled and edited by Harry P. Mostyn. 2 vols. 8vo. Sydney, 1859-68. MA 1 Q 45, 46

STUDENT INTERPRETER, A. [*See* CHINA.]

STUDENT OF THE INNER TEMPLE, A. [*See* CRIMINAL RECORDER.]

STUDENT'S ENCYCLOPÆDIA (THE) of Universal Knowledge. 6 vols. 4to. Lond., 1883. K 5 Q 31-36

STUDIA BIBLICA : Essays in Biblical Archæology and Criticism, and kindred Subjects; by Members of the University of Oxford. 8vo. Oxford, 1885. G 12 S 20

STÜDNITZ (ARTHUR VON). Gold; or, Legal Regulations for the Standard of Gold and Silver Wares in different Countries of the World. 8vo. Lond., 1877. F 5 S 30

STUDY OF THE PROLOGUE AND EPILOGUE in English Literature, from Shakespeare to Dryden ; by G. S. B. 8vo. Lond., 1884.   J 8 Q 20

STUKELEY (Rev. William), M.D. Itinerarium Curiosum ; or, an Account of the Antiquities and Remarkable Curiosities in Nature or Art, observed in Travels thro' Great Britain. 2 vols. (in 1) sm. fol. Lond., 1724–76.   B 15 S 9 ‡

STUMM (Capt. Hugo). Russia in Central Asia: Historical Sketch of Russia's Progress in the East up to 1873, and of the Incidents which led to the Campaign against Khiva. with Maps. 8vo. Lond., 1885.   B 12 U 4

STURGE (Mrs. George). Lord Beaconsfield. [*See* Brandes, G.]   C 9 V 13

STURGE (Joseph). Memoirs of; by Henry Richard. 8vo. Lond., 1864.   C 9 U 46

Visit to the United States in 1841. 8vo. Lond., 1842.   D 3 S 47

STURGESS (John). The Coaching Age. [*See* Harris, S.]   B 7 R 15

Ambassadors of Commerce. [*See* Allen, A. P.] J 1 U 9

STURM (Christoph Christian). Morning Communings with God; or, Devotional Meditations for Every Day in the Year; translated from the German, by W. Johnstone, A.M. New ed. 8vo. Lond., 1870.   G 16 Q 5

Reflections for Every Day in the Year, on the Works of God and of His Providence. 5th ed. 3 vols. 12mo. Lond., 1795.   G 8 U 17–19

STURROCK (A. C.) Australian Gardeners' Guide: an Epitome of Horticulture for the Colony of Victoria. New ed. 12mo. Melb., 1879.   MA 1 P 6

STURT (Capt. Charles), F.L.S., &c. Narrative of an Expedition into Central Australi, during the years 1844–46; together with a Notice of the Province of South Australia in 1847. 2 vols. 8vo. Lond., 1849.*   MD 3 U 30, 31

Two Expeditions into the Interior of Southern Australia, during the years 1828–31; with Observations on the Soil, Climate, and General Resources of the Colony of New South Wales. 2 vols. 8vo. Lond., 1833.*   MD 3 U 22, 23

Another copy. 2nd ed. 2 vols. 8vo. Lond., 1834.*   MD 3 U 26, 27

[Extracts from] Two Expeditions into the Interior of Southern Australia. 8vo. Lond., 1831.   MD 7 Q 51

STUTCHBURY (S.) Description of a new species of Plesiosaurus. (Pam. Cb.) 8vo. Lond., 1846.   A 16 U 25

On a new genus of Fossil Bivalve Shell. (Pam. Cb.) 8vo. Lond., 1842.   A 16 U 25

STUTFIELD (Hugh E. M.) El Maghreb: 1,200 Miles' Ride through Marocco. 8vo. Lond., 1886.   D 1 Q 2

STUTTERD (S.) [*See* Dzierzon, Dr. J.]

STYLES (Rev. John), D.D. The Animal Creation : its Claims on our Humanity stated and enforced. 8vo. Lond., 1839.   A 14 R 37

SUARD (—.) Notice sur la Vie de la Duc de la Rochefoucauld. [*See* La Rochefoucauld, F., Duc de.]

SUCCESS IN LIFE: a Book for Young Men. 12mo. Lond., 1852.   J 10 P 35

SUCKLING (Sir John). Aglaura. (Old Plays.) Sm. fol. Lond., 1638.   H 1 V 1

Life and Poems. of. [*See* Chalmers, A.]

Poems, Plays, and other Remains of. 2 vols. 12mo. Lond., 1874.   Libr.

SUDDS (Joseph), and THOMPSON (Patrick). Copy of the Record of Conviction of Joseph Sudds and Patrick Thompson, Privates of the 57th Regiment, who were convicted at the Quarter Sessions, at Sydney, New South Wales, on the 7th November, 1826, of stealing some Calico, and severally sentenced to seven years' transportation. (Parl. Docs., 6.) Fol. Lond., 1828.   MF 4 ‡

Return of all the Letters addressed by the Right Hon. the Secretary of State for the Colonies, in reply to Governor Darling's Despatches, relative to the Punishment and Death of Private Joseph Sudds, late of His Majesty's 57th Regiment, dated 4th and 12th December, 1826, and 20th April, and 28th May, 1829; also, portions of Mr. Wentworth's Letter of Impeachment. (Parl. Docs. 6.) Fol. Lond., 1832.   MF 4 ‡

[*See* Darling, Lieut.-Gen. Sir R.]

SUESS (Prof. E.) Die Entstehung der Alpen. 8vo. Wien, 1875.   A 24 U 6

SUETONIUS TRANQUILLUS (C.) Lives of the Twelve Cæsars, to which are added his Lives of the Grammarians, Rhetoricians, and Poets; the Translation of Alexander Thomson, M.D. 8vo. Lond., 1887.   C 4 P 9

Opera omnia, ex editione Baumgarten-Crusii ; cum Notis et Interpretatione in usum Delphini. 4 vols. 8vo. Lond., 1826.   J 13 S 29–32

SUFFOLK (Henrietta), Countess. Letters to and from Henrietta, Countess of Suffolk, and her Husband, the Hon. George Berkeley, 1712–67. 2 vols. 8vo. Lond., 1824.   C 9 T 46, 47

SUFFOLK and BERKSHIRE (Henry Charles Howard), Earl of. [*See* Racing.]   A 17 U 32

SUGAR CANE (The): a Monthly Magazine devoted to the Interests of the Sugar Cane Industry. 8vo. Manchester, 1874.   MA 1 Q 28

SUGERIUS (Abbas). Opuscula et Epistolæ. [*See* Migne, J. P., Series Latina, 186.]

SULEIMAN of Husn Keifa. [*See* Hall, I. H.] G 3 P 22 ‡

SULLIVAN (Capt. G. L.), R.N. Dhow-chasing in Zanzibar Waters and on the Eastern Coast of Africa. 8vo. Lond., 1873.   D 2 S 9

SULLIVAN (Sir Edward), Bart. Conquerors, Warriors, and Statesmen of India. 8vo. Lond., 1866.　B 10 U 28

SULLIVAN (Robert), LL.D., &c. Dictionary of Derivations; or, an Introduction to Etymology, or a new plan. 13th ed. 12mo. Lond., 1870.　K 11 U 26

SULLIVAN (William). Political Class-book, intended to instruct the Higher Classes in Schools in the Origin, Nature, and Use of Political Power; with Appendix, by G. B. Emerson. 8vo. Boston, 1836.　F 5 S 4

SULLIVAN (Prof. William K.), Ph.D., &c. Celtic Studies. [*See* Ebel, Dr. H.]

SULLY (James), M.A. Illusions: a Psychological Study. 8vo. Lond., 1881.　G 7 S 8

Outlines of Psychology, with special reference to the Theory of Education. 8vo. Lond., 1884.　G 12 S 5

Pessimism: a History and a Criticism. 8vo. Lond., 1877.　G 12 R 4

SULLY (Maximilian de Bethune), Duke de. Memoirs of, Prime Minister of Henry the Great; newly translated from the French Edition of [Pierre Mathurin] de l'Ecluse [des Loges]. 5 vols. 12mo. Edinb., 1773.　C 5 P 29–33

SULPICIA. Satire of Sulpicia. [*See* Juvenalis, D. J.]

SULPICIUS SEVERUS. Opera, ad MSS. codices emendata, notisque, observationibus et dissertationibus illustrata, studio et labore Hieronymi de Prato. 2 vols. 4to. Verona, 1741–54.　G 5 U 22, 23

SUMMER (Prof. James). English Outline Vocabulary. [*See* Bellows, J.]

SUMNER (Heywood). The Itchen Valley, from Tichborne to Southampton. Twenty-two Etchings. Imp. 4to. Lond., 1881.　D 4 U 12 ‡

SUN (The), and New South Wales Independent Press. Fol. Sydney, 1843.　ME

SUNDAY MAGAZINE (The), for 1865; edited by Thos. Guthrie, D.D. Imp. 8vo. Lond., 1865.　J 9 V 19

SUNDAY SCHOOL UNION. [*See* Van Diemen's Land Sunday School Union.]　MG 1 Q 39

SUNDERLAND (Countess of). Correspondence of Charles II with. [*See* Romney, Hon. Henry Sidney, Earl of.]　C 6 V 18, 19

SUNDERLAND LIBRARY. Bibliotheca Sunderlandiana: Sale Catalogue of the Library of Printed Books. Roy. 8vo. Lond., 1881.　K 8 Q 1

SUNDT (Eilert). Beretning om Fante-eller Landstrygerfolket i Norge. Bidrag til Kundskab om de laveste Samfundsforholde. Andet Oplag. 8vo. Christiania, 1852.　K 12 Q 43

SUNSHINE AND SEA: a Yachting Visit to the Channel Islands and Coast of Brittany; by "A Country Doctor." 8vo. Lond. 1885　D 7 R 49

SUPERINTENDENT OF THE *LAYTON*, THE. [*See* Emigration.]

SUPERNATURAL RELIGION: an Inquiry into the Reality of Divine Revelation. 2nd ed. 3 vols. 8vo. Lond., 1875–77.　G 8 T 14–16

SUPREME COURT. [*See* New South Wales; Victoria; *and* West Australia]

SURREBUTTER (Mr. John). [*See* Anstey, J.]

SURREY (Henry Howard), Earl of. Life and Poems of. [*See* Chalmers, A.]

SURREY (Henry Howard), Earl of, And Wyatt (Sir T.) Works of; edited by G. F. Nott. 2 vols. 4to. Lond., 1815–16.　J 8 R 9 10 †

SURTEES (William). Twenty-five in the Rifle Brigade. 8vo. Edinb., 1823.　C 4 Q 33

SURTEES (William Edward), D.C.L. Sketch of the Lives of Lords Stowell and Eldon. 8vo. Lond., 1846.　C 9 U 40

SURTEES SOCIETY. Publications of. 76 vols. 8vo. Lond., 1835–83.　E 2.41

SUSOOS. Religious Instruction for the Susoos. (Pam. Ea.) 12mo. Edinb., 1801.　MK 1 P 24

Spelling-book for the Susoos, and a Catechism for Little Children. (Pam. Ea.) 12mo. Edinb., 1802.　MK 1 P 24

SUSSEX ARCHÆOLOGICAL COLLECTIONS, illustrating the History and Antiquities of the County; with a General Index to vols. 1–25, by Henry Campkin, F.S.A. Published by the Sussex Archæological Society. 29 vols. 8vo. Lewes, 1848–78.　E 1.46

SUSSEX STREET RAGGED AND INDUSTRIAL SCHOOL. [*See* Ragged And Industrial School.]

SUTCLIFFE (Thomas). Sixteen Years in Chile and Peru, 1822–39; by "The Retired Governor of Juan Fernandez." 8vo. Lond., 1841.　D 4 Q 13

SUTHERLAND (Alexander). Achievements of the Knights of Malta. 2 vols. 12mo. Edinb., 1831.　B 14 Q 14, 15

Another copy. (Const. Misc.) 2 vols. 18mo. Edinb., 1831.　K 10 Q 51, 52

SUTHERLAND (Alexander), M.A. New Geography, for Australian Pupils. 12mo. Melb., 1885.　MD 6 P 36

SUTHERLAND (Alexander), M.A., and SUTHERLAND (George), M.A. History of Australia, 1606–1876. 12mo. Melb., 1877.*　MB 1 P 10

SUTHERLAND (George), M.A. Australia; or, England in the South. With Illustrations. 12mo. Lond, 1886.　MD 3 Q 5

[*See* Presbyterian Tracts.]

SUTHERLAND (George Granville Leveson Gower), Duke of. [*See* Gower, G. G. Leveson, Earl.]

SUTTA NIPÁTA; or, Dialogues and Discourses of Gotama Buddha; translated from the Páli, with Introduction and Notes, by Sir M. C. Swámy. 8vo. Lond., 1874.　J 11 S 29

SUTTER (ARCHIBALD), C.E. American Notes, 1881. 8vo. Edinb., 1882.　　　　　　　　　　D 3 Q 26

Per Mare, per Terras; being a visit to New Zealand, by Australia, for the examination of certain Lands there, during 1883–84, and in 1885. 12mo. Lond., 1887.　MD 1 Q 7

SUTTON (M. J.) Permanent and Temporary Pastures; with coloured Illustrations and botanical Descriptions of leading Natural Grasses and Clovers. 8vo. Lond., 1886.　　　　　　　　　　　　　　　　A 1 T 9

SUTTOR (BEVERLEY). Original Poetry. 12mo. Sydney, 1838.　　　　　　　　　　　　　　MH 1 R 46

SUTTOR (EDWIN C.) Australian Magistrate. [*See* PLUNKETT, J. H.]　　　　　　　　　　　MF 1 Q 8

Public Lands: Progressive Purchase, Fixed Price, Mixed Farming, Homestead Villages. 12mo. Sydney, 1871.　　　　　　　　　　　　　　　　MF 3 P 17

Another copy. 12mo. Sydney, 1871.　MJ 2 R 2

SUTTOR (GEORGE), F.L.S. Culture of the Grape Vine and the Orange in Australia and New Zealand; comprising Historical Notices; Instructions for Planting and Cultivation; Accounts, from personal observation, of the Vineyards of France and the Rhine; and Extracts concerning all the most celebrated Wines, from the Work of M. Jullien. 8vo. Lond., 1843.　　　MA 1 Q 5

Memoirs. Historical and Scientific, of the Rt. Hon. Sir Joseph Banks, Bart. 12mo. Parramatta, 1855.*　　　　　　　　　　　　　　　　MC 1 P 31

SUTTOR (W. H.) Australian Stories Retold, and Sketches of Country Life. 12mo. Bathurst, 1887.*　MJ 1 P 46

Old Time Sketches: a Bush Yarn about a Cattle Muster, and other things. (Newspaper Cuttings.) 8vo. Sydney, 1885.　　　　　　　　　　　　MJ 1 S 25

SUVA. [*See* FIJI.]

SWAAN (P.) [*See* AA, P. J. B. C. ROBIDE VAN DER.]

SWAINSON (REV. C.), M.A. Hand-book of Weather Folk-lore. 12mo. Edinb., 1873.　　　K 17 P 15

SWAINSON (REV. C. A.), D.D. Greek Liturgies, chiefly from original Authorities. 4to. Camb., 1884.　G 13 V 28

SWAINSON (WILLIAM). Animals in Menageries. (Lard. Cab. Cyclo.) 12mo. Lond., 1838.　K 1 U 8

Auckland, the Capital of New Zealand, and the Country adjacent, including some Account of the Gold Discovery in New Zealand. 8vo. Lond., 1853.*　MD 1 R 11

Exotic Conchology; or, Figures and Descriptions of Rare, Beautiful, or Undescribed Shells. 2nd ed., edited by Sylvanus Hanley, B.A., Oxford. Roy. 4to. Lond., 1841.　　　　　　　　　　　　　　A 2 R 6 t

Habits and Instincts of Animals. (Lard. Cab. Cyclo.) 12mo. Lond., 1840.　　　　　　K 1 U 17

SWAINSON (WILLIAM)—*continued.*

Natural Arrangement and Relations of the Family of Flycatchers, or Muscicapidae. (Nat. Lib., 13.) 12mo. Edinb., 1838.　　　　　　　　　　A 14 P 13

Natural History and Classification of Birds. (Lard. Cab. Cyclo.) 2 vols. 12mo. Lond., 1836–37.　K 1 U 9, 10

Natural History and Classification of Fishes, Amphibians, and Reptiles. (Lard. Cab. Cyclo.) 2 vols. 12mo. Lond., 1838–39.　　　　　　　K 1 U 12, 13

Natural History and Classification of Quadrupeds. (Lard. Cab. Cyclo.) 12mo. Lond., 1835.　K 1 U 20

Natural History of the Birds of Western Africa. (Nat. Lib., 7, 8.) 12mo. Edinb., 1837.　A 14 P 7, 8

New Zealand and its Colonization. With a Map. 8vo. Lond., 1859.*　　　　　　　　　MB 2 Q 10

New Zealand and the War. 8vo. Lond., 1862.*　　　　　　　　　　　　　　　MB 2 P 39

New Zealand: the Substance of Lectures on the Colonization of New Zealand; with Notes. 8vo. Lond., 1856.*　　　　　　　　　　　　MD 1 R 13

Observations on the Climate of New Zealand, principally with reference to its Sanative Character. 8vo. Lond., 1840.　　　　　　　　　　　　　MA 1 T 25

Preliminary Discourse on the Study of Natural History. (Lard. Cab. Cyclo.) 12mo. Lond., 1834.　K 1 U 7

Selection of the Birds of Brazil and Mexico. 8vo. Lond., 1841.　　　　　　　　　　A 13 U 28

Taxidermy, Bibliography, and Biography of Zoologists, &c. (Lard. Cab. Cyclo.) 12mo. Lond., 1840.　K 1 U 21

Treatise on Malacology; or, Shells and Shell-fish. (Lard. Cab. Cyclo.) 12mo. Lond., 1840.　K 1 U 19

Treatise on the Geography and Classification of Animals. (Lard. Cab. Cyclo.) 12mo. Lond., 1835.　K 1 U 14

SWAINSON (W.), AND SHUCKARD (W. E.) History and Natural Arrangements of Insects. (Lard. Cab. Cyclo.) 12mo. Lond., 1840.　　　　　　　K 1 U 18

SWÁMY (SIR MÚTU COOMÁRA). [*See* SUTTA NIPÁTA.]

SWAN RIVER SETTLEMENT. [*See* WESTERN AUSTRALIA.]

SWANK (JAMES M.) History of the Manufacture of Iron in all Ages, and particularly in the United States for three hundred years, 1585–1885. 8vo. Philad., 1885.　A 9 U 13

SWANWICK (ANNA). Dramas of Æschylus. [*See* ÆSCHYLUS.]　　　　　　　　　　H 4 P 13

Dramatic Works of Goethe. [*See* GOETHE, J. W. VON.]

SWART (JACOB). Journaal van de Reis naar het onbekende Zuidland, in den Jare 1642, door Abel Jansz. Tasman, met de Schepen *Heemskerck* en de *Zeehaen*. 8vo. Amsterdam, 1860.　　　　　　　　MD 5 U 31

SWARTZ (REV. CHRISTIAN FREDERICK). Memoirs of the Life and Correspondence of; by Hugh Pearson, D.D. 3rd ed. 2 vols. 8vo. Lond., 1839.　　　C 5 R 24, 25

SWASEY (J. B.) The American War; the Action of the American Government vindicated: a Lecture. 8vo. Melh., 1864. MJ 2 R 7

SWEDENBORG (EMANUEL): a Biography; by J. J. G. Wilkinson. 8vo. Lond., 1849. C 4 S 31

An Account of the Last Judgment, and the Babylon destroyed, and a continuation concerning the Last Judgment, and concerning the Spiritual World. 8vo. Lond., 1846. G 11 R 26

Angelic Wisdom, concerning the Divine Love and the Divine Wisdom. 8vo. Lond., 1859. G 11 R 2

Angelic Wisdom concerning the Divine Providence. 8vo. Lond., 1857. G 11 S 1

The Apocalypse Explained, according to the Spiritual Sense; and Index. 8vo. Lond., 1854–71. G 11 R 3–8

The Apocalypse Revealed, in which are disclosed the Arcana therein foretold. 8vo. Lond., 1851. G 11 R 9, 10

Arcana Cœlestia: the Heavenly Mysteries contained in the Holy Scripture; and Index. 8vo. Lond., 1840–60. G 11 R 11–24

A brief Exposition of the Doctrine of the New Church. 8vo. Lond., 1840. G 11 R 2

Conjugal Love and its Chaste Delights. 8vo. Lond., 1855. G 11 R 1

The Colonis; or, Appendix to the Work entitled "The True Christian Religion." 8vo. Lond., 1843. G 11 R 2

The Doctrine of the New Jerusalem concerning Charity. 8vo. Lond., 1840. G 11 R 26

The Earths in the Universe, and their Inhabitants. 8vo. Lond., 1860. G 11 R 28

The Four Leading Doctrines of the New Church. 8vo. Lond., 1846. G 11 R 29

The Generative Organs considered Anatomicaly, Physically, and Philosophically: a Posthumous Work; translated by J. J. G. Wilkinson. 8vo. Lond., 1852. A 26 T 17

Heaven and Hell; also the Intermediate State or World of Spirits. 8vo. Lond., 1856. G 11 R 25

On the Athanasian Creed, and subjects connected with it. 8vo. Lond., 1856. G 11 R 2

On the Divine Love and Divine Wisdom. 8vo. Lond., 1840. G 11 R 2

On the Doctrines of Baptism and Regeneration. 8vo. Lond., 1850. G 11 R 31

On the Intercourse between the Soul and the Body. 8vo. Lond., 1844. G 11 R 26

On the New Jerusalem and its Heavenly Doctrine. 8vo. Lond., 1859. G 11 R 27

On the White Horse mentioned in the Apocalypse; and an Appendix. 8vo. Lond., 1860. G 11 R 26

A Summary Exposition of the Internal Sense of the Prophetic Books of the Word of the Old Testament. 8vo. Lond., 1840. G 11 R 26

The True Christian Religion. 8vo. Lond., 1858. G 11 R 30

Vísdómur Englanna um hina Guddómlegu Elsku og hina Guddómlegu Speki. 8vo. Kaupmannahöfn, 1869. G 11 R 32

4 z

SWEET (HENRY), M.A. Anglo-Saxon Primer; with Grammar, Notes, and Glossary. 8vo. Oxford, 1882. K 11 T 2

Anglo-Saxon Reader, in Prose and Verse; with Grammatical Introduction, Notes, and Glossary. (Clar. Press.) 12mo. Oxford, 1876. K 16 P 48

Hand-book of Phonetics, including a Popular Exposition of the Principles of Spelling Reform. (Clar. Press.) 8vo. Oxford, 1877. K 16 P 49

History of English Sounds from the Earliest Period, including an Investigation of the General Laws of Sound, Change, and full Word Lists. 8vo. Lond., 1874. K 15 R 18

SWEET (J. M.) Newcastle Directory and Almanac, for the years 1880–81. 2 vols. 8vo. Newcastle, 1879–80. ME 3 S

SWEET (RODERT), F.L.S. Cistineæ: the Natural Order of Cistus, or Rock-Rose. Roy. 8vo. Lond., 1825–30. A 4 U 8

Flora Australasica; or, a Selection of Handsome, or Curious Plants, Natives of New Holland and the South Sea Islands; the Drawings by E. D. Smith, F.L.S. Roy. 8vo. Lond., 1827–28.* MA 1 U 9

SWEETSER (M. F.) Europe for Two Dollars a Day: a few Notes for the Assistance of Tourists of moderate Means; with some Personal Reminiscences of Travel. 12mo. Boston, 1875. A 10 R 31

SWETCHINE (MME. SOPHIE SOYMONOF). Correspondance du Rev. Père J. B. H. Lacordaire et de Madame Swetchine, publiées par le Comte de Falloux. 8vo. Paris, 1864. C 9 P 44

Journal de sa Conversion: Méditations et Prières, publiées par le Comte de Falloux. 8vo. Paris, 1863. C 9 P 45

Lettres de Madame Swetchine, publiées par le Comte de Falloux. 2 vols. 8vo. Paris, 1862. C 9 P 40, 41

Lettres inédites de Madame de Swetchine, publiées par le Comte de Falloux. 8vo. Paris, 1866. C 9 P 46

Sa Vie, et ses Œuvres, publiées par le Comte de Falloux. 4e éd. 2 vols. 8vo. Paris, 1861. C 9 P 42, 43

SWIFT (EDMUND LECHMERE). Life and Acts of Saint Patrick, the Archbishop, Primate, and Apostle of Ireland; now first translated from the original Latin of Jocelin, with the Elucidations of David Rothe, Bishop of Ossory. Imp. 8vo. Dublin, 1809. G 5 U 19

SWIFT (JONATHAN), D.D., DEAN OF ST. PATRICK'S. [A Biography]; by Leslie Stephen. (Eng. Men of Letts.) 8vo. Lond., 1882. C 1 U 34

Closing Years of Dean Swift's Life; with Remarks on Stella [Esther Johnson], and on some of his Writings hitherto unnoticed; by W. R. Wilde, M.R.I.A. 2nd ed. 8vo. Dublin, 1849. C 9 U 33

English Letters and Letter-writers. [See WILLIAMS, H.] C 2 V 29

Gulliver's Travels. [See CLASSIC TALES.]

Leaders of Public Opinion in Ireland. [See LECKY, W. E. H.] C 3 P 24

Life and Poems of. [See CHALMERS, A., and JOHNSON, S.]

SWIFT (JONATHAN), D.D., DEAN OF ST. PATRICK's—*contd.*
Life and Writings of Sir William Temple, Bart. [*See* TEMPLE, SIR W.*]

Life of; by Henry Craik, M.A. With Portrait. 8vo. Lond., 1882.   C 9 U 32

Life of; by John Forster. Vol. 1 (*all published*). 8vo. Lond., 1875.   C 11 P 35

Life of: by Sir W. Scott. 12mo. Edinb., 1870. J 1 Q 11

Memoirs of Capt. John Creichton. [*See* CREIGHTON, CAPT. J.*]   C 1 P 10

Tale of a Tub; written for the universal Improvement of Mankind. 8vo. Lond., 1882.   J 10 R 18

Travels into several remote Nations of the World, by "Lemuel Gulliver, first a Surgeon, and then a Captain of several Ships." 8vo. Lond., 1882.   J 10 R 17

Works of, containing additional Letters, Tracts, and Poems, not hitherto published; with Notes, and a Life of the Author, by Sir Walter Scott, Bart. 2nd ed. 19 vols. 8vo. Edinb., 1824.   J 8 S 1-19

SWINBURNE (ALGERNON CHARLES). A Midsummer Holiday, and other Poems. 8vo. Lond., 1884. H 8 T 8

Atalanta in Calydon.   H 8 T 9

Bibliography of Swinburne. [*See* SHEPHERD, R. H.*]

Bothwell: a Tragedy. 8vo. Lond., 1874.   H 8 T 16

Century of Roundels. 8vo. Lond., 1883.   H 8 T 1

Chastelard: a Tragedy. 8vo. Lond., 1878.   H 8 T 19

Erechtheus: a Tragedy. 2nd ed. 8vo. Lond., 1876.
                                                   H 8 T 15

Essays and Studies. 8vo. Lond., 1875.   J 9 U 21

Another copy. 2nd ed. 8vo. Lond., 1876.   J 9 U 22

George Chapman: a Critical Essay. 12mo. Lond., 1875.   C 2 S 9

Marino Faliero: a Tragedy. 8vo. Lond., 1885. H 8 T 2

Mary Stuart: a Tragedy. 8vo. Lond., 1881.   H 8 T 20

Miscellanies. 8vo. Lond., 1886.   J 9 U 20

Note of an English Republican on the Muscovite Crusade. 8vo. Lond., 1876.   J 9 U 19

Another copy. 8vo. Lond., 1876.   F 4 Q 1

Note on Charlotte Brontë. 8vo. Lond., 1877.   C 2 S 6

Notes on Poems and Reviews. 8vo. Lond., 1866.
                                                   J 9 U 19

Poems and Ballads. 12mo. Lond., 1871   H 8 T 7

Poems and Ballads. [1st and] 2nd series. 2 vols. 8vo. Lond., 1884-85.   H 8 T 3, 4

Queen Mother, and Rosamund. 2nd ed. 12mo. Lond., 1868.   H 8 T 11

Songs before Sunrise. 8vo. Lond., 1883.   H 8 T 12

Songs of the Springtides. 8vo. Lond., 1883. H 8 T 6

Another copy. 2nd ed. 8vo. Lond., 1880.   H 8 T 13

Songs of Two Nations. 8vo. Lond., 1875.   H 8 T 14

Studies in Song. 8vo. Lond., 1880.   H 8 T 10

Study of Victor Hugo. 12mo. Lond., 1886.   C 2 Q 18

SWINBURNE (ALGERNON CHARLES)—*continued.*
Study of Shakespeare. 8vo. Lond., 1880.   J 1 U 11

Tristram of Lyonesse, and other Poems. 2nd ed. 8vo. Lond., 1882.   H 8 Q 39

William Blake: a Critical Essay; with Illustrations from Blake's Designs in facsimile, coloured and plain. 2nd ed. 8vo. Lond., 1868.   C 10 P 9

SWINBURNE (HENRY). Courts of Europe at the Close of the last Century; edited by Charles White. 2 vols. 8vo. Lond., 1841.   C 8 U 48, 49

Travels in the Two Sicilies, 1777-80. 2 vols. 4to. Lond., 1783-85.   D 9 8 7, 8 †

Travels through Spain in the years 1775-76. 4to. Lond., 1779.   D 8 V 30

SWINDELL (JOHN GEORGE), A.R.I.B.A., AND BURNELL (GEORGE R.), C.E. Rudimentary Treatise on Wells and Well-sinking. (Weale.) 12mo. Lond., 1883. A 17 Q 62

Well-digging, Boring, and Pump-work. (Weale.) 5th ed. 12mo. Lond., 1872.   A 17 P 68

SWINNEY (ALFRED J. G.) Collieries, Coal-fields, and Minerals of New South Wales, Australia. 8vo. Lond., 1884.   MA 2 P 13

SWINTON (A. H.) Almanack of the Christian Era: a Record of the Past and Glimpse into the Future, based on Solar Physics. 4to. Lond., 1883.   A 3 U 23

Insect Variety: its Propagation and Distribution. 8vo. Lond., 1880.   A 14 T 28

SWITZERLAND. Gallery of Celebrated Landscapes of Switzerland. Roy. 8vo. Zurich, 1881.   D 8 V 4

SYDENHAM (RT. HON. CHARLES), LORD, G.C.B. Memoir of the Life of; with a Narrative of his Administration in Canada; edited by his brother, G. Poulett Scrope. 8vo. Lond., 1843.   C 10 P 30

SYDER (MINGAY), M.D. Voice of Truth in Defence of Nature; and Opinions antagonistic to those of Dr. Kilgour, upon the Effect of the Climate of Australia upon the European Constitution, in Health and Disease. New ed. 8vo. Geelong, 1861.   MA 2 S 38

SYDNEY (HON. ALGERNON). [*See* SIDNEY, HON. A.]

SYDNEY (CITY OF). An Act to declare the Town of Sydney to be a City, and to incorporate the Inhabitants thereof. With Plan of the City of Sydney, showing the Wards as laid down in the Bill. 8vo. Sydney, 1842.
                                                   MJ 2 8 3

Plan, showing the Site for the New Government House, Public Offices, Library, Circular Quay, and Improvements of Streets connected therewith. 12mo. Sydney, 1840.
                                                  MD 5 P 3 ‡

SYDNEY ART GALLERY. Opinions of the Art Press of London upon the Minute with reference to the formation of a Picture Gallery in Sydney, submitted to the Council of the New South Wales Academy of Art, by Mr. F. H. Thomas. (Pam. M.) 4to. Sydney, 1874.   MJ 2 S 4

SYDNEY BENEVOLENT ASYLUM.　Report from the Select Committee on the Benevolent Asylum, Sydney; togetner with the Proceeding of the Committee, Minutes of Evidence, and Appendix.　Fol.　Sydney, 1862.
　　　　　　　　　　　　　　　　　　　MF 10 Q 1 †

SYDNEY BETHEL UNION.　Annual Reports, 1849, 1852, 1855–57, 1863–64.　8vo.　Sydney, 1849–64. .
　　　　　　　　　　　　　　　　　　　MF 3 P 13

Annual Reports, 1851, 1853, 1855, 1857.　8vo.　Sydney, 1852–58.　　　　　　　　　　　　　　MJ 2 Q 10

SYDNEY BIBLE ASSOCIATION.　Third and Fifth Reports of the Committee.　12mo.　Sydney, 1823–25.
　　　　　　　　　　　　　　　　　　　MG 1 Q 28

SYDNEY CITY MISSION.　Annual Report for 1864. 8vo.　Sydney, 1864.　　　　　　　　MF 3 P 14

SYDNEY COLLEGE (The).　Annual Reports for, 1831–39. 12mo.　Sydney, 1831–39.　　　　　MG 1 P 37

Another copy.　12mo.　Sydney, 1831–39.　　MJ 2 Q 9

Annual Reports of, 1831–36.　8vo.　Sydney, 1831–36.
　　　　　　　　　　　　　　　　　　　MF 3 P 14

Prospectus; with a short Statement of the Proceedings of the Committee of Management.　12mo.　Sydney, 1830.
　　　　　　　　　　　　　　　　　　　MF 3 P 14

Another copy.　12mo.　Sydney, 1830.　　MG 1 P 37

SYDNEY COVE.　Report from the Committee on the proposed Quay at Sydney Cove; with the Minutes of Evidence. (Parl. Docs., 32.)　Fol.　Sydney, 1836.　　MF 4 †

SYDNEY DAILY TELEGRAPH (The).　17 vols.　fol. Sydney, 1879–87.　　　　　　　　　　　ME

SYDNEY DIOCESAN DIRECTORY (The), 1886. 12mo.　Sydney, 1886.　　　　　　　　ME 4 Q

SYDNEY DISPENSARY.　Reports of the Committee. 8vo.　Sydney, 1826–44.　　　　　MJ 2 Q 2

Another copy.　8vo.　Sydney, 1826–44.　　MJ 2 Q 21

Reports, 1835–37, 1841–42.　8vo.　Sydney, 1836–43.
　　　　　　　　　　　　　　　　　　　MF 3 P 13

SYDNEY DORCAS SOCIETY.　Reports, for the years 1862, 1864.　12mo.　Sydney, 1863–64.　　MF 3 P 10

SYDNEY EVENING MAIL (The).　Fol.　Sydney, 1859.　　　　　　　　　　　　　　　　ME

SYDNEY EXHIBITIONS.　Catalogue of Exhibits at the Metropolitan Intercolonial Exhibition, 1870.　8vo.　Sydney, 1870.　　　　　　　　　　　MK 1 R 43

Catalogue of the Victorian Exhibits to the Sydney Intercolonial Exhibition of 1870; together with the Awards of the Judges, the Report of the Commissioners, the Decision of the Wine Jurors, &c.　8vo.　Melb., 1870.　MK 1 P 1

Industrial Progress of New South Wales; being a Report of the Intercolonial Exhibition of 1870, at Sydney.　8vo. Sydney, 1871.*　　　　　　　　　MK 1 Q 6

Catalogue of the Metropolitan Intercolonial Exhibition, 1875.　8vo.　Sydney, 1875.　　　　MK 1 R 25

Report of the Canadian Commissioner at the Exhibition of Industry, held at Sydney, New South Wales, 1877. 8vo.　Ottawa, 1878.　·　　　　　MF 3 R 15

SYDNEY EXHIBITIONS—*continued.*

International Exhibition, 1879 :　Official Catalogue of the British Section.　8vo.　Lond., 1879.*　MK 1 Q 4

International Exhibition, 1879.　United States Court: Official Catalogue of Exhibits.　8vo.　Sydney, 1879.
　　　　　　　　　　　　　　　　　　　MK 1 R 28

International Exhibition, 1879.　Official Catalogues : New South Wales Court; Art Gallery; Straits Settlement Court; South Australian Court; United States Court; Exhibits, Government Printer's Department; Exhibits, India.　8vo.　Sydney, 1880.　　MK 1 Q 3

Official Record of the Sydney International Exhibition, 1879.　Roy. 8vo.　Sydney, 1881.*　　MK 1 S 1

SYDNEY FEMALE REFUGE SOCIETY.　Annual Reports of, 1848–49, 1860, 1863.　8vo.　Sydney, 1849–64.
　　　　　　　　　　　　　　　　　　　MG 1 Q 26

SYDNEY FREE PRESS (The).　Fol.　Sydney, 1841–42.
　　　　　　　　　　　　　　　　　　　ME

[*See* Free Press.]

SYDNEY GAZETTE (The), and New South Wales Advertiser.　40 vols. fol.　Sydney, 1803–42.　　ME

SYDNEY GENERAL TRADE LIST.　Nos. 1–6.　Fol. Sydney, 1828.　　　　　　　　　MF 1 U 14

SYDNEY GENERAL TRADE LIST AND MERCANTILE ADVERTISER.　Nos. 1–12, 14–20, 22–31.　Fol. Sydney, 1829–30.　　　　　　　MF 1 U 14

SYDNEY GENERAL TRADE LIST, MERCANTILE CHRONICLE, AND ADVERTISER.　New series, Nos. 1–3, Fol.　Sydney, 1830.　　MF 1 U 14

SYDNEY GYMNASIUM.　Prospectus, First Annual Rules, and Bye-laws.　8vo.　Sydney, 1861.　MF 3 P 14

Another copy.　8vo.　Sydney, 1861.　　MJ 2 Q 9

SYDNEY HERALD (The).　[*See* Sydney Morning Herald.]

SYDNEY HOMŒOPATHIC DISPENSARY.　Annual Reports, 1859, 1861.　8vo.　Sydney, 1859–61.
　　　　　　　　　　　　　　　　　　　MG 1 Q 26

SYDNEY INFIRMARY AND DISPENSARY.　Annual Reports, 1852–53, 1858, 1860–63.　8vo.　Sydney, 1853–64.　　　　　　　　　　　MF 3 P 13

Another copy, 1849, 1853–54.　8vo.　Sydney, 1850–54.　　　　　　　　　　　　　MJ 2 Q 9

Another copy, 1861.　8vo.　Sydney, 1862.　MJ 2 Q 10

Report, 1868.　8vo.　Sydney, 1868.　　MF 3 P 18

Rules and Regulations of.　8vo.　Sydney, 1853–64.
　　　　　　　　　　　　　　　　　　　MF 3 P 13

Another copy.　8vo.　Sydney, 1867.　　MF 3 P 18

[*See* Sydney Dispensary.]

SYDNEY LAW LIBRARY.　Catalogue of the.　(Pam. 10.)　8vo.　Sydney, 1843.　　　　MJ 2 Q 2

SYDNEY MAGAZINE (The) ; edited by G. R. Maclean, J.P.　8vo.　Sydney, 1878.*　　　　ME 3 R

SYDNEY MAGAZINE OF SCIENCE AND ART
(The); containing, by authority, the Proceedings of the
Australian Horticultural and Agricultural Society, and
the Philosophical Society of New South Wales; edited by
Joseph Dyer. 2 vols. 8vo. Sydney, 1858–59.*
                                                    MA 2 V 1, 2

SYDNEY MAIL (The), and New South Wales Advertiser. 28 vols. fol. Sydney, 1873–86.   ME

SYDNEY MALE ORPHAN INSTITUTION. [*See*
Male Orphan Institution.]

SYDNEY MECHANICS' SCHOOL OF ARTS. Annual
Report, 1867. 8vo. Sydney, 1868.   MF 3 P 22
Annual Reports, 1837, 1839–40, 1851, 1860–61, 1868,
1871. 8vo. Sydney, 1837–72.   MF 3 P 14
Annual Reports, 1872–74. 8vo. Sydney, 1873–75.
                                          MJ 2 P 28
Catalogue of the Library. 8vo. Sydney, 1837.
                                          MK 1 Q 13
Catalogue of the Works in the Library. 8vo. Sydney,
1862.   MK 1 Q 13
Catalogue of the Works in the Library. 8vo. Sydney,
1869   MK 1 R 38
Catalogue of the Works in the Library. 8vo. Sydney,
1885.   MK 1 R 39
Laws of; instituted 22nd March, 1833. 8vo. Sydney,
1833.   MF 3 P 14
Rules and By-laws. 8vo. Sydney, 1871.   MJ 2 P 28

SYDNEY MISSIONARY MEETING. Sydney Mis-
sionary Meeting, Sydney, December 20, 1813, to form a
Society for affording Protection to the Natives of the
South Sea Islands, and promoting their Civilization. Fol.
Sydney, 1813.   MJ 2 U 1

SYDNEY MONITOR (The). 10 vols. fol. Sydney,
1829–40.   ME
[*See* Monitor, The.]

SYDNEY MORNING HERALD (The). Sydney Herald,
1831–11 [*continued as* The Sydney Morning Herald,
1842–87.] 153 vols. fol. Sydney, 1831–87.   ME
Index to the Sydney Morning Herald's Reports of the
Debates in the Legislative Council of New South Wales,
Sessions, 1853–54. Fol. Sydney, 1854–55.   ME 10 Q †
The Centennial Supplement; together with Reports of
the principal Events in connection with the Celebration
of the Centenary of Australian Settlement. 4to. Sydney,
1888.   MB 2 U 8

SYDNEY OBSERVATORY. Fourth Report. Fol.
Sydney, 1861.   ME 10 Q 3 †

SYDNEY ONCE A WEEK (The); edited by C. H.
Barlee. 1st series, vol. 1, 1878. 8vo. Sydney, 1878.
                                          ME 3 Q

SYDNEY POST OFFICE. Opening of the New General
Post Office, Sydney, New South Wales. 1 September,
1874. 18mo. Sydney, 1874.   MJ 2 P 27

SYDNEY PROMISSORY NOTES, 1812–14. [*See*
Manuscripts and Portraits.]   MF 1 U 21

SYDNEY PROTESTANT MAGAZINE (The). Vol. 1,
Nos. 1–3, 6, and Vol. 2, No. 10. 8vo. Sydney, 1840–41.
                                          MJ 2 Q 7
Sydney Protestant Magazine. Vol. 1, No. 7. (Pam. H.)
8vo. Sydney, 1840.   ME 3 R

SYDNEY PUNCH (The), 1864–74, 1878–83. 28 vols.
(in 25) 4to. Sydney, 1864–83.   ME 20 T

SYDNEY RAGGED AND INDUSTRIAL SCHOOL.
Second Annual Report of. (Pam. 21.) Sydney, 1862.
                                          MJ 2 Q 10

SYDNEY RECORD (The). Fol. Sydney, 1843–44. ME

SYDNEY SAILORS' HOME. Second Report, read at
the Annual Meeting, 1864; with the Balance Sheet of
Receipts and Expenditure, and an Alphabetical Subscription List. 12mo. Sydney, 1864.   MF 3 P 10

SYDNEY SCHOOL OF INDUSTRY. Annual Reports,
1827, 1829, 1848–49, 1855, 1858, 1860–61, 1863. 12mo.
Sydney, 1827–63.   MF 3 P 12
Fourth Annual Report of. 12mo. Sydney, 1830.
                                          MJ 2 Q 21

SYDNEY SERIES OF MERCANTILE TRACTS. [*See*
Mercantile Tracts.]

SYDNEY TIMES. Fol. Sydney, 1834–35.   ME

SYDNEY TO SOUTHAMPTON. Recollections of a
Ramble from Sydney to Southampton, *via* South America,
Panama, the West Indies, the United States, and Niagara.
8vo. Lond., 1851.   D 10 R 12

SYDNEY UNIVERSITY. By-laws of the University.
8vo. Sydney, 1867.   MF 3 P 14
Calendars, 1852–54, 1856–63, 1865–68, 1870, 1874–86.
27 vols. 8vo. Sydney, 1852–86.   ME 5 S
Catalogue of the Library. Roy. 8vo. Sydney, 1860.
                                          MK 1 S 18
Church of England, and the Sydney University: Docu-
ments and Correspondence, reprinted from the *Sydney
Morning Herald*. 12mo. Sydney, 1852.   MJ 2 R 3
Inaugural Addresses. [*See* Nicholson, Sir C., *and*
Wooley, Prof. J.]

Manual of Public Examinations held by the University
of Sydney, for the year 1887, containing By-laws, Subjects
of Examination and Books recommended, Directions to
Candidates and Presiding Committees; also, the Papers
set in the year 1886, with a List of the successful Candidates. 8vo. Sydney, 1887.   ME 5 S

Musical Festival, a.d. 1859. The Creation: an Oratorio,
composed by Joseph Haydn, in the year 1798.—The
Messiah: a Sacred Oratorio, composed by George Frederic
Handel, in the year 1741. Roy. 8vo. Sydney, 1859.
                                          MJ 2 S 1

SYDNEY UNIVERSITY CRICKET CLUB ANNUAL, 1878. 12mo. Sydney, 1878. ME 5 Q

SYDNEY UNIVERSITY MAGAZINE (THE). Vol 1. 8vo. Sydney, 1855. ME 3 R

SYDNEY UNIVERSITY MAGAZINE (THE): a Literary, Scientific, and Educational Journal. Vols. 1, 2 (*all published*). 2 vols. 8vo. Sydney, 1878–79. ME 3 R
Another copy. 2 vols. (in 1) 8vo. Sydney, 1878–79.
ME 3 Q

SYDNEY UNIVERSITY REVIEW, November, 1881 to July, 1883. Nos. 1–5. (*All published.*) Roy. 8vo. Sydney, 1881–83. ME 3 Q

SYDNEY WATER SUPPLY. Report of the Commission appointed to inquire into the Supply of Water to Sydney and Suburbs. Fol. Sydney, 1869. ME 10 Q 4 †

SYED AHMED KHAN. [*See* AHMED KHAN.]

SYLVANUS. [*See* COLTON, R.]

SYME (DAVID). Outlines of an Industrial Science. 8vo. Lond., 1876. F 5 S 29

SYME (J. B.) Readings for Railways; or, Anecdotes and other short Stories. 12mo. Lond., 1850. J 7 Q 11

SYME (JOHN T. B.) English Botany. [*See* SOWERBY, J.] A 4 V 1–12

SYMEON (THESSALONICENSIS ARCHIEPISCOPUS). Opera omnia. [*See* MIGNE, J. P., SERIES GRÆCA, 155.]

SYMES (LIEUT.-COL. MICHAEL). Account of an Embassy to the Kingdom of Ava, in the year 1795; to which is now added, a Narrative of the late Military and Political Operations in the Birmese Empire. (Const. Misc.) 2 vols. 18mo. Edinb., 1827. K 10 P 47, 48

SYMINGTON (A. J.) Some Personal Reminiscences of Carlyle. 8vo. Paisley, 1886. C 4 T 5

SYMMONS (CHARLES). Native Grammar of Western Australia. [*See* MACFAULL, C.] ME 4 U

SYMONDS (JOHN ADDINGTON). Ben Jonson. (English Worthies.) 12mo. Lond., 1886. C 2 Q 37
Italian Byways. 8vo. Lond., 1883. D 8 Q 14
Renaissance in Italy. 7 vols. 8vo. Lond., 1875–86. B 30 U 1–7
1. The Age of the Despots.
2. The Revival of Learning.
3. The Fine Arts.
4, 5. Italian Literature.
6, 7. The Catholic Reaction.
Shakspere's Predecessors in the English Drama. 8vo. Lond., 1884. B 6 S 22
Shelley. (Eng. Men of Letts.) 8vo. Lond., 1878. C 1 U 29
Sir Philip Sidney. (Eng. Men of Letts.) 8vo. Lond., 1886. C 1 U 38
Vagabunduli Libellus. 8vo. Lond., 1884. H 7 P 35
[*See* CONINGTON, PROF. J.]

SYMONDS (REV. W. S.), F.G.S. Records of the Rocks; or, Notes on the Geology, Natural History, and Antiquities of North and South Wales, Devon, and Cornwall. 8vo. Lond., 1872. A 9 Q 36

SYMONDSON (F. W. H.) Two Years abaft the Mast; or, Life as a Sea Apprentice. 12mo. Edinb., 1876. D 10 Q 50

SYMONS (ARTHUR). An Introduction to the Study of Browning. 8vo. Lond., 1886. H 7 Q 25

SYMONS (BRENTON), F.C.S., &c. Sketch of the Geology of Cornwall, including a brief Description of the Mining Districts, and the Ores produced in them; with Geological Map of Cornwall. 8vo. Lond., 1884. A 9 P 5

SYMONS (JELINGER C.) Arts and Artisans at Home and Abroad; with Sketches of the Progress of Foreign Manufactures. 8vo. Edinb., 1839. F 5 U 10

SYNCELLUS (G.) [*See* BYZANTINÆ HIST. SCRIPT.]

SYNESIUS (PTOLEMAIDIS EPISCOPUS). Opera omnia. [*See* MIGNE, J. P., SERIES GRÆCA, 66.]

SYNTAX (DR.) [*See* COMBE, W.]

SZYRMA (COL. LACH). Revelations of Siberia. [*See* FELINSKA, EVA.] D 6 P 3, 4

T

T (I.) [*See* WASTE LANDS.]

T. (N. H.) [*See* MACHIAVELLI, N. DI B. DEI.]

T. (T. T.) [*See* LIFE IN CHINA.]

TAAFFE (JOHN). History of the Holy, Military, Sovereign Order of St. John of Jerusalem; or, Knights Hospitallers, Knights Templars, Knights of Rhodes, Knights of Malta. 4 vols. (in 2) 8vo. Lond., 1852.   G 10 R 4, 5

TABARI (ADOU-DJAFOR-MOHAMMED-BEN-DJARIR-BEN-YEZID). Chronique de Tabari; traduite sur la version persane, par H. Zotenberg. 4 vols. 8vo. Paris 1867–74.   B 1 P 14–17

TABERD (J. L.) Dictionarium Anamitico-Latinum te Latino-Anamiticum, primitus inceptum a P. J. Pigneaux, dein absolutum et editum a J. L. Taberd. 2 vols. 4to. Serampore, 1838.   K 15 U 12, 13

TACITUS (CAIUS CORNELIUS). Annals of (Latin Text); edited, with Notes, by Geo. O. Holbrooke, M.A. 8vo. Lond., 1882.   B 11 V 2

Cornelii Taciti Annalium ab excessu Divi Augusti Libri. The Annals of Tacitus; edited, with Notes, &c., by Henry Furneaux, M.A. Vol. 1, Books 1–6. (Clar. Press.) 8vo. Lond., 1884.   B 36 R 2

Opera omnia, ex Editione Oberliniana, cum Notis et Interpretatione in usum Delphini. 10 vols. 8vo. Lond., 1821.   J 14 Q 16–25

Works of; with an Essay on his Life and Genius, Notes, Supplements, &c., by Arthur Murphy. 8 vols. 8vo. Lond., 1811.   J 17 R 23–30

Works of; translated by A. Murphy. (Fam. Class. Lib.) 5 vols. 18mo. Lond., 1830–31.   J 15 P 41–45

[*See* SCRIPTORES ROMANI.]   J 13 T 35

TAGART (EDWARD). Memoir of the late Captain Peter Heywood, R.N.; with Extracts from his Diaries and Correspondence. 8vo. Lond., 1832.*   MC 1 R 28

TAGG (WILLIAM). Shakespere's Memorial, undertaken with a view to popularise Shakesperian Literature among all Classes. 12mo. Melb., 1861.   MH 1 R 43

TAHITIAN LANGUAGE. Grammar of the Tahitian Dialect of the Polynesian Language. (Pam. Ea.) 12mo. Tahiti, 1823.   MK 1 P 24

TAHITIAN MISSION. Report of the Windward Division, for the year 1824. Tahiti, 1824.   MF 3 P 10

TAINE (HYPPOLITE ADOLPHE), D.C.L., &c. English Positivism: a Study on John Stuart Mill; translated from the French, by T. D. Haye. 2nd ed. 12mo. Lond., 1873.   C 7 T 7

History of English Literature; translated by H. van Laun. 2nd ed. 2 vols. 8vo. Edinb., 1872.   B 6 S 16, 17

Notes on England; translated by W. F. Rae. 7th ed., reprinted from *The Daily News.* 8vo. Lond., 1876.   D 7 P 12

TAINE (HYPPOLITE ADOLPHE), D.C.L., &c.—*continued.* The Ancient Régime; translated by John Durand. 8vo. Lond., 1876.   B 8 U 30

The Revolution; translated by John Durand. 3 vols. 8vo. Lond., 1878–85.   B 8 S 1–3

TAIT (PROF. P. G.), M.A. Elementary Treatise on Quaternions. 2nd ed., enlarged. (Clar. Press.) 8vo. Oxford, 1873.   A 10 U 26

Heat. 8vo. Lond., 1884.   A 5 S 30

Lectures on some Recent Advances in Physical Science; with a Special Lecture on Force. 3rd ed. 8vo. Lond., 1885.   A 16 Q 7

Light. 8vo. Edinb., 1884.   A 5 R 43

Properties of Matter. 8vo. Edinb., 1885.   A 16 P 25

[*See* RANKINE, W. J. M.]   A 16 V 14

The Unseen Universe. [*See* STEWART, PROF. B.]

TAIT'S EDINBURGH MAGAZINE. 27 vols. roy. 8vo. Edinb., 1834–60.   E

TAKEN IN; being a Sketch of New Zealand Life, by "Hopeful." 12mo. Lond., 1887.   MD 1 P 6

TALBERT (B. J.) Examples of Ancient and Modern Furniture, Metal Work, Tapestries, Decorations, &c. L. 4to. Lond., 1876.   A 1 P 16 ‡

TALBOT (EDWARD ALLEN). Five Years' Residence in the Canadas, including a Tour through part of the United States of America in the year 1823. 2 vols. 8vo. Lond., 1824.   D 3 T 31 32

TALBOT (H. Fox). English Etymologies. 8vo. Lond., 1847.   K 15 Q 11

TALBOT (R.) The Serf: a Tragedy. (Cumberland's Eng. Theatre.) 12mo. Lond., 1829.   H 2 Q 9

TALES from Twelve Tongues; translated by "A British Museum Librarian." 8vo. Lond., 1882.   J 1 U 10

TALES OF THE EAST. [*See* WEBER, H.]

TALFOURD (SIR THOMAS NOON), D.C.L. Final Memorials of Charles Lamb, consisting chiefly of his Letters not before published, with Sketches of some of his Companions. 2 vols. 8vo. Lond., 1848.   C 4 S 11, 12

Letters of Charles Lamb; with some Account of the Writer, his Friends, and Correspondents. Revised by W. C. Hazlitt. 2 vols. 12mo. Lond., 1886.   C 2 S 26–27

[Tragedies and Sonnets.] 8vo. Lond., 1838–40.   H 3 S 19

Ion: a Tragedy; to which are added Sonnets. 4th ed. Glencoe; or, the Fate of the Macdonalds: a Tragedy. 2nd ed. The Athenian Captive: a Tragedy.

Vacation Rambles; comprising the Recollections of Three Continental Tours in the Vacations of 1841–43. 12mo. Lond., 1851.   D 10 P 4

TALLBOY. [*See* SONG OF SEPARATION.]

TALLEYRAND-PÉRIGORD (CHARLES MAURICE DE), PRINCE DE BENEVENTO. Historical Characters. [*See* DALLING AND BULWER, LORD.] C 8 Q 48, 49

Life of; translated from the French of Charles Maxime de Villemarest. With Portrait. 4 vols. 8vo. Lond., 1834–36. C 9 T 34–37

Another copy. 8vo. Philad., 1834. C 9 T 38

Reminiscences of; with Extracts from his Manuscripts, Speeches, and Political Writings. 2 vols. 8vo. Lond., 1848. C 4 R 44, 45

[*See* TIMBS, J.]

TALLEYRAND-PÉRIGORD (CHARLES MAURICE DE), PRINCE, AND LOUIS XVIII. Correspondence of, during the Congress of Vienna (hitherto unpublished); with Notes by M. G. Pallain. 2 vols. 8vo. Lond., 1881. C 9 T 49, 50

TALLIS (JOHN). History and Description of the Crystal Palace, and the Exhibition of the World's Industry in 1851. Illustrated. 3 vols. 4to. Lond. (n.d.) B 3 V 16–18

TAMIL LANGUAGE. Dictionary English and Tamil, [in two Parts.] 4to. Madras, 1852. K 14 S 12

Manual Dictionary of the Tamil Language. 8vo. Jaffna, 1842. K 12 R 13

TAMS (G.), M.D. Visit to Portuguese Possessions in Southwestern Africa; translated from the German, by H. Evans Lloyd. 2 vols. 8vo. Lond., 1845. D 1 R 17, 18

TANCOCK (REV. O. W.), M.A. English Grammar and Reading Book, for Lower Forms in Classical Schools. 2nd ed. (Clar. Press.) 12mo. Oxford, 1874. K 16 P 47

TANCREDE (PRINCE). Histoire de. [*See* GUIZOT, F. P. G., 23.]

TANGIER. Description of Tangier, the Country and People adjoining; with an Account of the Person and Government of Gayland, the present Usurper of the Kingdome of Fez; translated from the Spanish into English. 8vo. Lond., 1664. D 1 R 24

TANGYE (RICHARD), F.R.G.S. Notes of my Fourth Voyage to the Australian Colonies, including Australia, Tasmania, and New Zealand, 1886, for private circulation. 8vo. Birmingham, 1886. MD 1 V 8

Reminiscences of Travel in Australia, America, and Egypt. 8vo. Lond., 1883. MD 1 V 7

The Growth of a Great Industry—"One and All": an Autobiography of Richard Tangye, of the Cornwall Works, Birmingham. 8vo. Lond., 1889.* MC 1 P 44

TANGYE (RICHARD AND GEORGE). Old Wedgwood and Old Wedgwood Ware: Hand-book to the Collection formed by R. and G. Tangye; with Sketch of Wedgwood's Life &c., by F. Rathbone. 8vo. Lond. 1885. Libr.

TAOU-KWANG (EMPEROR OF CHINA). Life of; with Memoirs of the Court of Peking, by the Rev. Charles Gutzlaff. 8vo. Lond., 1852 C 4 U 33

TAPLEY (MARK), JUNR. [*See* STAMER, W.]

TAPLIN (REV. GEORGE). Folk-lore, Manners, Customs, and Languages of the South Australian Aborigines— 1st series. 8vo. Adelaide, 1879.* MA 1 R 10

Grammar of the Narrinyeri Tribe of Australian Aborigines. 8vo. Adelaide, 1878.* MA 1 R 10

The Narrinyeri: an Account of the Tribes of South Australian Aborigines inhabiting the Country around the Lakes Alexandrina, Albert, and Coorong, and the lower part of the River Murray. 8vo. Adelaide, 1874.* MA 1 R 2

Another copy. 8vo. Adelaide, 1874. MA 1 R 12

Tungarar Jehovald—Yarildewallin: Extracts from the Holy Scriptures in the Language of the Tribes inhabiting the Lakes and Lower Murray, and called the Narrinyeri. 12mo. Adelaide, 1864. MG 1 P 31

TARDIEU (A.) [*See* LA HARPE, J. F. DE.] D 8 P 12 ‡

TARGUMS (THE). [*See* ETHERIDGE, J. W.]

TARGINI (FRANCISCO BENTO MARIA), BARÃO DE SAÕ LAURENÇO. [*See* SAÕ, LOURENÇO F. B. M. T., BARÃO DE.]

TARLETON (SIR BANASTRE), BART. [*See* MACKENZIE, R.] B 1 S 14

TARLETON (FRANCIS A.), LL.D. Treatise on Dynamics. [*See* WILLIAMSON, B.] A 16 Q 8

TARLETON (W. W.), M.A. Collection of the Private Acts of practical utility in force in New South Wales; embracing the local Private Legislation, 1832–85. Roy. 8vo. Sydney, 1886.* MF 3 S 12

TARN (E. WYNDHAM), M.A. Elementary Treatise on the Construction of Roofs of Wood and Iron. (Weale.) 12mo. Lond., 1882. A 17 Q 55

Carpentry and Joinery. [*See* TREDGOLD, T.] A 2 T 34

TARTAR AND RUSSIAN GRAMMAR. 4to. St. Petersb., 1801. K 14 U 6

Another copy. 4to. St. Petersb., 1814. K 14 U 7

TARVER (E. J.) [*See* LONSDALE, H. W.] A 2 R 20 †

TARVER (J. C.) Theoretical and Practical Grammar of the French Language. [*See* LEVIZAC, J. P. V. L. DE.]

TASKER (REV. W.) Reminiscences of General Sir Thomas Makdougall Brisbane. 4to. Edinb., 1860. MC 4 P 1 †

TASMAN (ABEL JANSZ.) Discoveries on the Coast of South Terra Incognita. [*See* VOYAGES AND DISCOVERIES.]

Journaal van de Reis naar het onbekende Zuidland, in den Jare 1642. [*See* SWART, J.] MD 5 U 31

TASMANIA.

Copies of Despatches, with their Enclosures, relating to the Cases of Mr. Justice Montagu and Chief Justice Pedder; of Warrants for the issue of the Commissions to Chief Justice and Puisne Judge; of Commissions or Warrants for appointing the Members of the Legislative and Executive Councils of Van Diemen's Land; of Commission of Lieutenant-Governor of Van Diemen's Land; and of Petition, dated the 15th day of January, 1848, from certain Colonists of Van Diemen's Land. (Parl. Docs., 53.) Fol. Lond., 1848.   MF 4 ‡

Picturesque Tasmania : a Guide for Visitors. 8vo. Launceston, 1886.   MD 5 P 2

List of Districts into which the City is divided, for the purpose of Domiciliary Visitation, together with the Names of the Lady Visitors engaged in each District at the present date. 4to. Hobart, 1863.   MJ 2 U 3

ACTS OF PARLIAMENT.

Acts of the Parliament of; with an Index. 10 vols. sm. fol. Hobart, 1872–84.   E 2.46

Copies of the Laws and Ordinances passed by the Governor and Council of the Colony of Van Diemen's Land, 1826–30. (Parl. Docs., 7.) Fol. Lond., 1831.   MF

ADMINISTRATION OF JUSTICE.

In Van Diemen's Land. [*See* NEW SOUTH WALES.]

ANTI-STATE AID.

Northern Association for procuring cessation of State Support to Religion in Tasmania : Statement. 8vo. Launceston, 1857.   MG 1 Q 29

CENSUS.

Census, 1881 : General Report and Part 1. Fol. Hobart, 1882.   E 2.56

CHURCH ACT.

Act to enable the Bishops, Clergy, and Laity of the United Church of England and Ireland in Tasmania, to regulate the Affairs of the said Church. (Pam. A.) Fol. Hobart, 1858.   MJ 2 U 1

Appeal to the Members of the Legislative Council of Van Diemen's Land, against the "Church Act"; by "A Member of the Established Church of England." (Pam. 41.) 8vo. Launceston, 1837.   MJ 2 R 3

CLERGY AND SCHOOL LANDS.

Clergy and School Lands of Van Diemen's Land. [*See* NEW SOUTH WALES.]

CROWN LANDS.

Act to exempt Van Diemen's Land from the Provisions of an Act, intituled "An Act for regulating the Sale of Waste Land belonging to the Crown in the Australian Colonies." (Parl. Docs., 48.) Fol. Lond., 1845. MF 4 ‡

Copies of Royal Instructions to the Governors of New South Wales, Van Diemen's Land, and Western Australia, as to the mode to be adopted in disposing of Crown Lands. (Parl. Docs., 5.) Sm. fol. Lond., 1831.   MF 4 ‡

Papers relative to the Crown Lands in the Australian Colonies. (Parl. Docs., 59, 62 & 65, and) 3 vols. sm. fol. Lond., 1851–56.   MF 4 ‡

Return of the Alienations of Crown Lands in New South Wales and Van Diemen's Land respectively, during the last ten years. (Parl. Docs., 5.) Sm. fol. Lond., 1852.   MF 4 †

TASMANIA—*continued.*

FREE CHURCH.

Sustentation Fund : Statement issued by the Free Church Presbytery. 12mo. Hobart. (n.d.)   MG 1 P 42

HOBART.

View of Hobart Town, on the River Derwent; published by W. J. Huggins. 4to. Lond., 1830.   MD 2 P 18 ‡

View of the Country round Hobart Town, in Van Diemen's Land; reduced on Zinc by G. Scharf, from a Drawing by Lycet. 4to. Lond. (n.d.)   MD 2 P 18 ‡

PARIS UNIVERSAL EXHIBITIONS.

Tasmanian Contributions to the Universal Exhibition of Industry at Paris, 1855. Fol. Hobart, 1855. MK 1 Q 8 ‡

PARLIAMENT.

Journals and Printed Papers. 12 vols. fol. Hobart, 1884–87.   E 2.55

Journals of the Legislative Council ; with Papers. 18 vols. fol. Hobart, 1872–83.   E 2.55

PARLIAMENTARY LIBRARY.

Classified Catalogue of the Books, Magazines, and Newspapers. 8vo. Hobart, 1863.   MK 1 P 1

PENAL SETTLEMENTS.

Accounts relating to Receipt and Expenditure of Van Diemen's Land, and New South Wales. (Parl. Docs., 1.) Sm. fol. Lond., 1823.   MF 4 ‡

Returns of the Expenditure of the Colonies of New South Wales and Van Diemen's Land, from 1st January, 1830, to 1st January, 1831, specifying the expense of the Civil and Military Establishments, the Transportation of Convicts, and the support of them after their arrival; and of the number of Convicts sent to New South Wales, from 1st January, 1830, to 1st January, 1831. (Parl. Docs., 1.) Sm. fol. Lond., 1832.   MF 4 ‡

SALMON COMMISSIONERS.

Report of, for 1878. Fol. Hobart, 1879.   MJ 2 U 5

SHIPPING.

Account of Ships and their Tonnage which have cleared outwards to, and entered inwards from New South Wales and Van Diemen's Land, 1822–25. (Parl. Docs., 5) Sm. fol. Lond., 1825.   MF 4 ‡

STATISTICS.

Statistics of the Colony of, for the years 1875–85. 11 vols. fol. Hobart, 1876–86.   E 2.56

TASMANIAN (THE), March to December, 1827. Fol. Hobart, 1827.   ME

TASMANIAN AND AUSTRAL-ASIATIC REVIEW (THE), January to December, 1837. Fol. Hobart, 1837.   ME

TASMANIAN ATHENÆUM (THE); or, Journal of Science, Literature, and Art. 4to. Hobart, 1853. MJ 2 U 3

TASMANIAN JOURNAL (THE), of Natural Science, Agriculture, Statistics, &c. 3 vols. (*Imperfect*) 8vo. Hobart, 1842–49.   ME 3 R

TASMANIAN LADY, A.   [*See* TREASURES LOST AND FOUND.]

TASMANIAN MAGAZINE AND MASONIC REGISTER (THE). Vol. 1, No. 1. (Pam. G.) 8vo. Launceston, 1849.   ME 3 R

TASMANIAN COLONIAL MISSIONARY AND CHRISTIAN INSTRUCTION SOCIETY. Report of the, in connection with the Tasmanian Congregational Union. 8vo. Hobart, 1858.   MF 3 P 15

TASMANIAN PUBLIC LIBRARY. Catalogue of the Tasmanian Public Library and Reading Room; with the Rules, Regulations, Bye-laws, and List of Members. 8vo. Hobart, 1852.   MK 1 Q 13

Alphabetical and Classified Catalogue compiled by Murray Burgess; with the Rules, Regulations, and Bye-laws. 8vo. Hobart, 1855.   MK 1 Q 13

Alphabetical Catalogue; with the Rules, Regulations, and Bye-laws. 8vo. Hobart, 1862.   MK 1 R 22

Catalogue of Books, 1870. 8vo. Hobart, 1871.   MK 1 R 22

Report for the years 1871–72. Fol. Hobart, 1872–73.   MJ 2 U 1

Another copy. Fol. Hobart, 1872–73.   MJ 2 U 4

Report for the year 1878. Fol. Hobart, 1879.   MJ 2 U 1

Another copy. Fol. Hobart, 1879.   MJ 2 U 4

TASMANIAN STEAM NAVIGATION COMPANY. Deed of Co-partnership; with a List of the Directors, Officers, &c. 8vo. Hobart, 1852.   MJ 2 R 4

TASMANIAN SUNDAY-SCHOOL TEACHERS' MAGAZINE and Journal of Education. Vol. 2, No. 4. 8vo. Hobart, 1858.   MG 1 Q 29

TASSO (TORQUATO). Aminta. Fol. Firenze, 1804.   H 27 Q 23 ‡

Jerusalem Delivered: an Heroic Poem; translated from the Italian, by John Hoole. [*See* CHALMERS, A.]

Jerusalem Delivered: an Heroic Poem; translated from the Italian, by John Hoole. 8th ed., with Notes. 2 vols. imp. 8vo. Lond., 1803.   H 6 V 6, 7

Jerusalem Delivered; translated into English Spenserian Verse, from the Italian; with a Life of the Author, by J. H. Wiffen. 2nd ed. 3 vols. 8vo. Lond., 1826.   H 6 U 7–9

La Gerusalemme Liberata. 2 vols. fol. Pisa, 1807.   H 27 Q 20, 21 ‡

La Gerusalemme Liberata, e l' Aminta. 12mo. Paris, 1850.   H 7 P 23

Life of; by the Rev. R. Milman. 2 vols. 8vo. Lond., 1850.   C 4 R 42, 43

Trattato della Dignità, ed altri inediti Scritti di. 8vo. Torino, 1838.   J 17 P 22

5 A

TASSONI (ALESSANDRO). La Secchia Rapita: Poema eroicomico: colle Dichiarazioni di Gaspare Salviani, Romano; e le Annotazioni del Dottor Pellegrino Rossi, Modenese, rivedute, e ampliate. 12mo. Venezia, 1747.   H 7 P 20

La Secchia Rapita. Fol. Pisa, 1811.   H 27 Q 22 ‡

TATE (GEORGE), F.G.S. History of the Borough, Castle, and Barony of Alnwick. 2 vols. 8vo. Alnwick, 1866–69.   B 7 Q 3, 4

TATE (J.) [*See* HORATIUS FLACCUS, Q.]   H 8 U 37

TATE (RALPH). Appendix to the Manual of Mollusca. [*See* WOODWARD, S. P.]   A 14 Q 17

Rudimentary Treatise on Geology: Part 1. Physical Geology; Part 2. Historical Geology. (Weale.) 12mo. Lond., 1871.   A 17 P 37

TATE (WILLIAM). The Modern Cambist; forming a Manual of Foreign Exchanges in the operations of Bills of Exchange and Bullion, according to the practice of all Trading Nations; with Tables of Foreign Weights and Measures, and their Equivalents in English and French. 8vo. Lond., 1858.   F 4 S 10

TATHAM (W.) Political Economy of Inland Navigation, Irrigation, and Drainage. 4to. Lond., 1799.   F 8 P 14 †

TATTON (WILLIAM). Churchyard Musings, and other Poems. 8vo. Lond., 1858.   H 8 R 37

TAUBERT (CAPT.) On the Use of Field Artillery on Service, with special reference to that of an Army Corps; translated by H. H. Maxwell. (Weale.) 12mo. Lond., 1856.   A 17 P 55

TAULER (REV. DR. JOHN). History and Life of; with twenty-five of his Sermons (*temp.* 1340); translated from the German, by Susanna Winkworth. Sq. 8vo. Lond., 1857.   C 5 U 5

TAVERNIER (JEAN BAPTISTE). Les Six Voyages en Turquie, en Perse, et aux Indes. 3 vols. 18mo. Paris, 1679.   D 10 P 16–18

TAXATIO ECCLESIASTICA, Angliæ et Walliæ; Auct. P. Nicholai IV, circa A.D. 1291. At. fol. Lond., 1802.   F 24 S 12 ‡

TAYLER (JOHN JAMES), B.A. Retrospect of the Religious Life in England. 2nd ed. 8vo. Lond., 1876.   G 2 Q 25

TAYLER (WILLIAM). Thirty-eight Years in India, from Juggernath to Himalaya Mountains. 2 vols. 8vo. Lond., 1881–82.   C 9 V 22, 23

TAYLOR (A. G.) Law and Practice of New South Wales Letters Patent for Inventions and Improvements in the Arts and Manufactures. 8vo. Sydney, 1888.   MF 1 R 37

TAYLOR (ALFRED SWAINE), M.D., &c. Manual of Medical Jurisprudence. 8th ed. 12mo. Lond., 1866.   F 5 S 36

Another copy. 9th ed. (Churchill's Manuals.) 8vo. Lond., 1874.   F 5 S 37

On Poisons in relation to Medical Jurisprudence and Medicine. 3rd ed. 8vo. Lond., 1875.   A 12 P 35

TAYLOR (ANDREW T.), A.R.I.B.A. Towers and Steeples designed by Sir Christopher Wren. 8vo. Lond., 1881.
A 2 S 30

TAYLOR (BAYARD). Byeways of Europe. 2 vols. 8vo. Lond., 1869.   D 8 R 8, 9

Life and Letters of; edited by Marie Hansen-Taylor, and Horace E. Scudder. 2 vols. 8vo. Lond., 1884.
C 3 V 41, 42

Life, Travels, and Books of Alexander von Humboldt. [*See* HUMBOLDT, F. H. A. VON, BARON.]   C 3 Q 27

Studies in German Literature ; with an Introduction, by George H. Boker. 8vo. Lond., 1879.   B 9 R 11

Travels in Greece and Russia, with an Excursion to Crete. 8vo. Lond., 1859.   D 8 Q 1

Views Afoot; or, Europe seen with Knapsack and Staff. 12mo. Lond., 1874.   D 7 P 44

Visit to India, China, and Japan, in the year 1853. 8vo. Lond., 1855.   D 5 R 42

TAYLOR (CATHARINE). Letters from Italy to a Younger Sister. 2 vols. 8vo. Lond., 1842.   D 9 Q 40, 41

TAYLOR (CHARLES), M.B. The Angel in Disguise. 12mo. Parramatta, 1873.   MG 1 Q 39

TAYLOR (CHARLES), M.A. Introduction to the Ancient and Modern Geometry of Conics. 8vo. Camb., 1881.
A 10 T 26

TAYLOR (CHARLES). Calmet's Dictionary of the Holy Bible. [*See* CALMET, A.]

TAYLOR (EDGAR). German Popular Stories and Fairy Tales. [*See* GRIMM, J. L. AND W. K.]

TAYLOR (E. F.) Church and State. [*See* GEFFCKEN, H.]

TAYLOR (GEORGE LEDWELL). Autobiography of an Octogenarian Architect. 2 vols. roy. 4to. Lond., 1870-72.
A 24 U 24, 25

TAYLOR (G. L.), AND CRESY (E.) Architectural Antiquities of Rome. 2 vols. imp. fol. Lond., 1821-22.
A 1 R 8, 9 ‡

TAYLOR (Miss HELEN). Autobiography of J. S. Mill. [*See* MILL, J. S.]   C 8 R 41

Miscellaneous and Posthumous Works of T. Buckle. [*See* BUCKLE, H. T.]   J 15 S 11-13

TAYLOR (HENRY). Notes on Sketching Tours; by "An Architect." 8vo. Lond., 1880.   A 3 Q 8

TAYLOR (HENRY). Historic Notices, with Topographical and other Gleanings, descriptive of the Borough and and County-town of Flint. 8vo. Lond., 1883.   B 6 S 41

TAYLOR (SIR HENRY), K.C.M.G., &c. Autobiography of, 1800-75. 2 vols. 8vo. Lond., 1885.   C 7 U 54, 55

Philip van Artevelde: a Dramatic Romance. 2nd ed. 2 vols. 12mo. Lond., 1834.   H 1 Q 36, 37

The Statesman. 12mo. Lond., 1836.   F 1 P 23

TAYLOR (ISAAC), M.A. Ancient Christianity, and the Doctrines of the Oxford Tracts for the Times. 4th ed. 2 vols. 8vo. Lond., 1844.   G 10 R 21, 22

Elements of Thought; or, Concise Explanations of the Principal Terms employed in the several Branches of Intellectual Philosophy. 9th ed. 12mo. Lond., 1849.
G 9 Q 20

Etruscan Researches. 8vo. Lond., 1874.   B 11 V 26

Fanaticism. 8vo. Lond., 1833.   G 10 R 23

Greeks and Goths: a Study on the Runes. 8vo. Lond., 1879.   K 14 T 1

History of the Transmission of Ancient Books to Modern Times ; together with the Process of Historical Proof. 8vo. Lond., 1859.   B 14 Q 34

Loyola and Jesuitism in its Rudiments. 8vo. Lond., 1849.   G 2 T 18

Natural History of Enthusiasm. 6th ed. 8vo. Lond., 1832.   G 13 P 29

Physical Theory of another Life. 12mo. Lond., 1857.   G 10 P 13

Saturday Evening. 9th thousand. 12mo. Lond., 1852.   G 9 Q 16

Spiritual Despotism. 2nd ed. 8vo. Lond., 1835.
G 10 R 24

The Alphabet: an Account of the Origin and Development of Letters. 2 vols. 8vo. Lond., 1883. K 13 Q 36, 37
1. Semitic Alphabets.
2. Aryan Alphabets.

The Restoration of Belief. 8vo. Camb., 1855.   G 7 T 8

The World of Mind: an Elementary Book. 8vo. Lond., 1857.   G 7 T 9

Wesley and Methodism. 8vo. Lond., 1851.   G 10 R 25

TAYLOR (JAMES). [*See* LANDAUER, J.]   A 5 R 4

TAYLOR (JAMES), D.D., &c. Curling, the Ancient Scottish Game. With Illustrations by C. A. Doyle. 8vo. Edinb., 1884.   A 17 U 23

TAYLOR (RT. REV. JEREMY), D.D. Rule and Exercises of Holy Dying. 8vo. Lond., 1873.   G 10 R 10

Rule and Exercises of Holy Living. 8vo. Lond., 1873.   G 10 R 9

Whole Works of; with a Life of the Author, and a Critical Examination of his Writings, by Bishop Heber; revised by the Rev. C. P. Eden. 10 vols. 8vo. Lond., 1850-54.   G 10 R 11-20

Selections from the Works of. [*See* MONTAGU, B.]

TAYLOR (JOHN). British Gallery of Contemporary Portraits of Great Britain and Ireland; accompanied by short Biographical Notices. 2 vols. fol. Lond., 1822.   C 4 U 15, 16 ‡

TAYLOR (JOHN). Records of my Life. 2 vols. 8vo. Lond., 1832.   C 10 Q 44, 45

TAYLOR (JOHN). Works of John Taylor, the Water-Poet; edited by Charles Hindley, Esq. Imp. 8vo. Lond., 1872·
J 2 U 11

TAYLOR (JOHN). Bristol, Past and Present. [See NICHOLLS, J. F.]
B 2 T 36–38

TAYLOR (JOHN), D.D. Hebrew Concordance, adapted to the English Bible. 2 vols. fol. Lond., 1754–57.
K 35 Q 13, 14 ‡

TAYLOR (JOHN), LL.D. Summary of the Roman Law, taken from Dr. Taylor's "Elements of the Civil Law"; to which is prefixed, a Dissertation on Obligation. 8vo. Lond., 1772.
F 5 U 29

TAYLOR (JOHN EDWARD). Narrative of Events in Vienna. [See AUERBACH, B.]
D 7 P 23

TAYLOR (DR. JOHN E.), F.L.S., &c. Our Common British Fossils, and where to find them: a Hand-book for Students. 8vo. Lond., 1885.
A 9 S 22

Our Island-Continent: a Naturalist's Holiday in Australia. 12mo. Lond., 1886.
MD 1 T 51

[See ADALBERT OF PRUSSIA, PRINCE.]
D 9 T 21, 22

TAYLOR (JOHN GLANVILLE). United States and Cuba: Eight Years of Change and Travel. 8vo. Lond., 1851.
D 4 P 25

TAYLOR (JOHN SYDNEY). Comparative View of the Punishments annexed to Crime in the United States of America and in England. 8vo. Lond., 1831.
MF 1 Q 4

TAYLOR (MARIE HANSEN-), AND SCUDDER (HORACE E.) Life and Letters of Bayard Taylor. 2 vols. 8vo. Lond., 1884.
C 3 V 41, 42

TAYLOR (REV. MATTHEW), D.D. England's Bloody Tribunal; or, Popish Cruelty displayed. 4to. Lond., 1769.
G 6 V 19

TAYLOR (NORMAN), AND THOMSON (PROF. ALEXANDER M.) On the Occurrence of the Diamond near Mudgee; read before the Royal Society, 7th December, 1870. 8vo. Sydney, 1870.
MJ 2 R 14

TAYLOR (P. A.), M.P. The Vaccination Question: Speech of Mr. P. A. Taylor on Dr. Cameron's Resolution respecting Animal Vaccine. (Pam. Cp.) 8vo. Lond., 1880. A 12 S 34
Vaccination: a Letter to Dr. W. B. Carpenter, C.B., &c. (Pam. Cp.) 8vo. Lond., 1881.
A 12 S 34

TAYLOR (COL. PHILIP MEADOWS), C.S.I., &c. Story of my Life; edited by his Daughter. 2 vols. 8vo. Edinb., 1877.
C 5 Q 20, 21
Student's Manual of the History of India, from the Earliest Period to the Present. 3rd ed. 8vo. Lond., 1877.
B 10 Q 10

TAYLOR (PHILIP MEADOWS). Tobacco: a Farmer's Crop. 8vo. Lond., 1886.
A 1 P 26

TAYLOR (REV. RICHARD), M.A., &c. Past and Present of New Zealand; with its Prospect for the Future. With numerous Illustrations. 8vo. Lond., 1868.* MD 6 R 15
Te Ika a Maui; or, New Zealand and its Inhabitants. 2nd ed. 8vo. Lond., 1870.* MD 6 R 18

TAYLOR (RICHARD), F.S.A. Scientific Memoirs; selected from the Transactions of Foreign Academies of Science and Learned Societies, and from Foreign Journals. 3 vols. 8vo. Lond., 1837–41.
A 16 T 1–3

TAYLOR (DR. ROWLAND). Writings of. [See BRITISH REFORMERS.]

TAYLOR (R. W. C.) Introduction to a History of the Factory System. 8vo. Lond., 1886.
F 4 S 3

TAYLOR (SAMUEL). System of Stenography, or Shorthand Writing; with additional Notes and New Tables, revised and improved after considerable practice, by John Henry Cooke. New ed. 12mo. Lond., 1865.
K 11 U 24
Taylor's [Shorthand] improved. [See ODELL, G.]
Taylor's System of Shorthand. [See ANDERSON, T.]

TAYLOR (SAMUEL H.), LL.D. Classical Study; its value illustrated by Extracts from the Writings of Eminent Scholars; with an Introduction. 8vo. Andover, 1870.
J 12 U 12

TAYLOR (SEDLEY), M.A. Sound and Music: a non-mathematical Treatise on the Physical Constitution of Musical Sounds and Harmony, including the chief Acoustical Discoveries of Professor Helmholtz. 8vo. Lond., 1873.
A 7 P 14

TAYLOR (THEODORE). [See HOTTEN, J. C.]

TAYLOR (THOMAS). [See PORPHYRIUS.]
J 6 T 20

TAYLOR (TOM). Autobiographical Recollections; by the late Charles Robert Leslie, R.A. [See LESLIE, C. R. L.]
C 2 U 28, 29
Hand-book to the British Portrait Gallery, in the Art Treasures Exhibition. 8vo. Lond., 1857.
A 6 V 38
Hand-book to the Gallery of British Painters in the Art Treasures Exhibition. 8vo. Lond., 1857.
A 6 V 38
Hand-book to the Water Colours, Drawings and Engravings, in the Art Treasures Exhibition. 8vo. Lond., 1857.
A 6 V 38
Life of Benjamin Robert Haydon. [See HAYDON, B. R.]
C 3 T 28–30
Life of Sir Joshua Reynolds. [See LESLIE, C. R.]
C 9 P 35, 36

TAYLOR (WILLIAM) Historic Survey of German Poetry, interspersed with various Translations. 3 vols. 8vo. Lond., 1830.
H 8 V 15–17
Memoir of the Life and Writings of; compiled and edited by J. W. Robberds. 2 vols. 8vo. Lond., 1843. C 9 V 35, 36

TAYLOR (SERJ.-MAJOR WILLIAM). Life in the Ranks. 8vo. Lond., 1847.
J 9 R 38
Scenes and Adventures in Affghanistan. 8vo. Lond., 1842.
D 6 P 32

TAYLOR (REV. WILLIAM). Christian Adventures in South Africa. 8th thousand. 12mo. Lond., 1867.   D 1 T 1

TAYLOR (WILLIAM B. S.) History of the University of Dublin: its Origin, Progress, and Present Condition; with Biographical Notices of many Eminent Men educated therein. 8vo. Lond., 1845.   B 11 Q 9

Origin, Progress, and Present Condition of the Fine Arts in Great Britain and Ireland. 2 vols. 8vo. Lond., 1841.   A 6 V 13, 14

TAYLOR (WILLIAM CLARE). Jottings on Australia; with Remarks on the California Route to New York and Liverpool. 8vo. Lond., 1872.   MD 3 S 45

TAYLOR (WILLIAM COOKE), LL.D., &c. History of Mohammedanism and its Sects. 12mo. Lond., 1834.   G 10 P 18

History of the Civil Wars of Ireland, from Anglo-Norman Invasion till the Union of the Country with Great Britain. 2 vols. 12mo. Lond., 1831.   B 11 P 8, 9

Another copy. (Const. Misc.) 2 vols. 18mo. Edinb., 1831.   K 10 R 6, 7

Ireland. [*See* BEAUMONT, G. DE.]   B 11 P 16, 17

Popular History of British India, Commercial Intercourse with China, and the Insular Possessions of England in the Eastern Seas. 8vo. Lond., 1842.   B 10 Q 33

Revolutions, Insurrections, and Conspiracies of Europe. 2 vols. 8vo. Lond., 1843.   B 7 R 27, 28

Romantic Biography of the Age of Elizabeth; or, Sketches of Life from the Life from the Bye-ways of History, by the Benedictine Brethren of Glendalough. 2 vols. 8vo. Lond., 1842.   C 9 P 30, 31

Student's Manual of Ancient History. New ed. 8vo. Lond., 1877   B 14 Q 26

Student's Manual of Modern History. New ed. 8vo. Lond., 1872.   B 14 Q 27

TEA CYCLOPÆDIA (THE). Articles on Tea, Tea Science, Blights, Soils and Manures, Cultivation, Buildings, Manufacture, &c.; with Tea Statistics. Illustrated. 8vo. Calcutta, 1882.   K 17 U 7

TEA-PLANTER'S VADE MECUM. 8vo. Lond., 1886.   A 1 T 21

TEACHERS OF NEW SOUTH WALES. United Association of Teachers of New South Wales: Occasional Papers. 8vo. Sydney, 1866.   MJ 2 Q 10

Another copy. 8vo. Sydney, 1856.   MJ 2 R 5

TEALE (THOMAS PRIDGIN), M.A. Dangers to Health: a Pictorial Guide to Domestic Sanitary Defects. 3rd ed. 8vo. Lond., 1881.   A 2 S 34

TEATRO ESPAÑOL (TESORO DEL). [*See* OCHOA, E. DE.]

TEATRO NUEVO ESPAÑOL. Teatro Nuevo Español. 6 vols. 12mo. Madrid, 1800-1.   H 3 P 18-23

TEBBUTT (JOHN), F.R.A.S., &c. Gales of February, 1863. (Newspaper Cuttings, Pam. 28.) 8vo. Sydney, 1863.   MJ 2 Q 16

Letter on the Comet of 1862. 8vo. Windsor, 1862.   MJ 2 Q 16

On the Progress and Present State of Astronomical Science in New South Wales. 8vo. Sydney, 1870.   MJ 2 R 14

Results of Meteorological Observations made at the Private Observatory of John Tebbutt, "The Peninsula," Windsor, New South Wales, in the years 1863-81. 4 vols. imp. 8vo. Parramatta and Sydney, 1868-82.   MA 1 P 19-22 †

TECKLENBORG (H.) Internationales Wörterbuch der Marine über alle im Verkehr vorkommenden technischen Ausdrücke. 12mo. Bremen, 1870.   K 9 T 23

TEETOTALLER (THE), and General Newspaper. Fol. Sydney, 1842-43.   ME

TEGETMEIER (W. B.) Poultry-book; comprising the Breeding and Management of Profitable and Ornamental Poultry, their Qualities and Characteristics. Imp. 8vo. Lond., 1867.   A 14 V 10

TEGG (JAMES). Monthly Magazine. Vol. 1, March-July, 1836. [Containing an Account of "Fisher's Ghost."] 12mo. Sydney, 1836.*   MJ 2 P 38

Another copy. July, 1836. 8vo. Sydney, 1836.   ME 3 R

Tegg's New South Wales Pocket Almanac and Remembrancer, for the years 1836-44. 9 vols. (in 4) 16mo. Sydney, 1836-44.   ME 4 Q

Another copy, 1837-44. 8 vols. (in 2) 16mo. Sydney, 1837-44.   ME 4 R

TEGG (JAMES AND SAMUEL). List of Books published and sold by. 8vo. Sydney. (n.d.)   MK 1 Q 13

TEGG (WILLIAM). The Last Act; being the Funeral Rites of Nations and Individuals. 12mo. Lond., 1876.   G 16 P 29

TEGOBORSKI (LOUIS DE). Commentaries on the Productive Forces of Russia. 2 vols. 8vo. Lond.   B 12 U 8, 9

TEIGNMOUTH (JOHN), LORD. Memoir of the Life and Correspondence of; by his Son, Lord Teignmouth. 2 vols. 8vo. Lond., 1843.   C 9 Q 41, 42

Memoirs of the Life, Writings, and Correspondence of Sir William Jones. 4to. Lond., 1804.   C 2 W 14

Sketches of the Coasts and Islands of Scotland, and of the Isle of Man. 2 vols. 8vo. Lond., 1836.   D 7 R 9, 10

[*See* JONES, SIR W.]

TELANG (KÁSHINÁTH TRIMBAK), M.A. The Bhagavadgita. [*See* MÜLLER, PROF. F. M.]

TELFER (COMM. J. BUCHAN), R.N., &c. Strange Career of the Chevalier D'Eon de Beaumont, Minister Plenipotentiary from France to Great Britain, in 1763. With Portraits and Facsimile. 8vo. Lond., 1885.   C 6 Q 16

The Crimea and Transcaucasia. 2 vols. 8vo. Lond., 1876.   D 8 U 1, 2

TELFORD (THOMAS), C.E. Life of, written by himself, containing a Descriptive Narrative of his Professional Labours; edited by John Rickman. 8vo. Lond., 1838.
C 8 V 42

Atlas [to above]. Imp. fol. Lond., 1838.   C 21 P 18‡

TEMPERANCE ADVOCATE (THE), and Australasian Commercial and Agricultural Intelligencer. 2 vol. 4to. and fol. Sydney, 1840–41.   ME 19 T

Supplement to the Temperance Advocate, April 21st, 1841; containing the [New South Wales Temperance] Society's Report [for 1841]. Fol. Sydney, 1841.
MJ 1 P 45

TEMPERANCE PIONEER. [*See* VICTORIA TEMPERANCE PIONEER.]

TEMPERANCE SOCIETY. [*See* NEW SOUTH WALES TEMPERANCE SOCIETY.]

TEMPLE (SIR RICHARD), BART., &c. Asia; with Ethnological Appendix. [*See* KEANE, PROF. A. H.]   D 11 S 5

Cosmopolitan Essays. With Maps. 8vo. Lond., 1886.
F 10 R 30

India in 1880. 8vo. Lond., 1880.   D 6 R 6

Men and Events of my Time in India. 8vo. Lond., 1882.   B 10 S 35

Oriental Experience: a Selection of Essays and Addresses delivered on various Occasions. With Illustrations. 8vo. Lond., 1883.   D 6 R 7

TEMPLE (SIR WILLIAM), BART. Works of; to which is prefixed, some Account of the Life and Writings of the Author, by Dean Swift. 2 vols. fol. Lond., 1731.
B 36 Q 1, 2 ‡

TEMPLER (JOHN C.) Private Letters of Sir James Brooke, K.C.B., Rajah of Sarawak, narrating the Events of his Life, from 1838 to the Present Time. 3 vols. 8vo. Lond., 1853.   C 3 R 22–24

TEMPLETON (WILLIAM). Engineer's, Architect's, and Contractor's Pocket-book, for the year 1872. 12mo. Lond., 1872.   A 2 R 41

Engineer's, Millwright's, and Machinist's Practical Assistant. 4th ed. 18mo. Lond., 1868.   A 6 R 4

Locomotive Engine popularly explained and illustrated. 2nd ed. 8vo. Lond., 1848.   A 6 R 17

Millwright and Engineer's Pocket Companion, corrected by S. Maynard. 15th ed. 12mo. Lond., 1871. A 6 R 7

Practical Mechanic's Workshop Companion; revised, &c., by W. S. Hutton. 12mo. Lond., 1886.   A 11 P 10

TEMPSKY (G. F. VON). Mitla: a Narrative of Incidents and Personal Adventures on a Journey in Mexico, Guatemala, and Salvador, in the years 1853–55; edited by J. S. Bell. 8vo. Lond., 1858.   D 3 S 19

TEN BRINK (BERNHARD). Early English Literature (to Wiclif); translated from the German, by Horace M. Kennedy. (Translation revised by the Author.) 12mo. Lond., 1883.   B 3 P 22

TEN BROOK (ANDREW). History of the Thirty Years' War. [*See* GINDELY, A.]   B 7 T 33, 34

TEN KATE (L.) Aenleiding tot de kennisse van het verhevene deel der Nedurduitshe Spràke. 2 vols. 4to. Amsterdam, 1723.   K 13 T 21, 22

TENCH (CAPT. WATKIN). Complete Account of the Settlement at Port Jackson, in New South Wales, including an accurate Description of the Situation of the Colony; of the Natives; and of its Natural Productions. 4to. Lond., 1793.*   MB 1 U 8

Letter from. [*See* PHILLIP, CAPT. A.]

Narrative of the Expedition to Botany Bay; with an Account of New South Wales, its Productions, Inhabitants, &c. 3rd. ed. 8vo. Lond., 1789.*   MD 4 U 36

Voyages à la Baye Botanique, à la Nouvelle-Hollande, et au Nouveau Pays de Galles Méridional; traduits de l'Anglois, accompagnés de détails précieux relatifs à M. de la Peyrouse. 12mo. Liege, 1791.   Libr.

TENHOVE (NICHOLAS). Memoirs of the House of Medici, from its Origin to the Death of Francesco, the second Grand Duke of Tuscany, and of the Great Men who flourished in Tuscany within that Period; from the French, with Notes and Observations, by Sir Richard Clayton, Bart. 2 vols. 4to. Bath, 1797.   C 8 V 14, 15

TENISON–WOODS (REV. JULIAN EDMUND), F.G.S., &c. Census; with brief Descriptions of the Marine Shells of Tasmania and the adjacent Islands. 8vo. Hobart, 1877.
MA 2 Q 29

Description of new Tasmanian Shells. 8vo. Hobart, 1876.   MA 2 Q 29

Fish and Fisheries of New South Wales. Roy. 8vo. Sydney, 1882.*   MA 2 U 1

Geological Observations in South Australia, principally in the District south-east of Adelaide. 8vo. Lond., 1862.*   MA 2 Q 4

History of Australian Tertiary Geology. 8vo. Hobart, 1876.   MA 2 Q 29

History of the Discovery and Exploration of Australia; or, an Account of the Progress of Geographical Discovery in that Continent, from the Earliest Period to the Present Day. 2 vols. 8vo. Lond., 1865.*   MB 2 S 21, 22

Not quite as Old as the Hills: a Lecture on the Evidences of Man's Antiquity (delivered at Robe Town). Dedicated to the Members of the Gawler Institute. 8vo. Melb., 1864.   MA 2 Q 34

Another copy. 8vo. Melb., 1864.   MG 1 Q 37

Another copy. 8vo. Melb., 1864.   MJ 2 R 15

Notes on the Fossils referred to in "Further Notes on the Tertiary Marine Beds of Table Cape; by R. M. Johnston." 8vo. Sydney, 1876.   MA 2 Q 29

Notes on the Tertiary Fossils, Tasmania. 8vo. Hobart, 1876.   MA 2 Q 29

TENISON-WOODS (REV. JULIAN EDMUND), F.G.S.,
&c.—*continued.*

On a new genus of Nudibranchiata, fam. Elysiadæ, and
on some Tasmanian Patellidæ.   8vo.   Hobart, 1876.
MA 2 Q 29

On a new species of Ampullaria.   (Pam. Ch.)   8vo.
Hobart, 1876.   MA 2 Q 29

On some Australian Tertiary Corals.   8vo.   Sydney,
1877.   MJ 2 R 14

On some new Tasmanian Marine Shells.   (2nd series.)
Also on a new reversed Helix (*Helix Weldii*).   (Pam.
Cn.)   8vo.   Hobart, 1876.   MA 2 V 14

On the Freshwater Shells of Tasmania.   (Pam. Cg.)
8vo.   Hobart, 1875.   MA 2 V 8

On the genus Ferestella.   (Pam. Cg.)   8vo.   Hobart,
1875.   MA 2 V 8

Palæontology of New Zealand.   Part 4.   Corals and
Bryozoa of the Neozoic Period in New Zealand.   Roy.
8vo.   Wellington, 1880.   MA 2 R 34

[Scientific Papers of.]   2 vols. 8vo.   Sydney, &c., 1865–79.
MA 2 T 6, 7

  1. On some new Tasmanian Marine Shells.   On some Tertiary
Fossils from Table Cape.   On some new species of Tasmanian
Marine Shells.   On some new Marine Mollusca.   On some new
Australian Polyzoa.   On the Relations of the Brisbane Flora.
A Census of the Flora of Brisbane, by F. M. Bailey, F.L.S.,
&c., and the Rev. J. E. Tenison-Woods, F.L.S., &c.   On some
Tertiary Fossils.   On some new Marine Shells.   On some
Fresh-water Shells from New Guinea.   On the Extratropical
Corals of Australia.   On the Echini of Australia.   On some
Fossils from Levuka, Viti.   On some post-Tertiary Fossils
from New Caledonia.   On some Australian species of Trocho-
cardia.   On Heteropsammia Michellini, of Edwards and
Haime.   On a new species Distichopora.   On some new Marine
Shells from Moreton Bay.   On Araujia Albens, *Don.*   On some
Australian Tertiary Corals.   Palæontological Evidence of Aus-
tralian Tertiary Formations.   On some Australian Tertiary
Fossil Corals and Polyzoa.   The Molluscan Fauna of Tasmania.
On a new species of Millepora.

  2. On the genus Ferestella.   On the Fresh-water Shells of Tas-
mania.   On some new Tasmanian Marine Shells (2nd series);
also, on a new reversed Tasmanian Helix (*Helix Weldii*).   On
some Tertiary Fossils from Muddy Creek, Western Victoria.
Observations on the genus Risella.   Shells collected during the
Chevert Expedition, with Descriptions of the new species, by
J. Brazier, C.M.Z.S.   Description of new Tasmanian Shells.
Census: with brief Descriptions of the Marine Shells of Tasmania and the adjacent Islands.   On a new species of Nenera.
On a variety of Trigonia Lamarckii.   On a Tertiary Formation
at New Guinea.   The Echini of Australia (including those of
the *Chevert* Expedition).   On two new species of Land Shells.
On a new genus of Polyzoa.   On some Corals from Darnley
Island.   On some new Extratropical Corals.   On some Fresh-
water Shells from New Zealand.   On Bulimus Dufresnii.   On
three new genera and one new species of Madreporaria Corals.
On some Australian Shells described by Dr. A. Gould.   On
some new Marine Shells.   On some Tertiary Fossils from New
Guinea.   On an Australian variety of Neritina Pulligera, *Linn.*
On a new genus of Milleporidæ.   On a new species of Psam-
mocoria.   On a new species of Dennophyllum (D. Quinarium),
and a young stage of Cycloseris sinuosa.   On some Australian
Lithonidæ.   On the Tertiary Deposits of Australia.   On
some Fossil Corals from Aldinga.   On a new genus of Nudi-
branchiata, fam. Elysiadæ, and on some Tasmanian Patellidæ.
The Geology of Portland: two Lectures.   Tasmanian Forests;
their Botany and Economical Value.   On the genus Amathia,
of Lamouroux; with a Description of a new species.   History of
Australian Tertiary Geology.   Further Notes on the Tertiary
Marine Beds of Table Cape, Tasmania; by R. M. Johnson.
Notes on the Tertiary Fossils, Tasmania.   On a new species of
Ampullaria.

TENNANT (C.)   People's Blue Book: Taxation as it is,
and as it ought to be.   8vo.   Lond., 1857.   F 5 Q 19

TENNANT (ROBERT).   Sardinia and its Resources.   Roy.
8vo.   Roma, 1885.   D 8 V 21

TENNANT (REV. WILLIAM), LL.D., &c.   Indian Recreations; consisting chiefly of Strictures on the Domestic
and Rural Economy of the Mahomedans and Hindoos.
2nd ed.   2 vols. 8vo.   Lond., 1804.   D 6 P 11, 12

TENNEMAN (WILHELM GOTTLIEB).   Manual of the History of Philosophy; translated from the German, by the
Rev. Arthur Johnson, M.A.; revised, enlarged, and continued by J. R. Morell.   8vo.   Lond., 1873.   G 16 Q 22

TENNENT (SIR JAMES EMERSON), K.C.S., &c.   Belgium.
2 vols. 8vo.   Lond., 1841.   D 8 Q 22, 23

Ceylon: an Account of the Island, Physical, Historical,
and Topographical.   2 vols. roy. 8vo.   Lond., 1859.
D 4 T 36, 37

History of Modern Greece, from its Conquest by the
Romans, B.C. 146, to the Present Time.   2 vols. 8vo.
Lond., 1845.   B 9 T 13, 14

Sketches of the Natural History of Ceylon; with Narrative and Anecdotes.   8vo.   Lond., 1861.   A 14 S 10

The Wild Elephant, and the Method of Capturing and
Taming it in Ceylon.   12mo.   Lond., 1867.   A 14 S 7

[*See* EMERSON, J.]

TENNESSEE.   [*See* UNITED STATES.]

TENNESSEE STOCKBREEDERS' ASSOCIATION.
[*See* UNITED STATES.]

TENNYSON (ALFRED), BARON: a Biographical Sketch; by
H. J. Jennings.   With a Portrait.   8vo.   Lond., 1884.
C 4 Q 49

Ballads, and other Poems.   12mo.   Lond., 1880.   H 8 T 35

Becket.   8vo.   Lond., 1884.   H 8 T 27

Enoch Arden, &c.   12mo.   Lond., 1864.   H 8 T 38

Gareth and Lynette, &c.   12mo.   Lond., 1872.   H 8 T 30

Harold: a Drama.   8vo.   Lond., 1877.   H 8 T 25

In Memoriam.   2nd ed.   12mo.   Lond., 1850.   H 8 T 31

Locksley Hall, Sixty Years After, &c.   12mo.   Lond.,
1886.   H 8 T 26

Lyrical Poems by; selected and annotated by Francis T.
Palgrave.   12mo.   Lond., 1885.   H 8 T 29

Maud, and other Poems.   12mo.   Lond., 1855.   H 8 T 29

Poems by.   7th ed.   12mo.   Lond., 1851. H 8 T 32

Poetical Works of.   6 vols. 8vo.   Lond. 1873.   H 8 U 1–6

Queen Mary: a Drama.   12mo.   Lond., 1875.   H 8 T 24

The Cup, and the Falcon.   12mo.   Lond.,1884.   H 8 T 33

The Miller's Daughter.   Illustrated by A. L. Boyd.
4to.   Lond., 1857.   H 6 U 29

The Princess: a Medley.   6th ed.   12mo.   Lond.,
1854.   H 8 T 28

Tiresias, and other Poems.   12mo.   Lond., 1885.   H 8 T 37

Works of.   7 vols. 12mo.   Lond., 1884.   H 8 T 39–45

TENNYSON (FREDERICK). Days and Hours. 12mo. Lond., 1854. H 7 U 25

TEPPER (J. G. O.), F.L.S. Common Native Insects of South Australia: a Popular Guide to South Australian Entomology. Part 1. Coleoptera, or Beetles. Sm. 4to. Adelaide, 1887. MA 2 U 29

TERENTIUS AFER (PUBLIUS). Comedies of Terence, and the Fables of Phædrus; literally translated into English Prose, by Henry Thomas Riley, B.A.; to which is added, a Metrical Translation of Phædrus, by Christopher Smart, A.M. 8vo. Lond., 1872. H 1 Q 35

Comœdiæ Sex, ex Editione Westerhoviana, cum Notis et Interpretatione in usum Delphini. 4 vols. 8vo. Lond., 1824. J 13 T 1-4

TERRASSON (JEAN). Life of Sethos, taken from Private Memoirs of the Ancient Egyptians; translated from a Greek MS. into French, by Jean Terrasson, and now faithfully done into English from the Paris Edition, by Mr. Lediard. 2 vols. 8vo. Lond., 1732. J 10 R 4, 5

TERRESTRIAL MAGNETISM. Treatise upon. 8vo. Lond., 1871. A 5 T 33

TERRILL (EDWARD). Records of a Church of Christ, meeting in Broadmead, A.D. 1640-88; edited from the original MS., with Notes, by Nathaniel Haycroft, M.A. 8vo. Lond., 1865. G 10 Q 19

TERREIN DE LACOUPERIE (A. E. J. B.) Early History of the Chinese Civilization: a Lecture. 12mo. Lond., 1880. B 2 P 23

TERRY (CHARLES), F.R.S., &c. New Zealand: its Advantages and Prospects as a British Colony; with a full Account of the Land Claims, Sales of Crown Lands, Aborigines, &c. 8vo. Lond., 1842.* MD 5 U 38

TERRY (F. C.) The Parramatta River. Illustrated. Ob. 4to. Sydney, 1857. MD 6 P 7 †

TERSTEEGEN (GERHARD). Life and Character of; with Selections from his Letters and Writings, translated from the German, by Samuel Jackson. 4th ed. 12mo. Lond., 1846. G 2 P 3

TE WHITI (MAORI PROPHET). Wanderings of. [*See* WARD, J. P.]

TERTULLIANUS (QUINTUS SEPTIMUS FLORENS). Opera omnia. [*See* MIGNE, J. P., SERIES LATINA, 1-3.]

The Spirit of Tertullian. [*See* NEANDER, J. A. W.]

Tertullian: Apologetic and Practical Treatises; translated by the Rev. C. Dodgson, M.A. 8vo. Oxford, 1842. G 10 S 27

TESTA DE NEVILLE, sive Liber Fœdorum in Curia Scaccarii, temp. Hen. III, Edwd. I. Fol. Lond., 1807. B 24 S 13 ‡

TESTAMENTS. [*See* BIBLES.]

TETKA IZABELLA [a Russian Novel]. 3 vols. 12mo. Moscow, 1818. J 16 T 9-11

TEUCHER (L. H.) [*See* ANTONINUS LIBERALIS.] J 7 S 30

TEXAS. [*See* UNITED STATES.]

TEXIER (CHARLES). Description do l'Asie Mineure. 3 vols. imp. fol. Paris, 1839-49. D 7 P 4-6 ‡

TEXIER (CHARLES), AND PULLAN (R. P.). F.R.I.B.A. Byzantine Architecture, illustrated by Examples of Edifices erected in the East during the Earliest Ages of Christianity; with Historical and Archæological Descriptions. Imp. fol. Lond., 1864. A 4 Q 5 ‡

TEXT-BOOKS OF SCIENCE. 27 vols. 8vo. Lond., 1871-78. A 17 S 1-27

TEYSMANN (J. E.) [*See* AA, P. J. C. B. ROBIDE VAN DER.]

THACHER (JAMES), M.D., &c. History of the Town of Plymouth (U.S.), from 1620 to the Present Time. 12mo. Boston, 1835. B 1 Q 21

THACKERAY (REV. FRANCIS ST. JOHN). Eton College Library; reprinted from *Notes and Queries.* Sm. 4to. Eton, 1881. J 6 T 21

THACKERAY (WILLIAM MAKEPEACE) [A Biography]; by Anthony Trollope. (Eng. Men of Letts.) 8vo. Lond., 1879. C 1 U 35

Anecdote Life of. [*See* TIMBS, J.]

Bibliography of. [*See* SHEPHERD, R. H.] K 7 R 11

English Humourists of the 18th Century: a Series of Lectures. 12mo. Lond., 1858. C 1 R 37

Extracts from the Writings, chiefly Philosophical and Reflective. 8vo. Lond., 1881. J 2 P 24

Irish Sketch-book, 1842; by "Mr. M. A. Titmarsh.' 8vo. Lond., 1857. D 7 Q 31

The Kickleburys on the Rhine; by "Mr. M. A. Titmarsh." 3rd ed. 12mo. Lond., 1851. J 5 R 22

Miscellanies, Prose and Verse. 4 vols. 8vo. Lond., 1870. J 4 Q 30-33

Notes of a Journey from Cornhill to Grand Cairo; by "Mr. M. A. Titmarsh." 2nd ed. 12mo. Lond., 1846. D 1 T 9

Paris Sketch-book; by "Mr. M. A. Titmarsh." 2 vols. 8vo. Lond., 1840. D 7 R 29, 30

Sultan Stork, and other Stories and Sketches (1829-44); to which is added, the Bibliography of Thackeray. 8vo. Lond., 1887. J 2 P 23

Students' Quarter; or, Paris Five-and-thirty Years since. 8vo. Lond., 1876. D 7 Q 32

Thackeray and Cruikshank: on the Genius of George Cruikshank; reprinted verbatim from the *Westminster Review;* edited, with a prefatory Note on Thackeray as an Artist and Art-Critic, by W. E. Church. With Illustrations, including all the original Woodcuts. 8vo. Lond., 1884. C 7 R 48

THACKERAY (WILLIAM MAKEPEACE)—*continued*.

Thackeray, the Humourist and Man of Letters; by "Theodore Taylor" [John Camden Hotten]. 8vo. Lond., 1864.   C 4 S 44

Thackerayana : Notes and Anecdotes, illustrated by hundreds of Sketches. 8vo. Lond., 1875.   C 5 Q 19

Thackeray's London. [*See* RIDEING, W. H.]

Works of. With Illustrations by the Author, Richard Doyle, Fred. Walker, and Geo. Du Maurier. 22 vols. 8vo. Lond., 1869.   J 2 P 1–22

1, 2. Vanity Fair: a Novel without a Hero.

3, 4. The History of Pendennis : his Fortunes and Misfortunes, his Friends and his greatest Enemy.

5, 6. The Newcomes : Memoirs of a most Respectable Family ; edited by Arthur Pendennis, Esq.

7. The History of Henry Esmond, Esq., a Colonel in the Service of Her Majesty Queen Anne; written by himself.

8, 9. The Virginians: a Tale of the Last Century.

10, 11. The Adventures of Philip on his way through the World, showing who robbed him, who helped him, and who passed him by; to which is now prefixed, A Shabby Genteel Story.

12. The Paris Sketch-book of Mr. M. A. Titmarsh ; and the Memoirs of Mr. Charles J. Yellowplush.

13. The Memoirs of Barry Lyndon, Esq., written by himself; the History of Samuel Titmarsh, and the Great Hoggarty Diamond.

14. The Irish Sketch-book; and Notes of a Journey from Cornhill to Grand Cairo.

15. The Book of Snobs; and Sketches and Travels in London.

16. Burlesques; Novels by Eminent Hands; Jeames's Diary; Adventures of Major Gahagan; A Legend of the Rhine; Rebecca and Rowena; The History of the next French Revolution; Cox's Diary.

17. The Christmas Books of Mr. M. A. Titmarsh : Mrs. Perkins's Ball; Our Street; Dr. Birch; The Kickleburys on the Rhine; The Rose and the Ring.

18. Ballads and Tales.

19. The Four Georges; The English Humourists of the Eighteenth Century. With Portraits.

20. Roundabout Papers (from the *Cornhill Magazine*) ; to which is added, The Second Funeral of Napoleon.

21. Denis Duval; Lovel the Widower; and other Stories.

22. Catherine: a Story; Little Travels and Roadside Sketches, by Titmarsh; The Fitz-Boodle Papers; The Wolves and the Lamb.

THAER (A.) Principes Raisonnés d'Agriculture. 4 vols. (in 2) 4to. Paris, 1811–16.   A 1 T 25, 26

THAMES HAVEN DOCK AND RAILWAY ; with Observations on their anticipated Advantages. (Pam. 15.) 8vo. Lond., 1845.   MJ 2 Q 5

THATCHER (RICHMOND). An Australian Orator. [*See* BUCHANAN, D.]   MF 1 P 18

Life and Times of Jem Punch; with some Information respecting certain remarkable People of his Time, and containing a number of Historical Facts and Dates regarding New South Wales. 8vo. Sydney, 1885.   MC 1 P 35

Sydney and Suburban Hotel Guide and Licensed Victuallers' Directory, for 1886-87. 8vo. Sydney, 1886.*
                                                        ME 4 U

[*See* OUR CHRISTMAS BUDGET.]   MJ 2 R 17

THAUSING (MORIZ.) Albert Dürer: his Life and Works; translated from the German; edited by Fred. A. Eaton, M.A. 2 vols. 8vo. Lond., 1882.   C 10 V 13, 14

THAYER (WILLIAM M.) From the Tan-yard to the White House: the Story of President Grant's Life. With Portrait. 8vo. Lond., 1885.   C 2 T 36

THEAL (GEORGE MCCALL). Kaffir Folk-lore; or, a Selection from the Traditional Tales current among the People living on the Eastern Border of the Cape Colony ; with copious explanatory Notes. 8vo. Lond., 1882.   B 16 S 30

THEARLE (SAMUEL J. P.) Naval Architecture: a Treatise on Laying Off, and Building Wood, Iron, and Composite Ships. 8vo. Lond., 1876.   A 2 R 32

Plates to the above. 4to. Lond., 1876.   A 3 Q 17

THEATRICAL DICTIONARY (NEW); containing an Account of all the Dramatic Pieces that have appeared from the commencement of Theatrical Exhibitions to the Present Time. 8vo. Lond., 1792.   K 17 P 19

THEINER (AUGUSTINUS). Vetera Monumenta Hibernorum et Scotorum Historiam illustrantia quæ ex Vaticani, Neapolis ac Florentiæ tabulariis deprompsit et ordine chronologico disposuit, 1216–1547. Roy. fol. Rome, 1864.   B 12 U 1 ‡

THEIR REPORTER. [*See* GENERATION OF JUDGES. A.]

THEMISTOCLES. Dissertation on the Epistles of. [*See* BENTLEY, R.]

THEOBALD (W.) Burma : its People and Productions. [*See* MASSON, REV. F.]   D 5 V 4, 5

THEOCRITUS. The Idylls of Theocritus, Bion, and Moschus, and the War-songs of Tyrtæus; literally translated into English Prose by the Rev. J. Banks, M.A. 8vo. Lond., 1876.   H 5 S 34

Translations of. [*See* CHALMERS, A.]

THEODORE (KING OF ABYSSINIA). Narrative of the British Mission to. [*See* RASSAM, HORMUZD.] D 1 W 1, 2

THEODORETUS (CYRENSIS EPISCOPUS). Opera omnia. [*See* MIGNE, J. P., SERIES GRÆCA, 80–84.]

THEODORETUS (BISHOP OF CYRUS), AND EVAGRIUS. History of the Church, from A.D. 322, to the Death of Theodore of Mopsuestia, A.D. 427; and from A.D. 441 to A.D. 594; translated from the Greek, with Memoirs of the Authors. 8vo. Lond., 1854.   G 16 Q 6

THEODORUS [*See* NEW REFORMATION, THE.]

THEODORUS STUDITA (SANCTUS). Opera omnia. [*See* MIGNE, J. P., SERIES GRÆCA, 99.]

THEODULFUS (AURELIANENSIS EPISCOPUS). Opera omnia. [*See* MIGNE, J. P., SERIES LATINA, 105.]

THEOPHANES. [*See* BYZANTINE HIST. SCRIPT.]

THEOPHANES (SANCTUS). Chronographia. [*See* MIGNE, J. P., SERIES GRÆCA, 108.]

THEOPHANES CERAMEUS (Archiepiscopus Tauromenitanus). Homiliæ. [*See* Migne, J. P., Series Græca, 132.]

THEOPHRASTUS. Characters of; illustrated by Physiognomical Sketches. (Fam. Class. Lib.) 12mo. Lond., 1836. J 15 P 49

Les Caractères de Théophraste. [*See* La Bruyère, J. de.]

THEOPHRASTUS (Philippus), Bombast of Hohenheim. [*See* Paracelsus.]

THEOPHYLACTUS (Bulgariæ Archiepiscopus). Opera omnia. [*See* Migne, J. P., Series Græca, 123–126.]

[*See* Byzantinæ Hist. Script.]

THEOSOPHY. Five Years of Theosophy: Mystical, Philosophical, Historical, and Scientific Essays; selected from *The Theosophist.* 8vo. Lond., 1885. G 11 P 27

Introduction to. [*See* Fortescue, J. F.] G 9 Q 18

THEREMIN (Fra). Confessions of Adalbert. 12mo. Lond.; 1838. J 8 Q 39

THÉRÉSE (Sainte). Vie de. [*See* Capefigue, J. B. H. R.]

THERRY (Sir Roger), Knt. Appeal on behalf of the Roman Catholics of New South Wales, in a Letter to Edward Blount, Esq., M.P. for Steyning; with an Appendix. 8vo. Sydney, 1833. MG 1 P 5

Another copy. 8vo. Sydney, 1833. MG 1 R 16

Comparison between the Oratory of the House of Commons thirty years ago and the Present Time: a Lecture. 8vo. Sydney, 1856. MJ 1 T 38

Letter addressed to, by Bishop Broughton. [*See* Broughton, Rt. Rev. W. G.] MG 1 P 5

Letter to the Rt. Hon. G. Canning. [*See* Historical Pamphlets.] B 11 Q 1

Letter to the Rt. Hon. W. E. Gladstone, M.P. 8vo. Sydney. 1850. MF 3 P 3

Another copy. 8vo. Sydney 1850. MJ 2 R 20

Reminiscences of Thirty Years' Residence in New South Wales and Victoria. 8vo. Lond., 1863.* MB 1 R 1

Speeches of the Rt. Hon. George Canning; with Memoir of his Life. [*See* Canning, Rt. Hon. G.] F 13 P 12–17

Strictures upon a Letter written by. [*See* Fulton, Rev. H.] MG 1 P 5

THEVENOT (Jean de). Travels of Monsieur de Thevenot into the Levant. Fol. Lond., 1687. D 36 Q 7 ‡

[*See* Harris, J.]

THEY MIGHT HAVE BEEN TOGETHER TILL THE LAST: an Essay on Marriage and the Position of Women in England. 8vo. Lond., 1885. F 15 P 11

THIBAUDEAU (A. C.) Le Consulat et l'Empire; ou, l'Histoire de la France et de Napoléon Bonaparte, de 1799 à 1815. 8 vols. 8vo. Paris, 1834. B 8 P 27–34

THIÉBAULT (Dieudonné). Souvenirs de Vingt Ans Séjour à Berlin. [*See* Barrière, J. F., 23, 24.] C 1 T 23, 24

5 D

THIELMANN (Lieut. Max. von), Baron. Journey in the Caucasus, Persia, and Turkey in Asia; translated by Charles Heneage, F.R.G.S. 2 vols. 8vo. Lond., 1875. D 5 Q 13, 14

THIERCELIN (Dr. Henri). Chez les Anthropophages: aventures d'une Parisienne à la Nouvelle Calédonie. 12mo. Paris, 1872. MD 4 P 47

THIERRY (A.) History of the Conquest of England by the Normans. 3 vols. 8vo. Lond., 1825. B 5 P 36–38

THIERS (Louis Adolphe). History of the Consulate and the Empire of France under Napoleon; translated by D. F. Campbell. 20 vols. (in 10) 8vo. Lond., 1845–62. B 8 S 11–20

History of the French Revolution; translated, with Notes and Illustrations, by Fred. Shoberl. 5 vols. 8vo. Lond., 1838. B 8 S 6–10

THIRLWALL (Connop), D.D., Bishop of St. David's. History of Greece. (Lard. Cab. Cyclo.) 7 vols. 12mo. Lond., 1835–40. K 1 T 18–24

Another copy. 8vols. 8vo. Lond., 1845–55. B 9 T 3–10

History of Rome. [*See* Niebuhr, B. G.] B 12 R 13, 14

Letters, Literary and Theological; edited by the Very Rev. Stewart Perowne, D.D., and the Rev. Louis Stokes, B.A.; with Annotations and preliminary Memoirs by the Rev. Louis Stokes. 8vo. Lond., 1881. C 10 P 38

Letters to a Friend; edited by the Very Rev. Arthur Penrhyn Stanley, D.D. 8vo. Lond., 1881. C 10 P 39

THIRTY-SIX YEARS of a Seafaring Life; by "An Old Quarter-master." 8vo. Portsea, 1839. C 7 R 43

THISTLEWOOD (Arthur). [*See* Trials.]

THOM (Alexander). Official Directory of the United Kingdom of Great Britain and Ireland, for the year 1884. 8vo. Dublin, 1884. E

THOM (John Hamilton). Life of the Rev. Joseph Blanco White. 3 vols. 8vo. Lond., 1845. C 6 P 24–26

THOMAN (Fedor). Interest and Logarithmic Tables. [*See* Lintern, W.] A 6 R 35

Theory of Compound Interest and Annuities; with a Series of Logarithmic Tables. 3rd ed. (Weale.) 12mo. Lond., 1877. A 17 P 53

THOMAS (—.) [*See* Chapman.] MJ 2 R 4

THOMAS (Edward). Ancient Indian Weights. [*See* Numismata Orientalia, 1.] A 2 S 15 †

Chronicles of the Pathán Kings of Delhi, illustrated by Coins, Inscriptions, and other Antiquarian Remains. 8vo. Lond., 1871. B 10 V 23

Essays on Indian Antiquities. [*See* Prinsep, J.] B 10 T 34, 35

THOMAS (Ernest Chester). History of Materialism. [*See* Sange, F. A.]

THOMAS (F. H.) [*See* Sydney Art Gallery.]

THOMAS (FRANCIS SHEPPARD). Historical Notes, 1509–1714. 3 vols. roy. 8vo. Lond., 1856.   K 11 Q 4–6

THOMAS (H.) Guide for Excursionists from the Mainland to Tasmania. 12mo. Melb., 1869.   MD 2 Q 15

Guide to Excursionist between Australia and Tasmania. 12mo. Melb., 1878.   MD 2 Q 16

THOMAS (JENKIN). Jenkini Thomasii, Cambro-Britanni Dissertationes varii Argvmento. 12mo. Altdorfi, 1712.   G 12 R 19

THOMAS (JOHN JONES), B.A. "CARADDAEG." Britannia Antiquissima ; or, a Key to the Philology of History, (Sacred and Profane.) 2nd ed. 8vo. Melb., 1866.   MB 2 R 26

Another copy. 2nd ed. 8vo. Melb., 1866.   K 15 P 34

THOMAS (JOSEPH), M.D., &c. Complete Pronouncing Medical Dictionary. Roy. 8vo. Philad., 1886.   K 9 R 4

THOMAS (MRS. JULIA MARTHA). Murder of. [*See* WEBSTER, CATHERINE.]

THOMAS (JULIAN), "THE VAGABOND." Cannibals and Convicts : Notes of Personal Experience in the Western Pacific. 8vo. Lond., 1886.   MD 4 U 42

Occident and Orient : Sketches on both Sides of the Pacific. Vol. 1. 8vo. Melb., 1882.*   MD 6 P 16

The Vagabond Annual, Christmas 1877 ; dedicated to all Vagabonds in Australia. 7th thousand. 8vo. Sydney, 1877.   MJ 2 S 17

The Vagabond Papers : Sketches of Melbourne Life, in Light and Shade. Series 1–5. 5 vols. 12mo. Melb., 1877–78.   MJ 1 S 16–20

Another copy. Series 1–4 [only]. 4 vols. 12mo. Melb., 1877.   MJ 1 S 21–24

THOMAS (PASCOE). True and Impartial Journal of a Voyage to the South-Seas. and round the Globe, in H.M.S. *Centurion*, under the command of Commodore George Anson. 8vo. Lond., 1745.   D 10 R 30

THOMAS (RALPH), "OLPHAR HAMST." Aggravating Ladies; being a List of Works published under the Pseudonym of "A Lady"; with preliminary Suggestions on the Art of describing Books bibliographically. 8vo. Lond., 1880.   J 11 U 32

Hand-book of Fictitious Names : being a Guide to Authors, chiefly in the Lighter Literature of the 19th Century, who have written under Assumed Names. 8vo. Lond., 1868.   K 17 P 34

THOMAS (T. H.) [*See* SIKES. W. W.]   B 5 S 32

THOMAS (W. G.) On the Death of. [*See* PARLIAMENTARY PAPERS.]

THOMAS (W. K.), & CO. South Australia : an Account of its History, Progress, Resources, and Present Position ; reprinted from *The South Australian Register* of September 5, 1879 ; prepared specially for the Sydney Exhibition. 8vo. Adelaide, 1879.   MF 3 P 22

THOMÉ (OTTO W.) Text-book of Structural and Physiological Botany ; translated and edited by Alfred W. Bennett, M.A. (Text-books of Science.) 12mo. Lond., 1877.   A 17 S 23

THOMES (WILLIAM H.) The Belle of Australia ; or, Who am I ? (Corrected and revised from *Ballou's Monthly Magazine*.) Illustrated. 8vo. Boston, 1883.   MJ 1 R 33

The Bushrangers : a Yankee's Adventures during his Second Visit to Australia. 8vo. Chicago, 1884.   MJ 1 R 34

The Gold-hunter's Adventures ; or, Life in Australia. Illustrated. Chicago, 1886.   MJ 1 R 35

THOMMEREL (J. P.) Recherches sur la Fusion du Franco-Normand et de l'Anglo-Saxon. 8vo. Paris, 1841.   K 15 P 10

THOMPSON (AARON). [*See* GEOFFREY OF MONMOUTH.]

THOMPSON (CHARLES). The Gambler's Fate ; or, a Lapse of Twenty Years : a Drama. (Cumberland's Eng. Theatre.) 12mo. Lond., 1829.   H 2 Q 20

THOMPSON (DANIEL GREENLEAF). System of Psychology. 2 vols. 8vo. Lond., 1884.   G 10 S 1, 2

THOMPSON (CAPT. EDWARD). Life of Andrew Marvell. [*See* MARVELL, A.]   J 7 V 21–23

THOMPSON (EDWARD P.) Austria. 8vo. Lond., 1849.   D 8 Q 28

Life in Russia ; or, the Discipline of Despotism. 8vo. Lond., 1848.

Passions of Animals. 8vo. Lond., 1851.   A 14 R 46

THOMPSON (ELIZA). Wit and Wisdom of Don Quixote ; with a Biographical Sketch. [*See* CERVANTES SAAVEDRA, M. DE.]

THOMPSON (E. M.) [*See* SOPHOCLES.]

THOMPSON (GEORGE A.) Geographical and Historical Dictionary. [*See* ALCEDO, A. DE.]   D 9 R 20–24 †

THOMPSON (GEORGE CARSLAKE). Public Opinion and Lord Beaconsfield. 2 vols. 8vo. Lond., 1886.   F 4 P 7, 8

THOMPSON (HENRY), M.A. Life of Hannah More ; with Notices of her Sisters. 8vo. Lond., 1838.   C 4 P 13

THOMPSON (J.) Electric Telegraphs and Railways between Sydney and London not impossible. (Pam. 20.) 8vo. Sydney, 1855.   MJ 2 Q 9

Another copy. (Pam. 30.) 8vo. Sydney, 1855.   MJ 2 Q 18

THOMPSON (JAMES). New, improved, and authentic Life of James Allan, the celebrated Northumberland Piper. 8vo. Newcastle, 1828.   C 6 P 1

THOMPSON (JOHN), P.H. Shorthand, and how learn it in Twelve Lessons : being Exercises supplementary to "Pitman's Manual of Phonography." 12mo. Edinb., 1875.   K 11 U 24

THOMPSON (JOHN ASHBURTON), M.D. Report, containing Photographs of a Person suffering from Variola Discreta, and an Account of the Case. Fol. Sydney, 1886.　　　MA 1 R 23 ‡

THOMPSON (JOE). Life, Adventures, and Sporting Career of Joe Thompson, the King of the Ring; by "Tip and Tory." 8vo. Melb., 1878.　　　MJ 2 R 12

THOMAS (NATHAN), JUNR. Brief Description of Steam Machinery for building Boats. 8vo. New York, 1860.　　　A 11 U 10

THOMPSON (PATRICK). [*See* SUDDS, J.]

THOMPSON (RICHARD). Report of the Proceedings at the National Banquet, held at the Prince of Wales Theatre, Sydney, on the 17th of July, 1856, to celebrate the Establishment and Inauguration of Responsible Government in the Colony of New South Wales. 8vo. Sydney, 1856.　　　MF 1 Q 6

Another copy. 8vo. Sydney, 1856.　　　MF 3 Q 45

Another copy. 8vo. Sydney, 1856.　　　MJ 2 Q 9

Another copy. 8vo. Sydney, 1856.　　　MJ 2 Q 14

THOMPSON (STEPHEN). Hand-book to the Picture Gallery and Works of Art, Melbourne International Exhibition. 8vo. Melb., 1881.　　　MK 1 P 15

[*See* BRITISH MUSEUM.]　　　A 21 Q 1-9 ‡

THOMPSON (PROF. SILVANUS P.), B.A., &c. Philipp Reis, Inventor of the Telephone : a Biographical Sketch. 8vo. Lond., 1883.　　　C 9 Q 35

THOMPSON (LIEUT.-COL. T. PERRONET). Catechism on the Corn Laws; with a List of Fallacies and the Answers. 18th ed. 8vo. Lond., 1834.　　　F 6 V 10

Exercises, Political, and others. 2nd ed. 12mo. Lond., 1843.　　　F 1 P 24

THOMPSON (WILLIAM). Life and Poems of. [*See* CHALMERS, A.]

THOMPSON (WILLIAM HEPWORTH), M.A. Lectures on the History of Ancient Philosophy. [*See* BUTLER, PROF. W. A.]

THOMPSON (W. M.) The Holy Land, &c. [*See* BEDFORD, F.]　　　D 5 V 28

THOMS (WILLIAM JOHN), F.S.A. Collection of Early Prose Romances; edited by William J. Thoms. 3 vols. 12mo. Lond., 1828.　　　J 11 P 3-5

Hannah Lightfoot; Queen Charlotte and the Chevalier D'Eon; Dr. Wilmot's Polish Princess; reprinted, with some Additions, from *Notes and Queries.* 8vo. Lond., 1867.　　　B 6 P 43

[*See* WORSAAE, DR. J. J. A.]　　　B 2 R 8

THOMSEN (GRIMUR). The Northmen in Iceland : Remarks on a Treatise of George Webbe Dasent, Esq., D.C.L.; translated by Prof. G. Stephens. (Soc. Royale des Antiquaires du Nord.) (Pam. C.) Roy. 8vo. Copenhagen, 1859.　　　MJ 2 S 1

THOMSON (ADAM). Dissapointed Gallant; or, Buckram in Armour: a new Ballad Opera, written by "A Young Scots Gentleman." 12mo. Edinb., 1738.　　　H 1 R 26

THOMSON (ALEXANDER M.), D.Sc. Guide to Mineral Explorers, in distinguishing Minerals, Ores, and Gems. 8vo. Sydney, 1869.　　　MA 2 Q 30

Occurrence of the Diamond near Mudgee. [*See* TAYLOR, N.]

THOMSON (ANTHONY TODD), M.D., &c. Thomson's Conspectus, adapted to the British Pharmacopœia; edited by E. S. Birkett, M.D. New ed. 18mo. Lond., 1874.　　　K 9 P 1

Elements of Materia Medica and Therapeutics, including the recent Discoveries and Analysis of Medicines. 3rd ed. 8vo. Lond., 1843.　　　A 12 U 4

Introductory Lecture to the Course of Medical Jurisprudence. (Univ. of Lond.) 8vo. Lond., 1831.　　　J 5 8 8

London Dispensatory : a practical Synopsis of Materia Medica, Pharmacy, and Therapeutics. 11th ed. 8vo. Lond., 1852.　　　A 12 8 19

Philosophy of Magic. [*See* SALVERTE, E.]　　　A 10 R 3, 4

[*See* QUAIN, DR. J.]

THOMSON (ARTHUR S.), M.D. Story of New Zealand, Past and Present, Savage and Civilised. 2 vols. 8vo. Lond., 1859.*　　　MD 4 R 1, 2

THOMSON (MRS. CATHERINE). Celebrated Friendships. 2 vols. 8vo. Lond., 1861.　　　C 2 U 12, 13

Memoirs of Sarah, Duchess of Marlborough, and of the Court of Queen Anne. 2 vols. 8vo. Lond., 1839.　　　C 7 T 46, 47

THOMSON (MRS. CHARLES). Twelve Years in Canterbury, New Zealand (from a Lady's Journal). 12mo. Lond., 1867.　　　MD 6 P 35

THOMSON (SIR CHARLES WYVILLE), LL.D., &c. Depths of the Sea: an Account of the General Results of the Dredging Cruises of H.M.SS. *Porcupine* and *Lightning,* 1868-70. 8vo. Lond., 1873.　　　A 14 S 46

Voyage of the *Challenger.* The Atlantic: a preliminary Account of the General Results of the Exploring Voyage of H.M.S. *Challenger* during the year 1873, and the early part of the year 1876. 2 vols. 8vo. Lond., 1877.　　　D 9 U 18, 19

THOMSON (SIR C. WYVILLE), LL.D., &c., AND MURRAY (JOHN), F.R.S.E. Report on the Scientific Results of the Voyage of H.M.S. *Challenger* during the years 1873-76; prepared under the superintendence of the late Sir C. Wyville Thomson, Knt., &c., and now of John Murray, F.R.S.E. 31 vols. (in 37) roy. 4to. Lond., 1880-85.　　　A 6 P-R †

Zoology. (26 in 31.)　　　Botany. 2 vols.
Narrative. (2 in 3.)　　　Physics and Chemistry. 1 vol.

THOMSON (CHRISTOPHER). Autobiography of an Artisan. 8vo. Lond., 1847.　　　C 2 T 2

THOMSON (DAVID CROAL). Life and Labours of Hablôt Knight Browne, "Phiz." With 130 Illustrations. 4to. Lond., 1884.   C 2 W 1

Life and Works of Thomas Bewick; being an Account of his Career and Achievements in Art. 4to. Lond., 1882.   C 3 W 9

The Year's Art. [*See* HUISH, M. B.]

THOMSON (SIR EDWARD DEAS), KNT., C.B., &c. Chancellor's Address to the Sydney University, 1875. (Pam. M.) 4to. Sydney, 1875.   MJ 2 S 4

Corrected Report of the Speeches, delivered in the Legislative Legislative Council, on the First and Second Reading of the Bill for the Division of the Colony into Electoral Districts, in the First Session of 1851. 8vo. Sydney, 1851.   MF 3 P 3

Another copy. 8vo. Sydney, 1851.   MJ 2 S 4

Letter to certain Gentlemen interested in the Settlement of Port Phillip. [*See* MANUSCRIPTS AND PORTRAITS.]
                    MF 1 U 21

THOMSON (GEORGE M.), F.L.S. Ferns and Fern Allies of New Zealand; with Instructions for their Collections and Hints on their Cultivation. With five Plates. 8vo. Melb., 1882.   MA 1 V 11

THOMSON (JAMES). Financial Statements of the Colonial Treasuries of New South Wales, from the Introduction of Responsible Government on the 24th November, 1855, to the close of the Parliamentary Session of 1880–81, on the 6th April, 1881. 8vo. Sydney, 1881.*   MF 1 S 11

THOMSON (JAMES), A.M. Vindication of the Presbytery of Van Diemen's Land, and the Presbyterian Community, from the Charges contained in the Pamphlet, in defence of the Proceedings of the Rev. William Hutchins, Archdeacon of Van Diemen's Land. 8vo. Hobart, 1839.
                    MG 1 Q 21

THOMSON (JAMES). Edward and Eleonora: a Tragedy. (Bell's Brit. Theat.) 12mo. Lond., 1808.   H 2 P 4

Essays on the Lives and Writings of Fletcher of Saltoun, and the Poet Thomson, Biographical, Critical, and Political; by D. S., Earl of Buchan. 8vo. Lond., 1792.   C 8 P 9

Life and Poems of. [*See* BRITISH POETS; CHALMERS, A.; *and* JOHNSON, S.]

Poetical Works of; with the Life of the Author, by P. Murdoch, D.D. 12mo. Lond., 1803.   H 7 Q 8

The Seasons; embellished with Engravings on Wood, by Bewick, from Thurston's Designs. 8vo. Lond., 1805.
                    H 8 V 2

Tancred and Sigismunda: a Tragedy. (Bell's Brit. Theatre.) 18mo. Lond., 1792.   H 2 P 21

Another copy. (Brit. Theatre.) 12mo. Lond., 1808.
                    H 1 P 13

Another copy. (New Eng. Theatre.) 12mo. Lond., 1784.   H 1 P 17

Another copy. [*See* BRIT. DRAMA, 2.]

THOMSON (JAMES MAURICE). Registrum Magni Sigilii Regum Scotorum. [*See* SCOTLAND.]
                    B 13 S 18, 19

THOMSON (JOHN), F.R.G.S. Illustrations of China and its People: a Series of Two Hundred Photographs, with Letter-press descriptive of the Places and People represented. 4 vols. (in 2) fol. Lond., 1873–74. D 5 P 23, 24 ‡

Land and People of China: a short Account of the Geography, History, Religion, Social Life, Arts, Industries, and Government of China and its People. With Illustrations. 8vo. Lond., 1876.   D 5 P 43

[*See* DAVILLIER, BARON C.]   D 5 S 1 †

THOMSON (JOHN). New General Atlas of the Globe. At. fol. Edinb., 1827.   D 8 P 3 ‡

THOMSON (JOHN), M.D., &c. Account of the Life, Lectures, and Writings of William Cullen, M.D. 2 vols. 8vo. Edinb., 1859.   C 10 S 33, 34

Historical Sketch of the Opinions entertained by Medical Men respecting the Varieties and the Secondary Occurrence of Small-pox. 8vo. Lond., 1822.   A 12 S 30

THOMSON (JOHN COCKBURN). Queens of Society. [*See* THOMSON, MRS. KATHARINE.]   C 4 V 26, 27

THOMSON (JOHN TURNBULL). Rambles with a Philosopher; or, Views at the Antipodes; by "An Otagonian." 8vo. Dunedin, 1867.   MJ 1 R 27

THOMSON (JOSEPH), F.R.G.S. Through Masái Land: a Journey of Exploration among the Snowclad Volcanic Mountains and Strange Tribes of Eastern Equatorial Africa, 1883–84. 8vo. Lond., 1885.   D 2 S 10

To the Central African Lakes and Back: the Narrative of the Royal Geographical Society's East Central African Expedition, 1878–80; with a short biographical Notice of the late Mr. Keith Johnson, Portraits, and a Map. 2 vols. 8vo. Lond., 1881.   D 1 T 15, 16

THOMSON (JOSEPH T.), F.R.G.S. Translations from the Hakayit Abdulla (Bin Abdulkadar), Múnshi; with Comments. 8vo. Lond., 1874.   C 3 Q 22

THOMSON (MRS. KATHARINE AND JOHN). Queens of Society; by "Grace and Philip Wharton." 2 vols. 8vo. Lond., 1861.   C 4 V 26, 27

THOMSON (MAXWELL). Sketch First, of a Series of Sketches on the Evidence of the Christian Religion, originally delivered as Lectures. 12mo. Sydney, 1848.
                    MG 1 P 49

THOMSON (CAPT. MOWBRAY). The Story of Cawnpore. 8vo. Lond., 1859.   B 10 Q 27

THOMSON (P.) Cabinet-maker's Sketch-book : a Series of original Details for Modern Furniture. Fol. Glasgow, 1860.   A 23 Q 8 ‡

THOMSON (RICHARD). Chronicles of London Bridge: by
"An Antiquary." 8vo. Lond., 1827. B 4 P 7
Historical Essay on the Magna Charta of King John;
to which are added, the Great Charter, in Latin and
English, &c. 8vo. Lond., 1829. F 4 P 9
Illustrations of the History of Great Britain : an His-
torical View of the Manners and Customs, &c., of Great
Britain: (Const. Misc.) 2 vols. 18mo. Edinb., 1828.
K 10 Q 8, 9

THOMSON (ROBERT). Descriptive Catalogue of Collection
from Jamaica to Philadelphia International Exhibition,
1876. 8vo. Kingston, 1876. K 7 R 36

THOMSON (ROBERT DUNDAS), M.D., &c. Cyclopædia of
Chemistry ; with its Applications to Mineralogy, Physiology, and the Arts. 8vo. Lond., 1854. K 5 U 12

THOMSON (SPENCER), M.D., &c. Dictionary of Domestic
Medicine and Household Surgery. thoroughly revised and
brought down to the Present State of Medical Science;
with a Chapter on the Management of the Sick-room.
8vo. Lond,, 1866. K 9 Q 22

THOMSON (THOMAS), M.D., &c. Brewing and Distillation;
with Practical Instructions, by W. Stewart. 8vo. Edinb.,
1849. A 11 Q 26
System of Chemistry. 6th ed. 4 vols. 8vo. Lond.,
1820. A 6 P 10–13
[*See* ANNALS OF PHILOSOPHY.]

THOMSON (REV. THOMAS). Biographical Dictionary of
Eminent Scotsmen. [*See* CHAMBERS, R.] C 11 S 1–5
History of the Kirk of Scotland. [*See* CALDERWOOD, D.]
Life of James Hogg. [*See* HOGG, J.]

THOMSON (T. R. H.) Expedition to the River Niger.
[*See* ALLEN, CAPT. W.] D 2 T 13, 14

THOMSON (WILLIAM), F.R.C.S., &c. Bacon, not Shakespeare. 8vo. Melb., 1881. MH 1 S 21
Contagion alone the Cause of Typhoid Fever in Melbourne. 8vo. Melb.. 1880. MA 2 S 37
Digest of the Return, ordered by the Legislative Council,
of all the Deaths (2,143) from Phthisis in Melbourne and
Suburbs, during the years 1865–69, and first half of 1870,
forming a Sequel to the "Essay on Phthisis, &c." 8vo.
Melb., 1871. MA 2 S 37
Histochemistry and Pathogeny of Tubercle. 8vo. Melb.,
1876. MA 2 S 37
Not Man, but Man-like: a Reply to "Not like Man," of
the Professor of Anatomy in the University of Mel-
bourne. 8vo. Melb., 1874. MJ 2 R 12
On Phthisis and the supposed Influence of Climate;
being an Analysis of Statistics of Consumption in this
part of Australia. 8vo. Melb., 1879. MA 2 S 12
On Renascence Drama; or, History made Visible. 8vo.
Melb., 1880. MH 1 S 21
Political Allegories in the Renascence Drama of Francis
Bacon. 8vo. Melh., 1882. MH 1 S 21
Remarks on a Review of the Report on the Cause and
Extent of Typhoid Fever in Melbourne. 8vo. Melb.,
1879. MA 2 S 37

THOMSON (WILLIAM), F.R.C.S., &c.—*continued.*
Third Analysis of the Statistics of Phthisis in Victoria.
8vo. Melb., 1877. MA 2 S 12
Transversalis Pedis in the Foot of the Gorilla. 8vo.
Melb. (n.d.) MA 2 S 38
Typhoid Fever ; its Cause and Extent in Melbourne,
based on the Report of an Inquiry made by special request
of the Central Board of Health. 3rd ed., revised. 8vo.
Melb., 1878. MA 2 S 11
Another copy. 8vo. Melb., 1878. MA 2 S 37
William Shakespeare in Romance and Reality. 8vo.
Melh., 1881. MH 1 S 21

THOMSON (WILLIAS). Practical Treatise on the Cultivation of the Grape-vine. 8th ed., enlarged. 8vo. Edinb.,
1875. A 1 R 8

THOMSON (SIR WILLIAM), LL.D., &c. Electro-dynamic
Qualities of Metals. Part 6. Effects of Stress on Mag-
netization. (Roy. Soc. Pubs., 4.) 4to. Lond., 1876.
A 11 P 5 †
Mathematical and Physical Papers, collected from dif-
ferent Scientific Periodicals, from May, 1841 to the Present
Time. 2 vols. 8vo. Camb., 1882–84. A 10 U 23, 24
Notes of Lectures on Molecular Dynamics and the Wave
Theory of Light, delivered at the Johns Hopkins Univer-
sity, Baltimore. 4to. Baltimore, Md., 1884. A 15 U 7

THOMSON (WILLIAM M.), D.D. The Land and the Book:
Southern Palestine and Jerusalem. Sq. 8vo. Lond.,
1881. D 5 T 1
The Land and the Book : Central Palestine and Phœnicia. Sq. 8vo. Lond., 1883. D 5 T 2

THORBURN (GRANT). Forty Years' Residence in America;
or, the Doctrine of a particular Providence exemplified
in the Life of Grant Thorburn (the original Lawrie Todd).
12mo. Lond., 1834. C 1 R 36

THORBURN (S. S.) Bannú; or, Our Afghan Frontier.
8vo. Lond., 1876. B 10 T 6

THORBURN (MAJOR W. STEWART). Guide to the Coins
of Great Britain and Ireland, in Gold, Silver, and Copper,
with their Value. With Illustrations. 8vo. Lond.,
1884. A 13 S 25

THORESBY (RALPH), F.R.S. Diary of (1677–1724); now
first published from original Manuscript, by the Rev. Joseph
Hunter, F.S.A. 2 vols. 8vo. Lond., 1830. C 9 Q 43, 44
Ducatis Leodiensis ; or, the Topography of the Ancient
and Populous Town and Parish of Leedes. 2nd ed., with
Notes and Additions, &c. (and Life of the Author), by
T. D. Whitaker. Fol. Leeds, 1816. C 9 U 6 ‡
Letters of Eminent Men addressed to Ralph Thoresby,
F.R.S.; now first published from the Originals. 2 vols.
8vo. Lond., 1832. C 9 Q 45, 46

THORKELIN (GRIM JOHNSON), LL.D., &c. De Danorum
Rebus Gestis Secul. III et IV : Poëma Danicum Dialecto
Anglo-saxonica. 4to. Havniæ, 1815. H 6 U 19

THORNBURY (GEORGE WALTER). Shakspere's England; or, Sketches of our Social History in the Reign of Elizabeth. 2 vols. 8vo. Lond., 1856. B 4 R 27, 28

Criss-cross Journeys. 2 vols. 8vo. Lond., 1873. D 10 Q 25, 26

Haunted London, illustrated by F. W. Fairholt. 8vo. Lond., 1865. B 7 P 28

Life of J. M. W. Turner, R.A. 2 vols. 8vo. Lond., 1862. C 9 U 49, 50

THORNBURY (GEORGE WALTER), AND WALFORD (EDWARD). Old and New London : a Narrative of its History, its People, and its Places. Illustrated. 6 vols. 4to. Lond., 1873–78. B 3 U 1–6

THORNE (CHARLES). Silk Culture. [*See* BRADY, C.]

THORNE (E.) The Queen of the Colonies; or, Queensland as I knew it; by "An Eight Years' Resident." 8vo. Lond., 1876.* MD 4 V 6

THORNE (JAMES), F.S.A. Hand-book to the Environs of London. [*See* MURRAY, J.]

THORNHILL (GEORGIANA E.) Brief Memoir of; by Antoinette Powle. (Pam. 42.) 8vo. Hobart, 1853. MJ 2 R 4

THORNHILL (MARK). Personal Adventures and Experiences of a Magistrate during the Rise, Progress, and Suppression of the Indian Mutiny. 8vo. Lond., 1884. B 10 Q 46

THORNTON (EDWARD). Chapters of the Modern History of British India. 8vo. Lond., 1840. B 10 R 13

Gazetteer of the Territories under the Government of the East India Company, and of the Native States of the Continent of India. 8vo. Lond., 1857. D 11 T 15

Gazetteer of the Territories under the Government of the Viceroy of India; revised and edited by Sir Roper Lethbridge, C.I.E., and Arthur M. Wollaston, C.I.E. 8vo. Lond., 1886. D 11 T 16

History of the British Empire in India. 6 vols. 8vo. Lond., 1841–45. B 10 R 14–19

India; its State and Prospects. 8vo. Lond., 1835. B 10 It 12

THORNTON (PERCY M.) Foreign Secretaries of the 19th Century. 3 vols. 8vo. Lond., 1881–82. C N Q 11–13

Harrow School and its Surroundings. 8vo. Lond., 1885. B 6 S 15

THORNTON (ROBERT JOHN), M.D. New Family Herbal; or, Popular Account of the Natures and Properties of the various Plants used in Medicine, Diet, and the Arts. The Plants drawn from Nature, by Henderson; and engraved on Wood by Thomas Bewick. 8vo. Lond., 1810. A 5 P 28

New Illustration of the Sexual System of Carolus von Linnæus; comprehending an Elucidation of the several Parts of the Fructification; a Prize Dissertation on the Sexes of Plants, &c. At. fol. Lond., 1807. A 11 P 18 ‡

THORNTON (THOMAS). History of China, from the Earliest Records to the Treaty with Great Britain in 1842. Vol. 1 (*all published*). 8vo. Lond., 1844. B 2 Q 7

History of the Punjab, and the Rise, Progress, and Present Condition of the Sect and Nation of the Sikhs. 2 vols. 8vo. Lond., 1846. B 10 Q 44, 45

THORNTON (WILLIAM THOMAS), C.B. Indian Public Works, and cognate Indian Topics. 8vo. Lond., 1875. F 5 8 5

On Labour ; its Wrongful Claims and Rightful Dues, its actual Present and Possible Future. 8vo. Lond., 1869. F 4 8 7

THOROTON (ROBERT), M.D. Antiquities of Nottinghamshire ; republished, with Additions, by John Throsby. 2nd ed. 3 vols. 4to. Nottingham, 1790–97. B 6 V 22–25

THORPE (BENJAMIN). Cædmon's Paraphrase of Parts of the Holy Scriptures. [*See* CÆDMON, SAINT.]

Catalogue of the Library of the late Benjamin Thorpe. Lond. (n.d.)

Diplomatarium Anglicum Ævi Saxonici : a Collection of English Charters, from the Reign of King Æthelberth, of Kent, A.D. 605, to that of William the Conqueror. 8vo. Lond., 1865. F 4 S 11

Grammar of the Anglo-Saxon Tongue. [*See* RASK, PROF. E.]

Northern Mythology ; comprising the principal Popular Traditions and Superstitions of Scandinavia, North Germany, and the Netherlands. 3 vols. 8vo. Lond., 1851–52. B 9 S 3–5

Yule-Tide Stories: a Collection of Scandinavian and North German Popular Tales and Traditions, from the Swedish, Danish, and German. 8vo. Lond., 1875. B 20 Q 15

THORPE (MRS. MARY). Letters from Italy. [*See* LAVELEYE, E. DE.] D 9 Q 10

THORPE (PROF. T. E.), PH.D., &c. Absorption-Spectra of Bromide, &c. [*See* ROSCOE H. E.] A 11 P 5 †

Manual of Inorganic Chemistry. New ed. 2 vols. 8vo. Lond., 1877. A 5 R 6, 7

Quantitative Chemical Analysis. (Text-books of Science.) 8vo. Lond., 1873. A 17 S 13, 14

THORPE (PROF. T. E.), F.R.S., AND MUIR (M. M. P.) Qualitative Chemical Analysis and Laboratory Practice. 12mo. Lond., 1874. A 17 S 15

Another copy. 4th ed. 12mo. Lond., 1886. A 5 R 29

THORPE (PROF. T. E.), AND RÜCKER (PROF. A. W.), M.A. On the Expansion of Sea-water by Heat. (Roy. Soc. Pubs., 3.) 4to. Lond., 1876. A 11 P 4 †

THORPE (WILLIAM). Writings and Examinations of. [*See* BRITISH REFORMERS, 12.]

THORVALDSEN (BERTEL): his Life and Works ; by E. Plon ; translated by Mrs. Cashel Hoey. Illustrated. 8vo. Lond., 1874. C 8 V 41

THOUGHTS ON THE VALLEY; by "Viator." 8vo.
Melb. (n.d.) MG 1 Q 39

THOYRAS (P. DE RAPIN DE). [*See* RAPIN DE THOYRAS,
P. DE.]

THRASHER (J. S.) Island of Cuba. [*See* HUMBOLDT,
F. H. A. VON, BARON.] D 3 Q 60

THREE IRISH GLOSSARIES: Cormac's Glossary, Codex A (from a Manuscript in the Library of the Royal
Irish Academy); O'Davoren's Glossary (from a Manuscript
in the Library of the British Museum); and a Glossary
to the Calendar of Oingus, the Culdee (from a Manuscript
in the Library of Trinity College, Dublin); with a Preface
and Index, by W. S. 8vo. Lond., 1862. K 13 R 8

THREE WEEKS in Palestine and Lebanon. 8th ed.
12mo. Lond., 1839. D 5 P 21

THRELKELD (L. E.) Appeal to Common Sense; being a
Comparison of Mohammed and the Pope with the Messiah.
8vo. Lond., 1841. MG 1 Q 29

Australian Grammar; comprehending the Principles
and Natural Rules of the Language, as spoken by the
Aborigines in the vicinity of Hunter's River, Lake Macquarie, &c., New South Wales. 8vo. Sydney, 1834.
MK 1 Q 28

Key to the Structure of the Aboriginal Language spoken
by the Aborigines in the vicinity of Hunter River, Lake
Macquarie, N.S.W., &c. 8vo. Sydney, 1850.* MK 1 Q 28

[*See* ABORIGINES.]

THRESH (JOHN C.), F.C.S. Physics, Experimental and
Mathematical: a Hand-book for the Physical Laboratory,
and for Students preparing for the Science Examinations
of the London University. 12mo. Lond.(n.d.) A 16 P 19

THRING (REV. E.), M.A. On the Principles of Grammar.
(Clar. Press.) 12mo. Oxford, 1868. K 16 P 46

Exercises in Grammatical Analysis. (Clar. Press.)
12mo. Oxford, 1868. K 16 P 46

THROOP (M. H.) Civil Procedure of New York. 12mo.
Albany, 1885. F 1 T 7

THRUM (THOMAS G.) [*See* HAWAIIAN ALMANAC.]

THRUPP (JOHN). The Anglo-Saxon Home: a History of
the Domestic Institutions and Customs of England, from the
5th to the 11th Century. 8vo. Lond., 1862. B 5 S 23

THUCYDIDES. Analysis and Summary of Thucydides.
[*See* WHEELER, J. T.] B 9 S 15

De Bello Peloponnesiaco, libri octo, Græce et Latine, ad
Editionem Ios. Wasse, et Car. Andr. Dukeri. 6 vols. 8vo.
Biponti, 1788–89. B 9 S 38–43

History of the Peloponnesian War (Greek Text), illustrated by Maps; with Notes by Thomas Arnold, D.D.
7th ed. 3 vols. 8vo. Oxford, 1868. B 10 P 18–20

THUCYDIDES—*continued.*
Peloponnesian War; translated by William Smith, D.D.
(Fam. Class. Lib.) 3 vols. 18mo. Lond., 1831. J 15 P 46–48

Sicilian Expedition; being Books 6 and 7 of Thucydides;
with Notes, by the Rev. Percival Frost, M.A. 12mo.
Lond., 1877. B 9 S 14

Thucydides; translated into English, with an Introduction, &c., by B. Jowett. 2 vols. 8vo. Oxford, 1881.
B 9 V 19, 20

THUDICHUM (J. L. W.), M.D. On Wines; their Production, Treatment, and Use. (Cant. Lect., 9.) Roy.
8vo. Lond., 1873. A 15 U 21

THUDICHUM (J. L. W.), M.D., AND DUPRÉ (AUGUST),
PH.D. Treatise on the Origin, Nature, and Varieties of
Wine; being a complete Manual of Viticulture and Œnology.
Roy. 8vo. Lond., 1872. A 1 R 5

THUNBERG (CHARLES PETER), M.D. Flora Japonica,
sistens Plantas Insularum Japonicarum. 8vo. Lipsiæ,
1784. A 4 T 11

Travels in Europe, Africa, and Asia, made between the
years 1770–79. 3rd ed. 4 vols. 8vo. Lond., 1795–96.
D 10 R 7–10

THURBER (FRANCIS B.) Coffee; from Plantation to Cup:
a brief History of Coffee Production and Consumption.
8vo. New York, 1881. A 1 S 24

THURET (GUSTAVE), ET BORNET (DR. E.) Études Phycologiques: Analyses d'Algues Marines. Fol. Paris,
1878. A 23 Q 13 ‡

THURLOE (RT. HON. JOHN). Collection of the State
Papers of John Thurloe, Esq., Secretary to the Council,
of State, &c.; with a Life by T. Birch. 7 vols. fol.
Lond., 1742. B 18 T 1–7 ‡

THURN (EVERARD F. IM), M.A. Among the Indians of
Guiana; being Sketches, chiefly Anthropologic, from the
Interior of British Guiana. With Illustrations. 8vo.
Lond., 1883. D 4 Q 15

THURNEYSEN (RUDOLPHUS). Indices Glossarum et
Vocabulorum Hibernicorum. [*See* GÜTERBOCK, B.]

THURSTON (GEORGE H.) Pittsburgh and Allegheny in
the Centennial Year. 8vo. Pittsburgh, 1876. F 5 U 9

THURSTON (PROF. ROBERT H.), C.E., &c. Friction and
Lubrication: Determinations of the Laws and Co-Efficients
of Friction by new Methods and with new Apparatus.
8vo. Lond., 1879. A 11 Q 17

Materials of Engineering. 3 vols. 8vo. New York,
1883–84. A 6 T 1–3

Report on Copper-Tin Alloys. [*See* UNITED STATES.]
A 9 T 35

Report on Machinery and Manufactures; with an Ac-
count of European Manufacturing Districts. (Vienna
International Exhibition, 1873.) 8vo. Wash., 1875.
A 11 T 9

Stationary Steam-engines, especially as adapted to Electric
Lighting Purposes. 8vo. New York, 1884. A 11 P 22

THYER (ROBERT) Genuine Poetical Remains of Samuel Butler ; with Notes. [*See* BUTLER, S.]

TIBBINS (PROF. J.) [*See* FLEMING, PROF. C.] K 3 8 1, 2 †

TIBETAN TALES, derived from Indian Sources ; translated from the Tibetan of Kah-Gyur, by F. A. von Schiefner ; done into English from the German, with an Introduction, by W. R. S. Ralston, M.A. 8vo. Lond., 1882. B 20 S 2

TIBULLUS (ALBIUS). Albii Tibvlli Carmina, Libri tres cvm Libro qvarto svlpiciae, et aliorvm. Novis cvris castigavit Chr. G. Heyne. Editio altera, emendatior, et avctior. 8vo. Lipsiae, 1777. H 7 T 15

Erotica : the Poems of Catullus and Tibullus, and the Vigil of Venus : a literal Prose Translation ; with Notes by Walter K. Kelly. 8vo. Lond., 1878. H 3 T 50

Opera omnia, ex editione I. G. Huschkii, cum Notis et Interpretatione in usum Delphini. 2 vols. 8vo. Lond., 1822. J 13 T 5, 6

TICHBORNE ROMANCE (THE). Full and accurate Report of the Proceedings in the extraordinary and interesting Trial of Tichborne 1. Lushington, in the Court of Common Pleas, Westminster. (*Curious Trials.*) 8vo. Manchester, 1871. MF 2 R 19

Another copy. 8vo. Manchester, 1871. F 9 P 19

Another copy. 8vo. Manchester, 1871. F 13 R 1

TICHBORNE TRIAL (THE). Charge of the Lord Chief Justice of England in the Case of the Queen against Thomas Castro, otherwise Arthur Orton, otherwise Sir Roger Tichborne ; reprinted from the Official Copy taken from the Shorthand Writer's Notes ; corrected by the Lord Chief Justice. 2 vols. roy. 8vo. Lond.,1874-75. F 5 V 20, 21

Summing-up by the Lord Chief Justice of England ; together with the Addresses of the Judges, the Verdict, and the Sentence ; the whole accompanied by a History of the Case, and copious Alphabetical Index. 8vo. Lond., 1874. F 9 P 20

Another copy. (Pam. 8.) 8vo. Lond.,1874. F 13 R 1

Trial at Bar of Sir Roger C. D. Tichborne, Bart., in the Court of Queen's Bench at Westminster, before Lord Chief Justice Cockburn, Mr. Justice Mellor, and Mr. Justice Lush, for Perjury ; edited by Dr. Kenealy, M.P. 9 vols. fol. Lond., 1875-80. F 7 P 13-21 †

TICKELL (THOMAS). Works of J. Addison. [*See* ADDISON, J.] J 8 S 20-25

Life and Poems of. [*See* CHALMERS, A., *and* JOHNSON, S.]

TICKNOR (GEORGE). History of Spanish Literature. 3 vols. 8vo. Lond., 1849. B 13 T 18-20

Life, Letters, and Journals of. [Edited by G. S. Hillard, LL.D.] 2 vols. 8vo. Boston, 1876. C 9 R 34, 35

Report on the Bequests of G. Ticknor to the Boston Public Library. [*See* BOSTON PUBLIC LIBRARY.]

TIDMAN (PAUL F.) Gold and Silver Money. Part 1. A Plain Statement. Part 2. Objections answered. 8vo. Lond., 1882. F 5 S 26

TIECK (FRIEDRICH). Verzeichniss der antiken Bildhauerwerke des königlichen Museums zu Berlin. 8vo. Berlin, 1834. A 7 Q 21

TIECK (LUDWIG). Phantasus : eine sammlung von Mährchen, erzahlungen und Schauspielen. 2e auf. 3 vols. 8vo. Berlin, 1844-45. J 16 P 40-42

Tales by Musaeus, Tieck, Richter ; translated from the German, by Thomas Carlyle. 2 vols. 12mo. Lond.,1874. J 1 T 11, 12

TIELE (DR. C. P.) History of the Egyptian Religion ; translated from the Dutch, with the co-operation of the Author, by James Ballingall. 8vo. Lond., 1882. G 15 P 17

Outlines of the History of Religion, to the Spread of the the Universal Religions ; translated from the Dutch, by J. Estlin Carpenter, M.A. 8vo. Lond., 1877. G 9 S 18

TIERNEY (REV. M. A.), F.S.A. History and Antiquities of the Castle and Town of Arundel, including the Biography of its Earls, from the Conquest to the Present Time. 2 vols. roy. 8vo. Lond., 1834. B 3 V 1, 2

Church History of England. [*See* DODD, C.]

TIERNEY (SIR MATTHEW JOHN), BART., &c. Observation, on the Variola Vaccina, or Cow-pock, including a Statement of the formation of the first County Vaccine Institution, established in Sussex in 1804. 12mo. Brighton, 1845. A 12 P 2

TIGHE (MRS. HENRY). Psyche ; or, the Legend of Love : a Poem, in Six Cantos. [*See* APULEIUS, L.] J 16 T 23

TIGHE (ROBERT RICHARD), AND DAVIS (JAMES EDWARD). Annals of Windsor ; being a History of the Castle and Town, with some Account of Eton, and Places adjacent. 2 vols. roy. 8vo. Lond., 1858. B 2 T 39, 40

TILDEN (WILLIAM A.), F.C.S., &c. Introduction to the Study of Chemical Philosophy. (Text-books of Science.) 8vo. Lond., 1876. A 17 S 20

TILLEMONT (LOUIS SEBASTIAN LENAIN DE). Histoire des Empereurs, et des autres Princes, qui ont regné durant les premiers siècles de l'Eglise, &c. ; justifiée par les citations des Auteurs originaux. 6 vols. 4to. Paris, 1720-38. G 5 S 17-22

Mémoires pour servir à l'Histoire ecclésiastique des six premiers siècles. 2e éd. 16 vols. 4to. Paris, 1701-14. G 5 T 4-19

TILLEY (ARTHUR). Literature of the French Renaissance : an Introductory Essay. 8vo. Camb., 1885. B 9 P 1

TILLEY (HENRY ARTHUR). Japan, the Amoor, and the Pacific. With Illustrations. 8vo. Lond.,1861. D 5 S 19

TILLINGHAST (W. H.) Epitome of History. [*See* PLOETZ, C.] B 14 Q 24

TILLOTSON (JOHN). Picturesque Scenery in Wales. Illustrated. 4to. Lond., 1860.　　　　　　　　D 8 U 36

TILLOTSON (JOHN), D.D., ARCHBISHOP OF CANTERBURY. Works of; published from the Originals, by Ralph Barker. 3 vols. fol. Lond., 1735.　　　　　　　G 7 Q 14–17 †
Works of; containing Sermons on several subjects and occasions. 12 vols. 8vo. Lond., 1742–44.　G 14 S 1–12

TILLY (ALEXANDRE DE), COMTE. Mémoires. [*See* BARRIÈRE, J. F., 25.]　　　　　　　　　　C 1 T 25

TILTON (C. ROLLIN-). Morocco. [*See* AMICIS, E. DE.]　　　　　　　　　　　　　　　　D 2 U 2

TIMÆUS, THE SOPHIST. Lexicon vocum Platonicarum. [*See* MŒRIS ATTICISTA.]　　　　　　K 11 S 45

TIMBS (JOHN), F.S.A. Abbeys, Castles, and Ancient Halls of England and Wales; their Legendary Lore and Popular History; re-edited, revised, and enlarged by Alexander Gunn. 3 vols. 8vo. Lond., 1872–79.　　B 3 Q 5–7
Anecdote Biography: William Hogarth, Sir Joshua Reynolds, Thomas Gainsborough, Henry Fuseli, Sir Thomas Lawrence, and J. M. W. Turner. 8vo. Lond., 1860.　　　　　　　　　　　　　　　C 1 S 5
Anecdote Biography: William Pitt, Earl of Chatham, and Edmund Burke. 8vo. Lond., 1860.　C 1 S 6
Anecdote Lives of the later Wits and Humourists: Canning, Captain Morris, Curran, Coleridge, Lamb, Charles Mathews, Talleyrand, Jerrold, Rogers, Albert Smith, Hood, Maginn, Thackeray, Dickens, Poole, Leigh Hunt, Father Prout, &c. 2 vols. 8vo. Lond., 1874.　C 4 R 8, 9
Century of Anecdote, 1760–1860. 8vo. Lond. (n.d.)　　　　　　　　　　　　　　　　B 14 P 25
Clubs and Club-life in London; with Anecdotes of its famous Coffee-houses, Hostelries, and Taverns, from the 17th Century to the Present Time. 8vo. Lond., 1872.　　　　　　　　　　　　　　　　B 4 P 11
Curiosities of London, exhibiting the most rare and remarkable Objects of Interest in the Metropolis; with nearly Fifty Years' Personal Recollections. 12mo. Lond., 1855.　　　　　　　　　　　　　　D 11 Q 1
Doctors and Patients; or, Anecdotes of the Medical World, and Curiosities of Medicine. 2 vols. 8vo. Lond., 1873.　　　　　　　　　　　　A 13 P 18, 19
English Eccentrics and Eccentricities. 2 vols. 8vo. Lond., 1866.　　　　　　　　　　C 4 S 34, 35
London and Westminster, City and Suburb: Strange Events, Characteristics, and Changes of Metropolitan Life. 2 vols. 8vo. Lond., 1868.　　　B 4 Q 3, 4
Painting popularly explained. [*See* GULLICK, T. J.]
Romance of London: Strange Stories, Scenes, and Remarkable Persons of the Great Town. 2 vols. 12mo. Lond. (n.d.)　　　　　　　　　　　J 1 U 36, 37
Something for Everybody [and a Garland for the Year: a Book for House and Home]. 12mo. Lond., 1865.　　　　　　　　　　　　　　　　J 10 Q 34
Things not generally known: Curiosities of History, with new Lights. 12mo. Lond., 1857.　　B 14 P 45

5 c

TIMBS (JOHN), F.S.A.—*continued.*
Things not generally known: Curiosities of Science, Past and Present: a Book for Old and Young. [1st and] 2nd series. 5th ed. 2 vols. (in 1) 8vo. Lond., 1875.　　　　　　　　　　　　　　　A 16 P 1
Things not generally known familiarly explained: Curiosities of Science. 2nd series. 12mo. Lond., 1860.　　　　　　　　　　　　　　A 17 T 11
Things not generally known: Popular Errors explained and illustrated. New ed. 12mo. Lond., 1858.　A 17 T 12
Year-book of Facts in Science and Art, exhibiting the most important Discoveries and Improvements of the past years. 33 vols. 12mo. Lond., 1842–74.　　E
Year-book of Facts in the Great International Exhibitions of 1851 and 1862; their Origin and Progress, and Constructive Details of the Buildings, &c. 2 vols. 12mo. Lond., 1851–62.　　　　　　　　　　　E

TIMES (THE), for the 3rd October, 1798 (No. 4,298). [*Re printed.*] Fol. Lond., 1798.　　　　　　　E
Reprint from the *Times:* the Annual Summaries for a Quarter of a Century. 12mo. Lond., 1876.　E 2.21
The *Times* (weekly edition), for 1882–84. 3 vols. fol. Lond., 1882–84.　　　　　　　　　　E
The *Times* Register of Events in 1880–84. 5 vols. 8vo. Lond., 1881–85.　　　　　　　　　　E 2.21
Index to the *Times*, newspaper. [*See* PALMER, S.]

TIMOLEON. Life of. [*See* PLUTARCH.]

TIMON. [*See* CORMENIN, VISCOUNT DE.]

TIMPERLEY (C. H.) Encyclopædia of Literary and Typographical Anecdote, illustrative of the History of Literature and Printing. 2nd ed. Roy. 8vo. Lond., 1842.　　　　　　　　　　　　K 4 S 18

TIMPSON (REV. THOMAS). British Ecclesiastical History. 8vo. Lond., 1838.　　　　　　　　G 7 T 4
Memoirs of Mrs. Elizabeth Fry, including a History of her Labours in promoting the Reformation of Female Prisoners, and the Improvement of British Seamen. 8vo. Lond., 1847.　　　　　　　　C 3 S 45

TINDAL (N.) [*See* RAPIN DE THOYRAS, P. DE.]

TINDAL (WILLIAM). [*See* TYNDALE, W.]

TINGLE (JAMES). Country Directory and Gazetteer of New South Wales. [*See* SANDS, J.]

TINNE (J. ERNEST), M.A. Wonderland of the Antipodes; and other Sketches of Travel in the North Island of New Zealand. Roy. 8vo. Lond., 1873.　　MD 3 V 6

TINTORETTO (JACOPO ROBUSTI). Relation between Michael Angelo and Tintoret: Lectures on Sculpture; by John Ruskin. Orpington, 1879.　　　A 8 Q 32
Tintoretto; by W. R. Osler. (Great Artists.) 8vo. Lond., 1879.　　　　　　　　　　C 3 T 36

TIP AND TONY. [*See* THOMPSON, J.]

TIRABOSCHI (GIROLAMO). Stoiia della Letteiatuia Italiana. 16 vols. 8vo. Fiieize, 1805–13. B 30 T 7–22

TISCHENDORF (LOBEGOTT FRIEDRICH CONSTANTIN DE). Vetus Testamentum Giæca juxta LXX Inteipietes. [*See* BIBLES—GREEK.] G 10 S 8, 9

TISSANDIER (G.) Histoiy and Hand-book of Photogiaphy; edited by J. Thomson, F.R.G.S. Illustiated. 8vo. Lond., 1876. A 6 V 3

Royal Tieasuie-house of Knowledge: a Book of plain and healthful Studies, pleasing Expeiiments, and attiactive Pastimes, foi Family Amusement and Home Cultuie. Roy. 8vo. Sydney, 1887.* MA 2 V 19

Travels in the Aii. [*See* GLAISHER, J.] D 9 U 29

TISSOT (S. A.), M.D., &c. L'Onanisme: Dissertation sui les Maladies pioduits pai la Masturbation. 12mo. Lausanne, 1774. A 12 P 25

Practical Obseivations on the Small-pox, Apoplexy, and Diopsy, in a Seiies of Letteis to the Most Noble and Illustiious, Albeit Hallei. 8vo. Lond., 1772. A 12 S 28

TISSOT (VICTOR). Russians and Geimans; tianslated fiom Fieich, by Stephen L. Simeon. 8vo. Lond., 1882. B 12 U 13

TITCOMB (TIMOTHY). [*See* HOLLAND, J. G.]

TITE (WILLIAM), F.R.S., &c. Account of the Discoveiy of a Tessellated Pavement, 1854, undei the Vaults of the south-eastein aiea of the late Excise Office. Roy. 4to. Lond., 1853. B 18 S 5 ‡

TITIAN (TIZIANO VECELLIO). Life of; with Anecdotes of Distinguished Peisons of his Time, by J. Noithcote. 2 vols. 8vo. Lond., 1830. C 8 S 47, 48

Notices of the Life and Woiks of; by Sii A. Hume. 8vo. Lond., 1829. C 10 P 37

Titian: his Life and Times; with some Account of his Family, by J. A. Ciowe, and G. B. Cavalcaselle. 2 vols. 8vo. Lond., 1877. C 8 S 49, 50

Titian; by R. F. Heath, B.A. (Gieat Aitists.) 8vo. Lond., 1879. C 3 T 36

TITMARSH (MICHAEL ANGELO). [*See* THACKERAY. W. M.]

TITSINGH (ISAAC). Illustiations of Japan: Memoiis and Anecdotes, Desciiption of Feasts and Ceiemonies, Maiiiages and Funeials, &c. 4to. Lond., 1822. B 14 R 17 ‡

Nipon o dai itsi ran; ou, Annales des Empeieuis du Japon; tiaduites pai M. Isaac Titsingh, accompagné d'un Apeiçu de l'Histoiie Mythologique du Japon, pai J. Klapioth. 4to. Pajis, 1834. B 17 Q 12 ‡

TIZIANO VECELLIO. [*See* TITIAN.]

TOBIN (JOHN). The Honey Moon: a Comedy. (Biit. Theatre.) 12mo. Lond., 1808. H 1 P 25

The School foi Authois: a Comedy. [*See* FARCES, 7.]

TOCQUEVILLE (ALEXIS DE). Coiiespondence and Conveisations with Nassau W. Senioi, 1834–59; edited by M. C. M. Simpson. 2 vols. 8vo. Lond.,1872. C 5 P 1, 2

Demociacy in Ameiica; tianslated by H. Reeve. 2 vols. 8vo. Lond., 1862. F 4 S 1, 2

Memoii, Letteis, and Remains of; tianslated fiom the Fiench, with laige Additions. 2 vols. 8vo. Camb., 1861. C 5 P 3, 4

On the State of Society in Fiance befoie the Revolution of 1789, and on the Causes which led to that Event; tianslated by Heniy Reeve, D.C.L. 2nd ed., with seven additional Chapteis. 8vo. Lond., 1873. B 8 U 32

Peintentiaiy System in the United States. [*See* BEAUMONT, G. DE.]

TODD (ALPHEUS). On Pailiamentaiy Goveinment in England; its Oiigin, Development, and piactical Opeiation. 2 vols. 8vo. Lond., 1867–69. F 4 P 18, 19

Pailiamentaiy Goveinment in the Biitish Colonies. 8vo. Lond., 1880. MF 2 R 2

TODD (CHARLES BURR). Life and Letteis of Joel Bailow, LL.D., Poet, Statesman, and Philosophei. 8vo. New York, 1886. C 10 R 13

TODD (REV. HENRY JOHN), M.A., &c. Some Account of the Life of [Edmund] Speisei. [*See* SPENSER, E.]

Dictionaiy of the English Laiguage. [*See* JOHNSON, S.]

Memoiis of the Life and Writings of the Rt. Rev. Biian Walton, D.D.; to which is added, Di. Walton's own Vindication of the London Polyglot. 2 vols. 8vo. Lond., 1821. G 10 S 6, 7

Vindication of oui Authoiized Tianslation and Tianslatois of the Bible. 8vo. Lond., 1819. G 10 R 8

TODD (PROF. JAMES HENTHORN), D.D. St. Patiick, Apostle of Iieland: a Memoii of his Life and Mission. 8vo. Dublin, 1864. C 10 Q 40

TODD (REV. JOHN). Student's Manual, designed to aid in foiming and stiengthening the Intellectual and Moial Chaiactei and Habits of Students in all Piofessions; with a Pieface by the Rev. T. Binney. 12mo. Lond., 1869. J 1 V 42

TODD (LAWRIE). [*See* THORBURN, G.]

TODD (R. B.) Cyclopædia of Anatomy and Physiology. 5 vols. imp. 8vo. Lond., 1835–59. A 33 V 7–12

TODD (WILLIAM G.), D.D. The Iiish in England; iepiinted, with Additions, fiom the *Dublin Review.* 8vo. Lond., 1857. G 2 P 28

TODHUNTER (ISAAC), M.A., &c. Algebia, foi the use of Colleges and Schools. 5th ed. 8vo. Lond., 1871. A 10 S 13

Elementaiy Tieatise on Laplace's Functions, Lamé's Functions, and Bessel's Functions. 8vo. Lond., 1875. A 10 S 14

Histoiy of the Theoiy of Elasticity, and of the Stiength of Mateiials, fiom Galilei to the Piesent Time; edited and compiled by K. Peaison. Vol. I. 8vo. Camb., 1886. A 11 U 21

TODHUNTER (ISAAC), M.A., &c.—*continued.*
Key to Exercises in Euclid. 2nd ed. 8vo. Lond., 1882.   A 10 R 19

Mechanics for Beginners; with numerous Examples. 2nd ed. 12mo. Lond., 1870.   A 10 R 22

Plane Trigonometry, for the use of Colleges and Schools; with numerous Examples. 8th ed. 8vo. Lond., 1880.   A 10 R 15

Spherical Trigonometry, for the use of Colleges and Schools; with numerous Examples. 4th ed. 12mo. Lond., 1878.   A 10 R 16

Treatise on Analytical Statics; with numerous Examples. 3rd ed. 8vo. Lond., 1866.   A 10 S 10

Treatise on Plane Co-ordinate Geometry, as applied to the Straight Line and the Conic Sections. 4th ed. 8vo. Lond., 1867.   A 10 S 20

Treatise on the Differential Calculus; with numerous Examples. 5th ed. 8vo. Lond., 1871.   A 10 S 16

Treatise on the Integral Calculus and its Applications. 3rd ed. 8vo. Lond., 1868.   A 10 R 18

William Whewell, D.D., Master of Trinity College, Cambridge: an Account of his Writings; with Selections from his Literary and Scientific Correspondence. 2 vols. 8vo. Lond., 1876.   C 9 U 51, 52

TODIÈRE (L.) Guillaume le Conquérant. 8vo. Tours, 1856.   D 9 P 42

TODLEBEN (GEN. E. DE). Défense de Sébastopol; avec Exposé de la Guerre Souterraine, 1854–55, rédigé par M. Frolow. 3 vols. (in 5) imp. 8vo. St. Petersb., 1863–74.   B 12 V 2–6

Atlas topographique et Atlas armement [to the above]. 2 vols. el. fol. and ob. 4to. St. Petersb., 1863.   B 9 P 24, 25 ‡

TOHU (MAORI PROPHET). Wanderings of. [*See* WARD, J. P.]   MD 4 P 29

TOLAND (JOHN). Amyntor; or, a Defence of Milton's Life. 8vo. Lond., 1699.   G 3 P 1

Christianity not Mysterious; or, a Treatise shewing that there is nothing in the Gospel contrary to Reason, nor above it. 2nd ed. 8vo. Lond., 1696.   G 16 R 13

Life of James Harrington. [*See* HARRINGTON, J.]

TOLFREY (FREDERIC). Sportsman in France; comprising a Sporting Ramble through Picardy and Normandy, and Boar-shooting in Lower Brittany. 2 vols. 8vo. Lond., 1841.   A 17 W 31, 32

TOLHAUSEN (ALEXANDER), PH.D., &c. Technological Dictionary in the English, German, and French Languages. 3 vols. 8vo. Leipzig, 1876–78.   K 11 T 26–28
     1. English-German-French.
     2. Français-Allemand-Anglais.
     3. Deutsch-Englisch-Französich.

TOLLEMACHE (MRS. W. A.) Spanish Towns and Spanish Pictures: a Guide to the Galleries of Spain. 8vo. Lond., 1870.   D 7 Q 13

TOLMER (ALEXANDER). Reminiscences of an Adventurous and Chequered Career at Home and at the Antipodes. 2 vols. 8vo. Lond., 1882.   MC 1 P 4, 5

TOLMIE (W. FRASER), AND DAWSON (GEORGE M.), D.S., &c. Comparative Vocabularies of the Indian Tribes of British Columbia; with a Map illustrating Distribution. Roy. 8vo. Montreal, 1884.   K 12 T 24

TOMES (CHARLES S.), M.A. Development and Succession of the Poison-fangs of Snakes. (Roy. Soc. Pubs., 3.) 4to. Lond., 1876.   A 11 P 4 †

Development of the Teeth of Fishes (Elasmobranchii and Teleostei). (Roy. Soc. Pubs., 2.) 4to. Lond., 1876.   A 11 P 3 †

Development of the Teeth of Newt, Frog, Slow-worm, and Green Lizard; and on the Structure and Development of the Teeth of Ophidia. (Roy. Soc. Pubs., 1.) 4to. Lond., 1875.   A 11 P 2 †

Manual of Dental Anatomy, Human and Comparative. 2nd ed. Lond., 1882.   A 12 P 20

Structure and Development of Vascular Dentine. (Roy. Soc. Pubs., 5.) 4to. Lond., 1878.   A 11 P 6 †

TOMES (JOHN), F.R.S., AND TOMES (CHARLES S.), M.A. System of Dental Surgery. 2nd ed. (Churchill's Manuals.) 12mo. Lond., 1873.   A 13 P 35

TOMKINS (REV. H. G.) [*See* DYMOND, C. W.]

TOMKINS (P. W.) [*See* OTTLEY, W. Y.]

TOMLINE (G. P.) Memoirs of the Life of the Rt. Hon. William Pitt. 4th ed. 3 vols. 8vo. Lond., 1822.   C 9 Q 22–24

TOMLINS (THOMAS EDLYNE). Popular Law Dictionary, familiarly explaining the Terms and Nature of English Law. 8vo. Lond., 1838.   K 11 R 1

TOMLINSON (CHARLES), F.C.S. Biographical Sketch of R. L. A. Davies. [*See* DAVIES, R. L. A.]   MH 1 P 9

Construction of Locks. [*See* HOBBS, A. C.]   A 17 P 35

Cyclopædia of Useful Arts, Mechanical and Chemical, Manufactures, Mining, and Engineering. 3 vols. imp. 8vo. Lond., 1868.   K 6 S 16–18

Experimental Essays on the Motions of Camphor on Water, &c., and History of the Modern Theory of Dew. (Weale.) 12mo. Lond., 1863.   A 17 Q 6

Introduction to the Study of Natural Philosophy. (Weale.) 8th ed. 12mo. Lond., 1870.   A 17 P 46

Pneumatics for the use of Beginners. (Weale.) 3rd ed. 12mo. Lond., 1866.   A 17 P 39

Rudimentary Mechanics; being a concise Exposition of the General Principles of Mechanical Science, and their Applications. 11th ed. (Weale.) 12mo. Lond., 1872.   A 17 P 39

Another copy. (Weale.) 12mo. Lond., 1872. A 17 Q 33

Rudimentary Treatise on Warming and Ventilation. (Weale.) 12mo. Lond., 1870.   A 17 P 19

TOMPSON (CHARLES), JUNR. Wild Notes from the Lyre of a Native Minstrel. 4to. Sydney, 1826.* MH 1 T 1

TONE (THEOBALD WOLFE). Life of; written by himself; edited by W. T. W. Tone. (Autobiog., 19.) 18mo. Lond., 1828. C 1 P 14

TONE (WILLIAM THEOBALD WOLFE). Life of Theobald Wolfe Tone. [*See* TONE, T. W.]

TOOKE (ANDREW), A.M. The Pantheon, representing the Fabulous Histories of the Heathen Gods and most illustrious Heroes. 34th ed. 8vo. Lond., 1819. B 14 P 5

TOOKE (JOHN HORNE). Epea Pteroenta; or, the Diversions of Purley. 2nd ed. 2 vols. 4to. Lond., 1798. K 15 T 1, 2
[*See* BARCLAY, J.]

TOOKE (THOMAS), F.R.S. History of Prices, and of the State of the Circulation, 1793-1856. 6 vols. 8vo. Lond., 1838-57. F 4 P 12-17

TOOKE (WILLIAM), F.R.S. Life of Catherine II, Empress of Russia. 3 vols. 8vo. Lond., 1798. C 6 R 27-29
[*See* BOYDELL, J.]

TOOVEY (JAMES). Catalogue of an extensive and extraordinary Assemblage of the Productions of the Aldine Press, from its first establishment at Venice in 1494, together with Lyonese and Venetian Counterfeits, the Giunta, and other Works illustrative of the Series. 8vo. Lond., 1880. K 7 R 16

TOPINARD (DR. PAUL). Etude sur les Races Indigènes de l'Australie. 8vo. Paris, 1872. MA 1 S 7

TORONTO ESTATE. Plans, Views, and Particulars of the Toronto Estate, Lake Macquarie. Ob. 4to. Sydney, 1887. MD 4 P 32 †

TORONTO PUBLIC LIBRARY. Catalogue of the Circulating Library. 8vo. Toronto, 1884. K 7 R 12

TORRENS (COL. ROBERT), F.R.S. Colonization of South Australia. 8vo. Lond., 1835.* MF 2 P 25
Letter to NassauWilliam Senior, Esq., in reply to the Article, "Free Trade and Retaliation," in the *Edinburgh Review*; with Letters on Free Trade and Reciprocity. 8vo. Lond., 1843. F 6 V 10

TORRENS (SIR ROBERT R.), K.C.M.G. Hand-book on the Real Property Act of South Australia; containing a succinct Account of that Measure, compiled from authentic Documents, with full Information and Examples for the guidance of Persons dealing; also, an Index to the Act. 12mo. Adelaide (n.d.) MJ 2 R 1
South Australian System of Conveyancing by Registration of Title; with Instructions for the guidance of Parties dealing, illustrated by Copies of the Books and Forms in use in the Lands Titles Office; to which is added, the South Australian Real Property Act, as amended in the Sessions of 1858, with a copious index, by Henry Gawler, Esq. 8vo. Adelaide, 1859. MF 1 Q 18

TORRENS (W. M.), M.P. Empire in Asia; how we came by it: a Book of Confessions. 8vo. Lond.,1872. B 10 T 4
Imperial and Colonial Partnership in Emigration. 8vo. Lond., 1881. MF 2 P 19
Marquess Wellesley, Architect of Empire: an Historic Portrait. 8vo. Lond., 1880. C 9 V 49
Memoirs of the Rt. Hon. William 2nd Viscount Melbourne. With a Portrait. 2 vols. 8vo. Lond., 1878. C 8 R 39, 40

TORREY (JOSEPH). General History of the Christian Religion and Church. [*See* NEANDER, DR. J. A. W.]

TOSCANI (PROF. GIOVANNI). Italian Conversational Course: a new Method of Teaching the Italian Language, both theoretically and practically. 5th ed. 8vo. Lond., 1875. K 11 T 43

TOTT (FRANÇOIS), BARON DE. Memoirs of, containing the State of the Turkish Empire and the Crimea, during the late War with Russia. 2nd ed., translated from the French. 2 vols. 8vo. Lond., 1786. C 5 U 7, 8

TOUCHSTONE (THE). A Word to Sceptics of all Denominations, and the seven Churches of Sydney brought to the Touchstone; by "A Labouring Mechanic." 8vo. Sydney (n.d.) MG 1 Q 31

TOULMIN (JOSHUA), D.D. Life of Daniel Neal, M.A. [*See* NEAL, D.]

TOURIST IN WALES (THE): a Series of Views of Picturesque Scenery, Towns, Castles, Antiquities, &c. with Historical and Topographical Notices. Roy. 8vo. Lond., 1851. D 7 V 30

TOURNEFORT (JOSEPH PITTON DE). Voyage into the Levant. Illustrated. 3 vols. 8vo. Lond.,1751. D 7 U 5-7

TOVEY (LIEUT.-COL. HAMILTON), R.E. Martial Law. 8vo. Lond., 1886. F 5 P 27

TOWLE (G. M.) Timely Topics: England and Russia in Asia. With Maps. 12mo. Boston, 1885. F 2 P 27

TOWLER (J.), M.D. The Silver Sunbeam: a Practical and Theoretical Text-book on Sun-drawing and Photographic Printing. 8th ed. 8vo. New York, 1873. A 6 V 4

TOWN (MRS. W.) [*See* WOOLLS, REV. W.]

TOWN AND COUNTRY JOURNAL (THE). Fol. Sydney, 1870-87. E

TOWN AND COUNTRY MAGAZINE (THE), 1769-90. 19 vols. 8vo. Lond., 1769-90. E 1.36

TOWNEND (REV. JOSEPH). Autobiography of; with Reminiscences of his Missionary Labours in Australia. 2nd ed. 8vo. Lond., 1869. MC 1 P 12

TOWNEND (WILLIAM). Descendants of the Stuarts: an Unchronicled Page in England's History. 8vo. Lond., 1858. C 9 T 43

TOWNLEY (REV. JAMES). Illustrations of Biblical Literature. 3 vols. 8vo. Lond., 1821. G 10 S 3-5

TOWNSEND (REV. GEORGE), M.A. Notes on the Contributions to the new edition of "Fox's Martyrology." [*See* MAITLAND, REV. S. R.]

TOWNSEND (GEORGE H.) Manual of Dates: a Dictionary of Reference of the most important Facts and Events in the History of the World. 5th ed., edited by Frederick Martin. 8vo. Lond., 1877. K 11 P 16

Men of the Time: a Dictionary of Contemporaries, containing biographical Notices of Eminent Characters of both Sexes. 7th ed. 8vo. Lond., 1868. C 4 U 9

TOWNSEND (JOSEPH PHIPPS). Rambles and Observations in New South Wales. 8vo. Lond., 1849.* MD 3 Q 14

TOWNSEND (LEONARD). Alphabetical Chronology of Remarkable Events; with Notes. 8vo. Lond. (n.d.) B 15 P 32

TOWNSEND (PAULINE D.) Life of Mozart. [*See* JAHN, O.] C 7 S 19–21

TOWNSEND (T.) [*See* SOLIS, A. DE.] B 17 S 14 ‡

TOWNSEND (WILLIAM). [*See* NETHERBY GAZETTE.] MJ 2 R 8

TOWNSEND (WILLIAM C.), A.M. History of the House of Commons, from the Convention Parliament of 1688–89, to the passing of the Reform Bill in 1832. 2 vols. 8vo. Lond., 1843–44. B 7 Q 19, 20

Lives of Twelve Eminent Judges of the Last and of the Present Century. 2 vols. 8vo. Lond., 1846. C 10 P 31, 32

Modern State Trials; revised and illustrated, with Essays and Notes. 2 vols. 8vo. Lond., 1850. F 4 P 10, 11

TOWNSHEND (REV. C. H.), A.M. Facts in Mesmerism; with Reasons for a dispassionate Inquiry into it. 2nd ed. 8vo. Lond., 1844. A 12 S 26

TOWNSHEND (F. TRENCH), B.A. Wild Life in Florida, with a Visit to Cuba. 8vo. Lond., 1875. D 4 Q 40

TOWNSHEND (GEORGE). Adventures and Sufferings of an Old Colonist of forty years standing, on board of the *Great Britain*, on her Voyage from Liverpool to Melbourne, in 1866. 8vo. Melb., 1866. MJ 2 R 8

TOWNSHEND (J. K.) Sporting Excursions in the Rocky Mountains, including Journey to the Columbia River, Visit to Sandwich Islands, &c. 2 vols. 8vo. Lond., 1840. D 4 P 43, 44

TOWNSON (ROBERT), LL.D. Tracts and Observations in Natural History and Physiology. 8vo. Lond., 1799. A 16 T 4

TOYNBEE (ARNOLD). Lectures on the Industrial Revolution in England: Popular Addresses, Notes, and other Fragments; together with a short Memoir, by B. Jowett. 8vo. Lond., 1884. F 4 S 12

TOZER (REV. HENRY FANSHAWE), M.A., &c. Turkish Armenia and Eastern Asia Minor. 8vo. Lond., 1881. D 4 T 39

[*See* FINLAY, G.] B 9 T 24–28

TOZER (HORACE). Memorandum and Articles of Association of the Caledonian United Gold-mining Company, Limited; drawn and registered by Horace Tozer, Solicitor, Gympie. 8vo. Gympie, 1885. MF 2 P 4

TRACTS FOR THE TIMES; by Members of the University of Oxford, 1833–37. 4 vols. 8vo. Lond., 1838–39. G 16 S 9–12

TRACTS OF SCOTLAND. [*See* SCOTLAND.]

TRACY (DR. R. T.) Portrait of. [*See* MANUSCRIPTS AND PORTRAITS.]

TRADES' UNION CONGRESS (INTERCOLONIAL). First Intercolonial Trades' Union Congress: Report of Proceedings during Session, commencing on October 6th, 1879, in the Lecture Hall of the Mechanics' School of Arts, Sydney. (Pam. Jb.) 8vo. Sydney, 1879. MF 3 P 21

TRAILL (MRS. CATHERINE PARR). Backwoods of Canada: being Letters from the Wife of an Emigrant Officer. (Lib. Ent. Know.) 12mo. Lond., 1836. K 10 R 19

TRAILL (H. D.) Coleridge. (Eng. Men of Letts.) 8vo. Lond., 1884. C 1 U 37

Shaftesbury (the 1st Earl). (Eng. Worthies.) 8vo. Lond., 1886. C 2 T 35

Sterne. (Eng. Men of Letts.) 8vo. Lond., 1882. C 1 U 33

TRAILL (T. S.) [*See* SCHLEGEL, H.]

TRAILL (THOMAS W.), C.E., &c. Chain Cables and Chains; comprising Sizes and Curves of Links, Studs, &c.; with numerous Tables, Illustrations, and Lithographic Drawings. Fol. Lond., 1885. A 23 R 26 ‡

TRAIN (GEORGE FRANCIS). Speech in commemoration of the 82nd Anniversary of the Declaration of American Independence. 12mo. Lond., 1858. MJ 2 P 33

The Merchant abroad in Europe, Asia, and Australia: a series of Letters. 8vo. Lond., 1857. MD 1 W 16

Young America abroad in Europe, Asia, and Australia: a series of Letters. 8vo. Lond., 1857. MD 1 W 15

TRAITS OF SCOTTISH LIFE, and Pictures of Scenes and Characters. 3 vols. 12mo. Lond., 1830. J 5 P 20–22

TRANSPORT Voyage to the Mauritius. [*See* MAURITIUS.]

TRANSPORTATION. Memoir of Proceedings taken by the Colonists in connexion with the proposed cessation of Transportation to Van Diemen's Land. Roy. 8vo. Launceston, 1847. MJ 2 S 1

Remarks against the Revival of Transportation. (M.S.) Fol. Sydney (n.d.) MJ 2 U 1

Reply to "A Letter to the Householders of Hobarton on the Effects of Transportation upon the Morals, and Moral Condition of the Colony; by a Man and a Brother." 12mo. Hobart, 1847. MJ 2 P 30

Report from the Select Committee on Transportation. (Parl. Docs., 1.) Fol. Lond., 1812. MF 4 ‡

TRANSPORTATION— *continued.*
Report from the Select Committee on Transportation; together with the Minutes of Evidence, Appendix, and Index. Lond., 1837.* MF 2 U 14

Report from the Select Committee on Transportation; together with the Minutes of Evidence, Appendix, and Index. (Parl. Docs., 20, 21.) 2 vols. fol. Lond., 1837-38. MF 4 ‡

The Question of Transportation considered, in a Letter to the Rt. Hon. Lord Goderich, Principal Secretary of State for the Colonies, &c.; by "A Colonist of New South Wales." 8vo. Lond., 1832. MF 3 Q 40

The Transportation Question considered. 8vo. Hobart, 1847. MF 3 P 6

Another copy. 8vo. Hobart, 1847. MJ 2 R 13

Van Diemen's Land: Circular and Declaration. (Pam. B.) Fol. Hobart, 1852. MJ 2 U 2

[*See* ABOLITIONISTS; ANTI-TRANSPORTATION; ARTHUR, SIR G.; ATKINSON, J. R.; BANNISTER, S.; BLOSSEVILLE, MARQ. DE; CHISHOLM, MRS. C.; CONVICTS; CRIMINAL RECORDER; FRY, H. P.; HALE, M. B.; *and* LACKLAND, J.]

TRATTLE (MARMADUKE). Catalogue of the Collection of Coins and Medals, in Gold, Silver, and Copper, of Marmaduke Trattle, Esq. 8vo. Lond., 1832. A 13 S 41

TRAUTWINE (JOHN C.), C.E. Civil Engineer's Pocketbook of Mensuration, Trigonometry, Surveying, Hydraulics, Hydrostatics, Instruments and their Adjustments, Strength of Materials. 12mo. New York, 1855. A G R 5

Field Practice of laying out of Circular Curves for Railroads. 11th ed. 12mo. Philad., 1882. A G R 23

Field Practice. [*See* SIMMS, F.]

New Method of Calculating the Cubic Contents of Excavations and Embankments by the aid of Diagrams; together with Directions for Estimating the Cost of Earthwork. 7th ed. 8vo. Philad., 1881. A 10 T 25

TRAVELLER, A. [*See* CAMPBELL, J. F.]

TRAVELLER from New Zealand, A. [*See* ROUGH, D.]

TRAVELLING BACHELOR, A. [*See* COOPER, J. F.]

TRAVERS (HENRY). Notes on Birds. [*See* HUTTON, CAPT. F. W.]

TRAVERS (W. T. L.), F.L.S. New Zealand, Graphic and Descriptive. [*See* BARRAUD, C. D.] MD 1 P 8 ‡

TRAVIS (HENRY), M.D. Effectual Reform in Man and Society. 8vo. Lond., 1875. G 7 P 1

TREASURES LOST AND FOUND: a Story of Life in Tasmania; by "A Tasmanian Lady." 12mo. Lond., 1872. MJ 1 Q 23

TREASURY OF BIOGRAPHY. [*See* MAUNDER, S.]

TREBECK (GEORGE). Travels in the Himalaya Provinces of Hindustan and the Punjab. [*See* MOORCROFT, W.] D 6 S 4, 5

TREDGOLD (THOMAS), C.E. Construction of Roofs. [*See* ROBISON, J.] A 17 P 57

Elementary Principles of Carpentry; with Practical Rules and Examples. 5th ed., corrected and enlarged by P. Barlow. 4to. Lond., 1870. A 1 S 14 †

Another copy. 6th ed., revised and considerably enlarged by E. Wyndham Tarn, M.A. 4to. Lond., 1885. A 2 T 34

Principles of Warming and Ventilating Public Buildings, Dwelling-houses, Manufactories, Hospitals, Hot-houses, Conservatories, &c. 2nd ed. 8vo. Lond., 1824. A 2 S 36

TREDGOLD (THOMAS), C.E., AND TARN (E. W.), M.A. Carpentry and Joinery. (Weale.) 12mo. Lond., 1873. A 17 Q 28

Atlas of Engravings [to the above.] 4to. Lond., 1873. A 2 T 33

TREDWELL (DANIEL M.) Monograph on privately-illustrated Books: a Plea for Bibliomania. 8vo. Brooklyn, 1881. J 11 V 21

TRÉGANCE (LOUIS). Narrative of. [*See* NEW GUINEA.]

TREGEAR (EDWARD). The Aryan Maori. 8vo. Wellington, 1885.* MA 1 R 19

TREGELLAS (WALTER H.) Cornish Worthies: Sketches of some Eminent Cornish Men and Families. 2 vols. 8vo. Lond., 1884. C 10 S 22, 23

TRELAWNY (E. J.) Recollections of the Last Days of Shelley and Byron. 8vo. Lond., 1858. C 3 U 39

TRELEASE (W.) [*See* POULSEN, V. A.] A 5 S 21

TRELOAR (W. P.) Ludgate Hill, Past and Present: a Narrative concerning the People, Places, Legends, and Changes of the Great London Highway. 8vo. Lond., 1881. B 3 R 12

TREMENHEERE (COL. C. W.), R.E., C.B., &c. Kuriacbu Harbour Report; with an Atlas. Fol. Bombay, 1864. E 2.24

Description of the mode adopted in taking Observations to determine the velocity of and amount of solid matter in Water at different depths in the Indus and Canals of Sinde. Fol. Bombay, 1864. E 2.24

TREMENHEERE (HUGH SEYMOUR). Notes on Public Subjects, made during a Tour in the United States and in Canada. 8vo. Lond., 1852. F 5 T 3

TRENCH (MOST REV. RICHARD CHENEVIX), D.D., ARCHBISHOP OF DUBLIN. English, Past and Present: Eight Lectures. 8th ed., revised. 12mo. Lond., 1873. K 11 U 23

On the Study of Words. 14th ed., revised. 12mo. Lond., 1872. K 20 Q 39

TRENCK (FREDERIC), BARON VON. Life of; containing his Adventures during Ten Years' Imprisonment at the Fortress of Madgeburg; translated by Thomas Holcroft. 4th ed. 3 vols. 8vo. Lond., 1817. C 4 P 36-38

TRENDELENBURG (FRIDERICUS ADOLPHUS). [*See* ARISTOTELES.]　　　　　G 16 S 21

TRESEDER (JOHN G., AND THOMAS). The Garden. 8vo. Sydney, 1880.　　　　　MA 1 P 9

TREVELYAN (GEORGE OTTO), M.P. Cawnpore. 8vo. Lond., 1865.　　　　　B 10 Q 32

The Competition Wallah. 8vo. Lond., 1864.　　J 11 S 31

Early History of Charles James Fox. 8vo. Lond., 1880.　　　　　C 11 P 36

Life and Letters of Lord Macaulay. 2 vols. 8vo. Lond., 1876.　　　　　C 7 S 38, 39

Index [to the above.] [*See* CLARK, P.]　　C 7 S 40

Selections from the Writings of Lord Macaulay. [*See* MACAULAY, T. B., LORD.]

TREVELYAN (PAULINA JERMYN), LADY. Selections from the Literary and Artistic Remains of; edited by David Wooster. 8vo. Lond., 1879.　　J 2 S 4

[*See* MACAULAY, T. B., LORD.]

TREVES (EMILIO), AND STRAFFORELLO (GUSTAVO). Dizionario Universale di Geografia: Storia e Biografia. 4ª ed. 2 vols. roy. 8vo. Milano, 1882–84. D 12 V 1, 2

TRIAL (THE). Trial of the most Notable Lawsuit of Ancient or Modern Times; the Incorporated Scientific Era Protection Society *v.* Paul Christman and others, in the Court of Common Reason, before Lord Penetrating Impartiality and a Special Jury; Issue, "Did Christ rise from the Dead?" *Verbatim* Report by "A Shorthand Writer." 8vo. Lond., 1882.　　　　G 16 S 22

TRIAL BY JURY, and a Representative Assembly in New South Wales: Debate in the House of Commons, Thursday, 28th June, 1832. 8vo. Lond., 1832.　　MF 1 Q 4

TRIALS. Celebrated Trials and remarkable Cases of Criminal Jurisprudence, to 1825. 6 vols. 8vo. Lond., 1825.　　　　　F 5 U 13–18

Complete Collection of State Trials, from the Earliest Period, 1163, to the year 1820; compiled by W. Cobbett, T. B. Howell, and T. J. Howell; Index, by D. Jardine. 34 vols. roy. 8vo. Lond., 1816–28.　　F 2 S 1–T 16

Trial of Colonel E. M. Despard, 1803; Arthur Thistlewood, Gent.; James Watson, the elder, Surgeon; Thomas Preston, Cordwainer; and John Hooper, Labourer, for High Treason. 8vo. Lond., 1803–17.　　F 5 U 1

Queen *v.* Hayes; Queen *v.* Joseph; Proceeding on the Trials of these Informations in the Supreme Court of the Colony of Victoria. Fol. Melb., 1855.　　MF 2 U 6

[*See* STATE TRIALS.]

TRIBUNE (THE), and News of the Week. 4 vols. fol. Sydney, 1882–84.　　　　　ME

TRIGAUT (NICOLAS). De Christianis apud Japonios Triumphis, sive de gravissima ibidem contra Christi Fidem persecutione exorta anno MDCXII usq. ad annum MDCXX, libri quinq. Sm. 4to. Monachii, 1623.　　　　G 8 U 3

TRIMEN (HENRY), M.B., &c. Medicinal Plants. [*See* BENTLEY, R.]　　　　　A 5 P 29–32

TRINITY of Italy (The). [*See* ITALY.]

TRIPPLIN (JULIAN). [*See* SAUNIER, C.]　　A 11 V 1

TRISTRAM (REV. H. B.), LL.D., &c. Great Sahara: Wanderings South of the Atlas Mountains. 8vo. Lond., 1860.　　　　　D 1 P 17

Pathways of Palestine: a Descriptive Tour through the Holy Land. Illustrated with Photographs. 1st and 2nd series. 2 vols. roy. 4to. Lond., 1881–82.　D 5 V 2, 3

Survey of Western Palestine: Fauna and Flora of Palestine. [*See* PALESTINE EXPLORATION FUND.]　D 4 V 10

TROEDEL (CHARLES). Melbourne Album, containing a series of Views of Melbourne and Country Districts. Ob. 4to. Melb., 1864.　　　　　MD 3 Q 4 ‡

TROGNON (AUGUSTE). Fragment sur l'Histoire de France. [*See* GUIZOT, F. P. G. Hist. de France, 31.]

TROLLOPE (ANTHONY). An Autobiography. 2 vols. 8vo. Edinb., 1883.　　　　　C 4 V 43, 44

Australia and New Zealand. 2 vols. 8vo. Lond., 1873.　　　　　MD 1 V 30, 31

Harry Heathcote, of Gangoil: a Tale of Australian Bush Life. 2nd ed. 12mo. Lond., 1874.　　MJ 1 Q 42

Life of Cicero. 2 vols. 8vo. Lond., 1880.　C 3 T 2, 3

New South Wales and Queensland. 12mo. Lond., 1875.　　　　　MD 1 S 17

North America. 2 vols. 8vo. Lond., 1862.　D 4 Q 44, 45

South Africa. 2nd ed. 2 vols. 8vo. Lond., 1878.　　　　　D 1 P 11, 12

South Australia and Western Australia. New ed. 12mo. Lond., 1875.　　　　　MD 1 S 16

Thackeray. (Eng. Men Letts.) 8vo. Lond., 1879.　　　　　C 1 U 35

Victoria and Tasmania. New ed. 12mo. Lond., 1875.　　　　　MD 1 S 15

West Indies and the Spanish Main. 4th ed. 8vo. Lond., 1860.　　　　　D 3 R 40

One Story is Good till another is Told: a Reply to Mr. A. Trollope. [*See* CHUCK, T.]

TROLLOPE (MRS. FRANCES ELEANOR). Belgium and Western Germany in 1833. 2nd ed. 2 vols. 8vo. Lond., 1835.　　　　　D 8 Q 47, 48

Domestic Manners of the Americans. 5th ed. 12mo. Lond., 1839.　　　　　D 3 P 26

Paris and the Parisians in 1835. 2 vols. 8vo. Lond., 1836.　　　　　D 8 T 2, 3

Summer in Brittany. [*See* TROLLOPE, T. A.]　　　　　D 7 U 39, 40

Summer in Western France. [*See* TROLLOPE, T. A.]　　　　　D 7 U 41, 42

Vienna and the Austrians; with some Account of a Journey through Swabia, Bavaria, the Tyrol, and the Salzbourg. 2 vols. 8vo. Lond., 1838.　D 7 U 31, 32

Visit to Italy. 2 vols. 8vo. Lond., 1842.　D 8 T 25, 26

[*See* STIRLER, K.]　　　　　D 8 S 2 †

TROLLOPE (HENRY M.) The Salon of Madame Necker.
[*See* HAUSSONVILLE, O., VICOMTE DE.]   C 4 Q 21, 22

TROLLOPE (T. ADOLPHUS), B.A. History of the Commonwealth of Florence, from the Earliest Independence of the Commune to the Fall of the Republic, in 1531. 4 vols.
8vo. Lond., 1865.   B 11 R 22, 23
Papal Conclaves, as they were, and as they are. 8vo.
Lond., 1876.   B 12 R 38
Summer in Brittany; edited by Frances Trollope. 2
vols. 8vo. Lond., 1840.   D 7 U 39, 40
Summer in Western France; edited by Frances Trollope.
2 vols. 8vo. Lond., 1841.   D 7 U 41, 42
[*See* STIELER, K.]   D 5 S 2 †

TROLLOPE (REV. WILLIAM), M.A. Are the Catholics of
Port Phillip Tridentine Romanists?" an Enquiry founded
on the Anathema recently put forth in a "Vindication
of the Catholics, by N. J. Coffey, Dean." 8vo. Melb.,
1850.   MG 1 Q 31
Belgium since the Revolution of 1830. 8vo. Lond.,
1842.   D 8 S 36
Life of J. Jortin. [*See* JORTIN, REV. J.]   G 1 R 18, 19
[*See* O'FARRELL, P. A. C.]   MJ 2 R 12

TROMHOLT (SOPHUS). Under the Rays of the Aurora
Borealis: in the Land of the Lapps and Kvæns. Original
ed., with Illustrations. 2 vols. 8vo. Lond., 1885.
                                                D 7 S 10, 11

TROPICAL AGRICULTURIST (THE): a Monthly Record of Information for Planters; compiled by A. M.
and J. Ferguson, 1881–87. 6 vols. sm. 4to. Colombo,
1882–87.   E

TROSCHEL (PROF. F. H.) Handbuch der Zoologie. 8vo.
Berlin, 1871.   A 14 S 31

TROTTER (CAPT. H. D.) Expedition to the River Niger.
[*See* ALLEN, CAPT., W., AND THOMSON, T. R. H.]
                                                D 2 T 13, 14

TROTTER (CAPT. LIONEL J.) History of India under
Queen Victoria, 1836–80. 2 vols. 8vo. Lond., 1886.
                                                B 10 R 10, 11

TROTTER (MARCUS). Book-keeping. [*See* JACKSON, G.]
                                                   A 10 S 11

TROTTER (CAPT. PHILIP DURHAM). Our Mission to the
Court of Marocco in 1880, under Sir John Drummond Hay,
K.C.B. Illustrated. Sq. 8vo. Edinb., 1881. D 2 T 1

TROUBADOURS. Leben und Werke der. [*See* DIEZ, F.]
                                                    C 5 S 2

TROUESSART (E. L.) Microbes, Ferments, and Moulds.
8vo. Lond., 1886.   A 12 Q 42

TROUTBECK (REV. JOHN), M.A., AND DALE (REV.
R. F.) Music Primer for Schools. 2nd ed. (Clar. Press.)
8vo. Oxford, 1871.   A 17 T 48

TROW (J. F.) New York City Directory, for the year
ending May 1st, 1878. 8vo. New York, 1878.   E

TROWELL (T. J.) "The Stevenson Case": a Complete
Exposé of the System of alleged Frauds; also, a Self-
vindication of the Writer. 8vo. Melb., 1876. MJ 2 R 12

TROYER (ANTHONY). The Dabistan; or, School of Manners. [*See* DABISTAN, THE.]

TRÜBNER (C.) [*See* MARTIN, L. C.]   A 13 S 35

TRÜBNER (NICHOLAS). In Memoriam. Roy. 8vo. Lond.,
1884.   C 4 W 34
The Literature of American Aboriginal Languages.
[*See* LUDEWIG, H. E.]   K 17 Q 13
Trübner's Bibliographical Guide to American Literature.
8vo. Lond., 1859.   K 7 S 26

TRÜBNER & CO. Catalogue of Dictionaries and Gram-
mars of the principal Languages and Dialects of the World.
2nd ed. Lond., 1882.   Libr.
Scientific and Linguistic Publications of. 8vo. Lond.,
1871.   J 10 S 2

TRUE CATHOLIC (THE); or, Tasmanian Evangelical
Miscellany. 8vo. Hobart, 1843.   MG 1 Q 29
Another copy. . 8vo. Hobart, 1843.   MG 1 Q 39

TRUEBA Y COSIO (DON TELESFORO DE). History of
the Conquest of Peru by the Spaniards. (Const. Misc.)
18mo. Edinb., 1830.   K 10 Q 50
Life of Hernan Cortes. (Const. Misc.) 18mo. Edinb.,
1829.   K 10 Q 37

TRUMAN (MAJOR BENJAMIN CUMMINGS). The Field of
Honor: being a Complete and Comprehensive History
of Duelling in all Countries. 8vo. New York, 1884.
                                                  B 14 Q 2

TRUMBULL (BENJAMIN), D.D. Complete History of Connecticut, Civil and Ecclesiastical. 2 vols. 8vo. New
Haven, 1818.   B 1 R 29, 30

TRUMBULL (H. CLAY), D.D. Kadesh-Barnea, its Importance and Probable Site; including Studies of the Route
of the Exodus, and the Southern Boundary of the Holy
Land. 8vo. Lond., 1884.   B 2 R 50

TRUSLER (REV. DR. JOHN). Chronology; or, the Historian's Vade-mecum. 2 vols. 12mo. Lond., 1782.
                                                  B 3 P 3, 4
Descriptive Account of the Islands lately discovered in
the South Seas. 8vo. Lond., 1778.   MD 6 R 14

TRUSSEL (JOHN). Collection of the History of England.
[*See* DANIEL, S.]   B 16 Q 5 ‡

TRYON (GEORGE W.), JUNR. Manual of Conchology,
Structural and Systematic. [1st series.] Vols. 1–7. 7 vols.
roy. 8vo. Philad., 1879–86.   A 32 P 1–7
Manual of Conchology, Structural and Systematic. 2nd
series. 2 vols. roy. 8vo. Philad., 1885–86.   A 32 Q 1, 2
Structural and Systematic Conchology: an Introduction
to the Study of the Mollusca. 3 vols. (in 1) 8vo. Philad.,
1882–84.   A 14 T 2

TRYPHIODORUS. Tryphiodori Excidium Ilii. [*See* HESIOD.] H 6 V 29

TSCHÉMESSOFF (EVGRAF PETROVITSCH). Tschémessoff, Graveur Russe: elève de G. F. Schmidt son Œuvre, reproduit par le procédé de G. Scamoni. Fol. St. Petersburg, 1878. A 20 P 6 ‡

TSCHUDI (DR. J. J. VON). Travels in Peru, during the years 1838–42; translated by Thomasina Ross. 8vo. Lond., 1847. D 4 Q 14

TUCKER (ABRAHAM). The Light of Nature pursued; with some Account of the Life of the Author, by Sir H. P. St. John Mildmay, Bart. 2 vols. 8vo. Lond., 1837. G 14 Q 10, 11

TUCKER (G. A.) Lunacy in Many Lands; being an Introduction to the Reports on the Lunatic Asylums of various Countries, visited in 1882–85, by G. A. Tucker. 8vo. Birmingham, 1885.* MA 2 S 34

Another copy. Roy. 8vo. Sydney, 1887. MA 2 S 36

TUCKER (REV. HENRY WILLIAM). The English Church in other Lands. 12mo. Lond., 1886. G 7 T 5

TUCKER (J. H.), PH.D. Manual of Sugar Analysis, including the Application in general of Analytical Methods to the Sugar Industry; with an Introduction on the Chemistry of Cane-sugar, Dextrose, Levulose, and Milk-sugar. 8vo. New York, 1881. A 11 T 16

TUCKER (JEDEDIAH STEPHENS). Memoirs of Admiral the Rt. Hon. the Earl of St. Vincent, G.C.B. 2 vols. 8vo. Lond., 1844. C 9 S 27, 28

TUCKER (JOHN OWEN). The Golden Spring: a Tale of Tasmania, and other Poems. 12mo. Melb., 1865. MH 1 P 33

The Mute: a Poem of Victoria, and other Poems. 12mo. Melb., 1870. MH 1 R 51

TUCKER (ROBERT). [*See* CLIFFORD, W. K.] A 10 T 4

TUCKER (MISS SARAH). Abbeokuta; or, Sunrise within the Tropics: an Outline of the Origin and Progress of the Yoruba Mission. 5th ed. 12mo. Lond., 1856. D 1 V 3

The Southern Cross and Southern Crown; or, the Gospel in New Zealand. 12mo. Lond., 1855. MD 1 S 24

Another copy. 2nd ed. 12mo. Lond., 1855. MD 1 S 25

TUCKER (WILLIAM JAMES). Life and Society in Eastern Europe. 8vo. Lond., 1886. D 7 S 14

TUCKERMAN (BAYARD). History of English Prose Fiction, from Sir Thomas Malory to George Eliot. 8vo. Lond., 1882. B 4 S 23

TUCKERMAN (HENRY T.) Isabel; or, Sicily: a Pilgrimage. 8vo. Philad., 1839. J 12 Q 6

5 D

TUCKEY (LIEUT. J. H.), R.N. Account of a Voyage to establish a Colony at Port Phillip, in Bass's Strait, on the South Coast of New South Wales, in H.M.S. *Calcutta*, in the years 1802–4. 8vo. Lond., 1805.* MD 6 T 11

Bericht von einer Reise nach Neu-Süd-Wallis, um zu Port-Philipp, in der Bass's Strasse, eine Kolonie anzulegen. 8vo. Weimar, 1805. MD 6 T 14

TUDOR (HENRY). Narrative of a Tour in North America, comprising Mexico, &c., with an Excursion to the Island of Cuba, in a series of Letters, written in the years 1831–32. 2 vols. 8vo. Lond., 1834. D 3 Q 55, 56

TUDOR (JOHN R.) The Orkneys and Shetland; their Past and Present State; with Chapters on Geology, and Notes on the Flora of the Orkneys, and Notes on the Flora of Shetland. 8vo. Lond., 1883. D 7 R 15

TUDOR (WILLIAM). Letters on the Eastern States [of America]. 2nd ed. 8vo. Boston, 1821. J 5 S 18

TUER (ANDREW W.) Bartolozzi and his Works: a Biographical and Descriptive Account of the Life and Career of Francesco Bartolozzi, R.A. 2 vols. 4to. Lond., 1882. C 5 R 1, 2 †

Follies and Fashions of our Grandfathers, 1807. 8vo. Lond., 1886–87. A 7 Q 33

TUINMAN (CAROLUS). Fakkel der nederduitsche Taale; ontsteken byzonderlyk aan de Hebreeuwsche, Grieksche, en Latynsche spraaken, als ook de oude Duitsche, uit de overblyfzels der gryze aaloudheid, en die van laatere eeuwen. 4to. Leyden, 1722. K 15 P 31

TUKÁRÁM TÁTIÁ, F.T.S. The Yoga Philosophy. [*See* PANTANJALI.]

TUKE (DANIEL HACK), M.D., &c. Chapters in the History of the Insane in the British Isles. 8vo. Lond., 1882. A 12 S 18

TUKE (H.) Sentiments of the Society of Friends on Divine Worship and Gospel Ministry. 12mo. Hobart, 1837. MG 1 P 49

TULK (ALFRED). Lorenz Oken. [*See* ECKER, A.] C 5 Q 13

TULLOCH (COL. ALEXANDER M.) The Crimean Commission and the Chelsea Board. 8vo. Lond., 1857. F 4 S 5

Another copy. (Pam. 24.) 8vo. Lond., 1857. MJ 2 Q 12

TULLOCH (DAVID). [*See* KEARNEY, J.]

TULLOCH (REV. JOHN), D.D. Movements of Religious Thought in Britain during the 19th Century; being the Fifth Series of St. Giles' Lectures. 8vo. Lond., 1885. G 7 T 2

Theism, the Witness of Reason and Nature to an All-wise and Beneficent Creator. 8vo. Lond., 1855. G 3 P 4

TUNIS. History of the Conquest of Tunis and the Goletta by the Ottomans, A.H. 981 (A.D. 1573); translated from the Arabic into French, by A. Rousseau; and from the French, by J. T. Carletti. 8vo. Lond., 1883. B 1 P 32

TUPPER (MARTIN FARQUHAR), M.A., &c.   Half-a-dozen Ballads for Australian Emigrants, &c.   18mo.   Lond., 1853.   MH 1 R 46

Martin Tupper's Autobiography: my Life as an Author. 8vo. Lond., 1886.   C 8 Q 50

Paterfamilias's Diary of Everybody's Tour. 8vo. Lond., 1856.   D 7 P 46

Probabilities: an Aid to Faith; by the Author of "Proverbial Philosophy." 3rd ed., with Notes. 12mo. Lond., 1854.   G 7 T 3

Proverbial Philosophy: a Book of Thoughts and Arguments, originally treated. 12mo. Lond., 1852.   H 7 Q 3

Rides and Reveries of the late Mr. Æsop Smith; edited by "Peter Query, F.S.A." 8vo. Lond., 1858.   J 12 T 9

TURBERVILE (GEORGE).   Life and Poems of.   [*See* CHALMERS, A.]

TURENNE (HENRI DE LA TOUR D'AUVERGNE), VICOMTE DE. [Life of]; by H. M. Hozier. 8vo. Lond., 1885.   C 3 U 43

TURGOT (ANNE RODERT JACQUES).   [*See* ADAMS, J.]   B 15 R 15–17

TURGOT (SAINT), BISHOP OF ST. ANDREWS.   Life of St. Margaret, Queen of Scotland; translated from the Latin, by William Forbes-Leith, S.J.   2nd ed.   8vo.   Edinb., 1884.   C 4 Q 48

TURKEY.   Military Costume of Turkey; illustrated by Engravings (coloured), from drawings made on the spot. Roy. 4to. Lond., 1818.   A 23 S 15 ‡

Costume of Turkey.   [*See* DALVIMART, O.]

TURKISH SPY, A.   [*See* MARANA, G. P.]

TURNBULL (REV. ADAM).   [*See* SACRAMENTS, THE.]

TURNBULL (DAVID), M.A.   French Revolution of 1830. 8vo. Lond., 1830.   B 8 T 32

Travels in the West: Cuba; with Notices of Porto Rico and the Slave Trade. 8vo. Lond., 1840.   D 3 S 31

TURNBULL (JOHN).   Reise um die Welt, in den jahren 1800–4; aus dem Englischen übersetzt von Ph. Chr. Weyland. 8vo. Berlin, 1806.   MD 1 U 4

Voyage round the World, in the years 1800–4. 3 vols. 12mo. Lond., 1805.*   MD 1 T 28–30

Another copy. 2nd ed. 4to. Lond., 1813.* MD 7 P 23†

TURNBULL (PETER EVAN), F.R.S., &c.   Austria. Vol. 1. Narrative of Travels.   Vol. 2. Social and Political Condition. 2 vols. 8vo. Lond., 1840.   D 6 T 32, 33

TURNBULL (REV. ROBERT).   The Genius of Italy; being Sketches of Italian Life, Literature, and Religion. 8vo. Lond., 1849.   B 12 T 38

TURNBULL (WILLIAM B. D. D.)   [*See* CRANHAW, REV. R., *and* STUBBES, P.]

TURNBULL (W. P.)   [*See* COHN, H.]   A 12 U 18

TURNEBUS (A.)   [*See* PLINIUS SECUNDUS, C.]   A 16 S 2 ‡

TURNER (CHARLES EDWARD).   Studies in Russian Literature. 8vo. Lond., 1882.   B 31 Q 1

TURNER (CHARLES TENNYSON).   Collected Sonnets, Old and New. 12mo. Lond., 1880.   H 7 Q 2

TURNER (REV. DAWSON W.), M.A., &c.   Notes on Herodotus, original and selected from the best Commentators. 8vo. Oxford, 1848.   B 15 Q 34

Rules of Simple Hygiene, and Hints and Remedies for the Treatment of Common Accidents and Diseases. 6th ed. 8vo. Lond., 1872.   MA 2 S 38

Practical Grammar of the German Language.   [*See* AHN, DR. F.]

TURNER (E.), M.D., &c.   Elements of Chemistry, including the Actual State and Prevalent Doctrines of the Science; edited by Baron Liebig, and W. Gregory. 8vo. Lond., 1847.   A 5 U 7

TURNER (F. C.)   Short History of Art; with numerous Illustrations. 8vo. Lond., 1886.   A 8 Q 14

TURNER (REV. GEORGE), LL.D.   Nineteen Years in Polynesia: Missionary Life, Travels, and Researches in the Islands of the Pacific. 8vo. Lond., 1861.*   MD 6 R 5

Another copy. 2nd thousand. 8vo. Lond., 1861.   MD 6 R 8

Samoa a Hundred Years Ago, and long before; together with Notes on the Cults and Customs of twenty-three other Islands in the Pacific. 8vo. Lond., 1884.   MD 3 S 15

TURNER (REV. GEORGE E.)   Sermon, preached on Whit-Sunday, May 27th, 1849. 8vo. Sydney, 1849.   MG 1 P 1

TURNER (J. HORSFALL).   Ilkley, Ancient and Modern. [*See* COLLYER, REV. R.]   B 4 T 11

TURNER (JOSEPH MALLORD WILLIAM), R.A.   Anecdote Biography of.   [*See* THORNS, J.]   C 1 S 5

Liber Studiorum, reproduced in Autotype from the original Etchings. 3 vols. (in 1) imp. 4to. Lond., 1876.   A 23 P 22 ‡

Life of, founded on Letters and Papers furnished by his Friends and Fellow Academicians; by [George] Walter Thornbury. 2 vols. 8vo. Lond., 1862.   C 9 U 49, 50

Notes on the "Liber Studiorum." [*See* BROOKE, REV. S.]

Picturesque Views in England and Wales, reproduced in permanent Photography. 3 vols. imp. 4to. Lond., 1873.   D 4 U 6–8 ‡

Turner; by W. C. Monkhouse. (Great Artists.) 8vo. Lond., 1879.   C 3 T 33

Turner's Rivers of England: Sixteen Drawings by J. M. W. Turner, R.A., and three by Thomas Girtin, mezzotinted; with descriptions by Mrs. Holland. New ed., edited by W. Cosmo Monkhouse. Imp. fol. Lond., 1883.   D 5 R 20 †

Notes on the Turner Gallery. [*See* RUSKIN, J.]

TURNER (JOSEPH MALLORD WILLIAM), R.A.—*continued.*
Works of; with a Biographical Sketch and Critical and
Descriptive Notes, by James Dafforne. Roy. 4to. Lond.,
1877.   A 23 Q 2 ‡
Catalogue of the Drawings and Sketches by. [*See*
RUSKIN, J.]
Poetical Works of John Milton; with imaginative
Illustrations. [*See* MILTON, J.]
Poetical Works of Thomas Campbell; with Illustrations·
[*See* CAMPBELL, T.]
Italy: a Poem; by S. Rogers. Illustrated. [*See*
ROGERS, S.]

TURNER (MANSFIELD), AND HARRIS (WILLIAM). Guide
to the Institutions and Charities for the Blind in the United
Kingdom. 8vo. Lond., 1871.   F 9 P 22

TURNER (R.), JUNR., LL.D. Easy Introduction to the
Arts and Sciences. Illustrated. 18mo. Lond., 1804.
                                                   A 17 T 14

TURNER (SHARON), F.A.S., &c. History of England during
the Middle Ages. 3rd ed. 5 vols. 8vo. Lond., 1830.
                                                   B 5 R 16–20
History of the Anglo-Saxons, from the Earliest Period
to the Norman Conquest. 6th ed. 3 vols. 8vo. Lond.,
1836.   B 5 S 20–22
Modern History of England, Henry VIII–Elizabeth. 4
vols. 8vo. Lond., 1828–35.   B 5 R 21–24
Prolusions on the present Greatness of Britain; on
Modern Poetry; and on the present Aspect of the World.
12mo. Lond., 1819.   H 7 Q 4
Sacred History of the World, attempted to be philosophically considered, in a Series of Letters to a Son.
3 vols. 8vo. Lond., 1836.   G 10 R 1–3

TURNER (WILLIAM). Baxter Refuted; or, Louis Napoleon
not the destined Monarch of the World: a Lecture.
8vo. Beechworth, 1866.   MJ 2 R 15
Some Strictures on the Confession of Faith, addressed to
the Laity of the Presbyterian Church of Victoria. 8vo.
Melb., 1881.   MG 1 Q 39

TURNER (PROF. WILLIAM), M.B., &c. On the Placentation of the Apes; with a Comparison of the Structure
of their Placenta with that of the Human Female.
(Roy. Soc. Pubs., 6.) 4to. Lond., 1879.   A 11 P 7 ‡
On the Placentation of the Lemurs. (Roy. Soc. Pubs., 3.)
4to. Lond., 1876   A 11 P 4 †
[*See* ROLLESTON, PROF G.]   A 16 T 7, 8

TURNER (WILLIAM), M.D. Avium Præcipuarum, quarum
apud Plinium et Aristotelem mentio est, brevis et succincta
Historia. 18mo. Colon., 1544.   A 14 P 42

TURNER (WILLIAM H.) Selections from the Records of
the City of Oxford, illustrating the Municipal· History,
Henry VIII to Elizabeth (1509–83). 8vo. Oxford, 1880.
                                                   B 5 V 23

TURNER (PROF. WILLIAM W.) The Literature of
American Aboriginal Languages. [*See* LUDEWIG, H. E.]

TURNERELLI (EDWARD TRACY). Russia on the Borders
of Asia; Kazan, the Ancient Capital of the Tartar Khans.
2 vols. 8vo. Lond., 1854.   D 6 P 1, 2

TURNOR (HATTON). Astra Castra: Experiments and
Adventures in the Atmosphere. Roy. 4to. Lond., 1865.*
                                                   A 16 R 4 ‡

TURNURE (ARTHUR B.) Catalogue of the Art Department of the New England Manufacturers' and Mechanics'
Institute. 4to. Boston, 1883.   A 1 P 15 †

TUSON (PROF. R. V.), F.I.C. Cooley's Cyclopaedia of
Practical Receipts. [*See* COOLEY, A. J.]   K 1 Q 12, 13

TUSSAUD (MME.) Memoirs and Reminiscences of the
French Revolution. 2 vols. 8vo. Philad., 1839.   B 9 P 27, 28

TUTHILL (W. B.) The Suburban Cottage: its Design and
Construction. 8vo. New York, 1885.   A 2 S 20

TUTTLE (HERBERT). Brief Biographies: German Political
Leaders. Sq. 12mo. Lond., 1876.   C 2 R 15

TWAIN. [*See* IN SOUTHERN SEAS.]

TWAIN (MARK). [*See* CLEMENS, S. L.]

TWEED (JOHN). Glasghu Facies. [*See* McURE, J.]
                                                   B 13 P 20 21

TWEEDDALE (ARTHUR HAY), MARQUIS OF. Orni-
tho-
logical Works of; edited by Capt. Robert G. Wardlaw
Ramsay, F.L.S., &c. Roy. 4to. Lond., 1881. A 2 S 26 †

TWEEDIE (WILLIAM). Temperance Almanac for 1861–62.
12mo. Lond., 1861–62.   E 1.78

TWINING (LOUISA). Symbols and Emblems of Early and
Mediæval Christian Art. Illustrated. New ed. 8vo.
Lond., 1885.   A 8 P 26

TWINING (REV. THOMAS), M.A. Recreations and Studies
of a Country Clergyman of the 18th Century; being Selections from the Correspondence of the Rev. Thomas Twining,
M.A. 8vo. Lond., 1882.   J 4 P 28
Aristotle's Treatise on Poetry. [*See* ARISTOTELES.]
                                                   J 6 U 7

TWINING (THOMAS). Familiar Lessons on Food and Nutrition, intended to serve as a Hand-book to the Food
Department of the Parkes Museum of Hygiene. Part 1.
8vo. Lond., 1882.   A 17 T 57
Science Made Easy: a Series of Familiar Lectures on
the Elements of Scientific Knowledge most required in
Daily Life. 4to. Lond., 1876–78.   A 15 U 4
Technical Training; being a suggestive Sketch of a
National System of Industrial Instruction, founded on a
general diffusion of Practical Science among the People.
8vo. Lond., 1874.   G 17 Q 24

TWISDEN (Prof. John F.) Mathematics. [*See* Wylde, J.]

TWISS (Horace), Q.C. Public and Private Life of Lord Chancellor Eldon; with Selections from his Correspondence. 3 vols. 8vo. Lond., 1844. C 9 S 1-3

TWISS (Travers), D.C.L., &c. History of Rome. [*See* Niebuhr, B. G.] B 12 R 15

Law of Nations, considered as Independent Political Communities. 2 vols. 8vo. Oxford, 1861-63. F 4 S 8, 9

Oregon Question examined in respect to Facts and the Law of Nations. 8vo. Lond., 1846. B 1 T 26

View of the Progress of Political Economy in Europe, since the 16th Century. 8vo. Lond., 1847. F 4 S 6

TWOPENY (R. E. N.) Town Life in Australia. 8vo. Lond., 1883. MD 4 R 27

TWO BROTHERS. [*See* Hare, J. C. And A. W.]

TWO CHELAS in the Theosophical Society. [*See* Man.]

TWYFORD (Capt. A. W.), F.R.G.S. York and York Castle: an Appendix to the "Records of York Castle." 8vo. Lond., 1883. B 4 Q 28

TYCHO BRAHE. [*See* Brahe, T.]

TYCHSEN (T. C.) [*See* Quintus Smyrnæus.] H 7 T 32

TYERMAN (Rev. Daniel), And BENNET (George). Journal of Voyages and Travels by the Rev. Daniel Tyerman, and George Bennet, Esq., 1821-29; compiled by James Montgomery. 2 vols. 8vo. Lond., 1831.* MD 6 Q 20, 21

Another copy. 2nd ed. 8vo. Lond., 1840. MD 6 Q 24

TYERMAN (John). Plea for Free-thinkers; being a Letter to the Rt. Rev. Frederick Barker, D.D., Lord Bishop of Sydney. 12mo. Sydney, 1875. MG 1 Q 32

TYLER (J. Endell), B.D. Henry of Monmouth; or, Memoirs of the Life and Character of Henry v, as Prince of Wales and King of England. 2 vols. 8vo. Lond., 1838. C 8 Q 30, 31

TYLOR (Charles). Early Church History. [*See* Backhouse, E.]

Life and Labours of C. W. Walker. [*See* Backhouse, J.] MC 1 R 31

TYLOR (Edward B.), D.C.L., &c. Anahuac; or, Mexico and the Mexicans, Ancient and Modern. 8vo. Lond., 1861. D 1 Q 36

Anthropology: an Introduction to the Study of Man and Civilization; with Illustrations. 8vo. Lond., 1881. A 1 V 7

Primitive Culture: Researches into the Development of Mythology, Philosophy, Religion, Art, and Custom. 2 vols. 8vo. Lond., 1871. G 10 R 6, 7

Researches into the Early History of Mankind and the Development of Civilization. 3rd ed. 8vo. Lond., 1878. B 1 I S 5

TYMMS (W. R.) Art of Illuminating, as practised in Europe from the Earliest Times. 8vo. Lond., 1860. A 1 P 4 †

[*See* Westwood, J. O.] A 20 P 16 ‡

TYNDALE (William). Facsimile Texts: the First Printed English New Testament; translated by William Tyndale; edited by Edward Arber. Sm. 4to. Lond., 1871. G 5 Q 4

Five Books of Moses, called the Pentateuch: being a Verbatim Reprint of the edition of 1530; compared by the Rev. J. I. Mombert. Roy. 8vo. New York, 1884. G 5 S 4

Tyndale's Gospel. [*See* Bosworth, Rev. J.]

Writings of. [*See* British Reformers, 11.]

TYNDALL (Prof. John), D.C.L., &c. Contributions to Molecular Physics in the Domain of Radiant Heat. 8vo. Lond., 1872. A 5 U 22

Essays on the Floating-Matter of the Air in relation to Putrefaction and Infection. 8vo. Lond., 1881. A 12 Q 45

Faraday as a Discoverer. 8vo. Lond., 1868. C 5 R 15

Forms of Water in Clouds and Rivers, Ice and Glaciers. 8vo. Lond., 1873. A 3 S 22

Fragments of Science : a Series of detached Essays, Lectures, and Reviews. 4th ed. 8vo. Lond., 1872. A 17 V 8

Further Researches on the Deportment and Vital Persistence of Putrefactive and Infective Organisms, from a Physical Point of View. (Roy. Soc. Pubs., 4.) 4to. Lond., 1877. A 11 P 5 †

Heat, a Mode of Motion. 8vo. Lond., 1868. A 5 S 31

Hours of Exercise in the Alps. 8vo. Lond., 1871. D 8 Q 43

Inaugural Address delivered at the 44th Annual Meeting of the British Association for the Advancement of Science, 1874. (Reprinted from *Nature*.) 8vo. Melb., 1874. A 16 T 11

Another copy. 8vo. Melb., 1874. MJ 2 R 11

Lessons in Electricity, at the Royal Institution, 1875-76. 8vo. Lond., 1876. A 5 S 45

Lives of the Electricians. [*See* Jeans, W. T.] C 2 S 14

Notes of a Course of Seven Lectures on Electrical Phenomena and Theories, delivered at the Royal Institution of Great Britain, April 28th, June 9th, 1870. 8vo. Lond., 1870. A 5 S 50

Notes of a Course of Nine Lectures on Light. 4th ed. 8vo. Lond., 1872. A 5 R 37

Optical Deportment of the Atmosphere in relation to the Phenomena of Putrefaction and Infection. (Roy. Soc. Pubs., 2.) 4to. Lond., 1876. A 11 P 3 †

Researches on Diamagnetism and Magne-Crystallic Action, including the Question of Diamagnetic Polarity. 8vo. Lond., 1870. A 5 U 24

Six Lectures on Light, delivered in America in 1872-73. 2nd ed. 8vo. Lond., 1875. A 5 R 39

Sound : a Course of Eight Lectures, delivered at the Royal Institution of Great Britain. 2nd ed. 8vo. Lond., 1869. A 17 T 49

[*See* Helmholtz, Prof. H. L. F.]

TYPICAL Selections from the best English Writers; with Introductory Notices. (Clar. Press.) 2nd ed. 2 vols. (in 1) 12mo. Oxford, 1876. **J 1 T 29**

TYRCONNEL (RORY O'DONEL), EARL OF. Fate and Fortunes of Hugh O'Neill, Earl of Tyrone, and Rory O'Donel, Earl of Tyrconnel; their Flight from Ireland and Death in Exile; by the Rev. C. P. Meehan. 2nd ed. 8vo. Dublin, 1870. **C 4 R 5**

TYRONE (HUGH O'NEILL), EARL OF. Fate and Fortunes of Hugh O'Neill, Earl of Tyrone, and Rory O'Donel, Earl of Tyrconnel; their Flight from Ireland and Death in Exile; by the Rev. C. P. Meehan. 2nd ed. 8vo. Dublin, 1870. **C 4 R 5**

TYRRELL (ROBERT YELVERTON); M.A., &c. Correspondence of M. Tullius Cicero, arranged according to its chronological order; with a revision of the Text, a Commentary, and Introductory Essays on the Life of Cicero, and the Style of his Letters. Vols. 1, 2. 2nd ed. 8vo. Dublin, 1885–86. **C 14 U 6, 7**

Dublin Translations into Greek and Latin Verse. 8vo. Dublin, 1882. **H 8 U 7**

TYRRELL (RT. REV. W.), D.D., FIRST BISHOP OF NEW-CASTLE. Life and Labours of; by the Rev. R. G. Boodle. 8vo. Lond., 1881. **MC 1 Q 7**

Remarks on the Third Report of the Board of National Education in New South Wales, for the year 1850. 8vo. Sydney, 1851. **MG 1 Q 30**

TYRTÆUS. War Songs of, &c.; literally translated into English Prose by the Rev. J. Banks, M.A. 8vo. Lond., 1876. **H 5 S 34**

TYRWHITT (REV. RICHARD ST. JOHN), M.A. Greek and Gothic: Progress and Decay in the Three Arts of Architecture, Sculpture, and Painting. 8vo. Lond., 1881. **A 2 S 27**

TYRWHITT (REV. RICHARD ST. JOHN), M.A.—*continued.* Hand-book of Pictorial Art; with a Chapter on Perspective, by A. Macdonald. 2nd ed. (Clar. Press.) 8vo. Oxford, 1875. **A 23 U 7**

Our Sketching Club: Letters and Studies on Landscape Art. 8vo. Lond., 1874. **A 29 Q 42**

TYRWHITT (THOMAS). Poetical Works of Geoffrey Chaucer; with an Essay on his Language, &c.; with Notes and a Glossary. Roy. 8vo. Lond., 1871. **H 6 U 22**

TYRWHITT (WALTER S. S.), M.A. New Chum in the Queensland Bush. 8vo. Oxford, 1887. **MD 6 P 29**

TYSON (CAPT. GEORGE E.) Wonderful Drift on the Ice-floe. [*See* BLAKE, E. V.] **D 4 S 34**

TYTLER (ALEXANDER FRASER), LORD WOODHOUSELEE. [*See* WOODHOUSELEE, LORD.]

TYTLER (PATRICK FRASER), F.R.S.E. England under the Reigns of Edward VI, and Mary; with the Contemporary History of Europe. 2 vols. 8vo. Lond., 1839. **B 5 S 34, 35**

History of Scotland. 7 vols. 8vo. Edinb., 1828–40. **B 13 Q 11–17**

Life of the Admirable Crichton. 2nd ed. 12mo. Edinb., 1823. **C 2 Q 7**

Lives of Scottish Worthies. (Fam. Lib.) 3 vols. 12mo. Lond., 1831–33. **K 10 P 28–30**

TYTLER (SARAH). [*See* KEDDIE, MISS HENRIETTA.]

TYTLER (WILLIAM). Inquiry, Historical and Critical, into the Evidence against Mary, Queen of Scots. 2 vols. 8vo. Lond., 1790. **B 13 R 26, 27**

TZETZES (JOANNES). Antehomerica, &c. [*See* HESIOD.] **H 6 V 29**

U

UBICINI (A.) Aperçu historique sur la largue Roumaine. [*See* MIRCESCO, V.]

UCHTMANN (ALARDUS). Vox Clamantis in Deserto, ad doetissimum Juvenem Hadrianum Beverlandum Juris-peritum. 18mo. Medioburgi, 1679.   J 15 Q 11

UHLAND (JOHANN LUDWIG). Gedichte von Ludwig Uhland. 18e Auflage ; mit den Bildnisse des Verfassers. 8vo. Stuttgart, 1847.   H 7 P 14
Another copy. 9e Auflage. 18mo. Stuttgart, 1851.
                    H 6 P 25

UHLEMANN (MAX A.), PH.D. Handbuch der gesammten ägyptischen Alterthumskunde. 8vo. Leipsic, 1857–78.
                    B 2 R 37
Linguæ Copticæ Grammatica, in usum Scholarum Acade-micarum scripta cum Chrestomathia et Glossario. 8vo. Lipsiae, 1853.   K 13 Q 14

UHLHORN (DR. GERHARD). Conflict of Christianity with Heathenism. 8vo. Lond., 1879.   G 7 P 14

ULFILAS, ULPHILAS, OR GULPHILAS. [*See* UL-PHILAS.]

ULLATHORNE (RT. REV. W. B.), D.D. Few Words to the Rev. Henry Fulton, and his Readers ; with a Glance at the Archdeacon. 8vo. Sydney, 1833.   MG 1 P 5
Observations on the Use and Abuse of the Sacred Scrip-tures, as exhibited in the Discipline and Practice of the Protestant and Catholic Communions. 8vo. Sydney, 1831.   MG 1 P 5
Reply to Judge Burton, of the Supreme Court of New South Wales, on the State of Religion in the Colony. 8vo. Sydney, 1840.   MG 1 R 9
Another copy. 8vo. Sydney, 1840.   MJ 2 Q 9
Substance of a Sermon against Drunkenness, preached to the Catholics of divers parts of New South Wales. 8vo. Sydney (n.d.)   MG 1 P 1
[*See* FULTON, REV. H.]

ULLOA (DON ANTONIO DE). Noticias Secretas de America. [*See* JUAN Y SANTACILIA, DON J.]   B 16 R 18 ‡

ULLOA (DON ANTONIO DE), AND JUAN Y SANTACILIA (DON JORGE). Voyage to South America ; translated from the original Spanish, with Notes and Observations, and an Account of the Brazils, by John Adams. 4th ed. 2 vols. 8vo. Lond., 1806.   D 4 Q 1, 2

ULPHILAS. Opera omnia. [*See* MIGNE, J. P., SERIES LATINA, 18.]
Ulfilas Gothi che Bibelübersetzung die älteste Germanische Urkunde nach Ihr'ns. Text; ausgearbeitet von Fridrich Karl Fulda ; das Glossarium gearbeitet von W. F. H. Reinwald. 4to. Weissenfels, 1805.   K 14 U 5

Ulphilas, Apostle of the Goths. [*See* SCOTT, C. A. A.]

ULRICH (GEORGE H. F.), F.G.S., &c. Geology and Gold-fields of Otago. [*See* HUTTON, F. W.]   MA 2 Q 24
Geology of Victoria : a Descriptive Catalogue of the Specimens in the Industrial and Technological Museum (Melbourne). 8vo. Melb., 1875.   MA 2 Q 18
Intercolonial Exhibition Essays. [*See* SELWYN, A. R. C.]
                    MA 2 Q 35
Notes on the Physical Geography, &c., of Victoria. [*See* SELWYN, A. R. C.]   MF 1 Q 15
Observations on the Mode of Occurrence and the Treat-ment of Auriferous Lead, and Silver Ores, at Schemnitz, Upper Hungary. 8vo. Melb., 1868.   A 10 Q 6
[*See* SMYTH, R. B.]

UNDERWOOD (FRANCIS H.) Henry Wadsworth Long-fellow : a Biographical Sketch. 8vo. Lond., 1882. C 3 P 22
John Greenleaf Whittier : a Biography. 8vo. Lond., 1884.   C 1 U 49

UNGEWITTER (DR. F. H.) Australië en zijne Bewoners, volgens de nieuwste Ontdekkingen. 2 vols. (in 1) 8vo. Haarlem, 1854–56.   MD 4 W 18

UNIACKE (JOHN). Narrative of Mr. Oxley's Expedition to survey Port Curtis and Moreton Bay. [*See* FIELD, B.] [*See* PAMPHLET T.]

UNION BANK OF AUSTRALIA. Tenth Report of the Directors. 12mo. Lond., 1848.   MF 3 P 10

UNION OF RAILWAY SYSTEM OF N. S. WALES. [*See* NEW SOUTH WALES—RAILWAYS.]

UNITARIAN CHURCH, SYDNEY. Sixteenth Annual Report of the Committee. 12mo. Sydney, 1870.
                    MF 3 P 10
Another copy. 12mo. Sydney, 1870.   MG 1 Q 32

UNITED ASSOCIATION OF TEACHERS of New South Wales. Occasional Papers. No. 1. (Pam. 21.) 8vo. Sydney, 1856.   MJ 2 Q 10
Another copy. (Pam. 43.) 8vo. Sydney, 1856.
                    MJ 2 R 5

UNITED SERVICE MAGAZINE (COLBURN's). [*See* COLBURN'S UNITED SERVICE MAGAZINE.]

UNITED KINGDOM ALLIANCE for the Legislative Suppression of the Traffic in all Intoxicating Liquors as Beverages: Fifth Annual Report of the Dublin Auxiliary. 8vo. Dublin, 1859.   MG 1 Q 40

UNITED STATES OF AMERICA.
Document[s], accompanying Message[s] from the Presi-dent of the United States. 2 vols. 8vo. Wash., 1806–10.
                    F 5 T 16, 17

UNITED STATES OF AMERICA—*continued.*

Message[s] from the President[s] of the United States, 1811–12. 2 vols. 8vo. Wash., 1811–12.   F 5 T 18, 19

Index-Catalogue of the Library of the Surgeon-General's Office, United States Army: Authors and Subjects; with a List of Abbreviations of Titles of Periodicals. indexed. Vols. 1–7. Sm. fol. Wash., 1880–86.   K 8 S 2–8 †

Report on a Preliminary Investigation of the Properties of the Copper-Tin Alloys, made under the direction of the Committee on Metallic Alloys, United States Board to test Iron, Steel, and other Metals; Robert H. Thurston, Chairman. 8vo. Wash., 1879.   A 9 T 35

Report of Committee on the Naval Establishment. 8vo. Wash., 1811.   F 5 T 18

Alphabetical Catalogue of the War Department Library (including Law Library); compiled by D. Fitzgerald. Sm. fol. Wash., 1882.   K 9 P 17 †

Report of the Currency.   E

AGRICULTURE.

Reports of the Commissioner of Agriculture of the United States, 1862–87. 25 vols. 8vo. Wash., 1862–87.   E

CENSUS.

Compendium of the Ninth Census (June 1, 1870). Roy. 8vo. Wash., 1872.   F 3 R 14

Compendium of the Tenth Census (June 1, 1880). 2 vols. 8vo. Wash., 1883.   F 3 R 9, 10

Statistics of the Populations of the United States at the Tenth Census (June 1, 1880). 3 vols. roy. 4to. Wash., 1883.   K 8 Q 1–3 †

CONGRESS.

Dictionary of the United States Congress. [*See* LANMAN, C.]

Register of Debates in Congress. 3 vols. roy. 8vo. Wash., 1825–26.   F 1 R 16–18

CONSTITUTIONS.

Federal and State Constitutions, Colonial Charters, and other Organic Laws of the United States. 2nd ed. 2 vols. fol. Wash., 1878.   F 5 V 26, 27

CONSULAR REPORTS. Vols. 17, 18. 2 vols. 8vo. Wash., 1885–86.   E

EDUCATION.

American Education as described by the French Commission to the International Exhibition of 1876. 8vo. Wash., 1879.   F 7 Q 19

Bureau of Education, Circulars of Information : Value of Common School Education, of Common Labour, by Dr. E. Jarvis. 8vo. Wash., 1879.   F 7 Q 19

Co-education of the Sexes in the Public Schools of the United States. 8vo. Wash., 1883.   A 12 P 16

Training Schools of Cookery. 8vo. Wash., 1879.   F 7 Q 19

UNITED STATES OF AMERICA—*continued.*

EXPLORATIONS AND SURVEYS.

First Annual Report of the United States Entomological Commission, for the year 1877, relating to the Rocky Mountain Locust, and the best Methods of preventing its Injuries, and of guarding against its Invasions. With Maps and Illustrations. 8vo. Wash., 1878.   E

Geological Exploration of the 40th Parallel : Odontornithes ; by Prof. O. C. Marsh. Roy. 4to. Wash., 1810.   A 23 R 30 †

Report of the Superintendent [Prof. A. D. Bache] of the United States Coast Survey, showing the Progress of the Survey during the year 1853. 4to. Wash., 1854.   F 8 P 17 †

Report upon Geographical and Geological Explorations and Surveys west of the 100th Meridian : Zoology. 4to. Wash., 1875.   A 5 R 19 †

Reports of Explorations and Surveys; to ascertain the most practicable and economical Route for a Railroad from the Mississippi River to the Pacific Ocean, made in 1853–56. 12 vols. (in 13) 4to. Wash., 1855–60.   D 3 V 23–35

Scientific Results of the United States Arctic Expedition : Steamer *Polaris*, C. F. Hall, commanding. Vol. 1. Physical Observations ; by Emil Bessels. 4to. Wash., 1876.   D 1 S 10 †

United States Exploring Expedition, during the years 1838–42, under the command of Charles Wilkes, U.S.N. 15 vols. imp. 4to., and 5 vols. at. fol. Philad., 1845–76.   A 31 ‡

Narrative, and Atlas, by C. Wilkes.
Zoophytes, with an Atlas of 61 Plates, by James D. Dana.
Mammalogy and Ornithology, with an Atlas, by John Cassin.
Crustacea, with an Atlas, by James D. Dana.
Mollusca and Shells, with an Atlas of Plates, by Augustus A. Gould, M.D.
Geographical Distribution of Animals and Plants, by Charles Pickering, M.D. Part 1. History of the Introduction of Domestic Animals and Plants. Part 2. Plants in their Wild State.
Ethnography and Philology, by Horatio Hale.
Herpetology, with an Atlas of Plates, by Charles Girard.

FINANCES.

Annual Report on the State of the Finances to 1873; by William A. Richardson. (Pam. Dq.) 8vo. Wash., 1873.   F 4 R 7

Letter from the Secretary of the Treasury, transmitting a Statement of the several Banks in which the Public Monies are now deposited. 8vo. Wash., 1812.   F 5 T 19

GUIDES.

American Overland Route. (Pam. 39.) 12mo. New York, 1870.   MJ 2 R 1

LAND LAWS.

Existing Land Laws of the United States. 8vo. Wash., 1884.   F 3 R 11

Land Laws of the United States. 2 vols. 8vo. Wash., 1884.   F 3 R 12, 13

The Public Domain; its History, with Statistics. (Public Lands Commission on Codification.) 8vo. Wash., 1884.   F 3 T 3

UNITED STATES OF AMERICA—*continued.*

PATENTS.

Alphabetical Lists of Patentees and Inventions. 5 vols.
10y. 8vo. Wash., 1881–83.   E

Annual Reports of the Commissioner for Patents, for
the years 1847–71, and 1876–84. 75 vols. 10y. 8vo.
Wash., 1848–85.   E

Official Gazette of the United States Patent Office; with
Indexes for the years 1872–76. Vols. 1–30. Roy. 8vo.
Wash., 1871–85.   E

Patent Laws of the United States of America, passed 8th
July, 1870; with Revised Statutes, approved by Congress,
22nd June, 1874. Sm. 4to. Lond., 1876.   K 7 S 25

SANITARY COMMISSION.

United States Sanitary Commission: Bulletin and Documents. 4 vols. (in 3) 8vo. New York, 1866.   E

STATUTES.

Public and General Statutes of the United States of
America, 1789–1827; published under the inspection of
Joseph Story. 3 vols. 8vo. Boston, 1828.   F 12 R 3–5

CALIFORNIA.

Act of Incorporation and Ordinances of the City of San
Francisco. (Pam. 18.) 8vo. San Francisco, 1856.
                                                       F 12 P 10

All about California. 8vo. San Francisco, 1870.
                                                       D 4 Q 28

Biennial Report of the Surveyor-General of the State of
California, 1873–75. 8vo. Sacramento, 1875.   E

Biennial Reports of the Superintendent of Public Instruction of the State of California, for the school years
1866–67, and 1874–75. 2 vols. 8vo. San Francisco,
1867–75.   E

Civil Code of; compiled by Albert Hart. 12mo. San
Francisco, 1885.   F 2 P 1

Code of Civil Procedure; by Nathan Newmark. 12mo.
San Francisco, 1885.   F 2 P 2

Municipal Reports for the fiscal year 1874–75, ending
June 30, 1875. 8vo. San Francisco, 1875.   E

Penal Code of; annotated by Robert Desty. 12mo.
San Francisco, 1885.   F 2 P 3

Political Code of; by Nathan Newmark. 12mo. San
Francisco, 1885.   F 2 P 4

Report of the Debates in the Convention of California,
on the formation of the State Constitution, in 1849. 8vo.
Wash., 1850.

Report on the Business and Condition of the California
Trust Company, for 1870. 8vo. San Francisco, 1871.
                                                       D 4 Q 28

Report on the Condition of the Real Estate within the
Limits of the City of San Francisco. (Pam. 18.) 8vo.
San Francisco, 1851.   F 12 P 10

Report on the Subject of Land Titles in California; by
W. C. Jones. (Pam. 18.) 8vo. Wash., 1850. F 12 P 10

Reports of the Surveyor-General of California, from
1867–69. 8vo. San Francisco, 1869–70.   D 4 Q 28

UNITED STATES OF AMERICA—*continued.*

CALIFORNIA—*continued.*

Sixth Biennial Report of the Superintendent of Public
Instruction of the State of California. 8vo. Sacramento,
1875.   E

School Law of California, and Rules and Regulations
of the State Boards of Education and Examination. 8vo.
Sacramento, 1876.   G 17 R 13

Statutes of California, passed at the First Session of the
Legislature. 4to. San José, 1850.   F 8 P 19 †

Transactions of the California State Agricultural Society,
1859 and 1874. 2 vols. 8vo. Sacramento, 1860–75. E

CONNECTICUT.

Annual Reports of the Board of Education of the State
of Connecticut; together with the Annual Reports of the
Secretary of the Board. 3 vols. 8vo. Hartford and Newhaven, 1866–75.   E

ILLINOIS.

Annual Reports of the Board of Public Works to the
Common Council of the City of Chicago. 8vo. Camb.,
1871–76.   E

Annual Reports of the Board of Trustees of the Illinois
Industrial University, 1867–74. 7 vols. 8vo. Springfield,
1868–74.   E

Eighteenth Annual Report of the Trade and Commerce of
Chicago, for 1875. 8vo. Chicago, 1876.   E

Fifth Annual Report of the Railroad and Warehouse
Commission of the State of Illinois, for 1875. 8vo. Springfield, 1876.   E

Tenth Biennial Report of the Superintendent of Public
Instruction of the State of Illinois, 1873–74. 8vo.
Springfield, 1874.   E

Transactions of the Department of Agriculture of the
State of Illinois, with Reports from County Agricultural
Boards, for 1875. 8vo. Springfield, 1876.   E

INDIANA.

Annual Reports of the Officers of State of the State of
Indiana, 1875. 8vo. Indianapolis, 1876.   E

Twenty-second Report of the Superintendent of Public
Instruction of the State of Indiana. 8vo. Indianapolis,
1874.   E

IOWA.

Annual Report of the Iowa State Horticultural Society,
for 1875; Joseph L. Budd. 8vo. Des Moines, 1876. E

Report of the Secretary of the Iowa State Agricultural
Society, for the year 1870. 8vo. Des Moines, 1870–71. E

Thirteenth State Census of Iowa, as returned in the
year 1875. 8vo. Des Moines, 1875.   F 1 Q 22

KENTUCKY.

Annual Report of the Superintendent of Public Instruction, Kentucky, 1875. 8vo. Frankfort, 1875.   E

Message of Governor James B. McCreary to the General
Assembly of Kentucky, December 31st, 1875; Regular
Session of the Legislature of 1875–76. (Pam. Ja.) 8vo.
Frankfort, 1875.   F 7 S 21

Report of the Auditor of Public Accounts of the State
of Kentucky. 8vo. Frankfort, 1876.   E

UNITED STATES OF AMERICA— *continued.*

MAINE.

Annual Reports of the Superintendent of Common Schools of the State of Maine, 1869-75. 7 vols. 8vo. Augusta, 1869-76. E

Second Annual Report upon the Natural History and Geology of the State of Maine, 1862. E

MARYLAND.

Report[s] of the Commissioners of Fisheries of Maryland, 1876-77 and 1879-80. 8vo. Annapolis, 1876-80. E

MASSACHUSETTS.

Abstract of the Census, 1860 and 1865. 2 vols. 8vo. Boston, 1863-67. E

Abstract of the Certificates of Corporations organized under the General Laws of Massachusetts. 8vo. Boston, 1876. E

Annual Report of the Adjutant-General, for 1875. 8vo. Boston, 1876. E

Annual Report of the Commissioner of Savings Banks, 1875. 8vo. Boston, 1876. E

Annual Reports of the Board of Inspectors of the Massachusetts State Prison, October, 1875-January, 1876. (Pam. Dz.) 8vo. Boston, 1876. F 7 S 23

Annual Reports of the Bureau of Statistics of Labor. 5 vols. 8vo. Boston, 1876-84. E

Auditors' Reports of the Receipts and Expenditure of the City of Boston, 1824-73. 20 vols. 8vo. Boston, 1824-73.

Boston Board of Trade: Annual Reports, 1855-66, and 1869-72. 16 vols. 8vo. Boston, 1856-72. E

Census of Boston, 1845. 8vo. Boston, 1846. E

Census of Massachusetts, 1875. 2nd ed. 3 vols. roy. 8vo. Boston, 1876-77. E

Census System of, for 1875. 4to. Boston, 1876. E

Compendium of the Census of Massachusetts, 1875; prepared by Carroll D. Wright. Roy. 8vo. Boston, 1877. E

Discussions on the Constitution proposed to the People of Massachusetts by the Convention of 1853. 8vo. Boston, 1854. F 3 P 10

Fourteenth Annual Report of the Trustees of the State Lunatic Hospital at Northampton, October, 1869. (Pam. Ja.) Boston, 1870. F 7 S 24

History of the Massachusetts Insurance Department. 8vo. Boston, 1876. F 10 S 19

Massachusetts Institute of Technology : President's Reports for the years 1873-75; Eleventh Annual Catalogue of the Officers and Students, 1875-76. 8vo. Boston, 1873-76. E

Memorial of Joshua Bates. Imp. 8vo. Boston, 1865-66. C 3 W 3

Normal Institute of Physical Education, Boston, Massachusetts. (Pam. 37.) 8vo. Boston, 1863. MJ 2 Q 24

5 E

UNITED STATES OF AMERICA—*continued.*

MASSACHUSETTS—*continued.*

Prizes for Arboriculture, offered by the Trustees of the Massachusetts Society for promoting Agriculture. (Pam. Cl.) 8vo. Boston, 1876. A 16 U 21

Proceedings of the Eleventh Annual Meeting of the New England Cotton Manufacturers' Association, held at Boston, April 26, 1876. (Pam. Dx.) 8vo. Boston, 1876. F 3 T 17

Public Charities of Massachusetts : a Report made to the Massachusetts Centennial Commission, Feb. 1, 1876 ; Supplement to the Twelfth Annual Report. 8vo. Boston, 1876. E

Report of the Auditor of Accounts, for 1875. 8vo. Boston, 1876. E

Report of the Cochituate Water Board, to the City Council of Boston. 8vo. Boston, 1852. E

Report of the Commissioners on Inland Fisheries, 1872. 8vo. Boston, 1872. E

Report of the Commissioners on Inland Fisheries, for the year ending Janauary 1, 1876. (Pam. Ja.) 8vo. Boston, 1876. F 7 S 24

Report of the Treasurer and Receiver-General, for 1875. (Pam. Dz.) 8vo. Boston, 1876. F 7 S 23

Revised Statutes of the Commonwealth of Massachusetts. Roy. 8vo. Boston, 1836. F 8 T 12

Seventh Annual Report of the State Board of Health, January, 1876. Roy. 8vo. Boston, 1876. E

Summary of Seven Years' Work of the State Board of Health. Roy. 8vo. Boston, 1876. E

Thirty-ninth Annual Report of the Board of Education, together with the thirty-ninth Annual Report of the Secretary of the Board, 1874-75. 8vo. Boston, 1876. E

Thirty-third Report of the Legislature of Massachusetts, relating to the Registry and Return of Births, Marriages, and Deaths in the Commonwealth, for 1874. 8vo. Boston, 1876. E

Twelfth Annual Report of the Board of State Charities ; with an Appendix. 8vo. Boston, 1876. E

Twenty-first Annual Report of the Insurance Commissioner of the Commonwealth of Massachusetts, January 1, 1876. 2 vols. Boston, 1876. E

Twenty-second Annual Report of the Inspectors of the State Almshouse at Tewksbury, for the year ending September 30, 1875. (Pam. Ja.) 8vo. Boston, 1876. F 7 S 24

Twenty-second Annual Report of the Trustees of the State Lunatic Hospital at Taunton, 1875. 8vo. Boston, 1876. F 7 S 23

Twenty-third Annual Report of the Secretary of the Board of Agriculture, for 1875. 8vo. Boston, 1876. E

MICHIGAN.

Annual Reports of the State Board of Health. 3 vols. 8vo. Lansing, 1874-76. E

Annual Reports of the Superintendent of Public Instruction, 1855-73. 19 vols. 8vo. Lansing, 1858-64. E

UNITED STATES OF AMERICA—*continued.*

MICHIGAN—*continued.*

Census of the State of Michigan, 1874. 8vo. Lansing, 1875. F 1 R 7

Debates and Proceedings of the Constitutional Convention, convened at the City of Lansing, 1867. 2 vols. 4to. Lansing, 1867. E

Fifth Annual Report of the Secretary of the State Pomological Society, 1875. 8vo. Lansing, 1876. E

Fifth Annual Reports of the Secretary of State, relating to the Registry and Return of Births, Marraiges, and Deaths, for 1871. 8vo. Lansing, 1874. E

Fourteenth Annual Report of the Secretary of the State Board of Agriculture, for the year 1875. 8vo. Lansing, 1876. E

The State of Michigan, embracing Sketches of its History, Position, Resources and Industries; compiled under authority, by S. B. M'Cracken. 8vo. Lansing, 1876. F 1 T 11

Geological Survey of Michigan : Upper Peninsula, 1869–73. 4 vols. roy. 8vo. New York, 1873. A 9 U 7–10

School Funds and School Laws of Michigan ; with Notes and Forms. J. M. Gregory, Superintendent. 8vo. Lansing, 1859. G 17 R 16

The School Laws of Michigan ; with Explanatory Notes. Daniel B. Briggs, Superintendent. 8vo. Lansing, 1873. G 17 R 15

Third Annual Abstract of the Reports of Sheriffs relating to the Jails in the State of Michigan for 1875. (Pam. Dz.) 8vo. Lansing, 1876. F 7 S 23

Second Annual Abstract of Statistical Information relative to the Insane, Deaf, Dumb, and Blind, in the State of Michigan ; Abstract of the Annual Reports of the County Superintendents of the Poor of the State of Michigan, for 1874. (Pam. Dy.) 8vo. Lansing, 1875. MF 3 Q 1

Sixth Annual Report of the Commissioner of Insurance, 1875. Part 1. Fire and Marine Insurance. Part 2. Life Insurance. 2 vols. 8vo. Lansing, 1876.

State School at Coldwater: its Purposes and Aims ; by L. P. Alden. (Pam. Bs.) 8vo. Coldwater, 1876. MG 1 Q 31

Statistics of the State of Michigan, collected for the Ninth Census of the United States, 1870. 8vo. Lansing, 1873. F 1 R 6

MINNESOTA.

Executive Documents of the State of Minnesota, for the year 1875. 2 vols. 8vo. St. Paul, 1876. E

Geological and Natural History Survey of Minnesota : Annual Reports for 1872–83. 7 vols. 8vo. St. Paul, 1874–84. E

MISSOURI.

Report of the Geological Survey of the State of Missouri, including Field work of 1873–74. With Illustrations. 8vo. Jefferson City, 1874. E

MONTANA.

Annual Report of the Auditor and Treasurer to the Governor, Benjamin F. Potts, of Montana Territory, for 1874. (Pam. Dz.) 8vo. Virginia, 1875. F 7 S 23

UNITED STATES OF AMERICA—*continued.*

MONTANA—*continued.*

Biennial Report of Hon. Cornelius Hedges, Superintendent of Public Instruction for 1874–75. Roy. 8vo. Helena, 1876. F 3 T 17

Message of the Governor of Montana Territory, to the Extraordinary Session of the Legislative Assembly, commencing April 14, A.D. 1873. (Pam. Jb.) 8vo. Virginia, 1873. MF 3 P 21

NEW HAMPSHIRE.

Annual Reports of the Board of Agriculture to His Excellency the Governor. 3 vols. 8vo. Concord, 1873–75. E

NEW JERSEY.

Annual Announcement of the Stevens Institute of Technology. 8vo. Hoboken, 1876. E

Documents of the Ninety-ninth Session of Legislature of New Jersey, and Thirty-first under the New Constitution. 8vo. Camden, 1875. E

Report of the State Board of Education, and the State Superintendent of Public Instruction, for 1875. 8vo. Trenton, 1875. E

NEW YORK.

Reports of the Proceedings and Debates of the Convention of 1821 ; by H. Carter and W. L. Stone. 8vo. Albany, 1821. F 10 T 18

Trow's New York City Directory for 1878. 8vo. New York, 1878. E

NORTH CAROLINA.

Testimony taken by the Joint Select Committee to inquire into the Condition of Affairs in the late Insurrectionary States. 8vo. Wash., 1872. F 10 T 11

OHIO.

Cleveland Public Schools : Thirty-ninth Annual Report of the Board of Education for the School year ending August 31, 1875. 8vo. Cleveland, 1876. E

Pictorial Description of Ohio ; by J. B. Lossing. (Pam. 18.) 8vo. New York, 1849. F 12 P 10

Proceedings of the Seventh Annual Conference of Charities and Correction, held at Cleveland, 1880 ; edited by F. B. Sanborn. Roy. 8vo. Boston, 1880. MH 18 5

Twenty-ninth Annual Report of the Ohio State Board of Agriculture; with an Abstract of the Proceedings of the County Agricultural Societies to the General Assembly of Ohio. 8vo. Cincinnati, 1874. E

OREGON.

Biennial Report of the State Treasurer of the State of Oregon to the Legislative Assembly. 8vo. Salem, 1876. E

Biennial Report of the Superintendent of Public Instruction. 8vo. Salem, 1876. E

Report of the State Commissioner of Immigration, 1876. (Pam. Jb.) 8vo. Salem, 1876. MF 3 P 21

PENNSYLVANIA.

Charters of the Province of Pennsylvania and City of Philadelphia. Sm. fol. Philad., 1742. F 8 Q 13 †

Forty-third Annual Report of the Managers of the Pennsylvania Institution for the Instruction of the Blind, 1875. (Pam. Jb.) 8vo. Philad., 1876. MF 3 P 21

UNITED STATES OF AMERICA—*continued.*
PENNSYLVANIA—*continued.*
Philadelphia International Exhibition of 1876. [*See*
PHILADELPHIA INTERNATIONAL AND CENTENNIAL EXHI-
BITION.]
Mortality Experience of the Provident Life and Trust
Company of Philadelphia, 1866–85 ; prepared by Asa
S. Wing. Roy. 8vo. Philad., 1886. F 3 P 9
RHODE ISLAND.
Annual Report of the Adjutant-General of the State of
Rhode Island. (Pam. Ja.) 8vo. Providence, 1876.
F 7 S 24
Annual Report of the Commissioners on Inland Fisheries,
made to the General Assembly of the State of Rhode
Island, 1876. (Pam. Ja.) 8vo. Providence, 1876.
F 7 S 24
Annual Report of the Quartermaster-General, made to
the General Assembly of Rhode Island, January, 1876.
(Pam. Ja.) 8vo. Providence, 1876. F 7 S 24
Annual Reports of the Board of Education ; together
with the Annual Reports of the Commissioner of Public
Schools. 8 vols. 8vo. Providence, 1846–76. E
Annual Statement, exhibiting the Condition of the State
Banks of Rhode Island, 1875. (Pam. Ja.) 8vo. Provi-
dence, 1876. F 7 S 24
General Statutes of the State of Rhode Island and Provi-
dence Plantations. 8vo. Camb., 1872. E
History of Public Education in Rhode Island, 1636–1876 ;
compiled and edited by Thomas B. Stockwell. 8vo.
Providence, 1876. G 17 R 5
Manual, with Rules and Orders for the use of the General
Assembly, Rhode Island. 8vo. Providence, 1874.
F 5 S 6
Providence Directory, for the year commencing July 1,
1875. 8vo. Providence, 1875. E
Public Laws of the State of Rhode Island and Providence
Plantations. 8vo. Providence, 1876. • E
Rhode Island in the Continental Congress ; with the
Journal of the Convention that adopted the Consti-
tution, 1765–90, by Hon. William R. Staples, LL.D. ;
edited by R. A. Guild, A.M. 8vo. Providence, 1870.
F 4 R 3
Report and Documents relating to the Public Schools of
Rhode Island, for 1848. 8vo. Providence, 1849.
Report of the General Treasurer, January Session, A.D.
1876. (Pam. Ja.) 8vo. Providence, 1876. F 7 S 24
Report of the State Auditor, 1876. 8vo. (Pam. Dy.)
8vo. Providence, 1876. MF 3 Q 1
Report on the Condition and Improvement of the Public
Schools of Rhode Island, 1846. 8vo. Providence, 1846. E
Report upon the Census of Rhode Island, 1865 ; with
the Statistics of the Population, Agriculture, Fisheries,
and Manufactures of the State. 8vo. Providence, 1867.
F 12 R 2
Reports of Cases argued and determined in the Supreme
Court of Rhode Island. 5 vols. 8vo. Providence, 1862–75.
E
Reports to the General Assembly, relating to the Re-
gistry and Returns of Births, Marriages, and Deaths in
the State. 19 vols. 8vo. Providence, 1856–75. E

UNITED STATES OF AMERICA—*continued.*
RHODE ISLAND—*continued.*
School Laws of Rhode Island : Acts and Amendments
relating to the Public Schools. 8vo. Providence, 1855.
G 17 S 2
School Manual, containing the School Laws of Rhode
Island ; with Decisions, Remarks, and Forms. 12mo.
Providence, 1873. G 17 R 11
Report upon the Public Schools and Education in Rhode
Island, 1854 ; by E. R. Potter. 8vo. Providence, 1855.
G 17 S 2
Annual Report of the Commissioner of Public Schools
of Rhode Island ; by Robert Allen. 8vo. Providence,
1856. G 17 S 2
By-laws of the School Committee, and Regulations of
the Public Schools in the City of Providence. 8vo.
Providence, 1855. G 17 S 2
· Semi-Annual Report of the Railroad Commissioner, 1876.
(Pam. Dy.) 8vo. Providence, 1876. MF 3 Q 1
TENNESSEE.
Annual Report of the State Superintendent of Schools
for Tennessee, for 1875. 8vo. Nashville, 1876. E
Proceedings of the Tennessee Stockbreeders' Association,
held in Nashville, 1876 ; also, an Address delivered before
the Association by J. B. Killibrew. (Pam. Cl.) 8vo.
Nashville, 1876. A 16 U 21
Public School Laws of Tennessee, including all Acts
passed since March, 1873. (Pam. Bs.) 8vo. Nashville,
1876. MG 1 Q 34
TEXAS.
Fifth Annual Report of Public Instruction, 1875 ; by
O. N. Hollingsworth. (Pam. Cs.) 8vo. Houston, 1876.
MG 1 Q 34
WISCONSIN.
Annual Reports of the Superintendent of Public Instruc-
tion of the State of Wisconsin. 7 vols. 8vo. Madison,
1869–75. E
Historical Sketches of the Colleges of Wisconsin ; pre-
pared for the National Centennial Exposition, for 1876,
by A. L. Chapin. 8vo. Madison, 1876. G 17 R 17
Laws of Wisconsin relating to Common Schools, includ-
ing the Township and Free High School Law. 8vo.
Madison, 1876. G 17 R 14
Second Annual Report of the Railroad Commissioners of
the State of Wisconsin. 8vo. Madison, 1875. E
State of Wisconsin, embracing a brief Sketches of its History,
Position, Resources, and Industries, and a Catalogue of
its Exhibits at the Centennial at Philadelphia. 8vo.
Madison, 1876. F 4 S 20
Transactions of the Wisconsin Academy of Sciences, Arts,
and Letters, 1870–72. 8vo. Madison, 1872. E
Transactions of the Wisconsin State Agricultural Society ;
with Portions of the Correspondence of the Secretary,
Reports of the State Agricultural Society, &c. 9 vols.
8vo. Madison, 1853–76. E

UNITED STATES MAGAZINE and Democratic Review.
8vo. New York, 1843–45. J 10 V 13

UNIVERSAL HISTORY (AN), from the Earliest Account of Time; with Index and Chronological Tables. 21 vols. 8vo. Lond., 1747-54. **B 14 T 1-21**

Modern Part of an Universal History, from the Earliest Accounts to the Present Time. 42 vols. 8vo. Lond., 1780-84. **B 14 T 22-U 21**

UNIVERSAL INSTRUCTÓR (THE); or, Self-Culture for All. Illustrated. 3 vols. roy. 8vo. Lond., 1882-84. **K 9 U 26-28**

UNIVERSAL SONGSTER (THE); or, Museum of Mirth, forming the most complete, extensive and valuable Collection of Ancient and Modern Songs in the English Language; embellished with Wood Cuts by G. and R. Cruikshank. 3 vols. 8vo. Lond. (n.d.) **H 6 S 12-14**

UNIVERSITY MAGAZINE (DUBLIN). [*See* DUBLIN UNIVERSITY MAGAZINE.]

UNIVERSITY MAN, A. [*See* CARRINGTON, G.]

UNKNOWN, THE. [*See* AUSTRALIAN COLONIES.]

UNPAID MAGISTRATE, AN. [*See* HOLE AND CORNER PETITION.]

UNSER VATERLAND. In Wort und Bild geschildert von einem Verein deutscher und österreichischef Schriftsteller und Künstler. 4 vols. imp. 4to. Stuttgart (n.d.) **D 38 P 17-20**

1. Bayerisches Gebirge und Salzkammergut; geschildert von Herman von Schmid und Karl Stieler.
2. Tirol und Vorarlberg; geschildert von Ludwig von Hormann, Herman von Schmid, Ludwig Steub, Karl von Seyfflertitz, Ignaz Zingerle.
3. Wanderungen durch Steiermark und Kärnten; geschildert von P. K. Rosegger, Fritz Pichler, und U. von Rauschenfels.
4. Küstenfahrten an der Nord-und Ostsee; geschildert von Edmund Hoefer.

UNWIN (PROF. W. CAWTHORNE), B.Sc., &c. Elements of Machine Design. (Text-books of Science.) 8vo. Lond., 1877. **A 17 S 21**

Another copy. 3rd ed. 8vo. Lond., 1880. **A 11 P 20**

[*See* HYDRO-MECHANICS.] **A 11 U 7**

UPHAM (EDWARD). History of the Ottoman Empire, from its establishment till the year 1828. (Const. Misc.) 2 vols. 18mo. Edinb., 1829. **K 10 Q 28, 29**

Rameses: an Egyptian Tale; with Historical Notes of the Era of the Pharaohs. 3 vols. 8vo. Lond., 1824. **J 8 Q 35-37**

UPHAM (THOMAS C.) Life, Religious Opinions, and Experience of Madame de la Mothe Guyon; together with some Account of the Personal History and Religious Opinions of Fénélon, Archbishop of Cambray. 8vo. Lond., 1856. **C 3 R 41**

Archæologia Biblica. [*See* JAHN, J.]

UPPER TEN THOUSAND, Anecdotes of. [*See* BERKELEY, HON. G. F.]

URBAN II (PAPA). Epistolæ, Diplomata, et Sermones. [*See* MIGNE, J. P., SERIES LATINA, 151.]

URBINO (DUKES OF). Memoirs of. [*See* DENNISTOUN, J.]

URE (ANDREW), M.D., &c. Cotton Manufacture of Great Britain, systematically investigated. 2 vols 8vo. Lond., 1836. **A 11 R 17, 18**

New System of Geology, in which the Great Revolutions of the Earth and Animated Nature are reconciled at once to Modern Science and Sacred History. 8vo. Lond., 1829. **A 9 R 19**

Philosophy of Manufactures; or, an Exposition of the Scientific, Moral, and Commercial Economy of the Factory System of Great Britain. 8vo. Lond., 1835. **A 11 R 6**

Ure's Dictionary of Art, Manufactures, and Mines; with Supplement by Robert Hunt, F.R.S. Illustrated. 7th ed. 4 vols. 8vo. Lond., 1875-78. **K 18 Q 13-16**

URQUHART (DAVID). Manual of the Turkish Bath: Heat a Mode of Cure; edited by Sir Joseph Fife. 8vo. Lond., 1865. **A 12 Q 2**

Pillars of Hercules; or, a Narrative of Travels in Spain and Morocco in 1848. 2 vols. 8vo. Lond., 1850. **D 2 T 8, 9**

Spirit of the East, illustrated in a Journal of Travels through Roumeli, during an Eventful Period. 2 vols. 8vo. Lond., 1838. **D 8 T 40, 41**

URQUHART (J. W.), C.E. Electric Light; its Production and Use. With Illustrations. 8vo. Lond., 1880. **A 5 R 42**

Electro-plating: a Practical Hand-book, including the Practice of Electro-typing. 2nd ed. 8vo. Lond., 1880. **A 11 Q 36**

Sewing Machinery; being a Practical Manual of the Sewing Machine. With Illustrations. (Weale.) 12mo. Lond., 1881. **A 17 Q 46**

URQUHART (W. POLLARD). Life and Times of Francesco Sforza, Duke of Milan; with a preliminary Sketch of the History of Italy. 2 vols. 8vo. Edinb., 1852. **C 9 T 41, 42**

URSINS (ANNE MARIE DE LA TREMOUILLE), PRINCESSE DES. Secret Correspondence. [*See* MAINTENON, F. D'A., MARQUISE DE.] **C 8 Q 5-7**

URWICK (REV. W.), M.A. Indian Pictures, drawn with Pen and Pencil. Imp. 8vo. Lond. (n.d.) **D 5 V 34**

USE OF OIL AT SEA. Memorandum on the Use of Oil at Sea, for modifying the Effect of Breaking Waves, issued for the Information of Officers in general. 8vo. Sydney, 1887. **MA 1 T 22**

USHER (W.), M.D. Types of Mankind. [*See* NOTT, J. C.] **A 2 P 19**

USSHER (MOST REV. JAMES), D.D., ARCHBISHOP OF ARMAGH. Whole Works of; with the Life of the Author, and an Account of his Writings, by C. R. Elrington, D.D.; with an Index. 17 vols. 8vo. Dublin, 1847-64. **G 11 Q 1-17**

USSIEUX (MME. D'). [*See* CABINET DES FÉES, 36.]

USUARDUS (SANGERMANENSIS MONACHUS). Martyrologium. [*See* MIGNE, J. P., SERIES LATINA, 123, 124.]

UVA Revisited, and the Inauguration of the New Province; [by J. Ferguson.] 12mo. Colombo, 1886. **D 5 P 26**

V

VACCINATION. Historical Review of Nature and Results of Vaccination, as unfolded in Dr. Baron's "Life of Jenner;" by "Vigorniensis." 12mo. Lond., 1838.   A 12 P 2

Papers relating to the History and Practice of Vaccination. (General Board of Health.) Roy. 4to. Lond., 1857.   A 12 V 1

Reports of the National Vaccine Establishment. 8vo. Lond., 1811.   A 12 S 33

Vaccination Tracts. 12mo. Lond., 1877-79.   A 12 P 4
Preface and Supplement.
Cases of Disease, Suffering, and Death, reported by the Injured Families.
Compulsory Vaccination; a Desecration of Law, a Breaker of Homes, and Persecutor of the Poor.
Facts and Figures, showing that Vaccination has failed to stamp out, arrest, or mitigate Small-pox.
Historical and Critical Summary.
Letters and Opinions of Medical Men.
Opinions of Statesmen, Politicians, Publicists, Statisticians, and Sanitarians.
Propagation of Syphilis to Infants and Adults by Vaccination and Re-vaccination.
Vaccination; a Sign of the Decay of the Political and Medical Conscience in the Country.
Vaccination; Evil in its Principles, False in its Reasons, and Deadly in its Results.
Vaccination Laws a Scandal to Public Honesty and Religion.
Vaccination subverts Dentition, and is a Cause of the prevalent Deformity and Decay of the Teeth.

Vaccination Tracts. (Pam. Cp.) 8vo. Lond., 1880-81.   A 12 S 34
A Little Proclamation; reprinted from *Fun*, May 4th, 1881.
Analysis of the Parliamentary Return made by the Registrar-General to the House of Commons (No. 433, of 1878, published by *Hansard*, London), entitled "Vaccination Mortality"; by a Barrister-at-Law.
Benefits of Vaccination.
Latest Official Evidence of the Results of Vaccination.
Our Legislators on the Vaccination Question: a Record of Parliamentary and Extra-Parliamentary Utterances and Opinions. 1802-80.
Perils of Vaccination.
Slavery in the United States, and Tyranny in England: a Parallel.
Vaccination described by Dr. Jenner, Sir J. Paget, and Dr. Robinson.
Vaccination Quackery.

[*See* SMALLPOX.]

VACHER (S.) Fifteenth Century Italian Ornament, chiefly taken from Brocades and Stuffs found in Pictures in the National Gallery. Imp. fol. Lond., 1886.   A 11 P 15 ‡

VAGABOND, THE. [*See* THOMAS, J.]

VAILLANT (A. N.) Voyage autour du Monde, exécuté pendant les années 1836-37, sur la Corvette *La Bonite*. Zoologie, par MM. Eydoux et L. Souleyet. 2 vols. 8vo. Paris, 1841-52.   A 15 P 20, 21
Atlas [to the above]. Imp. fol. Paris, 1841-52.   A 23 Q 20 ‡

VAILLANT (J. A.) Grammaire, Dialogues, et Vocabulaire de la Langue des Bohémiens, ou Cigains. 8vo. Paris, 1868.   K 13 Q 12

VALENTIA (GEORGE), VISCOUNT. Voyages and Travels to India, Ceylon, the Red Sea, Abyssinia and Egypt, in the years 1802-6. 3 vols. 4to. Lond., 1809.   D 9 V 6-8

VALERIUS MAXIMUS. Factorum dictorumque memorabilium, libri novem ex editione Joannis Kappii, cum Notis et Interpretatione in usum Delphini. 3 vols. 8vo. Lond. 1823.   J 13 T 7-9

VALESIUS. Life of Eusebius. [*See* EUSEBIUS PAMPHILUS.]   G 14 P 16

VALLANCEY (GEN. CHARLES), LL.D. Collectanea de Rebus Hibernicis; published from the MSS. by General Charles Vallancey. 2nd ed., with Copper Plates. 6 vols. 8vo. Dublin, 1786-1804.   B 11 Q 10-15

VALLARSI (D.) [*See* HIERONYMUS, E.]   G 26 P 1-11 ‡

VALLÉE (LÉON). Bibliographie des Biographies. 2 Parts, with Supplement. 2 vols. roy. 8vo. Paris, 1883-87.   K 19 V 1, 2

VALLES (BARON DE LOS). Career of Don Carlos since the Death of Ferdinand VII. 8vo. Lond., 1835.   C 10 Q 16

VALLÈS (JULES). La Rue à Londres. Roy fol. Paris, 1884.   D 4 P 14 ‡

VALOR ECCLESIASTICUS, temp. Henry VIII, auctoritate Regia Institutus. 6 vols. (in 3) at. fol. Lond., 1810-34.   B 24 S 14-16 ‡
Introduction to. [*See* HUNTER, REV. J.]

VALPY (REV. A. J.) [*See* DELPHIN CLASSICS, *and* APULEIUS, LUCIUS.]

VALPY (REV. FRANCIS EDWARD JACKSON), M.A. The Course of Nature urged on Principles of Analogy, in vindication of particular Texts of Scripture from Sceptical Objections. 8vo. Lond., 1839.   G 10 P 12

VAMBÉRY (ARMINIUS). Central Asia and the Anglo-Russian Frontier Question: a Series of Political Papers. 8vo. Lond., .1874.   B 12 U 14

Coming Struggle for India; being an Account of the Encroachments of Russia in Central Asia, and of the Difficulties sure to arise therefrom to England. 8vo. Lond., 1885.   B 10 Q 1

His Life and Adventures; written by himself. With Portrait and Illustrations. 8vo. Lond., 1884.   C 9 T 51

History of Bokhara, from the Earliest Period down to the Present. 2nd ed. 8vo. Lond., 1873.   B 1 P 18

Sketches of Central Asia: Additional Chapters on my Travels, Adventures, and on the Ethnology of Central Asia. 8vo. Lond., 1868.   D 6 S 15

Travels in Central Asia, performed in the year 1863. 8vo. Lond., 1864.   D 6 S 14

VAN ARTEVELD (JAMES AND PHILIPP). [*See* ARTEVELD, J. AND P. VAN.]

VANBRUGH (SIR JOHN). Dramatic Works of. [*See* WYCHERLEY, W.] H 2 T 21

The City Wives' Confederacy : a Comedy. (Bell's Brit. Theatre.) 18mo. Lond., 1792. H 2 P 8

Another copy. (New Eng. Theatre.) 12mo. Lond., 1777. H 4 P 26

The Country House. [*See* BRIT. DRAMA 5.]

The Mistake : a Comedy. (Bell's Brit. Theatre.) 18mo. Lond., 1795. H 2 P 6

The Provoked Wife: a Comedy. (Bell's Brit. Theatre.) 18mo. Lond., 1794. H 2 P 14

Another copy. (Brit. Theatre.) 12mo. Lond., 1808. H 1 P 9

Another copy. (New Eng. Theatre.) 12mo. Lond., 1776. H 4 P 18

Another copy. [*See* BRIT. DRAMA 3.]

The Relapse ; or, Virtue in Danger : a Comedy. (Bell's Brit. Theatre.) 18mo. Lond., 1795. H 2 P 26

VANBRUGH (SIR JOHN), AND CIBBER (COLLEY). The Provoked Husband: a Comedy. (Bell's Brit. Theatre.) 18mo. Lond., 1791. H 2 P 33

Another copy. (Brit. Theatre.) 12mo. Lond., 1808. H 1 P 9

Another copy. (New Eng. Theatre.) 12mo. Lond., 1788. H 4 P 22

Another copy. [*See* BRIT. DRAMA, 4.]

VANCOUVER (CAPT. GEORGE). Voyage of Discovery to the North Pacific Ocean, and round the World, in the years 1790-95, in the *Discovery*, sloop of war, and armed tender, *Chatham*. Illustrated. 6 vols. 8vo. Lond., 1801. MD 1 U 22-27

Voyage de Découvertes, a l'Océan Pacifique du Nord, et autour du Monde, 1790-95; traduit de l'Anglais. 3 vols. 4to. Paris, 1800. MD 5 P 13-15 †

[Atlas to the above.] At. fol. Paris, 1800. MD 5 Q 4‡

VAN DALEN (ANTON). [*See* DALEN, A. VAN.]

VAN DER AA (P. J. B. C. ROBIDE). [*See* AA, P. J. B. C. ROBIDE VAN DER.]

VANDERBILTS (THE), and the Story of their Fortune ; by W. A. Croffut. 8vo. Lond., 1886. C 2 R 33

VANDERDECKEN. Yachts and Yachting. [*See* COOPER, W.]

VANDERKISTE (REV. R. W.) Lost, but not for Ever: my Personal Narrative of Starvation and Providence in the Australian Mountain Regions. 12mo. Lond., 1863. MD 2 R 11

Notes and Narratives of a Six Years' Mission, principally among the Dens of London. 12mo. Lond., 1863. F 15 Q 2

The Widow of East Angle. 12mo. Lond., 1870. G 2 P 1

VAN DER LINDE (DR. A.) [*See* LINDE, DR. A. VAN DER.]

VAN DER TUUK (H. N.) Outlines of a Grammar of the Malagasy Language. 8vo. Lond. (n.d.) K 15 P 3

VAN DIEMEN'S LAND. [*See* TASMANIA.]

VAN DIEMEN'S LAND COLONIAL MISSIONARY SOCIETY. Eighth Annual Report, 1843. 8vo. Hobart, 1844. MJ 2 R 13

VAN DIEMEN'S LAND COMPANY. List of Proprietors. 8vo. Lond., 1833. MF 2 P 38

Minutes of the intended Arrangements between Earl Bathurst, His Majesty's Secretary of State, and the proposed Van Diemen's Land Company. (Parl. Docs., 7.) Fol. Lond., 1825. MF 4 ‡

Proposals for the encouragement of Emigrants as Tenants to the Van Diemen's Land Company, 1823. 8vo. Lond., 1833.* MF 2 P 38

Reports, 1833, 1835. 8vo. Lond., 1833-35. MF 2 P 38

Another copy of Report for 1833. 8vo. Lond., 1833. MF 2 P 38

Report made to the Seventh Yearly General Meeting, held at the Company's Office, in Old Broad-street, the 13th March, 1832. 8vo. Lond., 1832. MJ 2 Q 19

Report made to the Eighth Yearly General Meeting, held at the Company's Office, in Old Broad-street, the 18th March, 1833. MF 2 P 40

VAN DIEMEN'S LAND MECHANICS' INSTITUTE. Catalogue of the Library. 8vo. Hobart, 1839. MF 3 P 15

Reports, 1838-39. 8vo. Hobart, 1839. MF 3 P 15

Rules and Orders. 8vo. Hobart, 1828. MF 3 P 15

Rules and Orders, revised. 8vo. Hobart, 1839. MF 3 P 15

Rules of, 1843. 8vo. Hobart, 1843. MF 3 P 15

To the Members of the Van Diemen's Land Mechanics' Institute [Address on Centrifugal Force]; by "A Member." 8vo. Hobart, 1847. MJ 2 R 4

VAN DIEMEN'S LAND MONTHLY MAGAZINE (THE), September-October, 1835. 8vo. Hobart, 1835. ME 3 R

Another copy. 8vo. Hobart, 1835. MJ 2 R 22

VAN DIEMEN'S LAND SUNDAY SCHOOL UNION. Seventh Annual Report. 8vo. Hobart, 1849. MG 1 Q 39

VAN DYCK (SIR ANTHONY). Sketches by Antonio van Dyck (1599-1641), comprising forty Portraits, engraved by E. Mitchell. Roy. 4to. Edinb., 1879. A 7 R 3 †

Van Dyck ; by P. R. Head. (Great Artists). 8vo. Lond., 1879. C 3 T 33

VAN DYKE (JOHN CHARLES). Books, and how to use them: some Hints to Readers and Students. 8vo. New York, 1883. J 11 U 29

VANE (Gen. Charles William), Marquis of Londonderry. [*See* Londonderry, Marquis of.]

VANE (Sir Henry). Life of. [*See* Mackintosh, Sir J.]
Brit. Statesm., 4.) 12mo. Lond., 1838. C 1 Q 37

VAN KERKWYK (L. C.) Sketch of the Public Works
in the Netherlands. (Inter. Exhib., Philad., 1876.) Roy.
8vo. Haarlem, 1876. F 1 S 28

VAN LAUN (Henri). [*See* Laun, H. van.]

VAN LENNEP (Henry J.), D.D. Bible Lands; their
Modern Customs and Manners illustrative of Scripture.
2 vols. 8vo. Lond., 1875. D 5 T 6, 7

VANN (John). Squatting Directory for New South Wales.
Roy. 8vo. Sydney, 1865. ME 4 V

VANNUCCI (Atto). Storia dell' Italia Antica. 4 vols.
roy. 8vo. Milano, 1873. B 11 T 21–24

VAPEREAU (Louis Gustave). Dictionaire Universel
des Contemporains. 5e éd. 8vo. Paris, 1880. C 11 V 19

VARCHI (Benedetto). Storia Fiorentina, con aggiunte e
Correzioni tratte dagli Autografi e corredata di note, per
cura e opera di Lelio Arbib. 3 vols. 8vo. Firenze,
1843–44. B 11 V 32–34

VARDY (William Lyndhurst). Lower Tribunals: a
Treatise upon the Present System of Administration of
Justice in Magisterial Courts in Australia. 8vo. Sydney,
1876* MF 3 Q 55

VARIGNY (Charles Crosnier de). Quatorze Ans aux
Iles Sandwich. 12mo. Paris, 1874. MD 4 T 38

VARIN (A. et E.) L'Architecture Pittoresque en Suisse;
ou, Choix de Construction Rustiques prises dans toutes les
Parties de la Suisse. Fol. Paris, 1873. A 23 P 33‡

VARLEY (Henry). Address delivered at the Town Hall,
Melbourne, on the Social Evil. 8vo. Melb., 1878.
MJ 2 R 15

VARNHAGEN (F. A. de). Amerigo Vespucci; son Caractère, ses Ecrits (même les moins authentiques), sa Vie, et
ses Navigations. Fol. Lima, 1865–70. C 23 S 31 ‡

VARNHAGEN VON ENSE (Karl August Ludwig
Philipp). Letters of Alexander von Humboldt, written
between the years 1827–58, to Varnhagen von Ense.
Authorized Translation from the German. 8vo. Lond.,
1860. C 7 P 2

Sketches of German Life, and Scenes from the War of
Liberation in Germany; selected and translated from the
Memoirs of Varnhagen von Ense, by Sir Alexander Duff
Gordon, Bart. 12mo. Lond., 1847. D 7 P 37

Another copy. (H. and C. Lib.) J 8 P 21

VARVATI (Constantin). Nouveau Dictionaire Français-Grec Moderne, à l'usage des Etablissements de l'Instruction Publique (4 parts in 2.) 2 vols. roy. 8vo.
Athènes, 1858–60. K 13 R 16, 17

VASARI (Giorgio). Lives of the most Eminent Painters,
Sculptors, and Architects; translated from the Italian, by
Mrs. Jonathan Foster, and Commentary by J. P. Richter,
Ph.D. 6 vols. 8vo. Lond., 1855–85. C 4 R 27–32

VASON (George). Authentic Narrative of Four Years'
Residence at Tongataboo. 8vo. Lond.,1810.* MD 5 S 15

VATTEL (Emmerich de). Law of Nations; or, Principles
of the Law of Nature applied to the Conduct and Affairs
of Nations and Sovereigns. Roy. 8vo. Lond., 1793.
F 4 R 16

Le Droit des Gens; ou, Principes de la Loi Naturelle
appliqués à la conduite et aux affaires des Nations et des
Souverains. 4to. Leyden, 1758. F 8 R 1 †

VAUBAN (Sebastian de Prestre de). Engineer Studies.
[*See* Lloyd, E. M.] A 6 S 14

VAUBLANC (Vincent Marie Viénot), Comte de. Mémoires de. [*See* Barrière, J. F., 13.] C 1 T 13

VAUGHAN (Charles) [*See* Smith, Rev. T.]

VAUGHAN (Prof. Henry Halford). New Readings
and New Renderings of Shakespeare's Tragedies. 2 vols.
8vo. Lond., 1878–81. H 3 R 13, 14

Answer to Prof. Vaughan's Strictures. [*See* Pusey, Prof.
E. B.]

VAUGHAN (Herbert). Year of Preparation for the
Vatican Council. 8vo. Lond., 1869. G 8 U 8

VAUGHAN (Rev. James). The Trident, the Crescent,
and the Cross. 8vo. Lond., 1876. G 12 T 21

VAUGHAN (J. D.) Manners and Customs of the Chinese
of the Straits Settlement. 8vo. Singapore,1879. D 5 U 2

VAUGHAN (Robert), D.D. Age of Great Cities; or,
Modern Civilization viewed in its relation to Intelligence,
Morals, and Religion. 8vo. Lond., 1843. G 12 T 22

Memorials of the Stuart Dynasty, including the Constitutional and Ecclesiastical History of England, from
the Decease of Elizabeth to the Abdication of James II.
2 vols. 8vo. Lond., 1831. B 6 P 30, 31

On the Study of General History: an Introductory Lecture. (Univ. of Lond.) 8vo. Lond., 1834. J 5 S 8

Protectorate of Oliver Cromwell, and the State of Europe
during the early part of the Reign of Louis XIV. 2 vols.
8vo. Lond., 1838. B 6 T 13, 14

Revolutions in English History. 2nd ed. 3 vols. 8vo.
Lond., 1867. B 5 R 37–39

Way to Rest: Results of a Life-search after Religious
Truth. 12mo. Lond., 1866. G 12 T 20
[*See* Vaughan, R. A.]

VAUGHAN (Robert Alfred). Essays and Remains of;
edited, with a Memoir, by Robert Vaughan, D.D. 2 vols.
12mo. Lond., 1858. J 6 P 25, 26

VAUGHAN (RT. REV. ROGER BEDE), ARCHBISHOP. First Advent Conference: the Church of Christ Indefectible. 8vo. Sydney, 1876. MG 1 Q 33

Fourth Advent Conference: the Church of Christ, the Catholic Church. 8vo. Sydney, 1876. MG 1 Q 41

Lenten Exercises, given in St. Mary's pro-Cathedral, Sydney, 1877. 8vo. Sydney, 1877. MG 1 Q 42

Life and Labours of S. Thomas of Aquin. 2 vols. 8vo. Lond., 1871–72. C 6 S 28, 29

Review of Lenten Discourses. [*See* BRIGHT, C.] MG 1 Q 34

VAUQUELIN (N. L.) Manuel de l'Essayeur. 4to. Paris, 1799. A 9 V 13

VAUVENARGUES (LUC DE CLAPIERS), MARQUIS DE. Œuvres choisies. [*See* LA ROCHEFOUCAULD, F., DUC DE.]

VAUX (F. W.) Rambles in the Pyrenees, and a Visit to San Sebastian. 8vo. Lond., 1838. D 9 Q 35

VAUX (JAMES HARDY). Memoirs of; written by himself [Edited by Barron Field.] 2 vols. 12mo. Lond., 1819 MC 1 P 18, 19

Another copy. 2nd ed. 18mo. Lond., 1827. MC 1 P 20

Another copy. 2nd ed. 18mo. Lond., 1827. C 1 P 11

VECELLIO (CESARE). Costumes Anciens et Modernes; suivis d'un Essai sur la gravure sur Bois, par Amb. Firmin. Didot. 2 vols. 8vo. Paris, 1859–63. A 7 R 9, 10

VECELLIO (TIZIANO). [*See* TITIAN.]

VEER (GERRIT DE). [*See* DE VEER, G.]

VEESMANN'S German, Latin, and Russian Dictionary 4to. St. Petersburg, 1782. K 15 S 1

VEESON (GEORGE). [*See* VASON, G.]

VEGA (GARCILASSO DE LA). [*See* GARCILASSO DE LA VEGA.] B 14 R 18

VEGA (JUAN DE). [*See* COCHRANE, CAPT. C.]

VEGA (LOPE FELIX DE CARPIO). Some Account of the Lives and Writings of Lope de Vega, and Guillen de Castro, by Henry Richard, Lord Holland. 2 vols. 8vo. Lond., 1817. C 3 P 42, 43

VEGETABLE PHYSIOLOGY. Popular Treatise on. 8vo. Philad., 1842. A 4 Q 5

VEGETABLE SUBSTANCES used in the Arts and in Domestic Economy: Timber Trees, Fruits. 2nd ed. (Lib. Ent. Know.) 8vo. Lond., 1830. K 10 R 46

Materials of Manufacture. (Lib. Ent. Know.) 8vo. Lond., 1833. K 10 R 48

VEHSE (DR. EDWARD). Memoirs of the Court of Prussia from the German; by Franz C. F. Demmler. 8vo. Lond., 1854. C 4 V 1

VEILLÉES PERSANES (LES); traduites de l'Arabe, par J. Cazotte, et D. Chavis. 4 vols. 8vo. Genève, 1793. J 15 R 38–41

VEITCH (PROF. JOHN), M.A. Institutes of Logic. 8vo. Edinb., 1885. G 7 T 12

Memoir of Sir William Hamilton, Bart. 8vo. Edinb., 1869. C 7 Q 26

VEITCH (WILLIAM), LL.D. Greek Verbs, Irregular and Defective; their Forms, Meaning, and Quantity, embracing all Tenses used by the Greek Writers, with reference to the Passages in which they are found. New ed. (Clar. Press.) 8vo. Oxford, 1871. K 20 R 7

VEITCH (WILLIAM), AND BRYSSON (GEORGE). Memoirs of Mr. William Veitch and George Brysson, written by themselves; to which are added, Biographical Sketches and Notes, by T. M'Crie, D.D. 8vo. Edinb., 1825. C 9 R 39

VEITELLE (I. DE). Mercantile Dictionary: a complete Vocabulary, in English, Spanish, and French. 8vo. Lond., 1864. K 9 T 19

VELARDE (MURILLO). [*See* MURILLO VELARDE P. P.]

VELASQUEZ DE LA CADENA (PROF. MARIANO). Dictionary of the Spanish and English Languages; in two parts. 1. Spanish–English. 2. English–Spanish. 12mo. Lond., 1878. K 11 U 38

Easy Introduction to Spanish Conversation. New ed., enlarged. 8vo. Lond., 1863. K 11 U 45

Pronouncing Dictionary of the Spanish and English Languages. 1. Spanish–English. 2. English–Spanish. 2 vols. (in 1) roy. 8vo. New York, 1877. K 16 R 1

VELASQUEZ DE LA CADENA (PROF. MARIANO), AND SIMONNE (PROF. T.) Key to the Exercises in Velasquez and Simonne's Method of learning Spanish, adapted to the Ollendorffian System. 8vo. Lond., 1876. K 11 U 37

New Method of learning to read, write, and speak the Spanish Language, adapted to the Ollendorffian System. 8vo. Lond., 1878. K 11 U 36

VELAZQUEZ (DON DIEGO RODRIGUEZ DE SILVA Y). Descriptive and Historical Catalogue of the Works of. [*See* CURTIS, C. B.] C 17 U 1

Velazquez and his Works; by W. Stirling. 8vo. Lond., 1855. C 1 R 38

Velazquez; by E. Stowe. (Great Artists.) 8vo. Lond., 1881. C 3 T 34

VELLEIUS PATERCULUS (C.) Historia Romana, ex editione J. C. H. Krausii, cum Notis et Interpretatione in usum Delphini. 8vo. Lond., 1822. J 13 T 10

[*See* SALLUSTIUS CRISPUS, C., *and* SCRIPTORES ROMANI.]

VENABLES (G. H.) Bleek's Introduction to the Old Testament. [*See* BLEEK, F.]

VENABLES (GEORGE STOVIN). The Italian War. [*See* LUSHINGTON, H.]

VENN (REV. HENRY), A.M. Complete Duty of Man; or, a System of Doctrinal and Practical Christianity. 8vo. Edinb., 1803. G 12 T 23

VENN (REV. JOHN), Sc.D., &c. Symbolic Logic. 8vo.
Lond., 1881.   G 7 T 10

VENTURA (FATHER GIOACCHINO). Funeral Oration of,
on the Death of the Liberator, preached at Rome, on June
28 and 30, 1847. (Pam.) 8vo. Dublin, 1847. C 14 R 22

VENUTI (RIDOLFINO). Accurata e Succincta Descrizione
Topografica del Antichità di Roma. 4to. Roma, 1803.
                                                A 2 T 25
VERAX. [*See* DUNCKLEY, H.]

VERBURG (ISAAC). Beschryving van de Regeringe der
Yncas, Koningen van Peru. [*See* FREZIER, A. F.]
                                                D 3 U 35
VERDEREVSKY (—.) Captivity of Two Russian Prin-
cesses in the Caucasus, including a Seven Months' Resi-
dence in Shamil's Seraglio; translated from the original
Russian, by H. Sutherland Edwards. 8vo. Lond., 1857.
                                                D 8 S 34
VERDON (SIR GEORGE FREDERIC), K.C.M.G. Present
and Future of Municipal Government in Victoria. 8vo.
Melb., 1858.   MF 3 P 5

VEREKER (LIEUT.-COL. THE HON. C. S.), M.A. Scenes
in the Sunny South, including the Atlas Mountains and
the Oases of the Sahara in Algeria. 2 vols. 8vo. Lond.,
1871.   D 1 S 3, 4

VERGILIUS (POLYDORUS). Historiæ Anglicæ, Libri 27,
accessit præteralia non nulla series Regum Angliæ à primis
initiis usque ad hanc ætatem. 8vo. Lugd. Bat., 1651.
                                                B 3 R 4
VERGNAUD (A. D.) Manuel de Chimie amusante, ou
nouvelles récréations chimiques. 18mo. Paris, 1829.
                                                A 21 P 7
VERGNIAUD (PIERRE VICTURNIEN). Life of [*See* LA-
MARTINE, A. DE.]   C 5 S 12

VERHANDLUNGEN der k. k. geologischen Reichsanstalt,
1867–85. 20 vols. roy. 8vo. Wien, 1869–85.   E

VERHEYK (H.) [*See* ANTONINUS LIBERALIS, *and* EUTRO-
PIUS.]

VERNER (CAPT. WILLIAM WILLOUGHBY COLE). Sketches
in the Soudan. Ob. 4to. Lond., 1885.   D 38 P 5 ‡

VERNET (HORACE). Horace Vernet; by J. R. Rees.
(Great Artists.) 8vo. Lond., 1880.   C 3 T 44

VERNEY (MAJOR GEORGE HOPE). Chess Eccentricities.
8vo. Lond., 1885.   A 17 U 12

VERNON (EDWARD). American Railroad Manual for the
United States and the Dominion. 8vo. New York,
1874.   E

VERNON (JAMES). Letters illustrative of the Reign of
William III, 1696–1708, addressed to the Duke of Shrewsbury; edited by G. P. R. James. 3 vols 8vo. Lond.,
1841.   C 9 S 40–42

5 F

VERNON (JOHN GEORGE WARREN), LORD. [*See* DANTE
ALIGHIERI.]

VERNON-HARCOURT (LEVESON FRANCIS). [*See* HAR-
COURT, L. F. V.-]

VERRALL (ARTHUR WOLLGAR), M.A. Studies, Literary
and Historical, in the Odes of Horace. 8vo. Lond.,
1884.   H 8 V 18
The Medea of Euripides. [*See* EURIPIDES.]

VERRILL (A. E.), AND SMITH (S. I.) Report upon the
Invertebrate Animals of Vineyard Sound and adjacent
Waters. 8vo. Wash., 1874.   A 14 U 23

VERRIUS FLACCUS (M.), quæ extant: et Sexti Pompeii
Festi Verborum significatione libri 20. ex editione A.
Dacerii in usum Delphini. 3 vols. 8vo. Lond., 1826.
                                                J 13 S 11–13
VERSTEGAN (RICHARD). Restitution of decayed Intelli-
gence in Antiquities concerning the most noble and re-
novvmed English Nation. Sm. 4to. Antwerp, 1605.
                                                B 21 S 23
VERTOT (RENÉ AUBERT), L'ABBÉ DE. Histoire des Cheva-
liers Hospitaliers de S. Jean de Jerusalem, appelez depuis
Chevaliers de Rhodes, et aujourd'hui Chevaliers de Malthe.
5 vols. 8vo. Paris, 1726.   G 8 P 19–23
Another copy. 4 vols. 4to. Paris, 1726.   G 12 Q 11–14

VERTUE (GEORGE). Anecdotes of Painting, and Catalogue
of Engravers. [*See* WALPOLE, H.]   C 2 Q 1–5

VERY (LIEUT. E. W.), U.S.N. Development of Armor
for Naval Use. 8vo. Annapolis, Md., 1883.   A 2 Q 8
Navies of the World, 1860–80. 8vo. Lond., 1880.
                                                A 2 Q 2
VESPUCCI (AMERIGO); son Caractère, ses Ecrits (même
les moins authentiques), par F. A. de Varnhagen. Fol.
Lima, 1865–70.   C 23 S 31 ‡

VETERAN, A. Reminiscences of. [*See* BUNBURY,
LIEUT.-COL. T.]

VETERAN COMPANIES. [*See* NEW SOUTH WALES.]

VETERINARIAN (THE): Monthly Journal of Veterinary
10 vols. 8vo. Lond., 1874–84.   E 1.50

VETROMILE (REV. EUGENE), D.D. Tour in both Hemispheres; or, Travels around the World. 8vo. New York,
1880.   D 10 R 44
Travels in Europe, Egypt, Arabia Petræa, Palestine, and
Syria. 2 vols. 8vo. New York, 1871.   D 9 S 19, 20

VIARDOT (LOUIS), AND OTHERS. Brief History of the
Painters of all Schools. Illustrated. Imp. 8vo. Lond.,
1877.   A 8 U 10

VIATOR. [*See* THOUGHTS ON THE VALLEY.]

VIBART (MAJOR HENRY MEREDITH), R.E. Military History of the Madras Engineers and Pioneers. 2 vols. 8vo.
Lond., 1881–83,   B 10 V 21, 22

VICARS (CAPT. HEDLEY). Memorials of [by Miss Catherine Marsh]. 12mo. Lond., 1856. C 1 R 39

[*See* SMITH, REV. T.]

VICARS (JOHN). Letters on the Tariff, and on Immigration and the Labour Question. 8vo. Sydney, 1873–77. MF 3 P 20

The Tariff, Immigration, and the Labour Question discussed. 8vo. Sydney, 1879. MF 3 P 21

VICE-ADMIRALTY COURTS. Rules and Regulations touching the Practice to be observed in Suits and Proceedings in the several Courts of Vice-Admiralty abroad. 4to. Sydney, 1842. MF 2 S 33

Table of Fees to be taken by the Judge, Registrar, Marshall, Advocates, and Proctors of the Vice-Admiralty Court at Van Dieman's Land. 4to. Sydney, 1842. MF 2 S 33

Vice-Admiralty Courts: Appendix to the Report of the Referees appointed to investigate and report on Fees, &c. 4to. Sydney, 1842. MF 2 S 33

VICENZA (ARMAND AUGUSTIN LOUIS DE CAULINCOURT), DUKE OF. Recollections of Caulincourt, Duke of Vicenza. 2 vols. 8vo. Lond., 1838. C 3 Q 18, 19

VICO (G.) Opere. 8 vols. 8vo. Napoli, 1858–65. G 12 T 11–18

1. Autobiographia della Anticrissima Sapienza degl' Italiani.
2. Dell 'Unico principio ed unico fine del Diritto Universale.
3. Della Castanza del Guirisprudente.
4, 5. Principj di una Scienza Nuova.
6. Opuscoli.
7. Istituzione oratorie e Scritti inediti.
8. Cinque orazioni Latine inediti.

VICTOR III (PAPA). Opera omnia. [*See* MIGNE, J. P., SERIES LATINA, 149.]

VICTOR SEXTUS. [*See* AURELIUS VICTOR, S.]

VICTORIA.
Democratic Government in Victoria. (*Reprinted from the Westminster Review.*) 8vo. Melb., 1868. MF 1 Q 3

Die Colonie Victoria in Australien; ihr Hilfsquellen und ihr physikalischer Charakter. 8vo. Melb., 1861. MD 7 Q 3

Future of Victoria; by "Acorn." 8vo. Melb. (n.d.) MF 1 Q 2

Guide to Sorrento. 8vo. Melb., 1876. MJ 2 R 10

History of the Crisis. 8vo. Melb., 1876. MF 1 Q 2

Homesteads for the People and Manhood Suffrage, in a series of Four Letters, from "Peter Papineau" to "Mr. John Bull," Bendigo. 8vo. Melb. (n.d.) MJ 2 R 21

Mallee District of Victoria. 8vo. Melb., 1880. MJ 2 R 15

Mallee Scrub Country; or, Mr. Dow's Delta. 8vo. Melb., 1880. MJ 2 R 15

Petition of the undersigned Total Abstainers from Intoxicating Drinks, and other Colonists of Victoria. (Pam. D.) 4to. Melb. (n.d.) MJ 2 U 3

VICTORIA—*continued.*
Political Crisis of Victoria, 1865–66; Recall of the Governor; the Despatches of His Excellency Sir Charles Darling, and the Replies from the Right Hon. Edward Cardwell, Her Majesty's Secretary of State for the Colonies. 8vo. Melb., 1867. MF 1 Q 2

(Port Phillip Bay): Illustrated Hand-book of the Bay. 12mo. Melb., 1876–77. MJ 2 P 31

Present and Future: Victoria as she is, and as she may be. 8vo. Melb., 1853. MJ 2 R 10

Rules and Regulations of the Savings' Bank of Port Phillip. 8vo. Melb., 1847. MJ 2 R 15

Squatters' Directory, Port Phillip. 8vo. Melb., 1849. MJ 2 R 15

Trip to Portland, the Watering-place of the West. 8vo. Melb., 1880. MJ 2 R 15

Victorian Commemoration: Australian Anthem composed in celebration of the glorious occasion of Separation. (Pam. E.) 4to. Melb., 1851. MJ 2 S 2

Victorian Government Prize Essays, 1860. 8vo. Melb., 1861.

ACTS OF PARLIAMENT.
Acts of Parliament of Victoria. 7 vols. 4to. Melb., 1867–84. E 2.49

AGRICULTURE.
Essay on the Agricultural Resources of Victoria, 1866–67. MK 1 R 33

First and Second Reports of the Secretary for Agriculture; to which is appended, the Report of the Inspector-General of Gardens, Parks, and Reserves. 2 vols. 8vo. Melb., 1873–74. ME 1 T

Proceedings of the Chamber of Commerce for promoting Agriculture, and settling the Waste Lands of the Colony. 8vo. Melb., 1855. MF 1 Q 3

ALMANACS AND DIRECTORIES.
Astronomical and Nautical (late Robinson's) Almanac, 1869, 1875. 12mo. Melb., 1869–75. ME 4 P

Directory for Shires and Road Boards in Victoria, 1867 by Heath and Cordell. 12mo. Melb., 1867. ME 4 P

Hamilton Spectator Directory and Almanac, 1875, 1877. 8vo. Hamilton (Vic.), 1875–77. ME 4 P

Melbourne Almanac and Port Phillip Directory, 1841–42; compiled by W. Kerr. 8vo. Melb., 1841–42. ME 4 U

Melbourne and Suburban Directory, 1864, 1875–76; by Sands and M'Dougall. 3 vols. 8vo. Melb. ME 11 P

Melbourne Directory and Almanac, 1853; by Pierce. 8vo. Melb. ME 4 Q

Port Phillip Almanac, 1843; by Kerr. 12mo. Melb., 1843. ME 4 P

Port Phillip Almanac and Directory, 1847; by Mouritz. 18mo. ME 4 P

Post Office Directory, 1884–85, comprising separate Alphabetical Directories for over 1,000 Townships, Boroughs, Cities, and Districts. Roy. 8vo. Melb., 1884. ME 10 P 17 †

VICTORIA—*continued.*
ALMANACS AND DIRECTORIES—*continued.*
Robinson's Almanac and Astronomical Ephemeris, 1864;
by White. 12mo. Melh., 1864.   ME 4 P
Stephens' Victorian Almanac, 1864, 1866. 12mo. Melh.,
1864–66.   ME 4 P
Victoria Nautical and Commercial Almanac, 1855; by
Murray. 12mo. Melh.   ME 4 Q
Victorian Almanac, 1864; by Bryant. 12mo. Avoca.
Victorian Almanac, 1864; by Franks. 12mo. Geelong.
Watmuff's Australian Almanac, 1871. 8vo. Melh.,
1871.   ME 4 P
ANTI-TRANSPORTATION LEAGUE. [*See* ANTI-TRANSPORTATION
LEAGUE.]
BALLOT IN VICTORIA.
Ballot in Victoria; Facts about the Ballot; Success of the
Ballot in Victoria, Australia. Roy. 8vo. Lond., 1857.
                                                MJ 2 S 5
BALLARAT TECHNOLOGICAL EXHIBITION.
Seventh Competitive Exhibition and Examinations. 8vo.
Ballarat, 1879.   A 16 U 23
BENEVOLENT ASYLUM.
Annual Reports of the Committee of Management of the
Benevolent Asylum, Melbourne; with the Rules of the
same, and a List of Subscriptions and Donations, for the
years 1861, 1863. 8vo. Melh., 1862–64.   MF 3 P 15
CENSUS.
Census of Victoria, 1881, Parts 1–8; with a General
Report by the Government Statist; Population enumerated
on the 3rd April, 1881. Fol. Melh., 1884.   E 2.54
CONSTITUTION.
Reform of the Constitution: Report of the Debates in
both Houses of Parliament. 8vo. Melb.,1878. MF 3 R 3
CONVENTION, 1857.
Resolutions, Proceedings, and Documents of the Vic-
torian Convention, assembled in Melbourne, July 15 to
August 6, 1857. 8vo. Melh., 1857.   MF 1 Q 2
Another copy. 8vo. Melh., 1857.   MF 3 P 5
CROWN LANDS.
Instructions as to Applications for a Title under the
Real Property Act. 8vo. Melh., 1862.   MF 3 P 5
Land Act, 1862. 8vo. Melh., 1862.   MJ 2 R 21
Land Act, 1884. 8vo. Melh., 1885.   MF 1 R 35
Land Bill; being a Letter addressed to the Members of
the Legislative Council, by "Moderation." 8vo. Melb.,
1860.   MF 1 Q 3
Land Question considered with reference to Pastoral
Occupation in Victoria. 8vo. Melb., 1867. MF 1 Q 3
New Idea on the Land Question. 8vo. Melh., 1853.
                                                MF 1 Q 3
Papers relative to Crown Lands in the Australian Colo-
nies. (Parl. Docs. 59, 62, 65.) 3 vols. fol. Lond.,
1851–56.   MF 4 ‡
Proceedings of the Melbourne Chamber of Commerce and
Special Committee, appointed to consider and report on
the best means of promoting Agriculture and settling the
Waste Lands of the Colony. 8vo. Melb., 1855.
                                                MF 1 Q 3

VICTORIA—*continued.*
CROWN LANDS—*continued.*
The Victorian Land Bill ; a Bill to regulate the Sale and
Occupation of Crown Lands. (Newspaper Cuttings.)
Roy. 8vo. Melh., 1857.   MJ 2 S 1
Correspondence [and Report from Select Committee] upon
Mr. Archibald McLachlan's claim upon the Victorian
Government. 8vo. Melb., 1861.   MF 1 Q 6
Opinions of Counsel on Rights of Pastoral Tenants of the
Crown. 8vo. Melh., 1856.   MJ 2 R 21
Statement of Case of Pastoral Tenants of the Crown. 8vo.
Melb., 1856.   MF 3 P 5
Regulations relating to the Occupation of Crown Lands.
8vo. Melh., 1848.   MJ 2 R 21
Reports of the Proceedings taken under the provisions
of the Land Act, 1862, and the Amending Land Act,
1868, up to the 31st December, 1868, and the Land Act,
1869, up the 31st December, 1875. Fol. Melb., 1866–76.
                                                MF 1 U 18
CROWN LAW OFFICES.
Catalogue of the Library. Roy. 8vo. Melh., 1878.
                                                MK 1 S 39
DEAF AND DUMB INSTITUTION. First Annual Report of the
Committee of the Victorian Deaf and Dumb Institution.
8vo. Melb., 1863.   MF 3 P 15
FRIENDLY SOCIETIES.
Sixth Annual Report, 1883. Sm. fol. Melb., 1885. E 2.54
GOLD-FIELDS.
Present Condition and Prospects of the Gold-fields in
Victoria, 1862. Fol. Lond., 1862.   MF 3 U 2
LEGISLATIVE ASSEMBLY.
Votes and Proceedings of the, and Papers. 107 vols.
fol. Melb., 1856–88.   E 2.47–54
LEGISLATIVE COUNCIL.
Votes and Proceedings of the. 10 vols. fol. Melh.,
1852–56.   E 2.47
MINES AND MINERAL STATISTICS.
Mineral Statistics of Victoria, for the year 1884: Report
of the Secretary for Mines. Fol. Melb.,1885. ME 10 Q 7 †
PARLIAMENTARY DEBATES.
Parliamentary Debates, Legislative Council and Legis-
lative Assembly. Vols. 1–33. 8vo. Melb.,1866–80. E 2.50
PARLIAMENTARY PAPERS.
Parliamentary Papers. Fol. Melb., 1883.   ME
    Hawthorn Railway Accident: Minutes of Evidence taken at
    the Inquest held by the Coroner, Dr. Youl, on the Death of
    William Cozens Tromas, 13th to 20th December, 1882.
    Royal Commission on Police: Special Report on the Detective
    Branch.
    Department of Industrial and Reformatory Schools: Report of
    of the Secretary, for the year 1881.
    Statistical Register of the Colony of Victoria, for the year 1881:
    compiled from Official Records in the Office of the Government
    Statist: Part 5. Interchange; Part 6. Law, Crime, &c.; Part
    7. Accumulation; Part 8. Production.
    Report of the Inspector of the Lunatic Asylums on the Hospitals
    for the Insane, for the year ending 31st December, 1881.
    Report on the Sanitary Station, for the year ending 31st De-
    cember, 1882.
    Land Act, 1869: Regulation; Order in Council.
    Public Works Temporary Advances Act, 1883.
    Railway Rolling-Stock and Permanent-Way: Estimate of Ex-
    penditure.
    Yan Yean Water Works Extension: Estimate of Expenditure.

VICTORIA—*continued.*
PARLIAMENTARY LIBRARY.
Catalogue. Part 1, Alphabetical Catalogue. Part 2, Classified Catalogue. Roy. 8vo. Melb., 1864–65.*
MK 1 R 11
Supplementary Catalogue of the. Roy. 8vo. Melb., 1871.
MK 1 R 13
Supplementary Classified Catalogue of the. Roy. 8vo. Melb., 1879.
MK 1 R 14
PASTORAL TENANTS.
Opinions of Counsel as to the Rights of the Pastoral Tenants of the Crown. 8vo. Melb., 1856.
MF 3 P 5
Statement of the Case of Pastoral Tenants of the Crown in Victoria. 8vo. Melb., 1856.
MF 3 P 5
Another copy. 8vo. Melb., 1856.
MJ 2 R 21
POLICE COMMISSION.
Minutes of Evidence, taken before the Royal Commission, on the Police Force of Victoria. Sm. fol. Melb., 1881.
E 2.54
RAILWAYS.
Union of the Railway Systems of New South Wales and Victoria: Celebration at Albury, on the 14th June, 1883. 8vo. Sydney, 1883.
MF 3 Q 17
Victoria Railways: [Map of] Melbourne and Suburbs. 4to. Melb., 1874.
MD 5 S 15 ‡
Victoria Railways: Report of the Board of Land and Works, for the year ending 31st December, 1877. Fol. Melb., 1878.
ME 9 Q 7 †
STATISTICS.
Statistical Summary of the Progress of the Colony of Victoria to the year 1865; compiled from Official Records in the Registrar-General's Office, Melbourne, for the Dublin International Exhibition of 1865. 8vo. Melb., 1865.
MF 3 P 8
STATUTES.
Public General Statutes of the Colony of Victoria. 4 vols. roy. 8vo. Melb., 1875–77.
E 2.49
Victorian Statutes. 3 vols. 4to. Melb., 1866.
E 2.49
SUPREME COURT.
Catalogue of the Library of the. 8vo. Lond., 1855.
MK 1 Q 13
Catalogue of the Library of. 2nd ed. Imp. 8vo. Melb., 1875.
MK 1 S 40
Comparative View of Court Fees and Attorney's Charges, under the late and present Rules of the Supreme Court of the Colony of Victoria, in reply to the Letter of the Acting Chief Justice to the Colonial Secretary in reference thereto, dated 21st March, 1854; to which are appended, the Letter of His Honor, and the new Scale of Charges. 8vo. Melb., 1854.
MF 3 P 5
Another copy. 8vo. Melb., 1854.
MJ 2 R 19
VICTORIA (HER MAJESTY THE QUEEN). Ancestry of Her Majesty Queen Victoria, and of His Royal Highness Prince Albert; by G. R. French. 8vo. Lond., 1841.
C 5 R 27
Earl Marshall's Orders concerning the Robes, Coronets, &c., to be observed at the Coronation of Her Most Sacred Majesty Queen Victoria. Sm. fol. Lond., 1838.
B 16 R 9 ‡
Fifty Years of a Good Queen's Reign: a Book for the Royal Jubilee of 1886–87; by A. H. Wall. 8vo. Lond., 1886.
C 5 R 31

VICTORIA (HER MAJESTY THE QUEEN)—*continued.*
Leaves from the Journal of our Life in the Highlands, 1848–62; edited by Arthur Helps. 8vo. Lond., 1868.
D 8 T 4
Life of Her Majesty Queen Victoria; compiled from all available Sources, by G. Barnett Smith. Jubilee edition. 8vo. Lond., 1887.
C 11 P 31
Memorial of the Royal Progress in Scotland. [*See* LAUDER, SIR T. D.]
D 6 T 27
Memoirs of the Courts and Cabinets of William IV and Victoria; from Original Family Documents, by the Duke of Buckingham and Chandos. 2 vols. 8vo. Lond., 1861.
B 3 S 13, 14
More Leaves from the Journal of a Life in the Highlands, 1862–82. 8vo. Lond., 1884.
D 8 T 5
Progresses of Her Majesty and Prince Albert in France, Belgium, and England. Illustrated. 4to. Lond., 1844.
J 8 R 7
Queen Victoria, from her Birth to her Bridal; by Agnes Strickland. 2 vols. 8vo. Lond., 1840.
C 5 R 28, 29
Queen Victoria: Scenes and Incidents in her Life and Reign; by T. Frederick Ball. 2nd ed. 12mo. Lond., 1886.
C 5 R 30
Speeches in Parliament, from her Accession to the Present Time: a Compendium of the History of Her Majesty's Reign told from the Throne; edited and compiled by F. Sydney Ensor. 8vo. Lond., 1882.
F 6 Q 7

VICTORIA INSTITUTE (THE). Journal of the Transactions of the Victoria Institute; or, Philosophical Society of Great Britain; edited by the Honorary Secretary, Capt. F. W. H. Petrie, F.R.S.L., &c. Vols. 1–15. 15 vols. 8vo. Lond., 1867–82.
E 1.46
Victoria Institute; or, Philosophical Society of Great Britain: Objects, &c.; with Preface. 8vo. Lond., 1878.
MG 1 Q 36
Another copy. (Pam. Cn.) 8vo. Lond., 1878.
MA 2 V 14

VICTORIA TEMPERANCE PIONEER (THE); or, Monthly Magazine, August, 1851. 8vo. Melb., 1851.
MG 1 Q 39

VICTORIAN CONVENTION. Resolutions, Proceedings, and Documents of the Victorian Convention, 1857. 8vo. Melb., 1857.
MF 1 Q 1

VICTORIAN EXHIBITION, 1861. Catalogue of the Victorian Exhibition, 1861; with Prefatory Essays. 8vo. Melb., 1861.*
MK 1 Q 15
Another copy. 4to. Melb., 1861.
MK 1 U 4
Die Colonie Victoria in Australien; ihr Fortschritt, ihre Hilfsquellen, und ihr physikalischer Charakter. Ins Deutsche übertragen von Benjamin Loewy. 8vo. Melb., 1861.
MD 7 Q 3
Another copy. 4to. Melb., 1861.
MF 3 S 14
Essais Divers, servant d'Introduction au Catalogue de l'Exposition des Produits de la Colonie de Victoria. 8vo. Melb., 1861.
MF 2 P 15
Another copy. 4to. Melb., 1861.
MF 3 S 15
[*See* MELBOURNE EXHIBITIONS.]

VICTORIAN GOVERNMENT PRIZE ESSAYS, 1860.
8vo. Melb., 1861.*   MJ 2 P 10

Acreson (Frederick), C.E.   Essay on the Collection and Storage of Water in Victoria.

Mayes (Charles), C.E.   Essay on the Manufactures immediately required for the Economical Development of the Resources of the Colony of Victoria.

Story (William).   Essay upon the Agriculture of Victoria.

Rosales (Henry), M.I.C.E.   Essay on the Origin and Distribution of Gold in Victoria.

VICTORIAN INSTITUTE FOR THE ADVANCEMENT OF SCIENCE.   [*See* ROYAL SOCIETY OF VICTORIA.]

VICTORIAN INTERCOLONIAL EXHIBITION, 1875.
.[*See* PHILADELPHIA INTERNATIONAL AND CENTENNIAL EXHIBITION, 1876.]

VICTORIAN MUNICIPAL DIRECTORY (THE), and Gazetteer, 1886. 12mo. Melb., 1886.   ME 3 S

VICTORIAN POETS. Lives of the. [*See* STEDMAN, E. C.]   C 13 R 14

VICTORIAN PRESS MANUAL (THE), and Advertiser's Hand-book, containing an Alphabetical List, with Particulars of all Newspapers published in the Colony of Victoria; also, Lists of the Newspapers published in New South Wales, Queensland, South Australia, Western Australia, Tasmania, and New Zealand. 2nd ed. 8vo. Melb., 1882.   ME 3 T

VICTORIAN REVIEW (THE); edited by H. Mortimer Franklyn. Vols. 1–4, Vol. 5, No. 28, and Vol. 8, No. 41. 6 vols. roy. 8vo. Melb., 1879–83.   ME 18 R

VIDA (MARCI GIROLAMO). Vida's Art of Poetry; translated by Pitt. [*See* CHALMERS, A.]

VIDAL (MRS. FRANCIS). Tales for the Bush. 4th ed. 12mo. Lond., 1852.   MJ 1 P 23

VIDOCQ (FRANÇOIS JULES), CHEF DE LA POLICE DE SURETÉ. Mémoires de. 4 vols. 8vo. Paris, 1828–29.   C 5 Q 22–25

Memoirs of; written by himself. (Autobiog., 25–28.) 4 vols. (in 2) 18mo. Lond., 1829.   C 1 P 18, 19

VIDYĀSĀGARA (ISVARACHANDRA). The Charitābali; or, Instructive Biography; with a Vocabulary, by J. F. Blumhardt. [In Sanskrit.] 12mo. Lond., 1884.   C 2 Q 9

VIENNA EXHIBITION, 1873: Report of William Robinson, Special Commissioner for the Crown Colonies, and Superintendent of the Colonial Section, upon the British Colonies represented at the Vienna Exhibition, 1873. 8vo. Lond., 1873.   MF 2 P 18

VIEUSSEUX (A.) History of Switzerland. (Lard. Cab. Cyclo.) 12mo. Lond., 1832.   K 1 U 1

Italy and the Italians in the 19th Century. 2 vols. 8vo. Lond., 1824.   B 12 Q 18, 19

VIEYRA (ANTONIO). Dictionary of the Portuguese and English Languages, in two Parts, Portuguese and English, and English and Portuguese. New ed. 2 vols. 8vo. Lond., 1840.   K 14 Q 23, 24

Grammar of the Portuguese Language. 13th ed. 8vo. Lond., 1869.   K 11 U 34

Novo Diccionario Portatil das Linguas Portugueza e Ingleza em duas Partes, Portugueza e Ingleza, Ingleza e Portugueza. Nova edição. 2 vols. 12mo. Paris, 1878.   K 11 8 33, 34

VIGA GLUM'S SAGA: the Story of Viga-Glum; translated from the Icelandic, with Notes and an Introduction, by the Rt. Hon. Sir Edmund Walker Head, Bart. 12mo. Lond., 1866.   B 20 P 14

VIGFUSSON (GUDBRAND), B.A. An Icelandic-English Dictionary. [*See* CLEASBY, R.]

VIGFUSSON (GUDBRAND), M.A., & POWELL (FREDERICK YORK), M.A. Corpus Poeticum Boreale: the Poetry of the Old Northern Tongue from the Earliest Times to the 13th Century. 2 vols. 8vo. Oxford, 1883.   H 8 V 11, 12

Grimm Centenary: Sigfred-Arminius, and other Papers. 8vo. Oxford, 1886.   B 36 R 8

VIGNE (GODFREY T.), F.C.S. Personal Narrative of a Visit to Ghuzni, Kabul, and Afghanistan. With Illustrations. 8vo. Lond., 1840.   D 5 T 11

Travels in Kashmir, Ladak, Iskardo, &c. 2 vols. 8vo. Lond., 1842.   D 6 8 18, 19

VIGNOLI (TITO). Myth and Science: an Essay. 8vo. Lond., 1882.   G 7 T 11

VIGNON (LOUIS). Les Colonies Françaises. 8vo. Paris, 1886.   MF 3 Q 2

VIGNY (ALFRED DE). Cinq-Mars; or, a Conspiracy under Louis XIII. Roy. 8vo. New York, 1847.   J 9 V 9

VIGORNIENSIS. [*See* VACCINATION.]

VIGORS (NICHOLAS AYLWARD), D.C.L. Inquiry into the Nature and Extent of Poetick Licence. 2nd ed. 8vo. Lond., 1813.   J 5 8 25

[*See* BEECHEY, CAPT. F. W.]   A 14 V 1

VILLAGE LAWYER (THE): a Farce. (Cumberland's Eng. Theatre.) 12mo. Lond., 1829.   H 2 Q 17

VILLANI (GIOVANNI). Cronica di, a Lezione ridotta coll' aiuto de' Testi a Penna. 8 vols. roy. 8vo. Firenze, 1823.   B 11 T 13–20

VILLANEUVA (DR. JOACHIMO LAURENTIO). Phœnician Ireland; translated, and illustrated with Notes, by H. O'Brien, B.A. 2nd ed. 8vo. Lond., 1837.   B 11 Q 3

VILLARI (MME. LINDA). [*See* VILLARI, PROF. P.]   C 3 U 20–23

VILLARI (PROF. PASQUALE). Niccolò Machiavelli and his Times; translated by Linda Villari. 4 vols. 8vo. Lond., 1878–83.   C 3 U 20–23

VILLARS (Montfaucon de), Abbé. Diverting History
of the Court de Gabalis. 2nd ed. 8vo. Lond., 1714.
                                                    G 2 P 10

VILLARS (P.) L'Angleterre, l'Ecosse, et l'Irlande. 4to.
Paris, 1886.   D 9 S 9 †

England, Scotland, and Ireland : a Picturesque Survey of
the United Kingdom and its Institutions ; translated by
H. Frith. 4to. Lond., 1887.   D 9 S 10 †

VILLE (Georges). Artificial Manures ; their Chemical
Selection and Scientific Application to Agriculture. 8vo.
Lond., 1879.   A 1 R 44

VILLEMAIN (Abel François). Essay on Pascal. [*See*
Pascal, B.*]   G 11 P 35

VILLEMAREST (Charles Maxime de). Life of Prince
Talleyrand. 4 vols. 8vo. Lond., 1834–36. C 9 T 34–37

Another copy. [American ed.] 8vo. Philad., 1834.
                                                    C 9 T 38

VILLENEUVE (Mme. de). La Belle et la Bête. [*See*
Cabinet des Fées, 26.]

VILLIERS (Rt. Hon. Charles Pelham), M.P. Free Trade
Speeches ; with a Political Memoir ; edited by "A Member
of the Cobden Club." 2 vols. 8vo. Lond., 1883.
                                                    F 4 S 13, 14

VILLIERS (George), First Duke of Buckingham. [*See*
Buckingham, Duke of.]

VILLON (Francis). Poems of ; now first done into English
Verse, in the original Forms, by John Payne. 8vo. Lond.,
1881.   H 8 R 36

[*See* Saintsbury, G. E. B.]

VILMORIN (Henri), and ANDRIEUX (M.) The
Vegetable Garden : Illustrations, Descriptions, and Cul-
ture of the Garden Vegetables of Cold and Temperate
Climates. Roy. 8vo. Lond., 1885.   A 1 S 13

VINCE (Rev. Samuel), A.M., &c. Complete System of Astronomy. 3 vols. 4to. Camb., 1797–1808. A 3 U 13–15

VINCENDON-DUMOULIN (Clément Adrien), et
DESGRAZ (C.) Iles Marquises ; ou, Nouka-Hiva : Histoire, Géographie, Mœurs, et Considérations Générales.
8vo. Paris, 1843.   MD 5 U 29

Physique-Hydrographie. [*See* Dumont D'Urville, Capt.
J. S. C.]

VINCENT (Augustine), Windsor Herald. Memoir of
Augustine Vincent, Windsor Herald [1617–24] ; by Sir
N. H. Nicolas. 8vo. Lond., 1827.   C 4 T 43

VINCENT (Benjamin). Dictionary of Biography, Past
and Present, containing the Chief Events in the Lives of
Eminent Persons of all Ages and Nations. (Haydn Series.)
8vo. Lond., 1880.   C 11 Q 12

Haydn's Dictionary of Dates. [*See* Haydn, J.]

VINCENT (Charles W.), F.R.S.E. [*See* Year-book of
Facts.]

VINCENT (Frank), Junr. Norsk, Lapp, and Finn ; or,
Travel Tracings from the Far North of Europe. 8vo.
Lond., 1881.   D 8 S 19

Through and through the Tropics : Thirty Thousand
Miles of Travel in Polynesia, Australasia, and India. 8vo.
Lond., 1876.   MD 1 S 31

VINCENT (Mrs. Charles Edward Howard). Forty
Thousand Miles over Land and Water. With Illustrations. 2 vols. 8vo. Lond., 1885.   MD 1 W 39, 40

VINCENT (H. D.), And TOWNSEND (W.) The Netherby
Gazette. [*See* Netherby Gazette.]   MJ 2 R 8

VINCENT (J. E. Matthew). Colonization of Greater
Britain : Viticulture, Fruit-farming, &c. in Australia ;
Irrigation Colonies in Victoria and South Australia, now
being carried out by the well-known firm of Chaffey
Brothers. Roy. 8vo. Melb., 1887.*   MA 1 Q 14

VINCENT (William), D.D. Periplus of the Erythrean Sea.
Parts 1, 2. 2 vols. 4to. Lond., 1800–5. D 5 V 15, 16

1. Containing an Account of the Navigation of the Ancients,
    from the Sea of Suez to the Coast of Zanguebar.
2. Containing an Account of the Navigation of the Ancients, from
    the Gulph of Elana, in the Red Sea, to the Island of Ceylon.

Voyage of Nearchus, from the Indus to the Euphrates.
4to. Lond., 1797.   D 5 V 14

Voyage of Nearchus, and the Periplus of the Erythrean
Sea ; translated from the Greek. (In Greek and English.)
4to. Oxford, 1809.   D 5 V 16

VINCENT DE PAUL (Sainte). Vie de. [*See* Capefigue,
J. B. H. R.]

VINCI (Leonardo da). Leonardo ; by Jean Paul Richter.
(Great Artists.) 8vo. Lond., 1880.   C 3 T 37

Literary Works of ; compiled and edited from the original
Manuscripts, by Jean Paul Richter, Ph.D. [In English
and Italian.] 2 vols. imp. 8vo. Lond., 1883. A 5 R 8, 9 †

VINE (Rev. F. T.) Cæsar in Kent : the Landing of Julius
Cæsar and his Battles with the Ancient Britons. 8vo.
Edinb., 1886.   B 4 P 19

VINES (Frederick). Cue to Prosperity ; or, Our Lands,
and how to get at them. 8vo. Melb., 1856. MF 1 Q 3

Another copy. 8vo. Melb., 1856.   MF 3 P 5

VINES (Sydney H.), M.A., &c. Botany. [*See* Bower,
Prof. F. O.]

Lectures on the Physiology of Plants. 8vo. Camb.,
1886.   A 4 S 6

VINNE (Theodore Low de). [*See* De Vinne, T. L.]

VINSAUF (Geoffrey de). [*See* Chronicles of the
Crusades.]

VIOLLET-LE-DUC (Eugène Emmanuel). Annals of a Fortress; translated by Benjamin Bucknall. 8vo. Lond., 1875.   A 6 S 18

Dictionaire Raisonné de l'Architecture Française, du XIᵉ au XVIᵉ Siècle. 10 vols. roy. 8vo. Paris, 1868–75.   A 2 Q 17–26

Dictionaire Raisonné du Mobilier Français de l'epoque Carlovingienne à la Renaissance. 6 vols. roy. 8vo. Paris, 1868–75.   A 2 Q 34–39

Habitations Modernes; recueillies avec le Concours des Membres du Comité de Rédation de l'Encyclopédie d'Architecture et la Collaboration de Félix Narjoux. 2 vols. imp. 4to. Paris, 1875–77.   A 1 Q 6, 7 ‡

Habitations of Man in all Ages; translated by B. Bucknall. 8vo. Lond., 1876.   A 2 S 40

How to build a House: an Architectural Novelette; translated by Benjamin Bucknall. 8vo. Lond., 1874.   A 2 S 14

Lectures on Architecture; translated from the French, by Benjamin Bucknall. Illustrated. 2 vols. roy. 8vo. Lond., 1877–81.   A 3 Q 14, 15

VION (Prof. Michel). Pierre l'Hermite et les Croisades. 12mo. Amiens, 1853.   G 7 U 2

VIRGILIUS (Polydorus). [*See* Vergilius Polydorus.]

VIRGILIUS MARO (Publius). Æneid of Virgil, Books 1–6; translated into English Blank Verse, by G. K. Rickards, M.A.; with an Index of Proper Names. 12mo. Edinb., 1871.   H 6 R 42

Æneid of Virgil; translated into English Verse, by John Conington, M.A. 3rd ed. 8vo. Lond., 1873.   H 7 S 24

English Version of the Eclogues of Virgil; by Samuel Palmer. With Illustrations by the Author. Fol. Lond., 1883.   H 3 P 23 †

First four Books of the Æneid of Virgil, in English Heroic Verse; by Richard Stanyhurst. 4to. Edinb., 1836.   H 5 V 19

Opera omnia, ex editione Heyniana; cum Notis et Interpretatione in usum Delphini, curante A. J. Valpy, A.M. 10 vols. 8vo. Lond., 1819.   J 13 T 11–20

Pub. Virgilii Maronis Bucolicorum Eclogæ Decem: the Bucolicks of Virgil; with an English Translation and Notes, by John Martyn, F.R.S. 4to. Lond., 1749.   H 5 V 8

Roman Poets of the Augustan Age. [*See* Sellar, Prof. W. Y.]

Virgil; the Eclogues, translated by Francis Wrangham; the Georgics, by William Sotheby; and the Æneid, by John Dryden. (Fam. Class. Lib.) 2 vols. 12mo. Lond., 1830.   J 15 P 50, 51

Virgil's Æneid; translated by Pitt. [*See* Chalmers, A., and Johnson, S.]

VIRGILIUS MARO (Publius)—*continued.*

Virgils Æneis, translated into Scottish Verse by Gawin Douglas; to which is added a large Glossary. Sm. fol. Edinb., 1710.   H 3 P 26 †

Virgil's Æneis travestirt. [*See* Blumauer, A.]

Virgil's Eclogues, 1, 4, 5–10, and Cæsar's Commentaries, Book 4, for the use of Schools. 12mo. Lond., MJ 1 P 18

Works of Virgil; containing his Pastorals, Georgics, and Æneis, translated into English Verse by J. Dryden. Fol. Lond., 1697.   H 22 S 3 ‡

Works of Virgil; translated by Dryden. [*See* Chalmers, A.]

VIRGIN ISLANDS (The). Letters from the Virgin Islands, illustrating Life and Manners in the West Indies. 8vo. Lond., 1843.   D 3 R 24

VIRI ILLUSTRES; edited by P. Geddes. 12mo. Edinb., 1884.   C 1 R 40

VISCONTI (Ennio Quirino). Iconographie Grecque. [1 vol. in 3 parts.] 3 vols. l. fol. Paris, 1808. B 12 P 11–13 ‡

Iconographie Romaine. [Vols. 2–4 by the Chevalier A. Mongez.] 4 vols. l. fol. Paris, 1817–26. B 12 P 11–17‡

VITALIS (Ordericus). [*See* Ordericus Vitalis.]

VITRIER (Jehan), And COLET (John), D.D., Dean of St. Paul's, London. Lives of; written in Latin by Erasmus, of Rotterdam; translated by J. H. Lupton, M.A. 12mo. Lond., 1883.   C 2 R 31

VITRUVIUS POLLIO (Marcus). Civil Architecture of Vitruvius. Imp. 4to. Lond., 1812.   A 23 R 19 ‡

Ten Books of Vitruvius. (Ancient Architecture.) (Weale.) 8vo. Lond., 1867.   A 17 P 64

VIVIAN (George). Scenery of Portugal and Spain. Imp. fol. Lond., 1839.   D 7 P 3 ‡

VIVIEN DE SAINT-MARTIN (Louis). Description Historique et Géographique de l'Asie Mineure, comprenant les Temps Anciens, le Moyen Age, et les Temps Modernes. 2 vols. 8vo. Paris, 1852.   D 5 T 4, 5

L'Année Géographique: Revue Annuelle des Voyages, des Explorations, &c., relatives aux Sciences Géographiques et Ethnographiques. 8vo. Paris, 1874.   E

VIVISECTION. Royal Society for the Prevention of Cruelty to Animals and the Royal Commission. 8vo. Lond., 1876.   A 12 R 24

VIZETELLY (Henry). Berlin under the New Empire; its Institutions, Inhabitants, Industry, Monuments, Museums, Social Life, Manners, and Amusements. 2 vols. 8vo. Lond., 1879.   D 8 U 30, 31

Facts about Champagne and other Sparkling Wines. 8vo. Lond., 1879.   A 1 P 9

VIZETELLY (HENRY)—*continued.*
Facts about Port and Madeira; with Notices of the Wines vintaged around Lisbon, and the Wines of Teneriffe. 8vo. Lond., 1880.   A 1 P 8

History of Champagne; with Notes on the other Sparkling Wines of France. Illustrated. 4to. Lond., 1882.   A 2 Q 5 †

Story of the Diamond Necklace told in detail for the First Time, chiefly by the aid of original Letters, Official and other Documents, and Contemporary Memoirs recently made public, and comprising a Sketch of the Life of the Countess de la Mothe, &c. 2 vols. 8vo. Lond., 1867.   B 8 P 10, 11

VLAMINGH (CAPT. WILLEM DE). Iets over de Reis van den Schipper-commandeur Willem de Vlamingh, naar Nieuw-Holland, in 1696 en 1705. 8vo. Amsterdam (n.d.)   MD 1 V 10

VLOTEN (J. VAN). Spinoza: an Essay. [*See* SPINOZA, B. DE.]   C 9 R 30

VOCABOLARIO degli Accademici Della Crusca impressione Napoletana secondo l'Ultima di Firenzi. 6 vols. fol. Napoli, 1746–48.   K 29 P 1–6 ‡

VOGEL (DR. HERMANN). Chemistry of Light and Photography in its application to Art, Science, and Industry. 8vo. Lond., 1875.   A 5 R 30

VOGEL (SIR JULIUS), K.C.M.G. New Zealand: Land and Farming in New Zealand; also, the Land Acts of 1877. With Maps. 8vo. Lond., 1879.   MF 1 R 45

Official Hand-book of New Zealand. 8vo. Lond., 1875.*   MD 7 Q 20

On the Federation of the British Empire. [*See* AUSTRALASIA.]

VOGT (C.) Lehrbuch der Geologie und Petrefactenkunde. 2 vols. 8vo. Braunsch, 1879.   A 9 R 27, 28

Embryologie des Salmones. [*See* AGASSIZ, PROF. L.]   A 14 V 48

VOGT (LIEUT.-COL. HERMANN). Egyptian War of 1882: a Translation; with a Map and Plans. 8vo. Lond., 1883.   B 2 S 13

VOGÜÉ (MELCHIOR), COMTE DE. Syrie Centrale. Architecture Civile et Religieuse du Iᵉʳ au VIIᵉ Siè. 2 vols. imp. 4to. Paris, 1865-77.   A 23 S 5, 6 ‡

Syrie Centrale. Inscriptions Sémitiques. Roy. 4to. Paris, 1868-77.   B 15 S 4 †

VOICE FROM THE DANUBE (A); or, the true state of the case between Austria and Hungary; by "An impartial Spectator." 8vo. Lond., 1859.   B 7 S 50

VOICE TO THE CHURCH; by "A Member of the Christian Church." 12mo. Hobart, 1852.   MG 1 P 49

Eighteen Thousand Souls in our City, at time of Census, 1851, found living in neglect of Public Worship. 8vo. Hobart, 1852.   MG 1 Q 29

VOLKNER (REV. C. S.) Murder of the Rev. C. S. Volkner, in New Zealand. 8vo. Lond., 1865.   MD 4 V 29

VOLNEY (CONSTANTIN FRANCOIS CHASSEBŒUF), COMTE DE. Travels through Syria and Egypt, 1783–85. Illustrated. 2nd ed. 2 vols. 8vo. Lond., 1788.   D 1 P 8, 9

The Ruins; or, a Survey of the Revolutions of the Empires; to which is added the Law of Nature. 5th ed. 8vo. Lond., 1807.   G 12 T 19

VOLTAIRE (FRANÇOIS MARIE AROUET DE). Works of. Translated from the French, with Notes, Historical and Critical, by Dr. Smollet, and others. 38 vols. 12mo. Lond., 1761–74.   J 1 S 1–38

Histoire de Charles XII, Roi de Suède. 18mo. Lond., 1832.   B 20 P 13

Histoire de l'Empire de Russie sous Pierre le Grand. 18mo. Lond., 1830.   B 31 P 1

Life and Times of François Marie Arouet, calling himself Voltaire; by F. Espinasse. Vol 1. 8vo. Lond., 1866.   C 9 R 36

Voltaire; by John Morley. 8vo. Lond., 1872.   C 8 P 25

Philosophical Dictionary; with a Biographical Memoir. 2 vols. 8vo. Lond. (n.d.)   G 13 Q 42, 43

Memoir of the Life of Voltaire; written by himself. (Autobiography I.) 12mo. Lond., 1826.   C 1 P 5

Life of; by James Parton. 2 vols. 8vo. Lond., 1881.   C 9 R 37–38

Voltaire. Bolingbroke: a Historical Study, and Voltaire in England; by John Churton Collins. 8vo. Lond., 1886.   C 5 R 5

Oeuvres complètes de. 64 vols. 8vo. Paris, 1819–22.   J 15 T 1–U 1

1–7. Théâtre.
8. La Henriade.
9. La Pucelle d'Orléans.
10. Poëmes.
11. Epîtres et stances.
12. Contes en vers, satires, et Poëstes mêlées.
13–16. Essai sur les mœurs et l'esprit des nations.
17–18. Siècle de Louis XIV.
19. Précis du Siècle de Louis XV.
20. Histoire de Charles XII.
21. Histoire de l'Empire de Russie.
22. Annales de l'Empire.
23. Histoire du Parlement de Paris.
24–25. Mélanges historiques.
26–27. Politique et Législation.
28. Physique.
29–31. Philosophie.
32. Dialogues et entretiens philosophiques.
33–38. Dictionnaire Philosophique.
39–40. Romans.
41. Facéties.
42–43. Mélanges Littéraires.
44–45. Commentaires sur Corneille.
46–57. Correspondance générale.
58–60. Correspondance avec le roi de Prusse, etc.
61. Correspondance avec l'Impératrice de Russie.
62. Correspondance avec de d'Alembert.
63. Lettres inédites.
64. Vie de Voltaire [par le Marquis de Condorcet.]

VOLUNTEER MILITARY FORCES. [*See* NEW SOUTH WALES.]

VOLUNTEER SERVICE GAZETTE (THE). Vol. 25. Nov. 1883–Oct. 1884. Fol. Lond., 1884.   E

VONDEL (JOOST VAN DEN). Milton and Vondel: a Curiosity of Literature. [*See* EDMUNDSON, G.]

VORSTERMAN VAN OYEN (A. A.) Dictionnaire Nobiliaire. Roy. 8vo. La Haye, 1884.   K 10 T 4

VOTES AND PROCEEDINGS OF PARLIAMENT. [*See* N. S. WALES, VICTORIA, NEW ZEALAND, QUEENSLAND, AND SOUTH AUSTRALIA.]

VOYAGES DE ROBERTSON aux Terres Australes. Traduit sur le Manuscrit Anglois. 12mo. Amsterdam, 1766–7.   MJ 1 P 34
Another copy. 12mo. Amsterdam, 1767.   MJ 1 P 35

VOYAGES AND DISCOVERIES. Account of several late Voyages and Discoveries; by Sir John Narborough, Captain Jasmen Tasmen, Captain John Wood, and Frederick Marten, of Hamburgh. 8vo. Lond., 1694.
                                                    MD 5 P 24
Collection of Voyages undertaken by the Dutch East India Company, for the improvement of Trade and Navigation. Translated into English. 8vo. Lond., 1703.
                                                    D 10 Q 36
Account of several late Voyages : 1. Sir John Narborough's Voyage to the South Sea. 2. Captain J. Tasman's Discoveries on the Coast of the South Terra Incognita. 3. Captain J. Wood's Attempt to Discover a North-east Passage to China. 4. F. Marten's Observations made in Greenland, and other Northern Countries. 8vo. Lond., 1711.   MD 5 P 25

VOYAGES AND DISCOVERIES—*continued.*
General Collection of Voyages, undertaken either for Discovery, Conquest, Settlement, or the opening of Trade, from the commencement of the Portuguese Discoveries to the present time. Vol. 1. (*All published.*) 8vo. Lond., 1789.   D 10 T 29
Account of the Most Remarkable Voyages, from the Discovery of America by Columbus to the Present Time. 12mo. Lond. (n.d.)   MD 1 T 17
Remarkable Voyages and Travels, consisting of Anson's Voyage Round the World, Stephen's Incidents of Travel in Greece, Turkey, Russia, and Poland, and Kaempfer's Account of Japan. Roy. 8vo. Lond. (n.d.)   D 9 U 13

VOYLE (MAJOR-GEN. G. E.), STEVENSON (CAPT. G. DE SAINT-CLAIR). Military Dictionary ; comprising Terms, Scientific and otherwise, connected with the Science of War. 3rd ed. 8vo. Lond., 1876.   A 29 Q 16

VRIES (DR. M. DE). [*See* DE VRIES, DR. M.]

VROMANS (PIETER). Tractaet de Foro Competenti, door H. van Middellant. Sm. 4to. Leyden, 1722. F 12 Q 5

VULCAN (B.) [*See* ARRIAN, F.]   B 16 R 12 ‡

VYSE (COL. HOWARD). Operations carried on at the Pyramids of Gizeh in 1837 ; with an Account of a Voyage into Upper Egypt, and an Appendix containing a Survey, by J. S. Perring, C.E. 3 vols. 4to. Lond., 1840–42.   D 2 V 16–18
Atlas of Plates. [*See* PERRING, J. S., AND ANDREWS, E. J.]   B 3 P 27, 28 ‡

W

W (F. F.) [*See* WYMAN, F. F.]

W.A.M. Description of the Quarantine Ground. [*See* NEW SOUTH WALES.]

Remarks upon the Language, &c., of the Aborigines of Australia. [*See* ABORIGINES.]   MJ 2 S 2

W.B.C. [*See* COLONIAL POLICY.]   MJ 2 P 36

W.B.L. [*See* KEY TO FORTUNE.]   MA 2 P 21

W.M.B. [*See* NARRATIVE OF EDWARD CREWE.] MJ 1 P 3

W.W. [*See* DETECTIVE'S ALBUM.]

WAAGEN (DR. GUSTAV FRIEDRICH). Galleries and Cabinets of Art in Great Britain, forming a Supplemental Volume to the "Treasures of Art in Great Britain." 8vo. Lond., 1857.   A 8 Q 13

Peter Paul Rubens; his Life and Genius; translated from the German, by Robert R. Noel, Esq.; edited by Mrs. Jameson. 8vo. Lond., 1840.   A 7 Q 22

Treasures of Art in Great Britain; being an Account of the Chief Collections of Paintings, Drawings, Sculptures, Illuminated MSS., &c. 3 vols. 8vo. Lond., 1854.
       A 8 Q 10–12

Verzeichniss der Gemälde-Sammlung des königlichen Museums zu Berlin. 8vo. Berlin, 1843.   A 7 Q 21

Works of Art and Artists in England. 3 vols. 8vo. Lond., 1838.   A 7 Q 26–28

WACE (REV. HENRY), M.A. Dictionary of Christian Biography. [*See* SMITH, W.]   C 11 S 9–12

WACHSMUTH (C.) [*See* LEIPZIGER STUDIEN.]
       K 19 S 5–11

WACHSMUTH (WILLIAM). Historical Antiquities of the Greeks, with reference to their Political Institutions. 2 vols. 8vo. Lond., 1837.   B 9 T 19, 20

WACKERNAGEL (WILHELM). Altdeutsches Handwörterbuch. (Deutsches Lesebuch.) 5° Auflage. Sq. 8vo. Basel, 1878.   K 15 R 7

WADDELL (REV. RUTHERFORD), M.A. Maoriland: an Illustrated Hand-book to New Zealand. [*See* WILSON, A.]   MD 5 Q 42

WADDINGTON (VERY REV. GEORGE), D.D. History of the Church, from the Earliest Ages to the Reformation. 2nd ed. 3 vols. 8vo. Lond., 1835.   G 4 S 17–19

History of the Reformation on the Continent. 3 vols. 8vo. Lond., 1841.   G 4 S 20–22

WADDINGTON (VERY REV. GEORGE), AND HANBURY (REV. BERNARD), A.M., &c. Journal of a Visit to some Parts of Ethiopia. With Maps and Engravings. 4to. Lond., 1822.   D 4 P 21 †

WADE (WILLIAM RICHARD). Journey in the Northern Island of New Zealand. 12mo. Hobart, 1842. MD 4 Q 23

WAFER (LIONEL). Nieuwe Reystogt en Beschryving van de Land-engte van Amerika. 8vo. 'sGravenhage, 1700.
       MD 1 U 1

Another copy. 8vo. Amsterdam, 1717.   MD 1 U 2

Reystogten rondom de Waereldt. [*See* DAMPIER, CAPT. W.]

WAGENAAR (J.) Vaderlandsche Historie, vervattende de Geschiedenissen der Vereenigde Nederlanden, inzonderheid die van Holland, van de vroegste Tyden af: uit de geloofwaardigste Schryvers en egte Gedenkstukken samengesteld. 21 vols. 8vo. Amsterd., 1752–59. B 12 S 17–37

WAGHORN (LIEUT. THOMAS), R.N., &c. Letter to the Rt. Hon. William Ewart Gladstone, M.P., Secretary of State for the Colonies, on the Extension of Steam Navigation from Singapore to Port Jackson, Australia. 8vo. Lond., 1846.   MF 2 P 16

Second Letter to the Rt. Hon. the Earl Grey, Secretary of State for the Colonies, on the Extension of Steam Navigation from Singapore to Port Jackson, Australia. 8vo. Lond., 1847.   MF 3 Q 73

WAGNER (DR. MORITZ). [*See* PULSZKY, F.] D 1 S 21

WÄGNER (DR. W.) Asgard and the Gods: Tales and Traditions of our Northern Ancestors; adapted by M. W. Macdowall, and edited by W. S. W. Anson. 8vo. Lond., 1882.   B 15 Q 6

WAGSTAFFE (W. W.), B.A., &c. Student's Guide to Human Osteology. 8vo. Lond., 1875.   A 12 P 27

WAHL (O. W.) Land of the Czar. 8vo. Lond., 1875.
       D 6 U 16

WAHL (WILLIAM H.) Techno-chemical Receipt Book. [*See* BRANNT, W. T.]

WAILLY (NATALIS DE). [*See* JOINVILLE, JOHN, LORD DE.]
       C 4 W 30

WAITE (A. E.) Mysteries of Magic: a Digest of the Writings of "Eliphas Levi" [A. L. Constant]; with Biographical and Critical Essay. 8vo. Lond., 1886. A 10 R 5

WAITE (J. M.) Lessons in Sabre, Singlestick, Sabre and Bayonet, and Sword Feats; or, how to use a Cut-and-Thrust Sword. With Illustrations. 12mo. Lond., 1880.
       A 17 U 18

WAIWERA. Waiwera (Hot Springs), near Auckland, New Zealand. 12mo. Auckland, 1878.   A 16 U 23

WAKE (C. STANILAND). Evolution of Morality; being a History of the Development of Moral Culture. 2 vols. 8vo. Lond., 1878.   G 7 T 13, 14

WAKEFIELD (EDWARD GIBBON). England and America. 8vo. Lond., 1833. F 3 P 11

Facts relating to the Punishment of Death in the Metropolis; with an Appendix, concerning Murder for the Sale of the Dead Body. 2nd ed. 8vo. Lond., 1832. F 5 U 8

Letter from Sydney, the principal Town of Australasia; together with the Outline of a System of Colonization; edited by Robert Gouger. 8vo. Lond., 1829.* MD 4 Q 35

New British Province of South Australia; or, a Description of the Country, illustrated by Charts and Views. 18mo. Lond., 1834. MD 1 P 9

Another copy. 2nd ed. 12mo. Lond., 1835.* MD 1 P 10

View of the Art of Colonization, with present reference to the British Empire, in Letters between a Statesman and a Colonist. 8vo. Lond., 1849.* MF 2 Q 12

WAKEFIELD (EDWARD JERNINGHAM). Adventure in New Zealand, from 1839–44. 2 vols. 8vo. Lond., 1845.* MD 5 T 13, 14

Illustrations to "Adventure in New Zealand." Lithographed from original Drawings (Coloured). At. fol. Lond., 1845.* MD 3 P 10 ‡

Another copy [uncoloured]. At. fol. Lond., 1845. MD 3 P 11 ‡

Hand-book for New Zealand; compiled by "A Late Magistrate of the Colony, who resided there during four years." 12mo. Lond., 1848. MD 1 P 12

WAKEFIELD (EDWARD JERNINGHAM), AND WARD (JOHN). British Colonization of New Zealand. 12mo. Lond., 1837.* MD 2 P 7

WAKEFIELD (GILBERT), B.A. Letter to Jacob Bryant, Esq., concerning his Dissertation on the War of Troy. (Pam.) 4to. Lond., 1797. B 18 R 13 ‡

Letter to William Wilberforce on the subject of his late Publication [Religious System of professed Christians]. (Pam. Bf.) 8vo. Lond., 1797. G 17 Q 20

[See LUCRETIUS CARUS, T.] J 13 R 6–9

WAKEFIELD (W.), M.D. Baths, Bathing, and Attractions of Aix-les-Bains, Savoy: its History, Geology, Mineral Waters, &c. 12mo. Lond., 1886. D 7 P 15

WAKEMAN (HENRY OFFLEY), AND HASSALL (A.), M.A. Essays introductory to the Study of English Constitutional History. 8vo. Lond., 1887. F 5 T 4

WALAFRIDUS STRABUS (FULDENSIS MONACHUS). Opera omnia. [See MIGNE, J. P., SERIES LATINA, 113, 114.]

WALCH (GARNET). Head over Heels: a Christmas Book of Fun and Fancy. 8vo. Melb., 1874. MH 1 R 17

The *Fireflash*—four Oars and a Coxswain: where they went, how they went, and why they went; and the Stories they told last Christmas Eve; by "One of the Crew." 8vo. Hobart, 1867. MJ 2 R 13

Victoria in 1880. With Illustrations on Stone and Wood, by Charles Turner. 4to. Melb., 1881.* MD 7 Q 4 †

WALCH (J.) Tasmanian Almanac and Guide to Tasmania, for 1863, 1865, 1869, and 1882; compiled from the most authentic Sources. 4 vols. 12mo. Hobart, 1863–82. ME 4 P

Tasmanian Guide-book : a Hand-book of Information for all parts of the Colony. 12mo. Hobart, 1871. MD 3 P 21

WALDECK (F. DE), ET BRASSEUR DE BOURBOURG (C. E.), L'ABBÉ. Monuments anciens du Mexique: Palenqué et autres Ruines de l'ancienne civilisation du Mexique. [Text only.] Imp. fol. Paris, 1860. B 15 S 3 ‡

Recherches sur les Ruines de Palenqué, et sur les origines de la civilisation du Mexique. Texte publié avec les dessins de M. de Waldeck. 2 vols. imp. fol. Paris, 1866. B 5 P 21, 22 ‡

WALDEGRAVE (JAMES), K.G., EARL. Memoirs, 1754–58. 4to. Lond., 1821. C 5 W 10

WALDEGRAVE (CAPT. HON. W.), R.N. Extracts from a Private Journal, kept on board H.M.S. *Seringapatam*, in the Pacific, in 1830. 8vo. Lond., 1834. MD 7 R 50

WALDIE (CHARLOTTE A.) Rome in the 19th Century; in a series of Letters written in 1817–18. 3 vols. 8vo. Edinb., 1826. B 12 Q 31–33

WALDSTEIN (ALBRECHT EUSEBIUS WENZESLAUS). [See FRIEDLAND, DUKE OF.]

WALDSTEIN (C.) Essays on the Art of Pheidias. 8vo. Camb., 1885. A 8 S 28

WALES. Ancient Laws and Institutes of; with Index and Glossary. Fol. Lond., 1841. F 24 Q 21 ‡

WALEY (JACOB). Davidson's Precedents. [See DAVIDSON, C.]

WALFORD (CORNELIUS), F.I.A., &c. Fairs, Past and Present: a Chapter in the History of Commerce. 8vo. Lond., 1883. B 7 U 25

WALFORD (EDWARD), M.A. Chapters from Family Chests. 2 vols. 8vo. Lond., 1887. B 2 S 34, 35

County Families of the United Kingdom. 6th ed. Imp. 8vo. Lond., 1871. E

Another copy. 13th Annual Publication. Imp. 8vo. Lond., 1873. E

Another copy. 16th Annual Publication. Roy. 8vo. Lond., 1876. E

Another copy. 24th Annual Publication. Roy. 8vo. Lond., 1884. E

Another copy. 26th Annual Publication. Roy. 8vo. Lond., 1886. E

Greater London: a Narrative of its History, its People, and its Places. Illustrated. 2 vols. imp. 8vo. 1884. B 3 U 7, 8

Hardwicke's Annual Biography, 1856–57; by E. Walford. 2 vols. 12mo. Lond., 1856–57. C 1 R 4, 5

WALFORD (EDWARD), M.A.—*continued.*
Life of the Prince Consort. 12mo. Lond., 1862.
                                              C 1 P 2

Analysis [of] an Exposition of the Creed, by John Pearson, D.D. [*See* PEARSON, PROF. J.]

Men of the Time: a Biographical Dictionary of Eminent Living Characters. New (5th) ed. 8vo. Lond., 1862.
                                              C 4 U 8

Old and New London. [*See* THORNBURY, W.]   B 3 U 1–6

Tales of our Great Families. 2nd series. 2 vols. 8vo. Lond., 1880.   B 35 Q 6, 7

Politics and Economics of Aristotle. [*See* ARISTOTELES.]
                                              F 5 S 51

[*See* ANTIQUARIAN MAGAZINE, *and* BRAYLEY, E. W.]

WALFORD (MAJOR NEVILLE LLOYD), R.A. Parliamentary Generals of the Great Civil War. (Military Biographies.) 8vo. Lond., 1886.   B 2 S 38

WALKER. [*See* JONES v. JENKINS.]

WALKER (ALEXANDER). Woman: physiologically considered as to Mind, Morals, Marriage, Matrimonial Slavery, Infidelity, and Divorce. 2nd ed. 8vo. Lond., 1840.   F 14 R 4

Documents and Dates of Modern Discoveries in the Nervous System. 8vo. Lond., 1834.   A 12 R 17

Intermarriage; or, the Natural Laws by which Beauty, Health, and Intellect result from certain unions, and Deformity, Disease, and Insanity from others. Illustrated. 2nd ed. 8vo. Lond., 1841.   A 12 P 43

Physiognomy, founded on Physiology, and applied to various Countries, Professions, and Individuals. 8vo. Lond., 1834.   A 13 P 30

Nervous System, Anatomical and Physiological. 8vo. Lond., 1834.   A 12 R 16

WALKER (MRS. ALEXANDER). Female Beauty, as preserved and improved by Regimen, Cleanliness, and Dress, and especially by the Adaptation, Colour, and arrangement of Dress, as variously influencing the Forms, Complexion, and Expression of each Individual, and rendering Cosmetic Impositions unnecessary. 8vo. Lond., 1837.   A 12 P 44

WALKER (HON. A.) Tracts on the Ballot; No. 5. Test of Experience; or, the Working of the Ballot in the United States. 8vo. Lond., 1855.   MJ 2 R 21

WALKER (Miss A. F.) Flowers of New South Wales. Painted and published by Miss A. F. Walker, of Rhodes, Ryde, Parramatta River, N.S.W. Roy. 4to. Sydney, 1887.*   MA 1 It 21 ‡

WALKER (CRITCHETT), C.M.G. New South Wales: Map, Illustration, and Descriptive Text. 4to. Sydney, 1881.*   MD 4 P 26 †

Railway Map of New South Wales; with a brief Account of the Character and Resources of the Colony. 8vo. Sydney, 1885.   MD 5 P 14 ‡

WALKER (DONALD). Walker's Manly Exercises; containing Rowing, Sailing, Riding, Driving, Racing, Hunting, Shooting, and other manly Sports; by "Craven." 8vo. Lond., 1878.   A 17 U 16

WALKER (F.) Brickwork; a Practical Treatise embodying the General and Higher Principles of Bricklaying, Cutting, and Setting. Illustrated. (Weale.) 12mo. Lond., 1885.   A 17 R 12

WALKER (FRANCIS A.) Compendium of the ninth Census (June 1st, 1870.) Roy. 8vo. Wash., 1872. F 3 R 14

A Brief Text-book of Political Economy. 8vo. Lond., 1883.   F 5 S 15

Political Economy. 8vo. Lond., 1883.   F 6 T 26

WALKER (FREDERICK). Works of W. M. Thackeray. [*See* THACKERAY, W. M.]

WALKER (GEORGE). Costume of Yorkshire in 1814. Illustrated. Imp. 4to. Leeds, 1885.   A 4 S 14 ‡

WALKER (GEORGE), M.A. Copious Latin Grammar. [*See* SCHELLER, I. J. G.]

WALKER (REV. GEORGE WASHINGTON). Friendly Counsel addressed to the Working Classes. (Pam., 39.) 12mo. Hobart, 1854.   MJ 2 R 1

Life and Labours of; by James Backhouse and Charles Tylor. 8vo. Lond., 1862.   MC 1 R 34

Addresses. [*See* BACKHOUSE, J.]   MG 1 P 9

WALKER (JOHN). Rhyming Dictionary of the English Language. Revised and enlarged by J. Longmuir, A.M., &c. 5th ed. 8vo. Lond., 1879.   K 11 U 13

Elements of Elocution. 2nd ed. 8vo. Lond., 1799.
                                              J 5 S 23

Critical Pronouncing Dictionary. 27th ed. 8vo. Lond., 1825.   K 15 Q 22

Walker remodelled. [*See* SMART, B. H.]

[*See* D'ROZARIO, P. S.]

WALKER (REV. JOHN). Selection of Curious Articles from the *Gentleman's Magazine.* 3rd ed. 4 vols. 8vo. Lond., 1814.   J 4 S 7–10

WALKER (JOSEPH COOPER). Historical Memoir on Italian Tragedy, from the Earliest Period to the Present Times, illustrated with Specimens and Analyses of the most Celebrated Tragedies. 4to. Lond., 1799.   J 8 R 6 †

WALKER (CAPT. J. H.) The Wreck, the Rescue, and the Massacre: an Account of the Barque *Thomas King,* on Cato's Reef, New Holland, in April, 1852. 18mo. Lond., 1853.   MD 2 P 44

WALKER (MRS. MARY ADELAIDE). Eastern Life and Scenery; with Excursions in Asia Minor, Mytilene, Crete, and Roumania. 2 vols. 8vo. Lond., 1886. D 5 Q 3, 4

WALKER (MARY GRACE). [*See* SMITH, TEENAR.] C 9 R 31

WALKER (ROBERT), F.R.G.S., &c. The Five Threes—
33,333 Miles by Land and Sea: Holiday Notes. 8vo.
Lond., 1884. MD 2 S 27

WALKER (ROBERT COOPER). Works on New South Wales;
compiled at the Free Public Library, Sydney, under the
direction of R. C. Walker, Principal Librarian. 8vo.
Sydney, 1878. MJ 2 R 17

Another copy. 8vo. Sydney, 1878. MK 1 S 7

WALKER (THOMAS), M.A. The Original: Essays, &c.
4th. ed. 8vo. Lond., 1838. J 4 S 20

WALKER (W.) Working Drawings and Designs in Mechanical Engineering, &c. [*See* BURN, R. S.] A 20 P 20 ‡

WALKER (WALTER FREDERICK). The Azores, or Western
Islands. 8vo. Lond., 1886. D 7 S 2

WALKER (WILLIAM). The Flood (1850): a Poem.
Fol. Windsor, 1860. MJ 2 U 1

Australian Literature: a Lecture. (Pam., J.) 8vo.
Sydney, 1864. MJ 1 T 38

Poems. Written in Youth. 8vo. Sydney, 1884.*
MH 1 Q 18

Miscellanies. 8vo. Windsor, 1884. MJ 1 T 19

An Account of the Great Flood at the Hawkesbury,
June, 1867. Reprinted, by permission, from the *Sydney
Morning Herald.* 8vo. Sydney, 1887.* MB 2 Q 31

Facts for Factories; being Letters on Practical Subjects,
suggested by experience in Bombay. (Pam., 24.) 8vo.
Bombay, 1857. MJ 2 Q 12

WALKER (W. H.) [*See* RANKEN, G.]

WALKER (WILLIAM B.) The Hand; by "Tom Cringle."
8vo. Melh., 1867. MJ 2 R 23

WALL (ABIATHAR). [*See* MACAULAY, J.] A 12 U 24

WALL (A. H.) Fifty Years of a Good Queen's Reign: a
Book for the Royal Jubilee of 1886–87. 8vo. Lond.,
1886. C 5 R 31

WALL (A. J.) M.D., &c. Indian Snake Poisons; their
Nature and Effects. 8vo. Lond., 1883. A 12 P 34

WALL (H. BERESFORD DE LA POER), M.A. Manual of
Physical Geography of Australia. 12mo. Melh., 1883.
MA 2 V 23

WALL (WILLIAM S.) History and Description of a new
Sperm Whale lately set up in the Australian Museum;
together with some Account of a new genus of Sperm
Whales called Euphysetes. Two Plates. 8vo. Sydney,
1851. MA 2 T 8

WALLACE (ALFRED RUSSEL), F.R.G.S. Australasia: with
Ethnological Appendix, by A. H. Keane, M.A.I. (Stanford's Compendium of Geography and Travel.) 8vo.
Lond., 1879. MD 1 U 29

Contributions to the Theory of Natural Selection: a
Series of Essays. 2nd ed. 8vo. Lond., 1871. A 17 T 42

WALLACE (ALFRED RUSSEL), F.R.G.S.—*continued.*
Geographical Distribution of Animals; with a Study
of the Relations of Living and Extinct Faunas. 2 vols.
8vo. Lond., 1876. A 14 U 1, 2

Island Life; or, the Phenomena and Causes of Insular
Faunas and Floras, including a Revision and attempted
Solution of the Problem of Geological Climates. 8vo.
Lond., 1880. A 16 V 21

Malay Archipelago; the Land of the Orang-Utan and the
Bird of Paradise. 2nd ed. 2 vols. 8vo. Lond., 1869.
D 6 P 39, 40

Narrative of Travels on the Amazon and Rio Negro; with
an Account of the Native Tribes. With Illustrations. 8vo.
Lond., 1853. D 3 T 10

WALLACE (D. MACKENZIE), M.A. Russia. 2nd ed. 2
vols. 8vo. Lond., 1877. D 6 U 23, 24

WALLACE (EDWARD J.) Oregon Question determined by
International Law. (Pam. 25.) 8vo. Lond., 1846.
MJ 2 P 37

WALLACE (EDWIN), M.A. Aristotle's Psychology. [*See*
ARISTOTELES.] G 4 R 24

WALLACE (GRACE MAXWELL), LADY. Beethoven's Letters
[*See* BEETHOVEN, L. VON.] C 3 Q 4, 5

Letters from Italy. [*See* MENDELSSOHN-BARTHOLDY, F.]
D 7 P 43

Letters of Distinguished Musicians: Gluck, Haydn, P. E.
Bach, Weber, Mendelssohn; translated from the German.
8vo. Lond., 1867. C 3 U 29

Letters of Felix Mendelssohn-Bartholdy. [*See* MENDELSSOHN-BARTHOLDY, F.] C 5 P 25

Letters of Wolfgang Amadeus Mozart. [*See* MOZART,
W. A.] C 3 V 33, 34

Reminiscences of Felix Mendelssohn-Bartholdy. [*See*
POLKO, E.] C 5 P 19

WALLACE (REV. JAMES). Description of the Isles of
Orkney. 8vo. Edinb., 1883. D 8 U 32

WALLACE (JOHN). Portrait of. [*See* MANUSCRIPTS AND
PORTRAITS.]

WALLACE (JOHN HOWARD). Manual of New Zealand
History. 8vo. Wellington, 1886.* MB 2 R 32

WALLACE (R. L.) British Cage Birds; containing full
Directions for Breeding, &c., various British Birds that can
be kept in confinement. 8vo. Lond., 1887. A 14 Q 44

WALLACE (WILLIAM). History of England. [*See* MACKINTOSH, SIR J.] K 1 S 42–T 5

WALLACE (WILLIAM). Laws which regulate the Deposition of Lead Ore in Veins. 8vo. Lond., 1861. A 9 S 19

WALLACE (WILLIAM), M.D. Infectious Diseases. [*See*
RUSSELL, J. B.] A 12 U 13

WALLACE (SIR WILLIAM). Early Days of; by John, Marquess of Bute, Knt. 4to. Paisley, 1876. B 13 P 18
Wallace; or, the Life and Acts of Sir W. Wallace. [*See* HENRY THE MINSTREL.]

Life of Sir William Wallace, of Elderslie; by J. D. Carrick. (Const. Misc.) 2 vols. 18mo. Edinb., 1830. K 10 Q 41, 42

Metrical History of Sir William Wallace, Knight of Ellerslie. [*See* HENRY THE MINSTREL.]

The Bruce; and Wallace. [*See* BARBOUR, J., *and* HENRY THE MINSTREL.]

WALLACE-DUNLOP (M. A.) [*See* DUNLOP, M. A. W.-]

WALLENSTEIN or WALDSTEIN (ALBRECHT EUSEBIUS WENZESLAUS). [*See* FRIEDLAND, A. E. W. WALLENSTEIN OR WALDSTEIN, DUKE OF.]

WALLER (EDMUND). Life and Poems of. [*See* CHALMERS, A., *and* JOHNSON, S.]

WALLER (REV. HORACE). Last Journals of David Livingstone. [*See* LIVINGSTONE, REV. D.]   D 1 W 9, 10

WALLEY (T.) Four Bovine Scourges. 8vo. Edinb., 1879.   A 1 T 15

WALLICH (NATHANIEL), M.D., &c. List of Indian Woods. (Pam. 2.) 8vo. Lond., 1831.   MJ 2 P 37
Plantæ Asiaticæ Rariores; or, Descriptions and Figures of a select number of unpublished East Indian Plants. 3 vols. roy. fol. Lond., 1830–32.   A 20 P 11–13 ‡

WALLINGTON (NEHEMIAH). Historical Notices of Events occuring in the Reign of Charles I. 2 vols. 8vo. Lond., 1869.   B 3 R 27, 28

WALLIS (GEORGE). Jewellery. (Brit. Man. Indust.) 12mo. Lond., 1876.   A 17 S 31

WALLIS (CAPT. JAMES). Historical Account of the Colony of New South Wales and its Dependent Settlements; in illustration of twelve Views, engraved by W. Preston, a Convict, from Drawings taken on the spot by Captain Wallis. Fol. Lond., 1821.   MD 1 R 27 ‡
[*See* HAWKESWORTH, J.]

WALLIS (JOHN D.D), Permutations and Combinations. [*See* BERNOULLI, J.]   A 10 U 12

WALLIS (W.) [*See* BIRMINGHAM MUSEUM AND ART GALLERY.]

WALMSLEY (HERBERT EDWARD). Cotton Spinning: a Practical Treatise. 8vo. Manchester, 1883. A 11 R 20
Cotton Spinning and Weaving: a Practical and Theoretical Treatise. 2nd ed. 8vo. Manchester, 1885.   A 11 R 21

WALMSLEY (HUGH MULLENEUX). Ruined Cities of Zululand. With Illustrations. 2 vols. 8vo. Lond., 1869.   D 1 Q 27, 28

WALPOLE (CHARLES GEORGE), M.A. Short History of the Kingdom of Ireland, from the Earliest Times to the Union with Great Britain. With Maps. 8vo. Lond., 1882.   B 11 P 11

WALPOLE (LIEUT. THE HON. FREDERICK), R.N. Four Years in the Pacific, in H.M.S. *Collingwood*, 1844–48. 2 vols. 8vo. Lond., 1849.   D 9 T 31, 32

WALPOLE (HON. HORACE), EARL OF ORFORD. Anecdotes of Painting in England. 5 vols. roy. 8vo. Lond., 1826–28.   C 8 V 24–28
Anecdotes of Painting in England; collected by George Virtue, digested by Hon. Horace Walpole. 5 vols. 12mo. Lond., 1782.   C 2 Q 1–5
The Castle of Otranto: a Gothic Story; with Portrait and Drawings. 8vo. Lond., 1883.   J 10 R 14
Catalogue of Engravers who have been born or resided in England; digested from the MSS. of Mr. George Virtue. With Portraits. Roy. 8vo. Lond., 1828. C 8 V 23
Catalogue of the Royal and Noble Authors of England, Scotland, and Ireland; with Lists of their Works; enlarged and continued by Thomas Park, F.S.A. 5 vols. 8vo. Lond., 1806.   C 6 S 21–25
Correspondence with George Montagu and others; with Illustrative Notes. 1735–97. 3 vols. 8vo. Lond., 1837.   C 10 P 42–44
Correspondence of; edited, with Notes, by the Rev. J. Mitford. 2 vols. 8vo. Lond., 1851.   C 10 P 47, 48
Historic Doubts on the Life and Reign of Richard III. 4to. Lond., 1768.   B 5 U 14
Horace Walpole and his World: Select Passages from his Letters; edited by L. B. Seeley, M.A. With Illustrations. 8vo. Lond., 1884.   C 4 T 9
Letters to Sir Horace Mann; now first published from the Originals in the possession of the Earl of Waldegrave; edited by Lord Dover. 3rd ed. 3 vols. 8vo. Lond., 1834.   C 9 S 29–31
Letters to Sir Horace Mann; concluding Series. 4 vols. 8vo. Lond., 1843–44.   C 9 S 32–35
Letters addressed to the Countess of Ossory, 1769–97; edited, with Notes, by the Rt. Hon. R. Vernon Smith. 2 vols. 8vo. Lond., 1848.   C 10 P 45, 46
Memoires of the last Ten Years of the Reign of George II. 2 vols. roy. 4to. Lond., 1822.   C 1 W 9, 10
The Works of. 9 vols. roy. 4to. Lond., 1798–1825.   J 3 Q 13–21 †

WALPOLE (J. K.), S.C.L. Recollections and Historical Notices of Cambridge. 12mo. Sydney, 1847. MJ 1 P 6

WALPOLE (SIR ROBERT), First Earl of Orford. Memoirs of the Life and Administration of; by William Coxe, M.A., &c. 4 vols. 8vo. Lond., 1816.   C 9 S 51–54

WALPOLE (S.) History of England, from the conclusion of the Great War in 1815. 2nd ed. 8vo. Lond., 1879–86.   B 5 P 41–45

WALROND (THEODORE). Letters of James, Eighth Earl of Elgin. [*See* ELGIN, JAMES, EIGHTH EARL OF.] C 7 R 1

WALSH (JOHN H.) "STONEHENGE." Modern Sportsman's Gun and Rifle. 8vo. Lond., 1882. A 11 U 19
British Rural Sports; comprising Shooting, Hunting, Coursing, &c. 15th ed. 8vo. Lond., 1881. A 17 W 46

WALSH (JOHN J.) The Black and White List; or, the Elector's Hansard. 8vo. Melb., 1871. MF 1 Q 2

WALSH (PETER). History and Vindication of the Loyal Formulary, or Irish Remonstrance, so graciously received by His Majesty, Anno 1661, against all Calumnies and Censures. In several Treatises. Fol. Lond., 1674. B 16 Q 4 ‡

WALSH (ROBERT), LL.D., &c. Didactics; Social, Literary, and Political. 2 vols. 8vo. Philad., 1836. J 5 Q 14, 15

WALSH (REV. ROBERT), LL.D., &c. Essay on Ancient Coins, Medals, and Gems, as illustrating the progress of Christianity in the Early Ages. 12mo. Lond., 1828. A 13 S 38
Residence at Constantinople during the Greek and Turkish Revolutions. 2 vols. 8vo. Lond., 1836. D 8 T 38, 39
History of the City of Dublin. [*See* WARBURTON, J.] B 15 Q 1, 2 ‡

WALSH (WILLIAM). Life and Poems of. [*See* CHALMERS A., *and* JOHNSON, S.]

WALSH (REV. WILLIAM HORATIO), M.A. Our Duty under recent Perversions to the Church of Rome : a Sermon. 8vo. Sydney, 1848. MG 1 Q 40
A Sermon, on the occasion of the Death of the Rev. G. W. Richardson. [*See* COWPER, VERY REV. W. M.]

WALSH (WALTER HAYLE), M.D. The Colloquial Faculty for Languages ; Cerebral Localization and the Nature of Genius. 2nd ed. 8vo. Lond., 1886. K 11 U 14

WALSINGHAM (THOMAS DE GREY), BARON, AND GALLWEY (SIR R. PAYNE). Shooting ; with contributions by the Hon. Gerald Lascelles, A. J. Stuart-Wortley, Lord Lovat, and Lord Charles Kerr. 2 vols. 8vo. Lond., 1886. A 17 U 33
1. Field and Covert.
2. Moor and Marsh.

WALTERS (REV. JOHN). English and Welsh Dictionary; with a Dissertation on the Welsh Language. 2 vols. (in 1) 4to. Dolgelley, 1815. K 16 S 5

WALTON (RT. REV. BRIAN), D.D., BISHOP OF CHESTER. Memoirs of the Life and Writings of; by the Rev. Henry John Todd, M.A., &c. 2 vols. 8vo. Lond., 1821. G 10 S 6, 7
Biblia Sacra Polyglotta. [*See* BIBLES, &c.]

WALTON (CHRISTOPHER). Notes and Materials for an adequate Biography of the celebrated Divine and Theosopher, William Law, comprising an Elucidation of the Writings of Jacob Böhme, and D. A. Freher. 8vo. Lond., 1854. G 14 P 17

WALTON (ELIJAH). Peaks in Pen and Pencil, for Students of Alpine Scenery. L. 4to. Lond., 1872. A 4 S 16 ‡

WALTON (IZAAK). Lives of Dr. John Donne, Sir Henry Wotton, Mr. Richard Hooker, Mr. George Herbert, and Dr. Robert Sanderson. 12mo. Lond., 1825. C 1 S 19
Another copy. New ed. 8vo. Lond., 1884. C 2 R 34

WALTON (IZAAK), AND COTTON (CHARLES). Complete Angler ; or, the Contemplative Man's Recreation ; with Lives of the Authors and Variorum Notes. 8vo. Lond., 1876. A 29 P 10

WALTON (THOMAS H.) Coal-mining Described and Illustrated. Roy. 4to. Philad., 1885. A 1 S 12 †

WALTON (WILLIAM). State of the Philippine Islands. [*See* COMYNS, T. DE.] D 6 T 7

WANDERER. A. [*See* PARKES, SIR H.]

WANG FOO. Po Koo T'oo : Chinese Antiquities. 16 vols. (in 3) sm. fol. China (n.d.) B 17 R 12–14 ‡

WANKLYN (JAMES ALFRED). Milk Analysis : a Practical Treatise on the Examination of Milk and its Derivatives, Cream, Butter, and Cheese. 8vo. Lond., 1874. A 5 S 4

WANKLYN (JAMES ALFRED), AND CHAPMAN (ERNEST THEOPHRON). Water Analysis : a Practical Treatise on Potable Water. 3rd ed. 8vo. Lond., 1874. A 5 R 36

WANLESS (THOMAS). Life of Thomas Wanless, Peasant. 8vo. Manchester, 1885. J 12 R 20

WANLEY (NATHANIEL), M.A. Wonders of the Little World ; or, a General History of Man. 2 vols. roy. 8vo. Lond., 1806. A 2 P 12, 13

WANLISS (T. D.) Constitutional Contest in Victoria. 8vo. Lond., 1879. MF 1 Q 6

WANSBROUGH (W. D.) The Portable Engine ; its Construction and Management. 8vo. Lond., 1887. A 11 Q 20

WARBURTON (ELIOT BARTHOLOMEW GEORGE). The Crescent and the Cross ; or, Romance and Realities of Eastern Travel. 9th ed. 8vo. Lond., 1852. D 5 Q 43
Darien ; or, the Merchant Prince : a Historical Romance. 8vo. Lond., 1852. J 11 R 6
Hochelaga. [*See* WARBURTON, MAJOR G.] D 3 Q 51, 52
Memoirs of Prince Rupert and the Cavaliers, including their Private Correspondence. 3 vols. 8vo. Lond., 1849. C 9 S 18–20

WARBURTON (MAJOR GEORGE). Conquest of Canada. 2 vols. 8vo. Lond., 1849. B 1 S 19, 20
Hochelaga ; or, England in the New World ; edited by Eliot Warburton. 3rd ed. 2 vols. 8vo. Lond., 1847. D 3 Q 51, 52
Memoir of Charles Mordaunt, Earl of Peterborough and Monmouth ; with Selections from his Correspondence. 2 vols. 8vo. Lond., 1853. C 3 T 18, 19

WARBURTON (John), WHITELAW (Rev. James), and WALSH (Rev. Robert), M.R.I.A. History of the City of Dublin, from the Earliest Accounts to the Present Time. 2 vols. 4to. Lond., 1818.   B 15 Q 1, 2 ‡

WARBURTON (Col. Peter Egerton), C.M.G. Journey across the Western Interior of Australia. 8vo. Lond., 1875.*   MD 4 W 10

WARBURTON (Rt. Rev. W.), D.D., Bishop of Gloucester. Works of; with some Account of the Life, Writings, and Character of the Author, by Bishop Richard Hurd. 12 vols. 8vo. Lond., 1811.   G 15 Q 1–12

WARBURTON (Rev. William Parsons). Edward III. 2nd ed., with three Maps. 12mo. Lond., 1876.   B 3 P 15

WARD (—.) New Zealand: Nelson, the latest Settlement of the New Zealand Company; by "Kappa." 8vo. Lond., 1842.   MJ 2 Q 2

WARD (Adolphus W.), M.A. Chaucer. (Eng. Men Letts.) 8vo. Lond., 1879.   C 1 U 8
Dickens. (Eng. Men Letts.) 8vo. Lond., 1882. C 1 U 13
History of English Dramatic Literature, to the Death of Queen Anne. 2 vols. 8vo. Lond., 1875. B 6 S 20, 21
Old English Drama. [*See* Marlowe, C.]

WARD (Artemus). [*See* Browne, C. F.]

WARD (Crosbie). Letter to the Right Honourable Lord Lyttelton, on the Relations of Great Britain with the Colonists and Aborigines of New Zealand. 8vo. Lond., 1863.   MD 1 U 21

WARD (Ebenezer). South-eastern District of South Australia; its Resources and Requirements. 8vo. Adelaide, 1869.   MD 5 R 28
Vineyards and Orchards of South Australia. 1st series. 8vo. Adelaide, 1862.   MA 1 Q 2

WARD (Capt. Edward W.), C.E. Report of Results obtained from Experiments on the Elasticity and Strength of Timber of New South Wales, procured through the Chief Commissioner of Railways, and tested at the Sydney Branch of the Royal Mint. (Votes and Proceedings, Vol. 2, 1858.) Fol. Sydney, 1858.   ME

WARD (Hon. Mrs. F. Marshall). The Microscope; or, Descriptions of various Objects of especial Interest and Beauty, adapted for Microscopic Observation. Illustrated. 3rd ed. 8vo. Lond., 1870.   A 17 T 15
The Telescope: a familiar Sketch, combining a special Notice of Objects coming within the range of a Small Telescope. Illustrated. 4th ed. 12mo. Lond., 1876.   A 3 R 17

WARD (Mrs. Harriet). Five Years in Kaffirland; with Sketches of the late War in that Country to the Conclusion of Peace. 2 vols. 8vo. Lond., 1848.   D 1 R 2, 2
[*See* Napier, Lieut.-Gen. E.]   D 1 S 35

WARD (Mrs. Humphry). Amiel's Journal. [*See* Amiel, H. F.]   C 2 R 1, 2

WARD (H. G.) Debate on his Resolutions on Colonization. [*See* Colonization.]   MJ 2 P 39

WARD (James). History of Gold as a Commodity and as a Measure of Value. Map. 12mo. Lond., 1852.   MA 2 P 14

WARD (Rev. John), A.M., Vicar of Stratford-upon-Avon. Diary of; extending from 1648–79. Arranged by Charles Severn. 8vo. Lond., 1839.   C 9 S 55

WARD (John). Information relative to New Zealand, for the use of Colonists. 8vo. Lond., 1839.* MD 5 T 33
Supplementary Information relative to New Zealand. 12mo. Lond., 1840.   MD 1 S 23
British Colonization of New Zealand. [*See* Wakefield, E. J.]   MD 2 P 7

WARD (John P.) Wanderings with the Maori Prophets, Te Whiti and Tohu (with Illustrations of each Chief). 8vo. Nelson, 1883.   MD 4 V 29

WARD (N. B.), F.L.S. On the growth of Plants in closely glazed Cases. 8vo. Lond., 1842.   A 1 S 20

WARD (Robert Plumer). Memoirs of the Political and Literary Life of; by the Hon. Edmund Phipps. 2 vols. 8vo. Lond., 1850.   C 9 R 40, 41
Enquiry into the Foundation and History of the Law of Nations in Europe, from the Time of the Greeks and Romans to the Age of Grotius. 2 vols. 8vo. Lond., 1795.   F 4 S 17, 18
Historical Essay on the real character and amount of the Precedent of the Revolution of 1688. 2 vols. 8vo. Lond., 1838.   B 2 S 36, 37

WARD (Samuel Ringgold). Autobiography of a Fugitive Negro: his Anti-Slavery Labours in the United States, Canada, and England. 8vo. Lond., 1855.   C 3 S 46

WARD (Thomas Humphry). Humphry Sandwith: a Memoir. 8vo. Lond., 1884.   C 6 U 22
Men of the Reign: a Biographical Dictionary of Eminent Persons of British and Colonial Birth, who have died during the Reign of Queen Victoria. 8vo. Lond., 1885.   C 4 U 12

WARD (William). View of the History, Literature, and Mythology of the Hindoos, including a minute Description of their Manners and Customs, and Translations from their Works. 3 vols. 8vo. Lond., 1822. B 10 S 22–24
The Story of. [*See* Marshman, J. C.]

WARD (Prof. William George), Ph.D. Essays on the Philosophy of Theism. Reprinted from the *Dublin Review.* Edited, with an Introduction, by Wilfrid Ward. 2 vols. 8vo. Lond., 1884.   G 4 S 10, 11

WARDLAW (Ralph), D.D. National Church Establishments examined. 8vo. Lond., 1839.   G 4 S 5

WARDLEY (EDWARD), M.R.C.S.L. Confessions of a Wavering Worthy; or, the Great Secret of Success in Life: an Ethical and Autobiographical Essay. 8vo. Sydney, 1864.   MJ 1 R 7

Abolition of Capital Punishment considered; by "Fiat Justitia." 8vo. Sydney, 1869.   MF 3 P 2

Another copy. 8vo. Sydney, 1869.   MJ 2 R 4

Lectiones Tarbanæ; or, Tall Talk at Tarban. 8vo. Sydney, 1870.*   MJ 1 T 28

Some Phases of Insanity and its Treatment, popularly considered. (Pam.; 43.) 8vo. Parramatta, 1871. MJ 2 R 5

WARE (SIR JAMES). The Whole Works of Sir James Ware concerning Ireland. Revised and improved by W. Harris. With Plates. 3 vols. (in 2) fol. Dublin, 1739–46.   B 16 R 1,2 ‡

Ancient Irish Histories. [*See* HANMER, M.]   B 11 R 8, 9

WARE (J. REDDING), AND MANN (R. K.) Life and Times of Colonel Fred. Burnaby, late Colonel-Commanding Royal Horse Guards—Blues. 8vo. Lond., 1885.
                                             C 4 S 3

WARE (REV. WILLIAM E.), "LUCIUS MANLIUS PISO." Letters from Palmyra, to his Friend Marcus Curtius, at Rome; now first translated and published. 2 vols. 8vo. Lond., 1838.   J 8 P 38, 39

WARING (EDWARD JOHN), M.D., &c. Manual of Practical Therapeutics, considered chiefly with reference to Articles of the Materia Medica. 3rd ed. (Churchill's Manuals.) 12mo. Lond., 1871.   A 13 P 34

Another copy. 4th ed. 12mo. Lond., 1886.   A 12 P 41

WARING (GEORGE), M.A. Gothic and Anglo-Saxon Gospels. [*See* BOSWORTH, REV. J.]

WARING (JOHN BURLEY). Illustrations of Architecture and Ornament. Fol. Lond., 1865.   A 23 R 21 ‡

Hand-book to the Museum of Ornamental Art in the Art Treasures Exhibition; to which is added "The Armoury," by J. R. Planché. 8vo. Lond., 1857. A 6 V 38

WARMAN (J. W.) The Organ; its compass, tablature, and short and incomplete octaves. 8vo. Lond., 1884.
                                             A 8 R 4

WARNE (CHARLES), F.S.A. Celtic Tumuli of Dorset: an Account of Personal and other Researches in the Sepulchral Mounds of the Durotriges. Fol. Lond., 1866.   B 14 S 19 ‡

WARNER (CHARLES DUDLEY). Washington Irving. (American Men of Letters.) 12mo. Lond., 1882.   C 1 R 15

My Summer in a Garden; with an Introduction, by Rev. Henry Ward Beecher. 12mo. Lond., 1876. J 12 S 9

Mummies and Moslems. 8vo. Lond., 1875.   D 2 Q 11

WARNER (FERDINANDO), LL.D. History of the Rebellion and Civil War in Ireland. 4to. Lond., 1767.   B 15 Q 19 ‡

5 H

WARNER (FRANCIS), M.D., &c. Physical Expression: its Modes and Principles. With Illustrations. 8vo. Lond., 1885.   A 12 Q 36

WARNER (OLIVER). Commonwealth of Massachusetts. Aggregates of Polls, Property, Taxes, &c., as assessed, May 1, 1875. (Pam., Ja.) 8vo. Boston, 1876. F 7 S 24

Abstract of the Census of Massachusets, 1860 and 1865. 2 vols. 8vo. Boston, 1863–67.   F 1 Q 20, 21

WARNER (RICHARD). Collection for the History of Hampshire, and the Bishopric of Winchester, including the Isles of Wight, Jersey, Guernsey, and Sarke, by D. Y.; with the original Domesday of the County, and an English Translation. Illustrated. 5 vols. (in 3) 4to. Lond., 1795.   B 6 V 13–15

Another copy. 5 vols. (in 3) 4to. Lond., 1795.
                                           B 10 P 5–9 †

WARNER (R.), F.L.S., &c., AND WILLIAMS (B. S.), F.L.S. Orchid Album. 5 vols. imp. 4to. Lond., 1882–86.
                                            A 14 P 1–5 †

WARNER (CAPT. S. A.) Fair Play's a Jewel: a Narrative of Circumstances connected with my Mode of National Defence against the whole World. 8vo. Lond., 1849.   F 14 S 15

WARNER (WILLIAM). Life and Poems of. [*See* CHALMERS, A.]

WARREN (COL. SIR CHARLES), G.C.M.G. Outlines of a Trigonometrical Survey of Western Palestine. [*See* FROME, LIEUT.-GEN. E.]

Recovery of Jerusalem. [*See* WILSON, COL. SIR C. W.]
                                             D 4 U 4

The Temple or the Tomb; giving further Evidence in favour of the authenticity of the present Site of the Holy Sepulchre, and pointing out some of the principal Misconceptions contained in Fergusson's "Holy Sepulchre," and "The Temples of the Jews." 8vo. Lond., 1880. B 10 P 22

Underground Jerusalem: an Account of some of the principal Difficulties encountered in its Exploration and the results obtained; with a Narrative of an Expedition through the Jordan Valley, and a Visit to the Samaritans. With Illustrations. 8vo. Lond., 1876.   D 4 T 40

WARREN (E. P.), AND CLEVERLY (C. F. M.) Wanderings of the *Beetle*. 4to. Lond., 1885.   D 8 V 3

WARREN (REV. F. E.), B.D., &c. The Leofric Missal, as used in the Cathedral of Exeter, during the Episcopate of its first Bishop, A.D. 1050–72. 4to. Oxford, 1883.   G 5 U 17

The Liturgy and Ritual of the Celtic Church. 8vo. Oxford, 1881.   G 4 R 29

WARREN (G. W.) [*See* BUNKER'S HILL MONUMENT ASSOCIATION.]   A 8 R 33

WARREN (HON. J. LEICESTER), M.A. Guide to the Study of Book-Plates (ex-libris). 8vo. Lond., 1880. J 10 T 30

WARREN (Samuel), F.R.S. Letter to the Queen on a late Court Martial. 8vo. Lond., 1850. F 5 U 31

Popular and Practical Introduction to Law Studies. 8vo. Lond., 1835. F 4 S 15

The Lily and the Bee; an Apologue of the Crystal Palace. 12mo. Edinb., 1851. J 1 T 2

WARREN (T. Robinson). Dust and Foam; or, three Oceans and two Continents; being Ten Years' Wanderings in Mexico, South America, Sandwich Islands, the East and West Indies, China, Philippines, Australia, and Polynesia. 8vo. New York, 1859. MD 4 Q 40

WARREN (Prof. William H.) Strength and Elasticity of New South Wales Timbers of Commercial Value. Roy. 8vo. Sydney, 1887. MA 1 V 51

WARREN (William Wilkins). Life on the Nile in a Dahabéeh, and Excursions on Shore between Cairo and Assouan; also, a Tour in Syria and Palestine, in 1866–67. 3rd ed. 12mo. Boston, 1883. D 1 T 5

WARRINGTON (William). History of Stained Glass, from the Earliest Period of the Art to the Present Time; illustrated by coloured Examples of entire Windows in the various styles. At. fol. Lond., 1848. A 20 P 15 ‡

WARRINGTON (Rev. William). History of Wales, in nine Books: with an Appendix. 2 vols. 8vo. Lond., 1788. B 3 P 25, 26

WARTER (John Wood), B.D. An Old Shropshire Oak; edited by R. Garnett, LL.D. Vols. 1, 2. 2 vols. 8vo. Lond., 1886. B 24 S 2, 3

Southey's Common-place Book. [*See* Southey, R.]

WARTON (Dr. Joseph). Life and Poems of. [*See* Chalmers, A.]

WARTON (Thomas), M.A. History of English Poetry, from the 11th to the 17th Century. 8vo. Lond., 1870. B 21 S 25

Life and Poems of. [*See* Chalmers, A.]

Life and Literary Remains of Ralph Bathurst, M.D., Dean of Wells, and President of Trinity College in Oxford. 8vo. Lond., 1761. C 3 U 8

Observations on Spenser's Fairy Queen. New ed. 2 vols. 8vo. Lond., 1807. H 8 U 29, 30

Poetical Works of; with Memoirs of his Life and Writings by Richard Mant, M.A. 5th ed. 2 vols. 8vo. Lond., 1802. H 6 U 11, 12

[*See* Huddersford, W.] C 1 V 11, 15

WARTON CLUB (The). Publications of. I vols. 8vo. Lond., 1855–56. E

WARWICK (Eden). [*See* Jabet, G. S.]

WARWICK (Sir Philip). Mémoires de. [*See* Guizot, F. P. G., I.]

WARWYCK (Vice-Adm. Wybrand van). Journael van de Schip-vaert op Oost-Indien. [*See* Neck, J. van.] D 5 Q 33

WASHBURN (Charles A.) History of Paraguay; with Notes of Personal Observations and Reminiscences of Diplomacy under Difficulties. 2 vols. 8vo. Boston, 1871 B 1 S 3, 4

WASHBURNE (Elihu B.) Franco-German War, and Insurrection of the Commune—Correspondence. 8vo. Wash., 1878. B 9 R 17

WASHBURN (Emelyn W.) Spanish Masters: an Outline of the History of Painting in Spain. 8vo. New York, 1884. A 8 P 32

WASHBOURNE (Henry). Book of Family Crests, comprising nearly every Bearing and its Blazonry, Surnames of Bearers, Dictionary of Mottos, British and Foreign Orders of Knightbood, Glossary of Terms, and Engravings illustrative of Peers, Baronets, and nearly every Family bearing Arms in England, Wales, Scotland, Ireland, and the Colonies, &c.; with Introduction, Mottos, Plates, Addenda, &c. 11th ed. 2 vols. 12mo. Lond., 1875. K 10 S 35, 36

WASHINGTON (Gen. George), First President U.S.A. Life of, and Atlas; by John Marshall. 2nd ed., revised. 2 vols. 8vo. Philad., 1832. C 6 T 27, 28

Life and Times of General Washington; by C. R. Edmonds. 2 vols. 18mo. Lond., 1835–36. C 1 P 36, 37

Washington; by F. P. G. Guizot, translated by Henry Reeve. 8vo. Lond., 1840. C 4 S 49

Monk and Washington : Historical Studies; by F. P. G. Guizot. 12mo. Lond., 1851. C 1 R 26

Life of George Washington; to which are added his Diaries and Speeches, and various Miscellaneous Papers relating to his Habits and Opinions; by Jared Sparkes. 2 vols. 8vo. Lond., 1839. C 9 Q 47, 48

Life of; by Washington Irving. 4 vols. 8vo. Lond., 1856–78. C 4 P 39–42

WASHINGTON (Capt. J.) On the Progress of Naval Architecture. [*See* Lond. Inter. Exhib., 1851.]

WASSE (Jos.), et DUKER (Cav. A.) De Bello Peloponnesiaco. [*See* Thucydides.] B 9 S 38–43

WATERHOUSE (E.) Fortescutus Illustratus; or, a Commentary on that Nervous Treatise De Laudibus Legum Angliæ. Sm. fol. Lond., 1663. F 8 Q 15 †

WATERHOUSE (G. R.) Natural History of Mammalia. 2 vols. 8vo. Tondi., 1846–48. A 15 P 11, 12

Natural History of Marsupialia, or Pouched Animals. (Nat. Lib., 26.) 12mo. Edinb., 1841. A 14 P 26

Mammalia. [*See* Darwin, C.] A 1 S 17 †

WATERTON (Charles). Wanderings in South America, the North-west of the United States, and the Antilles, in the years 1812, 1816, 1820, and 1824. 4to. Lond., 1825. D 3 V 20

Another copy. 5th ed. 12mo. Lond., 1852. D 3 P 5

Natural History—Essays; edited, with a Life of the Author, by Norman Moore, B.A. With Illustrations. 8vo. Lond., 1870. A 14 S 44

WATERWORTH (REV. WILLIAM). Church of St. Patrick; or, a History of the Origin, Doctrines, Liturgy, and Govermental System of the Ancient Church of Ireland. 8vo. Lond., 1869. G 7 T 15

WATHEN (G. H.) Arts, Antiquities, and Chronology of Ancient Egypt, from Observations in 1839. Roy. 8vo. Lond., 1843. A 3 Q 7

The Golden Colony; or, Victoria in 1854; with Remarks on the Geology of the Australian Gold-fields. Illustrated. 8vo. Lond., 1855.* MD 3 Q 8

WATKIN (W. T.) Roman Cheshire; or, a Description of Roman Remains in the County of Chester. 4to. Liverpool, 1886. B 2 U 8

WATKINS (JOHN L.), M.A. Crown Lands Acts of New South Wales, and the Regulations; with Notes and Index. 8vo. Sydney, 1880. MF 1 R 30

WATKINS (REV. MORGAN GEORGE). Gleanings from the Natural History of the Ancients. Roy. 8vo. Lond., 1885. A 16 V 15

WATMUFF (F.) Australian Almanac for 1871. 12mo. Melh., 1871. ME 4 P

WATNEY (HERBERT), M.A., &c. The Minute Anatomy of the Alimentary Canal. (Roy. Soc. Pubs., 3.) 4to. Lond., 1876. A 11 P 4†

WATSON (A. E. T.) [*See* RACING.] A 17 U 32

WATSON (DAVID), M.A. [*See* HORATIUS FLACCUS, Q.] H 8 V 36, 37

WATSON (DR. FORBES). Report on Cotton Gins, and on the Cleaning and Quality of Indian Cotton. 2 vols. imp. 8vo. Lond., 1879. A 17 V 7, 8

WATSON (GEORGE). England Preserved: a Tragedy. [*See* MODERN THEATRE, 8.]

WATSON (G. C.) Australian Colonies: Tasmania and its Railways, and the Commerce of Australia. 12mo. Ipswich, 1864. MJ 2 P 30

WATSON (HENRY). Lecture on South Australia; including Letters from J. B. Hack, Esq., and other Emigrants. 2nd ed. 8vo. Lond., 1838. MD 5 R 26

WATSON (HENRY WILLIAM), M.A. Elements of Plane and Solid Geometry. (Text-books of Science.) 2nd ed. 12mo. Lond., 1872. A 17 S 10

Treatise on the Kinetic Theory of Gases. (Clar. Press.) 8vo. Oxford, 1876. A 16 T 16

WATSON (H. W.), F.R.S., AND BURBURY (S. H.), M.A. Mathematical Theory of Electricity and Magnetism. Vol. 1. Electrostatics. (Clar. Press.) 8vo. Oxford, 1885. A 21 T 12

WATSON (JAMES). Watson's Choice Collection of Comic and Serious Scots Poems; the three parts, 1706, 1709, 1711, in one volume. 8vo. Glasgow, 1869. H 8 R 13

WATSON (JAMES). [*See* TRIALS.]

WATSON (PROF. JAMES C.) Theoretical Astronomy, relating to the Motions of the Heavenly Bodies revolving around the Sun, in accordance with the Law of Universal Gravitation. Roy. 8vo. Philad., 1881. A 3 S 4

WATSON (JEAN L.) The Songstresses of Scotland. [*See* KEDDIE, MISS HENRIETTA.] C 4 S 32, 33

WATSON (JOHN), M.A., &c. Kant and his English Critics. 8vo. Glasgow, 1881. G 4 S 6

WATSON (JOHN FANNING). Annals of Philadelphia. 8vo. New York, 1830. B 1 R 47

WATSON (JOHN FORBES), AND KAYE (SIR JOHN WILLIAM), K.C.S.I., &c. People of India: a Series of Photographic Illustrations; with Descriptive Letterpress of Races and Tribes of Hindustan, &c. 8 vols. roy. 4to. Lond., 1868. A 2 P 1–8†

WATSON (REV. JOHN SELBY), M.A. Justin, Cornelius Nepos, and Eutropius; literally translated. [*See* JUSTINUS.]

Biographies of John Wilkes and William Cobbett; with Portraits. 8vo. Lond., 1870. C 5 Q 30

Minor Works of Xenophon. [*See* XENOPHON.] B 9 S 17

Life and Letters of Cicero. [*See* JEANS, REV. G. E.] C 10 S 17

Quintilian's Institutes of Oratory. [*See* QUINTILIANUS, M. F.]

Cicero on Oratory and Orators. [*See* CICERO, M. T.]

Biographical Notice of Xenophon. [*See* XENOPHON.]

Iliad of Homer; with Notes, &c. [*See* HOMER.]

Odyessy of Homer; with Notes. [*See* HOMER.]

WATSON (REV. J. S.), AND DALE (REV. H.) The Cyropaedia of Xenophon. [*See* XENOPHON.] B 9 S 16

WATSON (PAUL BARRON), Life of Marcus Aurelius Antoninus. 8vo. Lond., 1884. C 8 T 2

WATSON (RT. REV. RICHARD), D.D., &c., BISHOP OF LANDAFF. Two Apologies: one for Christianity, in a Series of Letters addressed to Edward Gibbon, Esq.; the other for the Bible, in answer to Thomas Paine; to which are added two Sermons, and a charge in Defence of Revealed Religion. 8vo. Lond., 1816. G 4 S 7

A recdotes of the Life of; written by himself, and revised in 1814. 4to. Lond., 1817. C 4 W 37

A Collection of Theological Tracts. 2nd ed. 6 vols. 8vo. Lond., 1791. G 9 T 22–27

WATSON (RICHARD A.) Brown and Watson's, late Brown and Stansfield's Patent Self-discharging Concentrator, for Extracting the Pyrites or Sulphurets, and for saving the fine Gold, Quicksilver, and Amalgam, from Gold and Silver Ores, and also for the separation of Tin Ore. 8vo. Sydney, 1877. MA 2 Q 33

WATSON (Robert), LL.D. History of the Reign of
Phillip II, King of Spain. 3 vols. 8vo. Lond., 1812.
B 13 T 35–37

WATSON (Robert Grant). Spanish and Portuguese South
America during the Colonial Period. 2 vols. 8vo. Lond.,
1884.   B 2 P 13, 14

WATSON (Robert Spence). Visit to Wazan, the Sacred
City of Morocco. With Illustrations. 8vo. Lond.,
1880.   D 2 T 10

WATSON (Sir Thomas), Bart., M.D., &c. Lectures on
the Principles and Practice of Physic, delivered at King's
College, London. 5th ed. 2 vols. 8vo. Lond., 1871.
A 12 U 22, 23

WATSON, FERGUSON, & CO. Brisbane Post Office
Directory and Country Guide, 1883–86. 2 vols. 8vo.
Brisb., 1883–85.   ME 12 P

WATT (Alexander). Art of Leather Manufacture; being
a Practical Hand-book, in which the Operations of Tanning,
Currying, and Leather Dressing are fully described. With
Illustrations. 8vo. Lond., 1885.   A 11 P 1

Art of Soap-making: a Practical Hand-book of the
Manufacture of Hard and Soft Soaps, Toilet Soaps, &c.
With Illustrations. 8vo. Lond., 1884.   A 11 P 32

Electro-Deposition: a Practical Treatise on the Electro-
lysis of Gold and other Metals. Lond., 1886. A 9 Q 17

Electro-Metallurgy practically treated. 4th ed. (Weale.)
12mo. Lond., 1871.   A 17 P 27

History of a Lump of Gold, from the Mine to the Mint.
With Illustrations. 8vo. Lond., 1885.   A 9 P 35

WATT (James). Life of; with Selections from his Correspondence, by James Patrick Muirhead. With Portraits.
8vo. Lond., 1858.   C 9 R 45

Lives of Boulton and Watt, principally from the original
Soho MSS., by Samuel Smiles. 8vo. Lond., 1865. C 6 V 8

Origin and Progress of the Mechanical Invention of,
illustrated by his Correspondence with his Friends and
the Specifications of his Patents. 3 vols. 4to. Lond.,
1854.   A 11 U 1–3

WATT (Robert), M.D. Bibliotheca Britannica; or, General
Index to British and Foreign Literature. 4 vols. 4to.
Edinb., 1824.   K 17 S 6–9

WATTEAU (Jean Antoine). Watteau; by J. W.
Mollett. (Great Artists.) 8vo. Lond., 1883. C 3 T 39

WATTS (Alaric): a Narrative; by his Son, Alaric Alfred
Watts. With Portraits. 2 vols. 8vo. Lond., 1884.
C 5 Q 31, 32

WATTS (Alaric Alfred). Alaric Watts: a Narrative of his
Life; by his Son. 2 vols. 8vo. Lond., 1884. C 5 Q 31, 32

WATTS (R. H.) Municipal Records of Bath. [*See* King,
A. J.]   B 5 V 31

WATTS (Gilbert). Advancement and Proficience of
Learning. [*See* Bacon, Sir F.]

WATTS (Henry), F.R.S., &c. Chemical Technology. [*See*
Ronalds, Dr. E.]   A 5 U 8–13

Dictionary of Chemistry and the allied Branches of other
Sciences. 5 vols. roy. 8vo. Lond., 1869–71. K 9 P 8–12

[First] Second, and Third Supplements [to the above].
4 vols. roy. 8vo. Lond., 1872–81.   K 9 P 13–16

WATTS (Isaac). Cotton. (Brit. Manuf. Indust.) 12mo.
Lond., 1876.   A 17 S 37

Proposed Imperial Museum for India and the Colonies.
8vo. Lond., 1876.   MJ 2 R 12

WATTS (Isaac), D.D. The World to Come; or, Discourses
on the Joys or Sorrows of Departed Souls at Death. 8vo.
Lond., 1814.   MJ 2 R 22

Life and Poems of. [*See* Chalmers, A.; Johnson, S.;
and British Poets 3.]

WATTS (Lieut.) Journal of. [*See* Phillip, A.]

WATTS (William Lord). Snioland; or, Iceland, its Jökulls
and Fjalls. 8vo. Lond., 1875.   D 7 Q 20

WATTS (W. Marshall), D.Sc. Index to Spectra; with a
Preface by H. E. Roscoe, B.A., &c. 8vo. Lond., 1872.
A 6 P 14

WAUGH (James). Three Years' Practical Experience of a
Settler in New South Wales; being Extracts from Letters
to his Friends in Edinburgh, 1834–37. 3rd ed. 12mo.
Edinb., 1838.   MD 2 Q 6

Another copy. 6th ed. 8vo. Edinb., 1838.   MD 1 S 14

WAUGH (James William). Australian Settler's Hand-
book: the Farm; being Practical Hints for the Inex-
perienced on the most simple and profitable Method of
cultivating their Land. 12mo. Sydney, 1861.   MA 1 P 17

Waugh's Australian Almanac, 1858–63. 6 vols. (in 3)
12mo. Sydney, 1858–63.   ME 4 R

Waugh's Country Directory of New South Wales,
1862–63. 12mo. Lond., 1862.   ME 4 R

WAUGH & COX, Australian Almanac. 2 vols. (in 1)
12mo. Sydney, 1855–56.*   ME 4 T

Directory of Sydney and its Suburbs, 1855. 8vo.
Sydney, 1855.*   ME 10

WAUTERS (Prof. A. J.) Flemish School of Painting:
Ouvrage Couronné par l'Académie Royale de Belgique·
translated by Mrs. Henry Rossel. 8vo. Lond., 1885.
A 6 V 8

WAVE of Life (The): a Poem, in three Cantos; by
D. P. 16mo. Sydney, 1857.   MH 1 R 44

WAVERTREE (Oliver Mount). Home Life in England;
illustrated by Engravings on Steel. Roy. 4to. Lond.,
1876.   A 23 R 5 ‡

WAY (Arthur S.), M.A. The Iliad of Homer, done into
English Verse. [*See* Homer.]

WAY (GREGORY LEWIS). Tableaux ; or, Tales abridged from French Manuscripts of the 12th and 13th Centuries. [*See* LE GRAND D'AUSSY. P. J. B.]

WAY TO WEALTH (THE). Dedicated to all true Victorians, who intend making this Estate their adopted Country and Home; by "Junius." 8vo. Melb., 1856.
MJ 2 Q 16

WAYLEN (JAMES). House of Cromwell, and the Story of Dunkirk. Roy. 8vo. Lond., 1880. B 5 V 32

WAYNFLETE (WILLIAM), BISHOP OF WINCHESTER. Life of; collected from Records, Registers, Manuscripts, and other authentic Sources, by Richard Chandler, D.D. Roy. 8vo. Lond., 1811. C 7 V 48

WAYTE (GEORGE HODGSON), M.A. Prospecting; or, Eighteen Months in Australia, and New Zealand. 12mo. Lond., 1879.* MD 1 Q 5

WEALE (JOHN). Dictionary of Terms used in Architecture, Building, Engineering, Mining, Metallurgy, Archæology, the Fine Arts, &c. Edited by Robert Hunt, F.R.S. (Weale.) 12mo. Lond., 1873. A 17 P 30

WEALE (W. H. J.) Descriptive Catalogue of Rare Manuscripts and Printed Books, chiefly Liturgical. (Hist. Music Loan Exhib., 1885.) 8vo. Lond., 1886. K 7 S 12
Biographia Liturgica Catalogue Missalium Ritus Latini. 8vo. Lond., 1886. K 7 S 11

WEALE'S RUDIMENTARY SERIES. 162 vols. 12mo. Lond., 1852-85. A 17 P 1-R 14

WEATHERHEAD (G. H.), M.D. The Philosophical Rambler; or, Observations and Adventures of a Pedestrian Tourist through France and Italy. 8vo. Lond., 1834. D 8 T 11

WEAVER (O. W.) The Census System of Massachusetts for 1875. 4to. Boston, 1876. E

WEAVER (WILLIAM), C.E. Memoir of. Except Annual Report of the Institution of Civil Engineers, 1870-71. 8vo. Lond., 1871. MJ 2 P 28

WEBB (DANIEL CARLESS). Observations and Remarks during four Excursions, made to various parts of Great Britain in the years 1810 and 1811. 8vo. Lond., 1812. D 8 U 14

WEBB (GEORGE H. F.) Debate in the Legislative Council of the Colony of Victoria, on the Second Reading of the New Constitution Bill. 8vo. Melb., 1854. MF 1 Q 2

WEBB (REV. JOHN), M.A. Memorials of the Civil War between King Charles 1 and the Parliament of England, as it affected Herefordshire and the Adjacent Counties. 2 vols. 8vo. Lond., 1879. B 6 Q 13, 14

WEBB (JOHN HOLDEN), M.R.C.S., &c. Treatment of Spinal Curvature and Abscess by Inflation. 8vo. Melb., 1880. MA 2 S 38

WEBB (PHILLIP CARTERET), F.R.A.S. Account of a Copper Table, containing two Inscriptions in the Greek and Latin Tongues, discovered in the year 1732, near Heraclea, in the Bay of Tarentum, in Magna Graecia. (*Bound with Pennant's Literary Life.*) 4to. Lond., 1760. B 30 V 15

WEBB (PROF. THOMAS E.), LL.D. Faust; from the German of Goethe. [*See* GOETHE, J. W. VON.]
Veil of Isis : a Series of Essays on Idealism. 8vo. Lond., 1885. G 8 T 11

WEBB (REV. THOMAS WILLIAM), M.A., &c. Celestial Objects for the Common Telescopes. 8vo. Lond., 1873. A 3 R 18

WEBBE (CORNELIUS). Glances at Life in City and Suburb. 8vo. Lond., 1836. J 12 T 11

WEBBER (CHARLES W.) Adventures in the Camanche Country in search of a Gold Mine. 12mo. Glasgow, 1848. D 3 P 4

WEBBER (JAMES). Views in the South Seas, from Drawings by the late James Webber, Draftsman on board the *Resolution*, Captain James Cook, from the years 1776-80 ; with Letterpress, descriptive of the various Scenery, &c. Imp. 4to. Lond., 1808. MD 3 Q 6 ‡

WEBER (ALBRECHT). History of Indian Literature. 8vo. Lond., 1878. B 10 Q 19

WEBER (CARL MARI VON), BARON. Der Freischutz; or, the Seventh Bullet : an Opera. (Cumberland's Eng. Theatre.) 12mo. Lond., 1829. H 2 Q 15
Letters of. [*See* WALLACE, LADY.] C 3 U 29

WEBER (GEORG). Allgemeine Weltgeschichte. 2e auflage. Vols. 1-10. 8vo. Leipzig, 1882-86. B 35 U 1-10

WEBER (GOTTFRIED). Theory of Musical Composition; translated, with Notes. 2 vols. roy. 8vo. Lond., 1851. A 8 R 5, 6

WEBER (HENRY). Tales of the East ; comprising the most Popular Romances of Oriental Origin, and the best Imitations by European Authors; with new translations, and additional Tales, never before published. 3 vols. 8vo. Edinb., 1812. J 2 T 8-10
Metrical Romances of the Thirteenth, Fourteenth, and Fifteenth Centuries; from ancient MSS. 3 vols. 8vo. Edinb., 1810. H 8 R 8-10
[*See* BEAUMONT, F.] H 2 S 12-25

WEBER (JOSEPH). Memoirs of Marie Antoinetta, Archduchess of Austria, Queen of France and Navarre; including several important periods of the French Revolution. Translated by R. C. Dallas. 3 vols. roy. 8vo. Lond., 1805-12. C 5 W 12-14
Mémoires de. [*See* BARRIERE, J. F.] C 1 T 7

WEBER (WILHELM ERNST). Corpus Poetarum Latinorum, uno Volumine absolutum. Roy. 8vo. Francofurti, 1833.   H 7 V 19

WEBSTER (A.) Webster's Royal Red Book; or, Court and Fashionable Register. 8vo. Lond., 1870–83. E 2.4

WEBSTER (CATHERINE). Trial and Execution of, for the Murder of Mrs. Thomas, at Richmond, England. (Pam 8.) 8vo. Melb., 1878.   F 13 R 1

WEBSTER (DANIEL). Works of. 17th ed. 6 vols. 8vo. Boston, 1877.   F 6 V 1–6

WEBSTER (G. E.) Course of Analytical Chemistry. [*See* PINK, W. W.]   A 17 Q 13

WEBSTER (JOHN). Last Cruise of the *Wanderer*. 8vo. Sydney. 1852.   MD 3 S 16

WEBSTER (JOHN). Works of. Now first collected, with some account of the Author, and Notes, by the Rev. Alexander Dyce, B.A. 4 vols. 8vo. Lond., 1830. H 4 Q 5–8

Dramatic Works of; edited by William Hazlitt. 4 vols. 8vo. Lond., 1857.   H 4 Q 1–4

WEBSTER (NOAH), LL.D. Biography; by H. E. Scudder. (Amer. Men of Letts.) 12mo. Lond., 1882. C 1 R 41

Dictionary of the English Language. 2 vols. 4to. Lond., 1831–32.   K 15 T 19, 20

Another copy; thoroughly revised and improved by Chauncey A. Goodrich, D.D., and Noah Porter, D.D. New ed., with a Supplement of New Words, and an Additional Appendix of Biographical Names. 4to. Lond., 1880.   K 15 T 21

[*See* OGILVIE, J.]

WEBSTER (THOMAS), F.G.S., &c., AND PARKES (MRS.) Encyclopædia of Domestic Economy. New ed. 8vo. Lond., 1847.   K 5 U 4

WEBSTER (W. H. B.) Narrative of a Voyage to the Southern Atlantic Ocean, in the years 1828–30, performed in H.M. Sloop *Chanticleer*, under the command of the late Captain Foster, F.R.S. 2 vols. 8vo. Lond., 1834.   D 9 S 28, 29

WEDDELL (CAPT. JAMES), R.N. Voyage towards the South Pole, performed in the years 1822–24. 8vo. Lond., 1825.   D 4 R 26

WEDDERBURN (SIR DAVID), BART., M.P. Life of; compiled from his Journals and Writings, by his Sister, Mrs. E. H. Percival. 8vo. Lond., 1884.   C 9 V 37

WEDGE (JOHN HELDER). Letters of H. F. Gurner, respecting Mr. Wedge's Visit to Port Phillip in 1835. [*See* MANUSCRIPTS AND PORTRAITS.]   MF 1 U 21

On the Country around Port Philip, South Australia. 8vo. Lond., 1836.   MD 7 Q 51

WEDGWOOD (HENSLEIGH). Contested Etymologies in the Dictionary of the Rev. W. W. Skeat. 8vo. Lond., 1882.   K 12 P 25

Dictionary of English Etymology; with an Introduction on the Origin of Language. 2nd. ed. Roy. 8vo. Lond., 1872.   K 16 Q 2

Another copy.   3rd ed.   Roy. 8vo.   Lond., 1878. K 16 Q 3

WEDGWOOD (JOSIAH). Art of. [*See* METEYARD, E.] A 23 S 21 ‡

Life and Labours of, &c. [*See* TANGYE, R. & G.] Libr.

Life of, from his private Correspondence and Family Papers; by Eliza Meteyard. 2 vols. roy. 8vo. Lond., 1865.   C 9 V 38, 39

On the Clay of Sydney Cove; by F. Rathbone. 4to. Birmingham, 1885.   Libr.

Wedgwood and his Works; by Eliza Meteyard. Fol. Lond., 1873.   C 1 W 26

WEDMORE (FREDERICK). Four Masters of Etching. With original Etchings, by F. S. Haden, J. Jacquemart, J. A. M. Whistler, A. Legros. Roy. 4to. Lond., 1883. A 2 Q 20 †

Masters of Genre Painting; being an Introductory Hand-book to the Study of Genre Painting. With sixteen Illustrations. 8vo. Lond., 1880.   A 8 P 33

Studies in English Art. 8vo. Lond., 1876.   A 8 P 24

WEEKLY FREEMAN'S JOURNAL (THE). 2 vols. fol. Dublin, 1836–40.   E

WEEVER (JOHN). Ancient Funerall Monuments within the United Monarchie of Great Britaine, Ireland, and the Islands adjacent. Fol. Lond., 1631.   B 36 P 1 ‡

WEGELE (DR. F. X. VON). Geschichte der deutschen Historiographie seit dem Auftreten des Humanismus. 8vo. München, 1885.   A 17 V 35

WEIGAND (F. L. K.) Deutsches Wörterbuch. 2 vols. roy. 8vo. Giessen, 1857–60.   K 14 T 21, 22

WEIGEL (KARL), PH.D., &c. Neugriechisches teutsch-italiänisches Wörterbuch. 8vo. Leipzig, 1796. K 14 T 4

Teutsch-Neugriechisches Wörterbuch. 8vo. Leipzig, 1804.   K 14 T 5

WEINHOLD (ADOLF F.) Introduction to Experimental Physics, Theoretical and Practical; translated and edited by B. Loewy, F.R.A.S.; with Preface by G. C. Foster. 8vo. Lond., 1875.   A 16 T 12

WEINHOLD (DR. KARL). Grammatik der deutschen Mundarten. 2 vols. 8vo. Berlin, 1863–67. K 15 R 19, 20

WEINMANN (PROF. FREDERICK L.) Practical Grammar of the German Language. [*See* AHN, F.]   K 11 V 23

WEIR (ARCHIBALD). Historical Basis of Modern Europe (1760–1815). 8vo. Lond., 1886.   B 7 R 26

WEISBACH (JULIUS), PH.D. Manual of the Mechanics of Engineering and of the Construction of Machines; with an Introduction to the Calculus. 3 vols. roy. 8vo. Lond., 1877–84.　　　　　A 11 T 1–3

Principles of Mechanics of Machinery and Engineering. 2 vols. 8vo. Lond., 1847–48.　　　A 11 U 4, 5

WEISE (ARTHUR JAMES), M.A. Discoveries of America, to the year 1525. 8vo. Lond., 1884.　　B 1 U 14

WEISKE (BENJAMIN). Pleonasmi Græci. [*See* Bos. L.]　　　　　　　　　　　　K 12 S 34

WEISMANN (PROF. AUGUST). Studies in the Theory of Descent; with Notes and Additions. [Illustrated.] 2 vols. 8vo. Lond., 1880.　　　A 14 T 6, 7

WEISSE (JOHN A.), M.D. Origin, Progress, and Destiny of the English Language and Literature. 8vo. New York, 1879.　　　　　　　K 16 T 9

The Obelisk and Freemasonry, according to the Discoveries of Belzoni and Commander Gorringe; also, Egyptian Symbols compared with those discovered in American Mounds. With Illustrations. 8vo. New York, 1880.　　　　　　　　　　　　B 15 Q 33

WEISSER (PROF. LUDWIG). Bilder-Atlas zur Weltgeschichte nach Kunstwerken alter und neuer Zeit: 146 Tafeln mit über fünftausend Darstellungen; mit erläuterndem Text von Dr. Heinrich Merz. 3e auflage. At. fol. Stuttgart, 1884.　　　　　B 14 U 4 ‡

WEKEY (S.) Otago as it is; its Gold-mines and Natural Resources. 2nd ed. 8vo. Melb., 1863.　MD 1 U 21

WELCH (CHRISTOPHER), M.A. History of the Boehm Flute. 8vo. Lond., 1883.　　　A 7 U 5

WELCH (ROBERT P.), M.R.C.S., &c. Observations on Convict and Free Labour for New South Wales. 8vo. Lond., 1847.　　　　　　　MF 3 P 7

WELCKER (F. G.) [*See* MULLER, K. O.]

WELD (CHARLES RICHARD). Florence, the New Capital of Italy. 8vo. Lond., 1867.　　　D 8 Q 12

History of the Royal Society; with Memoirs of the Presidents. 2 vols. 8vo. Lond., 1848.　B 6 S 33, 34

Two Months in the Highlands, Orcadia, and Skye. 8vo. Lond., 1860.　　　　　　　D 9 P 1

Vacation Tour in the United States and Canada. 8vo. - Lond., 1855.　　　　　　　D 4 P 27

Vacations in Ireland. 8vo. Lond., 1857.　D 9 P 2

WELD (SIR FREDERICK ALOYSIUS). Hints to intending Sheep-farmers in New Zealand. 2nd ed. 8vo. Lond., 1853.　　　　　　　MD 6 T 3

Another copy. 4th ed. 12mo. Lond.,1864.　MA 1 P 24

WELDON & CO. Historical and Fancy Costumes, from the Earliest Period down to the Present Day. Obl. 4to. Lond., 1878.　　　　　　　A 2 P 10 ‡

WELLBANK (ISAAC). Australian Nautical Almanac and Coasters' Guide for the South and East Coasts, and part of the North-west and West Coasts of Australia, also the principal Ports and Harbours of Fiji. 2 vols. 8vo. Sydney, 1886–87.　　　　　　　ME 2 U

WELLDON (REV. JAMES EDWARD COWELL), M.A. Politics of Aristotle. [*See* ARISTOTELES.]

Rhetoric of Aristotle. [*See* ARISTOTELES.]　G 7 T 30

WELLER (EDWARD). Tasmania; or, Van Diemen's Land. (*Map.*) 8vo. Lond. (n.d.)　　MD 5 P 18 ‡

Victoria (Australia). (*Map.*) 8vo. Lond. (n.d.)　　　　　　　　MD 5 P 18 ‡

[*See* AGGAS, R.]　　　　　　D 33 P 4 ‡

WELLESLEY (RICHARD COLLEY), MARQUESS OF, K.P., K.G., &c. Despatches, Minutes, and Correspondence of, during his Administration in India; edited by Montgomery Martin. 5 vols. 8vo. Lond.,1840.　B 10 T 7–11

Irish Question considered in its Integrity. 8vo. Dublin, 1844.　　　　　　　B 11 R 18

Marquess Wellesley, Architect of Empire: an Historic Portrait; by W. M. Torrens, M.P. 8vo. Lond., 1880.　　　　　　　　　　　　C 9 V 49

Memoirs and Correspondence of ; comprising numerous Letters and Documents, now first published from original MSS., by R. R. Pearce. 3 vols. 8vo. Lond., 1846.　　　　　　　　　　　C 9 V 46–48

WELLINGTON (ARTHUR WELLESLEY), DUKE OF. Despatches of Field Marshal the Duke of Wellington during his various Campaigns, from 1799 to 1818. Edited by Lieut.-Col. Gurwood; with Index. 13 vols. 8vo. Lond., 1837–38.　　　　　　　　B 6 U 1–13

Supplementary Despatches, Correspondence, and Memoranda of Field Marshal Arthur, Duke of Wellington, K.G. Edited by his Son, the Duke of Wellington, K.G. 14 vols. 8vo. Lond., 1858–72.　B 6 U 14–27

Supplementary Despatches, Correspondence, and Memoranda of Field Marshal Arthur, Duke of Wellington, K.G. Edited by his Son, the Duke of Wellington, K.G. Vol. 15. Index to the Wellington Supplementary Despatches, vols. 1 to 14, with Chronological List of Letters, Memoranda, &c., published in the 1st (new) ed. of Gurwood, and in the Supplementary Despatches. 8vo. Lond., 1872.　　　　　　　B 6 U 28

Despatches, Correspondence, and Memoranda of Field Marshal Arthur, Duke of Wellington, K.G. Edited by his Son, the Duke of Wellington. (In continuation of the former Series.) Vols. 1–8. 8vo. Lond., 1867–80.　　　　　　　　　　　B 6 U 29–36

History of the Life of; by M. Brialmont; with Emendations and Additions, by the Rev. G. R. Gleig. 4 vols. 8vo. Lond., 1858–60.　　　　C 9 V 40–43

Life of Field Marshal His Grace the Duke of Wellington; by W. H. Maxwell. 3 vols. 8vo. Lond., 1839–40.　　　　　　　C 5 T 25–27

Life of the Duke of Wellington; by G. Soane. (Fam. Lib.) 2 vols. 12mo. Lond., 1839–40.　K 10 P 24, 25

WELLINGTON (ARTHUR WELLESLEY), DUKE OF—*contd.*
Life, Military and Civil, of the Duke of Wellington,
digested from the Materials of W. H. Maxwell, and in
part re-written by "An Old Soldier"; with some Account
of his Public Funeral. Illustrated. 8vo. Lond., 1877.
　　　　　　　　　　　　　　　　C 4 P 43

Speeches of, in Parliament, collected and arranged by
the late Col. Gurwood, C.B., K.C.T.S. 2 vols. 8vo.
Lond., 1854.　　　　　　　　　F 13 Q 18, 19

WELLS (B.) History of Taranaki. 8vo. New Plymouth,
1878.　　　　　　　　　　　　　MB 2 R 28

WELLS (DAVID AMESS), LL.D. Creed of Free Trade.
(Reprinted from the *Atlantic Monthly*.) 8vo. Lond.,
1875.　　　　　　　　　　　　　F 3 T 17

Another copy. (Reprinted, for the Cobden Club, from
the *Atlantic Monthly*, August, 1875.) (Pam., Dq.)
8vo. Lond., 1876.　　　　　　　F 4 R 7

Another copy. 8vo. Melb., 1875.　　MF 1 Q 6

Practical Economics. 8vo. N. York, 1885.　　F 12 R 1

Primer of Tariff Reform. 12mo. New York, 1884.
　　　　　　　　　　　　　　　　K 17 P 2

The Recent Financial, Industrial, and Commercial Ex-
periences of the United States: a Curious Chapter in
Politico-Economic History. [*See* COBDEN CLUB.]
　　　　　　　　　　　　　　　　F 10 T 15

WELLS (HENRY P.) Fly-Rods and Fly-Tackle: Suggestions as to their Manufacture and Use. Illustrated.
Squ. 4to. Lond., 1885.　　　　　A 29 R 5

American Salmon Fisherman. 8vo. Lond., 1886.
　　　　　　　　　　　　　　　　A 16 Q 30

WELLS (JAMES WILLIAM), C.E. Exploring and Travelling Three Thousand Miles through Brazil, from Rio
Janeiro to Maranhão. Illustrated. 2 vols. 8vo. Lond.,
1886.　　　　　　　　　　　　D 4 Q 6, 7

WELLS (WILLIAM HENRY). Map of the County of Cumberland, in the Colony of New South Wales. 8vo.
Sydney (n.d.)　　　　　　　　　MD 5 P 18 ‡

Geographical Dictionary; or, Gazetteer of the Australian Colonies: their Physical and Political Geography,
together with a brief Notice of all the Capitals, Principal
Towns, and Villages. 8vo. Sydney, 1848.* MD 7 Q 18

Keys to Well's Map of the City of Sydney, 1850.
12mo. Sydney, 1850.　　　　　MD 1 S 56

WELLSTED (LIEUT. J. R.), F.R.S., &c. Travels to the
City of the Caliphs, along the Shores of the Persian Gulf
and the Mediterranean. 2 vols. 8vo. Lond., 1840.
　　　　　　　　　　　　　　　D 5 S 22, 23

Travels in Arabia. 2 vols. 8vo. Lond., 1838.
　　　　　　　　　　　　　　　D 4 T 17, 18

WELSH (ALFRED H.), A.M., &c. Development of English Literature and Language. 2 vols. 8vo. Chicago,
1882.　　　　　　　　　　　　B 6 S 18, 19

WELSH (CHARLES). A Bookseller of Last Century; being
some Account of the Life of John Newbery, and of the
Books he published, &c. 8vo. Lond., 1885.　C 5 V 1

WELSH (REV. DAVID). Memoir of Thomas Brown, M.D.,
Author of Lectures on the Philosophy of the Human
Mind. [*See* BROWN, T.]　　　　　G 6 Q 18

WELSHMEN (EMINENT). Engwogion Cymru. Bio-
graphical Dictionary of Eminent Welshmen, from the
Earliest Times to the Present; by the Rev. Robert
Williams, M.A. 8vo. Llandovery, 1852.　C 11 Q 9

WEMYSS AND MARCH (FRANCIS WEMYSS CHARTERIS),
NINTH EARL OF. Letters on Military Organization.
8vo. Lond., 1871.　　　　　　　F 6 Q 4

WENCKSTERN (OTTO). [*See* SCHLESINGER, M.]

WENDEBORN (F. A.), LL.D. An Introduction to German Grammar. 4th ed. 12mo. Lond., 1803. K 11 U 32

WENDOVER (ROGER OF). [*See* ROGER OF WENDOVER.]

WENJUKOW (M.) Oberst Wenjukow Die russisch-
asiatischen Grenzlande aus dem Russischen übertragen,
von Kramer. 8vo. Leip., 1874.　　D 8 U 7

WENTWORTH (THOMAS), LORD RABY. [*See* STRAFFORD,
EARL OF.]

WENTWORTH (WILLIAM CHARLES). Statistical, His-
torical, and Political Description of the Colony of New
South Wales, and its dependent Settlements in Van
Diemen's Land. 8vo. Lond., 1819.*　MB 1 R 6

Another copy. 2nd ed., with a View of the Town of
Sydney, and a Map. 8vo. Lond., 1820.*　MB 1 R 10

Statistical Account of the British Settlements in Australasia, including the Colonies of New South Wales and
Van Diemen's Land. 3rd ed., with an Appendix, containing the Acts of Parliament, and other Documents
relating to these Settlements. With Maps, and a View
of Sydney. 2 vols. 8vo. Lond., 1824.* MB 1 R 13, 14

Papers explanatory of the charges brought against
Lieut.-Gen. Darling, by William Charles Wentworth,
Esq. (Parl. Doc., 6.) Fol. Lond., 1830.　MF 4 ‡

An Address to Mr. Wentworth relative to Resolutions
adopted at a Public Meeting, for the erection of a Statue
in Sydney, as a Memorial of the eminent services
rendered by him to the Colony. (Pam., A.) Fol.
Sydney (n.d.)　　　　　　　　　MJ 2 U 1

Public Funeral of the late W. C. Wentworth, Tuesday,
6th May, 1873. 8vo. Sydney, 1873.　MC 1 R 33

Another copy. 8vo. Sydney, 1873.　MF 1 Q 4

Lines on the Public Funeral of. [*See* COLERIDGE, D. M.]
　　　　　　　　　　　　　　　MH 1 Q 5

Mr. Wentworth's Letter of Impeachment relative to the
Punishment and Death of Private Joseph Sudds. [*See*
SUDDS, J., AND THOMPSON, P.]

[*See* MARSDEN, REV. S., AND WILSHIRE, J. R.]

WENGER (J.) Bengali Grammar. [*See* YATES, REV. W.]

WERNE (FERDINAND). Expedition to discover the Sources of the White Nile, in the years 1840–41; [translated] from the German, by C. W. O'Reilly. 2 vols. 8vo. Lond., 1849. D 1 R 20, 21

WERNER (CARL). Nile Sketches : painted from Nature during his Travels through Egypt. Gustav W. Seitz, Water Colour Facsimiles. With accompanying Text, by Dr. A. E. Breim and Dr. Johannes Dümichen. Pantographic edition, Seitz Patent. 4to. Wandsbeck, 1882. D 5 Q 9 †

WERNER (FRIEDRICH LUDWIG ZACHARIAS). The Templars in Cyprus : a Dramatic Poem. Translated by E. A. M. Lewis. 12mo. Lond., 1886. H 4 P 30

WERNER (DR. KARL). Geschichte der katholischen Theologie. (Ges. der Wiss. in Deutsch., 6.) 8vo. München, 1866. A 17 V 20

WERNERIAN NATURAL HISTORY SOCIETY. Memoirs of, 1808–37. 7 vols. 8vo. Edinb., 1811–38. E

WERSHOVEN (F. J.), D.Sc. Technological Dictionary of the Physical, Mechanical, and Chemical Sciences. English, French, German, Italian, Spanish. Vol. 1— English–German. 12mo. Lond., 1885. K 13 T 32

WESEHAM (VERY REV. ROGER DE), DEAN OF LINCOLN, &c. Memoirs of the Life of; by Samuel Pegge, A.M. 4to. Lond., 1761. C 4 W 7

WESLEY (REV. CHARLES), M.A. Life of; comprising a Review of his Poetry, Sketches of the Rise and Progress of Methodism, &c.; by Thomas Jackson. 2 vols. 8vo. Lond., 1841. C 6 R 18, 19

WESLEY (REV. JOHN). Life of; and Rise and Progress of Methodism, by Robert Southey. 2 vols. 8vo. Lond., 1846. C 6 R 20, 21

Extract of the Journal of ; together with Tracts illustrative of the Doctrines and Discipline of Methodism, and an Account of his Family, Education, and Death ; by the late Rev. J. Benson. 6 vols. 8vo. Lond., 1825. C 10 Q 46–51

Compendium of Natural Philosophy ; being a Survey of the Wisdom of God in the Creation. Revised, &c., by Robert Mudie. (Fam. Lib.) 3 vols. 12mo. Lond., 1836. K 10 P 21–23

Wesley and Methodism. [*See* TAYLOR, J.]

WESLEY (SUSANNA). [Life of] ; by Eliza Clarke. (Eminent Women.) 8vo. Lond., 1886. C 2 S 39

WESLEYAN AUXILIARY MISSIONARY SOCIETY OF NEW SOUTH WALES. Reports of, for 1821–22, 1824, 1828–30, 1837–45. 8vo. Sydney, 1822–45. MG 1 Q 27

Reports for 1825–27. 12mo. Sydney, 1826–28. MJ 2 Q 21

WESLEYAN METHODIST MISSIONARY AUXILIARY SOCIETY. Report for the Liverpool District for 1819. 8vo. Liverpool, 1820. MG 1 Q 27

5 I

WESLEYAN METHODIST MISSIONARY SOCIETY. Report, 1824. 8vo., Lond., 1824. MG 1 Q 27

WESSELY (JOSEF). Les richesses Forestieres de l'Autriche et leur Exportation. (Pam., 34.) 8vo. Vienne, 1867. J 12 U 26

WEST (A.) Collection of Views in New South Wales. Roy. 4to. Sydney, 1813–14. MD 7 Q 2 †

WEST (ALBERT E.) Tasmania, Queen of Southern Isles : a Jubilee Volume of Poems. 12mo. Sydney, 1887. MH 1 P 31

WEST (CHARLES), M.D. Nice and its Climate. [*See* BARÉTY, DR. A.] D 7 P 17

WEST (E. W.) Pahlavi Tents. [*See* MÜLLER, PROF. F. M.]

WEST (GILBERT), LL.D. Life and Poems of. [*See* CHALMERS, A., *and* JOHNSON, S.]

WEST (HANS). Raisonneret Catalog over Consul West's Samling af Malerier med Indledning samt Liste over Haandtegninger, Figurer, Kobberstik og trykte Værker Samlingen tilhörende. 8vo. Kiöbenhavn, 1807. A 7 Q 20

WEST (REV. JOHN). History of Tasmania. 2 vols. 8vo. Launceston, 1852.* MB 2 Q 22, 23

WEST (REV. THOMAS). Ten Years in South-Central Polynesia; being Reminiscences of a Personal Mission to the Friendly Islands and their Dependencies. 8vo. Lond., 1865.* MD 4 U 14

WEST (THOMAS D.) Moulder's Text-book; being Part 2 of American Foundry Practice. 8vo. New York, 1885. A 11 Q 27

WESTALL (WM.) Russia under the Tzars. 8vo. Lond., B 12 T 33, 34

WESTCOT (REDMAN). [*See* SELDEN, J.] B 2 T 45

WESTCOTT (W. WYNN), M.B. Suicide: its History, Literature, Jurisprudence, Causation, and Prevention. (A Social Science Treatise.) 12mo. Lond., 1885. F 5 S 14

WESTERGAARD (N. L.) Zendavesta; or, the Religious Books of the Zoroastrians. [*See* ZOROASTER.]

WESTERHOVIUS (A. H.) [*See* TERENTIUS AFER P.]

WESTERN AUSTRALIA. A Bill to provide for a limited time for the government of His Majesty's Settlements in Western Australia, on the West Coast of New Holland. (Parl. Doc., 5.) Fol. Lond., 1829. MF 4 ‡

Catalogue of Exhibits in the Western Australian Court, Melbourne International Exhibition, 1880. 8vo. Melbourne, 1880. MJ 2 R 16

Copies of the Correspondence of the Colonial Department with certain Gentlemen proposing to form a Settlement in the neighbourhood of the Swan River, in Western Australia. (Parl. Docs., 7.) Fol. Lond., 1829. MF 4 ‡

WESTERN AUSTRALIA—*continued.*

Copies of a Statistical Report of the Colony of Western Australia; the Land Regulations contained in the Appendix, addressed to the Secretary of State for the Colonies; and Copy of a Despatch from the Governor of Western Australia to Lord Glenelg, dated 3rd December, 1837. (Parl. Doc., 36.) Fol. Lond., 1838.   MF 4.‡

Extract of a Despatch from Lieut.-Gov. Stirling to the Rt. Hon. Sir G. Murray, dated 20th Jan., 1830, containing Information relative to the Progress of the Settlement at Swan River. (Parl. Docs. 7.) Fol. Lond.,1830. MF 4 ‡

Northern Territory of West Australia. 8vo. Perth, 1864.   MJ 2 R 16

North-western Australia : its Soil, Climate, and Capacity for Pastoral Enterprise. 8vo. Melb., 1864.
                                               MD 5 T 27

Another copy. 8vo. Melb., 1864.   MJ 2 R 16

Western Australia : containing a Statement of the Condition and Prospects of the Colony, and some Account of the Western Australian Company's Settlement of Australind; with a Map. 8vo. Lond., 1842.*   MD 4 Q 49

Western Australian Almanack, for the year 1842; with an Appendix containing a Native Grammar, by Charles Symmons. 8vo. Perth, 1842.   ME 4 U

Western Australian Almanac : The *Herald* Western Australian Almanack and Commercial Directory, for 1874 and 1885. 2 vols. 8vo. Freemantle, 1874–85. ME 3 T

ACTS.
An Act to continue until the 31st day of December, 1842, and until the end of the then next Session of Parliament; an Act 10 George IV, for providing for the government of His Majesty's Settlements in Western Australia, on the Coast of New Holland. (Parl. Docs. 42.) Fol. Lond., 1841.   MF 4 ‡

Acts of Council 41 Vict., 1877. 4to. Perth, 1877.
                                               E 2.62

BLUE BOOKS.
Blue Books, for the years 1875, 1878, 1883, and 1884. Sm. fol. Perth, 1876–85.   E 2.62

CENSUS.
Census of the Colony, taken on 31st March, 1870 : and also the General Statistics of the Colony, for the Ten Years ending 31st December, 1869. Compiled by W. Knight. Fol. Perth, 1870.   E 2.62

CROWN LANDS.
Copies of the Royal Instructions to the Governors of New South Wales, Van Diemen's Land, and Western Australia, as to the mode to be adopted in disposing of Crown Lands. (Parl. Docs., 5.) Fol. Lond., 1831.
                                               MF 4 ‡

Papers relative to Crown Lands in the Australian Colonies. (Parl. Docs., 59, 62, 65.) 3 vols. fol. Lond., 1851–56.
                                               MF 4 ‡

GOVERNMENT GAZETTE.
Government Gazette. 7 vols. fol. Perth, 1873–83. E 2.62

WESTERN AUSTRALIA—*continued.*

LEGISLATIVE COUNCIL.
Parliamentary Debates, Legislative Council. Roy. 8vo. Perth, 1877.   E 2.62

Votes and Proceedings of the Legislative Council during the Session of 1876, 1877, 1882, 1884. With Papers presented to the Council by command of His Excellency the Governor, and Copies of the various Documents ordered by the Council to be printed. 4 vols. fol. Perth, 1876–84.   E 2.62

SUPREME COURT.
Supreme Court Act, 1880, and Rules of Court; with a Table of Contents, a Time-table, and an Index. 4to. Perth, 1881.   MF 1 U 30

WESTERN PALESTINE. Survey of. [*See* PALESTINE EXPLORATION FUND.]

WESTGARTH (WILLIAM). Anniversary Address of the Chairman of the Chamber of Commerce to the Members of the Association, 1852. 12mo. Melb., 1852. MJ 2 P 30

Australia Felix; or, a Historical and Descriptive Account of the Settlements of Port Phillip, New South Wales. 8vo. Edinb., 1848.*   MB 2 S 14

Australia; its Rise, Progress, and Present Condition. 12mo. Edinb., 1861.*   MD 4 R 33

Colony of Victoria; its History, Commerce, and Goldmining; its Social and Political Institutions, down to the end of 1863. 8vo. Lond., 1864.*   MD 4 W 19

Commerce and Statistics of Victoria, from the commencement of the Colony. (Pam. C.) Roy. 8vo. Melb., 1856.
                                               MJ 2 S 1

Commercial, Statistical, and General Report on the District of Port Phillip, New South Wales, for the half-year ended 31st July, 1845. 8vo. Lond., 1845. MJ 2 R 18

Commercial, Statistical, and General Report on the District of Port Phillip, for the half-year ended 31st Jan., 1846. 8vo. Melb., 1846.   MJ 2 Q 6

Another copy. 8vo. Melb., 1846.   MJ 2 Q 8

Another copy. (Pam. 19.) 8vo. Melb., 1846. MJ 2 R 18

Essays on the Street Re-alignment, Re-construction, and Sanitation of Central London. [*See* LONDON.] A 6 T 21

Remarks upon the proposed Branch of the Royal Mint about to be commenced in Sydney; with an Estimate of its probable relations to Colonial Commerce. 8vo. Melb., 1854.   MB 3 P 5

Report, Commercial, Statistical, and General, on the District of Port Phillip, for the half-year ended 31st July, 1846. 8vo. Melb., 1846.   MF 3 P 15

Another copy. 8vo. Melb., 1846.   MJ 2 R 10

Another copy. 8vo. Melb., 1846.   MJ 2 R 18

Report on the Condition, Capabilities, and Prospects of the Australian Aborigines. 8vo. Melb., 1846. MA 1 R 2

Another copy. 8vo. Melb., 1846.   MF 2 R 22

Tracks of McKinlay and Party across Australia. [*See* DAVIS, J.]   MD 2 V 2

WESTGARTH (WILLIAM)—*continued.*
Victoria and the Australian Gold-mines in 1857 ; with Notes on the Overland Route from Australia, *viâ* Suez. 8vo. Lond., 1857.*		MD 4 R 35

Victoria, late Australia Felix ; or, Port Phillip District of New South Wales; being an Historical and Descriptive Account of the Colony and its Gold-mines. 8vo. Edinb., 1853.*		MB 2 S 18

[*See* MACKINTOSH, W.]		MJ 2 R 22

WESTHEAD (J. P.) Letter to the Rt. Hon. Robert Peel, Bart., on the Corn Laws. (Pam. 19.) 8vo. Lond., 1839.		MJ 2 Q 8

WESTLEYS & CLARK. Trade List of Price for Book-binding. (Pam. A.) Fol. Lond. (n.d.)		MJ 2 U 1

WESTMINSTER ABBEY. [*See* COMBE, W.]

WESTMINSTER CONFESSION OF FAITH (THE). People's Edition of. 8vo. Melb., 1881.		MG 1 Q 39
The Confession of Faith, together with the Larger and Lesser Catechismes composed by the Reverend Assembly of Divines sitting at Westminster. 8vo. Lond., 1658.		G 9 T 4

[*See* TURNER, W.]		MG 1 Q 39

WESTMINSTER HALL. Catalogue of the Cartoons sent in pursuant to the Notices issued by H.M. Commissioners on the Fine Arts, for exhibition. 12mo. Lond., 1843.		A 7 P 32

Hand-book Guide to the Cartoons now exhibiting in Westminster Hall; by H. C. Clarke. 12mo. Lond., 1843.		A 7 P 32

WESTMINSTER, MATTHEW OF. [*See* MATTHEW OF WESTMINSTER.]

WESTMINSTER REVIEW (THE). 111 vols. 8vo. Lond., 1825–85.		E 2.9

WESTPHAL (RUDOLF). Vergleichende Grammatik der indogermanischen Sprachen. Band 1. 8vo. Jena, 1873.		K 16 Q 22

WESTROPP (HODDER M.) Early and Imperal Rome; or, Promenade Lectures on the Archæology of Rome. 8vo. Lond., 1884.		B 11 S 1
Hand-book of Pottery and Porcelain; or, History of those Arts from the Earliest Period. With Illustrations. Sq. 12mo. Lond., 1880.		A 11 Q 14
Pre-Historic Phases ; or, Introductory Essays on Pre-Historic Archæology. With Illustrations. 8vo. Lond., 1872.		B 14 U 22

WESTWOOD (JOSEPH JEWELL). Journal of J. J. West-wood (Evangelist); or, an Account of Eight Years' Itineracy to the Townships and Squatting Stations of Victoria, New South Wales, South Australia, and Tas-mania. With Portrait. 8vo. Melb., 1865.	MD 1 U 28

WESTWOOD (J. O.), F.L.S., &c. Arcana Entomologica ; or, Illustrations of New, Rare, and Interesting Insects. 2 vols. roy. 8vo. Lond., 1845.		A 13 U 5, 6
Fac-similes of the Miniatures and Ornaments of Anglo-Saxon and Irish Manuscripts. Drawn on Stone, by W. R. Tymms. Chromo-lithographed by Day and Son. Sm. fol. Lond., 1868.		A 20 P 16 ‡
Index Entomologicus. [*See* WOOD, W.]		A 13 U 4
Exotic Entomology. [*See* DRURY, D.]		A 14 V 11–13

WESTWOOD (T.), AND SATCHELL (THOMAS). Biblio-theca Piscatoria : a Catalogue of Books on Angling, and Fisheries, and Fish-Culture. 8vo. Lond., 1883.	K 18 Q 4

WETTON (—.), AND JARVIS (—.) Portraits of Illus-trions Persons. Twenty-nine Plates. 4to. Lond., 1820–30.		C 1 S 13 †

WEY (FRANCIS). Rome; containing Engravings on Wood, designed by the most celebrated Artists, and a Plan of Rome. Imp. 4to. Lond., 1872.		D 5 S 4 †

WEYLAND (P. C.) Reise um die Welt. [*See* TURN-BULL, J.]		MD 1 U 4

WHALLEY (THOMAS SEDGEWICK), D.D. Journals and Correspondence of ; edited, with a Memoir and Illustra-tive Notes, by the Rev. Hill Wickham, M.A. 2 vols. 8vo. Lond., 1863.		C 9 P 47, 48

WHARNCLIFFE (RT. HON. JOHN STUART WORTLEY), LORD. Letters and Works of Lady Mary Wortley Montagu. Edited by her Great Grandson, Lord Wharncliffe. 3 vols. 8vo. Lond., 1837.		C 4 V 8–10

WHARTON (C. J.) [*See* DU MONCEL, TH., COUNT, AND GERALDY, FRANK.]		A 5 R 62

WHARTON (GRACE AND PHILLIP). [*See* THOMSON, MRS. KATHERINE AND JOHN.]

WHARTON (HENRY THORNTON), M.A. Sappho: Memoir, Text, Selected Renderings, and a literal Translation. [*See* SAPPHO.]

WHARTON (JOHN J. S.), M.A. Law Lexicon ; or, Dic-tionary of Jurisprudence, explaining the technical words and phrases employed in the several departments of Eng-lish Law. 5th ed., revised and enlarged, by J. Shiress Will. Imp. 8vo. Lond., 1872.		K 11 R 8

WHARTON (CAPT. W. J. L.), R.N. Hydrographical Surveying : a Description of the Means and Methods employed in constructing Marine Charts. 8vo. Lond., 1882.		A 6 S 30

WHARTON (W. R.) [*See* BAINES, E.]		B 6 V 21, 22

WHAT IS MERIT? A Question in a Letter to the Earl of Clarendon. (Pam. Dd.) 8vo. Lond., 1855.	F 12 P 22

WHAT PUT MY PIPE OUT; or, Incidents in the Life of a Clergyman. 8vo. Lond., 1863.		J 9 P 36

WHATELY (E. JANE). Life and Correspondence of Richard Whately, D.D., late Archbishop of Dublin. 2 vols. 8vo. Lond., 1866.   C 9 R 47, 48

WHATELY (M. L.) Among the Huts in Egypt: Scenes from Real Life. 8vo. Lond., 1871.   D 1 T 20

WHATELY (MOST REV. RICHARD), D.D., ARCHBISHOP OF DUBLIN. Thoughts on Secondary Punishments, in a Letter to Earl Grey; to which are appended two Articles on Transportation to New South Wales, and on Secondary Punishments, and some Observations on Colonization. 8vo. Lond., 1832.   MF 2 P 12

Remarks on Transportation, and on a recent Defence of the System, in a second Letter to Earl Grey. 8vo. Lond., 1834.   MF 2 P 13

Account of an Expedition to the Interior of New Holland; edited by Lady Mary Fox. (*Fictitious.*) 12mo. Lond., 1837.*   MJ 1 S 1

Account of an Expedition to the Interior of New Holland. 2nd ed. 12mo. Lond., 1849.   MJ 1 S 3

Substance of a Speech on Transportation, delivered in the House of Lords, on the 19th of May, 1840. 8vo. Lond., 1840.   MF 2 P 14

The Southlanders: an Account of an Expedition to the Interior of New Holland. Edited by Lady Mary Fox. 3rd ed., revised. 12mo. Lond., 1860. MJ 1 S 4

Elements of Logic. 8th ed. 8vo. Lond., 1844.
                                           G 12 T 30

Elements of Rhetoric. 4th ed. 8vo. Oxford, 1832.
                                              J 5 S 15

Introductory Lectures on Political Economy. 8vo. Lond., 1831.   F 3 P 7

Charges and other Tracts. 8vo. Lond., 1836. G 12 T 32

Essays, 1st series: on some of the peculiarities of the Christian Religion; 2nd series: on some of the Difficulties in the Writings of the Apostle Paul; 3rd series: on the Errors of Romanism. 3 vols. 8vo. Lond., 1837.   G 12 T 25-27

Selections from the Writings of. Thoughts and Apophthegms—Miscellaneous. 12mo. Lond., 1856. G 10 P 11

Sermons on various subjects. 8vo. Lond., 1835. G 12 T 31

The use and abuse of Party Feeling in matters of Religion; in Eight Sermons. 3rd ed. 8vo. Lond., 1833. G 12 T 28

Life and Correspondence of Richard Whately, D.D., late Archbishop of Dublin; by E. Jane Whately. 2 vols. 8vo. Lond., 1866.   C 9 R 47, 48

View of the Scripture Revelations concerning a Future State; by "A Country Pastor." 8vo. Lond., 1837.
                                               G 7 U 1

Bacon's Essays; with Annotations. [*See* BACON, SIR F.]

WHATLEY (STEPHEN). England's Gazetteer; or, an Accurate Description of all the Cities, Towns, and Villages of the Kingdom. 3 vols. 12mo. Lond., 1751. D 11 Q 3-5

WHEARE (D.) Method and Order of Reading both Civil and Ecclesiastical Histories. 12mo. Lond., 1685. B 14 Q 20

WHEATLEY (HENRY B.), F.S.A. Hand-book of Decorative Art in Gold, Silver, Enamel on Metal, Porcelain, and Earthenware. Illustrated. 8vo. Lond., 1884. A 7 T 16

How to Form a Library. 12mo. Lond., 1886. J 10 Q 36

Samuel Pepys, and the World he lived in. 8vo. Lond., 1880.   C 9 P 23

What is an Index? a few Notes on Indexes and Indexers. 8vo. Lond., 1878.   J 3 S 26

WHEATLEY (HENRY B.), F.S.A., AND DELAMOTTE (PHILIP H.) Art Work in Earthenware; Art Work in Gold and Silver.—Mediæval. (Hand-books of Practical Art.) 8vo. Lond., 1882.   A 7 S 28

WHEATLY (CHARLES), M.A., &c. Rational Illustration of the Book of Common Prayer, and Administration of the Sacraments, and other Rites and Ceremonies of the Church, according to the use of the Church of England. 8vo. Camb., 1858.   G 12 T 24

WHEATON (HENRY), LL.D. Digest of the Law of Maritime Captures and Prizes. 8vo. New York, 1815.
                                              F 4 S 19

Elements of International Law. 2 vols. 8vo. Lond., 1836.   F 4 S 22, 23

WHEATSTONE (PROF. CHARLES). Lives of the Electricians. [*See* JEANS, W. T.]   C 2 S 14

WHEELER (ALEXANDER). Vaccination opposed to Science, and a Disgrace to English Law. (Pam. Cp.) 8vo. Lond., 1879.   A 12 S 34

WHEELER (DANIEL). Extracts from the Letters and Journal of Daniel Wheeler, now engaged in a Religious Visit to the Inhabitants of some of the Islands of the Pacific Ocean, Van Diemen's Land, and New South Wales. Part 1. 8vo. Lond., 1839.   MD 7 P 23

Memoirs of the Life and Gospel Labours of [by his Son, Daniel Wheeler]. Roy. 8vo. Lond., 1842. MC 1 R 24

WHEELER (DANIEL), JUNR. Memoirs of the Life and Labours of Daniel Wheeler; by his Son. 8vo. Lond., 1842.   MC 1 R 24

WHEELER (J. TALBOYS), F.R.G.S. Analysis and Summary of Herodotus; with a Syncronistical Table of Principal Events, Tables of Weights, Measures, Money, and Distances, an Outline of the History and Geography, and the Dates, completed from Gaisford, Bachr, &c. 2nd ed. 8vo. Lond., 1877.   B 14 Q 48

Analysis and Summary of Thucydides; with a Chronological Table of principal Events, Money, Distances, &c., reduced to English Terms, a Skeleton Outline of the Geography, Abstracts of all the Speeches, Index, &c. 8vo. Lond., 1876.   B 9 S 15

Early Records of British India: a History of the English Settlements in India. Roy. 8vo. Lond., 1878. B 10 V 10

Geography of Herodotus. With Maps and Plans. 8vo. Lond., 1854.   D 12 U 22

History of India, from the Earliest Ages. 4 vols. (in 5) 8vo. Lond., 1867-81.   B 10 R 20-24

India under British Rule, from the Foundation of the East India Company. 8vo. Lond., 1886.   B 4 S 1

WHEELER (William Adolphus), M.A. Dictionary of the Noted Names of Fiction; including also, Familiar Pseudonyms, Surnames bestowed on Eminent Men, and analogous Popular Appellations often referred to in Literature and Conversation. 12mo. Lond., 1866.   K 17 P 6

WHEELER (William A. and Charles G.) Familiar Allusions: a Hand-book of Miscellaneous Information, including the Names of Celebrated Statues, Paintings, Palaces, Country-seats, Ruins, Churches, Ships, Streets, Clubs, Natural Curiosities, and the like. 8vo. Lond., 1882.   K 9 P 6

WHEELWRIGHT (Rev. C. A.), M.A. [*See* Aristophanes *and* Pindar.]

WHEELWRIGHT (Horace W.), "The Old Bushman." Bush Wanderings of a Naturalist; or, Notes on the Field Sports and Fauna of Australia Felix. 12mo. Lond., 1861.*   MA 2 T 23
Natural History Sketches. With Illustrations. New ed. 12mo. Lond., 1871.   MA 2 T 26
Sporting Sketches at Home and Abroad. 12mo. Lond., 1866.   MA 2 V 22
Another copy. 12mo. Lond., 1866.   A 17 U 3
Ten Years in Sweden; being a Description of the Landscape, Climate, Domestic Life, Forests, Mines, Agriculture, Field Sports, and Fauna of Scandinavia. 8vo. Lond., 1865.   D 7 T 38

WHEILDON (W. W.) [*See* Bunker Hill Monument Association.]   A 8 R 33

WHELAN (Peter). Numismatic Atlas of the Roman Empire. 8vo. Lond., 1864.   A 13 S 46
Numismatic Dictionary; or, a Collection of the Names of all the Coins known, from the Earliest Period up to the Present Day, with their Countries, Values, Multiples, Divisions, &c. 12mo. Lond. (n.d.)   K 7 Q 1

WHERE SHALL I DINE? a Farsetta. (Cumberland's Eng. Theatre.) 12mo. Lond., 1829.   H 2 Q 22

WHERRY (Rev. E. M.), M.A. Comprehensive Commentary on the Qurán; comprising Sale's Translation and Preliminary Discourse, with Additional Notes and Emendations. 4 vols. 8vo. Lond., 1882-86.   G 15 P 1-4

WHETHAM (J. W. Boddam-). Pearls of the Pacific. 8vo. Lond., 1876.*   MD 5 S 33

WHETSTONE (George). Mirror of Treue Honnour and Christian Nobilitie: exposing the Life, Death, and Divine Vertues of the most Noble and Godly Lorde Francis Earle of Bedford, Baron Russell. [*See* Park, T.]

WHEWELL (Rev. William), D.D. Astronomy and General Physics, considered with reference to Natural Theology. 8vo. Lond., 1834.   A 3 S 11
History of the Inductive Sciences, from the earliest to the present times. 3 vols. 8vo. Lond., 1837.   A 17 V 11-13
Philosophy of the Inductive Sciences, founded upon their History. 2 vols. 8vo. Lond., 1840.   G 2 S 27, 28

WHEWELL (Rev. William), D.D.—*continued.*
On the Principles of English University Education. 2nd ed. 8vo. Lond., 1838.   G 17 P 11
On the Philosophy of Discovery: Chapters Historical and Critical. 8vo. Lond., 1860.   G 16 P 28
Of the Plurality of Worlds: an Essay. 12mo. Lond., 1854.   A 3 R 20
Elements of Morality, including Polity. 2 vols. 12mo. Lond., 1848.   G 17 T 16, 17
History of Scientific Ideas. 3rd ed. 2 vols. 12mo. Lond., 1858.   A 16 Q 5, 6
Indications of the Creator: Extracts bearing upon Theology, from the History and the Philosophy of the Inductive Sciences. 2nd ed. 8vo. Lond., 1846.   G 2 P 23
An Account of his Writings; with Selections from his Literary and Scientific Correspondence; by J. Todhunter, M.A. 2 vols. 8vo. Lond., 1876.   C 9 U 51-52
Strictures on Dr. Whewell's "History of the Inductive Sciences." (Pam., 19.) 8vo. Lond., 1847.   MJ 2 Q 8
Life and Selections from the Correspondence of William Whewell, D.D.; by Mrs. Stair Douglas. 8vo. Lond., 1881.   C 9 R 46
General Bearing of the Great Exhibition on the Progress of Arts and Sciences. [*See* Lond. Internat. Exhib., 1851.]   A 16 Q 22
[*See* Education.]

WHIG, A. [*See* Present Crisis, The.]

WHINFIELD (E. H.), M.A. The Quatrains of Omar Khayyám. [*See* Omar Khayyám.]

WHINYATES (Col. F. A.) From Coruña to Sevastopol: the History of "C" Battery, "A" Brigade (late "C" Troop), Royal Horse Artillery. 8vo. Lond., 1884.   B 5 U 15

WHISHAW (Francis), C.E. Railways of Great Britain and Ireland, practically described and illustrated. 4to. Lond., 1840-41.   A 1 Q 6 †

WHISTLER (J. A. M.) [*See* Wedmore, F.]   A 2 Q 20 †

WHISTON (William), M.A. Historical Memoirs of the Life of Dr. Samuel Clarke. 8vo. Lond., 1730.   C 4 T 3

WHITAKER (John), B.D. Ancient Cathedral of Cornwall; historically surveyed. 2 vols. 4to. Lond., 1804.*   B 17 Q 13, 14 ‡
Mary Queen of Scots Vindicated. 2nd ed., enlarged. 3 vols. 8vo. Lond., 1790.   C 5 U 2-4

WHITAKER (Joseph), F.S.A. Almanack for the years 1881-85. 5 vols. 8vo. Lond., 1880-84.   E
Reference Catalogue[s] of Current Literature, containing the full Titles of Books now in print and on sale; with the prices at which they may be obtained of all Booksellers; and Index[es], 1874-75, 1877, 1880, 1885. 5 vols. 8vo. Lond., 1874-85.   Libr.

WHITAKER (THOMAS DUNHAM), LL.D., &c. Ducatus Leodiensis; or, the Topography of the Town and Parish of Leedes; by Ralph Thoresby; with Notes and Additions, &c. (and Life of the Author). 2nd ed. Fol. Leeds, 1816.   B 15 U 6 ‡

Loidis and Elmete; or, History of Leeds; with Appendix. Fol. Leeds, 1816.   B 15 U 7 ‡

WHITE (ANDREW DICKSON), LL.D. Paper Money Inflation in France; how it came, what it brought, and how it ended. (Economic Tracts.) 12mo. New York, 1882.   A 12 P 38

Warfare of Science; with Prefatory Note by Prof. Tyndall. 12mo. Lond., 1876.   A 17 T 16

WHITE (REV. CHARLES), D.D., "MARTINGALE." Sporting Scenes and Country Characters; with numerous Illustrations on Wood. 8vo. Lond., 1840.   A 17 U 30

English Country Life. 8vo. Lond., 1843.   D 7 R 39

WHITE (CHARLES). Three Years in Constantinople; or, Domestic Manners of the Turks in 1844. 3 vols. 8vo. Lond., 1845.   D 9 P 31–33

Courts of Europe. [*See* SWINBURNE, H.]

WHITE (MRS. ELLEN G.) The Great Controversy between Christ and Satan: the Spirit of Prophecy. 3 vols. 12mo. Battle Creek, Mich., 1870–72.   G 7 T 18–20

Life Sketch of. [*See* WHITE, J.]

Sketches from the Life of Paul. 12mo. Battle Creek, Mich., 1883.   G 7 T 22

WHITE (E. J.) Astronomical and Nautical (late Robinson's) Almanac for 1869 and 1875. 2 vols. (in 1). 12mo. Melb., 1869–75.   ME 4 P

[*See* ROBINSON, E. L.]

WHITE (ERNEST WILLIAM), F.Z.S. Cameos from the Silver-Land; or, the Experiences of a young Naturalist in the Argentine Republic. With Map. 2 vols. 8vo. Lond., 1881–82.   D 3 S 5, 6

WHITE (GEORGE S.) Memoir of Samuel Slater, the Father of American Manufactures, connected with a History of the rise and progress of the Cotton Manufacture in England and America. 2nd ed. 8vo. Philad., 1836.   C 9 V 32

WHITE (REV. GILBERT). Natural History and Antiquities of Selborne. With Notes. 8vo. Lond., 1877.   A 17 V 6

Natural History of Selborne. (Const. Misc.) 18mo. Lond., 1832.   K 10 Q 33

WHITE (HENRY), M.A. [*See* D'AUBIGNÉ, J. H. M.]

WHITE (HENRY KIRKE). Remains of; with an Account of his Life, by Robert Southey. 9th ed. 2 vols. 8vo. Lond., 1821.   J G T 6, 7

Life and Remains of. 12mo. Lond., 1825.   J 9 P 8

[*See* BRITISH POETS, 2.]

WHITE (JAMES). Life Sketches: Ancestry, early Life, Christian Experience, and extensive Labours of Elder James White, and his Wife, Mrs. Ellen G. White. 12mo. Battle Creek, Mich., 1880.   G 7 T 21

Sketches of the Christian Life and Public Labours of William Miller. 12mo. Battle Creek, Mich., 1875.   G 7 T 23

WHITE (JAMES). Treatise on Veterinary Medicine. 4 vols. 8vo. Lond., 1820–21.   A 1 P 31–34

WHITE (JOHN). Ancient History of the Maori; his Mythology and Tradition. Horo-Utu; or, Taki-Tumu Migration. (English and Maori.) 2 vols. 8vo. Wellington, 1887*   MB 2 T 7, 8

Te Rou; or, the Maori at Home: a Tale, exhibiting the Social Life, Manners, and Customs of the Maori Race of New Zealand prior to the Introduction of Civilization amongst them. 12mo. Lond., 1874.*   MJ 1 R 23

WHITE (JOHN), SURGEON-GENERAL. Journal of a Voyage to New South Wales. 4to. Lond., 1790.* MD 4 Q 6 †

Voyage à Nouvelle Galles du Sud, à Botany-Bay, au Port Jackson, en 1787–89; traduite de l'Anglais par Charles Pougens. 8vo. Paris, 1795.   MD 3 Q 32

WHITE (JOHN H.) Queensland as an Emigration Field; being a Reprint of Letters to the *Christian World*, with Notes. 12mo. Grimsby, 1882.   MD 2 Q 34

WHITE (REV. JOSEPH BLANCO). Life of, written by himself; with portions of his Correspondence edited by J. H. Thom. 3 vols. 8vo. Lond., 1845.   C 6 P 24–26

WHITE (NATHANIEL). Handy-book on the Law of Friendly, Industrial and Provident Building and Loan Societies. (Weale.) 12mo. Lond., 1867.   F 5 S 20

WHITE (RICHARD GRANT). Every-day English: a Sequel to "Words and their Uses." 8vo. Boston, 1880. K 12 P 22

Studies from Shakespeare. 8vo. Lond., 1885. J 9 S 17

Words and their Uses, Past and Present: a Study of the English Language. 3rd ed., revised and corrected. 8vo. Boston, 1881.   K 12 P 21

WHITE (COL. S. DEWÉ). Complete History of the Indian Mutiny. 8vo. Weston-super-Mare, 1885.   B 10 S 7

WHITE (LIEUT.-COL. THOMAS PILKINGTON), R.E., &c. Ordnance Survey of the United Kingdom. 8vo. Edinb., 1886.   A 6 R 31

WHITE (WALTER). Holidays in Tyrol Kufstein, Klobenstein, and Paneveggio. 8vo. Lond., 1876.   D 7 R 1

Holidays in Tyrol, Klobenstein, Paneveggio, and Obladio. 12mo. Leipzig, 1881.   D 7 P 14

July Holiday in Saxony, Bohemia, and Silesia. 8vo. Lond., 1857.   D 8 Q 50

Londoner's Walk to the Land's End. 8vo. Lond., 1855.   D 7 R 38

Month in Yorkshire. 8vo. Lond., 1858.   D 8 It 30

Rhymes. 8vo. Lond., 1873.   H 8 V 23

Report on the East Anglian Earthquake. [*See* MELDOLA, R.]   A 9 S 12

WHITE (Sergt. William), R.A. Memoirs of Sergeant William Marjouram, Royal Artillery; including Six Years' Service in New Zealand, during the late Maori War. 12mo. Lond., 1861.* MC 1 P 23

WHITE (William Hale). Ethic demonstrated in Geometrical Order. [*See* Spinoza, B. de.]

WHITEFIELD (George), A.B. Journal of a Voyage from London to Savannah, in Georgia. 12mo. Lond., 1826. C 1 P 7

Life of; by the Rev. Samuel Kent. (Pam. Bb.) 12mo. Sydney. (n.d.) MG 1 P 49

WHITEHEAD (C.) Reports on Insects injurious to Hop Plants, Corn Crops, and Fruit Crops in Great Britain. 3 vols. (in 1) roy. 8vo. Lond., 1885–86. A 13 U 12

WHITEHEAD (John). Davidson's Precedents. [*See* Davidson, C.]

WHITEHEAD (Paul). Life and Poems of. [*See* Chalmers, A., *and* Johnson, S.]

WHITEHEAD (William). Creusa, Queen of Athens: a Tragedy. (Bell's Brit. Theatre.) 18mo. Lond., 1797. H 2 P 45

Another copy. [*See* Brit. Drama 2.]

The Roman Father: a Tragedy. (Bell's Brit. Theatre.) 18mo. Lond., 1792. H 2 P 40

Another copy. (Brit. Theatre.) 12mo. Lond., 1808. H 1 P 14

Another copy. (New Eng. Theatre.) 12mo. Lond., 1788. H 4 P 27

Another copy. [*See* Brit. Drama 2.]

The School for Lovers: a Comedy. (Bell's Brit. Theatre.) 18mo. Lond., 1793. H 2 P 25

Another copy. [*See.* Brit. Drama 4.]

Life and Poems of. [*See* Chalmers, A.]

WHITEHURST (Felix M.) My Private Diary during the Siege of Paris. 2 vols. 8vo. Lond., 1875. B 8 S 36, 37

WHITELAW (Rev. J.), M.R.I.A. History of the City of Dublin. [*See* Warburton, J.] B 15 Q 1, 2 ‡

WHITELOCK (R. H.) Lectures on Modern History. [*See* Schlegel, F.] B 14 P 1

WHITELOCKE (Sir Bulstrode). Journal of the Swedish Ambassy, in the years 1653–54, from the Commonwealth of England, Scotland, and Ireland; written by the Ambassador, the Lord Commissioner Whitelocke. 2 vols. 4to. Lond., 1772. B 2 T 9, 10

Memorials of the English Affairs; or, an Historical Account of what passed from the Beginning of the Reign of King Charles I, to King Charles II, his happy Restauration. Roy. fol. Lond., 1732. B 19 U 3 ‡

Notes upon the King's Writt for choosing Members of Parlement; published by Charles Morton, M.D.; with Index. 2 vols. 4to. Lond., 1766. B 2 T 17, 18

WHITELY (J.) Centennial Geography of New South Wales, designed for use in Public Schools. 12mo. Sydney, 1888. MD 1 T 43

WHITEMAN (John). Sparks and Sounds from a Colonial Anvil. 12mo. Melb., 1873. MH 1 R 30

WHITESIDE (James), A.M., &c. Italy in the 19th Century, contrasted with its Past Condition. 3 vols. 8vo. Lond., 1848. B 12 R 21–23

WHITFORD (W. C.), A.M. Historical Sketch of Education in Wisconsin; prepared for the National Centennial of 1876. 8vo. Madison, Wis., 1876. G 17 R 2

WHITGIFT (John), D.D., Archbishop of Canterbury. Life and Acts of. [*See* Strype, J., 3–5.]

WHITING (George). Products and Resources of Tasmania, as illustrated in the International Exhibition, 1862. 8vo. Hobart, 1862. MF 3 P 8

WHITING (William). War Powers under the Constitution of the United States, Military Arrests, Reconstruction, and Military Government; also War Claims of Aliens. With Notes, &c. 43rd ed. 8vo. Boston, 1871. F 3 P 12

WHITMAN (C. O.) Methods of Research in Microscopical Anatomy and Embryology. 8vo. Boston, 1885. A 27 U 31

WHITMAN (J.) Cameron's proposed Monthly Line of Steamers between Panama and Australia. (Pam., 30.) 8vo. New York, 1855. MJ 2 Q 18

WHITMAN (Walter). Walt Whitman, Poet and Democrat; by John Robertson. (Round Table Series.) 8vo. Edinb., 1884. C 6 U 28

Walt Whitman; by Richard Maurice Bucke, M.D. 8vo. Philad., 1883. C 4 S 45

Another copy; to which is added English Critics on Walt Whitman. Edited by Prof. E. Dowden. 8vo. Glasgow, 1884. C 4 S 46

[*See* Essays from the Critic.]

WHITNEY (Geffrey). "Choice of Emblems." A Facsimile Reprint; edited by Henry Green, M.A.; with an Introductory Dissertation, Essays, Literary and Bibliographical, and Explanatory Notes. 4to. Lond., 1866. J 8 V 7

WHITNEY (Rev. George H.), D.D. Hand-book of Bible Geography. Illustrated by nearly one hundred Engravings and forty Maps and Plans. 8vo. New York. 1875. D 11 R 12

WHITNEY (James Lyman). A Modern Proteus; or, a List of Books published under more than One Title. 12mo. New York, 1884. K 17 P 3

WHITNEY (Josiah D.), LL.D. Climatic Changes of Later Geological Times: a Discussion based on Observation made in the Cordilleras of North America. 4to. Cambridge, 1882. A 2 S 27 †

WHITNEY (PROF. WILLIAM DWIGHT), Ph.D., &c.　Life and Growth of Language. 8vo. Lond., 1875.　K 11 U 7

Index Verborum to the published Text of the Atharva-Veda.　Imp. 8vo.　New Haven, 1881.　K 14 R 3

Compendious German Grammar.　4th ed., with Supplement. 8vo. Lond., 1877.　K 11 V 26

WHITSON (T. W.)　Maoriland.　[*See* WILSON, A.]　MD 5 Q 42

WHITTIER (JOHN GREENLEAF).　A Biography; by Francis H. Underwood.　8vo.　Lond., 1884.　C 1 U 49

Poetical Works of.　Complete edition.　3 vols. 8vo. Boston, 1882–84.　H 8 R 14–16

Prose Works of. 2 vols. 8vo.　Boston, 1886.　J 12 T 4, 5

WHITTINGHAM (MAJOR C. B.)　Personal Recollections of a Ten Months' Residence in Berlin; also, Extracts from a Journal kept in Paris during the Crisis of 1839. 8vo. Lond., 1846.　D 6 T 10

WHITTOCK (NATHANIEL).　On the Construction and Decoration of the Shop Fronts of London.　Illustrated. 4to. Lond., 1840.　A 2 T 28

History of the County of Surrey.　[*See* ALLEN, T.]　B 4 U 20, 21

History of the County of York.　Views.　[*See* ALLEN, T.]　B 4 V 1–3, B 6 R 8–13

WHITTON (JOHN).　Description of the Lines and Works of Construction on the Railways of New South Wales. Sm. fol. Sydney, 1876.*　MA 1 P 1 †

New South Wales Railways: Section of the Great Southern Railway—Sydney to Albury; Section of the Great Western Railway—Sydney to Orange; Section of the Great Northern Railway—Newcastle to Tamworth. 3 vols. ob. fol. Sydney, 1877.　MA 1 P 1–3 ‡

Report to the Hon. the Secretary for Public Works on the Railways in course of Construction, and the Trial Surveys for proposed Extensions in the Colony of New South Wales, 1 June, 1878.　Fol.　Sydney, 1878.　MA 1 P 1 ‡

Report on the Trial Surveys for proposed Railway Extensions. Fol. Sydney, 1879.　MJ 2 U 5

Map showing the Railways of New South Wales. 8vo. Sydney, 1883.　MD 5 P 13 ‡

WHITWORTH (CHARLES), LORD.　Account of Russia as it was in 1710. 12mo. Strawberry Hill, 1758. D 7 P 21

WHITWORTH (GEORGE CLIFFORD).　An Anglo-Indian Dictionary: a Glossary of Indian Terms used in English and of such English or other Non-Indian Terms as have obtained Special Meanings in India.　8vo.　Lond., 1885.　C 15 P 7

WHITWORTH (ROBERT P.)　Stories told round the Camp Fire; compiled from the Note-book of "Mr. Daniel Digwell" [R. P. Whitworth].　[*See* EVANS, G. C.] MJ 1 U 8

Baillière's New South Wales Gazetteer.　[*See* BALLIÈRE, F. F.]

Baillière's Victorian Gazetteer.　[*See* BALLIÈRE, F. F.]

WHYMPER (EDWARD).　Scrambles amongst the Alps, in the years 1860–69. With Illustrations. 8vo. Lond., 1871.　D 6 T 25

WHYMPER (F.)　The Sea: its Stirring Story of Adventure, Peril, and Heroism.　Illustrated.　4 vols. imp. 8vo.　Lond., 1878–81.　J 2 U 6–9

Fisheries of the World: an illustrated and Descriptive Record of the International Fisheries Exhibition, 1883. Imp. 8vo.　Lond., 1884.　A 15 S 17

WICHMANN (A.)　Geologic Ost-Asiens und Australiens. [*See* GEOLOGISCHEN REICHS-MUSEUMS IN LEIDEN.]

WICKES (C.), ARCHITECT.　Handy-book on Villa Architecture. 8vo. Lond., 1862.　A 2 U 6

WICKES (E. W.)　Brief Outline of English Grammar; adapted for Australian Beginners, also for the use of Pupils who are able to devote only a short time to the study of Grammar.　18mo.　Adelaide, 1864.　MJ 2 P 34

Brief Outline of the History of England.　4th ed. 18mo. Adelaide, 1865.　MJ 2 P 34

Geography for Australian Beginners; with Notices of Australian Discovery and Exploration; Sacred Geography; and Maps. 18mo. Adelaide, 1865.　MJ 2 P 34

WICKHAM (CAPT. E. H.), R.A.　Influence of Firearms on Tactics.　[*See* INFLUENCE.]　A 16 T 27

WICKHAM (REV. HILL).　Journals of T. S. Whalley. [*See* WHALLEY, T. S.]　C 9 P 47, 48

WICLIF OR WYCLIFFE (JOHN), D.D.　Joannis Wiclefi, Viri undiquaque piissimi, Dialogorum Libri Quatuor, quorum primus Divinitatem et Ideas tractat.　4to. Francofurti, 1753.　G 4 R 25

Wycklyffe's Wycket: whych he made in Kyng Rychards Days the Second.　Imprynted at Norenburch, 1546. Reprinted by Thos. P. Pantin. Sm. 4to. Oxford, 1828.　G 8 P 12

John Wycliffe and his English Precursors; by Prof. Lechler, D.D.; translated from the German by the late Prof. Lorimer, D.D.　8vo.　Lond., 1878.　C 6 U 29

De Ortu ac Progressu Hæresum J. Witclefi in Angli Presbyteri.　[*See* GRASSI, P. M.]

Wiclif and Hus.　[*See* LOSERTH, PROF. J.]

Writings of.　[*See* BRITISH REFORMERS, 12.]

Wycliffite Version of the Books of Job, Psalms, &c. [*See* BIBLES, &c.]

[*See* BOSWORTH, REV. J.]

WIDOWSON (HENRY).　Present State of Van Diemen's Land; comprising an Account of its Agricultural Capabilities.　8vo.　Lond., 1829.*　MD 4 V 9

WIEDEMANN (F. J.)　[*See* SJÖGREN, J. A.]

WIEDERSHEIM (R.)　Elements of the Comparative Anatomy of Vertebrates; translated by W. N. Parker. Roy. 8vo. Lond., 1886.　A 27 U 29

WIELAND (CHRISTOPHER MARTIN VON). Les Aventures Merveilleuses. [*See* CABINET DES FÉES, 36.]

Oberon: a Poem; from the German of Wieland, by W. Sotheby. 3rd ed. 2 vols. 12mo. Lond., 1826.
H 8 R 6, 7

Oberon : a Romantic Fairy Tale. (Cumberland's Eng. Theatre.) 12mo. Lond., 1829.   H 2 Q 13

Republic of Fools ; being a History of the State and People of Abdera, in Thrace ; translated by Henry Christmas, M.A. 2 vols. 8vo. Lond.,1861. J 4 R 19, 20

WIESENER (LOUIS). Youth of Queen Elizabeth, 1533–58 ; edited by Charlotte M. Yonge. 2 vols. 8vo. Lond., 1879.   C 2 P 11, 12

WIFE OF AN OFFICER IN THE 16TH FOOT, The. [*See* ASHMORE, MRS. HARRIETTE.]

WIFFEN (J. H.) Life of Tasso. [*See* TASSO, T.]

WIGAN FREE PUBLIC LIBRARY. Index Catalogue of Books and Papers relating to Mining, Metallurgy, and Manufactures; by Henry Tennyson Folkard, Reference Department. Roy. 8vo. Southport, 1880.   K 8 Q 17

WIGGINS (JOHN), F.G.S. "Monster" Misery of Ireland: a Practical Treatise on the relation of Landlord and Tenant. 8vo. Lond., 1844.   F 5 T 14

Practice of Embanking Lands from the Sea. New ed. (Weale.) ' 12mo. Lond., 1867.   A 17 P 13

WIGHT (GEORGE). Queensland, the Field for British Labour and Enterprise, and the Source of England's Cotton Supply. 2nd ed. 12mo. Lond., 1862.*   MD 4 Q 19

WIGHT (THOMAS). History of the Rise and Progress of the People called Quakers in Ireland, 1653–1700; afterwards revised and continued to 1751 by John Rutty. 4th ed. 8vo. Lond., 1811.   G 15 Q 20

WIGHTWICK (GEORGE). Hints to Young Architects; revised and enlarged by G. H. Guillaume. (Weale.) 12mo. Lond., 1875.   A 17 Q 31

WIGNER (G. W.), F.C.S. Sugar-growing and Refining. [*See* LOCK, C. G. W.]

WIGRAM (REV. SPENCER ROBERT), M.A. Chronicles of the Abbey of Elstow; with some Notes on the Architecture of the Church, by M. J. Buckley. 8vo. Oxford, 1885.   B 7 Q 7

WILBERFORCE (EDWARD). Social Life in Munich. 8vo. Lond., 1863.   D 8 Q 42

Statute Law: the Principles which govern the Construction and Operation of Statutes. 8vo. Lond., 1881.
F 10 P 21

WILBERFORCE (REGINALD G.) Life of the Rt. Rev. Samuel Wilberforce. [*See* ASHWELL, A. R.] C 9 R 42–44

WILBERFORCE (ROBERT ISAAC AND REV. SAMUEL). Life of William Wilberforce; by his Sons. 5 vols. 8vo. Lond., 1838.   C 4 U 34–38

5 K

WILBERFORCE (RT. REV. SAMUEL), BISHOP OF WINCHESTER. Life of; with Selections from his Diaries and Correspondence, by A. R. Ashwell, M.A., and Reginald G. Wilberforce. 2 vols. 8vo. Lond.,1880–82. C 9 R 42–44
[*See* WILBERFORCE, R. I.]

WILBERFORCE (WILLIAM). Letter to the Gentlemen, Clergy, and Freeholders of Yorkshire. (Pam. Dd.) 8vo. Lond., 1807.   F 12 P 22

Life of; by his Sons, Robert Isaac Wilberforce, and Samuel Wilberforce. 5 vols. 8vo. Lond., 1838. C 4 U 34–38

Practical View of the prevailing Religious Systems of professed Christians in the Higher and Middle Classes in this Country. 8vo. Lond., 1805.   G 15 R 2

Letter to William Wilberforce [on the above]. [*See* WAKEFIELD, G.]

WILCOCKE (SAMUEL HULL). New Pocket Dictionary of the English-Dutch and Dutch-English Languages. Sq. 18mo. Lond., 1811.   K 11 S 18

WILCOCKS (J. C.) The Sea-Fisherman ; comprising the chief Methods of Hook and Line Fishing in the British and other Seas, and Remarks on Nets, Boats, and Boating. 4th ed. 12mo. Lond., 1884.   A 16 P 22

WILD (CHARLES). Cathedrals of Canterbury and York: a Series of Views. Imp. 4to. Lond., 1809.   A 4 P 9 ‡

Illustration of the Architecture and Sculpture of the Cathedral Church of Lincoln. Imp. 4to. Lond., 1819.
A 4 P 9 ‡

Illustration of the Architecture and Sculpture of the Cathedral Church of Worcester. Imp. 4to. Lond., 1823.
A 1 P 8 ‡

Illustration of the Architecture of the Cathedral Church of Chester. Imp. 4to. Lond., 1813.   A 4 P 9 ‡

Illustration of the Architecture of the Cathedral Church of Lichfield. Imp. 4to. Lond., 1813.   A 4 P 9 ‡

Views of Metropolitan Church of Canterbury. Imp. 4to. Lond., 1809.   A 4 P 9 ‡

Views of Metropolitan Church of York. Imp. 4to. Lond., 1809.   A 4 P 9 ‡

WILD (MRS. E.), "BESS OF THE FOREST, THE LINCOLNSHIRE LASS." Long Bay. 18mo. Sydney, 1865. MJ 1 P 16

Squire Brown and Mr. Robinson's Ride. 16mo. Sydney, 1865.   MJ 1 P 16

The Arrival of Squire Turner and Lady Lucy; Mr. Robinson's Courtship. 16mo. Sydney,1865.   MJ 1 P 16

The Landscape. 16mo. Sydney, 1865.   MJ 1 P 16

The Fortune-Teller. 16mo. Sydney, 1865.   MJ 1 P 16

WILD (JOHN JAMES), PH.D., &c. At Anchor: a Narrative of Experiences Afloat and Ashore during the Voyage of H.M.S. *Challenger*, 1872–76. Imp. 4to. Lond., 1878.
MD 2 P 5 ‡

WILDE (JACOB DE). Selecta Numismata Antiqua, ex Musæo Jacobi de Wilde. 4to. Amsterd., 1692.   A 13 S 39

WILDE (JANE FRANCESCA SPERANZA), LADY, "SPERANZA."
Ancient Legends, Mystic Charms, and Superstitions of
Ireland. 2 vols. 8vo. Lond., 1887.   B 11 P 26, 27

Driftwood from Scandinavia. 8vo. Lond., 1884.
                                                D 8 S 42

WILDE (SIR WILLIAM R.), M.D., &c. Austria; its Literary,
Scientific, and Medical Institutions. 8vo. Dublin, 1843.
                                                D 8 R 32

Closing Years of Dean Swift's Life; with Remarks on
Stella, and on some of his Writings hitherto unnoticed.
8vo. Dublin, 1849.   C 9 U 33

Memoirs of Gabriel Beranger, and his Labours in the
Cause of Irish Art and Antiquities, 1760–80. With
Illustrations. Roy. 8vo. Dublin, 1880.   C 3 W 4

Narrative of a Voyage to Madeira, Teneriffe and along
the Shores of the Mediterranean. 2 vols. 8vo. Dublin,
1840.   D 9 S 26, 27

WILDEY (CAPT.) Treatise on Chinese Labourers as compared with Europeans, the Tribes of Africa, and the
various Castes of Asiatics. (Pam 2.) 8vo. Lond.,
1836.   MJ 2 P 37

WILDEY (WILLIAM BRACKLEY). Australasia and the
Oceanic Region; with some Notice of New Guinea. 8vo.
Melb., 1876.   MD 4 R 25

WILHELM (CAPT. THOMAS). Military Dictionary and
Gazetteer. Revised ed. Roy. 8vo. Philad., 1881.
                                            A 29 V 12

WILHELMI (CHARLES). Manners and Customs of the
Australian Natives. 8vo. Melb., 1862.   MD 1 V 9

WILKES (ADMIRAL CHARLES), U.S.N. Narrative of the
United States Exploring Expedition, during the years
1838–42. Text and Atlas. 6 vols. imp. 4to. Philad.,
1845.   D 31 P 1–6.‡

Another copy; condensed and abridged Roy. 8vo. Lond.,
1845.*   MD 3 V 12

WILKES (GEORGE). Shakespeare, from an American
point of view, including an inquiry as to his Religious
Faith and his knowledge of Law; with the Baconian
Theory considered. 8vo. Lond., 1877.   C 9 R 23

WILKES (JOHN), LORD MAYOR OF LONDON. Biographies
of John Wilkes and W. Cobbett; by J. S. Watson.
With Portrait. 8vo. Lond., 1870.   C 5 Q 30

Speeches in the House of Commons, 1775–87. 8vo.
Lond., 1786–87.   F 4 U 16

English Liberty; being a Collection of interesting Tracts,
from the year 1762 to 1769, containing the Private
Correspondence, Public Letters, Speeches, and Addresses
of John Wilkes, Esq. Sm. fol. Lond., 1771. B 18 Q 1‡

WILKIE (SIR DAVID): a Biography; by J. W. Mollett,
B.A. (Great Artists.) 8vo. Lond., 1881.   C 3 T 3‡

Life of; with his Journals, Tours, and Critical Remarks
on Works of Art, and a Selection from his Correspondence;
by Allan Cunningham. 3 vols. 8vo. Lond., 1843.
                                            C 9 S 37–39

WILKIE (SIR DAVID)—*continued.*
Observations on the Communication of, Relative to the
National Gallery. [*See* GWILT, C. P.]   A 7 Q 13

Etchings by Sir David Wilkie, R.A., and by Andrew
Geddes, A.R.A.; with Biographical Sketches, by David
Laing, F.S.A.S. Sm. fol. Edinb., 1875.   A 23 R 11‡

WILKIE (WILLIAM), D.D. Life and Poems of. [*See*
CHALMERS, A.]

WILKIN (SIMON), F.L.S. Sir Thomas Browne's Works.
[*See* BROWNE, SIR T.]   J 10 T 22–25

WILKINS (SIR CHARLES), KNT., &c. The Bhāgvăt Gēĕtā;
or, Dialogues of Krēĕshnā and Arjŏŏn, in eighteen Lectures, with Notes. Roy. 4to. Lond., 1785.   G 12 R 4†

WILKINS (DAVID), S.T.P. Concilia Magnæ Brittanniæ
et Hiberniæ, a Synodo Verolamiensi A.D. 446, ad Londi-
nensem A.D. 1717. 4 vols. imp. fol. Lond., 1737.
                                            G 35 Q 9–12‡

Leges Anglo-Saxonicæ Ecclesiasticæ et Civiles; accedunt
Leges Edvardi Latinæ, Guilielmi Conquestoris Gallo-
Normannicæ, et Henrici I Latinæ. Fol. Lond., 1721.
                                            F 29 P 12‡

WILKINS (GEORGE), M.A. Growth of the Homeric
Poems: a Discussion on their Origin and Authorship.
8vo. Dublin, 1885.   J 12 V 3

WILKINS (WILLIAM), M.A., &c. On the Change in the
line of Front of the Buildings for the National Gallery.
8vo. Lond., 1833.   A 7 Q 13

Prolusiones Architectonicæ; or, Essays on subjects
connected with Grecian and Roman Architecture. 4to.
Lond., 1837.   A 2 U 27

Civil Architecture of Vitruvius. [*See* VITRUVIUS.]
                                            A 23 R 19‡

WILKIN (W.) Geography of New South Wales; new ed.,
revised. 12mo. Sydney, 1881.   MD 1 T 38

Principles that underlie the Art of Teaching : six Lectures,
delivered at the Technical College, Sydney, under
the auspices of the Board of Technical Education. 8vo.
Sydney, 1886.   MG 1 R 8

Australasia: a Descriptive and Pictorial Account of
the Australian and New Zealand Colonies, Tasmania,
and the adjacent Lands. 8vo. Lond., 1888.* MD 1 R 1

WILKINS (A. S.) [*See* CURTIUS, G.]

WILKINS (W. WALKER). Political Ballads of the
Seventeenth and Eighteenth Centuries; annotated.
2 vols. 8vo. Lond., 1860.   H 8 R 21, 22

WILKINSON (ALFRED J.) The Australian Cook : a
Complete Manual of Cookery suitable for the Australian
Colonies ; with especial reference to the Gas Cooking
Stove. 2nd ed. 12mo. Melb., 1877.*   MA 1 V 37

WILKINSON (REV. C. A.) Reminiscences of the Court
and Times of King Ernest of Hanover. 2 vols. 8vo.
Lond., 1886.   B 9 Q 35, 36

WILKINSON (C. S.), F.G.S., &c. Notes on the Geology of New Soutı Wales. 4to. Sydney, 1882. MA 2 R 8

WILKINSON (GEORGE BLAKISTON). Soutı Australia: its Advantages and Resources; being a Description of tıat Colony, and a Manual of Information for Emigrants. 8vo. Lond., 1848.* MD 5 Q 21

Working Man's Hand-book to Soutı Australia. 12mo. Lond., 1849. MD 2 Q 56

WILKINSON (GEORGE). Practical Geology and Ancient Arcıitecture of Ireland. Roy. 8vo. Lond., 1845. A 9 U 11

WILKINSON (JAMES JOHN GARTH). Compulsory Vaccination, its Wickedness to the Poor. (Pam., Cp.) 8vo. Lond. (n.d.) A 12 S 34

Emanuel Swedenborg: a Biograpıy. 8vo. Lond., 1849. C 4 S 31

Small-pox and Vaccination. (Pam., Cp.) 8vo. Lond., 1871. A 12 S 34

The Generative Organs. [*See* SWEDENBORG, E.]

WILKINSON (REV. JOHN F.) Friendly Society Movement: its Origin, Rise, and Growtı; its Social, Moral, and Educational Influences. 8vo. Lond., 1886. F 5 S 16

WILKINSON (SIR JOHN GARDNER), F.R.S., &c. Dalmatia and Montenegro; witı a Journey to Mostar, in Herzgovina, and Remarks on the Slavonic Nations; the History of Dalmatia and Ragusa; the Uscocs, &c., &c. 2 vols. 8vo. Lond., 1848. B 7 T 35, 36

Modern Egypt and Tıebes; being a Description of Egypt. 2 vols. 8vo. Lond., 1843. D 2 Q 14, 15

Manners and Customs of the Ancient Egyptians. First and Second Series; witı Index and Plates. 6 vols. 8vo. Lond., 1837–41. B 2 R 28–33

Materia Hieroglyphica; containing the Egyptian Pantıeon, and the succession of the Pıaraoıs. 8vo. Malta, 1828. B 2 S 4

Topograpıy of Tıebes, and general view of Egypt. 8vo. Lond., 1835. D 11 U 17

WILKINSON (ROBERT). Londina Illustrata—Tıeatrum Illustrata: Grapıic and Historic Memorials of Monasteries, Cıurcıes, Cıapels, Scıools, Tıeatres, &c., in the Cities and Suburbs of London and Westminister. 2 vols. imp. 4to. Lond., 1808–34. B 19 T 7, 8 ‡

Atlas Classica; being a Collection of Maps of the Countries mentioned by the Ancient Autıors, botı Sacred and Profane. Imp. 4to. Lond., 1830. D 33 Q 7 ‡

WILKINSON (T. T.), F.R.A.S., &c. Lancasıire Legends, &c. [*See* HARLAND, J.] B 3 R 11

WILKINSON (WILLIAM HATTAM). Australian Magistrate. 3rd ed. Roy. 8vo. Sydney, 1876. MF 1 Q 10

Anotıer copy. 4th ed. 8vo. Sydney, 1881. MF 1 Q 11

Anotıer copy. 5th ed. 8vo. Sydney, 1885. MF 1 Q 12

Reports of Cases. [*See* NEW SOUTH WALES SUPREME COURT.

Plunkett's Australian Magistrate. [*See* PLUNKETT, J. H.] MF 1 Q 9

WILKS (MARK). The Tıree Arcıbisıops. [*See* WILKS, WASHINGTON.] C 2 U 7

WILKS (REV. THEODORE C.), M.A. History of Hampsıire. [*See* WOODWARD, B. B.] B 2 U 5–7

WILKS (WASHINGTON AND MARK). The Tıree Arcıbisıops: Lanfranc, Anselm, a'Beckett. 8vo. Lond., 1858. C 2 U 7

WILL (J. SHIRESS). Wıarton's Law Lexicon. [*See* WHARTON, J. J. S.]

WILLDENOW (D. C.) Principles of Botany and of Vegetable Pıysiology. 8vo. Edinb., 1805. A 4 Q 2

WILLEMÖES-SUHM (R. VON), PH.D., &c. On the Development of Cirripedia. (Roy. Soc. Pubs., 2.) 4to. Lond., 1876. A 11 P 3 †

WILLERT (P. F.), M.A. Reign of Lewis XI. 8vo. Lond., 1876. B 9 P 12

WILLIAM I (KING OF ENGLAND). Guillaume le Conquérant. [*See* TODIÈRE, L.]

William the Conqueror and ıis Companions; by J. R. Plancıé. 2 vols. 8vo. Lond., 1874. B 7 Q 10, 11

LAWS of. [*See* KELHAM, R.]

WILLIAM I (EMPEROR OF GERMANY AND KING OF PRUSSIA). The Emperor William and ıis Reign; from the Frencı of Edouard Simon. 2 vols. 8vo. Lond., 1886. C 7 U 57, 58

WILLIAM III (KING OF ENGLAND). Letters illustrative of the Reign of William III, 1696–1708, addressed to the Duke of Sırewsbury, by J. Vernon; edited by G. P. R. James. 3 vols. 8vo. Lond., 1841. C 9 S 40–42

Letters of William III and Louis XIV. [*See* GRIMBLOT, P.]

WILLIAM IV (KING OF ENGLAND). Life and Reign of William IV; by the Rev. G. N. Wright, M.A. 2 vols. 8vo. Lond., 1837. C 9 S 43, 44

Life and Times of William IV; including a View of Social Life and Manners during ıis Reign, by Percy Fitzgerald. 2 vols. 8vo. Lond., 1884. C 9 S 45, 46

Memoirs of the Courts and Cabinets of William IV and Queen Victoria; by the Duke of Buckingıam and Cıandos. 2 vols. 8vo. Lond., 1861. B 3 S 13, 14

WILLIAM OF MALMESBURY. Cıronicle of the Kings of England, to the Reign of King Stepıen; witı Notes by J. A. Giles. 12mo. Lond., 1866. B 3 P 12

Gesta Regum Anglorum atque Historia Novella, ad fidem codicum Manuscriptorum recensuit Tıomas Duffus Hardy. 2 vols. 8vo. Lond., 1840. B 5 T 32, 33

History of the Kings of England, and the Modern History of William of Malmesbury; translated from the Latin, by the Rev. Joın Sıarpe, B.A. 4to. Lond., 1815. B 2 U 34

Opera omnia. [*See* MIGNE, J. P., SERIES LATINA, 179.]

WILLIAM HENRY (PRINCE), DUKE OF GLOUCESTER. Queen Anne's Son: Memoirs of William Henry, Duke of Gloucester ; reprinted from a Tract (by Jenkin Lewis) published in 1789, and edited by W. J. Loftie. 12mo. Lond., 1881.   C 1 R 30

WILLIAMS (A. LUKYN), B.A. Famines in India ; their Causes and possible Prevention. (Prize Essay, 1875.) 8vo. Lond., 1876.   F 5 S 17

WILLIAMS (BENJAMIN SAMUEL), F.L.S., &c. Orchid Album. [*See* WARNER, R.]

Orchid-grower's Manual. 6th ed. 8vo. Lond., 1885.   A 4 Q 23

WILLIAMS (CHARLES). The First Week of Time; or, Scripture in Harmony with Science. 12mo. Lond., 1863.   G 9 Q 6

WILLIAMS (C. GREVILLE). Hand-book of Chemical Manipulation. 8vo. Lond., 1857.   A 5 S 3

WILLIAMS (CHARLES H.), AND MANDY (H. C.) Ecclesiastical Manual for New South Wales. Fol. Sydney, 1882.*   MF 1 U 15

WILLIAMS (CHARLES J. B.), M.D., &c. Memoirs of Life and Work. 8vo. Lond., 1884.   C 9 Q 49

WILLIAMS (CHARLES P.) Southern Sunbeams: an Australian Annual for the Field, the River, and the Home Circle. Illustrated. 8vo. Melb., 1879.   MJ 1 T 46

WILLIAMS (C. WYE), A.I.C.E. Elementary Treatise on the Combustion of Coal, and the Prevention of Smoke, chemically and practically considered. (Weale.) 12mo. Lond., 1858.   A 17 P 62
[*See* CLARK, D. K.]

WILLIAMS (REV. EDWARD A.), M.A. Cruise of the *Pearl* round the World; with an Account of the Operations of the Naval Brigade in India. 8vo. Lond., 1859. D 10 R 26

WILLIAMS (EDWARD H.) [*See* BURNHAM, G.]   A 9 P 2 †

WILLIAMS (E. M.) [*See* MASTERS, M. T.]   A 4 S 3

WILLIAMS (FRANCIS H.) [*See* BRUNTON, T. L.] A 12 U 6

WILLIAMS (FREDERICK S.) Our Iron Roads; their History, Construction, and Social Influences. 8vo. Lond., 1852.   A 6 S 8

Our Iron Roads; their History, Construction, and Administration. 5th ed. 8vo. Lond., 1884.   A 6 S 9

WILLIAMS (REV. GEORGE), M.A. The Holy City; or, Historical and Topographical Notices of Jerusalem; with Illustrations from Sketches by the Rev. W. F. Witts. 8vo. Lond., 1845.   B 10 P 30

WILLIAMS (GEORGE W.) History of the Negro Race in America, 1619–1880: Negroes as Slaves, as Soldiers and as Citizens. 2 vols. 8vo. New York, 1883. B 1 T 36, 37

WILLIAMS (HARTLEY), JUDGE. Religion without Superstition. 8vo. Melb., 1885.*   MG 1 P 23

Another copy. 3rd ed., revised. 8vo. Melb., 1885.   MG 1 P 25

WILLIAMS (HELEN MARIA). Travels to the Equinoctial Regions of the New Continent. [*See* HUMBOLDT, F. H. A. VON, BARON, AND BONPLAND, A.] D 3 T 19–24

Researches concerning the Institutions and Monuments of the Ancient Inhabitants of America. [*See* HUMBOLDT, F. H. A. VON, BARON.]

WILLIAMS (REV. HENRY), ARCHDEACON OF WAIMATE. Life of : by Hugh Carleton. 2 vols. 8vo. Auckland, 1874–77.   MC 1 Q 11, 12

WILLIAMS (HENRY L.) Selections from Poetical Works of Victor Hugo. [*See* HUGO, V. M.]

WILLIAMS (HOWARD), M.A. English Letters and Letter-writers of the 18th Century. 1st Series. Swift and Pope. 8vo. Lond., 1886.   C 2 V 29

WILLIAMS (REV. JAMES). System of Shorthand. [*See* ANDERSON, T.]

WILLIAMS (REV. JOHN). Life and Actions of Alexander the Great. 2nd ed. 12mo. Lond., 1829.   C 1 P 4

WILLIAMS (REV. JOHN). Memoirs of the Life of ; by Ebenezer Prout. 3rd thousand. 8vo. Lond., 1843.   C 11 P 19

Another copy. 3rd thousand. 8vo. Lond., 1843.   MC 1 R 26

Narrative of Missionary Enterprise in the South Sea Islands; with Remarks upon the Natural History of the Islands, Origin, Languages, Traditions, and Usages of the Inhabitants. Illustrated. 8vo. Lond., 1837. MD 6 Q 1

Another copy. 6th thousand. 8vo. Lond., 1837.*   MD 6 Q 2

Another copy. 6th thousand. 8vo. Lond., 1838.   MD 6 Q 4

Another copy. 27th thousand. Roy. 8vo. Lond., 1840.   MD 6 Q 5

WILLIAMS (JOHN BUTLER), C.E., &c. Practical Geodesy ; comprising Chain Surveying, and the use of Surveying Instruments, Levelling and Tracing of Contours. 3rd ed. 8vo. Lond., 1855.   A 6 T 25

WILLIAMS (JOHN CARVEL). Disestablishment. [*See* RICHARD, H.]

WILLIAMS (JOSHUA). Law of Real Property. 11th ed., edited by T. C. Williams. 8vo. Lond., 1882. F 3 P 2

WILLIAMS (DR. JOSIAH), F.R.G.S. Life in the Soudan: Adventures among the Tribes, and Travels in Egypt, in 1881–82. Illustrated. 8vo. Lond., 1884. D 2 R 12

WILLIAMS (SIR MONIER), K.C.S.I., M.A., &c. Indian Wisdom; or, Examples of the Religious, Philosophical, and Ethical Doctrines of the Hindūs. 8vo. Lond., 1875. G 4 S 13

Modern India and the Indians; being a Series of Impressions, Notes, and Essays. 3rd ed. 8vo. Lond., 1879. D 6 Q 32

Religious Thought and Life in India: an Account of the Religions of the Indian Peoples, based on a Life's Study of their Literature, and on Personal Investigations in their own Country. Part 1. Vedism, Brāhmanism, and Hindūism. 8vo. Lond., 1883. G 4 S 23

WILLIAMS (REV. ROBERT), M.A. Enwogion Cymru: a Biographical Dictionary of Eminent Welshmen, from the earliest times. 8vo. Llandovery, 1852. C 11 Q 9

WILLIAMS (ROBERT), B.A. Nichomachean Ethics of Aristotle. [*See* ARISTOTELES.]

WILLIAMS (PROF. ROBERT FOLKESTONE). Lives of the English Cardinals; including Historical Notices of the Papal Court, from Nicholas Breakspear (Pope Adrian IV) to Thomas Wolsey, Cardinal Legate. 2 vols. 8vo. Lond., 1868. C 10 Q 23, 24

Shakespeare and his Friends; or, the "Golden Age" of Merry England. 3 vols. 8vo. Lond., 1838. J 4 R 24–26

Court and Times of James the First. [*See* BIRCH, REV. T.] C 10 S 37, 38

Court and Times of Charles the First. [*See* BIRCH, REV. T.] C 10 S 39, 40

WILLIAMS (SAMUEL), LL.D. Natural and Civil History of Vermont. 2nd ed. 2 vols. 8vo. Burlington, 1809. B 1 T 27, 28

WILLIAMS (PROF. SAMUEL WELLS), LL.D. The Middle Kingdom: a Survey of the Geography, Government, Literature, Social Life, Arts, and History of the Chinese Empire and its Inhabitants. Revised ed. 2 vols. 8vo. Lond., 1883. D 5 T 31, 32

Syllabic Dictionary of the Chinese Language; arranged according to the Wu-Fang Yuen Yin, with the Pronunciation of the Characters as heard in Peking, Canton, Amoy, and Shanghai. Roy. 4to. Shanghai, 1874. K 13 U 10

WILLIAMS (THOMAS), AND CALVERT (JAMES). Fiji and Fijians: the Islands and their Inhabitants. 2 vols. 12mo. Lond., 1858. MD 4 R 11, 12

WILLIAMS (THOMAS C.) New Zealand; the Manawatu Purchase completed; or, the Treaty of Waitangi broken. 8vo. Lond., 1868. MF 2 P 11

WILLIAMS (RT. REV. WILLIAM), D.C.L., BISHOP OF WAIAPU. Dictionary of the New Zealand Language, and a concise Grammar. 2nd ed. 8vo. Lond., 1852.* MK 1 P 31

Dictionary of the New Zealand Language. 3rd ed., with Additions by the Ven. W. L. Williams, B.A. 8vo. Lond., 1871. MK 1 Q 26

Christianity among the New Zealanders. With Illustrations. 8vo. Lond., 1867.* MG 1 P 34

WILLIAMS (W.) Manual of Telegraphy. Illustrated. 8vo. Lond., 1885. A 5 R 53

WILLIAMS (WILLIAM). Secondary Punishments discussed; by "Humanitas, an Emigrant of 1821." Sydney, 1834. (*Reprinted.*) Lond., 1835. MF 1 Q 15

WILLIAMS (WILLIAM ELLIS HUME). Irish Parliament, from the year 1782 to 1800. 8vo. Lond., 1879. B 11 R 13

WILLIAM (WILLIAM FRITH). Historical and Statistical Account of the Bermudas, from their discovery to the present time. 8vo. Lond., 1848. B 1 R 11

WILLIAMS (REV. WILLIAM F.) Syrian Antilegomena Epistles. [*See* HALL, I. H.] G 3 P 22 †

WILLIAMS (VEN. WILLIAM LEONARD), B.A. First Lessons in the Maori Language; with a short Vocabulary. 18mo. Auckland, 1872. MK 1 P 36

Lessons in the English Language for Maori Schools. 8vo. Wellington, 1875.* MK 1 P 37

[*See* WILLIAMS, RT. REV. W.]

WILLIAMS (W. M.), F.C.S., &c. Iron and Steel. (Brit. Manuf. Indust.) 12mo. Lond., 1876. A 17 S 34

Oils and Candles. (Brit. Manuf. Indust.) 12mo. Lond., 1876. A 17 S 36

Explosive Compounds. (Brit. Manuf. Indust.) 12mo. Lond., 1876. A 17 S 38

WILLIAMSON (ALEXANDER W.) Chemistry for Students. (Clar. Press.) 3rd ed. 8vo. Oxford, 1873. A 21 P 5

WILLIAMSON (PROF. BENJAMIN), M.A., &c., AND TARLETON (FRANCIS A.), LL.D. Elementary Treatise on Dynamics; containing Applications to Thermodynamics. 8vo. Lond., 1885. A 16 Q 8

WILLIAMSON (WILLIAM C.), F.R.S. Organization of the Fossil Plants of the Coal Measures. Part 7. (Roy. Soc. Pubs., 2.) 4to. Lond., 1876. A 11 P 3 †

Organization of the Fossil Plants of the Coal Measures. Parts 8, 9. (Roy. Soc. Pubs., 4, 5.) 4to. Lond., 1877–79. A 11 P 5, 6 †

WILLIE'S FIRST ENGLISH BOOK, written for Young Maoris who can read their own Maori Tongue, and who wish to learn the English Language. 12mo. Wellington, 1872. MK 1 P 35

WILLIS (ALFRED). Wanderings among the High Alps. 8vo. Lond., 1856. D 9 Q 33

WILLIS (ARTHUR), GANN & CO. New Zealand Circular. Assisted Passages for Good Labourers and Mechanics to the Province of Canterbury. Free Grants of Land 40 to 500 acres and upwards in the Province of Auckland. 12mo. Lond. (n.d.) MJ 2 P 32

New Zealand Hand-book; or, Emigrant's Bradshaw; being a complete Guide to the Britain of the South. 12mo. Lond., 1859. MD 2 P 46

WILLIS (BROWNE), LL.D. Notitia Parliamentaria; containing an Account of the First Returns and Incorporations of the Cities, Towns, and Boroughs in England and Wales that send Members to Parliament. 8vo. Lond., 1750.   F 5 T 7

WILLIS (C. J.), M.D. Persia, as it is; being Sketches of Modern Persian Life and Character. 8vo. Lond., 1886.   D 5 U 8

WILLIS (REV. FRANCIS). Portrait of Dr. Willis. [*See* MANUSCRIPTS AND PORTRAITS.]   MF 1 U 21

WILLIS (J. A. C.) Map of Port Jackson and City of Sydney, showing the adjacent Municipalities. 8vo. Sydney, 1867.   MD 5 P 11 ‡

WILLIS (JOHN WALPOLE). Notes on the acquisition of New Zealand as a Dependency of New South Wales, with reference to Lands obtained by British Subjects from the Aborigines. (MS.—Pam. A.) Fol. Sydney, 1840.   MJ 2 U 1

WILLIS (NATHANIEL PARKER). Health Trip to the Tropics. 8vo. Lond., 1854.   D 3 R 51

Letters from under a Bridge, and Poems. Sm. 4to. Lond., 1840.   J 4 T 8

Life of E. A. Poe. [*See* POE, E. A.]

Loiterings of Travel. 3 vols. 8vo. Lond., 1840.   J 8 R 5-7

Canadian Scenery Illustrated; from Drawings, by W. H. Bartlett. 2 vols. 4to. Lond., 1842.   D 3 V 2, 3

WILLIS (ROBERT), M.D. Benedict de Spinoza; his Life, Correspondence, and Ethics. 8vo. Lond., 1870.   C 9 R 32

WILLIS (REV. ROBERT). Architectural History of the University of Cambridge; enlarged by J. C. Clark. 8vo. Camb., 1886.   A 3 Q 10-13

Machines and Tools for working in Metal, Wood, and other Materials. [*See* LOND. INTERN. EXHIB. 1851.]   A 16 Q 22

WILLIS AND SOTHERAN. Catalogue of Ancient and Modern Books. 8vo. Lond., 1862.   K 7 S 21

WILLIS (T. R. H.) Mortality and Management of Infants. [*See* AUSTRALASIAN HEALTH SOC.] MA 2 S 23

WILLIS-BUND (PROF. J. W.) [*See* BUND, PROF. J. W. WILLIS-.]

WILLISON (REV. JOHN). A Prophecy of the French Revolution and the downfall of Antichrist: Two Sermons. (Pam. Br.) 8vo. Lond., 1793.   C 16 S 18

WILLM (J.) Education of the People; with a preliminary Dissertation by J. P. Nichol. 2nd ed. 8vo. Edinb., 1859.   G 17 P 25

WILLMER (GEORGE). The Draper in Australia; being a Narrative of Three Years' Adventures and Experience at the Gold-fields, in the Bush, and in the chief Cities of Victoria and New South Wales. 12mo. Lond., 1856.   MD 2 R 22

WILLMET (JOHN). Lexicon Linguae Arabicae, in Coranum Haririum, et Vitam Timuri. 4to. Lugd. Bat., 1784.   K 16 S 24

WILLMOTT (REV. ROBERT ARIS). Pleasures of Literature. 5th ed., enlarged. 12mo. Lond., 1860.   J 1 W 33

WILLOUGHBY (HOWARD). Australian Pictures: drawn with Pen and Pencil; with a Map and 107 Illustrations. 4to. Lond., 1886.*   MA 7 P 25 †

WILLOUGHBY (PEREGRINE), LORD. Life of. [*See* BERTIE, LADY G.]   C 10 V 37

WILLOUGHBY-OSBORNE (MRS.) [*See* OSBORNE, MRS. WILLOUGHBY-]

WILLS (WILLIAM JOHN). Burke and Wills Exploring Expedition. [*See* BURKE, R. O'H.]   MJ 2 Q 23

Expedition in Search of Burke and Wills. [*See* BOURNE, G.]   MD 3 U 18

Expedition in Search of Burke and Wills. [*See* LANDSBOROUGH, W.]   MD 3 U 19

Portrait of. [*See* MANUSCRIPTS AND PORTRAITS.]

Successful Exploration through the Interior of Australia, from Melbourne to the Gulf of Carpentaria. 8vo. Lond., 1863.*   MD 2 T 29

WILLSON (HUGH BOWLBY). Currency; or, the Fundamental Principles of Monetary Science postulated, explained, and applied. 8vo. N. York, 1882.   F 5 S 27

WILLSON (RT. REV. R. W.), BISHOP OF HOBART. Application to the Imperial Government for Pension, or other Assistance, &c. (Pam. 26.) 8vo. Hobart, 1860. MJ 2 Q 14

WILMOT (CHARLES O. EARDLEY). Advice to Immigrants, in the shape of a few Familiar Chapters, pointing out their Duties towards their Employers, and towards each other. 2nd ed. (Pam. 39.) 12mo. Hobart, 1855. MJ 2 R 1

Six Letters on Subjects of Colonial Interest; being Letters addressed to the *Advertiser*, altered and added to. (Pam. 42.) 8vo. Hobart, 1855.   MJ 2 R 4

WILMOT (JAMES), D.D. "Dr. Wilmot's Polish Princes." [*See* THOMS, W. J.]   B 6 P 43

WILMOT (SIR JOHN C. EARDLEY), BART. Correspondence between the Secretary of State and Sir Eardley Wilmot, Bart., relative to the Recall of the latter from the Government of Van Diemen's Land. (Parl. Docs., 60.) Fol. Lond., 1847.   MF 4 ‡

WILMOT (SIR JOHN E. EARDLEY), BART. Reminiscences of the late Thomas Assheton Smith; or, the Pursuits of an English Country Gentleman. 8vo. Lond., 1860. C 9 U 26

WILSEN (F. C.) Bôrô Boedoor op het Eiland Java. [*See* LEEMANS, DR. C.]

WILSHIRE (J. R.) Letter to W. C. Wentworth Esq., M.C., on the subject of Municipal Revenue, as prayed for by the Corporation of the City of Sydney. (Parl. Docs., 41.) Fol. Sydney, 1844. MF 4 ‡

Letter to W. C. Wentworth, Esq., M.C., on the subject of Police Administration, as prayed for by the Corporation of the City of Sydney. (Parl. Docs., 41.) Fol. Sydney, 1844· MF 4 ‡

WILSON (ALEXANDER), AND BONAPARTE (C. L.) American Ornithology; or, the Natural History of the Birds of the United States. (Const. Misc.) 4 vols. 18mo. Edinb., 1831. K 10 R 1-4

WILSON (ALEXANDER), WADDELL (RUTHERFORD), AND WHITSON (T. W.) Maoriland: an Illustrated Hand-book to New Zealand, issued by the Union Steamship Company of New Zealand. 12mo. Melb., 1884.* MD 5 Q 42

WILSON (A. J.) Dictionary of Commerce and Commercial Navigation. [*See* MACCULLOCH, J. R.]

WILSON (ALEXANDER JOHNSTONE). Reciprocity, Bi-Metallism, and Land-Tenure Reform. 8vo. Lond., 1880. F 4 S 21

Resources of Modern Countries: Essays towards an Estimate of the Economic Position of Nations, and British Trade Prospects. 2 vols. 8vo. Lond., 1878. F 3 P 3, 4

WILSON (ALEXANDER STEPHEN). A Bushel of Corn. With Illustrations. 8vo. Edinb., 1833. F 5 S 1

WILSON (ANDREW), PH.D., &c. Chapters on Evolution. 8vo. Lond., 1883. A 14 S 35

Studies in Life and Sense. 8vo. Lond., 1877. G 7 T 29

The Abode of Snow: Observations on a Journey from Chinese Thibet to the Indian Caucasus, through the Upper Valleys of the Himalaya. 8vo. Edinb., 1875. D 5 T 36

WILSON (CHARLES HEATH). Life and Works of Michel-angelo Buonarroti. Roy. 8vo. Lond., 1876. C 9 V 28

WILSON (REV. CHARLES THOMAS), M.A., &c., AND FELKIN (R. W.), F.R.G.S., &c. Uganda and the Egyptian Soudan. 2 vols. 8vo. Lond., 1882. D 1 R 28, 29

WILSON (LIEUT.-COL. CHARLES TOWNSHEND). Duke of Berwick, Marshal of France. 1702-34. 8vo. Lond., 1883. C 8 S 10

James the Second and the Duke of Berwick. 8vo. Lond., 1876. B 6 P 47

WILSON (COL. SIR CHARLES WILLIAM), K.C.B., &c. From Korti to Khartum: a Journal of the Desert March from Korti to Gabat, and of the ascent of the Nile in General Gordon's Steamers. 8vo. Edinb., 1885. D 1 Q 1

WILSON (COL. SIR CHARLES WILLIAM), K.C.B., AND PALMER (CAPT. HENRY SPENCE), R.E. Ordnance Survey of the Peninsula of Sinai. In 3 parts. 5 vols. fol. Southampton, 1869. D 4 S 1-5 ‡

WILSON (COL. SIR CHARLES WILLIAM), K.C.B., &c., AND WARREN (COL. SIR CHARLES), G.C.M.G., &c. Recovery of Jerusalem: Narrative of Exploration and Discovery in the City and the Holy Land. 8vo. Lond., 1871. D 4 U 4

WILSON (MRS. CORNWELL BARON-) Memoirs of Harriot, Duchess of St. Albans. 2 vols. 8vo. Lond., 1839. C 3 U 40, 41

WILSON (FELIX). [*See* MOORE, J. S.]

WILSON (PROF. SIR DANIEL), KNT., LL.D. Archæology and Pre-historic Annals of Scotland. Roy. 8vo. Edinb., 1851. B 12 V 31

Memorials of Edinburgh in the Olden Time. Roy. 4to. Edinb., 1875. B 16 R 11 ‡

WILSON (RT. REV. DANIEL), D.D., BISHOP OF CALCUTTA. The Apostolical Commission: a Sermon, delivered at the Cathedral Church of St. John, Calcutta. 2nd ed. (Pam., Be.) 8vo. Madras, 1835. G 16 S 18

Two Charges delivered to the Clergy in the Diocese of Calcutta. (Pam Be.) 8vo. Madras, 1835. G 16 S 18

WILSON (D. M.) Elements of Thermal Chemistry. [*See* MUIR, M. M. P.]

WILSON (EDWARD). Squatters' Directory; containing a List of all the Occupants of Crown Lands in the intermediate Unsettled Districts of Port Phillip. 8vo. Melb., 1849. MJ 2 R 15

Enquiry into the Principles of Representation: a Reprint of several Letters and Leading Articles from the *Argus* Newspaper. 8vo. Melb., 1857. MF 1 Q 3

Another copy. MJ 2 Q 14

Rambles at the Antipodes: a Series of Sketches of Moreton Bay, New Zealand, the Murray River, and South Australia, and the Overland Route. 8vo. Lond., 1859.* MD 1 S 42

Acclimatisation; read before the Royal Colonial Institute. (Pam. Ch.) 8vo. Lond., 1875. MA 2 Q 29

Another copy. (Pam. Co.) 8vo. Lond., 1875. A 16 U 23

Another copy. (Pam. Cg.) 8vo. Lond 1875. MA 2 V 8

Another copy. 8vo. Lond., 1875 MJ 2 R 9

[*See* ARGUS LIBEL CASE.] F 1 Q 1

WILSON (REV. F. R. M.) Memoir of the Rev. Irving Hetherington, Scots' Church, Melbourne; including Sketches of the History of Presbyterianism in New South Wales and Victoria. 8vo. Melb., 1876. MC 1 Q

WILSON (REV. CANON FREDERICK SYDNEY). Australian Songs and Poems. 12mo. Sydney, 1870. MH 1 P 43

[*See* DUBBO HOME WORDS, THE.] ME 3

WILSON (PROF. GEORGE), M.D., &c. Five Gateways of
Knowledge. 2nd ed. 12mo. Camb., 1857.   G 9 P 36

WILSON (GEORGE H.) Ena; or, the Ancient Maori.
8vo. Lond., 1874.   MJ 1 R 28

WILSON (HENRY). History of the Rise and Fall of the
Slave Power in America. 3 vols. 8vo. Boston, 1872–
77.   B 1 S 10–12

WILSON (CAPT. HENRY). Account of the Pelew Islands.
[*See* KEATE, GEORGE.]   MD 6 P 20 †
Supplement to an Account of the Pelew Islands. [*See*
HOCKIN, REV. J. P.]   MD 6 P 20 †

WILSON (HENRY), AND CAULFIELD (JAMES). Book
of Wonderful Characters, Memoirs and Anecdotes of
Remarkable and Eccentric Persons in all Ages and
Countries. 8vo. Lond., 1869.   C 3 U 2

WILSON (PROF. HORACE HAYMAN), M.A., &c. Dictionary, Sanscrit and English. Roy. 4to. Calcutta,
1819.   K 3 S 21 †
Introduction to the Grammar of the Sanscrit Language,
for the use of Early Students. 2nd ed. 8vo. Lond.,
1847.   K 12 S 32 †
Essays and Lectures, chiefly on the Religion of the
Hindus. 2 vols. 8vo. Lond., 1862.   G 4 S 8, 9
Ariana Antiqua: a Descriptive Account of the Anti-
quities and Coins of Afghanistan. 4to. Lond., 1841.
                                                B 17 Q 2 ‡
Vishnu Purana: a system of Hindu Mythology and
Tradition. Roy. 4to. Lond., 1840.   B 14 R 13 ‡
Rig-Veda Sanhitá: a Collection of Ancient Hindu
Hymns. 2nd ed. 4 vols. 8vo. Lond., 1866. G 4 Q 32–35
Manual of Universal History and Chronology. 12mo.
Lond., 1835.   B 14 Q 32
Select Specimens of the Theatre of the Hindus. 3rd ed.
2 vols. 8vo. Lond., 1871.   H 3 S 6, 7
History of British India. [*See* MILL, J.] D 10 S 13–21
The Mégha Dúta: a Poem. [*See* KÁLIDÁSA.]

WILSON (J.) Aperçu Statistique de l'Agriculture, de la
Sylviculture, et des Pêcheries en Russie. Imp. 8vo.
St. Pétersbourg, 1876.   F 7 U 13

WILSON (JAMES). Letter to the Rev. the Moderator.
[*See* SIMSON, R.]

WILSON (CAPT. JAMES). Missionary Voyage to the
South ern Pacific Ocean, performed in the years 1796–98,
in the Ship *Duff*, commanded by Capt. James Wilson.
4to. Lond., 1799.*   MD 6 P 22 †
[*See* VASON, G.]

WILSON (JAMES), F.R.S.E., &c. Voyage round the
Coasts of Scotland and the Isles. 2 vols. 8vo. Ediob.,
1842.   D 9 P 3, 4
British India. [*See* MURRAY, H.]   B 10 Q 16–18

WILSON (MRS. JAMES GLENNIE). Lays from an Australian
Lyre; by "Austral." 12mo. Lond., 1882.   MH 1 R 3

WILSON (JAMES GRANT). Bryant and his Friends: some
Reminiscences of the Knickerbocker Writers. 8vo. New
York, 1886.   C 3 S 10

WILSON (JAMES M.), M.A., &c. Hand-book of Double
Stars. [*See* CROSSLEY, E.]

WILSON (JASPER). Letter, Commercial and Political, addressed to the Rt. Hon. William Pitt. 8vo. Lond.,
1793.   F 6 T 2

WILSON (PROF. JOHN), "CHRISTOPHER NORTH." Memoir
of John Wilson; compiled from Family Papers, &c., by
his Daughter, Mrs. Gordon. 2 vols. 8vo. Edinb.,
1862.   C 4 R 2, 3
Poems by. 2 vols. 8vo. Lond., 1825.   H 8 R 11, 12
Works of. Edited by his Son-in-law, Prof. Ferrier.
12 vols. 8vo. Lond., 1865–70.   J 6 Q 20–31

WILSON (JOHN). Studies of Modern Mind and Character, at several European Epochs. 8vo. Lond., 1881.
                                                B 7 U 28

WILSON (JOHN ALEXANDER). Immortality of the Universe considered in relation to the Persistence of its
Motive Powers. 8vo. Mell., 1875.   MA 2 V 17

WILSON (HON. JOHN BOWIE). Report on the Present
State and Future Prospects of Lord Howe Island. 4to.
Sydney, 1882.*   MD 6 P 26 †

WILSON (PROF. JOHN MATTHIAS), B.D., AND FOWLER
(PROF. THOMAS), M.A. Principles of Morals. 8vo.
Oxford, 1886.   G 13 P 9

WILSON (REV. JOSEPH). French and English Dictionary.
Roy. 8vo. Lond., 1837.   K 16 S 4

WILSON (JOSEPH). Memorabilia Cantabrigiæ; or, an Account of the different Colleges in Cambridge: Biographical
Sketches of the Founders, and Eminent Men. 8vo. Lond.,
1803.   B 23 S 4

WILSON (MRS. ROBERT). New Zealand, and other Poems.
12mo. Lond., 1851.   MH 1 R 50

WILSON (SIR SAMUEL). Salmon at the Antipodes; being
an Account of the successful Introduction of Salmon and
Trout into Australian Waters. 12mo. Lond., 1879.
                                               MA 2 T 18
The Angora Goat; with an Account of its Introduction
into Victoria, and a Report on the Flock belonging to the
Zoological and Acclimatisation Society of Victoria. 8vo.
Melb., 1873.   MA 2 U 17
[*See* MELBOURNE UNIVERSITY.]   MB 2 S 1

WILSON (T. B.), M.D., R.N. Narrative of a Voyage round
the World. 8vo. Lond., 1835.   MD 7 Q 46
Narrative of Voyage round the World; comprehending
an Account of the Wreck of the Ship *Governor Ready*, in
Torres Straits, a Description of the British Settlements on
the Coasts of New Holland, &c. 8vo. Lond., 1835.*
                                                A D 2 V 24

WILSON (WALTER MONRO). Taxation by One Chamber or Two; or, the Council, the Assembly, and the Ministry: a View of the present Constitutional Difficulties. 8vo. Melb., 1865.   MF 1 Q 3

WILSON (WILLIAM P.), M.A.   Lecture on the Conservation of Energy. [*See* MELBOURNE PUBLIC LIBRARY.]

WILSON (REV. WILLIAM), D.D. Memorials of Robert Smith Candlish, D.D., Minister of St. George's Free Church, and Principal of the New College, Edinburgh; with concluding Chapter, by Prof. Robert Rainy, D.D. 8vo. Lond., 1880.   C 8 U 14

WILSON (SIR WILLIAM JAMES ERASMUS), F.R.C.S., &c. Anatomist's Vade Mecum: a System of Human Anatomy. 9th ed. (Churchill's Manuals.) 8vo. Lond., 1873.   A 13 P 36

Egypt of the Past.   With Illustrations.   8vo. Lond., 1881.   B 2 S 14

Lectures on Dermatology : a Synopsis of Diseases of the Skin. 8vo. Lond., 1871.   A 12 R 31

On Diseases of the Skin. 2nd ed. 8vo. Lond., 1847.   A 12 R 29

On Diseases of the Skin : a System of Cutaneous Medicine. 6th ed. 8vo. Lond., 1867.   A 12 R 30

[*See* QUAIN, J.]   A 1 S 8–10 ‡

WILSON & MACKINNON. [*See* ARGUS LIBEL CASE.]

WILTON (REV. C. PLEYDELL N.), M.A.   Twelve Plain Discourses, addressed to the Prisoners of the Crown, in the Colony of New South Wales. 8vo. Sydney, 1834.   MG 1 P 1

[*See* AUSTRALIAN QUARTERLY JOURNAL.]

WILTSHIRE. Memoirs illustrative of the History and Antiquities of Wiltshire and the City of Salisbury; communicated to the Archaeological Institute of Great Britain and Ireland, 1849. 8vo. Lond., 1851.·   B 7 P 9

WIMBLEDON (GEN. SIR EDWARD CECIL), VISCOUNT. Life and Times of; by Charles Dalton, F.R.G.S. 2 vols. 8vo. Lond., 1885.   C 10 S 2, 3

WIMMER (LUDV. F. A.) Oldnordisk Formlære til brug ved Undervisning og Selvstudium. 8vo. Kobenhavn, 1870.   K 12 Q 17

Oldnordisk Læsebog med Anmærkninger og Ordsamling. 2ª Udgave. 8vo. Kobenhavn, 1877.   K 12 Q 18

WINCHELL (PROF. ALEXANDER), LL.D.   Pre-Adamites; or, a Demonstration of the Existence of Men before Adam. Sq. 8vo. Chicago, 1880.   A 1 W 20

World-Life ; or, Comparative Geology. 8vo. Chicago, 1883.   A 9 Q 18

WINCKELMANN OR WINKELMANN (JOHANN JOACHIM). Histoire de l'Art chez les Anciens. 3 vols. (in 2) 4to. Paris, 1802–3.   A 8 S 24, 25

Monumenti Antichi Inediti, Spiegati, ed Illustrati. 2nd ed. 3 vols. fol. Roma, 1821.   A 4 Q 14–16 ‡

Storia delle Arti del Disegno, presso gli Antichi. 3 vols. 4to. Roma, 1783–84.   A 1 R 8–10 †

5 L

WIND CHARTS. [*See* BOARD OF TRADE.]   D 8 P 13 ‡

WINDEYER (SIR WILLIAM), KNT., &c.   Commemorative Address on the Celebration of Fiftieth Anniversary of the Sydney Mechanics' School of Arts. Roy. 8vo.   Sydney, 1883.*   MJ 2 S 25

WINDHAM (RT. HON. WILLIAM). Diary of (1784–1810); edited by Mrs. Henry Baring. 8vo. Lond.,1866. C 10 P 40

Speeches in Parliament; to which is prefixed, some Account of his Life, by Thomas Amyot, Esq. 3 vols. 8vo. Lond., 1812.   F 13 Q 20–22

WINDISCH (PROF. WILLIAM OSCAR ERNST). Concise Irish Grammar; with Pieces for Reading; translated from the German by Norman Moore, M.D. 8vo.   Camb., 1882.   K 11 U 3

WINDSOR (ARTHUR LLOYD). Ethica; or, Characteristics of Men, Manners, and Books. 8vo. Lond.,1860. G 9 S 21

WINDSOR REVIEW (THE): a Monthly Magazine of Literature, Science, and Art. (Pam. G.) 8vo. Sydney, 1857.   ME 3 R

WINE. Extracts from an English Book on Wine; reprinted from the *Argus*, 30th December, 1876. 12mo. Melb., 1877.   MJ 2 S 23

WINES (REV. ENOCH COBB), LL.D., &c. State of Prisons and of Child-saving Institutions in the Civilized World. Roy. 8vo. Camb., 1880.   F 1 T 10

Two Years and a Half in the American Navy ; comprising a Journal of a Cruise in the years 1829–31. 2 vols. 8vo. Lond., 1833.   D 10 Q 42, 43

WING (ASA S.) [*See* PROVIDENT LIFE AND TRUST CO.]

WINGFIELD (HON. L. S.) Notes on Civil Costume in England, from the Conquest to the Regency. 8vo. Lond., 1884.   A 8 T 25

Under the Palms in Algeria and Tunis. 2 vols. 12mo. Lond., 1868.   D 1 S 1, 2

WINKELMANN (J. J.) [*See* WINCKELMANN, J. J.]

WINKLER (PROF. CLEMENS), PH.D.   Hand-book of Technical Gas Analysis, containing Concise Instructions for carrying out Gas-Analytical Methods of proved utility. 8vo. Lond., 1885.   A 6 Q 6

WINKLES (B.) Architectural and Picturesque Illustrations of the Cathedral Churches of England and Wales; with Historical and Descriptive Accounts. 3 vols. 4to. Lond., 1836–42.   A 2 T 14–16

French Cathedrals; from Drawings by R. Garland. 4to. Lond., 1837.   A 2 T 17

WINKWORTH (SUSANNA). History and Life of the Rev. Doctor John Tauler, of Strasbourg; with twenty-five of his Sermons (*temp.* 1340). Sq. 8vo. Lond., 1857. C 5 U 5

WINSLOW (Forbes), M.D.　Physic and Physicians: a Medical Sketch-book. 2 vols. 8vo Lond.,1839.　C 4 T 30, 31

WINSLOW (Mrs. Mary).　Domestic Receipt Book for 1864.　8vo.　Boston, 1864.　　　　　　　MA 2 S 38

Life in Jesus: a Memoir of Mrs. Mary Winslow; by her Son, Octavius Winslow, D.D.　8vo.　Lond., 1863. G 11 P 25

WINSLOW (Octavius), D.D.　Life in Jesus: a Memoir of Mrs. Mary Winslow.　8vo.　Lond., 1863.　G 11 P 25

WINSOR (J.)　Narrative and Critical History of America. Vols. 2–4.　3 vols. imp. 8vo.　Lond., 1886.　B 17 U 2–4

WINTER (John).　Portrait of.　[*See* Manuscripts and Portraits.]

WINTER (Richard).　New Zealand Industries: an Essay. [*See* New Zealand Exhibitions.]　　　　　MK 1 S 16

WINTON (John G.)　Modern Workshop Practice. (Weale.) 12mo.　Lond., 1870.　　　　　　　　A 17 Q 19

WIRGMAN (Lieut.-Col. Theodore), LL.B.　Russians in Central Asia.　[*See* Hellwald, F. von.]　D 5 P 53

WISCONSIN.　[*See* United States.]

WISE (B. R.)　Australian Economic Association Papers: No. 1. The Mutual Relations of Imports and Exports. (Read at a Meeting of the Association, on the evening of Tuesday, 30th August, 1887.)　8vo.　Sydney, 1887.* MF 3 Q 35

Facts and Fallacies of Modern Protection.　8vo. Lond., 1879.　　　　　　　　　　　　　　F 5 S 34

WISE (B. R.), and DAVIES (Hanbury), B.A.　Bankruptcy Act, 1887, Rules and Forms; with Introduction, Commentary, Notes of Cases, and Index.　8vo.　Sydney, 1888.*　　　　　　　　　　　　　　MF 3 Q 12

WISE (Edward).　Letter to the Colonial Secretary, suggesting the appointment of Law Reporters.　(MS. Pam. A.)　Fol.　Sydney, 1861.　　　　　　　MJ 2 U 1

WISE (Henry) & CO.　New Zealand Post Office Directory, 1875–76, 1878, 1880–81, 1883–84, 1885–86.　5 vols. imp. 8vo.　Dunedin, 1875–86.*　　　　　ME 10 P 6–12 †

WISE (Thomas Alexander), M.D., &c.　History of Paganism in Caledonia.　4to.　Lond., 1884.　　　　B 12 V 19

WISE, CAFFIN, & CO.　New South Wales Post Office Directory, 1886–87.　Imp. 8vo.　Sydney, 1886. ME 10 P 15 †

WISEMAN (Nicholas Patrick Stephen), Cardinal. Essays on Various Subjects.　3 vols. 8vo.　Lond., 1853. G 4 R 26–28

High Church Claims; or, a Series of Papers on the Oxford Controversy; the High-Church Theory of Dogmatical Authority; Anglican Claim to Apostolical Succession, &c. (Pam. Br.)　8vo.　Lond. (n.d.)　　　　MG 1 Q 35

WISEMAN (Nicholas Patrick Stephen), Cardinal—*contd.* Horæ Syriacæ, seu Commentationes et Anecdota Res vel Litteras Syriacas spectantia　8vo.　Romæ, 1828.　J 13 T 33

Recollections of the last Four Popes, and of Rome in their Times.　8vo.　Lond., 1858.　　　　C 9 P 20

Twelve Lectures on the connexion between Science and Revealed Religion.　2 vols. 8vo.　Lond., 1836. G 14 Q 16, 17

WISHART (Rt. Rev. George), Bishop of Edinburgh. Memoirs of the most renowned James Graham, Marquis of Montrose; translated from the Latin.　8vo.　Edinb., 1819.　　　　　　　　　　　　　　C 5 T 16

WISLICENUS (Dr. J.)　[*See* Strecker, A.]　A 6 Q 4

WISSENSCHAFTEN IN DEUTSCHLAND.　[*See* Geschichte der Wissenschaften in Deutschland.]

WITCH OF THE WAVE.　(Illustrated Story-teller.) Roy. 8vo.　Lond. (n.d.)　　　　　　　　　J 9 V 9

WITCHCRAFT.　Collection of rare and curious Tracts on Witchcraft and the Second Sight; with an original Essay on Witchcraft.　8vo.　Lond., 1820.　　G 9 T 11

WITCOMB (C. and H.)　New Guide to Modern Conversations in English and Spanish.　New ed.　18mo.　Paris (n.d.)　　　　　　　　　　　　　　　K 11 S 5

WITHEROW (Thomas).　Historical and Literary Memorials of Presbyterianism in Ireland (1623–1731).　8vo.　Lond., 1879.　　　　　　　　　　　　　　G 7 T 28

WITHERS (William Bramwell).　History of Ballarat, from the first Pastoral Settlement to the Present Time; with Plans and Illustrations.　8vo.　Ballarat, 1870. MB 2 Q 33

Another copy.　2nd ed.　8vo.　Ballarat, 1887.　MB 2 Q 34

WITNESS (The) and Australian Presbyterian.　12 vols. (in 10) fol.　Sydney, 1874–84.　　　　　　　ME

WITS AND HUMOURISTS.　Anecdote Lives of.　[*See* Timbs, J.]

WITT (Mme. Henriette de).　Monsieur Guizot in Private Life, 1787–1874.　Translated by M. C. M. Simpson. 8vo.　Lond., 1880.　　　　　　　　　C 7 P 12

WITT (John de).　Life of.　[*See* Pontalis, A. L.]

WITTSTEIN (Dr. G. C.), and MUELLER (Sir Ferd. von), Baron, K.C.M.G.　Organic Constituents of Plants and Vegetable Substances, and their Chemical Analysis. 8vo.　Melb., 1878.*　　　　　　　　　　MA 1 V 8

WOERMANN (Dr. Karl).　History of Painting.　[*See* Woltmann, Dr. A.]　　　　　　　　A 7 V 21, 22

WOFFINGTON (Margaret).　Life and Adventures of Peg Woffington; with Pictures of the Period in which she lived, by J. F. Molloy.　2 vols. 8vo.　Lond., 1885. C 2 R 35, 36

WÖHLER (FREIDRICH). Hand-book of Inorganic Analysis. 8vo. Lond., 1854. A 5 S 38

WOIDE (CARL GOTTFRIED). Notitia Codiois Alexandrini, cvm variis eivs Lectionibvs omnibvs. 8vo. Lipsiæ, 1788. G 2 P 24

WOLCOTT (JOHN), M.D., "PETER PINDAR." Works of. 5 vols. 8vo. Lond., 1794-1801. H 8 U 22-26

WOLF (JOHANN CHRISTOPH). Bibliotheca Hebræa. Accedit in calce Jacobi Gaffarelli Index Codicum Cabbalistic. 4 vols. 4to. Hamburgi, 1715-33. K 13 S 30-33

Casauboniana. [*See* CASAUBON, I.]

WOLF (LUCIEN). Sir Moses Montefiore: a Centennial Biography; with Extracts from Letters and Journals. With Portrait. 8vo. Lond., 1884. C 5 S 29

WOLF (RUDOLF). Geschichte der Astronomie. (Gesch. der Wiss.) 8vo. München, 1877. A 17 V 30

WOLFE (REV. CHARLES), A.B. Remains of; with a Brief Memoir of his Life, by the Rev. J. A. Russell. 2nd ed. 8vo. Lond., 1826. G 15 R 12

WOLFE (GEN. JAMES). Montcalm and Wolfe; by Francis Parkman. 2 vols. 8vo. Lond., 1884. C 5 S 21, 22

Another copy. 6th ed. 2 vols. 8vo. Lond., 1885. C 5 S 23, 24

WOLFF (A. R.) The Windmill as a Prime Mover. 8vo. New York, 1885. A 11 U 17

WOLFF (SIR HENRY DRUMMOND), G.C.M.G. Madrilenia; or, Pictures of Spanish Life. 8vo. Lond., 1851. D 8 S 18

WOLFF (REV. JOSEPH), D.D., &c. Narrative of a Mission to Bokhara, 1843-45, to ascertain the fate of Col. Stoddart and Capt. Conolly. 2 vols. 8vo. Lond., 1845. D 6 Q 5, 6

WOLFF (DR. O. L. B.) Hausschatz deutscher Prosa. Sq. 8vo. Leipzig, 1856. B 27 T 1

Poetischer Hausschatz des deutschen Volkes: ein Buch für Schule und Haus. 8vo. Leipzig, 1853. H 5 U 30

WOLFINGHAM; or, the Convict-settler of Jervis Bay: a Tale of the Church in Australia. 12mo. Lond., 1860. MJ 1 P 17

WOLKENBERG (REV. M.) The Pentateuch according to the Talmud. [*See* HERSHON, P. I.]

WOLLASTON (ARTHUR N.), C.I.E. English-Persian Dictionary. 8vo. Lond., 1882. K 13 P 12

Gazetteer of India. [*See* THORNTON, E.] D 11 T 16

WOLLASTON (H. N.) Christ, or Plato? The Immortality of Man and his future Punishment briefly examined in three Sermons. 12mo. Melb. (n.d.) MG 2 P 8

WOLLASTON (WILLIAM). The Religion of Nature delineated. 6th ed. 4to. Lond., 1738. G 15 T 10

WOLSELEY (GENERAL SIR GARNET JOSEPH), VISCOUNT. Narrative of the War with China in 1860. 8vo. Lond., 1862. B 2 P 36

WOLSEY (THOMAS), CARDINAL. Life of; by G. Cavendish, from the original Autograph Manuscript. 2nd ed., with Notes and Illustrations, by S. W. Singer, F.S.A. 8vo. Lond., 1827. C 10 P 41

Negotiations of Thomas Woolsey, the Great Cardinall of England; containing his Life and Death; composed by George Cavendish. Sq. 8vo. Lond., 1641. C 3 P 46

Life of. [*See* MACKINTOSH, SIR J.]

WOLTMANN (DR. ALFRED FRIEDRICH GOTTFRIED ALBERT), AND WOERMAN (DR. KARL). History of Painting. From the German. Edited by Prof. Sydney Colvin, M.A. 2 vols. imp. 8vo. Lond., 1880. A 7 V 21, 22

WOLVERHAMPTON FREE LIBRARY. Eighth Annual Report. (Pam., P.) Sm. fol. Wolverhampton, 1877. MJ 2 U 4

Ninth and Tenth Annual Report. (Pam., Q.) Sm. fol. Wolverhampton, 1878-79. MJ 2 U 5

WOLZOGEN (ALFRED), BARON VON. Raphael Santi. His Life and his Works. Translated by F. E. Bunnètt. 8vo. Lond., 1866. C 5 R 22

WOMEN OF THE DAY: a Biographical Dictionary of Notable Contemporaries; by Frances Hays. 8vo. Lond., 1885. C 11 Q 3

WONDERFUL MAGAZINE (THE), and Marvellous Chronicle of Extraordinary Productions, &c. 5 vols. (in 3) 8vo. Lond., 1793. J 2 R 17-19

Another copy. 5 vols. 8vo. Lond. (n.d.) J 2 R 22-26

WONDERFUL MAGAZINE (THE NEW). Illustrated with Portraits, Engravings Wood-Cuts, &c. 2 vols. 8vo. Lond. (n.d.) J 2 R 20, 21

WONTNER (—) Old Bailey Experience: Criminal Jurisprudence, and the actual working of our Penal Code of Laws; also an Essay on Prison Discipline, &c. 8vo. Lond., 1833. F 3 P 6

WOOD (ANTHONY A'), M.A. History and Antiquities of the Colleges and Halls in the University of Oxford. 4to. Oxford, 1786. B 6 V 6

Athenæ Oxonienses: an exact History of all the Writers and Bishops who have had their education in the most Antient and Famous University of Oxford, from 1500 to 1695; with the Fasti, or Annals of the said University. 2 vols. fol. Lond., 1721. C 1 W 3, 4

Lives of those eminent Antiquaries John Leland, Thomas Hearne, and Anthony A'Wood; by W. Huddersford and T. Warton. 2 vols. 8vo. Oxford, 1772. C 1 V 14, 15

WOOD (C. F.) A Yachting Cruise in the South Seas. 8vo. Lond., 1875. MD 7 P 26

WOOD (CHARLES W.) Under the Northern Skies; with Illustrations. 8vo. Lond., 1886. D 7 S 37

WOOD (GEORGE). Concise and Poetic Description of the Proceedings and Speeches at the late Memorable Meeting, December 22nd, 1862, of the Subscribers to the Lancashire Relief Fund. 12mo. Sydney, 1862.   MH 1 P 17

Drinkamania: an Appeal against the Licensed Obstructives to the Moral, Social, and Commercial Progress of New South Wales. 18mo. Sydney, 1864. MH 1 R 46

Loyalty in Sydney, as demonstrated on the memorable occasion of the Marriage of H.R.H. the Prince of Wales with H.R.H. the Princess Alexandra. 8vo. Sydney, 1866.   MH 1 P 36

WOOD (GEORGE B.) Household Practice of Medicine, Hygiene and Surgery. Edited by Frederick A. Castle, M.D. 2 vols. roy. 8vo. Lond., 1881.   A 12 V 7, 8

WOOD (HARRIE). Mineral Products of New South Wales. 4to. Sydney, 1882.   MA 2 R 8

WOOD (HENRY). Change for the American Notes; in Letters from London to New York; by "An American Lady." 8vo. Lond., 1843.   D 9 P 39

WOOD (HENRY T.) Reports of the Colonial Sections of the Colonial and Indian Exhibition, London, 1886. 8vo. Lond., 1887.   A 17 W 24

WOOD (HERBERT). Shores of Lake Arall. 8vo. Lond., 1876.   D 6 R 16

WOOD (REV. JAMES). Religions of India. [*See* BARTH, A.]

WOOD (JAMES). Van Diemen's Land Royal Kalendar, Colonial Register, and Almanack. 16mo. Launceston, 1848.   ME 4 P

Tasmanian Royal Kalendar, Colonial Register, and Almanack. 12mo. Launceston, 1849.   ME 4 P

Royal Southern Kalendar, Tasmanian Register, and General Australasian and East Indian Official Directory, 1850. 12mo. Launceston, 1850.*   ME 4 P

Tasmanian Almanack, 1851, 1856-57. 3 vols. (in 1). 12mo. Launceston, 1851-57.   ME 4 P

WOOD (JAMES), D.D. Elements of Algebra; originally designed for the use of Students in the Universities. New ed., re-modelled, simplified, &c., by Thomas Lund, B.D. 8vo. Lond., 1876.   A 10 S 3

WOOD (CAPT. JOHN). Voyage to Spitzbergen. [*See* VOYAGES AND DISCOVERIES.]   MD 6 P 24

Attempt to Discover a North-east Passage to China. [*See* VOYAGES AND DISCOVERIES.]   MD 5 P 25

WOOD (LIEUT. JOHN), I.N. Twelve Months in Wellington, Port Nicolson; or, Notes for the Public and the New Zealand Company. (Pam. 10.) 8vo. Lond., 1843.   MJ 2 Q 2

Personal Narrative of a Journey to the Source of the River Oxus, by the Route of the Indus, Kabul, and Badakhshan, in 1836-38. 8vo. Lond., 1841.   D 6 R 26

WOOD (JOHN DENNISTOUN). Address to the Electors of Beechworth, delivered at the Beechworth Athenæum, on the 26th March, 1859. 8vo. Beechworth, 1859.   MF 1 Q 2

Laws of the Australasian Colonies as to the Administration and Distribution of the Estate of Deceased Persons. 8vo. Lond., 1884.   MF 1 Q 19

WOOD (REV. JOHN G.), M.A., &c. Strange Dwellings; being a Description of the Habitations of Animals. New ed. 8vo. Lond., 1873.   A 14 Q 18

Trespassers: showing how the Inhabitants of Earth, Air, and Water are enabled to trespass on Domains not their own. 8vo. Lond., 1875.   A 14 T 18

Homes without Hands; being a Description of the Habitations of Animals, classed according to their principal of construction. 8vo. Lond., 1875.   A 15 P 9

Insects at Home; being a popular Account of British Insects, their Structure, Habits, and Transformations. 8vo. Lond., 1872.   A 15 P 10

Man and Beast; here and hereafter. Illustrated by Original Anecdotes. 2 vols. 8vo. Lond., 1874.   G 3 P 6, 7

Insects Abroad; being a popular Account of Foreign Insects. 8vo. Lond., 1874.   A 14 R 28

Out of Doors: a Selection of Original Articles on Practical Natural History. 8vo. Lond., 1874.   A 14 Q 10

Common Objects of the Seashore; including Hints for an Aquarium. 12mo. Lond., 1858.   A 14 P 58

Common Objects of the Country. 12mo. Lond., 1858.   A 14 P 59

Natural History of Man. 2 vols. imp. 8vo. Lond., 1868-70.   A 2 P 6, 7

Illustrated Natural History.—Vol. 1. Reptiles, Fishes, Molluscs, &c. Vol. 2. Mammalia. Vol. 3. Birds. 3 vols. imp. 8vo. Lond., 1863-67.   A 13 V 2-4

Horse and Man. 8vo. Lond., 1855.   A 1 R 28

Man and his Handiwork. 8vo. Lond., 1886.   A 1 V 18

[*See* RENNIE, J.]   A 14 P 45

WOOD (JOHN TURTLE), F.S.A., &c. Discoveries at Ephesus, including the site and remains of the Great Temple of Diana. With Illustrations. Imp. 8vo. Lond., 1877.   B 13 V 11

WOOD (MARY ANNE EVERETT). Letters of Royal and Illustrious Ladies of Great Britain, from the Commencement of the 12th Century to the Close of the Reign of Queen Mary. 3 vols. 8vo. Lond., 1846.   C 4 R 10-12

WOOD (NICHOLAS). Practical Treatise on Railroads and Interior Communication in general. 8vo. Lond., 1838.   A 6 S 7

WOOD (ROBERT). Ruins of Palmyra, otherwise Tedmore in the Desert. Imp. fol. Lond., 1753.   B 20 P 7 ‡

Ruins of Balbec, otherwise Heliopolis in Coelosyria. Imp. fol. Lond., 1757.   B 20 P 8 ‡

WOOD (SAMUEL). Tree Planter and Plant Propagator. (Weale.) 12mo. Lond., 1880.   A 17 Q 38

Tree Pruner; being a Practical Manual on the Pruning of Fruit Trees, &c. (Weale.) 12mo. Lond., 1880. A 17 Q 37

WOOD (DR. W.) Twenty Styles of Architecture. Illustrated. Imp. 8vo. Lond., 1881. .   A 3 Q 2

WOOD (WILLIAM), F.R.S., &c. Index Entomologicus; or, a complete illustrated Catalogue of the Lepidopterous Insects of Great Britain : a new and revised ed., with Supplement; by J. O. Westwood, F.L.S. Roy. 8vo. Lond., 1854.   A 13 U 4

Index Testaceologicus; or, a Catalogue of Shells, British and Foreign. 2nd ed. 8vo. Lond., 1828.   A 14 S 50

Supplement to the Index Testaceologicus. 8vo. Lond., 1828.   A 14 S 50

WOOD (RT. HON. WILLIAM PAGE). [*See* HATHERLEY, RT. HON. W. P. WOOD, BARON.]

WOOD (W. S.) Eastern Afterglow; or, Present Aspect of Sacred Scenery. 8vo. Cambridge, 1880.   D 1 W 20

WOODBERRY (GEORGE EDWARD). History of Wood-engraving. Illustrated. 8vo. Lond., 1883.   A 7 S 11

WOODHEAD (G. S.), AND HARE (A. W.) Pathological Mycology: an Enquiry into the Etiology of Infective Diseases. 8vo. Lond., 1885.   A 12 U 21

WOODHOUSELEE (ALEXANDER FRASER TYTLER), LORD. Elements of General History, Ancient and Modern. New ed., with the History brought down to the close of the year 1871. 12mo. Edinb., 1872.   B 14 P 25

Essay on Military Law, and the Practice of Courts Martial. 8vo. Lond., 1814.   F 4 S 4

Memoirs of the Life and Writings of the Hon. Henry Home, of Kames (Lord Kames). 2 vols. 4to. Edinb., 1807. -   C 3 W 15, 16

Universal History, from the Creation of the World to the Beginning of the 18th Century. (Fam. Lib.) 6 vols. 12mo. Lond., 1834.   K 10 P 12–17

WOODHULL (MICHAEL). [Tragedies of] Euripides. [*See* GREEK TRAGIC THEATRE.]

WOOD-MARTIN (MAJOR W. G.) History of Sligo, County and Town, from the Earliest Ages to the Close of the Reign of Queen Elizabeth. 8vo. Dublin, 1882.   B 11 Q 20

Lake-dwellings of Ireland; or, Ancient Lacustrine Habitations of Erin, commonly called Crannogs. Roy. 8vo. Dublin, 1886.   B 11 R 20

WOODS (DANIEL B.) Sixteen Months at the Gold Diggings. 8vo. Lond., 1851.   D 3 Q 42

WOODS (REV. F. H.), B.D. Sweden and Norway. With Illustrations. 8vo. Lond., 1882.   D 7 P 24

WOODS (REV. GEORGE), M.A. Latin Grammar for the use of Schools. [*See* MADVIG, PROF. I. N.]

WOODS (J. D.) Narrative of a Visit of H.R.H. the Duke of Edinburgh, K.G., to South Australia. 8vo. Adelaide, 1868·   MB 2 P 32

Native Tribes of South Australia. [*See* ABORIGINES.]   MA 1 R 12

WOODS (JAMES CHAPMAN). Old and Rare Books: an Elementary Lecture. 8vo. Lond., 1885.   J 2 S 16

WOODS (REV. JULIAN E. TENISON-). [*See* TENISON-WOODS, REV. J. E.]

WOODS (N. A.) The Past Campaign: a Sketch of the War in the East, from the Departure of Lord Raglan to the Capture of Sevastopol. 2 vols. 8vo. Lond., 1855.   B 12 U 18, 19

WOODWARD (BERNARD BOLINGBROKE), B.A. History of Wales, from the Earliest Times to its final Incorporation with the Kingdom of England. 2 vols. roy. 8vo. Lond., 1853.   B 5 V 12, 13

Treasury of Knowledge and Library of Reference. [*See* MAUNDER, S.]   K 9 T 15

WOODWARD (BERNARD BOLINGBROKE), B.A., AND CATES (W. L. R.) Encyclopædia of Chronology, Historical and Biographical. 8vo. Lond., 1872.   K 5 U 5

WOODWARD (BERNARD BOLINGBROKE), B.A., &c., WILKS (REV. THEODORE CHAMBERS), M.A., AND LOCKHART (CHARLES), B.A. General History of Hampshire; or, the County of Southampton, including the Isle of Wight. With Illustrations. 3 vols. 4to. Lond., 1870.   B 2 U 5–7

WOODWARD (REV. CHARLES), B.C.L. Analysis of Paley's Horæ Paulinæ; or, the Truth of the Scripture History of St. Paul evinced. 2nd ed. (Pam. 40.) 12mo. Sydney, 1850.   MJ 2 R 2

WOODWARD (G. P. M.), M.D. New South Wales Railways Ambulance Hand-book : Accidents and their Treatment, Aids in Cases of Injuries, Sudden Illness, &c. Illustrated. 12mo. Sydney, 1887.   MA 2 S 21

WOODWARD (HORACE B.), F.G.S. Geology of England and Wales: a Concise Account of the Lithological Characters, Leading Fossils, and Economic Products of the Rocks. 8vo. Lond., 1876.   A 9 Q 1

WOODWARD (J. J.) Hospital of the Medical Department, United States Army, 1876. [*See* PHILADELPHIA INTER. EXHIB.]

WOODWARD (S. P.), A.L.S., &c. Manual of the Mollusca; being a Treatise on Recent and Fossil Shells. 2nd ed.; with Appendix, by Ralph Tate, F.G.S., &c. (Weale.) 8vo. Lond., 1871.   A 17 P 25

Another copy. 3rd ed.; with Appendix, by Ralph Tate, F.G.S., &c. 8vo. Lond., 1875.   A 14 Q 17

WOOLHOUSE (W. S. B.), F.R.A.S., &c. Elements of the Differential Calculus. (Weale.) 5th ed. 12mo. Lond. (n.d.)   A 17 P 47

Measures, Weights, and Moneys of all Nations. (Weale.) 5th ed. 12mo. Lond., 1872.   A 17 P 48

WOOLLAHRA PENNY BANK (THE). Prospectus, and First Report. (Pam. 35.) 8vo. Sydney, 1863.   MJ 2 Q 22

WOOLLETT (W.) Catalogue Raisonné of the Engraved Works of. [*See* FAGAN, F.]   K 9 P 1 †

WOOLLETT (WILLIAM M.) Old Homes made New; being a Collection of Plans, &c. illustrating the Alteration of Suburban Residences. Ob. 8vo. New York, 1878.
　　　　　　　　　　　　　　　　　　　　　A 2 R 22

WOOLLEY (PROF. JOHN), D.C.L. Idylls of the King: a Lecture (Pam. J.) 8vo. Sydney, 1861. MJ 1 T 38

Inaugural Address, delivered on the Opening of the University of Sydney. [*See* NICHOLSON, SIR C.] MJ 2 S 2

Inaugural Address, delivered to the Members of the Maitland School of Arts. 8vo. Maitland, 1857. MJ 2 R 14

Lectures delivered in Australia. 8vo. Camb., 1862.*
　　　　　　　　　　　　　　　　　　　　　MJ 1 U 18

Schools of Art and Colonial Nationality: a Lecture. (Pam. J.) 8vo. Sydney, 1861. MJ 1 T 38

Sermon on behalf of the Northern Missions. 8vo. Sydney, 1853. MG 1 P 1

Social Use of Schools of Art: a Lecture. 12mo. Sydney, 1860. MJ 2 R 1

Another copy. 12mo. Sydney, 1860. MJ 2 R 14

Two Lectures: Oral Instruction and Self-Culture; and, The Office of Christian Associations towards the State and Church. (Pam. J.) 8vo. Sydney, 1855. MJ 1 T 38

WOOLLEY (RICHARD). Railways: by whom shall they be made and managed? Four Letters. 8vo. Melb., 1855.
　　　　　　　　　　　　　　　　　　　　　MF 1 Q 2

Another copy. (Pam. 28.) 8vo. Melb., 1855. MJ 2 Q 16

WOOLLEY (THOMAS). Reminiscences of the Life of a Busman; or, How to make Happiness, Abundance, and Profit, the Results of emigrating to Australia. 12mo. Lond., 1850. MD 3 Q 28

WOOLLS (REV. WILLIAM), PH.D., &c. Contribution to the Flora of Australia. 8vo. Sydney, 1867.* MA 1 V 12

Lectures on the Vegetable Kingdom, with special reference to the Flora of Australia. 8vo. Sydney, 1879.*
　　　　　　　　　　　　　　　　　　　　　MA 1 V 14

Letter, addressed in 1839, to the Students of the Sydney College. 12mo. Sydney, 1842. MG 1 P 18

Lines written to commemorate the passing of a "Bill to incorporate and endow a University, to be called the 'University of Sydney,' 14 Vic., 1850." 2nd ed. 12mo. Parramatta, 1851. MH 1 P 17

Miscellanies, in Prose and Verse. 12mo. Sydney, 1838.*
　　　　　　　　　　　　　　　　　　　　　MJ 1 Q 18

Plants indigenous in the Neighbourhood of Sydney, arranged according to the System of Baron F. von Mueller, K.C.M.G., &c. 8vo. Sydney, 1880. MA 1 V 16

Another copy. (Pam. Co.) 8vo. Sydney, 1880.
　　　　　　　　　　　　　　　　　　　　　A 16 U 23

Plants of New South Wales, according to the Census of Baron F. von Mueller, K.C.M.G., F.R.S., &c., Government Botanist of Victoria. 8vo. Sydney, 1885.* MA 1 V 17

Postscript to the "Tract for the Times, addressed to the Laity of New South Wales." 12mo. Parramatta, 1850.
　　　　　　　　　　　　　　　　　　　　　MG 1 P 18

WOOLLS (REV. WILLIAM), PH.D., &c.—*continued.*

Progress of Botanical Discovery in Australia: a Lecture. (Pam. 44.) 12mo. Sydney, 1869. MJ 2 R 6

Sermon on the Character of Christ, &c., 12mo. Sydney, 1879. MG 1 Q 35

Sermon, preached in St. Peter's Church, Richmond. 8vo. Windsor, 1874. MG 1 Q 35

Sermon, preached in St. Philip's Church, North Richmond, on the occasion of Mrs. W. Town's Death. (*For private circulation only.*) 8vo. Sydney, 1886. MG 1 Q 23

Short Account of the Character and Labours of the Rev. Samuel Marsden. 12mo. Parramatta, 1844. MG 1 P 18

Another copy. 12mo. Parramatta, 1844. MG 1 P 49

Species Plantarum Parramattensium, secundem Ordines Naturales disposuit. 8vo. Gottingen, 1871. MA 2 V 6

Tract for the Times, addressed to the Laity of New South Wales. 12mo. Parramatta, 1850. MG 1 P 18

Another copy. 12mo. Parramatta, 1850. MG 1 P 48

WOOLNER (THOMAS). My Beautiful Lady: [a Poem.] 2nd ed. 12mo. Lond., 1864. H 8 R 5

Pygmalion. 8vo. Lond., 1881. H 8 R 32

WOOLNOTH (W.) Ancient Castles. [*See* BRAYLEY, E. W.] B 7 Q 5, 6

WOOLNOUGH (C. W.) The Whole Art of Marbling, as applied to Paper, Book-edges, &c. 8vo. Lond., 1881.
　　　　　　　　　　　　　　　　　　　　　A 11 Q 21

WOOLS. Catalogue of Wools for the London International Exhibition of 1862, and for competition for Messrs. Mort and Co.'s Gold Medals. Fol. Sydney, 1862. MJ 2 S 2

WOOLSON (MRS. ABBA LOUISA). George Eliot and her Heroines: a Study. 12mo. New York, 1886. C 4 P 8

WOOL TRADE. Abstracts of the Evidence taken before the Select Committee of the House of Lords appointed to take into consideration the state of the British Wool Trade. (Pam., 31.) 8vo. Lond., 1828. MJ 2 Q 19

WOOLSEY (THOMAS), CARDINAL. [*See* WOLSEY, THOMAS, CARDINAL.]

WOORE (THOMAS). Australian Railways and the Sydney University Magazine. (Pam., 39.) 12mo. Sydney, (n.d.) MJ 2 R 1

Substance of a Lecture on Railways, delivered at the Goulburn Mechanics' Institute, July 6, 1855. 12mo. Sydney, 1855. MJ 2 Q 1

Another copy. 12mo. Lond., 1855. MJ 2 Q 10

Warragamba Water Scheme. (Pam., 43.) 8vo. Sydney, 1872. MJ 2 R 5

Errors in the Great Western Railroad, New South Wales, exposed. (Pam., N.) 8vo. Goulburn, 1876.
　　　　　　　　　　　　　　　　　　　　　MJ 2 P 29

Remarks on what New South Wales might become by introducing the Light of Science into it. (Pam., G.) 8vo. Goulburn, 1876. MA 2 V 7

WOORE (THOMAS)—*continued.*
Supply of Water from the Warragamba River, Sewerage of Sydney, Irrigation of Cumberland, Relief of the Hawkesbury, Suburban Railway, and Defence of the North Shore of Botany Bay,—combined in one scheme. (Pam. Cj.) 8vo. Sydney, 1876.   MA 2 V 7
Comments on Mr. W. Clark's Report on Water-supply to Sydney. (Pam., Cj.) 8vo. Goulburn, 1877.   MA 2 V 7
Australian Railways and the Sydney University Magazine. (Pam. 21.) 8vo. Sydney (n.d.)   MJ 2 Q 10
Another copy. (Pam., 39.) 12mo. Sydney (n.d.)
                                                MJ 2 R 1

WOOSTER (DAVID). Selections from the Literary and Artistic Remains of Pauline Jermyn Trevelyan. [*See* TREVELYAN, LADY.]

WOOTON (EDWIN). Guide to Degrees in Arts, Science, Literature, Law, Music, and Divinity, in the United Kingdom, the Colonies, the Continent, and the United States. 8vo. Lond., 1883.   G 18 R 1

WORCESTER (EDWARD SOMERSET), SECOND MARQUIS OF. Life, Times, and Scientific Labours of; to which is added a reprint of his "Century of Inventions," 1663. 8vo. Lond., 1865.   C 8 V 43

WORCESTER (FLORENCE OF). [*See* FLORENCE OF WORCESTER.]

WORCESTER (JOSEPH EMERSON), LL.D. Dictionary of the English Language; with Supplement. New ed. 4to. Philad., 1881.   K 15 U 4

WORDSWORTH (RT. REV. CHARLES), D.C.L. Greek Primer for the use of Beginners in that Language. (Clar. Press.) 5th ed. 12mo. Oxford, 1875.   K 16 P 43

WORDSWORTH (CHARLES FAVELL FORTH), Q.C., A.I.C.E. Law and Practice of Elections, as altered by the Reform Acts. 8vo. Lond., 1835.   F 3 P 1

WORDSWORTH (REV. CHRISTOPHER), D.D. Ecclesiastical Biography; or, Lives of Eminent Men connected with the History of Religion in England. 3rd ed. 4 vols. 8vo. Lond., 1839.   G 4 S 1–4

WORDSWORTH (RT. REV. CHRISTOPHER), D.D., BISHOP OF LINCOLN. A Church History to A.D. 451. 4 vols. 8vo. Lond., 1881–83.   G 7 T 24–27
Correspondence of Richard Bentley. [*See* BENTLEY, R.]
                                            C 8 S 26, 27
Greece: Pictorial, Descriptive, and Historical. Roy. 8vo. Lond., 1840.   B 9 V 34
Memoirs of William Wordsworth, Poet Laureate, D.C.L. 2 vols. 8vo. Lond., 1851.   C 9 S 47, 48
Miscellanies: Literary and Religious. 3 vols. 8vo. Lond., 1879.   J 6 T 14–16

WORDSWORTH (DOROTHY). Recollections of a Tour made in Scotland, A.D. 1803. 8vo. Edinb., 1874. D 7 P 4

WORDSWORTH (JOHN), M.A. Fragments and Specimens of early Latin; with Introductions and Notes. (Clar. Press.) 8vo. Oxford, 1874.   K 20 U 4

WORDSWORTH (WILLIAM), D.C.L. William Wordsworth: a Biography: by Edwin Paxton Hood. 8vo. Lond., 1851.   C 4 U 39
Memoir of W. Wordsworth, Poet Laureate; by C. Wordsworth, D.D. 2 vols. 8vo. Lond., 1851.   C 9 S 47, 48
The Prelude; or, Growth of a Poet's Mind: an Autobiographical Poem. 8vo. Lond., 1850.   H 6 U 10
Poetical Works of. 6 vols. 12mo. Lond., 1836–37.
                                            H 8 R 26–31
[A Biography]; by F. W. H. Myers. (Eng. Men of Letts.) 8vo. Lond., 1881.   C 1 U 36
On the Platonism of Wordsworth. [*See* SHORTHOUSE, J. H.]

WORDSWORTH SOCIETY. Transactions of, 1882–86. 5 vols. 8vo. Lond., 1882–87.   E

WORKING DRAWINGS AND DESIGNS. [*See* BURN, R. S.]

WORKING MEN'S BOOK SOCIETY. Report, 1864. 8vo. Sydney, 1864.   MG 1 Q 26

WORKING MEN'S CLUB. Rules of the Working Men's Club, Hobart Town, Tasmania. 12mo. Hobart, 1865.
                                            MG 1 Q 31
Depositor's Book, Working Men's Club Penny Bank. 32mo. Hobart, 1865.   MG 1 Q 31
[*See* NIXON, REV. T. R.]

WORKING MEN'S EDUCATIONAL UNION. Report. 8vo. Lond., 1856.   MF 3 P 15

WORKMAN'S DWELLINGS AND HUTS; or, Dwellings of our Agricultural Labourers, &c. (Newspaper Cuttings.—Pam., C.) 8vo. Sydney and Leeds, 1859.
                                            MJ 2 U 1
Workman's Dwellings and Model Lodging Houses. (Pam., C.) 8vo. Lond. (n.d.)   MJ 2 U 1

WORKSHOP (THE): a Monthly Journal, devoted to Progress of the Useful Arts. (Text and Plates.) 2 vols. 4to. Lond., 1868–69.   A 3 S 15, 16 †

WORMALD (R. B.) [*See* STAUNTON, H.]   A 17 U 11

WORMELL (R.), D.Sc., &c. Principles of Dynamics: an Elementary Text-book for Science Students. 8vo. Lond., 1876.   A 10 R 29

WORNUM (RALPH NICHOLSON). Some Account of the Life and Works of Hans Holbein, Painter, of Augsburg. Imp. 8vo. Lond., 1867.   C 3 W 13

WORRELL (GEORGE). Trial of, for the Murder of Frederick Fisher. [*See* MANUSCRIPTS AND PORTRAITS.]
                                            MF 1 U 21

WORSAAE (JENS JAKOB ASMUSSEN), HON.F.S.A., &c. Industrial Arts of Denmark, from the Earliest Times to the Danish Conquest of England. In two Parts. [*See* SOUTH KENSINGTON MUSEUM, 21.]

Primeval Antiquities of Denmark. Translated by William J. Thoms. 8vo. Lond., 1849.   B 2 R 8

Pre-history of the North, based on contemporary Memorials. Translated, with Memoir, by H. F. M. Simpson. 8vo. Lond., 1886.   B 7 S 44

WORSLEY (RT. HON. RICHARD), BART. History of the Isle of Wight. Roy. 4to. Lond., 1781.   B 2 U 35

WORSNOP (THOMAS). History of the City of Adelaide, from the Foundation of the Province of South Australia in 1836, to the end of the Municipal Year, 1877. 8vo. Adelaide, 1878.   MB 3 Q 29

Adelaide and its Environs: a Descriptive Guide to Adelaide and Places in its Vicinity. 12mo. Adelaide, 1880.   MD 1 T 57

WORTH (RICHARD NICHOLLS), F.G.S. History of Devonshire; with Sketches of its Leading Worthies. 8vo. Lond., 1886.   B 3 T 12

WORTHAM (REV. B. HALE), B.A., &c. Satakas of Bhartrihari. [*See* BHARTRIHARI.]   G 15 P 8

WORTHINGTON (MAJOR). The Old Field Officer. [*See* STOCKQUELER, J. H.]

WORTHINGTON (T. LOCKE). Historical Account and Illustrated Description of the Cathedral Church of Manchester. 4to. Manchester, 1884.   B 5 V 11

WORTLEY (EMMELINE STUART), LADY. [*See* STUART-WORTLEY, A. J.]

WOTTON (SIR HENRY). Life of; by Izaak Walton. 12mo. Lond., 1825.   C 1 S 19

Another copy. New ed. 12mo. Lond.,1884.   C 2 R 34

WOUVERMANS, OR WOUVERMENS (PHILIP). Oeuvres de Ph. Wouvermens Hollandois. Gravées d'après ses meilleurs Tableaux. 2 vols. el. fol. Paris, 1737-62.   A 11 P 19, 20 ‡

WRANGELL (ADM. FERDINAND VON). Narrative of an Expedition to the Polar Sea, in the years 1820-23. Edited by Major E. Sabine. 8vo. Lond., 1840.   D 4 S 1

WRANGHAM (REV. DIGBY STRANGEWAYS), M.A. [*See* ADAM OF ST. VICTOR.]   H 8 R 17-19

WRANGHAM (REV. FRANCIS). Eclogues of Virgil. [*See* VIRGILIUS MARO P.]   J 15 P 50, 51

The Pleiad : a Series of Abridgements from seven distinguished Writers on the Evidence of Christianity. (Const. Misc.) 18mo. Edinb., 1828.   K 10 Q 14

See LANGHORNE, J. AND W.]   C 7 U 48-53

WRAXALL (SIR C. F. LASCELLES), BART. Life and Times of Her Majesty Caroline Matilda, Queen of Denmark and Norway. 3 vols. 8vo. Lond., 1864.   C 10 P 20-22

Recollections of Russia. [*See* RUSSIA.]   D 7 P 49

WRAXALL (SIR N. WILLIAM), BART. History of France, from the Accession of Henry III, in 1574, to the Death of Henry IV, in 1610; with a view of the state of Europe at the Accession of Louis XIII. 6 vols. 8vo. Lond., 1814.   B 8 P 14-19

Historical Memoirs of my own Time—1772 to 1784. 2nd ed. 2 vols. 8vo. Lond., 1815.   C 6 R 23, 26

Posthumous Memoirs of his own Times. 3 vols. 8vo. Lond., 1836.   C 5 U 17-19

Tour round the Baltic, through the Northern Countries of Europe, particularly Denmark, Sweden, Finland, Russia, and Prussia. 4th ed. 8vo. Lond., 1807.   D 8 T 30

WRAY (COL. HENRY), C.M.G., &c. Some Applications of Theory to the Practice of Construction; with Examples. 8vo. Lond., 1880.   A 6 U 9

WRAY (LEONARD). Practical Sugar-planter: a complete Account of the Cultivation and Manufacture of the Sugar-cane. 8vo. Lond., 1848.   A 1 R 10

WRECK OF THE SHIP *ALL SERENE*. [*See* ALL SERENE.]   MD 1 V 9

WREN (SIR CHRISTOPHER). Towers and Steeples designed by Sir C. Wren: a Descriptive, Historical, and Critical Essay; with Illustrations, by Andrew T. Taylor, A.R.I.B.A. 8vo. Lond., 1881.   A 2 S 30

Sir Christopher Wren: his Family and his Times; with Original Letters, and a Discourse on Architecture hitherto unpublished, 1585-1723; by Lucy Phillimore. 8vo. Lond., 1881.   C 9 P 50

Parentalia. [*See* WRENS, FAMILY OF THE.]   C 23 S 33 ‡

WRENS (FAMILY OF THE). Parentalia; or, Memoirs of the Family of the Wrens, chiefly of Sir Christopher Wren; compiled by his Son, Christopher Wren. Sm. fol. Lond., 1750.   C 23 S 33 ‡

WRIGHT (CARROL D.) Ninth Annual Report of the Bureau of Statistics of Labour. [*See* UNITED STATES.] E

WRIGHT (ELIZUR). Fables of La Fontaine; translated from the French. [*See* LA FONTAINE, J. DE.]

WRIGHT (REV. GEORGE NEWNHAM), M.A. Life and Reign of William IV. 2 vols. 8vo. Lond., 1837.   C 9 S 43, 44

China; in a Series of Views. [*See* ALLOM, THOMAS.]

France Illustrated. [*See* ALLOM, THOMAS.]   D 6 V 1, 2

Topographical Dictionary. [*See* GORTON, JOHN.]   D 12 U 16-18

WRIGHT (GEORGE R.), F.S.A. Local Lays and Legends, Fantastic and Imaginary. Sm. 4to. Lond., 1885. J 12 V 8

WRIGHT (J. H.) [*See* COLLIGNON, M.] A 6 V 25

WRIGHT (J. M. F.), A.B. Commentary on Newton's Principia; with a supplementary volume. 2 vols. 8vo. Lond., 1833. A 10 U 14, 15

WRIGHT (JOHN). Biographical Memoir of the Rt. Hon. William Huskisson. Roy. 8vo. Lond., 1831. C 10 V 39

WRIGHT (JOSEPH). Life and Works; by W. Bemrose. Fol. Lond., 1885. C 23 P 18 ‡

WRIGHT (LEWIS). Brahma Fowl: a Monograph. 3rd ed. 8vo. Lond., 1873. A 14 Q 49
Illustrated Book of Poultry ; with practical schedules for judging, constructed from actual analysis of the best modern decisions. Illustrated. 4to. Lond., 1877. A 2 Q 7 †
Practical Poultry-keeper: a complete and standard Guide to the Management of Poultry. 9th ed. 8vo. Lond., 1877. A 1 P 43
Light: a Course of Experimental Optics, chiefly with the Lantern. 8vo. Lond., 1882. A 5 R 40

WRIGHT (O. W.) History of Modern Philosophy. [*See* COUSIN, V.]

WRIGHT (ROBERT SAMUEL), M.A. Golden Treasury of Ancient Greek Poetry. (Clar. Press.) 8vo. Oxford, 1847. H 8 P 41

WRIGHT (ROBERT SAMUEL), M.A., AND SHADWELL (J. E. L.), M.A. Golden Treasury of Greek Prose. (Clar. Press.) 8vo. Oxford, 1870. J 1 T 37

WRIGHT (MARCUS J.) Memoirs of Lee. [*See* LONG, A. L.] C 5 W 11

WRIGHT (THOMAS), M.D. Comparative Anatomy. [*See* AGASSIZ, PROF. L. J. R., AND GOULD, A. A.]

WRIGHT (THOMAS), M.A., &c. Alfred the Great. [*See* PAULI, DR. R.] C 8 T 1
Anglo-Saxon and Old English Vocabularies. 2nd ed ; edited by R. P. Wülcker. 2 vols. 8vo. Lond., 1884. K 14 Q 21, 22
Biographia Britannica Literaria; or, Biography of Literary Characters of Great Britain and Ireland. 2 vols. 8vo. Lond., 1842–46. C 8 S 1, 2
Dictionary of Obsolete and Provincial English. 2 vols. 12mo. Lond., 1869. K 11 U 4, 5
Early Travels in Palestine. [*See* PALESTINE.] D 5 Q 17
England under the House of Hanover; its History and Condition during the Reigns of the Three Georges. 2 vols. 8vo. Lond., 1848. B 5 R 41, 42
Feudal Manuals of English History: a Series of Sketches of our National History. Sm. 4to. Lond., 1872. B 5 R 40
Historical Works of Giraldus Cambrensis. [*See* BARRI, G.]
History and Antiquities of London. [*See* ALLEN, T.] B 7 P 16–20
History and Topography of the County of Essex; comprising its Ancient and Modern History. Drawings by Bartlett. 2 vols. 4to. Lond., 1836. B 2 U 9, 10

5 M

WRIGHT (THOMAS), M.A., &c.—*continued.*
History of Caricature and Grotesque in Literature and Art. With Illustrations. 8vo. Lond., 1864. B 14 S 21
History of Fulk Fitz Warine, an Outlawed Baron in the Reign of King John. (Warton Club.) 8vo. Lond., 1855. E
History of Ireland, from the Earliest Period of the Irish Annals to the Present Time. Illustrated. 3 vols. imp. 8vo. Lond., 1852. B 10 P 2–4 †
History of Ludlow and its Neighbourhood. 8vo. Ludlow, 1841. B 6 R 34
Memorials of Cambridge. [*See* LE KEUX, J.] B 6 S 17
Songs and Carols, from a Manuscript in the British Museum of the 15th Century. (Warton Club.) 8vo. Lond., 1856. E
The Celt, the Roman, and the Saxon: a History of the Early Inhabitants of Britain, down to the Conversion of the Anglo-Saxons to Christianity. 8vo. Lond., 1875. B 4 Q 19
Town of Cowper; or, the Literary and Historical Associations of Olney and its Neighbourhood. With Engravings. 8vo. Lond., 1886. B 4 P 22
Travels of Marco Polo. [*See* POLO, MARCO.] B 10 Q 35
University of Cambridge. [*See* FULLER, T.] B 6 R 30
Volume of Vocabularies. 8vo. Lond., 1857. K 12 T 20
Womankind in Western Europe, from the Earliest Times to the 17th Century. Sm. 4to. Lond., 1869. B 7 T 29
Vision and Creed of Piers Ploughman. [*See* LANGLEY, W.]

[*See* FAIRHOLT; F. W., *and* MALORY, SIR T.]

WRIGHT (THOMAS), F.S.A., AND EVANS (R. H.) Historical and Descriptive Account of the Caricatures of James Gillray, comprising a Political and Humorous History of the latter part of the Reign of George III. 8vo. Lond., 1851. A 7 S 4

WRIGHT (THOMAS COOKE). Davidson's Precedents. [*See* DAVIDSON, C.]

WRIGHT (WILLIAM), B.A., &c. Empire of the Hittites; with Decipherment of Hittite Inscriptions, by Prof. A. H. Sayce, LL.D.; and a complete Set of Hittite Inscriptions, revised by Mr. W. H. Rylands, F.S.A. 8vo. Lond., 1884. B 2 R 49

WRIGHT (WILLIAM ALDIS), M.A. Select Plays of Shakespeare. [*See* SHAKESPEARE, W.]
Advancement of Learning. [*See* BACON, SIR F.]

WRIGHTSON (PROF. JOHN) Agricultural Machinery. (Brit. Manuf. Indust.) 12mo. Lond., 1876. A 17 S 29

WRIGHTSON (REV. W. G.), M.A. Examination of the Functional Elements of an English Sentence; together with a New System of Analytic Marks. 8vo. Lond., 1882. K 11 V 1

WRIXON (ARTHUR N.) Electoral Law of New South Wales and Victoria. 8vo. Sydney, 1831. MF 3 Q 19

WRIXON (H. J.) Condition and Prospects of Australia as compared with Older Lands: a Lecture. 8vo. Melb., 1869. MJ 2 R 7

WROTTESLEY (LIEUT.-COL. THE HON. GEORGE). Life and Correspondence of Field-Marshal the Rt. Hon. Sir John Burgoyne, Bart.; by his Son-in-Law. 2 vols. 8vo. Lond., 1873. C 8 U 9, 10

WÜLCKER (RICHARD PAUL). Anglo-Saxon and Old English Vocabularies. [*See* WRIGHT, T.]

WÜLLERSTORF-URBAIR (COMM. B. VON). Circumnavigation of the Globe, by the Austrian Frigate *Novara.* [*See* SCHERZER, DR. KARL.] D 9 U 21–23

WUNDT (W.) Grundzüge der physiologischen Psychologie. 2 vols. roy. 8vo. Leip., 1880. A 12 U 7, 8
Philosophische Studien. Bande 1–3. 3 vol. 8vo. Leipzig, 1883–86. G 6 T 1–3

WURM (CHRISTIAN FRIEDRICH LUDWIG). Wörterbuch der deutschen Sprache von der Druckerfindung bis zum heutigen Tage. Erster Band. (*All published.*) 8vo. Freiburg, 1858. K 15 S 30

WURTZ (CHARLES ADOLPHE). Atomic Theory. 8vo. Lond., 1880. A 5 R 34
History of Chemical Theory, from the Age of Lavoisier to the present time. 8vo. Lond., 1869. A 5 S 55
Die Atomistische Theorie. 8vo. Leipzig, 1879. A 5 S 24

WYAT OR WYATT (SIR THOMAS). Life and Poems of. [*See* CHALMERS, A.]
Works of. [*See* SURREY, EARL OF.]

WYATT (SIR MATTHEW DIGBY), M.A., &c. Fine Art: a Sketch of its History, Theory, Practice, and application to Industry. 8vo. Lond., 1870. A 7 Q 4
Art of Illuminating. [*See* TYMMS, W. R.] A 1 R 4 †
Industrial Arts of the 19th Century: a series of Illustrations of the Choicest Specimens produced by every Nation at the Great Exhibition, 1851. 2 vols. fol. Lond., 1851–53. A 2 P 2, 3 ‡

WYATT (CAPT. WALTER J.) History of Prussia, from the earliest times to the present day. 2 vols. 8vo. Lond., 1876. B 9 R 8, 9

WYATT (DR. WILLIAM), J.P. Some Account of the Manners and Superstitions of the Adelaide and Encounter Bay Aboriginal Tribes. With a Vocabulary of their Languages, Names of Persons and Places, &c. (Native Tribes of South Australia.) 8vo. Adelaide, 1879.* MA 1 R 12

WYATVILLE (SIR JEFFRY), R.A. Illustrations of Windsor Castle. 2 vols. el. fol. Lond., 1841. A 10 P 11, 12 ‡

WYCHE (SIR P.) Life of Don John de Castro. [*See* ANDRADA, JACINTO FREIRE DE.] C 7 V 46

WYCHERLEY (WILLIAM). The Country Girl: a Comedy; altered from Wycherley's "Country Wife," by David Garrick. (Bell's Brit. Theatre.) 18mo. Lond., 1791. H 2 P 20
Another copy. (New Eng. Theatre.) 12mo. Lond., 1790. H 4 P 26
Another copy. (Brit. Theatre.) 12mo. Lond., 1808. H 1 P 16
The Plain Dealer: a Comedy; altered and adapted by by Isaac Bickerstaff. (Bell's Brit. Theatre.) 18mo. Lond., 1796. H 2 P 12
Another copy. [*See* BRIT. DRAMA, 3.]

WYCHERLEY (W.), CONGREVE (W.), VANBRUGH (J.), AND FARQUHAR (G.) Dramatic Works of. With Biographical and Critical Notices, by L. Hunt. Roy. 8vo. Lond., 1855. H 2 T 21

WYCLIFFE (JOHN). [*See* WICLIF, J.]

WYKEHAM (WILLIAM), BISHOP OF WINCHESTER. Life of Robert Lowth, D.D. 3rd ed., corrected. 8vo. Oxford, 1777. C 9 P 49

WYLD (JAMES). Map of Australia; compiled from the Nautical Surveys made by Order of the Admiralty and other authentic Documents. 4to. Lond. (n.d.) MD5S18‡
Province of Queensland. (Map.) 8vo. Lond. (n.d.) MD 5 P 16 ‡
Notes on the Distribution of Gold throughout the World, including Australia, California, and Russia. With four Maps. 8vo. Lond., 1852.* MA 2 Q 11
Another copy. 8vo. Lond., 1852. MA 2 Q 35
Maps and Plans, showing the principal Movements, Battles, and Sieges of the British Army during the War, from 1808 to 1814, in the Spanish Peninsula and South of France. El. fol. Lond., 1841. B 8 P 15‡
Memoir (annexed to the above.) Roy. 4to. Lond., 1841. B 8 P 16 ‡
Military Map of the Countries between Odessa and Perekop; with the Stations of the Russian Troops. (Sheet.) Sm. fol. Lond., 1855. D 33 P 2 ‡
Map of China. (Sheet.) Sm. fol. Lond., 1840. D 33 P 2 ‡

WYLDE (MRS. FLORA FRANCES). Life of Flora M'Donald. Written by her Grand-daughter. 8vo. Lond., 1875. C 1 S 32

WYLDE (JAMES). Mathematics, Pure and Applied; including Arithmetic, Algebra, Geometry, Trigonometry (plane and spherical), Logarithms, Logarithmic Tables, Mensuration, &c. Imp. 8vo. Lond., 1873. A 1 R 11 †
Magic of Science: a Manual of amusing and instructive Scientific Experiments. 3rd ed. 8vo. Lond. (n.d.) A 16 P 5

WYLIE (JAMES HAMILTON), M.A. History of England
under Henry the Fourth. Vol. 1 (1399–1404). 8vo.
Lond., 1884. B 4 P 23

WYLIE (WILLIAM HOWIE). Thomas Carlyle: the Man
and his Books. Illustrated. 8vo. Lond., 1881. C 2 T 12

WYLLIE (JOHN WILLIAM SHAW), M.A., &c. Essays on
the External Policy of India; edited, with a brief Life,
by W. W. Hunter, B.A., &c. 8vo. Lond., 1875. B 10 T 12

WYMAN (C. W. H.) List of Technical Terms relating
to Printing Machinery. 12mo. Lond., 1882. A 11 P 17
Bibliography of Printing. [*See* BIGMORE, E. C.]

WYMAN (F. F.) From Calcutta to the Snowy Range;
being the Narrative of a Trip through the Provinces of
India to the Himalays; by "An Old Indian" [F. F. W.]
8vo. Lond., 1866. D 6 P 18

WYMAN (W. H.) Bibliography of the Bacon-Shakespeare Controversy; with Notes and Extracts. 8vo.
Cincinnati, 1884. K 17 Q 25

WYMAN & SONS. [*See* FURNITURE, OLD.] A 2 U 23

WYNDHAM (GEORGE). Letter to Sir John Bull, Bart.,
upon the Disposal of Crown Lands in the Colonies; by
"A Squatter." 8vo. Sydney, 1847. MF 3 P 2
Another copy. 8vo. Sydney, 1847. MJ 2 Q 8
Impending Crisis. Fellow Colonists:—Meet and discuss,
an' it please you, but before you meet, read and digest
this much from Blackstone upon Squatting; and oblige
your obedient humble servant. (Pam. 19.) 12mo.
Maitland, 1847. MJ 2 Q 8
Letter addressed to the Squatters of New South Wales,
on the Transportation and Labour Questions; by "A
Squatter." (Pam. 19.) 8vo. Sydney, 1851. MJ 2 Q 8

WYNDHAM (HENRY P.) [*See* DODINGTON, G. B.] C 1 P 16

WYNDHAM (JOHN). The Land Question: Address to
the President of the Hunter River Agricultural and
Horticultural Association, Maitland, September 22, 1873.
(Pam. Ds.) 12mo. Sydney, 1873. MF 3 P 17
Photographs of the Dalwood Vineyards, near Branxton,
New South Wales, Australia. Imp. 4to. Branxton,
1886. MD 3 Q 9 ‡

WYNTER (ANDREW), M.D., &c. Borderlands of Insanity,
and other allied Papers. 8vo. Lond., 1875. A 12 Q 24
Subtle Brains and Lissom Fingers; being some of the
Chisel-marks of our Industrial and Scientific Progress.
2nd ed. 8vo. Lond., 1864. J 12 U 19
Our Social Bees. 2nd series. 8vo. Lond., 1866.
J 8 R 31
Peeps into the Human Hive. 2 vols. 8vo. Lond.,
A 17 T 25, 26

WYNTER (REV. JAMES CECIL), M.A. Hints on Church
Colonization. 12mo. Lond., 1850. MJ 1 Q 38

WYNTOUN (ANDROW OF). De Orygynale Cronykil of
Scotland, be Androw of Wyntown, Priowr of Sanct
Serfis Ynche in Loch Levyn. 2 vols. 8vo. Edinb.,
B 13 T 1, 2
Another copy. Vols. 1, 2; edited by David Laing.
(Historians of Scotland.) 2 vols. 8vo. Edinb., 1874.
B 13 P 46, 47

WYON (FREDERICK W.) History of Great Britain during
the Reign of Queen Anne. 2 vols. 8vo. Lond., 1876.
B 23 U 1, 2

WYSE (RT. HON. SIR THOMAS), K.C.B. Excursion in
the Peloponnesus, in the year 1858. With Illustra-
tions. 2 vols. roy. 8vo. Lond., 1865. D 7 V 2, 3
Impressions of Greece. 8vo. Lond., 1871. D 7 T 27
Education Reform; or, the necessity of a National
System of Education. Vol. 1. (*All published.*) 8vo.
Lond., 1836. G 17 R 7

X

XENOPHON. [Works of.] Vol. 1. Anabasis; [or, Ex-
pedition of Cyrus into Persia;] translated by Edward
Spelman.   Vol. 2. The Cyropædia; [or, Institution of
Cyrus;] translated by the Hon. M. A. Cooper. (Fam.
Class Lib.) 2 vols. 18mo. Lond., 1830. J 15 P 52, 53

Anabasis; or, Expedition of Cyrus; and the Memorabilia
of Socrates; literally translated from the Greek, by the Rev.
J. S. Watson, M.A., &c. 8vo. Lond., 1878.   B 9 S 18

Cyropædia, or Institutions of Cyrus and the Hellenics;
or, Grecian History; literally translated from the Greek,
by the Rev. J. S. Watson, M.A., and the Rev. Henry
Dale, M.A.; with Biographical Notice [by the Rev. J. S.
Watson, M.A.], Chronological Table, and Index.   8vo.
Lond., 1876.   B 9 S 16

Life of Socrates; collected from the "Memorabilia" of
Xenophon. [*See* COOPER, J. G.]   C 10 Q 41

Memoirs of Socrates for English Readers. New Translation from Xenophon's "Memorabilia," with illustrative
Notes, by Edward Levien, M.A. 18mo. Lond., 1872.
                                                   C 1 P 35

XENOPHON—*continued.*
Minor Works; literally translated from the Greek, with
Notes and Illustrations, by the Rev. J. S. Watson, M.A.,
&c. 8vo. Lond., 1877.   B 9 S 17

Whole Works of. 8vo. Lond., 1847.   J 17 Q 22

Xenophontis de Cyri Institutione, Libri octo; edit Thomas
Hutchinson, A.M. 8vo. Lond., 1790.   B 27 U 13

XENOPHON EPHESIUS.   De Amoribus Anthae et
Abrocomae Libri 5. [*See* SCRIPTORES EROTICI GRAECI.]

XENOS (STEPHANOS).   The Devil in Turkey; or, Scenes in
Constantinople; translated from the Author's unpublished
Greek Manuscript, by Henry Corpe, M.C.P. 1st series.
3 vols. 8vo. Lond., 1851.   J 4 P 20-22

XIPHILINUS (JOANNES). Opera omnia. [*See* MIGNE,
J. P., SERIES GRÆCA, 120.]

[*See* DION CASSIUS.]   B 12 P 32, 33

XYLANDER (W.) [*See* ANTONIUS LIBERALIS.] J 7 S 30

Y

Y. (D.) History of Hampshire, &c. [*See* WARNER, REV. R.]
B 6 V 13-15

YALDEN (THOMAS). Life and Poems of. [*See* JOHNSON, S.; *and* CHALMERS, A.]

YAPP (G. W.) Art Industry: Furniture, House Fittings, and Decorations, Illustrative of the Arts of the Carpenter, Joiner, Cabinet Maker, Painter, Decorator, and Upholsterer. With about 1,200 Engravings and Diagrams. Imp. 4to. Lond., 1883. A 23 P 8 ‡

YARRELL (WILLIAM), V.P.Z.S., &c. History of British Fishes. Illustrated; with Supplements. 2 vols. 8vo. Lond., 1836-39. A 14 U 31, 32

YARRINGTON (REV. W. H. H.), M.A. University Prize Poems ["Captain Cook meditating on Australia's Future"], and other Verses. 12mo. West Maitland, 1880. MH 1 P 44

YARROW (DR. H. C.) List of Skeletons and Crania in the Section of Comparative Anatomy of Philadelphia International Exhibition, 1876. 8vo. Philad., 1876. A 16 U 21

YASS GRAMMAR SCHOOL MAGAZINE. Devoted to Literature, Science, and Sport. (*All published.*) Sm. 4to. Yass, 1872. MJ 2 S 4

YATE (LIEUT. A. C.) England and Russia Face to Face in Asia: Afghan Boundary Commission. With Illustrations. 8vo. Edinb., 1887. D 4 T 35

YATE (REV. WILLIAM). Account of New Zealand, and of the Formation and Progress of the Church Missionary Society's Mission in the Northern Island. 8vo. Lond., 1835.*
MD 3 R 37
Letter to the Parishioners of St. James Church, Sydney; suggested by the approaching Confirmation. 8vo. Sydney, 1836. MG 2 Q 31
Another copy. 8vo. Sydney, 1836.* MJ 2 R 22

YATES (MRS. ASHTON). Letters written during a Journey to Switzerland, 1841. 2 vols. 8vo. Lond., 1843. D 8 S 31, 32

YATES (EDMUND). Celebrities at Home. Reprinted from *The World.* First-Third Series. 8vo. Lond., 1877-79. C 10-T 2-5
Edmund Yates: his Recollections and Experiences. [Written by himself.] 2 vols. 8vo. Lond., 1884. C 9 T 53-54
The Ball; or, a Glance at Almack's in 1829. 8vo. Lond., 1829. J 11 S 3

YATES (EDWARD), B.A., &c. Elements of the Science of Grammar, illustrated by a Comparison of the Structure of the English and Turkish Languages. 8vo. Lond., 1857. K 12 Q 39

YATES (REV. W.), D.D. Introduction to the Bengáli Language; edited by J. Wenger. 2 vols. 8vo. Calcutta, 1847. K 13 Q 19, 20
Bengáli Grammar. Reprinted, with Improvements, from his Introduction to the Bengáli Language; edited by J. Wenger. 12mo. Calcutta, 1864. K 11 V 21

YEAR-BOOK OF FACTS (THE). In Science and the Useful Arts. 42 vols. 12mo. Lond., 1842-80. E

YEAR-BOOK OF NEW ZEALAND, 1885-87; compiled by G. V. Stewart, T. S. Jones, and H. C. Cooper. 2 vols. 8vo. Lond., 1885-86. ME 14 P

YEAR-BOOK OF SCIENTIFIC AND LEARNED SOCIETIES, 1884-86. 3 vols. 8vo. Lond., 1884-86. E 1.59

YEAR'S SPORT (THE) for 1885. 8vo. Lond., 1886. E 1.78

YEARSLEY (JAMES), M.D., &c. Throat Ailments: more especially the Enlarged Tonsil and Elongated Uvula, in connection with Defects of Voice, Speech, Hearing, Deglutition, Respiration, Cough, Nasal Obstruction, and the imperfect development of Health, Strength, and Growth in young Persons. 8th ed. 8vo. Lond., 1867. A 13 R 15

YEATS (JOHN), LL.D., &c. Growth and Vicissitudes of Commerce, from B.C. 1500 to A.D. 1789. (Technical, Industrial, Trade Education.) 8vo. Lond., 1872. F 6 Q 5
Manual of recent and existing Commerce, from the year 1789 to 1872. (Technical, Industrial, and Trade Education.) 8vo. Lond., 1872. F 6 Q 6
Technical History of Commerce. 8vo. Lond., 1871. F 5 S 13
Yesterdays with Authors. New illustrated ed., by James T. Fields. 8vo. Lond., 1881. C 5 S 27

YELDHAM (CAPT. WALTER), "ALIPH CHEEM." Lays of Ind. New ed. 8vo. Bombay, 1876. H 7 S 26

YELVERTON (THERESE), COUNTESS AVONMORE. Teresina Peregrina; or, Fifty Thousand Miles of Travel round the World. 2 vols. 8vo. Lond., 1874. D 10 R 13, 14
Yes or No? 8vo. Lond., 1852. MF 1 R 17

YEOMAN (THE). Yeoman and Australian Acclimatiser. 3 vols fol. Melb., 1861-64. ME

YOE (SHWAY). [*See* SCOTT, J. G.]

YOLLAND (CAPT. WILLIAM). Ordnance Survey Account of the Measurement of the Lough Foyle Base in Ireland. Roy. 4to. Lond., 1847. A 2 Q 10 †

YONGE (CHARLES DUKE), M.A. Constitutional History of England, from 1760 to 1860. 8vo. Lond., 1882. B 5 R 36
History of the British Navy, from the earliest period to the present time. 2 vols. 8vo. Lond., 1863. B 6 Q 31, 32

YONGE (CHARLES DUKE), M.A.—*continued.*
Three Centuries of English Literature. 8vo. Lond.,
1872.   B 4 R 30
Academic Questions of M. T. Cicero. [*See* CICERO,
M. T.]
Works of Philo-Judaeus. [*See* PHILO-JUDAEUS.]
Life of Marie Antoinette, Queen of France. 2 vols.
8vo. Lond., 1876.   C 3 P 27, 28
Life and Administration of Robert Banks, Second Earl
of Liverpool, K.G. 3 vols. 8vo. Lond., 1868. C 7 S 4–6
Roman History. [*See* AMMIANUS MARCELLUS.] B12P22
The Deipnosophists; or, Banquet of the Learned. [*See*
ATHENAEUS OF NAUCRATUS.]   J 10 P 2–4
Flowers of History. [*See* MATTHEW OF WEST-
MINISTER.]   B 3 P 8, 9
Lives and Opinions of Eminent Philosophers. [*See*
DIOGENES LAERTIUS.]   C 1 S 34

YONGE (CHARLOTTE MARY). Cameos from English History. First to Fifth Series. 5 vols. 12mo. Lond.,
1883–87.   B 23 P 7–11
The Danvers Papers: an Invention. 12mo. Lond.,
1867.   J 7 Q 19
Life of John Coleridge Patteson, Missionary Bishop of
the Melanesian Islands. 2nd ed. 2 vols. 8vo. Lond.,
1874.   MC 1 R 16, 17
Youth of Queen Elizabeth. [*See* WIESNER, L.]
                                                  C 2 P 11, 12
Memoirs of Marshal Bugeaud. [*See* D'IDEVILLE,
COUNT H.]   C 8 U 11, 12
[*See* BEUGNOT, COUNT J. C.]

YORK. Accurate Description and History of the Cathedral
and Metropolitical Church of St. Peter of York. 12mo.
York, 1768.   B 4 P 3

YORK GATE LIBRARY. Catalogue of the York Gate
Geographical and Colonial Library. Roy. 8vo. Lond.,
1882.   K 8 Q 4
Catalogue of the York Gate Library, formed by S.
W. Silver: an Index to the Literature of Geography,
Maritime and Inland Discovery, Commerce, and Colo-
nization; by E. A. Petherick. 2nd ed. Imp. 8vo.
Lond., 1886.   MK 1 U 21

YORKE (COL. PHILLIP), F.R.S. Life of Baron Von
Muffling. [*See* MUFFLING, BARON VON.]   C 7 U 47

YOSY (A.) Switzerland, as now divided into Nineteen
Cantons; with Picturesque Representations of the Dress
and Manners of the Swiss. 2 vols. roy. 8vo. Lond.,
1815.   D 8 V 15, 16

YOUATT (WILLIAM). Cattle; their Breeds, Management,
and Diseases; with Index. 8vo. Lond., 1834. A 1 R 3
Sheep; their Breeds, Management, and Diseases, &c.
8vo. Lond., 1837.   A 1 S 9
The Horse; with a Treatise on Draught. 8vo. Lond.,
1868.   A 1 R 26
The Dog. 8vo. Lond., 1867.   A 1 R 14

YOUATT (WILLIAM), AND SIDNEY (SAMUEL). The Pig;
comprising Modern Pigs, Breeding, Feeding, Ancient History, Natural History, Medical Information. With Illustrations. 8vo. Lond., 1860.   A 1 P 19

YOUL (REV. JOHN). Circular Letter, relating to the Dis-
tribution of Bibles and Testaments in the Colony by the
Agents of the Bible Society. (MS. Pam. E.)
Sydney, 1819.   MJ 2 S 2

YOUL (RICHARD), M.D., &c. [*See* VICTORIA—PARLIA-
MENTARY PAPERS.]

YOUNG (ALEXANDER). Short History of the Netherlands
(Holland and Belgium). 8vo. Lond., 1886.   B 12 T 1

YOUNG (ARTHUR). Six Months' Tour through the North
of England. 4 vols. 8vo. Lond., 1770. A 1 Q 39–42
The Farmer's Letters; containing the Sentiments of a
Practical Husbandman on various Subjects of great Im-
portance. 3rd ed., corrected and enlarged. 2 vols. 8vo.
Lond., 1771.   A 1 Q 47, 48
The Farmer's Tour through the East of England. 4 vols.
8vo. Lond., 1771.   A 1 Q 43–46
Travels during the years 1787–89. 2 vols. 4to. Bury St.
Edmunds, 1794.   D 7 V 14, 15
Another copy. 2nd ed. 2 vols. 4to. Lond., 1794.
                                                  D 7 V 16, 17

YOUNG (PROF. CHARLES A.), PH.D., &c. The Sun. With
Illustrations. 8vo. Lond., 1882.   A 3 S 32

YOUNG (CHARLES MAYNE). Memoir of, Tragedian; with
Extracts from his Son's Journal, by the Rev. Julian Charles
Young. 2 vols. 8vo. Lond., 1871.   C 3 P 47, 48

YOUNG (DAVID). Account of the Capture, Trial, and
Execution of. [*See* DAYLESFORD MURDER.]   MF 2 S 1

YOUNG (EDWARD), PH.D. Labor in Europe and America:
a Special Report on the Rates of Wages, the Cost of Sub-
sistence, and the Condition of the Working Classes in Great
Britain, Germany, France, Belgium, and other Countries of
Europe; also, in the United States and British America.
Roy. 8vo. Wash., 1876.   F 3 P 8

YOUNG (EDWARD), LL.D. The Brothers: a Tragedy.
(Bell's Brit. Theatre.) 18mo. Lond., 1797. H 2 P 45
Another copy. (New Eng. Theatre.) 12mo. Lond.,
1777.   H 4 P 27
Busiris, King of Egypt: a Tragedy. (Bell's Brit. Theatre.)
18mo. Lond., 1796.   H 2 P 2
Life and Poems of. [*See* CHALMERS, A., *and* JOHNSON, S.]
Poetical Works of. 2 vols. 8vo. Boston, 1859.
                                                  H 8 R 34, 35
The Revenge: a Tragedy. (Bell's Brit. Theatre.)
Lond., 1792.   H 2 P 22
Another copy. (New Eng. Theatre.) 12mo. Lond., 1788.
                                                  H 4 P 17
Another copy. (Brit. Theatre.) 12mo. Lond., 1808.
                                                  H 1 P 12
Another copy. [*See* BRIT. DRAMA, 1.]

YOUNG (EDWARD D.), R.N. Nyassa: a Journal of Adventures whilst exploring Lake Nyassa, Central Africa, and establishing the Settlement of "Livingstonia"; revised by Rev. Horace Waller, F.R.G.S. With Maps. 2nd ed. 8vo. Lond., 1877. D 1 R 15

YOUNG (FRANCIS), M.C.P. Cassell's Historical, Political, and Commercial Map of Europe. 4to. Lond., 1858. D 33 Q 16 ‡

YOUNG (FREDERICK). Imperial Federation of Great Britain and her Colonies. Roy. 8vo. Lond., 1876. MF 2 S 28

Another copy. Roy. 8vo. Lond., 1876. F 3 P 16

YOUNG (SIR GEORGE). Fac-simile of a Proposal for a Settlement on the Coast of South Wales, 1785; from a Copy in the possession of the Publishers. Sm. fol. Sydney, 1888.* MB 3 P 6 †

YOUNG (GERARD). Voyage of the *Wanderer.* [*See* LAMBERT, C. AND S.] D 9 U 32

YOUNG (I. S. HUNTER). Victorian Geographical and Biographical Charades. Sm. 4to. Melb., 1870. MJ 2 P 17

YOUNG (JENNIE J.) Ceramic Art: a Compendium of the History and Manufacture of Pottery and Porcelain. With Illustrations. Roy. 8vo. Lond., 1879. A 11 T 18

YOUNG (JOHN), M.D., &c. Physical Geography. 8vo. Lond., 1874. A 29 P 15

YOUNG (PROF. JOHN RADFORD). Analysis and Solution of Cubic and Biquadratic Equations. 8vo. Lond., 1842. A 10 S 13

Introduction to Algebra, and to the Solution of Numerical Equations; with full Explanations of the Theory, and numerous Examples for exercise. 12mo. Lond., 1851. A 10 S 5

Key to "Introduction to Algebra," containing Solutions in full. Lond., 1854. A 10 S 5

Key to Rudimentary Treatise on Arithmetic. (Weale.) 12mo. Lond., 1882. A 17 P 4

Mathematical Dissertations, for the use of Students in the Modern Analysis; with Improvements in the Practice of Sturm's Theorem, in the Theory of Curvature, and in the Summation of Infinite Series. 8vo. Lond., 1841. A 10 T 20

Mathematics. [*See* WYLDE, J.]

Navigation and Nautical Astronomy, in Theory and Practice. (Weale.) 12mo. Lond., 1872. A 17 P 12

Rudimentary Treatise on Arithmetic. 10th ed. (Weale.) 12mo. Lond., 1882. A 17 P 4

Tables intended to facilitate the Operations of Navigation and Nautical Astronomy. (Weale.) 12mo. Lond., 1872. A 17 P 12

Another copy. (Weale.) 12mo. Lond., 1884. A 17 R 8

Theory and Solution of Algebraical Equations of the Higher Orders. 2nd ed., enlarged. 8vo. Lond., 1843. A 10 T 20

[*See* HANN, J.]

YOUNG (JOHN RUSSELL). Around the World with General Grant: a Narrative of the Visit of General U. S. Grant, ex-President of the United States, to various Countries in Europe, Asia, and Africa, in 1877–79. 2 vols. imp. 8vo. New York, 1879. D 10 T 26, 27

YOUNG (REV. JULIAN CHARLES). Memoir of Charles Mayne Young, Tragedian; with Extracts from his Son's Journal. 2 vols. 8vo. Lond., 1871. C 3 P 47, 48

YOUNG (ROBERT), LL.D. Dictionary and Concordance. of Bible Words and Synonyms. 8vo. Edinb., 1883. K 18 R 9

YOUNG (REV. ROBERT). Southern World: Journal of a Deputation from the Wesleyan Conference to Australia and Polynesia. 8vo. Lond., 1855. MD 1 W 22

Southern World : Australia and Tasmania. 4th ed. 12mo. Lond., 1858. MD 1 W 23

Southern World: New Zealand and Polynesia. 4th ed. 12mo. Lond., 1858. MD 1 W 24

YOUNG (THOMAS). Narrative of a Residence on the Mosquito Shore, during the years 1839–41. 8vo. Lond., 1842. D 3 P 62

YOUNG (W.) Great Increase of Small-pox in London. 8vo. Lond., 1881. A 12 S 34

Fable about the Hospital Nurses saved from Small-pox by re-Vaccination. (Pam. Cp.) 8vo. Lond., 1880. A 12 S 34

Vaccination Statistics. (Pam. Cp.) 8vo. Lond., 1881. A 12 S 34

Vaccination ; the Fallacy of the Mitigation Dogma. (Pam. Cp.) 8vo. Lond., 1881. A 12 S 34

YOUNG MEN'S WESLEYAN MUTUAL IMPROVEMENT SOCIETY. Rules. 18mo. Sydney, 1869. MJ 2 P 27

YOUNG VICTORIA: a Contribution in aid of National Education; by J.B.A. 8vo. Melb., 1871. MG 1 Q 38

YRIARTE (CHARLES). Florence; its History, the Medici, the Humanists, Letters, Arts. Imp. 4to. Lond., 1882. B 19 U 2 ‡

Venise; Histoire, Art, Industrie, la Ville, la Vie. Imp. 4to. Paris, 1878. D 4 P 6 ‡

YULE (COMM. CHARLES B.), R.N. [*See* AUSTRALIA DIRECTORY.]

YULE (COL. HENRY), C.B. [*See* POLO, MARCO.]

YULE (COL. H.), AND BURNELL (A. C.) Hobson-Jobson; being a Glossary of Anglo-Indian Colloquial Words and Phrases and of Kindred Terms. 8vo. Lond., 1886. K 14 T 30

YVAN (DR. M.) China, &c. [*See* CALLERY, J. M.] B 2 P 29

YVES (SAINTE) ÉVÊQUE DE CHARTRES. Opera Omnia. [*See* MIGNE, J. P., SERIES LATINA, 161, 162.]

Z

ZADKIEL. [*See* MORRISON, LIEUT. R. J.]   A 24 U 6

ZAEHNSDORF (JOSEPH W.) The Art of Bookbinding.
Illustrated. 8vo. Lond., 1880.   A 11 R 4

ZAMOYSKI, OR ZAMOYSCI (JOHANN SAVIUS). Collectanea Vitam Resque Gestas J. Zamoyscii. Illustrantia ; edit A. T. C. de K. Dzialynski. Imp. 4to.
Posnaniae, 1861.   C 7 R 4 †

ZARNCKE (F.) [*See* BENECKE, G. F.]

ZEITSCHRIFT FUR WISSENSCHAFTLICHE ZOO-
LOGIE. Band 27–43. 17 vols. 8vo. Leipzig, 1876–
86.   E 1.37

ZELLER (PROF. EDWARD). History of Eclecticism in
Greek Philosophy. 8vo. Lond., 1883.   G 7 T 32

History of Greek Philosophy, from the Earliest Period
to the Time of Socrates. 2 vols. 8vo. Lond., 1881.
          G 7 T 33, 34

David Friedrich Strauss in his Life and Writings.
With a Portrait. 8vo. Lond., 1874.   C 4 Q 47

Die Philosophie der Griechen. 3e auflage. 8vo.
Leipzig, 1880.   G 2 T 15

Strauss · and Renan : an Essay. 8vo. Lond., 1866.
          G 10 Q 17

Geschichte der deutschen Philosophie, seit Leibnitz.
(Ges. der Wiss, 13.) 8vo. München, 1873.   A 17 V 27

Outlines of .the History of Greek Philosophy. 8vo.
Lond., 1886.   G 7 T 35

ZELTER (KARL F.) [*See* GOETHE, J. W. VON.] C 1 S 29

ZENDAVESTA ; or, the Religious Books of the Zoroastrians ; edited and translated by N. L. Westergaard.
Vol. I. The Zend Texts (*all published*). 4to. Copenhagen, 1852-54.   G 5 U 21

ZENO (SANCTUS), VERONENSIS EPISCOPUS. Opera omnia.
[*See* MIGNE, J. P., SERIES LATINA, 11.]

ZETA. [*See* INDIA.]

ZETZSCHE (DR. KARL EDUARD). Kurzer Abriss der
Geschichte der elektrischen Telegraphie. Roy. 8vo.
Berlin, 1874.   A 5 R 60

ZEUNE (J. C.) [*See* HORATIUS FLACCUS, Q.] J 13 Q 12–16

ZEUSS (J. C.), PH.D. Grammatica Celtica e Monumentis Vetustis tam Hibernicae Linguae quam Brittani-
carum Dialectorum Cambricae Cornicae Aremoricae
comparatis Gallicae priscae reliquiis. Editio altera
curavit H. Ebel. Imp. 8vo. Berolini, 1871. K 14 U 1

ZEUSS (J. C.), PH.D.—*continued.*
Index Nominum et Vocabulorum Hibernicorum quae
in I. C. Zeussii Grammatica Celtica reperiuntur ; con-
struxit I. O. Molloy. (*All published.*) 8vo. Eblanae,
1878.   K 14 U 2

Indices Glossarum et Vocabulorum Hibernicorum quae
in Grammaticae Celticae editione altera explanantur.
Composuerunt B. Güterbock et R. Thurneysen. Roy.
8vo. Lipsiae, 1881.   K 14 S 11

ZIEMANN (ADOLF). Mittelhochdeutsches Wörterbuch
zum Handgebrauch. Nebst grammatischer Einleitung.
8vo. Quedlinburg, 1838.   K 13 Q 41

ZIEMSSEN (PROF. HUGO WILHELM VON). Cyclopædia of
the Practice of Medicine. Albert H. Buck, M.D., Editor
of English Translation. Vols. 1–17. Roy. 8vo. Lond.,
1875–80.   K 9 Q 1–17

ZINCKE (REV. F. BARHAM). Egypt of the Pharaohs and
of the Kedivé. 8vo. Lond., 1871.   D 2 P 22

A Walk in the Grisons ; being a third month in
Switzerland. 8vo. Lond., 1875.   D 8 R 13

ZINGERLE (IGNAZ). Tirol und Vorarlberg. [*See* UNSER
VATERLAND.]   D 38 P 18 ‡

ZIRKEL (DR. FERDINAND). Lehrbuch der Petrographie.
2 vols. 8vo.. Bonn, 1866.   A 10 Q 10, 11

ZITTEL (PROF. K. A.) Aus der Urzeit ; Bilder aus der
Schöpfungsgeschichte. 2 vols. 12mo. München, 1871–72.
          A 9 P 50, 51

Hand-buch der Palæontologie Band 1–2 Palæozoologic.
2 vols. München, 1876–85.   A 9 U 34, 35

ZLATAGORSKOÏ (E.) Essai d'un Dictionnaire des
Homonymes de la Langue Française, avec la Traduction
Allemande, Russe, et Anglaise, et des Exemples tirés des
meilleurs Auteurs. 8vo. Leipzig, 1862.   K 12 R 17

ZÖLLNER (PROF. JOHANN CARL FRIEDRICH) Transcendental Physics : an Account of Experimental Investigations, from the Scientific Treatises of Johann Carl
Friedrich Zöllner. Translated by C. C. Massey. 1st ed.
8vo. Lond., 1880.   A 16 S 18

Another copy. 2nd ed. Lond., 1882.   A 16 S 19

ZOLLTARIF. Die Zolltarife des In-und Auslandes. 4to.
Berlin, 1884.   F 5 V 25

Alphabetisches Waaren-Verzeichniss zum Braunshäuser
Elb-zoll-tarif. 8vo. Hanover, 1845.   MJ 2 Q 25

ZONARAS (JOHANNES). Opera omnia. [*See* MIGNE,
J. P., SERIES GRÆCA, 134–136.]

ZONDRAS (J.) [*See* BYZANTINAE HIST. SCRIPT.]

ZOOLOGICAL AND ACCLIMATISATION SOCIETY OF VICTORIA. Proceedings and Reports. 5 vols. 8vo. Melb., 1872–78.* ME I P
First, Fourth, Fifth, Sixth, and Seventh Reports of the Acclimatisation Society. 8vo. Melh., 1862–71. ME 1 Q
[*See* ACCLIMATISATION SOCIETY.]

ZOOLOGICAL RECORD (THE). Record of Zoological Literature, 1864–85. Edited by Edward Caldwell Rye, F.Z.S., M.E.S. Vols. 22. 8vo. Lond., 1865–86. E

ZOOLOGICAL SOCIETY OF LONDON. Indexes, 1830–80. 3 vols. 8vo. Lond., 1866–82. E 1.47
Proceedings of the Scientific Meetings of the Zoological Society of London, for the years 1830–85. 39 vols. 8vo. Lond., 1830–86. E 1.47
Transactions. 11 vols. 4to. Lond., 1835–85. E

ZOOLOGISCHE STATION ZU NEAPEL. Fauna und Flora des Golfes von Neapel. 2 vols. 4to. Leipzig, 1880–85. E 2.6
Zoologischer Jaresbericht herausgegeben von der Zoologischen Station zu Neapel, 1879–84. 6 vols. 8vo. Leipzig, 1880–86. E 1.39

ZORLIN (ROSINA M.) Recreations in Geology. 2nd ed. 12mo. Lond., 1841. A 9 P 12

ZOROASTER. Zend-Avesta, ouvrage de Zoroastre ; traduit en François sur l'original Zend, avec des Remarques ; et accompagné de plusieurs Tratés propres à éclaircir les matières qui en sont l'objet ; par Abraiam Hyacinthe Anquetil du Perron. 3 vols. 4to. Paris, 1771. G 3 V 11–13

ZOSIMUS. [*See* BYZANTINAE HIST. SCRIPT.]

ZOTENBERG (HERMANN). Chronique de. [*See* TABARI, ABON-DJAFOR-MOHAMMED BEN-DJARIR-BEN-YEZID.] B 1 P 14–17

ZSCHOKKE (HEINRICH). Autobiography of. 8vo. Lond.* 1845. C 9 Q 50

ZUALLARDO (GIOVANNI). Il Devotissimo Viaggio di Gierusalemme, Aggiontiui i disegni in Rame di varij Luoghi di Terra S. e altri Paesi. 12mo. Roma, 1595. D 5 P 18

ZUCCARINI (DR. J. G.) [*See* SIEBOLD, P. F. DE.] A 4 V 3, 4 ‡

ZULU IZAGA, that is, Proverbs, or Out-of-the-Way Sayings of the Zulus; collected, translated, and interpreted by "A Zulu Missionary"; reprinted from the *Natal Colonist*, Newspaper. 8vo. Natal, 1880. K 12 Q 17

ZULU MISSIONARY, A. [*See* ZULU IZAGA.]

ZUÑIGA (MARTINEZ DE). Historical View of the Philippine Islands. 2nd ed. 2 vols. (in 1) 8vo. Lond.,1814. B 10 S 8

Sydney : Charles Potter, Government Printer. — 1895.

.

Lightning Source UK Ltd.
Milton Keynes UK
UKHW051530120219
337100UK00020B/1318/P